LITERARY CULTURES OF
LATIN AMERICA

A COMPARATIVE HISTORY

LITERARY HISTORY PROJECT

UNDER THE AUSPICES OF THE SOCIAL SCIENCES
AND HUMANITIES RESEARCH COUNCIL OF CANADA
AND THE UNIVERSITY OF TORONTO

RESEARCH DIRECTOR
Mario J. Valdés, University of Toronto

CODIRECTOR
Linda Hutcheon, University of Toronto

Hutcheon, Linda, and Mario J. Valdés, eds.
Rethinking Literary History: A Dialogue on Theory.
New York: Oxford University Press, 2002.

Valdés, Mario J., and Djelal Kadir, eds.
Literary Cultures of Latin America: A Comparative History.
3 vols. New York: Oxford University Press, 2004.

Cornis-Pope, Marcel, and John Neubauer, eds.
History of Literary Cultures in East-Central Europe.
Forthcoming.

LITERARY CULTURES OF
LATIN AMERICA

A COMPARATIVE HISTORY

Mario J. Valdés
and
Djelal Kadir
Editors

Volume II
INSTITUTIONAL MODES AND
CULTURAL MODALITIES

OXFORD
UNIVERSITY PRESS
2004

Page Design & Production
Publication Services

Project Manager
Susan Yates

Designer
Lori Martinsek

Editorial Manager
Rob Siedenburg

Editorial Staff
Jerome Colburn, Al Davis, Philip D. Hamer, David Mason, Jennifer Putman,
Scott Stocking, Rebecca Taylor

Production Manager
Foti Kutil

Production Staff
Kelly Applegate, Pamela J. Broderick-Rhoades, Elisa Laird, Carol McGilliuray,
Paul Mitchell, Steven Sansone, James Torbit, Eric R. Tucker

Indexing Staff
Alysia Cooley, Benjamin Moreland, Louise Toft, Joyce Wiehagen,
Debora Mori Benencase Ayers, Neil Ching

Art
Ben Coblentz, Jason Pankoke, Guoliang Wu

OXFORD
University Press

Oxford   New York
Auckland   Bangkok   Buenos Aires   Cape Town   Chennai
Dar es Salaam   Delhi   Hong Kong   Istanbul   Karachi   Kolkata
Kuala Lumpur   Madrid   Melbourne   Mexico City   Mumbai
Nairobi   São Paulo   Shanghai   Taipei   Tokyo   Toronto

Copyright © 2004 by Oxford University Press, Inc.

Published by Oxford University Press, Inc.
198 Madison Avenue, New York, New York, 10016
http://www.oup.com/us

Oxford is a registered trademark of Oxford University Press

Library of Congress Cataloging-in-Publication Data

Literary cultures of Latin America : a comparative history / edited by
Mario J. Valdés and Djelal Kadir.
     v. ; cm.
  Includes bibliographical references and index.
  Contents: v. 1 Configurations of literary culture -- v. 2
Institutional modes and cultural modalities -- v. 3 Latin American
literary culture.
  ISBN 0-19-512621-1 (set : alk. paper) -- ISBN 0-19-517540-9 (v. 1 :
alk. paper) -- ISBN 0-19-517541-7 (v. 2 : alk. paper) -- ISBN
0-19-517542-5 (v. 3 : alk. paper)
  1. Latin American literature--History and criticism. 2. Literature
and society--Latin America. I. Valdés, Mario J. II. Kadir, Djelal.
  PQ7081.A1L525 2004
  860.9'98--dc22

                          2003027353

Printing Number: 9 8 7 6 5 4 3 2 1

Printed in the United States of America
on acid-free paper

CONTENTS OF VOLUME II

Institutional Modes and Cultural Modalities

INTRODUCTION
Walter D. Mignolo   xv

PART ONE

CULTURAL INSTITUTIONS

INTRODUCTION
Lisa Block de Behar and Tania Franco Carvalhal   1

SECTION I: BOOKS AND READERS IN LATIN AMERICA

1. Books, Myths, and the Reading Public in Spanish America during the Sixteenth Century
   Luigi Avonto   7

2. The Book in Brazil: Libraries and Presses
   José Mindlin   23

3. Document: Oswald: Free Book
   Augusto de Campos   28

SECTION II: CULTURAL INSTITUTIONS

4. Cultural Institutions in Latin America
   K. Alfons Knauth   33

5. Cultural Institutions and Intellectual Life in Brazil
   Luiz Roberto Cairo   50

6. Cultural Models of Representation in Seventeenth-Century Brazil
   João Adolfo Hansen   57

7. Museums in Latin America
   Maria de Lourdes Parreiras-Horta   65

8. Education in Brazil: Omissions, Advances, and Future Perspectives
   Célio da Cunha   69

9. Brazilian Literature in the 1970s: Censorship and the Culture Industry
   Cíntia Schwantes and Rildo Cosson   79

10. State Sponsorship and Control of Publishing in Brazil
    Fábio Lucas   83

SECTION III: CULTURAL JOURNALISM

11. Cultural Journalism in Spanish America: An Overview
    Aníbal González-Pérez   87

12. Criticism and Literature in Brazilian Periodicals of the Romantic Period
    Luiz Roberto Cairo   92

13. From Journalism to Foundational Text: *Os Sertões* [*Rebellion in the Backlands*]
    Jorge Coli   98

14. Literary Journalism in Brazil during the First Half of the Twentieth Century
    Ivia Alves   101

15. Literary Periodicals of the 1960s: Proposals for Re-reading
    Luz Rodríguez-Carranza   108

16. Criticism and Cultural Journalism in Contemporary Brazil
    Maria Lucia de Barros Camargo   119

SECTION IV: TRANSLATION AS A CULTURAL INSTITUTION

17. Translation as a Literary Institution
    László Scholz   129

18. The Development of a Translation Paideuma and
    Poetics in Brazil: The Campos Brothers
    Else Ribeiro Pires Vieira   140

PART TWO

TEXTUAL MODELS AND THEIR TRANSFORMATIONS

INTRODUCTION
Randolph D. Pope and Flora Süssekind   145

SECTION I: FORM AND FIGURATION

19. The Book and the Format of the Novel
    Jussara Menezes Quadros   147

20. The Representation of Nature in Nineteenth-Century
    Narrative and Iconography
    Luz Aurora Pimentel   156

SECTION II: POETIC MODELS AND THE CULTURAL IMAGINARY

21. Poetic Exchange and Epic Landscapes
    Gwen Kirkpatrick   173

22. An Emerging Poetry
    Noé Jitrik   188

SECTION III: FORMS OF DISCOURSE IN TESTIMONIO, AUTOBIOGRAPHY, AND LETTER WRITING

23. In the Web of Reality: Latin American Testimonio
    Elzbieta Sklodowska   197

24. Document: From the Spoken to the Written Word
    Elena Poniatowska   209

25. The Epistolary Genre and Brazilian Modernism
    Júlio Castañon Guimarães   216

SECTION IV: THE ESSAY AND ITS COROLLARIES

26. The Comparative Drive in the Latin American Essay
    Randolph D. Pope   227

27. Satire and Temporal Heterogeneity
    Flora Süssekind   241

28. The Sermon in the Seventeenth Century
    Alcir Pécora   258

SECTION V: THE NOVEL

29. The *Feuilleton* and European Models in the
    Making of the Brazilian Novel
    Marlyse Meyer   267

30. Novel and Journalism: Strategic Interchanges
    Aníbal González Pérez   278

31. The Making of the Latin American Novel
    Roberto González Echevarría   289

PART THREE

THE CULTURAL CENTERS OF LATIN AMERICA

INTRODUCTION
Eduardo F. Coutinho and Victoria Peralta   307

SECTION I: NORTHERN MEXICO AND THE BORDER

32. Threshold without Frontier: Cultural Limits and
    Cultural Intervals on the Mexico-U.S. Border
    José Manuel Valenzuela Arce   313

SECTION II: MESOAMERICA

33. Enlightened Neighborhood: Mexico City as a
    Cultural Center
    Carlos Monsiváis   335

34. The Cultural Centers of Central America
    Nicasio Urbina and Laura Barbas Rhoden   351

SECTION III: THE CARIBBEAN

INTRODUCTION
Marcelino Juan Canino Salgado   365

35. Havana
     Luisa Campuzano   369

36. Santo Domingo: Center of Innovation, Transition,
     and Change
     William Luis   381

37. Puerto Rico: Caribbean Cultural Center
     Marcelino Juan Canino Salgado   392

SECTION IV: ANDEAN REGION

INTRODUCTION
Consuelo Triviño Anzola   405

38. Caracas
     Alexis Márquez Rodríguez   413

39. Lima: A Blurred Centrality
     Sara Castro-Klaren   426

40. Bogotá: From Colonial Hamlet to Cosmopolitan
     Metropolis
     Victoria Peralta   444

41. Convent in the Clouds: Quito as a Cultural Center
     Regina Harrison   462

42. La Paz–Chukiyawu Marka
     Elizabeth Monasterios   474

SECTION V: AMAZONIA

INTRODUCTION
Nicomedes Suárez Araúz   499

43. Belém: Cultural Center
     Benedito Nunes   505

44. Document: The View from Manaus
     Milton Hatoum   516

45. Amazonian Cultural Centers of Bolivia
     Nicomedes Suárez Araúz   525

SECTION VI: EAST AND CENTRAL BRAZIL

INTRODUCTION
Ângela Maria Dias   531

46. Recife as a Cultural Center
     César Leal   539

47. Bahia: Colonization and Cultures
     Eneida Leal Cunha, Jeferson Bacelar, and
     Lizir Arcanjo Alves   551

48. Rio de Janeiro: Capital City
     Renato Cordeiro Gomes, Margarida de Souza Neves,
     and Mónica Pimento Velloso   566

49. São Paulo: The Cultural Laboratory and
     Its Close
     Nicolau Sevcenko   585

50. Ouro Preto, Belo Horizonte, Brasília: The Utopia
     of Modernity
     Maria Zilda Ferreira Cury   597

SECTION VII: THE PAMPAS, THE SOUTHERN BORDERLANDS

INTRODUCTION
Mario J. Valdés   615

51. Asunción as a Cultural Center
     Olga V. Araujo-Mendieta   617

52. Porto Alegre: Cultural Center of
     Southern Brazil
     Rita Terezinha Schmidt   626

SECTION VIII: RIO DE LA PLATA AND CHILE

INTRODUCTION
Richard J. Walter   639

53. Montevideo: From Frontier City to Mercosur
     Hugo Achugar   644

54. Buenos Aires: Cultural Center of River Plate
     Noemí Ulla   658

55. Santiago
     Marcela Orellana   670

SECTION IX: LATIN AMERICAN CULTURE IN NEW YORK AND PARIS

56. New York City: Center and Transit Point for
     Hispanic Cultural Nomadism
     Dionisio Cañas, with contributions by
     Orlando Hernández, Doris Schnabel,
     and Luisa García Conde   679

57. Paris and Latin Americans, Nineteenth and
     Twentieth Centuries: From Cultural Metropolis to
     Cultural Museum?
     Denis Rolland   703

CONTENTS OF OTHER VOLUMES

Volume I
Configurations of Literary Culture

INTRODUCTION: BEYOND LITERARY HISTORY
Mario J. Valdés

SERIES OVERVIEW: RETHINKING LITERARY
HISTORY–COMPARATIVELY
Mario J. Valdés and Linda Hutcheon

COEDITOR'S INTRODUCTION:
HISTORY AFTER HISTORY
Djelal Kadir

INTRODUCTION TO VOLUME I: FOR A MORE INCLUSIVE
LITERARY HISTORY OF LATIN AMERICA
Luisa Campuzano

PART ONE

PARAMETERS OF LITERARY CULTURE

INTRODUCTION: PARAMETERS OF LITERARY CULTURE
Mario J. Valdés

SECTION I: GEOGRAPHIC FACTORS AND THE
FORMATION OF CULTURAL TERRAIN FOR LITERARY
PRODUCTION

1. The Formation of a Cultural Territory
   Hervé Théry

2. From the New Spain of Cortés to the Mexican, Central
   American, and Caribbean Mosaic
   Alain Musset

3. The Andean Countries
   Jean-Paul Deler

4. Brazil: A Continent, An Archipelago
   Hervé Théry

5. The Southern Cone
   Sébastian Velut

6. The Amazon: The Forgotten Heart
   Emmanuel Lézy

SECTION II: DEMOGRAPHICS AND THE FORMATION OF
CULTURAL CENTERS

7. Demography, Language, and Cultural Centers
   Nicolás Sánchez Albornoz

SECTION III: LINGUISTIC DIVERSITY OF LATIN AMERICAN
LITERARY CULTURES

8. Linguistic Diversity in Mexico
   Beatriz Garza Cuarón

9. Document: Tzotzil Text
   Juan González Hernández

10. Document: Zapotec Text
    Santiago Fábian

11. Linguistic Diversity in Venezuela
    Marie-Claude Mattéi Muller

12. Linguistic Diversity in Colombia
    Jon Landaburu

13. Linguistic Diversity in the Andean Countries (Argentina, Bolivia,
    Chile, Ecuador, Peru) and Paraguay
    Willem F. H. Adelaar

14. The Portuguese Language in Brazil
    Marianne Akerberg

SECTION IV: HISTORY OF THE PRODUCTION OF LITERARY
CULTURES IN COLONIAL LATIN AMERICA

15. The Production of Literary Culture in New Spain
    José Joaquin Blanco

16. The Context of Literary Culture in the Caribbean
    Jorge Luis Camacho

17. The Foundations of Brazilian Literary Culture
    Tania Franco Carvalhal

18. Literary Culture during the Peruvian Viceroyalty
    Luis Millones

SECTION V: ACCESS AND PARTICIPATION IN THE LITERARY
CULTURES OF LATIN AMERICA

19. Social History of the Latin American Writer
    Mario J. Valdés

20. Reading as a Historical Practice in Latin America: The First
    Colonial Period to the Nineteenth Century
    Juan Poblete

21. Literary Nationalism in Latin America
    Leyla Perrone-Moisés

PART TWO

FROM THE MARGINS OF LITERARY HISTORY

INTRODUCTION
Cynthia Steele, Heloisa Buarque de Hollanda, Marlyse Meyer,
and Beatriz Resende

SECTION I: CONFIGURATIONS OF SOCIOECONOMIC, RACIAL,
AND ETHNIC ALTERITY IN LITERARY HISTORY

22. Poverty in the History of Literary Cultures
    Kathleen Newman

23. First Nations, First Writers: Indigenous Mexican Literary History
    Cynthia Steele

24. Recent Mayan Incursions into Guatemalan Literary
    Historiography
    Gail Ament

25. Andean Indigenous Expression: Resisting Marginality
    Regina Harrison

26. Brazil's Indigenous Textualities
    Claudia Neiva de Matos

27. Afro-Hispanic Writers in Latin American Literary History
    Rosemary Geisdorfer Feal

28. Black Presence in Brazilian Literature: From the Colonial Period
    to the Twentieth Century
    Heloisa Toller Gomes, Gizelda Melo do Nascimento, and
    Leda Maria Martins

29. Jewish Literary Culture in Spanish America
    Saúl Sosnowski

30. Displacement and Disregard: Brazilian-Jewish Writing and the
    Search for Narrative Identity
    Nelson H. Vieira

SECTION II: GENDER AND SEXUAL ORIENTATION IN THE
HISTORICAL FORMATION OF THE CULTURAL IMAGINARY

31. Women Writers during the Viceroyalty
    Josefina Muriel

32. Saints or Sinners? Life Writings and Colonial Latin American
    Women
    Kathleen Ann Myers

33. Mystics and Visionaries: Women's Writing in Eighteenth-
    Century Portuguese America
    Leila Mezan Algranti

34. Exclusions in Latin American Literary History
    Debra A. Castillo

35. Women Writing in Nontraditional Genres
    María Elena de Valdés

36. Brazilian Women: Literature from the Nineteenth to the
    Twentieth Centuries
    Lucia Helena, Sylvia Oroz, Sylvia Paixão

37. Constructing the Place of Woman in Brazil's Northeastern
    Region
    Luzilá Gonçalves Ferreira

38. Writing against the Grain: An Overview of Twentieth-Century
    Lesbian Literature in Latin America
    Elena M. Martínez

39. Secrets and Truths
    Daniel Balderston

40. Notes toward a History of Homotextuality in Brazilian Literature
    Denilson Lopes

PART THREE

PLURALITY OF DISCOURSE IN LATIN AMERICAN CULTURE

SECTION I: POLITICAL, SCIENTIFIC, AND RELIGIOUS DISCOURSES

INTRODUCTION
Eneida Maria de Souza and Raúl Antelo

41. The Rhetoric of Latin American Nationalism from the Colonial Period to Independence
Silvia Delfino

42. The Rhetoric of Citizenship in Modernity
Adriana Rodríguez Pérsico

43. The Struggle Over the Printed Word: The Catholic Church in Brazil and Social Discourse
Aparecida Paiva

44. Scientific Discourse in Brazil and Intellectual Exchange
Rachel Esteves Lima

45. Bio-Policies Undergoing Transformation: Bodies and Ideas of American Identity
Claudia Gilman

SECTION II: ORALITY AND LITERATURE

INTRODUCTION
Eugenia Meyer

46. The History of Oral Literature in Mexico
Leonardo Manrique Castañeda

47. African Orality in the Literary Culture of the Caribbean
Luz María Martínez Montiel

48. Orality and Literature in the Peruvian Andean Zone
José Antonio Giménez Micó

49. Argentina, Chile, and Uruguay: A History of Literary Orality
Eva Grosser Lerner and Eduardo Lucio Molina y Vedia

50. Oral Literature in Brazil
Jerusa Pires Ferreira

51. Textuality and Territoriality in Brazilian Oral Discourse
Ivete Lara Camargos Walty

SECTION III: THE MULTIPLICITY AND DIVERSITY OF DISCOURSES AND THEATRICALITIES

INTRODUCTION
Juan Villegas

52. The Theater in Pre-Hispanic America
Juan Villegas

53. Contemporary Mayan Theater
Tamara Underiner

54. Plurality and Diversity of Theater Discourse
Juan Villegas

55. Afro-Latin American Theater
Juan Villegas

56. Theatrical Forms and Their Social Dimensions in Nineteenth-Century Brazil
João Roberto Faria

57. Dramaturgies and Theatricalities: Aspects of the Twentieth-Century Brazilian Literary Scene
Maria Helena Werneck and Victor Hugo Adler Pereira

SECTION IV: TRANSFORMATIONS IN POPULAR CULTURE

INTRODUCTION
Mario J. Valdés

58. Laughing through One's Tears: Popular Culture in Mexico
Carlos Monsiváis

59. Mass Culture and Literature in Latin America
Ana María Amar Sánchez

60. *Literatura de Cordel*: Literature for Market and Voice
Idelette Muzart Fonseca dos Santos

61. Religious Celebrations in Brazilian Cultural History
Marlyse Meyer

62. Carnival
Félix Coluccio and Marta Isabel Coluccio

63. Popular Memory and the Collective Imagination in Latin American Soap Operas
Jesús Martín-Barbero

64. The Popular in the Confused Republics?
Carlos Monsiváis

SECTION V: CINEMA: CULTURAL DIALOGUES AND THE PROCESS OF MODERNITY

65. Cultural Dialogues and the Process of Modernity
Julianne Burton-Carvajal and Zuzana M. Pick

Volume III

Latin American Literary Culture:

Subject to History

INTRODUCTION
Wander Melo Miranda

PART ONE

FISSURED FOUNDATIONS: NOSTALGIA AND NEW BEGINNINGS

INTRODUCTION
Doris Sommer and Maria Consuelo Cunha Campos

SECTION I: EPIC VOICES: ENCOUNTERS AND FOUNDATIONS

1. Epic Voices: Non-encounters and Foundation Myths
   José Antonio Mazzotti

2. Fragment and Totality: Narrating Colonial Encounters
   Guillermo Giucci and Marcelo Rocha Wanderley

**SECTION II: THE DISCOURSE OF MELANCHOLY:
A CULTURE OF LOSS**

3. Spectacular Cityscapes of Baroque Spanish America
   Stephanie Merrim

4. The Discourse of Melancholy in a Culture of Loss
   Maria Consuelo Cunha Campos

**SECTION III: NARRATIVES OF LEGITIMATION:
THE DISCOURSE OF HEGEMONY AND THE HERMENEUTICS
OF GLOBALIZATION**

5. Narratives of Legitimation: The Invention of
   History-Monument and the Nation-State
   Beatriz González Stephan

6. Creating the National Imaginary
   Vera Follain de Figueiredo

SECTION IV: DISCOURSES OF MODERNITY

7. National Installments: The Erotics of Modernity in
   Spanish America
   Doris Sommer

8. In the Public Eye: Naturalism and Brazilian Letters
   Victor Hugo Adler Pereira

PART TWO

INTERNAL BORDERS: CULTURAL CONFLICTS AND STATE DISCOURSE

INTRODUCTION
Alberto Moreiras

SECTION I: LETTERED MEDIATIONS

9. Documents of the First Encounter of Europeans with the New
   World: Lexicons, Missions, Voyages, and Resistances
   Ettore Finazzi-Agrò

10. Indigenous, *Mestizo,* and Imperial Reason
    Marco Luis Dorfsman and Lori Hopkins

11. "A Very Subtle Idolatry":
    Estanislao de Vega Bazán's Authentic Testimony
    of Colonial Andean Religion
    Kenneth Mills

12. The Three Faces of the Baroque in Mexico and
    the Caribbean
    Iris M. Zavala

13. The Baroque and Transculturation
    Mabel Moraña

14. The Baroque Gaze
    Raúl Antelo

15. Francisco Xavier Clavijero and the
    Enlightenment in Mexico
    José Emilio Pacheco

16. New Thinking: From the Enlightenment to
    Independence
    Susana Rotker

17. Literary *Criollismo* and Indigenism
Horacio Legrás

SECTION II: PEOPLES, COMMUNITIES, AND NATION BUILDING

18. Projects of Latin American Emancipation:
The Caribbean, 1800–1850
Sibylle Fischer

19. Transculturation and the Discourse of Liberation
Graciela Montaldo

20. Transculturation and Nationhood
Idelber Avelar

21. The Brazilian Construction of Nationalism
Adriana Romeiro

SECTION III: THE INVERSION OF SOCIAL DARWINISM

22. *Negrismo*: The American "Real"
Elzbieta Sklodowska

23. The Literary Culture of the "New Order":
Mexico 1867–1910
Leopoldo Zea

24. The Transcultural Mirror of Science: Race and
Self-Representation in Latin America
Gabriela Nouzeilles

25. Literary Education and the Making of
State Knowledge
Juan Poblete

26. *Mestizaje* and the Inversion of Social Darwinism in
Spanish American Fiction
Julie Taylor and George Yúdice

SECTION IV: MODERNIZATION AND THE FORMATION OF
CULTURAL IDENTITIES

27. Mexico-U.S. Border Transculturation and
State Discourses: Nineteenth and
Twentieth Centuries
Marcus Embry

28. A Paradigm for Modernity: The Concept of
Crisis in *Modernismo*
Jorge Luis Camacho

29. Textual Transcultural Mediations and the
Formation of Regional Identity
Ileana Rodríguez

30. Anatomy of the Latin American "Boom" Novel
Brett Levinson

31. The Modern Imaginary and Transculturation
Eneida Maria de Souza

PART THREE

LIMINALITY AND CENTRALITY OF
LITERARY CULTURES IN THE TWENTIETH CENTURY

SECTION I: AMERINDIAN LITERARY CULTURES

INTRODUCTION
Elizabeth Monasterios

32. Literatures of Mesoamerica
Miguel León Portilla

33. The Nature of Indigenous Literaturesin the Andes
Denise Y. Arnold and Juan de Dios Yapita

SECTION II: HISPANIC CULTURES IN THE UNITED STATES:
DIVERSITY, HYBRIDISM, AND CONSTANT TRANSFORMATION

INTRODUCTION
Juan Villegas

34. Reinventing America:
The Chicano Literary Tradition
María Herrera-Sobek

35. Chicano/Latino Theater Today
Claudia Villegas-Silva

36. Puerto Rican Literature in
the United States
Carmen Dolores Hernández

37. Construction of New Cultural Identities:
Puerto Rican Theater in New York
Grace Dávila-López

38. Colonial Figures in Motion: Translocality,
Tropicalism, and Translation in Contemporary
Puerto Rican Literature in the United States
Arnaldo Cruz Malavé

39. Cuban Theater in the United States
José A. Escarpanter

40. Cuban American Prose: 1975–2000
María Cristina García

PART FOUR

LITERARY CULTURE IN THE TWENTIETH CENTURY

INTRODUCTION
Renato Cordeiro Gomes, Djelal Kadir, and
Marília Rothier Cardoso

SECTION I: HISTORIC DISPLACEMENTS

41. Historic Displacements in Twentieth-Century
    Brazilian Literary Culture
    Renato Cordeiro Gomes, Ana Lúcia Almeida Gazolla,
    Ana Maria de Alencar, Antonio Arnoni Prado,
    Edson Rosa da Silva, Eneida Leal Cunha,
    Everardo Rocha, João Cezar de Castro Rocha,
    Marília Rothier Cardoso, and Nádia Battella Gotlib

42. Signs of Identity:
    Latin American Immigration and Exile
    Clara E. Lida and Francisco Zapata

43. Exile in the Narrative of the
    Spanish American Diaspora in the
    Twentieth Century
    Ivan Almeida and Cristina Parodi

44. Political Exclusion / Literary Inclusion:
    Argentine and Uruguayan Writers
    Saul Sosnowski

45. Writers under (and after) the Chilean
    Military Dictatorship
    Javier Campos

SECTION II: MODERNITY, MODERNISMS, AND THEIR AVATARS

46. Nations of Modernity
    Javier Lasarte Valcárcel

47. Aesthetics of Rupture
    Eneida Maria de Souza

48. The Postmodern in Brazilian Literary
    Theory and Criticism
    Italo Moriconi

SECTION III: IDEOLOGIES AND IMAGINARIES

49. Literature and Revolution in
    Latin America
    Hermann Herlinghaus

50. Imagining Narrative Territories
    Lucille Kerr

51. Utopic Theories in Brazil
    Vera Follain de Figueiredo

52. Conservatism and Modernization
    in Brazil
    Victor Hugo Adler Pereira

53. Post-Utopian Imaginaries
    Flavio Carneiro

SECTION IV: BY WAY OF CODA: IN ANTICIPATION

54. Scenes of the Twenty-first Century:
    The Routes of the New
    Julio Ortega

NAMES AND INDEX

List of Contributors

List of Persons Included in *Literary Cultures of Latin
America* with Birth and Death Dates

Index: Volumes I, II, and III

INTRODUCTION TO VOLUME II

Walter D. Mignolo

To situate the scope of my introductory comments, I would begin by reminding the reader that until about the decade of the 1970s literary histories were written in specific frames of reference. One of these frames was the macronarrative of "Western Civilization" ("literature" as "poetry" and literary studies as poetics were therefore said to have begun in Greece). Another of these paradigms was grounded in the national languages and, indirectly, in the formation of the bourgeois nation-states after the French Revolution. This frame included a given national language and a series of authors organized by periods and by literary movements or schools. It was assumed that the historical model to be used for language, literature, and cultures was not only national but also natural (see Hutcheon 2001). The interest that those literary histories have for us, today, is to remind us of things past and mainly of the end of an era when "histories" were assumed to be linear narratives of chronologically arranged events. Between approximately 1950 and 1980 literary histories responded, directly or indirectly, to René Wellek's complaint that literary histories were neither histories of *literature* nor *histories* of literature (see Valdés 2001). Wellek was here adapting to literary history a dictum that Roman Jakobson and the Russian Formalists formulated around 1920, offering an analogy between literary studies and a policeman who arrested everybody who crossed his path, just in case he or she was guilty. Literary studies, according to Jakobson and the Formalists, followed the same path, since literary critics were not analyzing a literary work *qua* work, but talking about everything possible and imaginable around it. After almost thirty years under the dominance of the linguistic and the discoursive "turns"–and of trying to sort out what makes a given discourse a literary work of art and how to write histories of such artifacts–we are now starting to focus on cultural and institutional concerns. These are being accompanied by the *spatialization* of (literary) histories, and, I would add, a spatialization across the "colonial difference" that mapped and still maps the modern or colonial world. My assumption is that coloniality is constitutive of modernity–that there is no modernity without coloniality. However, this idea is still somewhat alien to the English language, so alien that the spelling checker in my computer underlines "coloniality" in red but doesn't have any problem with "modernity" (see Mignolo 2000, 3–48).

The volume that readers have in their hands is one of the three volumes devoted to the comparative history of Latin-American literary cultures. However, this set of three volumes is in its turn one unit out of three devoted to the idea of comparative literary history. The first is *Rethinking Literary History: A Dialogue on Theory* and the last is *A Comparative History of the Literary Cultures of East Central Europe: Junctures and Disjunctures in the 19th and 20th Centuries*. The entire project is grounded in a basic set of principles that sustains its coherence and supports

its originality within current research in the humanities. First of all, the project examines and then contests the inherited concepts of "literature" and the "national," that is, of national literature. In the programmatic statement explaining the entire enterprise, the term *rethinking* in the phrase "rethinking literary history comparatively" means not just to "think again" but mainly to "think anew." And to "rethink comparatively" means also to do so beyond those national literary units on which even the discipline of comparative literature has been founded. To compare, then, beyond national frames, in a global world, acquires a new meaning, and that is precisely one of the consequences of "thinking anew": A comparative enterprise in a global world changes its old shape and enters into an open process of circulation, in which comparison loses its role as go-between for static units (the national literatures being compared). However, in this circulation, literature itself loses its previous meaning, since it is no longer the text alone that counts, but the entire process of production, distribution, readership, institutional setting, and so on. Rethinking literary history, comparatively, then becomes looking at literature in circulation, linked to technological artifacts, to migration, and to all aspects of global flow.

The present volume should be introduced in the larger frame of previous attempts to rewrite literary history. A recent project, which I will call transitional in the sense that it openly *faced* the restrictions of writing a literary history of Latin America, was the project led by the late Uruguayan critic Angel Rama and the Chilean literary critic Ana Pizarro and published by Memorial de América Latina in São Paulo, Brazil (see also Luisa Campuzano's introduction to Volume I of this history). As a literary history proper, this project was a failure; however, its failure was simultaneously its victory. The title of the three volumes is *America Latina. Palavra, literatura e cultura* [*Latin America: Word, Literature, and Culture*]. The title is revealing of the uncomfortable situation in which a distinguished group of scholars (Angel Rama, Antonio Candido, Domingo Miliani, Ana Pizarro, Gutiérrez Girardot, and Beatriz Sarlo, among others) met and discussed the project for about ten years before its completion. The situation was not clear at the time, but, in retrospect, it could be interpreted as the result of a tension between the emergence of transnational corporations and the demise of the ideology of nation (translated into subcontinental ideology, e.g., Latin America) under which literary histories were usually written. The title then bears witness to this situation in two complementary ways. First, it does not direct the reader to something that happened exclusively in Latin America. It suggests, on the contrary, that Latin America was part of the process whose history (*palavra, literatura, cultura*) was being narrated. Second, *palavra* ("word") introduced into the project the oral dimension, departing from the traditional idea that literary history was the history of something written. Literature comes from "littera," a Latin word that designates letter (of the alphabet). In a geo-historical space like Latin America, with a long memory of oral narratives among its Amerindian and Afro-American communities, limiting literature to the written would have meant reproducing the historical violence of a lettered elite that counted as texts only those written in Spanish and Portuguese; that is, literary history in the past reproduced the colonial power installed by the colonial model and continued by the internalized colonialism of nation-builders (see Mignolo 2001). No Amerindian or black Creole Caribbean literatures were considered worthy of recognition. Finally, the word *culture* extended the reach of discursive practices–oral or written–into the wider domain of the semiotic and the conflictive sphere of the political, that is, of the colonial configuration of power (which ended between 1810 and 1820) and the internal colonialism enacted during the period of nation building (1820–1845). Thus, *America Latina. Palavra, literatura e cultura* was imagined and published during the period in which national ideals were no longer taken for granted and when the vocabulary of globalization was not yet fully in place.

The entire project of rethinking literary history comparatively goes beyond the literary history of Latin America proper. The model for this project has been provided by French historian Fernand Braudel, particularly in his three-volume *Civilization matérielle, économie et capitalisme, 15e–18e siècles* [1979; *Civilization and Capitalism, 15th–18th century*, 1981–1982]. Braudel's description of his project as being comparative and dialectical at the same time also applies to the present project. If, indeed, a history of capitalism between the fifteenth and the eighteenth centuries cannot but be comparative (since capitalism was transnational from its very inception), it also needs to be imbedded in time, in the dialectic between the past and the present.

> A "comparative" literary history would not only try to keep in the foreground this dialectic hermeneutic movement between past and present, but would try to do something analogous to what Braudel and the *Annales* school accomplished in their moving of history's emphasis from the events of politics and diplomacy to, on the one hand, a study of the broader circumstances (demographic, geographical, climactic, etc.) conditioning such events and, on the other, a parallel and very detailed scrutiny of the concrete material data (quantified) of life of the past. (Valdés and Hutcheon 2–3)

The frame of the present project corresponds to the particular history of the Americas. The first major step was to break with the distinction between Latin and Anglo America, with the Caribbean in the middle, and to take the Americas as a whole. What the Americas have in common (besides their aboriginal histories) is the historical process that began in the sixteenth century, with the coming into being of the Atlantic commercial circuit. The Atlantic was under the control of Spain and Portugal in the sixteenth and seventeenth centuries and of England, Holland, and France from the eighteenth to the early twentieth century. However, since 1848 (but mainly after the 1898 Spanish-American War), the United States began to be a distinctive force in relation to Europe and a new colonial force in relation to Latin America. Latin America is thus being remapped, in this project, and situated at the intersection of the colonial and the imperial differences in the modern or colonial world.

What is at stake in the present comparative history at this point, at the end of the Cold War, in a post-national (not necessarily post-state) frame of mind? The oft-mentioned weakening of the nation-state should be considered separately, since the weakening of the *state* is in contradiction to the rising power of *nation*alism. Indeed, the most striking sign of such "weakening" is that what was assumed to be one double entity (the nation-state) is being uncoupled now in complex ways: On the one hand, the state is changing as an administrative and managerial unit; on the other, "nations" are more difficult to imagine as homogenous groups of people united by a language, a literature, a border, a culture, a history. Mass migration and mass-mediation (to use Appadurai's expression) are eroding the belief in homogenous languages and cultures. This history of literary cultures offers the possibility of unlinking language, literature, and culture from the constraints of the "national." By the same token, it invites us to think and imagine "pluri-languaging" (Mignolo 2000, 250–77) in a transnational frame, although from the perspective of existing local histories in the process of transformation. These two goals imply that the "Americas" are to be looked at in their common colonial history–a common history that does not hide, however, the asymmetry of power embedded in both the imperial (i.e., America as seen from the United States in relation to Europe and Latin America) and the colonial differences (i.e., America as seen from Latin American perspectives in relation to the United States, Europe, Africa, and Asia). The monocultural and territorial conceptualization of the two Americas–one Bolívar's and the other Jefferson's imaginary–is broken up in this project by its focus on the materiality of reading and writing cultures rather than on the structure of the literary works. Such is, precisely, one of the symptoms and demands of the global era and the postcolonial or national critical perspectives on globalization to which literary histories must respond.

This second volume, *Institutional Modes and Cultural Modalities*, contributes to the *materialization* of the entire project in several interesting ways. Part I of Volume II, devoted to "Cultural Institutions," underlines the relevance of publishing houses and readers, education, academies, and government incentives to cultural production. Institutions and public policy have been complicitous with the Spanish and Portuguese languages insofar as both, either in their colonial or national incarnation, accomplished a function of distinguishing and controlling the small percentage of the population that–in colonial domains and ex-colonial countries–was literate. Literary practices were, in Spanish and Portuguese America, both an echo of the "mother [language] countries" and yet also a move toward autonomy. Section I of this volume shows this tension at different levels (printing presses, audience, journalism, literary criticism, and translation) and in two political periods: the colonial and the nation-building (i.e., internal colonialism).

Translation is one telling sign of the complex histories of literary cultures and institutions in colonial and ex-colonial countries. In the Colonial period, translation contributed to the imposition of alphabetic writing (see Boone 2000; Boone and Mignolo 1994). Although translations were done from colonial to indigenous languages and vice versa, they were never operative in the oral domain. Translations were indeed heavily monotopic, since they contributed to imposing not only alphabetic literacy but also the colonial languages. After decolonization and during the nation-building period, translation went in a different direction and acquired different emphasis. Amerindian languages were no longer a prime concern. The coloniality of power shifted, and the Spanish and Portuguese languages drifted to a position of subalternity in relation to French (mainly), English, and German. Translation at this point truly operated in one direction: from French, English, and German to Spanish and Portuguese. There was little translation in the other direction. The South had much to learn from the North, but any learning in the reverse direction was deemed irrelevant; while the intellectual elite of Latin America was proud of its efforts to achieve the goals of civilization and modernization, the European intellectual elite had other concerns and was not particularly interested in what emerging Latin American nations had to say. France was the exception, and its concerns were political. How to stop the United States advancing toward the South? "Latinidad" was imposed as an ideological and cultural "translation" of Bolivarian republican ideals into French national and imperial designs.

Part II, "Textual Models and Their Transformations," could also be read as a kind of translation of genres and of media (translating painting into literature or vice versa). However, the technical aspects of translations should not overshadow the relations of power in the colonial horizon of modernity from which the very notion of America (Latin and Anglo) takes its meaning. It is precisely the frame established by the coloniality of power that could help in getting away from the national ideology focused on interior memories (i.e., interior memories as defined by the ideologues of nation building and, previously, by the ideology of Spanish exceptionalism and Portuguese imperial dreams). During the Colonial period, textual models and their transformations constituted a complicated issue, given the models of Amerindian semiotic practices that were "textual" in the sense of alphabetically written (see Boone 2000; Mignolo 1995; Edmonson; Adorno). There were complicated shifts that went in at least four different directions: One of these was the reflection, in the colonies, of textual models and their transformation in Spain, Portugal, and Italy; another was the parallel transformation of textual models in the colony itself; the third one was the transformation of Amerindian models when translated by Amerindian intellectuals into textual models governed by alphabetic literacy; the fourth was perhaps the most dramatic—the marginalization and silencing to which Amerindian "textual models" were subjected and that, consequently, slowed down their own transformation vis-à-vis the dominant colonial models. There is a parallel here, certainly, between translation at the level of languages and at the level of genres.

During the nation-state period (1820–1945), the transformation of textual models followed a path parallel to that of translation in the narrow sense (i.e., from French and English to Spanish and Portuguese). But a series of specific phenomena also emerged, growing out of internal colonialism and intellectual dependency on Europe, particularly until the beginning of the Cold War (in the 1950s) and the advent of the Cuban Revolution (1959). In a sense we could suggest that Latin American ideas on continental identity and its sense of marginalization with regard to Europe ended only with the Second World War. Perhaps the most telling phenomenon in the realm of the transformation of literary models in the nation-building period was the emergence of the historical novel in Latin America—parallel to and simultaneously different from its manifestation in Europe (in England, France, Spain, and Portugal). The historical novel in Latin America appeared at the intersection of a multiple transformation: It displaced the other dominant historical narratives in the colonial period and introduced the fictional mode in complicity

with nation building (see White; Sommer); second, the historical novel contributed to the transformation of the Renaissance system of genres modeled on rhetoric and on the *trivium* as a scholarly system of forms and knowledge. History as a genre was refashioned in the Renaissance and then again in the Enlightenment; however, both transformations contributed to its canonization and the fixing of its "origin" in Greece. This "origin" became a measuring stick with which to judge people who were not aware either of history or of history as a Greek invention. Historical fiction in Latin America was an imitation of the European form, but, simultaneously, an effective way of building national ideologies. European novels were translated in Latin America, either from French or English into Spanish or Portuguese, or were adapted into popular fictional narratives with local content. (The opposite did not happen: There were no novels translated from Latin-American languages into French or English.)

In the twentieth century the Latin-American novel acquired its maturity, and the literary "boom" was recognized as the sign of this achievement. This triumph did not mean that the colonial structures of power vanished. On the contrary, that triumph during the Cold War period was a response to the transformation of the intellectual field after World War II and the division of the world into First, Second, and Third Worlds. If the nineteenth century saw the novel as the literary genre complementing the transformation underway in the fields of ethics, philosophy, and theology and on into the social sciences, the second half of the twentieth century witnessed the success of the Third World novel in parallel to the rise of the social sciences and of area studies in the United States. The Third World was not supposed or expected to produce scientific knowledge, either in the natural or the social sciences; but it *was* expected to produce culture, and that was precisely what the literary boom did.

The essay as a genre in Latin America is the peculiar manifestation of a form common in Europe, particularly after the early pioneer work of the French intellectual Michel de Montaigne. In the European tradition it became a particular genre of philosophy as a discipline, of which Leibniz's essay on human understanding is a good example. The difference between Montaigne's and Leibniz's essays is that the former operates as an unframed genre, while the latter has been framed within the discipline of philosophy. The Latin-American essay is unframed like that of Montaigne, but for different reasons. In Montaigne's hands, the genre was a *nova reperta* in relation to the tyranny of Renaissance cultures of scholarship, dominated by the *trivium* and by rhetorical norms. The essay in Latin America offers an example of how the margin of the modern or colonial world responded to its needs and to the emergence of the social sciences in Europe, a genre in which history, sociology, philosophy, aesthetics, and psychology found their home. Although there were *cátedras* (academic chairs) of social sciences in major universities in Latin America, university programs in those areas did not find a place until after World War Two (see Romero Pittari; Marini and Millán). Not coincidentally, the last manifestations of the essay as a dominant genre can be located in the decade of the 1950s; from the 1960s on, the social sciences began to dominate the scene, creating a situation parallel to the literary boom. The rise of the genres of the *testimonio* and the essay could be explained and understood within the general framework of the sociopolitical and intellectual transformations of the world order. *Testimonio* marks a transformation of fictional narratives that simulate documentary histories and yet still bear witness to social reality. *Testimonio* opened the doors of literature to those who were not part of the elite of "writers" representing the literary institution. To make a long and complex story short, two new social and literary actors emerged with *testimonio*. On the one hand, members of "civil society," either from *criollo* or immigrant descent, who were victims of dictatorial regimes in the Southern Cone (Carmen Castillo, Hiber Conteris) or were revolutionary agents (Roque Dalton, Omar Cabezas, or Manlio Argueta) in Central America turned to *testimonio* as a principal means of communication. On the other hand, members of "political society" (ethnically marginalized from "civil society") of indigenous descent, such as Domitila Barrios de Chungara and Rigoberta Menchú, wrote *testimonios* that were more than a transformation of the historical and fictional genres of the nineteenth century: These were transformations of colonial genres, too, almost forgotten but created by the members of the indigenous colonial elite at the end of the sixteenth and the beginning of the seventeenth century. Alvarado Tezozomoc or Alva Ixtlilxochitl in Mesoamerica or Guaman Poma de Ayala and Pachacuti Yapanki in the Andes are indeed the distant ancestors of Domitila Barrios de Chungara and Rigoberta Menchú. Both the indigenous historians and chroniclers of the late sixteenth century and Chungara and Menchú conveyed a transformation from subaltern positions, that is, from subaltern languages and subaltern systems of genres. They did it by transforming at once dominant genres and the genres of their own tradition. Although Chungara and Menchú are very different from one another, it is appropriate in both cases to note the transformation of oral narratives into a written genre and the transformations and translations of indigenous languages into the official language of the nation.

Part III of Volume II, "The Cultural Centers of Latin America," introduces a new concern to literary history: the historic formation of cultural centers in the Americas from a Latin American perspective. Paris and New York, as well as the border between Mexico and the United States, are considered cultural centers of Hispanic and Luso-Brazilian *latinidad*. (It is telling that Part III opens up with Northern Mexico and the Border and ends up with New York and Paris.) Beyond the traditional narratives of Latin American artists and intellectuals living in Paris or New York, this section gives us new lenses through which to look at an old issue. While current stories of Latin Americans in those cities have been narrated from the triumphal or nostalgic locations of national ideologies, Part III frames the issue from the "borders" rather than from the "territory." Consequently, the "Latin American perspective" introduced in this section is no longer that of Latin America as an essentialized entity but, rather, as a constant borderland–from the sixteenth to the twenty-first century. Furthermore, by displacing the Latin American perspective from the "territory" of national and continental ideology to the "borderlands" of the modern or colonial world, the "Cultural Centers" section, dealing with geopolitical phenomena, displaces the notion of *region* as well, and thus the link to the national and subcontinental imaginary. While "region" is generally taken to mean a part of the nation or the continent, "cultural centers" are points of intersection in the global flow of the modern or colonial world as well as in transnational and transcontinental historical processes. In fact, each of the cultural centers described here can be understood in its interdependence within the Atlantic economy and its map of the

modern or colonial world: The modern or colonial world goes together with the emergence of the Atlantic commercial circuit, which did not exist until the sixteenth century. This perspective, of course, dilutes the modern debate over whether Columbus was the "first to arrive or discover" the New World. Whether he was the first or not may be a question of national pride, but it is inconsequential for the world order and world economy. What is indisputable is that there was no previous economic circuit in the Atlantic that had the force and power this one acquired in the sixteenth century. Modernity and coloniality came together with the expansion of capitalism.

Looking at the formation and transformation of cultural centers invites us to look at the flow of people, goods, and capital. Looking at the formation and transformation of regions invites us, instead, to look at the particularity of a given geo-historical space within a larger whole, in this case the Americas. While each of the cultural centers identified here acquired its singularity within the singularities of its "region," the features of each region were not formed by any internal regional history, but through interaction with the colonial powers. Thus, Mesoamerica and the Andes acquired their "Mesoamericanness" and "Andeanness" because of the classifications provided by colonial discourses–those of missionaries, archeologists, or anthropologists. Amerindians did not have the chance to identify the cultural centers formed in the making of the modern or colonial world with the names they used to designate their dwelling places (Anahuac and Tawantinsuyu, respectively). A similar argument can be made about the Caribbean, a name that itself emanated from Columbus's confusion and bad ear (see Hulme). However, the Caribbean acquired its singularity through the plantation economy and through being the maritime center of the slave trade, as well as the place where the successive colonial entities established a power base: Spain (Santo Domingo, Havana, and San Juan), Portugal (Bahia), France (Martinique, Guadaloupe), England (Barbados, Jamaica, Antigua), Holland (Suriname). Consequently, contrary to the Andes and Mesoamerica–where Spanish interacted with Amerindian languages–the Caribbean became a cultural center in which the dominance of colonial languages gave rise to French and English Creole.

Thus, if Bahia, in northeast Brazil, contributes to the Caribbean as a cultural center, it differs significantly from Manaus and Belem, also part of Brazil's North and Northeast. While there are connections between the three centers because of Portuguese colonial possession, the Portuguese language, and, later on, the ideology of the nation-state, it is also true that these centers have been characterized by the economic relations established during the formation and transformation of the modern or colonial world. The possibility of identifying these centers, today, is not the consequence of the essentializing forces of Amazonía, the Caribbean, or the national spirit that contributed to the distinguishing of Brazil from Bolivia. Amazonía's cultural centers connect transnationally: Brazil, Bolivia, Perú, Venezuela, and Colombia.

In summary, *Literary Cultures of Latin America* has all the elements to move the reader away from the national framework in which literary histories have been written in the past. Furthermore, since the national model of language and literature was built on the image of European nations as disseminated through their languages and literatures, the colonized areas were inevitably seen as deficient when they came to write their own literary histories. Projects such as this and the others in progress (such as the South Asia project, coordinated by Sheldon Pollock at the University of Chicago) are truly departures in "rethinking" at once literature, history, and comparative studies. The most compelling aspect of these projects is, in my view, the spatialization of history (considering the borderlands of the modern colonial world) and the interaction between European (colonial) and indigenous American, African, and Asian languages. While early comparative literary studies were founded on the comparison between the languages and literatures of emerging European nations, the comparative work in these projects points toward a wider sphere of linguistic and semiotic practices that can no longer ignore the borderlands of colonial difference. It may also free literary studies from a presumed universality of linguistic codes and human communication. Instead of starting from some kind of abstract universals and then moving to their concretization in history, the process is here being inverted. In this transformation, the "literary text" is no longer the center, as concretization of either a national consciousness or a universal grammar. Beyond the colonial model and beyond the universal model of the sciences, what is left for the future is the search for a critical cosmopolitanism, not the cosmopolitanism promoted by economic and technological globalization, but the cosmopolitanism of the critical turn in the humanities, to which this project contributes. It hopes to maintain the critical (epistemic, ethical, political) role of the humanities at the moment in which knowledge tends more and more to be confused with expertise and with information, rather than with thinking. It is, in the final analysis, the future of the humanities–rather than the future of literature–that is at stake.

Works Cited

Adorno, Rolena. 1982. *Guaman Poma de Ayala: Writing and Resistance in Colonial Peru.* Austin: University of Texas Press.

Appadurai, Arjun. 2000. "Anxieties of Tradition in the Era of Globalization." *Time in the Making and Possible Futures.* Ed. Cándido Méndez and Enrique Rodríguez Larreta. Rio de Janeiro: UNESCO-ISSC-EDUCAM. 29–67.

Boone, Elizabeth Hill. 2000. *Stories in Red and Black: Pictorial Histories of the Aztecs and Mixtecs.* Austin: University of Texas Press.

Boone, Elizabeth Hill, and Walter D. Mignolo, eds. 1994. *Writing Without Words: Alternative Literacies in Mesoamerica and the Andes.* Durham: Duke University Press.

Braudel, Fernand. 1981–1984. *Civilization and Capitalism, 15th–18th Century.* Trans. Sian Reynolds. 3 vols. New York: Harper and Row.

Campuzano, Luisa. 2001. "Introduction." Vol. I. *Configurations of Literary Culture. Comparative History of Latin American Literary Cultures.* Ed. Mario J. Valdés and Djelal Kadir. New York: Oxford University Press.

Edmonson, Munro S., ed. 1985. "Literatures." *Supplement to the Handbook of Middle American Indians.* Austin: University of Texas Press.

Hulme, Peter. 1986. *Colonial Encounters: Europe and the Native Caribbean, 1492–1797.* London: Methuen.

Hutcheon, Linda. 2002. "Rethinking the National Model." *Rethinking Literary History: A Dialogue on Theory.* Ed. Linda Hutcheon and Mario J. Valdés. New York: Oxford University Press. 3–49.

Hutcheon, Linda, and Mario J. Valdés. 2002. "Preface: Theorizing Literary History in Dialogue." *Rethinking Literary History: A Dialogue on Theory.* Ed. Linda Hutcheon and Mario J. Valdés. New York: Oxford University Press. ix–xiii.

Jakobson, Roman. 1966. [1921]. "Du réalisme artistique." *Théorie de la littérature.* Ed. T. Todorov. Paris: Seuil. 98–108.

Marini, Mauro, and Márgara Millán, eds. 1994. *La teoría social latinoamericana. Los orígenes.* Vol. 1. Mexico City: Ediciones del Caballito.

Mignolo, Walter D. 1995. *The Darker Side of the Renaissance: Literacy, Territoriality and Colonization.* Ann Arbor: University of Michigan Press.

——. 2000. *Local Histories/Global Designs: Coloniality, Subaltern Knowledge and Border Thinking.* Princeton: Princeton University Press.

——. 2001. "Rethinking the Colonial Model." *Rethinking Literary History: A Forum on the Problematics, Old and New.* Ed. Linda Hutcheon and Mario J. Valdés. New York: Oxford University Press. 155–193.

Pizarro, Ana, ed. 1993–1995. *América Latina. Palavra, Literatura e Cultura.* 3 vols. Sao Paulo: Memorial de América Latina.

Pollock, Sheldon (2003). "Introduction." *Literary Cultures in History: Reconstructions from South Asia.* Berkeley: University of California Press.

Romero Pittari, Salvador. 1997. *La recepción académica de la sociología en Bolivia.* La Paz: Facultad de Ciencias Sociales.

Sommer, Doris. 1991. *Foundational Fictions: The National Romances in Latin America.* Berkeley: University of California Press.

Valdés, Mario J. 2002. "Rethinking the History of Literary History." *Rethinking Literary History: A Dialogue on Theory.* Ed. Linda Hutcheon and Mario J. Valdés. New York: Oxford University Press. 63–115.

Valdés, Mario J., and Linda Hutcheon. 1994. "Rethinking Literary History–Comparatively." *American Council of Learned Societies,* ACLS Occasional Paper. No. 27.

Welleck, René. 1963. "Literary Theory, Criticism and History." *Concepts and Criticism.* New Haven: Yale University Press. 1–20.

White, Hayden. 1978. *Tropics of Discourse.* Baltimore: Johns Hopkins University Press.

Literary Cultures of
Latin America

A Comparative History

PART ONE

CULTURAL INSTITUTIONS
INTRODUCTION

Lisa Block de Behar and Tania Franco Carvalhal

This part of Volume II of *Literary Cultures of Latin America* explores the role of cultural institutions in the constitution, preservation, and reproduction of the forms of literary culture in Latin America. Considering that institutional processes can be responsible for social exclusion and for the formation of canons, we have endeavored to appraise their repercussions and effects on the forming of literary systems. Thus, the institutional structure becomes a significant dimension for the analysis of cultural phenomena and practices. Although our aim is not to be exhaustive, we consider certain questions that are specific to the Latin American cultural context and are, therefore, representative of the cultural variety characterizing the continent, a variety often synthesized in the now commonplace expressions *cultural pluralism* and *cultural diversity*. By pointing out the differences that coexist together within the continent, we will stress the plural nature of literary culture in Latin America. The essays that compose this section are grouped into four main themes: "Books and Readers in Latin America," "Cultural Institutions," "Cultural Journalism," and "Translation as Cultural Institution"–understood as an essential element of cultural mediation.

The first section of Part I is composed of three essays. Backed by extensive research, Luigi Avonto's text "Books, Myths, and the Reading Public in Spanish America during the Sixteenth Century" deals with the books of fiction and other writings that were read by the European conquerors, thus linking the literary forms of fantasy to the "unconscious instigating stimuli of the actions" they carried out. According to Luigi Avonto, the Conquest of America included, among other cultural transfers, the overseas re-emergence of several frontiers disputed for so many centuries by Christians and Muslims in the Iberian peninsula, such as the most auspicious space for evangelization to be promoted–as a modern version of the Crusades–even if the conquerors' minds were more medieval than modern. Without doubt, their readings of chivalric romances also exerted an enormous influence on their sense of adventure: Once more, fiction became history. Luigi Avonto traces information about the reading and books of the men who traveled to America, especially during the first years of the Conquest, finding several factors that influenced the conquerors' thought and behavior and that inspired their actions and explorations: the genre of the chronicles (which were often likely to include narratives of unrestrained fantasy); and their preference for chivalric romances that, once published, had a wide circulation in several vernacular languages. Books in general had a great impact on the societies in which the reverence and prestige of the written word were very strong, because books were the monopoly of select minorities, particularly

books that (during the sixteenth century) revived the medieval European ideal of a universal monarchy. All conquerors shared a belief in the marvelous (and their popular literature fed them with what was necessary to keep such faith). The exploration of unknown territories, which corresponded neither to known data nor to geographic schema, contributed to the enthusiastic acceptance of and interest in the search for an Earthly Paradise, the Kingdom of Prester John, the City of the Caesars, the dwelling of the Amazons, and so on. Evidence of the influence that these readings had on those who traveled to the New World has been assessed and vehemently condemned because of the negative consequences that some cultured Spanish critics attributed to them. José Mindlin, the renowned Brazilian book collector, offers an informative article about "The Book in Brazil: Libraries and Presses," in which he discusses the disparity between the early emergence of the printing press in Spanish America and its rather late introduction to Brazil–in 1808, when the Portuguese court moved from Lisbon to the colony, fleeing the Napoleonic invasion of the Peninsula. Illustrated by photographs from his private collection, Mindlin's article examines the history of the book from the time of the arrival of the Jesuits in 1549. We can thus see the valuable contribution of this and other religious orders, such as that of the Benedictines and the Franciscans, to the cultural development of early Brazil. Also discussed are the establishment of the first libraries, the opening of typesetting shops, and the role played by French editors who transformed the cultural outlook of the country and helped to ensure the dynamism of its incipient cultural development.

Brazilian publishing came of age in the middle of the modernist movement, in the aftermath of 1922. It is in this context that Augusto de Campos, on contemplating the edition of the *Primeiro caderno do alumno de poesia* [*First Notebook of the Poetry Student*] by Oswald de Andrade (1927), will state that "[it] is possibly the most beautiful book of our Modernist poetry. It is also the most beautiful coherent set of poems, in its risk-taking and boldness in language, as much as in the book's formal and material conception."

According to Augusto de Campos, this edition is related to "a concept of reformulating the visual language of the book." Thus, he defines it as a "free book, which would begin to be written collectively in our century." Going even further in his essay, de Campos links Oswald and Tarsila's books to other graphic, plastic, and musical ideas that characterized the century. Opening toward the future, Oswald's free book illuminates the continuity of the search and consolidation process, which characterizes the history of the book in Brazil and, by extension, in Latin America.

The second section of Part I deals with Latin American cultural institutions analyzed as central elements for the development and formation of the cultural outlook of the region. In "Cultural Institutions in Latin America," Alfons Knauth offers a broad survey of a number of institutional manifestations within the Spanish context of Latin America. He gives an extensive but succinct view of the institutional landscape of the continent, including schools, universities, academies and anti-academies, societies, social gatherings, workshops, parties and commemorations, libraries, museums, and prizes—all of which contributed to forming the collective imaginary of Latin American societies, especially in relation to literature. Knauth analyzes the nature of these institutions, their historical development and changes throughout the four periods defined by the author as pre-Colonial, Colonial, neo-Colonial, and post-Colonial. After enumerating and describing the pre-Colonial antecedents, Knauth suggests that European penetration implied a translation or transplantation process of European cultural institutions to America, which gave rise to a "relative advance of the acculturation process in the school system." Universities were frequently plurilingual during the Colonial period; from their earliest stages, universities contributed to developing cultural syncretism (also enhanced by Colonial religious celebrations), which has specific Latin American features and which today leans toward regional and supranational perspectives. Throughout the twentieth century, such syncretic processes gave rise to indigenous and Afro-American academies and societies. Less frequently, they influenced social gatherings in bookstores and coffee shops, which became very popular during the second half of the nineteenth century and the first of the twentieth. In other cases this syncretism was constantly renewed by means of modern literary workshops, which found their antecedents in the rhetorical exercises of imitation of classical models practiced in Colonial colleges, but which also contributed to the popularization of culture and literature. Popular celebrations, such as the carnival, also became institutions where popular and high culture (including literature) authentically converged. Libraries and museums were also transplanted European institutions; the paradox is that the same zeal that led to the destruction of indigenous writing also transplanted the book culture to Latin America (and thus created libraries), whereas museums offer singular examples of cultural syncretism and have moved all the Americas toward the preservation of the past for the future.

Luiz Roberto Cairo's essay "Cultural Institutions and Intellectual Life in Brazil" studies the role of the Jesuits from their arrival during the period of cultural "transference" up to the eighteenth century. He also outlines the emergence, in the nineteenth century, of significant institutions such as the Brazilian Historic and Geographical Institute and the Brazilian Academy of Letters in Rio de Janeiro; the Literary Parthenon Society in Porto Alegre; the Recife School in Pernambuco; the Student's Phoenix, the Popular School, and the French Academy in Ceará; and finally the first University Faculties of Letters, which were introduced during the 1930s. This essay thereby explores the significant role played by the cultural and educational associations and institutions in Brazilian literary culture.

In order to understand Brazilian cultural development, it is important to analyze the links with Portugal from the beginnings of colonization. João Adolfo Hansen's essay "Cultural Models of Representation in Seventeenth-Century Brazil" explores the relationships with the metropolis and the Brazilian appropriation of European cultural elements. The essay helps not only to understand Luso-Brazilian colonial remains, the cultural models which structured the mental universe of Colonial Brazil, but also to appreciate the theological and political categories that guided the qualitative notion of temporality, the rhetorical-poetic instruments that allowed the exploitation of the distortions in Colonial artistic representations, and the contemporary use-values of the notion of "Baroque." Following this foundational text on cultural practices during the Colonial period, the essay by Maria de Lourdes Parreiras Horta, "Museums in Latin America," articulates Brazilian and Spanish-American contexts for the establishment of museums and provides an extensive view of this fundamental institution in the cultural development of the continent. The author starts from European models that were transplanted in American lands and became the distanced and discriminatory look at American culture, flora, and fauna that—under the shield of science—prevailed as Eurocentric exotica during the nineteenth century, known as the era of spectacle. The author describes the creation of the first private collections within the context of what had become the "cultural interpenetration" of two worlds and recognizes the irrecoverable loss of historical artifacts through ignorance and indifference. Her study emphasizes the role the museum plays in the contemporary formation of cultural identity.

If, together with Pierre Bourdieu, we consider that apart from museums, schools, and universities are also "instances of consecration," Célio da Cunha's essay "Education in Brazil: Omissions, Advances, and Future Perspectives" is a necessary complement to the present picture. The essay deals with educational policies and pedagogical ideas in Brazil, from the early Jesuits up to the present, and explores the educational renewal introduced in the country by João VI, with the establishment of the Military Academy, the Public Library, the National Museum, and the Botanical Gardens, as well as regular lectures on surgery and anatomy, which were the bases for the future development of higher medical education as well as the renewal movement of the 1920s at the New School.

The issue of censorship is the subject of Cíntia Schwantes and Rildo Cosson's essay, which traces the country's situation during the 1970s and brings to light several aspects, including the political situation—the socioeconomic and cultural transformations that opened the way to modernity—and the contemporary consolidation of the cultural industry, following the laws of the free market. Censorship has had a strong impact on the direction of the Brazilian literary system not only because of the works and authors banned, but also—and above all—because of the detrimental effects of self-censorship that eliminates artistic freedom. This second section concludes with a seminal article on the related issue of State sponsorship and control of publishing in Brazil by Fábio Lucas.

The section on cultural journalism opens with the text by Aníbal González-Pérez, which gives a much needed general overview of cultural journalism in Spanish America. The importance and far-reaching effects of cultural journalism cannot be overestimated. In a continent where more than 60 percent of the population is economically limited, the access to books has always been seriously constrained, and if it were not for cultural journalism, there would not be a Latin American literary culture. Dating from the mid-nineteenth century to the present, the cultural imaginary of Latin America has been to a very large extent the work of cultural journalism.

The next essay, written by Luiz Roberto Cairo, "Criticism and Literature in Brazilian Periodicals of the Romantic Period," assesses a form of literary journalism that has been characteristic of Latin America and that has been present since the early Romantic period. The author studies the relationship between criticism and literature in the period's newspapers, emphasizing the biographical and sociological features that prevailed over literary elements, as well as the construction of a sense of nationality. He concentrates on the role played by Minerva Brasiliense in the creation of the journal of the "Biblioteca Brasílica" and several periodicals. For the author there is an organic relationship between journalism and literature, which is the result of the symbiosis of writers who have simultaneously played the role of literary men and journalists, in journals and newspapers; they have thus supplemented the limited book circulation of a developing society. Euclides da Cunha's novel, *Os Sertões*, is a good example of the work of a journalist who acquires literary stature. The essay written by Jorge Coli analyzes this work in order to explore both da Cunha's observation skills—which came from his job as a reporter—and the rhetorical and poetic devices he employed. From this strange symbiosis between journalism and literature developed a very particular style that brings together lyricism and precision. In the essays of this section, the figure of Euclides da Cunha becomes the synthesis of the intellectual who united a sense of commitment with a creative output, a process that allowed him to write his own version of reality.

In "Literary Journalism in Brazil during the First Half of the Twentieth Century," Ivia Alves completes the picture outlined by the discussions on Romero, Araripe, and Verissimo, and explores the modifications undergone by Brazilian critical thought as it appeared in the pages of the newspapers. Thus, if during the 1920s and 1930s the emphasis fell on a critical attitude, during the following years there was a preference for theoretical analyses centered on the use of language and on the text itself. In "Literary Periodicals of the Sixties: Proposals for Re-reading," Luz Rodríguez-Carranza offers a subtle and agile analysis of the periodicals of that decade. She proposes a second reading of the literary periodicals that were contemporary with the Latin American literary boom. She suggests that such periodicals helped to promote (by exalting "the new") and canonize (by recurrently mentioning a not very large group of authors, titles, critics, journals, and "value judgments") the boom authors, many of whom continue to be appreciated by the reading public in general. In the same way, Rodríguez-Carranza notices that later periodicals were established before the previous ones had satisfactorily overcome the categorizations and selections promoted by the same group of people (using notions of what is modern and cosmopolitan as criteria to indicate literary quality, the recurrent concern for certain subjects or names, the hierarchical approval of certain publications and the scorn for others). Among those people, there are still many living authors and critics who tend to put forward a condemnation that—while it is true that it showed interest in studying such periodicals as "agents of consecration"—also evaluate them in absolute terms of value and no value at all. In the last instance such binaries reflect their political positions or their lining up behind editors who represent a counter-current: Rodríguez Monegal, Ángel Rama, and Fernández Retamar, for example. For

Rodríguez-Carranza, such interpretations of Latin American literary culture create anew a "master narrative" to substitute for that of the 1960s (although not very different from it). This still dominant dualism is unsatisfactory, because it does not respect the reality of far greater nuance and complexity in Latin American literature. She considers that a new reading of such periodicals–neither isolated from the body of local publications that constitute the "corpus" nor outside the period's framework and the place in which they were written (thus considered as documents)–will help to understand the fact that the 1960s journals are not as univocal as is usually believed: The editorials do not always reflect the plurality of the contents, for instance, some journals with a clear political line can, in fact, in the contents differ much in the opinions expressed, and what seems to be a hegemonic discourse may signify something very different, according to who is enunciating it, the place in which it occurs, and the immediate aims of the authors. Even the reappearance of the same critics and writers in different kinds of periodicals becomes relative once the function of the texts is analyzed. Thus, apparently continental agendas acquire different meanings in different contexts or else are reappropriated by local conflicting sectors in different places. What is purportedly universal would then become much more local than expected; in fact, a continental dialogue among periodicals can be an "indirect transposition of internal debates of the editors of each" and the debates themselves can be, above all, local arguments, counter-arguments, and publications, which are now forgotten, rarely mentioned, left out in the original articles, and in later revisions. Maria Lucia Camargo's "Criticism and Cultural Journalism in Contemporary Brazil" complements the studies dealing with contemporary Brazilian criticism and literature. Taking as its point of departure the 1960s, her study parallels that of Luz Rodríguez-Carranza in its analysis of the variety of cultural and literary journals of the period. She concentrates on the cultural supplements of the big newspapers, the literary and cultural journals, and the so-called *small press* publications that arose as a form of resistance against censorship and the dictatorial political system. The examination of this rich material leads to a critical reading of today's cultural journalism in the most influential newspapers of the country.

The fourth section, "Translation as Cultural Institution," includes two texts: "Translation as a Literary Institution" by László Scholz and "The Development of a Translation Paideuma and Poetics in Brazil: The Campos Brothers" by Else Ribeiro Pires Vieira. Considering (and emphasizing) the influence of translation upon the configuration of the cultural and literary, Scholz studies the significance of a phenomenon that has become central to Latin American literature. Related both to aesthetic principles and to the "dynamics of the literary institution" in particular, translation activities and production are much more important than in other literary traditions and other languages. According to Scholz, translation is an ever-present activity throughout the history of the continent. Thus, by offering some examples taken from Colonial times, others from relatively recent periods, and some more from the present, he studies the most outstanding writers of the region to whom has been committed the task of translating, an activity that—because of the extraordinary nature of its performers—has given rise to many literary forms. According to Scholz, if a narrow mimetic criterion is rejected in analysis of these translations, the texts become valuable sources for the study of the aesthetic and ideological outlooks of the diverse periods and for the understanding of the parameters that define a period's canon. According to him it is necessary to pose strict critical questions—with sound theoretical foundations—in order to grasp the role of such a determining literary institution and the kind of central questioning necessary for understanding Latin America. Among other considerations, he explores the development of the discipline through the work of El Inca Garcilaso de la Vega and Guamán Poma de Ayala in the sixteenth century; of Andrés Bello at the start of the nineteenth; of the vast French influence in the late nineteenth century, an influence that served to impose French values and interests by means of indirect translations via Paris; Arguedas's "narrative transculturation of the Andean universe"; and the most recent role of translations from the English language, as well as examples of literary intralinguistic translation. He acknowledges that serious studies on translation are scarce and that it is necessary to formulate a systematic theory of translation that includes the monumental works and reflections of Alfonso Reyes, Octavio Paz, Jorge Luis Borges, and Julio Cortázar.

Else Vieira makes reference to the influential work of translation and theorization carried out since the 1950s by Augusto and Haroldo de Campos and Decio Pignatari, who—from the start of the poetical Concretist movement—consolidated the foundations of a Brazilian poetics, which has universalized the plurality of its own aesthetic criteria. Haroldo's translations shake the foundations of shared references that are not widely known in the Portuguese-speaking world. His language not only has a scholarly referent, but offers a substantial linguistic and literary transformation by means of the "transorchestrations" of the Bible, the "transhelenization" of the Homeric poems, the "transilluminations" of Dante's cantos, the "transluciferations" of Goethe's Faust, up to the visualisations of Mallarmé's verses, Pound's cantos, the poetry of Marina Tsvetaieva or Maiakovsky, or the work of Octavio Paz. In its turn, the work of Augusto de Campos brings to the Portuguese language the work of controversial, marginalized authors, thus bringing to the surface half-forgotten issues of a literary history that acquires a new dimension in the light of Augusto's approach. In both cases the Campos brothers make use of new cybernetic techniques, demanding an "iconogrammical" aesthetic of their own, which brings together the artistic and the theoretical.

Constructing an autonomous theoretical framework for translation within a wider cultural space constitutes a singularity of Latin America's cultural and literary tradition, as can be seen in the significant figures of Jorge Luis Borges and Octavio Paz, who, according to Else Vieira, renewed the most important literary works of the continent—works that are sustained by a critical background, which in turn has played an important role in defining twentieth-century world literature. Thanks to the Campos brothers, translating literary texts becomes a process of recreation or parallel creation—a transcreation—according to the term they have coined to describe the multilateral transformation and absorption of texts that belong to different cultures. The transcreation process implies a rewriting that interweaves, according to Haroldo de Campos, the semantization with the corporeality of signs; it penetrates into the organization of the works, establishing morphological and grammatical correspondences that reveal the sound by means of a "hyperfidelity" contrary to the restrictions of literalism. According to these poet-translators, the task of translation is to assert the cultural identity and the

historical sense of belonging of the translator within a tradition that comes across in the translated text, establishing a dialogue between languages and cultures by means of texts that take part in the reconfiguration of literary tradition and thus build an alternative tradition.

To conclude, it is important to reconsider the issue of the transfer of institutions from the centers of Europe and the United States to Latin America as an oscillation that overflows linguistic limits, as a transit phenomenon that aims at a shared (id)entity. To consider translation from a strictly linguistic perspective limits the subject; it should be approached as an act of transference that goes far beyond merely translating a text from one language into another; instead, it translates major cultural events in which texts are inscribed. Translation is in fact a textual and verbal action that involves the displacement of references and institutions, a transaction that establishes the continent's creation, determines its territories, and, at the same time, travels across borders, instituting spaces of tolerance, which permeate reciprocal forms of curiosity between cultures that are in touch. Just as we have considered the origin of human institutions in relation to the origin of languages, it would be legitimate to study it in relation to translation. In this sense, translating texts that belong to Northern languages constitutes the most complete metaphor of that transference. It is in fact a metaphor of itself—a double metaphor—because it is "transport," "transference," as well as tropisms, which lead to the adventures of the imagination in which foreign cultures interplay, recreated them by means of these exchanges. When Haroldo de Campos translates texts from Hebrew, Aramaic, or Greek into Portuguese, he transforms Portuguese, making it Hebrew- or Homer-like. At the same time the original language does not remain unchanged: The signals of each new reading modify the writing of origin. The transference does not move in a single direction anymore: It moves in the multiple directions of circulation. Translation is thus a metaphor of the models built by those institutions that, once they are transferred to America, did not remain the same. We must stress that transference symbolized by the imposition of a culture also implied a reflux, a kind of return, a modification carried out—because of a bilateral influence—both in the receiving culture and in the producing culture.

From the moment of the establishment of ministries of culture and education, libraries, and museums under a national, ecclesiastical, municipal, or university jurisdiction, the choice and gathering of books and works of art, as well as the patronage that sponsored or limited them—together with the endowments, foundations, academies, competitions, grants and prizes, publishing houses, and the specialized newspaper supplements—the literary culture of Latin America has been institutionalized. These institutions have collectively set the conditions of the creation of art and literature, but they have also given rise to focused forms of resistance in the form of a rebelling counter-power. There are therefore institutional structures that concentrate on the production, transmission, divulgation, and imposition of selected knowledge. From the Empire to the Colony, the geopolitical reason of conquest is inclined toward a universality that questions the conflict between the past and the present, between continuity and rupture, between unity and diversity, between the known and strange. Institutionalization endeavors to solve those confrontations in time and space, by means of a juridical body that normalizes dissidence by attempting to make it disappear, attenuates difference through a policy that foresees and organizes knowledge, creation, and culture. Society cannot dispense with the institutional strategies–strategies that strengthen conventions that favor or affect invention. Excesses of and impediments to a proposal that has been debated for a long time seem to be inevitable–the impossibility of eluding the categorization even when attempting to transgress it. The difference that affects the models and their modes of expansion becomes obviously aporetic, an application with no way out but its own transformation.

Translation by Nair María Anaya Ferreira

CHAPTER 1

BOOKS, MYTHS, AND THE READING PUBLIC IN SPANISH AMERICA DURING THE SIXTEENTH CENTURY

Luigi Avonto

The principal aim of this section is to draw the attention of those interested in the cultural aspect of the initial phase of the Europeanization of the New World to works of popular fiction that inspired the imagination of the conquistadores and their descendants in Spanish America during the sixteenth century. As Irving A. Leonard has rightly emphasized in some of his important and illuminating work on books and the reading public during the Spanish Conquest and Colonial period in Spanish America (*Romances of Chivalry, Books of the Brave, Baroque Times in Old Mexico*), various books published by creative individuals "played a silent, but not wholly passive part" (1964, vii) in the development of events in the New World; their influence is still an unwritten chapter in the history of the Europeanization of the American continent.

Guillermo Céspedes del Castillo (b. 1920) has stressed that the overseas frontier that the conquistador sailed toward in the sixteenth century was *new* for various fundamental reasons. Primarily he was dealing with a physical world very different from that of Mediterranean Europe. While the latter was relatively small and familiar, the geographical area of America was immense and unknown (38). However, it was the inhabitants that made it truly new: men who were evidently human beings but with completely different concepts of and approaches to life. Their physical and human otherness, when compared with the world of the Spanish conquistador, was what characterized this new world, conferring on it the most extraordinary novelty. All these facts are worth taking into account in the search for a more precise understanding of the conquistadores' considerable enthusiasm for works of fiction, since together they give credence to a certain vision of reality, notably a medieval sense of the marvelous that was highly prized in these texts.

Before focusing on the books favored by the conquistadores, I must point out that while, during the first phase of the Conquest, the taste for reading imaginative works such as chivalric romances clearly predominated among those who voyaged to the Indies, during the second phase (that of the Kingdoms of the Indies) the inclination for such writings, though still strong, had begun to diminish slowly in favor of two tendencies that indicated the gradual replacement of the

cultural legacy of the Middle Ages with an increasingly strong affiliation with new ideals and values. In other words, there was a greater preference for certain literary works of a more humanistic bent that were perhaps initially accepted as works that still bore some relation to the traditional genre of chivalry (for example, the Spanish translations of works by Lodovico Ariosto, Prietro Bembo and Torquato Tasso, plus *Il Cortegiano* of Baldassare Castiglione). At the same time there was a growing interest in spiritually orientated literature inspired by the humanist Renaissance of patently Erasmian character. This latter has been studied by Marcel Bataillon in his erudite works on Erasmus and the New World (1932; 1986). However, such themes transcend the limits of the current study, since our focus here is principally on sixteenth-century literary works, notably tales of chivalry that were capable of stimulating a longing for adventure in men who traveled to the other side of the ocean during the period of the Conquest.

It is now recognized that the popularity of these novels in sixteenth-century Spain was a revival, or perhaps more of a continuation, of the medieval passion for tales of knight errantry. In fact, some of the same fantastic and idealizing elements glorified in such stories could be found in popular Spanish romances that still fascinated the less educated during the Conquest period (see ch. 1 of Menéndez Pidal). The success of this newest version of the narrative genre (whose prestige, based on authenticity, was derived from the use of historical facts) is clear; it had also become extremely popular among the aristocratic levels of Peninsular society. Moreover, with the gradual movement southward toward the Moslem frontier, where the struggles between Christians and Moors provided so much thematic material for artistic expression, prose chronicles assumed an increasingly descriptive character; from this emerged a poetic and chivalric invention that proceeded to indissolubly fuse historical truth with fiction (see chs. 8–10 of Ticknor). The fertile territory from which later tales of chivalry, written between the end of the fifteenth and the first half of the sixteenth century, took their inspiration permitted this genre to present itself with the same prestige based on authenticity that was attributed to the chronicles. The multiplying effect of the printing press also enabled a broader (and considerably more influential) circulation in society than that achieved by manuscript texts that until then had only been read by the more powerful social strata.

If it is undeniable that the printing press initiated the broader circulation of books among increasingly wide sectors of the public, then it is also clear that the multiplication of the printed text did not immediately change the traditional belief that a book was an infallible source of knowledge and an irrefutable verification of the truth. When we consider that popular works, such as the romances of knight errantry, not only appeared at the moment in which the printing press began its work of circulation, but also were presented in the vernacular (ancient manuscripts and works of theological or speculative content were almost always written in Latin and their reading continued to be the privilege of erudite churchmen and aristocrats), the reasons for the growing popularity of these fictional works and their overwhelming success on different social levels are obvious. Leonard has pointed out that "the apparent historicity of these tales, together with the enormous expansion of the physical horizons brought about by the recent discoveries in Africa and the New World, gave plausibility to the wildest notions with which writers might season their stories. The vast possibilities that the earthly globe thus seemed to offer stirred the fevered imagination of readers to a high pitch of excitement and moved the more adventurous to seek out the mysterious wonders and the untold treasure with which the unknown lands were endowed so authoritatively" (1964, 19).

Despite its fundamentally popular character, this frivolous fiction rapidly made headway among readers of the educated and aristocratic classes. Suffice it to note, among many possible examples, those of Don Fernando Colón (1488–1539), son of the admiral, whose splendid library housed many of the chivalric romances most in vogue in his time (Thacher 422–50) and the even more revealing example of the Emperor Charles V, whose passionate devotion to such books is well known. It is said the monarch's enthusiasm for the adventures of *Belíanis de Grecia* occasioned the author of this work to write a sequel (Thomas 149) and that, when the Emperor abdicated the throne and retired to the monastery of Yuste, he took with him various books of knight errantry for his personal entertainment (Stirling 316–17). The Emperor's liking for books of chivalric romance suggests a not entirely fortuitous relationship between the imperial expansion of Spain and contemporary works of fiction.

The great discoveries realized in America during Charles's reign gave rise to the conviction among his contemporaries that the Emperor fully incarnated the imperial idea. Thanks to the conquistadores as emissaries of Charles V, Europe had discovered a new world destined to stimulate more interest than that stirred by Portuguese activity in the East Indies during the first years of the sixteenth century. The possessor of the imperial title was not the Portuguese but the Spanish monarch, a fact that had contributed to the widespread belief that Spanish imperial expansion beyond Europe enjoyed a special divine dispensation that implied a global mandate. The image of the empire of Charles V as a dynamic entity in continuous expansion was also supported by a particularly persuasive symbolic iconography whose point of greatest strength lay in the imperial heraldic emblem. Circulating in the European culture of the 1500s was an interpretation of the Hapsburg *Plus Ultra* that tended to accord more privilege to its geopolitical than its moral connotation. This limiting of the significance of the imperial emblem probably derived from Charles's failure to contain the Moslem advance and reestablish a solid religious unity within the confines of the Empire—in contrast with the successes achieved in America. The philo-imperial intellectuals tended to interpret the value of *Plus Ultra* almost exclusively in the context of Hapsburg expansionism toward the distant and unknown lands beyond the ocean. It is interesting to note some important antecedents to this universalist approach of the imperial Hapsburg myth and in particular the "transoceanic" aspect: These include the interpretation of the reconquest of Granada as heralding the final triumph over Islam; the foreign policy of Ferdinand the Catholic with special reference to Italy, North Africa, and the Mediterranean; and, in the Spanish expansion in the new American lands, the beginning of the evangelization of the Indians, understood as the renovation of the crusade against the infidel. These antecedents had already begun to be manifest in the Spain of the Catholic Kings in the last years of Ferdinand's reign, and coincided exactly with the period in which *Amadís de Gaula* (1508) and *Las Sergas de Esplandián* (1510) first appeared. We need only recall in this respect the frequency with which contemporary humanists, such as the Italian Peter Martyr of Anghiera (1457–1526), resident at the court of the Catholic Kings, Antonio de Nebrija (1444?–1522), and the chronicler Andrés Bernáldez (d. 1513), all insisted in their writings precisely on those aspects seen as among the more "universalist" in Fernando's policy (Avonto 1995, 201; Ballesteros Beretta 68). As we will see later, it is not happenstance that these are explicit references in *Las Sergas de Esplandián* to the new regions situated "on the right hand of the Indies" (539) inhabited by the pagan queen of the Amazons, or in the long narrative that follows concerning the tremendous battle that Esplandián, his father Amadís, and other Christian knights undertook against the Turks and their Amazon allies in defense of the Emperor of Constantinople and those Christians under siege by the infidels (540–46). Indeed the principal heroes that join battle under the imperial standard already appear in a light similar to that which supporters of the subsequent imperial Hapsburg myth would envelop the conquistadores who were presented as emissaries of the Emperor. In the Spain of the Catholic Kings, there existed an important tradition that could support such an imperial dream and exercise its suggestive force on the authors of chivalric romances such as *Amadís* and *Las Sergas de Esplandián*.

Proceeding to the central theme of this section, we must now try to answer a question that has considerable relevance: Did the conquistadores read chivalric romances? If we note the purported frivolity and negative influence on contemporary readers that was attributed to these fictional works by moralists of the period, an affirmative reply might appear irrelevant. Nevertheless, various scholars have frequently suggested that there was a connection between these narratives and the conquistadores; yet there have been few up to now, with the notable exception of Irving A. Leonard in some works previously cited, who have dedicated themselves to elucidating this specific problem that is so intimately related to the fascinating and subtle interactions that frequently exist between literature and human action. It is generally admitted that books of chivalry had an influence on the heroic nature of the Conquest, given the wide circulation of these works, both spoken and written, among the conquistadores (for example, Rojas III, 26, 103; Madariaga 233–41; Gayangos), but any proof to support such assertions is left implicitly to the intuition of the reader interested in the subject, with no precise data that might dissipate eventual doubt. There is, as we shall see, some clear and conclusive evidence.

Bernal Díaz del Castillo (1492–1584), the chronicler and conquistador, described an incident in 1519 when Hernán Cortés (1485–1547) was sailing along the Mexican coast toward San Juan de Ulúa. Alonso Hernández Puertocarrero, one of the companions who already knew that the terrain possessed mountains and rivers, approached his leader and, after quoting a verse from an old ballad, said: "And I say to you: You are looking on rich lands. May you know how to govern them well!" (83). Cortés, who had understood well the reason for the exhortation, replied: "May God give us the same good fortune in fighting, as he gave to the paladin Roland. For the rest, with you, sir, and these other gentlemen as my captains, I shall know how to acquit myself" (83). To confirm the celebrated conquistador's familiarity with the chivalric literature in vogue at the time, a researcher in the nineteenth century recounts that, along with Cortés's twelve captains, there was a group of *Doce Pares* who made solemn vows to fight like knights errant "to defend the Holy Catholic Faith, to right wrongs, and to aid Spaniards and friendly natives" (Leonard 1964, 42).

An analogous appearance of these "Twelve Pairs" from chivalric fiction occurred in 1536 during the expedition of Pedro de Mendoza to the River Plate. One of the expeditionaries, who had been sentenced to death for insubordination, protested to his superiors, pointing out that "One day what God wishes will come to pass and the *doce pares* will reign again" (Rojas I, 280). These words clearly indicate the speaker's knowledge of some book of chivalric romance from the Carolingian cycle, for example the *Historia del emperador Carlomagno y de los doce pares de Francia* [History of the Emperor Charlemagne and the Twelve Pairs of France], published a few years earlier in 1525. Even Bartolomé de las Casas (1474–1566), in his enthusiasm to obtain volunteers to realize his plan of peaceful colonization and evangelization on the Coast of Paria in 1519–1520 (Giménez Fernández 831; Avonto 1981, 18–37) petitioned the King to grant his followers the title of *Caballeros de Espuelas Doradas* [Knights of the Golden Spurs], confident that it would be enormously attractive to "the New World adventurers [who] clearly read [the romances of chivalry] with passionate enthusiasm" (Leonard 1964, 67).

Explicit reference to the irresistible attraction that the fables of these books held for those who crossed to the New World is also found in the work of Gonzalo Fernández de Oviedo (1478–1557), conquistador and celebrated chronicler of the Indies. The evidence offered by his *Historia general y natural de las Indias* [1535, 1537; General and Natural History of the Indies] is extremely important, given that not only did he know the chivalric literature extremely well but he also made his writing debut in 1519 with the publication of his own chivalric romance entitled *Claribalte*. In the preface to Book XVIII of his *Historia de las Indias,* his wide experience in the Indies and his awareness of advancing age persuaded him to set the true "histories" of the Indies against the "fables" of the chivalric romances such as *Amadís, Esplandián* and others, adding that these were patronized by the devil, father of lies. A penitent Fernández de Oviedo, repenting of his previous writings and indignant at those who had been seduced by them, passionately denounced fictional works and the marked tendency of many contemporary readers to approach

Spanish American reality through the fables contained in chivalric romances: He now turned to what he considered historical truth, to

> . . . write without any exaggeration or fear what I have seen and understood of these marvelous histories [the true histories of the Indies] that are so unfamiliar and so deserving of being heard. Let the vain then lend their ears to the books of Amadís and Esplandián and those stories that are derived from what is already such an infinite generation of fables; indeed I am ashamed to hear that in Spain they wrote so many of these trivialities that make one forget those of the Greeks. Evil is he who writes such things and he who reads such fictions, according to the words of the Evangelists that teach us that the devil is the father of lies. Free me, O Lord, from such a great sin and inspire my pen in the path of truth so that it always writes what conforms to truth and serves and praises the same truth which is God. (II, 182)

Another chronicler of the Indies who took a similar line on chivalric romance was the Inca Garcilaso de la Vega (1539–1616), son of a Spanish conquistador and an Inca princess and author of the celebrated *Comentarios Reales* (1609). Even though he condemns such fictions, in *La Florida*, proclaiming in contrast the truth of his own narrative, he also confesses his youthful enthusiasm for stories of knight errantry read in distant Cuzco, thus confirming that the Spanish conquistadores had brought these tales to the rugged mountain ranges of Peru. His early passion for such fiction, adds the Inca, had been later changed into aversion on reading Pedro Mexía's (1496?–1552?) censure of those who read and wrote such books:

> . . . con verdad podré negar que [*La Florida*] sea ficción mía, porque toda mi vida–sacada la buena poesía–fui enemigo de ficciones como son libros de cavallerías y otras semejantes. Las gracias desto devo dar al illustre cavallero Pedro Mexía, de Sevilla, porque con una reprehensión, que en la *Heroica obra de los Césares* [o sea, la *Historia imperial y cesárea* de Pedro Mexía, Sevilla, 1545] haze a los que se ocupan en leer y componer los tale libros, me quitó el amor que como muchacho les podía tener y me hizo aborrecerlos para siempre. (Vega 1988, 220–21)

> I, . . . truthfully declare that this account [*La Florida*] is not a fabric of my imagination. In fact all of my life I have been an enemy of such fiction as one finds in books of knight-hood and the like, good poetry excepted. For this attitude I am indebted to the illustrious cavalier, Pedro Mexía, since with the censure that he applies in his heroic treatise on the Caesars [that is Pedro Mexía's *History of the Empire of the Caesars,* Seville 1545] to those who occupy themselves with reading and composing such books, he took from me the love that I had for them as a boy and thus made me abhor them forever. (Vega 1951, 158–59)

Nevertheless in another passage of *Florida* the Inca makes it clear that something of his old attraction to chivalric romance still remains, since he compares the arrogant remarks of the Indian leader Vitacucho to the words of "the bravest knights that the divine Ariosto and the enlightened and much loved Count Mattheo María Boyardo, his predecessor, introduced in their works" (201). The names of these two Italian authors, whose poems were then habitually associated with the traditional vein of courtly romances, frequently recur in documents connected with the circulation of books in the New World, along with the names of the authors of the chivalric novels that were most in vogue during the sixteenth century.

The most conclusive evidence that the conquistadores read tales of chivalry is provided by the previously mentioned Bernal Díaz del Castillo, a soldier of Cortés who participated in the conquest of Mexico and author of the *Verdadera historia de la conquista de la Nueva España* [1632; The Discovery and Conquest of Mexico 1517–1521]. This firsthand account, though ranked over other chronicles because of its realism, still conserves in many aspects an element of the enchantment and spirit of adventure of so many knightly romances. It is enough to remember, for example, his enthusiastic comparison of the Aztec capital, as seen by the Spaniards for the first time, with the cities described in the book *Amadís*, an impression that his companions must have shared:

> And when we saw all those cities and villages built in the water, and other great towns on dry land, and that straight and level causeway leading to Mexico, we were astounded. These great towns and causeways and buildings rising from the water, all made of stone, *seemed like an enchanted vision from the tale of Amadís.* Indeed some of our soldiers asked if it was not all a dream. It is not surprising that I should write in this vein since it was all so wonderful that I do not know how to describe it. . . .
> (178; italics added)

The emotion that vibrates in this passage by Bernal Díaz makes it clear that his allusions to the book of Amadís were no literary affectation but rather "spontaneous and almost involuntary exclamations of one who is suddenly reminded of what he and his comrades had so often talked about" (Leonard 1964, 43). Before leaving for the New World or soon after their arrival, Bernal and his companions had certainly read some books of chivalry and it is very possible, adds Leonard, "that copies of these fantastic tales, probably much the worse for wear, lay about the soldiers' camps and served to divert the more literate in the lulls between campaigns" (1964, 43–44). Indeed, those who could not read also certainly had the opportunity to familiarize themselves with the stories, since there would be no lack of people who could read, surrounded by "more than thirty" of their comrades, dreaming of adventures and marvels like Miguel de Cervantes's (1547–1616) harvesters (218). If the owner of the fictional inn in Spain heard with special pleasure of the "furious and terrible blows of the knights" (218), then one does not need to make any great effort to imagine how the companions of Bernal Díaz would have been excited when faced with the enchantment of marvelous cities and strange lands that evoked the fantastic descriptions of their favorite reading. As Leonard observes, it is worth noting, in the passage from Bernal Díaz quoted above, the indistinct use of the personal pronoun:

> Where the plural *we* is employed it clearly indicates that Bernal Díaz, in alluding to the comparison of the scene before the Spaniards with descriptions found in *Amadís of Gaul* and its successors, did not express himself in terms of his own reading alone, but was conveying an impression shared by his companions who were also familiar with these novels. As they pushed inland on their spectacular conquest these bold adventurers doubtless talked of Amadís and Esplandián, and as they marched along they reminded one another of incidents and scenes described in the romances read or listened to. And thus they eagerly projected from their own minds into the exotic landscape about them the imaged evoked by their acquaintance with this literature of fantasy. (1964, 43)

The reference to the book of Amadís is not the only one in the Bernal Díaz's work. On two other occasions the author reveals his precise knowledge of that novel through his mentioning of Captain Pedro de Ircio. He recalls his sobriquet "Agrajes," the name of a character in *Amadís* that Bernal Díaz employs ironically to indicate boastfulness, a meaning that the

name went on to accrue in the proverbial phrase of popular speech: "Ya lo veredes, dijo Agrajes" (Riquer 53) ("Now you see it, said Agrajes"). In the first of the two quotations referring to Pedro de Ircio, the chronicler describes him in the following manner: "Pasó un Pedro de Ircio: era ardid de corazón y era algo de mediana estatura, y hablaba mucho que haría y acontecería por su persona, y no era para nada; y llamábamosle que era otro *Agrajes sin obras,* por su mucho hablar; fue capitán en el real de Sandoval" (Díaz del Castillo 583) ("One Pedro de Ircio came: He was cunning at heart and talked much about what he would do and bring about, and it was all hot air; and we said that he was another *Agrajes sin obras* (Agrajes with no deeds to his name) on account of his fondness for talking; he was a captain in Sandoval's camp"). Later Díaz repeats and rounds off his description: "El capitán Pedro de Ircio era de mediana estatura y paticorto, y tenía el rostro alegre, e muy plático en demasía, que así acontecería, que siempre contaba cuentos de Don Pedro Girón y del conde de Ureña, e era ardid, y a esta causa le llamábamos *Agrajes; sin obrar e sin hacer cosas que de contar sean,* murió en Méjico" (598) ("Captain Pedro de Ircio was of medium stature and short-legged with a cheerful face and given to talking in excess and projecting into the future. He always told stories of Don Pedro Girón and the Count of Ureña and he was a trickster. For this reason we nicknamed him *Agrajes,* 'with no deeds or fulfillment of those acts that he talked about,' he died in Mexico"). So why did Bernal Díaz and his companions give Captain Pedro Ircio the nickname of "*Agrajes sin obras*" ("Agrajes with no deeds")? Martínez Ruiz, after describing Agrajes, Amadís's valiant cousin, concluded: "Such is the figure of Agrajes of *Amadís.* In *Agrajes sin obras* as mentioned by the chronicler Bernal Díaz del Castillo, we see the antithesis of the chivalric hero, since his continuous talking and boasting was not translated into anything practical" (119). Marcel Bataillon takes the theme further:

> Il semble bien que, dans les deux passages, Bernal Díaz précise le mode habituel de "mucho hablar" de Pedro de Ircio: "il parlait pour dire ce qu'il ferait et ce qu'il adviendrait de sa personne," "il abusait des propos annonçant ce qui allait se passer?" Nous sommes amenés à compléter ces expressions elliptiques en suppléant: "y nunca respondían las obras a las palabras," et à en rapprocher le modisme: "*Ahora lo veredes, dijo Agrajes.*"
> (Bataillon 1962, 31)

> It clearly seems that, in the two passages, Bernal Díaz describes the usual talkative way of Pedro de Ircio: "He talked to say what he would do and what would happen to him." We are inclined to complete his elliptical expressions by adding, "and his deeds never matched his words," and thus give credence to the expression: "Now you will see it, said Agrajes."

Bataillon's comments certainly seem convincing. But, as Martín de Riquer (b. 1914) rightly observes, one must admit that "those in the Indies who bestowed this soubriquet on Pedro de Ircio did so very much in the style of *Amadís de Gaula.* The note placed in the hero's swaddling clothes when abandoned in a chest shortly after his birth read: 'This is Amadís *Sin Tiempo,* the King's son,' while Agrajes' uncle is often dubbed '*Galvanes Sin Tierra*'" (51). Riquer considers that the name *Agrajes sin obras,* in the style of *Amadís,* "must have been invented by Pedro de Ircio's companions-in-arms to mock his wordiness unaccompanied by action and perhaps (why not?) because the short-legged captain was accustomed to use the saying '*Agora lo veredes*'" (51). Since this proverbial phrase does not appear in Montalvo's adaptation of *Amadís,* Martín de Riquer shrewdly concludes that, in the original *Amadís,* Agrajes pronunciaba una o varias veces la frase amenazadora "Agora lo veredes," suprimida por Montalvo, quien no la suprimió, y la modernizó en "Agora lo vereys," en boca del adversario de Gandales . . . , en boca de *Amadís* . . . , ni en boca de los caballeros del perverso Arcalaus . . . Por razones diversas el "Agora lo veredes" dicho por Agrajes llamó la atención de los lectores del *Amadís* primitivo y se repitió tanto que se convirtió en una expresión popular, por lo general utilizada irónicamente. (52–53)

pronounced the threatening phrase "*Agora lo veredes*" once or various times. Deleted by Montalvo, it was actually not suppressed entirely but instead modernized into "*Agora lo vereys*" spoken by Gandales's adversary . . . , by Amadís . . . , but not by the knights of the perverse Arcalaus. . . . For diverse reasons "*Agora lo veredes*" as uttered by Agrajes drew the attention of the readers of the original *Amadís* and was repeated so often that it became a popular expression, generally used ironically.

If, as we have seen, direct proof exists that the conquistadores did effectively read or listen to readings of the fantastic tales contained in the books of chivalric romance, no less significant is the evidence that confirms the influence of these works on the development of the myth of the Amazons, one of the most powerful and durable mythic inventions in the history of the American conquest. The history of the "discoveries" and of Spanish penetration into the New World would be incomprehensible without studying the numerous attractive myths and legends that inflamed the fantasy of the conquistadores, brought American geography to life, and frequently constructed a reality distorted by imagination and distance. Those myths and legends, some originating from classical and medieval antiquity, others emerging after Columbus's first voyage as a consequence of an encounter that could be defined as a basic event of Euro-American syncretism, enormously stimulated the penetration of the conquering armies into the interior of the continent. Here is not the place to make a study of the numerous myths and legends that drove generations of Spaniards and other Europeans into delusional adventures through vast unexplored areas of the New World (see Gandía; Gil; Bartra). We must now focus on the myth most directly related to the influence of chivalric romances on the conquistadores.

It is generally accepted that the myth of the Amazons, a legacy from the classical world, was revitalized by the Europeans' first encounter with America and had wide circulation at all levels of Spanish society on both sides of the ocean between the end of the fifteenth and the first half of the sixteenth century. Initially set in the Antilles and later in the basin of the eponymous Amazon River, this was without doubt the legend that suffered the greatest number of adaptations, if not deformations. The hope of finding these mythical female warriors of ancient times was considerably revived by Columbus himself from the moment of his first contact with the new lands on the other side of the ocean. For many centuries, writers (including medieval travelers) had vaguely located them in different unexplored or semi-explored areas away from the referential axis of the Europeans in compliance with the longstanding mytho-poetic tradition whereby the limits of the world had to be inhabited by monstrous or fantastic beings (Avonto 1995, 75–76, 91–110). The navigator suggested that various Amazons might live separately in some islands of the Caribbean, access to which was impeded by strong winds; he also imagined that other specimens of such elusive and masculine women might be found on dry land once the regions inhabited by cannibals had been conquered.

These fantastic rumors were spread among cultivated classes by Pedro Martyr of Anghiera (1457–1526), the sophisticated Italian humanist, councilor to the Catholic Kings and later to Emperor Charles V, whose celebrated verses *De Orbe Novo* were composed over many years and had a wide circulation in manuscript form before the publication of the first edition in 1530. Another confirmation of the truth of the Amazon myth was offered by the Spanish translation of the apocryphal *Travels* of Sir John Mandeville published in 1521, the same year that Cortés conquered Mexico. Only a few years later the story of Magellan's great voyage, as narrated by Antonio Pigafetta (ca. 1480/91–ca. 1534), appeared, locating the home of the Amazons "in the Island of Ocloros, below Java" (Pigafetta 132). While similar stories about the Amazons circulated in Spain and other European countries, it is doubtful whether these works would have been standard reading for soldiers or those in the lower echelons of society who, generally speaking, did not even know of their existence. As Leonard has rightly observed, the most popular literature was the chivalric romances "and to them it is logical to turn as a possible source of inspiration for the renewed interest in the classical myth" (1964, 38). An episode involving Calafia, Queen of the Amazons, who lived on a craggy island bearing the significant name of "California," appears in *Las Sergas de Esplandián*, the sequel to the first four books of *Amadís de Gaula*. The origin of the name "Calafia" could harken back to the *Victorial*, written by the chronicler Gutierre Diez de Games (ca. 1379–ca. 1450), in which appears a Queen Taléstride (the Taléstrida of Alfonso X), whose name is transformed into Calestia. As Juan Gil suggests, this latter "is closer both to Calafia as well as California" (II:74). Given that the main theme of *Las Sergas de Esplandián* does not appear until after the Amazon episode; perhaps Montalvo, the author of the book, had changed his original plan to exploit the attraction of this resurrected classical legend Leonard explains, "While he was engaged in writing this tale it is possible that there reached his ears an echo of Columbus's report of Amazon-like women on some islands past which he had cruised and of their alleged proximity to the Earthly Paradise" (Leonard 1964, 39). The Admiral supposed he had arrived at such a place and wrote about it with feverish excitement in his report to the Spanish monarchs on his voyage (see Columbus 1982c, 204–21). This hypothesis not only seems confirmed by the tone of amazement and profound emotion that characterizes both the start of Montalvo's Amazon episode and Columbus's report but also by some expressions that even at first sight suggest a certain relationship between the two texts. Here is Rodríguez de Montalvo commenting on the Island of California that he locates on the edge of the Earthly Paradise:

> Quiero agora que sepais una cosa la más extraña que nunca por escriptura ni por memoria de gente en ningún caso hallar se pudo. . . . Sabed que a la diestra mano de las Indias hubo una isla, llamada *California*, muy llegada a la parte del Paraíso Terrenal, la cual fue poblada de mujeres negras, sin que algún varón entre ellas hubiese, que casi como las Amazonas era su estilo de vivir. . . . Estas eran de valientes cuerpos y esforzados y ardientes corazones y de grandes fuerzas; la ínsula en si la más fuerte de riscos y bravas peñas que en el mundo se hallaba; las sus armas eran todas de oro, y también las guarniciones de las bestias fieras, en que, después de las haber amansado, cabalgaban; que en toda la isla no había otro metal alguno. Moraban en cuevas muy bien labradas. (1950, 539)

Now I wish you to know about the strangest thing ever found anywhere in written texts or in human memory. . . . I tell you that on the right hand of the Indies there was an island called California, which was very close to the region of the Earthly Paradise. This island was inhabited by black women and there were no males among them at all, for their life style was similar to that of the Amazons. . . . These women had energetic bodies and courageous, ardent hearts, and they were very strong. The island was made up of the wildest cliffs and the sharpest precipices found anywhere in the world. Their armor was made entirely of gold–which was the only metal found on the island–as were the trappings on the fierce beasts that they rode once they were tamed. There was no other kind of metal in all the island. They lived in very well-designed caves. (1992, 456)

Columbus likewise writes on his discovery of the region where supposedly the Earthly Paradise was located (see **Figure 1**):

Ya no hallo ni jamás he hallado escriptura de latinos ni de griegos que certificadamente diga al, sino en este mundo, del Paraíso Terrenal, ni he visto en ningún mapamundo, salvo situado con autoridad de argumento. Algunos le ponían allí donde son las fuentes del Nilo en Ethiopía, mas otros anduvieron todas estas tierras y no hallaron conformidad d'ello. . . . Ya dixe lo que yo hallava d'este hemisperio y de la hechura . . . y creo que . . . allí es el Paraíso Terrenal, adonde no puede llegar nadie salvo por voluntad divina. Y cero qu' esta tierra que agora mandaron descubrir Vuestras Altezas sea grandíssima y aya otras muchas . . . , de que jamás se ovo notiçia. . . . Grandes indiçios son estos del Paraíso Terrenal, porqu'el sitio es conforme a la opinión d'estos sanctos e sacros theólogos. Y asimismo las señales son muy conformes. (Columbus 1982c, 217–18)

I do not find in any of the writings by the Romans or Greeks anything that truly establishes the location of this Earthly Paradise. Nor have I seen it authoritatively placed on any map of the world. Some locate it at the sources of the Nile in Ethiopia while others have explored all these lands and not found any evidence of it. . . . I declare that I found it in this hemisphere and as described . . . ; I believe that there is the Terrestrial Paradise that no-one can arrive at except by divine will. And I believe that this land that now Your Highnesses ordered to be discovered is large and that there are many others . . . of which there has never been report. . . . There are great indications that this is the Earthly Paradise because the location accords with the opinion of those holy and sacred theologians. And also the signs are very much in agreement.

The strong emotion expressed by the Admiral is perfectly understandable. During his third voyage Columbus arrived at the mouth of the Orinoco; when he understood that such a great river could only come from a continent and one that did not fit into any geographical schema known in his epoch, he believed he had found the Terrestrial Paradise. In fact, the Admiral thought he had arrived in the East, a land that was not just a vast country of spices, silk, gold, and precious stones; in the context of complex medieval philosophy to which Columbus was heir, the East was also the highest ground on earth and thus the most sacred and perfect, privileged as the location of the rising of the sun, source of life and divine expression. It is no coincidence that the medieval maps represent the East as being situated on high ground. Here the Earthly Paradise was drawn in, positioned on a high mountain from which ran the four sacred rivers, the Ganges, the Tigris, the Euphrates, and the Zeon. Jerusalem, the center of the world, was located at the gates of the East. Between Jerusalem and the Terrestrial Paradise existed the kingdom of Prester John, while beyond lay a series of fantastic regions, replete with monsters and hazards, as well as other real lands,

Figure 1.

Letter of the first voyage and discovery of Isla Española (Santo Domingo) by Christophoro Colombo (Christopher Columbus) published by Johanes de Olpe in Basle, 1494. (Archive of the author)

ancient knowledge of which had survived in the geographical concepts of the Middle Ages. These regions constituted a kind of defensive barrier to the entrance to the Earthly Paradise, a place of delights forbidden to humankind as a result of Original Sin. Many legends attribute to saintly travelers the desire to reach the Terrestrial Paradise, but only few succeeded and those only through divine will and after various tremendously difficult trials. When faced with the conundrum represented by this land that he had discovered, Columbus could not envisage any solution, bar that of speculating on the whimsical literary geography of the traditional debates over where might be Paradise, the same geography with which his contemporary Rodríguez de Montalvo was certainly familiar. He thus was able to convince himself that he had arrived at the Earthly Paradise, recording what he wrote on pages burning in an almost mystical fervor.

In the section of *Las Sergas de Esplandián* mentioned above, the author located the home of the bellicose Amazons in the recently discovered regions of the Indies, despite the fact that the novel's extravagant geography makes these islands accessible by sea from Constantinople and Asia Minor. In fact, during the period in which Rodríguez de Montalvo (fl. 1500) was writing, many still thought that Columbus had discovered a new route to Asia. On reporting his first discoveries in the Antilles on his first voyage, Columbus himself had explicitly revived the ancient classical legend of the Amazons, situating the possible home of this female tribe on an island that the Indians called Matininó (most probably modern Martinique) and which they claimed was rich in gold. In various parts of his ship's log as well as in the famous letter to Luis de Santángel written during his return from the first voyage and immediately circulated thanks to the printing press (with nine editions appearing of the Latin version of Leandro de Cosco during the two-year period 1493–1494), the Admiral had mentioned the legendary female warriors with enthusiastic references to the great quantity of gold they possessed, a fact destined to excite the most fevered dreams of the numerous conquistadores and adventurers who would set out in search of them over various decades in the most remote and inaccessible places of the New World: "Concerning the Island of Matininó, that Indian said that it was totally populated with women without men and that there is much *tuob* there, which is gold" (Columbus 1982a, 115). Later he wrote:

> Así que monstruos no he hallado ni noticia, salvo de una isla que es Carib, la segunda a la entrada de las Indias, que es poblada de una iente que tienen en todas las islas por muy ferozes, los cuales comen carne humana. . . . Estos son aquellos que tratan con las mugeres de Matinino, que es la primera isla partiendo de España para las Indias que se falla, en la cual no ay hombre ninguno. Ellas no usan exercicio femenil salvo arcos y flechas . . . , y se arman y cobigan con launes de arambre, de que tienen mucho. . . . En esta [isla] ay oro sin cuento (Columbus 1982b, 144–45)

> As I have found no monsters, so I have had no report of any, except in an island "Quaris," which is the second at the coming into the Indies, and which is inhabited by a people who are regarded in all the islands as very fierce and who eat human flesh. . . . These are they who have intercourse with the women of "Martinio," which is the first island met on the way from Spain to the Indies, in which there is not a man. These women engage in no feminine occupation, but use bows and arrows of cane, . . . and they arm and protect themselves with plates of copper, of which they have much. . . . In it [this island] there is gold incalculable. (1970, 263–64)

After reading these passages by Columbus it is not so strange to read that the Amazons of Montalvo lived in an island "situated at the right hand of the Indies" and carried weapons made entirely of gold or dominated cruel cannibals of black and Indian parentage, an allusion in some way to those "very fierce" tribes that ate human flesh and dealt with the women of Matinino mentioned by the Admiral:

> En esta isla, California llamada, había muchos grifos . . . los cuales en ninguna parate del mundo eran hallados; y en el tiempo que tenían hijos, iban estas mujeres con artificios para los tomar, cubiertas todas de muy gruesos cueros, y traíanlos a sus cuevas, y allí los criaban. Y siendo ya igualados, *cebábanlos en aquellos hombres y en los niños que parían.* (Rodríguez de Montalvo 1950, 539)

> On this island called California, there were many griffins . . . that were not found in any other part of the world. When the griffins had offspring, in order to capture the young, these women ingenuously covered themselves in coarse hides; then they took them back to their caves where they raised them. When their plumage was even, they fed them so often and so cleverly with the captured men and the boys they bore. (Rodríguez de Montalvo 1992, 458)

In all probability the author of *Las Sergas de Esplandián*, inspired by the meager facts provided by Columbus, rounded out his prolix description by changing the name of the Amazons' island from the ugly Matininó that appears in the Admiral's writings for the more attractive and euphonic California (Olschki 382). The statement that the weapons of the Amazons were all of gold because "there was not other metal in the island" convinced his readers that those who

might discover this place would find a fabulous fortune. Thus Montalvo dressed up the facts provided by Columbus and, from then on, the conquerors of America always associated the Amazons with boundless wealth.

It is notorious that the popularity achieved by the first books of chivalry was followed by that of a long sequence of novels on the successive descendants of Amadís and Esplandián. Thus in the first *Lisuate de Grecia* published in 1514, four years after *Esplandián*, Queen Calafia of California makes another appearance, this time fighting at the side of the Christian knights against the Turks; in the previous novel the warlike queen, conquered by the skill of Amadís and by the beauty of Esplandián, had been converted to Christianity. As Leonard comments, it is interesting to observe that the first edition of *Las Sergas de Esplandián* was published in 1510 by the Cromberger press in Seville, which in 1525 went on to publish the only edition of *Lisuarte de Grecia* known after the first edition of 1514 (even though it is possible that others were published between these two dates). This is most significant, given that most of the expeditions to the Indies set sail from Seville (Leonard 1964, 41). Thus it is possible that the expeditionaries who voyaged during these years had read the two books that contain the episodes concerning Queen Calafia of California even before leaving Spain. However, one fact is certain. When Grijalva explored the Mexican coast from the Yucatan to the River Panuco in 1518, the Amazons made another appearance: The cleric Juan Díaz who accompanied the expedition wrote in his chronicle that the Spaniards found a "very beautiful tower on a point which it is said was inhabited by women who live without men; it was believed they belonged to the Amazon race" (García Icazbalceta 288).

In the same way, Cortés's *Fourth Letter* reports that one of the objectives of the expedition composed of four ships that left in 1524 for the islands of the West under the command of Alvaro de Saavedra Cerón was precisely that of exploring an island that had been talked about by the *caciques* of Ciguatán as being "toda poblada de mujeres sin varón ninguno, y que en ciertos tiempos van de la tierra firme hombres, con los cuales han acceso; y las que quedan preñadas, si paren mujeres, las guardan, y si hombres los echan de su compañía. . . . Dícenme asimismo que es muy rica de perlas y oro" (1945, 254) ("inhabited only by women, without a single man, and that at certain times men go over from the mainland and they have intercourse with them; the females born to those who conceive are kept, but the males are sent away. . . . They also told me that it was very rich in pearls and gold") (1986, 298). Clearly, after Magellan's voyage, Cortés was shifting Columbus's experiences in the Atlantic to the Pacific area, but these are the same concepts that *Las Sergas de Esplandián* had undoubtedly helped to circulate among the conquistadores of New Spain. This is all perfectly understandable. Was not New Spain situated to the east of India in a region that could correspond to the spot where Montalvo had located the Island of California "on the right hand of the Indies"? Inevitably the name of the Amazons resonated in this way, once again heralding the proximity of fabulous treasure.

But more was to come. In the same year, 1524, the conqueror of Mexico assigned to his relative Francisco Cortés the command of an expedition to investigate some reports concerning the coast near the province of Colima. These reports apparently claimed that in this zone "there was much wealth and in these parts is a place inhabited by women without men who have a way of reproducing as described for the Amazons in the old histories" (*Colección* xxvi, 153). The special interest of this document lies in Cortés's subsequent statement that his knowledge of the Amazons came from the reading of "old histories," a phrase that was then applied to both historical chronicles and tales of chivalry, since these latter frequently included the terms "history" or "chronicle" in their titles. The lack of care with which these definitions were applied to tales of fact or fiction "produced confusion in the minds of general readers as to the nature of what they were reading; consequently, the more interesting they found a book, the more inclined they were to believe in its veracity" (Leonard 1962, 50).

It does not therefore seem coincidental that in 1542, when *Las Sergas de Esplandián* and *Lisuarte de Grecia* were still popular, the expedition of Juan Rodríguez Cabrillo would have registered in the ship's log the peninsula on the Pacific coast of New Spain (long believed by the Spaniards to be an island) by the name California after *Amadís*. This would indicate that this title "had now been firmly established" (Rivera Novo and Martín Merás 238–39), given that the peninsula was located "on the right hand of the Indies," just as Montalvo had stated in his book. In the documented history and literature of travel and exploration in the sixteenth century, examples of repeated recounting of the Amazon legend and the ceaseless search for their habitation throughout the Americas are innumerable. For the sake of brevity only some of the most interesting examples during the period of discovery and first decades of the conquest of the New World can be mentioned here. However, it is clear that a diffuse faith in the marvelous, inspired by a medieval legacy and fed by contemporary fiction, played a part in all the expeditions that set off for the New World during the sixteenth century. When it was finally realized that neither Amazons nor the waters of Eternal Life nor enchanted cities like the Seven Cities of Cíbola existed in New Spain, the conquistadores naturally shifted the possible location of these fantastic realms and mythic personages to regions even more mysterious and distant from the mainland. Thus the hallucinatory search for Paradise, El Dorado, the City of the Caesars, and the Amazons that had so excited the greed and illusions of the romantic conquistadores continued in South America. The most famous and symbolic of the Spanish enterprises in South America provides a classic example: the incredible voyage undertaken by Francisco de Orellana and his companions in 1542 through the vastness of the Amazon basin, a place that owes its name to these men's unquenchable faith in the old legend of the female tribe possessed of incalculable riches. With the advance of the conquistadores into different regions in the interior of this immense continent, the fantastic kingdom of the Amazons that had once been conceived of as an island was subsequently transformed into hinterland. But this never altered the isolated character of these elusive warriors, and their name continued to be associated with the idea of the countless riches spoken of by Columbus and Rodríguez Montalvo.

If the examples mentioned above sufficiently prove the conquistador's enthusiasm for books of chivalry and the influence these had on their actions, further and equally significant evidence of the connection between the popular reading of the period and the deeds of such readers is clear in the frequent hostility that moralists and religious and secular authorities manifested against the "mendacious stories" read so enthusiastically by the adventurers of the New World. Among those who opposed the literary fashion for chivalric romance was the celebrated humanist Juan Luis Vives (1492–1540), whose attacks on this frivolous reading, which according to him corrupted young minds and morals, began in 1524 with his *Instrucción de la mujer cristiana* [Education of the Christian Woman] and was reiterated in successive works such as *De disciplinis* [1531; On Discipline] and *De ratione dicendi* [1532; Art of Rhetoric]. Vives, who was familiar with contemporary literature in Spain, France, and the Low Countries, included in his reprimand all kinds of fiction. Among the Spanish examples were *Amadís* and its sequel *La Celestina* [1499; *Celestina* "the mother bawd of all evil"] and the *Cárcel de Amor* [1492; Prison of Love]. He cited *Lanzarote del Lago* [Sir Launcelot of the Lake], *Paris y Viana* [Paris and Viana], *Ponto y Sidonia* [Pontus and Sidon], *Pedro de Provenza* [Pedro of Provence], and *Magalona y Melusina* [Magdalene and Melusine] as French examples and from the Low Countries *Flores y Blancaflor* [Flores and Blancaflor], *Leonela y Vanamor* [Leonela and Vanamor], *Curias y Floreta* [Curias and Floreta], and *Píramo y Tisbe* [Pyramus and Thisbe] (Vives 36). To these Vives added the translations of the Early Italian Renaissance works such as the *Facecias* by Poggio, and in his *De disciplinis* he catalogued Ariosto's *Orlando furioso* [1532; Orlando Enraged] with the chivalric romances. All this kind of reading, wrote Vives, should not be put in the hands of young people if one wanted "their morals to be healthy" (36). What could be written about love stories, whether pleasant or tragic, asked the humanist from Valencia, other than their sensual aspect? Directing his offensive in particular against books of chivalric romance, he mocked these heroes that were able to kill twenty or thirty enemies single-handed (36). Censured as immoral and mendacious literature, these two principal accusations were repeated throughout the sixteenth century by other intellectuals, including Antonio de Guevara (d. 1545), Bishop of Guadix and spiritual counselor to Charles V as well as the author of *Reloj de príncipes* [1529; Guide to Princes]; Pedro Mexía, author of *Historia imperial y cesárea* [1545; Imperial History], already mentioned in the context of the Inca Garcilaso's fondness for chivalric romances; and Diego Gracian, translator of Plutarch and Xenophanes (1548) who railed against the discredit that fell on worthy writers as a result of the public's incapacity to discriminate between reality and fiction–for which he blamed these tales.

These examples reveal the opposition within the cultivated elements of Spanish society to popular literature, largely based on the apparently negative consequences that this genre provoked in its readers. However, the most conclusive evidence of the enormous popularity of tales of chivalry among those who traveled to the New World can be deduced from the prohibitive legislation that the metropolitan authorities had to adopt repeatedly under pressure from moralists and ecclesiastics. In a royal decree of 4 April 1531, the Queen, in the absence of her husband, thus instructed the officials of the *Casa de Contratación* (Tribunal of Commerical Affairs with the Indies): "Yo he seydo ynformada que se pasan a las Yndias muchos libros de Romance y de ystorias vanas y de profanidad como son el Amadís y otros desta calidad, y por que este es mal exercicio para los yndios e cosa en que no es bien que se ocupen ni lean, por ende yo vos mando que de aquí adelante no consyntays ni deys lugar a persona alguna pasar a las Yndias libros ningunos de ystorias y cosas profanas." (*Colección* xlii, 466–67) ("I have been informed that many books of Romance and vain and profane stories are sent to the Indies such as *Amadís* and others of similar quality and this is a bad thing for the Indians and it is not good that they should spend time reading them, for which reason I charge you that from henceforth you neither consent nor give room to any person taking books of stories or profane matters to the Indies").

Despite the force of law intimated by this decree, a few years afterwards the same Queen was complaining that the competent authorities had not been sufficiently vigilant in the execution of her previous orders and thus that it was necessary to repeat them with a new decree dated 14 July 1536 that alluded to some instructions sent to the first Viceroy of Mexico, Antonio de Mendoza:

> Algunos días ha que el Emperador y Rey, mi Señor, proveyó que no se llevasen a esas partes libros de Romance de materias profanas y fabulosas, por que los indios que sopiesen leer no se diesen a ellos, dejando los libros de sana y buena doctrina, y leyéndolos no aprendiesen en ellos malas costumbres y vicios; . . . y porque creemos que en la execución desto no a abido el cuidado que debía, mucho vos encargamos y mandamos proveais, como de aquí adelante no se vendan libros algunos desta calidad, ni se trayan de nuevo, porque cesen estos incombinientes. (*Colección* xxiii, 457–58)

> Some days ago my Lord, the Emperor and King, decreed that books of Romance containing profane and fabulous material should not be taken to these lands so the Indians who can read do not turn to these and abandon books of good and healthy doctrine, nor learn bad habits and vices from them; . . . and because we believe that insufficient attention has been paid to the execution of this command, we charge and command that you see that from henceforth no books of this quality are sold or brought again, so that this inconvenience comes to a stop.

It is all too evident that the Queen's orders were not observed with the scrupulousness they deserved, given that seven years later, on 13 September 1543, her son, the Prince and future king, Philip II, sent new instructions to the *Casa de Contratación* reiterating orders of a similar tenor regarding books sent out to the Indies:

> Sabed que de llevarse a las dichas Yndias libros de Romance y materias profanas y fábulas ansí como son *libros de Amadís y otros desta calidad de mentirosas ystorias* se siguen muchos ynconvenientes porque los indios que supieren leer, dándose a ellos, dexarán los libros de sana y buena doctrina y, leyendo los de mentirosas y storias, deprenderán en ellos malas costumbres y vicios . . . , yo vos mando que no consintays ni deis lugar que en ninguna manera pasen a las dichas nuestras Indias libros algunos de los susodichos. (Medina 1958–62, xxvi–xxvii)

> Know that the taking books of romance and profane and materials and fables to the Indies such as the books of Amadís and other mendacious stories continues to be highly inconvenient since Indians who know how to read, giving themselves over to them, abandoning books of good and healthy doctrine and reading those fabricated stories, are inspired to bad habits and vices . . . , I charge you not to agree or permit that books of this kind arrive in our Indies.

A few days later, rather briefer instructions in a similar vein were sent to the *Audiencias* in Lima and Santo Domingo. On 5 September 1550, it was decreed "that they be listed specifically, not generally, in the registers for all books sent to the Indies" (Madariaga 238).

However much the repetition of similar decrees roundly proves that the orders they contained were not observed and that the "profane and mendacious stories" arrived in the Indies without any difficulty, there is a fact of greater importance inherent in this prohibitive legislation that deserves the most considered attention. The intention behind the promulgation of

these laws was not to prevent Spaniards and their descendants in America from reading works of fiction. Rather it was to prevent their Indian subjects, for whose Christian education the monarchs felt profoundly responsible, from losing their new faith under the influence of profane works or from confusing scriptural truths with the vanities of frivolous literature, as result of their ignorance of Spanish customs. The Inquisition, so often accused of the worst kind of cultural obscurantism, was on the contrary notably indulgent and tolerant when it came to popular tastes in literature and its vigilance with regard to forbidden books was limited almost exclusively to Bibles in the vernacular and Lutheran and Protestant tracts in general, both in Spain and in the Indies. In addition, there is evidence that the officials of the Inquisition had precise orders to make their "visits" to the ships lying at anchor in the ports of embarkation in Spain and on arrival in the Indies with the greatest deference possible to avoid complaints by Peninsular and Colonial merchants about interferences and delays in the traffic of books. Such an activity was surely lucrative, since the printed material was practically exempt from export tariffs that were applied to the majority of other articles sent to the Indies. When the *avería* tax was introduced to finance the expenses of providing an armed escort for the merchant fleets that were continually under threat from corsairs and pirates, the fiscal duty paid on books was very moderate (between 1 and 7 percent) and only reached the maximum level during times of severe international instability.

It must be added that such tariffs were frequently avoided, thanks to smuggling by merchants and ships' captains and the lack of attention (and venality) of customs agents; the officials of the Inquisition were also no exception. Censorship, if well established in 1550, had hardly any effect until 1583 when Quiroga's corrected and extended "Index of Prohibited Books" was promulgated. It is worth emphasizing that only the books listed in this Index were proscribed, since their heretical content meant they were considered to be dangerous for the Catholic faith. In fact the registers for the freighting of books destined for the Indies and the documentation known to date concerning their sale and circulation (see Leonard 1964, 208–61, 281–315; also see "documento I-IX" in the Spanish translation of Leonard 1953, 271–358) prove unquestionably that the most important works of Spanish literature were very easily exported to the Indies and often in the same year as their publication in Spain. This clearly confirms that the Spanish possessions in the Indies were at that time an extension of the mother country and more generally of European culture. Of course religious publications predominate in almost all surviving inventories of books made during the Colonial period; all these belong to the last decades of the sixteenth century when it was obligatory to mention each title in the bill of lading. This should not lead to erroneous conclusions, given that these works constituted a literature that could be described as professional and usually used for the instruction of the clergy and for teaching. Such works filled monastic and convent libraries where, at times, they survived the destructive impact of time. Meanwhile, works of the creative imagination (poetry and history in the broad meaning of the term) were not only read and perused more continually by the public, but also passed from one avid reader to another with considerably more frequency than serious theological works and pious tracts. This circulation also contributed to their greater deterioration and more rapid dispersion.

The study of these book inventories proves that, thanks to their existence and to the linguistic unity assured by the use of Spanish in these overseas possessions, and despite imagined and theoretical restrictions decreed by political and religious power, the American Viceroyalties of the sixteenth century were ideologically situated in the context of Renaissance Spain. In addition, their inhabitants in practical terms had virtually the same access to imaginative and spiritual works as the supposedly more privileged subjects in the Peninsula. For reasons of space, it is not possible to make a detailed examination of all available documentation illustrating the literary tastes that flourished in the last decades of the sixteenth century—the period of the inventories and lists of works that have been conserved in different archives. Even so, a quick reading of a list of books that circulated, for example in the Lima market in 1591, could be sufficiently indicative of a general situation reflected in other parts of Spanish America, since it is confirmed by similar documentation in Mexico and other places.

This list from Lima, comprising 1186 titles (Leonard 1964, 286–94) confirms above all that the sixteenth century was basically a period of narrative literature in which chronicles, histories, novels, and epic poems could count on a wide readership. In addition, the document provides clear proof not only that the attacks of the moralists and religious authorities against the "mendacious stories" of chivalric fiction were ineffective but also that these stories continued to arouse enormous interest in the children and grandchildren of the conquistadores. The list includes various copies of *Amadís de Gaula* and its sequel *Las Sergas de Esplandián*, as well as other examples of the same genre such as *El Caballero de Febo, Don Florisel de Niquea*, and *Belianis de Grecia* that soon would be firmly replaced in the public's favor by Cervantes's *Quijote*. La *Crónica de Don Rodrigo con la destruición de España* [1400; The Chronicle of Don Rodrigo and the Destruction of Spain] by Pedro de Corral, who lived between the fourteenth and fifteenth centuries, could be included in this category, despite its pretensions to being a true story, along with some verse chivalric romances such as *Celión de Iberia* [Celión of Iberia] and *Don Florando de Castilla* [Don Florando of Castille] that were favorites of those who still enjoyed tales of chivalry. There were, however, clear indications that the literary tastes of the conquistadores' descendants were evolving, since alongside the above-mentioned titles we also find some pastoral novels such as *Ninfas y pastores de Henares* [1587; Nymphs and Shepherds of Henares] by Bernardo Gonzalez de Bobadilla (d. 1587) and *Desengaño de celos* [1586; Disillusion of Jealousy] by Bartolomé López de Enciso (fl. 1586). Long verse narratives by Italian poets of the Renaissance like Ariosto and Tasso, such as the latter's *Gerusalemme liberata*, also enjoyed great popularity, most probably because of their obvious affinity with the chivalric Spanish vein. The *Celestina* provides a notable contrast to this literature of fiction and fantasy, even if this masterwork of Spanish Realism was already a century old. Finally the Lima document allows one to see the slow replacement of polemical tracts on theology by pious and devotional homilies.

On the other hand, a list of books for Mexico in the year 1600 (Leonard 1964, 301–15) provides the opportunity to appreciate clearer changes in literary taste in the last decade of the sixteenth century as well as the survival of earlier works. These 678 books, new and old, scientific and superstitious, cover virtually all fields of knowledge, confirming again that New Spain, like other Spanish possessions in America,

was an extension of the mother country and of Hispanic and European culture. The titles give a surprisingly complete picture of diverse currents of what was very decidedly Renaissance thought during the sixteenth century; they include a significantly high number of Italian authors, followed by other European writers of different nationalities. Alongside works by classical authors such as Euclid, Archimedes, and Sacrobosco appear the writings of Peuerbach, the corrector of Ptolemy and his disciple Regiomontano. Ancient history is represented by various classics and general history by authors such as Gilbert Génébrand, Florian de Ocampo (1499?–1555?) with his *Crónica general* [1543; General Chronicle] and Antonio de Nebrija's (1444–1522) *Décadas*. Italian, French, and Austrian history books are listed as well as works on political science, law, and biography by authors such as Plutarch, Giovio, and Hotman. Among the legal tomes it is surprising to come across the *Dialéctica juris civilis Otomani* by François Hotman, the Calvinist author and critic of absolute monarchy. Once more this confirms that the vigilance of the Inquisition over the books that arrived in the Indies was not quite as efficacious as one might suppose. From the interpretation of other surviving documents, one would also imagine that similar cases were not so uncommon.

Belles lettres, the favorite reading of the period, are of particular interest in this context since they contribute valuable clues regarding the literary taste of the general public. Works of poetry and rhetoric dominate the list, both ancient and modern, featuring, for example, Lazaro Cardona's (fl. 1550) writing on Sannazaro, those of Guastarini on Tasso's *Gerusalemme liberata*, and Tasso's own *Discorsi*. Numerous volumes of Greek and Latin literature, works by Petrarch, Teofilo Folengo, and Alciati, collections of Erasmus's epistles, as well as select works by Bembo Pontano, Poliziano, and Aeneas Silvius also figure. Among the listed books of chivalry and pastoral literature are featured *Hermosura de Angélica* [1586; The Beauty of Angelica] by Luis Barahona de Soto (1548?–1595), *Orlando furioso* by Lodovico Ariosto, the *Pastor de Iberia* [The Shepherd of Iberia] of Bernardo de la Vega (mid-sixteenth to early seventeenth centuries), and *La enamorada Elisea* [1594; Elisea in Love] by Jerónimo de Covarrubias Herrera (late sixteenth to early seventeenth centuries). On the dramatic side are featured Juan de la Cueva's (1543–1612) *Comedias y tragedias* [1583; Comedies and Tragedies] and various Italian plays, in particular the comedies of Dolci. The popularity enjoyed by Italian literature is made evident by the presence of the prose writings of Boccaccio, Sannazaro (*Arcadia*), Bembo (*Asolani*), and Castiglione (*Il Cortegiano*), apart from miscellaneous works by Doni, Calmo, and Guicciardini. The writings of Dante, Petrarch (both in Italian and in Spanish translations), Alammani (*Opere toscane*), Annibal Caro, and other Renaissance authors are there in abundance. Seen as a whole, this list features the most select and erudite literature that was being read in Europe. Indeed to give the lie once more to the often repeated idea that the censorship of the Inquisition was responsible for dragging the intellectual life of Hispanic America into darkness, many titles cited in the Index of Quiroga (1583) by authors such as Erasmus, Génébrand, Alberto Pio, François Hotman, Javellus, and others actually appear in this Mexican list.

We are now obviously in another age and another historical moment. But chivalric and fictional literature that had fed the dreams and adventurous exploits of those in the New World (who had tried to emulate the deeds of the knights errant) did not entirely die out. In the same way that the real or fictitious heroes of the Spanish *reconquista* contributed enormously to the fascinating legacy of popular Spanish folklore, once the Conquest was complete, tales of the heroic knights of chivalric fiction and the conquistadores who wished to emulate them in the New World gradually passed into the collective and timeless memory of the Hispanic peoples of America. Evidence for this lies in the survival up to the present day of themes, fables, and popular verse in the most unimaginable and distant places of the continent whose origin is undoubtedly rooted, as various studies have proved (Schevill 173–96; Menéndez Pidal 47–53; Carrizo 63–83; Coll y Toste 87–93), in the fictional and recreational literature of the sixteenth century that accompanied the conquistadores–whose deeds often appear to be suspended somewhere between reality and fantasy.

The cultural vicissitudes of Spanish America in the sixteenth century analyzed in the course of the present study lead inevitably to the acknowledgment that the intellectual history of the continent during this foundation period was, without doubt, an imported one. Similarly, reflection on the next long phase of the Spanish Empire in America, that of the Kingdoms of the Indies, leads to the recognition that this same imported history largely predominated until the eve of the struggles for independence by the Hispanic peoples. In fact, when we accept that Spanish America was intellectually a region of Western culture from the beginning, it seems inconceivable to imagine an intellectual history of this region separate from that of Europe. Moreover, this same Occidental culture would be incomplete without that of America. Given that the intellectual history of Spanish America began as an imported history, it is logical to next ask when this culture really succeeded in becoming independent. The answer to this all-consuming question will be dealt with in what follows, proposed to the reader as an open conclusion to the task undertaken here of delineating a synthetic vision of the whole complex of Spanish American intellectual history in the two centuries that followed the cultural transferral realized by Spain and Europe during the 1500s. One must take into account three fundamental elements in this process: (a) the transplanting of ideas and cultural tools; (b) those who used the imported culture; and (c) the reflection, maturation process, and re-creation of the imported culture.

With regard to the first of these elements, we have seen that the importation of books or ideas from Europe began from the very moment of Columbus's encounter with the New World, thereby originating an intellectual history that is essentially and unavoidably the history of a transferal of those books and ideas from one continent to another. As Juan Marichal comments in this respect, in Spanish America "such movement is in fact one, and perhaps the major, thread that allow us to trace the coherence of its intellectual history" (21), a history of Spanish America that for three centuries (from the sixteenth to the eighteenth) is characterized by a cultural and ideological unity that is nothing more than a "direct reflection of the religious unity of the Iberian Peninsula" (22) faced with the threat represented by the triumphant Protestantism in the countries of Northern Europe. As we will see later, "it is not however credible to suppose that imported books were read in a substantially different way by their European readers" (22).

Let us take a look at some of the most significant evidence for this cultural transferal that took place during the long period between the first exploration and Conquest of America and the struggle for independence. In this respect, a brief examination of the books that circulated in the Kingdoms of the Indies and the receptivity of their readers can help enormously in the understanding of the most salient characteristics of the cultural life of these countries in the long period preceding Spanish American independence. Notarial information, library inventories, wills, and commercial documents provide extremely useful (if not revelatory) information, allowing the reconstruction of important aspects of the cultural life in Spain's American possessions. Books are by no means the only elements to be reckoned with in this kind of research. The existence and varied activities of universities must also be taken into consideration (since those of Santo Domingo, Lima, and Mexico were established early on, being founded in 1538, 1551, and 1553, respectively) as well as that of the colleges, religious institutions, and the centers of power represented by the viceregal courts. These entities and their activities not only assured the religious, cultural, political, and ideological unity of the Colonial world with the motherland but also, from an early stage, promoted, among other practical requirements, the introduction into Spanish America of a cultural medium as powerful as the printing press.

In fact, Juan de Zumárraga (1468–1548), Bishop of Mexico, wrote to Charles V in 1533 that "it might be useful and convenient to have there a press and paper mill" (Baudot 316). Shortly afterward, in 1535, the year in which Antonio de Mendoza became viceroy, the first printing press in America was installed in Mexico with the support and authorization of Bishop Zumárraga. This was thanks to the printer Juan Cromberger, based in Seville, who obtained exclusive rights for Mexico and sent an Italian, Juan Pablos (Johannes Pauli or Paoli), to act as his representative there. As the Mexican chronicler Father Agustín Dávila Padilla (1562–1604) reported, Pablos was the "first printer who came to this land" (Baudot 317). In 1539 he published the first book printed in America, the *Doctrina christiana en lengua mexicana y castellana* [Christian Doctrine in the Mexican and Spanish Language] under contract to Bishop Zumárraga. The printing press arrived somewhat later in Peru (1582), this time thanks to Antonio Ricardi, an Italian printer from Piedmont, who moved to Lima from Mexico, bringing his own machine with him. The first book to appear in Peru was *Doctrina cristiana o catecismo* [Christian Doctrine or Catechism], approved by the Third Council of Lima (1582–1583), rapidly followed by the publication of *Arte y vocabulario Quechua* [General Principles of the Vocabulary of the Quechuan Language]. An idea of the importance of the role played by the printing press after its introduction into Spanish America is provided by the mention, in an inventory over a century later (1689), that around twenty presses existed in Mexico City alone, with approximately 2000 published titles during the seventeenth century that included more than 600 devotional tracts and sermons and twenty-two works on indigenous languages as well as a respectable number of texts on medicine, astronomy, and literature (Maza 58). Certainly the great majority of books printed during the seventeenth and eighteenth centuries were destined for the use of the numerous clergy that inhabited the Kingdoms of the Indies for the purposes of instruction and catechism. A good example is the work of the Jesuit Andrés Pérez de Ribas's history of the Jesuit missions in northern Mexico (see **Figure** 2). However, the continuous development of the medium in Spain's overseas possessions, along with the importing of books from Spain and Europe, played an undoubtedly important role in the process of consolidating the strong link between the colonies and the mother country from the time of the Conquest.

Figure 2.

Andrés Pérez de Ribas, History of the Triumph of Our Holy Faith *published in Madrid by Alonso de Paredes in 1645. The original is in the Ayer Collection of the Newberry Library, Chicago. (Archive of the author)*

It has been established that the most important centers of cultural life, such as the viceregal capitals of Mexico and Lima (and others to a lesser extent), had no lack of printed material; nor was this material limited to the needs of the Church, though it constituted the most important customer for books within the colonial community. If works of a religious nature, whether from local presses or imported from Spain, dominated all other genres in the libraries of Spanish America, surprising quantities of purely secular works of fiction, poetry, drama, history, and other works of the imagination were sold, not only to the lay public of the viceregal capitals but also to many clerics who found such reading recreational. As Leonard has remarked, "Many of the convents and monasteries possessed rich libraries which steadily grew in size and variety, while the lordly officials of the state, merchants, wealthy Creoles, and even individuals in humbler categories, owned book collections of impressive proportions"(1959, 80).

In 1620, for example, one Simon García Becerril of Mexico City submitted an inventory of his own small library to the Inquisition as part of a routine investigation on their part. Particularly interesting was the discovery, among the listed works of imaginative literature, of various Italian texts in their original language that, as Leonard rightly emphasizes, "testifies to the close cultural and political ties of the Spanish and Italian peninsulars since the fifteenth century and earlier" (1959, 81). The importance of these works in García Becerril's

collection "lies in the fidelity with which it reflects the current tastes of the mother country in a remote center of the New World" (Leonard 1959, 81). Apart from a *Diccionario de la lengua toscana* [Dictionary of the Tuscan Language] and works by Boccaccio such as *De claris mulieribus* [1350; On Illustrious Women] and the *Laberinto de amor* [1546; Labyrinth of Love], the inventory included *La Cortegiana* (1524), a comedy by an author similar to Pietro Aretino who would later figure in the *Indice último de los libros prohibidos y mandados expurgar para todos los reynos y señoríos* [1790; Definitive Index of Forbidden and Expurgated Books for all Kingdoms and Communities], the *Tragedia de Fedra* [Tragedy of Fedra] by the more well-known Francesco Boza Candioto, *Arcadia* by Sannazaro (a pastoral novel widely circulated in Europe), Ariosto's *Orlando furioso,* and *Gerusalemme liberata* by Torquato Tasso. Among the books of pious verse owned by García Becerril was a copy of *Vergel de flores divinas* [1582; Garden of Divine Flowers] by Juan López de Ubeda (fl. 1579–1582) from Toledo and *Flores de poetas ilustres de España* [1605; Anthology of Illustrious Poets of Spain], a work that "in some respects, opened the era of Baroque verse" (Leonard 1959, 82).

Even more interesting is another catalogue of 1663 volumes belonging to the private library of Melchor Pérez de Soto, native of Mexico and one of the builders of the Cathedral there, who was examined by the Holy Office in 1655 under suspicion of heresy. The inventory made by the officers of the Inquisition who examined Pérez de Soto's library included "not only an amazing diversity of religious literature, secular nonfiction, and belles lettres in such different languages as Latin, Italian, French, Flemish, Dutch, and even English, but much in the owner's native Spanish" (Leonard 1959, 93). The constant presence of Italian authors and others writing in the Italian style, already noted in the private library of García Becerril, is substantially confirmed here by the existence of works by Dante, Petrarch, Sannazaro, Guarini, Ariosto, Guicciardini, Castiglione, and various others. Religious literature takes up a third of the total number of books, notably the homiletic writings of Saint Teresa of Avila, Saint John of the Cross, Fray Luis de León, Fray Luis de Granada, and many others.

A far more important quantity of works can be found in the category defined by Leonard as "secular nonfiction" (1959, 93), represented by works of history, philosophy, architecture, sculpture, music, medicine, mathematics, navigation, astrology, astronomy, and military strategy, along with numerous treatises on such topics as mining, agriculture, carpentry, and horsemanship. There are more than 150 titles on the history of the world from its beginnings to the period contemporary with Pérez de Soto. Worthy of note among the books on astronomy are works by Copernicus and Kepler, authors regarded with suspicion by the Catholic world of the time. Indeed, writes Leonard, "at the mid-point of the seventeenth century when the Baroque age was in full flower, when the neomedieval culture of theology and scholasticism seemed all pervasive, particularly in the overseas possessions of Spain, such an abundance of scientific, mathematical and technical literature in the library of an artisan with no apparent connection to the intellectual circles of viceregal society is surprising" (1959, 93–94).

Literary works including poetry, fables, and essays comprise the third category of books owned by Pérez de Soto, representing a fifth of his entire library; this includes works by the most widely read and popular writers in the

Spanish-speaking world. These books were of the kind that passed from hand to hand and for this reason merit special attention. Many chivalric romances are featured such as *Amadís de Gaula, Lisuate de Grecia, Amadís de Grecia, Don Florisel de Niquea, Palmerín de Oliva, Palmerín de Inglaterra, Don Belianís de Grecia,* and various others of the same genre. The appearance of the pastoral novel is also consistent, represented by a good number of works such as Sannazaro's *Arcadia* (in both Italian and Spanish), the *Pastor Fido* by Guarini, and *Diana* (1559) by Jorge de Montemayor (1520–1561). The picaresque novel, the other extreme of prose fiction, figures in Pérez de Soto's library in the form of the second part of *Guzmán de Alfarache* [1599; The Life of Guzmán de Alfarache] by Mateo Alemán (1547–1615) and *Historia de la vida del Buscón* [1603–1604; Story of the Life of the Buscón] by Francisco de Quevedo (1580–1645). Collections of short stories are also represented, in particular the group of moral tales from the fourteenth century known as *El Conde Lucanor*. When it comes to poetry, the library of the Creole builder, according to Leonard, "almost provides an index from the fifteenth to the seventeenth centuries" (1959, 96) in which the works of Luis de Góngora (1561–1627), revered model of innumerable good and bad baroque poets, especially in Spanish America, make an expected appearance. Among the many authors of histories appears the name of the Inca Garcilaso de la Vega, who has a particular interest for Colonial literature in that, as a scion of Spanish and indigenous ancestors, he dealt with specifically American themes.

The existence of this very complete library (despite the inexplicable absence of *Quijote*) in the hands of a secular member of society of relatively humble social status and in a region far from the cultural centers of Europe would suggest that Pérez de Soto made his purchases gradually in local bookshops. Men of his standing rarely imported directly from Peninsular booksellers, who generally dealt wholesale with colonial merchants. Travelers from Spain frequently brought books for sale in their baggage to defray the costs of the journey; perhaps the Creole bibliophile had acquired some works in this way. According to Leonard the facts of the Inquisitorial investigation into Pérez de Soto "support this theory of local purchase, since one of the witnesses against him, Antonio Calderón, son of the proprietor of the best-established printing and bookshop in the capital, testified that the architect often came to his parent's store where he chatted about his astrological interests" (Leonard 1959, 97). Even though contraband in forbidden books was not rare, it is probable that the Mexican bibliophile acquired the majority of his collection by legal means. Libraries like that of Pérez Soto were not likely the exception in Spanish America. The library of García Becerril mentioned above, though less conspicuous, seems to confirm this. If one individual of modest resources, such as the artisan Pérez de Soto, could amass such a large and varied quantity of books, then it is almost certain, writes Leonard, "that wealthier members of the community, laymen as well as clergymen, brought together even richer assortments" (Leonard 1959, 97). On the other side, notarized archives, edited and unedited, from various regions of Spanish America evidence the truth of this statement and it is scarcely necessary to offer other proof of the inefficacy of legislation against the free circulation of books; its application was clearly frequently wrongly interpreted. The presence of so much imaginative literature and informative lay works in colonial book catalogues, of which the inventory of Pérez

Soto is only one of the more interesting, is an indication of the limited obstacles that the Inquisition put in the way of the acquisition and reading of books, excepting those that contained opinions considered heretical from the point of view of orthodox Catholicism. With the exception of the volumes on astrology, it is noteworthy that the Holy Office returned to the widow of Pérez de Soto (who had died a little after the start of the Inquisitorial process) the entire library he had amassed (Leonard 1959, 98).

In terms of the consumers of imported culture, the case of Mexico describes a situation with sufficient clarity that it was not likely very different from that of other important cities of Spanish America. In the 1680s a population of around 400,000 lived in the capital. Even though the mixing of races had progressed during the preceding century and a half, 72,000 individuals were considered to have pure European blood. Of these, 22,000 were male Spaniards who lived in the city with their families; another 20,000 men were travelers or temporary residents, while the female white population was calculated at 30,000. Indigenous inhabitants were estimated at 80,000, though many more were entering or leaving the city on a continual basis. A minority of 10,000 blacks and mulattos, both slaves and free men, existed who acted generally as domestic servants or retail and door-to-door salesmen. Various kinds of *mestizos* made up the rest of the population (Waffer 453–57). Socially, the *criollo* class was the most affluent, having notably increased both in number and economic power over the course of the century. During this period the cultural life of the capital was particularly vigorous. In 1683, for example, one of the most elaborate poetic tournaments was celebrated in the University of Mexico, complete with processions, pageantry, oratory, and theatrical representations (Leonard 1959, 162). Plays were written and produced. The celebrated Sor Juana Inés de la Cruz (1648–1695) was at the time composing the best poetry of the period in Spanish and many books were imported and read.

The religious orders had by then accrued large book collections that were rich in important volumes and rare manuscripts. The College of the Carmelitas Descalzas (Barefoot Carmelites) in the remote convent of San Angel could boast of a library "among the best in the Indies," endowed with "around twelve thousand volumes" (Gemelli Careri 67); other seminaries and schools could make equal claims. Many collections were semi-public and accessible to various interested individuals and foreign visitors of a certain social standing and culture. Other less conspicuous libraries belonged to individuals, lesser officials, professors, lawyers, doctors, merchants, and other secular members of society who, like Simón García Becerril and Melchór Pérez de Soto, regularly acquired volumes imported by local booksellers, many of them lightweight and read for recreational purposes (Leonard 1959, 162–63). During these years, the great scholar of the University of Mexico, Carlos Sigüenza y Góngora (1645–1700), eagerly collected manuscripts and diverse material connected with the indigenous past, mathematics, astronomy, engineering, history, and philosophy, for a library that was considered one of the best of the Colonial period. The buying public for books was so large that the number of merchants in this sector continually increased to a surprising degree. They were generally owners of local printing workshops who also imported printed books on a large scale. Perhaps the most important of all was the bookshop belonging to the widow of Bernardo Benavides de Calderón. Founded half a century earlier by a native of Alcalá de Henares, this bookshop grew rapidly and in 1683 produced a considerable percentage of the printed material in the locality (Medina 1907, cxxviii; Leonard 1959, 162–63).

An inventory of 266 titles arranged alphabetically according to author was part of this enterprise, providing edifying information regarding the reading preferences and cultural interests of the Mexican public toward the end of the seventeenth century. Unfortunately, the number of examples of each title has been omitted, thereby preventing an analysis of the relative popularity of each work. The books appearing in this inventory can be divided up into various categories: religious writing, secular literature (not novels), and belles lettres. Approximately half of the titles belong to the category of religious writings, for reasons already mentioned, but the works of fiction certainly would have enjoyed greater popularity since they were passed from hand to hand and probably had the widest public.

What singled out a gentleman was his knowledge of classics and history. The inventory abounded with the works of Latin authors such as Cicero, Virgil, Seneca, and Ovid. The inclusion of the poetic works of Luis de Góngora was no surprise; his enormous influence was evident in the numerous poetic tournaments celebrated in the university. Spain could boast a great popular theater in the seventeenth century; it is therefore not strange that the *corrales de comedias* (open air dramatic performances) in Mexico City were fully attended on an almost daily basis, while the printed versions of these plays delighted their readers equally. From the beginning of the century the *Partes* or pamphlets, each one with a dozen plays, introduced works by Peninsular dramatists on a continual basis to an enthusiastic public in America. Such works also meant a thriving trade for both printers and booksellers.

The list of Benavides's widow is headed by Pedro Calderón de la Barca (1600–1681), the dramatist who incarnated perfectly the most enduring spirit of the Baroque period. This inventory includes his *Quinta parte* [Fifth Partition] or *Colección de comedias* [Collection of Plays], published in Madrid in 1677. Though the reading of plays was fashionable in the Hispanic world of the seventeenth century, plays by no means replaced the prose novel in its various forms. However, there existed a general tendency to insert didactic elements, which meant the genre was less popular than the brilliant verse plays. During the 1680s enthusiasm for the chivalric romances of the 1500s, still perceptible in the library of Pérez de Soto in 1655, had ceased totally, but another two genres of opposite character survived, notably syrupy pastoral fiction and the picaresque tale, notorious for its knavery and venomous satire. Evidently cultured Mexicans in populous New Spain had a rich and diversified supply of entertaining books to choose from, and their tastes did not much differ from their Peninsular contemporaries. It is not surprising therefore that the period produced spirits as restless and talented as the great poet Sor Juana Inés de la Cruz in Mexico and the enlightened investigative writer Pedro de Peralta y Barnuevo (1663–1743) in Lima, two figures that certainly occupy an influential place not only in the colonial literature of their time but also in the greater sphere of Hispanic culture. In fact the Baroque period was one of particular splendor for all genres of Spanish American literature, including epic poetry, drama, and prose. As José Miguel Oviedo (b. 1934) commented, during this period there is a "flowering of great creative personalities, whose projects and aesthetic visions have a grade of complexity, grandeur and originality that is perhaps surprising in an environment that had only been introduced to the Spanish language and begun to organize its cultural life a century earlier" (173). Individuals such as the Inca Garcilaso in the first half of the seventeenth century, Sor Juana Inés de la Cruz in the second half, and Pedro de Peralta y Barnuevo (1663–1743) from the end of that century into the first decades of the eighteenth century, give the "general impression of maturity, affirmation and inner certainty" (173). At the same time it must not be forgotten that these writers "were surrounded by numerous talents of considerable consequence who gave colonial literature a very defined profile" (173).

This brilliance in seventeenth-century America is sometimes considered as an obvious reflection of the Peninsular culture of the Golden Age. To a certain degree this is true, notes José Miguel Oviedo, given that the hegemony of the mother country was both spiritual and aesthetic, and "estos ecos ultramarinos y periféricos de la cultura central . . . no eran sino confirmaciones de un vigor que se desbordaba por sus fronteras físicas" (1:174) ("these overseas echoes on the periphery of the central culture . . . were no more than confirmations of a vigor that overflowed its physical borders"). But, adds the critic, this is only partially true, pointing out that "lo cierto es que, si los escritores de América . . . crearon estimulados por las obras de los grande nombres que venían desde España–Lope, Cervantes, Calderón, Quevedo y tantos pocos–, lo hicieron con un creciente sentido, no de subordinación, sino de *comunidad estética*, de la que ellos eran protagonistas con un rango en nada inferior a los peninsulares" (1: 174) ("it is undeniable that if the writers of America . . . created from the stimulus of works by the great names that came from Spain–Lope de Vega, Miguel de Cervantes, Pedro Calderón de la Barca, Francisco de Quevedo and many others–, they did so with a growing sense, not of subordination, but of belonging to an *aesthetic community*, in which they were protagonists on a level equal to the Penisulars").

At the beginning of the eighteenth century, the Spanish crown passed into the hands of the Bourbons with Phillip V, grandson of Louis XIV of France, who took power as a consequence of the long War of Spanish Succession. This struggle had put two political philosophies at loggerheads: "mientras España se había ido replegando sobre sí misma, encerrándose en la triple fortaleza del pensamiento escolástico, el nacionalismo a ultranza y la rigidez contrarreformista, Francia representaba la tendencia hacia el funcionalismo, la apertura europeísta y las ideas nuevas del iluminismo" (Oviedo 1: 282) ("while Spain had folded in on herself, locked up in the triple fortress of scholastic thought, nationalism at all costs, and rigid adherence to the Counter Reformation, France represented a tendency towards functionalism, a European openness and the new ideas of the Enlightenment").

The Bourbons brought the fresh air of European reform to Spain and thus began a complex task of renovation, fostered by the authoritarian and paternalist reformism known as "enlightened despotism." This French influence revealed Spain's backwardness in comparison with the most important European nations and thus Spanish authorities eagerly attempted to modernize the nation with the aim of recovering universal prestige and standing. But as has been rightly observed, "the new universality that began to fascinate Peninsular minds did no more than reveal the inevitable decadence of their empire and provide the tools for analyzing the reasons behind her crisis" (Oviedo 282). For the critics of Spanish America, these tools soon transformed into effective weapons with which they would win independence. In this new context journalism and societies inspired by ideas of the Enlightenment merit particular attention since, stimulated by the new reformist debate at the end of the eighteenth century, these groups opened the way to freedom of thought that would bring American independence in its wake. Following the examples of gatherings inspired by the Enlightenment that proliferated in the Peninsula in deference to the new fashions from France, American subjects founded similar institutions "as a symbol of both the intellectual maturity and cultural identity of their respective territories; the idea of a nation, as a reality distinct from that of Spain . . . was bred in the core of these societies" (Oviedo 332). Among the most important of such associations that emerged during this period were the Sociedad Académica de Amantes de Lima [1790; Academic Society for the Love of Lima], the Cuban Real Sociedad Patriótica [1793; Royal Patriotic Society], the Arcadia Mexicana [1808; Mexican Arcadia], and the Sociedad Económica de Amigos del País [Economic Society of the Friends of the Nation] in Quito.

Journalism was the great passion of the period, given that it allowed for the rapid diffusion of information and culture, thereby lessening the barriers between the lettered elite and the public in general. In the last decades of the eighteenth century and even more at the beginning of the nineteenth, "a large part of intellectual and creative activity would be transmitted through newspapers and journals. A considerable number of writers directed and promoted these media or were enthusiastic collaborators" (Oviedo 333). Particularly outstanding among the journalistic media of the time were the glorious biweekly *Mercurio Peruano*, which from 1791 to 1795 realized the great achievement of publishing more than 600 issues; the *Gaceta de México* (1784–1809); the *Gacetas de Literatura de México* (1788–1795); *El Papel Periódico de La Habana* (1790–1804); the *Primicias de la Cultura de Quito* (1791); *El Telégrafo Mercantil* (Buenos Aires 1801–1802); the *Seminario del Nuevo Reino de Granada* (1808–1811) in Bogotá; and the *Gaceta de Caracas* (1808).

At the same time, between the last decades of the eighteenth century and the first years of the nineteenth century, the imported book and above all the prolific writings of the philosophers responsible for the *Encyclopedia* and the Enlightenment, took on a new character and began to be read as an incitement to reform individual and collective ways of life. The library of Bishop Manuel de Azamor y Ramírez (1733–1796), today part of the National Library of Buenos Aires, was a case in point, for it included Rousseau's *Social Contract*, the works of Voltaire and Montesquieu, Bayle's Dictionary, and other equally scandalous examples of heterodoxy. In a similar vein, the inventory of books belonging to Francisco Ortega (1793–1849) in Montevideo, drawn up in 1790, featured twenty-eight volumes of the *Encyclopedia* and works by Voltaire, Montesquieu, Robertson, and Marmontel (Leguizamón 72). This is the moment when a vast intellectual movement among the lettered classes of Spanish America was being outlined; it had a clearly political agenda and generated a literature that would not be out of place defined as committed (see Oviedo). This is the moment, in other words, that initiated the period in the intellectual history of Spanish America so well defined in Juan Bautista Alberdi's (1810–1884) phrase: "America practices what Europe thinks." This is the period, to answer the question proposed at the beginning of these concluding considerations with respect

to an intellectual history of Spanish America, during which this culture embarked on its great effort to free itself and arrive at true independence.

Moreover, as Juan Marichal has clearly stated in a 1985 article on the significance of the intellectual history of Spanish America, from this time onward one notes "a marked regional variety in the selection of imported books. In other words, intellectual history from the end of the eighteenth century lacks the uniformity of the previous centuries. Thus the European book was no longer an object that remained unaltered in the hands of its American readers. The personalities of these countries and their differing circumstances were responsible for very different ways of interpreting and experiencing the European texts" (22). Proceeding from Alberdi's comment quoted above, the scholarly Spaniard therefore identified the main thread of the intellectual history of Spanish America from independence to today as being located in the freedom of thought at the end of the eighteenth century and the beginning of the nineteenth century and reveals how, at this crucial moment, European thinking began to assume a new character in America, thereby achieving "what could be called the circumstantial transmutation (in the Ortegan sense of circumstance) of imported ideas" (Marichal 22). According to Marichal's lucid analysis, the main thread of the intellectual history of Spanish America from Independence to the modern day consists in the "circumstantial transmutation" of imported books and ideas. Once on American soil, these imported ideas acquired a character that perhaps constituted a feature of the intellectual history of Spanish America, what Marichal defines as the "biographical incarnation" of ideas brought in from outside (24). Indeed certain imported ideas took on a much more effective life in America in the "biographical incarnations" of those that "practiced" them, as Alberdi would say, and the intellectual history of Spanish America "shows the application of new meanings to these foreign ideas, given that the reading that enthusiasts of *Quijote* (in the strict sense of profound readers) gave imported books clarified them to a degree superior to that of its European readers" (25).

From Miranda to Bolívar and from Alberdi to Octavio Paz (1914–1998), many Spanish American intellectuals have been without doubt "Quixotic" readers in accordance with Marichal's clear interpretation of the word. Many have been driven off course, but as Marichal rightly points out, the history of their "projectist" dreams in the political and moral field "is the history of the continuity of a faith, and as such is a constant stimulus to create history" (25)–in other words, an act of faith in the future of the people of Spanish America and humanity itself.

Translation by Jessica Johnson

Works Cited

Amadís de Gaula. 1950. *Libros de caballerías*. Ed. Pascual de Gayangos. Madrid: Atlas.

Anghiera, Pietro Martire d'. 1912. *De orbe novo: Eight Decades*. 2 vols. Trans. and Ed. Francis Augustus MacNutt. New York: Putnam.

Avonto, Luigi. 1981. *Mercurino Arborio di Gattinara e l'America: Documenti inediti per la storia delle Indie Nuove nell'archivio del Gran Cancelliere di Carlo V.* Vercelli: Società Stoárica Vercellese.

———. 1995. *Mirando al Otro: América en la literatura de viajes de los italianos (siglos XV–XVI)*. Montevideo: Universidad de la República, Facultad de Humanidades y Ciencias de la Educación.

Ballesteros Beretta, Antonio. 1947. *Figuras imperiales*. Buenos Aires: Espasa-Calpe.

Bartra, Roger. 1992. *El salvaje en el espejo*. Mexico City: Universidad Nacional Autónoma de México.

Bataillon, Marcel. 1932. "Erasme au Méxique." *Deuxième Congrès International des Sciences Historiques.* 14–16 April 1930. Alger. 31–44.

——. 1962. "Agrajes sin obras." *Studi ispanici* I. Pisa: Università degli Studi." 18–32.

——. 1986. "Erasmo y el Nuevo Mundo." *Erasmo y España.* 3rd ed. Trans. Antonio Alatorre. Rpt. Mexico City: Fondo de Cultura Económica. 807–31.

Baudot, Georges. 1983. *La vida cotidiana en la América española en tiempos de Felipe II. Siglo XVI.* Trans. Stella Mastrangelo. Mexico City: Fondo de Cultura Económica.

Carrizo, Juan Alfonso. 1945. *Antecedentes hispano-medievales de la poesía tradicional argentina.* Buenos Aires: Publicaciones de Estudios Hispánicos.

Castiglione, Baldassare. 1884. *Il Cortegiano.* Firenze: Sansoni.

Cervantes, Miguel de. 1987. *Don Quijote de la Mancha.* Barcelona: Edicomunicación.

Céspedes del Castillo, Guillermo. 1988. "Raíces peninsulares y asentamiento indiano: los hombres de las fronteras." *Proceso histórico al conquistador.* Ed. Francisco de Solano. Madrid: Alianza Editorial. 37–50.

Colección de documentos inéditos relativos al descubrimiento, conquista y colonización de las posesiones españolas de América y Oceanía. 1864–1884. 42 vols. Ed. Joaquín F. Pacheco, Francisco de Cárdenas and Luis Torres de Mendoza. Madrid: Real Academia de la Historia.

Coll y Toste, Cayetano. 1967. *Leyendas puertorriqueñas.* Mexico City: Orion.

Columbus, Christopher. 1970. *The Voyages of Christopher Columbus.* Trans. and Ed. Cecil Jane. New York: Argonaut Press.

——. 1982a. "Diario del Primer Viaje." *Textos y documentos completos.* Ed. Consuelo Varela. Madrid: Alianza Editorial. 15–138.

——. 1982b. "Carta a Luis de Santángel." *Textos y documentos completos.* Ed.Consuelo Varela. Madrid: Alianza Editorial. 139–46.

——. 1982c. "Relación del Tercer Viaje." *Textos y documentos completos.* Ed. Consuelo Varela. Madrid: Alianza Editorial. 204–21.

Cortés, Hernán. 1945. "Carta cuarta." *Cartas de relación de la conquista de Méjico.* Buenos Aires:Espasa-Calpe. Col. Austral. 241–86.

——. 1986. *Letters from Mexico.* Trans. and Ed. Anthony Pagden. New Haven and London: Yale University Press.

Díaz del Castillo, Bernal. 1982. *Historia verdadera de la conquista de la Nueva España.* 5th ed. Madrid: Espasa-Calpe. Col. Austral.

Fernández de Oviedo, Gonzalo. 1959 [1535]. *Historia general y natural de las Indias.* Madrid: Ediciones Atlas.

Gandía, Enrique de. 1929. *Historia crítica de los mitos de la conquista americana.* Buenos Aires: Juan Roldán y Cía.

García Icazbalceta, Joaquín. 1866. *Colección de documentos para la historia de México.* Vol. 2. Mexico City: Librería de J.M. Andrade.

Garcilaso de la Vega, El Inca. 1951. *The Florida of the Inca.* Trans and ed. John Grier Varner and Jeannette Johnson Varner. Austin: University of Texas Press.

Gayangos, Pascual de. 1857. Prólogo. *Libros de caballerías.* Madrid: Biblioteca de Autores Españoles. Rpt. 1950. Madrid: Atlas. V–LV.

Gemelli Careri, Giovanni Francesco. 1976 [1697]. *Viaje a la Nueva España.* Trans. Francisca Perujo. Mexico City: Universidad Nacional Autónoma de México.

Gil, Juan. 1989. *Mitos y utopías del descubrimiento.* 3 vols. Madrid: Alianza Editorial.

Giménez Fernández, Manuel. 1960. *Bartolomé de las Casas.* Vol. 2. Sevilla: Escuela de Estudios Hispano-Americanos.

Leguizamón, Julio. 1945. *Historia de la literatura hispanoamericana.* Vol.1. Buenos Aires: Ed. Reunidas.

Leonard, Irving A. 1933. *Romances of Chivalry in the Spanish Indies.* Berkeley: University of California Press.

——. 1953. *Los libros del conquistador.* Trans. Mario Monteforte Toledo. Mexico City: Fondo de Cultura Económica.

——. 1959. *Baroque Times in Old Mexico: Seventeenth-Century Persons, Places, and Practices.* Ann Arbor : University of Michigan Press.

——. 1964. *Books of the Brave.* New York: Gordian Press.

——. 1990. "Conquistador y cronista: Bernal Díaz del Castillo." *Ensayos y semblanzas: Bosquejos históricos y literarios de la América Latina colonial.* Trans. Juan José Utrilla. Mexico City: Fondo de Cultura Económica. 47–53.

Madariaga, Salvador de. 1945. *Cuadro histórico de las Indias.* Buenos Aires: Editorial Sudamericana.

Marichal, Juan. 1985. "La significación de la historia intelectual de la América Latina." *Rábida* [Huelva] 2: 20–25.

Martínez Ruiz, Juan. 1959. "Un 'Agrajes sin obras' entre los conquistadores de Méjico." *Iberida* (Río de Janeiro) 2:103–30.

Maza, Francisco de la. 1968. *La ciudad de México en el siglo XVI.* Mexico City: Universidad Nacional Autónoma de México.

Medina, José Toribio. 1907. *La imprenta en México, 1539–1821.* Vol 1. Santiago de Chile: Imprenta Universitaria. Rpt. 1965. Amsterdam: N. Israël.

——. 1958–1962. *Biblioteca Hispano Americana (1493–1810).* Vol. 6. Santiago de Chile: Fondo Histórico y Bibliográfico José Toribio Medina.

Menéndez Pidal, Ramón. 1939. *Los romances de América y otros estudios.* Buenos Aires: Espasa-Calpe. Col. Austral.

Olschki, Leo. 1941. "Ponce de León's Fountain of Youth: History of a Geographic Myth." *Hispanic American Historical Review.* 21.3: 364–83.

Oviedo, José Miguel. 1995. *Historia de la literatura hispanoamericana. De los orígenes a la Emancipación.* Vol.1. Madrid: Alianza Editorial.

Pigafetta, Antonio. 1988. *Primer viaje alrededor del globo.* Madrid: Ed. Grech.

Riquer, Martín de. 1987. *Estudios sobre el Amadís de Gaula.* Barcelona: Sirmio.

Rivera Novo, Belén, and Luisa Martín Merás. 1992. *Cuatro siglos de cartografía en América.* Madrid: Ed. Mapfre.

Rodríguez de Montalvo, Garci. 1950 [1510]. *Las Sergas de Esplandián: Libros de caballerías.* Ed. Pascual de Gayangos. Madrid: Atlas.

——. 1992. *The Labors of the Very Brave Knight Esplandián.* Trans. William Thomas Little. Binghamton: Center for Medieval and Early Renaissance Studies, State University of New York at Binghamton.

Rojas, Ricardo. 1924–25. *Historia de la literatura argentina.* 8 vols. 2nd ed. Buenos Aires: La Facultad.

Schevill, Rudolph. 1943. "La novela histórica, las crónicas de Indias y los libros de cavallería." *Revista de Indias* (Bogota) 2nd ser. 59–60: 173–96.

Stirling Maxwell, William. 1853. *The Cloister Life of the Emperor Charles V.* Boston: Crosby, Nichols & Co.

Thacher, John Boyd. 1904. *Christopher Columbus: His Life, His Works, His Remains.* 3 vols. New York: G.P. Putnam's Sons.

Thomas, Henry. 1920. *Spanish and Portuguese Romances of Chivalry.* Cambridge: Cambridge University Press.

Ticknor, George. 1851. *Historia de la literatura española.* Vol. 1. Trans. Pascual de Gayangos y Enrique de Vedia. Madrid: Imprenta de la Publicidad.

——. 1988. *La Florida.* Madrid: Alianza Editorial.

Vives, Juan Luis. 1940. *Instrucción de la mujer cristiana.* Buenos Aires: Espasa-Calpe. Col. Austral.

Waffer, Leonel. 1939. *La ciudad de México en 1678.* Mexico City: Universidad Nacional Autónoma de México.

CHAPTER 2

THE BOOK IN BRAZIL
LIBRARIES AND PRESSES

José Mindlin

The history of the book and the press in Brazil is very different from that in Spanish America, for books in Spanish were already being published in the New World in the sixteenth century, while Brazil was to wait more than two centuries. Printing came only as a consequence of the transference of the Portuguese royal family to Brazil in 1808, as a result of the French invasion of Portugal. Only then was the Imprensa Régia (Royal Press) created. Before that, the possible subversive power of the press had been seen as a threat by the metropolis, and the only publishing attempt that is historically documented, that of Antônio Isidro de Fonseca, in Rio de Janeiro in 1747, was frustrated by the severe repressive measures imposed by the authorities: The press was impounded and the printer was deported to Lisbon. The few known publications of Isidro de Fonseca were quite innocent, the most famous being the *Relação da entrada do bispo* [Story of the Bishop's Entrance], but the fact of its being inoffensive did not diminish the fear that the mere existence of a printing press represented a danger to the security of the Colonial institutions. There was also another example that predated the Imprensa Régia, a pamphlet called *Canto encomiástico de Diogo Pereira Ribeiro de Vasconcellos* [Eulogy of Diogo Pereira Ribeiro de Vasconcellos], written by Father José Joaquim Viegas de Menezes and printed in 1806 in Vila Rica (today Ouro Preto), but it was an etching on copper of the whole pamphlet and printed calchographically. It is not, therefore, properly speaking a printed book in that it was not printed with movable type. (This pamphlet, which is extremely rare, had a facsimile edition made in 1986 by the National Library.)

With some generosity, one could say that there were some books published in the eighteenth century in what is now Brazilian territory. They were printed in Paraguay, in the Jesuit Missions, which encompassed a large part of the state of Rio Grande do Sul, the north of Argentina, and Paraguay itself. These are extremely rare editions of books written to catechize the Indians, and were printed by the Indians themselves who had learned to set type, though everything was, of course, under the guidance and supervision of the Jesuits. The number of printings must have been minimal, and it has taken me a few decades to get hold of two of these works: the *Arte de la lengua guarani* [Art of the Guarani Language] by Father Ruiz de Montoya (1585–1652) and the *Explicación del catecismo en la lengua guarani* [Explanation of the Catechism in the Guarani Language] by the Indian Nicolas Yapuguay; both were printed in 1724 in Santa Maria la Mayor. I believe it justifiable for Brazil to claim at least part of the credit for these publications, since some of the Jesuits were Portuguese. It does not seem very likely that there were other publications before 1808; in any case, none is known.

Though the introduction of the press was extremely late in Colonial Brazil, books and libraries existed there from its earliest colonization. The presence of the book goes back to the sixteenth century, already brought in by the Jesuits in 1549, who arrived in that year, led by Manoel da Nóbrega (1517–

1570). They brought books, although always in insufficient supply, for the schools they founded in several parts of the Colony. Even so, in the Colégio de Salvador there was already in the sixteenth century a library installed in a special room, as well as the same in Rio de Janeiro, São Paulo, and Espírito Santo. The library of the Colégio do Rio de Janeiro received at the beginning of the seventeenth century half of the books left behind by the Official Visitor Bartolomeu Simóes Pereira, who came to Brazil in 1577, bringing his personal library from Portugal. (I don't believe anyone knows what became of the other half.) In the seventeenth century, these libraries grew, and Father Antônio Vieira (1608–1697) could claim regarding the Colégio do Maranhão, that it was a very good library. It was well set up, in a special room with a capacity for up to 5000 volumes. This praise is significant coming from Antônio Vieira, a great friend of books, who at his own request took charge of the libraries of all the convents through which he passed. All this bibliographic wealth suffered the consequences, however, of the expulsion of the Jesuits in 1759, and a good part of the libraries in various convents was irretrievably lost.

With respect to other religious orders, the existing information on Franciscan and Benedictine monasteries reveals the existence of book collections of great importance, making a significant contribution to education. Practically all the religious orders had libraries in their monasteries and in the adjacent schools, where they taught basic education and, of course, higher-level courses for the instruction of priests. The Franciscans, in the field of education, reformulated their pedagogical methods in 1776, in accordance with the reform of the Marquis of Pombal at the University of Coimbra. The Franciscans of Bahia, Rio de Janeiro, Minas Gerais, and Pernambuco owned good libraries, some of them, like that of São Paulo, with works of encyclopedists and philosophers, thus revealing a surprising openness of mind. Great men were trained in these monasteries: for example, Frei José Mariano da Conceição Veloso, botanist and polymath, who directed, at the beginning of the nineteenth century, the Arco do Cego Press in Lisbon and was known for scientific works of major importance.

The same can be said of the Benedictine monasteries in Rio de Janeiro, Bahia, Pernambuco, and São Paulo, which also had excellent libraries, if local limitations are taken into consideration. Unfortunately, most of the records of books existing in Brazil before 1810 were lost because of the primitive conditions of life in the colony, but the existence of books and libraries is more than proved by the significant Brazilian intellectual production of this period, all of it published in Portugal and today well known, thanks mainly to the bibliographical research of Rubens Borba de Moraes. These works could not have been produced without its authors being well versed in all the themes they discussed. Furthermore, the nearly two thousand Brazilian students who studied in Europe in the eighteenth and beginning of the nineteenth centuries (basically in Coimbra, Lisbon, and Paris, but also in Montpelier, England, and Scotland) brought back books from Europe. In spite of the conditions of life, literary activity was considerable in the eighteenth century. Academies existed in several *capitanias*, the "captaincies" or large administrative estates; one of the most renowned was the Academia dos Esquecidos e a dos Renascidos [Academy of the Forgotten and of the Reborn]. Intellectuals gathered in these academies to read their work and discuss the latest books from Europe; works of surprising quality emerged. The poets of the Inconfidência Mineira of 1789 (an unsuccessful attempt to establish Brazilian Independence) deserve to be emphasized: Thomaz Antônio Gonzaga (1744–1807?), author of *Marília de Dirceu* (1792); Claudio Manoel da Costa (1729–1789); Manoel Inácio da Silva Alvarenga (1749–1814); Basílio da Gama (1740–1795), author of *Uraguay* (1769); Frei José de Santa Rita Durão (1720?–1784), author of *Caramuru* (1781); and Ignácio José de Alvarenga Peixoto (1748–1798). An important institution was the Arcádia Ultramarina, a branch of the Arcádia de Roma, whose very existence has been challenged in heated debates from the beginning of the nineteenth century to our own time, for, although several of the authors I have mentioned called themselves members of the Arcádia Ultramarina, no document is known that might prove that it actually existed. It is known that Basílio da Gama belonged to the Arcádia de Roma, but the reference to the Arcádia Ultramarina came to be considered a simple claim of status and not indication of a real institution. (The mystery was cleared up when I obtained a diploma of the Roman Arcádia in Portugal, granted to Joaquim Ignácio de Seixas Brandão, cousin of "Marília de Dirceu," admitted through the nomination of Basílio da Gama. This diploma, in addition to the signature of Sotto-Custode of the Roman Arcádia, also bears the signature of the representative of the *Fondazione della Colonia Oltramarina*.)

There is also evidence of the existence of some private libraries of great importance in Colonial Brazil, like that of Father Francisco Agostinho Gomes of Bahia, who collected thousands of volumes later donated to the Public Library of Bahia; that of Manoel Inácio da Silva Alvarenga, who owned around 1600 volumes, more than half being works of general culture and many censored books; the library of Luiz Vieira da Silva, in Minas Gerais, which served as source material for the book by the erudite critic Eduardo Frieiro, *O diabo na livraria do cônego* [The Devil in the Canon's Library]; and that of Pedro Gomes Ferrão de Castello Branco, of Salvador. These are merely a few names among the many who formed the lettered elite of Colonial Brazil. The major event, however, in the history of Brazilian libraries was the establishment of the National Library in Rio de Janeiro. The National Library, created by decree in 1810, housed the entire Royal Library brought to Brazil in 1808 by Dom João VI and consisted mainly of the Barbosa Machado (author of the *Biblioteca Lusitana*) Collection, printed in the eighteenth century and even today a reference work of fundamental importance. Numerous collections were incorporated in the course of the nineteenth and twentieth centuries: the collection of Frei José Mariano da Conceição Veloso (1742–1811), with his works of botany; the Conde da Barca collection, with over 6000 volumes from the seventeenth and eighteenth centuries; the collection of Angelis, with nearly 3000 volumes and 1300 manuscripts, dedicated especially to the Jesuit Missions of Paraguay (which, as mentioned above, included the greater part of the state of Rio Grande do Sul); the Salvador de

Medonça collection, specialized in material from the seventeenth century on the Dutch occupation in northeastern Brazil; the José Antonio Marques collection, with an emphasis on Colonial Brazil and on works by and on Camóes; the Teresa Cristina collection, donated by D. Pedro II, then in exile, with close to 50,000 volumes and more than 1000 printed maps and manuscripts, the largest collection received by the Library; the Benedito Ottoni collection, which belonged to José Carlos Rodrigues, an exceptional collection of Brasiliana, listed in the Catalogue of Rare Works published in 1907 (this catalogue is itself a classic of Brazilian bibliography); the archive from the Casa dos Contos, with about 50,000 precious documents for the study of the history of gold and diamond mining, as well as the *bandeiras*, or inland expeditions, and of the Inconfidência Mineira (1789); the Alexandre Rodrigues Ferreira collection, related to the journey of this distinguished naturalist to the Captaincies of Grão Pará, Rio Negro, Mato Grosso, and Cuiabá between 1783 and 1792, with its extraordinary series of watercolors, most of them unpublished (but about to be published in an edition worthy of them); the Abraão de Carvalho collection, dedicated to musical literature and musical scores, including rare works from the seventeenth and eighteenth centuries, totalling around 17,000 pieces; and the Morgado de Matteus collection, whose origin is the Casa de Matteus, with nearly 9000 original documents referring to the administration of the Captaincy of São Paulo by Morgado in the eighteenth century. There are also many treasures in the National Library, especially a beautiful evangelistary (a book of gospel citations to be read at the Roman Catholic Mass) from the eleventh and twelfth centuries; two copies of the Moguncia Bible, printed in 1462 by Fust & Schoeffer; the only known copy of the *Gramática da língua portuguesa* [Grammar of the Portuguese Language] of João de Barros (1496–1570), printed in 1539; the first edition of *Os Lusíadas* [The Lusiads] of 1572; the *Cultura e opulência do Brasil* [Culture and Opulence of Brazil] of Antonil, also known as João Antônio Andreoni (1650–1716), printed in Lisbon in 1711 and suppressed by the crown, which, although only six copies survived, was fortunately republished in the nineteenth century; and the *Arte da gramática da lingua mais usada na costa do Brasil* [Grammatical Art of the Language Most Used on the Coast of Brazil] by Father José de Anchieta (1534–1597), printed in Lisbon in 1595, of which very few copies are known. (In my own library [see **Figure 1**], however, there are copies of the latter work, as well as the first edition of *Os Lusíadas*–in fact, both versions of the same date, called Edition E and Edition E.E.)

However, a clarification in this review of libraries is necessary. The first library actually founded in Brazil was in Salvador, Bahia in 1811; the National Library was founded *de jure* in 1810, but it really was the relocation of the Royal Library of Portugal, that is, the transferring of a preexisting collection to Brazil. The initiative for the Library of Bahia came from sugar plantation owner Pedro Gomes Ferrão de Castello Branco, who conceived of the library as a fundamental institution to promote the education of the people. Castello Branco formulated a project that he called a "Plan for the establishment of a public library in the city of S. Salvador, Bahia de Todos os Santos," and submitted it for the approval of the "Illustrious Gentleman Conde dos Arcos, Governor and Captain-General of this Captaincy." The "Plan," dated 26 April 1811, was approved by Conde dos Arcos on April 30; its publication was authorized for purposes of public notice and the obtaining

Figure 1.

José Mindlin in his personal library, São Paulo, Brazil. (Archive of the author)

of donations on May 8. The printing was done on the press of Silva Serva, one of the first print jobs ever done in Bahia. The Conde dos Arcos himself donated eighty volumes, and the publication of the Plan resulted in the donation by private citizens of nearly 3000 volumes (which proves the existence of other private libraries in the northeast). The books of Conde dos Arcos were, however, merely loaned, as a way of attracting the donations of others, since they were later returned to the owner's library. The inauguration took place at the old Colégio dos Jesuítas on 4 August 1811. In 1818, when Conde dos Arcos left the government, the library had 7821 volumes. In that year a catalogue was published (the first to be printed in Brazil), which also came from the press of Silva Serva. The presence of censored books in the collection is important for an understanding of the Brazilian literary culture of the period, as are the holdings of the *Correio Brasiliense* [Brazilian Mail] and the *Investigador Português em Inglaterra* [Portuguese Investigator in England], since both journals were prohibited. The censored books and the banned periodicals are not listed in the catalogue for obvious reasons. The Portuguese government had consistently been concerned about the diffusion of new ideas in the colony; this policy obviously explains the delay in introducing print to Brazil.

Important libraries were established in the nineteenth century in Rio de Janeiro, including the Royal Portuguese Reading Room, and in other cities. The most important of these were in Salvador (Bahia), Recife, and Belém do Pará, and in the law schools of Olinda and São Paulo (the law schools were founded in 1827; there were also numerous municipal reading rooms in the interior of several states. At the start of the twenty-first century, Brazil can count around 5000 libraries, the majority of these being municipal and public, but there are also some university libraries throughout the country, many of them with appreciable collections of rare works.

Besides those already mentioned, the following specialized libraries are also important: in Rio de Janeiro: the Library of the Ministry of Foreign Affairs (Palácio do Itamaraty), the National Archive, the Brazilian Historical and Geographical Institute, and the Casa de Rui Barbosa Foundation, with its excellent literary collection, one of the best in Brazil, assembled by the bibliophile Plínio Doyle. In various Brazilian states, there are also the libraries of the Historical and Geographical Institutes and of the State Archives, especially those in Bahia, Minas Gerais, Pará, Pernambuco, Rio Grande do Sul, and São Paulo, which deserve mention. Concerning university libraries, the library of the Institute of Brazilian Studies of the University of São Paulo is especially important for its collection of specialized historical sources. Of the private libraries, the most important of the nineteenth century were incorporated into the collections of the National Library. Many private libraries of the twentieth century were dispersed, a fact that if, on one hand lamentable, on the other may be contributed to the formation of a number of other libraries that exist today (such as, for example, the present author's); many were acquired by universities or foreign libraries in Britain, the United States, and Australia (like the famous collection of Brazilian literature of Adir Guimarães, which is now in Australia). Others remained in Brazil: the Brasiliana collection of Carlos Rodrigues went to the National Library and the José Felix Pacheco library was acquired by the Municipal Library of São Paulo (today the Mário de Andrade Library); the important Brasiliana collections of Yan de Almeida Prado and Alberto Lamego are part of the collection of the Institute of Brazilian Studies, which contains the libraries, archives, and art collections of Mário de Andrade (1893–1945) and several other major writers, including Guimarães Rosa (1908–1967). Other universities, like those of Brasília, Campinas, and other states today also house important collections. UNICAMP, the University of Campinas, deserves to be mentioned for its efforts in developing an important bibliographical complex, which already has the libraries and archives of Sérgio Buarque de Hollanda (1902–1982), Paulo Duarte (1899–1984), Alexandre Eulálio (1932–1988), and Oswald de Andrade (1890–1954), among others. Much more, of course, could be said about libraries, were it not for the limitation of space and the need for synthesis in a work of this nature. The list of works cited will allow those interested to deepen their studies.

We now proceed on to the history of publishers and presses, which in the nineteenth century was chaotic; the available information is quite ample, but for the same reasons mentioned above, I must restrict this discussion to only its main aspects. The response to the freedom of the press was at first timid, but gained in momentum beginning with Independence, and subsequent decades saw an explosion in demand, with a significant increase in the number of publishers and presses. When one thinks of Brazilian publishing in the early decades of the nineteenth century, with the high rate of illiteracy in the country, this explosion in demand is surprising, revealing on the one hand a thirst for knowledge and the existence of cultural centers, and on the other the need for recreational reading material. Together these forces created a demand that is far superior to what would have been expected. Works of every kind–literary, scientific, religious, and political–were being published; newspapers and magazines appeared in profusion, not only in the Court but in the provinces. The second half of the nineteenth century turned out to be a period of vast diffusion of the most varied kinds of knowledge. In literature, at first, translation predominated, primarily of French and English works: Alexander Pope and Jeremy Bentham were among the most sought-after authors, but French novels like Victor Hugo's *Notre-Dame de Paris* (1831) and Balzac's *Eugénie Grandet* (1833) were popular, as were those novels that were published as *feuilletons* in Europe and became well known in Brazil in the 1830s and 1840s.

In the decade preceding Independence, the publication of books in Rio de Janeiro was limited by the monopoly of the Imprensa Régia, but by 1821 two private presses had appeared: the Nova Officina Typographica and the Typographia de Moreira e Garcez. On the eve of Independence in 1822, four more appeared: Silva Porto & Cia., Officina dos Annaes Fluminenses, Typographia do Diário, and Typographia de Torres & Costa. From then on, the presses multiplied, reaching several hundred by the end of the nineteenth century. Similar to what was going on in Rio de Janeiro, presses were being set up in the provinces, the first of these being that of Manoel Antônio da Silva Serva, as early as 1811, in Salvador (Bahia). In Minas Gerais, the first presses appeared in the 1820s in São João del Rey (1827) and Diamantina (1828), soon followed by Ouro Preto, and so on. A major change that markedly affected publishing was the very rapid development of a female reading public from the 1830s on; before this, illiteracy among women was general, mainly a strategy of *machismo*: It was thought that by keeping women illiterate they could be kept chaste. (Apparently, Brazilian women were victorious both in learning to read and in managing amorous intrigues.) Another important factor for the growth of the book marketplace was the abolition of censorship by a decree of 1821.

Let us begin this survey with the most important presses and publishers in Rio de Janeiro. Besides official publications, the Imprensa Régia published a varied selection, although it is difficult to determine any criterion for that selection. Its scope is extensive: from literature to astronomy and trigonometry, medicine and public health, the history of the Mexican empire, scientific and philosophical works, poetry, and newspapers; exaggerating just a little, one could claim to find a cross-section of everything imaginable in the publishing lists of the Imprensa Régia. *Paul e Virginie, As Aventuras do Barão de Munkausen* [The Adventures of the Baron of Munkausen], the *Diabo Coxo* [The Devil Upon Two Sticks] of Le Sage, works by Ovid, Virgil, Racine, and Voltaire, the "Ensaios Morais" [Moral Essays] and the "Essay on Criticism" by Alexander Pope (in a magnificent format), *Marília de Dirceu* by Thomaz Antônio Gonzaga, *Uraguay* by Basílio da Gama, and the collection of *O Patriota* are only some of the titles among the hundreds of examples of the eclecticism of the published list. Among the special items of note is the Letter of Pero Vaz de Caminha, a core document of Brazilian nationality, which was published for the first time in 1817 by the Imprensa Régia in the *Corografia Brasílica* of Ayres do Casal (1754?–1801?). The list is not only varied, it is huge. The publishing program of the Imprensa Régia encompassed legal works from Portugal and France; Adam Smith's *The Wealth of Nations*; treatises on agriculture, international trade, natural sciences, history, and philosophy; theatrical works (operas as well as plays); children's literature; sacred oratory; the most varied political and scientific pamphlets; and the popular serial literature of the *cordel* [chapbooks], in addition to newspapers, such as *O Patriota* and *A Gazeta do Rio de Janeiro*. The first publication to

emerge from this press on the very day (13 May 1808) that it was established was the "Report of the Dispatches Published in the Court by the Secretary of State of Foreign Trade and War." These final dispatches had not been published for lack of type! Of the "report," only three copies are known, one in the National Library, another in the library of Rubens Borba de Moraes, and a third in my own. There are other very rare publications, for example, the *Diabo Coxo* and *Marília de Dirceu*, both from 1810, the latter of which only five or six copies are known, despite the unusually large printing of 2000 copies. Rubens Borba de Moraes (1899–1987) completed and corrected the work of the great bibliographer of the Imprensa Régia, Alfredo do Valle Cabral, and fortunately concluded this task before his death in 1987, and with the assistance of the historian Ana Maria Camargo, it was published posthumously in 1993. For the information of scholars, it should be pointed out that the Imprensa Régia (or Impressão Régia) afterward adopted the names Régia Officina Typographica, Typographia Imperial e Nacional, Typographia Nacional, Typographia Real, and, finally today, Imprensa Nacional.

Of the hundreds of presses established in Rio de Janeiro in the nineteenth century, some deserve special mention: in the 1820s, Plancher-Seignot, which in the following decade came to be called Typographia Imperial de E. Saignot-Plancher, and, in the same decade, of the press of the great French printers, the Imprimerie de Gueffier & Cie., which published Masonic and anti-Jesuitic texts; the Typographia Imperial E Constitucional de J. Villeneuve & Comp. of B. Ogier, who Borba de Moraes considered the best typesetter in Brazil, and the Imprimerie et Chalcographie directed by G.H. Fourcy, which in 1839–1840 published the *Revue Française*, a number of French literary texts with beautiful engravings. At the same time, the Typographia Fluminense de Brito & Cia, of Francisco de Paula Brito, appeared and operated from 1831 to 1875, run for the last thirteen years, after the death of Paula Brito, by his widow. This press operated under several names: Tipografia Fluminense de Brito & Cia; Tipografia Imparcial de Brito; Tipografia Teixeira & Cia.; Tipografia de Paula Brito; Empresa Tipográfica Dois de Dezembro, of Paula Brito; Impressor da Casa Imperial; and Tipografia Paula Brito, Paula Brito Viúva & Genro. Francisco de Paula Brito was a major figure in nineteenth-century Brazilian publishing; he himself was a minor poet, the author of several prose works, and the translator of a dozen or so French novels. He was also the proprietor successively of five newspapers and over the years the publisher of more than eighty newspapers and magazines and nearly 400 books and pamphlets. He is also distinguished for having been the publisher of the first works of Machado de Assis (1839–1908), *A Queda que as Mulheres têm para os Tolos* [Women's Attraction to Fools], and *Desencantos* [Disenchantments], both in 1861. Machado de Assis was, in fact, Paula Brito's printer's apprentice. Paula Brito was also the publisher and editor of works of Joaquim Manoel de Macedo (1820–1882), Domingos José Gonçalves de Magalhães (1811–1882) (first edition of *A Confederação dos Tamoyos* [The Confederation of the Tamoyos], in 1856), Casimiro de Abreu (1839–1860) (first edition of *As Primaveras* [Spring], in 1859), Teixeira e Souza (1812–1861), Martins Penna (1815–1848), Mello Moraes (1816–1882), Gonçalves Dias (1823–1864), and many others.

The works of José de Alencar (1829–1877) had at least nine publishers: the Empreza Nacional do Diário published the first edition of *O Guarani* in 1857, of which only three copies are known to exist; the other publishers were B.L. Garnier and his Typographia Franco Americana, Typographia de Santos Cardoso & Irmão, Typographia Perseverança, Typographia Acadêmica, Typographia da República, and Imprensa Industrial, Typographia Cosmopolita. The works of Machado de Assis were printed, besides Paula Brito, mainly by B.L. Garnier e H. Garnier, but also by the Typographia Nacional, Typographia do Imperial Instituto Artístico, Lombaerts & Cie., by Typographia do Diário do Rio de Janeiro, Typographia do Globo (but the publisher was Gomes de Oliveira & Cia.), and by Typographia do Cruzeiro (though published by G. Vianna & Cia.).

It should be remembered that most works published by French publishers in Brazil were in good part printed in France, or, when the printing was done in Brazil, it was done by French printers, which explains the many errors in Portuguese. It is obvious, however, that on the whole these French editors had a beneficial influence as far as culture was concerned. The following nineteenth-century publishers should also be mentioned as excellent craftsmen: Hyppolito Garnier, S.A., Sisson, Eduardo and Henrique Laemmert, and J. Cremière. One must also mention the press of the Typographia do Jornal do Comércio of José Carlos Rodrigues, who published the newspaper *O Novo Mundo* in New York from 1870 to 1879 and the Typographia Brasileira of Maximiano Gomes Ribeiro, who in 1854 published the *Memórias de um Sargento de Milícias* [Memoirs of a Sergeant of the Militia] by Manoel Antônio de Almeida (1831–1861). This is an arbitrary list, for, as noted above, presses in Rio de Janeiro in the nineteenth century were extremely numerous. By the mid-twentieth century, the outstanding presses were still Livraria Garnier, succeeded by F. Briguiet; Livraria Francisco Alves; Civilização Brasileira, of Enio Silveira; and José Olympio (who rose from clerk of the Casa Garraus in São Paulo to become publisher of the principal Brazilian authors between 1930 and 1970).

In the provinces, in the nineteenth century, besides Silva Serva in Salvador (Bahia) and the presses of Minas Gerais, there were two distinguished printers from S. Luiz do Maranhão: José Maria Corrêa de Frias and Belarmino de Mattos, whose work was recognized as outstanding, fully justifying the title of the Brazilian Athens for S. Luiz de Maranhão. In addition to first-rate printing, Belarmino de Mattos published the Brazilian translation of Victor Hugo's *Les Misérables* in 1862, in the same year as the original edition. It is impossible to detail the development of printing throughout the country after the proclamation of the Republic, given the limitations of space of this essay; suffice it to say that presses were established in Bahia in 1811, in Pernambuco in 1817, in Maranhão in 1822, in Minas Gerais, in 1827, in Pará in 1828, in Ceará

in 1864, in São Paulo in 1836, in Rio Grande do Sul in 1835, in Santa Catarina between 1836 and 1838, in Amazonas by 1852 at least, in Paraná at least by 1855, in Goiás by 1837 at least—all of which shows the vitality of publishing in Brazil throughout the nineteenth century. In the twentieth century, printing and publishing existed in every state, but were concentrated in São Paulo, where the outstanding names were the publishing house of Monteiro Lobato; Companhia Editorial Nacional, founded by Octales Marcondes Ferreira; Companhia Melhoramentos; Editora José de Barros Martins; Editora Perspectiva; Brasiliense; Companhia das Letras; Ática; Illuminuras; Duas Cidades; Hucitec; Edusp; Cultura; and Paz e Terra, among many others. I should also mention here Editora Globo, run by Henrique Bertazo and Érico Veríssimo, which in Rio Grande do Sul has done excellent work and today operates in Rio de Janeiro under a different directorship.

In the works cited following this essay can be found more detailed information both about publishers and presses from 1808 to the present day and about libraries in Brazil. These sources of information are recommended for scholars on the subject. The approach to the topics of this text had to be done *à vol d'oiseau*, but I have attempted to give an idea of the vitality of the publishing process in Brazil throughout the nineteenth century, a vitality which continues today. Besides publishing Brazilian authors, with printings that in certain cases go beyond 100,000 copies, the presses have been publishing a growing number of translations, thus allowing the Brazilian public and that of other Portuguese-speaking countries adequate access to important materials.

Translation by Thomas LaBorie Burns and Gláucia Renate Gonçalves

Works Cited

Cabral, Alfredo do Valle. 1881. *Annaes da Imprensa Nacional do Rio de Janeiro de 1808 a 1822*. Rio de Janeiro: Typographia Nacional.

Frias, José Maria Côrrea de. 1978 [1866]. *Memória sobre a tipografia maranhense*. 2nd ed. São Luís: SIOGE.

Moraes, Rubens Borba de. 1969. *Bibliografia brasileira do período colonial*. São Paulo: IEB-USP.

———. 1979. *Livros e bibliotecas no Brasil colonial*. Rio de Janeiro: LCT/SCCT; São Paulo: Secretaria da Cultura.

———. 1983. *Bibliographia Brasiliana: Rare Books about Brazil Published from 1504 to 1900 and Works by Brazilian Authors of the Colonial Period*. 2 vols. 2nd ed. Los Angeles: UCLA Latin American Center Publications; Rio de Janeiro: Livraria Kosmos Editora.

———. 1993. *Bibliografia da Impressão Regia do Rio de Janeiro*. São Paulo: IEB-USP and Vitae.

CHAPTER 3

DOCUMENT: OSWALD
FREE BOOK

Augusto de Campos

When I visited Oswald de Andrade (1890–1954) in 1949, in the company of Décio Pignatari (b. 1927), Haroldo de Campos (1929–2003), and Nilo Odália (b. 1929), I did not expect to be given a magnificent gift. At one point, encouraged by the conversation with these young writers, Oswald went out for a minute and returned with four copies of *Poesias Reunidas O. Andrade* [1945; Collected Poems of O. Andrade], Edições Gaveta, in wide format, with illustrations by Tarsila, Segall, and the author, and offered them, with his autograph, to each of us. (No. 136 of this edition of just 200 copies fell to me.) The books, what remained of the 1945 edition, were piled up, if I remember correctly, on the top of a cabinet in an inner room of the apartment. Oswald handed them out in this generous way to a few friends and supporters. Such was the solitude of the poet, by now nearly in his sixties, that, "with torch on high, playing Trotsky, in a soliloquy with the permanent revolution," as Patricia Galvão (1910–1962) had described him a year before (183), he continued to vociferate against everything and everybody in defense of Modernism and "Anthropophagy," waiting to be redeemed by future generations.

The *Poesias Reunidas* consisted of the only two books of poems previously published by Oswald, *Pau Brasil* [1925; Brazilwood] and *Primeiro Caderno do Aluno de Poesia Oswald de Andrade* [1927; First Notebook of the Student of Poetry Oswald de Andrade], plus the unpublished "Cântico dos Cânticos para Flauta e Violão" [1942; Canticle of Canticles for Flute and Guitar] and a few "Poemas Menores" ["Minor Poems"]. Of the first book there is no printing record; the second had only 300 copies. Twenty years later, the whole publishing fortune of Oswald's poetry was reduced to this small harvest, and his work would only begin to be recovered with the publication, in 1966, of the new *Poesias Reunidas*, to which would be added the poem "O Escaravelho de Ouro" [1946; The Gold Scarab]. The fortune of the novels *Memórias Sentimentais de João Miramar* [1924; Sentimental Memoirs of João Miramar] and *Serafim Ponte Grande* [1933; Seraphim Grosse Pointe], or of the plays *O Homen e o Cavalo* [1934; The Man and the Horse], *A Morta* [The Dead Woman], *O Rei da Vela* [1937; The King of the Candle] has not been any better, since they have not been republished and at that point the plays had not been staged.

Nevertheless, this *Primeiro Caderno do Aluno de Poesia Oswald de Andrade*, printed at the press on Rua Santo Antonio, No. 19, in the wide format of 26.5 by 21.5 centimeters, with cover by Tarsila and drawings by Oswald, type in two colors (all the titles in red), is possibly the most beautiful book of our Modernist poetry. (See **Figure 1.**) It is also the most beautiful coherent set of poems, in its risk-taking and boldness in language, as much as in the book's formal and material conception. The edition put together by Oswald and Tarsila has something to do not only with poetry itself, but with a concept of reformulating the visual language of the book; this puts it in contact with the great undertakings of the European avant-garde, in the path opened up by Mallarmé in *Un coup de*

dés jamais n'abolira le hasard [1897; A Dice Throw Will Never Do Away with Chance], and in the preface that Mallarmé added to the poem: "Aujourd'hui ou sans présumer de l'avenir qui sortira d'ici, rien ou presque un art, reconnaissons aisément que la tentative participe, avec imprév" (1951, 158) ("Today or without presuming upon the future which will come out of this, nothing or almost an art, let as readily acknowledge that the endeavor has an unforseen part") (1977, 257). This hypothetical book was a free book, which would begin to be written collectively in our century.

To stick to only a few examples, it would suffice to remember, as a group phenomenon, the editions of the Russian cubist-futurist or constructivist books, which linked poets such as Khlebnikov, Mayakovski, Krutchonik, Kamenski, and Iliazd with important artists like Malyevich, Rodchenko, Rotzanova, Gontchovora, Laryonov, and El Lissitski, and even incorporated the enthusiasm of critics such as Roman Jákobson, who, under the pseudonym of Aliagrov, took part as a poet, with Krutchonik, in 1915 in a remarkable book *Zaúm*: On the col-

Figure 1.

Cover page of the first edition, 1927, of Oswald de Andrade's notebook. (Archive of the author)

lage cover, a red cardboard heart with a shirt button glued on; on the inside, between the poems, colorful engravings of the playing cards of Olga Rotzanova. In *Pro Eto* [Of This] of 1923, the poems of Mayakovski appear joined to the photo montages of Rodtchenko; in *Dliá Gólossa* [For Voice], of the same year, Mayakovski's poems are definitively integrated into the visual project by Lissitski with only typographical resources, in two colors (red and black), as a functional reading guide.

In this way, the poetic texts were liberated from conventional printing restrictions, at the same time that the idea of illustration evolved in the sense of a greater interpenetration with the poem and of a deeper accommodation to the book as a whole. Another example, certainly dear to Brazilian Modernists—Paulo Prado (1869–1943) owned one of the rare copies, No. 119, dedicated by the author to him and to "*tous les amis de San-Paolo*" in 1924—was *Prose du Transsibérien et de la Petite Jeanne de France* [The Prose of the Trans-Siberian and of Little Jeanne of France] of Blaise Cendrars (1887–1961), a volume printed in several tones and illustrated with "simultaneous colors" by Sonia Delaunay in 1913: an accordion-book, which (when opened up) was about two meters long (linked together, the 150 copies of the announced printing, it was said, would reach the height of the Eiffel Tower). Brazilian Modernist periodicals, especially *Klaxon*, from the visual point of view, would attempt to respond to the provocations of its peers—*Lacerba*, *Dada*, *Blast*, and so many others. In the book projects, however, visual boldness tended to be restricted to the cover, with no adventuring into inner programming.

It was Oswald, with the aid of Tarsila, who gave the most significant response—a little in *Pau Brasil* and a lot in this *Primeiro Caderno*—which would inspire at least one other exception: the amateurish but provocative "lbum de Pagu" written and drawn by the 18-year-old in 1929, a unique book which, handed over to Tarsila, was only rediscovered and disseminated in the 1970s, almost half a century later. It was a response to a new tradition, that of the visual appreciation of the book, distinct from the deluxe edition and only occasionally similar to the artist's book, which would begin to be lost in the 1930s. One of the last expressive examples would be the first edition, in 1931, of *Cobra Norato* [The Snake Norato], of Raul Bopp (1898–1984), with a cover by Flávio de Carvalho. The latter would still maintain the Modernist enthusiasm in issue No. 1 of *RASM* (*Revista Anual do Salão do Maio*) [Annual Magazine of the May Salon], published in 1939, with its brutal aluminum cover that incorporated something of the Futurist experiments of the *libromacchina bullonato* (Depero/Azari, 1927) and the *libro di lata* (Marinetti/Albissola, 1932). As a defined, collective project, this tradition would only be resumed in the visual poetry of the 1950s.

It is essential, however, to redeem this other innovative aspect of the poet's rich personality, by reproducing the original book in facsimile, with its formatting, dimensions, colors and types, design, and drawings: the "free book" of Oswald de Andrade. He, by the way, did not only "illustrate" the work, he played a decisive role in its graphic organization, as proven by the recently released document belonging to the private files of Rudá de Andrade (b. 1930), a student notebook (see **Figure 2**) on whose cover Oswald marked in his own hand some of his changes, modifying the names of the states on the coats-of-arms and making drafts of the title and the credits: "Caderno de Exercicios pertencente ao aluno de poesia Oswald de Andrade. Começado em 1925. Acabado em 1926. Capa de Tarsila. Autoilustrações do autor" ("Notebook of

Figure 2.

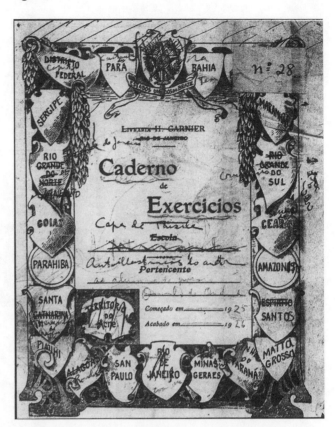

Cover page of the original notebook. (Archive of the author)

Exercises belonging to the student of poetry Oswald de Andrade. Begun in 1925. Finished in 1926. Cover by Tarsila. Illustrations by the author"). There is here a sketch of the layout to show that the conception of the cover was the poet's.

In the generous space of the original edition, which the play between red and black type illuminates, the poems respond in a livelier and more functional way to the intertextual illustrations. They are inseparable from these drawings, just as the "Hotel Esplanada," with its amorous elevator, seemed already indissociable from the graphic poem "não funciona" ["it doesn't work"], which happily has accompanied it in later re-editions. Here, the synthesis-poems "Fazenda" ["Farm"], "Crônica" ["Chronicle"], and "O Pirata" ["The Pirate"] recover their definitive shape, each one taking up a full page. Here, the poem "Amor" ["Love"] (title in red) reinvigorates the amplified silence of the page, with its strange and insinuating abstracted drawing that, to increase the reader's perplexity, will appear inverted in the edition of the *Poesias Reunidas*: Is it a mushroom? A tree? A ferris wheel? (See **Figure 3.**) (According to Rudá de Andrade, the correct position of the drawing would be as it was in the first edition. He recalls a comment by Nonê, Oswald de Andrade Junior, in which he claims that the image represents a cannon from the First World War): love, humor, poetry, "a descoberta/das coisas que eu nunca vi" ("the discovery/of things I've never seen").

By emphasizing the material recovery of the whole-body-Oswald of the original edition, I see that I have said little about his poetry or his poetics. Yet, that has already been recovered, beginning in the 1960s: Oswald is now a part of the bloodstream of Brazilian poetry. All are Oswaldians. It

Figure 3.

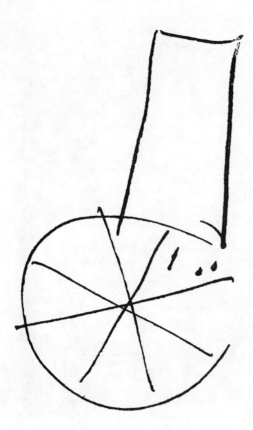

A René Bacharach

Amor

Drawing by Oswald de Andrade from the notebook. (Archive of the author)

would be idle perhaps, although it does not seem irrelevant, to remember here the re-oxygenizing operation performed by Oswald within the ranks of Modernism on the exhausted poetics of post-Parnassian conventionalism. The radicalized post-symbolism of a Pedro Kilkerry (1885–1917) or an Ernani Rosas (1886–1955) would maintain reserves of modernity to be explored in other veins, in the future. "The Age Demanded." The Age demanded the rupture of the metrical hairshirt, the abandonment of the *sermo nobilis,* of a rhetoric pitched in academicisms, and it urgently demanded the draught of daily language, the immediacy of the newspaper and the cinema—imagination without the puppeteer's strings, words in freedom, as the futurists preached before all. To these demands our Modernists would come to respond, in their time.

Oswald, radical in everything, sought in the uncivility of the cannibal (the bad savage) and in the mischief of childhood ("O netinho jogou os óculos/na latrina") ("The little grandson threw the spectacles/into the latrine") the metaphor-weapons to proceed to his own corresponding antidote to brainwashing, his "zero degree of writing," his zero limit. The "Manifesto Pau-Brasil" [1924; Brazilwood Manifesto] and, soon afterward, the

"Manifesto Antropófago" [1928; Cannibalist Manifesto] are in full harmony with the poetry that he practiced and clarify it more than illustrate it: they allow one "ver con olhos livres" ("to see with free eyes"). Everything is already there: from the "contribuição milionária de todos os erros" ("millionaire contribution of all errors") to the "sintese" ("synthesis"), the "invenção" ("invention"), and the "surpresa" ("surprise"). Between the poetry of *Pau Brasil* and that of the *Primeiro Caderno* there is not perhaps any essential difference, except in degree. Paulo Prado explained Oswald's poetics in his introduction to *Pau Brasil* as "Em comprimidos, minutos de poesia" ("In pills, minutes of poetry"). Already a practitioner of the minute-poem, Oswald advances in the *Caderno,* radicalizing the radical, even the instantaneous poem, or flash-poem, of two or three lines, and associating himself with the few Modernists who have successfully attempted the mini-epigram, Cendrars, Pound, Mayakovski, Ungaretti, and Cummings. And he arrives at the poem-in-one-note, a synthesis of syntheses: "amor-humor." Seed of other revolutions, this radical gesture recalls the more significant ruptures with tradition in painting—the "White Square on White" of Malievitch, soon answered by the "Black on Black" of Rodtchenko, in 1918–although the poetics of Oswald, powered by laughter and action, is not exhausted in this practice and does not systematize such a limiting gesture. On defining Oswald's poetry as "a ready-made poetry," Décio Pignatari reminds us of another kind of radicalism, that of Marcel Duchamp, perhaps more in tune with the typology of Oswaldian humor.

Taking the comparison to the field of music—and such similes clearly do not translate into exact identity but rather into points of reference and inter-illumination—I would recall the personality of the poet-composer Erik Satie, whom Oswald admired ("Se houve ultimamente um gênio em França, esse se chamou Erik Satie" ("If there was a genius in France of late, he was called Erik Satie") (1943–1944, 113). Like Oswald, Satie went through a long process of discredit until he was rehabilitated in the 1950s by the undisciplined voice of John Cage. One should emphasize here Oswald's nearness to the plainness, the "*retour à la simplicité*" (Cocteau) and especially (to resort to Picabia's anagram) the "satierik" face: the subversive laughter against "serious" work, shown in musical epigrams that metamorphize the cliché into nonsense. And, specifically with respect to the *Primeiro Caderno,* of interest is the Satie of "*Sports et Divertissements*" (1914), an uninterrupted sequence of anecdote-compositions that mixes very short texts and musical notes in poem-scores, handwritten in black and red, also requiring us to see a facsimile, since the design is part of the creation.

Oswald's poetic *oeuvre* seems to have most in common with Satie the absolute disdain for "artistic" values; there is more connection there than with the work of Villa-Lobos, whose prolixity is at the antipodes of Oswald's synthetic verve—in spite of the Modernist Villa-Lobos works of the 1920s, the "Noneto" and the "Choros" (No. 3, of 1925 dedicated to Oswald and Tarsila). Oswald the poet (in this aspect, distinct from the post-Machadian prose writer) is not a craftsman, like Mallarmé. There is in his poetry—averse as it is to all literary stylization and yet open to the elementary nature of raw language, to brutalizing collage, and to the malapropisms of daily speech—a natural adherence to everything that is by definition "non-poetic," such as noise (already incorporated by Satie in the creation of "Parade" in 1917, whose score conceived even sirens, gunshots, and the clatter of typewriters). This interest in the apparently "non-musical" is a critical refusal that appears to be both Satie's fierce and humorous renunciation ("*J'emmerde l'art*") and Duchamp's (when he abandoned "retinal" painting). This is another key to understanding Oswald's "free book." To match his seeing-with-free-eyes, there would have to correspond a hearing-with-free-ears.

To complete the pleasure of this definitive re-encounter with Oswald's poetry, it would be necessary to hear the recording he made of some of his poems, including "Balada do Esplanada" ["Ballad of the Esplanade"] and "Soidão" ["Solitude"] from the *Primeiro Caderno*. The technical precariousness of these records, which were made unpretentiously and privately in Oswald's final years of life, hardly matters. Whoever hears the poet speaking the opening passage of the "Canticle of Canticles for Flute and Guitar," with his voice slightly halting with emotion in the line "cais da minha vida quebrada" ("quay of my broken life"), will not forget it and cannot but feel the presence of this untameable poetry, which a version not "corrected" by conventional standards brings even closer to us.

—**Folha de S. Paulo, February 8, 1992, pp. 6–10**

Translation by Thomas LaBorie Burns and Gláucia Renate Gonçalves

Works Cited

Andrade, Oswald de. 1943–1944. *Ponta de Lança*. São Paulo: Martins.

——. 1945. *Poesias reunidas*. São Paulo: Edições Gavete.

——. 1966. *Poesias reunidas O. Andrade*. Intro. and ed. Haroldo de Campos. São Paulo: Difusão Européia do Livro.

Campos, Augusto. 1992. "Poesias Reunidas: Oswald de Andrade." *Folha de Sâo Paulo*, (February 8), 6–10.

Galvão, Patricia. 1982. "Contribuição ao Julgamento do Congresso de Poesia 1948." *Pagú: Vida-Obra*. Ed. Augusto de Campos. São Paulo: Brasilense. 182–84.

Mallarmé, Stéphane. 1951. "Preface. Un coup de dés jamais n'abolira le hasard." *Poems*. Trans. Roger Fry. New York: Vail-Ballou P. 156–58.

——. 1977. "Preface. Un coup de dés jamais n' abolira le hasard. Poëme/A Dice Throw Will Never Do Away with Chance. A Poem." *Poems: A Bilingual Edition*. Trans. Keith Bosley. Harmondsworth: Penguin Books. 254–57.

Pignatari, Décio. 1971. "Marco Zero de Andrade (1964)." *Contracomunicação*. São Paulo: Perspectiva. 141–55.

CHAPTER 4

CULTURAL INSTITUTIONS IN LATIN AMERICA

K. Alfons Knauth

This essay deals with the diverse cultural institutions that promote literature: schools, colleges, universities, academies, societies, literary gatherings, workshops, festivals, libraries, museums, competitions, and prizes. These institutions perform various functions regarding literature: conservation (libraries and museums), reception and reproduction (schools, colleges, universities, academies), creative production (workshops, literary gatherings, and academies), stimulation (literary prizes), and public implementation or production (performances, recitals, and festival competitions). There is often a certain amount of overlap between institutional functions, such as reception and production in universities, academies, and literary gatherings, or between stimulation and implementation in festival competitions. The overreaching function of the literary institutions is to contribute, through its multiplying effect, to shaping the collective awareness of literature as part of society. This process of forging identity through the institutions operates simultaneously through the opposing principles of durability and dynamism, sameness and otherness.

The establishment and functioning of literary and cultural institutions will be dealt with from the point of view of their historical development. This development will be considered on the basis of the following basic divisions: (1) the pre-Colonial period (before 1492), (2) the Colonial period (from 1492 to roughly the early nineteenth century), (3) independence and the neo-Colonial period (from about the early nineteenth century to the early twentieth century), and (4) the post-Colonial period (from the early twentieth century to the present). Some of the periods overlap, particularly the neo- and post-Colonial periods. This division is the result of a certain dialectic that transcends any linear progression of dependence–independence–interdependence, a dialectic especially relevant to the Colonial, neo-Colonial, and post-Colonial periods.

Schools and Colleges

The complex structure of the Amerindian cultures included a sophisticated system of underlying scholastic institutions. Due to the shortage of primary documents, however, knowledge of these pre-Colonial institutions is at best hypothetical. It would appear that in the Incan, Aztec, and Mayan cultures, there was a dual system of education for the elite and the masses. The aristocratic elite was trained at palace schools such as the *calmécac* of the Aztecs (León-Portilla 223–30) or

the *yachaywaci*, the Incas' "houses of knowledge" (Valcárcel 27). The master who presided over the *yachaywaci* was the wise *amauta* (Garcilaso 4:19), a term that reemerged in the twentieth century in the title of the Amerindian journal founded in 1928 by Mariátegui. Palace schools taught the hierarchical and hieratic principles of Amerindian cultures, Mayan and Aztec hieroglyphics and calendars, mythology, history, law, music, and epic, lyrical, and dramatic poetry, together with the mnemonics typical of predominantly oral cultures (Garcilaso 2:27; León-Portilla 226–27). The tradition of the *harawi* Quechua poems was maintained for many centuries, spawning numerous Latin American variations, and appeared once again in *Los ríos profundos* [1958; Deep Rivers] by José María Arguedas (1911–1969). The extraordinary memory of the Amerindian rhapsodists, such as the Incan *harávec*, is recalled to this day, albeit obliquely, in "Funes el memorioso" [1942; "Funes, the Memorious"], Borges's (1899–1986) Amerindianized short story. The Mayan writing taught at the palace schools had such prestige, due to its hieratic nature, that many sovereigns awarded themselves a title denoting their literary competence (Grube 40). In addition to the palace schools, there were common schools, called *telpochcalli* in Mexico, that offered a military, physical, and technical as well as a basic cultural education. Basic culture involved learning the general language, such as Quechua in the Incan empire of the *Tahuantinsuyu* (Garcilaso 6:35), reading (in the Mayan and Aztec schools) religion, and morals, together with the pedagogical principles of reciprocity and perspectivism, among others (Grube 39–40; Thompson 191, 194).

In tribal civilizations (such as the *pajé* [Câmara 660–62] or *piai* of the Brazilian Amerindians), cultural instruction was organized around the central figure of the shaman. In addition to his basic role as a physician, the *piai* was—and still is—a transmitter of cultural practices and organizer of the rites and festivals of *Pindorama* (Métraux 1967, 83–85). There were also female shamans with similar functions, such as the *machi* who presided over Araucanian fiestas (Lindig and Münzel 124). Female education was of a predominantly domestic nature, however, and was therefore undertaken in the family home. Yet there was a special form of education for the *aclla*, the chosen Incan women, in the *acllawaci*, or "houses of knowledge," where they were taught by the *mamacuna*, the highest of the high teachers, the female equivalent of the *amauta*. Only the *Coya*, the Incan queen, was entitled to enter the *acllawaci.* The *mamacuna,* or "matron," as the Inca Garcilaso de la Vega (1539–1616) translated the term, taught the *aclla* divine worship (Inca Garcilaso de la Vega 4:1) and all the sacred handicrafts associated with it. There was a similar institution for the daughters of Aztec nobles (Rojas 50). From an extremely modern, oblique, and transcultural point of view, the Chilean Diamela Eltit (b. 1949) renews and renovates the Incan tradition of female pedagogy through the workshop on social theater organized by the protagonist Coyacoa in her novel *Por la patria* [1984, For the Fatherland]. One can well say that in this respect the past has yet to come.

The military conquest of America was accompanied from the outset by a spiritual conquest. The bell towers of the Catholic monks summoning their pupils to indoctrination in the monastery schools were built on the ruins of the Amerindian schools. Attempts were made to implement a European religious educational system, a policy evoked by the Andeans in the traumatic myth of the foreign, alienating school (Jara and Spadaccini 74–75), with its barbaric acculturative power. In the face of the resistance it elicited, the strategy of forced acculturation was moderated and sometimes transformed into an attempt at apparent or genuine transculturation. The first missionary and convent schools were founded in the early sixteenth century in Santo Domingo, the Franciscan school in 1502, and that of the Dominicans in 1509. From 1524 onward, these were followed by the Franciscan schools in Mexico, founded by Bernardino de Sahagún (1500?–1590), Pedro de Gent (1500?–1572?), and Gerónimo de Mendieta (1525–1604). Since the lay apostolate imposed on the *encomenderos* (landowners) by Queen Isabella of Castile in the late fifteenth century failed, the religious orders took over the mission and the general task of teaching (Konetzke 1965, 245–47). The Catholic Church therefore had all the more reason to transfer its pedagogical hegemony, jeopardized in Europe by humanism and subsequently by Protestantism, to the New World. The state supported the pedagogical process with the requirement that a school be established in every division, a demand reiterated by the Viceroy of Peru, Francisco de Toledo, in 1578 (Pottier 20). A map of the schools shows that priority was given to urban centers, although certain missionary epicenters, such as the Jesuit settlements of Lake Titicaca and Paraguay, were also extremely important as far as schools were concerned.

Reading, writing, and arithmetic were the basic subjects in elementary education, which served as the basis for religious and intellectual instruction. In the Jesuit schools particularly, music was added to these primary subjects, serving both as the universal language and as an inductive teaching method (Hesse 51, 57). As regards the Franciscan schools, it is worth noting the pedagogy of humility and solidarity of Pedro de Gent, the founder of the educational system of New Spain, who rejected the post of archbishop and introduced the Canticle of St. Francis of Assisi as a canonical text for education in Mexico (Steger 1967, 96). A certain transcultural mentality can be discerned in the adoption of a Náhuatl name by the Franciscan Motolinía (meaning "poor," like the "poverello" St. Francis of Assisi). The question of language was crucial in teaching. It was difficult to impose Spanish or Portuguese monolingualism at all social, regional, and educational levels. Despite the respective decrees for Spanish America in 1770 and Brazil in 1727, monolingualism (in the colonizers' languages) was never imposed on Amerindian communities, and in many cases, even a rudimentary knowledge of these languages failed to be achieved. For this reason, an ambivalent strategy regarding linguistic colonization was adopted from the outset. Missionaries were obliged to learn the languages of the Amerindians in their care, or at least the general language of the region. In exchange, the Amerindians had to learn the Iberian language as far as possible, in addition to their local general language (witness the decrees and laws of 1516, 1550, 1575; see Pottier 20–21). In the Jesuit settlements of Paraguay, only Guaraní was spoken (Steger 1965, 40).

The education of the settlers and *criollos,* in addition to the important oral culture provided by the women of the house (Pumar Martínez 26), was primarily undertaken in the predominantly religious colleges, which had one section for primary education and another for higher education, reflecting a system of pedagogical dualism and a profound social and even ethnic division. From the mid-sixteenth century onward, the Jesuits achieved a degree of hegemony in higher education whose consequences can be felt to this day, despite their long absence from America between their expulsion in 1759/1767 and their gradual return, albeit on a smaller scale, throughout the nineteenth and twentieth centuries. The most prestigious Jesuit colleges in Brazil were those of Salvador da Bahia (1553); São Paulo in Piratininga, the nucleus of the city of the same name, founded by the Provincial Manuel da Nóbrega (1554); Río de Janeiro (1568); and Olinda (1576). In Spanish America, they included the Colegio Máximo de San Pedro and San Pablo in Mexico (1568), which in 1618 merged with the famous Colegio de San Ildefonso, and the Colegio Máximo in Córdoba, built in 1613 on the initiative of Diego de Torres, who also established the first Jesuit settlements in Paraguay. Education in the Jesuit colleges was free, and the colleges were financed through donations (such as those of Alonso de Villasecas in Mexico), through ecclesiastic and state contributions (such as the *redízima* of the ten-cent silver coins in Brazil, granted by King Sebastião; see Buarque de Hollanda 141–42), or through the *hacienda* economy together with international trade (Steger 1967, 187–88). Jesuit education was based on the principles laid down for various centuries in the *ratio studiorum* of 1599 (see Steger 1974).

To optimize the acculturation process, it was essential to incorporate the Amerindian elite, which is why the colleges for *caciques* were built. The first was the Colegio de Santa Cruz in Tlatelolco, founded by the first bishop of New Spain, Juan de Zumárraga, in 1536; the Franciscan Bernardino de Sahagún was one of its most eminent professors, but there were also Amerindian teachers, and in 1552, even the dean was Amerindian. Another *caciques'* college of great renown was the Jesuit college San Francisco de Borja, founded in Lima in 1620 (Valcárcel 103). The Amerindians were taught Latin, rhetoric, philosophy, theology, music, and tropical medicine. Educated Amerindians taught the priests the Amerindian languages and cultures (Pottier 27). The Amerindian students at these colleges made significant contributions to the works of European teachers (such as Sahagún and Anchieta) on the Amerindian languages and cultures (Gómez Canedo 176). Basic education for women was domestic and undertaken by their families. The nuns' convents also provided a certain amount of intellectual training within a religious framework. The first secular college for women in New Spain, with strict religious supervision, was the Colegio de las Vizcaínas in Mexico, whose foundation in 1752 was promoted by the Jesuits. This may have been the first concession to the demands for intellectual training for women, expressed by

Sor Juana Inés de la Cruz (1648–1695) in a letter to her Jesuit confessor in the late seventeenth century. The Jesuits also founded a college for Amerindian women, the Colegio Guadalupe, in Mexico, in 1740 (Pérez 394).

Following the independence of the American states, education became progressively secularized and nationalized. The idea of popular education arose, promoted by the Argentinian Domingo Faustino Sarmiento (1811–1888), exiled in Chile, and subsequently by the Uruguayan José Pedro Varela (1845–1879), who, under the influence of Sarmiento, created the Society of the Friends of Popular Education (1869) and drafted the Uruguayan Law of Common Education in 1877 (Zum Felde 251–62). Yet schooling was still generally restricted to a few years at school, and that only in a handful of geographical regions. In Chile, training of future teachers and professors was also institutionalized in the Normal School in keeping with the Napoleonic system, with Sarmiento as its first director. The acculturation of the Amerindians proceeded more methodically, often with a distinctly Christian orientation. This acculturative spirit can be discerned in the title of the work by the Bolivian priest Carlos Felipe Beltrán, published in the collection *Civilización del indio* [1890; Indian Civilization]: "Escuela indiana o Método para enseñar a leer y escribir a los indiecitos en quichua y castellano" ["Indian School or Method for Teaching the Indians to Read and Write in Quechua and Spanish"] (Pottier 337–39). Secondary education in the colleges began to be modernized with the introduction of the new technical, historical, and social disciplines and modern languages, which gradually challenged the traditional hegemony of Latin. In Chile, the foundation of the Pedagogical Institute for training secondary teachers in 1889 and Rudolf Lenz's so-called German Reform led to the development of the paradigm of national cultures regarding both the Chilean language (and the literary canon) and the introduction of the inductive method of reasoning from the particular to the general (Poblete 25–27). Despite the innovative idea of popular education, the dual system persisted, with a marked discrepancy between a generally neglected elementary education and a rigorous secondary and higher education.

Toward the end of the nineteenth century, a specifically female civil education began to emerge with the establishment of schools for and by women, such as the first Institute for Young Ladies in Santo Domingo, established by the poet Salomé Ureña de Henríquez (1850–1897) in 1881, or the first female colleges in Chile with a humanistic orientation, founded by Antonia Tarragó in 1864 and by Isabel Le Brun de Pinochet in 1872. In 1877, thanks to the initiative of these teachers, the Ministry of Public Education in Chile declared women's right to secondary and higher education (Labarca 162–63).

During the twentieth century, popular education advanced considerably with the establishment of an extensive network of primary schools in both urban and rural areas, compulsory schooling (albeit restricted to an average of five years and not always enforced), and literacy campaigns, the most outstanding and influential being those of the Mexican and Cuban revolutions. High schooling rates in Argentina, Chile, and Uruguay were already traditional by the late nineteenth century. Driven primarily by the consciousness-raising strategy of Paulo Freire's "pedagogy of the oppressed" (Schrader 388), the Adult Education Campaign (1947), various literary campaigns from the 1950s to the 1980s (Fausto 384–85), and the introduction of eight years of primary school in 1971, schooling

also increased considerably in Brazil, though with sharp regional and social differences (Schrader 388–96).

One of the main achievements of the post-Colonial period was a relative advance in the acculturation process in the school system. In the wake of the study of Amerindian culture at the beginning of the twentieth century, and revived at the end of the twentieth century at around the time of the Fifth Centenary (1492–1992), there was a renaissance in the study of Amerindian cultures (Allebrand and Bernecker 22). This renaissance was expressed in the constitutional guarantee of "ethno-development" in several countries (such as Brazil, Colombia, Guatemala, Mexico, and Peru), including the promotion of indigenous languages and bilingual schooling, although it proved difficult to enforce in practice (Allebrand and Bernecker 23; Masferrer 282–83; Cojtí 157–58). Cultural pluralism combined with Guaraní-Spanish bilingualism was already traditional in Paraguay, where it was a result of the pro-Guaraní policy adopted by the Jesuits in the settlements. In reality, however, this bilingualism was a form of diglossia with marked social, regional, and cultural differences. Guaraní, apart from a short Quechua period during the 1970s in Peru (Pottier 348–49), was the only co-official Amerindian language in Latin America and as such also figured in the international discourse of the Mercosur, albeit marginally.

Universities

During the process of *translatio studii* (the transfer of cultural institutions from Europe to America), universities, with their virtual monopoly on universal knowledge for 500 years, were the institutions with the greatest duration and scope. In the beginning, the *translatio* was a colonizing act and, over the centuries, was gradually transformed into an emancipating activity, creating a relatively autonomous structure. Universities developed from affirmative to critical institutions within society. During the early stages of the Colonial period, universities were generally established on the basis of already existing Dominican, Franciscan, or Jesuit schools (Konetzke 1968, 166). There were two types of universities that anticipated the current dualism of national and private institutions: the universities with a royal or imperial statute and those with a pontifical statute—with links and overlappings between the two (Steger 1967, 96). In Brazil, there were no universities at all during the Colonial period; students and future leaders were obliged to travel to Coimbra to pursue higher studies, particularly in law and medicine. In Latin America, the numerous universities founded during the Colonial period (Rodríguez Cruz 313–17) were distributed according to the importance of the cities with government headquarters or high courts. The first establishments were the Universidad Santo Tomás de Aquino in Santo Domingo, run by the Dominicans, with a pontifical statute, founded in 1538; the Universities of Lima and Mexico, with imperial statutes, both founded in 1551; and the Universities of Santa Fé de Bogotá and Córdoba, founded in 1621 and run by the Jesuits. Universities were also established in Quito (1586), Charcas (Chuquisaca, Sucre) (1621), Cuzco (1621), Guatemala (1676), Caracas (1725), Havana (1728), and Santiago, Chile (1747). The majority of these universities were run by the Jesuits, with some run by the Dominicans. From the eighteenth century onward, however, there was a tendency to found universities independently of religious institutions, such as the Universidad General in Santiago, Chile (1747), and the Real Universidad Literaria in Guadalajara, Mexico, which also had chairs in medicine and surgery (1791) (Konetzke 1968, 167; Rodríguez Cruz 278–79).

The Jesuit colleges in Brazil were virtually university-level, particularly in the humanities, philosophy, and theology; yet they were denied a university statute, which implied, among other things the *ius ubique docendi*, for political reasons. Following the expulsion of the Jesuits by the Marquis do Pombal (1759), the college at Olinda (Pernambuco) was established as the center of Pombalian modernization in Brazil. Following the transfer of the Portuguese court to Brazil in 1808, modern colleges or professional schools of economics, medicine, navigation, mining, and agriculture were founded in Bahia, São Paulo, Río de Janeiro, and Ouro Preto. In Latin America, the Enlightenment led to the establishment of scientific institutions such as the College of Medicine in Mexico (1768), the Anatomical Amphitheater in Lima (1792), the College of Surgery in Guatemala (1804), and the College of Mining (1792) and the Botanical Garden (1788) in Mexico, which also included a scientific institute and a university chair (Trabulse 23). Latin American science, whose high level was emphasized by Alexander von Humboldt, shifted from the traditional universities, regarded as the repositories of the medieval, speculative, and scholastic spirit, toward the colleges and institutes, with their enlightened, empirical, and pragmatic stamp.

The aim of higher education in the universities, colleges, and institutes was to train the administrative, clerical, intellectual, military, medical, and technical *criollo* elites. However, the training of the chiefs of staff, who had to be of Spanish origin and pure-blooded, was undertaken at European universities. One of the main sociological functions of universities was vertical mobility, within set limits. Intellectual graduation permitted social promotion for *mestizos* and sometimes for Amerindians, particularly in the cultural field. The best-known examples of the interaction of the university and social promotion were the Amerindian writers Hernando de Ixtlixóchitl (1500–1531) (sixteenth-century Mexico), Juan de Espinosa Medrano (1620?–1688?) (seventeenth-century Peru), and Francisco de Santa Cruz y Espejo (1747–1795) (the son of an Amerindian and a mulatto woman in eighteenth-century Ecuador). The chairs in Amerindian languages, at the universities of Mexico, Guatemala, Lima, Cuzco, and Quito and the semi-university colleges of Bahia, Pernambuco, São Paulo de Piratininga, and Mexico's Santa Cruz de Tlatelolco ("a university for Amerindians," Carreño 65), favored the promotion of Amerindian culture and its practitioners to a certain extent.

The transfer to America of the European university system led to the implementation of a humanistic and literary culture through the liberal arts, study of which was compulsory for all students and which formed the basis of higher studies in philosophy, theology, civil law, canon law, and medicine (the latter remaining relatively neglected until the end of the eighteenth century). Within liberal arts, the *Trivium*, consisting of grammar, rhetoric, and dialectic, implied the study of languages, literature, and history. The prevailing pedagogy was that of the Jesuits' *ratio studiorum*, promulgated in 1599, with its methodical rationalism, its sophisticated didactic progress, its universalism combined with localism and syncretism, its religious and humanistic spirit, its casuistry and aestheticism, and its orientation toward the ultimate objective of the spiritual conquest imposed by the Council of Trent, occasionally modified by either theocratic or ecumenical tendencies.

Together with liberal arts, the values of European literature were transferred to America: the oratorical institution of ancient rhetoric, adapted to modern discourse; the humanistic canon of classical and modern authors; the system of literary genres and styles; and the principle of emulous imitation. The latter translated into a creative didactic and literary exercises in the genres of argument, dialogue, public discourse, sermons, epigrams, satire, fables, eclogues, panegyric hymns, and theater. The principle of syncretism, practiced primarily by the Jesuit pedagogues, permitted a certain degree of mixing among the genres and languages, such as the incorporation of Amerindian songs and dances into religious theater. The performance of Amerindian roles by European actors and European roles by Amerindian actors was one of the methods used in Jesuit education and produced a genuine transcultural theater.

As far as linguistic culture was concerned, American universities were characterized by a marked multilingualism. Latin was the erudite language and was used in teaching and elaborate communication; Spanish or Portuguese was employed for colloquial communication outside the colleges; the Amerindian languages learned for contact with the Amerindians replaced the Greek of European faculties, to such an extent that Tupí in Brazil was known as *o grego da terra*. From the seventeenth century onward, however, ancient Greek was added, as well as Hebrew (Letite 1:75, 2:561, 7:161–62). Father Antonio Vieira (1608–1697) noted the pentecostal polyglottism of the Jesuits, trained for the evangelization of the Amazonian Babel, regarding it as superior to that of the apostles (Epiphany Sermon, 1662). The universities, convents, and colleges of America were "like an immense linguistics classroom" (Furlong, *El trasplante social* 135). The interculturalism of a significant sector of American intellectuals modified the process of *translatio studii,* turning the concept of acculturation into a concept of transculturation. It represented a more highly differentiated study and denoted the beginnings of a hegemonic shift in studies and in culture. Certain repercussions of this syncretism can be found in the *mestizo* works of the Jesuit José de Anchieta (1534–1597) and Sor Juana Inés de la Cruz.

The *traslatio studii* operated primarily through the university or semi-university institutions and subsequently carried over into literary life. The teaching of literature, closely linked to the Christian mission, was therefore undertaken in a pedagogical sphere, where some of the first works of Latin American literature emerged. Just as Brazilian literature began during the second half of the sixteenth century with the Amerindian plays of Father Anchieta, the first Latin American play was performed on a Jesuit stage. In 1640, the *Comedia de San Francisco de Borja* [The Play of St. Francisco of Borja], a hagiographic work by Father Matías de Bocanegra (1612–1688) on the founder of the Jesuit province in Mexico, was performed by students of the college in Puebla. As far as women's higher education was concerned, one should recall that women were excluded from university during the entire Colonial period. The exemplary case of Sor Juana shows that in order to obtain intellectual training, women had to resort to convent libraries and self-teaching or employ a sort of sexual quid pro quo, posing as men, as Sor Juana planned, following the art of disguise of the seventeenth-century lieutenant nun Catalina Arauso (Pumar Martínez 85–99).

After independence, throughout the nineteenth century, universities closed down or were remodeled; some of them were not fully reopened until the twentieth century, such as the University of Mexico. The universities, now republican, basically became nationalized and secularized. There were only a few new establishments, such as the University of Buenos Aires (1821) and the University of the Republic in Montevideo (1849), that, following the lengthy intellectual and commercial isolation of the River Plate region during the Colonial period, now became centers of notable scientific development. In 1883, the national poet (Cosse 338) of Uruguay, Juan Zorrilla de San Martín (1855–1931), inaugurated the first chair of literature at the newly founded university (Paris et al. 77). The University of Chile (remodeled in 1842), with statutes drawn up by Andrés Bello (1781–1865), its dean from 1854 onward, served as the model for the university of lawyers, which prevailed in the nineteenth century, giving jurists a virtual monopoly over public discourse (Steger 1967, 253). Repercussions of this spirit were even felt in surrealist poetry: The co-founder of the Chilean group La Mandrágora, the lawyer and poet Enrique Gómez-Correa (1915–1995), called his most recent collection of poems *Las cosas al parecer perdidas* [1996; Things Seemingly Lost], the title of an article taken from the Civil Code drafted by Andrés Bello.

Instead of large, integrated universities, independent faculties of various disciplines were established, together with several professional and polytechnic institutes, based on the French model of *Grandes . . . Écoles,* such as the . . . *École normale supérieure* or the specialized . . . *École des Mines* or the encyclopedic . . . *École polytechnique.* Particularly in Brazil, which continued to have no university as such throughout the nineteenth century, faculties and polytechnic institutes, also known as *escolas,* multiplied, such as the *Escola de Minas* in Ouro Preto (1877), whose founding director was a Frenchman (Azevedo 225). In both the modernized universities and the polytechnic institutes of Latin America, the ideology of French positivism was implanted, with scientific, technical, economic, and social progress being the objective of national education. Auguste Comte's famous slogan was even incorporated into the Brazilian coat of arms, proposing and promising the people *ordem e progresso.* The function of the Brazilian *bacharel* corresponded to that of the Spanish American *licenciado* as the principal representative of public discourse. The only major college of humanities established during the empire in Brazil was the prestigious *Colégio Imperial Dom Pedro II* in Río de Janeiro (1837) (Azevedo 333). Higher education institutions also operated as a factor in relative social mobility. Through studies at both the recently created *escolas* and the colleges of humanities, *mestizos* and mulattos obtained a certain degree of social promotion in Brazil (Azevedo 338); this is exemplified by the naturalistic novel *O mulato* [1881; The Mulatto] by Aluísio Azevedo (1857–1913), by the rise of the Luso-Afro-Amerindian poet Antônio Gonçalves Diaz (1823–1864), who held the Latin and Brazilian history chairs at the *Colégio Imperial Dom Pedro II,* and by the public career of the national writer Machado de Assis (1839–1908), a mulatto who was the first president of the Academia Brasileira de Letras.

The 1918 Córdoba Reform, preceded by the Uruguayan Reform, effective since the 1908 Organic Law (Traversoni and Piotti 123), ushered in the post-Colonial era in the history of Latin American universities. The Reform of the University of Córdoba (Argentina), one of the oldest universities in the continent, introduced the principle of university autonomy and joint government—and even joint student management, as well as free studies—which spread throughout Latin American during the course of the century. Joint student management can be regarded as a genuinely Latin America innovation (Weimberg 441), dispensing with the primitive statutes of medieval universities, such as those of Bologna. After the Córdoba Reform, most Latin American universities were granted statutes of autonomy, such as the University of Mexico, re-inaugurated in 1910, which became autonomous in 1929 and was renamed UNAM (Universidad Nacional Autónoma de México [National Autonomous University of Mexico]). The Reform led to the profound politicization of the university—which sometimes combined with its poeticization, as in the case of the avant-garde university of Estridentópolis in Xalapa, Mexico (1926), inspired by the great Estridentista simile of Manuel Maples Arce (1898–1981), a graduate of the *Escuela Libre de Derecho* and revolutionary superpoet (Schneider 132–34, 140–44). The political function, in the broadest sense, was revived by most current universities, particularly against the background of dictatorial experiences. Revolutionary radicalization, institutionalized at the University of Cuba, produced dissent between fundamentalists and pluralists (Real de Azúa 34–35, 69–70, 158–61).

This period saw the founding of the first universities in Brazil. The first was the Universidade do Rio de Janeiro (1931), which was followed by the Universidade de São Paulo (USP), with the first literature faculty (1934), and the Universidade Federal do Rio Grande do Sul in Porto Alegre (1936). The "prince" of Brazilian poets, Manuel Bandeira (1886–1968), occupied the first chair in Latin American Literature at the Universidade do Brasil in Rio de Janeiro (1943). The Universidade de Brasília, with the anthropologist Darcy Ribeiro (1922–1997) as its founding rector (1962), was the first comprehensive Brazilian university. The statutes of the USP stipulate the triple function of the university: research, teaching, and the dissemination of science and its progress. Its critical and democratic functions were concomitant obligations, not codified in the statutes, yet expressed, for example, in the title of the book compiling the articles of Afrânio Coutinho (1911–2000): *Universidade, instituição crítica* [1977; The University, a Critical Institution]. The statutes establishing the autonomy of Brazilian universities were drafted between 1945 and 1966.

Parallel to the national universities, an increasing number of private universities were founded, particularly those of a technological or religious nature, with Catholic universities being primarily administered by the Jesuits (Albornoz 37). Major Catholic universities included the remodeled Pontificia Universidad Javeriana in Bogotá (1937), the Pontificia Universidade Católica (PUC) in Río de Janeiro (1946), and the Pontificia Universidade (PUC) in São Paulo (1946). Despite offering a certain undeniable scientific success, it proved difficult for private universities to reconcile their particularism and their ideological or financial dependency with the principles of scientific autonomy and "universal" training in a democratic society (Gutiérrez 240–50).

The creation of polytechnic universities, whether private or state-funded, was due to the rapid expansion of technology and globalization. The Universidade Estadual de Campinas (UNICAMPI) became one of Brazil's centers for technological and agricultural research (Jacob 406–7). Collaboration with North American universities and financial support from the United States was common in this field. Thus, the foundation of the Universidad de los Andes in Bogotá (1948) was made possible by support from the Rockefeller Foundation, and its curricula were based on the North American model. The Instituto Tecnológico y de Estudios Superiores in Monterrey, Mexico (1943), one of the most highly renowned in Latin America, has been closely linked to its neighbors in Texas, since it is an extraterritorial member of the Association of Texas Colleges (Steger 1965, 68). Moreover, the Instituto Tecnológico is structurally different from other universities, given the integration of its traditional and technological faculties. The emphasis it places on literary culture is borne out by its library holdings, which include a fine collection of historical and indigenous works on the sixteenth century, together with an impressive collection of two thousand editions of *Don Quixote.*

The media revolution led to the establishment of new faculties and institutes at various universities, such as the Escola de Comunicações e Artes at the Universidade de São Paulo or the Ciencias de la Comunicación institutes of both the Universidad de la República and the Universidad Católica de Montevideo. Parallel to this, the new paradigm of cultural studies, which became the dominant intellectual base for many, was developed, thereby marginalizing traditional philology, regarded as excessively specialized and elitist (Sarlo 33–36). This accentuation of mass culture also corresponded to the marked democratization of universities, which, thanks to the growing number of students, were already becoming mass cultural institutions; witness the National Autonomous University of Mexico, which, at the end of the twentieth century, had 300,000 students. In the case of Cuba, the impressive extension of scientific training during the Socialist Revolution, the "universalization of the university" (Franzbach 200), was accompanied by the loss of university autonomy (Albornoz 49).

Together with the relative democratization of universities and the progressive emancipation of women from the beginning of the twentieth century onward, there was a greater presence of women, particularly among students and to a lesser extent among faculty. Following the emergence of the first female professors, such as the Chilean pedagogue Amanda Labarca (1923) (Manny 2–15), the number of female professors, particularly in the humanities, rose significantly, although modestly, during the last decades of the twentieth century. The *alma mater* is currently reviewing its purely allegorical statute.

A fundamental trend in universities and semi-university institutions in Latin America is the growing supranational and regional approach to Latin American culture, renewing Bolívar's ideal of a continental university. This was first postulated by the Chilean Francisco Bilbao (1823–1865) in 1856, and in about 1930 by the Argentinian Julio R. Barcos (1883–1960), eventually leading to the formulation of statutes for a Universidad de la Cultura Americana at the International Convention for American Teachers in Montevideo (Roig 69–70, 74–76). It was not until the last decades of the century, however, that these projects were even partially implemented, through the creation of centers and studies. Foremost among these was the Centro de Estudios Latinoamericanos at the National Autonomous University of Mexico, initially at the Political and Social Science Faculty (1960) and subsequently at the Philosophy and Literature Faculty (1966). The headquarters of the Centro Coordinador y Difusor de Estudios Latinamericanos (1979), in whose creation Leopoldo Zea (b. 1912) played a leading role (Zea 8–9), were established at UNAM. The recently created Centro de Estudios Latinoamericanos Rómulo Gallegos (CELARG) in Caracas is another institution specializing in this field. In Brazil, the Centro de Estudos Latino-Americanos of the Memorial da América Latina was founded in São Paulo and since 1989 has been devoted to

continental culture in the tradition of Bolívar and Martí (see 'Museums' in this essay). Virtually simultaneously, the Programa da Integração da América Latina was launched at the Universidade de São Paulo (1988), with a graduate course in the new discipline (Chiampi 62–63).

The Universidad Iberoamericana in Mexico, established by the Jesuits in 1943 (Pérez 421–24) follows Latin American interests in keeping with continental and universal Catholicism, while the Casa de las Américas in Cuba (1959), with its Centro de Investigaciones Literarias, orients its Latin American studies toward socialist internationalism.

In addition to universities, there are institutes devoted primarily to research, such as the aforementioned Centro de Investigaciones Literarias in Cuba (see Instituto 196); El Colegio de México (1939), based on the Collège de France; or the Instituto Caro y Cuervo near Bogotá, created in 1942 by the Colombian Congress to celebrate the centenary of the birth of the two eminent Colombian philologists after whom it was named, to pursue state-of-the-art philological research (Páramo 138; Steger 1965, 77). In addition, the Fundação Rui Barbosa (Rui Barbosa Foundation) in Rio de Janeiro must be cited as one of the most important cultural research institutes in Brazil. From its beginning in 1927, its research activities have involved the examination of various issues of jurisprudence and the human sciences in the tradition of Rui Caetano Barbosa de Oliveira (1848–1923), after whom it is named.

Academies, Societies, Athenaeums, Literary Gatherings

The famous *Iconología,* written by Cesare Ripa (1560?–1623?) in approximately 1600, features the allegory of academia, represented by a highly civilized woman dressed like a vestal, holding laurel and lime leaves (Ripa 2). A few pages further on, the allegory of America appears, portrayed as a barbarous, virtually naked Amazon carrying a bow and arrow, with an iguana and a human head at her feet. At the same time, in about 1600, the first academy in America, the so-called Academia Antártica, was founded in Lima. A highly cultured woman, the Peruvian poetess and Petrarchan Francisca Briviesca (Rössner 49), participated in its creation.

There are basically three types of academies: scientific academies (comprising all kinds of science), literary academies (resembling literary gatherings), and pedagogical academies (rather like schools). Literary academies may be intended to be either permanent, in which case they have legal status, or purely circumstantial, created on the occasion of a politicocultural event or a literary contest. They tend to be combined with scientific or philological academies. Scientific academies may involve a single scientific field, a combination of fields, or all scientific fields. This essay shall not deal with scholastic academies, which are fairly multifaceted and prolific, since *academy* is not an exclusive term. To a certain extent, the term *academy* extends to universities, since these are usually described as academic. On the other hand, an academy lacks the status of a university, since it is not authorized to grant academic degrees.

Academies have had a longer tradition than universities and indeed were their forerunners as scientific institutions. They group together the scientific, literary, or artistic elite of a nation, as well as the scientific elite of universities. The prototype of the academy is the ancient Platonic Academy (c. 385 BCE), revived by the Accademia Platonica of Italian neo-Platonism (1474) and continued by both the academies of languages and literature and by the scientific academies of Italy, Germany, France, Spain, Portugal, and England: the Accademia della Crusca (1582), the Accademia dei Lincei (1603), Die Fruchtbringende Gesellschaft (1617), the Académie Française (1635), the Academia dos Generosos (1649), The Royal Society (1660), Die Akademie der Wissenschaften (1700), and the Real Academia Española de la Lengua, created as a result of a literary gathering in 1713 (Jacobs 10–19, 43). From 1600 onward, as part of the *traslatio studii* process, the institution of the academy was transferred from Europe to America. A century later, the first signs of a hegemonic shift in intellectual enlightenment could already be observed: *Sol oriens in occiduo* [sun rising in the west] was the proud motto of the Academia Brasílica dos Esquecidos in 1724 (Castello 107).

During the Colonial period, literary academies–combined, however, with scientific activities–prevailed. The most outstanding academies were the aforementioned Academia Antártica in Lima (c. 1600); the Academia de Palacio, founded by the Peruvian viceroy (c. 1700); the Academia Brasílica dos Esquecidos (1724) and the Academia dos Renascidos (1759), both in Bahia; and the Academia dos Felizes (1736), the Academia dos Seletos (1753), and the Academia Científica (1771), all in Río de Janeiro (Castello 97–118). The Academia Científica was an academy with proper statutes, whereas the others were of a more circumstantial nature. Imitation, together with creative emulation, made up the aesthetic principles of literary academies following the European tradition. Consequently, the genres of epic verse and amatory poetry, both ancient and modern, were cultivated. The poetic efforts of the Academia Antártica produced *Las armas antárticas* [1604?–1614?; Antarctic Weapons] by Juan de Miramontes y Zuázola (fl.1600), an epic on the Spanish Conquest created as an ideological and literary response to Alonso Ercilla's (1533–1594) *Araucana* (1569–1589) and the epic on the spiritual conquest *La Cristiada* [1611; The Christian Epic], by the Dominican Diego de Hojeda. Academy members competed with Ovid and Petrarch, already a patriarch of modern poetry. Through *El Parnaso antártico de obras amatorias* [1608; The Antarctic Parnassus of Love Poetry] by Diego Mejía de Fernángil (1565–c. 1620) and the *Miscelánea austral* (1602) by Diego Dávalos y Figueroa (1550?–1608?) and his wife, the poet Francisca Briviesca (1550?–1610?), Petrarchan laurels were transported to Andean surroundings, where they soon hybridized with the tropical rhetorical flora. The Americanism of the academies was not only translated through their mottoes, such as *Sol oriens in occiduo*, but also through their literary and scientific products. The Júbilos de América, organized by the president of the Academia dos Seletos, the Jesuit Francisco de Faria (b. 1653), shows signs of a certain degree of maritime transport in the relocation of the Lusíadas to Brazil, with sails and seas swollen with Brazilian enthusiasm (Castello 117). Not only were rhetorical flowers cultivated; botanical research also flourished, particularly with *La Flora Fluminense* [1790; The Flora of Rio de Janeiro] by Frei José Mariano da Conceição Veloso (1742–1811), inspired by the Academia Cientifica in Rio de Janeiro. *História da América Portuguêsa* [1730; History of Portuguese America] by Sebastião Rocha Pita (1660–1738), a member of the Academia Brasílica dos Esquecidos, is one of the masterpieces of early Brazilian historiography.

The enlightened and emancipating tendencies of the last decades of the eighteenth century led to a new type of academy, the society, based on the Spanish model of the Sociedades de los Amigos del País, whose objective was to modernize the country (Jacobs 52–62). Outstanding examples included the Sociedad Académica de Amantes del País in Lima, which published the *Mercurio Peruano;* the Sociedade Literaria of Rio de Janeiro (1786), involved in the political conspiracies that heralded the *Inconfidência mineira* of 1789; and the Sociedad Patriótica del Nuevo Reino de Granada (1801), organized with the collaboration of the illustrious naturalist Celestino Mutis. The Sociedad Económica de Amigos del País, founded in Havana during the French Revolution (1793), lasted, paradoxically, until the Cuban Revolution of 1959 (Instituto 978–80).

After independence, cultural *criollismo* initially prevailed in the academies. In 1835, the Academia de la Lengua was founded in Mexico, with collaborators such as the Americanist journalist Quintana Roo, after whom a Mexican state was named. The Academia de Letrán (1834–1856) was dedicated to the cultivation of Mexican literature, while in Buenos Aires, the Academia Argentina (1876) was devoted to fostering national culture and opposing the cosmopolitanism of the Círculo Científico y Literario. In order to counteract academic *criollismo,* the Academias de Lengua, which depended on and corresponded to the Real Academia Española de la Lengua, were founded from 1871 onward. The latter practiced cultural neo-colonialism to compensate for the lost colonies, using language as an "instrument of domination" (León Galindo de Vera [1819–1889] [Bochmann 348]). The academies, however, had a number of eminent collaborators, such as the philologist Miguel Antonio Caro, the first chairman of the Academia Colombiana de la Lengua (1872); and the writer Ricardo Palma (1833–1919), the author of *Tradiciones peruanas* [1872–1883, Peruvian Traditions] and founder of the Academia Peruana de la Lengua (1887). The 1892 Proclamation, organized by seven Latin American ministers, elicited a great literary confederation comprising all the peoples who speak Spanish both there and overseas. Other Latin American countries, such as Argentina, resisted this "literary" re-colonization, as Juan Bautista Alberdi (1810–1884) called it (Bochmann 351). The Academia Mexicana de la Lengua, founded in 1875, would subsequently have the collaboration of such cosmopolitan figures as Alfonso Reyes (1899–1959) and writers such as Juan Rulfo (1918–1986).

During the twentieth century, post-colonial tendencies would predominate in the national academies. These would be expressed, however, in structural oppositions, such as those between conservative academicism and academic or anti-academic avant-gardism. The founder and first president of the Academia Brasileira de Letras, founded in 1896, was Machado de Assis (see **Figure 1**), while its members included Eça de Queiros, Émile Zola, Theodor Mommsen, and Tolstoy. Moreover, each chair was assigned the name of a literary figure from the Brazilian literary tradition, such as Grégorio de Matos (1633?–1696), Gonçalves Dias (1823–1864), José de Alencar (1829–1877), and Castro Alves (1847–1871), (see **Figure 2**). The joint founder and subsequent president of the Academia Brasileira, Graça Aranha (1868–1931), promoted the Modernist movement, choosing a lecture on the "Week of Modern Art" in São Paulo (1922) to inaugurate the event that marked the emancipation of Latin American culture with such nerve and verve, both ironic and iconoclastic. However, a conflict arose between academic conservatism and the "Modern Spirit" (1924). Graça Aranha continued to defend projects to modernize the Academia, which were so vehemently

Figure 1.

Brazilian author Machado de Assis. (Archive of the author)

Figure 2.

Building of the Brazilian Academy of Letters, constructed by the French government as its pavilion in the centennial celebration of Brazilian independence in 1922. (Archive of the author)

rejected that he resigned in protest. National academies often worshiped tradition to excess, such as the Academia Argentina de Letras (1931), whose stated spirit of purity would later become the parodied "Purity!" of Cortázar's *Rayuela* [1963, *Hopscotch*, 1966]. At the same time, attempts to reconcile the traditional with the modern continued, as in the case of the Academia Nacional de Letras de Uruguay, founded in 1943, in which Lisa Block de Behar had organized an avant-garde, intercultural program since the 1980s. All Latin American academies, together with the Real Academia Española, belong to the Asociación de Academias, which held its First Congress of Academies in Mexico in 1951.

In Cuba, academic and revolutionary issues formed an unusual alliance. The Academia Nacional de Artes y Letras (1910–1960) was replaced by revolutionary organizations such as the Academia de Ciencias de Cuba (1962), a research institution, in keeping with the Junta Central de Planificación, comprising institutes grouped together according to the various scientific disciplines, such as the Instituto de Literatura y Lingüística. Founded in 1959, the Casa de las Américas, an institution for the dissemination and promotion of the cultural and social revolution on an international (especially Latin American) scale, operates in politicocultural coordination with the Academia. The Casa publishes a homonymous journal, currently directed by Roberto Fernández Retamar (b. 1930),

who replaced a Latin American editorial board that consisted of the Mexican Juan José Arreola (1918–2001) and the Argentineans Ezequiel Martínez Estrada (1895–1964) and Julio Cortázar (1914–1984).

A major academic event has always been the awarding of literary prizes, following the tradition of courtly and university competitions. The most famous of all academic contests was perhaps the eclogue competition between Tomás de Iriarte and Meléndez Valdés at the Real Academia de la Lengua in 1780, which Juan Pablo Forner accompanied with a *Cotejo de églogas que ha premiado la Real Academia de la Lengua* (Collection of Prize-winning Eclogues from the Royal Academy of the Language), emphasizing the historical quarrel between Iriarte and Forner. Nowadays, the Real Academia Española grants the most prestigious prize for literature in Spanish, the Miguel Cervantes Prize, which since its creation in 1975 has been won by a pleiad of American authors such as Carpentier (1976), Borges (together with Gerardo Diego in 1978), Onetti (1980), Paz (1981), Ernesto Sábato (1984), Fuentes (1987), Roa Bastos (1989), Bioy Casares (1990), Dulce María Loynaz (1992), Mario Vargas Llosa (1994), Cabrera Infante (1997), Jorge Edwards (1999), and Alvaro Mutis (2001). National prizes in Latin American countries are awarded by the respective ministries of culture or education. The Spanish Minister of Culture also presides over the jury for the Cervantes Prize. Prizes are generally distributed according to genre (such as poetry, novels, etc.). Thus, since 1917, the Academia Brasileira de Letras has awarded the Bilac Prize (for poetry), the Coelho Neto Prize (for novels), the Artur Azevedo Prize (for theater), and the Machado de Assis Prize (the highest prize for a complete work or a set of works). Among the most highly sought-after prizes in Latin America are those presented by the Casa de las Américas, likewise awarded for different literary genres.

Also worth mentioning are the semi-academic organizations, such as the institution of the athenaeum, which has a literary and rhetorical tradition dating back to ancient times and which was revived by the French Revolution and the progressive, Liberal culture of the nineteenth century. Based on the French *athénées* and the Ateneo Científico y Literario de Madrid (1835), the Ateneo de Montevideo, founded in 1877, grouped together an entire generation of Liberal politicians and intellectuals of turn-of-the-century Uruguay (Zum Felde 272–75) and continues to organize scientific, literary, and pedagogical programs to this day. Mexico's historic Ateneo de la Juventud only lasted from 1907 to 1914, although it was the cradle of Latin American idealism and cosmopolitanism, encouraged by Antonio Caso, who taught José Vasconcelos (1881–1959), Alfonso Reyes, and the Dominican Pedro Henríquez Ureña (1884–1946)–classical representatives of the cultural historiography of Latin America, inspired by the *Arielismo* of the Uruguayan José Enrique Rodó (1871–1917) [1900, *Ariel*]. Another athenaeum of international fame was the Ateneo Iberoamericano in Buenos Aires, created in 1912, whose inaugural meeting was attended by the Nicaraguan poet Rubén Darío (1867–1916) and the Spanish writer Vicente Blasco Ibáñez (1867–1928). There was also a trend toward popular athenaeums, such as the Ateneo Popular de la Boca (1926) (Santillán 1:293), following the model of the nineteenth-century popular, working-class athenaeums in Barcelona or the first Universidad Popular, created on the initiative of the Ateneo de la Juventud in Mexico (Álvarez 2:662).

Amerindian and Afro-American academies, societies, and institutes were an important post-colonial innovation. They arose within the traditionally Amerindian or *mestizo* framework of Paraguay and Mexico, as well as in the relatively traditional Afro-Americanist tradition of Cuba and Brazil, and subsequently in the context of the renaissance of Amerindian awareness around the time of the Fifth Centenary. The Academia de la Lengua y Cultura Guaraní was founded in Paraguay in 1949, the Instituto Nacional Indigenista in Mexico in 1948, and the Academia de Lenguas Mayas in Guatemala in 1990, albeit with an extremely limited budget (Cojtí 156). The Sociedad de Estudios Afrocubanos (Association of Afro-Cuban Studies), founded in 1936 by Fernando Ortiz (1881–1969), devised the concept of transculturation and cultural miscegenation, which at times overlapped with the cultural philosophy of the *Raza cósmica* [1925; The Cosmic Race] of the Mexican José Vasconcelos. The future national poet and chairman of the UNEAC (Unión de Escritores y Artistas de Cuba, 1961), Nicolás Guillén (1902–1989), had already made a significant poetic and ideological contribution to this concept from his early journalistic activities and the poems of *Sóngoro Cosongo* (1931), with its programmatic prologue. In Brazil, the Afro-Brazilian studies at the Universidade Federal da Bahia, organized by researchers such as Pierre Verger and Júlio Braga, in collaboration with poets and essayists such as the literary shaman António Risério, were particularly noteworthy.

After they became excessively academic, the academies produced an institution known as the anti-academy. From the sixteenth century onward, the academies of the *Insensati* (1561), the *Oziosi* (1563), and the *Fantastici* (1625) (Moisés 9) sprang up in Italy. Rubén Darío's parodical formula "Deliver us from the Academies, oh Lord" was adopted as the motto of the Anti-Academia Nicaragüense (1931) (Wentzlaff-Eggebert 251–52). This did not, however, prevent its protagonist, the professor and avant-garde poet Pablo Antonio Cuadra (1912–2002), from subsequently assuming the chairmanship of the Academia Nicaragüense de la Lengua and becoming a conservative writer, thereby following the opposite route from the one taken by José Pereira da Graça Aranha (1868–1931), who resigned as chairperson of the Academia Brasileira de Letras to work on behalf of avant-gardism. The Academia Lunfarda in Buenos Aires was founded to offset the traditional purism of the Academias de la Lengua, particularly the Academia Nacional de Letras in Argentina. The contemporary Academias da Cachaça in Brazil and Portugal were animated by a lively spirit whose Dionysian inspiration served to counterbalance the dry rationalism of official academies.

The counterpoints to these academies, apart from the anti-academies, were the literary gatherings from which they had emerged before becoming official institutions. Literary gatherings, informal and sometimes libertarian institutions, continued to accompany the academies and, with the liberalization of culture following the Enlightenment, installed themselves in the public spaces of cafés, bars, saloons, bookshops, café-bookshops, and television shows. Their activities were characterized by a spirit that was more playful than methodical, based more on trial and error than on a particular system. They substituted logophilia for philology. These were institutions that facilitated the reception, promotion, and realization of literature. Due to their spontaneity, however, they were more ephemeral at the individual level. As a social phenomenon of a particular period, literary gatherings proved more permanent, as was the case of the literary cafés that proliferated during the second half of the nineteenth century and the first half of the twentieth. The history of literary circles and cafés virtually coincides with the history of the literature of that period; for this reason, I shall only mention a few of the cafés that stood out as places of literary communication. The Café de Nadie in Xalapa, evoked in the homonymous short story (1926) by Arqueles Vela (1899–1978), was the headquarters of the Mexican Estridentistas (Schneider 166–67, 257, 261). In the Gruta de Zaratustra circle, whose discourse is reflected in Jose Asunción Silva's (1865–1896) novel *De sobremesa* [1896; After-Dinner Conversation], some of the first Colombian *modernistas* emerged. "Los Nuevos" of the 1920s, including Jorge Zalamea (1905–1969), León de Greiff (1895–1976), and Germán Arcieniegas (1900–1999), frequented the Café de Windsor and the Café Rivière in Bogotá, with their unique blend of coffee and the literary (Rodríguez Morales 234–35). The Café Colombo in Rio de Janeiro, founded in 1896, served as both the writing desk and the scenario for much of Brazilian literature until the advent of modernism. The cafés of Buenos Aires served as the forum for the literary discourse of Macedonio Fernández (1874–1952), when he was not in a state of mental absorption. Like the cast of characters in the international cafés depicted by the narrator of *Rayuela* [*Hopscotch*, Chap. 132] or by Enrique Jardiel Poncela (1901–1952) in the colophon to his novel *Amor se escribe sin hache* [1929; Love Is Written Without an H], Macedonio

Fernández–that itinerant writer evoked by a fellow member of his literary circle, Borges–would have been able to draw an urban map of the cafés of the Argentinean capital that gave rise to the production of his work. The open institution of cafés, with the flow of ideas within and between them, may have contributed to the creation of the "open book" genre, the first example of which was the mobile and multiple *Museo de la novela de la eterna* [1967; Museum of the Novel of Eterna], as its narrator states in the *Prólogo final*.

Literary Workshops

Literary workshops are institutions for creative production, with methodological and pedagogical components that distinguish them from literary gatherings and with alternative components that distinguish them from public schools. They are twentieth-century institutions, but date back to ancient scholastic traditions, particularly the *exercitationes* of rhetoric (Lausberg 470). The *exercitationes* method was taken up by Jesuit colleges and institutionalized as an exercise for applying rhetorical principles together with the imitation of ancient and modern models, such as the traditional exercise involving the recreation of Aesop's fables (which continued until the creative pedagogy of the twentieth century), which had a history of over 2000 years. The tradition of the rhetorical workshops at the colleges had an equivalent in the literary practice of Incan and Aztec schools, as already mentioned. The coincidence between these traditions probably fostered the conservation of the Quechua fable, the *haranway* (Carrillo 47, 56, 80; Garcilaso 2:27), and the Aztec adaptation of Aesopian fables in *Esopo mexicano* (*Aesop* 48), continued to a certain extent by the enlightened *Fables* (1817) of the "Pensador Mexicano," Fernández de Lizardi (1776–1827), a former student of both the old and the new (1814) Jesuit college of San Ildefonso.

Modern workshops are based on, in addition to the European and American scholastic tradition, both active and alternative pedagogy and the technological, technical, and socialistic ideology inherent in the very name given to these laboratories. Workshops suggest a more popular and democratic tradition, in keeping with the tradition of Tretjakov and Brecht, particularly the numerous literary workshops of revolutionary Cuba (Instituto 995–97) but also those of Chile (Miranda 231–33) and much of Latin America in recent decades. The short story workshop organized by the Mexican writer Juan José Arreola (1918–2001), for example, is clearly based on the rhetorical tradition of the *exercitationes* of fables, the author's *Confabulario* being a work-in-progress since 1952 and winning him the National Prize for Literature in 1979. It would seem that the *Fábula del tiburón y las sardinas* [1956; *The Shark and the Sardines*, 1961] by the former president of Guatemala Juan José Arévalo (1904–1990), *El gran zoo* [1967; The Great Zoo] by Nicolás Guillén, and *Los cuentos, fábulas y anti-fábulas* [1992; Stories, Fables and Anti-Fables] of another Guatemalan writer, Max Araújo (b. 1950), are the result of the same oratorical institutions.

Many workshops arose in response to dictatorships. This was true of the Teatro do Oprimido (1974), with its "Latin American Techniques for Popular Theater," organized by Augusto Boal (b. 1931) in Brazil and among Latin American exiles. By the 1960s, the Movimento de Cultura Popular and the Centros de Cultura Popular had already been created in Brazil on the initiative of the politically committed poet Ferreira Gullar (b. 1930). Both Gianfrancesco Gualtieri's Teatro de Arena and Zé Celso Martínez Correia's Teatro Oficina

contributed to the popularization of culture, through the famous theatrical and cinematographic recreation of Oswald de Andrade's (1890–1954) *O rei da vela* (1937) (King of the Candle) in the public spaces of São Paulo and Rio de Janeiro (1982) (Schumann 120–22). In addition to their popular and democratic orientation, the workshops had Amerindian, collective, and international components, such as the Latin American and Amerindian workshop at the Centro Libre de Experimentación Teatral y Artística (CLETA, Center of Free Theatrical and Artistic Experimentation) during the 1960s. Within this context, the UNAM theater group created its Aztec-inspired piece *Las tandas de tlancualejo* [1975; The Acts of the Tlancualejo] (Adler 504–5). One of the most enduring movements was the popular theater created by César Rengifo in Venezuela in 1945, which, by the 1970s, had three hundred theater groups (Borsò 453–54). Literary workshops were also created in major libraries, such as the Biblioteca Pública Piloto de Medellín, founded on the initiative of UNESCO (see "Libraries").

Finally, it is worth noting the private workshops of individual poets, including those held in Mexico during the 1970s or the workshops organized by the Casas de Poesía, such as the exemplary "Casa de Poesía Silva" founded in 1986 in Bogotá. The latter paved the way for a type of institution that was both conservative and creative, which spread to other Latin American cities such as Caracas, Mexico City, and Quito, through the establishment of similar Casas de Poesía (Jaramillo 141–42).

Festivals

Popular religious, scholastic, academic, courtly, and republican festivals have constituted a cultural institution that has fostered literary and artistic production, while at the same time generating its own products. This institution functions either periodically or occasionally. In cultural terms, the most important periodic festivals during the Colonial period were the feast of Corpus Christi and the various patron saints' days, since they gave rise to the creation and representation of allegorical plays. Thus, the allegorical play *As onze mil virgens* [11,000 Virgins], performed on a sailing-ship on land, which paraded down the streets of Bahia on 21 October 1584, the feast of Santa Úrsula (Cradim and Leite 2:608–9), anticipated the numerous naval floats that would parade in the Brazilian carnivals of the Rio de Janeiro Sambadrome or the streets of Porto Alegre and São Paulo representing, for example, the story of the Conquest or slavery (Knauth 1992, 126). In Mexico, the Franciscan Toribio de Motolinía (1490?–1565?) describes the performance of allegorical plays on the occasion of the feasts of Corpus Christi and St. John (Bellini 156–57) in his *Historia de los indios de la Nueva España* [c. 1550; History of the Indians of New Spain]. These allegorical plays constituted an oral prologue, so to speak, to the new written Mexican theater, which began, as mentioned earlier, with seventeenth-century Jesuit theater. Likewise, church festivals gave rise to poetic competitions, such as the contest organized by the University of Mexico for the Immaculate Conception in 1682. Among the more than seventy poets participating in this contest were Sor Juana Inés de la Cruz and Carlos de Sigüenza y Góngora (1645–1700) (Laferl 72–73). The Catholic rite was therefore the institutional framework for the production and performance of an incidental form of literature that occasionally proved to be an essential part of the literary culture.

The events that spawned feasts and a festive literature in colonial America were either political or ecclesiastical: glorification of the throne, the arrival of viceroys, the promotion of governors, investitures of bishops, beatifications, and canonizations. One of the most remarkable feasts was the one held in Mexico to celebrate the arrival of the viceroy, the Marquis de la Laguna, in New Spain in 1680. The "Triumphal Arches" through which the viceroy entered the city were conceived of by the most eminent literati in Mexico, Sor Juana and Carlos de Sigüenza y Góngora, who also wrote the *Neptuno alegórico* [1680; Allegorical Neptune] and the *Teatro de virtudes políticas* [1680; Theater of Political Virtues], respectively (Laferl 72–73), in honor of the viceroy (as was customary). In Brazil, the appointment of the governor of Bahia as the "Mestre de Campo General" responsible for the demarcation of Portuguese and Spanish dominions in South America as a result of the Treaty of Madrid (1750) was the reason for the ostentatious celebration of the aforementioned "Júbilos da América" (1754) with their "Brazilian" poetry (Castello 115–18). This festivity also served as an "Ato Acadêmico Panegírico" and, as such, formed part of the academies' institutional culture.

Religious feast days constituted the institutional framework within which a significant cultural syncretism arose, expressed in both cultured and popular theater. *El divino narciso* [1690; The Divine Narcissus] by Sor Juana, created as an *auto sacramental* [mystery play] for the feast of Corpus Christi, displays a marked generic, thematic, and linguistic syncretism of Hispanic and indigenous cultures, as did Peruvian and Mexican theater dedicated to the Virgin of Copacabana and the Virgin of Guadalupe, performed in public squares on the occasion of the respective commemorative feasts for a predominantly Amerindian public (Gisbert 1992, 642–45). The Corpus Christi processions in sixteenth-century Cuzco described by the Inca Garcilaso in his *Comentarios reales* [1609; The Royal Commentaries of Peru 8:1] revealed significant participation by the *caciques* and Amerindians of various "nations" with their own songs in their respective languages, their icons, and even totemic disguises, condor's wings and lion skins. The Amerindians disguised as monsters, notes Garcilaso, pretended to be mad and foolish. It seems that the Christian system only accepted the pagan rite *sub specie carnavalis*; its fictions led the historian to believe that they were people who were aware of the falseness of their previous heathendom. These same totemic masks have in fact featured in the carnival at Oruro, Bolivia, until the present in the Amerindian dances known as Condors' Dances (Gisbert 1989, 27). Beyond mere syncretism, Catholic festivals often produced veritable attempts at cultural subversion. This trend was noticed, for example, in the festivities to celebrate the beatification of St. Ignatius of Loyola in Cuzco in 1610, where Incan plays were performed and there were public recitals of *harawis*–poems in honor of Incan heroes, disguised as Catholic rites, such as "the Invocation of the Infant Christ, dressed as an Inca" (Métraux 1989, 45). These were subsequently forbidden.

African culture was also characterized by syncretism within religious rites. It has survived to this day, for example, in the ceremonies and land and sea parades in honor of Yemanjá and the Virgin of the Sea, on the occasion of the Catholic feast of the Immaculate Conception, Candlemas, or the Virgin of Regla, in both Brazil and Cuba (Knauth 1992, 127). These parades constituted an elementary nautical theater that has a great affinity with the naval floats of the allegorical plays mentioned earlier, as well as with carnivals. Ideologically, their allegories are rooted in the transatlantic spirit, in the two meanings that this had for the descendants of either European settlers or slaves: the joy of the promised land together with nostalgia for the land they had left. Political components are sometimes added to contemporary religious celebrations. Thus, in the traditional Vía Crucis of Holy Week in Mexico, the Passion of Christ represented in the processions throughout the country is frequently associated with the social suffering of the Mexican people, as in the poem by Héctor Kiev ("Tacho") "Vida, pasión y muerte del mexicano" ["The Life, Passion, and Death of the Mexican"], published in the newspaper *Novedades de Quintana Roo* (31 March 1997).

The majority of popular festivals are linked to religious feast days, dating back to the rites of nature which, on the one hand, survived in indigenous cultures and, on the other, were syncretized by the Christian religion. Thus the carnival is a secularized festival of the rites of spring celebrating Dionysian fertility and happiness. In the Catholic calendar, it precedes the liturgical cycle of Lent, beginning with Ash Wednesday. In Brazil, the "anthropophagous" Modernists declared the carnival an institution of national culture that religiously celebrates the "barbarous" miscegenation of Amerindian, Afro-American, and European cultures (Oswald de Andrade, *Manifesto da poesía Pau-Brasil*, 1924). It is the cultural institution where the meeting between popular and highbrow culture proves most authentic. The carnival parades are meticulously prepared by the Samba Schools, often in collaboration with the social associations of the respective districts–as is the case, for example, of the "Beija Flor" of Joãzinho Trinta–thereby eliminating secret financing of luxury carnivals. Also visible and represented are the literary topics drawn from the novels of Jorge Amado (1912–2001) and the concrete poetry or the other multifaceted work of Chico Buarque de Hollanda (b. 1944). The latter won the 1998 carnival championship with the "Mangueira" Samba School, together with the "Beija Flor" School, which in 1989 won second prize with the poetic-political theme "Lixo Luxo," inspired by the homonymous poem by Augusto de Campos (b. 1931) and disseminated by the song of the *samba enredo* of the "Beija Flor" (Knauth 1989, 5–9).

Fairs and markets constitute another institutional framework for the production and realization of popular culture. In 1991, the Fiesta da Uva in Caixas do Sul (Brazil, Río Grande do Sul), one of the largest fairs in South America, was the scene of a series of parades with floats depicting viticulture, whose Dionysian and biblical symbolism was commented on by the writer Moacyr Scliar (b. 1937) in the newspaper *Zero Hora* (Porto Alegre 16 February 1991). Traditionally, fairs were the scene of literary and musical competitions in the form of *pelejas* (contests), in which singers or narrators would be confronted with the sometimes improvised presentation of their compositions (Diégues 42–49). In Brazil, these compositions, recited in the form of a dialogue, and others recited as monologues in the public square or in cafés, were often published in the monthly installments of *literatura de cordel* [chapbooks]. One of the most famous singers was the renowned Cego (The Blindman) Alderado, whose *peleja* with Zé Pretinho do Tucum was published in several versions (1946, 1962). The best-known contemporary representative of this popular poetry is the Brazilian Patativa do Assaré. The Argentinean equivalent of the Brazilian *peleja* is the *payada* or *contrapunteo,* described by José Hernández (1834–1886) in *La vuelta de Martín Fierro* [1879; The Return of Martín Fierro] (Canto XXX) and responded to by Borges in the short story "El fin" (*Ficciones*) [1944; "The End," *Fictions*]. The setting for the *payadas* was portrayed by the artist Carlos Morel in his painting *La Pulpería*. The classic Argentinean *payador,* clearly identifiable in Borges' story, was the dark-skinned Gabino Ezeiza (1858–1916), whose work is compiled in *El cantor argentino* [1896; The Argentinean Singer].

Amerindian and Afro-American cultures also have a well-established tradition of popular narrators, such as the *hablador* of Peruvian Amazonia, the theme of Vargas Llosa's (b. 1936) homonymous novel (1987); and the *akpalô* or *negra velha* of the Afro-Brazilians, who features in the "sugar mill" novel *Menino de engenho* [1932; Plantation Boy] by José Lins do Rego (1901–1957) (Diégues 37). The black female narrator also plays an important role in Afro-Cuban culture, where she blends with the figure of the *Santería* priestess. The same is true of the female storyteller Ma'Lucia in the novel *Biografía de un cimarrón* [1966; *The Autobiography of a Runaway Slave*] by Miguel Barnet (b. 1940). Male and female black storytellers with their stories, fables, and proverbs serve as teachers in the Afro-Latin American oral culture, as confirmed by the writer Maryse Condé (b. 1937) in her essay *La civilisation du bossale* (1978, 27–45), and the anthropologist Lydia Cabrera (351), as well as the old narrator in the testimonial *Biografía de un cimarrón*: "They taught me a lot even though they couldn't read or write" (Barnet 154). The equivalent to the Afro-Cuban storyteller in the French Antilles is the narrator, personified by the protagonist of Condé's novel *Moi, Tituba sorcière* [1986; *I, Tituba, Black Witch of Salem,* 1992], which revives the tradition of the African *griots*. Amerindian and Afro-American rites are also the sphere where specific poetic genres are produced, such as the hymns *araweté* or yoruba, the *marci marak,* and the *oriki,* whose impressive verbal skills are described by Antonio Risério (b. 1953) in his essay "De Oriquis" (36–46) and *Poéticas extraocidentais nos trópicos brasileiros* (85–89) [Poetics of the Far West in the Brazilian Tropics]. The *Ilê Aiyê* [Our World] of the Casa de Benin in Salvador de Bahia is an institution that produces non-Western culture through the Afro-Brazilian song of the "Banda Reflexu," whose *Serpente negra* [1988, Black Serpent] was heard throughout Brazil on the occasion of the centenary of Abolition. From its sociocultural center in a district of Salvador da Bahia, the Olodum group exported its poetic-political creations all over the world, in the wake of the tropical songs (by Gilberto Gil [b. 1942], Caetano Veloso [b. 1942], etc.) that were mainly drawn from non-Western institutions and ritual practices. At the same time, in his "total novel" *Las palabras perdidas* [1992; Lost Words], the Cuban writer Jesús Díaz Rodríguez (b. 1941) proposes a new concept of imagination based on the verbal magic of Afro-Cuban rites, practiced to this day in Cuba, yet linked to universal literature.

The cultural institution of indigenous and Afro-American rites, with or without syncretism, has survived slavery, persecution, and acculturation. It was preserved and transmitted through the Brazilian *ilê* (where *candombe* dances are held, *terreiro, pejí*; Câmara 705) and in the Cuban *ilé* (*santero,* or place where *santería* ceremonies are held; Castellanos 81–83), in the brotherhoods (Grube 62; Thiemer-Sachse 608; Furlong, *El trasplante social* 534–36), in societies for blacks—whether secret (Carpentier 210), public (Barnet 72–76), or private (Carpentier 35–41)—in the huts and enclosures of fugitive slaves, in the *tabas* or hideouts of Brazilian Amerindians, and sometimes with the support of national authorities, such as the Instituto

Nacional Indigenista in Mexico (García Canclini 135). The rites and rhythms, whether hidden or highbrow, of these cultural institutions, demonstrate the resistance of non-European civilizations, confirming not only their survival but also their abundance of vitality, albeit harnessed to the hegemonic culture (Gisbert 1992, 629–77; García Canclini 28–30, 142–47).

After independence, a new type of festival was institutionalized—national and Republican holidays, including acts to commemorate independence itself. The most memorable commemoration, owing to its cultural performance, was undoubtedly the First Centenary of Brazilian Independence in 1922, which culminated in a Week of Modern Art in São Paulo. The "Week" demonstrated the absolute autonomy of Brazilian culture, which had become avant-garde and even hegemonic for the first time: "Poesía Pau-Brasil, de exportacão" (Oswald de Andrade, *Manifesto de poesía Pau-Brasil,* 1924). São Paulo realized that, like Rome, it was built on seven hills and that it had achieved the *translatio studii* on its own, as Mário de Andrade (1893–1945) suggests in *Macunaíma* (1928).

The voyages of discovery had been generally celebrated since the sixteenth century with the dances and songs of the feather dances (Thiemer-Sachse 609) and the maritime performances representing the arrival of the sailors or the Moors (Mário de Andrade 94–126). From the Third Centenary onward, however, official commemorations produced major politico-cultural conflicts. In 1792, the Americanism that anticipated independence expressed its demands for cultural autonomy through Juan Pablo Vizcayo's *Carta a los españoles americanos* [Letter to the Spanish Americans]. The Fifth Centenary in 1992 generated a protest against the very institution of the commemorative celebration by numerous Amerindian and Afro-American organizations (Allebrand and Bernecker 19–21) and led to a general reconsideration of Latin American identity (repercussions of which can be found in these volumes). At the same time, there were attempts to revalue French culture in the formation of Latin America. This was the case of the commemoration of the Fifth Centenary by the Academia Nacional de Letras de Uruguay (National Academy of Uruguayan Literature) through a homage to the Franco-Uruguayan poets Jules Laforgue (1860–1887) and Isidore Ducassa, Comte de Lautréamont (1846–1870) (Block de Behar et al.), which highlighted the degree of contact between the two cultures to which these authors belonged. Another type of secular festival is the celebration to mark social solidarity, such as the *Guelaguetza* (the Zapotec term for mutual assistance) in Oaxaca, introduced by the Mexican state to contribute to raising awareness and valuing of *mestizo* culture (Thiemer-Sachse 609), or the celebration of the Cuban Revolution, which gives rise at the end of each year to a mass representation of Revolutionary culture, including the politically committed songs of the *nueva trova,* such as Carlos Puebla, Pablo Milanés, and Silvio Rodríguez.

Libraries

Until the end of the twentieth century, libraries ensured the preservation of written culture in its entirety. They constituted society's material memory. The libraries of New Spain were built on the ashes of Aztec and Mayan libraries, whose purportedly satanic books were burnt by the Christians as the first stage of spiritual conquest. The most conspicuous bonfires were those that the bishops Francisco de Zumárraga and Diego de Landa ordered lit in Tlatelolco, Tenochtitlan, and

Yucatán. The core of a culture was thereby annihilated. Setting fire to these Amerindian books proved more destructive than the historical burning of the ancient Library of Alexandria, since only a couple of codices were preserved as testimonies of entire civilizations. However, the loss of the codices was partly offset by the Amerindians' extraordinary ability to memorize, which enabled them to reconstruct, through alphabetic script, at least part of what had been lost. Pre-Hispanic literatures outside New Spain were characterized by an almost total lack of books, due to their predominantly oral nature. European bibles and libraries were transported to this despoiled America, lacking any written culture, in the ships of the spiritual conquerors in a lengthy maritime procession. The first library transferred to New Spain was that of Fr. Alonso de la Veracruz in 1536. Since the mid-sixteenth century, the new American printing presses increased the stock of libraries transported from Europe. The first book printed in America was a bilingual Spanish/Náhuatl catechism (1539). There were no printing presses in Brazil before the nineteenth century.

During the Colonial period, the largest libraries were to be found in the great monasteries, colleges, and universities, where the foundations of Christian and humanistic culture were preserved. There were also the well-stocked libraries of the viceregal courts and a few valuable private libraries belonging to clerics or literati such as Juan de Palafox y Mendoza (1600–1659), the Bishop of Puebla, Carlos de Sigüenza y Góngora, Sor Juana Inés de la Cruz, and Santa Cruz y Espejo. The catalogues and inventories of both libraries and book traders (and the ships that transported them) (Furlong, *El trasplante cultural: Arte* 30–32, 46–47), together with the literary canon of educational institutions, enable us to reconstruct the intellectual horizon of the time on the basis of this infrastructure. Some of the most valuable catalogues include those of the monastic libraries of the Franciscans in San Francisco, California, the Dominicans of Santo Domingo, and the College of *caciques* in Tlatelolco. The records of the Jesuit colleges in both Brazil and Spanish America amply document the vast knowledge stored in American libraries, comparable to the stock of European libraries (Furlong, *El trasplante cultural: Arte* 36–38). However, one should recall that this knowledge carried the lingering negative stamp of a conquering spirit.

The second half of the eighteenth century saw, in addition to the growing local production, the widespread importation of illustrated books, much of it contraband, which gradually modernized American libraries. One of history's greatest ironies was the recycling of the ideology of the noble savage and its revolutionary derivatives, particularly through Rousseau's *Discours* and *Contrat social,* which became the bedside book of an entire generation of revolutionaries and liberators (Arciniegas 306–14, 325–29). The transportation across the Atlantic of a printing press, complete with guillotine, in the ship of the French revolutionary Victor Hugues, narrated by Alejo Carpentier (1904–1980) in his novel *El siglo de las luces* [1962; *Explosion in a Cathedral*], illustrates this modern version of *translatio studii* through the force of law: Europe sought to impose a freedom and happiness on America which the latter had already known, in different terms, before its conquest by the Europeans (Oswald de Andrade, *Manifesto antropófago,* 1928).

Another of history's ironies was the transfer of one of the most prestigious libraries in the Portuguese Empire from the metropolis to the colonies: The Royal Library was transported from Lisbon to Rio de Janeiro in 1808 following the threat of Napoleonic invasion. This library, opened to the public in 1814, constituted the basic stock of the Biblioteca Nacional do Brazil (1878).

Following independence, the great national libraries were founded, preceded by the first public libraries, such as those of Santa Fé in Bogotá (1777), Buenos Aires (1794), and Rio de Janeiro (1814). The earliest national libraries were those of Argentina, in Buenos Aires (1810); Peru, in Lima (1821); and Colombia, in Bogotá (1823). The core of the national libraries consisted of the books confiscated from the Jesuits and other religious orders; royal libraries, such as the library of the King of Portugal, José I, and the Real Biblioteca Pública of Bogotá, which in turn had inherited the Jesuits' books; as well as private donations, such as the library of the naturalist José Celestino Mutis in Bogotá (1808) or that of Bishop Azamor in Buenos Aires (1796). Some national library directors were eminent writers such as Ricardo Palma (appointed 1883) and his successor Manuel González Prada (appointed 1912) in Peru, Jorge Luis Borges in Argentina (appointed 1955), or the philologist Miguel Antonio Caro in Colombia (appointed 1880); Caro's private library was donated to the national library of that country (1939), while Borges's Biblioteca de Babel was bequeathed to the Biblioteca Universal.

Likewise, university libraries took advantage of the dissolution of Jesuit libraries and the monastic libraries of other orders during the Enlightenment and Independence. They subsequently expanded their stock using national (or private) funds for promoting higher education and research, at varying rates, depending on the country, the political regime, the economic situation, and the media constellations. One of the most important university libraries in Latin America is that of UNAM, with over a million volumes. The specialized libraries of the various institutes are added or incorporated into the central university libraries.

The democratization of culture led to the establishment of popular libraries from the second half of the nineteenth century onward–from 1870, in Argentina, on the initiative of President Sarmiento, and from 1881, in Colombia. The Mexican Revolution, with its emphasis on popular culture, led to the creation of public libraries, subsequently promoted by José Vasconcelos, rector of the National University (1920–1921) and Minister of Public Education in Mexico (1921–1924), as part of his literacy campaign. The 1983 National Public Library Program revived this initiative, planning a municipal library for every Mexican city. The same happened in Colombia with the Instituto Colombiano de Cultura (Colcultura), founded in 1968, which began a national program for the creation of public libraries. UNESCO had already launched a similar program for the whole of Latin America, involving mobile libraries in the form of buses. To this end, the Biblioteca Pública Piloto, conceived of as a model for Latin America, was founded in Medellín in 1954 (Espitaleta 135–36).

With the expansion of the mass media, both national and university libraries were equipped with new units such as newspaper libraries, press rooms, sound-film libraries, and film or video libraries. The new communications technology led to the establishment of an interlibrary network system, through a computerized data bank service (the Secobi at UNAM) and Internet connections. Library activities extended beyond the basic functions of the preservation and lending of books and the publication of bibliographies, catalogues, annals, and bulletins. They were expanded to include literary, artistic, critical, and teaching programs for general culture, which included conferences, recitals, exhibitions, and literary workshops. The increasingly transnational approach of Latin American libraries translated into the creation of the respective institutions, such as the Biblioteca Iberoamericana in Mexico, founded on the initiative of Vasconcelos in the 1920s, or the Biblioteca de América Latina of the Memorial da América Latina in São Paulo, inaugurated in 1989.

Museums

We shall be dealing here specifically with museums that are significantly linked to literature. There are museums that contain "libraries" that contain "museums" that are libraries, in other words, literary collections. Thus, the Museo Nacional de Arqueología in Mexico contains the Biblioteca Nacional de Arqueología of Mexico, which contains El Museo de ambas Américas (1842), which contains an extensive summary of Incidents of Travel in Central America, Chiapas, and Yucatán (1841) by the North American archaeologist John L. Stephens. This "mise en abîme" illustrates the degree of overlap that exists between the concepts of "museum" and "library." The overlap is either metaphorical—the most outstanding example being the "library-museum" of the Museo de la Novela de la Eterna (Museum of the Novel of Eterna) belonging to Macedonio Fernández—or referential. In fact, museums tend to acquire specialized libraries, while libraries tend to present themselves as showy museums—like the UNAM library, whose façade is covered in an immense, multicolored and multicultural mosaic by the Mexican artist Edmundo O'Gorman. Nowadays, the frequent association between the two institutions is due to an educational and aesthetic concept: Both museums and libraries, in addition to being "conservatories" of the past, tend to form integrated centers of living culture and, as such, offer a broad range of cultural activities, including graphic and literary workshops, lectures, concerts, films, and plays. There is also a natural symbiosis between museums and literature in the case of museums on national poets or in the case of combinations of words and images exhibited in museums. Verbal-visual products are created, on the one hand, through inscriptions on monuments, walls, sculptures, stelae, posters, or paintings, and on the other hand, through visual poetry.

The earliest Latin American museums date from the first decade of independence. They were based on collections of pre-Columbian antiquities, such as the private collection confiscated from Boturini in 1747, which was subsequently kept by the University of Mexico and in 1825 became the first national museum (named the Museo Mexicano in 1834). Both the casual combination of sculptures, ceramics, and codices from the Boturini collection and the connection between the Museo Mexicano and the Chair of Ancient Mexican History, established at the same time to research these antiquities, demonstrate the additive nature of the institution. Integrated, multifunctional museums are a twentieth-century institution. At the beginning of the twentieth century they were based on the simultaneity of distinct periods exhibited in the same space, and subsequently on the totalization of artistic space, such as in André Malraux's Musée imaginaire, a concept which had begun in the nineteenth century, and culminated in the various globalizations of the twentieth century and finally in the contemporary use of multimedia, which is an extension of historical simultaneity.

Other paradigmatic examples will suffice to illustrate the institution of multifunctional museums. The recently founded Memorial da América Latina (1989) in São Paulo is one of the most perfect models of a modern museum. Its cultural conception was planned by the anthropologist and founding dean of the University of Brasilia, Darcy Ribeiro, and its architectural concept by Oscar Niemeyer, the architect who designed Brasilia (Nader 40, 42). The memorial is devoted to the cultural integration of Latin America and consists of historical, anthropological, and artistic museums and monuments from all over Latin America, in addition to a Biblioteca da América Latina with a stock of both rare and contemporary books, a sound-film library, and a video library, all linked to the central theme of the memorial. There are areas for all kinds of cultural activities, ranging from concerts, ballet, popular art, and plays to conferences and seminars. The museum publishes a partially bilingual journal, based on José Martí's supranational concept: Nossa América, Nuestra América. The Centro de Estudos Latino-Americanos, responsible for research into regional integration, organizes the debates held at the institution, such as the talk on "A palavra poética da América Latina" [The Poetic Word of Latin America], intended to promote "uma idea de região cultural, a latino-americana" (Costa 27) ("an idea of a cultural region, Latin America"). As a result, the museum implements a double discursive strategy; it preserves the past as a memory and, as a memorial, orients it toward the future. The link among the muses of the verbal-vocal-visual is perfectly expressed in the Museo de Arte Moderno La Tertulia in Cali, Colombia, beginning with the name of the museum. This mix of museum and literary gathering was founded in 1956 and combines plastic arts, literary colloquia, theater, cinema, a workshop-school, and folk dances within the same cultural space (Martínez 316).

The major archaeological museums of Mexico and Guatemala, including the true museum-temples or museum-cities of the Maya and Aztecs, contain the most characteristic examples of the natural syncretism between art and literature, as suggested by the name of the Temple of the Inscriptions in Tikal and the Temple of the Inscriptions in Palenque, whose glyphs narrate the chronicle of the seventh-century Pacal dynasty (Coe 206–7). Archaeological museums, from their origins in the era of Independence until today, have proved crucial to the identity of Latin America, since by emphasizing the heterogeneity of ancient Amerindian culture, they have affirmed both the diversity and the uniqueness of current culture.

Museums exclusively devoted to literature are rare but include house-museums devoted to literati of national importance, such as the Casa de Poesía Silva in Bogotá, (see **Figure 3**) the Casa Jorge Amado in Salvador de Bahia, the Casa José Martí in Havana, the Casa Nicolás Guillén in Camagüey, the Museo Juan Zorrilla de San Martín in Montevideo, and the Museo Pablo Neruda in Santiago, Chile. Both the Museo Pablo Neruda and the Casa de Poesía Silva are characterized by their polyvalent nature; in addition to preserving the memory of the poet through the library, pictures, a sound-film library, lectures, or colloquia, they are dedicated to encouraging creativity through literary workshops or awards. Instead of merely worshiping a national poet, they attempt to foster the culture of contemporary poets by directly or indirectly inspiring them through the genius loci of the museum.

In addition to actual museums, there are literary exhibitions. These are characterized by spectacular products, such as the heterogeneous books of visual poetry. Their numerous exhibitions already constitute an extensive, imaginary museum. Foremost

Figure 3.

Courtyard of the Casa José Asunción Silva in Bogota. (Courtesy of Victoria Peralta)

among these are the Exposição Nacional de Arte Concreta, organized in 1956 by the "Noigandres" group in the Museu de Arte Moderna in São Paulo and transferred in 1957 to the Ministério da Educação e Cultura of Rio de Janeiro. This historic exhibition officially inaugurated the Brazilian "Poesía Concreta" movement, which was later disseminated throughout the world, promoting a new type of polyglot literature. The poetic institution of "Palabras," similar to "Fonobrás" in the world of songs, contributed to making Brazil a significant exporter of "Pau-Brasil" culture and helped reverse the traditional direction of *translatio studii* (Knauth 1996, 157–58). At this stage, as one can see, literary institutions have already begun to merge with the institution of literature, which is the subject of other chapters.

Translation by Suzanne D. Stephen

Works Cited

Adler, Heidrun. 1996. "Theater in Mexiko." *Mexiko heute: Politik, Wirtschaft, Kultur.* Ed. Dietrich Briesemeister and Klaus Zimmermann. 2nd ed. Frankfurt: Vervuert. 504–14.

Aesop in Mexico. 1987. *Die Fabeln des Aesop in aztekischer Sprache: A 16th-Century Aztec Version of Aesop's Fables.* Vol. 3. Ed. Gordon Brotherston and Günter Vollmer. Berlin: Gebr. Mann.

Ainsa, Fernando. 1992. *De la edad de oro a El Dorado: Génesis del discurso utópico americano.* Mexico City: Fondo de Cultura Económica.

Albornoz, Orlando. 1971. *La universidad latinoamericana: La crisis del desarrollo.* Santiago de Chile: Instituto Latinoamericano de Investigaciones Sociales.

Allebrand, Raimund, and Walther L. Bernecker. 1996. "Zwischen Widerstand und ethnischem Aufbruch: Indianische Renaissance in Lateinamerika." *Aus Politik und Zeitgeschichte: Das Parlament* 48–49: 19–29.

Álvarez, José Rogelio, ed. 1987. *Enciclopedia de México.* Mexico City: Enciclopedia de México, Secretaría de Educación Pública.

Andrade, Mário de. 1982. *Danças dramáticas do Brasil.* Vol. 1. Belo Horizonte: Itatiaia.

Arciniegas, Germán. 1965. *El continente en siete colores: Historia de la cultura en América Latina.* Buenos Aires: Sudamericana.

Azevedo, Fernando de. 1944. *A cultura brasileira: Introdução ao estudo da cultura no Brasil.* São Paulo: Companhia Editora Nacional.

Barnet, Miguel. 1980. *Biografía de un Cimarrón.* Havana: Letras Cubanas.

Bellini, Giuseppe. 1997. *Nueva historia de la literatura hispanoamericana.* 3rd ed. rev. Madrid: Castalia.

Block de Behar, Lisa, François Caradec, and Daniel Lefort, eds. 1993. *Lautréamont & Laforgue. La cuestión de los orígenes: La quête des origines.* Montevideo: Academia Nacional de Letras.

Bochmann, Klaus, ed. 1993. *Sprachpolitik in der Romania.* Berlin: Walter de Gruyter.

Borsò, Vittoria. 1995. "Kolumbien und Venezuela: Violencia und Aufbau einer demokratischen Identität." *Lateinamerikanische Literaturgeschichte.* Ed. Michael Rössner. Stuttgart: Metzler. 443–54.

Buarque de Hollanda, Sérgio, ed. 1960. *História geral da civilização brasileira.* São Paulo: Difusão Européia do Livro.

Cabrera, Lydia. 1974. "Oye Ogbó. Refranes y ejemplos. Cómo enseñaban a sus hijos los viejos lucumíes y taitas criollos" *La Enciclopedia de Cuba. Prosa de guerra. Geografía. Folklore. Educación. Economía.* Vol. 6. Ed. Vicente Báez. Madrid: Enciclopedia y Clásicos Cubanos. 349–82.

Câmara Cascudo, Luís da. 1972. *Dicionário do folclore brasileiro.* Rio de Janeiro: Ediouro-Coquetel.

Carpentier, Alejo. 1989. *Ecue-Yamba-O.* Madrid: Alianza.

Carreño, Alberto María. 1961. *La real y pontificia Universidad de México: 1536–1865.* Mexico City: Universidad Nacional Autónoma de Mexico.

Carrillo, Francisco. 1986. *Literatura quechua clásica.* Lima: Horizonte.

Castellanos, Jorge, and Isabel Castellanos. 1992. *Cultura Afrocubana. Las religiones y las lenguas.* Vol 3. Miami: Universal.

Castello, Aderaldo José. 1965. *Manifestações literárias da Era Colonial (1500–1808/1836).* São Paulo: Cultrix.

Chiampi, Irlemar. 1989. "A emergência da integração." *Nossa América, Nuestra América: Revista do Memorial da América Latina* (São Paulo) 1: 62–63.

Coe, Michael D. 1992. *Breaking the Maya Code.* New York: Thames and Hudson.

Cojtí Cuxil, Demetrio. 1997. "Eine Politik für mein Volk." *Die Erben der Maya: Indianischer Aufbruch in Guatemala.* Ed. Raimund Allebrand. Bad Honnef: Horlemann. 136–71.

Condé, Maryse. 1978. *La civilisation du bossale: Réflexions sur la littérature orale de la Guadeloupe et de la Martinique.* Paris: L'Harmattan.

Cosse, Rómulo. 1987. "Juan Zorrilla de San Martín." *Historia de la literatura hispanoamericana. Del neoclasicismo al modernismo.* Vol. 2. Ed. Luis Iñigo Madrigal. Madrid: Cátedra. 337-44.

Costa, Horácio, ed. 1992. *A palavra poética na América Latina: Avaliação de uma geração.* São Paulo: Fundação da América Latina.

Coutinho, Afrânio. 1977. *Universidade, instituição crítica.* Rio de Janeiro: Civilização Brasileira.

Diégues, Manuel, Jr., et al., eds. 1986. *Estudos: Literatura popular em verso.* São Paulo: Itatiaia.

Espitaleta de Villegas, Lina. 1993. "Las bibliotecas en Colombia." *Gran Enciclopedia de Colombia. Cultura.* Vol. 5. Ed. Darío Jaramillo Agudelo. Bogota: Círculo de Lectores. 129–40.

Fausto, Boris, ed. 1984. *História geral da civilização brasileira.* São Paulo: Difel.

Franzbach, Martin. 1979. "Unterentwicklung als Erziehungsproblem." *Iberische Halbinsel und Lateinamerika: Bildung und Ausbildung in der Romania.* Ed. Rolf Kloepfer et al. München: Fink. 3: 195–205.

Furlong, Guillermo. 1969. *Historia social y cultural del Río de la Plata 1536–1810. El trasplante cultural: Arte; El trasplante cultural: Ciencia; El trasplante social.* 3 vols. Buenos Aires: Tipográfica Editora Argentina.

García Canclini, Néstor. 1982. *Las culturas populares en el capitalismo.* Havana: Casa de las Américas.

Gisbert, Teresa. 1989. "La máscara y el Carnaval de Oruro." *Encuentro: Revista Boliviana de Cultura* (La Paz) 2.5: 23–31.

——. 1992. "Art and Resistance in the Andean World." *Amerindian Images and the Legacy of Columbus.* Ed. René Jara and Nicholas Spadaccini. Minneapolis: University of Minnesota Press. 629–77.

Garcilaso de la Vega, el Inca. 1963. *Comentarios reales de los Incas: Obras completas.* 4 vols. Ed. Carmelo Saénz de Santa María. Madrid: Atlas.

Gómez Canedo, Lino. 1982. *La educación de los marginados durante la época colonial: Escuelas y colegios para indios y mestizos en la Nueva España.* Mexico City: Porrúa.

Grube, Nikolai. 1997. "Die Geschichte der Maismenschen." *Die Erben der Maya: Indianischer Aufbruch in Guatemala.* Ed. Raimund Allebrand. Bad Honnef: Horlemann. 20–68.

Gutiérrez Girardot, Rafael. 1965. "Zehn Thesen zum Thema Privat-Universität und Unterentwicklung." *Grundzüge des lateinamerikanischen Hochschulwesens: Eine Einführung in seine Probleme.* Ed. Hanns-Albert Steger. Baden-Baden: Nomos. 237–51.

Hesse, Axel. 1993. "Jahre Musik im Jesuitenstaat und ihr Nachhall." *Diálogo y conflicto de culturas: Estudios comparativos de procesos transculturales entre Europa y América Latina.* Ed. Hans-Otto Dill and Gabriele Knauer. Frankfurt: Vervuert. 47–70.

Instituto de Literatura y Lingüística de la Academia de Ciencias de Cuba. 1980. *Diccionario de la Literatura Cubana.* 2 vols. Havana: Letras Cubanas.

Jacob, Gerhard. 1994. "Universitäten, Wissenschaft und Forschung in Brasilien." *Brasilien heute: Politik, Wirtschaft, Kultur.* Ed. Dietrich Briesemeister et al. Frankfurt: Vervuert. 404–20.

Jacobs, Helmut C. 1996. *Organisation und Institutionalisierung der Künste und Wissenschaften: Die Akademiegründungen der spanischen Aufklärung in der Tradition der europäischen Akademiebewegung.* Frankfurt: Vervuert.

Jara, René, and Nicholas Spadaccini, eds. 1992. *Amerindian Images and the Legacy of Columbus.* Minneapolis: University of Minnesota Press.

Jaramillo Agudelo, Darío, ed. 1992–1993. *Gran Enciclopedia de Colombia.* Vols. 5–6. Bogotá: Círculo de Lectores.

Knauth, K. Alfons. 1989. "Konkrete Poesie und Karneval." *Dichtungsring* (Bonn) 9: 5–15.

——. 1992. "Planken, die die Welt bedeuten: Zum Zusammenhang von Schiffahrt und Schauspiel." *Entgrenzungen: Studien zur Geschichte kultureller Grenzüberschreitungen.* Ed. Rudolf Behrens and U do L. Figge. Würzburg: Königshausen & Neumann. 123–41.

——. 1996. "Palabrás: The Haroldic Emblem." *Experimental-Visual-Concrete: Avant-garde Poetry since the 1960s.* Ed. K. David Jackson, Eric Vos, and Johanna Drucker. Amsterdam: Rodopi. 157–72.

Konetzke, Richard. 1968. "L'Implantation de l'université européenne en Amérique espagnole pendant l'époque coloniale." *La Découverte de l'Amérique.* Ed. Pierre Mesnard. Paris: Vrin. 157–81.

——. 1965. *Die Indianerkulturen Altamerikas und die spanisch-portugiesische Kolonialherrschaft.* Frankfurt: Fischer.

Labarca, Amanda. 1939. *Historia de la enseñanza en Chile.* Santiago: Imprenta Universitaria.

Laferl, Christopher. 1995. Öffentliche und private Literatur im Vizekönigreich Neu-Spanien." *Lateinamerikanische Literaturgeschichte.* Ed. Michael Rössner. Stuttgart: Metzler. 70–83.

Lausberg, Heinrich. 1963. *Elemente der literarischen Rhetorik.* München: Hueber

Leite, Serafim. 1938–1950. *História da Companhia de Jesus.* 10 vols. Lisboa: Portugália

León-Portilla, Miguel. 1966. *La filosofía náhuatl estudiada en sus fuentes.* Mexico City: Universidad Autónoma de México, Instituto de Investigaciones Históricas.

Lindig, Wolfgang, and Mark Münzel, eds. 1985. *Kulturen und Geschichte der Indianer Nord. Mittel- und Südamerikas.* Vol. 2. München: Deutscher Taschenbuch.

Manny Paul, Catharine. 1968. *Amanda Labarca H.: Educator to the Women of Chile.* Mexico City: Centro Intercultural de Documentación.

Martí, José. 1993. "Nuestra América." *Fuentes de la cultura latinoamericana.* Ed. Leopoldo Zea. Mexico City: Fondo de Cultura Económica. 1: 121–27.

Martínez Rivera, María Clara. 1993. "El arte en los museos: Guía e historia." *Gran Enciclopedia de Colombia. Arte.* Vol. 6. Ed. Darío Jaramillo Agudelo. Bogotá: Círculo de Lectores. 301–20.

Masferrer Kan, Elio. 1994. "Die Indianer in Mexico." *Mexiko heute: Politik, Wirtschaft, Kultur.* 2nd ed. Ed. Dietrich Briesemeister and Klaus Zimmermann. Frankfurt: Vervuert. 272–91.

Métraux, Alfred. 1967. *Religions et magies indiennes d'Amérique du Sud.* Paris: Gallimard.

——. 1989. *Los incas.* Trans. Víctor Manuel Suárez Molina. Mexico City: Fondo de Cultura Económica.

Miranda Sallorenzo, Manuel. 1979. "Educación popular en la presidencia de Salvador Allende." *Iberische Halbinsel und Lateinamerika: Bildung und Ausbildung in der Romania.* Ed. Rolf Kloepfer Rolf et al. München: Fink. 3: 224–33.

Moisés, Massaud. 1985. *Dicionário de termos literários.* São Paulo: Cultrix.

Nader, Alceu. 1989. "O símbolo da integração." *Nossa América, Nuestra América: Revista do Memorial da América Latina* (São Paulo) 1: 34–43.

Páramo Pomareda, Jorge. 1993. "El Instituto Caro y Cuervo." *Gran Enciclopedia de Colombia. Cultura.* Vol. 5. Ed. Darío Jaramillo Agudelo. Bogotá: Círculo de Lectores. 138.

París, M. Blanca, Roque Faraone, and Juan Oddone, eds. 1997. *Cronología comparada de la Historia del Uruguay.* Montevideo: Universidad de la República.

Pérez, Alonso, and Manuel Ignacio, eds. 1975. *La Compañía de Jesús en México: Cuatro siglos de labor cultural (1572–1972).* Mexico City: Jus.

Poblete, Juan. 1997. "El castellano: La nueva disciplina y el texto nacional en el fin de siglo chileno." *Revista de Crítica Cultural* (Santiago de Chile) 15: 22–27.

Pottier, Bernard, ed. 1983. *América Latina en sus lenguas indígenas.* Caracas: UNESCO/Monte Ávila.

Pumar Martínez, Carmen. 1988. *Españolas en Indias: Mujeres-soldado, adelantadas y gobernadoras.* Madrid: Anaya.

Real de Azúa, Carlos. 1992. *La Universidad.* Montevideo: CELADU.

Ripa, Cesare. 1643. *Iconologie.* Trans. I. Baudoin. Paris: n.p.

Risério, António. 1993. *Textos e tribos: Poéticas extraocidentais nos trópicos brasileiros.* Rio de Janeiro: Imago.

——. 1992. "De Oriquis." *Afro-Ásia* (Publicação do Centro de Estudos Afro-Orientais da Universidade Federal da Bahia em Co-edição com a Edições Ianamá) 15: 36–55.

Rodríguez Cruz, Águeda María. 1992. *La universidad en la América Hispánica*. Madrid: MAPFRE.

Rodríguez Morales, Ricardo. 1993. "Cafés y tertulias literarias." *Gran Enciclopedia de Colombia. Cultura*. Vol. 5. Ed. Darío Jaramillo Agudelo. Bogotá: Círculo de Lectores. 229–44.

Roig, Arturo Andrés. 1993. "Los ideales bolivarianos y la propuesta de una universidad latinoamericana continental." *Fuentes de la cultura latinoamericana*. Ed. Leopoldo Zea. Mexico City: Fondo de Cultura Económica. 1: 69–80.

Rojas, José Luis de. 1988. *Los aztecas entre el Dios de la lluvia y el de la guerra*. Madrid: Anaya.

Rössner, Michael, ed. 1995. *Lateinamerikanische Literaturgeschichte*. Stuttgart: Metzler.

Santillán, Diego A. de, ed. 1956. *Gran Enciclopedia Argentina*. Buenos Aires: Ediar.

Sarlo, Beatriz. 1997. "Los estudios culturales y la crítica literaria en la encrucijada valorativa." *Revista de Crítica Cultural* (Santiago de Chile) 15: 32–38.

Schneider, Luis Mario. 1970. *El estridentismo o Una literatura de la estrategia*. Mexico City: Instituto Nacional de Bellas Artes, Departamento de Literatura.

Schrader, Achim. 1994. "Bildung." *Brasilien heute: Politik, Wirtschaft, Kultur*. Ed. Dietrich Briesemeister et al. Frankfurt: Vervuert. 384–403.

Schumann, Peter B. 1988. *Handbuch des brasilianischen Films*. Frankfurt: Vervuert.

Steger, Hanns-Albert, ed. 1965. *Grundzüge des lateinamerikanischen Hochschulwesens, eine Einführung in seine Probleme*. Baden-Baden: Nomos.

——. 1967. *Die Universitäten in der gesellschaftlichen Entwicklung Lateinamerikas: Wissenschaftstheorie, Wissenschaftspolitik*. Gütersloh: n.p.

——. 1974. *Las universidades en el desarrollo social de América Latina*. Mexico City: Fondo de Cultura Económica.

Thiemer-Sachse, Ursula. 1996. "Traditionelle Volkskultur." *Mexiko heute: Politik, Wirtschaft, Kultur*. 2nd ed. Ed. Dietrich Briesemeister and Klaus Zimmermann. Frankfurt: Vervuert. 591–615.

Thompson, J. Eric S. 1995. *Grandeza y decadencia de los mayas*. Trans. Lauro J. Zavala. Mexico City: Fondo de Cultura Económica.

Trabulse, Elías, ed. 1994. *Historia de la ciencia en México: Estudios y textos. Siglo XVIII*. Vol. 3. Mexico City: Fondo de Cultura Económica.

Traversoni, Alfredo, and Diosma Piotti. 1993. *Historia del Uruguay Siglo XX*. Montevideo: Plaza.

Valcárcel, Carlos Daniel. 1975. *Breve historia de la educación peruana*. Lima: Educación.

Weinberg, Gregorio. 1986. "El universo de la educación como sistema de ideas en América Latina." *América Latina en sus ideas*. Ed. Leopoldo Zea. Mexico City: Siglo XXI. 432–45.

Wentzlaff-Eggebert, Harald. 1995. "Die hispanoamerikanischen Avantgardebewegungen: Ein Überblick." *Lateinamerikanische Literaturgeschichte*. Ed. Michael Rössner. Stuttgart: Metzler. 236–54.

Zea, Leopoldo, ed. 1993. *Fuentes de la cultura latinoamericana*. Vol.1. Mexico City: Fondo de Cultura Económica.

Zum Felde, Alberto. 1991. *Proceso histórico del Uruguay*. Montevideo: Arca.

CHAPTER 5

CULTURAL INSTITUTIONS AND INTELLECTUAL LIFE IN BRAZIL

Luiz Roberto Cairo

The year 1556 may be considered highly significant for the cultural institutions around which Brazilian intellectuals developed a literary life; this is the year in which the Jesuits created the course in Letters at the Colégio (secondary school), which was founded in Bahia after the opening of the church–a course that sought to attend to a clientele made up of the children of the Indians and the Portuguese colonists. At this moment, which the Bahian historian Pedro Calmon called the period of "transferência" (transference) from culture to colony, the Jesuits "acumularam as funções de apóstolos–para o culto, de catequistas–para a conversão do gentio, de professores–para a educação da juventude, de políticos–para o governo espiritual, a administração, a paz interna, nesta terra dominada, sem contraste, por sua imensa autoridade" (Calmon 13–14) ("accumulated for themselves the functions of apostles, for church worship; of catechism-instructors, for the conversion of the gentiles; of teachers, for the education of youth; of politicians, for spiritual government, administration, and internal peace, in this land dominated, with no competition, by its immense authority"). The Jesuits' Colégio, besides offering the elementary course for children and the congregation, included three course-programs: Letters (Latin, grammar, rhetoric, poetry, and history), which lasted three years; Arts (philosophy and science, or physics and applied science), with the more refined character of a humanities seminar, completed by the School of Philosophy, lasting three years and meant to be an introduction to the University of Coimbra; and Theology (moral and speculative), addressed to ecclesiastics or young men "with a special ambition for knowledge." In 1575, the first bachelors graduated from the Arts course, and in addition to receiving the title of Master, they enjoyed the same privileges as those who had attended universities in Portugal. These privileges were assured years later through the regulations in the Royal Charter of 1688.

Before this time, many missionaries had requested the co-validation of these graduate credentials with those belonging to graduates from established universities, and in 1592, Father Beliarte even considered "não somente justa, como indispensável, a instalação, na Bahia, de uma Universidade, à maneira do México, de Santo Domingo, do Peru, de Córdova" ("not only just, but indispensable, the establishment of a university in Bahia, in the manner of Mexico, Santo Domingo, Peru, Cordoba"). Nevertheless, "o Rei cautelosamente se recusou sempre a consentir que na colônia crescesse instituição rival ou concorrente de Coimbra" (Calmon 15) ("the King has always cautiously refused to permit development of a rival or competitive institution to Coimbra be allowed to grow in the colony"). Unfortunately, the most these graduates managed to obtain, at the request of the Council and by the provision of 16 July 1675, was "que aos estudantes de filosofia e retórica" ("that the work of students of philosophy and rhetoric") one year of Arts "se levasse em conta nas Universidades de Coimbra, Évora" (Calmon 15) ("be taken into consideration at the universities of Coimbra and…vora"). Around the Colégio,

therefore, were priests who, besides being teachers, were also confessors, booksellers, and preachers, plus students and "homens letrados, que liam fartamente os seus velhos autores–alguns com forte cheiro de impiedade, como lhes invetivou o Santo Ofício" (Calmon 13) ("men of letters, who read assiduously all the ancient authors–some with a strong smell of impiety, as the Holy Office has designated").

Through the initiative of the Jesuits, in the northeast region of Brazil–Recife and Olinda in Pernambuco–there were important centers disseminating colonial literary life. The historian João Capistrano de Abreu (1853–1927) used to say that Pernambuco was "o lugar em que abrolhou a flor literária em nossa pátria" (Brito Broca 1979, 19) ("the place where the literary flower of our nation blossomed"), owing to the prosperity displayed early in the captaincy of Duarte Coelho. In the seventeenth century, according to Pierre Moreau, in Francisco Augusto Pereira da Costa's (1851–1923) *Anais Pernambucanos* [Annals of Pernambuco], when the Dutch took over Pernambuco, they planned the foundation of a "Universidade da América de todas as artes e ciências" ("University of America in all the arts and sciences") in Recife, and because of this "já cuidavam de propagar a instrução entre os chamados 'Brasilienses e Tapuias'" ("already took care to propagate education among the so-called 'Brazilians and Indians'") (Brito Broca 1979, 21–22). Moreau also informs us that several times the Supreme Council of the Government of Brazil requested a printing press from the directors of the West Indies Company, feeling it was particularly needed for the diffusion of culture in the colony. The 1642 arrival in Pernambuco of the printer Pieter Janszoon was registered, and it was announced that he would be disposed to begin work in the colony "if certain conditions were met." Unfortunately, he died before this could occur. It seems that the difficulty in finding a printer to replace Janszoon, however, was due to the fact that the West Indies Company did not recommend the setting up of a press in the colony because "enquanto a conquista não estivesse consolidada, tão perigosa arma pareceria a imprensa naquela época para quem tentasse uma aventura político-militar" (Brito Broca 1979, 22) ("as long as the conquest had not been perfectly consolidated, the press would appear to be a dangerous weapon in that period for anyone wishing to attempt some politico-military adventure").

In the eighteenth century, the so-called Gold Circuit caused a shift of the center of literary life in Brazil: from the captaincies of the northeast to Vila Rica in the captaincy of Minas Gerais, and subsequently, in the nineteenth century, to Rio de Janeiro. If we were to attempt to sketch literary life in Brazil, we would see, as the critic José Brito Broca has lucidly observed, that "a literatura do Brasil se desenvolveu no sentido Norte-Sul: Olinda-Recife, Bahia, Minas Gerais, Rio de Janeiro. Apenas com o Romantismo, depois de 1830, ela se deslocaria para São Paulo" (Brito Broca 1979, 24) ("the literature of Brazil developed in the north–south direction: from

Olinda-Recife, to Bahia, to Minas Gerais, then to Rio de Janeiro, and only with Romanticism, after 1830, did it shift to São Paulo").

Despite the attempts to found university education in the Colonial period, this would only begin in Brazil after the arrival of the royal Portuguese family in 1808, and even then, the attempts made to create a university during the empire and the early days of the republic were not successful. The first Brazilian university was only founded on 7 September 1931, in Rio de Janeiro, and was constituted by grouping three previously existing colleges: Law, Engineering, and Medicine. The first true university was the University of São Paulo, founded on 25 January 1934. The Letras (Letters) course was relegated to a subordinate level, with (according to the critic and literary historian Massaud Moisés) a certain negative influence on literary activity, which took place "mais à luz do improviso e do talento que do estudo e da meditação sistemática" (Moisés and Paes 420) ("more on the basis of improvisation and talent than on scholarship and systematic thinking"). The first College of Philosophy, Sciences, and Letters, based on the experience of the College of Philosophy of São Bento (of 1908), was founded in 1934, together with the University of São Paulo. In fact, Brazil was the last of the American countries to found its own university.

On the other hand, as Antônio Cândido (b. 1918) argues, the Brazilian literary system came into existence with the literary works produced at the Academias dos Seletos e dos Renascidos [lit. Academies of the Select and the Reborn] in about 1750 (Cândido 1:25). In the history of Brazilian literature, the periods of greatest productivity were connected to the response of writers coming together around a certain cause. From the nineteenth century on, literary life centered on a few cultural and educational institutions. In this sense, it is worth noting the role played in the nineteenth century not only by the Instituto Histórico e Geográfico Brasileiro (Brazilian Historical and Geographical Institute), but also by other institutions, such as the Colégio Pedro II, the Escola Politécnica (Polytechnic School), and the Academia Brasileira de Letras (Brazilian Academy of Letters) in Rio de Janeiro; the Faculdade de Direito (Law School) of the Largo de São Francisco in São Paulo; the Escola de Recife (School of Recife) in Pernambuco; the Escola de Medicina (School of Medicine) in Bahia; the Partenon Literário (Literary Parthenon) in Rio Grande do Sul; the Fênix Renascida (Phoenix Reborn), the Academia Francesa (French Academy), the Escola Popular (Popular School), and the Padaria Espiritual (Spiritual Bakery) in Ceará; and many other associations and societies that were responsible for the circulation and constant renewal of the literary life in the country.

With the emergence of the Brazilian nation, and in response to writers and intellectuals from Portugal who refused to acknowledge the existence of a Brazilian literature (since, they argued, the texts produced in Brazil did not express *brasilidade* (Brazilianness) in an explicit way and were written in the Portuguese language, which these writers considered a privilege of their own), Brazilian authors felt they had in some way to idealize a model that would affirm their nationality. European Romantic ideas favored the spread of national sentiment and consequently allowed for the creation of a concept of a national literature as the greatest expression of the spiritual evolution of a nation. This met the priorities of young Brazilians, who made every effort to discover what features of the texts produced in the former colony were shared

in order to be considered Brazilian. They also worked very hard at defining who the Brazilian writers were so that they might trace those writers who would constitute a tradition, without clashing with the concept of national literature that was being constructed at the time. Given this intention, a curious alliance developed between Romanticism, independence, and nationalism in order to make European models fit Brazilian reality. This effort surpassed the limits of the individual initiative of Brazilian writers and took on an institutional character, insofar as it had at its service the associations, societies, and groups mentioned above, as well as the support of the emperor.

At the time of the establishment of the royal government in Brazil (1831–1889), a movement emerged that was dedicated to promoting the modernization and progress of national culture. With it, inevitably, Brazil imported the practice of "philomatic" societies, institutions devoted to promote learning. As the critic Antonio Soares Amora says, these societies were "organizadas para proporcionar, aos sócios e a quem estivesse sob sua ação, a oportunidade de se porem a par do estado atual de todos os conhecimentos, particularmente os chamados conhecimentos úteis" (6) ("organized to offer both to members and anyone under their sway the opportunity to be on a par with the current state of all knowledge, especially the so-called useful kind"). Before this, the law schools of Olinda and São Paulo were inaugurated by a decree of 11 August 1827. In spite of the precariousness of cultural life in São Paulo, the literary activities of the law school, better known as the Academia do Largo de São Francisco, flourished precisely in this pre-Romantic phase, as was the case at the Sociedade Filomática (Philomatic Society), founded by teachers and students of the school in 1832—earlier than the famous law school of Olinda, later of Recife, whose ebullient literary life flourished in the second half of the nineteenth century. The Philomatic Society did not last more than two years, but it left a significant legacy through the *Revista da Sociedade Filomática* [Review of the Philomatic Society], whose six issues were published in São Paulo by the Novo Farol Paulistano press. Antonio Soares Amora observes that the review aimed to take a decisive part "na formação dos 'princípios ativos' (era a expressão da época) de nossa literatura, então empenhada em encontrar o seu caráter nacional e valores à altura dos valores de consagradas literaturas européias, antigas e modernas" (6) ("in the formation of the 'active principles' (the expression of the period) of our literature, then devoted to discovering its national character and values, on a par with the values of acclaimed European literatures, ancient and modern"). Justiniano José da Rocha Lima (1812–1862), Francisco Bernardino Ribeiro (1814–1837), and Antonio Augusto Queiroga (1811–1855) were among those who contributed to this short-lived but highy influential periodical.

Other societies had similar functions to those of the Philomatic Society, publishing and consolidating the new ideas in the periodicals connected with them. In order to establish themselves, these societies "precisaram contar com o amparo de um órgão institucional que oficializasse a reforma, e, ao mesmo tempo, garantisse a continuidade do projeto nacionalístico-romântico. O Instituto Histórico foi esse órgão institucional, cujos sócios, não por um acaso, quase sempre eram os mesmos que colaboravam na Niterói, na Minerva, n'O Guanabara" (Azevedo 134) ("needed to count on the protection of an institution that espoused the Reform movement, and at the same time furthered the Nationalist-Romantic project. The Historical Institute was such an institution, and its members, not by chance, were nearly always the same writers who contributed to the *Niterói*, the *Minerva*, the *O Guanabara*"). The idea of creating the Brazilian Historical and Geographical Institute came from the members of the Sociedade Auxiliadora da Indústria Nacional (SAIN) (Society in Support of National Industry), founded in 1827 and inspired by the Enlightenment ideas of European institutions of the seventeenth and eighteenth centuries; it was established for the purpose of stimulating Brazilian progress and development. In the first half of the nineteenth century, the Brazilian Historical and Geographical Institute was mainly responsible for the dual project of "dar conta de uma gênese da Nação brasileira, inserindo-a contudo numa tradição de civilização e progresso, tão caras ao iluminismo. A Nação, cujo retrato o instituto se propõe traçar, deve, portando, surgir como o desdobramento, nos trópicos de uma civilização branca e eruropéia. Tarefa sem dúvida a exigir esforços imensos, devido à realidade social brasileira, muito diversa daquela que se tem como modelo" (Guimarães 8) ("accounting for the genesis of the Brazilian nation, and placing it in a tradition of civilization and progress, so dear to the Enlightenment. The nation, whose portrait the institute proposed to trace, must therefore emerge as the unfolding of the white, European civilization in the tropics. This was no doubt a task that demanded immense effort, owing to Brazilian social reality, so different from its model").

Founded in 1838, mainly through the initiative of two members of the Society in Support of National Industry–the soldier Raimundo José da Cunha Matos and the canon Januário da Cunha Barbosa (1780–1846)–the Historical Institute was located on the premises of the above-mentioned society and had as its model the Institut historique de Paris; thus, besides serving as agent of legitimacy, the Paris model would also supply the Brazilians with the parameters for their historiographical work. According to the statutes, the Brazilian Historical and Geographical Institute consisted of fifty full-fledged members (twenty-five in the historical section and twenty-five in the geographical) and a great number of foreign and national corresponding members, as well as honorary members. With D. Pedro II as their patron, the members of the institute had the task of researching both Brazilian history and the development of a national identity through Brazilian letters. For this reason, writers of the period read "lerem suas memórias sobre fatos da história brasileira nas sessões" (Azevedo 135) ("their memoirs about Brazilian history in the institute's sessions"); this symbolized, for the critic Sílvia Maria Azevedo, "a aliança que acabou se firmando entre o programa nacionalista e um órgão oficial do Império, o Instituto Histórico" (135) ("the alliance that developed between the nationalist program and an official institute of the Empire, the Historical Institute").

The nationalist program was put forth both by the *Revista do Instituto Histórico* and other important periodicals edited by members of other writers' associations, the same people who wrote in turn for the *Niterói, Revista Brasiliense* [1836; Niteroi, Brazilian Journal], published in Paris; the *Minerva Brasiliense, Jornal de Ciências, Letras e Artes* [1843–1845; The Brazilian Minerva, Journal of the Sciences, Letters, and Arts]; *O Guanabara: Revista Mensal Artística, Científica e Literária* [1849–1856; The Guanabara: Artistic, Scientific, and Literary Monthly Review]; and the *Revista Popular* [1859–1862; Popular

Review], published in Rio de Janeiro. The contributors were Francisco Sales Torres Homem (1812–1876), Domingos José Gonçalves de Magalhães (1811–1882), Manuel de Araújo Porto Alegre (1806–1879), Santiago Nunes Ribeiro (d. 1847), Joaquim Norberto de Sousa e Silva (1820–1891), Carlos Emílio Adet (1818–1867), canon Joaquim Fernandes Pinheiro (1825–1876), canon Januário da Cunha Barbosa, Antônio Gonçalves Teixeira e Sousa (1812–1861), Antônio Francisco Dutra e Melo (1823–1846), Antônio Gonçalves Dias (1823–1864), and Joaquim Manuel de Macedo (1820–1882), among others.

At the end of the 1860s, when Romantic ideas began to decline throughout the country, the south of Brazil, which during the height of Romantic splendor had lived through the harsh times of the River Plate wars, became the site of an active literary life, again centered on the cultural associations and literary periodicals. Within these associations, the importance of the Sociedade Partenon Literário (Parthenon Literary Society) should be noted, an association founded in Porto Alegre on 18 June 1868 on the premises of the Sociedade Firmeza e Esperança (Hope and Strength Society), situated on the old Rua de Bragança, now Marechal Floriano, by a group of young men headed by José Antonio do Vale Caldre e Fião (1821–1876) and Apolinário Porto Alegre (1884–1904). The name of the association came from "do desejo de homenagear e fazer reviver no Rio Grande do Sul a beleza do templo grego e de toda uma cultura, pertencente ao passado heleno" (Baumgarten and Silveira 17) ("the desire to pay homage to and revive in Rio Grande do Sul the beauty of the Greek temple and of an entire culture belonging to the Hellenic past"). The Sociedade Partenon Literário had a surprising influence on the life of the province, according to the historian and critic Guilhermino César–"quer pelo que realizou como entidade de fins culturais, quer pelo que fizeram individualmente os seus agremiados, cujos nomes passaram a capitanear a vida mental do Rio Grande, no livro, no jornal, na tribuna, bem como na luta pela Abolição e pela República" (172) ("both by what it did as an organ with cultural objectives, and by what its members did individually, as their names came to head the intellectual life of Rio Grande, in books, newspapers, the courts, as well as in the struggle for Abolition and the Republic"). After assimilating Romantic ideas, the members tried to introduce them into the region, thus beginning "o ciclo da literatura regionalista, dita gauchesca, como consequência de uma atitude mental necessariamente combativa" (173) ("the cycle of regionalist, so-called gaucho literature, as a consequence of a necessarily combative mental attitude"). The rustic hero replaces the Indian and the Negro in the "literatura liberal que desde Macedo enfartara as letras do centro e do norte do país" (174) ("liberal literature, which since Macedo had filled the literature of the center and north of the country"). Like the societies developing in the center of the country, the "Parthenon" founded a journal, the *Revista Mensal da Sociedade Partenon Literário* [Monthly Review of the Parthenon Literary Society], which, with a few interruptions, published the literary production of several of its members for ten years. Besides the men already mentioned (Apolinário Porto Alegre and Caldre e Fião), Múcio Teixeira (1858–1926), Carlos von Koseritz (1834–1890), Bernardo Taveira Júnior (1836–1892), and Amália dos Passos Figueirôa (1845–1878), among others, were also members of the Society.

In the 1870s, the great expansion of science and scientific methods into all disciplines led Brazilian historical writers and critics to concern themselves with the evolution of artistic forms, rigorously applying the laws and principles that determined their origins. This concern was expressed in a language imbued with scientific expressions taken mainly from biology, physics, mathematics, chemistry, and psychology and invoked as much as possible through the methods borrowed from these sciences. It was felt that it was important to confer a scientific character on the history of literature and on literary criticism. Critics now had to use the scientific method and base their analysis on it, so that literary criticism would lose its character of mere interpretive speculation and gain the stamp of seriousness and truthfulness, which characterized scientific knowledge. Once more, a European model of thought was loosely adapted to the tropics.

The development of Brazilian intellectuals of the nineteenth century varied from region to region because of the kind of associations and spontaneous groups mentioned above, which arose wherever there was literary activity. The influence of Auguste Comte's positivism on the intellectuals of Rio de Janeiro, for example, was not the same as it was on those of the northeast, where subtle differences existed between what took place at the Escola de Recife in Pernambuco and at the so-called Academia Francesa of Ceará, not to mention other areas. If, in Rio de Janeiro, the orthodox, religious positivism of Comte ruled—by way of Miguel Lemos (1854–1917)—in the northeast, the Comtean model was modified by the significant impact of scientificist historians and philosophers, influenced mainly by the positivism of Buckle, Taine, and Spencer, not to mention the Germans, such as Haeckel, whose ideas were diffused in Recife by Tobias Barreto (1839–1889) and in Porto Alegre by Carlos von Koseritz. In Ceará, the Academia Francesa was an informal association without a board of directors or a place of its own, since its members met in their own homes for lectures or the presentation of theoretical discussions on any subject. Founded in 1872, it was preceded by the Fenix Estudantil (Student Phoenix) of 1870, which assembled youths from fifteen to twenty years of age, former students of the Atheneu in the 1860s. Rocha Lima, Capistrano de Abreu, and Araripe Júnior (1848–1911) all took part in it.

Capistrano de Abreu, an ardent Comtean, describes the Academia Francesa in his *Ensaios e Estudos* [Essays and Studies] (1st series) in this way:

Era em casa de Rocha Lima que se reuniam os membros do que chamávamos Academia Francesa. Quanta ilusão! Quanta mocidade! França Leite [Nicolau] advogava os direitos do comtismo puro, e sustentava que o Système de Politique era o complemento do Cours de Philosophie. Melo [Antônio José de] descrevia a anatomia do cérebro, com a exatidão do sábio e o estro do poeta. Pompeu Filho [Tomás] dissertava sobre a filosofia alemã e sobre a India, citava Laurent e combatia Taine. Varela—o garboso, abnegado paladino—enristava lanças a favor do racionalismo. Araripe Júnior encobria com a máscara de Falstaff a alma dorida de René. Felino Barroso [pai de Gustavo Barroso] falava da Revolução Francesa com o arrebatamento de Camille Desmoulins. Lopes [João, pai dos escritores Tomás e Oscar Lopes], ora candente com um raio de sol, ora lôbrego como uma noite de Walpurgis, dava asas a seu humor colossal. Por vezes, das margens do Amazonas chegava o eco de uma voz, doce como a poesia das suas águas sem fim—a de Xilderico de Faria. O mais moço de todos, Rocha Lima, era um dos que mais se distinguiam. A sua inteligência plástica e compreensiva assimilava as diferentes teorias de maneira admirável. A sua palavra espirituosa destacava aspectos novos nas questões mais abstrusas. As objeções que apresentava, as sugestões que oferecia, limitando o campo do debate, encaminhavam muitas vezes as conclusões por todos admitidas. Além disso, o seu caráter tão lhano, como firme, sabia afagar as susceptividades, e evitar choques e divergências fatais em sociedades de tal orgem. (Lins 115)

It was at the home of Rocha Lima that the members of what we called the Academia Francesa gathered. Such illusion! Such youth! França Leite [Nicolau] advocated the rights of pure Comtism, and sustained that the *Système de politique* was the complement of the *Cours de philosophie*. Melo [Antonio José de] described the anatomy of the brain, with the exactitude of the scholar and the passion of the poet. Pompeu Filho [Tomás] spoke on German philosophy and on India, cited Laurent, and contested Taine. Varela—the unselfish, elegant paladine—tilted lances in favor of rationalism. Araripe Júnior covered the sorrowful soul of René with the mask of Falstaff. Felino Barroso [Gustavo Barroso's father] spoke of the French Revolution with the rapture of Camille Desmoulins. Lopes [João, father of the writers Tomás and Oscar Lopes], sometimes fiery as a ray of the sun, sometimes as dark as a Walpurgis night, gave wings to his colossal humor. Occasionally, the echo of a voice, sweet as the poetry of its endless waters, was heard from the margins of the Amazon—that of Xilderico de Faria. The youngest of all, Rocha Lima, was one of those who most distinguished themselves. His subtle and comprehensive intelligence assimilated the different theories in an astonishing way. His witty words pointed out new aspects in the most abstruse questions. The objections he put forward, the suggestions he offered, limiting the field of debate, often led to conclusions that were accepted by everyone. Also, his character, both sincere and strong, knew how to appease sensibilities and avoid clashes and fatal differences in societies of this type.

Later, the Fênix Estudantil and the Academia Francesa continued their mission in the Escola Popular (which was inaugurated on 31 May 1874, also in Ceará), "fiel à preocupação de Augusto Comte com a formação intelectual do proletariado" (Lins 116) ("faithful to the concern of Auguste Comte with the intellectual formation of the proletariat").

The historian Ivan Lins, in the *História do positivismo no Brasil* [History of Positivism in Brazil], further records some notes of Capistrano de Abreu on the Escola Popular:

Aludindo à Escola Popular, escreve Capistrano: 'os que tiveram ocasião de visitá-la, recordam-se da animação, da cordialidade, do estímulo, que ali reinavam, e corriam parelhas com o desinteresse dos jovens professores'. E acrescenta haver sido grande a sua influência, 'não só sobre as classes a que se destinava, como sobre a sociedade cearense em geral, por intermédio de conferências ali feitas, em que o ideal moderno era apregoado por pessoas altamente convencidas da sua excelência', sendo, 'maior a influência da Escola sobre os espíritos audazes e juvenis, que congregou, reuniu e fecundou uns pelos outros.' (116–17)

Alluding to the Escola Popular, Capistrano writes: "those who had occasion to visit it, recall the excitement, the cordiality, the stimulation that ruled there, and that ran neck-and-neck with the intense interest of the young teachers." And he adds that its influence has been great, "not only on the classes it was meant for, but on Ceará society in general, through the lectures given there, in which the modern ideal was preached by people highly convinced of its excellence," with "the influence of the Escola" being "greater on young, bold spirits who gathered, joined and planted some ideals on the others."

Afrânio Coutinho (1911–2000), in *A formação de Capistrano crítico* [1935; The Formation of Capistrano as Critic], calls attention to the fact that Fortaleza, at the beginning of the

1870s, was "um centro, no qual, no que concerne à atividade espiritual, as condições eram de franco progresso e autonomia. Estava em moda a tertúlia intelectual" (1981, 102) ("a center whose conditions, concerning cultural activity, were frankly progressive and autonomous. The intellectual gathering was in style").

In Pernambuco, there was the Escola de Recife [School of Recife], which had a "ressonância maior devido à Faculdade de Direito, que agia como centro de agitação e debate intelectual" (Coutinho 1969, 22) ("greater resonance due to the Law School, which acted as a center of intellectual ferment and debate"). The Escola de Recife experienced a predominantly German influence because of its head, Tobias Barreto, and the impact of the monism of Haeckel (and the evolutionism of Spencer), which, along with orthodox (and heterodox) positivism and the scientific movement in general, formed its intellectual basis. It was also, according to Coutinho, improperly called a school, since it did not possess either the "unity of thought" or "literary coloring" that usually characterize literary and philosophical schools. For this reason, he reduces the role of the Escola de Recife to a center of intellectual ferment similar to those that existed around the law schools of São Paulo and Olinda and the School of Medicine of Bahia.

It is curious to note that when Coutinho speaks of these associations, it is in the context of an analysis of the reigning educational system in Brazil in the nineteenth century, where he argues the efficiency of this system in relation to its objectives:

> Um sistema de educação só deve julgado de acordo com o seu objetivo. E os objetivos do trabalho educacional não são impostos pelo educador, mas pelo tipo de civilização e pelos valores que a caracterizam e que ela tem que defender e transmitir. O problema da educação é, pois, organizar um currículo que esteja de acordo com aqueles objetivos. O que importa não é saber se um sistema é bom, mas para que ele é bom. A política educacional resulta do que a cultura julga que é importante. (1981, 98)

> A system of education should only be judged according to its aims. And the aims of education are not imposed by the educator, but by the type of civilization and values that characterize it and that it has to defend and transmit. The major problem of education is therefore to organize a curriculum that is in accordance with those objectives. What matters is not if a system is good in the abstract, but what it is good for. Educational policy results from what the culture considers important.

This theory, which was in fact inherited from the Jesuits, had as its aim the formation of an intelligentsia of the lettered and learned, and this aim it achieved:

> Era, por certo, um sistema educacional construído sobre o indivíduo como alicerce sem atenção adequada ao aspecto social. Era uma educação para um pequeno número de indivíduos seletos. Mas assim se fazia no mundo inteiro, pois a preocupação social em educação não surgiu antes da metade do século XIX. O principal era o treino intelectual, feito de modo isolado, para o bem exclusivo do indivíduo, era uma educação individualista e não social, para criar indivíduos auto-suficientes e não tipos cooperantes. Deve a educação visar à formação de homens de espírito superior, ou deve pretender a elevação da massa? Eis a questão fundamental, que só encontra resposta adequada levando-se em conta o tipo da civilização a que procura servir. (Coutinho 1981, 98-99)

> It was, truly, an educational system built on the individual as a foundation, without giving much attention to the social aspects. It was an education for a small number of select individuals. But it was done that way all over the Jesuits' world; social concerns in education did not emerge until the middle of the nineteenth century. The main thing was intellectual training, done in a concentrated way, exclusively for the good of the individual; it was an individualistic and not a social education, aiming at creating self-sufficient leaders and not cooperative types. Was education to form men of a superior spirit, or to attempt to educate the masses? Here is the fundamental question, which only finds an adequate answer by taking into consideration the type of civilization which it seeks to serve.

This important observation leads to a reflection on the goals to be achieved by the present Brazilian educational system in contrast to that of the past. In fact, the current one is extremely inefficient, for it neither forms persons of spirit nor succeeds in (in)forming the masse; it levels all society downward.

Much of the cultural ferment of the nineteenth century was thanks to the existence of good private schools:

> A instrução progredira sobretudo graças aos colégios particulares. Bibliotecas surgiram. Discutia-se filosofia, literatura, ciência, história. O enciclopedismo inspirava os espíritos. Voltaire, Kant, Comte, Darwin, Buckle, sobretudo Spencer, eram os luzeiros. Portugal cedera o lugar à França como orientação intelectual, e de Portugal só o que estivesse de acordo com as novas correntes, isto é, em vez dos clássicos os modernos da polêmica coimbrã. (Coutinho 1981, 102)

> Instruction had progressed above all thanks to the private schools. Libraries came into being. Philosophy, literature, science, history were discussed. Encyclopedism inspired minds. Voltaire, Kant, Comte, Darwin, Buckle, especially Spencer, were the luminaries. Portugal had yielded to France its intellectual leadership and sent to Brazil only what was in accordance with the new trends in France, that is, instead of the classics, the moderns of Coimbra's polemics.

The Brazilian educational system of the nineteenth century was, in fact, responsible for the formation of associations like the Escola de Recife and the Academia Francesa. It was not a question of homogenizing the educational system, and this is clear not only in the philosophical differences between associations, but also in the developing of diverse currents of thought within the groups.

Another aspect that needs to be clarified is that the Escola de Recife existed simultaneously with the Academia Francesa of Ceará, without one influencing the other, in spite of the exchanges between some of the members, mainly those men of Ceará who studied at the Law School of Recife. Clóvis Beviláqua even states that the School of Recife did not have a fixed set of principles, a definitive systematization of ideas, but rather more a progressive philosophical direction (see Coutinho 1981, 107). The German influence, mainly of Haeckel, was what most differentiated the men of Pernambuco from those of Ceará, who were more influenced by the French, as the name of the association itself indicates. Along with the German influence, the Escola de Recife favored Spencerian evolutionism and Positivism, while the Academia Francesa added Spencerian evolutionism and Buckle's determinism to the French thought of Taine and Comte. These facts cannot be ignored when one speaks of the formation of Brazilian intellectuals in the nineteenth century, since realist critics, such as José Veríssimo (1857–1916), Sílvio Romero (1851–1914), and Araripe Júnior, though living in Rio de Janeiro at the height of their careers, had been educated in their, respectively, northern (Pará) and northeastern (Pernambuco/ Sergipe and Ceará) Brazilian provinces; and it was in this formative period that the ideas that they later developed were first planted, allowing each of them separately to articulate values that could provide new ideas and allow more or less receptiveness to new ideologies. In the specific case of Araripe Júnior, who took part, along with Rocha Lima and Capistrano de Abreu, in the Academia Francesa and also the Escola Popular of Ceará (where Tobias Barreto and Sílvio Romero worked), there were, in addition to the notable influence of Taine, other influences as well: Spencer's evolutionism and the scientificism of Émile Hennequin, not to mention other influences that gave a rather special character to the Tainean basis of his thought. Sílvio Romero, for his part, influenced the works of Carlos von Koseritz in the south of Brazil, making Tobias Barreto's ideas (and consequently those of the Escola de Recife) very well-known in Rio Grande do Sul (César 251).

Before the turn of the century (in 1896) the writer Machado de Assis (1839–1908) founded in Rio de Janeiro the Academia Brasileira de Letras (Brazilian Academy of Letters), following the Parisian model of the French Academy, for the purpose of cultivating the national language and literature, trying to "conservar, no meio da federação política, a unidade literária" (Machado de Assis 926) ("preserve, amidst the political federation, literary unity"), thus giving continuity to the project of developing a national literature that had been initiated at the Brazilian Historical and Geographical Institute. The Brazilian Academy of Letters consisted of forty members, twenty-five of whom lived in Rio de Janeiro, as well as twenty additional corresponding members. By the statutes, "só podem ser membros da Academia os brasileiros que tenham, em qualquer dos gêneros da Literatura, publicado obras de reconhecido mérito, ou fora desses gêneros, livro de valor literário. As mesmas condições, menos a de nacionalidade, exigem-se para os correspondentes" (Moisés and Paes 17) ("only those may be members of the Academy who have, in any of the genres of literature, published works of acknowledged merit, or outside these genres, a book of literary value. The same conditions, except that of nationality, are required for the correspondents").

Machado de Assis presided over the first board of directors of the Brazilian Academy of Letters, formed by Joaquim Nabuco as General Secretary, Rodrigo Otávio as First Secretary, and Inglês de Sousa as Treasurer. In an address made to the closing session of the academy's meeting, on 7 December 1897, Machado de Assis said: "Brasileira de Letras tem de ser o que são as associações análogas: uma torre de marfim, onde acolham espíritos literários, com a unica preocupação literária, e de onde estendendo os olhos para todos os lados, vejam claro e quieto. Homens daqui podem escrever páginas de história, mas a história faz-se lá fora." (927) ("Founded among serious circumstances of public order, the Brazilian Academy of Letters has to be what analogous associations are: an ivory tower, which harbors literary spirits, with only a literary concern, and from which men, casting their eyes on all sides, see clearly and quietly. Men from here may write pages of history, but history is made outside.") With respect to the function of guardian of the language, he observed: "A Academia, trabalhando pelo conhecimento desses fenômenos buscará ser, com o tempo, a guarda da nossa língua. . . . Guardar não é impor; nenhum de vós tem para si que a Academia decrete fórmulas. E depois para guardar uma língua, é preciso que ela se guarde também a si mesma, e o melhor dos processos é ainda a composição e a conservação de obras clássicas." (Machado de Assis 927–28)("The Academy, working for the knowledge of these phenomena, will try to be in time the guardian of our language. . . . To guard is not to impose; none of you believe that the Academy decrees formulae. And, furthermore, in order to guard a language it is necessary for it to guard itself, and the best process is still the composition and preservation of classic works.") In this (slightly conservative) spirit, each state of the union came to have its own Academy of Letters, around which the literary life of the region revolved.

In the 1930s, with the coming of the French mission to the Faculdade de Filosofia (School of Philosophy) of the University of São Paulo, a vigorous new renaissance in the literary life of Brazil can be seen, now that a new generation of middle-class intellectuals from São Paulo had been formed; this made up the Brazilian intellectual elite at the end of the millenium. The appearance of the first Faculdades de Letras (College of Letters) in the 1940s and the attempt to create the figure of the professional man of letters—a move that caused a controversy, headed by Afrânio Coutinho, regarding who should write about literature in Brazil. The inclusion of the so-called footnote critics of the newspapers, such as the emblematic figure of Álvaro Lins (1912–1970), would give continuity to this now traditional role of nourishing literary life that the cultural and educational institutions had been playing. Today, we can also see the results of the consolidation of the Colleges of Letters, which, in a general way, have been mainly responsible for the ferment in academic and literary production, especially through the relevant research projects developed in the postgraduate programs connected with them and maintained by funds from federal (CAPES and CNPq) and state financing organs, in the case of the Foundations for Research Support in some states of the union. Literary life in Brazil continues to revolve around institutions such as ABRALIC, Associação Brasileira de Literatura Comparada (Brazilian Association of Comparative Literature); ANPOLL, Associação Nacional de Pós-Graduação e Pesquisa em Letras e Linguística (National Association of Post-Graduate Research in Letters and Linguistics); and the SBPC, Sociedade Brasileira para o Progresso da Ciência (Brazilian Society for the Progress of Science), among the most important ones.

Translation by Thomas LaBorie Burns and Glàucia Renate Gonçalves

Works Cited

Amora, Antonio Soares. 1977. "Um precioso documento." *Revista da Sociedade Philomática.* São Paulo: Typographia do Novo Farol Paulistano; Metal Leve, Ed. facsimile.

Araripe Júnior, Tristão de Alencar. 1958. *Obra crítica.* Vol. 1. Ed. Afrânio Coutinho. Rio de Janeiro: MEC–Casa de Rui Barbosa.

Azevedo, Silvia Maria. 1996. "Joaquim Norberto: O nacional e a história." *Continente Sul Sur* (Porto Alegre) 2 (November): 133–48.

Baumgarten, Carlos A., Carmen C. Silveira, and Regina Zilberman. 1980. *O Partenon Literário: Prosa e poesia–Antologia.* Porto Alegre: Escola Superior de Teologia São Lourenço de Brindes–Instituto Cultural Português.

Brito Broca, José. 1975. *A vida literária no Brasil–1900.* 3rd ed. Rio de Janeiro: José Olympio–Departamento de Cultura da Guanabara.

———. 1979. *Românticos, pré-românticos, ultra-românticos: Vida literária e Romantismo brasileiro.* São Paulo: Polis; Brasília: INL.

Cairo, Luiz Roberto. 1996. *O salto por cima da própria sombra.* São Paulo: Annablume.

Calmon, Pedro. 1949. *História da literatura baiana.* 2nd ed. Salvador: Publicação da Prefeitura Municipal do Salvador; Rio de Janeiro: José Olympio.

Cândido, Antônio. 1971. *Formação da literatura brasileira: Momentos decisivos.* 4th ed. 2 vols. São Paulo: Martins.

Castello, José Aderaldo. 1975. *Manifestações literárias do período colonial: 1500–1808/1836.* 3rd ed. São Paulo: Cultrix–EDUSP.

César, Guilhermino. 1956. *História da literatura do Rio Grande do Sul.* Porto Alegre: Globo.

Costa, Francisco Augusto Pereira da. 1951–1966. *Anais pernambucanos.* Vol. 1, *1493–1590.* Vol. 2, *1591–1634.* Vol. 3, *1635–1665.* Vol. 4, *1666–1700.* Vol. 5, *1701–1739.* Vol. 6, *1740–1794.* Vol. 7, *1795–1817.* Vol. 8, *1818–1823.* Vol. 9, *1824–1833.* Vol. 10, *1834–1850.* Recife: Arquivo Público Estadual.

Coutinho, Afrânio. 1969. *A literatura no Brasil.* Vol. 3. Rio de Janeiro: Sul-Americana.

———. 1981. *Conceito de literatura brasileira.* Petrópolis-RJ: Vozes.

Guimarães, Manoel Luís Salgado. 1988. "Nação e civilização nos trópicos: O Instituto Histórico e Geográfico Brasileiro e o projeto de uma história nacional." *Estudos Históricos* (Rio de Janeiro: Associação de Pesquisa e Documentação Histórica) 1: 5–27.

Lins, Ivan. 1967. *História do positivismo no Brasil.* 2nd ed. São Paulo: Companhia Editora Nacional.

Machado De Assis, Joaquim Maria. 1962. *Obra completa.* 2nd ed. Vol. 3. Ed. Afrânio Coutinho. Rio de Janeiro: Aguilar.

Moisés, Massaud, and José Paulo Paes, eds. 1980. *Pequeno dicionário de literatura brasileira.* 2nd ed. São Paulo: Cultrix.

CHAPTER 6

CULTURAL MODELS OF REPRESENTATION IN SEVENTEENTH-CENTURY BRAZIL

João Adolfo Hansen

A historical study of Brazil's seventeenth-century literary culture undertaken at the end of the twentieth century benefits from the current use of the term *Baroque*, but it is also circumscribed through our awareness that this past is the product of our literary archaeology that has constituted it. The colonial remnants today are principally those poetic, oratorical, historical, and narrative texts that are part of the literary canon, including the satire attributed to Gregório de Matos e Guerra (1633?–1696); the sermons, correspondence, and prophetic works of Fr. Antônio Vieira (1608–1697); various historical speeches from sessions of the Academia dos Esquecidos [1724; Academy of the Forgotten] and of the Renascidos [1759; Resurrected], as well as the *História da América Portuguesa* [1730; History of Portuguese America] by Sebastião da Rocha Pita (1660–1738); and novels such as Gaspar Pires de Rebelo's *Os Infortunios Trágicos de Constante Florinda* [1625; Tragic Misfortunes of Constant Florinda] or works such as Nuno Marques Pereira's (1652–1731) *Compêndio narrativo do peregrino da América* [1728; Narrative Compendium of the Pilgrim of America]. We could add the municipal council's minutes and letters to the Inquisition, royal orders, governors' statutes, descriptive treatises, pragmatics of dress and address, texts of counsel to princes, chronicles of the Dutch Wars, legislation of "just wars against the Indians," descriptions of festivities, books of the brotherhoods, and so on. The list is evidently inexhaustible, and serves here merely to indicate materials for organizing the reconstruction of homologies and categories that govern Luso-Brazilian colonial representation.

In discussing the present, it is necessary to reestablish the chain of appropriations of these colonial remains in order to examine the contemporary use-value of the notion of Baroque. A reconstitution of the Colonial period shows that, since Romantic poet Domingos José Gonçalves de Magalhães's (1811–1882) nationalist program of 1836, writers and works have either been included or excluded from the canon according to the teleology of a literary historiography that conceives past forms unilaterally as fixed stages for the construction of a narrative structure for literary history. In the appropriation of colonial letters, the evolutionary assumption of this historiography is the universalizing use of critical categories taken from the Hegelian and Romantic continuum: expression, authorship, psychological subjectivity, plagiarism, the aesthetic, originality, aesthetic break, progress, criticism, utopia, negative rationalization of form, revolution, public, literate/illiterate, etc. When retrospectively applied to representations invented through other categories of thought, transmitted by different technical means and material supports, and consumed according to other concepts of the public (with other meanings of experience of history), the categories are completely anachronistic. To avoid comparison

with evolutionist ideology or post-utopian aesthetization, the core criterion for establishing the historical value of colonial texts, we propose, is the communication or intersubjective relationship established in and through the works. It is not a matter of studying them as a means of achieving empirical relations of intersubjectivity but of studying them as formalized practices of representation and as representations of contemporary practices of their time. It is not useful to reduce them to Jakobson's half-dozen functions of language, which may be viable in the linguistic description of forms but is inadequate to account for their function in colonial cultural practices that depend upon extratextual criteria (such as the exclusive metropolitan social hierarchy, the Inquisition, and the institution of slavery). The very concept of Baroque, through which seventeenth-century Brazilian letters are anachronized by Wölfflin and D'Ors, also requires some commentary. The doctrine of *ut pictura poesis*–when applied to Brazilian colonial art and literature–takes up selected fragments of works rather than the creative process as a whole and therefore says more about the addressee than of the literary culture; this applies not only in terms of semantic meaning but also with regard to the concerns of the historian as the primary agent of appropriation of the cultural materials of the past. Such work is cited, for example, as grounds for the selection and ordering of historical materials for the seventeenth century according to various degrees of application of the idea of the sharp-witted conceit. For this very reason, a critique of the universalization of Enlightenment categories applied to colonial remains must hold to the need to define colonial representations as metonymies or remnants of historical practices of representation and, simultaneously, recognize that, in their time, they were included in actual systems of representation. Like Louis Marin, I take *representation* to signify four basic articulations: (1) the use of symbols in the place of something else; (2) the presence of the absent thing produced in the substitution; (3) the appearance or symbolic form of this presence; (4) the position staged in this form and, obviously, the conflicting positions of the representations. That is to say, it signifies history.

In the search to determine the structure and function of colonial representations (so understood), it is not valid to use the images that they themselves offer, but rather it is necessary to reconstruct the precepts of their production and consumption (Chartier 1994, 140). As representations of practices, colonial remains are ordered by cultural models that organize the *forma mentis* of lettered men and artisans. The archeology of the models establishes homologies between various references, both of discursive and plastic expression, fictitious or not, reconstructing the structure and function of their theological-political-ethical-rhetorical categories. Archeology relates structures and uses, deducing the structures of the various differentiated uses. In this operation, the differential nature of the (self-)representations of the uses and their historical agents is specified as particular appropriations of socially common, anonymous, collectivized structures. In Brazil, however, studies of these relations are just beginning, and it is still necessary to determine the cultural differences in the uses of common structures through the analysis of their material means and institutional supports, correspondences, and internal fluxes of the personal and group initiatives of colonial lettered men and artisans.

Here, the designation *seventeenth century* serves to classify a lengthy period whose boundaries may be more or less determined by the dates 1580 (when Portugal came under the Spanish Hapsburg rule of Philip II, who reigned from 1556 to 1598) and 1750 (marking the death of João V, who reigned from 1706 to 1750), including the political and cultural transformations of the Marquis of Pombal's (1699–1782) "Catholic Enlightenment" (1750–1777). These boundaries are as arbitrary as any others; they take into account, however, the predominance of Italian and Spanish cultural models, which made colonial lettered men and artisans contemporaries of other lettered men and artisans living in Paris or in New Spain. Thus 1580 (the date of the beginning of the Iberian Union) marks the subordination of Portuguese letters to Italian standards, principally those of the Counter-Reformation appropriation of sixteenth-century *Mannerism*, which subordinated artistic programs to the opposition "life of devotion/life of libertinism," and Spanish models, such as the poetry of Luis de Góngora (1561–1627) and Francisco Quevedo (1580–1645), the theater of Lope de Vega (1562–1635) and Calderón de la Barca (1600–1681), as well as the oratory of the Italian Paravicino. As for 1750, the year of João V's death, it marks the beginning of the Marquis of Pombal's "Catholic Enlightenment" and the decline and abandonment of the absolutist court's rationalist modes, such as the penchant sharp-witted debate, dissimulation, and courtly techniques of political prudence. Obviously, these dates can be pushed forward or back through consideration of the various temporalities of the historical period concepts appropriated by lettered men and artisans—for example, classical Greek and Latin, medieval, Renaissance, Baroque—which, at times, go beyond conventional chronological boundaries of general history.

During this period, rhetoric regulated all representations and allowed lettered men and artisans to apply a wide variety of styles in imitation or emulation of Renaissance, medieval, Latin, or Greek models of extremely long standing by adapting them prescriptively to local and material circumstances of consumption. The same plurality of styles renders historically untenable any unification of representations produced at that time under generic labels, such as "seventeenth century" or "Baroque." After the Portuguese Wars of Restoration, Spain's recognition of Portugal's independence in 1660 and the reign of João IV, Duke of Bragança from 1640 to 1656, came the brief government of Afonso VI, deposed in 1667 by the coup d'état organized by his brother Prince Peter, who married his sister-in-law Marie Françoise of Savoy and became regent and, later, king (as Peter II) until 1706, when his son João V ascended the throne. Several crises distinguished the period. Beginning in 1675, customs restrictions imposed by England, France, and Holland upon the distribution and sale of Brazilian sugar on European markets caused supplies to pile up in the warehouses of Lisbon. Hoping to make Brazilian sugar

competitive, the crown ordered the reduction of prices. In Bahia and in Pernambuco, the drop immediately affected clerical and bureaucratic payrolls, and raised the value and price of slaves and other materials indispensable to the plantations, leading to the nonpayment of debts to bankruptcies and to the *fogo morto*; it also affected tax collection, donations, and tithes as well as intensifying the poverty of an already chronically impoverished population. The crisis was further intensified when metropolitan gold and silver was fixed at a face value inferior to that of the currency circulating in Brazil, leading to the flight of metals to Portugal, accompanied by an increase in the price of commodities (see Hanson). In 1688, after the 20 percent devaluation of the Spanish *pataca* (copper coin), Portuguese hard currency became more vulnerable to contraband and other practices such as cut edges of coins and the melting of shavings or leftovers, transformed by the goldsmiths of Bahia into metal bars, tableware, and sumptuary objects, which, along with tobacco and spirits, were traded for Africans in Angola and in the Gulf of Guinea. Also during the period extending from 1680 to 1700, in Bahia and other regions of the northeast, there was a high mortality among slaves caused by the *bicha* (literally "the beast")–the yellow fever brought over on the slave ships. This critical situation was characterized by widespread rumors, the sedition of soldiers, slave rebellions, and attacks by Indians and pirates. The rise of merchants and members of the artisan guilds into positions of lower aristocracy was ferociously combated by sectors of the nobility allied to the Holy Office of the Inquisition headed by Dominicans, leading to an intensification of the repressive measures against Jews and "New Christians." During this period the ruling hierarchy suffered constant threats, which were expressed in innumerable conflicts in representation. Between 1690 and 1700 the *bandeirante* (backland explorer) penetration of the *sertão* (backlands) led to the discovery of gold in the Vila Rica region and diamonds in Arraial do Tijuco; this ensured the luxury of João V's court, the construction of the palace-convent at Mafra, and the continued Portuguese importation of architects, painters, musicians, and Italian men of letters, who reactivated sixteenth- and seventeenth-century schemes of representation. Architecture, sculpture, painting, poetry, oratory, drama, and music once more turned to Borromini, Palladio, Scamozzi, Serlio, Pozzo, Ripa, Possevino, Peregrini, Pallavicino, Tesauro, Gilio, Marino, Guarini, Bernini, and Monteverdi. In Brazil, the same schemes were reactivated in the academies, founded after 1724 as attempts at a systematic organization of Brazilian culture. After 1750, the neo-Scholastic politicotheological schemes of the seventeenth-century Counter-Reformation still dominant in Brazil are criticized by such authors as Verney and Cândido Lusitano; they had been replaced, in Portugal, by French neo-Classical and Italian pastoral models. In Colonial Brazil, however, they continued to flourish, principally in the Baroque architecture of Minas Gerais–at least until the French mission brought over, through the initiative of João VI, the neo-Classical style in 1817.

Presupposing the synchrony of Brazil with the African and Asian colonies of Portugal, the colonies of Spain, and various European cultural centers (such as Rome, Naples, Paris, Vienna, Prague, and Augsburg), colonial representation may initially be described as a result of technical-political processes of integration of various cultural codes through the "Pombal" model of rationalism of the absolutist court. The fact that the majority of the colonial population was illiterate, that there were no universities until the twentieth century, that there were no printing presses until 1808, and that books were severely censored constitutes an overwhelming restriction on written production. However, we should remember that there were other forms of circulation and appropriation of written discourse that did not necessarily depend on reading. There were written discourses that presupposed other forms of organization of time and memory, adapting diffusion to the everyday life of the streets and squares. It was customary to read aloud to an illiterate public all documents and notices written according to the erudite standards of lettered high culture. Sheets of paper were nailed to church doors or circulated in looseleaf form; there were the satires written by Gregório de Matos that dramatized erudite topics of Latin letters, such as those from the poetry of Ovid, Horace, Lucan, and Juvenal, or of Portuguese and Spanish poetry of the fifteenth, sixteenth, and seventeenth centuries, such as Garcia de Resende's (1470–ca.1536) *Cancioneiro Geral* [1516; General Anthology] and the poetry of Luiz de Camões (1524?–1580), Quevedo, Góngora, and Lope de Vega. These poems have a loose, predictable plot constructed through stereotyped topoi of the genre, usually in imitation of orality. Such schemes were easily memorized and reapplied in other circumstances, according to the needs of the moment, as evidenced by variants of poems, some of which contain important alterations of meaning of the Gregorian codices, currently housed in the National Library in Rio de Janeiro.

The integration of various cultural codes takes place with the production of local use-value for the neo-Scholastic doctrine then diffused in Portugal by such academic institutions as the University of Coimbra and in Brazil by the Jesuit colleges. The internationalization of the court rationalism of the Iberian absolutist monarchies thus means that the lettered men and artisans of Rome, Naples, Spain, Portugal, New Spain, Peru, and Brazil, principally, came to share the same rhetorical-theological-political points of reference. The doctrine of Pombal's "Catholic policy" was taught, imposed, imitated, and deformed in an attempt to guarantee the centralizing orthodoxy of cultural unification operating within the various instances that integrated the catechized indigenous populations, enslaved Africans, and judicially differentiated social levels of Iberian culture from plebeians to nobles. In countless circumstances, the applications and deformations of the doctrine appear as conflicts of representation that stage the generalities of both the Crown's and local private interests. The works of the principal Colonial poets, orators, and prose writers of the period, such as Manuel Botelho de Oliveira (1636–1711), Gregório de Matos e Guerra, Antônio Vieira, Sebastião da Rocha Pita, and Nuno Marques Pereira, and artisans such as Francisco Xavier de Brito (d. 1751), Antônio Francisco Lisboa (1730–1814), and Manuel da Costa Athayde (1762–1830), presuppose the same teleological-political unity of doctrine as the foundation for the rhetorical-poetical processes of invention. In this sense, there is a basic model for specifying the structure, uses, and values of the representations and self-representations of lettered men and artisans in Colonial society. In it, neo-Scholastic memory, will, and intelligence define the "person" as a result of the soul's participation in the metaphysical substance of God. In its turn, social position is ruled by the juridically codified privileges of a person's association with one social order or another, more than by individual psychological attributes.

One of the principal factors in the colonial diffusion of these models is the education of the lettered men, whose *forma mentis* is organized by topoi and the arguments of canon law. The imaginary of jurisprudence articulated in cultural representations naturally includes them in the corporative concept of society ruled by law founded in the teleology of a *telos*, or Final Cause—God—who determines the hierarchy of all created species according to the analogy of proportion of participation. In neo-scholastic terms, the concept of law in Portugal presupposed that, prior to being "will" (*voluntas*), the law was reason (such as *ratio, proportio, commensuratio, ordo, ius, judgment,* and *prudence*). Thus there was a consensus that natural law existed independently, prior to its volition by the king; its knowledge and application depended on a specific knowledge to be repeated by the specific class of lettered men that people established in the bureaucracy of the state. After Machiavelli, when the Catholic world faced the problem of the efficacy of continuing to theorize power ethically, the doctrine of the "reason of the state" would adapt itself to the new developments of the seventeenth century, affirming often that natural law was included in it. But the traditional notion of Royal Authority endured, constituting itself around the notion of legitimacy of the king's central power by means of legal control in the courts and by the idea that the king could not govern without juridical counsel. If he did so, he was against the *ratio juris*. Consequently, representation of the lettered man as an influential, powerful, or superior type was supported by jurisprudence. In addition to this the slowness of the Portuguese legal machine in the colony, always jammed with appeals, suits, and claims, and the extremely wide discretional margin of arbitration given to arbitrators and judges, made possible by the doctrinaire and bureaucratic structure of legal knowledge, are constitutive elements in the centrality of the social place of lettered men in Luso-Brazilian colonial society, as well as in the forms of its thought, diffused throughout the entire "political body" as a model of distinction to be imitated by all.

Lettered men then living in Brazil were nearly always members of the bureaucracy and the clergy, generally educated in canon law at the University of Coimbra. Like the artisans who worked for fraternities, brotherhoods, and religious orders, they depended directly upon sponsors. Starting with the Academia dos Esquecidos (Academy of the Forgotten) in 1724, typical institutional partnerships were dispensed with by viceroys. Colonial lettered man did not yet warrant a social imaginary (Viala 51–52): he was not an author or writer in the Enlightenment and post-Enlightenment sense of the terms; he was no longer the "scribe" of a medieval guild of trades. His social identity was first defined within fields other than that of letters. Proof of this was the extremely small number of iconographical documents that portray the figure of the writer; another indicator was the nonexistence of work categories such as author, writer, or man of letters in the Portuguese legal and administrative system. The lettered status was determined by social and professional categories of the state, not through authorial autonomy, personal expression, or literary originality and invention as we understand them today. The archeology of seventeenth-century letters ought to therefore include institutional and material boundaries generally not considered in analyses of writers and works.

In a slave owner's society organized according to a stereotype of natural inequality based on purity of blood, the fact that lettered men were not defined as writers and were almost always bureaucratic or clerical employees, generally white or so classified, when added to the censorship of books and the absence of both specialized knowledge and a cultural market for the work of schools, contrasts with the fact that artist and artisans were almost invariably mulattos, *mamelucos,* or Africans; this established a double standard in the place given to the various forms of cultural production. In the case of letters, integration into society functioned predominantly from the top down and, in the plastic arts, from the bottom up. For example, satirical poems circulating in Bahia between 1680 and 1700, adapted from the Aristotelian rhetorical-poetical prescriptions but written in African *banto* or Amerindian *tupi,* are considered barbaric. Genre thus became an instrument for constituting the natural inferiority of blacks, mulattos, and *mamelucos* by disparaging the contributions made by these groups. In art, a basic classification of works became the way of distinguishing nobility and radically disqualifying manual labor, relegating it to the work of plebeians and slaves. Contempt for manual labor meant that the Colonial visual arts were almost always produced by black, mulatto, and *mameluco* artisans. The *búzios* created by black or mulatto artisans for the carved altars of the Church of Saint Iphigenia in Vila Rica offer good examples of "bottom-up" appropriation of aesthetic models. As an ornament, the *búzio* condenses erudite reference and ancient iconography (such as the myth of Aphrodite's birth) along with Christian references in which the labyrinthine form of the snail allegorizes the mysteries of love in the Incarnation of Mary. In a church for blacks who worshiped a black saint, the *búzios* probably had a ritual value analogous to that which they have today in *candomblé* (see Silva).

The representations produced by lettered men and artisans were mimetic, Aristotelically ordered as *conceit, emulation, judgment, proportion, sharp-wittedness, verisimilitude, prudence,* and *decorum.* Resulting from the application of anonymous and collectivized supra-individual rhetorical techniques, they emulated models of authority, adapting them to the themes dominant in the colonial frame of reference. These adaptations produced stylistic deformations of varying degrees that systematically repeated the prescriptions of the common rhetorical rules and simultaneously evinced the particularity of a practice that classified the work not as being individually authored, but as the signature of a performance that emulated the *auctoritas* of its genre. In this case, it may be useful to maintain the author-work-public sociological schema currently in use in works of literary historiography—as long as it is emptied of all evolutionist, illuminist, or post-utopian character.

Since it is mimetic and assumes a different concept of the meaning of both history and subjectivity, the mode of colonial representation did not recognize authorship as individualized expression; it did not define works as literature, nor did it install any notion of a reading public. As we have seen, authorship was the *auctoritas* of a non-psychological rationalism that applied to the specific characters and passions of various genres. Therefore, style was absolutely prescribed. Always assuming the imitation of traditional topoi, such works do not foresee criticism in the sense of the term's politically transformative negativity according to the Kantian and post-Kantian aesthetic evaluation. Literary works are objects of the judgment of lettered reception, which theoretically accepts the same protocol as the enunciation's *auctoritas*; thus they are evaluated according to their suitability and adherence to the models of genre and to the decorum of their application in certain circumstances. There was no public in

the sense of public opinion theoretically endowed with free critical initiative. In this case the public appeared as a witness to representation (as in the theater); it was heterogeneous but unified *by* representation *in* representation *as* representation (Chartier 1990, 48). The survey of techniques through which representation constitutes the addressee evinces the particularity of evaluative criteria that this historical formation used to produce and validate what it said and wrote. Obviously mutable and differential criteria allowed the specification of standards of order(ing) and discursive distribution of texts of fiction, once homology with events figured in other contemporary discourses has been established. This is one way to avoid both the generic contentism of realist doctrine and the trans-historical formalism of the postmodern, for this necessarily includes (as a principle of value) the mediation of a public in the works' reception. Evidently, the public by definition was not unitary but, rather, culturally ordered as a consuming audience by generalized standards and schemes of intelligibility and use. It is useful to discard our notion of a "literary reading" that retrospectively generalizes the current standard of judgment to works written before the nineteenth century. Anchieta's autos, Vieira's sermons, and the satire attributed to Gregório de Matos were not necessarily directed to a literate public; nor do they even assume the act of reading. In fact, literacy, shared among the elite as an obvious and defining criterion since the Enlightenment, is not pertinent to pre-eighteenth-century historical formations in which other forms organize memory, time, history, and languages, and that do not depend directly on received values inscribed in writing. Literacy becomes a basic assumption from the time of Pero Vaz de Caminha's (fifteenth-century) *Carta* [1 May 1500; Letter] as the recycled standard of a tradition of especially Latin works (such as Plinius, Tacitus, Cicero, Virgil, Ovid, Horace, and Juvenal) emulated by local writers. Another anachronistic criterion to be abandoned is that of the distinction between popular and erudite, principally when proposed as two opposite and non-communicating spheres: the popular, always humorous and critical of the elite, to which are attributed the low genres; and the erudite, always serious and pompous, to which are attributed the high genres. With a kind of critical reductionism verging on caricature, the idea of defining laughter as a privilege of the lower classes obviously does not take into consideration Bakhtin's categories of contradiction or of the circularity of culture. Authorial initiative is, after all, part of the cultural social whole; there is at this time no notion of modernist aesthetic originality or of postmodern dematerialization. Representation as a cultural phenomenon in the seventeenth century obviously does not recognize the Enlightenment's division of discursive practices. There is no literature in the Kantian sense of a discursive practice that is the object of disinterested aesthetic contemplation; for writers of this time, *belles lettres* possess an immediately utilitarian function: to celebrate or to denigrate. Thus colonial representation may be redistributed into two large groups: solemn works for situations that celebrate hierarchy, and works of polemical intent that attack individuals and groups constituted as threats to the common good. The possible pertinence of this classification arises from its pragmatism and includes the material conditions of representation and the ends for which writing is produced. It also implies the immediate connection of the pragmatic to the suitability of the works' rhetorical-poetical genre to the decorum of hierarchy.

Works for solemn circumstances are those that celebrate manifestations of monarchical power in various local institutions according to the specific authority of each one. The ceremonies are related to the church's liturgy and to solemn processions, celebration of holy days, the Inquisitions' auto-da-fe and the arrival of bishops, as well as public events that celebrate the nobility and the royal family, and encomiastic occasions (such as birthdays, births, weddings, occasions of mourning, commendations, and burials). More often public celebrations were manifestations of monarchic power (arrivals and departures of the governors, and celebrations of victories against seditions, pirates, Indians, and rebel slaves). As for polemical works, the most obvious is probably that of Gregório de Matos, to whom an extensive colonial corpus of satires was attributed; but it is also necessary to refer to the anonymous pamphlets against entire groups such as the New Christians and people of varying social positions, including the governors, Gregório de Matos himself, plantation owners, lawyers, nuns, mulattos, Indians, and slaves characterized by clichés of low comic genres adapted to local refractions of "the common good" (Campos 77).

Even in the absence of immediate links with government institutions, colonial culture's monopolistic exclusion of the common citizen placed the lettered man within the orbit of the apparatuses of both central power and local power. In the exercise of power, the lettered man was generally oriented to the court, almost always a member of one of the administrative or religious institutions, and, more rarely, someone with no direct relation to the institutions but with influence. In most cases he belonged to the clergy, often having studied theology, like Vieira; or else he was a member of the militia (like Colonel Sebastião da Rocha Pita), a member of the Tribunal da Relação (Court of Appeal), a graduate in civil law, like countless members of the Academia Brasílica dos Esquecidos (Brazilian Academy of the Forgotten) and dos Renacidos (of the Resurrected), or a Coimbra graduate in canon law with no apparent connection to any of the institutions, such as Gregório de Matos. Thus his intellectual activity reflected the crown's interests, often in opposition to local concerns in a tense and conflict-ridden quotidian reality frequently expressed as a univocal determination of textual meaning. An absolute sense of decorum prescribed what, how, when, and for what (to what end or purpose) the lettered man could pronounce, and, theoretically, this precluded any illusion of autonomy. Thus in order to be "public" in the aforementioned sense, representation had to be immediately subordinated to the orthodoxy of institutions in such a way that its formulation did not include, for example, those doctrines deemed heretical and dangerous to the "common good," such as Lutheranism, Calvinism; the ideas of Erasmus, Descartes, or Machiavelli; or anything taken from Judaism. Sanctioned representation only refers to heterodoxies negatively in order to combat them. This would appear to align it with the orthodoxy of central power.

We would do well to remember that, even though limited by rigid institutional prescription such as inquisitorial and royal censorship, many works succeeded in including a variety of controversial topics and interests precisely because of the use of figurative formulations that condense or allegorically integrate various conflictive themes. Antônio Vieira is an exemplary case. His sermons, his História do Futuro [1664 (manuscript), 1718 (first printed edition); History of the Future] and even the various manuscript copies of his prophetic work in Latin, Clavis Prophetarum, state contradictory positions that converge on the Jewish presence, including the ideas of the Jesuits, New Christians, local nobles, the Roman curate, the crown, and the Dominicans.

In order to be more specific about the commemorative and polemical functions of colonial representation historically, we must relate the Catholic doctrine of the natural light of innate Grace (man is created in the image of God with original sins as the only determent) to the model of courtly discretion and its preferred form of diction, the sharp-witted conceit. As we know, one of the principal theses published by Luther in Wittenberg in 1517 stated that Original Sin corrupts human nature, rendering men incapable of recognizing the *verum Deum absconditum* and, as a result, driving societies to the most radical anomie, if God does not send the king who rules "by divine right" to impose order. Against Luther, Portuguese canonical law reaffirmed the Catholic dogma established at the Council of Trent by theologians and jurists, such as Cardinal Roberto Bellarmino and Domingo de Soto. According to Catholic doctrine, the corruption of sin is not total. Revived by Francisco Suárez against James I of England in the *Defensio fidei* of 1614, the doctrine stated that there is hope in the works of men, which can also be perfected by the arts. The natural light of innate Grace shines upon man's conscience as the "spark of consciousness" of divine enlightenment. Indicating goodness in occasions of free choice, natural light provides judgment with ethical guidance in *agibilium*, things that can be acted upon, and technically counsels things that can be done (*factibilium*). It was therefore held that the rhetorical-political decorum of the representational style externalizes or metaphorizes the ethical rightness of judgment enlightened by natural light.

Politically contrary to the Lutheran thesis of "divine right," the doctrine of natural light establishes the origin of the state in a pact of subjection (*pactum subiectionis*) through which the entire community, as a single mystical body of unified wills, gives up its sovereignty, investing it in the mystical person (*persona mystica*) of the king. In the contract, established according to the legal model of slavery (*quasi alienatio*), subjects are hierarchized through the bestowal of privileges, from the "head," the king, to the soles of the "feet," the slaves. In representations, the hierarchical integration of the state thus conceived was characterized by a dramatization of the king's sacred place (hypostasis of the Trinity). As a fixed point of virtue, the ultimate meaning of representation derives from his *persona mystica*. Every act is subordinated to the three teleological primordials (Power of the Father, Love of the Spirit, and Knowledge of the Son) that define the royal mystique. Colonial representation appears hierarchized according to the metaphor that Saint Thomas Aquinas uses in the *Summa Theologica* to theorize the third way to the unity of the human body. Scholarly definition of the body proposes that its perfection results from the integration of its various members and functions as an instrument for the superior principle, the soul. The unity of the body presupposes the plurality of its members and the diversity of functions as *ordo* (order). In the doctrine of power, the *corpus hominis naturalis* is, by analogy, a term of comparison for the doctrine of the political body of the state, defined as the hierarchical harmonization of individuals, governing assemblies, and social and religious orders. Systematized as the "reason of the State" in *Della ragion di Stato* (1588) by the Jesuit Giovanni Botero, this doctrine was then taught at Coimbra's course in canon law and established throughout Brazil by the administration of governors, tribunals, and court reports, by the Society of Jesus and other religious orders, as well as lettered men and artisans who allegorized them in their works. Botero suggests that there is an "interest" in maintaining harmony and peace in the kingdom by controlling individual appetites and the friendship of all the orders of the state, since they ensure the common good. As one of the principal foundations of Portuguese mercantilism, Boterian "interest" is radically opposed to Machiavelli's thesis of "war of all against all," then identified with the devil. Staging the harmonious integration of individuals, governing assemblies, and royal orders in the mercantilist common good, even the obscene polemical genres (such as satire) that circulated throughout Bahia between 1680 and 1700 foresaw the Aristotelian-Stoic system of virtues prudently composed by the correction of abuses that reinstated good Christian usage. Therefore, the rhetorical-poetic order of the sharp-witted conceit in practices of representation was always a dramatization of the theological-political conceit of the civilizing standard transposed to the tropics and deformed by various registers and material means. In the sharp-witted conceit, colonial representation updated the fifteenth-century Italian assimilation of logic (as dialectic) and art (as rhetoric). In this case, artistic activity was the technique of expressing an interior model through a sharp-witted metaphor. Metaphor's first postulate, then, is the universal nature of the *design*, or *disegno*, theologically defined as *segno di Dio*, *God's sign* or *design* in the mind. According to this concept, the interior discourse that takes place in the mind through discrete judgment, illuminated by the natural light of synderesis, is a composition of metaphors, as reflections on truth provided by the divine Substance. Exterior discourse is therefore an order of signs that copy them as metaphors of metaphors. Here, the neo-scholastic updating of Aristotle implies that plastic, verbal, and musical signs be understood as illustrated definition, as presented by Cesare Ripa (1560?–1623?) in the *Iconologia* of 1593, signifying that representation is the allegory of visualizing effects ordered by the technical operations of judgment. It is of major consequence that, instead of an "aesthetic," there was the "technique" of a non-psychological rationalism.

All representation was thus defined as the *theatrum sacrum* indoctrinated into Brazilian men of letters by the Jesuits since the sixteenth century. As a dramatization of the techniques of conquering, maintaining, and expanding power, the anti-heresy positions of the *theatrum sacrum* can never be dissociated from Aristotelian-Christian ethics, formulated in letters of advisement and countless ethical-political treatises, "princely mirrors," or "loyal counselors," such as Giovanni Della Casa's *Galateo*, which was read in the Jesuit colleges of Brazil. In these Greek, Roman, medieval, and Renaissance topoi regarding those virtues that defined the perfect Christian gentleman are recycled. One of the most important of these, arms and letters, is characteristic of the bellical-poetic heroism of the seventeenth-century courtier, proposing the universal man of Baldassare Castiglione's treatise as a model. According to this view, honor, heroism, honest dissimulation, subtlety, and prudence define the representation of excellence, as could be read in the final chapter of Baltasar Gracián's (1601–1658) *El Discreto* [1646; The Compleat Gentleman].

The principal cultural model of human excellence in these texts was that of the *discreto* (gentleman) or *entendido* (expert). As a courtly ideal, the gentleman was also an intellectual category and a character in the interlocutionary process of representations,

defined by his expression—subtle, prudent, discrete, and molded by Aristotelian rhetoric as renewed by sharp-witted conceit. These prescriptions allowed one to demonstrate a discrete identity defined within the discipline of striking a pose appropriate to the occasion. The ability to choose and apply an occasion-specific decorum defines the writer's social superiority suited to his place in the hierarchy, for freedom is defined as subordination to royal power; thus, such distinction—as excellence and power—comes from the form of representation integrated hierarchically. It is the sharp-witted conceit, seen as the representation of natural light and good judgment, that distinguishes it from the vulgar in the ingenious and tendentially hermetic application to the proper themes of the writer's social position, ladies, letters, politics, and arms. In other words, subtlety, prudence, and judgment are indoctrinated as correct means for the production and consumption of representations of a programmatic difficulty or hermeticism that distinguish the best from the common. Colonial appropriations of models of gentlemanliness and vulgarity produce conflicting representations in which social types and categories—such as black, mulatto, Indian, New Christian, Jew, merchant, whore, priest, sodomite, and so on—are identified either with vulgarity or are offered as the opposite of the appropriate expression of gentlemanliness (which together impose the negative classifications of society). The *gentlemanly/vulgar* pair thus specifies the verisimilitude and decorum of various genres, since it operates as a pragmatic mechanism for the constitution and attribution of social positions. With the subtlety (or sharp-wittedness) of discourses and the etiquette of gentlemanly manners, there was almost always an attempt to emulate the Salon de Rambouillet, perhaps the most famous of the seventeenth century's witty salons, during the reign of João V. Pedro II's first wife, Maria Sophia, was a princess of the House of Savoy, a cousin of Louis XIV, always interested in establishing at the court of Lisbon the standards of good taste of the gallant *honnêtes hommes* of Versailles.

Rhetorically and poetically, the theological-political principle that integrated cultural diversity in the seventeenth century appeared as a corrective Counter-Reformation appropriation of sixteenth-century Mannerism. In the plastic arts, Mannerism composed space as a disaggregation and multiplicity of perspectives; in literature, it ordered a thematic, discursive plurality that led to semantic incongruence. Appropriating Mannerism, the Jesuit representation of the *theatrum sacrum* redirected it as a sharp-witted imitation of rhetorical cases as filtered by the providentialist truth of sacred history. These representations illustrated the metaphysical unity of the one, God, mirroring this in the royal mystique and making it proliferate in the stylistic accumulation of species sensitive to its effects.

For the sake of convenient classification, the term *Baroque* in Brazil may be interpreted as the Counter-Reformation program of combating against heresies, converting the gentry, and subordinating dominated cultures such as those of the Indians and Africans, dominated by mercantilist interests and founded on the dogma of natural light. Staged in representations of the *theatrum sacrum*, this program made metaphysical unity proliferate in the variety of its species, individuals, and senses, evincing in all of them the presence of divine light that saturated and totally integrated discursive or plastic material. In this case, the Court was the geometric place of hierarchies (Le Roy Ladurie xiv), staged as participation in the divine light. The "good use" of this dramatized hierarchy updated the medieval portrayal of Christian virtues, adapting them to the colony's new ends as a standard of civilization that assumed and implied the psycho-social internalization of external violence (see Elias).

Thus it is necessary to remember that the theological-political categories of the state's mystical body always implied a qualitative definition of temporality as being analogous to or an emanation of the divine. In colonial representation, time advanced in a straight line, as orthodox Catholic temporality; and, just as today, every moment was understood as diverse and different from all the preceding ones. But unlike today, the social structure of representation at the time proposed that all moments resemble one another because of the divine presence that is a part of them as the absolute identity of its first cause; this makes them effects and signs of participation in the mystical body. According to this concept, history and nature form a double book, which is to be interpreted by the hermeneutic techniques of patristic and scholastic factual allegory. Antonio Vieira's *História do futuro* is a good example; today it seems paradoxical in the light of the *philosophes* and the French Revolution announcement of the death of God. In the qualitative concept of temporality, which subordinates all historical figures and events to time, history is an emanation of the divine substance and, as such, is the nucleus of fundamental traditionalism of seventeenth-century Luso-Brazilian historical practices of representation, seeking past models that prophesize the advent of events.

Analogy is included in this dominant theological-political Colonial mode of representation—neo-Scholastically defined as the metaphysical and logical participation of languages in the divine. The principal rhetorical-political instrument modeled by the analogy is the *dialectical ornament* or *sharp wit* developed by sixteenth-century Italian theorists such as Giovanni Andrea Gilio (fl. 1564) and Antonio Possevino (1533–1611), and seventeenth-century ones such as Peregrini, Pallavicino, and Tesauro. The three scholastic types of analogy redefined in the seventeenth-century modes of dialectical ornamentation are attribution or the discernment of inherent quality, symmetry, and proportionality, which together allow for same specification regarding the degree of artistic deformation operative in Colonial art as well as the use-values of their employment. It may be said, following Weimann, that sharp-wittedness is a social process generalized as a double-function technique, mimetic-representative and judicial-evaluative (190–233). By staging materials, subjects, and themes of contemporary discourses, representation simultaneously traces for the addressee an evaluative perspective that implies the formalization of an appropriate point of view from which the meaning of the representation becomes explicit as verisimilitude and decorum. The gentlemanly addressee partakes both of the effects and the technical mastery used to produce them, as opposed to vulgar readers, who allow themselves to be led by the sensual effects of representation. In this sense, the witticisms also evince, in the effected incongruities, the superior perspective of gentlemanly judgment of sharp-witted prudence that makes them up. According to Count Emanuele Tesauro (1592–1675), one of the greatest adepts of the period, they are proportionate disproportions or convenient inconveniences. A survey of homologies in the Luso-Brazilian colonial world shows that they are made with a limited but significant purpose in mind: the reconstruction of a general semantic field created by lettered men and artisans as they simultaneously engaged in the invention of representative and judicial works.

Through the analogy of attribution, lettered men of the seventeenth century understood that the only being that is absolutely and fully constituted is God; all else are but mere images or resemblances of Him as signs and effects, of sorts. By logically producing the attribution, they would establish a relationship between two mental images or two metaphors by means of a third term common to both: A (snow): B (lily): C (whiteness). In composing poetry, for instance, they would suggest an equivalence between snow and lily through using an attribute common to both, such as whiteness. This allowed them to make up sharp-witted, fantastic, and tendentiously incongruent metaphors (saying, for example, that snow is the lily of winter or that the lily is the snow of spring). The metaphor of attribution, however, is easily understood, and colonial lettered men preferred to demonstrate the erudition typical of gentlemen by approximating distant conceits through the analogy of proportion. Metaphysically, proportion establishes the hierarchic degrees of participation of the beings created in the uncreated Being; logically, it establishes a relationship of resemblance between two forms common to two species: is to B as C is to D, as in a verse attributed to Gregório de Matos, "Discreta e formosíssima Maria" ("Discrete and most beautiful Maria"), which emulates a poem by Góngora, "Mientras por competir con tu cabello" ("While competing with your hair") "que o tempo trota a toda ligeireza" ("time passes so swiftly"), in which a proportional relation is established between the destructive passage of time and the movement of a horse. Proportionality, the third mode of dialectical ornamentation brings extremely distant conceits closer together to form hard-to-decipher, fantastic, incongruous, and hermetic images, making addressees as sharp-witted and ingenious as the author. A good example in another genre is the sermon preached circa 1700 in Salvador by Franciscan Friar Antônio do Rosário, who established the allegorical proportionality between more than twenty names of tropical fruits and the mysteries of the Virgin of the Rosary (Rosário 21).

In the end, the ingenious intellectualism of colonial representation does not arise from word play, excess, thematic nihilism, affectation or from aesthetic rupture, originality, and formal revolution, as has been (and continues to be) suggested by the criticism of the Enlightenment, of neo-Classicism, of Romanticism, of evolutionism, of nationalism, or of post-utopianism. It stems, rather, from representation as the understanding of an indirect participation by the lettered man and artisan's *forma mentis* with the not-yet-created but virtual embodiment in God, just as the model imitated by them is defined as a concept analogous to Being—in Colonial life as governed by the courtly models of the Iberian Counter-Reformation Catholic policy.

Translation by Stephen A. Berg

Works Cited

Campos, João da Silva. 1941. *Procissões tradicionais da Bahia*. Obra póstuma. Preface by Arnaldo Pimenta da Cunha. Bahia: Museu da Bahia/Secretaria de Educação e Saúde.

Chartier, Roger. 1990. *Les origines culturelles de la révolution française*. Paris: Seuil.

——. 1994. "Historia y prácticas culturales [Entrevista a Roger Chartier por Noemi Goldman y Leonor Arfuch]." *Entrepasados. Revista de Historia* (Buenos Aires) 4.7: 133–48.

Elias, Norbert. 1985. *La société de cour*. Preface by Roger Chartier. Paris: Flammarion.

Hanson, Carl. 1986. *Economia e sociedade no Portugal barroco 1668–1703.* Lisboa: Publicações Dom Quixote.

Hespanha, António Manuel, and Ângela Barreto Xavier. 1992. "Paradigmas políticos e tradições literárias." *História de Portugal: O antigo regime.* Ed. José Mattoso and António Manuel Hespanha. Lisboa: Editorial Estampa. 121–55.

Le Roy Ladurie, Emmanuel. 1985. "Réflexions sur l'essence et le fonctionnement de la monarchie classique (XVIe–XVIIIe siècles)." *L'État baroque 1610–1652: Regards sur la pensée politique de la France du premier XVIIe siècle.* Ed. Henry Mechoulan. Paris: Librairie Philosophique J. Vrin. vii–xxxv.

Marin, Louis. 1987. "Introduction." *Portrait of the King.* Trans. Martha M. Houle. Minneapolis: University of Minnesota Press. 3–15.

Rosário, Frei Antônio do. 1701. *Frutas do Brasil numa nova e ascetica monarchia, consagrada a santissima senhora do Rosario.* Lisboa: António Pedroso Galram.

Silva, Lázaro Francisco da. 1995. "Conjuração Negra em Minas." *Revista do IFAC.* Ouro Preto: Instituto de Filosofia, Artes e Cultura, Universidade Federal do Ouro Preto. 2: 68–78.

Tesauro, Emanuele. 1670. *Il cannocchiale Aristotelico.* 5th ed. Torino: Zavatta.

Viala, Alain. 1989. "Du caractère d'écrivain à l'âge classique." *Textuel–Images de l'écrivain.* Paris: Université de Paris VII. 22: 51–57.

Weimann, Robert. 1984. "Metaphor and Historical Criticism." *Structure and Society in Literary History: Studies in the History and Theory of Historical Criticism.* Expanded ed. Baltimore and London: Johns Hopkins University Press. 190–233.

CHAPTER 7

MUSEUMS IN LATIN AMERICA

Maria de Lourdes Parreiras-Horta

A few years ago Brasília witnessed an intense controversy surrounding the installation of a museum of contemporary art in the beautiful edifice originally created by Oscar Niemeyer to house a National Museum for Native Peoples. When the debate between advocates for the native museum and partisans of contemporary high art reached an impasse, a well-meaning representative of the media decided to seek out the opinions of the natives themselves. Aboriginal leaders replied quickly and conclusively: "Let them do what they want with the building. Museums are for white people." Yet the tenure of the Museum of Contemporary Art in Niemeyer's building proved short-lived. A decade after the episode, Brasília witnessed the inauguration of the Brazilian Museum for Native Peoples. Its rich collection and conceptual guidelines reflect the legacy of anthropologist Berta Ribeiro, who dedicated her life to furthering the comprehension and appreciation of cultures indigenous to the country.

We may take this episode and its conclusion as an exemplary parable of the character, history, and role of museums in Brazil's social, cultural, and political landscape—and by extension of museums' trajectory in the other Latin American nations over the last centuries. Within these multifaceted contexts, museums can be read as texts or intertexts that reflect—through their vocabulary, grammar, syntax, and semantics—dominant and hegemonic discourses that permeate the contour, disposition, and interrelation of the different groups that make up the societies throughout this vast continent. If we were to analyze Brazil's system of museums past and present with an eye to comparing it with the functioning of museums in other Latin American countries, we might start by taking note of its pre-history or origin in the process of European territorial conquest and colonization in the sixteenth century. The native chief's summation proves a masterful synthesis of this predicament: "Museums are for white people," or rather, for the Europeans who "discovered" the New World.

In the South American continent the idea and model for museums that began to take shape corresponded to the model disseminated in Europe at the end of the Middle Ages, an elitist model that reserved for the delight of Renaissance princes and noblemen cabinets of curiosities and chambers of marvels. These held marvels and curiosities collected by voyagers to distant lands or by the distinguished masters of alchemy, each article a gift or purchase worth its weight in gold for the purpose of private exhibition to guests and friends. European encounter with the Americas brought incalculable growth to collections of exotic, rare specimens and unexpected riches, much to the amazement of the noblemen from the north. Infamously, Pedro Álvaro Cabral's fleet brought back from Brazil, among animals and plants never before beheld in Europe, some half-naked individuals adorned with war paint and feathers. Most would not survive the long voyage, but the few who did were exhibited in royal galleries as trophies and evidence of conquest. Later in the sixteenth century the French brought back from their settlement in Rio live examples of Brazil's primitive inhabitants and made them parade in splendid festivities, a spectacle registered in the Gobelin

tapestries on display today in European museums. Living examples of the inhabitants of the Americas were still paraded as ethnographic curiosities during the vogue for universal exhibitions in the nineteenth century. Under the auspices of science and the European's distanced and discriminating eye, the exhibition of live specimens from the New World would reach its prime during the century social scientists have termed the Age of Spectacle. Today, due to an irony of fate or perhaps to the law of eternal return, Germans, Italians, Danes, and the French themselves are often seen parading in feathers and headdresses among the ranks of the Samba schools in Rio de Janeiro.

From the outset, European strategies for the conquest of new territories rested on the main axes of land demarcation and the inventory of resources both human and mineral. The main purpose for the missions of exploration that immediately followed the conquest encompassed the description and naming of the areas and elements found. Out of these meticulous reports, and in accordance with precise rules, arose the corpus of travel literature whose importance has not yet been sufficiently recognized and explored, as Daniel Defert notes in an essay on "la collection du monde" for Switzerland's Musée d'Ethnographie de Neuchâtel. We could venture that these travel chronicles constitute the birth certificate of a vast Museum of the American Imaginary, signaling the moment that it both virtually and concretely came into being. In this light one might explain the existence in European archives and museums of an original collection of fundamental importance for the history and culture of South American peoples, re-collected in their original forms and manifestations at the moment of conquest. One need only recall that the earliest examples of crafts from the Tikuna of the Upper Amazon are located in German and Austrian archives and museums, far from the eyes of Brazilian anthropologists and the natives who now seek to recuperate their cultural roots and traditions.

The Text (or Hyper-Text)

The authors of the first lines of the Latin American museological text can be traced in the reigns of Portugal and Spain over the colonies to groups possessing specific economic, political, and religious power and capital. Religious and missionary orders were the first to disseminate the taste for culture, literature, and the arts of their countries of origin in the autochthonous communities, from the "ajuntamientos," or gatherings, of the interior to the distinctly *mestizo* urban nuclei that began to spread rapidly throughout the continent. The phenomenon of Jesuit missions among the Guaraní only serves to attest to the transference of cultural and artistic forms and standards. This transference of values would give rise to the first hybrid manifestations of a local and distinctly American cultural production, having its own elements and traits. This unique cultural interpenetration of Old and New worlds in the continent's south is still present today in the missionary museums of Argentina, Brazil, and Paraguay, as well as in the traditions still extant in some regions of Bolivia.

In South America the private collections of the minor aristocracy and economic elites were essentially composed of objects and goods imported from the metropolis in accordance with the fashion and style of the time, and served above all as a symbolic mark of distinction within the colonies' class system and social categories. The provinces imported not only goods from Europe, but also structural attitudes: codes of dress and behavior, interests, and expectations. These required the production of portraits and coats-of-arms, among other symbols of pomp, custom-made by foreign artists established there or by their native apprentices who learned the skill and technique.

Vocabulary and Grammar

During the first centuries of colonization in Latin America, cultural and artistic production in the colonies reflected in style and content the characteristics of the visual and material encyclopedia of the imperial centers. The more the local cultural production approximated the technical quality and formal refinement of the imported models, the more it was valued and appreciated. Throughout the continent, aristocratic residences were crammed full of goods and instruments that denoted wealth and power, mostly commissioned directly from the producers that catered to the residences and palaces of European nobility: crockery from China, France, and England; abacuses inlaid with ivory; jewelry and ornamented silverware; dyed Persian fabrics; tapestry and lace from Flanders; and adornments made across the Atlantic, albeit with raw material from silver, gold, and diamond mines in the colonies. Gradually stylized or adorned furniture made out of Brazil's precious woods comes to be manufactured locally, though based on the sketches and models brought by Portuguese masters. Likewise, mulatto goldsmiths and silversmiths, who first developed their talents in the service of religious brotherhoods responsible for Brazil's first trade guilds, perfected their craft in the markets of Rio de Janeiro and Salvador. Brazil's churches and monasteries still boast the legacy of *mestizo* sculptors, woodcarvers, and composers of genius, a phenomenon also observed in the former Spanish colonies along the Andes and the River Plate.

It is from these diverse objects, representative of a segment of colonial society and its stratified relations, that the original holdings of art galleries and historical museums were derived and later augmented by the broken and rusty trophies of the struggles for independence. If we can speak of a museological thesaurus that systematically and symptomatically shapes the nature and pertinence of the collections accumulated and exhibited in the continent's first institutionalized museums in the late eighteenth and early nineteenth centuries, war and power would be its keywords. Absent in these collections are objects representative of the anonymous population masses that gradually occupied the vast territories, be they native to the continent or imported following the dictates of commerce and the slave economy. This absence is explained not merely as a function of the social and cultural stratification that still determines the structure of Latin American societies to this day, but there is also a more basic reason: the extreme poverty and almost total destitution of most people during this period, which forbade the possession of objects both of use and ostentation. As inventories of household items in seventeenth- and eighteenth-century Brazil demonstrate, even middle-class families possessing some hectares of land and a handful of slaves lived a life of extreme simplicity and

austerity. Typically these families possessed only a table, a few stools and rare chairs, some trunks and boxes, perhaps a rustic cupboard to house muskets, and a few belongings. Surviving on a subsistence economy based on the trade of goods and grain, colonial society–in its lowest spheres–did not take part in what we today term a consumer society.

Each social group makes use of a vocabulary of objects and images (no less than one of words) corresponding to the ideas and concepts of a mental encyclopedia that structures its members' thoughts, values, and manners. It is thus possible to imagine that the museological encyclopedia found in Latin American museums is far from adequate in its representation of these societies during their formative periods. If a great share of this vocabulary is lost or, rather, was not collected throughout its history and evolution, this phenomenon may nonetheless be understood in light of the work of Ferdinand de Saussure, whose formulation of the concepts of language and speech can explain what happened and still happens in the universe of museums in the continent. If a common language–Tupí-Guaraní mixed with Portuguese or Spanish–was spoken by merchants as well as the greater part of the population in rural areas, villages, and towns, and if the *banto* or the *nagô* were spoken freely in the streets of Rio, Salvador, or Vila Rica in Minas Gerais, only the dominant speech was officially registered in the texts and documents of archives and museums–the only historical sources recognized in these countries until quite recently. An analysis of this speech in its texts and intertexts–as embodied by the institutional discourse of Latin American museums–reveals with few exceptions the remarkable permanence today of a cultural configuration that transcends formal and apparent changes in the social process (to use the notion of configuration coined by Ruth Benedict in 1934). The persistence of dominant speech and of a lacuna in the representation of vanquished and dominated groups poses the greatest challenge to a museological practice that would fashion itself as democratic, in the service of society and its complex web of relations.

The Syntax

The systematic organization of this material vocabulary collected and preserved in museums throughout the continent begins at the dawn of the nineteenth century, parallel to the process of political and administrative emancipation of Latin American countries and the formation of national identities. The relocation to Brazil in 1808–not only of the Portuguese court but also of the royal treasures of Queen D. Maria and of the prince regent, the future King D. João VI of Portugal, Brazil, and the Algarve–gave rise to the first Royal Museum installed in Rio. Its collections formed the embryo of the current National Museum (of Science and Ethnography) and of the National Museum of Fine Art. Two previous attempts at expressing a native museology possess a singular significance: the pavilions of Xavier dos Pàssaros and of Xavier das Conchas, artists who created installations with their own materials to enchant the frequent visitors to Rio's Passeio Publico (Public Walks). Though no visual documents of these museological constructions survive, contemporary accounts describe the exceptional art and creativity of the two artists, whose popular language and syntax do not shy away from evoking the taste for allegory and exoticism of the eighteenth-century European court. In retrospect these installations take on the significance of what we would today term the avant-garde, challenging as they did (either through intuition or ignorance) the dominant models originated by Linnaeus in Europe's museums of natural history. Auguste Comte's philosophical positivism and its application to experimental science gave a new and unique character to museums the world over, privileging the study of nature and life as laboratories for the investigation and systematization of knowledge. Museum becomes synonymous with scientific inquiry, with the classifying and naming of the universe. As the repositories of the legacy of Descartes and of the Enlightenment, museums were catapulted to the highest level among the system of institutions that also encompassed schools and universities, designated by Pierre Bourdieu as "authorities of consecration." Within the panorama of Latin America, these institutions consequently could be seen as taking on the role of "authorities of exclusion," or at least of differentiation.

The nineteenth century is the epoch of the great expeditions of naturalists and scientists of all disciplines who perceived the New World as the paradisiacal domain for their discoveries. Latin America thus had its entrails explored and classified by these heroic individuals, a mixture of artists, scientists, and adventurers whose saga fed a new series of accounts and images of their voyages. This travel literature in turn contributed to the Romantic and cultured imaginary of the European intelligentsia, constituting configurations that would be unquestioningly absorbed by their disciples south of the Equator. At a time when the social sciences (and ethnography in particular) emerged and developed in Europe, the world's museums classified their specimens and pinned peoples like butterflies into precise places and categories. By contiguity, this syndrome of classification and systematization contaminated museums of history and art, and by extension what we may term the syntax of the museological sentence: the organization, classification, and exhibition of collections. This was the epoch of the encyclopedic museums that displayed heterogeneous collections in homogeneous groupings and arbitrary categories based on formal, stylistic, or even functional criteria, irrespective of content and meaning: halls devoted to porcelain, furniture, glassware, silverware, images, muskets, and decorations, and galleries dedicated to the monotonous and repetitious procession of images of the nation's leaders alongside their innumerable generals. There was no sign of those who perished in battle—beyond the doubtful ashes housed in a mausoleum in an Ouro Preto museum of martyrs of the "Inconfidência Mineira," antiimperialist revolutionaries exiled and executed in eighteenth-century Minas Gerais.

Perhaps even the idea of syntax beyond the purely grammatical fails to do justice to a descriptive and comparative process of enumeration that boasted an almost infinite series of identical elements, stripped as they were of any meaning beyond their exemplarity as objects. Museums of art became display cases for the academy, for official salons and their travel prizes, and for an academicism that took its cue from foreign masters as to what were to be the recognized norms and values of civilization. In Latin America the museological sentence of museums of all kinds clearly betrayed the model and language of elite culture, an erudite and specialized jargon understood only by the small circle of initiates with access to the universes of science, history, and art. The institutional differentiation between cultures was evident in the relegation of the testimony of native cultures to raw material for study in museums of ethnography and natural history, and the relegation (even in the twentieth century) of expressions of popular art and culture to museums of folklore. Thus one should not be surprised to find that traditional museums still remain empty, attracting merely those already interested or initiated in their hermetic language. Following the 1972 Santiago statement of principle, museums in Latin America (as throughout the world) have proposed a veritable revolution in favor of integrating museums into the life of the community. Nonetheless, the realm of museums still remains indecipherable to the majority of common citizens who do not possess the specific codes sanctified by professional practice and who do not recognize themselves in the rhetoric and expository discourses offered them.

The Semantics of Discourse

A reevaluation of museological discourse and practice in Latin America would only take place after World War II, as a repercussion of the destruction of contemporary society's imperturbable assurance in heritage and museums and of the debates that raged in the nations most afflicted by this world catastrophe. The loss and destruction of a heritage accumulated over the centuries in the cathedrals of history and art, hitherto considered a birthright in affluent societies, provoked the inevitable revision of the truths accepted as sacred and intuitive in the realm of the museum. In a great share of institutions the permanent pedagogical mission came to reflect a preoccupation with the subject rather than with the object of culture. In South America and throughout the developing world, the consolidation of regional and national identity—coupled with democratic emancipation—lead to a greater awareness of the need to question the role and social function of museums among other public institutions.

In a 1997 lecture delivered on the occasion of Uruguay's national meeting of museum directors, Gabriel Peluffo, architect and director of Montevideo's National Museum of Fine Art, developed a shrewd and appealing approach to the ethical question of the role of the museum in an era of cultural globalization. Some of his observations deserve to be considered here at length, given their great pertinence to the Latin American museological panorama. "The museological practice in our countries," Peluffo affirms, "while under pressure from the rules of the game of the 'global museum,' is also subject to the social and cultural conditions of the regional 'enclave,' inherited from a tradition that is born with the configuration of nation-states in the nineteenth century." Today museums need to represent new collective imaginaries, both trans-territorial and trans-cultural, while under the pressure of the demands of the trends and competition imposed by the metropolitan models.

"This pressing need," the author claims, "appears nonetheless at a time when these countries have not been able to process their own identity crises, both in the realm of ideology and in the museum. While the canonical concept of the National Museum still prevails, these crises called into question the old internal hegemonies and put in their place a complex map of diversity." For Peluffo, the question can no longer be that of the imaginary museum of modernity, constructed on the basis of a centralizing vision, but rather the imaginaries of the museum, constituted by the diverse constructions of culture and identity that the museum is capable of producing from its collections and from its institutional conception. Citing Luis Gerardo Morales, Peluffo notes that the historical-political construction of a homeland is the fruit of a long gestation marked by a positivistic and liberal philosophy:

"Rather than pursuing the objective of salvaging a passive object before it is absorbed into history, the American museum is propelled by the need to construct an active imaginary subject, given the great promise of the emergence of new nationalities. In the Americas the museum was born above all to satisfy the need to construct a national space (even at the cost of the assassination of the other–as in the dramatic case of the incorporation in the collection of the Museum of La Plata of the indigenous chiefs who survived General Roca's military campaign as live exhibits," claims Marta Dujovne (116).

In the case of his own field of fine art, Peluffo notes that museum's essentially static "foundational imaginary" incorporates the new concept of the museum as an ideal of modernity and hence as a dynamic entity, as well as the mission of establishing closer historical ties to the Eurocentric model of a universal museum. Interestingly, the author considers São Paulo's biannual exhibitions of art, first instituted in the 1950s, as the first great ripple of postwar cultural and economic globalization in the region's artistic scene and traditional museological order. An immediate result of this new stage is a qualitative change in the mounting pressures exerted by the main industrial sponsors over their peripheral voice in museum policy. This scenario contributes to the public debate over existing museological structures and practices, in addition to the possible democratization of aesthetic experience, as evident, for example, in the new proposals for street art or even for a street museum.

In the 1970s and 1980s, the decline of military regimes in Latin America and the accompanying restoration of democracy brought to light new conflicts in museological theory and practice. Peluffo notes in particular the predicament of historical and ethnographic museums (normally within the state's sphere), which had to rethink their projects of regional representation at a time of national crisis. On the other hand, art galleries and museums (often operated privately and virtually disconnected from other museums) relished their symbolic role as agents of cultural modernization and their promotion of international artistic developments as mechanisms of legitimation. This increased demand on the international circuit in turn diminished, according to Peluffo, the chances for these art museums to carry out on a regional scale the renovation of a specific cultural project. In this regard the same author adds that one cannot ignore the existence of a concentric structure of power in the international system of museums that effectively determines the norm in force for the rest. No analysis of Latin American museological practice can neglect the disequilibrium caused by globalization, whereby cultural decentralization and pluralism are balanced by a strong redistribution of power through new mechanisms of cultural discrimination. According to this concentric logic of power, museums of the first order give financial preference and legitimation only to other institutions of the first order–a criterion established on the basis of technological structure, the international value of their collections, and the sophistication of their staging and set design. In this predicament, one can host a great international exhibition only if one's museums possess air-conditioned halls. We need only cite the example of Rio's National Museum of Fine Arts, which was only able to host an exhibit of the work of Monet thanks to a million-dollar grant from the Ministry of Culture for the air-conditioning of its galleries. The risk inherent in this process, as Peluffo affirms in his analysis, is of an ever-greater discrepancy between museums of the first order and those that risk obsolescence due to their inability to insert themselves into the international circuit, either because of a scarcity of resources or the prioritization of cultural tasks that tends to the discursive and critical needs of cultural production in the regional enclave. In Peluffo's estimation, Latin American museums of art have yet to set in motion a dialogic labor that would prove both educational and receptive to a region's diverse cultural fabrics. Rather, they too often have contented themselves with lending legitimacy to great exhibitions supported by the instruments of mass media and conceived as sophisticated spectacles of mass as well as academic consumption.

As an exemplary case of this quandary one may cite a reporter's interview with a woman who waited with her young son for more than four hours in the queue for the Monet exhibit in Rio. Asked why she was in line, and what her motivation was in coming out to see the Monet works, she replied she had no idea who this Monet was but, since there was so much interest, he must be important for the future of her son. Clearly, this answer lends itself to divergent interpretations, like a double-edged sword. Perhaps the crucial questions to be posed with respect to the realm of Latin American museums at the start of the new millennium would be: What duties and role would museological institutions possess within the heart of Latin American communities bound closer together through mass communication and the ties of common economic and cultural markets, common threats and challenges, and ever more convergent hopes and expectations? How could museums prove themselves as instruments of both change (and development) and the preservation of cultural integrity, in sum, of the construction of a better future for children?

Translation by Paulo Horta

Works Cited

Benedict, Ruth. 1934. *Patterns of Culture*. Lisboa: Livros do Brasil.

Bourdieu, Pierre. 1982. *Le Marché des biens symbolique*. Trans. S. Miceli. São Paulo: Ed. Perspectiva.

Defert, Daniel. 1982. "La collection du monde–Pour une étude des récits de voyages du XVIe au XVIIIe siècle." *Collections de Passion*. Ed. Jacques Hainard and Roland Kaehr. Neuchâtel: Musée d'Ethnographie de Neuchâtel. 17–31.

Dujovne, Marta. 1995. *Entre musas y musarañas: Una visita al museo*. Buenos Aires: Fondo de Cultura Económica.

Morales, Luis Gerardo. 1994. *Orígenes de la museología mexicana: Fuentes para el estudio histórico del Museo Nacional (1780–1940)*. Mexico City: Universidad Iberoamericana.

Peluffo, Gabriel. 1997. "Ética museológica y globalización cultural–una perspectiva subregional latinoamericana." 2nd Encuentro Nacional de Directores de Museos. Atlantida–Canelones. Ministerio de Educación y Cultura. Montevideo. 8, 9, 10 August.

Saussure, Ferdinand de. 1949 [1916]. *Cours de Linguistique Générale*. Paris: Payot.

CHAPTER 8

EDUCATION IN BRAZIL
OMISSIONS, ADVANCES, AND FUTURE PERSPECTIVES

Célio da Cunha

This essay offers a synthesis of the Brazilian educational policies and pedagogic ideas, from the time of the Jesuits to the present day. The educational system is an important part of any history of literary culture, but in Latin America in general and Brazil in particular, it is central to even the most basic understanding of their cultural kaleidoscope at the start of the twenty-first century. The focus will especially be on the successive omissions of the government, which can greatly explain the shortcomings that the Brazilian educational system has accumulated throughout its history, and the heavy burden that it carries today.

Educational Policy and Jesuit Pedagogy

The Jesuits first arrived in the northeastern state of Bahia in 1549 and had complete control of education in Brazil for the next two centuries. To have an accurate sense of the significance and reach of Jesuit educational policy and the pedagogical ideas on which it was based, one must take into account the impact of the Reformation and the Counter-Reformation. The pedagogical ideals of the Reformation were, one cannot deny, progressive for the time, even including the education of the popular classes. As Manacorda very appropriately said of Martin Luther: "foi ele especialmente quem deu impulso prático e força à programação de um novo sistema escolar voltado também à instrução de meninos, destinados não à continuação dos estudos, mas ao trabalho" (196) ("He especially was the one who provided a practical impulse and incentive for creating a new school system that included the instruction of boys who were to join the work force"). This view was shared by the leaders of the Reformation. Luther's 1524 letter is a pioneering document, because it championed the education of boys and girls from childhood. The quick dissemination and acceptance of the ideals of the Reformation provoked an immediate reaction on the part of the Catholic Church and an all-out effort to guarantee a Catholic monopoly on education. The Council of Trent (1545–1563) was vehemently opposed to the main thesis of the dissemination of knowledge, which was central to the Protestant reformers. One of the bishops of the Council went so far as to venture that books were unnecessary (see Manacorda 201). Manacorda, however, points out that the future of education took a very different direction from this.

The Order of Saint Ignatius of Loyola was founded in 1534 with the objective of becoming the central thrust behind the Catholic response to the Reformation: It was created to stem the rapid spread of Protestantism, which (as far as Catholics were concerned) was heresy. It was Durkheim who argued that it was in order to fight heresy that Ignatius de Loyola founded his innovating organization, one that broke away from the realm of the cloisters and concentrated on action. It was an attempt to work among the people in order to exert influence over them (Durkheim 217). This spirit behind the Jesuit initiative left a long-lasting legacy in Brazil.

Their first Jesuit grammar school was inaugurated in Bahia, and the Order's activities soon spread to reach the south of Brazil, Porto Seguro, Espírito Santo, São Vicente, and São Paulo. By the time the Jesuit Order was expelled from Brazil on the orders of the Marquis de Pombal in 1759, 210 years after having arrived, the educational system they had established comprised seventeen major schools and thirty-six missions, a number of smaller seminaries, and grammar schools.

Jesuit pedagogy was an effective combination of the ideas of Saint Thomas Aquinas and the tenets of Greco-Roman culture. One should keep in mind that the University of Paris in the sixteenth century, one of the principal sources for the Society of Jesus's pedagogic plan (*Ratio Studiorum*), was heavily involved in a movement of Thomist Restoration, so that the educational ideal that guided its pedagogical activities "was the complete fulfillment of human nature, elevated to the level of the sublime according to Divine design" (Franca 78). Their administration and educational policy excelled in terms of organization and the extraordinary individual and collective courage and dedication that were the hallmark of the Society. The Jesuits studied and learned the indigenous languages and penetrated the lands in the interior of the colony; although they founded a great number of grammar schools, their main concern was to reach the youth. This led them to concentrate their efforts on secondary education, and it became the high point of the school system they established. M. L. Santos Ribeiro explains that in the initial colonizing and educational phase the Jesuits did in fact pay attention to primary education, and turned their main emphasis toward secondary school education after the "Constituições da Companhia de Jesus" [1556; Constitutions of the Society of Jesus] and the "Ratio Studiorum" (1599) were approved. The program outlined in these two documents centers on the teaching of elements of European culture, and shows a disinterest in or alludes to the difficulties in instructing natives; this served from here on to underline the elitist character of Jesuit education. In other words, "os instruídos serão descendentes dos colonizadores. Os indígenas serão apenas catequizados" (Maria Ribeiro 7) ("instruction will be given to the descendents of the colonizers, whereas natives will only be given catechism"). Thus it is that the pedagogy first introduced by Manuel da Nóbrega (1517–1570), João Azpilcueta Navarro (d. 1557), and José de Anchieta (1534–1597) (which marked the initial period of education in Brazil) suffered a great shift with the intervention of the *Ratio*'s directives–a shift that can be characterized as being retrogressive in every respect. It was a change of lasting effect that set the bounds for years to come; its impact had grave consequences for the future of Brazilian education.

The Jesuit régime was cut short by the Marquis de Pombal, Prime Minister to the King Dom José I and committed follower of Enlightenment ideals, who expelled the Order from the Portuguese Empire in 1759. It was alleged that Jesuit pedagogy did not serve Portugal in attaining a place for itself as a modern European nation. These ambitions were translated into Enlightenment ideology with a good deal of attention given to renewing and contesting inherited traditions. Notwithstanding the role of Enlightenment philosophy, which surely was important, there were also economic factors. Dom José I and the Marquis de Pombal's policy had placing Portugal "numa situação econômica capaz de competir com as potências estrangeiras" (Carvalho 100) ("in an economic situation which would enable the nation to compete with foreign powers") as its objective. The growing economic power of the Jesuit presence in the Brazilian colony was seen as an obstacle to this aim. In other words, there were two states, the one run from Lisbon and the other from Rome, and the latter, it was feared, was getting the upper hand.

Pombal's action had another important aspect to it: It marked the direct intervention of the state in education, a trend that was to become generalized in Europe after the French Revolution in 1789. The educational reforms enacted by Pombal were, however, resounding failures both in Portugal and in Brazil, with the sole exception of a few innovations that were actually carried out at the University of Coimbra. The Brazilian colony saw the levy of a tax named "Literary Subsidy" on certain articles, such as cigars and alcoholic beverages, which was intended to finance education but in practice turned out to be impossible to enforce, defeating its purpose. The Marquis's actions provided ample ground for controversy, and the ensuing passionate engagement in the polemics distorted the issue further. The conservative pedagogy of the Jesuits, impervious to the innovating ideals of the Enlightenment, was an obstacle to the Crown's ambition to modernize Portuguese culture. In Brazil, however, Robert Southey, an English historian of the period and author of a voluminous history of Brazil, made an observation worthy of note: "[T]hey [the Jesuits] were incapable (like their Spanish brethren) of bequeathing their knowledge to posterity: their painful acquirements therefore perished with them" (3:547).

In fact, over two centuries of knowledge—based on the experience of daily struggle with all sorts of difficulties—"perished with them" (Southey 3:547). They were expelled one and all (590 priests left the colony), and a great emptiness settled in their place. The sporadic *aulas régias* (lectures) that were then instituted meant the beginning of a period of extreme chaos and disorganization of the colonial educational system that was to continue through into the empire and the republic. The Jesuit schools had this organization, by contrast, and their teachers were among the most highly trained in the Americas of their time. Although criticism of the conservative content of their pedagogy may have been warranted, in terms of effective organization of schools and of teaching individual self-reliance, the Jesuits offered a rich experience that was suddenly abandoned—to the severe detriment of Brazil.

Dom João VI's Educational Reform

The period that covers the interim from the exit of the Jesuits in 1759 to the arrival of the Portuguese royal family in 1808 did not make any real contributions to education. Portugal was still a poor nation and Brazil's educational program had been cut short. The Methuen Treaty (1703) had subjected Portugal to an extreme dependence on England. Dom José I and the Marquis de Pombal's plan to reverse the situation had run aground and brought about negative consequences for the colony. The *ciclo de mineração* (mining period) and the discovery of gold and other mineral riches in Brazil mark the Portuguese effort to recover a financial equilibrium. Nevertheless, most of this wealth found its way to England. Two facts ought to be noted with respect to education. The first was the 1792 *Inconfidência Mineira* (the rebellion in the mineral rich region of *Minas Gerais*), which planned to create a university on the model of the University of Coimbra, a dream that saw its demise when the uprising was crushed. The second was the foundation of the *Seminário de Olinda* (Olinda Seminary) in Pernambuco by the Bishop Azeredo Coutinho. The seminary offered secondary education, introduced new teaching methods, and changed the curriculum to confer greater emphasis on the sciences, previously ignored in the Jesuit system, which favored the humanities and the classics instead.

The arrival of the Portuguese royal family in 1808, provoked by the invasion of Portuguese lands by Napoleon's troops, meant a period of cultural and educational renewal for Brazil. The Portuguese court numbered over fifteen thousand members, and it became necessary to provide the new seat of the kingdom with the minimal cultural conditions demanded by the new situation. A great many institutions were created concurrently in the field of education and culture, among them Academia Real Militar (The Royal Military Academy) in 1810 (now Escola Nacional de Engenharia [The National School of Engineering]); the Curso de Cirurgia (School of Surgery) in Bahia, and the Curso de Cirurgia e Anatomia (School of Surgery and Anatomy) in Rio de Janeiro in 1808, which inaugurated higher studies in medicine; specialized courses for technical training in economics, commerce, agriculture, chemistry, mineralogy, and technical design in Bahia and Rio de Janeiro; the Public Library in 1810; the National Museum in 1818; the *Gazeta do Rio de Janeiro* [Rio de Janeiro Gazette] in 1811; and the Botanical Gardens in Rio de Janeiro in 1810. These are but a few of the examples of the cultural and educational legacy of Dom João VI in Brazil. "O que a Colônia não obtivera em três séculos obteria em uma década" ("What the colony had not obtained in three centuries it would attain in a decade") was the enthusiastic observation of Cruz Costa (53). The presence of the Portuguese court in Brazil would, in a sense, accelerate the process of independence, echoing events in neighboring Latin American nations. The end of the Colonial period was fast approaching. As articulated by Cruz Costa, the court's move to Brazil was, in fact, the last stage in the dismantling of the nation's colonial status, a dismantling that was long in the making and would be catalyzed by Napoleon's army and English economic interests (61).

Before entering into the period of Independence, we must highlight the fact that Dom João VI's accomplishments in the field of university education were to have an enduring legacy. He did not create universities or research institutions; rather, he created independent institutes for technical education, thereby establishing a model that survives to this day. The presence of the royal family did not, however, bring about any changes in primary education. The population of Brazil at the time numbered 3,300,000 inhabitants, of which approximately 1,000,000 were slaves, and less than 1 percent of the free population went to primary school (circa 20,000 pupils).

Independent Brazil: The Educational Exclusion Continues

The Declaration of Independence in 1822 raised hopes that the reality of exclusion in primary education would come to an end; after all, Europe, the United States, and Canada were on the path to universal primary education. The 1823 Project for the Constitution, presented to the Constitutional Assembly, included in one of its articles broad educational measures: "haverá no Império escolas primárias em cada termo, ginásios em cada comarca e universidades nos mais apropriados locais" (Peixoto 219) [("the Empire will have primary schools in every *term* [subdivision of a jurisdiction], secondary schools in every *comarca* [jurisdiction], and universities wherever most appropriate"). The Constitutional Assembly was, however, dissolved, and a new constitution was instated in 1824. Even so, the new constitutional document was able to maintain in part the intention to provide all citizens with free education; it preserved, at least, a concern for the education of the masses.

In 1827 a law was passed with the intent of combating the educational exclusion of the greater part of the population. This law mandated the creation of primary schools in all cities, villages, and places with a higher concentration of population in the empire. It would have been the equivalent to the *Lei Áurea* (the law to abolish slavery) of Brazilian education (Lima 1996, 79) if only it had been fully enacted. Seven years later (1834) saw the promulgation of the *Ato Adicional* (Additional Act), which delegated the responsibility for primary education legislation to the provinces. Valnir Chagas states that the motivation for instating the *Ato Adicional* was found in Liberalism itself, an ideology present in the *Grito do Ipiranga* (Dom Pedro I's Declaration of Independence), which, with the sometimes coherent logic of the absurd, promulgated a decentralization of what was yet to be unified, in name of the organization of the nation (13). The *Ato Adicional* single-handedly set back the future of primary education in Brazil.

The 1834 decentralization meant that Brazilian educational policy was to go through its evolution without being able to count on a coordinating center or a master plan. Chagas has observed: "O que viria em seguida, seria uma decorrência desse indiferente lavar de mãos" (16) ("What was to follow was but a consequence of this indifferent washing of hands"). In other words, this marked the complete absence of the Brazilian state with respect to lay or mass-based education. These facts conspired to keep the issue of primary education on the margins of government concerns during the empire. Higher education fared better; in 1827 the colleges of law of Olinda and Sao Paulo were created, and these became the main sources for educated political leaders during the imperial period. As for technology, half a century was to elapse before the Emperor Pedro II created the Escola de Minas de Ouro Preto (the Ouro Preto Mining School) in 1875 as a way to guarantee the state the knowledge and exploitation of mineral wealth.

As for secondary education, the most important act was the creation of Colégio Pedro II (Pedro II School) in 1837, as well as the appearance of the first schools intended to train teachers, the *escolas normais* in Niterói (1835), Bahia (1836), Ceará (1845), and Sao Paulo (1846). Although these schools could only boast a rudimentary kind of organization, they nevertheless constituted an important initiative in the face of the overwhelming lack of teachers. In 1857 Brazil had an estimated population of 8,500,000, of which approximately 1,500,000 were slaves. Rui Barbosa states that enrolled students in primary schools numbered 70,244 out of a population of 7,000,000 free men and women; only 1.04 percent were enrolled in primary education (14).

The consequences of the decentralization of 1834 became visible to Antônio Gonçalves Dias (1823–1864), one of the greatest Brazilian poets of the Romantic period, on the occasion of his inspection of the northern provinces of the nation. He noted that the educational system lacked "a unifying center for action" (qtd. in Larroyo 2:954). Similar criticisms were made by intellectuals and politicians, including Liberato Barroso, Tavares Bastos, and Paulino José de Souza. Their voices protested the absence of the state in primary educational policy. The result of this absence was that Brazil continued to regress in educational policy and to pay the cultural consequences.

In sum, the entire Imperial period–as far as education was concerned–could be characterized as lethargic. The few reforms carried out were limited in scope to the institutions of the court, because the empire itself had no commitment to the education of the country. As Rui Barbosa calculated in his famous study on primary education in Brazil (1882), at the rate it was going it would take Brazil 799 years to reach the goal of full school attendance for primary school-age children, an aim that had already become the standard in some nations at the time (Barbosa 17).

Rui Barbosa (1848–1923), one of the most lucid thinkers of the time, after conducting a detailed study of the educational system of many countries, proposed wide ranging reforms. His efforts reflected to a certain extent the new ideas that were crossing the border into Brazil in the decades of 1870s and 1880s. As Cruz Costa put it, "o positivismo, o naturalismo, o evolucionismo, enfim, todas as modalidades do pensamento europeu do século XIX–vão se exprimir agora no pensamento nacional e determinar um notável progresso do espírito crítico" (115) ("Positivism, Naturalism, Evolutionism, all the different modalities of nineteenth-century European thought were to find expression in Brazilian thought, and foment a remarkable advance in critical thinking"). This movement, sometimes referred to as the *Ilustração Brazileira* (Brazilian Enlightenment), played a role in rousing the nation, in speeding up the abolition of slavery and the beginning of the republic. In Barros's words: "Os homens das décadas de setenta, se propõem, realmente, a 'ilustrar' o país; a 'iluminá-lo' pela ciência e pela cultura; a fazer das escolas 'focos de luz,' donde haveria de sair uma nação transformada" (9–10) ("Men of the seventies took it on themselves to educate the nation, to enlighten it through science and culture, to make of schools 'beacons of light,' by which a transformed nation would arise"). It was hoped that, in this context of intellectual effervescence, accompanied by a positive economic outlook, "é nesta época que o Brasil toma pela primeira vez conhecimento do que é progresso moderno e uma certa riqueza de bem-estar material" (C. Prado Junior, qtd. in Cruz Costa 115) ("it is the first time that Brazil had a direct experience of modern progress and a certain wealth and material comfort"), and thus that the Brazilian state would be able to make a commitment in favor of a general educational reform.

The end of the empire and the new republic encouraged hopes for this long-awaited educational reform. The republic went so far as to create the Ministério da Educação, Correios e Telégrafos (Ministry for Education, Mail and Telegraph); the first Republican Constitution, however, held virtually no guarantees for education and was a step back from the 1824 constitution, which at least ordained primary education for all. Added to this lack of foresight, the abolition of slavery was enacted without any policies for social integration, abandoning the enormous contingent of the black population to their own resources, as "um simples bagaço do antigo sistema de produção" (Fernandes qtd. in Federico 3) ("a simple exhausted relic of the old system of production"). At this moment in Brazilian history, the new republic had to contend with an illiteracy rate of 67 percent.

The Reform Movement of the 1920s and the Pioneer Manifesto

There were no significant initiatives in the first few decades of the new political regime. Primary education continued to be at the margins of national policies, in spite of several speeches denouncing government inaction, such as the ones given in 1903 by Manoel Bomfim, who saw primary education as a national priority: "como o meio para curar os nossos males essenciais" (22) ("a medium to cure our fundamental ills"). The surge of new ideas and pedagogic practices in favor of educational reform was to come about only in the very last decade of the First Republic. This movement was named *Escolanovismo* (new school politics), because its intellectual proponents in Brazil were influenced by different pedagogical movements from the United States and Europe that came under the denomination of the New School. This movement, though not without a few shortcomings, was to fill the void that existed in education. One aspect worthy of note of the Brazilian *Escolanovismo* was that it came to power at the state level, since the federal government, still under the aegis of the 1834 *Ato Adicional*, was conspicuously absent. States such as Sao Paulo, Pernambuco, Ceará, Rio Grande do Sul, Rio de Janeiro, Minas, and Paraná, to mention only a few, carried out educational reforms inspired by the New School's pedagogical theories. Strictly speaking, New School ideas had long been known in Brazil. Some of the basic premises behind Rui Barbosa's 1880 reform proposal were inspired in the New School and Liberal ideas. However, as Nagle aptly observed, up until 1920 their effect was merely one of clearing the way; it was only after that decade that there would be "não havia condições sociais e pedagógicas que estimulassem o desenvolvimento da nova forma de entender a escolarização" (240) ("the necessary social and pedagogic conditions to stimulate the development of a new education policy").

There were several factors that contributed to the *Escolanovista* movement and its unprecedented dynamism. The 1920s were characterized by a greater critical awareness of Brazilian reality. Euclides da Cunha's (1866–1909) *Os Sertões* [1902; *Rebellion in the Backlands,* 1944] carried a message to a nation traditionally content to look across the ocean to Europe, to turn to the interior of the nation instead. Writers such as Mario de Andrade (1893–1945), José Bento Monteiro Lobato (1882–1948), and Oswald de Andrade (1890–1954) began to reform the Brazilian nation. The 1922 Semana de Arte Moderna (Modern Art Week) became a watershed for the culture of the nation to Brazilians. The foundation of the Communist Party and the first conference on primary education were among the many indicators that "refletem ou acusam a existência de desajustamento entre as forças sociais dominantes e as novas forças sociais em emergência" (Nagle 242) ("reflected the distance between the political authorities in power and the new emerging social forces"). The urgency to renew the combat with the authoritarian practices of the Old Republic found its main sustenance in the ideology of Liberalism. The atmosphere of change was heightened by the commemorations for the Centennial of Independence, which coincided with the attempt to implement the pedagogical ideals

of the New School. Heitor Lira created the Associação Brasileira de Educação [Brazilian Association for Education] in 1924, which was to act as a catalyst of the movement. The pioneering Liberal leaders of the New School movement met with strong opposition and intense public debate especially from Catholics, since the notion of lay schools had not yet won general approval.

The education reform movement saw the Revolution of 1930 and the ascent of Getúlio Vargas to power as an unprecedented opportunity to push for an organic educational policy that would finally give Brazil a national educational system and guidelines for the future. The beginning of the 1930s saw the creation of the Ministério de Educação e Saúde (Ministry for Education and Health), headed by Francisco Campos, who, together with Mario Casasanta, had previously conducted one of the most important educational reforms of the New School movement in the state of Minas Gerais (in 1927). The initial optimism over the choice of the head of the new ministry soon gave way to fear, as president Vargas hesitated in keeping his promise to give Brazil a constitution. As Fernando de Azevedo noted, the new political administrators of the nation came to power without a plan and/or guidelines and seemed to hesitate between the different possibilities open to them. It was in this context that educators wrote a manifesto in which these guidelines were defined, one that would eventually determine the new educational policy (n.d. 85). Getúlio Vargas himself had, during a meeting of the Associação Brasileira de Educação, called for a plan to reorganize education at a national level (Azevedo n.d., 86). It was after this meeting that Fernando de Azevedo was given the task of writing a manifesto in such a way as to consolidate—in a single document, for widespread dissemination—a proposal for a new national educational policy.

The Manifesto dos Pioneiros da Educação Nova [Pioneers of the New Education Manifesto] was presented to the people and to the government in March of 1932, and it had resounding repercussions in public opinion. The most notable educators of the time had signed the manifesto—Lourenço Filho, Anísio Teixeira, Fernando de Azevedo, Almeida Junior, and Frota Pessoa. However, the manifesto had many contradictions, which mirrored the different pedagogical beliefs held by the followers of the New School. In spite of its many flaws, there is no doubt of its political and social significance. One great virtue of the manifesto was to bring the state back into a role of prominence in education policy, with the understanding that education has a social and eminently public function that the state must carry out with the cooperation of various institutions (Azevedo n.d., 66). This was the turning point, thanks to the state's long-standing absence from the creation and implementation of educational policies. The manifesto proposed an organic and integrated educational policy comprising all levels and modes of teaching, as well as a division of responsibilities between the union, the states, and the municipalities. The manifesto opens with a statement that establishes outright the importance of the political dimension of education: "na hierarquia dos problemas educacionais, nenhum sobreleva em importância e gravidade ao da educação" (Azevedo n.d., 59) ("in the hierarchy of (national) problems, none exceeds the importance or the gravity of education"). In spite of vehement opposition from conservative Catholics, the manifesto, a culminating point of the movement for educational reform in the 1920s, was implemented in the Constitution of 1934. The Constitution's chapter on education was groundbreaking in Brazilian history, and it included an unprecedented amount of attention to mobilizing resources for education.

On the whole, the cultural effervescence in the 1920s and 1930s can be considered to have resulted in a positive outcome. It saw the creation of the Ministry for Education, and it was the first time that educational issues were presented in a comprehensive document to open public debate (in other words, in a manifesto). This period also witnessed the emergence of the first Brazilian universities: Rio de Janeiro (statute 1920; operation 1931), Minas Gerais (statute 1927; operation 1931), Porto Alegre (statute 1934; operation 1936), and São Paulo (statute and operation in 1934). São Paulo especially–the first Brazilian integrated university–became an important agent for critical thought in the nation. It would be responsible for the first Brazilian generations to receive an education in science, a fact that would lead to a gradual disclosure and explanation of the nation's cultural and educational backwardness. During this same period, seminal works on Brazil were published, such as Gilberto Freyre's (1900–1987) *Casa Grande e Senzala* [1933; *The Masters and the Slaves,* 1946], Caio Prado Junior's (1907–1990) *Evolução Política do Brasil* [1933; Political Evolution of Brazil], and Sergio Buarque de Hollanda's (1902–1982) *Raízes do Brasil* [1936; Roots of Brazil].

It is true that, as far as education was concerned, the debate carried out at the time, while indisputably pioneering, lacked a firm grounding–something that would only come about once university-level research was under way. The pedagogical concepts had been important, and whatever their merits, they needed to be examined critically and in light of the local geographical, demographic, and cultural context. Nagle observes that, in this respect, New School policy and the way it was implemented opted for emphasis on the technical dimension in place of the juridical political dimension of education, which meant adopting a more focused model for what was the perceived scope of educational issues (259). The New School movement without doubt was a major contribution to the advent of critical thinking in Brazilian education, as exemplified in the work of renowned educators such as Anísio Teixeira, Fernando de Azevedo, and Lourenço Filho, to name a few of the movement's principal exponents. It is also true, however, that the statistics were not encouraging: at the time, only 27 percent of school-age children (between 7 and 14 years of age) were enrolled in school, and the illiteracy rate was of approximately 60 percent.

The efforts of the Liberal pioneers during the 1920s and 1930s to bring a viable new primary school educational policy into being were not successful. Popular unrest, political strife, and the nation's internal dichotomies, allied to the strengthening of Fascism and Nazism in Europe, eventually led to the Estado Novo Regime takeover in 1937. The democratic constitution of 1934 was eliminated in favor of a fascist one that made Getúlio Vargas the plenipotentiary ruler. It marked the beginning of the dictatorship and the exclusion of Liberal democracy as well as the idealism of the New School from public life–which lasted until the Estado Novo's fall and the nation's return to democracy in 1945.

The Struggle for Public Schools Resumes

The Estado Novo meant a regression in educational policy and practice. On the one hand, it can be credited with having formally reorganized the educational system by establishing organic laws on schooling. On the other hand, the head of the Ministry for Education, Gustavo Capanema, persecuted and aborted the innovative project for the Universidade do Distrito Federal (University of the Federal District) as it was conceived by Anísio Teixeira, and which was destined to perform a role similar to the one the Universidade de São Paulo had already begun for Brazilian cultural life. The Estado Novo also excluded a generation of new educators who had been trained in the ideals of the New School from contributing to a new educational policy.

The Estado Novo's fall in 1945 meant that a new constitution was promulgated in 1946 to restore democratic freedoms. The union was now constitutionally empowered to establish the guidelines and foundations for a national educational system. This led to the elaborating of a project by specialists in the field, among whom many educators of the New School movement reappeared. The project was sent to the Câmara Federal (Congress) and was stopped in its tracks by a restricting intervention of the then member of Congress Gustavo Capanema, who had been head of the Ministry for Education during the Estado Novo. The intervention sent the project into a long period of hibernation, but it spurred the proponents of public schooling and progressive forces in education to open public debates of the issue. Again, leading New School educators, such as Anísio Teixeira, Almeida Junior and Lourenço Filho, made themselves heard. The guidelines and foundations project were in favor of decentralization and the strengthening of the public school system, which came into direct conflict with the interests of the private sector.

Brazil had, however, a different profile in the 1950s, quite distant from the nation it had been in the 1930s. Some of the indicators that the nation was now on the threshold of a period of greater clarity and increased critical thinking included the presence of a middle class, the growth of a literate working class, the strengthening of nationalism, and a growing consciousness of the importance of the public school. In the face of the void in legislation, the educational sector began to react through educational campaigns, including the demand for the expansion of secondary education (CADES), the concerted effort for the improvement of university level skills (CAPES), and the push for the eradication of illiteracy and the expansion of commercial schooling (CAEC). Chagas notes that these campaigns engendered a new consciousness and a new style, one well grounded in the reality of the nation.

The most auspicious development of the period was, however, the outcome of the public debate regarding public schools. Member of Congress Carlos Lacerda, a polemic politician who represented Right-wing interests, proposed legislation that conceded ample powers to private schooling, bringing the public debate to a head. Educators defending public education forwarded their own legislation in 1959. This was followed by a widespread campaign in favor of public schools led by numerous intellectuals. At the height of the campaign, Azevedo, the author of the manifesto of 1932, was called to write the *Manifesto dos Educadores*, addressed to the people and the government (in July 1959). The manifesto of 1959, a summing up of the campaign's propositions, was signed by 189 highly regarded members of the Brazilian intellectual class, many of whom had already signed the *Manifesto dos Pioneiros* of 1932; among these were Anísio Teixeira, Mario Casasanta, Delgado de Carvalho, Nóbrega da Cunha, Cecilia Meirelles, A. Alvarez Alberto, and Paschoal Lemme, as well as numerous persons recognized for their contributions to the nation's intellectual independence, including: Fernando Henrique Cardoso, Antonio Cândido de Melo e Souza, Cesar Lattes, Paulo Duarte, Sergio Buarque de Hollanda, Joel Martins, Caio Prado Junior, Jose Arthur Gionotti, Florestan Fernandes, Afrânio Coutinho, J. Leite Lopes, Celso de Rui Beisiegel, and Frota Pessoa.

The critical issue of primary and popular education was one of the basic premises of the *Manifesto dos Educadores*:

Se se considerear ainda que ultrapassa de 50% da pupulação geral o número de analfabetos no país e que, de uma população em idade escolar (isto é, de 7 a14 anos) de 12 milhões de crianças, não frequentam a escola senão menos da metade ou, mais precisamente, 5. 728. 000, nada será preciso acrescentar, pois se terá, com isso, um quadro sombrio demais para lhe carregarmos cores e desolador demais para detemos a indagação melancólica de outros fatos e detalhes. (Azevedo 59)

If one takes into consideration that more than 50% of the population is illiterate, and that of the total school age population (between 7 and 14 years of age) numbering 12 million children, less than half are enrolled in school, 5,728,000 to be precise, we need add nothing else. It is a somber enough fact that can speak for itself and a situation desolate enough to forgo *minutiae*.

The campaign in favor of public schooling finally led to the approval of the Lei de Diretrizes e Bases (Lei 4.024/61) (Guidelines and Foundations Law)–a partial victory, but a victory nevertheless, in the words of Anísio Teixeira.

As Maciel Barros wrote, the campaign in favor of public schooling had the fundamental value of bringing out into the open, in unequivocal terms, the relations between national development, democracy, and the improvement of living conditions, on the one hand; and, on the other, the intensive effort for the instruction of the Brazilian people, which could only be promoted by the state (xvii). It also served to create a consciousness in the nation of the relevance of popular, public education, as was proved by the involvement of workers and students in the issue of education. The UNE, União Nacional dos Estudantes (National Student Union), meeting held in Bahia in May 1960 asked for universities to be open to the people (and not discriminate on the basis of wealth), to promote literacy by teaching basic skills, to offer courses to foster the communication skills of union leaders, and even to train construction workers (Poerner 198).

This was the same spirit that saw the creation of the Universidade de Brasilia in 1961. It was conceived of as a national center for thought and studies. It was to develop a mature and critical awareness of the problems of the nation, and to search for lines of action that would enable the people to reach the fulfillment of their historically repressed potential. The student movement was also reflected in Álvaro Vieira Pinto's book *Questão da Universidade* [The University Issue], which centered on the problematic of the marginalized masses (see Cunha 1987, 241). The book proposed a university that belonged to the people instead of to the elites. As such, his proposition stated that the reform could not be led by professors, since their interests clashed with opening the universities to the masses, and since the professors could not transmit culture to the masses from their own perspective. Students ought to have their own project for the university.

The 1960s were a period of political effervescence for Brazil. The resignation of president Jânio Quadros and the rise to power of Jango Goulart (then vice-president) encouraged debate over the nation's backwardness and social inequalities.

The years 1962 and 1963 witnessed numerous events and demonstrations in city squares on the topic of fundamental reform, such as in the agrarian sector, the banking system, and the universities. This was the context in which Paulo de Tarso, head of the Ministry for Education, following Darcy Ribeiro's suggestion, invited the educator Paulo Freire (1921–1997) to create a national literacy plan. Freire was a relatively unknown educator at the time, but he was to become internationally famous as a spokesman for civil rights. He developed his first experiments in Angicos in the State of Rio Grande do Norte, where he was able to teach field workers to read and write in 45 days. Based on this experience he proposed to teach two million Brazilians to read and write through the creation of twenty thousand *círculos de cultura* (circles of culture).

Paulo Freire's method was revolutionary. It was based on teaching words that had existential meaning for the student, in order to establish an alliance between the text and the person's context. It was his aim to make the teaching process a part of the student's growing awareness of his or her place in the world. Learning to read and write, as Lima commented regarding Freire's method, instead of being seen as a foreign interference in the world of the illiterate person, was to become a natural result of the adjustment the student made when gaining a lucid consciousness of the limitations of illiteracy (1996, 79). The military coup of 1964, as Gadotti notes (72), landed Freire in prison for 75 days under the accusation of being *"subversivo e ignorante"* (subversive and ignorant), and he was sent into exile. That was the beginning of his long trajectory, across many Latin American nations, Europe, and Africa, writing and serving as an educational consultant to governments. His most famous book, *Pedagogia do oprimido* [*Pedagogy of the Oppressed*], published in 1970, called the attention of intellectuals and researchers to the educational disenfranchisement of the masses, and was the first step in the career that earned him respect and admiration throughout the world. His legacy was honored when, soon after his death in July 1997, UNESCO held a meeting in Hamburg, Germany, and published its Final Declaration on the Education of Adults, which recognized him; in his honor the Paulo Freire International Prize was established.

Another Reversal

The military coup of 1964 had a negative impact on public education. In keeping with what happened to Paulo Freire, other educators and intellectuals were forced into exile, and the ones remaining were constrained to a culture of silence. The Plano Trienal de Educação (Triennial Plan for Education) and the Plano Nacional de Alfabetização (National Literacy Plan), created and initiated during Jango Goulart's presidency, were abandoned. Both plans had been based on the promise of a significant increase in funds for education. The innovative Universidade de Brasilia suffered the greatest setback, since it was the object of intense persecution leading to more than 200 professors being forced out of the institution: "configurando-se um crime sem precedentes na história cultural do país" (Cunha 1987, 238) ("[it was] an unprecedented crime in the cultural history of the nation"). In 1964, "depois de assaltada por tropas militarizadas, a universidade de Brasilia teve diversos professores presos, levados a um pátio militar para serem ali desnudos e assim permanecerem por toda a tarde" (Darcy Ribeiro 85) ("after being invaded by military troops, several professors of the University of Brasília were imprisoned, taken out to a yard in the military quarters, rid of their clothes and left naked for an entire afternoon").

More generally, the 1964 military takeover promulgated two fascist constitutions, one in 1964 and another in 1969, and promoted a reform of primary and secondary education [Law 5.692/71] as well as of higher education [Law 5.540/68]. The first law was an attempt at professionalizing secondary schools, a move that was eventually evaluated as a mistake and revoked. Higher education, however, did make some progress, especially with respect to postgraduate education. The government's support of postgraduate education allowed for the establishing of long-lasting national plans and the organization of a competent postgraduate system. Primary education, on the contrary, floundered. An expansion policy created the *salário-educação* (fund for education wages); this was a new fund based on taxation of corporate income. Although this fund promoted an increase in primary school teachers, it did nothing to improve the quality of education; and an ever-increasing number of students failed to pass the school year and were obliged to take it over again, thus creating an even more serious problem. There was therefore no connection between the number of children enrolled in school and the number of children graduating, since a large number of them left school in the interim after successive failures. This form of social exclusion became a mechanism to accelerate the children's loss of self-esteem, and it had serious consequences for the future of Brazil. As for the crushing problem of illiteracy, the military regime tried to attenuate the problem by instituting the Movimento Brasileiro de Alfabetização (MOBRAL) (Brazilian Literacy Movement) program in 1970, but soon found its efforts ill planned and inadequate and therefore abandoned it. From the 1980s on, the results of the social and economic policies enacted by the military regime began to show signs of fragility, and there began a slow return to democracy by a gradual restoration of democratic freedoms to the nation. A national campaign for the people's right to vote directly in the presidential elections (a system of partial elections was already in place) gained wide support in the Brazilian civilian society and mobilized the most important sectors of the nation. The movement culminated in the creation of the Constitutional Assembly and in 1988 in the promulgation of a new constitution, the most democratic of all Brazilian constitutions.

New Times and New Issues

During the period in which the 1988 Constitution was being written, Brazil's rate of total illiteracy was 18.3 percent of the population older than 15 years of age. The rate of enrollment in schools for the population between 7 and 14 years of age (considered obligatory education) was 86.9 percent. The national expenditure in education, as a ratio of the PIB [GNP], was approximately 4.3 percent. The high index of repetition of the school year meant that it took the average student 11.4 years to complete the obligatory 8 years of schooling. No educational policy could allow such wastefulness. One should add that the expansion of the primary school system was undertaken without changing the extremely poor quality of primary school teaching described above, which was the direct consequence of the systematic reduction of teachers' incomes to the point that—in many regions of the nation—the monthly wage was less than fifty dollars. Secondary education fared not much better. Due to the high incidence of school year repetition, few students went beyond primary school. At the end of the 1980s Brazil had one of the lowest levels of enrollment in secondary education in Latin America and the Caribbean. No more than 20 percent of children in the appropriate age group (15 to 19 years of age) were enrolled in secondary schools.

As noted above, higher education developed differently. Thanks to the support of the government and international loans to universities, especially the public universities, much improvement came about for both the technical and scientific infrastructure and for professors' incomes and careers during the second half of the 1980s. Two important governmental agencies for financing research contributed greatly to the improvement of higher education: the CNPq, Conselho Nacional de Desenvolvimento Científico e Tecnológico, (National Council for Scientific and Technological Development) and CAPES, Coordenação de Aperfeiçoamento do Pessoal de Nível Superior, (Coordination for the Improvement of Graduate and Post-Graduate Education). One of the reasons for this progress was that these agencies were always managed by members of the academic community and not the military regime—a decisive factor in the public credibility they attained.

The 1988 Constitution, called the Citizenship Constitution because of its incorporation of long-standing social demands, has a chapter devoted to education in which ideas that had been put forward since the *Manifesto dos Pioneiros* in 1932 were finally adopted. The constitution was committed to eliminating illiteracy within a period of ten years, as well as guaranteeing all children, youth, and adults a fundamental eight years of schooling. It is important to take into account, however, that the constitution was approved a year before the fall of Russian socialism and the regime in Eastern Europe, events that were to have numerous political and economic consequences. The acceleration of economic globalization, allied to the neo-Liberal model, became an obstacle for developing some of the most important advances of the constitution.

In 1989 Brazil elected president Fernando Collor de Mello, who took office at the beginning of 1990 and inaugurated a turbulent administration of neo-Liberal inspiration. The turbulence was such that his mandate was cut short by impeachment halfway through his term in office. The impeachment process was riddled with denunciations of all sorts of irregularities that had been occurring in the nation; problems regarding ethics, citizenship, and corruption were widely debated in civil society. The public discussion of these topics was heightened in the face of the striking social inequalities and enormous disparity in the distribution of wealth that revealed the full inequities of the nation's reality. Educational issues were part of this debate: Educational penury, to borrow the title of a classic book on Brazilian education (see Werebe) was brought out in public and generated growing perplexity within the ranks of the ruling elite, among businessmen, and in the press in general.

When Congress approved the impeachment and the new president Itamar Franco took office, it was a time of celebration in Brazil, since the nation had been able to oust a president who had broken rules of ethics and honesty through juridical procedure; but it also meant that the new government faced even greater challenges due to the new vigilance awakened in society toward governmental conduct. The only relevant contribution the deposed president had made toward education was the Plano Nacional de Alfabetização e Cidadania (PNAC) (National Plan for Citizenship and Illiteracy), which had the sole merit of bringing the issue of illiteracy into public debate. The new government, through the Ministry of Education, took up the challenge of education for all, as it was announced in UNESCO's Jomtien Meeting, held in Thailand. Education for all meant a ten-year plan for universal education, adopting a methodology of widespread participation of civil society through its most representative institutions. In the spirit of the Jomtien, Thailand, declaration, the Ten-Year Plan comprised pre-school education from 3 to 6 years of age, basic education from 7 to14 years of age, and that of youth and adults. The plan gradually gained credibility and defined a minimal agenda for the reform of basic education. Its guiding principles were equity, quality, school for all, and the recognition of teachers. There was an agreement between the government and the teachers' union to guarantee a standard minimum salary in order to end the exploitation of the profession through low salaries and to improve the quality of teaching.

The public debate engendered by the Ten-Year Plan was vital for harnessing the will and the interest, energy, and resources of the various states, municipalities, and even civil society as a whole. It was a strategy to make up for lost time and to set the pace of the nation for the coming years. There was a clear understanding that without a deliberate joint effort on the part of the government and civil society, the Brazilian educational problems would never be solved. In 1995 Fernando Henrique Cardoso took office; this meant that the policy on education changed and the Ten-Year Plan was only partially upheld. One of the high points of the Cardoso government's educational policy was the creation of the FUNDEF, Fundo de Valorização do Magistério e Desenvolvimento da Educação Fundamental, (Fund for the Recognition of the Teaching Profession and Development of Basic Education). It was an instrument of accounting to guarantee the fair distribution of financial resources destined for basic education, in which the student was the criteria for distribution. In other words, money was directed to where the students were, and 60 percent of the fund's resources went toward teachers' payrolls. The plan is still in its first years, and as of yet it is not possible to evaluate properly its repercussions. A recent study on the FUNDEF conducted by the University of São Paulo's FIPE, Instituto de Pesquisas Econômicas, (Institute for Economic Research) indicates that there has been an improvement in teacher salaries and the pedagogical infrastructure of schools, especially in the poorer areas of the country. On the other hand, the study also registers a strong criticism with regard to the amount of funds devoted to education. It is currently at US$190 per student each year, and should in fact be approximately US$300 according to the law that created the FUNDEF. There have been other measures of unquestionable outreach, such as the creation of TV Escola (School Television), which uses satellite transmission and offers the school system modern and updated programs in various areas of the curriculum for basic education. One should also mention the program "Toda Criança na Escola" ["All Children to School"], which, as a mobilization strategy, resulted in an increase in school-age enrollment. There are many experiments regarding the quality of education being conducted at this moment, and there are already indications that the number of students repeating school years is down. There has also been a general improvement in the quality and distribution of textbooks. Specialists have been evaluating the methodology available and excluding books that fall below par or are outdated. Textbooks are also being updated in accordance with issues of discrimination, and there is increased training in ethics and citizenship.

Largely as an outcome of these measures, Brazil now has approximately 96 percent of school-age children enrolled in basic schooling (circa 36 million students), and the number is likely to rise. New educational mechanisms, such as the *bolsa-escola* (scholarships for schools) and *renda minima* (minimum income) destined for low-income families that guarantee to keep their children in school, are now being adopted in various states and municipalities. This means that Brazil is close to accomplishing universal access to the eight years of obligatory schooling. The enrollment rate in secondary school began to rise, thanks to the lowering of the rate of primary school year repetitions; from 3,770,000 students enrolled in 1991, the number has risen to roughly 7,767,000 in the year 2000, which accounts for 33 percent of the population between 15 and 19 years of age. The plan is to continue to expand secondary schooling in the next few years, and has the ultimate aim of guaranteeing the entire age group universal access to the classroom. It is important to note, however, that most of this expansion is under way in night courses (70 percent of total enrollment), where the quality of education leaves much room for improvement.

There is reason to believe the education policies for basic and secondary education are fulfilling their aims, especially with respect to basic schooling (which is the government's priority). The same does not apply to higher education, or to the education of young adults and infant and pre-school care. The government is not devoting the same attention to higher education it is awarding to basic and secondary education, at times justifying its policy with the comparatively elevated cost of higher education. Although there has been a great expansion of the student population (enrollment in universities increased from 1,540,000 at the beginning of the 1990s to 2,377,715 in the year 2000), university teacher unions have voiced frequent criticisms of governmental policy, especially regarding salaries, the control of expenditures, and the autonomy of federal universities. In 1998 a debilitating three-month strike by university faculty called attention to the fact that salaries had not been adjusted for inflation in the past four years. Recent years have witnessed a sharp decline in the investment in technical and scientific infrastructure, with clear consequences for the quality of teaching, research, and postgraduate education. It is feared that the policy of excluding universities from their share of the education budget could result in the serious deterioration of the postgraduate study and research infrastructure, which had been constructed so carefully during the previous decades. In 1999 Brazil had 2066 programs in postgraduate studies (master's and doctorate programs) in which 82,800 students were enrolled. Approximately 4700 Ph.D. candidates graduate a year. The year 2000 also witnessed the creation of sector-specific funds in the area of science and technology, which could mean a significant influx of new resources for the exact sciences.

The most pressing challenge for Brazilian educational policies, however, remains the education of youths and adults. The country has today about 15 million people categorized as absolute illiterates. If we adjust this to include the reality of functional illiteracy, the number doubles to 30 million, and no government to this day has been bold enough to face the problem in its entirety. It is a great educational deficit accumulated through a history of neglect, omission, and exclusion. To face the magnitude of the problem would mean mobilizing society as well as bringing in additional resources, something the current model of national development will not allow. The biggest program in action today, Alfabetização Solidária (Literacy Through Solidarity), organized and managed by the government with the participation of businessmen and civil society, has already reached approximately 1,500,000 students. The results, however, are quite disappointing: It has a success rate of no more than 25 percent, largely because of the brief period of time allotted to instruction (four months). The program suffers the added vulnerability that there is no clear plan for continuing studies, making it weak from the point of view of a pedagogy of learning. The situation with pre-schools and day care is practically identical. Brazil's pre-schools serve about 51.2 percent of children whose ages range from 4 to 6 years (with 4,102,000 enrolled). The perspective for broadening the attendance is bleak. The business sector has started up some initiatives, but its efforts have limited effect because of the nation's social inequality in income distribution and extreme, out-of-reach poverty.

In a final summary of the omissions that occurred in the evolution of Brazilian education, it should be noted that the Ten-Year Plan, the "Plano Decenal de Decca para Todos," marks the first time the Brazilian state has taken a firm position in formulating and coordinating educational policy. This has encouraged and facilitated the coordination and division of responsibilities with states and municipalities. There is much progress, although most of it is quantitative, not qualitative. There has been a noteworthy expansion of the population enrolled in primary, secondary, and higher education. But, as we have repeatedly indicated, these improvements in enrollment cannot be called an improvement in the quality of education. The dimension of the problem of quality is well illustrated in a 1998 UNESCO study on language and mathematics, conducted with primary school students of third and fourth grades in thirteen nations in Latin America. The study demonstrated that "el rendimiento de los alumnos de la mitad más baja de Cuba, es significativamente superior al rendimiento de la mitad más alta de los países que le siguen inmediatamente" ("the lowest half of the scores in Cuba were significantly higher than the scores of the top half of the following nations"): Brazil, Colombia, Chile, and Argentina. This discouraging result (from the standpoint of these latter four countries) was ratified by evaluations conducted in Brazil by INEP, Instituto Nacional de Estudos e Pesquisas Educacionais, (National Institute for Research in Education). Taking Portuguese scores as an example, on a scale of 0 to 500, tests resulted in only 39.7 percent of eighth-grade students scoring above 300.

Quality in education is therefore the most important challenge for Brazilian education on all educational levels. One can argue that a successful educational system starts in pre-school. We have seen that Brazil only serves 51.2 percent of the children in this age group, a fact that means this challenge cannot be met in the short term. It cannot be stated too often that a policy of improvement in education means mobilizing the corresponding financial resources, and Brazil, despite its most recent efforts, still invests relatively very little in education. One should, finally, have a clear understanding that there are no such things as miracles in the field of education. Progress is the result of the continuous and uninterrupted efforts of all participants in the field over a number of years. Brazil has amassed a number of educational deficits and shortcomings in its centuries of neglect and omission. Neither miracles nor revolutions will overcome them. On the one hand, there must be an educational policy that is discussed nationally and reflects the legitimate aspirations of all sectors of the country, so that the government and civil society may effectively join efforts; and on the other hand, since personal as well as national destinies are ever more subjected to the influence of international forces–as was opportunely noted in the *Relatório Jacques Delors* [Jacques Delors Report] (16)–it is important to heed the admonition voiced by the ex–Director General of UNESCO, Federico Mayor, that it is necessary to control globalization. A world in which globalization is carried out by the few and suffered by the masses is inadmissible. The future of education, like that of so many things, rests on the development of a new universal ethics to humanize development. It is not clear yet whether such a thing is possible in Brazil. What we do know is that there is a limit to the subjugation of human dignity to the vicissitudes and volatility of the world markets.

Translation by Lis Horta Moriconi

Works Cited

Azevedo, Fernando. n.d. *A educação entre dois mundos*. São Paulo: Melhoramentos.

——. 1960. "Manifesto dos Educadores." *Diretrizes e bases*. Ed. Roque Spencer Maciel de Barros. São Paulo: Pioneira. xvii, 59–62.

Barbosa, Rui. 1947 [1883]. "Cálculo do americano Henry Hill." *Reforma do ensino primario e varias instituições complementares da instrucção publica*. Rio de Janeiro: Ministério da Educação e Cultura. 13–17.

Barros, Roque Spencer Maciel de. 1986. *A Ilustração brasileira e a idéia de universidade*. São Paulo: Convívio, Editora da Universidade de São Paulo.

Bomfim, Manoel José do. n.d. *A América latina, males de origem*. 2nd ed. Rio de Janeiro: Noite.

Carvalho, Laerte R. 1979. *As reformas pombalinas da instrução pública*. São Paulo: Saraiva, Editora da Universidade de São Paulo.

Chagas, Valnir. 1978. *Educação brasileira: O ensino de 11 e 21 Graus*. São Paulo: Saraiva.

Cruz Costa, João. 1967. *Contribuição à história das idéias no Brasil*. 2nd ed. Rio de Janeiro: Civilização Brasileira.

Cunha, Célio da. 1987. "Universidade e regionalização. Campinas: Faculdade de Educação da Unicamp." Diss. University of Campinas.

Delors, Jacques, et al. 1998. *Educação: Um tesouro a descobrir*. Trans. José Carlos Eufrázio. São Paulo: Cortez; Brasília: United Nations Educational, Scientific and Cultural Organization, Ministerio da Educação e Cultura.

Durkheim, Émile. 1995. *A evolução pedagógica*. Trans. Bruno Charles Magne. Porto Alegre: Artes Médicas.

Federico, Celso. 1998. "Florestan, Jornalista." *Caderno Especial de Resenhas, Folha de São Paulo* (September 12): 3.

Franca, Leonel. 1952. *O método pedagógico dos jesuítas*. Rio de Janeiro: Agir.

Gadotti, Moacir. 1996. *Paulo Freire: Uma biobliografia*. São Paulo: Cortez; Brasilia: United Nations Educational, Scientific and Cultural Organization.

INEP. 2000. *Instituto Nacional de Estudos e Congressos Educacionais*. Brasilia: Instituto Nacional de Estudos e Pesquisas Educacionais.

Larroyo, Francisco. 1970. *História geral da pedagogia: A educação no Brasil*. 2 vols. São Paulo: M. Jou.

Lima, Lauro de Oliveira. 1974. *Estórias da educação no Brasil: De Pombal a Passarinho*. Brasilia: Ed. Brasília.

——. 1996. "O método Paulo Freire." *Paulo Freire: uma biobibliografia*. Ed. Moacir Gadotti. São Paulo: Cortez, United Nations Educational, Scientific and Cultural Organization. 79.

Manacorda, Mário Alighiero. 1989. *História da educação*. Trans. Gaetano Lo Monaco. São Paulo: Cortez, Autores Asociados.

Nagle, Jorge. 1974. *Educação e sociedade na Primeira República*. São Paulo: Editora Pedagógica e Universitária.

Peixoto, Afrânio. 1933. "Projeto de Constituição apresentado à Constituinte de 1823. Art. 250." *Noções de história da educação*. São Paulo: Companhia Editora Nacional. 219.

Poerner, Arthur José. 1979. *O grande poder jovem*. 2nd ed. Rio de Janeiro: Civilização Brasileira.

Ribeiro, Darcy. 1978. *Universidade de Brasília: Invenção e descaminho*. Rio de Janeiro. Avenir.

Ribeiro, Maria Luísa Santos. 1978. *História da educação brasileira: A organização escolar*. São Paulo: Cortez & Moraes.

Southey, Robert. 1817–1819. *History of Brazil*. 3 vols. London: Longman, Hurst, Rees, Orme, and Brown.

Unesco, Oreal. 1998. *Primeiro estudo internacional comparativo: Laboratório Latinoamericano de la Calidad de la Educación*. Santiago: United Nations Educational, Scientific and Cultural Organization; Oficina Regional para América Latina e o Caribe.

Werebe, Maria José Garcia. 1994. *Grandezas e misérias do ensino no Brasil*. 2nd ed. São Paulo: Ática.

CHAPTER 9

BRAZILIAN LITERATURE IN THE 1970s
CENSORSHIP AND THE CULTURE INDUSTRY

Cíntia Schwantes and Rildo Cosson

In a series of three lectures on censorship in Brazil and in Latin America he delivered at Cambridge University in 1974, Antônio Callado (1917–1997) says that the literature of Borges is not representative of Latin America. "Unless," says the Brazilian writer, "we see in his scholarly, phantasmagorical fiction the very essence of Latin American literature, above or beyond censorship, or even, God help us, drawing strength from censorship" (13). Callado's words reflect a common view among Latin American critics and writers, whose fiction and criticism are permeated by the conviction that literature cannot be separated from the political history of their countries–a history in which censorship and other mechanisms of repression have always made their power felt on artists. But if censorship and its political correlates are old acquaintances, the result of their coercive action is never mere silence. Literature has always responded in many forms and in many ways to censorship and other repressive measures imposed by the state. This is why, whether above or beyond censorship (or even drawing its strength from it), Brazilian literature has much to tell about the strange and disturbing situation during the 1970s. (For a corresponding study of censorship during the same period in Chile, see Javier Campos [Vol. 3, Chapter 45], Ed.)

Literature and Dictatorship in the 1970s

A two-part division is normally proposed to articulate Brazil's many contrasts during the rise and fall of the military dictatorship that controlled the country since 1964. The decade begins with guerrilla warfare and ends with the formation of grassroots neighborhood associations as a form of political resistance. The dictatorial government, which at first made widespread use of torture, eventually granted amnesty to exiled political opponents. The economic success of the first years of the dictatorship gave way to growing inflation by the decade's end. In literature the contrast is provided by an initial period of apparent silence and lethargy, dubbed a cultural void by critics and characterized by the nonparticipation and introspection of a large number of writers, which was succinctly expressed in the slogan "*Brasil, ame-o ou deixe-o*" [Brazil: love it or leave it]. In the second half of the decade, however, literature awakened, exploded, and became the front line of resistance to and condemnation of the dictatorship. One of the ways of explaining this contrast has been through the examination of the dictatorship's cultural policy, which also divides the decade in two parts. The first was almost exclusively dedicated to the repression or elimination of any political opposition to the regime and corresponds to the years 1968 through 1974 and to the hard-line governments of Costa e Silva, the military *junta*, and Emilio Garrastazú Médici. The general opinion is that after an early relative tolerance to opposition manifestations by students and intellectuals, the regime became a true dictatorship, censoring writers (its most

visible instrument of coercion), though the government did not disdain other, more punitive strategies, which include forced retirement, layoffs, exile, imprisonment, torture, and, finally, the disappearance of those who dared to raise their voices against Brazil "que vai pra frente" ("which moves forward"). The second half of the decade begins in 1975 with the Geisel and Figueiredo governments of relative liberalization, extending through to the decade's end. During this period, censorship continued to be the state's most visible weapon against writers, but it already divided its functions of controlling the production and the circulation of cultural products and information with a National Cultural Policy that rewarded supporters and, in general, was a policy of sponsorship and political co-optation.

Of all the dictatorship's instruments of repression, censorship received the most attention from literary critics. It is both an emblematic and dominant feature of the decade. Censorship appears to assign a special, if not contradictory, role to literature. In the first place, in comparison with the systematic silencing and sometimes brutal suppression of the press, the artistic scene, and the mass communications media, the direct action of censorship upon literature appears to have been relatively minor. According to Domingos Pellegrini, Jr., it was a very bad decade for writers and producers of theater, but not so bad for those who wrote short stories. As the decade progressed, paradoxically, censorship began to act more directly upon literature, just as the general process of liberalization of mass communication and cultural activity began, as may be observed by the suspension of prepublication censorship of newspapers and magazines beginning in 1975; yet this was also the time of the 1975 prohibition of José Louzeiro's (b. 1932) *Aracelli meu amor* [Aracelli My Love] and Ignácio Loyola Brandão's (b. 1936) *Zero* (1976), which had already circulated freely for almost a year. The only recorded case of a writer's arrest because of his work also belongs to this period. Renato Tapajós (b. 1943) was imprisoned for one month because his book *Em Câmara Lenta* [1977; In Slow Motion] was judged to be a dangerous manual for subversive activity.

All things considered, the various critical assessments of the period characterize the literary narrative of the 1970s as being dominated by a plurality of aesthetic proposals that make it difficult to provide a unifying synthesis and a strong link with the nation's political history. Apparently, the documentary, allegorical, confessional, fragmentary, experimental, testimonial, and political nature of the period's fictional narratives is, to a large extent, the response to the conditions of cultural production under the military dictatorship. Specifically, censorship was principally responsible for the proactive function taken on by literature (in contrast to the noninvolvement of journalism), which eventually distinguished the decade in the literary history of Brazil.

Censorship in the Canon

The vicarious role of Brazilian literature in the 1970s was an escape valve for cultural production in this period and has been explained by critics as the consequence of two factors. In the first place, literature, with its small number of readers, did not represent as great a threat to the military *junta* as mass communications media, with its millions of viewers. Besides this, individual reading and the absence of immediate contact between readers and writers did not have the same mobilizing force as theater or cinema. The second factor that influenced the military regime was the fact that literature was published in small editions of three thousand copies in a nation of millions of readers. The censors' indifference was such that, as Ignácio Loyola Brandão has observed, publishers did not obey the law of prepublication censorship that was in force for all the arts and, even so, suffered practically no sanctions. In his opinion the government did not oppose such resistance; on the contrary, "it knew about it and permitted it to continue because the vigilance over television, radio, cinema, popular music and theater was great, that they could be more flexible with regard to literature" (177). Such elasticity would soon be noticed by the various cultural producers who, having been repressed in other areas, sought their lost freedom of expression in literature. Hence the migration of journalists and professionals from other media to literature, a move that would eventually augment the commitment to the documentary nature of the literature of the period (see Hollanda and Gonçalves; Santiago 1980).

Consequently, during this decade of censorship, literature took on greater importance within the cultural arena, as evidenced by the growing number of new authors and an obvious commitment to political realism. Literature functioned vicariously to reveal a Brazil that had been hidden or erased from the general public by mass media censorship. Through literary texts, readers could experience part of the world that had been banned from radio, cinema, and television. The growth of literature as a realistic option among writers and readers was also recognized by the censors, who, in a reversal of form, once other means of artistic expression had been silenced or controlled, began to devote much more attention to literary phenomena. The apparent contradiction between the exemption from prepublication censorship and the censors' increased vigilance of literature can thus be explained as a change from indifference to what was first considered an elite minority's indulgence to a recognition of the latent power of literature. Besides prompting literature to serve as a cultural escape valve, censorship may be indirectly related to other characteristics of the Brazilian literary production of the period. Silviano Santiago (1982) calls attention to the fact that censorship did not necessarily prevent an artist from writing but that, by restricting the number of works published, it led to the sterility of the cultural scene. Thus, in addition to the physical violence inflicted against writers themselves, censorship committed its greatest artistic transgression in controlling society, preventing citizens from freely choosing and assessing those creative elements that will make up their world view. In this sense it might be said that censorship indirectly influenced the adaptation of new forms, such as Latin American magical realism and the nonfiction novel. Santiago is not proposing that there is a direct causal relationship between these two types of texts and censorship but, rather, that these were some of the options permitted or suggested to writers, especially younger ones, and those who saw in literature the opportunity to engage in a less intensely scrutinized form of expression. Among the formal innovations that resulted from censorship, two can be pointed out: On one hand, a fragmented, metaphorical discourse developed that sought to disguise any facts that might be censurable and, on the other hand, a quasi-journalistic documentary discourse emerged denouncing and criticizing the arbitrariness of the state whenever possible. Literary criticism also developed a mode of allegorical reading in order to construct a bridge from the hermetic to the concrete and from the singular to the general (see Arrigucci).

In short, and despite having been enormously destructive and impoverishing to society, censorship unwittingly redirected the course of Brazilian literature in the 1970s. Its effect may be measured by the large number of writer-journalists who came to occupy the literary field and promote a fusion between politics and literature, as well as in the period's aesthetic options that sought to reconcile allegory and realism or simply to split literary discourse into two distant modes, the documentary and the fantastic. Nevertheless, the overall effect of censorship on Brazilian society has undoubtedly been negative for, as critics have frequently emphasized, censorship led to a sacrifice of aesthetic quality in favor of a univocal direct communication with the reading public, a trait closer to journalism than to literature (see Sussekind and Lucas). Still, there is more to be said about the relationship between censorship and literature during the 1970s. A reading that takes into consideration not only the canon, upon which critics have preferentially concentrated, but also the literary system as a whole shows that censorship did not act alone during the period in question; there were often other factors that contributed to the changes just described.

Censorship in the Literary System

From a systemic perspective (see Even-Zohar), three points should be observed in reading the literature of the 1970s. The first concerns journalistic migration to literature and the space of freedom represented by literature (see Angelo). Even so, one cannot forget that journalists had other options to continue writing. One such option was the alternative (or underground) press. The chronology of censorship is also important here. A simple date check reveals that the expansion of literature began just as censorship was being lifted from the newspapers. Thus, with or without censorship, there were many more writers who took part in this general expansion of the Brazilian literary system during the period. The consolidation of the culture industry is an important element in the literary system of the period, both in the sense of organizing cultural production according to a market mentality or as a marked resistance to it. The former would be of greater relevance for narrative works, especially those of social criticism, and the latter for poetry, notably so-called marginal or alternative poetry, which remained far removed from the culture industry and the commentary on current events.

Emblematically represented by the hegemony of television as a mass communications medium, the culture industry also reveals itself in the alterations made in the production, circulation, and consumption of books and other printed materials. First, there was an expansion and fragmentation of the publishing industry with the appearance of new publishing houses (see Hallewell) and the increase in publication (to more than one book per inhabitant per year). There was a concomitant growth in the number of readers, as evinced by a 10 percent drop in the illiteracy rate (from 39 percent in the first year of the decade to 29 percent in the last year) and by the growth of higher education, which raised the number of college and university students from one hundred thousand to nearly one million over the decade. The opening of new venues for the sale of books, previously restricted to bookstores, now offered a significant increase of sales in stationary shops, newsstands, train stations, and other places (see Reimão). In literary genres there was an unprecedented increase in short story writing, previously a minor and hard-to-commercialize form. There was also the resurgence of literary magazines and, finally, a tremendous growth of children's literature (see Machado), along with a clear preference for Brazilian writers; even formerly unknown Brazilian writers were in demand. Apparently, the effects of the economic miracle, though brief and tardy, began to have an effect in the editorial market.

General facts of socioeconomic transformation should also be considered, such as demographic growth, the rise of the cities, and the country's thriving industrialization. In tracing this panorama it should not be forgotten that, whether we consider books or any other segment of communication and the arts, the fundamental distinction of this consolidation of the culture industry in 1970s Brazil was an economic rationalization of the market and cultural production according to consumerism (see Ortiz). Second, the cultural void in the early years of the decade was more of a comparative effect caused by the contrasting expansion experienced in its second half than a true downturn. Without neglecting the violent climate of fear and self-censorship that would dominate any society at such moments, the truth was that Brazilian literature survived the dictatorship with its previous characteristics practically intact. This can be observed in the continued publication of renowned writers. The period produced new works of note like *Avalovara* (1974) and *A Rainha dos Cárceres da Grécia* [1976; The Queen of the Prisons of Greece] by Osman Lins (1924–1978), *Os Sinos da Agonia* [1974; The Bells of Agony] by Autran Dourado (b. 1926), and *Incidente em Antares* [1971; Incident at Antares] by Érico Veríssimo (1905–1975). The use of the particular themes and styles of acclaimed writers such as Graciliano Ramos (1892–1953), Jorge Amado (1912–2001), Guimarães Rosa (1908–1967), Murilo Rubião (1916–1991), and Clarice Lispector (1925–1977) was very much in evidence throughout the fictional narratives of the 1970s (see Candido). Such continuity confirms that literature suffered direct attacks of censorship much less than other areas, especially theater and cinema. If well-known writers suffered little, even among the newer ones interference was limited to a few titles, normally and even in these cases only after these had already circulated in a first edition. (Rubem Fonseca's [b. 1925] *Feliz Ano Novo* [1975; Happy New Year] was censored after almost a year of circulation.)

Though unofficial, the list of censored titles in the 1970s presented by Deonísio da Silva can serve as the basis for examining the effects of censorship upon the literary system of those years. The list includes 434 titles, of which 76.4 percent have clearly erotic content and 17.2 percent explicitly political connotations. The remaining 6.2 percent are made up of titles that suggest no obvious reason why they were censored. Among this 6.2 percent, one-fifth were essays of a scientific or philosophical nature and the remaining four-fifths

were works of fiction. The reason given for this censorship was that the works in question offended morality; one thus perceives that censors had a marked preference for reading erotic or pornographic works. But it was not only content that offended public morality; José Louzeiro's *Aracelli meu amor* and Rubem Fonseca's *Feliz Ano Novo* were banned because of offensive language. Therefore, the sexual censorship was much greater than that of political or ideological works. The basic criterion for censorship was the purported defense of morality, since the majority of the titles on the list of censored works during the decade have some erotic connotation. It should also be kept in mind that not all the censored books were works of literature. The list also included political texts, like those of Che Guevara, Mao Tse-tung, and Fernando Henrique Cardoso, as well as nonfiction books dealing with sexuality or eroticism, such as the *Hite Report* by Shere Hite and *Erotika Biblion* by Mirabeau. Among the works of narrative fiction, critics are correct in pointing out that relatively few works by established authors were censored. The great majority of the works banned by the censors were popular or mass-culture erotic literature, whether translated or by Brazilian authors. Among established writers there were only a few prohibited books. The exceptions were Adelaide Carraro, who had eleven works censored, and Cassandra Rios, who had fifteen titles banned—a number that amounted to practically the whole output of the two authors.

Upon examining the list of censored titles, one inevitably concludes that an entire genre of publications was hard hit: erotic or pornographic literature (the borderline between them is tenuous at best, and the action of the censors only helped to obscure it further). Attracting readers beyond the traditional public of "serious" literature, erotic literature was not only one of the most lucrative genres in the publishing market, but it represented a significant number of Brazilian authors along with a number of works in translation. Within the Brazilian literary system, the erotic subsystem was therefore active on two fronts: one that was common to all mass literature, aiming to increase the number of readers; and another pointing toward a process of nationalization of that system, as it sought to replace or at least to compete with similar imported texts. However, this nationalization of erotica was not successful. After the suspension of censorship at the end of the decade, the subsystem of erotic literature quickly reasserted its place in the market. The market for erotica was flooded with publications that more fully satisfied their consumers, as was the case with magazines that combined text with photography. In addition, the economic crisis of the 1980s led publishing companies to give preference to international titles, which provided a safer guarantee of profit.

In conclusion, the presence of censorship in the Brazilian literary system had multiple consequences. In the first place, the action of censorship cannot be disassociated from the nationalized consolidation of the culture industry. This industry was developed under government auspices within the country's project of modernity. The dictatorship controlled the culture industry *directly* in the form of incentives, as well as with direct ties between the government and the mass communications media, and *indirectly* as a collateral effect of economic expansion that, among other things, increased the consumer-public of cultural products (see Caparelli and Miceli). The connection between censorship and the culture industry is contradictory, for the former cut off one of the greatest sources of profit of that industry, precisely that which is represented by the publication of erotic literature. Nonetheless, once censorship had blocked the subsystem of erotic literature, the editorial market was not long in seeking out and offering alternatives for their consumers. Censorship precipitates the short story boom, the expansion of children's literature, and the increase in political fiction. Finally, the repression of traditional genres prompts writers to adapt new hybrid forms like the journalistic novel or transcribed oral histories and biographies. Literary criticism (which was for the most part skeptical of these new forms) emphasized a continuity between the last accomplishments of Brazilian modernism, such as the work of Guimarães Rosa and Clarice Lispector, and the works of this decade. The contrast was striking, however, and the literary production of the 1970s appeared mediocre and lacking in great aesthetic or political accomplishment.

Officially revoked in 1978 with the end of AI-5, censorship did not completely disappear from the Brazilian cultural scene. The Lei de Segurança Nacional (National Security Law) continued to be at the disposal of the authorities, along with other legal devices. Once the period of arbitrariness had ended, however, the balance of the relationship between censorship and literature during the 1970s may be seen, in canonical terms, as an unwitting promotion of formal and thematic deviations from the literary production of the period. It may also be read as a time when literature appears to have taken a vicarious function. In literary systemic terms, the momentary exclusion of the subsystem of erotic literature contributed to the strangulation of national production in the area, but the market was flooded with foreign erotica in translation. On the whole, and despite the fact that criticism restricted its attention to canonical literature, it cannot be denied that the action of censorship within the context of the dictatorship was a determinant factor in the course taken by the Brazilian literary system.

Translation by Stephen A. Berg

Works Cited

Angelo, Ivan. 1994. "Nós que amávamos tanto a literatura." *Brasil: O trânsito da memória.* Ed. Saúl Sosnowski and Jorge Schwartz. São Paulo: EDUSP. 69–73.

Arrigucci, Davi. 1979. "Jornal, realismo, alegoria: O romance brasileiro recente." *Achados e perdidos: Ensaios de crítica.* São Paulo: Pólis. 79–115.

Brandão, Ignácio de Loyola. 1994. "Literatura e resistência." *Brasil: O trânsito da memória.* Ed. Saúl Sosnowski and Jorge Schwartz. São Paulo: EDUSP. 175–84.

Callado, Antonio. 1974. "Censorship and Other Problems of Latin American Writers." Working paper, University of Cambridge.

Candido, Antonio. 1987. "A Nova Narrativa." *A Educação pela noite e outros ensaios.* São Paulo: Ática. 199–215.

Caparelli, Sérgio. 1989. *Ditaduras indústrias culturais no Brasil, na Argentina, no Chile e no Uruguai.* Porto Alegre: Ed. Universidade/UFRGS.

Carraro, Adelaide. 1976. *Escritora Maldita?* São Paulo: L. Oren.

Even-Zohar, Itamar. 1990. "Polysystem Theory." Special Issue, *Polysystem Studies.* Ed. Itamar Even-Zohar. *Poetics Today* 11.1: 9–26.

Hallewell, Laurence. 1985. *O livro no Brasil: Sua história.* São Paulo: T. A. Queiroz, EDUSP.

Hollanda, Heloísa Buarque de, and Marcos Augusto Gonçalves. 1980. "Política e literatura: A ficção da realidade Brasileira." *Anos 70.* Ed. Adauto Novaes. Rio de Janeiro: Europa. 7–81.

Lucas, Fábio. 1994. "A crise da cultura literária no Brasil pós-64." *Brasil: O trânsito da memória.* Ed. Saúl Sosnowski and Jorge Schwartz. São Paulo: EDUSP. 131–40.

Machado, Ana Maria. 1994. "Da Resistência à Transição: A Literatura na Encruzilhada." *Brasil: O trânsito da memória.* Ed. Saúl Sosnowski and Jorge Schwartz. São Paulo: EDUSP. 75–90.

Miceli, Sérgio. 1994. "O papel político dos meios de comunicação de massa." *Brasil: O trânsito da memória.* Ed. Saúl Sosnowski and Jorge Schwartz. São Paulo: EDUSP. 41–68.

Ortiz, Renato. 1991. *A moderna tradição brasileira: Cultura brasileira e indústria cultural.* 3rd ed. São Paulo: Brasiliense.

Pellegrini, Domingos. 1980. "A literatura entre a ficção e a história." *Folhetim–Folha de São Paulo* (January 13): 7.

Reimão, Sandra. 1993. "Brasil, anos 70: Mercado editorial e literatura ficcional brasileira." *Comunicação e Sociedade* 12.20: 73–88.

Santiago, Silviano. 1980. "Uma década de onze anos." *Folhetim–Folha de São Paulo* (January 13): 2.

———. 1982. "Repressão e censura no campo das artes na década de 70." *Vale quanto pesa (Ensaios sobre questões político-culturais).* Rio de Janeiro: Paz e Terra. 47–56.

Silva, Deonísio da. 1989. *Nos bastidores da censura: Sexualidade, literatura e repressão pós-64.* São Paulo: Estação Liberdade.

Sussekind, Flora. 1985. *Literatura e vida literária.* Rio de Janeiro: Jorge Zahar.

CHAPTER 10

STATE SPONSORSHIP AND CONTROL OF PUBLISHING IN BRAZIL

Fábio Lucas

The idea of the sponsorship of the arts and letters in contemporary societies is identified as one of the social functions of government by which the state is responsible for both social well-being and cultural development. Without state intervention, certain artistic and literary manifestations would be unable to survive financially, because market demand has been insufficient either to initiate or to maintain them. Ballet, sculpture, symphony orchestras, theater, (some) film, museums, public archives, opera, and public libraries are often unable to survive on their own. Historically, state sponsorship is a variant of patronage. As we know, Caius Cilnius Maecenas, the friend of Augustus, became celebrated as a patron of letters and literati. A loyal helper of Octavian from 43 B.C. on, he was associated with many poets (among them Virgil, Horace, Propertius, and Varro). Over time, his name has been permanently associated with protective initiatives for the arts and letters. The Latin poet Martial (Marcus Valerius Martialis, 40?–104?) expressed it succinctly: "Well, give me a Maecenas and I'll soon find you a Virgil" (8.56: 249). With the diminishment of feudalism in Europe and the rise of the capitalist system of production, state intervention became necessary to mitigate the rigor of economic laws and to conserve the cultural patrimony (as well as the cultivation of the humanities).

However, under the cover of intellectual direction, sponsorship is frequently censorship in disguise. This is demonstrated not only in the protectionism that favors certain groups over others, but also in the excessive taxation imposed on initiatives not considered valuable by the government in power. Brazil has experienced both direct and indirect censorship, particularly during periods of dictatorship (under Vargas from 1937 to 1945 and under the military from 1964 to 1985). During the first, lengthy period of development as an agricultural economy–extending from the Colonial period to the middle of the twentieth century–cultural sponsorship, granted by the power of the state, was indistinguishable from the concessions granted to the monocultural and latifundiary organization of the Portuguese cultural elite (who were masters of agricultural production). Authoritarian power mixed with the arbitrary granting of favors was the social reality. The state expected legitimation and praise of its power in return for sponsorship. Subordinated to the interests of landed power, writers tended to propagate the dominant ideology of a slave economy. The historical exception to this was the gold and diamond era of Minas Gerais–industrial in nature and urban in concentration–which produced an urban middle class with a certain degree of social mobility, as well as intellectual independence and aspirations for political and social freedom. Even so, the most dynamic group, that of the Minas Gerais Arcadians, only became known thanks to the protection of the Marquis of Pombal. Thus the group's characteristic style (known as "Pombaline") was permeated by the political substrata of the Enlightenment favored by Pombal.

A century later, in the midst of the industrial period that followed the Revolution of 1930, patronage of the arts came exclusively from the Vargas dictatorship, which used it to reinforce the nationalist ideology of the government. There is no tradition of private patronage of the arts in Brazilian society. On the contrary, the private sector would appear to hold aesthetic activity in contempt. Cultural sponsorship is scarce even among businesses that exercise activities related to the fields of artistic or literary production. There have been no intensive, lasting initiatives from the private sector toward stimulating the refinement of culture and aesthetic achievement. Brazilian publishing development has taken place through interventionist policies in place since 1930, when the Getúlio Vargas government created an agency to protect the nation's historical and artistic patrimony and, simultaneously, through Decree-Law No. 93 of 21 December 1937, when the Instituto Nacional do Livro (INL) (National Book Institute) was charged with stimulating literary production. Thanks to the activity of the INL, Brazilians were given access to Brazilian and foreign works which, though of core cultural importance, had no economic appeal for the commercial publishing houses. Private sponsorship for book publication has recently experienced a slight turnaround as a result of initiatives such as the co-editions system. Initially adopted by the military dictatorship's Instituto Nacional do Livro in 1970, it was later extended to several other state agencies. From 1971 to 1986 the INL published over two thousand titles under the co-edition system.

Among the cultural and scientific organizations that developed similar editorial procedures are CNPq, Conselho Nacional de Desenvolvimento Científico e Tecnológico, (National Council for Scientific and Technological Development); Unicamp, Universidade Estadual de Campinas, (State University of Campinas); the Fundação Cultural do Estado da Bahia (Cultural Foundation of the State of Bahia); Fapesp, Fundação de Amparo à Pesquisa do Estado de São Paulo, (São Paulo State Foundation for Support of Research), almost always through writing grants; the Escola Federal de Engenharia de Itajubá, Minas Gerais (Federal School of Engineering of Itajubá, Minas Gerais); Eletrobrás; and Edusp, Editora da Universidade de São Paulo, (São Paulo University Press), which initiated the system in 1964. The fact is, however, that political biases have carried significant weight in sponsorship programs. The U.S.-influenced military coup had also hoped to have an impact on public opinion through specific publications in support of U.S. foreign policy. This explains the United States Information Agency's (USIA) part in the installation of Geil's Executive Group, created by the Brazilian executive branch's Decree-Law of 9 June 1959. After it was closed down in March 1971, the Emílio Garrastazu Médici government absorbed it into the INL.

Insofar as books were concerned, the USIA often furnished original texts or at least guided the selection of works and was instrumental in helping obtain translation rights and even in paying North American writers, going so far as to collaborate directly in production costs. In particular, the USIA encouraged the publication of political works that praised the virtues of capitalism and condemned communism. From 1971 to 1976 it co-sponsored 264 editions. Among Brazilian publishers favored were Agir, Artenova, Atlas, Bloch, O Cruzeiro, Cultrix, Expressão e Cultura, Forense, Forum, Freitas Bastos, Fundação Getúlio Vargas, Ibrasa, Lidador, Victor, and Zahar (Hallewell 318).

Stimulus to editorial production is evidently concomitant with the imposition of state censorship. Official didactic book lists were controlled by the Conselho Nacional do Livro Didático (National Council for Educational Books), established by Decree-Law No. 1.006 of 30 December 1938. The military dictatorship later created the Comissão Nacional do Livro Técnico e Didático (Colted) (National Commission for Didactic and Technical Books) through Decree No. 59.355 of 4 October 1966, jointly financed by the Ministry of Education and USAID (the United States Agency for International Development) with the collaboration of the Sindicato Nacional dos Editores de Livros (also known as Snel) (National Book Publishers Union). Intermittent confiscation of literary works took place under both dictatorships as did harassment and threats to authors, publishers, and book distributors. For example, in 1941 all copies (an entire printing) of the Editora Martins edition of Jorge Amado's (1912–2001) *ABC de Castro Alves* were confiscated. After the publisher appealed this decision in court the book was restored to circulation later that year, but not until the publisher agreed that the book would not be reviewed or advertised in any way, including in book shop window displays.

In *Vida de Luis Carlos Prestes, o cavaleiro da esperança* [1942; The Life of Luis Carlos Prestes, the Knight of Hope], Jorge Amado lists the following inventory of so-called communist works by himself, José Lins do Rêgo, and others apprehended and publicly burned in Bahia by order of Colonel Antônio Fernandes Dantas, commander of the 6th Military Region on 19 November 1937, at Editora Baiana, Catilina, and Sousand bookstores. Works by Jorge Amado included "808 copies of *Capitães de Areia* [1937; *Captains of the Sands,* 1988], 223 of *Mar Morto* [1936; *Sea of Death,* 1984], 89 of *Cacau* (1933), 93 of *Suor* [1934; Slums], 214 of *O País do Carnaval* [1934; The Country of Carnival]; and 15 of *Doidinho* [1933; *Doidinho,* 1966], 26 of *Pureza* [1937; *Pureza, a Brazilian Novel,* 1947], 4 of *O Moleque Ricardo* [1935; Little Richard], 14 of *Menino de Engenho* [1932; *Plantation Boy,* 1966] by José Lins do Rêgo (1901–1957); 23 of *Educação para a Democracia* [1936; *Democracy and Its Creative Achievement,* 1965] by Anísio Teixeira (1900–1971), 6 of *Idolos Tombados* [1937; Fallen Idols] by Maia dos Santos, 2 of *Idéias, Homens e Fatos* [1937; Ideas, Men and Facts] also by Maia dos Santos; 25 of *Doutor Geraldo* [1937; Dr. Geraldo], 4 of *O Nacional Socialismo Germano* [German National Socialism] and 1 of *Miséria através a polícia* [Misery by Way of the Police]" (Amado 365).

Following this, the 1964 military coup appointed Flávio Suplicy de Lacerda, dean of the University of Paraná, as Minister of Education. The record shows that in order to uphold morality and *"bons costumes"* (good social customs), this former member of the Nazi-fascist Integralist Party ordered university librarians to tear pages from works by Emile Zola (1840–1902), Benito Pérez Galdós (1843–1920), and Eça de Queirós

(1845–1900) as an anti-obscenity measure. He also ordered the expurgation of works by Graciliano Ramos (1892–1953), Jorge Amado, Guerra Junqueiro (1850–1923), and even a collection of the *Revista Anhembi.* The Garrastazu Médici government's Decree-Law No. 1077 went into effect on 2 February 1970, establishing prepublication censorship of works on themes referring to sex and public immorality. Any publication featuring erotic subject matter, crime, violence, amorous adventures, horror, or spicy humor could only be sold in resistant, opaque wrappers bearing the warning "sale forbidden to minors."

The subsequent government of General Ernesto Geisel had a picturesque censor in Armando Falçao. He applied Decree No. 427 of 1977, which widened the scope of prepublication censorship and extended it to imported publications. According to Laurence Hallewell, "[b]y late 1978 there were some five hundred books banned in Brazil" (365). This was the inspiration for Deonísio da Silva's (b. 1948) *Nos bastidores da censura–sexualidade, literatura e repressão pós-64* [1984; Behind the Censorship Scene–Sexuality, Literature and Repression after 1964], which examines the alleged reasons for censorship of Rubem Fonseca's (b. 1925) work and includes extensive documentation of the official case against his novel *Feliz Ano Novo* [1975; Happy New Year].

Incentives and Censorship: The Current Situation

According to Eduardo Vieira Manso (b. 1931) copyright law differs from personal law and personal property law. It is not, therefore, a sort of property right. It results from the public right to safeguard access to culture and to development, and therefore extends beyond the singular protection of individual rights. Its only basis is original intellectual creation. Patrimonial rights and moral rights are both observed in the exercise of copyright. The first Brazilian copyright law was No. 496 of 1 August 1896, known as the Medeiros de Albuquerque Law in recognition of that author's efforts. The military dictatorship produced the confused, ambiguous, and badly interpreted law No. 5.988 of 12 December 1973, which superseded the Civil Code of 1917 and in turn was replaced by No. 9.610 of 19 February 1998, altering, updating, and consolidating Brazilian legislation on copyright laws. Its content is attuned to the progress of electronic communications and encompasses new conceptual aspects. Passed under pressure from the United States government (President Bill Clinton came to Brazil personally to speed up voting on the new law) and business organizations, it includes some redresses to copyright protection. Artistic and literary organizations succeeded in inhibiting certain items considered harmful to artists and writers in the drafting of the law. The União Brasileira de Escritores (Brazilian Writers Union) was present during the visit made by writers' and artists' organizations to the President of the Senate during the elaboration of the law. On many points, the interests of the culture industry prevailed, establishing a distance between authors and their works based on negotiation of the publishing contract. Beyond this, the publisher's obligation to number editions was eliminated in order to allow for greater author control over the commercialization of the work and to clarify the collection of authorial rights.

At the start of the twenty-first century the Brazilian book industry is alive and well. The 16 November 1996 edition of *Idéias* (*Jornal do Brasil*'s literary supplement) transcribed the results of a British Euromonitors poll appearing in *Publishers Weekly,* according to which the United States reported a world-leading US$25.5 billion in sales, followed by Japan with US$10.5 billion. According to the same source, the highest per capita index belongs to Western Europe (US$64.70 as opposed to US$45.90 for the Americas). Brazil closed out the year as second-largest market in the Americas with US$2.5 billion, followed by Canada with US$1.3 billion. The 7 August 1998 edition of *Folha de São Paulo* published the results of a survey of Brazilian cultural production taken by Fundação João Pinheiro (João Pinheiro Foundation) of Minas Gerais at the Ministry of Culture's request. It showed that in 1997 Brazil spent R$6.5 billion on culture (the equivalent to 1 percent of its gross national product). Data included entertainment services (radio, movie theaters, theaters, and so forth); the record industry; the production of tapes, film, and records; musical equipment; and book publishing. In an attempt to relativize the results contained in the Fundação João Pinheiro survey, *Folha de São Paulo* noted that, together, 1997 grosses for the record industry, the editorial market, and the four principal television networks (Globo, Bandeirantes, SBT, and Record) totaled R$6.3 billion. According to the survey, private sector expenses primarily targeted gains in institutional image (on a scale of 65.04 percent).

The following factors have determined the growth of book production in Brazil: (1) urbanization, resulting from industrial progress beginning with the revolution of 1930, followed by a greater expansion of the school system; (2) the development (and autonomy) of literature for children and adolescents; (3) the expansion of public, school, and university libraries; (4) the modernization of printing equipment through the creation of GEIL (the Grupo Executivo da Indústria do Livro) by the executive branch—a joint venture with the United States Information Agency (USIA) (according to some of the program's critics, its ultimate purpose was the dissemination of works of political content—attacks on communism and academic discussion of underdevelopment; its unintended results were, however, beneficial to the country); (5) the (INL) Instituto Nacional do Livro's (National Book Institute) publication of works of exceptional cultural value (but scant economic interest) through the development of co-editions with the private sector and aiding in the acquisition of works to stock public libraries and those of the primary and secondary school systems (the latter activity was passed on to the (FAE) Fundação de Assistência ao Estudante [Foundation for Student Assistance], currently the largest book purchasing agency in Brazil; the Collor government closed the Instituto Nacional do Livro and replaced it with the Secretaria Nacional do Livro [National Book Office], a division of the Fundação Biblioteca Nacional [National Library Foundation]); (6) the expansion of communication and information media that indirectly contributed to making books more accessible to the public; (7) the creation of the Book Biennials in Rio de Janeiro and São Paulo, as well as the Book Fairs of Porto Alegre, Belo Horizonte, Fortaleza, and other Brazilian cities (in São Paulo, the Bienal do Livro [Book Biennial] attendance has numbered upward of one million visitors).

Translation by Stephen A. Berg

Works Cited

Amado, Jorge. 1945 [1942]. *Vida de Luis Carlos Prestes, o cavaleiro da esperança.* São Paulo: Livraria Martins Editora.

Hallewell, Laurence. 1982. *Books in Brazil: A History of the Publishing Trade.* Lanham, MD: Scarecrow Press.

Martial, Marcus Valerius. 1924. *The Twelve Books of Epigrams.* Trans. J. A. Pott and F. A. Wright. Ed. F. A. Wright. London: Routledge.

Silva, Deonísio da. 1984. *Nos bastidores da censura—Sexualidade, literatura e repressão pós-64.* São Paulo: Estação Liberdade.

CHAPTER 11

CULTURAL JOURNALISM IN SPANISH AMERICA

AN OVERVIEW

Aníbal González-Pérez

A brief overview such as this one cannot hope to do justice to the variety and abundance of Spanish American cultural journalism. However, even lengthier historical accounts of this subject often degenerate because of the sheer number of texts spanning four centuries and nineteen national literary traditions into mere country-by-country listings of periodicals and their dates of publication or into a kind of schematic political history of the continent (e.g., "with the rise in Colombia of the liberal government of X, new journals and newspapers began to appear"). In either case, a broader perspective on the content and meaning of journalism in Spanish America is lost. To avoid some of these pitfalls, I will offer instead some general comments regarding the development of cultural journalism in Spanish America and will list only a few selected publications of source material.

The origin of cultural journalism as such in Spanish America dates back only to *modernismo* and the turn of the nineteenth century, and its flowering is a twentieth-century phenomenon. Before then, the borderlines between the discourses of journalism, literature, politics, economics, history, and the natural sciences, among others, were too fluid to allow such specific classifications. Indeed, Spanish American journalism from the Colonial period through the first half of the nineteenth century was divided into two broad currents: the economic or mercantile and the political. Periodicals of the former type were produced by and for merchants and entrepreneurs. Meant to be read in the quiet of the study, or at most over the table at a coffee house, these contained notices on the departure and arrival of ships and their type of cargo, plus essays (on political economy, medicine, and natural history), letters to the editor, occasional works of poetry, government proclamations (newspapers of this sort tended to be officious), and very brief bulletins on newsworthy events from around the globe. The very first daily newspapers in Spanish America, the *Diario Erudito, Económico y Comercial* (published in Lima [1790–1793]), and the *Diario de México* (1805–1814), belong to this category, as do the earlier weekly or quarterly journals such as the *Gaceta de México* (1728–38) and *Gacetas de Literatura de México* (1788–1795), the *Mercurio Peruano* (1791–1795), and the *Papel Periódico de La Habana* (1790–1804).

The term *literature* was used rather loosely in those days, and much of what was published under that heading in, for example, the *Gacetas de Literatura de México*, was actually information pertaining to natural history, agriculture, economy, and antiquities (such as the Mexican ruins of Xochicalco). The *Diario de México*, however, did print poetry, essays on manners, and theater reviews. The latter commented more on the performance than on the texts, but they did provide a glimpse into what was at times a fairly active artistic milieu. Much of the poetry published in the *Diario de México* was produced by members of the "Arcadia de México," one of the various "poetic academies" that arose in Spanish America toward the mid-1700s in imitation of similar European institutions. In Spanish America these academies served not only to establish standards of poetic taste, but also to disseminate Enlightenment ideas and to foment patriotic feelings (such was the case with the *Sociedad Patriótica y Literaria* in Buenos Aires and the *Tertulia Eutrapélica* in Bogotá).

The "political" dailies, weeklies, pamphlets, and gazettes that also proliferated during the latter years of the Colonial period and the turbulent decades of Independence were no less varied in content than the mercantile publications. Although they specialized in the rowdiest forms of political polemic and commentary, often the form that commentary took would be considered "literary" by today's standards. Suffice it to recall that it was precisely journalism of this sort that José Joaquín Fernández de Lizardi (1776–1827), the author of *El Periquillo Sarniento* [1816; *The Itching Parrot*, 1942], practiced in Mexico in the early nineteenth century. With brazenly partisan and polemic titles such as *El Patriota, El Constitucional, El Fénix de la Libertad, El Amigo del País,* and *El Conductor Eléctrico,* many of these journals and gazettes were addressed to a broader public and therefore made use of a plainer language that was more open to Spanish American idioms. Many of their articles show the stylistic influence of oratory and drama (in their use of the dialogue form) and were clearly meant to be read aloud to the illiterate masses that gathered in taverns and public squares.

The scant literary criticism that appears in early Spanish American periodicals is usually in the letters addressed to the editor by some of the readers. In these, comments on the poetry published in previous issues or discussion on matters of literary taste can be found. These comments are generally prescriptive and attempt to follow the dictates of neo-Classical poetics, such as those of Nicholas Boileau or Ignacio de Luzán. Propriety, idealization, reasonableness, conformity to rules, and avoidance of Latinisms or obscure words–indeed, an overt anti-Gongorism–are the literary values stressed in this criticism. Occasionally there are expressions of an incipient literary regionalism, as when Manuel del Socorro Rodríguez (1758–1818), in the *Semanario de Nueva Granada*, defends the poetry written in the viceroyalty of New Granada from charges that it is inferior to that written in Mexico or Peru.

The style and content of the late colonial journals and dailies generally reflected the lofty ideals and educational propensities of the European Enlightenment. Although much of this late eighteenth-century Spanish American literary production appears today excessively pedantic, constrained, and conservative, it was perceived quite differently at the time. Instead, it was seen as part of a broad movement of sociopolitical and cultural renewal launched by the French-inspired reformism of the Spanish monarch Charles III. Many of the stuffy neo-Classical versifiers and critics who published in the *Diario de México* or the *Papel Periódico de La Habana* were young men, members of the *criollo* elite, who shared a growing cosmopolitan attitude and a hunger for new ideas. This same modernizing spirit continued in the early Romantic dailies and journals of the 1820s and 1930s. Again, despite their designation at the time as literary publications, these were hetereogeneous in content. Erudite journals such as Andrés Bello's (1781–1865) *Biblioteca Americana* (1823) and *Repertorio Americano* (1826–1827), which were published in England, as well as more general-interest magazines such as *El Iris* (1826), founded by José María Heredia y Heredia (1803–1839) in Mexico, offered their readers not only literary works (poems, essays on manners, critical essays), but also notes on fashion, natural history, and political commentary. To avoid government censorship, the latter was often done under the guise of literary criticism, a tradition that has continued in Spanish America to this day. For example, the notorious controversy between the liberal Domingo Faustino Sarmiento (1811–1888) and the more conservative Andrés Bello in Chile in 1842 took place as a debate about Romanticism and linguistic usage in the pages of the daily *El Mercurio*.

Nation building was of course a concern for most of the Spanish American literati of the mid-nineteenth century. While journalism's role in this process is rarely as central as theorists such as Benedict Anderson contend (history abounds in examples of nations constituted without the aid of print media), Spanish American writers and intellectuals did make enthusiastic use of periodical publications to disseminate their ideas about how the newly founded nations should be constituted. For example, the Mexican journal *El Renacimiento* (1869), founded by Ignacio Manuel Altamirano (1834–1893), was explicitly designed to encourage a new burst of intellectual activity in that country after its victorious struggle against French domination. Even in Cuba, which remained a Spanish colony through all of the nineteenth century, journals with a highly patriotic as well as literary content were founded, such as the *Revista Bimestre Cubana* (1831–1835), which was modeled on the *Edinburgh Review*. Costumbrismo, the Romantics' version of the eighteenth-century essay on manners, was one of the staples of literary journalism in Spanish America during much of the nineteenth century. Essays on manners modeled after those of the Spaniards Mariano José de Larra (1809–1837) and Ramón de Mesonero

Romanos (1803–1882) proliferated in Spanish American journals and dailies, with their sometimes nostalgic, sometimes satirical evocations of local customs and institutions. In Peru, *La Revista de Lima* (1859–1863) featured some of Ricardo Palma's (1833–1919) early *tradiciones* [traditions]. Satirical journals and newspapers with earthy-sounding titles such as *La Chinaca* (1862) and *La Cuchara* (1862–1863) in Mexico or, in Peru, *El Diablo* (1848), *El Burro* (1852), *La Zamacueca Política* (1859), and *La Broma* (1877, founded by Ricardo Palma), which were direct descendants of the political gazettes of the Independence period, also served as outlets for *costumbrismo* and its collection of "national types": the Argentinean *gauchos*, the Chilean *huasos*, the Mexican *charros* and *chinas*, and the Peruvian *cholos*.

As the nineteenth century continued, with the arrival of technological improvements such as the steam-powered press and the telegraph and commercial innovations such as the penny newspaper, which increased journalism's audience enormously, the major Spanish American newspapers such as Chile's *El Mercurio* (founded 1827), Lima's *El Comercio* (founded 1839), and Argentina's *La Nación* (founded 1870) not only grew in influence and power, but also became more specialized. By the latter third of the nineteenth century (from the 1870s through the 1890s), Spanish American journalism, like its English, French, and North American counterparts, had become a mass phenomenon and a purely money-making enterprise. The telegraph allowed newspapers to increase their coverage of newsworthy events not only at the local but at the national and international levels, and the institution of the reporter came into existence. As a result, the material in the newspapers and journals was segregated according to its subject matter: Journalism of opinion was confined to what today are called op-ed pages, and the front page was taken over by the short news bulletin transmitted via telegraph from the scenes of events. This naturally led to the abandonment of the more literary or oratorical model of journalistic style favored in the nineteenth century and to the rise of a more condensed telegraphic style. Moreover, the explicitly cultural and literary content of the newspapers was concentrated in specific and clearly identified cultural sections. No longer were the *folletines*, or serial novels, placed in a strip at the bottom of the front page, as had been the case earlier in the nineteenth century; but now, when there were serial novels at all, these were placed in a literary page, where they vied for space with the increasingly popular genre of the short story and newly created genres such as the *crónica*. Poetry continued to be a staple of these sections, but it too was more restricted in space.

The need for autonomous and more specialized cultural journals grew evident as the daily newspapers in Spanish America gave less room in their pages to literary and cultural subjects. The 1880s saw the founding throughout the continent, first under the aegis of Positivist philosophy and later of *modernismo*, of a series of journals whose sometimes austere titles gave notice of their explicitly cultural purpose: among others, the *Revista Venezolana* (1881), founded by the *modernista* José Martí (1853–1895); the *Revista de Artes y Letras* (1884–1890) of Chile, where the *modernista* Rubén Darío (1867–1916) was a collaborator; the *Revista Nacional de Letras y Ciencias* (1889–1890) of Mexico, directed by the Positivist historian Justo Sierra (1848–1912) and the *modernista* poet Manuel Gutiérrez Nájera (1859–1895); and *El Peru Ilustrado* (1887–1897) of Peru, directed after 1889 by the novelist and precursor of *indigenismo* (Indigenism), Clorinda Matto de Turner (1852–1909). However, as noted earlier, the first great age of cultural journalism in Spanish America owes its existence primarily to the *modernistas*, who founded, directed, and collaborated in a series of journals characterized by their strict devotion to literature and the arts coupled with a wide-ranging cosmopolitan spirit (indeed, one of the salient *modernista* journals in Venezuela bore the title of *Cosmópolis*, 1894–1895). Among the chief precursors of this trend was *La Habana Elegante* (1883–1896), in which the *modernista* Julián del Casal (1863–1893) published much of his work. As might be expected, the list of *modernista* journals is extensive. In consonance with that literary movement's more urban emphasis, these journals were usually founded in their countries' capital cities, and at the turn of the nineteenth century there were *modernista* journals in all of the major capitals of Spanish America: the *Revista Gris* (1892–1896) in Bogota, the *Revista de América* (1894) and *La Biblioteca* (1896–1898) in Buenos Aires, *El Cojo Ilustrado* (1892–1915) in Caracas, the *Revista Azul* (1894–1896) and *Revista Moderna* (1898–1911) in Mexico City, and the *Revista Nacional de Literatura y Ciencias Sociales* (1895–1897) in Montevideo.

Freed from the urgency of nation building, these cultural journals were devoted to defending, to varying degrees, the dignity and autonomy of art vis-à-vis politics and science. This attitude was frequently misunderstood as pure aestheticism or art for art's sake, but it in fact simply reflected the *modernistas*' desire to systematize their knowledge about art and literature and raise the contemporary standard of taste. The *modernistas* were less interested in "building" countries than in "building" Literature (with a capital *L*). The exception that proves the rule is, of course, Martí, but even he understood the hierarchical difference between the political and the literary spheres, as the following, oft-quoted passage from his notebooks attests: "No hay letras, que son expresión, hasta que no hay esencia que expresar en ellas. Ni habrá literatura hispanoamericana, hasta que no haya Hispanoamérica" (21:164) ("There is no writing, which is a form of expression, until there is an essence to be expressed by it. Nor will there be Spanish American literature until there is Spanish America"). Martí's words also prefigure the *modernistas*' main contribution, after the crisis of 1898, to the ideological background of Spanish American literature: the search for a compact, clear-cut concept of Spanish American culture (an "essence," in Martí's terms) from which Spanish American writing springs and through which Spanish American writing ensures its uniqueness and originality. The *modernistas* saw culture as artifice, as a product of conscious human endeavor. Unlike the Romantics, the *modernistas* did not view national culture as a process of spontaneous, natural generation from obscure, folkloric roots. Without forsaking altogether the organic metaphors of Romantic philology, the *modernistas*, like their French Symbolist and decadent counterparts, regarded national culture (including literature and the arts) as highly refined end-products of a laborious and deliberate historical process. This idea of culture is best summarized by a quotation from a speech by Ernest Renan found in one of Martí's "Escenas europeas" (1884): "No es la historia humana un capítulo de Zoología. El hombre es ser racional y ser moral. La libre voluntad está por encima de las sugestiones ruines del espíritu de raza. Una nación es un alma, un principio espiritual, elaborada de lo pasado, con vida en lo presente, y toda gran junta de hombres con mentes saludables y corazones generosos puede crear la conciencia moral que constituye una nación" (14:449–50) ("Human history is not a chapter in Zoology. Man is a rational and moral being. Free will stands above the base influence of the *Volksgeist*. A nation is a soul, a spiritual principle created out of the past, with its life in the present, and any great assemblage of men of sound minds and generous hearts can create the moral consciousness that constitutes a nation"). Although the *modernistas* tended to focus on what would later be termed *high culture* in their journals, their emphasis on the importance of culture would lead in time to broader, more inclusive notions of that concept.

The prestige of the *modernista* journals, along with their cosmpolitanism, paved the way for the subsequent flowering of powerful and highly influential cultural journals in Spanish America from the 1920s through the 1960s. Indeed, the *modernista* journals were the immediate precursors of the explosion of Spanish American avant-garde journals in the first two decades of the twentieth century. Most of these journals, which often bore geometric-sounding one-word names such as *Prisma* (Argentina, 1921–1922), *Elipse* (Chile, 1922), *Irradiador* (Mexico, 1923), and *Vórtice* (Puerto Rico, 1922), were ephemeral, lasting only as long as the short-lived literary movements whose manifestos they carried. However, as their numbers grew, the roll call of Spanish American cultural journals began to include longer-lasting publications of international importance, many of which became cultural monuments in their own right. Leaving aside distinguished academic journals such as *Revista de Filología Hispánica* (1939–1946) and *Nueva Revista de Filología Hispánica* (founded 1947), which, because of their specialized nature, fall outside the scope of this essay, these publications are *Amauta* (Peru, 1926–1930), *Revista de Avance* (Cuba, 1927–1930), *Contemporáneos* (México, 1928–1931), *Sur* (Argentina, 1931–1970), *Marcha* (Uruguay, 1939–1974), *Orígenes* (Cuba, 1944–1956), *Asomante* (Puerto Rico, 1945–1970), *Cuadernos Americanos* (Mexico City, founded 1941), *Casa de las Américas* (Cuba, founded 1960), *Mundo Nuevo* (Paris, 1966–1968), and *Vuelta* (Mexico City, 1976–1999).

Amauta and *Revista de Avance* shared a more broadly cultural and openly political approach than the other avant-garde journals. Founded and directed by the Marxist José Carlos Mariátegui (1894–1930), *Amauta* affirmed the intrinsic value of the art and culture of Peru's Indians, while the *Revista de Avance*, which had among its founders Alejo Carpentier (1904–1980), Jorge Mañach (1898–1961), and Juan Marinello (1898–1977), espoused a similar neoprimitivist and authochtonous stance with regard to Afro-Cuban art and music. *Contemporáneos*, on the other hand, although deeply concerned about Mexican and Latin American issues, displayed a less stridently nationalistic tone than was typical of Mexico's intellectual and political life at the time. Like *Amauta* and the *Revista de Avance*, however, the roster of writers who collaborated in *Contemporáneos* reads like a "who's who" of Mexican letters of the 1930s: Jorge Cuesta (1903–1942), José Gorostiza (1901–1973), Salvador Novo (1904–1974), Carlos Pellicer (1899–1977), Xavier Villaurrutia (1903–1950), and many others.

The journals *Sur*, *Orígenes*, and *Asomante* had in common not only their longevity, but also their cosmopolitan refinement, elitism, and a generally critical and skeptical attitude toward politics. Modeled to a large extent on the Spaniard José Ortega y Gasset's (1883–1955) highly influential *Revista de Occidente* (1923–1936), these journals revolved around the wide-ranging and polyglot literary tastes of their founders and directors. While Victoria Ocampo (1890–1979) in *Sur* and Nilita Vientós Gastón (1903–1989) in *Asomante* were content to set a general tone of intellectual refinement, José Lezama Lima (1910–1976), with his daunting neo-Baroque poetry and poetics, exerted a stronger influence on *Orígenes* and its collaborators. Events such as the Spanish Civil War and World War II, which led many intellectuals from Spain and the rest of Europe to go into exile in the Americas, as well as these journals' own open and eclectic attitude, contributed to their international dissemination. Along with Argentinean, Cuban, and Puerto Rican writers, they also featured in their pages collaborations by writers from Spain such as Ortega y Gasset, Jorge Guillén, Pedro Salinas, and Juan Ramón Jiménez, as well as U.S. and European literary figures such as T.S. Eliot, William Faulkner, André Gide, Count Keyserling, André Malraux, and Wallace Stevens, among many others. It should be stressed that although literature (in the form of short fiction and poetry) was always prominent in these periodicals, their culturalist approach also led them to publish essays in fields such as anthropology, history, philosophy, the visual arts, and music.

In contrast to the conservative political bent of *Sur, Orígenes,* and *Asomante,* the journals *Marcha, Cuadernos Americanos,* and *Casa de las Américas* were decidedly left-wing in their orientation. Their respective styles and formats were quite different, however: *Cuadernos Americanos,* founded by Jesús Silva Herzog, followed a *Revista de Occidente*-like format in which articles in sociology, economics, politics, and history were often more prominent than works of poetry, fiction, or literary criticism. *Marcha,* on the other hand, was a weekly newspaper devoted mainly to political and social commentary, but it featured a literary section that was at various times directed by important writers such as the novelist Juan Carlos Onetti (1909–1994) and the literary critic Angel Rama. The newspaper *Marcha* itself was directed from 1943 to 1960 by another major literary critic, Emir Rodríguez Monegal. Both *Cuadernos Americanos* and *Marcha* were independent leftist publications, and their coverage of artistic and literary subjects was cosmopolitan and interdisciplinary, linking literary criticism with art and film criticism, as well as politics and sociology. By contrast, *Casa de las Américas* was from its inception linked to the cultural institution of the same name, which was directly sponsored by the Cuban Revolutionary government. Eclectic in its political and artistic content during the 1960s, *Casa* became more politically rigid during the 1970s and 1980s, as ideological controversies erupted over the Cuban Revolution and some of the Spanish American writers who had supported it through their contributions in the journal and their participation in the conferences, panels, and literary contests organized by the Casa de las Américas.

Marcha and *Casa de las Américas* were active in the promotion and support of the Spanish American narrative "boom" of the 1960s in its early stages, but it is the journal *Mundo Nuevo,* founded and directed in Paris by Emir Rodríguez Monegal, that remains indelibly associated with that literary phenomenon. Although the "boom" was not a movement in the same sense as *modernismo, Mundo Nuevo* helped to focus attention on the explosion of literary creativity in Spanish America during the 1960s and 1970s, particularly in the field of narrative. *Mundo Nuevo*'s approach to Spanish American literature tended to avoid nationalism or regionalism, emphasizing instead the quality of the literary production. Its articles

on literary criticism, for example, evaluated Spanish American works without apology or condescension with the same rigor and erudition usually applied to European literature. At the same time, *Mundo Nuevo* showcased the short fiction, novel excerpts, and interviews of most of the best writers of the "boom" and their precursors: from Borges (1899–1986) and Lezama Lima through Carlos Fuentes (b. 1928) and Gabriel García Márquez (b. 1927) to Manuel Puig (1932–1990) and Severo Sarduy (1937–1993). The fiery political and aesthetic conflicts of the decade also engulfed *Mundo Nuevo* when the journal and its founder were unfairly accused in 1966 by writers from *Marcha* and *Casa de las Américas* of being instruments of the Central Intelligence Agency. In retrospect, *Mundo Nuevo,* like the *modernista* and avant-garde literary reviews of the 1920s and 1930s, was perhaps too closely intertwined with the literary phenomenon it promoted. As the "boom" narrative began to evolve and the sense of cohesion and solidarity among its writers disappeared, Rodríguez Monegal's mercurial interests changed and the journal lost its reason for being.

The Mexican journal *Vuelta* was conceived as a longer-lasting venture. Although its layout was similar to that of a popular magazine, *Vuelta* was in the tradition of the general cultural journals that followed the *Revista de Occidente* model. Its tone was nonacademic, addressed to a readership assumed to be made up of highly cultivated nonspecialists. It featured a mixture of essays on political, historical, and philosophical subjects not circumscribed by Mexico or Latin America, along with cultural notes and comments, book reviews, poetry selections and, very rarely, short fiction. From its inception, like so many other Spanish American cultural journals, *Vuelta* strongly reflected the political and aesthetic views of its founder, Nobel Prize winner Octavio Paz (1914–1998), particularly his commitment to a cosmopolitan outlook, intellectual freedom, and anti-authoritarianism. Not unexpectedly, *Vuelta* did not survive very long after the death of Paz. Controversies among Paz's collaborators led to the journal's closing in 1999.

At its best, Spanish American cultural journalism has been both a creative and enlivening force and a witness to the vitality of the region's cultural production. Among its shortcomings have been a lack of sustained effort along with an excessive personalism and idiosyncrasy. Few Spanish American cultural journals have survived the departure or the demise of their founders. One misses in the Spanish American milieu the more durable and institutionalized types of cultural journals one finds in other parts of the world: There are no Spanish-American analogues to *The New Yorker* or, on another level, *Les temps modernes.* Undoubtedly, Spanish American cultural journalism, like all journalism in the region, has all too often had to contend with censorship and repression, and this helps to account for its frequently ephemeral nature. An additional issue is the steadily diminishing cultural coverage in Spanish American daily newspapers through the last four decades. Their "literary pages," which once featured poetry, essays, short fiction, and serialized novels, have been mostly given over to book reviews. At most, newspaper readers encounter occasional *crónicas* (chronicles) by a few major national and international Spanish American writers—as in the "Grandes Firmas" series distributed by the Spanish press agency EFE in the 1980s—but these texts are often inconsequential. Given the region's turbulent history, the wonder is that Spanish American writers and intellectuals have been so persistent, inventive, and fecund in the pursuit of cultural journalism. With the recent advent of the Internet a whole new wave (and a new modality) of cultural journals in Spanish America has begun to emerge, with titles such as *Cyberayllu*, *El Cuarto del Quenepón*, *Internauta Poesía*, *La Habana Elegante (Segunda Epoca)*, and *Revista Electrónica de Literatura Mexicana*. It is still far too early, however, to predict what final shape, if any, they will take.

(In pursuance of the general principle behind this comparative history of literary cultures–to facilitate the interested reader's investigative trajectory through the enormity of the archive–Aníbal González-Pérez has listed the most important contemporary sources of primary material rather than the primary matter itself. The reader might also want to consult the related text by Juan Poblete in Chapter 20 of Volume I and the texts in this volume by Luiz Roberto Velloso Cairo [Chapter 12], Ivia Alves [Chapter 14], Maria Lucia de Barrios Camargo [Chapter 16], and especially the text by Luz Rodríguez-Carranza [Chapter 15].)

Works Cited

González, Aníbal. 1993. *Journalism and the Development of Spanish American Narrative.* Cambridge: Cambridge University Press.

Martí, José. 1964. *Obras completas.* Vols. 14 and 21. Havana: Editorial Nacional de Cuba.

CRITICISM AND LITERATURE IN BRAZILIAN PERIODICALS OF THE ROMANTIC PERIOD

Luiz Roberto Cairo

Before the arrival of the Portuguese royal family in Brazil in 1808, Lisbon controlled all cultural venues. There was no "tipografia nem livraria e qualquer espécie de papel impresso só podia vir de Portugal, depois de passar pelo crivo da censura" (Brito Broca 42) ("printing-press or bookshops and any kind of printed material could only come from Portugal, after passing through the sieve of censorship"). The Brazilians read only what the Portuguese government allowed them to read or what they could acquire by illegal means. Thus the cultured colonials clandestinely read the works of Voltaire, Rousseau, and the French encyclopedists. Every attempt to establish a press in Brazil until that time had been unsuccessful. Only by a decree on 13 May 1808, the date of King Dom João VI's birthday, the press finally came into existence, with its origin and development being much more literary than journalistic. This literary influence is explained by the fact that the Brazilian press, from the beginning, was in the hands of a lettered elite who gave Brazilian journalism a literary flavor, and in time, both their literature and literary criticism incorporated journalistic features. In counter-distinction to other Latin American countries, where literature was influenced by journalism from the start, in Brazil, literature preceded journalism by several centuries, but it began asserting its autonomy from Portugal simultaneously with the beginning of journalistic activity (i.e., with the introduction of printing in 1808). This meant that a symbiosis existed between the two kinds of writing by the same people who, as writers, published their literary works—poems, chronicles, novellas, serial novels, stories, and essays—in newspapers. As journalists, their news reports were written in a highly lyrical style. Since the choice of the subject and emphasis in journalistic discourse is directly connected to the public's expectations, and since everything depends on its interest, acceptance, and understanding (because of the link that exists between transmitter and receiver), a fact that in the end determines journalism's informative, objective, and easily assimilated character, the literary discourse of Brazilian writers was also mixed up with these didactic objectives. Their objective included both the easy understanding of the message and the satisfaction of the emerging reading public's taste for elegant language.

Thus journalism and Brazilian literature (as distinct from colonial Portuguese literature) developed side by side, resulting in the mainly informative and markedly superficial character of the literary criticism produced in Brazil until at least the end of the 1920s, as João Luiz Lafetá (b. 1946) notes in his analysis of the critical works of Agripino Grieco (1888–1968), whose critical discourse is a good example of this literary-journalistic symbiosis:

> Sua palavra fácil, seu estilo eloqüente, a presença constante do humor, facilitariam a adaptação a um métier, que hoje designaríamos pelo nome de colunismo, jornalismo, noticiário literário ou mesmo crônica literária, mas nunca de crítica. De fato, se havia àquela época (refiro-me à década de 20), entre a maioria dos escritores que comentavam os livros surgidos, qualquer intenção de crítica, esta ficava apenas na intenção. (31)

His easy language, his eloquent style, and the constant good humor facilitated the adaptation to a *métier* which today we would call column-writing journalism, literary news, or even literary chronicle, but never literary criticism. In fact, if there was at that time (I refer to the 1920s) any intention of criticism among most of the writers who commented on the new books, it was merely an intention.

All things taken into consideration, one may say that Lafetá's comment on the critic from Rio de Janeiro applied as well to all nineteenth-century Brazilian literary critics. This notable feature of the criticism of the 1920s is, in fact, an inheritance from nineteenth-century Brazilian criticism: Literary criticism was meant to "informar ao público de que tratava o livro" (Lafetá 31) ("inform the public what the book was about"), through a summary of the plot and a biography of the author. An analysis of the text or the author's ideas did not usually occur. Thus it is that the informative character of journalistic discourse transformed literary criticism into book news, which generally consisted of a paraphrase of the featured work. It was what Lafetá quite appropriately called *book news/criticism*, which sometimes meant no more than digressions on any subject at all. At the same time, there existed another form of criticism, namely the essay, in which the critic was more interested in his own writing itself than in writing about any particular work, and the result was simply a display of style and personality. While this mode of criticism was transformed into literature, these features, sometimes so strong that they seem to dissociate the writer from his role as a literary critic, at least in the nineteenth and first decade of the twentieth century, did not in any way invalidate the intellectual aim of this writing.

Until the eighteenth century, there was almost no reading public for Brazilian literature. What Brazilian writers produced was a literature aimed at Portuguese readers and, in some few cases, we can find rare manifestations of a literature aimed at a home audience. In discussing these examples of Brazilian literature, the critic Antonio Cândido explains that the existence of a literature presupposes one pole that produces, another that receives, and a means of transmission, and that this did not exist in Brazil until the end of the eighteenth century (see Cândido 1971). A conscious concern for a literature directed to the Brazilian public would develop only after political independence, when the Brazilian people effectively emerged as a people. Before this, only isolated works had such a concern, but they were not "um sistema vivo de obras agindo umas sobre as outras e sobre os leitores" (Cândido 1973, 74) ("a living system of works acting on each other and on readers"). With national independence in the nineteenth century, an incipient public for Brazilian literature began to appear. Writers had as their mission the implementing of the circulation of literary works written in Brazil so as to form what could later become Brazilian literature. For this purpose they made use of any means that aroused an interest in reading, which was not an easy task, as Luiz Costa Lima brilliantly argued in his discussion of the intellectual system in Brazil:

Assim, embora o romantismo já tivesse tipografias à sua disposição, a literatura continuava fundamentalmente cúmplice da oralidade. E a maneira de converter a página escrita em forma oral consistia em oferecer uma leitura fácil, fluente, embalada pela ritmicidade dos versos iguais (Gonçalves Dias) e pela prosa digestiva, de tema nativista e/ou sentimental. É bastante sugestiva, para entendermos a imagem do leitor pela qual se guiava o romancista, a maneira como Alencar imagina o seu: '. . . embalando-se na macia e cômoda rede', na 'hora mais ardente da sesta', folheando as páginas de seu escrito, 'para desenfastiar o espíritu das cousas graves que o trazem ocupado' ('Prólogo' de *Iracema*). Quando o tema não favorece tal relaxamento, o escritor há de se esforçar em não cansar seu leitor, pois doutro modo as revistas e jornais da família, consumidas pelo público femenino e pelos jovens ainda não iniciados, não se interessariam por suas crônicas e folhetins. (7)

Thus, although by the high point of Romanticism, writers already had printing-presses at their disposal, literature basically continued to be disseminated through orality. And the manner of converting the written page into oral form consisted of offering an easy, fluent reading style swayed by the rhythmic quality of equal verses (Gonçalves Dias) or the easily assimilated stories of nativist and/or sentimental themes. The way Alencar imagined his reader is rather suggestive, if we are to understand that this is the image of the reader by which the novelist was guided: ". . . swaying in the soft, comfortable hammock, in the hottest hour of the siesta, turning over the pages of the text, to relieve the spirit from serious things that worry him" (Prologue of *Iracema*). When the theme does not favor such relaxation, the writer must make an effort not to tire his reader, for otherwise the family magazines and newspapers, consumed by the newly constituted feminine public and by the still uninitiated young, would not be interested in his chronicles and *feuilleton* novels.

This situation lasted for a long time. Not only José de Alencar (1829–1877), but also Joaquim Machado de Assis (1839–1908) had to contend with this reading public, as can be seen by the way the author addresses his readers.

If the author of fictional works had to make use of such resources, there fell to the literary critic, the commentator on these works, an even more difficult task: the formation of two types of public, namely the first reader of fictional works and the experienced reader of criticism. Thus the critic's discourse had to awaken an interest in reading the works to be analyzed and motivate the discussion, analysis, and evaluation of the works that were, and would hopefully be, read. For this reason he made use of forms such as the newspaper column and the *crônico* (chronicle). The news aspect of criticism was therefore as important as the analytic, insofar as it informed the public and aroused the curiosity that would lead to the reading of the work. If this did not happen, the work in question was not heard of again. The chronicle aspect flourished naturally in the discourse of nineteenth-century Brazilian criticism in the *bacharelesca* (law school) eloquence that constituted another characteristic feature of the style of this period's generation of critics. It is difficult to escape this kind of rhetoric, since intellectual life in Brazil was centered on the law schools, which imparted a particular florid eloquence to its

students. The journalists of the time were writers, but most of them had law degrees. In the chronicle, the norm was to write a text that was easy to read, with moving words and *bacharelesca* eloquence (introduced into Brazil by the Jesuits) intended to emotionally move the mass public. The chronicle thrived in nineteenth-century Brazil, and through it, it was possible to introduce serious problems to the reader in a seductive, easily assimilated language—and this was indeed one of the objectives of literary criticism addressed to a public still in process of formation.

One of the most significant cultural traits of the Brazilian intellectual system was orality. Luis Costa Lima referred to it as *auditividade* (auditive quality), to avoid any possible confusion with the oral culture tradition:

Ao contrário, em sua versão romântica e moderna, o estilo auditivo é sedutor, não por horrorizar, por inspirar gestos de pesado arrependimento, que levariam a ser imediatamente engrossadas as filas dos confesssionários, mas por seu tom a cariciante, de conversa à beira da rede ou ao pé do fogo, de conversa despreocupada. A crônica, tão bem aclimatada ao Brasil, é o seu gênero por excelência. A cultura auditiva é portanto fundamentalmente uma cultura que se transmite sem cadeias demonstrativas. (16-17)

On the contrary, in its Romantic and Modern versions, the auditive style is seductive, not because it terrifies or inspires acts of great regret, which would lead to the long lines at the confessional, but for its soothing tone, that of a conversation beside the hammock or the stove, a casual conversation. The chronicle, so well adapted to Brazil, is its genre *par excellence*. The audible culture is therefore fundamentally one that is transmitted without demonstrative links.

Today, it seems odd that a critical discourse often privileged book news and journalistic aspects at the expense of the analysis of the work, but one should not forget that the concern for the work in itself and literariness is to a certain extent a recent twentieth-century concern. Criticism of that time was interested in the personality of the author of the work and the society that produced and consumed it.

Afrânio Coutinho has made an observation that is an important reminder for any scholar of nineteenth-century Brazilian criticism: "Na constituição desse sistema entravam elementos oriundos das ciências, o que era a norma na sua época, mormente das ciências naturais, biológicas e sociais. Eram critérios, portando, de cunho e orígem extraliterária. A compreensão de que aos fatos literários há que julgar com critérios literários, é noção que se esperaria ainda algum tempo para admitir" (1981, 155) ("This system was comprised of elements originating in the sciences, what at the time was the norm, the natural, biological, and social sciences. Therefore criteria were of an extra-literary nature and origin. The understanding that literary facts have to be judged according to literary criteria is a notion that would only be grasped later"). If such was the discourse of nineteenth-century criticism, from the thematic viewpoint what one notes is a discourse directed toward the construction of nationalism. Because of this concern about creating a national literature, writers, critics, and journalists published their texts mainly in periodicals and, occasionally, later in books.

A brief retrospective of cultural periodicals in Brazil in the Romantic period must begin with the first Brazilian journal known—a literary one, published in 1812, in Bahia. It was called *Variedades ou Ensaios de Literatura* and had a short existence and very little impact (Moisés and Paes 359). Later, faculty and students of the São Paulo Academy of Law, members of the Sociedade Filomática (Philomatic Society), published the *Revista de Sociedade Filomática* from June through December 1833. Printed by the Novo Farol Paulistano press, this periodical commanded a mostly regional circulation for its six issues. It hoped to participate in the development of the basic principles of Brazilian literature; it was dedicated to finding what was then called the Brazilian national character and thus establishing Brazilian letters at the same level as the European literatures, both ancient and modern (see Amora). Its editors were Francisco Bernardino Ribeiro, J. I. Silveira da Mota, C. Carneiro Campos, Antonio Augusto de Queiroga, and Justiniano José da Rocha (1812–1862). The latter was the only one later to become well known as a journalist and writer of fiction.

In 1836, *Niterói, Revista Brasiliense* was published; this was the first periodical of importance that introduced Romantic ideas into Brazil, setting in motion the process of creating Brazilian literary nationalism. Even without listing the names of directors or editors, it is self-evident that *Niterói, Revista Brasiliense* was directed by Domingos José Gonçalves de Magalhães (1811–1882), Francisco de Sales Torres Homem (1812–1876), and Manuel de Araújo Porto-Alegre (1806–1879). There were only two issues, which were published and edited in Paris in 1836 by Dauvin et Fontaine, Libraires (Passage des Panoramas, 35), and printed at the Imprimérie de Baulé et Jubin (rue de Monceau Saint-Gervais, 8) (Doyle 5). In spite of the brief existence of this periodical, it featured texts of great significance for Brazilian literary historiography, such as the "Ensaio sobre a história da literatura do Brasil" ["Essay on the History of the Literature of Brazil"] by Gonçalves de Magalhães, and "Estudos sobre a literatura" ["Studies on Literature"] by João Manuel Pereira da Silva (1817–1898).

In 1839, the *Revista do Instituto Histórico e Geográfico Brasileiro* was founded by the members of that institute, an official organ of the empire; it was directed toward research on Brazilian history and on the creation of a national literature. This periodical is an important source for our understanding of the literature produced in Brazil during the Romantic period, given that it disseminated the nationalist ideas of the imperial project. Even though it was not exclusively a literary periodical, a great amount of literary material was published in it, mainly during 1839–1869, featuring biographies of Brazilian poets and writers, studies of poetic works and literary institutions, poetry and poetic compositions of an elegiac tone by authors like Antônio Gonçalves Dias (1823–1864), Joaquim Manoel de Macedo (1820–1882), Juanuário da Cunha Barbosa (1780–1846), Santiago Nunes Ribeiro (d. 1847), João Manuel Pereira da Silva, Francisco Adolfo Varnhagen (1816–1878), Joaquim Norberto de Sousa e Silva (1820–1891), and Joaquim Caetano Fernandes Pinheiro (1825–1876) (see Pillar).

For a short period between 1843 and 1845, the *Minerva Brasiliense*, a journal of science, letters, and the arts, was published in Rio de Janeiro by an association of writers. This periodical should not be mistaken for another small-format biweekly of the same name that circulated in Bahia from April to December 1821. The *Minerva Brasiliense* from Rio was a fortnightly newspaper published on the first and fifteenth of every month, and seems to have existed for thirty-one issues, subsequently gathered in three volumes. This journal had two phases. In the first phase, whose initial number is dated 1 November 1843, it was printed at the press of J. E. S. Cabral, located at Rua do Hospício, 66 in Rio de Janeiro; its editor-in-chief was Francisco de Sales Torres Homem. In his other journalism, Torres Homem found himself involved in political disputes in *O Maiorista* (1841–1842) with Justiniano José da Rocha, director of the newspaper *O Brasil* (1840–1852) and a conservative spokesman, who was considered by some historians to be the nation's greatest journalist, known for having begun "a conjugação entre imprensa e literatura que se firma então" (Sodré 183) ("the close ties between the press and literature"). In the first issue of *Minerva Brasiliense*, Torres Homem published the article "Progresso do século atual" ["Progress of the Current Century"], a kind of program manifesto in which the advances of the nineteenth century in the various branches of human knowledge were celebrated, recognizing and proclaiming that the duty of his generation was to work for future generations. Even though its appeal was more scientific than literary, it is curious that the newspaper would become more notable in the area of letters. In fact, the essay "Da nacionalidade da literatura brasileira" ["On the Nationality of Brazilian Literature"] by Santiago Nunes Ribeiro, published in the same issue, caused some controversy and ended up serving as a manifesto both of Brazilian Romantic literature and of the newspaper itself.

The journal dealt with a wide variety of subjects: astronomy, medicine, botany, zoology, chemistry, physics, history, and literature. In the sciences, contributors included Francisco Freire Alemão, Pedro de Alcântara Bellegarde, Cândido de Azevedo Coutinho, and Emílio Joaquim da Silva Maia. In the literary section, besides Francisco Sales Torres Homem and Santiago Nunes Ribeiro, contributors included Carlos Emílio Adet (1818–1867), Antônio Gonçalves Teixeira e Sousa (1812–1861), Antônio Francisco Dutra e Melo (1823–1846), Luís Antonio Burgain (1812–1877), and Joaquim Manoel de Macedo, among others. With number 24, on 15 October 1844, the first phase of the *Minerva Brasiliense* was over. In fact, from number 22 (of 15 September of that year), it had already been under the supervision of Santiago Nunes Ribeiro. The first issue of the second phase, which would eventually make up volume III, was released on 15 November 1844. The journal began to be printed at the Tipografia Austral, situated at the Beco de Bragança, 15 in Rio de Janeiro, and underwent some reformulation in its editorial policy, as can be perceived in reading Santiago Nunes Ribeiro's "Introduction," whose lead read "Grandes fases da civilização brasileira: antecedentes e caráter dos progressos literários e sociais" ("Great Phases of Brazilian Civilization: the precedents and character of literary and social progress").

> Até o presente, neste como em outros países, o máximo número de leitores era o dos homens de letras, estudiosos, e as pessoas que sem o serem de profissão, haviam recebido uma educação literária. Hoje porém, além destas que tem em maior grau, o gosto da leitura se acha na parte sã de todas as classes, e singularmente nas duas mais úteis do Estado, a dos negociantes e fazendeiros, pois que são como as artérias do corpo social nas quais gira a riqueza pública. (2)

> Until the present, in this country, the majority of readers have been men of letters, scholars, and people who, though not engaged in the profession, have received a literary education. Today, however, besides these people who have a love of reading in the highest degree, the taste for reading is also found in a good part of all social classes, and especially in the two most useful to the state, the businessmen and the estate owners, for they are like the arteries of the social body in which the public wealth circulates.

This passage is curious since, in addition to describing the profile of the reading public of the journal and the incipient reading public in Brazil (and even defining the horizon of expectations of the latter), it ends up by portraying the Brazilian elite of the time.

Among the notable reforms that took place in the journal during this second phase was the important attempt to democratize information without overt radicalism:

> Para estes, bem como para outros muitos leitores, a instrução deve ser mais recreativa que científica na forma, por que não lêem, como os homens de profissão, para entender o que há de geral e abstrato, isto é, de filosófico nas ciências, ou nas particularidades, isto é, de filosófico nas ciências, ou nas particularidades, aquilo que por ser técnico só interessa a quem estuda a ciência, ou exerce a arte. Isto posto, e sabido que o nosso fim é dar uma instrução sólida, substancial e divertida, os nossos leitores podem contar com artigos mais variados e recreativos que os da *Minerva* do ano findo, sem que porém se entenda que esta publicação vai descer tanto que se nivele com alguns Magazines, ou armazéns de notícias e descrições nimiamente superficias e populares. Tão longe estamos de querer tornar a *Minerva* em extremo democrática, que não duvidaremos inserir um ou outro artigo de ciência ou erudição, dos que interessam aos professores respectivos. (Ribeiro 2–3)

> For many other readers, instruction must be more recreational than scientific because they do not read, as those in the literary profession do, to understand what is general and abstract, that is, philosophical in the sciences, or in the particularities, which only interests one who studies science or practices art. Having said this, and making it clear that our goal is to provide solid, substantial, and interesting information, our readers can count on the most varied and amusing articles such as those *Minerva* published last year, which is not to say that this publication will sink to the same level as other magazines that provide news and superficial and popular descriptions. We are so far from wishing to make the *Minerva* radically democratic that we will not hesitate to include one or another article of science or erudition of the type that interests professors and other professionals.

Another important fact of Brazil's nineteenth-century literary culture was the creation of the "*Biblioteca Brasílica, ou coleção de obras originais, ou traduzidas de autores célebres*" ("*Brazilian Library*, or collection of original works, or translated works of celebrated authors"), a collection of significant books that was the result of the reforms proposed by Santiago Nunes Ribeiro to offer the readers of the journal the chance of purchasing, in even-numbered issues, literary works at reasonable prices. In this sense, he says:

> Observando a escassez de algumas obras e o preço exorbitante delas, entendemos conveniente dar em 12 números alternados da *Minerva*, reimpressões das ditas obras ou traduções de novelas, viagens, ou quaisquer outras que preencham nossos fins. Todas quantas pessoas temos consultado sobre esta idéia de um dos nossos colegas mais ilustrados e zelosos, lhe dão assenso e louvor sem restrição. Resulta disto que os nossos assinantes terão por 340 reis um volume de 56 páginas dos que se vendem por 1$000 a 2$000 nas livrarias. (Ribeiro 3)

> Given the scarcity of some works and their outrageous price, we find it fitting to offer, in 12 alternate issues of *Minerva*, reprintings of the aforementioned works or translations of novels, travelogues, or any others that fulfill our purposes. As many people as we consulted on this idea introduced by one of our most illustrious and industrious colleagues have given it their unrestricted assent and praise. As a result of this, our subscribers will have a 56-page volume each issue of those works that sell for 1000 to 2000 reis for only 340 reis.

The introductory text of the *Brazilian Library*, by Santiago Nunes Ribeiro, has an epigraph appropriate to the intentions of the publication: "Après avoir nivellé les droits, il faut niveller autant que possible les intelligences" ("After making rights common to all, one must also make intelligence common to all as far as possible"). In the Introduction, Santiago Nunes Ribeiro argues that:

> Ápovo não pode exercer os seus direitos constitucionais, se vive na ignorância. Só um povo instruído estará capacitado de governar-se. A religião, outrora elemento conservador e base da sociedade, desprestigiada como está na sociedade atual só poderá recuperar a sua força quando as inteligências se esclarecerem. É necessário despertar o amor à leitura e ao estudo, porque sem ele tudo quanto se fizer redundará em vão. (qtd. in Lopes 37)

> the people cannot exercise their constitutional rights, if they live in ignorance. Only an educated people will be fit to govern itself. Religion, at one time a conservative element and the basis of society, but without prestige in the present society, can only recover its strength when people's minds are enlightened. It is necessary to arouse the love of reading and study, because without it everything that is done will be in vain.

It seems that, of the twelve issues planned for the *Brazilian Library*, only five actually came out, for the second phase of the *Minerva* had only twelve issues. Numbers 1, 3, 5, 7, 9, 11, and 12 are regular editions of the journal and make up volume III. Numbers 2, 4, 6, 8, and 9 are issues of the *Brazilian Library*. Number 2 (1 December 1844) includes the "Introduction" to the *Brazilian Library* and the poem "O Uruguay" by Basílio da Gama, then in its fourth edition, followed by the text "Breve notícia sobre a vida de José Basílio da Gama" ("A brief note on the life of José Basílio da Gama"). Both the introduction and note are signed by Santiago Nunes Ribeiro.

Number 4 (1 January 1845) published a little work by the Rio de Janeiro writer Feliciano Joaquim de Sousa Nunes (1734–1808), author of the text "Do estado conjugal, discurso político e moral" ["On the married state, a political and moral discourse"], dedicated to the Marquis do Pombal. Since the text took up only twenty-four pages, Feliciano Joaquim de Sousa Nunes's translation of the six initial chapters of Hoffman's *O Morgado* [The Wealthy Man] was included, thus filling the required fifty-six pages of the issue. Santiago Nunes Ribeiro justified the publication of the little work by arguing that it was a rarity, and the inclusion of Hoffman's story because it was a masterpiece of the fantastic. Number 6 (1 February 1845) continued the publication of Hoffman's translated story: chapters VII to XXI, and a conclusion. Numbers 8 and 9 (1 March and 1 April 1845, respectively) published *Cartas Chilenas* [Chilean Letters] by Tomás Antônio Gonzaga (1744–1807?). This is the first edition of Gonzaga's satirical poem. It must be said that this is an incomplete edition, since it consists of only seven letters–which is not the case in the 1863 edition by Francisco Luís Saturnino da Veiga and H. Laemmert, who published eleven complete letters as well as fragments of two others.

Number 10 of the *Brazilian Library* ended up being the last issue released; it should have come out as number 9, thus breaking the sequence that had been followed by issues of odd numbers for the periodical *Minerva Brasiliense* and even numbers for the *Brazilian Library*. Number 11 came out on 15 April 1845, and after a break of two months number 12 was published on 15 June 1845, thus closing the second and last phase of the *Minerva Brasiliense*.

In December, 1845, an old contributor to the journal, the Peruvian D. José Manuel Valdez y Palácios (1812–1854), author of *Viagem da cidade de Cusco ao Grã-Pará pelos rios Vilcamayo*,

Ucayli e Amazonas [Journey from the City of Cuzco to Grã-Pará by the Vicamayo, Ucayli, and Amazon Rivers], reviewed by Santiago Nunes Ribeiro in number 17 of the first phase of the *Minerva Brasiliense*, decided to publish a journal that would provide continuity by founding *A Nova Minerva*, which spanned six months. This was the third phase of the *Minerva Brasiliense*, and had twenty-four issues of sixteen to twenty pages. The journal was weekly and aimed at being a periodical also dedicated to the sciences, arts, literature, and culture.

From 1 December 1849 to March 1856, *O Guanabara*, a monthly artistic, scientific, and literary journal, edited by an association of lettered men and directed by Manuel de Araújo Porto-Alegre, Antônio Gonçalves Dias, and Joaquim Manoel de Macedo, was published in Rio de Janeiro. It began being printed at the Tipografia Guanabarense of L.A.F. de Meneses, situated at Rua São José, 45, but the dissatisfaction of the editors with the work of this press, especially concerning distribution, led them to contract the services of Francisco de Paulo Brito (Lopes 53). It seems that this magazine had thirty-seven published issues, which are bound in three volumes; the first and second volumes each contained twelve issues and the third volume thirteen.

Following the same policy as the *Minerva Brasiliense* and taking on the role of disseminating the nationalist project of the Brazilian Historical and Geographical Institute, the journal *O Guanabara* published articles on a variety of subjects and had on its staff list of editors and contributors the same names that had contributed earlier to the *Minerva*, except for Santiago Nunes Ribeiro, who died around 1845. Like *Minerva Brasiliense*, *O Guanabara* had its *Biblioteca Guanabarense*, which issued the following works: the novel *Rosa* (1849) by Joaquim Manoel de Macedo; the comedy *A estátua amazônica* [1851; The Amazon Statue] by Manuel de Araújo Porto-Alegre; *Cobé* (1852), a five-act drama by Joaquim Manoel de Macedo; *O Cavaleiro teutônico ou A freira de Marienburg* [1855; The Teutonic Horseman or The Nun of Marienburg], a tragedy in five acts by Antônio Gonçalves Teixeira e Sousa; and *Amador Bueno ou Á fidelidade paulistana* [1855; Amador Bueno or São Paulo Fidelity], an historical drama in five acts by Joaquim Norberto de Sousa e Silva.

The *Revista Popular*, a Romantic publication considered the "centro dinâmico na renovação das idéias literárias" (Martins 1:135) ("dynamic center in the renewal of literary ideas"), offered sixteen issues between 5 January 1859 and 20 December 1862. Following the tradition of the *Minerva Brasiliense*, it was a journal of book news on scientific, industrial, historical, literary, artistic, biographical, anecdotal, and musical works. It also took the format of an illustrated newspaper and endorsed the nationalist program of the Historical Institute, as can be seen mainly in the articles signed by Joaquim Norberto de Sousa e Silva, who published in this magazine the famous introductory chapters of what would have been a "History of Brazilian Literature," if it had been completed and published as a book. These focused on three themes: "a tendência dos selvagens para a poesia, a questão da nacionalidade e da originalidade da literatura brasileira e a história literária" (Moreira 77) ("the tendency of savages to poetry, the question of nationality and the originality of Brazilian literature, and literary history"). The editorship of the *Revista Popular* was in the hands of Joaquim Norberto de Sousa e Silva, Luís de Castro (1863–1920), José da Rocha Leão Júnior (b. 1823), Duarte Paranhos Schutel (1837–1901), Joaquim Manoel de Macedo, Joaquim Caetano Fernandes Pinheiro

(1825–1876), and others. For contributors, it had Lino de Almeida, Casimiro de Abreu (1839–1860), Luís Antonio Burgain, Luís Delfino (1834–1910), Maciel Monteiro (1804–1868), José Joaquim Cândido de Macedo Júnior (1842–1860), Juvenal Galeno (1836–1931), José Alexandre Teixeira de Melo (1833–1907), Faustino Xavier de Novais (1820–1869), Domingos José Gonçalves de Magalhães, Bruno Seabra (1837–1876), Augusto Fausto de Sousa (1835–1890), Augusto Emílio Zaluar (1825–1882), among others. Published in Rio de Janeiro by B.L. Garnier, the journal was replaced in 1863 by the *Jornal das Famílias* (1863–1878), by the same publisher (Coutinho and Sousa 2:1145). In addition to these, during the Romantic period, the following periodicals were issued in Rio de Jaineio: *Óris* (1848–1849), *Anais da Academia Filosófica* (1858), *O Espelho* (1859–1860), *Revista Brasileira* (first phase 1857–1860, second phase 1869–1881, third phase 1895–1899), *Revista Mensal de Ensaios Literários* (1863–1865, 1872–1874), and several others of literary or eclectic interest.

Outside the Brazilian northeast/southeast axis, the south of Brazil was also undergoing a certain cultural ferment. São Pedro do Rio Grande, Pelotas, and Porto Alegre stood out as foci of literary life in the region, for this is where periodicals such as *Arcádia* and the *Revista Mensal da Sociedade Partenon Literário* were issued. The *Arcádia*, an illustrated literary, historical, and biographical newspaper, belonged to the Portuguese editor Antonio Joaquim Dias, who published it between 1867 and 1870. With a total of four series, the journal had the first three series published in Rio Grande do Sul and the fourth in Pelotas. Referring to the *Arcádia*, the critic Carlos Alexandre Baumgarten stated: "Dedicando-se exclusivamente à difusão da literatura, publicou este periódico literário poesias de nossos autores mais representativos, bem como romances, contos, textos críticos e correspondência entre homens ligados ao movimento cultural da Província" (Baumgarten 26) ("Dedicating itself exclusively to the spread of literature, this periodical published poetry by our most representative authors, as well as novels, stories, critical texts, and correspondence between men connected to the cultural movement of the Province"). Contributors to the *Arcádia* were Bernardo Taveira Júnior (1836–1892), Apolinário Porto-Alegre (1844–1904) and Aquiles Porto-Alegre (1848–1926), Aurélio Veríssimo de Bittencourt (1849–1919), and Frederico Ernesto Estrela de Villeroy (1837–1897), among others. Ideologically, the *Arcádia* showed some affinities with the project for the construction of a national literature, along the same lines as *Minerva Brasiliense*.

In 1869, the *Revista Mensal da Sociedade Partenon Literário* began circulation; it was edited by the Partenon Literário and founded 18 June 1868 at the seat of the Sociedade Firmeza e Esperança, in Porto Alegre. Both journal and society owe much to Apolinário Porto Alegre and José Antonio do Vale Caldre e Fião (1821–1876). The journal circulated in four phases: the first from March to December 1869, the second from July 1872 to May 1873, the third from August 1877 to 1878, and the fourth from April to September 1879. Besides the two writers cited above, other contributors were João da Cunha Lobo Barreto (1853–1875), Aurélio Veríssimo de Bittencourt, Amália dos Passos Figueiroa (1845–1878), Afonso Marques (1847–1872), Aquiles Porto-Alegre, Carlos von Koseritz (1834–1890), Bernardo Taveira Júnior, Múcio Teixeira (1858–1926), João Damasceno Vieira Fernandes (1850–1910), and Alberto Coelho da Cunha (1853–1939) (Cesar 176). The journal had as its primary aim the dissemination of the ideas held by the Parthenon Society's members, who were the most representative group in the history of Romantic literature of Rio Grande do Sul (Moreira 156).

In concluding this retrospective on the cultural periodicals of the Romantic period in Brazil, I would like to underscore what the critic Léa Masina has stated in a 1996 article, commenting on the organic relation between literature and journalism, the result of the symbiosis of writers who, in newspapers and magazines, played the simultaneous roles of men of letters, politicians, and journalists, and in this way filled the gap caused by the low circulation of books in a society still in formation (Masina 228).

**Translation by Thomas LaBorie Burns and
Gláucia Renate Gonçalves**

Works Cited

Amora, Antonio Soares. 1977. "Um precioso documento." *Revista da Sociedade Philomática*. São Paulo: Typographia do Novo Farol Paulistano. Facsimile ed.

Baumgarten, Carlos Alexandre. 1982. *Literatura e crítica na imprensa do Rio Grande do Sul: 1868–1880*. Porto Alegre: Escola Superior de Teologia São Lourenço de Brindes.

Brito Broca, José. 1979. *Românticos, pré-românticos, ultra-românticos: Vida literária e Romantismo brasileiro*. São Paulo: Polis.

Cândido, Antonio. 1971. *Formação da literatura brasileira: Momentos decisivos*. 4th ed. 2 vols. São Paulo: Martins.

——. 1973. *Literatura e sociedade: Estudos de teoria e história literária*. São Paulo: Companhia Editora Nacional.

César, Guilhermino. 1956. *História da literatura do Rio Grande do Sul*. Porto Alegre: Globo.

Coutinho, Afrânio. 1981. *Conceito de literatura brasileira*. Petrópolis: Vozes.

Coutinho, Afrânio, and J. Galante de Sousa, ed. 1989–1990. *Enciclopédia de literatura brasileira*. 2 vols. Rio de Janeiro: MEC–Fundação de Assistência ao Estudante.

Doyle, Plínio. 1976. *História de revistas e jornais literários*. Vol 1. Rio de Janeiro: MEC–Fundação Casa de Rui Barbosa.

Lafetá, João Luiz. 1974. *1930: A crítica e o modernismo*. São Paulo: Duas Cidades.

Lima, Luiz Costa. 1981. *Dispersa demanda: Ensaios sobre literatura e teoria*. Rio de Janeiro: Francisco Alves.

Lopes, Hélio. 1978. *A divisão das águas: Contribuição ao estudo das revistas românticas* Minerva Brasiliense *(1843–1845) e* Guanabara *(1849–1856)*. São Paulo: Conselho Estadual de de Artes e Ciências Humanas.

Martins, Wilson. 1983. *A crítica literária no Brasil*. 2 vols. Rio de Janeiro: Francisco Alves.

Masina, Léa. 1996. "Periodismo cultural no início do século." *Continente sul/sur* (Porto Alegre) 2: 227–35.

Moisés, Massaud, and José Paulo Paes, eds. 1980. *Pequeno dicionário de literatura brasileira*. 2nd ed. São Paulo: Cultrix.

Moreira, Maria Eunice. 1991. *Nacionalismo literário e crítica romântica*. Porto Alegre: IEL.

Pillar, Thanira Chayb de. 1996. "A literatura na *Revista do Instituto Histórico e Geográfico Brasileiro* de 1839 a 1869." *Letras de Hoje*. Porto Alegre: EDIPUCRS. (December) 31.4: 37–40.

Ribeiro, Santiago Nunes. 1844. "Introdução." *Minerva Brasiliense*. Rio de Janeiro: Tipografia Austral 3.1 (15 November): 1–4.

Sodré, Nelson Werneck. 1983. *História da imprensa no Brasil*. 3rd ed. São Paulo: Martins Fontes.

CHAPTER 13

FROM JOURNALISM TO FOUNDATIONAL TEXT

OS SERTÕES
[*REBELLION IN THE BACKLANDS*]

Jorge Coli

Euclides da Cunha's *Os Sertões* [1902; *Rebellion in the Backlands,* 1944] is unique for several reasons, the most important of which is the metamorphosis of its initial journalistic project into a prodigious critical epic at the heart of Latin American culture. Euclides da Cunha was reporter and author–simultaneously and dialectically. The reporter's methods of observation clash with the author's interpretive procedures, destroying concepts and preconceptions while creating conditions for a meditation on the nature of civilization and barbarism in the continent. The reporter's words become the means of reflection, penetrating the author's mental structures.

A general insidious subversion of preconceived ideas of civilization and barbarism that draws strength from a unique fusion of lyricism and precision allows Euclides da Cunha (1866–1909) to sharpen his exceptional analytic intelligence. His hybrid journalistic style defies definition or summary classification. His rich, antithetical sentences and Hugoesque metaphors swell toward the final stop, to the insistent silence of the ellipsis; yet elsewhere the phrase is sharp and incisive, bringing to life the smallest of objects as well as the large masses of land and humanity. Thanks to his journalistic powers of observation and his interpretive powers of evocation, Euclides da Cunha builds a highly complex foundational myth. His narrative is based on an *original crime,* which he records and denounces. This is a different perspective from that of another denunciation of modern times, Zola's *Rougon-Macquart* or *La Débâcle.* Zola speaks of the new France emerging from the mud of the Second Empire as a tree that sprouts branches anew after an old branch is cut off, a France freed from its murderous utopias and cured of the Commune. Euclides da Cunha is more complex, more circumspect than Zola. He rejects the fanaticism of Canudos–a town located inland in the Brazilian northeast–but denounces the massacres perpetrated by the Republican forces much more vigorously than does Zola in his description of the massacres of the Commune. It is because of the journalist in him that the center of the book becomes not the uprising itself, but its suppression. He openly admires the *sertanejo* (man of the *sertão,* or backlands), who ought to be educated, step by step, in the perspective of the Enlightenment, rather than massacred or exterminated by "civilizing" forces.

The very evolution of da Cunha's thought within his project is significant: The impassioned Republican, initially convinced that he will find a barbarian conspiracy, is quickly nauseated by the imbecility and gratuitous ferocity of the Republican forces. In this, through analysis, he shuffles the very categories upon which he depends, thus displacing his most fundamental concepts. While recording savagery, popular mysticism, and blind modernity, he risks contradicting his own theory of history. He mocks the "lettered city's" fears and ghosts. He notes the incompetence of politicians and of the military, who send thou-

sands off to be massacred; similar to the way in which Machado de Assis (1839–1908) in *O alienista* [1881; *The Psychiatrist,* 1963] sets reason and madness together, leading to combat and annihilation, da Cunha places the fanaticism of soldiers who shout "Viva a República!" ("Long live the Republic!") and that of the insurrectionists into a game where each is the mirror image of the other. Such writing is quite rare. Instead of simply producing journalism for immediate effect, the author perceives that he himself possesses the intellectual means to transform a journalistic account of that highly critical moment in Brazilian history into a fundamental instrument for understanding his country. This is how *Os Sertões* came about. In the journey from journalism to the foundational book of Brazilian identity, a curious and exemplary epistemological turnaround took place. From a common central nucleus, the account of an event (the uprising) expanded to become a meditation on the implications of suppression.

The uniqueness of *Os Sertões* has often been noted. It is a book that belongs to no particular genre; nor could its procedures be repeated in subsequent works, for it depended upon the encounter between an exceptional event and an exceptional writer. The specific event was the confrontation of two disparate forces: the regular army of a secular republic and the believing inhabitants of a theocratic city. The former possessed enormous resources with which to meet its enemies and won in spite of a total lack of discipline, enormous waste, and fatal ingenuousness. The latter possessed an almost organic knowledge of their environment, as well as a rigor, economy, and intelligence of the conflicts, which, though they lost, rendered them exemplary. The book's origin lies in a perplexing question: How was it possible for a band of backward fanatics without modern weapons or military training to resist the organized forces of a nation for so long? This initial query did not take into account the different *natures* of the combatants; it presupposed only a matter of relative military strength. How was it possible for the weak to resist the strong? Euclides da Cunha's answers clearly distinguish the diverse natures of the two worlds. And in having to explain Canudos and the Republican army, he asks the crucial questions: What is archaic? What is modern? What is savage? What is civilized? To penetrate to the heart of these questions, the author employs a precise tool: the objective description of detail–a reporter's instrument. However, he still possesses the theoretical methods of the humanities disciplines, which wanted then–and want today–to be human sciences. He makes use of yet another instrument, surely not considered by the author himself on the same level as the previously mentioned elements of reportage and philosophical reflection, but just as important: his style of writing. It possesses a power that some call demiurgic and others heuristic. It can be considered demiurgic because it installs a world: Canudos, its men, its region, its battles, appear to the reader as tangible realities. This is not only because every historical event exists only through historical accounts and interpretations, but because da Cunha bestowed the event with unprecedented greatness and complexity, and projected it into the heart of Brazilian culture with great resonance.

In Euclides da Cunha's *Os Sertões*, Canudos is made with words, and these words become Canudos for an entire nation. Highly pertinent in this sense is a brief passage by Antônio Medina Rodrigues that reminds us of the role played by language in *Os Sertões* and of the mistaken distinction between conceptual content and stylistic form and, therefore, the separation of interpretation and formal analysis: "O fantástico mundo verbal de Euclides não pode ser tratado como uma retórica à parte, que sirva de invólucro ao quadro histórico e geográfico" (3) ("Euclides's fantastic verbal world cannot be treated as a separate rhetoric, which serves as a wrapping for the historical and geographical portrait"). It is quite true that the great historical works of the nineteenth century had developed an admirable principle of writing of high stylistic quality in order to narrate the events with intelligence and analysis. Literary writing was then conceived as the primordial achievement of the human sciences: Taine, Renan, and Michelet are clearly noticeable in the background of *Os Sertões*. The book, however, is not reducible to these precedents, but distances itself from all its great models with distinction. Euclides da Cunha's writing depicts the people, the land, and the struggle in a style that eludes summary classification. His incisive sentences are crammed with antithesis and metaphor. And the force of the words brings with it the interpretive flux.

Besides being a war epic, *Os Sertões* is a scientific epic. It matters little, in this case, that its science was largely false. The universe of scientific knowledge that fascinated da Cunha (the inexorable chain of causalities, the obsession with precise response, the funneling and expansion of factors that link the private and the general) function unexpectedly as dynamic elements of a poetics and achieve memorably paroxysmal moments:

> É natural que estas camadas profundas de nossa estratificação étnica se sublevassem numa anticlinal extraordinária–Antônio Conselheiro. . . . [O] infeliz, destinado à solicitude dos médicos, veio, impelido por uma potência superior, bater de encontro a uma civilização, indo para a história como poderia ter ido para o hospício. Porque ele, para o historiador, não foi um desequilibrado. Apareceu como integração de caracteres diferenciais–vagos, indecisos, mal percibidos quando dispersos da multidão, mas enérgicos e definidos, quando resumidos numa individualidade. (117–18)

> It was natural that the deep-lying layers of our ethnic stratification should have cast up so extraordinary a case as Antônio Conselheiro. . . . [T]his unfortunate individual, a fit subject for medical attention, was impelled by a power stronger than himself to enter into conflict with a civilization and to go down in history when he should have gone to a hospital. For, to the historian, he is not only an unbalanced character but rather appears as the integration of various social traits–vague, indecisive, not readily perceived when lost in the multitude, but well defined and forceful when thus summed up in the individual human personality.

See too his contemplation of a soldier's dead body:

> E estava intacto. Murchara apenas. Mumificara, conservando os traços fisionômicos, de modo a incutir a ilusão exata de um lutador cansado, retemperando-se em tranqüilo sono, à sombra daquela árvore benfazeja. Nem um verme–o mais vulgar dos trágicos analistas da matéria–lhe maculara os tecidos. Volvia ao turbilhão

da vida sem decomposição repugnante, numa exaustão imperceptível. Era um aprelho revelando de modo absoluto, mas sugestivo, a secura extrema dos ares. (24)

> His body was intact. It had dried out a little, that was all, had undergone a mummification which had preserved the lines of his physiognomy to such an extent as to give the precise illusion of a tired fighter taking a peaceful nap in the shade of that benevolent tree. Not even a worm–most vulgar of the tragic solvents of matter–had defiled his tissues. He had returned to life's melting-pot without any unseemly decomposition, through an imperceptible draining-off process. In brief, here was an apparatus that revealed, absolutely and in the most suggestive manner, the extreme aridity of the atmosphere.

It is a mere step from paroxysm to delirium. J. M. de Montremy, one of the analysts who studied the French translation of *Os Sertões* (an impressive critical success published in 1993, with a paperback edition that followed at the end of 1997) does not hesitate: "The superb war story of Canudos also tells of the confrontation between two follies: the lettered madness of Euclides allows itself to be overtaken by his poetic madness" (17).

A causal explanatory flux of sentences and words that become entangled in immense chains carry the conviction of the objective word *and* delirious truth. It is with them that Euclides da Cunha weaves the moving fabric of his world.

But the demiurgic word is also a heuristic word, for it provokes a revealing, implacably rigorous gaze. In a perfect analysis, another French critic, Gilles Lapouge, writes:

> The mestizos [in Os Sertões] are weak, degenerate, physically contorted and convulsed. Psychotic or neurotic, they lost, in the course of generations, the white man's virtues without acquiring the black man's vigor. They are incurable. It is not surprising that these uneasy, lazy, lethargic, near idiots allowed themselves to be fooled by the first lunatic who stood up against the Republic and science, behaving like savages! Conselheiro's barbarous eloquence is of no interest whatsoever to Euclides da Cunha, who goes so far as to surmise that there may be a Jewish influence behind his mention of the golden age–horrors!

> And so? Leaning on futilities of this order, how does the book succeed in being so beautiful and intelligent? By burning itself as it is written. The book weaves its own *auto-da-fé*. While telling the epic of Canudos, Euclides discovers, unawares, or better yet, with rage, the intractable greatness of the "incurable," the "degenerate," the "hysteria" of Canudos. Against his own certainties, he concedes that the mulattos whom he classifies as the last class of men are heroic and noble. He discovers the beauty of the mestizo. He admires their ability, their generosity, their dignity, their glory, and their beautiful hope. A metamorphosis takes place before our eyes: the scientist of dry ideas comes to worship that which he had intended to detest. His song of hatred becomes a love song to those whom he believed he hated. (32)

"Dry ideas," writes Gilles Lapouge, of the criticism. The year of Canudos's centennial saw the publication of various essays and articles, many of which, disturbed by the complexity required for an understanding of Euclides da Cunha, declared that the author had changed his mind upon discovering the terrifying events he witnessed.

But Euclides da Cunha did not change his mind–and, at any rate, whether he did or did not is of no importance, for *Os Sertões* leads us into a deeper probe of intelligence to which our pseudoscience had rendered us unaccustomed, and this is an understanding of convictions, of ideas, of concepts, which is not the same as saying these words in oral or written expression. The apparent simple clarity of some words can rapidly become opaque. Da Cunha had his political and scientific convictions, which certainly he did not give up. As those of a Republican imbued with racist theories, his interpretations may sound outdated, but the rigorous descriptive language brings with it a rigor of analysis. And the penetrating subversion of the text itself is permanent. This subversion derives its strength from a unique fusion of lyricism and precision that allows the writer to sharpen his exceptional analytic intelligence: Here is the *auto-da-fé* of the self to which Lapouge refers. In this sense, the illuminating word catches fire in the specifics. And as it greatly contradicts generality, it also contradicts itself. Thus, the writer who rejects the fanaticism of Canudos also denounces the massacres perpetrated by the Republican forces. In reality, as we have seen, his narrative is centered not upon the uprising but on its suppression. And the theoretically archaic and savage *sertanejo* becomes the manifest object of his admiration. In the detailed description of the campaigns, the military forces, however, appear by turns absurd, ridiculous, pathetic, and criminal.

Euclides da Cunha himself is the finest example of the displaced perspective. The passionate Republican, convinced that he was to witness a monarchist conspiracy, a backlands Vendée (to borrow his image), is quickly sickened by the stupidity and needless violence of the Republican forces. Against cruel stupidity he sets the prodigious cleverness, the intelligence, and the admirable appropriateness of the insurrectionists' relationship to their environment. And it is impossible not to contrast Conselheiro's purity, strength of character, and tragic grandeur (as revealed to us by the author) with the civilized and rationalist barbarism of his exhumation and decapitation. It is the alleged barbarians who possess higher qualities that are absent in the world of purported reason, order, and modernity. Is it necessary to remember that Euclides da Cunha left for Canudos knowing clearly what civilization and barbarism were, convinced that the Republican army stood for the defense of scientific and civilizing forces? And that, in asking himself about barbarism, he found it where he had not expected to, conjuring up formidable phantoms of brutality, which he makes no attempt to disguise?

The book's ending depicts a ritual of abominable savagery, where civilized men dance a horrid sarabande before an ignoble trophy:

> Restituíram-no [o Conselheiro] à cova. Pensaram, porém, em guardar sua cabeça, tantas vezes maldita—e como fora malbaratar tempo exumando-o de novo, uma faca, jeitosamente brandida, naquela mesma atitude, cortou-lha; e faca horrenda, empastada de escaras e de sânie, apareceu mais uma vez ante aqueles triunfadores. . . . Trouxeram depois para o litoral, onde deliravam multidões em festa, aquele crânio. (476)

Then they put him [Conselheiro] back in his grave. Later, however, the thought occurred to them that they should have preserved the head, that head on which so many curses had been heaped—and, since it was a waste of time to exhume the body once more, a knife cleverly wielded at the right point did the trick; the corpse was decapitated, and that horrible face, sticky with scars and pus,

once more appeared before the victors' gaze. . . . After that they took the head to the seashore, where it was greeted by delirious multitudes with carnival joy.

Euclides da Cunha contradicts his own hypotheses; he cancels one side out with the other, condemning two opposing barbarisms: latter-day mysticism and blind modernity. He mocks the city's artificially grown terrors; he scorns the incompetence of politicians and the military who, devoid of any realism or common sense, send millions off to slaughter; he continually points out the dubious conjectures that always led the Republicans to misunderstand the real cause of Canudos; he confronts and annihilates reason with madness, bringing the fanatic military cries of "Long live the Republic!" face to face with the insurrectionists' messianism.

In doing so he corrodes the very theories upon which he had based his position and upsets his own most fundamental beliefs. Thus, for instance, in an example of this kind of subversive incoherence, while he opposes the backlands' "race" in the making to the country's generalized miscegenation, he insists upon the racial diversity of the female prisoners taken at Canudos. Conversely, in the battle's final stages, when the soldiers lose their uniforms, it becomes impossible to tell them apart from the backlanders. Euclides da Cunha therefore precludes the very use of definitions, axioms, or concepts, which he himself affirms emphatically but precisely, with such excessive emphasis that it means going beyond his own theoretical point of departure. In exemplary fashion, he points to the narrow-mindedness and false reasoning emanating from a prori theoretical hypotheses, unshakable conviction, and proclaimed truths—procedures frequently still present within the humanities.

Os Sertões thus moves us through an unexpected epistemological configuration: Starting from the reporter's ephemeral, intellectually unambitious yet demanding verification of the facts, it rises above reportage to become a meditation on civilization and barbarism unequaled in Brazilian culture to this day. Torn apart by bombardment, drowned by water, Canudos becomes indestructible and inexorable, present, immense—thanks to a book whose wholeness leaps out at us but that is built upon the ambiguities of its contradictions.

Translation by Stephen A. Berg

Works Cited

Cunha, Euclides da. 1944. *Rebellion in the Backlands.* Trans. Samuel Putman. Chicago: University of Chicago Press.

———. 1995 [1902]. *Os sertões: Campanha de Canudos.* 37th ed. Ed. Anamaria Skinner. Rio de Janeiro: Francisco Alves Editora.

Lapouge, Gilles. 1993. "Os sertões." *Le Monde* (Paris) 26 March.

Montremy, J. M. de. 1993. "Os sertões." *La Croix* (Paris) 5 April.

Rodrigues, Antônio Medina. 1993. "Estilo de Euclides da Cunha é pictórico." *Cultura, o Estado de São Paulo* (literary suppl.) 23 May: 3.

Zola, Emile. 1969–1970. [1871–1893] *Les Rougon-Macquart.* Ed. Pierre Cogny. Paris: Éditions du Seuil.

CHAPTER 14

LITERARY JOURNALISM IN BRAZIL DURING THE FIRST HALF OF THE TWENTIETH CENTURY

Ivia Alves

As newspapers became an everyday commodity, it became necessary for them to expand their various sections and columns in order to hold the interest of a diverse reading public. If, in the preceding century, it was the serial (or *feuilleton*) that had stimulated consumption by the middle-class reading public, by the twentieth century these had become the entertainment of the popular classes, and daily newspapers dedicated pages of *crônicas* (byline columns), short stories, and news articles aimed at the middle-class reader. Newspapers have traditionally allotted space to literary criticism in designated columns, *rodapés* (serial publication at the bottom of the newspaper page), and also entire supplements that serve as a barometer for what takes place in literature and in cultural life. The shape, language, and perspective of journalistic criticism were modified over the years as it followed trends and provided a contextual framework for literary culture. The changes in and tendencies of literary taste are clearly presented through contemporary journalistic criticism in the pages of a daily newspaper.

We may see at a glance that during the 1920s and 1930s criticism consisted primarily of value judgments, while succeeding decades reveal a gradual preference for critical approaches and theories centered upon language, textuality, the work of art. Slowly, journalistic criticism relinquished its interest in the writer to concern itself primarily with the text. During the early 1920s, the period in which this outline begins, the principal critics and intellectuals of the nineteenth century, those whose studies had determined the shape of Brazilian literature, had already left the scene: Araripe Júnior (1848–1911), Silvio Romero (1851–1914), and José Veríssimo (1857–1916). (See **Figures 1** and **2.**) This left a great vacuum that would eventually be filled by critics of diverse orientations, but what predominated was evaluative impressionism. A few survivors of the nineteenth century still wrote, but they were interested in pointing out grammatical mistakes or commenting on philological details. By and large, literary criticism was taken over by younger intellectuals with nineteenth-century education who, in a reaction to objective (scientific) methods, preferred impressionistic criticism; these critics therefore presented their sentiments and impressions with regard to the writers they reviewed. They frequently combined their impressions with biographism (impressionistic biography) and psychologism, emphasizing the person and the external circumstances that contributed to the writing. All the critics of the day privileged personal evaluation, giving a description of the writer's personality as a way of casting light upon the work. The effect of a work's impression upon the critic was the central part of this criticism, as well as the relevance of the work to what the critic considered to be everyday reality. All this was written in a pleasant manner, which provided the public with easy reading, in the light but acrimonious prose of these impressionists.

Figure 1.

foto G. Huebner & Amaral

ARARIPE JUNIOR

Figure 2.

JOSÉ VERISSIMO

Whether the critic was discussing the literary performance of Levi Carneiro (1882–1971) or commenting on minor authors, the following fragments reveal Agrippino Grieco (1888–1968) himself to be at the center of his own criticism:

Alguém, definindo os dois mais ferozes panfletários lusitanos dos Ultimos tempos, falou na águia do Alentejo e no galo do "Pimpão." O primeiro era o grande Fialho [de Almeida] e o segundo o bem menor Silva Pinto, talvez um simples pintainho atacado de gosma incurável. Porque enquanto o autor das "Pasquinadas" investia, de garra e bico afiados, contra o soberano em exercício ou contra o perigoso concorrente que se chamava Eça de Queirós, o verineiro daquela revista humorística só se atirava, de esporão frágil, à sátira miúda a comentadores e corregedores de duvidosa importância na história do burlesco universal.

Mas, de qualquer modo, esse pequeno galináceo da crítica não deixa de possuir os seus aspectos curiosos. Foi Oscar Wilde–creio–quem acentuou não serem nunca os escritores de categoria elevada os tipos mais interessantes das respectivas literaturas. Mais interessantes são sempre os escritores de quarta ou quinta classe. E Silva Pinto, não indo muito além desta baixa classificação, era, dentro do terreno anedótico, cem vezes mais sugestivo que um Eça ou um Ramalho. (Grieco 209)

In defining two of the fiercest Portuguese pamphleteers of recent times, someone had spoken of the eagle of the Alentejo and the cock of the "Pimpão." The great Fialho (de Almeida) was the former, and the much lesser Silva Pinto the latter, perhaps a mere baby chick afflicted with an incurable chicken pip. For, whilst the author of "Pasquinadas" [Pasquinades], sharp of beak and claw, attacked the ruler in power or that dangerous competitor Eça de Queirós [1845–1900], the lampooner of that comic review dedicated himself exclusively to the minor satire of commentators and magistrates of doubtful importance in the history of the universal burlesque.

At any rate, this tiny chick of criticism still possessed curious aspects. I believe it was Oscar Wilde who insisted it was never writers of a high category who were most interesting in any given literature. Fourth- or fifth-class writers are always more interesting. And Silva Pinto, not going too far beyond this classification, was, within the field of the anecdotal, one hundred times more suggestive than an Eça or a Ramalho.

His column in the 1930s on Graciliano Ramos's (1892–1953) novel *Caetés* (1947) deserves to be singled out as a clear example of his manner of making a value judgment:

Muitos romancistas ficam indignados quando lhes constatamos a inferioridade da obra que apresentam. E lá vem desaforo em cima do crítico. . . . Da minha parte, não tenho prazer algum em registrar mau tempo nas letras. Sinto-me, ao contrário, alegríssimo quando de um belo dia a desfrutar de pronto.

É o caso deste admirável romance do Sr. Graciliano Ramos, intitulado *Caetés*. Conheci o autor em Maceió. Passava eu por lá, em direção a Recife, quando José Lins do Rego, Valdemar Cavalcanti, Aloísio Branco e o Sr. Graciliano me foram buscar a bordo, para, nas duas ou três horas de parada do navio, correr à cidade, comer um sururu e ver as formosas igrejas da terra. Mas uma das coisas que vi com mais gosto foi o romancista dos *Caetés,* alto, magro, pouco palrador, sem nenhum talento no sorriso, com um jeito de revisor suplente de jornal aqui do Rio, dos que recebem sempre em atraso. . . . Leio-lhe agora o volume de estréia e verifico que tal romance é bem de tal homem. Nada de gastar saliva inutilmente. nada de consumir papel quando não seja para dizer qualquer coisa realmente proveitosa ao gosto ou à s ensibilidade dos demais.

Mas é estranho como esse patrício se conservou assim discreto, pouco verboso, pouco gesticulante, numa zona de derramados, de criaturas que gostam de despejar metáforas às carretas nos livros. (Grieco 42–43)

Many novelists become indignant when we establish the inferiority of a work they present. And insults are piled upon the critic. . . . As for myself, I have no pleasure at all in recording heavy literary weather. On the contrary, I am overjoyed when allowed straight away to enjoy a lovely day.

Such is the case of Mr. Graciliano Ramos's admirable novel *Caetés.* I met the author in Maceió. I was passing through there on my way to Recife, when José Lins do Rego [1901–1957], Valdemar Cavalcanti [1912–1982], Aloísio Branco and Mr. Graciliano came aboard to fetch me so that, during the ship's two or three hour stopover, we might see the city, eat sururu, and visit the handsome local churches. One of the persons it gave me great pleasure to see was the tall, thin, taciturn novelist of *Caetés,* his unsmiling manner suggesting that of a substitute proofreader for a Rio newspaper, the one whose paychecks are always late. . . . I am reading his first novel and it is typical of such a man. No wasted saliva, no wasting of paper except to say something truly profitable to the taste or sensibility of others.

Yet it is strange the way this fellow-countryman has kept himself discreet, with great economy of words and gesture in this land of excess, of creatures who lay on the metaphors with a shovel.

Superficial and judgmental this may be, yet efficiently pleasant and easy to digest, with a light touch of humor. Very little has remained of such criticism, which has become dated and riddled with local and contemporary references and facts that were lost in time.

Beginning in the 1920s and continuing throughout the 1930s and 1940s, Agrippino Grieco was the most familiar figure in journalistic criticism. A product of the nineteenth century, his journalistic career was a long one (1920–1950). According to J. L. Lafetá, he is an important critic "porque está sempre presente nas colunas de jornal e, dotado de agilidade mental e da versatilidade que caracterizam bem certo estilo de colunismo literário, influi de maneira ponderável no quadro geral das atividades da época" (Lafetá 29) ("because, with his constant presence in news columns, as well as the mental agility and versatility which characterize a certain style of journalism, he exerts considerable influence on the general scheme of the period's activities"). His preoccupation with cultivating the public's taste led him to develop a highly influential kind of criticism through the superficial promotion of the works, mixed with biographism wrapped in eloquent language, rich in images and shot through with irony and satire. Published in newspapers (particularly, his own column in *O Jornal*) and reviews, his articles dominated the literary scene from 1920 to 1950. Well read and ironic, almost sarcastic, Agrippino Grieco had strong Eurocentric sentiments.

Felizes as nações como a França que, além de ter tido Rivarol, têm o seu champanha para distribuir ao mundo.

E quando a nós outros, pobres filhos de uma terra sem vinhos, não há mal algum em que leiamos todas as noites um epigrama de Rivarol e bebamos, ao menos uma vez por semana, meia taça de chamapanha. (Grieco 23)

Happy are those nations which, like France, in addition to having had Rivarol, have their champagne to distribute to the world.

As for the rest of us, poor sons of a land without wines, there is no harm at all in nightly reading an epigram by Rivarol and drinking, at least once a week, half a glass of champagne.

Some of his work reveals the misfit critic who was to dominate for a long while until reaction came with the critics of the 1960s.

Stylistics, or criticism concerned with poetic language, had been fueled by Luís Gonzaga Duque Estrada (1863–1911) and

João Ribeiro (1860–1934), among others. Nestor Victor (1868–1932) and José Cândido Andrade Muricy (1895–1984) completed the picture, although they were more concerned with Symbolist, end-of-the-century production rather than with contemporary letters. João Ribeiro may be counted as one of the most highly regarded of the remaining nineteenth-century critics. Here is Aurélio Buarque de Holanda Ferreira's (1910–1989) assessment of Ribeiro's articles in the preface to *O Fabordão*:

> O maior encanto do nosso comércio com João Ribeiro é a variedade, o imprevisto, a amplidão de horizonte cultural que ele vai devassando, entre obstinado e volúvel, aos olhos do leitor, quando esse não se contenta com a primeira leitura e rumina o livro lido, para marcar alguns trechos da sua preferência. . . . Numa fase de vacas magras, de gramática emperrada, com exclusiva orientação normativa nos estudos filológicos, João Ribeiro deu na província do Brasil o exemplo da mais arejada objetividade no trato dessas questões, que procurava temperar quase sempre de prudência avisada e bastante ironia. (Ribeiro viii)

> The most delightful aspect of our dealings with João Ribeiro is the unexpected variety and breadth of the cultural horizon he obstinately and voluably reveals to the reader who, not contented with a first reading, ponders over a book to mark a few favorite passages. . . . In this stubbornly limited period of linguistic commentary with its slim pickings and strictly philological standards, João Ribeiro affords Brazilian letters the most objective examples of those subjects which he nearly always sought to temper with sense and prudence and plenty of irony.

Humberto de Campos was yet another impressionist critic whose column, begun in 1928, was written in Rio and distributed to the provincial newspapers; he thus occupied an important place in literary journalism in the 1930s. He was born in Maranhão and became a critic near the end of his life—as he himself states, because of the scarcity of intellectuals in the field. According to João Pacheco (1910–1966), his criticism combines impressions and reminiscences with superficial considerations that alternate with general concepts interlaced with scholarly digressions (Pacheco 64).

The first twelve years of Tristão de Athayde's (1893–1983) journalistic criticism were contemporaneous with the modernist experiments in São Paulo. Out of open-mindedness rather than through spiritual affinity, Tristão de Athayde recorded or, better yet, bore witness to the advance of modernist ideas and groups that, touched by the energy of the São Paulo movements, spread throughout the provinces, through the publication of numerous books and reviews. As for his own approach, Tristão de Athayde understood the inadequacy of critical impressionism and sought to provide an analytical method that might combine intuition and analysis, proposing a critical method divided into three stages: (1) identification of the author's "soul," (2) dissection of the work's elements (theme, language), and (3) concluding synthesis—an evaluation of its aesthetic value (see Lafetá 87–89). Thus he followed closely the modernist publications of the "heroic phase." In the next decade, after his conversion to Catholicism, his interests leaned toward more abstract general subjects. Having set literature aside during the 1930s, he returned occasionally to literary criticism, as in his study of Raquel de Queiroz's (b. 1910) *O Quinze* (1930; "1815") (see Lafetá 87–89).

Of all his contemporaries, Athayde was among those most interested in and concerned with textual analysis. His European education, however, prevented him from recognizing a movement directed toward a specifically Brazilian reality. As

transcribed by Wilson Martins (b. 1921), Mário de Andrade's (1893–1945) assessment of Athayde is symptomatic: "a quase dolorosa incompreensão poética; a conversão sistemática de todos os nossos valores individuais e movimentos a fenômenos de mera importação; e, o que é pior, a sujeição das opiniões artísticas dele à *coup d'amour* européia. Outro dos seus defeitos seria a falta de sutileza de análise" ("the almost painful lack of any poetic understanding, the systematic conversion of all Brazilian values and movements to imported phenomena, and, worse, the subordination of his artistic opinions to the European *coup d'amour*. Another of his faults is his lack of analytical subtlety"). Martins concurs with this evaluation and concludes:

> Colocando em face de um movimento que foi regionalizante e, por isso mesmo, ganglionar, e que, apesar das suas fontes livrescas e estrangeiras, ambicionava encarnar a "realidade" ou "as realidades" brasileiras, Tristão de Athayde exerceu uma crítica universal e sintetizadora, pouco brasileira e menos sociológica que filosófica, generalizando em lugar de analisar e negando-se, com isso, inconscientemente, a reconhecer a originalidade voluntária do Modernismo. (606–7)

> Faced with a regionalizing and, for this very reason, a centralizing movement which, despite its bookish, foreign sources, sought to embody Brazilian "reality" or "realities," Tristão de Athayde practiced a not uncommon Brazilian, universalist, synthesizing criticism, more philosophical than sociological, general rather than analytic, and thus unconsciously refused to acknowledge Modernism's originality.

The active critics of the 1920s were unaware of the profound transformation that Modernism was bringing about in literature. The majority of the critics based in Rio de Janeiro—which, then the country's capital, held cultural power–preferred to ignore it and had no measure of its repercussions. Benevolent toward the movement, Ronald de Carvalho (1893–1935) and João Ribeiro were among those dominant journalists who had homeopathically promoted and reported on what was new in the provinces. From his Symbolist stronghold, Nestor Victor uneasily watched the spread of São Paulo Modernism. At once condescending and benevolent toward new writers, João Ribeiro was likewise unable to grasp the transformation that was to take place with the new experimentation.

Modernism was not a homogeneous movement. It began in São Paulo and then spread in waves throughout all the provinces, which, in turn, established their own divergences and tensions with the São Paulo movement. Nor did the early Modernist *Klaxon* magazine (see **Figure 3**) group remain united, having split up into various other groupings, each with its own specific aesthetic project supported by ideological norms that spanned a representative arc from Leftist propositions to those of the Right with strong totalitarian coloring. Throughout the decade, Modernism presented a wide literary range from the most radical formal experiments to a thematic search for Brazilian identity. This moment was accompanied by the publication of reviews that represented the direction to be followed by each splinter group. A brief analysis reveals many points of contact, especially in the revision of authors of the past, allied with an emphasis on the analysis of contemporary production. In other words, this meant that, within the bastions of their reviews, the new writers not only experimented with creative writing, but also sought to evaluate previously existing literature as well as contemporary authors.

Figure 3.

Cover of the first issue of the Modernist literary magazine Klaxon, *1922, São Paulo. (Archive of the author)*

The reviews became the centers of these groups, even for those that rose up against experimentation.

Though Cassiano Ricardo (1895–1974) and Antônio Alcântara Machado (1901–1935) also wrote, Mário de Andrade was the catalyzing figure of Modernism; he became a journalistic critic at the end of the 1930s, an activity he performed until his death in 1945. He started with a column in the *Diário de Notícias,* and many of the pieces he wrote for it are collected in *Aspectos da literatura brasileira* [1943; Aspects of Brazilian Literature]. Giving methodological preference to psychologism, his work served as a reference point and orientation to critics of later decades. Because of his method rather than his actual perceptions, some of his judgments frequently gave way first to objections and then to refutation.

The 1930s were dominated by ideological criticism and the clash between groups gathered in cliques. Critics assessed the value of published work more in terms of what it represented to the "country's sociopolitical plan" than for its aesthetic merits. The decade is thus characterized by a hierarchy of political tendencies that, as personal ideology, direct the individual to entrench himself in groups whose members are treated with distinction and kept cohesive through mutual compliments, while the work of adversaries is insulted.

According to Wilson Martins, criticism came to reflect political concerns, replacing its "'sociological' scale of values with a 'sociopolitical one'." "A literatura, que tinha sido um meio de conhecimento, de interpretação ou de expressão da terra, transforma-se em instrumento de convicções políticas. O romance, a poesia, estimam-se pelo seu conteúdo "revolucionário–já agora politicamente, e não mais literariamente revolucionário" (620) ("Literature, which had been a way of knowledge, of interpretation or of national expression, becomes an instrument of political convictions. Poetry and novels are regarded for their "revolutionary" political [rather than literary] content"). According to Brito Broca (1903–1961), the cliques (or *capelinhas*) wove "os fios de uma tediosa política literária" ("the threads of a tedious literary politics") and came together through spiritual affinity or sometimes less elevated circumstantial convenience. Much reciprocally overvalued criticism arose from this situation (Broca 11).

At the end of the decade, some scholars came on the scene who would be predominant during the 1940s and 1950s, when a critical breakthrough took place, creating journalism centered on the actual work of literature and more concerned with anchoring itself in literary theories and critical approaches. With the new generation of critics, already formed within the parameters of Modernism, Brazilian criticism reached a new level of achievement. There was a new visibility, and cultural legitimacy was the issue debated through the publication of various specialized reviews and newspapers with different, smaller formats (the tabloids) or separate literary supplements. Two generations shared the same space, though the focused examination and appreciation of the literary work of art prevailed. Thus *do Branca, Boletim de Ariel, Leitura, Revista do Globo* (edited in Porto Alegre, but with nationwide circulation), and the weekly *Dom Casmurro* joined the *Revista do Brasil* and *Revista Brasileira.* Edited by Gastão Cruls (1888–1959) and Agrippino Grieco, *Boletim de Ariel* was intended to be a popularizing magazine (Broca 103) with the aim of increasing the number of readers interested in literature. Moyses Velhinho (1902–1980) and Lúcia Miguel Pereira (1901–1959), among others from this group of critics, moved on to the dailies. Founded in 1937 by Brito Broca after the manner of Parisian literary periodicals such as *Les nouvelles littéraires* (see Broca 104), *Dom Casmurro* housed young critics like Franklin de Oliveira, Josué Montello, Joel Silveira, José Conde, Wilson Louzada, and Eugenio Gomes, some of the most representative critics and specialists of the second half of the 1940s.

With the end of the World War II, the 1940s significantly transformed the country's social and political life as well as the literary and cultural scenes. The expansion of printing was accelerated by the appearance of new publishing houses; this, in turn, paved the way for a greater number of translations. As the axis of cultural influence shifted from France to the United States, the publication of critical essays and literary supplements grew. If the first five years were dominated by the founding of reviews and the "Autores & Livros" ("Authors & Books") supplement of the daily *A Manhã* (a newspaper with government ties), after the war another supplement, under the title of "Letras e Artes" ("Letters and Arts"), was to compete with many others. The *Correio da Manhã* supplement began its activity with sections and columns dedicated to the visual arts, music, theater, and literature but aimed at a more specialized readership (Broca 105).

Literary criticism in Brazil had been changing since the end of the 1930s, with the arrival of the first specialists who inaugurated the essay format and published monothematic publications, anchored by new literary theories. Some of these critics would come to dominate the scene in the 1940s, collaborating in the daily newspapers; their articles contained far more analysis than value judgment. Concerned with focusing on the work as opposed to the man, they began to elaborate new readings of already canonical writers. In mapping this rich and diversified decade, one must also take into account the arrival of European critics who sought refuge in Brazil from the war and who would, after a fashion, broaden the horizons of critical militants, more attuned to local interests. Spurred on by the reading public's eagerness for foreign writers, and especially for those writing in English, publishing houses invested in translations while creating reviews that began to occupy themselves with essays on foreign authors, making way for the emergence of critics interested in other cultures. Specialists predominated; commenting on Eugenio Gomes's (1897–1972) book *Prata da casa*, Hildon Rocha called attention to this type of criticism in the newspaper supplements: "O especialista tende a estudar uma determinada literatura, em tais ou quais autores, pelo menos a ponto de nos oferecer dessa dedicação especial e apaixonada, um estudo definitivo, um livro a que tivesse confiado todo o seu conhecimento de um autor ou de um gênero específico. Um estudo de interpretação que se possa ter como fonte de consulta e de esclarecimento" (Rocha 1954)("The specialist tends to study a given literature through this or that author, at least to the point of affording us a definitive study from this special and passionate dedication, a book to which he entrusted all his knowledge of a specific author or genre. These interpretations of texts can be held as a source of reference and enlightenment").

Readers too began to demand a wider spectrum of subjects and to read attentively the critical analyses of contemporary works as well as reading writers of the past from new perspectives. In Antonio Cândido's terms: "Formaram-se então novos laços entre escritor e público, com uma tendência crescente para a redução dos laços que antes o prendiam aos grupos restritos de diletantes e "conhecedores." Mas este novo público, à medida que crescia, ia sendo rapidamente conquistado pelo grande desenvolvimento dos novos meios de comunicação" (1967, 159–60)("Thus new ties were forged between writer and public, with a growing tendency toward the reduction of (those) ties which previously bound him to restricted groups of dilettantes and so-called experts. But, as it grew, this new public was quickly won over by the tremendous development of new media"). Eduardo Portella adds:

A crítica brasileira agarrou-se ao esquema francês de XIX e construiu a sorte–uma sorte um tanto lotérica–dos nossos livros, dos nossos autores da nossa literatura.

Por isto se fez necessário o estabelecimento imediato de uma nova ordem. Todos, os lúcidos, os que não se marginalizaram, reconheciam a falência do antigo sistema. O ambiente se tornou propício à instauração do novo regime crítico. Apoderava-se do País uma mentalidade nova, a do conhecimento aparelhado, da conclusão científica. A fase do amadorismo estava definitivamente sepultada. Afrânio Coutinho foi o principal servidor desta causa: da reformulação crítica, da renovação metodológica. Ele se inscrevia num movimento de âmbito universal pela renovação dos processos e métodos de pesquisa e investigação literária. E não tardou para que essa consciência e esse ímpeto renovador conquistassem toda a nossa motivação crítica, transformando por completo o nosso modo de operar criticamente e repercutindo, de maneira particular e positiva, em nossa própria concepção do fenômeno literário. (51–61)

Brazilian literary criticism had held fast to the French schematic arrangements of the nineteenth century and had cast with lottery-like luck into obsolete categories our books, our authors, all our literature.

Because of this, the immediate establishment of a new order became necessary. Everyone, the lucid, those who were not marginalized, acknowledged the bankruptcy of the old system. The environment became conducive to the beginning of a new critical regime. A new mentality took hold of the country, that of informed knowledge, of scientific conclusions. The amateur phase was permanently put to rest. Afrânio Coutinho [1911–2000] was the principal servant of this cause of critical reformulation and methodological renewal. He was part of a worldwide movement for the renewal of research methodology and procedures for literary investigation. And it was not long before this awareness and rejuvenating thrust conquered all of our critical motivation, utterly transforming our ways of critical operation and affecting, in a particular and positive manner, our very conception of the literary phenomenon.

Thus critics of various orientations coexisted in the daily newspapers, which devoted space to the exercise of literary criticism by intellectuals, militant critics, and the first generation of graduates from various university philosophy departments. In language stripped bare of adjectives, value judgments were made in a vehicle that limited great flights but fashioned a criticism that was both consensual and accessible. Even beyond the fact that the articles were distinguished by the absence of specific theoretical jargon that would have hampered their understanding, these essays were designed to involve the greatest possible number of specialized readers. As Wilson Martins has stated, the 1940s were basically dominated by critics who were products of Modernism and who therefore understood the primacy of the text over the author's life, of the search for distance and a comprehensible language (meta-language) with which to examine the literary text, but also one that allowed a depth of interpretation. The decade was greatly affected by the arrival of scholars who, by appropriating methods from the field of literary theory, succeeded in giving literary studies their due maturity.

The reorganization of the country's political and economic life demanded a new reading of the country and its cultural manifestations as well as its claims to be part of Western culture, furnishing support for the unfolding of a nationalist line both in life and in the arts. In literature, the debate about cultural dependency was stirred up over the label of Brazil as an "underdeveloped country" versus the awareness of being a colonized people. Some of Antônio Cândido's texts of this period, such as the following one, can give us a sense of the moment:

No decênio de 1930 predominava entre nós a noção de "país novo" que ainda não pudera realizar-se mas que atribuía a si mesmo grandes possibilidades de progresso futuro. Sem ter havido modificação essencial na distância que nos separa dos países ricos, o que predomina agora é a noção de "país subdesenvolvido." Ora, dada esta ligação causal–'terra bela–pátria grande' não é difícil ver a repercussão que traria a consciência do subdesenvolvimento como mudança de perspectiva, que evidenciou a realidade dos solos pobres, das técnicas arcaicas, da miséria pasmosa das populações, da sua inculta paralisante. A visão que resulta é pessimista quanto ao presente e problemática quanto ao futuro. (Cândido 1987, 140–41)

The concept of a "new country," as yet unfulfilled but which attributed to itself great possibilities for future progress, prevailed among us during the thirties. With no essential change in the distance which separates us from rich nations, what prevails now is the idea of the "underdeveloped country."

Given this causal connection ("beautiful land–great nation"), it is not difficult to see the repercussion brought about by an awareness of underdevelopment which witnessed the reality of the poor soil, of archaic techniques, of the astonishing poverty of its population, of its paralyzing lack of culture. The resulting vision is pessimistic with regard to the present and problematic with regard to the past.

This highly critical group grew larger as the 1950s unfolded, with the debate being about cultural dependency, which, in a way, was already a way of signaling the difference between the appropriations of literatures of the center and their mere imitation. Several comparatists began to appear on the scene; Eugênio Gomes (1897–1972) and Augusto Meyer (1902–1970) were foremost among them.

However, it was critic Álvaro Lins (1912–1970) who dominated the scene during the 1940s, positioning himself independently from the cliques; he claimed he would not allow himself to be "dominar por qualquer circunstância estranha à literatura" (Martins 620) ("dominated by any consideration foreign to literature"). Curious and instinctive, Lins succeeded, despite his inability to cast off impressionism, in restricting himself exclusively to the work's aesthetic merits. In 1948 his literary criticism suffered a demolishing attack at the hands of Afrânio Coutinho, who, upon his return from the United States, took upon himself the task of introducing North American "New Criticism" to Brazil. Eugenio Gomes gives this account:

> Os métodos, muito mais que os críticos, eis o que tinha especialmente em vista, mas é claro que, combatendo aqueles, estes não podiam sofrer a paciência de assistir à derrocada de seus princípios, e, em conseqüência, a luta revestiu-se às vezes de um aspecto que a desviava lastimavelmente do campo apropriado. Quaisquer, porém, que sejam as razões de um lado e de outro, será injustiça deixar de reconhecer que o inconformismo afirmativo de Afrânio Coutinho teve o mérito de atrair a atenção geral do país para um corpo vibrátil de idéias, cuja ausência de nossos debates em torno da crítica estética seria inconcebível. (1961)

> It was methods he had in mind, far more than individual critics, although, of course, the latter did not suffer the patience of seeing the demolition of their own critical principles and, consequently, the struggle was sometimes endowed with an aspect which sidetracked it most regrettably from its appropriate field of literary criticism. Whatever the reasons of one side or the other, it would be unfair not to acknowledge that Afrânio Coutinho's affirmative non-conformism possessed the merit of drawing the country's attention to a vibrant body of ideas whose absence from our debate on aesthetic criticism would be inconceivable.

Thus, Brito Broca (1903–1961), Homero Senna (b. 1919), Wilson Martins (b. 1921), Antonio Cândido (b. 1918), Afrânio Coutinho, Fábio Frexieiro (1931–1984), Fábio Lucas (b. 1931), Adalmir Cunha (b. 1930), Lúcia Miguel Pereira (1901–1959), and Joel Pontes (1926–1977), as well as visitors like Otto Maria Carpeaux (1900–1978) and Paulo Ronai (1907–1992), exist in the records alongside the historicist scholars. The arrival of foreign critics for extended visits afforded more intimate contact with other literatures besides the French, as was the case with Otto Maria Carpeaux's study of the work of Franz Kafka. Among the many new directions introduced at this time, we should point out the study of primary sources through the original documents of writers of the national past, as well as comparative literature based on German and French theory and the North American interventions of Czech scholar Rene Wellek. An embryonic genetic criticism still based on philological methodology also began to blossom. By the end of the

1950s, literature as object, along with its theory and methods, stood at the center of debate, and the revision of the canon through literary historiography was concretized with the publication of countless histories of literature. Antônio Cândido gives an account of this time of rapid change:

> Daí as modernas tendências estetizantes aparecem ao sociólogo e ao historiador da cultura como reação de defesa e ajustamento às novas condições da vida intelectual; uma delimitação de campo que para o crítico, é principalmente uma tendência ao formalismo, e por vezes à gratuidade e ao solipsismo literário. Tanto para o crítico quanto para o estudioso da cultura e da sociedade, ela é, contudo, uma elaboração de novos meios expressivos e um desenvolvimento de nova consciência artesanal. (1967, 162)

> Hence modern aestheticizing tendencies appear to the sociologist and to the cultural historian as defensive reactions or adjustments to the new conditions of intellectual life; a delimitation of the field which, to the critic, is chiefly a tendency toward formalism and sometimes toward gratuitousness and literary solipsism. To the critic as much as to the scholar of culture and society it is, however, an elaboration of new means of expression and the development of a new awareness of craft.

At the decade's end Eduardo Portella (b. 1932) made his entrance, and literary theory became a regular offering in departments of literature throughout the country. At the close of the 1950s, the publication of two historiographical studies offered new perspectives on the founding models of twentieth-century historiography, as wrought by José Veríssimo, Silvio Romero, and Araripe Júnior: the publication of Afrânio Coutinho's *A literatura no Brasil* [1955; Literature in Brazil] and Antônio Cândido's *Formação da literatura brasileira* [1959; The Making of Brazilian Literature]. In addition to Massaud Moisés's *História da literatura brasileira* [1983; History of Brazilian Literature], Antônio Cândido's *Formação* was to be a new re-reading of the founding moment, dialoguing with Sílvio Romero, and presenting an articulation of the sociological and the aesthetic.

From another perspective, incorporating Araripe Júnior's model, *A literatura no Brasil* was published between 1956 and 1958 as a collective effort. Initially directed by Afrânio Coutinho (its creator) with the collaboration of Eugênio Gomes and Barreto Filho, it counted among its participants the principal critics of the day: Wilton Cardoso, Antonio Cândido, Wilson Martins, Sílvio Castro, Eugênio Gomes, José Aderaldo Castello, Soares Amora, Waltensir Dutra, Luís Costa Lima, Cassiano Ricardo, Emanuel de Morais, Heron de Alencar, Josué Montello, Moysés Velhinho, Péricles Eugênio da Silva Ramos, Barreto Filho, Franklin de Oliveira, Otávio de Faria, Peregrino Júnior, Adonias Filho, Wilson Louzada, Edgar Cavalheiro, Augusto Meyer, Andrade Muricy, Xavier Placer, Darci Damasceno, Alceu Amoroso Lima (Tristão de Athayde), Mário da Silva Filho, Mário Chamie, Dirce Cortes Riedel, Bandeira de Melo, Herman Lima, Moraes Filho, Afonso Arinos de Melo Franco, and intellectuals specialized in other fields, such as Câmara Cascudo, Fernando de Azevedo, Segismundo Spina, Cândido Jucá Filho, Carlos Kopke, Luís Viana Filho, Aderbal Jurema, and Américo Lacombe. Most of the scholars of the day, regardless of age, ideology, or critical apparatus, were recognized in this comprehensive yet uneven work, which, nonetheless, has become a reference book on text and styles and is a good barometer to Brazilian intellectual and critical dynamism during the last quarter of the twentieth century.

Translation by Stephen A. Berg

Works Cited

Broca, Brito. 1993. *Teatro das letras*. Campinas: Ed. UNICAMP.

Cândido, Antonio. 1967. *Literatura e sociedade: Estudos de teoria e história literária*. 2nd ed. São Paulo: Companhia Editora Nacional.

———. 1987. *A educação pela noite & outros ensaios*. São Paulo: Ática.

Coutinho, Afrânio, ed. 1986. *A literatura no Brasil*. Rio de Janeiro: J. Olympio.

Gomes, Eugenio. 1961. "Lição de inconformismo." *O Globo* (Rio de Janeiro) 25 March.

Grieco, Agrippino. 1935. *Gente nova no Brasil*. Rio de Janeiro: J. Olympio.

Lafetá, J. L. 1974. *1930: A crítica e o modernismo*. São Paulo: Duas Cidades.

Martins, Wilson. 1986. "A crítica modernista." *A literatura no Brasil*. Vol 5. Ed. Afrânio Coutinho. Rio de Janeiro: J. Olympio.

Pacheco, João. 1967. *O realismo. (A Literatura Brasileira)*. São Paulo: Cultrix.

Portella, Eduardo. 1971. *Literatura e realidade*. Rio de Janeiro: Tempo Brasileiro.

Ribeiro, João. 1964. *O Farbodão*. Rio de Janeiro: S. José.

Rocha, Hildon. 1954. "Homens & Obras: O crítico e as especializações." *A Noite* (Rio de Janeiro) 5 October.

CHAPTER 15

LITERARY PERIODICALS OF THE 1960s
PROPOSALS FOR RE-READING

Luz Rodríguez-Carranza

In any historiographic study, including those resolutely inscribed under the New Historicism (Veeser ix), it might sound rather contradictory to propose that we re-read–or, even more so, re-write–history that is still in the making, such as that of the literary and cultural periodicals of the 1960s. We have been fervent readers of these periodicals; many of the younger contributors are still among us, and their memories offer legitimate interpretations. A more modest proposal would thus be to give a panoramic overview. When memories are presented as a whole and are successfully transmitted, however, they weave versions that inevitably leave an indelible mark on future interpretations. Despite their proximity in time, two very solid narratives written in the 1960s and 1970s, which Carlos Mangone calls the cultural and the political decade respectively (196), have already been interposed between us and the periodicals. The first is that of the Boom, an onomatopoeic term coined by the weekly *Primera Plana* (Buenos Aires, 1962–1971) to baptize the symbolic and commercial success of the novels of Julio Cortázar (1914–1984), Gabriel García Márquez (b. 1927), Carlos Fuentes (b. 1928), Mario Vargas Llosa (b. 1936) (Rodríguez Monegal 1972, 24). The second is that of the post-Boom, which challenged the ideological stance adopted by authors and texts of the dominant Boom model, whose success was attributed to international marketing strategies.

The former narrative affirmed and the latter confirmed the extraordinary burgeoning of periodical publications during those years. In his prescriptive essay of 1972, *El boom de la novela latinoamericana* [The Boom of the Latin American Novel], Emir Rodríguez Monegal foregrounded particularly the decisive role of periodicals and their proliferation, as did Ángel Rama (1926–1983) in a 1981 text that has become a key reference work for anyone studying the 1960s, "El boom en perspectiva" ["The Boom in Perspective"]. The literary supplements of the leading newspapers competed with the publications sponsored by the State and with those financed by foundations; academic journals hastened to bring themselves up to date; public and private publishing houses launched their bulletins; modern magazines imitating *Time* or *Newsweek* had a circulation of over 50,000 copies; writers and critics founded innumerable publications on specific topics in the form of deluxe editions or laboriously mimeographed pamphlets. However, that incredibly rich production is still classified in omni-explanatory binary syntheses. If we propose to reconstruct the complexity of voices, dialogues and controversies of a period no less hybrid than that of the start of the twenty-first century, it is essential that we unearth its roots.

Genealogies I: Readings of the Boom

The hegemony of the model of the so-called new novel was imposed by an academic discourse using the same method used when imposing the grand narratives of the past: a systematic reiteration of value judgments. It is worth noting that this took just a decade to achieve, because the first selection/interpretation of the works was contemporaneous, and thus either simultaneous with the production that it attempted to systematize or, at times, even prior to it. As Claudia Gilman points out, in the 1960s "se configura, tal vez con la misma fuerza e igual voluntarismo que durante el período modernista, una 'idea' (o la necesidad de una idea) de América Latina" ("an 'idea' (or the need for an idea) of Latin America was outlined with perhaps the same strength and willfulness as during the *modernista* period"), and "se trató entonces de detectar y aislar las contribuciones progresivas que el campo intelectual fue realizando en la construcción conceptual de una literatura nueva en un mundo nuevo" ("an attempt was made to discern and isolate the intellectuals' progressive contributions to the conceptual construction of a new literature in a new world") (1997, 174). What we might call Latin-Americanization was advocated as actively by the cultural policy of the Cuban Revolution as by that of the United States of America in its attempt to institutionalize an inter-American system (the Inter-American Treaty of Reciprocal Assistance in Rio in 1947; the creation of the Organization of American States in 1958; and the Alliance for Progress).

From the early sixties on, there was a worldwide demand to know more about Latin American literary production, and intellectuals enjoyed exceptional communication conditions. Meetings, colloquia, round-table discussions and congresses with funding from different sources were organized throughout the sixties. Despite all this, it was, in fact, lack of communication that was the main theme of one of the first meetings, held in Concepción, Chile, in 1962 and presided over by such figures as Pablo Neruda (1904–1973), José María Arguedas (1911–1969), Augusto Roa Bastos (b. 1917), Carlos Fuentes, Alejo Carpentier (1904–1980), José Miguel Oviedo (b. 1934), and José Bianco (1908–1986). Latin Americans were well versed in European and U.S. literature, as well as that of their own individual countries, but had little knowledge of other literatures on their continent (Donoso 1972). Bonds were created: Critics and writers developed an awareness of their common history and a mode for writing it. Their interest in the culture of other countries naturally led to a conscious and willing exchange of views concerning Latin America, foreign models (Sartre, Faulkner, Camus, Dos Passos, Moravia, Capote, Proust, Mann), and the texts themselves.

The communication initiated at these congresses was consolidated by correspondence and, above all, by an increasingly coherent network of literary and cultural periodicals. *Casa de las Américas* (Havana, 1960–), *Mundo Nuevo* during its first period (Paris, 1966–1968), *Marcha* (Montevideo, 1939–1974), *Primera Plana* (Buenos Aires, 1962–1971), *El Escarabajo de Oro* (Buenos Aires, 1961–1974), *La Cultura en México* (supplement of *Siempre!* Mexico, 1962–1972), *Imagen* (Caracas,

1967–1969 and 1971–1974), and *Zona Franca* (Caracas, 1964–1984) shared contributors, reprinted articles, and designed sections for the purposes of advertising each other's work, engaging in polemics, and exchanging information. All this made way for literary prizes–commented on fully in the periodicals: the *Formentor*, the *Primera Plana* and *Losada* (Buenos Aires), the *Seix Barral* (Barcelona), and the *Casa de las Américas* (Cuba)–and then the first Rómulo Gallegos prize of Caracas (1967), awarded for the best Latin American novel written in Spanish during the previous five years.

As the Gallegos prize revealed, the adjective **new** referred to the modern novel, defined and systematized by Mariana Frenk as the new novel in the Spanish-speaking regions of Latin America (Frenk 85). When explaining the revolutionary nature of Juan Rulfo's (1918–1986) writing, Frenk selects and explains the salient characteristics of this new novel, such as its themes, the technique and language of the naturalist novel and the psychological novel, and then uses these to analyze *Pedro Páramo* (1955) (Frenk 90–95). Although he does not cite Frenk, Carlos Fuentes uses the same term in 1964 in his article entitled "La nueva novela latinoamericana" ["The New Latin American Novel"] written for *La Cultura en México*; he confirms Rulfo as the first really new novelist by establishing a genealogy from Mariano Azuela's (1873–1952) *Los de abajo* [1915; *The Underdogs*, 1971] and placing Carpentier, Vargas Llosa, and Cortázar within this new trend. Fuentes published a longer version of this essay, including a consideration of Juan Goytisolo, in book form in 1969 as *La nueva novela hispanoamericana* [The New Hispanic-American Novel]. The model was defined a little later in Emir Rodríguez Monegal's prescriptive monographic study (1972), which included Fuentes and the Brazilian Guimarães Rosa (1908–1967) in the list of new novelists.

The criteria for assessing the quality of this novel were very precise: It had to be an absolutely fictitious rendering; it should rewrite the history of the continent in a mythical code and transform language. This final criterion included specific devices. First of all, the use of different kinds of Latin-American Spanish endowed their prose with a different lexicon and different semantic fields for the same words, thus permitting a transculturation of the Joycean model. Similarly, the syntax of indigenous languages and urban slang subtly transformed the rhythm of Spanish. Second, the simultaneous overlaying of temporal planes exacted the reader's active participation. A third device was the narration by characters and focalization through them; their use of direct and free indirect discourse resembled recordings, because the narrator was so anonymous. Thus, the omniscient third-person narrator, who could provide the only valid interpretation of the story, was replaced by a mosaic of voices; the readers, as producers rather than consumers of meaning, had to reconstruct the new stories from the pieces at their disposal.

The articles and reviews advocating this new model reveal that there was also a transformation in style that was directly influenced by the works analyzed and by the journalistic techniques of modern magazines. Rodríguez Monegal wrote magnificent portraits of the Boom writers in *Nuevo Mundo*, spiced with novelistic details about their personalities. These characters, like those in their novels, were all made to use direct discourse. In the articles written by Jorge Rufinelli (*Marcha*), Ernesto Shoo and Tomás Eloy Martínez (*Primera Plana*), Emmanuel Carballo, Carlos Monsiváis and Elena Poniatowska (*La Cultura en México*), dialogue is presented directly without narrative intervention; there is often an exchange of letters,

but the interview is the dominant genre, and the tape recorder–which accompanies the journalist like a fetish,–is a symbol constantly mentioned. It is worth noting, however, that even though the narrator gives voice to the characters, they only say what he or she wishes them to say: Meticulously creating a montage, he or she chooses the exact phrases, directs the discussion, and even intervenes, as does the narrator of Fuentes' *Cambio de Piel* [1967; *Change of Skin*, 1968]. These new critics constructed new worlds: They ran and contributed to periodicals, chose the cultural events and happenings and their mode of temporal representation, and, indeed, organized a literary system.

Almost at the same time that congresses, prizes, and periodicals were canonizing this model, the process of selecting representative articles to explain them began. The first studies to appear in book form at the end of the 1960s and the beginning of the 1970s were anthologies of essays published in the periodicals of this network, which were now established as the breeding ground for renovation. This publishing formula was the only reaction possible on the part of the critics to a vertiginous situation. Not only were journalists responding to best-sellers, thereby collaborating in establishing their economic value, but critics also wrote essays in cultural and literary periodicals declaring their support for modernity and the revolutionary aesthetic quality of the texts in vogue. This symbolic bonus, so to speak, included the relation explicitly established by Fuentes between the social and the literary language revolution. The new man and the new novel were considered a syntagma that could be read using the same code; this explains the immediate demand for editions and interpretations on the part of intellectuals in general and of students of literature in particular–all of which were reproduced in the United States of America and Europe during the following decade.

In an attempt to meet the demands of the new readership, the publishing houses created a hybrid product, the compilation of articles. This solution had two variants: On the one hand, critics would make a selection of their studies of authors and their work and write an introduction that generally set down the norms. Examples of this trend include Luis Harss (b. 1936) *Los nuestros* [1966; *Into the Mainstream*, 1967], Mario Benedetti (b. 1920) *Letras del continente mestizo* [1967; Literature of the Mestizo Continent], Fernando Alegría (b. 1918) *La novela hispanoamericana* [1967; The Spanish American Novel], Julio Ortega (b. 1924) *La contemplación y la fiesta* [1968; Contemplation and Celebration], Carlos Fuentes *La nueva novela hispanoamericana* [1969; The New Hispanic American Novel], Alejo Carpentier (1904–1980) *Tientos y diferencias* [1964; Attempts and Differences], and Ariel Dorfman (b. 1942) *Imaginación y violencia en América Latina* [1970; Imagination and Violence in Latin America]. At the beginning of the 1970s, on the other hand, university professors began to compile collections of studies written by different critics, based, of course, on the same list of authors now held in ever higher esteem. These include: Angel Flores and Raúl Silva Cáceres' *La novela hispanoamericana actual* [1971; The Contemporary Spanish American Novel], Pupo Walker's *El cuento hispanoamericano* [1973; The Spanish American Short-Story], Jorge Lafforgue's *Nueva novela hispanoamericana* in two volumes [1969; The New Hispanic American Novel], Juan Loveluck's *La novela hispanoamericana* [1963; The Hispanic American Novel], and *Novelistas hispanoamericanas de hoy* [1976; Hispanic American Novelists Today], Aurora Ocampo de Gómez's *La crítica de la novela iberoamericana actual* [1973; Criticism of the Contemporary

Ibero-American Novel], Rodríguez Alcalá's *Narrativa hispan-oamericana* [1973; Hispanic American Narrative] and Joaquín Roy's *Narrativa y crítica de nuestra América* [1978; Narrative and Criticism of Our America]. The most monumental products of this trend were the *Homenajes* (*Homages*) by Helmy Giacoman, which were deluxe anthologies dedicated to the star authors.

The same critics' names appeared time and again in these compilations. Just as the same writers–Fuentes, Cortázar, and Vargas Llosa–were generally discussed, so the commentators were gradually becoming the major authorities in the field. These included such critical voices as Fernando Alegría, Mario Benedetti, Roberto Fernández Retamar, Luis Leal, Juan Liscano, Fausto Massó, Alfred McAdam, Seymour Menton, José Miguel Oviedo, Enrique Pezzoni, Angel Rama, Richard Reeve, Mercedes Rein, Emir Rodríguez Monegal, Alfredo Roggiano, Jorge Rufinelli, Ivan Schulman, Raúl Silva Cáceres and Guillermo Sucre. The compilers of the collections undertook the first task of selecting the critical material, and academics working on bibliographies were responsible for confirming it. Since the material from the periodicals of the so-called network proved to be insufficient, other publications were consulted, such as the *Anales de la Universidad de Chile* (1843–), the Peruvian *Amaru* (1967–1971), the Chilean *Atenea* (1924–), the Colombian *Eco* (1969–1983), the Argentinian *Sur* (1931–1978), the Puerto Rican *Asomante* (1944–1970) and *Sin Nombre* (1970–1984), *Revista Mexicana de Literatura* (1956–1965), the Uruguayan *Número* (1949–1955 and 1963–1964) and *Temas* (1965–1968), and the *Revista Iberoamericana* (1939–) of Pittsburgh. The articles compiled in one volume might have been written at different times, and their juxtaposition would thus reveal the evolution of prescriptive criteria and the differences among positions. García Márquez, for example, was not appreciated by everyone for the same reasons, and the same critic might radically change his opinion concerning a writer, as Ángel Rama did concerning Roa Bastos.

If these differences of opinion were still obvious when a homogeneous criterion was used to select texts, the disagreements must clearly have been much more acute at the date of their original publication in the periodicals. In the research project I directed in Louvain-Leuven between 1987 and 1990 on the periodicals of the 1960s, we proved, for example, that whereas *Casa de las Américas* had been organizing discussions, talks, and colloquia on the new novel since 1964 (see Verschoote), the *Revista Iberoamericana* had focused attention on *modernista* poetry (see Coignez and Jongbloet). Similarly, the *Revista Nacional de Cultura* in Venezuela had little regard for the new novel, describing it as mass literature written for the market (see Ledegen and Van Hecke). *Asomante*, edited by Nilita Vientós Gastón, held the opinion that the essence of Puerto Rican-ness lay in its Spanish heritage, and it was thus principally interested in canonical Spanish literature (see Sioen). *Zona Franca*, edited in Caracas, was more journalistic than academic and decided to focus on the young generation of poets from Venezuela and other Latin American countries, taking the modern and elitist line (and many of the contributors) of the waning Argentinian journal *Sur* (1931–1978). *Zona Franca* even questioned the Rómulo Gallegos Prize of 1967 awarded in Caracas to Vargas Llosa (see Sas), which was, in turn, greeted with acclaim by *Imagen* (see Laurijssen). *Primera Plana* had triumphantly announced the appearance of the new novel (see Gabriels and Van Doren); *Marcha* criticized it harshly while continuing to discuss it (see Colpaert) and *Mundo Nuevo* canonized it, establishing it as a model between 1966 and 1967 (see Opsomer).

The Rómulo Gallegos Prize of 1972 was awarded in a very different climate. In Venezuela, the *Revista Nacional de Cultura* dedicated a special number to the new novel; the differences of opinion between Rodríguez Monegal and Rama were published in both *Imagen* and *Zona Franca*. *Casa de las Américas*, in turn, censored every reference to the "writers sold out to imperialism" after the Padilla case. In Puerto Rico *Asomante* had been replaced by *Sin Nombre*, which contained articles on Latin-Americanization, Cuba and the Antilles; and the *Revista Iberoamericana* commissioned Rodríguez Monegal, who had left *Mundo Nuevo* to work as a university professor in the United States, to edit an issue on the new novel. The Boom had become an academic and publishing enterprise, and militant and populist anti-intellectualism had replaced the new novel in many cultural periodicals (see Gilman 1993). The new trend was to advocate a more social reading of literature, a rediscovery of marginalized literary production and of popular genres, as well as a return to realism.

Genealogies II: Readings of the Post-Boom

Political commitment and militancy, repression and exile: In the 1970s the new novel was sold and studied abroad, but the Latin American intellectuals had other concerns. Toward the end of the decade researchers, particularly in Mexico City, Caracas, and several North American universities, embarked upon an extraordinary critical and historiographic enterprise, one upon which Ángel Rama, as teacher and writer, exerted a profound influence. To those in exile–and those in internal exile, so to speak, since their work was published much later–we owe not only the first and crucial re-readings of the literatures of the nineteenth century, of the avant-garde of the 1920s and, more recently, of the Colonial period, but also the immense task of publishing rediscovered texts forgotten by earlier literary histories. At the same time, they wrote an extensive body of work in which contemporary production was recorded and interpreted; although placed under the umbrella term of post-Boom writing, this corpus included such different genres as the new historical novel, mass literature, popular genres, literature written by women, testimonial literature, and so forth. This collective effort, marked by its openness and its questioning of established criteria, also made it difficult to rewrite the grand narrative of the Boom.

Very few original or differently focused studies have been written on this topic in Latin America since Viñas's *Más allá del boom: literatura o mercado* (Beyond the Boom: Literature or Market); a re-reading of this book is, in my opinion, essential to an understanding of the approach taken by the first studies of the periodicals of the 1960s. Containing lectures and discussions, this volume is the proceedings of the meeting held in October 1979 at the Latin American Program of the Woodrow Wilson International Center for Scholars. One of the first meetings to be organized in a North American academic center, thanks to the enthusiasm of Saúl Sosnowski, editor of *Hispamérica* (1973–) and professor at the University of Maryland (where Ángel Rama worked), its purpose was to give writers and critics–whether in exile within or without–the opportunity to discuss, exchange opinions, and reflect upon matters in a place far from the tensions and repression that made communication impossible in their home countries (see Sosnowski 1987 and 1988). The focus of the interventions at this meeting had been delimited to "dentro de una convergencia en torno a los análisis sociales de la cultura" (Rama 1981b, 9) [a convergence concerning social analyses of culture]. From this perspective, the participants outlined two main objectives: (a) to understand and explain the phenomenon of the Boom, and (b) to contest reductionism by rediscovering works unjustly marginalized. This second objective was the theme running through Sosnowski's lecture; he had started this task of rediscovery in the first numbers of his journal in 1973 by including a section entitled "the marginalized." The participation of what we might call the other, or ex-centric, writers in the discussion also met this purpose, and Antonio Cándido's study of Brazilian literature completed the panorama. The text that best responded to the first objective of the meeting was unquestionably Rama's "El boom en perspectiva." The other participants were by no means in agreement with the abundance of data and the innuendoes implied in his approach, however. The historian Tulio Halperín Donghi defined the framework for interpreting the novelists' project as a dynamic constituent element of a developmental continental discourse, which erroneously believed that Latin America was "a punto de ingresar como interlocutora de pleno derecho en la historia universal" ("on the point of entering universal history as a full interlocutor"). Despite the fact that the writers of the new novel supported the Cuban Revolution, they were tolerated in the United States and in the Soviet Union as "versión moderna de la Narrenfreiheit, de la irresponsable libertad del bufón" (Halperín Donghi 148) ("a modern version of the *Narrenfreiheit*, of the irresponsible freedom of the fool.")

The critics and writers at the meeting agreed with Halperín Donghi, and they expatiated on the "memorial de agravios" ("record of grievances,") as Rama termed the list of personal confrontations and ethical and ideological judgments passed on the Boom writers (Rama 1981a, 73). There was a general consensus that the new novelists had produced myths useful for imperialism and detrimental to Latin America; moreover, they sold themselves on the market with the support of publishers and critics. Once again Rama viewed the complexity of "un fenómeno sociológico enteramente nuevo en el continente . . . como es la demanda masiva de obras literarias" ("an entirely new sociological phenomenon on the continent . . . as is the mass demand for literary works") from a different perspective (1981a, 58). He thus placed the cultural publishers in a positive light by emphasizing their non-commercial practices—they produced collections of poetry and difficult new works; they went bankrupt, he explained, because "pensaron más en el desarrollo de una literatura que en la contabilidad" (1981a 68) ("they thought more about the development of literature than about their bank balance.") "Las revistas" ("Periodicals,") in turn, "fueron instrumento capital de la modernización y de la jerarquización de la actividad literaria sustituyendo las publicaciones especializadas destinadas sólo al restricto público culto . . . establecieron una comunicación con un público mayor" (Rama 1981a, 57) ("were a decisive factor in the modernization and hierarchical arrangement of literary activity as they substituted . . . communication with a larger readership for the specialized publications addressed purely to the educated few.") The marginalized writers at the 1979 meeting could only see these suggestions in a negative light. Viñas was contemptuous of "aquellas revistas à la page de tapas tan barnizadas como horteras" (30) ("those periodicals with covers as shiny as the glossies"), and many agreed that their critics were responsible for having imposed an elitist and formalist model, which disdained the work of others who were more realistic and committed to social problems.

Rama warned of the dangers of continuing this line of attack, which "que tendió a repudiar tanto el sistema como a los escritores que él utilizaba" (Rama 1981a, 54) ("tended to repudiate as much the system as the writers it used.") The Uruguayan critic's call for moderation apparently fell on deaf ears, as did his suggestions concerning literary periodization. Elizabeth Garrels's summary of the discussion is particularly interesting:

> Un racismo de palabras se formó gradualmente alrededor del concepto de universal: cosmopolita, metrópolis, abstracto, unificado, homogéneo, ontología, mito, hegemonía, dominante, burguesía, imperialismo, purismo, clásico, humanista, racional (estas tres últimas de la ponencia de Desnoes), y–las más persistentes de todas–Latinoamérica y el boom. Las encarnaciones de lo particular fueron: pluralidad, transcultural, realidad, histórico, anómico (trabajo de Corradi), surrealista e histérico (trabajo de Sánchez), miope (Skármeta), neorealismo, regionalismo, sub-regionalismo, ideoléctico, clase social, y los silenciados y excluidos. Todas estas palabras representaron valores y posiciones . . . . Formaron el discurso del debate. (Garrels 309–10)

> A racism of words gradually formed itself around the concept of the universal: cosmopolitan, metropolis, abstract, unified, homogeneous, ontology, myth, hegemony, dominant, bourgeoisie, imperialism, purism, classical, humanist, rational [these last three from Desnoes' lecture], and the most persistent of all, Latin America and the Boom. The embodiment of the particular were plurality, transculturation, reality, history, anomy [Corradi's study], surrealism and hysteria [Sánchez's study], short-sightedness [Skármeta], new realism, regionalism, subregionalism, idiolect, social class, the muted and the excluded. This conglomeration of words represented values and positions . . . . They shaped the discourse of the debate.]

Few paragraphs express better than this the way in which the vocabulary used to narrate literary history changed at the beginning of the 1980s. Nevertheless, Rama had insisted on renewing conventional concepts, proposing that both the cosmopolitans and the transculturists were avant-garde (Garrels 312). The summary of the discussions and the later silence on the part of Latin American literary historians concerning the new novel–other than to declare it a narrative of power and to question it ideologically–make it quite clear, however, that this meeting had produced a new parting of the waters, one which was as divisive as that Fuentes and Rodríguez Monegal had established between traditional and innovatory writing practices. What was lost was the effect of Sosnowski's lecture and the repeated declarations of various participants: the need to demonstrate the coexistence of and interrelations between different and apparently incompatible models, to rediscover the models obscured by that of the new novel, and thus to restore the density and complexity to the literature of the period.

In the 1980s, researchers' awareness of institutional responsibility for the imposition of cultural models made them even more interested in literary periodicals. Carlos Altamirano and Beatriz Sarlo dedicated an important space to them in the second part of their seminal study of the beginning of the 1980s: *Literatura/Sociedad* (Literature/Society) (61–130). As if scholars were responding to a call, studies on the topic burgeoned during the mid-1980s. Surprisingly, the hierarchy established during the sixties did not change, and the most distinguished periodicals once more exerted the greatest influence throughout the continent. The difference was that the collections on the so-called new novel did not select a single traditional text that they could not turn to their advantage, while the analyses of the eighties created an ideological division–based on the editors' positions and sources of funding–which determined the literary model for each periodical.

These new readings of the periodicals provided the necessary information and denunciations, but the 1960s were still sketched in black and white in a clear binary opposition. There were two hegemonic cultural policies: the U.S. Alliance for Progress and the Cuban Revolution. The former was financed by the CIA, first through anti-Communist institutions, of which the Congress for Cultural Freedom was the most visible exponent (see Coleman, Vanneste, Opsomer, Grimon, Vanden Berghe 1997), and then through the Rockefeller and Ford Foundations, among others. According to the analysts, this financing was a principal factor in determining the editorial line of *Zona Franca, Imagen, Cuadernos* (1953–1965), *Temas*, the former *Sur* and, first and foremost, *Mundo Nuevo*. The second cultural policy, the Cuban, was that of *Casa de las Américas* (see Weiss), which was reflected in the Montevideo periodical *Marcha* (see Roca; Gilman 1993), in the Argentinian periodicals following a "Sartrean commitment"–*El Grillo de Papel* (1959–1960), *Escarabajo de Oro* (1961–1974) (Scalabrini Ortiz Seminar 186) and in the Venezuelan *Tabla Redonda* (1959–1965) (see Vandorpe). The most important magazines–the Buenos Aires *Primera Plana, La Cultura en México*–acted like a real mafia business, protecting the interests of the publishing houses and of the star writers (see Vanden Berghe 1989). Some of the editors, in a typically 1970s' gesture, even became self-critical, as did Tomás Eloy Martínez (editor in the nineties of *Primera Plana*, the cultural supplement of the Buenos Aires newspaper *Página 12*) when speaking of his work as assistant editor of *Primera Plana* for many years: "La infección de los semanarios de noticias (mea culpa, espero que a tiempo) ha contribuido a desorientar las pocas veletas bien calibradas que moraban en la Argentina" (qtd. in Rodríguez-Carranza 1996, 87) ("The infection of the weeklies (mea culpa, I hope on time) has helped to make the few wellcalibrated weather cocks residing in Argentina lose their bearings.")

Studies on periodicals generally still confirm the selection of publications and their ideological adhesion to one or the other group, represented by the editors of *Mundo Nuevo* (Rodríguez Monegal) and *Casa de las Américas* (Roberto Fernández Retamar), which was supported by the editor of the literary section of *Marcha* (Ángel Rama). The analyses of the polemics among these star critics and among the writers (Cortázar, Collazos, Vargas Llosa, Arguedas, etc.) divide the field of interpretation. Most researchers agree, however, that the different positions held during the period seemingly vanished when it came to determining the criteria for assessing the literary quality of the modern novel and the topics to be covered, which were apparently the same throughout the continent. Topics included Sartre; the end of the Cold War; the Cuban Revolution; the role of the intellectual and the relations between the intellectual and the political avantgarde; international writers' congresses; the CIA's sponsorship and the penetration of U.S. imperialism; the death of Che Guevara; censorship, including specific cases (the abrupt dismissals of Orfila Reynal from the Mexican publishing house Fondo de Cultura Económica and of the Spivakow's team from EUDEBA; the Soviet dissidents Solzhenitsyn, Sinyavski and Daniel; Pablo Neruda; Guillermo Cabrera Infante; Heberto Padilla); and, finally, the literary prizes. Latin-Americanization is here indisputable and the history of the periodicals of these years might well be summarized under the Greimasean binary schemes: opponents, helpers, senders, receivers.

Re-Reading

New Historicist discontent is likely inevitable. From the 1980s onward, have we not repeated time and again–and I include my own research during this period–the grand narrative of the sixties, simply replacing the positive appreciation of the new novel (as a reaction against the traditional novel) for a negative judgment, embodied in the word, "Boom," which was contested by the muted, the excluded, and the transculturists? The same has happened with the periodicals, read as univocal discourses based on preconceived categories. Thus, as in the Spanish *posadas*, one finds what one wishes to find in editorials, in articles that concur with them, in the sources of funding for publications, and in current declarations made by former editors-in-chief and editors, whose memories construct a definitive interpretation. This attitude seems inevitable: The readings of the materials and narratives depend on the historian's discursive positioning, his or her beliefs and knowledge, as well as on the institutional space in which the discourses under study are uttered. Oscar Terán makes this clear in his reading of the Argentinean periodicals from 1955 to 1965 when he states explicitly that he has opted for a genealogical reconstruction of what had become an intellectual hegemonic discourse by the end of the 1980s: "Hegemónico, es cierto, no significa exclusivo. Que hubo otras propuestas y otras trayectorias me parce indudable (y los ecos de algunas de ellas serán audibles en este estudio), sólo que no creo que hayan tenido los alcances de la que aquí investigo, y por fin, no formaron parte de hecho del área de mis análisis e intereses" (Terán 12) ("Hegemonic certainly does not mean exclusive. There is no doubt that there were other proposals and approaches (the echoes of several reverberate throughout this study), but I do not think that they have been as influential as that which I am researching here, and in the end, they do not form part of my field of interest and analysis.")

The hegemonic discourse of the 1950s referred to by Oscar Terán, which in time became dominant but never exclusive, was the contribution of Argentinean critical intellectuals who challenged and questioned the liberal writers' monopoly on cultural capital, from the Martin Fierro movement to *Sur, Contorno* (1953–1959), which was the meeting-point of all the genealogies. This discourse, which sustained the intellectuals' commitment and the Cuban Revolution of the 1960s (*El Escarabajo de Oro*), became more radical at the beginning of the seventies (*Los Libros* 1969–1976) and maintained its critical stance under the Argentinean dictatorship (*Punto de Vista* 1980–). We could go further and state that this discourse was heard in Argentinean cultural institutions from 1983 onward, and that at the present time it contends on the cultural scene with that of the intellectuals baptized by Beatriz Sarlo as the "neopopulistas massmediáticos del menemismo" (see Rodríguez-Carranza 1997a) [Menem mass-media neopopulists]. It would also be very easy to identify it with the stance of *Marcha* at the end of the 1960s, with the Cuban proposals from 1968 onward and during the "grey quinquennium," with the most significant opinions expressed at the 1979 meeting in Washington (among the founding editors there were Halperín Donghi and David Viñas of *Contorno* and Ángel Rama of *Marcha*), and, indeed, with the hegemonic stance of Latin American literary historiography of the eighties, given that Caracas, Mexico City, and certain U.S. universities became the main sanctuaries for Argentinian, Uruguayan and Chilean exiles, who developed a discourse of dependency there (see Vidal). We might go even further and indicate the points in common between the Latin American discourses and the first manifestations of postmodernist and postcolonial discourses in the United States of America. What is fascinating is that *Diacritics* (Cornell University, 1970–) published during its early years (1971–1974) interviews with Julio Cortázar, Octavio Paz (1914–1998) and Severo Sarduy (1937–1993), thereby disclosing its commitment to the model established by Rodríguez Monegal (who wrote about Borges). At the same time, it published articles by Roberto González Echevarría, Rolena Adorno, Ihab Hassan, Frederic Jameson, Edward Said, and Jacques Derrida. In the 1990s, the ideas of Jameson and Said have been used in the *Revista Iberoamericana* to vindicate the discourses of dependency: those of Franz Fanon, Roberto Fernández Retamar, Enrique Dussel, Roberto Kusch, for example (see Mignolo).

The genealogy I have outlined above covers more than forty years, the same span of time as Fuentes covered in his genealogy of innovatory writing from Azuela's *Los de abajo* to the 1960s. This resistant discourse had finally become the dominant mode and replaced the universalist discourse, which had, in turn, replaced the traditional and the regional type of discourse. Once more we have fallen into the evolutionary trap and all that remains for us to do is to write history from the conquerors' perspective, because we can hardly return to a pristine and innocent past: We are conditioned by the narratives we question. The historians' rediscovery of forgotten texts during the 1980s might, however, by analogy suggest a method of analysis that challenges these binary syntheses. This is precisely what several researchers have been engaged in during the last few years.

1. The first thing that these recent readings have perceived is that the periodicals are by no means univocal. The institutions that sponsored them could not completely control the texts: A convincing example is the work of Manuel Maldonado Denis. This critic, whose stance on political independence was well known in Puerto Rico, even expressed his left-wing opinions outside his country. In 1966 he wrote to Ángel Rama expressing his solidarity with Rama's campaign in *Marcha* against *Mundo Nuevo*, the periodical edited by Emir Rodríguez Monegal. Rama's accusation was that the CIA was funding Mundo Nuevo through the Ford Foundation. The Ford Foundation had granted Maldonado Denis a scholarship in 1963 to travel to Santo Domingo and had financed his trip to Cuba in 1967. His articles about this trip supporting the Cuban Revolution were published in Caribbean Studies, the journal of the Caribbean Studies Institute, funded once more by the Ford Foundation (Rodríguez Carranza and Lie 149).

The editorials do not always coincide with the multiplicity of discourses often interfused in the same article. Kristine Vanden Berghe's study of *Cadernos Brasileiros* (1959–1970)–a periodical sponsored by the Congress for Cultural Freedom, one of the screens for CIA donations–reveals the differences in relation to the discourse on the "end of ideologies" and Pan-Americanism:

El analisis de los editoriales mostró que los editorialistas querian introducir ambos principios, básicos en el pensamiento político del C.L.C. internacional, en su revista. Pero el estudio de las demas contribuciones realzó que los autores brasileños consideran que el panamericanismo es poco mas que una quimera y que continúan pensando en términos de izquierda y derecha o de pueblo y élite. Por consiguiente, para ellos el fin de las ideologias no significa lo mismo que para los congresistas europeos y estadounidenses. (Vanden Berghe 1997, 241)

An analysis of editorials showed that the editors wanted to introduce both of the principles central to the political thought of the international CCF in their periodical. A study of the other contributions revealed that the Brazilian authors regarded Pan-Americanism as little more than a chimera and they continued to think in terms of right and left, of the people and the elite. Therefore, the end of ideologies did not mean the same to them as it did to the European and U.S. members of the Congress.

The democratic and pacifist editorial line of Quijano, editor in chief of *Marcha*, does not coincide at all, as Gilman has demonstrated so clearly, with the militant discourse of many of the contributors in favor of direct action (see Gilman 1993). *Cultura en México*, the supplement of *Siempre!*, seems to be totally opposed to its own magazine (Vanden Berghe 1989, 49). There is a sharp contrast between the articles in the Cinema and Theater sections of *Primera Plana* and the explicitly liberal and pro-military line of the political and economic articles and Mariano Grondona's columns (see Rodríguez-Carranza 1996). Thus, as Vanden Berghe points out, although "la produccion del equipo de la redacción es mas de una vez considerada como una '*mise-en-abîme*' del discurso global" (1997, 240) ("the editors' production has more than once been regarded as a '*mise-en-abîme*' of global discourse"), it cannot be taken as representative of the whole periodical. I would add the warning that the same happens with the memory of certain advisory and contributing editors.

2. A second observation is that what seems to be hegemonic subject matter–that is, the agenda that determines what should be discussed–is totally different, depending on the enunciative situation and the immediate and local objectives of the contributors who exploit them. The obligatory topics are "pluriacentuables" ("multi-accented"), but they are "monoacentualizados por grupos competidores que se afanan por imponer 'su' interpretación" (Lie 15). ("accented in one way by competing groups who strive to impose 'their' interpretation"). This can be exemplified on all levels: within the same periodical, among periodicals in the same cultural space, or in different spaces across the continent. An example of the first level is the modernizing discourse of *Primera Plana*, which insists on efficiency, dialogue, tolerance, and change as antidotes against repression, prejudice, resistance to change, lack of communication, and conformity. In 1963 these values were used to defend democracy and the end of the Cold War (in the political columns and sections) as much as openness to and exploration of new expressive possibilities (in the cultural sections); by 1966 the former used the terms of efficiency and change to demand Onganía's staging of a *coup d'état*, while in the latter "dialogue" subtly opened the doors to an interest in communication, happenings, and psychoanalysis. In 1969 the political columns appropriated the theme of communication for the purposes of criticizing the government's failure to understand the student-workers' movement in Cordobazo, utilizing change, in this case, to demand the replacement of Onganía (see Rodríguez-Carranza 1996).

An example of the second level is the so-called obligatory agenda of the 1960s and 1970s in Puerto Rico. The defense of the Spanish language was at that time a vindication shared by Hispanic academics and left-wing independents, while "transculturation" was used to refer exclusively to the U.S. cultural invasion of the island. The word transculturation, which stood for the rediscovery of indigenous cultures through Arguedas' modern narrative techniques in the Uruguayan *Marcha*, changed in meaning in the seventies–in accordance with the new sense given to it by Fernando Ortiz (1881–1969) and Angel Rama–and was used to attack racism among Hispanists. Paradoxically, it also blended in those years with the Western cosmopolitanism of *La Torre* and of the periodicals written in English on the island (*Caribbean Review, Caribbean Studies*) that identified the linguistic problem with "backwardness," "modernization" with the Pan-American "dialogue" of liberalism, and "mestizaje" and "transculturation" with U.S. sociological theories of the melting pot (Rodríguez-Carranza and Lie 152–53).

This kind of subject matter was treated in the same manner across the continent. No example is more interesting as a topic of discussion than that of Jean-Paul Sartre, whose "commitment" waned depending on its use within a spectrum which ran from commitment to revolution, the proletariat, peasants, the people, and Latin America to commitment to art, creative independence, the soul, or humanity (often considered Western and Christian by contributors to *Sur*). Sartrian alienation was an even more flexible topic: Any discursive enemy can be the cause, whether it be bourgeois ideology, the petty bourgeoisie, or totalitarian regimes of whatever persuasion. As a humanist and phenomenologist or as a Marxist and Lacanian, Sartre's significance lay not in his presence but in particular translation codes that positioned him in concrete power games.

3. The collaboration of the same critics and writers in different periodicals is also relative when one analyzes the function of the text in each space. Thus, Lie demonstrates that the "Arrufat discourse" of *Casa de las Américas* imported Latin American texts in order to indicate the prudent self-censure of Cuban writers (Lie 139–53). *La Torre*, the renowned journal of the University of Puerto Rico that sustained the westernized theses of its editor-in-chief Jaime Benítez, published articles both by Gordon K. Lewis, the most distinguished Marxist at the university, who insisted on the reactionary character of nationalism, and by Manuel Maldonado Denis, the figurehead of the left-wing independence movement. Not only was the presence of these intellectuals a test of tolerance and openness, but also their essays paradoxically provided powerful arguments against independence and nationalism (Rodríguez-Carranza and Lie 152–53).

4. Researchers who have attempted to analyze the major periodicals across the continent, thus isolating them from local discussion, have learned from bitter experience that this practice cannot be sustained. As soon as certain unknown rhetorical adversaries appear in the discourses, the international referents become irrelevant. One has to read strictly local publications, which do not exist within the grand narrative of the 1960s: They are not included in anthologies or mentioned in studies; they have been cast from the memory of the protagonists. The most impressive case, at least to my knowledge, is that of the articles of Lisandro Otero and

Jorge Serguera published in *Revolución y Cultura*, an organ of the Cuban National Council of Culture in 1967. When Nadia Lie examined these articles, she discovered an identifiable "counterlocutor" and understood many formerly inexplicable transformations in the discourses of the *Casa de las Américas* (Lie 180–85). Her study also makes us aware of the importance of *Lunes de Revolución*: this supplement had, according to K.S. Karol (qtd. in Lie 123, n21), a circulation of 250,000 copies.

5. The new dimensions of the publications within a specific cultural space also disclose some rare gems, which cannot be classified under the established categories. Such is the case of the Peruvian magazine *Oiga* (1948–1996), the design and outlay of which was identical to that of *Primera Plana* of Buenos Aires during the 1960s; *Newsweek* was the model followed, with a large photograph on the cover and on the left margin. Like *Primera Plana*, it supported the Nassarean faction of the armed forces, wanted to present a modern image, and called for change. But there the similarities end. In all its sections, *Oiga* appropriated the discourse of the Peruvian Revolution of Velasco Alvarado in 1968, which was very different from that of Onganía during the same period. It was, moreover, a nationalist magazine, expressing anti-imperialist, pro-Cuban, progressive and developmental sentiments. The editorial project of defining a new Peruvian identity and rewriting national history (see Churampi Ramírez) could hardly be further from that of the cosmopolitan cultural pages of the Argentinian weekly. When rereading *Primera Plana* in the light of the revealing expression of Nassarean discourse in *Oiga*, we discover the subtle polemic launched in 1969 in its financial section, using military discourse.

6. The periodical researcher soon grows aware that it is impossible to work alone. Our material may provide us with "robot-portraits," voices interweaving with those that we are analyzing, but their identification often comes from others' work. The most interesting case is that of the youth counterculture periodicals, which can only be discovered by reading the brief, derisive, and ironic comments made about them in the mainstream periodicals. The Venezuelan *Revista Nacional de Cultura* (1938–) never mentioned *Sardio* (1958–1961), but criticized it indirectly in *Techo de la Ballena* (1961–1965), another review in which the *Sardio* followers later wrote (see Ledegen and Van Hecke). From my study of *Primera Plana* and the first *Los Libros*, I began to realize that the rivalry was not between these two publications–one liberal and the other left-wing–or even between these and the populist magazines. They had a common enemy, which I provisionally termed "youth" (see Rodriguez-Carranza 1996). It was only after consulting Carlos Mangone's research that I could identify the enemy: a beatnik discourse evident in *Eco Contemporáneo* and the critics' target in *El Escarabajo de Oro*. Three or more periodicals of the sixties from Buenos Aires, which had different ideological leanings, focused their attacks on a marginal project: Their presence and importance in the period necessitated reassessment. Thus, other genealogies began to appear.

7. Although the most interesting studies of periodicals are undoubtedly those that make a synchronic comparison of several local publications (see for instance, Warley 1993, Mangone, Vandorpe), they are the most demanding

because they imply a change in mentality. Not only does one have to identify the author-enunciator precisely, but one has to abandon the illusion about the authorial institution; one has to accept that the enunciating instance is not the periodical, but discourses that drift from one publication to another. The genres and styles used are particularly significant, whereas the tone of periodicals subsidized by oil companies is didactic, paternalistic, and omniscient (see Vandorpe). Liberal cultural supplements and militant magazines are full of interviews and testimonial writing with hardly any apparent editorial intervention.

8. As I mentioned above, when other voices are rediscovered, other genealogies appear. Yasmine Vandorpe's discovery is particularly interesting. *Shell* (1952–1962) and *El Farol* (1939–1975), organs of propaganda for two multinational companies, launched a crusade to affirm Venezuelan identity, regional culture, ethnicity, and folklore using a discourse that is generically similar to that of many current academic publications. Viñas's long diatribe in 1979 against structure and in favor of consciousness was a settling of old scores with Oscar Masotta, his former colleague at *Contorno*. The discourses of Oscar del Barco, Héctor Schmucler, and Germán L. García in the first *Los Libros* (see Bosteels) reappeared in *Literal* (1973–1977), in which Masotta and García also wrote (see Capdevila and Giordano), and in the *Babel* review (1988–1991) at the end of the eighties (see Bosteels and Rodríguez-Carranza). No longer the popular magazine of the seventies, *Crisis* (1973–1976) was now actively involved in the task of re-reading national history (Cohen Imach 282), following a procedure similar to that of the Peruvian *Oiga*, while at the same time expressing much interest in counterculture and the modernity of the mass media. Hence, this was one of the first platforms for several researchers who, by appearing on radio and television or fleeing to Mexico or France during the dictatorship (like Schmucler, Steinburg, or Verón), spearheaded Latin American semiotics.

9. Apart from local discussions, one can perceive other similarities. The international network of periodicals that had extolled the model of the new novel and become engaged in ideological debates was intertwined with other threads that should be unraveled. Taking a corpus of sixteen periodicals from different countries and periodicity during 1967 as his test case, Bart Lauwereins analyzed three types of relations: publicity for each other's work, articles, and contributors in common. This 1992 study not only confirms the dominant role played by *Mundo Nuevo* and *Casa de las Américas*, but also reveals other interconnections. One is that of the countless poetry magazines of the decade, which surprisingly include *Casa de las Américas*, *El Escarabajo de Oro*, *Asomante*, and *Cuadernos Americanos* (Mexico City 1942–). The mainstream periodicals engage in dialogue with others generally forgotten today, such as the Colombian *Espiral* (1944–1975), the Chilean *Trilce* (1964–1966), *Trilce de Poesía* (1966–1973), *Orfeo* (1963–1968), and *Cormorán y Delfín* (1963–1973), the Argentinian *Eco Contemporáneo*, the Uruguayan *Aquí Poesía* (1962–1966), the Venezuelan *Arbol de Fuego* (1968–1977), the Nicaraguan *El Pez y la Serpiente* (1961–1991), and the Mexican *El Corno Emplumado* (1961–1969) and *Pájaro Cascabel* (1959–1966).

This network, perhaps even more solid than that discussed earlier, established a mandatory page for advertising each other's work in insets which were reproduced in all these publications.

10. During the 1960s and 1970s the dictatorships in Argentina, Chile, Uruguay, and Brazil did not coincide, and the intellectuals in exile transplanted their discourses. A conversation with María Lucia de Barros Camargo, who directs a project on Brazilian periodicals at the University of Santa Catarina, shows just how essential it is to compare periodicals written in Portuguese with those written in Spanish. The correlations are striking: publications with the same name, adapted subject-matter, authors in common, similar discourses and genres, and so forth. Brazilian cultural, and particularly literary, periodicals flourished in the mid-seventies on account of the gradual dismantling of the dictatorship and the slow process of returning to democracy. How can we not compare the articles of Antonio Cándido (b. 1918) in *Argumento* (1973–1974) with those of Ángel Rama, who also published in this magazine, or the proposals of *Escrita* (1976–1988) with those of the Argentinian *Crisis*? Most interesting in this comparison are the transformations and differences, however. Up to 1976 Tropicalism and counterculture were issues generally explored in the tabloids; only later were they adopted by the countless new Brazilian periodicals. Most people were aware of their existence like *Onda* in Mexico City, but the situation in Argentina was different: The tabloids were conservative until the beginning of the 1970s, and the local youth counterculture was similarly silenced by the periodicals. *Crisis* expressed interest in Brazilian Tropicalism. In order to speak about an apparently taboo topic–the hippies and rock represented the decadent culture of imperialism–this Argentinean periodical followed the procedure used by Arrufat during the early years of *Casa de las Américas* of speaking about what was happening in other countries. Paradoxically, it was under the dictatorship (1978–1983) that the underground publications flourished with a circulation of over 1000 copies (Warley 1993, 202).

Re-Writing

Critical re-reading and re-writing do not imply sweeping aside former interpretations, and none of the young researchers cited have proposed starting from tabula rasa. Such a task would be absurd because the existing histories provide essential and very useful information; it would, moreover, be impossible unless we were struck with an attack of amnesia like that in *Cien años de soledad* [1967; *One Hundred Years of Solitude*, 1970]. The inhabitants of Macondo put name tags on objects, and our situation is somewhat similar: The names are there, in the narratives that the institutions of cultural reproduction have decided to legitimize. What has been lost, however, is the weight of the labels chosen and interpreted as data and their dialogue with other practices of the period. This is what Jean Bessière has designated as "the contemporary": "dans lequel les éléments qui forment ensemble sont ceux qui se produisent à ce moment, ceux qui sont disponibles dans ce moment et actualisés d'une manière ou d'une autre" (78) ("in which the elements that make a whole are those produced at this moment, those which are available at this moment and those which are, one way or another, actualized at this moment"). Bessière opposes this concept to that of "the synchronic," which is the historian's task: to map systems and interpret how they work (see Schmidt).

The narrative of the new novel selected certain data and constructed an interpretative system, which was then presented as objective and scientific. The post-Boom questioned this supposed transparency and held the historian responsible for the ideology. The rewriting that I propose is based on an epistemological hypothesis concerning the material: The relations among the data are established contemporaneously through a daily dialogue with the texts. The periodicals are essential sources for detecting this dynamic, but they must be analyzed as "monuments" and not as "documents" of institutional power (Foucault 15), as rhetorical constructions of interpretations of reality and not as transparent data that are only meaningful in the historian's narrative (see, for more, Rodríguez-Carranza 1997b). The echoes of alternative proposals and developments to those of the grand narratives are to be found in the same material that has been used up to now: One only has to look for whatever resists being pigeonholed in the models, the signs of polemic, of relevant alliances and implicit dissidence. The interplay is multiple, and a researcher working on his or her own may well discover and interpret some of the threads; however, it is only through collective work that he or she will really advance from re-reading to re-writing in this task of detective reconstruction.

The most effective stages in a critical re-reading are those I have summarized in this essay: those of the hypothesis. First of all, one should start with the known, which are, in this case, the continental readings in the former narratives, and trace their genealogy in the material under scrutiny. A second methodological step entails an examination of the local dialogic context of the periodicals. In the case of the 1960s, even though the mandatory subject matter may seem continental and the names of the mainstream critics may be found in important periodicals in different countries, we can prove that the concepts, themes, and authors represent symbolic anomic commodities. Universality and Latin Americanism are codes that have very different meanings in different cultural spaces, depending on their specificity in concrete struggles for the power of the word. It is as essential to analyze the marginal periodicals as it was for the historians of the eighties to rediscover ex-centric literary works; one can detect projects in them which the filters of the dominant narratives have prevented us from perceiving in the major publications. Only in this way can we compare the successive stages in our research: establish other relations through the circulation of discursive practices in different contexts and situations, perceive the rewritings that appropriate these alien discourses, and, finally, analyze the transformations.

If Borges, with Pierre Ménard, suggested that every text rewrites others, but is at once new and unique, our historiographic venture is precisely that of detecting rewritings. The material read sends us to other texts which, in turn, deconstruct the first readings. If comparative study is understood in this way, it is a Sisyphean task, which forces us to renounce all cartographic dreams in order to interpret particular cases by analogy—and not by equivalence—and to compare the unclassifiable element that challenges our former hypotheses. My conclusion is a confirmation, somewhat anarchic I must confess, of a failure: that of omni-explicative systems. What needs to be discovered is why a given discourse, which has a specific efficacy when it employs given genres and styles, is chosen. In sum, we need a pragmatic perspective in order to discover not only what is being spoken and written about, and who is doing this, but also in favor of what, against whom, and for what purpose the power of the word has been used. This approach will perhaps enable us to understand what happened to our dreams of the 1960s and 1970s, what we transformed them into, and in what manner they have survived in our current words and attitudes. This is a plural research project; it is a call to those zealous enough to go on quests without prejudice or compass, because there are things in periodicals that escape our pitiable understanding.

Translation by Charlotte Broad

Works Cited

Alegría, Fernando. 1967. *La novela hispanoamericana. Siglo XX.* Buenos Aires: Centro Editor.

Altamirano, Carlos and Beatriz Sarlo. 1983. *Literatura/Sociedad.* Buenos Aires: Hachette.

Benedetti, Mario. 1967. *Letras del continente mestizo.* Montevideo: Arca.

Bessière, Jean. 1987. "Synchronie et contemporain: L'actualité démocratique du littéraire." *Oeuvres et Critiques* 12.2: 77–90.

Bosteels, Wouter. 1995. "Análisis de un discurso enamorado. Barthes y Althusser en *Los Libros.*" *Literatura y Poder.* Ed. C. De Paepe, et al. Leuven: Leuven UP. 271–79.

Bosteels, Wouter and Luz Rodríguez-Carranza. 1995. "El objeto Sade. Genealogía de un discurso crítico: de *Babel, revista de libros* (1989–1991) a *Los Libros* (1969–1971)." *Culturas del Río de la Plata (1973–1995). Transgresión e intercambio.* Ed. Roland Spiller. Frankfurt am Main: Vervuert Verlag. 313–38.

Capdevila, Analía and Alberto Giordano. 1996. "Al pie de la letra *Literal*, una revista de vanguardia." *América; Cahiers du CRICCAL* 15–16: 421–31.

Carpentier, Alejo. 1967. *Tientos y diferencias.* Montevideo: Arca.

Churampi Ramírez, Adriana. 1997. "Yo también me llamo Perú." Diss. Rijks Universiteit Leiden.

Cohen Imach, Victoria. 1994. *De utopías y desencantos. Campo intelectual y periferia en la Argentina de los sesenta.* Tucumán: Universidad Nacional de Tucumán, Facultad de Filosofía y Letras, Instituto Interdisciplinario de Estudios Latinoamericanos.

Coignez, Veerle and Ingeborg Jongbloet. 1988. "*Revista Iberoamericana*, 1960–1975. La canonización del cambio." Diss. Katholieke Universiteit Leuven.

Coleman, Peter. 1989. *The Liberal Conspiracy. The Congress for Cultural Freedom and the Struggle for the Mind of Postwar Europe.* New York: The Free P.

Colpaert, Ina. 1989. "Entre boom y transculturación. *Marcha* 1967–1969." Diss. Katholieke Universiteit Leuven.

Donoso, José. 1972. *Historia personal del boom.* Barcelona: Seix Barral.

Dorfman, Ariel. 1970. *Imaginación y violencia en América.* Santiago de Chile: Editorial Universitaria.

Flores, Angel and Raúl Silva Cáceres. 1971. *La novela hispanoamericana actual.* New York: Las Américas.

Foucault, Michel. 1969. *L'archéologie du savoir.* Paris: Gallimard.

Frenk, Mariana. 1969. "Pedro Páramo." *Recopilación de textos sobre Juan Rulfo.* Ed. A. B. R. Havana: Instituto de Letras Casa de Las Américas. 84–95.

Fuentes, Carlos. 1964. "La nueva novela latinoamericana." *La Cultura en México* (Suplemento de *Siempre!*) 128 (July 29): ii–vii and xiv–xvi.

——. 1969. *La nueva novela hispanoamericana.* Mexico City: Joaquín Mortiz.

Gabriels, An and Inge Van Doren. 1990. "Buenos Aires, el mundo. El discurso cultural en *Primera Plana*, 1965-1969." Diss. Katholieke Universiteit Leuven.

Garrels, Elisabeth. 1981. "Resumen de la discusión." *Más allá del boom: Literatura y mercado*. Ed. David Viñas. Mexico City: Marcha editores. 287–326.

Gilman, Claudia. 1993. "Política y cultura: *Marcha* a partir de los años 60." *Nuevo Texto Crítico* 6.11: 153–86.

———. 1997. "La situación del escritor latinoamericano: a voluntad de politización." *Cultura y política en los '60*. Ed. Enrique Oteiza et al. Buenos Aires: Instituto de Investigaciones Gino Germani. 171–86.

Grimon, Annick. 1992. "*Cuadernos* (1953–1957): desde el miedo hacia la libertad." Diss. Katholieke Universiteit Leuven.

Halperín Donghi, Tulio. 1981. "Nueva narrativa y ciencias sociales en la década del sesenta." *Más allá del boom: Literatura y mercado*. Ed. David Viñas, et al. Mexico City: Marcha editores. 144–65.

Harss, Luis. 1966. *Los nuestros*. Buenos Aires: Sudamericana.

Lafforgue, Jorge. 1969. *Nueva novela hispanoamericana*. 2 vols. Buenos Aires: Paidós.

Laurijssen, Lieve. 1991. "Análisis de la revista *Imagen*, de Venezuela, 1967–1970." Diss. Katholieke Universiteit Leuven.

Lauwereins, Bart. 1992. "Una red de revistas." Diss. Katholieke Universiteit Leuven.

Ledegen, Inge and An Van Hecke. 1990. "El poder de la cultura oficial. *Revista nacional de cultura*: un análisis polisistémico." Diss. Katholieke Universiteit Leuven.

Lie, Nadia. 1996. *Transición y transacción: la revista cubana Casa de las Américas 1960–1976*. Gaithersburg: Leuven UP.

Loveluck, Juan. 1963. *La novela hispanoamericana*. Santiago: Editorial Universitaria.

———. 1976. *Novelistas hispanoamericanos de hoy*. Madrid: Taurus.

Mangone, Carlos. 1997. "Revolución Cubana y compromiso político en las revistas culturales." *Cultura y política en los años '60*. Ed. Enrique Oteiza. Buenos Aires: Universidad de Buenos Aires, Oficina de Publicaciones del C.B.C. 187–205.

Mignolo, Walter. 1996. "Posocidentalismo: las epistemologías fronterizas y el dilema de los estudios (latinoamericanos) de áreas." *Revista Iberoamericana* 62:176–77; 679–96.

Ocampo de Gómez, Aurora. 1973. *La crítica de la novela iberoamericana actual. Antología*. Mexico City: Universidad Nacional Autónoma de México.

Opsomer, An. 1992. "Dos revistas y un nombre. Un análisis discursivo de la revista *Mundo Nuevo*." Diss. Katholieke Universiteit Leuven.

Ortega, Julio. 1968. *La contemplación y la fiesta*. Lima: Editora universitaria.

Otero, Lisandro. 1967. "Che: la razón en caballería." *Revolución y Cultura* 2: 2–4.

Pupo Walker, Enrique. 1973. *El cuento hispanoamericano ante la crítica*. Madrid: Castalia.

Rama, Angel. 1981a. "El boom en perspectiva." *Más allá del boom: Literatura y mercado*. Ed. David Viñas, et al. Mexico City: Marcha editores. 51-110.

———. 1981b. "Nota introductoria." *Más allá del boom: Literatura y mercado*. Ed. David Viñas, et al. Mexico City: Marcha editores. 7–10.

Roca, Pablo. 1993. "35 años en Marcha. Escritura y ambiente literario en Marcha y en el Uruguay, 1939–1974." *Nuevo texto crítico* 6.11: 3–151.

Rodríguez Alcalá, Hugo. 1973. *Narrativa hispanoamericana*. Madrid: Gredos.

Rodríguez-Carranza, Luz. 1991. "Comparatismo latinoamericano: una perspectiva pragmática." *Términos de comparación: los estudios literarios entre historias y teorías*. Ed. Lisa Block de Behar. Montevideo: Academia Nacional de Letras del Uruguay. 171–91.

———. 1996. "Los demonios inútiles. El discurso sobre la juventud en *Primera Plana* y *Los Libros*." Ed. L. Area, L. Pérez, and P. Rogieri. *Fin de un siglo: las fronteras de la cultura*. Rosario: Homo Sapiens Ediciones. 87–102.

———. 1997a. "Argentina, años '90: el intelectual y los medios." *Continente Sul/Sur (Revista do Instituto Estadual do Livro)* 2: 23–34.

———. 1997b. "De la retórica a la historia literaria." *La Torre, Revista de la Universidad de Puerto Rico* 2: 391–406.

Rodríguez-Carranza, Luz and Nadia Lie. 1994. "A Comparative Analysis of Caribbean Literary Magazines: 1960–1980." *A History of Literature in the Caribbean*. Vol 3: *Cross Cultural Studies*. Ed. Arnold James. Amsterdam: Benjamins. 119–60.

Rodríguez Monegal, Emir. 1972. *El boom de la novela latinoamericana*. Caracas: Tiempo Nuevo.

———. 1996. "Papel del escritor en América Latina." *Mundo Nuevo* (5 noviembre): 25–35.

Roy, Joaquín. 1978. *Narrativa y crítica de nuestra América*. Madrid: Castalia.

Sas, Kristien. 1988. "La torre de marfil de los poetas. Análisis de la revista venezolana *Zona Franca*, 1964–1968." Diss. Katholieke Universiteit Leuven.

Schmidt, Siegfried J. 1980. *Grundriss der Empirischen Literaturwissenchaft*. Braunschweig, Wiesbaden: Vieweg.

Serguera, Jorge. 1967. "El intelectual y la Revolución." *Revolución y Cultura* 2: 6–17.

Sioen, Lieven. 1991. "Análisis de la revista *Asomante* de Puerto Rico." Diss. Katholieke Universiteit Leuven.

Sosnowski, Saúl. 1987. *Represión, exilio y democracia: la cultura uruguaya*. Montevideo: Ed. de la Banda Oriental.

———. ed. 1988. *Represión y reconstrucción de la cultura: el caso argentino*. Buenos Aires: Editorial Universitaria de Buenos Aires.

Terán, Oscar. 1989. *Nuestros años sesentas: la formación de la nueva izquierda intelectual en la Argentina, 1956–1966*. Buenos Aires: Puntosur.

Vanden Berghe, Kristine. 1989. "*La cultura en México* (1959–1972) en dos suplementos." Diss. Universidad Nacional Autónoma de México.

———. 1997. *Intelectuales y anticomunismo. La revista 'Cadernos Brasileiros' (1959–1970)*. Leuven: Leuven UP.

Vandorpe, Yasmine-Sigrid. 1997. "Los senderos que se cruzan y se bifurcan." Diss. Katholieke Universiteit Leuven.

Vanneste, Tine. 1991. "*Cuadernos* 1962–1965: las paradojas de la democracia." Diss. Katholieke Universiteit Leuven.

Veeser, H. Aram. 1989. "Introduction." *The New Historicism*. Ed. H. Aram Veeser. New York: Routledge. ix–xvi.

Verschoote, Ingrid. 1988. "Análisis polisistémico de la revista cubana *Casa de las Américas*. El sistema literario-cultural cubano entre 1960 y 1965." Diss. Katholieke Universiteit Leuven.

Vidal, Hernán. 1976. *Literatura hispanoamericana e ideología liberal: surgimiento y crisis. (Una problemática sobre la dependencia en torno a la narrativa del boom)*. Buenos Aires: Hispamérica.

Viñas, David. 1981. "Pareceres y digresiones en torno a la nueva narrativa latinoamericana." *Más allá del boom: Literatura y mercado.* By David Viñas et al. Mexico City: Marcha editores. 13–50.

Warley, Jorge. 1987. "Las revistas político-culturales en la década del setenta." *Claves del periodismo argentino actual.* Ed. Jorge Bernardo Rivera and Eduardo Romano. Buenos Aires: Ediciones Tarso. 83–96.

———. 1993. "Las revistas culturales de dos decadas (1970–1990) en la cultura argentina de la dictadura a la democracia." *Cuadernos hispanoamericanos* 517–519 (July–Sept.): 195–207.

Weiss, Judith. 1977. *Casa de las Américas: an Intellectual Review in the Cuban Revolution.* Chapel Hill: Estudios de Hispanófila; Madrid: Castalia.

CHAPTER 16

CRITICISM AND CULTURAL JOURNALISM IN CONTEMPORARY BRAZIL

Maria Lucia de Barros Camargo

Something new seems to be emerging in Brazilian literary culture which goes against the widespread notion that this is an age when the printed text is obsolete: A number of cultural and literary journals are being sold in bookshops and newspaper stands. Of a varied nature, and emerging from different interests–either critical, academic, aesthetic, ideological, graphical, or merely commercial projects–the launching of these new journals, especially after 1995, has been the undertaking of big printing houses, and their circulation seems to indicate a good reception on the part of a reading public which is certainly not homogeneous.

Titles such as *Cult, Azougue, Bravo, O Carioca, Inimigo Rumor, Livro Aberto, Libertárias, Morcego Cego, Praga, Crítica Marxista, Cadernos de Literatura Brasileira, Range Rede, Gragoatá, Literatura e Sociedade,* and *Imagens* join some older ones that continue to be printed: *Revista USP, Ponto & Virgula, Exu, Tempo Brasileiro, Lua Nova, Novos Estudos–CEBRAP, Teoria e Debate, Remate de Males, Revista de Letras, Organon, Travessia,* and the almost century-old *Revista de Cultura Vozes.* The variety of formats is immense, ranging from editions that can be very sophisticated or very simple, which vary between high-technology graphics and works of expert craftsmanship, to very simple printings, which range from large circulation to very small editions. In brief, these literary journals have a very wide variety of profiles and range from a wide to a more restricted distribution, but whatever the venue the fact is that a new cultural phenomenon has emerged in Brazil at the end of the twentieth century.

It is not an exaggeration to say that such movement parallels another, two decades before, which had a similar effervescence but a different motivation and context. The new publications seem to occupy the space taken by certain journals and reviews during the late 1970s and which disappeared throughout the 1980s. Who can forget titles such as *Escrita, José, Almanaque, Inéditos, Código, Poesia em G, Ficções, Através, Qorpo Estranho, Polímica, Oitenta, Bondinho, Malasarte, Ýnima, Revista de Poesia e Crítica, Leia Livros,* or, certainly, the tabloids *O Pasquim, Opinião, Movimento, Versus, Ex,* and *Beijo*? Then, as now, their random roles point to a diversity of projects and productions. Brazil's literary culture then and now is one of pluralities and heterogeneities.

It is not by chance that the late 1970s, when most of these journals began, were years of transition in Brazilian cultural history. This was a time in which two processes coexisted, a process of "uncovering", or of a loosening of military repression, and a process of rapidly augmented international travel and communication, both in politics and in the literary and intellectual worlds. We can assert that throughout the closing decades of the twentieth century, Brazilian cultural life underwent moments of great agony and violent repression as well as moments of prosperity and euphoria, followed by severe depression. Critical and literary currents which arose during these decades were consolidated; others were created; and others still either dispersed or were reassembled or silenced. There was a revision of critical and aesthetic values frequently discussed through a heated counterpointed debate concerning the role of the intellectual, of literature and the arts, all as part of a rapidly changing sociopolitical scene dominated by relationships with a consumer society and a mass culture–transformations which become evident in the interwoven discourses that constitute the diversity of the journals and periodicals.

Strategic Retrogression: The 1960s

To be able to reflect upon the significance of the pages of those cultural journals, especially those of the late 1970s and of the 1990s, it is necessary to look back to the convoluted decade of the 1960s, which inherited a developing and modernizing euphoria symbolically represented in the inauguration of the new federal capital Brasília, on 21 April 1961.

The 1960s inherited some of the cultural supplements of the major newspapers–such as, among others, *Diário de Notícias* and *Jornal do Brasil* in Rio de Janeiro, and in São Paulo *O Estado de São Paulo*–which stood out during the 1950s when "conheceu o auge dos suplementos literários, especialmente no Rio de Janeiro, onde representavam uma tradição do jornalismo literário e apresentavam uma grande variedade de artigos, poemas, crônicas, ensaios, contos" (Abreu 19) [literary supplements reached a climax, especially in Rio de Janeiro, where they represented a significant tradition of literary journalism and offered a large variety of articles, poems, chronicles, essays, and short stories].

The literary supplement of the conservative *Diário de Notícias* was the platform of an intense debate about literary criticism, especially as a result of the impact produced by the column "Correntes Cruzadas" [Cross Currents] in which Afrânio Coutinho (1911–2000), apart from making New Criticism of the United States known in Brazil, proposed methodological and conceptual changes and promoted a kind of intrinsic criticism and analytical methodology concentrating on the formal aspects of aesthetic composition. If such a debate originated on the pages of newspapers, its very nature removed it from there and took it to the universities and to the field of specialized publications. The *Suplemento Dominical do Jornal do Brasil* (SDJB), created in 1956 and published every week until 1962, also stood out with an avant-garde spirit that sheltered the concretist movement and its first critics. The supplement *O Estado de S. Paulo*, the well known *Suplemento do Estadão*, was also founded in 1956, survived for almost 20 years, and became the major literary supplement of the 1960s.

It is not an exaggeration to say that, throughout the 1960s, literary criticism in Brazil actually took place in the supplementary pages of the major newspapers, the main example being the *Suplemento do Estadão*, which became the vehicle for the production of the "uspian" group (a group associated with the University of São Paulo), founded in the 1940s within the magazine *Clima*. Antônio Cândido (b. 1918) created and planned the supplement, and Décio de Almeida Prado (1917–2000) was its director for ten years, during its most important and productive stage, from October 1956 to April 1967.

It is interesting to point out that if in general the debates on literary criticism which took place in Rio de Janeiro eventually lost their space in the newspaper and had to move toward the specialized university media, the opposite actually occurred in the pages of the *Suplemento do Estadão*. Alzira A. de Abreu confirms the links it had established with the University of São Paulo:

> Diferentemente do Rio de Janeiro, onde se encontravam os melhores suplementos do país, São Paulo se caracterizava por ter o melhor centro universitário do país. *O Estadão*, em sua nova orientação, deveria refletir essa marca. A seção cultural de *O Estado de S. Paulo*, reformulada como suplemento, foi concebida, segundo palavras de Antonio Candido, 'como uma espécie de cruza entre o suplemento e a revista literária, isto porque São Paulo não tinha uma boa revista literária'. (Abreu 53)

> [Whereas the country's best literary supplements could be found in Rio de Janeiro, São Paulo had the best university, and *O Estadão*, with its new outlook, took this into consideration. The cultural section of *O Estado de S. Paulo*, reshaped as a supplement, was conceived, according to Antônio Cândido, 'as a kind of crossbreed between a supplement and a literary journal because São Paulo did not have a good literary magazine'.]

Under Antônio Cândido, the *Suplemento* undoubtedly and effectively played the role of a literary journal, imposing a new line of criticism, creating a specific theoretical lineage and exerting a significant pedagogical and civilizing influence. Such an educational function was part of the supplement's nature, according to Antônio Cândido in an interview given to Marilene Weinhardt:

> ... Outra idéia que eu lancei é que nós não deveríamos procurar fazer suplementos literários como havia alguns no Rio de Janeiro, que eram muito combativos, muito brilhantes, muito movimentados, cheios de polêmicas, porque eu dizia: até o momento o que São Paulo contribuiu realmente para a cultura brasileira foi a Universidade. [...] esse suplemento, sendo embora literário, vai refletir um pouco o tom da intelligentsia paulista, que é um tom de estudo, de ensaio, de reflexão. (Weinhardt 2:450)

> [One of my ideas was that we should not produce literary supplements like those of Rio de Janeiro, which were too combative, too brilliant, too colorful, full of fascinating disputes, because in my view São Paulo's contribution to Brazilian culture up to that moment had been its university [...] this supplement, in spite of its literary nature, was going to reflect some elements of São Paulo's 'intelligentsia', including its mood of study, of reflection.]

As a space that represents the triumph and consolidation of a specialized university criticism, the Supplement marked the moment of birth of modern Brazilian criticism, as Flora Süssekind names it, which was based at the University of São Paulo and which stands out by its process of canonizing Brazilian modernism as well as by its consolidation of a sociological and dialectic criticism which has in Antônio Cândido its main representative. Furthermore, the supplement defined the profile of other literary supplements of the 1960s and distinguished itself from the more journalistic supplements of the 1950s of which the *SDJB*, which disappeared in 1962, was their best and most daring example.

If it is possible to say that the 1960s inherited the power of this supplement journalism from the developmental era, it is also true that there was a consolidation of literary criticism in the supplements: The supplements became the privileged conveyors of the critical word. This sense of privilege is even more significant when we remember that a supplement like that published by the *Estadão* allowed a wide and heterogeneous reading public to have access to literary culture, thanks to their extensive circulation, much larger than that of any magazine. Supplements multiplied and gained importance outside Rio de Janeiro and São Paulo; such was the case of the *Caderno de Sábado*, the supplement of the *Correio do Povo* in Porto Alegre, which offered a major critical framework thanks to the contributions of Guilhermino Cesar (1908–1993), as Tânia Carvalhal has shown. Another major supplement was that of Minas Gerais, the official newspaper of the homonymous state. Following the example of the *Estadão*, it promoted contemporary criticism, although it was not exclusively avantgarde. It was criticism aimed at a specialized readership, but which also searched for the universal; a criticism from which controversies arose and which maintained a place for interpretative analysis and, beyond the specifics, a place of literary criticism itself in the educated spheres of Brazil; a criticism based on clear values even though it started from nonconsensual theoretical and critical assumptions.

The institutional *Revista do Livro*–a contemporary of the *Estadão's* supplement–was also a result of the developmental project of the 1950s and fulfilled a similar pedagogical and civilizing function. Even though it was addressed to a narrower audience–as usually occurs with specialized journals–the *Revista do Livro* was published between 1956 and 1970 by the National Book Institute (an organ of the Ministry of Education created during the New State but eliminated by the Collor administration in the 1990s). It performed the role of

> funcionou como uma faculdade à distância, na medida em que levava para vários cantos do país a crítica abalizada de figuras do porte de Augusto Meyer, Rodrigues Lapa, Adolfo Casais Monteiro, Augusto Magne, Osman Lins, Edson Nery da Fonseca, Alexandre Eulálio, Eugênio Gomes, José Galante de Sousa, Afrânio Coutinho, Oswaldino Marques, Plínio Doyle, alguns de seus colaboradores ao longo de quase 15 anos. ... a *Revista do Livro* declara, em depoimento inicial, ...que seu objetivo é o da "democratização da cultura", tendo como ponto de fuga, a brasileira, sem "exacerbação nacionalista." (Dimas 42)

> [a kind of open, external faculty insofar as it took to the farthest corners of the country the renowned criticism of figures such as Augusto Meyer, Rodrigues Lapa, Adolfo Casais Monteiro, Augusto Magne, Osman Lins, Edson Nery da Fonseca, Alexandre Eulálio, Eugênio Gomes, José Galante de Sousa, Afrânio Coutinho, Oswaldino Marques, and Plínio Doyle, who were some of its contributors throughout its almost 15 years. ... the *Revista do Livro* declared, in its opening statement ... that its aim was 'the democratization of culture,' having as a point of departure Brazilian culture, but without a 'nationalist exacerbation.']

Parallel to these supplements and official journals, during the 1960s other literary and/or cultural journals were published which, having a variety of partisan links and contacts, fully demonstrated the tensions between different currents of thought and criticism. Good examples of these are the avantgarde *Invenção* and the dissident journal *Praxis*.

It can be said that *Invenção* was the official organ of the concretist movement, the vehicle of diffusion of the São Paulo group Noigandres, consolidating critical space for concretism and its followers, who were well known during the 1950s thanks to the *SDJB*. The pages of *Invenção* published the group's production–such as the first edition of Haroldo de Campos's (1929–2003) "Galáxias"–and introduced new poets like Paulo Leminski (1944–1989), who gained credibility and recognition there. As the consolidation stage of the concretista movement, *Invenção* became the instrument for the institutionalization of the last and belated avant-garde current in Brazil, as well as the last new literary journal in the strict sense of the word, that is, a journal understood as a periodical publication, generally ephemeral and with a limited edition, and committed to expressing or defending the political and aesthetic principles of a certain group.

Even though other literary journals emerged afterwards (during the late 1970s *Poesia em G, Código, Muda,* and *Qorpo Estranho*), they were all followers of *Invenção* and have all disappeared and can be read today as cultural residues which were born at a time when the avant-garde movements–including self-styled Brazilian avant-garde–had already fulfilled their historical contribution to Brazilian literature. They were signs of exhaustion of avant-garde ideas.

The journal *Invenção* must be read as the intellectual voice of the concretists and their tendencies, which gave them the reputation of being cosmopolitan, modernizing, and internationalist; it can also be read as a sign of the cultural tensions that arose during the early 1960s between the aesthetic project, which was exacerbated within the group, and the defense of the revolutionary popular art that characterized a great deal of the nationalist, left-wing production. Taken to the extremes, this articulated the opposition between commitment and alienation, between form and content, which fed the debates of the period and were clearly permeated by the nationalist question. In fact, it was precisely this issue of nationalism–vindicated by both the right and the left–that became one of the strong discursive elements characteristic of the tensions in Brazilian culture during the 1960s and 1970s. Once it was removed from center stage, it could be seen to represent the changes of critical perspectives regarding the issues underlying cultural criticism after the 1980s.

The main political event of the decade was the 1964 military coup, which imposed a dictatorial regime and deeply wounded all cultural activities in Brazil. Resistance to the dictatorship became the cohesive element among a significant number of Brazilian intellectuals, and it produced, almost immediately, the first periodical to describe itself as a journal of resistance–the *Revista Civilização Brasileira*. Founded in 1964 and published by the Editora Civilização Brasileira, which occupied a significant cultural space and possessed a notable catalogue, its explicit aim was to criticize the recently established military regime, which called itself "revolution" and was ironically referred to by dissidents, even within the pages of the *Revista*, as "the redeemer."

The discourse of the *Revista* openly opposed the government and was marked by a militant and propagandistic register, as can be seen in the "Primeira epístola ao Marechal: sobre o Delito de Opinião" [First Epistle to the Field Marshall: on the Crime of Opinion]–an ironic and harsh open letter to Field Marshall Castelo Branco, then President of the Republic, published in the third issue, dated July 1965, and written by Ênio Silveira, the first editor of the journal and owner-manager of the Editora Civilização Brasileira. The letter conveys the author's defense of individual rights, his nationalism, his opposition to the military regime, and his historical

struggle; it describes his recent detentions for committing "crimes of opinion" and defends the issues which turned him into a "subversive" person in the eyes of the Field Marshall's government. He concludes the long letter saying: "'O delito de opinião,' Senhor Marechal, é o crime que devemos todos praticar diariamente, sejam quais forem os riscos. Se deixarmos de ser 'criminosos', nesse campo, seremos inocentes . . . e carneiros" (Silveira 11) [The 'crime of opinion', Honourable Field Marshall, is a crime which we must all commit every day, no matter what the risks are. If, regarding this issue, we stop being 'criminals' we will be innocent . . . and lambs]. The "crime" of opinion, honourable readers, is the trademark of this journal.

As an activity of resistance, the *Revista Civilização Brasileira* became the vehicle for the commited intellectual, who took responsibility for the j'accuse! Among its collaborators one can find the names of a variety of renowned figures who took part in different aspects of Brazil's cultural and political world and in diverse newspapers and institutional organs, varying from universities to the top levels of government. I am referring to intellectuals such as Octavio Ianni, Francisco Weffort, Antonio Houaiss (1916–1999), Paul Singer, Jânio de Freitas, Paulo Francis, Ferreira Gullar, Fernando Henrique Cardoso, Francisco de Oliveira, Otto Maria Carpeaux, and Nelson Werneck Sodré (1911–1999), all of whom were invariably identified as belonging to the left and who shared a single purpose: to resist. And in this case to resist implied two complementary movements: to denounce fascism and to support democracy.

Quite explicitly, the journal attacked the military regime and endlessly denounced its arbitrary acts, such as the forfeiting of books and journals, interrogations, compulsory retirements, persecutions, imprisonments, especially of university people, and the closing of universities themselves. In essays and analytical texts dealing with different issues and areas of knowledge, the journal fulfilled a pedagogical and explanatory function without losing, evidently, its political line. It pioneered the discussion of certain subjects such as mass culture and cultural industries, as well as the translation of fundamental texts and authors central to modernity such as Walter Benjamin. It was a strong, homogeneous, and coherent journal.

The first issues presented fixed sections–National Politics, International Politics, Economics, Social and Political Issues, Literature, Fine Arts, Cinema, Theater, Cultural and Philosophical Issues, Science and Technology, Music, Popular Culture, and Documentaries–but this division disappeared after the first ten issues, even though the subjects discussed preserved their planned organization and purposes.

In the section "Literature", apart from the critical essays, poems, and short stories, there was a fixed column that appeared in all of the journal's issues and seemed to reflect with reasonable precision the critical outlook of the journal where literature was concerned. Signed by Nélson Werneck Sodré of the Editorial Committee, the column emerged in the first two issues with the title "Notes of criticism"; from Number 3 it was called "The Literary Moment", making allusion to the 1905 book in which writers were interviewed by João do Rio and which was published in Paris by the Garnier publishing house. Raúl Antelo points out that this book "salienta em implacável galeria de grotescos a inserção compulsória do Brasil na nova ordem mundial: art nouveau, armamentismo, nacionalismo" (16) [brings to the surface, in an inexorable grotesque gallery, the compulsory insertion of Brazil into the new world order: art nouveau, the armament race, nationalism]. If art nouveau had already become completely kitsch, the other elements of the new order were more than contemporary half a century later.

Werneck Sodré's column, "The Literary Moment", always opened with an introductory paragraph in which the author dealt with the situation of Brazilian literature and culture within the political moment of the country and, by doing so, analyzed the existence and purpose of the journal itself. It emphasized the idea of art and culture as a direct occurrence of the historical context, severely denouncing both the increasing abuses and repression of the dictatorial regime against cultural activities and the meek submission of a number of intellectuals to the status quo. Using the same denunciatory register, "The Literary Moment" explained its positions and systematically criticized publications from the right, especially newspapers, and also often dealt with the situation of literary journals of the country, as was already shown in the second issue, May 1965:

> Temos poucas revistas de cultura, e as que temos não se distinguem pelo alto nível. Há motivos para isso, evidentemente. Não é aqui o momento e o lugar de expô-los e discuti-los. O aparecimento desta *Revista*, aliás, pretende ser uma resposta à situação. Ora, a atividade intelectual, e a literária em particular, em todos os países de desenvolvimento cultural razoável, faz-se muito através das revistas deste tipo. Estamos apenas começando, nesse campo, assim. As revistas têm muitos aspectos positivos, prestam uma variedade de serviços. E um deles consiste no intercâmbio com outros países e outras literaturas. Por diversos motivos funcionam mais do que os livros. Ora, vem acontecendo, pela nossa deficiência em revistas, anomalia curiosa, que merece atenção. (Sodré 166)

> [We have few cultural journals, and those we have are not distinguished by their high level. There are, evidently, reasons for this, although this is neither the place nor the time to discuss them. The creation of this journal, however, intends to be an answer to this situation. In all countries with a reasonable cultural evolution, intellectual and literary activities are largely carried out in journals of this kind. We are, indeed, just beginning to take part in this area. Journals offer many positive aspects, and they offer a variety of services, one of which is to establish connections with other countries and other literatures. Journals work better than books for several reasons, including accessibility and dissemination. And precisely because of our lack of journals–strange anomaly which deserves our attention–they are now beginning to emerge.]

Certainly, among the specialized journals, so generically and anonymously referred to, one can mention *Tempo Brasileiro* which was also launched in Rio de Janeiro in 1962 and still continues to be published today, always under the direction of Eduardo Portella, critic and university professor linked to Afrânio Coutinho, and who years later became Minister of Education under the last military president. *Tempo Brasileiro* is presented in its editorials as an "órgão de militância, intransigentemente comprometido com a condição humana e a causa Brasil" (num.1, 3) [militant organ, obstinately committed to the human condition and to the cause of Brazil]. Founded two years before the military coup, the journal survived unscathed by the dictatorship, only suffering a short interruption in 1964 which was explained in these terms in the editorial of number 7 (1965): "Como dizíamos ontem: a nossa revista teve a sua caminhada perturbada pelas contingências sombrias de abril. Ao optar por uma compreensão aberta e livre dos seres e do mundo, assumimos logo um compromisso de luta que se rege por tábuas de valores que nada possuem de dogmática ou sectária." (3-4) [As we were saying

yesterday, the development of our journal was disturbed by the sombre contingencies of April. By choosing an open and sympathetic understanding of human beings and of the world in general, our commitment to fight is ruled by values which are neither dogmatic nor sectarian]. It was a clearly defined option.

If both *Tempo Brasileiro* and *Revista Civilização Brasileira* share as point of departure a nationalist attitude–and the adjective "Brazilian" in their names (which also corresponds to their publishing houses)–neither is gratuitous nor arbitrary. Their ideological position, their critical-theoretical outlook, and their aims are completely different. *Tempo Brasileiro* follows a nonintellectual nationalism which promotes an undiscriminated and vague Brazilian evolution, whereas for the *Revista Civilização Brasileira* nationalism is seen as an element to strengthen national identity, as a means to overcome dependency, as a political project that could transform the situation of the times. In both, however, a militancy in favor of Brazil marked the discourse of a number of generations, legitimating certain positions that were equally authoritarian both to the right and to the left, and within several cultural areas, as can be seen in the debate that emerged toward the late 1960s around the subject of the purity of Brazilian popular music when electric guitars were introduced by the tropicalismo movement. This was but a sign of what was to come. However, let us return to Werneck Sodré.

Miserly in its praise, but prodigal in its attacks, *O Momento Literário* had as its favorite target the anomaly mentioned above, that is, the *Revista de Cultura Brasileira,* which was then published in Madrid and was directed by Afrânio Coutinho, who was never mentioned by name in the column . . . a revealing omission. Werneck Sodré harshly criticized, for example, the special issue about avant-garde literature published by the Brazilian Embassy in Spain. Sodré even questioned the choice of people interviewed, among whom the critic barely recognizes that there are some "legitimate individuals" who were able to give "intelligent answers", such as Murilo Mendes (1901–1975), "renowned poet," and some "arguable but respectable" poets like Haroldo de Campos (1929–2003) and Augusto de Campos (b. 1931), Décio Pignatari (b. 1927), and Mário Chamie (b. 1933). The other interviewees, who were not named, are dismissed because they "carecem totalmente de significação, de autoridade" [absolutely lack any authority, any significance] and lead this critic to wonder "que se está pensando da atividade literária, em nosso país, quando tal leviandade preside a iniciativas culturais?" (Sodré 166–67) [what is happening within Brazil's literary activity, when such flippancy conducts the cultural initiatives of the country?]. This was, as can be seen, a sectarian, inflamed criticism against *Revista Civilização Brasileira*.

Many other journals were similarly criticized, like *América Latina* ("it reveals an incurable weakness"); *Revista do Livro* ("insignificant"); *Azor* ("as bad as all the others"); *Ilha* ("inadequate critical approach, weak material; and regarding cultural issues, its position is nonexistent"); *Praxis* ("continues in its endeavor to explain the thought of a movement in which Mario Chamie is the main figure"); *Convivium* (". . . a Mr. José Francisco Coelho asks why almost all Brazilian intellectuals belong to the left. This disturbs him. He tries to explain, and asserts that this happens because intellectuals, in countries like ours, have a 'significant role in the liberation of the oppressed classes, and in their commitment to human rights in the community.' It looks like a sufficient reason, or doesn't it?"). And so on. For Werneck Sodré nothing can be rescued from Brazilian cultural production in journalism, apart from the fact that adverse political conditions give rise to feebleness: "Fracas as revistas e jornais especializados em literatura e artes outras. É natural que assim aconteça, quando a cultura é vista como algo insólito, que merece ser acompanhado de perto pela autoridade policial e severamente controlado." (Sodré num. 7, 164) [That magazines and journals specialized in literature and other arts are very weak is only natural since culture is considered as something eccentric, which has to be closely watched by the police and severely controlled by the State].

The target of the attacks of *O Momento Literário* was not only the authoritarian state; another object of ridicule was the so-called university criticism, harshly reprimanded for being an "old criticism", using obsolete processes and methods, being ill informed, and having a precarious scale of values. To this old criticism which was even practiced, according to Werneck Sodré, by Antônio Cândido, he opposed the "new criticism" practiced by students, at the beginning of 1968 in a

> fase ainda de transição, em que velhos conceitos e velhos processos estão desmoralizados, e continuam a vigorar, entretando, nas cátedras universitárias, nas revistas especializadas, nos rodapés de jornais, enquanto novos conceitos e processos começam a surgir, mas não se generalizaram ainda. Como a crise do ensino universitário força a juventude, hoje, a procurar o caminho do autodidatismo, a crítica nova começa a firmar-se em trabalhos como o de Carlos Nelson Coutinho. (Sodré num. 17, 196)
>
> [transition stage in which old concepts and old processes are demoralized but continue to be in effect in university lectures, in specialized journals, in newspaper articles, whereas new concepts and processes begin to emerge but are not yet generalized. Just as young people are forced to look towards the paths of self-instruction as a result of the crisis in university teaching, so is new criticism emerging in the work of people like Carlos Nelson Coutinho.]

This fragment shows the tensions which arose within the field of literary criticism and inside the university, repeating the old opposition between old and new and echoing the debates, which had originated in the 1950s, between specialized (university) criticism and impressionist criticism. Now, the person who represents "the new" is a marxist critic, translator of Georg Lukács and Lucien Goldmann, who was quite far from the defenders of "New Criticism"—among whom Afrânio Coutinho was the main representative—but certainly much closer to the sociological and dialectical criticism of Antônio Cândido. This was the kind of marxist criticism that imprinted its mark in the literary section of the *Revista Civilização Brasileira*.

If the "First Letter to the Field Marshall" does not leave any doubts as to the purposes of the journal—and it is not necessary to repeat the problems faced by its directors, all of whom were considered subversive by the military regime—the increasingly harsh attitude of the government, sheltered in the implicit violence of the Fifth Institutional Act (Ato Institutional Número 5, or AI-5) sealed its destiny: The journal stopped publication in 1969. With it, the explicit discourse of resistance also disappeared.

Ebbs and Tides: The Mutant 1970s

The cultural production of the last fifty years was decidedly marked by the long dictatorship, which lasted from 1964 until 1984 and implemented actions of repression and censorship, as well as by the expansion, consolidation, and state control of the cultural industry, especially of the mass media. As a period of transition, the 1970s (which really started in 1968) went from a strong repression to the gradual opening of the regime, which ended up granting wide, general, and unrestricted amnesty in 1979. The slow redemocratization–linked to the neoliberal politics and to the market economy as well as to the process of globalization of the economy–had deeply affected the cultural industry, which had not yet managed to overcome the impact of redemocratization after twenty years of repression.

Cultural journalism underwent profound changes, especially after the AI-5 law was decreed on 13 December 1968, suppressing individual rights and freedom of speech. The fact that after 1968 cultural activities were closely followed by the police and that there was a strong censorship, even within editorial rooms, caused some newspapers to close or to make drastic changes in style: Allegory was substituted for direct commentary, and all direct criticism was replaced by puns and conceits, which had the aim of meaning one thing for the censor and another for the audience. The front page of the *Jornal do Brasil* of 14 December 1968, is emblematic of this kind of discursive transformation. According to Zuenir Ventura, "Apesar do sol de dezembro, por exemplo, a previsão meteorológica anunciava no alto à esquerda da primeira página: 'Tempo negro. Temperatura sufocante. O ar está irrespirável. O país está sendo varrido por fortes ventos'" (288–89) [In spite of the stable weather and the hot December sun, for instance, the top lefthand side of the front page offered the weather forecast: 'Rough weather. Stifling heat. The air is unbreathable. Strong winds are sweeping the country'].

During the following years, there was a diversity of textual strategies developed in order to evade the censors and denounce censorship. Major newspapers such as *O Estado de S. Paulo,* for instance, filled the gaps left by the censors' scissors with fragments of Camões' *Os Luisíadas* or, in the case of the *Jornal da Tarde,* with cooking recipes. Thus, the nonsense of these absolutely hybrid texts acquired a full meaning when each reader exerted his own exegesis, thus becoming an accomplice in free speech. The attempt to convey to the reader forbidden information or vetoed subjects gave rise to a whole culture of the pun, in newspapers and journals, in the lyrics of popular music, and in literature, as an exercise of resistance.

This kind of language characterized, for instance, *O Pasquim* (1969–1985), the first newspaper to take part in this exercise, although, unlike the *Revista Civilização Brasileira*, it had not been created with the aim of opposing the regime. It was born as a humorous tabloid and was concerned with criticizing manners, an aspect that includes counterculture. However, its problems with censorship—which went beyond the political sphere and into the field of morality—turned it into a joyful and steady vehicle of political resistance. The year 1972 saw the publication of a single issue of the journal *Navilouca* which, in spite of having other editorial aims, also served as a showcase for emerging attitudes and practices of literary and cultural expression. Concerning *Navilouca*, Ana Cristina Cesar says

> A revista *Navilouca* é a mais importante publicação do grupo do pós-tropicalismo. Organizada por Torquato Neto e Wally Sailormoon, reúne textos literários de diversos poetas, além de contribuições de artistas plásticos, músicos e cineastas. Num clima de fragmentação, desagregação e contradições, a intervenção cultural do pós-tropicalismo se faz múltipla e polivalente. Os

produtores 'atacam' em várias frentes, diversificam-se profissionalmente. A valorização da técnica e do moderno integram-se num sentido anárquico de subversão.

O nome *Navilouca* já revela uma relação entre viagem (percurso cultural, mutação constante ou transe do drogado), artista e louco. Na revista está presente a preocupação com uma "nova sensibilidade", que incentiva um tipo de trabalho coletivo e múltiplo, empenhado fundamentalmente na experimentação radical de linguagens inovadoras, como "estratégia de vida", e na recusa das formas acadêmicas e institucionais da racionalidade. Era preciso mudar a linguagem e o comportamento, recusar as relações dadas como prontas, "viajar", tornar-se "mutante". . . . o nome desta publicação foi sugerido pelo Stultifera Navis. . . . *Navilouca*, a revista, recolhe também a intelectualidade desgarrada, louca, cuja marginalidade é vivida e definida por conceitos produzidos pela ordem institucional; seus viajantes estão, portando, fora, mas o mesmo tempo dentro do sistema. Essa ambigüidade é evidente no própio projeto da revista: aos textos marcados pela fragmentação e pela crítica anárquica, junta-se o tratamento gráfico dos mais sofisticados, tecnicamente equiparando-se neste nível, às revistas industriais. (Cesar 130-31)

The magazine *Navilouca* is the most important publication of the post-tropicalismo group. It was organized by Torquato Neto and Wally Sailormoon and brought together literary texts of a number of poets, as well as contributions by artists, musicians, and filmmakers. In a climate of fragmentation, disintegration of accepted concepts and contradiction, the cultural intervention of post–tropicalism was multiple and pluralistic. Creators "attacked" on several fronts, and they were professionally diversified. The significance of technical aspects and of modern features became integrated in an anarchic sense of subversion.

The name itself, *Navilouca*, reveals a relationship between a journey (a cultural exchange, a constant mutation, or a drug addict's trance) of an artist and a madman. The magazine is concerned with a "new sensibility" which promotes a kind of collective and multiple work, committed to radical experimentation of innovative languages, as a "life strategy", and to the denial of academic and institutional forms of rationalism. It was necessary to transform language and behavior, to reject given relations, to "travel", to become a "mutant" . . . . the name of this publication was suggested by Stultifera Navis. . . . *Navilouca*, the journal, also brought together a torn, mad intellectual life whose marginality had been lived and defined by concepts produced by the institutional order of the State; the travelers were, therefore, outside even if they were inside the system. This ambiguity is obvious in the very project of the journal: Texts marked by fragmentation and anarchic criticism were accompanied by highly sophisticated graphic work which could be technically compared to that implemented in the best journals of the culture industry.]

The 1970s saw the emergence of other tabloids which resisted censorship and the military regime, and thus suffered the abuse of official and unofficial repression. From this kind of printing press, nicknamed in Portuguese "nanica", certain newspapers such as *Opinião* stood out in the cultural field. This paper discussed the debate on literary theory, specifically structuralism, which was usually undertaken in universities, especially in the Pontifical Catholic University of Rio de Janeiro. Founded in 1972, *Opinião* suffered constant persecution but managed to survive throughout the period most difficult for the regime's opposition. The journal undergoing rigorous censorship, which included huge and absurd cuts, at a time when other journals were already free from them; the economic pressure finally made it unprofitable for the journal to continue, and in April 1977 the editorial committee

decided to interrupt all activities until censorship was completely removed in Brazil. Censorship ended some years later, but *Opinião* never returned. The journal's final decision was corroborated by the contributors' committee in a document signed by Antônio Cândido, Fernando Henrique Cardoso (b. 1931), Millôr Fernandes (b. 1924), Celso Furtado (b. 1920), and Paulo Emílio Salles Gomes (1916–1977), among others. They were the same contributors who took part in many other journals, including the *Revista Civilização Brasileira* and *Argumento*; that is, the same group that started with *Clima*. *Opinião* disappeared just at the time that the military regime was beginning its slow and gradual political opening, precisely when a number of new literary journals began to emerge.

Regarding literary and cultural journals, the early 1970s saw the disappearance of almost all which had been created during the 1950s and 1960s, whatever their political tendency. Apart from the *Revista Civilização Brasileira*, most others were closed, like the institutional *Revista do Livro*, and the avant-garde *Invenção* and *Praxis*, which had an intense rivalry between them. There were other contributing factors besides that led to closing of these publications. There were, in fact, deeper sociocultural transformations that can be perceived in the emergence of certain movements such as *tropicalismo*, as well as in behavioral changes linked to counterculture, to rock and roll, to feminism, to drugs, to the new sexuality resulting from the pill, to mass culture and mass media, and so on; that is, the typical transformations that arose out of the accelerated and contradictory process of urbanization and modernization of the period. This process gave rise to countless tensions, even within the left, which were overshadowed by the need to be united against a common enemy: the military dictatorship and its repression. There seemed to be no readers among this new sociocultural profile; in other words, certain types of literary publications seemed to lack a market. During this period, among the few journals that survived were *Tempo Brasileiro*, which did not have "subversive" features and had an academic profile, and *Vozes*, which was supported by the Catholic Church and became, during the 1970s, the voice of Liberation Theology.

It was a symptomatic trait: Both the *Revista do Livro* and the *Suplemento do Estadão* disappeared in the early 1970s, and the latter was replaced by *Cultura*, a supplement that stopped being exclusively literary and critical in order to deal with news of recent developments in various fields of culture, understood in a wider sense. Similarly, the space devoted to literature in newspapers was reduced. The issue now is the specificity of the question of what is literary. Therefore, in this evolution of the newspapers a wider movement occurred: the reduction and the later disappearance of the literary supplements and their replacement with cultural supplements, in which literature (reviews, literary criticism, and the space for new poets and prose writers) shares space with theater, cinema, painting, philosophy, politics, and the diffusion of science. In a second stage, and fulfilling what Paul de Man had already announced in the 1970s in his *Allegories of Reading*, there is a blurring of the distinction between criticism and literature; the space that had been given to literature is filled by theoretical and critical essays, and the publication of poems, short stories, or narrative fragments, especially by new authors, disappears. The only exception to the rule occurs in the occasional translation and/or publication of unpublished pieces by renowned authors, as can be seen in *Mais*, the current

Sunday supplement of the *Folha de São Paulo,* which had replaced *Letras,* which in turn had replaced *Folhetim.*

Without really belonging to the field of the "deviant behaviors" as Ana Cristina Cesar would call them, a new journal was born: *Argumento–*revista mensal de cultura, a monthly journal of which only four issues were published between October 1973 and February 1974, and whose last issue did not even appear on the streets, because it was confiscated on the newsstands shortly after its distribution. Using the slogan "Against the fact there is Argument", the magazine defined the place of resistance: It was situated within the field of ideas, but used an argumentative discourse less explicit and less sectarian than that of the *Revista Civilização Brasileira,* although both journals shared some of their contributors, such as Fernando Henrique Cardoso and Francisco Weffort (b. 1937), both of whom were members of the Editorial Committee of *Argumento.* Both journals were also similar in their profile and in the theoretical and critical approach given to a number of issues.

As to the difference in discourse, credit can be given partly to the sober style of one of *Argumento's* main contributors and one of its creators, Antônio Cândido, as well as to the participation of people like Celso Furtado, Anatol Rosenfeld (1912–1973) (who died between the publication of issues 2 and 3, and was honored in number 4), Luciano Martins (b. 1934) and Paulo Emílio Salles Gomes, under the direction of Barbosa Lima Sobrinho (1897–2000). Certainly, the change between the state of affairs before and after the AI-5 did not leave much room for explicitness, although the editors still managed to publish quite courageous articles, as can be seen in José Arthur Giannotti's (b. 1930) essay on the relationship between the intellectuals and the State, or in the one which questioned the banning of the play "Calabar, elogio da traição" [Calabar, in Praise of Treason]. Resistance to censorship led to the publication of these cultural journals, which could be clearly identified as belonging to the opposition, both because of their daring texts and because of their contributors, clearly marked as leftist. In a way, this profile guaranteed a kind of symbolic recognition and, more than that, the material survival of the papers or even their prosperity and long life, as was the case with *O Pasquim.* (It has to be said that this long life lasted until the end of the military regime in 1984).

Throughout the first half of the 1970s, *Argumento* stood out by the quality of the writing and the importance of the subjects explored; there are essays such as Antônio Cândido's "Literatura e subdesenvolvimento" ["Literature and Underdevelopment"], published in the first issue, or the important contribution by Ángel Rama (1926–1983), "Um processo autonômico: das literaturas nacionais à literatura latino-americana" ["An Autonomous Process: From National Literatures to Latin American Literature"], in which, as a response to Cândido's work, Rama transcends the discussion of the national, which was still so relevant in other journals of the time. Among the journal's goals declared in the opening editorial, *Argumento* aimed at becoming a meeting place for foreign thought, especially that of Latin America. Thus, its explicit goal was to conceive and set up a Latin American integration founded upon symbolic exchange and not upon the establishment of common markets, as well as to covertly criticize the situation in Brazil by denouncing similar cases of repression in other Latin American countries. In order to fulfil its aim of resisting the regime and to promote its theoretical and critical concern for the relation between texts and the

society that shapes them, there is a marked preference for the works and authors renowned for their commitment: in cinema, (the New Cinema prevailed); in theater, several articles devoted to the works of Dias Gomes (1922–1999), and the staging of the play "Calabar, o elogio da traição", written by Ruy Guerra (b. 1932) and Chico Buarque de Hollanda (b. 1944) and which was banned on the eve of its premiere; in plastic arts, the criticism to the XII São Paulo Biennial and its "anti-art". Television is only explored in one text, in which playwright Jorge de Andrade is interviewed: "Theatre or television?" The journal already shows the possibility of future combinations between certain disciplines which were up to then quite different where academic work was concerned.

Considered from a more strictly literary point of view, it can be said that although *Argumento* followed up the line initiated by the journal *Clima* and continued by the *Suplemento Literário d'O Estado de S. Paulo,* it also introduced a new generation of critics trained or studying at the University of São Paulo, under the direction of Antônio Cândido. I refer to Davi Arrigucci Jr., João Luiz Lafetá, Lígia Chiappini Moraes Leite, Flávio Aguiar, and Roberto Schwarz. Thus, Antônio Cândido's critical current–a sociological and dialectic criticism–was consolidated, keeping alive the productive collaboration between the university and cultural journalism, two institutions which serve to legitimate and acknowledge, and which complement, each other.

It cannot be said that *Argumento* is a strictly literary journal. Like most of the journals which emerged in that period, it defined itself as a cultural journal where culture could be understood not only as a set of artistic and intellectual activities performed by and for an elite, but "also as all the 'signifying practices'–from language, passing through philosophy and arts, and including journalism, fashion, and advertising–which now constitute this complex and necessarily extensive field" (Williams 13), even though, as we have seen, the concept's range was not yet absorbed by intellectuals, something that only started to happen toward the end of the decade. It is perhaps possible to say that the main issue for *Argumento* was politics and related themes such as underdevelopment, censorship and freedom, racial relations, socialism, and capitalism–dangerous issues, in those years, in spite of the prestige of those who dealt with them. In the meantime, it seems that the risks were calculated, or at least foreseen; the limitation of our field can still be restricted, ponders the editorial written for the journal's launching; and it was. The fact that *Argumento* had to close demonstrates the notable decrease in publishing texts which opposed the military regime in the early 1970s. But, still, some works were published.

If during the first half of the 1970s the repressive apparatus of the authoritarian State operated widely and with impunity, curtailing all resistance initiatives, it was also, paradoxically, a period in which the *nanica* tabloids flourished and the creativity of textual strategies produced double meanings, incorporating humor and illustration; a period in which, paradoxically, there was a discourse of the cultural vacuum, as if these years had produced nothing of interest. *Argumento* justified its own creation as a means to fill the existing cultural vacuum–a correct idea if we consider the empty space left by the *Revista Civilização Brasileira,* or the loss of the *Suplemento Literário d'O Estado de S. Paulo,* which was not the same after 1967. In spite of the great cultural activity of those years, references to the vacuum were repeated up to the early 1980s, because critics did not take into consideration alternative or marginal works that remained outside of institutionalized circuits. The article about marginal poetry published by Heloísa Buarque de Hollanda and Antonio Carlos de Brito in *Argumento* is the exception which confirms the rule, because this new poetry was given the role of political resistance, which inserted it into the arguments of *Argumento*.

Even though the amnesty law and the end of censorship only took place in 1979, and the end of the military regime in 1984, the expectations of freedom seemed to give rise to new cultural manifestations much earlier, at the same time that the big tabloids or *nanicos* began to decline, together with the discourses of resistance. New issues began to be incorporated into the cultural agenda and, even in the consolidated groups, criticism began to unfold with greater diversity. In the tabloids, for instance, internal dissent within *Opinião* generated two newspapers: *Movimento* in São Paulo and *Beijo* in Rio de Janeiro. The distinction in their titles is significant–there is a dislocation from the conceptual to the body, from reason to feeling. However, if *Opinião* had a longer life, from 1972 to 1977, *Beijo* was as ephemeral as a kiss: It did not even reach ten issues.

In "Para projeto da Revista" ["For a Journal's Project"], unpublished text written by Ana Cristina Cesar (1952–1983), who also left *Opinião* in order to become part of the team of the recently-created journal–or was it a magazine?–one can find *Beijo's* guidelines: (1) desecration; (2) role of undervaluation; (3) decentralization; (4) emergence of contradictions; (5) language; (6) competence; (7) strategy; and (8) political practice and everyday life (between affection and strategy). Thus, the changes of approach and of the priorities of cultural production were quite clear in this project, in the same way as the symptoms of the loss of cohesion of the different groups of the left became manifest to the extent that the common enemy, which served to diffuse the differences, tended to disappear. The new, Foucaultian agenda gave priority to the questioning of power, to an antiauthoritarianism, to the dislocation from the center, to the search for another alternative language, different from the language of the press and that of the university. In the opinion of Ana Cristina Cesar the aim was to give voice to issues and registers that had been emphasized mainly within the insular left. And we could add also to dislocate purported certainty and to incorporate desires. *Beijo* did not last long, but the issues that it brought forward endured and recorded the debate which has prevailed for a long time.

Perhaps encouraged by new perspectives, *Escrita* was born in 1975, in São Paulo, as a specifically literary journal devoted to the diffusion of literature and, in particular, of Brazilian writers. It was not linked to specific aesthetic groups or tendencies, and its aim was to open up spaces for a wider circulation of the literary text, promoting the formation of new readers or, rather, the widening of a literary market at a time when the mass media and the editorial market were expanding and becoming consolidated. It was sold at newspaper stands, and it had a dynamic national circulation: it was sold in a number of states, and contributors wrote by means of a system of correspondents located in various state capitals of the country. It promoted national contests of poetry, short stories, novels, and essays, and endeavored to make the winners well known, especially during its first three years, a period at the beginning during which it managed to keep its periodicity monthly, changing later to bimonthly. After this, there were some delays, and after number 33, published in 1983, circulation was interrupted. Between 1986 and 1988, an additional five issues appeared, but the journal closed definitely with number 39. These figures show that the journal's active and most productive period actually took place between 1975 and 1979; in fact, during its first year, it also published as supplements some numbers of *Escrita-ficção* and *Escrita ensaio*. *Escrita* did not perish at the hand of censorship, which no longer existed; it had to yield to the hard rules of the mass market.

In order to fulfill its role of literary diffusion, *Escrita* published both new and well known writers and tried to keep in tune with Brazilian literary activities. It did not promote big theoretical or critical debates, defending a rather commonplace idea of literary value. In fact, its polemic nucleus lies in the issues of the professionalization of the writer and the tensions arising between the cultural industry and the market of cultural goods. How to promote the product, books, and the merchandise, literature, without going into the formula of the best-seller? How can literature compete with television, which had already settled in the country and transmitted soap operas on national networks? The journal's contradictory concerns with the media are intense and appear reflected in a number of articles that fluctuate between total satanization of television and a coy appeal to collaborate.

Although *Escrita* seriously defended national literature, it did not get mixed up with issues of national identity. More than once, it dealt with the search for recognition of the Brazilian writer abroad–as symbolic capital–and with the search for new markets for literature produced in Brazil–real capital. In this sense, the ambivalence of the journal is exemplary: On the one hand, it opened its space to harbor Spanish-American literature, thus establishing a purported fraternity between colonized countries; on the other, the references to the Spanish-American boom in Europe and English North America revealed an undisguised spite.

Escrita did not really contribute to critical discussions or innovations; its merit was in its literary diffusion and the promotion of new writers. Unfortunately, it did not manage to solve the problems of its times, of our times; not just because they are, perhaps, issues without solution, but especially because the journal did not endeavor to discuss them with new criteria and categories. Anyway, the question of the complex relationship between literature and a mass consumer society was definitely put forward, unlike the proposals of the other two literary journals launched that same year–*PoesiaemG* and *Código*–both of which were the remains of the concretist movement.

A number of literary journals: *Inéditos*, in Belo Horizonte; *Ficções*, *Ânima*, and *José* in Rio de Janeiro; *Revista de poesia e crítica*, in Brasília; *Qorpo Estranho* (which in the 1983 issue became *Corpo Extranho*) and *Almanaque* in São Paulo, just to mention a few examples, emerged in 1976. By way of describing the kinds of issues they discussed, I want to single out *José* and *Almanaque*.

Based in Rio de Janeiro, *José–literatura, crítica & arte* was really a poetry journal, and its name, which paid homage to the famous Carlos Drummond de Andrade's (1902–1987) poem "José", echoed the refrain "E Agora, José?" ["And now, José?"]. Both poet and poem seemed to outline the paradigm and the riddle of the journal. The paradigm: The journal offered good poetry and, consequently, it linked good literature to modernist creation, already canonized, which had in Carlos Drummond de Andrade (and even more so in the Carlos Drummond de Andrade of the 1930s) its major poet.

The riddle: Is it still possible to write modernist poetry in 1976? And now, José? Which way to turn?

However, if the modernist paradigm was confirmed in other signs, the riddle unfolded when José looked toward its own time and published, apart from new poems from new poets, the transcription of the debates promoted by the journal and which had one point in common: the lack of consensus on literary value and the difficulties critics encountered in trying to judge recent production. The first debate dealt with the publication of an anthology of poems organized by Heloísa Buarque de Hollanda: 26 poetas hoje ("26 poets today"), which collected examples of marginal poetry.

The second debate was even more crucial, for it concerned the journal itself, and its own significance. The debate took part in the penultimate issue of the journal, with the participation of the editors and guests such as Silviano Santiago (b. 1936) and Ferreira Gullar (b. 1930), and it put forward very serious doubts and misgivings which led, ultimately, to closing the journal with the next issue. In sum, the questions were: How to sell journals? How to survive in the market? Who is our reading public? With regard to the issues, they were: How to judge what is literary today? How to compete with *Pasquim* and *Folhetim*? Or with *Escrita*? How not to be *Almanaque*? What constitutes and what is the use of a literary journal which is neither academic nor avant-garde? What is the journal's project? Has it got a project? How to survive without facing a clear enemy?

For so many unanswered questions it is possible to see that the choice of Drummond's poem, with its refrain–And now, *José?*–marked from the start the end of the party. It became a criticism of its own times, a self-criticism, an awareness of the changes the Brazilian literary culture was undergoing and of the impossibility of continuing. Between the market's requirements and the lack of projects, the journal died, in awe of life. And, symbolically, its last issue mourned in a posthumous homage to Otto Maria Carpeaux, who had just died. And now, *José?* How to confront modernity and postmodernity?

If *José* seemed to turn toward the past, recording the perplexities in which it was fatally inserted, it is also necessary to consider *Almanaque–cadernos de literatura e ensaio*, which was published in São Paulo from 1976 to 1982 by the then powerful Editora Brasiliense. Its editors were two professors from the University of São Paulo–Bento Prado Jr., professor of philosophy, and Walnice Nogueira Galvão, professor of literary theory and disciple of Antônio Cândido. Among its frequent contributors were Roberto Schwarz and Lígia Chiappini Moraes Leite, who had also written in *Argumento*. The journal was placed, therefore, within the range of the inheritors of *Clima*.

Considered as academic (that is, "uspiana"–from the University of São Paulo) by the group from *José*, and having indeed that kind of outlook, *Almanaque* came as a double surprise because of the humorous irony with which it satirized its own academic production and as a result of its entry into the field as a literary journal starting from a simple title: an almanac which can speak about everything and anything, a book which can include many trivialities. Thus, it satirically reconsidered the discussions about the place of criticism and, sometimes a bit uncomfortably, dealt with the relationships between literature and the press, between the elite and the masses, and questioned the role of the critic. Some of its contributors, like Ana Cristina Cesar and Heloísa Buarque de Hollanda, also worked in *José*. The journal criticized the structuralists of the faculties of literature, which reminds us of Luiz

Costa Lima (b. 1937) and the disputes between Rio and São Paulo, and conveyed its own self-irony in the publication of its specialized, typically academic essays.

When confronting *José* and *Almanaque*, we see that the doubts and misgivings posed by it were quite extensive: *Almanaque* confirmed the lack of a program, the absence of projects, albeit as a virtue; it proposed the criticism of culture instead of the habit of cultivating theoretical texts which were increasingly dense at the expense of increasingly sparse hair. Thus, it belonged to post-modernity, not so much because of its happy insertion into the market, but rather because it ironically questioned these relations.

Even if we throw a distrustful glimpse at the ironies and jokes of *Almanaque*, what can be confirmed in the conversation established among *Almanaque, Escrita*, and *José* is the definite death of the enlightening and enlightened mission of literary journals: the death of their pedagogical and educative function; the death of the privileged place of the intellectual and the poet; the death of the center of reference; the death of the reforming utopias.

A Brief Conclusion

In spite of the fact that the cultural activists of the 1970s had to live amidst the censorship instituted by the military regime and its slow process of relaxation which eventually led to the 1979 amnesty act and the 1984 indirect election of a civilian president, they found in the newspapers a significant vehicle of expression. Reconsidered today, the launching of the magazines and journals of that period actually indicates the existence of a strong cultural production and questions the idea of a vacuum or whether a cultural vacuum prevailed among Brazilian intellectuals at that time. Apart from this, or perhaps as a result of this, Silviano Santiago (1998) considered those years, and more precisely the years between 1979 and 1981, as the moment of transition toward the end of the twentieth century in Brazil, and identified some signs of that passage: the end of the silent and gloomy resistance to the military regime in favor of the celebration of democracy; the end of the cohesion of the various groups of the left, a cohesion which had been attained thanks to a common enemy–repression, censorship, the torture of political prisoners imposed by the dictatorship after 1964–but whose disappearance led to the emergence of differences and internal conflicts; the birth of a dominant cultural and anthropological trait in Brazilian art which is no longer predominantly literary and sociological; the closure of the gap between high, popular, and mass culture as objects of critical reflection.

Regarding the three years that marked the beginning of the Brazil of the end of the century Santiago stated:

> . . . a luta das esquerdas contra a ditadura militar deixa de ser questão hegemônica no cenário cultural e artístico brasileiro, abrindo espaço para novos problemas e reflexões inspirados pela democratização no país (insisto: no país, e não do país). A transição deste século para o seu fim se define pelo luto dos que saem, apoiados pelo companheiros de luta e pela lembrança dos fatos políticos recentes, e, ao mesmo tempo, pela audácia da nova geração que entra, arrombando a porta como impotentes e desmemoriados radicais da atualidade. (12)

[. . . the struggle of the left against the military dictatorship had stopped being a hegemonic question in the cultural and artistic field of Brazil, thus opening the way to new problems and reflections inspired by the process of democratization in the country (I insist, in the country, and not of the country). The transition toward the end of the century is defined by the mourning of those who leave, supported by their comrades in arms and by the memories of recent political events and, at the same time, is characterized by the audacity of the members of the new generation who come in knocking down doors like today's impotent and forgetful radicals.]

Now that the 1980s have gone by, a decade which was indeed characterized by the emptiness of cultural activities, we have arrived at the end of the century and are able to witness what seems to be a new renaissance. The cultural market is there, definitely settled, and the old misgivings and the old riddles seem not to disturb the new cultural producers. Side by side with the older ones, it is possible to detect a variety of tendencies and new currents and, from the thirteen journals mentioned at the beginning of this essay, eight were exclusively devoted to literature, so that they can be rightly defined as literary journals. The new journals, both as a group and individually, announce a plurality of perspectives and values. Is this a sign of the new times?

Translation by Nair María Anaya-Ferreira

Works Cited

Abreu, Alzira Alves de. 1996. "Os suplementos literários: os intelectuais e a imprensa nos anos 50." *A Imprensa em transição: o jornalismo brasileiro nos anos 50*. Rio de Janeiro: Editora Fundação Getúlio Vargas. 13–58.

Antelo, Raúl. 1997. "Introdução." *A alma encantadora das ruas. João do Rio*. Ed. Raúl Antelo. São Paulo: Companhia das Letras. 9–26.

Carvalhal, Tânia, ed. 1994. *Notícia do Rio Grande: literatura. Guilhermino Cesar*. Porto Alegre: Instituto Estadual do Livro/Editora da UFRGS.

Cesar, Ana Cristina. 1993. "Literatura marginal e o comportamento desviante." *Escritos no Rio*. São Paulo: Brasiliense/Rio de Janeiro: Editora da UFRJ. 123–134.

de Man, Paul. 1979. *Allegories of Reading*. New Haven: Yale UP.

Dimas, Antonio. 1996. "Um suplemento carnudo." *Continente Sul/Sur*. 2:35–45.

Santiago, Silviano. 1998. "Democratização no Brasil – 1979–1981 (Cultura versus Arte)." *Declínio da Arte/Ascensão da Cultura*. Ed. Raúl Antelo et al. Florianópolis: Letras Contemporâneas, ABRALIC. 11–23.

Silveira, Ênio. 1965. "Primeira epístola ao Marechal: sobre o delito de opinião." *Revista Civilização Brasileira*. 3: 3–11.

Sodré, Nélson Werneck. 1965–1968. "O momento literário." *Revista Civilização Brasileira*. 3–10; 14–22.

Süssekind, Flora. 1993. "Rodapés, tratados e ensaios: A formação da crítica brasileira moderna." *Papéis colados*. Rio de Janeiro. Editora da UFRJ. 13–33.

Ventura, Zuenir. 1988. *1968: O ano que não terminou*. Rio de Janeiro: Nova Fronteira.

Weinhardt, Marilene. 1987. *O Suplemento Literário d'O Estado de S. Paulo: 1956–1967*. 2 Vols. Brasília: Instituto Nacional do Livro.

Williams, Raymond. 1992. *Cultura*. Trans. Lólio Lourenço de Oliveira. Rio de Janeiro: Paz e Terra.

CHAPTER 17

TRANSLATION AS A LITERARY INSTITUTION

László Scholz

Although current literary histories ignore it and relevant theoretical approaches pay it scant attention, the phenomenon of translation has always had a strong presence in Latin American literature. In fact, it is one of the few cultural constants in tradition throughout all the epochs and across all the regions of Latin America. The inventory of examples is, as we will see, lengthy and extremely varied; it presents itself to us like an open fan stretching from the zero degree of nontranslation that can be seen, for example, in the infamous "*requerimiento*" (the proclamation read to the American natives upon first contact) (Spitta 73) and in the burning of the Mesoamerican codices during the Conquest, on the one hand, to texts written as pure translations–such as those written in French by Vicente Huidobro (1893–1948)–without Spanish originals, on the other. Between these two extremes we will find Mayan versions of more than forty-seven of Aesop's fables, translated from the Latin by way of Spanish in the sixteenth century; Quechua songs on Catholic themes rendered into Spanish by José María Arguedas (1911–1969); translated from standard Spanish to the colloquial Spanish of Cuba of a Benito Pérez Galdós's (1843–1920) novel effected by Fernando Ortiz (1881–1969); as well as the free translations by Guillermo Valencia (1873–1943) of French, English, Arabic, and Chinese poems; the Spanish version of *Maldición eterna a quien lea estas páginas* [1980; *Eternal Curse on the Reader of These Pages*], which Manuel Puig (1932–1990) originally wrote in English; and the renditions of William Faulkner's *Wild Palms*, Oscar Wilde's *The Happy Prince*, and Virginia Woolf's *Orlando* realized by no less a figure than Jorge Luis Borges (1899–1986). We will find all these, without forgetting the paraliterary transpositions of the Bible into florid prose, or the ballet-theater of the evangelization, or Julio Cortázar's (1914–1984) attempts to transmute verbal discourse into a pictorial system in *Prosa del observatorio* [1972, *Prose from the Observatory*] or in *Territorios* [1978, *Territories*].

Not only is the variety of translations bewildering, but so too is the quantity. Without having comprehensive statistics for the entire Hispanic world at our disposal, and recognizing that illegal translations, even in countries like the United States, can reach up to 15 percent, let us consider a number of isolated figures. According to UNESCO, 508 literary works were translated into Spanish in Argentina in 1954; in Brazil a total of 1331 translations were made in 1984, of which 507 were literary; and in Spain, whose publishing industry is closely tied to those of Latin America, 38,405 titles were published in 1986, with one in four being a translation (see *Index Translationum, The Bowker Annual Library and Book Trade Almanac, UNESCO Statistical Yearbook*). Here the role played by literary journals and reviews cannot be overestimated, because in Latin America the majority of foreign authors, to a degree far exceeding that in other cultures, are published only in journals and reviews. And in every epoch of Latin American letters these have been numerous: Between 1900 and 1938 there were eighty-five literary journals in Mexico alone; Argentina counted 1700 journals in 1942, of which 135 were of a cultural nature, including thirty-one institutionally affiliated literary publications (Carter 1959, 18–19, 24).

The presence and importance of translators in Latin American culture is no less surprising. From the first contact the so-called *lenguas* or *tongues* played a decisive role in the conquest; between 1529 and 1680, no less than twenty-nine decrees were promulgated in the mother country in order to ensure translators' loyal service (Lefevere et al. 148–49; Arnaud 2–5). The first post-Columbian translator, Malinche, is still routinely referred to in present-day historical-cultural discourses as the traitress, the intermediary, or mother of the *mestizos* (Spitta 191; Bowen 261–62, Bassnett 1993, 153). And in every epoch of its literature, the most distinguished Hispanic American authors were translators. We have only to recall El Inca Garcilaso de la Vega (1539–1616), Andrés Bello (1781–1865), José Martí (1853–1895), Rubén Darío (1867–1916), Alfonso Reyes (1899–1959), Pablo Neruda (1904–1973), Ernesto Cardenal (b. 1925), and Julio Cortázar, each of whom made fundamental contributions to the tradition with their versions of León Hebreo, Horace, Emerson, Baudelaire, Mallarmé, Whitman, or Poe.

Above and beyond these factors, however, there is a further aspect of translation that reveals its primordial function: the fact that almost all of the concepts employed by literary criticism in its description of the intrinsic nature of Latin American letters are based upon approaches implying one or another form of communication between, or the fusion of, two or more systems. The famous category of transculturation invented by Fernando Ortiz–and endorsed by Bronislaw Malinowski in the 1940s, and later applied by, among others, Ángel Rama to the realm of literature–by definition implies the notion of a dialectical movement between two distinct worlds, either, for example, between Hispanic and African cultures in Cuba, or between the cultural worlds of the high-lands and the littoral in Peru. The concept and theory of het-erogeneity, as we see it applied, for example, in the works of Antonio Cornejo Polar (1936–1997), stems from "the duplic-ity or plurality of sociocultural signs" which creates "of necessity a zone of ambiguity and conflict" (73). The critical series of dichotomies between civilization and barbarism, urban and rural, Hispanicism and nativism (*indigenismo*), cen-ter and periphery, has inevitably been reinforced by the real or virtual mediations that are to be found between these poles. The postcolonial concepts of hybridism, syncretism, mimicry, and "contact-zones," employed by figures such as García Canclini, Abdul Jan Mohammed, Gayatri Chakra-vorty Spivak, and Mary Louise Pratt to highlight the process and result of unequal relations between two or more cultures, attest to this wider cultural use of the concept of translation. Other critics have explicitly employed the term *translation* to define the literary idiosyncrasies of a particular nation or of the continent as a whole. A few years ago Gustavo Pérez Fir-mat, for example, characterized Cuban culture as more "translational" than "foundational" at a conference of profes-sional translators organized by the State University of New York at Binghamton under the title *Translating Latin America: Culture as Text*. The Puerto Rican writer Luis R. Sánchez (b. 1936) spoke on the subject of "Literature as Cultural Transla-tion" (Sánchez 23–24). At the same conference, in a brilliant intervention on the subject of the translation into English of [Huidobro's] *Altazor* (1919), José Quiroga advanced the notion that Latin America has always been in the process of translating itself from an oral to a written culture (317–23). Susan Bassnett (151), for her part, employing a vocabulary developed by Walter Benjamin, spoke of Latin America as a kind of translation of Europe in the manner of a survival or continuation–its afterlife, if you will. In each of these formu-lations what is patently lacking is the notion of homogeneity; addressing themselves to the question of the dominance of a genetic or teleological system, each proposes literary transla-tion as a protagonist in the task of establishing new forms. As we will see–and this is the central thesis of this essay–once we separate the phenomenon of translation from its relations with conventional mimetic representation, translation acquires the privilege of almost transcendental importance. The mimetic notion of representation has traditionally viewed the phenomenon of translation with reference to the categories of fidelity and infidelity, adequacy and inade-quacy, liberty and servitude, loyalty and betrayal, as well as in relation to the concept of a humanistic dialogue or balance between the I and the you, or as an interchange without loss (see Ortega y Gasset 434; Kelly 2–3; Steiner 47). If, however, we accept that there is no univocal origin (with Derrida), that in the linguistic sign the signified, both "original" and trans-lated, is defined by its transference to another sign (Jakob-son), and that the hybrid nature of a translation system entails asymmetric and unequal relations (see Niranjana), then the phenomenon of translation becomes an emblem of great value for understanding the entire dynamic of the liter-ary institution. As such, it offers us a unique lens through which to view the motive forces, both ideological and aes-thetic, that define the canon in a given epoch. It is in this sense, then, that Claudio Guillén's well-known claim about translation can be advanced: "no genre of writing so exposes the theoretical, social, and ideological foundations of the lit-erary phenomenon" (355).

By way of illustrating this concept, let us briefly consider the case of Andrés Bello, who not only translated a great vari-ety of texts into Spanish but did so according to changing cri-teria. While still a university student, and in an effort to learn English, Bello translated Locke's *An Essay Concerning Human Understanding*. Later, he translated into Spanish fragments of the vast work of Alexander Humboldt (whom the young Bello had accompanied on some of his Venezuelan expedi-tions), fragments which, out of a clear interest in the dissemi-nation of scientific discoveries, Bello published in *El Censor Americano* [*The American Critic*] and in the *Repertorio Americano* [*Compendium of the Americas*]. During the years 1806–1808 he composed neoclassical poems in free imitation of the ancients, poems like "Egloga" ["Eclogue"] (after Virgil) and "A la nave" ["To the Ship"], whose subtitle is "Ode in imita-tion of Horace or *Navis, referent*.]" Although twenty years later, in 1827, Bello translated two poems by Jacques Delille ("Les trois règnes de la Nature" ["The Three Kingdoms of Nature"] and "Les jardins" ["The Gardens"]) with such fidelity that these versions are practically literal renditions, the five poems he translated from Victor Hugo in the 1840s ("Les fantômes" ["Los fantasmas"; "The Phantasms"], "À Olympe" ["A Olimpo"; "To Olympus"], "La prière pour tous" ["Invo-cación a todos"; "Invocation for Everyone"], "Les Djinns" ["Los duendes"; "The Sprites"], and "Moïse sur le Nil" ["Moi-ses salvado de las aguas"; "Moses Rescued from the Waters"]) were virtually free re-creations. In addition to all of the above, Bello also translated dramatic works, the *Rudens* of Plautus, Alexandre Dumas's *Teresa*, and a part of Byron's *Sardanapalus*; he also spent four decades preparing an exceedingly liberal version of Boiardo's epic (refashioned by Berni), *Orlando innamorato*. This notion of variable criteria can also be found in Bello's notes and critical texts (see Bello 82). To the poem "Les Djinns" he added an explanatory commentary stating that "All that I have taken from the original is the general idea, some of its notions, and the progressive rise and fall of its metre." The French composition is entitled: "Les Lutins" ["The Sprites"]. While in his commentary to a translation from Homer (Bello 380–87) he rails against the several classes of infidelity he will not permit himself with respect to *The Iliad*, he reaffirms, in a summary of a translation by Sarmiento, his views with respect to the Bible that "scrupu-lous fidelity is the first of a translator's obligations" (392–94).

Bello's theoretical and practical labors in the field of poetic translation, which with good reason can be considered incon-sistent or, perhaps, even contradictory, are today justified in a number of distinct ways, because of the differing genres being translated, due to personal preferences or eclecticism, or sim-ply by declaration, such as that of Rodríguez Monegal, that true poetry is always "above poetic credos." It appears, how-ever, that the different attitudes that we have seen in Bello's various translations do not stem so much from the already mentioned personal factors as from the dynamic of Latin American letters vis-à-vis the dominant discourse of the moment. The classical imitations that Bello produced at the beginning of the nineteenth century can be seen as "unfaithful" because they were written in the context of a neo-Classical canon that granted full liberty to the practice of *imitatio*. Simi-larly, Bello's literal renditions of the late 1820s took place in the context of a different ambience: Neo-Classical canons having been overturned by Romanticism, Bello, in his fully faithful translations of Delille's neo-Classical poems, opted in fact to put into practice the new tendencies, which were by and large English, and relegated the French poet to a secondary or peripheral status. Here Bello's excessive fidelity is that of a scholar, or better, of a museum curator describing, in the most objective manner possible, a number of objects from the past (in actual fact, Bello changed only Delille's misspellings of scientific terms); this indirect Romanticism can also be seen in Bello's critical texts from the same era citing Byron, Blair, and Blake (Rodríguez Monegal 110–12). Bello's versions of Hugo, published paradoxically during the famous polemic of 1842–43, already constitute an explicit advertisement for what will come to be the new canon. They are Romantic texts of a consecrated French idol translated with Romantic liberty–which is to say Bello pays little attention to the original structure, and like Avellaneda (Aparicio 34), he modifies the meter (Rodríguez Monegal 337), adds a considerable number of verses and, above all, interpolates a series of painful biographical digressions of a Byronic character (Rodríguez Monegal 330–36). Again, the same attitudes can be perceived in his critical writings of the period: Bello published articles on Hugo, Michelet, Sainte-Beuve, and Chateaubriand in *El Araucano* [*The Araucanian*], wrote about Hermosilla, translated from the French, and commented on Villemain's biography of Byron. Finally, the excessive liberties taken in his version of the monumental *Orlando innamorato* can also be justified by reference to his desire to be accepted by the newly emerging canon. In this work Bello not only reduced the first fifteen cantos to fourteen, not only added his own verses to the beginnings of various cantos, but also allowed himself, once again, to intercalate autobiographical sections in a style taken from Byron's *Don Juan* (Rodríguez Monegal 120–23), giving to the whole a highly Romantic justification of the past. In this *modus operandi* we have one of the most convincing proofs of the existence of the other Andrés Bello, who for decades had been en route toward the new canon.

In all these labors the real differences, therefore, were not between literal and free translation, but rather between the various attitudes adopted vis-à-vis the changing panorama of the literary system: The decisive option was one of choosing to support or to change the existing canon. In other words, the individual liberties that Bello took in translating Horace, Hugo, and Boiardo were, from the point of view of the institutional criteria of literature, very particular liberties more reflective of Latin American letters in the first half of the nineteenth century than of one or another of Bello's own aesthetic principles. Bello's case is by no means exceptional or rare in Hispanic letters. We have only to think of Fray Luis de León, who when translating from Latin worked very freely, while when translating from Hebrew opted for a word by word approach, or of Moratín, whose translation of *Hamlet* could not be more literal, and whose translations of Molière could not be more Spanish (Gallego Roca 118–22), or even, in the opposite sense, of various European translations of the picaresque novel, first in literal versions, and later in more liberal and moralizing ones (Gorp 136–48).

It is in this light that we shall analyze the multiple phenomena of literary translation in Latin America. Arguments will not be developed on the basis of mimetic principles of equivalence; nor will a chronological panorama of works translated be offered. Rather we shall present a series of cases in which a translation enters, either from inside or outside, the literary manifold or polysystem and becomes an important player in the dynamics of the literary institution. Methodologically, we have opted to employ the theory of the polysystem invented and developed by Itamar Even-Zohar, Gideon Toury, José Lambert, and Hendrik van Gorp, not only because it situates the translation in a stratified, heterogeneous, and changing context, but also because the basic categories of the theory coincide with the multiplicity and hybrid nature of Latin American letters. This account will center on two groups of examples, the first consisting of cases in which a translation arises out of an interior dynamic and reaches into a dominant discourse principally ruled by relations of power, and the second consisting of cases in which the emphasis is more on attempts arising from an exterior dynamic and directed toward a dominant discourse principally ruled by relations of prestige.

Translation is never merely an opening onto a distinct world: It always implies the explicit or implicit intention to penetrate, dominate, or subvert. In Latin America, language was deemed, for centuries, the indispensable instrument of conquest and colonization. Recall Nebrija's own proclamation that Castilian was the "companion of imperialism" (Klor de Alva 144–45)–and it was for this reason that the powerful were loathe to let it out of their grip. And, in fact, the first translators were considered key figures in the enterprise, in a sense both guides and counselors, and their activities were closely monitored: Columbus, for example, captured natives with the aim of training them as "tongues," and in order to forestall any ideas of escape, he kept them and their wives under guard (Bowen 261–62); in Seville dozens of royal letters patent were issued decreeing the organization and regulation of the imperial interpreters. And in 1542 Núñez Cabeza de Vaca did not hesitate to have "proclaimed to his troops the statutes and ordinances to which the "translators" were obliged to adhere" (Arnaud 27; see also 86–90). As Vicente Rafael has pointed out (7), "to translate" was defined in the Colonial discourse as sharing a common root with the verbs "to conquer" and "to convert," and reflected with perfect clarity the asymmetrical and unequal relations that then prevailed in society. Because translations from native languages into Spanish were few, translations between native languages were practically nonexistent, and the selection of texts translated into native languages, to put it mildly, strategic (catechisms, hagiographies, dictionaries, etc.), books translated from Spanish had an unquestionable influence and predominance. Even today, as editorial statistics attest (Hale 20–23; Jacquemond 139–58; Stoberski 21–28; Sayers Peden 27–30; Steenmeijer, Mantecón Navasal, Shur), this paradigm has not really changed; only the terminology employed has changed (developed and underdeveloped nations, first and third worlds, North and South). In 1991, 67,628 and 48,146 books were published in Great Britain and the United States, respectively, of which only about 3 percent were translations; in the same year the percentage for Denmark was 50 percent, the Netherlands 40 percent, Italy 26 percent, Spain 25 percent, and France 18 percent. In France in 1986, 529 books were published on various aspects of Arab culture, of which only twenty-nine were translations. The U.S. publisher Knopf, which has always made a point of introducing new foreign authors to the reading public, published only six Latin American titles in the years 1940–1960, six more between 1961 and 1965, seventeen during the height of the Latin American literary boom (1966–1970), and six again between 1971 and 1975. Under a State cultural regime, the USSR published no more than two or three foreign titles per year from 1917 to 1959. By way of comparison, a quick glance at Mexican statistics shows that 118 translations were published in 1959, and the annual catalogues of Losada, Siglo XXI, Fondo de Cultura Económica, or Seix Barral demonstrate that this figure was far from anomalous.

It is in this context that we shall examine the productions of two emblematic figures of Hispanic American literature, El Inca Garcilaso de la Vega and Guamán Poma de Ayala (1524?–1613), in whose works translations constitute a tentative means of escape. As is well known, in 1590 Garcilaso translated into Spanish Leon Hebreo's *Dialoghi d'amore* [*The Philosophy of Love*]. For a long time critics viewed Garcilaso's translations as a preparatory phase, a kind of literary exercise that brought him to the threshold of his magnum opus, *Los comentarios reales* [1609; *The Royal Commentaries of Peru*]. In fact, this view is not without some basis, for Garcilaso himself wrote in a letter to Emperor Maxmillian II of the Holy Roman Empire that he had translated the dialogues because they "como parecerme cosa tal como ellos dirán de sí y por deleitarme más en la suavidad y dulzura de su filosofía y lindezas que tratan" (xli) ("seemed to say to me the same as they would say to themselves and also to take further delight in the sweetness and light of their philosophy and the charms of which they discourse"). However, as Susana Jákfalvi-Leiva has demonstrated in an exemplary analysis (13), Garcilaso worked on the *Diálogos de amor* and his own works simultaneously, and thus the aforementioned translation project formed part of a plan whose scope was far greater: Much more than a possible literary initiation, translation for Garcilaso was the means by which he attempted to penetrate the cultural space of the conquerors. His strategy was: First, assimilate the codes of the dominant discourse (genre, form, language, etc.) and apply them in a minor text in order to gain admittance at a secondary rank to the literary polysystem; then, once inside, infiltrate into the highest strata of the literary hierarchy so as to effect through translation a "de-Hispanicization of Inca history" (Jákfalvi 58). Garcilaso's first translation was a wise choice: This was a text enjoying a wide currency that, although its linguistic origins were obscure, came to Garcilaso in an Italian translation, which is to say, in a consecrated idiom in the then dominant discourse of Spain. There were, moreover, two previous Spanish translations of the text (1548 and 1582), an important factor because such precedents would lessen the implicit political risks of Garcilaso's project (risks that were in no manner of speaking unfounded: The *Diálogos* were eventually placed on the Index of the Inquisition). Garcilaso produced his translation, "fielmente por las mismas palabras que su autor escribió en el italiano, sin añadirle otras superfluas" (xli) ("faithfully [rendering the text] with the same words that its author had written in Italian, without adding other superfluities"), and thereby legitimated himself in the literary domain—an objective he could not have realized with one of his own works nor with a translation from another language such as, for example, Quechua. The sequel is well known: In *Los comentarios reales* Garcilaso both fulfilled the requirements of the dominant discourse and at the same time took advantage of the framework created to refashion himself as another translator, the interpreter of and commentator on the subjugated world and the silenced common language of Peru. This time his translation went far beyond merely seeking approbation: It aimed to transgress, subvert, and delegitimize the dominant discourse. Garcilaso's presence in the Spanish text of this and his other translations from Quechua (speeches, proverbs, songs, poems, myths,

etc.) represents much more than the arrival of a *mestizo* writer from the periphery into the letters of the mother country; it constitutes a political act that also questions the status of power. The most eloquent proof of this was the subsequent prohibition of his works.

In 1615 the compatriot and contemporary of Garcilaso, Felipe Guamán Poma de Ayala, produced a radically different text, the *Nueva corónica y buen gobierno* [New Chronicle and Good Government]. Poma did not forsake his homeland, or attempt to produce a literary work in Spanish, but rather opted for a more straightforward approach: Writing directly to the king, he unleashed a descriptive denunciation of colonization and a ferocious critique of Christian morality. In this text the notion of translation operates on a number of distinct levels. On the linguistic level, Poma produced a polyglot admixture of languages, including both indigenous dialects and Spanish; on the level of genre, Poma, reconciling forms belonging to the world of the conquerors with those belonging to the conquered (particularly in his description of historical stages), created a singular amalgam; and on the level of communication, Poma reiterated his verbal message with some 400 illustrative drawings. On all these levels the "translation" constituted a multiple violation of the existing canon, and it was this offense that predetermined the fate of the text: Not only was it not accepted, not even at the margins, into the literary polysystem of the epoch, but it was subjected to the scorn of total silence for more than three centuries.

The linguistic pluralism of Poma's text has proved to be, even after the fact, highly relevant. On the one hand, Poma's linguistically plural text objectifies a Colonial reality that could be stigmatized, according to distinct criteria, as unstable, marginal, heterogeneous, and chaotic, but the text, by the very fact of its existence, unavoidably implies a critical attitude in its methodical disturbance of any monolinguistic continuum. On the other hand, the text is also a sign that translation in the opposite direction was in fact possible, as indeed was that between native languages. These latter options imply a negation of a kind of the conquistador and his language, and represent a return to the translation practices of the pre-Columbian era (Brotherston 402–3). The phenomenon of the nontranslation of certain textual elements, however, is even more revealing. As Rolena Adorno has pointed out (75–6), the native words intercalated without translation in the Spanish text magnify the distance between Poma and the king, while narrowing that between the author and his Quechua-speaking readers. Poma's most original use of nontranslation occurs when he satirizes the Quechua sermons of the Spanish priests. These are quoted without translation, thus depriving them of their own idiom; that is to say, he administers to the sermons the same dispossession that they imposed on the conquered.

On the level of genre, mediating between Christian and native forms, Poma again produced an apparently chaotic plurality in which various distinct elements, such as myths, cosmologies, allegories, sermons, chronicles, catechisms, and biographies, were intermixed. His interpretation, nonetheless, conveys a functional character in at least two ways. The intermixing produced in the text is clearly that of someone unlettered, a representative of the oral, popular culture who did not and could not accept the dominant discourse of the Golden Age and who challenged it from the margins of the literary polysystem. At the same time, Poma did not merely imitate but also stylized the forms he adopted, and, as Rolena Adorno, basing her claims on Bakhtin, points out, this stylization implies an element of appropriation (76); that is to say, Poma in fact appropriated various means from the dominant discourse so that some of the criteria belonging to the dominated would prevail. In this sense, the author-translator of the *Nueva corónica y buen gobierno* was not a mediator but rather a transformer or, in Ángel Rama's terminology, a "transculturator."

The pictorial translation of the text, which Frances Aparicio has with reason called intersemiotic (see 149–73), also highlights the aforementioned heterogeneity. Intricately mixing Andean symbols with European visual elements, Poma's composition takes advantage of a spatial distribution that permits a parallel and at times multiple reading of its drawings (Pratt 35). But even more important is the fact that the images that visually translate the text, and the original intention of the author, open up a new dimension of signification that not only criticizes and, in a specific sense, disqualifies the linguistic level of reading, but also questions the concept of literature itself as presupposed by the dominant system. Poma's transgression aims at a form of nonverbal communication, more than justified from the point of view of the illiterate Andean public, but which to his Spanish readers would have clearly constituted an out-and-out rejection of their cultural codes.

The processes of translation in a bi- or multilingual context can take a number of forms somewhat different from those we have mentioned. In the case of Spain's other colony, the Philippines, for example, the Spanish language rose rapidly to the rank of dominance, imposing itself over Tagalog even in written discourse, despite the existence of the local "Baybayin" writing system (Rafael 44–46). Curiously, the superiority of Spanish also manifested itself in the nontranslation of the key terms of the evangelization (*Dios, Espíritu Santo, Virgen, Cruz* [God, Holy Spirit, Virgin, Cross]) into the language of the conquered, a practice of incalculable importance (Rafael 29). Contemporary with the works of Garcilaso de la Vega and Guamán Poma, a book of bilingual poems was published in Manila with a most unique form of translation: In each verse, the first part appeared in Tagalog and the second in Spanish. Although the Spanish part of the line was an approximate translation of the preceding words in Tagalog, the rhythm and rhymes of each part gave the whole the form of two parallel vertical columns. The *auit* from which Rafael quotes commences:

> Anong dico toua, Como no he de holgarme;
> Con hapot, omaga, la mañana y tarde;
> dili napahamac, que no salio en balde;
> itong gaua co, aqueste mi lance;
> madla ang naalaman; y a mil cossas saben;
> nitong aquing alagad, los mil escolares;

Translating this literally into English, Rafael (60) writes:

> Oh, how happy I am, why shouldn't I make merry,
> when afternoon and morning, morning and afternoon
> no danger occurs, it was not in vain,
> this work of mine, this my transaction.
> So much will be known, and a thousand things will be known
> by my followers, those my students.

Although Tomas Pinpin, the author of the aforementioned book, invented this method in order to teach Spanish to the natives, in fact he created a model that goes far beyond that didactic framework, for this translation, among its other functions, limits the language of the conquerors by enclosing it in a culturally local, linguistic, and poetic system. At the same time the presence of Spanish in the verse produces, from the Tagalog point of view, a syncopated rhythm that, as Rafael's sound analysis demonstrates (62), is full of multiple political meanings, among which stands out a denunciation of the threat that the conquerors posed. Clearly, Pinpin took advantage of the translation to appear to reinforce the dominant language, while in reality undermining it.

Returning to the Americas, and leaping from the Colonial era to the beginning of the twentieth century, let us now turn to another equally exceptional case, that of an interlingual literary translation, from Spanish to Spanish. In 1909–1910, Fernando Ortiz published a "translation" of Pérez Galdós' *El caballero encantado* [*The Enchanted Knight*] under the title: *El caballero encantado y la moza esquiva (Versión libre y americana de una novela española de D. Benito Pérez Galdós)* [*The Enchanted Knight and the Shy Servant (Free and American Translation from Pérez Galdós's Spanish Novel)*]. The first explanation of this curious work would be that Ortiz converted the peninsular Spanish of the original into the Spanish spoken in Cuba, which is to say Americanizing it throughout; however—as Gustavo Pérez Firmat (31, 36–46), in a brilliant analysis, explains—Ortiz discloses in his preface to the work that his text requires a double reading, "once scanning the lines on the page, and another more deliberate, reading between its lines." And in fact, Ortiz's conversion of the original aims precisely at the creation of a variant which permits a different reading: an Americanist interpretation of the original pan-Hispanism of Galdós.

By definition, an intralingual translation ought to be free (Pérez Firmat 4–5). Ortiz, however, was not content with such a simple solution and took with his version what may be called excessive liberties. Changing, reducing, and manipulating the text and language of the original, he added and removed aspects of the characters, and, in order to flesh out his vision, allowed himself to append to the conclusion a number of fabricated letters that did not exist in Galdós's novel. By these means Ortiz actualized a conspicuous distance between the two versions, between the translator and the author, and between the ex colony and the mother country. However, the most striking element of his attempt was the fact of translation itself, the act in which Ortiz's explicit conviction was made manifest: If a work of peninsular Spanish must be translated in the Americas, the supposed linguistic, historical, and political unity of the Spanish world is an illusion. Fernando Ortiz, Cuban author, ethnographer, and anthropologist, fashioned himself a translator in order to reject, from the periphery, a centrist political principle propagated by the most consecrated writer of his time in Spain.

Several decades later, there appeared in the Andean region another author-anthropologist-ethnographer who invented solutions even more novel. In the works of José María Arguedas, we encounter, at the very least, two translators: Arguedas-the-ethnographer who collected and translated into Spanish a whole series of Quechua narratives, poems, and songs; and Arguedas-the-creator (in the fullest sense of the word), the figure who in a singularly original manner "transcultured" the Andean world in his narratives. In his translations of folkloric texts he was guided, as he himself stipulates, by the principle of maximum fidelity: "he permanecido fiel al contenido y a la forma de los cuentos que traduje. He intentado una traducción fiel no literaria" (in Rama 220) ("I have remained loyal to the content and the form of the tales I translate. My intention was to offer a faithful, not a literary, translation"). In the same essay he offers a very characteristic example: While the Quechua phrase *pin kanki hora*, literally translated, means "Who are you hour," Arguedas instead proposes "the hour at which it is no longer possible to see peoples' faces and that at which it is necessary to ask Who are you?" This exactitude is not that of the creator but that of the scientist who seeks to legitimize his discoveries according to the protocols of his discipline.

In his narrative works, however, another translator appears. Much like El Inca Garcilaso, this translator enters into the dominant discourse, writes stories and novels, and writes them in Spanish. But Arguedas enters this language in order to de-Hispanicize the texts. His strategies are various: On the one hand, he introduces fragments of songs, poems, and dances in Quechua immediately followed by a translation. His *huaynos* (or traditional ballads) and his *yaravíes* (traditional Andean poetic form) open a number of communicative channels that radically change the aesthetic panorama, because, by such means, elements of another literary system (Quechua, popular poetry, orality) are introduced into the dominant discourse. Their presence is highly marked and, thanks to the translation, also unavoidable. What Arguedas succeeds in creating are, in fact, polyphonic texts, polyphonic not in the sense of the multiplicity of voices employed or manipulated by post-Boom narrators, but rather in the sense of an organic union of distinctly different worlds. The effect is unique: The peripheral system is liberated from dependence at the same time that the dominant discourse undergoes a number of enriching alterations. What is even more remarkable is the fact that this enrichment results precisely from the introduction of supposedly traditional or conservative elements (folklore, orality) which, by their presence, make visible the dialectic of primary and secondary strata within the dynamic of the polysystem (Even-Zohar 45–51).

Arguedas's other solution is even more profound. In certain parts of his narrative texts he puts into commission a Spanish syntax that is the literal translation of his Quechua phrases, which is to say he "omits" the verb, "drops" articles, "offends" in his overuse of the gerund, and so forth. By means of this mechanism, the Andean system is relocated at the very foundation, in the deep structures of the Spanish language, effecting once again an essential and unavoidable alteration in the Hispanic discourse. The translation of the underlying linguistic code of Quechua into the language of literary Spanish is a veritable transculturation in the sense proposed by Fernando Ortiz, which is to say: mutual influence, movement in both directions between the two cultures. In Spanish discourse the presence of a world for centuries ignored and marginalized can be felt in its full profundity, while the Andean system occupies center stage behind the "mask" of a Spanish lexicon. In the hands of Arguedas, translation no longer operates according to the schema of faithful/free or, and this is key, under the paradigm of colonizer/colonized (Spitta 167); rather, translation becomes, among other things, the privileged medium by which the narrative transculturation of the Andean universe is achieved.

We have seen from previous examples how the transposition of certain oral strata into the literary written code can be an important element in the processes of translation. In certain genres, however, this phenomenon is a decisive factor. I refer to ethnographic or anthropological literature, which intersects in more than a few places with testimonial literature. While the intentions of the translators of these genres will naturally be influenced by a large number of factors (scientific attitude, colonialist appropriation, political-cultural vindications or grievances, etc.), the fundamental dilemma they confront is the same: How can a corpus originally conceived in non–aesthetic terms be made literary? The means applied to the solution of this problem are numerous and double-edged. Let us consider two illustrative examples from out of the vast Hispano-American narrative reserve. The *Autobiografía* [Autobiography] of Juan Francisco Manzano (1797–1854) was written in Cuba in 1835 and, like all such works in which the author is the protagonist, it would not in principle seem to be complicated by the problem of external influence (Niranjana 82–83). However, it so happened that the text, written at the prompting of Domingo del Monte (1804–1853), a nineteenth-century publisher of slave poetry, was immediately revised and corrected by Anselmo Suárez y Romero. According to the research of William Luis (12–15), the correction of the manuscript was in fact a translation, from Spanish to Spanish, of an original that was considered defective because its spelling and syntax did not meet the standards of the dominant discourse of the era. Here again political motives intervened: The reviser of the manuscript sought to produce a document that would be useful to the British reformer, Richard Madden, and help to bolster his arguments against slavery. Suárez y Romero excised, inserted, and reordered certain episodes of the biography, changed important rhetorical points, inserted phrases in quotation marks, reconjugated certain passages from the singular to the plural, eliminated a number of English names, and suppressed Manzano's (positive) references to his proprietress. This version was the basis for Madden's English translation, published in London in 1840; as for the original, it slipped into oblivion until the 1970s, although the historian José Luciano Franco published a version of the *Autobiografía* in 1937 that, while much closer to the original, was not without its own liberties.

Although in each of these versions a political intention can be discerned and the subject imposing his mastery on Manzano's authorial "I" can be named, what is most interesting is the route the text has traversed over time: It has taken more than a century for this work, born on the social, political, and literary margins, to pass from mere acceptance to consecration, and for its original elements to exercise a noticeable influence on the center of the literary polysystem. What in the first instance could appear in the cultural space only in the guise of a translation, would later become part of a new canon and produce its innovative effects–without translation. The translated avatars of the *Autobiografía* secured its acceptance and presence, the nontranslation, its legitimacy.

A more recent case of note is Miguel Barnet's (b. 1940) 1966 work, *Biografía de un cimarrón* [*The Autobiography of a Runaway Slave*], telling of the life of the Cuban ex-slave Esteban Montejo. The book appeared at a time when its subject matter squared perfectly with current political ideas; Barnet himself made use of the terminology of the state newspaper, *Granma*, in speaking of giving voice to those without history (1969, 99–123), or emphasizing, in the prologue, the revolutionary spirit of the protagonist who "a los 105 años de edad constituye un buen ejemplo de conducta y calidad revolucionarias" (1980, 11) ("at 105 years of age is a fine example of revolutionary qualities and conduct"). At the same time, however, Barnet had scientific objectives in mind when he published his extensive interviews with Esteban Montejo in this form; and, in fact, the first edition of the *Biografía* was published by the Cuban Academy of Sciences. Equally apparent are Barnet's aesthetic motives, not only because Barnet was essentially a poet and creative individual, but also because the organization of the text is (consciously or unconsciously) guided by aesthetic criteria: in the prologue, for example, Barnet says that "poner a hablar a un informante es, en cierta medida, hacer literatura. Pero no intentamos nosotros crear un documento literario, una novela" (1980, 9) ("to set an informant talking is, in a certain manner of speaking, to produce literature. And yet our intention has not been to create a literary document or novel"). There is, in addition, a further motive that is not usually or often not mentioned or acknowledged: Barnet produced literature by publishing testimonials because in those years in Cuba it was not possible to publish truly creative works (one has only to recall the plight of Cabrera Infante, or that of the many "testimonial" authors of Eastern Europe). All these factors shaped Barnet's elaboration of Montejo's oral account: Barnet highlighted ideological elements, emphasizing their conformity with the mind-set of the moment; he altered, manipulated, and domesticated the terminology of his protagonist with a view to his readers' expectations (Martínez-Echazabal 61); and he imposed the historian's chronology, abbreviated the digressions of his informant, and clearly adjusted his style to the requirements of genre.

Nothing put the rapid admission and acceptance of *Biografía de un cimarrón* into the center of the literary polysystem at risk, because Barnet had composed the work according to the aesthetic-ideological criteria of the epoch; had he not proceeded in this manner, it would have been impossible to publish it. What could not be achieved with his translation, however, was that the biography of the ex-slave Esteban Montejo acquire a primary value or innovative status. A work entirely in harmony with the prevailing literary discourse, a work acceptable to contemporary institutions, can only be a predictable, conservative, and secondary work from the point of view of the dynamics of the literary system (Even-Zohar 46–49). In order to have advanced an innovative work, on some level, Barnet would have had to publish his interviews in their entirety, without any translation, or have translated them in such a manner that the conflicting elements of their form and content remained salient. Of course, as we well know, these two options were equally impossible in the Cuban cultural context of the 1960s, and thus resulted the situation in which the dominant discourse, qualifying itself as "revolutionary," propagated as its own a rather conservative work—a not infrequent occurrence in literary history. It was only on the political level, and again in a very paradoxical manner, that Barnet's text brought about anything in the way of a positive result: The fact of its presence in the literary system, even at the cost of severe translation, suggested to many Cuban readers that there existed a genre, that of the testimonial and of the truth, that would one day also speak of their own epoch. It is not Barnet's fault that many of the foreign translations of his translation often place their accent on the supposed historical and novelistic character of the work: The title of the Hungarian version—*Fekete sors az Antillák gyöngyén*, or "Black Destiny in the Pearl of the Antilles"—illustrates this point, as does listening to the musical adaptation made by Hans Werner Henze, *Rezital für 4 Musiker* (based on a translation by Hans Magnus Enzensberger).

Beyond the phenomena discussed above or, more precisely, parallel with them, translations played an equally decisive role in the relations of the larger polysystem (Even-Zohar 47–48) when new models entered the system from outside and when the dominant discourse was less beholden to the powers that be and more open to aesthetic currents, prestige, and fashion. In the Victorian era, for example, there was no political or ideological motive in English-Italian relations that would have justified the situation in which "[t]hrough much of the Victorian period, both Her Majesty and Covent Garden restricted themselves to opera in Italian for their main seasons. German, French, Russian, and even English operas had to be translated before they would be presented" (Apter and Herman 27). Sarmiento's famous phrase—"you have today neither authors nor writers, nor anything of value . . . you here and we over there, both of us translate" (in Paz 1973a, 115–16)—aimed its critique not at political dependence but rather at the cultural servility that subordinated the Hispanic world to France.

It is a fact worth recalling that great periods of literature have in general preceded or been accompanied by an intense activity of imitations and translations (Woodsworth 68). In the Spain of the Golden Age, for example, ninety-seven classic works were translated between 1550 and 1574 (Barras 192–95; Beardsley), and eighty-eight between 1600 and 1624; in the first decades of the nineteenth century there existed in the French theater a kind of symbiosis between creation and translation (Gorp 136–48), such that at times it was not even mentioned on the title page that the work at hand was a translation; and in twentieth-century Hungary, the glorious poetic generation grouped around the journal *Nyugat* published translated volumes as an integral part of their creative labors. As Even-Zohar (45–51) has observed, foreign models and translations have an even greater weight in those literatures that are "young" and are thus incapable of producing major works in all the genres at the same time, and those that have literary institutions that are less developed or in crisis. Latin American letters are no exception: Modernismo would have been unthinkable without the translation of the French Parnassians and Symbolists, just as would the Latin American avant-garde without knowledge of European Surrealism. The most extensive period of this kind of translation took place between Latin America and France in the nineteenth century, with its effects lasting well into the twentieth century. In fact, "the French hour" of influence in post-Independence Latin American culture surpassed in extension and intensity all the other foreign models combined.

Because Latin American culture is a culture of journals, and only a small fraction of the texts published in the periodicals eventually appear in book form (Carter 1959, 18–19, 24), the distribution of translations in any given epoch is symptomatic. Taking a representative nineteenth-century journal like *El Siglo XIX* (published in Mexico) as a source, what sort of picture do we get? According to Carter's statistics (1959, 15–17), between 1845 and 1896 *El Siglo XIX* published 579 foreign authors of which 231 were Spanish, 148 other Latin American, 134 French, 20 English, 12 from the United States, 9 German, and 7 Italian. Among non-Hispanic authors, the number of French writers was three times that of all the others. Let us compare these figures with those from a modern journal of undeniably cosmopolitan credentials, *Sur*, published in Buenos Aires: between 1931 and 1950 the numerical breakdown of writers was 180 Latin American, 80 French, 55 English, 41 Spanish, 35 from the United States, 15 German, 14 Italian, 11 Russian, 5 Swiss, and 2 Belgian. The change in representation between the peninsular Spanish and Latin American writers is salient, as is the parity between anglophone and francophone writers, although these latter continued to maintain a firm presence.

In the publication of books of poetry and first books of translation, we can also verify the canonization of French literature in Latin America, evidence of which can be seen in the fact that not only the outstanding figures were translated, but the secondary figures as well. According to Max Henríquez Ureña's (1885–1970) *Breve historia del modernismo* [1954; Brief History of *Modernismo*], Abelardo Varela in Chile published translations from Verlaine, Rollinet, Richepin, and Bauville; Carlos Ortiz in Argentina translated Baudelaire, Moréas, and Samain; Aniceto Valdivia and Eulogio Hostos in the Caribbean translated Hugo, Barbier, and Mallarmé; Leopoldo Díaz included in his 1897 volume *Traducciones* [*Translations*] Zola, Leconte de Lisle, and Hugo, among many others; Enrique González Martínez dedicated an entire volume to French poetry in his 1915 anthology *Jardines de Francia* [Gardens of France] which included authors like Heredia, Samain, Verlaine, Raynaud, and Vivien; and Ismael Enrique Arciniegas in Colombia published a book of *Traducciones poéticas* [*Poetic Translations*] in 1926, a version of Heredia's *Trophées* [*Trophies*] in 1934, and a version of Géraldy's *Toi et moi* [*You and I*] in 1936.

It was not only a question of knowing and making known French idols in the Latin American context. The aim, or at least the desire, to adapt and to enrich with a view to future original creations is constantly repeated in the prologues, notes, and critical texts. Gutiérrez Nájera, for example, employed the term "intersection" in his insistence that Latin American writers had to be aware of foreign models in order to be able "to revive old beauties, still young . . . that their poetry would be invigorated by the intersection" (Aparicio 34). Other writers employed terminology that in itself implied that translation shared a family resemblance with creation and made equal use of inspiration, experiment, and enrichment. Gertrudis Gómez de Avellaneda added various subheadings to the titles of her Romantically inspired translations: "imitation" ("Farewell to the Lyre" by Lamartine), "translation" ("The Poet" by Hugo), "free translation" ("Love's Law" by Parmy), "paraphrase" ("Miserere"), as well as "fantasia," "improvisation," or "composition inspired by . . ." Several decades later, in the fin-de-siècle twilight, two Colombian poets would be even more specific: Guillermo Valencia qualified translation as an autonomous literary process (Aparicio 37–38), and Miguel Antonio Caro, for his part, spoke of a complex process: "Translation is the excruciating mixed labor of imitation and adaptation, recasting and correspondence" (Santoyo 186).

This notion of translation surfaces with even more clarity when we consider the veritable proliferation of versions of the same poem, at times made by the same translator. Different versions of Mallarmé's "*Apparition*," for example, were published by Guillermo Valencia (766–68) in his *Ritos* [*Rites*] (1898); by Leopoldo Díaz (1901); by various Spanish poets (Teodoro Llorante, Juan Pablo Rivas), and also by Alfonso Reyes (see Aparicio 55–63). Reyes also elaborated three versions of "El abanico de Mademoiselle Mallarmé" ["Mademoiselle Mallarmé's Fan"] (55–59), versions which, according to the author, take the differing forms of a literal version in prose, a rhythmic translation with slight infidelities, and a re-creation. Reyes produced similar multiples from José María Heredia's poem "El estoque" ["The Rapier"]. When Max Henríquez Ureña prepared his complete translation of Heredia's *Los Trofeos*

[*Trophies*], there already existed, at least in fragments, numerous versions of the sonnet cycle translated by the Colombian Miguel Antonio Caro (1891), the Argentines Emilio Berisso and Leopoldo Díaz (1897 and 1934), the Ecuadorian César Borja, the Mexican Justo Sierra (1899), the Chilean Francisco Contreras (1906), the Cuban Francisco J. Pichardo (1908), the Salvadoran Román Mayorga Rivas (1915), the Mexican Enrique González Martínez (1915), and the Argentine Leopoldo Lugones (1919). Some fifty odd other poems also had been translated (Heredia 124–28). The ramifications of this proliferation were considerable for the peripheral literatures. On the one hand, as Reyes himself has correctly pointed out (40), while each new translation is affected by its antecedents, inasmuch as it seeks to distance itself from them, these relations of influence also necessarily alter the relation between the translation and the original. The multiple translations of a given work form an autonomous corpus whose members create a set of complex relations which can obscure their correspondence to the original and thus, also, the original's intentions and relations. On the other hand, the excessive multiplication of translations in an epoch of continuing dependence often leads, in the target literature, to a sense of anachronism: Without knowing the originals, the Hispano-American reader might very well believe that Hugo, Verlaine, and Mallarmé, for example, all belonged to the same literary current. In the case of Hungary, which also lived through its "French hour" of influence, the poetic discourses of Mallarmé and Rimbaud are inextricably mixed, and Verlaine's verse, for many, sounds like Baudelaire's (Karáston 165–82).

Further evidence of the unequal relations between center and periphery in the larger polysystem during the "French hour" is confirmed by the fact that many non-French or even non-European works have made their way to Latin America via Paris by means of indirect translations. A given work may be of major or minor importance, of primary or secondary interest, but if it is translated in France it acquires in Latin America an immediate relevance. To give another central European example, a number of poems by Huidobro, Borges, Maples Arce, and J. Abril were first translated into Hungarian, probably from French, during the period 1921–27, because some Hungarian poet by chance discovered them in a French journal during the obligatory pilgrimage to Paris (Scholz 440–47). From among the many possible Latin American examples, let me mention only two: Valencia's oriental translations and the vicissitudes of the works of Edgar Allan Poe. Valencia's 1929 collection *Catay* [*Cathay*] brought together 120 Chinese poems, from various epochs, and five translations from the Arabic. In his prologue (215–18), Valencia explained that he was publishing "un libro preterista" ("a book of bygone times"), based on the French prose translations of Franz Toussaint, and that in his experience Chinese poetry was often marked by a narrative character and phrases so pedestrian "que uno se siente cohibido y opta, al fin, por sacrificar la distinción a la fidelidad" ("that one felt oneself constrained, and opted in the end to sacrifice distinction to fidelity"). However, the decisive feature of his volume is the underlying longing to participate in the Parisian vogue for the mysterious, the sensual, and the refined, which is to say, the great Orientalist tide. The metaphor Valencia employs for his translation says it all:

de aquel té, con tanto esmero cultivado en los monasterios de la montaña de Uí, brindó perfumada taza un hijo de Francia a los sinófilos de Europa. Feliz de mí si, después de someter a segunda infusión esas mismas hojas, puedo ofrecerla, aunque no en vaso azul de Ni-Ging, a aficionados curiosos. (218)

of that tea, cultivated with such refinement in the monasteries of the mountains of *Uï,* this child of France raised a perfumed cup to the Sinophiles of Europe. Fortunate would I be if, after having submitted those same leaves to a second infusion, I could offer it, even without a *Ni-Ging* blue vessel, to eager enthusiasts.

Edgar Allan Poe exercised a profound influence on Hispano-American literature (Englekirk 146) and he did it via Paris, thanks to Baudelaire's translations. While there were Hispano-American translations before *modernismo* (1880–1920)–the early versions of Carlos Olivera, Eduardo Wilde, and Eduardo de la Barra, for example–it was only decades after the French (1845–1857) and the Spanish (1858–1868) waves that the Latin American epidemic broke out. Once the *modernistas* had discovered Poe through Baudelaire's versions, the translation machine was set in motion: The literary journals were inundated with multiple versions of "Annabel Lee," "To Helen," "The Bells," and, of course, "The Raven." This last poem was the subject of eight translations, the first of which was made by José Antonio Pérez Bonalde in 1887. (Pérez Bonalde's subtitle, "Direct translation from the English by J. A. Pérez Bonalde," is revealing as it highlights the fact that the previous versions had been indirect.) In 1893, more than forty years after his death, Latin American letters canonized Poe: Rubén Darío included him in *Los raros* [1896; *Exceptional Men*].

Although no other foreign model could compete with the French with respect to the duration, intensity, and disproportion of its influence, other models did manage to penetrate Latin American letters by means of translation. Let me mention two illustrative cases from U.S. literature, both of which entailed major changes in the long term, but not without first experiencing a very bumpy ride. The poetry of Walt Whitman achieved a definite presence in Latin America in the *modernista* period: José Martí wrote a famous article (255–71); Darío dedicated a sonnet to him; Amado Nervo (1870–1919), Juan José Tablada (1871–1945), José Santos Chocano (1875–1934), and Leopoldo Lugones (1874–1938) all knew his work intimately; and González Prada translated the poem "A Woman Waits for Me." These are only a few of the instances cited by Fernando Alegría. Whitman's presence was, however, only partial, based on a fragmentary knowledge that, in a certain manner of speaking, was misguided because his aesthetic principles did not coincide with the dominant discourse that came from France. It was only in the twilight of Latin American *modernismo* that his voice acquired its power; it was not until twenty years after his death and more than sixty years after the first publication of *Leaves of Grass* that Whitman's name was affixed to the standard of the new Latin American poetry. In 1912 Whitman's *Poemas* [*Poems*] appeared in a translation by the Uruguayan Armando Vasseur, and they then began to play a decisive role. This was further evidence of the law that between the quality and the effect of a translation there may be no necessary connection, for Vasseur's versions were rather lame: Fernando Alegría in some twenty pages tallies the errors, including flawed vocabulary, conceptual mistakes, and dubious interpretations (353–73). These shortcomings notwithstanding, a Whitman school (C. Sabat Ercasty, E. Martínez Estrada, L. F. Franco) sprang up almost immediately in Argentina, Uruguay, and Chile. With the subsequent rise of the avant-garde movement, Whitman was displaced from the center of concern and his influence suspended for a brief period, while the avant-garde flame burned bright; however, once that movement had spent its energies, Whitman returned to the stage, in a new context of the larger polysystem, and this time he was to exercise a profound and

prolonged influence. New spokesmen stepped forward on his behalf (Alegría 417–18), and multiple translations appeared from writers of stature like Jorge Luis Borges, José Coronel Urtecho (1906–1994), Fernando Alegría (b. 1918), León Felipe (1884–1968), and Arturo Torres-Rioseco (1897–1971). Torres-Rioseco, to cite only one example of the late proliferation of Whitman translations, produced two versions of the poem "When Lilacs Last in the Dooryard Bloomed," in 1922 and 1946, and, as Alegría has observed, the two versions are so distinct "they appear to be based upon texts from two different poets" (273). In this third and prolonged appearance, Whitman's influence would prove to be central: Without his voice, his free verse, his cosmic sweep, the works of Vicente Huidobro (1893–1948), Pablo de Rokha (1894–1968), and Pablo Neruda are, I believe, unthinkable.

Decades later a practically identical scenario of halting acceptance played itself out with respect to the work of William Faulkner. Faulkner already had a dozen books in print when the first Spanish translation appeared in 1934: the Cuban Lino Novás Calvo's (1905–1983) version of *Sanctuary.* However, even at this late date Novás Calvo's *Santuario* was a Faulkner misinterpreted and badly translated, and it showed evidence of only an indirect contact with the writer's work. Published in Spain by Espasa Calpe as a social-documentary novel, the book was selected for translation largely on the basis of the success of the film version and because of the polemics surrounding the French translation (Chapman 127–31). According to Tanya Fayen (xi), the Hispanic image of Faulkner at this time was much more a product of the French existentialists' vision–that of an "angelic" but "fatalistic" and "tragic" writer, preoccupied above all with liberty and destiny–than of any reception or evaluation in the United States. Because Novás Calvo's translation was severely abridged and critical reception negative enough, Faulkner's discourse did not succeed in entering the Hispano-American literary system in the 1930s. For this, it had to wait another decade until, in the new international context, a second attempt was made to establish him in Latin America. Between 1939, when *Dry September* appeared in *Sur,* and 1949, when Faulkner was awarded the Nobel Prize, six of his works were published in Latin America (Fayen 80–81). Here again Latin America followed the lead of France where, between 1934 and 1940, Faulkner's most important works were translated, and where Faulkner enthusiasts included such eminent figures as Valéry Larbaud and Jean-Paul Sartre. Although Faulkner did this time enter the main current of Latin American letters, almost all the translations made in this period were to a greater or lesser degree falsifications. Compromising their texts with the discourse prevalent in the target language, the translators changed, modified, and distorted the originals unscrupulously. This was not merely a case of changing the titles and the sequence of the stories in *These Thirteen* (José Blaya Lozano, for example, opted to publish only twelve of the stories under the title *Victoria y otros cuentos* [*Victoria and Other Stories*]), but was rather a matter of "improvements": "domesticating" the style, ignoring (or being ignorant of) the neologisms, completing "incomplete" sentences, naming enigmatic pronominal subjects, clarifying obscurities (Fayen 221–27). In these practices the translators professed a concept of translation that adhered rigidly to canonized norms, granting to Faulkner only a limited influence. This situation changed only at the end of the 1940s, when Faulkner was internationally consecrated: The Latin American literary polysystem experienced an opening, and

Faulkner was received into its heart. The translations that followed, now twenty or thirty years after Faulkner's rise to fame, managed to communicate the innovations of form and content that had distinguished the originals; they even inaugurated a number of highly characteristic "faulknerisms": Between 1950 and 1952, for example, the greatest supporters of the "misogynist" Faulkner were a group of women translators (Chapman 144). This fruitful period came unexpectedly to an end in the late 1950s with the change of paradigm known as the Boom.

The examples I have enumerated in the preceding pages testify to the stature and singular importance of the phenomenon of translation, both from the point of view of aesthetic principles and from that of the dynamics of the literary institution. To date, however, precious little criticism has addressed this phenomenon in Latin America. No systematic theory has yet attempted to take on or surpass the consecrated theoretical texts of Alfonso Reyes, Octavio Paz (1914–1998), Jorge Luis Borges, or Julio Cortázar; nor have translators produced many analyses of individual works, although there are a few, ranging from brief articles by R. Ferré, M. E. Bravo, C. Eshleman, N. Lindstrom, N. Th. Di Giovanni, and A. MacAdam, to the extensive monographs, some of which I have cited, of A. Reyes, M. Henríquez Ureña, S. J. Levine, and J. Felstiner. To my mind the most useful approaches are those that advance their textual analyses within a consistent theoretical frame, works like Aparicio's book on Paz, Borges, and Cortázar, and above all Jákfalvi's work on El Inca Garcilaso and Fayen's on Faulkner. These latter works allow us a glimpse of the road by which we might, one day, approach the full amplitude of translation in the literary system.

Translation by Colman Hogan

Works Cited

Adorno, Rolena. 1986. *Guaman Poma: Writing and Resistance in Colonial Peru*. Austin: University of Texas Press.

Alegría, Fernando. 1954. *Walt Whitman en Hispanoamérica*. Mexico City: Studium.

Aparicio, Frances R. 1991. *Versiones, interpretaciones y creaciones: Instancias de la traducción literaria en Hispanoamérica en el siglo veinte*. Gaithersburg, MD: Hispamérica.

Apter, Ronnie, and Mark Herman. 1995. "The Worst Translations: Almost Any Opera in English." *Translation Review* 48–49: 26–32.

Arguedas, José Maria. 1949. *Canciones y cuentos del pueblo quechua*. Selección, traducción y notas de José Maria Arguedas. Lima: Editorial Huascará, 1949.

Arnaud, Vicente Guillermo. 1950. *Los intérpretes en el descubrimiento, conquista y colonización del Río de la Plata*. Buenos Aires: Hachette.

Barnet, Miguel. 1980 [1966]. *Biografía de un cimarrón*. Havana: Letras Cubanas.

——. 1972. *Fekete sors az Antillák gyöngyén*. Trans. István Dely. Budapest: Magvető.

——. 1969. "La novela testimonio: socio-literatura." *Unión* 4: 99–123.

Barras, Tine. 1978. "The Function of Translated Literature within a National Literature: The Example of 16th Century Spain." *Literature and Translation*. Ed. J. Holmes, J. Lambert, and A. Lefevere. Louvain: ACCO. 181–202.

Bassnett, Susan. 1993. *Comparative Literature: A Critical Introduction*. Oxford: Blackwell.

Beardsley, Th. S. 1970. *Hispano-Classical Translations*. Pittsburgh: Duquesne University Press.

Bello, Andrés. 1979. *Obra literaria*. Caracas: Ayacucho.

Borges, Jorge Luis. 1974. "Las versiones homéricas." *Obras completas*. Buenos Aires: Emecé. 239–243.

——. 1974. "Los traductores de las 1001 noches." *Obras completas*. Buenos Aires: Emecé. 397–413.

Bowen, Margareta, et al. 1995. "Interpreters and the Making of History." *Translators through History*. Ed. Jean Delisle and Judith Woodsworth. Amsterdam: John Benjamins. 245–77.

The Bowker Annual Library and Book Trade Almanac. 1994. New Jersey: P.R. Bowker.

Bravo, María Elena. 1985. "Borges traductor: el caso de *The Wild Palms* de William Faulkner." *Insula* 40.462: 11–12.

Brotherston, Gordon. 1992. *Book of the Fourth World*. Cambridge: Cambridge University Press.

Carter, Boyd G. 1968. *Historia de la literatura hispanoamericana a través de sus revistas*. Mexico City: Andrea.

——. 1959. *Las revistas literarias de Hispanoamérica*. Mexico City: Andrea.

Chapman, Arnold. 1966. *The Spanish American Reception of United States Fiction*. Berkeley: University of California Press.

Cornejo Polar, Antonio. 1982. "El indigenismo y las literaturas heterogéneas: Su doble estatuto socio-cultural." *Sobre literatura y crítica latinoamericanas*. Caracas: UCV. 67–85.

Cortázar, Julio. 1980. "No hay peor sordo." La vuelta al día en ochenta mundos. México: XXI. 93–100.

Englekirk, John Eugene. 1934. *Edgar Allan Poe in Hispanic Literature*. New York: Instituto de las Españas en los EE.UU.

Eshleman, Clayton. 1968/69. "Translating César Vallejo: An Evolution." *Tri-Quarterly* 13–14: 55–82.

Even-Zohar, Itamar. 1990. "Polysystem Theory." *Poetics Today* 11.1: 1–96.

Fayen, Tanya T. 1995. *In Search of the Latin American Faulkner*. Lanham: University Press of America.

Felstiner, John. 1980. *Translating Neruda: The Way to Macchu Picchu*. Stanford: Stanford University Press.

Ferré, Rosario. 1990. "Ofelia a la deriva en las aguas de la memoria." *El coloquio de las perras*. Harrisonburg, VA: Cultural. 67–82.

Franco, José Luciano, ed. 1937. *Autobiografía, cartas y versos de Juan Francisco Manzano*. Havana: Municipio de La Habana.

Gallego Roca, Miguel. 1994. *Traducción y literatura: Los estudios literarios ante las obras traducidas*. Madrid: Jucar.

Garcilaso de la Vega, El Inca. 1965. *Obras completas*. Vol. 1. Madrid: BAE.

Giovanni, Norman Thomas di. 1970–71. "At Work with Borges." *The Antioch Review* 30.3–4: 290–298.

Gómez de Avellaneda, Gertrudis. 1869. *Obras literarias*. Vol. 1. Madrid: Rivadeneyra.

Gorp, Hendrik van. 1985. "Translation and Literary Genre. The European Picaresque Novel in the Seventeenth and Eighteenth Century." *The Manipulation of Literature*. Ed. Theo Hermans. New York: St. Martin's Press. 136–48.

Guillén, Claudio. 1985. *Entre lo uno y lo diverso*. Barcelona: Crítica.

Hale, Terry. 1996. "Traducción e identidad nacional en Gran Bretaña." *Voces* 28: 20–23.

Henríquez Ureña, Max. 1954. *Breve historia del modernismo*. Mexico City: Fondo de Cultura Económica.

Henze, Hans Werner. 1972. *El cimarrón: Biographie des geflohenen Sklaven Esteban Montejo. Rezital für 4 Musiker*. New York: Schott.

Heredia, José María de. 1938. *Los Trofeos*. Trans. Max Henríquez Ureña. Santiago de Chile: Ercilla.

Index translationum. International Bibliography of Translations. Paris: UNESCO.

Jacquemond, Richard. 1992. "Translation and Cultural Hegemony: The Case of French-Arabic Translation." *Rethinking Translation*. Ed. L. Venuti. London: Routledge. 139–158.

Jákfalvi-Leiva, Susana. 1984. *Traducción, escritura y violencia colonizadora: un estudio de la obra del Inca Garcilaso*. Syracuse: Syracuse University Press.

Karáston, A. 1982. "The Translation and Refraction of Symbolism: A Survey of the Hungarian Example." *The Symbolist Movement in the Literature of European Languages*. Ed. Anna Balakian. Budapest: Akadémiai Kiadó. 165–82.

Kelly, L.G. 1979. *The True Interpreter*. New York: Blackwell.

Klor de Alva, J. Jorge. 1983. "Language, Politics and Translation: Colonial Discourse and Classic Nahuatl in New Spain." *The Art of Translation*. Ed. R. Warren. Boston: Northeastern University Press. 143–62.

Lambert, J., L. D'hulst, and K. van Bragt. 1985. "Translated Literature in France (1800–1850)." *The Manipulation of Literature: Studies in Literary Translation*. Ed. Theo Hermans. New York: St. Martin's Press. 149–163.

Lambert, José, and Hendrik van Gorp. 1985. "On Describing Translations." *The Manipulation of Literature: Studies in Literary Translation*. Ed. Theo Hermans. New York: St. Martin's Press. 42–53.

Lefevere, André et al. 1995. "Translators and the Reins of Power." *Translators through History*. Ed. Jean Delisle and Judith Woodsworth. Amsterdam: John Benjamins. 131–55.

Levine, Suzanne Jill. 1991. *The Subversive Scribe*. St. Paul: Graywolf.

Lindstrom, Naomi. 1984. "On the Translation of Unnatural Language." *Translation Review* 15: 40–43.

Luis, William. 1991. "Culture as Text: The Cuban/Caribbean Connection." *Translating Latin America*. Ed. William Luis and Julio Rodríguez-Luis. Binghamton: Center for Research in Translation, State University of New York at Binghamton. 7–20.

MacAdam, Alfred. 1991. "Rebirth of a Novel." *Translating Latin America*. Ed. William Luis and Julio Rodríguez-Luis. Binghamton: Center for Research in Translation, State University of New York at Binghamton. 337–42.

Mantecón Navasal, José Ignacio. 1964. *Indice de las traducciones impresas en México, 1959*. Mexico City: Biblioteca Nacional.

Manzano, Juan Francisco. 1937. *Autobiografía, cartas y versos de Juan Francisco Manzano*. Ed. José Luciano Franco. Havana: Municipio de la Habana.

———. 1981. *The Life and Poems of a Cuban Slave: Juan Francisco Manzano, 1797–1854*. Ed. Edward J. Mullen. Hamden, Connecticut: Archon Books. Previously published as *Poems by a Slave in the Island of Cuba*. 1840. Ed. and trans. R. R. Madden.

Martí, José. 1972. "El poeta Walt Whitman." *Antología mínima*. Vol. 2. Havana: Editorial de Ciencias Sociales. 255–71.

Martínez-Echazabal, Lourdes. 1991. "Testimonial Novel: Translating Culture while Narrowing the Genre Gap." *Translating Latin America*. Ed. William Luis and Julio Rodríguez-Luis. Binghamton: Center for Research in Translation, State University of New York at Binghamton. 57–65.

Niranjana, Tejaswini. 1992. *Siting Translation: History, Post-structuralism, and the Colonial Context*. Berkeley: University of California Press.

Ortega y Gasset, José. 1962. "Miseria y esplendor de la traducción." *Obras completas*. Madrid: Revista de Occidente. 5: 441–52.

Ortiz, Fernando. 1910. *El caballero encantado y la moza esquiva (versión libre y americana de una novela española de D. Benito Pérez Galdos*. Havana: Editorial Letras Cubanas.

Paz, Octavio. 1973a. *Los hijos del limo*. Barcelona: Seix Barral.

———. 1973b. "Teoría y práctica de la traducción." *El signo y el garabato*. Mexico City: Joaquín Mortiz. 57–109.

Pérez Firmat, Gustavo. 1989. *The Cuban Condition: Translation and Identity in Modern Cuban Literature*. Cambridge: Cambridge University Press.

Pérez Galdós, Benito. 1977. *El caballero encantado*. Ed. Julio Rodriguez-Puértolas. Madrid: Catedra.

Pratt, Mary Louise. 1994. "Transculturation and Autoethnography: Peru 1615/1980." *Colonial Discourse/Postcolonial Theory*. Ed. F. Barker. Manchester: Manchester University Press. 24–46.

Quiroga, José. 1991. "Translating Vowels and the Defeat of Sounds." *Translating Latin America*. Ed. William Luis and Julio Rodríguez-Luis. Binghamton: Center for Research in Translation, State University of New York at Binghamton. 317–23.

Rafael, Vicente L. 1988. *Contracting Colonialism*. Ithaca: Cornell University Press.

Rama, Ángel. 1982. *Transculturación narrativa en América Latina*. Mexico City: Siglo XXI.

Reyes, Alfonso. 1938. *Mallarmé entre nosotros*. Buenos Aires: Destiempo.

Rodríguez Monegal, Emir. 1969. *El otro Andrés Bello*. Caracas: Monte Avila.

Sánchez, Luis Rafael. 1991. "La literatura como traducción de una cultura." *Translating Latin America: Culture as Text*. Ed. William Luis and Julio Rodríguez-Luis. Binghamton: Center for Research in Translation, State University of New York at Binghamton. 23–33.

Santoyo, Julio-César. 1987. *Teoría y crítica de la traducción: antología*. Barcelona: Universitat Autónoma de Barcelona.

Sayers Peden, Margaret. 1996. "Knopf, Knopf: Who's There?" *Translation Review* 50: 27–30.

Scholz, László. 1984. "Del fenómeno internacional de las vanguardias." *Acta Litteraria Academiae Scientiarum Hungariacae* 26: 440–47.

Shur, L.A. 1966. *Literatura latinoamericana en la imprenta rusa*. Moscow: Kniga.

Spitta, Silvia. 1995. *Between Two Waters: Narratives of Transculturation in Latin America*. Houston: Rice University Press.

Steenmeijer, Maarten. 1991. *Bibliografía de las traducciones de la literatura española e hispanoamericana, 1946–1990*. Tübingen: Niemeyer.

Steiner, George. 1998. *After Babel*. Oxford: Oxford University Press.

Stoberski, Zygmunt. 1972. "The Role of Translations in the Development of World Culture." *Babel* 18.4: 21–28.

Toury, Gideon. 1981. "Translated Literature: System, Norm, Performance." *Poetics Today* 2.4: 9–27.

——— ed. 1987. *Translation across Cultures*. New Delhi: Bakri.

UNESCO Statistical Yearbook. 1995. Lanham: UNESCO Publications and Bernan P.

Valencia, Guillermo. 1948. *Obras poéticas completas*. Madrid: Aguilar.

Woodsworth, Judith, et al. 1995. "Translators and the Emergence of National Literature." *Translators through History*. Eds. Jean Delisle and Judith Woodsworth. Amsterdam: John Benjamins. 67–98.

CHAPTER 18

THE DEVELOPMENT OF A TRANSLATION PAIDEUMA AND POETICS IN BRAZIL
THE CAMPOS BROTHERS

Else Ribeiro Pires Vieira

Illuminating interfaces between cultural history and literature surface when broached through the phenomenon of translation: what is and what is not translated, who translates what and how, which new translation theories are established, and so on. In the nineteenth century in Brazil, the translation of plays and novels was outstanding and extensive, and the name of Machado de Assis (1839–1908), for example, comes to mind as a great contributor to translation, predominantly for the theater. The 1940s and 1950s have been called the golden age of translation, when distinguished Brazilian writers *cum* translators such as Érico Veríssimo (1905–1975), Carlos Drummond de Andrade (1902–1987), and Cecília Meireles (1901–1965) rendered everything from the works of Nobel Prize winners to canonical fiction into Portuguese (Paes 1990, 27–8). Censorship during the military dictatorship (1964–1984) led to a period of intense translation of plays, particularly Brecht's, as a vehicle of safe expression (Benn-Ibler). In the later stages of the dictatorship, there was a notable opening up of the régime and a relaxation of cultural restrictions, but there was no decrease in the number of foreign works translated into Brazilian Portuguese, which leads us to hypothesize that the construction of an alternative past free of the arbitrary constraints of limited access and state interference was becoming a possibility (Vieira 1998b, 53–75). In general, translation has become increasingly conspicuous in Brazil, as further evidenced by the recent boom of poetry translation in the 1980s and 1990s.

This essay concentrates on the contemporary Brazilian translators and theorists Haroldo de Campos (1929–2003) and his brother Augusto de Campos (b. 1931), both main exponents of translation and its theorizing in Latin America. In the 1950s, something more substantial than the mere translation of great books by equally great Brazilian writers was happening. This is when the brothers Campos and a constellation of equally distinguished avant-garde poets, gathered around the Concretist movement, began to translate prolifically. Augusto de Campos, Haroldo de Campos, and Décio Pignatari (b. 1927) were leading names in the movement of these years, which took up once again the question of dependence on foreign literary models. They set out to change the nature of poetry in Brazil and ended up having a great impact abroad as well. The Concretist poets also enhanced experimentalism in Brazilian poetry, expanding poetic sensibility through the focus on visuality. Haroldo de Campos had stressed that the antinormative tradition in Brazilian contemporary poetry is what has informed the Concretist movement, in that it articulates differences, both appropriated and reclaimed, as the patrimony of a peripheral literature, thus both criticizing and remaking a poetics (1986, 51). Out of the attempt of São Paulo's Concretist poets of the

1950s to theorize and create a Brazilian poetics, there emerged a continuous translation activity of re-/trans- creation related to that of Ezra Pound and his view of translation as criticism; while translating Pound's *Cantos* themselves, these poets were nourished by and then able to apply Pound's own criterion of creative translation (1992, 42). A series of translations followed–of e.e. cummings, the German avant-garde, Japanese *haikus*, Dante, Joyce–whose "fragile and apparently unreachable beauty" had its entrails dissected and then revitalized as part of the body of a foreign language and poetics (1992, 43). The translation of creative texts, Haroldo de Campos argued, is always re-creation or parallel creation; the opposite of a literal translation, it is always reciprocal, an operation in which it is not only the meaning that is translated but the sign itself in all its corporeality (sound properties, visual imagery, all that makes up the iconicity of the aesthetic sign) (1992, 35). With Pound, translation is seen as criticism, insofar as it attempts theoretically to anticipate creation; it chooses; it eliminates repetitions; it organizes knowledge in such a way that the next generation may find only the still living part. Pound's well-known "Make it new" is thus recast by Haroldo de Campos as the revitalization of the past via translation (1992, 36).

The complexity of the issues dealt with by the Concretist poets enables translation to mean more than the interpretation or the re-codification of a text into another language. Translation became a project, a visible cultural and literary phenomenon: It established a canon, thereby contributing to the reconfiguration of tradition or the construction of an alternative one. Moreover, the Campos brothers introduced a (variously labeled) poetics of translation as re-creation that broadens the poetic resources of the receiving language and literature. More specifically, Haroldo and Augusto de Campos renewed thinking on translation, devised a translation poetics, and triggered questions of reading cross-culturally– while redrawing the relations between the local and the international. João Alexandre Barbosa corroborates the view that, as translators, they created an ample repertoire for young groups interested in poetry and established a canon as they radically chose some authors over others. This was an important move insofar as they made these works available to the Portuguese language and Brazilian culture (qtd. in Schwartz 5). José Paulo Paes highlights the Concretists' broadening of the horizons of the Brazilian readership, also remarking that Augusto de Campos, Haroldo de Campos, Décio Pignatari, and José Lino Grünewald deserve special mention in that they formulated a theory of translation and a poetics of re-creation of the highest formal complexity (1983, 8–11). Yet, relatively little has been written internationally on the Campos brothers, compared with the response of writers worldwide to the play on translation and its cultural possibilities by such writers as Salman Rushdie and Jorge Luis Borges, for instance.

In Brazil, their translations have often been reviewed in the important newspapers and journals, a site also for the publication of their own views on translation, operational procedures, and metalanguage. The Brazilian contribution to translation theory has been outstanding, and the Campos brothers have established the pattern in this respect. Their metalanguage, in general, mixes critical discourse with the use of metaphors, simultaneously introducing new registers and praxes. They thus situate translation studies in Brazil within the postmodern and poststructuralist agenda. Translation, criticism, and creativity can be seen to weave a fabric that resists dichotomies and the hierarchies of primary and secondary discourses, stressing, rather, a relation grounded not in binary oppositions but one operating at the threshold of fusion and distinction, assimilation and expropriation. Metaphors, in the brothers Campos's metalanguage in general, convey a sense of bilaterality (such as the digestive metaphor and that of "blood transfusion"). These metaphors thus move translation beyond obvious polarizations such as source/target, superior/inferior.

This development fits into the rich context of translation in Latin America, even though the Brazilian phenomenon has its own specificity. This contrasts with the Anglo-Saxon world where, Lawrence Venuti contends, the translator has a shadowy existence. In Brazil and in Spanish America translation is a visible practice, and translators produce both translations and translation commentary and criticism. What Venuti has remarked in relation to poststructuralism applies to the poetics developed foremost by the Campos brothers: Their contribution liberates the translation from its subordination to the foreign text and enables the development of a hermeneutic that reads the translation as a text in its own right (i–viii). A great amount of high-quality literary translation is produced in Brazil and the rest of Latin America along with translators' commentaries and theorizations. The region's construction of an autonomous theoretical framework for translation has contributed to the revitalization of thinking in this area, as is evident with the outstanding case of Jorge Luis Borges (1899–1986). The mention of this Argentine writer prompts a parenthesis to highlight another important aspect of translation theorization in Latin America, which has been labeled "the fictional turn in translation studies" (by Vieira 1998a) and which stems from a distinctive contribution of that literature. For example, Borges's well-known "Pierre Menard," like his other pieces, halfway between scientific and fictional discourses, deconstructs many of our inherited assumptions about translation; these works have become a point of reference in Latin America and throughout the world (see Vieira 1998a). In fact, Borges's recurrent use of characters who are translators or critics of translation highlights the role played by translation since the dawn of Western literature. Borges thought of translation as creation and as a way of enriching the language and transmitting stylistic procedures, new poetic forms, and narrative models (Wordsworth 89–91). Of course, he does not stand alone in Argentina or in Latin America; many have contributed to the development of thought about translation, most obviously in the twentieth century. Among fiction writers who have reflected upon the processes of translation one could mention, besides Borges, the names of Julio Cortázar (1914–1984), Ricardo Piglia (b. 1941; Argentina), Cabrera Infante (b. 1929; Cuba) and Gabriel García Márquez (b. 1927; Colombia).

A Poetics of Re-Creation

New modalities introduced in the 1970s and 1980s in Brazil by the Campos brothers can be seen to problematize specularity, break with the one-way flow theory of translation, and reconceptualize the notion of origin. Augusto de Campos introduced in 1978 the term *intradução/intranslation* to describe his theory and praxis–a fusion of *introdução* (introduction) and *tradução* (translation), with the idea of "introduction" metamorphosing into "translating within." Haroldo de Campos's terminology has been changing in consonance with his theoretical mode of working with the particular text he is translating in order to derive his metalanguage. One term he coined in this way was *transtextualization* for the two-way amalgam of original and national literature, part of his project of transcreation. Broadly speaking, these neologisms convey the interweaving both of the original and of native Brazilian elements in the translated text; translation is thus seen as transformation and bilateral absorption. Illuminating for this perspective is the notion of double capture, advanced by Gilles Deleuze as a way of describing a process of becoming whereby each term in a relation takes on the properties of the other and transforms itself, while still keeping its own identity. In this light, a more dynamic relation obtains between original and translation; both are donors and receivers; the original becomes one with the translation and the translation becomes one with the original, so neither are the same again. This dual trajectory points to an ambiguous space of absorption collateral with self-expression.

The sense of duality and growth attendant upon the encounter of the one and the other via translation are well exemplified in Augusto de Campos's famous translation of John Donne's "The Apparition." Donne's lines:

> Then shall my ghost come to thy bed,
> And thee, fain'd vestall, in worse armes shall see; (83)

are recast by Augusto de Campos (1977) as:

> Meu fantasma virá ter ao seu leito
> Onde serás, falsa vestal, uma mulher
> Qualquer nos braços de um outro qualquer.(86)

> My ghost will return to your bed
> Where you shall be, false virgin,
> Just another woman in the arms of another man.

The insertion of lines from Lupicínio Rodrigues (1914–1974), a name associated with popular music, not 'high art,' into his translation produces an interesting intertextual and intercultural play with political implications. Transcending the conventional power hierarchy between original and translation or, ultimately, between the superiority of an established and central culture and the consequent inferiority of a peripheral one, and at the same time breaking with the high low culture polarization, Augusto de Campos heralds a new axiomatics of translation in that there is a shift away from sacred textuality toward textualized otherness. Translation is thus seen as a process of rewriting that also asserts the translator's cultural identity and her or his historical embeddedness. A more politicized slant also emerges in the delimitation of an authorial space for the translator, and in the consequent redistribution of authorship and authority.

Augusto de Campos also interweaves different languages in his translations and is well known for what he called an *iconogramic version* of William Blake's "The Sick Rose." Blake's

142 ELSE RIBEIRO PIRES VIEIRA

text, which is originally linearly laid out, is metamorphosed in the translation into a concrete poem. He does not translate Blake only into the Portuguese language but also into Brazilian literature, that is, his own kind of concrete poetry. Voices and discourses interweave–the writer's, the translator's, English literature, Brazilian literature, verbal discourse, nonverbal discourse, and so on. Another example of Augusto de Campos's re-creation through visual translation, aimed at revitalizing poetry, articulates text and translation through technology, which attunes his project to our technological era. It further refers back to the Concretist bias, as the translation says, of organizing the line in such a way as to highlight the relation between graphic and phonic values, thereby revitalizing the word from its basic materiality (1996, 8). Here the best example is Augusto de Campos and Arnaldo Antunes' creative computer-aided translation of Rimbaud's "*Voyelles*," which can be said to improvise from the translation of "The Sick Rose."

Another example of this interweaving is afforded by Haroldo de Campos's translation of the Hebrew Bible. Transculturating both the sacred and the diabolic, being both irreverent and reverent–indeed, moving beyond essentialist binarisms–Haroldo de Campos *aportuguesa* ("portugueses") the Hebrew language and *hebraiza* ("hebraizes") the Portuguese language, stressing bilateral movements in his translation, one that depends on semantic homology and, at the same time, inscribes difference in tradition. The Hebrew Bible, he explains, presents a proverbial and aphoristic style in which the solemn and the colloquial intermingle in a markedly poetic form. Subscribing to Walter Benjamin's view that fidelity relates to the signifying form beyond the transmission of a communicative content, he further stresses the resources he used, specifically from Brazilian Portuguese. Focusing on the fact that the literary emergence of Brazilian Portuguese occurred during the Baroque period, he argues that the transposed language counteracted the constraints of a European and long-standing rationalist tradition, despite all the efforts of the purists; the language was shaken by the subversion of speech, of orality in its several registers, not to mention its several lexical inventions; it is a plastic idiom that has opened its sounds and its syntax to the fertilizing impact of the foreign language. In order to render the original's interplay of the oracular and the familiar/colloquial, whereby the voice of God is heard alongside that of man, he transtextualizes the Hebrew text into the corresponding existing tradition of Brazilian writers–such as Guimarães Rosa (1908–1967) in *Grande Sertão: Veredas* [1956; *The Devil to Pay in the Backlands*], or João Cabral de Melo Neto (1920–1999) in *Autos* [1950; *Plays*]–who have, in their turn, fed on the popular oral tradition, as well as the innovation and revitalization of the arcane in popular speech (Haroldo de Campos 1992, 31–5; 1991).

A theoretical view of translation as re-creation and as a locus of duality, conveyed by Haroldo de Campos in his seminal essay, "Da Tradução como criação e como crítica" [1992; "On Translation as Recreation and Criticism"], is related to the construction of a paideuma and a poetics. He establishes his own relationship with Ezra Pound's project and those of Brazilian precursors such as Manuel Odorico Mendes (1799–1864), highlighting further dimensions of translation theorized as a critical operation and as rewriting. The view of translation as re-creation that he elaborates throughout that essay prefigures the wealth of neologisms for

and concepts of translation later advanced by Haroldo de Campos: translation as "verse making," "reinvention," a "project of recreation," "transilluminations" (stemming from his translation of Dante), as "transtextualization," as "transcreation," as "transluciferation" (from his translation of Goethe's *Faust*), as "transhelenization" (from his translation of *The Iliad* of Homer), as "poetic reorchestration" (from his rendering of the Hebrew Bible into Brazilian Portuguese). "New Transilluminations/"Novas Transiluminuras" (as explained in a 1998b interview) describes a section in Haroldo de Campos's latest book, *Crisantempo* (1998a), where he collects translations that would not fit into a specific book–some Horace, some Japanese poetry, and modern Israeli poets: In terms of form, these tend more toward a paraphrase (1998b, 25). Such a view of translation as re-creation was later cast by Haroldo de Campos under the rubric of a "poetics of Transcreation."

"Re" and "trans" are recurrent prefixes in his thought that locate translation at a remove from monological truth, moving it in the direction of the transformative re-creation of inherited tradition. "Transcreation," Haroldo de Campos argues, is a radical translation praxis. To transcreate is not to try to reproduce the original's form understood as a sound pattern, but to appropriate the translator's contemporaries' best poetry, to exploit the local existing tradition (1981, 185). As such, for him, to transcreate means also to take nourishment from local sources, nourishment that simultaneously limits the universality of the original and inscribes the difference. Translation is a reading of the universal tradition, he claims, but also of local literary production, because if the translator does not have a stock of the best poetry of his time to work from, he cannot reshape–synchronically and diachronically–the best poetry of the past (1981, 185). Translation, as such, relates to his utilization of parody as a "parallel canto," a dialogue not only with the original's voice, but with other textual voices or, as he encapsulates it, "Translation: transtextualization" (1981: 191, 200). Translation as transtextualization or transcreation demythifies the ideology of fidelity. If translation transtextualizes, it is no longer a one-way flow. Transcreation–the poetics that disrupts the primacy of the one model–is a rupture and a recourse to both the one and the other.

More recently, Haroldo de Campos has stressed that transcreation is not a free translation heedless of the original; he considers it "hyper-faithful" to the original because, besides fidelity to content, it structurally integrates this content into a semantization that may occur even in phonemes; the internal organization, the sound plays, and the morphological and grammatical correspondences must be re-created (1998b, 25). Transcreation or the act of translation cannot be separated from the act of writing; it has further a devilish dimension that he now theorizes as an act of usurpation (1997, 47) with an anthropophagic dimension of textual revitalization, of feeding on the text he is translating in order to derive his own metalanguage. In contrast, "reimagination" is a term used in very special cases, such as in his translations of Chinese poetry, which tend to be more paraphrases, insofar as the Chinese language, a tonal language, cannot be rendered into any Western language. So what Haroldo de Campos does is to reimagine these tones like a form of orchestration, in free verse with an occasional rhyme, and what gets translated are the grammatical plays (1998, 25).

The Campos Brothers' Dialogue with Tradition and with Ezra Pound

Both Haroldo and Augusto de Campos, in their respective ways, share with Pound the project of making world literature known. Augusto de Campos's dialogue with Pound emerges through the metaphor of the mask. In fact, this is a move that he makes explicit in a passage that also provides alternative ways of looking into the relationship between translation and original. This new axiomatics of translation is suggested by the cluster of metaphors that involve the actor and the dressing up in "another's skin." As he says in the introduction, further establishing the connection with Fernando Pessoa and his several identities:

> A tradução para mim é *persona*. Quase heterônimo. Entrar dentro da pele do fingidor para refingir tudo de novo, dor por dor, som por som, cor por cor. Por isso nunca me propus traduzir tudo. Só aquilo que sinto. Só aquilo que minto. Ou que minto que sinto, como diria, ainda uma vez, Pessoa em sua própia *persona*. (Augusto de Campos 1978, 7)

> Translation for me is a *persona*. Nearly a heteronym. It is to get into the pretender's skin to re-pretend everything again, each pain, each sound, each colour. This is why I never set out to translate everything. Only what I feel. Only what I lie about. Or what I lie that I feel, as Pessoa would say once more in his own *persona* (my translation).

Another link with Pound is the occasion for broadening the definition of translation: "tradução é crítica, como viu Pound melhor que ninguém. Uma das melhores formas de crítica" (1978, 7) ("translation is criticism, as Pound saw better than anybody else. One of the best forms of criticism"). In fact, the inextricability of literary, translational, and critical discourses is a prominent feature of Augusto de Campos's text. The title of his groundbreaking book, *Verso, Reverso, Countroverso* [1978; Verse, Reverse, Controverse] with its play on the word "verse" relates to Augusto de Campos's translation paideuma: What he sets out to do is to present and translate the texts that, at the time of their creation or even now, are the reverse of canonized and acknowledged literature and, as such, were or are subject to controversy. To re-read, to re-write, to re-create, to re-evaluate the past, all are subsumed under "reverse," a term that not only encompasses Augusto de Campos's project, but also lends it a marked cannibalistic and postmodern contour, for in both the question of tradition emerges fully, not necessarily as a refusal, but as a reevaluation, a rewriting of the past.

Augusto de Campos's early translation paideuma also correlates in part with Pound's. The book includes a series of translations of medieval Provençal poetry, English metaphysical poetry, Italian Baroque poetry, Hopkins, Laforgue, and others, each with an introduction. Together with these, there are critical essays on medieval Portuguese satirical poetry, Portuguese erotic and satirical poetry throughout the ages, and literatura de cordel, a popular form of oral literature from the Northeast of Brazil. What binds these together is a marked reevaluation of the past, a presentation of the reverse side of the coin. Most of these texts, unpublished or only partially published, or even censored at the time of composition and subsequently, offer a distorted or incomplete picture of the literature they were/are connected to. Some of these were also misunderstood in their time (English metaphysical poetry being a case in point). There is also the case of literary production conventionally deemed marginal, such as cordel literature. So

Augusto de Campos's project, as far as tradition is concerned, has been not to reject the past, but rather to pay homage and do justice to it by rewriting it. There is a lot to learn from their striking modernity and novelty, he claims, even though many of the texts are medieval ones.

Haroldo and Augusto de Campos in part share a common theory of art in their translations of Pound (1960, *Cantares* [*Cantos*]), James Joyce (1971, *Panorama do Finnegan's Wake* [*Finnegan's Wake*]), Vladimir Mayakovsky (1987, *Poesia russa moderna* [1985; Modern Russian Poetry]), Stéphane Mallarmé (1975, *Mallarmé*). With Pound, both develop the idea of a world-wide family tied by literary affinities. In their respective trajectories, however, they have followed different itineraries. If Augusto tends to rehabilitate the literature of once marginalized writers, Haroldo de Campos, as becomes apparent in his metalanguage, as well, tends toward the classics in world literature: Homer, Dante, Goethe, the Hebrew Bible, and Chinese poetry make up his paideuma. He also stresses that his affinities also contrast with Pound's: He followed the German avant-garde, in which Pound was not interested; nor was Pound interested in Petrarch, Virgil, or Russian poetry (1998, 22). But his concept of the universal tradition also leads him to his own home country. It is in the Brazilian Baroque, when the "rule of anthropophagy" develops, deconstructing the logocentrism inherited from the West (1986, 49), that he pinpoints the first practitioner of Anthropophagous translation, Gregório de Matos, in whose translation of Góngora, he argues, one finds a very distinctive trace, articulating alterity in the gaps of a universal code (1986, 48). But he claims in the same essay that the first actual theorist of translation, and more specifically of creative translation, is the pre-Romantic Manuel Odorico Mendes. Haroldo de Campos explains that in his translation of the *Odyssey*, Odorico Mendes synthesized 12,106 lines into 9,302, perhaps in order to accommodate in pentameters Homer's hexameters or to avoid the monotony of transposing the sound effects typical of a language with declensions to an analytical one. He further made up compound words in Portuguese to translate Homer's metaphors; "anthropophagically," he interpolates lines from other poets such as Camões into Homer (1992, 38–9). More recently, Haroldo de Campos has stressed the importance of an ethnographic dimension in a translation paideuma; this has been the stimulus to his publishing with Perspectiva (the publishing house for which he is the director of the Signos series) the translation by Antônio Risério, from the Yoruba language, of the book *Oriki Orixá*. He has further emphasized the importance of the work carried out by Josely Vianna Baptista with the Tupi-Guarani Indians; it is his belief that this tradition should be incorporated into the Brazilian archive.

Haroldo de Campos's reactivation of parody as "parallel song" marks his rereading of the Faustian tradition. Transilluminations of Dante's *Paradise* and transorchestrations of the Hebrew Bible coexist with a movement toward a counter-sublime, the daemonization of translation apparent in the "bad savages" who take nourishment from Goethe by translating him (as brought out in the paratext to Haroldo de Campos's translation of *Faustus* [*Faust*] in 1979 and published in 1981). Goethe is quoted defending himself against the accusation of plagiarism on the grounds that one can only produce great works by appropriating others' treasures–a view shared by Eliot and Pound, who argued that great poets borrow or steal from their forerunners and contemporaries and light their own light at the top of the mountain (1981, 74). Plagioentropy, a related notion Campos also advances, calls attention to the etymology of "plagios" as "oblique," "transverse," meaning the translation of tradition. Semiotically speaking, this is an unlimited semiosis (as theorized in Peirce and Eco), and has to do with the etymological meaning of parody as "parallel song" to designate the nonlinear transformation of texts throughout history (1981, 75–6).

Also in the early 1980s, Haroldo de Campos conveyed a reading of tradition through translation as parricidal dis-memory that "intends to erase the origin, to obliterate the original" (1981, 209); yet, it stands to reason that the very thrust of translating implies a gesture of acknowledgment. He highlights the satanic implications of "every translation that refuses to serve a content, that refuses the tyranny of a pre-ordered Logos, breaks with the metaphysical closure of presence (as Derrida would say)" (1981, 180). The "critical devouring of the universal heritage is formulated not from the insipid, resigned perspective of the 'noble savage' . . . but from the point of view of the 'bad savage,' devourer of whites–the cannibal" (1986, 44); there is nothing more alien to it than submission, for translation implies fidelity not so much to the original, but to another form. The pragmatics of translation, he claims, involves translating a poem's form, "rewriting it . . . in the translator's language in order to get to the transcreated poem as an isomorphic re-project of the originating poem" (1981, 181).

For the brothers Campos, it can be said that translation unsettles the single reference, "the logocentric tyranny of the original"; it has the "devilish dimension of usurpation" (Haroldo de Campos 1997, 33–59); it disturbs linear flows and power hierarchies. These are daemonic dimensions that coexist with the a priori gesture of tribute to the other inherent in translating and the giving of one's own vitality to the other.

Works Cited

Benn-Ibler, Veronika. 1998. "Textos-leitores-contextos: Brecht no Brasil, uma leitura reversa da história." *Discursos de tradición y contemporaneidad.* Ed. Horacio Crespo. Córdoba, Argentina: Centro de Estudos Avanzados. 71–8.

Campos, Augusto de. 1977. "John Donne, O Dom e A Danação." *O anticrítico.* São Paulo: Companhia das Letras. 83.

——. 1978. *Verso, reverso, controverso.* 2nd ed. rev. São Paulo: Perspectiva.

Campos, Augusto de, Haroldo de Campos and Décio Pignatari. 1996. "Concretismo: A certeza da influência." *Folha de São Paulo* (Dec. 8).

Campos, Haroldo de. 1981. *Deus e o Diabo no Fausto de Goethe.* São Paulo: Perspectiva.

——. 1986. "The Rule of Anthopophagy: Europe Under the Sign of Devoration." Trans. Maria Thai Wolff. *Latin American Literary Review* 14.27: 42–60.

——. 1991. *Qohélet = O-que-sabe: Eclesiastes: poema sapiencial.* Trans. Haroldo de Campos with J. Guinsburg. São Paulo: Perspectiva.

——. 1992. "Da Tradução como criação e como crítica." *Metalinguagem e outras metas: ensaios de teoria e crítica literária.* 4th ed. rev. São Paulo: Perspectiva. 31–48.

——. 1997. *O Arco-Íris Branco: Ensaios de literatura e cultura.* Rio de Janeiro: Imago Editora.

——. 1998a. *Crisantempo.* São Paulo: Perspectiva.

——. 1998b. "Entrevista: Haroldo de Campos fala sobre *Crisantempo.*" *CULT: Revista Brasileira de Literatura* (August): 18–27.

Donne, John. 1968. "Apparition." *The Complete Poetry of John Donne.* Ed. John T. Shawcross. New York: New York University Press. 83–4.

Paes, José Paulo. 1983. "A tradução no Brasil." *Folhetim* (São Paulo). Sept. 18. 8–11.

——. 1990. *Tradução a ponte necessária: Aspectos e problemas da arte de traduzir.* São Paulo: Editora Ática and Secretaria de Estado de Cultura de São Paulo.

Risério, Antonio. 1996. *Oriki Orixá.* São Paulo: Perspectiva.

Schwartz, Adriano. 1998. "Apaixonados e Furiosos: Poetas e críticos expõem suas concordâncias e divergências em relação ao movimento." *Folha de São Paulo* (Dec. 8): 5.

Venuti, Lawrence. 1992. "Introduction." *Rethinking Translation: Discourse, Subjectivity, Ideology.* New York: Routledge. i–xi.

Vieira, Else Ribeiro Pires. 1998a. "New Registers in Translation for Latin America." *Rimbaud's Rainbow: Literary Translation and Higher Education.* Ed. Kirsten Malmkjaer and Peter Bush. Amsterdam: John Benjamins. 171–96.

——. 1998b. "Um Mundo Metafísico nos Trópicos." *Revista Ilha do Desterro: English Renaissance and Drama* 34 (Jan.–June): 53–75.

Wordsworth, Judith and Jean Delisle, eds. 1995. *Translators through History.* Amsterdam: John Benjamins.

PART TWO

TEXTUAL MODELS AND THEIR TRANSFORMATIONS

INTRODUCTION

Randolph D. Pope and Flora Süssekind

When authors set out to write a work of literature, they invariably have a model in mind, a form that makes it possible for the writer to imagine the text-in-the-making, be it sonnet, novel, or essay. These established formal categories are historical in nature, and they evolve, changing in detail but also sometimes subject to radical distortion, as for example in parodic forms and counter-genres. Over the 500 years of literature that concerns us in this history of Latin American literary cultures–ranging from Renaissance Spain and Portugal and pre-Conquest Native America to the end of the twentieth century–the basic characteristics of European literary genres have remained relatively stable and have enjoyed remarkable continuity and flexibility in adaptation to radically new circumstances in Latin America.

Literary models can be compared to the urban grid of Spanish Renaissance city planning that was implemented throughout Spanish America or to Baron Haussman's modernization of Paris that was imitated in Latin America from Mexico City to Rio de Janeiro. These models were entirely European in design and historical development, and they were transferred to the Americas by master artists. In the case of literary form in Latin America, these artists are primarily Italian (Petrarch), Spanish (Garcilaso de la Vega, Cervantes), Portuguese (Camões), or French (Montaigne), for example. Writers are always subject to the vicissitudes of geography and the contingencies of birth, but whatever their historicity may be as writers, they work within a cultural past that simultaneously conditions their work and limits it.

The thirteen essays in this section probe into the continuous struggle with and at times dependence on the lettered tradition. In Latin America writers have both appropriated and rejected European, Anglo-American, and pre-Hispanic literary forms, which surfaced immediately when the writing began; it is for this reason that both the traditional genres of narrative prose and poetry, as well as the personal or popular genres–such as autobiography, epistolaries, debates, satire, sermons, the essay, and (in the last half-century) *testimonio*, as well as the *folletin* (or serial novel)–have all been treated by our group. Theater, as a complex union of text and performance and historically linked to religious and state public spectacles, has an entire subsection devoted to its development in Volume I.

There has been no attempt by us to be exhaustive in dealing with all the formal mutations of literary communication. Instead, we offer significant examples that permit us to address the main issue of the fundamental tension between imitation of a model and the appropriation of its characteristics and the creation of new configurations; this is the ever-present tension between possibility and reality that is always in play in writing and reading. We also want to stress that in our approach we do not trace influence or lines of development; nor do we outline the historical vicissitudes of Colonial dependence and subordination, for this is treated fully in Volume III. Our aim in this section has been to describe literary form as a dynamic part of the history of Latin American literary culture. We propose that, far from being a fixed base, the generic model be considered as part of a continuous dialogue and contestation within and especially between Europe and Latin America. In the same way that Mexican church architecture appropriated European models and transformed them into an incontestably new expression–related to but different from their European prototypes (through the syncretic fusion of pre-Hispanic symbolic elements)–so too did José Martí and José Carlos Mariátegui make the Latin American essay an autochthonous genre that responded to the anomaly of cultures that were simultaneously ancient and new. It is in the same vein of appropriation that we examine Domingo Sarmiento's autobiography or Gabriel García Márquez's remaking of the novel.

Writers in the twenty-first century must begin their work with both an incentive and barrier: the work of Jorge Luis Borges, Julio Cortázar, Guimarães Rosa, Clarice Lispector, and Elena Poniatowska has created a situation similar to that of Latin America's best writers a century ago, when faced with Victor Hugo and, later, Emile Zola. Comparative Literature, however, has taught us not to restrict the orbit of texts and authors that make up a writer's repertoire in a national or regional way. Today in the midst of postmodern globalization, in which literary canons are constantly being challenged and restored, it is impossible–more than ever before–to determine with any certainty which generic models are behind a text. Perhaps a novel has been written with a film as its model, or a poem is inspired by a video clip; new texts from India and Japan or from Africa and Australia are available in translations in Rio de Janeiro, Buenos Aires, Mexico City, Quito, or Managua, while at the same time authors from the past are no longer only available through libraries; there are new editions every day of classic authors, as well as rediscovered authors from the past.

What we as a group can affirm is that writing continues to be the implementation of textual models and consequently will continue to be a process of dynamic transformation. The thirteen essays that follow explore this intertextual process that is part of the writing, distribution, and reception of literature; in other words, it is this process of appropriation that mediates and makes possible the exchange of the cultural symbolic. The basic question we ask is to what extent imported models have taken American roots that have developed into a Latin-American cultural modality. There is no doubt that José Marmol's *Amalia,* José Hernández's *Martín Rivas,* and José Eustacio Rivera's *La vorágine*–to name but a few well-known novels–are unique and express a profound reality quite different from that which stood behind their European prototypes, be it in Romanticism, Realism, or Decadentism. Our affirmation does not deny the very real links with European generic models; what we explore is the range of appropriation and mutation of literary form. These essays examine in detail selected specific aspects of this dialogue of literary cultures, which has been an integral part of both the long Colonial process and the explosive post-Colonial period that at the start of the twenty-first century has become more complex and fluid–not only because of globalization of capital resources and the expansion of multinational corporations, but also and above all because of the unprecedented growth in richness and diversity of Latin American literary culture.

CHAPTER 19

THE BOOK AND THE FORMAT OF THE NOVEL

Jussara Menezes Quadros

A small vignette decorated the frontispiece of the original, now rare, edition (1844) of *A Moreninha* [The Little Brunette], a Brazilian novel by Joaquim Manoel de Macedo (1820– 1882). The images, on a small scale and set between the middle and the lower part of the page next to the printing information, was more than a decorative piece in the eyes of the reader. Within its curved lines, which outlined treetops in a forest, one discerns the figure of a young woman taking a solitary walk and holding a small book in her left hand. This was not a publisher's logo or even an allegorical motif; on the contrary, the allegories still found in the few illustrated Brazilian books at the time gave way to a representation of female reading, demarcated by clear conventions of Romantic sentimentality. This was a cliché originating in the realm of European books that, nevertheless, in the context of the late appearance of the novel in Brazil, took on the role of a frontispiece that signaled to the reader, and especially to the female reader, her admittance to the domain of the book and of the genre itself. In the practical ordering of the page, the vignette was subjected to a vertical hierarchy, being thus subordinate to the title above it, to which it served as a visual complement. But this page, also called *bela página* [beautiful page] in typography, was seen as a whole, and the aesthetic arrangement of its elements constituted in itself another artifice: As it emphasized the visual qualities of the page as a unit, the graphic variation, with its symmetrical proportions, in the end revealed a logic of interdependency that controlled each element and its position on the page, providing for a reading of both letter and image, itself a field of latent diversity of meanings.

In the case of *A Moreninha*'s frontispiece, the central position of the epigraph implies a connection between the upper half of the page that associated the work directly with the name of the author and the lower half that descended from the vignette to the printer's address, associating the work with its condition as a book and its material status as an object. Macedo had chosen the following verses from the poem "Les ombres" ["The Shadows"], by Jean-Baptiste-Louis Gresset (1709–1777), as epigraph to the novel: "Trop occupé pour corriger,/Je vous livre mes rêveries/. . ./J'en fais pour me désennuyer" ("Too busy to correct, I offer you my reveries, . . . I do it in order to amuse myself"). On the one hand, this quotation refers to the topos of literary creation as a disinterested spiritual activity, deprived of practicality or usefulness, exhibition or self-exhibition, with a totally subjective motivation: an author's amusement and not

his profession. On the other hand, the authorial voice puts into practice, from the beginning, a tactical dramatization of writing in the development of a second topos: that of the *captatio benevolentia*, aimed at the reading audience.

This was the first step toward a new reading protocol that formed itself around the epigraph and the vignette, through the figure of a female reader, and consisted of using symbolic inscription for a combined effect with what might come to the surface in a first reading of Gresset's verses: Both in the reference to (not) correcting the writing in its initial line as well as in the possibility of a double meaning of the verb *livrer* used in the first person, clearly what has not been corrected and what is now being reflexively offered to readers is a book. The epigraph thus anticipates and extends a thread of meaning forming the remaining paratexts; the preface reaffirms this reflexivity, enlarging the original scope of writing (this time noting its genesis within the novel genre), and the postscript (found only in this edition and left out of the following ones) makes explicit that which was merely alluded to: the transition from literary composition to the material existence of the book. A little *cul-de-lampe* with an inkholder, a pen, and an unfolded sheet of paper, placed immediately after the preface and repeated as a decorative item at the opening of the postscript, serves as a sign of connection between these spaces at the beginning and end of the book. These are signs of writing, which punctuate the spaces where the author unveils his presence, and, at the same time, they are a visual representation of the handwritten origin of the printed text. One inferred from this *cul-de-lampe*, in its position after the preface, direct references to the writing of the novel and the metaphorical play with the book itself. Note the definition of the genre that appears in the novel's first lines: "Eis aí vão algumas páginas escritas, às quais me atrevi a dar o nome de, romance" ("Here are a few written pages, which I dared to call a novel"). And note the rhetorical description of its origin related in a careless tone ("trinta noites garatujando o que por aí vai" ["thirty nights scribbling what you see here"]) and the reference to writing tools: "as penas dos autores" ("the authors' sorrows"), the "berço de carteira" ("desk cradle") of the Little Brunette, which was nothing other than his notebook, his manuscript, as it was referred to at the time (Macedo 1844, 4). And the title itself is appropriate to the predominant topos in the preface, namely, that of treating the work like a child.

The preface enlarged the scope of the author's declared intention, already announced in the epigraph, to guide the reader through a benevolent reading with respect to imperfections and serious defects that had not been corrected in the literary composition of a writer making his first attempt in a genre without an established tradition in Brazil: "Pode ser que me acusem por não tê-la conservado debaixo de minhas vistas mais tempo para corrigir suas imperfeições, e mostrá-la depois digna do amor dos leitores . . . porém esta menina saiu tão travessa, tão impertinente, que não pude mais sofrê-la no seu berço de carteira, e para ver-me livre dela, venho depositá-la nas mãos do público, de cuja benignidade e paciência tenho ouvido grandes elogios" (4) ("I may be accused of not having kept [the work] to myself longer in order to improve its imperfections and only then unveil it, so as to be worthy of the readers' affection . . . but this little girl is so naughty, so impertinent, that I could no longer keep her in her cradle, and, to get rid of her, I come to place her in the hands of the audience, of whose kindness and patience I have heard many compliments").

The same appeal, although in a very different tone, is made in the postscript, where faults are directly explained as a certain inexperience in publishing:

> Doce e forçoso me é aqui agradecer aos meus amigos, e colegas, o muito que fizeram para a publicação deste romance. A eles e a todos os leitores rogo que fechem os olhos aos señores e defeitos da primeira obra, que me atrevi a fazer imprimir. Sobretudo notar-se-ão inumeráveis erros de ortografia, que a pesar meu escaparam; mas nos últimos meses de um ano letivo tão trabalhoso, como o em que estou, mal pude atender devidamente a todos os erros, que formigavam nos capítulos do romance copiados por diversas pessoas, cada uma das quais talvez segue ortografia diferente: perdão e desculpa, pois. (n.p.)

> Sweet and imperative it is for me to thank my friends and colleagues for all they have done toward the publication of this novel. To them all and to all my readers, I pray that they shut their eyes to the faults and defects of my first work, which I dared to have printed. Above all, the several spelling errors that I have overlooked will be noted; but in the last few months of an arduous year, such as the one I am presently living, I could hardly catch all the errors that abound in the novel whose chapters were copied by many people, each of whom perhaps followed different spelling rules: forgive me, then.

Placed on the last page, after the colophon—that is, the printer's (or press's) name and address (Tipografia Francesa, in Rio de Janeiro)—Macedo's postscript occupies a space usually reserved for errata and the printer's list of misprints. On the upper part of the page, the inkstand, pen, and paper act as signs of authorial writing, this time subject to an unstable demarcation, where the errors of the various copies and copyists are listed. If the postscript indicates the series of interferences that characterized the passage from handwritten manuscript to typographical imprint, it suggests, moreover, in the way that Joaquim Manoel de Macedo thanks his friends for their help in publishing the work he "dared to have printed," that the postscript also took the place of the usual list of subscribers.

Although more commonly associated with the publication of a more prestigious genre such as poetry, the need, by the 1840s, to obtain subscribers beforehand revealed the reality of a literary environment with only a recent acquaintance with editorial practices: We must keep in mind that the press started its legal activities only after 1808, upon the arrival of the Portuguese royal family in Brazil. An editorial market and a regular commerce of books were still being established under almost exclusively foreign control (mostly booksellers and printers from France and Portugal). The importation and easy pirating of European works provided the economic basis for a national readership, but to nationalize reading habits became a task especially for Brazilian Romantic writers, who had to deal with the unequal conditions in Brazil compared to Europe, a situation that imposed serious limits on the publishing of national works. Advertisements in Rio de Janeiro's newspapers attest to the ongoing circulation of handwritten literary works, an anachronism that continued in spite of a significant increase in the number of printed books and periodicals, even during the last years of the 1830s. In 1832, in his *Manual da tipografia Brasiliense* [Brazilian Typography Manual], the Frenchman René Ogier, who owned a press in Rio de Janeiro, was concerned with standardizing the art of typography by adapting European rules and guidelines and including in his manual everything from the techniques of making imprints to the proper relations with authors. Ogier omitted, however, mention of the possibility of the coexistence of free and slave labor in Brazilian printshops, in the same way that he would not refer to the modern contracts that in Europe had long defined in legal terms the relations between authors and editors, guaranteeing a high degree of professionalism in the literary market.

Thus, throughout the first half of the nineteenth century and even later, the absence of contracts and the practice of printing at the author's request described one side of the Brazilian editorial market, in contrast to the other, which was characterized by more frequent and quantitatively greater editorial initiatives that primarily involved translations and the publication of foreign works. Practices such as subscription and sponsorship, the former being a slight variation on the latter, guaranteed the publication of a large part of the works by Brazilian authors at the time, showing the persistence of traditional relations of patronage and protection alongside a transition to new market relations. Nevertheless, one must note the unique character of these relations in Brazil: A poet like Domingos José Gonçalves de Magalhães (1811–1882) could announce the sponsorship of the monarch D. Pedro II himself as an honor bestowed on him; the long lists of subscribers that concluded the books of poems of Antônio Gonçalves Teixeira e Sousa (1812–1861) revealed his humble social origin, an embarrassment that would lead to the tendency to transfer to paratexts, using literary formulas of gratitude, anything that might resemble acknowledgments of patronage. A good example of this is the strategic use of the many dedications below the title, in a different kind of print, that appeared in Antônio Gonçalves Dias's (1823–1864) first book of poems, entitled *Primeiros cantos* [1846; First Songs].

Yet what was true of poetry, historical works, and tragedies did not apply to the novel, which appeared late and, long into the century, and retained an ambiguous status. It could not count on any kind of patronage and, as the postscript to *A Moreninha* demonstrates, the decision to print the work required direct involvement by the author in the different stages of the printing. The figure of the author as novelist was established without hiding the material requirement of printing and without avoiding a certain overlapping of authorial and editorial roles. But in the absence of other records and documentation beyond the book itself, how, in the first edition of *A Moreninha*, can one draw the line between the initiatives of the author and those of the supervisor of the typographical tasks to which every printed work of the time was subject? The two roles in fact merge into one. Placed in context, this first edition of Joaquim Manoel de Macedo's novel distinguished itself precisely because it went against common practice and introduced substantial changes in the procedures of publication of prose fiction in Brazil. It was published without an editor (who would appear only in the second edition in 1845) and, certainly financing the costs of publication himself and with the help of friends, Macedo had unprecedented albeit relative control over editorial decisions, for economic reasons if nothing else. The most significant of these decisions was the choice of materials for the book and its format, which European editorial conventions still associated with the status of the work in the hierarchical classification of literary genres. If in Europe after 1820 the novel had left behind the smaller formats, and publication would soon include books whose extraordinary dimensions were determined by a large investment in images and the use of graphic space, in Brazil, on the other hand, publication of prose fiction survived through the publication of short stories and novellas that came out in booklet format, as well as through the publication of Portuguese language novels in France. It was from these French publications that Macedo must have gotten the idea for the first edition of *A Moreninha*.

It is of some importance to remember that between 1835 and 1845, the translation of novels into Portuguese in Paris by José Ignácio Roquette (1801–1870), E. O. da Câmera, José da Fonseca (1788–1866), and Brazilian Caetano Lopes de Moura (1780–1860)–published mostly by Casa Aillaud but also by Pillêt Aîné and Livraria Européia de Baudry–represent a significantly large portion of the books available in Brazil (see Ramos). This double addition of both Portuguese language novels and Portuguese translations of French novels published in France created a distinction between these books and all the other imported books to be found on the Brazilian market. These French publications were closer to the readers because of the language. From 1837 on, there was great interest in them, as is evident from the simultaneous advertisement of their availability by the main booksellers in Rio de Janeiro: the Portuguese Albino Jordão in his Casa do Livro Azul and A. F. Guimarães e Cia.; the office of Junes Villeneuve, owner of the *Jornal do Comércio*; Eduardo and Henrique Laemmert's Livraria Universal; the reading room of Edouard Mongie, who also sold books; and Paula Brito's Tipografia Imparcial, among others. The almost daily presence of these advertisements up to the middle of the 1840s indicates that the number of imported copies of these editions, which to a certain extent could be called French-Portuguese, was much greater than the average of other foreign books. With the exception of Eugène Sue and Alexandre Dumas, in 1844–1845 foreign books were rarely distributed in such a systematic manner. The consistent advertising, taking into account the cost of the advertisements, suggests that these editions maintained a steady rate of sales in a bookselling market that at the time was still attempting to form its reading audience.

In 1837, Laemmert announced the release of *O Talisman, ou Ricardo na Palestina* [The Talisman, or Richard in Palestine] by Walter Scott, translated by Caetano Lopes de Moura and published by Aillaud in Paris in the same year: "As obras de nenhum autor podem gabar-se de terem sido recebidas com tanto entusiasmo como as de W. Scott que, tanto no original inglês, como nas traduções feitas na Alemanha, França, etc.

têm sido espalhadas por todas as nações cultas, num número de mais de meio milhão de exemplares" (*Jornal do Comércio*, 19 May 1837) ("No other author's works can claim to have been welcomed with such enthusiasm as those of W. Scott, which, both in the English original as well as in the translations made in Germany, France, etc., have circulated in all cultured nations, totaling over half a million copies"). The reference to Scott alludes to the irresistible growth of the international publishing of the novel genre in the 1830s. Part of this expansion, and Walter Scott's case is paradigmatic of what occurred with all successful novelists, was due to the absence of any regulated control of authorial rights in many countries. Thus, between the original and the probably authorized translations, a wide space opened up for the dissemination of numerous illegal editions. This phenomenon helps us understand the repertory of novels that were published by Pille Aîne, Aillaud, and Baudry, going directly from Paris to the Portuguese and Brazilian markets. There was a clear preference for English novelists. Between 1837 and 1844, Aillaud published seven novels by Walter Scott, and Pillet Aîne published works by Jonathan Swift, Daniel Defoe, Thomas Moore, and U.S. novelists like James Fenimore Cooper, while clearly avoiding French novels written by living authors, who were protected by law. In an essay that precedes the bibliographical survey of these editions, Victor Ramos points out the inexplicable absence of works by Victor Hugo and Balzac. The legal protection of living French authors' works did not extend to any other country or even to the deceased French authors; this accounts for the significant presence of titles from French literature from the eighteenth and seventeenth centuries, and from the Spanish picaresque tradition. Ramos considers Pillet Aîne's, Baudry's, and Aillaud's editorial enterprises to be a sort of imperialism in the field of publishing. They no longer reflected, in their repertory, the political orientation of the Liberal Portuguese emigrants who had been prominent in the pre-1835 period of their French exile. Strictly economic interests now guided their editorial policy; they set out to dominate the market and no longer counted on the deficiencies of Portuguese and Brazilian publishing houses, and therefore on the weak competition French books would find in those countries.

In relation to the European editorial market from which they originated, novels in small format (*duodecimo*, sixteen*mo*, eighteen*mo*, and, even the tiny thirty-two*mo*) seemed clearly outdated. They were poor, faded versions of the small deluxe editions of the end of the eighteenth century, which had joined fineness of form with easy handling. Small-format, inexpensive books had been replaced with large, illustrated books, which were luxury items aimed at the affluent upper middle class. In the past, the small formats included both sentimental and chivalrous novels and books on devotion and morality, as well as seditious and libertine literature. Such flexible adaptation to different registers did not mean an absence of some mode of distinguishing between them: A qualitative scale in format corresponded to a genre hierarchy. The richer or poorer binding, the artistic value of the illustrations commissioned from prestigious artists, the author's reputation in the literary environment, these were reflected in the typographical display; all of these represented nuances were capable of singling out and ennobling a book previously considered "minor" because of its genre. Or, in a version of the same logic, but turned around, "one tacitly admitted that a cheap format was the natural bibliophilic expression of cheap content" (Charvat 8). This relation of correspondence and conformity, which strongly associated the value of the written text to its material appearance as object and which characterized the condition of manufacture and reception in the old regime, was not abandoned but rather was restored on a more complex basis in the nineteenth century. Among other things, the mixture of genres itself, defended by Romanticism, began to destabilize the older system of conventions and its excessively strict character of exclusions and inclusions. At the same time, the introduction of modern industrial processes into paper manufacturing eventually freed publications from fixed paper dimensions and from a standardized format. A notable change was the eighteenth-century convention of the almost mandatory use of the small format for the publication of novels. Gradually, between 1820 and 1830, novels began to appear in octavo or quarto forms, a format that had previously been used only for the publication of the so-called higher genres. What both publishers and writers continued to look for was an identification of the works with traditional values through the material quality of the books. Stendhal is reported to have disdainfully referred to little novels in duodecimo as appropriate for the hired help when he published *Le Rouge et Le Noir* in the medium-sized octavo format (Genette 20–25), demonstrating how, in the materiality of the book, hierarchies of genre and hierarchies of class converged; we can also see the effort it took for writers to free the novel from previous publishing conventions in order to claim a higher status for the genre.

The little book that the female reader carried in *A Moreninha*'s vignette referred to another time; it also displayed a habit acquired by Europeans during the previous centuries, namely, that of private, solitary reading. In Joaquim Manoel de Macedo's presentation of the new Brazilian novel, the genre was established through the rhetoric of his preface by associating writing with idleness, and reading with leisure. Far from intending to establish the seriousness of the genre, what this edition of *A Moreninha* achieved in 1844 was a late liberation of the novel from the book format to which it had been relegated. Its material form had a certain correspondence with, and was indeed influenced by, novels published by the Paris firms of Pillet Aîné and Aillaud, a fact that was even more evident in its second, illustrated edition of 1845. By establishing this material link (since the Paris novels were treated in a way notably superior to the poor means then characteristic of national publication practices in Brazil), Macedo also made the point that literature in Portuguese deserved the same treatment as that usually reserved for French books. Many of these books in Portuguese, printed in Paris (as it was usually advertised), had illustrations, good-quality French binding, and an emphasis on illustration that often exceeded the advertising of the works and authors themselves. The illustrations, however, were restricted to a small number of extra-textual pictures that were still under eighteenth-century norms of representation; this gave them an old-fashioned look that did not conform to the French Romantic editions of the period, which had transformed the techniques and artistic conceptions of books and, of course, were not unknown in Brazil. Illustrated books began to arrive in Brazil in 1837, beginning with travel literature or large history books with over 500 pictures, but illustrated books were only occasionally advertised; it was not until 1844–1845 that French Romantic editions were put on sale by book dealers in Rio de Janeiro. These books were sold as deluxe editions at high prices, whereas in France they could be purchased in separate installments at moderate prices; their importation into Brazil was restricted to a small number of copies aimed at a small elite within the reading public, even if one takes into account that their readership was increased by their availability in reading rooms. In the 1840s, some of the regular advertisers of French illustrated editions were those establishments under the supervision of Frenchmen living in Rio de Janeiro, such as those of Cremière, Edouard Mongie, Mlle. Edet's reading room, or the Libraire Belge-Française, all of which offered books for sale or rent.

Meanwhile, the European Romantic illustrated book contrasted markedly with the Brazilian editions. There was a notable difference between the central role of artistic and technical reproduction of images in Europe and the limited resources available in Brazil. If this kind of book quality remained an unattainable goal, in time the strategic nature of illustration would end up becoming a publishing challenge, a concern for the Brazilian literary environment over most of the nineteenth century. It is in this light that the intermediate position of Portuguese language illustrated editions coming from France must be considered; they were outdated by European standards, but far superior to Brazilian editions. They offered novelists a possibility that the 1844 edition of *A Moreninha* by Joaquim Manoel de Macedo made concrete at a time when pamphlets, not books, were the main vehicle for prose fiction in Brazil.

The Novel Preceded the Book

From 1837 to 1844, the year when *A Moreninha* was published, the literary collections released by Junes Villeneuve, owner of Rio de Janeiro's *Jornal do Comércio*, by his main rival, Eduardo and Henrique Laemmert's Tipografia Universal, and by the Tipografia Associação do Despertador, under the direction of Sales Torres Homem, together would account for the largest number of Brazilian publications at the time. Their graphic features, however, revealed their dependence on, and complicity with, the printed page of the newspaper. Previous publication of literary texts in the daily press or in illustrated magazines and periodicals conditioned their inclusion in the collections, and they took the form not of books, but rather of pamphlets. Their format was small, and so was the number of pages; they were simple and barely decorated, with tiny fonts and very low-quality paper. These features made them resemble those collections of European popular texts of the so-called *littérature de colportage*. Works such as *A história da Donzela Theodora* [1735; The Story of the Maiden Theodora], *A história de João de Calais* [1867; The Story of Jean de Calais], *Leocádia ou a inocente vítima do crime* [Leocadia, or the Innocent Crime Victim], or *Confissão de marujo* [1880?; Sailor's Confession], included in Villeneuve's and the brothers Laemmert's collections of the end of the 1830s, did not conceal their origin. From the 1840s on, the repertory followed the rise of the French *feuilleton* novel that appeared in the pages of the daily newspapers, but, while their greatest successes were subsequently published as books and in several volumes, the shorter texts of Alexandre Dumas, Eugène Scribe, George Sand, and Prosper Merimée, among others, would only be released as pamphlets, using the same typographical material from the daily press in order to reduce publication costs.

It was amidst the precarious conditions of these collections, distinguished only by their steady publication, that one discerns the first attempts at producing the Brazilian novel.

There was, however, some uncertainty in these early attempts at fictional writing, as can be seen from the references to genre added to the titles; in the classifications that wavered between novella, historical chronicle, and historical novel; and without any distinctions made between original creations, translations, and rewritings. This allowed, for instance, Justiniano José da Rocha (1812–1862) to claim for himself the authorship of one of E. T. A. Hoffman's short stories without even mentioning him and justified Paula Brito's question, in the preface to *O pontífice e os carbonários* [1839; The Bishop and the Rebels], on publishing an adapted translation of a text by Alexandre Dumas: "But what difference does it make to the reading audience who the author is?" (2). This murky line between appropriation and plagiarism might be explained, first, by the earlier appearance of these novellas in the pages of newspapers and magazines, where the original authors' names were often lost among a plethora of anonymous writers and pseudonyms. But what was even more unstable in claims to authorship was not their registry, but rather their authenticity. How could one identify the original and grant it credence when the daily press and publishing firms continuously filled their pages with a steady stream of what writers in Lisbon pejoratively called the products of "French piracy" in Brazil? The absence of international copyright laws had made translation into strategic theft. For the Brazilian press of the time, the expenses of translators of novellas and *feuilleton* novels, correspondents in Paris, and subscriptions to foreign periodicals had become substantial. It was the high point of compilations and unscrupulous rewritings, of multiple appropriations, when translations could hardly be recognized in relation to their original authorships.

What also encouraged translator-authors (translators who claimed authorship) like Justiniano José da Rocha and Francisco de Paula Brito (1809–1861) was the widespread idea that the re-creation of texts was legitimate; of even more weight was the notion that this re-creation represented the opportunity to practice European fiction writing and thus incorporate something of their own into the still undefined profile of national fiction. As Flora Süssekind points out:

> [I]t is in the "Miscellanea," in the "*Feuilleton*" and "Appendices," or in the "Leisure Supplement," alongside the *feuilleton* novels and foreign histories (serials or not), that local writers rehearsed their own fiction writing. For this reason, it is not so painful for someone like Justiniano José da Rocha or someone like Paula Brito to cross the thin line dividing a literal version and an adaptation, a difference that existed in the very same novellas or in the *feuilleton* that they translated for newspapers, especially when the affirmation of authorial originality and the incorporation of national peculiarities seemed so crucial. But it is through a relatively close, though unavoidable exchange with foreign newspapers, novels, and *feuilletons*, that these writers seem to view the possibility of literary activity in Brazil at the time. (99)

At the same time, in this exchange, publication in the pre-formatted space of the newspaper involved rather restrictive conditions: for instance, the loss of the literary text's unity (dispersed as it was among the variety of writings with which it shared the printed page), the interruption of its continuity in the case of serial publications, and, especially, its adaptation to a graphic display of measured dimensions, its delimitation by lines and columns under the headings "Miscellanea," "Appendices," "Varieties," "Feuilleton." When transferred from the pages of the *Jornal do Comércio* to the collection released by Villeneuve, such works as *O Aniversário de D.*

Miguel em 1828 [1839; D. Miguel's Birthday in 1828] by João Manuel Pereira da Silva (1817–1898) (a feeble attempt at an original historical novel) and *Os Assassinos Misteriosos ou a paixão dos diamantes* [1839; The Mysterious Assassins or the Passion for Diamonds], by Justiniano José da Rocha with their 36 pages and 29 pages, respectively, clearly revealed the convergence of the material limitations of newspaper columns and those of the small format of pamphlets. The imposed concision of the first Brazilian works of fiction accentuated their incomplete, unfinished nature and made difficult any attempt to relate them to the novel genre. The minor status of the *feuilleton*, a kind of poor substitute for the book, as well as the installment publication in periodicals that was at its origin, did not grant the texts any autonomy; the collection imposed an equally collective identity on whatever authorial intentions there might have been to individualize literary works. Many other fictional attempts of these years by Brazilian writers were confined to literary, fashion, and variety periodicals. That was the case, for example, with Luís Carlos Martins Pena's (1815–1848) and Josino do Nascimento e Silva's (1811–1866) narratives in the *Correio das Modas* (1839–1840), published amid French lithographs of fashion plates and accounts of court balls, as well as with Gonçalves de Magalhães's *Amância* and Joaquim Norberto de Souza e Silva's (1820–1891) "Brazilian novel" *Maria ou vinte anos depois* [Maria, or Twenty Years Later], both featured in the magazine *Minerva Brasiliense*, respectively in 1843 and 1844.

With the publication of Teixeira e Sousa's *O Filho do Pescador* [The Fisherman's Son] by Paula Brito's Tipografia Imparcial in 1843, the gap between these publications and the book apparently began to close, which contributed, to a certain extent, to its being regarded as the first Brazilian novel. What this book added to Brazilian letters was the first full adaptation of a literary text to the requirements of the genre, as Antonio Cândido (b. 1918) suggests in *Formação da literatura Brasileira: Momentos decisivos* [1959; The Development of Brazilian Literature: Decisive Moments]: "Em 1843 aparece *O Filho do Pescador* de Teixeira e Sousa, considerado geralmente o primeiro brasileiro, já que os outros, apesar de trazerem por vezes esta designação, têm dimensões de conto ou novela"(II:120) ("In 1843 Teixeira e Sousa's *O Filho do Pescador* appears; it is generally considered the first Brazilian novel because the others, although sometimes classified as such, have the proportions of a short story or novella"). That these proportions also implied an adaptation of the literary composition to the printing restrictions of the newspaper is demonstrated in Joaquim Norberto de Souza e Silva's *Maria ou vinte anos depois* of that same year. Instead of a short story or a novella, Cândido classifies it as a "lightning-novel," because it consisted of plot, character development, and description condensed into only eleven pages of the magazine *Minerva Brasiliense*.

O Filho do Pescador was published directly as a book, without previous publication in newspapers or magazines, and for the first time a Brazilian fictional text took the form of a full-length novel. It is significant, however, that in advertisements at the time it was presented to the public not as a novel, but as a novella, and not as a book, but as a pamphlet: *O Filho do Pescador*. Novela feita para entretenimento de uma moça bonita, cuja ação se passa no Rio de Janeiro, no lugar chamado Copacabana; vende-se um lindo folheto com 152 páginas, por 1000 réis, na loja de Paula Brito, onde há *Um Roubo na pavuna*, por 800 rs, *As Duas infelizes*, por 320 rs; *Juiz de paz na roça* por 400 rs; e *Noivo em mangas de camisa*, por 400 rs (*Jornal do*

Comércio 26 January 1844) ("*The Fisherman's Son.* A novella written with the aim of entertaining a pretty lady, whose plot is set in Rio de Janeiro, in a place called Copacabana; this beautiful pamphlet of 152 pages is sold for 1000 *réis*, in Paula Brito's shop, where one also finds *Um roubo na pavuna* [A Robbery in the Valley], for 800 réis; *As duas infelizes* [Two Unhappy Ladies], for 320 réis; *Juiz de paz na roça* [Country Judge] for 400 réis; and *Noivo em mangas de camisa* [Bridegroom in Shirtsleeves], for 400 réis"). Since the National Library does not have this first edition, nor do any collectors, it is very likely that none of the copies was preserved, and that even in the nineteenth century it was considered a rare book. That may perhaps explain the fact that the characteristics described in its first advertisement are unlike those of the edition known today, which is based on the 1859 edition. According to the advertisement, it was a novella originally of 152 pages, but the 1859 edition has 248 pages; it was perhaps only then that Sousa added the subtitle "original Brazilian novel." It was probably a revised edition, with the 1843 original text being promoted from *feuilleton* to octavo format size, with a considerable increase of 96 pages, which likely indicates the existence of extensive unpublished material.

Similarly, in 1852, Joaquim Norberto de Souza e Silva gathered his works of fiction that had previously been "dispersos por vários jornais de efêmera existência e limitada circulação" (viii) ("dispersed among several newspapers of brief existence and limited circulation") and published them as books. Prologues and notes were added, aimed at an evaluation of his work in a new context as novels. This development was directly associated with the success of Joaquim Manoel de Macedo's *A Moreninha* and his other works published in the 1840s. Norberto praised Macedo as "coroa de romancista distinto que orna a lira do autor de *Moreninha* e *Moço Loiro*" (viii) ("the distinguished novelist who wrote *A Moreninha* and *O Moço Loiro* [1845; The Fair Gentleman]") because his novel had contributed to a retroactive reevaluation of the fictional work of Norberto, of Pereira da Silva, and of Teixeira e Sousa, the feeble attempts of the past, which were now viewed as evidence of earlier experiments on the way toward a Brazilian novel. A similar sign of the recognition of Macedo's prestige among the youth of the 1840s, especially university audiences, can be found in the memoirs of the novelist José de Alencar (1829–1877), who was then a young student at the Law School of São Paulo: "Que estranho sentir não despertava em meu coração adolescente a notícia dessas homenagens de admiração e respeito tributados ao jovem autor dí *A Moreninha*!" (37–38) ("What an odd feeling I had as a young man when I learned the many expressions of admiration and respect toward the young author of *A Moreninha*!"). For Alencar and others of his generation, Macedo's example served as a decisive motivation in that it demonstrated the possibility of individual success in a literary career; but even more important, it demonstrated for the first time that success could be achieved with the novel, a genre that until then had been little esteemed.

Establishing this genre required the material solidity of the book, and it fell to Macedo's novel, in 1844, to accomplish this transition, a transition that was even more significant because it took place in the middle of a period of increasing literary imports. Whether or not *A Moreninha*'s first edition was up to the publishing standards of European novels, its true significance for Brazil emerged in contrast with national publishing practices up to that time. Joaquim Manoel de

Macedo's first book ended up having a greater impact than any work of fiction that had come before bypassing, from the beginning, the precarious stage of newspaper publication that still functioned as a limit on Brazilian fiction. Macedo dismissed the periodical press, where almost all prose fiction production took place (and thus remained inferior to foreign books), and he made *A Moreninha* definitively surpass the mere *feuilleton*, breaking with the graphic constraints on all previous attempts at a Brazilian novel. Joaquim Manoel de Macedo's changes to the material presentation of literary texts in Brazil had an extraordinary effect on the market in a short span of time. He transformed the general conditions of publication and reception by using the format of the illustrated book in the 1845 second edition of *A Moreninha,* incorporating other graphic features similar to those of European novels of the time in his new novel *O Moço Loiro* of the same year; they were published as two-volume sets in the octavo format.

It is generally agreed that *A Moreninha* created an impact on the reading public of the time; Cândido, in fact, calls it a little revolution. From a different point of view, the critic and literary historian José Veríssimo, (see **Figure 1**) trying to diagnose the decreasing popularity of Brazilian fiction at the end of the nineteenth century, used Macedo's book as an example of a certain success in communication achieved in the past that began to be seen as unrepeatable: "Um sucesso como o da "*Moreninha*" de Macedo, é quase inconcebível hoje. O sucesso em literatura, como no vestuário, vem de Paris ja feito" (Veríssimo 1978, 64) ("A success like Macedo's *Moreninha* is nearly inconceivable today. Success in literature, as in attire, comes already made from Paris"). In 1844, Brazilian booksellers had available Eugène Sue's *Os Mistérios de Paris* [The Mysteries of Paris], Balzac's *César Birotteau* [The Rise and Fall of César Birotteau], Dumas's *A Capela Gótica* [The Gothic Chapel], among others, from a long list of European novels published as *feuilletons* by the presses of Rio de Janeiro and the provinces, or advertised in books during that year by bookdealers and reading rooms (Meyer 281–88). This was the situation at the end of the nineteenth century, when Veríssimo referred to the circumstances of Brazilian writers of his age as largely affected by market relations: "[N]ós não podemos competir diante dos nossos leitores com o que eles de lá (da Europa) recebem em primeira mão, oferecendo-lhes um produto similar em segunda" (1978, 65) ("We cannot compete in the eyes of our readers with what they receive first-hand from Europe by offering them a similar product second-hand").

The language of merchandising comes to the surface in Veríssimo's historiographical analysis of the relations between readers and Brazilian books in the nineteenth century. Successes like *A Moreninha* could be accounted for by their belonging to the earlier period from 1835 to 1865, when nationalism helped to disguise weaknesses and make the works welcome to the public in an exaggerated preference for the nation's literature. After 1865, the effectiveness of nationalism for selling books declined rapidly. As it declined, denationalization supposedly revealed the many deficiencies of Brazilian works, and they were forced more and more to compete with foreign books for the public–without any ideological protection. In the market what made the works sell was novelty, a factor that remained unnamed but coercive in the "denationalization" emphasized by Veríssimo. Works from the past–those that with the passing of time had not become "dead books"–eventually found a place in the literary canon and in literary histories; their value was historical. Nationalism still played an important cohesive and

Figure 1.

Literary critic and historian José Veríssimo, c. 1887. (Archive of the author)

structuring role, but it did not sell books. There was a cautious restraint since, at the core of this building of a national literature, criticism threatened to cause ruptures as works underwent closer scrutiny and interpretation. This was to be the fate of *A Moreninha*, the obsession of Brazilian literary history with the foundation of the Brazilian novel did not prevent this same system from making negative aesthetic evaluations, pointing to the outdated prose of Macedo's novel and the contrived nature of his Romantic formulas.

Macedo's texts no longer resisted the new developments of the novel, which soon were made the norm in literary historiography, thanks to the naturalist scientificity defended by Silvio Romero (see **Figure 2**) between 1870 and 1890 and the existence of exclusively artistic writing as an instrument of culture, defended by José Veríssimo during the same period. These novels, on the other hand, in relation to the book and the book market, continued to have resonance: Macedo was the Brazilian writer with the largest number of editions and re-editions throughout the whole nineteenth century. Soon after his death in 1882, according to press commentary, those readers he still had, lived in the interior or were children. His books had fallen from favor and supposedly no longer spoke to the average urban reader, but rather only to those in the backlands, where reading was slow, or to children, who could read without time constraints—or even more notably to the unlettered, who could still follow the story read aloud to them. It was a disgraceful response considered in relation to what Macedo's work had represented in the past; but one must note a similar response, in Europe and in the Americas,

Figure 2.

Literary critic Silvio Romero. (Archive of the author)

to prominent Romantic novels, such as those written by Walter Scott, Charles Dickens, James Fenimore Cooper, and Victor Hugo. What seemed a kind of last frontier in the decline of the Romantic novel was the refuge offered in popular libraries—a faith that also demonstrated that there was a still unexhausted expansionist development possible for literature, similar to what had been experienced in the first decades of the nineteenth century, when changes in print technology had given fiction access to a greater market.

José Veríssimo described the years between 1835 and 1865 as a nationalist period that had allowed for the success of novels such as *A Moreninha*, as well as of José de Alencar's historical novels and novels of manners, emphasizing a context in which nationalism strongly influenced reception. The same years roughly correspond to developments in Europe and the United States, when the modernization of printing, as well as the introduction of Romantic aesthetic innovations into the graphic arts of book production, resulted in the illustrated Romantic book, as well as serial publication. The book market, from the Romantic period on, began to experience an increase in international exchange; this stimulated the use of similar strategies in the publishing practices of different countries and activated a relatively integrated circulation that made possible the international character of the illustrated Romantic edition. One may note, in the advertisements of

Rio de Janeiro's *Jornal do Comércio*, that some of the most important of French Romantic publications were available through book dealers in the same year as *A Moreninha*'s release. In July 1844, Villeneuve, the owner of *Jornal do Comércio*, announced the sales of Goldsmith's *Le Vicaire de Wakefield* [*The Vicar of Wakefield*], illustrated by Tony Johannot, whom Théophile Gautier referred to as the French king of illustration, with a preface by Charles Nodier; and also Louis Michelant's *Faits mémorables de l'histoire de France* [Memorable Events in the History of France], with 120 engravings based on Victor Adam's drawings. These were books that the advertisement recommended both for their content and for the sumptuousness of the editions.

In the same month, the Belge-Française bookstore also established a reading room on Rua dos Ourives, and put on sale large-format documentaries, such as Eugène Pacini's *La marine* and Léon Galibert's *L'histoire de L'Algérie*, which were representative of a highly descriptive genre that allowed for an abundance of illustrations. In *La marine*, Isabey, a renowned artist of the beginning of the century, considered a precursor in the transition from a neo-Classical style to a Romantic illustration style, signed thirty watercolor illustrations; in *L'histoire de l'Algérie*, Raffet, famous for his illustrations of military life, contributed drawings of the French army in Africa. There were also three other books of significance in this bookstore's list (which contained some of the best graphic achievements of French publishing during 1843): *Chants e chansons populaires de la France*, edited by Delloye; *L'été à Paris*, by Jules Janin, published by Curmer; and Silvio Pellico's *Mes Prisons*, announced in Brazil in the same year it came out in Paris. Among the imported French Romantic books, we should add the great illustrated books like *La grande ville*, announced by the reading room of Mlle. Edet; and *Les Français peints par eux-mêmes* and *La vie privée des animaux*, sold by Mongie. This year also marked the high point in the publication of French *feuilleton* novels, marked by the notable success of Eugène Sue's *Os misterios de Paris* [*Mysteries of Paris*], which was published in the pages of the *Jornal do Comércio*.

Both publications revealed a close relation between the European book market and the Brazilian press, a relation based on imports, imitation, or piracy, and made possible by the predominance of foreigners in the book trade, as directors of presses and controllers of newspapers and periodicals. To consider this context, its scope and implications, would surely institute a new kind of thinking about Brazilian literature and perhaps offer a solution to the paradox that in the end led to the duality nationalism-denationalization, which, according to Veríssimo, culminated in the following formula: "De sorte que, pode-se dizer, . . . foi o desenvolvimento de nossa cultura que prejudicou nossa evolução literária. Parece um paradoxo, mas é simplesmente verdade. Defeituosa e falha, essa cultura foi ainda assim bastante para revelar ao público ledor a inferioridade de nossos escritores, não mais contrabalançando este sentimento pelo ardor patriótico do período de formação da nacionalidade" (1978, 64–65) ("One may say, . . . it was the development of our culture that impaired our literary evolution. It appears to be a paradox, but it is simply the truth. Flawed and imperfect, this culture was still enough to reveal to the reading public the inferiority of our writers, no longer counterbalancing this feeling with the patriotic passion of the formative period of nationalism").

This literary culture that developed in opposition to the literature written in Brazil was the product of an inequality between what an international book market could offer its readers and the publication conditions available to writers in Brazil. A success like *A Moreninha* in 1844, which marked the literary début of Joaquim Manoel de Macedo and a new direction for the Brazilian novel, undoubtedly had the advantage of the strong links between literature and nationalism at the time, those that are inscribed in the text itself and those that were later conferred on it by literary historiography. But *A Moreninha* was above all a book; its "little revolution" also took place because of the way its first material appearance stood out against a background of *feuilletons* and serial publications and, in its re-edition of 1845, its later incarnation as an illustrated book. This success needs to be understood in comparison with other publications in Brazil at the time, such as illustrated magazines, lithographic books, and even caricature newspapers, taking into account the concerted attempt to overcome the distance between Brazil and its European rivals, the attempts at approximation to and strategies of appropriation of, even with modest and inferior results, the new techniques for reproducing images and of the new art forms that Romanticism had introduced into the book.

**Translation by Thomas LaBorie Burns
and Gláucia Renate Gonçalves**

Works Cited

Alencar, José de. 1990. *Como e porque sou Romancista*. Campinas: Pontes.

Brito, Francisco de Paula. 1839. *O pontífice e os carbonários*. Rio de Janeiro: Typ. Imp. e Const. J. Villeneuve e Comp.

Cândido, Antonio. 1981. *Formação da literatura Brasileira: Momentos decisivos*. 2 vols. Belo Horizonte: Ed. Itatiaia.

Charvat, William. 1992. *The Profession of Authorship in America, 1800–1870*. New York: Columbia University Press.

Genette, Gérard. 1987. *Seuils*. Paris: Seuil.

Gresset, Jean-Baptiste-Louis. 1883. "Les ombres." *Poésies choisies de Gresset*. Ed. L. Derome. Paris: A. Quantin. 221–32.

Hallewell, Laurence. 1985. *O livro no Brasil (sua história)*. São Paulo: Editora da Universidade de São Paulo.

Macedo, Joaquim Manoel de. 1844. *A Moreninha*. 1st ed. Rio de Janeiro: Tip. Francesa.

———. 1845. *A Moreninha*. 2nd ed. Rio de Janeiro: Tip. Americana de I. P. da Costa.

———. 1845. *O Moço Loiro*. 2 vols. Rio de Janeiro: Tip. de Carlos Haring.

Melo, Antonio Francisco Dutra e. 1844. "A Moreninha." *Minerva Brasiliense* 2.24 (Oct. 15): 746–51.

Meyer, Marlyse. 1996. *Folhetim: Uma história*. São Paulo: Companhia das Letras.

Ogier, René. 1832. *Manual da typographia Brasiliense*. Rio de Janeiro: Tip. de R. Ogier.

Ramos, Vitor. 1972. *A edição de língua portuguesa em França, 1800–1850*. Paris: Fundação Calouste Gulbenkian.

Rocha, Justiniano José da. 1839. *Os assassinos misteriosos ou a paixão dos diamantes: Novela histórica*. Rio de Janeiro: Typ. Imp. e Const. de J. Villeneuve e Comp.

Romero, Silvio. 1980. *História da literatura Brasileira*. Vols. 4 and 5. Rio de Janeiro/Brasília: José Olympio Editora/INL.

Silva, Joaquim Norberto de Sousa e. 1852. *Romances e Novelas.* Niteroi: Typ. Fluminense de Candido Martins Lopes.

Silva, João Manuel Pereira da. 1839. *O aniversário de D. Miguel em 1828: Romance histórico.* Rio de Janeiro: Typ. Imp. e Const. de J. Villeneuve e Comp.

Sousa, Antonio Gonçalves Teixeira e. 1977. *O filho do pescador: Romance brasileiro original.* São Paulo/Brasília: Ed. Melhoramentos/INL.

Süssekind, Flora. 1990. *O Brasil não é longe daqui: O narrador, a viagem.* São Paulo: Companhia das Letras.

Veríssimo, José. 1978. *Teoria, crítica, história literária.* Ed. João Alexandre Barbosa. Rio de Janeiro: LTC/Editora da Universidade de São Paulo.

———. 1981. *História da literatura brasileira.* Brasília: Editora Universidade de Brasília.

THE REPRESENTATION OF NATURE IN NINETEENTH-CENTURY NARRATIVE AND ICONOGRAPHY

Luz Aurora Pimentel

Canon or Canons?

In most histories of Latin American nineteenth-century narrative, there is a sort of running leitmotif that labels novels in terms of an opposition between the derivative and the authentic. According to this point of view, the literary influence from Europe is what makes novels artificial, while a supposedly direct observation of nature and life in Latin America confers upon them a seal of authenticity, originality, or even a national character. Most literary histories or critical accounts will always name Bernardin de Saint-Pierre and Chateaubriand as central influences to establish a sort of lineage, as when Anderson Imbert says of Jorge Isaacs's (1837–1895) *María* (1867) that it "pertenece a esa familia literaria" (159) ("belongs to that literary family," 278). But because only the family resemblance is focused on, similarity or difference will be valued or disparaged according to the critic's ideological stance; praise or criticism will be evenly handed out from the heights of the critic's or the literary historian's authority. Some will declare that *María*, for example, is infinitely better than its French predecessors, since Isaacs's descriptions of nature are more authentic and personal, the result of direct observation; others may condemn Latin American Romantic narrative–partially (Jean Franco) or as a whole (Vargas Llosa, for example)–on grounds of inadequacy: "With the exception of *María*, novels were partial or wholly failures in their attempts to express American experience, since they failed to express this in a significant form" (Franco 91).

Despite the literary historian's insistence on the European models at the basis of nineteenth-century Latin American narrative, the ways in which the parent model is transformed are seldom examined closely; nor is the value of the model itself assessed from the perspective of its own dependence on and/ or transformation of other models. These are the limitations imposed by an approach to literary history that is both authoritative (or even authoritarian) and derivative. Even when a comparative perspective is taken, it will be the artificial approach of *influence* and *literary fortune*–a pair of terms that, for years, guarded the methodological doors of the old French school of comparative studies (cf. Balakian)–a set of procedures usually entrenched in a world of facts and proofs, leading to a one-to-one relationship, a definite set of similarities and differences, and a definitive label of success or failure stuck onto the literary work in question. The result is a petrified, framed object, ready to be placed as an exhibit inside the labeled glass case of some museum of canonized literature. Other very influential critical works, such as Mario Vargas Llosa's (b. 1936) "Novela primitiva y novela de creación" [1969; "Primitive Novel and Creative Novel"], have also contributed to this summary dismissal of nineteenth-century Latin American novels. He classifies narrative in three

moments: the imitative novel (*novela refleja*), lasting till the end of the nineteenth century; the primitive novel (*novela primitiva*), from the last decade of the nineteenth century well into the first half of the twentieth; and the creative novel (*novela de creación*), starting from the second half of this century. But Vargas Llosa's taxonomic effort also operates as so many rigid labels, for it is not merely a chronological scheme but one plagued with peremptory generalizations. He dismisses the whole lot of "*novelas reflejas*" as merely imitative. With a fine irony, the now successful Peruvian writer claims that Ricardo Palma (1833–1919) "inventó un pasado versallesco al Perú" (184) ("invented a versaillesque past for Peru") in his famous *Tradiciones Peruanas* [1872; Peruvian Traditions]. In similarly ironic terms, Vargas Llosa says that Isaacs, in *María* (1867), only "aclimató Chateaubriand y Bernardin de Saint-Pierre a la geografía y la sensiblería americanas" (184) ("acclimatized Chateaubriand and Bernardin de Saint-Pierre to the Latin American geography and melodramatic sensibility"). The full weight of Vargas Llosa's contempt is to be felt in that one word, *sensiblería*:

> Pero ninguno de nuestros narradores románticos o realistas fraguó un mundo literario universalmente válido, una representación de la realidad, fiel o infiel, pero dotada de un poder de persuasión verbal suficiente para imponerse al lector como creación autónoma. El interés de sus novelas es histórico, no estético, e incluso su valor documental es reducido; reflejas, sin punto de vista propio, nos informan más sobre lo que sus autores leían que sobre lo que veían, más sobre los vacíos culturales de una sociedad que sobre sus problemas concretos. (184)

> But none of our Romantic or Realist novelists ever did create a universally valid literary world, a representation of truth–whether faithful or unfaithful–endowed with enough power of verbal persuasion to impose itself on the reader as an autonomous creation. Whatever interest there still is in these novels lies in their purely historical, not aesthetic value; even their documentary value is limited. Like a reflecting surface, without a point of view of their own, they tell us more about what their authors read than about what they saw, more about society's cultural emptiness than about its concrete problems.

Let me sound the voice of the past to counter Vargas Llosa's opinion, with a judgment that may be just as biased, or as valid–it always depends on the elusive argument of fidelity to the real–as the comments from the Peruvian novelist, a writer who is as acclaimed today as Isaacs himself once was, and, curiously, for very similar reasons: their truthful portrayal of life. In 1890, only twenty-three years after the publication of *María*, for Rollo Ogden's translation of the novel, Thomas A. Janvier wrote an introduction containing these enthusiastic remarks: He claims that "the dominant characteristic [of the novel] is entire truthfulness to nature," and to prove his assertion he offers his own personal experience of life in Latin America: "But the side of the story which comes nearest to my own heart . . . is its beautiful and its absolutely truthful portrayal of life in a Spanish-American home. . . . Homes of this sort, my own experience has convinced me, are not the exception but the rule in Spanish-America" (x). What has changed is both our perception of the real, and what we consider the right conventions to represent reality faithfully. Janvier's enthusiastic remarks sound almost as a kind of retrospective response to Vargas Llosa's contemptuous dismissal of the nineteenth-century Latin American novel. Thus, literary histories as institutions and as influential judgments, however subjective and arbitrary, become the building blocks of the canonical walls inside which texts are imprisoned, while those remaining outside are also (canonically forgotten).

In recent years what has now come to be called "the Western canon" has been attacked by the champions of multiculturalism, as though it were the one monolithic enemy to be fought. Nonetheless, the notion of canonical literature is both elusive and delusive, because the making of a canon—Western or otherwise—depends on a system of inclusions and exclusions, operating not on one but on various levels, and determined by the particular perspective and power stronghold of the different cultures and literary institutions in interaction. Furthermore, this dynamic system of inclusions and exclusions is not restricted to changing perspectives within the one all-powerful canon, as T. S. Eliot described the phenomenon for the English literary tradition. It is not only a question of changing values triggered by the appearance of a new writer or new readings of old texts; most important, it is a question of power relations established on different levels and among different cultures, leading to the ideologically charged opposition between *central* and *peripheral* literatures.

In his *The Western Canon*, Harold Bloom contends that "the Western Canon is a kind of survivor's list," that inclusion is won purely on aesthetic grounds, and that "aesthetic value emanates from the struggle between texts" (36). But on looking closely at a sample of his own list, it is clear that the English-American survivors most definitely outnumber those from all other literary traditions, including the other purportedly central literary traditions of Europe. Furthermore, the non–English-speaking authors included are mostly those who have conspicuously influenced the *English* tradition: Homer, Virgil, Dante, Cervantes, Montaigne, Goethe, Ibsen, Tolstoy, and so on. So what is so grandly referred to as the *Western* canon boils down to an affirmation/confirmation of the centrality and cultural domination of the *English-American* canon. Bloom insists that the choice is aesthetic and results from a solitary struggle between the author and tradition (*whose* tradition is, of course, a question he never asks); therefore, the Western canon is "a choice among texts struggling with one another for survival, whether you interpret the choice as being made by dominant social groups, institutions of education, traditions of criticism, or, as I do, by late-coming authors who feel themselves chosen by particular ancestral figures" (19). But Bloom's baker's dozen is, ironically, a demonstration of the first option, not of his own, for it is clearly biased by the English tradition that has ignored the aesthetic value of the innumerable foreign authors who happen not to have come to its attention, and who often—it might be equally contended—have a greater aesthetic value than many of the ones he does include in his canonizing discussions. Why, one wonders, is Smollett included and not Diderot? Is Aldous Huxley

really better than Gide or Céline? Why is Swinburne included and Rubén Darío (1867–1916) excluded, considering—with Bloom's same criteria, questionable as they are–that Darío's influence has been so much greater and lasting? The same goes for Harriet Beecher Stowe's curious presence, occupying a space worth allotting to a more influential figure, say Chateaubriand, who is not even mentioned. Why Fletcher and not Corneille? Is Willa Cather all that much better than Emilia Pardo Bazán? Why Norman Mailer and not Goytisolo or Cela? Why Theodore Dreiser and not Rómulo Gallegos? And, to expose the absurdity of this competitive game, one could also ask why should all these alternatives—which the writer of the present essay has proposed out of sheer ignorance of other, potentially valuable, literary traditions—be any better than any other baker's dozen? And so on, ad infinitum.

Despite Bloom's influential book, the powerful attacks on the centrality of the Western canon have made the frontiers shift, or at least the binary opposition itself has been put into question, so that if nothing is central anymore, nothing can be pushed into the margins, for at this point in cultural history margins are to be found everywhere and nowhere since—for better or for worse—the center cannot hold. Until recent times, Latin American literature had been considered peripheral in relation to the Western canon, but the so-called Latin American boom has brought it more toward that ideal and idealized center of the scene. For some, this may be part and parcel of the story of multiculturalism; however, it is interesting that, in the past, the same canonical play has been staged even within the sphere of the supposedly marginal literatures. For, still operating at a supranational level, Latin American literature was also institutionalized then, in order to build an artificial entity in which labels were just as rigid and the system of inclusions and exclusions just as arbitrary as the ones in the Western canon—or rather, just as dependent on the power relations defined by that central and centralizing canon. In fact, the Western canon has always dictated the rules as to which writers are to be included in the hierarchically dependent canon of Latin American literature: Only he or she who has been successful in Europe, or at least in the whole of Latin America and/or the United States, will figure in the official canon, which in turn becomes central, with the local literary traditions of the Latin American countries taking up the marginal position. As may be seen, the same power scheme is simply repeated on a Latin American scale. Centrality, however, is relative and illusory, because the Latin American canon has been built in strict dependence on the power of Western opinion: Inclusion is conditioned by international success.

Now, if the lens is focused on the local literary traditions–the peripheral within the peripheral–the same process of institutionalization is seen to be at work, except that, at this level, *nationalism* versus *internationalism* becomes the dominant criterion on the battlefield of inclusion/exclusion. At times, defense of national literatures may even border on chauvinism, praising national or Latin American writers excessively for the sake of the attributed value—or even respectability—of the local canon. One could even say that this was the dominant practice in nineteenth-century Latin American criticism. For instance, Ignacio Altamirano's (1834–1893) book review of *María*, in 1881, is an extreme illustration of this defensive attitude. Isaacs's novel is of course declared superior to *Paul et Virginie* and *Atala*, in the absence of any close reading of the three texts involved. The descriptions of the American scene, Altamirano claims, are original and true. Furthermore, he insists that the Colombian novel is close, in spirit, to tragedy.

Sentí al leerla y meditar sobre ella, algo de esa extraña impresión indefinible que sobrecoge al espíritu cuando se lee una tragedia de Esquilo o de Sófocles, cuando se piensa en la desdicha de Ofelia, cuando se contemplan las desgracias de los seres débiles y dulces, cuando se encuentra uno frente a frente de ese inmenso poder que se llamó fatalidad en los antiguos tiempos y que proyecta siempre su sombra misteriosa tendida como una red traidora y terrible a los pies de la humanidad. (194)

As I read (*María*) and thought about it, I felt something of that strange, undefinable sensation that seizes the spirit with awe when one reads a tragedy by Aeschylus or Sophocles; when one thinks of Ophelia; when one contemplates the miseries of the weak and the meek; when one is faced with that vast power, named Fate in ancient times, which will always cast its mysterious shadow, like some treacherous and terrible net, at the feet of humanity.

In Altamirano's appreciation of *María*, an interesting paradox of the national literary canon comes to the surface: The national or continental value is emphasized on grounds of authenticity and originality; at the same time, for the work to acquire full value, it must be inscribed in the highest layers of the Western canon, so *María* is said to bring to life the spirit of Greek tragedy. Joaquín Arcadio Pagaza (1839–1918) will be the Mexican Virgil, Florencio María del Castillo (1828–1863) the Mexican Balzac, and so on. Thus, what was twice marginal has, in this mirage of power, become central. Nevertheless, this alleged centrality is an illusion, because the local canonization of the authors is modeled on the hierarchies that organize the all-powerful Western canon. Therefore, writers will be valued and/or included in the national canon if they fulfill two conditions: being true to the national experience and fitting the *Ur-Canon*.

A Comparative Approach Based on the Provisional and the Exploratory

It is clear that the price to pay for canonization is reification: Authoritative, definitive readings and evaluations of literary works become the straitjackets of opinion that impoverish a potentially refreshing reading experience, even of canonical texts. Reading in the univocal direction of influence and literary fortune, for example, distorts both the influencing and the influenced works, because it promotes the uncritical assumption that the first text is a model in more than one sense, for it is not only a formal but an evaluative, moral, and aesthetic model. The second text is simply forced through the grid of the first: What does not fit the shape of the grid is either discarded or highlighted in the competitive spirit of a sort of literary football game played out to see who wins, who is superior. And because this or that interpretation is proposed as the *true meaning* of the text, the relative arbitrariness and limitations of the interpretive grid are concealed; in this kind of criticism, even the grid itself is made to appear as nonexistent.

When one rereads texts from the perspective of the cultural horizon of the present in a meaningful interaction with that of the past, as a phenomenon of both intertextuality and transculturation, it is no longer a question of including or excluding but of *exploring*, with all the provisionality, the limitations, and the risks that any exploration entails. In the comparative approach I have taken, the goal is, therefore, not to propose a parallel system of inclusions and exclusions–I am certainly not about to exclude canonical texts–but to explore a few verbal and iconic texts with the help of a formal model created ad hoc for the purpose of this provisional exploration.

I believe that the experimental nature of the model and the interartistic approach prevents reification, since all claims to authority or exhaustiveness have been abandoned, thereby stressing the relativity of all reading and interpretation. Considering that this is only an analytical construct, the critical position of the analyst/historian/explorer is defined as a zone of indeterminacy, as a temporary playground for meanings to be deployed. Therefore, the components of the literary model are as much part and parcel of the literary tradition of the West as an act of selection from the intellectual, historical, and ideological perspective of the explorer, thus attesting not only to the provisional nature of the selection but also to the degree of subjectivity and arbitrariness informing the model itself and the consequent readings of iconographic and narrative texts.

Traces of an International, Transhistorical Literary Model in Nineteenth-Century Latin American Narrative and Iconography

Much has been said about the varied and rich intertextual pressures on the descriptions of the new continent during the age of discovery. Paraphrasing Vargas Llosa, one could say that the descriptions of America of Columbus, Cortés, Díaz del Castillo, Harriot, or Raleigh tell us more about what these men read than about what they saw–"wanderlust overtaken by nostalgia," as Harry Levin would say (60). But these descriptions tell us something else; in their chronicles Utopia has been given a local habitation and a name, as it were, for many of the rhetorical, poetic, and narrative devices of the pastoral genres, the medieval romances, and the folklore around the myth of the golden age and the myth of the savage–both wild and noble–make their presence felt in these descriptions. "Life at its barest and least sophisticated was somehow decked out with a set of trappings inherited from the learned conventions of literature" (Levin 60). Or, as Leo Marx has so aptly put it, "in the age of discovery . . . a note of topographical realism entered the pastoral" (47). But, conversely, we could also say that a note of the pastoral modified the perception of the new reality. Latin American narrative has had to come to grips with this note of topographical realism, and it has been a question of working *in* and *against* the grain of previous textual models for the verbal and iconic representations of this "new" world. These textual models may be derived not only from literary texts but also from chronicles, travel books, reports, and the many other texts that have contributed to the representation of nature in the American continent. The best example of a highly influential account of America is Alexander von Humboldt's "thirty-volume voyage," as Mary Louise Pratt has called this titanic intellectual enterprise (115).

One of the threads guiding me in the labyrinths of this textual and iconic exploration is a literary scheme of extraordinary resilience and capacity for transformation: the classical topos of the *locus amoenus*, an idealized space in which all the dreams of a harmonious relationship between man and nature are played out, where the concepts of *nature* and *nurture* converge and become almost synonymous. For Ernst Robert Curtius (1:122–59, 263–89), who has done extensive and profound work on this subject, topoi are schemes of thought, extended metaphors, or descriptive strategies that have become more or less fixed in the literary tradition of the West, from Homer to the modern age (1:122–23). As a discoursive scheme, the components of *locus amoenus* may reach a high degree of fixation (1:280ff), even at the lexical level, thus becoming conventionalized set pieces or expressions employed as a resource for the composition of subsequent texts belonging to the same genre, usually the pastoral. But I believe that the scheme may be further abstracted and reduced to seven basic components, regardless of their explicit verbal formulation: water, grass, trees, flowers, fruits, birds, and domestic or tame animals. What is striking about this scheme is that all of its constituent parts may be located in the middle range on the scale of intensity, so that a common semantic feature to all of them could be abstracted as *mildness*: In this idealized world it is always spring; the temperature is never too hot or too cold; water is thirst quenching, fresh, crystal clear, and warbles or murmurs as it flows; there is never a strong wind but a mild, caressing breeze; grass is always qualified as lush, soft, comfortable, a thick carpet to sit or lie on; trees offer humankind their fruits, but also their shade and shelter; meadows and trees are covered with colorful flowers; birds sing happily while peaceful animals, usually cows, sheep, or very tame goats, graze contentedly nearby; if there are insects, they are bound to be harmless—colorful butterflies or industrious bees (without, of course, any mention of their potentially aggressive sting).

All these elements orbit around human beings, the centerpieces in this idyllic world, to enhance their life, to nurture and protect them. In turn, humans relate to this world in the same middle range of intensity, creating harmony and balance in all their activities: Their meals are frugal, their health perfect; their time is spent in ease and happiness. *Otium*, once the privilege of Virgil's shepherd, Tityrus, has become the defining mark of this idyllic world; idleness as a prerequisite for the contemplation of nature. It must be noted that there is a predictable lexical and semantic reiteration that goes together with all of the components of *locus amoenus*: silence or melodious, soft sounds; peace, fertility, softness, protection, sweetness, warmth, light, freshness, and so on.

Bernard Le Bovier Fontenelle (1657–1757), in his "Discours sur la nature de l'eclogue" [1688; "Discourse on the Nature of the Eclogue"], makes an interesting syllogistic remark on the pastoral: "He assumes that 'all men would be happy, and that too at an easy rate.' From this premise he deduces the proposition that pastoral poetry, if it is to make men happy, must present 'a concurrence of the two strongest passions, laziness and love'" (Congleton and Brogan 887). Even work, when and if it makes an appearance in this idyllic world, should be toned down, like all the other components, to the middle range of pleasure and ease—*ease*, the twin brother of *otium*. As a set piece, then, this topos was extensively used in pastoral poetry, from which it took its schematic form, but it tends to reappear—under one guise or another—in most verbal representations of nature throughout the ages; the result is that this scheme has grown beyond its rhetorical sphere to become an all-pervading myth in the Western imagination, considering a myth, with Pierre Brunel, as "toute image capable d'exprimer dynamiquement un élément ou un conflit de la psychologie collective" (1131) ("any image capable of expressing dynamically an element or a conflict in the collective psychology"). One could even say that the myth of the *locus amoenus* is, in fact, the spatial/topographical side of the timeless yet time-bound myth of the golden age (see Levin 7ff, 58–83). If the contemplative dimension of the myth is already present in the old pastoral genres in the figure of the idle shepherd, nature as a *spectacle* is an eighteenth-century phenomenon. In the age of the grand tour, people living in towns and cities deliberately assumed the passive role of the spectator when confronted with nature; no wonder they found it *spectacular*:

> Today it is difficult to realize that Europeans have not always looked upon the landscape as an object of aesthetic interest and delight. But the fact is that landscape painting emerged as a distinct genre only during the Renaissance, and it did not achieve real popularity until the eighteenth century, when aesthetic interest in natural scenery reached something of a climax. One writer has suggested, in fact, that the arts of travel, poetry, painting, architecture, and gardening might be regarded as having been fused, in this era, into a single art of landscape.... On both sides of the Atlantic ladies and gentlemen traveled great distances to gaze at inspiring vistas. Often they carried Claude glasses, pieces of tinted, framed glass with handles named after Claude Lorrain, who after his death in 1682 had become the most popular landscape painter of the age. When a viewer used the Claude glass the landscape was transformed into a provisional work of art, framed and suffused by a golden tone like that of the master's paintings. The significant fact is that the glass helped to create a pastoral illusion. (Marx 89)

In a world in which art imitates nature and nature is made to imitate art, the frontier between the two becomes blurred. Furthermore, if those early tourists were creating what we might call "plastic happenings" with their Claude glasses, garden designers were seriously trying to make this painterly ideal come true by creating more permanent natural tableaux. Kent, an English landscape architect of the time, designed gardens as if they were pictorial compositions; his aspiration was to create a garden that could be composed like a Poussin painting (Hautecoeur 171ff). Furthermore, in this mirrorlike relationship between painting and landscape, the human eye brought in another reflecting surface: In nature the human found his/her own self, so nature thus became not only a mirror but an extension of the soul. Therefore, all the elements that went into landscape composition were designed to create a certain mood and facilitate the contemplative act. Rousseau had stressed the civilizing power of nature; he believed that all intercourse with nature could only foster good feelings, at the individual and the social level. But, unlike many of his followers, Rousseau was aware that the savage within us—that utopian natural state—is an imaginary construct, a heuristic device to search into our soul, "a state which no longer is, which may never have been, and will probably never will be, but about which it is, nonetheless, essential to have a clear notion in order to do justice to our present" (see Bartra's discussion of this idea, 171ff). Nature as mentor and mirror is our only guide in that voyage within. For the Romantics, then, meditation on and in nature could be conceived as a sort of sentimental and social education, but also an aesthetic education since nature itself had become an object of contemplation.

In the light of such a heritage, it is not insignificant that the notion, even the term *pathetic fallacy* should be a nineteenth-century invention: To contemplate nature with heightened emotion and believe that nature responds to that emotion, to imagine that primitive life is essentially good, and to place a greater value on the feelings fostered by nature—this was the Romantic ideal for life and, as was to be expected, it greatly affected not only verbal and pictorial representations of nature but also the ways in which people actually perceived nature. Once trapped in this hall of mirrors, one wonders to what an extent Vargas Llosa has been misled by his own prejudices, that is, whether indeed all those sentimental descriptions of nature tell us only about what the authors read and not about what they saw, considering that what they did see was already mediated by art. Significantly, one of the recurring words, both in nineteenth-century fiction and in the critical commentaries about it, is the term *picturesque*. Placed in the world of nature, the eye of the beholder–our own, biologically built-in Claude glass–makes a picture not only for spiritual but for aesthetic contemplation.

One last element to be considered in the gradual transformation of the locus amoenus myth is the cultural phenomenon of *exoticism*, which makes its appearance in fictional narrative with Bernardin de Saint-Pierre's *Paul et Virginie*. In most histories of French literature the critical assessment of the descriptive value of this text is almost unanimous: Saint-Pierre has *painted* a new nature. Even Lanson, who is so mercilessly critical of him (claiming, for example, that as a disciple of Rousseau, Saint-Pierre repeats his master's lessons mechanically, as an unintelligent pupil), lavishes his praise on Saint-Pierre's descriptions of nature, calling them picturesque: "Pas de rhétorique, mais un impressionisme sincère et puissant. Des mots propres inouïs, bizarres, palmistes, tacamaques, papayers, dressent devant les imaginations françaises toute une nature insoupçonnée et saisissante" (832) ("No rhetoric, but a sincere and powerful impressionism. Unheard-of, *bizarre* proper names, like palmistes, tacamaques, papayers, conjure a whole unsuspected nature for the French imagination" [my emphasis]). Two aspects must be highlighted here. On the one hand, the taste for the exotic is so strong, the names so bizarre and colorful, that they successfully conceal–even from Lanson's keen eye–the pervading presence of the old descriptive strategies. On the other hand, the emphasis is clearly put on the receptive end of the narrative process: Nature is a spectacle–the picturesque again–for the *French* imagination. The profile of the implicit reader is decisive in the structure of this text; it is for him that this nature is exotic, it is to him that the unknown *other* has to be explained, that is, the unknown is simply forced into the comfortable mold of the familiar. To illustrate these procedures, here are two descriptions of nature in *Paul et Virginie*. One is Virginia's fountain spring, the other, the narrator's cabin.

Il naquit de ces deux fruits deux cocotiers qui formaient toutes les archives de ces deux familles: l'un se nommait l'arbre de Paul, et l'autre l'arbre de Virginie. (54)

Excepté cette plantation, on avait laissé cet enfoncement du rocher tel que la nature l'avait orné. Sur ses flancs bruns et humides rayonnaient en étoiles vertes et noires de larges capillaires, et flottaient au gré des vents des touffes de scolopendre suspendues comme de longs rubans d'un vert pourpré. Près de là croissaient des lisières de pervenche, dont les fleurs sont presque semblables à celles de la giroflée rouge, et des piments, dont les gousses, couleur de sang, sont plus éclatantes que le corail. Aux environs, l'herbe de baume, dont les feuilles sont en coeur, et les basilics à odeur de girofle exhalaient les plus doux parfums. Du haut de l'escarpement de la montagne pendaient des lianes semblables à des draperies flottantes, qui formaient sur les flancs des rochers de grandes courtines de verdure. Les oiseaux de mer, attirés par ces retraites paisibles, y venaient passer la nuit. (54–5)

La rivière qui coule devant ma porte passe en ligne droite à travers les bois, en sorte qu'elle me présente un long canal ombragé d'arbres de toute sorte de feuillages: il y a des tatamaques, des bois d'ébène, et de ceux qu'on appelle ici bois de pomme, bois d'olive et bois de cannelle; des bosquets de palmistes élèvent çà et là leurs colonnes nues et longues de plus de cent pieds, surmontées à leurs sommets d'un bouquet de palmes, et paraissent au-dessus des autres arbres, comme une forêt plantée sur une autre forêt. Il s'y joint des lianes de divers feuillages, qui, s'enlaçant d'un arbre à l'autre, forment ici des arcades de fleurs, là de longues courtines de verdure. (127)

These nuts produced two cocoa-trees [*sic*], which formed the only records of the two families; one was called Paul's tree, the other, Virginia's. (80)

With the exception of these two trees, this nook of the rock was left as it had been decorated by nature. On its embrowned and moist sides broad plants of maiden-hair glistened with their green and dark stars; and tufts of wave-leaved hart's tongue, suspended like long ribands of purpled green, floated on the wind. Near this grew a chain of the Madagascar periwinkle, the flowers of which resemble the red gillyflower; and the long-podded capsicum, the seed-vessels of which are of the colour of blood, and more resplendent than coral. Near them, the herb balm, with its heart-shaped leaves, and the sweet basil, which has the odour of the clove, exhaled the most delicious perfume. From the precipitous side of the mountain hung the graceful lianas, like floating draperies, forming magnificent canopies of verdure on the face of the rocks. The sea-birds, allured by the stillness of these retreats, resorted here to pass the night. (83)

The river which glides before my door passes in a straight line across the woods, looking like a long canal shaded by all kinds of trees. Among them are the gum tree, the ebony tree, and that which is here called bois de pomme, with olive and cinnamon-wood trees; while in some parts the cabbage-palm trees raise their naked stems more than a hundred feet high, their summits crowned with a cluster of leaves, and towering above the woods like one forest piled upon another. Lianas, of various foliage, intertwining themselves among the trees, form, here, arcades of foliage, there, long canopies of verdure. (157)

Notwithstanding the many faults of the English translation, we may observe that behind the *clematides, tatamaques, scolopenders*, and *palm trees* lurks the old, familiar *locus amoenus*. As was to be expected, in this faraway island in the middle of the Indian Ocean, vegetation is luscious, the trees, in all the beauty of their shady foliage, are laden with fruit. But each of the components of the myth has been expanded into an inventory that furnishes this world with strange exotic birds and plants, brooks, and trees. Nonetheless, the scheme continues to be the same, while the potentially decentering, otherwise alienating power of these exotic verbal creatures is kept in check by the explanations and analogies appended to each term, so that it becomes not only intelligible but sensuous and imaginatively iconic . . . to the French imagination, at least. The procedure will be followed later by Chateaubriand, becoming a common practice in most Latin American nineteenth-century narrative: New, semantically *empty* names will be listed at the end of the novel in a glossary, or else defined, either in footnotes or in analogies running in apposition to those names. These elaborate paratextual and metatextual practices are carried out exclusively for the sake of that implicit reader, who does *not* belong to the same cultural community as that being described and is usually identified with the European reader. "Papayers," for example, would need no explanation or iconic analogy for Latin American readers, but it does for Saint-Pierre's contemporary European readers. Yet explanations, analogies, and glossaries are means not only for decoding the exotic but for appropriating it culturally from a position of power. If the text told us that *tatamaques* resemble *casahuates*, or that *clematide* was a sort of red *cempazuchitl*, it

Figure 1.

Girodet, "Passage au torrent," drawing for the Édition Didot, 1806, of Paul et Virginie. *(Archive of the author)*

Figure 2.

Hipólito Salazar, "Juventud de Pablo y Virginia," illustration for the 1843 edition of Pablo y Virginia. *Mexico City: Casa Editora de Lara. (Archive of the author)*

would make sense to a Mexican reader, but then that would not be nearly as exotic as the Mauritian specimens are for the Europeans.

From the perspective of this strange mixture of cultural power, distance, and ignorance, the exotic paradoxically acquires a sort of formless, synonymic character, since the new, therefore incomprehensible object/name may be replaced by any other equally new item and yet create the same effect: Notice the term *cocoa* to signify "coco," the tropical fruit-bearing palm tree, in the 1856 English translation of Saint-Pierre's novel. This is even *visually* evident in many nineteenth-century illustrations of *Paul et Virginie*. In most of them, palm or banana trees will always figure as tokens of the new and exotic, putting a spicy touch, or even defamiliarizing the rigidity of the academic neo-Classical or Romantic compositions in which they often appear. Witness Girodet's drawing of Paul and Virginia crossing the stream with just a few palm trees in the background as a reminder that this is a primitive, exotic world (see **Figure 1**). In the 1843 Mexican edition of Saint-Pierre's novel, Hipólito Salazar also offers an interesting combination of the academic and of the exotic in his illustrations. The recurrent, almost trite motif of the lovers framed by a flowery or leafy bower (see **Figure 2**) conjures a host of other lovers from other nineteenth-century novels in the same idyllic pose.

One could even set Salazar's illustration side by side with another of María and Efraín (see **Figure 3**) in an Argentinean edition of Isaacs's novel *María* (this one from Buenos Aires's Editorial Castelar): While the compositional pattern is very similar in both, what varies are the figurative elements. María and Efraín are dressed in elegant European clothes, and,

although the flowers that frame them are not drawn in great detail, they still achieve the effect of a conventional bower in a very tame, well-groomed *English* garden. In fact, we might say that in its lithographic component, this Argentinean edition of *María* is visually anglicized; not a single note of the American scene is captured by Raul Ramauge's illustrations. The tiger hunt scene could figure in any English painting of the time; even the tiger itself looks more Asian than American (see **Figures 4** and **5**). This is a great irony, considering that the novel is set in Colombia, in the heart of the wild Cauca region. However, and paradoxically, the lithographic artist does do justice to the novel, because a visual body has been given to the European element in the narrative, elements that constitute one of the many worlds that make up the variegated, often unstable fictional world of *Maria*.

But, returning to the 1843 Mexican edition of *Paul et Virginie*, it is the appearance of this framed couple, not the composition itself, that is supposed to make the same exotic: The two young lovers are barefoot, poorly dressed, and slightly disheveled–though very slightly so–to convey the impression of the simplicity and primitiveness of their happy lives. But their clothes, features, expression, and pose are European enough for the purposes of reader identification. Curiously, the only note of realism is in the drawing of the vegetation that replaces the flowers in the conventional bower scene, for this is clearly tropical vegetation, the tropical vegetation of Central and South American rain forests. This impression is reinforced in another illustration by Hipólito Salazar (see **Figure 6**), in which a very Mexican-looking

Figure 3.

Raúl Ramauge's illustration of Isaacs's María. *Buenos Aires: Editorial Castelar, n.d. (Archive of the author)*

Figure 4.

Raúl Ramauge's illustration of Isaacs's María. *Buenos Aires: Editorial Castelar, n.d. (Archive of the author)*

maguey–almost a national symbol–spreads a disturbing presence in the foreground of an otherwise nondescript landscape. But was not an island off the coast of Madagascar (at the time called *L'Île de France*) supposed to be the setting of *Paul et Virginie*? That does not seem to matter, not even to the literary historian, for some actually say that the action of *Paul et Virginie* is set somewhere in the American continent! So, therefore, a maguey should surprise no one, since it is equally exotic and will perform the same function as any other specifically Mauritian plant. Still, one might wonder what reading/visual impact the lithographic dimension of this book could have had for a nineteenth-century *Mexican* reader. It is clear that the natural scene is composed with these iconic token signs throughout the book; the reader is invited to decode them as exotic, and yet for a Mexican reader they would be a familiar landscape. What would be the effect of such a reading program on a Mexican audience? Would the encoded signs defamiliarize the familiar? Moreover–and this is a more disturbing question–is the representation of nature so very conventionalized even in its exotic features that it easily lends itself to lithographic plagiarism? I was forced to pose this question because of the discovery of two claims of iconographic authenticity: The 1843 Mexican edition claims to have original illustrations made by Salazar, yet the idyllic scene of Paul and Virginia under the bower (though not, significantly, the landscape with the maguey) is the exact same illustration attributed to Tony Johannot in the 1838 Curmer edition. All these enigmas, I think, might be an

interesting avenue of research into both plagiarism and reception studies. But, for the time being, suffice it to say that the paradox at the heart of this procedure is unsettling because precisely those signs that are the most concrete, both verbally and iconically, the ones with the strongest referential value–and, therefore, the supposed marks of fidelity to the real–end up acquiring abstract value and meanings within this uniform and convertible notion of exoticism (a notion so uniform that it may be borrowed with no compunction). If the pictorial and literary schemes that organize the representation of nature are general (due to their bookish, conventional nature), the figurative elements, endowed with transient novelty, are contradictorily abstract too (given their semantic function as markers of exoticism). That is why Romantic nature may often take on such strong allegorical overtones.

As was to be expected in the forerunner of this kind of natural scene, this is what happens in the narrative of *Paul et Virginie*. Nature, as the extension of the human soul, is played out almost as an allegory of the course of human life; the myth of the *locus amoenus* dynamically interacts with its opposite, the wasteland, as two poles in this pre-Romantic meditation on nature. For instance, the initial unity and perfection of Virginia's fountain spring, with the two palm trees representing the two children, is later turned upside down (another of the classical topoi is "the world turned upside down") by the violence of a tropical storm that pollutes the spring. But this defiling action of nature is only a mirrorlike reflection/premonition of the lovers' impending separation and, obliquely, of Virginia's growing

Figure 5.

Raúl Ramauge's illustration of Isaacs's María. *Buenos Aires: Editorial Castelar, n.d. (Archive of the author)*

Figure 6.

Hipólito Salazar's illustration of Maurician landscape for the 1843 edition of Pablo y Virginia. *México: Casa Editora Lara. (Archive of the author)*

into maidenhood—the contamination of the spring as a metaphor for Virginia's menstrual blood that has begun to pollute her body, even though this fact of life is only demurely alluded to. Appropriately, the novel ends with a description of nature that works as the rhetorical antithesis of the *locus amoenus*, a vision of the wasteland in which, significantly, what little remains of the idyllic world has now been expelled from the paradisiacal middle course: Goats, for example, have become wild, while the only birds that are left, mostly birds of prey, sing in a shrill voice.

Thus, it is evident that the old literary scheme of the *locus amoenus* is the organizing principle in Saint-Pierre's depiction of nature, even though the lexical furnishings are new—a fact that may easily lead readers to think that because the natural scene described is new, the form of representing it is also new, the product of *direct* observation. The reception contemporaneous to the writing of this book was unanimous in its acclaim of the novelty of the descriptive procedures; by contrast, our own contemporary reading of *Paul et Virginie*, given our cultural horizon, immediately highlights the intertextual and highly artificial character of the depicted natural scene. The abstract relationship between the stability or even permanence of the model and the novelty of its furnishings is not devoid of moral and ideological implications.

These, I think, are clear in Chateaubriand's prologue to *Atala.* He says that the advantages of making Chactas, his narrator-hero, half savage, half civilized (he knows both the living

and the dead languages of Europe) are that he can create a character "en le faisant parler en Sauvage dans la peinture des moeurs, et en Européen dans le drame et la narration" (43) ("by having him speak like a savage when painting the customs of the land, and as a European in the drama and the narrative"). What is clearly involved in these comments is the writer's reluctance or, perhaps, incapacity to conceive the other as *other*, except in his *picturesque* externals: Chactas fixes his age in terms of so many snowstorms; his face is painted red and blue; he is dressed in beaver furs, eats bear ham and maple syrup, and, as a baby, was rocked in a moss cradle suspended high up from the branches of a maple tree. The moral and ideological implications are clear: The picturesque (and, by implication, the culture of the other) is merely ornamental and therefore superficial and unimportant; the fundamentals of life, by contrast—the drama, the narrative—can only be conceived in terms of European culture. That is why, even though Chactas is an Indian/savage by blood, he finds in López the spiritual father who will give him his moral and intellectual credentials as a civilized man, as a European. The same is true of Atala herself. Only half her blood is European, since she is the bastard daughter of that same López, while Christianity has made her whole soul and body belong to the West. This comes up again and again in the pictorial representations of Atala: Although she is half Indian, she is always depicted as a white, sensuous woman. Likewise, Chactas, even though the color of his skin varies, is always given European features.

In this alternation between the familiar and the strange, the "important" and the "picturesque," Chateaubriand is actually following an old pictorial convention for the representation of nature and life in the New World, dating from the second half of the sixteenth century. In the very famous travel books printed by De Bry, the visual counterpart to the chronicles mounts the exotic jewels of the Indian figures in the familiar frame of European conventions. For example, John White, illustrating Thomas Harriot's account of the Virginia plantation, depicts the Algonquin Indians with a particular emphasis on details of dress and activities that have an undeniable ethnographic value, for White was a reasonably competent artist and his watercolors were done from direct observation. But direct observation does not mean unmediated perception of reality. J. H. Elliott observes in his prologue to *America* (DeBry 9) that John White's work is informed by ideological mediating structures such as the ideals of physical beauty and decorum that he shared with his contemporaries. The result is a series of watercolors that display Indian bodies in a kind of gallery of Greco-Roman statues (see **Figures 7, 8,** and **9**).

As we have seen, the role of language and the formal descriptive schemes is paramount in the representation of nature: Words make up worlds, but they may also distort the ones they set out to (re)present. What has been said about *descriptive* schemes also holds for *narrative* schemes and the lexical stock that is associated with them. We have seen that in the domain of description, the exotic is marked by the display of new, unfamiliar objects/words that furnish the new world; likewise, the strain of exoticism *in the action* often goes hand in hand with a pseudo-epic style. For Jorge Isaacs, it is not the American but the *African* scene that is treated in this self-conscious exotic vein; appropriately, when he tells

the story of the family slaves Nair and Sinar, born in Africa, Isaacs immediately switches to this pseudo-epic style: "Indecisa aún la victoria, Magmahu, resplandeciente de oro y terrible en su furor, recorría las huestes animándolas con su intrepidez" (Chapter 40) ("Victory still uncertain, Magmahu, resplendent in gold and terrible in wrath, moved among his troops encouraging them with his daring"). All the epic furnishings are there: The hero is always accompanied by epithets that elevate his stature–Magmahu is "resplendent in gold and terrible in wrath"–his warriors are called "hosts" ("huestes"), and his courage is called "valor" ("intrepidez"). The opening participial phrase has all the flavor of a battle scene from the *Iliad*–"Indecisa aún la victoria . . ." ("Victory still uncertain . . ."). In the world that these words evoke, all that needs to be done is to exchange Magmahu's name for Agamemnon or Charlemagne in order to have access to a "new world," which will turn out to be the same–the déjà vu experience. Something similar is at work in the description of the family relationships in *María*, despite Janvier's naive claim of he truthfulness of the portrayal. Again, even though some of the furnishings of this hacienda are clearly Latin American, the *words* often used to describe the family relationships inscribe its members in the moral, social, and intellectual climate of Europe, even feudal Europe (at one point, a black youth, attendant on his young master, Efraín, is designated as a *paje* or "page").

Figure 7.

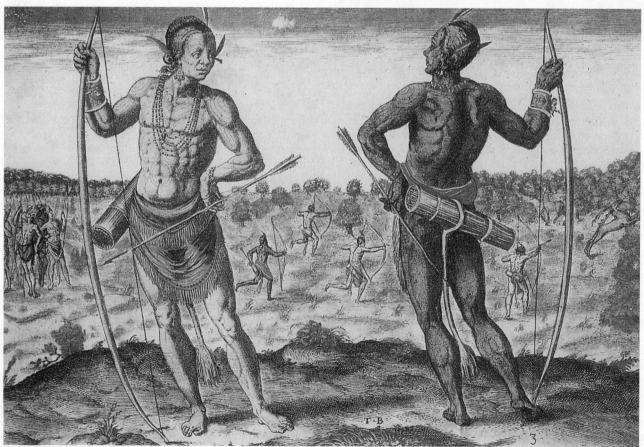

John White's illustration in Book One of America *by De Bry. Madrid: Ediciones Siruela, 1992. "Retrato de los príncipes y señores de Virginia" (20). (Archive of the author)*

Figure 8.

John White's illustration in Book One of America *by De Bry. Madrid: Ediciones Siruela, 1992. "El Nigromante o Mago" (30). (Archive of the author)*

Figure 9.

John White's illustration in Book One of America *by De Bry. Madrid: Ediciones Siruela, 1992. "De cómo suelen las mujeres de Dasamonquepeuc llevar a sus hijos" (29). (Archive of the author)*

In the nineteenth-century imagination, primitive, exotic peoples were often put side by side the ancient heroes of classical epic poetry, and so their feats and prowess were narrated and described in an appropriately elevated style. For Chateaubriand, who turns his Natchez into epic heroes, a bayonet becomes a glaive from Bayonne, a rifle an inflamed tube. This is a stylistic procedure that was condemned as ridiculous even in his own time, but Chateaubriand's influence was powerful; we have seen, in the example from *Maria*, how this pseudo-epic style became a literary convention in the Latin-American Romantic novel too. Another striking example of this are the early Indianist narratives, the Romantic precursors of the indigenist novels. José María Lacunza's (1809–1869) *Netzula* (1837), one of the first Mexican historical novels dealing with the theme of life and war at the time of the Conquest, is set in the last days of Moctezuma's reign, and written in an epic style: "Eran los últimos dias de Moctezuma: el imperio volaba a su ruina, i la espada de los españoles hacia estremecer el trono del monarca; donde quiera se escuchaban sus victorias, i los hijos de América doblaban el cuello a la cadena de los conquistadores" (15) ("These were the last days of Moctezuma: The empire was heading to its destruction, and the Spaniards' swords shook the monarch's throne; cries of victory were heard everywhere and the sons of America bent their necks to the conquerors' chains").

The heroes are the Indians themselves, so that the story is allegedly told from their point of view. And yet, just as the heroic natives are called "los hijos de América" ("the sons of America"), the Spaniards are always referred to by the epic epithet of "los hijos del océano" ("the sons of the ocean"); in fact, these Indians think, feel, and behave like Europeans, or rather, like Greek heroes. Strangely, though darts and arrows are also mentioned at some point, these native warriors end up wielding swords, like their enemies. Something similar

occurs in Eulalio María Ortega's (1820–1875) *La batalla de Otumba* [1837; The Battle of Otumba], also narrated from the point of view of the natives; nonetheless, the warriors are described as wearing helmets (*yelmos*, not *penachos*, it must be noted).

Yet, even as I allude to these two works of fiction, I am aware to what extent I myself am bound to words and their world-making capacity. By referring to this period as Moctezuma's reign, or even empire, I have allowed words to impose a perspective of the world that is totally alien to the pre-Hispanic cultures. Even though the Aztec *tlatoanis* ruled in ways that may be approximately equated to the notion of *king* or *emperor*, it is only approximately so. Calling Moctezuma an "emperor" is already seeing and assessing him from the outside, from this side of the "other." Nevertheless, Lacunza's and Ortega's epic heroes are in keeping with a view that was very popular in the eighteenth and nineteenth centuries, though one might trace it back to Montaigne: the notion that these primitive peoples have in them the makings of epic heroes, and that, as Humboldt advised, the regeneration of all the races of the world was necessary if mankind was to witness universal progress. Montaigne himself had put the inhabitants of the New World in the sphere of the Greco-Roman world when, in his essay "On the Cannibals," he made the fantastic claim that the natives' language (notice, not "languages" but "language"; again the uniformity imposed by distance and ignorance) is sweet and pleasing to the ear, with a cadence similar to Greek.

In the frontispiece of Humboldt's book *A Critical Examination of the History and Geography of the New Continent*, the following allegorical illustration seems to make precisely that ideological statement (see **Figure 10**). In the background, Mount Chimborazo is drawn with some detail, yet *nopaleras* (cactuses) and a vaguely Egyptian-looking pyramid in a desert setting with equally Egyptian-looking palm trees—all supposed to represent Cholula—are sprinkled about in impossible contiguity, as impossible as the implicit geographic superimposition of Mexico and Ecuador. In Mary Louise Pratt's *Imperial Eyes:*

Figure 10.

Frontispiece of Humboldt's Atlas of America. *"Humanity, Knowledge, Economy." See Mary Louise Pratt.* Imperial Eyes: Travel Writing and Transculturation. *London: Routledge. 1992. 139. (Archive of the author)*

Figure 11.

Frontispiece of Book One of America *by De Bry (15). (Archive of the author)*

Travel Writing and Transculturation, this illustration is captioned as follows: "The allegory depicts a defeated Aztec warrior prince being consoled by Athena, goddess of wisdom, and Hermes, god of trade. At the bottom lies a smashed statue. In the background stands a mountain modeled on Chimborazo and the pyramid of Cholula in Ecuador in Mexico [*sic*]. The caption reads 'Humanity, Knowledge, Economy" (139). In the foreground of the illustration we do see a very neo-Classical character composition, with the defeated Indian hero being consoled by Greek gods. But the overthrown prince's sandals are very much like those of Hermes, as is his muscular build and his facial features. Pallas Athena is handing him a twig from an olive tree (rather than a *nopal* or the disheveled branch from a palm tree, as the background landscape might lead us to expect). The Indian prince's latticed tunic, his collar, helmet, shield, and spear look like some exotic blend of the Greek, the Roman, and the Aztec, with a faint flavor of the circus. Even the feathers look more like ostrich than quetzal feathers. In this exotic mixture, Chimborazo and Popocatépetl may be just as interchangeable as Mexico and Ecuador, as a pre-Hispanic and an Egyptian pyramid, as the Greeks and the Aztecs, or as *nopales* and laurels. This visual *syncretism* is interesting because it tells the ideological story of the time. While some of the items in the landscape are represented with as much realism as observation can master, the composition itself, the pose and the expression of the characters involved place them all under the influence of

Western culture. The implication is that the contiguity with Western myths not only informs but confers value on the native culture. Examples of this ideologically charged visual syncretism can be easily multiplied; a few may be highlighted to confirm the ideological proposition. One is constituted by the frontispieces in De Bry's various books on America (see **Figures 11** and **12**). The Indians are portrayed in some detail, emphasizing the exotic feathers and ornaments, and even their cannibalistic habits, but these figures are grotesquely set in the niches of neo-Classical buildings, as though the Western architectural frame was the only means of conferring meaning upon these exotic creatures. Another example of this "framing" assimilation into Western culture is G. G. Ancira's portrait of Benito Juárez (see **Figure 13**). The Mexican hero is surrounded by a number of significant Mexican emblems (the eagle eating a serpent, the cactus plants, the ribbon and book alluding to the 1857 Constitution and Reformation laws), but he is also conspicuously flanked by two Greek goddesses. The same visual syncretism–with an added touch of Bernini–is apparent in the illustration of the "Salto del agua" fountain in Mexico City (see **Figure 14**) that appears in the frontispiece of the 1864 edition of *México y sus alrededores* [Mexico and Its Surroundings]. The eagle certainly looks more Austrian than Mexican. Again, Pallas Athena presides over the architectonic composition, and, as in the illustration on Humboldt's book, the Aztec hero–probably

Figure 12.

Frontispiece of Book Three of America *by De Bry (113). (Archive of the author)*

Figure 13.

"Ciudadano Benito Juárez Presidente de los Estados Unidos Mejicanos," by G.G. Ancira. José Ma. Vigil and Juan B. Híjar. Ensayo histórico del Ejército de Occidente. *Guadalajara, Mexico City: Imprenta de Ignacio Cumplido, Taller litográfico de Loreto y D. Rodríguez, 1874.* Nación de imágenes. La litografía mexicana del siglo XIX. *Mexico City: Consejo Nacional para la Cultura y las Artes, 1994. (Archive of the author)*

Cuauhtémoc or Moctezuma–is elevated to the same exalted position as the goddess, as if only Greek contiguity could confer value upon Aztec culture. The visual ideological statement is clear: Only by being assimilated into the European ideal of civilization can the culture of the "other" accede to the dignity of that name.

This alienation by assimilation is even more apparent in the lithographic illustration of Moctezuma by Joaquín Heredia (see **Figure 15**). Here, not even a token of exotic realism remains; not even the eagle ornamenting his coronet/helmet/*penacho*, for this is not the Aztec serpent-eating predator, but the imperial eagle of the Romans. So too is Moctezuma's outfit Roman, from the vaguely rococo leather cuirass to that impossible, massive sword, with an elaborate eagle's head on the hilt, and the suggestion of an equally elaborate scabbard. And let us not even speak of the blatantly Spanish facial features, hair, and beard that are part of the representation of this Moctezuma, in whom not a single drop of Indian blood has been left.

Thus, the verbal and visual representation of the world at a given moment in the history of a culture sets this reversible phenomenon in motion: If words and iconic signs have a capacity for world making, in turn, the "encyclopaedia of the world," as Eco would call it, informs the meaning of those signs. For Latin America, language–be it Portuguese or Spanish–was an imported reality; so too were the literary and pictorial schemes used in the representation of the real, not to speak of the political, social, intellectual, and domestic networks that organized life in the colonized lands.

Locus Amoenus: A Ghost in the Jungle

If it is true that European descriptive, narrative, and iconic schemes organized the representation of the new American reality, this has not been without creative tensions. As Jean Franco observes, echoing a generalized opinion on the subject, "it was difficult to idealize Latin American nature, which was infinitely more ferocious and savage than anything known in Europe" (88). Difficult, yes, but not impossible, for Latin Americans also seem to have had their own built-in Claude glass, so that they too could delight in aesthetic and spiritual contemplation of their own natural wonders, even though

Figure 14.

Frontispiece of México y sus alrededores. *Carlos Monsiváis et al.*
Casimiro Castro y su taller. *Mexico City: Fomento Cultural
Banamex, A.C., 1996. (Archive of the author)*

framed by a Western sensibility. Isaacs's *María* is, in many ways, a
synthesis of these tensions. Many critics have pointed out that
nature is idealized in the presence, both physical and spiritual, of
María, while in her absence the violence of nature is what comes
to the foreground. But a close reading tells a more subtle, complex story. It is unquestionably true that the immediate surroundings of the hacienda are described as an extension of María.
Flowers, ponds, trees, and bowers metonymically refer to her in
their beauty and freshness. Outside the family estate "ferocious"
nature begins. But this dichotomy is not as clear cut as the canonical descriptions would have it, for, from the very beginning,
nature is also described in terms of Efraín's moods and his social
surroundings. It is not only when María is in his mind that nature
has this idyllic quality; when he is alone nature becomes a mirror
of his soul, but, most of all, of his desire. At times, one could even
say that certain narrative situations are forced into the descriptive
grid of convention, as attested to by the very masculine bathing
sequence that follows the visit to don Ignacio's *potreros* [pasture for
colts]–a veritable *cuadro costumbrista* [sketch of customs], one of
the many that, mosaic-like, dot the novel from beginning to end.
Again, this is supposed to be the "fierce" nature outside the hacienda, yet the situation of rest and contemplation immediately
calls upon the *locus amoenus* scheme to filter experience. But let us
look more closely at these two instances of idyllic nature outside
the hacienda and in the absence of María.

Figure 15.

"Moctezuma," attributed to Joaquín Heredia. William H. Prescott.
Historia antigua de México y la de su conquista. *Mexico City:
Imprenta de Ignacio Cumplido, 1846. Nación de imágenes. (Archive
of the author)*

At the beginning of the novel, even before he has fallen in
love with María–in fact, even before María has appeared–
Efraín describes the landscape before his eyes in such a way
that we feel as though he has adjusted his Claude glass: His
idealized vision passes through the tinted lens of both perceptual and aesthetic conventions. The following tableau is verbally constructed:

El cielo tenía un *tinte azul pálido*; hacia el oriente y sobre las
crestas altísimas de las montañas medio *enlutadas* aún, vagaban
algunas *nubecillas de oro, como las gasas del turbante de una bailarina,*
esparcidas por un aliento amoroso. Hacia el sur flotaban las
nieblas que durante la noche habían embozado los montes
lejanos. Cruzaba *planicies alfombradas* de verdes gramales, regadas
por *riachuelos* cuyo paso me obstruían *hermosas vacadas,* que
abandonaban sus sesteaderos para internarse en las lagunas o
sendas abovedadas por florecidos pisamos e higuerones frondosos. Mis
ojos se habían fijado con avidez en aquellos sitios medio ocultos
al viajero por las copas de añosos *guaduales;* en aquellos cortijos
donde había dejado gentes virtuosas y amigas. En tales momentos
no habrían conmovido mi corazón las más sentidas arias del

piano de U***. Si los perfumes que aspiraba eran tan gratos comparados con el de los vestidos de ella..., si el *canto de aquellas aves* sin nombre tenía armonías tan dulces a mi corazón. (7–8, italics mine)

Levantéme al día siguiente cuando amanecía. Los resplandores que delineaban hacia el Oriente las cúspides de la cordillera central *doraban* en semicírculos sobre ella algunas nubes ligeras que se desataban las unas sobre las otras para alejarse y desaparecer. Las *verdes pampas y bosques frondosos* del valle, se veían como *al través de un vidrio azulado*, y en medio de ellos algunas *cabañas blancas, humaredas* de los bosques recién quemados elevándose en espiral y alguna vez las revueltas de un río. La cordillera de Occidente, *con sus pliegues y senos*, semejaba *mantos de terciopelo azul oscuro* suspendidos de sus centros por manos de genios *velados por las nieblas*. (17, italics mine)

The sky was a *pale blue*, towards the east, and above the highest peaks, still half veiled *in mourning (enlutadas)*, floated little *clouds of gold, like the gauze of a dancer's turban* stirred by an amorous breath. In the south hung the mists which had cloaked the mountains during the night. I was crossing *plains carpeted* with the greenest grass and watered by *little brooks*, the sorts of droves of *beautiful (hermosas)* cattle which had left their resting-places for a plunge in the pools, or for browsing along *paths arched over by trees thick with leaves and blossoms* (of *pisamos and leafy higuerones*). My eyes turned eagerly to those spots, half hidden to the traveller by clumps of old giant-reeds, where were the houses of goods friends of mine. My heart would have been unmoved then by the arias of U--'s piano; the perfumes I was drinking in were sweeter than those that clung to her rich garments, and captivating to my soul was *the song of the numberless birds*. (2–3, italics mine)

I rose the next morning at daybreak. The flush that was outlining in the east the peaks of the central cordillera was *gilding* a few light clouds that hung round the mountains, and that now began to separate, slowly move away, and disappear. The green meadows and *leafy (frondoso;* notice the insistence on this word, of which the translator seems oblivious) woods of the valley appeared *as if seen through blue-tinted glass*, and among them one caught sight of *white cabins*, spiral clouds of *smoke* rolling up the mountains recently burned over, and here and there the gleam of a river. The western cordillera, with *its folds and hollows (senos—breasts in English—is translated hollow)*, looked like a succession of *dark blue velvet mantles* held at their centers by the hands of genii hidden *(veiled)* by the clouds. (20–21, italics mine)

The painterly intention in these descriptive passages is evident, from the careful balance between light and darkness (the golden tint in the clouds and the fog), creating special *chiaroscuro* effects, to the trichromatic compositions in green, blue, and gray/white, and all these examples speak of temporal and cultural adjustments in the sensitive hues of the spiritual Claude glass of the late-nineteenth-century sensibility. This composition might just as well be called "symphony in green and blue," with all the corresponding decadent overtones, but the emphasized words and phrases not only point to the subjective tone that animates this description, but also call attention to the pervading presence of the *locus amoenus* myth, down to the lexical predictability of "carpeted" meadows, "leafy" trees, "sweet-voiced" birds, and beautiful cows [*hermosa vacada*], interspersed with the local, exotic specimens from the vegetal world: *guaduales* or *pisamos*. Beyond this basic spatial principle of organization, this tableau is the mirror of Efraín's desire, not a metonymical extension of María. In this descriptive passage—undoubtedly guilty of the crime of "pathetic fallacy"—there is a clear feminization of nature: The undulating shapes of the mountains are compared to a

woman's breasts, and clouds spread out like the gauze on some ballerina's headpiece, with the wind as a lover, synecdochically personified by his "loving breath." Yet one cannot say that the feminization of nature is due to María's influence. The spiritual process at work here is noteworthy because of the power of reversibility that the mirror possesses. Efraín shifts the image of his desire from his previous infatuation with some city lady, vaguely designated as U***, to a revitalizing contact with nature. At the same time, it is almost as though this contact was preparing him for María, whom, significantly, he has not seen yet. Therefore, this description of nature looks back to the sophisticated women in the city: The ballerina image, the dark blue velvet covering the mountain's breasts, or U***'s perfume and singing ability are unfavorably compared to their correspondent equivalents in nature. But it also looks forward to María. Nature is often qualified as virginal (*naturaleza virgen* is, in fact, the Spanish equivalent of "wilderness"); so too is María. Efraín's desire focuses on the half-hidden objects that the natural scene presents him, and this motif of desire and partial concealment will be central in the development of the lovers' relationship. Finally, the natural scene is also premonitory: Nature is constantly ringing an ominous note of mourning ("montañas medio enlutadas"), which prefigures María's early death. Here, it is the clouds on top of the mountains that are described as being in mourning; elsewhere the ominous signs will be impending storms and, particularly, the repeated presence of a black bird.

Let us now turn to the bathing sequence after the rodeo.

El sitio escogido por Emigdio en el río era el más adecuado para disfrutar del baño que las aguas del Amaime ofrecen en el verano, especialmente a la hora en que llegamos a su orilla. *Guabos churimos*, sobre cuyas flores revoloteaban millares de *esmeraldas*, nos ofrecían bajo densa sombra *acolchonada hojarasca*, donde extendimos las ruanas. En el fondo del *profundo remanso* que estaba a nuestros pies se veían hasta los más pequeños guijarros y *jugueteaban sardinas plateadas*. Abajo, sobre las piedras que no cubrían las corrientes, *garzones azules y garcitas blancas* pescaban espiando o se peinaban el plumero. En la playa de enfrente rumiaban acostadas *hermosas vacas, guacamayas* escondidas en los follajes de los cachimbos charlaban *a media voz*, y tendida en las ramas altas dormía una partida de monos en *perezoso abandono*. Las chicharras hacían resonar por dondequiera sus *cantos monótonos*. Alguna ardilla asomaba por entre el cañaveral y desaparecía velozmente. Hacia el interior de la selva oíamos de rato en rato el *trino melancólico* de las chilacoas. (42, italics mine)

The part of the river chosen by Emigdio was the best place to be found in the whole Amaime for a bath at that time of year, especially at that time of day. *Guabos churimos* over whose flowers thousands of insects (*esmeraldas*) were hovering furnished us *dense shade and leafy couches* on which to lay our cloaks. On the bottom of the *deep pool (remanso)* at our feet we could distinguish the smallest pebble, and silvered sardines playing about. Farther down the stream, upon the rocks sticking out of the water, were *blue and white herons* watching for fish, or preening their feathers. On the opposite shore *beautiful (hermosas)* cows lay chewing their cud. Macaws, hidden among the leaves of the *cachimbos*, chattered *sleepily (a media voz)*; and high up on the topmost branches a troop of *monkeys dozed in lazy abandon*. On all sides the cicadas were giving their *monotonous calls*. Here and there, a curious squirrel would peer over the edge of the gorge, and then swiftly disappear. From within the forest could be heard from time to time the *melancholy trill* of the *chilacoas*. (62, italics mine)

The point is not to argue–to use Mary Louise Pratt's words about Humboldt's descriptions of American nature–that Isaacs's representation is "somehow implausible or lacking in verisimilitude" (127); what must be argued is that it is not inevitable, that verisimilitude is filtered through a grid–that of the *locus amoenus*–that will not let anything else pass. Undoubtedly the *esmeraldas* are authentic insects inhabiting the Cauca region, but they have been chosen for their beauty, their harmlessness, and their mildness, and, perhaps, even because of their name. There must have also been spiders or *tambochas*–those deadly ants described in *La Vorágine*–but the *locus amoenus* grid is too fine to let such frightful beasts pass through. The *guabos churimos* are exotic enough creatures to certify their authenticity, but their tree life is confined to the lexical previsibility and spatial contiguities demanded by the topos: They offer their shade and, at their foot, the ground is carpeted with *acolchonada hojarasca*. Even *guacamayas*, *chicharras*, and monkeys, whose strident voices are well known, modulate their voices to fit that middle range of intensity required by the literary model. Even the *hermosas vacas* are there, as are most of the components, in short, of the *locus amoenus* scheme: water, grass, trees, flowers, birds, and domestic or tame animals.

Locus amoenus, nonetheless, is not the only habitat in this many-layered world: idyllic, epic, realist, *costumbrista* [narrative of customs and manners], *regionalista* [regionalist], and *modernista*. But nowhere is the composite character of this fictional world more evident than in the representation of nature: Spatially, the European, the Colombian, the Jewish, and the African worlds coexist in a precarious contiguity, almost as if they were ignorant of one another's presence. We have seen how Africa enters this world, through the vein of exoticism, as an epic world; we have also seen how the graphic artist of the Argentinean edition draws his inspiration from the anglicized aspects of the garden, while the hunting scenes are described as a sort of conventional *pukha sahib* tiger hunting expedition in India. The panoramic descriptions of nature, seen through the now blue-tinted Claude glass of an Impressionist sensibility, evoke a very European fin-de-siècle world, a world that, in turn, could not be more different from the one created, for example, in the description of Efraín's bath, carefully and lovingly prepared by María. The ritual of an open bath in an oriental-looking pool, whose waters have been delicately perfumed with flower petals, is an intimate allusion to the Jewish strain in the novel, which again contrasts with the world of the dangerous Colombian jungle and rapids that must be traversed in order to come back home. But even wild, dangerous nature, when seen from afar and in a particular mood, can be filtered through the chromatic, painterly models of Parnassian and Symbolist descriptions of the world, a tableau that we might call "*locus amoenus* in decadent green and blue."

Thus, nature is represented in *María* as an aesthetic composition in (and from) the eye of the beholder. Often nature becomes a metonymic representation of Woman–that Romantic projection of the masculine ideal of the "Eternal Feminine"–all in the colors and patterns of the time, woven into the different strains that have gone into the writing of this novel: Impressionistic, Parnassian, and Symbolist images, dyed in the soft hues of oriental-Jewish sensuality and the more exuberant colors of the Colombian natural scene. This composite image is, nonetheless, still pastoral; there is still, as Fontenelle would say, "a concurrence of the two strongest passions, laziness and love" (Congleton and Brogan 887). Only idyllic nature can be a setting for contemplation; however, the "ferocity" of Latin American nature puts an enormous pressure on contemplation, for it demands action. The central tension in *María*, and an important moment in the transformation of the literary model, is the tension between contemplation and action. This informs its opening and its closing. *María* begins with descriptions of nature as an object of contemplation and ends in a voyage full of hardships in which the expertise of man is called to account; nature refuses to be contemplated and demands interaction–demands to be acted upon and against–if human beings are to reach their goal or even to survive.

Running parallel to the *locus amoenus* myth, there is another European scheme for the representation of nature: Alexander von Humboldt's highly influential account of America.

> As the titles of his writings suggest, Alexander von Humboldt reinvented South America first and foremost as nature. Not the accessible, collectible, recognizable, categorizable nature of the Linnaens, however, but a dramatic, extraordinary nature, a spectacle capable of overwhelming human knowledge and understanding. Not a nature that sits waiting to be know [*sic*] and possessed, but a nature in motion, powered by life forces many of which are invisible to the human eye; a nature that dwarfs humans, commands their being, arouses their passions, defies their powers of perception. (Pratt 120)

This is a dramatic not an analytical representation of nature, not the passive, "collectible nature" that may be subjected to punctual analysis but the active nature of drama, animated by hidden forces, always ready to fight against humanity. And yet, Humboldt's "reinvention" does not cease to be a spectacle, a model of perception/representation that mediates the two opposite attitudes to nature: contemplation and action.

At the end of *María*, for example, "ferocious" nature takes over, but this is still Humboldtian nature: dangerous rapids, impenetrable forests, and a group of men fighting against these hidden forces with all their might, though not without zest and knowledge. Despite the mournful tone of these last pages, despite the obstacles that nature presents Efraín in his desperate voyage toward the dying María, there is a sense of exultation in the fight–so much so that the interest in the love story as such fades considerably in the presence of the natural scene, thus cleaving the novel in two schizophrenic parts, the pastoral (contemplation) and the realist (action), which are never quite reconciled. There is an attempt to merge the two strains in Efraín, as the ideal mediator between both worlds, but he has been too much on the Romantic side of contemplation, and, physically, he has been abroad too long to make his knowledge and expertise of jungle life credible.

It is interesting that Humboldt's dramatic model, like the *locus amoenus*, also has a set of fixed constituents:

> From Humboldt's *Views of Nature* and its sequel *Views of the C ordilleras*, European and South American reading publics selected the basic repertoire of images that came to signify "South America" during the momentous transition period of 1810–1850. Three images in particular, all canonized by Humboldt's *Views*, combined to form the standard metonymic representation of the "new continent": superabundant tropical forests (the Amazon and the Orinoco), snow-capped mountains (the Andean Cordillera and the volcanoes of Mexico), and vast interior plains (the Venezuelan *llanos* and the Argentine pampas). (Pratt 125)

But this "iconic triad of mountain, plain, and jungle," unlike the components of the *locus amoenus*, must be located at the very top of the scale of intensity. Exuberance, vastness, luxuriance . . . : If the *locus amoenus* myth calls for a poetics of the middle course, Humboldt's triadic model could be inscribed in a poetics of excess. Both, however, occupy the same place in the tonal and axiological scales: euphoria/magnificence—toned down in the scale of intensity to a moderate delight in the locus amoenus, Romantically heightened almost to ecstasy in Humboldt's triad. For even dangerous, impenetrable forests are for him an exhilarating spectacle: dramatic nature leading to dramatic pleasure. It has taken more than "one hundred years of solitude" in the jungle to tilt the balance to the other pole of this tonal/axiological scale, to present us with a disphoric experience of nature. But, paradoxically, the depths of the green prison have incorporated and transformed these previous models of the representation of nature, with the *locus amoenus* at times projected, like a film negative, onto the horrors of the jungle. This is apparent in José Eustacio Rivera's (1888–1928) *La Vorágine*, a novel that works out all the disphoric potential of nature. In the descriptions, the ghost of the *locus amoenus* lurks nostalgically, filtering negatively the details that must be registered:

> Entre tanto, la tierra cumple las sucesivas renovaciones: al pie del coloso que se derrumba, el germen que brota; en medio de los miasmas, el polen que vuela; y por todas partes el hálito del fermento, los vapores calientes de la penumbra, el sopor de la muerte, el marasmo de la procreación.
>
> ¿Cuál es aquí la poesía de los retiros, dónde están las mariposas que parecen flores traslúcidas, los pájaros mágicos, el arroyo cantor? ¡Pobre fantasía de los poetas que sólo conocen las soledades domesticadas!
>
> ¡Nada de ruiseñores enamorados, nada de jardín versallesco, nada de panoramas sentimentales! Aquí, los responsos de sapos hidrópicos, las malezas de cerros misántropos, los rebalses de caños podridos. Aquí la parásita afrodisíaca que llena el suelo de abejas muertas; la diversidad de flores inmundas que se contraen con sexuales palpitaciones y su olor pegajoso emborracha como una droga; la liana maligna cuya pelusa enceguece los animales; la "pringamosa" que inflama la piel, la pepa del "curují" que parece irisado globo y sólo contiene ceniza cáustica, la uva purgante, el corozo amargo. (104)

In the meantime, the earth undergoes successive renewals: the sprout at the feet of the fallen colossus; in the midst of miasma, the breath of ferment, the hot vapors from the darkness, the lethargy of death, the apathy of breeding.

Where is the poetry of secluded places here, where are those butterflies like translucid flowers, the magic birds, the warbling streams? Poor fantasy of poets who only know of domesticated wilderness!

No loving nightingales, no Versaillesque gardens, no sentimental landscapes! Here, only the funeral prayers of dropsical toads, the brambly undergrowth of misanthropic hills, the pools made by rotten streams. Here, the aphrodisiac parasitic flower that scatters the ground with dead bees; the diversity of filthy flowers contracting with sexual palpitation, whose sticky odor intoxicates one like a drug; the evil liana whose fuzz blinds animals; the skin swelling "pringamosa," the seed of the "curují" that looks like an iridescent globe but only contains caustic ashes, the purgative grapes, the bitter cohune palm.

The *locus amoenus* is still lurking in the jungle, still filtering, even though negatively, the materials that go into the representation of Nature. Ghosts take time to really die; Latin American narrative will have to wait until the middle of the

twentieth century to explore nature from the perspective of aboriginal myths and representational schemes in such narrative works as Miguel Angel Asturia's (1899–1974) *Hombres de maíz* [1949; Men of Maize] or Juan Rulfo's (1918–1986) *Pedro Páramo* (1955).

Works Cited

Altamirano, Ignacio Manuel. 1988 [1881]. "María. Novela Americana por Jorge Isaacs." *Escritos de literatura y arte: Obras completas*. Ed. José Luis Martínez. Mexico City: Secretaria de Educación Pública. 2: 191–96.

Anderson Imbert, Enrique. 1954. *Historia de la literatura hispanoamericana*. Vol. 1. Col. Breviarios. Mexico City: Fondo de Cultura Económica.

——. 1969. *Spanish American Literature: A History*. Vol 1. Trans. John V. Falconieri. Detroit: Wayne State University Press.

Balakian, Anna. 1962. "Influence and Literary Fortune." *Yearbook of Comparative and General Literature*. Bloomington: Indiana University Press. 11: 24–31.

Bartra, Roger. 1992. *El salvaje en el espejo*. Mexico City: Ediciones Era.

——. 1997. *El salvaje artificial*. Mexico City: Ediciones Era.

Bloom, Harold. 1994. *The Western Canon: The Books and School of the Ages*. New York: Riverhead Books.

Brunel, Pierre, ed. 1988. *Dictionnaire des mythes littéraires*. Monaco: Editions du Rocher.

Chateaubriand, François-René de. 1964 [1801]. *Atala. René*. Paris: Garnier-Flammarion.

Congleton, J. E., and T. V. F. Brogan. 1993. "Pastoral." *The New Princeton Encyclopedia of Poetry and Poetics*. Ed. Alex Preminger and T. V. F. Brogan. Princeton: Princeton University Press. 885–88.

Curtius, Ernst Robert. 1955 [1948]. *Literatura europea y Edad Media latina*. Vol. 1. Trans. Margit Frenk Alatorre and Antonio Alatorre. Mexico City: Fondo de Cultura Económica.

De Bry, Teodoro. 1992. *América (1590–1634)*. Intro. John H. Elliott. Ed. Gereon Sievernich. Trans. Adán Kovacsics. Madrid: Ediciones Siruela.

Franco, Jean. 1969. *An Introduction to Spanish-American Literature*. Cambridge: Cambridge University Press.

Hautecoeur, Louis. 1959. *Les jardins des dieux et des hommes*. Paris: Hachette.

Humboldt, Alexander von. 1818–1829. *Personal Narrative of Travels to the Equinoctial Regions of the New Continent during the Years 1799–1804*. 7 vols. Trans. Helen Maria Williams. London: Longman, Hurst, Ress, Orme and Brown.

Isaacs, Jorge. 1938 [1867]. *María: Novela americana*. Buenos Aires: Editorial Sopena.

——. 1890. *María*. Trans. Rollo Ogden. Intro. Thomas A. Janvier. New York: Harper and Brothers.

Lacunza, José María. 1996 [1837]. *Netzula: El año nuevo de 1837*. Vol. 1. Facsimile ed. Mexico City: Universidad Nacional Autónoma de México.

Lanson, Gustave. 1898. *Histoire de la littérature française*. Paris: Hachette.

Levin, Harry. 1969. *The Myth of the Golden Age in the Renaissance*. Bloomington: Indiana University Press.

Marx, Leo. 1967 [1964]. *The Machine in the Garden: Technology and the Pastoral Ideal in America*. London: Oxford University Press.

Montaigne, Michel de. 1991. "On the Cannibals." *The Essays of Michel de Montaigne*. Ed. and trans. M. A. Screech. London: Allen Lane. 228–41.

Ortega, Eulalio María. 1996 [1837]. *La batalla de Otumba. El año nuevo de 1837*. Vol. 1. Facsimile ed. Mexico City: Universidad Autónoma de México.

Ortega, Eulalio María. 1996 [1837]. *La batalla de Otumba. El año nuevo de 1837.* Vol. 1. Facsimile ed. Mexico City: Universidad Autónoma de México.Pratt, Mary Louise. 1992. *Imperial Eyes: Travel Writing and Transculturation.* London: Routledge.

Rivera, José Eustasio. 1980. *La vorágine.* Mexico City: Porrúa.

Saint-Pierre, Bernardin de. [1787] n.d. *Paul et Virginie.* Paris: Éditions Jules Tallandier.

———. 1856. *Paul and Virginia: With a Memoir of the Author.* No trans. Philadelphia: H. C. Peck and Theo. Bliss.

———. 1787 [1843]. *Pablo y Virginia.* No trans. Ilustrations by Hipólito Salazar. Mexico City: Casa Editora de Lara.

Vargas Llosa, Mario. 1973 [1969]. "Novela primitiva y novela de creación en América Latina." *La crítica de la novela iberoamericana contemporánea. Antología.* Ed. Aurora M. Ocampo. Mexico City: Universidad Autónoma de México. 182–97.

POETIC MODELS AND THE CULTURAL IMAGINARY

POETIC EXCHANGE AND EPIC LANDSCAPES

Gwen Kirkpatrick

En América dondequiera que surge posibilidad de paisaje tiene que existir posibilidad de cultura. El más frénético proseso de la mimesis de lo europeo, se licúa si el paisaje que lo acompaña tiene su espíritu y lo ofrece, y conversamos con él siquiera sea en el sueño. El valle de México, las coordenadas coincidentes en la bahía de La Habana, la zona andina sobre la que operó el barroco, es decir la cultura cuzqueña ¿la pampa es paisaje o naturaleza?, la constitución de la imagen en paisaje, línea que va desde el calabozo de Francisco de Miranda hasta la muerte de José Martí, son todas ellas formas del paisaje, es decir, en la lucha de la naturaleza y el hombre, se constituyó en paisaje de cultura como triunfo del hombre en el tiempo histórico.

—Lezama Lima 105

In the Americas wherever there is the possibility of landscape there exists the possibility of culture. The most possessive European mimesis completely evaporates if the perceived landscape retains its spirit and offers it to us so that we can converse. The valley of Mexico, the district coordinates of Havana harbor, the Baroque Andean region that is the culture of Cuzco. Is the Pampas nature or landscape? The expression of landscape in the Americas has a heritage stretching from the prison cell of Francisco de Miranda to the death of José Martí; altogether these images make up the landscape of culture which at the very core is man's triumph in the struggle with nature and is part of man's history.

and though,
There is no harder prison than writing verse,
What's poetry, if it is worth its salt,
But a phrase men can pass from hand to mouth?
From hand to mouth, across the centuries,
The bread that lasts when systems have decayed

—Walcott 377

Nineteenth-Century Latin America

What do we see when we survey the poetic landscapes of the nineteenth century in Latin America, and how does this compare with the graphic mappings of poetic desire as well as the geopolitical desires of territorial acquisition and influence? In both a literal and a figurative sense, the notion of landscape within this time frame must include not just the idealized ruins, such as those evoked by Rubén Darío (1867–1916) in 1896, in "Palabras liminares" ["Liminal Words"] of *Prosas profanas* [Profane Prose]: "Si hay poesía en nuestra América, ella está en las cosas viejas: en Palenke y Tutlatlan, en el indio legendario y el inca sensual y fino, y en el gran Moctezuma de la silla de oro. Lo demás es tuyo, demócrata Walt Whitman" (180) ("If there is poetry in our America, it is to be found in ancient works: Palenque and Tutlatlan, in the legendary Indian, in the sensual and elegant Inca, in the great Moctezuma of the golden throne. The rest is yours, democrat Walt Whitman"). It must include as well the earlier meditative poetry on the history of pre-Conquest America, such as that of José Joaquín de Olmedo (1780–1847) in "La victoria de Junin" [1825; "The Victory of Junín"] or José María Heredia's

(1803–1839) "El teocalli de Cholula" [1832; "Cholula's Teocalli"]; and also the later evocations of the urban landscape as another stage for meditation on the ruins of empires and dreams, as in Julián del Casal's (1863–1893) "impure love" for the cities. Landscape construction paints history as well as geographic space, and its poetic representation in Latin America gives a vantage point from which to examine literary and social exchange with other parts of the world.

Landscape as metaphor might seem inadequate and too tame to convey the moving tableaux of the turbulent nineteenth century in Latin America. But its visual dimensions and its value as a unit of social space give us a way to frame a vast stretch of history and complex literary production. Framing, of course, implies selection, trimming, and omission, as well as imposing a certain perspective on the scene. Despite the limitations of landscape as metaphor, however, it can be a fruitful way of organizing literary history. One of its advantages is that it allows us to bypass the history of European literary movements as a framing narration of Latin American poetry, a narration that has usually served to point up the "belatedness" of such movements in Latin America. And metaphorically, landscape can anchor us more closely to the particularities of the American scene by foregrounding features not present in European models.

The tradition of landscape representation–its emblematic nature, historical connotations, and its role in nationalist discourses–can help us to understand the complexity and dynamism of Latin American literature during the turbulent nineteenth century. Landscape is not just a representation of nature, but also a changing social space. Exploring its traditions can reveal complex cultural and poetic conventions. As José Lezama Lima (1910–1976) asks in the opening epigraph, "Is the pampa landscape or nature?" He understands the formation of landscape as an exchange or conversation between people and nature, not as a framed scene frozen in time. Because landscape implies stylization and not just realistic inclusion, conceptually it offers a metaphor for how Latin American writers chose to frame their specific terrains, histories, and future visions for public presentation. It is important to note what is included and excluded from landscape depiction, understanding the tradition as a mobile social space as well as a calculated representation of nature within complex cultural and poetic conventions.

In its origins, the term *landscape* denoted a unit of human occupation, and thus its heritage is that of a shared culture, a "tradition built from a rich deposit of myths, memories, and obsessions" (Schama 10, 14). Or as Lezama eloquently states, we are constantly engaged in dialogue with landscape, even though "only in dreams." Just as Lezama stresses landscape framing as a form of human dominance, so other observers have associated landscape with imperial expansion (Mitchell) or the mystique of a national "homeland" (Schama). While exclusivist claims to places–nationalist or regionalist–fix them as "sites of nostalgia, the opting out from Progress and History" (Massey 4–5), the definition of landscape as a space constructed out of social relations opens them up to mobility and shifting boundaries. Modernity increasingly "tears space away from place by fostering relations between 'absent' others. . . . [I]n conditions of modernity, locales are thoroughly penetrated and shaped in terms of social influences quite distant from them" (Giddens qtd. in Massey 6). Thus Latin America, whether it consciously embraced or rejected the signs of modernity, was entwined in the modern world economy. Its colonial legacies, such as the slave trade, *latifundia,* and clientelism, were a necessary complement to faraway hegemonic countries–not simply the antithesis to modernity, but an essential part of its underpinnings (Schwartz 12–17).

The representation of landscape is central to an understanding of Latin American poetry, as has been witnessed in the efforts of colonial poets to describe the New World, partly for their far distant readers and partly to form local consciousness. Yet the nineteenth century increases the primacy of landscape even more. While landscape construction has been associated largely with European Romanticism, especially with Wordsworth's reflective poems, using geographic sites as physical correlatives of mental and spiritual reflections, its function in Latin American poetry acquires even greater importance, especially as it relates to an integration of the historical dimension. Landscape framing and composition have received extraordinary attention from art historians and cultural critics in recent years, with an increase in our awareness of the social and political forces involved in artistic renderings of terrain and the people who inhabit it (see Mitchell; Pratt; Schama). Yet it is difficult, even knowing the primacy of the

conventions of landscape painting and literature in the nineteenth century, to comprehend its importance for Latin America. Because of the landscape genre's surge in popularity in Europe during the late eighteenth and nineteenth centuries, it has been referred to as the dreamwork of imperialism, in the terms of W. J. T. Mitchell, marking the change from previously popularized battle scenes to landscape scenes, where the geography takes a primary role over the actors. Nonetheless, Mitchell's interpretation through the lens of British imperialism cannot fully apply to the Americas. Although landscape did become more prominent as a poetic staging in Latin American poetry, the early abundance of colonial examples (such as Bernardo de Balbuena's [1563?–1627] Baroque stylized *Grandeza mexicana* [Mexican Greatness]) only reinforces the impression that representations of nature, particularly framed as landscape, carried even more symbolic weight than their European counterparts. Geographic sites were correlatives not just of internal emotion but particularly of historical reflection.

Transnationalism, free trade, and mass migrations bring to mind a late-twentieth-century scene of globalization, but one must remember that colonialism itself, the slave trade, and postcolonial realignments created massive shifts in populations and resources. Just as Latin America engaged in economic trade with the rest of the world, so its literary and cultural life was in constant journeying and transformation. The words of António Cândido concerning Brazilian literary relations are relevant to all of Latin America: "estudar literatura brasileira é estudar literatura comparada" (211) ("to study Brazilian literature is to study comparative literature"). The constant referencing of oneself to external models gave a comfortable sense of parentage, in an intellectual world where "a imitação era timbre de glória" ("imitation was a sound of glory"). A desire to belong to a larger family, in this case a family that would extend much farther than the limits of the paternalistic world of Portuguese colonialism, has echoes in large parts of Latin America, especially in the nineteenth century, when almost all the Spanish colonies in the hemisphere (except for Cuba and Puerto Rico) had won their political, if not cultural, independence from Spain. Insistence on originality and organic culture, as Roberto Schwarz reminds us, arises from a Romantic vision that gained cultural force at the same time as the rise of imperialism and organized science, which rendered obsolete any dream of a harmonious and auto-centered national culture (39–44). The very nature of entwined and journeying economies, peoples, and cultures, not to mention the dispersion of printed materials far from their original contexts, makes the topic of imitation and originality a constant preoccupation of literary histories in Latin America. Literary theories of dependency, neocolonialism, transculturation, *mestizaje*, hybridity, or Brazilian Modernism's *antropofagia,* among many others, show a constant preoccupation with the question of models or "original" forms and their imitation, transformation, or refusal. This dialectic of perceived inside and outside forces gives shape to many histories of Latin American literature. It is an essential component of any recounting of Latin America's literary legacy, but it is worth remembering that many of these approaches are derived from the imperative that sees cultural life as an organic totality, with specific origins and subsequent growth and transformation. Acting on a world stage where economic and commercial movements made exchanges inevitable, Latin Americans were inextricably bound up in a number of cultural and artistic systems, making complete autonomy or total originality an impossibility.

The Public Role of Poetry

A genre of great public resonance, poetry had a vibrant life in nineteenth-century Latin America. At least until late in the century, it was linked to social practice in a way inconceivable to contemporary readers. As inheritors of the Romantic tradition, modern readers tend to see poetry as an interior genre or an inspired form, arising from the deepest currents of the human and social psyches, or in contemporary terms, from the social imaginary. This tradition sees the poetic impulse as part of a prelogical, premodern intuitive connection between mind and world. This apprehension works quite well when we apply it to the work of some Latin American poets–such as the *Trilce* by César Vallejo (1892–1938), Darío's "Nocturnos," the work of Delmira Agustini (1886–1914), much of Neruda (1904–1973), José Martí's (1853–1895) *Versos libres*, and a great deal of contemporary poetry, especially that which concentrates on desire and the body. It even focuses a great deal of our critical readings of the poetry by Sor Juana Inés de la Cruz (1648–1695), as we seek to decipher the puzzles of her as a female speaking subject in the late seventeenth century. Yet such a vision of almost daimonic poetic power is harder to maintain when one looks at other important poets, especially in previous centuries. Does one feel that Bernardo de Balbuena was illuminated by lyric fire when he set out his vision of Mexico City in the seventeenth century? Or what about Andrés Bello's (1781–1865) founding odes and liras to celebrate early nationhood? José Hernández's (1834–1886) *Martín Fierro* [1872; The Gaucho Martín Fierro] is, after all, a verse narrative, as is *Tabaré* (1888), a Romantic Indianist epic by Juan Zorrilla de San Martín (1855–1931). Even Pablo Neruda and César Vallejo's books on the Spanish Civil War, or a great part of what we call political poetry, resist being read as manifestations of individual inspiration. The long narrative poem reflected confidence in the role of poetry in the social realm, a faith in its ability to represent and to shape visions of past, present, and future.

In considering the *public* role of poetry in Latin America, it is important to make a distinction between public and popular. Even though a great deal of poetry aimed at the public forum did indeed become popular, or found its roots in popular legend or tradition, one cannot associate "public" with "popular" without erasing significant differences. Without question, the tradition of popular poetry in Latin America remains alive and well. Writers of "popular" forms, including the gauchesque, the *corridos*, and their contemporary adaptations, combined truly popular forms, such as the legacy of the romancero or *cordel*, with the distribution techniques of print culture to create some of Latin America's most enduring literary legacies–for example, Bartolomé Hidalgo's (1788–1822) irreverent and musical "cielitos" ("Cielito, cielo qua sí/ guárdense su chocolate,/aquí somos indios puros/y sólo tomamos mate" [qtd. in Carilla 1979a, 102] ["*cielito* (piece of heaven), yes,/you can keep your chocolate,/we are all pure Indians here,/and all we drink is mate"]), *Martín Fierro* (1872), Martí's *Versos sencillos* (1891), Neruda's *Canto General* (1950) and Cabral de Melo Neto's (1920–1999) *Morte e vida severina* [1956; Severe Death and Life]. While literary adaptations of popular poetry are not unique to Latin America, this hybrid process produced distinctive forms that have been integrated widely into public consciousness and have–as in the case of gauchesque poetry, the *cordel*, and the *corrido*–come to form cornerstones of national traditions. Especially significant is the combination of popular forms with the long narrative poem, such as *Martín Fierro*, *Canto General*, and *Morte e vida severina*.

During the first two decades of the century the Spanish colonial empire collapsed in the face of widespread revolution, and the number of new nations created was not equaled until the mid-twentieth century, when European colonial empires withdrew from Africa and Asia. Brazil, under Portuguese rule, did not follow the same revolutionary process, but the move of the imperial capital from Lisbon to Brazil (owing to the French invasion of Portugal), rapid interior development, and the slave system set the stage for its full independence later in the century. The shocks of long-term wars and financial ruin limited many of the utopian social plans envisioned by the young republics, which were constructing national states despite extraordinary obstacles. The fervent belief in literacy and education as tools for creating citizens (though limited by class, gender, and race) guided many of the social and cultural programs. The dream of a common language, in the wider cultural sense, endured well beyond the initial utopian republican ideals. Faced with diverse cultural and linguistic groups, marked by the colonial hierarchical caste system, the hope of linguistic and cultural unity seemed a more accessible goal than political unity. And despite the difficulties of communication and travel, it must be remembered that ideas, theories, and publications did travel on both sides of the Atlantic (see Pratt; Sussekind). Although in nineteenth-century Latin America only Mexico could boast a true publishing center, the rise of the periodical press had already begun to change the face of intellectual relations.

Bolívar's dreams of a united Spanish America were set against inevitable fissures caused by vast geographic, racial, and cultural difference. But men of letters in the early nineteenth century generally were also men of action, many of whom, through forced exile or the privilege of education, were steeped in European culture and had discovered poetry's public usefulness, especially in the Independence period. Women, whose public and print space was minimal, found in poetry an acceptable outlet for expression in an age where female education and real literacy were very limited, and the preferred "feminine" genres were autobiography, letters, and poetry (see Molloy). Nonetheless, as public education became one of the glories of the liberal state in Latin America, women's participation in the lettered sphere increased, both as readers of and writers for periodicals in particular (Masiello; Greenberg 174–76).

Although most Western critics date the end of poetry's role in the public sphere with the death of Victor Hugo (1885) and Baudelaire's struggles as a poet within a rapidly changing modern world, the cultural matrix of Latin America did not produce the same results in every sphere. Well into the nineteenth century in Latin America, verse forms, whether dramatic works or epic or lyric production (odes, heroic hymns, elegies, madrigals, epigrams, fables) dominated literary production. As has often been noted, the publication of novels in the Spanish colonies was illegal, prohibited by laws of 1532 and 1543 against works of "pure imagination" (Henríquez Ureña 1978, 180)–although it is clear that novels, especially the *Quijote*, circulated widely. In 1816 the Mexican writer José Joaquín Fernández de Lizardi (1776–1827) published the first novel in Latin America, *El periquillo sarniento* [The Itching Parrot], whose very title indicates its resistance to following the heroic mode.

The late appearance of the novel, however, cannot explain the greater relative importance assigned to poetry. In *Las corrientes literarias en América Hispánica* [Literary Currents in Hispanic America], Pedro Henríquez Ureña laments the dominance of poetry in the early nineteenth century: "[E]l prejuicio en favor de la poesia seguía siendo demasiado grande en la America hispanica" (121) ("[T]he prejudice in favor of poetry continued to be too inclusive in Hispanic America"). Contemporary readers might find the notion of poetry's priority over other genres incomprehensible, given poetry's retreat from the public sphere over the past century (unless one includes lyrics from popular songs). But as a contemporary U.S. critic has noted, the contemporary discussion of the "marginalization" of poetry, in a very literal sense, implies the existence of the "master page" (Perelman 79). What could this "master page" be for the history of Latin American literature in the nineteenth century? In terms of genre, poetry was still a genre of great prestige; in terms of literary models, the situation was more complicated. Despite linguistic and cultural ties with Spain and Portugal, in most of Spanish America models from the *madre patria* (motherland) were so intertwined with the colonial yoke that the new republics would not claim patrimony. And in Brazil, although the move away from Portugal was less violent, writers increasingly sought to differentiate themselves from the models of a tattered empire. Would the master page be the undeniable influence of French literature, marked by its political revolution, on emerging national literatures, the heritage of Rousseau mixed with the prophetic vision of Victor Hugo? As England gained economic hegemony in much of Latin America soon after the Wars of Independence, would its literatures of empire–Kipling, Tennyson, and others–dominate? As its neighbor to the north, the United States, "the giant in seven league boots" or the "tiger in waiting," in the words of José Martí's "Nuestra América" [1891; "Our America"], moved to annex half of Mexico and exert its power increasingly in the Caribbean and Central America, especially after Spain's defeat in 1898, would its culture become dominant? U.S. literature had an undeniable impact, especially Emerson, Longfellow, Poe, and Whitman, but the routes of exchange traveled both ways.

Late-nineteenth-century Spanish American poetic *modernismo*, although usually characterized as an inward-turning movement, nonetheless was not homogeneous in this aspect; nor did it erase long-standing traditions of poetry in the public sphere, both popular and learned, and their inevitable exchanges, often circuitous, via Europe, until later in the century. Remembering this early prejudice toward poetry in rethinking literary history in Latin America might help us to clarify some of its problematic issues, specifically the late emergence of a full-fledged novelistic tradition and a persistent anxiety about the belated arrival of European models of literature, whether it be the Romantic tradition or the Realist novel. Focusing on poetry would not necessarily allay concerns of anxieties of influence or belatedness, common preoccupations of postcolonial societies, but it might make more comprehensible a literature that, without denying its obvious dynamic exchange with external models, could reflect better the glories and vicissitudes of its new development. Perhaps the detailed letters, diaries, reports, histories, and fiction of some of these public figures reveal more truly their plans and hopes, but it is also true that they invested poetry with their future dreams as well as their revisions of history. For many, poetry was understood as an important, immediate means of communicating with their public, however constrained that audience might be by the exigencies of poetry itself.

Poetry and Narrative

The situation in which the new republican leaders (almost exclusively *criollo* men of letters) found themselves made necessary a vision of the future that could harmonize the troubling memories of their ancestors' victimization of the indigenous peoples with their own claim to "Americanness" and property rights, property that included human slaves. How could they claim the American past as their own space of origin and legitimacy, while at the same time forging political and legal structures that would maintain their dominance? Revolutionary leaders were often anxious about legitimizing the political and cultural project of creating new nations, freed from the *madre patria* but with the inevitable ties brought by their largely *criollo* (of European descent, born in the Americas) origins. As traced by Tulio Halperín-Donghi, this anxiety of origins arises from the revolutionaries' doubts concerning the legitimacy of their claims to govern the new nations. Their doubts are based not on their queasiness about the break with empire, but about their own intermediate status as descendants of the Spaniards who usurped control from its previous rulers. Simón Bolívar (1783–1830) himself, great general of the Revolution and architect of a failed plan to unify the new republics, was troubled by this contradictory position of espousing liberty while subjugating others. He identifies his own group as neither Indian nor European, but "una especie media entre los legítimos propietarios del país y los usurpadores españoles" (qtd. in Halperín-Donghi 747) ("a species midway between the legitimate masters of the country and the Spanish usurpers"). What Halperín calls this "defecto de origen" (748) ("originary defect") occupies a prominent place in Latin American reflections on the constitution of nations and identities, and this originary defect forces a search for a defense of the legitimacy of the new republics. Bolívar searched for a model in the classical tradition, finding both North American and current European models to be inadequate for the particularities of the Spanish American situation. Compounding the problem of establishing successful new republican forms was the legacy of Spanish colonial domination, denounced as an aging remnant of a tattered feudal tradition, out of step with Western reforms.

It is important to remember that at the same time the new nations of Latin America were struggling to develop new societies and to forge cultural traditions that would integrate these societies into modern states, cultural forms were rising and falling in prestige and importance. As Lamartine, founder of the Romantic poetic tradition in France, said in regard to the chaos of standards created in the July Revolution in 1848, "The catalog is jumbled" (qtd. in Geertz 221). A return to archaic traditions was celebrated, even while an emphasis was being placed on the importance of the natural or individual voice. National traditions were being rediscovered or invented through the collection of oral tradition and national epics (Appiah 282–85); scholars assiduously collected folk traditions, tales, and music. And later, at the same time the Realist novel flourished, we see the beginnings of the Symbolist poetic movement, and Naturalist fiction is developed in line with Positivism, through the scientific and medical discoveries of the nineteenth century. In connection with the revival of the nationalist epic, the long semi-narrative poem became prominent. One only has to think of Victor Hugo, Wordsworth, Byron, Elizabeth Barrett Browning, Pushkin, Tennyson, Espronceda, and Zorrilla to find correlatives in Europe for the composition taking place in Latin America.

Many theorists (Auerbach, Lukács, Bakhtin) have found that the mid-nineteenth century is the point when epic composition in verse became impossible, given that the stringency of archaic forms cannot accommodate the voice needed for the modern work in epic spirit. The novel and also drama (see Brecht) have been seen as the most likely vehicles for expressing the epic sweep of societies in flux. Yet the long poem of narrative scope did not disappear, and often it bore the mark of the epic impulse (see Bernstein). We might remember that many theorists have found some of the origins of the modern novel in the epic, those long narrative poems that told the stories of heroism and the founding of nations, and forged identities at the origins of the modern nation-state—common examples being the *Chanson de Roland*, Camoes's *Os Lusiadas*, Spain's *El canto del mío Cid*, and many others, especially those that were written to celebrate the conquests of empire and the annexation of territories. Epic, however, has been considered an unlikely form for modern times. In a recent study David Quint reminds us of the double-edged sword of epic and romance: "To the victors belongs epic, with its linear teleology; to the losers belongs romance, with its random of circular wandering. Put another way, the victors experience history as a coherent, end-directed story told by their own power; the losers experience a contingency that they are powerless to shape to their own ends" (9). He also notes the inevitable interplay between the winners' and losers' narratives and the vision of each that the other

projects, using as an example one of the sources for Neruda's own epic narrative, Alonso de Ercilla's *La Araucana* (1569), where the losers (the Araucanians) attract the sympathies and admiration of the victors. Thus part of the promise of epic genre is the idea that "those who have been victimized losers in history somehow have the right to become victimizing winners, in turn" (18).

Compared to the poetry of predecessors such as Balbuena, the praise of Mexico's natural wonders develops into a more recognizable landscape description with Rafael Landivar's (1731–1793) *Rusticatio mexicana* [1781, 1782; Mexican Country Scenes]. Written originally in Latin, it describes the landscape of Mexico and Guatemala, as well as the survival of indigenous cultures. Circulated widely in its time in its original language, it began to be translated to Spanish in the nineteenth century–first by the Cuban poet José Heredia (1803–1859), whose own landscape poems ("Niagara" [1824] and "El teocalli de Cholula" [1820]) were important shapers of the modern vision of American landscape. In designing an emblematic field for recognizing American singularity, poets made landscape a vehicle for recording history as well as nature. It is within this framework that the predominance of ruins assumes a central part in reminding readers of the depth of historical tradition within the new republics. While the notion of ruins, leftovers from scattered empires and peoples, is a feature of European writings of the period, the particularity of the American historical landscape necessitated a reincorporation of pre-Conquest cultures within the historical imagination of the new republicans. (See **Figure 1.**)

Contemplation, such as that of José Heredia's "El teocalli de Cholula," produces equal parts historical reflection (on the ruins of the Aztec Empire and on the Wars for Independence) and individual soul searching. Heredia himself, in exile from a still Spanish-controlled Cuba, views not just from the promontory

Figure 1.

Peru-Bolivian Family. Pampa de La Paz. Lithograph by Juan Mauricio Rugendas. (Archive of the author)

of historical distance but from physical exile. Or later in the century, the Mexican Juan de Dios Peza (1852–1910) reads the book of nature as the physical remains of an empire disappeared:

Del palacio la grandeza:
Del templo la pompa extraña;
La azul y abrupta montaña
Convertida en fortaleza;
Todo respira tristeza,
Olvido, luto, orfandad;
¡aun del sol la claridad
Se torna opaca y medrosa
En la puerta misteriosa
De la negra eternidad!

(qtd. in Zaid 1982, 440)

From the palace greatness:
From the temple unknown pomp;
The blue and abrupt mountain
Turned into a fortress;
Everything breathes of sadness,
Oblivion, mourning, neglect;
even the sun of clarity
Becomes dark and timid
In the mysterious door
Of black eternity!

Gregorio Gutiérrez González (1826–1872) mixed descriptions of nature with scenes of local customs in his "Memoria sobre el cultivo de maíz en Antioquia" [1868; "Memoir on Maize Cultivation in Antioqui"]. While not as grand in intention (or geographic scope) as Bello's "Oda a la agricultura de la zona tórrida" ["Ode to the Agriculture of the Tropics"], it is nonetheless an anchoring of landscape with local custom. (See **Figure 2**.) Like some of the poems on similar themes by the Brazilian Antonio Gonçalves Dias, it was the result of its author being invited on a scientific expedition to explore Colombia's interior. Gonçalves Dias (1823–1864) also is credited with the founding of Indianist studies in Brazil, based in large part on his linguistic and ethnographic work. He published the first dictionary of the Tupí language in 1857, inspiring José de Alencar in his famous novels *Guarani* [1856; The Guarani Indian] and *Iracema* [1865; *Iracema, Honeylips: A Legend of Brazil*] (Henríquez Ureña 1949, 126).

Slavery and Poetry

Distance, rather than proximity, inspired some of Latin America's most famous poems of nature. Gertrudis Gómez de Avellaneda (1814–1873) departed from Cuba as a young woman for Spain, where she became one of the most notable literary figures of her time; yet the evocation of Cuba and her crusade for the abolition of slavery determined a great deal of her writing. Famous as a poet, she is today more recognized for her antislavery novel *Sab* (1841). César Vallejo, in his *El romanticismo en la poesía castellana* [Romanticism in Spanish Poetry], notes that this Cuban poet, "honra y prez de la cultura cubana" (58) ("honor and glory of Cuban culture"), marks a definite change in the poetry of the second third of the century. Vallejo attributes to the Spanish Romantic José Zorrilla the indelible influence of social Romanticism in Latin America, in Avellaneda as well as in the work of "Plácido, el mulato cubano [Gabriel de la Concepción Valdés], en cuya sangre palpitaban más enérgicamente los ideales fervorosos de autonomía americana, y de protesta contra la organización

Figure 2.

"Carretero," lithograph by Juan Mauricio Rugendas, 1858. (Archive of the author)

social aristocática" (59) ("Plácido, the Cuban mulatto, in whose blood the fervent ideals of American autonomy and the protest against social aristocracy pulse energetically").

Abolition of slavery was a cause sounded through poetry in many parts of Latin America, especially in the Spanish Antilles and in Brazil. (Slavery was not abolished in Brazil until 1881, in Puerto Rico until 1872, and in Cuba until 1880, whereas in most parts of Latin America it had been abolished, at least in the letter of the law, by mid-century.) A Cuban poet more widely recognized today for his celebrated autobiography is Juan Francisco Manzano (1797–1854), a mulatto slave who earned his manumission by the sale of his autobiography, commissioned by Domingo del Monte and a group of abolitionists and first published in English in 1840, translated by Richard Madden (who would appear later in Borges's "El jardín de senderos que se bifurcan" ["The Garden of the Forking Paths"] (Balderston 79–82). But previous to writing his autobiography (not published in Spanish until 1937), Manzano had published two volumes of poetry, *Poesías líricas* [1821; Lyrical Poetry] and *Flores pasajeras* [1830; Fading Flowers] (Lewis Galanes 32–43). Ramos records a fascinating case of a slave writer, Mascimo Hero de Neiba from Trinidad, Cuba, whose volume of poetry, *Murmurios del Tavaba: Poesías* [1865; Memoirs of Tayaba: Poems] begins with a statement asserting the economic necessity of receiving fair publication rights for his work, pointing to his profits as a route to his manumission: "Al publicar mis pobres concepciones,/Manumitirme solamente espero;/Por eso ruego abiertas suscriciones" (1994, 214) ("By publishing my humble words,/I hope to obtain my manumission,/and that is why I plead for subscriptions"). The theme of manumission also appears, surprisingly enough, in a poem by Sor Juana, "Rumba de las princesas de guinea por la Asuncion" ["Rumba of the Princesses of Guinea through Asunción"], which is written in a satiric patois of African speech (qtd. in Zaid 1982, 398).

In Brazil, abolitionist poetry had its best-known exponent in the Bahian poet Antônio de Castro Alves (1847–1871). His poetry espousing abolition was heavily influenced by the tenets of Romanticism and modeled on a series of poems on Victor Hugo's epic *La legende des siècles* [The Legend of the Centuries]. One of them, "The Slave Ship," was very well known (Rodríguez Monegal 207). Eulogized in Neruda's own epic, *Canto General* (Canto IV, "Los libertadores" xxix), Castro Alves is singled out as a writer in a gallery of voices almost exclusively of Revolutionary leaders. His narrative poem, "O Navio Negreiro (Tragedia do Mar)" [1868; "The Slaveship (Tragedy at Sea)"] dramatically portrays the slave ship:

Era um sonho dantesco! . . . o tombadilho
Que das luzemas vermelha o brilho,
Em sangue a se banhar.
Tinir de ferros . . . estalar de acólite . . .
Legiáes de homens negros como a noite,
Horrendos a dansar.

(14)

As in a vision of Dante,
I saw the quarterdeck, slippery with blood,
The skylight washed with crimson.
The clanking irons . . . the crack of a whip . . .
Legions of men black as the night,
Dancing their horrible death-dance.

(15)

Landscape and the Indigenous Past

Nineteenth-century landscape poetry responds both to the celebratory tradition of the colonial poets who tried to capture the New World bounties of nature, and its native populations and their often incomprehensible, and thus dramatically rendered, cultures. It also takes its cue from the tropes of Romanticism and the wonderment expressed in scientific expeditions of the previous century, particularly through the impact of Humboldt's writings. Yet as even a review of Mexico's own colonial poetry shows, Humboldt was not the prime shaper of this vision, but one of its inheritors. The previous recorders of the New World had established their visions and transmitted them to several generations of Europeans, who found in part what they had been directed to see by earlier chroniclers and poets.

As indigenous oral traditions were supplanted by the officialization of alphabetic writing for legal, administrative, and political processes within the years of colonization, these oral traditions became distinctly minority cultures, just as the indigenous peoples themselves were eliminated or relegated to castes and shadow systems under the dominance of the European and *criollo* tradition (Lienhard 35). Indigenous culture, for the purposes of mainstream Latin American poetry since the early nineteenth century, was converted to Romanticized historical drama or landscape, as in Olmedo's "Victoria de Junín" (1825), which celebrated Bolívar's critical victory in Peru. Olmedo, in an extensive poem of over nine hundred verses, exalts the cause of independence and recruits the ghost of the last Inca, Huayna Capac, to predict the final victory of the Revolutionary cause at Ayacucho. The Andes themselves, "the enormous, stupendous/mounds resting upon

golden bases," like everything American, "will never move" and will conquer the "fierce Spaniard" and incorporate past, present, and future into a sublime landscape where "sacred Liberty/was placed within the Temple of the Sun" (Rodríguez Monegal 199). This incorporative (cannibalistic, Oswald de Andrade might say) gesture is repeated in countless ways throughout the history of Latin American literature in dealing with the Indian past. In Spanish America's first great epic poem, *La Araucana* (1569, 1578, 1589), Alonso de Ercilla exalts the courage and nobility of the Araucanian warriors with whom he and his Spanish comrades must battle, likening them in dreams and visions to the heroes of classical mythology. His epic foreshadows a long poetic tradition of mythologizing the Indian presence or romanticizing it, often incorporating the Indian past within a landscape tradition of ruins and artifacts, managing both the spatial and historical indigenous experience within a naturalized canvas of continental scope. Although this idealized conversion of cultures resistant to assimilation within the new republican vision of an American landscape might find affinities with the Western tradition of Romantic folklore, specifically the *cuadros de costumbres* [sketches of customs and manners] so popular in Spain in the early nineteenth century, the political and social stakes are much higher. Not too distant from battles for independence are the memories of the late-eighteenth-century indigenous revolts against Spanish colonial administrators led by Tupac Amaru (José Gabriel Condorcanqui, Peru, 1740–1781), who became a symbolic leader for later independence fighters ("Tupamaros").

This renewal of interest, often called Indianism, was most prominent in Mexico (see Brading), and in other areas its variations were based on the degree of distance its writers felt from these cultures. Some of the best examples in poetry include the previously mentioned works of Gonçalves Dias, *Jicotencal* by Cuba's "Plácido" (Gabriel de la Concepción Valdés [1809–1844]), *En boca del último inca* [The Mouth of the Last Inca] by José Eusebio Caro (1817–1853), and Rodriguez Galván's (1816–1842) *Profecia de Guatimoc* [Prophecy of Guatimoc]. In the second half of the century, long narrative poems such as *Tabaré* often highlighted Indian themes, such as Bolivia's José D. Barrios's poems *Choriguilla o la Virgen de Potosi* [1875; Choriguilla or the Virgin of Potosi], the *Fantasias indigenas* [1877; Indigenous Fantasies] by José Joaquín Pérez (1845–1900) of Santo Domingo, and Mexico's Guillermo Prieto (1818–1897), whose *Romancero nacional* [1885; National Book of Ballads] recounts Mexican history in eighty *romances* (Seluja-Cecin 12–14). Increasingly, it was the novel that developed Indianist themes, such as that of José de Alencar, Gómez de Avellaneda's *Guatimozin* (1846), *Cumandá* by Ecuador's Juan León Mera (1832–1894), and the classic *Enriquillo* (1879–1882) by the Dominican Manuel de Jesús Galvan (1834–1911).

Although Indian uprisings were not uncommon in the nineteenth century, republics created from the earlier viceroyalties, New Spain and Peru, had longer histories of domination and control over indigenous populations, despite the latter's greater numbers. Thus, it is not surprising that in Peru Mariano Melgar (1790–1815) was a pioneer in adapting Indian, writing *yaravíes* in Spanish in the Quechuan manner (Cornejo-Polar 1994). Such efforts forecast the more widely known Peruvian efforts in the twentieth century to recapture Quechuan tradition, like the movement of *indigenismo* initiated by writers such as Manuel González-Prada (1844–1918) and developed more fully in the 1920s by José Carlos

Mariátegui (1894–1930) and the *Amauta* group, and later the passionate endeavor of José María Arguedas (1911–1969) in his novels and ethnographic studies (Cornejo-Polar 1994). In Mexico José Joaquín Pesado (1801–1861) translated many versions of Nahuatl poems such as *Cantos del Emperador Netzahualcoyotl* [Poems of the Emperor Netzahualcoyotl] (Carilla 1979a, 225). Pesada recasts Moctezuma in "Leyenda del vaticinio" ["Legend of the Prophecy"] as a monarch indifferent to the sufferings of his people, and unheeding of the prophesies of the disaster that would await him. Early warnings of danger from other sources were forecast by Mexico's Ignacio Rodríguez Galván (1816–1842) in heptasyllables in "Al baile del señor Presidente" ["To the President's Dance"], an uncanny forecast of Mexico's territorial losses in 1848 to the United States, as well as a condemnation of Mexico's treatment of its people:

> Bailad mientras que llora
> El pueblo dolorido,
> Bailad hasta la aurora
> Al compás del gemido
> Que a vuestra puerta el huérfano
> Hambriento lanzará.
> ¡Bailad! ¡Bailad!
> . . .
> Ya por Texas avanza
> El invasor astuto,
> Su grito de venganza
> Anuncia triste luto
> A la infeliz república
> Que al abismo arrastráis:
> ¡Bailad! ¡Bailad!
> . . .
> Europa se aprovecha
> De nuestra inculta vida,
> Cual tigre nos acecha,
> Con la garra tendida,
> A nuestra ruina próxima
> Ya celebrando está.
> ¡Bailad! ¡Bailad!

> *(qtd. in Zaid 1986, 426–27)*

> Dance while a wounded
> People cry,
> Dance until dawn
> To the beat of the groan
> Thrown at your doorstep
> By the hungry orphan.
> Dance! Dance!
> . . .
> The astute invader
> Marches through Texas:
> His cry of vengeance
> Announces the sad mourning
> Of an unhappy republic
> Being dragged to the abyss:
> Dance! Dance!
> . . .
> Europe takes advantage
> Of our uncultivated life,
> Like a tiger stalking us,
> With claws extended,
> Already celebrating
> Our coming ruin.
> Dance! Dance!

Rodríguez Galván uses many of the same dramatic metaphors; "las garras del tigre" is one also used by Domingo Faustino Sarmiento in his *Facundo* [1845; Facundo, or Civilization and Barbarism] and by José Martí in his classic essay "Nuestra América" of 1891. The "tiger's claws" are a metaphor for different threats faced by the Mexican poet, the combined threat of the United States and Europe–for Sarmiento, the "barbarism" inherent in the Gaucho Facundo; and for Marti, the adulation of the foreign, which was *far* more "barbarian" than the native peoples.

In republics emerging from the newer viceroyalties, specifically Argentina, the romanticism of Indianism was of a very different nature. In Argentina, engaged throughout the century in conquering territories from the Indians, its poets painted different landscapes, where the romanticization of the gaucho, fighter of the Indians, became the defining force in creating a national tradition. The battles against indigenous peoples culminated in the "Desert Campaign" of the 1880s, which effectively subdued or eliminated these groups in a manner similar to the U.S. battles in the Western frontier.

Not all writers admit even a bit of the romanticization of the Indian in their writings, especially where European conquest is incomplete and uneasy. Argentina's Esteban Echeverría (1805–1851), one of the authors of the "Dogma socialista" ["Socialist Dogma"] and an espouser of Liberal, democratic values, presents portraits of the "salvajes" in his narrative poem "La cautiva" [1837; The Captive], Argentina's foremost example of the captivity tale, a genre also prominent in U.S. frontier fiction (see Iglesia and Schvartzman; Masiello 1993). Beginning a section of "La cautiva" with an epigraph from Victor Hugo, Echeverría makes known his intention in "El desierto" [The Desert] to show the rural landscape of the Argentine pampa as equal in grandeur, and in dramatic action, to Old World counterparts:

> A veces la tribu errante,
> sobre el potro rozagante,
> cuyas crines altaneras
> flotan al viento ligeras,
> lo cruza cual torbellino,
> y pasa; o su toldería
> sobre la grama frondosa
> asienta, esperando el día
> duerme, tranquila reposa,
> sigue veloz su camino.

> *(62–63)*

> Sometimes the errant tribe,
> on the magnificent colt,
> whose arrogant mane
> floats lightly in the air,
> crosses like a whirlwind,
> past the encampment;
> on the lush grasslands
> awaiting daybreak, settled
> in its tranquil sleep,
> and continues its rush past.

In Part 11 of "La cautiva," however, in "El festín," he presents savage portraits of the Indians as bloodthirsty vampires:

> En torno al fuego sentados
> unos lo atizan y ceban;
> . . .
> como sedientes vampiros
> sorben, chupan, saborean

la sangre haciendo murmullo
y de sangre se rellenan.

(68–69)

Seated around the fire
some stir the fire and eat;
. . .
like thirsty vampires
they suck, swallow, and savor
the blood making a ripple
and they gorge themselves with blood.

Later Argentine poets, in particular José Hernández in his gaucho epic *Martín Fierro* (1872) and *La vuelta de Martín Fierro* (1879), writing in the midst of the "Campaña del desierto" [Desert Campaign] to eradicate the Indians, shows them as cruel and bloodthirsty:

Hacían el robo a su gusto
y después se iban de arriba,
se llevaban las cautivas
y nos contaban que a veces
les descarnaban los pieses,
a las pobrecitas, vivas.

(105)

They robbed at their pleasure
and would then take off,
taking the captives with them
and they told us that they sometimes
would pull the flesh off
the little victims while they were still alive.

Martín Fierro is part of an extensive tradition of gauchesque literature, initiated by Bartolomé Hidalgo (1788–1822) and including *Fausto* (1866) by Estanislao del Campo (1834–1880), *Los tres gauchos orientales* [The Three Gauchos from the East] by Antonio Lussich (1848–1928), as well as novels by Eduardo Gutiérrez (1851–1889) such as *Juan Moreira* (1880). Brazil also, though to a lesser extent, produced a gauchesque literature, including José Martiniano de Alencar's (1829–1877) novel *O gaucho* [1870; The Gaucho] and poems by Mucio Scevola Lopes Teixeira (1858–1926).

Juan Zorrilla de San Martín's *Tabaré* (1888) is a particularly striking case of the Indianist poetic narrative that served as a foundational national text for Uruguay. Widely acclaimed in its time, *Tabaré* evokes a nostalgic portrait of a *mestizo* survivor who must disappear in the face of Western civilization. Notable for its combination of romanticized legend and narrative of "progress and civilization," it has become canonized as a symbol of Uruguayan nationality, although most indigenist traces were erased from the country. In a literary sense it is also remarkable. Its publication coincided with Rubén Darío's *Azul*, the volume that marks a watershed in poetry in Spanish. The publication of *Azul* effectively limits the possibility of Zorrilla's Romantic type of poetic national narrative. Most subsequent writers will only approach the long narrative poem with irony or subversive intent, such as in Vicente Huidobro's (1893–1948) *Altazor* [1930; Altazor, or A Voyage in a Parachute]. Darío's presence marks the end of an era, and his work is a bridge between the two centuries. In the words of Jorge Luis Borges (1899–1986), "Todo lo renovó Darío: la materia, el vocabulario, la métrica, la magia peculiar de ciertas palabras, la sensibilidad del poeta y de sus lectores. Su labor no ha ni cesará. Quienes alguna vez lo combatimos comprendemos hoy que lo continuamos. Lo podemos llamar el libertador" (qtd. in Cobo Borda 17) ("Darío renewed everything: the content, the vocabulary, the meter, the particular magic of certain words, the sensitivity of the poet and his readers. His work has not ended and will not end. Those of us who at times fought him, today understand that we continue his work. We can call him the liberator").

The Other America

The United States presents an important comparative case in dealing with the "newness" of national states, and Rubén Darío's work traces the changes in the reception of U.S. political and literary influences. Like his predecessors, the young Darío celebrated important writers like Ernest Wadsworth Longfellow (1845–1921) and Walt Whitman (1819–1892). As the century drew to a close, Darío, like many of his fellow Latin Americans, expressed rejection of U.S. expansionist aims (particularly after 1898), famously expressed in his "Salutación al Aguila" [1905; "Salutation to the Eagle"]. José Enrique Rodó's (1871–1917) *Ariel* (1900), with its characterization of the United States as a materialistic "Caliban," influenced Latin American thought for many decades. Yet earlier, especially after independence, many Latin Americans, particularly Sarmiento in Argentina, identified with the United States; José María de Heredia, for example, dedicated a long celebratory poem to Washington. Like Latin America, the United States was engaged in its own problems of internal stability, expansionism, technological modernization, and attempts to define national culture under a coherent symbolic assemblage. Civil wars, abolitionist struggles, and, at least in some regions, warfare against indigenous groups presented other similarities. Nonetheless, representation of an Indian past took very different paths in many regions, especially in Mexico, Central America, and the Andean region, where large populations of indigenous peoples and cultures were suppressed rather than exterminated.

Despite the indifference with which his work is regarded today, Longfellow was a towering literary figure in his time, and his popularity is evidence of the prominence of a poetry, especially the long dramatic poem, less cultivated today. His works were translated into Spanish by such eminent writers as Bartolomé Mitre (1821–1906), Rafael María Merchán (1844–1905), the Chilean Carlos Morla Vicuña (1846–1901), and the Mexican Joaquín Casasús (1858–1916). Longfellow himself translated and adapted numerous works from Spanish, as well as from a variety of other languages. His "Song of Hiawatha" (1855) was modeled on the Finnish epic *Kalevala* and, like "The Courtship of Miles Standish," is an extensive poem combining some of the same impulses of landscape presentation, dramatic monologue, and epic impulse common in that period in Latin America. With "Hiawatha," the utopian vision of the Indian is hardly interrupted by the arrival of the "'Pale-Face," and Hiawatha moves west of his own will, called by unseen forces, rather than in the forced westward march known as the Trail of Tears.

It is hard to underestimate the importance of Edgar Allan Poe (1809–1849) to Latin American literature, both in poetry and in prose. The Venezuelan poet Juan Antonio Pérez Bonalde (1846–1892), who influenced a whole generation of poets through his incorporations of poetry in other languages, translated Poe's work, as well as that of Heine (Picón-Salas 119–20). Although much of Poe's importance is attributed to his being championed in France, especially by Baudelaire, Poe's own criticisms of Longfellow are revealing. They can illustrate why Poe was important for Latin Americans, especially the *modernistas,* who had tired of heroic nationalism and Romantic grandiloquence. In his "Longfellow and Other Plagiarists," Poe attacks his borrowings and adaptations from other cultures. Poe's vehement denunciation of colonial influence ("We have snapped asunder the leading-strings of our British Grandmama") and his assertion of the necessity of a literature grounded in the New World, and not built upon European versions of America, can explain his extraordinary influence among other "new" cultures.

While U.S. readers hold Poe in less reverence than his French and Latin American readers, his work nonetheless helped to change the course of literature around the world. An unorthodox critique by the poet William Carlos Williams (1883–1963) in 1925 can help to explain his extraordinary influence: "Poe gives the sense for the first time in America that literature is *serious,* not a matter of courtesy but of truth" (216). Despite the absence of specifically American settings in his work, Poe, for Williams, is to be the true American genius: "It is NOT culture to *oppress* a novel environment with the stale, if symmetrical, castoffs of another battle. . . . Poe could look at France, Spain, Greece and NOT be impelled to copy. He could do this BECAUSE he had the sense within him of a locality of his own, capable of cultivation. . . . He was–the first to realize that the hard, sardonic, truculent mass of the New World, hot, angry–was, in fact, not a thing to pain over, to smear, to destroy–for it WOULD not be destroyed, it was too powerful,–it smiled" (225).

Andrés Bello (1781–1865), as writer and statesman, is the paradigmatic forerunner of several generations of writers in the new nations. In "Alocución a la poesía" [1823; "Allocution to Poetry"] of his *Silvas americanas,* Bello, a great intellectual force in the first half of the nineteenth century in Latin America, apostrophizes "Divina Poesía" ["Divine Poetry"] to abandon Europe and turn its face toward America:

tiempo es que dejes ya la culta Europa,
que tu nativa rustiquez desama,
y dirijas al vuelo adonde te abre
el mundo de Colón su grande escena.

(in Carilla 1979a, 40)

it is time for you to leave effete Europe,
no lover of your native rustic charms,
and fly to where Columbus's world
opens its great scene before your eyes.

(Bello 70)

Bello then paints his own American scene in over eight hundred verses, a vast panorama of the natural beauty and fecundity of the land and its people. (See **Figure 3**.) He stressed specific geographic and historical detail, especially of its capital cities and revolutionary heroes, as well as legendary indigenous leaders such as Manco Capac and Moctezuma. His poem maps out an ambitious literary and social program for American writers in justifying local landscapes and history as worthy of the attention of "Divine Poetry." In a similar vein several decades later, Walt Whitman urges poetry to leave behind European attachments in "Song of the Exposition" (1855):

Come Muse migrate from Greece and Ionia,
Cross out please those immensely overpaid accounts,
That matter of Troy and Achilles' wrath, and Aeneas', Odysseus'

wanderings, Place
Placard "Removed" and "To Let" on the rocks of your snowy Parnassus . . .

. . .

For know a better, fresher, busier sphere, a wide, untried domain
Awaits, demands you.

(196)

Just as Bello incorporated into his *Silvas americanas* some of the spirit of the first verse epic in Spanish in America (Alonso Ercilla y Zúñiga's sixteenth-century *La araucana*), so a modern poet, Pablo Neruda, would take up again the challenge of praising the possibilities of Latin America in *Canto General,* his verse epic of 1950, whose initial structure and themes obviously owe much to Bello's inspiration. The continent's most recent history of revolution against Spanish colonialism (still under way in 1823) supplies the backbone of Bello's narrative. Yet his important gesture asks for a change of gaze rather than a profound reworking of literary precepts. To the list of classical heroes ("Regulo, Trasea, Marco Bruto Decio" [55]) he would add the names of American heroes such as "Padilla, honor del nombre casrellano; Caupolican y Cuaicaipuro aitivo" (55) and Lecount–the glories of the heroes of Independence. The inherent contradictions in Bello's argument–the appeal to the new, wrought in classical form–are repeated many times by subsequent writers in Latin America. His claim for a New World poetics and intellectual independence is presented through precepts inherited from his classical education, more specifically, in the "silvas" preferred in Spanish neo-Classicism.

Figure 3.

Drawing by W. Kuhnert of a young Indian woman in "De la poésia y elocuencia del las tribus de América" in La literatura de mayo *(Buenos Aires, 1871) by Juan MaríaGutiérrez. (Courtesy of the John P. Robarts Research Library, University of Toronto)*

For Bello the poet is to be the painter of this young world:

Si tus colores los más ricos mueles
y tomas el mejor de tus pinceles,
podrás los climas retratar, que entero
el vigor guardan genital primero
con que la voz omnipotente, oída
del hondo caos, hinchió la tierra, apenas
sobre su informe faz aparecida,
y de verdura la cubrió y de vida.

   (in Carilla 1979a, 43)

If you prepare your richest colors,
if you take up your best of brushes,
you can paint climes that keep entire
their old primordial vigor at the time
when God's omnipotent voice,
heard in the abyss of chaos,
swelled the earth, newly created
out of the void, and covered it with verdure
and with life.

   (Bello 11)

Abundant references to the extraordinary vegetation of the continent make clear that these lands can claim to be more closely related to Eden or Utopia ("América, del Sol joven esposa" [41] ["America, young wife of the sun"]) than to the worn-out and decrepit Europe.

Bello's trope of Europe as exhausted or corrupt found wide currency in manifestos of the American spirit, where it is compared with the fresher (female) spirit embodied as America, the sun's "joven esposa" in Bello's poem or the "virgin lands" of countless writers. Antonio de Castro Alves (1847–1871) later in the century paints an even more politically charged picture of Europe as degenerate. The old continent is corrupt and seductive, and the promoter of African slavery:

Europa—e sempre Europa, a gloriosa!...
A mullier deslumbrante e caprichosa,
   Rainha e cortezã.
Artista—corta o marmor de Carrara;
Poetisa—tange os hymn os de Ferrara.
No glorioso afan! . . .
   . . .
O Universo apos elle—doudo amante
Segue captivo o passo delirante
Da grande meretriz.

   (2–4)

Europe—is always Europe, the glorious one! . . .
The seductive and willful woman,
   A queen and courtesan.
Artist—cut[s] the marble of Carrara;
Poet—strum[s] the hymns of Ferrara,
Toiling for her glory!
   . . .
The Universe pursues her—an excited lover
Captive to the dizzying steps
Of the noble whore.

His piercing rebuke to Europe lays bare the economic and social systems, undergirded by the slave trade, that allowed economic and cultural domination from afar.

In Brazil, shortly after Bello wrote his *Silvas*, José Gonçalves de Magalhães (1811–1882), known as Romanticism's first exponent in Brazil, mocks the pretensions of his compatriots in his *Ensaio* of 1836: "La poesía de Brasil no es una india civilizada, es una griega vestida a la francesa y a la portuguesa y aclimatada en el Brasil; . . . los poetas brasileños . . . olvidaron las sencillas imágenes que una naturaleza virgen les ofrecía tan profusamente" (in Carilla 1979b, xxxiv) ("Brazilian poetry is not a civilized Indian, she is a Greek woman dressed in Spanish and Portuguese fashion and acclimatized to Brazil; . . . Brazilian poets . . . have forgotten the simple images that virgin nature offered them so profusely"). No one understood as well as Bello the importance of language in setting the foundations of the new nations, and as educator, statesman, poet, journalist, linguist, and jurist, he was critical in bridging old and new traditions within the public ideals of his time, both in his adopted Chile and in the rest of Latin America (Jáksic xxviii). For educated men of his time, "Liberty . . . had been absorbed by writing and was impossible without it" (Rama 43); thus education and respect for literacy were major projects of the new nations.

Although Bello's poem shows the marks of Rousseau's ideal of nature or Romantic calls to nationhood, its evocation of American energies envisions orderly channels for the development of nature and new citizens. This New World, then, is not to be a radical break with European tradition, but instead will incorporate the vast diversity of nature and peoples within a framework forged by its enlightened citizens. Poetry, as one of the most elevated arts, can channel and mold these natural energies by elevating and educating its audience. Yet, just as the calling forth of untamed natural forces seems to strain the bounds of his long poem, giving a surplus energy to the contained expression, so other writers would seek to celebrate and also to subvert the very traditions they inherited, crafting new forms to consolidate consensus and to suggest alternative visions. Writers like Bello were aware of the possible power granted to poetry. His praise of patriots, some of whom became Bolívar's enemies, and his less-than-effusive praise of the "Libertador" apparently cost him the appointment he desired in the new government of Colombia, leaving him to accept the position offered in Chile, where he would spend the rest of his life (Cussen 140–41). Literature and writing, although not always explicitly tied to state power, nonetheless were closely linked to those who exercised power during most of the century (Ramos 1989). Bello, who advocated the primacy of Spanish over Latin in formal education, and who dedicated enormous energies to the task of defining American Spanish, nonetheless witnessed the "disintegration of the classical model of empire and culture" with nostalgia, as one exiled from the ancient empires (Cussen 177).

Literary Institutions

The first poetic anthologies of the new nations appeared early on, partly inspired by Enlightenment interests in classification, and partly as a sign of national or regional cultural independence. In Brazil, in 1831 Januario da Cunha Barbosa (1780–1846) published *Parnaso brasileiro* [Brazilian Parnassus]. Two early collections were *La lira argentina* [1824; Argentine Lyre] and *El Parnaso oriental* [1835–1837; Parnussus of the Banda Oriental (Uruguay)]. Juan María Gutiérrez (1809–1878), famous as a cultural historian and also as poet of the gauchos and of idealized portraits of the Indians ("Iruperya, Caicobe," "Las flores del Lipu"), compiled a systematic anthology of Spanish American poetry in the nineteenth century, *América poética* [1846; Poetic America]. Gutiérrez also wrote extensively about colonial poetry and reprinted many such works. In his essay "La literatura de Mayo" ["Literature of May"], Gutiérrez is very emphatic about the absence in the Rio de la Plata of the baleful influences of popular poetry: "El Rio de la Plata carecía de poesía popular y no estaba habituado, como lo estaban Méjico y el Perú, a la villana degradación de la musa. Los europeos no encontraron entre nosotros el pábulo que ofrecen a la sensualidad de las razas esclavizadas y serviles" (1941, 7) ("The Rio de la Plata lacked popular poetry and was not accustomed, like Mexico and Peru, to the rustic degradation of the muse. The Europeans did not find among us the encouragement which the sensuality of the enslaved and servile races had to offer").

Later anthologies often stressed regional or thematic links, such as *Lira americana: Colección de poesías de los mejores poetas del Peru, Chile y Bolivia* [American Lyre: Collection of Poems of the Best Poets from Perú, Chile and Bolivia], edited in 1865 by Ricardo Palma (1833–1919). Later in the century, as anthologies proliferated and traditions of national literatures became established, nearly all countries established national academies to maintain linguistic unity; these were, with the exception of Argentina and Brazil, directly linked to the Spanish Royal Academy (Rama 59–60). Most successful was the Colombian academy, founded by Miguel Antonio Caro (1843–1909), the essayist, classicist, and poet who became president of his country (Rama 60).

Landscape of Modernity

The second half of the nineteenth century saw massive though uneven changes in Latin America. Tragic wars, like the War of the Triple Alliance (against Paraguay) in 1865–1870, which devastated the population of young males, and the War of the Pacific in 1879–1884, in which both Bolivia and Peru lost territory to Chile, showed that the ideals of Latin American unity were far distant. Caudillism and Liberalism shared places in many national capitals. In countries such as Argentina, Brazil, and Mexico, the last decades of the century witnessed extraordinary technological advances, at least in urban areas. Railroads facilitated commerce and migration. In the Mexico of Porfirio Díaz, who ruled from 1876 to 1911, technology and science were exalted, to the extent that his closest advisers were called "Los Científicos" ["The Scientists"]. Cities such as Buenos Aires and São Paulo, late in the century, swelled by new immigrants, became economic powers and true urban centers. With immigration and uneven urbanization came new political influences, such as anarchism and socialism from southern Europe. Notwithstanding new political and social movements, the goals of Positivism, based on progress, order, and scientific and medical achievement, dominated social policy and legal systems, with scientific racism incorporated into government doctrines.

Education had created new classes of readers and writers; in some areas a professional middle class (many of the *modernista* writers came from this class, especially in Mexico and the Southern Cone). Writers were not always statesmen, and increasingly they were not always men. From the beginnings of the periodical press in Latin America, women had been involved in writing and publishing, although on a limited scale. Important female writers in the nineteenth century included Gómez de Avellaneda (1814–1873), Clorinda Matto de Turner (1852–1909), Juana Manuela Gorriti (1816–1892), Juana Manso (1819–1875), Adela Zamudio (Bolivia 1854–1928), and lesser-known poets such as Dolores Veintimilla de Galindo (Ecuador 1830–1857) and Laura Méndez de Cuenca (Mexico 1853–1928), among many others. Writers such as Gorriti established important literary salons and literary journals. Exiled from her native Argentina, she moved to Bolivia and then to Peru. In Lima she initiated *El Album* with

Carolina Freire de Jaimes (1844–1916) and founded *La Alborada* with the poet Numa Pompilio Llona (1832–1907), and later in Argentina established *La Alborada del Plata*. Particularly important were the literary salons, "Veladas Literarias" (1876–1877), she organized in Lima, which included writers such as Mercedes Cabello de Carbonera (1845–1909), Ricardo Palma (1833–1919), and Carolina Freire de Jaimes, and gave a public space to new groups. In the words of one of her contemporaries, Alejandro Cerdena: "Pero faltaba en el seno de nuestra sociedad un círculo literario donde la mujer, ser privilegiado por la naturaleza, hallara abierto el campo de sus aspiraciones a ilustrar su entendimiento por medio del estudio de las ciencias y de la literatura" (in Gorriti 319) ("There was an absence at the heart of our society of a literary circle where women, being so privileged by nature, would be able to find a place to pursue their aspirations and enlighten their understanding through the study of the sciences and literature"). A number of these women writers conducted intense drives for women's rights. For example, Juana Manso is known as the architect of many of Sarmiento's programs for women's education (see Garrels). Zamudio, an autodidact, herself was a member of a growing class of literate women who had been trained as schoolteachers. Her poem "Nacer hombre" ["Born Male"] reflects frustration over the limits of citizenship: "Con tal que aprenda a firmar/puede votar un idiota,/¡Porque es un hombre!" (Flores and Flores 124) ("As long as he can learn to sign his name/even an idiot can vote/because he is a man!").

The emergence of more women in the public sphere is related to the heightened emphasis on the female body in *modernista* poetry. Anxieties about women's expanded visibility and changing public roles showed up in the uneasy representation of the female in turn-of-the-century literature. The iconic presentation of the female figure as an image prized for its possession, status, and above all, rich possibilities was subverted by an increased attention to the dangers of eroticism. *Modernista* poetry is filled with images of femmes fatales who show late-nineteenth-century society's obsessive preoccupation with the dangers of female sexuality. Increased attention to eroticism accompanies a kind of voyeuristic gaze, which increasingly focuses on a limited and interior space. In contrast to the wide expanses seen in much previous landscape poetry, *modernismo* accentuates interior spaces.

Delmira Agustini (1886–1914) and her poetic production offer a case unimaginable a century earlier. Celebrated widely for her poetry, she was a latecomer to the famous generation of intellectuals called the Uruguayan "Generación del 900," which included Rodó, Julio Herrera y Reissig (1875–1910), Horacio Quiroga (1878–1937), Florencio Sánchez (1875–1910), Javier de Viana (1868–1926), Carlos Vaz Ferreira (1872–1958), and Maria Eugenia Vaz Ferreira (1875–1924). Agustini, like many of her *modernista* contemporaries, focused on eroticism and interiority and employed many of the same images as her contemporaries, but alternated the beautiful with exaggeration and the grotesque. This slippage between the sublime and the monstrous is a constant in much of her poetry. It can be traced in part to a Romantic poetic heritage, but the speaker and the receiver—the nebulous "tú" whom she address so often—are unstable entities, detached signifiers that realign themselves at every turn. History does not exist, except as classical references. There is enough violent physical imagery in Agustini's poetry to confuse any reader searching for certainties, for an informing ideology or aesthetic. Even more memorably, she took the image of the swan, so closely associated with Darío's aesthetics, and stained it (and writing itself) with blood. As Sylvia Molloy has discussed, Agustini turned around Darío's symbolic constructions of beauty and the contemplation of the female form.

Although *modernismo* is striking for its excesses, both in subject matter and form, its innovations clearly marked a major change in the role literature, especially poetry, would play in public life. A self-consciousness about the need for revolutionary change, whether understood as political or literary, marked most turn-of-the-century writers. The movement of poetic *modernismo* has often been characterized as an escapist tendency, although Octavio Paz has qualified this "evasión de la realidad americana. Mas cierto sería decir que fue una fuga de la actualidad local . . . en busca de una actualidad universal, la única y verdadera actualidad" (1969, 9) ("evasion of the Latin American reality. It would be more accurate to say that it was a flight from the local present reality . . . in search of a universal present-day reality, the one true reality"). While recent readers of *modernista* poetry have come to no agreement about what constitutes a universal reality in poetic terms, most have come to accept that all interpretations of *modernismo* are inherently paradoxical. Highly attentive to poetic experimentation, especially in the French tradition, they understood possibilities of the incorporative impulse. Writers like Martí, Darío, Julián del Casal, José Asunción Silva (1865–1896), Manuel Gutiérrez Nájera (1859–1895), Leopoldo Lugones (1874–1938), Julio Herrera y Reissig (1875–1910), and Delmira Agustini showed their creative dexterity in assimilating a wide range of poetic styles, sometimes simultaneously. Notable innovators, like Martí and Darío, have marked the poetry of the twentieth century as well by their insistence on the renewal of form—in the case of Martí by the reintroduction of the popular octosyllablic line in serious poetry, and in Darío's case by attention to musicality, rhythm, and the renewal of forgotten verse forms. These writers were clearly in dialogue with Europe and the United States and forced a reassessment of common cultural values. Recent critics like Gerard Aching have stressed the historical importance of the *modernista* writers who, by "presenting their readers with postcolonial, hyper-real versions and European culture and traditions . . . [,] were the first to create a collectively derived discursive space of Spanish American cultural identity" (159). An important element in this discursive space is the substitution of a "spiritual community" of Latin America for a political one. While some *modernista* writers, such as Martí and Manuel González Prada, were notable political figures, the majority of these writers were peripheral to the centers of power. While writers could reach a much broader public than those earlier in the century, the dream of poetry as a useful public tool was severely reduced.

Rapidity of communication and technological change is praised and lamented by writers like Martí, Gutiérrez Nájera, Darío, Lugones, and Díaz Rodríguez. In "Amor de ciudad grande" ["Love of the Large City"] Martí mourns the loss of innocence in the face of urban life (his model is New York), while Lugones writes ecstatically in 1899 of the railroad ("gran caballo negro al cual no se ve sudar" [99] ["huge black horse whose sweat cannot be seen"]). *Modernismo*, contemporary with the rise of Naturalistic fiction in Latin America, also shares Naturalism's emphasis on the body and on the underside of the apparently beautiful. These sometimes contradictory aesthetics are joined in the poems and stories of Darío's *Azul* (1888). It is

primarily at the beginning of the twentieth century that technology begins to be overtly questioned in literary discourse. Rodó's *Ariel*, as previously discussed, gave usable imagery–Ariel and Caliban–around which to mold opinion concerning the onrush of technology and the increasingly powerful United States. *Modernista* writers ended the earlier preference for long narrative poems, landscape poetry related to history and heroics, and the very notion of poetry as a more public genre. Lugones's *Lunario sentimental* [1909; Sentimental Lunar Cycle], with its parodic introduction of the urban middle class as part of the poetic landscape, as well as its motley assembly of shopworn mythic figures, is a self-conscious farewell to a vision of poetry–and the poet–as a major public force. In addition, led by innovations like free verse and Darío's introduction of archaic verse forms and emphasis on musicality, the very backbone of poetic discourse had changed.

By the second decade of the twentieth century, *modernismo* as a poetic style was devalued, and young writers like César Vallejo, Pablo Neruda, Vicente Huidobro, Ramón López Velarde (1888–1921), Gabriela Mistral (1889–1957), Oliverio Girondo (1891–1967), and Jorge Luis Borges were changing again the nature of poetic language in Spanish–most indelibly by Vallejo and Huidobro. Even less unity could be found among the impulses, themes, and styles of the new generation. Poetry as a genre of public resonance disappeared, or at least was greatly diminished. Yet the difficulties of sorting out tendencies in Latin American poetry in the early decades of the twentieth century–vanguardist experimentation exists alongside, and even includes, regional evocation–should not lead us to dismiss its impact in the larger cultural sphere. Although poetry survived less as a celebratory, expansive genre and more as a private, "hand to mouth" force, to use Walcott's terms, the slippages between poetry and prose point up poetry's changed functions. If literature does indeed have a public presence in the twentieth century, it is unquestionably through the novel, but the novel as a form that has inherited some of poetry's other functions: the wide sweep of historical representation, the epic force of heroes and nations, and the evocation of natural space. But the reintroduction of political poetry, especially with the Spanish Civil War (1936–1939), sparked anew the dream of poetry as a public medium. Neruda, Vallejo, and Nicolás Guillén (1902–1989), among others, wrote books of poetry united by the narrative of a political struggle. Later, major poets like Neruda, Cabral de Melo Neto, and Mistral return to the long narrative poem, often informed by landscape continuities, to tell new stories for the twentieth century. Even in mid-century, Neruda and Cabral de Melo Neto venture forth with extensive narrative poems, *Canto General* and *Morte e vida severina*, which recover many of poetry's most ancient functions, such as prophecy, social denunciation, mythic scope, and landscapes filled with natural beauties and human sorrows. Returning to ancient forms such as the epic and the *auto natal*, but with contemporary preoccupations, these works illustrate possibilities of reclaiming for poetry its resonance as a forceful public medium.

Works Cited

Aching, Gerard. 1997. *The Politics of Spanish American Modernismo: By Exquisite Design.* Cambridge: Cambridge University Press.

Alves, Antonio de Castro. 1990. *The Major Abolitionist Poems.* Ed. and trans. Amy A. Peterson. New York: Garland.

Appiah, Kwame Anthony. 1990. "Race." *Critical Terms for Literary Study*. Ed. Frank Lentricchia and T. McLaughlin. Chicago: University of Chicago Press. 274–87.

Auerbach, Erich. 1953. *Mimesis: The Representation of Reality in Western Literature*. Trans. Willard R. Trask. Princeton, NJ: Princeton University Press.

Bakhtin, Mikhail. 1981. *The Dialogic Imagination: Four Essays*. Trans. Caryl Emerson and Michael Holquist. Austin: University of Texas Press.

Balbuena, Bernardo de. 1941. *Grandeza mexicana y fragmentos del Siglo de Oro y El Bernardo*. Ed. Francisco Monterde. Mexico City: Universidad Nacional Autónoma de México.

Balderston, Daniel. 1996.*¿Fuera de contexto? Referencialidad histórica y expresión de la realidad en Borges*. Buenos Aires: Beatriz Viterbo Editora.

Bello, Andrés. 1997. *Selected Writings*. Ed. Iván Jáksic. Trans. Frances M. López-Morillas. New York: Oxford University Press.

Bernstein, Michael Andre. 1980. *Tales of the Tribe*. Princeton, NJ: Princeton University Press.

Brading, D. A. 1985. *The Origins of Mexican Nationalism*. Cambridge: Centre of Latin American Studies.

Brecht, Bertolt. 1983. *Mother Courage and Her Children*. Trans. John Willet. London: Methuen.

Cabral de Melo Neto, João. 1968. *Morte e severina, e outros poemas em voz alta*. Rio de Janeiro: Sabiá.

Cândido, António. 1993. *Recortes*. São Paulo: Companhia das Letras.

Carilla, Emilio, ed. 1979a. *Poesía de la independencia*. Caracas: Biblioteca Ayacucho.

——. 1979b. "Prólogo." *Poesía de la independencia*. Ed. Emilio Carilla. Caracas: Biblioteca Ayacucho. ix–xxxv.

Cobo Borda, Juan Gustavo. 1985. *Antología de la poesía hispanoamericana*. 1st ed. Mexico City: Fondo de Cultura Económica.

Cussen, Anthony. 1992. *Bello and Bolívar: Poetry and Poetics in the Spanish American Revolution*. Cambridge: Cambridge University Press.

Darío, Rubén. 1977. "Nocturno." *Rubén Darío: Poesía*. Ed. Ernesto Mejía Sánchez. Caracas: Biblioteca Ayacucho. 270.

——. 1977. "Prosas profanas y otros poemas [1896–1901]." *Rubén Darío: Poesía*. Ed. Ernesto Mejía Sánchez. Caracas: Biblioteca Ayacucho. 179–241.

Echeverría, Esteban. 1991. *Obras escogidas*. Ed. Beatriz Sarlo and Carlos Altamirano. Caracas: Biblioteca Ayacucho.

Ercilla y Zuñiga, Alonso de. 1803. *La Araucana*. 2 vols. Madrid: Imp. De Mateo Repullés.

Flores, Angel, and Kate Flores. 1984. *Poesía feminista del mundo hispánico*. Mexico City: Siglo Veintiuno Editores.

Garrels, Elizabeth. 1994. "Sarmiento and the Woman Question: From 1839 to the *Facundo*." *Sarmiento: Author of a Nation*. Ed. T. Halperín-Donghi, Ivan Jaksic, Gwen Kirkpatrick, and Francine Masiello. Berkeley: University of California Press. 272–93.

Geertz, Clifford. 1973. *The Interpretation of Cultures*. New York: Basic Books.

Gorriti, Juana Manuela. 1892. *Veladas literarias de Lima, 1876–1877*. Vol. I. Buenos Aires: Imprenta Europea.

Greenberg, Janet. 1986. "The Divided Self: Forms of Autobiography in the Writing of Victoria Ocampo." Diss. University of California, Berkeley.

Gutiérrez, Juan María. 1846. *América poética: Colección escogida de composiciones en verso*. Valparaíso: Imprenta del Mercurio.

Gutiérrez, Juan María. 1979 [1871]. *La literatura de Mayo y otras páginas críticas*. Ed. Beatriz Sarlo. Buenos Aires: Centro Editor de América Latina.

——. 1941. *Los poetas de la revolución*. Buenos Aires: Academia Argentina de Letras.

Halperín-Donghi, Tulio. 1993. "Hispanoamérica en el espejo. (Reflexiones hispanoamericanas sobre Hispanoamérica, de Simón Bolívar a Hernando de Soto)." *Historia Mexicana* 42.3: 745–87.

Henríquez Ureña, Pedro.1949. *Las corrientes literarias en la América hispánica*. Mexico City: Fondo de Cultura Económica.

——. 1978. *La utopía de América*. Caracas: Biblioteca Ayacucho.

Heredia, José María. 1945. "El teocalli de Cholula." *Antología herediana: Selección de las mejores poesías líricas. Los últimos romanos de José María Heredia*. Ed. Emilio Valdés y de Latorre. Montevideo: C. García. 80–85.

Hernández, José. 1917. *Martín Fierro: La vuelta de Martín Fierro*. 3rd ed. Buenos Aires: La Cultura Argentina.

——. 1972. *Martín Fierro*. Ed. Emilio Carilla. Barcelona: Editorial Labor.

Humboldt, Alexander von, and Aimé Bonpland. 1941–1942 [1799–1804]. *Viaje a las regiones equinocciales del nuevo continente*. Trans. Lisandro Alvarado, Eduardo Rohl, and José Nucete-Sardi. 5 Vols. Caracas: Ediciones del Ministerio de educación nacional.

Iglesia, Cristina, and Julio Schvarztman. 1987. *Cautivos y misioneros: Mitos blancos de la conquista*. Buenos Aires: Catálogos Editora.

Jáksic, Iván. 1997. "Introduction." *Selected Writings of Andrés Bello*. Ed. Iván Jáksic. Trans. Frances M. López-Morillas. New York: Oxford University Press. i–lvi.

Lezama Lima, José. 1969. "Sumas críticas del americano." *La expresión americana y otros ensayos*. Montevideo: Arca. 96–116.

Lienhard, Martín. 1992. *La voz y su huella: Escritura y conflicto étnico-cultural en América Latina, 1492–1988*. Lima: Editorial Horizonte.

Longfellow, Henry Wadsworth. 1875. *The Poetical Works*. Boston: James R. Osgood & Co.

Lukacs, George. 1983. *The Historical Novel*. Trans. Hannah and Stanley Mitchell. Lincoln: University of Nebraska Press.

Manzano, Juan Francisco. 1991. *Poesías de J. F. Manzano, esclavo en la isla de Cuba*. Ed. Adriana Lewis Galanes. Madrid: Editorial Betania.

Martí, José. 1970. *Versos libres*. Ed. Ivan A. Schulman. Barcelona: Editorial Labor.

Masiello, Francine. 1992. *Between Civilization and Barbarism*. Lincoln: University of Nebraska Press.

——, ed. 1994. *La mujer y el espacio público: El periodismo femenino en la Argentina del siglo XIX*. Buenos Aires: Feminaria.

Massey, Doreen. 1994. *Space, Place and Gender*. Minneapolis: University of Minnesota Press.

Melgar, Mariano. 1975. *Antología poética*. Ed. Antonio Cornejo-Polar. Lima: Editorial Universo.

Mitchell, W. J. T. 1994. "Imperial Landscape." *Landscape and Power*. Ed. W. J. T. Mitchell. Chicago and London: University of Chicago Press. 5–34.

Molloy, Sylvia. 1991. *At Face Value: Autobiographical Writing in Spanish America*. New York: Cambridge University Press.

Neruda, Pablo. 1990. *Canto General*. Ed. Enrico Mario Santi. Madrid: Cátedra.

Olmedo, José Joaquín. 1960. "La victoria de Junín: Canto a Bolívar." *José Joaquín Olmedo: Poesía, Prosa*. Puebla, Mexico City: Editorial J. M. Cajica Jr. S. A. 101–36.

Paz, Octavio. 1969. *Cuadrivio*. Mexico City: Joaquín Mortiz.

Perelman, Bob. 1996. *The Marginalization of Poetry*. Princeton, NJ: Princeton University Press.

Picón-Salas, Mariano. 1984. *Formación y proceso de la literatura venezolana*. Caracas: Monte Avila.

Pratt, Mary Louise. 1992. *Imperial Eyes: Travel Writing and Transculturation*. London and New York: Routledge.

Quint, Eric. 1993. *Epic and Empire*. Princeton, NJ: Princeton University Press.

Rama, Angel. 1996. *The Lettered City.* Trans. John Charles Chastain. Durham, NC: Duke University Press.

Ramos, Julio. 1989. *Desencuentros de la modernidad en América Latina.* Mexico City: Fondo de Cultura Económica.

——. 1994. "La ley es otra: Literatura y constitución del sujeto jurídico María Antonia Mandinga en el archivo de la ley." *Esplendores y miserías del siglo XIX: Cultura y sociedad en América Latina.* Ed. Beatriz González-Stephan et al. Caracas: Monte Avila. 193–215.

Rodríguez Monegal, Emir, ed. 1984. *The Borzoi Anthology of Latin American Literature from the Time of Columbus to the Twentieth Century.* Vol. I. New York: Alfred A. Knopf.

Schama, Simon. 1996. *Landscape and Memory.* New York: Vintage Books.

Schwarz, Roberto. 1987. *Que horas são?: Ensaios.* São Paulo: Companhia das Letras.

Seluja Cecín, Antonio. 1984. "Estudio preliminar." *Tabaré.* Montevideo: Universidad de la República. 12–90.

Sussekind, Flora. 1990. *O Brasil não é longe daqui: O narrador, a viagem.* São Paulo: Companhia das Letras.

Vallejo, César. 1954. *El romanticismo en la poesía castellana.* Lima: Juan Mejía Baca & P. L. Villanueva Editores.

——. 1991. *Trilce.* Madrid: Cátedra.

Walcott, Derek. 1986. *Collected Poems 1948–1984.* New York: Noonday P; Farrar, Straus & Giroux.

Whitman, Walt. 1965. *Leaves of Grass.* New York: Norton.

Williams, William Carlos. 1956 [1925]. *In the American Grain.* New York: New Directions.

Zaid, Gabriel, ed. 1982. *Omnibus de poesía mexicana, siglos XIV a XX.* 9th ed. Mexico City: Siglo XXI.

——. 1986. *Omnibus de poesía mexicana, siglos XIV a XX.* 12th ed. Mexico City: Siglo XXI.

Zorrilla de San Martín, Juan. 1984. *Tabaré.* Ed. Antonio Seluja Cecín. Montevideo: Universidad de la República.

CHAPTER 22

AN EMERGING POETRY

Noé Jitrik

After all the reflection on the matter, at times steeped in skepticism, at others in rapturous enthusiasm, there can be no doubt that *modernismo* constituted a decisive inflection in Latin American poetry. The fact that it would be proclaimed at virtually the end of the nineteenth century, produce in those early years the most representative and influential works of what might be considered its repertoire, and only assert itself as a dominant cultural force shortly after the beginning of the twentieth century—confers on modernismo its markedly transitional quality. In some sense modernismo takes the form of a vehicle passing from one era to another.

By 1900, Latin American countries had already changed markedly from their colonial past, and, in particular, those having undergone the most dramatic changes were Mexico, Argentina, Peru, Colombia, Cuba, Uruguay, Nicaragua, and Chile. Although there were differences in the rates of change and degrees of conviction, all were at the doorstep of modernity: aspiring to define their own cultural structures as if they were the peers of the metropolitan nations, experiencing the euphoria afforded by the proliferation of raw materials and, of course, the bewilderment generated by the immense wealth of the few who, intoxicated with fantasies of possession, attempted to and succeeded in modifying the outward appearance of what were to become great cities. Very few had the prescience to realize that such an entrance to modernity (and by such means) would demand a cost so exorbitant that almost none of these countries would be able to pay the price—for many decades.

However, now is not the time to assess such transitions, however important they may be, or the role that poetry may have played in assisting them in specific ways, or whether it was, as some critics have maintained somewhat accusingly, a symbolic contributor to sociopolitical projects, or even whether it constituted, on the contrary, a space of resistance against precisely such projects. In any event, what is known is that whatever inspirational effect poetry may have had on society, it has never had pragmatic—direct and immediate—consequences. In the worst cases, it has been the explicit accessory of a social process, conscientious and obliging, celebratory and reverential; in the best of cases, and this may be one reading of modernismo, it has constituted a homologous system, apparently autonomous but in fact subjected to the demands of the sociopolitical structure or a product of it. Our interpretation of modernismo only partly shares this view: Tempering these views, it appears to us that modernismo's central premise of innovation actually designs a kind of model, albeit virtual, of the possibility of reorienting the productive system of society as a whole. A semiotic gloss of its components, which some call aesthetic—for example, the idea of the serial and quasi-systematic production of poems (which does not exclude significant individual or stylistic aspects)—could furnish, by contrast, the image of an economic system of industrial proportions. This would be a system differently organized from the dominant one, and very far advanced from the ruralism that still occupied the entire economic and mental space at the beginning of the twentieth century and

upon whose returns the land-owning classes erected their ostentatious (and only in this respect modernizing) caprices.

Any sensible approach to modernismo ought to take this ideal-model dimension into account as well as its imaginary and perfect productive system. Doing so would allow us to distance ourselves from both the simplistic critiques of an obvious and reviled Europeanism and the nebulous criticism of achievements, and thus to clear the air of the figurative incense that is still burned whenever great poetry is discussed. Without ignoring modernismo's interplay with other poetries or its achievements, but rather fixing both in the looking glass of an "incomplete" society, it can perhaps be seen what it was that modernismo glimpsed: the pure image of a perfect society in which every social system would function as brilliantly and as excellently as the poetic one. Since their work was rooted in a formal rigor—considered by many to be *préciosité*, virtuosity or technical play—that previous poetry ignored or disdained, José Martí (1853–1895), Leopoldo Lugones (1874–1938), Manuel Gutiérrez Nájera (1859–1895), and, above all, Rubén Darío (1867–1916) were neither prophets nor precursors but the theoretical practitioners of a highly paradoxical liberation. Earlier poetry, whether Romantic, post-Romantic, epic-lyrical, confessional, or public-private, privileged a vaguely sublime and rhetorically simplistic content that never surpassed the rustic eulogies with which even Rubén Darío began.

Thus, at times drawing from Castilian poetry, at others from the reckless gambles into which European poetry had submerged itself since the middle of the nineteenth century—Parnassianism, Symbolism, Decadence, pre-Raphaelitism—free-verse modernismo stipulates as part of its aesthetics or poetics that the central operation of writing resides in the defining units of the line and the stanza and thus exploits all of their rhythmic and metrical possibilities. Hence, the first paradox: the figure of the poet is that of an artist-inventor and, by virtue of the exquisiteness of his work, also that of an outcast or exile, in part a legatee of bohemian Romanticism and in part as a martyr to the passage of culture into modernity. The paradox is completed when, as was demonstrated by Ramón del Valle Inclán's (1866–1936) *Luces de bohemia* [1920 and 1924; Bohemian Lights] and Manuel Gálvez's (1882–1962) novel *El mal metafísico* [1916; Metaphysical Vice], the poet no longer appears as mere victim but rather as the greatest critic a hypocritical society can have, a society that not only misunderstands art but fails to grasp the extent of its own miseries and limitations.

Further, this extreme rigor, this discipline that at times transforms a referential void or virtual void into an elevated poetic utterance, opens the door to a realm of freedom that subsequent poetry will embrace with a fecundity indicting every attempt at didacticism. So great was the power of the modernist revolution's conviction that, in no time at all, its poetics became absolutely inescapable, tracing a divide from the past in such a way that to write poetry, and to a certain extent prose, without heeding its own dictates implied on the one hand falling into an erroneous anachronism, or on the other hand, falling prey to consecration as living classics. In less that two decades modernismo became academic, and it can be said that, in being taken up by the academy and in gaining acceptance, it accepts in its turn all the rules against which it rose up in revolt. What had been open was now closed; repetition lay in wait; poetry and the ludic spirit became commonplace; those whom modernismo had authorized began to write against it; other theories of poetry began to emerge.

Thus, the key to modernismo resides in the poetic scene itself and in what began to happen once the medley of manifestations that goes by the name of the "modernista movement" authorized and legitimized all manner of new verbal operations. Some prolonged the movement–Enrique Banchs (1888–1968), Julio Herrera y Reissig (1875–1910), and Enrique González Martínez (1871–1952); others refuted or repudiated it–Baldomero Fernández Moreno (1886–1950), Vicente Huidobro (1893–1948), and Jorge Luis Borges (1899–1986); still others reinterpreted it–José Juan Tablada (1871–1945), Leopoldo Lugones (1874–1938), and César Vallejo (1892–1938)–and/or strengthened and developed it–Ezequiel Martínez Estrada (1895–1964) and Ramón López Velarde (1888–1921). But they could not have been understood in their enormous diversity had not this extraordinary irruption taken place earlier. This is how history works: Certain events set others in motion, and only in rare cases are there absolute discontinuities; at most, as we will see when the avant-gardes are invoked, such discontinuities are consciously solicited, thus demonstrating the extent to which continuities prevail.

Hence, every attempt to describe the transformations of poetry in Latin America in the twentieth century must begin with modernismo. Out of it and against it, as we have seen, a process was shaped stretching right up to the present, but whose culminating moment–José Gorostiza's (1901–1973) *Muerte sin fin* [1939; Death Without End] or Pablo Neruda's (1904–1973) *Canto General* (1950), to name but two works– was perhaps witnessed in the 1950s. This is not to imply that thereafter the poetic force languished or that what followed did not have a relevance analogous to the phenomena witnessed between, say, 1900 and 1950. It is merely to state that this decade was overflowing with great names and great works, from Vicente Huidobro (1893–1948) to Alberto Girri (1919–1991), passing by way of Manuel Maples Arce (1898–1981), Luis Palés Matos (1898–1959), Emilio Adolfo Westphalen (1911–2001), Augusto de Campos (b. 1931), José Gorostiza (1901–1973), José Lezama Lima (1910–1976), Jorge Luis Borges (1899–1986), and Joâo Cabral de Melo Neto (1920–1999), to name but a few of the innumerable who could be mentioned.

Two Streams: Consequence and Rupture

Imposing a certain order on the descriptions of the mass of expressions that characterize the poetic process of the twentieth century, we can say that irrupting from modernismo and radiating outward, two streams emerged, comprised of texts like *Versos sencillos* [1891; Plain Poems], *Prosas profanas* [1896 and 1901; Profane Prose], *Los crepúsculos del jardín* [1905; Twilights in the Garden], *Peregrino de piedra* [1914; Stone Pilgrim], "La duquesa Job" [1884; "The Duchess Job"], *"Nocturno"* ["Nocturne"], to cite only the most definitively modernista works: the stream of consequence or, that which, with variations, pursues the poetic lived experience, and the stream, we might call of "ruptures" with its iconoclastic negativity. Every

dualistic schema is dangerous: It implies a confrontation of terms that erases nuances and, therefore, dilutes particularities. This double channeling of outcomes and ruptures, however, by virtue of its vast scope, endeavors to sidestep the hazards and salvage innumerable and interesting differences. To begin with, I will say that it encompasses the four elements to which modernismo apparently gave rise: extension, reinterpretation, refutation, and negation. If we were to examine each one of these, bearing in mind the previous categories, over a trajectory of four or five decades, we could trace a map of the most important aspects of twentieth-century Latin American poetry, and perhaps understand the peculiarity of the positions occupied by its respective representative texts. This would allow us, at the same time, to avoid having to take sides–the somewhat inevitable outcome of adopting the two-stream schema and merely limiting ourselves to ascribing value to one or the other of the currents. If, for example, focusing on the "academicization" of modernismo, we were to examine the poetry of Ramón López Velarde, a writer who unquestionably continued in the vein of modernismo, and were to compare his work with the work of Vicente Huidobro, who repudiated it, we would be left with no other option than to choose Huidobro's work, attributing to it a value that we would be unable to concede to López Velarde's. Such schema are, of course, misleading: For what is at stake is a process that at times can be found in the work of a single poet (for example, in that of César Vallejo, at times) and for the most part, in a larger group, which is to say among poets who, influenced by different and even opposing poetic principles, allow us to understand the relation that is struck between a poet and his times. Oliverio Girondo (1891–1967) is as modern as Xavier Villaurrutia (1903–1950); Pablo Neruda is as much a modern poet as José Lezama Lima, and equally representative.

Whatever the paths we take to describe the process of Latin American poetry during the first half of the twentieth century, taken as a whole it can be said to contain an affirmation of identity, not as a reflection or reproduction of feelings of belonging, nor as a conviction or ideology of identity, but rather as an expression of the ownership, the possession of a particular idiom and a structured language. If we add to this description another register, such as popular poetry, which traces a trajectory parallel to that of cultured, written poetry (the register on which our argument here is based), we are made aware that ownership, possession, or identity also concerns and comprises the dimension of speech: tenancy and title, not in the sense of a linguistically self-conscious or stylized representation, but in the sense of a sure and certain handling or fluidity, as if language and its registers were already a material safely secured, but malleable and pliant and not, as it was understood and felt to be by the nineteenth-century Romantics and many pre-*modernista* poets, an object of inquiry and affirmation. To experiment, therefore, propounding ruptures or pursuing perfection, as in a certain sense modernismo advocated, did not, however, run the risk of severing ties with a series of poetic appropriations; rather, these were legitimate assays on a material already grasped and possessed. Although Pedro Henríquez Ureña's (1884–1946) proposal, namely, for a Latin American literature in search of its own expression, was no longer a problem with respect to expression itself, there continued to be, just as he thought, a problem with respect to the content of such expressions, about which deep doubts and contradictions still remained. I refer to the conflict between the centrifugal and the centripetal, embodied in the controversial concepts of universalism and particularism that, in more recent times, have found new and original responses in Borges or Octavio Paz (1914–1998). I refer also to the supposed debate as to whether something like national literatures exist, or whether there is only one Latin American literature.

Permanent Interaction Between the Streams

Modernismo proudly resisted or haughtily assumed the accusations of tending to favor foreign ways, as Rubén Darío's credo in *Los raros* [1896; The Uncommon Ones] makes clear. But even before the reverberations caused by the modernista irruption had subsided, José Juan Tablada, asserting the right not only to certain poetic models but to certain contemporary life styles or forms of culture, had begun exploring a territory barely hinted at by Darío: the old Parnassian tradition of orientalism. Focusing on the formal rather than the imagistic, he discovered the Japanese haiku and incorporated it once and for all into the formal universe of the Spanish language, just as the sonnet, imported from Italy, had been incorporated many years earlier. Whether the haiku revives an exotic image or whether it is an exercise in poetic dexterity need not concern us: Its incorporation into the Spanish language merely records the fecundity of an opening and the possible scope of its compass; above all, it created the conditions for the revision of the poetic code. If, perchance, this example had not been followed by others, and subsequent (or contemporary) poets such as Enrique Banchs (1888–1968), Leopoldo Díaz (1862–1947), Amado Nervo (1870–1919), or Delmira Agustini (1886–1914) had limited themselves to extracting the greatest sonorous and rhythmic possibilities from the innovations already incorporated, this would not have lessened the interest of Tablada's attempted application of a productive model. By placing so much emphasis on the strophic and subjecting his verse to such rigid discipline, it could be said that his poetry projected toward a greater beyond that seemed more than a little dispersed and disintegrated. While one of the currents that *modernismo* had not fully exhausted–sonority–continued to offer possibilities (Herrera y Reissig published his *Peregrino de piedra* [1914; Stone Pilgrim]), Tablada burst in abruptly, placing the accent elsewhere, in the transformation effected by a numerical concept, a set number of syllables, and in the creation of a single, concentrated, explosively unexpected image that was enigmatic and in no way narrative.

However, this restlessness animating Tablada, this shooting for the greater beyond, was not a personal idiosyncrasy: It was in the air. One proof was Leopoldo Lugones's poetic essay *Lunario sentimental* [1905; Sentimental Tide Table], in whose poems there is not only a scathing attack on the thematic of Romantic exaltation, but a singular torsion that, despite its apparent extravagance and open affiliation with Laforgue, appears to be the positive result of a recently acquired freedom based on an immensely formal rigor. Tablada and Lugones, one might say accordingly, continued what modernismo had staged, albeit remodeling it. Lugones, for his part, took off in two directions, different from Tablada and apparently opposed to each other. From this proto-avant-garde practice, and by means of a self-imposed celebrating image responding to an ideological intention, what one might call a modernista certainty began to take root: its academic triumph, its canonical projection, and its emergence as the "official poetry" characteristic of a social system that regarded poetry

as an appropriate means of sustaining the symbolic. Something similar can perhaps be said of Enrique González Martínez, of the poetic beginnings (soon abandoned) of Horacio Quiroga (1878–1937), of the Romantic regressions of Amado Nervo (1870–1919), and even of Porfirio Barba Jacob (1883–1942). To return to Lugones, evidence of this certainty can be found in his *Odas seculares* [1910; Secular Odes] and *Poemas solariegos* [1927; Ancestral Poems], as well as in the first poetic assays of Alfonso Reyes (1889–1959). In prose, conversely, Lugones continued to experiment. He not only wrote fantastic tales, *Las fuerzas extrañas* [1906; Strange Forces], but also, as a means of reinforcing his affiliation with Tablada, the *Cuentos fatales* [1926; Fatal Tales], exotic orientalist narratives, a kind of final residue of the spirit of decadence. While Tablada continued to rummage in the Japanese poetic universe and Lugones was inspired by Arab legends and traditions, of far greater consequence was the Baroque prose of *La guerra gaucha* [1905; The Gaucho War], for it demonstrated both how much ground modernismo had gained and, continuing to delineate the original aims of the movement, the extent to which it could impose both a syntax and a lexical universe.

Continuities and Alterations

In addition to these complex vicissitudes, there were clearer examples of the prolongation of modernismo, more linear, and more faithful to the original project (albeit with their own diverse ingredients) in the works of Delmira Agustini, Enrique Banchs, Ezequiel Martínez Estrada, Carlos Pezoa Véliz (1879–1908), and even in the Puerto Rican Carmela Eulate Sanjurjo (1871–1961) in *La muñeca* [1895; The Doll] (although the latter is primarily a prose writer). Moreover, this continuity can be seen in the popular poetry of various countries, above all in the musical libretti of the tango, the bolero, and the *danzón*. These follow modernista prescriptions virtually to the letter, although they are perhaps inspired or endorsed by the facility for versification that in the songs of Agustín Lara (1900–1970), for example, constitutes an irreplaceable social orthopedics: fine lines well accented, rich opportune rhymes, stanzas that lend themselves to the singing voice, and an exquisite vocabulary suggesting, with a most agreeable and characteristic swagger, a touch of social climbing.

One figure who began at this point but who quickly took things to extremes was Vallejo, whose development is highly illustrative. His first poems (*Los heraldos negros* [1918; The Black Heralds]) bear a modernista stamp; yet he soon passed on to other regions of poetic discourse and joined, despite their all too obvious differences, the project in which at this time Vicente Huidobro, from another perspective, had already become involved. In *Trilce* (1922), Vallejo formulated a poetic that was at the same time proto- and post-avant-garde; secluded in Trujillo, far from any talk of an avant-garde program, he spontaneously set his poetic "concepts" in motion. Unlike Huidobro, who sought to initiate a poetic era by glorying in historical consciousness, fully aware of what he opposed and clearly lucid about what he was aiming at, Vallejo did not limit himself to consolidating a program or a trend. While the purpose or aim of his poems is always clear, each reaches, nevertheless, exquisitely elevated registers, a form of expression that accords with his obsessive images of flight (birds and airplanes), and is essential to any history of Latin American poetry.

If the notion implied by the word *precursor* were not so feeble and hackneyed, then it would be an appropriate term for

Vicente Huidobro's relation to the avant-garde, although the well-defined and abiding compass of his poetic praxis rules it out. From the outset, and unlike Tablada, who realized a reinterpretation and a derivation of modernismo, Huidobro in effect articulated an avant-garde idea and practice as clearly defined as those of the European avant-garde, and with conceptual and poetic results that were similar, if not even more praiseworthy, considering all poetic seeds that were sown on his many journeys and that blossomed in his wake. In any event, both writers paved the way for the new era and inaugurated the next chapter of Latin American poetry, which, in general terms, can be described by two complementary words, *rupture* and *innovation*, to borrow a phrase from Guillaume Apollinaire, a writer whose poetics was so close to Huidobro's. Perhaps understanding this confluence and discovering in it common features of attitude and of consequence, a musician as refined and as representative of the contemporary avant-garde as Edgar Varèse (1883–1965) was inspired by the poems of Tablada and Huidobro to compose his *Offrandes* [Offertory]. Here, again, is evidence of the extent to which (and the means by which) not only what may be called the avant-garde was taking shape, but also the arrival at a modernity understood as universal was being prepared.

As for Huidobro in particular, he theorized both outside and in his poems. The formula "the poet is a little god" formed the basis of his creationism ("the poem must not imitate the creations of nature but must be created in the same way that nature creates") and opened the doors to a poetic explosion that can certainly lay claim to incarnating the symbol of modernity, at least with respect to the place occupied by symbolic processes in relation to material production. In the creationist credo, the modern would be an extension of the natural, the conjunction of culture and nature. It is not surprising, therefore, that Huidobro, reproducing the modernista gesture of the journey, should have sown so many ideas in his wake, first in Argentina (in the anthology he published with Alberto Hidalgo [1897–1967] and Jorge Luis Borges), later in Spain (in the constitution of *ultraísmo*) and, finally, both with and against Paul Réverdy, in Paris itself, the crucible of the avant-garde, the city through which Walter Benjamin at that very moment was rummaging and which he regarded as the embodiment of modernity itself.

An Interval of Calm: Digression on the Referent

Before the 1920s these attempts did not, however, constitute the entire range of poetry; nor were they absolutely authoritative. In Argentine letters, to begin with, and, seemingly at least, as a result of a confusion that might be called referential, a new kind of poetry began to develop in relation to a powerful urban reality experienced as highly complex. In its maximal form, it was realized in the work of a kind of prophet called Almafuerte (1854–1917), whose half-anarchic, half-Christian verses foretold of vast social and moral upheavals. As a prophet, he was followed, more modestly, by Evaristo Carriego (1883–1912), who spoke of "the soul of slums" and its humble personages, and about whom Borges wrote a sort of biographical epic. In its minimal form, this new poetry was realized in what became known as *sencillismo* ("minimalism"), whose prime example was Baldomero Fernández Moreno. To a certain extent, and with regard to such an intimate and immediate referent, this poetry could be linked with certain aspects of the work of Ramón López Velarde, the Velarde of the "provincial light" verses, although this work is somewhat

Gabriela Mistral (Lucila Godoy Alcayaga), photograph c. 1949. (Archive of the author)

indebted to the virtues of Leopoldo Lugones, particularly with respect to the sonority–limpid in the Mexican, more artistic in the Argentine. We might even place the early work of Gabriela Mistral (1889–1957) (see **Figure 1**) in a similar category–with its deep emotions, rigorous observations, controlled but not experimental expression, a direct poetry that speaks to the feelings, the eyes, and the heart–as well as that of Alfonsina Storni (1892–1938) and even the early work of Pablo Neruda. And if Almafuerte, with his exclamatory and righteous poetry, is a voice that we cannot stop listening to, perhaps it is because it has, despite being crossbred with the conceptual conquests of the avant-garde, something to do with a subsequent phenomenon, always regarded as being in opposition to Huidobro's and Neruda's command of the poetic scene: the insolent and impudent practice of taking on the world that cannot but be recognized in the work of Pablo de Rokha (1894–1968), with his political and moral inflections, expounded in an equally arrogant claim of ever-expanding spatiality.

Certainly, this poetry is no longer modernista, although and it is in no sense avant-garde. Despite its reserve and apparent renunciation of all expressionism and stridency, it is certainly opposed to the current that Huidobro set in motion and which extended itself throughout the continent between 1920 and 1930. Neither could it be said that sencillismo exhausted itself in the aforementioned expressions; rather, it was prolonged in projects like that of Raúl González Tuñón (1905–1974) in the 1930s, and in Nicanor Parra's (b. 1914) later endeavor throughout the 1950s. Parra called his an "anti-poetry," and while direct links cannot be established between this proposition and that of Fernández Moreno, for example, neither can one deny that they share something of a common attitude, namely, a greater emphasis on the poetic vehicle that transports an image than on verbal image itself. Sencillismo, as implied by the idea of "anti-poems," reemerges in the so-called colloquial or conversational poetry that prevailed from the 1950s and which has representatives or exponents throughout Latin America, from Mario Benedetti (b. 1920) to Roberto Fernández Retamar (b. 1930), passing by way of Roque Dalton (1935–1975), César Fernández Moreno (1919–1985), Juan Gelman (b. 1930), Efraín Huerta (1914–1982), and many others.

The Avant-Garde Storm

What was begun by Huidobro, as an effective disseminator of his ideas, and by Vallejo, as the silent practitioner (since *Trilce* became incorporated into this roster by virtue of subsequent interpretations), was reinforced from the outside, both as a kind of international avant-garde duty, manifest in all its declarations, and also through the emergence of multiple models that were rapidly accepted. However, before proceeding down this stream, mention should be made of those threshold poetic positions that sought not to situate themselves in any particular stream but that allowed or authorized a passage to other very different currents. I refer to the work of Macedonio Fernández (1874–1952), quite solitary in its time, but which incorporated, much as German Romanticism once did, a philosophical material both in subject matter and in its metapoetical dimension that in previous poets was either underground (Darío) or declarative (Huidobro). Within this same category, we ought also, perhaps, to include José Lezama Lima, somewhat less lonely than Macedonio Fernández, perhaps because, after the work of José Gorostiza, and given his connections with the ideas of Paul Valéry, Jorge Guillén, Giuseppe Ungaretti, and even the penultimate Juan Ramón Jiménez, writing a poetry that referred to itself was no longer an anomaly or an expression of rupture.

However, to return to the avant-garde, the models furnished by Futurism, Cubism, and Surrealism encountered enthusiastic and imitative rejoinders, above all in the matter of images reflecting the external face of modernity: mechanization, urbanization, and abstraction. The acceptance of these models was widespread–from Argentina to Mexico, including at least the Dominican Republic, Cuba, Puerto Rico, Nicaragua, and Venezuela. Everywhere, not only could one find identical images (automobiles, telegraph wires, trains, planes, and submarines) whose referents seemed hypervalued in relation to the reality from which they might have emerged, but also a certain exaltation that we may call "representativist." The best example of this has to be Mexican *estridentismo* ("stridentism"), which linked its revolutionary propositions to the Mexican Revolution itself, as if the modernizing yowls and proclamations (*gritos*) of this poetic movement could have had the same form as the political one. If the Mexican Revolution changed social structures, estridentismo, rebelling against forms of language and poetry characteristic of the world the revolution overturned, claimed to be making something similar, a revolution in poetry.

However, the models that arrived from Europe–and whose presence seemed so determinant that it suggests, were it not for Huidobro and Vallejo, a veritable subordination, above all in thematics–were not exclusive; the United States also provided a wealth of material in this extremely busy literary traffic. Although Pedro Henríquez Ureña, while attending a U.S. university, understood what was implied by the "New Poetry" and

what use its conceptions could be put to, it was Salvador Novo (1904–1974), with his *Antología de la nueva poesía norteamericana* [Anthology of New North American Poetry] in 1922, who made the U.S. poetic explosion known in his own country. At the same time Salomón de la Selva (1893–1959) introduced these new ideas into Nicaragua, thereby marking out, perhaps definitively, the direction poetry would take in that country. And the work of José Coronel Urtecho (1906–1994) could also be read within this tradition. Thus, it would be right to maintain that there is an unquestionable relation between the avant-garde and modernity insofar as the two sources of the avant-garde are intimately linked, especially and specifically in the U.S. avant-garde, to social processes of a clearly modernizing stamp. The U.S. impact on the avant-garde underlies what will later be the Latin American "conversational poetry" that results not from the mere application of a model but from the confluence of the two streams.

Salvador Novo quickly abandoned this U.S. vein with his resolute entry into "*Los contemporáneos*" [The Contemporaries], a group poetics that were less pronouncedly avant-garde and more inclined, in the work of Gorostiza, Carlos Pellicer (1899–1977), Villaurrutia, and Jorge Cuesta (1903–1942), toward a metaphysical order embodied by poets like Rilke and Valéry in Europe. With regard to this tendency, it may also be said that the poetic position of José Lezama Lima and the *Orígenes* [Origins] group had a similar scope, although more dedicated to a metapoetics in Lima's case, and more inclined to the construction of a universe of meanings in that of Cintio Vitier (b. 1921) and Eliseo Diego (1920–1994), both working from a position that, faced with the rise of the *negrista* movement, proposed new homologues with other cultural forms. We can consider the poetry of both the *Orígenes* and *Los contemporáneos* groups as emergent philosophical poetry, recognizing that behind their work stood the rich achievement of the Spanish generation of 1927, particularly the works of Pedro Salinas, Luis Cernuda, and Jorge Guillén, to which we might add an ever more hermetic Juan Ramón Jiménez. Initially inspired by Dilthey, but soon discovering and exploring the mysteries that Heidegger's philosophy sought to embrace, *Orígenes* and *Los contemporáneos* were symptoms of and responses to the need to recover a concept of poetry that inquired into being (mystically, if necessary), or that at least harvested the knowledge gained from experience. Is it possible to read Alberto Girri (1919–1991)–hermetic in line, rigorous in concentration, and philosophical in his referential interest–from this perspective? Probably, although such a reading would not seek to classify his poetry, since that would perhaps trivialize it, but rather to understand the forces that come together in his poetics and lend it historicity.

As emergent poets, they can also be related to the obvious desire to reclaim a sort of Apollonian distance and an ethics of verse that was implied by the position of the so-called generation of 1940 in Argentina; or they can even be linked to the course taken by post-Surrealism in the works of Braulio Arenas (1913–1988) and, above all, Gonzalo Rojas (b. 1917) in Chile. One must also consider, in this context, the work of Juan Sánchez Peláez (b. 1922) in Venezuela, undergoing the aftereffects of *El techo de la ballena* [The Whale's Roof]; Olga Orozco (1920–1999) in Argentina, supported by post–generation-of-1940 poets Enrique Molina (1910–1997) and an Oliverio Girondo (1891–1967) who were part of what could be considered a logical response of the youngest poets to the impact of *En la masmédula* [1956; In the Deepest Marrow]. Those effects could be felt in both the journals that revived the old Surrealist passion and in the work of Aldo Pellegrini (1903–1973), Edgar Bayley (1919–1990), and Francisco Madariaga (1927–2000).

From the Kingdom of Sonority to Spatiality

In this poetic process, the link with the experience of a not-too-distant, innovative past is a relation worthy of consideration. It may be seen as a kind of antibody that goes on high alert when seemingly overwhelming poetic models appear on the horizon: In every case inflections are produced, giving rise to original formulations undoubtedly linked to the universal process of innovation, the most important element of which is the doors they open, the acquisitions they reveal. It would be enough to invoke the impressive cases of Pablo Neruda and Jorge Luis Borges to give some idea of this. However, even more revealing are manifestations such as Puerto Rican *diepalismo* and, from another point of view, the infusions Latin American poetry has received from the poetic expressions of *ultraísmo* in Argentina, *estridentismo* and *Los contemporáneos* in Mexico, *the Orígenes* group in Cuba, Surrealism in Chile and Peru, as well as from a multitude of poets whose attitude to the past ranges from an apparently unlimited support to one of independence, always forging syntheses and harmonies, as if the essential *modernista* lesson had not been forgotten.

If what matters is the process of poetic creation and not only what its final achievements might be (as variable as the changing results of equally changing interpretations), then the case of diepalismo is of great interest, despite its ephemeral existence, and its small body of work. Diepalismo did not appear to be avant-garde in intent: the duo of José Diego Padró (1896–1974) and Luis Palés Matos (1898–1959)–whence the eponym "die-pal"–sought to compose poetry by reproducing or imitating, as far as possible, the noises and sounds of the fertile Puerto Rican natural ambiance. On the one hand, they seemingly subjected sonority–the quality that had defined poetry up until the better-known avant-garde trends (Cubism, for example) exploited and made evident the spatial character of writing–to a hypertrophy or distention; however, since onomatopoeia does not create words, the text they produced, *Orquestación diepálica* [Diepalic Orchestration], was not readable. There was nothing else to do with it but look at it, spread over a smooth surface, much like Huidobro's paper work "La capilla aldeana" ["The Village Chapel"], in which the physical, visible form reproduces a cultural form in addition to referring to it. As if following Huidobro's example, they attempted to recreate nature itself in poetry. The experiment might have ended there, perhaps, but very quickly it proved its effectiveness when the onomatopoetic attraction shifted toward speech and, in the fervor of perceiving the ethnic reverberations, it transformed into *negrismo*. This time, there was a rational syntactic structure that made certain linguistic practices, particularly those of the Caribbean, an object of recovery and vindication and the product of highly elaborate poetic conceptions. In this way, the poetry of Nicolás Guillén (1902–1989) and Emilio Ballagas (1908–1954), and even the later works of Palés Matos himself, were integrated into the general Latin American poetic process, entirely consonant with the currents flooding the continent's poetic discourse as a whole.

Diepalismo, seeking to recuperate poetry from one of the components of the sign, addressed itself to the aural signifier and thereby deposed the previously sovereign word; this objective was carried out by sacking the signified and leaving the signifier intact. What resulted from this procedure was the appearance of a word without the word itself, something Oliverio Girondo was to effect much later, on the other side of the continent, in his *En las masmédula*. In this work, the simultaneous disassembly and refashioning of words not only produces a significant vertigo, in the sense that since the words themselves are incomprehensible and what is understood is a powerful "something else," but also thrusts a "feismo," or aesthetics of the ugly, onto center stage, implying a confrontation with the prevailing aesthetic of beauty inherited from Symbolism through modernismo. The piece manifests an essentially constructive possibility, since the internal games to which its broken wordplay gives rise demonstrate that language is in a state of permanent flux, seething with semiosis, and that poetry, by its articulations and by the parody it engenders, can make sense of it all. This constructivist arc was carried even further by the Brazilian concrete poetry movement; in the footsteps of Mallarmé, and building on the momentum created by the São Paulo "Modern Art Week" exhibitions, Augusto de Campos (b. 1931) proposed an extreme spatialization in which not only words but signs themselves become fragmented: Syllables break down phrases, typographic orchestration and a purified graphics convey one to the edge of a precipice, and the unity that is lost to a comprehension without a future resides in the "look" or the "view."

Various Syntheses

Pablo Neruda (see **Figure 2**) and Jorge Luis Borges evolved in a curious fashion, as did Octavio Paz, who traced a similar trajectory. For one thing, their evolutions supposed the privileged position of the poetic word; their names function something like a promise of being or a guarantee of existence, a reasoning that is connected to the immense problems of identity that have besieged Latin American culture since the processes of national autonomy were initiated in the various countries. It is not that local figures personifying the same level of achievement were lacking; what stands out is that the trajectories of these three manifest not only an evolution from initiation to maturity in their own discourse, but also a synthesis of tendencies. Each constitutes a space in which decisions are resolved, a place where attempts to give poetry a form are enfolded and refolded, offering a repository of poetic problems that many other Latin American poets, more partially perhaps, would also confront.

As is well known, Borges was initially puzzled by the novelty of the incipient avant-garde, although he established a peculiar sort of pact with it nonetheless. Since *ultraísmo* had been defined by what it ought to include (the kingdom of metaphor) and to exclude (the unnecessary, what were called "ornamental trifles"), it placed its imagination at the service of a recuperation of both a cultural and poetic tradition and an immediate civic concern. The early poetry of Borges is one of journeys and reconnaissance, rather than of the spatial figurations advanced by his ultraist coreligionists Alfredo Brandán Caraffa (1898–1987) or Oliverio Girondo. That he would have been taken for a member of the avant-garde is borne out by the fact that he promoted iconoclastic declarations and journals of that stripe, as well as by the fact that he was seen as such by Huidobro, with whom he put together an anthology that was as explicit and combative as could be expected in this moment of enthusiastic faith in poetic renovation. In this sense his subsequent evolution was predictable; it can be seen

Figure 2.

Pablo Neruda (Neftalí Ricardo Reyes Basoalto), photograph c. 1960. (Archive of the author)

Figure 3.

Photograph of Machu Picchu, the Inca city that inspired "Alturas de Machu Picchu" published in Canto general *by Pablo Neruda. (Photograph by Mario J. Valdés)*

as faithful to this early experience and, at the same time, as a search for other modes and jurisdictions. Thus, his poetry became gradually more traditional in form and more metaphysical in its premises and propositions, an evolution whose constancy is as admirable as was Borges's sixty years of poetic searching.

This notion of constancy is a guiding thread in Latin American poetry in general. Without meaning exactly the same thing, we can speak of poetic constancy in referring to Alfonso Reyes, Ricardo Molinari (1898–1996), Emilio Westphalen, Enrique Molina, Eliseo Diego, Juan L. Ortíz (1896–1978), Cintio Vitier, Carlos Pellicer, Dulce María Loynaz (1902–1997), Carlos Drummond de Andrade (1902–1987), and León de Greiff (1895–1976), among others, not because they had a common poetics, but because they shared a similar faith in the poetic work–some by way of interrogating the word, others the emotional word or the intelligence, still others by means of an unshakable confidence in the power of poetry and its place in the most intimate orders of signification.

It can be said that Pablo Neruda began his poetic labors timidly, amid Romantic and modernista reminiscences. Quite rapidly he revealed his talent in all his possibilities, its collaboration with a Surrealist-inspired avant-garde that opened to him a perspective he would never relinquish: faith both in the

poem as a unit and in what an exploration of expression could yield. Neruda traveled a different route than Huidobro: His trajectory described a kind of referential kaleidoscope in which even a cursory glance shows both matters of great human import, in *Canto general*, 1950 and the simple and artless, in *Odas elementales* [1954; Elemental Odes], explored with the same passion for discovery. A miner of reality and history, he quarried in a kind of secret land and attempted to extract all the riches it contained. In this gesture, Neruda's work traces a vast parabola and, as one would expect from a talent as powerful as his, has had a decisive impact on the poets who followed him: Jorge Enrique Ramponi (1907–1977) and Thiago de Mello (b. 1926). However, and quite naturally, if this decisive impact operates in a larger context, then Neruda obviously shares this with César Vallejo, whose imprint on Latin American poetry was very deep and acknowledged by many subsequent poets. (See **Figure 3.**)

In the case of Octavio Paz, it is possible to speak of his poetic evolution, and also of his intellectual and cultural leadership, but undoubtedly it is in the culminating moments of his verse linked to a metapoetic preoccupation that we find his mastery. If the avant-garde poets were perhaps more explicit in what they advocated than in what they sought, Paz attempted to bind his poetry to a perhaps changing poetic, but one always marked by a lucidity sensual and intellectual: a lucidity of verse and poem, a lucidity of ideas, a lucidity of what might be called the theory of writing poetry. *Blanco* is in this respect an excellent synthesis or, if one would rather not see it this way, a demonstration of the extent to which an attentiveness to what transpires in the realm of poetic theory can be ingested and processed. Paz's poetry is distinct in two ways: On the one hand, it is marked by an obvious intellectual structure, a trait perhaps inherited from the *Los contemporáneos* poets to whom he was so closely linked and which is well demonstrated in the homage that is Laurel's *Antología de la poesía moderna* [1941; Anthology of Modern Poetry], as well as in so many other of his diverse reflections on the Latin American and global poetic process; and his work is also marked, on the other hand, by a great faith in the poetic word, which explains why so many excellent poets have followed in his footsteps, feel an affiliation for his teachings, or can recognize themselves in a similar atmosphere: Roberto Juárroz (1925–1995), Jorge Eduardo Eielson (b. 1924), Alejandra Pizarnik (1936–1972), José Emilio Pacheco (b. 1939), Ida Vitale (b. 1926), Enrique Fierro (b. 1942), and a myriad of poets whose work spans the 1950s and 1960s.

Conclusion

It is not easy to speak of epochs and to give them a precise meaning in an essay that has attempted to give a brief account of such diverse poetic practices. The interactions between phenomena go beyond individual contours; the methods of modifying models differ and, later, when the results of such modifications appear, they exert an impact and authority, shaping the whole into a highly complex network full of resonances and connections. It is, in fact, a question of a reading practice that allows us to move in all directions without having to resort to the overly normative idea of movements, tendencies, or schools, or to the even more objectionable (critically speaking) and overly protective idea of influence. The objective, whose historicizing and historicist nuances should be evident, would be to understand the discursive universe both horizontally, which is to say, by tracing the framework erected between the various, contemporaneously emergent poetic endeavors, and vertically, in the relations established at every moment with external models, with poetics that might have been paralyzing yet proved to be both inspiring and fertile. Would this not be a mode specific to Latin American culture, or rather to Latin American writing?

Be that as it may, and even before examining the texts themselves, it may have been possible to sense (perhaps even more than observe) that what emerges from a map such as we have drawn here is a constant and well-grounded force. And if, at the same time, we could explore these texts, devoting ourselves to what goes by the name of aesthetic feeling, then we would have an even greater appreciation of the consistency and the import of a process that, by means of certain articulations and modes of association, we have attempted to illustrate. Perhaps the notion of constancy is the unique feature that characterizes this fragment of history. Neither obstinacy nor persistence, constancy is both fidelity and self-awareness, two essential qualities that are buttressed by an indubitable sense of adventure, a certainty in the instrument, not in achievements. Thus poetry, which in the modernista period sought to be a model for society as a whole, kept on tendering a center of resistance: an imposing rock amidst the storms that tend to dissolve discourse and to reduce the human word to a mere farm tool in a land that wishes to remain fallow.

Writing poetry at the end of the nineteenth century and writing poetry in the first decades of the twentieth century were two very different things. Poetry in the earlier era faced an expectation about what would emerge from its socially situated (if desperate) practice, as though, despite the primary nature of the cultural apparatus by which it endeavored to operate, something decisive was expected of it. For this reason, its excesses and deviations, or its errors, were perhaps feared; once detected, by means of reading practices that can today be seen as rather insufficient, they were marked as veritable transgressions of the spirit under construction, a spirit in which the notion of identity was key. In little more than a century the situation has changed—although the desperation remains (if not, in fact, on the increase). However, in spite of this desperation and the spasmodic outbursts it may occasion, it is not at all clear what may be gained from a discursive war. Yet this notion of "writing poetry at the end of the century" does not permeate the poetic material we have tried to situate; perhaps that is a necessary historicist precision. Things changed for poetry at a specific time—perhaps it was the death of Neruda—although that change has paralyzed no one; nor has it interrupted a flow that appears to be constant. Perhaps we should recall Adorno's remark about poetry after Auschwitz: Latin American life has been visited with so many murders that to believe poetry was invulnerable, and that its ancient values would continue to guide the creativity of society, could well be naive or vain. Poetry has been vulnerable, but it has also constituted an unending front of resistance: It shall continue to surprise us with new forms of creativity.

Translation by Colman Hogan

CHAPTER 23

IN THE WEB OF REALITY
LATIN AMERICAN TESTIMONIO

Elzbieta Sklodowska

Definitions

Within the vast constellation of Latin American texts written on behalf of the other—which range from the explanations of the New World in the chronicles of discovery to a variety of recent life-story narratives—*testimonio* is being presented as an innovative and original form that arises from a deep dissatisfaction with the ways in which Latin American writing had depicted the world of the disenfranchised. Since the publication in 1966 of Miguel Barnet's (b. 1940)/Esteban Montejo's (1860–1973) *Biografía de un cimarrón* [*The Autobiography of a Runaway Slave,* 1994], there has also been a consistent effort on the part of the critics and Latin American writers to ascribe a distinct literary identity to nonfictional texts labeled as *testimonio*. For readers familiar with the plethora of "ghost-written" autobiographies of fugitive slaves in the United States, Barnet's project may not seem as radically novel as some critics have claimed. Moreover, most of the ideological, formal, and ethical questions pertinent to such documentary texts as *Biografía de un cimarrón* seem to have been exhausted in the United States in the 1960s and 1970s, in the course of lively debates surrounding the so-called nonfiction or new journalism of Truman Capote, Joan Didion, and Norman Mailer, as well as Oscar Lewis's "life stories" (see Foley; Hellman; Hollowell; Zavarzadeh).

In the context of Latin American letters, *Biografía de un cimarrón* remains nonetheless a text of exceptional resonance that continues to appeal to the contemporary preoccupations of literary critics, historians, and anthropologists. The only other known personal testimony of a slave to emerge from Latin America and therefore the most obvious ancestor of Montejo's narrative is Juan Francisco Manzano's (1797–1854) *Autobiography* (written in 1835, published in England in 1840 and in Cuba in 1937). In addition to being a unique human document, Barnet's/Montejo's text is regarded as a foundational *testimonio,* even though evaluations of the book itself vary widely from critic to critic.

My invocation of the nonfictional novel and the new journalism as a means of framing *testimonio* has less to do with comparing techniques or establishing points of contact (particularly in light of existing studies by Dorfman, Foster, Fraire, and Gale Chevigny) than with stating the fact that these roughly coterminous forms of writing emerged as a response to a similar challenge: that of "trying to understand, and then describe, and then make *credible* much of the American reality" (Roth qtd. in Hellmann 414). Consequently, in all of these cases, the notion of literary genre is "historically derived" rather than "logically prescribed" (Lohafer 11). However, it is also my view that specific texts written in answer to this challenge were as different as was the historical experience of Mailer or Capote and that of their Latin American counterparts. The most striking difference between *testimonio* and other texts that qualify as testimonial by conventional understanding—such as the nonfictional novel, the new journalism, the documentary novel, autobiographies, memoirs, and diaries—consists in the mediated character of the *testimonio*: The witness is both the subject and the object of the narrative, with the editor positioned as mediator between story and discourse. Consequently, the "intertwined issues of authorship, representation, and self-reflection" (Logan 203) should be of particular interest to readers and critics of *testimonio*.

To be sure, the term *testimonio,* as used in the present study, denotes only those narratives whose production "involves the recording and/or transcription and editing of an oral account by an interlocutor who is a journalist, writer, or social activist" (Beverley and Zimmerman 173). While this narrowing of focus enables me to mark the *testimonio* as a distinct form of writing, it is not intended to place the questions of genealogy out of the scope of critical interest. In order not to replicate, however, what others have already said, I would direct readers seeking an overview of the Latin American testimonial archive to Beverley's "The Margin at the Center," which, in addition to the most obvious examples, lists colonial *crónicas,* the *costumbrista* essay *Facundo* (1845), *Os sertões* [1939; *Rebellion in the Backlands,* 1944], the *diarios de campaña* (war diaries) of, for example, Bolívar or Martí, or the Romantic biography, a key genre of Latin American liberalism (1989, 25).

Simply to claim to have found traces of testimonial mechanisms in a mediated account is still too broad a base on which to build a definition. On the other hand, to attempt a more detailed classification could lead us, at best, to a quasi-Borgesian taxonomy. To elide this double bind, we may want to remember that *testimonio* lends itself almost inevitably to transdisciplinary approaches as it unsettles the boundaries between the fictional and the factual, the oral and the written, anthropology and literature. Its allegiance to the political left, on one hand, and its formal cross-fertilization, on the other, invite reflections from political activists, social scientists, and literary critics alike. For the latter–bound by the customs of their discipline–the question as to how the aesthetic value of *testimonio* can be measured has become of paramount importance. Even though, in the face of postmodern erosion of the Western criteria of art, this question is also one most likely to remain unanswered, Latinamericanists tempted to give *testimonio* an expressly literary rather than a simply sociological character may find themselves in agreement with the Polish critic Michal Glowinski, who argues that "literariness is a constitutive, not just an accidental or ornamental element" in Oscar Lewis's anthropological works (388). Glowinski further distinguishes between "belletrisation" and "novelization": While the first term designates "the accidental, nonsystematic use of approaches and procedures proper to the narrative literary forms, primarily the novel, in texts designated as social documents," the second one, in contrast, offers "a systematic shaping of such a text on the model and likeness on the novel" (389).

Because of its binarism, Glowinski's proposal generates a further question: Have literary critics developed the methodological tools necessary to study the interwoven formal, political, and ethical strands of *testimonio*? Even though the complex issues surrounding the production of mediated testimonials inform some of the most compelling studies, the focus on truth and authenticity often seems to take precedence over discursive analysis per se. For George Yúdice, for example, *testimonio*

> may be defined as an authentic narrative, told by a witness who is moved to narrate by the urgency of a situation (e.g., war, oppression, revolution, etc.). Emphasizing popular, oral discourse, the witness portrays his or her own experience as an agent (rather than a representative) of a collective memory and identity. Truth is summoned in the cause of denouncing a present situation of exploitation and oppression or in exorcising and setting aright official history. (17)

This action-oriented definition assumes that the testimonial word that emerges from oppression offers a legitimate challenge to what Milan Kundera (b. 1929) once called "organized forgetting." In this view, the word of the victim has the unquestioned power and right to summon truth, denounce, exorcise, and set aright official history. As George L. Dillon has shown, whenever an emphasis on experience is linked with persuasion, we enter the domain of rhetoric, "where style is not viewed as an end but as a means of achieving the main aim–as strategic–and voice leads one to ethos, another of the means of persuading. Assuming a persuasive purpose tends to narrow and simplify the critic's expectations about how the writing works: one is not looking for subtle exploration of the doing and undoing of language and representation. Language in persuasion is harnessed to the world" (197).

In a recent powerful rereading of *Me llamo Rigoberta Menchú y así me nació la conciencia*, 1983 [*I, Rigoberta Menchú: An Indian Woman in Guatemala*, 1984], Brett Levinson broaches the question of critics' reluctance to de-idealize or de-mythify Rigoberta's testimony by arguing that avoiding close reading rests on a rigid understanding of political commitment:

> Indeed, the critics who have authored the most powerful interpretations of *I, Rigoberta Menchú* have also deployed the text as a key political device: as a means to rethink the question of

colonial/post-colonial oppression, the role of literature and writing in the new Latin American social movements, and the politics of Latin American studies. To offer a fundamentally new reading of *I, Rigoberta Menchú*, therefore, is also potentially to upset the delicate balance between hermeneutics and politics. (33)

Obviously, when answering the question of what counts as *testimonio*, not all critics share Yúdice's belief in the unique power of testimonial texts as an outlet for redressing sociopolitical grievances. As a matter of fact, there are a great variety of opinions on this matter, simply because criticism on *testimonio* has centered as much around the positions and counter-positions of the scholars as on the texts per se. While some readers may agree that testimonial narratives not only register but also affect social processes, they also resist the idea that the objective of advocacy should eliminate any literary concerns. Without abandoning their extra-literary interest, critics such as Hugo Achugar, Juan Duchesne, Mempo Giardinelli, Jorge Narváez, Françoise Perus, and Antonio Vera-León describe *testimonio* in terms of its rhetorical characteristics, while also highlighting its aesthetic facets. More specifically, these approaches favor the use of family resemblance, whereby this arguably new literary form is described by its likeness to what is already established. *Testimonio*, so the argument runs, relies as much on its links to the *Bildungsroman* and the picaresque or to legal patterns of argumentation as on the narrative conventions of the realist novel. We are also told that *testimonio*'s use of the life story–inspired by the writings of Oscar Lewis–is creative rather than scientific.

The family resemblance method does not always succeed in disentangling *testimonio* from neighboring forms and genres. Nonetheless, some approaches appear to provide at least a point of departure. Such is the case with the succinct yet precise definition proposed by Beverley and Zimmerman: *Testimonio* is "a novel or novella-length narrative, told in the first person by a narrator who is also the actual protagonist or witness of the events she or he recounts. The unit of narration is usually a life or a significant life episode (e.g., the experience of being a prisoner)" (173). By and large, the metaphor of family resemblance is helpful in delineating the contours of *testimonio*, but it does not account for what perhaps another metaphor–that of cannibalism–would capture better: the process of disintegration, reappropriation, and absorption of recognizable conventions into a new form, that of *testimonio* (see Kilgour on cannibalism and its discursive ramifications). In view of the fact that mediated testimonials are not reducible to a common formal denominator, a single element that draws together the otherwise disparate definitions belongs to the realm of ideology rather than rhetoric. Despite their considerable differences in tone and focus, each of the critics I have mentioned so far underscores *testimonio*'s premise to recover the unspeakable experience of the oppressed and the unspoken world of the disenfranchised that would otherwise be muted or forgotten. With its eyes set on communities and individuals excluded from official historiography, *testimonio* reminds us that, along with the history of remembering, there also comes a politics of forgetting.

If there are difficulties in defining the intrinsic characteristics of *testimonio* and tracing its Latin American genealogy, the question of transnational links is no less vexing. While it is not my intention to claim that Latin American *testimonio* is only a belated articulation of some of the European or North American experiments, I would point to what may be the missing link in *testimonio*'s trajectory, namely the substantial contributions to the documentary literature of solidarity and resistance collected and transcribed by intellectuals in the United States (testimonies of former slaves), France, Germany, the Soviet Union, and Scandinavia in the 1920s and 1930s. Clas Zilliacus's (100–102) informative study demonstrates how the original model for recording words "from the lips of the people themselves" might be traced back to Henry Mayhew's monumental *London Labour and the London Poor* (1861–1862) (xv) and how it becomes epitomized in Studs Terkel's *Working*. Zilliacus also shows how the consolidation of this impulse into a political and discursive pact occurred in the Soviet Union in the 1920s, during a project spearheaded by Sergey Tretyakov and implemented by writers associated with the Left Front of the Arts (LEF):

> The new Soviet reality was to be documented as it emerged. On the one hand were those who did the work that made it emerge; these, the "data bearers," had the insight and the experience but lacked the means to articulate them. On the other was a cadre of writers professedly willing to dedicate themselves to articulating them. The task of the writer was to join the workers as interviewer, literary secretary (a term with Balzacian connotations), or "constructor" of the raw material with which he was confronted. Tretyakov's desire was to create a literature of fact (*literatura facta*). (107)

We can safely assume that, while there is no direct "influence" of *literatura facta* on Latin American *testimonio*, there is a forging of alliances with other subjects that became an important site of enunciation for Latin American intellectuals in the 1960s. As Beverley reminds us, following the Cuban Revolution, "one of the richest sources of testimonial material has been the interaction of intellectuals, peasants, and working people in literacy campaigns" (1989, 26). All these encounters are wrought with tensions and point to the limits of cross-cultural understanding in the modern era. What is important to note—particularly given the "transnational" frame of this text—is what Michael Taussig finds as the embodiment of the modern era, precisely "the encounter between strikingly different narrators . . . different on just about any criterion you care to select: economic class, urban/rural, skin color, generation, education, diet, body build, understanding of labor, of gossip, of sorcery" (349). The mediation that ensues is, obviously, a cornerstone of modern anthropology and is crucial to the testimonial pact.

At this point some thinkers will be quick to warn us, however, that in recent times testimony—whether direct or mediated—has lost its appeal altogether. According to Gianni Vattimo, the disintegration of the bourgeois/Christian notion of the subject—defined in terms of the hegemony of consciousness—has severed the relationship between the individual and truth, so vital to the testimonial contract: "The notion of testimony goes 'out of date' as a result of the inversion of the traditional hierarchy of the elements of the individual psyche. This inversion has meant an increasingly dominant role for the unconscious" (47). Vattimo's words may speak to late-twentieth-century or early-twenty-first-century concerns in general, but they are of limited applicability to Latin America, where the flourishing of *testimonio* took place precisely at a time when in Europe "any appeal to the ideal of testimony" was considered "anachronistic" (Vattimo 40). One could argue, of course, that personal testimonies are generated and sustained by violent events of which the people of Latin America have had more than their share and that the 1970s and early 1980s—when *testimonio* was canonized—saw the

entire continent swept by waves of extreme authoritarianism. Under such circumstances the urge to testify becomes an ethical obligation, since, as Jean François Lyotard has argued, in the testimonial contract, "the phrase replaced by silence would be a negative one. Negated by it is at least one of the four instances that constitute a phrase universe: the addressee, the referent, the sense, the addressor" (13). Lyotard's position runs counter to the prevailing postmodern opinion—such as Vattimo's—that *testimonio*'s value can be dismissed because of the fallible nature of language and the disintegration of the subject. (I will return to Lyotard's argument in my discussion of specific testimonial texts.)

Canonization of *Testimonio*

In hindsight, it appears that *testimonio*'s institutional legitimation took place with the simultaneous waning of the formal experimentation of the "new novel." This process of canonization resulted from a constellation of factors. For one, the critics' compensatory effort to bring texts previously considered marginal or nonliterary to center stage was reinforced by the authors and editors themselves (see Miguel Barnet 1981; Elena Poniatowska 1969–both highlighted the innovative and creative facets of their testimonial projects). In 1970 the prestigious Cuban cultural institution, Casa de las Américas, added the category of testimonial narrative to its literary competition. With Havana established as a center for dissemination of *testimonio*, the role of the new genre as a counterpoint to self-centered artifacts of the boom became more evident than ever. The shaping forces of canon formation—such as the role of the community of literary professionals, authorial statements (interviews, prefaces), placement in the curricula, and nonacademic readership—have not been studied thoroughly in relation to *testimonio*. Nonetheless, even a schematic examination of *testimonio*'s trajectory shows certain omissions or distortions. To give just one obvious example: Even though Carolina Maria de Jesus's (1914–1977) *Child of the Dark*, 1962 (originally published as *Quarto de Despejo*, 1960) gained immediate international recognition, it is not included among the "foundational" texts of Latin American *testimonio*. The fact that this diary of a woman from a Brazilian *favela* is seldom mentioned by the critics along with testimonial texts in Spanish is most probably due to the prevailing marginalization of Brazil vis-à-vis the Spanish-speaking countries. However, its absence from the volume dedicated to Brazilian literature in the recently published *Cambridge History of Latin American Literature* is more difficult to explain. Robert Levine's hypothesis that de Jesus's refusal to "conform to prevailing social values" (56) enraged and alienated everybody in Brazil, from politicians on the right to intellectuals on the left, offers an important insight into the intricate mechanisms of recognition and rejection that seem to have shaped this case.

In pursuing the relation of *testimonio* to the social institutions that both restrict and enable its production, it may be helpful to take a brief look at the possible linkage between literary invention and critical fashion. According to Murray Krieger, one can interpret the recent history of theoretical fashion in U.S. universities as a series of movements:

> Each movement, as a would-be empire, can be seen as deriving its force for change more from the kind of literary culture it wishes to bring into being than from its commitment to advance its internally directed argument toward theoretical truth. It is thus related to literary change as the latter stimulates the rise and fall of literary

fashions, with a subservient literary criticism anxious to defend and expand the influence of a particular brand of literary invention. (184)

For a student of Latin American literature Hernán Vidal's polemical article on postcolonialism offers a more familiar frame for Krieger's argument. Vidal argues that over the last three decades the field of Latin American studies has been plagued by an ideological split between a technocratic and a culture-oriented criticism. Whereas the first trend draws inspiration from a variety of imported theories that ignore the social problems of the cultures being studied, says Vidal, the second one "sets as its goal direct contributions to the cultures from which its material for study comes, addressing itself to the academic establishment only as a very secondary interlocutor" (115). Vidal offers an indictment of the first trend, which he perceives as obsessed with endless innovation for innovation's sake and concerned only with its own perpetuation rather than with "Latin American social needs" (116).

If we were to combine Krieger's and Vidal's insights for the purpose of this essay, we could say that in the late 1970s the critical empire of "technocratic deviations" (in Vidal's sense) entered its third stage, that "of the empire in decline" (Krieger's term). At the same time, the rise of "culture-oriented" studies marked the first stage of the empire-to-be, which defined its territory in the academic marketplace by focusing on the notion of otherness. It is beyond dispute that it was this awareness of difference that led to the absorption into the literary canon not only of testimonio, but of other previously unrecognized or underrepresented areas of Latin American letters as well, including women's writing and minority autobiographies. And, last but not least, the fact that most of the initial studies of testimonio were published in the United States adds yet another ironic twist to the "imperialist" terminology proposed by Krieger and Vidal. During this first stage of consolidation, critics–myself included–followed the stimulus of the official register of testimonial texts. For the most part, reading against the grain of testimonio's editorial voice was avoided for fear of destabilizing its founding political assumptions. With the 1986 publication of René Jara's and Hernán Vidal's Testimonio y literatura, although short of becoming some kind of annus mirabilis, that year marks a turning point in testimonio criticism. In the most general terms, it closes the period of recognition and opens up the stage of consecration. This pioneering monograph also demonstrates how critics in this area defined their turf in the intellectual marketplace by arguing that, unlike any other discourse, testimonio's truth claims are not captive in the prisonhouse of language.

Testimonio was thus canonized as a unique literary form, one that represented both the creative vitality of Latin American culture and its power to change the paradigm of subaltern representation. All this was happening at a time when two disciplines that bear "family resemblance" to testimonial writing–history and anthropology–had already been involved in an intense process of self-interrogation. In the early 1970s Clifford Geertz and Hayden White admitted, respectively, that the ethnographer's and historian's activities consist of producing texts. Consequently, they suggested that rhetorical analysis should take precedence over scientific truth claims, and White went almost as far as the Derridean negation of the "hors texte" (outside the text) when he declared that "truth remains captive of the linguistic mode" (xi). In contrast, while some of the sociologically oriented Latin American testimonies

(such as the Brazilian Memórias do exílio [Memoirs of Exile]) encompass a discursive spectrum that extends from methodological considerations to serious editorial interventions, most writers of testimonio have opted for avoiding the self-reflexive examination of their own modus operandi. As Kathleen Logan observes, even the editors of personal testimonies published in recent years "rarely discuss the significant part played by the recorder-editor in creating the structure of the final document. Nor is much said about the social relationship between the authors of the testimonies and those who record and edit them" (203). Logan illustrates her point with two mediated women's testimonials: Este es mi testimonio: María Teresa Tula, luchadora pro-derechos humanos de El Salvador [1994; Hear My Testimony: María Teresa Tula, Human Rights Activist of El Salvador] and Celsa's World: Conversations with a Mexican Peasant Woman (1994, Tirado 1991).

Even though I would hesitate to follow Joe Kicheloe's lead and call such reluctance to write self-reflexively "the modernist paranoia" (70), I would note that the approach that prevailed in testimonio criticism until the mid-1980s also tended to eschew self-questioning by tacitly assuming the transparency of language within authentic narratives. Among the studies that viewed testimonio through the lens of its documentary value and that revalidated the notion of the subject repressed by poststructuralism are the early works by Beverley, Yúdice, and Zimmerman, together with the studies by Duchesne, René Jara, Renato Prada Oropeza, Margaret Randall, Ileana Rodríguez, and Vidal. It was not until the late 1980s that a number of critical works by Achugar, Rosemary Geisdorfer Feal, Lucille Kerr, Alberto Moreiras, Doris Sommer, Cynthia Steele, and Vera-León, as well as new approaches by Beverley, Yúdice, and Zimmerman, began to effectively challenge the original presupposition that revealing testimonio's rhetorical workings would "convict" it politically. This shift in focus is perhaps best illustrated by The Real Thing: Testimonial Discourses and Latin America, a collection of essays that covers the last decade of work on the topic. While building on existing studies, The Real Thing takes a step forward in testimonio criticism in that it brings some much-needed methodological rigor (by Beverley, Alberto Moreiras, Sommer, and Gareth Williams). In contrast to earlier monographic studies (such as the 1991 issue of Latin American Perspectives), The Real Thing seeks to reinscribe some of the basic tenets of testimonio criticism within a changing sociopolitical context. By juxtaposing different approaches and allowing the critics to reexamine their own presuppositions (compare the "early" and "later" articles by Beverley), the editor of the volume, Georg M. Gugelberger, has set the stage for a critically productive dialogue. Framed by a thoughtful introduction, The Real Thing certainly exemplifies the evolving recognition that sociopolitical aspects of testimonio should go hand in hand with textual analysis; but it also reminds us that we are well into the third stage of testimonio's trajectory, with its textual productivity in decline and critical enterprise somewhat fossilized.

Testimonial Paradigms: Religion, Anthropology, Psychoanalysis, Law

Even though, as we have just seen, in contemporary critical parlance, by testimonio we mean in Latin America a first-person narrative elicited by a bona fide intellectual from a marginalized witness and then further transformed through rhetorical strategies, the task of rethinking the testimonial mode within a larger project of comparative literary history has to transcend this specific format and place in time. To be sure, the 1970s and 1980s saw eyewitness narratives emerge from the margins of literature. However, even a cursory historical overview will remind us that testimonial writing is probably the most enduring tradition in Latin American letters. Rather than subject the reader to a lengthy catalogue of texts that extend—or may be stretched over—a broad spectrum of testifying, my approach here is to examine some of the discursive patterns used to produce the testimonial effect. More specifically, I will seek to show how contemporary *testimonio* conflates and puts into play four deep-rooted orders of discourse: the religious, the anthropological, the psychoanalytic, and the legal. To be sure, I was guided here by Roberto González Echevarría's innovative study *Myth and Archive* that proposes to see Latin American narrative as dominated by "three manifestations of Western hegemonic discourse: the law in the colonial period, the scientific discourse of the many naturalists who ranged over the American continent in the nineteenth century, and anthropology, which supplies a dominant version of Latin American culture in the modern period" (172).

While I do not intend to overdo or misuse the metaphor of cannibalization—which has recently become something of a keyword in postcolonial discourse (Kilgour)—I would argue that Latin American *testimonio* could function at some point as an effective political tool due to, among other factors, its subversive reappropriation of recognizable paradigms. Whether "the master's tools"—no matter how defiantly wielded—can or cannot "dismantle the master's house" (in Andre Lorde's phrase) is a question I would like to keep in mind while discussing those different "tools" or paradigms of the Western tradition: religion, anthropology, psychoanalysis, and law.

To begin with Paul Ricoeur's (b. 1913) helpful analysis of religious testimony, we should remember that in the Western tradition testimony begins as a confession of truth. In his essay on hermeneutics, Ricoeur takes us as far back as the Book of Exodus and demonstrates how the claim of biblical scribes to provide reliable testimony hinges upon the authority of the eyewitness and the etymological link between the word "witness" and its root word "martyr": "When the test of conviction becomes the price of life, the witness changes his name; he is called a martyr. . . . *Martus* in Greek means witness" (129). Julia Kristeva makes a similar point in her study of confession in Christian tradition: "*Omologeo* and *martireo*, I *acknowledge* and I *bear witness*: in those terms Christians *confess*, hence avow their faith in Christ, as they will later their trinitary faith. . . . The avowal of faith is thus from the very start tied to persecution and suffering. This pain, moreover, has wholly permeated the word "martyr," giving it its basic, ordinary meaning, that of torture rather than testimony" (129).

The act of testifying as an act of faith—with the overtones of suffering and persecution—is clearly exemplified by one of the best-known Latin American *testimonios*—Rigoberta Menchú's 1983 account of the victimization of the indigenous population of Guatemala. The vast corpus of both direct and mediated testimonies from the Southern Cone, denouncing torture and persecution, also belongs here, with well-known accounts of Alicia Portnoy (b. 1955), Jacobo Timerman (1923–1999), and Hernán Valdés (b. 1937), among many others. The depictions of political violence often follow the bifurcating paths of interviews, fragmentary manuscripts, and scraps of memory, as in the Brazilian collective *Memórias do exílio de muitos caminhos* [Memoirs of Exile Along Many Paths] and *Memórias das mulheres do exílio (depoimentos)* [Memoirs of Women in Exile (Testimonies)]. On the other side of the Atlantic, the massive human suffering of the Holocaust and the Gulags has also stimulated an outpouring of testimonial writings on the part of survivors. In all of these cases, writing in response to the unspeakable crimes—which in the plans of the perpetrators were to remain untold—draws meaning from the same semantic sphere of confession and has the emblematic value of "martyrdom" testimony. As a way of modifying and enriching this approach we may want to consider Gareth Williams's persuasive reading of *testimonio* as "the discursive reconfiguration of personal and collective experience . . . facilitated by a movement of mourning in which loss of original selfhood is fought against and reconciled to itself by its absorption and translation into the very basis of cultural resistance and survival" (97).

Within the multilayered discursive memory of *testimonio*, the presence of anthropology may not be as deep-seated as that of religion, but it appears to be more tangible. In view of the fact that the ethnographic process of making the experience of the other "palatable to our sapience, and amenable to our interests" (Tyler 96) is mentioned quite explicitly in most archetypical testimonials, it is anthropological discourse that gives *testimonio* a semblance of cohesiveness. Barnet, for example, remarks in his preface to *Biografía de un cimarrón* that, as editor, he had to "paraphrase a good deal" of Montejo's testimony in order to avoid confusion and repetition. In a similar vein, Burgos-Debray candidly admits to have reorganized Menchú's words: "I followed my original chronological outline, even though our conversations had not done so, so as to make the text more accessible to the reader" (xx). Both statements provide the most persuasive illustration for Tyler's argument that the ethnographer's task "to achieve in writing what speech has created" (197) is a paradoxical one. In a parallel vein, the specific conjunction of anthropology and *testimonio* is the focus of *The Anthropological Imagination in Latin American Literature* by Amy Fass Emery (see, in particular, the chapter "The Voice of the Other: Anthropological Discourse and the *Testimonio* in *Biografía de un cimarrón* and *Canto de sirena*," 70–92). The link between *testimonio* and anthropology becomes somewhat more nuanced in the light of Michel de Certeau's notion of heterology as an art—or science—attempting to capture a voice reaching us from across a range of cultural, ethnic, and gender boundaries:

> The heterological operations seem to depend on the fulfillment of two conditions: an object, defined as "fable," and an instrument, translation. To define the position of the other (primitive, religious, mad, childlike, or popular) as a "fable" is not merely to identify it with "what speaks" but with a speech that "does not know" what it says. . . . The fable is thus a word full of meaning, but what is says "implicitly" becomes "explicit" only through scholarly exegesis. (1986, 160)

Exploring the tacit clauses of heterology makes us realize to what extent testimonial mediation actually resembles not only an encounter between an anthropologist and a native informant, but also the one between an analyst and a patient. *Biografía de un cimarrón* may well serve as an example of this similarity. Barnet's celebrated book creates a fable of a mutually constructed reality through dialogue and "translation." The oral testimony of a 105-year-old illiterate former slave is recorded and then transcribed by a young Cuban ethnologist who has no direct knowledge of the facts he is assembling into discourse. By sifting a wealth of data, Barnet is performing a contradictory role: On the one hand, he is a researcher, an engaged participant, whose own theoretical biases and sympathetic gaze should not interfere with the making of an ordered scientific record; on the other hand, he is a literary writer who–despite his explicit disavowal of all aesthetic intentions–seeks to construct a readable tale. And from both of these points of view, the informant's life story requires rewriting in order to be valued as "literary," even though Montejo is an exceptional raconteur. After all, "Who would want to read unimproved fieldnotes?" (59)–asks James Clifford in a recent essay on ethnographic writing. The actual extent to which the editor might have imposed his own narrative devices on Montejo's account is impossible to assess. Even though Barnet takes us behind the scenes of the production of the testimony, in the introduction he talks about it in a somewhat oblique manner. In the text per se, the editor leaves no fingerprints, except for an occasional footnote and a glossary. What he discloses, however, indicates his dissatisfaction with Montejo's disjointed style, replete with digressions and repetitions: "I have necessarily had to paraphrase a good deal of what he told me. If I had transcribed his story word for word it would have been confusing and repetitive. I have kept the story within fixed time-limits, not being concerned to recreate the period in minute detail of time and place" (8). What remains even more obscure than the specific details of Barnet's editing technique is, of course, what Montejo said and what he withheld. In view of the fact that Doris Sommer has lucidly analyzed similar "secrets" in Rigoberta Menchú's testimony, here I will limit myself to a more general question that we may want to consider throughout a changing history of Latin American testimonials: To what extent does the memory of inquisitorial techniques of confession determine in these texts the complex interplay between disclosure and concealment?

Yet, as we weave together different strands of the heterological tradition, for a different take on Barnet's preface, it may prove helpful to pair it with Sigmund Freud's introduction to what is probably his best-known "case history"–that of Dora. As Steven Marcus has demonstrated, when Freud "proceeds to specify what it is that is wrong with the stories his patients tell him . . . [t]he difficulties are in the first instance formal shortcomings of *narrative*: the connections, 'even the ostensible ones–are for the most part incoherent,' obscured and unclear; 'and the sequence of different events is uncertain'" (55). Among various types of narrative insufficiency, Marcus continues, Freud lists "amnesias and paramnesias of several kinds and various other means of severing connections and altering chronologies" (163). In a similar vein, Barnet underscores the problem of Montejo's failing memory as related to his inability to tell a coherent, chronological story. "In many cases my informant was unable to remember precisely," he states on one occasion, and elaborates further: "Esteban's life in the forest is a remote and confused period in his memory" (8). The superseding voice of the editor is there to bring a restoration of order, narrative harmonization, and a tidy closure. Even though the analogy between Freud and Barnet may be far-fetched, in both cases the act of bearing witness calls for a guided dialogue; the fragmentation of the original account gradually acquires the overall coherence of the final discourse, and the role of the informant has to fit the script of the discipline.

After the enormous success of *Biografía*, Barnet formulated a theory of *testimonio* in his influential essay, "La novela-testimonio: socio-literatura" ["The Testimonial Novel: Socio-literature"]. Originally conceived as a lecture, the text was appended to his testimonial novel *Canción de Rachel* [1969; *Rachel's Song*, 1991], thus inspiring a series of critical debates concerning the amorphous identity of the genre. By following the designation "testimonial novel" affixed to *Canción de Rachel* by the author, readers are more likely to focus on the literary aspect of the text than on the hierarchically structured dialogue between a sympathetic intellectual and a marginalized witness-protagonist–in this case a lower-class woman born to immigrant parents. In a manner similar to another well-known testimonial novel of the period–Elena Poniatowska's *Hasta no verte Jesús mío* [1969; *Here's to You, Jesusa!*, 2001]–*Canción* moves away from the conventions of the first-person deposition and appears closer to the realm of fiction. It is only in light of Barnet's commentary, appended to the Spanish edition of *Canción de Rachel*, that the reader becomes aware of the novel's complex ties with multiple narrative paradigms: life story, confession, and memoir.

Edward H. Friedman's analysis of ways in which the raw material of a life story is transformed in *Hasta no verte Jesús mío* is also helpful in understanding the hybridity of *Canción de Rachel*: "The writer uses a real informant and encodes the material of her interviews to produce a persona, Jesusa Palancares. The account vacillates between the unmediated narration of documentary and the self-conscious reinvention of a nonfictional character through narrative and rhetorical strategies" (170–71). Yet, as enlightening as these remarks might be, they fall short of providing a working definition of the testimonial novel. Dillon has suggested, in a different but related context, that in the absence of explicit negotiations with the reader, "default assumptions will hold according to the genre" (200). Given the importance of texts surrounding the testimony, on one hand, and the considerable differences in this respect between various editions and translations, on the other, readers end up negotiating different testimonial contracts. Consider, for example, the translator's preface to the more recent English translation of *Biografía de un cimarrón*, in which W. Nick Hill says: "The first English translation of Montejo's story took as its title *Autobiography of a Runaway Slave* (U.S. edition, 1968) in recognition of its formal structure, but in so doing it failed to recognize the complex process of reproducing the text. The current translation goes back to the original title of *Biography*" (12). Hill does not talk about other differences, such as the substitution of Barnet's original introduction accompanying many Spanish editions with an essay titled "The Alchemy of Memory," appended to *Biography* as an afterword.

"Difference" seems to be a keyword when approaching *testimonio* and its incarnations. The lack of normative models is such that dealing with texts labeled as *testimonios* or "testimonial novels" is like dealing with multiple selves, and we have to develop a set of instruments for each text under scrutiny by teasing out its formal components. In pursuing this point, let us go back to *Hasta no verte Jesús mío* and *Canción de Rachel*. Unlike Poniatowska's story of Jesusa Palancares, Barnet's text establishes its pact with the reader of the Spanish edition through authorial commentary. In his essay Barnet tells how he interviewed six Cuban women–all of them former actresses in cabaret-style theaters of the Republican period–and then interlinked their selected confessions with materials drawn directly from the Cuban press (1902–1930). In addition, he incorporated into *Canción* several accounts of secondary witnesses. Barnet highlights the fact that he fused six identities into one. We may add that once Rachel becomes a literary creation, her "testimony" ultimately hinges upon dispossessing the real witnesses of their voices. Here, Dillon's analysis of the use of "composite case histories" in advice books offers a curious parallel with Barnet's technique of amalgamation of real witnesses into a fictional persona.

Unlike *Biografía de un cimarrón*–which allocates testimonial authority to one narrator and bears the authenticating seal of a real witness–*Canción de Rachel* evolves around the erosion of identity and subjectivity. And because testimonial texts base their claims to truth primarily on the credibility of the witness, the testimonial word of a woman "whose name was not Rachel" can quite easily be deemed unreliable. Subjecthood, Kamala Visweswaran tells us, "requires a category or name" (60). However, "the naming process itself suggests a juridical or inquisitorial model of history, one that interrogates the subject beginning with the first question: 'What is your name?'" (60). Latin American testimonials are rife with naming, renaming, and refusing a name. Rachel, as we have seen, is "baptized" as she is invented by Barnet; so is Jesusa Palancares, whose real name, according to Poniatowska, was Josefina Borque. In Montejo's case there is a discrepancy between his "real" name and the one he chooses to use: "One of my surnames is Montejo," he explains, "after my mother, who was a slave of French origin. The other is Mera. But hardly anyone knows this. Well, why should I tell people, since it is false anyway? It should really be Mesa, but what happened is that they changed it in the archives" (17). And Rigoberta Menchú, as we remember, refuses to name her protective spirit: "I can't tell you what my *nahual* is because that is one of my secrets" (20).

Numerous studies point to the tenuous nature of the testifying process even when the name and the identity of the witness are "real." Lorraine Code, for example, attributes the fragility of testimony to its indirect, dialogical format: "a testimonial report looks to its listener(s) for evidence of comprehension, acknowledgment. For testimony is, inherently, a form of address in which epistemic interaction, intersubjectivity are explicitly invoked" (65). A similar argument is offered by Ricoeur, albeit with a clearly judicial twist. Since "we cannot claim to have certainty but only probability, and the probable is only pursued through a struggle of opinion" (125), in Ricoeur's view persuading the opposition becomes a complex technique, which should "take into consideration the dispositions of the audience and the character of the orator" (127).

Code's and Ricoeur's ideas cast another light on the precarious condition of Rachel as a witness. She is portrayed by secondary (male) informants in the novel as untrustworthy not only because of her much-disputed reputation as a woman, but also because of her narrative incompetence. She is perceived as an unreliable narrator, whose reconstruction of the past is tainted by her failing memory and willful fabrication. Furthermore, she is guilty of narrative sloppiness, which manifests itself in forgoing causal explanation and linear notions of history. Rachel has no credibility to begin with because–as a foreigner, an actress, and a woman of ill repute–she does not fit the stereotype of a reliable witness. Her narrative incompetence discredits her altogether, for it clearly positions her as a "hysterical female." Mary Ann Doane has noted in a similar context that inconsistencies in women's discourse have traditionally been associated with hysteria: "The woman's narrative acumen is thus transformed into the symptom of illness. Her narrative cannot stand on its own, it must be interpreted. . . .The

logic seems to be this: if a woman must assume the agency of speech, of narration, let her do so within the well-regulated context of an institutionalized dialogue–psychoanalysis, the hospital, the court of law" (165).

Regarded from a "literary" point of view, *Canción de Rachel* is a tribute to modern perspectivism, allowing us to glean a few bits and pieces of fragmented lives and selves rather than a complete story of a unified and stable subject. But from the testimonial perspective, it dramatizes the fact that for the belief in the power of a personal testimony to crumble, it is enough not to grant the witness the right to tell her own story. When the fictional Rachel makes her alleged "confession" in a room full of photos and newspaper clippings, the real Rachels are lost forever, outside of the time and the space of the novel that never quite becomes testimonial.

The Case of *Operación masacre*: The Rhetoric of the Differend

Although much can be learned from the recognition that there are many facets to any testimonial paradigm and that none of them provides unmediated truth, I would like to avoid what Mary E. Hawkesworth calls "the slide into relativism that results from too facile a conflation of world and text" (555). In my search for a mode of analysis that would not lock us into a duality of context versus text, Lyotard's work on the protocols governing testimonial contract began to look particularly promising. Although Lyotard's *The Differend* is essentially a defense of testimonials, his project does not see such texts as monolithic monuments of authenticity and truth. Rather, his approach points to possible ways in which to remain sensitive to the complexities of representation, while being aware of the fact that social experience cannot be reduced to a linguistic sign. Lyotard stresses what I would call a forward-looking quality of testimonial discourse as part of the ongoing task of rewriting human experience. This task, in Lyotard's words, calls for instituting "new addressees, new addressors, new significations, and new referents in order for the wrong to find an expression and for the plaintiff to cease being a victim. This requires new rules for the formation and linking of phrases. No one doubts that language is capable of admitting these new phrase families or new genres of discourse. Every wrong ought to be able to be put into phrases" (13).

Four elements are required, according to Lyotard, to build a phrase universe of a *testimonial contract* as a truth-believing paradigm. First, we need an addressee–someone not only willing to listen and accept the reality of the referent, but also worthy of being spoken to. Then there is an addressor, a witness who not only is a survivor but who also refuses to remain silent. Third, we have to find a language capable of signifying the referent. And finally, the referent emerges, demanding "to be put into phrases, and suffers from the wrong of not being able to be put into phrases right away" (13). The referent, continues Lyotard, may be obliterated if silence results from the denial of one or several of the preceding three elements (14). In other words, testimony takes place only if the reality of a referent is established and, in order for this to happen, all silent negations must be withdrawn and the authority/credibility of the witness, the addressee's competence/credulity, and language's ability to signify must be assured. Dori Laub's remark on the fragility of the testimonial process reinforces Lyotard's point: "The absence of an empathic listener, or more radically, the absence of an *addressable other*, an other who can hear the anguish of one's memories and thus affirm and recognize their realness, annihilates the story" (Felman and Laub 68). As a way of illustrating these somewhat abstract points, let us think about the case of Anita Hill and Clarence Thomas in the 1991 U.S. Senate hearings. According to Kimberle Crenshaw, Hill's testimony met with incredulity because she as a witness did not comply with the dominant presumptions concerning credibility: "the particularities of black female subordination are suppressed as the terms of racial and gender discrimination law require that we mold our experience into that of either white women or black men in order to be legally recognized" (qtd. in Code 61).

From the standpoint of literary criticism, the usefulness of Lyotard's subject positioning consists in underscoring the importance of language in persuasion and representation. The reason I suggest that we take cue from Lyotard's proposal when approaching *testimonio* is, while it remains politically principled, this obvious "commitment" does not detract from exploring the fault lines of language and *testimonio*'s contradictory workings. Lyotard reminds us over and over again that there is a fine line between transposing human suffering into nothing but text and acknowledging, self-critically, that there is no discourse that makes sense of everything, that "what remains to be phrased exceeds what we can presently phrase" (13). In the following reading of *Operación masacre* [Operation Massacre], I shall attempt to address some of the issues so poignantly discussed by Lyotard. I have let the concept of the "differend" guide my thinking here in order to see how the process of producing the testimonial effect is shaped through a series of "tangled negotiations" in a "power-saturated" context (Code 67). *Operación masacre* is arguably the only Latin American mediated testimonial recognized as "canonical" that does not attempt to gloss over its own contradictions. Rather, it incorporates its own critique into the creative process, unmasks its own status as a second-order retelling of events, and signals that "facts" may always be refuted or airbrushed.

Originally published in 1957, Rodolfo Walsh's (1927–1977) account of a massacre of a group of alleged supporters of a Peronist uprising in June 1956 underwent numerous revisions. In what is regarded as the final version, the book consists of a prologue; Part I, detailing the activities of the victims on the night of the arrest; Part II, focusing on the arrest and the massacre; and Part III, recreating the court case on behalf of the five dead and seven survivors of the massacre. The figure of the journalist/editor becomes crucial in the endeavor to recover the history—which was meant by the military authorities to be erased without a trace. Walsh's position resembles that of an ancient *histôr*—described by François Hartog—as it evolved in the antiquity from its initial sense as eyewitness to that of an investigator, a judge, and a wordsmith (Hartog 87).

In his introduction to the third edition of the book (1969) Walsh explains how he was able to create a situation of enunciation—a "rhetorical space" in Code's terminology—that would allow the victims to attest in the most compelling way to what had happened. What Walsh/the *histôr* knows is not grounded in what he saw, but in what he heard in the process of his painstaking and often perilous investigation. His credulity empowers the victims: "Livarga me cuenta su historia increíble; le creo en el acto. Así nace aquella investigación, este libro. La larga noche del 9 de junio vuelve sobre mí, por segunda vez me saca de 'las suaves, tranquilas estaciones" (11) ("Livarga tells me his incredible story; at once I believe him and that is how my research and this book began. The long night of 9 June comes back to me, and once again forces me out of my calm and tranquility"). Livarga, shot through the

face, not only survives the massacre but, along with Walsh, fights against forgetting. "Será el único" ("He must be the only one"), says Walsh, "entre los sobrevivientes y familiares de las víctimas, que se atreve a presentarse para reclamar justicia" (49) ("among the survivors and the families of the victims who dares to demand justice"). In Lyotard's terms, it is Walsh's investigative journalism that makes the testimonial phrase regimen possible by assuming the following: that the situation in question (the massacre) falls within his competence; that it indeed happened; that it can be signified; and, last but not least, that it is the survivor's business to be talking about it (Lyotard 14).

Yet, as Kathleen Newman has pointed out in one of the most incisive analyses of Walsh's work, the focus on the author's transformation from an apolitical intellectual into a committed reporter is the flipside of the testimonial account: "the fact that Walsh the author is to be a protagonist as much as the men whose encounter with death he is going to narrate, changes the purpose of the narrative. Walsh will become, like them, a hero" (201). Walsh's status within the discourse can be perceived as disquieting and it certainly begs the question of what is at stake when a committed intellectual uses his own political agenda to assure the tellability of a story based on other people's experiences. Despite the usual misgivings in relation to testimonial mediation—as occurring at the intersection of unequal power, knowledge, and authority—it does not seem essential to elaborate here on the pitfalls of the account given through the filter of investigative reporting, mainly because the writer himself begins by setting forth two intertwined modes of reading—the testimonial and the self-critical (meta-testimonial). Perhaps the most significant difference between Walsh and other editors of well-known mediated stories (Barnet or Burgos-Debray) is that he does not deflect the focus away from his own persona. On the contrary, by inscribing himself into the text, he cannot claim to be an unobtrusive interviewer or a self-effacing editor. Whereas Barnet and Burgos practice what Algidras J. Greimas calls the strategy of "objectivizing camouflage" (685) whereby all "marks of enunciation" are erased, Walsh does not obliterate the context of the primary discourse. Rather than trying to create a simulacrum of a seamless text, he subjects bits and pieces of testimonies to a relentless negotiation of meaning between the listener and the testifier.

Throughout this process of testimony building Walsh reflects openly on the fact that the memory of events has been restructured and there are quite a few blanks in the text. When commenting, quite un-self-critically, on the lack of information about one of the victims, he concludes bitterly: "En estas dos instantáneas puede resumirse toda la vida de un hombre" ("the entire life of a man is reduced to these two snapshots"). The entire account is interspersed with remarks such as: "No hay testigos de lo que hablan. Sólo podemos formular conjeturas" (30) ("There are no witnesses to what was said. We can only guess"); "De Garibotti no volveremos a tener referencias ciertas" (31) ("We will not have any more certain traces of Garibotti"); "Será difícil encontrar a un testigo que recuerde a todos; los que podrían hacerlo están ausentes o muertos" (55) ("It will be difficult to find a witness who can remember them all. Those who could have, have either disappeared or are dead"). At the close of the first part, significantly titled "Las incógnitas" ["Doubts"], the narrator confesses to what he does not know: "Con respecto a estos dos hombres, nuestra búsqueda ha concluído en un callejón sin salida" (55) ("With respect to these two men, our search ended in a blind alley"). According to David William Foster this segment can be read as "the narrator's cry of frustration" (44). Yet I would argue that it also reveals the constitutive strength of testimony: its resistance to establishing closure and its ability to contest silence from new perspectives and with new evidence. What the testimony does not offer, Felman and Laub remind us in their book on post-Holocaust testimonials, is "a completed statement, a totalizable account of . . . events. In the testimony, language is in process and on trial, it does not possess itself as a conclusion, as the constatation of a verdict or the self-transparency of knowledge" (5).

Walsh's tedious search for evidence against the corrupt establishment and against the silence of the victims also implies a search for a language capable of signifying the differend, that is "the case where the plaintiff is divested of the means to argue and becomes for that reason a victim" (9). A case of a differend between two parties, explains Lyotard, takes place when "the 'regulation' of the conflict that opposes them is done in the idiom of one of the parties while the wrong suffered by the other is not signified in that idiom" (9). In the case recounted by Walsh this hegemonic idiom is the one of law. Since *Operación masacre* has to signify the wrong suffered by "the other" in the idiom of law, some of the rhetorical ploys used by Walsh have little to do with the rules of literary tellability. Such is the case with his reconstruction of the exact time at which the radio station stopped playing music and announced martial law. Careful attention to tangible details (e.g., time, place, and identity) becomes paramount in Walsh's argument, as it enables him to prove that the massacre had taken place before the imposition of martial law and therefore could not be legally justified. Here is how he presents the results of his inquiry: "Este, pues, es el documento al que tiene que responder, y no responderá jamás, la revolución libertadora. Prueba todo lo que afirmé en mis artículos de 'Mayoría' y en la primera edición de este libro: que se detuvo a un grupo de hombres antes de entrar en vigencia la ley marcial; que no se les instruyó proceso; no se averiguó quiénes eran; no se les dictó sentencia; y se los masacró en un descampado" (170) ("This then is the document to which the 'liberating revolution' must respond and does not. It proves what I state in my articles of 'Mayoría' and in the first edition of this book: that a group of men were detained before martial law was declared; that they were never arraigned; that they were never identified; that they were never sentenced; and that they were massacred in an open field").

Let us consider another example of where the differend has to be signified in the parlance of law in order to be vindicated. When reviewing the "órdenes de encarcelación" ["orders of imprisonment"] that one of the survivors, Giunta, was given upon his release from jail, Walsh notes: "En la de Giunta, en el rubro 'causa,' había una expresiva línea de guiones escritos a máquina. Sin causa, en efecto, se había pretendido fusilarlo. Sin causa, se le había torturado moralmente hasta los límites de la resistencia humana. Sin causa, se lo había condenado al hambre y la sed. Sin causa, se lo había engrillado y esposado. Y ahora, sin causa, en virtud de un simple decreto que llevaba el No. 14.975, se lo restituía al mundo" (134) ("In the case of Giunta, under the heading of 'cause,' there was a most expressive line of hyphens typed in. There was in effect no cause. It had been determined that he would be executed. Without cause, he had been tortured to

the very limits of human endurance. Without cause, he had been condemned to hunger and thirst. Without cause, he had been shackled and handcuffed. And now, without cause, by virtue of a simple decree number 14.975, he had been released"). It seems obvious that no "cause" should justify torture, brutality, or death, but Walsh has to speak with a forked tongue in order to enter the "phrase regimen" of the law and challenge it from within. This tactic–which has been analyzed from different points of view by Foster, Newman, and Aníbal Ford–is a double-edged one, since it may be perceived as reproducing the dominant discourse rather than reconfiguring it. Nonetheless, it is precisely this method that enables Walsh to conclude the final version of his book with the following refutation: "No habrá ya malabarismos capaces de borrar la terrible evidencia de que el gobierno de la revolución libertadora aplicó retroactivamente, a hombres detenidos el 9 de junio, una ley marcial promulgada el 10 de junio. Y eso no es fusilamiento. Es un asesinato" (191–92) ("There would be no more juggling of facts that could possibly erase the damning evidence that the government of the "liberating revolution" had retroactively applied martial law invoked on June 10 to a group of men detained on June 9. This was not execution. It was assassination").

As Walsh carves out a rhetorical space that will legitimate and foster his witnesses' words, he shows in practice what Code has argued on a theoretical level: That which is at stake in the testimonial process is not so much "the nature and status of empirical evidence" as the distribution of power and "cognitive authority" (62). Thus, as a form projecting faith, presence, and truth, any testimonial format presents a paradox: It can be used both as an institutional model to control the other *and* as a form of transgression and resistance on the part of the victim.

Throughout his search for evidence and a language to signify it, Walsh appeared to have warned his countrymen against collective oblivion. On 25 March 1977, after having written an open letter denouncing the crimes of the military junta, the writer was kidnapped and "disappeared." Six years later, when reflecting upon European amnesia vis-à-vis the Holocaust, Lyotard wrote the following words that could serve both as a postscript to Walsh's work and an epitaph:

> The "perfect crime" does not consist in killing the victim or the witness (that adds new crimes to the first one and aggravates the difficulty of effacing everything), but rather in obtaining the silence of the witnesses, the deafness of the judges, and the inconsistency (insanity) of the testimony. You neutralize the addressor, the addressee, and the sense of the testimony; then everything is as if there were no referent (no damages). If there is nobody to adduce the proof, nobody to admit it, and/or if the argument which upholds it is judged to be absurd, then the plaintiff is dismissed, the wrong he or she complains of cannot be attested. He or she becomes a victim. (13)

So far, nobody has been able to do on behalf of Walsh what he himself had done in *Operación masacre*: to adduce the proof, to admit it, to uphold it and, ultimately, to offer a redemptive testimonial retelling of the horror of his disappearance.

Conclusions

As we have seen, most Latin American writers and Latinamericanists have agreed by now–to varying degrees–that truth in *testimonio* is produced rather than told. As we live through an era labeled as postmodern, the testimonial function that acquired canonicity through *testimonio* appears to be extending over a wider spectrum of texts. On the one hand–and quite predictably, if we agree with the theory of literary evolution proposed by the Russian Formalists–the recognition of *testimonio* has set the stage for outright parodies of its conventions. On the other, the reexamination of *testimonio's* presuppositions has produced texts such as Ruth Behar's *Translated Woman: Crossing the Border with Esperanza's Story* (1993), whose unmitigated self-consciousness appeals to our postmodern sense without the side effect of deconstructing the testimonial pact altogether. Still, critics differ in their assessment of Behar's work as testimony. In Logan's judgment, Behar not only "explores the terrain of self versus other or distinctions between subject and object that usually determine the structure of testimonial literature," but also "takes care to link her reflections to the existing literature on testimonies and also to the current fiction and poetry being written by Latin American women" (203–4). According to Logan, Behar has created "a path-breaking melange of advocacy, reflection, oral literature, and social science" (203–4). I tend to agree, however, with Moreiras's more nuanced assessment of the paradoxes produced by Behar's extreme use of self-reflection:

> It is a maddening text: it problematizes the authorial position because it takes to an extreme the irreducible conflict between political desire and epistemic constraints; it pretends to translate without ignoring the fact that translation shows the original to be dead, that it in fact kills the original; it allegorizes the relationship between anthropologist and subject as that between a wetback and her coyote, maybe even the worst kind of coyote; it calls itself redemptive ethnography knowing full well that there is no redemption actually happening anywhere; it denounces its own malinchismo; it purports to go beyond the self/other division without actually bothering the self/other division. (223)

While we may be inclined to lament the demise of "the dialogue essential to testimonial discourse" due, in part, "to the retrenchment of the left" (Sanjinés 254), we should bear in mind that the loss of *testimonio's* critical potential is quite likely to open spaces for previously unheard voices and alternative venues of representation. Tellingly, the most recent perspectives on the topic depart from *testimonio* "as we know it." These newer approaches demonstrate, as Jill Brody observes, the diminishing role of testimonial mediation and "increased appreciation of indigenous authorship and growing concern about preserving and documenting endangered and disappearing languages" (250). Rather than becoming nostalgic custodians of *testimonio*, which, in Beverley's words, "runs the risk of becoming a new form of *costumbrismo*" (1996, 281), we have to consider new ways of mobilizing public memory in the era of powerful global transformations and virtual realities.

Works Cited

Achugar, Hugo. 1992. "Historias paralelas/Historias ejemplares: La historia y la voz del otro." *Revista de Crítica Literaria Latinoamericana* 36: 49–71.

Amar Sánchez, Ana María. 1986. "La propuesta de una escritura: En homenaje a Rodolfo Walsh." *Revista Iberoamericana* 135–36: 431–45.

—. 1990. "La ficción del testimonio." *Revista Iberoamericana* 151: 447–62.

Barnet, Miguel. 1966. *Biografía de un cimarrón*. La Habana: Instituto de Etnología y Folklore.

—. 1969. *Canción de Rachel*. La Habana: Instituto del Libro.

—. 1981. "The Documentary Novel." *Cuban Studies/Estudios Cubanos* 11.1: 19–32.

—. 1991. *Rachel's Song*. Trans. W. Nick Hill. Willimantic, CT: Curbstone Press.

—. 1994. *Biography of a Runaway Slave*. Trans. W. Nick Hill. Willimantic, CT: Curbstone Press.

Behar, Ruth. 1993. *Translated Woman: Crossing the Border with Esperanza's Story*. Boston: Beacon.

Beverley, John. 1989. "The Margin at the Center: On *Testimonio* (Testimonial Narrative)." *Modern Fiction Studies* 35.1: 11–28.

—. 1991. "'Through All Things Modern': Second Thoughts on Testimonio." *boundary 2*, 18.2: 1–21.

—. 1996. "The Real Thing." *The Real Thing: Testimonial Discourse and Latin America*. Ed. Georg M. Gugelberger. Durham and London: Duke University Press. 266–86.

Beverley, John, and Marc Zimmerman. 1990. *Literature and Politics in the Central American Revolutions*. Austin: University of Texas Press.

Brodzky, Bella, and Celeste Schenck, eds. 1988. *Life/Lines: Theorizing Women's Autobiography*. Ithaca: Cornell University Press.

Brody, Jill. 1994. "Performance and Discourse: Transcribing Latin American Languages and Cultures." *Latin American Research Review* 29.3: 249–56.

Carey-Webb, Allen, and Stephen Benz. 1996. *Teaching and Testimony: Rigoberta Menchú and North American Classroom*. Albany: SUNY Press.

Cavalcanti, Pedro, Celso Uchôa, and Jovelino Ramos, eds. 1978. *Memórias do exílio: Brazil 1964–19??. De muitos caminhos*. Vol. I. Sao Paulo: Livramento.

Certeau, Michel de. 1984. *The Practice of Everyday Life*. Trans. Steven F. Randall. Berkeley: University of California Press.

—. 1986. *Heterologies: Discourse on the Other*. Trans. Brian Massumi. Minneapolis: University of Minnesota Press.

Chevigny, Bell Gale. 1986. "Twice-Told Tales and the Meaning of History: Testimonial Novels by Miguel Barnet and Norman Mailer." *Centennial Review* 30.2: 181–95.

Clifford, James. 1990. "Notes on (Field) Notes." *Fieldnotes: The Making of Anthropology*. Ed. Roger Sanjek. Ithaca and London: Cornell University Press. 47–70.

Code, Lorraine. 1995. *Rhetorical Spaces: Essays on Gendered Locations*. New York and London: Routledge.

Craft, Linda J. 1997. *Novels of Testimony and Resistance from Central America*. Gainesville: University of Florida Press.

Dillon, George L. 1989. "Fiction in Persuasion: Personal Experience as Evidence and as Art." *Literary Nonfiction: Theory, Criticism, Pedagogy*. Ed. Chris Anderson. Carbondale/Edwardsville: Southern Illinois University Press.

Doane, Mary Ann. 1986. "The Clinical Eye: Medical Discourse in the 'Woman's Film' of the 1940s." *The Female Body in Western Culture: Contemporary Perspectives*. Ed. Susan Rubin Suleiman. Cambridge: Harvard University Press. 152–74.

Dorfman, Ariel. 1966. "La última obra de Capote: Un nuevo género literario?" *Anales de la Universidad de Chile* 124: 94–117.

Duchesne Winter, Juan. 1992. *La narrativa de testimonio en América Latina: Cinco estudios*. Río Piedras: Universidad de Puerto Rico.

Emery, Amy Fass. 1996. *The Anthropological Imagination in Latin American Literature*. Columbia and London: University of Missouri Press.

Feal, Rosemary Geisdorfer. 1990. "Spanish American Ethnobiography and the Slave Narrative Tradition: *Biografía de un cimarrón* and *Me llamo Rigoberta Menchú*." *Modern Language Studies* 20.1: 100–111.

Felman, Shoshana, and Dori Laub. 1992. *Testimony: Crisis of Witnessing Literature, Psychoanalysis and History*. New York and London: Routledge.

Foley, Barbara. 1980. "History, Fiction, and the Ground Between: The Uses of the Documentary Mode in Black Literature." *PMLA* 95.3: 389–403.

Ford, Aníbal. 1972. "Walsh: la reconstrucción de los hechos." *Nueva novela latinoamericana*. Ed. Jorge Lafforgue. Buenos Aires: Paidós. 2: 272–322.

Foster, David William. 1984. "Latin American Documentary Narrative." *PMLA* 99.1: 41–55.

Fraire, Isabel. 1983. "Testimonial Literature: A New Window on Reality." *The American Book Review* (September–October): 5–6.

Friedman, Edward H. 1987. *The Antiheroine's Voice: Narrative Discourse and Transformations of the Picaresque*. Columbia: University of Missouri Press.

Geertz, Clifford. 1973. *The Interpretation of Cultures: Selected Essays*. New York: Basic Books.

Giardinelli, Mempo. 1989. "Novela, testimonio y *Non-Fiction Novel*: Una opinión." *Puro Cuento* (May–June) 16: 28–31.

Glowinski, Michal. 1987. "Document as Novel." *New Literary History* 18.2: 385–401.

Gluck, Sherna Berger, and Daphne Patai, eds. 1991. *Women's Words: The Feminist Practice of Oral History*. New York: Routledge.

González Echevarría, Roberto. 1990. *Myth and Archive: A Theory of Latin American Narrative*. Cambridge: Cambridge University Press.

González Echevarría, Roberto, and Enrique Pupo-Walker, eds. 1996. *The Cambridge History of Latin American Literature*. 3 vols. Cambridge: Cambridge University Press.

Greimas, Algirdas Julien. 1989. "The Veridiction Contract." *New Literary History* 20.3: 651–60.

Gugelberger, Georg M., ed. 1996. *The Real Thing: Testimonial Discourses and Latin America*. Durham and London: Duke University Press.

Hartman, Geoffrey H. 1993. "Public Memory and Modern Experience." *Yale Journal of Criticism* 6.2: 239–247.

Hartog, François. 1992. "On Historiographical Operation." *Diacritics* 22.2: 83–93.

Hawkesworth, Mary. 1989. "Knowers, Knowing, Known: Feminist Theory and Claims of Truth." *Signs: Journal of Women in Culture and Society* 14.31: 533–57.

Hellmann, John. 1977. "Fables of Fact: New Journalism Reconsidered." *Centennial Review* 21: 414–32.

Hill, W. Nick. 1994. "Preface." *Biography of a Runaway Slave*. Trans. W. Nick Hill. Willimantic, CT: Curbstone Press. 11–13.

Hollowell, John. 1977. *Fact and Fiction: The New Journalism and the Nonfiction Novel*. Chapel Hill: University of North Carolina Press.

Jara, René, and Hernán Vidal, eds. 1986. *Testimonio y literatura*. Minneapolis: Institute of Ideologies and Literature.

Jesus, Carolina Maria de. 1962. *Quarto de Despejo*. Sao Paulo: Livraria Francisco Alves.

—. 1963. *Child of the Dark: The Diary of Carolina María de Jesus*. Trans. David St. Clair. New York: Dutton.

Kilgour, Maggie. 1990. *From Communion to Cannibalism: An Anatomy of Metaphors of Incorporation*. Princeton: Princeton University Press.

Kincheloe, Joe. 1997. "Fiction Formulas: Critical Constructivism and the Representation of Reality." *Representation and the Text: Re-framing the Narrative Voice*. Ed. William G. Tierney and Yvonna S. Lincoln. Albany: SUNY Press. 57–80.

Krieger, Murray. 1992. "Literary Invention, Critical Fashion, and the Impulse to Theoretical Change: 'Or Whether Revolution Be the Same.'" *Studies in Historical Change*. Ed. Ralph Cohen. Charlottesville and London: University of Virginia Press. 179–206.

Kristeva, Julia. 1982. *Powers of Horror: An Essay on Abjection*. Trans. Leon S. Roudiez. New York: Columbia University Press.

Kundera, Milan. 1981. *The Book of Laughter and Forgetting*. Trans. Michael Henry Heim. New York: Penguin.

Langness, L. L. 1965. *The Life History in Anthropological Science*. New York: Holt, Rinehard and Winston.

Levine, Robert M. 1994. "The Cautionary Tale of Carolina Maria de Jesús." *Latin American Research Review* 29.1: 55–83.

Levinson, Brett. 1996. "Neopatriarchy and After: *I, Rigoberta Menchú* as Allegory of Death." *Journal of Latin American Cultural Studies* 5.1: 33–50.

Logan, Kathleen. 1997. "Personal Testimony: Latin American Women Telling Their Lives." *Latin American Research Review* 32.1: 199–211.

Lohafer, Susan. 1983. *Coming to Terms with the Short Story*. Baton Rouge: Louisiana State University.

Lorde, Audre. 1984. *Sister Outsider: Essays and Speeches by Audre Lorde*. Trumansburg, CA: Crossing Press.

Lyotard, Jean François. 1988. *The Differend: Phrases in Dispute*. Trans. Georges Van Den Abbeele. Minneapolis: University of Minnesota Press.

Marcus, Steven. 1993. "Freud and Dora: Story, History, Case History." *Essential Papers on Literature and Psychoanalysis*. Ed. Emanuel Berman. New York: New York University Press. 36–80.

Mascia-Lees, Frances, Patricia Sharpe, and Colleen Ballerino Cohen. 1989. "The Postmodernist Turn in Anthropology: Cautions from a Feminist Perspective." *Signs: Journal of Women in Culture and Society* 15.1: 7–33.

Mayhew, Henry. 1861–1862. *London Labour and the London Poor: The Condition and Earnings of those that Will Work, Cannot Work, and Will Not Work*. 4 vols. London: C. Griffin.

Menchú, Rigoberta. 1983. *Me llamo Rigoberta Menchú y así me nació la conciencia*. Mexico: Siglo XXI.

—. 1984. *I , Rigoberta Menchú: An Indian Woman in Guatemala*. Ed. Elisabeth Burgos-Debray. Trans. Ann Wright. London: Verso.

Montejo, Esteban. 1968. *The Autobiography of a Runaway Slave*. Ed. Miguel Barnet. Trans. Jocasta Innes. New York: Pantheon Books.

Moreiras, Alberto. 1996. "The Aura of Testimonio." *The Real Thing: Testimonial Discourse and Latin America*. Ed. Georg M. Gugelberger. Durham and London: Duke University Press. 192–224.

Narváez, Jorge. 1983. *El testimonio 1972–82: Transformación de un sistema literario*. Santiago de Chile: CENECA.

Newman, Kathleen. 1983. *The Argentine Political Novel: Determination in Discourse*. Diss. Stanford University. Ann Arbor: University of Michigan.

Oliveira Costa, Albertina de, et al., eds. 1980. *Memórias das mulheres do exílio (depoimentos)*. Vol. 2. Rio de Janeiro: Editora Paz e Terra S.A..

Patai, Daphne. 1988. *Brazilian Women Speak: Contemporary Life Stories*. New Brunswick, NJ and London: Rutgers University Press.

Perus, Françoise. 1989. "El 'otro' del testimonio." *Casa de las Américas* 174: 134–37.

Poniatowska, Elena. 1969. *Hasta no verte Jesús mío*. Mexico City: Era.

—. 2001. *Here's to you, Jesusa*. Trans. Deanna Heikkinen. New York: Farrar, Straus & Giroux.

Randall, Margaret. 1985. *Testimonios: A Guide to Oral History*. Toronto: Participatory Research Group.

Ricoeur, Paul. 1980. "The Hermeneutics of Testimony." *Essays on Biblical Interpretation*. Ed. Lewis S. Mudge. Philadelphia: Fortress Press. 119–54.

Rodríguez, Ileana. 1982. "Organizaciones populares y literatura testimonial: Los años treinta en Nicaragua y El Salvador." *Literatures in Transition: The Many Voices of the Caribbean Area*. Ed. Rose Minc. Gaithersburg, MD: Montclair State College/Hispamérica. 85–96.

Sanjinés, Javier C. 1996. "Beyond Testimonial Discourse: New Popular Trends in Bolivia." *The Real Thing: Testimonial Discourse and Latin America*. Ed. Georg M. Gugelberger. Durham and London: Duke University Press. 254–65.

Sommer, Doris. 1992. "Sin secretos." *Revista de Crítica Literaria Latinoamericana* 36: 135–54.

Steele, Cynthia. 1992. "Testimonio y autoridad en *Hasta no verte Jesús mío*, de Elena Poniatowska." *Revista de Crítica Literaria Latinoamericana* 36: 155–80.

Taussig, Michael. 1996. "The Construction of America: The Anthropologist as Columbus." *Culture/Contexture: Explorations in Anthropology and Literary Studies*. Berkeley: University of California Press. 323–56.

Terkel, Studs. 1974. *Working: People Talk about What They Do All Day and How They Feel About What They Do*. New York: Pantheon Books.

Tirado, Thomas Charles. 1991. *Celsa's World: Conversations with a Mexican Peasant Woman*. Tempe: Center for Latin American Studies, Arizona State University at Tempe.

Tula, María Teresa. 1994. *Hear My Testimony: María Teresa Tula, Human Rights Activist of El Salvador*. Ed. and trans. Lynn Stephen. Boston: South End Press.

Tyler, Stephen. 1987. *The Unspeakable: Discourse, Dialogue, and Rhetoric in the Postmodern World*. Madison: University of Wisconsin Press.

Vidal, Hernán. 1993. "The Concept of Colonial and Postcolonial Discourse: A Perspective from Literary Criticism." *Latin American Research Review* 28.3: 113–119.

Vattimo, Gianni. 1993. "The Decline of the Subject and the Problem of Testimony." *The Adventure of Difference: Philosophy after Nietzsche and Heidegger*. Baltimore: Johns Hopkins University Press. 40–60.

Vera-León, Antonio. 1992. "Hacer hablar: La transcripción testimonial." *Revista de Crítica Literaria Latinoamericana* 18.36: 181–99.

Visweswaran, Kamala. 1994. *Fictions of Feminist Ethnography*. Minneapolis: University of Minnesota Press.

Walsh, Rodolfo. 1972. *Operación masacre*. 3rd ed. Buenos Aires: La Flor.

White, Hayden. 1973. *Metahistory: The Historical Imagination in Nineteenth-Century Europe*. Baltimore: Johns Hopkins University Press.

Williams, Gareth. 1993. "Translation and Mourning: The Cultural Challenge of Latin American Testimonial Autobiography." *Latin American Literary Review* 21.41: 79–99.

Yúdice, George. 1991. "*Testimonio* and Postmodernism." *Voices of the Voiceless in Testimonial Literature*. Ed. Georg Gugelberger and Michael Kearney. Special issue of *Latin American Perspectives* 18.3: 15–31.

Zavarzadeh, Mas'ud. 1976. *The Mythopoeic Reality: The Postwar American Nonfiction Novel*. Urbana: University of Illinois Press.

Zilliacus, Clas. 1979. "Radical Naturalism: First Person Documentary Literature." *Comparative Literature* 31.2: 97–112.

CHAPTER 24

DOCUMENT: FROM THE SPOKEN TO THE WRITTEN WORD

Elena Poniatowska

Foreword by Elzbieta Sklodowska

Novelist Elena Poniatowska's text highlights both the elusive nature of Latin American testimonio and its continuing vitality. Unlike critical studies that tend to attest to their truth and validity through copious footnotes and vast theoretical apparatus, this text stands out as a unique testimony in itself: The testimony of a woman writer and of a Latin American intellectual whose commitment to speak the unspeakable has been both symbolic and exemplary. Poniatowska reminds us that Latin American testimonio resists definition, because it occupies a space somewhere between literature, investigative journalism, anthropology, and oral history. This formal indeterminacy of testimonial texts makes them, inevitably, an easy target for manipulation according to different political and methodological agendas. One of the most evident examples of such manipulation is the controversy (in spring 1999) surrounding Rigoberta Menchú's testimony and David Stoll's book Rigoberta Menchú and the Story of All Poor Guatemalans.

Rather than engage in a debate over testimonios' marks of identity, Poniatowska tells us that this form of writing is first and foremost a vehicle for solidarity: It allows us to summon voices, experiences, and events for which we have no "mainstream" forms of representation. As I mention in my essay in this volume, "In the Web of Reality: Latin American Testimonio": "Forging alliances with other subjects became an important site of enunciation for Latin American intellectuals in the 1960s." Hence, testimonio stands for what would otherwise have been reviled, silenced, or obliterated, just like the Maya Indians in Chiapas, "Mexico's most forgotten people." Within a broader spectrum of literary history, Poniatowska's text captures both the urgency of the moment and the awareness of traditions unrelated to the Western heritage that remain buried beneath the foundation of contemporary Latin America: "We keep stepping on our remains; we carry them with us on the soles of our shoes." In Poniatowska's succinct words, Latin American testimonio is a function of ethics, politics, and aesthetics: It responds to a necessity. This pragmatic aesthetic shows how reality and action—often disassociated from art—can find a viable aesthetic form in testimonial writing. And, as Poniatowska points out, such merging of aesthetics and politics has produced an impressive array of texts, from Ricardo Pozas' Juan Pérez Jolote *(1948) and Carolina Maria de Jesús's* Quarto de despejo *(1960) to the statements and manifestos of the Zapatistas in the 1990s.*

By addressing the ethical and political functions of testimonio, Poniatowska also brings an awareness of constant change fueled by an ongoing search for discursive forms capable of mobilizing both outrage and solidarity. Testimonio is open to change (the use of the cyberspace by the Zapatistas could serve as a prime example of such discursive [r]evolution) and it rescues voices that would likely go unheard in the attrition of postmodern cacophony, like the voice of María Sabina, the medicine woman from the mountains of Oaxaca. Poniatowska's text aptly highlights the orality of textimonio, which, as I mention in my essay, occurs in the liminal space between the literary and the scientific, between imagination and discipline.

Since one of testimonio's strengths lies in its open-ended format, it creates a space for performance, where the substance remembered is as important as the interplay between recall and account, reality and magic. Testimonio's resistance to closure allows for its ability to rewrite, counter, and conjure, but, as Poniatowska points out, it also creates a realm of resistance for the witness, for his or her "secrets" and silences. In my contribution to this volume I stress the fact that the encounters between intellectuals engaged in a testimonial project and their "witnesses" *are inevitable, "wrought with tensions, and point to the limits of cross-cultural understanding in the modern era." Speaking from her experience with Jesusa Palancares, Poniatowska shows how her witness will never conform to the model we try to construct for her: "Jesusa never submits, despite the harshness of her circumstances. Not even the book written about her life is a form of subjection."*

Most importantly, perhaps, Poniatowska's text vindicates the conviction—not easy to sustain in the era of postmodern simulacra—that there is a corresponding reality outside of discourse and that signs and symbols stand as surrogates for a very real referent. "Everyday life," says Poniatowska, "comes into one's creation because it is impossible to set reality aside." What evolves, of course, is the discourse itself. Poniatowska's text shows this awareness of ever-changing forms of representing reality and points to new ways in which Latin American testimonial writing can continue to preserve individual and public memory in the era of vertiginous, global transformations.

From the Spoken to the Written Word

Scientists have told us that there are two kinds of realities in the world: one based on individual consciousness, *mine* or *yours*, and the reality of *others*, the existence of everything else we think as essential to our lives. If our minds die or are destroyed, our lives lose meaning. Without consciousness we lose everything, and there remains little point in continuing to live. Our minds, encapsulated in our brains, play the most essential role in our lives, as well as the most essential role in the universe for us. This continent includes nineteen Spanish- and Portuguese-speaking countries and 400 million inhabitants. Like Africa, Latin America is a continent plagued by economic disasters, including famine. Famine could be avoided through the existence, and the exercise, of various liberties and political rights, including the freedom of expression, according to the 1996 Nobel Prize winner in Economics, Amartya Sen. Indeed, as Sen noted, one of the remarkable facts in the terrible history of famine is that no serious famine has ever occurred in a country with a democratic government and a relatively free press. Instead, this particular form of disaster has stricken ancient kingdoms and contemporary authoritarian societies, primitive tribal communities and modern technocratic dictatorships, colonial economies controlled by imperialists from the north and newly independent countries of the south, run by despotic national leaders or intolerant single parties. But, argues Sen, famines have never afflicted any country that is independent, holds open and regular elections, has opposition parties to voice criticism, and permits newspapers to report freely and to question the wisdom of government policies without extensive censorship. Poor countries whose people die of hunger—as when more than 30 million Chinese died between the years 1958 and 1960—necessarily live different realities than those of North American countries. According to UNICEF, 5,400 children were killed by hurricane "Mitch" in Central America. We in North America are unfamiliar with the vulnerability that comes of such deprivation. Sometimes we know nothing about these vulnerable people; they seem so far away. Yet they are part of the life of the world, and, as such, they are part of ourselves.

It seems to me that literature as a whole might also be the product of two modes of existence, two realities. Mexico has never really produced a *nouveau roman* like France, although some Mexican writers do reflect on their inner souls and states of mind in their work. Others reflect on and analyze the reality or existence of the majority; at least, that is what they try to do. Of course, relativity plays a great part in the choice of their themes, because what they choose to write about has a definite influence on their lives and marks them until the day they die. It is almost impossible to forget oneself. Everyday life comes into one's creation, because it is impossible to set reality aside. Octavio Paz (1914–1998) was Octavio Paz, but he was also a part of Mexico: His grandfather fought in the Mexican revolution, his mother came from Spain, and in his blood flowed the ancestry of pre-Columbian and Western civilizations. That is why he was, himself, a bridge, and his writings have built bridges to link Mexico with other countries, bridges over the Atlantic and the Pacific Oceans and over the rivers of India, France, England, the United States, and Japan, bridges connecting these distant places with our country: Mexico. The same could be said of another Mexican writer, the extraordinary and cosmopolitan novelist Carlos Fuentes (b. 1928). Even Juan Rulfo (1918–1986), who wrote only two books and behaved like an *arriero*, a peasant, a man of the earth, embodied a combination of various cultures; he was tightly bound to his origins; the marks of his birth are also at the origin of his particular vision of the world.

Like Egypt, Mexico is a country of pyramids. There are pyramids near our capital, Mexico City, at Teotihuacan; pyramids in Oaxaca, at Monte Albán and Mitla; and pyramids in Yucatán, at Chichen Itza and Uxmal. Under every colonial church there is a pyramid, buried deep beneath its foundations. Little idols and shards of ceramics bloom like ancient flowers behind Mexican altars. Anita Brenner was right when she wrote her book, *Idols behind Altars.* Maybe she should have chosen the word *under.* We keep stepping on our remains; we carry them with us on the soles of our shoes. These three writers Paz, Rulfo, and Fuentes are, socially and intellectually speaking, on the top of the pyramid. The peak of the pyramid, its apex, is their thought, their contribution to universal knowledge, and their way of life. Our political and social life is certainly pyramidal in shape. At its bottom lie the voices of the people, and without them the top would not exist. On some occasions, the top can erupt, politically, transforming the pyramid into a volcano. Swiss investigators seized 114 million dollars from Raul Salinas, the uncomfortable brother of Mexico's former President, Salinas de Gortari. Incredible fortunes are made at the top of the pyramid, built on the backs of those who carry the stones–the same cannon fodder as always, the majority inhabitants of countries with huge peasant populations.

Since I became a journalist, I have always listened to voices. Where does a reporter get her voices? I got them first in jail, then in the streets, then at the moment of a natural disaster. Why under these circumstances? Because it is in extreme situations that people feel the urge to be with others. They suddenly have time for themselves and for others, and they speak out. In a way they attempt a new communication with their fellow men and women, they improvise their conduct, in a moment when barriers and prejudices have been demolished. In doing so they acquire a torrent of new knowledge. For instance, on 19 September 1985, fifteen years ago, Carlos Monsiváis and I began our stay in the streets, which lasted for three months and witnessed how Mexico City underwent one of the noblest transfers of power in its history, a power that greatly transcended the limits of mere solidarity: the transformation of the people into a government and of official disorder into civilian order. Democracy can suddenly bring importance to individuals who were previously invisible.

From Truman Capote (1924–1984) and his *In Cold Blood* (1965) on, reports, *récits de vie*, or true stories have acquired the status of literature in the sense that they make as good reading as fiction. The commonplace that reality surpasses fiction in its capacity to produce compelling tales is borne out by writers who portray reality and become chroniclers of what they see, hear, and feel. This is why Bernal Díaz del Castillo (1496–1584) is such a good novelist. This is why Carlos Monsiváis (b. 1938) does not need novels to transmit his immense creative capacity and narrative talent. Oscar Lewis (1914–1970) was a researcher who stood by anthropology but produced tales as powerful as well-crafted fiction, like *The Children of Sánchez* (1961).

Juan Pérez Jolote, by Ricardo Pozas (1912–1994), appeared in 1948, before *The Children of Sánchez,* and is probably the spiritual father of testimonial literature in our countries. *Juan Pérez Jolote* tells the story of a Chamula Indian from the state of Chiapas, where the poor rose up in arms on 1 January 1994. Because he also spoke Spanish, Juan Pérez Jolote served as an interpreter to Mexican anthropologist Ricardo Pozas. One day, as it was raining, they were forced to take shelter in a cave, so Pozas asked Jolote about his life. Thus the very extraordinary *Juan Pérez Jolote* was born, and it has come to serve as a model for other books, such as *Hasta no verte Jesús mío* [1969; *Here's to You, Jesusa!,* 2001], the true story of the life of a Mexican woman who took part in the Revolution of 1910.

Testimonial literature inevitably merges with politics. Ricardo Pozas was political in his denunciation of liquor vendors, landowners, politicians, and agrarian leaders in the state of Chiapas; Oscar Lewis's books on Mexico were political in that he revealed poverty. His book on prostitution in Puerto Rico, *La vida* (1966), was political and created great controversy. Domitila Barrios de Chungara (b. 1937) was political in condemning the owners of mines in Bolivia; Rigoberta Menchú's (b. 1959) exposure of social injustices in Guatemala was political; Benita Galeana (1905–1995), a member of the Communist Party who denounced the Communists for never caring to find out if she knew how to read and write and never taking the trouble to teach her, was political; Judith Friedlander's (1944) book about the town of Hueyapan, Mexico, was political; Ana Gutiérrez was political in her work about the living conditions of servants in Cuzco, Perú, *Se necesita muchacha* [1983; Servant Needed].

A new political and social reality in Mexico took us by surprise on 1 January 1994. This was the uprising of the Maya Indians in Chiapas. We had been told repeatedly by the Mexican government that we were entering into modernity, that NAFTA was lifting us out of the ranks of the Third World and transforming us into a member of the First World, that our economy was extraordinary, that we had to learn how to administer our riches, and suddenly, out of a cold blue sky, the Maya Indians in Chiapas, "Mexico's most forgotten people," the smallest of the little people, reminded us that there are 10 million Indians in Mexico who live exactly the same way that they did when the Spanish *conquistador* Hernán Cortés set foot on the new continent in 1519. The Mayans, who were the creators of the most powerful and astonishing culture in Mexico and Central America, the creators of the pyramids of Yucatán, Palenque, and Tikal, the astronomers who, in the fourth and fifth centuries, invented a calendar far more precise than the Gregorian one used today, are, in the twentieth century, the most forsaken of all American Indians. These are people who do not have running water or electricity, people who must carry wood on their shoulders, people who die of curable diseases like smallpox, cholera, and every kind of intestinal infection imaginable.

These Maya Indians, mostly peasants, mostly malnourished and illiterate, were led by one man, who had been living with them, sharing their critical conditions in the jungle for more than sixteen years. A university professor with a big nose, a pipe, and a good sense of humor, who at first was mistaken for a priest, is their *Subcomandante* Marcos; his real name, given out by the Mexican Police, who got it from the FBI, is Rafael Guillén, from the city of Tampico, in the state of Tamaulipas, in the north of the Mexican republic. Why does he call himself *Subcomandante* [Subcommander]? Why not *Comandante*? Some people say that the real *Comandante* is the bishop, don Samuel Ruiz, who was a member of the conventional church hierarchy of León, Guanajuato, a very conservative state in Mexico, but who changed radically when confronted with the reality of Chiapas and then chose to become the *tata*, or father, of the Indians. But this cannot be true, because the bishop and Marcos have had their differences. Others say that the *Comandante* may be a woman, and that to me sounds fascinating, but it has not been proven. I like to imagine *Comandante* Ramona, a tiny Indian woman, who speaks beautifully and has very powerful things to say about the relationship between men and women (unheard of in indigenous customs). She states that she wants to be able to look into the eyes of the man she chooses and not be given to him by her parents in exchange for a bottle of liquor, as tradition demands, and to have the children she wants–in other words, to be the owner of her body and herself. (See **Figure 1.**)

Subcomandante Marcos and his men call themselves *Zapatistas* in remembrance of Emiliano Zapata, the hero of the Mexican Revolution of 1910. Zapata never demanded power for himself, but instead asked for *tierra y libertad* [land and freedom]. *Subcomandante* Marcos has also proven that he has no personal ambition and desires to be nothing more than what he already is: a man with no face and no future. Rather, he is forever handing over power to civil society, to sympathizers who are willing to participate in Mexico's civic life and to take decisions independent of political parties. The *Zapatistas* bought arms with money raised from the sale of their own cattle. They have nothing to lose but their lives. University students travel to Chiapas with food, clothing, and books. Without their brigades, named "Ricardo Pozas" for the anthropologist author of *Juan Pérez Jolote*, the *Zapatistas* would receive no help at all. One of the *Subcomandante*'s proposals to Mexican citizens ("civil society" as he calls it) was the creation of a cultural space, a library in the jungle. Marcos and his *Zapatistas* provided the raw material, young people contributed several thousand books, and a number of university students travelled to the Lacandon jungle to work as librarians. The first thing the Mexican army did in 1996 was to burn the library down. Were the soldiers trying to erase the symbol of the *Zapatistas*, whose very first petition is for culture?

At least 3000 volumes were gathered, many of them "how to" books on how to preserve, build, and repair. The Mexican Army destroyed not only the wooden library constructed by

Figure 1.

Photograph of Subcomandante Marcos of the EZLN (Ejército zapatista de liberación nacional), c. 1994. (Archive of the author)

the *Zapatistas*, but all the books as well, reminding us of acts committed in Chile when Salvador Allende was murdered by the army in Moneda Palace. Books were burned then because they were considered dangerous propaganda by the military; thank God the poet Pablo Neruda was too ill to be there to see how Cervantes, Tolstoy, Walt Whitman, and Edgar Allan Poe went up in flames.

When ex-President Salinas declared that he was willing to forgive the *Zapatista* Indians who had declared war on 1 January 1994, Marcos answered:

¿De qué tenemos que pedir perdón? ¿De qué nos van a perdonar? ¿De no morirnos de hambre? ¿De no callarnos en nuestra miseria? ¿De no haber aceptado humildemente la gigantesca carga histórica de desprecio y abandono? ¿De habernos levantado en armas cuando encontramos todos los otros caminos cerrados? ¿De no habernos atenido al Código Penal de Chiapas, el más absurdo y represivo del que se tenga memoria? ¿De haber demostrado al resto del país y al mundo entero que la dignidad humana vive aún y está en sus habitantes más empobrecidos? ¿De habernos preparado bien y a conciencia antes de iniciar? ¿De haber llevado fusiles al combate, en lugar de arcos y flechas? ¿De haber aprendido a pelear antes de hacerlo? ¿De ser mexicanos todos? ¿De ser mayoritariamente indígenas? ¿De llamar al pueblo mexicano todo a luchar de todas las formas posibles, por lo que les pertenece? ¿De luchar por libertad, democracia y justicia? ¿De no seguir los patrones de las guerrillas anteriores? ¿De no rendirnos? ¿De no vendernos? ¿De no traicionarnos?

¿Quién tiene que pedir perdón y quién puede otorgarlo? . . . ¿Los que nos llenaron las bolsas y el alma de declaraciones y promesas? ¿Los muertos, nuestros muertos, tan mortalmente muertos de muerte "natural", es decir, de sarampión, tosferina, dengue cólera, tifoidea, mononucleosis, tétanos, pulmonía, paludismo y otras lindezas gastrointestinales y pulmonares? . . . ¿Los que nos tratan como extranjeros en nuestra propia tierra y nos piden papeles y obediencia a una ley cuya existencia y justeza ignoramos? ¿Los que nos torturaron, apresaron, asesinaron y desaparecieron por el grave "delito" de querer un pedazo de tierra, no un pedazo grande, no un pedazo chico, sólo un pedazo al que se le pudiera sacar algo para completar el estómago?

¿Quién tiene que pedir perdón y quién puede otorgarlo?
(EZLN 14344)

Why should we ask for pardon? What are you to pardon us for? For not dying of hunger? For not being quiet about our misery? For not humbly accepting the gigantic historic burden of contempt and abandonment? For having taken up arms when all other ways were closed to us? For ignoring the penal code of Chiapas, the most absurd and repressive penal code in living memory? For having demonstrated to the rest of the country, and to the whole world, that human dignity is alive and can be found dwelling in its poorest inhabitants? For having prepared ourselves well and conscientiously before we began? For carrying guns into battle instead of bows and arrows? For having previously learned how to fight? For all of us being Mexicans? For most of us being Indians? For calling on Mexicans to fight in every possible way to defend what is theirs? For fighting for freedom, democracy and justice? For not following the path of conduct of previous guerrilla groups? For not giving up? For not selling out? For not betraying each other?

Who should ask for pardon, and who is to grant it? . . . Those who fill their pockets and their souls with declarations and promises? The dead, our dead, dead of a "natural" death from measles, whooping cough, dengue, cholera, typhoid, mononucleosis, tetanus, pneumonia, and gastrointestinal and pulmonary diseases?. . . .Those who treat us like foreigners in our own land and ask us for our papers and our obedience to a law of whose existence and justice we know nothing? Those who tortured us, put us in jail, murdered us and made us disappear for wanting a piece of land, not a big one, just a piece of land on which we could produce something to fill our stomachs?

Who should ask for pardon, and who is to grant it?

Some books that could be described as testimonials are *Quarto de despejo* (1960) or *Beyond All Pity* (1962) by Carolina Maria de Jesús (1914–1977), a hungry, uneducated woman whose book sold 100,000 copies in her country, Brazil, and was translated into sixteen languages; *El Peso mocho* [c. 1979; Benita] by Benita Galeana who, without knowing how to read, much less write, managed to tell of her life as a political fighter; *Si me permiten hablar* [1978; *Let Me Speak!*] by Domitila Barrios de Chungara and Moema Viezzer; and *Yo me llamo Rigoberta Menchú y así me nació la consciencia* [1983; *I, Rigoberta Menchú: An Indian Woman in Guatemala*], written by Rigoberta Menchú and Elizabeth Burgos-Debray. These books have converted their authors and protagonists–the Bolivian Domitila Barrios de Chungara and the Guatemalan Rigoberta Menchú–into two advocates for social justice, who today travel to attend international forums and defend their people: Domitila the miners, and Rigoberta the poorest of the poor, the Guatemalan *campesinos*.

Domitila made one of the most striking speeches as a woman from the Bolivian Andes, wife of a mine worker and mother of seven children, who came to Mexico to speak at a forum organized by the United Nations in Mexico in 1975. Domitila was denouncing the hunger in Bolivia and the situation of the miners, when the president of the Mexican delegation interrupted her: "Hablaremos de nosotras, señora. . . . Nosotras somos mujeres. Mire, señora, olvídese usted del sufrimiento de su pueblo. Por un momento, olvídese de las masacres. Ya hemos hablado bastante de esto. Ya la hemos escuchado bastante. Hablaremos de nosotras. . . de usted y de mí. . . de la mujer, pues" (1988, 225) ("Let's speak about us. . . .We're women. Look, señora, forget the suffering of your people. For a moment, forget the massacres. We've talked enough about that. We've heard you enough. Let's talk about us . . . of you and me . . . well, about women") (1978, 202).
To this, Domitila replied:

> Muy bien, hablaremos de las dos. Pero, si me permite, voy a empezar. Señora, hace una semana que yo la conozco a usted. Cada mañana usted llega con un traje diferente; y sin embargo, yo no. Cada día llega usted pintada y peinada como quien tiene tiempo de pasar en una peluquería bien elegante y puede gastar buena plata en eso; y, sin embargo, yo no. Yo veo que usted tiene cada tarde un chofer en un carro esperándola a la puerta de este local para recogerla a su casa; y, sin embargo, yo no. Y para presentarse aquí como se presenta, estoy segura de que usted vive en una vivienda bien elegante, en un barrio también elegante, ¿no? Y, sin embargo, nosotras mujeres de los mineros, tenemos solamente una pequeña vivienda prestada y cuando se muere nuestro esposo o se enferma o lo retiran de la empresa, tenemos noventa días para abandonar la vivienda y estamos en la calle.
>
> Ahora, señora, dígame: ¿tiene usted algo semejante a mi situación? ¿Tengo yo algo semejante a su situación de usted? Entonces, ¿de qué igualdad vamos a hablar entre nosotras? ¿Si usted y yo no nos parecemos, si usted y yo somos tan diferentes? Nosotras no podemos, en este momento, ser iguales, aun como mujeres, ¿no le parece? (1988, 225)

> All right, let's talk about the two of us. But if you'll let me, I will begin. Señora, I have known you for a week. Every morning you show up in a different outfit; and, on the other hand, I don't. Every day you show up all made up and combed like someone who has time to spend in an elegant beauty parlor and who can spend money on that, and yet I don't. I see that each afternoon you have a chauffeur in a car waiting at the door of this place to take you home, and yet I don't. And in order to show up here like you do, I'm sure you live in a really elegant house, in an elegant neighborhood, no? And yet we miners' wives only have a small house on loan to us, and when our husbands die or get sick or are fired from the company, we have ninety days to leave the house and then we're in the street.
>
> Now, señora, tell me: is your situation at all similar to mine?
>
> Is my situation at all similar to yours? So what equality are we going to speak of between the two of us? If you and I aren't alike, if you and I are so different? We can't, at this moment, be equal, even as women, don't you think? (1978, 202-3)

Real Life

It never bothered Truman Capote to be called a reporter, that is, a nonfiction writer, when he produced *In Cold Blood* (1965). Miguel Barnet, his Spanish translator, published one year later, in 1966, the *Biografía de un cimarrón* [*The Autobiography of a Runaway Slave*, 1966], the biography of a black slave, now considered a classic of Cuban literature. During these years I have asked myself, "Is it of any use to talk about and divulge the extent of misery in Latin America?" Does testimonial literature impoverish current Latin American literature, with its accounts of its social struggles, lost battles, famine, catastrophes, missing persons in dungeons, like Haroldo Conti (1925–1976?) or Rodolfo Walsh (1927–1977), downed by a bullet? Does it undermine our exotic, tropical literature, our literature of palm trees, coconuts, bananas, and drums? What is the meaning of the story of a fugitive Cuban slave or a woman from Oaxaca who becomes a camp follower? Should those stories be confined to the anthropological annals, to be read only by sociologists?

Once again, it is the turn of those who have no voice, the fugitives, the Jesusas, the Domitilas of the world, the Pérez Jolotes, all those who in our countries suffer from internal colonialism. Jesusa lived in a city in Mexico, which sank lower and lower, fit only for the dogs, until it was leveled to the ground, covered over with cardboard roofing, made into swamps, the electric light stolen by a wire device, deprived of drainage or services, accessed by dirt roads. But these popular personalities like Jesusa are not defeated people. One must listen to Benita Galeana who, at the age of eighty, states:

Now I am learning to be old, so that I don't feel disappointed by old age. As a child I enjoyed everything, good and bad, and life has compensated me in all areas. Like a ball it hits me, but I catch it and carry it with me, and I throw it to the others who also want to play . . . . I am giving life to my life, I am fertilizing it so that I do not end up bitter. As I say: learn to be old. I was and I am. Lots of old folks, men and women alike, ask me to teach them how to live. It's that they didn't have hard lives, they restricted themselves to their homes and routines, and when the weight of the years overtook them, they didn't know what to do when faced with life. They tell me, "Well, Benita, you go out to do the shopping and walk very upright." I answer them, "Ah! And why would I stoop if I don't owe life anything? I haven't robbed anyone. I must walk upright because life needs life.

(Personal interview with Elena Poniatowska)

Testimonial literature sets forth political problems; it talks of massacres, belongs to the ghettos, pokes around in the garbage, shakes the flea-infested mattresses, and gathers together the voices of those who are slowly migrating to the United States. Finally, I feel that men and women who do not have a voice are those who possess the most powerful voice, because it is unknown, unlikely, imaginative, terrifying, unpredictable: a voice that has not been carved with a chisel into formalities, a voice modulated only by the earth. No woman has ever said to me what I have heard from Jesusa, no one else shares her particular courage, no one else has given me what she gave; nor does anyone else display her level of poise, what the Spanish people call *casta* (breeding). I fall into place beside her: She knows what no one knows and what no one can teach; her wisdom is of the corn and the wind. Collecting old rags, paper, pieces of metal, and bricks to build her house, she picks herself up, while I debate with myself on the psychiatrist's couch. Jesusa never stops. To be a camp follower is to march with the troops, prepare the food, fight in the battles. Jesusa, for example, gallops at the side of her husband, Pedro Aguilar; while he is firing, she loads the Mauser. When he dies, she is the one who fires. She gives us fiery and unforgettable images of what war signifies. In Mexico life isn't worth anything, and Pedro Aguilar falls off his horse without Jesusa noticing: "Yo todavía le tendí el máuser cargado, y como no lo recibía, volteé a ver y Pedro ya no estaba en el caballo" (128) ("I kept trying to hand him the loaded Mauser and when he didn't take it, I turned around to see that Pedro was no longer on the horse"). Death is as simple as that.

Jesusa never submits, despite the harshness of her circumstances. Not even the book written about her life is a form of subjection. Jesusa lives her daily life and an imaginary one, the life of her reincarnations, her life of prodigious truths, her life of prodigious lies, because as Antonio Machado says: "Se miente más de la cuenta por falta de fantasía, también la verdad se inventa" ("We embroider on stories for lack of fantasy: the truth is also invented"). One afternoon when I told her I was going to be away for six months, she responded:

Algún día que venga ya no me va a encontrar; se topará nomás con el puro viento. Llegará ese día y cuando llegue, no habrá ni quien le dé una razón. Y pensará que todo ha sido mentira. Es verdad, estamos aquí de a mentiras; lo que cuentan en la radio son mentiras, mentiras las que dicen los vecinos y mentira que me va a sentir. Si ya no le sirvo para nada,)qué carajos va a extrañar? Y en el taller tampoco ¿Quién quiere usted que me extrañe si ni adioses voy a mandar? (8)

Some day when you come to see me you won't find me; you'll only run headlong into the wind. This day will arrive, and when it comes, there will be no one to tell you what happened to me. And you will think that everything has been a lie. It's the truth, we are here living a lie, what they say on the radio are lies, lies are what the neighbors tell you and it is a lie that you will miss me. If I'm no longer of any use, what in hell are you going to miss? Not even in the workshop: for who do you think will miss me if I'm not even going to say goodbye?

One must conclude that testimonial literature responds to a necessity: It reveals and documents the hidden; it inscribes the story of those who don't apparently have one. Those who don't have the slightest opportunity to make themselves heard have biographers, men and women, who are interested in social problems: dogs dictating to their owners, the reversal of the classic situation. If in 1960 Carolina María de Jesús wrote from a Rio de Janeiro slum about her life, and Benita Galeana did the same in Mexico in 1940, then it is to be expected that other Benitas, Jesusas, and Domitilas will write their own biographies. In this sense, many feminine voices have integrated themselves into the huge stream of testimony, which is already a literary phenomenon.

While conditions of oppression, misery, and social exclusion exist in our countries, a testimony will be the only way in which the reader can become aware of unsuspected experiences. Readers are very often hostile to this new reality. The voices of testimony are not only linked to literature, but are themselves literary. On 2 October 1968, more than 200 people were killed on the Plaza of the Three Cultures in Tlatelolco; thus ended the Mexican Students' Movement, in a massacre 10 days before the World Olympic Games were due to begin. For more than a year I interviewed students involved in this movement; the ages of the young men and women imprisoned following this demonstration ranged from 18 to 25. In *Massacre in Mexico* [1991; *La noche de Tlatelolco* (1971)], María del Carmen Rodríguez, a student of Spanish literature at the Iberoamerican University, recalled:

Lo vi como nunca antes. Vi sus manos muy blancas, como de cera, con las venas azules, su barba de candado que siempre le pedí que se dejara: "¡Déjatela, déjatela!", porque lo hacía verse mayor que sus veintiún años, vi sus ojos azules muy sumidos en sus cuencas (Èl siempre ha tenido una expresión triste) y sentí su cuerpo tibio junto al mío. Los dos estábamos empapados por la lluvia y porque nos tiramos al suelo tantas veces en el agua, y sin embargo yo sentía su brazo cálido sobre mis hombros. Entonces por primera vez desde que andamos juntos le dije que sí, que cuando nos dejaran salir los soldados que me llevara con Él, que al cabo y al fin, nos íbamos a morir, sí, tarde o temprano y que yo quería vivir, y que ahora sí, le decía que sí, sí, sí quiero, sí te quiero, sí, lo que tú quieras, yo también quiero, sí, sí, ahora soy yo la que quiero, sí . . .(1971, 226)

I suddenly saw him as I had never seen him before. I saw his very pale hands, as white as wax, with blue veins, his little goatee that I had kept begging him not to shave off: 'Leave it, please!' because it made him look older than he really was, twenty-one; I saw his deep-set blue eyes (they've always had a very sad look in them) and felt his warm body next to mine. Both of us were soaking wet from the rain and from having fallen into so many puddles every time we flung ourselves to the ground, yet his arm felt nice and warm around my shoulders. Then, for the first time since we had been going together, I told him yes, that when the Army troops let us go I'd live with him, that we were going to die some day, sooner or later, and that I wanted to live, that I was saying yes, yes, I love you, I really really love you, I'll do whatever you want, I'm in love with you too, yes, yes, I'm in love too, yes . . . (1975, 269)

This paragraph bears a striking resemblance to another, which I am sure you will recognize: "I asked him with my eyes to ask again, yes, and then he asked me would I say yes to say yes my mountain flower and first I put my arms around him yes and drew him down to me so he could feel my breasts all perfume yes and his heart was going like mad and yes I said yes I will yes" (Joyce 783).

Augusto Roa Bastos (b. 1917) from Paraguay says that when a book appears on our continent it is as if it had been written by the entire people. He says this of Latin American literature, because our books weave our voices, genealogies, legends, whispers, landscapes, secrets, and customs together as if we belonged to the same huge country. The novel of dictatorship has been written by García Márquez (b. 1927), Roa Bastos, Alejo Carpentier (1904–1980), Carlos Fuentes (b. 1928), Juan Rulfo (1918–1986), in works such as *Cien años de soledad* [1967; *One Hundred Years of Solitude,* 1970], *Yo el supremo* [1974; *I, The Supreme,* 1986], *El recurso del método* [1974; *Reasons of State,* 1977], *El otoño del patriarca* [1975; *The Autumn of the Patriarch*], *La muerte de Artemio Cruz* [1962; *The Death of Artemio Cruz,* 1964] and *Pedro Páramo* (1955). While these last two novels are not about dictatorship, they do have a lot in common with the others, portraying characters who are, to say the least, the most original, apocalyptic personalities of our continent. In their excesses they transcend Latin America's flora and fauna, which as everyone knows are already delirious. In this way, in García Márquez's *Cien años de soledad,* Melquiades, the Gypsy, makes his appearance in Macondo, with the greatest invention of all time. He enters into our 100 years of backwardness with a block of ice that dazzles us.

To write in Latin America means something different than it does in the United States or in Europe. I suppose that the same thing happens in Africa: Latin American reality invades, possesses, interferes, and works its way into the smallest cracks. Latin America is always out there, behind the window, watching, spying, ready to jump. The street enters through the door, people find their way in, look at you while you are sleeping, eating, or making love. The path is public. In great cities of the United States everyone has something to do: People go somewhere, walk quickly, never turn their heads to look at their neighbors. In Latin America, in Mexico, no one has anywhere to go; thousands and thousands of people with nothing for themselves. Nothing. Not a single opportunity. Their empty hands hang near their bodies, in front of their mouths, on the tops of their knees, their waiting hands, useless. All this human energy is there, wasted. They look, they wait, they fall asleep, and they wait some more. Nobody loves them, nobody misses them, they are not needed anywhere. They are nobody. They do not exist. So much to do in the world, and there is no place for them—so much lost energy. There is no one to tell them, "Let's get up, Let's get going, Let's save, Let's build." Outside my window, the multitude is always present, ready to burst in. Life is very resistant. People, the same cannon fodder that nourishes great universal misfortunes, *Les Condamnés de la terre,* the damned of the earth, "the wretched of the earth," as Frantz Fanon called them. Suddenly, during an earthquake, one of them saves your life. You have no idea who he or she is, what his or her name is, no way to thank them, and they don't expect to be thanked. We never see them again; they saved our lives and they vanished. Yet they are frighteningly present.

As Carlos Fuentes puts it, the 1,600-mile border (2,000 kilometers) between Mexico and the United States is the only visible border between the developed and the developing worlds. It is also the border between Anglo-America and Latin America. The immigrant workers are so desperate that they are willing to die rather than stay on the Latin-American side. Arriving mostly from Mexico, but also from Central America, as far south as Colombia, and from the Caribbean, they enter the United States for reasons of economic necessity. The main motivation is hunger: Their own countries are not capable of feeding them. There are now more than 30 million Hispanics in the United States; the vast majority of these are of Mexican origin, but there are also many from Puerto Rico, Cuba, and Central and South America. The Hispanics are the fastest-growing minority in the United States, and as we all know, for the time being, they are doing the jobs that citizens of the United States don't want to do. Even if you only speak Spanish, you can make yourself understood in Los Angeles, the largest Spanish-speaking city in the United States; in Miami, where the population is predominantly Cuban; and in San Antonio, which, integrated by Mexicans, has been a bilingual city for 150 years. A whole civilization with Hispanic origins has been created in the United States: Selena, the Mexican-American folk-country singer who was murdered in Corpus Christi, Texas, could be a symbol of Hispanic or Latino power, which, by the way, aspires to the status of cultural power.

Noam Chomsky has often said it would be impossible for a Third World country like Panama to defend itself, because it would be crushed by the military might of the world's superpowers. The only recourse has to be to fight back, politically and using every political opportunity that offers itself. The *Zapatistas* have learned their lesson. Latin America is recovering many of its territories through migrant tactics, as Mexicans and Central and South Americans come to settle in the United States. Are we still being conquered? In many ways we are, through our own local dictatorships; we are still being conquered by our own ignorance, our lack of technology, corrupt politicians, political backwardness, political parties, bad philosophies, own misery, lack of opportunities, the very heavy weight of the Catholic religion that teaches us that we will be happy in heaven and that we should revere tradition. Christian Spain lives in our countries, but the Anglo-Saxon United States also has a very definite influence.

Our culture is universal. Jorge Luis Borges (1899–1986) and, in a minor way, Alfonso Reyes (1889–1959) created a humanistic space in which all literatures and philosophies meet. Octavio Paz did the same. Carlos Fuentes tries to explain our countries to Europe. Nevertheless, only very few Latin Americans have access to education, much less to culture. I always remember a young Mexican peasant girl who once asked, "Why do I have to go to school if I'm going to continue eating beans?" It was difficult to convince her, in her dirt-floored house, that if she went to school, she would be able to eat something else.

I would have loved to end on a happier note, but the time has not yet come for rejoicing. Jesusa Palancares, the heroine of *Hasta no verte Jesús mío* [*Here's to You, Jesusa*] thinks very little of herself. She says:

> Soy como los húngaros: de ninguna parte. No me siento mexicana ni reconozco a los mexicanos. Aquí no existe más que pura conveniencia y puro interés. Si yo tuviera dinero y bienes, sería mexicana, pero somo soy peor que la basura, pues no soy nada. Soy basura a la que el perro le echa una miada y sigue adelante. Viene el aire y se la lleva y se acabó todo. . . .Soy basura porque no puedo ser otra cosa. Yo nunca he servido para nada. Toda mi vida he sido el mismo microbio que ve. (218)

> I am like the gypsies, from nowhere. I don't feel Mexican, and I don't recognize Mexicans. If I had money, I would be considered Mexican, but I am worse than dirt, I am nothing. That's right, that's what I am: garbage for the dogs to pee on and keep walking. The wind comes and blows it away, and that's the end of it. There's nothing else for me to be. I've never been worth anything. My whole life I've been this same good-for-nothing germ you're looking at right now.

Yet there is hope, because Mexicans have a powerful voice. Under the influence of the ceremony of sacred mushrooms, which she ate in the mountains of Oaxaca, where she acted as a priestess, the Indian Medicine woman, María Sabina, spoke in the ancient voice of the earth and chanted while giving way to the psilocybin that, in Switzerland, was transformed into LSD. She said:

> Porque soy la mujer estrella-Dios
> La mujer estrella cruz
> Porque puedo nadar en lo grandioso
> Porque soy la mujer sabia en medicina
> soy mujer piedra del sol sagrada
> soy mujer que mira hacia adentro
> soy la mujer Jesucristo,
> soy la mujer Jesucristo,
> soy la mujer Jesucristo.
> Soy mujer que truena
> soy mujer estrella grande
> soy mujer estrella cruz,
> soy mujer de luz.

> Because I am the star-god woman,
> I am the cross star woman
> because I can swim in infinity,
> because I am the wise medicine woman
> I am the sacred stone sun woman,
> I am the woman who looks within,
> I am the Jesus Christ woman,
> I am the Jesus Christ woman,
> I am the Jesus Christ woman.
> I am the thunder woman
> I am the big star woman
> I am the cross star woman
> I am a woman of light.

Works Cited

Barrios de Chungara with Moema Viezzer. 1978. *Let me Speak!: Testimony of Domitila, a Woman of the Bolivian Mines*. Trans. Victoria Ortiz. New York: Monthly Review Press.

—. 1988 [1977]. "*Si me permiten hablar. . .": Testimonio de Domitila, una mujer de las minas de Bolivia*. 12th ed. Mexico City: Siglo XXI editores.

Brenner, Anita. 1928. *Idols Behind Altars*. New York: Biblo and Tannen.

Capote, Truman. 1965. *In Cold Blood: A True Account of a Multiple Murder and Its Consequences*. New York: Random House.

EZLN [Ejército Zapatista de Liberación Nacional]. 1994. *Chiapas: la palabra de los armados de verdad y fuego (Entrevistas, cartas y comunicados del EZLN hasta el 4 de marzo de 1994)*. Barcelona: Serbal

Friedlander, Judith. 1975. *Being Indian in Hueyapan: A Study of Forced Identity in Contemporary Mexico*. New York: St. Martin's Press.

Galeana, Benita. 1979. *El peso mocho*. Mexico City: Editorial Extemporáneos.

—. 1993. *Benita*. Trans. Amy Diane Prince. Pittsburgh: Latin American Literary Review Press.

Gutiérrez, Ana. 1983. *Se necesita muchacha*. Prologue by Elena Poniatowska. Mexico City: Fondo de Cultura Económica.

Jesus, Carolina Maria de. 1960. *Quarto de despejo: diário de uma favelada*. São Paulo: Livraria Francisco Alves.

—. 1962. *Beyond All Pity*. Trans. David St. Clair. London: Souvenir Press.

Joyce, James. 1961. *Ulysses*. New York: Modern Library.

Lewis, Oscar. 1961. *The Children of Sánchez: Autobiography of a Mexican Family*. New York: Vintage Books.

—. 1966. *La vida: A Puerto Rican Family in the Culture of Poverty–San Juan and New York*. New York: Random House.

Menchú, Rigoberta, and Elizabeth Burgos-Debray. 1983. *Me llamo Rigoberta Menchú y así me nació la conciencia*. Barcelona: Argos Vergara.

—. 1984. *I, Rigoberta Menchú: An Indian Woman in Guatemala*. Trans. Ann Wright. London: Verso.

Montejo, Esteban. 1966. *The Autobiography of a Runaway Slave*. Ed. Miguel Barnet. Trans. Jocasta Innes. London: Bodley Head.

—. 1966. *Biografía de un cimarrón*. Ed. Miguel Barnet. Havana: Instituto de Etnología y Folklore.

Poniatowska, Elena. 1969. *Hasta no verte, Jesús mío*. Mexico City: Ediciones Era.

—. 2001. *Here's to you, Jesusa!* Trans. Deanna Heikkinen. New York: Farrar, Straus and Giroux.

—. 1971. *La noche de Tlatelolco*. Mexico City: Ediciones Era.

—. 1975. *Massacre in Mexico*. Trans. Helen R. Lane. New York: The Viking Press.

Pozas Arciniegas, Ricardo. 1962. *Juan the Chamula: An Ethnological Re-Creation of the Life of a Mexican Indian*. Trans. Lysander Kemp. Berkeley: University of California Press.

—. 1969. *Juan Pérez Jolote* [1948]. Havana: Casa de las Américas.

CHAPTER 25

THE EPISTOLARY GENRE AND BRAZILIAN MODERNISM

Júlio Castañon Guimarães

Letter Writing in Brazil

The first document referring to the history of Brazil is a letter of 1500, written by Pero Vaz de Caminha, chronicler of Pedro Álvares Cabral's naval fleet. In the letter he gave D. Manuel, King of Portugal, were details of the journey and the discovery of the new land, and a description of the inhabitants they had found there. This document represents the first European gaze on Brazil. On the one hand, the letter is a private document, since it contains a request for a personal favor (a favor for a son-in-law); on the other hand, however, it contains considerable information of a historical and ethnographic nature. There are few collections of letters from the Colonial period that are worthy of note; generally speaking, they comment on the colony in a descriptive and informative tone. Father Antônio Vieira's (1608–1697) letters, however, are quite significant: He not only reasserts his concern to give information about the colony, but also describes its several aspects, as if attempting to extend the process of discovery itself. The letters written by Vieira during the time he was a missionary in Maranhão and Pará are good examples: As he describes his travels around the area, comments on the administrative and political situation, and proposes missionary strategies, he also provides in these writings many details about the land and its inhabitants.

This attempt to explore—in the sense of discovering and making good use of an inhospitable place—seen in the letters from the Colonial period, changes in the nineteenth century. This change is connected to historical and cultural shifts the country was undergoing (it became independent in 1822). Throughout the nineteenth century, there are few significant sets of letters of literary quality. Antônio Gonçalves Dias's (1823–1864) correspondence begins to show a different view on Brazil. In a sense he continues the earlier mode of discovery in his letters about the Amazon, but there is also a discussion of problems with a view to try to change the country, an attitude that one finds more often later, during the era of Modernism. It is no longer a matter, whether from a missionary or a colonial point of view, of imposing on the country conditions typical of the metropolitan perspective. In this sense, the letters Gonçalves Dias wrote from Europe have a special importance as a reversal of the usual direction. His accounts of European things ultimately lead to a reflection on Brazil, which, seen from Europe, is no longer a simple object of discovery, but rather a space open to a new project. Gonçalves Dias's letters also deal with personal questions, but, as in those later written by Mário de Andrade (1893–1945), there is a constant interaction between his life and work and reflections on the cultural level. Dias's letters are a significant example both of the epistolary genre's flexibility and of the beginning of a forward movement that will result in Modernism.

If the letter is a manifestation of interpersonal relations, it is also a space in which textual plurality thrives, insofar as epistolary misunderstanding does take place, as Vincent Kaufmann concludes in his thesis on the correspondence of writers. According to Kaufmann, instead of contributing to a sense of nearness and communication, the epistolary genre creates a distance "in which writers find the chance to become writers" (4). This is a way to read for a literary text within the letter, a text in effect constituted by, or associated with, the letter. In broad terms, one can speak of the "instability of its forms," "of its ceaseless movement," of the "essentially hybrid nature of the genre," and of a "border genre" (Haroche-Bouzinac 3, 11, 14). Owing to this flexible character, therefore, a variety of approaches makes possible different interpretations and of connections to the letter genre. A survey of the epistolary form in Brazilian literature reveals how productive it is in terms of its function within other genres that are to a greater or lesser degree associated with it—the chronicle, the novel, and poetry. On the other hand, this literary use of the letter results both from its fruitfulness as a genre and its significant function as a space for discussion, as can be seen in a very special way in the development of the Modernist project.

Correspondence and Other Genres

In Brazilian literature, the literary epistle emerges first as poetry, in a few, though diversified, examples. The most famous is perhaps the satiric poem "Cartas Chilenas" [1863; "Chilean Letters"] by Tomás Antônio Gonzaga (1744–1807). In Carlos Drummond de Andrade's (1902–1987) work, there are three poems with titles containing the word *letter.* Two of them are simply called "Carta" ["Letter"], and the third is "Carta a Stalingrado" ["Letter to Stalingrad"]. The first of the two letters entitled "Carta," from the collection *Claro enigma* [1951; Clear Enigma], describes what a letter should be like—a letter gradually written in the poem itself. The last line reads: "Contudo, esta é uma carta" (297) ("Yet, this is a letter"). The second poem with this title, from the collection *Lição de coisas* [1962; Lesson of Things], has an addressee, which itself is a feature of a letter. Its first line makes use of the same resource found in all correspondences "Há muito tempo, sim, que não te escrevo" (391) ("It has been a long time since I last wrote"). The poem "Carta a Stalingrado," from the collection *A rosa do povo* [1945; The Rose of the People], also has an addressee—in this case, the city of Stalingrad. Manuel Bandeira (1886–1968) also explicitly links the letter and the poem in his title "Carta-poema" ["Letter-Poem"], from his book of occasional verse *Mafuá do malungo* [1948; Comrade's Celebration]. In the "Carta-poema," the poet addresses "Excelentíssimo Prefeito/Senhor Hildebrando de Góis" (1:530) ("Your Honor, the Mayor, Mr. Hildebrando de Góis"). On another level, letters are also the theme of another poem, "Cartas de meu avô" (1:27) ["Letters from My Grandfather"] from the collection *A cinza das horas* [1917; The Ashes of Time]. Here, the poem is a reading of the correspondence sent by his grandfather to his grandmother, through the resulting emotions of the poet, as is to be expected.

The letter as a literary genre, though, flourishes more in prose than in verse. It appears as an element of fiction in two ways: First, it can be a part of the narrative, in the sense of moving the story line forward. This is the case, for example, of Machado de Assis's (1839–1908) *A mão e a luva* [1874; The Hand and the Glove], in which a character's reaction is triggered by a letter. The letter has the ability to move from fiction to nonfiction, a movement that is in fact the theme of this particular passage of the novel. The chapter entitled "Revelação" ["Revelation"] thus begins: "Meia hora depois, indo a abrir o livro para continuar a leitura, viu Guiomar a cartinha de Jorge" (63) ("Half an hour later, as Guiomar opened the book to continue her reading, she came across Jorge's little letter"). A little further on in the novel, after a few brief reflections on the part of the character, one reads: "A moça ficou algum tempo quieta, a olhar para o papel, sem o querer ler, como a hesitar entre queimá-lo ou restituí-lo intacto a seu autor" (64) ("The young lady remained quiet for a while, looking at the piece of paper, trying not to read it, as if hesitating between burning it or returning it to its writer. But curiosity overcame her; Guiomar unfolded the sheet and read the following lines"). Jorge speaks of his passion for Guiomar in the letter. After reading it, "pôs a carta de lado, abriu o livro e continuou o romance. Mas o espírito, que não ficara tão indiferente como o coração, entrou a fugir-lhe do romance para a vida" (64) ("she put the letter aside, opened the book and went on with her reading of the novel. But her spirit, which did not react as indifferently as her heart, fled from the novel into life"). Here one encounters an example of how the letter represents life in fiction, the real as opposed to the fictive (the book Guiomar is reading).

In another novel by Machado de Assis, *Quincas Borba* [1891; *Quincas Borba*, 1998], it is from a letter that Rubião learns about the situation of his friend Quincas Borba. Chapter 10 begins: "Sete semanas depois, chegou a Barbacena esta carta, datada do Rio de Janeiro, toda do punho do Quincas Borba" (1979, 651) ("Seven weeks later this letter postmarked Rio de Janeiro arrived in Barbacena, all in Quincas Borba's handwriting" [1998, 18]). Following the letter, one reads: "Rubião mal sustinha o papel nos dedos. Passados alguns segundos, advertiu que podia ser um gracejo do amigo, e releu a carta; mas a segunda leitura confirmou a primeira impressão. Não havia dúvida; estava doudo" (1979, 652) ("Rubião could barely hold the piece of paper in his hands. After a few seconds he sensed that is might be one of his friend's japes, and he reread the letter. But the second reading confirmed his first impression. There was no doubt about it, he was crazy" [1998, 19]). Soon after, the doctor arrives and asks for news, explaining that the postman had told him a letter had arrived. Rubião hides the letter, saying it only contained private matters: "Dizendo isto, Rubião meteu a carta no bolso; o médico saiu, ele respirou. Escapara ao perigo de publicar tão grave documento, por onde se podia provar o estado mental de Quincas Borba" (1979, 652) ("Saying that, Rubião put the letter in his pocket. The doctor left. He breathed deeply. He'd escaped the danger of making public such a dangerous document by which it would be possible to prove Quincas Borba's mental condition" [1998, 19]). Here is an example of several aspects of the letter: Through its status as a document, it travels between the private and the public; and with respect to narrative economy, there is a situation in which a letter's contents are known by one character and not by others, as well as another in which the letter is addressed to one and not to others, though this does not prevent it from having an effect, whether in reality or in fiction.

In addition to being an element of the narrative, the epistle can become the narrative itself, as is the case with epistolary novels. There are not many such novels in Brazilian literature; Antonio Candido refers to one of them, namely João do Rio's 1918 *Correspondência de uma estação de cura* [Correspondence from a Sanatorium], as "dos raríssimos romances epistolares da nossa literatura" (xii) ("one of the rare instances of the epistolary novel in our literature"). He also states that "antes do romance de João do Rio, só lembro o de Júlia Lopes de Almeida (1862–1934), *Correio da Roça*, publicado em 1914" (xvi) ("before João do Rio's novel, the only other example I can recall is Júlia Lopes de Almeida's *Correio da Roça* [Rural Mail], published in 1914"). There was, however, another earlier epistolary novel, as Flora Süssekind has pointed out: *O Marido da Adúltera* [1882; The Husband of the Adulteress], by Lúcio de Mendonça (1854–1909).

Antonio Candido calls our attention to the fact that "entre as diversas modalidades de narrativa epistolar (um estudioso chega a identificar doze), a escolhida por João do Rio (1881–1921) é das mais raras: diversas pessoas escrevem a amigos que não respondem" (xvi) ("among the many forms of the epistolary narrative, the one chosen by João do Rio is one of the rarest: in it, several people write to friends who do not reply"). He refers to what he calls a "truque de verossimilhança" (xvi) ("trick of verisimilitude"), a rather uncommon device: The letters were in fact never delivered, since they were retained by a crazy clerk, which thus puts the set of letters in the hands of a single person, a dispatcher, who then makes them public. Candido concludes: "Não havendo primeira pessoa privilegiada que escreve nem editor fictício que organiza as cartas e pode manifestar-se sobre elas no prefácio ou nas notas, este livro é um exemplo puro de técnica epitolar funcionando pela própria força; têm palavra apenas os missivistas" (xvi) ("Since this book has no first-person writer or fictitious editor who collects the letters and discusses them in the introduction or the afterword, it is a clear example of the epistolary technique working on its own strength; only the letter-writers have the word"). Flora Süssekind comments: "Dessa maneira, cartas sem resposta impressa, sem interlocutor direto, os diversos relatos funcionam efetivamente como ficção, capítulos desse romance anotado em livro comercial" (222) ("As such, letters with no printed reply or no direct interlocutor, these accounts in effect function as fiction, as chapters of this novel embedded in a commercial book"). She adds that the "[n]arrador que não diferencia as diferentes correspondências, padroniza-as em registro identicamente fiel, em pequenas reportagens assinadas, como se fosse, ele mesmo, um jornal" (222) ("narrator who cannot distinguish between the different kinds of correspondence generalizes them as equally faithful registers, as brief signed accounts, as if the letter writer were himself a newspaper").

As she analyzes the novel, Süssekind notes that although "o fato de não se ter constituído uma tradição epistolar forte no romance brasileiro" ("a strong epistolary tradition did not develop in Brazilian literature"), there was a "a súbita voga das cartas no início do século" ("sudden fashion for letters at the beginning of the twentieth century") (Süssekind 211). Concerning such popularity, in his *A Vida Literária no Brasil–1900* [Literary Life in Brazil–1900], Brito Broca mentions "umas colunas de prosa melíflua com os 'bilhetinhos a Míriam', gênero sub-simbolista com larga aceitação na época" (228–29) ("some newspaper sections offering the purple prose of 'notes to Míriam,' which was well received at the time"). Commenting on this passage, Broca states: "Esse gênero epistolar tornava-se comum, e como tudo em nossas letras teria vindo da literatura francesa. . . . Entre as crônicas epistolares que se multiplicaram em nossas revistas, basta citar as 'Cartas de Mulher', de *Iracema*, na *Revista da Semana*" (228–29) ("This epistolary genre was becoming popular, and like everything else in our written tradition it originated in French literature. . . . Among the epistolary chronicles that flourished in our journals, one needs only mention 'Cartas de Mulher' [Woman's Letters], in *Iracema* (1865) (by José de Alencar [1829–1877]) featured in the *Revista da Semana* [Weekly Review]"). Lúcio de Mendonça's novel was composed of letters sent to a newspaper, and Süssekind comments that "já pelo modo como foi publicado, *O Marido da Adúltera*, de Lúcio de Mendonça, estabelece uma ligação estreita entre a escolha do gênero epistolar e sua veiculação como folhetim de jornal" (214) ("the way in which Lúcio Mendonça's *O Marido da Adúltera* was published shows a close connection between the choice of the epistolary genre and its publication as a serial"). In this novel the letters "funcionam ao mesmo tempo como capítulos tradicionais e como meios de se cortar sem maiores problemas a ação narrativa para obedecer à exigência de publicação periódica do folhetim" (214) ("function as conventional chapters and as a means of interrupting the narrative without affecting the unfolding of events, which makes it possible for the novel to follow the norms of publication in periodicals"). One can see how the letter was both a private and a public means of communication: "A carta impressa e o romance em cartas têm o dom de apagar também a oposição entre criação pessoal e intransferível e conteúdo público no interior da produção literária" (Süssekind 212) ("The printed letter and the epistolary novel blur the distinction between private and public contents within literary production").

Aluísio de Azevedo's (1857–1913) novel *Mattos, Malta ou Matta?* [Mattos, Malta or Matta?] was also composed, in part, of letters sent to a newspaper. Azevedo's novel was published as a serial in the periodical *A Semana* [The Week], beginning on 3 January 1885 and was later collected and published as a book. Approximately half of the novel is composed of letters sent to the editor of *A Semana*. Referring to the "estratagema de supostas cartas dirigidas à redação de *A Semana*" ("strategy of letters supposedly addressed to the editor of *A Semana*"), Alexandre Eulálio observed that "não é impossível que Aluizio, soprado por Valentim Magalhães, houvesse tratado de parodiar, ou pelo menos reaproveitar de forma grotesca, a sugestão do polêmico romance epistolar de Lúcio de Mendonça *O Marido da Adúltera, crônica fluminense*" (Eulálio 174) ("it was not impossible that Aluízio de Azevedo, following the suggestion of Valentim Magalhães, tried to parody, or at least make satirical use of Lúcio de Mendonça's controversial epistolary novel *O Marido da Adúltera, crônica fluminense* [The Husband of the Adulteress, a Chronicle of Rio]"). From a certain point on, however, the narrative develops as the quill flowed, as the text itself indicates. If, on the one hand, this fact emphasizes the narrative nature of the letters, on the other hand, it also reveals the peculiarities of the narrative conditions of the letter. Withdrawing from the epistolary form at a certain point in the novel allows the narrative to unfold faster, to be closer to the facts of the story, at times even taking place

in the present time. Regarding this change, Alexandre Eulálio says: "A mesma narrativa, já vimos que se encaminha, sem transição alguma, das *cartas* do missivista que dialoga como o Redator de *A Semana*, para o raconto corrido, no qual o protagonista passa a se dirigir ao público da folha sem mediador algum. Um texto portando uno e múltiplo em si mesmo, no qual, à fragmentação calculada da narrativa epistolar, faz suceder o fluxo narrativo corrente" (166) ("The same narrative abruptly moves from the sender's letters to the Editor of *A Semana* to an uninterrupted account, in which the protagonist starts to address the newspaper readers without any mediation. It is in itself therefore a single and multiple text, in which the narrative flow follows the calculated fragmentation of the epistolary narrative").

A novel such as Júlia Lopes de Almeida's *Correio da Roça* is connected to the popularity of the epistolary form and the slight flourishing of epistolary novels, but it adds the telegram to the genre. Its organization is quite simple: There is an exchange of letters between identified senders and receivers in a customary sequence of letters and replies. One might see in the use of certain postal resources–such as telegrams and postal notes–new forms, both of realism and of creating new narrative possibilities. Thus a chapter composed of a brief telegram can interrupt the narrative flow, while another chapter composed of a small postal note likewise introduces a break in the narrative to allow for a reflection or a comment. In fact, however, the novel's plot becomes rather frayed; the novel is an account of the difficulties in adapting that a family encounters as it begins to make a living from the fields. In this sense, in this epistolary novel the letter perhaps is more than a first-person narration used to construct the novel: It is closer to the chronicle through the opportunity it gives the letter writer to express personal opinion. Although not published in a newspaper (and indeed with no) fictional claim to be letters sent to a newspaper, as was the case of the novels discussed above, *Correio da Roça* may well have been printed in periodicals as a succession of chronicles in praise of rural life.

Brito Broca has said that, since writers have used letters not only as fiction but also as chronicles, one must deal with this generic fact that various kinds of articles and chronicles have been published as letters. One need only recall, for example, Adolfo Caminha's (1867–1897) *Cartas literárias* [1895; Literary Letters], which were in fact short commentaries on literature. Another example is Rui Barbosa's (1849–1923) *Cartas de Inglaterra* [Letters from England] of 1896; it contained articles on history and politics, but in this case written from exile, giving them the status of open letters; that is, they were clearly intended for publication, with a public readership in mind, instead of a private one. In 1896, Luís Gonzaga Duque (1863–1911) published "Três cartas íntimas" ["Three Private Letters"] in Rio de Janeiro's Symbolist periodical *Galáxias* [Galaxies]. His "intenção parece ser discutir os rumos do movimento, suas relações e questões, a partir de uma carta fictícia" (Lins 1998, 97) ("intention seems to be, through a fictitious letter, to discuss the course of the Symbolist movement, its relations and main issues"). Thus it is that in order to reveal publicly through the press questions related to a literary movement, the author resorted to a private vehicle, namely the letter–even emphasizing its private nature in the title itself. On the one hand, this procedure is associated with Gonzaga Duque's aesthetic ideas and the significance he attributed to the literary manifestations of the inner self. On the other hand, however, it is ironic that privacy is emphasized only to be made public, thus revealing what a complex and contradictory entity the epistolary text is.

Somewhat related to this use of the letter form are those epistles written in effect to a private addressee but nevertheless published in the press. There are also letters written to a private addressee and actually delivered, although clearly written in order to compose an essay on a particular topic; later on, when collected and published, they take on the shape of an essay. This is the nonfiction counterpart to the serial novel. Worthy of mention are examples like Valle Cabral's (1851–1894) *Cartas bibliográficas* [Bibliographical Letters]; Francisco Adolfo Varnhagen's (1816–1878) *Cartas sobre a "Prosopopéia" de Bento Teixeira Pinto e sobre "O Peregrino da América" de Nuno Marques Pereira* [Letters on Bento Teixeira Pinto's "Prosopopeia" and Nuno Marques Pereira's (1652–1731) "America's Pilgrim"]; José de Alencar's (1829–1877) *Cartas sobre a Confederação dos Tamoios* [Letters on the Tamoios Confederacy], published in a newspaper under a pseudonym; José de Alencar's letters to Joaquim Serra, at first published by the addressee in a newspaper and later collected in a book under the title *O nosso cancioneiro* [Our Book of Ballads], since they deal with popular literature; and the letters exchanged between José de Alencar and Machado de Assis about Castro Alves (1847–1871) that were later featured in a newspaper. What is notable is that with this approximation to the forms of the chronicle and even criticism, despite the limitations imposed by the private addressee, many editions of letters are collected in books that append other, related texts. This is the case of Castro Alves's *Correspondência e crítica* [Correspondence and Criticism] and Lima Barreto's (1881–1922) *Um longo sonho de futuro* [A Long Future Dream] (diaries, letters, interviews, and various confessions).

In Mário de Andrade's (1893–1945) *Macunaíma*'s (1928) chapter IX, entitled "Carta pras Icamiabas" ["Letter to the Icamiabas"], there is another example of the epistolary form used as an element of fiction. What one finds in this novel is a rather peculiar use of it, which in fact was the topic of much heated discussion even at the time it was being written. (See, for example, Manuel Bandeira's letter of November 1927.) In Andrade's work, the letter breaks the narrative flow, which is not presented in epistolary form. There is also a change in narrative point of view, from narrator to hero or protagonist. More important than the meaning of the letter within the narrative structure is how the epistolary model operates. Maria Augusta Fonseca notes: "A Carta, aparentemente, demonstra a necessidade de Macunaíma adaptar-se ao modelo, fazendo com que a língua e a cultura européia sobressaiam na formação do missivista de improviso" (281) ("The Letter, apparently, demonstrates the need for *Macunaíma* to adjust to a model, illustrating the use of the European language and culture by the improvised letter writer"). She adds:

> Na Carta, o herói prende-se a um modo tradicional de narrar. Mas constrói um texto inteiramente descaracterizado por força do não-comprometimento cultural, variando o tema na superfície. Sem poder assimilar o aprendido dentro de um novo padrão, sua carta passa a estampar uma sucessão não digerida de frases, trechos de poesia, discursos verborrágicos, citações em língua estrangeira, denominações em latim, citações de autores e obras, desentranhados do aprendizado 'de orelha'. (281)

In the Letter, the hero/protagonist is caught in a conventional mode of narration. But he constructs a text that is not entirely characterized by his cultural noncommitment, changing the theme, at least on the surface. Without assimilating what he has learned within a new pattern, his letter contains a series of undigested sentences, passages of poetry, windy speeches, quotations in foreign languages, Latin terms, citations of authors and works, that have been acquired from his learning from book flaps.

One sees that the letter does not quite have the usual epistolary function of exchanging information between characters (and thus a narrative role in the novel), but rather in its condition as fluid text, it allows the character to express new things he has learned. In other words the epistolary model is used to allow a change in point of view. Moreover, in Andrade's novel the letter has yet another characteristic: It is not within the realm of the private, insofar as it is an account of the protagonist's view of a new world that he intends to make public. In this sense it is similar to open letters published in newspapers or even to chronicles.

If in these texts the epistolary form kept few of its original characteristics and barely deserved to be called such, it became even more distant from the original model as the literary tradition evolved. On the one hand, the first example of further modification is Lúcio Cardoso's (1913–1968) *Crônica da casa assassinada* [1959; Chronicle of the Murdered House]. This novel is a collection of excerpts from diaries, letters, confessions, reports, memoirs, and narratives; these are indeed the classifications used in the titles of its chapters. The variety of types of texts collected in the novel brings the epistolary narrative closer to the realm of the intimate and the private, which explicitly connects the letter to forms like the memoir and the diary—in short, to forms from the sphere of autobiography. On the other hand, the fragmented nature of *Crônica da casa assassinada*, made up of multiple, alternating narratives, causes a spatial and temporal fragmentation whose complexity requires minute attention to its many details—such as, for instance, temporal and spatial signs—in order for the reader to put the fragments together. Given this feature, the letters contained in the novel take on certain peculiarities. The titles of the chapters that are composed of letters indicate the names of the sender and receiver, but the letters are never answered: The addressee does not reply. This does not come as a surprise, since they are inserted in a narrative that connects many different kinds of writing. The novel thus emphasizes the letter as a pure element of the narrative: The "replies" to the letters constitute the narrative progression itself. A reply is not necessary, since what the reader in fact finds are explanations within one particular letter concerning another or passages from diaries by yet a third character about that letter. These are all part of a larger narrative that weaves the private texts into the novel's plot.

One no longer encounters the play between public and private; there is, instead, an emphasis on reclusive spaces, on settings of disintegration, and on the intimate, created by the fact that all manifestations of intimacy are handwritten. One occasionally finds comments such as "Escrito com letra diferente à margem do caderno" ("Written in a different handwriting in the margin of the page"); "Escrito à margem do Diário, com tinta diferente" ("Written in the margin of the diary, in different ink"); or "Pós-escrito à margem do papel" ("Postscript on the margin of the sheet"). There is a clear distinction between this highly complex formal use and the earlier use of the letter by the press and its interplay of the private and the public. Here, the letter is again used essentially as a private resource in the development of a narrative for which the press is no longer a possible vehicle—as it used to be for serialized novels. Altogether, the devices used in the construction of *Crônica da casa assassinada* emphasize the precariousness of testimonies, as well as their fragmented state. This becomes clear through the additions, which are pointed out as having been written in the margins, as well as through the titles of chapters, such as "Do livro de memórias de Timóteo" ["From Timóteo's Book of Memoirs"]. Another point worth mentioning is that fragmentation does not take place only because the narrative is scattered throughout various kinds of documents or because these texts have been damaged; it also occurs on the temporal level, because the various texts originate at different times or present gaps in continuity. One cannot overlook the fact that the fragmentation and precariousness of the texts that form the narrative parallel the novel's plot; deterioration and weaknesses occur on different levels: psychological, economic, and social.

In Sergio Milliet's (1898–1966) *Duas cartas no meu destino* [1941; Two Letters in my Destiny], the narrative includes a series of excerpts from private texts. At a certain point near the beginning of the novel, the narrator states: "Contada assim, você não pode ter uma idéia bastante clara da evolução dessa aventura. Tenho porém arquivado grande número de documentos elucidativos, meu diário íntimo, cópia de cartas minhas, bilhetinhos enviados por Ana Maria. Para facilitar essa confissão tremenda que me impus, vou mostrar-lhe alguns desses papéis. Há coisas difíceis de dizer, que a simples exibição de um documento esclarece" (15) ("Told in this way, you cannot picture clearly enough the development of this adventure. However, I have collected a large number of explanatory documents, my private diary, copies of my letters, notes sent by Ana Maria. In order to make it easier for you to understand the remarkable confession I am determined to make, I will show you some of these papers. Some things are hard to say, and the mere revelation of a document clarifies everything"). Here one notes the documentary value of the letter, instead of its literary nature, as a narrative device. The novel is permeated by comments such as: "Antes de continuar, meu amigo, quero ler uma carta que escrevi mais ou menos nessa época, a Ana Maria" (21) ("Before proceeding, my friend, let me read a letter that I wrote to Ana Maria about that time"); "Entre cartas, conversas, encontros fortuitos, passaram-se muitos dias" (25) ("Between letters, conversations, chance encounters, several days passed"); "Talvez lhe pareça deslocada a inclusão aqui de um techo de uma carta de Ana Maria" (27) ("It may seem odd to include here a passage from a letter by Ana Maria"); "Trecho de meu diário" (35) ("Passage from my diary"). Here one is dealing with the kind of narrative in which the narrator addresses a reader and develops his narrative with the help of excerpts from "documents," which are actually other narratives inserted in the composition of the novel as a whole. The novel is also composed in the absence of letters, through the gaps left, as in the passage in which the narrator reveals: "Escrevi duas cartas que rasguei" (43) ("I wrote two letters but tore them up").

In Rosário Fusco's (1910–1977) *Carta à noiva* [1954; Letter to the Bride] the indeterminate novel advances its action without ever revealing the contents of notes that are read: "O bilhete lido confirmava o acabado de ouvir, além de recomendar-lhe o bar do estabelecimento como ponto de referência" (89) ("The note he just read confirmed what he had heard, besides recommending the bar as a point of reference"), or "Deixo um bilhete para me comprometer e comprometê-la. . . . Minutos depois, porém, vinha implorar à empregada que lhe vendesse o bilhete" (108) ("I am leaving a note so as to involve myself and involve her. . . . A few minutes later, however, he was begging the housekeeper to sell him the note"). The novel ends with the "plan" for a letter: "Acende a lâmpada: mas só a alvorada lhe fornecerá a luz que os olhos pedem para escrever a carta à noiva" (250) ("He turns on the light: but only dawn will bring the light that his eyes need to write the letter to the bride"). This plan had been hinted at a certain point in the text when, as the character was "[f]olheava a revista de modas, detinha-se nas páginas de correspondência sentimental" (126) ("[b]rowsing, through a fashion magazine, his attention was caught by the section containing love letters").

In Antonio Callado's (1917–1997) *Reflexos do Baile* [1976; Thoughts of the Ball], the excerpts from diaries and letters that make up the novel present an addressee, but no letter writer. In this way readers have to link up the facts themselves and identify the characters, a process parallel to the investigation of the clandestine activities that are being narrated (the resistance and its repression during the military dictatorship in Brazil from 1964 is the main subject). A device employed in this novel is the introduction of letters written in English followed by their translation, with footnotes by the translator. This device is similar to that of adding references that concern the handwritten nature of letters in other works, such as in Lúcio Cardoso's novel. In Callado's novel, the device actually involves various moves: the "real" existence of the letter (in English), proved by its translation; the interference of a character in the writing of the correspondents—in this case, the translator, editor, or author; the very act of translating, which implies writing, interpreting, and adding data to clarify the odd and faulty parts of the narrative.

Modernist Correspondence

With Modernism, literary correspondence in Brazil undergoes significant changes. Besides the aesthetic transformations sought and achieved by the movement, there was much intense discussion and reflection. One of the sources of such discussion was undoubtedly the correspondence between writers in different cities, like Mário de Andrade in São Paulo, Manuel Bandeira in Rio de Janeiro, and Carlos Drummond de Andrade in Belo Horizonte. The aesthetic changes brought by Modernism included freedom with respect to established models, the search for national characteristics, and so on. The correspondence reflects these aspects, both in the discussions and in its own formulations. The letter now loses the formality it once had; as an effective if somewhat formal substitute for conversation, it makes possible the exchange of ideas and information. Without a doubt, this change fostered a greater expressive freedom, so that beyond dealing with literary questions the letter also served as a vehicle for personal artistic expressions, as well as for the more traditional private information about people involved in the literary life.

The central figure in terms of literary correspondence during the years of Brazilian Modernism is Mário de Andrade. He is central for several reasons: first, because of his importance as a writer of poetry, fiction, literary criticism, art, and music criticism; second, because of the large number of letters he wrote during his lifetime; and finally, for having exchanged letters with people related to all the aforementioned fields and with a large number of Brazilian intellectuals during those years. For this reason, any investigation of the literary correspondence of Brazilian Modernism inevitably means studying Mário de Andrade's correspondence. However, it is worth recalling some of the problems faced in the study of this correspondence, as well as the existence of other, equally significant sets of letters, among which may be included the letters exchanged between Manuel Bandeira and Carlos Drummond de Andrade; between Murilo Mendes (1901–1975) and Carlos Drummond de Andrade; between Manuel Bandeira and Ribeiro Couto (1898–1963); between Carlos Drummond de Andrade and Rodrigo Melo Franco de Andrade (1898–1969); and between Carlos Drummond de Andrade and Abgar Renault (1908–1995).

A few figures will give an idea of the extent of the material available. The 91 letters written by Mário de Andrade to Carlos Drummond de Andrade are among the most important published. Those written by Abgar Renault to Carlos Drummond de Andrade are still unpublished, but number 453 letters. There are other large sets of letters written to Carlos Drummond de Andrade: 110 letters by Rodrigo Melo Franco de Andrade; 127 letters by Ciro dos Anjos (1906–1994); 49 letters by Ribeiro Couto; and 32 by Manuel Bandeira. There are 64 letters written by Ribeiro Couto to Manuel Bandeira, and 426 by Manuel Bandeira in return. This tremendous difference in the numbers is a perfect example of a problem in preservation, because it is clear that Manuel Bandeira would not have written so often to Ribeiro Couto unless he replied nearly as often. The conclusion must be that Manuel Bandeira's archives did not preserve all of his papers. There are, in contrast, over ten books collecting Mário de Andrade's correspondence. Many volumes containing the correspondence between Mário de Andrade and Manuel Bandeira, Carlos Drummond de Andrade, Cândido Portinari (1903–1962), Murilo Miranda (1912–1971), Oneyda Alvarenga (1911–1984), Pedro Nava (1903–1984), Murilo Rubião (1916–1991), Henriqueta Lisboa (1904–1985), Anita Malfatti (1889–1964), Rodrigo Melo Franco de Andrade, Fernando Sabino (b. 1923), Paulo Duarte (1899–1984), among others, have been published. Correspondence turns out to be made up not only of precariousness and gaps, but also of multiplication, repetition, and trivia.

Many of these letters, however, are unpublished; in some cases they are available in archives. In this case, to study them one must begin by deciphering the authors' handwriting, organizing them chronologically, verifying if there are any missing letters, and so on. In the case of published letters, there are other problems such as deletions, missing letters, and so on. Much of Mário de Andrade's correspondence may have been published, but the problems persist: from a lack of uniformity in the author's peculiar use of language (as Marcos Moraes has noted, in "Diálogo" ["Dialogue"]), to various problems that prevent one's access to interrelated aspects. Mário de Andrade's correspondence remained sealed until fifty years after his death, so this correspondence will gradually have to be organized and made public (as long as its respective authors and heirs do not oppose the idea). With respect to Ribeiro Couto's letters kept as a part of Manuel Bandeira's archives, the inventory states: (1) "Há cartas incompletas" ("There are incomplete letters"); (2) "Algumas cartas são documentos reservados e só poderão ser abertas a consultas em 2015" ("Some letters are private documents and will only be available for consultation in 2015") (36).

In these collections of letters, one notes that many of them have a relatively small number of foreign correspondents. In most cases there are a few very short letters that merely provided requested information. It is noteworthy that this is also the case with respect to Spanish American writers: In the archives of authors such as Manuel Bandeira, Carlos Drummond de Andrade, or Ribeiro Couto, there are very few letters by Spanish Americans. In the case of a vast archive, such as the correspondence of Carlos Drummond de Andrade, one might suppose that the number of Spanish American letters would not be so small, but one should note that most of these letters were written by representatives of publishing houses or periodicals, and they do not comprise significant groupings. What one finds instead are occasional letters, which do not form a lasting epistolary exchange. This does not mean there is nothing significant in these letters; what I mean to emphasize is the fragmentary and occasional nature of these exchanges of only two or three letters.

The same thing happens with Manuel Bandeira's archives, although one needs to take into account the fact that he himself was neglectful in preserving of documents. In his archives, for instance, there are only three letters from Alfonso Reyes (1889–1959), who lived in Brazil for some time. Reyes was deemed worthy of mention in Manuel Bandeira's famous poem "Rondó dos cavalinhos" ["Rondo of the Little Horses"] (featured in *Estrela da Manhã* [Morning Star]), in the following stanza: "Os cavalinhos correndo,/E nós cavalões, comendo . . ./Alfonso Reyes partindo,/E tanta gente ficando" (1:261) ("The little horses prancing,/And we, the big horses, eating . . ./Alfonso Reyes leaving,/And so many people staying"). The three letters featured in the archives are short and the most significant information in them is the author's comments on his *Libro Jubilar* [Jubilee Book], which has references to Manuel Bandeira.

In another extensive archive of letters, such as Ribeiro Couto's, the lack of Spanish American correspondents is similar. Here, however, the exchange with the Mexican writer Alfonso Reyes is notable for the number of letters–twenty-six–which, in comparative terms, is large, but they are all relatively short letters, with brief, general information by the sender. This set of letters offers no evidence of the great letter writer Reyes was, for example, in the correspondence with his fellow countryman, José Vasconcelos (1881–1959), which spans the years 1916 to 1959 and is composed of forty-nine letters, a figure that deserves attention. Of these forty-nine, thirty-seven are written by Vasconcelos, but only twelve by Reyes; the difference can likely be explained by the fact that Vasconcelos did not keep the letters he received. Other important letters by Reyes indicate a greater frequency in writing, like his correspondence with Pedro Henríquez Ureña (1884–1946) and with Genaro Estrada (1887–1937). The editor of the correspondence between Vasconcelos and Reyes had access to copies preserved by Reyes himself. This set of letters also reveals a certain difference in pace in the exchange, such as during a time when the writers were going through highly productive periods, and a final period in which the exchange became occasional and the letters brief, as both writers were traveling around the world as part of their work. As the editor states, "as cartas já não são mais que meros pretextos para agradecimentos por livros trocados ou pequenos serviços prestados" (33) ("the letters are now no more than pretexts to acknowledge books that were exchanged or other small favors done"). He adds that, despite these characteristics, the letters from this period are important since they offer information about certain dates that Vasconcelos does not seem to recall with precision in his memoirs. The Reyes-Vasconcelos correspondence is therefore a good example of several aspects of letter exchanges that should be taken into account to make their study more productive.

In terms of the interrelations among correspondences, the best examples to study are in Mário de Andrade's total correspondence. His unceasing dedication to work of all kind increased his overwhelming correspondence, in itself comprising multiple volumes that undoubtedly (and inevitably) count as a part of his *oeuvre*. This great body of texts grows every time a new set of letters is made public. In a letter to Sousa da Silveira (1883–1967) from 15 February 1935, Mário de Andrade seems to sum up his *oeuvre*'s multiplicity: "Não havia folclore musical brasileiro. Não havia crítica de arte em São Paulo, e a pouca brasileira existente era mais que péssima. Fiz crítica de arte. Não havia tratado de poética, moderno, adaptável ao tempo. Fiz um. Não havia história da música em nossa língua. As existentes eram simplesmente porcas. Fiz uma, bem melhor que as outras, Etc." (119) ("There was no Brazilian musical folklore. There was no art criticism in São Paulo, and whatever little criticism there was in Brazil was extremely poor. I wrote art criticism. There was no modern, time-situated treatise on poetry. I created one. There was no music history in our language. The few that existed were pitiful. I wrote one, much better than the others. Etc."). Despite this inclusive spirit, this awareness of his work, and especially this full consciousness of his contribution, there were nevertheless several projects he never had a chance to complete. The letters also reveal possible inconsistencies in or even discouragement with such a generally positive outlook.

Finally, correspondence implies a two-way exchange, in which writers complement each other. If Mário de Andrade hesitated about publishing his letters, sometimes agreeing to have some of his letters to Drummond de Andrade published, at others asking Bandeira not to publish them, either way reveals how aware he was of the significance of letters. In 1944 Drummond published long excerpts from letters he received from Mário de Andrade in the *Folha Carioca* [Rio News], and Mário de Andrade did not object; on the contrary, he even appeared to be moved by it, as Drummond indicates in his introduction to the collected letters. In that same year Mário de Andrade agreed to have his letters to Cecíla Meireles published. In a letter to Manuel Bandeira, however, he stated his opposition to the publication of his letters to Bandeira. He also saved all the letters he received and, being confident of their eventual value, even decided on the date when they should be made public–which was the same for the letters he himself had written. About the possibility of not publishing Mário de Andrade's letters, Drummond wrote in the introduction to his edition of the collected letters:

A obediência implicaria sonegação de documentos de inegável significação para a história literária do Brasil. Não só os praticantes da literatura perderiam com a falta de divulgação de cartas que esclarecem ou suscitam questões relevantes de crítica, estética literária e psicologia da composição. Os interessados em assuntos relativos à caracterização da fisionomia social do Brasil também se veriam lesados pela ignorância de valiosas reflexões abrangentes de diversos aspectos da antropologia cultural. (ix)

To obey that would mean to withhold documents of undeniable importance for the literary history of Brazil. Not only the writers of literature would lose out by the withholding of letters that clarify or raise relevant questions concerning criticism, literary aesthetics, and the psychology of composition. Those interested in

topics related to the social character of Brazil would also lose out by not having access to valuable reflections on various aspects of cultural anthropology.

In the letter addressed to Sousa da Silveira, Mário de Andrade said: "não há um só gesto significativo em mim que não seja uma atitude destinada, um ato consciente de vontade" (119) ("there is not a single significant gesture of mine that is not a premeditated attitude, a conscious act of will"). It is not difficult to perceive the irony of this statement: It was made in a letter, a space of privacy and at the same time of disclosure, appropriate not so much for confessions as for all sorts of indirections and insinuations that cannot be avoided even with the most attentive and careful control. Through the fissures of this statement, apparently a positive one, many silences emerge, such as these, to which must be added those Mário de Andrade himself intentionally created. The enormous volume of his letters, the editing of which may never reach completion, thus remains a work in progress for archivists and scholars. The possible readings of such texts continue to multiply, readings no longer done by his addressees, but instead by a larger public that turns its attention to the work of the author as a whole.

An initial silence can be found in the passive voice correspondence, whose time for release has come, although it will certainly be a while before those of greater interest are available to the public (that is, before the long work of preparing them for publication is completed). Another silence is the one found in Mário de Andrade's own letters that have not yet been made available to the public, or those that perhaps never will, whether because they were not preserved by their addressees or because the addressees themselves are not interested in the disclosure of letters that only contain personal matters. There are yet other silences. Several names have been omitted in the letters addressed to Oneyda Alvarenga, as she explains in her introduction to the collection: "Onde a discrição o exigia, omiti na correspondência os nomes de pessoas vivas e dos mortos ainda muito presentes na memória intelectual do país. Alguns poucos trechos, mesmo se cortados os nomes das pessoas, traziam em seu próprio conteúdo um endereço tão nítido, que precisei suprimi-los" (15) ("Whenever discretion called for it, I have omitted from the correspondence the names of living people and of those deceased who are still very much present in the intellectual memory of the country. A few passages, even when the names were omitted, contained such an obvious referent that I had to suppress them. Letters that stand alone and ellipses between parentheses indicate such cases"). Manuel Bandeira himself only published the letters he received from Mário de Andrade up to 1935, and, as he stated, he even suppressed some passages from them. The original letters Bandeira preserved are marked by him in pencil, indicating which passages should be left out–the visible marks of imposed silences. Some of the letters to Bandeira after 1935 were probably lost, and many of the ones prior to 1935 that had deletions were also lost, so that the parts that were suppressed are forever irretrievable. These are only signs of many other silences. In an undated letter, probably written on 24 October 1927 to Rosário Fusco, for instance, Mário de Andrade makes the following comment right at the beginning: "Lamento que minha carta registrada contendo escrita longa e 'Caso de cascata' pra *Verde* não tenha chegado aí" (14) ("I am sorry to hear that my registered letter containing a long piece of writing and 'Caso da cascata' [The Case of the Water-fall] for *Verde* never made it to you"). In a note to this same letter, Rosário Fusco says: "O resto da carta se perdeu" (15) ("The rest of the letter was lost"). In a single example, then, one finds an instance of the precariousness a letter is subject to and the gaps that also compose part of a correspondence.

The relation between the letter and the chronicle has been the subject of a few studies. Cecília de Lara has compared Antônio de Alcántara Machado's (1901–1935) letters sent from abroad and his travel chronicles included in *Pathé-Baby*. Although the comparisons are at first on the factual level, they can serve as a way of evaluating transpositions between texts of a different nature: "Além das informações biográficas, que possam oferecer, estas cartas e cartões se revestem de importância maior, pois permitem um confronto de textos sem cunho literário com a transposição para o plano da criação, nas crônicas de jornal e do livro" (Lara 37) ("Besides the biographical information they provide, these letters and cards are important in that they allow a comparison of non-literary texts with those conceived on a creative level, for newspaper and book chronicles"). From another point of view, the connection between the letter and the chronicle can also be seen in the work of Mário de Andrade. While investigating the beginning of his journalistic writings, which appeared in the magazine *Ilustração Brasileira* in 1920, Telê Ancona Lopez observed:

> É na segunda crônica, todavia, que Mário de Andrade vai refletir sobre seu papel de cronista (dezembro, 1920). Imbuindose de tarefa de correspondente, rotulará seu texto de 'cartas', definindo-se: 'Nestas cartas para a *Ilustração Brasileira* dois são os meus propósitos. Procurarei realiza-los pouco a pouco, si para tanto o engenho me sobrar. A todo este larguíssimo Brasil, que a revista abraçará, ao mesmo tempo que tenciono mostrar o movimento artístico e literário de gente paulista, é intuito meu explicar a enigmática cidade. (175)

> It is in the second chronicle, however, that Mário de Andrade reflects upon his role as a writer of chronicles (December 1920). Taking on the role of correspondent, he labels his texts as "letters," with this explanation: "In these letters for *Ilustração Brasileira* I have two aims in mind. I will try to accomplish them little by little, if I have enough skill left to do so. At the same time that I intend to show the artistic and literary movement of the people from São Paulo, I also intend to explain this enigmatic city to the rest of the people in this vast Brazil, whom the magazine may reach."

Lopez connects the chronicle and the letter form: "Porém, mais interessante é comentar essa idéia sua de cronista que envia 'cartas'. As cartas estão, na verdade, muito ligadas à tarefa de historiar, mas, sob o ângulo de quem as está escrevendo e que, algumas vezes pode se comportar como o cronista-historiador, ou do cronista-ficcionista de costumes" (175) ("However, what is even more interesting is to comment on his idea of being a writer of chronicles who sends 'letters.' The letters have, in fact, a close connection with the work of writing history, but from the perspective of someone who is writing them and who, at times, may behave as chronicler-historiographer, or chronicler-fiction writer of manners"). These connections between chronicle, fiction, and letter point to another web of relations around the letter, beyond that web of personal writings, like diaries and memoirs.

With regard to Malazarte's chronicles, published in *América Brasileira*, Telê Ancona Lopez states that they are "um campo de experimentação aberto. Vão admitir o conto e a carta" (185) ("an open field for experimentation, embracing the short-story and the letter"). Lopez considers Chronicle IX (a letter to Ribeiro Couto) as an example of this connection between the chronicle and the letter: "uma conversa com o amigo que se torna pública, tecendo a crítica do livro *A cidade do vício e da graça*. A carta ao colega de letras, ao leitor, continuará aparecendo anos a fio na crônica de Mário de Andrade" (186) ("a conversation with a friend that was made public about a critique of the book *A cidade do vício e da graça* [City of Vice and Grace]. The letter to the colleague, to the reader, will keep appearing for years and years in Mário de Andrade's chronicles"). Upon analyzing this chronicle-letter, Lopez notes that, as a chronicle, it has two parts, and can in fact be compared in structure and tone to many letters that Mário de Andrade sent to writers who requested his opinion: "Linguagem informal, afetiva, crítica severa, porém externando a condenação com tolerância e simplicidade e entusiasmando-se vivamente com os acertos" (Lopez 186) ("Informal, affective language, sharp criticism, yet showing his condemnations with tolerance and simplicity and openly displaying enthusiasm over successes"). In an undated letter (but written in 1925), a passage suggests his self-consciousness on this count:

> Sou um fenômeno culto, sei disso e não me afasto disso. Agora: numas cartas escritas alegremente pra amigos, por brincadeira, com intenção evidentemente pitoresca uso exageros de pângega, pra rir. Isto não quer dizer que vá escrever sempre assim nos meus artigos. Não. Por mais que eu escreva agora direto e simples, ainda faço distinção entre escrever pra público e pra amigos. As cartas que mando pra você são suas. Si eu morrer amanhã não quero que você as publique. Nem depois da morte de nós dois, quero um volume como o epistolário Wagner-Liszt. (226)

> I am a cultured phenomenon; I know this and I don't avoid it. Now: in some letters written gaily, jokingly, or with an explicitly picturesque intention to friends, I have exaggerated in the fun to cause laughter. This doesn't mean that I will always write like this in my articles. No. No matter how direct and plain my writing is at the moment, I still make a distinction between writing for the general public and writing to my friends. The letters I send to you are really yours. If I die tomorrow, I don't want you to publish them. Not even after both of us are dead do I want to see a book like the collected Wagner-Liszt letters.

Here are all the elements we have discussed: the possible informality of letters, the distinction between letters and articles, the distinction between private and public, and the privacy of letters.

Several other aspects of Mário de Andrade's texts, however, redefine these points. In a letter of 22 July 1926 to Manuel Bandeira, Mário de Andrade wrote: "Tinha muito que conversar com você . . . agora creio que só irei conversando aos poucos" (298) ("I had a lot to say to you . . . but now I think I will just talk about it little by little"). The letter as a form of conversation, or dialogue, is here emphasized. In a letter of 10 November 1926, however, one reads: "Tenho certeza que si eu perguntar em carta ou artigo pra êle quem que está fazendo arte negra, si eu, êle secundará que não sou eu" (320) ("I am sure that if I ask him in a letter or in an article who is producing black art, he will reply that it is not me"). Here, as on many other occasions, there is again an association made between the letter and the article. This association is not made merely in a single reference, as in this specific case, but occurs in almost all of his letters. In some rather extreme cases, the letter could be mistaken for an(other) text, an essay. This is the case of two letters from 1935, one of which opens as if with a dictionary entry: "Embolada: Fórmula poético-musical, específica" (275) ("*Embolada*: a poetic-musical composition, specific"). In a comment on the letter, Manuel Bandeira explains: "Mário responde nesta carta às consultas que lhe fiz sobre a definição de termos da música brasileira para os respectivos verbetes do *Pequeno dicionário Brasileiro da língua Portuguesa*. Todas as suas definições foram introduzidas por mim no dicionário e mantidas nas edições seguintes" (275) ("In this letter Mário answers some questions I asked him about the definition of some terms of Brazilian music for entries in the *Pequeno dicionário Brasileiro da língua Portuguesa* [Abridged Brazilian Dictionary of the Portuguese Language]. All of his definitions were used by me in the dictionary and maintained in subsequent editions"). In a later letter, the procedure is nearly the same, the only difference being a brief introduction: "recebi a carta agorinha, desta vez a resposta é mais fácil: *Samba*: Dança (287) ("I have just received the letter, and this time the answer is easier: *Samba*: Dance").

The same thing occurred in many of the letters to Oneyda Alvarenga. In a letter of 2 February 1935, he wrote a brief introduction and immediately launched into technical questions: "começo agora respondendo a todas as perguntas das suas cartas. Vamos a ver se dou conta de tudo agora mesmo, nesta tarde de Sábado de quem está desta forma fazendo a sua semana-inglesa. Primeiro as perguntas bibliográficas. O tambor de que fala Lévy-Bruhl é Quilaut. Eu aconselharia você a escrever assim: quilô" (58) ("I will now begin to answer all of the questions in your letters. Let's see if I can do it all at once, on a Saturday afternoon for someone who is therefore having his English-week. First the questions concerning bibliography. The drum that Lévy-Bruhl speaks of is the *Quilaut*. I would advise you to spell it like this: *quilô*"). Mário de Andrade's letter of 27 February 1940 to Alvarenga opens with a proposal: "Vamos iniciar o nosso trabalho de colaboração pros seus estudos iniciais relativos à sua futura 'História social da música'. Antes de mais nada está claro que você precisa estudar um bocado de sociología fundamental, cujos princípios você aplicará para exposição dos fatos históricos musicais e sua crítica" (79) ("Let's begin our collaborative work for the early studies of your upcoming 'História Social da Música' [Social History of Music]. Before anything else, it seems clear that you need to study quite a lot of basic sociology, whose principles you can apply to the discussion of historical and musical facts and the criticism on these"). Here one finds another aspect of Mário de Andrade's letters: The different addressees require distinctive epistolary formulations. Oneyda Alvarenga is a student to whom the letters are like lessons; Manuel Bandeira is a friend to whom Mário de Andrade submits his poems; Drummond is the younger poet to whom he offers advice.

These distinctions established, the correspondence with Rodrigo Melo Franco de Andrade reveals yet other characteristics. Their correspondence is very important for evaluating Mário de Andrade's role in the matter of historical heritage; furthermore, it shows how the responsibility of his work caused him to give friendship a secondary priority, making the letters documents too easily confused with administrative papers. His collected letters have a significant title: work letters. Also significant is the subtitle to the section in which the correspondence is transcribed: letters, documents, and reports. Mário de Andrade's letters often refer to a piling up of work; other than that, they span the variety of subjects already mentioned, such

as patrimony, music, literature, visual arts, and so forth. The closeness in them between his work and personal, affectionate comments once again suggests other forms of writing similar to letters—articles, chronicles, and diaries. A letter can function as a laboratory of multiple texts. It also functions as a center, both because it reveals Mário de Andrade's central (at times centralizing) role and because in it one finds the characteristics of an aesthetic movement. If, in the letter cited to Rodrigo Melo Franco de Andrade, what is at issue is homage to Manuel Bandeira, in an undated letter (but from 1930) to Bandeira himself, one reads: "Mas adorei a página sobre *Alguma Poesia*. Quem elogia êsse livro, até me parece que me elogia a mim, tanto que insisti pro Carlos publicálo, com carinhos, persuasões e fixando abertamente a minha admiração pelas coisas dele, até que enfim saiu e tive mesmo um alegrão" (446) ("But I loved the piece on *Alguma Poesia* [Some Poetry]. When someone pays a compliment to this book, it feels like he's complimenting me, so much so that I insisted, with affection, persuasiveness, and in an open statement of my admiration for his writings, that Carlos publish it, until finally it was released and I was quite happy"). The letters are thus a kind of intersection for various figures of Modernism, just as the letters themselves intersect. After all, Carlos Drummond de Andrade was another great correspondent of Mário de Andrade's, to whom Drummond submitted the poems that later appeared in his first book, *Alguma Poesia* [Some Poetry].

Carlos Drummond de Andrade's edition of the letters sent to him by Mário de Andrade is of great importance in that they contain detailed notes with the purpose of clarifying the letters, sometimes referring to other exchanges. Just as is the case of Manuel Bandeira's correspondence, the discussions are usually on literary subjects—both concerning Modernism in general and specifically concerning the texts that the correspondents were writing. In them one finds a considerable portion of Mário de Andrade's critical thinking about poetry. While the letters written by Modernists illustrate the turmoil caused by changes in various aspects of cultural, historical, and political life, they also occasionally show signs that the letter-writing process itself is undergoing changes. The improvement of postal service led to an increase in the exchange of letters, but, on the other hand, telephone communication did not diminish it. And yet, while the use of facsimile communication (fax) has recently led to a return to written communication, the Internet now begins to introduce other changes. As Walnice Nogueira Galvão has noted, "Talvez, então, a epistolografia não esteja propriamente desaparecendo, mas meramente efetuando uma transferência de suporte e de visualidade, enquanto mantém sua função de comunicação interpessoal" (162) ("Maybe, then, the epistolary tradition is not exactly disappearing, but rather undergoing a change in medium and in visual aspect, while it maintains its function of promoting interpersonal communication"). Before these changes the correspondence of the Modernists was the last great moment of the genre in Brazilian literature, not only because of the possibility of connecting it directly with the literary works of Modernism and for the information we glean about the epistolary genre itself, but also because it was a fundamental vehicle for building an important part of a decisive movement in Brazilian culture.

**Translation by Thomas LaBorie Burns
and Gláucia Renate Gonçalves**

Works Cited

Alencar, José Martiniano de. 1962. *O nosso cancioneiro (cartas ao senhor Joaquim Serra)*. Ed. Manuel Esteves and M. Cavalcanti Proença. Rio de Janeiro: São Jose.

——. 1971. *Cartas sobre a Confederação dos Tamoios*. By I. G. (pseud.). Rio de Janeiro: Diario.

Alencar, José de, and Machado de Assis. *Cartas sobre Castro Alves.* N.p: n.p.

Almeida, Guilherme de. 1931. *Carta a minha noiva.* São Paulo: Companhia Editora Nacional.

Almeida, Júlia Lopes de. 1913. *Correio da roça.* Rio de Janeiro: Francisco Alves; Paris: Aillaud, Alves.

Alvarenga, Oneyda. 1974. *Mario de Andrade, um pouco.* Rio de Janeiro: José Olympio.

Alves, Castro. 1920. *Correspondência e crítica.* Rio de Janeiro: Editora H. Antunes e Cia.

Andrade, Ana Isabel de Sousa Leão. 1983. *Catálogo da correspondência de José Américo de Almeida (Cartas: 1915–1952).* Vol 1. João Pessoa: Fundação Casa de José Américo.

Andrade, Ana Isabel de Sousa Leão, and Carmen Lúcia de Souza Leão Rêgo. 1978. *Catálogo da Correspondência de Joaquim Nabuco (1865–1884).* Vol 1. Recife: Instituto Joaquim Nabuco de Pesquisas Sociais.

Andrade, Ana Isabel de Sousa Leão, Carmen Lúcia de Souza Leão Rêgo, and Tereza Cristina de Sousa Dantas. 1980. *Catálogo da Correspondência de Joaquim Nabuco (1885–1889).* Vol 2. Recife: Fundação Joaquim Nabuco.

Andrade, Carlos Drummond de. 1979. *Poesia completa e prosa.* Rio de Janeiro: Aguilar.

——. 1976. "O projeto da carta." *Jornal do Brasil* (January 27): 2.

Andrade, Mário de. 1964. "Cartas a Sousa da Silveira." *Revista do Livro* 26: 113–33.

——. 1967. *Cartas a Manuel Bandeira.* Rio de Janeiro: Edições de Ouro.

——. 1968. *Mário de Andrade escreve cartas a Alceu, Meyer e outros.* Ed. Lygia Fernandes. Rio de Janeiro: Editora do Autor.

——. 1981a. *Cartas a Murilo Miranda, 1943–1945.* Rio de Janeiro: Nova Fronteira.

——. 1981b. *Cartas a um Jovem Escritor: Cartas de Mário de Andrade a Fernando Sabino.* Rio de Janeiro: Record.

——. 1981c. *Cartas de Trabalho: Correspondência com Rodrigo Mello Franco de Andrade (1936–1945).* Brasília: Serviço do Patrimônio Histórico e Artístico Nacional; Fundação Pró-Memória.

——. 1982a. *A Lição do Amigo: Cartas de Mário de Andrade a Carlos Drummond de Andrade.* Rio de Janeiro: José Olympio.

——. 1982b. *Correspondente contumaz: Cartas a Pedro Nava.* Rio de Janeiro: Nova Fronteira.

——. 1983. *Cartas de Mário de Andrade a Álvaro Lins.* Ed. Ivan Cavalcanti Proença and José César Borba e Marco Morel. Rio de Janeiro: José Olympio.

——. 1985. *Cartas de Mário de Andrade a Prudente de Morais Neto.* Rio de Janeiro: Nova Fronteira.

——. 1988a. *Macunaíma.* Ed. Telê Porto Ancona Lopez. Paris: Association Archives de la Littérature latino-américaine, des Caraïbes et africaines du XXe. Siècle; Brasília: Conselho Nacional de Desenvolvimento Científico e Tecnológico.

——. 1988b. *Mário de Andrade Escreve cartas a Alceu, Meyer e outros.* Ed. Lygia Fernandes. Rio de Janeiro: Ed. do Autor.

——. 1989a. *A Lição do Guru (Cartas a Guilherme de Figueiredo) (1937–1945).* Rio de Janeiro: Civilização Brasileira.

——. 1989b. *Cartas a Anita Malfatti.* Rio de Janeiro: Forense.

——. 1990a. *Cartas de Mário de Andrade a Henriqueta Lisboa.* Rio de Janeiro: José Olympio.

——. 1990b. *Querida Henriqueta: Cartas de Mário de Andrade a Henriqueta Lisboa.* Rio de Janeiro: José Olympio.

——. 1991. *Cartas de Mário de Andrade a Luís da Comara Cascudo.* Belo Horizonte: Villa Rica.

——. 1994. *Cartas do irmão maior: Cartas de Mário de Andrade a João Etieme Filho.* Belo Horizonte: Mazza, Belas Artes Liberdade.

——. 1995. *Portinari, amico mio: Cartas de Mário de Andrade a Cândido Portinari.* Ed. Annateresa Fabris. Campinas: Mercado de Letras: Autores Associados.

——. n.d. *71 cartas de Mário da Andrade.* Ed. Lygia Fernandes. Rio de Janeiro: São José.

——. n.d. *Cartas a Rosário Fusco.* Exemplar único, provas tipográficas da biblioteca Plínio Doyle, Fundação Casa de Rui Barbosa. N.p: n.p.

Andrade, Mário de, and Oneyda Alvarenga. 1983. *Cartas.* São Paulo: Duas Cidades.

Andrade, Mário de, and Manuel Bandeira. 1974. *Itinerários (Cartas a Alphonsus de Guimaraens Filho).* São Paulo: Duas Cidades.

——. 2000. *Correspondência.* Ed. Marcos Antônio de Moraes. São Paulo: Editora da Universidade de São Paulo; Instituto de Estudos Brasileiros, USP.

Assis, Machado de. 1979. *Quincas Borba: Obras Completas.* Vol 1. Rio de Janeiro: Aguilar.

——. 1988. *A mão e a luva.* Rio de Janeiro-Belo Horizonte: Garnier.

——. 1998. *Quincas Borba.* Trans. Gregory Rabassa. New York: Oxford University Press.

Azevedo, Aluísio. 1985. *Mattos, Malta ou Matta?* Rio de Janeiro: Nova Fronteira, Fundação Casa de Rui Barbosa.

Bandeira, Manuel. 1958. *Poesia e prosa.* 2 vols. Rio de Janeiro: Aguilar.

Barbosa, Rui. 1896. *Cartas de Inglaterra.* Rio de Janeiro: Typ. Leuzinger.

Barreto, Lima. 1993. *Um longo sonho do futuro: Diários, cartas, entrevistas e confissões dispersas.* Rio de Janeiro: Graphia Editorial.

Broca, Brito. 1956. *A vida literária no Brasil.* Rio de Janeiro: Serviço de Documentação, Ministério da Educação e Cultura.

Cabral, Valle. n.d. *Cartas bibliographicas.* N.p: n.p.

Callado, Antônio. 1976. *Reflexos do baile.* Rio de Janeiro: Paz e Terra.

Caminha, Adolpho. 1895. *Cartas litterárias.* Rio de Janeiro: n.p.

Caminha, Pero Vaz de. 1943. "Carta." *A Carta de Pero Vaz de Caminha.* Ed. Jaime Cortesão. Rio de Janeiro: Livros de Portugal. 193–241.

Cândido, Antônio. 1922. "Atualidade de um romance inatual." *A correspondência de uma estação de cura.* Ed. João do Rio. Rio de Janeiro: Fundação Casa de Rui Barbosa; São Paulo: Scipione/Instituto Moreira Salles. ix–xviii.

Cardoso, Lúcio. 1991. *Crônica da casa assassinada.* Ed. Júlio Castañon Guimarães. Madrid: Archivos.

Dias, Antônio Gonçalves. 1971. *Correspondência ativa de Antônio Gonçalves Dias.* Rio de Janeiro: Biblioteca Nacional.

——. 1998. "Correspondência." *Poesia e prosa completas.* Ed. Alexei Bueno. Rio de Janeiro: Nova Aguilar. 1033–144.

Duarte, Paulo. 1985. *Mário de Andrade por ele mesmo.* São Paulo: Hucitec.

Eulalio, Alexandre. 1985. "Depois do romance." *Mattos, Malta ou Matta?* Ed. Aluísio Azevedo. Rio de Janeiro: Nova Fronteira, Fundação Casa de Rui Barbosa. 161–87.

Ferreira, Ascenso. 1989. *Cartas de Ascenso Ferreira a Veríssimo de Melo.* Natal: Academia Norte-Rio-Grandense de Letras.

Figueiredo, Jackson de. 1948. *Cartas.* Rio de Janeiro: Centro Dom Vital.

Fonseca, Maria Augusta. 1988. "A carta pras icamiabas." *Macunaíma*. Ed. Mário de Andrade. Paris: Association Archives de la Littérature Latino-américaine, des Caraïbes et Africaine du xx. Siècle; Brasília: Conselho Nacional de Desenvolvimento Científico e Tecnológico. 278–94.

Freitas, Newton. 1975. "Correspondência de Mário de Andrade." *Revista do Instituto de Estudos Brasileiros* 17: 91–120.

Fusco, Rosario. 1954. *Carta à Noiva (Romance)*. Rio de Janeiro: Organização Simões.

Galvão, Walnice Nogueira. 1998. "¿ margem da carta." *Desconversa*: *Ensaios críticos*. Rio de Janeiro: Editora da Universidade Federal do Rio de Janeiro. 154–63.

Gonzaga, Tomás Antônio. 1996. *Cartas Chilenas*. São Paulo: Companhia das Letras.

Guimarães, Júlio Castañon. 1996. *Distribuição de Papéis: Murilo Mendes escreve a Carlos Drummond de Andrade e a Lúcio Cardoso*. Rio de Janeiro: Fundação Casa de Rui Barbosa.

Haroche-Bouzinac, Geneviève. 1995. *L'épistolaire*. Paris: Hachette.

Inventário do arquivo Carlos Drummond de Andrade. 1989. Rio de Janeiro: Fundação Casa de Rui Barbosa.

Kaufmann, Vincent. 1994. *Post Scripts: The Writer's Workshop*. Trans. Deborah Triesman. Paris: Minuit.

Lara, Cecília de. 1986. "Da realidade contada à transposição no texto literário. Pathé-Baby: Correspondência e Crônicas de Viagem." *Revista do Instituto de Estudos Brasileiros*. Universidade de São Paulo. 35–45.

Lins, Vera. 1997. *Ribeiro Couto, uma questão de olhar*. Rio de Janeiro: Fundação Casa de Rui Barbosa.

—. 1998. *Novos pierrôs, velhos saltimbancos*. Curitiba: Secretaria de Estado da Cultura.

Lobato, Monteiro. 1959. *Cartas escolhidas*. São Paulo: Brasiliense.

Lopez, Telê Porto Ancona. 1992. "A crônica de Mário de Andrade: Impressões que historiam." *A crônica: O gênero, sua fixação e suas transformações no Brasil*. Ed. Antônio Cândido et al. Campinas: Editora da Unicamp; Rio de Janeiro: Fundação Casa de Rui Barbosa. 165–88.

Machado, Antônio de Alcântara. 1963. *Pathé-Baby e prosa turística: O viajante europeu e platino*. Ed. Cecília de Lara. Rio de Janeiro: Civilização Brasileira.

—. 1997. *Pressão afetiva e aquecimento intelectual (Cartas de Antônio de Alcântara Machado a Prudente de Moraes, neto)*. Ed. Cecília de Lara. São Paulo: Giordano: Lemos: Educ.

Mendes, Manuel Odorico. 1989. *Cartas*. Rio de Janeiro: Academia Brasileira de Letras.

Mendes, Murilo. 1990. "Seis Cartas de Murilo Mendes a Carlos Drummond de Andrade." *Revista do Brasil* 5.11: 79–84.

Mendonça, Lúcio de. 1882. O *marido da adúltera*. Campanha: Typ. de M. de Oliveira Andrade.

Milliet, Sergio. 1941. *Duas Cartas no Meu Destino*. Curitiba: Editora Guaíra.

Moraes, Marcos Antonio de. 1995. "Diálogo multiplicado." *Gênese e memória*. IV Encontro internacional de pesquisadores de manuscritos e de edições. São Paulo. Associação de Pesquisadores do Manuscrito Literário, Annablume. 253–59.

Rio, João do. 1992. *A correspondência de uma estação de cura*. Rio de Janeiro: Fundação Casa de Rui Barbosa; São Paulo: Scipione, Instituto Moreira Salles.

Süssekind, Flora. 1993. "O romance epistolar e a virada do século: Lúcio Mendonça e João do Rio." *Papéis colados*. Rio de Janeiro: Editora Universidade Federal do Rio de Janeiro. 211–25.

Varnhagen, Francisco Adolpho. 1929. *Cartas sobre a "Prosopopéia", de Bento Teixeira Pinto e sobre "O Peregrino da América" de Nuno Marques Pereira*. Rio de Janeiro: Separata do volume XXVI das Publicações do Arquivo Nacional.

Vasconcelos, José, and Alfonso Reyes. 1995. *La amistad en el dolor: Correspondencia entre José Vasconcelos y Alfonso Reyes, 1916–1959*. Ed. Claude Fell. Mexico City: El Colegio Nacional.

Vieira, Antônio. 1854. *Cartas*. Lisboa: Editores, J. M. C. Seabra and T. Q. Antunes.

CHAPTER 26

THE COMPARATIVE DRIVE IN THE LATIN AMERICAN ESSAY

Randolph D. Pope

A Place of Origin

Location is as important for the essay as it is for real estate. While it is consoling to pretend that the literary page takes off on its own merits to welcoming readers the world over–an idea often propagated by hegemonic cultures–in practice, any text remains entangled with a gendered and ethnic body, a national origin, a geographical location, and a language and its tradition–all determining greatly its reception. If there is a Latin American essay distinct from a European essay, the vital difference is not to be found in its subject, style, or inter-textual references, since the libraries of essayists on both sides of the Atlantic look much the same. But at the point of its origin, because these essays are written by a Latin American, often a difference emerges in the way the text is conceived, and in how and where it circulates.

The essay, seen comparatively, is similar to an international conversation that Europeans have long dominated. When the Peruvian or Brazilian essayist attempts to join in, the authoritative voices of Hume and Adam Smith, Gobineau and Weber, Rousseau and Nietzsche, Marx and Freud, Montaigne and Ortega, Derrida and Lacan, Kristeva and Irigaray, among many others, crowd the stage, leaving little if any room for newcomers from Latin America. It could be argued that the importance of such essayists as José Martí (1853–1895), José Carlos Mariátegui (1894–1930), and Octavio Paz (1914–1998), to give three well-known examples, should prove the value of Latin American essayists, and it does in a way, but that does little to bolster their international circulation or their regular insertion in the debate of ideas. In this aspect, as in others, one can apply what Octavio Paz affirmed in his acceptance speech for the Nobel prize: "The consciousness of being separate is a constant feature of our spiritual history" (1991, 10). Further, the predominance of the European and North American cultural centers has produced a corrosive feeling of belatedness, as if ideas had to come into existence first in Paris to acquire reality. Again, in the words of Octavio Paz: "For us Spanish Americans this present was not in our own countries: It was the time lived by others–by the English, the French, the Germans. It was the time of New York, Paris, London. We had to go and look for it and bring it back home" (16); "the modern was outside and had to be imported" (19). This process was facilitated by the constant expansion of the European and North American markets into Latin America. Gilberto Freyre (1900–1987)

recalls in *Interpretación del Brasil* [1945; Interpretation of Brazil] that the British exported to Brazil items such as heavy blankets and ice skates. This, according to Freyre, reflects the ideals and the interests of the producers of consumer goods and ideas, who wish the world were divided into two large sectors: one formed by the imperial regions, where articles and ideas are produced to satisfy the needs of the people who live there; the other, the colonial region, where people must consume products and accept ideas provided by the imperial region, be they adequate or not to local conditions (75–77). It is not a reciprocal relation, and Martí denounced it roundly as "la importación excesiva de las ideas y fórmulas ajenas" (90) ("the excessive importing of foreign ideas and formulae"), ideas and behaviors that the Argentinian Ezequiel Martínez Estrada (1895–1964) called "un panal comprado" (2:52) ("a purchased honeycomb"), noting that they did not correspond to the organic evolution of the native society.

In previous centuries, as in today's practice, footnotes and bibliographies of Latin American essays frequently invoke and seldom question effectively the authority of the European authors and, more recently, those from the United States. They are brought into the home of the Latin American essay with admiring hospitality, while Latin American names only rarely figure prominently in the essays of their European or North American counterparts. From the very beginning, to write essays in Latin America has meant to read and incorporate metropolitan thought, but seldom to be admitted there as an agent of speech. Ironically, in the late twentieth century, at exactly the time when Europe begins to be challenged and eclipsed by foreign essayists, doctrines such as deconstruction and postmodernism take hold, in which originality is debunked and the author erased. Too many subalterns have joined the party, so it is called off.

When Simón Bolívar (1783–1830) recalled in 1825 his education, he claimed to have studied closely "Locke, Condillac, Buffon, Dalembert, Helvetius, Montesquieu, Mably, Filangieri, Lalande, Rousseau, Voltaire, Rollin, Berthot" (19), plus many other European writers from the classics to the modern. While one may suspect some exaggeration in Bolívar's enumeration, what matters is that these names were exchanged with his interlocutor as icons of a defensive learning, with the fear of being caught short in an intellectual economy with which they both were familiar and where European values prevailed. There is a nakedness to be dissimulated, and the fear, mocked by Martí in "Nuestra América" is that the bottom may be revealed uncovered, in "nuestra América mestiza, en los pueblos de pierna desnuda y casaca de París" (89) ("our mestizo America, in the villages of naked legs and Parisian frock coat"). While Bolívar notes that he learned foreign languages–associated a few lines later by contiguity with other social skills, such as fencing, dancing, and riding–under private tutors in Madrid, we can feel fairly certain that these languages did not include any of the native languages of Latin America. This neglect was not because they were not considered foreign, but because they did not have any immediate role in the education of a gentleman.

Bolívar despaired of the divisive and contentious nature of the new nations, and much of his writing is addressed to them as a call for concerted action. His essays are, at their best, inflammatory prose pieces, strung together by an imperative of liberation, as in the concluding lines of his "Manifiesto de Cartagena" ["Manifesto of Cartagena"] of 1812: "Id veloces a vengar al muerto, a dar vida al moribundo, soltura al oprimido y libertad a todos" (57) ("Go rapidly to take revenge for the dead, resuscitate the dying, liberty to the oppressed and freedom to all"). Yet this freedom for all could not but open up a much vaster library than the one he knew from his education in Caracas and Madrid, and his travels to Italy, France, and England; it was the library of kipus and Mayan glyphs, of body painting in the Amazon, of Guaraní legends in Paraguay, and much more. When he writes from Kingston, on 6 September 1815, his famous "Contestación de un Americano Meridional a un caballero de esta isla" ["Response from a South American to a Gentleman of this Island"], he declares himself aware of his lack of books and experience: "Así, me encuentro en un conflicto, entre el deseo de corresponder a la confianza con que Vd. me favorece, y el impedimento de satisfacerla, tanto por la falta de documentos y libros, como por los limitados conocimientos que poseo de un país tan inmenso, variado y desconocido, como el Nuevo Mundo" (61) ("Thus it is that I find myself in a quandary between my desire to reciprocate the trust you have shown me and the impediments I have in satisfying it–not only a lack of documents and books, but also my most limited knowledge of such an immense, varied, and unknown country like the new world").

The European library could neither account for nor express the polyglossia of the Americas. Bolívar wandered into what for him was a quagmire, with ideas gathered from Bentham, Montesquieu, and Rousseau, proposing vainly as a model the British constitution and toying with the ideal of a centralizing and authoritarian government. His essays aimed not only to describe but also to transform reality so that it accorded with his readings. This was a Quixotic quest, noble and destined to frustration. Bolívar, in his letter from Jamaica, railed against Spain and her transformation from mother to cruel stepmother, and took his revenge by cutting her away from the rest of the continent: "¿Y la Europa civilizada, comerciante y amante de la libertad, permite que una vieja serpiente, por solo satisfacer su saña envenenada, devore la más bella parte de nuestro globo? ¡Qué! ¿Está la Europa sorda al clamor de su propio interés?" (66) ("How can a civilized Europe that engages in trade and loves liberty permit an old serpent to devour the most beautiful part of our world just to satisfy its venomous rage. What! Is Europe deaf to the sound of its own interests?"). This characteristic grabbing of the reader's attention with a sequence of questions and exclamations slashes

Spain away from civilization, in the first question, by opposing her to the "Europa civilizada" ("civilized Europe"), and then proceeds, in the second, to erase the "old snake"–the spoiler of Paradise–altogether from Europe. The problem is that what is left, "las naciones cultas" (67) ("civilized nations"), do not rush to the rescue. From their point of view, Bolívar notes bitterly, "somos un pequeño género humano; poseemos un mundo aparte" (69) ("we are but a small part of humanity, we are a separate world"). The narrow and uncomfortable range to which this isolated "we" applies is revealed a few lines later: "no somos indios ni europeos, sino una especie media entre los legítimos propietarios del país y los usurpadores españoles" (69) ("we are neither Indians nor Europeans, but rather a people midway between the legitimate owners of this country and usurping Spaniards")–an idea he repeats later in the "Discurso de Angostura" (96) ["Declaration of Angostura"]. He ends with a stark image: "La América está encontrada entre sí, porque se halla abandonada de todas las naciones; aislada en medio del universo" (84) ("America finds itself in conflict with itself, because it has been abandoned by all nations, isolated in middle of the universe"). America finds itself (se encuentra) in a situation of internecine conflict (encontrada entre sí), as if language itself were warping and deteriorating with the tensions of the new freedom, and being in the ideal geographical situation, at the center of the universe in the most beautiful spot on the globe, is no consolation. In fact, implicit in the comparison of the new countries with Icarus, lurks the mapping of America as a labyrinth from which it is impossible to escape: "¿Se puede concebir que un pueblo recientemente desencadenado se lance a la esfera de la libertad, sin que, como a Icaro, se le deshagan las alas y recaiga en el abismo? Tal prodigio es inconcebible, nunca visto. Por consiguiente, no hay un raciocinio verosímil que nos halague con esta esperanza" (76) ("Is it conceivable that a people only recently freed from its chains could throw itself into liberty without, like Icarus, falling into the abyss when its wings fail? Such a wonder is inconceivable, never before seen. Consequently there is no rational argument that can lift our spirits with this hope").

Bolívar, steeped after all in the Enlightenment and in Romantic ideas, will not be deterred by the limits of the rational. In 1819 he quotes Rousseau to the effect that freedom is "un alimento suculento, pero de difícil digestión" (98) ("a succulent food that is difficult to digest"). If Bolívar's essays flicker between somber disappointment and radiant hope, it is because he believes there are sublime reserves in the human spirit that can overcome unbelievable limitations. What better example than the Greeks of a people who start with scant resources, a smattering of rival cities, and yet face invading armies, expand their reach with commerce, and create a lasting cultural heritage? Can't we imitate them? But when Bolívar introduces this hope, he undercuts it by expressing the obstacles he sees against attaining it:

> Es una idea grandiosa pretender formar de todo el Mundo Nuevo una sola nación con un solo vínculo que ligue sus partes entre sí y con el todo. Ya que tiene un origen, una lengua, unas costumbres y una religión debería, por consiguiente, tener un solo gobierno que confederase los diferentes estados que hayan de formarse; mas no es posible, porque climas remotos, situaciones diversas, intereses opuestos, caracteres desemejantes dividen a la América. ¡Qué bello sería que el istmo de Panamá fuese para nosotros lo que el de Corinto para los griegos! (81)

It is a grandiose idea to dream of forming one nation of the whole new world with one law to link all its parts among each other and into one nation. It already has a common origin, language, customs, and religion; it should therefore have only one government to bring together in confederation the different states that will come to be; but it is not possible because there are too many diverse climates and situations, opposing interests, incompatible characters that divide America. How beautiful it would be if the isthmus of Panama would be for us what Corinth was to the Greeks.

But the distance is not easy to bridge. Centuries later, Pedro Henríquez Ureña's (1884–1946) first consideration was geographic when he attempted in 1928 to define what is "La América española y su originalidad" ("Hispanic America and its originality") in *Seis ensayos en busca de nuestra expresión* [1952; Six Essays in Search of Our Expression]. America is far away from Europe, he asserts, and adds a striking comparison: "[A] distancia mayor sólo se hallan, dentro de la civilización occidental, los dominios ingleses de Australia y Nueva Zelandia" (32) ("[O]nly the British dominions of Australia and New Zealand in Western civilization are further away"). His map measures distance *away* from Europe, and totally ignores the other possible maps that also exist in America, where the center is in Cuzco or the Orinoco, in Africa, China, or the Middle East. The off-handed clause "in Western civilization" is not unimportant, because it makes the fundamental assertion that Henríquez Ureña wishes to let pass unchallenged that America is *Spanish* and part of the Western tradition. The comparison of America with Australia and New Zealand, British dominions, is a parallel that evinces the postcolonial situation. While politically the Spanish American countries are independent, the lingering economic superiority of Europe and the United States confirms for many the truth of an internalized cultural predominance of Paris, London, or New York in terms of originality, depth, and universality. Therefore, Henríquez Ureña continues with a lament that distills centuries of failed salesmanship: "Las naciones de nuestra América, aun las superiores en población y territorio, no alcanzan todavía importancia política y económica suficiente para que el mundo se pregunte cuál es el espíritu que las anima, cuál es su personalidad real" (32) ("The nations of our America, even those with larger population and territory, have not yet achieved the political and economic importance for the world to ask about the spirit that moves them, inquire about their true personality").

The categories of extension and population (whereby Mexico, Brazil, or Argentina would outrank any European country) are subordinated to political and economic might. Henríquez Ureña's hopeful "no alcanzan todavía" ("have not yet achieved") implies, as a sort of incantation, that in the future America will fully develop, emerge, and join the first world. Yet the distance to cover can be measured by his juxtaposition of "nuestra América" ("our America") and "el mundo" ("the world"). Outside of the world, unknown, ignored, misconstrued, Spanish America does not form part of the "important" reality defined by the other shore. As Octavio Paz put it in *El laberinto de la soledad* [(1950), 1993; *The Labyrinth of Solitude*, 1961], "Para un europeo, México es un país al margen de la Historia universal" (72) ("For a European, Mexico is a country at the margins of universal History").

Comparing Race

From a postcolonial perspective, Bolívar's assumption that all people in Latin America have one origin and one language,

plus identical mores and religion, seems wrong-headed. He excluded Portuguese from the New World, not to mention the many indigenous nations and languages. But, in fact, in a famous public letter written the same month as the one just discussed, he acknowledged that of fifteen to twenty million inhabitants–his statistics were far from exact–distributed throughout the continent, whites represented a distinct minority compared to native Americans, people of African origin, and mixed races. Yet the "temor de los colores" (87) ("fear of colors") he observed around him should diminish, he claims, because the whites were more active, the Indians were passive and mild, and the blacks respected their owners. He was acutely aware of the plural and only partially mixed nature of America. His "one origin" is disingenuous, therefore, and, even more, a form of what Freud called "screen memory." When a traumatic episode makes remembering it painful, it is displaced and substituted by another, safer, more comfortable one that satisfies the urge for origins and locks out from consciousness the truly original and disturbing event. The wide swerve away from Latin America to Greece in the final thought of the quoted paragraph revealed more, then, than a simple classical reminiscence. Here, Corinth obstructed with its harmonious glow the emergence of the challenging origins, tongues, mores, and religions of Latin America. The "fear of colors" returned once again when Bolívar attempted to assuage it with the same appeal to the classical: There was nothing to fear, he assured his readers, from being so few whites in a vast continent peopled by slaves and oppressed nations: "¿En Atenas no eran los esclavos cuatro veces más que los ciudadanos? ¿Los campos de Esparta no los cultivaban los ilotas?" (89) ("Were there not four times as many slaves as citizens in Athens? Were not the fields of Sparta farmed by the Ilotas?"). Comparing here is more an act of denial than of illumination. His deep concern about the confusing effect of the racial intermingling comes through in the "Discurso de Angostura," in which he proposes the adoption of a new constitution for the emerging state. He affirms:

> Séame permitido llamar la atención del Congreso sobre una materia que puede ser de una importancia vital. Tengamos presente que nuestro Pueblo no es el Europeo, ni el Americano del Norte, que más bien es un compuesto de Africa y de América, que una emanación de la Europa; pues que hasta la España misma, deja de ser Europa por su sangre africana, por sus Instituciones, y por su carácter. Es imposible asignar con propiedad, a qué familia humana pertenecemos. La mayor parte del indígena se ha aniquilado, el Europeo se ha mezclado con el Americano y con el Africano, y éste se ha mezclado con el Indio y con el Europeo. Nacidos todos del seno de una misma Madre, nuestros Padres diferentes en origen y en sangre, son extranjeros, y todos difieren visiblemente en la epidermis; esta desemejanza trae un reato de la mayor trascendencia. (103)

May I be permitted to call the attention of the Congress to an issue that may be of vital importance. Let us keep in mind that our people are not Europeans or from English North America, that our population is largely made up of African and Amerindian people more so than European for even Spain itself is not European because of its African blood, because of its institutions and its character. It is impossible to properly designate to what human family we belong. A large part of the Indian population has been annihilated; Europeans have mixed with *criollos* and African Americans, and these people have in turn mixed with the indigenous and with the recently arrived European. We have all been born of the same mother but of different fathers differing in origin and blood; they are strangers and they differ visibly in the color of their skin; this dissimilarity brings with it a residual burden of some consequence.

The common land acts as the bond between the disparate races, becoming a figurative mother that whitens out all the real mothers that keep passing on the discordant traits of race to their descendants. Bolívar's observation about the African elements in Spanish culture remind us that the issues discussed in his essays are not unique to America; nor are they altogether resolved today. The furor that Américo Castro's books and essays caused in proposing that Spain had not emerged until Christians, moors, and Jews interacted in the Middle Ages, along with the unremitting tensions with Basques and Catalans within the Iberian peninsula even today, show that the Romantic idea of the ancestral nation dies hard. Gilberto Freyre, in *Interpretación del Brasil*, used precisely this composite character of Spain and Portugal–their diversity in ethnic groups, religions, languages, geography, and climate–to explain the special resilience of the Portuguese colonizers and their adaptability in America, and to conclude that the European roots of Brazil, via Portugal and Spain, were partly African and Asiatic.

Bolívar saw in a blending of all bloods and cultures the only solution to chaos: "Unidad, Unidad, Unidad debe ser nuestra divisa" (116) ("Unity, Unity, Unity should be our goal"). That this well-meaning unification could only result in the loss of some minority or subordinated cultures was a price that he was willing to pay to avoid chaos. It will not happen in his lifetime. In 1830 he wrote from Barranquilla some of the best-known lines of Latin American literature–a literature that has always been immersed in the political, sociological, and utopian–lines that have haunted essayists ever since:

> Vd. sabe que yo he mandado veinte años, y de ellos no he sacado más que pocos resultados ciertos: 1, la América es ingobernable para nosotros; 2, el que sirve una revolución ara en el mar; 3, la única cosa que se puede hacer en América es emigrar; 4, este país caerá infaliblemente en manos de la multitud desenfrenada para después pasar a tiranuelos casi imperceptibles de todos colores y razas; 5, devorados por todos los crímenes y extinguidos por la ferocidad, los europeos no se dignarán conquistarnos; 6, si fuera posible que una parte del mundo volviera al caos primitivo, éste sería el último período de la América. (169)

> As you know, I have been in command for twenty years and I have only come upon a few certain conclusions: (1) America is for us ungovernable; (2) he who serves a revolution plows the sea; (3) the only thing one can do in America is emigrate; (4) this country will without any doubt fall into the hands of an undisciplined mob only to pass to petty dictators of all colors and races; (5) devoured by crime and exhausted by ferocious violence, the Europeans will not dignify us by conquering us again; (6) if it were possible for a part of the world to revert to the most primitive chaos, this would be the final period in the history of America.

In a few pages here we cannot follow in detail the fortunes of the debate on race in Latin America. Significant is José Vasconcelos's (1881–1959) *La raza cósmica* [(1925), 1948; *The Cosmic Race*, 1997], because his prominence as an intellectual of the Mexican Revolution and the vehemence of his prose assured this conflictive text a wide distribution. It starts out with a chapter in which he develops the fanciful theory that the human race began with a red race, who populated the vanished island of Atlantis and left its traces in Chichén Itza and Palenque, from where its secrets were carried over to Egypt. The importance of his new myth was that it was a

reply to the irritation of being discovered and new, postponed, and neglected: "Si, pues somos antiguos geológicamente y también en lo que respecta a la tradición, ¿cómo podremos seguir aceptando esta ficción inventada por nuestros padres europeos de la novedad de un continente, que existía desde antes de que apareciese la tierra de donde procedían descubridores y reconquistadores?" (2–3) ("If our land is ancient geologically and our traditions are also ancient, how can we continue to accept the fiction invented by our European fathers that this continent is new, since it existed before the land from which the discoverers and conquerors came?").

Vasconcelos accepts the importance of precedence and invents a new history for America. And he does not rest there. He sees as descendants of the red people the black, the Indian, the Mongol, and the white, who now has only temporarily taken control. The tide of history, according to Vasconcelos, leads inexorably to a fifth race, a cosmic race, that will have its origin and stronghold in Latin America. He is not alone in his opinion: Gilberto Freyre in *Interpretación del Brasil* echoes Vasconcelos when he affirms that the "tipo extra-europeo de civilización" (159) ("the extra-European form of civilization") that was being developed in Brazil by incorporating all races would be the nation's unique contribution to the development of the human personality in the modern world.

Like Bolívar, Vasconcelos lamented the loss of unity of the continent that blocked the realization of his ideal and projected it to the future. He also found debilitating the break with Spain. Once the blending attained the unity of the new race, "se verá en seguida que somos nosotros de mañana, en tanto que ellos [the American whites] van siendo de ayer" (18) ("it will be immediately seen that we are of tomorrow, while they [the American whites] are of yesterday"). This self-affirming theory would have only a curiosity value if it did not reflect the Latin American contest to redefine the terms of its encounter with Europe and the United States, traditionally seen as degrading. Vasconcelos's passion can be appreciated in a conversation he had with an American scientist of Hungarian origin aboard a ship taking him to Brazil. The scientist, who was a disciple of Darwin, asserted that all future cities would follow in their evolution the model of New York. Vasconcelos retorted that "toda civilización verdadera se empeñará en no imitar a Nueva York, que es la patria de Mammon y una lacra del mundo; . . . el arquetipo del futuro está en Rio Janeiro [*sic*] y está en Buenos Aires" (48) ("all true civilization will be determined not to imitate New York, which is the fatherland of Mammon and a black mark on the world; . . . the archetype of the future is in Rio de Janeiro, is in Buenos Aires"). The rest of *La raza cósmica* is taken over by a trip Vasconcelos made representing his country to Brazil, Uruguay, Argentina, and Chile. This became the testing ground for his ideas and we watch them go from assured confirmation in Brazil to defiant frustration in Chile. In the comparative scheme that is familiar:

> Por fin apareció en el horizonte un resplandor, el anuncio nocturno de toda gran ciudad, resplandor tibio de París que promete goces sensuales; resplandor estridente de Nueva York, que ofusca un instante y en seguida desilusiona; resplandor gris de Chicago, envuelto en un manto de humo, que vicia la atmósfera diez leguas a la redonda. El resplandor de Rio era un resplandor claro, se diría una gran ciudad en la que el tráfico, los servicios de todos dependieran de la electricidad y no ya del carbón; una urbe posterior a la etapa monstruosa del coke. (52)

Finally a radiance appeared on the horizon, the nocturnal notice of all great cities, a warm radiance in Paris that promises sensual pleasures, a strident light in New York that for a moment dazzles then disappoints, a gray brilliance in Chicago, enveloped in a blanket of smoke that contaminates everything within an area of ten leagues round. The splendor of Rio de Janeiro is a clear radiance, almost as if it were a great city in which the traffic, the public services all powered by electricity and not by fossil fuel, a city beyond the monstrous age of coal.

Vasconcelos presents beautifully the aura of the city, the glare of its lights on the night sky over the horizon. It is a scene of anticipation, which brings to his cosmopolitan memory a triad of other cities, well known to him. Paris promises sensuous delights, New York disappoints, Chicago poisons the air; instead Rio can be imagined as a city beyond coal and crude exploitation, silently and cleanly run by electricity. A second look at the paragraph shows that Vasconcelos is making three affirmations and one supposition. He has not yet seen Rio; he is only envisioning it refulgent to correspond to his yearning for Latin American superiority. The reality will be less exhilarating–he has some unkind words for Rio's architecture–even if the people and the geography confirm his optimism. Given the country's resources, "Ni duda cabe: el porvenir es del Brasil" (74) ("There is no doubt the future belongs to Brazil"), "el Brasil será la potencia mundial del futuro" (137) ("Brazil will be the world power of the future"). The horizon keeps receding and it has become narrower. It is not now a whole new race that will emerge to bring together all the Latin American continent; it is one nation.

The rest of the trip proves even more corrosive. In Uruguay he finds a literature that is Frenchified, while business is beholden to England and international politics to the United States (146). In Buenos Aires there is much to praise: He affirms defiantly that "Buenos Aires es nuestro París, la capital de nuestra América" (239) ("Buenos Aires is our Paris, the capital of our America"). But he runs into a bronze statue of Sarmiento, sculptured by Rodin, that raises his hackles. This becomes an occasion for him to rebuke the European gaze of the Latin American: "[S]e encargan estas estatuas a escultores mercenarios que ni saben ni les importa saber del personaje que falsifican; se les da un retrato, y ellos lo copian, y probablemente aún se permiten ironías a costa de aquellos que, en su ignorancia, catalogan como un oscuro héroe americano. Cualquier escultor argentino hubiera hecho mejor estatua de Sarmiento, el santo, que esta de Rodin, el célebre" (160) ("[S]culptures are ordered from these mercenary sculptors who neither know nor care to know anything about the personages they falsify; they are given a photograph and they copy it and probably permit themselves some irony at the expense of those who in their ignorance they catalogue as an obscure American hero. Any Argentine sculptor could have made a better statue of Sarmiento, the saint, than this one made by the famous Rodin").

It should be clear by now that Vasconcelos was fighting to wrestle the representation of America from European and Yankee hands. His essay is a continuation of the revolution, polemical, distrustful, unfair, but generous and illuminated. He had no proof to imagine that European sculptors would indulge in an ironic casting of the honored hero, nor that they would always falsify him or classify him as obscure. Clearly, while Rodin's statue may be faulty, it is a stretch to affirm that any Argentinean sculptor would have done it better. And yet, through Vasconcelos's irascible sentences spoke a long Latin American experience, so they ring true. The last part of his trip takes him to Chile, where his ideas of Pan-Americanism are met with distrust and even open rebuke, when he dares suggest that Chile should drop its contentious attitude toward Bolivia and Peru. The cosmic race seems now, as he retraces his steps over the Andes, a very far away glow of an impossible city.

More recent essays have stressed the effects of the colonial attitude within Latin America, denouncing the oppression, misperception, and neglect of Indian cultures, perceived by the dominant white culture as a drag on the drive to modernity. Néstor García Canclini (b. 1939) has oriented his work to highlight and revalue all forms of hybridity that resist the unifying thrust of hegemonic forces, supporting what he calls in *Culturas híbridas* [1992; Hybrid Cultures] "la *heterogeneidad multitemporal* de cada nación" (15, italics in original) ("the *multitemporal heterogeneity* of each nation"). Guillermo Bonfil Batalla (1935–1991), for example, asserts in *Pensar nuestra cultura* [1991; Meditation on Our Culture] that for the 40 million Indians and their 400 ethnic groups there is a profound continuity with the past, not wholly interrupted or canceled by Spanish colonialism. He speaks against cultural uniformity, which does not truly mix but instead substitutes and erases differences, and is wary about the effects of globalization, proposing instead striving in 1987 to vitalize Mexicans' own civilization based in the profound values, mores, and ideas of the Indian cultures. In his *México profundo: Reclaiming a civilization*, 1996, he denounces the groups that have held power in Mexico since independence as having had a distorted view of the country, based on a Western framework and suffocating the profound living roots of Mexican culture (xvi–xvii). As if answering Vasconcelos's melting-pot project, Bonfil Batalla proposes a diversified culture in *Pensar nuestra cultura*:

> La cultura nacional no puede ser otra cosa que la organización de nuestras capacidades para convivir en una sociedad pluricultural, diversificada, en la que cada grupo portador de una cultura histórica pueda desarrollarse y desarrollarla al máximo de su potencialidad, sin opresión y con el estímulo del diálogo constante con las demás culturas. No es pues, la cultura nacional, un todo uniforme y compartido, *sino un espacio construido para el florecimiento de la diversidad*. (122, italics in original)

> The national culture cannot be other than the organization of our capacity to live together in a diversified pluricultural society in which each group heir to a historical culture can develop and develop its culture to its maximum potential without opposition and with the stimulation of constant dialogue with other cultures. Therefore, the national culture is not a uniform whole shared by all, but *rather a space that has been designed for the nurturing of diversity.*

Comparing National Psychologies

An offshoot of this comparative approach is the indulgence in essays about national psychology. The dangers of reductionism, stereotyping, and exclusion are seldom avoided, and yet the results have the fascination of the self-portrait, presenting an amalgam of fact and fancy, reality and desire. The Countess of Merlin (1789–1852), writing in French but born in Cuba, which she left for Europe when she was 12, provides invaluable observations about social life, but creates a portrait of the woman from Havana that cannot but be fanciful. Could Cuban women have "the tiny and delicate limbs of a child . . . [and a] voluptuous head"? (Meyer 14).

Fernando de Azevedo (1894–1974) reached the following conclusions in his 1943 *A cultura brasileira* [Brazilian Culture]: "To sum up, Brazilians are altruistic, sentimental, and generous, capable of impulsive passions, violent but not very tenacious, lovers of life more than order, peaceful, hospitable but suspicious, and tolerant both by temperament and by lack of concern. . . . Brazilians have an acute sensibility, a rare intellectual vivacity, and an imagination rich in invention, which predisposes them more to letters and the arts than to the sciences" (quoted in Summ 8).

While this reads like a horoscope—who will not accept that she or he has a rare intellectual vivacity and is tolerant?—the most interesting aspect of these essays is in the anecdotes used to buttress the argument and offer a rare glimpse into what is considered significant by each nation. An example of this is Clodomir Vianna Moog's (1906–1988) *Bandeirantes e pioneros: Paralelo entre duas culturas* ["Bandeirantes" and Pioneers: A Parallel of Two Cultures], first published in 1954 and frequently reedited and translated, where the other culture in question is the United States. (He is also the author of *Novas cartas persas* [1937; New Persian Letters] in the tradition of Montesquieu.) His basic question is shared all over the continent—applied to different nations—but is particularly well expressed by Vianna Moog:

De há muito que esta pergunta anda no ar em busca de uma resposta em grande: como foi possível aos Estados Unidos, país mais nôvo do que o Brasil e menor em superfície continental contínua, realizar o progresso quase milagroso que realizaram e chegar aos nossos dias, à vanguarda das nações, como a prodigiosa realidade do presente, sob muitos aspectos a mais estupenda e prodigiosa realidade de todos os tempos, quando o nosso país . . . ainda se apresenta, mesmo à luz de interpretações e profecias mais optimistas, apenas como o incerto país do futuro? (xiii)

For some time now the question has been floating in the air in search of an all-encompassing answer. How is it possible that the United States, a country younger than Brazil and smaller in continental land mass, can achieve almost unprecedented progress that in our days places it in the vanguard of nations? Such is the prodigious reality of all aspects of this most stupendous and prodigious achievement of all time. In contrast, our country . . . is still today, even in the light of the more optimistic interpretations and predictions, merely an uncertain country of the future.

In search for an answer for this long-standing question, Vianna Moog denounces quite rightly the off-the-cuff answers contained in previous essays that provided no supporting scientific data for their conclusions—in the tradition of the essay that, according to Ortega, offers the conclusions without the proofs, biological, sociological, anthropological, or historical: "Bastava a palavra. Era tudo sob palavra" (5) ("To give one's word was enough. Everything was about one's word"). His book, therefore, provides numerous case studies from which to examine previous theories, mostly discardable, and possible answers. For example, to reply to those who believe that the backwardness of Brazil comes from its Portuguese ancestry and the mix with black and Indian, he adduces a couple of marvelously narrated instances of the failure of white North Americans in Brazil. The first one is Henry Ford's experiment of cultivating rubber trees in Brazil under controlled conditions, with the trees in neat rows and easily accessible. The description of this failure (19–26), told with relish and dramatic vigor, proves to him that the Brazilian nature is not as easily exploitable as the more welcoming plains and forests of the United States, regardless of the race of the enterprising agent. A second example, equally compelling, is the story of white Anglo-Americans who came to Brazil after the U.S.

Civil War. They were plantation owners of the South, and they expected to transfer their skills easily but instead were defeated by the harsher conditions they encountered, and their story ended in frustration and failure (31–38). Faced with an uncooperative geography, concludes Moog, the inheritance of the Portuguese has obstructed the emergence of a truly modern economy.

Equally fascinating is Paulo Prado's (1869–1943) *Retrato do Brasil: Ensaio sobre a tristeza brasileira* [1928; Portrait of Brazil: Essay on Brazilian Sadness], which starts with the pithy aphorism "Numa terra radiosa vive um povo triste" (9) ("In a radiant land there lives a sad people"). With this assessment concurs another distinguished Brazilian essayist already mentioned, Gilberto Freyre—educated partly in the United States, at Columbia University, where he received his doctorate in sociology and studied with the anthropologist Franz Boas. He affirms, in *New World in the Tropics: The Culture of Modern Brazil* (1959), that "the sadness expressed in Brazilian folk music and guitar songs is explained by a trauma in the social past of a large part of the population: slavery" (in Summ 89). But Prado has a different diagnosis: "Numa terra radiosa vive um povo triste. Legaram-lhe essa melancolia os descobridores que a revelaram ao mundo e a povoaram. O esplendido dynamismo dessa gente rude obedecia a dois grandes impulsos que dominam toda a psychologia da descoberta e nunca foram generadores de alegria: a ambição do ouro e a sensualidade livre" (9) ("In a radiant country there lives a sad people. The European conquerors bequeathed onto them this melancholy by exposing them to the world and by colonizing them. The splendid dynamism of these uncultivated people responded to the main impulses that dominate the entire psychology of the European domination, which were never generators of happiness but only for the ambition of gold and unbridled sensuality").

It is possible to surmise behind these interpretations a Freudian configuration of the archeology of the national mind: The country is seen as a person and its psyche plumbed for the traumatic and repressed. A more intriguing attempt to capture a nation's psychology is the Cuban Fernando Ortiz's (1881–1969) *Contrapunteo cubano del tabaco y el azúcar* [1940; Cuban Counterpoint, Tobacco and Sugar, 1947], where he uses these national products to symbolize many aspects of his society. Beyond the oppositions between dark and white, stable and processed, aromatic or not, he is a good observer who can make fleeting vignettes curiously concrete and representative at the same time. Probably the most famous example of a controversial national portrait is Octavio Paz's *El laberinto de la soledad*. Partly a response to Samuel Ramos's (1897–1959) earlier *El perfil del hombre y la cultura en México* [1934; Profile of Man and Culture in Mexico, 1962], which explained much of Mexico through Adler's inferiority complex theory, Paz's approach is to offer a series of brief portraits that illustrate national traits, such as reticence, solitude, enjoyment of popular festivities, and dissimulation. The experience that motivated writing the essay was a two-year stay in the United States, where he observed the marked differences between that society and the Mexican, including the Mexican community of Los Angeles. While most of his statements are too general to hold and highly impressionistic, his essay contains lines of great beauty that probably, when applied to Paz himself, are trenchant and revealing: "La historia de México es la del hombre que busca su filiación, su origen. Sucesivamente afrancesado, hispanista, indigenista, 'pocho,' cruza la historia como un cometa de jade, que de vez en cuando relampaguea. En su excéntrica carrera, ¿qué persigue?

Va tras su catástrofe: quiere volver a ser sol, volver al centro de la vida de donde un día–¿en la Conquista o en la Independencia?–fue desprendido" (23) ("This history of Mexico is the history of the people who seek a sense of belonging, of origin. Successive identities–francophile, hispanic, indigenist, 'pocho'–cross the horizon of history like a jade comet with an occasional lightning. In its eccentric race, what does it pursue? It seeks its own catastrophe: It wants to be the sun once more, it wants to return to the center of life from where one day–in Conquest or Independence–it was cut off").

Recent essays, such as Roger Bartra's (b. 1942) *The Cage of Melancholy,* have taken a more sophisticated approach, recognizing that national character "enjoys only a literary and mythological existence" (3), pervasive in its social effects, but molded by special interests of selection and exclusion, and therefore also deconstructable. Probably the most subtle descriptions of the Mexican are the chronicles of Elena Poniatowska (b. 1933), who, perhaps because she avoids generalization and essayistic grandstanding, provides a penetrating and nuanced portrayal. Her work blurs the genre categories of novel, reportage, autobiography, and essay, making her editorial voice almost imperceptible behind those she reinvents in her texts.

Describing Land and Society

Bolívar's comparison of the emergent nations to Icarus, with echoes of Prometheus, is one of many with which essayists have attempted to capture the essence of the New World in order to convey it to a broader audience. The letters of Cortés had already lured Europe into a recognition of the American continent by translating it into familiar terms. Cortés recognized the need to awaken and sustain the interest of a distant interlocutor who was only narrowly interested in the new land. This selling of America, its reaffirmation as an equal, and its framing in familiar terms for European readers are constants in the Latin American essay. The terms *Latin America, Iberian America,* and *Hispanic America,* or even *Afro-Indo-Latin America,* are traces of this marketing of the new under the guise of the familiar. The founding of many cities that echoed in their names European counterparts–such as Santiago, mirroring the Galician pilgrimage center–in places as far apart as Chile and Cuba, corresponds to many essayists' laboring to rename the new and the different they encountered in America with well-worn European labels. Alejo Carpentier (1904–1980) indicates in *Tientos y diferencias* [(1964) 1970; Flourishes and Differences] that a European writer does not need to elaborate on most of the words he employs, since they are well known abroad–pine or chestnut trees are easy to imagine for Latin American readers–while familiar words such as *ceiba* would draw an exotic blank for a French reader (35).

In opposition to Bolívar's pessimism, a group of essayists were doing the opposite of emigrating: immersing themselves in the new territories, describing it minutely, mapping it, classifying its flora and fauna, charting the seas, and introducing scientific thought. That this was not always easy in colonial Latin America is seen in the famous letter of Sor Juana Inés de la Cruz (1648–1695), in which she describes her continuous reading, experimenting, and questioning. In salons, study groups, civic societies, and periodicals, created on the European models of the Enlightenment, and later in the official academies that were founded in the Independence period, numerous essayists were translating the continent into numbers, tables, graphs, illustrations, and learned treatises. Of

these, we can highlight here the Mexican Carlos de Sigüenza y Góngora's (1645–1700) *Libra astronómica y filosófica* [1690; Astronomic and Philosophical Libra] and the work of the Peruvian Hipolito Unanue (1755–1833). Sigüenza y Góngora discussed the significance of comets, the polemic originating in the responses to a comet observed in November 1680. Tearing away the astrological and religious superstition that accompanied these visitations (which produced terror and apocalyptic fear), and framing the discussion in purely scientific terms, thus laying the ground for modern astronomy, Sigüenza y Góngora's was part of a larger movement on both sides of the Atlantic but his text was particularly elegant, detailed, and well argued. He was well informed and up-to-date, but his insistence on experimentation and observation shows that this was not just a bookish enterprise: He participated in the spirit of Bacon, Gassendi, and all the other philosophers and scientists who were at the time redefining the known world, teasing faith away from knowledge, opinion from truth. For example, he affirms that "ociosos son los preceptos cuando no se acompañan con ejemplos que los comprueben" (121) ("precepts that are not accompanied by examples that prove their validity are in vain"). And he continues, even more forcibly:

> Hasta aquí el contexto del autor [the one he is refuting] con sus palabras mismas; pero antes de examinarlo, advierto que ni su reverencia, ni otro algún matemático, aunque sea el mismo Ptolomeo, puede asentar dogmas en estas ciencias, porque en ellas no sirve de cosa alguna la autoridad, sino las pruebas y la demostración. . . . Advierto también que las observaciones hechas sin instrumento, sino con la vista y estimación, es cosa indigna pensar que se puede concluir cosa alguna de consideración en materia tan primorosa como la que aquí se ventila. (123)

> Up to this point I have presented the author's argument [that he is refuting] in his own words; but before examining it, I want to insist that neither his reverence nor any other mathematician, including Ptolemy himself, can assert dogma in science, because in science authority is worthless if it is not accompanied by proof and demonstration. . . . I also want to point out that observation made by sight and estimate without scientific instruments are worthless. It is beneath contempt to think that such observations are of any use on the important subject we are considering.

What was being aired here was not only the precision of the observations of the Mexican but also their value in the international scientific community, because Sigüenza y Góngora felt slighted by his European counterparts. The following paragraph, in which he talks about his main rival in describing the comet, narrates an experience so frustrating, representative, and dramatic that is worth reproducing in full:

> Y aunque por haberse hecho a la vela [el padre jesuita Eusebio Francisco Kino, jesuíta, quien venía de Alemania] desde la ciudad de Cádiz para la Nueva España, a fines de enero de este año, dice que careció de observaciones hechas en Francia, Italia y Germania, para combinarlas con las suyas y definir la menor o mayor distancia del cometa a nosotros, bien sabe su reverencia que absolutamente no le faltaron, cuando luego que llegó a esta ciudad le ofrecí las mías porque me comunicase las suyas, cosa que jamás conseguí, pues aunque me mostró un cuaderno en que estaban señaladas para los primeros días de enero las ascensiones rectas y declinaciones del cometa, no era eso lo que yo quería saber, sino las alturas, azimutes o distancias a las fijas, en que lo había observado para carearlas con las mías y de ello sacar las ilaciones que me importasen; y no sólo le ofrecí las mías, sino las que hasta el día 12 de enero hizo en el puerto de San Francisco de Campeche el muy erudito matemático don Martín de la Torre.

Pero no solicitándolas, o no haciendo caso de unas y de otras, discurro que sería porque no estaban hechas en Alemania, o porque los observadores no habían estudiado las matemáticas en la Universidad de Ingolstadio. Pero del contexto de este mi escrito podrá prácticamente reconocer haber también matemáticos fuera de Alemania, aunque metidos entre los carrizales y espadañas de la mexicana laguna. (119)

And because he, the German Jesuit Eusebio Francisco Kino, sailed from Cadiz to New Spain at the end of January of this year, he says that he lacked the observations made in France, Italy, and Germany in order to compare with his own and thus establish the lesser or greater distance of the comet from earth, although as your reverence knows, he did not lack for observations. When he arrived in this city I offered him my observations in exchange for his own which I never received, for although he showed me a notebook in which he had the calculations for the ascent and decline of the comet during the first days of January, this was not the data I required. I asked for calculations on the height, the azimuth, or fixed distances of the comet from what he had observed in order to compare them to mine and thereby derive the illations that interested me. Not only did I offer him my calculations but also the ones made in San Francisco de Campeche on 12 January by the erudite mathematician don Martín de la Torre. But by not accepting them or rather not taking into account either Martín de la Torre's calculations or mine, I surmise that it must be because they were not made in Germany or because the observers had not studied mathematics at the University of Ingolstadio. But based on this text he might recognize that there are mathematicians outside of Germany even amidst the reeds and bulrushes of the Mexican lagoon.

Not only were there scientists among the Mexican reeds and bulrushes, but they were working tenaciously all over America. In Perú, for example, the polygraph Hipólito Unanue, who taught in Lima the brave new science of anatomy, performing autopsies, and advocating the scientific method, wrote the exemplary *Observaciones sobre el clima de Lima y su influencia en los seres organizados, en especial el hombre* [1806; Observations on the Climate of Lima and Its Influence on Organized Beings, Especially Man]. His accomplishments as a teacher of medicine, geography, statistics, and botany, and his participation in politics during the transition to Independence are monumental; important too is his participation in the publication *El Mercurio Peruano* and in the founding of the learned society *Sociedad Amantes del País* ("Society of Friends of the Nation"). He met Humboldt when the German scientist went through Lima, and provided him much information. His ecological perception of nature—he saw everything as interrelated—makes his *Observaciones* as good or better a description of life in Lima than any realist novel.

Also distinguished is the Ecuadorian Francisco Javier Eugenio Santa Cruz y Espejo (1747–1795), who, by openly criticizing the educational system of the time and satirizing scholasticism and Baroque expression, came to be known as America's Lucan and opened the way for scientific thought and straightforward prose. His work was informed by the ideas of European Enlightenment, yet his ancestry made him defensive to grand claims of universalism, since his father was of Indian origin. He was twice imprisoned, the second time for almost a year in complete isolation, for his independentist ideas (which he had developed from reading about the United States and the French Revolution). A doctor, librarian, secretary of the *Sociedad económica de amigos del país* [Economic Society of Friends of the Country], and editor of the first newspaper published in Quito, *Las Primicias de la Cultura de*

Quito [The Beginnings of the Culture in Quito], Espejo was an essayist with clout, but his ideas and mixed race made his condition always precarious. Inspired by the Spaniard José Francisco de Isla's (1703–1781) *Fray Gerundio de Campazas*, Espejo took it upon himself to ridicule the Baroque style of preaching of the Ecuadorian clergy in a work entitled *El nuevo Luciano* [The New Lucian] that circulated in manuscript. In the inaugural issue of *Las Primicias*, he urges his compatriots to observe nature, make original observations, and publish them, and follows this call with a candid declaration of the fears that could assault a fledgling intellectual in the backwaters of the empire:

> Que juzguen nuestros émulos . . . que estamos en el ángulo más remoto y oscuro de la tierra, a donde apenas llegan algunos pocos rayos de refracción desprendidos de la inmensa luz que baña a regiones privilegiadas: que nos faltan libros, instrumentos, medios, y maestros que nos indiquen los elementos de las facultades, y que nos enseñen el método de aprenderlas. Todo esto nada importa, o no nos impide el que demos a conocer que sabemos pensar, que somos racionales, que hemos nacido para la sociedad. (7–8)

> Let our colleagues judge . . . that we are in the most remote and darkest corner of the world, where only a few rays of refracted light from the immense brilliance of the privileged regions reaches us: that we lack books, instruments, and other means and that we also lack teachers to indicate the proper subject matter for our faculties and who could teach us the methods for studying them. All of this however, does not matter or rather it does not impede us from letting them know that we know how to think, that we are rational, that we have been born to live in civilized society.

Among those who know how to think, Espejo included women, and several times he wrote using a female persona–for example, in number three of *Primicias*, where he signed himself Erophilia, and in his *Cartas riobambenses* [1787; Letters from Rio Bamba], where the author of most letters, Manuelita, reveals great wit, a modern outlook, and a scathing opinion of her life in the provinces, where she rebels against somber and repressive traditions. For an enlightened essay about gender issues, though, it is worth studying the Cuban Gertrudis Gómez de Avellaneda's (1814–1873) "Women," published in the *Album Cubano de lo Bueno y lo Bello* [1860; Cuban Album of the Good and the Beautiful] (Meyer 25–39). Here, the comparison is with men, who she concedes have greater physical strength, but in feeling she thinks woman is undisputedly superior. The pain of childbirth elevates her, conceding her special grace. Women are brave, as proven by many examples from the scriptures and history. And they do all this without special training! Gómez de Avellaneda takes courage from this to move on to claim not equality, but the superiority of women in government. If they are less successful in the sciences it is only because they are barred from the universities, but they have excelled in literature. This is a truly revolutionary essay, brash and lively. Equally impressive is the Colombian Soledad Acosta de Samper's (1833–1913) reflections on "The Mission of the Woman Writer in Spanish America" (see Meyer 71–76), where she calls for the creation of a uniquely American literature written by women, avoiding "the wicked ways imported to our societies from the corrupt civilization of Europe" (75). While her vision of the United States is too idyllic and her conception of a sanitized novel not compelling, the vigor and concern with which she addresses the issue of a literature appropriate for the new nations are evident. Victoria Ocampo (1890–1979) compares the situation of women in South America with others who live in "great countries" (Meyer 133) in her "Woman and Her Expression," making the point that they are doubly marginalized, by being women and by living in South America, but that this challenge can be overcome by international solidarity.

On the other hand, for an example of the many outlandish concepts expressed about women in the Latin American essay, see Octavio Paz's *El laberinto de la soledad*, where he describes what he considers the Spanish, Mexican, and North American perceptions of women, saying, for example, that "La mexicana simplemente no tiene voluntad. Su cuerpo duerme y sólo se enciende si alguien lo despierta. Nunca es pregunta, sino respuesta, materia fácil y vibrante que la imaginación y la sensualidad masculina esculpen" (41) ("Mexican women simply do not have will. Her body is asleep and only comes to life if someone else awakens her. She is never a question, but rather a response, facile and vibrant matter she is shaped by masculine imagination and sensuality").

Geography as Destiny and Project

American nature has often been seen in contrast to the European, as in the following evocation by Paulo Prado: "Nos capuchinhos de la Ravardière, já tocados pelo humanismo da Renascença rabelaiseana, ao começar o seculo XVII e ao pisarem o solo ardente do Maranhão, vamos a porém encontrar a revelaçao desse mundo novo, com e qual nunca tinham sonhado nas cellulas tristes do seu convento de Paris" (21) ("The Capuchins of the Ravadière, already touched by the humanism of the Rabelaisian Renaissance, at the beginning of the seventeenth century, upon stepping onto the burning soil of Maranhão, find the revelation of that new world of which they had dreamed in the sad cells of their convent in Paris"). Especially the Parisian monks could not imagine the unbridled sexuality that went with the paradisaic landscape. Prado presents numerous testimonies of the European's surprise and joy at the availability of naked women they could take at any time and use for their own satisfaction, as if they were gifts of the land: "Era uma simples machina de gozo e trabalho" (53) ("Women were simple machines of pleasure and work"). Prado blames equally the Portuguese's rapacity and the Indian women's sensuality. For him there was also the addition of the "passividade infantil da negra africana, que veiu facilitar e desenvolver a superexcitação erotica em que vivia o conquistador" (54) ("the childlike passivity of the black African woman, who came to facilitate further and develop the erotic superexcitability in which the conquerers lived"), which contributed to the formation of a culture where manly prowess matters: "só o macho contava" (54) ("only the male counted"). That his text itself, by a strikingly one-sided presentation of this encounter, reveals the depth and persistence of the point of view of the man, as opposite to the woman it pretends to describe, is not surprising but representative.

The land also offered gold and emeralds. For Prado, this unleashed greed, *cubiça*, which brought the devil into paradise; but the land itself proved resourceful and reticent in her riches: "O ouro brasileiro defendia-se, entretando, pelos obtaculos naturaes que surgiam deante dos passos dos mineradores: escondia-se traiçoeiro na trama impenetravel das mattas do deserto" ("The Brazilian gold defended itself; with natural obstacles that impeded the miners, it treacherously hid itself in the impenetrable reaches of the desert"). But, as with persistent scorned lovers, "nem perigos, fadigas ou desillusões esmoreciam a paixão dos aventureiros" (86) ("neither danger, fatigue or disillusionment would discourage the adventurers' passion"). Gold and diamonds seduce and distract, as Prado sees it, from the more necessary agriculture and industry. What we witness here is the reconfiguration of the process of expansion, exploitation, and destruction in terms of cardinal sins and the passion of love. For Prado the "drama do ouro" (103) ("drama of gold") has made the "drama de conquista e povoamento" ("drama of the conquest and settlement") (113) different in Brazil and the United States, where the pilgrims longed only for freedom to practice their religion and left an indelible imprint on the character of the nation (109–13). Prado applies a clinical eye to the sick body of his nation, arriving at the following shrill conclusion: "No Brasil a tristeza succedeu á intensa vida sexual do colono, desviada para as perversões eroticas, e de um fundo accentuadamente atavico. ... [U]ma entidade morbida, uma doença do espirito, com seus symptomas, suas causas e evolução. Pode absorver toda a energia psychica, sem remedios para o seu desenvolvimento, sem cura para os seus males" (124) ("In Brazil sadness followed the colonist's intense sexual life, sidetracked by erotic perversity that was fundamentally atavistic. ... [I]t is a morbid entity, a sickness of the spirit, with its own symptoms, causes, and evolution. It can absorb all of one's psychic energy, without there being any remedy to arrest its development, without a cure for its evils"). This may be no more than an extrapolation of the *saudade* ("yearning") for long considered a Portuguese national trait, a form of reaffirming the inheritance that Prado wishes to denounce, even if, or precisely because, he affirms that Portugal is "um ser alegre quando comparado com o descendente tropical" (127) ("a happy individual when compared to its tropical descendant"). Set to it, we will outdo the metropolis even in its defects. Prado's book is fanciful and at times perverse–it blames much of the moral corruption he finds in society on the slaves (140–41)–but his unremittingly critical examination of society exemplifies the exasperation of an essayist confronted by official sugarcoating and retrograde obstructionism. He leaves his readers affirming that he has "a confiança no futuro que não póde ser peior do que o passado" (216) ("confidence in a future that cannot be worse than the past").

The difficulty of the task of domesticating an intractable nature is expressed often in the Latin American essay. Briefly put by Jesús Silva Herzog (1891–1985) in *El mexicano y su morada* [1960; The Mexican and his Dwelling Place]:

El pueblo de México ha tenido y tiene una morada hostil, una morada en la cual se han acumulado innúmeras dificultades. No es que el mexicano sea inferior a tal o cual habitante de la tierra, es que al mexicano le ha tocado una morada donde el desafío de la naturaleza ha sido constante y formidable. Por eso hemos ido evolucionando lentamente. Nuestra historia, nuestra realidad, nuestra pobreza, se explican en gran medida por la morada que nos ha tocado en suerte habitar. (19)

The Mexican people have had and have a hostile dwelling place, a place in which innumerable difficulties have accumulated. It is not that the Mexican is inferior to any other people on earth; it is that it has been the Mexican's lot in life to live in a place where the challenge of nature has been constant and formidable. That is why we have evolved slowly. Our history, our reality, our poverty can to a large extent be explained by the dwelling place it has been our lot to live in.

Going Overboard: To Be *Europeizante*

To define this reality, essayists have had little choice but to borrow, recycle, adapt, and locally contest European models–in turn, of course, the product of vast amalgams and intersections–such as Catholicism, the Enlightenment, positivism, Romanticism, the avant-garde, Existentialism, Marxism, and the like. Significantly, José Carlos Mariátegui begins his highly influential *7 ensayos de interpretación de la realidad peruana* [*Seven Interpretive Essays on Peruvian Reality*, 1971], first published in 1928, with a quote, in German, from Nietzsche, followed immediately after with a vehement defense of his European categories of interpretation: "No faltan quienes me suponen un europeizante, ajeno a los hechos y a las cuestiones de mi país. Que mi obra se encargue de justificarme, contra esta barata e interesada conjetura. He hecho en Europa mi mejor aprendizaje. Y creo que no hay salvación para Indo-América sin la ciencia y el pensamiento europeos u occidentales" (12) ("There is no lack of people who judge me to be a Europeanizer, a stranger to the needs and issues of my country. I will let my work speak for itself against this cheap and self-interested attack. I have indeed taken my apprenticeship in Europe. And I believe that there is no salvation possible for Indo-America without European and Western science and philosophy"). The easy slippage between "European" and "Western," identified by Mariátegui as one and the same, leaves Indo-America as a liminal patient or sinner awaiting salvation from abroad. Among the changes he sees in his contemporary society, he notes that, due to the opening of the Panama Canal, the distance between Peru and Europe has diminished what he had called an "enorme distancia" (19) ("an enormous distance"). With this new route, "mejora notablemente nuestra posición geográfica, [y] se acelera el proceso de incorporación del Perú en la civilización occidental" (26) ("our geographic position improves notably and the process of the incorporation of Peru into Western civilization is greatly accelerated"). His assured and insightful analysis focuses on the economy, because for him "el hecho económico es más complejo y trascendental de lo que parece" (21) ("economics is much more complex and transcendental than it might appear"); but precisely in this field of globalization, capitalist or otherwise, it is difficult to account for the local. His brief and glowing description of the Inca rule reads as a projection onto the past of Marx's future communist society, and his prescription for addressing *el problema del indio* [the problem of the Indian] is to change the property of the land to give them real economical clout. In an extensive footnote, he attempts to defend his designation of the Inca society as communist. He notes that the historical evidence is incontestable, but that some critics object to the Inca's despotism. Here, Mariátegui entertains a comparative perspective, conceding first that "el comunismo moderno es una cosa distinta del comunismo inkaico" (78) ("modern communism is different from Inca communism"). They are, he affirms, the product of different human experiences and they correspond to different stages of society, agrarian and industrial. He draws a blunt conclusion: "Es absurdo, por ende, confrontar las formas y las instituciones de uno y otro comunismo" (78) ("It is therefore absurd to confront the forms and institutions of one and the other form of communism"). What is left, a reader may well ask, to compare, once *formas* (implementations, strategies, behavior?) are bracketed?

Mariátegui continues with a vague methodological recommendation: "Lo único que puede confrontarse es su incorpórea semejanza esencial, dentro de la diferencia esencial y material de tiempo y espacio" (78) ("The only thing that can be compared is the essential incorporeal similarity within the basic essential and material difference of time and space"). He then calls for some degree of historical relativism that would allow the researcher to concede that freedom becomes prioritized as a value only with liberal individualism. The Incas could well be happy without feeling any need for individual freedom. Nor were they egged on by other needs: "La vida y el espíritu del indio no estaban atormentados por el afán de especulación y de creación intelectuales" (79) ("the life and spirit of the Indian were not tormented by the need to have intellectual speculation and creation"). The need for individual freedom, the drive to philosophizing and to intellectual creation, to engaging in commerce–these are all, according to Mariátegui, "los progresos morales de la sociedad moderna" (79) ("the moral progress of modern society"). The point here is not the ultimate truth of Mariátegui's analysis, but the anxiety revealed by this extensive footnote that runs at the bottom of several pages. The essayist's need is similar to that of several missionaries who found forms of proto-Christianity in the religions of native Americans. This comparison aims to establish a continuity of past and present, and to dignify the Incas, rescuing them from anachronism and revealing their position as precursors, but it ends up mired in the realization that as precursors they are behind the times by the universalizing European clock.

Mariátegui has an assured voice, buttressed by footnotes, expressed in straightforward affirmations, and frequently reaching numbered conclusions that are forceful and proactive. What raises his writing to a level above the pamphlet or the political tract is his awareness of the frailty of this authorial stance. For example, in an essay about schooling, he determines that the Spanish inheritance and the French and North American influences have molded the Peruvian educational system. He starts a paragraph with his usual urge to label and classify, but then his confidence crumbles: "La historia de la instrucción pública en el Perú se divide así en los tres períodos que señalan estas tres influencias. Los límites de cada período no son muy precisos. Pero en el Perú este es un defecto común a casi todos los fenómenos y a casi todas las cosas. Hasta en los hombres rara vez se observa un contorno neto, un perfil categórico. Todo aparece siempre un poco borroso, un poco confuso" (105) ("The history of public education in Peru is thus divided into three periods that are marked by these three influences. The limits of each period are not very precise. But in Peru this is a common defect in almost all phenomena and almost all things. Even among men one rarely observes a sharp outline, a categorical profile. Everything is always a bit murky, a bit confused"). One can surmise that the underlying comparison that triggers these beautiful and uneasy sentences is the European *elsewhere,* a realm where categories and people appear clearly and without confusion. Therefore, for Mariátegui, mixed races, especially if they involved African or Chinese blood, were cut loose from the moorings of myth and sensibility peculiar to the "civilización europea o blanca" (343–44) ("European or white civilization") or the Incas. Almost a century later, postmodern readers can see in this crossbred and hybrid nature of Latin America a positive value (see García Canclini), but a distinguished Peruvian critic, Antonio Cornejo-Polar (1936–1997), has countered with the observation–more in the spirit of Mariátegui–that these designations tend to falsify the conflictive and fragmented nature of society. Cornejo-Polar denounces as "falaz armonía" (341) ("fallacious harmony") what others celebrate as the mixing of many races, cultures, and languages.

José Martí (1853–1895) brilliantly diagnosed the need for a radical independence of thought that would accompany political liberation, but he was acutely aware of the difficulties. In his essays he highlights the American and avoids European comparisons. And yet, he describes in a letter of 1878 how the Latin American intellectual is forced by repressive political conditions at home and the allure of the European into an alienated glowing monstrosity:

> Es nuestra tierra, tú lo sabes bien, un nido de águilas; y como no hay aire allí para las águilas; como cerca de los cadalsos no viven bien más que los cuervos, tendemos, apenas nacidos, el vuelo impaciente a los peñascos de Heidelberg, a los frisos del Partenón, a la casa de Plinio, a la altiva Sorbona, a la agrietada y muerta Salamanca. Hambrientos de cultura, la tomamos donde la hallamos más brillante. Como nos vedan lo nuestro, nos empapamos en lo ajeno. Así, cubanos, henos trocados, por nuestra forzada educación viciosa, en griegos, romanos, españoles, franceses, alemanes. (188)

> Our country, you know it well, is an eagle's nest; and since there is no air for the eagles to fly; and since only crows live well near scaffolds, from birth we tend toward an impatient flight to the rocky heights of Heidelberg, the friezes of the Parthenon, the house of Pliny, the proud Sorbonne, the cracked and dead buildings of Salamanca. Hungry for culture we take it from where we find it most brilliant. Since they deny us our own, we soak up the foreign. Thus, it is that Cubans, because of a vicious education forced on us are turned into Greeks, Romans, Spaniards, Frenchman, Germans.

This lament is highly ambiguous. The harsh-sounding "peñascos" ("rocky heights"), the perception of the Sorbonne as "altiva" ("proud"), and the double cannonade of "agrietada" ("cracked") and "muerta" ("dead") for Salamanca, plus the adjective "viciosa" ("vicious"), all reveal that this impatient flight away from the native and into the European blaze can be destructive. Because he believes that "ni el libro europeo, ni el libro yankee daban la clave del enigma latinoamericano" (91) ("neither the European book nor the yankee book give the key to the Latin American enigma"), he reacts fiercely against what he sees as the slight of Americans rejecting their homeland for Europe: "¡Estos hijos de carpintero, que se avergüenzan de que su padre sea carpintero! ¡Esos nacidos en América, que se avergüenzan, porque llevan delantal indio, de la madre que los crió . . . !" (87) ("Those sons of carpenters who are ashamed that their father was a carpenter! Those born in America who are ashamed of the Indian dress, of the mother who nurtured them . . . !").

Roberto Fernández Retamar (b. 1930) in *Calibán* (1971) continued this attack, clearly recognizing his debt to Martí. After quoting Borges's opinion that the Latin American tradition is based in Europe, he proceeds to identify this European flavor as typically Latin American, but of a culture that he would like to see end: "Borges es un típico escritor colonial, representante entre nosotros de una clase ya sin fuerzas, cuyo acto de escritura . . . se parece más a un acto de lectura" (60) ("Borges is a typical colonial writer, representative among us of a class already devoid of strength, whose act of writing is closer to an act of reading"). This opinion coincides with the more general and lapidary observation by Ezequiel Martínez Estrada (1895–1964) in *Radiografía de la pampa* [1946; *X-ray of the Pampas,* 1971]: "Para el porteño, mirar al interior es mirar hacia afuera; al exterior. Interior para él es Europa" (II, 17) ("For the porteño (person from Buenos Aires), to look within is to look toward the outside, the exterior. Interior for him is

Europe"). Borges (1899–1986) in "El escritor argentino y la tradición" [The Argentinean Writer and Tradition], Alejo Carpentier, Julio Cortázar (1914–1984), and many others defended in the contemporary period a passion for European culture that is not incompatible with a deep concern for Latin America. In fact, Carpentier in *Tientos y diferencias* [(1964) 1970; Flourishes and Differences] affirms that "el enfoque asiduo de culturas extranjeras, del presente o del pasado, lejos de significar un *subdesarrollo* intelectual, [es], por el contrario, una posibilidad de *universalización* para el escritor latinoamericano" (30, italics in original) ("the assiduous focus on foreign cultures, of the present and the past, far from signifying intellectual underdevelopment, on the contrary, offers the possibility of universalization for the Latin American writer"). One strategy has been simply to appropriate world culture, confidently, and here the Mexican Alfonso Reyes (1889–1959) is especially distinguished. Next to insightful studies of *The Iliad* or Goethe, he devotes many pages to America. His delicate, profoundly respectful evocation of Tenotchtitlan in *Visión de Anáhuac* [(1917) 1960; Vision of Anáhuac] has something of the antiquarian, but has become a classic. In *Ultima Tule* (1941) he provides a detailed reconstruction of the period preceding the discovery of America by the Europeans and shows that the continent was born under a set of expectations that were utopian, addressing more obviously European frustrations than American reality.

Also important, as seen in other sections here as well, was Oswald de Andrade's (1890–1954) "Manifesto Antropófago" [1928; Anthropophagous Manifesto], a manifesto where he inveighed against "all the importers of the canned conscience" (Stavans 97) and proposed to get rid of cultural icons and the rut of memory by absorbing the competing European culture in a ritual form of anthropophagy. Samuel Ramos tried to mediate in this conflict between nationalists and Europeanizers in *El perfil del hombre y la cultura en México* [1934; *Profile of Man and Culture in Mexico,* 1962], by declaring both wrong; the nationalists would cut away Mexico from Europe and isolate it dangerously, while chasing the impossible dream of a willed originality, while the Europeanizers all fail to see Europe from a Mexican viewpoint: "Instead, they see Mexico from the viewpoint of Europe" (98). But Ramos does not offer a viable way out of these warring alternatives except by proposing a "creole culture" inspired by naturally superior men who have transcended their inferiority complex (180).

If there is any doubt as to the effect of the centuries of colonialism and European worship decried in *Calibán*, it would fade when considering how the zone of the "real" is mapped by some major Latin American intellectuals. In an example of blindness and insight, Andrés Bello (1781–1865) dealt in 1826 with the issue of location in the description of his project for a Latin American journal based in London. "Given the present state of America and Europe," he asserted, "London is perhaps the best place to publish this periodical" (3). There is some hesitation–the conflicted nature of his *perhaps* should not be overlooked–but in this replacement and displacement of his original country, Venezuela, as the foundational place for an enlightened Latin America (he had tried there before, and failed), there is a sober acknowledgment of the economical underpinnings of culture: "[England's] commercial relations with the countries on the other side of the Atlantic make it, in a sense, the center of them all, and the aid given to literary circulation by industrial circulation is too obvious to need description" (3–4). And yet he proceeds immediately to wave aside the ability of these resources to grant a culture the golden halo of assurance and good taste by dramatically inverting these factors and proclaiming that it is because England is culturally superior that it attracts the attention and investment of other nations: "But London is not only the metropolis of trade; in no part of the globe are the causes that vivify and nourish the human spirit as active as they are in Great Britain. Nowhere are researches bolder, the flight of genius freer, scientific speculations more profound, experiments in the arts more spirited. Rich in herself, Great Britain draws to herself the riches of her neighbors" (4).

The *locus amoenus Europeus*, be it Rome, London, Paris, or Berlin, vivifies and nourishes the human spirit, while the designation *Lima la horrible* [1964; Lima the Horrible] by Sebastian Salazar Bondy (1924–1965) could stand as a typical title for a significant number of essays in which the Latin American cities are denigrated, often in contrast with the real or imagined European metropolis. For some Latin American essayists, the real exile was from their mistaken Latin American destiny.

Alberto Zum Felde's (1889–1976) notable *Indice crítico de la literatura hispanoamericana: Los ensayistas* [1954; Critical Index of Spanish American Literature: The Essayists] is possibly still the most informative book on this topic, but it is permeated by his reverent attitude toward European culture. Few if any other critics have read as widely as the Uruguayan, and yet his unquestioned assumption was that the Latin American essay is local, while the European is universal. The following paragraph, from the introduction, is characteristic of this fallacy:

> La vida europea se desenvuelve de modo específico en el clima humano de la cultura, esencial y formalmente universal, ecuménico, en su mayor parte; por tanto, su ensayística nacional puede ser, también en amplio grado, de significación e interés universales, ecuménicos. La vida hispanoamericana, en cambio, se produce y desenvuelve en un clima social predominantemente condicionado–y limitado–por los factores histórico–geográficos propios, a veces regionales, lo que restringe en mucho, casi siempre, su significación y su interés, al ámbito mismo continental; o sólo al nacional, a veces. (8)

> In a very specific way European life develops in a human climate of culture that, for the most part, is essentially and formally universal and ecumenical; therefore, its national essay can be, to a large degree, of universal significance and interest. Life in Hispanic America, in contrast, is produced and develops in a social climate that is primarily conditioned–and limited–by its historical-geographic factors, sometimes even by regional considerations that almost always restrict its significance and interest to the same part of the continent or sometimes only to the national contours.

Zum Felde's many hesitations ("en su mayor parte" ["for the most part"], "en amplio grado" ["to a large degree"], "casi siempre" ["almost always"], "a veces" ["sometimes"]) reveal the magnitude of his assertion. Why the European essay can be of universal interest and applicable worldwide remains puzzling even if the reader considers the examples Zum Felde hastens to provide: If a Spanish essayist, he claims (and why not a Latin American essayist?), studies the Spanish Middle Ages, his conclusions interest not only Spain, but also Europe and the whole Western world, because those peninsular events influenced wide-ranging developments in the West. Here, again, one sees a substitution of the Western world for

the universe, and the hurried and anxious attempt to be included even under the category of the local within this prestigious European mantle. Much more damning even is the next step in Zum Felde's argument:

> E igualmente ocurre si esos estudios se refieren a la crisis contemporánea de los valores históricos de la cultura en cualquiera de sus formas, lo cual aun cuando se refieran al campo de experiencias nacionales de algunos de esos países, alcanza, por analogía e influencia, a todos los otros de Occidente. En cambio, estudios sobre fenómenos típicamente hispanoamericanos,– herencias caracterológicas del coloniaje, problema del indio, militarismo político, imperialismo económico, dialéctica de civilización y barbarie, el barroquismo o el modernismo literarios, el americanismo cultural–, son temas que interesan fundamentalmente a la intelectualidad americana, pero no trascienden los límites nacionales o continentales, no se incorporan a la problemática universal, ecuménica, de Occidente. (8–9)

> And the same thing happens in those studies that refer to the contemporary crisis in the historical values of culture in any of its manifestations, which even when they treat national issues of some of those nations do so in such a way that by analogy and influence reach all other Western nations. In turn, studies on issues that are typically Hispanic American–characterological colonial legacies, the Amerindian problem, political militarism, economic imperialism, and the dialectic of civilization and barbarism, baroque or *modernista* literature, cultural Americanism– are subjects that profoundly interest the Hispanic American intellectual, but these issues do not transcend national or continental limits, do not become part of universal, ecumenical problematic of the West.

Once this premise is affirmed, the next step is to find reasons for this lack of transcendence. Returning to Henríquez Ureña in his *Seis Ensayos en busca de nuestra expresión* [1928, 1952; Six Essays in Search of Our Expression], he, like many others, proceeds to discuss the importance of race. After a spirited defense of the equality of all races, he engages in two lines of argument that are hardly reassuring. On the one hand, he claims that the indigenous population saw its best accomplishments destroyed by the conquest, thus placing their pinnacle of achievement in the past and rescuing the race, while condemning its present representatives: "No hay incapacidad; pero la conquista decapitó la cultura del indio, destruyendo sus formas superiores . . . respetando sólo las formas populares y familiares" (33) ("There is no incapacity; however, the conquest destroyed the Indian's culture, destroying its leading modes . . . leaving only popular and familiar forms"). In spite of his admiration for these lingering accomplishments, the categories of the popular and the familiar–aligned with the feminine–cannot compete with European high culture and its virile accomplishments in the economy, industry, and war. The second line of argument is that there is some similarity between the present creativity of the indigenous population and superior accomplishments of Europe, but, not surprisingly, the comparison is of the Latin American present with the European past, ancient Greece, or medieval Spain. Significantly, two footnotes bring back the full anxiety of location. In the first one, he gives examples of Indians who have received a European education and excelled–for example, the Mexican Fernando de Alba Ixtlilxóchitl (1578–1650), who is nicknamed, presumably as a high form of praise, "el Tito Livio del Anáhuac" ("The Titus Livius of Anáhac"). Bolívar had called Quetzalcoatl "el Hermes o Buda de la América del Sur" ("the Hermes or Buddha of America"), adding that he was not well known among the Mexican people, "porque tal es la suerte de los vencidos, aunque sean dioses" (82) ("because that is the fortune of the defeated, even among gods"). The comparative, and ultimately subtly disparaging perception–would anyone say that Titus Livius was the Alba Ixtlilxóchitl of the Tiber–makes of the Mexican an echo or faint reproduction of the Roman. Henríquez Ureña also highlights people of mixed race, from the Inca Garcilaso (1539–1616) to Rubén Darío (1867–1916). It is not race that matters, but the incorporation of the European. More recently, Beatriz Sarlo, in *Escenas de la vida posmoderna* [1994; *Scenes from Postmodern Life,* 2001], has written eloquently about how these intellectuals who had "la pasión de lo universal" (174) ("a passion for the universal") are now being displaced by a universe in which their voices grow dim and inconsequential.

The Essay as a Call for Action

Few essayists have commanded Martí's talent to express his cause–independence and justice–with such dramatic immediacy, unforgettable images, and pithy sentences. "El presidio político en Cuba" [Political Prison in Cuba], for example, remains unsurpassed as a denunciation of the abuses of imperial power. The alternation of agile narrative with abundant use of dialogue, recrimination, and a call to action cannot fail to move the reader. Here, among other cases of gross injustice, he describes the abuses to which an old, sick, and beaten prisoner is submitted. The reader sees him first lying on the ground, from where he is lifted onto a cart that bounces and tumbles down the road, as if all of nature contrived against the prisoner. But Martí elevates the abused body even higher, by implicitly equating this road with the Calvary: "Golpeaba la cabeza en el carro. Asomaba el cuerpo a cada bote.... ¡Miserables! Olvidaban que en aquel hombre iba Dios" (13–14) ("His head banged against the side of the cart. His body bounced with every bump.... Miserable men! They had forgotten that God was in that man"). This body, revealed only in suffering fragments and disquieting glimpses, demands action, as most of Martí's essays do. In a letter of 1882 he claimed he abhorred words that are not accompanied by deeds (28). This instrumentality of the essay form adds urgency and nobility to many Latin American essays, such as those of Juan Montalvo (1832–1889) who opposed unremittingly two Ecuadorian dictators. The Peruvian Manuel González Prada (1844–1918) also left a political legacy of vibrant social criticism leading to action. The Uruguayan Eduardo Galeano's (b. 1940) *Las venas abiertas de América Latina* [1971; *Open Veins of Latin America: Five Centuries of the Pillage of a Continent,* 1973] offers "una historia del saqueo [de América] y a la vez contar cómo funcionan los mecanismos actuales del despojo" (13) ("a history of plunder [of Latin America] as well as a present-day account of the mechanism of dispossession"), in order to counter foreign imperialism and the national oligarchies' complicity. The early model, and one of the most illustrious or infamous (according to where the reader stands regarding the Spanish conquest), is that of Fray Bartolomé de las Casas (1474–1566), and, in modern times, Domingo Faustino Sarmiento (1811–1888), especially with his *Facundo* (1845). His description of the Argentinean land, the different types of people that inhabit it, and its recent history is couched in terms of European objective science, but under each sentence fumes a hardly repressed anger

against the contemporary conditions of Argentina and, especially, against the government of Juan Manuel de Rosas (1793–1877). The complexity of this book depends, in part, on the vast learning that Sarmiento weaves into his story, raising it from the local to a conflict of cosmic proportions, as the struggle between order and chaos, civilization and barbarism. Allusions to Machiavelli, the Sphinx, and the Inquisition in the first three pages show that the struggle for power between Good and Evil is not restricted to America but pervasive everywhere. And yet Sarmiento, as a good journalist and polemicist, is not beyond simplifying–by placing Africa, Spain, and some regions of the interior of Argentina closer to the reign of darkness. His dazzling rhetorical questions for which the reader is merely a foil, his many exclamations, the many categorical affirmations, the sprinkling of the sublime and tragic, the personification of a lofty nature, all speak of the Romantic period, but serve him well in his attempt to lead his reader to a revulsion that will lead to action. There can be no doubt that *Facundo* mesmerizes even today, but his battle cry in favor of the city and a European education that "liga al mundo civilizado" (217) ("unites the civilized world") has become less convincing. By collapsing the violence of some people into a demonizing of some regions of Argentina and some of its people, he ultimately fell into the same strategy of appropriating the symbolic of which Rosas was master. When, in closing the book, he adduces the reasons why Europe should help depose Rosas, the dangers and shortcomings of his program become clear: "¿Quiere la Inglaterra consumidores cualquiera que el gobierno de un país sea? Pero ¿qué han de consumir seiscientos mil gauchos pobres, sin industrias como sin necesidades, bajo un gobierno que, extinguiendo las costumbres y gustos europeos, disminuye necesariamente el consumo de productos europeos?" (228) ("Does England want consumers whatever government a nation may have? What are six hundred thousand poor *gauchos*, without any industry, without even the basic necessities, going to consume under a government that destroys European customs and tastes and therefore reduces necessarily the consumption of European products?").

While being ignored as producers and consumers, relegated to the past or postponed to the future, and condemned either to eccentricity or imitation has riled Latin American essayists, the deep fear of falling altogether away from Western civilization and of being relegated with the barbarians beyond the pale of European culture has also been a constant anxiety. This explains the genius of Sarmiento's strategic displacement onto the Latin American soil of a tension that had been felt before between Europe and America. Sarmiento, by transferring the *barbarie* to the gauchos of the interior and the roving Indian tribes, asserted that the educated citizens of Buenos Aires or Córdoba, plus the many European immigrants that would come later, were in fact part of civilization. There have been innumerable discussions about Sarmiento's ideas, about the success (or not) of the immigration and the educational program to which they led. His extremely negative opinion of the Indians, whom he wanted extinguished as the most pure carriers of the virus of barbarism, is indefensible. What matters is that this essay, *Facundo*, whether one agrees or not with it, had a profound influence on policy and on the representation of national history. The bipolar terms of civilization and barbarism became popular, bringing with them the attendant blindness and insight.

José Enrique Rodó (1871–1917) was reacting in *Ariel* [(1900), 1985] to the immigration that Sarmiento had implemented, since Rodó feared a "degeneración democrática" (25) ("democratic degeneration") from the combined forces of the new masses coming from Europe and the materialism exported by the United States. Taking on the voice of a teacher to all the youth of America (when he still had not reached 30), he extols the values of optimism and the ideals represented by Greek society. He would like youth to resist the imitation of the utilitarian United States, where freedom is practiced but the beautiful is not loved passionately and any truth that cannot be applied is shunned (41). Tacit, but easily recognizable by any reader, is the fact that this text is written after the Cuban American War of 1898, which made of the United States a blatantly colonial power for Spanish-speaking countries. With a barrage of quotations from French authors and many Greek references, Rodó downplays the accomplishments of the United States and, comparatively, rescues for the future of Latin America a more true-to-its-nature function of conserving and developing high culture with intelligence and magnanimity. This was a satisfying message and it enjoyed great success among the reading public, but its message soon came under fire for, on the one hand, its elitist undercurrents and, on the other, its unrealistic neglect of the importance of material conditions.

A direct response to *Ariel* is Roberto Fernández Retamar's *Calibán: apuntes sobre la cultura en nuestra América* [1974; *Caliban and Other Essays,* 1989], which starts out with a question posed to the author by a European journalist: "Does a Latin American culture exist?" Fernández Retamar perceives another implicit, more incisive, interrogation: "Do you exist?" Coming little over a decade after the Cuban Revolution, this question was particularly timely and irritating, since cultural dependence, in which countries become an echo of what happens first elsewhere, is part of the colonial condition from which Cuba wanted to break away. What characterizes Cuban culture, according to Fernández Retamar, is its being racially mixed, even if it must use, like Caliban, the language of its oppressors. Like the Shakespearean character, it is misperceived as monstrous by the colonizers who unify the continent's diversity in their possessive gaze. Fernández Retamar concludes that, in order for a Latin American culture to truly exist, all forms of colonialism must end. There is no doubt that the essays considered here have addressed the issue of colonialism in different ways, but with equal concern. Therefore, the drive to compare and compete with other cultures and literatures has remained constant. Perhaps in a truly postcolonial and postmodern future, the comparative urge will fade away as one of the pivotal forces of the Latin American essay.

Works Cited

Bartra, Roger. 1992. *The Cage of Melancholy: Identity and Metamorphosis in the Mexican Character.* Trans. Christopher J. Hall. New Brunswick, NJ: Rutgers University Press.

Bello, Andrés. 1997. *Selected Writings.* Trans. Frances López-Morillas. Ed. Iván Jaksic. New York: Oxford University Press.

Bolívar, Simón. 1975. *Escritos políticos.* 3rd ed. Selected and introduced by Graciela Soriano. Madrid: Alianza Editorial.

Bonfil Batalla, Guillermo. 1991. *Pensar nuestra cultura.* Mexico City: Alianza Editorial, 1991.

———. 1996. *México profundo: Reclaiming a Civilization.* Trans. Philip A. Dennis. Austin: University of Texas Press.

Carpentier, Alejo. 1970. *Tientos y diferencias.* Montevideo: Arca.

Cornejo-Polar, Antonio. 1997. "Mestizaje e hibridez: Los riesgos de las metáforas. Apuntes." *Revista Iberoamericana* 58: 341–44.

Fernández Retamar, Roberto. 1974. *Calibán: Apuntes sobre la cultura en nuestra América.* 2nd ed. Mexico City: Diógenes.

Freyre, Gilberto. 1945. *Interpretación del Brasil.* Mexico City: Fondo de Cultura Económica.

Galeano, Eduardo. 1973. *Open Veins of Latin America: Five Centuries of the Pillage of a Continent* Trans. Cedric Belfrage. New York: Monthly Review Press.

———. 1979 [1971]. *Las venas abiertas de América Latina.* 23rd ed. Mexico City: Fondo de Cultura Económica.

García Canclini, Néstor. 1992. *Culturas híbridas: Estrategias para entrar y salir de la modernidad.* Buenos Aires: Sudamericana.

Henríquez Ureña, Pedro. 1952. *Seis Ensayos en busca de nuestra expresión.* Buenos Aires: Raigal.

Mariátegui, José Carlos. 1978. *7 ensayos de interpretación de la realidad peruana.* 38th ed. Lima: Amauta.

Martí, José. 1972. *Sus mejores páginas.* 2nd ed. Mexico City: Porrúa.

Martínez Estrada, Ezequiel. 1946. *Radiografía de la pampa.* 2 vols. Buenos Aires: Losada.

Meyer, Doris. 1995. *Rereading the Spanish American Essay: Translations of 19th and 20th Century Women's Essays.* Austin: University of Texas Press.

Moog, Clodomir Vianna. 1964. *Bandeirantes e pioneiros: Paralelo entre duas Culturas.* 7th ed. Rio de Janeiro: Editôra Civilização Brasileira.

Paz, Octavio. 1991. *In Search of the Present: 1990 Nobel Lecture.* Bilingual edition. Trans. Anthony Stanton. San Diego: Harcourt Brace Jovanovich.

———. 1993. *El laberinto de la soledad. Postdata. Vuelta a El laberinto de la soledad.* 2nd ed. Mexico City: Fondo de Cultura Económica.

Prado, Paulo. 1928. *Retrato do Brasil: Ensaio sobre a tristeza brasileira.* São Paulo: Duprat-Mayença.

Ramos, Samuel. 1962. *Profile of Man and Culture in Mexico.* Trans. Peter G. Earle. Austin: University of Texas Press.

Reyes, Alfonso. 1960a. *Última Tule. Obras completas.* Vol 11. Mexico City: Fondo de Cultura Económica.

———. 1960b. *Visión de Anáhuac. Obras completas.* Vol. 2. Mexico City: Fondo de Cultura Económica.

Rodó, José Enrique. 1985. *Ariel: Motivos de Proteo.* 2nd ed. Intro. Carlos Real de Azúa. Ed. Angel Rama. Cáracas: Biblioteca Ayacucho.

Santa Cruz y Espejo, Francisco Javier Eugenio. 1912. *Escritos.* 2 vols. Quito: Imprenta Municipal.

Sarlo, Beatriz. 1994. *Escenas de la vida posmoderna: Intelectuales, arte y videocultura en la Argentina.* Buenos Aires: Ariel.

Sarmiento, Domingo Faustino. 1970. *Facundo.* 4th ed. Buenos Aires: Losada.

Sigüenza y Góngora, Carlos de. 1959. *Libra astronómica y filosófica.* Ed. José Gaos and Bernabé Navarro. Mexico City: Centro de Estudios Filosóficos, Universidad Nacional Autónoma de México.

Silva Herzog, Jesús. 1960. *El mexicano y su morada, y otros ensayos.* Mexico City: Ediciones Cuadernos Americanos.

Stavans, Ilan, ed. 1995. *The Oxford Book of Latin American Essays.* New York: Oxford University Press.

Summ, Harvey G., ed. *Brazilian Mosaic: Portraits of a Diverse People and Culture.* Wilmington, DE: SR Books.

Vasconcelos, José. 1948. *La raza cósmica: Misión de la raza iberoamericana; Notas de viajes a la América del Sur.* Mexico City: Espasa-Calpe Mexicana.

Zum Felde, Alberto. 1954. *Indice crítico de la literatura hispanoamericana: Los ensayistas.* Mexico City: Editorial Guarania.

CHAPTER 27

SATIRE AND TEMPORAL HETEROGENEITY

Flora Süssekind

Contrary to the position of Alfred MacAdam, who associates the persistence of a satirical vein in Latin America with a sort of structural flaw related to the region's "colonial condition" (16), characterized by its lack of a "specific sense of history" (20), a "historiographic core" (16), it is perhaps possible to see satire not as a "transitory form" (289), a compensatory shortcut for cultures unable to produce "genres" in the proper sense of the term. Rather, it could be seen as a strategy that is particularly appropriate for embodying the region's tensions and social uncertainties, the conflicts arising from the persistent coexistence of ideas from different historical periods and the practices of cultural hybridization and appropriation of foreign and domestic, traditional, and contemporary models—processes that define and distinguish the historical and artistic experience of Latin America. In this sense but with no expectation that reliance on a given form of expression will generate homogeneous effects, the examination of four modern Latin American novels with a clearly satirical orientation—Oswald de Andrade's (1890–1954) *Memórias sentimentais de João Miramar* [1924; *Sentimental Memoirs of John Seaborne*, 1971] and *Serafim Ponte Grande* [1933; *Serafim Grosse Pointe,* 1979], Macedonio Fernández's (1874–1952) *Museo de la novela de la eterna* [posthumously 1967; Museum of the Novel of Eternal], and Guillermo Cabrera Infante's (b. 1929) *Tres tristes tigres* [1967; *Three Trapped Tigers,* 1971]—will perhaps bring out some elements and functions on the basis of which this alternative, discontinuous, but persistent tradition of Latin American cultural systems can be investigated.

Although the four novels in question resort to a deliberate mixture of different genre strategies, the dominance of satire immediately is apparent in Macedonio Fernández's option for an anatomy of narrative, in Cabrera Infante's nocturnal transfiguration of the symposium, and in Oswald de Andrade's ironical narration of adventures and travels. The three authors resort to traditional forms of satire, characteristic examples of which are Burton's *Anatomy of Melancholy*, in Macedonio's case, Falstaff's excesses in Shakespeare's *Henry IV* plays—explicitly mentioned, in fact, by Cabrera Infante in the "Bachata" section of *Tres tristes tigres* (311)—and Lucian's *True History* in Andrade's travel accounts. Also characteristically satirical are the structural procedures used in the four novels. Take, for instance, the digression in *Museo de la novela de la eterna*. Here there are fifty-nine prologues, one post-prologue, and three sections of final considerations, although the actual chapters number no more than twenty. Parentheses unfold within other parentheses; postponement, sidetracking, and reelaboration are constant; there are frequent dialogues between the characters, the author, and the readers, such as the proposal, at the close of Chapter 5, to save readers from their own lives, inviting them to step into the narrative and lose themselves there. Such elements point to a poetics of indeterminacy, nondiscursiveness, and deactualization of the very form of the novel. For, as Oscar del Barco observes, it is precisely "what cannot be a novel" that "Macedonio

paradoxically calls a novel" (469). In his book, there is always "the beginning of one more prologue, of an interminable sequence of prologues explaining what the novel ought to be like, introducing the characters, offering ideas about every conceivable topic, and soon leading to another prologue" (471). In satires, incompleteness and digressiveness tend to be common features of prefaces, parentheses, summaries, and interpolations, as in Swift's *A Tale of a Tub*, in which "the digression, although recognized by the ancients as a component of the formal oration," becomes "the epitome of modern form, or, more precisely, the modern departure from form," as Leon Guilhamet observes in his study of satire (129).

Oswald de Andrade's Modernist novels include such elements as a pseudo-preface signed by one Machado Penumbra (*Memórias sentimentais de João Miramar*) and a long, digressive series between the fourth and ninth chapters of *Serafim Ponte Grande* (H. de Campos 1984, 163–4), but in this particular case it could be said that the basis of the author's satirical effect is his peculiar use of ellipsis. Antonio Candido rightly observes that "o tom melhor de Oswald" ("Andrade's most effective tone") occurs when there is "a sua fusão com a poesia, sobretudo pela extensão de processos poéticos a contextos quaisquer. Sarcasmo-poesia, e não sarcasmo-sarcasmo" ("fusion with poetry, particularly through the extension of poetic processes to all kinds of contexts. This is poetic sarcasm, not sarcasm for its own sake") (1995, 93). Hence the sections converted into poetry, such as "Casa da Patarroxa" ["House of Patarroxa"] in *Miramar* or the variations on the homecoming topos in the "Fim de Serafim" ["The End of Serafim"] section of *Serafim*; the rhythmical use of blank space, making quasi-stanzas out of autonomous blocks of prose, as in the "Intermezzo" in *Serafim*; the recurrent reliance on microchapters, sometimes reduced to a single sentence, such as the "Natal" ["Christmas"] chapter of *Miramar*, which reads, in its entirety: "Minha sogra ficou avó" ("My mother-in-law turned grandmother"). Hence, too, the general structure of *Miramar* as a sequence of 163 very brief fragments, or the unexpected verse form of quite prosaic bits of information, as in Chapter 44, "Mont-Cenes," in the same book: "O alpinista/de alpenstock/desceu/nos alpes" ("The alpinist/with an alpenstock/landed on the Alps") (Andrade 1990, 8). This passage is marked by the repetition of "alp," an effect that alludes to poetry but is so gratuitous that its ultimate effect is comic. In addition to these satirico-poetical forms of ellipsis, Oswald de Andrade's Modernist prose also resorts to "poignant metaphors" ("O trem a manhã e a chuva eram um corador de roupa branca" (1990, 94) ("The train the morning and the rain were white linen bleaching on a clothesline") that contrast with deliberate clichés (night descending like a bird, the "poetic" hissing of the wind, and so on), and to exercises in imagery, such as "O silêncio vermelho" ("The red silence") (1984, 122), and paratactic constructions as in the passage in which, describing the return to Brazil, the movement of the ship and the passage of time are presented in the form of a list. This is made obvious in the closing paragraph of "Os esplendores do Oriente" ["The Splendors of the Orient"], in *Serafim Ponte Grande*: "O Oriente fechou-se. Tudo desapareceu como a cidade no mar, seus brilhos, seus brancos, suas pontas de terra, esfinges, caftãs, fezes, camelos, dragomãs, pirâmides, haréns, abaias, pilafs, desertos, mesquitas, templos, tapetes, acrópoles, ingleses, inglesas" (1984, 123) ("The East is closed. Everything is gone, like the city under the sea, its gleams, its blanks, its capes, sphinxes, caftans, fezzes, camels, dragomen, pyramids, harems, minarets, abayas, pilafs, deserts, mosques, temples, carpets, acropolises, Englishmen, Englishwomen").

In *Tres tristes tigres*, the structuring principle seems to be transformation. This is already apparent in the way new words are created, throughout the book, in the metamorphoses of proper names. Transformations curiously similar to the onomastic process used by Sousândrade (Joaquim de Sousa Andrade [1833–1902]) in Brazilian nineteenth-century poetry. In his narrative poem *O Guesa*, he creates composite expressions such as Roma-Manhattan, Sul-Serafim (South-Serafim), Hércules-Guttenbergs, Deus-deserto (God-desert), Copo-d'Água-Deus (Glass-of-Water-God). In Cabrera's satirical novel, Arsênio Cué, for example, becomes, successively, Arsenietzsche Cué, Arseniostradamus, Narciso Cué, Cuery Grant, Buster Cué, Le Cuerbusier, Capitan Kuedd. This transformation principle is equally present in the variations of accent and dialect, and in the nocturnal wanderings through the streets of Havana of the voices that, juxtaposed, make up the book; in Bustrófedon's various rewritings of "Muerte de Trotsky" ["Death of Trotsky"] parodying the styles of José Martí (1853–1895), José Lezama Lima (1910–1976), Virgilio Piñera (1912–1979), Lydia Cabrera (1899–1991), Lino Novás (1905–1983), Alejo Carpentier (1904–1980), and Nicolás Guillén (1902–1989); and in the contradictions concerning the "História de un baston" ["Story of a Cane"], according to the Campbells. This can also be seen in the translations, usually with comic effect. A particularly striking example is the novel's multilingual "Prólogo" ["Prologue"]; in the series of corrections that often follow even the most casual observation, such as an abrupt comparison with the character Philip Marlowe, who turns into "Montgomery-Marlowe-Chandler," clearly to specify the literary and cinematic reference; and, again, in the graphic changes that sometimes have the effect of representing the story being told in the most literal way, as in the "Rompecabeza" ["Jigsaw Puzzle"] section, where the metaphor of writing as a "trick with mirrors," present throughout the book, is materialized; or in the section "Algunas revelaciones" ["Some Revelations"], where a text and its mirror image are reproduced on opposite pages. This principle of change, dominant in *Tres tristes tigres*, is no less fundamental to the constitution of a possible identity of satire as a genre, in which the appropriation and the deformation of variable rhetorical and genre structures are converted into "part of the dynamic of generic satire" (Guilhamet 54).

Quite aside from the singularities of composition of each, all four books under discussion suggest not only a redefinition of satire, as the genre that "transforms such miscellany into a generic structure" (Guilhamet 17), but also of its seemingly close relations with structural elements of Latin American intellectual systems—a fact that partly explains the preference for the genre and the transformations it necessarily goes through, given the diversity of the concrete historical relations with which it dialogues. On the basis of Cabrera Infante, Fernández,

and Andrade, one might then establish a few generic traits that are potentially interchangeable between satire as a form of expression and Latin American cultural processes. The first of these would be an inevitable hybridization, because Latin American societies are marked by processes of cultural imposition and dependence, while satire is a form that "emerges from the combustible dynamic of mixed literary styles" (Guilhamet 17), which, even when mimicked and apparently preserving their own internal traits, lose their formal identities in the context of this new structuring, which is of a "protean nature" (Kernan 1962, 7), of a recurrent "deforming ironic pattern" (Guilhamet 165–66). In this way, mobility and a sort of instability are constitutive traits of satire.

Thus the combination of sarcasm and poetry, telegraphic-journalistic prose and private diary, in Oswald de Andrade's *Miramar* and *Serafim*, of digressiveness and monothematicism in Macedonio Fernández's *Museo*, of linguistic, narrative, stylistic-parodistic variation and quotation in Infante's *Tres tristes tigres*; and, in all three cases, of reference and deformation of genre and intertextual structures, of historical information and appropriate contemporary and traditional elements—each in its own way, all of these elements point to a "movimento de desvio da norma, ativo e destruidor" ("active, destructive swerving from the norm") and to an activity of "contaminação" ("contamination") and "transfiguração" ("transfiguration") of the "elementos feitos e imutáveis" ("given and immutable elements") that are perhaps, as Silviano Santiago observes in "O entre-lugar do discurso latino-americano" [1978; "The In-Between of Latin American Discourse"], the fundamental contribution of the most critical productions of Latin American cultures toward the "a destruição sistemática dos conceitos de unidade e pureza" (Santiago 1978, 18) ("systematic destruction of the concepts of unity and purity"). It also may be a significant response to "a representação do modelo dominante" ("the representation of the dominant model") that it inevitably embodies in itself, which takes place through difference, through "o suplemento de leitura e criação" ("the supplement of reading and creation"), "no própio nível da fabulação" ("on the very level of fabulation") (Santiago 1982, 23).

Another satirical element that plays a fundamental role in *Tres tristes tigres*, *Museo de la novela de la eterna*, and in *Miramar* and *Serafim* is the perception of narrative activity itself as problematic, the tendency to the exacerbation of formal and ethical self-consciousness. For if, as Michael Rosenblum writes, following an old tradition, satire is the "bastard genre," the "mixed dish," "without the style and unity of the more elevated genres" (29), which chooses to deal with the "deformed," the "vicious," the "absurd" (Rosenblum 28), it is diametrically opposite to moral and aesthetic self-justification. Hence the reflexive tone, the self-exhibition, and sometimes the self-analysis—as in Sterne's *Tristram Shandy* or Machado de Assis's *Memórias póstumas de Brás Cubas* [*Posthumous Memoirs of Brás Cubas*, 1997]—that seem inherent to the genre, to its need for self-justification, and, in the cases of Cabrera Infante, Fernández, and Andrade, also to the specific conditions of intellectual work in Latin American countries. For in Latin America the reading public is limited by widespread illiteracy and a lack of access to (or of identification with) cultural productions. There is "sem um campo cultural autônomo" ("no autonomous cultural field"), as Néstor García Canclini observes (75), and there is an inevitable unease brought about by the simultaneous need to assert national singularities and one's own spiritual freedom, on the one hand, and to keep up with metropolitan standards, on the other.

However, there are various forms of satirical self-exhibition to be found in Cabrera Infante, Fernández, and Andrade. One of them takes place somewhat perversely by means of the disclosure of expressive procedures against which they devise, ironically, their own means of expression. Thus Andrade constantly comments on the vapid, academic literature that was dominant in Brazil before Modernism; through Bustrófedon, in *Tres tristes tigres*, Cabrera Infante parodies what he sees as certain stylistic mannerisms of modern Cuban literature; and Fernández's rejection of true and "hallucinatory" realism and didacticism leads him to write simultaneously a more or less conventional novel, *Adriana Buenos Aires*, and an antinovel, *Museo*, so that a parallel reading of the two would itself function as a critical device.

On the other hand, there is a disclosure of the very process of writing and a sort of anticipatory dramatization of its reading. In *Museo*, the book itself is presented as an account of its own elaboration and as an exercise in the fictionalization of its own reception. At one point, the "nonskipping" reader is ousted: "Fora, leitor de desenlaces!" (408) ("Out, you reader of dénouements!"). In *Miramar*, in addition to the many rhetorical exercises with other voices (Machado Penumbra, Pôncio Pilatos da Glória, Mandarim Pedroso, Fíleas, and Minão da Silva), the narrator defines himself ironically as a "young poet" and quotes enthusiastic praise from Penumbra and Dr. Pilatos, which should be read, as Haroldo de Campos has observed, as covert manifestos by Andrade himself; the same may be said of the final comment in *Miramar*. "O meu livro lembrou-lhe Virgílio, apenas um pouco mais nervoso no estilo" (107) ("My book reminded him of Virgil, seeming only a bit more nervous in its style"). This seems to underscore a structural tension in the text between the prose of the self, on the one hand, and the deadpan "telegraphic style," on the other.

In *Serafim* self-exhibition becomes more direct, and at times the narrative switches to the present: "A paisagem desta capital apodrece. Apreço ao leitor. Pelotari. Personagem através de um vidraça" (15) ("The setting of this capital is rotting. I show myself to the reader. Pelotari. Character seen through a windowpane"). At other times, the third person is adopted; narrative and protagonist draw apart and are converted into objects of observation—"Serafim some pelo escapamento" (78) ("Serafim disappears through the exhaust pipe")—or fictional control, as in the episode in which Pinto Calçudo is thrown out of the novel, when, Serafim having asked him who is the real protagonist of the book, he simply "com toda a força um traque" (71) ("lets out a thunderous fart").

In *Tres tristes tigres*, in addition to a constant self-ironic treatment of the literary (in favor of movies and songs) and of modern works—including the works of Joyce, with which the book itself dialogues—the hesitations of the writing process are graphically represented as erasures, individual words that are crossed out in Campbell's story. There are also countless parentheses and appeals to the reader, as well as sudden stylistic strictures ("Linda frase, verdad? Lástima que no sea mía" [1967, 224] ["A nice sentence, ain't it? Too bad it's not mine"] [1971, 233]) that underscore the parodistic imagination driving the narrative onward and function as a fundamental strategy of a poetics based on jokes, randomness, inversion, and change, personified by Bustrófedon and synthesized in the "Rompecabeza" section of *Tres tristes tigres*.

But as the literary experience is unveiled through these devices, the historical experience is presented as well. "Eu, Serafim Ponte Grande, empregado de uma Repartição Federal

saqueada e pai de diversas crianças desaparecidas" (45) ("I, Serafim Ponte Grande, an official working at a looted department of the Federal Government and the father of several missing children") is the melancholic self-description given by the narrator-protagonist of Oswald de Andrade's novel, in a blatant contrast with the phrase "our hero," often used to refer to him in the third-person passages of the book; the hero in question invariably involves himself in one ludicrous scrape after another, culminating in a random rooftop sniping that leads to his death. "Modéstia à parte, eu mesmo sou um símbolo nacional. Tenho um canhão e não sei atirar" (46) ("If I may be allowed to boast a bit, I really am a national symbol. I have a cannon but don't know how to shoot"), he says, combining hyperbole and derision, and underscoring his difficulty in achieving self-representation outside of satire. This same difficulty, at the end of the book, has the effect of driving mad the painter commissioned to paint his posthumous portrait because some minute detail is always missing from the painting.

The difficulty of figuration also is featured in *Tres tristes tigres*, notably in Ribot's attempted self-description through negatives after a failed attempt to get a raise: "ni artista ni técnico ni artesano ni obrero ni científico ni lumpen ni puta: un híbrido, una cruza, un engendro, un parturiunt montes (como dirías tú, Silvestre, hablando latín con acento oriental) nascetur ridiculus mus" (Cabrera Infante 1967, 48) ("neither artist nor technician nor artisan nor worker nor scientist nor *lumpenproletariat* nor prostitute: a hybrid, a half-caste, an abortion, a *parturiunt montes* [as you would say, Silvestre, speaking Latin with a Cuban accent] *nascetur ridiculus mus*") (Cabrera Infante 1971, 42). This indefiniteness is reaffirmed by Silvestre himself–"en Cuba nadie es escritor: Esa profesión no existe, como me dijo una bebliotecaria de la Biblioteca Nacional" (Cabrera Infante 1967, 339) ("in Cuba nobody can be a writer: That's not a *profession*! the librarian at the National Library told me one day") (Cabrera Infante 1971, 367)–by the fate of Arsenio Cué, who tries to work as a playwright and ends up as a television actor, and by that of Ribot himself, a translator. Or Bustrófedon, who refuses to write and who, in the book, has no voice of his own, operating as a transforming principle exerted on other voices and forms–somewhat like satire itself, as if such deformation and such indetermination were inescapable facts: "Te ríes? Es el signo de Cuba. Aquí siempre tiene uno que dar a las verdades un aire de boutade para que sean aceptadas" (Cabrera Infante 1967, 342) ("You're laughing. Just like a Cuban. People here always have to turn anything that's true into a joke. To extract truth with laughing gas") (Cabrera Infante 1971, 370). This is the explanation given in the book's "Bachata" section. And in place of a culturalized style of the sort that Bustrófedon parodies in the various versions of "Death of Trotsky," which "seemed absurdly out of place when compared to the degraded reality" (Franco 418) of Havana in the 1950s, *Tres tristes tigres* apparently points to the conversion of this unease, this asynchrony, this "sense of a cultural chasm" (Franco 419) between the writer and his public–in the case of Cabrera Infante, through transformation, derision, the dismemberment of form–into the principle of literary work proper, of fabulation marked by discontinuity and interweaving, and of a narration in various voices and *in perpetuum mobile*.

It seems only proper, then, that the characters of *Museo*, led by the President, after leaving the *estancia* [country house] "The Novel" in order to attempt "la conquista de Buenos

Aires para la belleza y el mistério" ("to win Buenos Aires for beauty and mystery"), should attribute, through indirect allusion, a fundamental role to a recurrent figure in the satirical tradition–the cynical philosopher Diogenes–in the definition of some of the tactics of occupation: the lantern carried by a messenger in search of an artist in want of light, or the candle that a semi-paralyzed trombone player can neither blow out nor let go of, so that he looks for someone who can do it for him (Fernández 353). Here there is a search with a lantern all over town not for a man, as in the anecdote traditionally told about Diogenes, but for an artist. This is reminiscent of the authorial figuration in *Tres tristes tigres* and in Oswald de Andrade's novels. The narrative voice also seems to be engaged in a dialogue with the movement of self-exhibition and with the expressive self-consciousness that in satire functions in association with the metamorphic or pressure that, nevertheless, is constitutive of it. This is a form characterized by a sort of imminent suspension, a resistance to formalization, an in-betweenness, the recurrence of which in modern Latin American literature may bring satire closer to some of the dilemmas of structuring that are typical of the most significant works produced in the field of the visual arts in these countries. As Rodrigo Naves writes in *A forma difícil*, there is "uma relutância em estruturar fortemente os trabalhos, e com isso, entregá-los a uma convivência mais positiva e conflituada com o mundo" ("a reluctance to give a strong structure to the work so that it is forced into a more positive and conflictive relation with the world"), and this invests such works with "um movimento íntimo e retraído, distante do caráter prospectivo de parcela considerável da arte moderna" ("an intimate, timid movement, quite different from the forward-looking character of much modern art"); their "natureza remissiva" ("allusive nature") evokes "uma sociabilidade de ordem semelhante, pouco definida" ("a similarly ill-defined sociability") (21).

If this "social indecisiveness" is at times manifested as "formal reluctance," it also can be associated with "radical indefiniteness," a transformation of the difficulty of formalization into a "difficult form." "The malaise of this out-of-step social dynamic," writes Rodrigo Naves, "is formally incorporated into some works, which reveal in their structure the dubious, dragging movement of a society marked by asynchronicity and ambiguity" (22). It is not difficult to see that this double way of dealing with formal indetermination is also present in the way modern Latin American cultures appropriate satire–a form intrinsically characterized by indefiniteness and mixture that at times tries to point to only external referents, aiming at a realism that transforms it into a simple mirror of social ambiguity and at other times remains locked up in its own self, so that the intertextual sphere becomes the exclusive space of a literature conceived as logocentric play. Such exclusive paths point, in the case of satire, not to a "difficult form" but to an impasse in the task of formalization. But the rarefaction of a discourse that "records and records and records" and the multiplication of blank spaces in the "Epilogue" of *Tres tristes tigres*; the dénouement of *Miramar*, in which the reminiscing narrator suddenly gives up his story; the end of *Serafim*, in which the ship *El Durasno* is left permanently adrift with Pinto Calçudo aboard; and the structural incompleteness of *Museo*–all suggest not reluctance but a formal choice. And the transformation of their unstable, composite nature into a unique structuring principle with its discontinuity and constitutive discrepancies is particularly

adequate for depicting the Latin American temporal experience, marked as it is by heterogeneity and the simultaneity of the non-simultaneous.

Thus there is a reason for the "temporal disturbances" in the prose of Macedonio Fernández, Cabrera Infante, and Oswald de Andrade. In Macedonio Fernández, a repeated postponement achieved by a series of prologues makes back-and-forth digressiveness the novel's dominant temporal principle. This, however, in a way contrasts with the linearity suggested by the chapters dealing with the history of the President, the Eterna, the *estancia* called "The Novel." In *Tres tristes tigres*, the temporal organization of the work seems to be oriented by the tension between proliferation and rarefaction, between expansion and structural disjunction, and between the rhythmic repetition of voices, the themes of the Havana night, and the extreme inner variation to which the smallest elements that make up these narrative blocs are subjected.

In the case of *Serafim*, what is particularly evident from the outset is the lack of continuity, as Haroldo de Campos observes in "Serafim: Um grande não-livro" ["Serafim: The Big Non-Book"]: "há um hiato cronológico, uma intercalação parentética, que fratura o tempo narrativo (1984, 162) ("there is a chronological hiatus, a parenthetical interpolation, that fractures narrative time"). He continues: "Entre o 'Cômputo' (em IV)–título que carreira a idéia de cálculo final, de balanço–e o 'Fim de Serafim' (IX) abrius-se um enorme parêntese, operou-se um corte tmético como aqueles famosos, do *Tristram Shandy*, que correm por páginas e páginas, permitindo a expansão do material intercalado" (164) ("Between 'Cômputo' ['Tally'] (in IV)–a title that suggests the idea of a final balance–and 'Fim de Serafim' (IX) [The End of Serafim], there lies a long parenthesis, a tmesis similar to the famous breaks in *Tristram Shandy*, extending for pages and more pages, allowing the expansion of the interpolated material"). This temporal fracture is underscored by the change of narrative voice from the first to the third person singular, to which a further development might be added, one mentioned by Kenneth D. Jackson in *A prosa vanguardista na literatura brasileira: Oswald de Andrade* (1978): "existem in *Serafim* dois esquemas de tempo principais que espelham as estruturas horizontal (diacrônica) e a vertical (sincrônica) e a dupla interpretação de Serafim como personagem" (92) ("in *Serafim* there are two main time schemata mirroring the horizontal [diachronic] and the vertical [synchronic] structures and the double interpretation of Serafim as a character").

Thus we have, on the one hand, a chronological level, with the life and travels of Serafim, and on the other, the reference to "different historical times and styles," so that each of the novel's major sections seem to suggest a new, hypothetical text: a romantic narrative that takes off Camilo Castelo Branco (1825–1890) in "Cérebro, coração e pavio" ["Brain, Heart and Wick"]; an imitation of a child speaking in "Alpendre"; something approaching the stage directions of a play in "Recitativo" ["Recitative"]; a moral drama in "Vacina obrigatória" ["Compulsory Vaccine"]; an intimate diary in "Folhinha conjugal" ["Conjugal Calendar"]; a sixteenth-century chronicle in "Elemento sedativo" ["Sedative Element"]; a cloak-and-sword novella in "O meridiano de Greenwich" ["Greenwich Meridian"]. These takeoffs, veritable books within a book, make up not only a stylistic masquerade but also a particularly intense intersection of periods with historical and literary references. Each section has its own differentiated rhythm, seemingly in conflict with the book's general orientation toward the memoir. In this way, a complex, heterogeneous temporality is established, tuned to "a consciência dilacerada de seu autor" ("the shattered consciousness of its author"), "no limiar de uma assunção crítica e de uma definida investidura ideológica" ("on the verge of a critical stance and a definite ideological position") (Campos 1984, 171)—with regard to the tension, typical of Brazilian Modernism (see Candido 1985, 109–26), between the impulse to modernize and adopt current European artistic standards and the urge to redefine nationality—and to the "heterogeneidade sociocultural" ("sociocultural heterogeneity"), the "conflitos entre temporalidades históricas" ("conflicts between historical temporalities"), and "tradições culturais que convivem e se contradizem o tempo todo" ("cultural traditions that are in constant coexistence and contradiction") (García Canclini 1997, 70–83) within Latin American societies.

These temporal disturbances, in turn, are attuned to satirical discourse itself, marked as it is by discontinuity, digressiveness, and a characteristic rejection of linear progression, often expressed in the tension between form and the search for form, story, and episode. Gilbert Highet writes of satirical narratives: "If they are long, they are usually episodic. Although the satirist pretends to be telling a continuous story and gives his fiction a single unifying title, he is less interested in developing a plot with preparation, suspense, and climax, than in displaying many different aspects of an idea" (206). This display is of fundamental importance, for instance, in the composition of *Tristram Shandy*, in the tension between "tragic plot" and "comic life" and between the desire that "his chronicle [should] fit the patterns of tragedy," with "a beginning, a middle, and an end," and the fact that, try as the narrator may, "every event is inseparable from an endless series of trivialities going before and through it" (Kernan 96). Or, in the case of Machado de Assis's (1839–1908) *Memórias póstumas de Brás Cubas*, not only in regard to the temporal inversion—the attribution of authorship to a "*defunto autor*," a dead man who writes—that directs the narrative, but also in the digressive structure, in the constant dialogues with the reader, in the expressive self-consciousness, and in the narrator's mobility, attuned to the figure of the "mobile protagonist asking questions" (Paulson 135), characteristic of Lucian's satire, like Diogenes in *Dialogues of the Dead*.

Temporal disjunction is then a vital constitutive component in such a form as satire, which results exactly from the "dynamics" of a series of different styles, registers, elements, genres, and times in a tense coexistence. As appropriated by Latin American cultures, it often seems to serve the function of telescoping the experience of various times into a single time, stressing the simultaneity of contrasting temporalities and rhythms that characterizes the literary consciousness and historical experiences of these countries. Given this fact, it is hardly surprising that Antonio Candido in "Dialética da malandragem" ["Dialectic of Roguery"] should have relied precisely on a satirical countercurrent of Brazilian literature to propose a historiographical approach based not on the "lei da sucessão temporal homogênea" ("law of homogeneous temporal succession") but on a consideration of "diferentes ritmos temporais" ("different temporal rhythms") (qtd. in Pizarro 26 and 43), of relations between works not exactly synchronous. Hence his suggestion of a discontinuous comical lineage skipping various historical periods (Candido 1993c) and including the folk hero Pedro Malasarte, the figure of the satirical Baroque poet Gregório de Matos (1633?–1696), Mário de

Andrade's (1893–1945) *Macunaíma* (1928), and Oswald de Andrade's *Serafim Ponte Grande*, with Pantagruelian developments in the second Romantic generation in Brazil, as well as including Manuel Antônio de Almeida's (1831–1861) use of popular elements, the burlesque stylistic mélange of José Sousa Caldas's *Carta marítima* [Letter from the Sea, written in 1790 but first published in 1821], and the satirical poetry of Sapateiro Silva (Silva the Cobbler) between the late eighteenth and early nineteenth centuries, poised somewhere between high and popular cultures. (See **Figure 1**.)

This view of satire, however, does more than suggest changes in historiographical approaches from a diachronic perspective: It also invites contrastive rereadings and different critical approaches on the synchronic plane. It seems only natural that the breakup of the canon of genres (H. Campos 1979, 286–89), the discontinuous style, the linguistic and discoursive mixture, and the satire of genres it incorporates should have led to Augusto and Haroldo de Campos's revision of Sousândrade's poetry within Brazilian Romanticism. And the same is true of the fact that the study of satirical works in nineteenth-century Brazil underscores an intensification of the dialogue between literature and newspaper illustration, between fictional character and political caricature, and between the genres that were practiced in the period and the almost simultaneous development of their humorous counterparts. An example of this is Manuel de Araújo Porto-Alegre's (1806–1879) parody of travel writing, *Excertos das memórias e viagens do Coronel Bonifácio de Amarante* [1848; Excerpts from the Travel Memoirs of Colonel Bonifacio de Amarante]; another is Joaquim Manuel de Macedo's (1820–1882) *Memórias do sobrinho do meu tio* [1867; Memories of My Uncle's Nephew], a

Figure 1.

Mário de Andrade por Di Cavalcanti, 1928

Caricature of Mario de Andrade by DiCavalcanti, 1928. (Archive of the author)

satire on narrators of novels, which came at a time when the novel was a fledgling genre in Brazilian fiction and Macedo himself was one of its earliest practitioners. Other examples are the anti-lyrical dimension of part of the poetry of Bernardo Guimarães (1825–1884), Laurindo Rabelo (1826–1864), and Luís Gama (1830–1882) and the demolition of moral plays, then dominant in Brazilian drama, by Qorpo Santo's (the pseudonym for José Joaquim de Campos Leão [1829–1883]) self-mocking theatrical pieces.

The satirical strain in Brazilian Romanticism perhaps may be associated–keeping in mind the evident differences–with what Borges observed about the Baroque in his "Prologue to the 1954 Edition" of *Historia universal de la infamia* [Universal History of Infamy]: "aquel estilo que deliberadamente agota (o quiere agotar) sus posibilidades y que linda con su propia caricatura" (291) ("that style which exhausts [or would exhaust] its possibilities and that borders on its own caricature"). This is indeed reminiscent of nineteenth-century Brazil, with its estrangement from its own language, its "gravitação cotidiana das idéias e perspectivas práticas" (Schwarz 1977, 24) ("everyday gravitation of ideas and practical perspectives"), a country where "um latifúndio pouco modificado" ("a relatively untouched latifundio structure") was preserved, as Roberto Schwarz notes, even as "passarem as maneiras barroca, neoclássica, romântica, naturalista, modernista e outras" ("the Baroque, neo-Classical, Romantic, Naturalistic, Modernistic and other manners came and went") (Schwarz 1977, 21–22)–an estrangement that satirical expression helps to make visible.

Satire does not necessarily imply a break with literary convention: Witness the case of Gregório de Matos (1633?–1696), who remained faithful to the rhetorical tradition dominant in the seventeenth century. And often satire's incisiveness must remain within the bounds of the inner conflicts of the ruling class, as in Tomás Antônio Gonzaga's (1744–1807?) *Cartas chilenas* [Letters from Chile]. But nineteenth-century satire seems almost invariably associated with a mocking attitude toward writing itself and toward the hierarchy of genres respected by writers in their own practice, so that the same authors (for instance, Araújo Porto-Alegre) produce both epic works and illustrated newspaper satire, both lyrical and fescennine poetry (for example, Bernardo Guimarães). But effective critical interference did not always develop between these different registers, so that each remained within its own well-defined boundaries. There were exceptions: Álvares de Azevedo's (1831–1852) *Macário* (1853–1855) is a sort of Faustian caricature, part drama, part tale, part literary dialogue; Gonçalves Dias (1823–1864), in his "Sextilhas de Frei Antão" ["Sextains by Father Antão"] adopted a purposely anachronistic diction and appropriated, somewhat perversely, Portuguese prosody and the model of historical narrative; and Sousândrade's (1833–1902) *O Guesa* (1877) is an epic poem pervaded by stylistic admixture, its opposites, incompleteness, and by the possibility of dissolution suggested in the "infernal episodes," particularly through a frantic interweaving of epic and mock-epic. Sousândrade's multiple perspective, like Machado de Assis's (1839–1908) narrative *perpetuum mobile*, allows these authors to use the resources proper to satire so as to turn it against literary practice itself. This, in the field of Latin American historiography rather than exclusively in nineteenth-century literature, perhaps may be intensified by means of discontinuity and rhythmic variation at work in diachronic exercises, and by the contrastive unfolding of the "nonsimultaneous" read as simultaneous in the same period or within the same genre.

"What Does Brazil Want from Me, That It Should Pursue Me So?"

On the one hand, we must underscore a certain metahistorical conceptualization of satire in the context of Latin American literary cultures, taking into account in particular the structural interrelations (hybridization, metamorphic pressure, problematic character of the form, and dilemmas of structuring) between this textual model (which emerges from the dynamics of mixed times and styles) and the organization of these cultural systems (marked by processes of cultural dependence and imposition); on the other hand, we note the dominance in the makeup of both satirical forms and these systematic cultural data and of a temporality characterized by the experience of simultaneity of the non-simultaneous through a fundamental chronological heterogeneity. Given this, even these recurrent and potentially interchangeable (between textual model and cultural system) traits seem to point also to distinct changes and functions, to different kinds of satire, bearing in mind the concrete historical relations and the specific cultural processes with which they dialogue. In this sense it might be interesting to contrast Gregório de Matos's Baroque satire in seventeenth-century Brazil with the heroicomic poems, *glosas,* and satires of the eighteenth century, the Arcadian period of letters in the Portuguese colony, a time when Brazilian literature was beginning to take shape as an "sistema articulado" ("articulated system"), when "encorpando o processo formativo, que vinha de antes e continuou depois" ("the formative process, which had already begun and was to continue afterwards, gained momentum"), as Antonio Candido wrote in *Formação da literatura brasileira* (1975, I:16).

In the case of Gregório de Matos–the son of the owner of a sugarcane plantation, who studied law in Coimbra, Portugal, and rose to the position of judge and first treasurer–perhaps the first question (next to the problematic attribution of much of his work) to be raised in connection with his long-term dedication to satire, which earned him the nickname "Boca do Inferno" ["Devil's Mouthpiece"], concerns the social locus in which his satire arises. This locus is marked by the fact that Matos had close ties to the rural gentry at a time when the sugar economy was in a crisis due to the depressed price of sugar (and when merchants recently arrived from Portugal were gaining financial and social status) and by the fact that Matos had a degree in law and was therefore a "náufrago erudito" ("literate castaway") in a society characterized by low educational standards, by "farsa das instituições jurídicas" ("farcical juridical institutions") (Wisnik 15), and by the social contradictions that "se embrenham" ("penetrate") his poetry. These made it, as José Miguel Wisnik writes, a battlefield for the "luta de duas sociedades, cada uma delas absurda perante a outra" (18) ("struggle between two societies, each absurd in the eyes of the other"): one "saudada nostalgicamente" ("nostalgically yearned") in encomiastical visions, the other "amaldiçoada" ("cursed") (19) and represented parodically.

Matos's poetry is full of invectives against those who "não sabem governar sua cozinha,/e podem governar o mundo inteiro" (I:33) ("cannot govern their own kitchens/and can govern the whole world"), the judge who makes "o direito torto" (I:374–75) ("right into wrong"), the "fidalgo de solar" ("manor house lord") who steals "o ventre sustentar" ("to fill his belly"), the "donzela amancebada" ("kept damsel") who prefers "ter saia, que ser honrada" (I:35) ("finery to honesty"), the scribe who "mal lê" (I:376) ("can hardly read"), the abbot who "rouba as rendas do convento" (I:37) ("steals the monastery's revenue"), those who learn about "calundus" ("hexes") and "feitiços" ("jinxes") from runaway slaves (I:42), and a man who "deixa a mulher em couros,/e traz os filhos famintos" ("leaves his wife without a stitch/and his children famished") but whose mistress "há de andar como um palmito" ("must go about like a flowered palm frond") (I:50). At times the attacks are directed not at types but at specific human targets, as in the numerous caricatures of governor Antônio de Souza Menezes. Many of his satires are bitterly critical of Bahia, portrayed as the epitome of all vice; in some of them the region confesses "os pecados" ("the sins") it both "faz" ("commits") and "patrocina" ("sponsors"), so that it becomes "inferno" ("hell") "para os bons" ("to the good") and "para os maus paraíso" ("paradise to the evil"). Sometimes he contrasts the two aspects of "Sra. Dona Bahia" ("Mistress Bahia"), its "triste" ("melancholy") condition after it was ruined by "máquina mercante" ("the merchant machine") ("se a frota não traz nada,/por que razão leva tudo?" [I:339] ["if the fleet brings in nothing/why take everything away?"]). Bahia is as impoverished as the poet himself ("Pobre te vejo a ti, tu a mi empenhado" [I:333] ["Poor I find you, in arrears you find me"]), who believes that, like the other "filhos da terra" ("children of this land"), he is left behind while foreigners go "com tripa cheia" ("full-bellied"), merchants who "em Portugal são ratinhos/e cá no Brasil são gatos" (I:357) ("were as mice in Portugal/but in Brazil are changed to cats"), made rich at the expense of his once "nobre e opulenta cidade" ("noble and opulent city") and its "povo com pança oca" ("empty-bellied people"). "Que os brasileiros são bestas" ("Brazilians are beasts of burden"), he writes in another poem, "e estarão a trabalhar/toda a vida por manter/maganos de Portugal" (II:1172) ("and will forever be toiling/to keep in comfort and larded/these villainous Portuguese").

When, however, Gregório de Matos is exiled to Angola, the boundaries of his satire seem to expand so as to encompass the entire colony; at one point he writes: "Que me quer o Brasil, que me persegue?" (II:1163) ("What does Brazil want from me, that it should pursue me so?"). Here Bahia and Brazil function as embodiments of the traditional topos of the world upside down: a "terra tão grosseira e crassa" ("land so gross and crass"), a "cidade tão suja" ("city so filthy"), and an "pátria ingrata" ("ungrateful fatherland"), where "honram os mofinos" ("the miserly are flattered") and "mofam dos liberais" (II:1172) ("the freehanded are mocked"), where the "canalha perseguidora" ("persecuting scoundrels") expels "homens sábios" ("men of wisdom") who are "beneméritos" ("praiseworthy") from a land where nobility "consiste em muito dinheiro" (II:1172) ("rests on having money aplenty") rather than "no bom procedimento" ("on good conduct"). A land that is "avesso de todo o mundo,/só direita em se entortar" (II:1173) ("like all the world reversed/can be put to right only if un-crooked"). These reversals are used as an ordering principle, to assert, by means of antithesis, an "arte da prudência" (Hansen 1989, 107) ("art of prudence") and a "ideal hierárquico" (Hansen 1989, 30) ("hierarchical ideal"). This ideal excludes not only rogues, nouveau riche merchants, and foreigners, but also mulattos, blacks, Jews, Turks, "infiéis e outros gentios" ("infidels and other heathens"), and sodomites, all of whom, Matos believes, might threaten the integrity of the good order he describes, antithetically, through satire.

In Gregório de Matos, "com uma prática fundamentalmente integrativa" ("with his fundamentally integrative practice"), as João Adolfo Hansen writes, "a sátira emanava do lugar sagrado do rei-hipóstase de Deus" (Hansen 1999, 5) ("satire emanated from the sacred place of the king as hypostasis of God") and from a "tipologia semântica de virtudes e vícios" ("semantic typology of virtues and vices") that amounted in fact to "uma topologia pragmática de posições hierárquicas" (Hansen 1999, 6) ("a pragmatic topology of hierarchical positions") and the praise of the "virtudes heróicas" ("heroic virtues" [prudence and ingenuity]) "do perfeito cavaleiro cristão" ("of the perfect Christian knight"). Side by side with the depiction of Bahia, Brasil, Pernambuco ("pouco urbano" ["hardly urban"]) and Angola ("armazém de pena e dor" ["emporium of suffering and pain"]) as "mundos às avessas" ("worlds upside down"), inhabited by such types as mixed-bloods, misers, and heathens, together with the "excessos malditos" ("cursed excesses") of all orders, in Matos's satire one also finds poems concerned with the poet himself and his form of expression. In one of these, having passed "in dishabille"–in a rough coat and stocking cap–by his beloved's door, not knowing that wherever he saw Betica he was expected to act as though he were in "Corte" ("Court"), the poet says: "quero-me satirizar" (II:731) ("I want to satirize myself"). Then he calls himself a "magano" ("villain"), a "patife" ("scoundrel"), a "mariola" ("blackguard"), a "sátiro" ("satyr"), a "salvajola" ("savage"), and so on. But this has the reverse effect of acting as the assertion of an ideal of gentlemanliness and of a rule of good taste. In the same way, when he lists possible imperfections of his own literary method– "não falo em cultos modos,/mas em frase corriqueira" (I:306) ("I speak not in cultured modes,/but instead in homely phrases")–he simultaneously argues for the adequacy of the register he adopts ("a narração há de igualar ao caso" [I:366] ["the telling must be suited to the tale"]) to the purpose of opening up "a testa" ("the heads") of his interlocutors so as to "encaixar-vos, que é prudência" (I:368) ("to make you wise, which is prudent"). It was the duty of his "Musa praguejadora" ("cursing Muse") to tell "verdades" ("truths") like "água" ("water"), in such a way that "por que todos entendais" (I:368) ("all of you should understand").

But even these considerations of the rudeness of satirical language seem to point to a traditional rhetorical topos: that of the connection between truthfulness and straightforwardness, which underscores the "lugar institucional" ("institutional locus") from which seventeenth-century Brazilian satire seems to emerge, anchored in "repertórios de lugares-comuns, argumentos e formas da tradição retórico-poética e suas transformações locais" (Hansen 1989, 29) ("repertoires of commonplaces, arguments and forms of rhetorical-poetical tradition, and the local changes suffered by them"). Emphasizing that the satirical poet tends to "pirata do verso alheio" (Hansen 1989, 47) ("prey on other people's poetry") and rely on imitation, with the recombination of traditional models, motifs, types, and situations as his characteristic procedure of composition, João Adolfo Hansen defines the "sátira barroca produzida na Bahia" ("Baroque satire produced in Bahia") not as "oposição aos poderes constituídos de interditos morais e sexuais" (Hansen 1989, 29) ("opposition to the powers that be, though it violently attacks specific representatives of these powers," nor as "a liberator of moral and sexual prohibitions"), but rather as a "conjunto de lugares-comuns mais ou menos petrificados que se reativam num estilo engenhoso pelo investimento semântico local: misoginia, crítica à simonia, glutoneria, usura e luxúria do clero, crítica dos judeus, do dinheiro, do mundo às avessas, etc." (Hansen 1989, 30) ("set of more or less petrified commonplaces reactivated in an ingenious style through local semantic investment: misogyny, criticism of the clergy's simony, gluttony, usury and lust, criticism of Jews, money, the world upside down, etc."). These are meant as "correção das maneiras, da moral e da boa ordem política" ("correction of manners, morals, and good political order") and "interpretação da ocasião histórica em termos escolásticos" (Hansen 1989, 31) ("interpretation of the historical moment in scholastic terms").

Consideration of the rhetorical-institutional bases that partly shape colonial Baroque poetry also points to a reevaluation of two critical topoi regarding Matos's satire: the issue of "plagiarism" (debatable particularly when one takes into account the Baroque technique of permutation), usually brought up in connection with his appropriation of Quevedo and Góngora, and the problem of authorial attribution (which takes on a new dimension when one bears in mind the combinatorial character of these texts, their reactualization of poetical formulas). But if even the social tensions of colonial life and the conflicts of a "filho d'algo em apuros" ("gentleman in trouble") who "não tolera o comerciante forâneo nem o desenvolto mercador cristão novo" ("cannot suffer the foreign merchant or the uninhibited New Christian merchants"), the "netos de Caramuru" ("grandchildren of Caramuru") (i.e., descendants of Indians), or the "mestiços forros" (Bosi 101–6) ("mixed-blood freedmen"), the conflicts of a lawyer-poet connected to the sugarcane culture in a society marked by the sugar crisis, the weakening of local power, and the disrespect of the law, seem reshaped by the deformations and contrasts posed by a scholastic rationality (a presupposed poetical device), then it is perhaps possible to see, in its combinatorial method and in its appropriation of the Baroque problematic sense, the trail of a temporal plot in which rhetorical opposites point not only to the poet's ingenuity but also to the tense coexistence, in Matos's poetry, of asynchronous times and viewpoints.

In this sense, Matos's lyrical poetry may contribute to an understanding of the multitemporal perspective of his satire. Particularly relevant are three poems in which the subject, in a dialogue with various landscapes, contrasts the course of his life with that of a river. In one of them, a sonnet to the Caipe River (I:426–27), the lyrical voice establishes some correspondences (between the river's mouth and his own death and between the waters and shoals in the river and the poet's tears that mix with them) and searches for sympathy in the natural environment ("contra amor me dá socorro" ["against love it gives me succor"]), after he has been abandoned by "sua senhora" ("his lady"); on the other hand, he eventually acknowledges the futility of his pleas–"Suspende o curso, ó Rio" ("Suspend thy course, O River"), "Não corras lisonjeiro" ("Flow not so flattering"), "Não corras, não te alegres, não te rias" (I:426) ("Flow not, joy not, laugh not")–and of such a unity between poet and nature ("Que não é bem, que tuas águas frias,/Sendo o pranto chorado dos meus olhos,/Tenham que rir em minhas agonias" [II:426] [It is not proper that your waters cold,/Being the tears that pour out of mine eyes,/Should laugh even as I grieve"]). In this poem the change in the poet's life is in sad contrast with the impossibility of changing the river's course; in another poem, this one concerning the "fluxo e refluxo da maré" (II:768) ("ebb and flow

of the tide"), it is precisely the landscape that is transformed ("Muda-se o tempo, e suas temperanças./Até o céu se muda, a terra, os mares,/E tudo está sujeito a mil mudanças" [II:768] ["The weather changes, and its mildness too./So does the welkin, the earth and the sea,/Subject are all to mutability"]), in contrast with the poet's apparently unchanging isolation and fate ("Só eu, que todo o fim de meus pesares/Eram de algum minguante as esperanças,/Nunca o minguante vi de meus azares" [II:768] ["Myself alone, the end of all whose sorrows/Were ever the expiration of some hope,/Have never seen the ebb of my mishaps"]), reinforced by this distinction. They also are reinforced by the opposition–in this particular case, not suggested by the love motif–between "corrente arrebatada de um caudaloso rio" ("the impetuous current of a mighty river") ("Vai-te, mas tornas a vir" ["Thou goest, but ever returnest"], "vazas, e tornas a encher" ["thou ebbest, and flowest again"]) and "o curso da vida humana" ["the course of human life"] ("eu vou, e não torno mais" ["I go, and come not back"], "tudo em mim é acabar" ["all in me is extinction"]) that was to provide the theme for another dialogue between poet and river (II:769–72). Here another changing landscape contrasts not with apparent immutability, as in the description of the tide, but with a distinct form of movement without the cyclical rhythm, the returns, that are typical of the river, characterized instead by dissipation and by the awareness of mortality. Thus the time of the subject is different from that of the landscape, so that these dialogues with the tide and the river function as a sort of *ars moriendi*. This trait directly points to the Baroque universe; however, it also underscores not only an overlapping of times, a division in the temporal consciousness that organizes them, but also a perceptible asynchrony between poet and nature.

This asynchrony became a fundamental component in the makeup of Matos's satirical perspective. Unlike the colonial chroniclers, and in contrast with the descriptive perspective of many of his contemporaries (a good example of which is Botelho de Oliveira's [1636–1711] "À Ilha de Maré" ["Maré Isle"]), Matos "rejeit[a] a contemplação anestesiada do natural" ("rejects the anaesthetized contemplation of the natural"), "dando as costas para o natural" ("turns his back on nature"), as Antônio Dimas observes (345), and concentrates instead on "vasculhar os interstícios da sociedade" ("rummaging in the nooks and crannies of society") and "encarar o país a partir da sociedade mal-ajambrada que aqui se constituía" ("considering the country in terms of the shabby society being established here"). To a certain extent, this option explains the importance of the satirical diction in Matos's work. It was reinforced by the possibility of inserting in such miscellaneous genre the various times that coexisted in the colonial temporal dimension, in addition to the tensions of forms of cultural expression that seem to emerge outside an autonomous cultural field.

For if Matos's poetry seems to rely on models and motifs taken from the European tradition, on Christian norms and Baroque rhetoric, and if in his explicit appropriations of Francisco de Quevedo (1580–1645) and Luis de Góngora's (1561–1627) poems or in combinatorial exercises based on them, he attempts to display his own command of the discursive rules of his time, his texts nonetheless seem to contain an internal destabilizing movement beyond what can be ascribed to the Baroque. This movement is apparent in his meter (which conjoins traditional Portuguese versification, conspicuous in the dominance of *redondilha maior*, heptasyllabic verse, and the so-called "new measure," the Italian *decassilabo*), in his vocabulary (which combines a cultured European register with morphological and semantic archaisms, words from Tupi and African languages, vulgar language, and Brazilianisms), in his use of a register that undermines the boundaries between oral and written languages, and in his various ways of visualizing the dissimilitude to be found in the range of the apparently similar. Hence Matos's variants of Spanish Baroque lyricism, his taste for ambiguities arising from prosodic variants or puns based on homophony, in which clichéd phrases suddenly yield a quite different meaning, as Augusto de Campos observed in his analysis of "Regra de Bem Viver" (93–97) ["Rules for a Good Life"].

This also explains Matos's simultaneous use of idealization and colloquialism within a single love poem, a mixture that generates "uma alteração muito expressiva do lirismo amoroso em língua portuguesa" ("a very expressive alteration of the Portuguese-language love lyric"), violating, as José Guilherme Merquior notes, "as convenções literárias que o repeliam desde o verso dos trovadores" ("the literary conventions that had disallowed [simultaneity of idealization and colloquialism] ever since troubadour poetry") and desublimating "a grandiloqüência do verso erótico dos melhores autores seiscentistas" (21) ("the grandiloquence of the erotic verse of the best seventeenth-century poets"). This can be seen, for instance, in the sonnet analyzed by Merquior concerning a "sonho em flaso" ("false dream"), addressed to the mulatto woman Custódia (and derived from Quevedo's *Ay, Floralba! Soñé que te . . . dirélo?* ["Oh, Floralba! I dreamt that . . . shall I say it?"]), in which Matos "equilibra as metáforas *nobres*" ("balances the *noble* metaphors") against "a vivacidade da narrativa e a reflexão prosaica, desidealizada" (Merquior 21) ("vivid narrative and prosaic, unidealized reflection"). This sort of interplay of registers and of tension between the poetic and the prosaic was to be expressively exploited in a systematic manner in Brazilian lyricism only in the modern period. In the case of Matos's poetry, it seems to indicate that his emphasis on satire is no mere rhetorical device; rather, satire in his hands becomes a protean form, reluctant, sometimes rhythmically heterogeneous and sometimes conjoining apparently incompatible dictions, and the tensions between them seem to dialogue with those that characterized the exercise of cultural activities in a discouraging milieu, and with the colonial historical experience in general.

Epistolary Satire

By the eighteenth century, the dominant themes in Brazilian satire are the cultural milieu, education, the functioning of Portuguese universities, the satirical genre itself, and one of its relatively new forms, the heroicomic poem. Such is the case of several texts by Manuel Inácio da Silva Alvarenga (1749–1814)–for instance, "Às Artes" ["The Arts"], which describes the "os dias horrorosos/de escuros nevoeiros" (1864, I:331) ("awful days/of murky fog") before Pombal's reforms, a time when "as artes gemeram desprezadas" (1864, I:331) ("arts did moan, neglected") and their later resurrection, even "até nestes confins do Novo Mundo" (1864, I:331) ("in this distant corner of the New World"); or "Os vícios" ["The Vices"], a satire concerning the history of satire; or *O desertor das letras* [1774; Deserter of Letters], about a group of runaway students in Coimbra–in the preface to which the author defines and defends the heroicomic genre. Another instance of this is a satire in the same genre, *O Reino da Estupidez* [1785; The Kingdom

of Stupidity], by Francisco de Melo Franco (1757–1823), on the revolt of Stupidity against Progress and its attempt, aided by Fanaticism, Hypocrisy, and Superstition, to reconquer Portugal. Also noteworthy are José Bonifácio's (1763–1838) "Epístola escrita de Coimbra no começo da primavera de 1785" ["Epistolary Written from Coimbra at the Beginning of Spring of 1785"] in which "Estupidez afável" ("affable Stupidity") clashes with "Verdade espavorida" ("frightened Truth"); "O Entrudo" ["The Intruder"], a satire attributed to Basílio da Gama in which, upon the occasion of the singer Anna Zamparine's appearance in Lisbon, the poet attacks some of those who wrote poems to her and "a irresistível raça dos Pedantes" ("the irresistible race of Pedants"), who, "à custa de maus versos" ("on the strength of their bad verses"), of their "orelhas de aço, tímpanos de bronze" ("steel ears and bronze eardrums"), see themselves as "Homeros e Virgílios" ("Homers and Virgils"); and the "Carta dirigida a meu amigo João de Deus Pires Ferreira, em que lhe descrevo a minha viagem por mar até Gênova" [1790; "A Letter Addressed to my Friend João de Deus Pires Ferreira, in which I Describe My Voyage by Sea to Genova"], where Sousa Caldas, alternating prose and verse, varying the meter and combining "o elemento ideológico com o elemento fabulativo" (Candido 1993a, 211) ("ideology and fabulation"), denounces "o sistema de educação que os Europeus têm adotado" ("the educational system that Europeans have been adopting"), which "extraviado do caminho das ciências" ("strays from the path of the sciences"), being based on "decorar coisas muitas vezes inúteis" ("the memorization of often useless things") and on knowledge of mythology, "recheado mais de nomes que de coisas" ("containing more names than things").

One noticeable fact about some of these satires is that they are addressed to a specific person; in fact, some of them are explicitly epistolary. Such is the case of José Bonifácio's epistle to Francisco de Melo Franco, of Sousa Caldas's to Pires Ferreira, and also of another work, not a satire but a reflection on stylistics and a panegyric on the "laws of nature," from Silva Alvarenga to Basílio da Gama. Another example is Tomás Antônio Gonzaga's *Cartas chilenas*, a satire on Luís da Cunha Meneses's administration of Vila Rica, probably written between 1786 and May 1789. The work is made up of thirteen letters in blank verse, addressed to Doroteu, a friend supposedly in Spain, by Critilo (a name that alludes to Baltasar Gracián's *Criticón*), concerning the transgressions and misconduct of Fanfarrão Minésio, governor of a "Strange Kingdom," a fictional Chile. Appended to these letters is an epistle to Critilo by Cláudio Manuel da Costa. Epistolary form in Gonzaga's *Cartas chilenas* seems to function as an "importante recurso retórico" ("important rhetorical device"), as Joaci Pereira Furtado writes, in that it implies that there is a relevant subject to be discussed, allowing the adoption of "um tom mais informal e intimista" ("a more informal and intimate tone") and opening the way "para o exercício da naturalidade preconizada pelos cânones poéticos da época" (35) ("to the exercise of the naturalness recommended by the poetic canons of the day"). But if one takes into account other representatives in eighteenth-century Brazil of satirical letters as a genre, and, more generally, other texts with a specific addressee, these functions are expanded. According to Antonio Candido, "grande parte da poesia setecentista é endereçada, é uma conversa poética, quando não é francamente comemorativa" ("much of eighteenth-century poetry is directed to an addressee, amounting to poetic conversation, even when it is not explicitly celebratory"), a fact that points to a "cunho altamente sociável" (1975, I:52–53) ("highly sociable tone"), "um amplo movimento de elogio mútuo, graças ao qual maracavam-se e reforçavam-se as posições dos membros" (1975, I:82) ("an ample movement of mutual praise, which affirmed and reinforced the positions of the members").

The use of an addressee signals a search for alliances, not just against the target of the satire but also in the constitution of a common perspective of meaning. That is why José Bonifácio indirectly mentions *O Reino da Estupidez* and its author, Melo Franco, whose satires are said to be "worthy of Pope," in his 1785 "Epístola escrita de Coimbra" ["Epistolary Written from Coimbra"]. Another example is Doroteu's reply to Critilo, an affirmation of the didactic purpose of satire, "que nos defeitos de um castiga a tantos" (Gonzaga 48) ("which the faults of one chastises many") and makes us "buscar nos fazes/da cândida virtude a sã doutrina" (Gonzaga 48) ("search in the workings/of chastest virtue for the sound doctrine"). Here the author seems to echo Gonzaga's contemporary comments on instruction through exposure of "ações indignas" ("unseemly actions") in the "Dedicatória," and his observations, in the "Prólogo," concerning the possibility of an exemplary caricature "such as Fanfarrão Minésio" being able to "corrigir a desordem de um Governador despótico" (36) ("correct the disorder of a despotic Governor").

The same could be said of the frequent use of apostrophe, of direct references to the interlocutor, and of dramatization of possible dialogues, throughout the series of Critilo's letters. "Que é isso Doroteu? Tu já retiras/Os olhos do papel? Tu já desmaias? (Gonzaga 94) ("How now, Doroteu? Dost already take/This sheet away from thy sight? Feel'st thou faint?") the poet asks at the end of the third letter. "Amigo Doroteu" ("Friend Doroteu"), he writes in the fifth letter, "Ah! Tu não podes/pesar o desconcerto desta Carta" (115) ("Oh that thou couldst conceive/The derangement of this Letter"). In another passage, Critilo simultaneously affirms the distance of the addressee and the possibility of reaching him through his letter:

e o teu Critilo,
Que não encontra aqui com quem murmure,
Quando só murmurar lhe pede o gênio,
Pega na pena, e desta sorte voa,
De cá tão longe a murmurar contigo.

and thy Critilo,
Not finding any here to whisper to,
When whispering is all my spirit will,
Takes up his pen, and thus away he flies
From his far nook, to whisper unto you.

(82)

In this way, satire seems to be transformed into a form of poetic conversation and of asserting the satirical persona's group bonds, reinforced by references to mutual friends: "o nosso Amigo Alceu" ("our Friend Alceu"), "o velho Altimedonte" ("old Altimedonte"), "o nosso bom Dirceu" ("our good Dirceu"), "o terno Floridoro" ("the gentle Floridoro"), "o nosso Damião" ("our Damião"), "o gordo Josefino" ("fat Josefino"). The list of names seems to stress the intimacy between Critilo and Doroteu, while the association of some of them with reading or writing activities also affirms social identification as members of a literate set.

Altimedonte, for instance, is described as handling "os grandes, grossos livros" ("the large, thick books") and in terms of "c'os dedos inda sujos de tabaco/ajunta ao mau processo muitas folhas" (81–82) ("his fingers with tobacco soiled and stained/to the foul lawsuit adds many a leaf"); Dirceu "metido no capote a ler gostoso/o seu Virgílio, o seu Camões, e Tasso" (82) ("wrapped in his cloak cozily sits and reads/his Virgil, his Camões, and his Tasso"). The narrator describes himself as "absorbed" in his "já roto, destroncado Ovídio" (198) ("torn and dismembered Ovid"), and several times explicitly refers to his own identity as a writer. He constantly mentions the act of writing, speaks of taking up and sharpening his pen, folding the paper, "compor sentidos versos" ("composing heartfelt verses"), and says his hand trembles with exhaustion. In his second letter, he describes his house, saying that there are no "colchas matizadas" ("multicolored bedspreads") and "dourados leitos" ("golden beds") in "casa mal provida de um Poeta" (66) ("a Poet's badly-appointed home"). Later on he tells Doroteu about a dinner party he failed to attend, imagining it in detail "só para escrever mais uma carta" ("only to write one letter more"), and curses "o vício de um poeta" ("the poet's vice") that "priva/de encher o seu bandulho pelo gosto/de fazer quatro versos" (97) ("deprives him/of opportunities to eat his fill/for the sake of writing four lines of verse").

But Critilo does not deal only with the material aspects of writing and the poet's everyday existence. In addition to his mention of pens, paper and reading, his assertions of his identity as a *littérateur*, he occasionally expounds his poetic precepts. Ronald Polito, in his study of Gonzaga (195–236), focuses on some of these principles: the tension between reason and feeling, a standard of beauty based on the "idea of truth" ("Não sei, prezado Amigo, o que te escrevo./Só sei que o que te escrevo são verdades" [68] ["I know not, dear Friend, what I write to you./I only know that all I write is true"], Critilo says in the second letter), the moral concept of satire (meant to stir up indignation, not laughter), the Horatian model present in the constant "identificação da poesia à pintura" (52) ("identification of poetry with painting"), in the "compromisso entre imitação e originalidade" ("compromise between imitation and originality"), and in the ideal of "sábia proporção" (84) ("wise proportion"), conspicuous in its absence in the caricature of Fanfarrão Minésio.

It is by inversion also that Critilo sometimes depicts himself as a *littérateur*. The quintessential antimodel here is Robério, a poet in the service of Minésio, whose caricature is marked by disproportional traits that contrast with those of a model (wide face versus short stature, thin legs versus fat belly, wide shoulders versus short neck, Parnassus versus lame verses). It is relevant to Gonzaga's process of self-awareness that even Fanfarrão Minésio should be seen, at a certain point, as a sort of fake *littérateur*, with his "virgem livraria" ("virgin library"), his handwriting consisting of "rabiscos" ("scrawls"), his "frase moura" (Polito 208) ("Moorish turn of phrase"). Because the formation of a cultural identity for men of letters in eighteenth-century Brazil included the image of "como cidadão, homem da polis, a quem incumbe difundir as *luzes*" (Candido 1985, 79) ("a citizen, a man of the polis, whose task it is to disseminate *Enlightenment*"), it makes sense that even Critilo's antagonist should be portrayed as a combination of *littérateur* and politician.

On the one hand, the attacks against Minésio seem to reinforce, by means of satire, the incipient process by means of which men of letters achieved a degree of autonomy in eighteenth-century Luso-Brazilian society, through association with Pombal's patronage, the rise of academies and a movement of "laicização da inteligência" (Candido 1975, I:169–74) ("secularization of intelligence"). But they also can be seen in quite a different light if emphasis is placed on their implicit praise of the "old habits" and the hierarchical ideal and loyalty to the Portuguese crown (not respected by the Governor), and the privileges of the Old State (before Pombal's reforms). For although "o século XVIII luso-brasileiro" ("the Luso-Brazilian eighteenth century")—as João Adolfo Hansen observes—"assiste ao desenvolvimento de instituições letradas surgidas no XVII" ("saw the rise of literary institutions created in the seventeenth century") and the appearance of "um extremamente tímido mercado metropolitano para as obras" ("an extremely reduced metropolitan market for their works"), which contributed "para formação da identidade social dos letrados" ("to the formation of the social identity of littérateurs"), there still lived on the "velhos padrões hierárquicos do Antigo Estado, fundados nos privilégios do pacto de sujeição . . . que une rei e súditos como 'corpo místico'" ("old hierarchical patterns of the Old State, founded on the privileges of the pact of subjection . . . that unites king and subjects in a 'mystical body'"), functioning "como limite da autonomia autoral e estética que o letrado e seu produto possam ter" (Hansen 1997, 17) ("as a limit on whatever authorial and aesthetic autonomy the littérateur and his product may have").

The nature of this limit is not exclusively aesthetic or political, but also has to do with implicit criteria for the *littérateur*'s self-identification and group belonging. These criteria range from the rejection of those who express themselves "em tosca frase do país somente" ("in the coarse language of the land alone"), as is said of Robério in the *Cartas chilenas*, or of the "mísero copista" ("miserable copyist") and the "rimador grosseiro" ("crude rhymester") mentioned by Silva Alvarenga, to rejection of motifs ("o que se fez vulgar perdeu a estimação" ["what has turned common no longer has worth"], writes Alvarenga) and genres, such as the epigram, mocked not only by Gonzaga but also by Silva Alvarenga, who in his epistle to Basílio da Gama criticizes "alambicadas frases e agudos epigramas" ("precious phrases and sharp epigrams") in favor of naturalness of expression (1977, 175–79).

Another aspect of this limit can be seen in the case of another late-eighteenth-century poet, Joaquim José da Silva (1775–1825), known as Sapateiro Silva (Silva the Cobbler), who from the "Arcadian" viewpoint simply could have never been seen as a *littérateur*. His sonnets and *glosas* functioned, in fact, as a sort of counter-literature that often relied precisely on satire of the literary hierarchies and conventions of the time. But Silva also made use of the conventions of satire itself, such as hybridization of people and fruit (thus he speaks of a certain "Também se acho certo salafrário/Com cara mais inchada que turanja" ["scoundrel/Whose face is all swollen, like a grapefruit"], qtd. in Süssekind and Valença 132), reduction of human attributes to things (emotion converted into the clapper of a bell), self-satirization (he depicts himself in "fralda rota" ["ragged shirttails"] and "chinelo" ["slippers"], as "chavelho velho" ["old and doddering"], full of "mazela" ["infirmities"], "comendo caldo em panela" ["eating broth out of the pot"]), and caricature (as the following description of a nose in one of his *décimas*: "Um tal frade frei Gregório/Nas ventas do seu naria/Tem um letreiro que diz:/*Alminhas do Purgatório*" ["There's a certain Friar Gregory/In whose nostrils is a sign/Bearing this inscription fine:/*Little Souls in Purgatory*"]; see Süssekind and Valença 151). He also works with traditional formulas, resorting to, for instance, mythological figures and references to Greco-Roman civilization so dear to neo-Classicism: Dido, Hero, Plutarch, the Cyclops, Eros, the Roman Capitol, and Mars are found in his texts. But they appear side by side with extremely prosaic references to Afro-Brazilian dances, the sidewalks of the Lapa district of Rio, or the backlands of Pernambuco, and to such everyday characters and situations of his time as Friar Tobias, a pastry cook, Father Paulo, a fisherman, Friar Honório, the Easter Saturday street celebrations, promenades about the city, and festivals.

The same might be said of his poems addressed to specific persons, but in a quite different sense from their counterparts by the Arcadian poets. One of these poems is a complaint motivated by a badly made pair of breeches, sent to a "Master Tailor" said to be in fact a "botcher." An ironical sonnet explains why he failed to deliver on time a pair of women's shoes, and promises to do so "in three Hail Marys." Unlike the addressed poems of the Arcadians, these texts have nothing to do with mutual praising or affirmation of a group identity. Instead, they underscore an antagonism between two kinds of tradesman—the cobbler and the tailor—and between the tradesman and his customers, such as the girl with the satin shoes, whom he threatens with "as botas do Grão-Duque de Aquitânia" (qtd. in Süssekind and Valença 131) ("the Grand-Duke of Aquitaine's boots").

Another appropriation with inversion of meaning occurs when Silva compares sonnets to "pares de sapatos" (in Süssekind and Valença 128) ("pairs of shoes") or to last evening's "ceia" ("supper"), with the qualification that "molhinho de lampreia" ("a bit of lamprey sauce") might be more appreciated (qtd. in Süssekind and Valença 130). The satirical operation lies less in these prosaic analogies than in the use of a plebeian vocabulary and humorous nonsense in fixed poetic forms with rhythmic structures that are elementary, permutational, and deliberately poor. Silva himself called such operations, in one of his sonnets, his "desencaixes meus" ("displacements") underscoring the unidealistic singularity of "tal humor" ("such humor"):

> Ao menos o bom Rio de Janeiro
> Não possuiu um gênio desta casta,
> Por mais e mais que corra o seu roteiro.
> Tem possuído alguns de afasta-afasta:
> Porém nunca um Poeta sapateiro,
> Que tenha um tal humor; adeus, que basta.
>
> In Rio de Janeiro, as I know it,
> Ne'er has a genius of this kind there been,
> As far back as its history may show it.
> A few of little consequence, I ween,
> But not one both a cobbler and a Poet
> Endowed with such a humor as I mean

(in Süssekind and Valença 130)

This satirical nonsense functions as a sort of counter-genre, particularly when contrasted with the concept of satire adopted by the Arcadians and in the heroicomic literature of the period.

This point is brought sharply into focus when Silva's poetry is contrasted with two passages from the *Cartas chilenas*. Critilo advises Doroteu: "Não esperes, amigo, não esperes,/por mais galantes casos que te conte,/mostrar no teu ssemblante um ar de riso" (114) ("Expect not, dearest friend, however many/Gay anecdotes I may perchance tell thee,/Aught like a smile be imprinted on thy face"), stressing the seriousness and the moral and didactic character of his satire, which is not meant to raise a laugh. "Não hás de/Duvidar do que leres, bem que sejam/Desordens, que preçam impossíveis" (Gonzaga 200) ("Thou shalt not/Doubt what thou readest, though it be such rank/Disorder that it seem hard to believe"), he writes in the tenth letter, emphasizing his commitment to truth even to the point of implausibility. The apparent disorder is to be submitted to Critilo's reordering judicial and hierarchical perspective, whereas Silva's displacements are to remain as such. The *Cartas chilenas* are offered as serious satire, quite different from the cobbler-poet's singular "humor."

In Silva's *glosas* and humorous sonnets both the juridical-religious sphere, in which Critilo opposes Minésio, and the literary plane, on which a literary identification is defined in the *Cartas chilenas*, are presented as absurd elements among others. Friar Tobias is a pastry cook; Friar Gregório has a sign hanging from his nose; Friar Honório has a taste for lamprey sauce; the Judge of Santarém "estala da paixão" ("is bursting with passion"). The newspapers report "que pariu a porca um burro" (qtd. in Süssekind and Valença 146) ("that a sow gave birth to an ass"); the traditions "se dão a ler às Nações/num grosso livro de fólio" ("handed down to all Nations/In a thick folio book") mention "um pé de cajuru" ("a *cajuru* palm tree") growing "do Monte Sião" ("by Mount Zion"), Methuselah scorning two hundred years of lifetime, "Deus vendado" ("God blindfolded") "com a funda de Davi" ("with David's sling"), comes from the Orient, a Spanish midwife "montada num baiacu" ("riding on the back of a blowfish"), one "Admiral Balão" giving a "tremendo cachação" ("solid spanking") to his daughter Floripes "no tempo dos três Filipes" ("in the time of the three Philips") (qtd. in Süssekind and Valença 149–50).

Thus at the time when an articulated cultural system was being formed and an incipient process of literary self-awareness was taking place in Colonial Brazil, in the late eighteenth century, these mechanisms of identification also were being lacerated, as evidenced by the asynchrony between the literary practices of Silva the Cobbler and those of his contemporaries, the Arcadians. So it comes as no surprise that, in contrast with Critilo's constant authorial self-portraits or Silva Alvarenga's self-justifying reflections on art or the heroicomic genre, Silva should eschew not only depersonalization and pastoral names but also the very possibility of univocal identification as a poet. He defines himself, analogously to the satirical mixture he practices, as a hybrid: "Primaz da Parnasal sapataria" ("Archbishop of the Parnassus Shoe Store"), "Poeta Sapateiro" ("Cobbler Poet"), "Todos me lêem nas costas–sapateiro" ("'Tis written on my very back: a cobbler"). This double nature partly explains his choice, in the sphere of satire, of a form contrary to "unity" and "hierarchization" (Ávila 187), such as nonsense; it also further complicates the already problematic "situação do intelectual de cultura européia num país semibárbaro" (Candido 1975, I:65) ("position of the intellectual with a European education in a semibarbarous country"), which is how eighteenth-century Brazilian *littérateurs* seemed to see themselves. This complication, however, was to turn into a concrete factor of literary practice, particularly by means of the "choque entre formas opostas de visualização" (Costa Lima 425) ("shock between opposite forms of visualization") that was to characterize the poetic experience of Sousândrade, the "desidentificação sistemática de si mesmo" ("systematic self-deidentification") and the "idéias e formas à disposição de um homem culto do tempo" ("ideas and forms at the disposal of a cultured man of the period") which in this way "ficam relativizadas (e também estereotipadas e barateadas)" (Schwarz 1990, 32) ("are relativized [and also

stereotyped and cheapened]"). This movement was to become a formal principle of the narrator-character in Machado de Assis's works, beginning with *Memórias póstumas de Brás Cubas*.

"Epitaph of What I Have Been"

Thus, in Brazilian literate culture, satirical devices seem to have had the recurrent function of providing writers with self-identification and literary self-awareness in the midst of the dilemmas of the colonial historical experience. This can be seen, with the corresponding differences, in the seventeenth-century body of work attributed to Gregório de Matos and in the heroicomic poetry of the eighteenth century, which is commented on, at a certain remove, by the humorous sonnets and *décimas* of Silva the Cobbler. However, there was a certain formal diversification, an expansion of the range of the critical effects of this means of expression, particularly once a true literary system had been established: Hence, the dissemination of satire in the eighteenth century, when the tensions between particularism and cosmopolitanism, regional singularization and universalistic affirmation, and redefinitions of the national, local and globalizing trend came sharply into view, functioning not only as privileged motifs but also exerting pressure on the formal plane within texts, bringing about disjunction, hybridization, and temporal disturbances no longer accidental but explicit and purposeful, transformed into structural principles. It is then only natural that two of the periods in which the formal multiplicity of Brazilian satire was most marked were Romanticism (from the 1830s to the 1870s) and Modernism (from the 1920s to the 1940s). These two periods, as Antonio Candido notes in "Literatura e Cultura de 1900 a 1945" [1985; "Literature and Culture from 1900 to 1945"], "inspirados no exemplo europeu" ("inspired by the European example"), "representam fases culminantes de particularismo literário na dialética do local e do cosmopolita" (1985, 112) ("are culminating phases of literary particularism in the dialectics of the local and the cosmopolitan"). In both periods, the mixed language of satire seems to have played a significant role in the search for "um tipo ao mesmo tempo local e universal de expressão" (Candido 1985, 121) ("a form of expression that was simultaneously local and universal").

This is quite evident in some of the most characteristic Modernist devices. One of these is the juxtaposition of archaic, folk, and popular material with modern artistic processes, a strategy adopted in such works as Mário de Andrade's (1893–1945) *Macunaíma* (1928), Raul Bopp's (1898–1984) *Cobra Norato* (1931), and Oswald de Andrade's "Brazilwood" poetry. Another is the parodistic intertextual dialogue of the kind used particularly by Oswald, Mário, and Alcântara Machado (1901–1935) in the prose of the 1920s. Yet another is the macaronic text of Juó Bananére (pseudonym Alexandre Ribeiro Marcondes Machado; 1892–1933) in his "Cartas d'Abax'O Piques" (a satirical political column based on a suggestion by Oswald de Andrade) in the magazine *O Pirralho*, and in such books as *Galabaro* and the anthology *La Divina Increnca* [1915; The Divine Muddle]. In the anthology, the author does macaronic spoofs of classical Brazilian writers (Machado de Assis in "Círgolo Viziozo" ["Vicious Circle"], Gonçalves Dias in "Migna Terra" ["My Land"], Casimiro de Abreu [1839–1860] in "Os Meus Otto Anno" ["My Eight Years"], Olavo Bilac [1865–1918] in "Uvi Strella" ["Listen to Strella"], and their foreign models (Luis de Camões [1524?–1580] in "Sunetto Crassico" ["Classic 'Sunnet'"], Edgar Allan Poe

[1809–1849] in "O Gorvo" ["The Raven"]), and also on the Modernists (see his "Sunetto Futuriste" ["Futurist 'Sunnet'"]). He also mocked "a linguagem dos jornais italianos publicados em São Paulo" (Chalmers 209) ("the language of the newspapers published in Italian in São Paulo") at the time, providing humorous comments on the growing political role of Italian immigrants, the increasing affluence of Italian-Paulistas and the social ambiguities that characterized the early decades of the twentieth century in Brazil. The three strategies–parody, collage of contradictory elements and macaronic text–seem to point directly to a temporal tension (updating, revision of the past) and distinct dictions within the range of Modernist satirical expression.

A similarly significant example is the *poema-piada* (joke poem), an anti-lyrical form of poetic writing that is typical of Modernism and its critical mockery of academicism and the nineteenth-century literary canon that remained the official standard in the early decades of twentieth-century Brazil. This form, a product of the increasing tendency towards prosaism and synthesis that characterized Brazilian poetry in the 1920s and 1930s, also underscored in its own unique way the process of satirical hybridization, juxtaposing oral and written registers, street slang and bookish language, the commonplace and the literary, and the collective and the individual. (See **Figure 2**.) Also, the joke poem with its explicit humor and formal compression expressed the emphasis on a critical awareness of the possibilities of the cultural praxis of Brazil at that time.

In nineteenth-century culture, the dissemination and diversification of satire–from comedies and satirical novels to outright political attacks, from the "poema miscelânea" ("miscellaneous poem") to "disparates rimados" ("rhymed nonsense"), from burlesque quatrains to literary hoaxes–seem to function, as we have seen, as a kind of critical counterpart of the development of an "articulado" ("articulated") literary system "de escritores, obras e leitores ou auditores, reciprocamente atuantes, dando lugar ao fenômeno capital da formação de uma tradição literária" (Candido 1985, 90) ("of writers, works, and readers or listeners, acting reciprocally on one another, giving rise to the crucial phenomenon of the formation of a literary tradition") in the country. Although conventional historiography attributes to the second Romantic generation a sort of monopoly on satire, the self-assertion of Romanticism and of some of its characteristic discursive strategies from the 1830s and onward seems to include a corresponding movement toward self-caricature.

Take, for instance, the literal reports concerning travels to or around Brazil, such as the Visconde de Taunay's (1843–1899) trips or Gonçalves Dias's expedition to the Negro River, or Varnhagen's (1816–1878) 1840 romanced paraphrase of Pero Vaz Caminha's fifteenth-century letter *Crônica do descobrimento do Brasil* [Chronicle of the Discovery of Brazil], or the countless publications and republications of travel journals and colonial descriptive treatises (such as those by Pero de Magalhães Gândavo [d. 1576], Pero Lopes de Sousa [1500–1539], André João Antonil [1650–1716] or Fernão Cardim [d. 1625]) of the earlier half of the nineteenth century, or the footnotes full of references to this descriptive literature that can be found in José de Alencar's (1829–1877) Indianist novels. These examples are countered by a series of contemporary texts, from Araújo Porto-Alegre's fanciful adventures of Bonifácio de Amarante to Sousândrade's wandering *Guesa*; from Álvares de Azevedo's "O Poema do Frade" ["The

Figure 2.

A OBSESSÃO DO SABIO

"A obsessão do sabio" ["Intellectual obsession"], an example of mockery of the intellectual's self-importance. (Archive of the author)

Monk's Poem"], in which a "narrador-cavaleiro andante" ("knight-errant-narrator") is involved in a "peregrinação pelos terrenos dos diversos gêneros literários" ("pilgrimage through the territories of the diverse literary genres"), as Cilaine Alves observes (Alves 169), to the constant digressions of the "narrador-cronista" ("chronicler-narrator") of *Um passeio pela cidade do Rio de Janeiro* [A Stroll Through the City of Rio de Janeiro] and of the "sobrinho-do-tio" ("uncle's nephew") in *A carteira de meu tio* [My Uncle's Wallet], two works by Joaquim Manuel de Macedo.

Also, the first half of the nineteenth century was marked by novels and satires on the novel, the formation and deformation of the new genre. Macedo himself, whose *A moreninha* [1844; The Little Brunette] was a landmark in the establishing of the novel in Brazil, wrote some humorous, destabilizing narratives that pointed in the direction of other more digressive and meandering forms of composition. This was done particularly through the combination of weekly news and sketchy fictional plot in his column published in the *Jornal do Commercio* and through the combination of an unreliable narrator and caricature of a local *littérateur* in *A carteira de meu tio* and *Memórias do sobrinho de meu tio*, as well as in *A luneta mágica* [1868; The Magic Telescope], a book characterized by optical and moral deformations of perspective. Also relevant here is José de Alencar's humorous version of the historical novel–the genre he himself had developed both in his Indianist narratives and in a book such as *As minas de prata* [1865–1866; The Silver Mines]–in his "Alfarrábios" [1873; "Second-Hand Books"], particularly in *O Garatuja* [1873; The Scribbler].

Another contrast is established between dissemination of historicism and ironical linguistic and stylistic archaism, as well as the historical imposture of an invented author Friar Antão supposed to have written Gonçalves Dias's *Sextilhas de Frei Antão*. This text, a sort of "ensaio filológico" ("philological essay"), seems to be a direct response to Romantic medievalism, the "tendência genealógica" ("genealogical tendency") (to employ Antonio Candido's phrase) of Brazilian Romanticism, as well as history's privileged, central position in the nineteenth-century hierarchy of discourses. History, in fact, was given pride of place in Gonçalves Dias's own projects: Since 1847 he had been planning a "History of the Jesuits," for which, however, he went no further than compiling references and writing down a very few notes. The same tendency is apparent in some of his historiographic writings published in the journal of the Instituto Histórico e Geográfico Brasileiro, in his book *Brasil e Oceania* [Brazil and Oceania] and also in a historical play such as *Leonor de Mendonça*.

Equally characteristic of the dissemination of this satirizing process in nineteenth-century Brazilian culture is, as we have seen, the effect of the close relationship between literary production and visual humor, a consequence of the fact that a significant number of the writers of the period contributed to illustrated journals. This is another aspect in which Brazilian Romanticism and Modernism are similar. Just as there is a close relation between satirical writing and the cartoons of Henrique Fleuiss, Angelo Agostini, Pinheiro Guimarães, Rafael Bordalo Pinheiro, Flumen Junius, and others in the nineteenth century, the Modernist generation was clearly influenced by such illustrators as Antônio Paim Vieira, Emiliano Di Cavalcanti in his early work as magazine cartoonist and illustrator, and the caricaturists Belmonte (Benedito Bastos Barreto) and Voltolino (see Belluzo) and his work in such publications as *O Pirralho, O Parafuso,* and *O Saci,* the illustrated characters who carried on a direct dialogue with the characters in the writings of Juó Bananére and Alcântara Machado. However in the case of nineteenth-century literature, it is a significant fact that some of these *littérateurs* were also themselves caricaturists. Araújo Porto-Alegre (1806–1879), for instance, produced two series of prints, distributed as broadsides in the 1830s, that started the popularization of humorous lithographs in Brazil. And the novelist Aluíso Azevedo, in the last decades of the century, when Romanticism was already a spent force, found regular employment as a cartoonist in such magazines as *O Mosquito, Caras, caretas e carinhas contemporaneas,* and *O Mequetrefe.* But most of these nineteenth-century writers were active in the satirical press as editors. This was Porto-Alegre's function in *A Lanterna Mágica* (see **Figures 3, 4,** and 5) in the 1840s; there, with Rafael Mendes Carvalho, he transformed the Macaire-Bertrand duo from Daumier and Philippon's series in *Le Charivari* into Laverno and Belchior, characters that were later to reappear in one of his plays. Similarly, the poet Luís Gama published satirical texts in *Cabrião* in the 1860s and in *Coaraci* in 1875; in addition, he collaborated with the caricaturist Angelo Agostini in the magazine *Diabo Coxo* [The Lame Devil]. And another example is Luís Guimarães Júnior, who worked with the cartoonist Pinheiro Guimarães in *O Mundo da Lua* [The World of the Moon], but the case of Guimarães Júnior is illustrative of another characteristic aspect of nineteenth-century satire. This is a combination of social satire and verbal nonsense that, widening the scope of the comedy of manners and political satire of authors such as Martins Pena (1815–1848), França Júnior (1838–1890) and Joaquim Manuel de Macedo, focused both on genres not yet well established in the country and on characteristics already clearly marked of a cultural system that only recently had severed its direct links with Portugal.

Figure 3.

Cover page of humor magazine. (Archive of the author)

Figure 4.

Cover page of humor magazine. (Archive of the author)

Figure 5.

Cover of satirical magazine. (Archive of the author)

Thus it makes sense to see as a kind of exacerbated self-criticism, as part of the process of acquiring awareness of the dominant literary devices of nineteenth-century Brazil, the "rhymed nonsense" (which is reminiscent of Sapateiro Silva's "displacements") and Pantagruelian poetry of Bernardo Guimarães, the fescennine poetry of Laurindo Rabelo, the popular quatrains of Getulino (Luís Gama), and their takeoff on the poetic diction of the first Romantic generation, as well as the satirizing of the various sections of the newspaper, particularly the feuilleton novel itself, in *A família Agulha*, a humorous feuilleton by Luís Guimarães Júnior. The same applies to the author's self-portrayal as a gecko basking in the sun and a dying teal quacking in the hands of the cook in Álvares de Azevedo; as "the uncle's nephew" (that is, one who relies on patronage) in Joaquim Manuel de Macedo; as a man afflicted with a sort of structural instability (manifested in pratfalls and stumbles) in the poetry and drama of Qorpo Santo. The epitome of this sort of destabilization is Qorpo Santo's character "The Author," who, tired of writing the text of *As relações naturais* [1866; The Natural Relations] and after undergoing a series of metamorphoses (in the first act he is "Impertinent," then changes into "Truquetruque," next into "Malherbe," following that into a "cardboard figure"), changes into a doll whose arms, hat, and head are torn out; his body is totally disfigured and dismantled and is finally turned into a prop to be used as a weapon in the comedy's closing scene, a mêlée involving the author's servant, daughters, and wife.

Such disfigurements of the author's character were to play a fundamental role in Modernist satire. Examples would include João Miramar and Serafim Ponte Grande in Oswald de Andrade's novels; the pretentious discourse of the half-literate "Minão da Silva," the pompous preface, full of clichés, ornate turns of phrase, and oratorical tricks, signed by "Machado Penumbra," in *Memórias sentimentais de João Miramar*; and the ironical mishmash of the "Carta Pràs Icamiabas" proclaimed by "the great Emperor Macunaíma" in Mário de Andrade's novel, a sort of combinatory exercise in descriptive prose, pseudo-erudition, puristic Portuguese, praise of "the lesson of the classics," exclamatory style, apostrophe, and every kind of overblown eloquence.

In *Serafim Ponte Grande* there are abundant derogatory references to the protagonist's literary pretensions. Thus he mentions, in a passage full of grammatical mistakes, his wish to use a "pecedônimo" ("pseudonym") to sign the "romance" ("novel") he had considered "escrever" ("writing") (Andrade 1984, 30). When he announces that he has bought a fountain pen, he makes two comments, one prosaic–"a prestações" ("on the installment plan")–and the other disparaging–"não funciona muito bem" ("it doesn't work very well"). And he piles up a number of worn, exaggerated expressions to say he has decided "entregar à voracidade branca de uma folha de papel" ("to render unto the white voracity of a blank sheet of paper") the "comovidas lucubrações de última vontade" (Andrade 1984, 45) ("poignant lucubrations of [his] last will"). To this should be added his occupational ambiguity (as a teacher of geography and physical education and an amanuensis), his bouts of nausea, and his escape through the exhaust pipe, discrediting attributes that make him wonder, at a certain point, whether he has "com a escrita em dia" (Andrade 1984, 34) ("been keeping up [his] writing") or whether "neste livro" ("in this book") he really is "a personagem principal" (Andrade 1984, 108) ("the main character"). Such questions underscore a self-caricaturing that also is present in the introduction to the book added by Oswald de Andrade in 1933. In this text, the author says he is "enojado com tudo" ("disgusted with everything") he has written so far and with Modernist writing in general, which he defines as "literatura nova-rica da semicolônia" (Andrade 1984, 10) ("the *nouveau-riche* literature of this semicolony"), and with the novel *Serafim Ponte Grande*, a work he says interests him only as "necrológio da burguesia" ("an obituary of the bourgeoisie"), the depiction of "brasileiro à toa na maré alta da última etapa do capitalismo" (Andrade 1984, 11) ("a Brazilian wandering aimlessly in the high tide of the last stage of capitalism") and–once again stressing the aspect of self-caricature–as "epitáfo do que fui" (Andrade 1984, 11) ("the epitaph of what I once was").

Significantly, Romantic and Modernist instances of authorial disparagement–clearly mediated by the technique of the satirical narrator developed by Machado de Assis–at times share the very same models. One example is John Milton's (1608–1674) "Il Penseroso," taken up both by the Romantic Álvares de Azevedo in his *Macário* and by Oswald de Andrade in the 1920s in *Memórias sentimentais de João Miramar*. This shared reference points not only to another of Oswald's parodies of earlier authors and to the dialogue (founded on the differentiated repetition of the tension between particularization and cultural adaptation, and on the intensification, in both moments, of a process of formal and ethical self-awareness) that characterizes the relations between Romanticism and Modernism in Brazilian cultural history, but also, in particular, to a kind of problematic representation of the very cultural experience that left its mark both on *Memórias* and *Macário*.

In this context, it is important to point out that "Il Penseroso" is one half of a diptych– which is in its way problematic too. Milton wrote it as a structurally parallel and argumentatively contrasting companion piece to "L'Allegro," both dating from about 1631. The two conjoined poems, in a sort of scholastic exercise, are built on antithetical themes: "L'Allegro" is concerned with the joys of day and light, "Il Penseroso" with isolation, night, and darkness, amounting to a sort of exemplary image of the contemplative subject. It is thus understandable that Álvares de Azevedo should have made "Penseroso" one of the fictional extensions (the other being Satan) of the protagonist of *Macário*, a figuration of the agonies of the poetic conscience–the topic of this satirical combination of drama, tale, and narrative poem. It is by means of the dialogue between Macário and Penseroso that the defense of particularization and of literary nationalism is opposed to the emphasis on the expression of negative aspects of subjectivity, and the nativism of the first Romantic generation in Brazil to the subjectivism and Byronism of the second (to which Azevedo belonged). But if in *Macário* Satan and Penseroso are presented as characters distinct from the protagonist, there seems to be a sort of "unidade entre essas personagens" (Alves 126) ("unity joining these characters"), an implicit potential fusion ensured by the "teoria da binomia" ("theory of binomy") ("a coexistência e choque dos contrários, um dos pressupostos da estética romântica" ["the coexistence of and clash between contraries, one of the assumptions of Romantic aesthetics"], as Antonio Candido observes; see 1987, 11), which was made a fundamental poetic principle by Azevedo. "As seen from Álvares de Azevedo's perspective," writes Cilaine Alves in *O belo e o disforme*, "essas duas vozes distintas se fundem, formando uma seqüencia temática única" (Alves 126) ("these two distinct voices fuse together into a single thematic sequence"), so that they seem to stand for aspects not only of Azevedo's literary consciousness but also of the possibilities of nineteenth-century Brazilian poetry.

In Oswald de Andrade's use of "Il Penseroso," which reappears as the title of the first chapter-fragment of *Memórias sentimentais de João Miramar*, there is, to begin with, an indirect reference to the representation–recurrent in Brazilian literary criticism–of Álvares de Azevedo as an adolescent poet whose apparently meager amorous experience often is manifested in the wooden unreality of his female characters. So it is that the teenage Miramar of this opening section, evoking the stereotyped image of a melancholy Azevedo-Penseroso, sees in a nocturnal scene marked by religiosity, mannequins instead of women–mannequins "não têm pernas" ("without legs"): "Para que pernas nas mulheres, amém" (Andrade 1990, 45) ("Why should women have legs, amen"). But this passing reference to "Il Penseroso" is perhaps more than just another jab at Romanticism. And it is only fitting that it should reappear in a book marked by amorous escapades, by episodes concerning trips to Europe, and by its mixed nature as personal diary and telegraphic descriptive report written by a bohemian character whose very name (Miramar means literally "looks at the sea") suggests looking outward. Whereas *Macário* "Penseroso" stands for the Romantic desire to assert national singularity, in the *Memórias sentimentais de João Miramar* Oswald's Penseroso, "sob as ordens da mãe" ("under Mama's orders"), in the first chapter of the book, takes on, as José Paulo Paes observes, "o rosto histórico de um patriciado. . . cujo

cosmopolitismo bem viajado mal lhe escondia a condição semicolonial" (115) ("the historical visage of a patrician class . . . whose well-traveled cosmopolitanism can hardly disguise its semicolonial condition").

In spite of the inversion present in this refiguration of Milton's character, both Romantic and Modernist texts point not only to the tension between particularization and cultural adaptation, which is characteristic of both periods in Brazilian literary culture but also to a simultaneous dialogue between Oswald and nineteenth-century writing, as well as–within nineteenth-century literature–between Álvares de Azevedo in *Macário* and Byron's reappropriation of Milton's Satan, on the one hand, and, on the other hand, between Azevedo and the scholastically distinct figures contrasted by Milton in the pair Allegro-Penseroso. The difference is that what Milton treats as an antithetical pair is seen in *Macário* as the constitutive extension of a consciousness that, appropriately enough, seems to be associated with an imperious self-satire, a movement toward a form of expression that is internally problematic and inclusive–as in the "fragmentary compounds" of Álvares de Azevedo and Sousândrade, in the "sarcasm poetry" of *Memórias sentimentais de João Miramar*, and in the association between satirical expression and historical experience in Latin American literary cultures.

Translation by Paulo Henriques Britto

Works Cited

Alves, Cilaine. 1998. *O belo e o disforme*. São Paulo: FAPESP/EDUSP.

Andrade, Oswald de. 1990. *Memórias sentimentais de João Miramar*. São Paulo: Editora Globo.

——. 1984. *Serafim Ponte Grande*. São Paulo: Global Editora.

Ávila, Myriam. 1995. *Rima e solução*. São Paulo: Annablume Editora.

Azevedo, Álvares. 1987. *Macário*. Rio de Janeiro: Livraria Francisco Alves Editora.

Barco, Oscar del. 1996. "Macedonio Fernández o el milagro del ocultamiento." *Museo de la Novela de la Eterna* by Macedonio Fernández. 2nd ed. Ed. Ana María Camblong and Adolfo de Obieta. Collection Archives. Paris: ALLCA XX, Université Paris X. 463–72.

Belluzo, Ana Maria de Moraes. 1979. "Voltolino e as raízes do Modernismo." Master's thesis. São Paulo: ECA/USP.

Borges, Jorge Luis. 1975. *Obras conpletas*. Vol. 1. Buenos Aires: Emecé Editores.

Bosi, Alfredo. 1994. "Do Antigo Estado à máquina mercante." *Dialética da colonização*. São Paulo: Companhia das Letras. 94–118.

Cabrera Infante, Guillermo. 1967. *Tres tristes tigres*. Barcelona: Editorial Seix Barral.

——. 1971. *Three Trapped Tigers*. Trans. Donald Gardner and Suzanne Jill Levine. New York: Marlowe & Company.

Campos, Augusto de. 1978. "Da América que existe: Gregório de Matos." *Poesia. Antipoesia. Antropofagia*. São Paulo: Editora Cortez & Moraes. 91–106.

Campos, Haroldo de. 1979. "Ruptura dos gêneros na literatura latino-americana." *América Latina em sua literatura*. Ed. César Fernández Moreno. São Paulo: Perspectiva. 281–305.

——. 1984. "Serafim: Um grande não-livro." *Serafim Ponte Grande* by Oswald de Andrade. São Paulo: Global Editora. 143–72.

Candido, Antonio. 1975. *Formação da literatura brasileira (momentos decisivos)*. 2 vols. 5th ed. Belo Horizonte: Editora Itatiaia; São Paulo: EDUSP.

———. 1985. *Literatura e sociedade: Estudos de teoria e história literária*. 5th ed. São Paulo: Companhia Editora Nacional.

———. 1987. "A educação pela noite." *A educação pela noite e outros ensaios*. São Paulo: Ática. 10–22.

———. 1993a. "Carta marítima." *O discurso e a cidade*. São Paulo: Duas Cidades. 203–23.

———. 1993b. "Dialética da malandragem." *O discurso e a cidade*. São Paulo: Duas Cidades. 19–54.

———. 1993c. *O discurso e a cidade*. São Paulo: Duas Cidades.

———. 1995. "Digressão sentimental sobre Oswald de Andrade." *Vários escritos*. São Paulo: Livraria Duas Cidades. 67–103.

Chalmers, Vera. 1992. "A crônica humorística de *O Pirralho*." *A Crônica: O gênero, sua fixação e suas transformações no Brasil*. Ed. Setor de Filologia da Fundação Casa de Rui Barbosa. Rio de Janeiro: Fundação Casa de Rui Barbosa; Campinas, Editora da UNICAMP. 193–211.

Costa Lima, Luiz. 1982. "O campo visual de uma experiência antecipadora." *ReVisão de Sousândrade*. 2nd ed. Ed. Augusto and Haroldo de Campos. Rio de Janeiro: Nova Fronteira. 395–434.

Dimas, Antonio. 1993. "Gregório de Matos: Poesia e controvérsia." *América Latina: Palavra, literatura e cultura. A situação colonial*. Vol. 1. Ed. Ana Pizarro. São Paulo: Memorial da América Latina/Secretaria de Estado da Cultura; Campinas: Editora da UNICAMP. 335–57.

Fernández, Macedonio. 1995. *Museo de la novela de la eterna*. Ed. Fernando Rodríguez Lafuente. Madrid: Ediciones Cátedra.

Franco, Jean. 1986. *Historia de la literatura hispanoamericana*. Barcelona: Editorial Ariel.

Furtado, Joaci Pereira. 1997. *Uma república de leitores: História e memória na recepção das Cartas chilenas (1845–1989)*. São Paulo: Hucitec.

García, Canclini Néstor. 1997. "Contradições latino-americanas: Modernismo sem modernização?" *Culturas híbridas: Estratégias para entrar e sair da modernidade*. São Paulo: EDUSP. 67–97.

Gonzaga, Tomás Antônio. 1995. *Cartas chilenas*. 2nd ed. Ed. Joaci Pereira Furtado. São Paulo: Companhia das Letras.

Guilhamet, Leon. 1989. *Satire and the Transformation of Genre*. Philadelphia: University of Pennsylvania Press.

Hansen, João Adolfo. 1989. *A sátira e o engenho*. São Paulo: Companhia das Letras/Secretaria de Estado da Cultura.

———. 1997. "Prefácio." *Uma república de leitores: História e memória na recepção das Cartas chilenas (1845–1989)*. Ed. Joaci Pereira Furtado. São Paulo: Hucitec. 11–20.

———. 1999. "Floretes agudos e porretes grossos." *Folha de S. Paulo*, Oct. 20. Caderno *Mais*, 5–7.

Hegel, G. W. Friedrich. 1993. *Estética*. Trans. Alvaro Ribeiro and Orlando Vitorino. Lisbon: Guimarães Editora.

Highet, Gilbert. 1962. *The Anatomy of Satire*. Princeton: Princeton University Press.

Jackson, Kenneth D. 1978. "Serafim Ponte Grande e a revolta antropofágica." *A prosa vanguardista na literatura brasileira: Oswald de Andrade*. São Paulo: Editora Perspectiva. 65–101.

Kernan, Alvin B. 1962. *The Cankered Muse: Satire of the English Renaissance*. New Haven/London: Yale University Press.

———. 1965. *The Plot of Satire*. New Haven: Yale University Press.

MacAdam, Alfred J. 1977. *Modern Latin American Narratives: The Dreams of Reason*. Chicago: University of Chicago Press.

Matos, Gregório de. 1992. *Obra poética*. 2 vols. 3rd ed. Ed. James Amado. Rio de Janeiro: Record.

Merquior, José Guilherme. 1979. *De Anchieta a Euclides: Breve história da literatura brasileira*. Rio de Janeiro: Livraria José Olympio Editora.

Naves, Rodrigo. 1997. *A forma difícil: Ensaios sobre arte brasileira*. São Paulo: Editora Ática.

Paes, José Paulo. 1995. "A ruptura vanguardista: As grandes obras." *Palavra literatura e cultura. Vanguarda e modernidade*. Vol. 3. Ed. Ana Pizarro. Campinas: Editora da UNICAMP, São Paulo: Memorial da América Latina. 99–123.

Paulson, Ronald. 1967. *Satire and the Novel in Eighteenth-Century England*. New Haven: Yale University Press.

Pizarro, Ana. 1985. "Introducción" *La literatura latinoamericana como processo*. Ed. Ana Pizarro. Buenos Aires: Association pour l'étude socio-culturelle des arts, des littératures de l'Amérique latine/Centro Editor de America Latina. 13–67.

Polito, Ronald. 1990. "A persistência das idéias e das formas: um estudo sobre a obra de Tomás Antônio Gonzaga." Master's thesis. Niterói: Instituto de Ciências Humanas e Filosofia, Universidade Federal Fluminense.

Rosenblum, Michael. 1972. "Pope's Illusive Temple of Infamy." *The Satirist's Art*. Ed. H. James Jensen and Malvin R. Zincker. Bloomington: Indiana University Press. 28–54.

Santiago, Silviano. 1978. "O entre-lugar do discurso latino-americano." *Uma literatura nos trópicos*. São Paulo: Editora Perspectiva/Secretaria da Cultura, Ciência e Tecnologia do Estado de S. Paulo. 11–28.

———. 1982. "Apesar de dependente, universal." *Vale quanto pesa: Ensaios sobre questões político-culturais*. Rio de Janeiro: Editora Paz e Terra. 13–24.

Schwarz, Roberto. 1977. *Ao vencedor as batatas*. São Paulo: Duas Cidades.

———. 1990. *Um mestre na periferia do capitalismo: Machado de Assis*. São Paulo: Livraria Duas Cidades.

Silva Alvarenga, Manuel Inácio da. 1864. *Obras poéticas*. 2 vols. Ed. J. Norberto de Souza. Rio de Janeiro: H. Garnier.

———. 1977. "Epístola a José Basílio da Gama." *Presença da Literatura Brasileira. Das Orgens ao Romanticismo*. Vol. 1. 8th ed. Ed. Antonio Candido and José Aderaldo Castello. Rio de Janeiro: Difel. 175–79.

Süssekind, Flora, and Rachel Teixeira Valença. 1983. *O Sapateiro Silva*. Rio de Janeiro: Fundação Casa de Rui Barbosa.

Wisnik, José Miguel. 1976. "Introdução." *Poemas escolhidos* by Gregório de Matos. São Paulo: Editora Cultrix. 11–33.

CHAPTER 28

THE SERMON IN THE SEVENTEENTH CENTURY

Alcir Pécora

Broadly considered, the Iberian Catholic sermon as a genre in the New World reached its peak in the seventeenth century; it had a sacramental intentionality, which expressed the permanent projection of God onto the various forms of life in the universe. Everything was a reflection of God–"the 'visible signs' that are a testimony to God's majesty," in the words of the Jesuit biologist Eryc Wasmann (Miller 483). One cannot interpret the world without taking into account its historical specificity, but neither can one do without due regard to the divinity. It is a question of taking the reality of events as an effective discourse but one that contains what remains hidden within that reality. A fundamental element in this approach to Catholic thought is the notion of mystery, which is associated with mediation, according to three semantically inseparable aspects: first, the representation of the people before their God; second, the existence of an "institutional mechanism of mediation"; and third, the revelation of the future because the mediating mystery fosters an understanding and obedience to the hidden designs of Providence (Spicq 680–87). In any event, it is a question of recognizing the "mystery" at the core of nature itself (which is undeniable). The tendency was to emphasize the scientific burden of proof in acknowledging the natural "effects" of the world and the knowledge required for an adequate recognition of what makes natural phenomena occur, but also to understand what directs them. From these precepts results the notion that the real pertains to what is at the same time natural and supernatural.

The Catholic vocabulary on sacramental mystery is designed to account for the reality of humanity. The passing of time was itself considered a chronicle of Divine Providence that was constantly updated, and for this reason, historical events and their various causes need to be interpreted as elements of an account that was as inspired by God as were the Scriptures themselves. Thus, the importance of the mediating function of the Church and sacred orators, whose responsibility was the close correlation of history and science with the biblical Christian tradition as a science of the allegorical interpretation of scriptural meanings, and to a lesser degree with ancient rhetoric, which was limited to an analysis of persuasive enunciation. Moreover, according to those orators, exegetical interpretation essentially does not differ from the historical hermeneutics that interprets events because the historical events also appear in the Scriptures. In the Bible a sign connotes a thing, while a thing becomes a sign; thus it is that the interpreter encounters elements having the status of figures, types, or countertypes and that need to be interpreted both as historical facts and as providential signs.

In the sacramental form of sacred oratory, one perceives that theology, rhetoric, and politics form an indissoluble semantic whole, which operates at the core of salvation. The preacher who is worthy of being called such, must examine the signs of the divine in things, use them as discursive proofs capable of moving the will and reason of followers,

and organize them as a form of politics toward the historical triumph of the mystical body.

Therefore, in the Catholic mode of sacred oratory of the sixteenth and seventeenth centuries, the Scriptures are reinterpreted as events unfold, in such a way that what is taking place is interpreted in a specular, oratorical move into the most updated version of the Divine Text, in the sense that the very movement of historical succession implies a greater number of prophecies achieved; as history unfolds, it provides a basis that becomes more and more solid for new interpretations of the divine plan and purpose.

If, according to Auerbach's *Mimesis*, the biblical figuration of time in the Jewish religious context is projected onto the totality of history and forces it to "fit" inside itself (17), one may say that sacred orators of the seventeenth century assumed that historical facts, insofar as they are acts, reveal God's plans for men. They reveal this with propriety–and interpretative up-to-dateness. Thus properly interpreted, the holy Scriptures can decipher a great number of mysterious figures. God's truth always remains the same, but the varied, continuous discourse of history increasingly gathers a larger repertory of circumstantial references that contribute to an understanding of the mysterious figures used by God to communicate with men.

From this perspective, Auerbach's view that exegesis became for the medieval Christian a general method of apprehending reality (13) applies perfectly well to Counter-Reformation preachers, with one addition: the provision that it is not simply a matter of hermeneutics recovering the Truth announced in the Scriptures as historical facts, but that in dealing with the recording of contemporary facts in their historical progression, hermeneutics permits the Catholic historian to recognize the Truth more effectively than ever before. The Scriptures not only project themselves onto history, but history with its facts and events has a role to play in the interpretation of the Scriptures. The process of figuration, which controls the meanings encoded in the Scriptures, is accompanied by a realization of what is new in history–which for Maravall represents an unprecedented victory for Christianity (140).

From this perspective, historical inquiry is the best interpreter of the Scriptures. There is even a medieval topos–that of the dwarf on the shoulders of a giant, where the giant sees less than the dwarf despite the giant's greater size–which was appropriated by exegetical preachers to illustrate their advantageous position in relation to their greater predecessors.

In the case of the militant preaching of the missionaries, one thing should be made clear. God, who speaks through history, does so only to save humanity; that is, His historical utterance is clothed in the unmistakable purpose of salvation. The relevant issue in history is to point to the divine as Providence leading toward man's redemption. It is not the echo of transcendence as a single, incomprehensible Being, that can be read in history, but the signs of the historical development

258

of Christianity. This means that the best interpreters of these signs are the believers who are more involved in the conversion of men–among whom are first the preachers, followed by speculative theologians or contemplative mystics. Returning to the issue discussed above, one may say that in the context of missions the significant exegesis of preaching realizes and updates, according to the occasion, the signs of authentic divine militancy.

Thus, the sacramental form of preaching perpetuates the notion of truth in the sermon that is manifest in a double, irreducible moment of divine inspiration. The history of human actions cannot be understood by itself; it must be seen as an inspired account of an eternal, divine action which forms its basis. Nor is it possible to accept the reality of divine traces in the history of men without also accepting the idea of an entire reality, regardless of how removed or far from perfection this history may be. On the other hand, it is obvious that the meanings of the Scriptures also relate to the urgency of events and not only to doctrinal theory. Significant exegesis does not spiritualize the facts that are narrated in the Scriptures but is closely tied to them as facts. This dictum, obviously, does not reject the figurative aspect of biblical reading but aims to avoid the application of biblical meanings to an ahistorical or exclusively metaphysical aspect. As has been noted, the efficacy for men's conversion does not derive from the spiritual meaning of scriptural accounts but from their adjustment to those occasions in which history unfolds.

In the case of Christ, in which He Himself ontologically achieves the fusion of divine and human aspects, His actions must be interpreted by the preacher not only as signs of a metaphysical truth but also as acts capable of confronting the most delicate historical issues. Even more, Christ's acts, when interpreted correctly, are useful in the development of a Christian politics in history, especially with respect to the hierarchy of the Church and the state. Such acts are, thus, real documents for the princes, which must be accepted as such even by those who, like princes and politicians, are moved more by reason and prudence than by Christian faith.

It is true that among theologians and Catholic counselors the reason of state should not be dissociated from Christian virtues and from the government of the common good, but this does not imply the condemnation of political pragmatism. In the context of Counter-Reformation Catholicism, the notion of prudence generally is used to justify this kind of pragmatic calculation. Diego Saavedra Fajardo (1584–1648), who was one of the most prominent political writers of the seventeenth century, the secretary of the Spanish embassy in Rome, Sicily, and Naples, and the plenipotentiary for the "peace of Münster," wrote the following in his *Empresas políticas* [1640; Political Enterprises]: "Ninguna cosa mejor ni más provechosa a los mortales que la prudente difidencia. Custodia y guardia es de la hacienda y de la vida. La conservación propia nos obliga al recelo. Donde no le hay no hay prevención. Y sin ésta todo está expuesto al peligro" (501) ("Nothing is better or more profitable to mortal men than prudent diffidence. Watchfulness and carefulness are relevant to property and to life. Our own preservation forces us to be distrustful. Where this is lacking, there is no prevention. And all this is exposed to danger").

In the same way, in the sacramental form of sermons not only the signs of divinity in the earthly world are emphasized but also the adequacy of these signs in the guidance and government of this world. Theology is a form of politics.

The testimonies that divinity gives of itself do not dissolve worldly practices; rather, they reaffirm the possibility of gradually bringing together the world and Christianity. The mystery of the manifestation of the hidden divinity in earthly beings not only points to God but also makes us realize that in order to reach Him, there is a real trajectory within the world of men which must be followed. That is, just as one cannot understand the world without discovering in it the signs of a hidden God, one cannot realize what is hidden without carefully attending to what lies before one: Divine mystery by definition manifests itself in a variety of ways.

However, it is possible to specify more restricted domains for the revelation of the effects of the divine infinite on the historical finite. Few themes are so often enacted in sermons as those of the sacraments, and above all the sacrament of the Eucharist or Holy Communion. In fact, the mystery of the Eucharist, a central figure of divinity's hidden presence, summarizes Catholic weapons in the battle against the free individual examination of the Scriptures and the invisibility of the *congregatio fidelium* in the religion of the reformed church (Skinner 2:10–11). In an effort to strengthen the church as an institution, the mystery of the Eucharist does not suppose the representation of God but His integral presence in those hosts consecrated by the priest, who is responsible for the visual mediation between human and divine.

In order to understand this mediation strictly put in effect by the sacrament, the priesthood, and the sermon, it is worth pointing out that, among the basic topics associated with the Eucharist (the Last Supper, the presence of Christ in the consecrated host, the renewal of the divine presence in the communicant who receives Holy Communion, and the power of the divine presence), sermons often emphasize the sacrificial nature of the Eucharist or that which the exegetes of the Bible call a "memorial of expiatory death" (Stoeger 389–405). In this perspective, Christ, on sacrificing Himself, renewed the *via crucis* of Passion and Death, thereby renewing, at the same time, His voluntary surrender as an object of martyrdom for the salvation of the world. This interpretation of the sacrament, based on which Catholic preachers tend to construct strongly emotional arguments, is appropriate for its emphasis on the painful cost of Christ's sacrifice that validates the Eucharist. If in the Passion there is the great suffering of bodily wounds, in the sacrament of the Eucharist this suffering is intensified rather than suppressed by the preachers; it is the Body and Blood of Christ that is present through the mystery of transubstantiation.

The pathos of the transposition of the stations of the cross into the sacrament of the Eucharist may be interpreted as part of what Victor Tapié considers a characteristic of the Spanish model of statues and saints that spread throughout Catholic countries, including Rome, after the notorious sacking of the city (1527). According to the basic tenets of the Baroque, the representation of harmonious beauty, associated with the notion of an "Idea" that predominated in artistic practices during the Renaissance, is dramatically reworked so that the statues convey instead emotions like piety and suffering. In the same way, one cannot conceive of the triumph of the Counter-Reformation Church without taking into consideration the formation of an ostensible expiation through suffering. Be that as it may, a notable tendency in sermons was to draw together the New Testament notion of substitute expiation and the ancient sacrificial language of Hebrew rites, in which the primary effect was to dramatize the sacrament. This dramatization, in its turn, implied a basic artifice: that the hidden reason of the correspondences among objects, to be discovered through the sermon, is revealed only after pondering the difficulties that usually arise in establishing it. The rhetorical precept that best accounts for this process was written by the Aragonese Jesuit Baltasar Gracián (1601–1658), whose *Agudeza y arte de ingenio* [1642; Acuteness and the Art of Inventiveness] proposes the following: "[O]rdinario se va cortando a los principios de los discursos, y al fin se ata. Va con suspensión el auditorio aguardando en qué ha de venir a parar, que es más arte que el declararse luego al principio, y así de más gusto, como sucede en los empeños, que cuanto más se van dificultando, se goza más de la acertada salida" (471) ("[O]ne should start by leaving out principles from discourse, but in the end tie it all together. The audience is in suspense, not knowing where it would all end, because this shows more art than by stating what you mean right at the beginning, and so, it is with everything we put effort into, the more difficulties there are, the greater the pleasure in the end").

To which the following is added, in another passage of this masterwork of the period: "Es gran eminencia del ingenioso artificio llevar suspensa la mente del que atiende, y no luego declararse; especialmente entre grandes oradores, está muy válida esta arte. Comienza a empeñarse el concepto, deslumbra la expectación, o la lleva pendiente y deseosa de ver dónde va a parar el discurso, que es un bien sutil primor, y después viene a concluir con una ponderación impensada" (434) ("It is very important in this art to keep the audience in suspense, and not state what you have to say right away; especially among great orators, this is a most useful strategy. One starts to develop the concept, creates an expectation, leaves it suspended, with the audience wishing to know where the talk will lead, which is of great value to the orator, and then one should conclude with an unexpected conclusion").

The unexpected revelation of the deep correspondence among the issues dealt with in the sermon, presented as the solution to the difficulties the sermon puts at stake, intends to indicate the current manifestation of God's word at the time of preaching. The dramatic, sharp revelation follows the audience's expectation; in the sermon, this revelation functions as evidence of its perfection as a paraphrase of and commentary on God's original word.

This kind of argument, which often misinterprets the common sense of things in its attempt to uncover less conspicuous or probable relations, has been accused by those of a Romantic and Positivist stamp of being a mere "rhetorical" construct—in the pejorative sense of the word. In other words, its demonstrative method was considered a display of linguistic virtuosity or tortuous hyperbole, somewhat in fashion at the time, which limited itself to paying compliments to the mind's inventiveness, here understood as the ability to conclude with a difficult closing statement that relates opposite or incongruent objects. However, today apart from its historical reference, this kind of Positivist criticism is no longer relevant. It is clear that the preacher wanted to create certain effects in his audience, and there was an indisputable, pragmatic aspect to the sermon; preachers who had been raised in the militancy of the Counter-Reformation—and the Society of Jesus can be considered its "light cavalry" (see Dominique)—could not forget the pragmatic dimensions. But this search for rhetorical effect can by no means be thought of as frivolous, aiming simply at ornamentation, without a political or hermeneutic-theological purpose. For Catholic preachers at the time, the analogies that promote a correspondence between disparate objects (which is responsible for the highly dramatic style of sermons) cannot be conceived of as separate from the movement that is founded on the laws of nature, historical facts, and representations of the divine. To conceive of oratorical effects as a solely verbal strategy, in relation to both hermeneutics and politics, would be the same as the understanding that the divine aspect in matter could be merely the illusory appearance of matter, or that the identity of Being would be exhausted in the visible signs it leaves on matter. The acts of invention, which create formal adequacy, are legitimate only to the extent to which they maintain a specular relation with the communication of divine truth to men–which also, as has been noted, presupposes the revelation of precepts adequate to a Christian politics in history.

To sum up, the discourse of the preacher does not intend to give any new ontological insights or even new formal expression regarding God's creation. The game of analogies is the basis of the sermon; analogies are present everywhere in the complex world that can be used to convince the faithful that nothing can sustain itself without God. For preachers, to render the form of these effects autonomous and to remove the technique and the artifice of the natural end that guides them would be the same as conceiving of a heretical world–whether it be the heresy of thinking that matter is enough, rejecting the unnecessary presence of a God (a view similar to that of atheistic materialism), or the heresy of supposing that God exists within matter or that the soul of matter is equivalent to animated matter (a view similar to that of immanent animism).

From this perspective, one must reevaluate Padre Antonio Vieira's (1608–1697) noted reprimand in the 1655 *Sermão da Sexagésima* [Sermon of the Second Sunday before Lent] regarding the use of a cultured style by Dominican preachers in the *Paço* [Royal Residence], often interpreted in an anachronistic pre-Enlightenment way (as if Vieira were in favor of a more plain style and more good sense) or even pre-Romantic (as if he were speaking in defense of sincerity or the spontaneity of words). In fact, these anachronistic views lead to the equally common (though rather contrary to Jesuitical tradition) fact that Vieira himself did not follow his own advice, giving in to the games of ornamentation in his sermons.

Such readings of Vieira's sermons seem to misunderstand the issue: It is unlikely that Vieira would criticize discoursive ornamentation as such and consider it an inadequate rhetorical procedure *a priori*. First of all, he would not do so because figures of speech and rhetorical ornament are resources inherent in oratory, and knowing them well is part of mastering its available resources; a technically adept orator like Vieira could not consider such resources a negative unless their uses and effects were unsuccessful as a result of employing resources inadequate to the particular *decorum* of the genre of sacred oratory. The pulpit, he states, is mistaken for a dramatic stage by contemporary preachers, who disregard its seriousness:

Uma das felicidades que se contava entre as do tempo presente, era acabarem-se as comédias em Portugal, mas não foi assim. Não se acabaram, mudaram-se, passaram-se do teatro ao púlpito. Não cuideis que encareço em chamar comédias a muitas pregações das que hoje se usam. Tomara ter aqui as comédias de Plauto, de Terêncio, de Sêneca, e veríeis se não acháveis nelas muitos desenganos da vida e vaidade do mundo, muitos pontos de doutrina moral, muito mais verdadeiros e muito mais sólidos do que hoje se ouvem nos púlpitos. (1:86)

One of the joys of present times was to be the end of dramatic plays in Portugal, but it was not to be. They did not end; they moved; they went from the stage to the pulpit. Do not think that I am trying to refer to many of today's sermons as dramatic plays. I wish we had Plautus's, Terence's, Seneca's plays, and you would see that you may find in them many disillusions of life and vanities of the world, many aspects of moral doctrine, more true and more solid than what we hear today in pulpits.

With these words, Vieira does not intend to deny the art of the sermon, or the sermon as an art form. It is from within the terms of rhetoric as well as theology that he criticizes the modern styles. It is true that in the context of the Counter-Reformation, in an effort to re-Christianize the classical orator, and in the attempt to put an end to his secularization through classical eloquence as Margarida Vieira Mendes put it, he emphasizes "cautela devota contra os perigos da arte pagã e laica por excelência" (66) ("devoted caution against the dangers of pagan and secular art par excellence"). However, the arrival of the Jesuits altered the perspective on these concerns. With their pronounced humanistic formation, they were convinced that the apostolic sermon could not leave out art, and the matter was above all one of reconciling both traditions: to celebrate "o *orator* retoricamente competente, e, ao mesmo tempo, imitador de Cristo, dos Apóstolos e de S. Paulo" (Mendes 66) ("the rhetorically competent orator, and, at the same time, be an imitator of Christ, the Apostles, and St. Paul").

Vieira's recommendation that sacred oratory be practiced as an artless art (1:65) does not reject dialectical ornamentation or inventive concepts as adequate artistic resources; rather, he calls attention to the decorum of holy eloquence, that is, the appropriateness of person, place, and time, according to the genre. The loss of decorum prevented the sermon from bearing results, a failure that was likely to happen when the preacher did not have a solemn touch. Using the parable of the sower, which provides the theme (*Semen est verbum Dei*) for the *Sermão da Sexagésima*, Vieira lists the rules of "artless art" that he proposes in relation to the "substance" of invention, the "words" of elocution, and the appearance of spontaneity:

O trigo do semeador, ainda que caiu quatro vezes, só de três nasceu: para o sermão vir nascendo, há de ter três modos de cair. Há de cair com queda, há de cair com cadência, há de cair com caso. A queda é para as coisas, a cadência para as palavras, o caso para a disposição. A queda é para as coisas, porque hão de vir bem trazidas, em seu lugar, hão de ter queda. A cadência é para as palavras, porque não hão de ser escabrosas, nem dissonantes; hão de ter cadência. O caso é para a disposição, porque há de ser tão natural e tão desafetado que pareça caso e não estudo. (1:65)

The seed of the sower, even though it was sown in four places, only grew in three: For the sermon to grow, there are only three ways of sowing. It must be sown as appropriate to the situation; it must be sown with an appealing cadence; it must be sown with the appearance of spontaneity. Appropriateness is for things, cadence for words, spontaneity appearance for attitude. Appropriateness is for things because they ought to be in their proper place; they ought to happen. Cadence is for words because they ought not to be rough or dissonant; they ought to have cadence. The appearance of chance is for attitude because it ought to be so natural and spontaneous that it looks like chance and not study.

The strategic use of art in preaching does not diminish the dignity of the ecclesiastic orator, whose public value makes a difference in the effectiveness of his preaching for the congregation. The validity of the discourse, as can be seen, is a Christianized version of Aristotelian theory of the orator's character (175); Quintilian considered moral proof to be provided by the image of his habits, which can have great persuasive power on the public (262). For a Christian audience, this image of good habits is the first to be affected when the pulpit takes on the airs of a dramatic presentation.

There is a good reason why Vieira would not criticize rhetorical resources, except for their misuse: Considered in terms of their analogies, that is, as a revelation of the hidden relations of created things, adornments and figures of speech are also a part of nature and, therefore, of the logic behind its creation. What Vieira mostly criticizes in his *Sermão da Sexagésima* is precisely the rupture of the essential relation between ornament and its natural basis, between artful conceits and signs of divinity in the world, and between figures of speech of technical discourse and figures of the providential and teleological system. The fact that this rupture was much more in evidence in sermons given at the Royal Court than in missionary sermons would not be lost on Vieira or his public. However, the Dominicans in the Royal Residence, severely reprimanded by Vieira, do not warrant such condemnation for using embellished rhetoric and tropes. In their choice of devices, there is technique, but they are accused of breaking the fundamental link between the dialectic of ornamentation and the factual signs of the divine. From this perspective, they are preachers who no longer attempt to describe the hidden matter in these signs, the transcendental guidance that displays and explains them, but are content to treat such signs as autonomous verbal matter, whose mystery is dissipated in the exclusive use of rhetorical rules. In other words, it is the separation between rhetoric and the theological-salvational at the core of analogies that seems intolerable and improper:

Nesses lugares, nesses textos que alegais para prova do que dizeis, é esse o sentido em que Deus os disse? É isso o sentido em que os entendem os Padres da Igreja? É esse o sentido da própia gramática das palavras? Não, por certo, porque muitas vezes as tomais pelo que soam, e não pelo que significam, e talvez nem pelo que soam. Pois se não é esse o sentido das palavras de Deus, segue-se que não são palavras de Deus. E se não são palavras de Deus, que nos queixamos de que não façam fruto as pregações? Basta que havemos de trazer as palavras de Deus a que digam o que nós queremos, e não havemos de querer dizer o que elas dizem. (1:84)

These places, these texts that you claim are a proof of what you say, is this what God meant by them? Is this the meaning attributed to them by the Fathers of the Church? Is this the meaning of the words themselves? Certainly not, because you often choose words for what they sound like, and not for what they really mean. If this is not the meaning of God's words, then they are not God's words. And if they are not God's words, we cannot complain if the sermons have no effect.

Once decorum is lost and styles have become autonomous, outside of meaning, the audience's applause is the same as a condemnation, because in sacred oratory what bears false witness to God's words is to be condemned.

An analogous association can be made with regard to the meaning and the interest in the Eucharist, the climax of the Mass, which is reached precisely at the moment when the memory of Christ's acts are projected onto the bread and wine used in the ceremony. Liturgical ostentation–as well as rhetorical ornament (or discursive ostentation)–is a part of conversion and seems perfectly adapted to the theater of true faith. Nevertheless, the magnificence of the ceremony, as an application of appropriate doctrinal criteria, cannot be conceived outside of its role in the liturgy. Just as in the case of rhetorical tropes and figures of speech, the *discretio*–an Ignatian word par excellence–around which the Mass is organized associates it with the sacramental form of God's presence in material things. The dissociation between ostentation and its liturgical function, or between the liturgical function and the truth of God's presence, implies the complete failure of the ceremony and, in particular, the meaning of the mystery of the Eucharist.

The architecture of the churches designed by the most notable builders in the service of the Counter-Reformation, such as Jacopo Vignola and Giacomo Della Porta, closely associates the magnificence of the buildings with sacramental celebration: "[A] distribuição da luz feita pela maneira usada nos palcos, com acentuados contrastes entre as capelas laterais deixadas na penumbra e o fluxo de luz que da cúpula se derrama por sobre o altar-mór, exerce uma atração quase, diríamos, física sobre o visitante, que é arrastado em direção ao Santo Sacramento, e parece feita para por a alma de imediato em um estado de arrebatamento e de fé jubilosa" (Miller 467) ("[T]he lighting, done as it is on the stage, with sharp contrasts between the side chapels left in half-light and the stream of light originating in the dome that falls over the altar, draws the visitor almost physically toward the Holy Sacrament, and it seems to have been devised to lead one's soul to immediate ecstasy and jubilant faith").

Similarly acknowledging the integrative power of the mystery in the liturgy, Howard Hibbard has noted the cohesion of iconographic representations from chapel to chapel, as well as from the nave to the cross. For him, this cohesion is due to the effort of Counter-Reformation architects to organize the construction according to a *discretio*, similar to the one that serves as the base of the analogies of sermons: "*ut picturae sermones*" (40). Naturally, what this conclusion presupposes is the practice among the Jesuits of preaching as the main form of conversion and the salvation of souls (Sebastián 275).

At this point, in order to acknowledge the complexity of the sacramental form, keeping in mind especially the Eucharist as the doctrinally privileged figure, one must consider the recurrent argument that the *plus ultra* of the sacrament is a result of Holy Communion. Let us return to Antonio Vieira once more, as his sermons are by far the most spectacular writings in the Portuguese language during the Colonial period. Concerning Holy Communion, his speeches usually expand their significance by means of the rhetoric of Christ's sacrifice to attain the effect of the union at which the Eucharist aims. Here is an example of how he developed such topos:

> Quem come o meu corpo e bebe o meu sangue–diz Cristo–está em mim e eu estou nele. –Se perguntarmos aos intérpretes o entendimento destas palavras, todos respondem que significam uma união real e verdadeira, com que por meio da Comunhão ficamos unidos a Cristo. Isto dizem os expositores e os teólogos comumente, mas eu, com licença sua, tenho para mim que neste mistério não há uma só união, senão duas e essas mui diferentes: uma união com que Cristo nos quis unir consigo, e outra união com que nois quis unir conosco. O efeito da primeira união é estarmos unidos com Cristo; o efeito da segunda união é estarmos unidos entre nós. (15:280–81)

Whoever partakes of my body and my blood–says Christ–lives in me and I live in him. –If we ask the meaning of these words, all interpreters will say that they refer to the true and real union, which takes place by means of Holy Communion, which joins us to Christ. This is what theologians and interpreters usually say, but I, if you will allow me, believe that in this mystery there is not only one kind of union, but two, and these are somewhat different: a union between Christ and us and another one among ourselves. The effect of the first union is that we are united with Christ; the effect of the second one is that we are united among ourselves.

The so-called "formulae of reciprocal immanence"–that is, "He lives in me and I live in Him," typical of John's Gospel, which seeks precisely to avoid the "the expressions of identity of Hellenistic mysticism, since the integrity of one's personality is preserved" (Stoeger 404)–are here interpreted in a very different way, not in order to emphasize the distinction between the Being and created beings but to broaden the scope of identity among them:

> Reparo muito nesta duplicação de termos: ele em mim, e eu nele. Se Cristo na Comunhão pretendera somente unir-se conosco, uni destes termos bastava, e o outro era supérfluo. Provo. Porque para estas duas mãos estarem unidas, basta que a direita esteja na esquerda, ou a esquerda na direita. Da mesma maneira, para Cristo e nós estarmos unidos basta que nós estejamos em Cristo: *in me manet*–ou que Cristo esteja em nós: *et ego in illo*. Pois, se para explicar a união que há entre Cristo e o que comunga bastava qualquer destes termos, porque os dobra e multiplica Cristo? Por isso mesmo. Dobra Cristo e multiplica os termos porque também a união se dobra e multiplica. Se a união fora uma só, bastava dizer: *in me manet* ou ego *in illo*; mas diz *in me manet, et ego in illo* duplicadamente, para significar as duas uniões que obra aquele mistério: uma união imediata, com que nos unimos a Cristo, e outra união mediata, com que mediante Cristo nos unimos entre nós. (15:281)

I pay close attention to this doubling of terms: He in me, and I in Him. If Christ, in the Communion, only intended to become one with us, one of these terms would be enough, and the second one unnecessary. Let me prove that. In order for these two hands to be united, it suffices that the right hand be joined to the left, or the left to the right. Similarly, for Christ and us to be joined, it suffices that we live in Christ: *in me manet*–or that Christ live in us: *et ego in illo*. If, in order to explain the union between Christ and the person who partakes of the Holy Communion, only one of the terms is sufficient, why does Christ double and multiply them? For this very reason. He doubles and multiplies the terms because the union is also doubled and multiplied. If it were a single union, He would only need to say: *in me manet* or *ego in illo*, but He doubly says *in me manet, et ego in illo*, in order to indicate the two kinds of union that take place in the mystery: an immediate union, which unites us to Christ, and another mediated union, with which, by means of Christ, we unite ourselves to each other.

It is no longer the case, as in John's Gospel, of clearly distinguishing between the human and the divine aspects as far as the participation of the former in the latter is concerned, but of conceiving the divine as a mediation capable of overcoming differences between men or, more precisely, capable of conciliating men's differences in belief and individual desires around a divine identity of which all partake. Thus, sacramental communion not only creates the opportunity for contact between each man's soul and God, but above all, it strengthens the relations between men by means of investing God's presence in these relations. The argument is presented in terms of the double union: "Pela união que se termina de

Cristo a nós fica Cristo unido conosco; pela união que se termina de nós a Cristo ficamos nós unidos entre nós. Mais claro.
Pela união que se termina de Cristo a nós, fica Cristo unido a
cada um de nós, e como dividido de si; plea união que se termina de cada um de nós a Cristo, ficamos todos unidos com
Cristo e todos unidos entre nós" (15:281–82) ("By means of
Christ's union, He is united with us; by means of our union in
Christ, we are united among ourselves. To state this more
clearly: By means of Christ's union in us, He is united with
each one of us, thus multiplying Himself; by means of our
union in Christ, we are all united with Him and all united
among ourselves"). Therefore, the Holy Communion is not
fully achieved without the creation of a collective human identity, similar to each individual's relation to God: a natural,
rational and political body in which, nevertheless, the very
image of God appears more clearly. In other words, the mystical experience, through the sacramental mystery, places in a
specific relation of identity those men who equally desire to
participate in his Being. In order to demonstrate this, Vieira
makes use of the "etymological method" (Saraiva 16) widely
used in sermons during that time, whose purpose is to refer
back to the mysterious root of biblical words as the hidden
reason between the terms or objects of the historical present:

> Pregunto: que quer dizer comunhão? O nome comunhão–
> *communio*–não é inventado por homens, senão imposto por Deus
> e tirado das Escrituras sagradas em muitos lugares do Testamento
> Novo. E que quer dizer *communio*? Quer dizer *communis unio*:
> união comum. Assim explicam sua etimologia todos os
> intérpretes. De maneira que dando Cristo nome à Comunhão,
> não lhe pôs o nome da união particular que temos com ele,
> senão da união comum que causa entre nós. (15:282)

> I ask: What does communion mean? The word communion–
> *communio*–was not invented by men, but rather given by God and
> taken from the sacred Scriptures in several passages of the New
> Testament. And what does *communio* mean? It means *communis
> unio*: common union. This is the etymological explanation given
> by all interpreters. When Christ chose this name for the
> Communion, He did not name it according to the specific
> union we have with Him, but rather according to the common
> union that it causes in us.

The Sacrament therefore accomplishes the essential common
identity for all who individually look for the same God hidden in it. The analogy with the mystery of the Trinity, which
Vieira claims as evidence of this identity, can clarify the
strong meaning he gives to it:

> Só no mistério da Eucarista se pudera conseguir esta
> possibilidade, e só no mistério da Trindade se pudera achar esta
> semelhança. A maior maravilha do mistério da Trindade é haver
> nela multidão e unidade, muitas pessoas e uma essência. E o que
> faz no mistério da Trindade a unidade, faz no mistério da
> Eucaristia a união. A pessoa do Padre é distinta do Filho e do
> Espírito Santo; a pessoa do Filho é distinta do Espírito Santo e do
> Padre; a pessoa do Espírito Santo é distinta do Padre e do Filho, e,
> contudo, são um só Deus. Por quê? Porque se unem todas–não
> falo bem–porque se identificam todas em uma só essência.
> Identifica-se o Padre com a essência divina, o Filho com a
> essência divina, o Espírito Santo com a essência divina; e como a
> divina essência é uma só, e uníssima, como lhe chamou S.
> Bernardo, ainda que as três pessoas sejam realmente distintas,
> podem ser, e são uma só divindade, podem ser, e são só Deus. O
> mesmo passa no mistério soberano da Eucaristia, só com
> chamarmos aqui união o que lá se chama unidade. Chegam todos
> os homens àquela sagrada mesa: eu que comungo uno-me com
> Cristo, vós que comungais uni-vos com Cristo, o outro que

> comunga une-se com Cristo, e por meio desta união com Cristo
> ficamos unidos também entre nós: *Ut sint unum, sicut nos unum
> sumus*. (15:284)

> Only in the mystery of the Eucharist can one achieve this
> possibility, and only in the mystery of the Trinity can one find this
> similarity. The greatest wonder of the mystery of the Trinity is to
> find in it multitude and unity, many persons and one essence.
> And what constitutes unity in the mystery of the Trinity is what
> constitutes multitude in the mystery of the Eucharist. The Father
> is distinct from the Son and from the Holy Spirit; the Son is
> distinct from the Holy Spirit and from the Father; the Holy Spirit
> is distinct from the Father and from the Son and, yet, they are a
> single God. Why is that so? Because they are all united–it is hard
> to put this into words–and because they identify themselves with
> one single essence. The Father identifies himself with the divine
> essence, and so do the Son and the Holy Spirit; and since the
> divine essence is single and unique, as Saint Bernard has said,
> even though the three entities are distinct from one another they
> can be and in fact are a single divinity, they can be a single God.
> The same thing occurs in the sovereign mystery of the Eucharist,
> except that we call here union what we call there unity. All men
> come to the sacred table: As I commune I unite myself in God, as
> you commune you unite yourselves in Christ; another who
> communes unites himself in Christ, and this communion with
> Christ makes us united amongst ourselves: *Ut sint unum, sicut nos
> unum sumus*.

To sum up, the Holy Communion unveils the common being
among men, which cannot be explained outside of their relationship to Christ. That which is constituted by means of
union is deeply united with the Being which causes it through
the sacrament of the Eucharist.

This discovery of the essence of collectivity is a fundamental element of the sacred oratory of this period, and it is not
difficult to see that its terms are inseparably both theological
and political. The traditional topoi of the *unio mystica*
acknowledge the very organization of collectivity which, as it
gathers individual will into a single will, realizes the mystical
body par excellence. The divine essence of the man who lives
in God, according to Saint Bernard's or Guilherme de Saint-
Thierry's mystical theology, can be reinterpreted within the
concept of *universitas*, formulated by the Jesuit Francisco
Suárez, which refers to one's capacity to acknowledge the
common element within oneself and then be willing, as Skinner puts it, "to engage univocally in the performance of corporate legal acts" (2:165). In fact, a large part of the arguments
on the theme of the unifying purpose of the sacrament is
founded on the *via antiqua* of Thomism, taken up again by the
Dominican and Jesuit theologians who led the doctrinal
debate during the Counter-Reformation.

The necessary presupposition in this neo-Thomist formula
is that mankind in its natural state is not merely a body of
people, but people who share a common nature inasmuch as
it concerns beings irreducible among themselves. In this
sense, it is clear why for the sacramental form, the establishment of vertical and individualized relationships between
men and God is not sufficient, in the same way that the inner
certainty of the reformed man is not sufficient, for it is a matter of acknowledging and restoring the natural union between
men and of producing an intrinsically just and reasonable
assembly of beings, insofar as it has as an ontological basis the
communion with the Being.

On the other hand, from this model, in which the mediation between the human and the divine identifies the substance common to men's reason and will, derives the notion

that its development into a hierarchical and institutional ranking is natural. The coming together of men under a common identity develops in historical and political terms into a mystical body responsible for the legitimization of the Christian state. Particularly based on Suárez's position, Skinner thus comments on the question:

> But since the same moral characteristics are also possessed by all men in common, it is equally possible to think of the state of nature not as a community of individuals, but rather as "a single mystical body" in which all the members recognize the same obligations, follow the same rules, and are thus "capable of being regarded, from the moral point of view, as a single unified whole." . . . For the fact that they constitute a single mystical body implies that they must possess a single unified will–what Suárez calls "a special will or common volition existing in a single body of people." (2:165)

From this theological perspective, the sacramental form can radicalize, to a greater or lesser degree, the supernaturalization of the moral and voluntary identity of the mystical body. At times, the divine presence seems close to the political body to the point of continuously acting through it, on certain occasions, in order to favor its cohesion and maintenance. Furthermore, it can bring–much more than the doctrinal guidance that the Society of Jesus would recommend–the notion of the mystical body closer to a concept that confers full power on a particular Christian state, even though it does so invariably with a universal aim in mind. In Vieira's sermons, for instance, the essential community recognizes before anything else the formation of the Portuguese Catholic state. On the other hand, it is not reasonable to associate Vieira's tendency to acknowledge the *plenitude potestatis* of the Portuguese monarchy with Machiavellian theses in favor of the autonomous reason of state, that is, the thesis based on the idea of a separation between religion or moral and political pragmatics, or those in which state laws exclusively favor the prince or the government. On the contrary, Vieira's is an orthodox position which supposes that any political doctrine, whether or not it involves a contract among the members of the group to which it applies, must be based on the natural law established by God through the act of creation so as to not be outside of Grace. Besides, to be willing to participate in Christian concord has nothing to do with pessimistic compassion in the face of human misery after the Fall, because it means to seek a positive updating of the communion between man and his Creator. In terms of Christian virtues, there is nothing superior to this insertion in the natural society of men. In fact, to reject collectivity is equivalent to rejecting the God that supports it in a loving union through the sacrament.

There is one more issue that needs to be clarified with regard to the notion that Catholic preachers hold dear concerning the union of men both in theological and historical terms. First, the notion of union here points to a strong analogy with Divine Providence, which governs the world toward its end, and the voluntary act of men willing to improve themselves in this world in order to earn salvation. In other words, the Catholic topos of the union of men means, especially within the realm of Jesuit preaching, the exhortation of providential apostolic action, that is, the sense of a mission in the world. Second, to love one's neighbor, the exemplary pastoral motto of union, refers not only to a command given to the individual's conscience but, as has been noted, also claims the ontological founding of the institutional organization in which union historically is situated. This is to say that the motto

implies the idea of strengthening the Catholic state as a privileged place of communication and communion between the human and divine will.

Given all that, one can say that the union of men emphasizes the need for individuals to adhere to the providential action of Christianity, with its hierarchy and divisions, taken as natural within the realm of history. A Christian ethics of concord, love, or friendship in the sermons of this period cannot be understood outside of the context of an active insertion in a structure of power, determined to recover and unveil the hidden Being in the relations of men. There is thus a movement toward the consolidation of a Christian state, which closely resembles the monarchical organization of the Church, because, in this perspective, there can be no long-lasting state or even a future for humanity except when founded on God's will, which, by bringing men together in his "gentle love," makes it obligatory for them to love one another.

As traditional Catholic topos, gentle or disinterested love by definition is opposed to vulgar or common love. Cistercian writings, in particular, provide the basis of the vocabulary that was appropriated by sixteenth- and seventeenth-century preachers, but it already had been influenced by a fertile Ciceronian and Stoic quality. In it, the concept of love encompasses other notions such as *benevolentia*, that is, men's wish for the good of the loved one, for the loved one's sake and not his own, and *consensio*, which conceives of friendship as an essentially reciprocal good (Gilson 1983, 13). Such metaphors of love among Catholic preachers, far from being restricted to the individual affect, are basic concepts for the political theology that determines Christian duty according to the prudence of the state. Precisely for this reason, these concepts were embraced by political thinkers of the period. For instance, Saavedra Fajardo in the enterprise he called "*Concordiae cedunt,*" writes that "el valor de la concordia (é fazer) de muchas partes distintas un cuerpo unido y robusto" (2:830) ("the value of concord is [to turn] many different elements into a united and robust body"). In this same enterprise, whose symbol is the bodies of four soldiers side by side and on their raised shields the bodies of another four, attempting to reach the top of a high wall, he also states: "Todas las obras de la Naturaleza se mantienen con la amistad y concordia. Y en faltando desfallecen y mueren, no siendo otra la causa de la muerte que la disonancia y discordia de las partes que mantenían la vida. Así, pues, sucede en las repúblicas" (2:830) ("All of nature's works are maintained with friendship and concord. And when these are not present, nature's works fall apart and die, with dissonance and disharmony between the parts, that in their unity have kept them alive, being the cause of their death. The same thing happens with republics"). And soon he invokes the first analogy of the whole loving monarchy of men: "Como asistirá entre ellos Dios, que és la misma concordia, y la ama tanto que com ella mantiene (como dijo Job) su monarquía celestial?" (2:830–31) ("How can God be among us, He is concord Himself and loves to the point of having it as the basis (as Job would say) of his celestial monarchy?"). And then he authoritatively concludes: "debe el príncipe no dejar echar raíces a las discordias, procurando mantener su Estado en unión" (2:832) ("the prince should not allow disharmony to take root, always trying to maintain union in his state").

Generally speaking, truth, analogous to a theological essence, has sufficient potential attraction so as to impose itself politically, and by the same token institutions–legal instruments of love and power–cannot but sustain that very truth. That which is transcendent permeates history, and it is, for that reason, that history can be conceived only in terms of a mixture of the political and the theological. In other words, to historicize is proper to God when He speaks to men, and to look for the sacred in oneself is proper to history lived by men. Yet this is not all there is to the topos of men's union made possible by the sacrament. Vieira's sermons propose that collectivity, constituted in this way, is testimony to a common Incarnation, that is, to a second Incarnation in which the divine is made present in men's inclination toward union. In a *Sermão do Mandato* of 1655, Vieira stated the following as he compared the sacrament and Incarnation:

> É verdade que Deus na Encarnação não tomou a natureza humana em comum, senão uma humanidade particular [a de Cristo], mas essa mesma humanidade e essa mesma carne, unida à divindade, fê-la Cristo universal e comum, dando-a no Sacramento a todos es fiéis, e unindo-os realmente consigo; e como ficam unidos, e encarnados com Cristo, a mesma Encarnação do Verbo se estende e multiplica em todos nós. (7:101)

> It is true that God, in the Incarnation, did not take human nature in general, but instead a particular human nature [that of Christ], but this same humanity and this same flesh, united in divinity, was made universal and common by Christ, who gave it to all through the Sacrament. It is Christ who truly united all men among themselves; and since they stay united, in Christ, the same Incarnation of the Word reaches all of us and in us is multiplied.

From this perspective, God's infinite love for humanity would not be manifested so clearly in the Incarnation as it is in the Sacrament. In the latter, divine love reaches each individual at the same time that its presence consecrates the union of all people, so that as it becomes common among men, a single God is manifested in it.

One question worth asking is what kind of gathering of men would most appropriately comprise this "second Incarnation," more loving and universal than that which is restricted to Christ. The most appropriate community for this "second Incarnation" can be formed only by the *corpus mysticum* of the hierarchical, institutional Church–*principatus apostolicae sedis*–"which is destined to fulfill the mission which in the beginning has been entrusted to Peter" (Courtine 92). But, as we have seen, the definition of the *mystical body* is not limited to the Church or to the militant priesthood. The cornerstone of the Church, which is revealed as an inheritance in its visible hierarchy, extends naturally to the Catholic state. At this historical moment, there is no answer to the question of a collective Incarnation of Christ that does not lead to the discussion of the state's origin and sovereignty, whose historical acts are emphatically viewed as acts of Providence and in which the notion of Christianity and politics are not contradictory. Quite the opposite, the disparate movements of Church and state recover the hidden discourse of the common Being inscribed in them.

Vieira's sermons aptly illustrate this period of Catholic Counter-Reformation thought during which the full acceptance of Christ through the Eucharist leads to the union of political forces within the Christian kingdom (in this case, the Portuguese Empire) that are necessary for its defense, maintenance, and dissemination: "O corpo de Cristo, a quem comungamos, como é um só e o mesmo em todos os que o comungam, a mesma unidade que tem e conserva comido comunica aos que o comem. E assim todos, por mais e mais que sejam, ficam não já muitos, senão um só" (15:321) ("The body of Christ, with whom we commune, is a single one and the same for all who commune, its very unity is kept intact by those who drink and eat of it. And thus every one, regardless of how many they may be, are not many, but rather one").

Communion among men means both a theological movement, achieved through the gathering of men in God, and a historical and political act, which strengthens the Portuguese Empire in its wars, commerce, and religion (which were particularly difficult in Portugal at the time of the so-called Restoration): "A natureza da união é unir, a propriedade multiplicar, e para que a união faça de poucos muitos, é necessário que de muitos e de todos faça primeiro um só" (15:320) ("The purpose of union is to unite, to multiply, and for union to turn many into few it must first turn many and all into one alone"). It is important to note, though, that this union of men consecrated by God in the heart of the state can take place successfully only if it takes into account the hierarchy of social orders or traditional states of monarchy, which are not dissolved or made equal. Between one order and another, in fact, as Saavedra Fajardo has noted, the king sometimes needed to provoke disputes only to strengthen his authority:

> La discordia que condenamos por dañosa en las repúblicas es aquella hija del odio y aborrecimiento: pero no la aversión que unos estados de la república tienen contra otros, como el pueblo contra la nobleza, los soldados contra los artistas; porque esta repugnancia o emulación por la diversidad de sus naturalezas y fines tiene distintos los grados y esferas de la república, y la mantiene, no habiendo sediciones sino cuando los estados se unen y hacen comunes entre sí sus intereses, bien así como nacen las tempestades de la mescla de los elementos, y las avenidas de la unión de unos torrentes y ríos con otros. (2:833)

> The disharmony that we condemn as harmful for republics is that which derives from hatred and anger: but not the aversion that some states of the republic have for others, such as the people have against the nobility, soldiers against artists; because such aversion or emulation because of the diversity of their nature and aims occurs in various degrees and realms of the republic, and sustains it, there being no trouble when states come together and share interests, just as storms arise from the mixture of elements, and the avenues of the union, are formed with torrents and others with rivers.

And since harmony among social layers, maintained as such and not destroyed, is what is most convenient for the Christian prince, it then seems clear that concord must be primarily understood as an acceptance of hierarchy. Collective union, at the same time national and divine, can become unity only if, on the one hand, it encompasses the will of all orders (from the bottom to the top of the kingdom) as a united whole and, on the other hand, if this participation is determined by stable social segments or orders. This makes the top of the hierarchical pyramid or–to continue to use traditional metaphors of scholastic political institutions, still much *en vogue* at the time– the head of the mystical body, the best symbol of its unity.

This also clarifies the theological-political meaning, according to which a preacher like Vieira affirms: "[O]s príncipes e a nobreza é o tudo dos reinos. Escolheu Cristo aos nobres e senhores para que o tirassem do afrontoso suplício e fizessem as honras a seu corpo, porque honrar o corpo de Cristo afrontado, é ação que anda vinculada à nobreza. E quando assim trouxe a si a nobreza, diz que havia de trazer a si *onmia*, e não *omnes*, tudo, e não todos, porque os nobres não são todos, mas são tudo" (1:180–81) ("[T]he princes and the nobility are everything in kingdoms. Christ chose the nobility and the lords to relieve Him of offensive pain and honor His body, because honoring Christ's offended body is an act connected with nobility"). In a consecrated world, refuting hierarchies is not relevant because they are a testimony of the hierarchy of laws that govern the world since it was created, but it is indeed relevant to criticize its reformable vices and to reprimand its corrupt habits. In this light, one can see in sermons of this kind an ancient scholastic *topos* that claimed civil and spiritual nobility as equal: "[W]e must be prepared to recognize not merely 'godly' but also 'civil' nobility" (Skinner 1:60). This civil nobility, in Bartolus's words, "has been invented by us to be similar to, and an imitation of, godly nobility" (Skinner 1:60). In other words, there is an identification between, on the one hand, spiritual, divine, and moral nobility and, on the other, the nobility of blood and title inherited by the main lineages of the kingdom, and the relation between them is not arbitrary. Their main tendency is to admit that "[inherited] wealth is capable of promoting virtue" (Skinner 1:59). And, as Bartolus himself concludes, "anything which tends to promote virtue tends to promote nobility" (Skinner 1:59).

Nevertheless, the aim of Iberian preachers in the sixteenth and seventeenth centuries was not, in general terms, to favor the increase of the power of the nobility within the state. What they intended was to encourage the nobility's adherence to a centralizing, monarchic hierarchy and, in this sense, to promote its relative weakening, or greater dependence as a particular order, in relation to the king and his governmental machinery. The will of each one of the social orders of the mystical body of the state must converge toward this privileged place, for only the state, as has been noted, can conciliate private interests and the welfare of the political organism as a whole.

The viewpoint of these preachers obviously draws on Saint Thomas, for whom hereditary monarchy was the best form of government and the only one capable of looking after the common welfare, based on which rational organization is the basic principle of law; it is the only principle capable of avoiding the factions of certain groups and interests that threatened to destroy collectivity. In this Thomist and neo-Thomist context, to state that nobility is suitable for union certainly implies that nobility is to be persuaded that it must move toward accepting a state which legitimizes its status as nobility, both according to a model of Christian *virtus*, for which nobility is an example for other social orders, and according to its acceptance of the ideal of concord, which submits nobility to the higher power of the monarchy and the Church.

**Translation by Thomas LaBorie Burns
and Gláucia Renate Gonçalves**

Works Cited

Auerbach, Eric. 1987. *Mimesis*. São Paulo: Perspectiva.

Balthasar, Hans Urs von. 1960. *Teología de la historia*. Madrid: Ediciones Guadarrama.

Courtine, Jean-François. 1985. "L'héritage scolastique dans la problématique théologico-politique de l'âge classique." *L'État baroque: Regards sur la pensée politique de la France du premier XVIIe siécle*. Ed. Henry Méchoulan and Emmanuel Le Roy Ladurie. Paris: J. Vrin. 89–118.

Dominique, Pierre. n.d. *La politique des jésuites*. Paris: Bernard Grasset.

Gilson, Étienne. 1960. *Introduction à la philosophie chrétienne*. Paris: J. Vrin.

—. 1983. *La théologie mystique de saint Bernard*. Paris: J. Vrin.

Gracián, Baltasar. 1960. *Obras completas*. Madrid: Aguilar-Del Hoyo.

Green, Vivian Hubert Howard. 1984. *Renascimento e reforma a Europa entre 1450 a 1660*. Lisboa: Dom Quixote.

Hibbard, Howard. 1972. "Ut picturae sermones: The First Painted Decorations of the Gesù." *Baroque Art: The Jesuit Contribution*. Ed. Rudolf Wittkower and Irma B. Jaffe. New York: Fordham University Press. 29–49.

Maravall, José Antonio. 1986. *Antiguos y Modernos: Visión de la historia e idea de progreso hasta el Renacimiento*. Madrid: Alianza.

Mendes, Margarida Vieira. 1989. *A oratória barroca de Vieira*. Lisboa: Caminho.

Miller, René Fulöp. 1935. *Os jesuítas e o segredo de seu poder*. Porto Alegre: Globo.

Saavedra Fajardo, Diego. 1976. *Empresas políticas: Idea de un príncipe político-cristiano*. 2 vols. Madrid: Nacional.

Saraiva, António José. 1980. *O discurso engenhoso*. São Paulo: Perspectiva.

Sebastián, Santiago. 1985. *Contrarreforma y barroco: Leituras iconográficas e iconológicas*. Madrid: Alianza.

Skinner, Quentin. 1978. *The Foundations of Modern Political Thought*. 2 vols. Cambridge: Cambridge University Press.

Spicq, Ceslas. 1984. "Mediação." *Dicionário de Teologia Bíblica de Bauer*. 2 vols. Trans. Helmuth Alfredo Simon. São Paulo: Loyola. 680–87.

Stoeger, A. 1984. "Eucaristia." *Dicionário de Teologia Bíblica de Bauer*. 2 vols. Trans. Helmuth Alfredo Simon. São Paulo: Loyola. 389–405.

Tapié, Victor. 1961. *Le Baroque*. Paris: Presses Universitaires de France.

Vieira, Antonio. 1957–1959. *Sermões*. São Paulo: Editora das Américas.

—. 1982. *História do futuro*. Lisboa: Imprensa Nacional/Casa da Moeda.

SECTION V
THE NOVEL

CHAPTER 29

THE *FEUILLETON* AND EUROPEAN MODELS IN THE MAKING OF THE BRAZILIAN NOVEL

Marlyse Meyer

The Question of European Models

European models constitute a fundamental element in the making of Brazilian literary culture. Their role is irrefutable both in the elaboration of the national novel and in the correlative constitution of a reading/listening public ready to adopt new prose fiction that comes to replace or supplement the traditional orally transmitted narratives. After repeated attempts by those who have been designated precursors of the Brazilian novel, the genre was established in 1844 with the publication and success of Joaquim Manuel de Macedo's (1820–1882) *A Moreninha*. But models were not always taken from "high literature," as noted by Antonio Candido (one of Brazil's most important literary critics and historians whose work was the starting point for my own research): "In the decade of the 1930s the translation of serial *feuilletons* in newspapers or bound volumes published here or brought from Portugal and France was a primary incentive, creating in the public the habit of the novel and raising the interest of writers" (120–21).

In his autobiographical essay "Como e porque sou romancista" ["How and Why I Am a Novelist"], one of the founders of the Brazilian novel, José de Alencar (1829–1877), evokes the readings of childhood family gatherings: "Eu era quem lia . . . não somente as cartas e os jornais [note-se o registro do analfabetismo das mulheres que constituíam geralmente o auditório do menino], como os volumes de uma diminuta livraria romântica formada ao gosto do tempo. . . . Foi essa leitura contínua e repetida de novelas e romances que primeiro imprimiu em meu espírito a tendência para essa forma literária que é entre todas a de minha predileção?" (1987, 20, 23) ("I was the one who read . . . not only letters and newspapers to my family [note the illiteracy of the female relations that usually were the little boy's audience], but also the volumes of a minuscule romantic library conforming to the tastes of that time. . . . It was that continuous and repeated reading of novels and romances that first imprinted upon my spirit the inclination toward literature and the novel in particular").

My goal during years of research on the *feuilleton*–collected and published as *Folhetim, Uma História* (1996)–was to identify the "minuscule romantic library" of the little boy Alencar and to learn about the French form of the *feuilleton* and its presence in Brazil. The research showed that the books cited by Alencar did not fit in the category of French *feuilleton* novel.

From the start there was a difference: There are two strands of European fiction that arrived in Brazil (and in the whole of Latin America) in waves that succeed each other. First, I will examine Alencar's "little romantic library," and then I will take a brief look at the French *feuilleton* novel as it was disseminated in Brazil.

José de Alencar's essay gives us a unique glimpse at his childhood reading matter. Among those texts a significant one was *Sinclair das Ilhas ou os desterrados da ilha da Barra* [Saint-Clair of the Isles; Or the Outlaws of Barra–A Scottish Tradition]. (Barra is one of the Hebrides Islands, on the coast of Scotland.) *Sinclair das Ilhas* is also the favorite book of a number of characters in Machado de Assis's (1839–1908) novels and short stories, and the reading of it holds a major place in one of his most famous novels, *Quincas Borba* (1891). In Guimarães Rosa's (1908–1967) *Grande Sertão: Veredas* [1956; *The Devil to Pay in the Backlands*, 1963], the discovery and reading of *Sinclair das Ilhas* marks the initiation into the world for the narrator-protagonist, Riobaldo. It should also be mentioned that there was a rare Brazilian translation of *Sinclair* published in 1825 in Rio de Janeiro; it was published at a time of great political convulsions following the proclamation of Brazilian independence (1822). The reasons for publishing the translation were political as well as moral, as can be deduced from the preface as well as from an 1827 review done by a French journalist, Pierre Plancher.

The "Real Modern" Novels

The books evoked by José de Alencar were part of the romance in Europe from the latter half of the eighteenth century into the first quarter of the nineteenth. Published by specialized book dealers (especially by Minerva Press in London), they were the basis of the "circulating library" (invented around 1740 in England); these reading establishments rented books, volume by volume, to a growing and predominantly female public. Translated in Spain and Portugal, these novels crossed the Atlantic and reached Brazil through book dealers–especially French ones–who had established shops after 1808 when the Portuguese Crown moved the court to Rio de Janeiro in the flight from Napoleon. Abundant records are available about the circulation of these books from between 1810 and the 1840s–the date when the French *feuilleton* began to be translated and published in Brazilian newspapers. That year, 1808, is crucial in Brazilian history, for it marked the arrival of the Portuguese royal family headed by Reigning Prince D. João, the soon-to-be D. João VI, with a following of 10 to 15 thousand people who fled the Napoleonic invasion of Portugal. The royal court was established in Rio de Janeiro, thereby transforming the capital of the colony to the capital of what was (still) a vast Luso-Brazilian empire. Hence, the great and rapid change in the life of the small colonial town, which by 1820 had become an active center of political, commercial, economic, social, and cultural life.

Once the colonial laws that prohibited the immigration of foreigners were revoked, the opening of the ports brought hundreds from various parts of Europe and the Americas. The French were scattered all over the city, engaged in various trades, but they were primarily book dealers. And it was a French Liberal refugee, Pierre Plancher, who founded the newspaper *O Jornal do Comércio*, in addition to numerous other periodicals. The English dealt primarily in trade and represented the great British manufacturing establishments. Rio de Janeiro became a great consumer of European goods: It imported manufactured products from England, luxury items, furniture, beverages, and fabric from France, wheat from Argentina and the United States. There was a notable increase in the trade of slaves from West Africa. Teachers–especially English governesses–were also in great demand. The Brazilian elite was beginning to think about literacy and the education of young women according to European models. New schools were opened throughout the country but especially in the capital. A new look came to Rio, literary salons were opened in the new elegant houses. A new appreciation of the culture of the European elite brought about the Botanical Garden, the Royal Academy of Drawing, Painting, Sculpture, and Architecture, the Royal Press, the São José Theater. A French mission composed of artists, painters, and others was invited to Rio de Janeiro, and they would take on a decisive role in the development of the new city. Public libraries were founded in Rio and the provinces. And to crown it all, the love and the enthusiasm for opera took hold in Brazil. Besides the nobility from Portugal, a new middle class emerged and soon became the dominant social force, while all labor of any kind was completely carried out by the slave work force. It is into this fully transformed country, now free from the previous censorship, that books of all kinds entered, among them the popular French novels that were read and heard in public readings by the aspirants to the creation of a Brazilian national literature–as was the case with Alencar.

As of 1834 various facts suggest the beginning of a period in which literature came across the Atlantic fully transformed and marked by a rhythm more lively and more adequate to the transformations that were going on in Brazilian society and sensibility. Romanticism penetrated the country; theater began; a proliferation of literary magazines and newspapers took place. These venues published what were to be the first attempts at a national literature. The Liberal Revolution in Portugal in 1820 obliged King D. João VI to return to Portugal and reestablish the authority of the Crown. He left his son Pedro in Brazil as the reigning prince. Instigated by the Brazilian Party, Pedro proclaimed Brazilian independence on 7 September 1822. These were moments of concern about the political future of Brazil; these moments of upheaval were evoked in the preface to the Brazilian edition of *Sinclair das Ilhas*, whose patrons, "Brazilian patriots," were in opposition to D. Pedro I. He finally ended his reign (1822–1831), abdicating in favor of his son, D. Pedro II, who was still a child. Between 1831 and 1840 the government was led by the regency and faced yet another period of unrest; D. Pedro II's reign was declared in 1840 and lasted until 1889, the year when the republic was finally proclaimed and D. Pedro II went back to Portugal in exile.

In Brazil, books were distributed from Rio into the Brazilian provinces, as attested to by numerous ads in newspapers and by the catalogues of the country's public libraries. Franco-English popular novels and the French *feuilleton* chapbooks were very successful throughout the whole of Latin America, thanks to the same book-dealing circuit whose agents spread out all over Europe. Real modern novels translated from the French was the selling point for book dealers. French was, in fact, the intermediary language and not the first language for the versions of these novels in Portuguese (originally they were mostly English). These translations often simplified the original and made it more palatable for the incipient Brazilian readers. Translation from English to French and then, in abridged form, to Portuguese was the trajectory of these cultural transmigrations. Most of the authors of those popular novels were women, something to be credited to the social consequences of the Industrial Revolution in England. After all, it brought among, other things, the educated woman's liberation from domestic tasks, which generated the freedom necessary to write. Meanwhile, the reorganization of domestic, family, and conjugal life in England began to liberate women from the protective and restrictive traditions of the family. Those who did not get married–and even married women at times–began to enter the work force–hence all the women housekeepers, teachers, and novelists. They not only became reading clients, but also dared to write. Many of them were badly paid writers for publishers associated with the lending libraries; they were skillful connoisseurs of the market's taste, one whose voraciousness for fiction was at the same time instigated and satisfied by them. Being able to work for Minerva Press, for example, was a way to guarantee the daily bread for women thrown into the struggle for survival in industrialized England. Many had to write on assigned topics and themes–not much skill or imagination was needed, so redundant was the fiction offered for sale.

Mrs. Burney, Opie, Bennet, Inchbald, Lennox, the Lee sisters (much admired by Walter Scott), as well as the well-off and highly popular Mr. Radcliffe, were among the most read. Among them was Mrs. Elizabeth Helme (d. 1814?), a serious professional highly admired by her French translators: She wrote a good history of Scotland, many educational books, a great number of novels, and was a translator herself. Her novels were almost all best-sellers in English, French, Spanish, and Portuguese and not only at the time; they continued to be published well into the nineteenth century. One of them, *Louise, or the Cottage in the Moor* (1787), was cited in Brazilian catalogues as early as 1816. Mrs. Helme was also the author of *St. Clair of the Isles, or the Outlaws of Barra* (1803), despite its frequent attribution to Mme de Montolieu (author of the famous *Caroline de Lichfield*), who was in fact the book's French translator; this simple bookseller's error was repeated on numerous lists, and the catalogue at the Bibliothèque Nationale in Paris greatly contributed to the continuation of this error. Another best-selling woman writer, Regina Maria Roche (1764?–1845), is often cited in histories (for example, that of James Foster, *History of the Pre-Romantic Novel in England*) along with Helme as a best-seller. She is the author of *The Children of the Abbey* (1796), or *Amanda e Oscar*, which came into Portuguese from an excellent French translation by Abbott Morellet, a well-known man of letters who survived the French Revolution. In England and France these novels had an ambiguous status, still reflected by literary history today. Although the "implied reader" was the reading public of the popular *Minerva Press*, one of the first publishing houses to develop what would be called the culture industry, the serious critics from the famous *Edinburgh Review* severely criticized the Minerva Press, while occasionally recognizing one or another of its publications. Walter Scott admired many of those authors, to whom in fact he attributes his interest in writing historical novels.

In the state of cultural destitution of that time in Brazil, the arrival of foreign fiction could not be matched by any local production that could have reflected its own reality. This foreign fiction was adopted unambiguously as one of many civilizing products coming in from Europe. The list of book dealers selling "real modern novels" or "novels recently translated from the French" indiscriminately include "high" or "low" works from various European literatures, as the following list will attest: Fernando de Roja's (1470?–1541) *La Celestina* [1500; *Celestina* 1631], Bernardin de Saint Pierre's (1737–1814) *Paul et Virginia* [1787; *Paul and Virginia*, 1789], Miguel de Cervantes's (1547–1616) *El ingenioso hidalgo don Quijote de la Mancha* [1615; *The Story of Don Quixote*, 1620], Henry Fielding's (1707–1754) *Tom Jones* (1749), and *Clarissa, or, The History of a Young Lady* (1747–1748) by Samuel Richardson (1689–1761), and so on. A good example of this cultural displacement is the aforementioned 1825 Brazilian edition of *Sinclair das Ilhas*, which in Brazil was a moral and political guide to living, lending itself to vicarious reading, such as the one done years later in Machado de Assis's *Quincas Borba*. The Brazilian edition of *Sinclair das Ilhas* left deep marks on Brazilian literature, including in such writers as Guimarães Rosa.

We can thus conclude a few things regarding the multivalent meanings acquired by these Franco-English novels in the making of the young Brazilian society. They are, on the one hand, a commodity imported much like tea, pianos, tilbury, china, the latest fashion in Paris, and the English "governesses" who would educate hitherto illiterate young women. This was a commodity that earned a living for French book dealers and whose consumption (even in the form of a reading at a soirée) was a sign of status and "modernity" for the young woman who had just joined the court. It was also a generational dividing line. In the first Brazilian novels we witness elderly characters who read or hear traditional stories, whereas the young women, contrary to those elderly men, read "modern" novels. As a vehicle for good manners, for escapism, but also offering a worldview of modern ideology, these books led to an attempt to imitate locally a fictional European society. Furthermore, they provided a vehicle for the establishment of a model for Brazilian prose fiction. One is still left with not only the surprising fact of the massive presence of the Franco-English novel in Brazil by the first half of the nineteenth century, but also the astonishing preference for these texts that were already best-selling novels in their countries of origin, providing the seeds for another literature in a country certainly as exotic to Europeans as the Hebrides Isles were to Brazilians. Why did books like *Sinclair das Ilhas* (just one among hundreds that made it to Brazil) mark so vividly the memory of our major novelists? This question poses not so much the problem of imitation as the very specificity of the Brazilian imaginary.

The *Feuilleton* Offensive

The same question could be asked in regard to what fed the cultural imaginary following the invasion of Franco-English novels. The *roman-feuilleton*, or French chapbook, made its entrance into Brazil and Spanish America by the middle of the nineteenth century. Its massive presence coincides, in the Brazilian context, with the reign of Pedro II (1840–1889), a period of major social transformations in Brazilian society that, among other changes, brought a progressive growth in the reading public. A perusal of book-dealer ads of the period and the lists of publications of fiction in the newspapers themselves makes evident the gradual replacement of the aforementioned popular English and French novels with the *feuilleton* novel, which, little by little, took over the Brazilian reading public.

One can also trace changes in the newspapers that include a growth in size, a change in format, large-print headlines, and greater print runs, as announced in a *Jornal do Comércio* editorial in January of 1842. All these changes were in part due to the arrival of the *feuilleton* novel. The first explicit *feuilleton* novel to arrive in Brazil was *Capitan Paul* written by Alexandre Dumas (1802–1870) and published in 1838, in both France and Brazil. Between 1839 and 1842 the bottom half of *Jornal do Comércio* (and of other magazines and periodicals that multiplied at the time) successively published episodes of a *feuilleton* novel, translated day after day from the French, thereby introducing anguish and suspense with the fateful and ever present "to be continued." New French authors appeared who have since been forgotten, such as Lavergne, Berthet, Countess Dash, Soulié (the author of *Memories of the Devil*), as well as old names such as Ducange, connected to melodrama, or the always popular Paulo de Kock (whose work appears uninterruptedly from issues 132 to 161 of that newspaper). Other chapbooks published in newspapers include work by Charles Expilly—author of a book unflattering to Brazilian women—as well as some Brazilian works like *Pedro, O Noivo de Além Túmulo* [Peter, the Bridegroom from Beyond the Grave].

Eugène Sue's (1804–1857) *Mystères de Paris* [1842–43; *The Bohemians of Paris*, 1843] was immensely popular in France in 1844. It appeared in Brazil in a translation by a great publicist, Justiniano José da Rocha. Except for an interruption or two, it appeared daily, and occupied almost the entire Sunday supplement and the bottom half of the paper weekdays until 20 January 1845. But already in October 1844, for the first time in the paper's history, it announced the subsequent publication in large print of *Mysteries of Paris* as a book by the newspaper's press. From then on, Sue's *Le juif errant* [1844; *The Wandering Jew*, 1845], Alexandre Dumas's *Le comte de Monte Cristo* [1845–1846; *The Count of Monte Cristo*], and all the subsequent work of the author of *Les trois mousquetaires* [1844; *The Three Musketeers*] would inexorably follow. In 1859, with a great outburst of ads, claims, and propaganda, the Brazilian novel *Rocambole* was published. The adventures of the Ponson du Terrail invade the newspapers, the booksellers, the reading offices, and even theater, in the dramatic version by the great actor Furtado Coelho. Following *Rocambole*, new modalities of the genre appeared in the newspapers, with a momentum that would not level off until 1914. The French *feuilleton* continued to be published and republished in newspapers at least until 1950. Such a rapid penetration of the French *feuilleton* suggests that there was, during the decades of 1840 and 1850, a body of readers in Brazil who would consume these novels in numbers sufficient to make them a major factor in the sales of the newspapers. This is so even if sales were a true indicator of the numbers of reading public: "[E]ach subscriber represented on average ten readers, which gives a circulation of one hundred thousand readers when in fact the print runs don't go over the plateau of ten thousand copies" (Meyer 89). In the 1840s there was another definite indicator of the rapid growth of the reading public in the proliferation of private reading rooms and public libraries.

Along with the "real modern" novels and French *feuilleton,* the homegrown novels would emerge, such as Joaquim Manuel de Macedo's *Moreninha* [The Little Brunette] in 1844, his *feuilleton*-like *Moço Loiro* [The Blond Youth], and so many more. And by 1856–1857 the public throughout Brazil, but especially in Rio, would anxiously await their daily dose of José de Alencar's *O Guarani,* much like it had awaited *Le comte de Monte Cristo.* The French *feuilleton* started from the intelligent vision of French journalist Emile de Girardin after the July Revolution of 1830. He conceived of a cheaper newspaper that resorted to many expedients in order to boost sales so that it could be financed by the sale of advertising space. Among the resources utilized was the astute use of the space left vacant by Napoleonic censorship. It was to become the miscellaneous bottom of the page, filled with diverse amenities and the *feuilletons.* Taking advantage of a compulsive readership when novels appeared serialized, Girardin turned this space into the most popular part of the newspaper. The daily fiction insert would eventually be called "novel-*feuilleton,*" then simply *feuilleton.* To guarantee daily readership to the newspaper, the novel had to be published in well-conceived segments, so as to reinforce what is already appealing about the novel form: What is it that's going to happen next? Curiosity is thus sharpened and sales are guaranteed.

The novelty appeared on 5 August 1836 in *Le Siècle:* a translation of the Spanish picaresque novel *Lazarillo de Tormes* (1554). But the formula was not born ready-made. New authors were invited to write specifically for the newspaper, and to produce novels in short units; the first was Honoré de Balzac (1799–1850), with *La vieille fille* [The Spinster] in October 1836. The magic formula "to be continued in the next issue" only made its appearance at the end of the year of 1836. Alexandre Dumas, by then a renowned novelist and a famous playwright, observed the novelty with some suspicion. He only agreed to publish *Capitaine Paul* [Captain Paul] in segments in 1838, but this work definitely catapulted the *feuilleton* novel to runaway success, as well as granting the newspaper an increase of 5000 subscriptions in only three months. Dumas discovered that the essential technique of the *feuilleton* is to submerge the reader *in media res,* offer lively dialogue and typical, recognizable characters, and have a keen sense of where to best end an installment. It should be no surprise that the standard *feuilleton* form was developed by a playwright. The relationship between the *feuilleton* and the melodrama, a popular dramatic genre at the time, is close indeed, with its multiple and always surprising *coups de théâtre* and its skillful *chutes de rideaux.* Sue's *Mystères de Paris* was inspired by melodrama and, in turn, became a melodrama after the success of its newspaper publication. The decade of the 1840s marks the definitive constitution of the *feuilleton*

novel as a specific genre. Eugène Sue published the *Mystères de Paris* in *Journal de Débats* between 1842 and 1843; in 1844 the same Sue published *Le juif errant,* Dumas released *Les trois mousquetaires* and *Le comte de Monte Cristo,* and Balzac put out the *feuilleton* continuation of *Les illusions perdues* [Lost Illusions], that is, *Splendors* and *The Misery of Courtly Women.* This invention of Sue and Dumas turned into a recipe used by hundreds of authors throughout Europe and the Americas. The formula had another consequence, namely a conceptualization of a new publication method for the novel genre. Basically all the prose fiction from that time on begins to be written (if not published) as a *feuilleton,* that is, in daily newspaper fragments that are later compiled, depending on their success, in a bound volume. It is a form of publication also taken up by José de Alencar, Joaquim Manuel de Macedo, and Machado de Assis, Charles Dickens (1812–1870), Pérez Galdós (1843–1920), and many others. This mode, with its own demand for interruption and for fragments that nevertheless do not prevent a certain continuity, influenced the structure of the novel as such well into the century.

Notorious, Still and Always

The phenomenon of the *feuilleton* novel is present in all Rio de Janeiro newspapers in nineteenth-century Brazil. Even though the necessary research has not been carried out, due to the difficulty in obtaining data about publications and runs, there is enough evidence of a correlation between the *feuilleton* and newspapers' prosperity. The same data pointed out in the case of *Jornal do Comércio* are also available for other newspapers in Rio: There were successive transformations in the novel, changes in format and layout, always printed in bottom strips, and accompanied by ads. *Gazeta de Notícias* was founded in 1875 in opposition to *Jornal do Comércio,* whose director, Ferreira de Araújo, had a penchant for the literary and published many Portuguese writers including: Ramalho Ortigão (1836–1915), Eça de Queiroz (1845–1900), Machado de Assis, Capistrano de Abreu (1853–1927), José do Patrocínio (1853–1905), and T. A. Araripe Jr. (1848–1911). He also published Raul Pompéia's (1863–1895) *O Ateneu* in *feuilleton* format. Between December of 1879 and January of 1882, space was opened up to the controversial Tomás Alves, who had already appeared in the paper in polemic diatribes against Camilo Castelo Branco (1825–1890), and in caustic presentations of Brazilian poets in his *Cancioneiro alegre.* Tomás Alves published a number of short stories in the *feuilleton* format, with the pseudonym "Hop-Frog." Those stories were considered by some of his contemporaries one of the first manifestations of Brazilian naturalism. (Noteworthy is that another naturalistic text, Lúcio de Mendonça's [1854–1909] novel in the same vein, *O Marido da Adúltera* [The Adultress's Husband], came out during the same period, in 1881, in *feuilletons* published in the paper *O Colombo,* from Campanha, Minas Gerais.)

The proof that the fiction at the bottom of the page was indispensable for any new journalistic enterprise was to be found in *Jornal do Brasil,* a newspaper that was established in 1891 and enlisted many of the key writers in Brazilian letters and politics. It was, however, no exception to the rule; it published a number of *feuilletons.* And in the *Gazeta de Campinas,* for example, between 1869 and 1887 one finds on its pages novels by Bernardo Guimarães (1825–1884), Machado de Assis, Julio Ribeiro (1845–1890), Camilo Castelo Branco (1825–1890), Ramalho Ortigão, and Eça de Queiroz (*O Mistério da Estrada de Cintra* [The Mystery of the Road to Cintra]), Octave Feuillet (1821–1890), Maria Amália Vaz de Carvalho (1847–1921), and L. A. L. de Oliveira Bello's (1851–1914) *Esboço de um Romance Brasileiro, Os Farrapos* [Sketch of a Brazilian Novel: The Farrapos]. They accompany Alexandre Dumas, Richebourg, Mie d'Aghonne, Mery, Boisgobey, Ponson du Terrail, and George Ohnet's *Serge Panine* (in Dona Guilhermina Santos's version).

Women and Newspapers

Many were the nineteenth-century women who not only concerned themselves with achieving a place in public life through aspirations to creative and translation work, but also through disseminating their own ideas about the status of women either in existing newspapers or by founding new ones. Andradina América Andrada founded *O Escrínio* in Rio Grande do Sul in 1898 and the sisters Revocata Heloísa de Melo and Julieta de Melo Monteiro edited *O Corymbo* in the city of Rio Grande (1884–1944). Pedro Maia Soares observes an interesting fact about women writers and editors: They "are not isolated from one another, but on the contrary, they make up a sort of female network that encompasses the entire state and maintains connections with other centers in the country. . . . Among these women of letters are well-known feminists. Following Rio Grande do Sul, Ceará is the state with the highest number of collaborators" (142–46). This is confirmed by the diverse geographical origin of the collaborators on the foremost women's newspapers in Rio de Janeiro, whose reports on the female condition were compiled by Maria Thereza Caiuby Crescenti Bernardes (see Bernardes 111–75).

We take women's newspapers to mean those papers that, founded and directed by women, attempted in one way or another to pose questions of import to women. Editorials, headlines and their subtitles, and the personalities of directors and writers suggest very different social beliefs, but even a superficial perusal reveals that the entire operation was permeated with the question of education. This amounts to a "hygienist" approach to urbanize the old colonial family structure, and thus the household itself. This entailed a new definition of women's role and a consequent metamorphosis of the family as a social unit, as Jurandir Freire Costa has pointed out in his acute study in *Ordem médica e norma familiar* [1979; Medical Prescription and Familial Norm]. The contradiction—already experienced in her own life by the great pioneer Nisia Floresta (1809–1885)—was between the opening up of literature for women gaining emancipation from the "marital tyranny," access to politics, achievement of voting rights, and entry into the work force with full salary, on the one hand, and on the other, the impossibility of forgetting that women were mothers and the educators of their children—in a word, the center of life in the home. As a consequence, wrote Floresta, a "well-to-do woman should know how to receive her husband's guests, to be present at the dinner table, and engage in conversation. In parallel fashion, she should throw herself into her new social situation, and abandon her old habits, Europeanizing her body, her dress, and her manners (119).

Even if the novel and the *feuilleton* are always associated with contumacious frivolity of women, they did not go unutilized by the female press of a militant persuasion, for the reading of these genres had a role to play in the redefinition of the modern woman. Even leafing quickly through these papers, one notices that the novels and *feuilleton* that systematically

occupied the consecrated space of the bottom strip were mostly translations done by women or Brazilian texts often authored by those very women. The *Jornal das Senhoras*, with fashion, literature, fine arts, theater, and criticism, was published between 1 January 1852 and 30 December 1855. This Sunday paper, skillfully satisfying the "new" woman, was founded by Joana Paula Manso de Noronha, who was born in Argentina and was well traveled before settling down in Rio de Janeiro. She was a journalist, a teacher, a poet and playwright, and it was the latter activity that linked her to the original *feuilletons*: She was the author of *A Família Morel* [The Morel Family], a frank adaptation of *Mystères de Paris*, staged by some members of João Caetano's company in São Januário Theater, soon after the fire in the São Pedro Theater in September of 1851. (João Caetano's partner, Estela Sezefredo, garnered critical praise for her performance in *Correio Mercantil* [Commercial Mail] on 8 September 1851 [quoted in Prado 36].)

The founder of *Jornal das Senhoras* was also the paper's editor, and placed herself in front of the readers from day one; the newspaper's goal was to disseminate enlightenment and cooperate with all who sought the social betterment and moral emancipation of women. The newspaper invited all women to publish their literary works, anonymously if need be. It should be noted that all women's newspapers showed a great willingness to encourage local production, even for the paper's crucial bottom strip. *Jornal das Senhoras* offered a bit of everything: hygienic education that incorporated rigor and worldliness, beautiful images of fashion and detailed descriptions of them, and a feminist militancy that provoked numerous enraged letters by male readers. The newspaper opened up space for women to voice their opinion. An example of this was the young woman who demanded more justice in the marriage laws and repeatedly sent her articles to the paper. She argued that marriage laws had been written by men for men and that, in the end, what they sought was for women to make themselves obedient servants of their husbands, swearing to be their slaves and accepting the lie of inferiority.

Jornal das Senhoras systematically published fiction—novels that were either short or extended for several issues—and even showed some original achievement in terms of the beloved *feuilleton*, much like the one that begins in the paper's first issue. Taking advantage of her personal experience, Joana Paula Manso de Noronha, albeit anonymously, published *Misterios del Plata* [Mysteries from River Plate] over the course of several months, prefacing it with an epigraph taken from Michelet. It was a contemporary historical novel, insofar as its theme was indeed history, and a recent one at that: It narrated the defeat of the Argentine Rosas, a *caudillo* initially popular and later a bloody and chaotic despot, brought down at the Monte Caseros battle by the alliance of opposition forces composed of exiled Argentines—among them Sarmiento—the former federalist Urquiza's troops, and Brazilian and Uruguayan forces. In the novel, the opposition is symbolized by the heroic and historical figure of Alsina, who effectively returned to Buenos Aires, where he participated in the government as a venerated judge who declared the freedom of the press, established citizens' rights, and wrote the Argentinean penal code. He would also intervene long after the novel's last episode, where the author contented herself with announcing Alsina's entrance into the ministerial body. In November of 1852, she mentioned a letter from the minister inviting her to publish her novel. It is still unclear whether or not, as was common practice, the novel was published by the newspaper's printers simply as a separate volume.

Jornal das Senhoras also published *Karolina*, a "Polish novel," translated from the French by the "editor-in-chief" (from 22 August 1952 to 19 February 1953) and D. Carolina Coronado's *A Jarilla*. It published the earlier work *Amor, ciúme e vingança* [Love, Jealousy and Vengeance], a "Brazilian novel" by Pereira da Silva (1817–1898), and *Suicídio por amor* [Suicide for Love], also found in a women's paper from Pernambuco, *O Belo Sexo* (João Climaco Lobato's literary periodical from 1850). The same *O Belo Sexo* also published an early Indianist novel, *As duas amadas* [The Two Lovers], written by the paper's editor, and *Amélia*, a Pernambuco novel from 1849 set during the Revolution of 1848. To return to Rio and to *Jornal das Senhoras*, we should still highlight *Um amor de mulher* [A Woman's Love], a curious mix of an exaggerated Romantic hero's melodramatic love story and good-humored chronicle of manners. Throughout more than ten chapters, we stroll around Rio and São Paulo, from balls to meetings of Freemasons, from student jests to unrequited love. This is a highly readable *feuilleton* and one that even offers a parody of the genre.

Another periodical "dedicated to woman's interests" was *O Sexo Feminino*, initially published in Campanha, Minas Gerais, and (as of 1857) Rio de Janeiro. The founder and owner was Francisca Senhorinha da Mota Diniz, a teacher in Rio. After an interruption, the paper appeared again, after the Proclamation of the Republic in 1889, under the title *O Quinze de Novembro do Sexo Feminino* [The Fifteenth of November of the Female Sex]. In the section entitled *Folhetim do Sexo Feminino,* the paper published several novels, among which was *A Diva Isabela* [The Diva Isabela], an original novel by D. Elisa Diniz Machado Coelho, a novel that would be taken up by the pediatrician Dr. Carlos Costa's "scientific, illustrated, and literary" newspaper, *A Mãe de Família*, "designed for childhood education and family hygiene." In the first issue's editorial on 1 January 1871, the doctor explained that the paper was dedicated to the physical education of children. Hygienists were to him as necessary as pedagogues, and so the newspaper was directed toward disseminating the principles of hygiene.

Imitations and Influences of the *Feuilleton* Novel

To what extent did Brazilian *feuilleton* production match the European genre that was characterized by its unending and attractive peripeteia stretching out in time, developing an adventurous, cape-and-sword, historical, legal-detective, or sentimental-realist thematic (or a mixture of all of these)? Common to all of them, and rather important, were both suspense and the heartbreaking, handkerchief-provoking situations–not to mention the agile ways of sustaining an often unsophisticated readership, the adequate use of various tricks of emplotment to maintain the audience's faithfulness to the story, to the supplement, and then finally to the book. Whereas one or another of these Brazilian *feuilletons* is of some interest, as exemplified with Joana Noronha's *Mistérios do Prata*, they generally are as cumbersome as the novels by those precursors studied by José Aderaldo Castelo or edited by Barbosa Lima Sobrinho, or the admittedly *feuilleton*-esque novel by pioneer Teixeira e Souza. Late *feuilletons* are also awkward, although these authors already betray a certain acquired expertise. This is the case with *A Filha do Barão* [The Baron's Daughter] by Pedro Nolasco Maciel (1861–1909), published in *Diário de Alagoas* between 20 November and 24 December 1885, and January

and February of 1886. It was skillfully interrupted at a moment of greatest suspense and later completed and bound in a volume; only then was the enigma that had been left in the air resolved. It is considered the first novel of manners in the state of Alagoas, but the book is virtually unreadable, so scarce are its narrative attractions and so rudimentary its writing. It does not contain anything *feuilleton*-esque, except in the most derogatory sense of the word.

The same could be said of many authors who published their work in various provincial papers. Mysteries and miseries are multiplied in these texts without the excitement, the appeal, and the experience of their French models, even though they occasionally try to imitate some of these characteristics. This is the case, for example, of an author from the Paraíba Valley, Vicente Félix de Castro, born in Areias, and author of *Os Mistérios da Roça* [The Mysteries of the Countryside], published in the Guaratinguetá paper and taken up in a volume in 1861. The same novel with a different title, *Misérias da Atualidade* [Miseries of the Present], and in three bulky volumes was republished in São Paulo by the Azevedo Marques printer in 1864. The same author wrote *História do voluntário da pátria* [Bananal, 1896; Story of the Volunteer of the Fatherland], *Os dramas do sangue* [The Dramas of Blood], or *Os sofrimentos da escravidão* [The Sufferings of Slavery], published in two tomes, *A filha do mistério* [The Daughter of the Mystery] and *Herança usurpada* [Usurped Inheritance]. Eugène Sue's influence is clear in more than the title *Mistérios da Roça* (or *Misérias da Atualidade*). The Brazilian novel begins with the same somber atmosphere that opens *Mystères de Paris* and it is reinforced by threatening tropical storms; the mysterious element characteristic of Sue is never lacking as the entire scene suggests the menace of a catastrophe that will destroy the human race.

The *feuilleton* explicitly devoted to the preparation of food by Aluísio Azevedo (1857–1913) did not fare much better. It also attempted to unveil the *Os mistérios da Tijuca* [Mysteries of Tijuca] (published in 1882, in *Folha Nova*), which was the initial title of *Girândola dos Amores* [Girandole of Loves], a novel without any *feuilleton*-esque attractions, and in fact, I would say, without any attractions at all. Aluísio Azevedo situates his work, by constant narrative voice intrusions, vis-à-vis the edible novel, and is led to pose the question of the "high" and "low" novel. This makes the book interesting for criticism, but it would hardly be digested by the *feuilleton* aficionado, except, perhaps, for its light-hearted tone, as in the amusing Chapter LXI, "Onde o autor põe o nariz de fora" ("Where the author sticks out his nose") and addresses the reader: "Leitor! parece que te vás pouco a pouco adormecendo com o descaminho que demos ao filamento primordial deste romance" (172) ("Reader! It seems that you are little by little falling asleep with the winding road we imposed on the main stream of this novel").

Another instance of Aluísio Azevedo attempting to write for the gross public (or to the public grossness?) is *Memórias de um condenado* [Memories of a Condemned Man] (which is a title in Northeastern *cordel* literature), published in *feuilleton* format in the *Gazetinha* in 1882, and republished under the title *A Condessa Vesper* [The Countess Vesper]. And after the success of *O Cortiço* [The Slum], Azevedo published the *feuilleton A Mortalha de Alzira*, in *Gazeta das Notícias* in 1891, this time under the pseudonym of Victor Leal, so as not to harm his best-selling credibility. Victor Leal was also the name under which collective novels were published: for example, the famous *O Esqueleto* [The Skeleton], by Olavo Bilac (1865–1918) and Pardal Mallet (1846–1894), published in March of 1890 in *Diário das Notícias*, or the one that followed it in the same newspaper, *Paula Matos*, or *O Monte de Socorro* [The Hill of Protection], written by the same two partners along with Coelho Neto and Aluísio Azevedo. These are novels that can be designated as Brazilian versions of the *feuilleton*. Luís Guimarães Júnior (1845–1898) was an assiduous collaborator in *Diário do Rio de Janeiro* between 1869 and 1872, and also the author of a humorous *feuilleton* novel, *A Família Agulha*, that appeared in the same paper from January to April 1870, then published in a Garnier volume, and recently reedited by Flora Süssekind.

Exploring the caricature-like narrative sense that undoes itself as it follows the *feuilleton* linearity and its related expectations, Flora Süssekind highlights the "hallucinated figure of Bernardo José Anastácio Agulha, whose logic leads characters and readers to a realm of full *nonsense* [English in the original]" (17). And she subtly and acutely sees that the text's special comic flair:

> is connected directly to the possibility that these caricature-characters suddenly install another logic, another order, where eating the ear of a trolley passenger, or sadly biting someone's neck, or prohibiting guests from leaving a party, or waltzing to death, or stabbing a bundle of clothes with a knife do not appear to be absurd things. For this is, in fact, one of *Família Agulha*'s great merits: It is one of the rare texts from that period where laughter is not an exclusive fruit of the jest chronicle. (19)

It is this jocose vein that laughs as it treats the insignificant and anonymous lives of the Brazilian "nobodies" that we could relate to another *feuilleton* novel recently recovered by Plínio Doyle and published by Alexandre Eulálio: *Mattos, Malta, ou Matta? Romance ao correr da pena* [Mattos, Malta, or Matta? The Novel of the Unending Script], by Aluísio Azevedo. This *feuilleton* was anonymously published in 1885 in *Semana*, Valentim Magalhães's literary newspaper, but it was soon recognized that Aluísio Azevedo was the anonymous author. This is a little novel with a high-comic tone that arises out of a remarkable narrative of disorder as well as grotesque unexpected situations. These respond to our perception of a certain nonsensical quality of real life and the unbelievable incongruities of urban reality. This amusing *feuilleton* does not miss out on the opportunity to mock the genre itself: It mixes narrative foci, interrupts itself, and leaves action suspended; at the very moment when it unveils the identity of the one who was hiding behind the lofty and unfortunate hero, it unmasks the fiction-maker.

The imperial court under His Majesty Pedro II inspired a series of *feuilletons* that composed an amusing volume when they were extracted from their original newspapers: *O Monarca da Fuzarca: Três versões para um escândalo na corte* [The Monarch of Revelry: Three Possibilities for a Scandal at Court]. The plot consists of a theft of jewels from the crown in the palace of São Cristóvão. To make it worse, the jewels are found and the criminals are caught, initially incarcerated, and then released with the excuse that one of them, the Emperor's footman, was facilitating and organizing the Emperor's love encounters–preferably with nymphets. Sérgio Goes de Paula's book tells the story based on reports, articles, cartoons, and illustrations from the period's papers; it also reproduces the *feuilletons* inspired by it. The first, with a title that recalls its glorious ancestor (the Dumas of *Le Collier de la reine* [The Queen's Necklace]), was identified by Capistrano de Abreu as being the work of Raul Pompéia (1863–1895), then 19 years old. Arthur Azevedo (1855–1908) was undoubtedly the author of the second book, published in the *Gazetinha* between 31 March and 15 April 1882, as *Um Roubo no Olimpo* [A Robbery on Olympus]. Then there was *A Ponte do Catete* [The Bridge of Catete], published originally as a *feuilleton* in *Gazeta da Tarde* between 30 March and 12 October 1882, left unfinished, but signed G.P., initials that are meant to hide Giuseppe [*sic*] do Patrocínio. (This is a piece that does not compare with the other; it lacks grace and plot.) Raul Pompéia is the best exploiter of the genre's tricks. His works are full of suspense, good chapter cuts, a rape preceded by the classic soporific administered to the future disgraced woman, the beautiful and innocent virgin who will be undone by the nobleman's concupiscence, thanks to the footman's servility. All this is followed by incest, clocks striking midnight, deaths prevented just before the revelation of the family secret, subtle dialogues: The *feuilleton* novel by the young Raul Pompéia turns out to offer all this plus being a pearl of political satire and parody.

But if we consider the Brazilian *feuilleton* that explicitly imitates the grand European model, without disguises or parody (which was probably the only genre available to would-be novelists), we can concur with the verdict that they could well have remained unpublished. An honorable exception among Brazilian writers in this genre was the journalist and writer from Pernambuco, Carneiro Vilela (1846–1913), author of an excellent *feuilleton* novel of both regional theme and detective form, the captivating book: *A Emparedada da Rua Nova* [The Walled-In of Nova Street], that is among the very best by a Brazilian writer. This is a story of seduction with a dishonored father and husband and where the seducer is a strange mulatto character of unknown origins and much sought after by high society; it is the dishonored father who carries out the revenge insinuated in the title. The plot is well narrated and develops in the atmosphere proper to the Recife bourgeoisie, with the plantation houses owned by Portuguese tradesmen, the underworld of crime in Recife, and a gallery of well-developed characters: Zarolho ("cross-eyed"), Bigode de Arame ("barbed-wire moustache"), Jereba, and others. Founder of the Pernambuco Academy of Letters, Carneiro Vilela wrote poetry, drama, short stories, chronicles, pamphlets, and diverse fictions, all of which was published in newspapers, and all of it, judging from *A Emparedada*, deserves critical study. Let me point out two noteworthy titles: *Os Mistérios da Rua Aurora* [The Mysteries of Aurora Street] and *Os Mistérios do Recife* [The Mysteries of Recife]. The latter was released in installments in 1876 and divided into the following *feuilleton* sections: "O esqueleto do quartel de polícia" ["The Skeleton at the Police Headquarters"], "A vingança de um nobre" ["The Revenge of a Nobleman"], "Misérias do povo" ["Miseries of the People"], "Os amores de uma fidalga" ["The Loves of a Noblewoman"], "Testamento do misantropo" ["The Misanthropist's Will"].

But with the exception of *A Emparedada*, much of the Brazilian production of *feuilleton* novels fall in the same category of the fictional *A Maravilha* [The Marvel], by Ernesto Sousa; it is situated in a Paraíba Valley town and is a narrative of overflowing sentimentality, revenge, and above all, well-rewarded virtues and well-punished vices. *Maravilha* included an enrapturing ending, regarded with jealousy by many of the literati: "e um rubro fio de sangue correu do níveo seio da donzela apunhalada, como uma víbora de coral num mármore pagão" (in Lobato 110) ("and a scarlet stream of blood ran on the snowy breast of his stabbed mistress, like a rattlesnake on pagan ivory").

In 1908 Monteiro Lobato spoke of the "literary education" of these cities populated with those who do "the same things, sleep the same sleep, dream the same dreams, and talk about the same subjects day in day out" (10). They also read the same books: "the three books, venerated and worn-out by use, with their covers dirty, sprinkled with candle marks from being read and reread in long family soirées through successive generations. They are: Paulo de Kock's [1783–1871] *La mare d'Auteuil* [1852; The Sea of Auteuil], for those versed in French, some truncated volumes of *Rocambole*, for enrapturing the female imagination, and Bernardo Guimarães's [1825–1884] *Ilha Maldita* [1879; Cursed Island], for enjoyment of those with nationalist tastes" (10–11). It is certainly more interesting to examine the concrete French *feuilleton* influence on the making of the official Brazilian novel than to register the mere imitators. In terms of thematic influence, we could point out Macedo's *O Moço Loiro* [The Blond Boy], *Os dois amores* [The Two Loves], or even the adaptation of chapter headings from Alencar's *O Guarani* that managed to maintain the public's daily attention. Still in *O Guarani*, the characterization of the hero and the villain are *feuilleton*-esque, and the relationships of loyalty and betrayal are not far from the patriarchal relations that rule D. Antonio de Mariz's world. But there are instances–as with the title character in José de Alencar's *Lucíola*–when fate redeems the poor young woman without forcing her into high-class prostitution. Fate there operates by bringing her an inheritance that guarantees her future. Money brings more than happiness–it allows the beneficiary a chance to take a significant role in society, one that usually is incumbent upon men. An example of this is Cora in Xavier de Montépin's (1826?–1902) *Mulheres de Bronze* [Women of Bronze], who is daughter to a slave woman and rich man from plantations in the Antilles. His inheritance allows her to take justice into her own hands and take revenge for old humiliations.

Alencar himself experiments with the cape-and-sword *feuilleton* form with his *Minas de Prata* [1865; Silver Mines], a text that today could be called filmic in its extraordinary sense of movement and its cuts. An example, among many others, is the scene where Cristovão is threatened by five bandits and then saved, thanks to the intervention of a fantastic figure, João Fogaça. *Minas de Prata* is *feuilleton*-esque and skillful in its way of dealing with the reader's complicity. It also shows an acute sense of the *coup de théâtre*, as in the sudden revelation of the silver mines. The *feuilleton* imagination, with its details of scheming, not to mention its comic flair, was worthy of the best silent films. This is, then, a "modern" *feuilleton* interspersed with remembrances of a popular past, as in the twelve peers of France: twelve men, brave and fearless as lions, or in the same spirit of the remembrances of the old *Romanceiro* compilations, in the gracious imitation of the traditional Iberian romances. And in the fashion proper to the best Dumasian historical novels–how else did the general public learn about Louis XIII, Richelieu, and the English and French courts if not from the pages of *The Three Musketeers*?–it is through *Minas de Prata* that certain images of a Bahian everyday life remain: the vile Jesuits remind one of Eugène Sue's *Le Juif errant*, and the accomplishments of the young Bahians do not fall short of the brave musketeers.

We can find the *feuilleton* stamp on another of Alencar's characters: the heroine in *Senhora*, mentioned above. In the world of the *feuilleton* there are two major possibilities for women without means: If the woman is from the middle class or upper middle class, with no profession, having been deprived of education, and for whom working would be dishonorable, the only possible social integration is through marriage to a rich man; if the woman is, on the other hand, from the lower social classes, she is left with the option of being an embroiderer or a prostitute. There is a third, even lower, social plane, that of a factory-working woman who is barely able to maintain her humanity. As Valéria de Marco has pointed out, *Senhora* is more than an imitation of the genre, and is in fact a portrait of the disorder of Brazilian life in the nineteenth century, wrapped in a confusing web of intrigues and conflicts. The *feuilleton* mimes that reality. The adventure novel presents adventures that are not resolved (Marco 147–51).

It should not to be forgotten that Machado de Assis too knew how to use the narrative cut in his *feuilleton* short stories, always achieving effects such as abrupt endings with the necessary anticipation for the continuation of narrative sequences, as, for example, in *Quincas Borba*, a novel that had its origin in the installments of the newspaper *A Estação*. And when Aluísio Azevedo writes his installment novel, he resorts to Eugène Sue's method of writing for the general public (Azevedo 1985, 170).

Narrative Machinery and Thematic Diversity: *Feuilleton* and Melodrama

The *feuilleton*'s very commercial character was to benefit the authors: The newspaper became a permanently open platform for writers who wished to attempt a literary career and experiment writing novels. Unknown and established writers had an equal chance: Gonzalez, Countess Dash, Balzac, Soulié, Sue, Bernard, Scribe. Even François-René de Chateaubriand's *Memoires d'outre tombe* [An Autobiography] was published in *feuilleton* format in *La Presse* between 1848 and 1850. The derogatory connotation later associated with the *feuilleton* novel has obscured the fact that it is not a homogeneous and uniform genre, for there were good and bad *feuilleton* authors. The *feuilleton* novel, born in 1836, stretched approximately from 1838 to the first years of World War I (1914). It was born in full Romanticism, whose aesthetic inspired the "founding fathers": Eugène Sue, author of *Mystères de Paris* and other best-sellers, and Alexandre Dumas, author of, among others, *Le comte de Monte Cristo* and *Les trois mousquetaires*.

A "socialist" dimension of the *feuilleton* novel appeared for the first time with Eugène Sue, who gave the worker and the poor in general the stature of true characters; authorities went so far as to attribute the February Revolution of 1848 to Sue's incendiary ideas. Suspended as dangerous by Louis Napoleon after the 1851 coup, the *feuilleton* came back in the late 1850s and enjoyed great popularity until the end of the century. A name that stands out in the second phase of the Latin American *feuilleton* is Viscount Ponson du Terrail and the thirteen-year-long series (1857–1871) of *Rocambole*, whose success was such that the adjective derived from Rocambole became synonym with the *feuilleton*. After the French defeat in the Franco-Prussian War and the attempt at a worker's commune in Paris in 1871, which ended in a bloodbath, the *feuilleton* returned with the social criticism of Naturalism and, paradoxically, the conservative view of the ruling classes, who again feared disobedience from the working class. Not by chance, one of the labels attached to this *feuilleton* is "romance of the victim" or romance of the facts of life, and the victim is usually a woman.

The *roman-feuilleton*, indissociable from the newspaper, is a publication of fiction in fragments well chosen so as to fit the bottom strip and leave the reader's interest suspended from one issue to the next. The plots are entangled and the plot lines are either realist or fanciful, but they always aroused the interest of the reader. Countless tricks that film, radio dramas, and TV soaps (*telenovela*) would later appropriate such as the cuts, flashbacks, simple and typified characters, dialogue instead of description were first developed in the *feuilleton*.

It was this formidable narrative machine that enchanted Brazilians, Mexicans, Chileans, and Argentines alike for years. In its late phase, the *feuilleton* collected all the negative semantic charges attributed to the genre, including a confusion with melodrama. It constituted the stereotype of what would lead in Latin America to the *telenovelas*, a form marked by tears, excessive emotion, and generalized pathos; but it is a genre that also provides themes, situations, and types for modern fiction in Latin American cultures. It was not, in fact, by chance that melodrama and the *feuilleton* found such privileged terrain along Latin American latitudes. It is well known how Colombia, Mexico, and Argentina, from a very early period in the nineteenth century, much like Brazil, were flooded with the French *feuilletons* translated in the newspapers of the day. The heroes of *Mystères de Paris* enthralled literate Mexico during the late 1840s; the extensive *feuilleton* catalogues that circulated in Mexico demonstrate the widespread appreciation for the French popular novel (Covo 235–53).

The Mexican Manuel Payno (1810–1894)–who was in Paris between 1842 and 1844, where he followed Sue and Dumas's triumphal ascension with admiration–published in 1845 the first Mexican *feuilleton*, *El fistol del diablo* [The Devil's Necktie Pin], and later his greatest work *Los bandidos de Río Frío* [1888; The Bandits of Río Frío], both excellent examples of the best Mexican appropriation of the genre. *María* (1870), by the Colombian Jorge Isaacs (1837–1895), provoked the tears of generations of readers and thousands of illiterate listeners. This is a text close to Chateaubriand's mode of expressing sentiment. In Latin America this literature was a surrogate for modernity, insofar as it appeared to be French. The efforts of the first educated cadres of the young nations to create a national literature were thus legitimated. The *feuilleton* trained future novelists and constituted a reading public.

Over time this novelistic world, through the newspaper inserts and cutouts, was read and orally transmitted to the subaltern classes, the historically exploited and long-suffering Latin American masses, whose own oral popular tradition was now enriched by new voices. In these countries, where it is said that one tragedy is never enough, it was not surprising to have a vast audience for a novelistic genre that, besides captivating audiences and readers for its ingenious plots, also thematized substandard life conditions and exacerbated personal and family relations. Thus developed a paroxysm of situations and feelings, poorly channeled into conservative messages that intended to be conciliatory but that never erased completely their sense of protest, and cultivated a specific way of narrating the crudest facts of life, while at the same time lightening them up with fictional magic. An impudently expressive novelistic tradition developed along the same lines with an appreciation for the excessive gestures and convoluted words favored by illiterate populations. This is, then, a paroxystic reflection of their social disadvantage and permanent aspiration for a moral universe in which justice and love would finally reign.

A major part of Latin America's literary culture is reflected today in the pure love searched for in the reading of novels by the old jaguar hunter in the Amazon in the Chilean Luis Sepúlveda's (b. 1949) *Un viejo que leía historias de amor* [1989; The Old Man Who Read Love Stories]. During the night of vigil for the hunting of the wild jaguar, and to the astonishment of his partner, the old man reads in lamplight:

–Anda, lee un poquito más alto.
–¿En serio? ¿Te interesa?
–Vaya que sí. Una vez fui al cine, en Loja, y vi una película mexicana, de amor. Para qué le cuento, compadre. La de lágrimas que solté.
–Entonces, tengo que leerte desde el comienzo, para que sepas quiénes son los buenos y quiénes los malos. (1993b, 112–13)

"Come on, read louder."
"Are you really interested?"
"Of course I am. I once went to the movies in Loja, and saw a Mexican love film.
I don't know why I'm telling you, but I cried my heart out."
"In that case, I'll have to start at the beginning, so you can tell the good people from the bad." (1993a, 105)

Feuilleton and melodrama also appeal to the popular concept of the representation of justice. Hence, all the epilogues that do not automatically obey the desire for a happy ending go beyond the consoling structures pointed out by Umberto Eco (b. 1932) to impart a feeling of justice and morality. This is the sentiment that motivates the melodrama *A Guerra de Canudos* [1902; The War of Canudos] to correct history and insert the millenium's apocalyptic imaginary; in this work, Antônio Conselheiro (leader of the popular Canudos rebellion) does not die, as he did in Euclides da Cunha's (1866–1909) work. Instead we see him in a final apotheosis with his hands tied, among the victorious who sing in praise of Brazil and unfold the national flag.

Melodrama and the *feuilleton* invaded cinema too. From the beginning of Latin American cinema, melodrama fed the Brazilian and Latin American imaginary with emotion. Manuel Puig's (1932–1990) novels have transmitted this affinity perfectly, but one must also recall that Mexican cinema, as well as tango and Brazilian popular music, are essentially melodramatic and the *feuilleton*-melodrama became the matrix for the *telenovela*, a fact that was featured in Vargas Llosa's (b. 1936) *Pantaleón y las visitadoras* [1973; Captain Pantoja and the Secret Service]. In the first wave of Latin American *telenovela*, *El derecho de nacer* [The Right to be Born] came out of Cuba. All of us remember Albertinho Limonta and mother Dolores, much better perhaps than the name of their author, Felix Caignet. What we have are old archetypes: An illegitimate child of adultery is taken in and raised by a faithful servant, and eventually claims his birthright. The first Brazilian version on TV dates from 1964; its success went beyond classes and permeated the whole of society. That year, all of Brazil would stop for the *telenovela*, including the well-off bridge players or auction-goers. Whereas, in the most distant Minas Gerais village, ballads would sing of the suffering of Albertinho and Isabel, the bridge clubs would install TV sets for all to follow, in tears, the story of the same *telenovela*'s main characters.

In my view we should consider the *telenovela* the updated "translation" of an old genre that newspapers, magazines, and fascicles prolonged into the twentieth century and has been recycled in a new medium. In this new product, thanks to refined technology, one that is no longer related to the novel or theater or even cinema, we find again the same form and the same appeal: the series, the fragments, suspended time in a linear but broken narrative with multiple plots, connected to the main one, all of which makes up an intricate and seductive whole, open to the changes in the viewers' taste, so open in fact that the very interpreters know nothing of the destiny of their characters, much as in real life. The viewer that must remain suspended at all costs, tied by emotional hooks, and pulled in by suspense, is attracted by the expectation of diverse twists that trigger the plot. In the new product there is always a repetition of the old themes: twins separated at birth, good and ill fortune, identity usurped–in a word, everything we found in the *feuilleton* trajectory will again be found in the current, modern, and nationalized *telenovelas*. Their very distribution in different time slots corresponds to the different *feuilleton* modalities: adventure, comedy, serious drama, realism–all in such a way so as to satisfy the sponsor.

In the tradition of the late *feuilleton* we find the "realism" of everyday life depicted in the *telenovela*: The core of rich people is modulated in a hierarchy that goes from the sumptuousness of the "naturally" rich and well bred to the ostentation of those who fought their way up. They interact with the progressively poorer or, better said, lower middle class. Dignity is always on the side of the latter, but the rich offer that mirror to dreams and the snobbishness of which Gramsci speaks. The role of fashion, disseminating images of what good living (luxurious home, cars) and fashionable dress are, operates according to the differentiated standards of those hierarchies. The French champagne in the crystal glasses of Parisian *feuilletons* is replaced by the stereotyped sound of ice cubes in a glass of scotch. The same scenarios used to illustrate Brazilian fashion magazines in the nineteenth century and the prostitutes' houses, richly furnished by the political bosses. The Paris dream is replaced by the dreams of the south side of Rio or the gardens of São Paulo. The casualness and nonchalance that bring beauty to (but also veil) the "law of the jungle," the ideal world, and dreams of social ascent by those who watch it, but who often barely get by.

Yet, after recognizing the links between the old and the new, we must also note that the TV *feuilleton* lacks some of the audacity of its ancestors, which were indeed sugary, but where the moral lesson was never enough to obliterate the misery of poverty, wasted lives, and the everyday struggle to survive. Maybe the reality lived in these countries is already too melodramatic to be fictionally believable. The here and now of urban misery holds no mystery; its representation cannot overcome the barrier of the facts and seems to have no way of doing without the grandiloquent language of the *feuilleton* when it attempts to speak of this misery; in other words, the *telenovela* matches the *feuilleton* in its social impact. On the one hand, if in the *telenovela* the image's explicit concreteness on the small screen lends itself less to imaginative daydreaming than do the verbal images of reading, by the same token it makes more fallacious the identifications and projections of illusory "realist" make-believe.

But the modern avatar of the nineteenth-century "industrial literature," reread and retold through the new artifices of technology, and now fully part of mass communication and reaching a public of millions of people in all social strata, also abandons part of the old narrative modes: namely, all the old storytellers who could recount the *telenovela* story in the language appropriate to a public accustomed to other codes. For a good example, think of the truck drivers depicted by Guimarães Rosa, who retold the radio soaps to the official storyteller, who would then tell it "embroidered" for the usual listeners' circles; or think of the retelling of the *telenovela* at the hairdressers and other public and private spaces.

There is a piece of *cordel* literature that tells in verse the same story as *A Escrava Isaura* [1875; The Slave Girl Isaura] by Bernardo Guimarães; the author is a poet from Campina Grande (state of Paraíba), Caetano Cosme da Silva, author also of a best-selling title, *A Louca do Jardim* [The Crazy Woman of the Garden], and also *O Assassino de Sua Honra* [The Assassination of His Honor]. His source of inspiration was not, as one might imagine, the novel, and not even the *telenovela* based on the novel, but rather a storyteller's repertoire, the latter indeed inspired by the *telenovela*. This comes, then, full circle, but this is a circle that does not close, for *Escrava Isaura* has been traveling throughout the world winning the admiration of Europeans, Chinese, and Cubans. Much like the boundary-less novels of old, much like the reading room's Franco-English novel à la *Sinclair das Ilhas*, much like the imported *feuilleton* novel, this is a source of dreams. But this time it is Europe and the world that turn to Latin America, especially to Mexico and Brazil, the great providers and exporters of the old/new narrative raw material.

Translation by Idelber Avelar

Works Cited

Alencar, José de. 1987 [1893]. *Como e porque sou romancista*. Rio de Janeiro: Academia Brasileira de Letras.

Azevedo, Aluísio. 1882. *Mistério de Tijuca. Romance original*. Rio de Janeiro: Tipografia e Escritório da Folha Nova.

—. 1985. *Mattos, Malta ou Matta? Romance ao correr da pena*. Rio de Janeiro: Nova Fronteira/Fundação Casa de Rui Barbosa.

Bernardes, Maria Thereza Caiuby Crescenti. 1989. *Mulheres de Ontem–Rio de Janeiro Século XIX*. São Paulo: Editora T.A. Queiroz.

Candido, Antonio. 1959. *Formação da Literatura Brasileira*. Vol. 2. São Paulo: Companhia Editora Nacional.

Costa, Jurandir Freire. 1989. *Ordem Médica e Norma Familiar*. Rio de Janeiro: Editora Graal.

Covo, Jacqueline. 1975. "Le roman-feuilleton français au México: Influence et interprétation. *El fistol del diablo de Manuel Payno: Nationalisme et Cosmopolisme dans les littératures ibériques au XIXe siècle*. Ed. Martine Baruch. Lille: Université de Lille III. 235–53.

Floresta, Nisia, trans. 1989. Note in *Direito das mulheres e injustiça dos homens* by Mary Wollstonecraft. 4th ed. São Paulo: Cortez.

Gramsci, Antonio. 1975. *Quaderni del Carcere*. 4 vols. Turim: Einaudi.

Guimarães Júnior, Luís. 1987. *A Família Agulha (romance humorístico)*. 3rd ed. Ed. Flora Süssekind. Rio de Janeiro/Brasília: Editora Presença/Instituto Nacional do Livro.

Lobato, Monteiro. 1959. *Cidades Mortas*. São Paulo: Brasiliense.

Marco, Valéria de. 1993. *A perda das ilusões: O Romance histórico de José de Alencar*. Campinas: Editora Unicamp.

Meyer, Marlyse. 1993. *Caminhos do imaginário no Brasil.* São Paulo: EDUSP.

Prado, Décio de Almeida. 1972. *João Caetano: O ator, o empresário, o repertório.* São Paulo: Editora Perspectiva/Editora da Universidade de São Paulo.

Sepúlveda, Luis. 1993a. *The Old Man Who Read Love Stories.* Trans. Peter Bush. New York: Harcourt Brace.

———. 1993b. *Un viejo que leía novelas de amor.* Barcelona: Tusquets Editora.

Soares, Pedro Maia. 1980. "Feminismo no Rio Grande do Sul, primeiros apontamentos 1835–1945." *Vivência, Sexualidade e Imagens Femininas.* Vol. I. Ed. Maria Cristina A. Bruschini and Fúlvia Rosemberg. São Paulo: Fundação Carlos Chagas/Editora Brasiliense. 121–50.

Süssekind, Flora. 1987. "*A Família Agulha:* uma prosa em ziguezague." *A Família Agulha (romance humorístico)* by Luís Guimarães Júnior. 3rd ed. Ed. Flora Süssekind. Rio de Janeiro/Brasília: Editora Presença/Instituto Nacional do Livro. 9–21.

CHAPTER 30

NOVEL AND JOURNALISM
STRATEGIC INTERCHANGES

Aníbal González Pérez

Journalism's origins in Spanish America date from the sixteenth century, when the first printing press arrived in the New World (in New Spain in 1553) and the first printed broadsides appeared. These contained news that, though belated by today's standards (an earthquake in Guatemala the year before, for instance), still fulfilled the principal aim of journalistic discourse: to textualize current events, to produce a history of the present. On the other hand, the origins of the Spanish American novel, once thought to lie in the early nineteenth century, have been pushed back to the Colonial period by recent research. The notorious official prohibition of fiction writing in the viceroyalties, it is now known, was flaunted with increasing frequency throughout the seventeenth and eighteenth centuries in works that mixed historiography with satire and outright fiction, such as Juan Rodríguez Freyle's (1566–1642) *El carnero* [1638; The Conquest of New Granada], Carlos Sigüenza y Góngora's (1645–1700) *Infortunios de Alonso Ramírez* [1690; Misfortunes of Alonso Ramírez], Francisco Javier Santa Cruz y Espejo's (1747–1795) *El nuevo Luciano de Quito* [1779; The New Luciano of Quito], Alonso Carrió de La Vandera's (b. ca. 1706)) *Lazarillo de ciegos caminantes* [1775; Guide of Blind Travelers], and Pablo de Olavide's (1725–1803) *El evangelio en triunfo, o Historia de un filósofo desengañado* [1797–1798; The Triumph of the Gospel or The Story of a Disillusioned Philosopher]. It is true that none of these works openly proclaimed their fictional and novelistic nature, as did José Joaquín Fernández de Lizardi's (1776–1827) *El periquillo sarniento* [1816; The Mangy Parrot]; however, already in the aforementioned narrative works of the Colonial period one discerns a trait that Lizardi's novel would turn into one of its main themes, as well as its principal rhetorical trope and the key to its discursive strategy: dissimulation.

Dissimulation, with its associated concepts of simulation, mimeticism, and camouflage (see Sarduy 1982), is the trope that not only presides over the language and style of a great many works of narrative fiction in the Colonial period and the nineteenth century, but also is a strategy by means of which these works sought to evade censorship by the Church and the state. Narrative fiction, it is now generally recognized, is based less on an imitation of extratextual "reality" than on other texts and discourses. Novels in particular consistently try to pass themselves off as works in other genres, whether history, autobiography, diaries, or journalism. They also frequently make extensive use of the lexicon and rhetoric of the discourses regarded as most powerful in society, such as those of law, science, and religion. Conversely, as the novel became the preeminent example of narrative fiction, and as its prestige grew, the genres imitated by the novel began to imitate the novel in return, and a complex, almost inextricable web of interchanges arose between these prose forms. One of the oldest strands of that web, and perhaps the least difficult to trace, is the link between journalism and the novel. This brief account will focus mainly on the novel's side of that relationship, as this is principally an essay of literary, not journalistic,

history; but it must be kept in mind that journalism also constantly borrowed rhetorical and narrative strategies from the novel as well as from other forms of fiction, such as the theater (for instance, from melodrama).

The close historical relationship between the novel and journalism has essentially followed the same path on both sides of the Atlantic and in both North and South America. Ruled by dissimulation, it is a relationship based on the interplay of difference and resemblance, almost like a textual game of hide-and-seek, played out over many centuries and in many places. The novel and journalism share a number of important traits: Socially, both are linked to the rise of the bourgeoisie and to the bourgeois insistence on keeping account of facts as well as profits. Ideologically, they share the philosophical problematics of empiricism, giving primacy to the senses, particularly vision, in human understanding. In terms of their historical development, the two discourses have frequently imitated not only each other, but also other discoursive forms, such as letters, dialogues, diaries, *relaciones*, and so forth. Lastly, at the level of rhetoric, both use the same arsenal of tropes to produce an illusion of referentiality. The differences between the novel and journalistic discourse are less simple to enumerate in absolute terms. Although their aims are virtually opposite–journalism seeks to communicate verifiable facts, while narrative fiction seeks to organize facts into aesthetically coherent wholes–the distinguishing traits of both discourses are first and foremost conventional and historical. During a given historical period, there *are* differences between narrative fiction and journalism, although these are determined by convention and by prior stages of their interplay of difference and resemblance. This makes it possible, however, despite their mutual mimeticism, to discern traces of journalistic discourse in many literary works of a given period. These traces are numerous and varied; they range from the thematic evocation of journalism and journalists to the outright imitation of some or all aspects of what constitutes journalistic discourse at a certain period.

However, if it is easy to collapse both discourses linguistically into one another, it is nevertheless unquestionable that throughout history the sense of difference between journalism and the novel has been deliberately preserved, often on the basis of the greater or lesser degree of authority that has been assigned to either discourse. As Lennard Davis argues, until the late eighteenth century both journalism and narrative fiction were considered lowly or marginal genres. Moreover, they were considered interchangeable in terms of their epistemological value: In England, Davis argues, there was a common "news/novel discourse" shared by news ballads, newsbooks, and the novels of Defoe and Richardson (42–70 and passim). Novels and journalism began to be differentiated by the mid-eighteenth century. (Davis sees Fielding as an example of this trend [196–97]). By then, the fictional qualities of the novel had become firmly established, while journalism's empiricism and its claims of veracity became more pronounced. This allied journalism closely with the scientific trends of the period and gave it greater prestige than narrative fiction as a mode of representation. In fact, it may be argued that the novel maintained its own authority and prestige among the other literary genres of the late eighteenth and nineteenth centuries mostly by imitating the discourse of journalism, in an attempt to partake of journalism's truth-value. By the mid-nineteenth century, however, the prestige of the novel, although seemingly at its zenith in the work of the great masters of European "realist" fiction, was in fact being steadily eroded by the immense authority of science and technology, of which journalism had become the textual mouthpiece. Narrative fiction's claims to reveal truths of a higher order through art was severely put into question by the very existence of journalism, which aspired to uncover truth directly, without the mediation of rhetorical artifice. Nineteenth-century novelists and fiction writers in general were thus forced into direct confrontation with journalism. A great many of these authors, however, still shared some of the values and the epistemology of journalism and were reluctant to undertake a serious critique of its discourse.

But beyond a competition for textual authority during this period, there were also other motivations behind the mutual mimetic moves between the two discourses. The principal one was to serve as a strategy against censorship by shifting information from one regulated discourse to another that was less regulated and by often proposing a subversive counter-vigilance to that of religion, the law, and the state. From roughly the late seventeenth to the late nineteenth century, the novel and journalism found common cause, so to speak, in a struggle against the authoritarian discourses of religion, the law, and the state, which claimed to hold the monopoly of truth. From this perspective, a currently fashionable view proposing that both the novel and journalism in Spanish America during the nineteenth century were instruments in the task of nation building must be greatly nuanced or, in specific cases, questioned altogether. Most frequently, what one finds in Spanish American novels of the nineteenth century is not a constructive, positive prescription or model for nation building, but a series of feints, of moves and countermoves, that allowed authors to encode their ideological views defensively behind an apparently innocuous façade. This strategy of dissimulation, this back-and-forth between two discourses with fundamentally different aims (such as literature and journalism), is one of the key elements that contribute to the corrosive and profoundly self-critical makeup of the major Spanish American novels of the nineteenth century. The lasting value of novels such as *El periquillo sarniento* [1815; The Itching Parrot, 1942], *Amalia* (1851–1852), *Aves sin nido* [1889; Birds Without Nest], and *Tomóchic* (1894), among many others, probably resides less in their sometimes weak formal and stylistic qualities, or in their now-defunct doctrines, or in the information they provide about the manners and morals of a bygone era, than in the inherent drama of their rhetorical and discursive tensions. In their authors' struggle between what they wished to say and how they said it, between their desire to express and their need to conceal, these novels hold lessons that are still relevant to contemporary Spanish American narrative.

In the final months of 1815, pressured by censorship, the Mexican José Joaquín Fernández de Lizardi stopped publishing his two gazettes—*Alacena de Frioleras* and *El Caxoncito de la Alacena*—and devoted himself instead to writing a novel, *El periquillo sarniento*, which he published in serial form in 1816. As stated earlier, *El periquillo* is the first work of narrative

prose in Spanish America to openly proclaim itself a fiction and to associate itself with the novel. Elevated to a classic by the Spanish American critical tradition, *El periquillo*, like many such classics, is more talked about than read. Valued mostly for its depiction of the manners and mores of early-nineteenth-century Mexico (essentially as a precursor of *costumbrismo*), *El periquillo sarniento*'s figural elements have received scant attention. Readers of Lizardi's work have generally busied themselves with what the text signifies at an extratextual level—its literary and cultural allusions, the information it provides about society, politics, and language in Independence-era Mexico, or its thematic links with Lizardi's pamphleteering—and have not paid sufficient attention to the system of tropes through which Lizardi gives his text the illusion of coherence and narrative flow. While my ultimate aim here is to explore the relationship between *El periquillo* and Lizardi's journalism, I believe this should not be done without some attempt to read the text on its own terms, that is, in terms of its rhetoric and its strategies of representation.

An overly hasty linkage of Lizardi's discourse in *El periquillo* to that of Enlightenment texts has led to a largely unproblematic view of its use of language and representational strategies. To twenty-first–century readers, Lizardi's narrative voice, like that of Enlightenment authors such as Voltaire, Rousseau, and Diderot, already sounds modern and transparent; it speaks in a commonsensical, down-to-earth style that seeks a middle ground between the aristocratic and plebeian usages and emphasizes maximum communicative effectiveness. *El periquillo*'s discourse deliberately eschews many of the elements associated with Baroque style, particularly the use of Latin quotations but also the convoluted Latinate syntax of *culteranismo* and the ponderous metaphorical imagery of *conceptismo* [conceptism]. Nevertheless, *El periquillo* still clearly retains many Baroque elements in its discourse, beginning with its allusions to the Spanish picaresque tradition and to topics such as *desengaño* [disillusion]. It is furthermore naive to assume that because Enlightenment rhetorical norms emphasized linguistic clarity and effectiveness, such a use of language was devoid of tropes and metaphors of its own. *El periquillo*'s discourse is built around the tropes of simulation and dissimulation (both meanings of Lizardi's term *fingir*, which I will condense as "dissimulation"); these tropes are in turn connected with the image of the parrot, which is used to allude both to the text and to its protagonist, and they are also linked to the theme of hypocrisy, which runs through the text. Moreover, the image of the parrot recurs in Lizardi's journalistic work and is thus highly suggestive in terms of Lizardi's implicit theory of writing. The recurrent images of simulation, camouflage, and mimeticism in *El periquillo*, in addition, serve to elucidate how Lizardi viewed the relationship between his pamphleteering and his novelistic endeavors.

Although it was published episodically in pamphlets, *El periquillo sarniento* has a generally coherent and well-thought-out plot line, which its moralistic digressions (as the narrator insists time and time again) do not manage to lead astray. Unlike the *roman-feuilletons* of later decades (such as Eugène Sue's *Les mystères de Paris*, 1842–1843), the writing of *El periquillo* appears to have been little affected by any feedback from its readers, save in one significant instance—that of the state censor, who intervened to block the publication of the text's fourth volume because of its open polemic against slavery. External evidence of the premeditated nature of the structure of *El periquillo* may be seen in the fact that Lizardi published a prospectus of his text before beginning publication of the complete work (Spell 145). In the text itself, the reappearance at key moments of various characters, such as Januario, Aguilita, Don Antonio, and *el trapiento* (the Raggedy Man), signals Lizardi's intention of giving his work a coherent structure, even if it meant involving his protagonist in a series of improbably coincidental and repetitious encounters. Indeed, redundancy is a salient quality of this text, which often repeats the same message using different characters and scenes; for example, the moral lesson that "clothes do not make the man" is repeated countless times in Periquillo's experience, sometimes discursively, as in Don Antonio's advice upon leaving prison (193; see below), sometimes by example, as in the case of the Raggedy Man (in Chapter 8 of the second part).

The narrator's own nickname is fraught with allegorical resonances related to dissimulation. The first half—"Periquillo" [little parrot]—prefigures Pedro's mimetic propensities, his attempts to make a living through deception and simulation, but also his habit of falling under the spell of any reasonably persuasive person, whether good or bad. It also anticipates his verbal proclivities, his talkativeness, and his penchant for oratorical digressions late in life. The second half—"Sarniento" [mangy]—alludes not only to the character's poverty throughout most of his life, but also to the adage that whoever itches must scratch himself, which implicitly prefigures Pedro's restless, ambulatory life. In a typically picaresque movement, Periquillo goes from one master to another; nevertheless, far from remaining a mere servant, he learns to simulate the behavior and abilities of his masters to the point of taking their place, albeit temporarily. Thus he becomes, in quick succession, secretary to the notary lawyer Chanfaina, from whom he learns tricks of legalistic rhetoric ("el arte de la cábala con la pluma" [213] ["the art of cabalistic penmanship"]); apprentice to a barber (he never learns to shave others or do tooth extractions properly [224–28]); assistant to the druggist Don José, whom he impresses with his rudimentary knowledge of Latin and hypocritical behavior (231), until he accidentally poisons a customer (233); and lastly, assistant to the Molièresque Doctor Purgante, from whom he learns to use Latinate and Baroque medical jargon so convincingly that he is able to leave his master after stealing some of his books, diplomas, and clothing and pass himself off as doctor in the small town of Tula (235–47).

Periquillo's mimeticism expresses itself not only verbally and behaviorally, but in terms of dress as well. Each of his mutations is expressed by a different (dis)guise; the many rises and falls in his fortunes are marked by periodic changes of clothing, like an actor returning to his dressing room. Whenever he is down and out, his clothing immediately reflects this, of course, but even then there are gradations: Sometimes his rags are those of a white beggar or vagrant, and at other times he sinks lower in the social pyramid and ends up dressed like an Indian (397). But clothing is more than a mere reflection of his social status; Periquillo understands perfectly that in his society clothes *do* make the man, and he consciously uses them on many occasions to improve his social condition by simulating a status he does not possess (such as when he passes himself off as a doctor, wearing the robes and wigs he has stolen from Doctor Purgante). However, it is important to stress, as the narrator frequently does, the inadequacy of Periquillo's mimeticism: Despite his best efforts, he is in the end unmasked by circumstances or by his own clumsiness, and people always see through his disguise.

The close parallels between Periquillo and Lizardi are laid out quite explicitly near the end of the text. There, we learn that the fictional editor of Periquillo's manuscript is "El Pensador Mexicano" (Lizardi's pseudonym). Of this character, Periquillo says (with a wink to his readers) that "we have loved each other so much that I can safely say that I am one with *el Pensador* and he with me" (454). It becomes clear that most of Periquillo's attributes are shared by the Mexican pamphleteer who is the real-world author of his narrative, and that *El periquillo sarniento* can also be read as an allegorical discourse about writers and journalists in colonial Mexico. The clincher to this Periquillo-Lizardi connection may be the fact that Lizardi gave two of his late pamphlets titles that seem to allude to his novel: *La victoria del perico* [1823; The Parrot's Victory] and *El hermano del perico que cantaba la victoria* [1823; The Brother to the Parrot Who Sang Victory]. In the latter, as Jacobo Checinsky describes it, "[t]he author imagines . . . an enlightened parrot—the reincarnation of Pythagoras, no less—with whom he holds a series of dialogues in which the advantages of liberal federalism versus conservative centralism are discussed" (III:18).

What, then, is the allegorical message encoded in Periquillo, in his parrot-like imitativeness and his misadventures? What does the text have to tell us about writing, and journalistic writing in particular? In my view, one of the most explicit and condensed passages in this regard occurs when Periquillo tries to pass himself off as a count in the island of the "Chinese." Reflecting on how well he was treated by everyone because they thought he was someone important, Periquillo muses on the pros and cons of *fingir* (feigning):

[L]as más veces, aprecia a los hombres no por sus títulos reales, sino por los que dicen que tienen.

No por esto apruebo que sea bueno el fingir, por más que sea útil al que finge; también al lenón y droguero les son útiles sus disimulos y sus trácalas, y sin embargo no les son lícitas. Lo que quiero que saquéis por fruto de este cuento, es que advirtáis cuán expuestos vivimos a que nos engañe un pícaro astuto pintándonos gigantes de nobleza, talento, riqueza y valimiento. Nos creemos de su persuasión o de lo que llaman *labia*, nos estafa si puede, nos engaña siempre, y cunado conocemos la burla es cuando no podemos remediarla. En todo caso, hijos míos, estudiad al hombre, observadlo, penetradlo en su alma; ved sus operaciones, prescindiendo de lo exterior de su vestido, títulos ni rentas, y así que halléis alguno que siempre hable verdad y no se pegue al interés como al acero al imán, fiaos de él y decid: Este es hombre de bien, éste no me engañará ni por él se me seguirá ningún perjuicio. Pero para hallar a este hombre, pedidle a Diógenes prestada su lanterna. (768–69)

[T]he world most often values men not for their real titles but for those they claim to have.

Despite this, I do not say that to feign [*fingir*] is good, however useful it may be to those who feign. Cheats and go-betweens also find their tricks and dissimulations useful, yet they are not lawful. What I want you to get from this story is to realize how vulnerable we are to being tricked by any sly picaroon who makes us believe ourselves giants of nobility, talent, and wealth. We fall for his persuasion—what they call *labia* [winning eloquence]; he bilks us if he can, tricking us always, and we only realize we have been had when it is too late to stop it. In any case, my sons, you must study man, observe him, penetrate into his soul; watch the way he operates, disregarding the exteriors of dress, titles, and income, and as soon as you find one who always speaks truthfully and doesn't stick to his own advantage like iron to a magnet, trust him, and say: This is an honest man [*hombre de bien*]; this one will not trick me, nor will I be harmed by him. But in order to find this man, you will have to ask Diogenes for his lantern.

In this meditation on *fingir*, which is also a meditation on reading and interpreting, the narrator shows once again his awareness of the profoundly deceptive nature of language (and, indeed, of any communicative code), which can be harnessed to any purpose, good or bad. All language is liable to become alienated, corrupted, and perverted, like that of the parrot, torn from its origins or moorings in a rational consciousness—in other words, to become like writing. We must learn to read correctly, Lizardi states, in order not to be tricked by a hostile and devious world. Alarmingly, however, Lizardi also states that we will probably be tricked anyway. The essence of his lesson is a feeling of vulnerability, an awareness of the perils facing the reader in a world that abounds in people with *labia*, with eloquence, who will repeat and distort words in order to take advantage of others. Like Rousseau, Lizardi seems to regard writing as a "dangerous supplement," a double-faced activity that can help as well as hinder, improve as well as corrupt, and which must be kept in check by the application of an inner moral sense.

A narrative about dissimulation, *El periquillo sarniento* is itself an act of dissimulation, a textual camouflage. And like any good camouflage, it entails a modicum of self-revelation—a certain brazenness, such as that of the butterfly that hides itself by *displaying itself* as a leaf. There clearly are some autobiographical elements from Lizardi's life in *El periquillo*, but more importantly, there is in Lizardi's text a reflection on his own life and travails as a journalist, and indeed an attempt at self-justification. Periquillo's constant imitativeness, his desperate desire to be liked and accepted by all and to achieve success through simulation, exactly parallels Lizardi's own dependence on the public's fickleness and the authorities' tolerance toward his making a living as a pamphleteer. And although Lizardi, unlike Periquillo, does not seem to have sought wealth and status, he clearly understood the attraction of the peculiar form of power that is inherent in journalism, a power that emanates from the figural use of language, from simulation. In *El periquillo*, Lizardi presents an allegory of his own career as a pamphleteer in early-nineteenth-century Mexico: It is the journalist as *pícaro*, living by his wits, relying on many masters (his readers), using the figural, dissimulating powers of language to attract some readers and to protect himself from others. The facts of Lizardi's biography—his hand-to-mouth existence, his frequent troubles with the authorities, his imprisonments—tend to support such a view. The main difference between Periquillo and his author may lie in Lizardi's passionate engagement with politics, which Periquillo does not show, but which seems to have fueled Lizardi's vocation as a journalist. But even in political matters Lizardi was forced to dissemble like Periquillo, since his reformist views frequently put him at odds with the government and the Church.

Lizardi's greatest act of dissimulation, I would argue, is *El periquillo sarniento* itself: a text that is fundamentally a pamphlet passing itself off as a work of narrative fiction, as an "obra romancesca" (in Lizardi's own phrase) (7). Save for its plot, there is little to distinguish *El periquillo* from the hundreds of other pamphlets Lizardi had published and would continue to publish after the restrictions on his journalism were lifted in 1820. Any reader of Lizardi's newspapers, from *El Pensador Mexicano* (1812–1813), *Alacena de Frioleras*, and *El Caxoncito de la Alacena* (1815–1816) to *El Conductor Eléctrico* (1820), among others, cannot fail to notice the nearly absolute similarity between the writing of *El periquillo* and the dialogues, fables, narratives, and polemics about current events that compose the bulk of the material in these publications. Dialogues such as that between a young girl and "Tata Pablo" in Issue 13, Volume I of *El Pensador Mexicano* (*Obras III*, 114–18) and that between "El Tío Toribio" and his nephew Juanillo in Issue 6, Volume II (*Obras III*, 181–89) could easily have been included in the text of *El periquillo*, as well as the comments on the "abuses of fashion" in Volume II of the supplements to *El Pensador* (*Obras III*, 317–20) and the satirical poems and fables scattered throughout most of the issues of Lizardi's first important newspaper, to mention just a few examples. Needless to say, Lizardi's journalistic style was not particularly unique; other newspapers in Mexico and in the rest of the Hispanic world made use of genres currently considered "literary" in presenting their information, since, it must be recalled, journalism up to the late nineteenth century was less concerned with objectively communicating news than with self-expression, opinion, and ideological debate.

Even Lizardi's choice of the picaresque genre can be linked to his journalistic endeavor, not only because the picaresque novels and the early journalism of the sixteenth and seventeenth centuries have a common origin, or because the picaresque is an early form of Bildungsroman, but also, quite simply, because almost all journalists of the period in Spain and Spanish America frequently used pseudonyms that evoked lower-class, marginal, or regional characters: El Payo del Rosario, Fígaro, El Pobrecito Hablador, El Curioso Parlante, El Bachiller Cantaclaro, and El Gíbaro de Caguas, among others. Early-nineteenth-century journalists, including the costumbristas, often preferred to assume the protective persona of the country bumpkin or of the lazy, disinterested spectator when writing their polemical or critical articles. Although Lizardi's pseudonym was the decidedly un-picaresque "El Pensador Mexicano," "El Periquillo Sarniento" would not have been inappropriate, either as a pseudonym or as the title of one of the polemical pamphlets Lizardi loved to write. (Let us recall that one of Lizardi's last pamphlets was titled *La Victoria del Perico*.) Suffice it to say that on every level it is almost impossible to distinguish the discourse of *El periquillo sarniento* from that of the newspapers and gazettes of its day.

Nevertheless, Lizardi insists on *El periquillo*'s fictional nature, on its presumed difference from the journalism he was forbidden to write. *El periquillo sarniento* appears to confirm perfectly, in the Spanish American environment, Lennard Davis's thesis with regard to journalism and the origins of the English novel. Davis argues that

> The novel's fictionality is a ploy to mask the genuine ideological, reportorial commentative function of the novel. . . . [N]ovels came about partly as a complex reaction to the laws, statutes, and legal decisions that were aimed at restricting journalism. Therefore, novels may be seen as tangible forms of highly encoded and profoundly reflexive defenses against authority and power. The novel embodies the contradictory qualities of rebellion and conformity, of criminality and morality, of criticism and approbation of society, and so on. (213, 222)

This notion, although somewhat circular when applied to all novels in all epochs, describes perfectly what Lizardi does in early-nineteenth-century Mexico. When he insists that his text is an "obra romancesca," a work of narrative fiction, it is because already his Spanish American readers have a commonly accepted notion of what such a work must be like. Indeed, had Spanish American colonial readers (including the government censors) not had a certain idea of what a novel should look like, Lizardi's whole strategy would have failed. The narrator explicitly states in his prologue that his work "may be useful to those young men who lack, perhaps, better works from which to learn, or also to certain young (and not so young) men who are fond of reading little novels and comedies [*que sean amigos de leer novelitas y comedias*]" (5).

In writing *El periquillo*, Lizardi made use of the generic differentiation that had already taken place in his time between the novel and other forms of narrative. *El periquillo* mimics a novel not merely because Lizardi labels it as one, but because it incorporates characters, situations, and figures derived from the most easily recognizable novelistic genre of the day, the picaresque. *El periquillo* is a simulation in the very precise sense that Severo Sarduy (1937–1993) gives to this term: It is not a copy, but a work that uses the observer's (the reader's) position to produce an imposture (19). Lizardi's readers expected a novel to provide them with certain themes, characters, and situations, and he gave them what they expected. But he did more; he also tapped into a deeper level–that of rhetoric, a level in which the discourses of journalism and narrative fiction remain perpetually undifferentiated and undifferentiable. It was there, in the murky no-man's-land of figural language that is shared by all discourses, that Lizardi was able to inject the substance of his journalistic writings into the mold of a picaresque tale. Lizardi's journalism, let us recall, was a journalism of opinion and debate; in *El periquillo*, his opinions could be expressed as those of the fictional characters, with the layers of character, plot, and situation to shield Lizardi from his censors. Curiously, however, like Periquillo himself, Lizardi went too far in his imposture. He was easily uncovered by the censor when he tried to bring into the last volume of his novel the highly charged and controversial subject of slavery: The censor then forbade that section's publication, and subscribers to the first edition of *El periquillo* never got to read about the *pícaro*'s conversion into an upstanding citizen and a writer.

There is considerable irony in the realization that Spanish America's first self-proclaimed novel was actually a covert form of journalism, a pamphlet "in drag," passing itself off as a work of narrative fiction. To understand the oddity of Lizardi's situation, one need only imagine Thomas Paine (who, admittedly, was politically more radical than Lizardi) being forced to recast *Common Sense* (1776) as a short story, or Simón Bolívar (1783–1830) inserting his *Carta de Jamaica* (1815) into an epistolary novel. Or better still, one need only recall the numerous instances in which nineteenth- and twentieth-century works of narrative fiction have presented themselves as the opposite of what they are: as journalism, autobiography, or history. Clearly, *El periquillo* cannot be considered the "origin" of the modern Spanish American novel, whose roots, as said earlier, go back to colonial works such as Carlos de Sigüenza y Góngora's *Infortunios de Alonso Ramírez* and Alonso Carrió de la Vandera's *Lazarillo de ciegos caminantes*. The facts of literary history plainly show that the novel has been created and re-created in Spanish America many times in different places. If *El periquillo sarniento* inaugurates anything, it is, I would argue, an increased awareness and strategic use of the tropological (figural) nature of discourses in Spanish American writings, a figural nature that allows the same discourse to be read

as various, radically different, indeed sometimes antithetical, genres: pamphlet/novel, history/allegory, autobiography/fiction, etc. *El periquillo* marks the beginning of a tradition of discoursive dissimulation in which journalism, because of its own protean nature, plays a key role. Henceforth, journalism would be inscribed into virtually all major Spanish American works of narrative fiction as part of their strategy of textual dissimulation, of deliberately blurring discoursive boundaries. After *El periquillo*, we find in Spanish American narrative fiction simultaneous claims of truthfulness and verifiability and of utter fictionality, claims that mark this narrative's constant oscillation between journalistic and fictional discourses.

The same critical energy liberated in *El periquillo sarniento* is also found in José Mármol's (1817–1871) novel *Amalia*. What one might call "the law of dissimulation" exposed in Lizardi's novel, which rules over virtually all nineteenth-century Spanish American narrative, is somewhat obscured by Mármol's melodramatic and Manichaean storytelling, but it is still, I would posit, the main driving force behind the writing of Mármol's novel. *Amalia* began to be published in serial form in the newspaper *La Semana*, in Montevideo, in 1851. An activist against the dictatorship of Juan Manuel de Rosas in Argentina, José Mármol had fled to Uruguay in 1840. After the fall of Rosas's regime in 1852, the novel's serial publication was discontinued, and in 1855 a complete and definitive version was published in Buenos Aires. Mármol's Argentina had been torn for over three decades by a bloody civil war between Unitarians, who favored a strong central government based in Buenos Aires, and Federalists, who believed in greater autonomy for the provinces. But Unitarians and Federalists were also frequently identified with other cultural and even geographic divisions in Argentine society: the city versus the country, Buenos Aires versus the provinces, the elite versus the masses, Europeanization versus Americanism, and so on. Mármol, however, followed the principles of Esteban Echeverría's (1805–1851) "Asociación de Mayo," which was made up of young Unitarian intellectuals who, until they were persecuted by Rosas, sought to mediate between the two opposing camps, searching for a way out of the political impasse that had led to Rosas's Federalist dictatorship.

Most readings of *Amalia* have focused on its political and ideological aspects, seeing it as an example of the "national romance," that is, an allegorical narrative that encodes its author's ideas about nation building. Thus, its principal plotline, the ill-fated love story between the widow Amalia Sáenz and the dashing Eduardo Belgrano, aided by the wily Daniel Bello, has been seen as an allegory of Argentina's uncertain and static political situation after the fall of Rosas. At the end of the novel, Amalia again becomes a widow (since her husband Eduardo is killed by murderers sent by Rosas) like the Argentine nation she emblematizes, which remains bereft of its Independence-era leaders and of leaders from younger generations. But Amalia's condition as a political allegory also underscores the importance of dissimulation–particularly of the interplay between fictional and journalistic discourses–for the novel's very existence. If one considers that Mármol's main purpose was to attack Rosas's dictatorship and that he was safely in exile when he began in earnest his literary career, the question arises: Why write a novel at all? Why not write essays or articles in which his ideas could be openly presented and discussed? One answer would be, of course, that he did indeed write those essays or articles: Throughout the 1840s, Mármol wrote abundant political pieces for newspapers and journals in which he collaborated (*El Talismán*, *Muera Rosas!*, *El Comercio del Plata*) or that he founded (*El Album*, *El Conservador*, and *La Semana*; Fernández 158). Most of the ideas expressed in those articles are also found in *Amalia*. Thus, it is difficult to argue that Mármol's novel was, like Lizardi's, an attempt to evade censorship, although it is true that Mármol delayed publication of *Amalia*'s final version after Rosas's defeat because of the mood of reconciliation between Unitarians and Federalists that, for a while, pervaded the country.

I would propose, however, that aside from its somewhat dubious value as propaganda, or as a means of acquiring literary prestige (poetry was still more prestigious than the novel, as Mármol's own persistent efforts in this genre show), Mármol wrote *Amalia* for many of the same reasons that Lizardi wrote *El periquillo sarniento*: to analyze and experiment with the strategies of dissimulation. As Mármol and his anti-Rosista contemporaries Echeverría and Sarmiento were well aware, Rosas's power over Argentina was exerted not only (or merely) through the brute force of the *mazorca* (the Federalist vigilante groups), but largely through deceit and intrigue. Rosas's regime, which forced its citizens to wear a symbolic color (red) and other visible manifestations of their obedience to the dictator, also made appearances, simulacra, and mendacity the norm in Argentine society. *Amalia*, as many critics have pointed out, is one of the first dictator-novels in Spanish America, and in it one already finds the image of the dictator –as author, a sort of "evil twin" of the novelist, who, like the latter, grounds his power on the use and abuse of language, on the production of fictions that he attempts to impose on the real world.

Rosas is not the character who dominates this novel, however, and neither is Amalia or Eduardo. Instead, it is their friend Daniel Bello. Critics have always noted that Bello is the novel's hero, although, misled by the book's title, their interpretations have usually centered on the decidedly static characters of Amalia and Eduardo, relegating Bello to an auxiliary role. However, although Bello is clearly patterned after the stereotypical cloak-and-dagger heroes of the European serials, his profoundly ambivalent nature, which includes a good deal of self-reflexiveness, makes him by far the novel's most interesting figure, and the most telling in regard to Mármol's motivation in writing his novel. If the character of Amalia can be seen as an emblem of Argentina, that of Bello is an example of the synthesis between Unitarianism and Federalism that the "Asociación de Mayo" had wished to achieve and is, more generally speaking, emblematic of the dissimulation needed to survive in the Argentine society of the period–a dissimulation that also determines much of the structure and language of Mármol's novel. Another detail linking Bello with writing and literature can be discerned in his family name. If Eduardo Belgrano's family name connects him with the most illustrious leader of Argentine independence, Manuel Belgrano (of whom, we are told, he is a nephew), Bello's surname evokes the foremost literary figure of Spanish American independence, the Venezuelan Andrés Bello (1781–1865), who at the time lived and worked in Chile. The connection between a peace-loving man of letters and an adventure hero, though it may seem far-fetched or perverse, does reflect the paradox of what Mármol himself was attempting: to enlist the powers of literature for political activism.

The symbol of Daniel Bello's status as an allegory of the dissimulating and subversive writer is his weapon of choice, a device that Bello names in three languages: in English as a "life-preserver," in French as a *casse-tête*, and, translating the French term into Spanish (since he claims it has no special name in that language), as a *rompecabezas* (Mármol 260). Described as obviously phallic looking, the weapon consists of "a wicker handle one foot long and thin in the center, at whose ends were two iron balls of at least six ounces in weight, all covered by a fine net of soft leather. A weapon that, when taken by one of the balls, could be brandished without breaking the wicker, and whose other end tripled the weight and force of the slightest movement of the hand" (Mármol 260). The aristocratic, sword-wielding Belgrano sniffs at the "mysterious weapon" that Daniel carries in his breast pocket (Mármol 260), not only because of its phallic appearance but also because of its possible underworld provenance. Easily portable and discreet–dissimulating–and meant to be aimed mostly at the head and chest (and capable of amplifying "the slightest movement of the hand"), the *rompecabezas* resembles a writing instrument more closely than a sword or knife. Like the latter, however, it achieves its effect by breaking or separating objects into pieces. The term *rompecabezas* may thus be read as a pun that works on various levels, alluding not only to the head-cracking blows of the weapon, but also to a "puzzle" (another meaning of the Spanish term), which might in turn be seen as an allusion to the effect, produced both by Bello and by the text of which he is a part, on the reader. A serialized novel–that is, one that has been broken up into fragments for publication in a newspaper–*Amalia* also exhibits the rambling, heterogeneous discourse encouraged by its journalistic mode of publication. Such a mixture of fragmented discourses not only resembles a "puzzle," but its effect is also puzzling, meant to hide more than it reveals, like the broken patterns of a modern camouflage uniform.

Along with its discursive heterogeneity, *Amalia* offers allegorical elements that also further its textual dissimulation. Although allegory is frequently associated with the communication of doctrine (be it religious or political), it is no less true that there is always something enigmatic about it. If allegory is, in Calderón de la Barca's (1600–1681) trenchant formulation, that which "gives a body" to the concept ("*pues dando cuerpo al concepto,/ aún lo no visible animo*" [Parker 79]), it is still necessary for the allegory's reader to be familiar with the "concept" (the allegory's *logos*, its ultimate meaning) in order to decipher the "body." A highly visual trope, allegory bears strong affinities to dissimulation, for in both modes appearances can be deceiving. With its forbidding or simply confusing exterior, allegory can often serve to keep the uninitiated at a distance from the inner meanings it is meant to convey. In the case of *Amalia*, for example, an uninformed or unsympathetic reader might simply find it a boring, digressive work and remain oblivious to its potentially subversive aspects as a "national romance." Allegory does not suffice, however, to resolve *Amalia*'s inherent generic tension between history (including journalism) and fiction. Like Daniel Bello's mimetic camouflage, in which he paradoxically hides himself by *exposing* himself, the text of *Amalia* first presents itself boldly as a novel, a fiction, but soon begins to make claims that are rather more historical or journalistic. The clearest and most compact instance in this regard is the "Explicación" to which I have just alluded. This advertisement addressed to the reader employs a complex, zigzagging movement between times and genres from its very first lines: "Most of the historical characters of this novel still exist, and occupy the same political or social position as in the time in which the events you are about to read took place. But the author, by a deliberate fiction, writes his work as if several generations had passed" (4). Although, strictly speaking, all writing is about the past, here readers are invited to read about events of a decade before as if these events belonged to a more distant past. Since readers are reminded that many of the historical characters "still exist," the readers are essentially being asked to fictionalize them by distancing them further in time. Mármol's double claim here is paradoxical. He claims to be writing about relatively immediate people and events, that is, engaging in an essentially journalistic endeavor. Simultaneously, he states that he is writing as if these people were already dead and gone, thus creating a fiction. And it is no solution to say that he is writing an "historical novel," since the question of immediacy, raised by Mármol himself, persists: Can a "historical novel" still be "historical" when it deals with current events? Where does history end and journalistic reporting begin? In eighteenth-century England, the Stamp Act, which attempted to tax newspapers, led eventually to a pragmatic, legal definition of "news" as "a narrative of public events supplied by the posts and under one month old" (Davis 99). But these arbitrary definitions do little to solve the underlying philosophical problem of defining the present. Finding such a definition is less important in this case than the strategic use Mármol's narrative makes of this gray area, thus making his text much harder to pin down, leaving it free to pursue its subversive agenda.

Clearly, what is at stake here is the Romantic concept of literature as an expression of freedom and as freedom of expression. Reflecting a near-Heraclitean view of nature, the character of Daniel Bello probably voices Mármol's epistemological justification of this attitude when he states, "There is nothing, my dear Eduardo, that is more easily explained than my [erratic] character, because it's nothing more than a candid expression of the eternal laws of Nature. Everything in the physical world and in the moral order is inconstant, transitory and fleeting. It is contrast that creates all that is beautiful and harmonious that issues from God's hand. And nothing else displays best the infinite variety of the Universe than the human soul" (125). But, one might ask, if *Amalia*, as its critics and commentators have always stated, is meant to be an attack on Rosas's dictatorship and a statement of Mármol's political beliefs, why appeal to ambiguity, to the temporal confusion between past and present, and to the generic confusion between journalism and fiction? Again, why all this subterfuge? My reply once more would be that the use (and analysis) of subterfuge, of dissimulation, is the whole point of this novel. At the risk of sounding flippant, one might say that it's because in literature the best offense is always a good defense. Through its multiple techniques of dissimulation, the literary text moves "like the night" (to allude to the Homeric phrase used by Alejo Carpentier [1904–1980] in one of his fictions), launching its figurative missiles almost subliminally before the critical reader is even aware of what has happened.

As *El periquillo sarniento* and *Amalia* make abundantly clear, it makes little sense to speak of a conflictive relationship between fictional and journalistic discourses in the nineteenth century. On the contrary, despite their otherwise disparate aims, narrative fiction and journalism, as said earlier, found common cause in the struggle against other contemporaneous discourses that claimed a monopoly on the truth, such as those of religion, the law, and the state. To achieve this goal, by the second half of the nineteenth century certain modes of

narrative fiction, following the example of journalism, went so far as to subordinate fiction's hypercritical and unruly spirit to the claims of science. This was the case with the so-called naturalist fiction, which developed from French novels such as *Germinie Lacerteux* (1864) by brothers Goncourt and was brought to fruition by Emile Zola in his twenty-novel *Rougon-Macquart* cycle (1871–1893). In many ways, however, the naturalist vogue may be regarded as a moment when journalism (allied with science) reigned supreme over literature to an extent only surpassed by the testimonial and documentary narratives of the late twentieth century. That is why the remainder of this essay will be devoted to two novels in the naturalist mode: *Aves sin nido* and *Tomochic*.

Naturalist fiction is usually interpreted in reference to the scientific and ideological developments of the late nineteenth century, from Charles Darwin's evolutionism and Claude Bernard's biological determinism to the positivism of Auguste Comte and the socialism of Karl Marx. More innovative readings of Zola's brand of naturalism have also stressed his profound debt to the notion of entropy and in general to nineteenth-century theories of thermodynamics (see Serres). But it is important to remember that the naturalists' scientific penchant was almost always placed in the service of a project whose aims were rooted in the journalistic tradition: to uncover and denounce social oppression. Despite their Positivist-inspired rhetoric of dispassionate and "scientific" social analysis, the Naturalists' novels and narratives were passionate, ideological works that had much in common with the investigative journalism and crusading reportage pioneered by James Gordon Bennett in late-1830s New York newspapers (Stephens 242–52). Investigative reporting itself owed much, of course, in its approach and techniques, to scientific empiricism, but it was usually motivated by a highly unscientific sense of moral outrage and made use of blatantly literary techniques (such as melodrama) to move its readers.

In Naturalism we once again witness a strategic, dissimulating zigzag movement among discourses, similar to a shell game, that uses shifts among literary, journalistic, and scientific discourses to create a sense of ambiguity. Ambiguity is not a term generally associated with Naturalist novels, which, in their function as vehicles for propaganda and social critique, sometimes tended to resemble *romans à these*. However, an important difference between Naturalist novels and the *romans à these* is that the former were often less concerned with expounding a specific social or political program than with portraying and bringing to public discussion, in the manner of the journalistic exposé, the social problems their authors considered most urgent. Naturalist novels were thus profoundly moralistic works, despite their propensity to shock conventional sensibilities by their portrayal of social types and situations usually repressed by the ruling class (which ironically led them to be denounced by some as obscene or pornographic). Nevertheless, these novels' moralizing rarely provided concrete solutions for the problems they denounced. In this sense, they remained ambiguous. But an even deeper ambiguity lies in the Naturalist novels' use of dissimulation in order to "seduce" readers, so to speak—to entice them into accepting, or at least considering, the novels' critical message. Part of that dissimulating strategy is the aforementioned shell game played with the conventions of literary, scientific, and journalistic discourse. As will be seen in the analyses of *Aves sin nido* and *Tomochic*, the discourse of these novels constantly alternates among blatantly melodramatic or lyrical passages, the dry, clinical jargon of medicine or biology, and the sensationalism of yellow journalism and the crime story.

It hardly seems necessary to show how deeply *Aves sin nido* is embedded in a journalistic context. In the very same year that Matto de Turner (1852–1909) published her novel (1889), she was named director of *El Perú Ilustrado*, the country's premier literary and cultural journal. Matto thus crowned a lengthy career in journalism that began with the publication of her costumbristic pieces and "tradiciones" (following the example of Ricardo Palma) in the early 1870s. By the middle of that decade, Matto had become a sought-after journalist who published widely in Peruvian as well as foreign journals, such as *El Semanario del Pacífico, El Correo del Perú, La Ondina del Plata, El Porvenir, El Obrero, La Cartilla Popular, La Bolsa,* and *La Autonomía,* among others (Schneider ix). Beyond the circumstantial fact of Matto's success as a journalist, *Aves sin nido*'s thematic origins, as critics frequently point out, are to be found in the novels *El padre Horán* [1848; Father Horán] by Narciso Aréstegui (1824–1869) and *La trinidad del Indio, o Costumbres del interior* [1885; The Indian's Trinity or The Costumes of the Interior] by José T. Itolararres. Aréstegui's Romantic text, considered the first Peruvian novel, is based on the journalistic genre of the crime story: the murder of a woman by a friar, her ex-confessor, in Cuzco in 1836. Curiously, Matto de Turner's grandfather, Manuel Torres Matos, was prefect of Cuzco at the time and was involved in the investigation (Schneider xxi). This story, about a crime of passion committed by a man of the cloth (in which Horán, moreover, argues against celibacy and in favor of marriage for clerics), clearly affected Matto and helped shape her own strong views on the role of the clergy in Peruvian society. On the other hand, Torres y Lara's (pseudonym Itolararres) *La trinidad del Indio* called attention to the exploitation of the Indians in rural communities through the alliance of the priest, the governor, and the justice of the peace (the "Indian's Trinity" of the novel's ironic title). Texts such as this one, along with the pro-Indian speeches and essays of Peru's foremost turn-of-the-century intellectual, Manuel González Prada (1844–1918), provided the ideological underpinnings for Matto's first novel.

In addition to its links to the crime story and to the referential and "realist" discourse shared by both journalism and the philologically inspired works of González Prada, another important journalistic trait in *Aves sin nido* is its connection with sensationalist, crusading journalism. As said ealier, this so-called yellow journalism had much in common with Naturalist fiction; in fact, it would be hard to say which genre borrowed more from the other. Yellow journalism certainly pioneered the textualization of the seamier details of daily life, allied to a sense of outrage, but Naturalism pushed the boundaries of that textualization even further into areas that journalism had only dealt with euphemistically or moralistically, such as prostitution. The two issues that motivated Matto's crusade in *Aves sin nido* were almost as difficult to write about in Peru, at that time, as prostitution: the celibacy of priests and the abuses committed against the Indians. These two seemingly unrelated topics were connected, in Matto's view, by the priests' complicity in the oppression of the Indians by the civilian authorities. The priests' exploitation of the Indians was not only economic (as in the exorbitant fees the Indians had to pay for burial services) but also sexual, since Indian women would often be forced to serve as the priests' concubines. Needless to say, in turn-of-the-century

Spanish America the issue of priestly celibacy was highly charged and controversial, and to broach openly, in writing, the well-known fact that some priests had common-law wives and illegitimate children was sensationalistic, to say the least. For Matto, however, this sensational subject served primarily as a device to focus the Peruvian readers' attention on the social problems afflicting the country's Indians.

Another fundamental element of the discourse of *Aves sin nido* is one that naturalist fiction often tried (but failed) to avoid: melodrama. Like a similar work from an earlier time and a very different country, Harriet Beecher Stowe's *Uncle Tom's Cabin* (1852), *Aves sin nido* is an exercise in melodrama's "sentimental power" (to use Jane Tompkin's well-known phrase). In this regard, the melodramatic plotline of *Aves sin nido,* in which two young lovers, the *criollo* Manuel and the Indian Margarita (the two "birds without a nest" of the novel's title), discover that they are both children of bishop Pedro de Miranda y Claro from different mothers, is not a mere embellishment of or supplement to the novel, but fulfills an important function in Matto's narrative. Although to modern readers this plotline seems digressive in regard to Matto's own stated intention in the novel's prologue to denounce the exploitation of the Indians, it serves, in fact, as a dissimulating device to seduce the Peruvian readers of the time into reading about the Indians' plight. Clearly, Matto feared that a straightforward narrative centered exclusively on the Indians would not interest her readers, and despite her obviously strong views about priestly celibacy, she used this issue mainly as a lure for her readers and as a cover for the more far-reaching and potentially explosive issues of racial injustice in the countryside.

Given the prevalence of melodrama in *Aves sin nido,* one might wonder why this novel (its crusading aspect aside) has been linked with the naturalist novels of Zola and others. There seems to be scant "naturalism" in its discourse, aside from some scattered positivistic comments made by the character of Fernando Marín, who at one point offers the following analysis of the Indians' apparent "degeneracy":

> "There's something more, my child," said don Fernando [to his wife Lucía]; "it is a proven fact that the eating habits of the Indians have degenerated their cerebral functions. As you may have noticed already, these disinherited people rarely eat meat, and the advances of modern science teach us that the brain's activity and force are related to its nutrition. The Indian has been condemned to the most extravagant of vegetable diets, living off turnip leaves, boiled beans and quinoa leaves. Without albuminoids and organic salts, his brain has no way of getting phosphates and lecithin without psychic effort. He is merely fattening up his brain, which sinks his thoughts into darkness and makes him live at the same level as his draft animals." (59–60)

The text distances itself from these comments, however, by having don Fernando's wife immediately make gentle mockery of her husband's statements and by having the narrator note that "his wife's words made him realize he had just tried to give her a science lesson, which was probably pedantic and out of place" (60). Such ironic distancing from the most obvious traits of Naturalism is nonetheless common in Spanish and Spanish American novels in this mode. Naturalism was always critically received in the Hispanic world, where it coexisted with Spanish-American *modernismo* and its more influential "art for art's sake" attitude. Nevertheless, both Naturalism and journalism are fundamental pre-texts of *Aves sin nido,* since both serve as this novel's enabling discourses. Naturalism and journalism together lend Matto the combination of moral authority with relatively uncensored speech necessary to write in an openly critical and detailed manner about the Church and the abuses against the Indians. Melodrama, in this context, although a somewhat distracting presence, must be regarded as the dissimulating feint the novel uses to simultaneously protect and deliver its doctrinal message. At the risk of muddying the waters still further, it should also be remarked that the rhetoric of journalism in the nineteenth century was highly permeable to melodrama as well. Thus, its presence in *Aves sin nido* should probably not be considered antithetical to the novel's journalistic elements, but complementary to them.

This is also the case in the Mexican Heriberto Frías's (1870–1925) *Tomochic*. Critics have often derided the novel's amorous subplot, in which the protagonist, sublieutenant Miguel Mercado, falls in love with Julia, a girl from the rebel town of Tomochic, who later dies in his arms. This rather maudlin story, inlaid with touches of crude eroticism in the Naturalist style, has generally been regarded as an appendix to the novel's principal narrative: an account of the grinding military campaign to quell a rebellion in Tomochic, a village in the state of Chihuahua whose inhabitants, led by a religious sect, had risen up against the central government in 1892. The tale of *Tomochic*'s origins itself reads like a piece of melodramatic fiction, but it also underscores the novel's crusading thrust (see Brown xi–xii). One day, Frías, who was a veteran of the Tomochic campaign, came across a newspaper article whose account of the events he regarded as false. Indignantly, he quickly penned his own version of the events, which was critical of the government's role. This he sent to the editors of *El Demócrata*, who promptly began to publish Frías's text anonymously in installments. The serial publication of *Tomochic* caused widespread scandal, and the Díaz regime reacted by arresting the editors and shutting down the newspaper. Despite the novel's anonymity, the authorities suspected Frías of being the author, and he was soon incarcerated. He was saved from the firing squad by his quick-thinking mistress, who hid a letter to Frías from the editors of *El Demócrata* from the soldiers who came to search Frías's rooms. Later, during his military trial, a journalist friend of Frías broke into the closed-down offices of *El Demócrata* and destroyed the highly incriminating original manuscript of *Tomochic*, which was in Frías's handwriting on paper bearing the watermark of his own Ninth Battalion. Due to lack of evidence, Frías was acquitted, but he was discharged from the army and so was forced to make a living from journalism.

The Mexican historical incident described in Frías's text coincidentally resembles the 1889 Canudos rebellion in Brazil's northeast region portrayed in Euclides da Cunha's (1866–1909) classic *Os Sertões* [1902; *Rebellion in the Backlands*, 1944], a work that Frías probably never read. Nevertheless, a comparison of the two works proves illuminating in terms of the roles of journalism and fictional discourse in each. In *Os Sertões*, as is well known, Euclides attempts to offer a "scientific" explanation, as well as a journalistic account, of the Canudos rebellion. The Positivistic discourses of "scientific racism," geography, and criminology loom large in *Os Sertões*, almost overshadowing the story of the uprising itself, as if the text were trying to reenact, in its own discourse, the struggle between the Europeanized and modernizing Brazilian state, and the native and antimodern *jagunços* led by Antonio Conselheiro. Certain parts of *Os Sertões* therefore read like a sociological tract, while in others an intensely narrative, epic-like discourse predominates. Overall, however, an objectivist stance permeates Euclides's text.

This is not quite the case with *Tomochic*. As said before, the uprising described in *Tomochic* is eerily similar to that of Canudos. It was also led by a group of religious fanatics, and like Canudos, it was partly a reaction by the villagers to injustices committed by the government and partly a response to the secularism and the positivistic rhetoric of Porfirio Díaz's regime. However, Frías's novel, unlike Euclides's, is almost totally devoid of Positivistic rhetoric and sociohistorical digressions. Instead, it is essentially a narrative exposé, albeit focalized through the protagonist's subjectivity, of the tactical errors and the abuses committed by the military in their campaign. Indeed, a latent anti-Positivism—even subjectivism—and a heightened tendency toward fiction run in tandem with anti-Porfirian statements throughout Frías's novel. In the four subsequent editions (1894, 1899, 1906, and 1911) after the novel's first publication as a serial in the opposition newspaper *El Demócrata* in 1893, Frías not only rewrote the text to give it a more novelistic character, but also added more openly critical passages blaming the Díaz dictatorship for the disaster at Tomochic (Brown xviii–xxi). Arguably, Frías shows greater sympathy toward the Tomochic rebels than Euclides does towards the *jagunços*. Thus, despite their very similar subjects, *Tomochic* and *Os Sertões* may be seen as divergent in their approach: While Euclides conflates journalism with science to a very high degree, Frías tends to avoid journalistic rhetoric and gravitates more toward fictions of a particularly subjectivist and melodramatic cast. *Tomochic*'s subjectivism is manifested in the novel's tightly focused view of the events from the standpoint of the protagonist, Miguel. In many respects, Miguel is a typical *fin-de-siècle* character, in the mold of French decadent and Spanish American *modernista* fiction. Although his alcoholism makes him resemble some of Zola's Naturalist characters, his introspective and imaginative personality and sickly physique are like those of the artist-heroes of decadent and Modernist novels such as J.K. Huysman's *À rebours* [1884: *Against the Grain*, 1926], José Asunción Silva's (1865–1896) *De sobremesa* [1896; *After-Dinner Talk*], or Enrique Larreta's (1875–1961) *La gloria de Don Ramiro* [1905; *The Glory of Don Ramiro*, 1924].

Reading *Tomochic* as a Naturalist novel with strong *modernista* inflections allows us to better understand the inclusion of an amorous subplot in this novel about war. From this point of view, the subplot, far from being superfluous, performs a key function in the narrative: to convey in an oblique and allegorical fashion the narrator's ambivalence about the Tomochic rebels and their cult of the Saint of Cabora, as well as the war's effect on his personality and on his future vocation as an artist. Julia, Miguel's beloved, is the daughter of "San José" (the *nom de guerre* of one of the Saint of Cabora's followers) and the niece of Bernardo and also—as Miguel soon discovers to his horror—his concubine. The text's combination of Naturalism with *modernismo* in its discourse surfaces in the passages where the narrator refers openly to the degrading circumstances in which Julia lives: Bernardo, her uncle and common-law husband, is old, hairy, and filthy, with a long gray beard, and is insistently referred to as an "ogre" (19–21). Bernardo's wife also lives with them, a wizened old woman who is compared to a "harpy" (20). Julia herself is described as "the ogre's portion" [*la ración del ogro*, 19]. However, in a significant passage of rather purple prose, the narrator argues that, despite the abuse to which she has been subjected, Julia's soul remains "virginal":

Over the old bandit's concubine, over the flesh which was
blemished nightly without her enjoyment or excitement,
there shone, unknown and solitary, a virginal spirit. . . .

Nevertheless–charming consolation!–the monstrous violation
hardly dulled the girl's ineffably clear soul. The attempt left her
childlike spirit almost intact; the reddish creaking of the flesh did
not stain the elevated crystal of her serene and sad conscience. It
did not cloud her pupils with either horror or delight, nor
broaden her hips, nor soften her round, firm, small breasts. . . .

Her unbreakable resignation, her faith in the Virgin Mary, and
her constant activity, kept her body whole and kept lively the
melancholy grace of that lily of the hills.

The lovely Julia, the old drunkard's mistress, the bandit's woman,
the daughter of "San José," was indeed a holy girl, by a divine
miracle. . . . (28–29; the last ellipsis is Frías's)

The allusion to the "holy girl" is to the Saint of Cabora, the
young girl to whom miracles were attributed and whose
followers launched the Tomochic rebellion, and suggests
an allegorical parallel between the saint and Julia. Like the
saint, Julia remains "virginal" despite being used by men
for their own base purposes. The narrator's use of fairy-tale
terminology along with crude descriptions of immorality is
no doubt partly ironic, but it also marks a counterpoint in
Tomochic's discourse between the rough directness of Naturalism and the sublimating phraseology of *modernismo*. This
counterpoint or, to be more precise, vacillation between
crude realism and its artistic sublimation also occurs quite
shockingly at the level of the action when, after a brief
idyll, a drunken Miguel forces himself upon Julia, essentially placing himself at the same level as Bernardo. Miguel
even makes sacrilegious use of Julia's faith in the Saint of
Cabora (whose followers always invoked "God's Great
Power" [*el Gran Poder de Dios*]) in order to persuade her: "I
love you, you have my word of honor! I swear it to you by
the God's Great Power . . . ! You are my wife . . . God wills
it!" (42; Frías's ellipses). Miguel's alternately tender and
abusive attitude toward Julia may also be read, as said earlier, as emblematic of the narrator's posture toward the
Tomochic rebels. Clearly, Miguel's forcible seduction of
Julia in Chapter 13 parallels the government's crude
attempt to bring Tomochic to heel by means of military
violence. But also, despite its truculence, the romance
between Miguel and Julia functions in many ways as a
small-scale model of Frías's relation to his subject. Its
extreme ambivalence is mirrored in the way Frías tells the
story of the Tomochic rebellion: Just as the virtuous and
beautiful Julia is surrounded by ugliness and moral squalor, the tale of Tomochic is, on both sides of the struggle, a
panorama of foolhardiness, fanaticism, and destruction in
which are imbedded a few instances of honor and heroism.
Moreover, Tomochic becomes in the novel the crucible in
which Miguel's weak and vacillating self is tested and
becomes stronger, just as, for Frías, the experience of
Tomochic leads him ultimately to discover his literary
vocation.

In *Tomochic*, one is never completely certain whether Frías
is speaking about Tomochic or about himself. In other
words, one is never sure whether the novel's point is to
denounce the Díaz régime by portraying the suffering at
Tomochic–a suffering in which Miguel, Frías's alter ego,
plays a very minor role–or to recount the story of Miguel/
Frías's initiation into literature, for which the Tomochic

rebellion, however epic, simply serves as a backdrop. Ultimately, the two readings are irreconcilable. *Tomochic*
explores a number of borderlines as jagged as the Sierra
Madre mountains where the action takes place: between
state authority and dictatorial oppression, between spiritual
love and carnal desire, between literary subjectivity and
journalistic objectivity. Along with scathing critiques of Porfirio Díaz (added later, it is true, but still during the latter
days of Díaz's regime), one finds in it paeans to the military
and to its hierarchic worldview and, in the novel's melodramatic portions, contrasting instances of tenderness and of
physical abuse between men and women. These drastic
polar shifts in the novel's discourse also produce its dissimulating effect, turning the text into a sort of moving target
(like the soldiers and rebels who fire at each other in the
novel from varying positions) that is difficult to pin down in
terms of a clear-cut ideology.

Journalistic discourse is a fundamental presence in many
of the major Spanish American novels of the nineteenth
century. Its presence is significant, however, not in a deterministic way, but as an element in a broader strategy of
what I have called (following Severo Sarduy) "dissimulation": the systematic use of one or more discourses to hide
another through a sort of textual mimeticism that renders
the text's meaning ambiguous. From *El periquillo sarniento* to
Tomochic, we can see that Spanish American novels frequently made journalistic claims of veracity and verifiability, only to withdraw or obscure them by interweaving
them with fictional elements. These novels' juxtaposition of
journalism with forms usually linked with fiction (or that
are shared by both journalism and fiction, such as melodrama and sensationalism) serves to underscore how journalism and narrative fiction have imitated each other,
strategically, throughout history. Beyond such a truism,
however, lies the fact that Spanish American novels have
used this mutual mimesis as a paradoxical "cloak of invisibility" in their attempt to slip past the censors their messages of resistance or dissent.

Works Cited

Brown, James W. 1968. "Prólogo." *Tomochic.* by Heriberto Frías.
Mexico: Porrúa. viii–xxv.

Davis, Lennard J. 1983. *Factual Fictions: The Origins of the English
Novel.* New York: Columbia University Press.

Derrida, Jacques. 1981. *Dissemination.* Trans. Barbara Johnson.
Chicago: University of Chicago Press.

Fernández, Teodosio. 1987. "José Mármol." *Historia de la literatura
hispanoamericana. II. Del neoclasicismo al modernismo.* Ed. Luis Iñigo
Madrigal. Madrid: Cátedra. 155–62.

Fernández de Lizardi, José Joaquín. 1963. *Obras. I. Poesías y fábulas.*
Ed. Jacobo Checinsky and Luis Mario Schneider. Mexico City:
Universidad Nacional Autónoma de México.

—. 1968. *Obras. III. Periódicos. El Pensador Mexicano.* Ed. María Rosa
Palazón and Jacobo Checinsky. Prologue by Jacobo Chencinsky. Mexico
City: Universidad Nacional Autónoma de México.

—. 1970. *Obras. IV. Periódicos.* Ed. María Rosa Palazón. Mexico City:
Universidad Nacional Autónoma de México.

—. 1997. *El Periquillo Sarniento.* Ed. Carmen Ruiz Barrionuevo.
Madrid: Cátedra.

Frías, Heriberto. 1968. *Tomochic.* Mexico City: Porrúa.

Mármol, José. 1930. *Amalia: Novela histórica americana.* Barcelona: Ramón Sopena.

Matto de Turner, Clorinda. 1968. *Aves sin nido.* New York: Las Américas.

Parker, Alexander A. 1943. *The Allegorical Drama of Calderón: An Introduction to the Autos Sacramentales.* Oxford: Dolphin.

Sarduy, Severo. 1982. *La simulación.* Caracas: Monte Avila.

Schneider, Luis Mario. 1968. "Clorinda Matto de Turner." *Aves sin nido* by Clorinda Matto de Turner. New York: Las Américas. vii–liii.

Serres, Michel. 1975. *Feux et signaux de brume: Zola.* Paris: Grasset.

Spell, Jefferson Rea. 1971. *Bridging the Gap: Articles on Mexican Literature.* Mexico: Editorial Libros de México.

Stephens, Mitchell. 1988. *A History of News: From the Drum to the Satellite.* New York: Viking.

CHAPTER 31

THE MAKING OF THE LATIN AMERICAN NOVEL

Roberto González Echevarría

Readers of this text who know my work will recognize "The Novel as Myth and Archive: Ruins and Relics of Tlön" as the forerunner of these remarks. However, it is different, if for no other reason than the context of that publication was my long reflective essay on the Latin American narrative (1990), and the present text is part of "The Development of the Novel" within the section on "Textual Models and their Transformations," coordinated by Randolph Pope and Flora Süssekind in this volume of the Oxford history. I do not think it is satisfactory to treat the narrative as if it were a self-contained form of discourse, nor a raw reflection of sociopolitical conditions. In my view the relationships that the narrative establishes with nonliterary forms of discourse are much more productive and determining than those it has with its own tradition, with other forms of literature, or with the brute factuality of history. Narrative and poetry do not follow the same historical path, nor do they change at the same rhythm; hence I think it is a mistake to write literary history as if all genres moved together in the same direction like a vast river. Narrative is too profoundly affected by nonliterary forms to constitute a neat historical unit in the way that perhaps the lyric can. Conventional literary history, following a philological model, masks what I take as the true history of narrative prose. Domingo Faustino Sarmiento (1811–1888) and Euclides da Cunha (1866–1909) are more important in that history than José Mármol (1817–1871) or Jorge Isaacs (1837–1895). Only by mechanically applying a model of literary history drawn from European sources can *Amalia* (1855) and *María* (1867) play a significant role in the history of Latin American narrative. My views on narrative, one fully endorsed by the editors of this history, which can be ascertained by examining Part Three of Volume I, "Plurality of Discourse in Latin American Culture," coordinated by Raúl Antelo, Eugenia Meyer, Zuzana Pick, Eneida Maria de Souza, and Juan Villegas, will therefore be developed here as part of a collaborative rethinking of literary history.

In spite of its obvious debt to Sarmiento's *Facundo* (1845) and da Cunha's *Os Sertões* [1902; *Rebellion in the Backlands*], *Doña Bárbara* (1929) by Rómulo Gallegos (1884–1969) is a turning point. Latin American fiction is determined no longer by the Naturalists' conception of nature but by myths of cultural beginnings, and authority itself–the possibility of being an author–is predicated on being able to generate a discourse capable of containing and expressing those myths. A figure in modern Latin American fiction is the archive, or the repository of stories and myths, one of which is the story about collecting those stories and myths. The inaugural archival fiction in that recent tradition would be the other text that issued from traveling through Venezuela, Carpentier's (1904–1980) *Los pasos perdidos* [1953; *The Lost Steps*]. This tale of two texts–*Doña Bárbara* and *Los pasos perdidos*–contains the story of Latin American fiction in the modern period from the 1920s to the present. It is a story that centers on anthropology as the hegemonic discourse that makes the Latin American narrative

possible. Legitimacy now is obtained by mimicking the texts that constitute anthropological discourse, and the textual subplot of flight away from hegemony is from those anthropological texts. I shall first look at the sweep of that story and then at works by two very different authors who nevertheless strained the limits of the relationship between anthropology and narrative: Jorge Luis Borges (1899–1986) and Miguel Barnet (b. 1940). This is a story that has no satisfactory ending because it brings us to archival fictions, which make up the current mode of Latin American narrative, to which my own discourse probably belongs.

As a discipline, anthropology becomes a hegemonic discourse in Latin American narrative in the twentieth century, but the discipline itself had some of its beginnings during the Colonial period of what would become Latin America. This is so from the very moment of discovery. In 1494 Columbus left Fray Ramón Pané (d. 1571) in Hispaniola with the charge of learning the language of the native Taínos, finding out about their beliefs, and writing a report about his discoveries. The Spanish crown was interested in the natives' religion to gauge how difficult it would be to convert them to Christianity. Pané, a Catalan with an imperfect command of Spanish and no prior knowledge of the native population, dutifully went to the hills, lived among the Taínos, learned as much as he could of their language and religion, and by 1498 had written a truly extraordinary document, his *Relación acerca de las antigüedades de los indios* [An Account of the Antiquities of the Indians]. Pané's *Relación* anticipates many of the issues debated today by anthropologists, issues that also have been significant in modern Latin American fiction up to the very present–for instance, in Mario Vargas Llosa's (b. 1936) 1987 novel *El hablador* [*The Storyteller*]. Can one truly know the Other without doing violence to him or her and to his or her culture? Is contamination by Western culture desirable? Will it not bring about destruction? Is it possible to write about one's knowledge of the Other without distorting his or her culture beyond recognition? Is it impossible to avoid making fiction out of any such attempt? The bizarre fate of Pané's report, a story that reads as if it had been written by Borges, makes it an even more compelling textual phenomenon. Not only was the *Relación* written, one presumes, in faulty Spanish, but the original was lost–but not before Columbus's son Hernando had copied it and included it verbatim in the biography of his father that he wrote. But the manuscript of Hernando's book on the admiral also disappeared–but not before it was translated into Italian. The *Historie della vita e dei fatti dell'ammiraglio Don Cristoforo Colombo* [*The Life of the Admiral Christopher Columbus*], which appeared in Venice, in 1569, contained, of course, Pané's *Relación*, in Italian.

Contemporary scholars, most notably José J. Arrom, have sedulously translated Pané's text back into Spanish. I carefully avoid saying "back to the original" because modern versions, using our refined philological methods and greater knowledge of Arawak culture, are more faithful in transcribing the names of Taíno gods than Pané could have been, and the Spanish is, needless to say, flawless. The delicate textual archaeology that yielded these versions involved the cleansing of any trace of Italian from the names of those gods and the removing of the vestiges of sixteenth-century Italian that were left from when the *Relación* passed through that language. Pané added further confusion to his premonitory text by writing in a very self-conscious manner. He complains a number of times that he is unsure of the storyline of Taíno theogony because he has heard conflicting accounts from different informants, but adds that even if he had had the time or certainty about alternatives to rewrite his report, he was, like the protagonist of *Los pasos perdidos*, short on paper and hence could not make several drafts. All of these difficulties, and no doubt his own good will, led Pané to assume a charming and in many ways exemplary humility before the Taínos and their beliefs, and his report, for all its faults, remains a fundamental source of information about the religion of that exterminated people. At the same time, the variegated history of the text, its existence in several languages, none of which could be claimed either as the original or the definitive one, as well as the uncertainties introduced by Pané himself, make the *Relación* a good example of the kind of literariness that current anthropologists are claiming for their writings and of the attendant crisis in anthropology as a discipline. There is no doubt, from the point of view of Latin American literature, that Pané's *Relación* uncannily anticipates many of the topics that are fundamental in modern novels like *Los pasos perdidos* and *El hablador.*

Pané's efforts and report are but the beginning of a wide-ranging, controversial campaign to acquire knowledge about the New World's native populations, carried out in the sixteenth and seventeenth centuries both by members of religious orders and by government officials such as the *cronista mayor* (*Colección de documentos inéditos, relativos al descubrimiento, conquista y organización de las antiguas posesiones españolas de América y Oceanía sacados de los archivos del reino y muy especialmente del de las Indias* [Collection of Unpublished Documents Relative to the Discovery, Conquest, and Organization of the Former Spanish Possessions of America and East Asia Taken from the Archives of the Realm and Especially the Archive of Indies]). Works by Fray Bartolomé de las Casas (1474–1566) and Fray Bernardino de Sahagún (1500–1590), to mention only the most prominent, were written to prevent the Spaniards from enslaving the Indians by documenting the richness of their civilizations and hence their full-fledged membership in the human race. As is known, some friars, such as Toribio de Motolinía, took the side of the natives to the point of becoming one with them, even taking an Aztec name. Native writers like Fernando de Alva Ixtlilxochitl (1578–1648), El Inca Garcilaso de la Vega (1539–1616), and Felipe Guamán Poma de Ayala (1524?–1613) soon emerged to give characterizations of their own cultures (see Ricard 39–60). The polemic rages to this day because in some areas, such as Peru and Mexico, the destruction brought about by the Conquest has not led to a viable cultural or political synthesis. The bases for the discourse about the Other have changed, but not the fissure that makes that discourse necessary or even possible, as *El hablador* makes amply clear.

The knowledge-gathering activities of the friars as well as the natives' own testimonies and pleas had a tremendous political and intellectual impact in Spain and the New World. The debates about the right to seize territories and peoples divided the crown and its theological advisers, created turmoil in the colonies, and shook the ideological foundations of Western knowledge (Hanke; Simpson; El Inca, Garcilaso de la Vega). The work of the friars in particular is not only an invaluable source for, but a precursor of, modern anthropology, as much in method of research as in the manner of writing reports. There are, of course, many other texts from the Colonial period that offer as many premonitions as Pané's in terms of the future of anthropology and the Latin American narrative, most notably Alvar Núñez Cabeza de Vaca's (1490–1558) *Naufragios* [1542; Shipwrecks]. For the narrative, the problem of describing American cultures in a Western discourse created an important topic: that of writing about an Other whose culture is radically different from the author's, yet who is in possession of a knowledge that appears to be whole and functioning on its own in spite of the differences. In short, this is a story about an Other who can be other and human at the same time, a fact that threatens not only the right to hold power over him or her but erodes any self-assurance about the universal validity of the culture pretending to exercise control over his or hers. Las Casas was quite explicit on this point in his many moments of despair. The Latin American narrative returns to this topic in the modern period, spurred on precisely by modern anthropology, whose source is perhaps, in the non-Hispanic world, Montaigne's essay "On the Cannibals." Montaigne's well-known ironies were indictments in Las Casas, Sahagún, Motolinía (1490?–1565), and Guamán Poma, clearly because they were closer to the destruction and genocide. These authors did not write ethnographic reports, given that such a rhetorical vehicle was nonexistent in the sixteenth and seventeenth centuries. Their texts were, of necessity, part of the exchange of legal documents that prevailed in the Colonial period. It was the only way of saying what they had to say, and the most effective way to give their writings an immediate political impact. Hence, as with the description of nature, what later became a master narrative is already latent in Colonial times. What Pané lacked was the discourse of a discipline in which to see reflected the problematics of his own discourse. Modern anthropology would furnish that to Latin American writers.

The scientific travelers who swarmed over the New World from the eighteenth century onward not only knew the writings of Las Casas and others, which had been widely disseminated, but were themselves interested both in the European-like culture of cities in the crumbling Spanish Empire and in that of the non-European peoples who remained. Even though the natural world was the focus of the travelers' gaze, they provided a wealth of information about indigenous populations. Modern anthropology began as a branch of natural history; it grew out of the evolutionary conception of reality developed by nineteenth-century science. Human culture was perceived as a progression in which native American peoples stood somewhere in the early stages. Like nature in the New World, "contemporary savages" could furnish information about the ancestors of modern man; consequently American Indians were often the object of what George W. Stocking Jr. has called "Victorian anthropology" in an important book of the same name. This anthropology was ruled by a set of rhetorical guidelines whose function is comparable to the 1575 royal order the Spanish Crown sent to the Indies to regulate writing about "natives." Stocking writes:

At the same meeting, a committee was set up, with Lane Fox as secretary, to draw up brief forms of instruction "for travelers, ethnologists and other anthropological observers." By 1874, the committee, in which Tylor played a dominant intellectual role, had produced the first edition of *Notes and Queries on Anthropology, for the Use of Travellers and Residents in Uncivilized Lands.* Although the dropping of "ethnologists" from the intended audience of *Notes and Queries* suggests a settling back into the armchair, the men who in that little volume proudly labeled themselves "anthropologists" clearly anticipated a period of hard work and slow progress within an accepted framework, one that would be remembered as having established the new science on a solid empirical, theoretical and institutional footing. (258)

To describe the material culture and physical characteristics of these natives meant to follow the methods employed to analyze the flora and the fauna. Von Humboldt and his followers provided much knowledge about Indian and African cultures in the Americas but not on the scale of the chroniclers and friars, although some travelers became particularly interested in one or another human group. (Francis Bond Head wrote a detailed report on the *gauchos.*) Just as specimens of the flora and fauna were displayed in museums, "primitive cultures" became part of the entertainment of the *belle époque,* alongside circus freaks and other shows, such as the one in Brazil where Antonio Conselheiro's severed head was displayed to the delight of the multitudes (see Rearick). Travelers often had pictures of the natives made, both for scientific and entertainment purposes, just as they had pictures made of specimens from the natural world (see *Mexico ilustrado por Europa del renacimiento al romanticismo* [Mexico Illustrated by Europeans from the Renaissance to Romanticism]).

Latin American travelers, such as Lucio Mansilla (1831–1913) in Argentina and Cirilo Villaverde (1812–1894) in Cuba, to give but two examples, also wrote about non-Europeans in the New World–the first about Indians, the second about blacks in Cuba's sugar mills. These reports, however, were not written in an effort to incorporate those populations into a more inclusive culture or polity. On the contrary, and as can be readily ascertained in the works of Sarmiento and Euclides da Cunha, these reports often were permeated by a "scientific racism" that decried the deleterious influence non-European races had on the moral, intellectual, cultural, and material progress of Latin America. Inferior races could play a role, even if a negative one, in natural history but not in cultural history. The new republics, as known, often engaged in campaigns to exterminate the Indians, now under the banner of modernization. It might be remembered here that Charles Darwin met the Argentinean dictator Manuel Rosas in the pampas while the latter was leading a raid against Indians, and that Lucio Victorio Mansilla's (1831–1913) *Una escursión a los Indios Ranqueles* [1870; *An Expedition to the Ranquel Indians*] was not a mere fact-finding expedition but a military campaign, no matter how ironic and self-deprecating the colonel was or how critical of civilization (Stephan; Sarmiento; Stabb; Stocking). The urge to modernize moved the republics away from the Indian past and against the Indian present. Romantic literature, particularly poetry, made idealized figures of the natives, which had little in common with their current or past counterparts. These Indians came from Europe, mostly from the pen of Chateaubriand. In the Caribbean, where blacks occupied a position somewhat, but in reality not quite, analogous to that of Indians; the situation was similar, although the struggle against slavery generated some

early studies of African cultures. But no one thought, save in the most stylized and abstract Romantic poems or novels that invoked universal feelings such as love or grief, that the Indian or the black had anything to say that could be incorporated into Latin American culture, or that their history was anything but ancillary in the composition of the nascent independent states. They were not a source of stories that could express the innermost secrets of Latin American society; nor could their beliefs compete with the knowledge offered by "civilization" in general or by scientific reportage in particular. As can be seen in Esteban Echeverría's (1805–1851) *El matadero* [1838; *The Slaughter House*] and Sarmiento's *Facundo,* the stories told by the Spanish chronicles were left behind. The new story had to be of the present. In the present Indians and blacks appeared as part of nature, part of the violent becoming of the New World, but not its voice.

World War I, as we know, brought the nineteenth century to an end, tearing down the ideological certainties of the West. In Latin America this meant the demise of Positivism at the most visible level (Stabb 55–90). But it also meant disillusionment with nineteenth-century science. The crisis of the West, or the decline of the West (to give it Spengler's widely known title), removed natural science as the mediating discourse in Latin American narrative and made way for a new one, that of anthropology. But this was not an anthropology whose foundation was natural science anchored in the theory of evolution and its corollaries. The decline of Positivism in Europe itself had changed the foundations of Western anthropology. Stocking writes: "Although it reflected changes in the colonial situation and domestic ideological contexts of anthropology, this antievolutionary reaction was part of a more general 'revolt against Positivism' in European social thought. It involved both a reassertion of the role of 'irrational' factors in human life, and a critique of the methodological and epistemological grounding of prevailing scientific determinisms" (287). Such a reassertion also meant that European culture was no longer seen as the logical or even desirable goal of evolution; culture began to be conceived in a plural way, or rather, the idea that cultures, not culture, constituted the world, became a central tenet of the new anthropology. The shift is now precisely to what the native had to say. What the new discourse seeks is not so much knowledge about the Other as much as knowledge about the Other's knowledge. Anthropology appeared as a discipline capable of integrating into the polity as well as into Latin American consciousness the cultures of non-European peoples still very much present in the New World, that Other Within analyzed by Sarmiento and Euclides da Cunha. It was a totalizing discourse embracing all products of the human mind that promised to make whole political entities that were severely fragmented and often at war with themselves. Anthropology also offered those countries the possibility of claiming an origin different from that of the West–a fresh beginning that could lead away from the debacle of Western civilization. Anthropological knowledge could correct the errors of the conquest, atone for the crimes of the past, and make for a new history. Ironically this healing promise was a reflection of the role anthropology played in the West. Anthropology offered the West a mirror in which to look at its own battered culture to plot a new beginning, although, of course, in practice it was a legitimation of vast colonial enterprises that harked back to the nineteenth century (see Asad). Anthropology drew the veil of science over the violence of colonial occupation. It is this "prestige" of anthropology as a source of scientific knowledge about culture, as well as its complicity with modern art (particularly with the Surrealists) that made it a dominant form of discourse in Latin America.

Anthropological knowledge provided the Latin American narrative with a source of stories, as well as a master narrative about Latin American history. In fiction, Latin American history will now be cast in the form of myth, a form derived from anthropological studies. The relationship of the Latin American novel to anthropological discourse is homologous to its relationship in earlier periods to law and science. Revealingly, anthropologically mediated Latin American narratives lead, through a process analogous to one that takes place within anthropology itself, to a crisis in anthropological knowledge. If in the novel we move from a Gallegos to a Borges, a Carpentier, and a García Márquez (b. 1927), in anthropology we go from Bronislaw Malinowski and Marcel Griaule to Clifford Geertz, James Clifford, George Marcus, Talal Asad, Vincent Crapanzano, James Boon, Michael Taussig, and several others who are subjecting anthropological discourse to a radical critique. Latin American narrative may well be the design on the reverse side of the picture, or the mirror-image of the crisis in anthropology as a discipline.

The historical scheme I offer here for anthropology is derived from James Clifford's influential work, now available in *The Predicament of Culture*. The parallel plots of anthropology and Latin American narrative are as follows: The period between the wars is one in which authoritative texts are produced both in anthropology and the anthropologically mediated Latin American novel; after World War II, and in the case of the Latin American novel, after *Los pasos perdidos* (1953), the authority of anthropological discourse is voided. The evolution of anthropological discourse took the following path, according to Clifford:

> In the 1920s, the new field worker-theorist brought to completion a powerful new scientific and literary genre, the ethnography, a synthetic cultural description based on participant observation [which] may be briefly summarized [as follows]. . . . First, the persona of the field worker was validated, both publicly and professionally. In the popular domain, visible figures like Malinowsky, Mead, and Griaule communicated a vision of ethnography as both scientifically demanding and heroic. . . . T]he field worker was to live in the native village, use the vernacular, stay a sufficient (but seldom specified) length of time, investigate certain classic subjects. . . . The new ethnography was marked by an increased emphasis on the power of observation. Culture was construed as an ensemble of characteristic behaviours, ceremonies and gestures, susceptible to recording and explanation by a trained onlooker. . . . Certain powerful theoretical abstractions promised to help academic ethnographers "get to the heart" of a culture more rapidly. . . . The new ethnographer tended to focus thematically on particular institutions . . . . In the predominantly synechdochic rhetorical stance of the new ethnography, parts were assumed to be microcosms or analogies of wholes. This setting of institutional foregrounds against cultural backgrounds in the portrayal of a coherent world lent itself to realist literary conventions. (29–31)

These realist literary conventions in ethnography correspond to those of the regionalist or telluric novel in Latin American fiction, a kind of novel that prevails precisely between 1920 and 1950, cast essentially in a nineteenth-century realist mold. *Doña Bárbara* is, of course, the quintessential

telluric novel. Around 1950 there is, then, both in anthropology and in Latin American fiction a *crise de conscience*, provoked by a political awakening on the part of the object of anthropological study. The liberation of the postcolonial world and events in Latin America, such as the Cuban Revolution, undermined official stories such as the ones both literature and anthropology provided about Latin American culture or cultures. There was also an apparent complicity between anthropological conceptions of culture, their application to Latin America, and U.S. hegemony in Latin America that was vehemently denounced in the 1960s. This is the subject of Vargas Llosa's *El hablador*. In anthropology the crisis has generated a highly critical metadiscourse. Clifford writes:

> Henceforth, neither the experience nor the interpretive activity of the scientific researcher can be considered innocent. It becomes necessary to conceive ethnography, not as the experience and interpretation of a circumscribed "other" reality, but rather as a constructive negotiation involving at least two, and usually more, conscious, politically significant subjects. Paradigms of experience and interpretation are yielding to paradigms of discourse, of dialogue and polyphony. (41)

In Latin American narrative there is a parallel evolution to highly self-reflexive forms that turn back onto earlier narratives to reveal their literariness, rather than the validity of their knowledge about culture, annulling the anthropological mediation by showing it was a literary conceit all along. More recent forms then turn onto the metadiscourse itself to reveal its literariness. These are the archival fictions: *Terra Nostra* (1975), *Yo el Supremo* [1974; I, the Supreme], *De donde son los cantantes* [1967; From Cuba with a Song], *El arpa y la sombra* [1979; The Harp and the Shadow], *El libro de Manuel* [1973; A Manual for Manuel], *Rayuela* [1963; Hopscotch], and *Oppiano Licario* (1977), to name but a few. Of course, in the case of most practitioners of the metadiscourse among recent anthropologists–victims of the "epistemological hypochondria" of which Geertz speaks–they gladly avow the literary quality of anthropology (Geertz 71). "Literary" to these anthropologists means a discourse that does not assume method to be a transparent medium but is embedded in rhetoric and, as such, partaking of the general circulation of texts in a given epoch. It also means a nonauthoritative discourse containing several voices, including, most important, that of the object of study. Finally, it means a text with multiple, layered meanings that is never fixed, such as Pané's *Relación*.

So there is in the present a coincidence in the urge to declare anthropology literary both in anthropology itself and in the Latin American narrative. In the latter this turn constitutes the escape from the constraint of the model discourse by means of the legitimizing act of mimesis. In recent fiction this move takes the form of a return to the archive, the legal origin of the narrative in Latin America. The archive does not privilege the voice of anthropological knowledge; nor does it abide by the discourse of anthropology in method or practice. The archive questions authority by holding warring discourses in promiscuous and mutually contaminating contiguity, a contiguity that often erases the difference separating them. The archive absorbs the authority of the anthropological mediation. Later, of course, in the archival fictions, the archive is shown to be also a form of mythic discourse, not removed from the literary but a part of it. This swerve is, in turn, directed against the authority of the metadiscourse, by showing that the literary is not an independent category outside language, but language itself in its most vulnerable and self-revealing manifestation. Narrative invalidates the stance of the metadiscourse, showing that it is always part of the mythic. To realize this turn away from totalizing metadiscourse in cultural history is the aim of the present history of literary culture.

During the 1920s, in the wake of World War I, institutions were created in many Latin American countries to gather information about the cultures of indigenous or African peoples present in their territories. A powerful agent in bringing about this reversal was the Mexican Revolution, one of whose central programs was a vindication of the Indian legacy, as well as a recognition of the presence of Indian cultures in the makeup of modern Mexico (see Bernal). The state made a sustained effort in anthropology and related fields such as archaeology, founding museums, academies, schools, journals, and other institutions (see Henriquez Ureña 133–34). Although without undergoing a political upheaval as profound as Mexico's, Peru and neighboring Andean countries extolled the pre-Hispanic past and institutionalized the study of present indigenous cultures. The foundation of Alianza Popular Revolucionaria Americana and the rekindling of *indigenismo* are all part and parcel of this movement (Dorward 149–59; Kristal). In Argentina there was a rekindling of interest in *gauchesca* literature, while in the Caribbean attention was focused on blacks. The Afro-Antillean movement was promoted by anthropologists such as Fernando Ortiz (1881–1969), who was the first president of the Sociedad de Folklore Cubano in 1923, and founded the Institución Hispano-Cubana de Cultura in 1925 and in 1937 the Sociedad de Estudios Afrocubanos, which published the journal *Estudios Afrocubanos*. In Brazil, the Week of Modern Art in São Paulo (1922) celebrated the country's indigenous and African past and attempted a mock vindication of cannibalism as a cultural practice. The influence of these self-proclaimed *antropófagos* was far-reaching. They exemplify the convergence of avant-garde movements and the more widely accepted and institutional search for national identities. Mario de Andrade's (1893–1945) *Macunaíma* (1928) combines anthropology and avant-garde novelistic techniques to create a modern mythic hero. Both the institutions founded by the various governments and the avant-garde artists sought the discovery or creation of a national culture, a discourse, as it were, bespeaking the uniqueness of Latin America and of each individual subculture within it. The presence of anthropology in both as a mediating element and as an authoritative method delimiting the possibilities of discourse, is shockingly evident, and the participation of writers, artists, and intellectuals in general in this enterprise is a very significant episode in modern Latin American history. Concepts, methods, and often knowledge itself were derived either from the work of European-based anthropologists, or from that of European-trained native anthropologists, such as Ortiz himself and his disciple Lydia Cabrera. Anthropology as a set of given discursive possibilities, as the very possibility of writing about Latin American culture, is a given within and against which much of Latin American narrative is written in the twentieth century. There have been a number of writers who combined literature and anthropological research: Miguel Ángel Asturias (1899–1974), Alejo Carpentier, Severo Sarduy (1937–1993), Lydia Cabrera (1899–1991), José María Arguedas (1911–1969), Augusto Roa Bastos (b. 1917), Darcy Ribeiro (1922–1997), and the Mexican Juan Rulfo (1918–1986). But the point is that these writers make explicit a relationship between literature and anthropology that is implicit in the core of Latin American narrative in the modern period; in other words, Fernando Ortiz and Gilberto Freyre articulate in their scientific works what in the narrative is an inherent effort to represent culture that is ethnographic in its conception (see González Echevarría 1985).

The regionalist or telluric novel was conceived through this institutionalized anthropological grid. These novels are concerned with myth, religion, magic, language, genealogy, the impact of modern modes of production on traditional societies, retentions from earlier periods, in short, with the totality of a culture viewed and described from the outside, often through a narrator who follows a protagonist traveling to the jungle, the *llano*, or the *pampa*. As novels, these books generally adhered to the practices of nineteenth-century realism. The anthropological mediation is evident as much in the stories about the creation of each novel as in the actual text. These ancillary stories or pretexts serve to legitimize the persona of the novelist as a knowledgeable individual, much in the same way that the public and professional figures of anthropologists were legitimized by stories of their voyages and sojourns in the wild. One could call these stories fables of validation or legitimation. For instance, it is part of the tale always told about the composition of novels such as *Don Segundo Sombra* (1926) and *Doña Bárbara* that Ricardo Güiraldes (1886–1927) and Rómulo Gallegos traveled to the *pampa* and the *llano*, respectively, armed with notebook and pen to record unusual words, strange stories, customs regarding horsemanship and cattle ranching—in fact, everything that any self-respecting anthropologist doing fieldwork would note. In the most advanced statement on the telluric novel, Carlos J. Alonso convincingly has argued that the project of novelists like Rómulo Gallegos, Ricardo Güiraldes, and José Eustaquio Rivera was modern because of their critical perspective, which they sought to conceal, but was fundamental to their task: "The attempt to produce a text of autochthony places the writer in an eccentric perspective with respect to his or her own cultural circumstance; in the resulting displacement, the author necessarily becomes also a critic in spite of the unproblematic assumption of immediacy on which his project is predicated" (6). The critic that the novelist becomes is essentially an anthropologist because anthropology furnishes the only discourse capable of authoritatively analyzing and narrating the autochthonous—hence the fable of legitimation, and the various information-gathering activities to which they devoted themselves once in the field. Alonso's most productive insight is to realize that the "quest for identity" project implicit in telluric novels is itself a myth, a reflection, I would add, of the very discourse on which it is based. He writes:

> The Latin American quest for cultural identity could itself be regarded as a cultural myth of foundations; but a myth that narrates the story of an essential cultural schism, capable nonetheless of endowing the affairs of the collectivity with the requisite meaning and purpose. In the end, through this myth of permanent cultural crisis, Latin American intellectuals have paradoxically found an effective narrative of cultural identity. (36)

This reading is only possible from the perspective of the rereading of the telluric novels that more recent fiction has made possible, from the point of view of the archival fictions to which, ultimately, Alonso's own book belongs.

In *Los de abajo* [1915; *The Underdogs*], Mariano Azuela (1873–1952), in a stroke of genius, included the figure of the outside observer inside the novel: Dr. Cervantes (no less), who is forever frustrated in his efforts to understand the revolutionaries with whom he travels. A central concern of these so-called *novelas de la tierra* [novels of the earth] was to cull and record information about sectors of Latin American culture, which, while contemporary and part of that culture, were outside modernity; more important, these were illiterate populations, possessing essentially oral cultures, thus fulfilling an important prerequisite to be the object of an anthropological study. In his position as outsider, the anthropologist-author searched for the secret of his own uniqueness and the key to an originality that would be measured by its distance from the routines and commonplaces of the West. The insistence on being there–to use Clifford Geertz's formula–and being able to convince the reader of the authenticity of what is being written, takes a peculiar form in the case of the Latin American author because his conceit consists in affecting to have always been there, given that he is a native of the culture (Geertz 16). But, at the same time, he has to be outside to be able to record it, to inscribe it. Anthropology furnishes the novelists with the methodological instruments, the rhetoric or discourse to be both there and outside. On the most elementary level, as we saw, he or she carries a pad and pen to record what is out there. These efforts were not always as amateurish as they seem. If it is true that Güiraldes, Gallegos, and Rivera had really very little, if any, training in ethnography, other writers, particularly those more closely associated with the avant-garde, did have some, or by their extended stays "in the field" developed methods close to those of professionally trained anthropologists. One should remember here two further fables of validation or legitimation. Carpentier has written in *La música en Cuba* [1946; *Music in Cuba*] about how he attended Afro-Cuban rituals with reverence but also with notebook and pen to record the music as much as the story being acted out (236). The results are found in his 1933 novel *¡Ecué-Yamba-O!*, which includes the quite reliable transcription of an initiation ceremony (173–90). Another story is that of João Guimarães Rosa (1908–1967), who was not only a great Brazilian writer but also a medical doctor. Guimarães Rosa spent years caring for the dirt-poor people of the *sertão*. Since they could not pay him he would ask them to tell him stories in return for his services. From the stories that he collected he wrote many of his own short stories as well as his masterpiece *Grande sertão: Veredas* [1956; The Devil to Pay in the Backlands].

These novels are guided by a philological approach derived from nineteenth-century anthropology. The anthropologist-author aims to fix a text, containing a set of cultural practices and a group of stories. The study of this mythology is shrouded in the mystery of words, whose origin the anthropologist-author attempts to find and whose meaning he discovers and sets. Novels like *Don Segundo Sombra* or *Canaima* (1935) are philological works in this sense. Often, as in *Doña Bárbara*, *La vorágine* [1924; *The Vortex*], and *¡Ecué-Yamba-O!*, the books come equipped with glossaries, and Carpentier's novel even has illustrations. The narrative voice in these novels frequently contrasts a peculiar usage with the standard Spanish one. Gallegos, Güiraldes, and most regionalist novelists are experts in folklore and rural speech, and their novels show it. They are also at pains to reproduce through odd, presumably phonetic spelling, the peculiar pronunciation of their characters, creating an even stronger clash between their speech and the voice of the narrator. These books attempt to inscribe, to turn into writing, the oral culture or subculture in question, using the philological instruments of anthropology. Both in the actual creation of the novel and within the text, the trappings of method are present.

Anthropology as a form of hegemonic discourse is also evident in the regionalist novel because of the inordinate attention paid to matters of genealogy. Genealogy, as we know, is very much an element in the conventional novelistic tradition and could even be either a remnant of the epic or something willfully copied from the epic by novelists attempting to give their works an epic dimension. Be that as it may, genealogy is a fundamental element in modern Latin American fiction, not merely as a measure of time, or as a reflection of myth, but also because the regionalist novel studies the family as a group and how values are transmitted from generation to generation, as well as in social practices. The complex genealogical structure of *Doña Bárbara* has a mythic, theogonic dimension, but it is also a study of the clash between the conception of the family unit in rural Venezuela and urban Caracas. The apotheosis of genealogy one finds in *Cien años de soledad* [1967; *One Hundred Years of Solitude*] is a parody of this aspect of the regionalist novel. The study of myth and the family commingle and give the regionalist novel a peculiar character, but only because myth and the family are aspects of that synecdochical rhetoric that ethnography finds suitable for a holistic study of society.

Another aspect of anthropological discourse evident in the regionalist novel is the comparative method, which appears in these books mainly in contrasts between the oral subcultures and the dominant culture, although comparisons between oral subcultures also abound. Chronological contrasts also are drawn, pitting the state of a given group before the arrival of the Europeans against their present condition or chronicling the decline of a group as a result of a specific form of exploitation, as in the case of *La vorágine* with the rubber industry, *¡Ecué-Yamba-O!* with sugar production, or *Don Segundo Sombra* and *Doña Bárbara* with cattle ranching. There is a sense of loss in these telluric novels, a nostalgia for a past when traditional values prevailed and non-European cultures were true to their nonhistorical "essence." The recuperation of that state is the mission of the novels, a mission that can be achieved by finding a modern, all-encompassing myth that will make whole the disparate fragments of the present: one Venezuela, one Argentina, or one Mexico, united in an apotheosis of cross-cultural communion.

The most interesting and enduring among these novels explode under the pressure of their internal contradictions. These novels are not ideal subjects for myth criticism, as some have thought, but are themselves a form of myth criticism. The disparate mythic elements, the strands of various stories, plus the contemporary, historical plot involving the protagonists cannot coalesce under the all-embracing allegory or metamyth. In regionalist novels the language of the narrator is about magic, but it is not magical. In these texts the literary element is found precisely in their inchoate nature, which reveals the trappings as well as the inadequacies of method. These novels are mock anthropology that unmasks the conventionality of ethnography, its being a willful imposition on the material studied as an act of appropriation. This revelation, when it occurs as in *Doña Bárbara*, constitutes the flight of these texts from the hegemonic discourse that mediates them–a flight into literariness (González Echevarría 1985, 33–63).

The solution to this dilemma, still under the mediating influence of anthropology, was to write novels whose inner coherence imitated that of sacred texts, even including numerological and symbolic correspondences, and leaving no fissures between the world of the characters and that of the narrator. This was the great achievement of the Carpentier of *El reino de este mundo* [1949; *The Kingdom of this World*] and of Miguel Ángel Asturias's fiction in general. René Prieto has described Asturias's novelistic project in this way:"Like Joyce, who conceives *Ulysses* in terms of a complex narrative framework in which each chapter is linked with a section of the *Odyssey*, an hour of day, an organ of the body, an art, a color, and a musical instrument, Asturias builds his American idiom on the basis of layered relationships embracing elements, animals, colors and numbers (from Mayan lore) interlinked amongst themselves" (Prieto 191–92).

In 1927 Asturias (1899–1974) had translated, edited, and published the *Popol Vuh* in Paris; better yet, and closer to Pané and Borges, Asturias translated into Spanish Georges Raynaud's French translation. His novels, particularly *Hombres de maíz* [1949; *Men of Maize*], which is the one being discussed above by Prieto, profited from the knowledge he acquired in that anthropologicophilological restoration. Asturias's novels also gained from the various textual siftings that the Mayan material went through and from the traces that those siftings left in the final text. The Mayas had no writing and no books in the way the West conceives of them. They certainly had no novels. Their contemporary descendants write no novels either–unless they are called Miguel Ángel Asturias–and probably read very few of them. Spanish versions of Mayan myth are always translations, and the concoction of a numerological system bonding the contemporary plot of the novel with the rigid language of sacred lore is a product of the literary imagination, not of ritual. *Hombres de maíz* is a novel in the measure in which it pretends to be myth, not because it is myth.

José María Arguedas's answer to these dilemmas in his autobiographical novel *Los ríos profundos* [1958; Deep Rivers] is to narrate in the first person the life of a boy who, like him, lived among Indians and learned Quechua before Spanish. Very much like *The Portrait of the Artist as a Young Man*, *Los ríos profundos* is a *bildungsroman* in which the young protagonist is sent to a school where he is to learn to live in the society his parents have chosen for him. It is a deeply troubling experience because for Ernesto to learn from the Spanish-speaking priests and his classmates means to forget, or worse, to scorn the life of those who raised him. *Los ríos profundos* is almost an allegory about the conquest of Peru and the forced acculturation of the natives to Western civilization. It is not quite that, because its most profound message is precisely that the wounds of the Conquest have not healed; hence an overarching construct that will, as in Asturias, pretend to bind together the knowledge of the natives acquired by anthropological practice and their own knowledge of themselves is not possible. The disharmony at the core of Peruvian society is conveyed through the broken syntax of the narrator's discourse, which very often obeys the linguistic structures of Quechua. There are flashes of poetry in this fractured Spanish, catachreses created by the interference of another language. Moreover, as John Murra (an anthropologist) says about his colleague's fiction, for Arguedas the issue was "how to transmit to the reader of Spanish not only compassion for the oppressed, but a sense that the latter also had a perception, a world view of their own, in which people, mountains, animals,

the rain, truth, all had dimensions of their own, powerful, revealing, and utterly unlike the Iberian ones" (xi). *Los ríos profundos* represents through its very incompleteness and flaws the tense dialogue of cultures that makes up contemporary Peru, a dialogue in which the acquisition of knowledge about the other can still lead to genocide.

Given his unimpeachable credentials in anthropology, Arguedas's fable of legitimation is a much more dramatic one. By means of it, he clearly wanted to make a statement as much about his texts as about his life. When he killed himself in 1969, Arguedas was expressing the measure not only of his despair but also perhaps of his guilt for having made use of anthropological knowledge to approach a part of himself, a process that was already a kind of partial suicide. Feeling, perhaps, that he had stilled through inscription one of the voices within him, he felt that the proper thing to do was to annihilate the Other. In Arguedas the anthropological mediation is not bypassed, as in Asturias, by exposing its literariness, but by denouncing its violent, repressive nature, and by stressing the limitations inherent in the kind of knowledge that it can generate. For Arguedas, conquest and knowledge are still linked. Anthropology, which he practiced under the auspices of the sort of state organization to which I have alluded, was implicated in cultural genocide. He did not see a way out of the headlong rush to destruction that the arrival of the book and the cross in the Andes seemed to have started.

From early on, Borges has both profited from and offered a radical critique of anthropological discourse and its relationship to narrative. This is an aspect of Borges's work that easily can be overlooked because he wrote no novels and his fiction is considered to be inimical to the *novela de la tierra*. In "El jardín de senderos que se bifurcan" ["The Garden of Forking Paths"], there is a passage that appears to be a critique of any kind of discourse that attempts to contain a country or a culture in the way that regionalist novels do. The protagonist says: "Pensé que un hombre puede ser enemigo de otros hombres, de otros momentos de otros hombres, pero no de un país: no de luciérnagas, palabras, jardines, cursos de agua, ponientes" (475) ("I thought that a man might be an enemy of other men, of different moments of other men, but never an enemy of a country: not of fireflies, words, gardens, streams, or the West wind" [94]). Yet in May of 1940, Borges published a story that is to my mind his regionalist novel, "Tlön, Uqbar, Orbis Tertius." Given Borges's distaste for the novel in general and his disdain for realism and most forms of regionalism, it is not surprising that his *novela de la tierra* should be about a totally imaginary region. Borges was critical of regionalism and skeptical, if not mocking, of all efforts to define an independent Latin American consciousness or a unique Latin American literature. He positively was repelled by the link between such ideological enterprises and government programs. But he was hardly indifferent to these intellectual, cultural, and political enterprises. Borges himself began his literary career as a regionalist poet in *Fervor de Buenos Aires* [1923; Fervor of Buenos Aires] and worked closely with Ricardo Güiraldes. He also was fascinated by *gauchesca* literature, making quite a few valuable contributions himself in stories such as "El Sur" ["The South"] to a thematic that was essentially Argentine. (In fact, "El Sur" is, in some ways, a story about a fable of legitimation like the ones just seen in relation to the telluric novel.) In "El Aleph," furthermore, Carlos Argentino, who is bent on writing a national epic, is the quintessential telluric writer, and no matter how ironically he is portrayed, his project is important enough to be a central concern of the story.

In "Tlön, Uqbar, Orbis Tertius" Borges reveals the artifice of the regionalist novel by creating an entirely imaginary country described with the methodological precision of an ethnographer's report. In a sense, what Borges does is to turn the regionalist novel inside out, performing in the process a severe ideological critique of anthropological mediation. The style of the entry in the encyclopedia, where the narrator finds the information, is described as follows: "El pasaje recordado por Bioy era tal vez el único sorprendente. El resto parecía muy verosímil, muy ajustado al tono general de la obra y (como es natural) un poco aburrido. Releyéndolo, descubrimos bajo su rigurosa escritura una fundamental vaguedad" (432) ("The passage remembered by Bioy was perhaps the only startling one. The rest seemed probable enough, very much in keeping with the general tone of the work and, naturally, a little dull. Reading it over we discovered, beneath the rigorous writing, a fundamental vagueness" [19]). The key word here is the technical term *verosímil*, lost in the somewhat careless translation, which means realistic by virtue of the text's adherence to rhetorical norms for representing reality. The suggestion is clear: Regionalist novels are fantastic, not realistic; the methodology that legitimizes them is no more than a pretext to elaborate a cogent fictional world. Ethnography is always literature. The authoritative voice of method is as literary, as fantastic, as the stories that it uncovers.

Borges had anticipated this critique in a 1932 essay that is a direct answer to an anthropological treatise that had vast repercussions in Latin American literature, as well as many others, James G. Frazer's *The Golden Bough* (Borges 1996, 1:230–31). In this essay, "El arte narrativo y la magia," ["Narrative Art and Magic"], Borges writes about novels and stories and their relation to the "primitive mind." He contends, as he would on several occasions, that novels are as chaotic as the real world, unless they are constructed like detective novels. Such stories, he says, are carefully constructed worlds in which there are secret connections between events. Borges is interested in the secret of those connections, which we accept without blinking. For Borges causality is the most important element in his stories, but he asserts that causality in stories is as fantastic and as magical as the primitive cures described by Frazer, which depend on tropological relations between wound and cure, or between cure and the weapon that inflicted the wound. Primitive medicine is based on belief in such a system of metaphors; magic would be the efficacy of such a system in affecting reality. In reading and writing stories and in accepting detective stories as realistic, we indulge in the same kind of magic we assume to be typical of primitives. Hence, our "study" of primitives by means of anthropology and our writing about them using the literary conventions of ethnography reveals much about us, much that is a mirror image of the object we purport to describe or analyze. The links that we establish between events, our own metatexts about the primitive, are cast in a rhetorical mold that is not radically unlike his. Given these propositions, Borges's Others in "Tlön, Uqbar, Orbis Tertius" are not going to be "contemporary savages," like those of Victorian anthropology, but imaginary beings that inhabit a kind of metatextual utopia (Irby 411–419).

In "Tlön, Uqbar, Orbis Tertius" that metatext happens to be about a nonexistent realm, but the procedures and tropes that make it up are the same as those in ethnography; in fact,

one could say that the story actualizes the metadiscourse of ethnography. The fable of validation or legitimation in Borges's story has, therefore, been internalized, has been made a part of the narrative. Legitimation is not granted here by a journey to the wild, by "being there," but by the discovery in a pirated version of the *Britannica* of an article about Uqbar, a country that the narrator and his friend Bioy cannot find in any atlas. (Bioy is, of course, Adolfo Bioy Casares [1914–1999], an Argentinean writer of fantastic fiction, a detail that slips into the fiction of Borges's context at the time of writing.) Uqbar is a very odd place indeed, but it is described by the encyclopedia, as we saw, in the flat tone characteristic of such reference works. A second fable of validation is provided by the appearance of another encyclopedia, produced by a character who is drawn from the world of European expansion that generated modern anthropology. Legitimation in Borges does honor to the etymology of the word both as law and as reading. The textual space of the encyclopedia, which stands for all the knowledge in the West, a compendious and, at the same time, slightly frantic repository of information, is organized according to the most banal of conventions–the alphabet–yet can absorb anything, reducing to common knowledge the most distant and different cultural practices. Uqbar, knowledge of which the encyclopedia owes to the work of various German ethnographers and travelers, has a literature that obsessively is devoted to the description of two imaginary regions: Meljnas and Tlön. These are the telluric novels within the fictional telluric novel of Borges's story, the rest of which is about Tlön, one of those regions, which is as odd as Uqbar, if not more so. Information about Tlön is acquired from an *Encyclopedia of Tlön*, obtained from a blurry Englishman, appropriately named Herbert Ashe, who came to Argentina to work on the British-built railroads after some adventures in Brazil; he is obviously a figure of the European traveler, vaguely reminiscent of Francis Bond Head. Borges is notorious for the creation of this kind of *mise en abime* to underline the textual nature of most phenomena. In this case, however, the presence of the encyclopedia in a remote neighborhood of Buenos Aires–as far as Borges would travel from the city–and the role played by the English engineer, clearly point not only to the literary nature of ethnographic writing but also to the source of such discourse in institutions fostered by the British Empire. As we know, the growth of the *Britannica* during the nineteenth century paralleled the expansion of the Empire, culminating in the tenth edition, published in 1902, the date given in Borges's story for the encyclopedia. Herbert Ashe merely heightens the atmosphere of Victorian colonial life that permeates "Tlön, Uqbar, Orbis Tertius."

But Ashe is significant in another way. He transmits the *Encyclopedia of Tlön* to the narrator through death, as it were; it is a posthumous gift, a partial key to the secrets of that elusive region. There is something funereal about Ashe anyway, beginning with his very name. He is, according to the story, one of those Englishmen who suffer from "unreality." The point is that, like the Buendia who manages to translate Melquíades's manuscript in Gabriel Garcia Márquez's (b. 1927) in *Cien años de soledad*, Ashe establishes a link between knowledge and death that will be one of the main components of archival fictions. Death is a metaphor for the impossibility of knowledge or about the impossibility of there being any discourse about the Other that is not based on a potentially lethal power. Like Melquíades' manuscript and like all manuscripts found in the archive, the *Encyclopedia of Tlön* is a partial or unfinished work; Ashe is only able to produce one volume. Like ethnography, according to Clifford, this encyclopedia is predicated on synecdoche, only that here, the part can hardly be expected to produce a whole. The sum total knowledge about Tlön is hopelessly incomplete and is in need of further invention or investigation. But while knowledge may be fragmentary and partial, the fiction is all-encompassing, as the reader discovers in the epilogue, where it is revealed that Tlön may be the fabrication of an international sect of Tlönists. The inversion has been completed. From a discourse designed to describe and discover the codes of a given culture, ethnography becomes a mastercode to invent a society. Tlön is to Borges as Venezuela is to Gallegos. Hence, Venezuela is like Tlön. But Tlön is a negative culture; in it things seem not to add up but to "subtract down." While I am not unaware of the metaphysical implications of this, I am more taken by the way in which Borges has rewritten, or unwritten, the rules that govern the production of discourse about another culture, and also by how he has anticipated that Macondo would be like a house of mirrors and that the sources that Carpentier found in the Apure were always already stories.

Biografía de un cimarrón [*The Autobiography of a Runaway Slave*] was first published in 1966 by Cuba's Instituto de Etnología y Folklore, an entity whose origins are the Sociedad de Estudios Afrocubanos and other organizations founded by Fernando Ortiz. Miguel Barnet (b. 1940), once Ortiz's assistant, who helped him catalogue his library toward the end of the master's life, was among the original group of researchers when the Instituto de Etnología y Folklore opened its doors. He was on his way to becoming an anthropologist, perhaps Ortiz's successor. *Biografía de un cimarrón* which, as the institution that published it guaranteed, was intended as an ethnographic study, would change Barnet's life, perhaps as radically as *Doña Bárbara* changed Gallegos's. The enormous success of the book as a work of literature, both in Cuba and abroad, led Barnet to become an author both of various other testimonial narratives and of several books of poetry. Today he occupies a position at the Unión de Escritores y Artistas de Cuba, not at the Instituto de Etnología y Folklore (which has in any case been disbanded). Barnet's procedures are rather conventional. He interviews his subjects, researches the social and historical contexts in libraries and archives, and then writes a first-person account in chronological order. *Biografía de un cimarrón* was and continues to be an important book because it reached to the core of anthropological mediation and reopened issues that had been opened by Pané, Sahagún, Guamán Poma, and other chroniclers of the discovery and conquest of America. Barnet's book, in addition, seemed to cut through the ritualistic arguments about socialist realism and modernism, which had been rehearsed once again in the Cuba of the 1960s, and answered Carpentier's challenge in *Los pasos perdidos*. Moreover, in a local context that had nevertheless international repercussions, *Biografía de un cimarrón* returned to the questions around which Cuban literature had begun as a self-conscious activity and an institution in the 1830s. Barnet established a link with anti-slavery narratives of that period such as Manzano's *Autobiografía*, and with a whole tradition that is, as William Luis has demonstrated, at the evolving center of Cuban narrative since the first half of the nineteenth century. It was through anthropology that *Biografía de un cimarrón* tried to bypass the snares of the literary, but

anthropology is so ingrained in Latin American narrative that it was hardly an escape, and escaping is a theme of paramount importance in the book. If one looks at *Biografía de un cimarrón* as an object, one finds that outwardly it resembles as much a regionalist novel as an ethnographic monograph. There is a photograph of Manuel Montejo, an introduction, and a glossary at the end, very much like the ones found in novels such as *Doña Bárbara* and *¡Ecué-Yamba-O!*. It is true that the introduction and the first-person account have separated the voices of the narrator and the protagonist, but on the whole *Biografía de un cimarrón* appears as a logical sequel to the Latin American regionalist novel. But this is a sequel in which anthropological discourse is made evident to legitimize itself and the results of its research. What the book says is backed up by the Instituto de Etnología y Folklore.

This clash between the authorial voices of Montejo and Barnet is what constitues the book. It is a clash in which the narrators and their echoes and multiple reflections are often shuffled, shifted, and exchanged. Because if in this inaugural utterance Montejo plays the role of naive informant, in many others he plays that of knowledgeable, outside observer. One of Montejo's most remarkable traits is that he assumes an ethnographer's perspective vis-à-vis the ethnic groups that surround him, not only the Chinese and the whites (Galicians, natives of the Canary Islands, Turks—who are really Lebanese—and Jews) but also with respect to the various black nationalities represented among the slaves and former slaves, including his own. Montejo never marries and settles down. In his years as a maroon (from *cimarrón*, a runaway slave) he is constantly on the go. He is a perpetual traveler who is forced to join a slave community only when he is captured. He is never at home in any of these groups, however. Constant movement gives him a comparative perspective and trains him as a keen observer of others. This makes Montejo at once the best and the worst kind of informant: the best because of his powers of observation and his ability to establish a distance, the worst because he does not speak from inside any culture.

Montejo's most remarkable feature is not his penchant for communion with others but rather his yearning for solitude. He spends years in the wild alone, years in which he speaks to no one and retreats into a paleolithic lifestyle. It is an existence he comes to like, one in which he learns the language of nature and develops a rich inner life. Montejo is escaping the horrors of slavery, but at the same time he is delving deep into himself to find freedom from humankind in general. His journeys into the Cuban *manigua* are like those of the narrator-protagonist of *Los pasos perdidos*–a flight from history, a voyage back in time to a prelinguistic world, free from the fetters of existence as much as from the chains of slavery. This mythic journey, this death and resurrection, make him wiser and stronger. Silence teaches him about the questionable value of words and makes him intolerant of garrulousness. In his opinion the Chinese in Sagua la Grande babble in their incomprehensible tongue just to be a bother ("para joder," as he puts it [90]). Montejo was as evasive with other blacks as he may have been with Barnet: "Muchos negros querían ser amigos míos. Y me preguntaban qué hacia yo de cimarrón. Y yo les decía: 'Nada.' A mí siempre me ha gustado la independencia. La salsa y la escandalera no sirven. Yo estuve años sin conversar con nadie" (58) ("Many blacks who wanted to be my friends asked me what I did when I was a maroon. And I would say 'Nothing.' I've always liked being independent. Dancing around and carrying on are no good. I spent years without talking to anyone"). Montejo rejects rituals of communal bonding, rituals in which the various African ethnic groups strengthened their bonds. The culture Montejo develops in the wild is as negative as Tlön's: It is almost a reduction to the mere structure of culture and being, a system emptied of content and wound up to function as a mechanism for analysis that precludes participation. It is a negativity like the language of Tlön that in Montejo is expressed by the significant negativity of silence. Montejo is as much the ethnographer as Barnet.

Yet in a curious way Montejo's detached perspective, his memory being a sort of archive of different narrative possibilities—he can speak of and about the Congo or the Lucumí—is a reflection of neo-African culture in the Caribbean. Montejo moved among several ethnic groups who had different languages and religions, languages and religions that are still alive in Cuba today, as well as in New Jersey and Miami. It would be naive to think that these cultures and languages remained pure in Cuba and that they were not affected by their violent insertion into Western history. They were, indeed, profoundly affected, and neo-African culture in the Caribbean tends to be synchretic, absorbing even Catholicism. The resilience of neo-African culture is one of the most remarkable factors of Caribbean life and history. Languages, religions, and all sorts of cultural practices survived the horrors of slavery and later the scorn of racial and class discrimination. Neo-African culture also survived being turned into an object of ethnographic study.

The institution created by slaves to oppose slavery was the maroon society or *palenque*, some of which became impregnable citadels. But there were *palenques* of many sizes. Their chief function was to provide refuge to maroon slaves and resist the attempts to return them to the plantations. They were societies under siege, made up of individuals whose origins could be and often were very disparate. The *palenques* were as odd and as metadiscursive as Tlön. These were pluralistic societies harboring many languages and praying to many gods with the one common purpose: survival (see Price). Neo-African culture allowed gods from multiple theogonies to coexist, tacitly accepting a kind of religious pluralism and thus achieving a flexibility that also may go a long way to explain their survival. So, if one feature of neo-African society was (and is) its clandestinity, the other was its capacity to absorb parallel or conflicting theogonies, as well as a Babel of tongues. This, it seems to me, explains Montejo's relativistic wisdom, his being a storehouse of stories without giving preeminence to any of them. Montejo was a living archive, and the text of his story as much an archive as Melquíades's manuscript in *Cien años de soledad*.

In this regard Montejo and Barnet invoke a topic in Cuban literature that goes back to the anti-slavery narratives of the nineteenth century. When a slave became old and infirm, and therefore useless for productive work, he was often made into a *guardiero*. A *guardiero* was a keeper of the boundaries who lived on the frontiers between sugar plantations as a guard or gatekeeper. Because of their age and their commerce with many different people, these *guardieros* also became keepers of the traditions. These wise old men could be consulted on many matters, ranging from social practices and religious lore to the medicinal quality of plants and the whereabouts of somebody. The *guardieros* sat on the fence, as it were, straddling the divisions between African cultures and became ethnologists in their own right. I do not say this in a metaphorical

sense, or as a *boutade*. Anti-slavery narratives like Anselmo Suárez y Romero's (1818–1878) *Francisco* (1880) or Cirilo Villaverde's (1812–1894) *Cecilia Valdés* (1839) incorporated the *guardieros* and some of their knowledge. Both these authors traveled to the provinces to witness slave society in the sugar mills. By an astonishing turn of fate those novels figure among the most important sources of information in Fernando Ortiz's early work on African religions in Cuba (Ortiz 1973). Ortiz, as we have seen, was Barnet's mentor, and the knowledge and experience that he gathered from the *guardieros* is one of the voices in *Biografía de un cimarrón*, one that finds an echo in Montejo's own as well as in Barnet's.

Is there not in Montejo's story about his life as a maroon not only a tale about attaining a plural perspective but also an allegory of the text's escape from the mediation of the hegemonic discourse? Isn't his first-person account like that of the *pícaro* and other delinquents who live on the margins of the law and tell about their lives through the formulas of the notarial arts? Is Montejo's life not a return to the archive, not only those in Carpentier, Fuentes (b. 1928), and García Márquez, but the original of the sixteenth century? Montejo's story takes the form of the picaresque autobiography being told to someone in authority, in this case Barnet, the representative of the Instituto de Etnología y Folklore. Like the *pícaros*, Montejo escapes the constraints of hegemonic discourse by mimicking it and therefore absorbing it. Montejo shows that Barnet's method is literary from the start. Unlike the *pícaro*, however, and also unlike Ernesto in *Los ríos profundos*, Montejo is old, incredibly old. The delusions of innocence are not his. There is no fresh start, his age is capacious like the archive; it allows him to contain all the fresh starts, all the promises of a new beginning. Like Melquíades and Borges he is in possession of a knowledge that is at once all-inclusive and yet aware of the gaps and the unfinished stories.

The evolving nucleus of the Latin American narrative tradition is concerned with the uniqueness, difference, and autonomy of a cultural entity that defines itself within and yet against a powerful totality, real as well as invented, that could be called the discourse of the West. That tradition is generated in relation to three manifestations of Western hegemonic discourse: the law in the Colonial period, the scientific writings of the many Naturalists who ranged over the American continent in the nineteenth century, and anthropology, which supplies a dominant version of Latin American culture in the modern period both through the writings of Europeans and through the discourse of the state in the form of institutes of folklore, museums, and the like. The law in the Colonial period sets the structure of the relationship between Latin American narrative and dominant discourses. Legal writings deal with legitimacy, enfranchisement, and self-definition in the context of a patrimonial-bureaucratic state that controls writing and hence knowledge, which it safeguards in great storehouses like the Archive at Simancas and the Escorial, both created by Philip II. Like the emerging modern novel in its picaresque form, Latin American narrative in the Colonial period deals with delinquency and a general lack of legitimacy. These obstacles are circumvented through mimesis, the imitation of the forms of forensic rhetoric to gain freedom by showing the conventionality of legal language, its being a mere simulacrum to disguise arbitrary power. The performance of this mimetic act grants a momentary suspension of the censorious and punitive power of judicial language. This structure of constraint, imitation, and release is the master narrative of Latin America that prevails until the present, particularly in the other two major manifestations of hegemony.

The traveling Naturalists furnished a version of American uniqueness by their representation of time and change as conceived by evolutionary nineteenth-century European science. The Latin American narrative imitates their representation of Latin American specimens and takes advantage of their concept of mutation, as well as of the exceptional time in which this process takes place, to escape the dominant discourse by fusing with its transfiguring object. After the 1920s, ethnography, often aided by Latin American states, provided a way to represent the originality of Latin American stories, customs, speech, and other cultural phenomena. This is the discourse the Latin American narrative will imitate. The result was that *novela de la tierra* or telluric novel, that highly critical and hybrid product whose rhetorical model was furnished by anthropology, whose mastery it escaped also by fusing with its object of study, by showing the literariness of ethnography. A very self-conscious ethnography in the present is contemporaneous with a form of Latin American fiction that I call archival fictions, the most prominent manifestation of which is *Cien años de soledad.* It is a kind of novel that recovers the three previous mediations and hypostatizes their collecting function in the figure of the archive, which harks back to the founding mediation. The quintessential archive is Melquíades's room in the Buendía household, in which the gypsy writes the history of the family and Aureliano Babilonia later deciphers it with the aid of the encyclopedia and *The Thousand and One Nights.* These archival fictions, which are my hermeneutical model, constitute in some ways a dialogue between Foucault and Bakhtin, a counterpoint of prison and carnival.

Archival fictions are narratives that still attempt to define the cipher of Latin American culture and identity; hence they fall within the mediation provided by anthropological discourse. In the same manner as current ethnography, these books no longer accept the institutional discourse of method as a given, accepting the literariness of all representations of the Other, even, or perhaps especially, if it is an Other Within, as is the case with the Latin American narrative. Archival texts have not given up on the promise of anthropology, but they probe into anthropology itself, becoming a kind of ethnography of anthropology, as in Mario Vargas Llosa's novel *El hablador.* At the same time that they undermine the bases of anthropology, archival fictions privilege the language of literature in which both the novel and anthropology take refuge. This is a literature that aspires to have a function similar to that of myth in primitive societies and that in fact imitates the forms of myth as provided by anthropological discourse. The mutual mirroring between the discourse of method and its object here is seen not as antagonistic or conflictual but as part and parcel of that category, the literary, into which all forms of storytelling are displaced. So the difference between archival fictions and their predecessors is that they pretend to be literature, not any other form of hegemonic discourse; yet in doing so, they are in fact in a mimetic relationship with current anthropology. The obvious question, difficult to answer, is: Is anthropology still a form of hegemonic discourse, or is it being replaced by another discourse not yet apparent?

Archival fictions also remain within the anthropological mediation because through it narrative reaches back to the founding mediation, the discourse of the law. This is so because in anthropology the law stands for the primordial code of a given society, the master key to all of its codes. As the law, legal discourse is the basic medium for the exchange of values, the metaphor of metaphors, the most archaic rule—both the ruling rule, as it were, and the most ancient. That rule of rules contains all previous mediations, all the guises of the law as hegemonic discourse. In archival fictions all the previous simulacra of the law parade as in a ghostly procession, like the dynasty of bodies that Philip II brings to El Escorial in Fuentes's *Terra Nostra.* Emptied of power, the phantoms of previous mediations appear as in a wake of fictions. Myths from various theogonies also are found in the archive. As we saw, *Cien años de soledad* reflects, alludes, or remembers myths from several traditions. The archive is a myth of myths.

How are archival fictions mythic, and how is the archive a modern myth? First, the former are mythic because they deal with the origin both in a thematic and in what could be called a semiotic way. By the origin I mean the beginning of history, or a commonly accepted source of culture. Figures endowed with founding significance, like Columbus and Philip II, appear frequently in archival fictions, as do regions endowed with an originary aura, like the jungle or the village; activities like the founding of cities, the building of monuments, the redaction of histories occupy characters in archival fictions. Latin American history, as in *Cien años de soledad,* appears as made up of a series of high points common to the whole continent and reducible to a single, shared story. These thematic origins are important in the mythic constitution of archival fictions, but more so are what I call semiotic ones. Here I refer to the functions of the archive troped in these novels, like the gaps in the manuscripts, the floating texts, the storehouse function, in hoarding and accumulating. This accumulation function is semiotic in that it sorts the vestiges of previous mediations and displays them. Archival fictions are also mythic because, ultimately, they invest the figure of the archive with an arcane power that is clearly originary and impossible to express, a secret that is lodged in the very expression of the archive, not separate from it and hence impossible to render wholly discursive. This is why archival fictions incorporate death as a trope for the limits, for with death a sacralized, nondiscursive language becomes prevalent. This sacralized language cannot be sustained, however, for there is no hegemonic discourse to back it up, no authority to give it the proper intonation, or against which to establish a counterpoint. Nostalgia for this sacred language is evident in political doctrines that rewrite the past as teleological, apocalyptic, and leading to a single history. Such allegories remain outside the archive. The archive as myth is modern because it is multifarious, relativistic, and even thematizes relativism and pluralism as inherent qualities of literature, the language into which it escapes. Mythification is a version of the master narrative of escape from the strictures of the dominant discourse through fusion with one of the main objects of that discourse: myth. Heterogeneity of cultures, languages, sources, and beginnings is at the core of the archive's founding negativity, a pluralism that is a subversion or sub-version of the master plot. The archive culls and loses; it cannot brand or determine. The archive cannot coalesce as a national or cultural myth, although its makeup still reveals a longing for the creation of such a grandiose politicocultural meta-story.

Telluric novels were sustained by a pragmatic belief in the efficacy of literature as a political tool. Novelists like Gallegos had faith that once literature could express the essence of Latin

American culture, a national or continental myth could lead to a kind of political anagnorisis, a blinding revelation that would in turn become the basis of a useful political program. The complicity of anthropology and Latin American states is a testament to this belief and evidence of the existence of a coalition of political, literary, and scientific discourses. The only pragmatic quality of archival fictions is to turn the gaze of a new, nonauthoritarian ethnology onto that coalition to display its inner workings, its ideological supports, as well as its constitutive idealizations. But in doing so archival fictions cannot escape their own mystifications, which, as we have seen, lead to their own mythification, one that renders them, no doubt, less efficacious as purveyors of political programs. In a way, this may be due to a loss of faith among writers about their anointment as political messiahs in their roles as writers, a fact which has not stopped them, of course, from playing political roles as authors (that is, as public figures with a prestige and charisma that have political worth).

Archival fictions, then, return to the law as origin in order to delve into the structure of mediation as the constitutive structure of Latin American narrative, or perhaps of the Latin American imagination. These novels reach back to the legal origins of the narrative to pry into the relationship between power and knowledge, or better yet, the empowerment of knowledge through language in the legalistic, hence ritualistic, act of writing. This probe brings forth the violent, arbitrary nature of the act of empowerment and its link to punishment and incarceration. Narrative, be it novelistic or historical, often neutralizes this violence by thematizing the first escape from the strictures of hegemonic discourse, by fleeing the law, as in *Biografía de un cimarrón*. Archival fictions also deal with the accumulation of knowledge and the way in which knowledge is organized as culture. As storehouses of knowledge archival fictions are atavistic accumulations of the given. This is why archival fictions often are historical and consist of a complex intertextual web that incorporates the chronicles of the discovery and Conquest of America, other fictions, historical documents and characters, songs, poetry, scientific reports, literary figures, and myths—in short, a grab-bag of texts that have cultural significance. The organization of the archive defies conventional classification because classification is at issue, but it does not abandon this basic function of the archive to generate an inchoate, heteroglossic mass—a mass of documents and other texts that have not been totally (and sometimes not even partially) absorbed, that retain their raw, undisturbed original existence as evidence of the non-assimilation of the Other. The archive, as is evident in Carpentier's *El arpa y la sombra*, also stands for loss and for emptiness, frequently hypostatized as old age and death. In *El arpa y la sombra*, Columbus's bones, like the documents in the archive, are dispersed, linked by gaps. Archival fictions are also crypts, like the Escorial itself, a figure of the very book we read, monumental repositories of death's debris and documents lacking currency. If the archive's secret is that it has no secret other than this dialectic of gain and loss, this secret of secrets is uncovered through a set of figures and stories that characterize it like a subconscious of Latin American fiction.

Archival fictions are again concerned with the law because of their interest in the origins of the mediation process and the constitution of the narrative. The fact that the narrator-protagonist of *Los pasos perdidos*, the original archival fiction, writes his composition in notebooks destined to contain the first laws of Santa Mónica de los Venados suggests such a connection. So does the fact that the "case" on which *Crónica de una muerte anunciada* [1981; Chronicle of a Death Foretold] is based is culled from the brief drawn up many years before for the murder trial and gathered by the narrator from the flooded Palace of Justice of Riohacha. This remarkable passage in García Márquez's novella is the most meaningful expression of the archive in recent fiction. The passage recounts the narrator's search for the brief:

> Todo lo que sabemos de su carácter [the lawyer's] es aprendido en el sumario, que numerosas personas me ayudaron a buscar veinte años después del crimen en el Palacio de Justicia de Riohacha. No existía clasificación alguna en los archivos, y más de un siglo de expedientes estaban amontonados en el suelo del decrépito edificio colonial que fuera por dos días el cuartel general de Francis Drake. La planta baja se inundaba con el mar de leva, y los volúmenes descosidos flotaban en las oficinas desiertas. Yo mismo exploré muchas veces con las aguas hasta los tobillos aquel estanque de causas perdidas, y sólo una casualidad me permitió rescatar al cabo de cinco años de búsqueda unos 322 pliegos salteados de los más de 500 que debió tener el sumario. (1981, 129)

> Everything that we know about his character has been learned from the brief, which several people helped me look for twenty years later in the Palace of Justice in Riohacha. There was no classification of files whatever, and more than a century of cases was piled up on the floor of the decrepit colonial building that had been Sir Francis Drake's headquarters for two days. The ground floor would be flooded by high tides, and the unbound volumes floated about the deserted offices. I searched many times with water up to my ankles in that lagoon of lost causes, and after five years of rummaging around only chance let me rescue some 322 pages filched from the more than 500 that the brief must have contained. (1983, 98–99)

The dilapidated Palace of Justice, dating from colonial times, obviously alludes to the constitutive presence of the law in that founding period. Its decay recalls the time of the Naturalists—even the shaped stones that house the law will atrophy and become somewhat monstrous, as we shall see. The ruined palace stands, then, for the presence of the law as origin of the narrative, now hollowed out; it recalls the stage-set Palace of Justice in the first page of *Los pasos perdidos*, the Palacio de las Maravillas in *El arpa y la sombra*, and, of course, El Escorial in *Terra Nostra*. It even goes back to the ruined building cited by Cervantes in the last pages of the first part of *Don Quixote*, in which a manuscript containing the story of the mad hero is found. The construction of archives and the origins of the law are intricately connected, even etymologically. But here law as architecture, as arch-texture is a vestige. The fact that the Palace of Justice became the headquarters of a dashing and lawless Francis Drake suggests the reincarnation of the law as narrative. But there is more.

The volumes are unbound, unclassified and float through deserted offices because the power of the original archive is suspended. A ruined palace of justice, the archive functions as a sign, an allegory of the origin. Only the shell of the allegory remains, an empty form from which other meanings emanate, meanings that are unique to this specimen, which through change has evaded the uniformity of the law. *Descosidos* does not really mean unbound, in the sense that the documents are yet to be bound. In fact, *descosidos* could very well mean that these documents were once bound and have now literally fallen apart, become unsewn. If, indeed, the archive is like Borges's study, it is like Borges's study after that master demolisher of fictions is through thrashing the books. They only become volumes again when they are rewritten as novels by Fuentes, Carpentier, García Márquez, and others, as simulacra of the original archive. The absence of classification points to the importance of the unusual spaces between the documents. Here those gaps are filled with water. The documents float as opposed to being grounded, to being connected solidly to matter–to the earth–a condition that would provide them with a stable set of symbolic meanings, such as the ones in the *novela de la tierra*. (Earth, *tierra*, is, of course, a metaphor for the congealed ideology informing the surface project of telluric fiction.) The fact that the offices are now deserted, that the *letrados* have disappeared, further serves to withdraw authority from these papers. The *letrados* have left, leaving scattered traces of their foundational presence, as well as of their exit. They are a conspicuous and significant absence, like the ruined state of the Palace of Justice. Water could very well be the figure of time here, particularly since it is a water that ebbs and flows according to the laws of nature, to the tides. This *mar de leva* is a vestige of the naturalists' time machinery; in *Cien años de soledad* the most powerful vestige of the naturalists' time is the wind that razes the town at the end of the novel. The Palace of Justice is very much like the trash bin of Bogotá's *audiencia* in Rodríguez Freyle's (1566–1642) *El Carnero* [1636; The Conquest of New Granada], but it is a trash bin with a clock inside.

One cannot fail to notice that it was chance that allowed the narrator–a figure of the author–to find the documents that he did recover. It is chance, we might recall, that rules the life of Facundo Quiroga. The author recovers scattered documents. Hence, the story based on them and its ensuing arrangement is due to chance, not to any given rule or law. But chance also could be a reflection of fortune, the force that naturally rules the tragedy recounted in *Crónica de una muerte anunciada*, the elusive law of destiny that in earlier stories shaped the lives of Facundo Quiroga and Antonio Conselheiro. The story and the text that contains it duplicate each other on the sheen of the water that floods the Palace of Justice, turning its floor into a mirror, a reversed and illusory dome–an inverted law overarching yet undermining the constitution of the text. It is the mirage of a roof that does not shelter, that only reflects, that does not house. The floor, the ground, on the other hand, is here a watery mirror that reflects but cannot support anything.

The manuscript the narrator seeks to assemble is a *sumario*, technically a summary, but in any case a kind of adding up or summing up, and merely 322 "*pliegos salteados*" (my emphasis; this important adjective was left out of the translation); that is to say, the pages were not consecutive, there were gaps between them. Actually, *sumario* conveys a sense of incompletion at the origin, since it is a gathering up of relevant documents leading up to an eventual summation–not yet accomplished. The pages were slapped together to form the story, but then the story contains those gaps, the "*saltos*" that make it a series of "*pliegos salteados*." Furthermore, the ideal number of pages, the round 500 that the brief is understood to have originally contained, is now replaced by the very incomplete 322. But incomplete does not mean insignificant: The number 322 is also one that appears to open an infinite repetition of 2s, the sign of the initial repetition, the one that denies the originary power to 1. And 3, the opening, is full of mythic and tragic resonances. Furthermore, 322 also suggests a winding down, a diminution–not 2 3, but 3 2. The archive in its modern version does not add up, literally and

figuratively; it is not a *suma*, but a *resta*, an intermittent series of subtractions. Archival fictions reveal the constitutive gaps that shine between the documents on the watery floor of the Palace of Justice. In them, the archive is something between a ruin and a relic.

From the crumbling Palace of Justice in Riohacha we can move to national and even imperial archives in Asunción and El Escorial. The documents that Patiño supervises in *Yo el Supremo* are contained in the Paraguayan Archives of State, while in *Terra Nostra* the Escorial houses Philip II's papers, books, and body–indeed, it is a genealogy of real corpses. As in *Crónica de una muerte anunciada*, these are literalizations of the figure of the archive. One need not expect the figure always to be so legible. The manuscript that Consuelo keeps in a trunk and Felipe Montero restores and rewrites in Fuentes's *Aura* (1962) is another manifestation of the archive (Felipe Montero's name is etymologically a pleonasm, for *monteros* are lovers of horses but may very well also be an allusion to the original archivist, Philip II.) If Montero is a figure of the author of modern Latin American fiction, which I believe he is, his task is to rewrite the papers of the archive, to write an archival fiction, which he does. To do it he must fill the gaps. This *arca* has not only a figural link to the archive, but an etymological one as well. Like its distant predecessor in *Lazarillo de Tormes* [1554; The Life of Lazarillo of Tormes], it appears to be threatened by rats; the *arca* could leak, could lose some of its documents. It is significant that Consuelo's deceased husband, the author of the manuscript, was an officer in the French army of occupation; hence, though not directly related to the state and the law, his manuscript has its fictive origin close to the source of political power. As we shall see, it is significant that he is dead. Like the *letrados*, who have abandoned the Palace of Justice, the author here is also gone; all we have is his incomplete legacy.

The archive is at once capacious and incomplete. Capaciousness, which is related to safe keeping and the atavistic enclosure function of the archive, is a reflection of the totalizing force of the law. The law of laws would contain all. Melquíades's manuscript supposedly encompasses the entire history of the Buendía family, that is, of Macondo and the novel's whole fictional world. García Márquez's project recalls that of the *cronista mayor* in the Colonial period, particularly Herrera y Tordesillas. The national archive in *Yo el Supremo* presumably safeguards all of the nation's documents: the record of each of the transactions that together make up the power of the state. The manuscript blown away by the hurricane in *Oppiano Licario* is a *summa*. The size and capacity of the Vatican archive in *El arpa y la sombra* need not be belabored. The archive's capacity, its totalization, is an emblem of its power. The archive contains all knowledge; it is, therefore, the repository of all power. The crypt-like quality of the archive and its association with death is partly derived from this sense of completion. But it is also a vestige of former mediations, that is to say, of law as legitimation, science as the expression of time, and anthropology as the metacode capable of containing all codes, or a synecdochical expression of all codes. The archive is an image of the end of time. In *El arpa y la sombra*, Carpentier places a figure of the archive in the afterlife, in a circle of Dante's *Inferno*. The archive is apocalyptic; it is like a time capsule launched into infinity, but without hope of reaching eternity.

Capaciousness is sometimes reflected in the size of archival fictions, as in the case of the monumental *Terra Nostra*, but size is not always the measure of totalization, as is evident in the Ur-archival fiction "Tlön, Uqbar, Orbis Tertius" or in the relatively brief *El arpa y la sombra*. In some cases, in fact, as in *Cien años de soledad*, capaciousness is achieved through the reduction of all of history to a myth-like story, or, by centering, as in *El arpa y la sombra*, on a mythic figure of origin, like Columbus, who would contain all *ab ovo*. This tendency in recent Latin American fiction has led some critics and novelists to speak of a "*novela total*." Vargas Llosa says the following about *Cien años de soledad* in his book on García Márquez: "Fictitious reality is everything. It contains its own origin, he who creates and what is being created, he who narrates and what is being narrated. Thus, since the narrator's life is all of life, his death means the extinction of *everything*. The novel commits the same murder of god that the novelist wishes to perpetrate by exercising his vocation as writer. One ambition reflects the other" (1971, 542). Vargas Llosa and other critics are right in noticing the totalizing tendency, but they attribute it to the novel of the boom, when it is present since *Los pasos perdidos*. They fall prey to the illusion of totality without noticing that so-called total novels underscore their own incompleteness through some of the devices already seen earlier. They also fail to notice that the totalizing reduction of history to the language of myth is itself the reflection of an ethnographic discourse that still remains outside the totality, making its composition possible.

The archive is incomplete, as evidenced by the many unfinished or mutilated documents that it contains. This incompleteness generates the hoarding, the cumulative thrust of archival fictions. There are holes in Melquíades's manuscript that are not accounted for in the "final" version that we read. The lawyer in *Crónica* only recovers parts of the manuscript. The narrator-protagonist of *Los pasos perdidos* leaves his threnody unfinished. Felipe Montero must fill the gaps in order to rewrite General Llorente's manuscript in *Aura*. Consuelo tells him: "Son sus memorias inconclusas. Deben ser completadas. Antes de que yo muera" (20) ("They're his unfinished memoirs. They have to be completed before I die" [21]). The general's manuscript is not unfinished but has holes burned in it, "el descuido de una ceniza de tabaco" and stains, "manchados por las moscas" (54) ("some of them with holes where a careless ash had fallen, others heavily fly-specked" [55]). Columbus's manuscripts, like his scattered skeleton, are incomplete and hence are rewritten in *El arpa y la sombra* (since they really were written by Bartolomé de las Casas). This incompleteness appears as a blank, either at the end or elsewhere in the manuscript, and not only signals a lack of closure that works against the archive's capaciousness and desire for totalization, but more importantly underscores the fact that gaps are constitutive of the archive as much as is volume.

In addition to the unfinished or mutilated manuscripts, this fundamental discontinuity appears in other guises. The very notion of archive is based more on contiguity than continuity, separation and difference as much as culling and adding up, safekeeping, and bringing together. As with the encyclopedia, the principle of organization is not necessarily related to any intrinsic quality of the material in the archive. An exogenous agent sifts, ranks, and separates. The source of that agent's power is a secret the archive does not comprise, yet it is the most important. Hence there is a radical and foundational fault in the archive. That arbitrariness and incommensurateness often are represented in archival fictions by old age and death, as anticipated in the discussion of Borges and Barnet, that is, of Herbert Ashe and Manuel Montejo.

The presence of old, dying, or dead characters in current Latin American fiction is remarkable and significant. We have already seen several: Melquíades, Columbus, Montejo, and Consuelo. But there are many others, like Anselmo in *La casa verde* [1966; *The Green House*], the aging dictator in *El otoño del patriarca* [1975; *The Autumn of the Patriach*], Dr. Francia in *Yo el Supremo*, Florentino Daza in *El amor en los tiempos del cólera* [1985; *Love in the Time of Cholera*], the Señora in *Colibrí*, Cobra in the novel of that name, and Empress Carlota in Fernando del Paso's (b. 1935) *Noticias del Imperio* [1987; News from the Empire]. These oracular figures are links with the past and repositories of knowledge, like living archives. But their memories are faulty and selective. Senility is a figure for the gaps in these archival characters. Senility, curiously, here becomes a force for exuberant creativity, for originality. Senility is, in the context of this discussion, a metaphor for the incompleteness of the archive, but also for the force, the glue by which texts are bound together. There is a whimsical creativity in these characters' recollections that is parallel to how selection takes place in the archive in the creation of fiction and that is found in their lapses of memory. These often decrepit characters (dilapidated like the Palace of Justice) stand in opposition to the figure of the Romantic childlike poet, whose presumably fresh vision shapes much of modern literature, yet share with him a creative *élan* born not of remembrance as much as of forgetfulness. Their age also approximates death, one of the founding tropes of archival fictions. Death stands for the gap of gaps, the mastergap of the archive, both its opening and closing cipher. Consuelo's husband, author of the manuscript Felipe rewrites, is dead; so is Melquíades by the time his manuscript is read, and so are the narrators in *Pedro Páramo* (1955).

Sometimes, as in *El otoño del patriarca* or *Noticias del Imperio*, one of these terrible and capricious oldsters is the narrator, while in others, as in *Biografía de un cimarrón*, the old, oracular figure absorbs the author, who stands for method, for discipline, for institutional discourse. Felipe Montero also is absorbed by Consuelo and in fact becomes her dead husband-author of the manuscript, and in *Yo el Supremo*, old and cantankerous Dr. Francia and Patiño merge as the secretary ages and joins the ranks of dying yet living archives. Melquíades, always the paradigm, is old beyond age, and the narrator as well as his readers and rewriters have to struggle with his apocalyptic vision. Narrative self-reflexiveness is a figure of death. Self-historicizing brings forth the gap wherein these dead or dying figures spin their web of writing. So, like Ashe, that timid and funereal author, all of these internal historians are touched by death because they narrate the blank and the gaps; like their faulty memories they create from the discontinuities, from the breaks. Their narrative issues from the lapses. They are ruins at the origin, like the various crumbling buildings in Carpentier's fiction and the Palace of Justice in *Crónica de una muerte anunciada*. Creators of fictions, these figures wind up entombed in their own fictions, in their own archives; like Philip II in El Escorial they lead the parade of ghostly forms voided in the archive; they are the seat of theory. This theory unveils the workings of the mediation process whereby fiction has been engendered. They are the mediation.

Perhaps the most significant of these figures is not so much Melquíades as Bustrófedon, the character in Guillermo Cabrera Infante's (b. 1929) *Tres tristes tigres* [1967; *Three Trapped Tigers*]. Bustrófedon is dead when the novel begins, yet he is the source of the language games that the other characters play; he is not only an oracular source but the very source of language in the fiction. He inhabits the gap of gaps, having died of an aneurism of the brain, an interruption of his discursive powers that allowed him to break up language in his characteristic way. Bustrófedon's textual production is preserved in magnetic tapes, the sum total of which is the figure of the archive in this novel. Silvestre, Cué, and the others replay these tapes and repeat Bustrófedon in a manner similar to the process of translation and decoding of Melquíades's manuscript by the Buendías. The characters in Cabrera Infante's novel engage in an interpretation and commentary of Bustrófedon's textual legacy, mindful that it may contain a dark and important secret. That secret is the peculiar breakdown of language enacted by Bustrófedon. Death as gap is most evident in *Tres tristes tigres* because it is at the source; it is the voided presence of the production of language. The gaps we intuit in Melquíades's manuscripts are displayed as the foundation of the manuscript within *Tres tristes tigres*, a manuscript that here is figured as a voicescript. *Tres tristes tigres* is founded upon an archive of voices, much in the same way as is *Pedro Páramo*, another archival fiction. The same could be said of *Rayuela*, a novel that centers on the wake of Rocamadour, La Maga's child who brings together the figures of the Romantic child creator and the dead archival source in modern Latin American fiction. (In this novel, the figure of the archive is the shifting number of dispensable chapters, which contain the theory on which the novel is based.) Bustrófedon, Melquíades, Rocamadour, the dead narrators in *Pedro Páramo*, and Consuelo's dead husband install death as the violent origin of discontinuity, the discontinuity that makes up the archive.

These old, dying, or dead figures share with the ruined Palace of Justice at Riohacha the mark of time, of time as change, as mutation. In this they are also a vestige of the naturalist's mediation. These figures are often not only old or dead, but, like the manuscripts they sometimes hoard, they are mutilated, or monstrous in some other way. Time is written on their bodies as wrinkles, deformations, or disease. Much is made in *Terra Nostra* of Cervantes's mangled arm. In *Yo el Supremo* Patiño drags around his swollen foot; the patriarch in *El otoño del patriarca* must tow his enormous, herniated testicle; Consuelo, the very image of time, can transmute herself into a young Aura; Melquíades is a wizard. Bustrófedon, again, appears to be the most significant: His aneurism is literally an interruption of the natural flow of physical self, which is the source of the figurative deformations, the mutations of language in *Tres tristes tigres*. Through these physical ailments and deformations these characters reach back to Facundo Quiroga and Conselheiro, mutants of an earlier age who left an indelible imprint in archival fictions.

The lapse represented by death or by the faulty memory of old narrators does not signal an escape from the dominating discourse, but the opposite. The lapses and the lapse stand for the gaps and cuts, the proscription of language, the origin of the law. Death is a trope for interdiction and forgetfulness, for the creativity from within interdiction, which is the mark of the archive. This explains the seedlike function of Rocamadour and Bustrófedon, as well as of Dr. Francia, the dead narrators in *Pedro Páramo*, and the deathlike countenance of Ashe and his posthumous production of the book. The gap is the mediation, the founding hole, the limit of limits. Archival fictions return to the gap at the core of the archive because it is the very source

of fiction. This installment of death and old age as founding tropes to figure the Other, the power of hegemonic discourse, its originary and modeling force, is a mythification of the archive, the displacement of the language of method to the realm of myth and the sacred. Death tropes, mythifies the gap; its appearance in archival fictions is in no way a reveling in litteral death but a metaphor for the negativity of limit. Hence the archive is not a Bakhtinian carnival, but, if it is, it takes place within the confines of Foucault's prison.

Is there narrative beyond the archive? Do archival fictions give way to new kinds of narrative that announce a new master narrative? What would the new hegemonic discourse be? Can narrative ever really break the mimetic bond sealed by the law in the sixteenth century? Obviously, archival fictions continue to be produced in Latin America when one considers that *Noticias del Imperio*, which exhibits all of the major features outlined above, was published as recently as 1987. But there seems to exist a desire to break out of the archive, one that is no longer merely part of the economy of the archive itself. Is a move beyond the archive the end of narrative, or is it the beginning of another narrative? Could it be seen from within the Archive, or even from the subversions of the archive? Most probably not, but if one form of discourse appears to be acquiring hegemonic power, it is that of communication systems. Perhaps a new master plot will be determined by them, but it is difficult to tell with any degree of certainty from the archive.

Works Cited

Alonso, Carlos J. 1989. *The Spanish American Regional Novel: Modernity and Autochthony*. Cambridge: Cambridge University Press.

Andrade, Mario de. 1928. *Macunaima: O heroi sem nenhum caracter*. São Paulo: Oficinas gráficas de E. Cupolo.

Arguedas, José María. 1967. *Los ríos profundos*. Santiago de Chile: Editorial Universitaria.

Asad, Talal, ed. 1973. *Anthropology and the Colonial Encounter*. New York: Humanities Press.

Asturias, Miguel Ángel. 1949. *Hombres de maíz*. Buenos Aires: Editorial Losada.

Bakhtin, Mikhail M. 1981. *The Dialogic Imagination*. Trans. and ed. Michael Holquist. Austin: University of Texas Press.

——. 1984. *Rabelais and His World*. Trans. Hélène Iswolski. Bloomington: Indiana University Press.

Barnet, Miguel. 1966. *Biografía de un cimarrón*. Havana: Instituto de Etnología y Folklore.

Bernal, Ignacio. 1968. *The Mexican National Museum of Anthropology*. London: Thames and Hudson.

Borges, Jorge Luis. 1962. "The Garden of the Forking Paths." *Ficciones*. Ed. Anthony Kerrigan. Trans. Helen Temple and Ruthven Todd. New York: Grove Press. 89–101.

——. 1984. "Tlön, Uqbar, Orbis Tertius." *Ficciones*. Ed. Anthony Kerrigan. Trans. Alastair Raid. New York: Grove Press. 17–35.

——. 1996a. "El arte narrativo y la magia." *Obras completas*. Barcelona: Emecé. 1: 226–32.

——. 1996b. "El jardin de senderos que se bifurcan." *Obras completas*. Barcelona: Emecé. 1: 472–80.

——. 1996c. "Tlön, Uqbar, Orbis Tertius." *Obras completas*. Barcelona: Emecé. 1: 431–43.

Cabrera Infante, Guillermo. 1968. *Tres Tristes Tigres*. Barcelona: Seix Barral.

Carpentier, Alejo. 1933. *¡Eué-Yamba-O!* Madrid: Editorial España.

——. 1946. *La música en Cuba*. Mexico City: Fondo de Cultura Económica.

——. 1949. *El reino de este mundo*. Mexico City: Ibero Americana de Publicaciones.

——. 1979. *El arpa y la sombra*. Mexico City: Siglo XXI.

——. 1985. *Los pasos perdidos*. Ed. Roberto González Echevarría. Madrid: Cátedra.

Clifford, James. 1988. *The Predicament of Culture: Twentieth-Century Ethnography, Literature and Art*. Cambridge: Cambridge University Press.

Cortázar, Julio. 1966. *Rayuela*. Buenos Aires: Editorial Sudamericana.

Cunha, Euclides da. 1940. *Os Sertões (campanha de Canudos)*. Rio de Janeiro: Livraria Francisco Alves.

Dorward, Frances R. 1987. "The Evolution of Mexican *indigenista* Literature in the Twentieth Century." *Revista Interamericana de Bibliografía/Inter-American Review of Bibliography* 37.2: 145–59.

Echeverría, Esteban. 1986. "El matadero." *El cuento hispanoamericano. Antología crítico-histórica*. Ed. Seymour Menton. Mexico City: Fondo de Cultura Económica. 13–33.

Foucault, Michel. 1972. *The Archaeology of Knowledge and the Discourse on Language*. Trans. A. M. Sheridan Smith. New York: Pantheon Books.

Frazer, James G. 1981. *The Golden Bough: The Roots of Religion and Folklore*. New York: Avenal Books.

Fuentes, Carlos. 1975a. *Aura*. Bilingual ed. Trans. Lysander Kemp. New York: Farrar, Strauss and Giroux.

——. 1975b. *Terra Nostra*. Mexico City: Joaquín Mortiz.

Gallegos, Rómulo. 1933. *Doña Bárbara*. Barcelona: Araluce.

Garcilaso de la Vega, El Inca. 1966. *Royal Commentaries of the Incas and General History of Peru*. Trans. Harold V. Libermore. Austin: University of Texas Press.

García Márquez, Gabriel. 1970. *One Hundred Years of Solitude*. Trans. Gregory Rabassa. New York: Harper and Row.

——. 1975. *El otoño del patriarca*. Buenos Aires: Editorial Sudamericana.

——. 1981. *Crónica de una muerte anunciada*. Bogota: La oveja negra.

——. 1983. *Chronicle of a Death Foretold*. Trans. Gregory Rabassa. New York: Alfred A. Knopf.

——. 1984. *Cien años de soledad*. Ed. Jacques Joset. Madrid: Cátedra.

——. 1985. *El amor en los tiempos del cólera*. Barcelona: Bruguera.

——. 1988. *Love in the Time of Cholera*. Trans. Edith Grossman. New York: Alfred A. Knopf.

Geertz, Clifford. 1988. *Works and Lives: The Anthropologist as Author*. Stanford: Stanford University Press.

González Echevarría, Roberto. 1985. *The Voice of the Masters: Writing and Authority in Modern Latin American Literature*. Austin: University of Texas Press.

——. 1990. *Myth and Archive: A Theory of Latin American Narrative*. Cambridge: Cambridge University Press.

Hanke, Lewis. 1938. "The Requerimiento and its Interpreters." *Revista de Historia de América* 1: 25–34.

——. 1949. *The Spanish Struggle for Justice in the Conquest of America*. Philadelphia: University of Pennsylvania Press.

Head, Francis Bond. 1967. *Journeys Across the Pampas and Among the Andes*. Ed. C. Harvey Gardiner. Carbondale: Southern Illinois University Press.

Henríquez Ureña, Pedro. 1964. *Historia de la cultura en la América hispana*. Mexico City: Fondo de Cultura Económica.

Irvy, James E. 1971. "Borges and the Idea of Utopia." *Books Abroad* 45.3: 411–19.

Kristal, Efraín. 1987. *The Andes Viewed from the City: Literary and Political Discourse on the Indian in Peru 1848–1930*. New York: Peter Lang.

Lezama Lima, José. 1977. *Oppiano Licario*. Havana: Editorial Arte y Literatura.

Luis, William. 1990. *Literary Bondage: Slavery in Cuban Narrative*. Austin: University of Texas Press.

Mansilla, Lucio Vitorio. 1890. *Una escursión a los Indios Ranqueles*. Buenos Aires: Alsina.

México ilustrado por Europa del Renacimiento al Romanticismo. 1983. Catalogue of an exhibition presented at the Palacio de Iturbide. Mexico City (24 March–30 June).

Montaigne, Michel de. 1991. "On the Cannibals." *The Essays of Michel de Montaigne*. Ed. and trans. M. A. Screech. London: Allen Lane. 228–41.

Murra, John V. 1978. "Introduction." *Deep Rivers* by José María Arguedas. Trans. Frances Horning Barraclough. Austin: University of Texas Press. i–xv.

Museo Nacional de Antropología. 1986. *Guía oficial: Museo Nacional de Antropología*. Texts Carolina Baus de Czitrom, et al. Mexico City: Instituto Nacional de Antropología e Historia-Salvat.

Núñez Cabeza de Vaca, Alvar. 1990. *Naufragios*. Ed. Enrique Pupo-Walker. Madrid: Editorial Castalia.

Ortiz, Fernando. 1973. *Hampo afro-cubana. Los negros brujos. Apuntes para un estudio de etnología criminal*. Miami: Ediciones Universal.

Pané, Ramón. 1974 [1498]. *Relación acerca de las antigüedades de los indios: El primer tratado escrito en América*. Ed. José Juan Arrom. Mexico City: Siglo XXI.

Paso, Fernando del. 1987. *Noticias del Imperio*. Mexico City: Editorial Diana.

Price, Richard, ed. 1973. *Maroon Societies: Rebel Communities in the Americas*. New York: Anchor Books.

Prieto, René. 1988. "The New American Idiom of Miguel Angel Asturias." *Hispanic Review* 56: 191–208.

Rearick, Charles. 1985. *Pleasures of the Belle Epoque: Entertainment and Festivity in Turn-of-the-Century France*. New Haven: Yale University Press.

Ricard, Robert. 1966. *The Spiritual Conquest of Mexico: An Essay on the Apostolate and Evangelizing Methods of the Mendicant Orders in New Spain 1523–1572*. Trans. Lesley Byrd Simpson. Berkeley: University of California Press.

Roa Bastos, Augusto. 1974. *Yo, el Supremo*. Buenos Aires: Siglo XXI.

Rodríguez Freyle, Juan. 1973. *El carnero: Conquista y descubrimiento del Nuevo Reino de Granada, de las Indias Occidentales del Mar Océano*. Bogota: Bolsilibros Bodot.

Rosa, João Guimarães. 1956. *Grande sertão: Veredas*. Rio de Janeiro: J. Olympio.

Rulfo, Juan. 1955. *Pedro Páramo*. Mexico City: Fondo de Cultura Económica.

Sarduy, Severo. 1972. *Cobra*. Buenos Aires: Editorial Sudamericana.

——. 1984. *Colibrí*. Barcelona: Argos Vergara.

Sarmiento, Domingo Faustino. 1915. *Conflicto y armonías de las razas en América*. Buenos Aires: La cultura argentina.

——. 1955. *Facundo; o, Civilización y barbarie en las pampas argentinas*. Buenos Aires: Ediciones Peuser.

——. 1960. *Life in the Argentine Republic in the Days of the Tyrants; or, Civilization and Barbarism*. Trans. Mary Tyler Peabody Mann. New York: Hafner.

Simpson, Lesley Byrd. 1966. *The Encomienda in New Spain: The Beginnings of Spanish Mexico.* Berkeley: University of California Press.

Stabb, Martin S. 1967. "The Sick Continent and Its Diagnosticians." *Inquest of Identity: Patterns in the Spanish American Essay of Ideas, 1890–1960.* Chapel Hill: University of Carolina Press. 12–33.

Stephan, Nancy. 1982. *The Idea of Race in Science: Great Britain 1800–1960.* New Haven: Archon Books.

Stocking, George W., Jr. 1987. *Victorian Anthropology.* New York: The Free Press.

Vargas Llosa, Mario. 1966. *La casa verde.* Barcelona: Seix Barral.

——. 1971. *García Márquez: Historia de un deicidio.* Barcelona: Barral Editores.

——. 1987. *El hablador.* Barcelona: Seix Barral.

PART THREE

THE CULTURAL CENTERS OF LATIN AMERICA

INTRODUCTION

Eduardo F. Coutinho and Victoria Peralta

In the beginning of the first chapter of his book *La ciudad letrada* [1984; *The Lettered City*, 1996], Ángel Rama (1926–1983) makes an observation that seems crucial for the understanding of what will be here called *cultural centers* and of the role that these centers have played in the history of Latin American cultural formations. He says:

> Desde la remodelación de Tenochtitlán, luego de su destrucción por Hernán Cortés en 1521, hasta la inaguración en 1960 del más fabuloso sueño de urbe de que han sido capaces los americanos, la Brasilia de Lucio Costa y Oscar Niemeyer, la ciudad latinoamericana ha venido siendo básicamente un parto de la inteligencia, pues quedó inscripta en un ciclo de la cultura universal en que la ciudad pasó a ser el sueño de un orden y encontró en las tierras del Nuevo Continente, el único sitio propicio para encarnar. (1984, 1)

> From the remodeling of Tenochtitlán after its destruction by Hernán Cortés in 1521, to the 1960 inauguration of the most fabulous dream city of the Americas, Lúcio Costa's and Oscar Niemeyer's Brasília, Latin American cities have ever been creations of the human mind. The ideal of the city as the embodiment of social order corresponded to a moment in the development of Western civilization as a whole, but only the lands of the new continent afforded a propitious place for the dream of the "ordered city" to become a reality. (1996, 1)

If one conceives of Latin America as a great construction and of the cities therein created as multifaceted and polyphonic representations that have grown out of the colonialist enterprise into the complex and diversified formation of nations—always caught in a tension between the local and the universal—then it will be understood why this part, on the "Cultural Centers of Latin America," aims at examining the main centers where urban culture was produced, developed, and cultivated in this wide territory: It is in order to trace a kind of cultural mapping of the continent out of clearly delimited spatial and temporal selections. To achieve this, an attempt at a definition of what is here meant by *cultural center* must first be made, even if certainly in a problematic way.

Based on a colonizing process of more than three centuries and characterized in all its initial phase by the mere extraction of products (both agricultural and mineral), the Latin American economy has, throughout its history, been built around cycles of monoculture, which oscillate according to the interests of the international market. Since these cycles were created around specific, geographically located products, the organization of Latin American space was generally designed in accordance with these cycles, which gave rise to centers that formed and disseminated culture. Thus, near the

locales where a given mineral was found or where a certain agricultural product was cultivated, centers of control were founded; in most cases they developed until they acquired, centuries later, the shape of dynamic posts of cultural exchange. These were villages or small towns, inhabited by a number of literate men sent from the European capitals, which controlled the circulation of products and ensured the power of the Crown, constituting a kind of front line in the consolidation of the colonial process.

These villages or towns arose all over the continent, although in a very uneven fashion, and came to constitute the greatest urbanization enterprise in history; since the sixteenth century they made up the great foundations of the colonizing process, and, later in the nineteenth century, the sites where the formation of several Latin-American nations took place and their different constitutions were proclaimed, with many of them thus becoming the capitals of these nations. Built in general as the result of a political act–a decision of the Crown to control the resources originating in that locale–these towns were indispensable links between the centers of production and the distant metropolis, becoming from the beginning the locus *par excellence* of every type of contact and transaction between these two poles. Isolated, however, from each other, these villages did not come to develop networks of relations; rather, their mapping was constituted in the shape of islands or corridors, which extended from the axes of production to the European metropoles.

In this economic scheme (aimed always toward the outside), the ports or port cities played an important role from the beginning. They were the open door to the metropolis through which the products of the New World flowed, and at the same time the point of contact between these metropoles and the interior of the continent. Their importance was such that, in the cases in which the centers of production were far from the coast, a port in the nearest adequate place and a trail joining these two sites became necessary. This is what happened on a large scale along the Pacific coast, since the main mining centers were found in the mountain chain, and a basic corridor formed between the towns situated near the mining centers and the ports. While the majority of the main cities on the Atlantic coast were port cities, those on the Pacific were situated in the interior–near the main mining activity–a fact that demanded great vigilance on the part of the tax controllers and that created subsidiary port cities, often without any autonomous development. One needs only to remember cases like those of Santiago and Valparaíso in Chile or of Quito and Guayaquil in Ecuador, and Callao in Peru.

The economic system of exploitation was set up from the beginning of colonization and the model for the organization of space, based on the export of agricultural and mineral products–which formed an almost straight line from the interior to the coast (to the detriment of the development of a network of internal exchange of a continental scope)–conferred on Latin America the pulverized profile of an archipelago of local centers, disconnected from one another. The greatest expression of this atomization was, without doubt, the rise of a number of modern nations as economic and political units, each generally centered around a capital city that retained and controlled the mass of its economic and cultural production. Nevertheless, this atomization is not restricted to the international level. Nationally, one can observe, especially in the countries with the greatest territorial areas (Brazil, Colombia, or Argentina, for example), regional centers with economic and cultural features of their own that at times are even closer to foreign ones than to those of their own nation (although they remain politically linked to the capital city and subordinated to the centralized economy of the country).

In every case, however, what is found as a common denominator–at least in the Hispanic American world– from the beginning of colonization to our own days, is the presence of an urban center that functions as a hub that disseminates power. It was as such that the Spanish conceived the Colonial, Baroque city, with a definite design, constructed according to an ordering logic, which expressed a hierarchical social order. These cities were built on a geometric structure, based on the model that became known as that of the checkerboard, with the main plaza as the heart of the city–where the church or cathedral, the government palace, and the town hall were situated–followed by concentric blocks corresponding to neighborhoods, with perpendicular streets that extended to the outskirts and where the diverse levels of the population lived according to their socioeconomic status. Such cities were a kind of revival of the concept of the civilized Roman *polis*, which opposed itself to the barbarism of the nonurban. Besides being the points of concentration of the resources and wealth of the colonies, they were the sites where everything took place, from popular festivals–perhaps the most elaborate expressions of Baroque culture–to the great decisions of a political and administrative order. Also from the period of their first buildings, a constellation of lettered men (clergy, administrators, educators, professionals, writers, and various intellectuals) lived in them and enjoyed, according to Ángel Rama, an elevated status in society, which "obteniendo por lo tanto una parte nada despreciable de su abundante surplus económico" (1984, 24) ("naturally made them large consumers of the Colonies' economic surplus" 1996, 18). They carried out–with the advantages that the knowledge of letters gave them–the mission of *civilizing* their surroundings.

But if this was the dominant model in Hispanic America, in Brazil it began to be imposed only in the eighteenth century, when gold was extracted on a large scale in Minas Gerais, and this is no doubt one of the main differences between the processes of Spanish and Portuguese colonization. While the Spanish showed a clear intention of settling themselves on the new lands and wished to make the colony an organic extension of the metropolis, the Portuguese limited themselves in the first two centuries of colonization to the building of commercial enterprises, which had as a result a

predominance of rural over urban life and the rise of port cities, whose primary function was the defense of the territory and the outflow of its products. Thus, contrary to the geometrical rationale of Spanish American cities, the Brazilian cities developed spontaneously, according to the pace of daily circumstances and the immediacy of needs, without a plan defined or conceived *a priori*. They were what Sérgio Buarque de Hollanda (1902–1982) called, using with a beautiful image, in his famous *Raízes do Brasil* [1936; *Roots of Brazil*], "cities of sowers," in opposition to the "cities of bricklayers" of the Hispanic American context. Yet, if the mercantile, prudent, and realist profile of Portuguese colonization had as a corollary a type of "careless" city, "nenhum rigor, nenhum método, nenhuma previdência"(Hollanda 76) ("with no rigor, no method, no provision"), it also was inhabited by a significant caste of the lettered–at first representatives of the Portuguese Crown, and later the spokesmen of the local elites–who commanded the political and administrative scene.

The differences pointed out between the two types of cities are no doubt an important aspect in drawing a cultural map of the continent, but they evidently are not restricted to these particular ones. Another fundamental factor in the delineation of the profile of these urban centers is the heterogeneity of their population, resulting from the confluence of distinct ethnic groups–from the local inhabitants, with their highly differentiated cultures, to the colonizers, and even to the African slaves and the waves of more recent Asiatic and European immigrants, all with distinct origins and distinct ethnocultural formations. As these different population groups were distributed in an unequal manner through the various regions of the continent, the character of the cultural centers varied significantly according to the predominance of one or more of them and with the degree of miscegenation that took place in different regions. The anthropologist Darcy Ribeiro speaks, for example, of the coexistence of three large regions in Latin America: one consisting of the Andean countries, a large part of Central America, and Mexico, where a high indigenous population is noted; another consisting of the largest portion of Brazil, of the Antilles, and the Caribbean, where the African contingent is highly significant; and the third formed by Argentina, Uruguay, and the south of Brazil, where the European element predominates (100–14). In all these regions, a long and significant process of miscegenation has taken place, evidently in a varied manner and in different degrees–a fact that accentuates even more the heterogeneity and that leads to urban centers that are often quite distinct, even within a single region.

This ethnic and cultural diversity of Latin-American centers was even more accentuated throughout the history of the continent by a series of political measures of a homogenizing intent that were taken by the European metropoles, and the consequent reactions from the distinct segments of the population, developing (in some cases) strong resistance and generating interesting forms of syncretism. Among the most important of these measures were the policy for implanting European languages to the detriment of the indigenous tongues throughout all sectors of the "lettered city" and the hegemony of the Catholic religion, with the prohibition of any form of different religiosity or cultural practice related to it, such as music or dance. The politics of linguistic uniformity, already put into practice since the beginnings of colonization (according to the chronicles of the Conquest) by means of episodes like that of the letter of Cajamarca (Cornejo Polar

26–49), constituted in the nineteenth century one of the main tendencies in the construction of the Latin American nations; but it did not succeed, not even in its most radical moments, in stifling the languages spoken on the continent, not even those of the groups that arrived at a later period. The first languages continue to exist among an extremely numerous contingent of the Latin American population, as is the case of Nahuatl, Quechua, Aymara, and Guarani, the latter in fact raised to the status of official language alongside Spanish in Paraguay. And other tongues—in the cases in which they did not survive, like some African dialects that were introduced by the slaves—have left indelible marks on the official languages, as is proven today by research on the Spanish of certain regions of the Caribbean or of the Antilles and on the Portuguese of Brazil. One should mention as well—in the latter case and as a more recent phenomenon—the decisive influence of such languages as Italian on the Spanish of Buenos Aires or on the Portuguese of São Paulo.

Just as in the case of the policy of the homogenization of language, the implantation of the Catholic faith and the exclusion of every other type of religious practice generated varied reactions in Latin America, in the form of different types of syncretism. Witness the indigenous cults disguised as the Catholic religion in the countries with large indigenous populations, such as Mexico and Guatemala, especially the *santería* in Cuba and the Dominican Republic and *candomblé* in Brazil. The latter had a remarkable presence, mainly in cities like Salvador-Bahia and Rio de Janeiro, basic centers of colonial production, in which the African population played a significant role. Such prohibitions no doubt prevented—at least in places with greater control—the practice with autochthonous religious cults, but were not able to prevent instances of nominal adherence, which resulted in rich and varied syncretic manifestations and which were extended as well to other cultural sectors such as music and dance. One only needs to recall the popular music of various Latin American countries, with a strong indigenous influence, or Brazilian and Caribbean music, with its clearly African rhythm, as well as various types of dance—today so appreciated—which remained for a long time clandestine practices.

All these factors of various types caused the twentieth century to witness the survival not only of a great number of languages distinct from Spanish and Portuguese and of religions other than Catholicism, but also the most varied cultural manifestations of every type of activity such as music, dance, visual arts—including popular crafts, with their strong tradition—and literary production, from the lettered to oral expressions. These two latter manifestations offer, in fact, a wide and varied picture of the tensions that have dominated the continent, especially between a continuous hybridization, on the one hand, and the attempt to remain as untouched as possible, on the other. For example, there is a difference between forms of production that are clearly culturally mixed, like the Mexican mural paintings or the work of artists like Wifredo Lam (1902–1982) in Cuba or Emiliano Di Cavalcanti (1897–1976) in Brazil, and the production of indigenous groups such as the Quechua, Guarani, Aymara, or Nahua, with a minimum contact with other ethnic groups. And, in the case of literature, one may cite the opposition between the phenomenon of transculturation—so present in the twentieth century—with all its variations, and the production of indigenous groups such as those cited above or others, which is more and more coming to attention because of a revaluation of orality.

Another important factor, also crucial in the formation of Latin American cultural centers, was the mobility of its population, which always oscillated greatly—first as a result of economic cycles that ordered life in the colony and the very pioneering character of colonizers and adventurers (as in the case of the *bandeirantes*, in Brazil, responsible for the expansion of its territory to more than double its original size at the time of the Treaty of Tordesillas) and, more recently, owing to better living conditions in the regions with a more developed economy within the same nations or in neighboring countries. Yet, of all of these migratory waves that have occurred since Colonial times, the most significant has been the exodus to the cities, which took place throughout the twentieth century, mainly as a result of the process of industrialization. This phenomenon, verifiable in all Latin America and on a scale that often defies reason, has given rise to true megalopoles, today counted among the largest cities in the world, as is the case with Mexico City, São Paulo, Buenos Aires, and Rio de Janeiro. These megalopoles are characterized by contrasts of the most violent types—such as the coexistence of highly sophisticated residential neighborhoods and pockets of true misery or of high technology and the lack of a basic infrastructure; here, the most varied forms of culture and ideology live together in an unequal way, perhaps constituting today—by their unity within diversity—the most faithful portrait of Latin America.

In this scenario of disordered migrations, developed mainly during the twentieth century, the centralizing tradition of the colony has once more played an important role, since it privileged the capital city, creating a large gap between this and the other metropoles of the country. With rare exceptions, such as in the case of Brazil and Ecuador, in which the capitals are not the largest cities, the disparity of population density between the first and second city of the country is rather great. This situation has been changing a little in recent decades thanks to the exploitation of important natural resources in other areas outside the central metropolitan axis of each nation and due to the industrial diversification that has been taking place in several parts of the continent, not to speak of the cases in which the state itself has been trying to bring about a politics of decentralization; but it is still too early to evaluate to what extent these changes have already affected the hierarchy of Latin American urban centers, one of the deepest rooted structures of the continent. In any case, what cannot be ignored at present is the importance of secondary centers, which have been forming a true network in the context of each country, and of the recent attempts at regional integration among different nations, such as Mercosur and Alena, which have constantly called attention to regional specificities and raised alternative possibilities for studies that may take as their basis the cultural region instead of the old concept of *nation*, so arbitrarily materialized in the Latin American space.

These urban centers, both Hispanic American and Brazilian, which—in the Colonial period—constituted true arsenals of control of the colonizing process, did not lose, however, in either the era of nation building on the continent or their most recent phase of modernization throughout the twentieth century, the privileged position they had been granted in other times. It is true that some of them have gone into frank decline, caused by the devaluation or depletion of the product or products that had launched their development, and a few remain today only as historical sites for tourism. But in most cases these urban centers were converted into the seats of decision-making and the centers from which most spheres of human activity in Latin America have sprung; they thus constitute a kind of crossroads or point of convergence for ideas, images, and concepts. Furthermore, with the rural exodus that has occurred with industrialization and with the absorption of large groups of immigrants from other countries, especially Europe, these centers have grown in such a way that many of them have become megalopoles, characterized by a significant dialectic between the local and the universal–to use an expression of Antonio Candido (see 131–65)–and constituting a sort of potpourri of every type of tendency and ideology. Today, they are at once markets, centers of industry, economic power, and political decisions, hotbeds of scientific and philosophical ideas, and laboratories of artistic experiments, where all tensions generated by cultural and ideological differences can be seen in action.

As a result of the confluence of various aspects–historical, geographical, political, economic, social, ethnic, linguistic, demographic, and cultural–these urban centers of Latin America today have, according to Carpentier, in his *Literatura y conciencia política en América Latina* [1969; Literature and Political Conscience in Latin America], "el estilo de las cosas que no tienen estilo" (20) ("the style of things that have no style"), that is, of things that do not correspond to a homogeneous perspective with specific, sharply delineated features but are rather characterized precisely by a mixture, by the confluence of identities in constant conflict. It is this mixture of different elements–evidenced by the architecture–that perhaps constitutes the most significant feature of these centers, perhaps their greatest and unique common denominator. But if–in this context without a defined outline–a constant element can be located, it is also necessary to point out the differences that distinguish one from the other, for these are also the results of the same elements that gave them their identity. The aspects indicated above have not occurred in a similar manner in every part of the continent and, even less, in the same proportion; the consequence of this has been a plurality of distinct centers, each one with features of its own and at the same time some common to others. It is through this multiple perspective, as a kind of "diverse unity," that they will be approached in what follows, taking as a reference point, above all, the paradigmatic point of articulation between their geography and their history.

Cultural centers are magnetic poles of attraction of a symbolic-cultural order, exercised by a two-way movement–centrifugal and centripetal–in the interior region of a given country's region, but centered around an axis-city; therefore, they will be approached here mainly through two coordinates, spatial and temporal. From the spatial point of view, certain sites that occupy a position of importance–whether at a given moment in Latin American history or during its unfolding–will be taken as point of reference, and the cultural production and the role played by these locales in the panorama of the nation or the continent as a whole will be the focus. In this case we will see a greater recurrence of centers constituted around capital cities of present-day countries, given the importance these had in the centralized system that prevailed on the continent; but this does not at all make up a general rule, since there are even cases in which regional criteria will be privileged to the detriment of the division according to nations. This is what occurs, for example, in the case of the Amazon region, which encompasses several countries and is given a separate section here, or of other border regions, like that of the Plate or of the north of Mexico, which are also separate objects of study. The traditional geographical borders are taken into account here, but they are subordinated to matters of a cultural order. It is because of this that two essays referring to centers not located in Latin America will be included in the last section, for they are centers that had a predominant role not only in the formation of generations of Latin American intellectuals but also in the constitution of a Latin American diaspora: Paris and New York.

From the temporal point of view, a given moment in the development of the selected centers will be taken as a basis–their moment of greatest intellectual power and effervescence, marked by an expressive accumulation of quality production–which will function as a paradigmatic historical moment, and other periods will be discussed with respect to this one. In the approach to this moment, in which the place in question has effectively had the function of a magnetic pole characterized by the convergence of factors that allowed a dynamic of true exchange, other significant periods will be taken up and will emerge in simultaneous and no longer single lines. As the paradigmatic moment of each one of these centers will evidently vary according to the historical differences that formed them, what will result once again from the whole of this comparative history is a mobile and flexible design that ratifies the cultural diversity of the continent. To all this is also added a conscious commitment to the time of utterance, seeking to establish throughout the section what Fernand Braudel designated in his studies as a true dialectic between past and present (Braudel 25).

Just as the rigidity of geographical frontiers based on the concept of nation and the linear character of traditional historiography are here placed in check, so too the boundaries between academic fields do not count as fundamental reference points in the study of this constellation of cultural centers; a perspective that at the same time includes various areas of knowledge, such as sociology, anthropology, politics, and philosophy itself is adopted, in addition, of course, to that of literature and the arts, whose production constitutes the main element in the formation and characterization of the centers in question. In this sense we note that, when speaking of literature, that canonical product–traditionally covered by the concept of "literariness"–is not being exclusively denoted here. Instead, what is meant is a wider form of creative activity that includes the most varied verbal manifestations and that neutralizes dichotomies, such as popular versus erudite or written versus oral. In the same manner art is understood here as a form of cultural production that, far from being limited to the sphere of so-called *erudition*, takes in as well a vast gamut of expression, including popular crafts, music, and dance, as well as all of those forms of expression usually classified as folklore. By questioning the barriers erected by the official historiography of the continent, which was generally restricted only to the production of the elites descended from Spain and Portugal, this comparative study of Latin American cultural centers sets aside any monolithic vision of the continent in order to attempt to see it in its cultural heterogeneity, considering all the communities that inhabit it.

Taking into account all of these issues, and in tune with the spirit that informs this work as a whole, the section that follows is a comparative history of the literary culture produced in urban centers of Latin America–here seen in their similarities and especially their differences as a kind of microcosm of the continent. Seen as a whole, these centers offer us a panorama of the processes of development of the multiple, varied aspects of Latin American literary culture, from the place of the institutions that disseminate culture to the groups that constantly direct and reshape the picture of cultural manifestations in a dynamic context of transmission and reception. Nevertheless, given the differences in the constitution of these centers as a consequence of a set of distinct factors, the space/time relation mentioned above will be unique for each one of them, as well the perspective to be adopted. In this last case, a subdividing of the section was done on the basis of a broad definition of cultural regions, and among these a given number of centers was chosen to be dealt with separately, due to their relevant role in one or more periods of the history of the continent.

**Translation by Thomas LaBorie Burns
and Gláucia Gonçalves**

Works Cited

Braudel, Fernand. 1981. *Civilization and Capitalism 15th–18th Century.* Vol. 1: *The Structures of Everyday Life: The Limits of the Possible.* Trans. Sian Reynolds. London: Collins.

Buarque de Hollanda, Sérgio. 1971 [1936]. *Raízes do Brasil.* 6th ed. Rio de Janeiro: José Olympio.

Candido, Antonio. 1965. "Literatura e cultura de 1900 a 1945." *Literatura e sociedade.* São Paulo: Companhia Editora Nacional. 131–65.

Carpentier, Alejo. 1969. *Literatura y conciencia política en América Latina.* Madrid: Corazón.

Cornejo Polar, Antonio. 1994. *Escribir en el aire: ensayo sobre la heterogeneidad cultural de las literaturas andinas.* Lima: Horizonte.

Rama, Ángel. 1984. *La ciudad letrada.* Hanover, NH: Ediciones del Norte.

——. 1996. *The Lettered City.* Trans. John Charles Chasteen. Durham: Duke University Press.

Ribeiro, Darcy. 1970. *As Américas e a civilização. Processo de formação e causas do desenvolvimento desigual dos povos americanos.* Rio de Janeiro: Civilização Brasileira.

CHAPTER 32

THRESHOLD WITHOUT FRONTIER
CULTURAL LIMITS AND CULTURAL INTERVALS ON THE MEXICO-U.S. BORDER

José Manuel Valenzuela Arce

"Amanece. Amanece con siluetas que yo miro desde mi silla. Postes y cables. Alambradas. Pavimentos. Muladares. Techos de lámina. Casas de cartón prendidas en los cerros. Antenas de televisión arañando las barrancas. Basureros. Infinitos basureros. Latifundios de la basura. Perros. Que no se me acerquen. Y rumor de pies. Veloces. Cruzando la frontera. Abandonando la tierra. Buscando el mundo. Tierra y mundo, siempre. No tenemos otro hogar. Y yo sentado inmóvil, abandonado en la raya del olvido. ¿A qué país pertenezco? ¿A qué memoria? ¿A qué sangre? Oigo los pasos que me rodean. Me imagino al cabo que ellos me miran y al mirarme me inventan."

—Emiliano Barroso in "La raya del olvido" (Fuentes 1995, 123)

Sunrise. The sun rises with silhouettes I watch from my chair. Posts and cables. Barbed-wire fences. Pavements. Dung heaps. Tin roofs. Cardboard houses perched on the hillsides. Television antennas scratching the ravines. Garbagemen. Infinite numbers of garbagemen. Plantations of garbage. Dogs. Don't let them come near me. And the sound of feet. Swift. Crossing the border. Abandoning the earth. Seeking the world. Earth and world, always. We have no other home. And I sit here immobile, abandoned at the line of oblivion. Which country do I belong to? Which memory? Which blood? I hear the footsteps around me. Finally I imagine everyone looking at me and, as they look, inventing me.

—Emiliano Barroso in "The Line of Oblivion" (Fuentes 1997, 109)

The Sacrificed Nation

Site of interchanges and contrasts, the Mexico-U.S. border has been a fertile breeding ground for the shaping of stereotypes. More described than defined, and more censured than analyzed, the border has been spotlit as the stage where denationalizing forces are rooted and played out. The border is a field of social relations subject to constant flux. To understand the cultural processes that shape it requires passing beyond the inadequacies of dichotomous constructions–embracing neither the emphatic dimensions of change, rupture, or disjunction, nor those of continuity and contiguity. What is required of us are new approaches: We must advance toward the complex recreation of the singular cultural processes at work in the life and the sociocultural relations of the border, its dilemmas and representations.

The forms of Mexican-U.S. border-region community and social intercourse have been subject to constant mutations of such consequence that have called the notion of national boundaries into question. In addition to the redefinition of a number of the normative elements pertaining in the relation between the state and those it defines as its citizens (constitutional amendments, for example, that have allowed those Mexicans who are also foreign nationals to retain Mexican citizenship), the semantic web of meanings assigned to the notion of the threshold between Mexico and what lies north of the border manifests a number of important transformations that have overtaken the hermeneutics by which the cultural phenomena of the borderlands have traditionally been understood. Trans-border sociocultural intercourse includes

the social and familial networks that have markedly altered cross-border interaction and have produced processes of transculturation, re-creation, and resistance.

Three thousand one hundred kilometers in length, the Mexican-U.S. border is a zone of intense interaction; in 1995 alone, 75,496,000 arrivals and 95,555,000 departures were registered. These figures refer not only to the crossings made by individuals but also to the processes of interaction inscribed both in the framework of unequal social relations and in the diverse cultural matrices that inform the dynamics of border culture (Bringas Rábago). The population of the Mexican border region has doubled in the last twenty-five years. The 2,352,691 inhabitants of 1970 rose to over 5 million by 1995 (INEGI), including two cities of over one million, Tijuana and Ciudad Juárez (1,035,415 and 1,010,533 inhabitants, respectively), Mexicali with 695,805, and eight cities with populations between 100,000 and 500,000: Ensenada, San Luis Río Colorado, Nogales, Piedras Negras, Nuevo Laredo, Río Bravo, Reynosa, and Matamoros. The service sector is by far the largest component of the Mexican economy (retail and service industries employ 53 percent of the population), and for a number of cities in the northern border region, the service economy has been, and continues to be, their *raison d' être*–with the provisioning of U.S. visitors being one of the principal economic activities. In this sense, the retail, hotel, and restaurant trades in the states of Baja California, Sonora, Chihuahua, and Tamaulipas are the most significant sectors of their economies, while in the states of Coahuila and Nuevo León the service sector is second in importance after manufacturing.

The Border: Mexico from Outside

In 1819, when the Mexican struggle for independence was entering its final throes, Spain granted a parcel of Texas to the European and U.S. colonizers led by Moses Austin. This was the beginning of one of the most painful episodes in Mexican national history that would culminate in the signing of the Treaty of Guadalupe Hidalgo. In 1846 the United States declared war on Mexico, demanding recognition of both the independence of Texas and the Rio Bravo as the new border between the two nations. With the rout of the Mexican forces under the command of Santa Anna, Mexico signed the Tratado de Paz, Amistad y Límites de Guadalupe Hidalgo (Guadalupe Hidalgo Treaty of Peace, Friendship, and Boundaries) on 2 February 1848, recognizing the independence of Texas and accepting the Rio Bravo as the border. In the process, Mexico relinquished its claims to more than one and a half million square kilometers of arable land, rich in oil, minerals, and pasture lands. The treaty put an end to the misery, plunder, and murder that for almost two years had stalked the nation in the footsteps of the U.S. armies (see Bustamante; Roa Bárcena; Alcaraz).

The conquering and enslaving expansionism of the United States brought to awareness a scene incisively described by Antonio Castro Leal. In his preface to Roa Bárcena's essential work, he attempts to detail the complex of elements that influenced the Mexican defeat and defined the sense of doom that shadowed its troops:

> la imprevisión y el hambre, la falta de unidad de mando, la mala organización, la poca preparación humana y técnica, los elementos materiales insuficientes e inadecuados, la incapacidad de un esfuerzo continuado, la idea falsa–por exagerada–de nuestras fuerzas y recursos, las diferencias y las rencillas personales que aparecían en el fragor mismo de la batalla, la ambición del poder que relegaba a segundo término la salvación de la patria y ponía así en peligro lo mismo que codiciaba. (Castro Leal x)
>
> (the lack of foresight and the hunger, the disunity of the leadership, the disorganization, the weak human and technical preparation, the scarcity and inadequacy of materials, the inability to mount a continuous offensive, the false–by exaggeration–picture of our forces and resources, the personal squabbles and bickerings that arose in the heat of battle, the self-serving ambitions that relegated to second consideration the salvation of the nation and placed, thus, in jeopardy the very thing that was coveted.)

The seeds of the invasion began to germinate when the Spanish authorities and the Mexican administration of General Victoria granted a parcel of land to a group of U.S. citizens in 1819, thus authorizing the colonization of Texas. Isolated from the rest of the Mexican population and enjoying important privileges in the free use of land, without, however, having the right to do business with the Spanish-speaking Mexicans, these colonists were much closer culturally and politically to the slave-holding Anglo-Saxon society of the southern United States and bided their time for a pretext upon which to base their claims for independence from Mexico. The Monroe Doctrine of 1823 and the self-glorifying language of Manifest Destiny inspired in the Americans ambitious dreams of conquest: the desire to extend their territory to the south, to expand into Central America, and to reach the Pacific by means of a strategy that would include purchase, diplomatic manipulation, the exploitation of ambiguities in the definition of territorial boundaries, and war. In this way the United States was able to appropriate Louisiana, Florida, Oregon, Texas, California, New Mexico, Arizona, Utah, Nevada, and part of Colorado.

The U.S. government encouraged the migration of U.S. citizens to Texas, and the initial 3,000 who accompanied Moses Austin rapidly increased to 20,000 by 1829. Under the leadership of Austin and his son Stephen, these colonists took full advantage of the Colonization Law promulgated by the Coahuila legislature (to which the territory of Texas belonged) authorizing free grants of land and exempting the colonists from state taxes for a period of ten years. Although the foreigners "[que] deseasen establecerse en terrenos del Estado de Coahuila y Texas, eran libres para hacerlo, y se les invitaba a verificarlo en virtud de la ley general de 18 de agosto de 1824" (Alcaraz et al. 53) ("who desired to settle themselves in the territories of Coahuila and Texas were free to do so, and were encouraged to establish themselves by the common law of the 18th of August, 1824"), the colonists maintained only weak political and social links to Mexico (whose laws they flouted) and were much more inclined to the maintenance of slavery; indeed, the Mexican state's abolition and prohibition of slavery encouraged them to seek independence.

The insurrection of the colonists, backed by the United States, erupted when Mexico replaced its federal system by a centralized one. Mexico's response to the Texas insurrection was the dispatch of an army under the command of General Santa Anna. Despite the initial victories of the Mexican army, tarnished by a number of excesses and atrocities, Santa Anna was defeated and taken prisoner on 21 April 1836 during the Battle of San Jacinto. This defeat finalized the loss of Texas and spurred the drive of U.S. expansionism toward Mexican territories. Relations deteriorated when Texas demanded excessive war reparations from Mexico, and when U.S. President John Tyler proclaimed the annexation of Texas to the federation in 1845, a rupture between Mexico and the United States was effected, followed by a U.S. invasion in 1846.

Following the Battle of San Jacinto, the Mexican army withdrew to Matamoros until 1847. The conflict with her northern neighbor took place in the context of a recently independent Mexico that, having failed institutionally to channel the new national realities, already found herself embroiled in serious instabilities, internal conflicts, constant insurrections, and other problems that were to influence her ideas about reclaiming Texas and checking U.S. expansionism. Anastacio Bustamante, Mexican President from 1837 to 1841, faced a number of pressing problems, including the federalist uprisings, the separation of the Yucatan (which attained autonomy in 1841), and French aggression. Despite the great fanfares accompanying the military expeditionary force that would march north to reclaim Texas, the Mexican administration was unable to mount a serious campaign, and the expedition came to nought. On the contrary, internal divisions grew steadily and attempts to secure European backing for Mexico against the United States failed. As a result of these developments, Mexico found herself in a position of diplomatic isolation, economic precariousness, social fragility, and military vulnerability, faced with a powerful neighbor whose overt belligerence was shrouded in the proclamations of the Monroe Doctrine and Manifest Destiny.

This was the scene when a U.S. army under the command of Zachary Taylor marched on Saltillo and engaged the most important Mexican defenses at La Angustura. Taylor's army was later joined by that of John Wool, who had captured Chihuahua; a third army under the command of Stephen

Kearny, who had conquered New Mexico and California; and in March 1847 a force led by Winfield Scott, who had disembarked at Veracruz and advanced on Mexico City—which was abandoned by Santa Anna and his army on September 14 and taken by the Americans a few days later. In the wake of the battle at La Angustura, a chain reaction of disasters was unleashed, and internal conflicts made the bitterness of the defeats much more difficult to stomach. With the northern frontier undefended, the insurrection of San Luis gave way to that of General Paredes (whose charge it was to back up the northern defenses) and a consequent withdrawal of troops. The defenseless population had to take desperate measures: at Fronton, the townspeople burned their own houses in order to deprive the invaders of resources and quarters.

Despite the wishes of the troops and popular collaboration in the attack against the dispersing U.S. army, the order was given to withdraw and Matamoros fell without a fight. With the public rivalries between the generals of the Mexican army (such as the animosity between Ampudia and Arista in the north), fighting morale sank to a new low, and the rumours of betrayal and treason surrounding the same generals engendered an atmosphere of despondency, distrust, and paralysis. To this common climate of gloom was added poor or nonexistent military strategy, the promised backing and the reinforcements that never came, the changes in leadership, the induction of soldiers into the army without training, the misery and exhaustion of the troops, and the misappropriation of resources destined for the front lines of external defense by the various parties. Thus, despite a number of important examples of heroism and selflessness that were seen in the battles of La Angustura, Palo Alto, and El Topo, important cities such as Matamoros and Monterrey were captured. The description advanced by the authors of the *Apuntes* is incisive: "Monterrey quedó convertida en un gran cementerio. Los cadáveres insepultos, los animales muertos y corrompidos, la soledad de las calles, todo daba un aspecto pavoroso a aquella ciudad" (Alcaraz et al. 117) ("Monterrey was transformed into a huge cemetery. The unburied bodies, the dead and rotting animals, the vacant streets, everything combined to paint a terrifying picture of that city").

The occupation of (Upper) California also gave rise to examples of bravery on the part of a population facing the invasion of Fremont, who would capture the counties of Northern California, Monterrey, and Sonora. Following the occupation of Los Angeles, San Diego, Santa Barbara, and San Francisco by Freemont in August 1848, Commodore Stockton assumed the position of governor of the territory. On 23 September 1846, the under-armed population rose up against the occupiers, and, under the leadership of Captain Cérvulo Varela and backed by Don José María Flores, they lay siege to the city of Los Angeles and inflicted a number of defeats on the U.S. army. The forces coming to the rescue of the besieged Los Angeles were routed at Chino, and on September 30 the city was obliged to surrender. Mexican troops retook San Luis Obispo, Santa Barbara, Los Angeles, and San Diego from the Americans, local authorities were restored, and the army of Freemont was defeated to the north of Monterrey. However, despite their valor and their conviction, the Californians lacked the arms, resources, preparation, and numbers to withstand the U.S. invasion and were ultimately defeated when Los Angeles succumbed to U.S. troops on 10 January 1847.

In the middle of the war, in August 1846, a confrontation arose between the *puro* (or extreme) and the moderate parties. While Salas and Santa Anna both overtly supported the moderates, Santa Anna played both sides of the conflict. With the triumph of the *puros* in the December elections, Santa Anna was appointed president with a mandate to organize the national defenses, and Valentín Gómez Farías, the vice president, seeking to boost resources, devoted himself to the interests of the clergy and the other estates. On the battlefront, the defeats kept coming; the army abandoned Tampico and, following the Battle of Angustura, retreated to San Luis, leaving the population defenseless and incensed at the betrayal. Payno described the procession of military withdrawals as an army of starving, emaciated cadavers, with the sick and wounded abandoned to the dogs and the coyotes.

Attempts on the part of the *puros* and the presidency to undermine the economic and social power of the clergy produced stiff resistance, and backed by the moderate party (Mariano Otero stands out here), the clergy took legal action to block the initiatives that sought to abolish clerical privileges and to appropriate the mortmain properties of the Church as state property. The Church excommunicated and pronounced anathema those behind these attempts at divestiture and sought the aid of society, exhorting its parishioners to repel the "heretics." It was in this context that the Polko uprising broke out, supported by the Hidalgo, Victoria, Independencia, and Bravos brigades of the Federal District National Guard. Fully supporting the clergy and the monarchists, the Polkos harnessed the sympathies of the society dandies and enjoyed a fleeting glory crowned by the flowers that the ladies of high society threw in their path. To quell this movement Santa Anna left San Luis for the capital. On April 2 he set out for Veracruz, leaving Pedro María Anaya as interim president, and upon arrival took charge of the port's defenses in order to repulse a marine invasion by the U.S. army under the leadership of Winfield Scott.

The gloomy army advanced, losing El Paso and abandoning to misery and uncertainty Chihuahua on 28 February 1847; Veracruz fell on the March 27. Following the defeat at Cerro Gordo, the U.S. army occupied Perote, la Olla, Puebla, and Amozoc. Apparently unstoppable, the U.S. army advanced on Mexico City and, with Santa Anna unable to provide back-up, defeated the forces of General Valencia at the Battle of Padierna. Despite the resistance of Mexican troops, the routs continued at Puente and Convento de Churubusco, where on August 20 they succumbed to the armies of Twiggs and Worth. When the capital was on the point of falling to the U.S. army, the population, without the backing of the army, mounted a courageous defense that ended in a bloodbath. After the battles of El Molino del Rey and the storming of the Castillo de Chapultepec, Santa Anna ordered the evacuation of the city, even while the poor continued their fight in the streets. On 16 September 1847, Santa Anna relinquished his post as supreme commander and passed the presidency to Manuel de la Peña y Peña. With the withdrawal of Santa Anna from the scene, the majority of the wealthy barricaded themselves in their houses, while the poor and the middle classes continued to fight bravely without resources, a one-sided battle that would cost many lives. The Congress and the governors of the states convened at Querétaro and, only too aware of the parlous condition of the country, assumed responsibility for containing the state of national fragmentation characterized by a decimated and demoralized army, large portions of the nation under foreign occupation, an increasing number of civilian assassinations, and a chronic level of internal dissent that would not abate despite the climate of misery and uncertainty.

The New Border

The history of the border between the United States and Mexico begins with the painful memories of the war, in which, in addition to facing a large loss of human lives, Mexico was stripped of the territories of Arizona, California, New Mexico, Nevada, Utah, and part of Colorado in addition to Texas. The new border placed tens of thousands of Mexicans outside the new boundaries of the Mexican state, and as a result many had to emigrate to cities south of Rio Bravo. The line of the frontier not only instituted a demarcation between Anglo-Saxons and Mexicans, Protestants and Catholics, the white-skinned and the brown-skinned, immigrants and those whose social ties were pre-Hispanic, but it also divided families, social networks, and personal relationships. In the north of Mexico the population remained peripheral to the national processes of change defined at the center, while on the other side of the border, in the south of the United States, Mexicans, suddenly aliens in their own communities, were subject to a process of colonialization in which they were disadvantaged, stripped of their lands, and inscribed in a sociopolitical order that stereotyped them and discriminated against them. While the African American population of the United States suffered under slavery until abolition in 1863, the second half of the nineteenth century was marked by a profound oppression of the U.S. Mexican population. The first movements of social resistance began to express themselves in this context with the publication of periodicals taking up the ethnic cause, *la causa de La Raza*. During this time there also arose a number of social bandits who embodied the U.S. Mexican population's aspirations for restitution and compensation: figures such as Juan Nepomuceno Cortina, Gregorio Cortez, Elfego Vaca, Joaquín Murrieta, Tiburcio Vázquez, and others, who, in addition to operating on the social frontier between the rich and the poor (the traditional territory of bandits), also worked the racial and cultural lines differentiating Anglo-Saxons and Mexicans.

The Mexican, or Chicano, population of the United States was clear to articulate a number of fundamental traits that distinguished them from the Anglo-Saxons, such as their racial characteristics (skin color), their culture (principally defined in terms of language and religion), and their social status (as laborers situated at the bottom of the social hierarchy). From the perspective of the dominant group, the condition of social disadvantage borne by Mexicans and African Americans devolved upon a set of biological reasons that justified their designation as lazy, dirty, cruel, and cowardly—pejorative terms that also were applied to Asian immigrants. With the military conflict and subsequent proof of U.S. military superiority over Mexico, the American stereotyping of Mexicans acquired a new patent.

By the end of the nineteenth century the United States had consolidated its place in the world economy as an agricultural, mineral, and industrial giant. This situation led to a considerable migration of European and Asian workers, as well as a greater migration of Mexicans who, at the dawn of the twentieth century, numbered around half a million in the United States, one-fifth of whom were immigrants. With the new century, Mexican emigration continued to grow, stimulated by these economic developments (especially in industry and agriculture). During the reign of Porfirio Díaz (1876–1911), the policy of dispossessing the peasantry and (amassing their lands in large, privately held estates) left many peasants without land or resource, many of them became part of the burgeoning number of northern migrants who found work in the fields and ranches in the southwestern United States. The numbers of emigrants grew in tandem with the worsening of internal social conflicts and swelled during the time of the Mexican Revolution (1911–1917). In addition, World War I led to an increased demand for laborers in the United States, and this too influenced the migration patterns of the period. Mexicans began arriving in regions far from the U.S. Mexican frontier, such as Illinois and Ohio. By 1930, the U.S. Mexican population numbered 1,729,000, of which 640,000 were immigrants.

The increasing U.S. demand for agricultural laborers, resulting from industrial expansion and the movement of U.S. workers out of agriculture and into manufacturing, caused the U.S. government to take the interests of the agri-businesses and their demand for more field workers into account. In 1942 Mexico and the United States signed the Farm Labour Agreement (*Programa Bracero*), an accord on temporary Mexican contract labor authorizing the migration of thousands of Mexican workers to U.S. fields, mines, and road construction crews. This legal ingress of workers did not change the U.S. xenophobic and racist animus toward the Mexicans, who, with the termination of the *Programa Bracero* in 1964, numbered four million, who lived in degrading circumstances and whose lives were defined by the prevalence of a division of social opportunities marked by racism. Ignominious signs—posted in restaurants, buses, swimming pools, public parks, and residential neighborhoods—informed them (and African Americans) that they were excluded.

In the years following World War II the number of immigrants with permanent or temporary visas continued to increase, raising alarm bells among the U.S. population. The federal government responded with a massive campaign of deportations carried out by the Immigration and Naturalization Service and known as Operation Wetback, in which hundreds of thousands of Mexican laborers were expelled. Since then and until today, there has been a continual and constant emigration of Mexicans to the United States, based upon U.S. demands for manpower and the network of social ties fashioned over the previous century and a half.

The irruption of the Chicano movement in the 1960s facilitated the production of scholarly and artistic works by people of Mexican origin, works preoccupied with the redefinition of social, political, and cultural conditions and representations of the Chicanos in the United States. Coinciding with the African American Civil Rights movement and also premised on the breakdown of univocal positions that had undergirded assimilationism or the melting-pot ideology, the Chicano movement formed part of a generation of important changes in inter-ethnic relations. This generation also witnessed the rise of the youth and feminist movements as two of the principal agents of cultural change in the second half of the twentieth century. Together with these sociocultural changes these years were marked by a number of salient tendencies in the demographic profile of the United States, most notably for our purposes a large increase in the population of Latin American origin. According to the census of 1990, the U.S. population grew approximately 10 percent in the 1980s, reaching 248,709,873. Of this total, whites numbered 199,686,070, or 80.3 percent, with an increase of 6 percent from the previous decade; African Americans numbered 29,986,060, or 12.1 percent, with an increase of 13.2 percent; and Hispanics numbered 22,354,059, or 9 percent, with an increase of 53 percent.

The U.S. population of Mexican origin is characterized by its concentration in a small number of states and by its average age being ten years younger than the U.S. average. California has seen the largest increase in the Chicano population (25.7 percent), now totaling almost 8 million people, who represent 25.8 percent of the state total. Texas is home to 4,339,905 Chicanos, representing 25.5 percent of the total; New York has 2,214,026, representing 12.3 percent of the total; and Florida has 1,574,143, representing 12.2 percent of the total. In 1989, nine out of every ten Hispanics lived in only nine states of the United States, and 65 percent lived in only three: California, Texas, and New York (U.S. Department of Commerce). From the point of view of comparative demographic growth among different ethnic groups, it has been estimated that by the year 2000 with present rates of growth, Hispanics will number 25 million (taking immigration into account, this number could rise to 30.3 million), making the "Hispanic" community by the year 2050 larger than the African American community (Hayes Bautista 24).

The U.S. social structure is founded upon important ethnic inequalities, such that, still in 1987, the average annual income for Hispanic families was 62.73 percent of that of Anglo-Saxon families, while the average for African American families only amounted to 57.14 percent (U.S. Department of Commerce). Furthermore, gender inequality bears heavily upon the poor; Mexican women have a lower average annual income than Mexican men or the women of any other ethnic group.

The Other Side of the Line

From the 1920s until the present, the cities of the Mexican border region began to grow precipitously as a result of an influx of both internal migrants and those either frustrated in (or abandoning) their attempts to cross into the United States. The service sector in these cities also grew in the same period, orienting itself toward the provisioning of U.S. visitors who became more and more visible in this period, especially the younger among them who formed the thriving clientele of the bars, restaurants, and brothels of these cities. Within the cultural contexts of the Mexican-U.S. border, we can see an intense process of transculturation, re-creation, and cultural resistance. Transculturation involves a number of "cultural borrowings" between the members of different groups. We refer not so much to the everyday aspect of these borrowings as to the change in semantic associations undergone by the incorporation of particular elements in a new cultural matrix. These are dynamic processes incorporated within fields of power relations, such that to speak of transculturation in a context of a power inequality like that of the Mexican-U.S. border region is to take stock of the heightened potential for cultural conflict. In addition, the processes of transculturation involve different levels of re-creation, by means of which the new particulars are inserted in preexisting cultural constructions where they acquire new meanings.

In the border region there are a large number of cultural particulars that flow from one side to the other side of the line. This can be illustrated by means of a number of linguistic variations, such as the incorporation of Anglicisms in border-region Spanish, the discoursive re-creation that takes place in Mexico and in the United States, and the shaping of trans-border cultural expressions. Among the cultural particulars with important trans-border connotations, the life of the Mexican and Chicano neighborhoods has given rise to a number of processes bearing on the cultural re-creation, resistance, and invention of defining cultural traits that stand out from the common profile of Mexican cultural life as a whole. First among these would be Northern music, *la música norteña*, which, for a number of decades, has expressed the experience and fundamental values that constitute the limits of the identity attributed to Northern Mexicans. This is not to say, however, that that experience and those values directly modify the determining particulars of the world views of either side of the border. We also find in the border region important processes of cultural resistance: collective constructions of meaning based upon a number of defining symbolic elements of group identity that function as emblems reinforcing the collective identity, which is to say that the processes of cultural resistance fortify the symbolic contours of relevance and belonging. I do not share the point of view of those who consider that, in the border region, cultural processes circulate in a univocal manner from north to south. Neither am I in accord with those who reduce the complex processes of cultural interaction, present on both sides of the border, to the mere presence of an alterity that subsumes the ensemble of happenings on the other side of the border. The border presents several fundamental regional variations, among which number the diverse instantiations stemming from the various attributions of class, ethnicity, gender, and/or generation, such that to judge the ensemble of sociocultural processes that the border region produces as owing solely to U.S. influence would be a serious oversimplification. These variations come to light when we look at the cultural variations that are manifest in different border-region cities. This variability also influences any analysis of ethnic, class, gender, and generational differences.

There are a great number of cultural inequalities stemming from class distinctions, highlighting the greater predilection for things made in the United States as one goes up the socioeconomic ladder. Similarly, on the other side of the border, we can see that the desire to assimilate into Anglo-Saxon culture is greatest among the middle and upper classes, while the poor families that inhabit the Chicano quarters of southwestern U.S. cities manifest high levels of cultural retention. A further element that is fundamental to the delimitation of cultural identities is the differentiation of options stemming from the categorization of gender. This is based on the underlying fact of a symbolic universe where the social division of gender plays a central role both in the constitution of cultural identity and in one's social opportunities. According to the census of 1990, women of every ethnic group in the United States occupy the lowest rungs of social well-being, while in Mexico gender inequality continues to be manifest in the most outstanding manner in opportunities for employment, income expectations, the possibilities of socioeconomic mobility, as well as in the greater processes of sociopolitical participation.

It must be stated that the category of ethnicity continues to play a highly important role in the shaping of cultural identities. In the United States a sociocultural division of opportunities persists in which one's ethnic status plays a fundamental role. Thus, we see that visible minority groups live in a condition of cultural subordination, and that racism continues to have an important institutionalized presence in U.S. life. On the other side of the border, in Mexico, the condition of indigenous communities also can be inscribed within the frame of social disadvantage, and racism against these groups continues to take on an ignominious expression. This is the basis upon which a number of social, political, and cultural resistance movements have been built, such as the Zapatista National Liberation Army in the Mexican southeast.

The cultural structuration of the Mexican border region involves a juxtaposition and interaction with the United States. Nevertheless, happenings north of the border cannot fully explain the ensemble of cultural expressions manifest in Mexico, just as the Anglo-Saxon culture of the north has not accomplished an assimilation or cultural erasure of the broad sectors of the U.S. population of Mexican origin. U.S. culture is reproduced and recodified in a number of ways in the lived daily space of the border, characterized by inequalities, contrasts, similarities, assimilationist longings, and social and cultural resistances. Despite, however, the manifest social and economic disparities between Mexico and the United States (entailing differences, resistances, and conflicts in border region interactions), it is the popular cultures of the region that manifest the greatest ability to preserve and re-create a sense of cultural cohesion.

The border region presents a marked cultural heterogeneity in which emergent identities coexist with groups whose identity tends to be inscribed within older indigenous cultures. Of these latter, 400,000 live in the frontier states of Northern Mexico: 34,081 in Baja California; 4513 in Coahuila; 109,943 in Chihuahua; 5783 in Nuevo León; 233,078 in Sonora; and 10,489 in Tamaulipas. Native groups form a broad and diverse presence in this region and include the Pai Pai, the K'miai, the Kiliwas, the Cochimies, the Cucapás, the Yaquis, the Mayos, the Seris, the Pápagos, the Kikapús, and the Rarámuris. Some of these groups–the Yaquis and the Pápagos of Sonora and Arizona, the Kikapús of Coahuila and Oklahoma, and the Mascogos of Coahuila, who have some African roots–maintain a trans-border way of life. There is also an important immigration of Mixtecs, Zapotecs, and Mijes in the Northwest border region (Sonora and Baja California in Mexico; California in the United States), as well as of the Mazahuas in the state of Chihuahua. These trans-border movements highlight the importance of these peoples to a study of the border region and the necessity for a better comprehension of the specificity of the cultural processes in which they are involved.

The border region is also the site of a rich array of popular cultural expressions involving the youth cultural lifestyles of the *pachucos*, the *Cholos*, and the lowriders, as well as the punks and the rockers, all of whom have defined in an important way the urban scene of the border in the last few decades. Youth culture is one of the richest components of cultural re-creation and innovation, and the symbolic expressions of the youth of the working class neigborhoods stand out on these accounts.

In the history of the U.S. population with Mexican roots, of whom the Chicanos form a subset, there is marked overlapping of ethnic affiliation and social class. Traditionally, Mexican Americans have formed part of the working-class poor, and many Mexican American intellectuals have strong ties to and experience in agricultural labor, highway construction, and service or industrial jobs. These experiences run

deep and have had a profound impact on a number of Mexican American artistic expressions. It is for this reason that Chicano art is so closely tied to popular expressions founded on Mexican cultural capital that it renews through interface with the migratory experience and trans-border interactions; indeed all of these factors have been an important part of Chicano social, political, and cultural expression. In sum, the defining symbols of cultural identities cross the border and strike conspicuous roots in the barrios; in music (ballads [*corridos*], country and western [*canciones rancheras*], and *cumbias*) and dances; in theatrical or graphic expressions like murals and graffiti; in traditional medicine; in fiestas; in tales and oral traditions; in myths, legends, and games; and in New Age religions (*mística popular*), where figures like El Niño Fidencio, Pedrito Jaramillo, Juan Soldado, or Jesús Malverde enjoy a trans-border influence.

Early-nineteenth-century fascination in both the liberal and the conservative camps of Mexican political life with the social and economic development of the United States rapidly evaporated with the U.S. invasion in the middle of the century. Since then, the frequent threats of filibusters and freebooters have engendered apprehensions that have conferred a certain credibility to the popular refrain: "pobre México, tan lejos de Dios y tan cerca de Estados Unidos" ("Alas, Mexico: so far from God, so close to the United States"). The U.S. presence in Mexican life and thought has been a menacing and seducing specter; it is for this reason that it is thought to have contaminated those Mexican populations living in contiguity with the United States. This situation has been the subject of centralist caricatures disclaiming the possibility of cultural expressions in a North where, as the Eastern or Western Mexican tales would have it, culture ends and the barbecues (*el asado* [*o el cabrito*]) begin.

A number of the principal spokespersons who took part in shaping the vision of the border region in the twentieth century never completely eschewed the stereotypical and stereotyping currents that ran through the great debates of the era on the question of the national and the universal–nor did they lose the inferiority complex that labeled Mexicans as irremediable cultural juveniles. With the publication of Samuel Ramos's (1897–1959) *El perfil del hombre y la cultura en México* [1934; *Profile of Man and Culture in Mexico*, 1962], these currents became central to the discussion of what constituted the Mexican. At that time it was Europe and not the United States that constituted the Mexican alterity. For Ramos, Mexican nationalism was a manifestation of a rejection of the Europe that had formed Mexico and the Mexican character, since, he pointed out, the Mexican race was an offshoot of the European family tree; this nationalist rejection was a mask to conceal from ourselves a devaluation that tormented us, he wrote.

Agustín Yáñez (1904–1980), in his *Al filo de agua* [1947; *The Edge of the Storm*, 1963], re-created the caricaturizing perspective whereby the demonized features of the Northern Mexican became more accentuated when compared with those of Mexican from Central Mexico. From the perspective of those anchored in the Mexican tradition of convent, monastery, and cemetery, country towns peopled by women in mourning, and devout, plainspoken villagers, the Northerners were seen as profligate, uncouth, threatening figures. Even the young Jaliscan entrepreneurs without blemish, like Damián Limón, fall prey to the temptations and the dangers of the North, and no amount of blessings can save them from the black-widow women (*mujeres malasentrañas*) who entrap them, seduce them, and turn them into pitiable specimens of humanity (*malquerientes*). Even worse than the Northerners' "cock strutting ways" ("*parado de garza*"), by which they flaunt their lack of reserve and humility, the North is the accursed site from whence many do not return or, for those who do manage to do so, where the fundamental ties of the Mexican to his or her "Mexican-ness" are lost. The character Father Reyes underlines the belief that there are those who, because of their long trips north, succeed in corrupting themselves and losing the little religion that they had. Another character of the novel, Don Timoteo, makes the same point when he holds that Damian as a Northerner has no fear of God. If, as the popular refrain has it, the man who slips from righteousness falls all the way to the devil, then, from the perspective of Central Mexico, the North has been the repository of those who slip, of those who fall from the bosom of their families, their religion, their customs, and their values. In the section entitled "Los norteños" ["The Northerners"], Yáñez harshly describes this condition:

> Vientos que traen cizaña, cizaña ellos mismos, más perniciosa que la de los arrieros. (Ya no digamos la sangría en las familias, en los campos. No se sabe qué sea peor: la ausencia o el regreso.)
> "Peor es que vuelvan" dice la mayoría de las gentes.
> "Ni les luce lo que ganaron." "Y aunque les luzca, ya no se hallan a gusto en su tierra." "Muchos ya no quieren trabajar, todo se les va en presumir, en alegar, en criticar." "En dar mal ejemplo, burlándose de la religión, de la patria, de las costumbres."
> "En sembrar la duda, en hacer que se pierda el amor a la tierra, en alborotar a otros para que dejen 'la patria miserable y cochina.'"
> "Entonces son los que han traído las ideas de masonería, de socialismo, de espiritismo."
> "Y la falta de respeto a la mujer." (1955, 151)

Like plague-laden winds, themselves a plague, worse than the donkey-drivers. (It's hard to say which is worse, their absence or their return. . . . To say nothing of the families and fields deserted.)
> "It's worse when they come back," most people say.
> "And they gain nothing from their experience."
> "Even those who come back with money aren't satisfied here any longer."
> "Many of them don't want to work anymore; they just strut around, air their opinions, and criticize everything."
> "They're a bad example, making fun of religion, the country, the customs."
> "They sow doubt, undermine patriotism, and encourage others to leave this 'filthy, poverty-stricken country.'"
> "They're the ones who spread ideas of Masonry, Socialism, and Spiritism."
> "They've no respect for women." (1963, 135–36)

For the figures of Yáñez' fiction, Northerners undermine the Southerner's most dearly held values through their menacing presence, the social decomposition that they engender, and their shameful and disrespectful behavior toward everything that is sacred:

> "Son desobligados". "Viciosos". "Pendencieros". "Eso, eso principalmente, pendencieros". "Falsos de temor de Dios ¿para qué decir más?" "Y mientras más son, más se crecen, a nadie ya dejan vivir en paz: a los ricos por ricos, a los pobres por pobres; no quieren que nadie se les ponga por delante". "Pobre pueblo, pobre país". "Los más sabios son ellos, los más valientes, por unas palabras raras que revuelven con lengua de cristianos, aunque no sepan leer, como cuando se fueron". "Y porque traen dientes de oro, que andan pelando a toda hora". –"Porque vienen de zapatos

trompudos, con sombreros de fieltro, con pantalones de globito y camisas de puño, con mancuernillas relumbrantes". "Se hacen el pelo, como catrines, rasurados de atrás, melenudos". "Ni el bigote les gusta". "Son unos facetos". "Sí, facetos (con que al entenado de don Pedro Rubio, el pobre, se le había olvidado el nombre del atole!" "Pero no el meneadito". "¡Facetos!". "A mí lo que más me repatea es el modito con que se ríen y escupen por el colmillo". "¿Y dónde dejas el modo de hablar, que parece que se les olvidó el idioma que sus padres les enseñaron?". "Para que acabemos pronto, son unos traidores, que yo no sé si se adrede o por tarugos, el caso es que les sirven a los gringos como avanzadas para robarse lo que nos queda de tierra, lo que no se pudieron robar la otra vez". "Lo que no me explico es cómo las mujeres se vuelan con ellos." (1955, 151)

> "Nor sense of obligation at all."
> "They're vicious and quarrelsome, always ready to pick a fight."
> "They've lost the fear of God, that's the sum of it."
> "And there are more and more of them all the time. Nobody gets any peace. They meddle with everything–with the rich for being rich and with the poor for being poor. They have no respect for anyone."
> "Miserable people! Poor country!"
> "They think because they can roll off a few strange words they know more than anybody else and are a cut above other people, but they can't read a bit better than when they went away."
> "Just because they have some gold teeth and are always ready for a fight."
> "Because they come back with round-toed shoes, felt hats, wide-legged trousers, and shirts with wristbands and shiny cuff-links."
> "With their hair bushy in front and shaved behind."
> "They don't even have a mustache."
> "They're ridiculous."
> "They certainly are. When poor old Don Pedro Rubio's son-in-law came back and saw them stirring *atole*, he said he couldn't remember the word for it."
> "But he remembered how to stir up trouble all right."
> "They're ridiculous."
> "What gets me most is the way they laugh and brag."
> "How can anybody forget the language he's been brought up with?"
> "They're traitors, that's all there is to it. Whether they know it or not, they're the advance scouts of the gringos, sent to take our land away from us."
> "How women put up with them is more than I can see."
> (1963, 136)

The Northerner is a fallen angel, a sinner, and a cocksure arrogant man who, because of the suspicion with which he is viewed, can no longer integrate himself in the intimate web of sociality. Although born from the native soil, his fall has transformed him such that he can no longer be himself. He engenders suspicion; stories and rumors torment Bartolo, another of Yáñez's characters:

> ¿Quién pudo ser, sino un repatriado, el que mató de diecisiete puñaladas a la infeliz que hallaron hecha picadillo en el arroyo del Cahuixtre? Tenía metida en la boca una mascada de las que traen aquéllos y también la daga era gringa. ¿Y quiénes habían sido más que norteños los que habían robado muchachas a últimas fechas? (Bartolo temblaba con la ocurrencia de poder ser el primero a quien le quitaran la mujer.) (1955, 158)

> Who but one of the Northerners could have killed the poor woman found in the stream at Cahuixtle with seventeen dagger wounds? A scarf like those they bring from up there was stuffed into her mouth, and a gringo dagger had been used, too. Who but

the Northerners had been carrying off girls lately? (Bartolo trembled at the thought that he might be the first man whose wife was carried off.) (1963, 142)

Despite the misery and discouraging expectations of Northern Mexican life, the North is charged with a hope, a possibility, and a fate (*fatalidad*) that has not escaped the eye of Juan Rulfo (1918–1986) who in his "Paso del norte" ["Passage to the North"] (in *El llano en llamas* [The Burning Plain]) has presented the conflicted human condition that the decision to emigrate brings with it:

–Me voy, padre; por eso vengo a darle el aviso.

–¿Y pa onde te vas, si se puede saber?

–Me voy pal Norte.

–¿Y allá pos pa qué? ¿No tienes aquí tu negocio? ¿No estás metido en la merca de puercos?

–Estaba. Ora ya no. No deja. La semana pasada no conseguimos pa comer y en la antepasada comimos puros quelites. Hay hambre, padre, usté ni se las huele porque vive bien.

–¿Qué estás diciendo?

–Pos que hay hambre. Usté no lo siente. Usté vende sus cuetes y sus saltapericos y la pólvora y con eso la va pasando. Mientras haiga funciones, le lloverá el dinero; pero uno no, padre. Ya naide cría puercos en este tiempo. Y si los cría po se los come. Y si los vende, los vende caros. Y no hay dinero para mercarlos, demás de esto. Se acabó el negocio, padre.

–¿Qué diablos vas a hacer al Norte?

–Pos a ganar dinero. Ya ve usté, el Carmelo volvió rico, trajo hasta gramófono y cobra la música a cinco centavos. De a parejo, desde un danzón hasta la Anderson esa que canta canciones tristes; de a todo, por igual, y gana su buen dinerito y hasta hacen cola para oír. –Así que usté ve; no hay más que ir y volver. Por eso me voy.

–¿Y onde vas a guardar a tu mujer con los muchachos?

–Pos por eso vengo a darle el aviso, pa que usté se encargue de ellos. (1994, 131)

"I'm going a long way off, Father, that's why I've come to let you know."

"And where are you going, if one may ask?"

"I'm going up North."

"And why up there? Don't you have your business here? Aren't you still in the pig-buying business?"

"I was. But not any more. It doesn't bring in anything. Last week we didn't make enough to eat and the week before we ate pure weeds. We're hungry, Father; you can't even realize that because you have it so good."

"What are you saying?"

"That we're hungry. You don't feel it. You sell your skyrockets and firecrackers and gun powder and you make out all right with that. As long as there are fiestas, your money comes pouring in; but it's not the same for me, Father. Nobody's raising pigs now during this season. And if they do raise them, they eat them. And if they sell them, they sell them at a steep price. And there's no money to buy them with anyway. The business folded up, Father."

"And what the devil are you going to do up North?"

"Well, make money. You know Carmelo came back rich, even brought back a phonograph, and he charges five centavos to listen to the music. Five centavos for every number, from a Cuban dance to that Anderson woman who sings sad songs–the same for all of them–and he makes good money and they even line up to listen. So you see, you just have to go and come back. That's why I'm going."

"And where are you going to leave your wife and kids?"

"Well, that's why I've come to tell you, so you'll look after them." (1982, 147–48)

As in the work of Yáñez, for Rulfo ill fate and misfortune (*fatalidad*) is the traveling companion that pursues all those who take the road north, while return is marked by disillusion and tragedy:

–Padre, nos mataron.

–¿A quiénes?

–A nosotros. Al pasar el río. Nos zumbaron las balas hasta que nos mataron a todos.

–¿En dónde?

–Allá en el Paso del Norte, mientras nos encandilaban las liternas, cuando íbamos cruzando el río.

–¿Y por qué?

–Pos no lo supe, padre, ¿Se acuerda de Estanislado? Él fue el que me encampanó pa irnos pa allá. Me dijo cómo estaba el teje y maneje del asunto y nos fuimos primero a México y de allí al Paso. Y estábamos pasando el río cuando nos fusilaron con los máuseres. Me devolví porque él me dijo: "Sácame de aquí, paisano, no me dejes". Y entonces estaba ya panza arriba, con el cuerpo todo agujerado, sin músculos. Lo arrastré como pude, a tirones, haciéndomele a un lado a las linternas que nos alumbraban buscándonos. Le dije: "Estás vivo", y él me contestó: "Sácame de aquí, paisano". Y luego me dijo: "Me dieron". Yo tenía un brazo quebrado por un golpe de bala y el güeso se había ido de allí de donde se salta del codo. Por eso lo agarré con la mano buena y le dije: "Agárrate fuerte de aquí". Y se me murió en la orilla, frente a las luces de un lugar que le dicen la Ojinaga, ya de este lado, entre los tules que siguieron peinando el río como si nada hubiera pasado. (1994, 135–37)

"Father, they killed us."

"Who?"

"Us. When we crossed the river. They peppered us with bullets until they killed all of us."

"Where?"

"There, in El Paso del Norte, while they flashed the lights on us when we were crossing the river."

"Why?"

"Well, I don't know Father. You remember Estanislado? He's the one who got me to go up there. He told me how we could manage things and first we went to Mexico City and then from there to El Paso. And we were crossing the river when they shot at us with their rifles. I turned back because he said to me, 'Get me out of here, pal, don't leave me.' And then he was already on his back, his body full of holes, and gone slack. I dragged him the best I could, tugging him, trying to keep to one side of the lights they were flashing, looking for us. I said, 'Are you alive?' and he answered, 'Get me out of here, pal.' And then he said to me, 'They got me.' One of my arms was smashed by a bullet and the bone stuck out at my elbow. That's why I grabbed him with my good hand and said to him, 'Hold on tight here.' But he died on me by the shore, near the lights of a place they call Ojinaga, on this side, among the river reeds that continued combing the river as if nothing happened. (1982, 135–37)

The Solitude of the Labyrinth

The culture of the United States, as the alterity of the Mexican, has acquired a solidity, a power, and a major presence in Mexican national life that stems from the intensity of life in the border region, where adjacency determines the specific range of possible interactions. To this we can add the growth of Mexican–U.S. emigration associated with the revolutionary upheavals of 1910–1917 that resulted in a widespread displacement of the peasantry, the Farm Labor Agreement and the heightened demand for manual laborers produced by World War II, and the new forms of expression arising out of the youth culture of the Chicano and Mexican urban communities of the U.S. Southwest and the Mexican North. This new condition was recreated in a literary manner by Octavio Paz (1914–1998) in *El Laberinto de la Soledad* [1950; *The Labyrinth of Solitude*, 1961] , a book that has inspired and influenced countless works on the subject of Mexican culture.

Like Ramos, Paz believed that "el sentimiento de inferioridad influye en nuestra predilección por el análisis, y que la escasez de nuestras creaciones se explica no tanto por un crecimiento de las facultades críticas a expensas de las creadoras, como por una instintiva desconfianza acerca de nuestras capacidades" (1959, 10) ("an inferiority complex influenced our preference for analysis, and that the meagerness of our creative output was due not so much to the growth of our critical faculties at the expense of our creativity as it was to our instinctive doubts about our abilities" [1961, 10–11]). According to Paz the awareness of being Mexican is a diminished preserve, and the self-awareness of the Mexican is a minoritarian consciousness, the consciousness of those who know their numbers are limited. Inventing a literary manner of reading the Mexican, Paz constructed on the basis of Ramos's thesis a refined and sophisticated text whose analyses, despite their excellencies, were nevertheless cyclical in nature and removed from the cultural codes in which the practices and meanings of popular border life is shaped. Lacking a sense of these codes by which he might have drawn closer to these practices (clear in his analysis of the *pachucos* [Mexican masks]), Paz opts instead to invent from the point of view of the poetic.

For Paz, "Mexicanism" (*mexicanidad*) is a way of not being ourselves, "una reiterada manera de ser y vivir otra cosa en suma, a veces una máscara y otras una súbita determinación por buscarnos, un repetitivo abrirnos el pecho para encontrar nuestra voz más secreta" (1959, 151) ("a way of life that is not our own. Sometimes it is a mask; sometimes it is a sudden determination to find ourselves, to gash open our breasts in order to release our true and most secret voices" [1961, 169]). Mexicanism, according to Paz, is not in conformity with the symbolic thresholds of identity that delimit the different forms of belonging and participation in the national imagined community; rather, it is a mask that conceals. Underlying Paz's perspective we can see the old essentialist position that lurks behind the specific forms of the definition of identity. One of the principal problems with *El Laberinto de la Soledad*, beyond the problems of its cyclical and essentialist vision, is its lack of a relational perspective by which collective identities might be defined. This is manifest in a conspicuous manner in the chapter "El pachuco y otros extremos" ["The Pachuco and Other Extremes"], where Mexicanism is not framed in a sociocultural history marked by the condition of the subordination of the Mexican to the United States, where a sociocultural division of opportunities prevails.

When Paz claims that in Los Angeles, where "la mexicanidad 'flota en el aire' y digo que flota porque no se mezcla ni se funde con el otro mundo" (1959, 12) ("Mexicanism . . . floats in the air. I say 'floats' because it never mixes or unites with the other world" [1961, 13]), he forgets, in addition to the integration and cultural re-creation among different elements of the Anglo-Saxon and Mexican cultural matrices, the operative racism that has defined the kind of relations possible between the Mexican and Chicano communities in the United States with the Anglo-Saxon world. This condition includes social discrimination, spatial separation, and cultural contempt. Paz underestimates a long process of social and cultural resistance; many Chicanos, who are also U.S. citizens, desire to be treated as citizens. This does not imply that they seek to erase their cultural heritage; rather, it means that they wish that their cultural particularity not be the object of discrimination, and that they not be considered second-class citizens: "Algo semejante ocurre con los mexicanos que uno se encuentra en la calle. Aunque tengan muchos años de vivir allí, usen la misma ropa, hablen el mismo idioma y sientan vergüenza de su origen, nadie los confundiría con los norteamericanos auténticos" (1959, 12) ("Something of the same sort characterizes the Mexicans you see in the streets. They have lived in the city for many years, wearing the same clothes and speaking the same language as the other inhabitants, and they feel ashamed of their origin; yet no one would mistake them for authentic North Americans" [1961, 13]). Here things become complicated, and Paz is overtaken by his exclusivist logic, in which the authentic Americans (since it is not a question of the U.S. native population) are the Anglo-Saxons, a position that has been challenged in present-day debates on the question of U.S. cultural plurality and the arguments of postcolonialism.

The phenomenon of the *pachuco* arose in a U.S. context of deep racism, in an epoch when some restaurants prohibited entry to "dogs, Negroes, and Mexicans"; when Mexicans and African Americans were permitted to use public swimming pools only on the days when they were being washed; when African Americans and Latinos were restricted in their use of public transport and could not attend the same schools as the whites; and when Latinos were castigated for speaking Spanish, which was considered a bastard language. Given these facts, Paz's commentary, defining the *pachucos* as instinctive rebels, is disingenuous. Paz's analysis adopts a logic of dichotomy vis-à-vis the *pachuco* and Mexican Americans in general, in which the only choice is that between Mexican centralism and assimilation to the Anglo-Saxon: "El pachuco no quiere volver al origen mexicano, tampoco al menos en apariencia, desea fundirse a la vida norteamericana" (1959, 13) ("The *pachuco* does not want to become a Mexican again; at the same time he does not blend into the life of North America" [1961, 14]). Paz reiterates this dichotomous perspective when he points out: "Esta rebeldía no pasa de ser un gesto vano, pues es una exageración de los modelos contra los que pretende rebelarse y no una vuelta a los atavíos de sus antepasados o una invención de nuevos ropajes" (1959, 15) ("This rebelliousness is only an empty gesture, because it is an exaggeration of the models against which he is trying to rebel, rather than a return to the dress of forebears or the creation of a new style of his own" [1961, 16]). We encounter the same perspective when Paz voices his opinion on the African American population: "Otras comunidades reaccionan de modo distinto, los negros por ejemplo, perseguidos por la intolerancia racial, se esfuerzan por pasar la línea e ingresar a la sociedad" (1959, 13) ("Other groups react differently. The Negroes, for example, oppressed by racial intolerance, try to 'pass' as whites and thus enter society" [1961, 14]). Once again, society is seen as a structure exclusively defined by the Anglo-Saxons; Paz sees no need for proposals for a "new society"–nonexclusivist and multicultural, divested of the institutionalized reproduction of racism and social inequality. As we now realize, the African

American Civil Rights and the Chicano movements of the 1960s and 1970s have disqualified such interpretations.

Rather than seeing the *pachuco* as a form of sociocultural resistance produced by exclusion, Paz recognizes in him only an obsession with distinctiveness: "En muchas partes [del mundo] existen minorías que no gozan de las mismas oportunidades que el resto de la población. Lo característico del hecho reside en este obstinado querer ser distinto" (1959, 14) ("There are minorities in many parts of the world who do not enjoy the same opportunities as the rest of the population. The important thing is this stubborn desire to be different" [1961, 15]). Equally mistaken are Paz's comments stating that the *pachuco* has lost "toda su herencia: lengua, religión, costumbres, creencias" (1959, 14) ("his whole inheritance: language, religion, customs, beliefs" [1961, 15]), or that the clothing of the *pachuco* is simply a fashion, and that "al volver estético el traje corriente, el pachuco lo vuelve impráctico" (1959, 14) ("the *pachuco* by changing ordinary apparel into art, makes it 'impractical'" [1961, 15]). This is not the place to enter into a detailed refutation; suffice it to say that an important part of the *pachuco* symbol system is based upon a number of defining elements of the Mexican cultural profile. *Pachuquismo* was not a fashion–neither in the United States nor in Mexico–since it was an important form of identity that arose out of social resistance, taking precedence over the dimension of class in the case of the Mexicans, and over ethnic designation in the case of the United States. Finally, since the daily routines of the *pachuco* take their lead from the rhythms of the mambo or the boogie woogie, I only wish to underline what Carey McWilliams already said many years ago with respect to the functional character of the zoot suit, above all in reference to dancing: the roominess of the costume is entirely appropriate to its role in practice.

Paz's conclusion is a logical one when we consider that he constructs *pachuquismo* by abstracting the *pachuco* from historical and situational conditions. All that remains is a situation whereby the Mexican is guilty (in his characteristics) of the racism thrust upon him, and his victimization is his self-humiliating, impassive, sadistic, and sinister form of gaining admittance to U.S. society, or rather, of obtaining a certain recognition from the Anglo-Saxon population:

El pachuco es un Clown impasible y siniestro, que no intenta hacer reir y que procura atemorizar. Esta actitud sádica se alía a un deseo de autohumillación, que me parece constituir el fondo mismo de su carácter . . . busca atraer la persecución, el escándalo. Sólo así podrá establecer una relación más viva con la sociedad que provoca: víctima podrá ocupar un puesto en ese mundo que hasta hace poco lo ignoraba y el delincuente, será uno de sus héroes malditos. (1959, 15)

The *pachuco* is an impassive and sinister clown whose purpose is to cause terror instead of laughter. His sadistic attitude is allied with a desire for self-abasement which in my opinion constitutes the very foundation of his character; he seeks and attracts persecution and scandal. It is the only way he can establish a more vital relationship with the society he is antagonizing. As a victim, he can occupy a place in the world that previously had ignored him; as a delinquent, he can become one of its wicked heroes. (1961, 16)

In the same spirit of logic, Paz adds:

Por caminos secretos y arriesgados el "pachuco" intenta ingresar a la sociedad norteamericana. Más él mismo se veda el acceso. Desprendido de su cultura tradicional, el pachuco se afirma un instante como soledad y reto. Niega a la sociedad de la que procede y a la norteamericana. El "pachuco" se lanza al exterior,

pero no para fundirse con lo que lo rodea, sino para retarlo. Gesto suicida, pues el "pachuco" no afirma nada, no pretende nada, excepto su exasperada voluntad de no ser. (1959, 16)

The *pachuco* tries to enter North American society in secret and daring ways, but he impedes his own efforts. Having been cut off from his traditional culture, he asserts himself for a moment as a solitary and challenging figure. He denies both the society from which he originated and that of North America. When he thrusts himself forward, it is not to unite with what surrounds him but rather to defy it. This is a suicidal gesture, because the *pachuco* does not affirm or defend anything except his exasperated will-not-to-be. (1961, 17)

We beg to differ. The characteristic feature of the *pachuco* is not his naked singularity, but rather a singularity shaped by his identification as a Mexican, as a member of a stigmatized community.

The *pachuco*, as an extremity of what the Mexican can become, suffers, according to Paz, from a robust inferiority complex under which can be found his solitude, the solitude of being an orphan, dispossessed, in flight, always returning in his search of linkages to his origin. Paz's phrasing is much more beautiful:

La historia de México es la del hombre que busca su filiación, su origen. Sucesivamente afrancesado, hispanista, indigenista, "pocho", cruza la historia como un cometa de jade, que de vez en cuando relampaguea. En su excéntrica carrera ¿qué persigue? Va tras su catástrofe. . . . Nuestra soledad tiene las mismas raíces que el sentimiento religioso. Es una orfandad, una oscura conciencia de que hemos sido arrancados de todo y una ardiente búsqueda: una fuga y un regreso, tentativa por restablecer los lazos que nos unan a la creación. (1959, 18–19)

The history of Mexico is the history of a man seeking his parentage, his origins. He has been influenced at one time or another by France, Spain, the United States, and the militant indigenists of his own country, and he crosses history like a jade comet, now and then giving off flashes of lightning. What is he pursuing in his eccentric course? He wants to go back beyond the catastrophe he suffered. . . . Our solitude has the same roots as religious feelings. It is a form of orphanhood, an obscure awareness that we have been torn from the All, and an ardent search: a fight and a return, an effort to re-establish the bonds that unite us with the universe. (1961, 20)

It is in this condition of solitude that all the characteristic features of the Mexican are formed: his credulity; his love of myths and legends; his propensity–whether out of fantasy, despair, or to overcome the sordidness of life–for lying; his willingness to confess; his instinctive nihilism; his distrustfulness and suspiciousness; his melancholy and sarcastic temperament; his contemplativeness; his quietism; and his relish of his own afflictions.

When Paz speaks of "The Mexican" as a category, he neglects to take stock of the fine threads that are woven by the network of social interactions and the different ranges of identity within which these relations are expressed. It is only in this context that the devalorization of Mexican life and the Mexican inward-looking and unstable attitude, stemming from the Colonial period, make sense: "La situación del pueblo durante el periodo colonial sería así la raíz de nuestra actitud cerrada e inestable. Nuestra historia como nación independiente contribuiría también a perpetuar y hacer más neta esta psicología servil (puesto que no hemos logrado suprimir la miseria popular ni las exasperantes diferencias sociales)" (1959, 64) ("The situation that prevailed during the

Colonial period would thus be the source of our closed, unstable attitude. Our history as an independent nation would contribute to perpetuating and strengthening this servant psychology, for we have not succeeded in overcoming the misery of the common people and our exasperating social differences" [1961, 71]). Here Paz locates the source of the image or archetype of the *chingada*, which for Paz is "una madre mítica. . .la madre que ha sufrido, a la que se la han chingado . . . chingar es hacer violencia sobre otro. . . . Lo chingado es lo pasivo, abierto, inerte. . . . El chingón es el macho. . . . La chingada es la madre abierta, violada o burlada por la fuerza" (1959, 68–72) ("a mythical mother, the mother who has suffered, the mother who has been fucked. . . . *Chingar*, then, is to do violence to another. . . . The person who suffers this action is passive, inert and open. . . . The *chingón* is the *macho*, the male. . . . The *Chingada* is the Mother forcibly opened, violated or deceived" [1961, 75–79; translation modified]); the child of the *chingada* is the product of a violation, and the violated mother is associated, by Paz, with the Conquest "fue también una violación, no sólo en el sentido histórico, sino en la carne misma de las indias" (1959, 77) ("which was also a violation, not only in the historical sense but also in the very flesh of Native women" [1961, 86; translation modified]). The symbol of the surrender is Malinche, who represents for the Spaniards the fascinated, violated, or seduced Natives.

The corollary of Paz's argument is that the Mexican does not want, or does not dare, to be him or herself. Living in a state of self-denial and self-evasion, Paz recounts an anecdote that exemplifies this all-too-Mexican condition: "Recuerdo que una tarde, como oyera un leve ruído en el cuarto vecino al mío, pregunté en voz alta: ¿Quién anda por ahí? y la voz de una criada recién llegada de su pueblo contestó: No es nadie, señor, soy yo" (1959, 40) ("I remember the afternoon I heard a noise in the room next to mine, and asked loudly: 'Who is in there?' I was answered by the voice of a servant who had recently come to us from her village: 'No one, señor. I am'" [1961, 44]). Here Paz forgets to remember the relational and situational dimension of social identities, since his example does not demonstrate the self-negation of his employee, but rather the sense of belonging to different and profoundly unequal sociocultural domains represented by the categories of master and servant. Clearly this person, the servant, in the context of her village, her neighborhood, her own household, or in that of her horizontal social ties, has a name, a biography and is recognized as a person. If the same question had been asked of her by a kinswoman, a relative, or an acquaintance, she would have replied Doña Juanita, or some such name. To respond "No one, señor. I am" is to give voice to a relation of inequality that still exists in Mexico, a relation constructed inside a play of mirrors, where many are constrained to answer from a position of subordination and, often times, negation vis-à-vis the world of the masters.

Santiago Ramírez has taken up this issue of the pro-U.S. and anti-Mexican national attitudes prevalent in the Mexican upper classes and in some cultural spheres. He has pointed out that as one descends the ladder of social class from the top toward the bottom, identification with U.S. style and manner of life becomes more and more difficult, with attitudes becoming more finely graded, including even hostility and aggression, mockery or contempt for things foreign. According to Ramírez, the Mexicans' fear of losing their identity entails, in its search for a "forceful and vital" paternal figure, an adherence to a "non-existent and cruel" paternal figure, and creates

thus the figures of the *caudillo* and the hero. Another psychologist, Rogelio Díaz Guerrero, has underlined what he calls "the border effect," alluding to a partial assimilative acculturation of Mexican Americans to U.S. models or patterns paralleled by evidence of "un cierto grado de aculturación de los anglonorteamericanos de la frontera a los valores mexicanos" (120) ("a certain degree of acculturation among Anglo-Americans of the border region to Mexican values"). According to Díaz Guerrero, there exists a two-way traffic in cultural influences across the border, "un *efecto de frontera* en el que la gente de uno o de ambos lados de la misma, resultaron ser más diferentes que cualquiera de los patrones medulares, que éstos lo fueron entre sí" (120) ("a border effect such that the people on either side of the border become something quite different from either of the fundamental patterns or models is in itself").

In *La frontera de Cristal* [1998; *The Crystal Frontier*, 1997], Carlos Fuentes (b. 1928) explores a number of possibilities of border life. The characters of the novel shape and constitute the social fabric as well as the events that mark them. They learn not to trust the appearances that take shape on the other side of the crystal border, but rather they learn to survive, to despise themselves for being who they are, and to fall in love with the light the crystal border reflects back because they learn that away from the border and the English language and the immigration police, they possess the light which illuminates them, every one. The border is a site of rupture and a space of revisitation, as we see in the character Emilio Barroso, the "protagonist" of the section entitled "The Line of Oblivion." Barroso (whose name might be rendered in English as "Soiled"), is a figure who is paralyzed, hemorrhaging, and lost to himself, who cannot speak or move, but who can hear what happens around him. He does not know who he is because he has lost his memory and thus the moorings of his identity; he finds himself in an abyss facing the artificial line the migrants seek to cross, the line of the abyss that renders us mute and unable to recognize ourselves: Anglo-Saxon language and culture. Obstinate migrants living a life of self-absenteeism, dazed and bewildered, face the line waiting for the propitious moment to cross. While they wait, the imprints of identity gather force and the storm clouds of memory intensify; they are compelled to flush out their personal and collective points of reference from their mnemonic refuges. Doubt and equivocality run wild on the border and much of what transpires in the crossing is confounded. It is not exactly clear what to expect on the other side; what is undeniable is that the pathways traversed overwhelm with the smell of one's native soil and the charge of one's deepest emotions. There, at the border, Emilio Barroso recovers his memory, takes himself to task, and reestablishes a fix on the compass of his own identity-scape. At the line, displacement and losing one's way also engender a revisitation, above all when the razor wire, racism and intolerance, tear the crystal border to shreds.

To the North of the Line

Inter-ethnic relations in the United States have been conflictual principally because of their structural basis in a rigid division of sociocultural opportunities. The cultural borders between the two nations, particularly those of an ethnic and racial nature, have often been interpreted from the perspective of the dominant group that condemns those divested of power. Determinist approaches to the question of inter-ethnic relations hypostatise social and cultural differences by stressing that such relations arise from biological (or ecological) characteristics, and as such they assume the preexistence of groups that can be characterized as having inferior and/or superior traits. In this way, the supposed "innate" characteristics of a group determine their position in the social structure. Assimilationist and acculturation theories stress the cultural absorption of less developed groups by dominant groups or nations; on the one hand acculturation theories grow out of a dichotomous view of development and underdevelopment in which there is an inevitable assimilation of the less developed groups or nations and an acculturation of the so-called minorities by the dominant groups of the developed countries, who possess greater privileges, recognition, and power. On the other hand, the pluralist theory takes into consideration the inequality that stems from the processes maintaining institutionalization and cultural differences.

To counter these positions, a considerable number of studies have been undertaken, including those of the structuralists and the theorists of internal colonization, that locate the inequalities in the structure of social relations. This approach stresses the relations between groups with marked sociocultural differences, inscribed in schemas imposed by the dominant groups which reproduce the ethnic and cultural differences in the structure of labor relations. From this perspective, the Chicanos are considered to be a people colonized in their own (former) lands by the Anglo-Saxons, a situation that has created a structure of internal colonialism that reproduces a relation of subordination.

One of the literary testimonials that recreates the migratory process and the life conditions of the Mexican laborers in the United States is Daniel Venegas's (b. 1928) novel *Las aventuras de Don Chipote, o cuando los pericos mamen* [*The Adventures of Don Chipote, or, When Parrots Breast-Feed*, 2000], published in the Los Angeles periodical *El Heraldo de México* in 1928. This comic novel written in a colloquial idiom recreates the vicissitudes of the immigrants who abandon their families in order to work in the United States, and who, in the course of their travails, experience exploitation and appalling conditions. Venegas creates a trenchant irony through his cultural-convert characters like Pitasio, who, solely by crossing the line of the border, believes he can speak "la tatacha del toquinglés" ("the mumbo-jumbo of English talk"). Don Chipote and his dog "sufrelambre" ("bag o' bones") leave Doña Chipote and the little slap-abouts (*chipotitos*) and head north to the United States, where they undergo a series of exploitative, racist, and alienating experiences that force them to return to their own neck of the woods, coming to the acid conclusion that "los mexicanos se harán ricos en Estados Unidos: cuando los pericos mamen" (155) ("Mexicans will make millions in the United States, when parrots breast-feed").

The novel *Pocho* [1959; Spanglish Speaker], by the Los Angeles writer José Antonio Villarreal (b. 1924), tells a similar story, this time of an ex-supporter of Pancho Villa, Juan Rubio, who is obliged to forsake his country and head north to the United States (bearing the Revolution within him). In this work, Villarreal paints a picture of the exploitation of the Mexican workers in the produce fields of the United States, and, through Ricardo, the son of Juan Rubio, brings us face to face with the cultural and familial segregations inscribed in culturally discriminatory power relations and various linguistic preferences. Villarreal shows us the early conditions of apprenticeship whereby the Mexican children are labeled *Cholos*, or dirty Mexicans, and Ronnie, the Anglo-Saxon boy,

has interiorized these prejudices: "Mi madre tiene razón al juzgar este pueblo piojoso. No hay personas decentes, ¡sólo una bola de mexicanos y japoneses y no sé qué más mugre humana!" (205) ("My mother was right when she called these people scum. Not one of them is clean, only pack of Mexicans, Japanese, and I don't know what more human filth!"). Written at the end of the 1950s, *Pocho* raises to the level of literature a number of themes fundamental to the Mexican community in the United States, such as immigration, cultural change, racism, and *pachuquismo*.

The trans-border condition as a representation of cultural crossroads is taken up in an important manner by Miguel Méndez's (b. 1930) *Peregrinos de Aztlán* [1974; *Pilgrims in Aztlán*, 1992], a novel describing the Mexican, Native, wetback, and Chicano condition. The novel recounts, from the point of view of familiarity with marginalization, the experience of a wizened Yaqui sage who works as a window washer and the confrontation of indigenous ways with the modernity represented by the automobile. Born in Belen (Bethlehem), Sonora, he wanders the border region as Jesus, the Yaqui divinity. With a sharp ear Méndez represents the region's turns of phrase and slang, the migratory and laboring condition of its people. He does so from a point of view of the Chicano and Mexican sensibility that leads some of his characters to reflections of a totalizing nature: "y no se dan cuenta estos estúpidos que son ellos con su puerco dinero que lo pudren todo" (1991, 81) ("Those jerks don't realize that it's them and their shitty money that spoils everything" [1992, 66]). In Méndez's canvas, the pilgrimage is unending, and the pilgrims retain much of their popular traditions, their culture, and their forms of resistance, elements that, in the border region with its sordid stages of prostitution, drugs, and bars, combine in an intense way. Méndez constructs the future of the Chicano border people upon a recuperation of the past, a process of anamnesis that requires a return to what they were in order to know who they are and to get a bearing on the route they would follow forward: "¡Caballeros Tigres, caballeros águila, luchad por el destino de nuestros hijos! Sabed, los inmolados, que en esta región seréis alborada y también seréis río" (1991, 184) ("Tiger-knights, eagle-knights, fight for the destiny of your children! Know, those who have been immolated, for in this region you will be the dawn and you will also be the river" [1992, 178]). Only by recuperating their past will the Chicano be capable of reinventing themselves as a people:

> [O]ra como que apaño güergüenza, siempre camellando como un pinchi animal, ése, usté, que ha leyido tantos "comics", ¿qué somos slaves, nosotros la raza? Luego, ése . . . es como si le filerearan a uno los hígados. Allás, ése, pos es uno "greaser", un "Mexican", viene uno acá, ése, y quesque uno es "pocho"; me empieza a cuadrar que me llamen chicano, bato, me cai a toda madre, carnal, siquiera ya es uno algo, no cualesquier greaser o pocho ¿qué no? Usté que ha leyido tantos funnys, carnalito, ¿qué semos, ése? (1991, 37–38)

> Now it's almost like I felt ashamed, always scrounging around like an animal. You know what I mean, you've read a lot of comics. Are we just a bunch of slaves? It's just like they went and cut your liver up into pieces. You're nothing but a greaser, a spick, and then you come over here and you're nothing but a pocho. It really makes me happy when they call me a Chicano, pal. You don't have any idea what a thrill it gives me, brother. A man's somebody, not just a greaser or a pocho, right? You've read a lot of funny books, pal, what are we? (Méndez 1992, 20)

The Chicano pilgrimage of formative experiences has been a rich and profound one, and it is for this reason that a number of authors such as José Montoya (b. 1932) have chosen to emphasize their deep identity as Chicanos, inhabitants of the *Chicanación Casindia* (Chicano nation, almost Indian), full-blooded *Aztleños*.

Not only is the border region tied to questions of cultural heritage, it is imbricated in a world of myth, and Chicano literature is shot through with magical references. Rudolf A. Anaya's (b. 1937) novel *Bless Me, Ultima* (1972) develops the theme of the mythic with particular acumen in presenting a story of family rivalries and changes in a bucolic and supernatural world. The plot centers on the relationship between Antonio and Ultima, la Grande (the old and wise), a character endowed with curative powers, and on Antonio's quest to discover the history of his family and his people: "Luego vino el ferrocarril. El alambre de púas llegó también. Las canciones, los corridos, se hicieron tristes y el encuentro de la gente de Texas con mis antepasados fue sangriento, de asesinatos y de tragedia" (100) ("Then the railroad came. And with it the barbed wire. The encounter of my ancestors with the Texans was a bloody affair. Murder and tragedy; the songs and the ballads tell that sad story"). Through Ultima, Antonio's eyes are opened to the world of traditional wisdom, whose ancient gods are in the process of dying. He learns that immortality lies in the freedom of humanity and that the boundaries of "reality" limit our comprehension of the great cycle of life of which we are but a part: "'Las aguas son sólo una, Antonio.' Miré dentro de sus ojos brillantes y claros, y comprendí la verdad. Has estado viendo las partes—terminó—y no has visto más allá, hacia el gran ciclo que nos une a todos" (144) ("'All waters, Antonio, are one.' I looked into her brilliant clear eyes and understood the truth. 'You have only managed to look on the parts,' she concluded, 'you haven't seen beyond, to the great cycle that binds us to the all'"). A people's capacity to know itself as collective of individuals is put to its most severe test living on the political and cultural border where the sense of belonging is threatened at every turn. Ultima in her simple direct manner believes that understanding is nothing more or less than feeling love for people.

Beyond the well-documented history of the Chicano movement and its legendary figures—like César Chávez and the Farm Workers Union (*Sindicato de Trabajadores Agrícolas*), Reies López Tijerina and the Federal Alliance of Free Peoples (*Alianza Federal de Pueblos Libres*), Rodolfo "Corky" González (b. 1928) and the Crusade for Justice (*Cruzada por la Justicia*), or José Ángel Gutiérrez and the Racial Union Party (*Partido de la Raza Unida*)—the Chicano movement left a deep mark on the field of education. A number of departments of Chicano Studies were created at U.S. universities, as well as important organizations like the Aztlán Chicano Student Movement (*Movimiento Estudiantil Chicano Aztlán*, or MECHA) and the National Association of Chicano Studies (*Asociación Nacional de Estudios Chicanas y Chicanos*, or NACCS, formerly the NACS). Endowed with a rich cultural mix of numerous languages and cultural reference points, the United States is also a major Spanish-speaking nation, with a Latino population of about 30 million. Within this multicultural climate Latino culture possesses a conspicuous presence in a number of diverse areas—including music, dance, literature, the plastic arts, cuisine—a situation that has given rise to a number of important cultural hybrids and re-creations.

The experience of World War II and the intensification of inter-ethnic conflicts that were tied to it became highly visible with the persecution of the *pachucos* in the 1940s. In the years that followed, the Chicano movement and the rise in levels of literacy and urbanization among Mexican Americans influenced the development of literary production in which Chicano sociocultural oppression was highlighted and denounced. Underlying these works was a sense of the Chicano's colonial status and a search to recuperate Mexican and Native roots; in them portraits, scenes and vignettes were painted of the daily life of the barrios, the village, intimate life, and the network of mothers and fathers, grandmothers and grandfathers. Among the important works and developments of this period were the already mentioned *Pocho* (1959) by José Antonio Villarreal; Rodolfo "Corky" González's poem "I am Joaquín" (1954); and politico-satirical texts of José Montoya in *El Malcriado* [Bulletin of the Farm Workers Union], *Los poemas del barrio* [Barrio Poems] and the memorable "El Louie Rodríguez" (Montoya 76–79); the apparition of literary reviews like *El Grito* (1967) and *Chicano Riqueña* (1973); the editorial house Quinto Sol (1968), which published fundamental works of Chicano literature such as Tomás Rivera's (1935–1984) novel ...*Y no se lo tragó la tierra* [1971; ...*And the Earth Did Not Devour Him*, 1987]; the atmospheric novels of magic and traditional wisdom incarnated in "la Grande" in *Bless Me, Ultima* by Rudolfo Anaya, *Estampas del Valle y otras obras* [1973; Footprints of the Valley and Other Works] by Rolando Hinojosa-Smith (b. 1929), or *Lluvia de escorpiones* [1974; *Rain of Scorpions*, 1993] by Estela Portillo Trambley (b. 1936). Also published in 1974, as we have seen, were Miguel Méndez's *Peregrinos de Aztlán* [*Pilgrims in Aztlán*, 1992], taking up the theme of the northern border, and *Floricanto de Aztlán* [Floricanto from Aztlán] by Alurista (b. 1947). In the world of theater the most outstanding group was Teatro Campesino under the directorship of Luis Valdez (b. 1940), a group that took up the task of representing to the Mexican American community its own social and labor problems.

Beginning in the 1980s Chicano literature underwent a number of important changes, among the most important of which was the increasing presence of women. Without abandoning the fundamental anchorage derived from its position as a subordinated group in the United States, or the ethnic dimension, or the (re-)creation and deconstruction of symbols and icons based in the representation of the Mexican (such as the indigenous past, the thematics of the mythology of Aztlán, and the central masculinity of the Chicano nationalist discourse), Chicano literature forsook its previous binary stance and began to incorporate more complex analytic forms in which the centrality of gender and sexual orientation, the deconstruction of the masculinist discourse of the movement, and the impact of popular culture and religion rose to the fore. Together with new journals and spaces for literary discussion, the concerns of literature and gender become more and more visible. Among the writers who should be mentioned were Sandra Cisneros (b. 1954), Ana Castillo (b. 1945), Gloria Anzaldúa (b. 1942), Cherríe Moraga (b. 1952), Lucha Corpi (b. 1945), Helena María Viramontes (b. 1954), Denise Chávez (b. 1948), Angélica Vigil (b. 1949), Graciela Limón (b. 1938), Alejandro Morales (b. 1944), Norma Alarcón, Mary Helen Ponce (b. 1938), Norma Cantú (b. 1947), Angie Chabram (b. 1952), Rosaura Sánchez (b. 1941), José Antonio Burciaga (b. 1940), Francisco Alarcón (b. 1954), Cordelia Candelaria (b. 1943), Jimmy Santiago Baca (b. 1952), Norma

Klhan, María Herrera Sobek (b. 1942), Carlos Cumpián, Angela de Hoyos (b. 1945), Lorna Dee Cervantes (b. 1954), Rosemary Cotacalos, Rebeca González, Martín Espada (b. 1957), Ray González (b. 1952), Victor Hernández Cruz (b. 1949), and Carmen Tafolla (b. 1951). There are a number of works of fundamental importance for the broad reconstruction of Chicano literature, including those by Bruce-Novoa, Villanueva, Tatum, Candelaria, González, and Luis Leal.

In the last twenty years a number of important works have appeared that chart the sociocultural changes of the Chicano community. In the United States, postmodern perspectives, as well as theories of multiculturalism, have questioned the bases upon which the legitimation of the so-called superiority of the dominant culture has been founded. As a part of this trend, cultural discussion has prioritized the questioning of all manner of borders, whether they be ethnic, gender-based, generational, or having to do with sexual preference, and has placed a greater relevance on investigations of postmodernity, multiculturalism, postcolonialism, neocolonialism, and cultural studies. Much of this work has adopted nonessentialist positions and, following in the footsteps of Raymond Williams, advanced in the interpretation of the relations between the dominant, the residual, and the emergent. These works have also sought a discourse from and with the margins, the interstices, and the thresholds. Cultural borders do not reach a limit or conclude in ruptures, but rather, as Homi K. Bhabha has pointed out (1994), are themselves new horizons, fields where something is initiated, themselves intermediate spaces or interstices that impinge upon the definition of identity strategies and belonging (206–8).

The new debates on the issue of cultural borders take their expression from distinct approaches to the salient cultural processes at play as the new millennium arrives: identity, gender, youth culture, interculturalism, ethnicity, power, new social structures, the culture industry, the new audiovisual media, hybridism, the sociocultural diaspora, the center and the periphery, and the cultural interstices and thresholds. Renato Rosaldo has highlighted the fact that Chicano narratives are bearers of agreed upon borders as points of identitarian and cultural intersection (1991); this is given voice in the texts of Américo Paredes (1916–1999), Ernesto Galarza (1905–1984), Sandra Cisneros, and José Montoya that Rosaldo analyzes as liminal zones. Since the 1980s female writers have participated in a more intense manner in the greater process of the decodification of the previous prevailing narratives, incorporating into this work a profound reflection and a critical practice vis-à-vis gender relations, thus contesting the homogeneity of the masculine narrative. For these women, as Cherríe Moraga and Ana Castillo have pointed out, the notion of borders implies new racial, cultural, and feminist bridges (see Moraga and Castillo; Anzaldúa 1990).

Gloria Anzaldúa has advanced the analysis of the border by highlighting the fact that the condition of being a Chicano involves a series of multiple allegiances to different border identities, including Mexican, Native, and Anglo-Saxon. According to Anzaldúa, the women of the border region live on the threshold, in the interstices, at the margins; their consciousness is a border consciousness. Because border culture is the product of those who cross over the limits of normality, whether those limits are conceived in terms of nationality, ethnicity, race, or gender, Chicano and Chicana writers throw into relief the complex production of borders and the liminal. Angie Chabram adopts this perspective when she points out

that Chicano existential borders are multiple, marked as they are by complex historical and political contexts of survival. To cross over necessitates reinterpreting the qualities and constituents that take part and the thresholds that are shared. It is for this reason that Rosalinda Fregoso (1993) has analyzed the representation of women in the cinema, questioning the masculine centrality that reduces women to spectators, and has explored the work of women, like Agueda Martínez, Lourdes Portillo, Nina Serrano, Susana Muñoz, and others, who have advanced a repositioning of the representations and participations of women.

Distancing themselves from the centralist perspective that has constructed a single remote border, Chicano writers have taken to speaking from the plural borders. Writers like Sandra Cisneros, whose work has aimed at a literary re-creation of the family and neighborhood, have uncovered the ethnic dimensions linked to subordination and poverty, as well as the familial and gender dimensions present, for example, in looks, the broadening of the hips, or conjugal violence (although Sally, one of Cisneros's characters, is the subject of such violence, she pretends to justify it by saying "he doesn't hit me that hard" [1988, 85]). Borders take on a menacing aspect in language when the "no speak English" throws up distances between people, and this menace increases and becomes intolerable when it impedes communication with the children. These borders divide the neighborhoods, such that when the neighborhood begins to lose its dark complexion, the inhabitants become afraid. The neighborhood, for Cisneros, impresses us with its stamp, it inhabits us, and that is why Esperanza will always be contained in the image of Mango Street. Unlike the centralist perspective vis-à-vis the border and the migrants, for Cisneros and many border Chicanos, the border is a lived phenomenon, a site of meetings and exchanges, a place of positions and repositionings. In Cisneros's stories, distress is not attenuated, but rather empirically observed in Northern streets, factories, fields, and family biographies. Tragedy is known first-hand in, for example, the story "Gerardo No Last Name" (1984), where Cisneros tells us the story of a happy-go-lucky immigrant who loves to dance and dies without anyone ever knowing his surname or where he came from:

> But what difference does it make? He wasn't anything to her. He wasn't her boyfriend or anything like that. Just another *brazer* who didn't speak English. Just another wetback. You know the kind. The ones who always look ashamed.
>
> . . . They never saw the kitchenettes. They never knew about the two-room flats and sleeping rooms he rented, the weekly money orders sent home, the currency exchange. How could they?
>
> His name was Geraldo. And his home is in another country. The ones he left behind are far away. They will wonder. Shrug. Remember. Geraldo. He went north . . . we never heard from him again. (1988, 63)

For Chicanos, living as they do in and through borders, the imagined community of country has been a fragmented space that ceaselessly composes them. As Cherríe Moraga in *The Last Generation* (1993) has noted, "I am a Chicana nearing forty without a country,"(41) and, more sharply, in "Art in America," emphasizing the double inflection, "Los Estados Unidos es mi país, pero no es mi patria ("The United States is my country, but not my home"). I cannot flee the United States, my land resides beneath its borders" (54). Ana Castillo, who has thrown herself into the Chicano women's struggle through activism, cultural practice, and political battles, has taken up the task of defining the condition of Chicano women, the women without nation, the Mexic-Amerindians, or, in a more direct manner, defining what she calls "Xicanism," Chicano feminism (Castillo 1994). In her epistolary novel *Cartas de Mixquiahuala* [1986; Mixquiahuala Letters], Teresa interprets her own experience in her letters to Alicia through an existential reflection on the thresholds of gender, ethnicity, cosmography, and the world of the grandmothers and their ghosts. Her voyage of discovery of her complementary culture allows her to analyze her cultural distance from Mexico, as well as to confront the partisans of artistic machismo and sexism, as well as the vagaries of their relationships with her and thereby probes the limits of myth of the Mexican tradition. In the course of this development she understands that her language treats genders differently and that to be a Chicana exposes her to the stereotypes of being branded "loose." She learns that differences transcend the frontiers of identity, and thus begins to question traditional Mexican *machismo* and supposed male superiority in all aspects of life.

The cleavages of affections and attachments and cultural processes, pass beyond the limits of borders. For the Chicanos these cleavages take form as a lived existential certainty that is imbricated and integrated in their biographies, their blood and their epidermis, as well as in the markings that underwrite their identity. José Antonio Burciaga poetically re-creates this in his *Undocumented Love/Amor indocumentado*:

Para México con Cariño

Madre patria que acusaste
a tus hijos sin razón,
siendo tú la ocasión
quiero que recuerdes:
Que somos hijos de olvidados,
hijos de revolucionarios,
hijos de exiliados,
hijos de mojados,
hijos de braceros,
hijos de campesinos,
hijos que buscan pan,
hijos en busca de trabajo,
hijos of Sánchez que no educaste,
hijos que abandonaste,
hijos de padrastro gringo,
hijos de los de abajo,
hijos pochos,
hijos guachos,
hijos con el *Spanish* mocho,
hijos desamparados.
Recuerda que somos mexicanos,
somos chicanos,
sabemos inglés,
y como descendientes ausentes
recuérdanos como hijos pródigos.

To Mexico with Love,

Motherland accusing
your children without reason,
when the reason you were,
I want you to remember:
We are the forgotten children,
the children of revolutionaries,
the children of exiles,
the children of wetbacks,
the farm laborers' children,
the peasants' children,
the children who seek bread,
looking for work,
the children of Sanchez,
you abdicated, uneducated,
gringo step-fathered children,
the under-class, downtrodden,
discoloured Mexicans,
odd-sock orphans,
speaking one-armed Spanish,
helpless, defenseless.
Remember, we are Mexicans,
and also Chicanos,
we speak English,
and as absentee offspring
remember us as your prodigal, prodigious children.

(43)

The border is a field of intensified relations also entailing hatred, incomprehension, and intolerance, a mixture of sentiments well captured by Juan Felipe Herrera (b. 1948):

What if the U.S. was Mexico?
What if 200,000 Anglosaxicans
were to cross the border each month
to work as gardeners, waiters,
3rd chair musicians, movie extras,
bouncers, babysitters, chauffeurs,
syndicated cartoonists, feather-weight
boxers, fruit-pickers & anonymous poets?
What if they were called waspanos,
waspitos, wasperos or wasbacks?
What if we were the top dogs?
What if literature was life, eh.

(qtd. in Flores 224)

The border condition is also expressed in all its intensity, charged with necessity and absence, in the poem "El otro lado" ["The Other Side"], by the Salvadorean/Chicano writer Rubén Martínez:

El otro lado
The other side,
that's where I'm from,
el otro lado,
that's where you're from,
the other side
. . .Me oyes?
over there, por allá,
hear, me?
Here, me!
this me, this me,
desde este lado,
on this side, este yo
y no el yo del otro,
not your me.
But this me, the one
that wears all the colors
of the continent!

(81, 84)

In a manner similar to other writers, Guillermo Gómez-Peña (b. 1955) constructs his discourse as a constant crossing of borders, and in the process defines himself as a Mexican nomad, artist, and writer in the process of becoming Chicano. This stance is not only a spatial one but also involves a transit through linguistic domains of Spanish, Spanglish, and English. According to Gómez-Peña, U.S. culture is multi-centered and hybrid. In an epoch of ferocious changes, shifting borders, emptinesses, hatreds, losses, it is removal, migration, and deterritorialization that appear to be the only possible certainties, and thus one's home can only be here, somewhere else, and nowhere at all. As Guillermo Gómez-Peña states: "yo cargo la frontera conmigo y yo encuentro nuevas fronteras donde quiera que voy" (5) ("I carry the border with me and I encounter new borders wherever I go"). In this new-world border, the concept of *Mexamérica* acquires meaning as a conceptual nation that includes the northern states of Mexico and overlaps with a number of Native first nations. From this perspective, he held that Chicanos all are potential interlopers and cultural exiles, inhabitants of a "Hybridamerica and Transamerica" (6) in which hybridism is the cultural dominant. Since such Chicanos belong to the so-called Fourth World, constituted of Natives and diasporic communities, of intermixed nationalities without fixed identities, stripped of pure idioms and sacred cultural traditions: Members of the Fourth World live between and through multiple cultures, communities, and countries. The challenge of Fourth World artists and writers is derived from this kaleidoscopic perspective: to represent the new conjunction of myths, metaphors, and symbols that situates them in these cartographies in flux (Gómez-Peña 6–7). Unfortunately, the boundary crossings that Gómez-Peña proposes is unavailable for the majority of Chicanos and Chicanas and Mexican men and women who confront on a daily basis racism, discrimination, class exploitation, or seizure by the immigration police.

Special mention needs to be made of the work of a particular group of Chicana and Mexican women, who brought to fruition three conferences (in 1987, 1988, and 1989) under the title "Mexican and Chicano Women and Literature: Cultures in Contact" (López, Malagamba, and Urrutia). These conferences, organized by Aralia López and Elena Urrutia from the Programa Interdisciplinarios de Estudios de la Mujer (PIEM) of the Colegio de Mexico and Amelia Malagamba from the Departamento de Estudios Culturales of the Colegio de la Frontera Norte in Tijuana, Mexico, produced two volumes of conference papers edited by the coordinators. The conference on "Literatura escrita por mujeres Chicanas" ["Chicano Women's Literature"] was organized at the National Autonomous University of Mexico (UNAM) in Mexico City in 1993 with the same objective of opening up a dialogue. The conference proceedings were published in 1995 under the title *Las formas de nuestras voces: Chicana and Mexican Writers in Mexico*, under the editorship of Claire Joysmith. Despite the differences in racial and class objectives of the participants and their divergences in literary-political positions (the Chicanas were by and large more politically committed, and their points of reference more grounded in popular culture—evidence of a greater social and academic mobility), these conferences represented important attempts to shape the space of trans-border dialogue. These attempts at dialogue left many lessons to be mulled over, the most important of which was that there are innumerable borders that divide people, but for every border there also exists a bridge.

A Collage of Dreams

The literatures of the border region are comprised of a number of forms that include ancient expressions such as the narrations of the indigenous peoples, Colonial chronicles, and texts provoked by the U.S. conquest. They also include important popular narratives such as tales, stories, and, not to be overlooked, the ballads that began to be composed around the middle of the nineteenth century by writers like Juan Nepomuceno Cortina (1824–1894), Gregorio Cortés, and Joaquín Murrieta (1832–1853). These ballads, as well as popular legends, kept alive an important popular narrative that in many cases became a resource for sociocultural resistance.

José Javier Villareal has made an interesting survey of a number of northern writers, such as Brother Servando Teresa de Mier (1763–1827), who lived in Monterrey in the second half of the eighteenth century; Francisco González Bocanegra (1824–1861), from San Luis Potosí; Manuel Acuña (1849–1873), from Saltillo; Manuel José Othón (1858–1906), from San Luis Potosí; Ramón López Velarde (1888–1921), from Zacatecas; Julio Torri(1889–1970), from Coahuila; the great Alfonso Reyes (1889–1959) from Monterey; and Jesús E. Valenzuela (1856–1911), from Durango (Villareal). Among the most outstanding border writers in the second half of this century, one would include Edmundo Valadez, José Fuentes Mares (1919–1986), Carlos Montemayor (b. 1947), Federico Campbell (b. 1941), Jorge Aguilar Mora (b. 1946), José Vicente Anaya (b. 1947), Rafael Ramírez Heredia (b. 1942), Jesús Gardea (b. 1939), Alfredo Espinosa (b. 1954), Ricardo Elizondo (b. 1950), and Gerardo Cornejo.

Beginning in the 1970s, a new group of important writers came to public attention, bringing with them a wealth of new experiences. In addition to the traditional amatory, comic, erotic, and rural veins in writing, these writers worked into their fiction a new conception of the quotidian that included consideration of migration, factory work, and low-life environments. Among the many writers that could be cited here, let us mention Sergio Gómez Montero (b. 1945), Francisco Morales (b. 1940), Raúl Antonio Cota (b. 1949), Rosina Conde (b. 1954), José Javier Villarreal (b. 1959), Daniel Sada (b. 1953), Minerva Margarita Villarreal (b. 1957), Roberto Castillo (b. 1951), Luis Humberto Crosthwaite (b. 1962), José Manuel Di Bella (b. 1952), Guadalupe Aldaco, Francisco Luna (b. 1956), Mario Anteo (b. 1955), Francisco Amparán (b. 1957), Inés Martínez de Castro (b. 1954), Patricia Laurente, Margarita Oropeza, Rosario Sanmiguel, Micaela Solís, Regina Swain (b. 1967), Gabriel Trujillo (b. 1958), Oscar Hernández (b. 1974), and Federico Schafler.

The presence of the border as a literary theme and vital space began to be an important subject of discussion in the 1980s. While María Socorro Tabuenca (17) has considered it relevant to differentiate between the border in literature and the literature of the border, I prefer to work with representations of the border not as a geographic region but rather as an interstice of intensive human relations that participate in the definition of identifications, differences, and alterities and, as such, aid us in understanding the processes whereby new forms of self-construal vis-à-vis others are structured. In order to highlight perceptions of the border, Tabuenca points out some important differences: "[F]or Chicano literature the border is 'the Edenic paradise,' and as such an inexhaustible theme in those texts, whereas for Mexican border literature it is an everyday space, a site that is continually unrepresented and even unmentioned" (87). Adding to this distinction, she points out that "the border, perceived from the United States, is much more a textual–theoretical–border than a geographic one."

Chicano and Chicana writers have staked out more elaborate theoretical positions vis-à-vis the border, positions that permeate a large part of the creative and critical production of recent years. That said, however, we must recognize that their conception of the border has been constructed out of a living experience that is part and parcel of daily practice. Chicanos have been cut off and made mongrel by the border, and for many the experience of crossing remains tattooed deep in the consciousness. To cross over the border is to face disadvantages in the new society, the new culture, the new language, where every day the question of the practical and symbolic meaning of difference is a reality. For the Chicanos, to understand the border is a matter of existential necessity, since they live it as an indelible stigma. Miguel Méndez has traced the contours of this stigma with an admirable clarity:

–Apá, ¿Qué somos nosotros?

–Mexicanos, hijo.

–Mexicanos y no vivimos en México. ¿Entonces no somos americanos?

–Sí, hijito, también somos americanos.

–¿Por qué entonces, papá, en México nos llaman pochos y aquí Mexican Greasers? (1991, 176)

"Papa, who are we?"

"We're Mexicans, my son."

"Mexicans. But we don't live in Mexico . . . so does that make us Americans?"

"Yes, son, we're also Americans."

"But then why do they call us *pochos* in Mexico, papa, and Mexican Greasers here?" (1992, 170)

There has been no lack of revealing images to describe the life and conditions of the border regions: Di Bella's "collage of dreams," Romero's "translation space," or Tijuana writer Federico Campbell's view; he considers the border to be like a spatial metaphor, the one that evokes an intermediate world, a zone in which nothing is clearcut; it is a place of coming together and breaking apart, and it is above all a dividing line between reality and desire. The border as a theme in border region literature may have found its most youthful instantiation in the First Reunion of Young Border Region Prose Writers and Poets, held in Ciudad Juárez, Chihuahua, in 1986. Of the almost 300 poetic and narrative texts presented, only five alluded in any way to the life or circumstances of the border region. Of these five, a fragment of the poem "Topless" by the Ciudad Juárez resident Miguel Angel Chávez stands out.

TOPLESS

Coors and Budweiser, two little bitches
unconcerned, they travel the frontier
anguish is topless
a star in the flag, topless
life in the factories' shadow,
topless

(133)

The border is also a space where codes purveying certainties become blurred, an entryway into new fields of meaning where the possibility of being led astray lies waiting. The Nuevo Leon writer Sergio Ordóñez Camarena in his short story "Borderline" has for this reason compared the border to madness: "[H]e elegido ese nombre, en mis fugaces momentos de lucidez, para designar esa brumosa zona limítrofe, fuertemente custodiada, iluminada intermitentemente por poderosos haces de luz blanca, campo minado que divide brutalmente la realidad en dos mundos distintos y antagónicos; este lado y el otro. La frontera. La transición entre el sueño y la vigilia, entre el interior y el exterior, entre el equilibrio y la locura" (quoted in Vallarino 398) ("I've chosen that name, in my fleeting moments of lucidity, to designate that foggy border zone, intensely watched over, intermittently illuminated by beams of white light, the minefield brutally dividing reality in two distinct, antagonistic worlds; this side, that side. The border–transition point between dreams and wakefulness, the interior and the exterior, equilibrium and madness").

The plastic arts have also seen in recent years a wealth of important new productions and a number of exhibitions devoted to border or Chicano art, such as the Latin American exhibition in Houston in 1987 and the "Chicano Arte: Resistance and Affirmation, 1965–1985" (CARA) exhibit in the early 1990s, both of which acquired a special relevance. The CARA exhibit was accompanied by a manifesto describing Chicano art as "the modern and contemporary expression of the cultural, economic, and political struggle of the Mexican people in the United States, the affirmation of the complex identity and vitality of the Chicano people." A number of important visual arts projects have been realized on both sides of the border. Among these we can single out the Festival Internacional de la Raza, held in a number of different border cities between 1983 and 1993. The exhibitions of this international festival, coordinated by Amelia Malagamba of El Colegio de la Frontera Norte and Gilberto Cárdenas of the Galería Sin Fronteras, allowed for the production of art in binational, shared workshops with the important participation of Self Help Graphics of Los Angeles, Strike of San Antonio, and the Galería Sin Fronteras. The experience of the international festival brought together Mexican and Chicano artists in a number of projects that on certain occasions gave rise to discussions defining common thematics. Amelia Malagamba underlined the relevance of this cooperation: "Estas experiencias, integradas por exposiciones, murales y serigrafías, donde se ha recreado a la frontera, han hecho posible que surjan alternativas. Estas iconografías han sido reconocidas sin los formalismos y protocolos de la división política que se bautiza cotidianamente como *la línea*" (116) ("These experiments take the form of expositions, murals, and serigraphs that sought to recreate the border in artistic representations, and so have made a number of alternatives visible and possible. The images produced have been recognized and accepted without the formalities and protocols of the political divisions that on a daily basis fixes the line").

For his part, the academic and cultural animator Gilberto Cárdenas has stressed the regional dimension that characterizes border phenomena: "La cultura fronteriza en gran medida está constituida por una mezcla de cultura norteña de México, la cultura texana y la de los chicanos que viven fuera de Texas y de las áreas aledañas a la zona fronteriza" (91) ("Border culture is largely constituted by a mixture of cultures: Northern Mexican, Texan, and that of the Chicanos who live outside Texas and the areas adjoining the border zone . . . ultimately those who take up and give expression to border culture are the inhabitants of these regions"). Among the other events linking the artists of both sides of the border, the *Taller de arte Fronterizo* exposition, organized by the Centro Cultural La Raza (founded in 1970) and the Taller de Arte Fronterizo (founded in 1983), deserves mention. In this project thirty-seven artists, some with over twenty years experience in both

330 JOSÉ MANUEL VALENZUELA ARCE

countries, took up the task of crossing borders, conceptualizing the line as a confluence of cultures without geographic limits and the border as a precise nexus, as an authentic, culturally hybrid zone. To this end, they had recourse to collage as an artistic language for recreating fundamental aspects of border life such as self-determination, independence, and migration (Kanjo).

Chicano plastic arts are endowed with a fertile experimentalism, both in the mural tradition and in works highlighting the border dimension. Here the Texan artists Cármen Lomas Garza, César Augusto Martínez, Luis Jiménez, John Valades, and Malaquías Montoya, and the Californian Judy Baca, have all distinguished themselves.

Mass Media

The motion picture industry plays an important role in the calcification of inter-ethnic stereotypes and in the linguistic intensification of racial boundaries. U.S. movie production has markedly (re)presented Latinos as lazy, cunning, violent, disagreeable, and randy, while, from the other side of the border, Mexican productions have presented the border region as a sodomized space of gambling, prostitution, vice, and drug trafficking. On both sides priority has been given to low-budget and low-quality productions that tend to see the border region as a problem zone. This can be seen in the Hollywood films *Borderline* (1980), starring Charles Bronson, and *The Border* (1982), starring Jack Nicholson. Against such representations, a number of other works have been produced that, with varying degrees of quality, take a different perspective on the Chicano and border worlds. These films run the gamut from *Wet Back* (1953) by Alejandro Galindo, to productions by Chicano artists, such as *Raíces de Sangre* [1976; Blood Roots] by Jesús Traviño; *Zoot Suit* (1981) by Luis Valdez; *The Milagro Beanfield War* (1988) by Robert Redford; *La Balada de Gregorio Cortés* [1984; *The Ballad of Gregorio Cortés*] by Robert Young; *El Norte* [1983; North] by Gregory Nava; *Born in East L.A.* (1985) by Richard "Cheech" Marín; *La Bamba* (1987) by Luis Valdez; *Stand and Deliver* (1988) by Ramón Menéndez; *American Me* (1992) by Edward James Olmos; *Blood In, Blood Out: Bound By Honor* (1993) by Taylor Hackford; *My Family* (1995) by Gregory Nava; *Mi vida loca* [1993; *My Crazy Life*] by Allison Anders; *El Mariachi* (1993) and *Desperado* (1995) by Robert Rodríguez; and *Selena* (1996) by Gregory Nava. On the Mexican side, there have also been attempts at representing the processes of border life and culture, such as *Break of Dawn* (1988) by Isaac Artenstein, *El Jardín del Edén* [1995; *The Garden of Eden*] by María Novaro, and *Hasta Morir* [1995; Until Death] by Fernando Sariñana from a script by Marcel Fuentes-Beráin. These films can be characterized by their presentation of (or emphasis on) perspectives that differ from conventional cinema. They have taken up themes like migration and its vicissitudes (*Espalda Mojada, El Norte,* or *Born in East L.A.*), the exploitation of workers in the maquiladoras and the discrimination against Mexican Americans (*Raíces de Sangre*), the re-creation of Chicano and border historical figures and events (*La balada de Gregorio Cortés, Zoot Suit, La Bamba, Stand and Deliver,* or *Selena*) , or the life and culture of the *pachuco* and the *Cholo* (*Zoot Suit; American me; Blood In, Blood Out: Bound by Honor, My Family, Mi vida loca,* or *Hasta Morir*).

The Latin American presence in the United States spans a number of spheres of its history, society, and culture. In contrast to the situation in the nineteenth century, when great distances and the sparsity of communications magnified the sense of absence, the development of the means of communication and transport in the twentieth century has given shape to a number of areas of intensive relations. These areas are based on the possibility of moving back to one's birth place, on the density of border relations, and on the mediation of cultural industries (principally the Spanish communications media). In addition to the TV signals available from Mexico, whose reception is strongest in the border region, there are two television channels with national coverage in the United States: Univision, with an audience of approximately 24 million Latinos in the United States, and Telemundo, whose signal reaches 83 percent of the Latino homes in the country. From Mexico, the national channel, Galavision, is distributed on cable. In the realm of newspapers, there are ten dailies published in Spanish, the largest of which are *La Opinión* of Los Angeles and the *Nuevo Herald de Miami*, and both have print runs of approximately 110,000. Further, there are approximately 250 periodicals in existence, twenty-five distributed on a national level, and a number of academic journals highly relevant to the understanding of sociocultural processes of U.S. Latino life (such as *Aztlán* and *Latino Studies Journal*), 150 of which have a statewide or local distribution. There are about 300 radio stations in the United States broadcasting in Spanish, in addition to those located in the northern states of Mexico. According to a report by the Strategy Research Corporation in 1996, Hispanics over the age of 18 devote 60 percent more of their time to the watching of Spanish television than English television, while those under 18 watch almost twice as much English as Spanish. It was also noted that women watch more Spanish television than men. As an illustration of the increasing importance of the Latino presence in the United States, a report by Hispanic Business stated that in 1995 over 1 billion dollars was spent on advertisements directed at the Latino market (Díaz de Cosío, Orozco, and González 217–52).

This information points to the lie of the stereotyped discourse that characterizes the border region as inevitably destined for a complete Americanization. Rather, it corresponds to and reinforces the view that the cultural processes of the border region share the characteristics of reception seen in the northern Mexican states, where the levels of American assimilation are not as high as some would believe. This stereotypical image of the border can only be sustained with difficulty when we realize that border-region viewers show a marked preference for Mexican channels broadcasting in Spanish (see Valenzuela Arce). Two-thirds of Tijuana viewers opt for Mexican channels, and an equal number prefer channels broadcasting in Spanish. The reason for these preferences stems from a number of factors, among which we would have to include linguistic competence, the interest in and quality of programs, the presence of actors known to the viewing public, and habit—with language being the most salient factor. The preference for Mexican- and Spanish-language programming shows some correlation with social and gender factors: There is a higher preference among women and those of a lower and middle socioeconomic level than among the financially better off. (With respect to cinematic preferences, less than 10 percent prefer Spanish language films, 40 percent prefer foreign productions, and almost half have no preference at all. These figures notwithstanding, three-quarters of the population expressed a preference for

Mexican movie houses, while only 15 percent preferred Anglo-Saxon U.S. movie houses.)

Thresholds, Borders, and Interstices

In order to analyze the cultural processes of the border region, we ought to eschew a mechanical correspondence between economic processes and the goings-on in the cultural field; however, that does not mean we can ignore the objective elements expressed in social relations that influence the forms and practices of cultural production. Therefore the following elements should be incorporated into this analysis of border cultural phenomena.

Cultural intersection. The border is defined with respect to a number of fields of cultural intersection, in which an ensemble of cultural elements is shared by distinct groups located within different cultural matrices. The concept of cultural intersection entails processes of encounter and is composed of two levels: The first refers to a vertical cultural intersection (institutionalized/institutionalizing, both ascendent and descendent), where the dominant groups, by means of various processes of socialization, establish the cultural elements (characteristic or appropriate) that are taught and reproduced through the various legitimatized channels of socialization (as in the relation between dominant or hegemonic cultures and popular or subaltern cultures). The second level is a horizontal intersection, referring to the interaction of social groups that are linked to each other not by structural relations of domination but rather by networks of non-institutionalized interactions. Horizontal intersection is at work, for example, among diverse youth groups, between the various trans-border Native peoples, or between members of the same social class who, despite the existence of group identification based on the threshold of belonging and exclusion—identifications delimiting the members of the group into a "we" and a "you"—share recognizable cultural elements that they deem to be similar.

Neighborhood. The border is defined by neighborliness, a colloquial term much more illustrative of the relations rooted in border life than many more or less sophisticated concepts. More than adjacency, geographic privilege, or destiny, neighborhood, as Heidegger has pointed out, refers to the habitability of spaces within which intensive interactions take place: The neighbor is the one who lives in proximity to the other and with others (Derrida 65). Neighborliness necessitates a co-participation in a relational field. Yet U.S.-Mexican proximity is characterized by inequality, and it is for this reason that the perspective of shared destiny, expressing the idea that what is good for the United States is good for Mexico, is a fallacious perspective, as are official presumptions that effectively sanction the conditions of inequality on both sides of the border.

Cultural appropriation. Cultural appropriation implies an incorporation into a group's representative structure of cultural elements arising from another matrix of signification. The group appropriating these elements makes them theirs and grants them a legitimacy equal to the elements already at work in their proper signifying matrix. What defines this process is that the appropriation works in one direction only, independent of the will of the group or the groups in which the element in question originally belongs. In this sense, border cultures can be characterized by the appropriation of linguistic, gastronomic, and culturally consumable elements, elements that once integrated into the new cultural matrices, acquire new shades of meaning and significance.

Transculturation. Transculturation, a concept in circulation since the 1940s, refers to a double or multiple process of cultural appropriation in which the interacting groups exchange cultural elements. Transculturation is inscribed within fields of unequal relations where, frequently, groups, sectors, or nations employ strategies for the imposition of their cultural models upon less powerful groups. This situation has defined many of the existing relations between Mexico and the United States.

Innovation or cultural creation. Social groups are constantly producing new cultural forms in their response to new situations or in their negotiation with their pasts. This process is necessary to life itself and refers to the dynamic of cultural processes and their condition of unfolding, neither essentialist nor fixed.

Cultural re-creation. Cultural re-creation refers to the new signification that cultural products acquire once integrated into a signifying structure different from that in which they arose. This condition involves the re-marking of such products and as such, a new codification. This situation has been particularly conspicuous in the various forms in which the defining symbology of the Mexican cultural profile have been appropriated by the Chicano population in the United States, where, for example, the Virgin of Guadalupe and other native symbols have been inscribed in new fields of signification and sociocultural controversy.

Cultural resistance. Cultural resistance is produced within social relations when the members of a group mount an active response to the attempted imposition of cultural elements belonging to another group. There are two forms of such resistance. The first is the dominant, where the members of a dominant group react against the possible influences of subaltern or ethnic minority groups or against subordinated collectives (women, youth, etc.) with the aim of impeding their proposals and the cultural expressions of such groups that could contaminate them. Among the forms of dominant resistance we can single out activities of racial supremacists or racists, ideological offensives of the groups in power against ideas with which they are not in agreement, patriarchal responses against feminism, and reactions of the "moral majority" and other conservative groups against the voices of difference (homosexuals and advocates of gender relations not corresponding with the model of the nuclear family). The second form is anti-hegemonic resistance, referring to the collective actions undertaken by groups with the aim of stemming their cultural colonization by the more powerful groups in society. Among the forms of this type of resistance are those who have given form to the so-called new social movements, such as the ethnic, national liberation, feminist, youth, sexual liberation, ecological, and movements against oppression and class exploitation, etc. These groups have created forms of anti-colonial relations that take aim against those seeking to subject or control them, such as the Mexican "Mexico-only" authentic *coletos* movement, the U.S. white supremacists, and the "English only" movement, among others.

Interpretation. The border relation involves a constant process of representation and reintroducing each other by members of the different border groups. This is a process much more complex than mere translation, or co-translation, since deterritorialization/reterritorialization not only implies translating previous conditions but also that migrants know themselves to be inscribed within new fields of signification, and, as such, in addition to having recourse to the anterior points of reference, they attempt to interpret the relevance of their cultural matrix in the new context and assess the new possibilities that conjunction offers.

Cultural transference. Cultural transference is the projection and cultural reinterpretation or transformation that takes place with the aim of establishing a correspondence between cultural elements of the new social reality and other elements arising from another situation.

Cultural interstices. Diverse cultural interstices are expressed at the border, and these are processes with their own specificities and fields of wide-ranging influence that are rooted in the condition of national adjacency between Mexico and the United States.

Inclusion/exclusion. One important cultural characteristic of the border region is the presence of processes of inclusion and exclusion stemming from identifications shaped by the regions on both sides of the border. Inclusion refers to cultural aspects out of which border processes differentiate themselves vis-à-vis the conventional Mexican and U.S. imaginary. Similarly, central and southern Mexican processes create images of what typifies the Northerners. In the north the same takes place with respect to other national groups, and something similar occurs in relation to the different characteristics of what constitutes the United States.

Trans-border spheres relate to the processes of cultural intersection that take place between the populations on both sides of the border, where sociocultural phenomena are witnessed whose characteristics are the result of the specular play of mirrors and paradoxes at work in the context of border family life and its interaction with the dominant cultures of Mexico and the United States. The notion of the border allows us to recontextualize the center-margin relationship insofar as that relationship is structured by realities more linked to the notion of centrality principally in the field of national norms. To speak from the border is to locate oneself in a field that rejects centrality since the border is defined as that which is the limit. A limit is a beginning and an end, a rupture and a continuity, an up-until-here and a beyond. To situate oneself at the border necessitates positioning oneself in spheres of coexistence marked by a transgressive presence of limits, implicated in diverse social practices and acting in distinct spheres, intersections, or cultural interstices.

Border Thresholds

From the center of Mexico and the United States, the border represents the point of intersection, displacement, and crossing, the fortunate or painful experience of return, the landmarks of the road. Within the border region itself, international thresholds are the site of flight, marked on a daily basis by inequalities, the confrontation of differences, the specular play of mirrors, a site where the diasporic experience is made concrete and is brought to a head. A field of inter- and trans-cultural relations, the border is the place where national appearances standardize regional differences and the color of one's skin hints at one's social status. At the border, language is the visible manifestation of power. There, hope faces off against the territorial nation, offering the possibilities of outwitting its police and its military, of escaping its dogs, patrols, infra-red telescopes, computers, and electronic trackers. The social nation brings with it a sense of divided affections, trans-border community networks, and common

problems separated by absurd bureaucratic reciprocal red-tape whose purported aim is to better document the comings and goings of the neighbor.

The border is a represented space where cultural heritage and memory are purified and revealed, where fragmented identities are patched together, as it were, in flight. Site of linguistic intersections, inclusive grammars that identify levels of social tolerance, parti-colored compositions, and a constant re-reading of others, the border is a sphere of open significations, a field of intensity, of barbed darts that wound whole territories and humiliate entire peoples. The border is a test-case for tolerance; an interaction with the others among us; a polychrome work that colors our complexions, much of the tenor of our voices, the differences that complement us, the eyes with which we see, the eyes that give us visibility because with them we avoid going astray. The border is the glossary of synonyms that designate us, the image bank of mirrors that reflect us, the loving or horrifying image that one day we will leave behind in order to be with the others, the others who shape us, live within us, produce us in naming us: we, the others, with whom we (co-)produce ourselves in mutual relationships and representations. The borders are the social interstices where the inclusive dimension of plurality and heterogeneity acquires its full significance in conformity with the we/the others.

Translation by Colman Hogan

Works Cited

Alcaraz, Ramón, et al. 1991. *Apuntes para la historia de la guerra entre México y los Estados Unidos*. Mexico City: CONACULTA.

Alurista. 1971 *Floricanto en Aztlán*. Los Angeles: University of California in Los Angeles.

American Me. 1992. Dir. Edward James Olmos.

Anaya, Rodolfo A. 1972. *Bless me, Ultima*. Berkeley: Quinto Sol.

Anzaldúa, Gloria. 1987 *Borderlands/La frontera: The New Mestiza*. San Francisco: Spinters.

——, ed. 1990. *Making Face, Making Soul: Creative and Critical Perspectives by Women of Color*. San Francisco: Aunt Lute Foundation.

La Balada de Gregorio Cortés. 1984. Dir. Robert Young.

La Bamba 1987. Dir. Luis Valdez.

Berumen, Humberto Félix, ed. 1996. *El cuento contemporáneo en Baja California*. Mexicali: Universidad Autónoma de Baja California/Instituto de Cultura de Baja California.

Bhabha, Homi K., ed. 1990. *Nation and Narration*. New York: Routledge.

——. 1994. *The Location of Culture*. New York: Routledge.

Blood In, Blood Out: Bound By Honor. 1993. Dir. Taylor Hackford.

The Border. 1982. Dir. Tony Richardson.

Borderline. 1980. Dir. Jerrold Freedman.

Born in East L.A. 1985. Dir. Richard "Cheech" Marín.

Break of Dawn. 1988. Dir. Isaac Artenstein.

Bringas Rábago, Nora. 1997. "El turismo fronterizo en el marco de la integración comercial con Norteamérica." *Desarrollo fronterizo y globalización*. Ed. Alejandro Mungaray and María Guadalupe García de León. Mexico City: ANVIES/UNISON. 59–76.

Bruce-Novoa, Juan. 1983. *La literatura chicana a través de sus autores*. Mexico City: Siglo XXI.

Burciaga, José Antonio. 1992. *Undocumented Love/Amor indocumentado*. San Jose: Chusma House.

Bustamante, Carlos María de. 1990. *El nuevo Bernal Díaz del Castillo, o sea historia de la invasión de los angloamericanos en México*. Mexico City: CONACULTA.

Campbell, Federico. 1987. "La frontera como espacio literario." *La Opinión* (Los Angeles): 15 January, no. 347 (section "La comunidad").

Candelaria, Cordelia. 1984. *Ojo de la Cueva*. Colorado Springs: Maize Press.

———. 1986. *Chicano Poetry: A Critical Introduction*. Wesport, CT: Greenwood Press.

Cárdenas, Gilberto. 1988. "Cultura fronteriza, cultura de frontera: Muestra de arte chicano." *Encuentros: Los festivales internacionales de la raza*. Ed. Amelia Malagamba. Mexico City; Tijuana, Baja California: El Colegio de la Frontera Norte. 91–101.

Castillo, Ana. 1994 *Massacre of the Dreamers: Essays on Xicanisima*. Albuquerque: University of New Mexico Press.

———. 1994. *Las cartas de Mixquiahuala*. Mexico City: Grijalbo.

———. 1995. *My Father Was a Toltec and Selected Poems*. New York: Norton.

Castro Leal, Antonio. 1947. "Prólogo." *Recuerdos de la invasión norteamericana (1846–1847)* by José María Roa Barcenas. Vol 1. Mexico City: Porrúa. vii–xiii.

Chabram, Angie. 1986. *Chicano Literary Criticism: Directions and Development of an Emerging Critical Discourse*. Diss. University of California, San Diego. Ann Arbor: UMI, 1988. 8705632.

Chávez, Miguel Angel, ed. 1986. "Topless." *Primer encuentro de poetas y narradores jóvenes de la frontera norte*. Mexico City: SEP/Programa Cultural de las Fronteras. 133–34.

Cisneros, Sandra. 1987. *My Wicked Wicked Ways*. Bloomington, IN: Third Woman Press.

———. 1988. *The House on Mango Street*. Houston: Arte Público Press.

———. 1992. *Woman Hollering Creek and Other Stories*. New York: Vintage Books.

———. 1994. *Loose Woman*. New York: Knopf.

Cornejo, M. Gerardo. 1977. *La sierra y el viento*. Mexico: Arte y Literaria.

Derrida, Jacques. 1973. *Speech and Phenomena and Other Essays on Husserl's Theory of Signs*. Trans. David B. Allison. Evanston: Northwestern University Press.

Desperado. 1995. Dir. Robert Rodríguez.

Díaz de Cossío, Roger, Graciela Orozco, and Esther González. 1997. *Los mexicanos en Estados Unidos*. Mexico: Sistemas Técnicos de Edición.

Díaz Guerrero, Rogelio. 1983. *Psicología del mexicano*. Mexico City: Trillas.

Espalda Mojada. 1953. Dir. Alejandro Galindo.

Flores, Juan. 1993. *Divided Borders: Essays on Puerto Rican Identity*. Houston: Arte Público Press.

Foster, Hall. 1985. *La posmodernidad*. Barcelona: Kairós.

Fregoso, Rosalinda. 1993. *The Bronze Screen: Chicana and Chicano Film Culture*. Minneapolis: University of Minnesota Press.

Fuentes, Carlos. 1995. "La raya del olvido." *La frontera de cristal: Una novela en nueve cuentos*. Mexico City: Alfaguara. 107–35.

———. 1997. "The Line of Oblivion." *The Crystal Frontier: A Novel in Nine Stories*. Trans. Alfred MacAdam. New York: Farras, Straus and Giroux. 89–113.

García Canclini, Néstor, ed. 1994. *Los nuevos espectadores: Cine, televisión y video en México*. Mexico City: IMCINE.

Gómez-Peña, Guillermo. 1996. *The New World Border: Prophecies, Poems & Loqueras for the End of the Century*. San Francisco: City Lights.

González, Ray, ed. 1992. *After Aztlan: Latino Poets of the Nineties*. Boston: Godine.

Hasta Morir [Until Death]. 1995. Screenplay Marcel Fuentes-Beráin. Dir. Fernando Sariñana.

Hayes Bautista, David. 1988. *The Burden of Support: Young Latinos in an Aging Society, U.S.A.*. Stanford: Stanford University Press.

Herrera Sobek, María.1990. *The Mexican Corrido: A Feminist Analysis*. Bloomington, IN: Indiana University Press.

INEG [Instituto Nacional de Estadística, Geografía e Informática]. 1995. Mexico City: Centro de Población y Vivienda.

El Jardín del Edén [The Garden of Eden]. 1995. Dir. María Novaro.

Joysmith, Claire, ed. 1995. *Las formas de nuestras voces: Chicana and mexicana writers in Mexico*. Mexico City: Universidad Nacional Autónoma de México.

Kanjo, Kathryn, ed. 1993. *La frontera: The border. Art about the Mexico/United States Border Experience*. San Diego: Centro Cultural de la Raza.

Langley, Lester D. 1994. *MexAmérica: Dos países, un futuro*. Mexico City: Fondo de Cultura Económica.

Limón, Graciela. 1993. *In Search of Bernabé*. Houston: Arte Público Press.

López-González, Aralia, Amelia Malagamba, and Elena Urrutia, eds. 1988. *Mujer y literatura mexicana y chicana: Culturas en contacto*. Mexico City: El Colegio de México.

Malagamba, Amelia, ed. 1988. *Encuentros: Los festivales internacionales de la raza*. Mexico City: El Colegio de la Frontera Norte/Secretaría de Educación Pública.

El Mariachi. 1993. Dir. Robert Rodríguez.

Martínez, Rubén. 1992. *The Other Side*. New York: Verso.

Méndez, Miguel. 1991. *Peregrinos de Aztlán*. Tempe: Bilingual Press.

———. 1992. *Pilgrims in Aztlán*. Trans. David William Foster. Tempe, AZ: Bilingual Press/Editorial Bilingüe.

The Milagro Beanfield War. 1988. Dir. Robert Redford.

Mi vida loca [My Crazy Life]. 1993. Dir. Allison Anders.

Montoya, Jose. 1988. "El Louie Rodríguez." *Encuentros: Los festivales internacionales de la Raza*. Ed. Amelia Malagamba. Mexico City: El Colef/SEP/CREA.

Moraga, Cherríe. 1993. *The Last Generation: Prose and Poetry*. Boston: South End Press.

Moraga, Cherríe, and Ana Castillo, eds. 1988. *Este puente mi espalda: Voces de mujeres tercermundistas en los Estados Unidos*. San Francisco: Ism Press.

Morales, Alejandro. 1991. *Reto en el paraiso*. Mexico City: Grijalbo.

My Family. 1995. Dir. Gregory Nava.

El Norte [The North]. 1983. Dir. Gregory Nava.

Paredes, Américo. 1958. *With His Pistol in His Hand: A Border Ballad and Its Hero*. Austin: University of Texas Press.

———. 1976. *A Texas-Mexican Cancionero*. Urbana: University of Illinois Press.

———. 1993. *Folklore and Culture on the Texas-Mexican Border*. Austin: CMAS Books.

Paz, Octavio. 1959. *El laberinto de la soledad*. Mexico City: Lecturas Mexicanas.

———. 1961. *The Labyrinth of Solitude: Life and Thought in Mexico*. Trans. Lysander Kemp. New York: Grove Press.

Raíces de Sangre [Blood Roots]. 1976. Dir. Jesús Traviño.

Ramírez, Santiago. 1998. *El mexicano, psicología de sus motivaciones*. Mexico City: Grijalbo.

Ramos, Samuel. 1962. *Profile of Man and Culture in Mexico*. Trans. Peter G. Earle. Austin: University of Texas Press.

Roa Barcena, José María. 1947. *Recuerdos de la invasión norteamericana (1846–1848)*. Mexico City: Porrúa.

Rosaldo, Renato. 1991. *Cultura y verdad: Nueva propuesta de análisis social*. Mexico City: Grijalbo.

Rulfo, Juan. 1982. "Passage to the North." *The Burning Plain and Other Stories*. Trans. George Schade. Austin: University of Texas Press.

———.1994 [1953]. "Paso del Norte." *El llano en llamas*. Mexico City: Fondo de Cultura Económica.

Selena. 1996. Dir. Gregory Nava.

Stand and Deliver. 1988. Dir. Ramón Menéndez.

Tabuenca Córdova, María del Socorro. 1997. "Aproximaciones críticas sobre las literaturas de frontera." *Frontera Norte* 9.18: 85–110.

Tatum, Charles M., ed. 1982. *La literatura chicana.* Mexico City: Secretaría de Educación Pública.

———. 1986. *La literatura chicana.* Mexico City: Secretaría de Educación Pública.

Ulibarri, Sabine R. 1992. *Mi abuela fumaba puros.* Mexico City: Grijalbo.

United States Department of Commerce. 1991. "Census Bureau Complete Distribution of 1990 Re-Districting Tabulations to States." *News* 11March. Washingon, DC: U.S. Department of Commerce.

Valenzuela Arce, José Manuel. 1994. "Tijuana: La recepción audiovisual en la frontera." *Los neuvos espectadores: Cine, telvisión y video en México.* Ed. Néstor García Cancline. Mexico City: IMCINE/CONACULTA. 298–329.

Vallarino, Roberto. 1986. *Primer encuentro de poetas y narradores jóvenes de la frontera norte.* Mexico City: Programa Cultural de las Fronteras.

Venegas, Daniel. 1984. *Las aventuras de Don Chipote o cuando los pericos mamen.* Mexico City: Secretaría de Educación Pública.

Villanueva, Tino, ed. 1985. *Chicanos.* Mexico City: Fondo de Cultura Económica/Secretaría de Educación Pública.

Villareal, José Javier. 1987. *Primer foro de cultura contemporánea de la frontera norte de México.* Mexico City: Secretaría de Educación Pública.

Villarreal, José Antonio. 1959. *Pocho.* New York: Doubleday.

Williams, Raymond. 1980. *Marxismo y literatura.* Barcelona: Península.

———. 1963. *The Edge of the Storm.* Trans. Ethel Brinton. Austin: University of Texas Press.

Yáñez, Agustín. 1955. *Al filo del agua.* Mexico City: Porrúa.

Zoot Suit. 1981. Dir. Luis Valdéz.

ENLIGHTENED NEIGHBORHOOD
MEXICO CITY AS A CULTURAL CENTER

Carlos Monsiváis

The Nineteenth Century:
"If God Doesn't Exist, Then Someone Else
Should Award the Certificates"

It is to Bernardo de Balbuena (1563–1627) that we owe that wonderful inventory of hierarchies and beliefs, *Grandeza Mexicana*. In it, he provides useful advice for those interested in knowledge who also sought to become citizens: One who wishes to live and not remain dumb must deal with scholars, which means dealing with people removed from the slow-witted and uncouth–countryside. Praise of the court and scorn for village life was already apparent in the first expressions of New Spain in the group that Ángel Rama (1926–1983) labeled the Lettered City, a restrictive and drastically urban group that was initially responsible for preserving a set of values–ranging from Catholicism and Greco-Roman culture to social ceremonies and the practice of writing–in areas governed by illiteracy and a hatred of knowledge, which is also fear and reverence of the unknown. Despite the Bible's warnings–much study is a weariness of the flesh–these learned men observed the maxim attributed to St. Thomas, the patron saint of libraries: Distrust the man who has but one book.

During the viceroyalty, the Lettered City was a division of the ecclesiastical authority and thus of an orthodox, verbose interpretation of the canon and scripture. The wise, erudite doctors–who drew up laws, regulations, catechisms, proclamations, decrees, lives and miracles of saints, reminiscences of the astounding barbarity of the idolatrous, interminable propaganda of the faith, and delirious, servile versions of dogma–were prepared to serve God, the king, the viceroy, the bishop, and all representatives of the hierarchies. In the capital of New Spain, never very far from the monasteries, churches, and avenues dedicated to the splendor of the most Holy and the reverent spirits who accompanied Him, the few readers there showed their respect for the civil and earthly authorities and sought to find a space for the humanities. (See **Figure 1.**) They perceived what for others was a profound mystery: the distance between ceremonial writing and the spoken word, which, according to Rama, turned the Lettered City into a notarized city, reserved for a strict minority.

Figure 1.

Eighteenth-century lithograph panorama of Mexico City, Museum of the City of Mexico. (Photograph Mario J. Valdes)

The end of the Spanish Colonial government and the creation of the Mexican Republic renewed and complicated the Lettered City, which fragmented in keeping with political predilections (which are also cultural ideas). Although numerous priests fought for independence, university doctors who abhorred change were legion. And during the early decades of the nineteenth century, the Lettered City offered a contradictory scenario *par excellence*: It still occupied much of the territory of the former ecclesiastical city, but it became liberalized, or rather, progressively secularized in its habits, giving writing and lettered knowledge an increasing autonomy. The transition from an ecclesiastical to a secular culture (during the entry into the world communities or into the century of the Lettered City) involved several elements.

- There was a transformation of the constituent principle of the Lettered City–in other words, the unconditional respect for established order–and an increasingly conspicuous presence of dissenting or revolutionary political views.

- The precarious yet inexorable dissemination of reading matter became a reality. Remember that as late as the mid-eighteenth century the Bible was exclusively reserved for priests and that in the sixteenth and seventeenth centuries female reading was frowned upon: The popular saying was that a woman who knows Latin has neither a husband nor good intentions.

- The inevitable presence in governments of members of the Lettered City meant that they formulated the new public language on the basis of legal culture. Forensic codes and discourses spiritedly complemented the influence of the Gospels. Although lawyers set the verbal tone and provided the rhetorical emphasis, it was the notaries, copyists, and bureaucrats who proved extremely useful in the promotion of multiple legal forms, the inscribed sanctification of private property, the reglementation and containment of chaos, and the creation of an atmosphere in which a chosen few decided what was legitimate and legal. To this end, it was essential to uphold (without actually saying so) the pseudo-sacramental reverence for writing.

- Rhetoric and oratory were converted into extensions or derivations of ecclesiastical discourse and sacred oratory. In the Lettered City, the range of public enunciation had precise sites–the pulpit and the tribunal–with the figures of authority also clearly indicated–the priest and the lawyer. The figures of saints and virgins and the certainty of speaking in the name of eternal salvation were missing, but the functions of the discourse were similar. And the requirement that the Lettered City maintain an aura of classical knowledge was a defense and protection against the barbarians, which led to something that is still a cultural determinant today: the separation between public and private language. The generally petrified, cabalistic nature of the former was taken as an exorcism that freed the nation from its ignorance or protected the powerful from being (mis)understood by the populace.

- There was a widespread view of the need for the prestige that artistic or literary work gives a small society. The blunt phrase "in New Spain, there are more poets than dung" describes an environment in which the awareness of being a purely local voice exacerbates the desire to differentiate oneself through writing.

- And last but not least, there was a proliferation of academies, those substitutes for brotherhoods and religious orders, with their string of literary competitions, Parthenon-inspired triumphs, unrestrained displays of verbosity, panegyrics, heroic poems, odes, sonnets, and commentaries on indispensable books written by the commentators themselves. The first twentieth-century group of this lettered legacy was the Arcadia Mexicana, whose name epitomizes the classical mania and the pompous self-satisfaction required to be able to continue believing in their literary or cultural work despite general social indifference. While these self-serving exercises were being undertaken, the Lettered City was becoming politicized; it was filled with leaflets, handbills, and gazettes, while elegant coteries (that vital word that separated the lettered elite from everyday vulgarity) were flooded with references to books that were no longer prohibited, ideas of learned humanism, and the long-postponed sermons of the Enlightenment. Literary practices, however, were relatively unaffected by this ideological fervor. Although conservatives regarded change as an apocalyptic sign, Liberals did not necessarily support change in literary matters.

Even If the World Pays Us No Heed, Countrymen, Lend Me Your Ears

The central aim of a dominant sector of the Lettered City was to put an end to the psychological and cultural marginalization of Mexicans, to emancipate themselves, according to the discourse of the time, by constructing the literary and scientific equivalent of political independence. In pursuit of these goals, it was vital to remove the Lettered City from ecclesiastical control and to provide it with its own intellectual space. The first of these new secular spaces were the literary circles or *tertulias*, inevitably dominated by exchange or attentive reciprocity–You read my work, I'll read yours–which guaranteed literature a launching pad by the simple virtue of complicity. The members of these literary gatherings read their work aloud; this was writing intended for oral performance. Members of the *tertulia* were prepared, week after week, to assess ingenuity and erudition, to enthuse over the mere challenge of a blank sheet of paper, and to heap flowery praise on dirges and alexandrines of their fellow literati. Ever since the nineteenth century, there has undoubtedly been only one Lettered City in Mexico that has asphyxiated the rest of the country by brutally monopolizing cultural offerings. The provinces simply cannot compete. There have been groups of savants in Guadalajara, Veracruz, Oaxaca, and Puebla, usually priests versed in Greco-Roman topics. There have been scholars of encyclopedic learning who have boasted of their isolation and anonymity, as well as unexpected eccentrics (fully abreast of the latest novelties from France), unknown translators of French poetry, and real or armchair travelers to the Paris of writers and *demi-mondaines*. Yet, taken as a whole, these exceptions have been insignificant. Mexico City is irresistibly attractive, with its vast public and private libraries, its centers of higher education, its bookshops, and its intellectual freedom, which would be unthinkable in the provinces.

"Lord, Do Not Deliver Us from the Academies!"

The narrow area of what is now known as the historical center of Mexico City, only a few feet away from the *Zocalo* (main square) and the schools and monasteries where members of literary groups had studied, served as a meeting place for those who had perfected the art of fluent reading and elegant writing graced with perfect spelling. The street names have changed over the centuries, but successive generations of the lettered elite continued to frequent the same places, at least until 1955 or 1960. In the august shadow of the Colleges of San Gregorio or San Ildefonso, in the streets of La Cadena and Escalerillas, or in the Portal de Mercaderes, the Portal de Agustinos in the Alameda garden, or the Colegio de Letrán, scholars and lovers of the abstruse read poems to each other, exchanged books and news of books, learned to imitate each other and to petrify thought in the course of interminable debates, bearing their erudition like a shield, and, above all, discussed everything, since only thus, by debilitating the panorama of knowledge, did they become aware of its limits and possibilities. (See **Figure 2**.) In a nineteenth-century athenaeum, it was common to prepare speeches on morals, botany, agriculture, history, *belles-lettres*, jurisprudence, geography, and industry.

Belief in culture as a forum for spiritual redemption was so strong that both before and after the Reform Wars (1831–1857), and despite the havoc wrought by politics, athenaeum gatherings accepted both Liberals and Conservatives. Beyond political affiliation, being a member of a literary society was one of the few honors available to the citizens of the new republic, their highest duty being the cultivation of the language, to whose purity the Academia de la Lengua (Academy of Languages) was devoted. Founded on 8 March 1835, its multiple aims included publishing a series of classic texts,

Figure 2.

Nineteenth-century lithograph of the Alameda in Mexico City, Museum of the City of Mexico. (Photograph Mario J. Valdes)

compiling a Spanish-American dictionary and a dictionary for indigenous texts, and studying eloquence and poetry. In addition to the Masonic lodges, which had a great deal in common with athenaeums, academies such as the Sociedad Pública de Lectura (1820; Public Society of Reading), the Instituto Nacional (1826), the Academia de San Gregorio (1829), and the Sociedad de Literatos (1831; Society of Literary Scholars) sprang up in Mexico City and to a lesser extent in other major cities such as Veracruz and Puebla. Almost unbeknownst to the rest of the city, the Atheneists studied and committed works to memory, convinced that their task was to resist the philistines and barbarians. In deference to this conviction, in June 1836, in conjunction with his brother Juan, the scholar José María Lacunza, who lodged in a small room in the Colegio de Letrán (to which young people flocked admiringly), founded the Academia de Letrán, appointing the former insurgent Andrés Quintana Roo (1787–1851) its lifelong president. Most of the "academics" were young: Guillermo Prieto (1818–1897), Manuel Carpio (1791–1860), José Joaquín Pesado (1801–1861), Fernando Calderón (1809–1845), Ignacio Rodríguez Galván (1816–1842), Manuel Eduardo de Gorostiza (1789–1851), and Ignacio Ramírez (1818–1879). And yet there was a great deal of contact between the generations in a place that Prieto describes in his classic *Memorias de mis tiempos* [Memoirs of My Times] as being rather lugubrious: a dark, dirty entrance; bare, run-down, somber interiors; a library covered

in dust; and prostitutes of great renown all around. There the enlightened held discussions, read, corrected each other's work, became excited, and discovered the genius of someone who, only seconds earlier, had praised them for their restraint or greatness. They had but a single aim: to establish the conditions of a national literature and make it flourish and to revitalize the city and the nation in the process.

And Now That You Have Everything, There Is Only One Thing Missing: The Public

What was specifically Mexican about the nascent republic? Whether they accepted it or not, members of the *tertulias* of the first half of the nineteenth century were inspired by an extremely restricted and redundant idea of nation. What was Mexican was everything that Mexicans accepted as such, while an independent literature was the literature that incorporated the desires, concerns, and vehemence of those determined to write despite living in a large city that was not a metropolis. In short, what was Mexican was a blend of habit and social dreams, and for this reason, the Lettered City was characterized by its refusal to be affected by reality. One way of keeping the real city at bay was to demonize its inhabitants, the clods, as Carlos de Sigüenza y Góngora (1645–1700) did at the end of the seventeenth century. To him the rabble was beneath contempt. Like most of the lettered elite of this time, the rabble was identified by mixing ethnic indicators and class distinctions: Amerindians, Africans, Moors, and *mestizos* of all of the above and also what today would be called "white trash" to characterize the Spaniards from the lower levels of society, whom he considered to be the most despicable of all. I have no desire to settle accounts with the elitists of other centuries. I merely wish to point out their deep-seated hatred of what, in their view, was a degraded reality, found in the popular sectors, the Indian neighborhoods, and the craftsmen's districts. If the Lettered City was geographically restricted, it was partly to prevent it from being overwhelmed by the fetid, aggressive persistence of failure. Then, as now, circumscribing oneself olfactorily and visually ensured that taste was preserved.

Did the literature compensate writers for the misfortune of realizing that the other, the popular, city also exists? Yes and no. Writers and scholars were aware of the comparative advantages of participation, yet misery and relentless squalor reminded them of their everyday condition: They lived on the edges of the world and would never be read by the authors they venerated. The national literature they sought to influence had merely taken a first timid step toward world recognition. And poverty was identified with tragic destiny. In the words of poet Ignacio Rodríguez Galván, a Letrán academic, "Avaricia, no amor, el mundo rige/a quien la suerte vacilante aflije./Yo, que entre harapos trémulos nací, 'Te amo', le dije a la mujer. Revuelta,/Ella responde con la espalda vuelta:/'¡Mendigo, huye de aquí!'" ("Amor" 166) ("Greed, not love, rules the world/of those afflicted by irresolute destiny./I, who was born amid trembling rags/'I love you,' I said to the woman. Annoyed,/With her back turned, she replied:/'Beggar, get thee hence!'").

Atheism as Faith in the Unknown

Members of the Academia de Letrán wrote to establish themselves in their own eyes, held discussions to certify the existence of their ideas, lived in the humility of the periphery, and regarded themselves (with or without that name) as precursors.

This is why the act of provocation was so important to them, and it was the origin of the legend that the Academia de Letrán was a milestone in Mexico's intellectual life. In *Memorias de mis tiempos*, Prieto enthusiastically refers to an episode that took place in 1837. A young man, eighteen or twenty years old, looking shabby and dejected, entered the Academia de Letrán, that bastion of young men brought up on church culture:

> Ramírez sacó del bolsillo del costado, un puño de papeles de todos tamaños y colores; algunos, impresos por un lado, otros en tiras como recortes de moldes de vestido, y avisos de toros o de teatro. Arregló aquella baraja y leyó con voz segura e insolente el título, que decía: No hay Dios.
>
> El estallido inesperado de una bomba, la aparición de un monstruo, el durrumbe estrepitoso del techo, no hubieran producido mayor conmoción.
>
> Se levantó un clamor rabioso que se disolvió en altercados y disputas.
>
> Ramírez veía todo aquello con despreciativa inmovilidad. El Sr. Iturralde, Rector del Colegio, dijo: Yo no puedo permitir que aquí se lea eso; es un establecimiento de educación. (189–90)

> Ramírez drew a handful of papers of various sizes and colors out of his side pocket. Some were printed on one side, others were strips like cuttings from dress patterns, with theater or bullfight announcements. Carefully arranging this motley assortment of papers, in a confident, insolent voice, he read the title, which said: God does not exist.
>
> Neither the unexpected explosion of a bomb, nor the appearance of a monster, nor the deafening collapse of a roof could have created greater commotion. A furious uproar arose, which degenerated into squabbles and arguments. Ramírez regarded the scene with scornful detachment.
>
> Iturralde, the Dean of the College, said: "I cannot allow that to be read here; this is an educational establishment."

From the outset, Ignacio Ramírez (1818–1879) represented the modern spirit, which, according to Cyril Connolly (1903–1974), combines intellectual qualities inherited from the Enlightenment—lucidity, irony, skepticism, and intellectual curiosity—and the passionate intensity and exalted sensitivity of the Romantics, their rebellion and sense of technical experiment, and their awareness of living in a tragic era. And Ramírez was profoundly modern, by virtue of rigorously examining this inherited tradition of which he was inevitably a product. (He was born in 1818 in Guanajuato and studied at a seminary. A generation earlier, he would have wasted his talent, becoming embittered, but the Revolution of Independence [1810–1821] offered him alternatives.)

Because of the need to live differently, Ramírez spread the belief that he dared not say his name aloud. Thus, atheism did not mean indifference to or scorn of the images of eternal life but instead reflected a bellicose certainty: In republican society, moral standards would emerge from civilized consensus rather than from an absolute certainty that negotiates salvation with the Church on an everyday basis. Atheism and agnosticism were also alternative ways of experiencing the city. In nineteenth-century Latin America, a declared atheist was someone who, in the face of overwhelming prejudice, used moral concern as a means of civil training. Ramírez had a basic revolutionary thesis: God does not exist. The corollary was that humans and the natural world had their own biological and evolutionary development. This was stated not in Europe but rather in what has been characterized as an unenlightened, backward society, fanaticized by the secular empire of Spain. In Mexico at this time, this was a war cry against the institutional concept of God repeated from every pulpit and in every classroom on the authority of the infallible, divinely guided Roman Catholic Church. Reflective Mexicans shuddered in a foreboding of a social revolution that would shake up the still-intact old Colonial social structure and change Mexico forever.

In the nineteenth century, in cities barely worthy of the name or in the still-small Mexico City, clerics and members of the bourgeoisie publicly sought divine protection, for this is what distinguished them from the rabble. As Lucien Fèvre has shown in his magnificent analysis of Rabelais and sixteenth-century agnostic sentiment, the unthinkability of atheism formed part of social existence; it was an incontrovertible fact. Thus, the blunt statement "God does not exist" not only allows one to imply, through one individual, all those who share his attitude without daring to express it but, fundamentally, also draws us closer to the preamble to an urban culture through whose protective covering of inhibitions daring suddenly filtered. On its own, Ramírez's "God does not exist," still heretical in 1948, as Diego Rivera realized when he included it in his mural *Un domingo en la Alameda* [A Sunday in the Alameda Garden], only to erase it following a great political scandal, shows the mentality that emerges from Romirez's readings and from the reading of the city itself; add to this the fact that he had enough boldness to say what he thought. If, in 1837, the city was still subject to clerical influence and was governed by the oppressive megalomania of an elite class, then one can understand Ramírez's urban prophecy, which very possibly (what is unprovable is not necessarily inconceivable) also derives from the contemplation of the real city where lay life—lusty, wolfish, crafty, repressive, and religious at certain times—that was beginning to mature and become stronger. Ramírez merely commented on what was already true: that society no longer felt the fear of God that resulted in obedience toward the clergy and fear for enunciating the legitimacy of legal acts that were in accord with the clergy.

The Academia de Letrán was far more (and far less) than the triumphal appearance of Ignacio Ramírez. During its twenty years of existence, it mixed Liberals and Conservatives, disseminated poetry and rhetoric, and permitted exalted sessions and sessions of exhausting, bloodless knowledge. And in the small and, in some ways, marginalized city, the learned allowed themselves to be seen on avenues, in cafés and libraries, in spacious residences where their soirées were graced with works of art and the obligatory piano, and in theaters where hierarchies were as rigidly observed as in any viceregal court or religious procession. As persons with political lives, members of the Academia de Letrán fought, denounced, went into exile, and rebuked the authorities. As fellows of the Lettered City, they relied on readings, exchanges, admiration, and one certainty: that they were the beginning of a national literature. In order to reconcile opposites, they idealized the city as the seat of the Spirit and fraternal souls, and they regarded the real city as an inevitable nightmare. In 1836, the Academia de Letrán, which a few years earlier would have been a brotherhood, represented the eruption of religious temperaments in search of lay pulpits, of priests without churches, of priests with Latin but without mass, and of intellectuals and writers with few newspapers at their disposal, with no publishing industry and with a university reduced to the bare minimum. Together they constituted the first cultural public at their disposal: themselves. Oh valiant men, you loved your literary efforts unreservedly, only to prepare them for the oblivion of the coming generations!

The Restored Republic and the Dictatorship of Porfirio Díaz: If They Regard Us as Peripheral, Then Let Us Plagiarize the Soul of the Metropolises

In 1867 the triumph of the Liberals, together with the execution of the unsuccessful emperor Maximilian and the Conservative exodus, led to the proclamation of the Republic and the creation of a short-lived utopian dream of a nation free from internal strife and with no other aim save the consecration of humanism. And without anyone saying it in so many words, that nation was understood to be Mexico City, the only place with a guarantee of even minimal freedoms and a concentration of libraries and *tertulias* in a secular space. Achieving the utopian dream required issuing a call to unity and eliminating ideological enmities. A proven Liberal writer, Ignacio Manuel Altamirano (1834–1893), assumed responsibility for this task and called for reconciliation. His analysis explained the cultural backwardness as caused by "los huracanes de la guerra" ("the hurricanes of war"): "Era natural: todos los espíritus estaban bajo la influencia de las preocupaciones políticas, apenas había familia o individuo que no participase de la conmoción que agitaba a la nación entera, y en semejantes circunstancias, cómo consagrarse a las profundas tareas de la investigación histórica o a los blandos recreos de la poesía, que exigen un ánimo tranquilo y una conciencia desahogada y libre?" (*Renacimiento* 3) ("It was natural: All the leading writers were under the influence of political concerns. Hardly any family or individual had not taken part in the upheaval that shook the entire nation, and under these circumstances, how could one possibly devote oneself to the profound task of historical research or the gentle pursuit of poetry, which requires a calm spirit and a clear conscience?").

Altamirano called for national reconciliation between Liberals and Conservatives and between Classicists and Romantics, as well as between the supporters of Juárez and Maximilian. The aim was to counter the accusations of French writers who had labeled Mexico barbaric because of the defeat, capture, and execution of Maximilian and thereby to defend the honor of Mexico against such defamation. To this end, he published the journal *El Renacimiento*, creating a neutral territory, a kind of lay church open to all members of the Mexican family. Having demilitarized culture, he then proceeded to delimit the Lettered City, whose sphere of influence was regarded as transcending all party divisions. But within a few years, de-ideologization would give way to verbose, political, and disingenuous tributes to the dictator, Porfirio Díaz. There was no alternative; it was the unavoidable cost of the continued existence of the Lettered City.

The Porfirian City and the Republic of Letters

After the restored Republic (1867–1876), the cultural symbols of Juarez's Liberalism remained isolated in the city. They were respected writers without following, venerated names no longer relevant: Ignacio Ramírez, Ignacio Manuel Altamirano, Juan A. Mateos (1831–1913), Vicente Riva Palacio (1832–1896), and, above all, Guillermo Prieto, who had earned the affection of the multitudes and the esteem of the elite. No one challenged the priestly nature of the great Liberal writers, so typical of the Lettered City, according to Ángel Rama. They had succeeded in imposing their vision of a nation, maintaining the centrality of art and literature, and revitalizing a society that was fully aware of its marginality in the world. In the following generation, that of *modernista* poets supported by musicians and artists, the Liberals' "priestly" duties to culture were turned into the *modernista* hedonism of the "prophets of sensations." And it was the poets who revealed to all the great importance of a city that boasted such great talent. (Without this belief, society would have been even more wretched.) It was the era of an alternative religion of sentiments–through music and literature.

During the years of Porfirio Díaz's dictatorship (1876–1911, with a gap of four years), cultural life concentrated on celebrating the literati, particularly poets. They were the privileged *par excellence*, since poetry was the genre of genres, the only spiritual asset that, with its partial truths and heightened emotion, could be shared by civil servants, clerics, housewives, students, and professionals alike; even the illiterate were fond of oral performance. At literary evenings, at historical commemorations, at inaugurations of monuments, and on great occasions, poets read or declaimed from memory, electrifying their audiences. As part of the division of labor of this growing city, poetry was entrusted with the society's sensibility, in short, its spiritual dimension. Hence, in the city, poets were acknowledged as living monuments, signs of the greatness of language, who democratically conversed, walked through the streets, and read their work at special ceremonies. When a celebrated poet arrived in the city, the multitudes poured into the streets, cheering wildly and noisily proclaiming their faith in the power of a spiritual life outside the Church. The devotion to European culture, especially French, made the Mexican imitation of Parisian society a school of manners. For the upper classes, manners were to be based on those of Paris, since what was French was a sign of distinction, and its imitation demonstrated that living in Mexico was no obstacle to achieving class and refinement. Everything that was highly valued came from Paris: clothes, fashion, architecture, solemnity on the proscenium and in court, flower arrangement styles, the proper comportment for salons, fencing masters, and readings. A considerable number of writers were anxious to live in Mexico as if in Paris, and this sensation of bifurcation (belonging to two cities or making the city where one lives disappear through a utopian shift) culminated in the sense of "always being somewhere else." Rubén Darío (1867–1916) summed it up: "Mi esposa es de mi tierra, mi querida de París" ("My wife is from my country, my mistress from Paris"). And Manuel Gutiérrez Nájera (1859–1895), in the famous poem "La Duquesa Job" (1884), referred to the comings and goings of cultural fashion in the city:

> No tiene alhajas mi duquesita
> pero es tan guapa y es tan bonita
> y tiene un cuerpo tan *v'lan*, tan *pschutt*,
> de tal manera trasciende a Francia
> que no la igualan en elegancia
> Ni las clientas de Héléne Kossut.
> Desde las puertas de la Sorpresa
> hasta la esquina del Jockey Club,
> no hay española, yanqui o francesa,
> Ni más bonita, ni más traviesa
> que la duquesa del Duque Job.

> My little duchess has no jewels,
> but she is so pretty and so attractive
> and has such a v'lan, pschutt figure
> that so transcends France
> that none of Hélène Kossut's clients
> are even half as elegant.
> From the doors of La Sorpresa
> to the corner of the Jockey Club,

no Spanish, Yankee or French girl
is prettier or naughtier
than the duchess of Duke Job.

(19–23)

Keeping up to date with the latest magazines, poetry, and polemics and living mentally in Paris were a way to redeem oneself by resorting to an imaginative geography of admiration. In its ingenuous way, the cultural city crossed the Atlantic, and its arrival was well publicized. It was only through internal exile and one's psychological accommodation to the City of Light (a title passionately applied) that one could withstand the peripheral city, with its Paseo de la Reforma, so rank in parts, and its ignorance of the Symbolists. If writers and painters failed to enter a Parisian environment, they had to accept the fact that they were still in Mexico. The most destructive sedentary attitude was that of those who did not travel through the imagination. In *Impresiones y recuerdos* (1893), Federico Gamboa (1864–1939) describes the feeling of having arrived: "Y para mi coleto exclamé lo que D'Amicis al pisar Madrid:/¿Qué bien habré hecho en mi vida que Dios me permite conocer París?" (197) ("And I said to myself, as D'Amicis did when he first set foot in Madrid,/'What good must I have done for God to allow me to visit Paris?").

A bitter, distant cultural bureaucracy also emerged, dedicated to the care of institutions and excessive deference for respectability. Following the chaos of the civil wars and the despised figure of Antonio López de Santa Anna, "His Most Serene Highness" Don Porfirio called for stability, while the Porfirian social caste firmly established itself statutorily and received the tribute that its greatness warranted: It was then the city of living sculptural groups.

"Let Them Toast Europe/Since Their Fondness for Foreign Things Is Exquisite"

By the first decade of the *Porfiriato* (1876–1886), Mexico City possessed an undeniable wealth of talent, opportunity, stimulating atmosphere, cultural institutions, and brilliant coteries of legendary ability. The provinces had their share of scholars and savants, seminars with an excellent level in the humanities, eccentric creators, and poets deeply attached to their locality. Yet the capital was the only cultural center. During this period, priestly functions were undertaken by government officials, civil servant–writers, national glories of erudition, members of Language Academies, historians, and scholars. The most outstanding figure was don Justo Sierra (1848–1912): poet, historian, short-story writer, Minister of Public Education, and distinguished prose writer. The missionary zeal of this elite did not extend very far. It was not concerned with abolishing illiteracy; it admired the dictator and happily adjusted to its status as the proud emblem of knowledge amidst an unlettered environment. In politics, the most exalted cultural group was that of the former Comtean positivists, now "Los Científicos" ["The Scientists"]; this group around Porfirio Díaz was possessed by a "sense of breeding" that led them to scorn the pursuit of arts and letters and insist on the advantages of scientific reality (technical modernization) over lies and falsity (philosophy).

In contrast to the previous Liberal decade and despite its continued keen awareness of poetry, the city barely registered culture. Bohemians were responsible for most of the legends and mythical spaces, but institutional culture determined fame and positions in the hierarchy. One characteristic

Figure 3.

Song book cover José Guadalupe Pasada depicting the modernity of the railroad c. 1900.

of the *Porfiriato* was the weakness of the cultural environment; however, the strategy employed for its expansion was to regard it as already magnificent. Without this conscious adoption of "make believe," the country would have been unable to withstand the paucity of publications (most of the important books were published in Paris and Barcelona), the plethora of quarrels and resentments, the precariousness of state patronage, and the lack of readers. How did it manage to offset the distance of the metropolises? It did so through literary evenings attended by the Three Powers (the state, the Church, and the law school), through the admiration that transformed famous poets into para-religious institutions, and with readings as acts of consecration. And the cultural city developed around two formative institutions: the Escuela Nacional Preparatoria [National Preparatory School] in San Ildefonso and the School of Law. In *Pasado inmediato* [1941; Immediate Past], Alfonso Reyes (1899–1959) describes the Escuela Preparatoria in 1916 as "*alma mater* de tantas generaciones, que dio una fisonomía nueva al país; puesta después de la enseñanza primaria y antes de la profesional o especial, semejante en parte al bachillerato francés, y con un programa enciclopédico que recorría, peldaño a peldaño, la escala comtiana, desde la matemática abstracta y pura hasta las complejas lucubraciones sociales" (13) ("alma mater of so many generations, which changed the face of the country, inserted between secondary school and professional or training school, somewhat similar to the French Baccalauréat and comprising an encyclopedic program that climbed the Comtean ladder, step by step, from pure, abstract mathematics to complex social lucubrations").

The massive scale of the Escuela Preparatoria of today tends to obscure its former functions as an essential institution in the curriculum of all cultured men of the time. As Reyes notes, "[La preparatoria] no tenía por objeto el conducir a la carrera y a los títulos, aunque fuera puente indispensable para los estudios de abogados, ingenieros y médicos; sino el preparar ciudadanos -de ahí su nombre; gente apta para servir a la sociedad en los órdenes no profesionales. Sustituía a las humanidades eclesiásticas; llegaba a punto" (13) ("The aim of (La Preparatoria) was not to lead to a degree and qualifications, although it served as an essential bridge for the studies of lawyers, engineers, and physicians, but rather to prepare citizens, hence its name; people who would be able to serve society in the non-professional orders. It replaced ecclesiastical humanities, and it came at just the right moment"). And in the Lettered City, the School of Law served as the School of Humanities, the only one available.

"Only One Toast Was Missing: That of Arturo, the Pure Bohemian"

Live the city, counter the crass surrounding materialism, counter the ignorance of those who were stubbornly monolingual. While some acted like "Plenipotentiary Ambassadors of Academia," others swelled the ranks of the Bohemians, delighting in excess in the "sanctuaries of the muses." In *La bohemia de la muerte* [1929; The Bohemia of Death], Julio Sesto (1879–1960) chronicles the lives of certain *modernista* poets and their circle of musicians, painters, sculptors, and engravers. Their repertoire was predictable: absinthe, cigarettes, "incestuous" love for death (that frozen metaphor), esoteric tastes, worship of the night (the hours of imaginative splendor, gifts of inspiration, and pleasant company), venereal diseases, alcoholic self-destruction, and the depiction of prostitutes as the guardian angels of a poetry that is indifferent to what people might say. The Bohemians exalted sin, evil, and even atheism. In the words of Gutiérrez Nájera:

No moriré del todo, amiga mia.
De mi ondulante espíritu disperso
algo en la urna diáfana del verso
piadosa guardará la poesía.

I shall not completely die, my friend.
Of my undulating, scattered spirit,
Poetry will preserve something
in the diaphanous urn of verse.

(301)

The person who best described the urban experiences of marginalized poetry was a turn-of-the-century journalist, Guillermo Aguirre y Fierro (1887–1949). His poem *El brindis del Bohemio* [1928; The Bohemian's Toast], until recently a sanctuary of oral transmission in popular memory, provides a simple view of those who "live poetically":

En torno de una mesa de cantina,
una noche de invierno,
regocijadamente departían

seis alegres bohemios.
El eco de sus risas se escapaban
y de aquel barrio quieto
iban a interrumpir el imponente
y profundo silencio.
Sitting round a saloon bar table,
one winter's night,
six cheerful Bohemians
were happily conversing.
The echo of their laughter escaped
and from that calm neighborhood
interrupted the profound,
imposing silence.

(3)

Bohemia was that unfettered joy that continued to exist in the capital, which, in spite of it all, remained provincial. And journalism complemented and enhanced its nocturnal fervor. No writer and virtually no artist were able to avoid working for the press, either full-time or through the regular delivery of articles, poems, and drawings. A distinctive feature of the city, journalists ("galley slaves of the pen") were the network that linked the literate minorities to their exaggerated notion of importance to society (which gradually became a source of pride). By believing in the recognition afforded by the press, these artists valued their everyday life more because it was now a fact; it was in the newspaper. And it was this puffed-up newsworthiness that partially offset the limitations of living in a peripheral country.

The Ateneo de la Juventud

Virtually all the members of the most important literary and philosophical group in the Porfiriato–the Ateneo de la Juventud–were graduates of the School of Law. Its members– among others, Alfonso Reyes, José Vasconcelos (1881–1959), Martín Luis Guzmán (1887–1977), Pedro Henríquez Ureña (1884–1946), Julio Torri (1889–1970), Antonio Caso (1883–1946), Jesús T. Acevedo (1882–1918), Carlos González Peña (1885–1955), Rafael López (1875–1943), and Alfonso Cravioto (1884–1955)–observed the cultural deficiencies of the *modernista* poets, mocked the limitations of petrified academics, moderately opposed the positivist "Científicos," and, for literary reasons, brought the city an unexpected protest march. As Reyes notes in *Pasado inmediato*:

La manifestación en memoria de Guitiérrez Nájara. Por 1907, un oscuro aficionado quiso resucitar la *Revista azul* de Guitiérrez Nájera, para atacar precisamente las libertades de la poesía que proceden de Guitiérrez Nájera. No lo consentimos. El reto era franco, y lo aceptamos. Alzamos por las calles la bandera del arte libre. Trajimos bandas de música. Congregamos en la Alameda a la gente universitaria; los estudiantes acudieron en masa. Se dijeron versos y arengas desde el kiosco público. Por primera vez se vio desfilar a una juventud clamando por los fueros de la belleza, y dispuesta a defenderlos hasta con los puños. Ridiculizamos al mentecato que quería combatirnos, y enterramos con él a varias momias que andaban por ahí haciendo figura de hombres. Por la noche, en una velada. Urueta nos prestó sus mejores dardos y nos llamó "buenos hijos de Grecia." La *Revista Azul* pudo continuar su sueño inviolado. No nos dejamos arrebatar la enseña, y la gente aprendió a respetarnos. (49)

The manifestation in honor of Gutiérrez Nájera. About 1907, an obscure follower wished to revive Gutiérrez Nájera's *Revista Azul* precisely to attack the poetic freedoms originated by Gutiérrez

Nájera. We refused to allow it. It was an overt challenge, and we accepted it as such. We paraded the banner of free art through the city. We brought in musical bands. We drew university students to the Alameda; students came in droves. They recited poetry and speeches from the bandstand. For the first time ever, we saw young people clamoring for the privileges of beauty and prepared to defend it with their fists. The *Revista Azul* was able to preserve its dream intact. We did not allow our ensign to be torn away from us, and people began to respect us.

All this politicization around the name of a journal was a little strange, to say the least. And the clamor for "the privileges of beauty" had already repeatedly gone up for the exaltation of the poets. But this is how its primary role was perceived by an elite, happy to revive the city through, for example, homages to the positivist Gabino Barreda (1818–1881), the founder of the Escuela Preparatoria. In 1909, this homage, according to Reyes, was "la primera señal patente de una conciencia pública emancipada del régimen. . . . En el orden teórico, no es inexacto decir que allí amanecía la Revolución" (1941, 51) ("the first overt sign of a public awareness that had been emancipated from the regime. . . . In theory it was not inaccurate to say that that was where the Revolution had its beginnings"). Although this may be somewhat inaccurate, it is safe to say that one of the origins of the educational doctrine of the Revolution was the fact that the thirst for knowledge among small groups grew in direct proportion to the scarcity of opportunities. In the extraordinary correspondence between Reyes and Henríquez Ureña, the latter complained of the poverty of the city's library stock (9 February 1909):

¡Pero las cosas que suceden en estas bibliotecas! El sábado pensé aprovecharlo y despacharme los poetas italianos: fui a la Nacional y pedí unos líricos que había usado, y no los encontraron ni en su lugar ni en donde los ponen provisionalmente; pedí un tomo de Rivadeneyra, y no me lo dieron "porque habían sacado esos libros para revisarlos" pedí otro, y no se sabía por qué no se encontraba en el lugar en que estaba señalado. Al fin me dieron unos líricos italianos del siglo XVIII, muy malos, en quienes no encontré nada; la gente más importante allí eran Onofrio Minzoni e Innocenzio Frugoni, gentes cuyos nombres sabía por algunas traducciones de los seudoclásicos gachupines; tal para cual. Salí de ahí rumbo a la Jurisprudencia, y ahora se les ocurrió disponer que para el resto de las vacaciones no se abra sino de 9 a 12. Me dirijo a Preparatoria, pido líricos españoles, ¡y los tenía Urbina! La mayoría de los libros no se sabe allí donde están. Ese día reprimí la ira. (136–37)

You would never believe what goes on in these libraries! On Saturday, I thought I would take advantage of the day and finish off the Italian poets: I went to the National Library and asked for some lyrical poets I had used, but they couldn't find them where they were supposed to be or where they are kept provisionally. I asked for a volume of Rivadeneyra, which they did not give me "because they had taken out those books to check them." I asked for another one and they could not find it because it wasn't in the right place. Finally, they gave me some dreadful eighteenth-century Italian lyrical poets, in whom I could find nothing. The most important poets they had were Onofrio Minzoni and Innocenzio Frugoni, people whose names I knew from translations by Spanish pseudo-classicists–birds of a feather, so to speak. I walked out of there on my way to the School of Law, where it seems they have just decided to open from 9 to 12 during the holidays. I made my way to the Escuela Preparatoria and asked for Spanish lyrical poets, only to find that Luis Urbina had taken them out! They don't know where most of the books are. That day, I had to control my anger.

The City of the Revolution

The great political commotion, which has come to be called the Mexican Revolution (as an umbrella term for very different phenomena and movements and whose most intense stage took place between 1910 and 1930), typically and obviously had a profound effect on the cultural center. The group of the Ateneo de la Juventud was primarily divided between the advocates of change and those who supported Porfirio Díaz's reelection. (A minority were stubbornly Conservative.) And several of the finest wished to have nothing to do with the political life of the city, which furiously displaced all other forms of life there. About 1910, the capital decided to eliminate everything that was superfluous, which included the bookish, educated world, indifferent to political contingencies. Alfonso Reyes, son of the politician don Bernardo, one of the presumptive heirs to Porfirio Díaz, wrote to Henríquez Ureña on 6 May 1911: "Quisiera salirme de México para siempre: aquí corro riesgo de hacer lo que no debe ser el objeto de mi vida. Como no tengo entusiasmos juveniles por las cosas épicas y políticas, ni la intervención *yankee,* ni los conflictos me seducen gran cosa. Preferiría escribir y leer en paz y con desahogo. . . . De la ciudad nada tengo que contarte: nada sucede aquí en tu ausencia" (169) ("I would like to leave Mexico forever: Here I run the risk of making the object of my life what should not be. Since I lack youthful enthusiasm for epic adventures and political matters, I find neither Yankee intervention nor conflicts particularly attractive. I prefer to write and read in peace and at ease. . . . I have nothing of any significance to tell you about the city: Nothing has happened here in your absence").

See what Reyes then said on the eve of the triumph of the Revolution, when the city was in an uproar, in the midst of conspiracies and detentions. A month later, on June 6, don Alfonso continued his complaint: "He tenido más contrariedades de lo que puedes suponer. Los disturbios de México han llegado a molestar la vida privada de las gentes" (179) ("I have had more setbacks than you can imagine. The disturbances in Mexico have now upset people's private lives"). And yet, with extraordinary spirit, Reyes continued to be absorbed by his life of books and libraries. Other writers were brazenly apocalyptic. In the second series of *Mi diario,* in the entry for 26 May 1911, Federico Gamboa (1864–1939) feels sorry for himself with the perverse delight of a civilized man under threat of a barbarian invasion:

El servicio telegráfico de la prensa de aquí, me da la noticia: anteayer presentó el General Díaz su renuncia ante la Cámara de Diputados, que se admitió, menos un solo voto, por inverosímil mayoría absoluta!!!. . . ¡Parece mentira lo uno y lo otro!

En la misma noche, después de manifestaciones callejeras befatorias y canallescas, la salida rumbo a Veracruz del gran patriota y su familia, una salida con vagos perfiles de fuga, la ciudad en tumulto, las turbas plebeyas, escandalizando impunemente. Y en la vía del ferrocarril, el asalto a mano armada al tren que se lleva al caído. . . ¿Triste fin de presidenciada tan grande? ¿Nos amenazará la anarquía, la intervención yanqui tal vez, lo negro, lo pavoroso, lo horrrible?

¡Ah! Las siete Vacas Flacas de la Escritura se acercan bramando, a la zaga de las Siete Vacas Gordas que huyen despavoridas a hundirse en el vacío y en el recuerdo. Es la ley, la ley inmutable de la acción y la reacción, que por igual visita a los individuos que a los pueblos. ¿Qué será del país? . . . Y de tejas muy abajo, ¿qué será de mí? (376)

The telegraphic service of the press here gave me the news: The day before yesterday, General Díaz tendered his resignation to the Chamber of Deputies, which granted it to him, with the exception of one vote, by an unbelievable absolute majority!. . . Both things seem incredible.

That same night, following despicable, jeering street demonstrations, the great patriot and his family left for Veracruz, as though escaping, with the city in tumult and the plebeian masses making a fuss with impunity. And on the railway, armed assault on the train bearing away the fallen man. . . . A sad end to such a great presidential administration? Will we be threatened by anarchy, Yankee intervention, black, awful, and horrible things?

Oh! The Seven Thin Cows of the Scriptures approached bellowing, following the Seven Fat Cows, which fled terrified into the vacuum and into memory. Is it the law, the immutable law of action and reaction, which visits individuals and peoples alike? And what will happen to the country? . . .what will become of me?

In his reactionary sincerity, and in his undisguised hatred of the masses, Gamboa depicts a Lettered City that had grown frenetic at the collapse of the basis of its support and was convinced that the end of the world as it knew it was upon it. After a few months, the majority of known writers and intellectuals joined the relentless criticism of the Revolution and the government of Francisco I. Madero. All this took place amid the abrupt interruption of the usual offerings, such as theater, literary evenings, and the confident meeting of literary groups. Only a handful managed to continue working systematically: "Antonio Caso domina el panorama de México hasta el regreso de José Vasconcelos" (Reyes 1941, 58) ("Antonio Caso dominated the intellectual panorama of Mexico until the return of José Vasconcelos"). According to Reyes, the changes produced by the fall of the regime paved the way for action in other fields. As he writes in *Pasado inmediato*:

El 13 de diciembre de 1912, fundamos la Universidad Popular, escuadra volante que iba a buscar al pueblo en sus talleres y en sus centros, para llevar, a quienes no podían costearse estudios superiores ni tenían tiempo de concurrir a las escuelas, aquellos conocimientos ya indispensables que no cabían, sim embargo, en los programas de las primarias. Los periódicos nos ayudaron. Varias empresas nos ofrecieron auxilios. Nos obligamos a no recibir subsidios del Gobierno. . . . El escudo de la Universidad Popular tenía por lema una frase de Justo Sierra: "La Ciencia protege a la patria." (59–60)

On 13 December 1912, we founded the Universidad Popular, a flying squad that set out in search of the people in their workshops and centers to take to those who were unable to afford higher studies nor attend schools, the indispensable knowledge for which, however, there was no room in primary school curricula. The newspapers helped us. Several companies offered us assistance. We forced ourselves not to receive subsidies from the government. . . .The motto of the coat of arms of the Universidad Popular contained a phrase by Justo Sierra: "Science protects the Fatherland."

Writers who supported the dictatorship of Victoriano Huerta, who murdered President Madero and his vice-president, José María Pino Suárez, were legion. Among them were Enrique González Martínez (1871–1952), Salvador Díaz Mirón (1853–1928; perhaps the most servile), José Juan Tablada (1871–1945), and Federico Gamboa. Vasconcelos and Martín Luis Guzmán intervened briefly on the side of Villa. Yet despite this, in November and December 1913, in the bookshop owned by don Francisco Gamoneda, Antonio Caso and Henríquez Ureña organized a series of lectures whose titles

give some idea of the resistance to the totalizing significance of the Revolution. The repertoire of talks included "La literatura mexicana" [Mexican Literature] by Luis G. Urbina (1868–1934), "Filosofía de la intuición" [The Philosophy of Intuition] by Antonio Caso, "Don Juan Ruiz de Alarcón" by Pedro Henríquez Ureña, "Música popular Mexicana" [Popular Mexican Music] by Manuel M. Ponce (1882–1948), and "Novela Mexicana" [The Mexican Novel] by Federico Gamboa. Reyes, who had left for Europe three months earlier, notes, "Parece increíble, en efecto, que en aquellos días aciagos, Antonio Castro Leal escribiera revistas teatrales en pro de la *Cándida*, de Bernard Shaw, y que hubiera representaciones de Wilde; que el Marqués de San Francisco tuviera la calma de continuar sus investigaciones sobre la miniatura de México; o Julio Torri aprovechara el fuego mismo del incendio para armar sus trascendentales castillos de artificio" (1941, 63) ("It seems incredible that, during those fateful days, Antonio Castro Leal should have written theater reviews supporting Bernard Shaw's *Candida* and that Wilde's plays should have been performed; that the Marquis of San Francisco should have been able to continue his research on miniatures in Mexico; or that Julio Torri should have taken advantage of the heat of the conflagration to build his momentous mock castles").

The Mexico of Whose Existence We Were Unaware

In an essay published in 1927 and called "1915," Manuel Gómez Morín (1897–1972), the intellectual who, in 1939, founded the National Action Party (PAN), which concentrated the middle-class right, describes the impressions of the conservative elite during the Revolution and the shift from helplessness to mythology:

En el inolvidable curso de Estética de Altos Estudios y en las conferencias sobre el Cristianismo en la Universidad Popular, estaban (Enrique) González Martínez y Saturnino Herrán y Ramón López Velarde y otros más jóvenes. Todos llevados allí por el mismo impulso.

En esos días, Caso labraba su obra de maestro abriendo ventanas espirituales, imponiendo la supremacía del pensamiento, y con ese anticipo de visión propia del arte, en tono con las más hondas corrientes del momento, González Martínez recordaba el místico sentido profundo de la vida, Herrán pintaba a México, López Velarde cantaba un México que todos ignorábamos viviendo en él. (Gómez Morín 19–20)

The unforgettable Advanced Studies course on Aesthetics and the lectures on Christianity at the Universidad Popular were attended by Enrique González Martínez, Saturnino Herrán, and Ramón López Velarde, as well as other young men, all drawn by the same impulse.

During that time, Caso was working on his masterpiece, opening up spiritual windows, imposing the supremacy of thought, and with that foresight characteristic of art, in keeping with the most erudite currents of the moment, González Martínez recalled the profound mystical significance of life, Herrán painted Mexico, and López Velarde sang about a Mexico of whose existence we were all unaware, despite living there.

So far, events had followed the usual pattern: The Teacher was the ultimate spiritual trainer, who "expanded" the city by turning it into a stronghold of elective affinities. And no generation or group was able to avoid admiring a particular style of embodying humanism. But the Revolution was ubiquitous, and not even the elites were able to avoid it. During the early years of the civil war, the country was dominated by fear and the idea that all was lost. How did art and literature weather the storm? In 1914 Pedro Henríquez Ureña responded to the apocalyptic violence of the Revolution with the cry that Mexico had ceased to exist: There was no longer an effective government or any respect for private property. He and other members of the middle class felt that a community governed by laws had given way to the chaos of armed hordes. Millions of pesos' worth of property had been destroyed in Mexico City alone. This was a unique phenomenon in the civil wars of the Americas, since the U.S. Civil War was fought, for the most part, in the South. The Mexican Revolution inevitably reminded one of the destruction of order in the French Revolution. One could ponder seriously whether civilization would ever return to Mexico.

In order for civilization to return, one must have trust in native products and make nationalism the touchstone. This nationalism must not be founded on its exceptionality, but rather on the surprises it reserves for Mexicans who have minimized their cultural capacities. In the words of Gómez Morín:

> El aislamiento forzado en que estaba la República por el curso de la lucha militar, favoreció la manifestación de un sentido de autonomía. Poco podíamos recibir del extranjero. Razones militares y aun monetarias nos impedían el conocimiento diario y verídico de los sucesos exterirores y la importación de los habituales artículos europeos o yanquis de consumo material o intelectual. Tuvimos que buscar en nosotros mismos un medio de satisfacer nuestras necesidades de cuerpo y alma. Empezaron a inventarse elementales sustitutos de los antiguos productos importados. (20)

> The Republic's forced isolation as a result of the military struggle fostered the expression of a sense of autonomy. We were able to receive very little from abroad. Military and even monetary reasons prevented our obtaining a faithful, everyday version of external events, or importing the usual European or Yankee articles for material or intellectual consumption. We were obliged to find a means of satisfying the needs of body and soul within ourselves. People began to invent elementary substitutes for products that had traditionally been imported.

At this point, it is worth recalling an obvious fact: During the revolutionary period, although, in absolute terms, the city contained very small cultural nuclei and still depended, as it did during the *Porfiriato,* on self-consumption, its capacity for attraction developed out of proportion. The Revolution contributed a vast number of elements that simultaneously fostered a nationalistic art, an extremely ingenious and inventive popular culture, and an intellectual and artistic desire to match the realities and symbols generated by the armed struggle. And the cultural city perfected its strategy: Until the situation returned to normal, nationalism would be the forum for cultural normalization. The end of exile (both geographical and internal) and the return of the intellectuals and writers linked to the regimes of Porfirio Díaz and Victoriano Huerta saw the reestablishment of higher education centers and athenaeums and meant that it was now time to reconsider the evil of living with a lack of political freedom.

The Mexican Renaissance

In the years after 1920, the cultural city underwent surprising changes, undoubtedly prepared for the false, repressive, and fraudulent order of the dictatorship and the need to become rapidly incorporated into international life or, more specifically, to reproduce the mythology of the great urban centers (primarily Paris and London) on a smaller scale. The opportunity to abandon what was provincial and adopt what

was cosmopolitan was provided by the efforts of the Minister of Public Education (1921–1924), José Vasconcelos, with his emphasis on the spirit of the cosmic race, his call to the Revolution of culture and humanism, and, above all, his patronage of the muralist movement. Despite being deeply conservative, Vasconcelos was dominated by a Messianic impulse that shaped his goal: to lend the spirit (knowledge and the humanities) the support of a literate country. For Vasconcelos, teaching literacy skills involved imbuing a nation disintegrated by ignorance with an awareness of tradition and destiny. And teaching was also visual. Vasconcelos commissioned a group to paint the walls of the former monastery of San Ildefonso: Diego Rivera (1886–1957), José Clemente Orozco (1883–1949), David Alfaro Siqueiros (1896–1974), Jean Charlot (1896–1979), and Fernando Leal (1896–1964). The result was exceptional, and it obviously modified social perception of what was worth painting. The Right rejected muralism, was offended at the artists' anticlericalism, failed to understand the intellectual implications, and despaired at "Los Monotes" [cartoon figures]. But muralism was an avant-garde art that, virtually on its own and primarily as a result of Diego Rivera's personality, fostered an atmosphere of freedom ranging from the artistic to the personal. Rivera was the center of the movement; he was inevitably in the headlines, exhibited his private life, boasted of his communism and atheism, and portrayed his tormented relationships with Lupe Marín and the legendary Frida Kahlo (1907–1954) as heroic achievements. His quarrels, affairs, and outspoken remarks were the talk of the town. Rivera introduced the city to something that had hitherto been unknown: art and artists as objects of fascination for the masses.

At the same time, marginalized by journalism and ignored by politics, the literary avant-garde emerged. It made a rather late entry, but any earlier appearance would simply have been inconceivable. And one of the main themes of this avant-garde was the city as a cultural fact—the city that provided an avalanche of visual stimuli, allowed the discovery of the poetry inherent in technological development, and permitted the minimum personal freedoms, which, in contrast to the climate of repression, were turned into major freedoms. Poets constituted the avant-garde *par excellence*; a group of poets called the "Estridentistas" [strident] sought directly to provoke society. To this end, they published extremely provocative manifestos, in keeping with the period: "Viva el mole de guajalote!" "¡Muera el cura Hidalgo!" ["Long Live Turkey Mole!" "Death to Father Hidalgo!"] (Schneider 41; 50). Their vision of the city was derived from the worship of a radical metaphorical discourse that had hitherto been inconceivable:

> La ciudad insurrecta de anuncios luminosos
> Flota en los almanaques,
> Y allá de tarde en tarde
> Por la calle planchada se desgrana un eléctrico.

> The rebel city, of luminous advertisement
> Floats on the almanacs,
> And there, from evening to evening
> An electrical charge runs its course along the ironed street

(Schneider 73)

But the ones who established a new relationship with the city were not the Estridentistas but the poets associated with the *Contemporáneos* journal (1926–1929). They encouraged a new urban sensibility, introducing it as far as possible into a form of literature subject to rhyming verse, and, in the eyes of their small public, represented another form of urban modernity, which transmitted its alternative sensibility through images that would take time to be assimilated. The Contemporáneos–Carlos Pellicer (1899–1977), Xavier Villaurrutia (1903–1950), Salvador Novo (1904–1974), José Gorostiza (1901–1973), Jaime Torres Bodet (1902–1974), Jorge Cuesta (1903–1942), Gilberto Owen (1905–1952), Bernardo Ortiz de Montellanos (1899–1948), and Enrique González Rojo (1899–1939)–were the junior sector of the Lettered City that the Revolution had produced, less solemn than its extremely rigid Porfirian predecessors, yet cautious and uncertain regarding the transformations caused by the military and literary revolutions.

The cultural city offered a varied and indeed exhaustive range of activities: luncheons in honor of distinguished visitors or national celebrities, experimental theater, cinema clubs, literary gatherings in bookshops where traditional style was corrected by the need to accept the "new tremors," and meetings to exchange poems and congratulations. Those who regarded themselves as being exempt from the stupidity and philistinism (a key word) of a society that, at best, memorized *modernista* poets poorly here met with other intellectuals who were also convinced that murals educated the people in a revolutionary fashion. The government bureaucracy guaranteed their survival because the writers ghostwrote politicians' speeches, read the galleys of official publications, participated in educational campaigns, and shaped the state's first attempts at cultural dissemination. The inevitable political alliance between literary generations, while failing to reconcile marked differences in sensitivity, nonetheless supported an ambiguous sense of modernity that allowed those anxious writers to distance themselves from an oppressive cultural nationalism while still taking advantage of the energy of the Revolution. A double phenomenon took place: The literary establishment was consolidated and charged with both the explicit and the implicit canon, and more ostentatiously, in the capital of the Republic, a cosmopolitan trend began to develop, based on the propagandistic metamorphosis of wonder at the Revolution. The European, North American, and Latin American travelers who came to Mexico City understood the Mexican Renaissance as the artistic movement surrounding muralism. The name was obviously chosen as a means of encouraging a comparison between the Italian Renaissance and Revolutionary Mexico on the basis of a single point: The emergence of art subverts the idea of nation and the vision of the city. Travelers from the United States, Europe, Japan, and Russia fell under the spell of the violent and artistic metamorphosis of a people. What had failed to be attained during the intense revolutionary years was easily achieved through the murals and the atmosphere of gatherings, walks, and debates presided over by Diego Rivera. Thus, for example, during the 1920s and 1930s, Mexico was visited by the Soviets Vladimir Maiakovsky and Sergio Eisenstein, the North Americans Hart Crane, Edward Weston, John Dos Passos, Waldo Frank, and Frank Tannenbaum, the Englishmen D.H. Lawrence and Aldous Huxley, and the Frenchmen Antonin Artaud and André Breton. The sense of hospitality that immediately accepts those who are attracted by the sum of novelties was thus reinforced. Although the Mexican *modernista* poets had triumphantly received José Martí (1853–1895), the artists and writers of the 1920s and

1930s regarded openness to other countries as one of their main duties. For those who believed they were being subjected to an internal exile (the country fails to understand different forms of sensibility), the presence of cultural visitors proved extremely stimulating. Although the city did not become cosmopolitan, its artistic and intellectual elite sought to put its localism in the past.

"When All Acts Were Significant"

During the 1920s and 1930s, a group of prominent writers and painters in the cultural city were subjected to a moral lynching for their homosexuality, whether real or alleged. Participants in the campaign included politicians, journalists, sectors of both the Right and Left, writers, and painters. Following a series of shameful episodes (dismissal from government posts, the closure of a journal for using "bad language," etc.), however, neither prejudice nor homophobia stopped those attacked from being recognized or from engaging in social contact. Their very survival reflected the partial opening of the cultural city. (This was permitted in the "free territory" of the capital; elsewhere in the country it would have been unthinkable.) As institutions became consolidated, the scandal over the new sensibility gradually subsided. Forums of expression were expanded through literary journals, as were social spaces with the round of meetings and visits to cafés, restaurants, and cabarets. What was anticipated by José Juan Tablada in "El caballero de la yerbabuena" [1916; "Peppermint Gentleman"] went virtually unnoticed twenty years later: "En las más sincopada de las rumbas/préndeme tu vacuna, (oh mariguana!/Para universalizar el incidente" (522–23) ("In the most syncopated of all rumbas/give me a vaccination, oh marijuana,/To universalize the incident"). The sounds, technologies, and rhythms of the great city were incorporated into narrative and, to a lesser extent, poetry. Mexico City was a cultural center without the strong links to Europe of Buenos Aires in the same period, yet it possessed the popular overtones of the Revolution, which were enthusiastically embraced. In 1932 Salvador Novo wrote in "Diluvio":

Espaciosa sala de baile,
Alma y cerebro
dos orquestas, dos,
Baile de trajes
las palabras iban entrando
las vocales daban el brazo a las consonantes.

Spacious ballroom,
soul and brain
two orchestras, two
ball gowns
the words came in
and the vowels gave the consonants their arm.

(22–23)

A few journals, two or three publishing houses, the opportunity of having one's literary articles published, minor government posts, two or three libraries worthy of the name, few opportunities to travel for writers and painters, and extremely limited access to publications from other countries–the city did not offer much more than this, and yet it continued to attract visitors; its urban dynamism proved extremely rewarding, among other things, because of the constant contact among writers. In *Convergencias* (1991), Octavio Paz (1914–1998) evokes a Mexican scene from the 1930s and 1940s:

El Café París tuvo un carácter muy distinto. Su nombre no pertenece a la historia de la gastronomía y ni siquiera a la de las costumbres sino a la de la literatura y del arte. Mejor dicho, a esa historia, todavía por escribirse, de los grupos, las personas y las tendencias que componen la sociedad literaria y artística de una época. Una historia, más que de las ideas y las obras, de las formas de convivencia y, sobre todo, del *gusto*. Creo que los años del Café París han sido el único período en que hemos tenido lo que se ha llamdo "vida de café" como en Francia, España e Italia. El café fue una institución literaria que sustituyó al salón. Pero en México no tuvimos salones: los escritores se reunían en algunas librerías y los poetas modernistas en los bares. El Café París fue una sociedad dentro de la sociedad. Asimismo, una geografía. Cada mesa era una tertulia, cada tertulia una isla y una plaza fortificada. Las relaciones entre las islas eran, al mismo tiempo, frecuentes y arriesgadas. Siempre había algún intrépido-o algún inconsciente que iba de una mesa a otra. Unos eran mensajeros y otros desertores. (120)

The Café Paris had a very different atmosphere. Its name did not belong to the history of gastronomy or even to that of customs, but rather to that of literature and art. In fact, it belonged to the history, as yet unwritten, of the groups, people, and trends that compose the literary and artistic society of an era. A history, rather than of ideas and works, of the forms of coexistence and, above all, of taste. I think that the years of Café París were the only period when we had what is known as a "café life" as they do in France, Spain, and Italy. The café was a literary institution that replaced the salon. But in Mexico, we had no salons: Writers met in bookshops and *modernista* poets in bars. The Café París was a society within a society, as well as a piece of geography. Every table was a literary gathering, every literary gathering an island and a fortified square. Relations between the islands were both frequent and dangerous. There was always some foolhardy or scatterbrained individual who would flit from one table to the next. Some were messengers, others deserters.

"If Spain Falls (It's Just a Manner of Speaking)"

In 1936 in Latin America, the Spanish Civil War, that great forewarning of the advance of fascism, generated powerful loyalties and divided the intellectual sector. The majority supported the Republic, and in Mexico the government of Lázaro Cárdenas (1934–1940) gave the Republicans all the help it could. From 1938 onward, the exacerbation of the conflict forced tens of thousands of Republicans to emigrate, including artists, writers, architects, printers, set designers, musicians, publishers, scientists, and lawyers, who enriched the culture of Mexico, Venezuela, and Argentina. Among those who came to Mexico were the writers Emilio Prados (1899–1962), Manuel Altolaguirre (1905–1959), Ramón Gaya (b. 1910), Juan Gil-Albert (1904–1993), Luis Cernuda (1902–1963), Pedro Garfias (1901–1967), León Felipe (1884–1968), Max Aub (1903–1972), and Juan Rejano (1903–1976). A very large group of people working in cinema came as well, among whom Luis Buñuel (1900–1982) and the graphic designer Josep Renau (1907–1982) stood out; musicians such as Rodolfo Halffter, architects such as Félix Candela (1910–1997), philosophy professors José Gaos (1900–1969), Joaquín Xirau (1895–1946), and Adolfo Sánchez Vázquez, and very young writers such as Ramón Xirau (b. 1924) and Ramón Segovia (b. 1927) also came. Members of this group made an outstanding contribution to the publishing and graphic industry of the new cultural center that had developed in the city.

Spanish exiles are part of a varied migration that was seamlessly incorporated into the cultural city, where chauvinism was not an element of concern. The achievements of the Mexican Renaissance attracted artistic travelers from Europe and North America, radicals dazzled by the energy of popular armies of teachers and Vasconcelos's educational Messianism, and Latin American artists anxious to transfer the experience of muralism to their own countries. Between 1940 and 1970, these were joined by refugees from political persecutions, coups d'état, and the barbarity of military dictators. They came from Colombia, Peru, and Venezuela (including the deposed president Rómulo Gallegos [1884–1969] and the poet Andrés Eloy Blanco [1897–1955]) and from El Salvador, Nicaragua, and Guatemala (including the writers Luis Cardoza y Aragón [1904–1992], Augusto Monterroso [1921–2003], and Carlos Illescas [1918–1998]). Between 1948 and 1952, as a result of the pressure of the Cold War and, more specifically, McCarthyism, a group of North American Leftists settled in Mexico, including writers and screenplay writers (Alvah Bessie, Hugo Butler, and Dalton Trumbo). And during the revolutionary ferment of the time, Cuban exiles, led by Fidel Castro (b. 1927) and the Argentinian radical Ernesto Che Guevara (1928–1967), set sail from Veracruz to Cuba on the Granma. Other writers, such as the Colombians Gabriel García Márquez (b. 1927) and Álvaro Mutis (b. 1923), decided to settle in Mexico City because of its cultural ambiance.

During the 1970s, the strong-arm regimes sponsored by the U.S. government devastated South America and for a time set up Fascist military dictators in Argentina, Chile, Uruguay, and Bolivia. In 1973, General Augusto Pinochet's monstrous coup exiled a large group of Chileans who were mainly absorbed by Mexico's university centers; 1976 marked the beginning of the emigration of Argentinian and Uruguayan intellectuals, and since the late 1980s, Cuban writers, musicians, historians, and artists have flocked to Mexico City. Russian and Polish musicians, expelled from their countries following the breakdown of socialism, are now distributed among the various symphonic orchestras. These *transterrados* (transterritorialized, a term coined by José Gaos) have enlivened and diversified the culture of Mexico, linking it to another sphere of intellectual demands, now inseparable from the concern for human rights. The tradition of hospitality strengthened cultural development and organic entry into internationalization.

The Years of Institutionalism

Between 1940 and 1968, the Lettered City, whether it wanted it or not, became another sphere of republican ritual. The Institutional Revolutionary Party (PRI) predominated, and it fell to writers, academics, and artists to pay their respects and homage on great occasions. Cultural institutions developed parallel to state institutions. The Academia de la Lengua flourished, and in 1945, based on the Collège de France, the Colegio Nacional was created, attracting several leading intellectual, artistic, musical, and literary figures (such as José Clemente Orozco, Diego Rivera, Alfonso Reyes, Carlos Chávez, and Mariano Azuela). The National University of Mexico (UNAM) was strengthened, and the symbolic–or decorative, according to bureaucrats—importance of the humanities was emphasized. And in the Lettered City, a discreet minority organized the canon and the distribution of the levels of prestige, abiding by the judgment of literary journals and state mechanisms of consecration. At the same time, avant-garde movements no longer mattered, except as offshoots of a form of *costumbrismo* classified as esoteric by those who did not believe in artistic revolutions but who were vastly entertained by eccentricity. (This is not a bad way of taming avant-gardes, regarding them as "eccentric occurrences.") The journals that captured the life of the spirit included *Taller*, directed by Rafael Solana and Octavio Paz, *El Hijo Pródigo* (1940–1945), directed by Octavio Barreda with the notable participation of Spanish exiles, *Estaciones* (1957–1960), directed by Elías Nandino, and, during the final stage of this type of publication, *Revista Mexicana de Literatura*, directed in the early stages by Carlos Fuentes and Emmanuel Carballo and in the later stages by Tomás Segovia and Juan García Ponce. This was followed by a decline in strictly literary magazines.

During the heyday of these institutions, culture was an individual obsession that shaped both essential and superfluous knowledge. Moreover, for a long time, culture was the humanistic and artistic common property of the West, which, in any of its versions, enlivened hundreds and comforted tens of thousands. For three decades, a minority fought a passive battle against cultural nationalism and a vulgar Marxism that amused itself, without even intending to do so, with some of the achievements of the Mexican Revolution's regime. Alfonso Reyes's admonition that Latin should be taught to the working class can partly be explained as an attempt at finding a middle ground with the political populism: If higher education was for a chosen few, then let secondary school education, which is open to all, preserve classical culture. With a degree of discretion that went unnoticed at the time, Reyes pointed out to the regime what he regarded as one of its main faults: the lack of a humanistic dimension. However, his preaching went unheard, and there was no room for conciliation between the intellectual elite and the populists. (Today, don Alfonso might also demand Spanish language education for the Right, who have gladly exchanged it for their extremely limited and sectoral graduate business English.)

The 1930s were dominated by the struggle between those who wished to place the university fairly and squarely among the people and those who wished to keep UNAM in the cloisters as the sphere for those who contemplate academic freedom and those who look to university students for their radical orientation. In 1933, two philosophers, Antonio Caso and Vicente Lombardo Toledano, indulged in a well publicized polemic. According to Lombardo, there was no point in discussing eternal values when people were starving; in Caso's view, however, the open debate over ideas was the best way to preserve freedom. As is usually the case, the debate was resolved to the mutual self-satisfaction of both parties, and intellectual life grew lethargic under the somewhat mythomaniacal premise that knowledge was a matter for solitary appropriation, refined by dealing with one's peers. According to the intellectual elite, those who benefited from broad popular dissemination of culture would never penetrate genuine human achievement in the human sciences.

During the period of the greatest revolutionary sermonizing, a minority preached the value of great artistic creations, nearly always in journals with a very small print run, ranging from *Contemporáneos* to *El Hijo Pródigo*. Culture was defended rather than disseminated. In response to this defense of traditional culture, the Palace of Fine Arts was built and inaugurated in 1934. It then became the axis of cultural life, a site of initiation where the majority of the

public attended their first concert, their first opera, their first exhibition, or their first lecture. Thus, being a "cultured person" was generally associated with possession of a large library and politically conservative beliefs, being a member of the legal profession (although doctors and a few engineers were also accepted), and attendance at solemn and erudite gatherings. The government opted for pragmatism and the Left for anti-intellectualism, while higher education advanced slowly; only a mere handful supported the cult of books.

The Department of Fine (Ministry of Culture) Arts was virtually a utopian scheme in a society still attached to the decorative virtues of what was regarded as cultural. On 31 December 1946, the National Institute of Fine Arts (INBA) was created in order to "take care of, foster, sponsor, oversee and strengthen all the artistic ways in which the spirit of Mexico and universality is expressed and defined." From 1947 to 1952, the composer and conductor Carlos Chávez directed the INBA, with notable results, meaning that plays, concerts, and exhibitions began to be held. Then, as now, the state sponsored over 90 percent of cultural activities. Officially, literature, painting, music, and dance were no longer a matter for teaching but rather for pleasure. That was the goal: for the people to accept the obligation of culture with pleasure. Since 1947, the INBA has been fundamental for the cultured city, despite the fact that it has reinforced centralism. It serves to guarantee a project that, in the last analysis, has no party affiliations and is nonreligious. Yet centralism severely hampers the country's possibilities and, as far as culture is concerned, destroys the provinces' possibilities of growth. Among other things, centralism is responsible for the disproportionate concentration of cultural events in Mexico City (over 90 percent), the systematic depopulation of human resources in the provinces, the notion of the provinces as something irredeemably condemned to backwardness and vulgarity, neglect of the quality of secondary and higher education in the provinces, and the impossibility of true national productions from the center. To date, "national culture" has been virtually synonymous with what has been produced in the capital. The so-called provinces have reacted passively to intolerance and fanaticism; it has fallen to Mexico City to systematize spheres of tolerance and criticism. The capital has been the salvation of the spirit of Mexico's cultural participation on a world scale. The city's population explosion of recent decades has also contributed to the extremely high degree of cultural concentration.

The Other Side: Publishing Companies and Cultural Supplements

Disseminating culture is also the task of institutions of higher education, publishing houses, and publishers of newspaper literary supplements. Cultural supplements, virtually unnoticed at the outset, began to be published in the 1940s, thereby expanding the cultural public. As a result of these supplements, news of the arts, theater, dance (occasionally), history, and classical music systematically reached a public that was now delighted not only by these performances but also by the systematic information provided. This "normalization" of culture began with the supplement of *El Nacional* in the early 1940s and continued with *México en la Cultura* (1949–1961) in the newspaper *Novedades*. Following a battle against censorship that led *Novedades* to withdraw from publishing the supplement, *La Cultura en México* was taken up by the weekly *Siempre!* The director and enthusiastic promoter of these three publications was Fernando Benítez (1912–2000), who also promoted the expansion of the Mexican twentieth-century literary canon with new literature. Lengthy interviews were conducted with the survivors of the Ateneo de la Juventud and the Contemporáneos group, while the publication of novels, such as Carlos Fuentes' *La región más transparente* [*Where the Air Is Clear*] (with Benítez's headline "Whatever the destiny of Mexican books, they will no longer be fated to be ignored"), was considered front-page news; the sections on dance and music were also regarded as essential.

As a result of the intervention of these supplements, the cultural city understood its duties and privileges differently. The minority ("The 400 Educated Men") still presided over what had previously been the coteries and literary gatherings in bookshops (those of the Porrúa family having the highest repute), although the solemn, extremely civil literary evenings were gradually replaced by cocktail parties, which were somewhat more frivolous. Moreover, writers who were still attached to the government bureaucracy could now glimpse some slight possibility of alternatives: the film industry, journalism (without the destructive pressures of the *Porfiriato),* advertising (somewhat timidly), university chairs (albeit extremely poorly paid), cultural dissemination through the UNAM, and the publishing industry.

The Lettered City was primarily constructed by the publishing houses, however. In 1934, the Fondo de Cultura Económica, directed first by Daniel Cosío Villegas (1898–1976) and then by Arnaldo Orfila (1897–1997), embarked on its extraordinary literary task, so essential in Latin America. It soon added the dissemination of texts on economics, history, social science, and science, as well as literature. The 1950s marked the beginning of the publication of two outstanding collections: *Breviarios,* the first pocket books, and *Letras Mexicanas,* which published the books that would soon become classics. *El llano en llamas* [1953; *The Plain in Flames*] and *Pedro Páramo* (1955) by Juan Rulfo (1918–1986), *Varia Invención* and *Confabulario* [1949 and 1952; Confabulario and Other Inventions) by Juan José Arreola (1918–2001), *Balún Canán* (1957) by Rosario Castellanos (1925–1974), and Carlos Fuentes's (b. 1928) *La región más transparente* [1958; *Where the Air Is Clear*]. *Letras Mexicanas* even published one of the first bestsellers in the North American style, *Casi el paraíso* [1956; *Almost Paradise*] by Luis Spota (1925–1985). The Fondo de Cultura Económica (FCE) also published essays by Alfonso Reyes and poetry by Octavio Paz. Porrúa publishers, with their series *Sepan Cuántos . . .* and its collection of Mexican writers, disseminated international and national classics. And other publishing houses emerged in the 1960s: Joaquín Mortiz, Era, and Patria.

"And Buildings Will Be Both the Sign and the Classical Model for People's Modernity"

The year 1954 was one of drastic change. The UNAM faculties moved from the center, before it was regarded as historical, to the University City. The idea and practices of the university were radically modified. The banishment of tradition went virtually unnoticed (vacating such densely historical premises hastened the demise of a particular mode of

being), and at the same time, the notion of campus, already fully emancipated from the viceroyalty and the nineteenth century, led by sheer force of momentum to the new totem of modernity, which was the means of shaking off one's commitment to a past that seemed boring, hostile, and incriminating. Two archetypes or stereotypes were rejected for their anachronism: the post-viceregal, anti-revolutionary university student and the nationalistic, pre-modern university man; praise was heaped on dynamic images of the university, influenced by galloping Americanization and the need to install new mentalities in such modern buildings. Youth was already at that joyful stage, lacking the earlier duties of formalities and being free from worries. The *corpore sano* prophesied, by its very existence, the complementary nature of *mens sana,* and depoliticization was achieved through afternoon gatherings modeled after student associations in the United States.

For a number of years, from approximately 1954 to 1965, the UNAM Center for Cultural Dissemination (albeit under a different name) was in the vanguard, a role it played unexpectedly well. It was helped by the environment (with architecture that glorified progress and buildings that demanded new behavior) and benefited from the desire for novelty, which led to the quasi-religious adoption of culture (Mexican mystique with joy but without flagellation, the Lord moveth among booksellers and cinema clubs and museums). The message was aimed first and foremost at students and professionals and was conveyed through the *Revista de la Universidad* (which mixed literary texts and notes on art with historical dissemination and philosophical reflections), the University Radio Station (whose programming consisted virtually entirely of classical music) a few hours from Monday to Friday, and lectures by prominent figures, together with the odd concert or play. This was the unspoken creed: that culture was a delightful asset for professionals, which enhanced their lives or at least their after-dinner conversations. This new stage of cultural dissemination modified all criteria.

Why do I see a mystical tendency in this adoption of values? Because an expanding minority fervently devoted itself to readings, performances, the discovery of cinema classics, listening to opera and symphonies, and attending performances of dance companies. The exclusive club, which read Musil and Pavese, contemplated Fritz Lang and Eisenstein, listened to Berg and Stockhausen, Charlie Parker and Miles Davis, and rejoiced in the idea of the theater as entertainment without moral trappings, widened its membership. Over a period of eleven years (1954–1965), with Jaime García Terrés as director of Cultural Dissemination, the avant-garde impulse was concentrated in the UNAM, while knowledge began to be democratized. Of all the cultural transformations of the 1960s, only Alejandro Jodorovsky's theater group and the Nuevo Cine group, which promoted film culture and the thesis of "auteur" cinema, developed outside the university sphere. The concentration in the university was possible because, during the time when there was no freedom of political or artistic expression, the UNAM was a sort of free territory where the desire to be up-to-date reduced censorship to a minimum. Within this scheme, political issues were unimportant, although there was a marked disdain for the conservatism of the Right, as well as for official culture and its inertia and good manners (which made the administration at the time the source of both implicit dogmas and one explicit principle: rejection of any political and social dissidence, including that which already existed and that which could be eliminated before it emerged).

I do not think I am exaggerating. During the period from 1950–1970, prior to the rise of the cultural industry, the UNAM was primarily responsible for creating a new cultural public. In a city unaccustomed to modernity, cultural dissemination performed its task with a vengeance. It proposed a different and richer literary environment and different authors. Through theater, this modernity even changed the attitude of certain writers and forms of life. How can any description do justice to the spirit of those years, prior to the sudden increase in the range of cultural events available? The city seemed to shrink in order to promote what was happening in a few spheres. First nights made headlines, a number of writers, painters, and musicians were part of idealized autobiographical journalism eagerly consumed by their admirers, and lectures on philosophy, history, and literature were listened to from start to finish. Opposing censorship was considered one of the essential steps toward achieving urban freedom.

The Two Vanguards

In 1968, during the months of the student movement, the cultural and political vanguards coincided (long before the term "vanguard" acquired any funereal or pejorative connotations). The authoritarianism of the Díaz Ordaz (1964–1970) regime was resisted from diametrically opposed positions. The most frequent interpretation stressed the supremacy of political issues among students, the influence of the Mexican Left, and the political echoes of the guerrilla cult in Latin America ("No queremos olimpiadas, queremos revolución" ["We don't want the Olympics, we want revolution"]). This is only partly true, since it fails to take into account the strength of specifically cultural issues among broad sectors of society, disenchanted by the Mexican Revolution, and a new public devoted to novels, films, poems, philosophical essays, classical and rock music, and real (and not so imaginary) trips. Authoritarianism was also opposed by the urgent need to move far away from nationalistic suffocation. Both tendencies converged at one time, only to separate following the tragedy of 2 October, when the Army massacred a peaceful crowd at a student movement meeting in the Plaza de Tres Culturas.

In the cultural sphere, 1968 led to a number of consequences. On the one hand, it stimulated criticism and the revision of national history and reinforced critical distance from the regime. At the same time, the overt rejection of the government became a fetish (which afterwards, and in different ways, once the immense difficulties of dissidence had been revealed, made opportunism an adaptive necessity), imbuing the teaching of Marxism with a semireligious tone (complete with catechism—Marta Harnecker's books, for example, reached sixth-form students who were no longer familiar with Father Ripalda) and sanctifying the demagogic slogan "Universidad-Pueblo" [Universities for the People]. By training and temperament, President Gustavo Díaz Ordaz (1964–1970) loathed what he assumed the new university student to be: informal, nonnationalistic, radical or rebellious, an enemy of authority, lacking all respect for institutions, and influenced by the philosophers of destruction. President Luis Echevarría (1970–1976), equally authoritarian and repressive, perceived the change and strove to recapture the middle-class

sector that the massacre of 1968 had alienated from the political establishment (or whatever one calls the fatalistic perception of the political order). And in order to draw university students back into the official fold, Echevarría decided, among other assimilative tactics, to increase the budget for higher education by immediately creating institutes and faculties, doubling the size of university campuses throughout the country, and raising the number of full- and part-time researchers and professors.

The growth of the middle classes opened up markets for the cultural industry, which took over what the government and universities could not or would not do. Shops and supermarkets were flooded with highbrow music and reproductions of great paintings and classical literature, particularly from Spain and the United States. Despite the enormous range of cultural products available, the middle class failed to display its characteristic consumerism and instead appeared indecisive and snobbish, revealing a marked preference for what became kitsch (from Beethoven's "Ode to Joy" to Leonardo's "Last Supper," Picasso's "Quijotes," Dalí's Christs, and Neruda's *Veinte poemas de amor y una canción desesperada* [1924; *Twenty Love Poems and a Song of Despair*]). However, the rapid growth of higher education and certain developments in society itself changed the rules of the game. Pride in elitism lessened, and the public expanded and became consolidated with new demands, including the formal and informal demands of the masses who now regarded as their due access to what had formerly been the privilege of a chosen few (such as secondary and higher education, for a start, with a smattering of culture).

Between 1970 and the end of the century, cultural dissemination in Mexico was successful, achieving an infrastructure that was virtually unique in Latin America, such as the Undersecretariat of Culture and, during Carlos Salinas's administration (1988–1994), the National Council for Culture and the Arts (CONCULTURA). Despite the attendant difficulties, museums, cultural centers, galleries, radio stations, highbrow television (including two outstanding channels, Channel 22 and Channel 11), the National Arts Center, symphony orchestras, chamber music ensembles, dance groups, theater groups, and performances all multiplied. Grants and institutional support proved essential for many journals and numerous artistic creators. Moreover, in certain regions, and despite the endless abuse of centralism, cultural opportunities gradually increased as a result of budgetary increases in the universities, more available space in newspapers and magazines, or simply cultural internationalization. The idea of Mexico City as the only cultural center was weakened due to simultaneous free access to publications, recordings, and films, new mass ventures, and altered publishing attitudes and intellectual fashions throughout Mexico. And the new basic difference between the regions and Mexico City depended on the diversity and number of cultural offerings in the capital and the far greater restrictions of censorship (whether governmental, ecclesiastical, or entrepreneurial) in the provinces.

Competition was so great that it was absurd to believe in the indispensable nature of any particular enterprise. Moreover, as far as access to culture was concerned, an increasing number no longer required intermediaries. Supported by the vast cultural industry, there was an enormous increase in self-teaching (or that great variant of self-teaching, what one learns after leaving university). Freud and Jung, Proust and Virginia Woolf, Pasternak, Stravinsky, Mondrian and the Dadaists,

Alban Berg, Brecht, Beckett, Barthes, Derrida, Foucault, Eco, Lacan, Paz, Borges, Yourcenar, Paul Auster, Antonio Tabucchi, and Lezama Lima were all available to anyone who chose to approach them. And if they no longer serve as intermediaries at the highest level, what role is left for cultural dissemination and the cultural city, which is the capital of the Republic? Moreover, the cultural panorama is being totally modified by technology, particularly by the Internet. The need for different programs is met by intensifying the tried and true—symposia, lectures, concerts, university theater festivals, round tables, short courses—sand by adding something new: installation art and performance art. These formulae are partly effective, partly boring, but eventually come to constitute the educational landscape.

"When So Many People Come, No One Notices the Pictures Anymore"

The search for possible and impossible modernity during the period from 1940–1968 saw the emergence of an important novelty: the construction of an art market. Until the 1950s, there were only a handful of galleries to meet the scant demand: the Galería de Arte Mexicano, directed by Inés Amor, the Galería Proteo, the Galería de Lola Álvarez Bravo, the Galería Misrachi, and the Galería de Antonio Souza. By the early 1960s, these galleries were no longer able to meet the demand, since Mexican artists had fostered a sense of acquisitive pride among the bourgeoisie and middle classes. During the 1920s and 1930s, only a few, mainly U.S., collectors from Hollywood purchased the paintings of Diego Rivera, José Clemente Orozco, David Alfaro Siqueiros, and, somewhat surreptitiously, Frida Kahlo. The market subsequently expanded and Mexican collectors emerged, eager to purchase work by Rufino Tamayo, viceregal art, nineteenth-century Mexican painting (primarily José María Velasco), and pottery from Puebla—but little else. Subsequently, collectors' tastes expanded to include other painters, such as María Izquierdo, Alfonso Michel, Juan Soriano, and the photographer Manuel Alvarez Bravo. And following the collapse of Alfaro Siqueiros's thesis—No hay más ruta que la nuestra" ["There is no way other than ours"]—the value of abstract painting was acknowledged, resulting in a new enthusiasm for contemporary painting, represented in Mexico by artists such as Lilia Carrillo, Vicente Rojo, Pedro and Rafael Coronel, José Luis Cuevas, Manuel Felguérez, Francisco Toledo, Rodolfo Nieto, and Pedro Friedeberg. Understandably, international art was hardly sold at all. It was inaccessible in principle, too expensive, and, as far as taste was concerned, not really very well liked.

Yet the cultural city was governed by the fashion trends of the metropolises (invariably New York, Paris, and London, and also, as a result of the influence of cinema, Los Angeles). A vast social sector became internationalized, and to a certain extent the process also affected many more people as a result of television and cinema. Even though the cultural city was never as nationalistic as it was alleged to be, nationalism was pushed into the background from the 1980s onward and replaced by a national criterion that confined itself to celebrating what was produced in Mexico (since it was an authority on this issue). Internationalizing, in this respect, meant divulging the obligation to share both a taste for what was produced in the country (meaning the city) and a taste for what was metropolitan. And the success of international exhibitions gave ample evidence of Mexico's anxious abandoning

what was rustic and provincial. Hundreds of thousands filed past the exhibitions on Picasso, the Impressionists, Francis Bacon, David Hockney, Rodin, and the Italian futurists. And although the number of readers fell in relation to population growth, there too the desire to keep up to date prevailed. Having been engulfed by the urban monster of a Mexico City of twenty to twenty-two million inhabitants (fourteen million in the Federal District alone, the remainder in the outlying areas in the valley of Mexico), the cultural city finally renounced its proud tradition of being a minority and accepted that the world of the Internet and e-mail, congresses, and symposia were also sources of inspiration. Much of tradition has become a conceit, yet an intense intellectual link was retained with the past. In short, at the end of the twentieth century, the cultural city of Mexico was not equivalent to, and did not resemble or differ from, what it was in 1900 or 1910.

Translation by Suzanne D. Stephens

Works Cited

Aguirre y Fierro, Guillermo. 1928. *El brindis del bohemio: Monólogo en verso.* Mexico City: Librería teatral J. Lechuga.

Balbuena, Bernardo de. 1988. *Grandeza Mexicana.* Ed. José Carlos González Boixo. Roma: Bulzoni.

Gamboa, Federico.1922. *Impresiones y recuerdos.* Mexico City: E. Gómez de la Puente.

——. 1938. *Mi diario* Ser. II, vol 2. Mexico City: Ediciones Botas.

Goméz Morín, Manuel. *1915 y otros ensayos.* Mexico City: Editorial Jus.

Gutierrez Nájera, Manuel. 1953. *Poesías completas.* Vol. 2. Mexico City: Porrúa.

Henríquez Ureña, Pedro. 1977–1980. *Obras completas.* 10 vols. Santo Domingo: Universidad Nacional Pedro Henríquez Ureña.

Novo, Salvador. 1966. *Antología: 1925–1965.* Mexico City: Editorial Porrúa.

Paz, Octavio. 1991. *Convergencias.* Barcelona: Seix Barral.

Prieto, Guillermo. 1906. *Memorias de mis tiempos: 1828–1840.* Mexico City: Tipografía de la Viuda de Francisco Díaz de León.

Rama, Ángel. 1996. *The Lettered City.* Trans. and ed. John Charles Chasteen. Durham: Duke University Press.

El Renacimiento: Periódico Literario (México, 1869). 1993. Intr. Huberto Batis. Mexico City: Universidad Nacional Autonóma de Mexico.

Reyes, Alfonso. 1941. *Pasado inmediato y otros ensayos.* Mexico City: Colegio de Mexico.

——. Pedro Henríquez Ureña. 1986. *Correspondencia 1907–1914.* Mexico City: Fondo de Cultura Económica.

Rodríguez Galván, Ignacio. 1851. *Poesías.* Vol. 1. Mexico City: M. N. de la Vega.

Scheneider, Luis Mario, ed. 1985. *El estridentismo: México 1921–1927.* Mexico City: Universidad Autónoma de México.

Sesto, Julio. 1929. *La bohemia de la muerte: Biografías y anecdotario pintoresco de cien mexicanos célebres en el arte, muertos en la pobreza y el abandono, y estudio crítico de sus obras.* Mexico City: Editorial Tricolor.

Sigüenza y Góngora, Carlos. 1932. *Alboroto y motín de los indios de México: 30 de agosto de 1692.* Ed. Irving A. Leonard. Mexico City: Talleres Gráficos del Museo Nacional de Arqueología, Historia y Etnografía.

Tablada, José Juan. 1971. *Poesias.* Ed. Héctor Valdés. Vol. 1. of *Obras.* Mexico City: Universidad Nacional Autónoma de México, Centro de Estudios Literarios.

CHAPTER 34

THE CULTURAL CENTERS
OF CENTRAL AMERICA

Nicasio Urbina and Laura Barbas Rhoden

Cultural centers within Central America have changed during the approximately one thousand years of the region's recorded history, shifting from indigenous centers to provincial capitals in which were concentrated the majority of the *criollo* and peninsular Spanish population. The colonizers established administrative centers and ecclesiastical power bases that propagated Spanish culture among the conquered indigenous population. During the post-Independence period, at a national level, cultural life was concentrated in the capitals, which, as centers of political power, also monopolized the cultural life of the region. By means of schools and universities, theaters and literary groups, publishing houses and libraries, these urban centers succeeded once again in concentrating the meager cultural life of these countries while leaving the provincial cities and the countryside practically in a cultural limbo. It could be said that historically the regions in Central America have not changed much. Territorial control remains incomplete, given that the area today consists of an isthmus broken up into seven nation-states with one or two cultural centers per country, each with histories that are both shared and different, complementary and antagonistic. It was not always so.

The Mayan civilization of pre-Columbian Mesoamerica to a great extent determined the cultural map of the region not only during its classic period but also during the subsequent centuries before the Conquest. Apart from achieving impressive advances in architecture, mathematics, and fine arts, Mayan culture had a developed system of writing prior to the arrival of the Europeans. The first Mayan texts appeared around 300 CE on public monuments in the Petén area and provide important dates written in the calendrical system known as the Long Count (Bassie-Sweet 3). Evidence of writing appears at all the lowland Mayan sites, though the longest single example was discovered at Copán on the 2500-glyph-long Hieroglyphic Stairway. The inscriptions narrate the history of kings and the achievements of their reigns; they also note the dates of significant events and ceremonies in the Mayan calendar (Coe 65). Even though all these texts are carved on stone, it is thought that the Maya began to write using brush and paint (Love 3). Despite the fact that neither books nor codices survive from the classical period, various artifacts from the time show images of scribes and their work. The most well known can be seen on the murals of Bonampak, which provide evidence of the existence of a specialist elite responsible for recording their people's history (Coe 65). The chronicles written down in glyphic form and the archaeological evidence indicate that each city was situated in a strategic position on Mesoamerican trade routes. From this position they exercised a regional influence (Andrews 28). Commercial exchange took place within the Mayan region as well as between the Maya and other groups. For example, the Mayan cities of Uaxactún in the Petén and Teotihuacán in the Valley of Mexico exchanged goods, while sites in the Yucatan reveal a strong influence from the civilizations of central Mexico.

Figure 1.

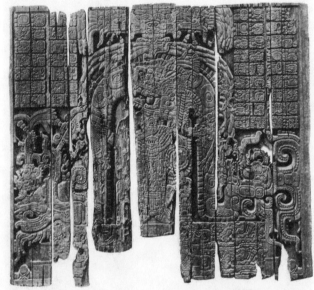

Carved wooden lintel from Temple IV, Tikal, Guatemala. Probably dedicated in CE 747, late Classic Period. (Photograph Mario J. Valdes 2000)

The Mayan cities, due to their location on trade routes and the enormous concentration not only of buildings but also of specialists, developed and spread Mayan culture throughout Mesoamerica. Indeed the hegemony of the Mayan region was cultural, never political, since each city-state maintained its autonomy and imposed its influence on the territory around its urban center. (See **Figures 1–5**.) The Mayan civilization was not an empire in the political sense, but a civilization based on a shared culture, cosmological vision, and social hierarchy. The inhabitants of the Mayan territory shared the same pantheon of major deities based on the natural world, a common diet, and an oral tradition that explained their racial origins. This cultural influence spread out from the city to the whole region. The concentration of people in a zone dedicated to the promotion of both divine and earthly interests resulted in the city emerging as the most important institution, not only in terms of the development and preservation of culture, but also for the spread of Mayan beliefs and practices throughout the sector. The city therefore became the focus for both a local and a regional dynamic with an exchange of goods and ideas throughout what is now modern Mexico and Central America. The only textual evidence for Mayan ideas is found in the few pre-Columbian codices that survived the wanton destruction of fanatical Spanish clerics. The Dresden, Peresianus, and Tro-Cortesianus (also known as the Madrid Codex) are three indisputably pre-Hispanic texts, all dating from the post-classic period. Some academics also consider the Grolier Codex as authentic (Stuart XV). The codices

Figure 2.

Drawing by A. Picken (1841) of "Casa de las monjas," Uxmal, published by Frederick Catherwood, 1844. (Courtesy of The Thomas Fisher Library, University of Toronto)

Figure 3.

Drawing by A. Picken (1841) of Stella at Copan published by Frederick Catherwood, 1844. (Courtesy of The Thomas Fisher Library, University of Toronto)

were painted using various colors and the glyphs were arranged in columns of regular tables (Bassie Sweet 4). The glyphs communicate the most important cultural information, including rules for ceremonies and religious practices, prophecies, and calendrical calculations. The Dresden Codex, for example, presents the calculations for the orbits of Mars and Venus (Villacorta and Villacorta 4). Even though very few of these fragile codices, made from the paper of the wild fig, escaped environmental deterioration and the Spanish Conquest, those that survive bear witness to the cultural and scientific achievements of this civilization. Like art, architecture, and town planning, Mayan science revolved around their theology and religious beliefs. In all the great cities, such as Mayapán, Tikal, Copán, and Chichén Itza, there is evidence of a lettered class solely dedicated to scientific research. It is thought that the Peresianus Codex, containing zodiacal drawings that reveal an intimate and sophisticated knowledge of astronomy, was written in Mayapán around 1450 CE (Freidel, Schele, and Parker 82–83; Love 13). The production of these codices in the post-classic period represents the culmination of years of scientific study.

Around 900 CE the Mayan civilization began to decline, for reasons still debated among academics. The different groups no longer built new centers or used the calendrical system.

Slowly the great ceremonial centers were abandoned to the tropical vegetation, even though the Mayan culture survived in a fragmented form among the peoples scattered throughout the region. The most famous book handed down from the Mayan tradition is the *Popol Vuh.* Also known as the *Book of Counsel,* it can be compared with the Bible to the extent that it recounts a creation story that includes various births and destructions of the human race. The version that has survived came from the Chichicastenango Manuscript that was discovered, copied, and translated into Spanish by Father Francisco Ximénez (1666–1722) at the beginning of the eighteenth century. Most of the credit for the diffusion of the *Popol Vuh* is due to the French translation by the Abbé Charles Etienne Brasseur de Bourbourg (1814–1874), which Miguel Angel Asturias (1899–1974) later translated to Spanish. From the once vast wealth of pre-Columbian literature unfortunately only the *Rabinal-Achí* remains, a ballet-drama that narrates in dialogue form the fight with, and subsequent capture and sacrifice of, Quiché-Achí by Rabinal-Achí (see Padial Guerchous and Vazquez-Bigi). As was the custom in such representations, the music, dance and costume were as important as the texts which between them formed a fascinating picture of the pre-Columbian Mayan culture. Other important texts from this tradition are the *Books of Chilam Balam,* the *Memorial of Tecpán-Atitlán,* the *Title of the Lords of Totonicapán* (Recinos) and the *Title of the Lords of Otzoya.*

Figure 4.

Drawing by W. Parrott (1841) of "Casa del Gobernador," Uxmal, published by Frederick Catherwood, 1844. (Courtesy of The Thomas Fisher Library, University of Toronto)

Figure 5.

Drawing by G. Moore (1841) of the east wing of "Las monjas," Chichen Itzá, published by Frederick Catherwood, 1844. (Courtesy of The Thomas Fisher Library, University of Toronto)

Despite their six-century-long domination, the Maya were not the only civilization to have a profound effect on what is now the isthmus of Central America. The Nahua culture, which also had a very great impact on the region, is defined in linguistic terms using a variation of Nahuatl as a classificatory criterion. This cultural group includes twenty-seven languages derived from the Uto-Aztecan group, including Nahua (no longer spoken today), Nahuatl, and Nicarao (Fowler 6; Stone 1977, 210). The Pipiles and Nicaraos of contemporary El Salvador and Nicaragua, respectively, who belong to the two largest Nahua groups, originate from migrations during pre-Columbian times (Fowler 3). The Nahua influence slowly spread through a series of southerly migrations of Nahua groups from central Mexico. The infiltration of the Central American isthmus possibly started in the ninth century CE and took place in various waves (Pérez Brignoli 38). During the Colonial period the conquistadors were surprised to encounter the same language and similar customs to those they had observed among the Mexicans and Aztecs of New Spain (Fowler 3). The Nahua preserved a very rich oral tradition based on their migrations. They explained to the Spaniards that they had left their land because they had been badly treated by their lords or had endured a long period of drought. Along with their language the Nahua brought with them their culture and ideology, including the pantheon of gods from the Valley of Mexico. For example, Chichén Itzá,

the center of post-classic Mayan civilization, reveals a strong influence from the Toltec culture of central Mexico in both its iconography and art. Thus the Nahuas demonstrated that, despite having maintained themselves as independent, they modified the religious practices of already established cultures in the isthmus. The Nahua culture was located to the south of the Mayan region, mainly in the area that is today El Salvador, Nicaragua, and Costa Rica.

When the Spaniards arrived on Central American soil, they were not long in founding their own urban and administrative centers, often appropriating indigenous sites and the materials of the buildings they destroyed. The colonization of the isthmus began as an extension of the settlement of the Caribbean, especially that of La Española (now the Dominican Republic and Haiti) (Woodward 26). The conquistadors founded cities to establish their supremacy in the region, aiming not only to subjugate the indigenous population but also to compete with their European rivals. Throughout the Colonial period, the culture of the area reflected this fragmentation and rivalry between different political and social centers. Pedro de Alvarado founded Santiago de Los Caballeros de Goathemala on the fringes of Iximiché, capital of the Cakchiquel kingdom. In 1527 the city was transferred to the Almolanga valley at the foot of the Agua volcano. However, in 1541 it was moved again because of floods in the Panchoy Valley where it remained until the earthquakes of 1773, the year in which the current Guatemala City was founded. The old city, known today as Antigua, is a jewel of colonial architecture and has become an important cultural center as the site for a series of artistic and cultural movements. When the Captaincy General of Guatemala became the seat of regional government, it gradually became the cultural center of the isthmus. In 1570 the jurisdiction of Guatemala ranged from Chiapas in Mexico to Costa Rica, constituting an area of economic, geographic, and cultural interest. In 1660 Guatemala boasted the first printing press to be installed in Central America, fourth after those of Mexico City, Puebla, and Lima. The press was largely dedicated to the publication of religious works, many in Latin, until the end of the eighteenth century (Woodward 62). The foundation of San Carlos University in 1681 also contributed greatly to the development of cultural life in Guatemala as Ricardo Castañeda Paganini has shown in his *Historia de la Real y Pontificia Universidad de San Carlos de Guatemala* [1947; History of the Royal Pontifical University of San Carlos of Guatemala]. At the end of the seventeenth century Guatemala City claimed 60,000 inhabitants, making it one of the largest and most populated in the continent. In 1729 the first issue of *La Gaceta de Guatemala* was published; the city at this time was home to a large number of artisans and artists organized in guilds that supplied hand-crafted and artistic works to a large proportion of the region included within the Captaincy General.

San Salvador was founded in 1525 and Sonsonate in 1552. Thanks to the boom in the export of aniline dye between 1770 and 1800, San Salvador became the largest and economically most important city of the Captaincy General and as a result began to demand more political and administrative autonomy. Granada and León, founded by Francisco Hernández de Córdoba in 1524, were the two main cultural centers in Nicaragua. León was moved to its current location in 1610, while the ruins of León Viejo are among the most important archaeological ruins in the country. Throughout their history a tremendous rivalry has existed between these two cities. Even though in 1527 León was named provincial capital and in 1531 became a seat of ecclesiastical authority, Granada exercised enormous commercial power due to its access to the Atlantic. Bartolomé de Las Casas preached in the city and founded a Dominican monastery during a brief stay there, before moving on to Guatemala in 1536.

Ciudad Trujillo, founded in 1525, was the first city to be built in Honduras, followed by Camayagua in 1537. Tegucigalpa owes its origins to the silver mines found in the locality, which, during the seventeenth century, were the source of substantial wealth. Even so, the geographic and demographic conditions of the country prejudiced the development of cultural centers. However, when the University of Honduras was founded in 1847, the intellectual life of Tegucigalpa little by little began to take on local importance. During the nineteenth century both Tegucigalpa and Comayagua fought over the right to be the capital city, a privilege that moved from one to the other until the government was finally established in Tegucigalpa. The Liberal reform of 1876 brought a certain amount of progress and intellectual development to the country, but at the end of the nineteenth century, Tegucigalpa still lacked a substantial cultural life.

Cultural activity in Costa Rica was originally concentrated in Cartago, founded in 1564, and the seat of colonial government. Later on three cities of average importance, Alajuela, Heredia, and San José, began to gain ground. During the Colonial period the cities of Costa Rica did not manifest any notable cultural or economic growth, a situation that changed with the cultural and educational expansion of the 1860s. In 1866 legislation about public education was passed that resulted in the foundation of a number of high schools and colleges of higher education. Even though Santo Tomás University was closed between 1888 and 1941, many institutes of higher education remained open.

Panama City was established in 1519, while Portobelo, the most important port on the shipping route, was founded in 1597. Vessels arrived in Panama carrying gold from Peru, which was later transferred on muleback to Portobelo, whence it continued its passage to Spain. When the output of the Peruvian mines began to decline, the route gradually lost importance until it fell into a kind of oblivion. Panama was part of the viceroyalty of New Granada (now Colombia) and was governed from Bogotá; however, its isolation (due to the tropical forest of Darien) meant that it had scant contact with the viceregal capital. This created a situation of decay, which only changed at the end of the nineteenth century, when the United States intervened and prompted independence in order to facilitate the construction of a canal.

In the colonial cities, monasteries and seats of ecclesiastical power were sources of political and economic authority as well as fonts of knowledge and depositories of scholarship. The greater part of the knowledge that we have of the period is derived from the works of friars and prelates who dedicated themselves to writing down and describing regional history and culture. Father Toribio de Benavente Motolinía (1490?–1565) wrote his *Historia de los Indios de la Nueva España* [History of the Indians of New Spain] around 1560. Father Miguel Agia (fl. 1563–1604) penned *Servidumbres personales de indios, sobre las encomiendas* [Personal Servitude of Indians with Reference to the Encomiendas] circa 1570. Father Estevan Aviles wrote his *Historia de Guatemala desde los tiempos de los indios hasta la fundación de la provincia de franciscanos; población de aquellas tierras, propagación, de los indios, sus ritos, ceremonias, policía y gobierno* [1633; History of Guatemala from the Time of the Indians to the Foundation of the Franciscan Province; the Population of this Territory, Propagation of the Indians, their Rituals, Ceremonies, Police and Government]. Father Fernando Espino (ca. 1597–1676) wrote the *Historia de la reducción y conversión de la provincia de Tegucigalpa con la vida, virtudes y prodigios de tres mártires* [1674; History of the Conquest and Conversion of the Province of Tegucigalpa with the Life, Virtues and Miracles of Three Martyrs].

The clergy in Central America was organized into four bishoprics: Chiapas, Guatemala, Honduras, and Nicaragua. The Archdiocese of Guatemala was established in 1742, and the historical record is full of examples of its power and how it was exercised. Even so, the power and cultural influence of the church suffered enormous setbacks, the most important perhaps being the expulsion of the Jesuits in 1767. The cultural weight of the clerics can be seen in the literary history of the region. The first great poem of Central America is *Rusticatio Mexicana* (1782) by the Jesuit Rafael Landívar (1731–1793). Written in Italy in Latin in the style of the *Georgics,* the poem is a rhapsody on the geography and landscape of Mexico and Guatemala, a hymn to the knowledge of these lands, their wealth and customs, pastimes, and productivity. Landívar's exquisite hexameters bring together a treasure trove of contemporary culture and learning. However, this work had no effect on the regional culture of the period, since it was not available in Spanish until the twentieth century.

The principal fiestas and cultural expressions of the Colonial period developed around religious ceremonies. The calendar of the Catholic Church gradually replaced that of the indigenous people and soon the most important fiestas, even those of patently indigenous origin, coincided with those celebrated by the Church. In Central America today there are more than a hundred festivities and celebrations that represent an extremely important aspect of the cultural life of the region. The majority of these events are in honor of the Virgin Mary or one of the patron saints and are a symbiosis of indigenous theater and Catholic ritual. The participants frequently wear masks, disguises, and every kind of allegorical adornment, dance to the sound of ceremonial rhythms and recite theatrical speeches that are more or less established by custom. Some of the most popular are the "Dance of the Conquest," "Moors and Christians," "The Deer Dance," "The Bull Dance," "*El Costeño*" ["The Coastal Dweller"], "The Giantess," "The Devil's Dance," and "Mexicans." Each one of these events involves a cultural organization that frequently includes pilgrimages to different towns and many months of planning. The relationship between these dances and the theater is undeniable and it would be impossible to understand the cultural life of Central America without taking into account their importance in the cultural development of the Mesoamerican people. Theater and dance were extremely popular among the pre-Hispanic indigenous population. For the Maya, drama was one of the most popular ways of transmitting knowledge. The Nahuas brought the dance tradition with them from Mexico, and they had a definitive influence on centers of cultural dissemination in Central America.

One of the most celebrated examples of colonial *mestizo* theater is *El Güegüense o Macho Ratón*, a comedy-ballet probably dating back to the middle of the sixteenth century, which represents a negotiation between Governor Tastuanes and the *mestizo* Güegüense who, by means of this, marries his son to the governor's daughter. The work is performed in the streets amidst a large number of the local population and is attended by members of different social levels. This performance takes place in the Carazo Department of Nicaragua during February and in Masaya in September, and involves elaborate preparations and long rehearsals. During the performance period the city fills with visitors that participate in the preparations and festivities. Carazo and Masaya become extremely important cultural centers not just for Nicaragua but for Latin-American theater, since *El Güegüense* is one of the few theatrical works that can claim to be purely *mestizo* and has enormous significance in terms of the power relationships that were established during Colonial times.

The influence of travelers and their observations has been particularly important throughout Latin America. In Central America they made an enormous contribution to knowledge about and study of indigenous and *mestizo* culture. Various Europeans and U.S. scholars traveled all over the continent studying the flora and fauna, collecting cultural materials, oral histories, and topographic descriptions, and thereby established important bases for the cultural history of Central America. Thomas Gage traveled the length and breadth of the region, bequeathing a lucid and valuable vision of Central American culture that was occasionally pitiless but nevertheless seminal for an understanding of the period. John Cockburn's *A Journey over Land, from the Gulf of Honduras to the Great South Sea* (1735) is worth mentioning for Honduras, along with *Exploration and Adventure in Honduras; Comprising Sketches of*

Travel in the Gold Regions of Olancho, and a Review of the History and General Resources of Central America (1857) by William Vincent Wells (1826–1876). E. G. Squier, first envoy of the United States government to Nicaragua, was responsible for the discovery of the anthropo-zoomorphic idols on the Island of Zapateras on Nicaragua's Great Lake. Daniel Garrison Brinton recovered, edited, and translated *El Güegüense*, while Karl Bovarious compiled the most important catalogues of Nicaraguan fauna. The contribution of these travelers to the cultural life was undeniable and such that, even today, they are consulted to discover who Central Americans were and how they ought to have been.

The ideas that arrived from France and other European countries soon took root among the *criollo* intelligentsia. In Central American cities cultural and political groups began to flourish that openly discussed the ideas of independence and equality that were filtering down from the north and the other side of the Atlantic. These new ideas simultaneously came together in Guatemala's San Carlos University and were disseminated outward. As John Tate Lanning points out: "From the methodological doubt of Descartes, or the theory of gravity of Sir Isaac Newton, to Benjamin Franklin's experiments in electricity, or the latest developments in hydraulics, there was scarcely a problem not defended or reviewed in some examination in the University of San Carlos de Guatemala in the last half of the eighteenth century" (115). The philosophy course at this university was extremely comprehensive and well attended, as José Mata Gavidia reveals in his *Temas de filosofía moderna sustentadas en 1785 en la Universidad de San Carlos de Guatemala* [1949; Topics of Modern Philosophy Discussed in 1785 in the University of San Carlos de Guatemala]. Between 1829 and 1830 printing presses were established in every province, resulting in a notable expansion in intellectual life. Men such as the Honduran José Cecilio del Valle (1777–1834), the Nicaraguan Miguel Larreynaga (1771–1847), the Guatemalans José Felipe Flores (1751–1814) and Pedro Molina (1777–1854), and the Costa Rican Father José Antonio de Liendo y Goicoechea (1735–1814) all contributed enormously to the development of the intellectual life of the region. Goicoechea wrote his *Memoria sobre los medios de destruir la mendacidad, y de socorrer los verdaderos pobres de esta capital* [Memoir on the Means of Abolishing Poverty and Giving Assistance to the Truly Poor of this Capital] published in New Guatemala in 1797. Pedro Molina published his *Ideas de derecho público* [1847; Ideas of Public Law], and Larreynaga left a vast legacy, including his *Discurso sobre las artes* [1798; Discourse on the Arts], a translation of Aristotle's *Rhetoric* published in 1799, *Método para extraer las causas* [1807; Methods for Distinguishing Causes], *Exposición dirigida a la Asamblea Nacional Constituyente* [1823; Report Addressed to the National Constituent Assembly], and *Prontuario de todas las cédulas reales, cartas acordadas y órdenes comunicadas a la Audiencia del Antiguo Reino de Guatemala, desde 1600 hasta 1818* [Catalogue of All the Royal Grants, Official Letters and Orders Communicated to the High Court of the Ancient Realm of Guatemala from 1600 to 1818], published in 1857. Despite economic difficulties and the isolation of the provinces, Guatemala enjoyed a vibrant intellectual life that was echoed in San Salvador, León, and Granada. The *Discurso que en el Aniversario de la Instalación de la Academia de Ciencias pronunció el Lic. C. Miguel Larreynaga* [Lecture Given by C. Miguel Larreynaga on the Anniversary of the Inauguration of the Academy of Sciences] is evidence of the intellectual and cultural activity of Central America.

Journalism was a central focus for the cultural life of the region. The lack of publishing houses and literary magazines meant that the newspapers were called upon to diffuse the culture and literary works of the region. In Guatemala journalism began with *La Gaceta de Guatemala* in 1729, of which a total of eighteen volumes were published. However, the newspaper that took on the greatest cultural responsibility was the *Diario de Centro-América*, founded in 1880, it published writers of the stature of Rubén Darío (1867–1916), Enrique Gómez Carrillo (1873–1927), Francisco Galindo (1850–1896?), and Alberto Masferrer (1868–1932). Around 1824, *El Seminario Político Mercantil* appeared in El Salvador, followed by *El Centinela*, founded in 1827, and *El Amigo del Pueblo*, in 1843. Other important newspapers were *El Faro de El Salvador* (1864–1871), edited by the Nicaraguan Pablo Buitrago, and, perhaps most important of all on a cultural level, the *Diario de El Salvador* (1896) under the editorship of another Nicaraguan, Ramón Mayorga Rivas (1862–1925). Finally, the *Diario Latino* (1885) featured at the center of political and intellectual life in the late nineteenth century. In Honduras José Cecilio del Valle founded *El Amigo de la Patria* in 1820, one of the most important organs of the independence movement. The great poet Juan Ramón Molina (1875–1908) ran the *Diario de Honduras* and *El Día*, both of which played an important role in the cultural life of Tegucigalpa and the country as a whole. Prominent among the newspapers of San José, Costa Rica, were *La República*, *El Comercio*, and *Costa Rica Ilustrada*.

The first Nicaraguan novel, written by José Dolores Gámez (1851–1918) and entitled *Amor y constancia* [Love and Loyalty], was published in installments in the weekly newspaper *El Termómetro de Rivas* between 15 February and 15 June 1878 under the editorship of the author. Similarly, in Guatemala and Costa Rica, José Batres Montúfar (1809–1844) and José Millá (1822–1882) published a large part of their work in periodicals and newspapers. Joaquín García Monge (1881–1958) rapidly established himself as the leader of Costa Rican *costumbrismo*. He was responsible for the publication of the review *Reperterio Americano* (1919–1958), a cultural institution of great quality and importance that was a vehicle for continental influence as well as the ideas and writings of the most prestigious authors of the period. In 1937 Froylán Turcios (1875–1943), who was at that time in San José, published his journal *Ariel*. As democratic institutions and the educational standards improved in Costa Rica, San José's importance as a cultural center developed in tandem with the establishment of new research centers and universities. *The Revista Histórico-Crítica de la Literatura Centroamericana*, founded in 1974 and published by the University of Costa Rica, was an important vehicle for critics and intellectuals of Central American literature. In Panama the reviews *El Bohemio* (1893) and *El Cosmos* (1896) were the first literary showcases for the writers of the region when it still belonged to Colombia. *El Heraldo del Istmo* (1904) was the first review of independent Panama, but *Nuevos Ritos* (1907–1917), published by the poet Ricardo Miró (1883–1940), established itself as the most professional. Rogelio Sinán (1904–1994), the other landmark writer in Panamanian literature, published his review *Antena*, which attested to the transformation from *modernista* literature to the avant-garde.

Prensa Libre, founded in 1951, is the main newspaper published in Guatemala today, competing with eight others, all of which are based in Guatemala City. There are five government-run and six educational radio stations, including Radio Cultural TGN, which, since 1950, has broadcast cultural and religious programs in English, Spanish, Cakchiquél, and Kekchí. Honduras today boasts four important newspapers with a print run of some 260,000, all with their central offices in Tegucigalpa. Some literary and cultural reviews, such as *Cultura para Todos* and *Revista Prisma*, are also published. A similar unequal concentration of journalistic resources is apparent in El Salvador, where the newspapers with the largest circulation, such as *El Diario de Hoy*, *La Prensa Gráfica*, and *El Mundo*, are based in San Salvador.

La Prensa is the oldest newspaper in Nicaragua still in circulation. Founded in 1926, *La Prensa* has played a considerable role in the political history of the country, distinguished by its critical spirit and independent line. For the last three decades its supplement, *La Prensa Literaria*, has been one of the main disseminators of culture in the country. *Barricada*, established in 1979, is the official organ of the Frente Sandinista de Liberación Nacional (Sandinista Front for National Liberation) and is edited in Managua in the same offices previously occupied by *Novedades*, the official newspaper of the Somoza dictatorship. In 1998 *Barricada* closed for two years; in April 2000 it began to publish once more, albeit on a weekly basis and with a reduced number of pages. *El Nuevo Diario*, a sensationalist newspaper that currently has the largest circulation in Nicaragua, also publishes a literary supplement entitled *Nuevo Amanecer Cultural*, whose contributors include some of the best writers in the country, such as Sergio Ramírez (b. 1942), Ernesto Cardenal (b. 1925), and Julio Valle Castillo (b. 1942).

Six daily newspapers are published in San José, the most important being *La Nación*. Costa Rica's economic growth combined with a large colony of immigrants from the United States who have settled in the country, and the internationalization of the culture can be seen in the publication of *The Tico Times*, a weekly newspaper in English. A total of four newspapers are published daily with a run of approximately 350,000. There is a 93 percent literacy rate, with 90 percent of eleven-year-olds attending school, giving the country the highest educational level in Central America. In Panama, news and cultural publications are obtained in Panama City. *El Siglo* and *La Estrella de Panamá* are the most important, with another twenty newspapers of lesser circulation. The most important cultural review is *Maga*, published by Enrique Jaramillo Levi (b. 1944).

The nineteenth-century optimism responsible for such a proliferation of journalism also resuscitated the idea of an inter-oceanic route. During the second half of the nineteenth century the existence of such a route through Nicaragua via the Great Lake, the San Juan River, and by railway, stimulated the economic and cultural life of the southern part of the country, generating a certain vitality in Greytown on the Atlantic coast and the Rivas isthmus on the Pacific. Even so, the possibility of another passage across the isthmus became a central concern of the Liberals in the post-Independence period. Even though a Franciscan friar was the first to mention such a project during the seventeenth century, the dream was not realized until the beginning of the twentieth century (Woodward 120). The construction of the inter-oceanic route in Panama affected the location of cultural centers in Central America, given that all commerce and the point of entry of merchandise, including cultural artifacts, shifted to Panama. In time, the effect diminished and Panama did not succeed in establishing itself as a cultural capital; the commercial character of the city came more to the fore. Even so, the canal had an impact on Panamanian narrative, with various novels dealing with the United States' presence in the region. *Luna verde* [1951; Green Moon] by Joaquín Beleño (b. 1922), *La isla mágica* [1979; Magic Island] by Rogelio Sinán (1904–1994), and *El último juego* [1977; Last Game] by Gloria Guardia (b. 1940) are some of the more well-known examples.

In the last two decades of the nineteenth century, *modernismo* emerged in Latin America, a cosmopolitan movement that revolved around the figure of the Nicaraguan Rubén Darío (1867–1916). As Darío's fame grew in the sphere of Spanish American literature, he attracted diverse groups of followers whose influence lasted until the second decade of the twentieth century. Darío spent the first part of his life in León, during a period when the arguments with Granada over the political hegemony of the country were still ongoing. From a very early age Darío showed evidence of poetic genius and cultural leadership, and on his return visits to Nicaragua, the city of León became the cultural capital not only of the country but also of the region. The first edition of *Azul* in 1888 had an immediate impact on Central America and was followed by a Guatemalan edition in 1890. His poet friends came from neighboring countries to meet and talk with him and wrote chronicles and articles that were later published in other countries. His journeys and sojourns, especially in San Salvador and Guatemala, had an enormously enlivening effect on the culture of those cities. During his second stay in San Salvador, Darío founded the short-lived newspaper *La Unión*, in which he wrote some memorable works. In Guatemala he directed *El Correo de la Tarde*, creating around him an important literary group that included the journalist and novelist Enrique Gómez Carrillo (1873–1927), author of the novels *Del amor, del dolor y del vicio* [1898; On Love, Pain, and Vice], *El evangelio del amor* [1922; The Gospel of Love] and the travel chronicle *Japón heroico y galante* [1912; Heroic and Urbane Japan]. José Tible Machado, Timoteo Miranda, and the Nicaraguan professor Santiago Argüello (1872–1940), author of *Divino Platón* [1934; Divine Plato] and many poems, books, and pamphlets, were also numbered among Darío's friends. In the latter's absence, Argüello adopted the role of the leader of the *modernista* movement in Nicaragua and exercised an enormous influence during his lifetime through his teaching and critical works.

In Honduras Juan Ramón Molina (1875–1908) was the central figure of the *modernista* revolution, but Froylán Turcios (1875–1943) exercised more influence, publishing Molina's poems after the latter's death in the volume *Tierras, mares y cielos* [1911; Lands, Seas, and Skies]. Not only was Turcios a fine writer, skilled in various genres, but he also performed a great literary service with his reviews and publications. Recently his short stories have been republished in *Cuentos del amor y de la muerte* [1991; Stories of Love and Death] and *Cuentos completos* [1995; Complete Short Stories]. In El Salvador Francisco Gavidia (1864–1955) was the precursor of major literary activity and a great teacher. His house and classroom established a cultural environment of great importance for Central American literature. Rubén Darío visited there and read his first attempts at versifying in French. Various generations of writers and an important current of Central American theater also originated there. Gavidia published his *Historia moderna de El Salvador* [Modern History of El Salvador] and *Cuentos y narraciones* [Stories and Narrations] between 1917 and 1918. In Panama the national cultural figure was Ricardo Miró (1883–

1940), whose review *Nuevos Ritos* was fundamental to the literary life of Panama and whose life and example molded the intellectual activity of the country. So important was the author of *Los segundos preludios* [1916; Second Preludes] in the Panamanian cultural panorama that the most notable national literary competition bears his name.

Parallel to the development of *modernismo* and at the height of the coffee export trade, Central American cities witnessed an economic growth that was accompanied by the modernization of the economy and a certain amount of industrial development. Even though the Central American capitals were not great modern metropolitan areas, they were regarded in their respective countries as centers of modernity and treasuries of Western culture (Ready 28). This urbanization, initiated on an economic level by new agricultural exports, reflected the improvement in living standards of a small percentage of the population and contributed to the development of cultural life. However, the majority of the inhabitants of the isthmus remained illiterate and continued to live in poverty. After the refined writing of the *modernista* movement, the literary groups that followed began to identify themselves more intimately with the social concerns of a region where the class differences had increased further as a result of modernization. At the beginning of the century there was an interest in popular culture that was reflected in the growth of regionalism and *criollismo*. In El Salvador, Salvador Salazar Arrué (1889–1975) (pseudonym Salarrué) wrote his *Cuentos de barro* [1933; Stories of Clay] and *Cuentos de cipotes* [1945; Stories of Urchins] in which he captured the popular voice of his people in traditional forms. Salarrué's studio in San Marcos became a meeting place for various artists, including the poet Carmen Brannon Vega (1899–1974), known by her pseudonym Claudia Lars, and the writers Serafín Quiteño (1906–1987), and Alberto Guerra Trigueros (1898–1950). In Nicaragua the poets Alfonso Cortés (1893–1969), Azarías Pallais (1884–1954), and Salomón de la Selva (1893–1959), precursors of the avant-garde, also began to write in these years.

At the beginning of the 1930s, avant-garde currents began to develop in Central America that were not only to revolutionize artistic aesthetic principles but also to give a further stimulus to urban cultural life. The best examples of this kind of movement can be seen in Guatemala and Nicaragua. In the former, the "Tepeus" group in the 1930s and "Acento" group in the 1940s were largely concerned with the status of the indigenous people. Despite their enthusiasm, it was not until after the revolution of 1944 that the artists of the Left eventually had an opportunity to influence the cultural politics of their country. The "Saker-Ti" group, composed of various writers, including Carlos Illescas (1918–1998) and the poets Raúl Leiva (b. 1934) and Otto Raúl González (b. 1921), published a review of the same name during this time and were able to disseminate their ideas on a broader basis through its literary pages (Rodríguez Mojón 17). Nevertheless, the most important twentieth-century figure in Guatemala is without doubt Miguel Angel Asturias (1899–1974), whose work and personality created an important cultural space in both his own country and in Latin America. All Asturias's work centers around the sociopolitical situation in Guatemala and, more specifically, the indigenous situation. This concern had been evident since his university thesis entitled *Sociología Guatemalteca* [1925; Sociology of Guatemala] and later permeated his entire narrative *oeuvre*. His most famous work, *El*

Señor Presidente, written in 1928 and not published until 1946, initiated the genre of the dictator novel in Latin America, a genre of singular importance in Latin American literature. The dictator novel is a major cultural mode of Central American narrative, a space where political vicissitudes and the spirit of the *caudillo* (political boss) in the Latin American continent converge. Another contribution of great importance is Miguel Angel Asturias's mythological Mayan world as developed in *Hombres de maíz* [1949; *Men of Maize,* 1975], in which poetic force meets with narrative invention to create one of the most magical and enigmatic texts of Latin American literature. This exploration of the Mayan mythos would be followed by *Mulata de tal* [1963; *The Mulatta and Mr. Fly,* 1963] and *Maladrón: Epopeya de los Andes verdes* [1969; Maladrón: Epic of the Green Andes]. Asturias is also responsible for developing a strong critical line against the United States' invasion of Guatemala, economic as much as military. His famous *bananera* ("banana company") trilogy, which includes *Viento fuerte* [1950; *Strong Wind,* 1968], *El Papa verde* [1954; *The Green Pope,* 1971], and *Los ojos de los enterrados* [1960; *The Eyes of the Interred,* 1973], represent the culmination of a series of narratives that are based on his concerns about the *bananeras.* *Weekend en Guatemala* [1956; Weekend in Guatemala] is a collection of short stories that reveals the violence of the United States' invasion of 1954, which led to the unseating of elected President Arbenz. With these texts Asturias consolidated his defense of the indigenous people and the people of Guatemala, showing the injustice and violence of the sociopolitical system. Even though Asturias did not live much of the time in Guatemala, it is clear that the country is the locus for his entire corpus of work. The fact that he was awarded the Nobel Prize in 1967 gave him an enormous prestige and authority that in turn redounded in honor of his country, consolidating its position as the nation producing the best fiction in Central America.

Returning to the avant-garde, it should be pointed out that the most important and active movement was that of Nicaragua, whose center of operations was the house of José Coronel Urtecho (1906–1994) and the tower of the Merced Church, both in Granada. During the 1930s Granada was the most important cultural center of Central America and it could be said that the tower of the Merced Church was the lighthouse from which the light of this cultural movement was spread. Around the poets Coronel Urtecho and Luis Alberto Cabrales (1902–1974) gathered other poets such as Pablo Antonio Cuadra (1912–2002), Manolo Cuadra (1907–1957), Octavio Rocha (1910–1985), Joaquín Pasos (1914–1947), and José Román (1906–1983). These poets declared themselves in revolt against the *modernista* and bourgeois aesthetic of their literary predecessors, forming the Anti-Academy of Arts and Letters in 1931 (Whisnant 153). The *Poemas Nicaragüenses, 1930–1933* [1934; Nicaraguan Poems, 1930–1933] and *Por los caminos van los campesinos* [1937; The Peasants Go Down the Road] by Pablo Antonio Cuadra come from this cultural period. Through their publications and manifestos as well as their iconoclastic stance and their literary meetings, this avant-garde group was the principal stimulus for the renewal of both Nicaraguan and Central American literature. In Nicaragua the next generation of writers, that of the 1940s, produced an impressive corpus of anti-Somoza literature. The most celebrated of these was Ernesto Cardenal, though the name of Carlos Martínez Rivas (1924–1998), author of *La insurrección solitaria* [1953; The Solitary Insurrection] should

not be omitted. During the 1960s a Leftist group was established around the publication *Ventana* and, in 1968, Grupo Praxis set up the magazine *Taller* (Whisnant 168). Other groups and affiliations also existed in Central America during this period, but their work was not as widely disseminated as that of the Guatemalan and Nicaraguan writers.

During the 1960s and 1970s an increasing number of women began to publish, following the example of authors such as Claudia Lars (pseudonym Carmen Brannon, 1899–1974), Eunice Odio (1922–1974), and Yolanda Oreamuno (1916–1956). Claribel Alegría (b. 1924) wrote *Cenizas de Izalco* [1966; Ashes of Izalco] with her husband Darwin Flakoll, a novel based on the 1932 massacre in El Salvador. Rosario Aguilar (b. 1938) published *Las doce y veintinueve* [1975; Twelve Twenty-Nine], which tells the story of the Managua earthquake of 1972 from a multiplicity of perspectives. Other women writers of the 1980s continued in the same vein of social conscience. In 1984 Irma Prego (b. 1933) published *Mensajes al más allá* [Messages to the Beyond], which gave literary expression to feminist concerns, while Carmen Naranjo (b. 1928) explored similar themes in the short stories appearing in *Ondina* (1985). Claribel Alegría and Gioconda Belli (b. 1948) took as their theme women guerrilla fighters in *No me agarran viva: La mujer salvadoreña en lucha* [1983; They Won't Take Me Alive: Salvadorean Women in Struggle for National Liberation] and *La mujer habitada* [1988; The Inhabited Woman], respectively. A strong current of erotic poetry written by authors such as Gioconda Belli, Michel Najlis (b. 1946), and others was also prevalent. The first works by Costa Rican writers Tatiana Lobo (b. 1939) and Linda Berrón (b. 1951) began to appear at the beginning of the 1990s. Their works probed into the colonial condition and the representation of women. Meanwhile, writers such as Prego, Alegría, and Belli continued to publish new work. A revival of interest in the Conquest and the Colonial period came with the 500th anniversary of Columbus's voyage as evidenced by Tatiana Lobo's *Asalto al paraíso* [1992; Assault on Paradise] and *La niña blanca y los pájaros sin pies* [1992; The White Girl and Birds Without Feet] by Rosario Aguilar (b. 1938).

Women also played an active part in the creation of protest literature that corresponded, both politically and culturally, to left-wing movements that opposed the military dictatorships in Central America. The boom of protest literature during the 1970s and 1980s was inspired by works with anti-imperialist themes such as *Prisión verde* [1950; Green Prison] by the Honduran writer Ramón Amaya-Amador (1916–1966) and *Mamita Yunai* (1941) by the Costa Rican Carlos Luis Fallas (1909–1966). *Murámonos, Federico* [1973; Let's Die, Federico] by another Costa Rican, Joaquín Gutiérrez (1918–2000), could also be included in this group. In general this protest literature as a whole tries to link social conscience with new aesthetic paradigms to create art of and for the people. Two genres associated with protest literature are *exteriorista* poetry and the *testimonio* (testimony). Protest poetry is an affirmation and glorification of people's power to resist the injustices of their oppressors. The guerrilla poetry and prose of Roque Dalton (1935–1975), author of *Las historias prohibidas del pulgarcito* [1974; The Forbidden Stories of Tom Thumb] and *Poemas clandestinos* [1980; Clandestine Poems], communicate this message of protest and consciousness raising. In Nicaragua the poetry of Gioconda Belli (b. 1948) in *Línea de fuego* [1978; Line of Fire] and Leonel Rugana (1949–1970) in *Poemas* [1981; Poems] is simple, with little technical complexity, and underlines the social urgency of the problems being expressed. Formal simplicity is also a characteristic of *exteriorista* poetry associated with Ernesto Cardenal in works such as *Canto nacional* [1973; National Canto] and *Oráculo sobre Managua* [1973; Oracle on Managua]. In his work, Cardenal proposes revolution as an act of love, inserting liberation theology, communism, and national myth in his verse.

Apart from poetry, the *testimonio* arose as an important weapon of protest, generally relating a significant event in the life of the protagonist/narrator in a context of political violence (Beverley and Zimmerman 173). The most famous of these is *Me llamo Rigoberta Menchú y así me nació la conciencia* [1983; I, Rigoberta Menchú: An Indian Woman in Guatemala, 1984], which tells the story of an indigenous Guatemalan. There is, however, a long list of testimonies by other authors, among which stand out *La Montaña es algo más que una inmensa estepa verde* [1982; Fire from the Mountain, 1985] by Omar Cabezas (b. 1950), *Carlos, el amanecer ya no es una tentación* [1976; Carlos, Now the Dawn Is No Fond Illusion] by Tomás Borge (b. 1930), *No me agarran viva* [1983; They Won't Take Me Alive] by Alegría and Flakoll, and Victor Montejo's (b. 1951) *Testimonio: Muerte de una comunidad indígena en Guatemala* [1987; Testimony: Death of a Guatemalan Village]. As with *exteriorista* poetry, the testimony is not concerned with literary form, but rather underlines the importance and urgency as a voice of protest.

These two forms of literary expression have achieved great international popularity, giving Central America a place in Latin American literature. Such notoriety has had a dual effect on the cultural centers of the region. On the one hand, considerable international attention has been focused on the countries and cities producing such literature, generating congresses and meetings of critics as well as monographs and articles. On the other hand, there is a noticeable shift from the capitals, where the cultural life of each country has been concentrated, toward the periphery, the real site of these texts. In this way indigenous and marginal themes come to the center of textual and critical discussion. The groups that are most relegated to the margins on a cultural level thus become cultural objects. This undoubtedly has an enormous effect on the location of cultural centers, and the consequences of this will continue into the twenty-first century.

Each country in Central America has various *institutional* cultural centers. Historically, the main center for higher education in the region was the University of San Carlos de Guatemala, founded by Royal Decree in 1676. The University of Granada was founded at the beginning of the nineteenth century (1811) followed by that of León (1815), both of which catered to the youth of not only Nicaragua but also Costa Rica and Honduras. Both the University of El Salvador and the Universidad Pontificia Santo Tomás in Costa Rica were founded in 1841; in 1847 Juan Lindo founded the University of Honduras. Thus by the mid-nineteenth century each Central American republic could count on at least one institution of higher education as well as various institutes and centers of higher learning. Rafael Heliodoro Valle confirms that halfway through the twentieth century, "The university social class has been aristocratic in the life of Central America; one that has not concerned itself with helping to solve the problems of their respective countries but rather has continually swelled the ranks of the bureaucracy" (Valle 121). If this is to be accepted as true, then it is also important to point out the active participation of the universities in the development of the social and political struggles of the region throughout the second half of the twentieth century. In Guatemala, El Salvador, Nicaragua, and other Central American countries the universities have been the principal home of new ideas as well as the breeding ground for militants supportive of revolutionary movements, carrying along with them not only political institutions but also cultural organizations. In this sense the universities have been not only cultural centers but also the inspiration behind the political and social life of the region.

Literary life in the cultural centers of Central America has developed in an informal manner through meetings of groups and *tertulias*. However, one should not underestimate the role played by the *ateneos* (cultural associations) and academies in the historical development of culture and the literary journals that have acted as cultural vehicles for countries lacking other editorial outlets. In Guatemala the Ateneo Batres Mantúfar, initiated in 1931, was a center of important literary activity in the capital. The *Revista de Guatemala*, founded by Luis Cardoza y Aragón in 1904, brought together a large majority of the Guatemalan intelligentsia. Finally, the journal *Universidad de San Carlos* (since 1945) has also been a seminal publication in the cultural life of Guatemala. In El Salvador the *Repertorio del Diario de El Salvador* and the review *Istmo*, founded in 1908 by Julio Enrique Avila and Raúl Andino, were focal points of literary activity. The *Revista del Ateneo de El Salvador* (1912) is another institution around which much of the cultural life of the country has developed. Founded in 1921, the Centro Intelectual Salvadoreño—in which the most important intellectuals of the period participated, such as Francisco Gavidia, Alberto Masferrer, and Arturo Ambrogi—was a vital part of Salvadorean culture. Among the most important reviews to be mentioned are *Cultura*, which has performed an exemplary task since 1955, and *Síntesis*, founded a year later.

The Academia Científico-Literaria de Honduras (1888), which hosted the most important literary meetings of the country, was founded at the end of the nineteenth century. The Ateneo de Honduras was established in 1913 and rapidly had a stimulating effect on the cultural life of the nation. In 1905 Froylán Turcios published the reviews *Esfinge*, *El Pensamiento*, and *La Revista Nueva*. In Nicaragua, Santiago Argüello published *La Torre de Marfil*, a review that addressed the aesthetic interests of the successors to the *modernista* poets. The avant-garde Nicaraguan Anti-Academy published their "Hoja de Vanguardia," in which members presented their writings. Around 1940 Pablo Antonio Cuadra began publishing the review *Cuadernos del Taller San Lucas*, which quickly became the epicenter of Nicaraguan cultural life. The *Revista del Pensamiento Centroamericano* (originally *Revista Conservadora del Pensamiento Centroamericano*) and *El Pez y la Serpiente* (1961–1981) were the two most important reviews, the first dedicated to a variety of themes and the second being purely literary, but both were responsible for a major contribution to the cultural life of the country. As a result of the financial difficulties of the 1980s *El Pez y la Serpiente* stopped publication, while the *Revista del Pensamiento Centroamericano* moved its offices to San José. At the end of the 1990s *Artefacto* began publication in Managua, a high-quality review with an iconoclastic approach to art and literature

Central America still does not have a professional commercial publishing house that publishes and efficiently distributes the work of its authors. Editorial Universitaria Centro Americana (EDUCA) is the most prestigious, functioning under the auspices of the Confederación Universitaria Centroamericana founded by Sergio Ramírez in San José, Costa Rica. EDUCA has produced over a hundred books of fine literary quality and at low cost from the Ciudad Universitaria Rodrigo Facio, an important intellectual center in itself. Among the published titles are Asturias's *Hombres de maíz* and *Azul* [Blue] by Rubén Darío. In part on account of budgetary reductions and in part because of bad administration, EDUCA was obliged to declare bankruptcy; however, at the time of writing (1999), it was once more in a process of restructuring. San José boasts about ten small publishing houses, of which the most notable is the Editorial Costa Rica.

Book production has been seriously limited in Honduras, which has shown a preference for the publication of journals and literary pages in the daily newspapers. The Editorial de la Universidad Autónoma de Honduras has been one of the principal publishing houses. During recent years Editorial Guaymuras has begun to publish some Honduran literary works of merit and to increase their circulation. The university's publishing arm has included in its titles *Memorías* [1980; Memoirs] by Froylán Turcios and *Antología: El poeta y sus señales* [1969; Anthology: The Poet and Her Signs] by Clementina Suárez (1902–1991). Those published by Editorial Guaymuras include the poem *El llanto de las cosas* [1995; The Lament of Things] by Roberto Sosa (b. 1930) and the anthology *Narradoras Hondureñas* [1990; Women Narrators from Honduras] edited by Hélen Umaña. In El Salvador the major publishing houses are found within the universities: for example, UCA Editores, responsible for the first edition of *Un día en la vida* [1980; One Day of Life] by Manlio Argueta (b. 1935), and Editorial Universitaria, both of which are main sources of cultural publications. Apart from literary works, the Editorial Universitaria also publishes volumes on the plastic arts such as *De la pintura en El Salvador: Panorama histórico crítico* [1986; On Painting in El Salvador: Historical-Critical Panorama] by José Roberto Cea (b. 1939). Clásicos Roxsil also plays a fairly important role in the literary and cultural life of the country.

In El Salvador at the beginning of the century, the Biblioteca Económica provided access to great works of literature in translation as well as works by Salvadoreans like *Cenizas de Izalco* [1966; *Ashes of Izalco,* 1989] by Alegría and Flakoll. Other notable efforts included the Biblioteca Cuscatlana and the Biblioteca de Autores Centroamericanos, edited by Arturo Ambrogi (1875–1936). Guatemala's Biblioteca del Pueblo, responsible for the publication of a good number of books that achieved wide distribution, also deserves mention. Other publishing houses of importance in the country include the Editorial Universitaria, which produces critical studies such as the *Historia crítica de la novela guatemalteca* [1985; Critical History of the Guatemalan Novel] by Seymour Menton as well as fiction, poetry, and drama. The Editorial Piedra Santa has also been an active source of literary production in Guatemala. Editorial Nueva Nicaragua published some books of literary quality during the 1980s in Nicaragua, but the distribution has been very poor, while chaotic administration has brought about bankruptcy. Banking institutions such as the Bank of America and the Central Bank have financed some important collections. The most important commercial enterprises include the Editorial Hospicio de León, the Editorial Alemana, and more recently Distribuidora Cultura, Hispamer, and Anamá, all based in Managua. Various critical editions of *El Güegüense,* the celebrated novel *Cosmapa* (1971) by José Román (1906–1983), *Héroes sin fusil* [1998; Heroes Without Guns] by Jorge Eduardo Arellano (b. 1946), and many more titles have issued from their presses.

The origins of plastic arts in Central America lie in the stupendous creations of the Mayas and the Nahuas. Later, during the Colonial period, artistic work was largely concentrated in the arts-and-craft-orientated guilds, particularly in Guatemala City, but also spreading throughout the other provinces. Sculptors and painters, musicians and metalworkers, silversmiths and watchmakers, all organized into guilds and regulated by the Audiencia de los Confines y los Ayuntamientos (Tribunal of Boundaries and Municipalities), were responsible for the development of the first works of art in colonial Central America (Samayoa Guevara 21). In 1778 the Escuela de Dibujo de Guatemala (Guatemala School of Drawing) and the Academia de Bellas Artes de San Carlos (San Carlos Academy of Fine Arts) both played an important role in the development of the plastic arts in Central America. But it was not until the twentieth century that the fine art schools and national museums were founded, which would also provide a stimulus to the region.

The ministries of culture have acted as state-run institutions dedicated to promoting the cultural and intellectual life of their respective countries. In many cases this work has been entrusted to the Education Ministry, as is the case in Panama today. El Salvador provides the most telling precedent; the Ministry of Culture was established in 1945 and two years later the Casa de Cultura (House of Culture). The Nicaraguan Ministry for Culture was organized by the Sandinista government in 1980 under the directorship of Ernesto Cardenal, undertaking very constructive work, especially in the area of street theater and poetry workshops. However in 1988 Ernesto Cardenal was removed from office for political reasons and the Ministry for Culture closed down. In 1999 a Nicaraguan Institute of Culture was operating, as well as the Asociación de Promotores de Cultura (Association for Promoters of Culture), whose membership was largely derived from the old Sandinista organizations. In Costa Rica, cultural activity at the official level is handled through the Ministerio de Cultura, Juventud y Deportes (Ministry of Culture, Youth, and Sports) and in Guatemala through the Ministerio de Cultura y Deportes (Ministry of Culture and Sports). In this manner Central American governments have attempted to control their national culture (though officializing culture is virtually always tantamount to destroying it) and in doing so have established an occasionally tense dynamic between intellectuals and governing officials.

Another interesting dimension to cultural centers is seen in the phenomenon of popular culture. In Central America this manifests itself in traditional form in folkloric music, regional dances, and handicrafts. However, it also includes local and imported mass media such as magazines, television programs, photo-novels, and illustrated comics. Even though in recent years there has been a debate on the binary opposition between popular and elite culture, the popular has customarily been identified with the masses and the elite with the upper class and bourgeoisie (Rowe and Schelling 2). Notwithstanding this debate, Central American artistic creativity is present at popular fairs, in the markets, and in the streets, where artisans sell their paintings and sculptures, and marimba trios play a *zapateado* (form of dance music). During the 1980s Nicaragua's Sandinista government tried to foster a variety of popular revolutionary culture. Poetry workshops, under the guidance of Ernesto Cardenal which promoted his *exteriorismo,* were organized by the Costa Rican Mayra Jiménez (b. 1938). Workers, youth, the military, and other citizens gathered in neighborhood workshops once a week to write and discuss their poetry. The Ministry of Culture and Sandinista cultural workers founded *casas de cultura* to promote popular culture. The workshops proved a good exercise in composition, but they did not produce the results dreamed of by Ernesto Cardenal. Despite this, the work of the poet and his community in Solentiname is an important cultural development in the history of Latin American literature. As a pictorial school, Nicaraguan *exteriorismo* found the appropriate conditions in Solentiname to develop into one of the important currents of Latin American culture. Solentiname is also a tragic site in the Latin American revolutionary struggle, immortalized in Julio Cortázar's short story "Apocalipsis de Solentiname." *Casas de cultura* have also been established in El Salvador with similar programs. Recently a popular theater has arisen among indigenous communities in Chiapas and Guatemala. Despite the disappearance of political conditions that emphasized the promotion of popular culture, it still exists as a dynamic phenomenon. The study of popular culture can reveal the constant negotiation between groups, interests, and aesthetic preferences at a given historical moment and provide the observer with new perspectives on the society responsible for its production.

With a population of 1,200,000, Guatemala City boasts a dynamic and expanding cultural life. Even taking into account the political problems of the last three decades of the twentieth century, the capital offers a multiplicity of cultural attractions as well as being the center of the country's intellectual life. The Academia Guatemalteca de Lengua organizes many events and presentations on literary and linguistic themes. Eight substantial libraries provide a good collection of material in various disciplines, while specializing in history and anthropology. Seven important universities cater to the student population, with those of San Carlos and Rafael Landívar being of particular note. Antigua is another important Guatemalan cultural center, boasting some beautiful museums such as the Museo Colonial, the Museo del Libro Antiguo, and the Museo de Santiago.

San Salvador has a population of only half a million inhabitants in a country with a total population of over five million; cities such as Soyapando, Santa Ana, and San Miguel thus assume demographic importance. However, despite this, San Salvador is the focus for the intellectual life of the nation. The six most notable libraries in the country are found in the capital, and the same can be said for the museums, of which the National Museum, founded in 1883, is the most important. The universities are also concentrated in San Salvador; the most noteworthy are the Universidad Centroamericana José Simeón Cañas and the El Salvador University. After ten years of bloodshed, the economy of the country at the end of the twentieth century was showing marked growth but the capital city was suffering serious social problems. Even so, there was a developing cultural life, and many writers and artists have returned from exile to contribute to the intellectual life of the nation.

Tegucigalpa has eight hundred thousand inhabitants and, as the seat of government, enjoys the culture provided by national institutions and the two most important universities in Honduras. San Pedro de Sula, the second city of the country, is more industrial and commercial. Honduras has around 70 percent literacy, and has fewer writers and artists than the other Central American countries. However, Tegucigalpa does provide a moderate intellectual and cultural life. The

Academia Hondureña (Honduran Academy), founded in 1949, provides interesting literary activities; five important libraries also perform cultural functions, while the National Museum has an interesting anthropological and historical collection. Featured among Honduras's cultural treasures are the ruins of Copán, evidence of Mayan cultural wealth, the Museo Regional de Arqueología Maya (Regional Museum of Mayan Archaeology), and the Museo Arqueológico e Histórico de Comayagua (Comayagua Archaeological and Historical Museum), the latter two housing some very important cultural treasures.

Managua was destroyed by both the earthquake of 1972 and the negligence of various military dictatorships. During the 1980s the population of the city grew disproportionately to one and a half million inhabitants, who now live on the fringes of the city and lack any kind of urban infrastructure. Despite the fact that the majority of cultural institutions are located in Managua, Granada and León enjoy a certain degree of cultural and intellectual life as well. Recently the old National Palace, the seat of Congress, was transformed into the Palacio de la Cultura (Palace of Culture) and now houses the National Library with its important collections. The Rubén Darío Theater is the focus of dramatic activity in the country and a series of literary cafés complete the cultural picture. The museums, the most outstanding being the National Museum in Managua, are very poor and badly run. The four most important universities are located in Managua, with the exception of the Universidad Nacional Autónoma de Nicaragua (National Autonomous University of Nicaragua), which is based in León.

San José in Costa Rica is currently a vibrant and rich cultural center. The high educational level of the population, the political stability provided by a reliable democracy dating from 1948, and a vigorous economy all provide suitable conditions for the development of the cultural and intellectual life of the city. The population of San José is estimated at a little under one million inhabitants and benefits from numerous theaters and libraries. Seven of the eight most important museums in the country are situated in the capital, providing a great variety of cultural activities. Particularly important for the preservation of the indigenous culture are the museums of gold and jade, whose collections are evidence of the wealth of pre-Columbian culture. With the exception of the Universidad Nacional (National University) in Heredia, the universities have their campuses in San José, thereby attracting a numerous student population from all over the country. On the other hand, the moderate climate and geographical location of San José contribute to the elegance and attractiveness of the city.

Less of a cultural center, Panama City is an important economic enclave within Latin America. The city houses seven hundred thousand inhabitants, three universities–including the Universidad de Panamá (Panama University)–and various specialized schools such as the Escuela Nacional de Música (National School of Music), the Escuela Nacional de Artes Plásticas (National School of Art), the Escuela Nacional de Danzas (National Dance School), and the Escuela Nacional de Teatro (National Theater School). The National Library, founded in 1892 , has a respectable collection of books and documents. The National Archive, Biblioteca Interamericana Simón Bolivar, the Biblioteca de Estudios del Canal Interoceánico (Panama Canal Research Library), and the Amador Washington Library are also worthy of mention. After the United States's invasion that deposed the dictator Manuel Antonio Noriega, the country has experienced a period of democratic development. During the 1990s President Valladares's ambitions for reelection were rejected by the popular will. The country also recently took over control of the Panama Canal.

At the end of the twentieth century Central American culture was experiencing a process of development and crisis. On the one hand the collapse of the liberation movements meant that left-wing groups and intellectuals were left without a solid platform from which to develop further. The long years of civil war, governmental corruption, and the high human cost of repression drained the population, the workers and *campesinos* in particular. On the other hand, neo-liberal policies and governments of the center-right that then took power were not able to give a satisfactory response to the social needs of the region. Even though the economies substantially recuperated, the standard of living continued to be very low while education and public health remained in crisis. The migration to the United States during the 1980s created two parallel phenomena: first, that of economic overdependence on the United States, given that the main source of income to the country now comes from the remittances sent by migrant workers back to their families, and second, a greater penetration of U.S. popular culture that now reaches even the lowest social levels. If U.S. popular culture once used to be a bourgeois legacy, now it has permeated the middle and lower classes, thus deforming the tastes and preferences of Central Americans. When we consider this phenomenon in the light of globalization and the development of communications, one can clearly see the transformations that are affecting these small, highly fragmented societies. Central American cities daily grow increasingly similar to urban areas in the United States, with a proliferation of U.S. apartment-style living quarters, shopping centers, and the inevitable ebb of people toward the periphery. The automobile is increasingly becoming an essential part of the culture, while television is the chief source of information and entertainment for the people at large. It is still too soon to see the effects of these social changes on literary production. Even so, works such as *Lobojack* by Rafael Vargaruiz (b. 1947) and *Road Movie y otros cuentos* [1996; Road Movie and Other Stories] by Leónel Delgado Aburto (b. 1965) point in the direction of change.

However, there is also a greater awareness of the need to maintain traditional values, recover indigenous culture, maintain ecosystems, and revitalize the communities from the ground up. The conservation of sites of archaeological interest improved in Central America when governments realized that they did not just represent an important cultural legacy but were also a substantial tourist attraction that in turn could generate significant income. Interest in economic development has forced many communities to look to themselves for solutions that neither the state nor the modern world has been able to supply. Hope exists that these stimuli might be superimposed on the crushing burden of modernization, maintaining the concept of sustainable development, and achieving a certain cultural balance. The governments, conscious of the weakness of their economies and institutions, have tried to follow the dream of Central American unification, a chimera that has tempted the imagination of the most distinguished Central Americans since 1821. Efforts have been made in this regard to create a Central American Parliament, a Secretariat of Central American Integration, and a Free Trade treaty, currently under negoti-

ation, that might continue the efforts of the Common Central American Market of the 1970s. All of the above could be very important factors in terms of the cultural map of the region in the twenty-first century, where indubitably the cultural centers will continue to evolve and thereby continue to fashion the rich and varied cultural profile of Central America.

Translation by Jessica Johnson

Works Cited

Agia, Miguel, Fray. 1946 [c.1570]. *Servidumbres personales de indios sobre las encomiendas.* Sevilla: Publicaciones de la Escuela de Estudios Hispano-Americanos de Sevilla.

Andrews, George F. 1975. *Maya Cities: Placemaking and Urbanization.* Norman: University of Oklahoma Press.

Asturias, Miguel Angel. 1955. *El señor presidente.* Buenos Aires: Losada.

——— .1957. *Hombre de maiz.* Buenos Aires: Losada.

Aviles, Estevan, Fray. 1633. *Historia de Guatemala desde los tiempos de los indios, hasta la fundación de la provincia de los franciscanos; población de aquellas tierras, propagación de los indios, sus ritos, ceremonias, policía y gobierno.* Guatemala City: José Pineda Ybarra.

Bassie-Sweet, Karen. 1991. *From the Mouth of the Dark Cave.* Norman: University of Oklahoma Press.

Beverley, John, and Marc Zimmerman. 1990. *Literature and Politics in the Central American Revolutions.* Austin: University of Texas Press.

Castañeda Paganini, Ricardo. 1947. *Historia de la Real Pontificia Universidad de San Carlos de Guatemala.* Guatemala City: n.p.

Cockburn, John. 1735. *A Journey over Land, from the Gulf of Honduras to the Great South-Sea.* London: Rivington.

Coe, Michael D. 1992. *Breaking the Maya Code.* New York: Thames and Hudson.

Espino, Fernando, Fray. 1674. *Historia de la reducción y conversión de la provincia de Tegucigalpa, con la vida, virtudes y prodigios de tres mártires.* Guatemala City: José Pineda Ybarra.

Fowler, William R. 1989. *Cultural Evolution of Ancient Nahua Civilizations.* Norman, : University of Oklahoma Press.

Freidel, David, Linda Schele, and Joy Parker. 1993. *Maya Cosmos.* New York: William Morrow and Company.

Gage, Thomas. 1648. *The English American; his Travail by Sea and Land.* London: R. Cotes.

———. 1987. *Viajes por la Nueva España y Guatemala.* Ed. and trans. Dionisia Tejera. Madrid: Historia 16.

El Güegüense. The Güegüense. A comedy-ballet in the Nahuatl-Spanish Dialect of Nicaragua. 1883. Ed. and trans. Daniel G. Brinton. Philadelphia: Brinton's Library of Aboriginal American Literature. Vol 3.

Landívar, Rafael. 1924 [1782]. *Rusticación mejicana.* Trans. of 2nd edition by Ignacio Loureda. Mexico City: Sociedad de Edición y Librería Franco Americana.

Lanning, John Tate. 1956. *The Eighteenth-Century Enlightenment in the University of San Carlos de Guatemala.* Ithaca: Cornell University Press.

El Libro de los libros de Chilam Balam. 1948 [1544-1811]. Ed. Alfredo Barrera Vásquez. Mexico City: Fondo de Cultura Económica.

Love, Bruce. 1994. *The Paris Codex: Handbook for a Maya Priest.* Intro. George E. Stewart. Austin: University of Texas Press.

Mata Gavidia, José, ed. 1949. *Temas de filosofía moderna sustentados en 1785 en la Universidad de San Carlos de Guatemala.* Guatemala City: Universidad de San Carlos de Guatemala, Facultad de Humanidades.

Memorial de Tecpán Atitlán. Por el Presbítero Celso Narciso Teletor. 1946. Guatemala City: Tipografía Nacional.

Motolinia, Toribio de Benavente. 1973. *History of the Indians of New Spain.* Ed. and trans. Elizabeth Andros Foster. Westport, CT.: Greenwood.

——. 1985. *Historia de los indios de Nueva España.* Ed. Georges Baudot. Madrid: Editorial Castalia.

Padial Guerchous, Anita, and Manuel Vázquez-Bigi. 1991. *Quiché Vinak: Tragedia. Nueva versión española y estudio histórico-literario del llamado 'Rabinal-Achí.'* Mexico City: Fondo de Cultura Económica.

Pérez Brignoli, Héctor. 1985. *Breve historia de Centroamérica.* Madrid: Alianza Editorial.

Popol Vuh. Las antiguas historias de Quiché. 1947. Trans. Adrián Recinos. Mexico City: Fondo de Cultura Económica.

Ready, Timothy. 1989. "Culture, Power, and Human Rights in Central America." *Culture, Human Rights and Peace in Central America.* Ed. George F. McLean, Raul Molina and Timothy Ready. Lanham: University Press of America. 25–34.

Recinos, Adrián, ed. 1980. *Título de los señores de Totonicapán.* Trans. Dionisio José Chonay. Guatemala City: Dirección General de Antropología e Historia: Editorial Piedra Santa.

Rodríguez Mojón, María Luisa, ed. 1970. *Poesía revolucionaria guatemalteca.* Madrid: Zero.

Rowe, William, and Vivian Schelling. 1991. *Memory and Modernity.* New York: Verso.

Samayoa Guevara, Héctor Humberto. 1978. *Los gremios de artesanos de la ciudad de Guatemala (1524–1821).* Guatemala City: Piedra Santa.

Squier, E. G. 1852. *Nicaragua: Its People, Scenery, Monuments and the Proposed Interoceanic Canal.* 2 vols. London: Longman, Brown, Green & Longmans.

Stone, Doris. 1977. *Pre-Columbian Man in Costa Rica.* Cambridge, MA: Peabody Museum Press.

Stuart, George E. 1994. "Introduction." *The Paris Codex: Handbook for a Maya Priest.* By Bruce Love. Austin: University of Texas Press. xv–xviii.

Valle, Rafael Heliodoro. 1960. *Historia de las ideas contemporáneas en Centroamérica.* Mexico City: Fondo de Cultura Económica.

Villacorta, J. Antonio, and Carlos A. Villacorta. 1976. *Códices mayas.* 2nd ed. Guatemala City: Tipografía Nacional.

Wells, William V. 1857. *Exploration and Adventure in Honduras: Comprising Sketches of Travel in the Gold Regions of Olancho, and a Review of the History and General Resources of Central America.* New York: Harper & Brothers.

Whisnant, David E. 1995. *Rascally Signs in Sacred Places.* Chapel Hill: University of North Carolina Press.

Woodward, Ralph Lee. 1985. *Central America: A Nation Divided.* 2nd ed. New York: Oxford University Press.

SECTION III
THE CARIBBEAN
INTRODUCTION

Marcelino Juan Canino Salgado

(Editors' Note: The Caribbean poses what is perhaps the most complex challenge to the historiographic aims of comparative literary history and its present reelaboration as a history of literary culture. The islands and mainland that comprise the region have been the political, economic, and social targets of the most ruthless exploitation ever devised by the European powers. Spain, England, France, and the Netherlands all engaged in a colonial process that amounted to genocide of the native Amerindians and the most barbaric enslavement of Africans, which necessitated a constant importation of more slaves because of the enormous death rate on the sugar plantations. The European powers imposed their language, laws, and religion on the usurped land: The zeal of the Spanish religious orders in converting the population and thereby establishing a nonjuridical legitimation for their actions was far greater than in the other colonial settlements. In all cases the European authorities attempted to abolish all traces of the native Amerindian and also the African cultures. It is against this historical background that one must approach the culture of the region, and with the understanding that the colonial authorities tried to make communication as difficult as possible among the enslaved Africans and between the various islands. The wide gap in communication that persists to this day and separates Trinidad from nearby Venezuela; Haiti from the Dominican Republic, with which it shares the island of Hispaniola; or Jamaica from Cuba, for example, can be explained only in the light of the historical evidence of centuries of enforced isolation. Yet in spite of these very real barriers, there is a pan-Caribbean popular culture, which we can only glimpse in the present work. We have asked the Puerto Rican philologist Marcelino Canino to give us a brief description of this Caribbean popular culture in his introduction. He calls our attention to the fact that a deeper study of this topic goes far beyond the limits of his introduction and, in fact, of this history.

In the twentieth century the role of the United States in the Caribbean has been that of military and economic cacique—first in Cuba and Puerto Rico, then in the Dominican Republic [the most recent invasion was in 1965], the tiny island of Grenada [120 square miles], and Panama. The attempt by the U.S. colonial authorities to impose English on Puerto Rico has been repeatedly resisted by the population. There are of course a large number of people from the Spanish Caribbean now living in the United States, who have created a unique literary culture that is now called Latino and that will be taken up in Volume III of this history and in the section on New York City in this section of the cultural centers.

With regard to the diversity and richness of the Caribbean region as a whole, we want to refer our readers to the three-volume history of the literatures of the Caribbean edited by A. James Arnold as part of the series on comparative literary history sponsored by the International Comparative Literature Association and published by Benjamins in Amsterdam [1994–2001]. This groundbreaking research took fifteen years to compile and write; it covers the literary cultures of the Caribbean in Spanish, French, English, Dutch, Creole, and Papamento.

The Caribbean mainland—Yucatan, Central America, and northern Venezuela and Colombia—has shared in the turmoil and natural disasters of the region, albeit with less ferocity than the Antilles, but it has also had extensive trade—both legal and contraband—that circulated a steady stream of popular and literary culture along with the European goods that the Colonial elites coveted.)

With the promulgation, by His Holiness Alexander VI on 3 May 1493, of the papal bull *Inter Caetera* favoring the Catholic kings of Spain, the way was cleared for the nascent Spanish Empire's supremacy in America. This bull gave the Spanish crown a free hand in the establishment of a lucrative political, religious, and commercial monopoly in the New World (Caro Costas 20). Despite the exclusivity with which the exploitation of the Americas was ceded to Spain by the Pope, Henry VIII of England ignored the papal injunction, and François I of France sarcastically and impiously demanded to be shown the "testament of Adam" that bequeathed an entire hemisphere to the Spanish (Parry 4). Ignoring papal authority, the enemies of Spain were anxious to avail themselves of the succulent fruit that the New World constituted in the minds of all Europeans, both Catholics and non-Catholics. The indigenous population of the Caribbean was practically exterminated in less than thirty years, and those few who survived were subjected to a rapid process of cultural and racial assimilation. The admonitory voice of Bartolomé de las Casas (1474–1566) took up the cause of the natives and advocated the introduction of black African slaves as a substitute for native manpower.

The strategic geographic location of the Caribbean Antilles attracted privateers, pirates, merchants, and adventurers of all types. The dream of fame and riches was an appetizing morsel tempting the enemies of Spain, who, in one manner or another, desired to establish their own bastions in the Caribbean, with all the military and economic glory that that implied. Overcoming great difficulties, Spain managed to maintain its political and cultural hegemony in the basin. Although by the end of the nineteenth century Cuba, the Dominican Republic, and Puerto Rico remained in Spanish hands, the majority of the other islands in the Greater Antilles had been sold, exchanged, or conquered by other powers. (The islands of Barbados, Jamaica, Trinidad and Tobago, Aruba, St. Martin, Bonaire, St. Eustache, Hispaniola [Haiti and the Dominican Republic], Cuba, and Puerto Rico all belonged to the ancient Arawak substratum; whereas Antigua, Grenada, St. Lucia, Guadeloupe, St. Thomas, St. John, and St. Croix belonged to the Caribbean substratum.) By the middle of the nineteenth century the islands of Antigua, Barbados, Dominica, Grenada, Guyana, Jamaica, St. Vincent, St. Lucia, Montserrat, Trinidad and Tobago, Jost van Dyke, Tortola, Guana, Virgin Gorda (these last four now part of the British Virgin Islands), and Grand Cayman had all come under English domination. For their part, the islands of Guadeloupe, Martinique, and Anguilla had passed into French hands. The Dutch Antilles—where Papiamento, Dutch, Spanish, Portuguese, and English are spoken—comprise the islands of Aruba, St. Martin, Bonaire, Curaçao, St. Eustache, and Saba. The U.S. Virgin Islands are St. Thomas, St. John, and St. Croix.

Despite being a multilingual, multicultural community of great ethnic diversity, miscegenation of every type predominates in the Caribbean. The indigenous substrata are highly diluted, and it is above all the various components of the diverse African cultures established in the Caribbean that have prevailed. The hectic maritime fluidity, the clandestine commerce, and the political and economic uncertainties have favored, in a certain sense, many of the cultural syncretisms that can be identified throughout the Caribbean as a whole. I would now like to outline in broad strokes a number of features characteristic of almost the entire Caribbean community, aspects such as customs, traditions, music, folkloric celebrations, cuisine, and recreations common to almost all the islands of the Antillean archipelago. These cultural components are but a sample of the ethnographic materials that could be studied in a multilingual aggregate, constituted by a cultural and ethnic diversity that maintains, nonetheless, communal ethos and Antillean solidarity.

The old refrain about the man who bit off more than he could chew helps metaphorically explain why, already by 1815, Spain had lost the majority of her overseas imperial possessions in the Antilles. In fact, long before the middle of the eighteenth century, the Spanish Crown had ceased to be the center of cohesion for the Caribbean Antilles, because the French, the English, and the Dutch had assumed control of a number of the territories claimed by Christopher Columbus and his successors. By the beginning of the nineteenth century, Spanish authority had been almost completely superseded by the new European strata that had taken control of and transformed the majority of the Antilles, and above all the Lesser Antilles. However, despite the cultural differences of the strata and superstrata that existed, a somewhat inexplicable element—expressed by means of signs and other extra-linguistic media, and even in relations of hostility and transcending in explanatory power both the indigenous substratum and the maritime fluidity of categories—kept the Antilles united in an indissoluble and tacit solidarity and made possible, despite the linguistic diversity, a continuing communication and commerce among all the peoples of the Caribbean. It was because of this ineffable factor that the majority of the ruling classes sympathetic to the imperial powers controlling the islands promoted policies of isolation between them, above all on the level of official visits between colonial governments, for it was well known that a number of these latter sympathized with the notion of a commonwealth of Caribbean peoples, laborers, and workers. Fishermen and sailors, adventurers and primitive globetrotters had maintained the inter-island connections of this virtual commonwealth by means of sea routes and maritime traffic, as well as by the cohesive force of a Caribbean tradition elaborated with elements that were both heterogeneous and common to all those who dwelled in the Antilles, where, by any reckoning, the black African element is fundamental, common, and obvious.

Arturo Morales Carrión (1913–1989) has more than demonstrated how the Hispanic and non-Hispanic Caribbean has been historically woven into a mosaic by the diversity of interests of the Spanish conquistadors, the Portuguese slave traders, the French and English pirates and privateers, the Dutch smugglers, and, finally, the U.S. profiteers. For purely geographic and subhistoric reasons, Puerto Rico, like the other Hispanic Antilles, was no exception to these heterogeneous influences, despite having been, by compulsion, the last island loyal and faithful to the Spanish Crown. The theory

formulated by Antonio S. Pedreira (1899–1939)—implying that a policy or tradition of insularity cut Puerto Rico off from the rest of the Antilles and the Caribbean conglomeration in general—has been overwhelmingly refuted by the vast documentation, showing that, historically, Puerto Rico played something of a central role in inter-Antillean commerce, as well as in the ideological interchange among the islands. From the beginning of the sixteenth century up until at least the first decades of the nineteenth century, Puerto Rico was guiding beacon in the *mare clausum* of the Caribbean.

This inter-relation of islands in a closed body of water encouraged the various imperial powers throughout the centuries not merely to seek possession of one or another isolated island, but, further, to entertain the ambition and intention of possessing the entire Caribbean, in order to guarantee thus undisputed sovereignty. U.S. sponsored archaeological explorations (The National History Survey of Puerto Rico and the Virgin Islands, 1913–1934) were not limited to Puerto Rico and the Virgin Islands but also encompassed sites in Cuba, the Dominican Republic, Haiti, Barbados, Jamaica, Grenada, Guadeloupe, the Bahamas, and others of lesser importance. This research into the Caribbean was connected to practices developed in the eighteenth century by various European powers, in which their most acclaimed naturalists and men of science were sent to the Antilles to study and catalogue the geographic characteristics and natural wonders, not only for scientific reasons but also for markedly political and economic ones. Although these studies, as well as the accounts of the voyages that made them possible, are of great benefit to contemporary scholars, they are really little more than a simple register of the data collected, and only on few occasions do they give any indication of the sociocultural surroundings of which these data formed a part. In light of the abstracting process operative in such accounts, the question proposes itself: How, despite the political and linguistic differences that stand between the various islands of the Caribbean, have they been able to retain a tacit solidarity with each other? What is the ethos that unites them?

Ethnographic Concomitances

How often is one astonished to realize that elements believed to be the exclusive prerogative of one island can also be found in other islands of the Caribbean? And if many of the elements that form part of the Puerto Rican, Cuban, Jamaican, or Dominican ethos can be found throughout the Caribbean, then we will have to seek what we might call the (national) essences of the present-day Caribbean in deeper roots—or perhaps we will have to concoct roots. In order to get a grip on this problem, it is imperative to begin with the fieldwork of collecting, cataloguing, and taxonomically classifying this experience, however arduous and humdrum it may be.

1. **Gastronomy**: Banana cake, cassava patties, *alcapurrias*, blood sausages, tripe, roast suckling pig, *cuchiflitos*, *mofongo*, among other exquisite and well-known dishes worshiped as works of the national genius, can all be found throughout the greater part of the Antilles. The *funche* that Puerto Ricans love so much (a kind of porridge made from corn flour, coconut milk, brown sugar, and spices) is not as Puerto Rican as one may think it is. Imagine my surprise when I discovered that it was a common, everyday delicacy in the Dutch Antilles (Aruba, Bonaire, Curaçao) known as *funchi*. The *caldo santo* that the coastal-dwelling Puerto Ricans make during religious holidays (a broth made from vegetables,

greens, fish, coconut milk, spices, and a pinch of corn meal) is the same *calaloo* consumed throughout practically all the French Antilles. I have had this same experience of recognition with *gofio* (a roasted maize meal, often stirred into coffee) and coconut pulp and cane syrup sweets, both as common as day throughout the Antilles.

2. **Carnivals**: With the exception of the U.S. Virgin Islands, the carnivals of the Caribbean maintain a series of common contact points. In my experience, what has been most remarkable is the tremendous similarity between the masks of the Montserrat and Nevis carnivals and those worn by the Knights of Santiago in Loiza Aldea; there is an equal similarity with the masks worn by the innocents and the *vegigantes* in the Hatillo y Camuy carnival in Puerto Rico.

3. **Music and dance**: A study of Caribbean music, more intensive and coordinated than those hitherto realized, is necessary if we are to go beyond the repetition of old stereotypes. To date, all such studies have highlighted the use of the pentatonic scale, percussive accompaniment, and syncopated rhythms. However, these characteristics are in fact far from particular to the Caribbean, since they can be found in the music of almost all the countries of the Western world. To repeat such clichés is to fall prey to simplification—as if the chromatic scale did not also predominate in Caribbean *sones*! On the other hand, we need to persevere in the labor of musical taxonomy and, further, undertake a comparative study of the great, common musical and choreographic heritage of the Caribbean. I have heard *plenas* rhythms and melodies in the Dutch and French Antilles, not to mention the black dances of Carriacou, Grenada, which are identical to the so-called *bomba* dances that exist throughout the Caribbean.

4. **Recreation**: The enthusiasm and frenzy of the spectators at a cockfight in St. Martin differs in no appreciable way from that to be experienced in the cockpits of Puerto Rico: Liquor is consumed, brawls break out over wagers, knife wounds are exchanged, and so forth.

5. **Esteem for domestic needlework**: In almost all the Dutch islands, and above all in the tiny island of Saba, the Spanish tradition of needlework is kept alive and highly regarded: hemstitch work, openwork, *enrejillado, calado,* and relief embroidery—the very same work done by the women of Aguadilla and Moca in Puerto Rico, as well as in the Dominican Republic.

6. **Mourning customs**: I have observed a vigil for the dead in St. Thomas, another in Aruba, and a burial in the Dominican Republic. Yes, I know that you will say that the common element is a corpse—no more and no less! Yet the responses to the departure of a loved one were identical to those I witnessed in the countryside and villages of Puerto Rico: cries of "You've gone and left me..." or "What am I to do without you!," beating of the breast, dizzy spells, hair pulling, orange leaf infusions—scenes of affliction that attempt to transcend the individual through the collective. The participants were not hired mourners, reminiscent of those ancient Spanish and Jewish funeral ceremonies. In addition, and above all in the Greater Antilles, cemetery architecture is virtually uniform. For example, the cemetery that occupies the Petionville Road in the center of Port-au-Prince is practically identical to the Palo Seco cemetery in Toa Baja, Puerto Rico.

7. **Popular religion**: Here again the similarities are striking. In Haiti, the Dominican Republic, Puerto Rico, and formerly in Cuba, it was customary to print loose sheets of paper with odd stamps or engravings of saints and the sayings particular to them. This practice has recently been the subject of a great deal of attention on the part of anthropologists who have produced a number of significant studies, such as the one by Nélida Agosto, a synchronic or structural description of possession rites in Haitian Voodoo. With respect to the religious aspects, however, there is a wealth of material remaining to be investigated by various disciplinary perspectives. One phenomenon that has not received the attention it deserves is that of the now extinct practice of the Dominican prophets of the Mana region near Baní in the south of the Dominican Republic: the striking similarity of Zacarias Arias and Bibiana de la Rosa to the development of the Puerto Rican deity, *Mita*, is astonishing.

8. **Architecture**: We can flesh out our catalogue by taking note of the formal coincidences and similarities between the architecture of San Juan, Puerto Rico, and the houses of Fort de France, Martinique; between the rural houses of Anguilla and St. Thomas, and those of Puerto Rico and the Dominican Republic; and between the wooden ornamental fretwork gracing the houses of Jamaica and those of the interior of Puerto Rico, the Dominican Republic, and Cuba.

All this listing is very entertaining, but nothing more than that. The upshot, it seems to me, is that if we truly wish to discover the underlying ethos that characterizes Caribbean cultural practices as both a variegated and diversified unity, on the one hand, and as indissoluble, on the other, then we are compelled to go beyond a purely classificatory and comparative methodology in our search for a diversified method that would be truly dialectical and illuminating. As we have already seen, typological taxonomies are not dialectical and thus do not lead us to any conclusions of immediate benefit, since they are a purely classificatory instrument. However, in the particular case of the Caribbean, we have to begin by collecting and appropriately classifying the data before we can take up the comparative work or apply an integrated method to the study of our materials.

It would be expedient to employ a geolinguistic and dialectological methodology in these cultural studies. To carry this out necessitates a command of the taxonomic concepts of substratum, adstratum, stratum, and superstratum, since most of the Antilles can be characterized by the common ethno-cultural substratum of formerly having been the seat of the Carib or Arawak cultures. (*Substratum* refers to elements or features of a language identified by linguists as responsible for change in another language that is otherwise dominant over it.) In addition, there is the common superstratum of the diverse African languages and cultures, and, at least in Haiti and the Dominican Republic, the obvious fact of linguistic change through influence by the neighboring idiom (adstratum). The islands that were originally Carib or Arawak later form part of the strata of the Spanish, English, French, Dutch, or U.S. cultures. However, both the substrata of Carib and Arawak, and the superstrata of black and Spanish gave rise to a highly original culture that we can label Creole: an intra-structure or characterizing element that would supersede the majority of the superficially manifest influences.

Sociolinguistic Categories and Language Barriers

As historical documentation has demonstrated, Puerto Rico was both officially and clandestinely a center of interchange and commercial contact with the other islands of the non-Hispanic Caribbean. While there exist literary historical documents from 1831 that testify to the presence of Papiamento-speaking groups of Africans in the southern region of the island of Puerto Rico, there is insufficient evidence to ascertain whether these people either affected or were influenced by the phenomenon of adstratum or whether they were multilingual. In any event, given that all the Antilleans in the Caribbean were capable of using two varieties of a single language (diglossia), it is possible that there existed a lingua franca or pidgin that facilitated inter-Antillean communication and trade among merchants. It is possible that this lingua franca disappeared in Puerto Rico, largely as a result of political and economic factors, but that residua of this pidgin can be found in the diasystemic modalities of some Creoles and in the Papiamento of the Dutch Antilles. (*Diasystem* refers to the linguistic macrosystem constructed by treating variants between dialects as part of a continuum of variations.) This seems to be the only way of explaining the presence of Spanish, English, Dutch, French, and Portuguese words in the Papiamento of Aruba, Bonaire, and Curaçao, and the surprising multilingual facility of the majority of the population of these islands. In this respect it could be said that the conservatism and Hispanophilia of colonial Puerto Rico were obstacles aiding the maintenance and development of a situation similar to that of the Dutch Antilles.

If there is no linguistic unity in the Caribbean, does it then follow that there is no Antillean solidarity? Impossible. Language—although the most important—is only one element of culture. And language is not culture. We can be neither bilingual nor multilingual and still be diglossal. This is to say that we can maneuver with absolute facility not only in the official national linguistic system, but also the diasystems that develop within the official idiom. We can possess a command of both the cultured idiom (the register of prestige) and the popular language and its categories, and our use and selection of the registers will be determined by the various sociocultural situations in which we as speakers find ourselves. If we can be diglossal, bilingual, and multilingual, can we also be pluricultural? Possibly. At the very least we are capable of incorporating into our culture elements that do not shatter or distort the system, which is to say, elements that enjoy precisely the same character as those that we can find in the diasystemic varieties.

Here we can now see the utility of taxonomies: The inventory of the associative and dissociative elements that we find in the cultural manifestations of the various islands of the Caribbean (without forgetting the diaphasic elements or individualized styles) will reveal to us whether the Caribbean in its entirety forms one single culturally integrated system, one system with several diasystems, or various systems with common characteristics that can only be fundamentally explained with reference to the indigenous substratum, the important and conspicuous African contribution, and the common, melting-pot amalgamation of Hispanic heritage. An investigation into the cultural reality of the Caribbean, in addition to orienting itself with reference to the synchronic and diachronic axes, will also have to establish levels of analysis that transcend the various commonplaces and strata. Only then will we have a global and detailed vision of the entire complex cultural ensemble of the Caribbean Antilles.

Translation by Colman Hogan

Works Cited

Agosto de Muñoz, Nélida. 1975. *El fenómeno de la posesión de la religión Vudú: Un estudio sobre la posesión por los espíritus y su relación con el ritual en el Vudú.* Río Pedras: Instituto de Estudios del Caribe, Universidad de Puerto Rico.

Arnold, A. James. 1994–2001. *A History of Literature in the Caribbean.* 3 vols. Amsterdam: John Benjamins.

Caro Costas, Aida. 1971. *Antología de lecturas de la historia de Puerto Rico.* San Juan: A. R. Caro Costas.

Morales Carrión, Arturo. 1995. *Puerto Rico y la lucha por la hegemonía en el Caribe.* Rio Piedras: Universidad de Puerto Rico.

Parry, John Horace. 1940. *The Spanish Theory of Empire in the Sixteenth Century.* Cambridge, England: Cambridge University Press.

Pedreira, Antonio S. 1957. *Insularismo (Ensayos de interpretación puertorriqueña).* San Juan: Biblioteca de Autores Puertorriqueños.

CHAPTER 35

HAVANA

Luisa Campuzano

The history of Cuba and of Havana as a cultural center has been largely determined by three factors that have influenced both the formation of the Cuban and Havanan mentality and the identity construction of both nation and capital: the island's strategic geographical position, the capital's condition of being both an isolated and a port city, and the character of the country's population. Thanks to the island's proximity to Europe, Columbus would encounter it on his first voyage; thanks to its centrality in the Gulf of Mexico, Cuba would become, by the mid-sixteenth century, the bridgehead for Spain's domination of the Americas. In the years that followed Havana would be established as the crossroads through which the fleets arriving from Spain and those returning from America, laden with riches, would pass; it would simultaneously serve as a bridge between two worlds, target of pirate attacks, and enclave coveted by other powers seeking to control the Caribbean and dominate the new continent.

When the great fleets disappeared and Cuba transformed into the sugar mill to the world, Havana's fidelity to the mother country would be sustained by colonial ties. Its harbor would continue to be the point of shipment for cargo boats and an obligatory stopover for travelers destined for, or returning from, the United States and Europe. Later, its high level of modernization vis-à-vis its immediate neighbors, the vitality of its cultural life, and, finally, the revolution would continue to make Havana an important center of literary creation and diffusion.

Havana: General Tendencies over the Long Term

Isolation, whether taken in its positive sense, as plenitude and totality (Lezama Lima 1953a, 45–46), or in a more resigned sense, as a manifestation of the natural solitude of the individual (Loynaz 78, 142–43), is a frequent theme in Cuban letters. It has also been interpreted as a form of marginalization and expression of the tragic destiny of the country. José Martí (1853–1895) contrasted the political fate of "las islas dolorosas del mar" ("the sorrowful islands of the sea") with that of "las naciones románticas del continente" ("the romantic nations of the continent") (1992a, 487); Virgilio Piñera (1912–1979) elaborated in La isla en peso (1943; The Island in the Balance) a cultural resignation to this misfortune; and the theme has been recently taken up again by the prose writer and dramatist Abilio Estévez (b. 1954) and the painter Sandra Ramos.

Seen in this way, isolation could be at the base of that separation anxiety, or continentalism, that would explain the early treatment of Latin American themes by such authors as José María Heredia (1803–1839) in "En el Teocalli de Cholula" [1820; "The Teocalli of Cholula"], Gabriel de la Concepción Valdés, Plácido (1809–1844) in "Jicotencal" (1838), Gertrudis Gómez de Avellaneda (1814–1873) in Guatimozín . . . (1846), as well as the works of Domingo del Monte (1804–1853) and José Antonio Saco (1797–1879) in the 1840s on Prescott's history of Mexico, or the studies of slavery in Brazil. This preoccupation can also be seen in the active participation of many Cuban exiles in the cultural and political life of numerous continental nations, whether in a direct manner, in

situ, as with Heredia and Pedro Santacilia (1826–1910) in Mexico, Antonio Zambrana (1846–1922) and José Joaquín Palma (1844–1911) in Central America, Manuel del Socorro Rodríguez (1758–1818) and Rafael María Merchán (1844–1905) in Colombia, or indirectly, from other centers of culture, such as Martí with his "letters" from New York destined for specific Hispano-American dailies. More recently this tendency has manifested itself in the attempts by José Antonio Portuondo and Roberto Fernández Retamar to found a theory of Latin American literature, and in the establishment of the Casa de las Américas, an institution created to, among other things, reedit the classics, stimulate young writers, broaden the canon by incorporating into it marginal testimonial voices and aboriginal textual productions, and integrate the literatures of Brazil and the Anglophone and Francophone Caribbean.

At the same time, this Latin Americanism, conceived in the nineteenth century as a counterweight to peninsular influence, coincided with the growing awareness of the necessity to construct, in the margins of political subordination to the metropole, a national identity. Almost from the beginning this energy took political expression in the publication of the El Habanero (Philadelphia–New York, 1824–1826), the promotion of Cuban schools (since 1833 employing Cuban texts), the heated polemics surrounding the creation of the Cuban Academy of Literature (1834), or the publication in 1836 of the first dictionary of Spanish Americanisms: the Diccionario provincial de voces cubanas, by Esteban Pichardo (1799–1879). In this self-recognition of a greater, cosmopolitan identity there lay not only a response to Cuba's exclusion from the independence movements of the continent, but also, and in the years to come, one of the bases for the elaboration of an anti-annexationism (see José Antonio Saco) and an anti-imperialism (see Martí) that have been key to the contested definition of Cuban national identity. It cannot be denied that "Cuba has been much more intimately tied to the United States than any other Latin American country," and that from the arrival of Félix Varela (1788–1853) and Heredia in the United States in 1823 until the triumph of the revolution, Cuba was "as if a link connecting the two cultures, playing the double role of interpreter and propagandist to both" (Manuel Pedro González 90-91). It is for this reason that "Cubans have been much more familiar with U.S. culture than their [Hispano-American] colleagues" (91). This familiarity has afforded them a knowledge of the virtues and shortcomings of their distinct and unequal neighbor–We love the land of Lincoln as much as we admire the land of Cutting," claimed Martí (1992b, 264)–that in cultural terms has been translated into that powerful attraction and violent rejection that has singularly marked the relations between the two nations.

On the other hand, blessed with a fortified port that has for centuries harbored hundreds of warships and their troops, Havana is still the principal garrison of the island. And from the days of the Spanish Armada to the Cuban Missile Crisis, it has always been involved in international conflicts that overflowed the frontiers of the continent and has thus necessarily kept abreast of events in the wider world. City of encounters and exchanges, of comings and goings, of immigrants and émigrés, of exiles from far and near, and as such an agglutinative and fragmented center, both receiver and emitter, Havana has known–before others–what is read, painted, sung, or has been in fashion elsewhere; it has assimilated or creatively sampled the booty that every packet boat, airplane, and passenger brought with them. It is hardly surprising, then, that at this crossroads there has arisen, in contrast to the invented marvels of Europe, the poetics of "translate America to the world" (Carpentier 1981, 57) and of "the marvelous-real of the Americas" (Carpentier 1987, 1–9); of the "mysterious echo" and of "the invisible showers and crystals" through which the culture of the metropole is filtered and transmuted into a Latin American idiom (Lezama Lima 1953, 62–97); and of the baroque as a counter-discourse, art of the counter-Conquest (Lezama Lima 1957, 32–54). Nor is it surprising that it was from Havana that Fernando Ortiz introduced into anthropology the category of transculturation (1983, 86–90), later taken up by literary criticism, a category he illustrated by making use of the paradigmatic strategy of irony in order to narrate how European metropoles adopted the diabolical tobacco of the colonies, the Havana cigar, with all the institutional compromises that that implied (Ramos 43, n.14).

The Cuban people are an amalgam of the descendants of the colonizers, immigrants from diverse regions of Spain, and of African slaves imported over more than three centuries: "a novel people" constituted out of "specific forms of ethnic domination [the enslavement of Africans] and productive organization [plantation culture] established under conditions of extreme social oppression and mandatory deculturation" (Ribeiro 163). They exhibit–in every facet of their culture–the symptoms of these relations of domination, the strategies of resistance developed against them, as well as the phobias, repressions, and projections whose tendencies are to make invisible or minimize the presence of the slaves or their descendants and their artistic legacy; included here would be the attempts to achieve a national integration without renunciations, whitewashes, or erasures. Whereas the greater part of nineteenth-century Cuban narrative production devoted itself, directly or indirectly, to finding a solution to the "negro problem," the linguistic politics of the slave traders and holders–separating the members of ethnic groups from one another and mixing them with other African nations in order to impede interslave communication–meant that the oral literature of Cuba has survived only in Spanish. And although riddles, refrains, and tales occupied but a small corner of the popular culture, in comparison with the wide currency of other Afro-Cuban cultural manifestations, it has been only since the 1930s that oral forms began to be incorporated in the literary canon by way of poetic (Nicolás Guillen, 1902–1989) or narrative and anthropological (Lydia Cabrera, 1899–1991) re-elaboration.

Havana: Political and Demographic History

Founded by Diego Velázquez in 1514 on the southern and favored shore of Cuba, then privileged by virtue of its proximity to the South American continent, the settlement of San Cristóbal changed places three times in five years. With the discovery of the Gulf Stream, promising to shorten the return voyage from the Indies to Spain, the settlement was relocated in 1518 on the northern shore, first at the mouth of the present-day Almendares River, soon after next to the port that, since 1508, mariners called *Carenas*. This was a splendid pocket-shaped bay with a wide and deep entrance and three ample inlets, situated at 231 degrees 8 minutes north and 821 degrees 24 minutes west, which would afford a protected anchorage for a large number of ships against both inclement weather and enemy attack. Almost from the beginning this harbor was known as *Habana*, an indigenous word; despite the utilization and dissemination of the name by the most diverse maps and *portolanos*, we should not underestimate the possible influence of its phonetic similarity to various words of German origin signifying "port": *Hafen, haven, havre, harbo(u)r*.

According to tradition, the first mass and the first municipal assembly of the village then called San Cristóbal de la Habana was celebrated on 16 November 1519 in the shadow of a silk-cotton (ceiba) tree, emblem of the future city. Beneath other ceibas, as monumental and hieratic in the architecture of their limbs as the sacred baobabs of Africa, the blacks who arrived with the conquistadors and were later captured as slaves to replace the exterminated aboriginal population began to observe their *orishas*. Havana remained an impoverished settlement, twice sacked by privateers, until the 1560s, when Philip II took charge of the organization, direction, and guardianship of the royal fleets. Rebuilt by decree, Havana saw the first outlines of streets and plazas, erected its first masonry dwellings, began the process of its fortification, financed by the well-heeled arriving from the viceregency of New Spain, and built its first aqueduct. This latter was to irrigate the region and, above all, to water the swelling population of hundreds, and later thousands, of officials and garrisoned troops–who for centuries would contribute to the increasingly unequal representation of males in the population of the future city–in addition to the thousands of mariners and infantry, functionaries, and voyagers stopping over en route to Mexico or the South American continent, or heading back to Spain. On the return voyage it was customary to stop over in the town for no fewer than three months, until the last of the ships for the Atlantic convoy arrived, and this exacerbated the demographic imbalance. The lodging and amusement of these men, as well as the production of foodstuffs for their stopover and crossing, were the principal economic activities of the heterogeneous Havana population that, by comparison with the remainder of the practically depopulated island, grew by leaps and bounds: The 700 inhabitants of 1554 rose to 4,000 in 1590 (Roig I, 67) and reached 8000 or 10,000 by 1660 (Pérez de la Riva 1975b, 304).

From the middle of the sixteenth to the middle of the eighteenth century Havana was transformed into one of the great fortified port and port-of-call cities of the world, characterized by a maritime and military culture and a service economy (Moreno Fraginals 1990, 2–5), and possessor of the finest dry docks, the best arsenal, and the most extensive system of fortifications in all the Americas. In 1592 the "city" was incorporated, and toward the middle of the seventeenth century, a coat of arms was conferred bearing the device of three castles and a key, symbols of the role that Havana played in the Spanish colonial regime, codified in the official mottos "Key to the New World" and "First Line of Defence of the West Indies." Although the governor, until the end of the Spanish domination almost always a military man, had resided in Havana since 1533, it was only in 1607 that Havana was designated the island's capital, an affront to the honor of Santiago de Cuba that would never be forgiven. Havana, whose northern frontier from 1565 to 1820 was the San Agustín River of the Florida peninsula, grew with its eyes ever to the sea and its back to the rest of the country. For its part, the remainder of the island devoted itself to the husbanding of animals and to primitive agriculture in order to subsist and to traffic in contraband with enemy ships, which, had they appeared before the batteries of the distant capital, would no doubt have received the full brunt of all the cannons.

The rapid profits that were reaped by the first planters and traders of the capital encouraged them to reinvest in other crops such as tobacco, sugar cane, and, later, coffee, all of which, given the fertility of the soil and the blessings of a subtropical climate, returned excellent harvests. Thus later, when the convoy system slowed to a trickle and began to die out, Havana could already count on a solid agricultural economy with a recognized presence in world markets. Although a tobacco monopoly (among other measures of administrative centralization) was imposed with the ascension of the Bourbons to the Spanish throne, this in fact only affected the producers outside of Havana and the small- and medium-sized planters of the capital–who rose up in rebellion three times between 1717 and 1723. For their part, the traders and grand plantation owners of the capital, on whom the king, since 1713, had begun to bestow the titles of nobility for services rendered to the governors and bishops, banded together in 1740 to found the Royal Havana Trading Company, presenting a share of their revenues to the crown. It was in this way that Havana, "the sole gateway for the ingress of slaves, the import of commodities and the export of tobacco and sugar; the only site where the Royal Company encouraged the augmentation of capital in any form" (Portuondo 188), earned the rancor of the entire island.

In 1762 Havana and its 50,000 inhabitants were seized by the English after Spain intervened on the side of France in the Seven Years War. Havana, whose economy was based upon slavery of a patriarchal nature and whose total population of slaves numbered no more than 5000, was then the third largest city in Spanish America, surpassed only by Mexico and Lima, capitals and viceregencies established on the ruins of imperial indigenous metropoles (Pérez de la Riva 1975b, 306). During the eleven months of English rule Havana tasted the benefits of free trade. Its active and profitable participation in the Thirteen Colonies' War of Independence, the uprising of the Dominican workers and the subsequent ruin of the Hispaniolan sugar planters, and the emigration to the west and central regions of Cuba of the former inhabitants of Louisiana–conquered by Spain in 1769 in a campaign launched from the great military enclave of Havana, ceded to Napoleon in 1802, and later sold to the newly created United States–established the bases for the impressive economic development of the fertile Havana-Matanzas plain during the final decades of the eighteenth and the first decades of the nineteenth century. It is worth recalling in this context that it was from the port of Havana that Charles III dispatched to the American colonists arms and munitions, some 12,000 men who were to fight on land and sea against the English, as well as cargo ships laden with Cuban goods. The economic boom in the Havana-Matanzas plain resulted, however, in only a limited increase in the population of the city and its outskirts, which, according to the census of 1791, did not exceed 55,000 inhabitants (Pérez de la Riva 1975b, 308), because the great rise in population was largely confined to the rural hubs, where the surge in production took place.

Founded upon a plantation economy and, with the authorization of unrestricted importation in 1789, the exploitation of large numbers of mostly male African slaves–exacerbating the extremely high ratio of males in the workers' quarters of the sugar mills–the sugar boom saw the emergence of a bourgeoisie that was by and large Creole and literate. These wealthy sugar or resource barons (see Moreno Fraginals 1978), who in a few years had become the world's largest sugar producers, achieved a higher standard of living and higher expectations than any other elite in the Americas. Although they desired to participate in the governance of the island (unlike the small group of separatist intellectuals and the less-favored classes), they did not seek independence. Rather, they feared that the numerical superiority of the slaves would lead in Cuba to the disturbances seen in Haiti. Thus they opted instead for a hypothetical program of reforms encouraged by the first election of Cuban deputies to the Spanish parliament in 1810, the proclamation of the Cadiz Constitution–abrogated in 1814 after only two years–its reestablishment in 1820, and the brief period in which Cubans once again enjoyed parliamentary representation (1821–1823).

In the 1830s Bolívar's forces were discouraged from landing in Cuba by the island's isolation from the South American continent, its proximity to the United States, and by U.S. insistence that under no circumstances would intervention in the island's affairs be tolerated. The U.S. considered it more expedient for its southern neighbor to remain in Spanish hands than for it to be free (lest it fall into English hands), even while weighing the possibility of purchasing the island outright. As political temperature rose as a consequence of the Spanish-American Wars of Independence, governors were invested with the absolute powers of military commanders under siege; civil courts gave way, following the restoration of Spanish absolutism in 1823, to military tribunals; and there was a marked increase in conspiratorial activities favoring the separatist option. Repression also rose to new levels, and the train of political expatriations that characterizes nineteenth-century Cuba began. From this period until the end of the nineteenth century–and the same would happen, though to a lesser extent and for different reasons, in the twentieth century–the greater and perhaps better part of Cuban literature is written in exile: in Mexico, Colombia, France, but above all in various cities in the United States. There, two poets imagined the literary and political emblems of the future nation: the palm (Heredia) and the flag (Miguel Teurbe Tolón).

The demographic disequilibrium favored by the Colonial government, by means of the illegal slave trade and the promotion of white immigration, the failure of the first movement toward reform, and the impossibility of achieving independence, gave rise to the development of two movements advocating the annexation of the island by the United States. The first, believing that the institution of political and economic liberties was impossible to achieve by any other means, opted for union with the U.S. northern states, and by consequence, for the abolition of slavery; the second, backed by the economic and political elites, advocated union with the U.S. south and the maintenance of slavery. An important sector of the Havana intelligentsia–frustrated by the same limitations to independence and reform, but vigorously opposed to annexation–promoted a variation in the separatist program that in the end proved to be effective: The intellectual formation, through the development of a

Cuban pedagogy, of the future achievers of a deferred independence, deferred until such time as the cessation of the slave trade (which they also sought to effect) or the caucasianization of the island they so desired, sanctioned a struggle for independence without risking a slave revolt.

Over the course of the following decades sugar production, having been extended to the entire island, continued to expand, and periods of relative calm were interrupted by moments of grave crisis. These included the expulsion of the parliamentary deputies and the promulgation of special laws for the governance of Cuba in 1837 (the same year in which, in the province of Havana, the first railway in the Spanish world was built), the Escalera Conspiracy in 1844 (the period in which rail lines linking Havana and Matanzas were laid down), various largely annexationist plots and uprisings linked to the Havana Club (1848–1855), and the consequent reprisals, imprisonments, banishments, and summary executions. Given the constant Spanish resistance to any type of reform and the continuation of the illegal slave trade—in 1841 demographic disequilibrium reached its highest point, with blacks comprising 58 percent of the population, and an even higher percent in the western regions—the political alternatives open to *criollo*, and especially Havana, society remained what they had always been.

However, if "sugar opened up the island," as one historian has alleged (Moreno Fraginals 1978, I:137–57), Cuba was also, as another has demonstrated, "an island of two histories" (Pérez de la Riva 1975c, 75–89). While the first independence battles erupted in eastern Cuba in 1868, it is now evident that the motivating causes of the insurrection were not to be found in the west, where the (ten-year) conflict never succeeded in catching on. Both regions were then experiencing a series of new conditions: the crisis occasioned by the definitive end of the slave trade, the liquidation of the old sugar manufactory, the waning of the *criollo* resource barons as a ruling class (accompanied by the rise to prominence of the commercial and financial elites), and the transfer of colonial hegemony from Madrid to Washington. With these changes the North American market assumed 60 percent of Cuban exports (Moreno Fraginals 1978, 2:197). However, it was the differences between the two regions, dating from the inception of colonialism and then reaching a maximal point, that were decisive. These two zones, which can be designated "Cuba A" and "Cuba B," demonstrated very different and unequal development processes. "Cuba A," comprising the red-dirt plain stretching from Artemisa to Colón that furnished the raw materials for the Havana economy, was principally dedicated to the production of sugar. While occupying only 30 percent of the nation's land, this region accounted for 65 percent of its total population, all of its plutocracy, and 60 percent of the elites, the immense majority of whom resided in the capital. "Cuba B," on the other hand, comprising the vast territories occupying the central and eastern parts of the island, occupying the remaining 70 percent of the island, but home to only 35 percent of the population, was dedicated to the raising of livestock, subsistence farming, and some sugar (Pérez de la Riva 1975c, 82–83). This economic disequilibrium can also be seen in a number of other factors. For example, while in "Cuba A" sugar was processed in modern steam-driven mills, "Cuba B" employed only simple ox-driven mills; "Cuba A" was home to 87 percent of all railroad miles, while "Cuba B" had 13 percent; slavery in "Cuba A" was largely of the plantation variety, while in "Cuba B" it

remained patriarchal in character. Of the 370,000 slaves enumerated in the 1861 census, 47.7 percent were tied to sugar production and 90 percent of those who worked in mills were to be found in "Cuba A." According to the same census, "Cuba A" produced 236 million pesos of the gross national product, "Cuba B" only 69 million; 89.9 percent of foreign trade passed through the ports of "Cuba A" and only 10.1 percent through the ports of "Cuba B"; 87 percent of tax revenues were collected from "Cuba A," while "Cuba B" accounted for only 13 percent (Pérez de la Riva 1975c, 83–84, 87).

In the first half of the 1860s a new Havana-based reformist movement got underway that, bolstered by its own political party and an influential newspaper, appeared to have greater chances of success. However, it too came to an untimely demise in the face of metropolitan reluctance to accept any changes to the status quo and the renewed upsurge, following the opening of hostilities, of the integrationists, advocates of the maintenance of Cuba's colonial status, and the fourth of the major nineteenth-century political factions. The integrationists coalesced around the recently established Spanish Club of Havana, whose members—the merchant and slave-trading proprietors of large land holdings, businesses, and publishing concerns—encouraged the enlargement and strengthening of the voluntary companies, the paramilitary militias, who took it upon themselves to discipline even the most minor offenses against the crown and whose most notorious crime was the execution of eight University of Havana medical students in 1871.

With the end of the rebellion in 1878 a new era dawned in which political parties and noninflammatory political propaganda were sanctioned, and in which progress began toward the gradual abolition of slavery (begun in 1800, it ended in 1886) and the opening up of the country to immigration. However, repeated petitions for reforms, then supported by large numbers of followers in the capital and formulated in the most radical of terms of autonomy, continued to go without response in the metropole. Moreover, the almost total economic dependence of Cuba on the North American market prompted the implementation of new tariffs against Cuban goods in 1894. The resulting drop in sugar prices was the detonator that reignited in early 1895 the war of independence, organized from the United States by José Martí (1853–1895) and begun once again in the east. Many from Havana enlisted in the Liberation Army, and although the capital neither joined the revolt nor was taken by the rebels, it did adopt a position of sympathy and solidarity with the cause. During the war Havana was site of concentration camps housing the starving peasantry uprooted from their lands in order to deprive the insurgents of *succor*; it also served as the stage setting for the opportune explosion of the battleship *Maine* in Havana harbor, the incident that brought the United States into the war and precipitated its end. After four years of rule by the occupying forces, and legitimated by a constitution that oversaw the installation of U.S. naval bases on Cuban soil as well as sanctioning the U.S. right to militarily intervene whenever it deemed the situation necessary, a republic of doctors, lawyers, and generals was established in 1902. This government managed a reconciliation of the various parties in the conflict: the *criollo* separatists, the annexationists or autonomists, Spanish integrationists, and U.S. interests—with the noted exception of the blacks, who continued to be relegated to the margins of power (Moreno Fraginals 1995, 295–300).

Initiated in the last third of the nineteenth century, the modernization of Havana fostered a period of accelerating and impressive growth. In 1871 the city occupied an area of approximately 4 square kilometers; this had reached 95 square kilometers by 1919, 116 in 1923 and 200 in 1953 (Le Riverend Brusone 1992, 213), although, according to a much more specialized source, the total area of greater Havana at the end of the 1950s was 478 square kilometers (Coyula 9). While the capital continued to be the political, financial, and cultural center of the country, enjoying the greatest influence in economic and commercial affairs, other areas in eastern and central Cuba began to be exploited with U.S. capital, Spanish immigrants, and West Indian labor. In the first three decades of the twentieth century the island's population, which had declined sharply during the war, grew rapidly, became increasingly white: after Argentina and Brazil, Cuba was the destination of choice for European immigrants—almost entirely Spaniards. However, these newcomers settled by and large in the interior. In 1899 the Cuban population reached 1,527,797 inhabitants, 67 percent white and 33 percent "colored," under which rubric were to be found not only blacks and *mestizos*, but also Chinese indentured laborers who, in great numbers since 1847 (and without wives), had for several decades come to Cuba to work under conditions practically equivalent to slavery. By 1931 the population had risen to 3,962,344, of which 73 percent were white. Greater Havana, which numbered 253,011 inhabitants in 1899, reached a population of more than 700,000 in 1931 and 1,216,762 in 1953 (Pérez de la Riva 1975b, 309–10). Havana was then one of the largest cities in the Americas and, in relation to the gross national population, "the most populated city in the world after London and Vienna" (Marrero 465, n.4).

When Fulgencio Batista launched his *coup d'état* on 10 March 1952, U.S. capital involvement in the economy and finances of Cuba was fundamental and was, in the context of the new tourist industry, soon in the process of converting Havana into a giant beach-front casino: the Las Vegas of the Caribbean. The revolutionary movement, once again arising in the east, received great support from the capital, whose large working class had been at the forefront of political and trade union struggles over the course of the century. Inspired by the audacious acts of the urban guerrillas against the Batista regime, including an attack on the Presidential Palace, the people of Havana joined in the fight or collaborated with the insurgents. On 8 January 1959, after the flight of Batista and the occupation of the capital by the troops of Camilo Cienfuegos and Che Guevara (having already liberated half of the island), Fidel Castro entered Havana at the head of a peasant army. An immense multitude turned out to greet them, filling the wide avenues and skyscrapers of a city that was then the most intensely modernized in Hispanic America.

The sweeping reforms and expropriations carried out by a markedly nationalist government meant, for many reasons, the beginning of the end of Havanan hegemony and the end to four centuries of inequality in every facet of Cuban life. Unlike the others, this third east-west invasion had not failed, and it initiated an intense process of miscegenation, migrations, and social mobility that completely altered the face of the capital. Nevertheless, Havana was more than ever the center of world attention and Cuba a territory fought over by the great powers. Besieged by the diplomatic, economic, media, and military campaigns that the United States unleashed in response to the reforms and nationalizations,

Cuba established alliances with the Soviet Union and other European and Asian nations, declared itself socialist, and, consequently, placed itself front and center in the Cold War, all the while pursuing its own program of national and international development. However, despite a constant fidelity to its original project of self-determination, Cuba was led by the force of circumstances toward an orthodox socialism. In 1972 Cuba became a member of Comecon and–little by little–began to adopt Soviet models in various economic and social analyses, a tendency that it began to abandon in the mid 1980s. With the advent of *perestroika*, Cuba's geographic location and insularity–but also (and principally) political and historical factors of a far greater importance–protected her from the chain reaction set off in the socialist countries of Eastern Europe. After a period of acute shortages, the crisis of "real socialism" ushered in the beginnings of a transition, controlled by the socialist state, to a mixed economy and then to Cuba's reentry into the world market system. These changes were essentially reflected in the reconversion of the capital into a grand tourist attraction, a principal site of investments, and therefore a magnet of internal migrations.

Despite the massive exodus of Havana's upper middle class and the entire social pyramid dependent upon them (almost uniformly) to Florida, the population of Havana reached 1,760,000 inhabitants in 1965, 22 percent of the national total (Pérez de la Riva 1975a, 466) and the highest percentage in the twentieth century. The baby boom, stimulated by the improving economy and the euphoria of the new era, as well as by the decline in the mortality rate and considerable internal migration, had compensated for the demographic effects of the exodus. However, these factors notwithstanding, Havana's 1995 population of 2,176,000 represented less than 20 percent of the national total. By this date the marked sexual demographic difference had also been cancelled out (see *Anuario* 1995) and there was a decline in the white population (62 percent) vis-à-vis blacks (12 percent) and Asians (0.1 percent), in favor of a rise in the number of *mestizos* (25 percent). Moreover–the paradox of a Third World nation with high levels of well-being, health, education, representation of women in the public sphere, and access to various forms of contraception–late twentieth-century Cuba demonstrated patterns of demographic behavior proper to far more economically developed nations: The median age of the population was thirty-four, the birth rate had fallen below the level necessary for the maintenance of existing population levels, and there had been a steady increase in the elderly population, such that by the first decades of the new century those over sixty years of age formed a larger group than those under fifteen (see Morejón).

Events, Institutions, and Transition Points: A Military and Maritime Culture

The first manifestations of Havanan culture in the sixteenth and seventeenth centuries were not great churches or ostentatious cathedrals, for there was no devotion to entomb; neither were they sculptures, altars, or polychrome *exvotos*, for there were no images of abomination to supplant; nor were they chronicles of a conquest, for there were no great exploits to record. Rather, they were of a merely economic nature. The artifacts left behind by the ancient people who inhabited the caves of the western part of the island gave evidence of their purely nomadic, hunter-gatherer existence that, with the exception of numerous *toponyms*, would contribute little to the culture of the nascent settlement. However, these prehistoric people were to influence in great measure the Tainos, from whom the Europeans, in their travels through Hispaniola and eastern Cuba, borrowed numerous names for the natural resources rapidly adopted by the *conquistadores*. These included names for foodstuffs, such as *cazabe* (cassava cake); for dwellings, such as *bohío* (wood and palm-thatched hut); for articles of clothing, such as *cutaras* (sandals); household furnishings, such as *hamacas* (hammocks); means of transport, such as *canoas* (canoes); and especially *toponyms*. This lexical assimilation would contribute to what one chronicler called "islands speech," the *koine* in which words of foreign origin and peninsular dialects were added to standard Spanish, as well as in which the lexicon of European flora, fauna, and, particularly in Cuban Spanish, nautical terms acquired other meanings. The nouns of this *koine*–sometimes with a modifying adjective, other times without–were employed to designate the novel things that by virtue of some likeness could be compared with old world items, but which were nevertheless distinct.

The splendid and imposing Renaissance fortresses that protected the harbor, the walls that girded the city, the boats constructed or carved from precious woods in the shipyard, or the navigation manuals written by resident savants promising "a cultural ambience as elevated or higher than that expressed in all the sonnets then composed in Lima or Mexico" (Moreno Fraginals 1990, 2)–these were the great testimonials to the arts and letters of the military and maritime city of Havana. Next to this high culture, frozen in time, another culture, ephemeral but much more permanent in its continual transformations, was being born. It arrived with the fleets, and formed itself out of the medley of European and African styles and sounds, from the cross-fertilization of the deep Spanish resonance of plucked strings–of *vihuelas*, guitars, *bandurrias*, and lutes–with the African percussive rhythms improvised on packing crates using nautical tholes, accompanying sexually symbolic ritual dances that were to attract the attention of the Inquisition, and with the licentious songs and verses alluded to in the farces and comedies of the Golden Age (Carpentier 1988, 51–62).

First intended as having a supporting role, music and dance have since then taken center stage in Havanan popular culture and have been the cultural expressions that have most influenced (and have been the most often featured theme) other Cuban artistic and literary forms. An entire artistic tradition has been built upon the appropriation of images and rhythms from these popular dance and musical forms as a means of enriching artistic textures and expressive registers or to connote an artist's conception of what is properly Havanan or Cuban. In the visual arts this would include nineteenth-century painters and etchers, by and large foreigners, with their representations of local customs and manners and, subsequently, visual artists, from the masters of the avant-garde to the most recent practitioners, as well as contemporary film makers, fascinated by the wealth, baroque aesthetic, ritualism, and indeed the autism or aphasia that on occasion these musical and dance expressions appear to manifest. In the realm of literature, this tradition would encompass eighteenth- and nineteenth-century journalistic chronicles, as well as nineteenth-century costume dramas, novels, tales, and even poems in which popular music and dance were execrated and designated as dangerous spaces or controversial zones of racial contamination (and yet of a contact impossible to avoid), in the face of which the only advisable behavior was abstention. In the twentieth century, however, from the *vanguardia* movement, whose highest literary expression are the *sones* of Nicolás Guillén, until the *posboom*, and long before the names of singers and bolero dancers were incorporated into the titles of dime-store fictions, the music and dance of Havana appeared in, among many other examples, the poetic texts of José Lezama Lima (1910–1976) or Fina García Marruz (b. 1923) on popular dance bands and *soneros*; the dramas of playwrights like Carlos Felipe (1914–1975); the novelistic characters of Alejo Carpentier (1904–1980) and Guillermo Cabrera Infante (b. 1929); or in one article or another by Severo Sarduy. Moreover, music has been the principal vehicle by which Cuban culture is known abroad and the form enjoying the greatest exposure in other cultures, from nineteenth-century habaneras to contemporary salsa, passing through the *danzón* and the bolero, whose characteristic rhythmic and instrumental components have influenced in equal measure the popular musical forms of jazz and the tango, as well as the operas of Bizet and the symphonic compositions of Stravinsky.

First Transition Point: Enlightenment, the Resource Barons, and the Literati

The accumulated fortunes of gold doubloons that the sailors, soldiers, functionaries, and voyagers who traveled with the fleets left behind in "the cheap taverns of the black *mondongueras*, in the gaming houses or tables set up by the generals and admirals in order to fleece the flush-with-cash, in places even less consecrated" (Ortiz 1984, 75), as well as in the pockets of provisioners and smugglers, consolidated the economy out of which arose the institutions by means of which Havanan literary culture was constructed toward the end of the eighteenth century. Because indigenous Cubans were considered primitive and, after several decades, their numbers were dwindling, it was not thought necessary to establish schools for them. The evangelization brought to bear by various religious orders upon the natives of Mexico, Colombia, or Paraguay would only find its equivalent in the Havanan sugar boom of the late eighteenth century with the publication of a catechism purposed to aid the masters and priests in explicating the Christian doctrine to the Africans by means of a comparison of the universal order and its diverse hierarchies with life in a sugar mill, transformed into an unconventional *Imago Mundi* (Moreno 1978, I:116–19). Thus, although by the end of the sixteenth century, the Franciscans and Dominicans had already established a seat of operations, where from the beginning of the seventeenth century they were teaching Latin, philosophy, and theology; in 1687, a century after the first Havanan school teacher was certified, the Governor would nevertheless write to the king that "we lack the fundamental: teachers... of reading, writing, and counting" (Portuondo 170). Only the Belemites, possessors of a school in their monastery, the houses of "friends" (private schools dedicated to teaching basic literacy to young girls), and the private tutors offered the school age population of Havana anything resembling the rudiments of learning. Toward the middle and the end of the seventeenth century, two convents were constructed for a city that had but few women: Santa Clara (1644), established by the nuns of Cartagena de Indias, and Santa Catalina (1688). In the final decades of the century a school for orphans and the poor, San Francisco de Sales, and the Seminario de San Ambrosio, for the elementary instruction of future priests, were established. Up until shortly after the arrival of the first printing press in the city in 1723, when the Dominicans founded the Real y Ponitificia Universidad de San Géronimo de la Habana (1728), higher education could only be acquired in New Spain, Santo Domingo, or the metropolis. Half a century later, the Seminario de San Carlos, amalgamated with San Ambrosio, settled into the premises vacated by the recently expelled Jesuits (1773). Like the university, the seminary was designed to impart higher, and no longer preliminary, instruction to those young men demonstrating purity of blood and belonging to the highest classes of society; for centuries, however, it would suffer from a backwardness resulting as much from the paucity of disciplines taught as from its pedagogic methods.

In the final decade of the century, "the Cuban Enlightenment" gave rise to the first point of transition in Havanan culture and literature, which since the middle of the century had been showing signs of interesting development. This antecedent period has hardly been studied, although the works of the historians Ribera, Morell de Santa Cruz, and Arrate y Urrutia deserve mention. It was during the final decade that the *Papel Periódico de la Habana* appeared (1792), modeled not on the official gazettes of the preceding decades, but rather designed as a modern newspaper containing every kind of mercantile, agricultural, and cultural information, as well as literary texts and criticism; its life span, under different names, extended into the middle of the nineteenth century. The same year saw the founding of Cuba's most important scientific and cultural institution, the Sociedad Económica de Amigos del País (SEAP; Economic Society of the Friends of the Country), active, save for a hiatus of thirty years, from 1792 until the present. This institution arose out of the mutual interest of the colonial government and the resource barons to incorporate into the accelerating material development of the capital region the knowledge and technologies that the Enlightenment had produced. It was a period favorable to the invention, diffusion, and application of the most novel devices, methods, and techniques that were to benefit the economy, stimulate the reform of higher education, and contribute to the maintenance of the vigorous intellectual climate that Havana was to enjoy in the first quarter of the nineteenth century. The founding of the "San Alejandro" Academy of Painting, Drawing and Sculpture and the "Santa Cecilia" Academy of Music, as well as the development of primary instruction and the publication of important monographs on various aspects of Cuban natural history, economy, society, and culture, were all stimulated by the SEAP, whose role in public affairs has been unparalleled.

During this same period new methods and modern ideas were introduced into seminary instruction by the reforms of the fathers Caballero and Varela. In the two brief periods of constitutional rule, censorship stopped and the political press multiplied; restrictions, however, were almost immediately reinstated and remained active until the 1880s–thus explaining the high frequency of "foreign" editions, printed in Havana with false, dated, or doctored particulars of publication (editorial house and seat), as well as the destruction or loss of manuscripts, that characterizes the Cuban literary institution (see Fornet). However, despite the prevalence of censorship, the number of dailies, weeklies, journals, and supplements related to literature published in Havana in the nineteenth century, almost always of brief duration, exceeded

200. And to these one would have to add the over 150 Cuban serial publications edited in the United States and Europe in which some literature appeared.

On the other hand, the exile of Varela and Heredia–prelude to the long series of exiles that will mark nineteenth-century Cuban literary culture–are the first signs of the political change of direction brought to bear by modifications within the power relations of the resource barons who, formerly the sole allies of the government, now found that they had to share their ever diminishing influence with the Spanish sugar merchants and slave traders. Despite the creation by the SEAP in 1830 of a Permanent Commission of Literature, which as the second item of its agenda took control of the Society's journal, renaming it, in a symbolic act of linguistic nationalism, the *Revista Bimestre Cubana*, the change of political direction became very much evident four years later when attempts by ideologues of the *criollo* oligarchy to create a Cuban Academy of Literature failed. The polemics produced around this affair, preceded by a prior ruckus over the poetry of Heredia, led to the termination of the journal and the exile of its editor, José A. Saco. From this point onward the elites of Havana curtailed their participation in public life and even their presence in the city. Their excursions multiplied, their epistolary contacts with the most distinguished intellectuals of New England or with friends and booksellers in Europe and North America, to whom they relay the latest news and events, grew; or they took refuge in the neighboring city of Matanzas, a sugar trading center that served as a comfortable, elegant, and discrete alternate space for a culture that, in relation to the Spanish, not only knew itself as *other* but discovered its own potential for political participation in the symbolic. In 1834 Domingo Del Monte (1804–1853) established his literary circle in Matanzas and, both during his residence there and after his return to the capital in 1836, he directed the literary production of the era with the aim of reining in the romantic current then in vogue, steering poetry and the theater toward social themes, while at the same time pioneering anti-slavery, ultra-abolitionist fiction, adversary of the already illegal trade that ever more "blackened" the moral reputation of the country at the same time that it multiplied the riches of the Spaniards who engaged in it with impunity. Linked with this circle were the mulatto poets Gabriel del la Concepción Valdés, "Plácido," (1809–1844) and Juan Franciso Manzano (1797–1854), a slave whose *Autobiografía* was written at the request of the group and who obtained his liberty with monies raised by its members. The two poets were to be victims of the suppression of the blacks begun in 1843 and unleashed the following year, an incident that convinced Del Monte to emigrate to Europe where he resided for the remainder of his life.

If the 1830s saw a veritable blossoming of literature in the genres, published in first class journals, the decades that followed, traditionally known as the years of "bad taste," saw both the rise of a populism that wished to be–and for many was–patriotic, and the introduction to Havana of what Sainte-Beuve would call "industrial literature." Two forms need to be mentioned here: on the one hand, the serialized publication of European novels in translation, occupying the major part of newspapers and journals, and, on the other, the outbreak (following a decline in the costs of book production that allowed many to consider themselves writers) of the "graphomania," which, in addition to receiving harsh criticism, became, like the "passion for dancing," a favorite term of the novels of customs and manners (Fornet 125). The writers Rafael Maria Mendive (1821–1886), Joaquin Lorenzo Luaces (1826–1867), and Ildefonso Estrada y Zenea (1826–1912), and the journals *Album de lo Bueno y de lo Bello*, the *Revista de La Habana*, and the *Revista Habanera* stood as exceptions to this trend.

In 1842 the University of Havana was secularized, and the chairs vacated by the departing Dominicans were occupied largely by Cuban professors who, little by little, adapted their instruction to the times and came to exert a substantial socio-political influence on the students. Moreover, with the passing of the 1844 Public Instruction Act, the first of its kind, the SEAP was divested of its educational obligations, and the management of public schools (which by 1864 numbered 122 in the region of Havana and its environs) passed to the municipalities. Of course, much earlier, the Cuban upper classes had set up their own private high schools, among the most notable of which were Carraguao and El Salvador in Havana–at different times under the superintendence of Luz y Caballero (Le Riverend Brusone 1960, 412–13, 420)–and La Empresa in Matanzas. These schools' utilization of textbook readers constituted an important innovation that would have a salutary influence on the dissemination and reception of the national literature and would at the same time contribute to the development of a sense of national identity. These readers consisted of a large number of literary texts, both for comprehension and analysis, by the most important contemporary Cuban writers. The Jesuits, for their part, reopened their school at Belén for the sons of the Spanish oligarchy.

Toward the middle of the 1860s the practice of cigar factory reading arose, a unique form of social adaptation and collective enjoyment, in which tobacco workers appointed from among their numbers someone to read aloud to them while they worked and whose daily wages they paid. However, despite the fact that the factory owners made the decisions about what was to be read, and that various press outlets and personalities celebrated the advent of this original form of cultural accession, there soon began a campaign against the practice, which led to its being banned in the following year, a prohibition that would not be lifted until after the Great War (1868–1878) and would once again be imposed with outbreak of the War of 1895. As has been pointed out, this practice enjoyed a broad acceptance among the Cuban tobacco workers of Florida, for whom military and literary figures as important as Máximo Gómez (1836–1905) and Manuel de la Cruz (1861–1896), encouraged by the Cuban Revolutionary Party, would write many memorable pages (Fornet 185–93). Tobacco readings are still, today, a daily custom in the cigar factories of the island.

Finally, during this period, Cuban dramatic literature, whose long "prehistory" has been noted (Leal I, 13–97), was to have a solid infrastructure of more than one hundred city-center theaters, in addition to the "comedy houses" and other theaters in the peripheral quarters of the city. These theaters were the stage for national and visiting international companies specializing in the Spanish classics, farces and revues with first-class actors, and offering seasons of ballet and French or Italian opera. Moreover, a body of combative theatrical criticism (well established in various journals) arose, which, while stimulating an abundant production of markedly nationalist theatrical works, was from the beginning of the Spanish American War of 1898 summarily dismissive of the Cuban comic theater and gave next to no space for discussion of the works of the most important dramatists–Milanés, Avellaneda, and Luaces.

Second Transition Point: Modernization, Modernism, and the Avant-Garde

At the end of a war that Spain was incapable of winning, the Cubans discovered that over the course of the hostilities, the nation had been consolidated and the people had formed a full consciousness of their identity. In the field of literature, this rise in consciousness had repercussions in a kind of archaeology of the "Cuban," whether learned or popular, that became manifest in the publication or reedition of the principal authors of the eighteenth century, the ideologues of the resource barons, the abolitionist writers, anthologies of poetry or the novels of customs and manners, as well as compilations of songs and folk dances. Moreover, the granting of provincial status to the island also had important reverberations in the cultural domain. The vitality of the recently legalized political parties, as well as the gradual disappearance of censorship, fostered the rise of a gamut of political literature taking the forms of oratory, essays, pamphlets, periodical articles, in addition to texts of a documentary, autobiographical, or narrative character that openly and lauditorily narrated tales of the heroes and the exploits of the war. Thus, at the same time as a full fledged critique of the colonial system was being disseminated, an heroic past was being celebrated that could be transformed into a model for the future.

In the 1880s, as a result of the rapid modernization of the country, the great Cuban (sugar producing and manufacturing) industrial revolution reached its peak (Moreno Fraginals 1995, 268). This moment of cresting had its literary institutional corollaries in the publication of the *Revista de Cuba* and the *Revista Cubana*, the development of scholarship, philosophy, and a literary criticism that enjoyed then one of its most brilliant epochs, and in the designation of contemporary French and English theoreticians and thinkers (and Parnassian and Symbolist poets and prose writers) as the models and mentors of the generation. For its part, the abolition of slavery inspired a number of plaintive anthropological studies, such as Francisco Calcagno's (1827–1903) pioneering *Antología de poetas de color* [Anthology of Poets of Color]. Political themes did find some echo in the literary circles of de Cortina, José María de Céspedes, and Nicolás Azcárate. However, the most politically inspired literary groups were the *Puentes Grandes* circle, meeting in Borrero's house, and those groups linked to the editorial boards of the new weeklies *La Habana Elegante* and *El Fígaro*, publishers of those Cuban and Hispano-American writers in large part influenced by French currents, the vehicles of the incipient modernism.

With the start of the new War of Independence in 1895 (First war 1868–1878), organized by José Martí, the majority of the intellectuals chose the separatist option and abandoned (or merely sustained without appetite) the plans already initiated, when they did not go into voluntary exile in order to dedicate themselves either to the fomentation of publications divulging the truth about Cuba or to marching straight to the battle front. With the establishment, in the new century, of a Cuban republic nursing vague hopes of being a U.S. protectorate, despondency took hold of the cultural milieu. The most brilliant writers were dead in the North or in the hills–Manuel de la Cruz and José Martí, principally–while others devoted themselves to the task of creating so as not to fall into despair. In the bleak intellectual climate of the first decade of the twentieth century the most productive literary genre was reflective prose devoted to the analysis of Cuban society. This can be immediately observed in the most important publication of the first quarter century, *Cuba Contemporánea*, a journal favoring articles of a moral or social persuasion, although it also concerned itself with contemporary literature and with the recuperation of hitherto unpublished nineteenth century texts.

Although the cream of the poetic crop was to be found in other cities, the essay and the novel, also having reached a great summit in the 1880s and 1890s, were the most representative genres of Havanan literature in the second decade of the twentieth century. Indeed, as we have seen, the title of Carlos Loveira's (1882–1928) work, *Generales y doctores* [1920; Generals and Doctors], comes to serve as the descriptive and affective denominator of that period. Women, for their part, in these years organizing their affairs and occupying a greater space in the life of the country to whose independence they had so notably contributed, received important recognition of their past and present literary production in the *Florilegio de escritoras cubanas* [Anthology of Cuban Women Writers], published in three volumes between 1910 and 1919 by Antonio González Curquejo. The collection comprises 120 authors and 1,500 texts, half of which are poetry, half narrative, running the gamut from the essayistic to the journalistic.

In 1923 two events occurred that mobilized a society that appeared to be lethargic, self-absorbed, and pessimistic: the University Reforms and the Protest of the Thirteen. While the first heralded the arrival of the grievances first aired by the movement initiated in Córdoba, grievances that in Havana encountered a tremendous echo and were to animate student struggles in the following decades, the second tested the resolve of intellectuals to abandon their position on the margins of social conflict. Out of a timely confrontation with a corrupt government and its irregularities, arose the group and the project that would, more than any other, revitalize Cuban culture in the first half of the century. The Grupo Minorista (the Minority Group), at first associated with the journal *Social*, and later with the *Revista de Avance*, assembled together representatives of distinct literary genres and cultural forms in order to introduce them into the literary and artistic–and political–avant-garde. In both the essays and modernist poetry of the Cuban *fin de siècle* and in the intellectual milieu of the first decades of the twentieth century in general, relations were increasingly often established with the rest of the Hispano-American world. Certain Hispano-American thinkers made a profound impression on Cuban society and ideas; a number of continental writers visited the island or published in the journals of the period. (The titles of some of these pieces give evidence of these links and influences.) Influenced by the European avant-garde, the Harlem Renaissance, anthropology, and above all by the ever more vigorous contribution of the African constituent to the popular urban culture and life of the city, the 1920s saw the reappearance of the black theme in Cuban letters. It had been present since the nineteenth century in the previously mentioned abolitionist narratives, in the caricatures of the comic theater and the manners and customs writers, and, from a naturalist or positivist perspective, in the approaches of the *fin-de-siècle* novelists and essayists.

The establishment of the republic was to entail a gradual educational reform at every level, as well as the creation of the National Library (1901), the National Academy of Arts and Letters (1910), and the Cuban Academy of Language (1926), each with its affiliated publications. Although the *Revista Bimestre* began republication under the auspices of the SEAP in 1910, Cuban literature–whose presumed nonexistence had engendered the polemics leading to the closing of that review in 1834–continued to be relegated to the status of providing examples for elementary school readers, and was only introduced as a subject of study in its own right in the universities in 1937. Fernando Ortiz, the great cultural animator of the period, not only directed the *Revista Bimestre*, then devoting some of its pages to literature, but was also instrumental in the founding of a number of seminal institutions: the Cuban Folklore Society in 1924, publisher of the *Archivos del Folklore Cubano*; the Hispano-Cuban Cultural Foundation in 1936, publisher of *Ultra*, "the review of reviews," and disseminator of the most important cultural products from other shores (as well as the Society for Afro-Cuban Studies in the following year). In 1936 the other great animator of Havanan cultural studies, Emilio Roig de Leuchsenring, created the City of Havana Historical Bureau, the promoter of numerous memorable conference series and widely respected editions.

For their part the women of the era, individually or collectively involved in various cultural projects and journals, founded the Lyceum in 1928. Given its broad mandate and excellent library, the Lyceum was destined to become one of the most dynamic Cuban cultural centers, as well as the meeting point for a series of conferences and courses that were to be extremely influential in the contemporary and future development of Cuban letters. From the end of the 1930s through the 1940s leftist writers and thinkers edited a number of journals of short duration, such as *Baraguá*, *Mediodía*, and *Gaceta del Caribe*, which published the early poems, short stories, and novel excerpts of some of Cuba's most important writers. In the 1950s *Our Time* was founded, a cultural society that–together with the Lyceum–would be one of the principal fora for prerevolutionary literary and artistic work. Spanish writers who visited the island both during the time of the Spanish Republic and, as exiles, during and after the Spanish Civil War, made stopovers in Havana or took up residence there for some time. A number, including Federico García Lorca, Juan Ramón Jiménez, María Zambrano, and Manuel Altolaguirre, were to exert, on various levels and in different ways, an important influence on the literary life of the city. Toward the middle of the 1940s a group of writers, who from the late 1930s had been involved in editing a number of journals of exacting literary standards and clear universalist intentions, came together around *Orígenes*. This new journal would demonstrate those characteristics in abundance, both in its high literary caliber and in the large number of foreign collaborators that it managed to bring together.

However, although there flourished in this period close to one hundred literary journals (some continuously, others much more briefly), and although almost all the newspapers contained important literary supplements (Instituto 1980, II: 749–73; 990–92), given their size limitations these publications were restricted to printing poems, short stories, and short essays. Furthermore, while a number of diverse, and principally private, institutions saw themselves as agencies for the promotion and development of Cuban letters, they almost always did so guided by specific interests. There did exist, of course, several publishing houses with a broad cultural mandate, but these firms by and large limited themselves to the production of all manner of school texts, many of which they exported to the other countries of Latin America and were little inclined to risk their capital on the publication of literature. The difficulties of literary publishing can also be seen in the context of the various competitions that, beginning in the eighteenth century, aimed to stimulate literary production in various genres. The SEAP, the Liceo de La Habana, various journals, and other private and later public institutions–the founding of the Office of Culture for the Secretary of Education in the early part of the twentieth century is important here (Instituto 1980, I:224–27)– all offered literary prizes, but it was only in rare cases that the winning work would see the light of publication. This resulted in the situation in which writers seeking to publish a book, in the majority of cases, had to finance its publication out of their own pockets; as a rule these editions were limited to less than 500 copies and given as gifts to friends. From the end of the nineteenth century continuing right through to the 1960s, one of the most expedient means of publishing literary works was in collections promoted by the journals, fine examples of which were the editions produced under the auspices of the *Revista de Avance* and *Orígenes* (Smorkaloff 51, 80–81). However, even in these cases the author frequently had to cover part of or all the costs of publication.

The modernization of the country and of Havana in particular also brought with it the construction of large theaters in the interwar period, the destinations of visiting foreign companies and home to opera and zarzuela seasons, as well as smaller theaters housing more local theatrical productions, such as those of Cuban-Chinese theatrical groups, for example (see **Figure** 1). With the exception of the markedly nationalist comic theater, which saw a rebirth in the 1980s but gave way to performances of an often much more pornographic character in the 1990s (Leal II: 157–229; 315), the only expansion of interest in dramatic literature would be tied to the rise of musical and choreographic productions that, from the early part of the century until the middle of the 1940s, were staged in the Alhambra Theater, as well as to individual plays by writers who also worked in other genres. In the first half of the century close to a dozen important theaters were erected largely for musical and variety shows that, just as had been the case in the late nineteenth century, attracted a clutch of international stars, including Bernhardt, Pavlova, and Caruso. It was only in the 1940s and the 1950s that Cuban dramatic literature began to renew itself, assisted by the efforts of, among other private initiatives, the Academy of Dramatic Arts, the Theatrical Foundation, and the University Theater. This renewal took form in the staging of European repertory and contemporary student works in tiny, weekend-only theaters, and in the emergence of the most important Cuban dramatists of the century (Instituto 1980, II: 1004–1005).

Cinema arrived in Havana in 1896, and the first film was shot in the capital the following year. However, despite the sporadic participation of the occasional writer in cinematic projects funded by the communists, literature's sole contribution to the screen in this period was an ill-fated version of *Cecilia Valdés*. Radio, first broadcast by Havanan aficionados in 1918 when only Russia, France, Great Britain, and the United States could count themselves as transmitting nations, received its official premiere in 1920. Thanks to the traditions of newspaper serials and tobacco factory readings, radio was to enjoy a tremendous success through its links to mass literature

Figure 1.

Art Nouveau Havana, 1931. (Archive of the author)

and to offer employment to a great number of writers dedicated to the dramatization of important international news stories and events, the adaptation of narrative classics, and especially the production of radio plays. By means of this new medium, many economically lower-class listeners, and especially the women of this group, were to experience their first encounter with literature. A pioneer in detective serials and radio novellas, Cuban radio was quickly to become the Hollywood of the medium (R. González 44), reaching listeners not only in the Hispano-American world, as history and fiction (see Mario Vargas Llosa's *La tía Julia y el escribidor* [1977; *Aunt Julia and the Script Writer: A Screenplay,* 1982]) have demonstrated, but listeners on other continents as well. Television, inaugurating its first regular transmissions in 1950, subsequently replayed in part the "literary" history of radio.

Third Transition Point: The Revolution

The Cuban Revolution fully opened the doors for Cuban writers and artists of every kind to a solicitous public. The numbers of these latter had swollen thanks to the literacy campaigns that in a single year (1961) presented the country with an enormous mass of potential readers, and to the development of a broad educational program that, from the elementary to the university level, multiplied both the number of schools and the number of teachers and professors. The explosion of schools for the training of new artists and teachers of the arts, the mushrooming of dozens of journals, tabloids, and weeklies (Le Riverend Brusone 1992, 272–73; Segre 249), as well as publishing houses, libraries, galleries, museums, theaters, and concert halls, in which contemporary works were presented and works of the past recuperated–all this contributed to the creation of an intellectual climate characterized by an abundance of polemics–ancients versus moderns, liberals versus reactionaries, partisans of the capital versus those of the provinces–but ultimately all oriented around the principle: "With the revolution, everything; against the revolution, nothing." The movement arising out of this fostered the creative development of national writers and artists, and the circulation, no longer merely among the elites, of world popular culture, largely because it also explicitly and emphatically rejected socialist realism even while, from the beginning of 1961, declaring itself socialist, and even though there continued to exist strong ties between the new Cuba and the former U.S.S.R. and the nations of Eastern Europe.

Havana in the 1960s, while beginning to lose its hegemonic grip on the country, simultaneously transformed itself into a kind of anti-dogmatic, leftist, and avant-garde capital. The ritual pilgrimage of European and Latin American intellectuals to the new revolutionary Mecca reached its acme with the May Salon (1967) and the Cultural Congress of Havana (1968), where many of the most noteworthy figures of the decade's cultural left were to come together. However, in the early 1970s with the First Congress of Education and Culture, a climate of intolerance, dogmatism, and isolation descended upon the island, as expressed in the famous, but no less lamentable, "Padilla case." Following the creation of the Ministry of Culture in 1976 and with the conclusion of the Second Congress of the Cuban Union of Artists and Writers, a retreat from previous political policies was initiated, a retreat which, since the second half of the 1980s and into the 1990s–and despite, or perhaps because of, the crisis suffered by the country–occasioned a remarkable opening up and return of a climate most favorable to the artistic and literary creation of the thousands of intellectuals who were shaped by the revolution. Either as exiles, politically opposed to the revolution, or as émigrés or part-time émigrés, many Cuban writers live and work in other countries. However, in the last few years, their works, which for decades have been kept out of the national canon, gradually and by diverse means–editions, journals, and anthologies–have been reincorporated into the mainstream of Cuban letters.

In addition to the steady improvement of all levels of instruction, the organization of a large network of libraries and bookstores, and the multiplication of literary workshops and prizes, three institutions were created in 1959 whose significance in the expansion of Cuban letters has been without parallel: the National Press (la Imprenta Nacional de Cuba), the Art and Motion Picture Industry Institute (el Instituto del Arte y la Industria Cinematográficos, or ICAIC), and the House of the Americas (la Casa de las Américas). The National Press took up the enormous task of book publishing in a country that, while lacking a publishing tradition and economically impeded from importing books from abroad, nonetheless experienced a growing demand for reading materials. Over the years the National Press of Cuba became the National Publishing House (Editorial Nacional) of Cuba and later the Cuban Institute of the Book, an amalgam of various specialized editorial divisions that in thirty years has produced several dozen million copies of books on every subject and literature under the sun for a highly diverse readership (Smorkaloff 191–231). Given the present economic crisis, various means have been sought to manage the shortages: smaller print runs than were previously seen, books of fewer pages, co-editions, anthologies, and the publication or republication of literary and cultural journals.

For its part, the ICAIC has not only benefited film directors, actors, designers, musicians, and photographers, but has also offered work to writers as scenarists and scriptwriters, literary consultants, and cinema critics, in addition to being a vehicle for their own works or those of their predecessors: Approximately one of every eight films produced in Cuba between 1959 and 1990 was based on a Cuban text (Douglas 270–78). Moreover, the founding of the Latin American New Cinema Festival in 1978, which has brought foreign directors to Cuba and facilitated the exhibition of foreign films that, for commercial reasons, would not otherwise be screened, as well as the establishment of the San Antonio de los Baños Film School in 1985, have fomented a climate of debate, creativity, and up-to-date cinematography. Given the multimedia character of cinema and the plurality both of the subjects it tackles and of the codes and languages it employs, Cuban cinema in this period has made up for many of the other information deficiencies and has promoted a rich intellectual dynamic.

The Casa de las Américas, envisioned as a forum for dialogue with the continent, has within a short span of years transformed itself into an important and dynamic center for the construction of a Latin American culture conceived as something more than the sum of national cultural productions. Devoted to the recuperation of tradition, the expansion of the canon, and the promotion of the new, the Casa de las Américas publishes one of the most prestigious journals in the Spanish language, hosts conferences attended by the most important writers and artists of the region, has played an instrumental role in the inauguration of the new Latin American narrative, as well as the genres of the protest song and the testimonial narrative, and has paid homage to numerous artists, all the while renovating the model of the engaged intellectual.

From the 1960s Havana has also been the site of a significant theatrical movement in large part characterized by the emergence and consolidation of important theater companies, the organization of national festivals, and the participation of Cuban companies in international festivals, all of which have had a positive influence on the development of dramatic literature. Finally, radio and television, the management of which was transferred to the state in order to expedite their use as vehicles of mass education, have offered many writers the possibility of exercising their literary interests in the adaptation to these media of Cuban and foreign, contemporary and classical works.

Translation by Colman Hogan

Works Cited

Anuario demográfico de Cuba, 1995. 1996. Havana: Oficina Nacional de Estadísticas.

Carpentier, Alejo. 1981. "América ante la joven literatura europea (1931)." *La novela latinoamericana en vísperas de un nuevo siglo y otros ensayos.* Mexico City: Editorial Siglo XXI. 51–57.

———. 1987 [1949]. Prologue. *El reino de este mundo.* Havana: Editorial Letras Cubanas. 1–9.

———. 1988. *La música en Cuba (1946).* Havana: Editorial Letras Cubanas.

Coyula, Mario. 1994. *La Habana de enero.* Facimile. Havana: [Grupo Desarrollo de La Habana]. 1–9.

Douglas, María Eulalia. 1996. *La tienda negra. El cine en Cuba (1897–1990).* Havana: Cinemateca de Cuba.

Fornet, Ambrosio. 1994. *El libro en Cuba, siglos XVIII y XIX.* Havana: Editorial de Letras Cubanas.

González, Manuel Pedro. 1939. "Las relaciones intelectuales entre los Estados Unidos e Hispano América." *Universidad de La Habana* 8.24–25: 84–110.

González, Reynaldo. 1988. *Llorar es un placer.* Havana: Editorial Letras Cubanas.

González Curquejo, Antonio. 1910. *Florilegio de escritoras cubanas.* Havana: La Moderna poesia.

Instituto de Literatura y Lingüística de la Academia de Ciencias de Cuba. 1980. *Diccionario de la literatura cubana.* 2 vols. Havana: Editorial Letras Cubanas.

Leal, Rine. 1975-1982. *La selva oscura (Historia del teatro cubano [...]).* 2 vols. Havana: Editorial Letras Cubanas.

Le Riverend Brusone, Julio J. 1960. *La Habana (Biografía de una provincia).* Havana: Academia de la Historia de Cuba.

———. 1992. *La Habana, espacio y vida.* Madrid: Editorial Mapfre.

Lezama Lima, José. 1953a [1937]. "Coloquio con Juan Ramón Jiménez." *Analecta del reloj.* Havana: Ucar y García. 40–61.

———. 1953b [1941]. "Julián del Casal." *Analecta del reloj.* Havana: Ucar y García. 62–97.

———. 1957. *La expresión americana.* Havana: Instituto Nacional de Cultura. 31–54.

Loveira, Carlos. 1965. *Generales y doctores.* Havana: Sociedad Editorial Cuba Contemporánea.

Loynaz, Dulce María. 1993. *Poesía completa.* Havana: Letras Cubanas.

Marrero, Leví. 1950. *Geografía de Cuba.* Havana: Talleres Tipográficos Alfa.

Martí, José. 1992a [1891]. "Nuestra América." *Obras escogidas en tres tomos.* Vol. 2: *1886-Octubre 1891.* Havana: Editorial de Ciencias Sociales. 480–87.

———. 1992b [1889]. "Vindicación de Cuba." *Obras escogidas en tres tomos.* Vol.2: *1886–Octubre 1891.* Havana: Editorial de Ciencias Sociales. 263–68.

Morejón, Blanca, ed. 1997. *Resultados de la encuesta nacional de migraciones internas a Ciudad de La Habana, 1995.* Havana: Centro de Estudios Demográficos.

Moreno Fraginals, Manuel. 1978. *El Ingenio: complejo económico social cubano de azúcar.* 2nd ed. 3 vols. Havana: Editorial de Ciencias Sociales.

———. 1990. "Claves de una cultura de servicios." *La Gaceta de Cuba* July: 2–5.

———. 1995. *Cuba/España, España/Cuba. Historia común.* Barcelona: Crítica.

Ortiz, Fernando. 1983 [1940]. *Contrapunteo cubano del tabaco y el azúcar.* Havana: Editorial de Ciencias Sociales.

———. 1984 [1935]. *La clave xilofónica de la música cubana.* Havana: Editorial Letras Cubanas.

Pérez de la Riva, Juan. 1975a [1967]. "La población de Cuba y sus problemas." *El barracón y otros ensayos.* Havana: Editorial de Ciencias Sociales. 435–53.

———. 1975b. "La población habanera." *El barracón y otros ensayos.* Havana: Editorial de Ciencias Sociales. 303–15.

———. 1975c [1968]. "Una isla con dos historias." *El barracón y otros ensayos.* Havana: Editorial de Ciencias Sociales. 75–89.

Pichardo y Tapia, Estéban. 1836. *Diccionario provincial de voces cubanas.* Matanzas: Imprenta de la Real Marina.

Piñera, Virgilio. 1998. *La isla en peso: obra poética.* Ed. Antón Arrufat. Havana: Ediciones Unión.

Portuondo, Fernando. 1957. *Historia de Cuba.* 7th ed. Havana: Editorial Minerva.

Ramos, Julio. 1996. *Paradojas de la letra.* Caracas: Ediciones eXcultura.

Ribeiro, Darcy. 1992. *Las Américas y la civilización. Proceso de formación y causas del desarrollo desigual de los pueblos americanos.* Havana: Casa de las Américas.

Roig de Leuchsenring, Emilio. 1963–1964. *La Habana. Apuntes históricos.* 2nd ed. 3 vols. Havana: Editora del Consejo Nacional de Cultura.

Segre, Roberto, Mario Coyula, and Joseph L. Scarpaci. 1997. *Havana: Two Faces of the Antillean Metropolis.* Chichester: Wiley.

Smorkaloff, Pamela Maria. 1987. *Literatura y edición de libros. La cultura literaria y el proceso social en Cuba (1900–1987).* Havana: Editorial Letras Cubanas.

Vargas Llosa, Mario. 1977. *La tía Julia y el escribidor.* Barcelona: Seix Baral.

CHAPTER 36

SANTO DOMINGO
CENTER OF INNOVATION, TRANSITION, AND CHANGE

William Luis

Ayer nací
a la tarde fui francés
a la noche etíope fui
hoy dicen que soy inglés:
¡no sé que será de mí!

I was born yesterday
In the afternoon I was French
by night I was Ethiopian
today they say I am English
I don't know what will be my fate!
–Juan Vázquez

Introduction

The Dominican Republic and its capital city, Santo Domingo, have the distinction of claiming multiple beginnings. The island of Hispaniola, which the Dominican Republic and Haiti have shared since the beginning of the nineteenth century, was visited by Columbus on his first voyage to the New World. The encounter between the two worlds is among the most important events of this millennium and of western civilization. Hispaniola was the first island to exhibit evidence of a significant Amerindian population and quantities of precious metals, one of the reasons that launched Columbus's enterprise. While on the island, everything the Spaniards did became a first. They built the fortress Navidad in 1492, the settlement La Isabela in 1493, and the port city of Santo Domingo in 1497, the first capital of the island and of the New World. As the center of social, religious, and administrative life, Santo Domingo housed all of the important early colonial structures. Some of these edifices include the first cathedral, Catedral de Santa María la Menor (1514–1520), and the oldest university in the western hemisphere, Universidad de Santo Tomás de Aquino, built in 1538. The city also became an avenue through which Spanish (and therefore European) ideas, culture, economy, government, religion, and jurisprudence first spread to the New World.

The island's notoriety also embodies a series of less fortunate events. On this island the Amerindians were first enslaved and made to work in the *repartimiento* and *encomienda*, systems devised to give Spaniards both land and Amerindian slaves. Many were massacred and others died from European diseases. When Columbus arrived on the island, there were some 400,000 Amerindians. By the time the 1508 census was taken, their numbers had diminished to approximately 60,000 (Moya Pons 1994, 26) and would decrease even more. By 1519 there were only 3,000 left to meet the growing demands of Spanish landowners. The first African slaves entered the island through the port city of Santo Domingo. They were brought to the New World to supplement the rapidly decreasing Amerindian population and thus to work in the mines and agriculture, particularly in the incipient and profitable sugarcane industry. The island also experienced the first Amerindian and African rebellions against their Spanish captors.

Just as quickly as the island and the port city acquired fame, they fell from grace when the Spaniards discovered more profitable lands and sailed to the island of Cuba and to the continent, to Mexico and Peru, where large deposits of gold and silver were found. The exodus to the mainland practically depopulated the island. In his *Manual de historia dominicana* [1977; Manual of Domincan History], Frank Moya Pons (b. 1944), arguably the most acclaimed Dominican historian in recent memory, states that by 1528 five towns had disappeared. Those that remained included Concepción, Santiago, Puerto Real, Higüey, Azua, San Juan de la Maguana, Santa María del Puerto, Salvatierra de la Sabana, and Yauana, with a total of 1000 inhabitants. Santo Domingo was the only town not affected by the emigration to the continent. On the contrary, it remained active as sugar became a much-desired commodity. Referring to a 1528 document, which mentions the thirty-three merchants living in Santo Domingo, Moya Pons describes the city and its people in the following manner:

> A pesar del monopolio que hacía subir los precios, en las calles de Santo domingo se veían las gentes enriquecidas vestir las sedas, tafetanes, bordados y brocados más caros importados a través de España de otras partes de Europa, y en las casas señoriales de los ingenios así como en las principales casas de los mercaderes se consumían alimentos y bebidas importadas a seis veces más su precio original. (1992, 34)

> In spite of the monopoly which made prices go up, on the streets of Santo Domingo the wealthy class could be seen wearing the most expensive imported silks, taffeta, embroidery and brocade which came from Europe through Spain, and in the aristocratic homes of the sugar plantations as well as in the manor houses of the merchants, the finest imported foods and beverages costing six times their original price were consumed.

The Dominican Republic is located between 17 and 20 degrees north latitude and 68 and 72 degrees west longitude in the Caribbean Sea and occupies two thirds of the island of Hispaniola, bordered by Haiti to the west and the Mona Canal to the east, separating it from the island of Puerto Rico. Hispaniola is one of the four islands of the Major Antilles and, after Cuba, the Dominican Republic is the second largest country of the Caribbean. The city of Santo Domingo, first named La Nueva Isabela, was founded by the Adelantado don Bartolomé Colón, the Admirante's brother, on 4 August 1496, on the eastern shore of the Ozama River, in the southern region of the island. In June of 1502 a hurricane destroyed the huts that had defined the city, and the following year governor Nicolás de Ovando ordered that the city be moved to the western shores of the river. Many of the conquerors of the New World departed from Santo Domingo, and it served as a base to support their enterprises on the continent. Though Santo Domingo became the official capital of the colony and, later, the republic, its privileged position would be challenged by other cities and regions. The northern Cibao region, known for its fertile lands used for agriculture, developed differently than that of the south. Home to some of the wealthiest families, who were able to demand high rents from their tenants, this was the site of the cultivation of tobacco and other agricultural crops that required more skill than cattle farming, and, as Fernando Ortiz's *Cuban Counterpoint: Tobacco and Sugar* (1940) shows, this represented a different way of using land. In some instances, Puerto Plata was in a competitive geographic position to receive immigrants. This was the case with Cuban exiles during the Ten Years' War (1868–1878), many of them professionals, businessmen, artisans, and craftsmen who sought refuge precisely in Puerto Plata. In fact, Santiago de los Caballeros has been known as the cultural capital of the country, and at times Puerto Plata held a similar distinction in business (Bell 114).

Dominican identity is intricately tied to those groups that have occupied the island, especially the eastern section. Most prominent are Amerindians, Spaniards, Haitians, and North Americans. It is also associated with multiple independence movements: one from France, two from Haiti, and three from Spain. In addition, the United States occupied the country from 1916 to 1924 and invaded it a second time in 1965. Dominicans have attempted to embrace or reject one or more of these occupational cultures, but to a lesser or greater degree, they have all had an impact on Dominican national culture and psyche. The coming and going of natives and foreigners has contributed to a multi-layered Dominican identity. This combination of cultures is best represented by the many names given to the island. When Columbus arrived in 1492, he encountered three autochthonous groups, namely the Arawaks, the Caribs, and the Ciboneys. The Arawaks called the island Hayti, land of the mountains; later the Tainos referred to it as Quisqueya, Mother Earth. The name would continue to change with the arrival of other cultures: The Spanish called it La Española (Hispaniola). After the Peace of Ryswick in 1697, in which Spain ceded the western portion of the island to France, it was named Saint-Domingue; the remaining Spanish territory would be known as Santo Domingo. And with the success of the slave rebellion against the French in 1791, the island changed names one more time, recovering in 1804 its original name, Haiti. And with the independence movement of 1844, the eastern part was renamed the Dominican Republic. Santo Domingo also suffered a change of names. It was first called La Nueva Isabela, as we have seen, and one year later, Santo Domingo. During Rafael Leonidas Trujillo's dictatorship (1930–1961), Santo Domingo was renamed Ciudad Trujillo. When his dictatorship came to an end, Joaquín Balaguer restored the original name of the country's capital city.

Santo Domingo and the Dominican Republic have been deeply marked by the Spanish colonization process. As the first capital of the New World, Santo Domingo was the first recipient of Spanish traditions in the New World. Spanish language, literature, culture, and the Roman Catholic religion became entrenched in the populations' cultural memory. After years of preparation, a comprehensive history of the literary culture of the Caribbean in Spanish, French, English, and Dutch has been published in three extensive volumes, which will be one of the principal sources of future scholarship (see A. James Arnold 1994). Dominican heritage distinguishes Dominicans from their neighbors: Dominicans are of European, but also African and Haitian, descent. Though some can be considered black, many do not identify themselves as such; for them Haitians are blacks, and this they reject in part because of the last Haitian occupation of the island. Instead, they prefer to claim a Spanish and pre-Columbian lineage, represented by the Amerindian groups that once lived on the island. As the capital of the New World, the island is the first landmass to appear extensively in Spanish writings. Columbus was the first to document his impressions of a world previously unseen by Europeans. In Columbus's *Diario de navegación* [The Journal of Christopher Columbus (During His First Voyage, 1492–1493)], which has been preserved with significant modifications by Bartolomé de las Casas (1474–1566), in his *Historia de las Indias* [1559; History of the Indies], the Almirante describes his experiences on the island, provides accounts of his interactions with the native population, and, to justify the voyage, despite not finding large deposits of precious metals, proposes to the Crown that the native inhabitants be converted into loyal subjects. Columbus's writings are characterized by his use of hyperboles, claiming, for example, that each island is more beautiful than the previous one.

The early period set the tone for the history that was to unfold well into the present. It was characterized by power struggles between Columbus and his numerous enemies. The new land would be the center of dispute not only between Spaniards and Amerindians, but also among the Spaniards themselves. In 1511 King Ferdinand established the Real Audiencia de Indias in Santo Domingo to prevent Columbus's family from governing independently of the Spanish Crown. Bernal de Pisa, the expedition's accountant, was the first in the New World to write against Columbus, accusing him of abuse of power. In his *Memorial*, he mentions that the Almirante created work and difficulties for everyone, and that they did not find the gold they had anticipated. Others, like the mayor of Isabela, Francisco Roldán Ximeno, challenged the Almirante's power. While Columbus was in Spain giving an account of his most recent discoveries of Cuba and Jamaica, Roldán took advantage of his absence and opposed first Bartolomé and later Diego Colón, the Almirante's brothers. He even depopulated La Isabela and moved his followers to Xaraguá. The Crown eventually removed Columbus from the position of Governor and named Francisco de Bobadilla to the post; when he in turn was not able to deal effectively with Roldán, he was replaced by Ovando, who was more effective in dealing with Roldán and his possible threat to the Crown's authority. Upon his arrival in 1502, Ovando returned Roldán to Spain, but he was shipwrecked outside the port. Roldán then wrote his *cartas* and *memoriales*, which give an account of his rebellion against Columbus (Vicioso 30–31).

The Conquest of Hispaniola and the New World was a military, economic, but also religious enterprise. Among the Franciscans who objected to the treatment of the native inhabitants was Fray Antonio Montesinos (1470–1520). During his sermon "Yo soy la voz que clama en el desierto" ("I Am the Voice That Cries Out in the Desert"), pronounced on 30 November 1511, he denounced the barbaric treatment of the Amerindians. When asked by the officials of the colony to retract his words, Montesino's restated his position in a second sermon, "Repetiré desde el principio mi saber y probaré que mis palabras son verdaderas" ("I Will Repeat My Truth from the Beginning and I Will Prove That I Speak the Truth").

Bartolomé de las Casas (1474–1566) is the best-known defender of the Amerindians. He represented a markedly different position from the one embodied by Spanish conquerors and explorers, one that was closely tied to his religious beliefs. In his *Historia de las Indias*, Las Casas records the injustices the Spaniards committed against the Amerindians, such as the abuse he attributed to Alonso de Hojeda, and others. He also writes about Valenzuela's mistreatment of the now famous Enriquillo, an Amerindian who accepted Catholicism but, reacting to his master's abuse, abandoned his Christian ways and led an uprising against the Spaniards. This story is retold by Manuel de Jesús Galván (1834–1911) in *Enriquillo* [1882; *The Cross and the Sword*, 1954], the Dominican Republic's nineteenth-century national novel. Spanish persecution, deception, torture, and killing of Amerindians like Guacanagarí, Caonabo, Anacaona, and their followers, led Las Casas to convince Carlos V that the court should save the Amerindians and substitute African slaves, advice Las Casas later regretted. For his tireless efforts to save and protect the Amerindians, in 1516 Cardinals Jiménez de Cisneros and Adriano de Utrech named Las Casas "Protector Universal de los Indios." Gonzalo Fernández de Oviedo (1478–1557), the Official Chronicler of the Indies, provided the prevailing perspective that supported the island's conquest. For example, in his *Historia general y natural de las Indias, islas y Tierra Firme del mar Océano* [1535; General and Natural History of the Indies, Islands and Mainland of the Ocean], Oviedo offers another interpretation surrounding Enriquillo's rebellion; Juan Méndez Nieto (b. 1530), in the *Discursos medicinales* [1607; Medical Discourses], describes his eight-year experience on the island.

The polemic unfolding in Santo Domingo regarding the treatment of Amerindians became a major object of concern in Spain. It culminated in the memorable debate in Valladolid (1550–1551) between Las Casas and the jurist Juan Ginés de Sepúlveda (1490–1573), whose ideas were made public in *Nuevas leyes de Indias* [1542; New Laws of the Indies] and are incorporated into his *Historia del Nuevo Mundo y México* [History of the New World and Mexico]. Las Casas argued that the Amerindians were human beings, while Sepúlveda supported the *repartimientos* (distributions of the natives) and *encomiendas* (royal land grants), and believed in the superiority of the Spaniards and the inferiority of the Indians. Even though Las Casas condemned the conquest of Amerindians and justified their rebellions, he emerged victorious against Sepúlveda.

But just as quickly as Hispaniola and Santo Domingo acquired prominence during the discovery and conquest of the New World, so they also lost it. The island and capital city were pushed to the margins of colonial activities, when Cuba and Puerto Rico emerged as the preferred ports of call on the oceanic routes. This fall from grace was further accentuated when the other two islands became strategically more important for the Spanish defense of the Caribbean. The shift in the island's importance would open it up to both foreign invaders and mismanagement. During the Colonial period, Santo Domingo had some fifty unmemorable governors and was attacked by foreign powers and pirates, including Francis Drake's 1586 siege and looting of Haina. Nevertheless, Spain made three attempts to gain effective control of its first Spanish-speaking colony: first, from 1492 to 1795, second, from 1809 to 1821, and the final one, from 1861 to 1865.

Foreign control of the northern part of Hispaniola, particularly of the cities of Puerto Plata, Bayajá, and La Yaguana, had a devastating effect on the economy, cultural development, and literary production of Santo Domingo. Due to the court's monopoly over commerce, many cattlemen, especially those from the fertile north and central regions, found it more profitable to trade with other European powers. Even business from the capital city fled to the north, thus also hampering the city's once lucrative commerce. In addition, contraband challenged ideological and religious loyalties Dominicans felt toward Spain, and the inhabitants of the northern region were already accepting a protestant way of life. To combat the Portuguese, Flemish, French, and British incursions, and as an effective strategy for combating the contraband problem, Baltazar López de Castro proposed the depopulation of the Banda del Norte. In 1598 López de Castro offered his *Primero memorial de arbitrio para el remedio de los rescates en la isla Española* [First Memorandum of Arbitration for the Rescue of the Island of Hispaniola] and his *Segundo memorial de arbitrio* [Second Memorandum of Arbitration], which contained a plan of action. López de Castro recognized the important role the port city of Santo Domingo played in the colony, because of its rich and prosperous trade with Spain, but he also acknowledged the adverse effect the foreign presence had on the economy and society. He therefore advocated that all the cattle and occupants of the northern region be moved to the surrounding areas of the capital city. López de Castro's evacuation plan was met with resistance, since many inhabitants of the region had accepted trade with foreigners as a way of life. But Governor Antonio de Osorio resisted pressure; in February of 1605 he put into effect the depopulation of the Banda del Norte. The depopulation of the north was not without its consequences, for it practically destroyed the island's economy. Prominent families of the region were ruined, and it became impossible to move all the cattle. The inhabitants of Bayahá rebelled against Osorio, and those living in Yaguana fled to Cuba. Slaves quickly seized the opportunity to escape to freedom. The depopulation of the Banda del Norte had a devastating effect on the island, and none of López de Castro's goals had been achieved. By the time Governor Diego de Sandoval took over from Osorio, the quality of life known in the previous century in Santo Domingo had also been affected. Even hunger was prevalent. There was a lack of cattle to export and little demand for imported goods. The few resources available were used for military campaigns during Spain's Thirty Year War and to fortify Santo Domingo's plaza.

Santo Domingo faced a difficult period, created by both nature and man, including the small pox epidemic of 1666, which killed many slaves, and the plague, which attacked the cacao trees. These disasters were followed by the 1669 epidemic, which killed more than 1500 people. Life in the capital city was reduced to a level of subsistence, and many were forced to move to the countryside to survive. A few years later the island was hit with other calamities, such as the hurricane of 1672, which destroyed the island's crops, and the earthquake of 1673, which demolished its existing structures. Abelardo Vicioso describes Santo Domingo's seventeenth-century decline, enumerating its causes as follows: "De manera que el yugo colonial, la miseria, la falta de incentivos, la represión ideológica, la escasez de público, la falta de instrucción y los obstáculos materiales que se oponían a la impresión y difusión de las obras, hacían que los intelectuales de esta tierra se sintieran minimizados con respecto a la creación literaria de los ingenios españoles" (181) ("The intellectuals of the island felt they were reduced to a minimal existence with respect to their counterparts in Spain owing to the colonial burden they had to bear as well as the economic misery, the lack of material incentives, the ideological repression, the lack of a reading public, the lack of public instruction, and the multiple material obstacles that made the printing and distribution of their work impossible").

The devastation and impoverishment of Santo Domingo was reflected in numerous ways, including the absence of significant writers. Although established Spanish writers traveled to Santo Domingo–Tirso de Molina (1579–1648) left for Santo Domingo in April of 1616 and is suspected of having conceived his *Burlador de Sevilla* (1627) there–the island did not have any major island-born writers until the mid eighteenth century, and a national literature did not develop until a century later.

The European presence in the northern part of the island, exemplified by the constant shift in control of Tortuga Island, culminated in 1655 with the British invasion of Hispaniola, through the city of Nizao, and the unsuccessful attempt to take over Santo Domingo. The Spanish retreat from the Tortuga led to the French occupation of that island, and under Bertrand d'Ogeron, whose men were looking for cattle, the French made incursions into the northern and western part of the island. Spain relinquished one third of the western part of the island to France in 1697. By importing African slaves to work in the sugar industry, the French turned their acquisition into an economically successful colony. In the eighteenth century the Spanish government paid more attention to the capital city, leaving the rest of the country to be ruled by *latifundios*, where owners governed their own lands and felt it more profitable to trade with their French neighbors. In comparison with the smaller but more prosperous French colony to the west, Santo Domingo was barely able to sustain a reduced population. Although the colony produced cotton, cacao, sugar, and tobacco, it only exported beef. Almost a century later, in 1795, the French forced the weakened Spanish Crown to sign a treaty, surrendering the eastern part of the island. The French were more successful than the Spanish in administering the newly acquired territory. With the enslavement of Africans they made Saint-Domingue the most prosperous colony of the eighteenth century. It was even rumored that the British were willing to trade their thirteen colonies for Saint-Domingue.

Events in Europe were to influence life in the colony. The French Revolution, whose leaders proclaimed the "Declaration of the Rights of Man and of the Citizen," provided the impetus for the slave rebellion in Saint-Domingue, and it became the first colony to be liberated from slavery. During the rebellion many French were killed and others were forced to flee to Cuba, Louisiana, and the United States. The successful uprising was the first of its kind and accentuated a fear of blacks, used in other countries (such as Cuba) to scare whites into even more oppression of slaves and freed blacks. Under Toussaint L'Ouverture's leadership, the island began to recover from the devastation of the war. However, Napoleon would not give up his prized possession and sent his brother-in-law General Leclerc to reclaim the island. Black leaders like L'Ouverture and Jacques Dessalines triumphed over the French. During this period L'Ouverture occupied Santo Domingo and, after his succession from Haiti, Dessalines and Henri Christophe attacked it. Haiti became the first black republic in 1804. The transition from slavery to freedom, from colony to independence and republic, is a major theme

of Alejo Carpentier's (1904–1980) *El reino de este mundo* [1949; *The Kingdom of this World,* 1957].

Haiti was turned into a European battleground for British, French, and Spanish interests. With help from the British, the Spaniards reconquered Santo Domingo and restored colonial rule in 1809, initiating the period known as *España Boba* [Foolish Spain]. As others had successfully done in most of Spanish America, José Núñez de Cáceres and other *criollo* leaders declared Santo Domingo's independence from an inept Spanish government in 1821. But the independence was short-lived. Like L'Ouverture before him, Haitian leader Jean Pierre Boyer invaded Santo Domingo and ended the last remnants of slavery on the island. Because of a lack of teachers and students, who had either left the island or joined the military, the University of Santo Domingo was closed. The Haitian occupation was felt mostly in Santo Domingo, and it was in this city that the nationalist movement was born. Dominicans trace their independence to 29 February 1844, when the Haitians surrendered control of Santo Domingo to the new Dominican authorities. With an increased nationalist sentiment and the help of Dominicans living in Venezuela, Juan Pablo Duarte expelled the Haitians and reclaimed Santo Domingo in a bloodless coup. The political events were also aided by natural disasters, such as the earthquake that destroyed Santiago and Cap Haïtien. Duarte was hailed as the founding father of the Dominican Republic. However, he hesitated to consolidate his power, and his rival, General Pedro Santana, with the support of the colonialists, took over the Junta Central Gubernativa. After Duarte's deportation Santana became the first President of the Republic. He and General Buenaventura Báez eliminated the opposition and dominated Dominican politics for the next forty-five years, taking the country not forward but backward to the sixteenth century, to the Spanish colonial model.

Political instability returned under Juan Isidro Jimenes and Horacio Vásquez, opponents of Heureaux, who now competed for power. The country plunged into further economic debt, creating an opportunity for the United States to intervene in the internal affairs of the Dominican Republic in 1908. After the success of the Spanish American War, in which the United States acquired Puerto Rico and the Philippines, dominated Cuba's economy, and later took over the Panama Canal, Theodore Roosevelt presided over a growing world power. He seized the opportunity to further promote ideas of Manifest Destiny and the Monroe Doctrine. Roosevelt negotiated a contract with President Carlos Morales to administer 55 percent of the country's export revenues and pay off foreign debts, which was extended to the administration of Ramón Cáceres who, like Heureaux, met with a violent death.

The U.S. military that invaded the Dominican Republic remained there from 1916 until 1924, when General Vázquez was elected to the presidency. During the occupation the United States increased its presence as the economic and political conditions of the country deteriorated, and Germany spread its influence to Haiti. The U.S. military and economic expansionism was met with opposition, especially from the eastern sugar provinces. After U.S. withdrawal its influence continued to be felt mainly in two areas: the U.S. control over the economy, and its training of the national guard, from which Trujillo emerged. Ramón Marrero Aristy's (1913–1959) *Over* (1939), is a response to the control North American sugar companies had over the economy, making low investments and extracting exaggerated profits. Under Vásquez, the Dominican Republic experienced relative stability and peace, but as in the past this too would come to an end, as rival groups planned to overthrow the government. Trujillo drew upon the strong-arm tactics of his predecessors. Having risen through the ranks of the national guard, Trujillo used his acquired powers to gain control of the government. He supported the rebels, eliminated his opposition, and seized the electoral process to win the presidency. Arguably one of the most heartless dictators of Latin America, Trujillo ran the country as if it were his own *latifundio*. He took advantage of every possible situation to further consolidate his power, whether it be a natural occurrence, like the hurricane of 1930, or man-made, like the market crash of 1929–1930. Trujillo believed that economic growth and development could only be obtained at the expense of political freedom. To this end, he increased his ties to the United States and allowed U.S. investments to control the Dominican economy. He presented himself as a staunch anti-communist, which helped him win favors with U.S. government officials. Although society did prosper (through public projects), Trujillo and his family multiplied their control of the country's resources, thus increasing their own economic wealth.

Trujillo relied upon the historical fear Dominicans have of Haitians in order to foster identity and a certain type of racist patriotism. In 1937 his army massacred some 15,000 Haitians living near the border, an event that became the theme of Freddy Prestol Castillo's (1914–1991) *El masacre se pasa a pie* [1973; Massacre is Passed on Foot]. In the decade of the 1950s, Trujillo invited the Japanese to settle in the Dominican Republic. The first arrived in 1956, and by 1986 they numbered 1459. During his reign, Trujillo accorded them housing, loans, and all the rights afforded to Dominican citizens. Some claimed that Trujillo wanted the Japanese to teach Dominicans how to work hard; others believed that he desired to "whiten" the population (Peguero 96). The dictator's decline resulted from his careless use of absolute powers. Trujillo crushed his opposition, even if his enemies lived in a foreign country like the United States, as with the murder of Andrés Francisco Requena (1908–1952), the author of *Cementerio sin cruces* [1949; Cemetery Without Crosses], or even if they were heads of state, as in the assassination attempt against Rómulo Betancourt, President of Venezuela. The latter event led to the U.S. withdrawal of support of Trujillo and a trade embargo against his government. This period was also accompanied by falling sugar prices and economic uncertainty. Trujillo attempted to hide his vulnerability and ordered the assassination of three of the four Mirabal sisters, who openly opposed the dictator. The death of the Mirabal sisters is the subject of Julia Álvarez's (b. 1951) *In the Time of the Butterflies* (1994). Sympathy for the Mirabals was accompanied by increased opposition to the dictator, and on 30 May 1961 a group of seven men murdered the dictator en route to visit one of his mistresses. Though Trujillo was dead, the institutions he created survived him and would play a significant role in the present and future political and economic development of the nation.

The fall of Trujillo created a unique opportunity for the Dominican Republic to start anew. The Council of State, which included the two surviving Trujillo assassins, received support from the military and the U.S. government. Trujillo's son Ramfis and one of his ministers, Joaquín Balaguer, attempted to retain power, but both were forced to leave the country. Political groups were then allowed to organize: the

two most important were Viriato Fiallo's National Civic Union (UCN), which represented business interests, and Juan Bosch's Dominican Revolutionary Party (PRD), which supported social democracy. Bosch, who by then had distinguished himself as a major short story writer, returned from exile and won a resounding victory in the 1962 elections. Bosch (1909–2001) was met with a unified opposition, made up of conservatives, the military, and U.S. government, which did not want another Cuba in the hemisphere. The military played a crucial role in his subsequent defeat since its leaders foresaw a change that would affect their best interests. In September 1963 Col. Elías Wessin y Wessin staged a bloodless coup, overthrew the democratically elected government, and imposed a civilian junta (led by Donald Reid Cabral), which favored conservatives and business interests. Reid Cabral's unpopularity in turn led to the PRD's own coup, in essence throwing the country into a civil war, which the popular pro-Bosch forces won; the rebels, who wanted to restore a democratically elected government, scored a resounding victory against the military. However, the attempt to restore Bosch to power was eclipsed by a second U.S. intervention, halting the resolution of the country's internal conflicts. On 28 April 1965 President Lyndon Johnson ordered a U.S. marine invasion of this sovereign nation. This invasion had an impact on the further development of the Dominican Republic through to the end of the twentieth century, as was reflected in Dominican literature and culture. This period is also marked by a slow but steady migration of Dominicans from Santo Domingo to New York City. Their numbers increased dramatically in the decades of the 1970s and 1980s.

Once the interim government of President García-Godoy was in place, the two factions, represented by Bosch and Balaguer, sought electoral support. With the fear of another Cuba in the background and with support from conservatives, the military and the U.S. government favored Balaguer, who won a decisive victory. He in turn became one of the most important politicians during the remaining years of the century. He was president from 1966 to 1978, during a period that saw high sugar prices, when many Dominicans enjoyed relative prosperity. Having been a minister under Trujillo, Balaguer was also familiar with the dictator's tactics, and he knew how to silence the opposition.

The world scenario continued to influence this small nation. A decline in sugar revenues, increased oil prices, and the Carter administration's insistence on promoting democracy gave the PRD, this time under Antonio Guzmán, reason to rejoin the electoral process it had boycotted. Under the watchful eye of the Carter government, Guzmán was elected president and assumed his official duties in August 1978. However, he did not enjoy the favorable economic conditions of the Balaguer period and even faced criticism from within his party. Unfortunately, Guzmán's accomplishments were modest at best; in fact, many Dominicans looked longingly to the recent past, to the period of economic growth under the Balaguer government.

Although Hispaniola and Santo Domingo were the first Spanish settlements, they soon lagged behind other parts of the colonial empire. While other Spanish American countries enjoyed the benefits of a printing press, this means of literary dissemination did not reach Santo Domingo until 1774. The first newspapers were not printed until 1821 and then only in response to the Haitian occupation. Early newspapers include *El Telégrafo Constitucional*, founded by Antonio

María Pineda, and *El Duende*, established by José Núñez de Cáceres, one of the most important political and literary figures of the period. Article 23 of the first Constitution of the Republic of 1844 made provisions for freedom of speech, but subsequent laws gave the government authority over censorship. Article 8, section 6 of the present Constitution guarantees freedom of expression, but the Congress or president can suspend these rights in the interest of peace. The law punished anyone, including journalists, involved in crime or who incited others to rebel: "Se prohibe toda propaganda subversiva, ya sea por anónimos o por cualquier otro medio de expresión que tenga por objeto provocar desobediencia a las leyes, sin que esto último pueda coartar el derecho a análisis o a crítica de los preceptos legales" ("All subversive propaganda is prohibited, be it by anonymous authors or by any other means of expression that has as its objective the incitement to disobey the law, without this prohibition in any way impeding the right of analysis and criticism of legal precepts").

During the reign of the many Dominican strong men, the press either became an accomplice of the government or was forced to desist. The first Dominican newspaper, *El Dominicano*, published by Pedro Antonio Bobea, became available in Santo Domingo one year after the founding of the republic. Other newspapers of the period include *Gaceta Oficial* (1851), *La Española Libre* (1852), *El Progreso* (1853), *El Porvenir* (1854), *El Eco del Pueblo* (1856), and *La República* (1856). However, journalism and newspapers were also important to and available in other cities, such as *El Correo del Cibao* (1851), *El Cibaeño* (1856), *El Progreso* (1861), *El Dominicano* (1872), and *El Orden* (1874) in Santiago de los Caballeros; *La Gaceta Oficial* (1858) in Cibao; and *El Porvenir* (1872) in Puerto Plata. Many of these and other newspapers had a short life span, but they provided an important medium for the exchange of ideas. Dominican writers and intellectuals of this and other periods were also journalists: Manuel de Jesús Galván directed *La Razón* (1862); Manuel de Jesús y Reynoso edited *El Dominicano*; Ulises Francisco Espaillat collaborated in *El Orden*; and Federico Henríquez y Carvajal wrote for *La Opinión* (1872).

The oldest and perhaps the most important Dominican newspaper is *Listín Diario*, published in 1889 by Arturo J. Pellerano Alfay and Julián Artiles in Santo Domingo during Heureaux's dictatorship. It began as a page, listing ships entering and leaving the port city and soon became the information lifeline of the country. Considered a moderate daily, it survived the Trujillo dictatorship by refraining from opposing the government. Nevertheless, the newspaper was closed in 1942 but resumed its responsibilities after Trujillo's death. Today it promotes literature, holds literary contests, and awards prizes. Also published in Santo Domingo is *El Caribe*, which has a greater circulation than *Listín Diario*. Founded in 1948, with support from Trujillo, it was run by Anselmo Paulino Álvarez. It was from this newspaper, under a variety of pseudonyms, that Trujillo attacked his enemies. Germán Ornes Coiscou bought *El Caribe* in 1954, and after Trujillo's assassination, the daily took a right-of-center position and opposed Juan Bosch's bid for the presidency of the republic.

In the twentieth century, *La Información*, which Rafael Vidal began to publish in the rival city of Santiago de los Caballeros in 1915, was the only newspaper to challenge in longevity the *Listín Diario*. During the Trujillo years, the magazine *La Opinión*, founded in 1927 by Abelardo René Nanita, was critical of the dictatorship and disappeared in 1940. In that year *La Nación*, which articulated the opinions of the regime, was born; it was published by Rafael Sánchez Lustrino, Rafael Vidal, Francisco Prats Ramírez, Manuel Amiama, and Ramón Marrero Aristy. The newspaper ceased to publish after Trujillo's assassination. At the same printing press *El Tiempo* was published in 1967 (Lebrón Saviñón 140–57). Other contemporary newspapers that should be mentioned are *La Noticia, El Nacional, El Siglo*, and *Hoy*, which publish literary supplements.

Education was an important institution that accompanied the settlement of Hispaniola. According to Mariano Lebrón Saviñón, the first schools date from 1502, and the founding of the Franciscan Colegio in the Convento de la Orden de San Francisco three years later. The efforts of Archbishop Sebastián Ramírez de Fuenleal, also governor and president of the Real Audiencia, led to the royal decree of 1529, founding in Santo Domingo the Colegio and the Universidad de Santo Tomás de Aquino. As in this and other periods, education reflected political events. Under the Haitian occupation all the schools were closed and replaced by new schools with Haitian teachers. In the republic, president Buenaventura Báez created the Colegio de San Buenaventura in 1852, and president Gen. José María Cabral initiated the opening of the Seminario Conciliar in 1866. These two institutions, along with the Colegio San Luis Gonzaga, founded by Father Francisco Billini in 1866, produced some of the most eminent figures of the period. Intellectuals also contributed to the Dominican educational system: During his second trip to the country, the Puerto Rican patriot Eugenio María de Hostos introduced additional changes to education in the Dominican Republic. He founded the Escuela Normal de Maestros in 1880 and reformed the curriculum, basing it on humanistic values. Salomé Ureña de Henríquez (1850–1897), one of the major intellectual figures in the country, expressed her concern for women by creating, along with others, the Instituto de Señoritas in 1881 (which, after her death, received its founder's name). Salomé Ureña also made many other contributions to Dominican culture.

Under the U.S. occupation the educational system underwent further reorganization. A Junta Directiva de Estudios was created in Santo Domingo, along with provincial juntas outside the capital city. During the Trujillo dictatorship there were measured changes in education. In the second year of the regime Max Henríquez Ureña was named Superintendente General de Enseñanza. One year later he was replaced by his brother Pedro Henríquez Ureña, who founded the Escuela Modelo and the Facultad Libre de Filosofía y Letras, later incorporated into the Universidad de Santo Domingo. Unfortunately, the Facultad lasted only one year before it was suppressed, and Pedro Henríquez Ureña's work remained inconclusive, since he was forced to leave the country (Lebrón Saviñón 125–40).

Primary, intermediate, and secondary education is currently under the supervision of the Secretaría de Estado de Educación, which provides instruction free of charge. However, it is not accessible to all. Many Dominicans have had to do without a formal education, but the situation is improving. Ian Bell interprets the 1970 census as follows:

> The census showed that, of more than 3.3 million Dominicans over the age of five, 1 million (including some 400,000 of school age in that year) had never been to school at all. Nevertheless, the fact that among Dominicans over thirty years of age nearly 38 per

cent had no education while among those under thirty only 28 per cent had none is a sign of progress. Within the younger age group upward of 1 million had received or were currently receiving primary education. Of these, however, only 10 per cent had reached sixth grade and gone on to intermediate and secondary levels . . . . The percentages of those educated up to primary, intermediate, and secondary levels were, respectively, 37.3, 5.8, and 3.8 in the older group and 45.5, 6.3, and 4.5 in the younger group. (161–62)

The university system is both public and private. While the Dominican Republic can boast of having the oldest university in the hemisphere, higher education did not begin to expand until the end of the Trujillo era. One year later, in 1962, the Universidad Católica Madre y Maestra was founded in Santiago. It has become a reputable center of higher education, drawing students from all regions of the country and indeed the Caribbean. Six years later the Universidad Nacional Pedro Henríquez Ureña was founded in Santo Domingo with private funding. In the decade of the 1970s, nine centers of higher learning were created, with another one appearing in the following decade. Most were inaugurated in Santo Domingo, but some were in the cities of Neiba, San Cristóbal, Santiago, and Bonao. During the Trujillo dictatorship the Universidad de Santo Domingo had been the only institution of higher learning in the Dominican Republic. It was conservative in its approach, requiring students to copy and repeat commonplace ideas. Professors also held government appointments and at times compromised their academic positions. After the fall of Trujillo, students expressed openly their opposition to the dictator and the institutions that supported him, including the UASD. Student activism, mainly in Santo Domingo but also in other cities, coincided with the student protest of the 1960s throughout the Western world. In the post-Trujillo era, the university has expanded to included other universities such as the much revered Universidad Católica Madre y Maestra, the Instituto Tecnológico de Santo Domingo, and the Universidad Nacional Pedro Henríquez Ureña. In recent decades these and other universities have attempted to follow the academic orientation of sister institutions in the United States and have become centers of research (Moya Pons 1986, 289–304).

Through their publishing houses, Dominican universities have played major roles in producing and circulating books. For example, Héctor Incháustegui Cabral (1912–1979) has written about the editorial successes of the books published by the newly founded Universidad Católica Madre y Maestra, which by 1973 had edited fifteen books in five years (229–33). Although the numbers were small by comparison to other publishers, all the copies were sold in less than one year. At that time, the press published Marcio Veloz Maggiolo's (b. 1936) *Cultura, teatro y relatos en Santo Domingo* [1962; Culture, Theatre and Narrative in Santo Domingo] and Emilio Rodríguez Demorizi's (1908–1986) *Poesía popular dominicana* [Popular Dominican Poetry].

Before this Antonio Sánchez Valverde (1734–1790) was the most important figure of the Colonial period. A rational thinker, considered the best orator and essayist of his time, Sánchez Valverde represented the interest of a nascent national bourgeoisie. His works included *Idea del valor de la isla Española y utilidades que de ella puede sacar su monarquía* [1785; The Idea of the Value of the Island of Hispaniola and the Uses Its Monarchy Can Make of It], which provided a clear and rational explanation of the court's abandonment of

the island and the historical reasons that led to that state of affairs, due to a large extent to the depopulation of the Banda del Norte. Sánchez Valverde affirms the value of the natural resources of the island and offered ways of restoring it to its splendor. He recognized the impact of the illegal trade with the French, who needed cattle and other goods to construct their sugar industry effectively, and of piracy on the port of Santo Domingo. He supported the development of cattle-raising and agriculture, as well as the need to import African slaves to foster development.

Dominican *literature* can be traced to the fall of Báez, and the restoration of the republic's sovereignty in 1873. Although literature tends to follow primarily literary patterns, the numerous political changes in the Dominican Republic also left their mark on artistic creation. The founding figures of Dominican literature, José Joaquín Pérez (1845–1900) and Salomé Ureña de Henríquez (1850–1897), were clearly influenced by the society in which they lived. Pérez began his poetic career as a reaction to the Spanish annexation and later looked to a romantic Amerindian past. Salomé Ureña founded a society for women and worked tirelessly in favor of the emancipation of the Dominican woman. She was also a poet of considerable merit. Of this early period is Galván's *Enriquillo*, a historical account that looks to the colonial past. If Salomé Ureña can be considered one of the leading literary figures of nineteenth-century Dominican literature, her children have subsequently also distinguished themselves. Certainly the Ureña family has been influential in Dominican literature from its inception to the present. Salomé and Francisco Henríquez y Carvajal had three children: Camila, Max, and Pedro Henríquez Ureña. At an early age Camila went to live in Cuba, where she stayed and contributed to Cuban culture. Like Camila, Max and Pedro lived for a time in Cuba, but they also resided in the United States and South America, among other places. Through their works, the latter two helped to define Dominican literature and culture. Max Henríquez Ureña (1885–1970) held various diplomatic and academic positions, but as a poet, he followed the *modernista* tradition. His works include *Los yankies en Santo Domingo* [1919; The Yankies in Santo Domingo], *Panorama histórico de la literatura dominicana* [1945; Historical Panorama of Dominican Literature], and *Episodios dominicanos* [1938, 1941, 1944, 1951; Dominican Episodes]. Like his younger brother, Pedro Henríquez Ureña (1884–1946) too was a poet and a professor and wrote works of philosophy, philology, and literary criticism. He was a humanist of considerable knowledge and the equal of any major literary figure of Latin America. Pedro authored works like *Ensayos críticos* [1905; Critical Essays], *Horas de estudio* [1910; Hours of Study], *Seis ensayos en busca de nuestra expresión* [1928; Six Essays in Search of Our Expression], *El español en Méjico, los Estados Unidos y la América Central* [1936; Spanish in Mexico, United States and Central America], *La cultura y las letras coloniales en Santo Domingo* [1936; Culture and Colonial Letters in Santo Domingo], and *El español en Santo Domingo* [1940; Spanish in Santo Domingo]. His accomplishments were publicly recognized when the Universidad Nacional Pedro Henríquez Ureña was named after him.

In the twentieth century both Joaquín Balaguer (1906–2002) and Juan Bosch (1909–2001), who later became political rivals and presidents of the republic, were among the most celebrated writers in the country. Each was affected by the Trujillo dictatorship–Balaguer positively, as a minister of the dictator, and Bosch negatively, as a member of the opposition forced to live in exile. Balaguer is known for the mastery of his poetry and essays, while Bosch is the country's best-known author, who defined the development of the short story. Like Bosch, the poet and narrator Pedro Mir (1913–2000) also lived in exile, where he wrote most of his works. In 1982 Mir was honored with the title of National Poet. In his years of power Trujillo had attempted to control all aspects of life, including culture and literature. The government sponsored literary and cultural journals, such as *Cuadernos Dominicanos de Cultura*, edited by Pedro René Contín Aybar (1907–1981), Héctor Incháustegui Cabral (1912–1979), Emilio Rodríguez Demorizi (1904–1986) and Rafael Díaz Niese (1897–1950); these expounded a certain kind of culture. This was also the case with the *Antología de la literatura dominicana* [1943; Anthology of Dominican Literature], which consecrated writers who defended the regime, and the *Albúm simbólico: poetas cantan a Trujillo* [1957; Symbolic Album: Poets Sing to Trujillo], which commemorates the twenty-fifth anniversary of the dictator's takeover of the government. After the Haitian massacre of 1937, intellectuals such as Manuel Arturo Peña Batlle (1902–1952) justified the government's actions, reducing Haitians to the level of animals, that is, a people without history, culture, or language. Similarly, Balaguer interpreted the deadly act as vengeance against the historical Haitian incursions into the Dominican Republic and as a way of recovering a lost Spanish heritage. Balaguer relied on similar tactics when he deported large numbers of Haitians across the border and attacked the candidacy of Peña Gómez. By identifying the *Other*, he preserved or conserved a popular interpretation of Dominican race and identity.

In the contemporary period the death of Trujillo and the U.S. marine invasion of the Dominican Republic influenced Dominican literature to the end of the twentieth century. A younger generation of writers emerged who rejected a past associated with the dictatorship and recreated in their works life under the regime. This is the case with Hilma Contrera's (b. 1913) short stories, and those of Virgilio Díaz Grullón (1924–2001), Marcio Veloz Maggiolo, and René del Risco Bermúdez (1937–1972), who denounced the dictatorship but were also known for their experimentation with narrative form. Four novels of considerable merit inspired by Trujillo's downfall are Veloz Maggiolo's *De abril en adelante* [1963; From April Onwards], Díaz Grullón's *Los algarrobos también sueñan* [1973; The Carobs Also Dream], Pedro Vergés's (b. 1945) *Sólo cenizas hallarás (bolero)* [1980; You Will Only Find Ashes (Bolero)], and Viriato Sención's (b. 1941) *Los que falsificaron la firma de Dios* [1992; They Forged the Signature of God, 1995]. According to the interviews conducted by Odalís G. Pérez (b. 1952), in his *Las ideas literarias en la República Dominicana* [1993; Literary Ideas in the Dominican Republic], Dominican writers summarize their country's literary movements of the twentieth century in the following manner: The Dominican poetic movement started with Vendrinismo, whose highest and perhaps only exponent was Orilio Virgil Díaz (1880–1961). Though free verse was already used by Rubén Darío (1867–1916) and other *modernistas* of Spanish America, it became a characteristic of Vendrinismo. Díaz, who lived in Paris, paid attention to his European environment, and often made references to Greek and Latin themes.

The first Dominican movement to treat truly national themes, however, is Postumismo, began in 1921 during the first U.S. occupation. Domingo Moreno Jimenes (1894–1986), along with Rafael Augusto Zorrilla (1892–1937) and Andrés

Avelino (1899–1974), were its best-known promoters. Unlike Vendrinismo, these poets turned their backs on European literary concerns and searched for national values. In 1935 Los Nuevos came into existence under the direction of Rubén Suro (1916–1999). The latter's poetry combines a traditional rhyme scheme with social and political interests. Born at a time when Afro-Cuban poetry was in vogue, Suro also wrote poems on the theme of race, years before it became associated with Manuel del Cabral's (1907–1999) poetry. Though Los Nuevos gathered different types of artists and intellectuals, the movement was short-lived. An important factor was its place of origin–not Santo Domingo, but the provincial capital of La Vega. Los Independientes del 40 followed Los Nuevos, insofar as they continued to develop national issues and underscored social and realist ideas. However, because Trujillo's repressive mechanisms were in full force, writers resorted to the use of elaborate literary tropes. Poets of the period included Pedro Mir, Héctor Incháustegui Cabral (1912–1979), Tomás Hernández Franco (1904–1952), and Manuel del Cabral. Juan Bosch and Juan Isidro Jimenes Grullón were forced into exile.

La Poesía Sorprendida (Surprised Poetry) is the nation's most important poetic movement. It is characterized by an abandonment of the local and folkloric, associated with the previous movement, and an acceptance of broader parameters, so that the work could be understood by anyone in the world. In fact, their poetry aimed to be a universal one. Dominican writers came into contact with other Caribbean, Latin American, and European writers, and some even followed the path of Surrealism of André Bretón, who had visited the country. The exponents of this include Domingo Moreno Jimenes (1894–1986), Mariano Lebrón Saviñón (b. 1922), Franklin Mieses Burgos (1907–1976), Freddy Gatón Arce (1920–1994), Manuel Rueda (1920–1994), Aída Cartagena Portalatín (1918–1994), Manuel Valerio (b. 1918), and the Chilean Alberto Baeza Flores (b. 1914). The Generación del 48 continued the universalizing ideas of La Poesía Sorprendida, but added a social element, to recreate a national Dominican reality. Writers like Abel Fernández Mejía (b. 1931) and Máximo Avilés (1931–1988) did so without coming into conflict with the Trujillo government. Nevertheless, poets like Víctor Villegas (b. 1924) and Rafael Valera Benítez (b. 1928) were jailed, not for their literature, but for political reasons.

The break with the government and the silent past acquires meaning with the activism of the younger Generación del 60. This is a period also influenced by European and U.S. literary currents. Writers defied the government and expressed openly their social and political ideas. Some like Miguel Alfonseca (1942–1994), René del Risco Bermúdez, and Virgilio Díaz Grullón were imprisoned. Writers of the subsequent Generation of 65 were marked by the April revolution and the U.S. invasion. Some of the poets of this generation identify with the victims of society and feel the need to reveal the harsh realities of the moment. Some introduce Marxist ideas into their works. Enriquillo Sánchez (b. 1947), Luis Manuel Ledesma (b. 1949), Soledad Álvarez (b. 1950), and Alexis Gómez Rosa (b. 1950) are among the poets of this generation.

Pluralismo is the name of the reaction against the all-encompassing political environment marked by the U.S. invasion. It favors a type of poetry with multiple signifiers, not immediately accessible to the average reader. Dominican poets found new intellectual directions in the work of French structuralists and the semiological and philosophical studies of writers of the Tel Quel group–Sollers, Derrida, Kristeva, and others–a direction other Latin American writers shared. Manuel Rueda (1920–1994) initiated this new mode of expression in Dominican poetry in 1974, and the group included other poets like Luis Manuel Ledesma and Gómez Rosa, as well as prose writers like Veloz Maggiolo and Diógenes Valdés (b. 1943).

These generational and group classifications are merely heuristic, and critics vary in their use of the terms. In his important *Antología histórica de la poesía dominicana del siglo xx (1912-1995)* [1995; Historical Anthology of Dominican Poetry of the Twentieth Century (1912–1995)], Franklin Gutiérrez (b. 1951), for example, does not recognize the idea of generation for the Generación del 48 and prefers to call them Grupo del 48. He also uses his own terminology with Los Independientes del 48. But what is not in question is the fact that among these writers are included Juan Sánchez Lamouth (1929–1968), Ramón Francisco (b. 1929), Rodolfo Coiscou Weber (b. 1924), and Veloz Maggiolo. Not all of the participants were poets, but were also musicians, historians, lawyers, painters, and playwrights. Gutiérrez also combines the Generación del 60 with the Generación del 65 under the broad heading "Generación del 60 y la poesía de la post-guerra" (57–59). In addition, Gutiérrez considers the Generación del 80 to be a tribute to the success of literary groups and workshops, and places their poetry closer to that of the Sorprendidos than to that of any of the previous ones. These writers were most concerned with the existence of humanity and attempted to bring philosophy and poetry together. This generation is also characterized by a number of women writers like Miriam Ventura (b. 1957), Marianela Medrano (b. 1964), Sabrina Román (b. 1956), and Mayra Alemás (b. 1957), all of whom question the traditional role of women (Gutiérrez 77–80).

Dominican theater can be traced to the Sociedad Dramática of the "La Filantrópica," founded by Dominican patriots fighting the Haitian occupation. Three plays were performed whose political content promoted the independence ideas expounded by Duarte's secret society, La Trinitaria. Dominican theater developed further in the Post-Independence period, in reaction to the historical conditions of the moment. The most important playwright of the period was Félix María del Monte (1819–1899), who wrote nonnativist plays like *El mendigo de la catedral de León* [The Beggar of the Cathedral of Leon] and *El último abencerraje* [1872; The Last Abencerraje], and the national tragedy *Antonio Duvergé o Las víctimas del 11 de abril* [1856; Antonio Duvergé or The Victims of April 11th], about Santana and the Spanish occupation. Other playwrights include Javier Angulo Guridi (1816–1884), who wrote the much celebrated *Iguaniona* (1867), about an impossible love between an Amerindian princess and a Spaniard. At the beginning of the twentieth century, Ulises Heureaux (1870–1938), son of the dictator, wrote short stories and two novels, *En la copa del árbol* [1906; In the Treetop] and *Amor que emigra* [1910; Love that Emigrates]. However, Heureaux was better known as a playwright: His plays include *Lo inmutable* [The Immutable], *Genoveva, Consuelo, El artículo 291* [Article 291], and *Alfonso XII.*

National themes were inspired by the government, with the founding of the Teatro Escuela de Arte Nacional, in 1946; but there were others writers who studied abroad. In the second half of the century Franklin Domínguez (b. 1931) emerged as the most important dramatist. Having studied theater at the University of Texas, he has authored more than three dozen works that include *Un amigo desconocido nos aguarda* [1957; An Unknown Friend Awaits Us], *El último instante* [1957; The Last Instant], *La broma del senador* [1958; The Senator's Joke], *La cena de las solteronas* [1960; The Spinsters' Dinner], *Espigas maduras* [1960; Ripe Spikes], *Antígona-Humor* (1961), and *Lisístrata odia la política* [1958; Lisístrata Hates Politics].

As in other countries, literary groups have played a necessary role in promoting literature in the Dominican Republic. The Grupo Literario 'La Cueva' provided a meeting place for a generation of writers that included Ramón Marrero Aristy, Perfiles Agrestes (b. 1941), Andrés Francisco Requena (1908–1952), and the famed Juan Bosch. Some of these writers suffered under the Trujillo dictatorship: Marrero Aristy both aided and conspired against the government, and died not in an accident, as reported, but was murdered; Requena, who had worked for the Embassy in Chile, fled to Cuba and lived in the United States, where he wrote his last novel, and where Trujillo had him assassinated in 1952; Bosch was jailed for writing *La mañosa* [1936; The Crafty Woman] and was forced into exile, where he remained until the dictator was killed. Other groups included the Movimiento Cultural Universitario (MCU) and the Movimiento Arte y Liberación. Trujillo's downfall, the April revolution, and the U.S. invasion created the conditions for an upsurge in literary activity. The first literary movement to appear was the Frente Cultural, which promoted art and literature. Others followed, like El Puño (1966), with writers like Iván García (b. 1938), Miguel Alfonseca (1942–1994), Enriquillo Sánchez, René del Risco Bermúdez, and Veloz Maggiolo; La Antorcha (1967), with Mateo Morrison (b. 1947), Soledad Álvarez (b. 1950), and Alexis Gómez Rosa; La Isla (1967), with Antonio Lockward Artiles (b. 1943), Wilfredo Lozano (b. 1950), and Norberto James Rawlings (b. 1945); and La Máscara (1968), with Aquiles Azar (b. 1932), Héctor Díaz Polanco (b. 1936), and Lourdes Billini Mejia (b. 1950). During this decade the Movimiento Cultural Universitario also held regular meetings. Literary circles were organized outside of Santo Domingo as well. For example, Manuel Mora Serrano (b. 1940) and Francisco Nolasco Cordero (b. 1932) founded the Grupo Admiversa in Pimentel, and Bruno Rosario Candelier (b. 1941) created the Grupo de escritores del Cibao in that same region (Gutiérrez 64–65). In the following decade the Movimiento Pluralista, influenced by Vicente Huidobro's (1893–1948) Creacionismo, came into being.

Certainly, the end of the Trujillo dictatorship represents a milestone in Dominican literature and culture. Frank Moya Pons's painstaking statistical research of Dominican works in libraries, both at home and abroad, encompassing the 170 years from 1820 to 1990, helps to determine the status of the country's publications. Moya Pons's charts show an increase in the number of works published to the present. The statistical breakdown is as follows: fifty-seven works from 1820 to 1890; 376 from 1901 to 1930; 938 from 1931 to 1960; and 1323 from 1961 to 1990. There is an obvious increase in the post-Trujillo era. As Moya Pons comments:

> Observen, por ejemplo, que el promedio de publicaciones anuales durante los primeros 30 años de este siglo fue de 62 obras cada cinco años, esto es, unas 12 obras anuales. Durante la Era de Trujillo, el promedio se duplicó hasta alcanzar las 156 obras cada cinco años, esto es, 30 obras anuales. Durante los treinta años siguientes a la caída de la Dictadura, el promedio subió a 220 obras cada cinco años, esto es, 44 obras anuales. (1994, 24–25)

Keep in mind that the average publication of books during the first thirty years of the twentieth century was 62 every five years, or that is some 12 works a year. During the Trujillo dictatorship the average doubled reaching 156 works a year, i.e. 30 a year. And during the thirty years that followed the fall of the dictatorship the average rose to 220 works every five years, i.e. 44 books a year.

Broken down into five-year periods, the last one from 1986 to 1990 produced the highest yield, with 330 works. After the period from 1931 to 1960 there was a significant increase in literary activity in all areas, except history and philosophy. Though poetry seemed to be the most popular genre, after Trujillo's fall the publication of novels, short stories, and plays increased dramatically over that of poetry. Moya Pons makes one final observation about works written by women, which also increased: 7 percent published from 1820 to 1900, 4.5 percent from 1901 to 1930, 9.8 percent from 1931 to 1960, and 10.5 percent from 1961 to 1990.

In recent years the Feria del Libro (Book Fair), celebrated in Santo Domingo, has been instrumental in publicizing and circulating literary works. The origin of the fair can be traced to Don Julio Postigo, whose efforts finally paid off. During and after the Trujillo years the fair saw intermittent success; but not until 1973 did the government create the Comisión Organizadora Permanente de la Feria del Libro (Permanent Organizing Commission of the Book Fair). That same year, the Secretaría de Educación (Ministry of Education), of which the Dirección General de Cultura (General Office of Culture) is a part, created the Premios Nacionales de Literatura (National Prizes of Literature). A law of 1985 confirmed a new commission, and a 1987 law transformed it into the Comisión Permanente de la Feria Nacional del Libro, under the auspices of the president but with autonomous powers. The fair received its latest change under the presidency of Leonel Fernández, whose decree also established a Comisión Permanente, presided over by José Rafael Lantigua. The fair has been held at the Plaza del Conservatorio, previously the Parque Zoológico y Botánico (Lantigua 13–16).

If part of Dominican history and culture is marked by the physical presence of the United States (during the two invasions and the economic ties between the two countries), the Dominican presence on the mainland offers a different interpretation of literature and culture today. With the mass migration of Dominicans to Puerto Rico and the United States, mainly in the decades of the 1970s and 1980s, those whose education has taken place abroad began to reconsider their country's treatment of women and race, influenced by the civil rights and the women's movements in the United States. To this end they have contributed to Dominican historiography and criticism by placing their country's history outside the context of a national discourse. They have begun to consider it not only alongside U.S., but also Haitian and Caribbean, history. In essence, this larger perspective offers a counter-discourse to the one expounded by the official promoters of Dominican culture. Some, like Blás Jiménez and James Rawlings, have looked at it along racial lines; others, like Chiqui Vicioso (b. 1948), influenced by the U.S. women's movement, have seen it along gender lines. Daisy Cocco de Filippis (b. 1949) has traced the feminist discourse to Salomé Ureña in the nineteenth century, for it was she who provided a women's discourse for use within the male dominant society.

A discussion of Santo Domingo and the Dominican Republic, as cultural centers, would not be complete without dedicating a paragraph to Dominican music. The island of Hispaniola can also claim the first musician born in the New World, Cristóbal de Llerena, the organist for the Cathedral of Santo Domingo; he helped to promote both the music brought from Spain and music written in the colonies. The island can also claim musicians who lived on the island but migrated to other lands, where they became successful, as was the case with the free slaves Micaela and Teodora Ginés, who lived in Santiago de Cuba. According to Alejo Carpentier, the latter was famous for her songs and became the subject of the song "La Má Teodora." This early *son*, which combines Spanish and African influences, provides a glimpse of popular Cuban music of the sixteenth century (Carpentier 1972, 41–49). Music and dance have been an essential part of Dominican life. According to Rodríguez Demorizi, Santana's men danced as they marched to war. As in Cuba and other Caribbean islands, music has been enriched by Spanish and African traditions, represented by the *fandango* and the *bomba*, respectively. The country's Dominican music includes compositions such as the *mangulina*, from Hicayagua; the *punto cibaeño*, from Cibao; the *carabiné*, of Haitian origin; the *tumba*, the national dance that has all but disappeared; the *criolla*, which has a slightly different manifestation in Cuba; and the internationally known Dominican *merengue*. Although the origin of the *merengue* continues to be uncertain, Pedro Henríquez Ureña traced it to the uprisings against the Haitian occupation: after the battle of Talanquera, Dominicans celebrated their victory with this type of composition (Lebrón Saviñón, 199–234). The *merengue* is still an integral part of Dominican life and culture. Its influence has reached the far corners of Spanish-speaking communities throughout the world.

There has been an upsurge of literary and cultural activities since the fall of Trujillo. The interest in culture and education is also influenced by events beyond the country's national borders: John F. Kennedy's Alliance for Progress, the triumph of the Cuban revolution, and the development of the Latin American Boom novel of the 1960s, which gave Latin American literature international recognition (see Luis). It is further enriched by the contact with and constant migration of Dominicans between the Dominican Republic and the United States. Many Dominican works are now also being published on the continent. Dominican literature and culture has transcended a national geographic space and has become part of Latin American literary culture.

Works Cited

Alvarez, Julia. 1994. *In the Time of Butterflies*. Chapel Hill, NC: Algonquin Books of Chapel Hill.

Arnold, A. James, ed. 1994. *A History of Literature in the Caribbean*. Vol. 1: *Hispanic and Francophone Regions*. Amsterdam: John Benjamins Publishing Company.

Balaguer, Joaquín. 1992. *Historia de la literatura dominicana*. Santo Domingo: Editora Corripio.

Bell, Ian. 1981. *The Dominican Republic*. Colorado: Westview Press.

Casas, Bartolomé de las. 1982. *Brevísima relación de la destrucción de las Indias*. Ed. André Saint-Lu. Madrid: Cátedra.

———. 1986. *Historia de las Indias*. Ed. André Saint-Lu. Caracas: Biblioteca Ayacucho.

Carpentier, Alejo. 1949. *El reino de este mundo*. Lima: n.p.

———. 1972. *La música en Cuba*. Mexico City: Fondo de Cultura Económica.

Céspedes, Diógenes, Soledad Álvarez, and Pedro Vergés, eds. 1994. *Ponencias del congreso crítico de literatura dominicana.* Santo Domingo: Editora de Colores.

Cocco de Felippis, Daisy. 1988. *Sin otro profeta que su canto: Antología de poesía escrita por dominicanas.* Santo Domingo: Editora Taller.

Columbus, Christopher. 1961. *Diario de navegación.* Havana: Ponciano.

Fernández de Oviedo y Valdés, Gonzalo. 1944–1945. *Historia general y natural de las Indias, islas y tierra-firme del mar océano.* Ed. José Amador de los Rios. Asunción: Editorial Guaranía.

Galván, Manuel de Jesús. 1975. *Manuel de Jesús Galvan's Enriquillo: The Cross and the Sword.* Trans. Robert Graves. New York: AMS Press.

Gutiérrez, Franklin, ed. 1995. *Antología histórica de la poesía dominicana del siglo xx (1912–1995).* New York: Ediciones Alcance.

Henríquez Ureña, Max. 1945. *Panorama histórico de la literatura dominicana.* Río de Janeiro: Companhia Brasileira de Artes Gráficas.

Henríquez Ureña, Pedro. 1936. *La cultura y las letras coloniales en Santo Domingo.* Buenos Aires: Imprenta de la Universidad de Buenos Aires.

———. 1945. *Literary Currents in Hispanic America.* Cambridge: Harvard University Press.

Incháustegui Cabral, Héctor. 1978. *Escritores y artistas dominicanos.* Santiago, D.R: Universidad Católica Madre y Maestra.

Lantigua, José Rafael. 1998. *Programa general de la primera Feria Internacional del Libro de Santo Domingo.* Santo Domingo: Impresora Intergráfica.

Las leyes nuevas, 1542–1543. Reproducción de los ejemplares existentes en la sección de patronato del Archivo general de Indias. 1945. Ed. Antonio Muro Orejón. Seville: Publicaciones de la Escuela de Estudios Hispano-Americanos de la Universidad de Sevilla.

Lebrón Saviñon, Mariano. 1982. *Historia de la cultura dominicana.* 5 vols. Santo Domingo: Universidad Nacional Pedro Henríquez Ureña.

Luis, William. 1991. "Culture as Text: The Cuban/Caribbean Connection." *Translating Latin America: Culture as Text.* Ed. William Luis and Julio Rodríguez Luis. *Translation Perspectives VI* (Binghamton, NY: SUNY Binghamton). 7–20.

Marrero Aristy, Ramón. 1993. *Over.* Santo Domingo: Ediciones de la Fundación Corripio.

Méndez Nieto, Juan. 1989. *Discursos medicinales.* Salamanca: Universidad de Salamanca; Junta de Castilla León.

Moya Pons, Frank. 1986. *El pasado dominicano.* Santo Domingo: Fundación J.A. Caro Alvarea.

———. 1992. *Manual de historia dominicana.* Santo Domingo: Caribbean Publishers.

———. 1994. "Biblioestadísticas de la literatura dominicana 1820–1990." *Ponencias del congreso crítico de literatura dominicana.* Ed. Diógenes Céspedes, Soledad Álvarez, and Pedro Vergés. Santo Domingo: Editora de Colores. 15–27.

———. 1995. *The Dominican Republic: A National History.* New Rochelle, NY: Hispaniola Books.

Ortiz, Fernando. 1947. *Cuban Counterpoint: Tobacco and Sugar.* Trans. Harriet de Onís. New York: A. A. Knopf.

Peguero, Valentina. 1990. "Japanese Settlement in the Dominican Republic: An Intercultural Exchange." *Caribbean Asians: Chinese, Indians, and Japanese Experience in Trinidad and the Dominican Republic.* Ed. Roger Sanjek. New York: Asian/American Center at Queens College, CUNY. 96–109.

Pérez, Odalís G, ed. 1993. *Las ideas literarias en la República Dominicana.* Santo Domingo: Editora Amigo del Hogar.

Prestol Castillo, Freddy. 1973. *El masacre se pasa a pie.* Santo Domingo: Taller.

Rodríguez Demorizi, Emilio. 1979. *Viajeros de Francia en Santo Domingo.* Santo Domingo: Editor del Caribe.

Sánchez Valverde, Antonio. 1785. *Idea del valor de la isla Española, y utilidades, que de ella puede sacar su monarquia.* Madrid: Imprenta Don Pedro Marin.

Sepúlveda, Juan Ginés de. 1993. *Historia del nuevo mundo y México.* Ed. and trans. Antonio Ramírez de Verger. Madrid: Alianza Editorial.

Tejera, Emiliano. 1878. *Los restos de Colón en Santo Domingo.* Santo Domingo: Imprenta de Garcia hermanos.

———. 1879. *Los dos restos de Cristóbal Colón exhumados de la catedral de Santo Domingo en 1795 e 1877.* Santo Domingo: Imprenta de Garcia hermanos.

Vicioso, Abelardo. 1979. *Santo Domingo en las letras coloniales: (1492–1800).* Santo Domingo: Editora de la UASD.

CHAPTER 37

PUERTO RICO
CARIBBEAN CULTURAL CENTER

Marcelino Juan Canino Salgado

Situated between longitude 65 degrees 35 minutes and 67 degrees 15 minutes West and latitude 17 degrees 55 minutes and 18 degrees 30 minutes North, the island of Puerto Rico occupies a central position in the submerged chain of mountains extending between the two Americas that forms the Antillean archipelago. Irregularly rectangular in shape, Puerto Rico, together with the islands of Vieques and Culebra, which form part of the territory, comprises 3435 square miles. It is the smallest of the Greater and the largest of the Lesser Antilles (Picó 77). There are two basic theories about the origins of the first indigenous peoples of Puerto Rico. The first claims they came from the Florida peninsula by way of Grand Bahama, Cuba, Jamaica, Hispaniola, and then on to Puerto Rico and the other islands (Veloz Maggiolo viii), while the second posits that, given the proximity of the Antillean island chain to the Yucatan and Central America, it is possible that the first indigenous peoples came to Puerto Rico from Mesoamerica (Rouse 234–42). However, the most recent archeological and ethnographic research in the Caribbean basin has pointed to a harmonization of the two theories, such that some indigenous groups are thought to have come from the north, while the majority are thought to have come from the south. As a result of these migrations, three groups established themselves in Puerto Rico and in the Antilles in general: the Archaic, the Arawak, and the Carib.

The Archaic were nomads and thus did not farm or produce ceramics. As coastal dwellers who gathered fish and mollusks, they made only very modest use of tools, mostly fabricated from flint and seashells. They did not practice cranial deformation. It is thought that the Archaic came to Puerto Rico from neighboring islands a little more than 20,000 years ago and remained there for approximately fifteen centuries. The ethno-cultural groups thought to have come to Puerto Rico from South America–putting aside the Archaic–are subdivided into three groups: the Igneri, the Sub-Taino, and the Taino. These classifications have been established by archeologists and anthropologists on the basis of differences in tool-making, ceramics, and the level of social and religious development. The Igneri were an Arawak people, coming from the south, who swept over the already resident Archaic in an invasion dated 200 CE (Alegría 1948, 233–46). It is thought they might have come from Venezuela, through Trinidad, and on through the Antilles to Puerto Rico and the eastern part of Hispaniola. The Igneri were cultivators and skillful ceramicists. Their pottery was made from choice clay, well baked, and decorated with elegant and attractive designs painted in red, white, black, yellow, and a number of shades of ochre. From out of the Igneri culture developed the subsequent Taino groups. The Taino were the insular people inhabiting the Antilles when the Spanish arrived in the fifteenth century. The Taino culture probably grew out of a harmonization of Archaic and Igneri cultures and an ever more sophisticated adaptation to the geo-environmental circumstances of the island and the Antilles in general. The

designation *Sub-Taino* refers to the culture that evolutionarily preceded the Taino, a Neolithic culture of stone polishers, cultivators, and ceramicists. The Taino language was widely spread throughout the Antilles and without doubt was directly descended from the South American Arawak language. The Taino name for the island of Puerto Rico was Boriquén, and in 1788 this was Hispanicized by Friar Iñigo Abbad to Borinquen.

Before the arrival of the Spanish the entire Caribbean basin from north to south was an active conglomeration of aboriginal transients and emigrants. The predominate language was Taino-Arawak, save in the Windward Islands and Trinidad, where Carib prevailed. The Cuban philologist, Juan Clemente Zamora, has pointed out that about a hundred Taino and Carib words are still commonly used in the Caribbean basin. Given their dispersed condition, the inhabitants of the Antilles were accomplished navigators and excellent builders of canoes, which they used in their trading activities. Twentieth-century archeological evidence has established that a thriving commercial intercourse existed between the Tainos of Boriquén and the island of Hispaniola.

Christopher Columbus landed on Puerto Rico on his second voyage on 19 November 1493. It was not until seven years later–in 1500–that the first effort to colonize the island was made by Vicente Yañez Pinzón. However, his attempt was abandoned and limited itself to the release of several pairs of pigs and goats on the coasts of Boriquén. Ponce de León arrived in Boriquén accompanied by fifty men on 12 August 1508 and quickly established a friendship with the principal chief of the island, Agüeybana, with whom, following the native custom, he exchanged names. The intrepid colonizer succeeded in establishing himself in the region of Caparra after various attempts near the banks of the Toa River (present day La Plata). King Ferdinand, having backed all of Ponce de León's previous undertakings, named him the governor of San Juan on 14 August 1509; given the site's amplitude and easy maritime access, the conquistador designated the harbor of the new settlement Puerto Rico. On orders from Ferdinand, Ponce de León awarded lands and natives to the colonizers accompanying him, as well as to thirty others dispatched from Seville to populate the island; so began the formal colonization of Boriquén.

For an important sector of the Puerto Rican intelligentsia the so-called Discovery of the New World or America was a reckless armed invasion on the part of the Spanish–and, later, the Europeans in general–of a world populated by distinct cultures and civilizations that the invaders called savages, primitives, or naturals. For another important intellectual sector, more conservative and Hispanophile, this invasion is referred to by the euphemism "the encounter of the two worlds." In Puerto Rico, as in other Spanish American countries, many intellectuals come from the privileged and dominant class. Those who are not Anglophiles are Hispanophiles, and among the latter there are those who still dream of overseas Austrian and Bourbon filiations. There also exists, on the other hand, two much more radical groups: the Tainophiles, or partisans of the aboriginal cause, and the Negrophiles, or partisans of the Afro-Boriquén cause. Without falling into the cowardice of evasion there also exists another group, more discrete and less bombastic, of a thoroughly nationalist persuasion. These latter, while refraining from joining in the cause of one or another of the various camps, do recognize the indelible impress of ethnic miscegenation and the originality of a culture whose general features, while being common to all the Hispanic peoples, are nonetheless specific to Puerto Rico's process of cultural syncretism.

In a now classic book written for the youth of the island, the renowned Puerto Rican archeologist and conservationist Dr. Ricardo E. Alegría stated very plainly: "The three great races of humanity–the mongoloid, represented by our aborigines; the white, represented by the Spanish colonizers; and the black, represented by the slaves brought here from Africa–have contributed over the course of the centuries to form the Puerto Rican people" (1969, ix). Alegría's theory has been repeated ad infinitum and yet there are still many who do not accept it as it was originally formulated, considering it to be a simplistic reduction. How different are the theories of Pedro Henríquez Ureña from those of this most respected anthropologist! This issue is still the topic of heated discussion. In general, all Puerto Rican intellectuals–at times sotto voce–accept that the colonizers exterminated the aborigines of Boriquén in the first twenty-seven to thirty-six years of the colony. The causes of this are widely known: forced labor, psychological maltreatment, and the hardly rational imposition of a policy of cultural assimilation. The Spanish chronicler, Gonzalo Fernández de Oviedo (1478–1557), in Book XVI, Chapter V, of his *Historia general y natural de las Indias* [1535 and 1537; General and Natural History of the Indies], narrates how between 1511 and 1515 the natives of Boriquén rebelled against the Spanish, how they put Don Cristóbal de Sotomayor to death, and, finally, how Juan González, the native-Spanish interpreter, escaped with his life. It appears that González learned Arawak in Quisqueya and thus made himself extremely useful in expediting communication between the colonizers and the natives.

The legend and myth of Spanish superiority over the weak Taino began with Juan González and Ponce de León. Spying on an assembly of Taino chieftains, planning a revolt against the Spanish (1511), González was surprised and attacked by the Tainos. Suffering from thirty-six poisoned arrow wounds, a spear wound in the ribs, a knife wound in the right shoulder, and four club blows to the head, González still managed to cross the central mountain range of the island and reach the north coast, where he warned the Spanish of the impending attack. Heroic exploits such as this are common in all the chronicles of the so-called Conquest of America, having the sole function, as already noted, of advancing the myth of Spanish superiority over the American natives, as well as justifying in this way their extermination. Common to these accounts is the prominent role played by a native woman who betrays her people. The paradigm of the young Indian princess, madly in love with the conquistador of lands and peoples, who reveals to her lover the ominous plans of her tribesmen, is also common in the chronicles. By these means, the Spanish chroniclers would have us believe that all the Spanish-Americans are illegitimate offspring. The late nineteenth-century Puerto Rican historian, Salvador Brau, has

noted with respect to this paradigm that "a native woman of Boriquén, moved by her affections, expressed the same sentiment of loyalty that had united the noble Marina and the gallant Hernán Cortés in Mexico" (Brau 1972, 161–62).

The Dominican friar Antonio de Montesinos (1470–1520) was the first to raise his voice in protest against the servitude and enslavement forced upon the natives in Puerto Rico. Already, in early 1511, Montesinos was preaching to the loyal colonialists that such enslavement constituted an injustice, since the natives were rational beings, capable of being converted to Christianity. Troubled by Friar Montesinos's criticisms, the colonialists sent the Franciscan Alonso de Espinal with a petition to the king. Upon hearing of the injuries and abuses suffered by the natives, Ferdinand ordered an assembly of distinguished theologians to study the matter. The assembly resolved and recognized that the natives had the right to enjoy their liberty and to be treated as human beings. However, it also stipulated that they must be placed under the tutelage of the Spanish and tied to lands granted to the colonizers, so that they could receive a Christian baptism.

Friar Bartolomé de las Casas (1474–1566) continued the work started by Antonio de Montesinos. Las Casas understood that, in order to save the natives from slavery, one could not in the same motion deprive the Spanish colonial estates of manpower or damage the economic basis of colonial society. The solution proposed by Las Casas was to introduce black slaves into the Antilles and America, since in those times "the savage blacks of the African continent were not considered human beings." Whether out of repentance, humanistic scruples, or because he had radically changed his ideas (it is not at all clear), Las Casas later revised his opinions of blacks and their suitability for enslavement in a short work written in the final years of his life entitled: *Brevísima relación de la destrucción de África* [c. 1559–1560; Very Brief Account of the Destruction of Africa]. The enslavement of black Africans in Puerto Rico existed from approximately 1518 until 22 May 1873. Almost all the censuses of the past, at least those that have been certified as historical documents, show Puerto Rico to have been a class society in which a minority of white Spanish colonists dominated a specific ethnic majority composed almost entirely of blacks and free or enslaved mulattos.

Toward the end of the sixteenth and beginning of the seventeenth century the island was on the point of being depopulated, above all by the feverish rush to the mainland in search of gold, then known by the phrase "May God take me to Peru." Salvador Brau has recounted how on 27 September 1644 Damián López de Haro wrote from his bishopric to Juan Díaz de la Calle (after noting that a mere 200 men remained in the capital) that only by including black women was the population brought up to over 4,000. The Hispanophiles have sought to reduce the contribution made by the black slaves and the *criollo* to a mere folkloric patrimony. However, the question is much more complex than it appears, since, on the one hand, the blacks were subjugated by the Spanish colonialists, while, on the other, ethnic intermarriage and intermixing between both races has given rise to a significant mulatto population, whose demographic presence is obvious. Because the black slaves came from regions of Africa whose cultural and linguistic differences were very great, it was often the case that, in general, communication between them suffered greatly from this obstacle, and this fact compelled them to learn the language of the dominant class: Spanish. It is for this reason that we can say that the use of

Spanish was the first stage of their acculturation. This situation notwithstanding, however, the beliefs, customs, traditions, and forms of life of the black slaves were gradually assimilated by the impoverished Puerto Rican peasantry. The foundations of cultural and economic infrastructure in Puerto Rico stemmed from the practices of these black slaves. In addition to the folkloric elements (for Hispanophiles, the sole and meager contribution of the blacks to culture), the profound contributions Afro-Boriquéns have made in a diverse array of areas, including music, literature, education, politics, the sciences, the visual arts, and craftsmanship, cannot be denied—at least in public—by the modern intellectual. And in recent times Hispanophiles have continued their attempts to reduce the contribution of the Puerto Rican blacks to the status of mere rhetorical trappings.

Commenting on the Antillean essence in a speech in Madrid in May 1988, the ex-governor of Puerto Rico, Rafael Hernández Colón, stated that present-day society in the Antilles is by and large the direct heir of the Spanish patrimony. Such declarations are hardly novel; what is surprising is that even such refined writers as José Isaac de Diego Padró have felt it necessary to make the point as here in 1932:

> Antilleanism, just like its basic components Creolism and Negroism, is nothing more than a geographic pipe dream. The Antillean intellectual type does not, properly speaking, exist, and to seek to steer all Antillean poetic activity through the slimy channels of Creolism and Negroism would be to lead our verse into a detestable species of hybridism. What our artists and thinkers ought to aspire to is to shake off the tropics and to express themselves more in accord with the universal and the sublime. (97)

Cultural development and cultural production during the first two centuries of Spanish colonization were practically nonexistent. Aside from the bishops and their entourages, who introduced books into the island largely with a view to their religious use, there did, however, from time to time arrive one or another book of history or Latin literature. This, for example, was the case when Miguel Manzo arrived on the island 10 October 1512 with a copy of Sallust [86–34 BCE] (Tanodi 155–56). Similarly, the first bishop sent to Puerto Rico, Alonso Manso, who disembarked here on 25 December 1512, brought with him among his many belongings a coffer containing 230 books. And Francisco de Quintanilla, a member of the prelate's entourage, brought with him a copy of Virgil and a Latin vocabulary (Tanodi 160–63).

It is to be imagined that in the midst of foreign and unknown lands music was a comforting balm for soothing the nostalgia for the distant homeland. On 11 December 1516 Juan Martín, a passenger on the San Juan, came ashore with the first guitar, introducing the instrument to the New World (Tanodi 338). Although these were but sporadic events in the long process of cultural formation, they continued over time, and through them we can glimpse in a certain manner the process whereby Spanish knowledge and erudition were transplanted to the island of Puerto Rico. During the first three centuries of Puerto Rican colonial life, the Puerto Rican-born sons of the Spanish colonists (that is to say, the *criollos*), as well as the *mestizos* (whatever their origins), received no formal education at all, save what their fathers crudely transmitted to them orally. Even at the end of the eighteenth century, the majority of the island's population was illiterate and submerged in the most profound ignorance (O'Reilly 388). While the Dominican fathers did make efforts to evangelize and provide primary instruction to children and adolescents in the capital region, the lack of official support made these efforts virtually fruitless. Motivated by piety and civic conscience, two of the city's residents, Antón Lucas (sometime before 1582, although the precise date is unknown) and Francisco Ruiz (in 1589) bequeathed modest sums (a little more than 200 ducats) for the support of instruction and above all for the creation of a professorship position for a grammar teacher. In 1647 the St. Thomas Aquinas Convent, a school for lay instruction at the university level, was founded. Two years later, in 1649, Friar Jorge Cambrero established his Casa de Estudios de Artes y Gramática (School for the Study of Arts and Grammar) for the novices and residents of the city. There were twenty-four students in grammar and twelve in the arts; the school's curriculum was, in a certain sense, a holdover from the medieval *trivium*: grammar, logic, rhetoric, and the Latin language (Coll y Toste 3–25).

In spite of the precariousness of instruction on the island, the sons of the landowners and the influential did manage to receive an education as public service officials, which is to say, as civil servants. However, many prominent *criollos* abandoned the island in search of a better future. In a celebrated *Memorandum* of 23 April 1647 Diego Torres Vargas, the Canon of the Holy Church of Puerto Rico, gave a detailed account to his correspondent, the Chronicler Gil González Dávila, of the prevailing state of affairs in the country upon his arrival there, passed judgment on the work of the governors and the bishops, and listed the famous Puerto Ricans who had abandoned the country only to distinguish themselves in the government and important offices of other lands such as Margarita, Florida, Cuba, Chiapas, Santo Domingo, New Spain, the Philippines, Venezuela, and even Spain (Caro Costas 288). One of the most illustrious Puerto Ricans of the seventeenth century was the first known poet, the priest Don Francisco de Ayerra y Santa María (1630–1708). The intellectual aridity of the Puerto Rico of those times obliged Francisco's parents to send him to New Spain for an education. He was received in Mexico by the religious orders and completed his bachelor's degree in Canon Law. It was also in Mexico that he would hold a number of important ecclesiastical offices: chaplain of the Royal Convent of Jesus and Mary, the first rector of the Tridentine Seminary, and inspector of the archbishopric. In addition, Ayerra y Santa María was a close friend of the distinguished Mexican savant Carlos de Sigüenza y Góngora (1645–1700), compiler of the anthology entitled: *Triunfo parténico que en gloria de María Santísima inmaculadamente concebida, celebró la Pontificia Imperial y Regia Academia Mexicana* [1683; Virginal Triumph of the Most Holy Mother, Immaculately Conceived, Celebrated by the Pontifical, Imperial, and Royal Academy of Mexico]. Four of Ayerra's poems figure in this anthology, two in Latin and two in Spanish. Influenced by the Gongorist [Luis de Gongora y Argote, 1561–1627] vogue for latinized, precious, highly metaphorical verse, Ayerra's poetic works circulated only among his closest friends during his lifetime and were hardly known by his contemporaries. Even today, they are little studied. All that remain of his works are three sonnets, three Latin epigrams, and a long cento inspired by one of Góngora's works (Rosa Nieves 19–24; Rivera de Alvarez I: 26–27).

It appears that the presence of bishop and poet Don Bernardo de Balbuena (1563–1627), residing in the island from 1620 to 1625 to oversee the religious life of the city, had little in the way of influence or impact on the population. The highly reputed poet of the *Grandeza mexicana* [1604; Mexican

Grandeur], *El siglo de oro en las selvas de Erífile* [1608; The Golden Age in the Wilderness of Erífile], and *El Bernardo o Victoria de Roncesvalles* [1624; Bernard or the Victory of Roncesvalles] suffered the misfortune of losing his excellent library as well as a number of his manuscripts when a pirate expedition captained by general Bowdoin Hendrick (Balduino Enrico) sacked the islet of San Juan Bautista de Puerto Rico from 25 September to 2 November 1625 (Caro Costas 355). Four of Balbuena's completed (and ready for the printer) manuscripts were lost in the fire that consumed his legendary library: "*Cosmografía Universal*" ["Universal Cosmography"], "*Divino Cristiados*" ["Divine Converts"], "*Alteza de Laura*" ["Laura Sublime"], and "*Arte Nuevo de Poesía*" ["New Art of Poetry"]. In 1893 Menéndez y Pelayo remarked of this incident: "Several of Lope de Vega's oft-repeated verses in *Laurel de Apolo* [*Apollo's Laurel*] alluded to this loss: 'And forever sweet shall your memory be,/Magnanimous Prelate,/Most Learned Bernardo de Balbuena./You held the bishop's staff and fate/Of Puerto Rico, when Hendrick the fierce,/Dutchman and ingrate,/Set your library aflame:/But your genius he could never claim'" (Menéndez y Pelayo 328–29).

With the ascension of Carlos III to the Spanish throne, the political and civil situation in the Antilles began to improve appreciably. Steeped in the theories of the Enlightenment, the king ordered Field Marshall Alejandro O'Reilly to undertake a full critical study of the island of Puerto Rico and to submit a report on the economic potential of the country. O'Reilly arrived in Puerto Rico in April 1765 and wasted no time executing the royal brief; by June 20 of the same year he had finished his study, and on September 20 the king authorized the reform project that O'Reilly had submitted. Among other reforms proposed was that of converting Puerto Rico into one of the major fortifications of the overseas empire. To expedite this project, and also on 20 September 1765, the engineer Colonel Tomás O'Daly was appointed to oversee the construction that would initially siphon off 100,000 pesos per annum from the Mexican treasury; later this figure would rise to 150,000 pesos per annum (Brau 1971, 159). This was the origin of one of the many debts of gratitude that the Puerto Rican people owe to the Mexicans. Lamentably, in those times the Caribbean Sea was infested with pirates and buccaneers of every nationality, and on many occasions the so-called "Mexican Security" never arrived. In O'Reilly's *Memorandum* he devotes a brief paragraph to the intellectual and pedagogic situation of the island in which he says:

> [C]onviene saber que en toda la isla . . . pocos saben leer, que cuentan, por épocas de los gobiernos, huracanes, visitas de obispo, arribo de flotas o situados: no entienden lo que son leguas; cada uno cuenta la jornada a proporción de su andar. (in Caro Costas 388)

> [I]t is as good to know that in the whole of the island . . . few learn how to read; that the people count the epochs with reference to the reign of the governors, hurricanes, the visits of the bishops, the arrivals of the fleets, or by blockades. No one can tell you what a league is; everyone measures the progress of their journey in proportion to the time elapsed.

Faced with such a sorry state of affairs, there were, beginning around 1770, several attempts to establish a university in Puerto Rico, above all after the cession of the Spanish part of the island of Hispaniola (Santo Domingo) to the French in 1795; however, these efforts came to naught. Previously, in 1788, Carlos III had authorized the Universidad de la Española in Santo Domingo to bestow degrees in philosophy and theology on the students graduating from the Colegio de Santo Tomás de Aquino and from the Monasterio de San Francisco; this practice would continue for fifty-one years. This concession entailed the frequent travel of students between the two neighboring islands and in this way fostered an incipient cultural interchange (Hostos 549). By the beginning of the nineteenth century the Puerto Rican cultural-educational panorama began to change. Motivated by enlightened reformism, local mayors became conscious of the importance of public education and, with public support, they began to pay school teachers to offer instruction to both male and female children at the primary level. In 1832, thanks to the efforts of Bishop Gutiérrez de Coz, the Seminario Conciliar de San Ildefonso was founded in the city of San Juan. On October 12 the Seminary opened its doors to twelve scholarship students, sponsored by the bishopric, and thirty-three paying students. The Seminary offered both religious and pre-university education. Some of the students would follow in the religious professions, while others went on to other careers, many of them in Spain, Cuba, France, Mexico, or the United States. In 1858 the Seminary passed into the hands of the Jesuits, who did a superb job running the school from 1859 until 1878 and graduated 221 recipients of the Bachelor of Arts. Two years later, in 1880, the governor of Puerto Rico, Don Eulogio Despujol, ordered a sweeping reorganization of the island's schools which resulted in, among other things, remunerative justice for the island's badly paid school teachers. Despujol's decree was approved by the crown on 1 February 1881 (Coll y Toste 137–38).

With the arrival of the printing press in Puerto Rico (between 1806 and 1807) the sociocultural, political, and economic situation of the island took on a number of new nuances. A French immigrant by the name of Delarue brought the press to the island; he did not, however, foresee the restrictions that the colonial government had put in place, or his prohibition as a foreigner from working as a printer. The then governor of the island, Toribio Montes, seeing the utility of the device, bought the press from Delarue and set up a printing office as an accessory to the General Captaincy. Montes ordered the publication of what would be the first Puerto Rican periodical, *La gaceta oficial de Puerto Rico,* a short-lived biweekly whose first issue was published 31 December 1807.

With the return of Fernando VII to the Spanish throne and the reinstallation of the Bourbon monarchy, the new constitution of 1812 promised to unite the Spaniards of both hemispheres in one single family. Even at that time, the reverberations of the Venezuelan Revolution and the events in Santo Domingo were heard, clandestinely, in Puerto Rico, where the burgeoning desire for liberty and emancipation began in to be manifest an embryonic manner in the timid proclamations of the Puerto Rican liberal bourgeoisie. The new constitution provided Puerto Ricans for the first time with a representative in the Cadiz parliament: Ramón Power. In the same era, although it had been agreed upon years earlier, a branch of the *Sociedad Económica de Amigos del País* was established in Puerto Rico for the promotion of the island's industry, agriculture, and commerce, as well as the propagation of scientific and cultural knowledge beneficial to its development. To these ends, and through the intercession of the intendant Alejandro Ramírez and the cooperation of an enlightened Puerto Rican, José Andino, the *El*

Diario Económico periodical was established to disseminate the principles of the new society. In addition, the *Cédula de Gracia* [Certificate of Privilege], signed into effect by the monarch on 1 August 1815, established (among other privileges): free trade with the United States and foreign colonies, provided the goods were transported by Spanish ships; an extension of the right to import slaves, machinery, and agricultural tools and devices; and the free admission of Catholic, foreign colonists, their servants and slaves, the concession of arable lands to these colonists, permission to bequeath property in full liberty, and authorization, after five years' residence, to return to the land of their origin with all the wealth and possessions they had acquired while in Puerto Rico (Brau 1971, 199). In the spirit of moderate liberalism, freedom of the press was decreed. The government printing press began to publish a series of periodicals that began with *El Investigador*, and later *El Cigarrón*, and *El Eco*, edited by Julián Blanco. According to the historian Salvador Brau, "While *El Eco* distinguished itself by its propriety, *El Investigador* surpassed it in influence, and was successful in obliging the metropolitan government to rectify the state of abandonment into which the public education system had fallen" (Brau 1971, 203).

Thirty-two years after the introduction of the printing press in Puerto Rico the *Boletín Mercantil* boasted in 1839 of having 300 subscribers. Given that at that time the population of the island numbered 358,836 (whites, free blacks, and slaves), the *Boletín*'s subscription represented less than .084 percent of the population. It was thus a periodical for the tiniest of minorities. In an exemplary and comprehensive study ("Nineteenth-Century Puerto Rico: Literature and Society") Iris M. Zavala analyzed the major portion of the nineteenth-century Puerto Rican periodicals and reviews published over seventy years, as well as the local and foreign literature that circulated in the country during this period. Her principal conclusions were that social concern in nineteenth-century Puerto Rico divided people into two distinct camps: a liberal, progressive group that employed the language of the peasantry in its writings in order to call into question the top-down imposition of reforms on the part of the ruling elites; and another, an urban group favoring the correct use of Spanish, advocating the conservative, Catholic, and royalist ideas of the dominant class. While *La gaceta oficial* popularized Spanish and foreign authors (the latter in translation), it only did so for those writings that could be affiliated with a Christian and excessively compliant Romanticism. Both *La gaceta* and the *Boletín* published only those authors and writings that had already appeared in the mother country's periodicals and reviews representing the same class and ideology. Freedom of the press was interpreted to mean freedom so long as it served the state's interests. For *El Investigador* this meant a subtle form of protest or admonition "in order to correct abuses, to attempt to reform customs, and to teach civility" (Zavala I: 13). But *El Investigador* also published the *supposed opinions* of peasants and farmers who mistrusted the intentions and decrees of the government. In this way it established an artificial dialogue between the city and the countryside in which the tension of contradictory forces began to manifest itself. Later *El Investigador* began to introduce innovative ideas, such as Saint-Simonist socialism, that were tolerated by the liberal-oriented people among the dominant class, both in Puerto Rico and in the mother country (Zavala I: 17).

The Warrant of 1815 also opened up an era of the free movement of books into Puerto Rico without government or customs censorship. Already by 1823 announcements were being made for informative and general interest books such as Guthrie's *Geografía Universal* [Universal Geography], the works of Say, Capmany, Quintana, Quintiliano, Navarrete, Genovesi, Virgil, and Nebrija, all of which could be purchased in Lorenzo Cayol's book shop on San Francisco Street in the capital. Toward the end of 1830 the Spaniard Santiago Dalmau, making the most of the necessity for books and aware of their prohibitive cost for many Puerto Ricans, established a bookshop and reading room at #8 Fortaleza Street in San Juan. This location became, for more than ten years, the cultural center of the city. By the end of the 1840s, the works of foreign—English, German, French, as well as Spanish—authors began to be disseminated in Puerto Rico, sometimes through newspaper serialization: Gray, Hugo, Dumas, Hoffman, Gessner, Humboldt, De Bonald, Weston, Joyce, Schiller, Goethe, Balzac, Cooper, Lamartine, Chateaubriand, and Balmes. Among the Spanish writers most circulated, both by *La gaceta* and the *Boletín*, were: Hartzenbuch (his plays, and above all his stories), Wenceslao Querol, Zorrilla, José Amador de los Ríos, Gabriel García Tassara, Francisco Javier de Burgos, Martínez de la Rosa, Eugenio de Ochoa, Salvador Bermúdez de Castro, Alberto Lista, Mora, Bretón de los Herreros, and Campoamor. Iris Zavala very pertinently underlines the fact that "almost all of these writers were exponents of Catholic Conservative ideas. Articles by Larra and Espronceda, on the other hand, never appeared; nor did social serials. The combative aspect of Romanticism remained in the shadows" (I: 22).

In an almost inadvertent manner the texts of the English economist Jeremy Bentham, father of utilitarianism, and those of the Frenchman Auguste Comte, founder of sociology and positivist philosophy, began circulating. Also surprising was that Gimbernat's bookshop began selling (in 1848) texts of the socialist writers Louis Blanc and Étienne Cabet, the founder of the communist school, and this in spite of the fact that the explicitly antisocialist, propagandistic texts of Balmes and Guizot had been circulating in Puerto Rico in 1847 (Zavala I: 23). As Zavala has pointed out, "the Puerto Rican reader was more or less fully informed, although the Christian writers always predominated" (24). This situation notwithstanding, what was undeniable was that all this literature only reached, as we have seen, an infinitesimal part of the population; most were largely oblivious of the cultural goings-on across the sea. All the intellectual sobriety and literary effervescence of ideologies that unfolded in the reviews and periodicals of the country certainly served as an influential model for the first wave of Puerto Rican writers: Ignacio Guasp Cervera (1810–1874), Fernando Roig (b. 1800), Martín J. Travieso (b. 1820), Francisco Vassallo Flores (1789–1849), María Bibiana Benítez (1783–1873), Santiago Vidarte (1828–1848), and Manuel Alonso y Pacheco (1822–1889). Of these figures, all were born in Puerto Rico, save Guasp, who identified with the problems of the country, although he was an ideological conservative.

The most distinguished of this group was Manuel Alonso y Pacheco, a doctor by profession and considered the father of Puerto Rican literature because of the claims that his work *El gíbaro* [The Rustic Peasant] was the first book published (1849) by a single author in the country. Although this primacy has been contested—many have pointed to the 1843 publication of *El Aguinaldo puertorriqueño* [The Puerto Rican Gift] and the 1844 publication of *El album puertorriqueño* [The Puerto Rican Album]–both these latter works were anthologies of the works of various authors. Alonso y Pacheco's book, as Zavala has explained, operates by means of two conceptions or expressions of the same term *jibaridad: el jíbaro*, the wild (animal) and the sullen, and *lo jíbaro*, the rustic. According to Zavala, *el jíbaro* is an emblem representing the "battle cry" of protest, the denunciation of social injustice, and the suspicion of official canons. *Lo jíbaro*, on the other hand, represents the picturesque, a social archetype, a concept that served as the pretext for the eradication of customs and what were thought to be vices. *El jíbaro* stands in opposition to the colonial order and asserts its own reality and aspirations, while *lo jíbaro*, in contrast, criticizes the typical, considering it to be an expression of an inferior culture. This dichotomy is up to a point an excellent means to a more clear awareness of Puerto Ricanness; in spite of the ideological ambiguities, this is in some sense a praiseworthy move. Alonso, as a medical doctor and colonial functionary, belonged to the dominant class; nonetheless, as a liberal reformer, he was a staunch opponent of the die-hard merchant capitalist, conservative, royalist, and illiterate Pablo Ubarri, who throughout his life opposed compulsory free education. Alonso remained to the end of his days the most responsible poet of his times, the poet, both in prose and in verse, of the Puerto Rican identity.

Juan González, editor of the fortnightly review *El Fomento de Puerto Rico*, wrote in 1863 that:

I[I]n Puerto Rico it has already been a long time now that the taste for reading has been in a state of awakening, so long in fact that, as has happened to every people, we have begun to take to frivolous reading, the reading of fiction and light poetry. To introduce a class of books other than these or the rudiments indispensable to learning would have been madness: to try and encounter readers for any other class of work would not have been possible, even in a utopia." (in Tapia y Rivera 1854, 19)

Every sort of sentimental, moralizing, idyllic, and in general Romantic novel was in circulation in Puerto Rico at this time, both in translation from the French or English, and as Hispanic-American novels that the customs censors considered innocuous. The *Boletín Mercantil*, the *Aguinaldo puertorriqueño* of 1843, and *El cancionero de Borinquen*, all published short novels by native and foreign authors, which only served to increase the market for the genre. From time to time, one or another critique of the regime in power or the monarchy would make its appearance in these works, veiled by a literary image.

In Puerto Rico the genre of the novel was linked to the *criollo*, Europeanized bourgeoisie. One of the results of the Certificate of Privilege of 1815 was that entire contingents of Corsicans, Frenchmen, Italians, and Northern Europeans arrived in Puerto Rico in search of a better livelihood, and this they found as plantation owners of coffee or sugar cane estates. However, in the process they also offered a luxurious and conspicuous-consumption life-style as their supreme avocation; this wealth was the product of their labors–and of the concealed exploitation of African slaves. For the writer and critic Alejandro Tapia y Rivera (1826–1882) the novel was slowly converting itself into an ontological vehicle in search of Puerto Rican identity. As a compiler and editor of historical documents relevant to Puerto Rico (*Biblioteca Histórica de Puerto Rico* [Historical Library of Puerto Rico], 1854), Tapia y Rivera developed a clear vision of the island's precarious cultural and economic future; yet it seems that the universalist models he became acquainted with in Spain in 1850 led him to a kind of Romantic evasion of the harsh and unacceptable reality that, in a certain manner, Manuel Alonso y Pacheco had become aware of. Nevertheless, I believe that Tapia overcame this evasion and in his novels and his plays sought the transcendent, not as a law or order imposed by the mother country, but rather as the supreme aspiration of individual liberty. His inquiry into Puerto Rican roots (*La palma del cacique* [1852; The Chieftain's Palm]) still did not bear fruit, since he continued to deem all things Spanish superior to those of Boriquén; but in *Cofresí* [1876; Casket], on the other hand, he took the direct path toward justice when he eulogized his marginalized hero. However, in the end, Tapia never confronted the true problem: government oppression and the exploitation of the peasantry. He was never able to transcend the simplistic concepts of Catholic social policies, and although he raised the question of the affliction of the downtrodden, he considered that such injustices could be rectified "without changing the nature and circumstances of society. The problem of social delinquency will only be resolved by the united efforts of fraternal cooperation and the improvements of capitalism." At the same time that Tapia was postulating these timid social palliatives in his works (1876), intellectuals like Eugenio María de Hostos (1839–1903) and Ramón Emeterio Betances (1827–1898) had already fired the first shots in the great anti-colonial battle by advocating for Puerto Rico a republican democracy (Zavala II: 17–18).

The revolutionary ideas that seeped into Puerto Rico following the events in Santo Domingo and Venezuela were taken up and brought to fruition in part by the liberals, but even more by the radicals alienated by the regime. The two most distinguished leaders of the revolutionary movement, Ramón Emeterio Betances and Segundo Ruiz Belvis (1829–1867), sought aid for their cause outside of Puerto Rico. Betances went to New York and later to Santo Domingo, from which he began to prepare an armed insurrection. Segundo Ruiz Belvis went south but tragically died in mysterious circumstances that have yet to be clarified, shortly before he was to reach Chile. Although a commission of Puerto Rican intellectuals had gone to Spain in 1867 in an effort to work out a solution to the Puerto Rican crisis, nothing came of it. The Lares Insurrection broke out 23 September 1867. Backed by a ragtag army of some 400 men, the people of Lares proclaimed themselves the Republic of Puerto Rico and established a provisional government composed of Francisco Ramírez Medina as president; Federico Valencia, Minister of Finance; Aurelio Méndez, Minister of Justice; and Clemente Millán, Minister of Foreign Affairs. The triumph of Lares notwithstanding, when the forces led by Manuel Rojas and Matías Brugman attempted the following morning to take the neighbouring town of San Sebastián del Pepino, they were met by Spanish troops and a hail of bullets, scuttling the revolutionary insurrection that even today fills Puerto Ricans with pride. With the proclamation of the first Spanish Republic in 1873, its liberalizing and reformist ideas extended to Puerto Rico. The most significant reform, erasing a shameful and inhuman past, was the abolition of slavery on March 22 of that year.

Although the idea of creating a space for the free interchange of culture and cultural ideas had been articulated by Alejandro Tapia in 1855, it was in reality Manuel Elzaburo, who surmounted the innumerable difficulties and succeeded in establishing on 29 June 1876 the Ateneo, the institution that would henceforth be the central clearing house for Puerto Rican culture, sciences, and arts and letters. At this time, and in a certain sense ever since, the government was suspicious of the institution, seeing it as a center of Leftist political agitation. From the very beginning the Ateneo sponsored annual courses in advanced study, competitions of every sort, cultural soirées, conferences, concerts, and ceremonies celebrating the contributions that Puerto Rican men and women made in every field of culture. It possesses an excellent library, with a special collection of Puerto Rican works, a portrait gallery of its founders, a valuable collection of art works, and a modest editorial house publishing their now classic review, as well as books, treatises pamphlets, and other necessary and interesting works. It is considered one of the most serious and respected institutions in Puerto Rico.

Román Baldorioty de Castro and Rafael María de Labra devoted all their energies to assembling in a single group all those who supported the already forgotten home-rule ideal that the old liberals had somewhat timidly advanced. The home-rule block sought a Puerto Rican government and the maintenance of union with Spain. The response from the despotic government of the Spanish general Romualdo Palacios was the merciless persecution of the partisans of home rule: A series of draconian practices aiming at crushing the movement were instituted by the government, including corporal punishment, imprisonment, rape, looting, and even assassination. As a result of this policy, the hands of the Spanish government were indelibly stained with blood. With the death of Román Baldorioty, Luis Muñoz Rivera took over the leadership of the home-rule movement. Although the protagonists of the movement were, as was the case in every colony, divided into various factions, Muñoz Rivera succeeded in forging a pact with Práxedes Mateo Sagasta who, upon winning the Spanish presidential election, obtained from the crown the concession of autonomy for Puerto Rico. The decree was approved in November 1897 and came into effect on 11 February 1898. Unfortunately, ten weeks later on 24 April the newly autonomous government was suspended by the imposition of martial law in response to the war that had broken out between Spain and the United States. The multiple aspirations of the Puerto Rican people once again were frustrated.

The Cuban struggle against Spain for absolute autonomy was a golden opportunity for the United States to intervene in Caribbean affairs. Following the contrived sinking of the *Maine* in Havana harbor, the United States declared war on Spain on 21 April 1898. On April 24 the U.S. invaded Cuba and attacked the Philippines, destroying the Spanish Pacific fleet in the port of Manila. On Sunday, 12 May 1898, U.S. vice-admiral Sampson bombarded for more than three hours the city of San Juan, which Puerto Rican and Spanish troops were defending. The U.S. fleet withdrew to Santiago de Cuba and routed the Spanish fleet under the command of Admiral Cervera, who was taken prisoner. Under the command of General Nelson A. Miles, U.S. troops stormed the port of Guánica on July 25 and so began the invasion and military occupation of Puerto Rico. With the signing of the Treaty of Paris on 12 August 1898, sovereignty of the island passed to the U.S., and on August 18 of the same year the first U.S. flag was raised at the Fortaleza palace.

The U.S. invasion of Puerto Rico produced an immediate disorientation, even chaos. Every civil and social institution in the country was thrown into confusion, and the population was in an obvious and heart-rending state of trauma. The Puerto Rican essayist Tomás Blanco (1896–1975) described the situation: "Contribuyeron también a la desorientación las protestas y promesas hechas por los Estados Unidos, por medio del general en jefe de la invasión, Nelson A. Miles, al pueblo de Puerto Rico: 'Venimos–decía–por la causa de la libertad, la justicia y la humanidad . . . a promover vuestra prosperidad . . . a dar a todos. . . las ventajas y bendiciones de la civilización ilustrada'" (62) ("Also contributing to the disorientation were the protests and promises to the Puerto Rican people made by the commander-in-chief of the invasion, general Nelson A. Miles, on behalf of his government: 'We come in the name of liberty, justice, and humanity . . . to promote your prosperity...and to confer on all . . . the blessings and benefits of enlightened civilization' "). Blanco adds that "Si no faltaron hijos del país que ofrecieron flores al invasor, la simpleza de ese gesto debe juzgarse no solo como resultado de la seducción ejercida por tan sonoras como vanas palabras, sino también como muestra de simpatía hacia quienes, aprentemente, no perseguían otra finalidad que socorrer a los patriotas del pueblo hermano en la consecución de sus derechos y libertades" (103) ("if there was no shortage of patriotic sons offering flowers to the invaders, the simplicity of this gesture ought to be judged not a result of the seduction exercised by such sonorous and vain words, but rather also as evidence of a sympathy toward those who, apparently, had no other aim in mind than that of giving aid to the patriots of a neighboring people in the acquisition of their rights and liberties"). The adverb employed by Blanco–*apparently*–was and continues to be a communal fiction. No one in Puerto Rico, save the recalcitrant Yankee-lovers, disputes the fact that the U.S. invasion initiated a prolonged paralysis in the development of the island's cultural struggle. The Puerto Rican musical historian Fernando Callejo wrote in 1915 that "No es práctica en Norte América, que el Estado se haga cargo directamente del fomento de las artes, y de ahí, que uno de los primeros actos del régimen [norteamericano] en Puerto Rico fuese la supresión de todas las subvenciones de carácter artístico" (67) ("direct state sponsorship of the arts and their development is not feasible, and thus it comes as no surprise that one of the first acts of the new [U.S.] regime in Puerto Rico was the abolition of all subsidies for artistic work").

The major blow dealt by the invaders and the U.S. administration against the Puerto Rican ethos was the attempt to acculturate everyone, to change the language that for more than 400 years had been the blood and the spirit of Hispanic world: Spanish. By means of the public education system, administered by the United States and now better funded than previously, an attempt was made to impose on the children and on the public in general the English language; ever since the U.S. invasion, the so-called language controversy has raged in Puerto Rico. This has been the most heroic of the many battles waged by the Puerto Rican people throughout its history (which, for reasons of space, we cannot go into here). The U.S. administration, anxious to acquire a detailed knowledge of all aspects of the life and natural history of its new Caribbean colony, and thus facilitate its assimilation into the union, undertook a comprehensive study of Puerto Rico and the Virgin Islands from 1899 until approximately 1918, known as the *Scientific Survey of Porto Rico and the Virgin Islands*.

The results of this survey, sponsored in part by The New York Academy of Sciences, were published in eighteen volumes and included geographic, topographic, hydrologic, botanical, zoological, icthyographic, and entomological studies. The anthropologist J. Alden Mason, who directed the ethnographic studies of the survey, also assembled one of the richest and most voluminous collections of Caribbean and, perhaps, Spanish American folkloric materials in existence. This material on Caribbean oral traditions was published in the *Journal of American Folk-lore*.

On 1 May 1900 the Foraker Bill came into effect, substituting military for civil rule in Puerto Rico; and in 1917 the Jones Bill granted U.S. citizenship to Puerto Ricans. At this time public opinion was divided into three camps: assimilationists (favoring annexation to the U.S.), the partisans of home rule, and the partisans of Independence. In light of Puerto Rican political history between 1900 and approximately 1936, the postulates of the first two groups came to be astonishingly similar. On the other hand, the partisans of Independence, in addition to being continuously persecuted by the colonial government, experienced a subtle internal division. From 1930 the Puerto Rican Nationalist Party, led by Dr. Pedro Albizu Campos, adopted the policy of claiming the absolute right to the complete liberation of Puerto Rico and did not rule out the possibility of violence to achieve that end. During the course of various hostilities and eruptions of violence between the nationalists and the colonial government, including the Ponce Massacre in 1937 and the nationalist rebellion of 1950, as well as the Washington incident, the Nationalist Party was mercilessly persecuted and Albizu Campos was incarcerated up until shortly before his death.

In November 1944 the new Popular Democratic Party, established by Luis Muñoz Marín, won a landslide victory, obtaining more than 63 percent of the vote, and in November 1948 Muñoz was elected governor, the first governor directly elected by the Puerto Rican people. Muñoz was a great social reformer who, under the slogan of "Bread, Land, and Liberty," managed to draw together the masses anxious for justice and dignity. Having been in his early youth a poet, a fiction writer, and a journalist, Muñoz took a special interest in the development of education and culture. Renouncing the Independence ideal that had been the subject of much discussion in the 1930s, Muñoz proposed a new form of autonomy from the U.S. (inspired, perhaps, by his father Luis Muñoz Rivera), much more limited in scope than the home rule conceded by Spain in 1897. Muñoz was a charismatic politician: By means of his new style of oratory, and the various effective and obviously beneficial reforms he pushed through, "*el Vate*" (the prophet, the bard), as he was affectionately known by the peasantry, maintained the respect and the support of the majority of the voters for some thirty years.

Over the years Puerto Ricans had been petitioning for the creation of a university in the island; to this clamor was added the experience of the Puerto Rican scientists and students in the U.S. who, in the course of their research, had come to realize the urgent necessity of having on the island an institution of higher learning for the education of school teachers. In 1900, under the initiative of the Commissioner of Education, Martin Brumbaugh, the Normal School was established for precisely this purpose. Originally located in the town of Fajardo and under the immediate supervision of the Commission, the Normal School was moved to Río Piedras in 1903 and was to become, in the years that followed, the University

of Puerto Rico and the alma mater of the majority of Puerto Rico's intellectuals and professionals. The University of Puerto Rico has reached a level of prestige and renown, not only in the natural and applied sciences, but also in the arts and letters. Its publishing house, as well as its journal, *La Torre*, founded by the then rector of the university, Jaime Benítez, have published works by the most famous and praiseworthy Puerto Rican and foreign intellectuals. To the cultural and educational labors of the University of Puerto Rico at Río Piedras and its many campuses have been added those of the various private universities that operate with an equal devotion to truth and excellence: the Universidad Interamericana de Puerto Rico (1907), the Universidad Católica Madre y Maestra in Ponce, the Dominican-run Universidad Central de Bayamón (1961), the Universidad del Sagrado Corazón in Santurce, and the Fundación Educativa Ana G. Méndez and its affiliates. All of these institutions of higher learning, irrespective of their academic preferences and specialties, publish cultural and professional journals of every type.

Through the efforts of the historians and university professors Arturo Morales Carrión and Ricardo E. Alegría, the Puerto Rican legislature adopted Bill 89 in 1955, creating the Instituto de Cultura de Puerto Rico. In addition to seeking to foster the maintenance of Puerto Rican culture, the bill also had the aim of conserving and restoring the Colonial historical-architectural patrimony. Since its foundation, the Institute has promoted the development of the visual arts, literature, music, and the theater; it has, in addition, funded hundreds of talented young people to enrich their particular studies both in and outside Puerto Rico. Further, the Institute has sponsored the publication and dissemination of Puerto Rico's classic and contemporary writers, as well as annual festivals of Puerto Rican and international theater, which have provided actors and performers with workshops and encouragement. Affiliated with the Institute are the National Archives, the National Library, and the Casa del Libro (Museum of the Book), this latter housing thousands of rare editions, incunabula, manuscripts, and illuminated manuscripts for the use of Puerto Rican and foreign scholars. Also under the umbrella of the Institute are a School of Plastic Arts, various archeological and historical museums, a journal, a center for popular and traditional arts, art galleries, a program of recitals and concerts, a string orchestra, the Banda de Puerto Rico, as well as the classical ballet company, the Ballets de San Juan, originally founded in 1954 by Gilda Navarra and Ana García as an independent entity. Under the leadership of its first director, Dr. Ricardo E. Alegría, the Institute sponsored cultural programs in all the municipalities of the country. The enormous and patriotic works of Dr. Alegría deserve the respect and approbation not only of the Puerto Rican people, but also our neighbors in culture, language, and tradition. The Institute is the custodian of an important art gallery housing a collection of valuable works by the most famous Puerto Rican painters from the eighteenth century to the present, as well as an extremely important collection of popular sculptures and carvings. It must be stated, however, that such government institutions have not taken as good care of this valuable cultural patrimony as they ought to have and that a number of the collections have deteriorated as a result of climatological conditions.

The Ponce Museum of Art, patronized by the millionaire businessman and ex-governor of Puerto Rico, Luis A. Ferré, has assembled a valuable collection of paintings, and to a lesser extent, of sculpture, that is truly a delight for the mind and spirit. This private institution also contains a restoration studio and is home to a number of experts in the practice, educated in the U.S. and Europe. Despite its size the Ponce Museum is a model of refinement and concern for the island's cultural legacy. The National Library of Puerto Rico, founded by Dr. Ricardo E. Alegría, is housed on the second floor of the historic building occupied by the National Archives. In addition to the somewhat small National Library, and the recently refurbished Carnegie Library in San Juan, there is also the José M. Lázaro Library in the Universidad de Puerto Rico in Río Piedras, the country's best and largest collection of books, documents, journals, maps, photographic and other scholarly materials. With every passing year the collection is augmented and patron services are improved by means of computerization (as well as retaining the traditional card catalogue). Maintaining these superb collections is a daily battle in a sub-tropical climate where humidity and book-eating larvae are a constant concern, making conservation a difficult and costly proposition.

Seeking to incorporate classical music into the "Operation Serenity" festival, Luis Muñoz Marín invited to Puerto Rico the renowned cellist and conductor Pablo Casals, who, although himself a Catalonian, had Puerto Rican roots through his mother. The first festival was held from 22 April to 8 May 1957 at the Universidad de Puerto Rico theater. This festival continues to this day at the modern facilities of the Puerto Rican Fine Arts Center, inaugurated in 1981. Casals's visit in 1956 awakened memories, among musical aficionados and professionals, of Antonio Paoli, the greatest Puerto Rican tenor of the nineteenth century, who, before his death in 1944, expressed the hope that one day Puerto Rico would have a music conservatory. Thanks to the efforts of the great amateur pianist and champion of Puerto Rican culture, Ernesto Ramos Antonini, a Conservatory of Music was established in Puerto Rico, opening its doors on 25 January 1960. The Puerto Rican Symphony Orchestra was created in the surge of interest that accompanied the founding of the Casals Festival and gave its first concert on 6 November 1958. In essence, the orchestra has been nourished by the graduates of the Conservatory. On the popular side Puerto Rican music has reached a position of indisputable prestige with the works of Pedro Flores, Edmundo Disdier, Bobby Capó, Sylvia Rexach, Guillermo Venegas, Johnny Rodríguez, and especially with the contributions made by the musician-poet Rafael Hernández, author of "El Cumbanchero" ["The Souse"], "Cachita," "Capullito de Alelí," as well as hundreds of other compositions known the world over.

In the last thirty years, and more specifically since the middle of the 1970s, Puerto Rican intellectuals have taken up in a more determined manner questions of national identity, the class problem and class consciousness, and the role of the intellectual in the sociopolitical situation of the country. Even the most conservative will agree that Puerto Rican intellectual life can be characterized by the existence of a number of essentially antagonistic, but harmoniously co-existing, social groups. José Luis González (1926–1997) took up this theme in his essay *El país de los cuatro pisos* [1980; *The Four-Storey Country*, 1990] and proposed the following thesis:

Puerto Rico está constituido por una sociedad dividida en clases donde coexisten dos culturas: la cultura de los opresores y la cultura de los oprimidos. Claro está que esas dos culturas,

precisamente porque coexisten, no son compartimientos estancos sino vasos intercomunicantes cuya existencia se caratariza por una constante influencia mutua. La naturaleza dialéctica de esa relación genera habitualmente la impresión de una homogeneidad esencial que en realidad no existe. Tal homogeneidad solo podría darse, en rigor, en una sociedad sin clases (y aún así, solo después de un largo proceso de consolidación). En toda sociedad dividida en clases, la relación real entre las dos culturas es una relación de dominación: la cultura de los opresores es la cultura dominante y la cultura de los oprimidos es la cultura dominada. Y lo que se presenta como cultura nacional, es, naturalmente la cultura dominante. (13)

Puerto Rican society is constituted by a class society in which two cultures can be found to co-exist: the culture of the oppressors and the culture of the oppressed. These two cultures are clearly not water-tight compartments but rather intercommunicating vessels whose mutual influence is constant. The dialectic character of this relation customarily generates the impression of a homogeneous essence that in reality does not exist. Such a homogeneity could, strictly speaking, only be produced in a classless society (and only, thus, after a long process of social consolidation). In every class society, the real relation between the two cultures is one of domination in which the culture of the oppressors dominates that of the oppressed. What in Puerto Rico presents itself as the national culture, is, in fact, the culture of the dominant.

Employing the ingenious metaphor of a four-story house, slowly constructed over time by a number of generations, each having its own points of reference, González has analyzed the formative process of Puerto Rican culture from within a Marxist theoretical framework and has clarified the thorny issue of Puerto Rican cultural and class divisions. Although there is no lack of opposition to his thesis among the Hispanophile elite, his work is a lucid and convincing synthesis of an historical process of cultural formation. According to González the foundation of the first Puerto Rican society was formed by the descendants of the *criollos* and the black slaves who were, he claims, already black Puerto Ricans: "De ahí mi convicción expresada en varias ocasiones para desconcierto e irritación de algunos de que los primeros puertorriqueños fueron en realidad puertorriqueños negros" (21) ("My conviction expressed on various occasions, much to the embarrassment and annoyance of some, is that the first Puerto Ricans were in fact black Puerto Ricans"). This assertion was in no way meant to discount the constitution of the first floor of Puerto Rican society by "campesinado blanco de esos primeros tiempos, o sea los primeros jíbaros, lo cierto es que era un campesinado pobre que se vio obligado a adoptar muchos de los hábitos de vida de los pobres que vivían desde antes en el país, vale decir los esclavos" (21) ("the white peasantry, or the first rustics [*jíbaros*], of colonial times. However, what cannot be denied is that they were an impoverished peasantry obliged to adopt many of the practices of the poor who had lived in the country prior to them, which is to say, the slaves"). One confirmation of González's thesis is the letter sent by Francisco Manuel de Lando to the King of Spain on 2 July 1534, in which de Lando pleads for the favor and liberty of this noble island now so depopulated that Spaniards are hardly to be seen, only blacks. It goes without saying that, in addition to the slaves, there were significant numbers of mulatto and white *criollos* scattered across the mountains and valleys of the island living in an abject and deplorable state of impoverishment (Figueroa I: 293; doc. 574). These peasants and their descendants cannot be excluded from what

González calls the first floor, the highly significant first stage of Puerto Rican cultural formation: "La cultura popular puertorriqueña, de carácter esencialmente afro-antillano nos hizo, durante los tres primeros siglos de nuestra historia pos-colombina, un pueblo caribeño más" (22) ("The essentially Afro-Antillean, Puerto Rican popular culture, made us over the first three centuries of our post-Colombian history a Caribbean people, above all"). The gastronomic traditions are a case in point. What in Puerto Rico is considered peasant food–bananas, vegetables, codfish, rice, and corn flour boiled in salt water (*funche*)–is in fact the cuisine common to the blacks of all the islands and coastal regions of the Caribbean basin. And Puerto Rican whites, like the majority of the whites in the Caribbean, have grown up eating this specially seasoned and spiced food because the cooks of the landowners were all blacks; over five centuries they acclimatized their masters' palates to the cuisine that is now eaten on a daily basis: Creole cooking.

Following the eruption of the revolutionary movement in Venezuela (10 April 1810), many of the Venezuelans loyal to the Spanish Crown–almost the entirety of the economic elite and those dependent upon them–sought refuge in Puerto Rico. The events in Venezuela inspired Puerto Rican separatists, above all in the town of San Germán, but these aspirations proved to be only the chimeric longings of individuals and were not translated into any collective achievement. The antirevolutionary propaganda of the emigrants who had suffered as a result of Bolívar's Independence movement found a welcoming and fertile ground among the pusillanimous royalists of Puerto Rico. The paternalistic ethos undergirding these warnings against revolutionary ideas was a kind of antecedent to the very similar ethos that animated the Cuban exiles who arrived in Puerto Rico in the 1960s. The Spanish exiles, who arrived as a consequence of the Spanish Civil War in the 1930s, were outwardly much more discrete. This wave was almost entirely composed of civil servants, academics, and artists of all kinds, who found a warm welcome and employment–sometimes at the highest levels–at the University of Puerto Rico. What never ceases to astonish is that these formerly republican and socialist Spanish exiles found the U.S. colonial government and its policy of suppressing Puerto Rican Independence to be perfectly acceptable.

The previously mentioned Certificate of 1815 acquired the popular tag "of Privilege" since it provided for a number of exceptions to the general economic regime whose objective was to increase the island's population, commerce, industry, and agriculture. In order to further these aims the Warrant authorized the free immigration of foreigners from all friendly nations irrespective of whether they were white, black, or free mulatto–always and only on the condition of being Catholics. All that was demanded was that they swear an oath of allegiance and loyalty to the reigning laws (see Figueroa I: 153 ff). The lure of economic benefits opened up to Spanish-Americans and Europeans by the Warrant translated into a stampede of immigrants largely from the Spanish colonies of Latin America who were at that time in the throes of various Independence struggles. The first wave of these immigrants was composed of the aforementioned Spanish American conservatives, as well as numerous foreigners–from England, France, the Netherlands, Ireland, the United States, and the Caribbean Antilles in general. Later, in the period up to the middle of the century, the majority of immigrants were Corsicans, Majorcans, and Catalans (see Cifre de Loubriel). The

socio-cultural impact of this immigration on the formation of the second floor of Puerto Rican culture can, following the amply justified analysis of José Luis González, be summarized as follows:

1. Inspired by the possibilities of enriching themselves, Spaniards and foreigners (Corsicans, Majorcans, and Catalans) took full advantage of the merciless colonial laws, not to mention the slavery regime, providing them with a servile and inexpensive labor force. The majority of these immigrants established themselves in the mountainous interior region of the island and dedicated their labor to the cultivation and exploitation of coffee.

2. These new landowners constituted one of the principal props of the Spanish colonial regime in Puerto Rico. Theirs was an aristocratic and foreign culture; the Mayorcan landowners spoke among themselves in Mayorcan and only used Spanish to make themselves understood by their Puerto Rican peasants.

3. The Puerto Rican poor always considered these immigrants to be foreigners; the Corsicans were still, at the end of the nineteenth century, considered to be French.

4. In their home country, many of the Mayorcans were considered to be Chuetas-Mayorcan, the descendants of converted Jews (González 23–24).

In light of these findings, González poses the question: "what social disposition or attitude can explain how it was that a minority, discriminated against in their place of origin, became in a very short space of time, and thanks to immigration, a privileged minority in their adopted country?" Further, we may well ask, how it was that the formerly persecuted became relentless exploiters of the Puerto Rican peasantry? At the end of the century the consequences of this maltreatment would surface in the contempt and hatred that the peasantry manifested toward the immigrants. According to González, "this hatred can explain, among other things, the marauding bands that attacked the haciendas of the highlands in 1898 (following the U.S. invasion)" (24). With that U.S. invasion of 25 July 1898, the third floor of the Puerto Rican cultural house began to take shape on top of the troubled foundations of the second floor. Following the U.S. occupation, the slow impoverishment of the Spanish and foreign landowners began, since they no longer had easy access to the U.S. market; their sons found that the only means of salvaging their social prestige and power was to dominate the lucrative university professions. It cannot be denied that, from their positions of academic and professional prestige, many descendants of the old impoverished landowners then made their way into political and public life in the new civil regime. It must be admitted that, somewhat naively, the Puerto Rican masses placed their hopes in the promises of justice and progress that the new U.S. regime and its local supporters broadcast among the afflicted. It is precisely for these reasons that José Luis González has stressed that what goes by the name of official Puerto Rican culture is nothing more than the foreign-looking culture of the privileged Spaniards and foreigners, who established their power base in Puerto Rico after a long historical process and above all in the last third of the nineteenth century.

Although Puerto Rican popular culture was never recognized by these elites, the cultural manifestations of the poor did not suffer a deterioration during the U.S. colonial regime, but rather a development. However uneven and troubled by vicissitudes, this development was, nonetheless, progressive (González 29). The ascension of cultural popularism in Puerto

Rico can be explained up to a point by the progressive dismantling effect that the transformations operative in society had on elite culture. More than an Americanization of society, the U.S. colonial regime effected an internal reversal of Puerto Rican cultural values. The void created by the breakdown of the culture of those at the top was not filled by an imposition or intrusion of U.S. culture, but rather by the ever more palpable ascension of the Puerto Rican culture that arose below (González 29).

The affirmations of González notwithstanding, it appears that Puerto Rican writers and intellectuals, above all the youngest in these groups, are in the habit of confusing and accepting as absolute synonyms the populist and lumpen elements. The reason for this is possibly the fact that many young writers and intellectuals have come from the economic or professional elites and thus have no intrinsic knowledge of the masses. On the other hand, those who have come out of the popular classes and risen up the social ladder tend to embrace a somewhat mythic vision of the culture of their roots, assigning to it attributes it does not possess.

According to González the fourth story began to appear in the 1940s and was the product of the belated rooting of U.S. capitalism in Puerto Rican society and the rise of opportunistic Puerto Rican populism. By the 1980s the fourth story had begun to fracture as a result of the collapse of the so-called Free Associate State (González 38). In fact, the supposed economic development promoted by the U.S. colonial regime merely aspired to create a society of consumption that would forget or withdraw itself from the traditional values that were characteristic of the patriarchal agricultural society. Stuck in a kind of cul-de-sac, Puerto Ricans are still struggling to come to terms with the colonial status of Puerto Rico: the last and oldest colony remaining in Latin America at the end of the twentieth century. The future is as unpredictable as it is uncertain. Collective confusion is becoming ever-more refined and the new intellectuals offer little in the way of substance.

Many of the younger generation of Puerto Rican intellectuals and writers, as well as Puerto Rican artists in general, have received their intellectual formation in U.S. universities; and it is undeniable that the influence of "the American way of life" as well as "American comfort" have come to form part of the stock of values and ideals of the new professional and creative classes in Puerto Rico. One obvious example of this can be seen in the manifesto of a group of professors and writers at the Universidad de Puerto Rico in Río Piedras that appeared in the monthly Diálogo in February 1997 (30–31). Entitled "Statehood from a Radical Democratic Perspective: Proposals for Discussion amongst all Puerto Ricans," the manifesto was signed by various Puerto Rican professors and writers working in both the United States and Puerto Rico. Acknowledging the liberal democracy and the plurality of races and cultures in the United States, the authors of the manifesto argue in favor of a liberalization of the rigid (and colonial in character) structures of Puerto Rican society. Dedicating themselves to fighting for Puerto Rican state status within the U.S. federation, the authors see annexation as a means of acquiring representation in the U.S. Congress and, from there, effecting social justice in Puerto Rico. In recent years our Spanish American traditions have begun to come apart at the seams, and the U.S. way of life has come to seem more and more as the only ideal way of life. However, the progressive disruption of the island's most time-honored cultural and spiritual values by U.S. economic temptations notwithstanding, Puerto Rico and its people are still a Spanish American nation: its writers, artists, intellectuals, troubadours, and poets all continue to sing and speak in the language of Cervantes.

If we reflect that Puerto Rico is the smallest of the Greater Antilles with limited natural resources, and has always been a colonial territory (first of Spain and later of the United States), then we ought not to be surprised when faced by the iron will of a people who, irrespective of political preference, continues to feel solidarity with and to be related to the greater Spanish American culture. Many Hispanophile purists among its neighbors have made acerbic critiques of the dialectal and phonetic variants of its Spanish without being completely informed about its political-cultural process. However, the Puerto Rican vernacular demonstrates no significant differences from that of the other Spanish-speaking peoples: The great quantity of Puerto Rican literary works published here and abroad confirms this. Puerto Ricans are a people with peculiarities all their own, but they also form an important part of the cultural choir of Spanish America. Puerto Rico's greatest resource is its people. As far back as the middle of the seventeenth century, Puerto Rican musicians were making their way to Santo Domingo and Cuba to fill the needs of the neighboring islands, a practice that continued right up until the final years of the nineteenth century. Similarly, from the end of the eighteenth to the beginning of the nineteenth century, the studio of the master painter José Campeche furnished every sort of religious painting that was required for worship or religious ornamentation for the entire Caribbean from Venezuela to Santo Domingo and Cuba. The cultural isolationism in which the Caribbean is submerged today—despite the multiple factors of ethnicity, culture, and history that unite the nations—is not of their making: It is, rather, a product of economic forces and political interests indifferent to their singularity.

Translation by Colman Hogan

Works Cited

Alegría, Ricardo E. 1948. "La población aborigen antillana y su relación con otras áreas de América." *Tercer Congreso Histórico Municipal Interamericano: Actas y Documentos*. San Juan: [n.p.]. 233–246.

——. 1969. *Descubrimiento, conquista y colonización de Puerto Rico 1493–1599*. San Juan, P.R.: Colección de Estudios Puertorriqueños.

Alonso Pacheco, Manuel. [n.d.] *El gíbaro* (1493–1599). Río Piedras, P.R.: Editorial Cultural.

Arrillaga, María. 1998. *Concierto de voces insurgentes: Tres autoras puertorriqueñas*. Río Piedras, Universidad de Puerto Rico: Isla Negra.

Blanco, Tomás. 1970. *Prontuario histórico de Puerto Rico*. San Juan, P.R.: Instituto de Cultura Puertorriqueña.

Brau y Asencio, Salvador. 1971. *Historia de Puerto Rico*. San Juan, P.R.: Ediciones Porta Coeli.

——. 1972. *Puerto Rico y su historia*. San Juan, P.R.: Editorial IV Centenario.

Callejo, Fernando. 1971. *Música y músicos puertorriqueños*. San Juan, P.R.: Editorial Coquí.

Caro Costas, Aida. 1971. *Antología de lecturas de historia de Puerto Rico*. San Juan, P.R.: A.R. Caro Costas.

Casas, Bartolomé de las. 1989. *Brevísima relación de la destrucción de África: preludio de la destrucción de Indias: primera defensa de los guanches y negros contra su esclavización*. Salamanca: Viceconsejería de Cultura y Deportes del Gobierno de Canarias; Editorial San Esteban.

Cifre de Loubriel, Estela. 1964. *La inmigración a Puerto Rico durante el siglo XIX.* San Juan, P.R.: I.C.P.R.

Coll y Toste, Cayetano. 1970. *Historia de la instrucción pública en Puerto Rico hasta el año de 1898.* Bilbao: Editorial Vasco Americano.

Diego Padró, José Isaac de. 1973. "Antillanismo, criollismo, negroidismo." *Luis Palés Matos y su trasmundo poético.* Río Piedras, P.R.: Ediciones Puerto. 93–97.

Fernández de Oviedo, Gonzalo. 1851–1855 [1535 and 1537]. *Historia general y natural de las Indias, islas y tierra-firme del mar Océano.* Ed. J. Amador de los Ríos. 4 vols. Madrid: Imprenta de la Real Academia de la Historia.

Figueroa, Loida. 1979. *Breve historia de Puerto Rico.* 2 vols. Río Piedras, P.R.: Edil.

González, José Luis. 1980. *El país de cuatro pisos y otros ensayos.* Río Piedras, P.R.: Huracán.

Hostos, Adolfo de. 1976. *Diccionario histórico bibliográfico comentado de Puerto Rico.* San Juan, P.R.: Academia Puertorriqueña de la Historia.

Menéndez y Pelayo, Marcelino. 1948. "Puerto Rico." *Historia de la poesía hispanoamericana.* Vol. 1. Madrid: Consejo Superior de Investigaciones Científicas. 325–46.

Morales Carrión, Arturo. 1995. *Puerto Rico y la lucha por la hegemonía en el Caribe.* Río Piedras: Universidad de Puerto Rico.

O'Reilly, Alejandro. 1972. "Memoria sobre la isla de Puerto Rico, 1765." *Antología.* Ed. Aida Caro Costas. 385–96.

Picó, Rafael. 1976. *Geografía: geografía de Puerto Rico.* Vol. 15. *La gran enciclopedia de Puerto Rico.* Ed. Vicente Báez. Madrid: Editorial Orbe.

Rivera de Alvarez, Josefina. 1969. *Historia de la literatura puertorriqueña.* Vol 1. San Juan, P.R.: Departamento de Instrucción Pública.

Rosa-Nieves, Cesáreo, 1948. *Francisco de Ayerra y Santa María: poeta puertorriqueño 1630–1708.* Río Piedras, P.R.: Editorial Universitaria.

Rouse, Irving. "Mesoamérica and the Eastern Caribbean Area." *Handbook of the Middle American Indians.* Vol. 4. Austin: University of Texas Press. 234–42

Tanodi, Aurelio. 1971. *Documentos de la Real Hacienda de Puerto Rico: 1510–1519.* Vol. 1. Río Piedras: Universidad de Puerto Rico.

Tapia y Rivera, Alejando. 1970. *Obras completas.* 3 vols. San Juan, P.R.: Instituto de Cultura Puertorriqueña.

Torres Vargas, Diego de. 1971. "Descripción de la Isla y Ciudad de Puerto Rico... 1647." *Antología.* Ed. Aida Caro. 251–89.

Veloz Maggiolo, Marcio. 1972. *Arqueología prehistórica de Santo Domingo.* Singapore: McGraw-Hill Far Eastern Publishers.

Zamora Munné, Juan Clemente. 1976. *Indigenismos en la lengua de los conquistadores.* Río Piedras: Universidad de Puerto Rico.

Zavala, Iris. 1977. "Puerto Rico, siglo XIX: literatura y sociedad." *Sin Nombre.* I: 7.4 ; II: 8.1 (San Juan, P.R): 7–26; 1–19.

ANDEAN REGION
INTRODUCTION
Consuelo Triviño Anzola

The Andean region, formerly dominated by the Inca Empire with its capital at Cuzco, today comprises Peru, Bolivia, and Ecuador, as well as large parts of Colombia, Argentina, and Venezuela, the nations grouped around the Andes mountain chain. Although the arrival of the Spanish devastated the native cultures of the region, it also unified, under the Spanish language, peoples who had little knowledge of each other's existence. Despite the cultural destruction accomplished by the colonizers, many of the region's traditions have survived, as can be seen in the conservation of native communities and languages, as well as in the importance of Quechua and Aymara in countries such as Ecuador, Peru, and Bolivia. From the perspective of developed nations, the Andean region has been seen as archaic, only with great difficulty adapting itself to the transformations of the Western world. This notion has been fueled by the backwardness of the region's cities as compared with Buenos Aires or Havana, the most cosmopolitan cities of Latin America at the beginning of the twentieth century. What is certain, however, as Ángel Rama (1926–1983) pointed out in his *Transculturación narrativa en América Latina* [1982; Narrative Transculturation in Latin America], is that the culture of the Andean region has developed a dual society, simultaneously anchored to the Spanish values imposed by the conquest and to those of the indigenous cultures, hidden behind innumerable masks, under which the various republics were established. It is precisely in this indigenous heritage that the specificity and particular accent of this culture is to be found.

The culture of the Andean region has been characterized by tremendous wealth, diversity, and complexity–far exceeding the standards of progress against which it is judged. The high and popular arts, literature, cinema, painting, and music of the region, weaving together various times and traditions, all attest to this fact. One has only to consider a paradigmatic figure such as César Vallejo (1892–1938), who in the early decades of the twentieth century was a leader of the Latin American avant-garde, to realize the astonishing renovation of the Spanish poetic idiom that has been carried out, continuing the tradition of radical innovation began by *modernistas* such as Rubén Darío (1867–1916). A similar story could be told in the visual arts, where, among the many who could be mentioned, such a figure as Osvaldo Guayasamín brought about the incorporation of emotion and protest into a body of work that has deeply influenced several generations of painters. Perhaps the most distinguishing features of Andean culture are its troubled miscegenation, its elitism, and its centuries-old centralism. It is for these reasons that it is necessary to approach its development from the point of view of its cities: hence the work of Victoria Peralta (Chapter 40); Elizabeth Monasterios (Chapter 42); Regina Harrison (Chapter 41); Sara Castro-Klaren (Chapter 39); and Alexis Márquez Rodríguez (Chapter 38). Each of these chapters, while making the above-mentioned aspects explicit, has also sought to illustrate the wealth and variety of the region's popular culture. And while painting a picture of a rich tradition that has survived through the centuries, each of these writers has refrained from laying down norms, since the official culture of these countries has traditionally been the exclusive preserve of their respective elites, who have attempted to uphold a false image of their histories and national realities. In short, the *criollo* bourgeoisies of these countries have accomplished nothing but the reproduction of the old colonial relations, both in their attitude to the popular classes–whom they have excluded from participation in social processes– and in relation to the European models to which they have demonstrated a timid and distressing submission.

In a nutshell this is the situation in the countries of the Andean region, although there are nuances of difference. Since the nineteenth century, various sectors of the national bourgeoisies have been locked in confrontation over the issue of whether society ought to adhere to Hispanic values–traditionalism, Catholicism, conservatis–or whether, out of sympathy for democratic principles, it ought to adopt the ideas of progress disseminated largely from England and France. Clearly influenced by the French Revolution, the Independence struggles of the Andean nations also gave rise to a change in the colonial mentality and an opening up of intellectual horizons to French ideas and culture. The principal achievement of these struggles was the overthrow of the Spanish monarchy's hold on Latin America and the disappearance of many of its institutions. While this period also witnessed the mobilization of significant groups of women and natives, as well as a break in the isolation of a number of regions, the cultural reference points of the epoch continued to be European–although it must be stated that a number of remote regions, abandoned by the powers that be, did manage to preserve their pre-Columbian traditions.

The Andean Cities

Today, by contrast, the posture of submission adopted by the national oligarchies of the region is in relation to the United States, whose lifestyle these oligarchies have adopted and imposed. As in the past, the privileged minorities of today continue to educate and define themselves by turning their backs on the plurality and diversity of their own cultures. In this manner they reproduce the colonial relations of yesterday, both feeding their contempt for what is particularly theirs and yearning for the idealized space that late nineteenth-century intellectuals hankered after, which is to say, that of modern Europe, and, increasingly today, that of the U.S. imperium. While proclaimed by some and deplored by others, none, it appears, can free themselves from the prerogatives of this space. The U.S. way of life has filtered into these countries by means of the mass communications media and has been incorporated into local images of the world to such an extent that it is no longer possible to speak of the autochthonous in the strict sense of the term.

Cultural elitism, with its consequent exclusion of large sectors of society, is a characteristic common to all the Andean region urban centers; it is from these centers that the political, economic, and pedagogical policies constituting the norms of life are laid down. This situation remained practically unchanged until the beginning of the twentieth century, when—influenced by modern currents of thought—the concept of nationalism rose to prominence. In 1928, in his *Siete ensayos de interpretación de la realidad peruana* [Seven Interpretative Essays of Peruvian Reality], José Carlos Mariátegui (1894–1930) explicated the Peruvian political condition from a Marxist point of view, identifying Peru's backwardness, its unjust treatment of the natives, and its centralism as the principal social evils to be addressed. Later, the generation that rose to maturity in the 1950s, influenced by the triumph of the Cuban Revolution in 1959, devoted itself to the task of social change in Latin America. It was this period that consolidated the figure of the committed intellectual whose integrity was measured by his or her adhesion to or rejection of the Revolution. This attitude expressed itself in a literature that called attention to social injustices and sought, through social commitment, an amelioration of the social conditions of the lower classes. A generation of writers, certain of their obligation to put their art in the service of the revolution, dedicated themselves to this task. These were the years of the "boom," during which Latin American literature reached its apogee of international recognition (with Julio Cortázar, Mario Vargas Llosa, Manuel Scorza, and Gabriel García Márquez, among others). This zenith of literary creation coincided with an increase in the activity of Leftist political groups and of armed organizations of a Marxist-Leninist or Maoist tendency.

And, in fact, following the social agitation of these groups (in many cases crushed by *coups d'état* and dictatorships), a tentative social opening began to be felt in the 1970s and 1980s. Access to university education began to include wide sectors of the middle classes; there was a noticeable increase in the enrollment of women (which had been previously almost nonexistent), and, most importantly, anthropologists and ethnologists began to take an interest in the indigenous communities and the marginalized urban classes, among whom they rediscovered a wealth and variety of traditions that had been forgotten. Already in the 1950s, José María Arguedas (1911–1969) had lived among the peasants and natives of the Mantaro Valley; from that experience he was able to demonstrate the persistence of colonial elements and "Quechua-colonial" values in the community, circumstances he used to explain their backwardness in his *Formación de una cultura nacional indoamericana* [1975; The Formation of a Native American National Culture].

The relative opening of society in the 1970s and 1980s in the countries of the Andean region was also manifest in the cultural demands of the masses for cinema, theater, radio, and television, as well as in the rising rates of literacy. Without this growing number of readers, phenomena such as the development of the publishing industry in Colombia (whose annual Book Fair is today one of the most important cultural events in Latin America) could hardly be explained. In order to foster the promotion and development of culture, cultural centers, museums, theaters, and publishing houses were created and traditional institutions were renovated. In Ecuador, for example, a "Cultural Front" (1965–1969) was created, bringing together intellectuals and workers. In Bolivia, on the other hand, a generation of Aymara leaders rose to the fore, who, from the late 1970s, reopened the question of a peasant union movement, something previously in the hands of the government. As Elizabeth Monasterios has noted, these organizations located in La Paz have created cultural centers such as the Centro Campesino Túpac Katari (1971) for the diffusion of Aymara culture. Despite these institutional innovations, however, much still remains to be done to overcome the entrenched elitism of Andean culture, since this cultural opening has not been accompanied by a change in attitude on the part of the elites toward the tradition; nor has there been a revision of their values.

Nevertheless, certain sectors of the population have established a consciousness of themselves as social actors, and this can be seen, for example, in the increasing numbers of oral storytellers who recount their lives and invoke parody, perhaps to an even greater degree, in the theater, cinema, and poetry. The cinema has criticized the violence exercised by society, in particular against children. Films like Víctor Manuel Gaviria's (b. 1955) *Rodrigo D.* (1989) and *La Vendedora de rosas* [1998; The Flower Girl] take us on a tour of the marginalized zones of the city of Medellín, inquiring as they go into the causes of violence and injustice—not from the point of view of political discourses, but rather from a poetic perspective; they thus portray a world of marginalization, pain, and tenderness that, in all essentials, is the common lot of many a Latin American city.

The majority of the inhabitants of the Andean region, almost 70 percent, are concentrated in the region's capital cities, which on average number between three and seven million inhabitants. This high rate of urban concentration has created a high level of social conflict: unemployment, misery, delinquency, child abandonment, an absence of the basic services that would contribute to the dignity of life, and a lack of incentives for the impoverished masses. Nevertheless, in this motley human canvas there does exist an infinite number of possible expressions and novel strategies of life. The capital cities of the region were established on an urban plan, based on the traditional Spanish checkerboard, that continues to this day: Quito in 1534; Lima in 1535; Bogotá in 1538; La Paz in 1548; and Caracas in 1567. The church, the government, and the army established their headquarters around a central "Plaza de armas" (central square); later viceroys, governors, presidents, courts, judges, priests, and much later universities and the tribunals of the Inquisition would follow suit, flushing out the apparatus of the hierarchical order that—from these centers—would impose the ruling principles of the Colonial society. This urban character of the Andean region reduced the outlying districts to the status of purveyors of raw materials for the provision of the capitals. Within this colonial order, the top of the social pyramid was occupied by Spaniards appointed directly by the mother country; next in line were the sons of the Spaniards born in America, followed by the *mestizos*, and finally the natives—a caste system of privileges relegating the natives to the periphery and the lowest rung on the ladder. So constituted, these cities imposed on the majority of the population a model of life alien to the sensibilities and needs of the mass of natives and peasants. All these factors had serious consequences that would hinder the consolidation of democratic governments, foster dictatorships and violence, and increase the dependence of these countries on the multinational corporations. The situation is now so far advanced that solutions to the poverty and marginalization of the greater part of the population are difficult even to imagine.

What in the Andean nations, and in all Latin America in general, is called *culture* traces its origins to what Ángel Rama has aptly called the *ciudad letrada* (lettered city), the organism that both developed and nourished itself by a simultaneous subjugation of the indigenous population and submission to European models. Although Independence brought about a rupture with the mother country, most of the colonial institutions remained intact. The founding fathers of Independence–Bolívar, Bello, and Martí–were not immune to these attitudes. In their writings they emphasized not only the importance of creating original models of governance adapted to the character of the peoples of the Americas, but also the necessity of liberating themselves from European cultural dependence. That said, however, they accepted the economic notion that Europe ought to be the destination of Latin American raw materials, since such exportations were, they thought, the only imaginable means of becoming part of the greater world, which for them meant the world established by the European powers.

As Ángel Rama pointed out in *La ciudad letrada* [1984; *The Lettered City*], the institution of writing, the composition of documents, and the presence of a corps of scribes who would bear witness to the authentication and execution of these orders was the sine qua non, legitimating the establishment of the Latin American cities. In this way the city and writing were mutually implicated from the very beginning in the consolidation of the colonial order. Alphabetic writing, thus, replaced the system of knotted strings for the recording of information (*quipu*) employed by the Incas for the administration of their empire. By virtue of its multiple functions, alphabetic writing achieved an enormous power: On the one hand, it transmitted the word of God in sacred texts; on the other, it gave testimony of what was done and to be done in His name. The composition of chronicles, one of the first manifestations of literacy in the Americas, was closely connected to the urgency of legitimating an undertaking that had given rise to numerous allegations of impropriety. Examples of the power of writing were the infamous *requerimientos*, documents by means of which the conquistadors formally took possession of the conquered lands, and proclaimed the protection or the subjugation of their new vassals.

Although the urban model of colonial life favored the institution of a caste system, the elites of the first generation of *mestizos* were, nonetheless, to play a decisive role in Andean society. The new society was erected on the basis of contempt for native cultures and an ignorance of its contributions. There were, however, exceptions, as was the case with El Inca Garcilaso de la Vega (1539–1616), who managed to integrate the two traditions in his own fashion. As José Miguel Oviedo (b. 1934) has proposed in his book, *Historia de la literatura hispanoamericana* [1995; History of Spanish-American Literature], El Inca Garcilaso de la Vega, both in his personality and in his works, constituted the clearest expression of the *mestizo* and *criollo* dilemma in that epoch. A child of the Renaissance, El Inca Garcilaso de la Vega was a humanist who attempted to represent poetically the most authentic historical truths and synthesize the Spanish and Inca cultures.

Mestizaje

As is well known, the conquistadors were unaccompanied by women, and as a result a *mestizo* population rapidly developed that, by 1570, constituted a significant fraction of the population. According to Angel Rosenblat (1902–1984), the *mestizo* population of the Viceroyalty of Peru, for example, numbered 100,000, compared with 38,000 whites and 1.5 to 2 million natives. However, the status of the *mestizos* was not uniformly the same and depended upon the circumstances of their birth, which is to say, whether they were recognized as legitimate children by their fathers, whether they remained in the fathers' households, and whether they received a Spanish education. One's belonging to a social group was subordinated, in the majority of cases, to one's racial origin, and this policy favored or restricted one's chances of social mobility. With the arrival of the slaves, Andean society was infused with another set of cultural elements. Africans were relegated to the very bottom of the social hierarchy, and the cultural inequality that maintained the separation of the Spaniards, the *mestizos*, the natives, and the blacks was established on the basis of the segregation of the education system, a situation that persisted until the nineteenth century. By similar means was Andean centralism established, and this has been historically one of the major obstacles to the economic development of the outlying regions.

The values of colonial society remained almost unaltered in the Andean cities until the early part of the twentieth century, not only because of the isolation and climatic conditions (cold, dampness, and high levels of precipitation) of these cities, but also because the economic models they adopted encouraged despotism (*cacicazgo*) and the consequent exploitation of the illiterate peasantry. By contrast, cities such as Buenos Aires, Havana, and even Barranquilla, by virtue of their commerce with Europe since colonial times, underwent a modification of their characters and characteristics. For with the trade in goods came books and new ideas, and these latter were to make the aforementioned cities the most cosmopolitan in the New World. After 1810, the independence movement spread like wildfire throughout the entire Spanish empire in the Americas. It has been documented that the ideological roots of emancipation were in the ideas of the Enlightenment and quite specifically the Declaration of the Rights of Man promulgated by the French Revolution. The Revolution had an immediate impact on the Caribbean islands, especially those that were French possessions, from which revolutionary zeal spread to other islands and, eventually, to the mainland. Because of its geographic location at the northern tip of South America and its close proximity to the Caribbean islands, Caracas became the principal port of entry of these ideas into South America and, as such, the center of the struggle for independence in South America. Simón Bolívar was, of course, a Caracan patriot.

Difficult-to-reach cities such as Bogotá, Quito, and La Paz, on the other hand, tended to remain permanently closed to the influences of cultural modernity. In Bogotá linguistic purism was the norm, imposed by the Hispanicized intellectual elite, whose monopoly on literary expression was their principal form of cultural activity. Literary creation was in the hands of a small minority of literate whites, who turned a deaf ear to every other form of cultural expression or to those coming from the peripheral regions of the country, such as Barranquilla, as happened in the beginning of the twentieth century. The fact that the concept of culture was firmly in the hands of a white, masculine elite and never extended to include natives, blacks, *mestizos*, or women–these groups representing, thus, "the other"–does not mean that these groups did not create or develop a culture. In fact, in times past, the natives, often aided by missionaries, recounted their history in their oral tradition and in theatrical performances. These pre-Hispanic theatrical forms have survived over the centuries. The most popular were short, satirical pieces representing the virtues and vices and local characters in both makeshift (*corrales*) and established theaters. The most famous actress in Peruvian colonial times was Micaela Villegas, known as La Perricholi, whose seductive dances won the attention of the Viceroy Manuel de Amat y Juniet

Satire was one of the most popular cultural forms in colonial society. Outside of the canonical literary models, and in a climate of oppression and repression, it is hardly surprising to find a wealth of satiric verse, in many cases anonymous. There was at the same time a significant development in painting that dates from the arrival of Íñigo de Loyola in Cuzco in 1545. Commissioned to fill the churches of the Viceroyalty with religious imagery, Loyola was also responsible for training a cadre of *mestizo* and native artists of talent in the European painting traditions. According to Elizabeth Monasterios, the existence of pre-Hispanic iconography in the works of this school–anthropomorphic creatures with rams' horns and hares' lips, "puma men," and so on–rather than being cultural expressions tolerated by the hegemonic class, were the result of specific theological strategies on the part of the religious orders for dealing with the problem of idolatry. She has further pointed out that the processes of transculturation, understood as a recuperation of values that had been submerged, traditionally rose to prominence in the consciousness of individual dissidents among the intellectual elites.

The opulence that came to characterize the *criollo* aristocracy was based upon the great wealth that was generated in the Americas by means of native and slave labor. Although this wealth, as is well known, filled the coffers of the Spanish crown, it also benefited land owners, merchants, and the literate *criollos* in general. In order to forestall the possibility of native insurrections, a program of mass ideological indoctrination was designed, employing the splendors of the baroque festival, representations of religious scenes, and an evangelizing propaganda in which the theater of New Spain played a decisive role. The urban literate class not only served the interests of the hegemonic powers but also created cultural models that were fundamental to the ideological cohesion of the dominant group. Festivals and celebrations, for example, were seen by the Spanish authorities as the most efficient means of binding the masses to their rule and of demonstrating the authorities' power over them, thus affirming and preserving it. In order to impart the image of power and glory, these ceremonies were celebrated with great pomp and ostentation. Lima, in particular, was a great center of concentration of this sort of Spanish political and cultural power and also for its diffusion in the rural areas of the empire.

It should come as no surprise that apart from economic realities, one of the most serious problems in the Andean region would be the inability of those stewarding the creation of national identities to face up to one of the principal constituents of their societies: the indigenous heritage. This problem is somewhat varied across the region, depending upon the level of miscegenation, which is higher in Colombia, and lower in Peru, Ecuador, and Bolivia, where the majority of the population is indigenous. The high level of intermarriage notwithstanding, Colombia has never accepted the native element within its social body or in its literature, the almost exclusive exceptions being José Eustasio Rivera (1888–1928), who somewhat superficially took up the theme of the native in his 1924 novel *La vorágine* [*The Vortex*, 1935], and later Eduardo Zalamea (1905–1963) in his 1934 work, *Cuatro años a bordo de mí mismo* [Four Years On Board Myself]. Nor was the theme of the native a preoccupation of the intellectuals in Colombia, although it has been addressed in Peru since the nineteenth century in the narratives of Clorinda Matto de Turner (1852–1909) and in the essays of Manuel González Prada (1844–1918), and in Bolivia in the 1919 novel by Alcides Arguedas (1879–1946), *Raza de Bronce* [Men of Bronze]. In the last two decades, however, Colombian native leaders have made some progress in opening up a space for their communities in society, which has led to some degree of awareness of their problems, or at the least of their existence within the social body.

The patent fact is that those stewarding the creation of national identities essentially consider themselves to be the children of the Spanish and feel not the slightest identification with the American natives who, they feel, either do not exist or are seen as an obstacle to progress, when they are not treated as slaves. The struggle that resulted from this incoherence can be traced in the current of thought that we call nativism (*indigenismo*). The theme of the native has been approached from various points of view and surfaces in accounts that pose the problem of the other. In the middle of the nineteenth century, a narrative subgenre idealizing the natives began to develop. These idealizations were intimately linked to the Romantic vision of the Americas put forth by authors like Chateaubriand, whose novel *Atala* was widely read and discussed in both Europe and the Americas. As a result of these intellectual currents, Latin American intellectuals began to question the unjust treatment of the natives, in many cases adopting anti-oligarchic and anti-Hispanic postures; such was the case with Manuel González Prada, whose provocative thesis of the "true Peru" of the natives was enunciated in 1888. Some of the positions adopted were clearly based upon positive stereotypes of race and of the power of natural forces over the human being. It goes without saying that in such cases the voice of the natives was neither heard nor understood, since raising the question of the condition of the natives also necessitated an ethical stance: that of attempting to enter their mentality and see the world from their point of view.

The Liberal urban oligarchy's domination of the popular classes during the era of state formation was the *criollo* version of the same process initiated during the Conquest, although it was cloaked in a modernizing discourse imitative of the European models they sought to implant in the countryside from the vantage point of the cities. However, not all intellectuals shared these views. Some essayists and thinkers–turning their attention to the natives–attempted to limn their features, as it were, from within. In this sense José María Arguedas' novel, *Los ríos profundos* [1958; *Deep Rivers*] was an undeniable achievement and the most sincere and moving expression of the native vision of the world, sensibility, relation to nature, and poetic sense of existence. Indigenous cultural expressions have been recovered from the oral tradition and collective memory where they were kept alive. Although it has been part of the hegemonic culture and clearly has a great life span, written culture has not been the only or principal means of combating oblivion and silence. The Andean region had a wide array of cultural practices. Quechua literature, for example, has produced a number of beautiful compositions, such as the love story *Manchay Puitu*, of which there exists two versions—one collected in Ricardo Palma's (1833–1919) *Tradiciones peruanas* [1872; Peruvian Traditions] and the other compiled by Jesús Lara (1898–1980) from numerous accounts in the *mestizo* and native villages of rural Bolivia and published for the first time in 1922. As discussions elsewhere in this volume explore, the poem clearly demonstrates a distinctly different attitude towards death and the sacred and cannot be judged on the basis of the parameters of Western culture.

Racism remains a largely unresolved social problem of some consequence. The violence and the acts of barbarism continue to be repeated in the racially motivated confrontations between social sectors. The arts have given expression to the suffering and the dislocations that result from social processes, such as the murder of natives, the exodus of peasants deprived of their lands, and the misery of the urban poor. Intellectuals alien to these cultures have not always been conscious of the ideological implications of the solutions they have proposed to the problems created by miscegenation, and in many cases their solutions worked more to the benefit of the national bourgeoisies than to that of the *mestizos*. The challenge of the next millennium will be, perhaps, to allow the natives to express themselves, as a Brazilian Desâna, Umusî Pãrõkumu, did in *Antes o mundo não existia* [Before the World Did Not Exist], an extraordinary testimony of origins that Ángel Rama considered a literary work of the "mythic genre."

The Native and Indianism

Indianism is one of the paradigms that runs through the Latin American cultural system since the days when El Inca Garcilaso de la Vega synthesized the two traditions of Renaissance humanism and that of the dualism manifest in the Inca organization of tribal communities [*ayllus*]. For some intellectuals, the native problem will be resolved only when the native disappears, integrated into the Western, capitalist world; for others, this resolution would only be possible by means of a thorough agrarian reform—one that has never been realized in the countries in question; for still others, much more extremist, the solution can only be on condition of a return to the *ayllu* communal system. Contrary to what happened in Europe, the cities of Latin America did not arise out of a process of the expansion and development of the rural economic system, which necessitated a center for the exchange of goods and commerce. Rather, it was from the Latin American cities themselves that the command for agricultural development arose, first, with the production of sugar and, later, of services, in order to provide for the maintenance and sustenance of the urban centers. These centers remained isolated in empty areas, separated from each other by vast inaccessible spaces; the supremacy of the cities over the conquered territories surrounding them was an emblem of the triumph of civilization over barbarism. This conception of the city as a focus of civilization prevailed until the time of Sarmiento, and

even up to the days of Gallegos, since the city was seen as the unique manifestation of European ideas that lay at the root of this conception and by which it was understood.

Centralism was one the themes touched on by Mariátegui when, in his *Siete ensayos de interpretación de la realidad peruana* [1928; *Seven Interpretative Essays of Peruvian Reality*], he advocated the urgent "reclamation of Peru by the Peruvians" ("peruanizar el Perú"). According to Mariátegui, the only way to guarantee the natives a life of dignity—health, housing, and education—was to incorporate them into the nation's economic processes, a project that passed for a policy of economic and political decentralization in Peru. However, in the 1980s the Neo-Liberal economic model began to be imposed, further exacerbating the enormous gulf between the rich and the poor. In Bolivia this model was introduced in 1979, after fifteen years of coups d'état and a military dictatorship; in Peru it was imposed under a dictatorial regime that legitimated its power by means of its war against the Sendero Luminoso; in Colombia it was imposed in the midst of a longrunning social confrontation that, while it had claimed thousands of lives, was no impediment to the exploitation of Colombian riches by multinational corporations. In this manner the peripheral regions of the Andean nations entered the world of globalization, despite the fact that such regions had been, for their centralist governments, previously nonexistent. The processes of modernization have sacrificed innumerable peasants and natives, evicted from their lands and condemned to a life of misery in the cities. This phenomenon happened once before, in the 1920s and 1930s, when foreign companies assumed control of the exploitation of the region's natural resources, leveling the jungle to establish rubber plantations, laying down absurd railways (with the sole aim of transporting mineral ores) and boring into the earth in search of petroleum. Literature has registered the violent impact of modernization in novels such as *La vorágine* [*The Vortex*] by José Eustasio Rivera and *Toá* and *Mancha de aceite* [1935; Oil Stain] by César Uribe Piedrahíta (1897–1951).

This is not to say that traditions have been totally annihilated: They survive in popular festivals and celebrations, whether Christian or pagan, in music, painting, the arts, and in the rituals and dances of the indigenous communities. During these times, the popular classes have created another culture that can be seen or heard, for example, in certain musical compositions, whose contrast with the official culture is clearly accented. Such compositions have successfully and forcefully expressed the popular classes' deepest sentiments of bitterness and humiliation. Translated into the terms of an amorous despair, such popular artists pour all their rage into a language that seeks either to wound, as in the *carrilera* or *guasca* musical forms of the Colombian highlands—"Si no me quieres te corto la cara. . ." ("If you say you don't love me I'll slash your face. . .")—or to move emotionally—". . . soy triste lamento, Yo soy basurita, que empuja el viento" (". . . I'm a mournful sob, a little piece of litter blowing in the wind").

If we accept that culture is the means by which individuals in society affirm and assert their personalities, and that the "I" expresses itself through a culture that is accessible and acceptable to it, then we can also say that the greater part of the population of the Andean region has not achieved this form of self-realization and affirmation, inasmuch as it finds itself operating within the models of an imposed culture and receives recognition or acceptance of its being from the greater social body. When a culture is not shared or adopted by all the members of a community, to protect itself it wraps itself in disguises and makes use of masks for its self-expression; it can also fall into patterns of self-destructive behavior and entertain notions of violent rebellion against all those who oppress it. The nonconformity of the greater part of the population of the Andean region vis-à-vis the elitism and centralism of official culture has resulted in cultural and artistic manifestations that document social injustices, violence against the peasantry and natives, and the poverty of the urban centers as well as the frivolity, unconsciousness, and cynicism of the local oligarchies. Since Colonial times, artistic forms have been cultivated and developed for the expression of the afflictions and injustices suffered by the indigenous populations during the Conquest. Incorporated by force into the new order, the natives brought to it their talents and creative capacities, one of the results of which was, as we have seen, the alteration of Christian iconography carried out by the Cuzco school's recreation of biblical themes and their extraordinary feminized archangels armed with harquebuses. In similar processes of incorporation, the theater of New Spain not only achieved a cohesion of the sense of belonging to the new society, but was also able to represent the memory of the indigenous past in works like *La tragedia del fin de Atahualpa* [1871; *The Tragedy of the Death of Atahualpa,* 1989] and *Ollantay* (1853), works subsequently prohibited by the colonial authorities.

Cultural Symbolism

Culture is constructed out of, among other things, symbols, sounds, and attitudes that have been assigned a significance. Clifford Geertz has defined culture as the signifying systems—composed, for example, of religious, political, or gendered symbols—that each society constructs in accord with its historical and cultural trajectory. In this conception, culture comprehends a number of distinct types of activities, and not merely the literary or artistic. Religious activity is equally part of culture in that religions incorporate a popular vision of the world, not as a theoretical understanding, but as a solid faith upon which all moral activity is grounded. Culture in the sense we have used in this history includes the scientific theories, artistic aesthetics, and industrial technologies that relate human beings to the world. Culture also comprises politics, which is to say, the relations of individuals amongst themselves, their relations as members of a national entity, and the relations of this entity with other peoples. In a similar manner, socioeconomic activity also forms part of culture, in that it concerns the relations of individuals to the utilization and elaboration of objects gathered from the exterior world.

In its earliest days the Andean culture revolved around the monasteries and the churches. Franciscan, Dominican, and Jesuit communities and their institutions established themselves in the urban centers and facilitated the creation of a political identity. Up until the eighteenth century, education was linked to the question of class and privilege; and within this aristocratic concept of culture primary education was very rudimentary. There was a dearth of teachers and a plethora of professors [*doctores*], and, since the state offered no subsidies, the cost of education was prohibitive. However, it was not only the natives who lacked access to education; both the middle class and commoners were effectively shut out. Further, books were not to be had. Despite being furnished with printing presses, the Viceroyalty of Peru, for example, did little to encourage the production of books. Although the first presses were established rather early in the histories of the colonies—in 1584 in Lima, in 1738 in Bogotá, and in 1760 in Quito-Ambato—most of the books in the region were imported and wound up in the hands of private collectors.

The tensions plaguing the Andean societies resulted not only from the confrontation between the Hispanic culture and that of the natives, whether Inca or Aymara, but also from a clash between traditional Spanish values and those of other European cultures, particularly the French, since the majority of the new ideas that stimulated change came from France. In the era leading up to the Independence struggles, these influences had shaken the foundations of the Colonial societies. Scientific expeditions, like those of Charles la Condamine and other members of the French Academy of Sciences, as well as that of Humboldt, left a profound impression on the enlightened classes of the colonies and in some sense opened their eyes to a knowledge of their own regions. The struggles for Independence would accentuate the differences and rivalries between the distinct regions of the Andean nations. The designation of new national capitals was a cause of controversy, as was the case with Quito, the Ecuadorian city most closely tied to the colonial past. The bases of the new society were the subject of heated discussions in literary circles, salons, and the *Amigos del País* economic societies. The development of journalism also facilitated the diffusion of new ideas and a burgeoning book trade, in which books moved from the port of Callao in Peru on to Lima and from there to Quito and La Paz. Nonconformity vis-à-vis the colonial regime was, in the Viceroyalty of Peru, very well reflected in the wealth of satiric verses, *pasquinades*, and pamphlets that expressed the popular sentiment. The issue of the oppression of the natives was recorded in the poetry of authors like Mariano Melgar (1790–1815) in Ecuador, who to some extent anticipated later native movements. Many years later, Narciso Aréstegui (1824–1869), a Cuzcan—educated in the College of Sciences and Arts founded by Bolívar—would denounce the hypocrisy of the Church and the abuses committed against the natives in his *El padre Horán: escenas de la vida del Cuzco* [1848; Father Horán: Scenes of Life in Cuzco].

At the end of the nineteenth and the beginning of the twentieth centuries, Latin America experienced one of its most intense crises in its process of Europeanizing society. In Colombia the confrontation between the radicals and the Church, allied with a Hispanicizing, hegemonic conservatism, the principal figures of which were the Catholic philologists Caro and Cuervo, resulted in a defeat of the radicals. As Victoria Peralta has pointed out, the oligarchy of the Andean region of Colombia, and in particular that of Bogotá, was influenced not only by Spanish ideas, but also those coming from France and England throughout the nineteenth century; some of these influences were politically institutionalized in, for example, the Napoleonic civil code and free-trade legislation. French Romanticism coexisted with English Liberalism. Many of the ideas that inspired the Colombian constitution of 1886 were picked up by Rafael Núñez (1825–1894) during his long residence in England. In literature, on the other hand, it was Victor Hugo (1802–1885) who reigned supreme, at least until the advent of *modernismo,* introduced in Colombia by José Asunción Silva, the poet who assimilated in the most essential and profound manner the new decadent currents, and produced an admirable prose narrative portraying the conflict between the artist and bourgeois society.

Toward the end of the nineteenth century, anti-Hispanic sentiment began to take root among certain groups of intellectuals in Latin America, and this fed into the then developing confrontations between those who advocated the necessity of change and those who held fast to tradition. Interestingly, both camps concluded that the natives constituted an obstacle to progress as they saw it. At this time the ideas of Comte began to be disseminated in Bolivia and were adopted by the dominant class. In 1899 the Geographic Society of La Paz was founded as an organ for the diffusion of scientific naturalism and Herbert Spencer's ideas. Although the Liberals and Conservatives saw themselves as opposed to each other, their differences were much more regional than ideological. In Peru, González Prada founded the Literary Circle, which later transformed into the National Union political party. Outlining the consequences of colonialism in Peruvian society from a Positivist point of view, González Prada explained how it was that Peru had lost the war with Chile, claiming that the defeat was due to the fact the natives–who constituted the majority of the population–had little reason to fight for a nation that exploited them and had never taken them into consideration as veritable citizens.

Along with the triumph of *modernismo* in the early years of the twentieth century, new roads were opened up, railways were laid down, the cities expanded–their faces changed by the erection of neo-Classical buildings on the foundations of the old colonial structures–and the countryside was assaulted by the influx of foreign capital. Electric light and the cinema arrived in Ecuador in 1906, the latter proving to be so popular in Guayaquil that by 1920 there were twenty cinemas, compared to only four in Quito. In Peru the old Colonial face of Lima was made over in the modern French style with circular plazas and spacious avenues. José Gálvez (1885–1957) recounted this process somewhat nostalgically in his work *Una Lima que se va* [1921; Lima, the City That Has Faded]. It was during these years that a number of educational reforms inspired by the ideas of Victor Raúl Haya de la Torre (1895–1979) were introduced, resulting in important changes in the Latin American universities, including the introduction of sociological studies and the complete renovation of legal studies. The Mexican Revolution had an indisputable impact on the changes underway in this era. For example, the Colombian students' union under Germán Arciniegas named Vasconcelos–the Mexican Minister of Education during the first revolutionary government–the "leader of our youth" ("maestro de las junvetudes").

Throughout the entire twentieth century, the countries of the Andean region have seen their natural resources pillaged by the powerful players in a world political economy that has assigned them the role of providers of raw materials to the privileged developed world. With the arrival of the multinational corporations in the region, the popular classes once again lost the opportunity to integrate themselves into the capitalist West and to enjoy the well being that such integration could provide. However, these economic barriers have never stopped the incessant production of culture in the most diverse areas, and it can be said that the popular cultures of the Andean region–those of the marginalized majorities–have never been as self-aware of their cultural diversity and wealth as they are now. This undeniably creative power of this self-awareness–manifest equally in music, theater, painting, and the cinema–could today teach the wider world, with all its splendors, that a new concept of culture is possible, one different from the erudite and elitist culture privileged by the intellectuals of yesteryear. In addition, it must be said that the awakening of certain indigenous communities has resulted in a strengthening of their languages, such that they are now capable of expressing in writing their sentiments with regard to the present and the past.

The figure of the Leftist intellectual inspired by Sartre, engaged with his political milieu and the conscience of his times, disappeared long before the Berlin Wall came tumbling down. Today, the poets do not give social orientation. Adopting a more modest role, the artist today documents the daily challenge of life or narrates from a position of perplexity induced by a complex world of great human variety and diversity. According to García Canclini, what is truly novel in this era called the *postmodern* is the advent of the contemporary artist of the borders: a producer of popular culture who, while adapting him- or herself to the global market of forms, is neither celebratory nor plaintive, but respectful of the past, and who incessantly modifies all that has until now been considered traditional and autochthonous by assigning it new and other values, offering hybrid productions that are the result of processes of appropriation and intertextuality. The power of this new cultural model would be unquestionable, should it find what it seems at times to be lacking: the rigorous application of an agile and vigilant criticism. Thus, at the frontier between indifference, uncertainty, hope, and doubt, and in a space unknown to the privileged classes stagnating in their conservative and frivolous postures, a different culture–at times unexpected and spontaneous, but above all more connected to life–has made its appearance. It is in the hands of this culture that the future of the Andean region can be glimpsed.

Translation by Colman Hogan

Works Cited

Aréstegui, Narciso. 1848. *El padre Horán; escenas de la vida del Cuzco.* Lima: Imp. del "Comercio" por J. María Monterola.

Arguedas, Alcides. 1945. *Raza de bronce.* Buenos Aires: Losada.

Arguedas, José María. 1958. *Los ríos profundos.* Buenos Aires: Editorial Losada.

——. 1975. *Formación de una cultura nacional indoamericana.* Sel., prologue by Angel Rama. Mexico City: Siglo Veintiuno Editores.

García Canclini, Néstor. 1991. *Culturas híbridas. Estrategias para entrar y salir de la modernidad.* Mexico City: CONALCULTA.

Garcilaso de la Vega. 1976. *Comentarios reales de los incas.* Caracas: Biblioteca Ayacucho.

Geertz, Clifford. 1973. *The Interpretation of Cultures: Selected Essays.* New York: Basic Books.

González Prada, Manuel. 1900. *Horas de lucha.* Lima: Librería Importadora Editora y Distribuidora Lima.

Haya de la Torre, Víctor Raúl. 1927. *Por la emancipación de América Latina: artículos, mensajes, discursos (1923–1927).* Buenos Aires: M. Gleizer.

Lara, Jesús, ed. 1973. *Mitos, leyendas y cuentos de los quechuas: antología.* La Paz: Editorial Los Amigos del Libro.

Mariátegui, José Carlos. 1975. *Siete ensayos de interpretación de la realidad peruana.* Havana: Casa de las Américas.

Matto de Turner, Clorinda. 1994. *Aves sin nido.* Caracas: Biblioteca Ayacucho.

Ollantay. 1973. Trans. José Sebastián Barranca, César Miró and Sebastián Salazar Bondy. Lima: Editorial Universo.

Oviedo, José Miguel. 1995. *Historia de la literatura hispanoamericana.* Madrid: Alianza.

Palma, Ricardo. 1973. *Tradiciones peruanas.* Mexico City: Editorial Porrúa.

Pãrõkumu Umusî and Tõrãmu Kehíri. 1995. *Antes o mundo não existia: mitologia dos antigos Desana-Kehíripõrã.* São João Batista do Rio Tiguié, Amazonas: UNIRT; São Gabriel da Cachoeira, Amazonas: FOIRN.

Rama, Ángel. 1984. *La ciudad letrada.* Montevideo: Fundación Ángel Rama.

———. 1982. *Transculturación narrativa en América Latina.* Mexico City: Siglo XXI.

Rivera, José Eustasio. 1976. *La vorágine.* Caracas: Biblioteca Ayacucho.

Rosenblat, Angel. 1954. *La población indígena y el mestizaje en América.* 2 Vols. Buenos Aires: Editorial Nova.

Tragedia del fin de Atawallpa. 1989. Ed. and trans. Jesús Lara. Buenos Aires: Ediciones del Sol.

Uribe Piedrahita, César. 1979. *Toá; Mancha de aceite.* Ed. J.G. Cobo Borda. Bogotá: Instituto Colombiano de Cultura.

Zalamea Borda, Eduardo. 1996. *Cuatro años a bordo de mi mismo.* Bogotá: Presidencia de la República.

CHAPTER 38

CARACAS

Alexis Márquez Rodríguez

The city of Santiago de León de Caracas was founded on 25 July 1567, by the Spanish Captain Diego de Losada. On two previous occasions the Spanish had tried to establish settlements at the same site, or very nearby, but these had only lasted a short time. The chosen site possessed optimal topographic and ideal climatic conditions: at the center of a long and narrow valley, 25 kilometers in length and 4 kilometers in width, and was blessed with a climate that was neither excessively hot nor overly cool with an average temperature of 25 degrees Celsius and a normal daily variation between 20 and 30 degrees, never exceeding the extremes of 14 and 34 degrees. Bordering this valley were three others, much smaller, that would in time permit the expansion of the city. The site was also traversed by one river and seven streams which, while not large enough to threaten floods, did guarantee a natural form of irrigation necessary for bountiful harvests and the provision of drinking water necessary for the livelihood of the population. To the north, the valley was ringed by a chain of mountains—whose highest peak reached 2,700 meters—of a consistent height that, although separating the recently established town from the sea, nonetheless permitted access to it without major difficulty by means of open pathways through the highlands. The city itself lay at an altitude of approximately 900 meters in the center and ranged between 870 and 1,043 meters toward the peripheries of the settlement. The city plan of Caracas drawn up in 1578 eleven years after the first settlement followed the traditional Spanish Colonial grid pattern (see **Figure 1**).

Figure 1.

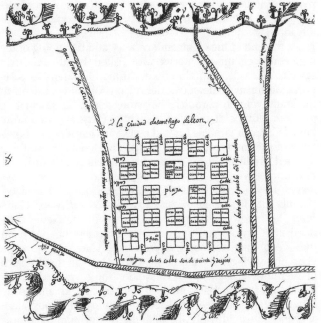

First city plan for Santiago de León de Caracas, 1578.
(Archive of the author)

The beauty of the countryside, the agreeableness of the climate, the fertility of the soil, and other natural endowments presaged a promising future for the settlement, and it was not long before the town began to develop. Various chronicles of this early era recount the gentle unfolding of its life, only sporadically interrupted by the incursion of pirates, never very numerous, who breached the mountains in order to fall on the town in search of booty, or by one or another skirmish with the natives of neighboring localities who, in the face of the plundering of their lands by the foreign invaders, nonetheless had not been completely pacified. These chronicles principally recount the domestic life of the settlers, the religious and other festivities in which they collectively participated, the small incidents that disturbed local tranquility, the agricultural and commercial goings on, etc. There is no mention of anything that could be considered a sign of important cultural activity.

Little by little the tiny city grew and developed. Although Coro was the *de jure* capital of the Province of Venezuela and remained so until 1602, in 1577 Caracas became the capital *de facto* where the political and administrative functions of the provincial government were really exercised when Governor Juan de Pimentel, and his entourage made the move from Coro. In 1591 the king of Spain conferred upon Caracas the rank of "The Most Noble and Very Loyal City of Santiago de León de Caracas" and an accompanying coat of arms. By 1723 the city had grown to a population of more than 6,000 inhabitants. The precise description both of the urban configuration and the life of the population of the city date from this epoch. In this same year, José de Oviedo y Baños (1671–1738) wrote his *Historia de la conquista y población de la provincia de Venezuela* [1824; History of the Conquest and Settlement of the Province of Venezuela], in which he gave a "report of the status reached by this city of Caracas" (1723):

En un hermoso valle, tan fértil como alegre y tan ameno como deleitable, que de Poniente a Oriente se dilata por cuatro leguas de longitud y poco más de media de latitud, en diez grados y medio de altura septentrional, al pie de unas altas sierras, que con distancia de cinco leguas la dividen del mar, en el recinto que forman cuatro ríos, que porque no le faltase circunstancia para acreditarla paraíso la cercan por todas partes, sin padecer sustos de que la aneguen, tiene su situación la ciudad de Caracas en un temperamento tan del cielo, que sin competencia es el mejor de cuantos tiene la América, pues además de ser muy saludable, parece que lo escogió la primavera para su habitación continua, pues en igual templanza todo el año ni el frío molesta, ni el calor enfada, ni los bochornos del estío fatigan, ni los rigores del invierno afligen: sus aguas son muchas, claras y delgadas, pues los cuatro ríos que la rodean, a competencia le ofrecen sus cristales, brindando al apetito en su regalo, pues sin reconocer violencias del verano, en el mayor rigor de la canícula mantienen su frescura, pasando en el diciembre a más que frías; sus calles son anchas, largas y derechas, con salida y correspondencia en igual proporción a todas partes, y como están pendientes y empedradas, ni mantienen polvos, ni consienten lodos; sus edificios los más son bajos, por recelo de los temblores, algunos de ladrillo, y lo común de tapias, pero bien dispuestos, y repartidos en su fábrica;

las casas son tan dilatadas en los sitios, que casi todas tienen espaciosos patios, jardines y huertas, que regadas con diferentes acequias que cruzan la ciudad, saliendo o encañadas del río Catuche, producen tanta variedad de flores, que admira su abundancia todo el año; hermoséanla cuatro plazas, las tres medianas y la principal bien grande, y en proporción cuadrada. (Gabaldón Márquez 171–72)

Situated in a splendid valley, as fertile as it is sunny and as pleasant as it is delightful, that from west to east stretches for four leagues in length and a little more than half that number in width; at ten and a half degrees latitude north, and at the foot of highlands that separate it from the sea five leagues distant; in an enclosure formed by four rivers that, while lacking no circumstance to vouch for it as paradise, does surround it on all sides, although without giving cause to fears that it may be overwhelmed, here lies the city of Caracas in a heavenly disposition, that without rival we may say is the best that is to be encountered in all the Americas, since, in addition to its salubriousness, it appears as if spring itself has chosen to make of it its continuous habitation, blessing it in equal moderation throughout the year, such that it suffers neither the inconveniences of cold nor the offenses of heat, and is neither wearied by the sultriness of summer nor aggrieved by the rigors of winter. Her waters are plentiful, clear, and delicate, since the rivers that gird round her, vying with each other to offer her their crystals, and satisfying the palette with their gifts, know not the violences of summer heat, maintaining on the hottest of days their freshness, and excelling in December with their bracing robustness. Her streets are broad, long, and straight, with issue and correspondence in equal proportion to every locality, and suffer neither dust nor mire since they are paved and inclined. Her buildings in the main are low, for fear of tremors, some of brick, though the most common of adobe, all of sound construction, and produced locally. The houses are so spread out in their allotments that almost all are furnished with ample patios and flower and vegetable gardens that, fed by a motley of irrigation ditches traversing the city, issuing from or draining into the Catuche River, bound forth with such a variety of flowers that their abundance is to be admired throughout the entire year; these adorn the city's three secondary and the one principal, rather large, quadrilateral plaza.

This is the first recorded description of the city of Caracas, written, as can be seen, in a grand style that reveals its author to be a well educated, mature writer, both historian and chronicler, as well as having an obvious literary calling. Oviedo y Baños was born in Santa Fe de Bogotá (Colombia; at that time the Province of Nueva Granada) and during his childhood lived for a time in Lima. Arriving in Caracas at age 15, he had still to complete his education, which is a good indication of the level of schooling on offer in the Caracas of that time. His uncle, the Archbishop of Caracas, don Diego de Baños y Sotomayor, a man of extensive culture, took charge of Oviedo y Baños's education. The inventory of his personal effects drawn up on his death in 1738 noted the existence in his household of an extremely well-stocked and choice collection of books. That was not the only known library of importance in colonial Caracas. The researches of contemporary historians allow us to state that in seventeenth- and eighteenth-century Caracas many books were read, that there were people of wide learning, and that a number of valuable personal libraries existed containing, in addition to the classics, books that in that epoch were true novelties even in Europe.

As to the people of Caracas, Oviedo y Baños tells us they were ". . . de agudos y prontos ingenios, corteses, afables y

políticos; hablan la lengua castellana con perfección, sin aquellos resabios con que la vician en los más puertos de las Indias; . . . siendo en general de espíritus bizarros y corazones briosos, y tan inclinados a todo lo que es política, que hasta los negros (siendo criollos) se desdeñan de no saber leer y escribir . . ." (Gabaldón Márquez 172) (". . . sharp and quick of wit, courteous, genial, and tactful; spoke Castilian with perfection, and without the unpleasant aftertaste that mars the Spanish spoken in the majority of the ports of these Indies; . . . being in general spirited of heart and generous of mind, with such a proclivity for political discourse that even the Blacks [Creoles] disdain themselves for not knowing how to read and write . . . .").

Lamentably, Oviedo y Baños's description of the cultural milieu and activities of the Caracas of his time was not as explicit, although he did minutely detail the developments of the Catholic religion and in particular the churches of the city and the festivities that were held in them. In speaking of the Seminario de Santa Rosa de Lima, however, he does say that classes in theology, philosophy, and grammar were given there, "donde cultivados los ingenios, como por naturaleza son claros y agudos, se crían sujetos muy cabales, así en lo escolástico y moral, como en lo expositivo" (Gabaldón Márquez 177) ("where they cultivate wits, which are by nature clear and sharp, and raise very consummate gentlemen, both in scholastics and morals, as well as in oratory").

The first event of cultural importance in Caracas was, in fact, the founding of the Seminario de Santa Rosa de Lima in 1696 after a series of steps taken by the authorities and the inhabitants dating back some years. In 1725 this seminary became the Real y Pontificia Universidad de Caracas, although it is to be supposed that there had to be some pedagogic activity of importance predating the seminary that justified its founding and shortly thereafter its conversion into a university. The details surrounding the foundation of the seminary are neither plentiful nor precise. However, what does appear to be clear is that insistent solicitations for the creation of a seminary and the fact that such solicitations were received, indicate that a sufficiently advanced system of elementary education was in existence to produce candidates for advanced study.

At the end of the eighteenth century and beginning of the nineteenth century, Caracas was visited by the German savant Alexander von Humboldt during his extensive peregrination through the equatorial regions of the continent. In the multi-volume chronicle he wrote about his fascinating journey, Humboldt spoke of the city of Caracas: "In a number of Caracan families I noted a taste for learning, a knowledge of the master works of French and Italian literature, a decided predilection for music that was cultivated with success and served—as the cultivation of the fine arts always serves—to bring together the different classes of society" (Humboldt, *Viaje a las regiones equinocciales del Nuevo Continente* [Voyage to the Equatorial Regions of the New Continent] 264). In the early years of the nineteenth century, on the eve of the Wars of Independence, Caracas enjoyed a vivid and variegated cultural life, particularly in the domains of literature and music. In addition, some small developments had taken place in the plastic arts, and interesting achievements had been realized in painting, religious statuary, and goldsmith work. In 1808 the first printing press was brought to Venezuela, well after it had made its appearance in the other colonial capitals of the continent. However, this press immediately became the center of a flurry of activity. In the same year, on October 24, the first Venezuelan periodical saw the light of day, the *Gazeta de Caracas*, the official publication of the Capitanía General of Venezuela, edited by the young Andrés Bello (1781–1864), a writer who would later distinguish himself as one of the most eminent Spanish American polymaths. Off this press would also come the first book to be published in Venezuela, the *Calendario manual y guía universal de forasteros en Venezuela para el año de 1810* [1959; Calendar Handbook and Universal Guide for Visitors to Venezuela for 1810], a publication which included a *Resumen de la historia de Venezuela* [1958; Summary of Venezuelan History], both written by Bello.

In the still tranquil and bucolic city of Caracas of those days, there existed an interesting intellectual movement principally comprised of practitioners of literature and music. A group of young intellectuals, among whom numbered the distinguished figures of Andrés Bello (1781–1865), Juan Germán Roscio (1763–1821), the brothers Francisco Javier and Miguel Ustáriz, Simón Bolívar (1783–1830), and others, would meet periodically to read poems and non-fiction on a diverse range of subjects, perform musical works, and discuss politics and other important issues. The chronicles of the epoch give an account of these salons, although they often excise any mention of the progressive political ideas that were to herald the events that, from 1810 on, would convulse not only the city of Caracas but also the country and ultimately the entire Spanish American continent.

In effect, the revolution got under way on Maundy Thursday, 19 April 1810, when a veritable rebellion erupted, led by young aristocrats with politically progressive ideas. This rebellion ignited an immediate popular reaction among the people gathered in the Plaza Mayor, ostensibly for religious celebration but also for political agitation, and popular pressure forced the Provincial Governor Vicente Emparan to step down and hand over the reigns of power to a *junta* that was established on the same day. Clearly, this Caracan populace did not erupt spontaneously but was whipped up by the young agitators of the recently formed Sociedad Patriótica (Patriotic Society) operating in their midst, and whose intentions went very much further–to total independence, which was finally declared in 1811. One of the most charismatic and ardent leaders of the Patriotic *junta* was the young Simón Bolívar. These events were precipitated by the arrival in Caracas of the news that Napoleon had invaded Spain, deposed the Spanish king Fernando VII and placed his own brother Joseph Bonaparte on the throne. Initially, the Caracan leaders and people repudiated the usurper king and pledged their allegiance to the monarch who had been forced to abdicate. It is for this reason that the *junta* at first took the name *Junta Defensora de los Derechos de Fernando VII* (The Committee Defending the Rights of Fernando VII), although one year later, on 5 July 1811, this proposition was superseded by the declaration of total autonomy and the advent of the Wars of Independence. In any event, what was most important about 19 April 1810, was that from this day on the Venezuelan *criollos* assumed the government and administration of the country, even if initially this was supposedly in the name of the Spanish Crown. The events of April 19 in Caracas, the first reaction in Latin America to the Napoleonic invasion and the deposition of the Spanish king, had immediate repercussions in the interior of the country and in a number of diverse cities wherein movements arose pledging their support to the *junta*

in Caracas. And it was not long afterward in the same year of 1810 that similar rebellions erupted throughout the Latin American continent: Buenos Aires (May 25), Bogotá (July 20), Quito (August 2), Mexico (September 15), and Santiago, Chile (September 18). All these rebellions were decisively influenced in a direct manner by events in Spain; in some of these cities there was news of happenings in Caracas, which must have had an impact on the political agitations then underway or about to explode.

The movement of emancipation that took shape throughout the length and breadth of the old regime of Spanish Colonial America in the 1810s had, as is well known, among other ideological sources, roots in the ideas of the Enlightenment. The French Revolution of 1789 had had an enormous influence on the Caribbean islands and especially those that were French possessions. From there, ideas of revolution spread to other islands and eventually the mainland. Given the privileged geographic position of Caracas at the extreme north end of the South American continent and very proximate to the Caribbean, the city was one of the principal ports of entry for these ideas, and from Caracas they spread to other localities on the continent. Although the Spanish Crown had prohibited the introduction of books into the Spanish American colonies, precisely out of fear that revolutionary and emancipatory ideas would be disseminated amongst the population, it is known that the so-called "Ships of the Enlightenment" contained many revolutionary books that were to make their way surreptitiously into Venezuela as contraband. This explains in part the early nineteenth-century advent in Caracas of a highly politicized group of young intellectuals familiar with the ideas emanating from the *Siglo de las Luces* [The Century of Lights]. It is known that at this time political meetings were held in which not only the idea of independence but also ideological texts were discussed, including the French Constitution and the *Declaration of the Rights of Man and Citizen of 1793*, of which there were various Caracan editions in circulation in the Caribbean, some of which reached the other Spanish colonies. It is also known that the leaders of the "Independence Generation" were very familiar with the works of Rousseau, Montesquieu, and other savants of the *Encyclopedia*. Further, there is now a sufficient historical consensus to back the claim that, contrary to what had been taken as absolute truth for a very long time, university education in Caracas in the final decades of the colony was not obscurantist and reactionary in its entirety, since the principle figures and ideological and philosophic movements of the times, those constituting a living presence in eighteenth- and early nineteenth-century Europe, were studied in the lecture halls of Caracas.

Even in those times there existed a strong link between literary affinities and revolutionary and ideological principles. The men of the "Independence Generation," principally comprised of young politicians, many of whom would soon become soldiers, were also men of letters, writers, and literati, whose intellectual vocation was in large part frustrated by the war in that it cut them off from the intellectual life. It is for this reason that their talents and sensibilities were often only realized in occasional texts: letters, discourses, proclamations, bills of legislation, and periodical articles. Their brevity and circumstantiality notwithstanding, these texts remain the testimony of a group of exceptional minds and progressive ideas and bear witness to an admirable integrative synthesis of their ideas and their aesthetics in an often coruscating language and style.

The Caracan culture of this epoch was not sequestered behind the geographic walls of the city's topography, those beautiful mountains that separate it from the rest of the country; Caracas was always a city from which cultural values radiated outward to the most diverse points of the horizon. As a seat of political power, Caracas always enjoyed a great prestige and admiration among Venezuelans at large. Many have seen it as distant and unattainable and have for that reason attempted to emulate what is done there. In addition, the privileges that stem from its status as the capital have acted as a powerful magnet for many people from the provinces who have cast their eye toward Caracas, dazzled by her power, riches, and glory. Caracas was the center where Venezuelans could fully realize their aspirations, whether in politics, commerce, the professions, the priesthood, or in the arts and letters. Thus, in the Caracan population there has always been a mix of peoples from the various provincial regions of the interior who have, in general stood out in those activities that have been characteristic of the capital. If there is anything of permanent applicability in Venezuela, it is the verses of the national anthem that, in the closing of one of its stanzas, proclaim: "seguid el ejemplo/que Caracas dio" ("follow the example/that Caracas set"). While these verses refer, of course, to the events of 19 April 1810, that culminated in the declaration of complete independence on 5 July 1811, in popular parlance their significance extends to include all activities in which Caracas has distinguished itself through the course of Venezuelan history.

Caracan cultural irradiation, which can be seen in other domains as well, extends to and beyond the national frontiers, manifesting itself in other regions, especially in the Caribbean, and in general in the adjoining countries and beyond. Caracas has always been a city of refuge for the politically persecuted of many other countries. In various epochs and for diverse reasons, exiles, whether forced or voluntary, have arrived in Caracas from Puerto Rico, Cuba, the Dominican Republic, Central America, Colombia, Peru, Chile, Argentina, Bolivia, Uruguay, Brazil, Spain, and a host of other places from around the world. Often, these have been intellectuals from a wide variety of occupations and tendencies: foreign writers, professors, politicians, journalists, and professionals representing the diverse branches of knowledge have all taken up residence in Caracas, some for a lengthy time, and there are even those who have remained there permanently. Among these refugees have been men and women of letters and artists who have made a profound impression on the intellectual, artistic, and literary life of the city in particular and the country in general. In addition, they have at the same time acted as conduits of communication with their countries of origin and, as such, have facilitated the cultural interaction between Caracas and Venezuela in its entirety, as well as other peoples and nations.

We ought also to note that many Venezuelans have themselves emigrated to other countries, frequently as a result of the persecutions that, for a long time, and in diverse periods of Venezuelan history, have been an ominous sign of Venezuelan political life. There are numerous Venezuelan artists and writers of note who in various moments of their lives have had to go into exile. Among this group have been Simón Rodríguez (1771–1854), Rómulo Gallegos (1884–1969) (see **Figure 2**), Andrés Eloy Blanco (1897–1955), José Rafael Pocaterra (1890–1955), Rufino Blanco Fombona (1874–1944), Carlos Augusto León

Figure 2.

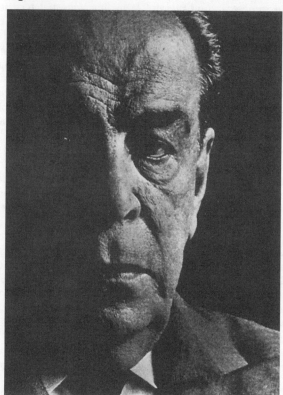

Venezuelan novelist Rómulo Gallegos (1884–1969) c. 1947. (Archive of the author)

(1914–1997), Mario Briceño Iragorri (1897–1958), Mariano Picón Salas (1901–1965), Arturo Uslar Pietri (1906–2001), Miguel Otero Silva (1908–1985), Pedro Beroes (b. 1912), Rafael Cadenas (b. 1930), Jesús Sanoja Hernández (b. 1930), Manuel Alfredo Rodríguez (b. 1929), Lucila Velásquez (b. 1928), and many others. Others have chosen to live outside the country voluntarily, either in search of new horizons suitable to their intellectual formation or as a result of their service in the diplomatic corps; for example, Andrés Bello left Venezuela in 1810 on a diplomatic mission and never returned to the country. Among these voluntary expatriates we would include: Fermín Toro (1807–1865), Rafael María Baralt (1810–1860), Teresa Carreño (1856–1917), Arturo Michelena (1863–1898), Cristóbal Rojas (1857–1890), Teresa de la Parra (1889–1936) (see **Figure 3**), Pedro Emilio Coll (1872–1947), José Antonio Ramos Sucre (1890–1930), Armando Reverón (1889–1954), Otto De Sola (1912–1975), Vicente Gerbasi (1913–1992), Jesús Rafael Soto (b. 1923), Carlos Cruz Diez (b. 1923), Héctor Poleo (1918–1989), Guillermo Sucre Figarella (b. 1933), José Francisco Sucre (b. 1931), Carlos Gottberg (b. 1929), Rafael Ángel Insausti (1916–1978), Guillermo Meneses (1911–1978), Juan Beroes (1914–1975), José Nucete Sardi (b. 1897), Julio Garmendia (1898–1977), Oscar Guaramato (1916–1987), Fernando Paz Castillo (1893–1981), Adriano González León (b. 1931) (see **Figure 4**), Jacobo Borges (b. 1931), Salvador Garmendia (1928–2001), Lucila Palacios (1902–1994), Eugenio Montejo (b. 1938), Francisco Salazar Martínez (b. 1925), Antonieta Madrid (b. 1939), Luz Machado (1916–1999), Ida Gramcko (1924–1994), Pedro Francisco Lizardo (b. 1920), Elisa Lerner (b. 1932).

Figure 3.

*The Venesuelan novelist Teresa de la Parra
(Ana Teresa Parra Sanojo) (1889–1936) c. 1930.
(Archive of the author)*

Figure 4.

*Professor and essayist Adriano González León (b. 1931).
(Archive of the author)*

During the nineteenth century, the development of journalism in Caracas reached a very high level of accomplishment. The already mentioned *Gazeta de Caracas*, Venezuela's first newspaper, had a long life, publishing continuously from its inception in 1808 until 1822. Its life was a stormy and contradictory one since, due to the vicissitudes of the Wars of Independence, the newspaper changed its orientation a number of times, according to the political stripe of the party dominating Caracas. In its first phase, as official organ of the Capitanía General, its outlook was royalist. Later, after the proclamation of independence, it served as mouthpiece for the patriotic government and the Republican cause. Still later, when the city of Caracas fell into the hands of the Royalists, the *Gazeta* returned to the Royalist position, and this phase was followed by a return to the independence cause after the city had changed hands once again and was under the rule of the patriots.

There were of course many other newspapers in circulation in Caracas in the nineteenth century. Among the most distinguished was the long-lived political newspaper *El Venezolano* founded by Antonio Leocadio Guzmán, one of the most eminent politicians of the Venezuelan nineteenth century, which served as a mouthpiece for the Liberal Party. On the conservative side was *El Nacional*, equally long-lived and distinguished, under the direction of Juan Vicente González, without a doubt the most brilliant and hard-nosed Venezuelan journalist of the nineteenth century. Juan Vicente González (1810–1866) was also an important writer whose *Biografía de José Félix Ribas* [1864; The Life of José Félix Ribas] is considered one of the fundamental works of Venezuelan letters and an exemplar of its times for its frequent intermixing of biographical and novelistic content within a Romantic conception of history and the novel.

In the larger literary scheme of things, the Venezuelan nineteenth century was a little on the gray side and, in any

event, with respect to the quality of the work produced, a less fertile epoch than that of many other countries. In poetry, for example, and this is true for the rest of the South American continent, there were no great figures nor literary movements of any real importance until the appearance, in the final decades of the century, of the *modernismo* movement. Only two nineteenth-century poets are relevant here, both Caracans, although one of them lived the major portion of his life outside Venezuela: Andrés Bello and José Antonio Pérez Bonalde (1846–1892). Bello developed as a writer in Caracas in the final decades of the Colonial era, and his first, Neoclassical-inspired verses and other writings published at this time manifest an indisputable command of Spanish versification. He left the city in 1810, when a diplomatic mission, comprised of Simón Bolívar and Luis López Méndez, with Bello as their secretary, was sent to London by the governing *junta* in order to solicit the backing of England and other powers for the Independence movement that was then taking shape in Venezuela. He remained in London until 1829 when, contracted by the newly independent government of Chile, he traveled to Santiago to undertake a reconstruction of the Chilean educational system. It was in Chile that Bello wrote his most important (and by far the greatest quantity) of his works, a series of publications touching on the most variegated areas of knowledge: poetry, grammar, literary historical criticism, philosophy, theater, jurisprudence, and so on.

Although Bello never returned to Caracas, he always remained a Caracan, nostalgic for his native city and its familiar surroundings and refused to give up his Venezuelan citizenship when he was offered Chilean citizenship in return. The Chilean government, however, made an exception in his case by allowing him to become a Chilean without renouncing his status as a Venezuelan. From the point of view of the aesthetic values of his time, Bello's poetry is very important. Although he was initially a partisan of the neo-Classical, later he became a practitioner of the Romantic aesthetic, influenced above all by Victor Hugo whom he imitated and translated.

As for Pérez Bonalde (1846–1892), he too lived many years outside of Venezuela. An indefatigable traveler who resided in the United States and toured numerous European countries, he always returned to Caracas. His poetry was oriented toward the Romantics, although it was not unrelated to the renovating currents that were the forerunners of the *modernismo* movement; in fact, he has been considered one of its precursors. He was well read in German poetry and was an excellent and respected translator of Heine, as well as having produced what has been considered one of the best Spanish translations of Edgar Allen Poe's *The Raven*. Pérez Bonalde was a dearly beloved Caracan, and it is to him that we owe a splendid poetic description of the Caracas of his time. In one of his best known and most celebrated poems, "Vuelta a la patria" (1880; "Return to the Native Land"), while recounting one of his homeward journeys to his native city, he contemplates the city from the mountains that dominate the approach to it and, deeply moved, exclaims:

¡Caracas, allí está! Sus techos rojos,
su blanca torre, sus azules lomas
y sus bandas de tímidas palomas
hacen nublar de lágrimas mis ojos.

There is Caracas! Its red roofs,
its white tower, its blue ridges
and its flocks of timid doves
becloud my eyes with tears.

Venezuelan literature of the nineteenth century was also rather weak in narrative forms. Except for the fact that the Venezuelan novel was born in this century with *Los mártires* [1842; The Martyrs], written by the Caracan Fermín Toro (1807–1865), the nineteenth century is a period of little importance in the development of narrative genres. Nevertheless, there were a few works of demonstrable value, such as the short stories and the first novels of Manuel Díaz Rodríguez (1871–1927), the best representative of Venezuelan *modernista* prose, and, on a different level, the first novels of Rufino Blanco Fombona, also under the influence of *modernismo*. In a similar manner, toward the end of the century, the *criollo* narrative was born in the work of Luis Manuel Urbaneja Achelpohl (1873–1937), Miguel Eduardo Pardo (1868–1905), Eduardo Blanco (1838–1912), and Manuel Vicente Romero García (1865–1917).

In contrast with the situation in poetry and narrative fiction, in the domain of expository and conceptual literature, the Venezuelan nineteenth century was marked by a number of great figures. Genres like the essay, the chronicle, the journalistic article, the epistle, and ecclesiastical and secular oratory were cultivated in nineteenth-century Caracas with great thematic and stylistic energy. Among the notable figures in these areas are Simón Bolívar (1783–1830), Francisco de Miranda (1750–1816), Andrés Bello (1781–1865), José Luis Ramos (1785–1849), Simón Rodríguez (1771–1854), Juan Germán Roscio (1763–1821), Manuel Palacios Fajardo (1784–1819), Francisco Javier Yánez (1777–1842), all members of the "Independence Generation," and later Fermín Toro (1807–1865), Juan Vicente González (1810–1866), Cecilio Acosta (1818–1881)–highly esteemed by José Martí (1853–1895)–Valentín Espinal (1803–1866), Luis López Méndez (1863–1891), and many others.

Independent of the greater or lesser quality of the literature produced in nineteenth-century Caracas, in the interior of the country literary production was much more scarce, both qualitatively and quantitatively, with the exception of journalism, which in this period underwent a healthy development. There had always been vigorous intellectual activity in the capital that was manifest in a number of diverse manners. One of these was book publishing. Since the introduction of the printing press in 1808, a publishing industry centered by and large in Caracas began to develop which, although rudimentary and corresponding to the level of development of the country as a whole, was also intense and continuous. Since the time of the Wars of Independence and despite the uncertainty and turmoil that followed in their wake, the presses of Caracas produced a number of extremely important books of very high quality. Not as recent a phenomenon as is commonly believed, the Venezuelan publishing industry is quite old. As noted, with the arrival of the printing press in 1808, Venezuelan book publishing began, and throughout the nineteenth century important works were published not only by Venezuelan authors but also by foreign writers, including translations from French and English. In 1839, for example, the *Complete Works* in three volumes of Mariano José de Larra (1809–1837), the premier representative of Spanish customs and manners (*costumbrista*) literature, were published in Caracas for the first time–before they were published in Spain. In an editorial note appended to the volumes, the publishers expressed their wish of producing an edition worthy of the eminent writer, one that would be read throughout the continent (since they imagined a market for their books not limited to Venezuela, but extending to the entirety of the Americas). This editorial note is a valuable document in that it illustrates that the vision of the Caracan editors was in harmony with the integrationist ideas of the great thinkers of the nineteenth century, with the four famous Caracans (Miranda, Bolívar, Bello, and Simón Rodríguez) leading the way. Not limited to national frontiers but envisaging the dissemination of literature and ideas to the entire continent, the nineteenth-century Caracan editorial houses published many books by the most important national and foreign writers. This editorial vision has acquired an even greater validity today in the face of immediate challenges.

One of the most significant literary publications produced in Caracas in the nineteenth century was *El Cojo Ilustrado* [1892; The Enlightened Cripple], a very prestigious review fundamental to the dissemination of the *modernismo* movement throughout the continent. *El Cojo Ilustrado* published the work of all the great poets and prose writers involved in or affiliated with *modernismo*: José Martí, Rubén Darío (1867–1916), Ismael Enrique Arciniegas (1865–1938), Salvador Díaz Mirón (1853–1928), Enrique Gómez Carrillo (1873–1927), Amado Nervo (1870–1919), J. M. Vargas Vila (1860–1933), José Santos Chocano (1875–1934), Ricardo Jaimes Freyre (1868–1933), Manuel Gutiérrez Nájera (1859–1895), Manuel José Othon (1858–1906), José Enrique Rodó (1871–1917), Leopoldo Lugones (1874–1938), José Asunción Silva (1865–1896), Enrique José Varona (1849–1933), Guillermo Valencia (1873–1943), Julián del Casal (1863–1893), José Juan Tablada (1871–1945), Baldomero Sanín Cano (1861–1957), Gonzalo Zaldumbide (1885–1965), Alberto Zérega Fombona (b. 1968), Alfonso Reyes (1889–1959), and others. In its pages could be found as well, in some cases quite regularly, original or republished pieces from numerous European or New World writers representing a diverse range of epochs and aesthetic or ideological persuasions. A partial listing of the writers published in this extraordinary journal indicates both the range and the level of the literary culture of Caracas during these years: Juan Montalvo, J. K. Huysmann, Arthur Conan Doyle, Azorín, Benito Pérez Galdós, Camille Flammarion, Alphonse Daudet, Catulle Mèndes, Charles Baudelaire, Alexander Pushkin, Eça de Queiroz, Emilio Castelar, Anatole France, Antonio Machado, Friedrich Nietzsche, Fyodor Dostoyevsky, Gabriele D'Anunnzio, Alfred de Vigny, Gustavo Adolfo Bécquer, Guy de Maupassant, Heinrich Heine, Clorinda Matto de Turner, Edgar Allan Poe, Ivan Turgenev, Jacinto Benavente, Maxim Gorky, John Keats, Miguel de Unamuno, Edmond de Goncourt, Pío Baroja, Jorge Isaacs, José María Pereda, Emilio Carrere, Giosuè Carducci, Juan Ramón Jiménez, George Sand, Jules Lemaitre, Emilia Pardo Bazán, Leo Tolstoy, Leopoldo Alas (Clarín), Jean Lorraine, Manuel González Prada, Juan Valera, Rémy de Gourmont, Mark Twain, Maurice Barrès, Maurice Maeterlinck, Nikolai Gogol, Novalis, Jules Renard, Oscar Wilde, Paul Bourget, Manuel Machado, Paul Groussac, Max Nordeau, Pierre Loti, Marcelino Menéndez y Pelayo, Paul Claudel, Vicente Blasco Ibáñez, Rudyard Kipling, Santiago Rusiñol, Victor Hugo, Théophile Gautier, Victor Coussin, Friedrich Schiller, Ramón del Valle Inclán, Selma Lagerlöf, Walt Whitman, Sully Proudhome, Rabindranath Tagore, and many others. *El Cojo Ilustrado* was also a veritable showcase of typographic art, utilizing the most modern printing and image- reproducing technology of the epoch. Its illustrations were truly *de luxe*, and even today, flipping through its pages, one experiences a genuine aesthetic pleasure. It was also exemplary with respect to reliability and perseverance, publishing fortnightly without a single lapse for a total of 559 issues over a period of almost twenty-three years, from 1 January 1892, to 1 April 1915, at which time the review closed as a result of the economic and other upheavals provoked by World War I.

Throughout the nineteenth century the links between political activity and Caracan—and Venezuelan, in general—literary movements were very important. In every epoch there have always been writers associated with the government of the day, irrespective of the greater or lesser degree of democratization that the government represented, although it should be noted that nineteenth-century Venezuelan political life was characterized by a predominance of dictatorial governments, whether *de jure* or *de facto*, and by an almost constant state of civil war. As a result of these circumstances, as it always seems to be the case, the majority of Venezuela's writers and intellectuals in general adopted an oppositional attitude. An exemplary instance was offered by Cecilio Acosta who, after having initially collaborated with the Guzmán Blanco regime in the drawing up of a novel set of progressive laws, in the final years of his life broke with the regime and bravely confronted it when he realized that Guzmán Blanco was merely one more despot, a corrupt authoritarian, hiding behind a mask of civilization and progressive politics. In January 1881 a young José Martí arrived in Caracas and soon espoused a profound admiration for Acosta, such that upon his death in July of that year, the Cuban revolutionary wrote a vibrant and moving obituary that was published in the second issue of the journal that Acosta had founded, the *Revista Venezolana*. This piece roused the dictator's anger, and Martí was ordered to leave the country immediately without, according to

his own account, having time to take his leave of his Caracan friends.

The anti-dictatorial and anti-Guzmán position of the Caracan intellectuals was also manifest in a much celebrated episode of Venezuelan intellectual history, known as *La delpiniada*, that took place in the principal theater of the city on Saint Florentina's Day, 14 March 1885. The performance was an absurd parodic ceremony satirizing the dictator. The organizers, a group of young writers and journalists, employed a peaceable but mentally unbalanced popular figure who, believing himself to be a poet, wrote raving nonsensical verses that provoked gales of laughter and mockery from the public. He was called, or pretended to be called Francisco Antonio Delpino y Lamas, a humble hat-factory worker, and was persuaded to attend the celebration, supposedly in his honor, in which he would be, among other things, crowned the Prince of Venezuelan Poetry. The ceremony was, of course, a satire of the Guzmán dictatorship, throwing into relief the tinsel, the corruption, and the megalomania of the president who believed himself to be a man of culture and a writer, as well as mocking the fawning entourage of men who applauded him.

Finally, to close this review of the nineteenth century, we should include a brief note of the other arts. The plastic arts and music underwent important developments in Caracas over the course of the nineteenth century. In painting, a number of figures stand out, such as Antonio Herrera Toro (1857–1914), Emilio Boggio (1857–1920), Cristóbal Rojas (1857–1890), and Arturo Michelena (1863–1898), among others. In music, Teresa Carreño (1856–1917) was without doubt the most important figure—a great pianist, a composer, and an orchestra conductor of international fame.

Throughout the twentieth century Caracas has continued to be the cultural center of Venezuela. The uneven development of Venezuela has contributed to a certain hypertrophy of the political center to the detriment of the progress of other cities, even though the bulk of economic activity has taken place far from the capital in provincial cities where the great petroleum ventures are located and where the majority of the wealth of the country has been generated. However, the political hegemony of Caracas over the rest of the country has meant that by far the largest share of intellectual activity is located there. This situation has begun to change in recent decades, such that today, in various cities of the interior and above all those where the universities are located, a tremendous cultural boom in the arts and letters is noticeable. This frank and healthy emulation of Caracas has resulted in a situation where, in some very specific domains, cultural production in the provinces has outstripped that of the capital. Of course, Caracas has had a lot to do with these changes. Writers, artists, and teachers emigrating from the capital in search of a modicum of tranquility—increasingly hard to come by in the Caracan metropolis—have taken up residence in a number of interior cities and especially those cities with a university. These internal emigrants have contributed much to the development of cultural activities in the cities of the interior: It is because they have retained contacts and links to the capital that the new arrivals have in many cases facilitated and bolstered cultural activity in their adopted cities. Often the provincial cultural centers have taken advantage of the presence in Caracas of foreign writers and artists, enticing them to come to the provinces to work on specialized projects. And it is no longer unheard of that this movement can go in the opposite direction, that provincial universities or cultural centers directly invite significant intellectuals from outside the country, who later pass through Caracas, or even return abroad without stopping over in the capital.

In the literary domain, twentieth-century Caracas has seen the growth and development of an important narrative movement. The first generation of mature Venezuelan novelists found its best expression in the so-called regional, rural, or *criollo* novel, a form linked both chronologically and stylistically to the *modernista* movement. Its principal exponent and one of the most important figures in twentieth-century Latin American letters was Rómulo Gallegos, followed by other important prose writers such as Manuel Díaz Rodríguez, Rufino Blanco Fombona, Luis Manuel Urbaneja Achelpohl, José Rafael Pocaterra, Teresa de la Parra, Julio Garmendia, Enrique Bernardo Núñez (1895–1964) (see **Figure 5**), and others, who were all Caracans or permanent residents of Caracas. Later, many other important short fiction writers and novelists were to appear, including Arturo Uslar Pietri (1906–2001) (see **Figure 6**), Miguel Otero Silva, Antonia Palacios (1915–2001), Guillermo Meneses (1911–1978), Gustavo Díaz Solís (b. 1920), Guillermo Morón (b. 1926), Salvador Garmendia, Orlando Araujo (1927–1987), Francisco Harare Duque (1929–1991), Adriano Gonzales León (b. 1931), Denzil Romero (1938–1999), Eduardo Land (b. 1941), Igor Delgado Senior (b. 1942), Carlos Noguera (b. 1943), Francisco Massiani (b. 1944), Orlando Chirinos (b. 1944), José Pulido (b. 1945), Ana Teresa Torres (b. 1945), Sael Ibáñez (b. 1948), Laura Antillano (b. 1950), Antonieta Madrid, Ángel Gustavo Infante (b. 1959), Israel Centeno (b. 1958), Milagros Mata Gil (b. 1951), Cristina Policastro

Figure 5.

Historian and novelist Enrique Bernardo Núñez (1895–1964) c. 1960. (Archive of the author)

Figure 6.

Novelist Arturo Uslar Pietri (1906–2001) c. 1976. (Archive of the author)

(b. 1955), Wilfredo Machado (b. 1956), Stefania Mosca (b. 1957), and others.

The narratives of these authors have gone through a number of diverse stages that can be characterized in a variety of ways: from the rural tale (although sometimes situated in an urban center, it is usually one so scarcely developed that there is little to differentiate it from a rustic milieu) to the urban story of the big city; or from the forthright, linear, and objective story without stylistic or experimental complications to the deeply introspective narrative, whether moving in psychoanalytic directions or not, often showing a marked Faulknerian influence; from a stark realism with strong social and political implications, whether influenced or not by Marxist or other sociopolitical doctrines, to the narrative constructions typical of magic realism or *lo real maravilloso* (the marvelous real); or, finally, from the limpidity and transparency of a style more or less bordering on the Classical, although deeply rooted in the Modern, to the characteristics of a Latin American Baroque, nourished, to be certain, by elements of the Spanish Baroque of the seventeenth century (and that of every age), although strongly accented with *criollo* and Latin American characteristics, stemming directly in some cases from the native heritage, but more commonly from the motley and piebald fountain of mestizo culture.

Developments in twentieth-century Venezuelan poetry were much the same. We have already remarked upon how nineteenth-century Venezuelan poetry was rather weak. In the first decades of the twentieth century, the generation of poetic modernists began to mature, without, however, the appearance of any major Venezuelan poets of an international reputation. Venezuelan poetry of the first third of the twentieth century was the product of an interface of aesthetic and stylistic currents like *modernismo*, nativism, and avant-gardism, but there were no poets of the stature of Vallejo, Neruda, Huidobro, or Borges. The first poetic movement of real importance in Venezuela was the "Generation of 18," a group of very distinguished poets who, within their limitations, were representative of a new kind of poetry and who have begun to be read and celebrated abroad. Among this group, the outstanding figures were José Antonio Ramos Sucre (1890–1930) (see **Figure 7**), Rodolfo Moleiro (1898–1970), Jacinto Fombona Pachano (1901–1951), José Tomás Arreaza Calatrava (1885–1970), Luis Barrios Cruz (1898–1968). Two important poets not belonging to the "Generation of 18" but who are chronologically of the same generation, deserve mention: José Antonio Ramos Sucre was a poet of importance who for a long time remained unknown, although in recent years he has begun to be read outside of Venezuela; and Enriqueta Arvelo Larriva (1886–1962), without a doubt the most accomplished female voice in Venezuelan poetry.

The poets of the "18" clearly had a transformative effect on Venezuelan poetry and were the precursors of the avant-garde movement that came to a head in the 1920s, and in particular in the second half of that decade. Paradoxically, the most enthusiastic proponent of avant-gardism in Venezuela was the *modernista* poet Alfredo Arvelo Larriva (1883–1934) who, without renouncing his *modernista* credentials, experimented with avant-garde techniques and above all persuaded the young poets of his time to adopt the new aesthetic canons. Among those who attended Larriva's talks were the most distinguished representatives of Venezuelan

Figure 7.

Poet José Antonio Ramos Sucre (1890–1930) c. 1924. (Archive of the author)

avant-garde poetry, such as Antonio Arráiz (1903–1962) and Pablo Rojas Guardia (1909–1978). The avant-garde movement would bear fruit somewhat later. Toward the end of the 1940s and the beginning of the 1950s, a poetic movement of great force got underway in Caracas, the *Grupo Viernes* (Friday Group). Active in this group were some of the most forceful and mature voices ever known to Venezuelan poetry, figures such as Vicente Gerbasi, Otto De Sola, Ángel Miguel Queremel (1900–1939), Luis Castro (1909–1933), and Pascual Venegas Filardo (1911–2003), among others, many of whom transcended the borders of the country, and some of whom have merited translation into foreign languages and publication by important editorial houses.

Later, between the 1940s and the 1990s, Venezuelan poetry continued to develop and renew itself with great vigor, although the absence of towering figures of the likes of Huidobro, Neruda, Lezama Lima, Octavio Paz (1914–1998), Nicolás Guillén (1902–1989), or Nicanor Parra (b. 1914), has persisted. In any event, the most important figures of this period, either born or resident in Caracas, are: Miguel Otero Silva (1908–1985), Juan Beroes (1914–1975), Carlos Augusto León (1914–1997), Juan Liscano (1915–2001) (see **Figure 8**), Luz Machado (1916–1999), Aquiles Nazoa (1920–1976)–the best Venezuelan humorist of all times, in verse or in prose, Luis Pastori (b. 1920), Pedro Francisco Lizardo (b. 1920), José Ramón Medina (b. 1921), Elizabeth Schön (b. 1921), Juan Sánchez Peláez (b. 1922), Ida Gramcko (1924–1994), Francisco Pérez Perdomo (b. 1930), Rafael Cadenas (b. 1930), Jesús Sanoja Hernández (b. 1930), Alfredo Silva Estrada (b. 1933), Guillermo Sucre (b. 1933), Ramón Palomares (b. 1935), Caupolicán Ovalles (b. 1936), Eugenio Montejo (b. 1938), Gustavo Pereira (b. 1940), Luis Alberto Crespo (b. 1941), Armando Rojas Guardia (b. 1949), Yolanda Pantin (b. 1955), Elena Vera (b. 1939), and Rafael Clemente Arráiz (1916–1996).

Throughout the twentieth century, the nineteenth-century traditions we have outlined–of the grand essayists, and, in general, of the cultivators of conceptual and expository literature–continued. Venezuela still produces estimable non-fiction writing in a diverse array of areas. In the domain of philosophy,

Figure 8.

Poet and essayist Juan Liscano (1915–2001) c. 1980. (Archive of the author)

a number of figures have stood out, including Pedro César Domínici (1873–1954), Juan David García Bacca (1901–1992), Ernesto Mayz Vallenilla (b. 1925), Juan Nuño Montes (1927–1995), Federico Ríu Farré (1925–1985), Alberto Rosales (b. 1931), Eduardo Vásquez (b. 1927); in philology and the linguistic sciences: Lisandro Alvarado (1858–1929), Ángel Rosenblat (1902–1984), María Teresa Rojas (b. 1902), María Josefina Tejera (b. 1930); in history and the social sciences: José Gil Fortoul (1861–1943), Laureano Vallenilla Lanz (1870–1936), Pedro Manuel Arcaya (1874–1958), Augusto Mijares (1897–1979), Miguel Acosta Saignes (1908–1989), Guillermo Morón (b. 1926), Germán Carrera Damas (b. 1930), Manuel Caballero (b. 1931), Luis Castro Leiva (1943–1999); and in theory and literary criticism: Jesús Semprún (1882–1931), Julio Planchart (1885–1948), Enrique Planchart (1894–1953), Mariano Picón Salas, Arturo Uslar Pietri, Pedro Pablo Barnola (1908–1986), Pedro Grases (b. 1909), Juan Liscano (1915–2001), Oscar Sambrano Urdaneta (b. 1929), Domingo Miliani (b. 1930), Manuel Bermúdez (b. 1930), Alexis Márquez Rodríguez (b. 1931), Guillermo Sucre, Francisco Rivera (b. 1933), Oscar Rodríguez Ortiz (b. 1944), Luis Barrera Linares (b. 1951), Carmen Bustillo, Miguel Gomes (b. 1964), Javier Lasarte (b. 1955), Alba Lía Barrios (b. 1943), Beatriz González Stephen (b. 1952), and Milagros Mata Gil.

The twentieth century saw important developments in Venezuelan theater that, while centered in Caracas, had ramifications in the country as a whole. The most significant Venezuelan dramatists of the century include Leopoldo Ayala Michelena (1897–1962), Luis Peraza (b. 1908), Isaac Chocrón (b. 1932), José Ignacio Cabrujas (1937–1995), Román Chalbaud (b. 1932), Pilar Romero, Rodolfo Santana (b. 1944). In the realm of theater history and criticism, mention should be made of Santiago Magariños (b. 1902), Leonardo Azparren (b. 1941), Enrique Izaguirre (b. 1929), and Rubén Monasterios (b. 1943); in the realm of performance, Juana Sujo (1913–1961), Luis Salazar (b. 1924), María Teresa Acosta (1906–1990), Hilda Vera (1923–1988), Flor Núñez, María Cristina Losada, Teresa Selma, Amalia Pérez Díaz (b. 1923), Orlando Urdaneta (b. 1950), Mimí Lazo, Carlota Sosa, Carlos Márquez (b. 1964), Franklin Virgüez; and in directing, Alberto de Paz y Mateos (1915–1967), Luis Peraza, Nicolás Curiel (b. 1928), Herman Lejter (b. 1935), Carlos Giménez (1945–1993), Armando Gota, Fausto Verdial. One of the great successes of the Venezuelan, and specifically Caracan, theater scene has been the International Theatre Festival sponsored by the Ateneo de Caracas, with significant financial support from the state through the National Council for Culture (CONAC: Consejo Nacional de la Cultura). Many theater groups from a range of countries representing every continent have participated in this great festival. There are today twelve principal permanent theaters in Caracas. In Colonial times the city already had a number of small sites where theatrical and other performances were presented. In the nineteenth century much larger, permanent, and more active theaters were established. The openings of two of these, the Teatro Coliseo, built in 1822, and the Teatro Caracas, built in 1854 and later destroyed by fire, were the subjects of great celebrations in their day. The nineteenth century also saw the construction in the old city center of a grandiose theater named after the dictator who ordered it built, Antonio Guzmán Blanco; later, in 1881, it was renamed the Teatro Municipal. This theater was extremely advanced for its day, equipped with all the most modern equipment and trappings for the presentation of theatrical spectacles, music, ballet, opera, and other performances of this kind. Still in existence, the Teatro Municipal was renovated in 1998, although with the growth of the city its seating capacity has become insufficient. The Teatro Nacional, built in 1904, also continues to operate, and it too suffers from the same problem of size. The principal theater of Caracas forms the nucleus of the Teresa Carreño Cultural Complex; the Sala Ríos Reyna is a large, multiple-use theatre of 4,000 seats, capable of staging grand theatrical, dance, ballet, opera, orchestral, and vocal musical performances. Technically speaking, the Sala Ríos Reyna is a showpiece of modernity: thanks to its completely computerized stage machinery, the transformation from one type of spectacle to another is possible in a matter of minutes. The Teresa Carreño Cultural Complex has a second, smaller theater of 400 seats, the Sala José Félix Ribas, also equipped with the latest in stage equipment.

The Central University of Caracas also has a number of important performance spaces for theater, concerts, ballet, dance, etc. The University's Great Hall or Aula Magna seats 2,000 people and is an extraordinary architectural work, with an enormous acoustic and decorative ceiling composed of large variously colored panels designed and personally installed by the famous artist, Alexander Calder. This installation is considered one of Calder's most important works. The Central University also boasts a spacious 400-seat Sala de Conciertos, and a number of smaller auditoriums, equally serviceable for meetings and cultural performances of all kinds, spread throughout its eleven faculties. The modern building housing the CELARG: Fundación Centro de Estudios Latinoamericanos Rómulo Gallegos (Rómulo Gallegos Central Foundation for Latin American Studies) also contains two spaces capable of staging a diverse assortment of cultural activities, one of which was specially conceived for theatrical representations. It contains, in addition, a number of other spaces with various seating capacities especially designed for conferences, forums, round tables, seminars, etc. The Centro Cultural Consolidado, belonging to the formerly named Banco Consolidado, now the Corp-Banca, is the principle privately-owned auditorium in the city. This theater, with its peculiar design, with two wings of seats placed at right angles to one another converging upon an ample proscenium stage, is capable of staging a variety of performances and cultural spectacles. There are, in addition to those already mentioned, a number of other state-sponsored and private institutions throughout the city containing ample and comfortable spaces for gatherings and cultural spectacles, almost always in modern buildings constructed expressly with these spaces in mind.

In the Colonial period and especially in the years preceding independence, interesting musical movements had developed in Caracas that would continue over the nineteenth and twentieth centuries. In the last century we find figures of high distinction like the composer and musical director Vicente Emilio Sojo (1887–1974), who was above all the inspiration for several generations of students at the Escuela Superior de Música (Conservatory) of which he was the director. Other eminent figures were the composers Antonio Estévez (1916–1988), still today the most outstanding figure of Venezuelan classical music, Evencio Castellanos (1915–1984), Gonzalo Castellano (b. 1926), Juan Vicente Lecuna (1891–1954), Juan Bautista Plaza (1898–1961), José Antonio Ríos Reyna (1905–1971), Moisés Moleiro (1905–1979), Juan Carlos Núñez (1895–1964), Modesta Bor (1926–1998), María Guinán, José

Antonio Abreu (b. 1939), Inocente Carreño (b. 1919), Pablo Castellanos (1917–1981), Josefina Benedetti–a number of whom are conductors and soloists of renown. In vocal music, the soprano Fedora Alemán, and the bass-baritone Pedro Liendo have distinguished themselves and are well known both inside and outside the country.

In recent decades Venezuelan ballet has reached an important level of development under the influence of a number of figures who have benefited from rigorous training abroad, especially in the United States. This has been the case with Sandra Rodríguez, the first great figure of Venezuelan ballet who, after a brilliant international career, returned to Caracas to devote herself not only to the training of young dancers but also to the organization and direction of ballet groups and companies. Another important figure in the world of Venezuelan ballet is Hercilia López. With respect to other dance forms, there has also been great interest, as well as modest growth, thanks to figures like Sonia Sanoja, Andreína Womut, and others.

Forty or fifty years ago there were very few public libraries in Venezuela. The only library in Caracas was the National Library whose modest collection and tranquil atmosphere made it almost exclusively the haunt of students, and in particular the students of the Central University since the library was housed in a wing of the old main block, next to the portion occupied by the University itself. Today the situation is completely different. In 1978 the National Library transformed itself into an autonomous institution, expressly conceived for the dissemination of reading materials and the establishment of libraries throughout the nation. As the result of an extraordinary effort, the National Library today maintains a number of large reading rooms in constant use, both in Caracas and in the interior. Every city of significance in Venezuela today contains a public library and an abundance of readers. In the more remote regions of the country the National Library provides access to its collections through regular deliveries to local elementary and high schools by means of specially furnished book-mobiles and even book-barges. The main branch in Caracas is housed in a modern building especially designed and constructed as a library and offers all the services that a modern library should to a wide variety of readers: researchers, teachers, students, professionals of all kinds, as well as the common reader and devoted book lovers. The National Library's collection now comprises nine million items, one third of which are books, including special collections of incunabula and rare books, and the remainder comprised of periodicals and newspapers, maps, musical scores, manuscripts, photographs, films, videos, transcripts, pamphlets, and loose-leaf fliers, etc.

As for book publishing, as already mentioned, there has existed in Venezuela a publishing industry since the beginning of the nineteenth century when the first press was introduced to Caracas. Today, the Caracan publishing industry is serviced by a number of technologically modern print works, binderies, and design and illustration studios of a very high caliber. Editorial houses are also quite numerous, of varied size, capacity, and editorial orientation, although almost all of them are relatively small, producing between ten and twenty titles on average per year. The largest, however, can be considered something of a giant. Monte Ávila Editores Latinoamericana C.A., while owned by the Venezuelan state, has been administered autonomously since its foundation in 1968 and thus operates by and large like a private corporation. Monte Ávila produces on average eighty to 120 titles per year, for a total of approximately 200,000 copies, ranging across a wide variety of genres and themes, written by authors of diverse nationalities (including several translations from different languages, many of which are done in the publisher's own translation branch). It is, in addition, the only Venezuelan publisher to export books abroad, by means of its excellent distribution network throughout the world, but especially in Spain, the United States, Mexico, Colombia, Argentina, Bolivia, and Puerto Rico, and by means of bookstores in all the countries of Latin America and in many other countries as well.

Beyond these publishing firms, a number of Venezuelan universities and some national academies, as well as a number of other private and public institutions are involved in the continuous and systematic publication of books. The average annual number of book copies published in Caracas is approximately 580,000.

In addition to numerous elementary and secondary schools, Caracas is home to five public and seven private universities. Total enrollment at the tertiary level numbers on average approximately 490,000 students, following a wide variety of academic, scientific, and technical programs. Beyond these universities, there are also in Caracas numerous public and private university institutes.

The oldest communications medium in Caracas is the print newspaper press. We have already seen that in the nineteenth century there were a number of periodicals published in Caracas. Today, the city is home to eleven large dailies, four tabloids, and a number of other standard-format newspapers, all produced in the modern manner, both in terms of design and layout as well as of printing. The contents of these publications are balanced between opinion and general information, the latter almost always arranged thematically under the rubrics of politics, events, government news, culture, sports, etc. and editorials. There are also in the city several weekly magazines and a number of publications of a specifically literary or cultural nature, some of which take the form of Sunday supplements to the various dailies, while others are autonomous publications.

Caracas was one of the first cities in the world to have a commercial radio network, beginning in 1926. Since then, radio broadcasting has seen considerable development and growth in the diffusion of broadcasts from Caracas to other parts of the country. Today, approximately twenty radio stations are located in Caracas, roughly divided between AM and FM frequencies, many of which are national in scope and audience. Almost all have a diverse range of programs that include news, opinion, music and entertainment, and the dissemination of economic, political, scientific, and sports information twenty-four hours a day. With the exception of the Radio Nacional de Venezuela, the state broadcaster, all are privately owned.

Although an excellent system of television networks has developed in Caracas, the excellence is a technical one. Caracas today has ten television channels, one of which is public, almost all of which broadcast nationally, and by satellite, internationally. There is a great diversity of programming: news, reportage on diverse subjects, individual and group opinion interviews, cinema, Venezuelan or internationally produced *telenovelas* (soap operas), sports, musicals, and programs disseminating scientific and cultural information.

There have also been developments in Venezuelan cinema, both in terms of production and in terms of exhibition. Despite major obstacles–especially financial–film production of every type (features, shorts, documentaries, etc.) has become more noticeable in recent decades, both numerically and qualitatively. State financial and technical support has been channeled into film production through the National Council for Cinema Funding (CNAL: Consejo Nacional de Asistencia al Cine), the body created especially for this purpose, although the degree of support has been far from what it should be. On the exhibition side, there are seventy-two commercial and seven publicly-funded movie houses in Caracas, in addition to a number of other small screening rooms that operate on a sporadic basis. Venezuelan and foreign films are freely shown without censorship, although there does exist a film classification system restricting, in certain cases, the age of entry. The open screening system is, however, frequently affected by economic factors stemming from the combination of bringing commercial cinemas into closed circuits of distribution, and their policy of answering only to financial interests. These cinemas are opposed, in as much as is possible, by a limited number of smaller, less robust, independent cinemas which, although they cannot compete with the powerful commercial distribution systems, do fulfill an important social role. The state-sponsored National Cinematheque in Caracas has become an important independent institution for the exhibition of films in which the screening criteria are fundamentally aesthetic and cultural, rather than economic. In addition to this role, the Cinematheque also fulfills important functions as an archive for the conservation of films, as well as intervening in the areas of film dissemination, training, and education in cinematic affairs.

At the start of the twenty-first century, the city of Santiago de León de Caracas continues to develop in all of the areas enumerated here. In the last few decades the city's growth has accelerated vertiginously, thanks to three principle factors. The first has been the rise in the birth rate combined with a fall in infant mortality and rising rates of life expectancy. The second has been an upswing in the number of immigrants, bringing people to the city from the many diverse countries of the Americas, Europe, and other continents, attracted, almost exclusively, by the economic bonanza that has resulted from the boom in oil production. This latter has noticeably diminished in recent years, without, however, a corresponding drop in the attractiveness of Venezuela for the populations of her neighbors, who by and large do not enjoy as high a standard of living. The bulk of these immigrants have settled in Caracas and its outlying metropolitan areas. The third factor has been the increasingly rapid rise in rates of internal migration from rural to urban areas, with Caracas as the principle pole of attraction. Combined with these increases in inhabitants, Caracas has experienced the (in general negative) consequences of a disproportionate and unplanned increase in its population. It is, however, unquestionable that the recent rise in population has been accompanied in the domain of culture by a truly extraordinary boom. (See **Figures 9** and **10**.)

Caracas is today one of the major Latin American capitals from a cultural point of view, presenting on a daily basis every type of cultural spectacle and activity from all the arts, many of them simultaneously across the city. With this boom in cultural activity, the city has also strengthened and amplified its status as a center of cultural diffusion, as much toward the interior of the country as toward specific localities in the exterior, principally, and naturally, toward its geographic neighbors. Venezuelan writers, as well as artistic

Figure 9.

Aerial view of the city of Caracas, 1999. (Archive of the author)

Figure 10.

Caracas from the surrounding hills, 1999. (Archive of the author)

groups and particular artists, now travel frequently outside the capital, both to the interior of the country and abroad, on missions of cultural exchange and dissemination. At the same time, the city also receives artists and artistic groups from both within and outside the country, in a reciprocal exchange. Like the country as a whole, Caracas has prepared itself for the new century and the next millennium, and while the present state of affairs is marked by signs of an acute economic, ethical and social crisis, it also permits optimism. Given the vast political courage of the Venezuelan people, diverse instances of which we have recounted in this history, and taking stock of the enormous natural wealth of the country, we can be optimistic that, in a future now closer than it is distant, the Venezuelan people will overcome their present difficulties, and, with Caracas leading the way, they will set off down that road of prosperity and well-being in which their cultural tradition will play an immensely important role.

Translation by Colman Hogan

Works Cited

Bello, Andrés. 1952. "Calendario manual y guía universal de forasteros en Venezuela para el año de 1810." *El primer libro impreso en Venezuela.* Ed. Pedro Grases. Caracas: Ministerio de Educación. 43–100.

———. 1952 [1810]. "Resumen de la historia de Venezuela." *El primer libro impreso en Venezuela.* Ed. Pedro Grases. Caracas: Ediciones del Ministerio de Educación. 55–90.

Gabaldón Márquez, Joaquín. 1948. *Muestrario de historiadores coloniales de Venezuela.* Caracas: Biblioteca Popular Venezolana.

González, Juan Vicente. 1990. *Biografía de José Felix Ribas.* Ed. Carlos Pacheco. Caracas: Venezuela: Monte Avila Editores.

Humboldt, Alexander von. 1956. *Viaje a las regiones equinocciales del Nuevo Continente.* Trans. Lisandro Alvarado. Vol. 2. Caracas: Ediciones del Ministerio de Educación.

Oviedo y Baños, José de. 1992. *Historia de la conquista y población de la provincia de Venezuela.* Caracas: Biblioteca Ayacucho.

Pérez Bonalde, Antonio. 1969. *Vuelta a la patria.* Caracas: Instituto Nacional de Cultura y Bellas Artes.

CHAPTER 39

LIMA
A BLURRED CENTRALITY

Sara Castro-Klaren

Lima is located on the banks of the Rimac River. In Quechua, the general language of the Inca empire (1400–1532), Rimac means "the one who speaks." However, the earliest archeological records indicate that the people who built Lima culture (200–800 CE) may be of Aymara origin. They may have come from Coquimbo in Chile and Tucuman in Argentina (Agurto Calvo 82). The Lima culture, to judge by the pottery samples in archeological sites, was in permanent communication with other cultures of the Central Andes: Moche, Nazca, Recuay, and Wari (Lumbreras 1974, 119). The pyramid of Maranga in the Rimac Valley shows structural similarities with the greater pyramids of the Moche Valley; polychrome murals have been found at most of the Lima pyramids. An estimated million tons of handmade adobe went into the construction of the Huaca Juliana, the Huaca Trujillo, and the Maranga pyramid, all of which are still standing in what is today the metropolitan radius of the city of Lima (Lumbreras 1990, 258–70). Pachacamac, to the south, in the Lurin valley, constitutes one of the most spectacular centers of Lima culture. This adoring site to the maker of the universe, later encompassed in the Inca cult of the Sun by the Inca Tupac Yupanqui (1471–1493), remained as the center of pilgrimages until the Spanish Conquest. The great complex faced the ocean and the entire edifice was painted in vermilion. The old temple enshrined the famous oracle of Pachacamac, represented in a bifrontal (back to back) deity. One side holds an ear of corn and his name is Vichama, god of daylight; the other holds feathers, and his name is Ichama-Pachacamac, the god of darkness. Hernando Pizarro destroyed this statue in 1533, but others, scattered in the region, survived (Silva Sifuentes 169–70; Watanabe 329–32; and Agurto 145–50, 153). Pachacamac shared many of the constitutive features of Wiracocha, the Wari deity posited as the maker of the universe, and it is for that reason that the temples in Pachacamac became a powerful center in Andean cults and pilgrimages (Agurto 106). According to María Rostworowski, the cult of Pachacamac as maker of the world (associated with earthquakes) maintained its force through the Colonial campaigns of the extermination of Andean religions. Pachacamac is in fact the deity inscribed within the popular contemporary cult to the Señor de los Milagros. It is Peru's pan-deity.

Colonial Semiosis

The arrival of the Spanish conquistadors in the Lima region on 18 January 1535, represents a second Andean urban foundation. It dislocates Cuzco's centrality, but it does not eclipse the former "navel" of the Inca empire. Lima's centrality, anchored on the power of the institutions that writing deployed, would constitute itself in a struggle for hegemony with other urban centers in the former Inca empire. The Spanish Colonial political system, resting on the concept of private property, saw the foundation of the city as the enactment of a ceremony by which the land was emptied out of all previous cultural practices and made ready for the inscription of land use specified in the Spanish urban grid. Surrounding the plaza and, as if facing each other,

the four major instruments in Colonial rule—Church, judiciary, executive, and pillory or *picota*–claimed land and built their edifices around the Plaza de armas. The streets which flowed out of the grid into the countryside and the Indian towns were the result of the huge land grants made to the early conquistadors and the different and competing evangelizing orders. An immense cathedral, great houses, meandering convents, and opulent churches, built by Indian labor and decorated by carvings and paintings from the hands of European, *mestizo*, and Indian artists, reconfigured the landscape of the Rimac Valley.

Despite the fact that the *quipu* (complex communication system of knotted cords) were widely and universally used through out the Inca empire, alphabetic writing displaced all Andean systems of recording memory and notation in official discourses (Millones 90). The Church's systematic destruction of the *quipu*, together with the priestly and administrative class who used them, did not eradicate their use in daily life. In practice it remained advantageous to continue using the *quipu* because they proved indispensable in the collection of tribute and taxes, as well as sins in the confessional. Nevertheless, writing in this colonial situation not only sustained the Spanish institutions founded upon its deployment but also produced a new class of Andean—*mestizo*, Indian, mulatto, and *criollo*–intellectuals. The two towering local intellectuals who stemmed from Andean families, Garcilaso de la Vega, Inca (1539–1616), and Guamán Poma de Ayala (1524?–1613), used alphabetic writing not only to compose in Spanish but, as in the case of Guaman Poma, also to record his writing in Quechua and Aymara. The fact that neither Garcilaso nor Guamán Poma was a resident of Lima speaks of the contested centrality of that city. (See **Figures 1** and **2**.)

After Pizarro's founding of Lima, the new urban space was often the site of military (and murderous) struggles for power among the conquistadors themselves and the several Crown officials dispatched from Spain with orders to establish a Colonial organization in which the Spanish Crown would play the paramount role. While the Spaniards fought for control of the unimaginable wealth and spoils of Conquest, the Andean population faced the compounded effects of invasion: endemic war, famine, rape, forced labor, loss of property, forced relocation, inducement into the *encomiendas* (royal land grants) and *repartimientos* (a system of land distribution), organizational breakdown, and cultural disruption. The consequences of conquest were disastrous and the holocaust the Andeans endured was expressed in Guamán Poma's refrain: "Qué no nos acabemos" ("Dear God keep us from extinction"). Historians estimate that the Andean holocaust involved a population decline from approximately nine million inhabitants in 1531 to one million by the time the New Laws reached Peru in 1543 (Klaren 49). By 1620, a few years after the death of Guamán Poma, the census registered a total of 700,000 Indians in the viceroyalty of Peru (Bakewell 151).

In order to supply the coastal *repartimientos*, *encomiendas*, and the great houses in the Spanish towns with labor for sugar and wine-making, as well as domestic service, African slaves

Figure 1.

Drawing by Guamán Poma de Ayala depicting the foundation of Santiago de Cuzco in 1534 from his book El primer nueva corónica y buen gobierno *(1615). (Courtesy of John P. Robarts Research Library, University of Toronto)*

Figure 2.

Drawing by Guamán Poma de Ayala depicting the foundation of Lima in 1533 from his book El primer nueva corónica y buen gobierno *(1615). (Courtesy of John P. Robarts Research Library, University of Toronto)*

were imported in large numbers. By 1586 Lima boasted 4,000 African slaves, a number which increased to 15,000 by 1640 (Millones 83). In comparison, Lima's non-African population was 2,000 in 1580 and 9,000 by 1630. Lima was not only the site of a large slave population but also of run-away and free slaves who mixed in with the thousands of vagabonds, beggars, and *picaros* of all ethnic backgrounds. The Colonial administration was hard-pressed to classify this multitude for taxing and tribute collecting purposes. They devised the grid of the *castas* by which all "mixtures and their offspring were obligated to pay tribute" (Millones 83). The reality of an uncontrollable *mestizaje* eventually gave the lie to a racist nomenclature developed as a control mechanism for fixing the population in geographical space, as well as in rigid social and economic niches.

In 1529 Charles V offered the Viceroyalty of New Spain (Mexico) to the Count of Oropesa, Don Francisco Alvarez de Toledo–who turned it down. Almost sixty years later (in 1569), one of his younger sons, Francisco de Toledo, arrived in Peru in order to organize the Colonial administration of the former Inca empire. During his years in Peru (1569–1581), Viceroy Toledo chose to travel and reconnoiter the country in order to pacify it and to dispose of the last Inca descendants

and all possible leaders of Indian or *mestizo* rebellions. On 24 September 1572, forty years after the foundation of Lima by Pizarro, Toledo had the last Inca, Tupac Amaru, executed in the great Plaza of Cuzco. This was only one of the many actions that Toledo took in order to "prove" that the Incas were "tyrants" and as such could not aspire to self-rule or joint rule with the Spanish. Toledo's purpose in decimating the Incan nobility was twofold: to destroy them physically in order not to have to negotiate with anyone and to invalidate Bartolomé de las Casas's (1474–1566) claims of Incan legitimacy as *señores naturales* (see **Figure 3**). With the execution of Tupac Amaru, Cuzco was decentralized and all eyes in the viceroyalty had to turn to Lima as the center of a new power game.

During his inspection the viceroy traveled with a phalanx of seventy men–jurists and clergy–whom he deployed for several tasks and whose reports and *cronicas* constructed a good part of what we now both know and ignore about the life and the history of the Andes. Toledo had been raised at the courts of Charles V and Philip II and he knew how to identify and motivate (by economic, social, and psychological rewards) the talented men whom he brought into his service. Among the people who collaborated with him were intellectuals such as

Figure 3.

Figure 4.

Drawing on the Inca Ataguapla in Caxamarca receiving Almagro, Pizarro and Fray Visente by Guamán Poma de Ayala from El primer nueva corónica y buen gobierno (1615). (Courtesy of John P. Robarts Research Library, University of Toronto)

Drawing by Guamán Poma de Ayala of an official scribe "Escrivano de cabildo" from El primer nueva corónica y buen gobierno (1615). (Courtesy of Rolena Adorno)

José de Acosta (1540–1600), Polo de Ondegardo (d. 1575), linguists and translators such as Diego González de Holguín (d. 1552), extricator of idolatries such as Cristóbal de Albornoz, adventurers such as Pedro de Sarmiento de Gamboa (1532?–1608?), and warriors such as Martín de Loyola (d. 1606). Even though he did not spend most of his time in Lima–his general inspection took five years to complete (1570–1575)–Toledo did set down the foundations for what was to evolve into an urban administrative center with an important courtly life in which Spanish jurists, clergymen and minor intellectuals, and poets and artists mixed with an ever increasing number of *mestizo* and even Indian clergy, lawyers, teachers, sculptors, and painters (see **Figure 4**). With the establishment of a printing press in 1583, Toledo gave impetus to San Marcos University (1551). He also approved the establishment of the Jesuit College for the sons of the Incan nobility and the building of the Franciscan, Augustinian, Dominican, and Mercederian monasteries. Lima began to acquire the physical and social capital necessary to fashion itself as the center of the Viceroyalty of Peru.

Toledo's labor legislation, based on *Gobierno del Perú* [1567; Government of Peru] by the Spanish jurist Juan de Matienzo (1520–1579), provided the ground rules for colonial exploitation

which would make possible (or impossible) the cultural life of Lima as a space of intense and, more often than not, asymmetrical cultural contact. The idea of grouping Indians into "repúblicas de Indios" where they could be controlled by the *corregidor* (chief magistrate) and supervised by the *curaca* (overseer) not only broke with the agricultural pattern of Andean population settlement, but it also gave rise to the Indian towns. These became new social spaces in which Andean culture would embark on an evolutionary post-conquest process of its own, marked by the predominant presence of the Church and seared by the campaigns for the extricator of idolatries. In 1609, driven by zealotry and personal interest, the clergyman Francisco de Ávila began making it public that, through confession in towns near Pachacamac, he had learned that many Indians, especially *curacas* and Andean priests, continued to worship the *huacas*. He proposed and won approval to conduct a campaign to discover the *huacas*, identify, and bring to trial (under the auspices of the Holy Inquisition) the leaders of the idolatries (Millones 113). With the *reducciones de Indios* (forced settlements) Toledo created a cultural contact situation which he did not anticipate: the possibility of governing the Indians had been left in the hands of the evangelizing clergy for they acted as the sole agents of cultural transformation. The priests not only made use of public ceremonies but they had also at their disposal the sacraments, all of which were key steps in the process of legitimization of the Andean peoples as subjects of the Crown. The entire life cycle of an Andean person was marked by the sacraments. However, despite the powerful weapons at the clergy's disposal, the Andean resisted the loss of their gods and rituals and, more often than not, the post-extirpation clergy decided that it was better to pretend to be unaware of the Andeanization of Christianity. As the Colonial process unfolded, it became evident that the persecution and destruction by Andean priests (*hechiceros*), which began as early as 1565 with the persecution of the Taqui Oncoy (dancing sickness) movement, did not benefit anyone (Millones 243–66). Even at the end of the eighteenth century, when the *curacas* were replaced with *alcaldes de indios* (Indian magistrates), named by the Spanish authorities, the power of the *hechiceros* had not diminished. The new leaders also needed the *huacas* in order to govern effectively (Millones 118).

Toledo also reconfigured the *mita* (system of forced labor) in order to provide labor for the mines. From then on, the Andean world revolved around the new centers of mineral production: silver in Potosi and mercury in Huancavelica. Lima's bureaucrats and traders benefited from the legislation that gave them control over the export of these minerals to Europe. Lima's cultural activity was dominated by the departure of the armed fleet during the months of April and June. Slowly, Lima gained the fruits of a *pax colonial* marked by an intense ceremonial life. The objective was to construct for the American subjects a visible sense of the power of the metropolitan center which, from a great distance, ruled their lives. A calendar with more than 150 celebrations was devised. The arrival and departure of viceroys, bishops, and other important figures in the colonial regime was marked by lengthy parades and other public events. Often, the Colonial order celebrated events in Spanish life that had already taken place some three to six months past. Invariably the Plaza de armas was chosen as the appropriate space for such state-sponsored spectacles of self affirmation and continuity. The Spanish authorities understood fiestas as an effective mode of mass communication in a society in which they needed to show the effects of their power as often as possible in order to conserve it. Visitors from all over the viceroyalty were simply awed by the pomp and pageantry and especially by the lengthy nature of the ceremonies and celebrations. The concentration of excess, the extravagant expenditure of precious resources, and the seemingly coextensive space with the metropolis constituted an image of the glory of power. In this sense Lima concentrated and irradiated great cultural and political power over the rural areas of the empire.

But the notion that the center of the Viceroyalty of Peru settled into a life of comfort dominated by a court of splendor is today challenged by new scholarship on the subject. The tropical climate was unhealthy to the many who lived in cramped quarters in a city without running water or sewage disposal. The hospitals, on the whole run by the charitable orders, were in fact centers for the spread of disease and death. Major earthquakes shook the city in 1655, 1687, and 1746, destroying several of its architectural jewels. Pirates and corsairs regularly raided the port of Callao. Such insecurities accentuated the intense ritual life already fostered by the many centers of religious life. Convents, monasteries, and schools absorbed and channeled almost all of the intellectual energy of the colonial city. These institutions were practically the only avenue for literacy and learning for *mestizos* and one of the few places where mulattos, *castas,* and women could escape a life of grinding physical labor and endless poverty. Spiritual life of all kinds found its way into the several institutions offered by the Church, from family worship and Sunday mass to *cofradias*, monastic contemplation, and even higher education. It is thus not surprising that the Colonial period produced more saints and holy people than secular intellectuals. Doña Inez Muñoz, wife and later widow to Martín de Alcántara, Pizarro's half brother, founded in 1573 a sumptuous monastery consecrated to the Virgin of the Immaculate Conception. The daughters and sisters of the *encomenderos* joined in droves. By 1688 the convent had 309 religious, fourteen novices, eighteen lay women, and twenty-seven *donadas* (servants). Rosa de Lima (1586–1617), the first American saint, was one of the many holy women and men who, during their own life, became objects of cults which attributed to them the power to perform miraculous cures. Santa Rosa's contemporary counterpart in popular devotion was the Dominican barber and servant Martín de Porras. The daughter of Spanish parents, Rosa de Lima was quickly canonized (1671), while the humble mulatto had to wait until the second half of the twentieth century to become the first black saint. Today they are revered as a pair, and their procession constitutes one of the largest public ceremonies in modern Lima.

Toward the end of the seventeenth century the population of Lima had grown to 37,234 people, 20 percent of whom belonged to some type of religious organization. The Holy Office of the Inquisition in Peru from 1569 to 1820 made sure that any deviation was met with severe discipline and punishment. Furthermore, the Church was not always happy with its saints, for they represented a thorny problem. On the one hand, their faith, life of sacrifice, and especially their Christian death could be construed as a monument to the success of the evangelizing mission and the transplantation of Spanish Counter-Reformation culture in the American dominions. On the other hand, that very same faith and especially its mystical raptures indicated the possibility of direct communication with God. The Church coped with its possible displacement by requiring all men and women embarked on the holy life to confess all visions, dreams, or revelations. Further, all faithful were under strict orders to denounce anyone suspected of heresy or heterodox practices. Even under such tight strictures, it was not always possible for the holy men or women to report visions that conformed to the Church's beliefs and many were tried, tortured, and burned at the stake (Millones 185). Such was the case of Francisco de la Cruz (1530–1578) who studied in Valladolid between 1558 and 1561 under the tutelage of Las Casas.

Born Isabel Flores de Oliva, the purposeful and delicate Rosa, took it as her mission to help the destitute Indians and blacks who came to die (unmercifully) in the Lima hospitals. But it was the deadly fasting and excruciating mortification of her young and beautiful body that made her famous in Lima and beyond. Rosa too was associated with a circle of mystics but when the Inquisition questioned her she responded by claiming complete ignorance and incapacity to understand what her visions meant. Her untimely death at the age of 31 allowed her to escape a full inquiry by the Holy Office. Her death was one of the great events of Lima history: Her body had to be moved several times in order to prevent members of her cult from cutting a finger or some other part of her sacralized body to keep as a holy relic.

Writing, confession, belonging to devotional circles, preaching, and thinking were all very dangerous acts to engage in within the confines of a Colonial regime anxious about Protestants, Jews, and Indians who, together, represented a projection of the fears, insecurities, and self-doubts of the colonial enterprise. In this climate of oppression and repression, it is not surprising to find literary expression confined to anonymous satirical verse, *autos sacramentales* (mystery plays), and sermons. In fact neither of the two great texts of this period were written in Lima. *Los comentarios reales* [Royal Commentaries of the Incas] by the *mestizo* exile Garcilaso de la Vega, Inca was published in Lisbon in 1609–1617 and the *Nueva crónica y buen gobierno* [New Cronicle [sic] and Good Government] finished in 1615 by Guamán Poma (lost until 1908 when the Americanist Richard A. Pietschmann found it in the Royal Library in Copenhagen) was published in Paris by Paul Rivet in 1936 (Castro-Klaren 1994, 229–44).

The colonial semiosis–which began in Cajamarca with the scene in which the Inca Atawalpa throws the Bible on the ground as a way of showing his displeasure with the Spanish claims that the Bible spoke the word of God–continued with the Counter-Reformation politics of evangelization. Visual representations–paintings and particularly *estampas* or prints–played as great a role in the colonization of the Andean imaginary as writing did in the establishment of discursive formations which organized thinking and feeling. The printing press brought to Lima in 1583 in conjunction with the three Concilios of Lima (1565, 1567, 1583) was instrumental in the establishment and advancement of a Colonial cultural policy which was two-pronged: the propagation of Christian belief by means of *estampas* or prints, etchings, and paintings together with the indoctrination of the catechism. The publication of *Doctrina cristiana y catecismo para la instrucción de los indios* [1584; Christian Doctrine and Catechism for the Indians' Instruction] and the *Confesionario para los curas de indios* [1585; Confessional Manual for Priests Who Minister to Indians], together with the arrival of Flemish and Italian master painters, mark key moments in the development of two of the most productive and original Colonial arts: painting and religious transculturation.

The Council of Trent (1545–1563) policies recommended the conversion of heretics through the use of visual texts. The Jesuits, leaders in the Catholic counter-offense against Protestantism, enthusiastically took up the idea of conversion in the Indies by means of the visual arts. Philip II gave them ample power over the education of the Indian elites, recognizing the special aptitude of the newly founded order for the evangelization of the American Indians (Lopez Baralt 174). The development of the Colonial schools of painting–in Cuzco, Lima, Chiquisaca, and Quito–as conveyors of the Christian themes selected as appropriate for catechization, responded strictly to the policies adopted in Trent. Painting thus had a didactic and highly ideologized purpose and, as such, it operated within very close strictures. Iñigo de Loyola, a Spanish painter, arrived in Cuzco in 1545, in order to populate with images the enormous churches being built all over the viceroyalty. However, his main mission was to train Indian and *mestizo* men of talent to produce images in the European manner. Other Spanish painters followed under the same conditions, and the Cuzco School of painting was born out of the transculturated style that the local artists produced in the several workshops of the Andes (see **Figure 5**). Seventy percent of the painters associated with the School of Cuzco,

founded by Diego Quispe Tito (1611–1681), were Indians (Gisbert 104), but not all the paintings done had religious themes; many were also portraits of prominent Spaniards and their families. And the rich *caciques* also paid to have their portraits done in either Spanish or post-Inca vestments. The *caciques* often paid as well to have paintings which recorded great ceremonies or fiestas (Fane 144–55 and 171–80), and these canvases remain a rich source of ethnographic data.

The iconography of the European Counter-Reformation underwent important alterations at the hands of the Indian and *mestizo* painters of the School of Cuzco. All topics pertaining to Mary were taken up with fervor. The themes of the Immaculate Conception and the Mother and Child dominated. Scenes in the life of the Christ Child adorned the walls of almost every church, with the return from Egypt as a particulate favorite. Scenes from the crucifixion, in which the torture of the flesh was powerfully depicted, found a home in churches, as well as on domestic altars. Despite the fact that the theme of the Trinity was excluded from the preaching done to the Indians for fear of misinterpretation and confusion with the Andean trinity (composed of father, son, and brother) (Gisbert 88), it was a topic *mestizo* and Indian artists

Figure 5.

Drawing by Guamán Poma de Ayala of a painter-artisan from El primer nueva corónica y buen gobierno *(1615). (Courtesy of Rolena Adorno)*

and their patrons found appealing. The God with three faces or three manifestations captured the imagination of the Andeans who deployed their very own readings of this iconography. Thus the Madonna became the outer casing of the great Apus–snowcapped mountains, sources of spring water– and Santiago was revalidated as a manifestation of the Illapa, the thunder god. Of course the most original and celebrated creations of the Cuzco School were the effeminate and delicate archangels armed with muskets, whose military uniforms were like those depicted in French military manuals (Bayón 1984, 742). The abundance of these delicious creatures was associated with the special role the Jesuits conferred upon angels as they catechized the Indians. The Jesuits were a newly created order and had no saints of their own, so they used the angels in military garb as an emblem of Christian Conquest and divine predilection for Spain (Gisbert 87).

In Lima, the Italians Bernardo Bitti (1548–1610) and Angelino Medoro (1547–1631) taught the basic techniques of European painting and thus established a Mannerist style and iconography (Mesa and Gisbert 1972, 9–10) that would be used practically until the end of the Colonial period (Stastny 32–34). In 1588 the Italian painter and engraver Mateo Pérez de Alesio (1547–1616) arrived in Lima with a huge number of prints of etchings and a *libro de dibujos* (book of drawings) by Durer (Mesa and Gisbert 1972, 64–68). Alesio was not the only painter to have arrived with an ample collection of prints which he used not only for instructive purposes but also as a kind of archive which contained models–clouds, trees, flowers, legs, faces, wings–which could quickly be put to the service of composition and rendition of any request made of the workshop. Baltasar de Figueroa (ca. 1560–1659) in Colombia left six books of prints (*estampas*) of lives of saints and some 1,800 other prints and motifs (Stastny 35). The iconographic and thematic archive of colonial painting was well-stocked by the printing presses and export houses of Amsterdam. By the middle of the seventeenth century, the export of paintings, etchings, prints, and fine furniture to America and the import of raw materials from Spanish America accounted for a fundamental transformation in the art business and the processes of transculturation on both sides of the Atlantic. It is thus not surprising to find in Colonial churches and private collections works by Zurbarán, Rubens and other Flemish and Spanish masters (Stastny 34).

In the late sixteenth century, the *Academia Antártica*, a group of Spanish and *criollo* poets, imitated the Academies which existed in Spain. A distinguished example of this group is Juan de Miramontes y Zuázola (1550–1614) whose epic poem *Armas antárticas* (1608) was one of the finest works of the Colonial period, as valuable as the much better known *La Araucana* (1569–1589). *Armas antárticas* had the same detailed documentation, as well as a sober neo-platonic orientation characteristic of the *Academia Antártica*. The programmatic collection *Discurso en loor de la poesía* [1608; Discourse in Praise of Poetry] is attributed to Amarilis, the female poet who also wrote a long love letter to the Spanish poet and playwright Lope de Vega (1562–1635). The *Discurso*, like much of the work of the poets of the *Academia Antártica*, indicates a close association with Spanish Petrarchism (Martín Adán 23–46).

Life in the colonies during the seventeenth century was characterized by corruption and contraband. Almost any office or title was for sale. The outcome of any encounter with the law was subject to games of influence and bribes. Some *criollos* were able to take advantage of the situation but, in general, they lost out to the Spanish-born elite which controlled all the sites of power in all the major institutions associated with writing. Personal advancement was virtually impossible. The sense of claustrophobia with which people lived was intensified by the Peninsula's own disillusionment after Spanish imperial ambitions suffered the major blow of the loss of the armada to England. The full impact of the Counter-Reformation and the onset of the Baroque in the metropolis had specific and very local manifestations in the colonies. Obliged to keep silent by virtue of the many royal decrees and the cultural policies of the Inquisition, the upper-class Colonial intellectuals who were not permitted to write novels or histories of the Indian peoples took up the tortuous route of Baroque prose and satirical verse (Costigan 29).

Chartered by Charles V in 1551, at the request of the Spanish colonists who wanted their sons to receive university titles in order that they may be eligible for positions in the high bureaucracy, San Marcos University, modeled after Salamanca, by 1570s boasted sixteen academic chairs, including one in Quechua. It maintained its place as the premier Colonial university offering training in the five major faculties necessary to rank as a major university: arts (philosophy), theology, medicine, civil law, and canon law. By 1678 it offered mathematics, but Quechua had been suspended. Although secularly endowed, the religious orders, who ran "Colegios" with college level instruction at the sites of their own convents and monasteries, also offered at San Marcos instruction in the writings of their most prominent theologians– St. Thomas Aquinas and St. Augustine. They thus gave the scholastic tradition in Spanish America a foundational role. But only San Marcos could confer baccalaureates, masters, licentiate, and doctoral degrees. San Marcos remained the focus of intellectual life for the Colonial elites. Until the end of the eighteenth century, it used the same textbooks approved for use (censored) in the entire Hispanic world and, in doing so, it contributed to the creation of a bifurcated pattern of cultural contact with Europe–for what the Spanish authorities put in the list of the forbidden (novels, philosophy, science, and history) came into the colonies by way of substantial book smuggling.

Of interest here is the fact that the number of men and women who lived in monasteries and nunneries during the seventeenth century in colonial cities was very large indeed. The population inside these institutions included not only the friars or nuns of the order, but also novices, brothers, students, lay brothers, servants, slaves, and artisans. By 1621 the Lima Audiencia estimated that there were 1,053 friars in the monasteries of the Franciscans, Dominicans, Mercedarias, Jesuits, Benedictines, and Augustinians. By far, the Jesuits had the largest number of students (170), while the Dominicans had thirty lay brothers. The monasteries had grown not only in size (they often occupied more than a square block), but in intellectual, social and economic importance. Their quarters often boasted beautiful architecture, patios tiled in Seville style, splendid churches decorated with the best of Colonial Baroque wood carvings, Cuzqueño or Lima school paintings, orchards, and of course legendary kitchens (Durán Montero 118–22).

However, male monasteries and schools paled in comparison with the women's convents and *beaterios* which housed lay women who took simple vows under the rules of the Third Order of the Franciscan Rule and other similar societies. Elementary schooling was offered to various classes of girls

(Lavrin 165–95; Bakewell 246). In 1625, a petition was made before the Audiencia to create a new convent of Santa Catalina in Lima. One of the reasons given was the population saturation in the existing convents and the unabated increase in new vocations. Such numbers, contrary to what might be expected, were perceived to be a problem. Charles II indicated his desire to see the number of women in convents curtailed because he had learned that the servants who, on the whole, were *mestizo*, mulatto, and black, were women of very "bad and despicable habits." They made it impossible really to keep cloister from the world (Durán Montero 123). The Lima convents for women were also disruptive to the Spanish city grid. As they extended the social formation processes taking place within the walls of their domain, they expanded physically, often occupying several city blocks. And indeed their efforts to extend over larger spaces were predicated on the fact that the crowded condition in which they lived caused many of the residents to die of tuberculosis (Durán Montero 124). The impossibility of entering the convents, either because of lack of space or the inability to pay the necessary dowry, saw the multiplication of the *beaterios*. These communities offered an ordered and simple life of prayer, routine, and spirituality. Many of these *beaterios* channeled their energies into social work and took in orphans, abused women, repentant prostitutes, and even Indian women inspired by a true vocation. The austerity of the *beaterios* contrasted with the luxury of some of the private cells in the cloistered convents. Relatively well-read nuns often disputed the meaning of the rule of their order and other interpretative matters with the bishop. The case of Maria Antonia Lucía del Espíritu Santo (1646–1709), founder of the Descalzas, is today as notable as it was then notorious (Bermúdez-Gallegos 25–28). Hagiography reading, writing, and commentary constituted the mainstays of the convent imaginary. All convents belonged to the contemplative orders; none belonged to the teaching orders, for the latter would not appear until the end of the eighteenth century (Bakewell 247).

The impact of an official world, organized by a set of enclosures, fixed hierarchies, and censorship, is most visible in the effects it had on the elite (*criollo*) Colonial intellectual. Pablo Macera (b. 1929) sees Baroque culture as a cultural formation traversed by dogmatic ideas, forms, and rules for action and belief (in Costigan 36; Macera 2: 400) which leave little room for alternate forms. In the scholastic atmosphere of the period, Colonial intellectuals had to hide their frustration and often wasted their energies contributing to the pageantry of ceremonies, poetry jousts, panegyrics, and other forms of court poetry. Gongorism, with its vocabulary and universe of reference steeped in Greek and Roman myth, history, legend, and literature, was then in vogue in Spain. Paradox, antithesis, inversion, and parallelism made up the rhetorical preferences of Gongorism, so the bulk of the Baroque poetry written under these circumstances was but an extravagant exercise in verbal pyrotechnics. Scholastic arguments, euphuistic poetry failed as a means of reflexivity or as the inscription lived reality. Gongorism, named after the Spanish poet Luis de Góngora, was practiced more as an instrument for ideological control than as a poetic form suitable for the exploration of subjectivity or the imaginary.

Before this impasse, the solution adopted by many was to distance themselves from privileged discursive forms. Their work came to constitute a kind of Baroque counter-culture (Costigan 39) practiced by itinerant and certainly part-time writers. John Beverly points out that what characterizes Gongorism in America is the way in which it was utilized in order to mystify, through its powerful stylistic and metaphorical alchemy, the Indian labor which was the real basis of wealth and of consumer goods (Beverly 90). Satirical verse, as in the case of *Diente del Parnaso* [ed. Ricardo Palma 1837; The Tooth of Parnasus], provides a good example of disenchanted distance but not of what we understand as modern critique. To a certain extent, Colonial satire recovered the ironic perspective of the general populace on the illusory game of official truth. Satire also began the work of incorporating Colonial usage into the lexicon in a move intended to record and represent the local universe. The idea of a new American literary discourse begins to emerge. Whether the poems were addressed to the members of the high court or the populace, the fact that they expressed dissent and disbelief in the official and pompous cultural forms offered a way to explore the incorporation of new historical subjects—*picaros*, pimps, whores, cardsharps, cuckolded husbands, fake virgins—who began to be incorporated into the Colonial discursive formations.

The case of Juan de Espinosa Medrano (1620?–1688), better known as Lunarejo, is pertinent here, even though he did not live in Lima. He was an illegitimate child whose "racial" parentage remains in doubt. What matters is that he wrote some of the most accomplished poetry in Góngora's style, achieving fame with the sermons he delivered in the Cuzco cathedral. Lunarejo was one of the most learned men of his time, usually remembered for his *Apologético en favor de D. Luis de Góngora, Principe de los poetas liricos de España* [Lima 1662; Apologetic in Favor of D. Luis de Góngora, Prince of the Lyrical Poets of Spain] which he wrote in order to defend the Spanish poet as well as Baroque aesthetics. Lunarejo argues that Góngora is quite entitled to write a poetry given to the beauty of rhetorical complication rather than to transcendental themes because Góngora's poetry is not epic or religious. Known also as the Doctor Sublime, the apologist himself was also highly regarded for his vast knowledge of the classics and for the dramas and comedies that he wrote in Quechua and Spanish. El Lunarejo studied in the Universidad de San Ignacio de Loyola in Cuzco and received his doctorate in 1654. In the *Apologético*, he expressed a clear self-identification with the New World and with men of letters who wrote *from* America. He questioned the commonplace idea that someone from the Indies could not be considered a good writer, capable of pleasing the Europeans, and he rejected the idea that satirical poetry was the only venue possible for an American: "Pero, que no puede haber bueno en las Indias? . . . . Sátiros nos juzgan, tritones nos presumen, que brutos de alma, en vano se alientan a desmetirnos mascaras de la humanidad" (qtd. in Chang-Rodríguez 118) ("What is this? There cannot be good writers in the Indies? They think us satyrs, trytons, brutes. In vain they encourage themselves to paint us as mere masks of humanity").

In the long run, in the development of Latin American letters, the questioning of the Eurocentric literary value system voiced from Cuzco would be more influential and long-lasting than the satirical moves of the poets associated with Lima's cultural milieu or the *Academia Antártica*. In the context of the life of El Lunarejo it is important also to underscore the role played by the sermon as a cultural form which mediated between certain types of orality and the more established written genres. Both the sermon and the theater, the principal Colonial verbal manifestations, assume the participation of a larger and more heterogeneous public than poetry or the essay do, despite the fact that the euphuistic sermon seduced a public which did not fully understand it. The seduction worked precisely because, as Antonio Gramsci might put it, the public found it too difficult to understand and therefore judged it to be good (Rodríguez-Garrido 154–55).

The "Barroco de Indias" refers to the *mestizo* architectural style that shaped every building and adorned the façades of temples and houses. Exuberant in size, color, and decorative motifs, the Spanish American Baroque of the highlands in contrast (Kubler and Soria 96) was heavy and imposing. The need for tremendous loads of local stone affected the Baroque in Lima which had no nearby quarry. Most of the decoration was reserved for the gold-leaf altars and *retablos* or niches inside the churches and the private chapels of the very wealthy. Art historians have demonstrated the clear imprint of Indian artisan traditions as well as Pre-Columbian iconography in Potosí, Pomata, Juli, and Arequipa (Bayón and Murillo Marx).

Local Knowledge and the Effects of the Enlightenment

The eighteenth century is often regarded as a period of transition in Colonial rule from the Hapsburg to the Bourbons (War of Spanish Succession 1700–1713) and the subsequent Bourbon reforms which brought, albeit slowly, great changes in the intellectual and artistic horizon of the Spanish American colonies. The Bourbons adopted a policy of increased independence from the Papacy. They also limited many of the privileges (*fueros*) previously granted to the Church and the clergy. They loosened the grip of scholasticism and fostered the expansion of knowledge in the natural sciences and favored economic reform. By 1723 the medical faculty in San Marcos accepted the scientific explanation of the circulation of the blood. The process of positive reception of the Enlightenment was launched by the Jesuits. The work of Decartes, Newton, and Leibnitz was being taught in the Jesuit colleges, and it was Francisco Javier Clavijero (1731–1787) who, in Mexico, launched the most powerful attack against scholasticism. The Jesuits were expelled from Spain and its colonies in 1767; in Lima, San Marcos stepped in to fill the vacuum left by the Company. Attention was also paid to the idea of creating a system in which education would be available to the general populace. The idea of accumulating and propagating scientific and economic knowledge lead to the creation of many *Sociedades económicas* or *Amigos del País*. The teaching of science found many obstacles—from religious orthodoxy to a lack of trained teachers. The *Sociedad de Amantes del País* published the *Mercurio Peruano* between 1791 and 1793, and the best minds of the high culture of Peruvian enlightenment wrote for it on economics, science, geography, philosophy, history, and even novels and theater. Contact with French intellectual and artistic life was intense and formative. The ample and lasting embrace of France in the intellectual and plastic arts began with the *afrancesados* (francophiles) of this period. The life of Pablo de Olavide (1725–1803) and his close association with Diderot, who wrote a biography of the Peruvian exile, serves as a telling example of the French connection.

On the whole, the eighteenth century is best characterized by the scientific expeditions which brought with them several of the new natural sciences—physics, botany, chemistry, archeology, and history. Scientific expeditions validated the local intellectuals' desire to know about themselves and their own territories and societies. Contact with cosmopolitan circles of men of knowledge was for the first time available directly to individuals. The French expedition to measure the geographical degree of latitude (begun in 1735) resulted in a comprehensive description of Peru. Jorge Juan and Antonio de Ulloa, the two Spanish scientists on the expedition produced a comprehensive and critical report of the viceregal administration. Ecclesiastical visits also gathered social and economic information. During six years of continuous visitations, the Bishop of Trujillo, Baltasar Jaime Martínez Campañón (1735–1797), gathered an enormous collection of paintings depicting with great accuracy the daily life of his parishioners. The Spanish doctor Cosme Bueno (1711–1798) published the *Descripciones geográficas del Virreinato del Peru* [Geographical Descriptions of the Viceroyalty of Peru] in a series of Lima almanacs (1763–1772 and 1774–1778). Historiography under the Bourbons lifted the censure against the writing of local history, and so urban and regional *petites histoires* made their appearance. Illustrious native sons engaged in the description of their region in order to advance economic and educational interests. Archeological expeditions initiated the rediscovery of the Incan and pre-Incan ruins; guides were published. These often dry descriptions did provide, however, a wealth of ethnographic information on the daily life of Indians in terms of customs and religious beliefs. Of course the most important single expedition (and personality) to explore Spanish America was that of Baron Alexander von Humboldt (1769–1859). In both Spanish America and Europe, his *Personal Narrative of Travels to the Equinoctial Regions of the New Continent during the Years 1799–1811,* and his *Ensayo político sobre el reino de la Nueva España* [1807–1811; Political Essay on the Kingdom of New Spain] bridged in one single stroke the "fissure that had opened between the European Enlightenment and American reality" (Brading 517).

Because of the great rebellion lead by José Gabriel Condorcanqui (1738?–1781) or Tupac Amaru II in 1780 the *ilustrados* (enlightened) here did not engage in the writing of Indian histories as Sigüenza y Góngora did in Mexico (Brading 483–91). This absence does not mean that Indian and *mestizos* were not themselves writing local history. As Luis Millones has demonstrated, the parades and theatrical presentations in town squares and plazas were deployed as the texts on which Andean *petites histoires* were being memorialized. Indeed, forms of Andean pre-Conquest theatrical representation survived until the end of the eighteenth century. The Spanish authorities associated the success of the Tupac Amaru II rebellion with abundant and regular staging of Andean dramas in Quechua. After the execution of Tupac Amaru II, secular drama in Quechua—plays such as *La tragedia del fin de Atahualpa*—were banned. But Quechua drama, such as *Ollantay*, continued to be composed and represented as late as 1780.

Clearly, in Lima, a city which adopted a Spanish self-identity, the most popular form of theater was the *sainete*, a short satirical piece which poked fun at local types and vices. *Sainetes* were performed in open air theaters or *corrales* and, later, in the larger coliseums with night lighting. Its most famous *limeña* actress was no doubt Micaela Villegas (1739–1819), better known as the Perricholi. Her seductive dance and passable *sainete* performances gained her the devoted attention of Viceroy Manuel de Amat y Juniet. The theater, together with Sunday mass and the parades and other public fiestas, remained as the chief cultural texts, despite the growth of print culture and the greater voice of local public intellectuals (Castro-Klaren 1996, 87–99). The Lettered City to which Ángel Rama assigned importance in the development of Latin American culture, at the end of the eighteenth century, was a very small affair indeed.

Pablo Macera writes that education during the eighteenth century remained stratified: It was a question of class privilege. Communication between the various educational sectors was at a standstill. An aristocratizing concept of culture informed those who saw themselves as illustrious reformers. While Colonial universities and colleges had no difficulty recruiting instructors–there was a surplus of doctors–school teachers were very hard to find. Primary school instruction was rudimentary: The Provision of 1789 required reading, writing, basic arithmetic, and catechism (Macera 2: 219–22). Complaints about the quality of the teachers, the low salary offered, and the poverty of the school conditions were endemic. Until the end of the eighteenth century, the sons of the *caciques* could, as boarders, receive relatively good schooling in the Colegio de San Borja in Cuzco and El Colegio del Príncipe in Lima. The cost of this education was obviously exorbitant, and the state did not provide any subsidies. However, the common Indians and the sons of the *curacas* were not the only sector of the population who had almost no access to education. Like all Colonial cities, Lima lived its life around the plaza, the market, and the church, not the school house. It is estimated that by the end of the eighteenth century there were 5,000 people enrolled in primary school (Macera 2:258), of which only 20 percent received a good education and most belonged to the nobility. Neither the middle class nor the masses could aspire to any education.

The state of books and printing presses in Peru at the end of the eighteenth century is indeed telling. Despite the fact that there were twenty-eight presses available, the book was mainly an imported object. These presses operated only partially and never managed to stay in business for very long. On the whole, the material conditions for the productions of books in Peru were missing: Paper had to be imported; at times, books were torn apart in order to reuse the paper. However, trade in books was good, and they were sold in the same shops as were nails and ribbons. But the best libraries in Lima were not built on such local commerce. Books came into collectors' hands by way of direct order from Europe. The most famous collector was the precocious intellectual and wealthy aristocrat, José de Baquíjano y Carrillo de Córdoba (1751–1817), who during the Wars of Independence remained loyal to the Spanish Crown (see Burkholder and Johnson). Nevertheless Lima, because of the import monopoly of the port of Callao, became the largest depository of books in the South American colonies. From Lima, Spanish books traveled to Santiago, Quito, and La Paz.

The private libraries in Peru could easily compete with their Spanish counterparts. However, the notion of public libraries was a long way off and this affected directly reading habits and the possible number of readers (Macera 1: 283–95) For the most part, the Colonial aristocracy did not read for pleasure. The best personal collections of bureaucrats and clergymen did not surpass 300 volumes. Among the best libraries of the period is one with 1,190 books bought by Hipólito Unanue (1755–1833) in 1798. The libraries in the monasteries far outweighed any private collection. Learning was clearly more a desire than a possibility. The foundation of two provincial universities–San Augustine in Arequipa in 1828 and La Universidad Nacional "La Libertad" in Trujillo in 1824–went a long way to turning desire into reality.

Independence

In the past historians taking Lima as Peru had argued that the Independence movement in Peru was a late arrival, forged in the end by the converging armies of San Martín and Bolívar. Historians now map a more complex, fragmented, and regional picture in which the Tupac Amaru II rebellion of 1780 plays a decisive precursor role. Satirical verse, the *pasquín* or "libelous pamphlet," expressed early nationalistic feelings (Bacacorzo 16–26). Arequipa's Mariano Melgar 1790–1815) wrote the most important civic poetry of the period. His progressive radicalism and concern for the oppressed Indian masses anticipated the several waves of the *Indigenista* movement. More than a poet, Melgar lived his life as a Romantic icon. His "Marcha patriótica" celebrated the entry of the revolutionary forces of Mateo Pumacahua in Arequipa in 1814, but the Spanish authorities summarily executed the poet for his participation in the rebellion. His popular poems and his patriotic struggle turned him into a martyr of Independence. "Carta a Sylvia" heralded a new pre-Romantic sensibility, though, it should also be associated with the *yaraví* (harawi), the popular, pre-Hispanic love songs adopted for the guitar. Melgar's *yaravís* mark an important step toward a genuinely emancipated literature (Higgins 56–61).

In the absence of a book-buying public or a flourishing book industry (Higgins 63), it is not surprising that the journalistic form of the *costumbrista* sketch came to dominate the cultural scene in Lima. The high-born Felipe Pardo y Aliaga (1806–1868), in his short-lived satirical journal *El Espejo de mi tierra* (1840), adopted a radically critical attitude toward the society of his day. He directed his satire against the *criollo* upper classes whose hereditary shortcomings–ignorance and indolence–disqualified them, he argued, to rule the chaos that the Republic with its democratic rhetoric had brought about. Pardo y Aliaga was not alone in conceiving of the theater as a pedagogical tool in the formation of a national literature concerned with local realities. His contemporary, Manuel Ascencio Segura (1805–1871), from the perspective of his own middle-class origins, with his "Catecismo para el pueblo" ["Catechism for the People"] wrote biting satires of every aspect of the country's political and cultural organization. Like most of the criticism voiced in satire, the Republican theater expressed its disillusionment in moral terms and continued the love of gossip and scandal which would eventually produce the *Tradiciones Peruanas* [1880, 1888; Peruvian Traditions] by Ricardo Palma (1833–1919).

A frustrated historian working in a cultural milieu where the idea of a nation had not yet emerged and in which historiography had not yet taken its first steps, Palma's love of the document as a shard of the past, together with his satirical and yet inoffensive laughter and his mastery of the piquant phrase lead him to compose his *Tradiciones* [1872; Traditional Tales]. Palma began as a derivative Romantic poet, but later his interest in the scandals of the recent past led him to write his *Anales de la Inquisición de Lima* [1863; Annals of the Lima Inquisition], the source for much of the information embodied in his *tradiciones*. One again, like the *sainete*, the *costumbrista* theater, and the *yaraví*, Palma's *tradiciones* honed in on the local event, crafting a distinct language of immediacy. Palma's awareness of being on the brink of something new was best captured in his linguistic work, the *Neologismos y Americanismos* [1896; Neologisms and Americanisms] and *Papeletas Lexicográficas* [1903; Lexicographic Papers], and in his indefatigable institutional work to have the Spanish Academy of the Language recognize his own work and American Spanish as true, if different, peers.

In marked contrast to the polished and amusing prose of the *tradiciones*, the amateurish novel *El Padre Horán* [Father Horán] appeared in serialized form in the Lima newspaper *El Comercio* in 1848. Its author, Narciso Aréstegui (1824–1869) was a *cusqueño* who studied in the Colegio Nacional de Ciencias y Artes founded by Simón Bolívar. Set in Cuzco, *El Padre Horán* narrates the seduction and the murder of the daughter of a liberal landowner by her confessor. (It is based on the actual murder of a young girl from a well-to-do Cuzco family.) Aréstegui anticipates several themes for the *indigenista* novel that was to come: the Church's hypocrisy, the central government's unwillingness and failure to stimulate local industry and agriculture, and the general disregard for the welfare of the nation's citizens. His ideas were consonant with the policies of the government of President Ramón Castilla (1797–1867), in office at the time of the publication of *El Padre Horán* (Kristal 44).

Clorinda Matto de Turner (1852–1909), the founder of the *indigenista* novel, had spent her literary apprenticeship refashioning Palma's work in *Tradiciones Cuzqueñas* [1879; Traditions from Cuzco]. In 1883 she traveled to Arequipa where she worked as chief editor of the newspaper *La Bolsa* and published both her historical tragedy *Hima-Sumac* (1892) and a text book for teaching literature to the "fair sex" (Delgado 89). In 1886, she returned to Lima where she found the doors open to the principal journals of the period: *La Revista Social* and *El Perú Ilustrado*, which eventually she headed. She became a member of *El Ateneo* and *El Círculo Literario*. With *Aves sin nido* [1889; Torn from the Nest], a novel squarely placed in the realist tradition, Matto de Turner overcame some of the rhetorical and aesthetic difficulties of the genre of *El Padre Horán*. The novel focused attention on the abuse of authority by the political superstructure, but it did not analyze the relationship of authority to the powerful economic interests which authority served. It seems to suggest that the appointment of enlightened and humanitarian officials would be enough to resolve the social and economic problems of the Peruvian highlands (Higgins 76). The vision that Matto de Turner gave of the Indians was certainly external, from an urban, centralist perspective.

In the aftermath of the War of the Pacific (1879–1883), Peru faced a profound and general upheaval. New institutions fostered the formation of Peruvian intellectuals whose ties to the socioeconomic hegemonic groups were neither solidaristic nor markedly dependent. These intellectuals proposed a thorough modernization of Peru; in the field of commercial and cultural affairs, they called for more contact with the outside world. Regarding the Indian question in the hinterland, they advocated establishing Indian ownership of the land that they worked. But this did not mean that Indians were to participate in national politics: They were considered an inferior race to be kept under the tutelage of an enlightened intelligentsia. Much of this national project emerged from the *Club Literario* founded by the *Amigos de las Letras* in the 1860s and their journal *La Revista de Lima*, of which Manuel González Prada (1844–1918) was the leading figure until 1886. In opposition, Ricardo Palma blamed the Indians for losing the war and the politicians in the

Partido Civil for causing it (Kristal 98). President Avelino Cáceres, a general in the Peruvian resistance, explained the defeat of Peru by the Chilean army and navy in terms of political disarray, underscoring the work of the Peruvian collaborationists. He did not attack the landed oligarchy–the target of the *indigenista* novel and González Prada's circle. Both Ricardo Palma and González Prada would spend a good part of their lives rebuilding the national library burned during the Chilean occupation.

As a dissenter, González Prada, together with other intellectuals, founded the *Círculo Literario*. Eventually this group became the political party La Unión Nacional (Kristal 108). Concurring with the general positivist thesis that ignorance and servitude arrest industrial progress, Gonzalez Prada in his famous *Politeama* speech of 1888 argued that Peru lost the war with Chile because the Indians, who comprised the majority of the country's population, felt no compelling reason to fight for a nation which in fact had never incorporated them as citizens and had mindlessly exploited them. In *Pájinas Libres* [1894; Freedom Pages] he thundered: "La mano brutal de Chile despedazó nuestra carne i machacó nuestros huesos; pero los verdaderos vencedores, las armas del enemigo, fueron nuestra ignorancia i nuestro espíritu de servidumbre" (49) ("Chile's hands mangled our flesh and crushed our bones, but the real weapons of the enemy were our ignorance and our system of servitude" [44]). He identified the judge, the governor, and the priest as the "trinity of [Indian] brutalization." Education, especially in science and other forms of secular learning, would set free not only the Indian, but the other equally ignorant classes that made up the Peruvian polity. In many ways, González Prada delineated the paths that the *indigenista* and the regionalist novel followed until the middle of the twentieth century.

Somewhat forgotten but straddling the period between the monumental work of César Vallejo (1892–1938) and the dismantling of the old order carried out by González Prada, stands the figure of Ventura García Calderón (1886–1959). Like many other influential Peruvians he spent most of his life in Europe. There he combined a career of diplomacy with journalism. He wrote fiction in Spanish–*La venganza del condor* [1924; Vengeance of the Condor]–and in French–*Danger de mort* [1926; Danger of Death] and *Couleur de sang* [1931; Color of Blood]. Embracing all three geographical regions of Peru, his stories attempt to recover cultural roots (Higgins 113). However, his influence on the formation of a national literature was more closely connected to his work as influential literary critic and to his right-wing politics. His racist views were constantly contested by the provincial intellectuals who founded new literary circles and journals: *Atusparia* in Huaráz, *Boletín Kuntur* in Sicuani, *Warakú* in Arequipa, *Boletín Titicaca* in Puno, *La Sierra* and *La revista Universitaria* in Cuzco. Here, provincial intellectuals put forth a project for Indian literacy in a newly negotiated citizenship contract. In 1938 the government of Peru asked García Calderón to edit the twelve-volume *Biblioteca de Cultura Peruana* [Library of Peruvian Culture] which has ironically played a normative role in the writing of twentieth-century histories of Peruvian literature.

The history of painting during the Republican period began with the diaspora of two generations of painters following the War of the Pacific. They went to Europe to improve their work and acquire technical knowledge. Often they were successful and even attained recognition in Paris or Rome (Lauer 34). Their pictorial language and topics tended to be universal or, rather, Eurocentric. Great Peruvian painters such as Ignacio Merino, Francisco Laso, Carlos Baca Flor, and Daniel Hernández lived, worked, and died in the metropolis. Their strong suit was portraiture: It is said that the most famous Parisian actresses posed for Reynaldo Luza. A generation later, Felipe Cossio del Pomar became famous as a painter of sumptuous, half-naked *gringas* or the famous "Vargas Girls." Mirko Lauer argues that one of the important effects of the diaspora was to break the dependency of the artist from the Limeño and provincial oligarchies (36) and to free the imaginary of painting from the received Colonial norms and tastes. However, despite this move to migration and residence in Europe, there was also a group of local painters whose work captured in portrait and murals the lived experience of the nineteenth century. Pancho Fierro's watercolors offer an example of such popular painting destined to be enjoyed by the very subjects depicted in the composition.

The Twentieth Century

In 1870 the walls that protected Lima from Indians and pirates were demolished by the U.S. engineer Henry Meiggs under contract with the Peruvian government. Lima's elites were dreaming of an elegant and open city in the modern French style. They wanted avenues, circular plazas, parks, and boulevards. Lima was enlarged and beautified. The passing from a Spanish spacial order to a modern urban complex was captured in the nostalgic *Una Lima que se va* [1921; Lima, the City That Has Faded] by the *cronista* José Gálvez (1885–1957) (Elmore 23–25). In his *Lima la horrible* [1964; Horrible Lima], the poet Sebastian Salazar Bondy (1924–1965) found that the *conspiración colonialista* (23–33; colonialist conspiracy) which Palma constructed, despite the dismantling work of José Carlos Mariátegui (1894–1930), remained alive in the myths that sustained the centrality and sophistication of Lima's lifestyle: to flatter fawningly, to please, to homogenize. For Salazar Bondy the myth of a Colonial arcadia on which Lima based its claims to hegemony rested in the cultural cycle of *satira-lisura-huachaferia* (satire–the fleetingly malicious phrase–the pastiche) (69–73). The task of getting through this culture of deception and amusement in order to uncover the realities which formed the country was to be the work of a varied but always multiplying cadre of intellectuals and artists coming from all areas of Peru to participate in a construction of the national center–a process which has, of course, not yet ended.

In a manner of speaking, the construction of a real center for a real country began with the publication of Peru's first literary history. José de la Riva Agüero (1885–1944) argued in *Carácter de la literatura en el Perú independiente* [1905; Characteristics of Literature in Independent Peru] that in responding to the question, "Is there a Peruvian Literature?", the answer had to be in the negative. For him, Peruvian literature, just like Latin American literature, was already irremediably inscribed within the borders of Western culture and thus Peruvian writers could not aspire to originality. They could only hope to achieve a certain accent or peculiarity (Delgado 7). At the same time as Riva Agüero was writing in Lima, intellectual activity in the provincial universities was producing irreversible changes in the production of knowledge and national subjects in Peru. The Universidad de San Antonio Abad in Cuzco led the way in university reform. Its students, inspired by the rediscovery of Machu Picchu in 1911 threw out the old-fashioned authorities, held elections for the first time, and chose the U.S. citizen Albert Giesecke as rector of the university. It is said that Cuzco and

Arequipa were closer to Buenos Aires and its spirit of modernity than to Lima. European magazines, newspapers, and books arrived directly in great numbers in Southern Peru. Many key cultural groups emerged at this time: "Resurgimiento" in Cuzco, "Orkopata" in Puno, and "La Bohemia" in Trujillo. Neither the recently founded School of Engineering (1896) nor the Agronomy School (1902) could accommodate all those who sought technical degrees. Many middle-class men and women went to Chile and Argentina in search of a better college and university education.

Lima was to be the recipient of these forces of renovation and innovation emerging from the different regions of the country. A few names and fields of endeavor make the point: Julio C. Tello (1880–1947), archeology (Huarochiri); Abraham Valdelomar (1888–1919), journalism, fiction (Ica); César Moro (1903–1956), and Oquendo de Amat (1899–1936), poetry (Puno); Alberto Hidalgo (1897–1967), poetry; Percy Gibson (1908–1969), theater (Arequipa); Jorge Basadre (1903–1980), history (Tacna); José Carlos Mariátegui (1894–1930), political theory; Luis E. Valcárcel (1891–1987), history (Moquegua); César Vallejo (1892–1938), poetry; Víctor Raúl Haya de la Torre (1895–1979) political theory, politician (La Libertad); Enrique López Albújar (1872–1966), narrative, journalism (Lambayeque); and Mariano Iberico (1892–1974), medicine (Cajamarca) (see Burga and Flores Galindo 1979, 169). There were also many readers of newspapers and magazines; the latter increased from 167 in 1918 to 473 in 1928. Most of the intellectuals mentioned above contributed to these regularly. The fact that Mariátegui published extensive portions of his *Siete ensayos de interpretación de la realidad peruana* [1928; Seven Interpretative Essays on Peruvian Reality] in journals is evidence of the confidence placed in the intellectual sophistication of the public (Manrique 215–19). Intellectuals writing in Lima or abroad now expected to have a national audience. The proliferation of intellectuals identified with liberal positions and strongly affected by both the Mexican and the Russian revolutions set off a reaction on the part of the old oligarchy in conjunction with the Catholic church: In 1917, they founded the Universidad Católica as a focus of resistance. By 1928 there were 2,290 university students in the country and 1,849 were enrolled in San Marcos. In 1919 an alliance of labor and intellectuals brought university reform to San Marcos. More than two-thirds of the students enrolled at San Marcos were born in the provinces. An unexpected great transformation was about to take place. These intellectuals were to enact a second modern national foundation, one in which Lima would take the central but always contested role of hegemony.

Contemporary Peruvian painting began with a formal break made with academic painting. The professional plastic arts are now local in inspiration. However, both the market as well as the institutions connected with the valorization and circulation of art were just beginning in Peru. The Museo de Historia Nacional directed by Max Uhle and the *Academia Concha* were in the 1920s the two major institutions concerned with art (Lauer 48). The Escuela Nacional de Bellas Artes would not have been possible without these two pioneering organizations. Local painters depicting their local landscapes began to foster the idea of paintings as objects of domestic decoration. Daniel Hernández was asked to direct the Escuela Nacional de Bellas Artes in 1919. Within three years the school roster showed among its students the group of painters that would create modern Peruvian painting: Julia Codesido, Elena Izcue, Ricardo Goyburo, Alejandro González, Emilio

Hohkpler, Carlos Quispez Asín, and Jorge Vinatea Reynosa (Lauer 67). The influence of the *indigenista* José Sabogal, was, however, the factor that would give the avant-garde its determining characteristics. The rediscovery of pre-Hispanic art, the arrival of nationalism, and the "isms" of the avant-garde mean that developments in painting parallel those in literature. The cultural nationalism of the 1920s can be summarized in Mariátegui's dictum "Let us make Peru Peruvian" (Lauer 81). However, no other artist embodied all the contradictions of this period better than José Sabogal. His work was not so much *indigenista* as a dedication to the rural town. With their colorful houses and patios, for the first time human figures of all classes and phenotypes (Lauer 103) were depicted. Sabogal did not like the *indigenista* label; he thought of the school he headed as a movement towards a rediscovery of Peruvian humanity (Lauer 113).

After World War I Europe was thought to be bankrupt, and artists and intellectuals, while not being parochial, turned their gaze to their immediate intellectual surroundings. During the nineteenth century, localized Romanticism, Naturalism, and especially Positivism had accumulated a vigorous legacy in Latin America. In Peru the initiator of the regional realistic novel was Abraham Valdelomar (1888–1919) whose short fiction attached a new emotive value to the evocation of simple and sunny provincial life. The recovery of the presence of the Indian continued with *Cuentos andinos* [1920; Andean Stories] and the novel *Matalaché* (1928) by Enrique López Albújar (1872–1966), narratives painting a wide and colorful image of rural life. Oral traditions and bilingual *mestizo* lore were skillfully woven in the representation of everyday life. This regionalist trend in fiction was also shaped by the consequences of the students' movement for university reform.

In *Peru, problema y posibilidad* [1931; Peru, Problem and Possibility], the historian Jorge Basadre (1903–1980) wrote that the Indian question and the problem of national identity had become indistinguishable. National identity transcended territorial and juridical issues and, instead, came to be understood as the negotiation of a series of contradictions (Elmore 100). Thus the electoral project labeled *La Nueva Patria* which swept Augusto B. Leguia (1863–1932) into the presidency responded to the demands made by, or on behalf of, the long neglected indigenous majority of Peru. Leguia created an Office for Indigenous Affairs, headed by the distinguished sociologist Hildebrando Castro Pozo (1890–1945). The dedication of an official holiday to the commemoration of the Indian (*el Día del Indio*) signaled the institutionalization of the assimilation of the largely rural indigenous population into the official and mainstream life of the nation. In history, sociology, anthropology, the arts, and politics, the concept of the "Indian," as a suppressed national subject, functioned as a pivotal locus for the re-elaboration of national and self-identities. Nevertheless, in literary salons, poetry readings, and Sunday literary pages, it was the noisy and sentimental verse of José Santos Chocano (1875–1934) which received official acclaim. The Symbolist verse of José María Eguren (1874–1942) was accorded a muffled and truncated reception; its impact would not be felt until after the change in sensibilities which emerged after World War II.

The publication of *Los heraldos negros* [1918; The Black Heralds] by César Vallejo (1892–1938) constitutes the major watershed in modern Peruvian literature and a major shift for poetry in the Spanish language as a whole. The *Colónida*

group of poets had already distanced itself from *modernismo*, emphasizing a simpler and more direct rhetoric. Alberto Hidalgo (1897–1967) had burst onto the scene with his avant-garde poetics in *Arenga lírica al Emperador de Alemania* [1916; Lyric Harangue to the Emperor of Germany]. But the full extent of the crisis of the old epistemology was not revealed until Vallejo began to publish. He depicted a numbed and bewildered humanity facing unceasing and senseless pain, as synthesized in the title poem: "Hay golpes en la vida, tan fuertes . . . Yo no sé" ("There are blows in life, so strong . . . I do not know"). This young provincial Peruvian, operating from a remote corner of the world, pursued a radical inquiry into language and metaphysics and established the fact that Spanish American artists no longer needed to emulate European models before finding the caliber and horizon for their own thinking. Vallejo was born in Santiago de Chuco, an isolated Andean village in northern Peru. But the geographical distance separating Santiago de Chuco from Lima and even Paris had already been shortened in both time and space. By the time Vallejo arrived in Lima in 1917, he had studied literature and law at the National University in Trujillo and had already fielded fully the challenge that modern science and philosophy posed for Romanticism and Christianity. Among the books that Vallejo received as university prizes in 1913 and 1914 were Hippolyte Taine's *Nineteenth-Century French Philosophy* (1857), Max Müeller's *History of Religion*, Ludwig Gumplowitc's *Social Philosophy* (1910), Gérard's *Attic Eloquence*, and Ernst Henri's *The Riddle of the Universe* (1900) (Franco 9). The shattering effect that evolutionary theory had on Vallejo's concept of the poet's and humanity's place in this crazed universe was evident in *Los heraldos negros*. During his years in Trujillo, he was a member of the Trujillo Bohemia, which had its counterpart in many other provincial cities; here Walt Whitman, Maeterlick, Emerson, Unamuno, Rodó, and an anthology of French Symbolist poetry were avidly read and discussed. Spanish and French literary magazines gave Vallejo a good sampling of the intellectual and artistic effervescence created by Aragon, Appollinaire, Tzara, Duhamel, and Claudel in Paris. *Claridad*, *Proa*, and other Argentinean magazines were also regularly received all over Peru. Contact with these liberating projects and practices made living in the colonial atmosphere of Trujillo all the more claustrophobic. In 1917 Vallejo, like thousands of other provincial intellectuals of the period, embarked for Lima, where he found a job as a school teacher. In the elegant and snobbish Lima of the time, he was lucky enough to be admitted to the literary circle of the Conde de Lemos, Valdelomar's literary pseudonym (Franco 15).

Vallejo's questioning of the Romantic myth of the poet deepened while in Lima. However, his interview with González Prada, now director of the National Library, proved encouraging; Vallejo felt reassured in his iconoclastic search for radical originality and regeneration. The fame he had gained with *Los heraldos negros* was not enough, however, to guarantee him employment or provide him with an adequate readership. When his absolutely genial and radically different *Trilce* appeared in 1922, its reception ranged from hostile to frigid. Influential reviewers deemed the book "incomprehensible" or weird (Franco 25). By the time he wrote *Trilce*, Vallejo had not only digested Kant, Rousseau, Spinoza, and Henri Barbusse, but he knew that philosophy furnished inadequate explanations for the problem of self and knowledge in a godless universe. If Vallejo cited the names of modern philosophers, it was not to gain authority for his thought on their work but rather to make a parodic comment on the insufficiency of their discourse. *Trilce* proved to be a revolutionary book devoted to the radical exploration and subversion of language. It embraces and wrestles with the results of the fall of the individual self and of the impossibility of knowledge. Vallejo's quest for an authentic language annihilated the possibility of the "I" type of enunciation: The individual's voice blurred into the regularity of nature's rhythms and humanity could no longer claim a privileged place in the workings of the universe. *Trilce* denied all possibility of transcendental design and purpose, and the poet was left as, Jean Franco has put it, with the "puzzle of his own motivation" (81). Already with *Los heraldos negros*, Vallejo had understood the destabilizing possibilities of ungrammatical or in-human language. In many ways, *Trilce* was ahead of its time and heralded the Derridean theory of language. Vallejo wrote against the grain: He gave a harsh edge to language, the very idea of expression, and the aspiration to making sense. This prescient move was perhaps linked to his knowledge of Quechua and the untranslatability of linguistic forms. Vallejo produced explosive and yet dense and resisting texts (Franco 91), in striking contrast with the poetry that preceded and surrounded his work. His dismantling of received poetics, together with the elaboration of his own horizon, constituted the appearance of the personal as the foundation in the national-universal and would be regarded as such by all who wrote after him.

Despite Vallejo's monumental status, literary history cannot ignore the other major poets whose profoundly innovative work made up the many layered legacy of the avant-garde in Peru. Like much of the Latin American avant-garde, Alejandro Peralta (1899–1973) in *Kollao* (1934), Carlos Oquendo de Amat (1899–1936) in *Cinco metros de poemas* [1927; Five Meters of Poems]; Emilio Adolpho Westphalen (1911–2001) with his *Abolición de la muerte* [1935; Abolition of Death], and César Moro (born Alfredo Quispez Asin, 1903–1956) in his Surrealist verse (written almost entirely in French) produced contestable texts which were simultaneously international and autochthonous. The avant-garde, stimulated and observed by José Carlos Mariátegui's critical eye, came to constitute a wide spectrum in artistic production; it cannot be regarded as the arbitrary appearance of genius but rather as the emergence of a cultural formation long in the making. *La casa de cartón* [1928; The Cardboard House] is the narrative masterwork of the avant-garde. Written by the brilliant poet Martín Adán (1908–1985), born Rafael de la Fuente Benavides, this version of the artist as a young man story relies on broken rhythms, sketchy character portrayal, and neologisms. It has no plot; the forty prose fragments (Unruh 105) evoke with a mixture of humor and nostalgia the relationship of a young man to his upper-class surroundings. Easy pleasure is mixed with the despair of the cultural desert in which his class navigates. The narrator is familiar with foreign writers and feels anxious about his facile but fragile acquisition of European culture. Tempted by the familiar option of a trip to and even residence in Paris and acting in spite of the family's pressure on him to give up his artistic aspirations, the narrator decides to stay in Lima and accept his artistic vocation. The world of literature, the cardboard house, remains his only possible world. This manifesto for an interior exile found very few readers, remaining only a literary curiosity. The influence of the recluse Martín Adán was to skip a generation.

The growth of capitalism with its concomitant destruction of the ancient Andean economies and ways of life aggravated the conditions of the Indians' life both in the cities, the haciendas, and the small towns which dot the Andean mountain ranges. Thus the Indian problem continued to command the attention of intellectuals. A radical *indigenista*, Luis E. Valcárcel (1891–1987), argued that the ancient Andean cultures were not dead, that the Indians' indigenous culture had survived the brutal process of conquest and colonization and that it was now poised to descend onto the more Hispanized coastal towns and cities and reconquer the country. Although such a thesis seemed to exaggerate the vitality of Indian culture, the demographic explosion and migration to the coastal cities that began in the 1930s in a way made good Valcárcel's prediction and connected his view with the findings made by archeology, anthropology, and history. The rediscovery of Machu Picchu in 1911, the work of Julio C. Tello (1880–1947) on the pre-Incan Paracas and Chavín civilizations, and the excavations of the city of Chán-Chán in Trujillo began to point to a very long and ancient history which needed to be dealt with as intellectuals struggled with the question of national identity. Uriel García (1884–1965), author of *El nuevo indio* [1929; The New Indian], remarked on the intersection of the *indigenista* movement in the 1930s and their contact with *The Decline of the West* by Oswald Spengler (Flores Galindo 43): There appeared to be a coincidence between Spengler's exultation of the order of rural life and its sublime relation to the environment and the indigenists' own sense of a beneficent and ordered rural world. Neither Henri Bergson, Nietzsche, nor Keiserling was absent from this panorama of the doubled construction of the autochthonous (Elmore 41).

José Carlos Mariátegui (1894–1930) and Víctor Raúl Haya de la Torre (1895–1979) formed part of this political and intellectual ferment which was in turn spurred by both the Mexican (1910) and the Russian (1917) revolutions. The possibility of constructing new societies, free of the exploitation of humanity by humanity that was implicit in capitalism, had spread around the world. While in Italy, Mariátegui observed and analyzed European culture with an ethnographic eye. He read in German, French, English, and, of course, Italian. For him, as for many other Peruvians–Pablo de Olavide, Ventura García Calderón, César Moro–to be *afrancesado* or intensely Europeanized was a way of being creatively Peruvian. Deep knowledge of all things European provided the critical distance for emancipation from the Eurocentric *religión del progreso* (religion of progress) (Flores Galindo 42–44). Upon his return from Italy, drawing on his experience with Antonio Gramsci's work, Mariátegui founded the newspaper *La Razón*, and with it he inaugurated analytical journalism. His critique of the fundamental assumptions by which the dominant classes had understood and ruled Peru was immediately perceived as a threat. Mariátegui disagreed with Leguía's project of assimilating the Indian "masses." He thought that the Indian cultures should have a chance to stand on their own. Leguía closed *La Razón*; Mariátegui then founded the journal *Amauta* (1926–1930) in whose pages were to appear the most distinguished Peruvian and Latin American thinkers and artists of the period. The impact of *Amauta* lasted well beyond the years of its publication. It created a new climate of opinion, a new concept of how Peru should be viewed within the context of the modern world. With the publication of *Siete ensayos de interpretación de la realidad peruana* (1928), Mariátegui was recognized as one of the most important political and cultural theoreticians of the twentieth century.

Mariátegui's analysis of Peruvian reality devolved on the relation of economic to social and cultural structures. For the first time the colonial feudal landowning oligarchy was seen as the force that held back the modern development of the economy and society as a whole. Among other things, Mariátegui concluded that the necessary emancipation of the Indian peasantry was to be achieved as part of a general agrarian reform which would restore the land to the Indians who worked it. He also analyzed literature in terms of its role in the formation of the nation-state and found the Peruvian situation deficient. Furthermore, in one of his most important essays, "Arte, revolución y decadencia" ["Art, Revolution, and Decadence"], Mariátegui argued that Ortega y Gasset's views on *La deshumanización del arte* [1925; The Dehumanization of Art] were fostering a misunderstanding about the nature of modern art in the Spanish-speaking world. For Mariátegui, the concept of dehumanization corresponded to modern art's detached (decadent) spirit which carried the kernel for engaged and revolutionary artistic practices (Unruh 25). Mariátegui called for a synthesis of technical innovation and critical engagement.

Like Mariátegui, Haya de la Torre also thought that the struggle for modernization and emancipation centered on a fight against capitalist imperialism. He found his defining moment during the university student marches and protests against the government and the calls for university reform. Haya emerged as a charismatic speaker capable of leading the emerging urban masses. In 1924, while in exile in Mexico, he founded the political party APRA (Alianza Popular Revolucionaria Americana) and began his lifelong ambition to revolutionize the political and social structures of life in Latin America. In 1927 he published his influential *Por la emancipación de América Latina* [For the Emancipation of Latin America]. His later *El antiimperialismo y el APRA* [1935; Anti-Imperialism and the APRA] offered a synthesis of his political thought and program for Peru. He spent a good part of his life in exile and his presidential ambitions were forever thwarted.

APRA played an important role in the life of many artists and intellectuals in Peru. Magda Portal (1903–1989), like many other *apristas,* suffered prison and exile, defining a new profile for women as a politician and writer. As a feminist she called attention to the precursor role of Flora Tristán (1803–1844), writing a biography of that Franco-Peruvian socialist. However, it is her autobiography *Ser mujer en el Perú* [1979; Being Woman in Peru] that is of greater interest today. Ciro Alegría (1909–1967) (see **Figure 6**), the father of the modern Peruvian novel, author of the prize-winning *El mundo es ancho y ajeno* [1941; Broad and Alien Is the World], was for many years an APRA party member. But José María Arguedas (1911–1969), considered the greatest of all Peruvian novelists, expressed a lack of confidence in APRA and its aspirations to represent the interests of either the working classes or the Indians in the haciendas and *ayllus* (Indian communities). Writing a few years after World War II, Arguedas mounted a serious critique of *indigenista* writers, for he felt that they spoke about a phantasmagoric Indian who in fact did not exist. The Indian of novels such as *Huasipungo* (1934) by Jorge Icaza (1906–1978) was an abject being, deprived of all subjectivity and intelligence. This image of the Indian was both hopeless and false, and his advocates did, in Arguedas's mind, more harm than good. In contrast, Arguedas's fiction did capture the

Indian perspective on the world and, in doing so, offered a sophisticated and rich tapestry of feeling, complex thought, and self-understanding heretofore unknown by those outside the Indian world. Arguedas's narrators are not outside observers of the Indians' suffering, joy, or tactical struggles. They either partake of Indian consciousness or struggle sympathetically to share visions and concerns in a mutual defense of life and cultural survival. In his first collection of short stories *Agua* [1935; Water], as well as his masterwork *Los ríos profundos* [1958; Deep Rivers], Arguedas narrates from within the density of the rural world.

Many if not most of these intellectuals came to Lima from the provinces in one or another of the successive migratory waves by which Lima was to lose its viceregal and Hispanic mythical character. Lima became the site of *cholo* (the not quite sophisticated or modernized subjects) occupation. During the 1940s Lima saw the arrival of 218,955 people from the provinces (Elmore 147). In the 1950s the city's population swelled by one third (364,000). Arequipa, Trujillo, and other coastal cities experienced a corresponding influx of migration from the highlands. This demographic revolution has not yet

Figure 6.

Novelist Ciro Alegría (1909–1967). (Archive of the author)

come to a halt and the economic, social, political, and cultural consequences have been unimaginable. Salazar Bondy in *Lima la horrible* had already pointed out that Lima's cultural essence was inauthenticity. A *kitsch* style of superficial and false imitation was in fact Lima's chief characteristic before the popular migrations. With these migratory waves Lima passed quickly from a false viceregal demeanor to the style of the squalor and hopelessness of a Third World capital. Lima's population at the start of the millennium exceeded the 7 million (Klaren 434, Table 3).

During this period the writing of history became more institutionalized. Raúl Porras Barrenechea (1897–1960), professor and diplomat, left behind a host of disciples. Though he never wrote a major work himself, his method of archival research trained many of the superb historians that were to come a generation later. Luis Alberto Sánchez (1900–1994) authored many books on Peruvian literature and taught for many years at a number of universities. He controlled the pages of several literary supplements, as well as access to fellowships for study abroad. However, the most comprehensive, intelligent, and objective account of the formation of the nation was written by Jorge Basadre (1903–1980) in his ten-volume *Historia de la república del Perú* [1949; History of the Republic of Peru] (Delgado 127–28). More and more fiction was written in Peru by a number of excellent novelists who focused on the teeming urban centers. Enrique Congrains (b. 1932) and Julio Ramón Ribeyro (1929–1994) captured the gray tones of Lima, the decaying odor of the old oligarchy, the daily erosion of the very order that Mariátegui had wanted to dismantle, and the despair of the middle classes. There appeared no horizon here beyond the routine frustration of marginal work, boring love-making, and the eternal duration of a spiritual fog that engulfs Lima's life. Carlos Eduardo Zavaleta (b. 1929), Luis Loayza (b. 1934), and Oswaldo Reynoso (b. 1932) have also finely examined the intricacies of a sad and subtly violent Limeño life.

With the accelerated crisis of the agricultural sector, social and political conflict overwhelmed all other concerns: Landscape, nature, and family have receded into the background. The generation of 1950, marked by the Cuban Revolution and the Cold War, responded in several different ways to both the aesthetic and political challenges before them. Anchored in the minuscule splintering Left, the social sciences produced towering figures such as Luis Lumbreras in archeology, Alfredo Torero in linguistics, Julio Cotler and Anibal Quijano in sociology, Pablo Macera and Carlos Aranibar in history, and Luis Millones, Manuel Burga, and Tito Flores Galindo in ethnographic history. Abimael Guzmán, the leader of *Sendero Luminoso* (The Shining Path), together with other intellectuals and artists who sought revolutionary change in Peru, also belong to this generation.

The cosmopolitization of poetry blurred the opposition between the pure poetry and the politically engaged poets. Washington Delgado (b. 1927) has observed that there seems to be an alternating current in Peruvian literary practice. Periods of fecund poetry writing seemed followed by explosions in novelistic innovation. In the 1960s the blending and distancing of pure poetry with socially committed verse in the work of Jorge Eielson (b. 1924), Sebastian Salazar Bondy, Javier Sologuren (b. 1921), Blanca Varela (b. 1926), Washington Delgado, and Juan Gonzalo Rose (1928–1983) achieved a radical revitalization of poetic form and language. Their poetics mark a high point in the tradition of

lucid skepticism. Carlos German Belli (b. 1927) with *Oh! Hada cibernetica* [1961; Oh, Cybernetic Spirit], *El pie sobre el cuello* [1964; Heel on the Neck], and many other collections represents this generation's return to a classic and yet colloquial language, capable of articulating themes of universal import in humble and mundane settings. James Higgins has called this a remarkable generation of poets whose standards are unmatched anywhere in Latin America (293). Younger poets such as Antonio Cisneros (b. 1942) with *Los comentarios reales* [1964; The Royal Commentaries] and *El libro de Dios y los hungaros* [1978; The Book of God and Gypsies], Rodolfo Hinostroza (b. 1941) with *Consejero del Lobo* [1965; The Wolf's Adviser], and, of course, the mourned guerrilla Javier Heraud (1942–1963), cultivated a matter-of-fact and yet lyrical language which expressed deep political commitment (in the line of César Vallejo) together with a serious inquiry into a poetics for a perilous and uncertain world. This period also saw a greater professionalization on the part of the artist. The literary presence of Kafka, Joyce, Huxley, and Faulkner (in translation) became generalized in the university literature curriculum. At the same time, an iconoclastic push for innovation and even radical change was once again emerging from the provincial sector. The "Grupo Renovador Alkamari" in Cuzco, the "Avanzada Sur" in Arequipa, the "Peña del Mar" and "Bahia" in Trujillo, and the "Raiz the Piedras" in Huancayo mobilized great political and cultural energies at a very high level of sophistication (Gutiérrez 49).

Three Peruvian fiction writers during these years achieved international acclaim and financial success. The first to leap to international attention was Mario Vargas Llosa (b. 1936) with his technically innovating, wrenching, and captivating *La ciudad y los perros* [1963; The Time of the Hero]. Almost a decade later, Alfredo Bryce Echenique (b. 1939) in *Un mundo para Julius* [1970; A World for Julius], with a light prose and subtle humor, would portray the happy ending of the world of the Peruvian ancient regime. Manuel Scorza (1928–1983) died soon after a long residence in Europe which launched his fiction onto the international market. His most notable achievement was the narrative cycle of five novels which began with *Redoble por Rancas* [1970; Drums for Rancas] and ended with *La tumba del relámpago* [1979; Lightning's Tomb]. Differing from Vargas Llosa, who strongly criticized *indigenismo*, and especially Arguedas for holding onto the vision of an archaic utopia, Scorza re-enacted *indigenismo*, while revising the traditional assumptions of realism.

This was a very rich period in Peruvian letters, music, theater, and art. The work of painters such as Fernando de Szyszlo (b. 1925), Armando Villegas (b. 1926), Victor Humareda (1920–1986), and Tilsa Tsuchiya (1936–1984) achieved international recognition. Because Peruvian presses did not distribute internationally or market their publications outside Peru, the fiction of many excellent writers remained at home: José Adolph (b. 1933), José Antonio Bravo (b. 1937), Cesar Calvo (b. 1940), Eduardo González Viaña (b. 1941), Miguel Gutiérrez (b. 1940), and Edgardo Rivera Martínez (b. 1934). The phenomenon of exile or simply migration began to show up in the publication of novels written about Peru by writers who left during their formative years. For the first time Peruvians of African ancestry broke into the mainstream of publication: Antonio Gálvez Ronceros (b. 1931) and Gregorio Martínez (b. 1942) were highly praised for the transgressive humor and linguistic play of their prose.

The towering figure of the period is Mario Vargas Llosa. He brought literary renovation to a stale realist art and has maintained an astonishing rhythm of publication. Like other Peruvian intellectuals, he has lived all his adult life in Europe. He has achieved bestseller status not only in Spanish, but in many of the other languages into which his novels and journalism have been translated. Despite the commercial success of novels like *La tía Julia y el escribidor* [1977; Aunt Julia and the Scriptwriter], his most important novel was *Conversación en la Catedral* [1969; Conversation in the Cathedral]. There he coupled his brilliant novelistic technique with his deepest reflection on human motivation and its relation to violence as a social organizing principle. His characters struggle naively, unknowingly, against a historically imbedded chain to the past that devastates their lives. In his later novels Vargas Llosa switched tone and attitude. The discrepancy between the characters' capacity to face the crushing forces of life and their insufficient awareness of their circumstances is no longer set in a tragic mode. Now the effect is one of humor. Like Miguel Gutiérrez in *La violencia del tiempo* [1991; The Violence of Time] and Edgardo Rivera Martínez in *El país de Jauja* [1993; The Land of Plenty], Vargas Llosa in his absorbing *La Guerra del fin del mundo* [1981; The War of the End of the World] participated in the marvelous revival of the historical novel in Peru and Latin America.

The last two decades of the twentieth century were a period of profound change in Peru. Twelve years of military dictatorship ushered in a panoply of long overdue but inexpertly carried out reforms. The agrarian reform that resulted in the peasants leaving the land and joining the urban poor brought forth a parallel informal society; change was deep, disturbing, and chaotic. As the country moved back into the game of electoral politics, the guerrilla *Sendero Luminoso* (Shining Path) intensified its terrorist campaign against the state, especially in Lima. Plagued by uncertainty, wage depression, protracted and deep unemployment, the death of thousands of its poorest citizens, and the inept and untold corruption of the Alan García administration, the country plunged into economic and social collapse. In 1987 Vargas Llosa, enjoying the prestige conveyed upon him by his brilliant international success as a writer of novels, decided to run for the presidency. The winner of the elections of 1990 was the then unknown Alberto Fujimori. As the country collapsed and massive shifts of power and identity were taking place in this new crisis, artistic and intellectual production did not, as one would have expected, come to a halt. In a disenchanted assessment of the loosely grouped generation of 1950, Miguel Gutiérrez questioned the social and historical analysis provided by historians, social scientists, and even poets of his generation in reference to the revolutionary struggle that defined Peruvian history during the latter part of the twentieth century. Writing during the height of the terror, Gutiérrez felt that the much admired Pablo Macera acted as a free shooter during the years when the generation split apart into several irreconcilable partisan sectors (Gutiérrez 207), thus denying the country appropriate political and intellectual leadership. He was equally critical of the uses that Aníbal Quijano made of Mariátegui. In the midst of the terror in the streets and the massacres carried out by the state in prisons and villages, Peruvians of all classes migrated to Europe, the United States, Canada, and even Australia.

However, among those who stayed, there emerged compact groups of younger generations of fiction writers, poets, and playwrights. In popular music, *chicha*–a blending of Andean rhythms and *cumbia*–and salsa invaded the country's airwaves and the dance halls. Short galvanizing plays were staged in the many theaters in Lima and other cities. Television journalism began to play an important role in the shaping of the citizens' awareness of the country's disastrous situation and its lack of future prospects. Many new national subjects made their entrance into the mainstream of the Peruvian public sphere: working-class women, peasants, youth leaders, shanty-town leaders, women journalists, judges, guerrillas, terrorists, new *beatas*, and saints.

More recently, the publication of thousands of poems in short-lived literary magazines, university gazettes, and literary journals occurred with greater intensity with the return to democratic forms of political expression. Poetic movements such as *Hora Zero* [1970–1973; Zero Hour] and *La Sagrada Familia* [1975; The Holy Family] rang iconoclastic bells. Carmen Ollé (b. 1947), the most respected feminine voice, was associated with the aesthetics of *Hora Zero* which, in a way, evokes the concept of *écriture* explored by Roland Barthes in his epoch-making *Writing Degree Zero* (1965). Very young female poets coalesced around the notion of *zafarrancho*–bricolage, makeshift work–as the appropriate description of the kind of writing possible at the end of a century in which everything seems to have been tried. Titles such as *Rosa fálica* [1983; Phallic Rose] by Sui Yun (b. 1955) and *Ese oficio no me gusta* [1987; I Don't Like that Job] by Rocío Silva Santisteban (b. 1963), capture the desire to write, together with the discomforting idea of being a poet.

In the last thirty years of the twentieth century, theater centered around very small stages like *Cuatrotablas*. Much work tended to be collective: The *Grupo Yuyachkani*, with their play *Los músicos ambulantes* [1979; Itinerant Musicians], was enormously successful. This theater was very timely: It staged plays with plots built around current important debates in national life, and in that way it competed successfully with the immediacy of radio and television. Because of its simultaneous appeal to various modes of perception, theater garnished the talents of painters, musicians, writers, actors, and producers, and thus it played an increasingly important role in galvanizing large groups of artists and intellectuals–a role which the more solitary exercise of writing or painting had not been able to play. University theater production (at San Marcos, La Universidad de Lima, la Universidad Católica) also played an important role in popularizing experimental theater (Higgins 300–304). Film in Peru had its beginnings in the 1920s with Luis Pardo and, like theater, it has recently achieved national and international success with the adaptation of historical themes–*El caso Huayanay* (1981) and *Tupac Amaru* (1984)–or classical novels such as *La ciudad y los perros* (1984) and *Yawar fiesta* (1986).

Radio has played a capital role in the conservation and the dissemination of Andean languages and music. Radio and television served to disseminate the work and personalties of writers, actors, singers, dancers, politicians, historians, and even literary critics. Radio stimulated the production and consumption of *huayno* and *yaraví* in the coastal cities and *marinera*, *cumbia*, *chicha*, *tondero*, and waltzes in the Andes. Both *criollo* and Andean music have produced a plethora of composers, musicians, singers, and dancers who perform with various degrees of commercial success. Just as in music, painting, political theory, and the social sciences, the arts and crafts in the twentieth century in Peru have experienced the impact of the provincial and lower classes at the previously dominant center. The result has been an unimaginable multiple enriching of the intellectual and artistic life of a sleepy and remote colonial region of the world in which vast creative powers of all races have transformed and continue to change the national cultural legacy.

Works Cited

Adán, Martín [Rafael de la Fuente Benavides]. 1928. *La casa de cartón*. Lima: Talleres de Impresiones y Encuadernaciones Perú.

——. 1968. *De lo barroco en el Perú*. Lima: Universidad Mayor de San Marcos.

Agurto Calvo, Santiago. 1984. *Lima pre-hispánica*. Lima: Finanpro.

Alegría, Ciro. 1941. *Broad and Alien Is the World*. Trans. Harriet de Onís. London: Merlin P.

——. 1941. *El mundo es ancho y ajeno*. Santiago: Ediciones Ercilla.

Arguedas, José María. 1935. *Agua*. Lima: CIP.

——. 1958. *Los ríos profundos*. Buenos Aires: Editorial Losada.

Bacacorzo, Javier. 1972. "El pasquín y su trascendencia en la lucha litertaria nacional." *Memoria del Congreso del Instituto Internacional de Literatura Iberoamericana: Literatura de la emancipación hispanoamericana y otros ensayos*. Lima: Universidad Nacional de San Marcos. 16–26.

Bakewell, Peter. 1997. *A History of Latin America: Empires and Sequels 1450–1930*. Oxford: Blackwell.

Basadre, Jorge. 1931. *Perú: Problema y posibilidad; ensayo de una síntesis de la evolución histórica del Perú*. Lima: F.y E. Rosay.

——. 1947. *Meditaciones sobre el destino histórico del Perú*. Lima: Ediciones Huascarán,

——. 1949. *Historia de la república del Perú*. 4th ed. Lima: Editorial Cultura Antártica.

Bayón, Damián. 1984. "The Architecture and Art of Colonial Spanish America." *Cambridge History of Latin America*. Ed. Leslie Bethell. Cambridge: Cambridge University Press. 2: 709–45.

—— and Murillo Marx. 1992. *History of South American Colonial Art and Architecture*. New York: Rizzoli.

Bermúdez-Gallegos, Marta. 1996. *Poder y transgresión: Perú, metáfora e historia*. Lima: Latinoamericana Editores.

Beverly, John. 1997. *Una modernidad obsoleta: Estudios sobre el barroco*. Caracas: Fondo Editorial A.L.E.M.

Brading, David. 1991. *The First America: The Spanish Monarchy, Creole Patriots and the Liberal State, 1492–1867*. Cambridge: Cambridge University Press.

Bryce Echenique, Alfredo. 1970. *Un mundo para Julius*. Barcelona: Seix Barral.

——. 1992. *A World for Julius*. Trans. Dick Gerdes. Austin: University of Texas Press.

Burga, Manuel and Alberto Flores Galindo. 1979. *Apogeo y crisis de la república aristocrática*. Lima: Rikchay Peru.

Burkholder, Mark A. and Lynman L. Johnson. 1998. *Colonial Latin America*. New York: Oxford University Press.

Castro-Klarén, Sara. 1990. *Understanding Mario Vargas Llosa*. Columbia: University of South Carolina Press.

——. 1994. "Writing Subalterity: Guaman Poma and Garcilaso de la Vega, Inca." *Dispositio/n* 19.46: 229–44.

——. 1996. "El siglo XVIII: Sujetos subalternos y el teatro del la Perricholi." *Razón, tradición, y modernidad: Re-visión de la ilustración hispánica*. Ed. Francisco La Rubia Prado and Jesús Tordecilla. Madrid: Tecnos. 87–99.

Chang-Rodríguez, Raquel. 1994. "La subversión del barroco en *Amar su propia muerte* de Juan de Espinosa Medrano." *Relecturas del Barroco de Indias*. Ed. Mabel Moraña. Hanover: Ediciones del Norte. 117–48.

Cisneros, Antonio. 1964. *Los comentarios reales*. Lima: Ediciones de la Rama Florida & Ediciones de la Biblioteca Universitaria.

——. 1978. *El libro de Dios y de los húngaros*. Lima: Libre-1.

Congrains, Enrique. 1954. *Lima hora cero*. Lima: Círculo de Novelistas Peruanos.

——. 1957. *No una, sino muchas muertes*. Lima: Populibros Peruanos.

Costigan, Lúcia Helena. 1991. *A sátira e o intelectual criollo na colônia: Gregorio de Matos e Juan del Valle y Caviedes*. Lima: Latinoamericana Editories.

Delgado, Washington. 1980. *Historia de la literatura republicana: Nuevo carácter de la literatura en el Perú independiente*. Lima: Ediciones Rikchay.

Durán Montero, María Antonia. 1994. *Lima en el siglo XVII: Arquitectura, urbanismo y vida cotidiana*. Sevilla: Diputación de Sevilla.

Elmore, Peter. 1993. *Los muros invisibles: Lima y la modernidad en la novela del Siglo XX*. Lima: Mosca Azul.

Espinosa Medrano, Juan de. 1662. *Apologético en favor de D. Luis de Góngora*. Lima: Imprenta de Juan de Quevedo y Zeirate.

Fane, Diana, ed. 1996. *Converging Cultures: Art and Identity in Spanish America*. Brooklyn: The Brooklyn Museum.

Flores Galindo, Alberto. 1980. *La agonía de Mariátegui: La polémica con la Komintern*. Lima: DESCO.

Franco, Jean. 1976. *César Vallejo: The Dialectics of Poetry and Silence*. Cambridge: Cambridge University Press.

Garcilaso de la Vega, Inca. 1976 [1609]. *Comentarios reales*. Ed. Aurelio Miró Quesada. Caracas: Biblioteca Ayacucho.

Gisbert, Teresa. 1980. *Iconografía y mitos indígenas en el arte*. La Paz: Gisbert y Cia.

González Prada, Manuel. 1966. [1894]. *Pájinas libres*. Lima: Thesis.

Guamán Poma de Ayala, Felipe. 1980 [1615]. *El primer nueva corónica y buen gobierno*. Eds. John Murra and Rolena Adorno. Mexico City: Siglo XXI.

Gutiérrez, Miguel. 1988. *La generación del 50: Un mundo dividido*. Lima: Sétimo Ensayo.

Haya de la Torre, Raúl. 1927. *Por la emancipación de América Latina*. Buenos Aires: M. Gleizer.

——. 1935. *El antimperialismo y el APRA*. Santiago de Chile: Ediciones Ercilla.

Heraud, Javier. 1961. *Estación reunida*. Lima: La Rama Florida.

——. 1963. *El río*. Lima: Cuadernos de Hontanar.

Hidalgo, Alberto. 1916. *Arenga lírica al emperador de Alemania*. Arequipa: Quiroz Hnos.

Higgins, James. 1987. *A History of Peruvian Literature*. Liverpool: Cairns.

Hinostroza, Rodolfo. 1965. *Consejero del lobo*. Lima: Fondo de Cultura Popular.

Holguín, Diego González. 1952 [1560]. *Vocabulario de la Lengua General de Todo el Peru Llamada Qquichua o del Inca*. Lima: Imprenta Santa María.

Icaza, Jorge. 1934. *Huasipungo*. Quito: Editorial Atahualpa.

Klaren, Peter. 2000. *Peru: Society and Nationhood in the Andes*. New York: Oxford University Press.

Kristal, Efraín. 1987. *The Andes Viewed from the City: Literary Discourse and Political Discourse on the Indian in Peru 1848–1930*. New York: Peter Lang.

Kubler, George and Martín Soria. 1969. *Art and Architecture in Spain and Portugal and their American Dominions, 1500–1800*. Baltimore: Penguin Books.

Lauer, Mirko. 1976. *Introducción a la pintura peruana del Siglo XX.* Lima: Mosca Azul.

Lavrin, Asunción. 1986. "Female Religious." *Cities and Society in Colonial Latin America.* Eds. Louisa Schell Hoberman and Susan Socolow. Albuquerque: University of New Mexico Press. 165–95.

López Albújar, Enrique. 1920. *Cuentos andinos, vida y costumbres indígenas.* Lima: Imprenta de la Opinión Nacional.

———. 1928. *Matalaché, novela retaguardista.* Piura: Taller de El Tiempo.

López-Baralt, Mercedes. 1988. *Icono y conquista: Guamán Poma de Ayala.* Madrid: Hiperión.

Lumbreras, Luis G. 1974. *The Peoples and Cultures of Ancient Peru.* Trans. Betty J. Meggers. Washington D.C.: Smithsonian Institution Press.

———. 1990. *Visión Arqueológica del Perú* Lima: Milenario.

Macera, Pablo. 1977. *Trabajos de historia.* Lima: Instituto Nacional de Cultura. 4 vols.

Manrique, Nelson. 1995. *Nuestra Historia. Historia de la República.* Lima: COFIDE.

Mariátegui, José Carlos. 1928. *Siete ensayos de interpretación de la realidad peruana.* Lima: Biblioteca Amauta.

———. 1971. *Seven Interpretative Essays of Peruvian Reality.* Trans. Marjory Urguidi. Austin: University of Texas Press.

Matienzo, Juan de. 1967 [1567] *Gobierno del Peru.* Ed. Guillermo Lohman Villena. Paris-Lima: Institute Francais.

Mesa, José de and Teresa Gisbert. 1972. *Mateo Pérez de Alesio.* La Paz: Instituto de Estudios Bolivianos.

Millones, Luis. 1995. *Nuestra Historia: Peru Colonial.* Lima: COFIDE.

Moro, César [Alfredo Quíspez Asín]. 1957 [1939]. *La tortuga Ecuestre, y otros poemas: 1924–1949.* Lima: Ediciones Tigrondine.

Oquendo de Amat, Carlos. 1969 [1927]. *Cinco metros de poemas.* Lima: Editorial Decantar.

Palma, Ricardo, ed. 1899 [1837]. *Diente del Parnaso.* By Juan de Caviedes. Lima: Jiménez.

Peralta, Alejandro. 1934. *Kollao.* Lima: Talleres de la Cía de Impresiones y Publicidad.

Portal, Magda. 1979. *Ser mujer en el Perú.* Lima: Topaku.

Ribeyro, Julio Ramón. 1960. *Crónica de San Gabriel.* Lima: Ediciones Tawantisuyu.

———. 1965. *Los geniecillos dominicales.* Lima: Populibros Peruanos.

Riva Agüero, José de la. 1962. *Obras completas.* Vol. 1: *Carácter de la literatura en el Perú independiente.* Lima: Universidad Católica.

Rodríguez-Garrido, José A. 1994. "Espinosa Medrano: La recepción del sermón barroco y la defensa de los americanos." *Relecturas del Barroco de Indias.* Ed. Mabel Moraña. Hanover: Ediciones del Norte. 149–72.

Rostworowski de Diez Canseco, María. 1992. *Pachacamac y el Señor de los Milagros.* Lima: Instituto de Estudios Peruanos.

Salazar Bondy, Sebastián. 1964. *Lima la horrible.* Lima: Populibros.

Sánchez, Luis Alberto. 1981. *La literatura peruana: Derrotero para una historia cultural del Perú.* 5th ed. Lima: Mejía Baca. 5 vols.

Scorza, Manuel. 1970. *Redoble por rancas.* Barcelona: Plaza & Janés.

Silva Santisteban, Rocío. 1987. *Ese oficio no me gusta.* Lima: Ediciones Cope.

Silva Sifuentes, Jorge. 1995. *Nuestra Historia: El Imperio de los cuatro suyos.* Lima: COFIDE.

Sologueren, Javier. 1981. *Antología general de la literatura peruana.* Mexico City: Fondo de Cultura Económica.

Soria, Martín, S. 1956. *La pintura del siglo XVI en Sudamérica.* Buenos Aires: Instituto de Arte Americano e Investigaciones Estéticas.

Stastny, Francisco. 1967. *Breve historia del arte en el Perú: La pintura precolombina, colonial y republicana.* Lima: Editorial Universo.

Valcárcel, Luis. 1927. *Tempestad en los Andes.* Lima: Editorial Minerva.

Valdelomar, Abraham. 1918. *El caballero Carmelo.* Ciudad de los Reyes del Perú: Talleres de la Penitenciaría de Lima.

———. 1921. *Los hijos del sol.* Lima: Ciudad de los Reyes: Euforion.

Vallejo, César. 1918. *Los heraldos negros.* Lima: [n.p].

———. 1930 [1922]. *Trilce.* Lima: Perú Nuevo.

Vargas Llosa, Mario. 1963. *La ciudad y los perros.* Barcelona: Editorial Seix Barral.

———. 1969. *Conversación en la Catedral.* Barcelona: Seix Barral.

———. 1977. *La Tia Julia y el escribidor.* Bogota: Círculo de Lectores.

———. 1981. *La guerra del fin del mundo.* Barcelona: Seix Barral.

Watanabe, Luis K. 1995. *Nuestra historia: Culturas preincas del Peru.* Lima: COFIDE.

Westphalen, Emilio Adolpho von. 1935. *Abolición de la muerte.* Lima: Ediciones Perú Actual.

Yun, Sui. 1983. *Rosa fálica.* Peru: Ediciones Loto.

CHAPTER 40

BOGOTÁ
FROM COLONIAL HAMLET TO COSMOPOLITAN METROPOLIS

Victoria Peralta

"There is no document of civilization which is not at the same time a document of barbarism."

–Walter Benjamin, 1940

Cultural studies have not demonstrated much in the way of interest in Bogotá as a cultural center. Despite this oversight, however, the most important coordinates shaping the role of culture in the history of the city are clear: its geographic location, its social organization in the post-Colonial period, and the coexistence since the time of the conquest of Spanish and indigenous cultures. These coordinates have shaped the culture of the city in four principal ways. First, the physical location of the city has isolated Bogotá from the mainstreams of modern culture, thus prolonging the Colonial legacy. Second, forms of social organization dating back to Colonial times have meant the predominance of Spanish culture and the suffocation of native cultures. Third, the material conditions (geographical, economical, social) of Bogotá have favored, until the twentieth century, the almost exclusive monopoly of literary expression over other cultural forms. And, fourth, the conjunction of, Spanish predominance and the monopoly of literary expression of the national cultural life have sanctioned with exclusion of all who do not belong to the limited and elitist white enclave. Thus, it has not been without cause that some of Colombia's most important cultural critics have characterized the culture of Bogotá as aristocratic, parochial, anachronistic, and imitative (Gutiérrez Girardot 1997, 177–187). However, to continue such a characterization would be to dismiss as inconsequential both a cultural expression that, by and large, has served certain civilizing sectors of society in their struggle against such a narrow vision and the cultural synthesis that is the product of that struggle and the culture of today's majority. Cultural limitations of this kind have spawned a number of diverse reactions, both on the part of opposition groups belonging to Bogotá's elite and on the part of groups marginal to it. It was not until the twentieth century, however, that the parochial and anachronistic culture of Bogotá entered into a state of crisis, when the struggles against its insularity, as well as demographic factors and rising levels of literacy, meant that the marginalized sectors of society could begin to express themselves in the same educated terms employed by the elites.

The cultural history of the Hispanicized village, made capital of the Viceroyalty of the New Kingdom of Granada in 1739 when its population numbered only 15,000 (Vargas Lesmes, 13), and today a metropolis of approximately 7.5 million people, is the history of reactions to the rigid limitations imposed on cultural expression from the very beginnings of the settlement. These reactions were the expression of the search for a cultural identity more in accord with modern Western culture and more in touch with the new sociopolitical reality; at the same time, they were manifestations of the struggle to move beyond the Colonial legacy and diversify the forms of cultural expression. They were and are the instantiations of Colombia's need to democratize and modernize its culture, a struggle for change that has been as arduous and as constant as the culture of the capital has been aristocratic, parochial, anachronistic, and imitative. The battles and the successes of this struggle, then, constitute the object of this study; through them can be witnessed the comings and goings of a culture still in the process of weaving its own history. However, the history of Bogotá specifically as a cultural center can be understood as a series of debates: between the conservation of Hispanism and the search for new horizons amenable to a modern and authentic culture; between literature and other forms of cultural expression; and between an elitist, parochial provincialism, and democratic cosmopolitanism. To what extent has this historical struggle attained its goals of cultural authenticity and originality, diversity of artistic expression, and the democratization of Colombian culture? The question of democratization, linked not only to culture, but also to political processes and movements for social change, will be treated in what follows in a tangential way, which is to say, seen not from a social or economic point of view but from the perspective of culture itself.

Santafé de Bogotá, or Bogotá for short, has always been a political and cultural center. Throughout its history Bogotá has been a temporary or permanent site of residence for people from every region and corner of the country. It has been a meeting point of interests through being a political capital from the days of the viceroyalty through to the time of the Republic and a cultural center whose sphere of influence grew ever more extensive, from the Andean highlands of its immediate environs in Colonial times to the national frontier in the twentieth century (Williams 75). In this essay, then, the term *modernismo* will be used to designate the late nineteenth-century Latin American literary movement. The term *modernity,* on the other hand, will be used to characterize the changes unleashed in Europe in the eighteenth and nineteenth centuries by the forces of the Enlightenment, the French Revolution, and scientific and technological innovations that were definitively to transform the continent–what the philosopher Leopoldo Zea (b. 1912) has identified in the history of the Americas as the civilizing process (257).

Cultural Coordinates: Space

Located toward the northern end of the Andean mountain range, Bogotá sits on a plateau ringed by mountains at 2,600 meters above sea level. This geographic situation has influenced two very important aspects of the culture of the city: the psychological makeup of its inhabitants, on the one hand, and the potential of the cultural infrastructure of the city, on the other. From pre-Columbian times until the arrival of the automobile and the airplane, to reach Bogotá one had to undertake a voyage of several days' duration, either from Honda, 145 kilometers distant, or from other ports on the Magdalena River, ascending high peaks and descending deep valleys. These geographic obstacles engendered a sense of isolation that was reinforced by the cold and rainy climate of the capital (Peralta 32). In Colonial times and in the first century of the republic (the nineteenth), the educated inhabitants of Bogotá passed the rainy afternoons by reading the few books that were to be had in sessions that became interminable. The inescapable monotony of the climate, brightened only by the sound of daily showers, imposed a self-absorption on the capital and its inhabitants that, rather than impeding, on the contrary was favorable to the formation of the literary circles that have proliferated throughout the history of Bogotá despite the pervasive difficulties. However, although these climatic and geographic conditions created an atmosphere of withdrawal propitious to the development of a literary culture, they were also to isolate the capital from more modern cultural currents and to shape the provincial and anachronistic character of its culture, as so many critics have stressed.

Since the first contact between the natives and the conquistadors and colonizers, this fact of isolation and the deficient communication to which it gave rise have conditioned cultural expression and encumbered both the renovation and the general dynamics of cultural production. Owing to distance from the principal fresh- and salt-water ports, and thus from the country's most important commercial actions, Bogotá was separated from the great migratory and ideological flux of the nineteenth century. Thus, unlike other Latin American cultural centers, which by virtue of their physical geography were more likely to be abreast of the cultural currents emanating from Europe or to a lesser extent from the United States, Bogotá did not enjoy the diverse cultural life and wealth of cultural production that were seen, for example, in Mexico City, Buenos Aires, or Havana. Although physical geography would hinder the dialogue between Bogotá and the rest of the world, the rich soil of the region, cultivated for centuries, did offer excellent agricultural conditions. Even the Chibcha name for the town, alluding to cultivation, gives evidence of this blessing (Abadía Morales 1983, 32). Both the natives and the first Europeans were to find here a productive and salutary natural environment for settlement, a situation that would, following Spanish colonization, contribute to the institution of aristocratic and oligarchic forms of the organization of production.

Origins

The term *origins* is employed here self-consciously to designate the moment of contact between the two cultures, native and Spanish, out of whose encounter would be forged the cultural traditions of the city. Since the number of blacks brought to work in Bogotá was small, African cultural influence would be very limited. Bogotá was founded on a plateau populated by the Muiscas (or Chibchas) in 1538 by Gonzalo Jiménez de Quesada, at the northern end of the Andean cordillera where various routes uniting the northern and southern parts of the South American continent cross. Inspired by the magnificence of the natural surroundings, Quesada, a jurist-conquistador as well as a poet, was to become the first Colombian dramatist (Antelo 142) and the inspiration behind the first poem, not only of Bogotá and Colombia, but, so the story goes, of the continent (Beutler 5; Rodríguez Demorizi 10). The "Romance

de Jiménez de Quesada" was written in the mother tongue by one of the companions in Quesada's band of conquistadors, 28 days after the conquest of the new land and the founding of the city. These facts suggest that poetry crossed the ocean with the Spanish fleet: "the ballad arrived first, singing in octosyllables the exploits of heroes ancient and modern" (Beutler 3). With this disembarkation of poetry, a literary form unknown to the Muiscas, verse compositions–not always original or of the highest caliber–multiplied, and the literary (and most important cultural) tradition of the isolated city of Bogotá was begun.

In addition to poetry, other characteristics of the Spanish world were to take root, not only in Bogotá but throughout Spanish America: medieval scholasticism, Catholicism, loyalty to the Spanish crown, the Spanish language, violence, and the arrogance of the conquistadors. Rafael Gutiérrez Girardot (b. 1928) states that "the monarchy lurking in the hearts of the majority of the Spanish Americans constituted, like their visceral Catholicism, a form of existence. And that hierarchical image of Catholicism underlying the feudal order nurtured monarchical ambitions" (1997, 174)–which is to say that, with the disembarkation, a rigidly hierarchizing and discriminatory social order also landed. Given its isolation, Bogotá is the Spanish American city where these traits, perhaps, struck the deepest roots and where they have remained for the longest time the most intransigent. For a number of reasons, neither the Spanish worldview nor the predominance of literature as a cultural expression was capable of opening Bogotá up to other cultures or diversifying it through other forms of expression. First among these reasons was the overwhelming weight of the Spanish religious culture and the indoctrination of the Muisca population, both of which conspired to asphyxiate the fragile pre-Columbian culture. Second, the strictures of the Inquisition, although less severe in Bogotá than in Cartagena, had an important impact on the censorship and circulation of books with modern or non-Hispanic ideas. Third, the colonial-bureaucratic apparatus of the city was reinforced with the elevation of Bogotá to the status of capital of the viceroyalty of New Granada in 1739, and, as a result, the sentiment of being a "royal" city, tied to the motherland, grew more entrenched. The Spanish language, while being the instrument by which municipal power was exercised, would at the same time constitute the protective seal of bureaucratic power–two factors that would bestow on the written language an uncommon prestige (Rama 1984, 33). Fourth, the scarcity of resources of both the city and the territory retarded the arrival (much more so than was the case in other Latin American cities) of books, musical instruments, scores, paintings, brushes, art and music instructors, as well as other means for the development of cultural expression other than the literary or for the opening of contacts to cultures distinct from the Hispanic. This poverty, pre-Columbian as well as Colonial, was an obstacle to the cultural diversification of Bogotá. It would mean that great architectural works, for example, such as had been built in Mexico City on the ruins of the rich pre-Columbian civilizations, works that could have gone a long way toward equalizing the relative weight of the literary and extra-literary cultures, would not be constructed in Bogotá. And finally, the most important factor favoring the long-term maintenance of the Hispanic heritage and the strong links between official Colombian discourse and the social and cultural characteristics of Spain was isolation.

Society

The Bacatá or Bogotá valley was inhabited by the Muiscas, the most politically and economically developed of the native groups to be found in what is today Colombia. Having reached the level of development that anthropologists call superior formative, the Muiscas were sedentary and hardworking cultivators, politically organized around a matrilineal chieftainship. The settlement of the first Spaniards was in the ample savannah of the valley: Their success in colonization was sustained by the fact that this was a strategic geographic base from which to pursue their incessant quest for *El Dorado* as well as by the fact that the Muiscas, already sedentary and less aggressive than many other previously encountered groups, were both docile and useful for the economic project of colonization. Even prior to the Conquest, the savannah of Bogotá had not been favorable to native political union, and the lack of linguistic unity (González de Pérez 60) among the various tribes of the plateau made Spanish cultural domination possible, and facilitated the submission of the natives to Spanish institutions. This linguistic diversity is one of the reasons why racial miscegenation was so widely embraced and why Hispanic culture was so thoroughly accepted in the city, to the detriment and the almost total destruction of the native cultures and languages. On 20 August 1550, Brother Jerónimo de San Miguel, the first guardian of the Franciscan province of Colombia, wrote to Charles V from Santafé de Bogotá stating: "no hablan todas la misma lengua, antes hay una gran diferencia entre ellas y tanto que en 50 leguas hay seis o siete lenguas: tienen todas una gran dificultad en la pronunciación y no hay español que sepa hablar una de ellas" (quoted in Tobón 51) (not all speak the same tongue. Rather so great is the difference between them that in 50 leagues six or seven languages are to be found–every one is understood only with great difficulty by the others and there is no Spaniard who knows how to speak any of them). Nor would there be need to speak native languages, for Spanish was rapidly being transformed not only into the common language of integration among the various native groups but also into the mechanism by means of which they were ceding their traditions and picking up the culture and the ways of the dominant society. By 1755, native languages were extinct in the province of Santafé de Bogotá (Moreno y Escandón 25).

The first Spanish settlers and their descendents, *encomenderos* (landholders) and functionaries, organized the institutions of the new colony for the benefit of a select minority. As Ángel Rama (1926–1983) has stated, "fue la distancia entre la letra rígida y la fuida palabra hablada, que hizo de la ciudad letrada una ciudad escrituraria" (Rama 1985, 3) (it was the disparity between the inflexible letter and the fluid spoken word that transformed the Lettered City into a Scriptural City). In Bogotá this condition of rigidity and elitism meant that language and grammar were identified with political power and social status (Deas 25–52). Respect for the written word did entail, however, that a small space would be opened for literate members of other social and racial groups to ascend to the political stage and the circles of social privilege. Examples of this social aperture were not numerous but there were some. Such was the case of the late eighteenth-century Cuban Manuel del Socorro Rodríguez (1758–1818) who, because of the untimely death of his father, supported his mother and sister by working as a cabinetmaker. A self-taught student of the humanities, Rodríguez excelled to the point of

Figure 1.

Drawing by Guamán Poma de Ayala depicting the foundation of Santa Fe de Bogota in 1538 from El primer nueva corónica y buen gobierno *(1615). (Courtesy of John P. Robarts Research Library, University of Toronto)*

making himself noticed by the governor of Havana, José de Ezpeleta. A short time later Ezpeleta was named viceroy of New Granada and brought Rodríguez to Bogotá as the librarian of the National Library. From a small study in the building where he was to live out the rest of his days, Manuel de Socorro inaugurated Colombian journalism when he established the *Papel Periódico*. He was also to inaugurate the "Europélica" salon (1791–1797) for the dissemination of ideas of the Enlightenment, as well as offering a meeting place for the most prominent political and social figures of the capital. Rodríguez's modest origins did not impede him from forging lasting friendships with members of the Bogotan elite; nor did they prevent his salon from influencing the political life of the capital, or deter history from conferring on him the title of father of Colombian journalism (Vélez 282). Other examples of this openness to upward mobility could be cited, such as the black poet Candelario Obeso (1849–1884) in the nineteenth century and President Marco Fidel Suárez at the beginning of the twentieth. Obviously, these examples are exceptions to the rule; however, it is important to clarify that in these cases knowledge of the Hispanic literary tradition opened the doors to social acceptance.

The cultural inequality underlying the separation of Spaniards, natives, *mestizos*, and blacks from each other was in large part a product of educational segregation. Although the statistics at the disposal of a cultural history of Bogotá are far from extensive, the limited educational system increasingly amplified social and cultural disparities between these groups. The percentage of Colombian children in elementary schools (by and large white children) rose only very slowly over the course of the nineteenth century: From 1.2 percent in 1835, it grew to 3.0 percent in 1873, 3.3 percent in 1897, reaching 6.1 percent in 1914 (Melo 124–26). The difference in literacy rates divided the various sectors of Bogotá's population and it was, obviously, the (white and educated) upper classes who would direct the cultural evolution of the city and, gradually, as their influence expanded, the country as a whole. The census of 1871 corroborated the elite character of Colombian society in general. While, of the 2,713,000 inhabitants enumerated, only 60,135 were in school, only 6,189 could be socially and culturally categorized as belonging to the learned, and a mere eighty-two were writers; the census also counted 14,390 artists and artisans (Pérez 1883, 166). The limited number of literates in the census allows us to draw a more strict correlation between culture and race, at least until the final years of the nineteenth century.

Racial and Cultural Miscegenation

While the cultural history of Bogotá can be faithfully characterized as being founded upon the predominance of Spanish culture, the monopoly of literature as the principal expression of cultural activity, and the exclusive possession of the latter by a tiny and elitist white group, it behooves us to ask what was happening in the distinct cultures of the other groups resident in the city in this era when the new city was in the process of establishing itself. Although the relation between culture and ethnicity in Bogotá has hardly been studied, various anthropological approaches have been able to throw some light on the question. The research of Peter Wade, for example, has analyzed the simplistic theory of opposition between a homogeneous white elite and their heterogeneous subalterns, and the cultural expressions arising out of and representing this social antagonism (Wade 87). Another approach, adopted by Gloria Triana, has regarded Colombian popular culture as a subaltern culture dominated and absorbed by an elitist, hegemonic, rootless, and foreign-looking culture (Triana 305). A third approach was that formulated by the German geographer Alfred Hettner, who, after visiting the city from 1882 to 1884 and observing the state of affairs, contended that the mestizos imitated the dominant culture: "estos han llegado hasta a prescindir de la ruana y del sombrero de paja, para imitar la indumentaria de estilo europeo de las capas superiores, así que para ellos a veces la calificación colectiva de 'gente de ruana' ya no le vale" (225) (in order to imitate the European style of apparel of the upper classes the mestizos have so renounced the poncho and straw hat, that to label them the 'ponchoed folk' is a qualification at times without validity).

In order to answer this question about the other cultures within Bogotan society we must first examine the *mestizo* situation. Demographically concerned about the diminution of royal revenues that was resulting from a decrease in the native population, the tax collector Francisco Antonio Moreno y Escandón wrote to the king in 1778: "El Nuevo Reino de Granada es cada vez más una nación de mestizos, y la desaparición de los indios por su conversión en éstos produce inquietudes" (31) (The Kingdom of New Granada is becoming a nation of *mestizos,* and the conversion, and consequent disappearance, of the natives is becoming worrying). The demographic report of the Parochial District of Santafé de Bogotá, tabled a few years later, corroborated that affirmation. According to the census of 1793, of the 17,725 inhabitants of the city, 38 percent were white, 52.7 percent *mestizo,* and only 3.6 percent pure-blooded natives. The high percentage of mestizos and the almost total absence of natives in the urban center of the city was a constant throughout its history. Hence, the surprise of Miguel Cané (1851–1905) when he entered Bogotá in 1882:

> La calle por donde el carruaje avanzaba con dificultad estaba materialmente cuajada de indios. Acababa de cruzar la plazuela de San Victorino, donde había encontrado un cuadro que no se me borrará nunca. . . . Los indios que impedían el tránsito del carruaje, tal era su número, presentaban el mismo aspecto. . . . Los bogotanos se reían mas tarde cuando les narraba la impresión de mi entrada y me explicaban la razón. Había llegado en viernes, que es el día de mercado. . .eran los jueves y viernes cuando los indios agricultores de la Sabana, de la tierra caliente y de los pequeños valles allende las montañas que abrigan a Bogotá, vienen con sus productos a la capital. (Cané 177)

> The road by which the carriage advanced with difficulty was swarming with Indians. Having crossed San Victorino Square, I came upon a scene that shall never be erased from my mind. . . . The Indians who blocked the path of the carriage, such were their numbers, all displayed an identical appearance. . . . Later, narrating the impression of my entrance, the Bogotans laughed heartily and explained to me the reason why. I had arrived on a Friday, which is to say market day. . . . Thursdays and Fridays were the days when the native farmers from the savannah, the lowlands, and the small valleys on the other side of the mountains that shelter Bogotá haul their produce to the capital.

As this episode suggests, although there were almost no natives living in the city, contact with natives and native culture was continuous.

During the Colonial period and until the twentieth century, the *mestizo* population was engaged in artisanal and commercial activity, either as owners of small stores and shops or as junior clerks in municipal offices (Hettner 225). This second-class employment, in addition to the differences in white and mestizo education, adds credence to Wade's position. However, historical examples of upward social mobility, such as the well-known cases of that black writer Candelario Obeso and the mestizo Eugenio Díaz (1804–1865), among others, suggest that the outlook assumed on the part of the mestizos was one of imitation. No longer being natives, the mestizos imitated a culture that was no longer particularly peninsular in character, but was rather, as Triana has proposed, rootless and foreign looking. In the case of Bogotá, as Raymond Williams has detailed, this culture was marked by a strong tendency toward Hispanism (Williams 42).

Can it be said then that the former terms of cultural diversity—indigenous versus Iberian—were superseded by a synthesis that homogenized the culture of the mestizos, Hispanicizing and uprooting them? With respect to the process undergone by Spanish music in the Americas, Pedro Henríquez Ureña (1884–1946) has stated that: "El mundo nuevo refluyó pronto sobre el antiguo iniciándose un juego de flujo y reflujo que persistirá, sin interrumpirse" (245) (The new world very quickly fed back into the old, initiating a play of flux and reflux that would persist without interruption). In this condition of feedback, Spanish culture was no longer the same as it had been previously, and there was no alternative for the mestizo population but to adapt themselves to the (also mutating) white culture, itself subject to the influence of new and foreign cultural modes. As Triana has stressed and as will be further explored in the following section, over time the culture of the Bogotan elite cut its roots with its own past and took on in its stead influences and traits of foreign origin. This pattern of cultural uprooting and imitation of the foreign was also adopted by the *mestizos*, a process that would be the end result of the ongoing battles to change the cultural standing of the origins, both native and Spanish.

In the following examples from the realm of the plastic arts and literature we can see how, in the tendency toward racial miscegenation, elements of both the Spanish and indigenous cultures (with emphasis on and precedence clearly for the former) were received and accepted. The first concerns the great metalwork tradition of the Muisca goldsmiths that in Colonial times melded its artistry with the equally millenarian tradition of Spanish silversmiths. Colonial smithery successfully evolved among the so-called silversmiths by conserving the forms of work that had been seen in Spanish silver, but all the while adapting native goldsmithing techniques. The fabrication itself was carried out by *mestizo* artisans, whose association was regulated since 1631 under the form of a medieval-style Spanish guild (Giraldo Jaramillo 323). Another interesting demonstration of aspects of this cultural miscegenation was that of the Sevillian painter Baltasar de Figueroa the Elder (born 1590), who, upon his arrival in the New Kingdom of Granada, spent a period painting religious works for the church of the town of Turmequé. There Figueroa married the native woman Inés de Turmequé; from that union and the craft of Figueroa was engendered not only a racial but an equally cultural miscegenation. The descendents of the painter constituted the artistic dynasty of the Figueroas, in whose Bogotan atelier many important painters of the Colonial era would receive their training. For its part, the indigenous artistic tradition would offer to the Colonial tradition many techniques developed by the Muiscas, such as the fabrication of brushes and pigments, and it was by means of such resources that Figueroa was able to extend the reach of his artistry. In spite of the important contributions made by the two traditions, the Colombian art historian Francisco Gil Tovar would clearly claim that the native contribution in painting, sculpture, ornamental carving, architectural decoration, weaving, and so on, is weak, and of little appreciable value in comparison with what can be seen in Mexico and Peru (247).

The same situation can be glimpsed in popular literary expressions where the heavy weight of the Spanish tradition also collaborated in the cultural miscegenation of Bogotá. In the nineteenth century the artisans' guild, racially linked to the mestizos, began to express itself through the same channels and in the same forms as the elites, which is to say by means of Spanish-language literature, although with different aims in mind. Poems of political harangue were written at this time, proposing the unification of the democratic societies and seeking to make their members conscious of their class condition and their relation to the elites. Such poems expressed "the shared sense of artisanal self-esteem" (Gutiérrez Sanín 39), as can be seen in: "A los ricos" ["To the Rich"], a poem appearing in the Bogotan newspaper *El Orden* in 1853:

Los ricos en otras partes
Merecen veneración
Prestando su protección
A los pobres, a las artes,
Dándoles ocupación.

The rich in other parts
Deserve veneration
Lending their protection
To the poor, to the arts
Giving them work.

Later in the same century the writer Jorge Isaacs (1837–1895) put together a compilation of the anonymous verses and popular songs of the epoch, studied and edited by the folklorist Guillermo Abadía (b. 1912). It is noteworthy, said Abadía in reference to the verses of the Bogotan region, how the expressions employed in the *bambuco* songs, as in airs adapted to dances and sketches, were not verses but rather erudite rhetorical forms, choice poems borrowed from the world repertoire, and, at times, from eminent poets like Juan Ramón Jiménez (1881–1958). Abadía illustrated this by quoting from the bambuco "Mañana de primavera" [Morning in Springtime], with music by Miguel Trespalacios (Abadía 1983, 156). These examples from the realm of popular literature confirm Gil Tovar's assertion that with respect to literature the indigenous element in the hybridization is weak and of little appreciable value.

In summary, then, the coordinates by which the culture of the city was shaped—geography, society, and the manner in which the culture developed—gave rise to a new culture with deep Hispanic roots. This new culture was characterized by a Spanish worldview that, abetted by a pattern of cultural imitation on the part of the *mestizos*, initially became stronger and more homogeneous, but which, coming under the constant influence of foreign ideas and practices during the Republic, progressively became uprooted, ultimately reaching a point of almost total crisis. In the twentieth century when the Bogotan rates of literacy made it possible for the formerly marginalized to express themselves as forcefully as the elites, the rising levels of education and the spread of telecommunications have also developed a culture of nondescript Hispanic American expression.

History

The history of Bogotá as a cultural center revolves around the battles waged by certain "civilizing" sectors of society (Zea 257) to loosen the iron grip that the aforementioned factors had upon the city's development. We have already mentioned that the culture of the capital has been characterized (by Gutiérrez Girardot; Peralta) as aristocratic, parochial, anachronistic, and imitative. It is from a historical perspective that the ongoing struggles between the defenders of the culture constructed in the "origins" and their diverse adversaries can best be seen. Among the latter group numbered people of every class, including members of the political elite, scientists, men of letters, and occasionally women, some of whom advanced French or English ideas, others European scientific, political, or literary notions. This generally antagonistic state of affairs was the basis for the cultural uprooting and widespread acceptance of foreign values that characterizes Bogotan cultural history, as well as for the instability of its cultural reference points. However, the questions return: Was this the only way to create a properly Bogotan and Colombian culture? To what extent did the campaigns of these cultural armies succor or abet the development of that culture?

We have, so far, only cursorily examined some of the cultural junctures in which the tensions between the discourse defending the tradition and the discourse seeking its transformation have changed the culture of the city. Before studying these junctures in greater detail, a number of methodological clarifications are necessary. First, given Bogotá's status, initially, as capital of the viceroyalty and later of the republic, certain cultural movements rooted in the locality would later become national issues; the character of these junctures must thus be seen as an amalgam of local, regional, and national elements. Second, these cultural junctures concern the contestation of the social, political, and cultural hegemony of the elite, and, as a consequence, political questions are intertwined with cultural questions. Third, in certain of these junctures some of the principal participants favored cultural change, while at other times they took a more conservative position. This was the case with Alberto Urdaneta (1845–1887), for example, who, while cultivating and modernizing the plastic arts as a legitimate form of cultural expression, would also uphold the traditional themes of the Hispanic culture of the city. Six well-known movements that served to galvanize the historical consolidation of Bogotá as a cultural center can be identified: the scientific, the political, the Anglophile/Francophile, and the restoration movements, the struggle between modernity and reaction, and finally, the advent of the masses or the crisis of Hispanicizing discourse.

The Scientific Movement

The cultural context in which Colombian modernizing discourses arose toward the end of the Colonial era, when church censorship still overshadowed the range of Colombian cultural expressions, has been accurately described by José María Vergara y Vergara (1831–1872) and quoted by José Ruiz Martínez (1873–1967):

> [E]staban entonces en su auge las excelentes bibliotecas de los conventos, en las que. . . .existían. . . . tesoros de verdadera s abiduría en los libros de los eminentes filósofos y expositores de la Iglesia, San Agustín, San Buenaventura, y sobre todo en los del admirable Tomás de Aquino, cuya liberal y elevada *Summa Theologica* era pasto de las inteligencias, que espantadas y aprisionadas por la inquisición, se refugiaban en sus páginas inmortales. . . . La iglesia católica era maternal protectora de las artes y de la ciencia. (quoted in Ruiz Martínez 599)

> In those days the excellent libraries of the monasteries were in full flower . . . where treasures of veritable wisdom could be found in the books of the eminent philosophers and expositors of the Church, such as Saint Augustine, Saint Bonaventure, and above all in the works of the admirable Thomas Aquinas, whose generous and lofty *Summa Theologica* was nourishment to the intellectual understanding, which, menaced and shackled by the Inquisition, found refuge in his immortal pages. . . . The Catholic Church was the maternal patron of the arts and the sciences.

So protective was the Catholic church of its cultural possessions and prerogatives that the Archbishop of Bogotá, Don Jaime Rodríguez Compañón, offered the impresario constructing the first theater in the city 40,000 pesos if he would desist from entertaining that iniquitous idea. Despite the obstacles, the theater did open its doors in 1792 (González Cajiao 68). In that restrictive climate, to characterize the infrastructural and cultural state of the city as backward is superfluous. However–and as the popular Bogotá oral refrain has

it–"no hay mal que dure cien años, ni cuerpo que lo resista" ("there is no evil that persists, nor carnal body that resists"); the appointment of José Celestino Mutis (1732–1808) in 1763 as botanist of the viceroy signaled a change in the cultural dynamic. A doctor and botanist by training and a scientist of some aptitude, Mutis would disseminate a discourse of scientific modernization that would precipitate the first major cultural movement and extensively modify the Colonial cultural state of affairs of the city in particular, and the viceroyalty in general. Mutis brought to the city not only Renaissance ideals but Newtonian and Enlightenment ideas: His critiques of scholastic impertinences resulted in the official acceptance of the Copernican astronomical system; and the botanical expeditions organized by him at La Nueva Granada, in 1783–1816, were in large part responsible for a cultural about-face in the Colombian view of the world, which until then had always been directed toward the memories and murmurs that arrived from Spain. The new outlook was formulated in the monasteries and directed toward the natural environment, a transition, as Carlos José Reyes (b. 1941) has called it, "from discovery to invention" (1993, 449). Reyes's characterization of this movement as "inventive" is perhaps somewhat overdone, but there is no doubt that a radical change of views did result.

The scientific movement inspired by Mutis can be seen as an anti-Hispanic modernizing discourse for a number of reasons. First, this new current of ideas that broke with the Spanish medieval philosophic thought that had characterized Colombian letters. In 1761 Mutis established the first chair of mathematics in Colombia at the Colegio Mayor de Nuestra Señora del Rosario (founded 1654), from which professorship Copernican astronomy and Newtonian physics were disseminated. Although these ideas can in no way be considered to have formed part of the intellectual stock of the capital, they were, however, not entirely unknown (Hernández de Alba and Martínez Briceño 1960, 55). There is evidence to suggest that the private library of 1060 volumes belonging to Father Fernando de Castro y Vargas had been in clandestine circulation since his death in 1664, and that this library contained a number of volumes prohibited by the Holy Office, such as the works of Erasmus and Copernicus's *On the Revolutions of the Heavenly Spheres* (1543). Second, the botanical expeditions of Mutis constituted a project of sociocultural modernization that opened the eyes of the Bogotans to what lay beyond the limits of the mountains that ringed the city, awakening them to a world they hardly knew existed, the world of nature's fauna and flora. Mutis's studies of the local natural environment and the repercussions of those studies for the medical, botanical, mineralogical, astronomical, and social sciences had the effect not only of establishing a tradition of scientific undertaking that would persist until this day, but also of rapidly bringing into common currency a number of basic scientific propositions and principles, both for those who followed the expeditions and for the inhabitants of the capital in general.

Third, the pictorial legacy of the expeditions began to break down the hegemony of literature over the cultural life of the colony. These expeditions produced a collection of herbaria whose illustrations numbered 5,393 plates representing 2,696 species and twenty-six varieties, plates now housed in the Royal Botanical Gardens in Madrid. The naturalist style of these drawings was an affront to the religious and Baroque canons of Colonial art that then prevailed in Bogotan painting (B. González 15). Fourth, the movement initiated by the efforts of Mutis served in its own way to democratize the culture. Although this was by and large an elitist movement, perhaps especially in its championing of scientific interests, the popular culture of Bogotá was involved in two very particular ways. From the beginning, the movement cast an anthropological eye on the customs and habits and daily lives of the various ethnic groups dwelling in the capital region. The best examples of this anthropological interest are the seven oil paintings left behind by the Quitonian artist Antonio Barrionuevo, one of the official painters of the expeditions, in which the depiction of the ethnic customs of the Cundinamarguesa region is outstanding. The other popular facet of the movement was the mixed social composition of the Bureau of Artists established by Mutis in Bogotá. First botanist to the king, Mutis worked closely with representatives of every stratum of society: *criollo* patricians, lower-class whites, *mestizos*, mulattos, and natives (B. González 6).

As a consequence of the reforms initiated by this movement, the last years of Bogotá's eighteenth century saw the consolidation for the first time of a solid cultural infrastructure. In the final forty years of the century a profound revolution in ideas and cultural institutions took place in a city that, prior to 1750, contained only monasteries and churches. In 1766 the first printing press was established; following the expulsion of the Jesuits it would be used to publish the annals of the botanical expedition. In 1777 the first public library was founded, The National Library, with 13,800 volumes from the former Jesuit library. Humboldt would describe the library at the disposal of the researchers under the directorship of Mutis and Caldas as unmatched in kind by any library in Europe (Henríquez Ureña 1979, 38). Increased by the arrival of a large group of painters from Quito who had come to collaborate with Mutis, the city's first school of drawing, The Royal Botanical Expedition Academy of Drawing, offered instruction between 1783 and 1816. The thirty-two graduates of the Academy, the majority from New Granada, were to constitute a prestigious pictorial school that would make a profound impression on the city's plastic arts tradition. 1785 saw the publication of the city's first newspaper and seven years later the controversial first theater of the city opened its doors; it was called "El Coliseo Ramírez" (The Ramírez Coliseum), after its tenacious manager and founder. During the wave of reforms inspired by the scientific spirit of the botanical expeditions, the Astronomical Observatory was established in 1803. At the beginning of the nineteenth century, and hard on the heels of this cultural-infrastructural construction boom, a new cultural movement appeared whose modernizing discourse would be much more political than scientific. It would initiate the overthrow of the principal political and cultural institutions that, up until 1810, had bolstered the Spanish Colonial discourse.

The Political Moment

Although the revolutionary wave that swept the South American continent in the early 1800s was a replica of that unleashed in France, it was nevertheless the first movement initiated and carried to term by the *criollos*. It was, however, by and large a political movement with little importance for the history of Bogotan artistic and literary creation (Jaramillo Uribe 1982, 120). In terms of the city's history, this revolutionary wave was threefold. First, it opened a door for the bold arrival and circulation of French Enlightenment ideas and culture, which then assumed the role of counterweight to

the archaic Spanish tradition. Second, it furthered the reforms and inaugurations of modern cultural institutions and, third, it propitiated the mobilization and integration of various groups, including women and natives, into the general political movement. The principal achievement of this movement was the abolition of the Spanish monarchy and the bulk of its institutions. In addition, with the high frequency and great quantities of information arriving in the capital from every city in South America, the independence era fostered a breakdown in the city's isolation. Joining Venezuela and Ecuador, New Granada became, until 1830, Greater Colombia (La Gran Colombia), with Bogotá as its capital. The world outside the capital now appeared in a new light.

During this period the modernization of cultural institutions continued unabated. Two new institutions deserve mention, the intellectual "salons" or *tertulias* and the periodical press. Salons modeled on the French Enlightenment example had been organized in Bogotá since the end of the eighteenth century. Bogotans and "enlightened" members of New Granadan society found in these salons a forum for the discussion of philosophic, literary, and political ideas and an arena in which they could be put into practice. In the final years of the colony and up until 1820, the most famous were the Europélica and the Buen Gusto Salons, the latter, under the patronage of Manuela Sanz de Santamaría de Manrique, having as much an "enlightened" as a political agenda. Also meeting regularly were scientific salons, the Tertulia del Observatorio Astronómico, founded in 1803, and the Casino Literario under the leadership of the politician Antonio Nariño. These salons played an important role in the political and cultural life of the city, in much the same way as French and English literary salons of the seventeenth century had, since they were a site of reunion, mutual information gathering, and participation for both enlightened aristocrats and the newly emerging and upwardly mobile classes (Habermas 70). The need to communicate the new ideas of this political and intellectual culture—with Rousseau, Montesquieu, and Voltaire being, naturally, the writers of preference—ushered in the era of the periodical presses, the creation and diffusion of which perhaps constitutes the major legacy of this political movement. The principal supporters of the modernizing movement were *El Zancudo* (1790–1791), a brilliant journal of caricatures and satires and the first serial publication, and a periodical whose political impact would be unparalleled, *El Papel Periódico de la ciudad* (1791–1797), edited by Manuel del Socorro Rodríguez, a forum for discussion of the arts and sciences, and initiator of the literary press—since sonnets, odes, *silvas*, eulogies, and *canciones reales* (royal songs) all appeared within its covers. Without going into too much detail, it is noteworthy that in the half century between 1790 and 1837, the year in which General Santander died and, by and large, the year that marked the end of the independence generation, 117 periodicals (all of short duration) were published in a city of only 35,000 inhabitants. By comparison, in the same period, the cities of Cartagena, Popayán, Cúcuta, Santa Marta, Tunja, Medellín, and Panamá were responsible for only sixty-eight periodicals (Reyes Posada 1994, 1011). From the very beginnings of the Bogotan periodical explosion there was a premonition that any future expansion or political amplification of this new means of communication would face a number of limitations and difficulties: limited print runs because of the high cost of production; a scarcity of readers, due to high levels of illiteracy (90 percent of the population);

the limitations on expression imposed by political censorship; and the competition resulting from a multitude of journals chasing a limited readership.

It was, however, upon these improved foundations for the dissemination of cultural expression that the initiative to achieve cultural autonomy moved forward. Here we need to mention the noted contributions of the Bogotan poet and dramatist Luis Vargas Tejada (1802–1829) and of the artist José María Espinosa (1796–1883). According to the critic William Ospina, in Vargas Tejada's work we are witness to a mastery of language only rarely encountered in nineteenth-century Colombian verse, and although Vargas Tejada's famous play *Las convulsiones* [1828; The Convulsions] is somewhat imitative of Lope de Vega and Albergati, his premature death nonetheless cut short the early development of a Colombian poetic voice (Carranza 106). From a less literary and more political point of view, Jaime Jaramillo Uribe has considered the patriotic and political poetry of the era, including that of Vargas Tejada, as being of little real merit.

Beginning with the realist painter José María Espinosa, the plastic arts of this era cleared their own path. Converting himself into a painter of customs and manners, Espinosa introduced into his painting a rupture with the calcified tradition of colonial painting. For his part, the art historian Francisco Gil Tovar labels Espinosa's work a portraitist-caricaturist art, claiming that the painters of this first part of the nineteenth century did not know how to paint because they had lost the will to develop the techniques of painting; it is for this reason that Tovar lumps these artists together with the naïve primitivists (Gil Tovar 1997, 323). Popular cultural participation was also to be found during this political movement, and was indeed prolific, especially in the composition of patriotic ballads and marches that accompanied the liberation armies on their campaigns. In conclusion, the space vacated by the Spanish in the period following independence opened a door to a new Anglo- and Francophilia. Bogotá, recently liberated from the weight of Spanish royal traditions, and searching for new material with which to nurture its construction of a more properly genuine culture, became receptive to English and French influences.

The Anglophile and Francophile Movement

Although Raymond L. Williams has stated that the Andean oligarchy of Colombia adopted and imitated, above all, the cultural values of the English and the Spanish (Williams 43), there is much evidence to support the assertion that French culture had its supporters, even during the most vigorous period of Anglophilia. According to Jaime Jaramillo Uribe, English influence peaked between 1810 and 1840, while French influence was ascendant in the following period between 1840 and 1880 (1977, 120). Frank Safford, in his *The Ideal of the Practical: Colombia's Struggle to Form a Technical Elite* (1976), contradicts Uribe's thesis and notes the large number of French scientists who visited Bogotá between 1822 and 1839 with the intention of carrying on the scientific ventures initiated by Mutis, but *à la française*. From this evidence it appears that in Bogotá, French and English influences coexisted with the Spanish legacy during almost the entire nineteenth century, even though the emphasis toward one or the other was greater in the specific periods indicated by Jaramillo Uribe. The struggle to implant or forcibly to uproot such influences was fought on the battlefields of the political institutions of the capital. In 1849 the Conservative Party was

born—a party that would by and large champion the Colonial cultural heritage. It was during this same period (1850–1860) that the liberal economic and political project, inspired by a mix of mostly English and to a lesser extent French political and economic institutions, enjoyed its greatest successes. For example, Andrés Bello's (1781–1865) translation of the Napoleonic civil code roughly coincided with the commercial bills inspired by English free-trade ideas; both pieces of legislation were tabled in the middle of the nineteenth century.

The Anglophile propensity found its justification in the English solidarity with the independence movement. English participation both in the battles and in the financial sector inspired the most important republican leaders to turn their attention to things English in the period after the Spanish withdrawal in 1816. And the fact that England was, in addition, the first to recognize Latin American independence led the patriots to a recognition of and an interest in English culture.

Rufino Cuervo (1801–1853), father of the eminent Hispanist Rufino José Cuervo (1844–1911), has characterized the post-independence Anglomania epoch as a great movement of Hispanic renunciation. Under the notable influence of the English philosopher Jeremy Bentham, English ideas began to make an impression on the thinking of the era's leaders. These ideas were promoted and disseminated in Bogotá and the nation not only by General Santander and his two administrations (ending in 1837), but also by a group of young liberal minds and some others not so liberal such as the Romantic poet José Eusebio Caro (1817–1853), father of Miguel Antonio Caro (1843–1909) (Jaramillo Uribe 1977, 121). To the influence of Benthamite ideas was added the advocacy of Juan García del Río (1794–1856), who championed the adoption of a spirit of enterprise and Anglo-Saxon ethics in commercial affairs. García del Río lived for a number of years in London where he collaborated with Andrés Bello in the editing of the famous London-published reviews, *La Biblioteca Americana* (1823) and *El Repertorio Americano* (1826). By means of these publications Bello's ideas on the worldview of the Americas began to circulate in the capital, thus linking it integrally to the bodies politic and cultural of the continent.

From 1840 until 1870, however, the anti-Hispanic example was set, above all, by French Romanticism. French Romanticism and English Liberalism, the latter still in vogue at this time, were the outlets by which individual liberties found cultural expression; they also made possible a final break with the authoritarian inflexibility imposed by the colonial order. These ruptures with the Spanish worldview and the opening up of new possibilities of expression would, however, as Antonio Cursio Altamar has pointed out (in Williams 68), still be insufficient for the literary and political culture of the capital to feel either that it had left off being a new replica, this time of English and French cultural models, or to feel itself authorized in the luster of its own originality. If Jeremy Bentham was the English thinker most influential in Colombian society up until 1850, the French Romantics Victor Hugo, Alphonse de Lamartine, and Eugène Sue would be the most read and admired writers in the period from 1850 to 1870. Conservatives criticized the awesome influence of Victor Hugo on Colombian liberal circles. The 1848 Revolution in France struck a new note of appeal for French cultural influence in the world, and Bogotá was no exception. The Romantic image of utopian socialism played itself out in the literature of the era, through the evocation of social themes and the sentiment of Christian charity. With *Les Misérables*, the orphan, the convict, the fallen woman, and the slave became the subjects of choice for poets within the orbit of Bogotá such as Manuel María Madiedo (1818–1888) and José Joaquín Ortiz (1814–1892) (Jaramillo Uribe 1977, 126). It is clear that Romanticism experienced fewer difficulties in being admitted to Bogotan culture, flourishing not only in literature but in general daily life, than Benthamite utilitarianism and the Anglo-Saxon mentality advocated by García del Río and others. As a philosophical doctrine placing the onus for action on the individual, utilitarianism was radically opposed to the Hispanic worldview founded upon Catholicism in which God was the center of all things in the universe. Utilitarianism not only aroused a great deal of opposition, but putting it into practice implied a total transformation of tradition and culture, whereas dreamy and idealistic Romanticism, on the other hand, was a much more comfortable and convenient form for expressing the predominant, aristocratically influenced, culture.

These nineteenth-century cultural currents were reflected in the composition of the National Library holdings. In 1855, of the 20,094 volumes in the only public collection in Bogotá, 32.98 percent were Latin texts, 24.79 percent in Spanish, and another 5.63 percent were on Colombia. The remaining 36.62 percent were books written in other European languages, French and English principally. By 1887 the total collection had risen to 22,100 volumes, and while the proportion of Latin texts had remained the same, the proportion of books in Spanish had fallen to 17.33 percent, the proportion of English and French texts having risen to make up the difference (Hernández de Alba and Botero Carrasquilla 1977, 111). The new possibilities of the book trade and the new taste for reading that arose from this Anglophile and Francophile movement paint a picture very different from the climate reigning at the time of the formation of Father Fernando de Castro y Vargas's library in 1664. In the nineteenth century the sale of books in Bogotá had increased considerably, as is evidenced by the output of the Echeverría Brothers' press. In this editorial enterprise, national (and especially liberal) writers found an assiduous publisher of their works (Castellanos 1996, 114). The Echeverría Brothers not only printed and distributed *El Tiempo*, the only newspaper to be distributed nationwide, with the greatest circulation between 1855 and 1872, but printed and distributed as well the lion's share of the books available on the Bogotan market. Of their total nonperiodical publications between 1855 and 1871, 3.7 percent were anticlerical texts, 6.9 percent books on history, philosophy, and national politics, 13.8 percent technical texts, the bulk of these commercial manuals, 16.1 percent official publications contracted by the government, 26.1 percent school textbooks, and 31.3 percent literary works. The high percentage of literary publications, almost a third of total output of the prestigious firm, is remarkable (Castellanos 1996, table 3).

A large number of the books in circulation at this time were imported, as can be seen from book-pages' advertisements for 2 March 1855 of the *Diario de Avisos,* a newspaper published by the commercial agents Pereira Gamba-Camacho Roldán and Company. Among the most notable titles that could be cited, titles that confirm the more cosmopolitan interest of the era are Alexander Bain's *Moral Science,* Jeremy Bentham's *The Defence of Usury* and *Legislation, Civil Government,* by John Locke; scores of novels by Voltaire, Victor Hugo, Eugène Sue, Alexandre Dumas, father and son, in addition to works by Lamartine; works in English promoting the Central American travels of John L. Stephens; a translation of the novels of Juvenal; *The History of Ireland* (1835), by Thomas Moore; the

complete works of Cervantes, Machiavelli, Napoleon, Molière, and so on; volumes on the history and geography of Colombia and of France, as well as on various subjects of European history. The French Revolution was well represented with the memoirs of Talleyrand and Guizot, and Napoleon's in Saint Helena. For reference there was a whole range of English and legal dictionaries, not to mention Latin and Spanish grammars; works seeking to resuscitate the Hispanic Colonial tradition such as the volume entitled *Aguinaldo Religioso* [Religious Epiphany], and a collection of selected essays on ethics, religion, and moral habits for the education of young women; finally, Josef Mamerto Hermosilla's (1771–1837) *Arte de hablar en prosa y verso* [1826; The Art of Speaking in Prose and Verse].

Of every 100 works advertised, seventy were imports from Europe, the majority from France and England, a minority from Spain; only 10 percent were by Colombian authors, 2 percent by other Latin Americans. By subject matter, the advertisements can be broken down into 28 percent juridical, legal, or political science, 22 percent literary, and 10 percent each on Colombian themes and accounting, agricultural, or general sciences. The remaining percentage is made up of dictionaries, grammars, bibles, and miscellaneous subjects. From this informal survey of a single issue of the *Diario de Avisos,* we can conclude that a Bogotan in 1855 could have been well informed on the most important French Romantics, given the availability of primary texts; but with respect to Latin American or Anglo-American questions, he or she would probably have been woefully uninformed. The 10 percent of book titles on technical and scientific subjects reflect perhaps the popular practical ideal, although it is to be noted that this percentage is smaller than that representing the number of legal and literary texts (*Diario de Avisos* 1–4).

Another of the achievements of this Anglo- and Francophilia movement, in addition to the greater cultural openness, came as a consequence of its liberal politics and the resulting social reforms. This spirit and these reforms brought to public attention the cultural expressions of marginalized and anonymous groups that until then had no voice in society–nor ears that would listen. These new voices belonged to the artisans who already participated, as did the peasantry and women, in the cultural life of the city. The journal *El Alacrán* was a recognition of this new artisanal standing. The quasi-ethnographic compilations of the writer Jorge Isaacs, collecting verses from every region of the country, including the peasant hamlets in the environs of Bogotá (Abadía 1985), gave an indication of the importance that this form of popular culture had at the time. Eugenio Díaz's novel *Manuela,* published in installments in the highly representative literary journal edited by José María Vergara y Vergara, *El Mosaico,* likewise reflects the opening of literary interests toward rural themes and subjects.

The positivist inspiration in the form of a will to institutionalization resulted in the creation of numerous scientific and cultural institutions with distinct and specific objectives. Scientists endeavored to keep the naturalist movement going begun by Mutis, while the community of letters sought to sustain Colombian national cultural expression. Some of the resulting institutions are still in existence today, such as the National Museum, founded in 1823 by Vice President Santander to stimulate knowledge of the arts and letters, while other institutions, such as the National Academy, established in 1826 but passing away with the political change of climate that followed the demise of Greater Colombia in 1830, had only a short lifetime. In 1870, José Manuel Marroquín (1827–1908) and José María Vergara y

Vergara founded the Academy of the Language, modeled on the Royal Spanish Academy and the first such institution in the Americas. As we shall see, this institution would adopt the role of the great champion of the royalist cause in the future restoration movement and the resurgence of Spanish influence.

During this period, creative expression continued to follow the example set by foreign patterns and models, offering further affirmation to Cursio Altamar's thesis of Colombian cultural "replication." Two very illustrative examples of this deficit of cultural originality come to mind. The first concerns Rafael Pombo (1833–1912), one of the most respected writers of his time, and indeed, in the history of Colombian literature. Pombo resided in New York, from 1855 to 1872, where he became acquainted with the variety of anonymous English nursery rhymes and lullabies. These songs and verses bear an enormous likeness to the fables that Pombo published under the names "Rinrín Renacuajo" and "Simón el Bobito," tales that are considered master works of Colombian children's literature (de Angeli 118, 126). This lack of originality can also be seen in the mid- to late-century boom of life narratives of customs and manners, portrait paintings and photographs, and feature articles. The most prolific portraits by representatives of this trend are the customs-and-manners watercolors and portraits by Ramón Torres Méndez (1809–1885), the work of the society photographer Luis García Hevia (1816–1887), the academic painter Epifanio Garay (1849–1903), as well as the most celebrated chronicler of the time, Ricardo Silva (1836–1887), José Caicedo Rojas (1816–1893), Soledad Acosta de Samper (1833–1913), and the best of the lot, José Maria Cordovez Moure (1835–1918). There appears to be a critical consensus that during this period Colombian culture did experience, through the medium of its poetry, a profound sense of cultural liberation, with the poet José Eusebio Caro being the most important exponent of this emancipatory fervor (Carranza 111). In the first 400 years of Bogotá's history, poetry was the expressive means by which a more representative, authentic, and properly Bogotan creativity was shaped. It is hardly surprising, then, that poets were the leaders of the following movement that sought to restore Spanish values in, and by means of, grammar, poetry, and politics.

The Restoration Movement

In 1843 Rufino Cuervo, father of Rufino José Cuervo, declared with the rare level-headedness that was his trademark, that "para un pueblo naciente era igualmente peligroso innovarlo todo, que mantenerlo todo en una situación estacionaria"(1843, 45–46) (it would be just as dangerous for a nascent people to adopt a stance of total innovation as it would be to remain stationary). Just as their predecessors had sought to modernize everything, however, the Restoration group, invoking the very different ideals of race and tradition, desired to restore everything. In his 1910 preface to *Idola Fori*, a work by the "Centenarista," Bogotan-influenced writer, Carlos Arturo Torres (1867–1911), José Enrique Rodó (1871–1917) remarked on these restitutory longings: "Diríase que el misterioso fondo sin consciencia donde se retraen y aguardan las cosas dormidas que parecen haber pasado para siempre en el alma de los hombres y los pueblos, se levantan a un conjuro, voces ancestrales, reclamos de la tradición, alardes del orgullo del linaje" (Rodó 17) (It could be said that the slumbering things which appear to have disappeared forever from the souls of men and peoples take their refuge and lie waiting in a mysterious

unconscious reservoir, and that it is from there that ancestral voices, the lures of tradition, and the braggadocios of the pride in one's descent can be conjured up). The new conservative constitution of 1886 dramatized these currents in a most representative way. In a thoroughly modern language, this document envisioned a resuscitation of the Spanish worldview that had been relegated to the shadows of history during the heydays of the Anglo- and Francophile movement. It was believed that this restitution was the only possible means of prevailing over the state of anarchy that had befallen the nation. The demands on the nation affected by the financial crisis, the social anarchy that prevailed, the facile desire of many Anglophile and Francophile Colombians to reform every social institution and the shape of culture itself were answered by the constitution of 1886, which was proclaimed as an ode to a new dawn.

Who were these new Hispanophiles? By and large they were the sons of former colonial functionaries who, although they had lost their privileges with the advent of the republic, had not abandoned tradition, the society of the book, and learned culture. They sought to lay hold of their birthright by political, juridical, constitutional, institutional, and cultural means, and plainly would not rule out the use of force to achieve it. The proliferation in this period of grammar manuals, dictionaries of Spanish orthography and etymology, apologies on behalf of classical learning, the purity of spoken Spanish and even Latin, and the founding of the Academies of the Language (1870) and of History (1903), all find their inspiration in this solicitude for the revival of an already indistinct Spanish heritage. Rufino José Cuervo toiled for thirty years in Paris on the "Diccionario de reconstrucción y régimen de la lengua española" [Dictionary of the Structure and Rules of the Spanish Language], a project that was only brought to completion by the Instituto Caro y Cuervo in 1997. The politician-poets Rafael Núñez (1825–1894), Miguel Antonio Caro (1843–1909), Manuel Marroquín (1827–1908), and Marco Fidel Suárez (1855–1927) were not only Colombian presidents, but also poets, grammarians, linguists, pedagogues, and essayists. As the careers of these figures make clear, politics, grammar, and poetry compounded, confirmed and supported one another in this era–known in Colombian political history as *La Regeneración* [The Reconstruction]. So strong was the cohesion of these elements that even the liberal Rafael Uribe Uribe (1859–1914) would author from his prison cell in 1885 a "Diccionario Abreviado de Galicismos, Provincialismos y Correcciones de Lenguaje" [Abridged Dictionary of Gallicisms, Provincialisms, and Corrections to the Spanish Language], a dense work of 376 pages and 300 explanatory notes. Uribe's honorable labors served him well, for he was one of the few liberals of this intensely conservative era to be recognized (Deas 25–26). Bogotá's renowned sponsorship of classical literary culture and Hispanism at this time led to its being baptized "the Athens of South America."

Naturally, the asphyxia that resulted from the hegemonic rule of these canons, these conservative politicians, and the Church gave rise to serious tensions between the apologists of Hispanism and the defenders of liberalism and modernization. It also led eventually, not only to a series of wars, but to the generalized impoverishment of the country. New cultural projects had little hope of receiving financial backing unless they were patronized by, or came under the auspices of, the reigning political figures; Presidents Núñez, Caro, Marroquín, and Suárez were obviously the official poets. One exception to this situation was the case of Alberto Urdaneta (1845–1887), a dynamic and aristocratic conservative with strong ties to the government, who, because of his enthusiastic support for literature and the nontraditional arts, was a respected patron of the arts. Urdaneta founded and financed in 1881 the *Papel Periódico Ilustrado*, the first newspaper in Colombia to be illustrated with woodcut prints; in 1884, with Julio Racines, he established one of the first photographic firms, Racines & Co. Under Urdaneta's leadership the Núñez government supported the establishment of The School of Fine Arts in 1885, and the first art exhibition, mounted at the Colegio de San Bartolomé, in 1885 (Moreno de Angel 1972, 156). The School of Fine Arts produced the most representative painters of the era, such as Epifanio Garay (1849–1903) and Ricardo Acevedo Bernal (1867–1930), both of whom personified the best of nineteenth-century Bogotan academic art. In 1964 the School was incorporated into the National University as the Faculty of Fine Arts, and thus its tradition is still present. While Urdaneta himself was a fine artist, and his illustrated newspaper disseminated information on the latest artistic techniques, the style of his own neoclassical work (although considered Bogotá's great innovation) had in fact already gone out of fashion in Europe a number of decades previously. Here, again, is another example of the temporal delay in Colombian artistic expression.

The elitist regime, hegemonic defender of medieval traditions, clearly had no intention of seeing the marginalized sectors of society participate in political and cultural activity, and created barriers to such participation. This may help to explain the continuing low levels of literacy (only 20 percent by the 1912 census), as well as the scarcity of women or blacks, with the sole exceptions of Soledad Acosta de Samper (1833–1913) and Candelario Obeso, in the ranks of the notables in the cultural history of the period (Carranza, 208). The regime's exclusion of opposing voices from political and public life was picked up by the famous and time-honored salons, new cultural journals, and by figures such as José Asunción Silva (1865–1896), Baldomero Sanín Cano (1861–1957), and others, leaders of the discourses of political or literary agitation and opponents of the monologue of Hispanism and of cultural isolation and backwardness. A number of writers' groups, renowned either for their support of the literary culture or for the pressure they exerted against the regime, should be mentioned. First among these would be the *El Mosaico* circle (whose publication bore the same name), founded in 1854 by José María Vergara y Vergara and the master of the customs-and-manners genre, Eugenio Díaz. The political tolerance of this group was singularly noteworthy, for it sheltered within its fold a wide range of customs-and-manners writers, irrespective of their political opinions. *El Mosaico* continued to meet regularly in the houses and shops of its members right through to the end of the century, and counted among its members Jorge Isaacs, José Manuel Marroquín, and many others. Other groups formed in the last years of the nineteenth and the first years of the twentieth century were *La Gruta Simbólica*, *Los Centenaristas*, and *Los Nuevos*, groups whose objectives were as political as they were literary. Politically they opposed the conservative regime; in literature they kept alive the well-known dispute between Rafael Maya (1898–1980) and other representatives of Hispanism and the critics of the cultural backwardness of the city, the *Modernistas*, whose leaders were José Asunción Silva and Baldomero Sanín Cano (Sánchez Lozano 1977, 7).

From the beginning of the twentieth century, cultural groups began to meet in more public spaces such as the famous Parisian-style cafés of Bogotá and/or in private clubs. As sites of encounter and assembly for writers, painters, and politicians, as well places for the exchange of books and information about cultural movements in Latin America and Europe, the cafés hosted the most diverse groups. Their members—and in some cases their founders—came from other cities of the country, were of varied social backgrounds, and had different political and cultural interests. Starting from 1920, the cafés began to play an important role in the political, literary, and cultural life of the city. The Café Windsor, famous throughout the 1920s and 1930s, saw assorted groups of intellectuals pass through its doors, including the anarchist León de Greiff (1895–1976), the socialist Luis Vidales (1904–1990), the conservative Rafael Maya (1897–1980), José Umaña Bernal (1900–1982), and Jorge Zalamea (1905–1969), all members of the *Los Nuevos* group. Also to be seen there were the liberal Germán Arciniegas (1900–1999), the fascist sympathizer Silvio Villegas (1902–1972), and, from time to time, the Centenaristas, who edited the journal *Los Alegres Compadres de Windsor* [Windsor's Merry Godfathers]. The cafés La Gran Vía and La Gaieté Gauloise were the headquarters for the *Gruta Simbólica* group, nicknamed the "Dandy's Bohemia" by Rafael Gutiérrez Girardot on account of the fact that the seventy-odd writers, men in the majority, who moved in its orbit were from the Bogotan upper and middle classes. Notable among this group were Julio Flórez (1867–1923), Luis María Mora (1869–1936), Aquilino Villegas (1879–1940), Max Grillo (1868–1949), Clímaco Soto Borda (1870–1919), Enrique Alvarez Henao (1871–1914), and Francisco Restrepo Gómez (1884–1924)—all liberals marginalized from politics and strong critics of the conservative hegemony. One member of this group, the cartoonist Ricardo Rendón (1894–1930), succeeded in capturing public opinion with his scathing satires and mobilizing it around the liberal cause against the regime.

Many of the salons, cafés, and learned societies were accompanied and backed by publications that reflected their ideologies and their positions vis-à-vis literature and politics. Toward the middle of the 1880s there were eleven publications of various types that chronicled the cultural life of the city, running the gamut from satirical, domestic, young women's, instructional, and local-color magazines to literary, didactic, and scientific monthlies. The most important of the cultural journals of the period, in terms of the ideas and the cultural identity sought to put forward, were: *El Repertorio Colombiano* (1878–1903), of conservative views, considered the mouthpiece par excellence of Hispanism; the *Papel Periódico Colombiano* (1881–1887), edited by A. Urdaneta, remarkable for its innovative use of the graphic arts, illustrations, and its promotion of a nonpartisan national identity; and *Gris* (1892–1896), a *modernista* review founded by Max Grillo (1868–1949), of which Rafael Gutiérrez Girardot has said: It "attempted" to be "modern," "attempted" to cast an eye on the Hispanic literature of the era from the distance of Bogotá, and "attempted" to make the literature of Bogotá known to the world outside the city and the nation, but finally remained only an attempt, above all an attempt lacking in criticism (1991, 17). *Contemporánea* (1904–1905), also "attempting" to be *modernista* and cosmopolitan, followed *Gris* in its intentions. It was run by Baldomero Sanín Cano, who through it attacked academicism and Hispanism when they were enjoying their greatest prestige. Finally, mention should be made of the review *Gruta* (1903–1904), the first journal to "attempt" to make a business or turn a profit by means of this medium. Toward the end of the "Restoration" period, in the 1920s, there were twenty publications of a cultural character to be found in Bogotá. This boom was due, in part, to the advent in 1923 of the "Weekly Novel," or serialized publication, which boosted the readership for these works (Williams 91), and in part to the relative peace and a growing economy.

Despite the vision of the world held by Caro and his Restoration companions–a vision that refused to accept the idea that a civilization based on technology, railroads, telegraphs, and machines could ever be desirable, a vision that, on the contrary, believed in the superiority of cultures like the Spanish because they extended their genius to the creation of artistic, religious, and metaphysical values (Jaramillo Uribe 1982, 92)–despite such a vision, advancements in the technology of communication did reach distant Bogotá in the first decades of the twentieth century. With the end of the War of a Thousand Days in 1903, difficulties in the transportation system began to be overcome. The first airline in the country, Scandia, was created in 1919, adding a network of air routes to the tiny network of railroads in the country, and it was from this date that the physical isolation of the city from the rest of the country, and consequently from the world, began to be definitively broken. In parallel to these new means of communication, there was a explosion of political, literary, and cultural discourses with the advent of the mass circulation dailies: *El Tiempo*, founded in 1911, and its cultural Sunday supplement, *Lecturas Dominicales*; *El Espectador*, founded in 1924. These are still today the most important newspapers in Colombia. Radio began broadcasting in 1925, and popular radio serials furthered the creation of a mass audience already initiated by the cinema, which had arrived in Bogotá in 1907. From the beginning, films were shown in Independence Park because the first theater devoted exclusively to the cinema, the Olimpia opened its doors only in 1912 at the corner of 25th Street and 9th Avenue (Martínez Pardo 22). These new, modern cultural institutions signaled the end of the monopoly that literature in general and poetry in particular enjoyed over other popular forms of cultural expression in the cultural life of the era. Radio, cinema, and nationally distributed mass-circulation dailies effected a democratization of information and culture, and through the aid of such audio-visual media, a decline in the serious problem of illiteracy was seen. However, despite efforts to educate the people, the literacy rate in 1948 had only reached 38 percent (Helg 121).

In my judgment, the Restoration movement had four principal consequences for the cultural history of Bogotá. The first has to do with the elevation in the status of literary culture and the Spanish language that was seen in this period, for the prestige that these then enjoyed would be of enormous benefit to future writers. Second, the zeal with which conservatives sought to implant their vision of the world aroused a fierce opposition that, backed by the influences of *modernismo*, was expressed in a number of original forms, all of which contributed to the shaping of a more properly Colombian cultural self-image. Third, the attempts to realize a cultural independence, attempts that Gutiérrez Girardot's critique of the *modernista* journals had described as "failures" of authenticity, originality, and so on, constituted nonetheless the first steps in the cultural history of Bogotá toward such autonomy. Opposition to the persistent maintenance of foreign, and above all

Spanish, cultural models was unquestionably a seed that would bear fruit in later decades. This is to say that Spanish American *modernismo* was an essential buttress or inspiration to the search for cultural authenticity and cosmopolitanism. Fourth, despite the resistance of Caro and other representatives of the Restoration to extra-literary culture, modernity did make an enormous impression on the city: Doors were opened to new forms of expression such as cartoons, magazines illustrated with drawings and paintings, radio serials, and the cinema, and as a result the first decades of the twentieth century offered the citizens of Bogotá a more extensive coverage of news and cultural events. Thus began an era in which the isolation of the city was broken, a less provincial attitude came into being, and the struggle for a less aristocratic society was unleashed, an era whose cultural aspirations envisioned the liberation of cultural expression from the rule of European canons.

The Struggle between Modernity and Reaction

A persistent pendulum movement between two clashing forces, the tendency toward economic backwardness and the tendency toward modernization mark the entire cultural history of Bogotá and Colombia. First proposed by the economic theorist A. Gerschenkron, this model of pendular movement has been applied to the social and cultural history of nineteenth-century Europe by the historian Arno J. Mayer in his book, *The Persistence of the Old Regime: Europe to the Great War* (1981). During the twentieth century this pendular phenomenon came to be more and more pronounced in Colombia owing to the fact that modernizing forces arrived in Bogotá from Europe and the United States. Carlos Sánchez Lozano, referring to the *Nadaismo* movement, in vogue between 1958 and 1974, has demonstrated that the traditional historical clash between the persistence of backward-looking ideas and the glimmers of forward-looking liberal enlightened ideas–in no way to be associated with the intellectual anemia of the Colombian Liberal Party–have produced an intellectual tradition of rescue in the cultural history of the city, a tradition that, clearly, the *Nadaismo* movement had not saved, but which on the contrary it had ignored all together (Sánchez Lozano 1989, 87).

In twentieth-century Bogotan culture, the problem of these simultaneously coexisting forces became more critical for two reasons: first, because of the collapse of some of the barriers that had clearly impeded the cultural development of the city, such as physical isolation and the extraordinarily high levels of illiteracy; and second, because, as Sánchez Lozano has pointed out, there was already a bivalent tradition of reclamation and rejection. Among the representatives of the recuperative tradition were José María Samper (1828–1888) and Miguel Samper (1825–1899), Ezequiel Uricoechea (1834–1880), Miguel Antonio Caro, Rufino José Cuervo, José Asunción Silva, and Carlos Arturo Torres (Sánchez Lozano 1989, 87). This situation of cultural-political bivalence imposed a more cautious disposition on all those involved in cultural endeavors. The fact that the new culture produced by the city's writers and artists was due to its close connections to, and dialogues with, the currents of European and Latin American culture, on the one hand, and to its integration of the cultural stock produced by those artists into the history of the city, on the other, constituted a challenge. It is clear that the task facing Bogotá's writers and artists, to further and bestow upon the local culture the capacity for change (a capacity that every socially embodied culture must possess) was made more difficult by the new situation. This suggests that the backing of responsible cultural institutions would be more necessary in this period than had been the case in previous eras.

Ramón Vinyes (1885–1952), the model for Gabriel García Márquez's (b. 1927) "sabio catalán" ("wise Catalonian") in *Cien años de soledad* [1967; *One Hundred Years of Solitude*], published in Barranquilla between 1917 and 1920 the journal *Voces*. In a fine summary of the conditions of cultural production in the capital published in the twenty-fifth issue of *Voces* (10 June 1918), Vinyes described his vision of Bogotan culture: "*Voces* ha protestado contra los señores que le deben a la política un excesivo nombre literario, contra los que han levantado un cenáculo para un intercambio de elogios. . . . contra los que llaman esnobismos a lo que va más allá de su limitadísimo círculo de conocimientos" (219) (*Voces* took exception to those gentlemen who give to politics an excessively literary gloss, to those who set a last-supper table for the exchange of eulogies . . . to those who label as snobbery all that which seeks to go beyond their miniscule circle of knowledge). At the same time that *Voces* criticized the cultural life of Bogotá for its excessive Hispanicizing and for its isolation from the modern currents of the world–deeming culture entirely without merit or validity (Gilard 36–40)–the journal also advocated jettisoning past models, searching for the beautiful beyond the doctrines of the schools, and, above all, seeking an authenticity rooted in the new society of the Americas. As ballast to Vinyes's vision, we would do well to ask ourselves what had changed between the cultural panorama traced by Vinyes in 1920 and that described by Vergara y Vergara in 1760? From the debut of the scientific movement to the end of the Restoration, 160 years had passed: What remained of those attempts to break the cultural narrow-mindedness, censorship, and second-hand status of Bogotá vis-à-vis Europe, and to loosen the stranglehold the élites maintained on culture–and thus the predominance of literature as the only legitimate form of cultural expression and the burden of institutionalized cultural Hispanism? And what remained of the cultural movements that had tried to modify the prevailing condition of cultural backwardness?

Seemingly, in Vinyes's eyes, little progress had been made; yet each cultural movement left its mark on the history of Bogotá. The principal problem, however, was the inability to keep alive the energies released in each struggle. Thus, although the botanical expedition left behind an agreeable memory that was continued with the Coronagraphic Commission in 1850, apart from these two expeditions there would be neither institutions nor botanical research to keep the vigor of their investigative spirit alive. Much the same happened to the political movement. After having brought to completion the political reforms inspired by the model of the French Enlightenment, the new nation was reorganized around new privileges in such a manner that the modernizing, liberal, and enlightened forces once again became impotent. Culture found itself in the position of having to make use of new yet archaic political institutions in order to express itself, institutions that in no way were to the benefit of the universalism, liberty, or tolerance in which the rational critique of cultural production must be inscribed. This critique, the praxis that facilitates dialogue so that it may dialectically create cultural progress, was suppressed, not in the manner of the ecclesiastical censorship of colonial times, but rather in a conservative hegemonic manner.

This situation might well be explained as an opening toward the breach effected in each one of these movements; once the fervor of the motivating circumstances had passed; however, a covering over, charged with forgetfulness, came into being. These overtures and foreclosures were due to the fact that the culture that had been harnessed to effect modernization–whether during the political movement or the movement of Anglo- and Francophilia–was a foreign, and principally European, culture; this link to a foreign culture meant that Bogotan cultural life was subject to the vicissitudes of cultural fashion and lacked a local system of roots. Both of these eventualities led to the situation where the local culture (that is, that produced by and for Bogotans) represented itself to itself as an ornament of a social class (Gutiérrez Girardot 1986, 66) and not as having emerged or taken shape as an instrument that, in a continuous manner, had stockpiled a reserve of cultural goods that could throw light upon the life of the individual in society. Local culture, having been considered a kind of fashion accessory of an individual, class, or political party, easily came to be forgotten since it did not correlate with the issues raised by local life as it was lived in Latin America, Colombia, or in far-flung Bogotá. This served to make the ensuing foreclosures charged with forgetfulness appear that much more accentuated. These circumstances would, by and large, mean that the incorporation of modern culture into the life of the city would be deferred, since the possibilities of recuperating and incorporating the stockpile of cultural tradition had become more difficult, especially given the fight against the persistence of oblivion.

In his book *Colombia: la modernidad postergada* [1994; Colombia: The Deferred Modernity], Rubén Jaramillo Vélez locates the cause of this deferment deep in the Spanish character: "La verdad es que la burguesía española no estaba preparada ni poseía una ideología universal" (The truth is that the Spanish bourgeoisie neither was competent nor possessed a universal ideology); this Spain, he continues, lacked a transformative ideology, and therefore, "el pensamiento español se enquistó en dogmas teológicos y la omnipresente inquisición arrancó todo brote de conciencia revolucionaria" (5) (Spanish thought shut itself up inside teleological dogmas and the omnipresent Inquisition rooted out every outbreak of revolutionary consciousness). Searching through 400 years of Latin American history, Gutiérrez Girardot claims that this new consciousness, free from the dogmas of the past, is hardly to be found:

La reciente historia de las sociedades hispánicas ha demostrado hasta la saciedad y la destrucción de sí mismas, que la sustancia dogmática que se les ha impuesto, que la 'astucia de la teología' sofocó las fuerzas creadoras y regeneradoras que desencadenó la Independencia, es decir, que impidió que se las asimilara y se las continuara y enriqueciera como se asimila y enriquece una tradición, es decir, que ellas se conviertieran en la nueva y propia tradición. (Gutiérrez Girardot 1986, 75).

The recent history of the Hispanic societies has more than demonstrated the destruction of those societies, that the dogmatic stamp that was imposed upon them, the "duplicity of theology," smothered the creative and regenerative energies that were unleashed by the independence movement. The assimilation of those energies was retarded, their furtherance and enrichment–as every tradition is enriched and imbibed–was impeded, and their transformation into the new and properly national tradition was obstructed by that imposed dogmatism.

However, according to Carlos Sánchez Lozano, and contrary to the view advanced by Vinyes in 1920, a stream of cultural plenty did flow into Bogotan tradition in spite of the dogma, the overtures and foreclosures that marked the advance of modern ideas, the "accessory" culture, and the historical amnesia (Sánchez Lozano 1989, 87). The endemic problems of Bogotan culture with respect to the struggle for independence, authenticity, and a modern culture did not stop some people and individual groups from realizing great successes; neither did they impede some traditionally marginalized sectors of society, such as the mestizos, from little by little integrating themselves into the dominant culture.

Among the outstanding achievements witnessed by the generations growing up in Bogotá in the first half of the twentieth century are two that deserve a fuller account. The first concerns what Gutiérrez Girardot has called the "storm" resulting from the poetic synthesis of the new with the Spanish 1927 movement made by the Bogotan poets known as the *Piedra y Cielo* [Stone and Sky] group. This storm broke when the poets Arturo Camacho Ramírez (1910–1982), Jorge Rojas (1911–1995), Darío Samper (1909–1984), and Eduardo Carranza (1913–1985) succeeded in creating, "sólo en la medida que sintetizaron varios ejemplos españoles" (only insofar as they synthesized a number of Spanish precedents), a brand new poetic language: "Con todo, suele reconocerse unánimemente, y con razón, que la literatura colombiana de primera mitad del siglo veinte se divide en dos. Antes de 'Piedra y Cielo' y después" (226) (in spite of everything, there exists a customary consensus of opinion, and not without reason, that Colombian literature of the first half of the twentieth century is marked by a watershed: before *Piedra y Cielo*, and after). Without *Piedra y Cielo*, Gabriel García Márquez's *Cien años de soledad* [*One Hundred Years of Solitude*] would not have been possible. This is not to say that García Márquez was an exponent of *Piedra y Cielo*. Rather, it is to say that *Piedra y Cielo* successfully purged the language of the rhetoric and recharged the Colombian poetic idiom, and that, without that example, García Márquez (who knew of the group first hand, as a schoolboy, from Carlos Martín [b. 1914], a minor member of the group) would not have had the springboard he did for the formation of his own language (Gutiérrez Girardot 1997, 226–28). The great achievement of the *Piedra y Cielo* group was to have woven a fabric of linguistic possibilities for the creation of national literary discourses in Bogotan letters, discourses that were no longer merely regional but rather endowed with the possibility of national and international diffusion; thus they helped terminate once and for all the physical isolation in which the capital had existed throughout its history. Local discourse emerged as national with the novelists J. A. Osorio Lizarazo (1900–1964), Jorge Zalamea Borda (1905–1969), and Eduardo Caballero Calderón (1910–1990), the historian Germán Arciniegas (1900–1999), whose 1945 *The Biography of the Caribbean* was an important milestone, and with, in addition to the members of the *Piedra y Cielo* group, the poet without peer, León de Greiff (1895–1976).

The second outstanding achievement realized in these generations was the eruption of a new discourse of liberal and revolutionary protest that unearthed the beautiful in the very soil of Bogotá's own Latin Americanness. Mention should be made here of the discourses of the novelists Antonio Osorio Lizarazo and César Uribe Piedrahíta (1897–1951), and that of the poets influenced by the Mexican Revolution but of a nativist inclination known as *Los Bachués*,

among whom numbered Darío Samper, as well as the plastic artists Pedro Nel Gómez and Gonzalo Ariza (Carranza 340). Of all the works portraying the social reality of Bogotan life in this period, the novels of Lizarazo and the paintings of Ariza are, perhaps, the most original and accomplished. This discourse of protest arising in literature was also manifest in political culture, with its own successes. This was the third great achievement of the era, for these discourses would make possible the triumph of twentieth-century political reforms and would also allow the (until then) marginalized sectors of society to begin to participate in the mainstream of the dominant culture. With all these successes, and in the middle of the bitter struggle between modernity and the persistence of a backward-looking ideology, the final years of the 1950s would be witness to a profound crisis in the Hispanicizing discourse.

The Advent of the Masses or the Crisis of Hispanicizing Discourse

In the twentieth century there are three significant developments in Colombian society that had an influence on the culture of Bogotá: population increase, political attempts to democratize culture, and the consequent strengthening of the cultural infrastructure; none of these, however, succeeded in completely liberating culture from the archaic ideological bonds of the past. Clearly, the demographic explosion that was seen throughout the entire twentieth century was very important: Bogotá's 100,000 inhabitants of 1905 had, by 1938, more than tripled to 338,000, and rocketed to over 1.6 million by 1964 (Pardo Pardo 508). These population increases, together with the relative rise in living standards, were obviously accompanied by an expansion in the market for books, periodicals, journals, musical instruments, concerts and theatrical performances, cinema screenings, radio, and later television serial productions. If we add to these demographic statistics the contributions made by social reforms, raising the level of literacy to about 90 percent in the 1980s for example, we should be able to conclude (were it not for the analyses of Gutiérrez Girardot and Sánchez Lozano) that much ground had been won for culture.

Although the social reform of the nation continued to be a dream, in Bogotá in particular a relative democratization began to take hold through education and public service. Perhaps the most important step toward the democratization of culture was the founding in 1930 of the Universidad Popular. The mandate of this limited liability corporation was to socialize education, and to that end it offered free primary instruction and night school courses. Among its professors were the writer Rafael Maya, lecturing on the history of art; Otto de Grieff, brother of the poet León, teaching the history of music; Luis López de Mesa (1884–1967), lecturing on popular culture; and Jorge Eliécer Gaitán (1898–1948), teaching criminal sociology (Uribe Celis 126). However, despite all the attempts to improve education, the gap between private education and public education at the end of the century continued to be abysmal.

These developments as well as advancements in the field of communications—everything from airplanes to cultural supplements of newspapers to telephones—contributed to the increase in the arrival and circulation of books, people, and ideas, and thus further reduced the physical isolation of the city. The effects of these social and economic changes were reflected in numerous new institutions. Throughout the twentieth century the breadth of cultural institutions and the services offered continued to increase, such that by 1956 Bogotá, whose population numbered 1 million, enjoyed twelve museums, thirteen universities, a philharmonic and a symphonic orchestra, forty-eight public libraries, three theaters, sixty-two cinemas, sixty-one bookstores, twenty-three publishers and editorial houses, eight art galleries, and 113 newspapers and journals. According to DANE (Departamento Administrativo Nacional de Estadística) statistics, in 1955 Bogotans saw 250 plays, 120 variety performances, and eighteen musical theater performances, as well as 62,245 film screenings, and thirty-five concerts (DANE 1955, 268–70). These figures paint the picture of a more robust cultural marketplace, even though the difference in quality and quantity of the offerings to be found in Bogotá and those seen in European cities or Mexico City in the same period continued to be very great. Bogotá still had a provincial culture, and although the differences between Europe and Bogotá had been narrowed—especially if we recall the situation in 1750 prior to the arrival of Mutis—a large distance between them still remained. In addition, the large number of public libraries did not accurately reflect the reality, for only two of them contained important collections: The National Library, containing about 100,000 volumes by the 1950s, and the Luis Ángel Arango Library, created in 1948, with a similar number of books.

The final decades of the century saw the creation of new institutions and continued investment in others, all crucial to their ability to openly promote the development and democratization of culture. In the publishing industry, almost exclusively located in Bogotá, 28 million copies of books were produced, of which only 2 million were foreign works. In 1997, 156 works were translated into Spanish, 102 from English. In this same year, 40 percent of the titles were in the field of social sciences, 25 percent literary works, 10 percent science and technology, and only 3 percent school texts (which, however, account for the large numbers of actual copies printed). Although the books produced in Bogotá were also for national distribution, the bulk (60 percent) were sold in the capital (*Portafolio* 1998, 16).

To round out this picture of the increase in book sales and production, we would do well to note that while 545 new titles were published in 1970, by 1989 that number had risen to 9,000 (DANE 1990, 556). The principal difference between the 1960s and the 1990s lay in the fact that the bulk of the books published in the 1960s were imprints of a single firm, the Tercer Mundo editorial house. In the 1970s the Spanish firm Plaza y Jánes began publishing in Bogotá; in the 1980s, La Oveja Negra, publisher of García Márquez, opened its doors. Together with Colcultura, Oveja Negra began to produce popular editions and paperbacks to fulfill their mandate of stocking the household libraries of the average Colombian. In the mid 1990s, eighty-one printing firms, distribution companies, and editorial houses were registered with the city of Bogotá, not to mention government publishing organizations (Cámara 1995). Since 1993, Planeta, one of the largest editorial houses in the country, has been publishing thirty Colombian literary titles per year, the lion's share originating in the capital.

Another important new institution has been the Bogotá Book Fair, financed by the publishing industry since 1996. The Book Fair has invited writers and critics from around to the world, putting students, writers, and the Bogotan reading public in direct contact with the most significant currents of world intellectual and cultural life. In addition to the Book Fair, the Ibero-American Festival of Theater, promoted since 1988 by the actress and impresario Fanny Mikey, has made an incomparable contribution to the cultural history of the city, bringing world and national theatrical works not only to the theaters of the capital, but also to its parks, squares, and streets—and thus into the daily lives of its millions of inhabitants. Interestingly, this festival has been held every other year during Holy Week, a scheduling unimaginable in the narrow-minded and conventional Bogotá of only a few decades ago, and an index of the secularization of Bogatan life.

With respect to the plastic arts, a remarkable development has been seen in this sector since the 1960s. Upon arriving in the city in 1960, Marta Traba (1930–1983), the Argentinean spouse of the writer Eduardo Zalamea Borda (1905–1963), remarked on the congenital backwardness of the Bogotan art scene. Her great knowledge of modern art, then largely unknown by the general public, was a great inspiration to Bogotá's modern artists. It is due to her arrival in the city and her efforts, as well as to the efforts made by the cultural promoter Gloria Zea in the founding of the Museum of Modern Art (MAM), that the painter Fernando Botero owed his success. Since the 1960s, the plastic arts have acquired an unprecedented profile in the cultural life of the capital.

This overwhelming evidence of an increasingly diversified and democratized culture is contradicted by a number of factors that highlight the continuing persistence, lurking within the forces of modernization, of a backward-looking mind-set. Among the most significant of these factors are the extremely low levels of education in the general population, the almost total nonexistence of objective cultural criticism, the feeble social implementation of scientific and cultural knowledge, and finally, the failure of libraries and bookstores to service the entire population. The low levels of education are reflected in the statistics on per capita book consumption. Annual per capita book consumption readers in our country continues to be very low: 0.8 percent in Colombia by comparison with 6.2 percent in England and 4.1 percent in Germany. This low level of consumption, when added to the extremely low ratio of books in Bogotá's two largest public libraries vis-à-vis the gross population (scarcely 3 million books for a population of 7.5 million people) (*Portafolio* 16), suggests that the purchase (and reading) of books is largely limited to the middle and upper classes, that is, to those able to afford the books they read. Furthermore, bookstores and libraries are by and large located in the city center, and not in the residential or more populous poorer districts, thus making participation in literacy and cultural life difficult for large sectors of society.

Bogotá's ongoing literary backwardness and book deficit has hindered the development of the kind of serious social criticism that could be effected by and through not only the small number of literate poor, but the intelligentsia in general, as well as the communications media. The absence of serious critique has been one of the underlying and perpetuating causes of the backwardness in social mentality. The universities continue to impart a scientific knowledge that is, according to Rubén Jaramillo Vélez, "alien, of no use to the solution of any problem, and for that very reason has never been applied" (47). Scientific knowledge, like cultural knowledge, has been only feebly implemented in Colombian society.

Seconding these remarks, we wish, however, to affirm that although the public, its education, and support systems have all been expanded in this period, the permanent social incorporation of the stock of cultural productions among the general public has continued to be deficient.

All of the foregoing is but a necessary consequence of the persistence of a traditional society unwilling to renounce its privileges. Traditionally, literary critics and academicians have been partisans of conservatism: Antonio Gómez Restrepo (1869–1947), José María Vergara y Vergara, and Gustavo Otero Muñoz (1894–1957), among others, have all enjoyed the social status requisite to discharging the role of literary and social legitimizers, a role traditionally associated with the oligarchy (the upper class, the university elites, and the Catholic Church). Literary criticism has involved the study of the Greek and Roman classics and philology, and has been dominated by men. In addition, it has played an "important legitimizing function" (Williams 43), since that legitimatizing power still continues to represent culture as the ornament of a class that persists in maintaining its privileges, even though the modernizing sectors of society become every year larger, more powerful, and more educated. This situation was in recent years subject to a trenchant exposé in the newspaper column of the writer and journalist Antonio Morales (b. 1955). Decrying the almost total lack of coverage in the Bogotá media of Víctor Manuel Gaviria (b. 1955) and Erwin Goggel, director and producer, respectively, of the Colombian film "La vendedora de rosas" [1998; The Flower Girl], which appeared at the Cannes Film Festival, Morales wrote that "the ass-kissing cultural-media elites" made no mention of the film, all the while lavishing excessive attention on Juan Carlos Botero (b. 1960) (son of the painter Fernando Botero): "being a third-rate scribbler [constitutes for this elite] a calling to the light-weight kingdom of fame, to the summits of Olympia and other places where the petty potentates of the lightweight kingdom of the arts and mediocrity repose in their spinelessness" (Morales 66). According to Morales, the legitimizing critical profession ignored Víctor Gaviria, as a member of one of the new modernizing sectors of society, without economic or social backing, because he did not represent the interests of the oligarchy. To the legitimating power wielded by the literary critics of yesteryear, one must now add, Morales points out, the new powers of the communications media, since many of these media are owned by families or economic interests that represent the persistent backward-looking mentality and society.

Gutiérrez Girardot poses a serious question when he asks: "¿Pero, cómo demostrar al que quiere ser ciego la importancia de la luz y de la vista?" (How can one demonstrate to a blind man the importance of light and the faculty of vision?) and then he answers: "se agrava si se tiene en cuenta que este 'corazón blindado guarda rencor', que rechaza las cosas y tiene su correlato inevitable en el velo con que se cubre y que hace posible la convivencia, es decir, en la frivolidad, esa otra forma de rechazar las cosas. Rencor y frivolidad 'barbarizan', 'primitivizan' la vida social" (1986, 47) (The question is made even more difficult when we consider that this 'armour-plated heart nurses a resentment' that rejects what it does not understand, and has its inevitable correlative in the shroud of ignorance with which it covers itself and which makes its sociality possible, which is to say the frivolousness that is that other form of rejecting what one does not understand. Resentment and frivolousness 'barbarize' and 'primitivize' social life). This situation notwithstanding, in the recent cultural history of the city some individuals have successfully managed to transcend the barriers of the trivial and achieved the recognition that their talents deserve. Thus, from out of the group linked to the journal *Revista MITO* (1955–1962), a number of names and works have arisen that have been a credit to the city's fine artistic tradition: Gabriel García Márquez, Rafael Gutiérrez Girardot, Jorge Gaitán Durán (1924–1962), Marta Traba, Álvaro Mutis (b. 1923), Fernando Charry Lara (b. 1920), and others. In political terms MITO opposed the Rojas Pinilla dictatorship, while in poetic terms the members assumed positions of clear cultural independence. This was expressed by the journal's managing editor Jorge Gaitán Durán in a declaration entitled "Tierra baldía" [Waste Land]: "Mi generación debe afrontar la crisis del poema. Crisis que, por cierto, se ha estado gestando en lo que va corrido del siglo . . . . A nosotros nos ha llegado el momento de romper el verso" (in Carranza 388) ("My generation has to confront the crisis of the poem, a crisis that, certainly, has been brewing continuously throughout the century so far. . . . For us, the time has come to smash the verse"). Among the individuals who deserve mention in this context are R. H. Moreno Durán (b. 1946) and Fanny Buitrago (b. 1943) in the novel, Jaime García Maffla (b. 1944), Giovanni Quessep (b. 1939), and Álvaro Rodríguez Torres (b. 1950) in poetry, Jorge Alí Triana and Santiago García (b. 1929) in theater, and Víctor Gaviria and Felipe Aljure in film.

Conclusions

Beginning in the 1970s Bogotá's demographic indicators began their precipitous rise, such that by the 1990s the population had reached 7 million inhabitants and the cityscape was dotted with factories. The cultural theorist John Storey has argued that industrialization and urbanization necessarily redraw the cultural map of industrialized societies (1997, 21); from recent research it appears that, although Bogotá is not completely industrialized neither is it an exception to the pattern. The question then proposes itself: What were the consequences for Bogotan culture that resulted from this new situation at the end of the twentieth century? And what were the consequences of the struggle of the first half of that century, between the forces that would maintain the old and those that would modernize the country? To attempt an answer to these questions we would have to be able, then, to speak of the advent of the masses. But to speak of a mass culture, would that not imply the recognition that the elitist culture of the Hispanicized city had been transformed for the sake of a culture of and for the greater public? The answer is yes, at least in part. On the one hand, there are a number of contemporary cultural institutions that have adapted themselves to the new population, the already mentioned purveyors of cultural services: the publishing industry, the entertainment industry (especially the theater), the book fair, and the electronic media, especially radio and television. These institutions as a group demonstrate the extent to which the old coordinates that have straitjacketed the culture of the city have been surpassed. Nevertheless, on the other hand, other factors have remained powerless to respond to the new situation, notably the libraries, the objective criticism of culture, and, especially, the system of education. The factors favoring cultural change and those that have failed support the coexistence of forward-looking and backward-looking sectors of society–their coexistence in a culturally amorphous space in which the struggle between the persistence of the old and the modernizing winds of change continues.

Translation by Colman Hogan

Works Cited

Abadía Morales, Guillermo. 1983. *Compendio general de folklore Colombiano.* Bogotá: Biblioteca Banco Popular.

——. ed. 1985. *Canciones y coplas populares de Jorge Isaacs.* Bogotá: Nueva Biblioteca Colombiana de Cultura, Procultura.

Antelo Iglesias, Antonio. 1980. *Perfil literario de Jiménez de Quesada.* Bogotá: Caro y Cuervo.

Beutler, Gisela. 1962. *'El romance' de Jiménez de Quesada: ¿El primer poeta colombiano?* Bogotá: Ed. Instituto Caro y Cuervo.

Cámara Colombiana del Libro. 1995. *Directorio de afiliados.* Bogotá: n.p.

Cané, Miguel. 1990. "Notas de viaje sobre Venezuela y Colombia" *Bogotá en los viajeros extranjeros del siglo XIX.* Ed. Mario Germán Romero. Bogotá: Villegas Editores. 177–200.

Carranza, María Mercedes, dir. 1991. *Historia de la poesía colombiana.* Bogotá: Casa de Poesía Silva.

Castellanos, Nelson. 1996. "'Impresores empresarios o políticos: la imprenta de Echeverría Hermanos.' en Bogota, 1851–1892" Tesis de Grado. Bogotá: Universidad Javeriana.

Cuervo, Rufino. 1843. *Memoria del secretario de hacienda de la Nueva Granada al Congreso de 1843.* Bogotá: Imprenta Cualla.

De Angeli, Marguerite. 1954. *Book of Nursery and Mother Goose Rhymes.* New York: Doubleday & Company.

Deas, Malcolm D. 1993. *Del poder y la gramática.* Bogotá: Tercer Mundo Editores. 25–60.

Departamento Administrativo Nacional de Estadística. 1955 & 1957. *Anuario Estadístico de Bogotá.* Bogotá: DANE. 268–73.

——. 1990. *Las estadísticas sociales en Colombia.* Bogotá: DANE.

Diario de Avisos. 1855. Bogotá: Agencia de Negocios Pereira Gamba-Camacho Roldán y Cia. March 2nd.

Gaviria, Victor, dir. 1998. *La vendedora de rosas.* Prod. Erwin Goggel.

Gerschenkron, Alexander. 1962. *Economic Backwardness in Historical Perspective.* Cambridge, Mass: Harvard.

Gil Tovar, Francisco. 1989. "Las artes plásticas durante el periodo colonial." *Nueva Historia de Colombia.* Dir. Jaime Jaramillo Uribe. Bogotá: Planeta. 1:239–52.

——. 1997. *Colombia en las artes.* Bogotá: Biblioteca Familiar Colombiana, Presidencia de la República.

Gilard, Jacques. 1989. *Entre los Andes y el Caribe, la obra americana de Ramón Vinyes,* Medellín: Universidad de Antioquia.

Giraldo Jaramillo, Gabriel. 1980. *Miniatura, pintura y grabado en Colombia.* Bogotá: Instituto Colombiano de Cultura.

González, Beatriz. 1996. "Los pintores de la expedición botánica." *Credencial Historia.* 74: 4–5.

González Cajiao, Fernando. 1986. *Historia del teatro en Colombia.* Bogotá: Colcultura.

González de Pérez, María Stella. 1980. *Trayectoria de los estudios sobre la lengua chibcha o muisca.* Bogotá: Instituto Caro y Cuervo.

Gutiérrez Girardot, Rafael. 1986. "Universidad y sociedad" *Argumentos* 14-15-16-17 :63–96.

——. 1991. "Tres revistas colombianas de fin de siglo *Boletín Cultural y Bibliográfico.* 28.27: 3–18.

——. 1997. "La crítica a la aristocracia bogotana en Gabriel García Márquez y R.H. Moreno-Durán" *Provocaciones.* Bogotá: Ariel. 173–200.

Gutiérrez Sanín, Francisco. 1995. *Curso y discurso del movimiento plebeyo 1849/1854.* Bogotá: El Ancora Editores.

Habermas, Jurgen. 1981. *Historia y crítica de la opinión pública. La Transformación estructural de la vida pública.* Barcelona: Gustavo Gili.

Helg, Aline. 1989. "La educación en Colombia 1846–1957." *Nueva Historia de Colombia.* Bogotá: Planeta. 4:111–34.

Henríquez Ureña, Pedro. 1978. "Música popular de América." *Textos sobre música y folklore.* Bogotá: Instituto Colombiano de Cultura.

——. 1979. *Historia de la cultura en la América Latina.* Mexico City: Fondo de Cultura Económica.

Hernández de Alba, Guillermo y Rafael Martínez Briceño. 1960. *Una biblioteca de Santafé de Bogotá en el siglo XVII.* Bogotá: Instituto Caro y Cuervo.

Hernández de Alba, Guillermo y Juan Botero Carrasquilla. 1977. *Historia de la biblioteca Nacional.* Bogotá: Instituto Caro y Cuervo.

Hettner, Alfred. 1990. "Viajes por los andes colombianos" *Extranjeros del Siglo XIX.* Ed. Mario Germán Romero. Bogotá: Villegas Editores. 201–38.

Jaramillo Uribe, Jaime. 1977. "Tres etapas de la historia intelectual de Colombia." *La personalidad histórica de Colombia y otros ensayos.* Bogotá: Colcultura. 105–30.

——. 1982. El pensamiento colombiano en el siglo XIX. Ed Temis.

Jaramillo Vélez, Rubén 1994. *Colombia: la modernidad postergada.* Bogotá: Ed. Temis.

Martínez Pardo, Hernando. 1978. *Historia del cine en Colombia.* Bogotá: Ed América Latina.

Mayer, Arno J. 1981. *The Persistence of the Old Regime: Europe to the Great War.* London: Croom Helm.

Melo, Jorge Orlando. 1987. "Las vicisitudes del modelo liberal: 1850–1899." *Historia Económica de Colombia.* Ed. José Antonio Ocampo. Bogotá: Siglo XXI. 119–72.

Morales, Antonio. 1998. "Literatura y sociedad" *Cambio 16 Colombia.* April 27, 354:66.

Moreno de Angel, Pilar. 1972. *Alberto Urdaneta.* Bogotá: Colcultura.

——. "Urdaneta, Paredes, Racines y la fotografía." *Credencial Historia.* 75: 8–11.

Moreno y Escandón, Francisco Antonio. 1985. *Indios y mestizos de la Nueva Granada del siglo XVIII.* Bogotá: Banco Popular.

Pardo Pardo, Alberto. 1972. *Geografía económica y humana de Colombia.* Bogotá: Eds. Tercer Mundo.

Peralta, Victoria. 1995. *El Ritmo lúdico y los placeres en Bogotá.* Bogotá: Ed. Planeta-Ariel.

Pérez, Felipe. 1883. *Geografía general, física, y política de los Estados Unidos de Colombia y Geografía particular de la ciudad de Bogotá.* Bogotá: Imprenta Echeverría Hermanos.

Portafolio. 1998. "Estancada la venta de libros". April 20: 16.

Rama, Ángel. 1984. "La ciudad letrada." *La ciudad Letrada.* Montevideo: Fundación Internacional Angel Rama. 31–45.

——. 1985. "La ciudad escrituraria." *La crítica de la cultura en América Latina.* Caracas: Biblioteca Ayacucho. 3–18.

Reyes Posada, Carlos José. 1993. "De los descubrimientos a la invención." *Senderos.* 5, 25–26: 444–52. Bogotá: Biblioteca Nacional de Colombia.

——. 1994. "Anaquel. Catálogo de Prensa del siglo XIX." *Senderos.* 7: 29–30: 1010–35. Bogotá: Biblioteca Nacional de Colombia.

Rodó, José Enrique. 1935. (1910). Prólogo. *Idola Fiori* de Carlos Arturo Torres. Bogotá: Minerva. 11–29.

Rodríguez Demorizi, E. 1943. *Del romancero dominicano.* Santiago: D.R. Editorial El Diario.

Ruiz Martínez, Eduardo. 1993. "Las bibliotecas neogranadinas durante la Ilustración." *Senderos.* 5, 25 & 26:587–612. Bogotá: Biblioteca Nacional de Colombia.

Safford, Frank. 1976. *The Ideal of the Practical. Colombia's Struggle to Form a Technical Elite.* Austin: University of Texas Press.

Sánchez Lozano, Carlos. 1989. "Nuestra joven miseria." El nadaismo colombiano: epílogo literario del Frente Nacional." *Revista Foro.* 8: 83–94.

——. 1997. "Rafael Maya y Baldomero Sanín Cano." *Gaceta.* 38–39: 7–10. Bogotá: Colcultura.

Storey, John. 1997. *An Introduction to Cultural Theory and Popular Culture.* London: Harvester Wheatsheaf.

Tobón, José. 1971. "Lenguas aborígenes." *Ayer y hoy de los indígenas colombianos.* Bogotá: DANE.

Triana, Gloria. 1989. "La cultura popular colombiana en el siglo veinte." *Nueva Historia de Colombia.* Dir. Alvaro Tirado Mejía. Bogotá: Editorial Planeta. 6:303–26.

Uribe Celis, Carlos. 1991. Los años veinte en Colombia. Bogotá: Ideología y Cultura, Eds. Alborada.

Vargas Lesmes, Julián. 1990. *La sociedad de Santafé colonial.* Bogotá: CINEP.

Vélez de Piedrahita, Rocío. 1995. *Literatura en la colonia: de Rodríguez Freile a Francisco José de Caldas.* Medellín: Biblioteca Pública Piloto de Medellín.

Voces. 1918. Barranquilla: (June 10) 2.25: 219.

Wade, Peter. 1997. "Entre la homogeneidad y la diversidad: la identidad nacional y la música costeña en Colombia." *Antropología en la Modernidad.* Ed. M.Victoria Uribe and Eduardo Restrepo. Bogotá: Instituto Colombiano de Antropología.

Williams, Raymond L. 1991. *Novela y poder en Colombia 1844–1987.* Bogotá: Tercer Mundo Editores.

Zea, Leopoldo. 1987. *Filosofía de la historia americana.* México: Fondo de Cultura Económica.

CHAPTER 41

CONVENT IN THE CLOUDS
QUITO AS A CULTURAL CENTER

Regina Harrison

In Ecuador, white cathedral bell towers compete with steel shafts of metal-clad office buildings in an effort to dominate the cultural landscape of the capital city, Quito. The views of traditional architecture alongside modernist construction are best seen from a vantage point of the neighboring mountain to the west, rugged Rucu Pichincha (4700 meters), or from the gentle slopes of nearby Panecillo in the southern sector of the city. In all, eighty-six churches exist in the city; some of the most spectacular cathedrals date from the earliest years of the Spanish invasion of the narrow Quito valley. With two deep gorges and a river cutting through the city of Quito, the landscape seemed so inhospitable that early visitors questioned the choice of the site for Spanish occupation. The laying out of the typical town grid was difficult due to the natural contours of the land. These same natural obstacles that were an impediment to Spanish settlement, however, also provided a measure of security and prevented attacks on the city. The Incan armies, occupying this territory a century before the Spanish invasion, left a legacy of fortresses ringing the city instead of erecting monumental stone ceremonial centers as in Peru. Atahualpa, the son of Inca Huayna Capac and a noble Quitu indigenous woman, lived with his descendants in the southern part of the city. As in other Incan settlements of the Andes, the city was divided into units of Hanan (upper) and Urin (lower). A deviation from the standard Incaic pattern occurred in Quito; the high noble class usually resided in the upper moiety (Hanan), but in Quito they lived in the southern (or lower) half of the city. Frank Salomon documents the existence of fifty-three Incan rulers in postconquest Quito (the lower half of the city), creating a mirror image of the spatial patternings that are so commonly found in the region of Cuzco (Ramón 60).

Cloisters, Conquerors, and Cabildos: The Sixteenth and Seventeenth Centuries

Sixty-seven Spanish conquerors first settled in the central Andean region of Riobamba in 1534; San Francisco de Quito became the second city founded in that same year, when 204 Spaniards were assigned plots of land in the city environs (Borchart de Moreno 184). (See **Figure 1**.) A map was drawn of the parcels, but unfortunately this drawing has not appeared in the archives. The earliest known map of Quito dates from 1573 in the *Relación de la ciudad de San Francisco de Quito* [Report on the City of San Francisco de Quito], now housed in the Biblioteca de la Real Academia de Historia, Madrid (Hardoy and Dos Santos 38). The descriptions of Quito written by the early chroniclers and historians dominate the literary landscape for several centuries: Quito was designated a bishopric in 1545, a royal audience in 1563 under the jurisdiction of the viceroyalty of Peru, and then part of the viceroyalty of Nueva Granada in 1717. These scholarly descriptions of legislative decrees and daily life in the cultural center of Quito reveal the harsh circumstances for the natives and the European settlers. Access to water was a right, subject to legislation: The Spaniard who stole supplies of water would be fined 30 pesos, but the Indian who diverted water for his

Figure 1.

Drawing by Guamán Poma de Ayla depicting the foundation of Quito in 1534 from El primer nueva corónica buen gobierno *(1615). (Courtesy of John P. Robarts Research Library, University of Toronto)*

own use would suffer the pain of having his nose cut by the authorities (Ospina 120).

The prominence of the historical descriptions of construction—of bridges, churches, and plazas—highlights Spanish efforts to "civilize" the natural contours of Quito and to curb the non-Christian behavior of the indigenous inhabitants. A large central plaza, now called the Plaza de Independencia, formed the nucleus of the city, while two other plazas to the east and west were also designated as sites for the Dominican and Franciscan convents and churches as early as 1535. The Cathedral, on the main plaza, was consecrated in 1572. The middle of the sixteenth century marked an intense period of frenetic religious construction, limited to a confined space between the ravines: the church of La Merced (1554), the church of Santo Domingo (1581), the Jesuit church of the Compañía (1605) (see **Figure** 2), the church of San Agustín (1580), the church of San Diego (1569), the church of Santa Bárbara (1550), the church of San Sebastián (1568), and the Conceptista Monastery (1575). Earthquakes and eruptions of the volcano Pichincha (in 1582 and in 1660) damaged many of these church towers and altars, yet the structures were piously rebuilt of more sturdy materials (see Peralta).

Parallel with the creation of a new political identity for Quito, a new literature emerged that reflected the conceptual and aesthetic perspectives of the Spanish masters. The Spanish invaders (Hernando Pizarro, Pedro Sánchez de la Hoz, and Francisco de Xerez) wrote accounts of the battles with the indigenous armies of Quito, of the internecine wars among the Spanish conquerors (Cieza de León), and of the exploratory expeditions of the vast new continent. The exploration of the Amazon River and its headwaters was a theme in many volumes in Ecuadorian literature and history. In February of 1541, an expeditionary force commissioned by Gonzalo Pizarro set off from Quito. The travails of the explorers were well documented in the sixteenth century by Toribio de Ortiguera (1581) and in the diary of Friar Gaspar de Carvajal (1504–1584), a Dominican who served as chaplain to Francisco de Orellana's men. Similarly, in the seventeenth century, Rafael Ferrer (1570–1611) and Cristóbal de Acuña

Figure 2.

Façade of the Church of the Compañia (Society of Jesus) Quito, Ecuador. Photograph by Graziano Gasparini c. 1940. (Archive of the author)

(1597–1675), both Jesuits, as well as José de Villamor Maldonaldo (d. 1652), a Franciscan, wrote about the "discovery" of the Amazon. Texts of spiritual hardship and miraculous enchantment, laden with realistic observation as well, comprise Ecuador's colonial heritage; these same texts influence a contemporary portrayal of the country.

Intellectuals, born in the colonies, were accorded some respect for their learning when they traveled to Spain. Gaspar de Villarroel (ca. 1587–1665), born in Quito, educated in the Colegio de San Martín in Lima and with his doctorate from the Universidad de Santo Tomás in Quito (1630), assured his position as an intellectual in Spain and Portugal. An elegant preacher and an ambitious writer, he proclaimed, "Compuse unos librillos, juzgando que cada uno había de ser un escalón para subir" (quoted in Barrera 162) (I wrote some minor compositions with the idea that they would be successive steps upward). An Augustinian, he was chosen as bishop of Santiago, a site far from his beloved Lima where he had spent his childhood. His residence in various parts of the viceroyalty of Peru and in the *Audiencia* of Quito, as well as in Europe, illustrates the cosmopolitan nature of the ecclesiastical networks that transcended official boundaries. Other learned men of the church forsook the activities of exploration; they stayed on in the "metropolis," dedicated to teaching the sons of Spanish and Indian leaders the arts of rhetoric and reasoning. Quito was a prominent educational center of the Spanish colonies, with the religious orders and the secular clergy accepting the task of pedagogy. Despite the common missionary goals shared by the religious orders, fierce rivalries existed among them. The Franciscans established the secondary school of San Andrés in 1552 for sons of Indian *caciques* and poverty-stricken children who were the result of the sexual encounters of the conquest. A report submitted to the Quito authorities in 1568 listed the plan of study: catechism instruction, classes in reading and writing, song, playing a musical instrument, Latin, and workshops in practical skills such as carpentry and bricklaying (Barrera 62; Villalba Freire 1992a, 451–52). The Augustine friars, however, replaced the Franciscans and administered the school from 1581. In 1603 this seminary became the short-lived University of San Fulgencio. The Jesuits, after their arrival in 1585, founded a seminary (the Colegio Máximo) in Quito (1589) and the University of San Gregorio in 1620. But royal approval for the Dominicans to establish the Real Colegio San Fernando and the Universidad de Santo Tomás in 1681 threatened to undermine the status of the Jesuit degrees. After much discussion in Rome and Madrid, the authorities declared that both institutions, that of the Dominicans and that of the Jesuits, were equal in privileges and importance; both could confer degrees (Villalba Freire 1992b, 431). The libraries were renowned; the Dominicans amassed 3500 volumes in the early Colonial period and the Jesuits housed 14,000 volumes in their libraries at the time of their expulsion in the eighteenth century.

While a small percentage of the male population was educated in Quito schools and universities, young women received a good part of their intellectual and religious training by entering a convent. There, in the confines of daily tasks and prayers, women were schooled by their mother superiors and their father confessors. Some convents were founded by petitions from well-connected women of the colonies, such as occurred in the creation of the convents of Santa Catalina (1592) and Santa Clara (1650). However, despite the endowment brought in by the founding mothers, strategic alliances with the Dominicans (Santa Catalina) and the Franciscans (Santa Clara) enabled the nuns more easily to gain economic support from the crown and clergy. By 1618 sixty nuns were engaged in good works in the convent of Santa Catalina, while Santa Clara housed seventy nuns in 1640. The first nunnery was the Convent of the Immaculate Conception (1575), a convent with which the venerated Santa Mariana de Jesús (1618–1645) [canonized 1950] had spiritual affiliations–although Jesuit advisors figured more prominently as theological advisers. Santa Mariana made a decision, after much thought and counsel, to remain in her own family house and claimed one room in which to perfect her spiritual exercises. According to the testimony of her Indian servant, Catalina de Paredes, Mariana practiced mortification of the flesh. In particular, in the manner of Christ, she crucified herself by tying her head, her hair, and her four extremities to a large wooden cross each Friday (Espinosa Pólit 286). Jesuit Jacinto Morán de Buitrón (1688–1749) wrote the history of Mariana's life in 1696, which was printed in Madrid in 1724; it contributed greatly to assuring her canonization. When the Convento de Carmen Alto was founded in 1661, it is specifically recorded that construction for the site bordered the house where Mariana had lived. A source of much inspiration–religious, historical, and literary–Mariana de Jesús was a focal point for cultural celebrations and intellectual fervor.

While much has been written about Mariana de Jesús, particularly testimonies for purposes of canonization, she left little written evidence of her existence. Two nuns in Quito convents, on the other hand, wrote exemplary manuscripts of their lives and their Christian devotion. The confines of the Santa Clara convent were described in Sor Getrudis de San Ildefonso's (1652–1709) three-volume work, *La perla mystica escondida en la concha de la humilidad . . .* [The Mystic Pearl Hidden in the Shell of Humility . . .], written with the collaboration of her confessor, Fray Martín de la Cruz. Although scholarship by Hernán Rodriguéz Castelo (b. 1933) has renewed interest in Sor Getrudis, the illustrated manuscript has not received the feminist and theoretical attention given to nuns' manuscripts in Mexico City, Chile, Lima, and Colombia. Laden with biblical allusions and theological argumentation, the text gives evidence of the state of knowledge at the close of the sixteenth century. Getrudis, with the aid of her confessor, gains insight into her mystical visions, which allows her to participate in the European heritage as written by San Juan de la Cruz. This nun's contribution to the volumes is forthright and direct, whereas Fray Martín's style is more *conceptista*, as seen in the following passage: "Pues ya se declaró el mysterio: ser esa mujer fuerte, esa Perla preciosa escondida en la concha de la humanidad, en el capullo cándido de la azucena que, desabontonando sus hojas, exhala aromas en virtudes; en lo cercado de espinas hallarse intacta rosa, con más colores que un carmín a los ojos divinos agradable (Rodríguez Castelo 383) (The mystery has been proclaimed: being that woman of fortitude, that precious pearl hidden in the shell of humility, in the stem of the innocence of the lily, which upon opening its leaves exudes the aroma of virtue; in the full rose protected by its thorns, with its vivid redness which is so agreeable to God's eyes).

While this relationship between priest confessor and his "spiritual daughter" was a success, one event in the seventeenth century–the revolt of the Santa Catalina nuns (1680)– revealed the conflict inherent in the collaboration between male and female religious orders. In the case of the Santa

Catalina convent, sixty of the ninety nuns chose to terminate their close ties with the Dominicans; they preferred to report only to the bishop. Peña Montenegro, the bishop, accepted the change, but the Dominicans and President Munive did not. An uproar ensued that involved throngs of residents in Quito. Despite a raging downpour that drenched them, the nuns took refuge in the diocese buildings and appealed for intervention by the king and the pope. These supreme authorities, notwithstanding the tumultuous event, decided in favor of the Dominicans (Villalba Freire 1992b, 434).

Another nun, just blocks away from the convent where Sor Getrudis lived and died, embarked upon writing an autobiography, "Secretos entre el alma y Dios" [Secrets Between the Soul and God], which was never published. Catalina Luisa Herrera (1717–1795), despite little formal schooling, dictated her thoughts in 150 notebooks, later carefully written out by Juan María Riera. Fortunately, Alfonso A. Jerves, in *Florilegio doctrinal* [1932; Doctrinal Anthology], published selections from the notebooks that reveal her fervor for communication: "Oh, si los mundanos probasen, Señor, tus amores, cómo de corrida dejarían los mundanos amores, que ellos llaman amores, no siendo la verdad sino amarguras, y se vendrían a meter en el vinos oforíferos de los tuyos, verdaderos!" (Jerves quoted in Barrera 334) (Oh, Lord, if the worldly could only taste of your love, they would rapidly abandon their worldly loves, that which they call love, which are not true but only bitterness, they would flock to enter into the divine adoration of your true love). Her poems include a *colloquio* between God and herself, where each verse she wrote was answered by the Divine Husband "doctrinal y en el mismo metro" (in religious doctrine and in the same meter). Yearning for solitude and union with the Divine, she complained in these verses of being forced to leave the comfort of her bare cell to encounter "donde la bulla y los peligros no me dejasen estar a solas contigo" (Jerves quoted in Barrera 336) (the worldly noise and dangers which do not permit me to attain solitude with you).

The nuns, of course, were not the only devout individuals penning texts behind the thick walls of the convents. A friendship of mentor and student existed among the Jesuits Antonio Bastidas (1615–1681) and Jacinto de Evia (b. 1629), both Guayaquileños by birth; they shared academic pursuits in the universities and *colegios* of Quito. The *Ramillete de varias flores poéticas, recogidas y cultivadas en los primeros abriles de sus años . . .* [Bouquet of Diverse Poetic Flowers, Gathered and Cultivated in Their Years of Youth . . .] was published in Madrid in 1675, the result of youthful poetic occasions when they wrote lyrics in praise of political figures or celebrations of events in Quito. These 400 pages reveal the influence of Góngora, a variety of poetic forms, and the youthful vigor of Evia and a fellow student, Hernando Domíngez Camargo (both were in classes with Bastidas in the Seminario de San Luis). Each poem (elegiac, lyric, sacred, amatory, and those of a satirical nature) is introduced with commentary. Among these verses are two poems dedicated to the founder of the Santa Clara convent (Francisca de Santa Clara) as well as to a nun in the Santa Catalina convent (Luisa Chaves).

Although the difficulties with the nuns of the Santa Catalina convent in 1680 marred his final years, Bishop Alonso de la Peña Montenegro (d. 1688) had provided strong leadership for thirty years in Quito. He is well known for his *Itinerario para párrocos de Indias* [1668; Guide for Parish Priests in the Indies], an erudite book that draws on scripture, theology, and royal decrees to best answer questions regarding the conversion and the conduct of the indigenous population. Requested to write a guide ("algunas reglas" [some rules]) by the Visitadores of Ibarra, Cuenca, and Guayaquil in the 1650s, the Bishop found that his explanations grew to 536 pages of double columns. Thirteen sections pertain to exemplary conduct of the missionaries; eight sections describe indigenous errors and customs; a long section is dedicated to the administration of the sacraments (confession and marriage) supplemented by precepts (fasting, tithes, and attending mass). The many European editions of the *Itinerario* (1678, 1698, 1726, 1754, and 1771) attest to the necessity for theological clarification, not only in the Andes, but for priests in Central America.

Ostentation and Outcry: Eighteenth-Century Quito

A number of official decrees worked to curtail the formation of a regional identity for Quiteños in the eighteenth century. In 1717, the Audience of Quito was subsumed in the new viceroyalty of the Nuevo Reino de Granada, and the latter was accorded all official functions (legislative, juridical, and military). Protest by Quiteños and the viceroy of Peru in 1720 caused the crown to return jurisdiction to Peru; yet, in 1739, a royal decree again placed the Audience of Quito in the hands of the Bogotaños of the viceroyalty of New Granada (Terán Najas 272–73). The eighteenth was not an exemplary century for contemplative literary pursuits either. The small world of the convents reflected the dangers and turmoil experienced in the colonies that began to chafe under Spanish-imposed authority. Notable was the Franciscan Riot of 1747–1748, where people of the San Roque *barrio* (originally designated as an Indian parish, but later a mixed parish) supported the Franciscans who refused entry to a Visitador sent from Lima and were thus excommunicated by him. In response, a commissary arrived from Lima and purged the order by jailing two priests. The incarceration of the two men (who were later freed) rallied support from the plebeians of San Roque, who staged a ritual procession mocking the church hierarchy. Further riots ensued in New Year's festivities when crowds stood watch at the church and convent of San Francisco; the authorities from Lima had to seek shelter with the Jesuits. A prison attack was launched by a twenty-five-person commando unit organized to free their neighbors of San Roque; several hundred people gathered in the streets to support this daring feat. Another disturbance that same year united the Quito parishes of San Roque, San Blas, and San Sebastián (all popular districts), which signaled each other through a code of firework displays. Martin Minchom categorizes these scandalous events as a moment when class antagonism was emphasized and played upon, a time when there was a decision to resist the status quo of colonial injustice and promotion of solidarity against nonlocal authority (Minchom 215–20).

In the great uprising of May 1765, the popular masses controlled the main square of Quito; peninsular Spaniards were temporarily banished from the city as well. One year later, calm was restored; but the uprising, described as the Quito Rebellion by historians, was seen as the first of the major insurrections that lead to the rebellion of Tupac Amaru in 1781. Unrest was triggered by a number of factors; Alto Peru was no longer buying cloth made in the Quito region because European textiles were arriving cheaply via Cape Horn; severe droughts and then frosts affected food production; and there were heavy casualties in measles epidemics (1693, 1720, 1740, 1759, and 1764) (Minchom 222–24).

Evidence of the widening economic divide separating the plebeian from the upper classes is seen in the inventory of goods left behind by the deceased wife of Pedro Vicente Maldonado. A selection of her items discloses a pair of pearl dotted mantillas, a coral and gold rosary, a short apron of green damask and silver lace, an organza dress, a cape of vivid red color brocade with golden fringe, and white lace sheets from England. (Barrera 276). Her possession of these goods is to be expected, as she was Maldonado's wife and he was a prominent member of the oligarchy. He accompanied the French Academy of Science expedition of 1736–1743 in Ecuador, which had arrived to measure the longitudinal degree of the meridian near Quito. The French clearly brought more than scientific research to the continent: Charles de la Condamine himself opened a store in one of the two rooms loaned him by the Jesuits and sold Dutch-made shirts, European cloth, buttons, stockings, exquisite Dutch handkerchiefs, and lace (Barrera 276).

The sumptuous dress, with excessive ornament, worn by the upper classes was well mirrored in the poetry fashionable in the eighteenth century. Exemplary is the *Colección de poesías varias, hecho por un ocioso en la ciudad de Faenza* [1790; Collection of Varied Poems, Compiled By a Man of Leisure in the City of Faenza], a collection totaling five volumes and 1500 pages, in which the Jesuit Juan de Velasco (1727–1792) meticulously copied poems written by his colleagues–Jesuits exiled from the Americas with the decree of 1767. Complexity of poetic expression was still paramount in the collection, yet there is considerable value also in the prose comparisons with Spanish poetry of earlier times, as well as in the descriptions of their exile in Italy. In particular, Mariano Andrade's (1734–1811) poem, "Despedida de Quito," reveals his nostalgia for the eternally green mountain city. Nevertheless, Velasco's efforts were better expended in his *Historia natural, antigua y moderna del Reino de Quito* [1789; Ancient and Modern Natural History of the Kingdom of Quito]. In a history that reads like a novel, Velasco speculates on Quiteño indigenous origins, the flora and fauna of the region, legends, and texts of the chroniclers. Often taken to task by historians for its flagrant inaccuracies, his work is now more appreciated as a cultural artifact with abundant examples from the oral tradition. For example, he narrates the legend of the Cantuña chapel, on the south side of the San Francisco cathedral, built with gold derived from Cantuña's pact with the devil. Father Velasco told this tale and others with such rhetorical skill that he is considered among the most distinguished authors of Ecuador's *belle-lettres*.

Velasco began writing the history in 1768, and his narrative cites sources that still have not surfaced from national or international archives. One text, among the many lost, was the history of Atahualpa and Huascar, written by the indigenous cacique Jacinto de Collahuazo (in the eighteenth century), and subsequently burned by the Corregidor of Ibarra (a northern province). Velasco asserts that he read a second version, rewritten by the elderly cacique (Pareja Diez Canseco xl). His Historia manuscript was never published in Velasco's lifetime; through the efforts of his nephew, also a Jesuit priest, the manuscript came out in print in 1792.

Although Mexico City had a printing press functioning in 1539 and one also existed in Lima in 1584, Bogotá was without a press until 1738 and Quito until 1760. *La Gaceta de Lima* (1715?–1780) is credited with being the first South American newspaper, but of some importance is the breadth shown by the *Diario de Lima* (1790–1793) with its range of articles (on economics, business, culture, and events), for it was read by slaves as well as by school children. Alexander Humboldt (1769–1859) chose the *Mercurio peruano* (1791–1794) to carry back with him to Berlin, where Goethe selected specific articles for translation (Lohmann Villena 111). The Cuban Manuel Socorro Rodríguez (1758–1818) edited the *Papel periódico de la Ciudad de Santafé de Bogotá*, a weekly publication, for the years 1791 to 1797; this is considered Colombia's first newspaper (Puyo 176). In the *Audiencia* of Quito, the Jesuits set up a press (1755) after much negotiation with authorities in a *colegio* in Ambato, aided by a recently arrived printer Juan Adán Schwartz, a Jesuit (Villalba Freire 1992b, 438). In Ambato, the first publication was a religious essay in Latin; in Quito, likewise the first publication was religious in theme (1760).

In 1792, however, the discourse of the printing presses would take on a political cast in Quito, as seen in the first newspaper, *Primicias de la cultura de Quito*, published biweekly for three months in 1792 by Francisco Javier Eugenio de Santa Cruz y Espejo (1747–1795). Pérez Calama, bishop from 1790 to 1792, paid for a supplement to the first edition of the *Primicias*, in which he advocated reforms in hygiene, grammatical usage, creation of literary prizes, and curricular reforms (Salvador Lara 1995, 257). Espejo, a physician, advocated liberal ideas for reform and imitated journalism in Lima and Bogotá, using broadsheets as well to disseminate his politics. His revolutionary advocacy was sharpened by his exile in Santafé de Bogotá from 1788 to 1790. The President of Quito, in writing to the viceroy of Nueva Granada, warned him of Espejo's influence: "Hierven las ideas liberales, no solamente en la cabeza de Espejo, sino en la de muchos literatos y pensadores de grande influencia, por lo que le remito a Bogotá, sin formularle causa alguna" (quoted in Barrera 311) ("liberal ideas boil over, not only in Espejo's head, but also in the many thinkers and literary authors of great influence [of his knowledge]. I send notice to you in Bogotá without any intention of originating a cause against him"). In exile, Espejo met with revolution-inspired Antonio Nariño, translator of texts on the rights of citizens from the French Revolution; when Nariño published these texts in 1794, he was exiled to Africa. Nariño eventually returned to New Granada and founded *La Bagatela*, a newspaper that was instrumental in unseating Jorge Tadeo Lozano, president in 1811 (Puyo 176). In Bogotá, Espejo also befriended the Quito-born Juan Pío Montufar; as the Marquis of Selva Alegre, Montufar afforded Espejo some political protection as well as encouragement to publish his tracts on reform. In "Escuela de Concordia," Espejo described a Quito in ruins and proclaimed the necessity for civil activism in the formation of a true *Patria* (fatherland); this essay, with its formula for change, was written at the behest of Montufar. Attuned to the events in Europe as well as in the viceroyalties, Espejo commented favorably on the Tupac-Amaru movement in Peru, as seen in his satirical "El retrato de Golilla" [The Portrait of Golilla] wherein the Spanish authorities were taken to task (Salvador Lara 1995, 264).

With the expulsion of the Jesuits in 1767, Quito acquired the richly endowed libraries of the order. A public library in Quito was opened in 1792 and Espejo was appointed as the director. A worthy appointee, Espejo (in conjunction with Bishop Pérez Calama) urged reorganization of the educational system. The Bishop, in his "Plan de estudios de la Real Universidad literaria de Quito" [1791; Plan of Studies of the Royal Literary University of Quito], consulted with Espejo for

suggestions for restructuring and the inclusion of a modernized bibliography for studies (Vargas 435). As an example of the new pedagogy, Pérez Calama sponsored the creation of a new professorship in Political Economy (Salvador Lara 1992, 134). Of course, Espejo's *Nuevo Luciano* [The New Lucian], published in 1799, had already been critical of Jesuit instruction and had favored a more open intellectual climate. The libraries of Quito, both public and private, were a source of envy for the Bogoteño José de Francisco Caldas (1768–1816), who was in Quito to collaborate on a botanical project with José Mejía Lequerica (1775–1813). Although Caldas criticized the city harshly in some writings, he did admit the cultural superiority in one domain–the books: "libros que no los pude ver en Santa Fe, los he encontrado aquí" (quoted in Barrera 476) (books I could not find in Bogotá, I have found here).

Eugenio Espejo characterized himself as a man of many talents and a monstrous capacity for understanding. His self-assessment is quite accurate; Espejo was highly regarded for his zeal for economic, pedagogical, and social reform. In scientific circles, Espejo is best known for his theoretical research on smallpox. Yet he did not neglect aesthetics; his *El nuevo Luciano de Quito* [1779; The New Luciano of Quito] served to ridicule the baroque tastes and lexical excesses common to this era. Espejo's own style was erudite, yet serious and forthright. The circumstances of his birth (grandson of an acculturated Indian named Chusic) are occasion for Ecuador to claim him as a "renowned Indian figure." In reality, Espejo fought very hard to minimize his Indian background and to join the ranks of the elite, according to M. Minchom. In a sense, Espejo reached the pinnacle of success, for he was a prominent member of the Sociedad Económica de los Amigos del País de Quito (Economic Society of the Friends of the Country of Quito), founded in 1791. With the influence of the Count of Casa Jijón and the newly appointed Bishop Pérez Calama, the Society united the aristocrats of the city who advocated goals of advancement in agriculture, science, arts, industry, commerce, politics, and fine arts. In this mission, the Quito Society paralleled the interests generally expressed by these organizations in other Latin American cities: "The Economic Societies, a reflection of Physiocrat influence and in principle among the more practical offshoots of Enlightenment thought, were centers for the exchange of social and political ideas ranging from the improvement of commerce and agriculture to politics and industry" (Minchom 236). Pressure from the church and a very traditional *cabildo* (municipal government) closed down the Society in November of 1793 with a royal decree–one way to quiet critical opinions. Espejo died after serving time in prison (1795), jailed because of his controversial and polemical attacks on society. His death was listed in the burial registry for *mestizos*, Indians, and blacks, not that of the whites, thus indicating his fall from grace.

Quito, the "city of cloisters," was receptive to the influence of the international scientific community when the French government obtained permission for Louis Godin and Pierre Bouger (mathematicians), Joseph de Jussien (a naturalist), and Charles de la Condamine to visit the South American continent. An enlightened cosmopolitanism on the part of Philip V opened up the colonies, formerly closed to foreign influence, to the measuring instruments of the French, who recorded all manner of matter. Spaniards Jorge Juan and Antonio de Ulloa were sent to accompany the expedition commissioned by the French Academy of Science; their observations are evident in the *Noticias secretas de América* [1826; Secret Notes from

America], a volume written to inform only the Spanish king about conditions abroad. As Mary Louise Pratt notes, there was an ambiguity in the interplay of diplomacy and science in the goals of the expeditions: "On the one hand, dominant ideologies made a clear distinction between the (interested) pursuit of wealth and the (disinterested) pursuit of knowledge; on the other hand, competition between nations continued to be the fuel for European expansion abroad" (18).

Pedro V. Maldonado (d. 1748) was an incorrigible traveler with a passion for exploring all regions of the Kingdom of Quito. His knowledge of the country is clear in his writing and in his maps. Maldonado was an ideal companion for the members of the French Academy. La Condamine published a *History of the Pyramids of Quito* (1751) and studies of curare, quinine, and rubber as a result of his extensive travel in the region. Maldonado, although he died at the age of thirty-eight, completed a geographical study of Quito and its provinces, which was detailed in a splendid map. He was highly regarded on both continents and he became a member of the French Academy of Science (Paris) in 1747. Antonio de Alcedo, born in Quito in 1734, assembled a reference work on the Americas that is considered the most accurate compilation of historical and geographic documentation in the eighteenth century. The five volumes of the *Diccionario Geográfico-Histórico de las Indias Occidentales o América* [1786–89; Geographical-Historical Dictionary of the West Indies or America] are more than a dry summary, for the author questions Eurocentric notions of civilization in commentary regarding human rights, the institution of slavery, and the problem of the aboriginal peoples.

In the field of science, Juan Bautista Aguirre (1725–1786), a scholar of humanities, as well, figured prominently as a professor of philosophy and theology at the Jesuit university of San Gregorio. Several of his texts demonstrate his enthusiasm for direct observation and experimentation, as seen in his "Disquisición sobre el agua" ["Treatise on Water"] from *Physica ad Aristotelis Mentem* (1757): "Sus partes no son perfectamente esféricas, sino un tanto elípticas como lo puede personalmente observar en al microscopio" (quoted in Pérez 56) (The parts of water are not perfectly spherical but rather elliptical as can be observed through a microscope). Aguirre is also recognized, although belatedly, as a significant Ecuadorian poet, despite the aspersions Espejo cast on Aguirre's poems in *El nuevo Luciano de Quito* (Pérez 209–10). In 1846, Juan María Gutiérrez (1809–1878), an Argentinean, called attention to Aguirre's poetic prowess in his *América poética* [Poetic America]. Aguirre had languished unnoticed by critics for a century until Gonzalo Zaldumbide (1885–1965), after reading Gutiérrez's book in a Paris library, unearthed more manuscripts in the research archives of Argentina. As a result of Zaldumbide's efforts, the collected works of Aguirre were published in 1943 in the third volume of *Colección de Clásicos Ecuatorianos* [Collection of Ecuadorian Classics], and has been much appreciated by literary scholars and intellectual historians. That same year, Emilio Carillo, using the same archive of Aguirre's papers, published his poems with the University of Buenos Aires (Barrera 406–7).

Another scientist who prevailed upon the Spanish king in the eighteenth century for permission to travel in the Andes was Alexander von Humboldt (1769–1859), who spent some six months in Quito at the turn of the century. European attention was drawn to Humboldt's attempt to scale Chimborazo while dressed in a frock coat and high-buttoned shoes, a feat that was written up in many of the foreign newspapers. Humboldt wrote prolifically, giving prose descriptions of deserts, *llanos* (prairies), and verdant jungles. He also experimented with the use of charts, tables, and graphs (Pratt 119). In particular, his drawing of Chimborazo depicted the crevices of the heavily snow-capped volcano and added numerous labels indicating vegetation niches on the 6300-meter-high mountain (Pratt 128). Humboldt had effusive praise for the work of Pedro Maldonado, stating that it was the most complete work of all the European colonies, save Egypt and some parts of the Grand Indies.

The same mountains that were applauded as marvels of nature were soon to inflict hardship on the troops fighting bravely for independence from Spain in the nineteenth century. The tumultuous years of pre-Independence when Juntas Superiores (High Juntas) established a *criollo* government in Quito (1808, 1810), still loyal to the Crown, were followed by years of more unrest and the War of Independence. Marked political division marred solidification of the former Andean *Audiencia* of Quito into one cohesive nation; Guayaquil and Cuenca displayed a regional factionalism, opposed to political alliances with Quito, and the country experienced one battle after another in border conflicts with what are now Peru and Colombia (despite the attempts by Simón Bolívar to impose order). The choice of the name "Ecuador" in 1830, rather than the use of "Quito," is indicative of both patriotic pride (a desire to separate from the past history with Spain) and an unwillingness to allow Quito a dominance over other regions. However, Quito was designated the capital in the constitutional assembly held in Riobamba that same year. Factionalism continued to split the country until the commanding presence of Gabriel García Moreno headed a conservative government that, by virtue of his autocratic rule, imposed calm from 1869 to 1875. García Moreno's strong hand on the reins of government inspired (differently) two Ambateño writers: Juan León Mera (1832–1894) lauded his governmental projects, but Juan Montalvo (1832–1889) censured his rule. García Moreno, while a student in Europe, had mastered both the arts and the sciences; he was, in fact, a professor of chemistry and physics, and President of Quito's Universidad Central (established in 1826). Another Ecuadorian who traveled extensively, not by his own choosing, was Juan Montalvo who, because of his strong opposition to García Moreno, was frequently writing in exile. Both men engaged in polemical disputes through pamphlets, newspapers, and magazines. Montalvo used the *Cosmopolita* to attack the president; García Moreno's supporters published harsh evaluations of Montalvo in *La Patria*.

Books, newspapers, magazines, art, and architecture all reflect the traditionalism of the theological orientation of this government in the mid-nineteenth century (1861–1865, 1869–1875); at the same time Quito underwent modern change, as was evident in the construction of the large prison in 1868 by the European architects Thomas Reed and Francisco Schmidt, who were teaching in Quito's Escuela Politécnica. Built in the style of La Santé prison, the panoptican featured a circular central space that functioned to control movement of prisoners (Peralta 148). Nearby, in the same southern section of the city, the San Diego cemetery was laid out in an ordered pattern of regular paths, despite a terrain that was hard to overcome. The chapels reflect a diversity of architectural styles, but Humberto Brúning's neoclassical structure is the most distinctive. The prison and the cemetery are apt symbols for the authoritarian control exerted by Ecuador's president, who commissioned these large monumental works. Intricate woodworking and sculpting, seen in the earliest Colonial *retablos* (altarpiece), were encouraged by the founding of the Escuela de Artes y Oficios (1871; School of Arts and Trades); García Moreno designated a site at the southern rim of the city for this technical academy (Navarro 243). García Moreno also founded the Academia de Bellas Artes (Academy of Fine Arts), where Rafael Salas began a nineteenth-century school of painting (1872–1875).

The coast and the mountain regions were separated from each other; for some six months of the year heavy rains hampered passage between Quito and Guayaquil in the 1860s (Kingman Garcés 131). Within the city of Quito, too, there existed similar sectors of isolation. Yet easier access north and south united the formerly separate sectors of the city; a bridge was built to span the Manchángara River, overseen by the Quito architect Mariano Aulestia (1860). The ease of passage through the city indicates, as well, the opening of Quito in other senses. The astronomical observatory, again drawn up by Francisco Schmidt and Thomas Reed, was built to trace the celestial patterns; archival holdings were planned for the first floor, as well as laboratory space for scientific observation. Santa Clara market, as well, represented a new concept in construction–a large enclosed and covered space for commerce built with imported materials (metal structures from Hamburg). A design competition was won by Francisco Schmidt and Gualberto Pérez, who conceived of their model based on the Les Halles market in Paris (Peralta 126). Construction began in 1879 and was finished in 1904, changing the face of the neighborhood, which was replete with convents and churches.

The concept of nation was, to some extent, defined by the monumental architecture of this period, in addition to the constant discussions restricting both democratic reforms and the inclusion of Ecuador's citizens in policy matters. Juan León Mera, a supporter of the Catholic president and Juan Montalvo's most ardent enemy, posited the origins of Ecuadorian lyric, and thus by extension Ecuadorian culture, in the Quichua verses of the indigenous inhabitants, as seen in his *Ojeada histórica-crítica de la poesía ecuatoriana* [1868; Historical-Critical Glimpse of Ecuatorian Poetry]. His emphasis on the indigenous populations in Ecuador, of course, was influenced by the European fashion of Chateaubriand and Marmontel, whose literature served as models for *Cumandá* (1879), Mera's novel set in the lush tropical forest. His *Antologia Ecuatoriana* of 1892 was to be a foundational text in the making of a national identity (see **Figure 3**). Consciousness building was at work: Pablo Herrera (1820–1896) published a history of Ecuadorian literature in 1860, which called attention to forgotten texts of Ecuador's past, while Pedro Fermín Cevallos (1812–1893) wrote a history of Ecuador that covered the period until 1845. However, Archbishop Federico González Suárez (1844–1917) was the intellectual who would define Ecuador's vision of the past (and the future). He amassed an impressive research library and founded the Ecuadorian Society of American Historical Studies, which, in 1909, became the National Academy of History. The *Boletín* published by these scholars was judged to be Ecuador's most intellectually serious publication (Barrera 1237). The Archbishop's Palace, off the Plaza de Independencia, was the site of intellectual fervor; Jacinto Jijón y Caamaño (1890–1950) (an archeologist and cultural historian), Carlos Manuel Larrea (a scientist and

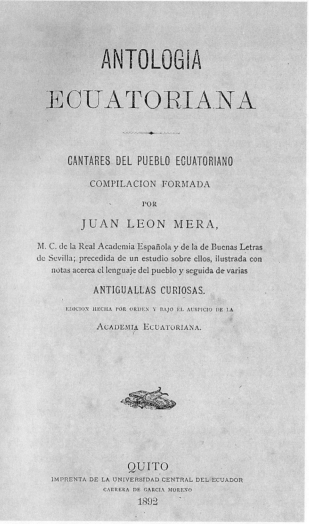

Figure 3.

Cover page Antología Ecuatoriana. *(Courtesy John P. Robarts Research Library, University of Toronto)*

bibliographer), and José Gabriel Navarro (an art historian) shared a scholarly passion for documenting their cultural heritage. The studies they wrote and the books they collected are deposited in the National Archive. Jijón's family home ("La Circasiana," restored in 1992) now houses the Instituto Nacional de Patrimonio Cultural [National Institute of Cultural Patrimony]. An equally accurate index of Ecuador's cultural and political activities was visible in the journal of the Sociedad Jurídico-Literaria (Rojas 93).

An indefatigable scholar, Federico González Suárez (1844–1917) conducted research in the archives of Spain, uncovered valuable documents in Ecuador, and participated in archeological excavations. These activities are reflected in the four volumes of the *Historia general de la República del Ecuador* [1890; General History of the Republic of Ecuador], which marks a radical departure from Velasco's Historia, published in mid-century. As historian and priest, González Suárez saw the value of researching the past as a means to heighten moral responsibility: "El fin de la historia debe ser más noble y elevado, pues ha de enseñar de qué manera pueden los pueblos adelantar y engrandecerse moralmente, y por qué caminos han ido hundiéndose algunos poco a poco en la degradación moral, hasta venir a parar en su ruina" (quoted in Barrera 844) (the aim of historiography should be more noble and elevated [than merely giving satisfaction to innate curiosity] for history must teach peoples the way in which progress can enhance their moral standards, and how, in contrast, the ways in which some nations have bit by bit sunk into moral degradation until arriving at decadence). Despite González Suárez's interest in the cultural history of archeological remains, his observations of contemporary Indians sharply outlined a program of change in the communities. For the nation to progress, he argued, Indians must be encouraged to better themselves:

Los indios tienen defectos de raza, notables y característicos; son, de suyo, muy dados a la inacción y a la pereza, y gustan de pasar el tiempo en estéril holganza; . . . sucios, desaseados, se dejan estar cubiertos de repugnantes harapos, sin hacer de la menor diligencia para mejorar de vestido; sus casas, aún a pesar de su pobreza, todavía pudieran ser menos incómodas y desgreñadas. Para gentes de semejante carácter, indolente y perezoso, el trabajo debió ser un tormento moralizador: condenemos los abusos, deploremos los excesos: pero reconozcamos que el trabajo no sólo es una fuente de riqueza, sino el medio más poderoso de la civilización. (447–48)

The Indians have notable racial defects that are characteristic; they are given to inaction and sloth and they choose to spend their days in sterile laziness . . . dirty, unkempt they persist in covering their bodies in the most repugnant rags without making even the slightest effort to better their clothes; their houses, in spite of their poverty, could be less uncomfortable and shabby. For people of such indolent and lazy character, work must be moralizing torture. Let us condemn the abuses and deplore the excesses, but let us also recognize that work is not only the source of wealth but also the most powerful civilizing force.

González Suárez's opinions regarding Indians were reiterated by Juan León Mera in an address to the Academia Nacional in Quito (1892), where he referred to them as "people sunk in abject poverty" (1892, 13); at the same time, however, Mera included Quichua poetry in the *Antología ecuatoriana* (1892), published by the press of the Universidad Central, Quito (Harrison 119). Inspired by nineteenth-century literary historians who equated nationhood with the preservation of folk poetry, Mera uncovered the most authentic indigenous lyric, "Atahualpa huañui," supposedly written by an Indian leader from Alangasí, near Quito. The poem, in a feminine narrative voice (Harrison 99–102), laments the barbaric slaying of Atahualpa, the last Incan ruler, at the hands of the Spanish and expresses the difficulty of continuing to exist and prosper under the rule of such fierce adversaries.

The condition of the natives, well noted by González Suárez and Mera, became part of a political platform with the arrival of the liberal leader, Eloy Alfaro, in Quito at the turn of the century. Fighting their way up from the coast, the Alfaro army successfully subverted the conservative politics that had united the church and state for half a century. As of 1861, Catholicism had been the only religion recognized in the constitution, and the Vatican had had power over censorship, ecclesiastic courts, and educational programs (Martz 63). Alfaro's efforts to better the lives of the Indians was seen in a decree of 12 April 1899, which insisted that Indians be paid no less than ten cents a day for their work (Rubio Orbe 67–69).

Modernity and Tradition: The Twentieth Century

This realistic, legislative view of the Indian was more accurate than the Romantic portrayal of Indians, which was often colored with legends and exotic archeology. In the beginnings of the twentieth century, the large landowners of the central Sierra were at the mercy of Alfaro's legislative reforms, which represented coastal attitudes toward commerce. Ecuador more readily conceptualized itself as a nation. Interaction between the two regions was facilitated by the completion of the Guayaquil–Quito railroad in 1908, a priority project for Alfaro. Daily newspapers also served to keep informed the dispersed regions of the country; national events were reported in *El Telégrafo* (Guayaquil 1884) and *El Comercio* in Quito (1904).

The arrival of the train was supplemented by another modern convenience, electric light, which lit up the Plaza Grande in 1899 (Kingman Garcés 146). The cultural scene was altered irrevocably with the showing of the first movie in Quito in 1906, brought by the Italian impresario Carlo Valenti to the Teatro Sucre. Guayaquil was much more enthusiastic about films, and in 1920 twenty theaters operated in the port city, whereas only four theaters existed in Quito. Although the films that first arrived in Ecuador involved foreign lands and events, soon a local context was projected on the screen: *Guayaquil en fiesta* [1921; Guayaquil in Celebration], *El tesoro de Atahualpa* [The Treasure of Atahualpa], and *Se necesita una guagua* [Baby Needed] were produced in 1924 by the Ecuadorian Film Company. The exotic representation of Indians was seen in a film directed by a Salesian priest of Italian descent, Father Carlos Crespi, who depicted the elaborate shrunken-head rituals of the Shuar peoples. A grant from UNESCO in 1995 enabled the Cinemateca of Ecuador to restore this 1926 film, *Los invencibles shuaras del Alto Amazonas* [The Invincible Shuaras from the Upper Amazon], from 2,500 meters of footage (Granda Noboa 97–102).

However, it was a book, not a film, that established Ecuador's cultural prominence in the twentieth century—the publication of Jorge Icaza's (1906–1978) *Huasipungo* (1934). Translated into seventeen languages in numerous editions, this novel, with its depiction of Indians on an *hacienda* who engage in an uprising to secure basic human rights, caused a stir inside and outside Ecuador. Set in the rural mountains, the novel describes unsanitary conditions and oppressive cruelty and thus formed public opinion to correct these abuses. Icaza, a solitary figure, stood apart from other literary groups formed in Quito to act on behalf of the indigenous population. A concerted effort was made in Quito by the National Association of Socialist Writers (Grupo ANDES), who, through the magazine *Nervio*, promoted a literary vanguardism that was revolutionary, not "without metaphors or verbal excesses" (Nuñez 134, quoted in Harrison 158). Gatherings of writers with a political agenda occurred in Cuenca and Loja, but the most active and prolific literary collective was the Grupo de Guayaquil, based on the coast. Alfredo Pareja y Diez Canseco (1908–1993), Enrique Gil Gilbert (1912–1973), Demetrio Aguilera Malta (1909–1981), and José de la Cuadra (1903–1941), in this decade and for many more to come, were internationally recognized Ecuadorian writers.

The surge in literary activity allowed for the commercial selling of books to the Quiteño population. Thus, Arsenio Briz Sanchez opened Artes Gráficas in 1927, in the old colonial sector of Quito, and later expanded his business to other

parts of the city. Librería América, owned by Antonio Lucio
Paredes, was responsible for selling the *Boletín* of the Academia de Historia, as well as selected works by González
Suárez, by subscription. Librería Científica, owned by Bruno
Moritz (of German origin), was complemented by the German immigrant Carlos Liebemann's Su Librería. Writers also
opened shops: the Agencia General de Publicaciones,
founded by Jorge Icaza and a Peruvian partner, became a
gathering spot for intellectuals while Augusto Arias combined
a bookstore with a cafe, an art gallery, and a variety of Argentine publications in his ambitious Librería Moderna. The Editorial Bolívar, set up by Alfonso and José Rumazo and dozens
of others, stands out for its printing of the *Biblioteca Ecuatoriana,* now out of print, and the *Serie Independiente,* with its more
contemporary perspective. Liebmann was influential in creating the Sociedad de Libreros in 1955, after a successful career
with Su Librería (Freire Rubio 103–39). Leonardo Muñoz
amassed a significant collection of Ecuadorian books in Quito,
some of them rare editions (Rojas 95).

Routes: Culture Moving North to the "New City"

With the creation of the Casa de la Cultura Ecuatoriana in
August 1944 while José María Velasco Ibarra was president,
the cultural focus of the city moved north into the New City.
The administrative offices, in a traditional style, were completed in 1944; however, the mirror-clad circle, an innovation
by René Denis Zaldumbide, was constructed over a period of
thirty years as a site for the large auditorium, a movie house,
library facilities, and Ecuador's National Museum. The impetus for creating the Casa de la Cultural Ecuatoriana is credited
to Benjamín Carrión (1898–1979), who insisted on Ecuador's
recovering from a profound sense of loss due to the terms of
the Río de Janeiro Protocol Agreement of 1942, when Peru
was the beneficiary of much of the tropical forest region. For
Carrión, the shrinking of the country's borders was no time
for passivity; this was the moment to "defend the *Patria*"
through artistic works and the democratic process, not by harboring a smoldering desire for vengeance. From this date forward, this complex of buildings has hosted artists from all
regions of the country as well as providing a site for international troupes, book fairs, symphony performances, and film
festivals (Ribadeneira 205–14).

With an upsurge in support of cultural creativity, attention
was again directed to the figure of the Indian. Camilo Egas
and Eduardo Kingman, graduates of the National School of
Fine Arts (founded in 1904), disseminated paintings of the
native peoples that depicted their customs and their plight.
Both were involved in the conception of Ecuador's pavilion in
the 1939 World's Fair in New York City (Weil 159). Their
early thematic work was carried on by Osvaldo Guayasamín
(1919–1999) (see **Figure 4**), an artist who, as a child, sold his
sketches on the streets of Quito. He studied with José Clemente Orozco (1883–1949) and incorporated the emotions of
protest and suffering in his work. The Museo Guayasamín in
northeast Quito houses a retrospective collection of the
painter's work and serves as a repository of his pre-Columbian
and Colonial collection.

Ecuador's extensive oil fields, which had been exploited
in the 1930s, acquired new importance in the decades of the
1960s and 1970s, with advances in processing techniques
and the high profit margin for petroleum. President Velasco
Ibarra drove a hard bargain with the Gulf–Texaco consor-
tium in 1969; higher royalties were paid, infrastructure

Figure 4.

*Photograph of the Ecuadorian painter Guayasamín and his work.
(Archive of the author)*

(roads and airports) was improved, and a TransAmazonian
pipeline to the coast was constructed. The city delighted in
the modern construction of hotels, restaurants, coffee shops,
and discotheques (one was housed in the body of an old airplane), which moved north accompanying the Casa de la
Cultura. The lingering importance of the old capitol, the
"Casco Colonial," the Quito of the years before oil revenues, is documented in Jorge Icaza's 1958 novel, *El chulla
Romero y Flores* [The Loner Romero y Flores]. In the seven
chapters, the protagonist Luis Alfonso Romero y Flores
attempts to carry out his task as accountant for a government agency. However, when he discovers the misuse of
government funds by the designated candidate for the presidency, he is persecuted by officials. This attempt to escape
the circumstances of his class origins, as well as his pursuers,
allows Icaza to paint a vivid picture of Quito: the prostitutes,
the beggars, the *chulla* (loner) for whom there is no escape
from the inner city: "Reliquia de la colonia. Cuatro varas de
ancho entre los tejados para mirar al cielo. Casas viejas car-
gadas de lepra, de telarañas, de recuerdos y de carcoma,
bajo el tedio de la humedad y del viento" (243) (Relic of
colonial times. Four yards wide between the roofs in order
to see the sky. Dilapidated houses, full of cobwebs, memories and dust beneath the tedium of dampness and the
wind). Significantly, the novel is anchored in the old streets,
with their musty smells in the disadvantaged barrios of San
Roque, San Sebastián, and San Juan.

The high-rise offices, sleek hotels, and the many-storied
condominiums built in the northern half of the city compete

with the international airport, the large campuses of the universities, and the numerous Protestant churches that also dot the landscape. Oil, and the subsequent infusion of funds into state coffers, made the economic boom possible. Attempts to adjust the growing economic disparity were evident in many social programs. Again in the 1960s large buildings demarcated government priorities, as they had in the 1860s: The Social Security Building was inaugurated in 1958 and the Ministry of Public Works in 1979, while the old city still housed the power base of the Ministry of Government and the Presidential Palace. The government's attempts to provide medical care, salaried employment, and land titles were replicated by the efforts of leftist writers who formed "Tzántzicos" (1962) and "Frente Cultural" (1965–1969), idealistic coalitions of intellectuals and workers. Theater production was aligned with activism, as "Grupo Ollantay" (a unit of the "Frente Cultural") wrote and performed "S + S = 41," a drama featuring Sherlock Holmes, Superman, and members of the Ecuadorian and Peruvian bourgeoisie. With audience participation consisting of improvised commentary, oil provides the structure to link the episodes:

> Porque la TEXACO tiene 350.000 hectáreas
> en nuestro oriente
> y domina la prensa, la radio, la televisión
> y puede comprarlo todo
> puede comprar ministros,
> coroneles, generales, gobernadores,
> hasta gobiernos enteros
>
> Because Texaco owns 350,000 hectares
> in our eastern provinces
> and controls the press, the radio, the television
> and can buy everything
> it can buy ministers,
> colonels, generals, governors
> even entire governments.
>
> *(Grupo Ollantay 116).*

The 1990s were colored by the massive Indian protests in Quito, demonstrations that halted traffic and hobbled political negotiations for several weeks. Social sector government spending was 4.2 percent of the gross domestic product (GDP) in 1990; the national income of Ecuador's poor dropped from 6.3 percent in 1965 to 2 percent in 1993. Structural adjustments, required by the World Bank and the Inter-American Development Bank, were put in place to offset the growing external debt of 37 percent of GDP (1983) as well as a fall in per capita income of 32 percent (Treakle 221–22). The Indian uprising in 1990, coordinated by CONAIE (the National Conference of Indian Nations in Ecuador), was compared to the common IMF riots in many countries in the early years of the new century, when people take to the streets to protest upheavals in the economy and structural adjustment (Treakle 223). This uprising was enacted to protest inaction on indigenous land claims, the high cost of living, and the low prices for produce grown by the indigenous populations in rural areas. Amid protest songs and celebrations of a Catholic mass, the Indians took center stage in the print media and television by occupying the colonial Santo Domingo church. With only one elected indigenous representative in congress as of 1994, the federation of regional Indian groups were militating for change and recognition of their own cultural heritage within the larger nation of Ecuador. Indians accepted television interviews to explain their plight and

were heard (and supported in their efforts) by the *mestizos* of the city (similar to the Zapatistas in Chiapas). Now, Indians seek urban apartments, university education, and participation in the nation-state in a manner that allows for their cultural survival *with* economic enrichment.

The success of this action in 1990, which led to open negotiations with the Ecuadorian government, did not produce significant change. Additional uprisings broke out in 1992 and 1994 as the Indian movement gained strength. World leaders and activist scholars have followed with interest subsequent meetings, especially the negotiations with the World Bank in 1993, when CONAIE and Acción Ecológica (an Ecuadorian organization) challenged projects in environmentally sensitive areas, often bordering indigenous communities. From a local grassroots action, the indigenous rights movement has become a global operation, centered in Quito. A precedent-setting case against the Texaco Oil Company for the environmental destruction in Ecuador's tropical forest (the leaking of 17 million gallons of crude oil and 30 billion of toxic waste) was waged by the Cofán Indians (Treakle 258). The Cofáns, directly affected by the waste, traveled to New York City to present their case. Quito is also the headquarters for COICA (Coordinator of Indigenous Organizations in the Amazon Basin) as of 1993, so that press releases and political sound bites originate in the capitol city. From Quito, e-mail, faxes, and press interviews discuss the slaying of Indians in the Amazon by gold miners or guerrilla groups, or the tack of native opposition to the Free Trade Act. The national Indian Federation CONAIE sponsors a biennial indigenous media festival, where Latin American directors tour Indian communities to show their films and discuss the aesthetic and political message of the visual texts. In addition, the video/film entries chosen for prizes are shown in Quito to further disseminate the results of the *concurso*. Thus, within cinema, cultural representation exists both *of* and *for* the indigenous communities and often involves their cooperation with the shaping of the material. From a Romantic symbolism that once relegated the Indians to an Incan past, television cameras in Quito now focus on Indians as active participants in the political process. Indians make appointments to seek redress in conversations with World Bank representatives as well as Ecuadorian officials. Thus, the closed claustral space, once dominated by prelates, in Quito opens up to a more inclusive expanse that promises a reconfiguration of the *barrios*, and a new definition of center and periphery.

Raymond Williams, in his cultural analysis of the image of country and city, described the former as representing an image of the past and the latter as a vision of the future. More important, however, he saw the space between the two as one of tension, a place where the histories of ideas conflict: "The pull of the idea of the country is towards old ways, human ways, natural ways. The pull of the idea of the city is towards progress, modernization, development. In what is then a tension, a present experienced as tension, we use the contrast of country and city to ratify an unresolved division and conflict of impulses, which it might be better to face in its own terms" (Williams 297). David Harvey, on the other hand, centers his discussion on expansive urbanization, noting that, in the beginning of the twentieth century, only sixteen cities had populations of more than a million inhabitants. In the twenty-first century, 500 cities will shelter persons in urban concentrations of one million inhabitants and one half of the world will live in an urban environment (403). The image of the city now incorporates reference to the passing of time. The past is comprised in "distinctive layers accumulated at different phases [of] . . . chaotic urban growth engendered by industrialization, colonial conquest, neocolonial domination, wave after wave of migration, as well as real-estate speculation and modernization" (Harvey 417). The attempt to plan for the future, to answer urban desires and needs, must be done without too much violence to the past, because the city embodies collective memory, political identity, and powerful symbolic meanings that are manifest in artistic expression of literature, music, and popular culture.

The efforts to preserve the colonial past in Quito have prohibited the construction of rapid-transit tunnels in the Old City, for fear of dislodging the aging foundations built on the steep hills. Instead, a system of trolleys sweep workers and tourists into the historical complex of plazas and palaces. In the large plaza in the New City, Indian painters sell their depictions of rural life (mountains with smiling faces, shepherds herding llamas into stone corrals, and so on) and, with the money earned, they purchase a television that plays sitcoms filmed in a faraway metropolis. This is now the urban landscape that is Quito, a place where past and future are fused in the present, as cultural and political institutions construct a means of accommodating the multicultural society that fills its streets.

Works Cited

Alcedo, Antonio de. 1786–1789. *Diccionario geográfico-histórico de las Indias occidentales ó América.* Madrid: Imprenta Benito Cano.

Barrera, Isaac A. 1960. *Historia de la literatura ecuatoriana.* Quito: Casa de la Cultura Ecuatoriana.

Borchart de Moreno, Christiana. 1981. "La conquista española." *Pichincha: Monografía histórica de la región nuclear ecuatoriana.* Ed. Segundo E. Moreno Yánez. Quito: Consejo Provincial de Pichincha. 177–95.

Cevallos, Pedro Fermín. 1870–1873. *Resumen de la historia del Ecuador desde su orijen hasta 1845.* Lima: Imprenta del Estado.

Cieza de León. 1941 [1553]. *La crónica del Perú.* Madrid: Espasa-Calpe.

Espinosa Pólit, Aurelio. 1967. *Santa Mariana de Jesús, hija de la Compañía de Jesús: Estudio histórico-ascético de su espiritualidad.* Quito: La Prensa Católica.

Freire Rubio, Edgar. 1994. "Esas viejas librerías de Quito!" *Quito: Panorama urbano y cultural.* Ed. Rosángela Adoum et al. Quito: Municipio de Quito/Agencia Española de Cooperación Internacional. 103–39.

González Suárez, Federico. 1969 [1890]. *Historia general de la República del Ecuador.* Vol. 2. Quito: Casa de la Cultura Ecuatoriana. 4 vols.

Granda Noboa, Wilma. 1995. *Cine silente en Ecuador (1895–1935).* Quito: Casa de la Cultura Ecuatoriana.

Grupo Ollantay. 1974. "S + S = 41." *Bufanda del sol* 6–7: 99–117.

Hardoy, Jorge E., and Mario R. Dos Santos. 1984. "Evolución histórica de la ciudad de Quito." *El centro histórico de Quito: Introducción al problema de su preservación y desarrollo.* By Hardoy and Dos Santos. Quito: Banco Central del Ecuador/Unesco. 39–55.

Harrison, Regina. 1996. *Entre el tronar épico y el llanto elegíaco: Simbología indígena en la poesía ecuatoriana de los siglos XIX–XX.* Quito: Abaya-Yala/ Universidad Andina Simón Bolívar.

Harvey, David. 1996. *Justice, Nature and the Geography of Difference.* Cambridge, MA: Blackwell.

Herrera, Pablo. 1895–1896. *Antología de prosistas ecuatorianos.* Quito: Imprenta del Gobierno.

Icaza, Jorge. 1959 [1958]. *El chulla Romero y Flores.* Quito: Rumiñahui.

———. 1997. *Huasipungo.* Madrid: Cátedra.

Kingman Garcés, Eduardo. 1992. "Quito, vida social y modificaciones urbanas." *Enfoques y estudios históricos: Quito a través de la historia.* Serie Quito. Quito: Dirección de Planificación I, Municipio de Quito, Consejería de Obras Públicas y Transporte, Junta de Andalucía, Ministerio de Asuntos Exteriores de España, Fundación TRAMA. 129–52.

Lohmann Villena, Guillermo. 1992. "La actividad artística." *Lima.* By Juan Gunther Doering and Guillermo Lohmann Villena. Madrid: Editorial Mapfre. 111–14.

Martz, John D. 1972. *Ecuador: Conflicting Political Culture and the Quest for Progress.* Boston: Allyn and Bacon.

Mera, Juan León. 1891. *Cumandá ó Un drama entre salvajes.* 2nd ed. Madrid: F. Fé.

———. 1892. "Discurso." *El Republicano* I, 1. 3 (29 October): 13.

———. 1892. *Antología Ecuatoriana: Cantares del pueblo Ecuatoriano.* Quito: Universidad Central de Ecuador.

———. 1893. *Ojeada histórico-crítica sobre la poesía ecuatoriana desde su época más remota hasta nuestros días.* 2nd ed. Barcelona: Imprenta de J. Cunil Sala.

Minchom, Martin. 1994. *The People of Quito, 1690–1810: Change and Unrest in the Underclass.* Boulder: Westview Press.

Morán de Buitrón, Jacinto. 1955 [1697]. *Vida de Santa Mariana de Jesús.* Quito: Imprenta Municipal.

Navarro, José Gabriel. 1985. *Artes plásticas ecuatorianas.* Quito: n.p.

Ospina, Pablo. 1992. "Quito en la colonia: Abastecimiento urbano y relaciones del poder local." *Enfoques y estudios históricos: Quito a través de la historia.* Serie Quito. Quito: Dirección de Planificación I, Municipio de Quito, Consejería de Obras Públicas y Transporte, Junta de Andalucía, Ministerio de Asuntos Exteriores de España, Fundación TRAMA. 107–26.

Pareja y Diez Canseco, Alfredo. 1981. Prólogo. *Historia del reino de Quito en la América Meridional.* By Juan de Velasco. Ed. Pareja y Diez Canseco. Caracas: Biblioteca Ayacucho. x1–1.

Peralta, Evelia. 1991. *Quito: Guía arquitectónica.* Quito: I. Municipio de Quito/Consejería de Obras Públicas y Transporte, Junta de Andalucía.

Pérez, Galo René. 1972. *Pensamiento y literatura en el Ecuador (Crítica y antología).* Quito: Casa de la Cultura Ecuatoriana.

Pratt, Mary Louise. 1992. *Imperial Eyes: Travel Writing and Transculturation.* New York: Routledge.

Puyo, Fabio. 1992. *Bogotá.* Madrid: Editorial Mapfre.

Ramón Valarezo, Galo. 1992. "Quito aborigen: Un balance de sus interpretaciones." *Enfoques y estudios históricos: Quito a través de la historia.* Serie Quito. Quito: Dirección de Planificación I, Municipio de Quito, Consejería de Obras Públicas y Transporte, Junta de Andalucía, Ministerio de Asuntos Exteriores de España, Fundación TRAMA. 29–64.

Ribadeneira M., Edmundo. 1994. "La Casa de la Cultura Ecuatoriana Benjamín Carrión." *Quito: Panorama urbano y cultural.* Ed. Rosángela Adoum et al. Quito: Municipio de Quito/Agencia Española de Cooperación Internacional. 205–14.

Rodríguez Castelo, Hernán. 1980. "Una gran mística quiteña." *Literatura en la Audiencia de Quito, siglo XVII.* By Rodríguez Castelo. Quito: Banco Central de Ecuador. 377–96.

Rojas, Angel F. n.d. *La novela ecuatoriana.* Quito: Ediciones Ariel.

Rubio Orbe, Alfredo. 1954. *Legislación indígena del Ecuador.* Mexico City: Instituto Indigenista Interamericano.

Salvador Lara, Jorge. 1995. *Breve historia contemporánea del Ecuador.* Mexico City: Fondo de Cultura Económica.

———. 1992. *Quito.* Madrid: Editorial Mapfre.

Santa Cruz y Espejo, Francisco Xavier Eugenio de. 1943. *El nuevo Luciano de Quito, 1779.* Quito: Imprenta del Ministerio de Gobierno.

Terán Najas, Rosemarie. 1991. "Sinópsis histórica del siglo XVIII." *Nueva historia del Ecuador,* 4. Ed. Enrique Ayala Mora. Quito: Corporación Editora Nacional/Grijalbo. 261–301.

Treakle, Kay. 1998. "Ecuador: Structural Adjustment and Indigenous and Environmental Resistance." *The Struggle for Accountability: The World Bank, NGOs, and Grassroots Movements.* Ed. Jonathan A. Fox and L. David Brown. Cambridge, MA: M.I.T. 219–65.

Vargas, José María. 1962. *Historia de la iglesia en el Ecuador.* Quito: Editorial Santo Domingo.

Villalba Freire, Jorge. 1992a. "Ecuador: La evangelización." *Historia de la Iglesia en Hispanoamérica y Filipinas (siglos XV–XIX).* Ed. Pedro Borges. Vol. 2. Biblioteca de Autores Cristianos. Madrid: Biblioteca de Autores Cristianos/ Quinto Centenario. 445–63.

———. 1992b. "Ecuador: La Iglesia diocesana." *Historia de la Iglesia en Hispanoamérica y Filipinas (siglos XV–XIX).* Ed. Pedro Borges. Vol. 2. Biblioteca de Autores Cristianos. Madrid: Biblioteca de Autores Cristianos/Quinto Centenario. 425–45.

Weil, Thomas E., et al. 1973. *Area Handbook for Ecuador.* Washington, DC: U.S. Government Printing Office.

Williams, Raymond. 1973. *The Country and the City.* New York: Oxford.

CHAPTER 42

LA PAZ–CHUKIYAWU MARKA

Elizabeth Monasterios

It is rare that a Latin American city has maintained and culti-vated the double cultural referent on which it was built—but La Paz is one of them. Split between its Aymaran and cosmo-politan aspects, La Paz presents a cultural spectacle in which the distinct expressions of the hegemonic culture have learned to coexist with the equally distinct expressions of Aymaran and popular culture. This coexistence goes all the way back to La Paz's origins in the sixteenth century when the first conquistador of the Viceroyalty of Peru, Pedro de La Gasca, ordered the founding of a settlement that would expe-dite the construction of the route connecting La Plata, Potosí, and Cuzco (see **Figure 1**) and at the same time ordered garri-son troops to put down insurrections, whether of natives or Spaniards (the precedent having been set by Gonzalo Pizarro who laid waste to the region from 1544 to 1548), which had plagued the territory of Charcas (present day Bolivia). La Gasca was also in all likelihood influenced in his decision by the information that Atahuallpa had informed Francisco Pizarro about gold mines in the Collao, the Inca term for the region inhabited by the multi-ethnic Colla culture, whose *lingua franca* was Aymara and whose most remote ancestors, the Pukina, had constructed the first city in the Bolivian Andes: Tihuanaku (1800 BCE–900 CE).

Alonzo de Mendoza, one of the conquistadors who had participated in the military campaigns led by Francisco Pizarro, was charged with the construction of the city. The first city, Nuestra Señora de La Paz, was founded at Laja on 20 October 1548; however, the original site's isolation and inhospitable climate led to a move, and the new site chosen was the valley of Chukiyawu, a strategic location between the Altiplano, the *Yungas* (tropical valleys), and the *Valles* (temper-ate valleys), that would allow for a broad surveillance of the region and was at the same time amenable to intense com-mercial and farming activity. These advantages notwithstand-ing, Chukiyawu did present the difficulty of not fitting into the urban design specified by the functionary Juan de Matienzo (1520–1579) and adopted as model by the crown. The model stipulated that new cities were to be built on unoccupied lands in order to demarcate the Republic of the Spanish from "Indian lands." This was not possible in the case of Chukiyawu because the region had been a prosperous terri-tory belonging to the Domain of Pacajes since pre-Inca times; even during the brief Inca occupation initiated by Tupac Yupanqui (1460?–1532), the Collas region had enjoyed a degree of autonomy within the Cuzcan empire. At the time of the conquest, the Aymarans of Chukiyawu constituted an important *marka* (cultural and commercial center) governed by *Mallcus* and *Jilacatas* (political leaders of the community's interests, subsequently known by the Inca term, *Kurakas*), organized on the basis of the *ayllu* system (social and political aggregations binding the population along family lineages and lines of production). Given the economic power of the Aymara leaders, it was in the Spanish interest to establish a colonial pact in which the indigenous communities organized in highly productive *ayllus* were incorporated into the colonial project on relatively liberal terms.

Figure 1.

Drawing by Guamán Poma de Ayala depicting the foundation of Chuquiiapo (La Paz) in El primer nueva coronica y buen gobierno *(1615). (Courtesy of John P. Robarts Research Library, University of Toronto)*

Chukiyawu was bordered by the Choqueyapu River which, in addition to irrigating the region and sustaining its agricultural ecology, abounded in gold deposits. Francisco Pizarro would appropriate lands on the banks of the Choqu-eyapu under an *encomienda* (royal land grant) in order to finance his war against Almagro. In addition to mineral extraction and commerce, the most lucrative activities in the region, Chukiyawu was also known for its ceramics, gold-smith work, *keros* (wooden ceremonial vessels), textiles, and its rich oral tradition. It was in this Aymara redoubt at 3,630 meters above sea level that Alonzo de Mendoza would tem-porarily place the city. It is striking how different the colonial concept of a city was from our present notion. Silva Arze and Rossana Barragán have pointed out that in the colonial epoch, cities were considered to be a kind of assembly constituted by occupants (the conquistadors and their descendants, all over-lords of *encomiendas*) and institutions (town councils, mayoral-ties, churches, etc.), and that the site where these were placed was considered to be of minor importance. This fact helps explain why many colonial cities first established in one place were later moved "lock, stock, and barrel" to a different loca-tion (Arze and Barragán 11).

It was only toward the end of 1549 that a site, both proxi-mate to the Aymara population and at the same time separate from it, was found which was deemed suitable for the defini-tive settlement of the city. The new site lay on the opposite side of the Choqueyapu River, which would henceforth remain the natural boundary between the Republic of the Spanish and the natives (Arze and Barragán 13). There the classical checkerboard plan that was a defining characteristic of the Spanish viceregal city was reproduced: a central official plaza bordered by the city's principal public buildings, and contiguous to this complex, also in a regular pattern ordered from above, the residences of the conquistadors and founders of the city. In contrast to this urban pragmatism, the native city, like most of the pre-Hispanic *markas*, was built with refer-ence to a symbolic-religious conception of geography and urban space, in which the human construction was a manifes-tation of the sacred and symbolized the cosmic order. Thus, the physical profile of Chukiyawu was an irregular one, spreading out from the central core in undulating narrow streets which followed the topography of the terrain and on which were constructed dwellings of a circular and rectangu-lar ground plan (Gisbert 1991, 29). The consolidation of a city with pretensions to Western urbanism interrupted the cultural development of the inhabitants of Chukiyawu who believed the only way to survive in their own space was to negotiate one's Aymara *persona* with the *non-persona* of the recently arrived foreigners. Xavier Albó has pointed out the funda-mental and still current opposition in Aymara culture between *jaqi* (Aymaran person; human being with a full com-plement of sociocultural attributes) and *q'ara* (literally: *pelados*, the term for non-Aymaran persons) (6–8). Over time this cul-tural duality became more and more accentuated. Far from passively assimilating themselves into the urban and civilizing project of the conquest, the inhabitants of Chukiyawu prob-lematized that project from within, converting La Paz into a city of contrary faces and forces, historically at odds with one another.

The question that arises in this context is: How did these two culturally and historically contrary forces continue to coex-ist? Further, how did each articulate its own cultural processes? The fact that not a single colonial author has left any descrip-tion of this double development (Mesa 329) is a symptom of the scant interest the peninsular Spanish had in the cultural practices of the Andean natives. Given this absence of docu-mentation it has been thought until recently that Chukiyawu was constituted by an ensemble of native villages that lay around the periphery of the new city. Today, however, thanks to the research of Saignes Thierry, we know that Chukiyawu maintained itself as an independent population until the eigh-teenth century, even while its ties to La Paz never ceased to interfere with its historical and cultural development. Of funda-mental importance in this context were the evangelization cam-paigns sponsored by the several religious orders which, from 1548, and according to various theological methods and orien-tations, made it their duty to indoctrinate the Aymarans and to exterminate their religious rites. In this tense climate of duality

and driven by the intense agricultural activity of the region, the blossoming of the silver industry, and the development of tex-tile production, La Paz began to acquire the characteristics of a thriving commercial center. The production of coca leaves, for example, surpassed that of Cuzco and attracted the attention of merchants from the mining center of Oruro y Potosí (a town which, following the discovery of the Porco and Sumac Orco mines in 1545, had transformed itself into the most important city in the viceroyalty, with a population of approximately 160,000 inhabitants, the majority of whom were Spaniards). All this activity was to produce a dramatic increase in the urban population of La Paz which, in addition to raising the level of economic activity, fostered the emergence of a new social strata that would sustain the economic structure of the city: the native-peasant, either Aymara or Quechua, dedicated to agri-cultural production.

With the aim of more closely regulating the economic development of the territory of present day Bolivia, the *Audi-encia de Charcas* (High Court of Charcas) was established in 1558 at La Plata (founded in 1538–1539 and also known as Chuquisaca). The juridical decree establishing the court helped to consolidate the prosperity of La Paz, since from this date forward the city formed part of an apparatus of gover-nance independent of Lima and with full judicial and execu-tive powers. Cultural practices in this period reflected the double register of the reality that was La Paz–Chukiyawu–and how could they not? During the early years of the city, the cultural and artistic activity of La Paz was limited to the cele-bration of religious festivities, while that of Chukiyawu pre-served, despite the intensification of evangelization, its pre-Hispanic forms. With the appointment of Francisco Toledo to Viceroy of Peru, however, there was a change in the direction of cultural processes in La Paz–Chukiyawu. From the moment of his arrival in Lima, on 30 November 1569, Toledo, consummate strategist of the colonial system, applied himself to the pacification of the region. His most significant political achievements were the execution of Tupac Amaru in 1572 and the subsequent suppression of the native resistance movement at Vilcabamba (1536–1572). Having consolidated the colonial system in Peru, Toledo made his way to Charcas with the aim of industrializing the mining production of Potosí. During the entire Colonial period he was the only viceroy to visit the Imperial City and had a profound impact on it. Thus Eduardo Arze Quiroga rightly observes that Toledo's administration closed the cycle of the conquest and initiated the era of the colony (323). (See **Figure 2.**)

Toledo arrived at Potosí on 23 December 1572, accom-panied by a retinue of intellectuals and priests; among his train figured old conquistadors like Polo de Ondegardo, chroniclers like Pedro Sarmiento de Gamboa and José de Acosta, monks, doctors, and native interpreters. Very quickly he brought to fruition his plans for the implementa-tion of a mercury-based silver extraction system, the organi-zation of the mining industry, and the legislation of colonial life. The success of his reforms was undeniable: The mer-cury technique produced a silver of the highest standard that augmented the profits of the crown and led to the cre-ation of the Casa de la Moneda (Treasury House), the gov-ernment mint and financial regulatory institution. At the same time, he initiated a campaign of acculturation aimed at rooting out, this time by means of laws and ordinances, Andean cultural practices. Toledo failed miserably, how-ever, in his project to exterminate the Chiriguana culture,

Figure 2.

Drawing by Guamán Poma de Ayala depicting the foundation of Potochi (Potosí) in El primer nueva coronica y buen gobierno *(1615). (Courtesy of John P. Robarts Research Library, University of Toronto)*

whose on-going mobilizations were threatening the security of the mining territories. Believing that he could crush the Chiriguana resistance in the same way that he had eliminated Inca resistance at Vilcabamba, Toledo did not count on the unpredictability of an Amazonian culture that had already frustrated Inca attempts at expansion. These failures notwithstanding, Toledo's impact on the cultural development of Charcas was decisive. Under his leadership the colonial system was consolidated and the evangelization missions were invigorated, thus encouraging the religious orders to sponsor a massive campaign of church construction. These churches would later be decorated with sculptures and paintings destined to facilitate the indoctrination of the natives and bring about the eradication of idolatry. During this period, many important artists and intellectuals began undertaking the journey from Lima to Charcas while others merely exported their works, creating a truly pan-Andean intellectual and artistic traffic. The most renowned artist of this epoch to live, paint, and sculpt in La Paz was the Jesuit Bernardo Bitti (1548–1610) who lived thirty years in the Viceroyalty of Peru and was one of the founders of the Cuzco school of painting and sculpture. Bitti is renowned in art history as one of the artists, along with Mateo Pérez de Alesio (1547–1616) and Angelino Medoro (1547–1631) (neither of whom painted in Charcas), responsible for the importation

of Italian Mannerism into the Americas. Inspired by Michelangelo, Raphael, and Flemish engraving, Bitti's Mannerism led to the creation of a classic art whose painted and sculpted representations inspired the Andes with an aesthetic ideal that destabilized the coordinates of the native arts, on the one hand, and led to the creation of a school and in some cases affected architectural currents, on the other. Among his disciples, the Cuzco sculptors Pedro de Vargas and Gregorio Gamarra (fl. 1600–1630) stand out, both of whom exported their works to La Paz. Not part of the Bitti school, but also working in the Mannerist tradition, was the Jesuit sculptor Gómez Hernández Galván who, after having worked on the principal altarpiece of the Lima Cathedral, completed the San Francisco altarpiece in La Paz.

Concurrent with these masters of the European tradition, both the Copacabana school of native sculptors and the sculptor Francisco Tito Yupanqui (1540?–1608?), not part of the school and at various times based in La Plata, Potosí, and La Paz, were making a name for themselves. An apprentice of the Spanish master Diego Ortiz de Guzmán resident in Potosí, Yupanqui was educated in the Mannerist tradition, but, unlike the European sculptors, who worked in cedar, he sculpted in the Agave plant. His virgins reveal something of the unforeseen and the disquieting; they announce a rupture with the equilibrium of the classical aesthetic without, however, capturing the rhythm of the pre-Hispanic arts, so much more abstract and lacking in realistic elements. His most celebrated work, the Virgin of Copacabana, is now housed in the museum of the same name. In addition to his accomplishments as a sculptor, Yupanqui is the sole artist of the epoch for whom we have an autobiography.

Between 1630 and 1640 a radical change swept through the arts of the viceroyalty that signaled the passing of Mannerism into the Baroque (see **Figure 3**). Gisbert has pointed to the arrival of the works of Francisco Zurbarán at Lima in the 1630s as the moment when the Baroque took hold in the Americas (1996, 173). As far as Charcas was concerned, the arrival in the city around the middle of the century of a group of Sevillian sculptors and joiners who had worked on the choir-stalls of the Lima cathedral was decisive. The principal members of this group were Gaspar de la Cueva, one of the last Mannerists of the viceroyalty, and Luis de Espíndola, Luis Ortiz Vargas, and Pedro Noguera, the first exponents of the Baroque in Charcas. With the arrival of this group, both the dominance of what we might call the first generation of European artists in La Paz (including those having apprenticed under European masters), as well as the relative artistic unity of the viceroyalty under the influence of Italian and Flemish Mannerism came to an end. From this point forward two principle schools of painting rose to predominance whose aesthetic projects were polarized between those who chose to cultivate the Spanish model of the artist, as well as his themes and styles (the Potosí school, whose major figure was Melchor Pérez de Holguín, [1660?–1732]) and a second group of artists that included a number of natives and *mestizos* who introduced into their works the iconography and techniques of the native tradition (the Lake Titicaca school). The precursor of the new modality in painting was the Spanish Jesuit Diego de la Puente (1586–1663), who worked in the Americas for forty years and whose most important works have been conserved in the Chapel of the Third Order in the National Museum of Art in La Paz. One of la Puente's earliest paintings, the Juli canvas (Peru), depicts an Epiphany in which one of the three

Figure 3.

Baroque sculpture of Arcangel in Potosi. (Archive of the author)

magi, Caspar, is portrayed as an Inca king. The Lake Titicaca school grew out of the studio of the master Leonardo Flores. Under the patronage of the Bishop of La Paz, Queipo del Llano y Valdez, Flores had painted a series of massive canvases in which elements of Bitti's aesthetic (elongated faces and figures draped in evanescent raiment) and Flemish engraving (the incorporation of anecdote and particulars into the work) were combined with a theme not previously seen in the seventeenth-century painting of the colony: triumphal carriages. Inspired by the vehicles that Rubens had painted for the Convento de las Descalzas Reales in Madrid, these triumphal carriages became the motif of choice in the viceregal cities for the constitution of a visual medium especially appropriate for indoctrination and for the celebration of religious festivals such as the Corpus Christi.

The favorite themes of the priests ministering to the natives in the territory were, without doubt, the passion of Christ and eschatology–the "four last things"–the latter taken up by another master of the Lake Titicaca school contemporary with Flores, José López de los Ríos (fl. 1684). López de los Ríos's works aim to sow in the conscience of the natives a disturbing concept of the world beyond and the horrors of the Christian hell. It is hardly surprising, then, that the natives appear in these narrative canvases in the role of the sinner or penitent. In addition to the theme of the "four last things," another Baroque motif began to make its appearance in viceregal painting at this time, a representation that, given its versatility in the interpretation of Christian iconography, as well as the ambivalence with which it was invested by artists like Caravaggio, was extremely

popular in Europe: angels. As Dominique Fernández has pointed out (93–95), innovation with respect to the representation of angels was thought to be so impossible that until recently the history of art ignored the viceregal contribution to the universal angelic tradition and excluded from catalogues and exhibitions the most outstanding exponent of the viceregal tradition, the master of Potosí, Melchor Pérez de Holguín. One of the best studies of this aspect of the viceregal arts is *El retorno de los ángeles: Barroco de las cumbres en Bolivia* [1996; The Return of Angels: The Summits of the Baroque in Bolivia], edited by Teresa Gisbert, José de Mesa, Edouard Pommirt, and Dominique Fernández. On the basis of this study it can be said that the originality of the viceregal angelic tradition lay in its capacity to negotiate the adolescent asexuality traditional in angelic representations with the semantic impertinence that such representations acquired in the works of artists who, like Caravaggio, charged their depictions with a sensuality and an eroticism that transgressed the conventional standards of decorum. In the second half of the seventeenth century, a series of paintings of what Gisbert and Mesa have called angelic suite endowed with these particular characteristics began to be produced, principally in La Paz and Cuzco. Even though a number of these works were unsigned, Gisbert and Mesa have established through comparative study that they belong to the school of López de los Ríos. The iconography of these works as a whole sought to consolidate the Christian conversion crusade and thus the representations of these supernatural beings were dressed according to the roles required of them in the scripts for proselytization. In some cases they accompany the Christian pantheon and function in a more or less purely aesthetic manner; in others, they are represented as incarnations of natural phenomena (with the aim of substituting for the Andean worship of heavenly bodies); a third category is made up of veritable celestial armies battling the devil. Common to all three categories are an exquisite elegance and a coquettish demeanor that, rather than suggesting the androgyny of supernatural creatures, makes one think of Baroque transvestites (Fernández 95). The best preserved series, housed in the Calamarca Church, which is one hour outside La Paz, has been described by specialists as the hierarchic and the musket angel series. This latter group is composed of ten well-armed and defiant angel-soldiers, a veritable theological militia. The unsigned work has been attributed to the master of Calamarca, a painter related to the López de los Ríos school (see **Figure 4**).

By shrewdly associating these representations with heavenly bodies and natural phenomena (objects worshipped in the Andean religions), the motif of the angel sank deep roots into native sensibilities where it has remained ever since, integrated into one of the most surprising (both for its originality and for the semantic impertinence that it represents) native cultural practices: the dance known as the devil's promenade (*diablada*), whose epicenter today is the Oruro carnival. Tracing its origins in all probability to the sixteenth-century movement of religious resistance known as the *Taqui Onqoy* (the black masquerade), the devil's promenade dancers present in a ritualized procession the entire hierarchy of demons lead by Lucifer. A fiendish Saint Michael battles against and defeats this host, whereupon he immediately is transformed into one of them. This extraordinary confrontation between angels and demons poses the question of how, in actuality, the Christian word was interpreted; as Luis Millones points out, the question continues to lack easy answers (12).

Figure 4.

Arquebusier angel, anonymous painting in the National Museum of Art, La Paz 18th century. (Archive of the author)

Complementing the cultural panorama of the Bolivian seventeenth century was the development of Baroque architecture that, in addition to replacing construction by adobe with that of stone, also replaced the Renaissance design of the first Bolivian churches (elongated ground plan with generally a single nave) with the Baroque model of a Latin cross ground plan and cupola. These new designs augmented the demand for sculptors, since in addition to images and altarpieces, the cupolas required painstaking sculptural ornamentation. It was in this epoch that the social and artistic status of the sculptor surpassed that of the painter. With the increased demand, European masters were supplemented by local, generally *criollo* or *mestizo*, artists, such that by the eighteenth century (when La Paz experienced the apogee of its urban development, and silversmith work reached a level of accomplishment similar to that seen in painting and sculpture) the great majority of La Paz's sculptors and joiners were natives who had learned their art in the workshops of the European masters. The members of this generation of sculptors were not considered by viceregal society to be artists but rather artisans, and as a result their names have fallen into anonymity (Mesa 445). In their works, the presence of native semantic content is highly accentuated within the Christian iconography, the most obvious case being the representations of Saint James (*Santiago*) as *Illapa*, the native god of thunder.

A parallel cross-fertilization can be seen in the domain of architecture with the late seventeenth-century style that certain historians have named Andean Baroque and others the *mestizo* style (categories equally applicable to painting and sculpture). In both cases the new modality is defined by the application of characteristic local ornamentation to European forms. Examples of this style incorporating pre-Hispanic iconography are the façade of the San Francisco church in La Paz, with its two rams as horned, harelipped anthropomorphic creatures, and the Casa de los Condes de Arana (today the National Museum) with its puma-men. These images are exemplars of an art born out of a transcultural friction. We would do well, however, to problematize this notion of transculturation and to consider that such works are, in the majority of cases, more than expressions of a culture that the institutions and authorities of the times tolerated: The presence of pre-Columbian motifs in these arts is the result of the specific theological strategies employed by the religious orders in their efforts to convert the infidels and in their responses to what they considered to be the problem of idolatry. The Dominicans, for example, maintained a position of radical intolerance, stipulating that "in order to remove the possibility of their return (as it is said) to their age-old deliriums and follies, nowhere in the native villages, neither in public nor in secret, is it permitted to paint the sun, the moon, or the stars" (Meléndez 2:62). In this fiat the profound recalcitrance of the colonial institution's most conservative and punitive attitudes is brought to light; and if we recall that this directive was one of the oldest in the region, we can grasp a sense of the impact of these strictures. Evidence of this can be seen in the art and architecture in which only Christian iconography (and preferably of the Marian variety) is worthy of representation. The Jesuits, in contrast, were more shrewd and founded their evangelization project upon a rigorous study of the culture of the pre-Hispanic past; armed with this knowledge, they harnessed it to the powerful projection of the image of the Christian God. In this way Jesuit theology sanctioned the use of indigenous iconography in official art with the purpose of demonstrating that the sun, the moon, the stars, and indeed any objects of Andean worship were, first of all, creaturely subjects of the Christian God. Under the mantle of this doctrine, artists like Diego de la Puente and members of the Lake Titicaca school were able to incorporate in their works openly indigenous iconography.

Within this scenario of prohibitions and permissions, the Augustinians exercised a special form of evangelization. Formed by Renaissance humanism and theologically inspired by the allegories of Augustine's *The City of God*, they took up the idea of clothing Christian content in a native iconography that they considered pagan. The most representative Augustinian theologians, the *criollo* Brother Antonio de la Calancha (1584–1654) and the Spaniard Brother Alonso Ramos Gavilán (in the late sixteenth or early seventeenth century) promoted the identification of the sun god (the Inca deity that had superseded the Aymara Viracocha and the Tunupa Tiwanacota) with the God of Christianity, and Copacabana (the ancient Aymara deity identified with Lake Titicaca, represented as an azure lacustrine monster) with the Virgin Mary. The singular manner in which the Augustinians promoted evangelization brought them into conflict with Dominican ideology and forced the Augustinians into a radical position that hindered an assessment of the coercive basis on which they operated. Subsequent analysis has highlighted, as a sign of cultural syncretism, the subversive presence of native icons within the official arts of the colony, to the detriment of the critical analysis that reveals the subordination of those icons to a unified signifying system. More than examples of cultural syncretism (presupposing the fusion of heterogeneous religious and philosophical elements without designating the criteria of their selection) or of "cultures in contact" (Adorno 33), these representations reveal the multiple shades of nuance operative within systems of cultural oppression that, in their determination to impose authoritative semantic content, go to great (and novel) lengths, such as these sanctioned manifestations of difference, only on the condition that they can stamp them with a seal of closure. In these conditions the indigenous consciousness was subjected to distorting effects and began to develop sentiments of subaltern that were already symptoms of the process of collective deterritorialization. From this perspective, concepts such as transculturation or cultural syncretism are less than satisfactory for the interpretation of the complexity of the colonial arts. One only need observe the condition of incommensurability surrounding the artistic codes that gave form to the viceregal Baroque to appreciate the inadequacy of such concepts.

We have already seen how in the pre-Hispanic cultural logic, geography and urban planning were conceived in a manner distinct from that of the West. With the conquest and the subsequent evangelization, a new geographic and architectural conception replaced the pre-Hispanic symbolic and religious coordinates, imposing a system of allegories (a conceptual category that did not exist prior to the conquest, given that access to the sacred operated without mediation) that precluded the indigenous logic. In its confrontations with the Christian allegorical system, the indigenous symbolic system operated at a disadvantage, being both degraded by the colonial institution and transformed in the experience of its artists (many of whom were Spanish-speaking natives). What we must not lose sight of, however, is that parallel to the processes of cultural deterritorialization unleashed by the conquest, there arose collective processes of cultural reterritorialization whose tendencies were to preserve continuity with the pre-Hispanic cultural logic. The cultural practices that consolidated this continuity were diverse. We have already seen how colonial sculpture and dance problematized and on occasion subverted the semantic integrity of Christian iconography. In what follows, we will examine how the reterritorializing function operated in the realms of collective memory (strategies for the preservation and divulgence of knowledge) and in oral literature (a cultural concept somewhat distinct from how the Western tradition views literature).

It is precisely through the byways of oral literature and collective memory that one of the most beautiful love poems in the Quechua language has come down to us. Composed in the eighteenth century, when the speaking of native languages was prohibited and subject to punishment by the Inquisition, the poem known as *Manchay Puytu* relates a singular love story lived and recounted by its protagonist, a native priest from Chayanta. There are two versions of the poem, the Palma (Peruvian) version, included in Ricardo Palma's *Tradiciones Peruanas* [1900?; Peruvian Traditions], and the Lara (Bolivian) version, compiled by Jesús Lara from recitations in various native and *mestizo* villages of Bolivia and published for the first time in 1922 in a Cochabamba newspaper. Perspicaciously, Lara pointed out that, although in broad strokes these are two versions of the same poem, there is clear evidence in the Palma version of an Hispanicization that mediates access to the indigenous world (126–36). The characters in the Peruvian version, for example, all have Spanish names and conform to the generic types of Spanish tradition and legend. In contrast, in the Bolivian version these characters are all Quechuan (despite the process of miscegenation that is already operative in it) and do not conform to Western traditional archetypes. This proximity to the native world in the Bolivian version allows the contemporary reader to perceive what in the Peruvian version has been neutralized: the dexterity with which the poem articulates an amorous discourse distinct from the amorous tradition introduced by the Spanish into the Americas. In the Bolivian version, neither the protagonists (a native priest and his beloved) nor the unfolding of their relations reproduce the tradition of courtly love: Here we have the death of the beloved–the priest profanes her tomb, abducts the body, and venerates her in silence; later he extracts from her corpse a tibia, with which he fashions a *quena* (native flute) and composes the music of the *Manchay Puytu* and the verses that accompany it. Not surprisingly, the Inquisition deemed the *Manchay Puytu* an act of heresy and promulgated a ban of excommunication on all who disseminated, sang, or possessed the music or the lyrics of a poem that, already from the time of the death of the priest, was considered by the natives of Potosí to be a work of great power and beauty.

Why did the Andean sensibility perceive apparently atrocious acts as poignant and beautiful? If we distance ourselves from a humanist and Christian epistemology and draw nearer an Andean one, there are ultimately no valid motives for questioning the beauty of these acts. To the Andean subject, neither the dead nor the proximity to them constitute causes of fear or gloom. To establish contact with the unknown realms of reality has always been conceived by the Andean sensibility as a sacred activity. One of the symbolic functions of the stones, caves, and springs that are still venerated in the Andes today is precisely that of facilitating contact with those realities that are not of this world. Even the amputation of a limb from a cadaver and the use of a human bone in the fabrication of a musical instrument, possibly the most repugnant acts imaginable from a Christian point of view, finds in the Andean logic their own place and function, since for the Andean culture human fat (and it is fat that fills bones) is considered to be a source of sonority.

This quick glance at the *Manchay Puytu* gives us an idea of the state of incommensurability in which the colonial artistic codes functioned and thus of the necessity of problematizing the notion of syncretism with which such processes are often explained. Much more suggestive in this regard is the reality of the already mentioned two republics that, in a condition of incommensurability and social disequilibrium, produced distinct artistic and historical registers. When these two registers came into contact, as in the case of the so-called viceregal Baroque, the vertical hierarchy of the epoch did not allow the indigenous presence to go beyond the merely formal or flourish outside the sanction of the official arts. While native sensibility did change colonial architectural expression, the colonial logic and its perception of the indigenous world remained what they had always been. Those who remained on the outside of the distinct cultural logic of the colony were the natives, and they had to learn to negotiate the cultural duality that the colony imposed on them. Facing toward La Paz, their artistic expressions were perceived to be contributions to the viceregal arts and forms of artisanship, folklore, and popular culture; facing toward Chukiyawu, however, they constituted expressions of struggle and cultural reterritorialization that in the long run would establish pretensions to officialdom, since their relations with the power structure would no longer be in terms of dependence or tribute. Perhaps it is better to say that these artistic expressions created a tension between one cultural order that sought to dominate and another that pursued survival.

In the literary domain, La Paz in this epoch did not experience any kind of explosion of "high" literature. The most distinguished intellectuals of the time arriving at Charcas wrote or conceived their works in La Plata (a city that since its founding was an important intellectual center and counted among its attractions, since 1624, the prestigious University of San Francisco Xavier) or in Potosí. The majority of their works were published in Spain or Lima, since Charcas had no printing press until after independence. One writer, however, did stand out, a writer linked to the group of humanists and poets residing in Lima that had founded the *Academia Antártica* (one of the first academies of the viceroyalty): the Sevillian Diego Dávalos y Figueroa (1550?–1608?). While residing in La Paz Dávalos wrote his *Miscelánea austral* [Southern Miscellany], which was published in Lima in 1602 by the viceregal printer, Antonio Ricardo. Several years previously, Miguel Cabello de Balboa's *Miscelánea Antártica* [1586; Antarctic Miscellany] had appeared, and in 1608 Diego de Mexía published his *Parnaso antártico* [Antarctic Parnassus]. The critical consensus is that Dávalos's *Miscellany* is "the most authentic document of American Petrarchism" (Colombí-Monguió 11) and "not only in the Viceroyalty but in all of Hispanic America, one of the most original sixteenth-century texts" (Mesa 365). This originality stems both from its formal elements (a Petrarchan verse colloquy between the author and his wife, Francisca de Briviesca y Arellano), as well as from its discoursive elements (i.e., its treatment, in addition to the amorous theme, of many aspects of the traditions, culture, and language of the sixteenth-century inhabitants of Charcas). Another Spanish intellectual resident in the region was the Augustinian theologian, Brother Alonso Ramos Gavilán (late sixteenth century–early seventeenth century), author of the celebrated *Historia de Copacabana* [The History of Copacabana], published in Lima in 1621 and probable source of inspiration for Calderón de la Barca's *La aurora en Copacabana* [1672; The Dawn in Copacabana]. Inspired by Augustine's allegories in *The City of God*, Ramos Gavilán (and the Augustinian order in general) conceived of clothing Christian content in the robes of an indigenous iconography. With this strategy in mind, Ramos Gavilán promoted the identification of Copacabana (the ancient Aymara marsh deity) with the Virgin Mary.

The cultural flux of the epoch and the intense activity of historical documentation demanded by the colonial project also drew into its orbit figures such as Pedro Cieza de León (1518–1554), who documented his observations on the Colla culture in chapters XCIX–CIX of the First Part of his *Crónica del Perú* [Chronicle of Peru]; Bernabé Cobo (1580–1657), whose interest in the Inca period took him to Tiwanacu and La Paz in search of information for his *Historia del Nuevo Mundo* [History of the New World]; and Alonso Barba, the first scientist educated in Charcas, who, while holding the posts of Ecclesiastic Magistrate and Curate of Ulloma and

Curawara de Pacajes, wrote his *Arte de los Metales* [The Art of Metals], published in Madrid in 1640. All these works were underwritten by the civilizing argument in which the only culture of importance was that of the peninsular and *criollo* elites and the sole religion was the Catholicism promulgated by the Council of Trent. As was seen to be the case in the realms of art and architecture, the other face of the city remained silent beneath the sign of a peripheral marginality, when not neutralized in folklore and artisanship, since the inhabitants of La Paz did not hesitate to incorporate in their celebrations native musical groups for the interpretation of sacred hymns and native dancing groups to add charm to popular festivals (Arze and Barragán 45). Only rarely did the inhabitants take an interest in the artistic criteria upon which indigenous musical scales were organized or the systems of symbolic representation evident in the variety of ceramics, textiles, and dances produced in Chukiyawu. The only cultural activity in which a genuine native participation was seen was in the theater, and this was because during the time of the conquest of Peru indigenous theater (basically a collective ritual taking the form of historical-religious dramas) had reached a stage of full development.

On the basis of information gathered by Bartolomé Arsanz de Orsúa y Vela, a picture has emerged of the theatrical culture that flourished during the first years of the conquest in Potosí (see **Figure 5**). Based on a repertory of eight comedies (as these dramatic representations were called at the time), publicly performed, some in Quechua and others in mixed verse (Quechua and Spanish), these anonymous, predominantly historical-religious works were performed with the aim of conserving the memory of the past and ritually reliving the death of the Inca. Over time, the various versions and representations of the end of Inca rule gave birth to a pan-Andean dramatic genre known as the *Atawallpap wañuynin* (Beyersdorff 189), enjoying a wide dissemination in the cities of Charcas, that was subsequently completely eradicated. A number of travelers' accounts mention that in 1781 (the year of the great Tupac Amaru uprising) a Quechua drama was staged in La Paz that was later prohibited. It is almost certain that this was an *Atawallpap wañuynin* performance which, thanks to the work of Jesús Lara, we now know to be the "Tragedia del fin de Atahuallpa" ["Tragedy of Atahuallpa's Death"]. The fusion that was produced between the pre-Hispanic commemorative and funeral rites and the representations, by means of these rites, of the death of the Inca was crucial to the development of Aymara culture in the period following the Conquest. A product of this fusion, *Atawallpap wañuynin* constituted a cultural strategy with multiple resonances, since, in addition to keeping alive the pre-Hispanic theatrical traditions, it allowed its creators and participants to come to grips with the trauma of the conquest: by means of a mechanism of historical memory articulating the past—symbolized in the capture and death of the Inca on the chaotic 15 November 1532—these survivors were able to measure the impact of the present and weigh the alternatives for their future. The importance of these performances helps to explain why, in Aymara memory, the Inca past (to which they only tangentially belong) is more vivid than the properly Aymara.

It was in years of the Tupac Amaru uprising that the first generation of literate natives arose who, in addition to making possible an underground network for the dissemination of rebel information and the intense production of satires and lampoons, also began the task of transcribing and compiling

Figure 5.

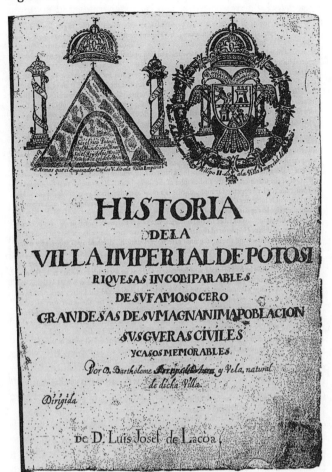

Cover page of Bartolomé Arzanz de Orsúa y Vela's Historia de la villa imperial de Potosí ms. 1736?. (Courtesy John P. Robarts Research Library, University of Toronto)

native texts, among which figured "The Death of Atahuallpa." Perceiving the enormous influence that the theater exercised in the social and cultural life of their Andean subjects, the Christian authorities adopted theatrical forms as an instrument of indoctrination. What they did not perceive, however, was the ritual function that the dramatic arts exercised in the pre-Hispanic cultures, the fact that, far from being merely a spectacular pastime, these performances dramatized the most transcendent events of life (Cáceres Romero 81; 158). With the eradication of these performances, the dramatic structure of the native theater survived by transforming itself into dance forms and dramatized fables; these same structures can be observed today in popular festivals such as the Lord of the Great Power festival, in the Entry of the Carnival, or in various manifestations of the oral tale.

With the eradication of the indigenous theater, the Colonial government instituted two modes of representation that would make the differences between the city of the Spanish and the Indian lands more pronounced: the parish theater, directed at the native population and inspired by Spanish medieval religious-allegorical theatrical forms, and the Golden Age theater, based on models established by Lope de Vega and Calderón de la Barca, and directed toward the Spanish, *criollo*, and *mestizo* populations. While the former was publicly performed in the vestibules and cemeteries of the native parishes, the latter necessitated the construction of *corrales de comedias* (open-air theaters) and *coliseos* (coliseum-like theatrical houses). The works staged there were generally of Spanish provenance and thus had the effect of greatly diminishing the possibilities of a local or *criollo* dramaturgy. This situation notwithstanding, a play written by Brother Diego de Ocaña (1565?–1608), *Comedia de Nuestra Señora de Guadalupe y sus milagros* [The Miracles of Our Lady of Guadalupe] was staged in Potosí in 1601 to great acclaim. Although many critics have categorized the play as an example of the religious theatrical genre then known as the miracle play, it would be much better described as a historical divinity drama, since it lacked those allegorical elements that would make it part of the mystery play tradition (Cáceres Romero 153; Mesa 357).

In order to complete this cultural panorama, we ought to take into account that educational instruction at this time was initially in the hands of the Jesuits and did not include the education of girls (which only began in 1774). In the realm of the arts, these same years saw the decline of the Baroque sculpture tradition, largely because the excessive demand for religious sculpture gave rise to industrialized workshops in which over time the sculpting of wood became a commercialized and artisanal practice lacking in artistic finesse. Analogously, Baroque styles experienced a loss of artistic prestige and were eventually displaced; in time they would be only practiced by *mestizo* and indigenous artists painting in the villages of the Altiplano. Liberated from what they had come to consider an art form in a state of decadence, the elites of La Paz adopted with enthusiasm the neo-Classical models that arrived with the reforms (1759–1788) of Carlos III. In 1767 the expulsion of Jesuits from the Spanish empire came as part of these reforms, with the explicit aim of separating the Church from the state, but it produced serious financial and educational problems in the Spanish American colonies. In La Plata it had the devastating effect of virtually paralyzing the San Francisco Xavier University, considered one of the most distinguished in the Americas. The colonial administration took advantage of this event to create an institution that would expand the ideology of the Enlightenment and at the same time function as a center for juridical studies. The new institution was founded in La Plata in 1776 with the name of Academia Carolina and was to become the *alma mater* of the enlightened elite of intellectuals and politicians who with time would become the intellectual leadership of the first Independence movement in Charcas which was proclaimed in La Plata on 25 May 1809. As Thibaud observes, this movement marks the beginning of a cultural, social, and political modernity which, although it opposed established sovereignty, did not offer anything more, since its members were reformers and supporters of political modernity, rather than precursors of independence and would, in the end, make up the ruling *criollo* elite of Chuquisaca and La Paz (40–56).

The second event that marked the cultural development of La Paz–Chukiyawu was the already mentioned native rebellion of 1781, without a doubt the most destabilizing episode of the eighteenth century and one that transformed La Paz into the command center of the rebels. Initially, the rebellion was led by José Gabriel Condorcanqui (Tupac Amaru) and Micaela Bastida in Cuzco, and the brothers Katari in Chayanta, to the north of Potosí. Approximately two million natives, in the majority Aymarans, rose up against the viceroyalty demanding the elimination of the *mita* (system of forced labor), the *corregimiento* (district governance of Indians), and the *repartimiento* (system of land distribution), the three institutions most directly responsible for the destruction of the integrity of the indigenous communities. Petitions were made as well for the creation of an indigenous government with *criollo* participation. And in fact, during the year of the insurrection, a native government did rule, the first independent government in Spanish America. In March 1781 the rebellion was put down by treachery, and on May 18 Tupac Amaru and his principal collaborators were executed in Cuzco. Almost immediately a new rebellion was unleashed in La Paz under the leadership of Julián Apaza (Tupac Katari) and Bartolina Sisa which, from its stronghold in Alto Potosí (the center from which the rebel armies of Cuzco and La Paz were coordinated), mobilized 40,000 Aymarans for the most spectacular sieges in the history of Charcas, the first lasting 109 days and the second seventy-three days. During the fighting (which lasted for six months and claimed 4,000 casualties), Katari's army devastated a large part of Chukiyawu where the confrontations took place, as well as large portions of La Paz abutting the walls that the magistrate Tadeo Diez de Medina had ordered constructed to defend the city. By the end of 1781 the Royalists had succeeded in suppressing the rebellion. Katari was betrayed—and quartered on 13 November 1781, in the plaza of Peñas (Ayo-Ayo). According to oral tradition his final words were: "Nayaw jiwtxa nayjarusti waranqa waranqanakaw kuttanipxani" ("Today I die, but tomorrow I will return transformed into thousands").

The physical and emotional impact of the insurrection left a profound impression on the historical perception that each of the protagonists retained of themselves. La Paz, which in these years based its identity on a consolidated *criollo* elite that had reached the acme of its splendor, had to confront its own fragility and begin reconstruction. In doing so, its *criollo* inhabitants reaffirmed themselves as the authentic lords of a city that had successfully defended itself against the ethnic attack of a "barbarous paganism." As a result of the insurrection, the prohibitions against indigenous theatrical performances remained strictly in effect and a period of the presentation of eulogies and encomia of the heroes of La Paz began. In the same year as the siege, the scientist Pedro Nolasco Crespo (1734–1807?) penned a jejune little play praising the exploits of the brigadier Don Sebastián Segurola which was performed in the Plaza Mayor under the title: "Encomium of the exploits of the Brigadier Don Sebastián Segurola, composed by way of *epitalamio*, by Don Pedro de Nolasco Crespo." A portrait of this defender of La Paz, accompanied by his wife María Josefa Ursula Rojas, still hangs in the Casa de Murillo Museum. Also related to the siege of La Paz, a famous painting of the city was completed in 1781; with the loss of the original, only the nineteenth-century copy made by Florentino Olivares has been conserved. For its part, Chukiyawu acquired a modern consciousness of its colonial status out of which it forged a logic of defiance still operative in Aymara cultural production and Aymara struggles for vindication (see Silvia Rivera Cusicanqui). In accordance with this logic, life is a permanent process of struggle whose major historical referent is the image of Tupac Katari. Over the years this image would be superseded by the emblematic figure of Atahualpa, and the notion of a historical reference point would constitute the zero degree of what Rivera Cusicanqui calls the long memory of the peasantry, which is to say, the vivid recollection of their anti-Colonial struggles.

With the restoration of the Colonial government, La Paz ceased to be a municipality run by magistrates and acquired the status of *Intendencia*, an institution of governance permitting greater autonomy within the viceroyalty and ruled over by a governor. At the end of the eighteenth century, when the productivity of Potosí and its satellite cities began to wane, La Paz recovered its status as the most important city in the *Audienicia de Charcas* (the administrative region of Charcas High Court) which, since 1776, had become part of the Viceroyalty of Río de la Plata. A document held in the National Historical Archives of Madrid (item # 21391) records that in 1808 during the Napoleonic Wars, Buenos Aires received one million pesos of patriotic aid: of these 100,000 from La Paz; 100,000 from Potosí; 50,000 from La Plata; 50,000 from Cochabamba; 30,000 from Córdoba; and 16,000 from Paraguay (Durand Flores 456). It was in this epoch that one of the greatest periods of civil and religious architecture was recorded, known as the neo-Classical age. It was also in these years that the scientific work of Nolasco Crespo, who had become a member of the "Amantes de París" Academic Society (founded in Lima in 1792), became known. Among his most important works were those published in the *Mercurio Peruano* (his discourse on Tihuanacu archeology, his study of quinine, and his "Dissertation on the Coca") and his meteorological and astronomical studies ("Letter on the Flux and Reflux of the Ocean" and "Letter against Copernicus"). In sum, the works of Crespo constituted the most distinguished scientific labor of the Bolivian eighteenth century and anticipated the enlightened conservatism and traditionalism that would characterize its nineteenth-century culture.

If the façade of La Paz for its intellectuals was one of cultural excellence and brilliance, internally, however, an acute process of decomposition was underway that would result in a political about-face for the *criollo* elites and sixteen years of Independence wars. In this climate, the viceregal arts and the work of its last master of painting, Diego del Carpio, were to stagnate. In contrast, there flourished literary lampoons and satires (including the *décima*, a ten-line stanza) and other literary forms demanding little in the way of aesthetic sophistication other than the ludic expression of open mockery of the Spanish authorities. Let me quote two examples of these satires, from Cáceres Romero's *Nueva Historia de la literatura boliviana* [1990; New History of Bolivian Literature] (III: 31):

Chaquetita verde
llena de botones
ya viene la muerte
para los chapetones
Ladronazo chapetón
os perderán las riquezas;
preparad vuestras cabezas,
ya viene la revolución

You with the green frock-coat
full of buttons
here comes the reaper
for Spaniards a-knocking
Thieving Spaniards your time is done
hold on to your britches
they'll strip you of riches,
now that the revolution has come

In the early months of 1809 a text known as *Diálogo entre Atahuallpa y Fernando VII en los Campos Elíseos* [Dialogue between Atahualpa and Fernando VII in the Elysium Fields] began circulating. This text was attributed to Bernardo

Monteagudo (1785–1825), one the most distinguished intellectuals who had graduated from Academia Carolina and the leader of the first independence uprising in Charcas which broke out in La Plata on 25 May 1809. In this parodic and intertextual work, the spirit of Atahualpa, who has been enjoying *las delicias francesas* (French delectations) for more than 300 years, encounters Fernando VII, wandering aimlessly and bewailing the Napoleonic invasion of his kingdom. The two have-nots strike up a conversation in which Atahualpa with irrefutable arguments invites Fernando VII to abdicate: "Off to the dead with you Fernando, adios! I, like Montezuma and the other kings of the Americas, am anxious to dispatch the good news that my subjects are already on the point of proclaiming 'Vive la liberté!'" Like many of the cultural productions of the Charcas tradition, this text forms part of a literary corpus that has not been studied with the attention it deserves.

During this period, social distinctions that had been in formation for over 200 years gave rise to tense differentiations of caste and ideology between the peninsular Spanish, the rich and poor *criollos*, and the *mestizos* (these latter considered by colonial society to be naturally inferior, and as such exempt from taxation and forced labor in the Colonial public works projects). The clash between these distinct social sectors, aggravated by the power vacuum that resulted from the Napoleonic invasion of the Iberian peninsula (1806–1807) and the recent independence campaigns in Haiti and the United States, were the preconditions that made the *criollo* revolt led by Pedro Domingo Murillo possible. Educated in Cuzco and Chuquisaca, Murillo had actively participated in the Spanish defense of Irupana during the native uprising of 1781 and had distinguished himself as a militarily savvy commander. On 16 July 1809, backed by a sector of the local *criollo* elite, Murillo made public his demand for Spanish-American independence in the name of Fernando VII. The paradox of imagining independence without renouncing the monarchy can be understood in two ways: either as a rhetorical formula for the legitimation of the movement or (and this appears more convincing) as a denunciation of the *criollo* incapacity of conceiving liberty in nonelitist and nonconservative terms. In fact, the maneuver found no echo in the villages of Chukiyawu, who considered Murillo an enemy. It is also to be supposed that news of English and U.S. financial backing for the new Independence movements had reached the ears of the (literate) Murillo.

Considered the first declaration of independence by a Spanish colony (despite the fact that months earlier, on May 25, a similar uprising had been unleashed in Chuquisaca), Murillo's revolt was rapidly suppressed by an army dispatched from Cuzco under the command of José Manuel de Goyeneche. In 1810 Murillo and his principal collaborators were condemned to the gallows. Murillo's residence in La Paz has been preserved as a museum, an exquisite neo-Classical building endowed with a sophisticated library that, considering the difficulties of acquiring books in this epoch, tells us much about Murillo's intellectual formation and well-to-do position in Colonial society. With the collapse of the urban *criollo* revolt led by Murillo, new foci of rebellion began to break out across Charcas. These movements of a largely rural character identified themselves as those of independence guerrillas. Unlike the leaders of 1809, the guerrilla leaders were *criollos* who had established political alliances with the *mestizos* and the natives. This situation became problematic in 1810 when, following their independence from Spain, the revolutionaries of Buenos Aires initiated an independence campaign in the territory of Charcas (which they called Alto Perú) in the belief that by this means they could wrest control of Potosí from Lima. To carry out that campaign the Argentines formed four reserve armies (that were later systematically routed) whose interests would come into conflict with those of the Charcan guerrillas, and especially with the interests of figures like Manuel Ascencio Padilla, Juana Azurduy de Padilla, and Ignacio Warnes, who had identified their struggle with that of the colonized. It was out of the guerrilla army of the Padillas that the most notable Quechua poet of the late eighteenth and early nineteenth century would arise: Juan Wallparrimachi Mayta (1793–1814). Systematically excluded from the anthologies and textbooks of Independence poetry, Wallparrimachi was not only a great poet, but he was the last of his generation who knew how to harness the Quechua lyric sense and give it expression in language, probably because he understood that the Quechua *aqoyraki* (misfortune) was inexpressible in the language of the conquerors. With Wallparrimachi an important cycle of Quechua poetry comes to an end; henceforward, from the Independence era up until the 1930s, the distorting effects of the Romantic aesthetic would dominate Bolivian poetry.

Velasco Flor (Manuel Ascencio Padilla's biographer and the copyist of two of Wallparrimachi's poems) has noted that for a long time Wallparrimachi's poetry lived in the collective memory, and that as late as the early 1870s his *yaravíes* were still being recited (in Lara 124). Lamentably, only twelve of Wallparrimachi's amorous poems have been conserved, the two that Velasco Flor recorded and ten recorded by José Armando Méndez. In 1947 Jesús Lara transcribed and compiled these poems in a volume entitled *La poesía quechua* [Quechua Poetry]. The excellence of Wallparrimachi's verse is evident in the following selection, from the final verses of "Imaynallatan atiyman" "("Why do I live now?"). It is to be noted that in the Quechuan amorous discourse, the loss of the beloved is not expressed in terms of abandonment, betrayal, or death (as it is in Spanish verse), but rather in what we may call an Andean sensibility in which the idea of amorous misfortune rends the subject because it alienates him from the earth, the water courses, and the trees:

Urpillay, ¿maypitaj kanki?
¿Ima wayq'o ima jallp'ataj
Ima sach'a, ima qaqátaj
sh'ikata pakaykusunki,
Nawiymanta suwasunki?
Qanllapi ñuqa yuyani
Qanmanta waqaspa kani.
¡Urpillay, kutínpuy ari!
Manachus janpunki chayri,
¿Imapajñátaj kausani?

Paloma mía, ¿dónde estás?
¿Qué tierra o qué barranco,
qué arbol o qué peñasco
de este modo te esconde
Y a mis ojos te roba?
Tú no te apartas de mi pensamiento
Y eres la causa de mi desventura
¡Paloma mía, vuelve!
Y si no has de volver,
¿Para qué vivo ya?

My dove, where are you now?
What soil or riverbank,
what forest or steep crag
conceals you in this way
and robs my eyes of you?
You cannot leave my thoughts,
Cause of my misfortune.
Come back, my dove, come back!
And if you must not return,
Why do I live now?

The Hispanicizing preconceptions of the Bolivian nineteenth-century elites, the Romantic vogue, and the arrogance with which these elites excluded Aymarans and Quechuans from the *criollo* cultural development, meant that the finest indigenous poet of the Independence generation was neither recognized nor integrated into the history of Bolivian literature. Gabriel René Moreno, for example, omitted Wallparrimachi from his *Estudios de literatura Boliviana* [1955; Studies in Bolivian Literature]. In contrast, the Peruvian poet Mariano Melgar (1790–1815), who wrote *yaravíes* in Spanish and submitted the singularity of the Quechuan lyric to the exigencies of Spanish verse, was canonized as an Independence poet and anthologized in works like Menéndez y Pelayo's *Antología* [Anthology], Angel Flores's *La literatura de la América Española* [Literature of Spanish America], Carrilla's *La poesía de la Independencia* [Independence Poetry], and Pedro Henríquez Ureña's *Corrientes literarias en Hispanoamérica* [Hispano-American Literary Currents].

Another text systematically excluded from the literary canon is the recently discovered (by Gunnar Mendoza) "Diario histórico de todos los sucesos ocurridos en las provincias de Sicasica y Ayopaya durante la guerra de la independencia americana, desde el año 1814 hasta el año 1825" ["Daily Chronicle of the Events that Took Place in the Provinces of Sicasica and Ayopaya during the War of Independence, 1814–1825"] by José Santos Vargas (1796–1853), the only known writer-guerrilla of the epoch. Santos Vargas's account has added to the few details known about the life of Juan Wallparrimachi and was published by the Siglo XXI editorial house in 1982 under the title: *Diario de un comandante de la independencia americana* [The Diary of a Bolivian Independence Commander].

It is hardly surprising that the consolidation of the indigenous Independence struggle went hand in glove with the acquisition of a complex historical consciousness of native cultural subaltern. The climate of political uncertainty that had created the guerrilla war became more acute with the wave of indigenous attacks on urban and rural centers. Up until this time these sectors of the population had only marginally integrated into the struggles for independence, and with these campaigns they began to act on their own behalf. As a result of this situation La Paz was transformed into the center of political and military agitation: It was the target of attacks by local Aymarans and of reprisals on the part of the Royalists who considered it to be in full insurrection against the Crown. In June 1811 an Aymara rebellion broke out, similar to the Tupac Amaru rebellion of 1781, which *criollo* collective memory had characterized as a revolt of the Indians and the *cholos* (half-breeds), a term used to designate those natives established in the cities and competent in the use of Spanish. In November Viceroy Abascal dispatched from Cuzco an army of 4,000 fusiliers and 30,000 Quechuans that would be responsible for one of the bloodiest exploits in the history of the city.

In 1816 both the guerrilla movements and the distinct indigenous insurrections suffered decisive defeats. Almost concurrently, Simón Bolívar (1783–1830) consolidated the Independence struggle in Venezuela, and Argentina declared independence from Spain; these events opened the era of the great military campaigns that would make Charcas an independent republic governed by its *criollo* elite. On 6 August 1825, with the consent of Antonio José de Sucre, the liberator of Charcas and hero of Ayacucho, the independence of the new republic was proclaimed in La Plata to the nations of the old world and the new. La Plata, also known at that time as Sucre, would be the capital from 1825 to 1899. Passing over the recommendations of Bolívar, who was more in favor of the territory joining with either Peru or Argentina, the creation of a republic satisfied the demands of the local *criollo* elites. In an act of compensation to the liberator they named the new republic Bolivia. For several months Bolívar was in charge of the government, but in actual fact the first president was Sucre who administered the new country from 1825 to 1828.

The first year of independence witnessed the publication of Bolivia's first newspapers, *El Cóndor de Bolivia* and *La Gaceta de Chuquisaca* and, at the request of Bolívar, Simón Rodríguez's arrival in Bolivia to take charge of the first Bolivian national cultural project: the "Model School." Convinced that neither monarchy nor republicanism suited every time and every place and that the most appropriate course for Spanish America would not be to import European or North American notions, but rather to develop original political and sociological solutions to its challenges, Rodríguez advocated the institution of governors for life while the country undertook the transformation of its people. The "Model School" program, incorporating universal education and the abolition of social differences, was designed to facilitate the attainment of these ideals. Rodríguez was ignorant, however, of the fact that ideological interests opposed to these projects already formed the basis of Bolivian society. With the foundering of the "Model School" project, a Liberal republican form of political governance, rooted in mercantilist ideas and directed by the generals and military leaders of the Wars of Independence, was instituted and remained in power until after the Pacific War (1879). This political system, which historians have called the *caudillo* or military strongman regime, was characterized by continuous military agitation and by the fact that political intrigue was the sole means of access to power. It should be noted that the militarism of these years was, in many cases, provoked and bolstered by the constant aggressions of Peru, Chile, and Argentina that obliged the government to divert a large percentage of the national budget to the maintenance of the army.

In this context of instability, the official national culture was affected in a number of ways. Perceived as practices proper to the old order, the painting and sculpture traditions of the colony gave way to the new tradition of national heroic portraiture, although colonial cultural processes continued unabated in terms of neo-Classicism in architecture and Romanticism in literature. Under the mantle of this latter movement a love poetry and a heroic epic tradition flourished whose most representative exponents were Ricardo José Bustamante (La Paz, 1821–1886), Néstor Galindo (Cochabamba, 1830–1865), María Josefa Mujía (Sucre, 1812–1888), Manuel José Tovar (Oruro, 1831–1869), and Adela Zamudio (1854–1928). Adela Zamudio was the first woman to venture into the patriarchal preserve of critical writing, but her work has not been recognized by literary historians. In contrast, the literary text that has been recognized from this period is the novel *Juan de la Rosa* (1885) by the Cochabamba writer Nataniel Aguirre (1843–1888) who, from the perspective of a soldier in the War of Independence, gave foundational status to a national imaginary which he proposed as a model for the nation. Of course, this national imaginary endorsed the interests of a *criollo-mestizo* liberalism as the national project and denied any place to women or to the Indian majority. Thus it was that the first national Bolivian narrative came forth as an intellectual exercise completely divorced from Bolivian reality in its pursuit of the ideals of the French Enlightenment.

Politically, the Republic maintained the colonial policy of taxing the natives, and the elites began soliciting foreign capital in order to reactivate the silver mines which, with Bolívar's decree eliminating the *mita* in 1825, had been facing serious financial difficulties. All in all, the triumphalist *criollo* elites wasted no time in tackling the challenge of governing a country in economic crisis (brought on by sixteen years of war and the collapse of the silver mining industry) and composed in its majority by the human groups they least appreciated: the natives and the *mestizos*. Sergio Almaraz (1928–1968) has described this situation with great precision: "the Republic was proclaimed on the foundation of a vacuum: its creators were all dead. The *criollos* thus found themselves in a country populated by a great mass of wretched and impoverished Indians, over whom they had total dominance, since the Indians by and large spoke no Spanish, but for whom they felt anything but affinity" (Almaraz 1969, 9).

It is important to point out that during the years the capital of the republic was located in Chuquisaca; the La Paz elites continued to exercise their traditional role of protagonist in the history of the country, since the control that they enjoyed over the Altiplano also made them proprietors of the nation's principle source of income: the silver mines. This financial predominance allowed La Paz to acquire from very early on a progressive hegemony over the other regions of the country and to shape itself as the principal modern city of Bolivia. Physically, the dual character of the urbanization that during the Colonial period had separated the Republic of the Spanish from Chukiyawu was in the process of disappearing, as La Paz expanded toward its peripheries. Socially and culturally, however, the difference between the whites and the natives, that *criollo* history would legitimize years later with social Darwinist arguments for the scientific ratification of indigenous inferiority, grew ever more pronounced. Only toward the middle of the twentieth century did political campaigns and cultural decolonization reverse–partially, and with great controversy–this state of affairs. In order to understand these processes, it will be necessary to revisit the conditions under which Chukiyawu was incorporated, first into the Liberal-Republican state, and later into the 1952 state.

The first congresses of the Bolivian Republic paid homage to the native communities and honored their titles to their property largely because the peasant merchant sector was the most productive in the new nation. However, as production decreased and the revenues from native taxation grew smaller, the political Liberals gained the upper hand, which meant a loss of lands and cultural integrity for the natives and the advent of a pre-capitalist market economy for the *criollos*. The Liberal republicanism of the elites never attempted to include the indigenous population in its political projects, almost exclusively oriented toward protecting the *criollo* economy by stabilizing silver production. This politics of exclusion found one of its most telling expressions in the first national census (taken in 1846 during the presidency of General José Ballivián) which reckoned the national population at 1.4 million inhabitants, with an estimated 700,000 "ungovernable Indians" (Klein 122). The various cultural initiatives undertaken in La Paz during the years of Republican government also indicated the extent to which these "ungovernable Indians" would remain excluded from the national cultural project, since the high culture that was disseminated by the urban literary societies and which intensified with the arrival of the wave of émigrés from the Rosas dictatorship in Argentina never imagined that it would reach or penetrate to the native population. One of these immigrants, Bartolomé Mitre (1821–1906), was the author of the first novel published in Bolivia, *Soledad* [1847; Solitude].

The interventions of Major-General Andrés de Santa Cruz during the decade 1829–1839 were decisive to the cultural development of La Paz. Santa Cruz sponsored the establishment of the Colegios de artes y ciencias (1831), the Universidad de San Andrés (1831), the Teachers' Training College (1835), the Teatro Municipal (1837), and the Municipal Library (1838), the completion of the Cathedral (originally designed by Manuel de Sanahuja but finished by the French architect Philippe Bertrés in 1843), and the construction of a Presidential Palace (1845), as well as numerous sumptuous residences constructed in a neo-Classical style that, while still retaining traces of the Baroque, had given up the *mestizo* element of the earlier era. Once again, the natives remained excluded from the benefits that these institutions offered the public. Even the Sucre Street market in La Paz, designed for the use of the rural peasantry and *mestizo* merchants, was oriented toward providing convenience to the metropolitan elites. Only in 1882 were the first government-sponsored indigenous schools established, although it must be stressed that these were intended to instruct the natives in a language that was not theirs and to civilize them in accordance with equally foreign pedagogical models, based as they were on the colonial theological and scholastic traditions. Paradoxically, as museums began to be instituted and constructed, an interest in the archeological study of pre-Hispanic societies was awakened. The Municipal or Public Museum, built in 1838, bears the inscription *Ayam Aru* (ancient word) above its entry and exhibits in its exposition halls archeological artifacts in the form of relics. What remained unacknowledged in institutions such as this was the fact that the mass of "ungovernable Indians" populating Chukiyawu descended in a direct line from that ancient word which *criollo* society could only incorporate into itself in the form of a curiosity from the past.

Unlike other Latin American countries, where the introduction of free market economics was intimately associated with the diffusionist logic of a Romantic civilization in alliance with the economic interests of the advanced capitalist nations, in Bolivia the free market system was the product of the concessionist policies that Melgarejo adopted with respect to the exploitation of the recently discovered guano and saltpeter deposits. Anxious for revenues with which to offset the deficit in national expenditures, Bolivia signed disastrous treaties with Peru (1865), Chile (1866), Argentina (1868), and Brazil (1868). In each of these documents Bolivia ceded territory (either as a concession or simply as a gift) and as a result lost a portion of its sovereignty. In the treaty with Chile, for example, Chile was not only entitled to the free use of Bolivian ports, but her exports and imports remained tariff-free. In part owing to the compliant nature of these concessions and in part as a symptom of its own economic expansionism, Chile developed a proprietary sentiment over certain Bolivian territories that provoked, in 1879, the Pacific War in which Bolivia, Chile, and Peru were embroiled in dispute.

Parallel with these events, the national elites experienced a profound transformation as a result of the diffusion of positivism and experimentalism in the natural sciences. In La Paz the outstanding figure was Agustín Aspiazu (1817–1897), author of close to 100 works, many of them published after the Pacific War, including *Curso de Física* [1858; Lectures in Physics], *Curso de Medicina Legal* [1862; Lectures in Forensic Medicine], and *Teoría de los Terremotos* [1868; Theory of Earthquakes]. The first center of positivist diffusion in the country was the Literary Circle (1876); the Circle's journal published the works of the German scientist Tadeo Haenke (1761–1817) who had directed one of the first European expeditions to the Spanish colonies, aiming to analyze their sources of wealth and thereby give a positivist basis to the policy of European expansionism. In 1877 this journal published *Haeckel y la teoría de la evolución en Alemania* [Haeckel and the Theory of Evolution in Germany], an event that marked the beginning of Darwinism in Bolivia. In these same years foreign geologists and paleontologists began the first archeological excavations in Tiwanacu; the first geographical dictionaries were published; and the Jesuits inaugurated the Colegio San Calixto, equipped with a meteorological, geographical, and seismic observatory.

Within this free market economic regime and positivist cultural climate, there was clearly no place for the natives or *mestizos* (*cholos*). The former remained relegated to the status of tax-paying peasants, while the latter were stereotyped as commercial retailers. The first serious attempt to confiscate native lands was made by Melgarejo. Realizing the importance that the urban merchants had acquired with the development of the mines, Melgarejo conceived the idea of confiscating indigenous lands in order to sell them to whites (the term applied to the *criollos* and those *mestizos* who aspired to form part of the social group that since the census of 1877 had begun to define itself as Spanish American), so that they could turn them into large profitable farms and in the process constitute a social sector that up until that time had not existed: the large estate landowners. The still embryonic condition in which the land-owning interests found themselves, combined with massive resistance on the part of the indigenous communities, hindered the realization of such projects.

Concurrent with these events, the first generation of literate La Paz intellectuals was taking shape, composed of *criollos*, *mestizos*, and some natives such as José Vicente Pasos Kanki (1779–1852?), one of the first journalists in Spanish America and the only native to have acquired the degree of Doctor and Professor at the University of Charcas. A fervent defender of the Republican system of government, Kanki got his start as a journalist with the *Gaceta de Buenos Aires* and became an active participant in the political life of Argentina. Among his many accomplishments were his membership in the New York Historical Society, his translations of the Independence Act and the four Gospels into Aymara, and his appointment as Consul-General of Bolivia in London during the Santa Cruz administration. Educated in the Rousseauistic

encyclopedism of the French Enlightenment and in traditional scholasticism, the members of this first generation of intellectuals lived and studied in England, France, and the United States, were well-versed in Greek and Latin, and were active participants in political life. When they took an interest in the natives and native culture, however, they did so from a kind of distorting, idealized, "noble-savage" point of view that impeded them from perceiving the sociocultural complexity of the indigenous reality. Yet, as a whole, they were persons of manifest brilliance and originality. Emeterio Villamil de Rada (1804–1880), for example, attempted to prove in his book *La lengua de Adán* [1888; The Tongue of Adam] that the original paradise was located in Sorata, that Tiwanacu was Babel, and that Aymara was the universal language. This Christianization of the pre-Hispanic past betrayed the epoch's insensitivity toward the alterability of the indigenous culture. Perhaps the sole intellectual of the nineteenth century to present a perspective distinct from the dominant conception was the Aymaran landowner Isaac Tamayo, friend and political colleague of Melgarejo. In his sociocritical essay, *Habla Melgarejo* [1836; Melgarejo Speaks], Tamayo addressed the problem of the Aymarans in a rhetoric that, while tinged with respect, was also in its fundamentals racist and paternalist, denying the natives the possibility of being historical subjectivities and bearers of their own culture. According to Tamayo, Bolivia was "a nation populated by the most energetic, strongest, restrained, warlike race, the race most suited to civilization and the most ready to assimilate the great knowledge of human progress" (53). The Pacific War (1879) temporarily placed political developments and the cultural process on hold and brought Bolivian politicians face to face with a species of national tragedy: The nation was bankrupt and the only viable sector of the economy, the guano and saltpeter deposits, were now Chilean possessions. With her rout in the Pacific War, Bolivia lost her only seacoast, becoming a landlocked nation, and the course of Bolivian history changed irrevocably.

Immediately following the defense of the 200 Indians involved in the Mohoza uprising, the positivist jurist Bautista Saavedra (1870–1939) became interested in researching the pre-Hispanic Aymara past in order to understand the motives for what he called Aymaran moral and psychological decadence. In order to carry out this research, Saavedra narrowed his focus to a study of the indigenous system of property. The results of his investigations were published in an essay entitled *El Ayllu* [1903; The Community], in which he concluded that the Andean system of property was the residue of the Bolivian society that would have to be exterminated. *El Ayllu* announced, as it were, the consolidation of Liberal positivism as the discourse rationalizing the status quo reality, and with it the country began, for the first time, to be conceived in terms of a modern nation-state. It was in this ideological climate that the natives began to be perceived as a destabilizing element within society that would either have to be integrated or destroyed in the name of progress. The same Liberal rhetoric declared native assimilation into "civilization" to be unviable on account of native intellectual feebleness, the costs that their education would incur, and the simple expediency of their extermination (Albarracín 246). Paradoxically, in the same years that these measures were being advocated, the country continued to be characterized by a large indigenous population (51 percent, at that time), overwhelmingly rural in character (more than 70 percent). The majority of these natives were speakers of Aymara or Quechua who had had, since the Declaration of Independence, no access to public schooling whatsoever. Although speaking the official language (Spanish), the bulk of the white and *mestizo* population was not that different: They too were largely illiterate, since public education had never functioned in an effective manner and the recently established private high schools were only open to the children of the well-to-do. And since the political elites had established that literacy was a precondition for exercising one's right of universal suffrage, practically 80 percent of the population was disqualified from political participation in elections. In the period following the Pando negotiations (during which time Bolivia lost the Acre War to Brazil), the Liberal ideology constituted itself as the national hegemonic discourse. The undisputed leader of the Liberals was Ismael Montes, twice president of the Republic (1904–1909, 1913–1917) and skillful leader of the opposition. The decisive factor in the consolidation of the Liberal regime was the forging of a political alliance between the Liberals and the new economic elite that took control of the mining industry around 1920. This elite would be commanded by three magnates known as the "tin barons."

The boom in tin production combined with the move to modernity and progress, promoted by the Liberal intelligentsia of La Paz, transformed the capital into the most prosperous city in the nation. By 1909 the population of La Paz had doubled; commercial and productive activities in the capital had surpassed those in the rest of the republic and accounted for more than 70 percent of the gross national product. In these years of prosperity the appearance of the city began to change radically vis-à-vis its original design. The urban core began expanding not only toward Chukiyawu but also toward zones previously considered to be rural. New neighborhoods, streets, avenues, and construction projects in neo-Classical or eclectic styles (the Legislature, the Courthouse, the City Hall) gave La Paz the modern edge that characterizes the capitals of Latin America. The architect Emilio Villanueva added a note of originality when, searching for a national style, he took Tiwanacota as his model and designed a number of highly innovative buildings including the Miraflores Stadium and the central block of the Universidad Mayor de San Andrés. Although this phase of La Paz's urban development emphasized the semantics of the names that were given to the new streets and avenues and the predominantly European styles the new buildings, it is to be noted that this growing national self-consciousness tended to inscribe in the urban geography the dates, names, and faces that celebrated the *criollo* origins of the modern, literate city.

During this urban and commercial boom that resulted from the political alliance of the mine owners and the landholders, the governing elite cultivated the self-image of a prosperous Bolivia whose modernization process depended, almost exclusively, upon the solutions that could be found to the "Indian problem" and to offset the disadvantageous position that Bolivia occupied in the geopolitical hierarchy. Fortunately for the governing elites, the census of 1909 indicated that the native population of La Paz had diminished in comparison with the census of 1902, while the number of "Bolivians" (the rubric applied exclusively to the whites) had increased. On the basis of these census figures the Liberal elites concocted the thesis that the native was a national blight in the process of extinction. What went completely unremarked upon was the fact that the very same census data showed that the *mestizo*

community was undergoing a rapid rate of expansion. Philosophically and ideologically, the Liberal state legitimized its racist discourse by means of the social Darwinist arguments–and its Comtean, Spencerian variants–promulgated by the Geographic Society of La Paz. The select group of intellectuals that constituted the Liberal intelligentsia of the epoch were all members of this institution. Educated in the positivist doxologies, they theorized the problems faced by *criollo* society in its confrontations with native society and offered positivist solutions to the crisis of education in Bolivia. At no point in their speculations did these intellectuals go beyond the ethnic, biological, psychological, and racist models with which they interpreted the society in which they lived; neither did they take any interest in the Weberian, Marxist, or other theories that, from 1903, began to be disseminated in the Agustín Aspiazu Society, theories which highlighted the role of the social in the relations of production.

One of the most celebrated intellectuals in the Bolivian positivist sociological and Liberal pedagogical traditions was Daniel Sánchez Bustamante (1871–1933), descendent of the conquistador Pedro Sánchez Bustamante and co-founder of the Geographic Society of La Paz. Even though not entirely in accord with positivist methodology and aware that the principal constituents of society were much more social than biological, Bustamante maintained a Spencerian line in sociology and a Comtean line in pedagogy. Entrusted by the regime in 1905 with carrying out a series of educational reforms designed to excise the theological and scholastic foundations on which Bolivian education was still based, Bustamante recommended the adoption of European and North American models as the sole means of modernizing the system. However, Bustamante's proposed reforms, as well as the political powers sponsoring those reforms were subject to scathing criticism by an anti-Hispanic and anti-positivist poet who had only recently been named the editor of the *El Diario* newspaper. Franz Tamayo (1879–1956) was the son of Isaac Tamayo and one of the most brilliant and best educated Liberal, anti-Conservative minds of his generation. Like his father, he had developed a peculiar notion of the Aymarans; however, unlike his father, Franz Tamayo's conception was not historically but rather racially and anthropologically conceived and highlighted the Aymaran's extraordinary vitality and will to survive in the face of adversity. On to this vision of the natives, the young Tamayo projected his philosophic cast of mind inspired by the works of Nietzsche, Goethe, and Schopenhauer. Rather than adopting the Liberal proposal of importing foreign models, Tamayo urgently advocated a return to roots, an awakening to life, and a re-creation of the nation on the basis of its most vital element: the full-blooded Indian. These ideas led to the foundation of the Radical Party and were later developed and articulated in the collection of Tamayo's periodical articles entitled *La creación de la pedagogía nacional* [1910; The Creation of a National Pedagogy].

In addition to calling into question the epistemological foundations of Bustamante's report, Tamayo also attacked Liberal society in its entirety. The land-owning elites, who as a result of the confiscation of native lands had been transformed into an economic spearhead, were denounced by Tamayo as a host of parasites. These verbal bombshells ignited a veritable national debate that forced the Liberal ideologues to confront a series of questions they had studiously avoided: What kind of nation was the Liberal positivist doctrine in the process of constructing? Was the Liberal regime a consolidated state that merely had recourse to the rationalizing discourse of positivism as a prop to its structure, or was the rationalizing discourse of positivism a structuring ideology that necessitated the formation of a state? The paradox of the Tamayan discourse was that, despite the success of its denunciations, it was able to articulate a genuinely nativist or, at least, alternate vision. For Tamayo the natives were desirable in their untouched state, which is to say, as they were in the remote past. In their actual condition, however, they were lacking in interest, and their sole possibility of survival lay in miscegenation with the whites. Like Vasconcelos in Mexico, Tamayo concluded that the symbiosis of the white race (whose calling was to educate) and the native race (whose calling was to be educated) was the *mestizo*, the only truly Bolivian possibility because it combined the intellect of the Europeans with the sentiment of the native Americans. As Albarracín Millán has suggested, the errors of this proposition are threefold: its inability to conceive the relations between the whites and the natives in terms of equality; its substitution of the classical analysis of white-native relations for a racial analysis; and its conception of political questions in isolation from economic and historical ones.

These weaknesses notwithstanding, the Liberal doctrine of 1910 was in no position to evaluate the inconsistencies of Tamayo's arguments, much less to articulate resolute responses to an attack that questioned its historical vision and national project. Politically, the Liberal camp disintegrated into a number of radical factions (out of which emerged the Radical Party of Tamayo) and a Conservative rump. Intellectually, it was destabilized by a group of young intellectuals–including Rigoberto Paredes (1870–1950), Alcides Arguedas (1879–1946), José Luis Tejada Sorzano (1882–1938), and Armando Chirveches (1883–1926)–who incarnated the implacable critical consciousness unleashed by Tamayo. Concurrent with this ideological uproar, a situation without precedent in Bolivian history, six books appeared almost simultaneously that have since become indispensable to the comprehension of the Bolivian cultural process. Rigoberto Paredes's *Política parlamentaria de Bolivia* [1907; Bolivian Parliamentary Politics] questioned the legitimacy of the Liberal political structure that he deemed a collective fraud. With respect to the natives, whom he perceived as abject and brutalized by the injustices of society, Paredes declared himself in favor of a social amelioration of their condition but placed his real hopes on the possibility of an increase in Caucasian immigration. Alcides Arguedas's *Pueblo Enfermo* [1909; The Afflicted People] denounced from a position of Lebonian and Tardean positivism the economic and psychological misery of a country he saw as suffering from the liberal regime of Montes. Arguedas openly disagreed with Tamayo on the native question, since by his diagnosis the native affliction was the worst manifestation of the general illness affecting society. Tamayo's own work, *Creación de la pedagogía nacional* [1910; Creation of National Pedagogy], as we have seen, examined and indicted the Bustamante reforms and proposed in their stead a purifying miscegenation. Armando Chirveches's naturalist novel *La Candidatura de Rojas* [1910; The Rojas Candidacy] advocated cultural renewal. The fifth book, Tejada Sorzano's *Después de la crisis* [1911; After the Crisis], examined the paradoxical reality of the Bolivian economy during the Montes regime–whose prosperity was no more than a boom, badly managed, in primary commodities and not in manufactured goods. Some years later Arguedas published *Raza de bronce* [1919; Men of Bronze], a novel that closed the book on the epoch of the Romantically inspired and idealized noble savage discourse (*indianismo*) of his predecessors and confirmed the advent of what criticism would later identify as the era of classical nativism. *Raza de bronce* engraved in narrative form Arguedas's positivist perception of the native condition in the era of the great landowners.

A careful analysis of these works reveals that their authors were ultimately consummate Liberals who, rather than offering original proposals, merely put forth liberal alternatives, substituting civilized expedients–the education of the natives, for example, and the creation of a more orderly and respectful relation between the constituent groups of society–for the vulgar expedients of the ruling oligarchy. In this sense Paredes, Arguedas, Tamayo, Chirveches, and Tejada Sorzano were the great reformers of the Liberal ideology. They discerned, with a penetrating critical consciousness, the exhaustion of the Liberal project to which they in one manner or another felt an attachment, and thus struggled to articulate the means by which it could be reanimated, although always within the theoretical frame of positivism and invariably conceiving social and cultural phenomenon from within the presuppositions of race. As Albarracín Millán has pointed out, one only needed to take note of the achievements of the businessman Patiño (whose *cholo-mestizo* background was evident) to realize that the concept of race counted for little in the context of international commerce (108).

The intellectual who most lucidly confronted his own limits was perhaps Alcides Arguedas. His novel *Raza de bronce* contains glimmers of an intuition and perhaps fear, that Liberalism as a rationalizing discourse of the status quo reality was already not viable and that, in the final instance, it would be the natives who were going to change the situation. Arguedas was unable, however, to say how or when such changes would occur because he lacked the means of truly understanding the natives and because the only means of expression open to his nativism was an authoritarian rhetoric that foreclosed actual indigenous discourse. This lack of intercourse between the discourse of nativism and the realities of the native subject characterized the literary and ethnographic nativism inaugurated by Jaime Mendoza (1874–1939) in his narrative works and by Paredes in his *Mitos, supersticiones y supervivencias populares de Bolivia* [1920; Myths, Superstitions and Survival of the Popular in Bolivia].

Also forming part of the liberal positivist and literary nativist intellectual ambiance was the only Bolivian modernist figure to achieve an international stature, Ricardo Jaimes Freyre (1868–1933). As Rama has pointed out, Freyre's *modernismo* is rigorously minoritarian and dedicated to a *modernista* ideal whose urban exemplar was Buenos Aires, the city where Freyre had belonged to the literary circle of Darío and Lugones, where he had founded with Darío the *Revista de América* (1894), and where he had published an extraordinarily beautiful book of poems, *Castalia bárbara* [1899; Barbarous Castalia] (135). This book received a warm critical reception that facilitated its incorporation into the literary canon basically because it was the first collection of Latin American poetry to explore the use of free verse in the Spanish language; Freyre later systematized its use in *Leyes de versificación castellana* [1912; The Rules of Castilian Versification]. Another factor that constantly stands out in the collection is the use it makes of Nordic mythology to express poetically the final days of a barbaric order and the arrival of a civilizing and

Christian one. The great paradox of *Castalia bárbara* is that the beauty and intensity of the barbarian aesthetic constantly surpasses the kindness of the civilizing order that would impose itself.

In sum, these writers constituted a vigorous generation of cultured intellectuals who–Freyre excepted–played a determining role in the deconstruction of the Liberal regime. The critiques they advanced and the debates they opened up, together with the fall in tin prices that had resulted from the economic instability of World War I and the constant native revolts against the land-owning class, provoked a crisis of legitimation so deep that the regime was destabilized and split into Liberal and Republican camps. The 1920s saw the advent of an era of Republican government that lasted until 1934. Further destabilizing events in this period included the deterioration of the tin mining industry; the burgeoning reception of Marxist ideas disseminated through the Agustín Aspiazu Society and the consequent reformulation of the Indian problem in terms of landlessness and exploitation; the rise of the first Leftist political parties and the first labor unions; the first debates about women's rights; and the articulation of the movement for university reform and the creation of native schools whose greatest accomplishment was the establishment of the community (*escuela-ayllu*) of Warisata in 1931 by the native professors Elizardo Pérez and Raúl Pérez.

Bolivia's defeat in the Chaco War (1932–1935) had profound repercussions on the social and cultural history of the nation. For the first time in its history, Bolivia was perceived in its multi-ethnic and underdeveloped complexity, and the idea of constructing the nation on the basis of the full participation of all its social sectors sank in. Although the cultural production that followed the end of the war lacked, in general, a high degree of artistic excellence, it did have documentary and accusatory value. Between 1920 and 1936 a number of documentary and feature films were produced (the majority of which were silent films) that, in addition to recording the military conflict, had the audacity to stretch the limits of the representable, portraying (sometimes in the role of protagonists) the native and *mestizo* face of the country. Among the most notable were *Hacia la gloria* [1932; Toward Glory] by Mario Camacho and José Jiménez with the collaboration of Raúl Durán and *La guerra del Chaco* [1934–1935; The Chaco War] by Luis Bazoberry. In the realm of literature, the young *mestizos* and whites who had in a wave of nationalist enthusiasm enlisted in the army, discovered upon their return from the war the corruption that the conflict had generated and the incompetence with which it had been fought. Known as the Chaco generation, these young men were the authors of the so-called Chaco narratives. Technically, these writers were part of the realist, naturalist, regionalist, and customs-and-manners (*costumbrista*) traditions of the previous generation (Chirveches, Arguedas, Mendoza), although they brought to their works a talent for articulating their indictment of society and their perplexed discovery of the other face of the country. The best work to come out of this generation was Augusto Céspedes's (1904–1996) *Sangre de mestizos* [1936; The Blood of the Mestizos], a collection of short stories in the realist style in which the critique of "Bolivian psychic and ethnic incoherence" was brought to fruition by means of finely crafted stories and fully realized characters. Oscar Cerruto's (1912–1981) novel, *Aluvión de fuego* [1935; Torrent of Fire], while not as narratively accomplished as Céspedes's stories, did present an expansive vision of the national reality transformed by the

emergence of the new historical agents of the proletariat and the peasantry who, while being unable to adopt the role of social protagonists, had already received their right of entry into society.

In the cultural context of the 1950s and 1960s, the National Revolutionary Movement (or MNR, Movimiento Nacionalista Revolucionario) played a determining role, since it was to change the orientation of Bolivian culture. The radical government of the MNR that had returned the confiscated lands to the natives and that had, at least in its first phase, included workers and peasants in the government, now found itself obliged to vindicate indigenous culture. In order to carry this out, the MNR advocated a cultural politics of integration with the masses that inspired artists, writers, and institutions to undertake the labor of cultural definition of the indigenous nation and its pre-Hispanic past. It was in this context that an official and retrograde nativist discourse (*indianismo*) arose proposing a return to the "earth mysticism" of the "ancestral-chthonic" as the only means of realizing a national culture. Fernando Diez de Medina brought these postulates to bear on the history of Bolivian literature in his 1953 volume, *Literatura Boliviana* [Bolivian Literature], in which he stressed that the literary origins of the country were more rooted in the pre-Hispanic Andean cosmogony and myths than in the Spanish tradition. The limits and contradictions of this work were evident in the pedagogic dimension, with the historical and reductive character (it studied only the Andean context) of the perspective it applied to the study of the indigenous context. For Diez de Medina the splendors of the Colla culture lay all in the past; in the present, it was historically decrepit (94). This diagnostic could not have been more eloquent, especially when one takes into account the state of assimilation and the loss of autonomy experienced by the Quechua peasantry during the Barrientos dictatorship (1966–1969).

Independently from the state's official cultural policies but well within the general thrust of its cultural politics, there emerged in the plastic arts the greatest exponents of Bolivian art in the twentieth century: the sculptor Marina Núñez del Prado; the muralist Walter Solón Romero; and the painters Cecilio Guzmán de Rojas, Lorgio Vaca, Enrique Arnal, Gil Imaná, Ricardo Pérez Alcalá, Gastón Ugalde, and Luis Zilvetti. Simultaneously, Bolivian music experienced a profound renovation, first as a result of the inauguration of the First Festival of Indigenous Music in La Paz (1956) and later with the presence of composers such as Alfredo Domínguez, Ernesto Cavour, Jaime Laredo, Gilberto Rojas, and Alberto Villalpando, who offered the daring and original proposition of incorporating into their works native musical themes and instruments. The state played an important supportive role in these activities with its funding of the Pedro Domingo Murillo prize. In addition to the excellence of these works, it is to be noted that with few exceptions these artists all utilized the representative guiding principle of translating the indigenous into artistic codes comprehensible to a nonindigenous public. When seen from the perspective of the indigenous society facing the state apparatus, however, this translation was highly problematic and exposed the cultural paradox of the MNR's intentions: to foment in the arts a spirit aiding and abetting the reconstruction of the national culture, all the while sustaining the colonizing and occidentalizing criteria that had led to the absence of indigenous participation in the official artistic scene. With the exception of music festivals, which rather than being considered artistic events were deemed folkloric ceremonies, native culture continued to be a subject configured by means of the various discoursivities in which it was narrated or represented.

In the 1970s other cultural domains, such as urbanization and architecture, reflected these paradoxes of the government rhetoric even more clearly. While private construction firms such as Luis and Alberto Iturralde (the Workers Hospital, the YPFB building, the CONAVI building), Roberto Muñóz (the Emusa building), Ernesto Pérez Ribero (the Villa Holguín, the Cerrado Coliseum, the Pedro Domingo Murillo Technical School), and Hugo López Videla (Hotel Crillón, the 6 de Agosto Cinema) modernized the city, they did so utilizing foreign designs that reflected little or nothing of the practical daily lives of the thousands of natives who lived there. There was nothing in these creative constructions that distinguished them as expressions of multiculturalism or which contributed to a shared national infrastructure. In tandem with these activities, a number of public institutions were established: the National Academy of Sciences (1960), the Universidad Católica Boliviana (1966), and, with the aim of monopolizing the communications media, the Undersecretary for the Press, Information, and Culture. As a subsection of this latter institution, the Bolivian Cinema Institute was founded (ICB in 1953) to finance the production of intensely political, documentary-testimonial cinema. Among the most notable products of this wave were the short films *Vuelve Sebastiana* [Ruiz 1953; Sebastiana Returns] and *Aysa* [Javier Sanjinés and Oscar Soria 1965], and Sanjinés's feature film *Ukamau* [1966; That's How It Is!], which became an instant classic of Latin American cinema and won both the Director's First Feature Prize at the Cannes Festival and the Flaherty Prize at the Locarno Festival the following year. Here again it must be stressed that these films were also marked by the limitations of having to formulate their scenarios within a representative schema allegorizing the indigenous reality. As Javier Sanjinés has remarked with reference to *Ukamau*, "the cinematography is both beautiful and memorable; however, it reproduces the Romantic stereotype of the peasant communities that the tradition of Bolivian folk music has disseminated in the local cities and has exported to the industrialized countries" (1992, 169).

Apart from these inconsistencies, however, this cinema and these directors were able to publicly effect a change in the semantic valuation of an image that, as was the case with the representation of the Aymara, had been stigmatized since colonial times as "barbarous" and "fearful." These genuine advances in the representation of the Aymaran world suggest that, at least in the cinema, the cultural politic of the MNR did play a foundational role. The same cannot be said with respect to literature. With the exception of a number of propagandistic works of dubious artistic merit, Bolivian literature was profoundly influenced by the deterritorializing experience of the revolutionary defeats. In reference to the literature of this period, Javier Sanjinés has spoken of the "literature of revolutionary frustration" (1992, 39) characterized by a repudiation of the utopian ideas engendered by the 1952 state. This literary response was in no sense univocal; nor did it produce a homogenous corpus of works. It did combine, however, a critical spirit–a characteristic trait of modern Bolivian letters–with an urgent desire to reformulate the narrative form, somewhat new to the tradition and as such constituted a veritable change of direction in Bolivian literature. Marcelo Quiroga Santa Cruz's (1931–1980) *Los deshabitados* [1957; The Deserted Ones] was perhaps the first Bolivian novel to break out of the nineteenth-century realist tradition.

By means of a sophisticated interior monologue and indirect free discourse, the author relates the ways in which the petty bourgeoisie internalized the collapse of the national revolution. While the novel achieves an admirable lucidity in its portrayal of the dimensions of the political shipwreck, its narrative is seen as limited by the absence of social agents capable of redeeming the crisis of the middle classes (Sanjinés 1992, 43–56).

Equally innovative with respect to its formal propositions and narrative strategies was Oscar Cerruto's short story collection *Cerco de penumbras* [1957; Siege of Shadows]; however, unlike *Los deshabitados*, Cerruto's work pried into far less visible zones of consciousness and reality and gave the impression of seeking to evade all questions of national social import. In *Cerco de penumbras* these issues were addressed in a philosophical sub-discourse that called into question the value of reason as the unique means of access to the real. Proceeding on the proposition that every system of ideological manipulation (and here those of the MNR are implied) negates or veils the existence of spatial incongruity in the construction of reality, Cerruto's fiction shows how the consciousness that becomes aware of the existence of these spaces will deconstruct every project that tries to "sell" it an inadequate description of reality. The eleven stories that constitute *Cerco de penumbras* dismantle the rhetoric of national unity and place the reader face to face with a series of marginal characters (madmen, the ailing, or the dead) who, nonetheless, live in a tangible reality that is of their own making. Rather than manifesting the "absence of the ordering coordinates of reality" (Sanjinés 1992, 80), the book sets in motion the dimensions of a reality crisis.

With the work of Jaime Sáenz (1921–1986), the project of subverting the authoritative discourses and semiotic systems reached its finest expression. Perceiving in authoritarian systems the symptoms of a logocentric and colonizing reason, Sáenz indicated (prior to Cerruto) the metaphysical propensity to evade difference (whether it be ethnic, cultural, linguistic, or epistemological) in the struggle to impose unity. Sáenz's first book, a poetic tale entitled *El escalpelo* [1955; The Scalpel], swept over his contemporaries like a cyclone. Still avid consumers of the realist and naturalist works of the customs-and-manners writers, society was little prepared to appreciate a discourse that exploded the use of quotidian language and realist coordinates as neutral instruments for the representation of reality. In a climate of nationalist and revolutionary fervor, when La Paz was proclaiming itself the very model of a modern capital, and the country was celebrating its economic progress with the inauguration of the Santa Cruz-Corumbá railway, Sáenz's poetic prose threw a spotlight on the ghosts of the city:

"Hay", me ha dicho alguien, "muchos espectros en la ciudad." Entre ellos, espectros que golpean reiteradamente una u otra puerta. . . "Son muchos", siguió diciéndome alguien, "incontables, los espectros que rondan en todos los ámbitos de la ciudad. . . Yo me remito a los cuerpos muertos de las ciudades, los cuales, tienen la mágica perseverancia de acercarse, de tocarme las costillas, de verme el esternón con sus menudos ojos. No hay duda de que esos cuerpos habrán de levantarse, alguna vez. Habrán de levantarse porque son gentiles, para amarrarle a uno el lazo de los zapatos. Habrán de levantarse para ejercer la venganza, porque la venganza se ejerce también con gentileza. (1975, 60–61).

"There are," somebody informed me, "a large number of specters in the city." Among others, specters who thump repeatedly on one door or another. . ."Yes, a great number," somebody continued, "in fact, the specters patrolling every corner of the city are innumerable." I am referring, of course, to all the perambulating corpses one comes across, the ones with the preposterous persistence of accosting you, poking you in the ribs, staring into your breastbone with their beady little eyes. Unquestionably these corpses will rise up in revolt, one day. They'll have to, because they're polite—they never hesitate to come to your aid and tie up your boot laces. You see, the reason they'll have to revolt is so they can wreak vengeance, because vengeance too is practiced with courtesy.

Twenty-four years later, in another poetic tale in the collection dedicated to the city of La Paz, *Imágenes Paceñas* [1979; Images of La Paz], Sáenz takes up these same preoccupations and formulates a poetic of the city by means of the characteristic ambivalence that has defined it since the Colonial period. In this work the semantic valuation of the two republics is transformed into a poetic code:

> Dado por sentado que la ciudad de la Paz tiene una doble fisonomía, y admitido que mientras una se exterioriza la otra se oculta, hemos querido dirigir nuestra atención a esta última.
>
> Presidida por el Illimani, por el mururata y el Huayna-Potosí. . . alzándose a una altura de 3.600 metros sobre el nivel del mar, con una población integrada en su gran mayoría por aymaras y descendientes de aymaras, La Paz asume un carácter altamente diferenciado. Las influencias del mundo actual, con múltiples desarrollos tecnológicos que desafían y sobrepasan todo lo imaginable, y de cuyas corrientes difícilmente podríamos substraernos, encuentran natural resistencia en estas alturas, pues dichas influencias aunque en algunos casos reportan beneficios, las más de las veces resultan nocivas, con normas, adelantos, divisas y aun costumbres que, decididamente, no cuncuerdan -por así decirlo- con nuestro modo de estar, y mucho menos con nuestro modo de ser. (1979, 10–11)
>
> Given that the city of La Paz has two faces and, admitting that while the one openly reveals itself the other keeps itself under wraps, we have sought to direct our attention toward the latter.
>
> Dominated by Illimani, by Mururata and Huayna-Potosí. . . and rising to an elevation of 3,600 meters above sea level, with a population composed by and large of Aymarans and the descendants of Aymarans, La Paz displays a highly distinctive character. In these heights, the influences of the world at large—its multiple technological developments challenging and exceeding the imaginable, whose currents we can resist only with difficulty—run up against a natural resistance, since such influences bring benefits only in certain cases; more often than not they are injurious, and their norms, improvements, emblems, and even their customs emphatically do not harmonize, so to speak, with our mode of living, and even less with our mode of being.

With this change of approach in the perception of La Paz–Chukiyawu and its inhabitants, Sáenz articulates a forceful cultural critique of modernity from a poetic point of view seemingly unconcerned with the political dimension. The city that interests him is ultimately Chukiyawu and its inhabitants, the Aymarans and the descendants of the Aymarans who, dwelling in a mysterious silence, scoff at "that other city responsible for their degradation" (Sáenz 1979, 149). Fortuitously, Sáenz imagines possibilities of Aymaran integration into the national culture that offer alternatives to the utopian nationalist vision. This is a decisive and original contribution to the cultural history of La Paz because the integrative vision imagined by Sáenz is not posed in terms of a pedagogy that would civilize the natives, or in terms of their insertion into a state that could assimilate them only rhetorically, or even in terms of their allegorical representation in the national

culture, as was the case with testimonial cinema. What animates Sáenz's vision is the incorporation of Aymara logic into the structure of the official culture.

Sáenz's works can be characterized by the peculiarity of his poetic language, the incorporation of oral strategies into his written discourse, his strange fascination with death, and the agonistic predisposition to death with which his characters confront their lives. A detailed examination of his oeuvre, however, reveals that these motifs are much more than eccentric literary choices when seen in the context of contact with a cultural logic that, like the Aymaran, formulates its notions of beauty, life, and death in ways that are highly distinct from the representative thought which the conquest and its consequences made possible in the Americas to which we have grown accustomed. While the cinema of Sanjinés recreates a stereotypical Aymara world, Sáenz's poetic works capture its sensibility and internal rhythm. Without necessarily appearing to be Aymaran, since they have been exposed to the distorting effects of modernity, his characters live, breathe, and expire within a cultural logic very distinct from that animating the official culture. They are the invisible faces of the city, consummately rendered in a gallery of characters that includes: the anonymous *aparapita* (an Aymaran who, having immigrated to La Paz, earns his living carrying baggage); shaman-philosophers like Juan de la Cruz Oblitas and Doña Urbana Zanzetenea de Toco y Pilla; and radically eccentric characters like Narciso Lima Achá, el Sr. Beltrán, el Sr. Peña y Lillo, Ramona Escalera, Nicolás Estefanic, and Felipe Delgado (the protagonist of a novel of the same name), all characters who, while not belonging to the Aymara culture, are bent on making contact with it by means of masquerade and who realize in the process that to be Aymara, one must live like the Aymarans. It was precisely this insight that the MNR state-sponsored cultural policy overlooked.

In addition to this unexpected about-face toward the Aymarans, Sáenz's works question with an extraordinary lucidity the realities of a country whose political machinations make it all but incomprehensible. In his 1979 work, *Felipe Delgado*, there is a pertinent discussion of the Bolivian condition during the period of the mining industry-landowners oligarchy:

> Con toda seguridad somos el país más rico del mundo en materia de minerales, pero sin embargo, los únicos beneficiados son tres potentados que manejan la nación como si fuera un campamento de pordioseros. Nos vemos obligados a pedir de rodillas un pequeño empréstito para construir un miserable edificio y para tender unos cuantos metros de cañería en esta ciudad. . . . En todo tiempo y en toda circunstancia algo ha marchado mal en Bolivia. Siempre y siempre. Todo tan inexplicable, todo tan lleno de contradicciones. Y sólo porque Dios es grande no pierde uno la fe. (170)
>
> It goes without saying that with respect to mineral resources we are the richest country in the world. However, the sole beneficiaries of this wealth are three magnates who rule the nation as if it were a paupers' shantytown. In this city, we're obliged to beg on our knees for money to construct a squalid building, to lay down a few meters of sewer-pipe. . . . Throughout all our history and in every circumstance, something has always gone wrong. Always, and forever. Everything so completely inexplicable, so riddled with contradictions. It's only because the Lord is great we do not lose faith.

Although Sáenz's narratives leave these questions hanging and underdeveloped—and, after all, this is more in keeping with a lived experience that confounds any rationalized reality—it is legitimate to rescue and reclaim his works as theoretical precedents useful to a discussion of the various contributions that have been made to the understanding of a culturally multi-ethnic society.

We have seen that what was lacking in the testimonial cinema of the 1970s was a sense of being anchored in the internal rhythms of the indigenous communities. *Ukamau* [That's How It Is!], as well as the film Sanjinés produced during the Barrientos military dictatorship, *Yawar Mallcu* [1969; Blood of the Condor] were cinematographic narratives still rooted in aesthetic traditions that were fundamentally alien to the natives. This alienation stemmed from the fact that these films portrayed collective history through a schema of fictionalized, individual character-heroes that distorted the communal and agonistic Aymara self-representation that inspires them to act—and struggle—en masse. Sanjinés remarked that, during the filming of *Yawar Mallcu*, he became aware that some sort of blockage or disagreement hindered him from harmonizing his directorial intentions with the sensibilities of his native actors. Later he was to realize that this disaccord stemmed from the cinematographic structure and even the script of his film. In his films of the 1970s, Sanjinés abandoned conventional narrative strategies for the representation of Aymaran history, replacing the Western modus operandi of personal protagonists and fictional story-lines with the living presence of the community that had figured in the events he sought to stage: the massacre of the Twentieth-Century Mining Co. workers in June 1967 during the presidency of the pacifier of the countryside and the mines, General René Barrientos. This film, *El coraje del pueblo* [1971; The Courage of the People], was produced by the Grupo Ukamau after Barrientos had already dissolved the ICB (the Instituto Cinematográfico Boliviano). *El coraje del pueblo* was the first Bolivian film to represent the Aymara miners without mediation and to anchor itself effectively in the intimate rhythms of the native communities. However, to speak of intimate rhythms is still to skirt the question of the mystery of *El coraje del pueblo* which lay in its having incorporated into the cinematic text the structure of orality and its methods of recording and registering for posterity the history of the community. The protagonists of the film are the same historical subjects who survived the massacre and who cathartically and symbolically relive it in the sights of a camera vigilant to the smallest details. The historical document is thereby enriched because, in addition to the knowledge of historical events the film affords the spectator, it recounts history with the living complicity of those who reproduce it—no longer as fiction but rather as a mechanism for the articulation of historical memory in which the past is able to affect the present. This process strikingly parallels how sixteenth-century Aymarans and Quechuans remembered and memorialized the death of Atahualpa. However, we should not lose sight of the fact that these achievements responded to the exigencies and urgencies of a political cinema that by necessity highlighted accusation, documentation, and testimonial chronicle to the detriment of an inquiry into the indigenous poetic substratum implicit in the structure of orality. However, what this cinema could not bring to representation (and it shares this deficit with the guerrilla literature of the 1970s and the testimonial reports written in the style of Domitila Barrios de Chungara (b. 1937)), is the poetic dimension of the indigenous cultural logic. Works such as those of Sáenz, which from the point of view of writing seek to reflect the perception of a properly Aymaran aesthetic, are in all

likelihood much more conducive to the representation of these indigenous intimacies. The question that now proposes itself is: To what extent have the social and aesthetic achievements of Sanjinés's cinema and the poetic successes of Sáenz's works paved the way for the constitution of a solid and grounded multi-ethnic culture?

The eighteen years of *coups d'état* and military dictatorships that followed the collapse of the Revolution, the nadir of which was the dictatorship of Hugo Banzer Suárez (1971–1978), took a devastating toll on the country in as much as they annulled the possibility of cultural continuity. The Bolivian intelligentsia was deprived of a space in which to dialogue with other ideas and, on that basis, to propose improvements or alternatives. The first assault on the possibility of cultural continuity came during the populist regime of General Barrientos (1966–1969) with the dismissal of Sanjinés from the ICB, the subsequent closing of that institution, and the creation in its stead of a National Broadcasting Network (Empresa Nacional de Televisión) and a Ministry of Culture charged with the diffusion of a state-sponsored cultural policy inspired by notions of "earth mysticism." Fernando Diez de Medina (then a private advisor to Barrientos) theorized this neo-idealist noble savage *indianista* rhetoric on the basis of an allegorical and ahistorical vision of the native represented as a prodigy of the past who had to be educated, civilized, and, as far as possible, eliminated. Relapsing into racist arguments, Diez de Medina proposed a miscegenation that would erase all differences, declaring that "leveling does not proceed downwards, as the Marxists suppose. On the contrary, leveling raises up. . . . With each passing year we will have fewer Indians and more mestizos, because the natural propensity and the leveling instruments of education march, as we have seen in Mexico, towards a fusion of races and cultures into a national type" (1969, 299).

Responses to this state-sponsored cultural policy were irregular, disjointed, and lacking in unanimity. Those put forward by Sanjinés—who, following his expulsion from the ICB, founded the Grupo Ukamau, the organization that produced his films *Yawar Mallcu* in 1969 and *El coraje del pueblo* in 1971—were severely critical, novel, and accusatory. We could also include here the work of Pedro Shimose whose *Poemas para un pueblo* [1968; Poems for a People] definitively opened the way toward the enunciation of a poetry accountable to the popular masses. Texts like Jaime Sáenz's *Visitante profundo* [1964; The Mysterious Visitor] and *El frío* [1967; The Cold] and Jesús Urzagasti's *Tirinea* (1969) also countered the assaults of the state-sponsored cultural policy with works that destabilized its cultural criteria. However, apart from these exceptions, the majority of the literary works in this era embraced an ethos of survival, more contentious than creative and which, sometimes from exile, sometimes from a position of social criticism, denounced the moral and civic vacuum that was being created in the middle-class imaginary by state militarism. This literature of protest, characterized by realism in prose and a language of crisis in poetry, ultimately lacked the instruments commensurate with its aims.

In the social sciences the only writer to undertake a substantive analysis of the political economy of the nation in these years was Sergio Almaraz in his books, *Petróleo en Bolivia* [1958; The Petroleum Industry in Bolivia], an exposition of the role the oil monopolies had played in the Chaco War; *El poder y la caída* [1967; Power and the Fall], a history of the mining oligarchy; and *Requiem para una república* [1969; Requiem for a Republic], a political and economic analysis of the collapse of the national revolution and the subsequent Barrientos dictatorship. In addition to these works, we should also note the existence of an extensive corpus of occasional essays and periodical articles that have yet to be published in book form.

The eruption of guerrilla activity in 1967 under the leadership of Ernesto "Che" Guevara and the brutal efficiency with which the Barrientos government crushed it gave rise to a novel form of literary expression, the guerrilla narrative, which as it developed also included the 1970 guerrilla experiences of Teoponte. In addition to its obvious thematic novelty, this literary form incorporated many of the narrative strategies that had been opened up during the Latin American boom of the 1960s and produced multiply nuanced works. In *Los fundadores del alba* [1969; The Progenitors of Dawn] by Renato Prada Oropez (b. 1937) a and *Después de las calles* [1971; After the Streets] by René Poppe (b. 1943), the guerrilla project, despite its collapse, is envisaged as a means to the historical ends distinct from the revolutionary nationalism of previous decades. Other novels such as *El ocaso de orión* [1972; The Decline of Orion] by Oscar Uzín Fernández or *Los vulnerables* [1973; The Vulnerable Ones] by Gaby Vallejo (b. 1941) limit themselves to recording the vacuum and the horror that remained after the dissipation of the guerrillas' utopian visions. A third tendency, markedly critical, sought to demystify the guerrilla mystique and found its finest expression in *Matías el apóstol suplente* [1971; Matthew, the Surrogate Apostle], by Julio de la Vega (b. 1924). Finally, government-sanctioned anti-guerrilla works were not lacking, of which *El guerrillero y la luna* [1972; The Guerrilla and the Moon] by Fernando Díez de Medina (1908–1990) and *Tiempo desesperado* [1978; The Time of Despair] by José Fellman Velarde (1922–1982) were the most notable.

In 1969 General Barrientos died mysteriously in a helicopter accident. His dictatorship was succeeded by a series of military administrations whose politics varied from the revolutionary reformism of Ovando Candia (1969–1970) and the Popular Assembly of Juan José Torres (1970–1971) (in which the first attempt to break with the hegemonic pattern established by the 1952 state was made) to the dictatorship of Hugo Banzer (1971–1978). The lack of coherence in the political behavior of the armed forces demonstrated that in the Bolivian case the army did not operate, as it had done in other Latin American countries, in a unified manner and did not represent a wholly organized entity. On the contrary, the army supported the most ideologically diverse and opposed policies. In this conjuncture of authoritarianism, dictatorship, and political risk-taking, Bolivia experienced a radical change in the composition of its social forces. The legacy of the Revolution, the socialist experiments of the Reformist and Leftist governments, and the Hispanicizing effects–that only then had begun to be felt–of the 1955 Educational Reforms and of the National Literacy Plan implemented by the Ovando Candia government converted large sections of the rural indigenous populace into a bilingual population that began to migrate to the cities. Since the end of the 1960s a new generation of Aymara leaders has arisen who have begun to reopen the issue of peasant syndicalism (co-opted by the Barrientos regime into an agent of the state-sponsored cultural policy) and to construct a series of ideological referents distinct from those employed by the revolutionary nationalists and the *criollo* Left. Parallel to these developments, Aymaran intellectuals resident in La Paz initiated the creation of cultural

institutions such as the Julián Apaza University Movement (1969), the Center for Rural Advancement and Coordination, and the Tupac Katari Farmers' Center (1971). These institutions began disseminating Aymara culture, for example, by means of Aymara radio broadcasts, and identifying their claims with the eighteenth-century anti-colonial struggles of the earlier Aymara chiefs. From these roots emerged in 1973 the *katarismo* movement, the first authentically Aymaran coalition dedicated to the articulation of rural and urban Aymaran culture and demands; the *katarismo* movement was to formulate a platform of political and cultural claims and grievances without precedent in the history of Bolivia (Rivera Cusicanqui 124–171). *El Manifiesto de Tiwanaku* [1973; The Tiwanaku Manifesto], produced in the midst of the Banzer years, set forth the political and cultural logic of the *katarismo* movement:

> Nosotros los campesinos quechuas y aymaras, lo mismo que los de otras culturas autóctonas del país. . . nos sentimos económicamente explotados y cultural y políticamente oprimidos. En Bolivia no ha habido una integración de culturas sino una superposición y dominación. . . no se han respetado nuestras virtudes ni nuestra propia visión del mundo y de la vida. . . no se ha respetado nuestra cultura ni comprendido nuestra mentalidad. . . (la educación que se nos impone) no sólo busca convertir al indio en una especie de mestizo sin definición ni personalidad, sino persigue igualmente su asimilación a la cultura occidental y capitalista.(216–17).

> We the Aymaran and Quechuan peasants, in solidarity with the other autochthonous cultures of the country. . . know ourselves to be economically exploited and culturally and politically oppressed. Bolivia has never had an integration of cultures, only a hierarchy and a domination. . . . our virtues and our vision of the world have never been respected. . . our culture or our mentality, either. . . . (The education that is imposed upon us) not only attempts to convert us into a species of mestizo without identity or personality, it uniformly aims at assimilating us into the Western capitalist culture.

The historical and cultural lucidity evident in this document reveals the extent to which the various literatures and cultural projects that had been proposed in Bolivia since independence had all failed to respond to the historical grievances upon which the *katarismo* movement was based. In essence these grievances centered on the vindication of indigenous ethnicities, both from a political perspective that would incorporate them into the nation as autonomous historical agents and also from a cultural perspective, incorporating them into the nation's cultures that, being distinct, desired to preserve their difference. However, above and beyond these proposals, what finally changed *criollo-mestizo* society's perception of the natives were the statistical data of the 1976 census. In La Paz alone, practically 50 percent of the population was composed of Aymarans who already formed an urban subculture and who had risen to a historical consciousness of their social marginality. For the first time since the Colonial epoch, the Aymarans constituted a politically and culturally organized nation with union leaders who, like Jenaro Flores and Macabeo Chila, demonstrated an extraordinary talent for negotiating the insertion of the peasantry into the labor movement and into Bolivian politics. One proof of this was the formation of an indigenously led political party, the Tupac Katari Revolutionary Movement, which in the 1985 elections won 2 percent of the national vote. The cultural demands of the natives centered on the decolonization of Andean cultural identity and the adoption of Quechua and Aymara as official languages.

So solid was the *katarismo* movement in these years that even the Banzer dictatorship was unable to crack it, and, in fact, the regime had to give way to the advances it made in alliance with the labor movement. In December 1977, four female miners led by Domitila Barrios de Chungara initiated a hunger strike that was almost immediately backed by the Bolivian Labor Federation, the National Federation of Peasant Workers of Bolivia, the *criollo* Left, and some sectors of the Catholic Church. The protest culminated in the obstreperous collapse of the Banzer regime (Rivera Cusicanqui 144–45). The artistic intelligentsia responded to these events (sometimes from exile and in the context of the closure of the universities) with works that sought to capture the native and popular pulse and articulate it in highly unconventional ways. This new wave of cultural production responded, in part, to what critics have called neo-nativism (*neoindigenismo*): An evolutionary phase of nativism that, doing away with both the idealized noble savage discourse of the native and the authoritarian rhetoric of classical nativism (*indigenismo*), opened up the possibility for works based upon a multicultural and multi-ethnic understanding of Bolivian culture. It was in this context that the Sudamericana editorial house published in 1977 Néstor Taboada Terán's (b. 1929) extraordinary novel *Manchay Puytu. El amor que quiso ocultar dios* [Manchay Puytu: The Love that God Would Conceal]. Based on the already mentioned eighteenth-century Quechua love poem that was transcribed by Jesús Lara in 1922, Terán's novel recreates the disturbing beauty of that amorous tale conceived and developed from an Andean aesthetic point of view. Later in 1995, Alberto Villalpando composed an opera based on this story, entitled *Manchay Puytu*, performed in 1995 at the Municipal Theater of La Paz.

Also in 1977, half a million city dwellers flooded to the cinemas to see the highest grossing Bolivian film ever: *Chuquiago,* by Antonio Eguino. Unlike Sanjinés, who had opted for exile, Eguino remained in La Paz during the dark years, and in the midst of the Banzer dictatorship produced a film that managed to reach out to the people, from the natives to the urban masses, who upon seeing themselves represented in their empirical daily lives began to acquire a critical consciousness of their relations with the La Paz upper classes, who were confronted on the screen by their own contradictions. Probably the greatest achievement of this film was to have consolidated the presence of Chukiyawu in the consciousness of La Paz's population. This perceptual reorientation vis-à-vis the multiethnic and multicultural bases of Bolivian society culminated with René Poppe's mining narrative, *El Koya loco* [1973; The Crazy Koya] and the testimonial of Domitila Barrios de Chungara (b. 1937), *Si me permiten hablar. Testimonio de Domitila una mujer de las minas de Bolivia* [1978; Let Me Speak! Testimony of Domitila, A Woman of the Bolivian Mines]. These two works were the first native cultural expressions to recount the story of the subjugation of the Aymara and Quechua peoples to the distorting effects of modernity and their conversion into the Bolivian mining proletariat. There is, however, a significant difference between the two works. While *El Koya loco* explores without mediation the mysterious and unknown world of the underground miners, the Testimonio of Domitila tackles, with aid of co-writer Moema Viezzer, the social reality of an open-pit miner's wife. In both these discourses, a predicament similar to the one discussed in relation to the cinema of Sanjinés and the poetic works of Sáenz is reproduced. While Domitila's testimony is a vivid and lacerating account of the miners' reality, it lacks the poetic dimension of

the tales of Poppe, who, like few Bolivian writers, has managed to capture in one fell swoop both the social exterior of the miners (strikes, massacres, etc.) and their troubled interior, both of which are expressed in the poetic logic of the underground that has little if anything in common with the Western rationality undergirding the hegemonic discourse of the *criollo-mestizo* culture. It is in this light that the inadequacy of describing these narratives in terms of neo-nativism becomes apparent: Although we might describe both these works as stories of mestizo protagonists (mestizos in as much they are natives permeated by Western culture), from a historical and cultural point of view these works really place the Andean cultural logic in the role of the protagonist in order to recount the confrontations with the hegemonic culture.

A major contributing factor to the consolidation of these discoursivities was the founding of the journal *Hipótesis* in 1977, as well as the presence of a new and vigorous generation of professional literary critics at the Literature Department of the Universidad Mayor de San Andrés (many of them contributors to *Hipótesis*). In the 1970s these critics had superseded the government-sanctioned traditionalist and philological orientation and had begun to incorporate a critical and revisionist vision of the Bolivian cultural processes into their works and their pedagogy. Almost immediately the testimony of Domitila and the demands of the *katarismo* movement were incorporated into curricula as cultural expressions that could not be ignored, either in actual discussions or in theory. Simultaneously, Juan de Dios Yapita and José Mendoza inaugurated a Native Language program in the San Andrés Department of Linguistics and institutions such as the CIPCA (Centro de Investigación y Promoción Campesiana [The Centre for Rural Research and Advancement]) and Radio San Gabriel sprung up, dedicated to the mass diffusion of Aymara culture.

However, while these transformations were operative in the universities and in a number of social sectors, outside of these realms there was a clear reluctance to face up to the multi-ethnic reality of the country. The political left and the political right, as well as public opinion in general, viewed the *katarismo* movement as a manifestation of anti-white racism. This disequilibrium in the social body was naturally a symptom of the colonial residua still present in Bolivian society; in addition it also indicated that before a solid national culture could be founded, it would be necessary to reconcile the various cultural tendencies that began to manifest themselves. The lack of an adequate space in which the different voices could enter into dialogue hindered, among other things, the consolidation of a national theater (Sanjinés 1985, 23).

Following the inconclusive elections of early 1979 (the first free elections in fifteen years), a military junta cut short the mandate of the caretaker government on All Souls' Day, 2 November 1979, initiating a civil war that would leave over 200 dead. The situation was unprecedented: Military dictatorships of the past had never been as unpopular as the junta was in the final days of 1979. A historic blockade of the nations' roads, organized by the peasants, and a general strike, called by the workers and massively supported by the population at large, broke the back of the junta. The efficacy with which the popular sectors defused the military *coup d'état* and safeguarded the continuity of the democratic process was ample evidence of the change that had taken place in the equilibrium of social forces in society.

It is particularly interesting to consider the various strategies employed by literature to digest these events. Let us consider in this light two paradigmatic texts, *Noviembre 79* [November '79] by Blanca Wiethüchter (b. 1947) and *La noche* [Night] by Jaime Sáenz. The first, published immediately after what Bolivian collective memory has dubbed the "All Souls' Massacre," is a book of minimalist poems that, from the point of view of an Andean aesthetic sensibility and employing metaphors of extraordinary creative amplitude, proposes the reconstruction of a collective ethic. Faced with the shock of "el alba/apuntando tanques" ("the dawn/sprouting tanks") and of "la sangre estupefacta" of "todos los vivos" ("the astonished blood" of "all the living"), the poem responds with verses of startling beauty:

Orgullo de ser
blanco
para una bala

Pride of being
white, like a target
for a bullet

The poem concludes: "No estamos solos/En este juego de rotaciones obstinadas/se tensan hostiles los polos de nuestra memoria/Será ésta la herida que nos nombra pueblo?" ("We are not alone/In the revolutions of this perpetual motion machine/the hostile termini of our memory are screwed down tight/Will these be the wounds that designate us a people?").

La noche, on the other hand, is a vast poem in which the events of November 1979 only enter into consideration in an indirect manner, in the section entitled "Intermedio" ["Interval"]. Going beyond the mimetic representation of history, Sáenz's poem offers a discourse whose intensity and violence translate the terror of those who lived through the massacre, at the same time that it functions as an apocalyptic prophecy sung by a poet before whose eyes the world (and human history) is smashed to pieces.

Sucedió una noche de noviembre.
Angustiosamente y con ojos extraviados me debatía en medio del tormento de cuatro días sin sueño,
cuando de pronto se escucharon atroces alaridos y voces y lamentos que llegaron a mis oídos desde lo hondo de un pozo fatídico,
y que dejaron adivinar horrores sin cuento,
por lo que me invadió el terror y me quedé mudo de espanto,
contemplando silenciosamente inmóviles aguas con una negrura reluciente,
que reflejaban formas fosforescentes de personajes depravados, de multitudes ensangrentadas, de ciudades asoladas, y de seres enloquecidos. (49)

One night in November it happened.
Anxiously, and with my eyes astray, I writhed in torment through four sleepless nights,
when suddenly, reaching my ears from the bottom of an ominous pit, atrocious shrieks and shouts and lamentations could be heard,
in which countless horrors were foretold,
and which steeped me in terror and struck me dumb with fear,
silently contemplating motionless waters of a gleaming blackness,
reflecting phosphorescent shapes of depraved characters, bloody multitudes, cities laid waste, and beings driven mad.

In both of these collections of poetry a number of the tensions in which the Bolivian culture continues to develop are openly manifest: a collective ethic of social reconstruction and a writing of the disaster tending toward a parody of the excesses of official history and a search for alternatives.

Politically, the Bolivian democratic process was only able to reestablish its viability in 1982, after a chaotic relapse into dictatorship and military government. The country made the transition to democracy while contending with a profound economic crisis, the growth of institutionalized corruption, and the illegal cocaine trade—all of which had been initiated under the previous military dictatorships. It has been in these same years also that an economic boom in the Bolivian Amazon has taken off and transformed Santa Cruz de la Sierra into the most prosperous city in the country; with this, the Amazon face of a country traditionally considered Andean will be perceived. The cultural process of the last two decades has been characterized by the transition to democracy, the socioeconomic crisis, the implantation of a neo-Liberal economic regime, and the fortification of the indigenous and popular cultures. The first democratic government (1982–1985) to follow the dictatorships formulated its agenda in what had been (since 1952) the traditional way, that is within the notion of the viability and desirability a state-historical project, and was sustained by a hyper-inflation that reached 81.79 percent. The legendary leader of the MNR Víctor Paz Estenssor succeeded this government when, by means of a series of political alliances, he managed to obtain his fourth presidential mandate. In less than a month Paz Estenssor had adopted the neo-Liberal structural adjustment policies that were to restructure the state and had initiated the privatization of public corporations, ushering Bolivia into the world of globalization. These restructuring reforms dismantled the nationalist-revolutionary model of the 1952 state and effectively declared that same state's cultural modernity project obsolete. In place of the old state's national vision of a Hispanicized *mestizo* population, the new government, inspired by the successes that the culturalist thesis had won in recent years in Europe and North America, adopted an official policy of multiculturalism. The paradox of these reforms is that the new multicultural policy was propounded from within the context of the ideological unilateralism of neo-Liberalism and the cultural logic of postmodernism whose theoretical scaffolding neutralized the social potential for conflict by postulating a consensus between subjects and cultures that, historically, had been deemed unequal. The consequence of this de-ideologization has been an increasing loss of articulation between the neo-Liberal state and the historical circumstances in which the multi-ethnic society developed. In addition, this multi-ethnic society, in its efforts to legitimate its cultural continuity, responded in a number of distinct manners to this type of ideological neutralization, and this too has been lost. It is by now clear that none of the subsequent governments have been able to extricate themselves from the cultural and economic prerogatives implanted in 1985. Thus, it is for this reason that the Bolivian cultural process of the final years of the twentieth century was characterized by a tension between the practice of a multiculturalism of postmodern inspiration (that, if it does produce genuinely new artistic creations, also runs the risk that every one of its intentions can be deemed artistically inspired) and an ethic of responsibility tending to reaffirm the cultural continuity of the indigenous and *mestizo* cultures.

In present-day Bolivia the debate continues between the various cultural projects of a society whose artists and intellectuals no longer perceive it as an homogenous and monolingual entity but rather as a controversially heterogeneous multi-ethnic and multilingual one. The proof of this plurality can be seen in a number of examples: the vigorous presence that indigenous cultural logic has in the cultural activities of the nation; the pressure that politically articulated popular movements have brought to bear on government policy; the formation of a substantive investigative and critical tradition, whose epicenters are the UMSA (Universidad Mayor de San Andrés), the ILCA (Instituto de Lengua y Cultura Aymara [Institute of Aymara Language and Culture]), the THOA (Taller de Historia Oral Andina [Andean Oral History Workshop]), and the San Gabriel Foundation; and the innovative initiatives of literary journals such as *Escarmenar, Puntos Suspendidos, La piedra Imán, La mariposa mundial* and so on.

Finally, it should be added that Bolivia's writers and filmmakers, while little known outside of the national frontiers, demonstrate a profound capacity for articulating new responses to the challenges that a multicultural society throws in the path of the nation.

Translation by Colman Hogan

Works Cited

Adorno, Rolena. "Cultures in Contact: Mesoamerica, the Andes, and the European Written Tradition." *The Cambridge History of Latin American Literature.* Ed. Roberto González Echevarría and Enrique Pupo Walker. Vol. 1: *Discovery to Modernism.* Cambridge: Cambridge University Press. 33–57.

Aguirre, Nataniel. 1981 [1885]. *Juan de la Rosa.* La Paz: Gisbert.

Albarracín Millán, Juan. 1978. *El gran debate (Positivismo e irracionalismo en el estudio de la sociedad boliviana.* La Paz: Empresa Editora "Universo."

Albó, Xavier. 1983. *Chukiyawu: La cara aymara de La Paz.* Vol. 3. La Paz: Cuadernos de Investigación CIPCA.

Almaraz, Sergio. 1958. *El petróleo en Bolivia.* La Paz: Editorial Juventud.

——. 1967. *El poder y la caída.* La Paz: Los Amigos del Libro.

——. 1969. *Requiem para una república.* La Paz: Universidad Mayor de San Andrés.

Arguedas, Alcides. 1909. *Pueblo enfermo.* Barcelona: Viuda de Luis Tasso.

——. 1945 [1919]. *Raza de bronce.* Buenos Aires: Ed. Losada.

Arzanz de Orsúa y Vela, Bartolomé. 1965. *Historia de la villa imperial de Potosí, riquezas de su incomparable cerro, grandeza de su magnífica población, sus guerras civiles y casos memorables.* Ed. Hanke Lewis and Gunnar Mendoza. Providence: Brown University Press. 3 vols.

——. 1970 [1872]. *Anales de la villa imperial de Potosí.* La Paz: Ministerio de Educación y Cultura.

Arze Quiroga, Eduardo. 1969. *Historia de Bolivia. Fases del proceso Hispano-americano: Orígenes de la sociedad boliviana en el siglo XVI.* La Paz-Cochabamba: Los Amigos del Libro.

Arze, Silvia and Rossana Barragán. 1988. *La Paz–Chuquiago. El escenario de la vida de la ciudad.* 2 vols. La Paz: Ediciones Casa de la Cultura.

Aspiazu, Agustín. 1959. *Obras completas.* La Paz: Burillo.

Barba, Alonzo. 1939 [1640]. *Arte de los metales.* La Paz: n.p.

Barrios de Chungara, Domitila y Moema Viezzer. 1997. *Si me permiten hablar. Testimonio de Domitila una mujer de las minas de Bolivia.* Mexico City: Siglo XXI.

Bazoberry, Luis, dir. 1934–1935. *La guerra del Chaco.*

Beyersdorff, Margot. 1998. *Historia y drama ritual en los andes bolivianos.* La Paz: Plural.

Cáceres Romero, Adolfo. 1990. *Nueva Historia de la literatura boliviana.* 3 vols. La Paz: Los Amigos del Libro.

Camacho, Mario and José Jiménez, dir. 1932. *Hacia la gloria.*

Carilla, Emilio. 1979. *La poesía de la Independencia.* Caracas: Biblioteca Ayacucho.

Cerruto, Oscar. 1935. *Aluvión de fuego.* Santiago: Ercilla.

——. 1957. *Cerco de penumbras.* La Paz: Industrial Gráfica E. Burillo & Cia.

Céspedes, Augusto. 1974. *Sangre de mestizos.* La Paz: Juventud.

——. 1946. *Metal del diablo.* La Paz: Ediciones La Calle.

Chirveches, Armando. 1970 [1908]. *La candidatura de Rojas.* La Paz: Editorial Juventud.

Cieza de León, Pedro de. 1971 [1553]. *La Crónica del Perú* . Bogotá: Ediciones de la Revista Ximénez de Quesada.

Cobo, Bernabé. 1943 [1653]. *Historia del nuevo mundo.* Madrid: Ediciones Atlas.

Colombí-Monguió, Alicia de. 1985. *Petrarquismo peruano: Diego Dávalos y Figueroa y la poesía de la "Miscelánea Austral."* London: Támesis.

Dávalos Figueroa, Diego. 1602. *Primera parte de la Miscelánea Austral.* Lima: A. Ricardo.

Díez de Medina, Fernando. 1969. *Mateo Montemayor.* La Paz–Cochabamba: Los Amigos del Libro.

——. 1972. *El guerrillero y la luna.* La Paz: Los Amigos del Libro.

——. 1981 [1953]. *Literatura Boliviana.* 4th ed. La Paz: Los Amigos del Libro.

Durand Flores, Luis. 1993. *El proceso de Independencia en el Sur andino. Cuzco y La Paz 1805.* Lima: Universidad de Lima.

Eguino, Antonio, dir. 1977. *Chuquiago.* Grupo Ukamau.

Escarmenar. Revista Boliviana de Estudios Culturales. 1995. La Paz: Plural.

Fellman Velarde, José. 1978. *Tiempo desesperado.* Cochabamba: Los Amigos del Libro.

Fernández, Dominique. 1996. "Donceles y soldados". *El retorno de los ángeles: Barroco de las cumbres en Bolivia.* Ed. Teresa Gisbert et al. Paris: Unión Latina. 93–95.

Flores, Angel. 1966. *The Literature of Spanish America: A Critical Anthology.* New York: Las Américas.

Gisbert, Teresa. 1980. *Iconografía y mitos indígenas en el arte.* La Paz: Gisbert.

——. 1991. *Historia de la vivienda y los conjuntos urbanos en Bolivia.* La Paz: Instituto Panamericano de Geografía e Historia y Academia Nacional de Ciencias de Bolivia.

Gisbert, Teresa et al. 1996. *El retorno de los ángeles: Barroco de las cumbres en Bolivia.* Paris: Unión Latina.

Henríquez Ureña, Pedro. 1964. *Corrientes literarias en Hispanoamérica.* 3rd ed. Mexico City: Fondo de Cultura Económica.

Jaimes Freyre, Ricardo. 1918 [1899]. *Castalia Bárbara.* 2nd ed. La Paz: Editorial Los Andes.

——. 1919 [1912]. *Leyes de versificación castellana.* 2nd ed. La Paz: González y Medina.

Klein, Herbert S. 1992. *Bolivia: The Evolution of a Multi-Ethnic Society.* New York: Oxford University Press.

Lara, Jesús. 1947. *La poesía Quechua.* Mexico City: Fondo de Cultura Económica.

—— "Manifiesto de Tiwanaku". 1981 [1973]. *Utopía y Revolución. El pensamiento político contemporáneo de los indios en América Latina.* Ed. Guillermo Bonfil. Mexico City: Nueva Imagen. 216–23.

Meléndez, Juan. Fray. 1681 [1671]. *Tesoros verdaderos de las Indias.* Vol. II. Rome: N.A. Tinassio.

Mendoza, Jaime. 1911. *En las tierras de Potosí.* Barcelona: Viuda de Luis Tasso.

Menéndez y Pelayo, Marcelino. 1893–1895. *Antología de poetas hispanoamericanos, publicada por la Real Academia Española.* Madrid: Sucesores de Rivadeneyra.

Mesa, José de. 1989. "La cultura en La Paz: Ensayos y análisis de temas prehispánicos, virreinales y republicanos." *La ciudad de La Paz: Su historia, su cultura.* La Paz: Alcaldía Municipal. 301–636.

Millones, Luis. 1998. *De la evangelización colonial a la religiosidad popular peruana: El culto a las imágenes sagradas.* Seville: Fundación El Norte.

Mitre, Bartolomé. 1933 [1847]. *Soledad.* Buenos Aires: J.C. Rovira.

Monteagudo Bernardo. 1973 [1808]. *Diálogo de Atahuallpa y Fernando VII en los Campos Elíseos.* La Paz: n.p.

Moreno, Gabriel René. 1956. *Estudios de literatura boliviana.* Potosí: Editorial Potosí.

Nolasco Crespo, Pedro. 1878 [1781]. *Loa que al mérito del Brigadier don Sebastián Segurola, compuso por vía de epitalamio don Pedro de Nolasco Crespo.* La Paz: José Rosendo Gutiérrez, comp.

Ocaña, Diego de. 1957 [1601]. *Comedia de Nuestra Señora de Guadalupe y sus milagros.* La Paz: Alcaldía Municipal.

Palma, Ricardo. 1997. *Tradiciones Peruanas.* Lima: Biblioteca Nacional del Perú.

Paredes, Rigoberto. 1911 [1907]. *Política Parlamentaria de Bolivia.* La Paz: Velarde Ediciones.

———. 1963 [1920]. *Mitos, supersticiones y supervivencias populares de Boliva.* 3rd ed. La Paz: Ediciones Isla.

Pasos Kanki, José Vicente. 1834. *Memorias histórico-políticas.* London: J. Moyes.

———. 1836. *El Evangelio de Jesu Christo según San Lucas en Aymará y español. Traducido de la Vulgata Latina.* London: J. Moyes.

Piedra Imán. 1997–2000. La Paz: Ediciones del Hombrecito Sentado.

Poppe, René. 1971. *Después de las calles.* La Paz: Camarlinghi.

———. 1973. *El Koya loco.* La Paz: Editorial Isla.

Prada Oropeza, Renato. 1969. *Los fundadores del alba.* La Paz–Cochabamba: Los Amigos del Libro.

Puntos Suspendidos. 1995–1998. La Paz: Plural.

Quiroga Santa Cruz, Marcelo. 1957. *Los deshabitados.* La Paz: Talleres Gráficos Bolivianos.

Rama, Ángel. 1982. *Transculturación narrativa en América latina.* Mexico City: Siglo XXI Editores.

Ramos Gavilán, Fray Alonso. 1976 [1621]. *Historia del célebre santuario de Nuestra Señora de Copacabana.* La Paz: Academia Boliviana de la Historia.

Rivera Cusicanqui, Silvia. 1984. *Oprimidos pero no vencidos. Luchas del campesinado aymara y qhechwa 1900–1980.* La Paz: CSUTCB-HISBOL.

Ruiz, Raúl, dir. 1953. *Vuelve Sebastiana.* Bolivia Films.

Saavedra, Bautista. 1902. *Proceso Mohoza. Defensa del abogado Bautista Saavedra pronunciada en la Audiencia del 12 de octubre de 1901.* La Paz: Tipográfica Velarde.

———. 1955 [1903]. *El Ayllu (Estudio sociológico).* La Paz: Editorial Gisbert.

Sáenz, Jaime. 1955. *El escalpelo.* La Paz: El Progreso.

———. 1975. *Obra poética.* La Paz: Biblioteca del Sesquicentenario de la República.

———. 1979. *Felipe Delgado.* La Paz: Difusión.

———. 1979. *Imágenes paceñas.* La Paz: Difusión.

———. 1984. *La noche.* La Paz: Talleres Escuela de Artes Gráficas.

Saignes, Thierry. 1985. *Los Andes Orientales. Historia de un olvido.* Cochabamba: CERES e IFEA.

———. 1986. *En busca del poblamiento étnico de los Andes Bolivianos.* La Paz: Museo Nacional de Etnografía y Folklore.

Sanjinés, Javier. 1985. "Introducción." *Tendencias actuales en la literatura boliviana.* Ed. Javier Sanjinés. Minneapolis: Institute for the Study of Ideologies and Literature; Valencia: Instituto de Cine y Radio-Televisión. 7–26.

———. 1992. *Literatura contemporánea y grotesco social en Bolivia.* La Paz: Fundación BHN, ILDIS.

Sanjinés, Jorge, dir. 1966. *Ukamau [(así es!].* Instituto Cinematográfico Boliviano.

———, dir. 1969. *Yawar Mallcu [sangre de cóndor].* Grupo Ukamau.

———, dir. 1971. *El coraje del pueblo.* Grupo Ukamau.

———, dir. 1989. *La nación clandestina.* Grupo Ukamau.

——— and Oscar Soria, dirs. 1965. *Aysa.* Instituto Cinematográfico Boliviano.

Santos Vargas, José. 1982. *Diario de un comandante de la Independencia americana (1814–1825).* Ed. Gunnar Mendoza. Mexico City: Siglo XXI.

Shimose, Pedro. 1968. *Poemas para un pueblo.* La Paz: Editorial Difusión.

Taboada Terán, Néstor. 1977. *Manchay Puytu. El amor que quiso ocultar Dios.* Buenos Aires: Editorial Sudamericana.

Tamayo, Franz. 1975 [1910]. *Creación de la pedagogía nacional.* La Paz: Biblioteca del Sesquicentenario de la República.

Tamayo, Isaac. 1914. *Habla Melgarejo.* La Paz: Puerta del Sol.

Tejada Sorzano, José Luis. 1911. *Después de la crisis.* La Paz: n.p.

Thibaud, Clément. 1997. "La Academia Carolina de Charcas: una 'escuela de dirigentes' para la Independencia." *El siglo XIX. Bolivia y América Latina.* Ed. Rossana Barragán, Dora Cajías and Seemin Qayum. La Paz: Instituto Francés de Estudios Andinos. 39–60.

Tragedia del fin de Atahuallpa. 1957. Ed. and trans. Jesús Lara. Cochabamba: Imprenta Universitaria.

Urzagasti, Jesús. 1969. *Tirinea.* Buenos Aires: Editorial Sudamericana.

———. 1987. *En el país del silencio.* La Paz: HISBOL.

Uzín, Oscar. 1972. *El ocaso de Orión.* La Paz–Cochabamba: Los Amigos del Libro.

Vallejo, Gaby. 1973. *Los vulnerables.* La Paz–Cochabamba: Los Amigos del Libro.

Vega, Julio de la. 1971. *Matías, el apóstol suplente.* La Paz: Los Amigos del Libro.

Villamil de Rada, Emeterio. 1988. *La lengua de Adán.* La Paz: Imprenta de la Razón.

Wiethüchter, Blanca. 1979. *Noviembre 79.* La Paz: Ediciones Piedra Libre.

Zamudio, Adela. 1913. *Intimas.* La Paz: Imprenta Velarde.

SECTION V
AMAZONIA
INTRODUCTION

Nicomedes Suárez Araúz

One can speak of "Amazonian literature" in the same sense in which one speaks of Peruvian, Chilean, Bolivian, Cuban or other literatures.

—Luis Hernán Ramírez

Ever since Francisco de Orellana in 1542 saw in awe the "river ocean" that he baptized with the name of a classical myth, the historical process of Amazonia has seemed irreversible. It cleared the way for the tragic decimation of indigenous groups, for the erosion and erasure of their cultures brought about by miscegenation and acculturation, and, ultimately, for the devastation of the region's natural wholeness. Today Amazonia is 87 percent ethnically and culturally *mestizo*, belying the image of it as terra incognita inhabited by "barbaric" tribes. The earlier vision of a region as a savage land, as represented in the 1571 map of Fernão Vaz Dourado (**Map 1**), persists today in the exoticized images of tourism and in the simplistic representations in news and entertainment media. European chroniclers, explorers, and naturalists provided the first Western visions of Amazonia. To them it was either benign or evil, a Paradise on earth or a living Inferno. In the nineteenth and twentieth centuries, writers reiterated both of those visions, giving them their own inflections. They also conceived the region in new metaphors: as lost paradise, green hell, green desert, vortex, chaos, promised land, immature land, green mansions, green architecture, and green plains of amnesia. The anthropologist Claude Lévi-Strauss labeled it a sad or melancholic tropical land; adventurers, developers, and government bureaucrats see is as a last frontier.

Map 1.

Map of the Amazon Region by Fernao Vaz Dourado, 1571. (Courtesy of Fundación Ptolomeo and the Central Bank of Ecuador)

A brief review of approaches to the literary history of the region will further illustrate the outsider and Eurocentric view of Amazonian culture. Spanish American critics have equated the earlier modern writing of the area with "The Novel of the Jungle," a label that incongruously conflates Spanish-, Portuguese-, and English-speaking works and includes diverse genres. For example, Lydia León de Hazera (b. 1927) lists, besides novels, the travelogues *De Bogotá al Atlántico* [1897; *Down the Orinoco in a Canoe,* 1902] by Santiago Pérez Triana (1858–1916) and *The Sea and the Jungle* (1912) by Henry Major Tomlinson (1873–1958), as well as the short-story collections *Inferno verde* [1908; Green Inferno] by Alberto Rangel (1871–1945) and *La venganza del cóndor* [1924; The Vengeance of the Condor] by Ventura García Calderón (1886–1959). Except for Ciro Alegría (1909–1967), born in Huamachuco, Peru, the authors León de Hazera mentions are not native to the region. To claim Amazonian "citizenship" for foreign writers such as Hudson or Tomlinson would be equivalent to labeling Joseph Conrad (1857–1924) an African writer or E. M. Forster (1879–1970) an Indian author.

Following similar criteria we can speak of "The Poetry of the Jungle," or, more comprehensively, group all genres together as "The Writing of the South American Amazonian Jungle." These classifications are based on a simplistic notion: *Selva* (from the Latin *silva*, meaning wild or savage)–the term for *jungle*–manifests a commonplace view of a barbaric social milieu, the product of a hostile natural environment. To be precise, however, the 7 million square kilometers of Amazonia overflow the limits of the jungle: The region spans vast savannahs, ascends into the sierra and, at its western limits, falls within the perimeters of Andean cities such as Quito and La Paz. Furthermore, some Amazonian writing since the 1930s has transcended traditional regional thematics.

A few critics use the term *Amazonian literature* to denote the indigenous oral traditions. Unlike most works in the former categories, these autochthonous works not only are set in or are about Amazonia but are born out of it. Their widespread omission from national anthologies of such work from most Amazonian-basin countries speaks to the perpetuation of old prejudices. The works' exclusion was the result of a cultural bias: the belief that these works were worthy solely of anthropological consideration. Critics, including the indigenist writer José Carlos Mariátegui (1894–1930), also disqualified them from literary status, basing their judgment on a strict definition of literature as *littera* ("letter"), that is, as written text (González Vigil 150). A debate persists as to whether Amazonian petroglyphs and hieroglyphs are genuine systems of writing (Ypiranga Monteiro 42). Significantly, after the 1920s, when Quechua and Aymara oral texts were accepted as foundational to the literature of the Andean countries of Bolivia, Ecuador, and Peru, their Amazonian counterparts continued to be ignored, revealing a hierarchical criterion of High Civilization and Low Civilization regions. Nonetheless, Amazonia has produced texts of remarkable merit, such as the *Moronguetá: um decameron indígena* [1967; Moronguetá: An Indigenist Decameron] by Manuel Nunes Pereira (b. 1893) from Brazil; the cosmogonic cycle of the Jurupari from Colombia and Brazil; or the creations of the Chimane and the Ayoreo from Bolivia and of the Huitoto and the Cashibo from Peru. These works, together with others of the nearly 400 linguistic groups of Amazonia, present a way to comprehend the complex Amazonian cosmological conception. The worldview appears to bear out a surprising ontological commonality among the groups (see Roe). Nonetheless, we should note that the phonetic transcription and translation of such works–with all the limitations and distortions that process implies–have been conducted mainly by anthropologists. Moreover, to claim this literature as the only legitimate Amazonian expression would be limiting. It would be equivalent to claiming that the oral traditions of the Sioux, Apache, Pueblo, Blackfoot, Iroquois, and other North American aboriginal nations are the only true literature of the United States, to the exclusion of English-speaking works.

Since the beginning of the twentieth century, authors native to Amazonia, as I mention above, have become the main contributors to what we may call Amazonian syncretic writing. This trend finds expression in either of the two major linguae francae of Amazonia: Spanish on the Hispanic side, Portuguese on the Brazilian side. Within this group there are a few Spanish- and Portuguese-speaking writers who, because of prolonged residence in Amazonia and an identification with it, have been active participants in the culture of "the nation of waters," to evoke the poetic phrase of the Brazilian poet Thiago de Mello (b. 1926)–a writer who has also tried his hand at composing poems in Spanish.

In pre-Colonial times there seems to have been an iterative Amazonian village (to evoke a notion of Antonio Benítez-Rojo (b. 1931) from his study of Caribbean culture, *The Repeating Island*). History has accrued variants on it, but some of its basic components persist. The uniformity of the cultural characteristics of Amazonia on the eve of the European invasion was remarkable, as Betty Meggers noted in reference to the approximately 1,400 ethnic groups extant at the time. Sociohistorical developments in the region since the European arrival in 1542 have superimposed two other key factors on its original autochthonous base. In the seventeenth and eighteenth centuries came the religious missions (mostly Jesuit); in the nineteenth century began the turbulent neo-Colonial economic cycles that reached their apotheosis with the Rubber Boom era (1860s–1920) and continued throughout the twentieth century. Cinchona, natural latex, Brazil nuts, gold, emeralds, woods, cattle, iron, and genetic resources spell out the signs of neo-Colonial exploiting practices of the last 140 years that have led to the present ecological crisis.

As Benedito Nunes, Milton Hatoum, and I note in our essays in this section, the syncretism of cultural texts in the history of Amazonia is evident in the development of its major urban centers. Belém and Manaus, the two largest cities of the basin, started as outposts of the Portuguese Conquest and were, in their beginnings, mostly populated by indigenous peoples who were the mainstay of the economy on which the colonizers depended. As in other regions of the Amazon basin, economic bonanzas based on the exploitation of native products (the rubber tree, *Hevea brasiliensis*), caused the expansion of the cities and brought to them European cultural elements. The signs of foreign influence are seen today, in Belém and Manaus, in the urban planning and in the neo-Classical, Baroque, and Art Nouveau architecture of the old sections of these cities. Belém, the older of the two centers, held sway until late in the twentieth century as the more progressive. Manaus strove to rival Belém's cosmopolitanism during the nineteenth century, and given Manaus' explosive economic growth during the Rubber Boom and its establishment in 1967 as a free-trade zone, it has become just as important an Amazonian metropolis as Belém. Yet in both cities, as Nunes and Hatoum point out, the architectural and other cultural signs evoking an older age mingle with the clamorous, and sometimes disturbing, echoes of continuing modernization.

The identification of Bolivia's eastern territory with the culture of the Greater Amazonia, which was an accepted notion in the nineteenth century, eroded in the twentieth century as the economic interdependency of Amazonian regions collapsed in 1920 with the end of the Rubber Boom. Since the 1980s, however, Bolivia's Amazonia, which had remained relatively isolated from the country's Andean centers of economic and political power, harked back to its lost Amazonian cultural identity. Riberalta, a city that began as a rubber-producing post, pointed the way. This Amazonian consciousness has spread to Trinidad, the capital of the state of Beni. With the intent of restoring their Amazonian identity, the citizens of Beni and of Pando, its neighboring northern department, are reclaiming their indigenous and *mestizo* past. An increase in economic links with other Amazonian regions, especially Brazil's, has induced Bolivian Amazonians to recognize a cultural commonality with the rest of the regions of the Amazon basin.

In the last three decades, traditional Amazonian towns and cities such as Iquitos in Peru, Leticia in Colombia, Manaus and Belém in Brazil, and Riberalta and Trinidad in Bolivia are undergoing a transformation into modern urban centers. In them, myriad cultural signs (which initially ascended the river in canoes, steamboats, and ocean liners) mix with local cultural manifestations that nonetheless reveal the muted presence of the indigenous peoples. These towns and cities are the new ultra-syncretic centers, where indigenous religion and lore mingle with Christian practices, where bows and arrows and AK assault guns are handled by natives, where oxcarts and jets coexist, and where cybernauts live side by side with shamans. The postmodern assemblage of cultural signs lends specific inflections to the various river cultures of Amazonia, depending on their ethnic mix and communication with the outside world. Nonetheless, the citizens of the various Amazonian regions have more in common with one another than with the inhabitants of the capital cities of their countries. Thus, a Bolivian Amazonian from the Mamoré River shares more with a Brazilian from Guajará Mirim, Manaus, or Belém than with a countryman from the highland cities of La Paz or Oruro.

Awareness of a similar culture and history spurred the countries of the region to create in 1987 the Union of Amazonian Universities, signaling an impulse toward unification. Several international treaties of economic cooperation in the development of Amazonia have been signed. A literary counterpart to this impulse, however, lags behind. The Center for Amazonian Literature and Culture was founded in 1993 at Smith College in the United States with the intention of being a catalyst to and a forum for a new understanding of Amazonia–one that restores its natural continuity of rivers, forests, savannahs, and sierras. (This continuity was first divided by the Treaty of Tordesillas of 1494, which apportioned the region's western section to Spain and eastern section to Portugal. It was further parceled out after the wars of Independence (1810–1825) and by regional strife among the countries that compose the Basin.) In 1998 the Center began publication of the *Amazonian Literary Review*, a journal devoted to the enhancement of the study of literature from the region. Questioning the existence and setting the parameters of Brazilian Amazonian literature, Mário Ypiranga Monteiro noted: "It wasn't until 1940 that people began speaking of an Amazonian literature as a convenient way of grouping writers. Meanwhile, Mário de

Andrade (1893–1945), and before him Joaquim de Sousa Andrade (1833–1902) and Antônio Gonçalves Dias (1823–1864), came to Amazonia in search of sources for their indigenist works" (in Suárez Araúz and Cutler 2).

Importantly, 1819 marks the beginning of modern Amazonian poetry in Brazil with the publication of Captain Henrique João Wilkens' epic poem, "A Muhuraida." Another foundational poem, *Cobra Norato* by Raul Bopp (1898–1984), is representative of the anthropophagic aesthetics of Brazil's *modernista* movement of the 1920s, whose aspirations had more in common with the Anglo American Modernism than with the earlier Spanish American *modernismo*, which was influenced by Parnassian and Symbolist writings. Benedito Nunes, noting the belatedness with which literary currents arrived in Brazilian Amazonia, wrote: "It was only in 1946 or 1947 that we came to know of *modernismo*" (see in Santiago 31). On 22 February 1954, an informal association, "O Clube da Madrugada," was founded in Manaus and has included such progressive writers as Luiz Bacellar (b. 1928), Antísthenes Pinto (b. 1929), Jorge Tufic (b. 1930), and Astrid Cabral (b. 1936)–all calling for a break from the earlier Parnassian poetry. It was preceded by the association "Norte," founded in Belém do Pará, where it published a magazine whose contributors included Benedito Nunes (b. 1929), Ruy Guilherme Barata (1920–1990), and others (Tufic 1984, 16).

In Bolivia as in Perú, writing from the Amazonian regions has, with a certain lag, followed the literary movements of the rest of Spanish America: from *modernismo* and its decline (1880–1920) to the inclusion of avant-garde currents (in Amazonia, since the 1930s). However, in a recent literary history of Peru, the stages of Peruvian Amazonian writing are periodized, significantly, in relation to key economic cycles: Período Cauchero ("Rubber Boom Period"), 1868–1920; Post Cauchero ("Post-Rubber Boom"), 1921–1970; Petrolero ("Oil Exploration Period"), 1970–1991 (Toro Montalvo 93). By such categorization, Toro Montalvo suggests that Amazonian literature in his country has no autonomy from economic developments: neo-Colonial exploiting conditions its periodization.

Like all regional literature, Amazonia's began by being centered on the motifs and themes suggested by its natural environment. Raúl Otero Reiche (1906–1976) from Bolivia voiced the ancient idea that the telluric was the power that inevitably determines the social psychology of human beings. This notion of Amazonian societies as *earth centered* was reiterated by Socorro Santiago in 1986: "Do rio e da floresta esse homem tira o necessário para o sustento do seu corpo" ("From the river and the forest, [an Amazonian] takes what is necessary for the sustenance of his body"). This environment, she adds, "gigantesco e misterioso, . . . imprime em seu sistema nervoso imagens e ficções estranhas, produto do medo, fruto da solidão" (Santiago 27) ("gigantic and mysterious, . . . impresses on his nervous system strange images, products of fear, fruit of his solitude"). Similarly, the *Encyclopédia de literatura brasileira* [*Encyclopedia of Brazilian Literature*] states:

> A Naturaleza, que é na Amazônia ao mesmo tempo terror, beleza e magia, explica a vocação lírica e a tendência mística do homen. . . . O caráter do habitante da planície é a saturação das suas própias inquietações. Comprimido entre duas terríveis melancolias: a do rio e a da floresta, ele se volve para si mesmo–e contraindo-se na angústia da introversão, foge à realidade cósmica pela imaginação, que gera os mitos e as lendas, os fantasmas e os talismãs, os espantos, os duendes, as supertições, todo o encantamento do fabulário caboclo do Inferno Verde. (Coutinho and Sousa 207)

Nature, which in Amazonia is at the same time terror, beauty, and magic, explains the lyric vocation of and the mystic tendency of Amazonians . . . . The character of the inhabitant of the plains derives from the saturation of his own anxiety. Caught between his two terrible melancholies, that of the river and that of the forest, he turns inward, and withdrawing into self-searching, he escapes to a cosmic reality by means of the imagination which invents myths and legends, phantoms, talismans, terrors, demons, superstitions—the whole enchantment of the *caboclo's* collection of fables of the Green Hell.

Whereas sea dwellers live out in the midst of a heartbeat of waters that speak in the plural, the river dweller lives in the apparent pure sound of a Heraclitean flow. The river's binary rhythm of droughts and floods seems to be that flow's only variant. Naturally, as Santiago points out, the urban dweller of cities such as Manaus is not as affected as the rural or jungle dweller who lives by the waters and, to a large extent, from them. Considering the ever-presence of the river, Socorro Santiago sees elemental water as the unifying theme in *Uma poética das águas* [A Poetics of the Waters], her study of poets from the state of Amazonas, which she appropriately grounds in Bachelardian phenomenology.

The presence of the region's indigenous cultures surfaces in its distinctive Amazonian *mestizo* imaginary space about which poet Paes Loureiro (b. 1939) writes in *A Cultura Amazônica: Uma poética do imaginário* [1995; Amazon Culture: A Poetic of the Imaginary]. Amazonian literature today visits that imaginary space that fuses past with present and speaks through myth the language of the individual and collective psyche. Thus, the living myth of the *boto*, the river dolphin capable of metamorphosis into human form and interaction with humans, surfaces in the poems of João de Jesus Paes Loureiro, Jorge Tufic, and Astrid Cabral. Tufic treats the myth of Jurupari, a polysemic figure who mediates and interconnects the human and natural realms. Some Amazonian myths are relatively recent or may have changed upon coming in contact with outside cultures. The Dolphin cycle, Luís da Câmara Cascudo notes, probably did not exist among the Indians of pre-Colonial Brazil (Slater 2). The Peruvian César Calvo (b. 1940) inverts the myth-making process in his poem "Amazona." In it he seems to transmute a personal relationship with a woman into the legendary elements of the Amazon River's inception. Amazona, both a real and a mythic person, gives mythogenetic birth to the river formed from her inconsolable and torrential weeping. This sense of the marvelous is also present in Elson Farias (b. 1936), who unveils in his poem "Rain Patterns" the mystery and ritual of water and in "The Medicine Man," the miraculous curative powers of a Shamanic healer.

Other poems elicit the myths and realities of the Conquest and El Dorado; still others touch on the ensuing colonialism and neocolonialism. Reflecting these concerns, Nicomedes Suárez Araúz (b. 1946), in his series of poems *Recetario Amazónico* [Amazonian Recipes], presents Amazonia in an extended ironic metaphor of the region and its people as edible dishes consumable by the outside world. Julio de la Vega (b. 1924) reiterates the image of the jungle vortex that vanquished intruders such as Francisco de Orellana, who, blinded by delusions of incalculable riches, died while attempting to navigate the Amazon a second time. Pedro Shimose (b. 1940) in "Moxitania" ("The Land of the Moxos Indians") aspires to that Edenic, pristine moment that preceded human presence, particularly that of the Europeans.

Shimose also evokes the brutish hordes of rubber tappers who brought, along with their greed, their garish vulgarity and murderous instincts. Paes Loureiro in "Workers" and "Bar do Parque" treats the urban theme of dehumanization. Otero Reiche voices the horrors of the war with Paraguay (1933–1936) that made his country's Amazonia bleed. Lequerica Perea (b. 1931) indirectly refers to the 1960s and 1970s—a period of bloody conflicts in Peru between socialist guerrillas and national government troops. Cabral, Paes Loureiro, and Shimose denounce the ecological devastation of the region.

As for foundational stylistic innovation, we should emphasize the role of Otero Reiche, Thiago de Mello, and Luiz Bacellar, outstanding figures who bridge the older styles of Amazonian writing and the new ones. From the 1930s on, Otero Reiche combined in his poetry expressionist and surrealist elements. Thiago de Mello (b. 1926) has incorporated international influences, including modern European traditions and the use of haiku. We perceive in these and other Amazonian writers, perhaps to a greater extent than in other Latin American writers, a tendency, even within a single poem, toward an amalgam of styles and intertexts. These are derived both from Amazonian and other poetic traditions. For example, in "The Forest," a poem written in the 1930s, Otero Reiche combines classical mythology, indigenous motifs, representations of nature by Chateaubriand and other Romantics, surreal and expressionist images, and the enumerative rhetoric of Whitman (which influenced Neruda during the same period).

Amazonian poetry can be faulted, especially in its beginnings, for its excessive rhetoricism. Under the influence of Euclides da Cunha (1866–1909), verbal inebriation became the fashion among Brazil's Amazonian writers of the nineteenth century; authors of Spanish American Amazonia, such as the Peruvian Juan Fabriciano Hernández Bustamante (1844–1890), echoed their grandiloquence. Amazonian writing adopted an arch-Romanticism, often tinged with Naturalism. *Tremendismo* (a thematic content that wallows in appallingly sordid acts) colors many of these early works. The modern Amazonian poets still manifest some of those characteristics; yet poems such as the sonnets by Otero Reiche and works by Lequerica Perea, Anibal Beçã (b. 1946), Cabral, Farias, Tufic, and others display both formal experimentation and a more restrained rhetoric.

The written history of Amazonia is yet to be pieced together–a process that may never be completed since large segments of the basin's historical puzzle disappear year-by-year, even before they are recorded. Darcy Ribeiro (1922–1997) noted that 100 indigenous groups became extinct between 1900 and 1970, the year of the publication of his classic book, *Os indios e a civilização* [The Indians and Civilization]. The disappearance of indigenous groups and their languages drains away a wealth of cultural knowledge. Not surprisingly, one of the key metaphors applied to the region has been "green plains of amnesia," an image which served as the pre-text to the apocryphal writings of *Los escribanos de Loén* [The Scribes of Loén] (Suárez Araúz 1982). The notion of a historical lacuna is a recurrent theme in regards to the literary production from Amazonia, possibly because the region's writings seem exiguous relative to its geographic immensity. The literary corpus by writers native to the region, nonetheless, is quite extensive, both in poetry and fiction.

Figure 1.

Photograph of anonymous nineteenth-century painting of Amazon river travel. (Archive of the author)

Amazonian history has been dependent on a inherited "discourse handed down in historical and literary texts" (Maligo 1998: 152). This practice began in its most extreme manner, with Amazonia's invention preceding its discovery. Echoing Edmundo O' Gorman's (1906–1995) pioneering work, *La invención de América* [1958; *The Invention of America*, 1961], Neide Gondim's *A invenção da Amazônia* [1994; The Invention of Amazonia] points out the intellectual processes by which the newly discovered region was integrated into the Western world. In some recent Amazonian novels the initial visions and motifs of the region's history and earlier literature are still present, as well as references to an imaginary space nourished by Indian and *mestizo* or *caboclo* lore. For example, César Calvo's (b. 1940) *Las tres mitades de Ino Moxo* [1981; *The Three Halves of Ino Moxo*, 1995] is an innovative mythopoetic narrative evoking shamanic practices to present a panorama of the transculturation and dialogue among its diverse ethnic and cultural components. Aspects of the early history of travel in the region are used by Márcio Souza (b. 1946) in his best-known works, *Galvez: Imperador do Acre: Folhetim* [1977; *The Emperor of the Amazon*, 1980] and *Mad Maria: Romance* (1980). (See **Figure 1.**) Like Souza's other works, these narratives are deft, burlesque allegories, featuring a comic flair and a sense of the absurd in reference to cultural confrontations that allow the author to reflect on the situation of his time. Milton Hatoum (b. 1952) launched a successful literary career with his first novel *Relato de um certo oriente* [1989; *The Tree of the Seventh*

Heaven, 1994], which explores, within the urban setting of contemporary Manaus, the conflictive experience of new immigrants to Amazonia.

Amazonian literature, then, as much as the region's cultural centers, bears the mark of Amazonia's historical incongruity which has resulted in an amalgam of influences–a phenomenon brought about primarily by the region's Colonial dependency. The foreign cultural signs evident in Amazonia's cities from a colorful and exciting patchwork that only partly covers the misery that overflows from the peripheries toward their center, or vice versa. Amazonian literature has often been a reflection and a criticism of such reality. Its authors write at the margins of the Western world, and sometimes even of their own national societies: Their texts stand as a courageous act of creation against the void of an invasive historical amnesia. Their cultural centers are symbols of a strong human will to withstand the hardships of a powerful nature and the general indifference from the outside world.

Works Cited

Coutinho, Afrânio, and José Galante de Sousa, eds. 1990. *Enciclopédia de literatura brasileira.* Rio de Janeiro: FAE–Ministerio de Educação.

Cunha, Euclides da. 1976. *Um paraíso perdido: Reunião de ensaios amazônicos.* Petropolis: MEC.

Gondim, Neide. 1994. *A invenção da Amazônia.* São Paulo: Editora Marco Zero.

González Vigil, Ricardo. 1990. *Retablo de autores peruanos*. Lima: Ediciones Arco Iris.

León de Hazera, Lydia. 1971. *La novela de la selva hispanoamericana*. Bogota: ICC.

Maligo, Pedro. 1998. *Land of Metaphorical Desires: The Representation of Amazonia in Brazilian Literature*. New York: Peter Lang.

Mandelbrot, Benoit. 1977. *The Fractal Geometry of Nature*. New York: Freeman.

Meggers, Betty. 1971. *Amazonia: Man and Culture in a Counterfeit Paradise*. Chicago: University of Chicago Press.

O' Gorman, Edmundo. 1958. *La invención de América*. Mexico City: Fondo de Cultura Económica.

Paes Loureiro, João de Jesus. 1995. *Cultura amazônica: Uma poética do imaginário*. Belém: Editora Cejup.

Ribeiro, Darcy. 1970. *Os indios e a civilização: a integração das populaçoes indigenas no Brasil moderno*. Rio de Janeiro: Civilização Brasileira.

Roe, Peter G. 1982. *The Cosmic Zygote: Cosmology in the Amazon Basin*. New Brunswick, NJ: Rutgers University Press.

Santiago, Socorro. 1986. *Uma poética das águas: a imagen do rio na poesia amazonense contemporánea*. Manaus: Edicões Puxirum.

Slater, Candace. 1994. *Dance of the Dolphin: Transformation and Disenchantment in the Amazonian Imagination*. Chicago: University of Chicago Press.

Suárez Araúz, Nicomedes. 1982. *Los escribanos de Loén*. 2nd ed. Housatonic: Lascaux Publishers.

——, and Charles Cutler. 1993. "Cuestionario/Questionário." Northhampton, Mass. Center for Amazonian Literature and Culture.

Toro Montalvo, César. 1996. *Historia de la literatura peruana*. Vol. 9: *Literatura amazónica*. Lima: A.F.A. Editores.

Tufic, Jorge. 1982. *Existe uma literatura amazonense?* Manaus: UBE-União Brasileira de escritores.

——. 1984. *Clube da madrugada: 30 anos*. Manaus: Impresa Oficial do Estado do Amazonas.

Ypiranga Monteiro, Mário. 1977. *Fases da literatura amazonense*. Manaus: Universidade do Amazonas.

CHAPTER 43

BELÉM
CULTURAL CENTER

Benedito Nunes

The Paris of old is there no more—
a city's pattern changes, alas,
more swiftly than the human heart—
—*Baudelaire 174*

In contributing to this literary history of Latin American cultural centers, I attempt to repay an old debt of mine to Belém, the subject of this study. My debt extends to the generation that experienced the city when it was still lovely between 1940 and 1960. Many of this generation are no longer with us. I am not concerned with rescuing Belém from the urban ravishment it has suffered for many years. Promises of rescues, both cultural and historical, are too often made. In the rhetoric of the state the term rescue is used and abused to the point of losing its import—our debt to Belém is too dear and impossible to be paid back. I merely sketch a freehand portrait of Belém from the reliable sources now available. In the past and still today I have had cause to feel close to texts by these authors: Vicente Salles, Roberto Santos, Fábio Castro, and the late Eidorfe Moreira, Augusto Meira Filho, and Ernesto Cruz. I dedicate my portrait of Belém to them. I have composed it from information gleaned from their studies, and colored it with the hues of my own tender recollection of Belém.

Father Vieira, Landi, and La Condamine

In 1616 the Portuguese captain Francisco Caldeira Castelo Branco founded Fort Presépio (so named after the Christmas tradition of the nativity scene) between the Guamá River and Guajará Bay, a secondary branch of the Amazon separated from that great river by the archipelago of Marajó. As an outlying post of the dominion of the United Crown of Portugal and Castille over the north of Brazil, Fort Presépio was meant to deter the foreign—primarily French—expansion already in evidence in São Luis, capital of the modern state of Maranhão. A Jesuit college and a Baroque church (dedicated to the Jesuit order) were established alongside the fort, which became the initial nucleus of the city of Belém. This area known as Felicitous Lusitania extended south along the margins of the Guamá River and north to the border with Guajará Bay, where the fort was separated from the continent by the marshy bayou of Pirí. (Technically Pirí or Piry constituted a *Cyperus Giganteus*, a great cyperaceous or sedge of submerged lowlands known much less formally in the continent as a *taboa* [see Vicente Chermont de Miranda 69]). But the Felicitous Lusitania that Father Antônio Vieira beheld upon his arrival in 1655 was far from thriving, and its population remained more indigenous than Portuguese due to the vast number of tribes native to the region.

At this time Belém constituted no more "than a modest assemblage of wattle and daub straw-thatched structures" (Moreira 1966, 34). In addition, the Portuguese adopted a mechanism of defense common to native villages, the *caiçara*–in principle less a fortress than a palisade–which at Fort Presépio served to encircle and protect not only the convent and the colonizers'

homes but also the villages of their native subjects. Already during his sojourn in Maranhão, Vieira had noted:

> The inhabitants of what we may term this new world are either Portuguese or Indians native to this land. Among the natives those who remain non-Christian live in the hinterland and possess an infinite number and diversity of languages. Those Indians who are for the most part Christian live among the Portuguese, some in freedom in their own villages and others in a state of partial captivity, living in Portuguese households and working on the plantations vital to their own sustenance and survival.
> (Vieira I, 297)

The entire fabric of the colonizers' material life was woven and given to them by the natives: from the rustic architecture of the colonizers' houses to the construction of their vessels, from the basic sustenance afforded by the cultivation of cassava to the practice of fishing, handpicking wild fruit, and the techniques for hunting turtles, alligators, and great cetaceans such as the *peixe-boi* (ox-fish). The Jesuit who accompanied Pedro Teixeira (ca. 1570–1610) on his Amazonian voyage had cause to remark: "There are so many Indians that a needle cannot drop to the ground" (J. Lúcio Azevedo 238).

Among the innumerable non-Christian groups native to the region Vieira named the Maimanás, Aruãs, Anajás, Mapuás, Paicacás, Guajarás, and Pixispixis–peoples that were mostly extinct by the end of the century. (Perplexed, the Jesuit noted the killing of 2 million natives over the span of forty years.) Preceded in the region by merchants and by the Franciscan order, the Jesuits aimed at what Vieira termed the spiritual conquest of these hundreds of thousands native souls. To that end Vieira argued that natives should be subject not to the governors and militia-governors who forced them into slave labor but exclusively to the Church, and he advocated the introduction (later effected by Maranhão's Commercial Company) of African slaves to the region (Salles 1971, 5). Native workers were nonetheless employed as rowers, bearers, fishermen, hunters, warriors, tobacco planters, laborers in civil and public works, and, in the nineteenth-century, also as extractors of latex from rubber trees. To the region's emergent *mestizo* culture the natives contributed many practices and customs, not least a cuisine centered on cassava and fish, ritual dances pertaining to the cult of birds, and the charms and rites of the *pagelança* cult. Despite the prohibition of the use of native languages by the Marquis of Pombal, these languages came to fertilize Portuguese in all its grammatical categories and to contribute to it many exclamations, nouns, verbs, and adjectives, as documented by José Veríssimo (1857–1916) in his 1886 glossary of Tupi-Guarani terms then in vogue in the Amazon (and as evidenced in this essay by the presence of many italicized terms from the Tupi-Guarani).

In his most daring voyage inland along the Tocantins River, undertaken soon after his arrival in Belém, Vieira briefly forsook his catechist concerns (whose juridical dimension was manifest in the policy of rescuing the natives–what the Portuguese termed *resgate* and the Spanish *encomienda*). Though Vieira does not display the anthropological sense we associate with Bartolomé de las Casas's (1474–1566) chronicles of the New World, one of his letters admiringly describes the natives' ability to build canoes exclusively from materials provided by the storehouse of nature: out of bark, vine, branch-wood, resin and tar the natives forged the boards, ropes, awning, sails, and insulation for their canoes. Not a single nail was employed to sustain the vessel's structure. Vieira notes that the colonizers' houses were themselves built by natives, who had access to nothing but the forest's simple raw materials; houses he describes as brutish and sad (Vieira 360ff). At the outset the Portuguese did not themselves have access to another technology.

It is only with the eighteenth-century administration of Francisco de Mendonça Furtado, a brother of the Marquis of Pombal who was concerned with implementing the Portuguese Crown's directives against the use of indigenous languages, that the latest European developments in civil and religious architecture reached this province. They arrived through architect and designer Giuseppe Landi, a native of Bologna who had first established himself in Barcelos in the neighboring state of Amazonas and who had from 1754 worked with the committee responsible for the demarcation of Portuguese and Spanish territory in accordance with the 1750 Treaty of Madrid.

Landi's influence predated the expedition of naturalist Alexandre Rodrigues Ferreira (1756–1815), whose *Viagem Filosófica* [1783–1792; Philosophical Voyage] chronicled in word and image the labors of nature and man along the route from the Island of Marajó to the Black River. A native of Bahia, Ferreira opened this route to visiting scientists from abroad, among them La Condamine (in the eighteenth century), and L. Agassiz, Daniel Kidder, and Henry Walter Bates (in the nineteenth century). From the moment Landi established himself in Belém (where he would marry a local woman and later die in 1791), he displayed a unique architectural style found in the Governmental Palace (erected in 1748) and the city's many prominent churches and chapels sketched or modified by him. This began with Landi's reconstruction of Belém's Governmental Palace and Cathedral (the Cathedral then bordered not only the Baroque church of the Jesuits but the church of Saint Francis Xavier, and later that of Saint Alexander). The palace gained a chapel and a façade leading to its interior garden. In a style reminiscent of his master Bibiena, Landi reconstructed the Cathedral's entrance and façade and adorned it with new towers. Landi's innovations further encompassed the Church of the Order of the Carmelites (today belonging to the Salesians) and (behind the palace) his masterpiece, Saint John the Baptist's chapel, with its distinctive eight-sided nave and bell tower. In the main passageways of Belém's center, then separated from the fort by the Pirí and known under the name of Campina, Landi's style was manifest in the convex façade of the Mercês Church, in the Mercedarios Church, in the Sant'Ana Church (where he was to be buried), and in the Pombo family's private chapel that

became a mandatory stop for religious processions. Landi's touch was to be felt as far away as the city's periphery and even to the margins of the Guamá in the form of the Murutucu Chapel, of which only ruins remain. Overall Landi's buildings display a style that is sober and neo-Classical without quite abandoning the Baroque and that further incorporates the Rococo of contemporary master and Minas Gerais native, Aleijadinho. Landi even designed an opera house that was to have been built in 1775. He was also a master of ceramics and a naturalist (Meira Filho [1976] lists sixty-seven of his extant prints of mammals, reptiles, and flora). In his capacity as botanist, Landi was responsible for the acclimatization of the Indian mango tree, which many years later would adorn most of the city's downtown streets (Meira Filho 1980, 4).

Even before Landi's work, Charles-Marie de La Condamine (1701–1774) felt he was transported to Europe when he beheld Belém after a sojourn in the Amazon forest. Thus La Condamine describes the Belém he visited from 1735 to 1745:

> We encountered a great city of well-aligned streets and magnificent churches, and of cheerful houses mostly built but three decades ago. A merchant fleet arrives from Lisbon every year and this trade allows the wealthy to provide for all their comforts with ease. European commodities are exchanged not only for gold-powder brought from the country's interior but for all manner of products brought to Belém via the Amazon or the rivers that flow into it: clover-wood bark, sarsaparilla, vanilla, sugar, coffee and above all cocoa, the source of the locals' riches, and the region's de facto currency. (La Condamine 107–108)

The market for these products was located at the heart of the sanctuary for the Virgin of Nazaré, the point of destination for traditional pilgrimages–the first of which was held by order of Governor Francisco de Souza Coutinho in 1790. The sanctuary was accessible only via a rustic path (later known as the road to Nazaré) that was surrounded by small ranches where the rich lived and tended their orchards. Today this site still attracts a rustic market and the annual procession in homage of Círio, a festivity that draws a mass of people in a state of religious fervor from both the interior and from Belém (Moreira 1971, 19). Since, at the time La Condamine wrote, Belém had barely undergone a process of urbanization, any comparison to the urban landscapes of Europe could not help but seem premature. It is only with the accentuation of certain urban features in the following century that a more limited comparison to Portugal, and to Lisbon in particular, becomes apt.

From Almost Venice to Almost Liverpool

Belém would only acquire its present shape at the end of the eighteenth century, when it was decisively reimagined along lines quite at odds with the fluvial nature of its topography. This was not due to the absence of a viable plan more in accordance with the dictates of nature. In fact, the engineer Gaspar João Gronfelts presented to governor Ataíde Teive the idea of opening canals following the contours of the Pirí, forging a harbor boasting stone piers and entrances alongside which fecund and decorative plants would be planted. Gronfelts's plan not only was technically feasible but might have made of Belém, as the engineer imagined, a new Venice. In rejecting this proposal the governor confirmed the policy (manifesting almost hydrophobia) shared by the city's successive administrations of making room for the city's spread by draining its numerous water courses. A systematic policy of arborization had already been pursued under the administration of the French with the establishment in 1781 of a botanical garden with specimens from Caiena (Penteado iii). In 1803 Count Arcos's administration initiated the process of converting the exuberant bayou of Pirí into a landfill, thus considerably advancing its land mass to the east. This in turn facilitated the extension of Belém's land to Campina and Nazaré, then the capital's outer limit. This expansion of Belém came at the time of the province's support for the fight for Brazilian independence in 1823 under the impetus of rebels (Felippe Patroni and Conego Batista Campos) and with the support of a fraction of the English fleet under the command of John Pascoe Grenfell.

Following the advent of Brazil's first empire, the explosion of pro-freedom and anti-Portuguese sentiment gathered new momentum in the form of what came to be known as the *cabanagem* of 1833–1836, in which the *mestizo* dwellers of the cabanas of the interior (*mestizos* whom the novelist Inglês de Sousa insisted on referring to as *tapuios*) revolted against landowners and the privileged. Only twelve years later, in 1848, would La Condamine's early impressions of Belém be superseded by the observations of naturalist Henry Walter Bates, who came to the Amazon in the company of Russell Wallace in search of empirical proof of Darwin's theory of evolution. Bates wrote:

> My first impressions of this first outing will never fade. Near the port we passed through some streets lined by tall and somber buildings not unlike convents, where soldiers in ragged uniforms idled carelessly bearing their muskets, and priests passed, as well as Negro women carrying on their heads pots of water, and Indian women bearing the weight of the naked infants on their hips with a melancholic air. . . .
>
> In our first excursions we limited ourselves to the city's periphery, located in a corner of land formed by the junction of the rivers Guamá and Pará (Guajará). . . . The forest that covers the whole region reaches into the city's streets. In truth the city was erected in a clearing in the middle of the woods, and only the government's constant care prevents the forest from reclaiming it. (Bates 14)

Signs of the golden age of the rubber boom to come were already evident from the first decades of the nineteenth century in the new forms of production that emerged in the extraction of sap from the *Hevea brasiliensis* or rubber tree, at a time in which rubber proved a highly prized and priced good in an international market which the Amazon, in the absence of competition, was predestined to supply exclusively. By 1848 (but particularly after 1854) what we might term the combustible effects of these new forms of production were already felt in Belém. The region's rapid and formidable enrichment culminated in the so-called golden age of 1890 to 1906, a period that appears to bear out the hypothesis of a causal (or dialectic) nexus between the renovation of the region's economic infrastructure as a function of the rubber boom and the renewal of its intellectual superstructure. According to this hypothesis the implementation of a new mode of production was accompanied by the establishment of a new social, political, and judicial way of life ideologically suited to rewarding and protecting capital but advantageous as well to the development of the arts and sciences. Yet while it seems to explain much, this reductive formula in fact explains nothing. If the financial and administrative system underlying the rubber boom's infrastructure proved as fragile as it appeared imposing, the boom's ensuing superstructure proved no more than the ephemeral fire of an artificial combustion ignited at the expense of the region's natural resources, slave labor, subjugated natives, and generally

destitute people. Weak government planning in the form of an administrative oversight determined the eventual decline of the region's rubber economy. The government of Pará allowed Henry Alexander Wickhan to send 70,000 seeds of *Hevea brasiliensis* to London, persuaded by the Englishman's claim that this amount of seed would be directed toward embellishing the botanical garden at Kew. Instead the seeds provided the genesis for the English rubber plantations in Malaysia, which in time were responsible for the fall in the price of rubber in international markets and for the gradual decline and final (1912) collapse of the financial system (both in Brazil and abroad) that had sustained the region's rubber boom (see Castro).

And yet Belém's process of urbanization and rise to the status of regional center had been greatly advanced already in the last decades of the eighteenth century, much before the rubber boom. A natural focal point along the Amazonian estuary–situated between river and forest, port and hinterland–Belém centralized the productive activities of the region's cities and villages in the eighteenth century. Belém's port was then the region's main site for national and international trade (including the slave market). After the destruction of the indigenous cultures and the subjugation of the surviving natives, the Portuguese looked to Belém for the dissemination of European civilization in the Amazon by force, more specifically through "the control over the source and course of the Amazon to Portugal's advantage" (Reis 1970 discusses this wave of imperial Conquest in his introduction to Amazon culture). During the Colonial period Belém ensured the maintenance of direct relations with Portugal, first as part of Maranhão and then as the capital of the Province of Pará and Rio Negro, a function it continued to fulfill after independence until 1850. Throughout this period Belém made possible a new wave of exploration and settlement known in Brazilian historiography (in deliberate contrast to the American model of pioneer expansionism) under the term *bandeirantismo* (Moreira 1966, 44). Long before its rubber boom, Belém had already acquired a distinctive profile of considerable aesthetic significance thanks to the profits from the sugar and cocoa plantations established during the period of the Marquis of Pombal. Albeit for different reasons, La Condamine and Henry Walter Bates were enchanted by the city that "due to its position and climate, vegetation and ecology, and due to the exuberance of the colors that surround it" proved "the most typical and representative of Brazilian tropical capitals" (Moreira 1966, 149–50). Belém's geographical location between river and forest, between the river's source and the ocean, had already predestined it to be the Amazon's cultural center, long before the mixed if not outright calamitous blessing of the affluence brought to the capital by the rubber boom. Nonetheless, during the industrial era of the expansion of the rubber economy Belém was indeed the center (Santos 42).

Once again involuntary indigenous labor proved integral to the region's mode of production. Natives were responsible for the extraction of latex from trees, a technique with which they were already familiar, and for the handicraft involved in making rubber replicas of European styles of leather shoes for export (particularly, as of 1820, to the United States). Later U.S. and other foreign manufacturers would send wooden molds to regulate production or simply leather shoes in need of rubber soles. Goodyear had not yet hit upon what is known in the industry as the process of vulcanization. At first the slow tempo of navigation abated the flow of raw materials to the capital and limited the exploitation of rubber to the forests close to Belém (ships were then still dependent on sails and even oars). Given that this limited mode of production encompassed merely the extraction of rubber rather than the final manufactured product that required industrialization, it exacerbated the sharp division of the boom's labor and rewards: Foreign banks administered capital and the means of transportation; local businessmen profitably arranged for carriers and export; the latex-extractors themselves remained poor. The forest provided latex, the rubber tapper extracted *pelotas* (balls) or *peles* (skins) of the raw material, foreign banks provided financing and generally also the ships, and the exporter transported the latex to interested nations such as England and the United States via intermediaries such as France, Italy, and Germany, all represented by consulates in Belém, which due to this activity even came to boast an Anglican Church and an English cemetery.

But at the outset it was not like this. Belém's late nineteenth-century rubber boom would not have been possible without the introduction of the steamboat in 1853. Under the pressure of the steam-powered and rapacious foreign powers that sought anchor at its northern ports, the Brazilian Empire granted a private monopoly to Amazonas's Navigational and Commercial Company under the direction of the Baron Mauá. Only in 1866 did the Brazilian government announce that it would open the Amazon basin to international trade the following year on the anniversary of its independence. When the emperor came to Belém for the festivities, a great pavilion was improvised opposite the bank of the Guajará, and the scene was registered by an amateur photographer who was among his official retinue, Felipe Augusto Fidanza, a native of what soon would become Italy. I mention Fidanza in passing because he did not return with Don Pedro II but rather set up an atelier on Santo Antônio Street, thus establishing the practice of the art of photography in Belém. Soon thereafter English companies established a regular commercial route between Belém and Liverpool. A little later Belém would be termed the new Liverpool, though it is difficult to tell if the joke was on the Brazilians or on the English.

Shillings (or Rather *Pichilingas*) Aplenty

Since England was a privileged client of the province of Pará, the export of latex earned that province millions of pounds per year, even if it did not catapult local industry to Liverpool's rates of industrial prosperity. By 1855 the pound sterling was used abundantly in Belém under the local slang *pichilinga*, quite likely an onomatopoeic variant of "shilling" (Santos 69). Never were there so many rich living amidst such destitution. With time, the natives were replaced in their capacity as rubber tappers by Northeasterners fleeing the great drought of 1870. This set the stage for the boom:

> Regional supply, at first limited to rudimentary and handcrafted goods made out of rubber, expanded at such a remarkable rate that by 1875 it required a massive organization of production and the use of slave labor, which was first (and mainly) provided by the natives. This mode of production entailed the mobilization of a vast quantity of laborers with only a relative increase in efficiency and physical productivity. Thus the process of rubber extraction, which required little more than 5,000 men in 1850, demanded by 1870 more than 31,000. (Santos 75)

Predictably the same financial mechanism made up of local exporters and foreign banks serviced the ceaseless importation of goods into Brazil. They exported rubber only to import everything from abroad—creating the same disequilibrium

that Paulo Prado refers to in the addendum to his famous *Retrato do Brasil* (1928): "In this land of plenty we import everything: from ideas to dresses, that is to say from the fashions of Paris to toothpicks and broomsticks. One would assume that in a well-adjusted country such massive imports would be balanced by formidable exports. Instead, for our toil and export of raw materials abroad, we suffer what the Germans call a loss of production" (Prado 1997, 204).

They imported everything. The Belém that boasted 91,307 free men and 26,975 slaves in 1833 was fed on a diet of stale local products and expensive imports such as those noted by La Condamine. As the population of the Amazon grew, the production of cocoa, coffee, and sugar declined and was virtually abandoned. Citizens of Belém ate bread made from the pure wheat of Europe, rather than from the cassava native to the region. The locals consumed butter, soap, and clothes from England and France. With the singular exceptions of improvements to cities here and there, such as Santarém or Óbidos, the Amazon as a whole did not profit from the new system. Only the metropolis benefited from the resources made available through foreign loans and local taxes and experienced a quickening of its process of urbanization. It is worth considering at length Bates's observations of these changes in 1859:

> I found Pará's city greatly changed, and for the better. It was no longer the backwater I had known in 1848 with its unpaved streets and derelict houses. Due to the influx of immigrants from Portugal, the Island of Madeira, and Germany, the population had increased to 20,000, and for some years the provincial government had spent the surplus of its considerable income to embellish the city. Where once there were streets made of sand and loose stones, now there were meticulously paved streets; where there were houses out of alignment, these had been demolished and replaced by more uniform buildings. Most of the old and abandoned houses had given way to beautiful edifices built above street level, and each boasted on its first floor an elegant and spacious verandah. The great plazas, once indistinguishable from marshland and no more than sad spectacles for the eyes, had been drained, weeded, and planted with rows of *amendoeira* and *casuarina* trees to great decorative effect for the entire city. Pleasure was sought after as eagerly as before, but more in accordance with the dictates of reason, as if the citizens of Pará now sought to imitate the customs not of Portugal but rather of the northern European nations. I am heartened to see various bookshops throughout the city, as well as a handsome building that serves as a library. (296–97)

Library, Opera House, and Newspapers (Including the Subversive Ones)

A permanent building to house the library was only inaugurated in 1870 with the requisite solemn speech by Bishop Marcelo Costa. Though construction on the opera house had begun a year earlier, it would only be ready in 1878, located in what was then known as the Pólvora (or Powder) Square, now the Plaza Republica. These two public buildings still stand today. The library is housed in a severe building with neo-Classical lines. In turn, the opera house, known under the name "Teatro da Paz" (Peace Theatre), is a sober yet imposing structure, whose entrance bears six rows of columns (before its modification in 1905 it bore seven, shielding the terrace). The architectural changes opened up the terrace above the gallery that leads to the entrance on the first floor, where each of the arts is represented in the form of a bust. The steep marble staircase leads past the iron gates to balconies delimited by colonnades, which also perform the function of supporting the ceiling. Instead of being illuminated by the traditional *andiroba* oil, these new buildings already boasted gas lighting, a technology available from the time of the outbreak of cholera in 1855. Soon after the Republic was proclaimed the opera house took the precaution of paving the theater's surroundings with rubber parallelepipeds (resembling the paving stones they replaced), so as to prevent the disturbance of performances by the clatter of passing coaches and carriages. Today the opera house is rocked by the maddening sonorous bombardment coming from the *trios elétricos* ("electric trios" that play loud popular music) across the square. Far less noise—merely the cracking of the coachman's whips—sufficed to instigate German philosopher Arthur Schopenhauer to direct formal and violent recriminations against the government of Dresden.

A new mode of transportation was introduced at the time of the unveiling of the library and opera house: the tram car or *bonde*, named after the first concessionaire of this service, a certain Mr. James Bond, representative of an English company which provided electricity to the city until 1940. Before this, local trams were pulled by donkeys. My childhood (and that of those of my generation) was marked by the sweet music of these electric trams—their mechanical purr. I can still remember the sparks falling from the tram's electrical lines on sharp turns, and the *kepi* on the head of the driver as he shifted among the vehicle's eight gears of speed.

Belém then boasted six dailies and four weeklies, and among these José Veríssimo contributed to: *O Liberal do Pará, O Diário do Grão Pará, A Gazeta do Norte, O Comércio, A Republica,* and *A Província do Pará.* I remember hearing the newspaper boys announcing Paulo Maranhão's daily *A Folha do Norte,* which lasted until the 1970s, but of course not the original *A Província do Pará,* whose offices were burnt down in 1912 in an event that sealed the fate of then director and future mayor Antônio Lemos. In accordance with the revolutionary impetus that marked the genesis of journalism in the province, these newspapers incited ideological debates that bore the stamp of ambitions specific to local political parties. Yet the coverage of these papers transcended arguments over political rights and obligations to encompass the dissemination of local poetry and prose and the practice of literary journalism with a renewed vigor following the introduction of a literary supplement to the *Folha do Norte* in 1946. In this spirit *O Diário de Belém* published the romantic lyrics of Santa Helena Magno, author of the 1869 *Harpejos Poéticos.* One should note that for too long the province's poets fell under the spell of the Parnassian school with its emphasis on metrical rigor and emotional restraint, often privileging the sonnet form. Here and there they sang of the Amazon, as in Acrísio Mota's *A Yara* and Paulinho de Brito's 1900 *Cantos Amazônicos.* One must acknowledge that from the writings of Bento de Figueiredo Tenreiro Aranha (1841–1918) to Modernism, prose rather than poetry provided the province's strongest literature.

At the outset of the nineteenth century only newspapers and official documents were printed in Pará. The type was set on wood blocks made locally. Both the press and printing press were introduced in the province by the erudite and talented Latinist and Sanskrit scholar Filippe Patroni (1789?–1866), who later published the 1851 *Cartilha Imperial* in accordance with the political orientation of Emperor Don Pedro II. Upon his 1822 return from Oporto's Constitutional Assembly, where he represented the province and obtained a printing press, Patroni published the province's first newspaper, *O Paraense,* which would soon come to be edited by the priest and Canon Batista Campos. In those days liberal ideas came from Caiena by means of the advocacy of Friar Luis Zagalo, a follower of Baboeuf since 1815 (Salles 1992, 96). Upon the occasion of the Confederation of Equador of 1824 and what became known as the Pernambuco movement, Patroni abandoned journalism and politics to dedicate himself to litigation at the court. Patroni and his family took the unusual measure of completing the journey to court on foot, a feat he would later record in a memoir *Viagem de 206 léguas.* With Patroni's retirement it was no surprise that Canon Batista Campos would be propelled by his connections to the directorship of the daily *O Paraense.*

Citizens of Pará were up to date with the most recent social and political ideas, including Marxism and the French socialism of Proudhon. As historian Vicente Salles records in his *Memorial da Cabanagem,* socialism arrived along with the 1860 wave of European immigration to the Amazon and soon took root in this land of craftsmen, serfs descended from enslaved natives, and African slaves who performed domestic labor or worked in the fields of Marajó and the pastures of the Lower Amazon. Tenreiro Aranha, son of the above mentioned poet, founded the first socialist nucleus in 1873, and in the spirit of the first International, Pará demanded workers' rights and preached the hegemony of labor. After *A Tribuna* forsook its erstwhile support of slavery for abolitionism, the popular children's writer Juvenal Tavares (author of *Seroes da Mãe Preta,* 1897) offered his services to the workers' cause in its pages (Salles 1992, 176). The cause was also taken up by Ignácio Baptista de Moura (1857–1929), author of the famous sonnet in praise of the workingman which commences: "É das mãos calosas do operário/ que a estátua do progresso há de surgir!" ("From the factory worker's callused hands/the statue of progress will come to be!"). A geographer by trade, Moura gave an account of his trip through the region of Tocantins in *De Belém a São João do Araguaya* (1910). Associated in this province with anarchism, socialism was a constant thorn in the side of the police and of republican governments, and its force was felt well into the 1920s in the form of general strikes. This helps explain why the titles of left-leaning papers such as *A Tribuna Operária* and *A Voz do Povo* were less likely to be cried out by the city's newspaper boys.

Positivism with a Touch of Grace

The first mayor (or intendant, as he was then known) to comprehend and administer Belém in the sum total of its urban needs and functions and to tend to the city's present and future without completely forsaking its past, was the above mentioned proprietor and director of the daily *A Província do Pará,* Antônio José de Lemos (1843–1913). Originally from the state of Maranhão, Lemos was a senator and a party president whose rise to the post of mayor coincided with the advent of the rubber boom and of the Republic. Though the province's fifteenth republican governor, Lauro Sodré (1858–1944) proved a political enemy to Mayor Lemos, their political visions were not so far apart. Sodré was the author of an apologia for scientific knowledge and for the positivist doctrine of August Comte—directly at odds with the teachings of the Catholic church (*Crencas e opiniões* [1896; Beliefs and Opinions]). I do not mean to suggest that in the manner of Sodré, the Catholic mayor fell under the spell of Benjamin Constant's positivism early in his youth. Nevertheless, Lemos found inspiration during his frequent trips to Paris for the reform of his city, and if he did not prove an intellectual himself, he succeeded in surrounding himself with the intellectuals of his day, in particular those affiliated with the daily *A Província do Pará*: Humberto de Campos (1886–1934), Ricardo Borges (1886–1975), Eliseu Cezar, Carlos Dias Fernandes (1874–1942), and Romeu Mariz. As a political creature, Lemos proved very much a hybrid: He was not only an advocate of the urban rationalism of Paris, but an aggressive champion of his political faction, an implacable administrator and political boss that many in his day likened to a northern and rustic Baron Haussmann. Even the great writer Euclides da Cunha came to praise Lemos upon the occasion of his visit to the Swiss scientist and Belém resident Emilio Goeldi.

Progress, according to positivist doctrine, demanded from society's luminaries and enlightened citizens assistance to the needy and the incapacitated, aid which in Belém took the form of improvements in the realms of health and hygiene and in the prevention of epidemics. Lemos built orphanages and asylums and oversaw the implementation of sewer systems, slaughter houses, and crematoria. In Brazil progress was linked to the idea of order (as stated by the motto of the national flag, "Ordem e progresso"), and accordingly Lemos redrew the plans for Belém, dividing it into great rectangular blocks, crisscrossed by broad avenues and roads, giving rise to new neighborhoods and extending the city limits to the Marco da Légua Patrimonial. As Euclides da Cunha attests in a letter addressed to his father in 1904, the writer came to know and admire the city remodeled by Lemos over the span of a decade:

> In Pará Senator Lemos made a speed boat available to me. There I spent two unforgettable hours, and I will never forget the surprise the city caused in me. Never will São Paulo or Rio boast avenues as monumental, forty meters wide and shaded by successive rows of enormous trees. Elsewhere in Brazil one cannot imagine Belém with its disproportionate large edifices, its incomparable plazas, and with its generous and gentlemanly citizens of European manner. (Euclides da Cunha 72)

Lemos's reform of the city followed the Art Nouveau style then in vogue, and his administration saw the emergence of a fish market made of steel, beautiful public buildings displaying exquisite railings, and palatial residences furnished in the same style with Limoges vases, bronze tables and jars, and stained-glass windows (see Bassalo's study on this subject). Typical of these lavish mansions was the residence of architect Francisco Bolonha that is often reproduced in books on the Brazilian art and architecture of that period.

Physiognomy and Images

A city's aesthetics is made up of a human and urban, as well as a natural environment: streets, squares, gardens, and public works define the city's physiognomy and lend it a unique character, a legible and interpretable face. A single public square with its characteristic cityscapes and physiognomic contours can reveal the city, as part of its expressive or even organic whole–if the comparison of urban space to an organism is still tenable. Belém's physiognomy and metropolitan aesthetic, once defined by its Baroque Jesuit churches, the monuments of Landi, the two-story houses decorated in tiles, and by the bars and stores in the manner of Lisbon, were transformed at the turn of the century by the introduction of *fin-de-siècle* architecture, street lamps, and clock towers and by the care paid to its now clean and unpolluted streets, sidewalks, gardens, and rows of trees. As a result the city's

physiognomy reconciles a multiplicity of different styles and periods which are harmonized through the recurrence of significant expressive traits. Without either its Baroque architecture or its vegetation Belém would lose its unique profile. Alongside the churches of Landi, the opera house, and the mango trees that form the city's characteristic images, I would like to single out what I deem to be the city's four other distinctive physiognomic landmarks: the Grand Hotel and Nazaré Park, now only accessible to us through photographs and personal memory, and the Rodrigues Alves Municipal Park and the Paris in America boutique, still among us albeit in a poor state of conservation (in the case of the former) or close to ruin (in the case of the latter).

In existence as a reserve within the Amazon forest since 1883, the Rodrigues Alves Municipal Forest was made into a European-style park in 1903 by Lemos (who had plans to establish fifteen other tropical forests). In it, European fashion was significantly accommodated to the tropics: Bridges and shelters were constructed among waterfalls, lakes, and under the majestically tall *hileia* trees with their voluminous trunks and falling vines. Straw-thatched huts were named after icons of both French and Brazilian cultures: Chateaubriand's Atala, Bernardin de Saint-Pierre's Paul and Virginie, and José de Alencar's (1829–1877) Ceci and Peri (though this last homage was likely paid not so much to Alencar but to master Carlos Gomes, who based his most celebrated opera on Alencar's novel *O Guarani* [1857]). Lemos's administration extended the concept of embellishing nature by means of artifice (which included even the construction of picturesque ruined castles) to its most exquisite square, the Plaza Batista Campos, in the form of the introduction of gazebos and pavilions. Thus the style of this square was strikingly different from that of plaza Republica with its paths converging before an elevated statue in an unmistakably republican allegory.

Lemos had a good reason to line the Plaza Batista Campos with mango trees: Their majestic crowns provided ample shade and–when intertwined across rows of other trees–formed natural domes observable not only in the square but along the city's principal avenues. In turn the city's ability to harmonize its tropical vegetation with that of the surrounding rainforest is best summed up in the Rodrigues Alves Park. There the sun shines through rows of trees of uneven stature to produce a chiaroscuro effect that is characteristic of Belém. But the park's claim to singularity rests on its threshold position between the urban and the natural, as if it were part of the adjacent nature to which it nonetheless remains irreducible and strange. This threshold condition speaks to the old and archaic if not ancestral process of formation, not only of the park, but of the nature glimpsed from current inhabitants' own backyards in houses that have now passed into the realm of memory.

At Nazaré the previously mentioned sanctuary underwent successive transformations from hut to chapel and finally to the sumptuous basilica there today. In turn the marketplace where the Círio procession was held would suffer alterations for more than a century, losing the appearance of a market and gaining that of an amusement park complete with food stalls, a carousel, and a ferris wheel (see Lobato). The Nazaré Square I remember had already been further remodeled with the introduction of an Art Nouveau clock ornamented with flowers made out of iron, a gazebo on each side, and the central Flora pavilion with its circular colonnade for recitals and open air concerts. And yet in the repressive climate of the

1970s, clock, gazebos, and pavilion all disappeared, swallowed up by an austere and ascetic concept of the nature and function of public celebration. Though the sanctuary remained, it was now surrounded by rails on all sides. Nonetheless to this day the square, once the site of youth's Dionysian energy, is still the focus of the people's fervent devotion during the Círio procession.

In turn the erstwhile sophisticated European boutique Paris in America still survives, although insignificant in its trade and virtually unrecognizable in terms of its architecture. It is next to the Bon Marché on one of the corners of Santo Antônio Street in that traditionally commercial district. Once the store imported not only the fine fabrics, but Europe's fashions themselves. One can still appreciate the masonry of its walls, the clock still ringing the hours, and the monumental cast iron staircase whose two sinuous curves meet at the mezzanine. Now picture, on the street west of the opera house, along the same square, a four-story building with a curved roof reminiscent of the buildings of Paris's Rue Rivoli. Imagine the large glass doors of its ground floor, the classical ordering of its balconies and windows on the upper floors. Place yourself on the sidewalk facing the entrance, next to the more than a dozen small stone tables and their many portable chairs, each table protected by a yellow umbrella. There you have the Grand Hotel, built at the end of the nineteenth century, still functioning in the 1970s when the festivities of Nazaré had faded, but which real-estate speculation has now eliminated from the urban landscape. These two icons that live on, more in photography than in living memory, nonetheless, speak to us like the text of a poem, conveying (like the two landmarks that still stand) the impalpable and imponderable atmosphere that once characterized Belém, however tenuous our apprehension and evocation of the city's past glory days.

Paris in America

In those days Belém reproduced the splendors of the *belle époque*. It became European, but not by imitating Lisbon or Liverpool, nor, as we have seen, by giving into the temptation of imitating Venice. Rather it emulated the nineteenth-century metropolis *par excellence*, its true capital, Paris. In a delicious summation Haroldo de Campos (1929–2003) once shared with me in conversation, "Belém do Pará" became "Belém de Paris." Thanks to their frequent sojourns in Paris the great landowners and rubber exporters who constituted Belém's upper class went so far as to confuse the two metropolises: They experienced not only Belém as Paris, but Paris as Belém. Yet, families had their clothes tailored in London and their books bound in Paris. On the Island of Marajó they could board ships straight for Europe, and some chose long sojourns of a year or two in Switzerland or Belgium, reasoning that it was cheaper than Paris, even once the costs of bringing along a cook and a nanny had been factored in. A society lady, however, is reported to have written to a friend back in Belém of the inconvenient love affairs of a young female acquaintance of theirs: "In Paris we speak of nothing else!"

In this spirit one of the age's great rubber exporters, Antônio José Pinho, presented one of his daughters with a trip to the French capital to witness Santos Dumont's flight at the Demoiselle and around the Eiffel Tower. According to tradition, Pinho possessed his own fleet of ships and agents in Liverpool to relay information on the processing of the raw material he exported. One of his sons, whom Pinho had intended to become a scholar in the City of Lights, died in one of his

many outings to the original Moulin Rouge. At Pinho's housewarming ball of 1897 the guests paraded the latest fashions from London and Paris through the three wings of his new mansion in Belém that boasted Portuguese tiles and even a chapel with a view of the Guamá River (see Bassalo). Foreign fashions provided the main subject for João Affonso's curious book on fashion in Belém up to the year of its tercentenary (1916, when the book was published). Boasting illustrations by the author, the book reserves only its final paragraphs to describe the attire of the common people and of black women and mulattas, in particular. Even Belém's pharmacies sold medicine imported from France or at least bearing French names: Gélineau tablets, Déhaut pills, Des Oiseaux laxative, Boyer water, and so forth (see Fábio Castro). This superimposition of Paris onto Brazil's northern metropolis infused the citizens of Belém with what Mário Faustino still referred to (in the 1950s) as *luteciomania*, an obsessive condition named after the Roman Empire's name for Paris, and which describes the process whereby a city's collective memory is haunted by visions of a splendid past and a utopian future.

Theater Follies–From Montmartre to the Nazaré Square

Landowners and rubber barons, journalists and politicians, intellectuals and members of the bourgeoisie all met at the Grand Hotel's large terrace, dotted with little tables, where they were joined by patrons of the Olympia Cinema (established in 1912), as well as of the many theaters then operating along Plaza Pólvora, such as the Politeama and the Palace. Belém's artistic and intellectual life was to be seen from the Paz Opera House to Nazaré Square. In 1927 Modernist novelist Mário de Andrade (1893–1945) came here for ice-cream in the heat of the afternoon and later wrote affectionately to Manuel Bandeira (1886–1968) of what he termed "the right to sit at that terrace, facing the mango-trees shading the Paz Opera House, sitting, that is all, savoring little by little an ice-cream made from *assaí* or *cupuaçu*" (1958, 164; 2000, 345). Such was the concentration of burlesque theaters, *cafés concert*, and vaudeville houses along Plaza Pólvora that–even before the building of the Grand Hotel and its terrace–journalists had nicknamed it Pará's *Montmartre*. Yet Belém's theatrical and operatic activity had commenced much earlier.

The opera house designed by Landi housed performances until 1812. Even the construction of the Teatro Providencia at Plaza Mercês (much before that of the Paz Opera House) would not have been viable had there not been already an audience for music, drama, and opera. Albeit rudimentary, this providential first stage attracted small traveling troupes of entertainers, mostly from Maranhão or Rio (and a few from Italy) who put on plays or abbreviated operas. Unfortunately these waves of traveling troupes sometimes coincided with the arrival of yellow fever, a disease which first plagued the city in 1861 and which even at the beginning of the twentieth century was responsible for the death of visiting Italian actors. In 1861 Adolfo José, an organist at the Sé Cathedral, organized in Belém the Society Phil' Euterpe (see Salles 1980). At the same time Henrique Eulálio Gurjão (1834–1885), the first to be granted a scholarship by the provincial government to study music abroad, returned from Europe with not only a diploma in composition and conducting, but also the score of his opera *Idália*. Pará's second composer and maestro José Candido de Gama Malcher (1853–1921) reached his creative peak during the early days of the Republic with *Burg-Jargal*, a youthful composition in the style of

Carlos Gomes that premiered at the Paz Opera House in 1890 and was later staged in Rio and São Paulo.

Since my days in primary school I have heard much of the Paz Opera House's sophisticated repertoire and of its cultured audience accustomed to the most refined and complex spectacles staged by the great European companies. I remember a still night in 1936 when the wind brought to my house a beautiful wave of sound from the opera house, and a family member remarked that it had to be Bidu Sayão singing at the Paz. And there, in the theater's corridor, alongside a mention of a performance by Pavlova in 1918, I find her name on a commemorative plaque. Despite the absence of exhaustive documentation we are able to recreate, as in a flashback, the opera seasons of 1881, 1882, and 1883. In the first season there is evidence of the success of the Italian repertoire (in particular *La traviata*, *Il trovatore*, and *Il barbiere di Siviglia*), in the second a note of the premiere of Gurjão's *Idália*, and in the third of the premiere of *Salvator Rosa* conducted by Carlos Gomes himself. Many other opera seasons followed, both before and after the proclamation of the Republic, most notably the season promoted by Carlos Gomes in 1883 despite the local outbreak of yellow fever (Salles 1994, I: 199). Following the end (in 1907) of this cycle of lyric operas, Belém witnessed a turn toward the operetta: A Portuguese group performed *Die lustige Witwe*, and local artists such as Helena and Ulisses Nobre provided the counterpoint of aria and recitative during the screening of the film of the same operetta at the Politeama Cinema.

The 1912 crash of the rubber economy interrupted the construction of the city's stock exchange, the ultimate symbol of its fortune, but it did not prevent entertainment houses including the Politeama Cinema and the local Moulin Rouge from underwriting the season at the Paz Opera House, which included acclaimed performances of zarzuelas by a Spanish company and of Rostand's *L' Aiglon* by a French troupe. One should note that, even before its gradual decline, the repertoire of the Paz Opera House was not necessarily as cosmopolitan and sophisticated as we remember it today. Its inauguration was marked by the performance of a mediocre five-act French drama, A. d'Ennery's *The Two Orphans*, which never returned to the playbill. Between opera seasons the stage was occupied by amateur bands of players; the repertoire was exclusively Portuguese and Brazilian, and the Paz's noble stage witnessed the presentation of someone who billed himself as the bullet man (the circus act of a man shot out of a canon). As to the great European companies I had heard so much about during my childhood, there is no evidence that any of the old continent's permanent opera companies performed at the Paz. The Paz was visited by the make-shift troupes that entrepreneurs, actors, and singers of note sometimes formed with the express purpose of coming to Belém, such as that headed by Tomás Passini and maestro Enrico Bernardi, and many a Brazilian, Spanish, French, and Italian entrepreneur and maestro found in Belém their favorite and most faithful clientele.

Its audience was not cultured in the sense of being able to cultivate artistic tastes with reference to one or more dramatic or musical genres given the continuity of what we term tradition. Perhaps Belém's opera-goers were afflicted by what José Veríssimo referred to in a similar case as *musicofilia*, a mania for music "that requires a lyric company once in a while–an expensive one" (Veríssimo 1894, 252). In purchasing expensive opera tickets they became peripheral participants in what sociology terms conspicuous consumerism: Thus members of the upper class were accompanied to the Paz by their middle-class associates and lower-class dependents. Prior to slavery's abolition in 1888, society ladies were said to be accompanied to the opera by the female slave attendants, who on the way to the Paz were responsible for lighting their mistress's path and holding the ends of their long skirts. The handmaidens would take the cheapest seats in the house, high up and furthest from the stage, in what opera-goers affectionately referred to as paradise.

The Republican period would nonetheless offer a spectacle for all classes, a mixture of public commemoration and consecration, in the form of the funeral procession for Carlos Gomes who died in Belém in 1896. Gomes's funeral procession marked the apogee of the *musicofilia* of Belém's beautiful epoch and, like the rubber boom itself, it achieved a Baroque grandeur. The long procession was led by Governor Lauro Sodré, Antônio Lemos, and the Bishop and was made up of representatives from the Church, press, military, government, gentleman's clubs, philantropic societies, and even primary schools–in sum, from all of Belém's civil society. Its trajectory was not short, and along its path all windows and doorframes and many rooftops overflowed with the enormous crowd. At each point the procession was greeted by banners and allegorical sketches, and there was no shortage of poets publicly declaiming their loss. Rhetoric was comparably well-served in the form of no less than forty speeches during the ceremony. Funeral rites were observed at the Chapel of the Soledade (Solitude) Cemetery, and the same procession accompanied the hearse to the margins of the Guajará to see the coffin off to the ship that would transport it to Santos and finally to Campinas. (Clovis Moraes Rego detailed this funeral procession in a series of articles for *Província do Pará* from 21 July 1996 to 14 December 1997.) The commemoration constituted an act of consecration, the final triumph if not the apotheosis of the maestro who only nominally directed the conservatory that was to be named after him, due to the advanced state of his illness when he reached Belém for the fourth and last time in May 1896. (On the subject of Carlos Gomes's last sojourn in Pará, see Marcus Góes.)

Of course not all of those present at Belém's first mass public gathering were lovers of opera, nor could they all have been familiar with the work of the composer of *O Guarani*. The crowd exceeded the sum of these audiences. One may assume that a significant number of those present attended not the Paz Opera House but rather the small theater houses of Nazaré, final destination of some of the productions that originated in Plaza Pólvora's Montmartre. At Nazaré's make-shift theaters they would have attended not only works pertaining to the European genres and the tradition we have discussed so far, but also the comedy, drama, music, and dance better suited to the region's general preference for folklore that were performed as part of a tradition dating back to the Círio festivities of 1873. It is not my intention to isolate two distinct cultures, the Amazonian and the European. The split between the audiences at the Paz and at Nazaré transcends the opposition of the erudite and the popular–its origin is not cultural but economic, for it corresponds to the stratification that results from social inequality. If it is difficult to avoid having recourse to the notion of class in a society as polarized as this, it is also impossible to forget that the ruling class only succeeds in imposing its will over the lower classes through a persuasive and symbolic discourse. In this manner the members of the lower class who glorified Carlos Gomes and accompanied his funeral procession had internalized the values of the ruling class. In turn, one should note that nothing performed at Nazaré's small theaters was purely popular: Dramatists and novelists known for their intelligence penned the popular comedies of manners, and allegorical and folkloric dances such as the *Boibumbá* betrayed the influence of the syncretism of the cultures of both masters and slaves; motifs of indigenous dances and legends celebrating animals and birds resurfaced in melodramas of an unmistakably European provenance. By the time these dances reached the stages at Nazaré, they had experienced a second erudite birth (see Moura).

Illustrious Emigrés and an Abundance of Books

Two of Brazil's best writers, José Veríssimo and Inglês de Sousa, likewise sought inspiration in the *mestizo* culture and customs of the *tapuias*, which were widely disseminated in the province's interior. Best known as a critic and historian of Brazilian literature, José Veríssimo (1857–1916) is not commonly appreciated for his contributions to the fields of ethnology, folklore, and pedagogy. What made him a central figure to the culture of his time was his ability to fuse regional and European traditions. Veríssimo wrote a salutation to the distinguished musician Carlos Gomes upon the occasion of his first visit to Belém in 1882. He also wrote about the ethnological formation of the people and collected the Amazonian legends which would inspire his own writing. He founded a society to promote instruction in the region, as well as his own school, which introduced the innovation of the kindergarten. He attended an anthropological conference in Paris in 1889, founded the magazine *Revista Amazonica*, and organized the Republican Club alongside Lauro Sodré. Later he went to Rio–from which he never returned.

Born in Óbidos (like José Veríssimo) Herculano Marcos Inglês de Sousa (1853–1918) moved with his parents to São Paulo at the age of six. Nonetheless, everything he wrote drew from his childhood memories and from the tales told to him by his father and his uncles. Sousa gathered his fiction under the general title *Cenas da vida Amazonica* [Scenes of Amazonian Life]: *Os contos Amazônicos* [Amazonian Tales], *O Cacaulista* [The Cocoalist], *História de um pescador* [Story of a Fisherman], *O Missionário* [The Missionary], and *O Coronel Sangrado* [Colonel Sangrado]. Written in a naturalistic vein, Sousa's novels constitute the first panorama of Belém's social and political history. While José Veríssimo pioneered ethnological and sociological study in the region, Inglês de Sousa provided the medium through which indigenous terms, already assimilated in the Portuguese spoken in the province, entered the realm of fiction. Both novelists were men of the interior who later emigrated, in this regard mirroring the fate of a pair of their notable contemporaries: the mathematician Aarão Reis, who along with Prado Lopes drew up the plans for the city of Belo Horizonte, and the biologist Gaspar Viana (1885–1914), a collaborator of Oswaldo Cruz (1872–1917), and Carlos Chagas (1878–1934) who discovered the cure for leishmaniasis.

Belém, the city which so prized the philosophy of Auguste Comte (1798–1857), offered at that time no room for advanced studies in mathematics and biology, the first and penultimate sciences according to his classification, nor for any other form of higher education. Nonetheless during its glory days, the city's teachers wrote and published a not insignificant number of textbooks (see Moreira 1979). Books were themselves never in scarce supply. Beautiful bookstores were up-to-date and well-stocked with books that arrived along with the latest fashions from Paris. From these stores books migrated to large private lending libraries and finally to the public libraries, as in the case of the donation of Lauro Sodré, or belatedly, due to disinterest on behalf of heirs, to second-hand bookshops, in the case of the collection of the first governor under the Republic, Justo Chermont. (There I have been able to salvage many of Chermont's volumes for my own private collection.)

Conclusion: Minerva's Owl and Don Sebastian

In spite of the social inequality mentioned above, Belém's role as centralizing cultural force in the realm of cultural production was furthered by these private and public libraries and through an intricate network of people formed at the turn of the century: theatrical entrepreneurs, actors, journalists, writers, singers, musicians, maestros, set designers, photographers, and painters, most notably among the latter Domenico de Angelis, famous for his work at the Cathedral and the foyer of the Paz Opera House. Working in the time of Don Antônio de Almeida Lustosa, himself the author of a fanciful history of the province's interior, de Angelis is reported to have been paid 100,000 gold francs for his labors, in which he was assisted by Sperindio Aliverti and Giovani Capranesi (see Leal 69–70). At the Sé Cathedral de Angelis's pastoral vistas decorate the dome of the main and ancillary chapels.

Already in the mid-nineteenth century a rising awareness about the necessity to chronicle the region's history led Antônio Baena (1782–1850) and Domingos Antônio Raiol (1830–1912) to pen, respectively, *O Compendio das eras das provincias do Pará* [1838; A Compendium of the Eras of the Provinces of Pará], a chronology of ephemeral facts, and *Motins politicos* [1865; Political Mutinies], a chronicle of regional insurrections both prior to and after independence, including the already mentioned revolution of the *cabanagem*. Later geographer Domingos Soares Ferreira Pena (1818–1888), author of a study of the areas of Tocantins and Anapu in 1864, founded Belém's Philomatic Society following the advice of Luiz Agassiz on a visit there in mid-1866. This society formed the nucleus of the city's museum of archeology, anthropology, and natural history, founded in 1871, and which would later acquire its definitive shape under the direction of Swiss naturalist Emilio Goeldi (whom Lauro Sodré had called to Belém in 1894).

Hegel wrote that Minerva's owl only flies at dusk. When the crash of Belém's rubber boom economy was already foreseeable, the city attracted a great number of distinguished Brazilian and foreign scientists, among them archeologist and ethnologist José Coelho da Gama e Abreu, geologist Charles Frederick Hart, zoologist Maria Elisabeth Emília Snethlage, ethnologist Carlos Estevão de Oliveira, botanist Paul Vincent Ledoux, and anthropologist

Walter Alberto Egler, in addition to Pena, who discovered the seven fluvial and oceanic *sambaquis* (prehistoric deposits of shells; see Bertho 77). Since then, Belém's Museum of Natural History and its Bulletin have remained central to the study of the region's soil and sub-soil, animal and plant species, and its remaining and vanquished indigenous tribes. The institution's botanical and zoological garden, known to members of my generation simply as the *Museu*, makes for the last (and fifth) urban icon I would like to single out. True historians combine an interpretation of historical evidence with a speculative or even creative imagination. This fusion characterizes the first study of the city's memory, Fábio Castro's *A cidade sebastiana: Era da borracha, memória e melancolia numa cidade na periferia da modernidade* [The Sebastian City: The Rubber Era, Melancholy and Memory in a City on the Periphery of Modernity]. Castro describes the city's obsession with its *belle époque* (the *luteciomania* referred to above) as an utopia inverted and projected onto the past, as a dream-like haunting that obfuscates our vision of the present and desensitizes us for the future. It is in this vein that he terms Belém a Sebastian city, a city that desires the return of its golden era, and that Castro reimagines the Portuguese mystical yearning for the return of King Sebastian, killed at Alkacerkibir, along the lines of Belém's yearning for the return of the grandeur of the rubber boom.

Though I acknowledge that this understanding of the city's past in the form of a single splendorous image is the product of the old upper class and am only too aware of the schism it represents for the individual's conscience, I admit that for me it still allows for an affectionate relationship to Belém. Today the lower class is formed by an anonymous mass of over 1.3 million people, and the upper class thrives on financial speculation that disconnects it from the city and that allows for no ideology other than that of short-term profit. This central city's urban landscape is in the process of being decentered from its own history. The city runs the risk of elimination of icons that guard its memory and guarantee the continuity of the present with the past at a time of great transformations and an uncertain future, when the younger generations are no longer frightened by the phantom described by Fábio Castro. If this is indeed the case, Belém runs the risk of losing its own cultural and historical identity.

Translation by Paulo Horta

Works Cited

Affonso, João. 1976. *Três Séculos de Modas*. Belém: Conselho Estadual de Cultura.

Andrade, Mário de. 1958. *Cartas*. Rio de Janeiro: Editora Simões.

——. 2000. *Correspondência: Mário de Andrade & Manuel Bandeira*. Ed. Marcos Antonio de Moraes. São Paulo: Universidade de São Paulo; Instituto de Estudos Brasileiros; Edusp.

Azevedo, J. Eustáquio. 1970. *Antologia Amazônica*. 3rd edition. Belém: Conselho Estadual de Cultura.

Azevedo, João Lúcio de. 1992. *História de António Vieira*. Lisbon: Clássica Editora.

Bassalo, Célia Coelho. 1984. *O "Arte Nouveau" em Belém*. Belém: FUNARTE/Secretaria de Cultura, Desporto e Turismo/Universidade Federal do Pará.

Bates, Henry Walter. 1979. *Um naturalista no rio Amazonas*. Trans. Regina Regis Junqueira. São Paulo: Editora Itatiaia/EDUSP.

Baudelaire, Charles. 1986. "Le Cygne." *Baudelaire: The Complete Verse*. Ed. and trans. Francis Scarfe. London: Anvil Press Poetry. 174–75.

Bertho, Angela Maria de Moraes. 1994. "Museu Paraense: A Antropologia na perspectiva de um saber sobre e na Amazônica (1886–1921)1st part." *Boletim do Museu Paraense Emílio Goeldi–Série Antropolgia* 9.1 (July): 55–111.

Castro, Fábio Fonseca de. 1994. "A cidade Sebastiana: Era da borracha, memória e melancolia numa cidade na periferia da modernidade." Diss. Universidade de Brasilia (UNB/COM).

Cunha, Euclides da. 1931. *Cartas de Machado de Assis e Euclydes da Cunha*. Ed. Renato Travassos. Rio de Janeiro: Waissman, Reis.

Góes, Marcus. 1996. *Carlos Gomes–A Força Indômita*. Belém: SECULT.

La Condamine, Charles-Marie de. 1992. *Viagem pelo Amazonas (1735–1745)*. São Paulo: Nova Fronteira/EDUSP.

Leal, Mons Américo. 1979. *A Igreja da Sé*. Belém: n.p.

Lobato, Manoel. 1970. "Teatro de Nazaré a 500 reis a entrada." *Antologia da cultura amazônica*. Ed. Carlos Roque and Arthur César Ferreira Reis. Vol. 7. Belém: Amazônia Edições Culturais. 115–19.

Meira Filho, Augusto. 1976. *Landi, esse desconhecido (o naturalista)*. Belém: Conselho Federal de Cultura.

——. 1980. *Antônio José Landi–Arquiteto Régio de Bolonha (esboço histórico)*. Belém: n.p.

Miranda, Vicente Chermont de. 1968. *Glossário Paraense (coleção de vocábulos peculiares à Amazônica e especialmente à Ilha de Marajó)*. Belém: Editora da Universidade Federal do Pará.

Moreira, Eidorfe. 1966. *Belém e sua expressão geográfica*. Belém: n.p.

——. 1971. *Visão geo-social do Círio*. Belém: Imprensa Universitária.

——. 1979. *O livro didático paraense (breve noticia histórica)*. Belém: Imprensa Universitária.

Moura, Carlos Eugênio Marcondes de. 1997. *O teatro que o povo cria–Cordão de Pássaros, Cordão de Bichos, Pássaros Juninos do Pará*. Belém: SECULT.

Patroni, Felippe. 1975. *Viagem de 206 léguas*. Obras escolhidas de Felippe Patroni. Belem:Conselho Estadual de Cultura.

Pena, Domingos Soares Ferreira. 1973. *Obras completas*. Belem: Conselho Estadual de Cultura.

Penteado, Antônio Rocha. 1968. *Belém–Estudo de Geografia Urbana*. Belém: Editora da Universidade Federal do Pará.

Prado, Paulo. 1997. *Retrato do Brasil: Ensaio sobre a tristeza brasileira*. Ed. Carlos Augusto Calil. São Paulo: Companhia das letras..

Raiol, Domingos Antônio. 1970. *Motins políticos: Ou, história dos principais acontecimentos políticos da provincia do Pará desde o ano 1821 até 1835*. Belem: Universidade Federal do Pará.

Reis, Arthur Cézar Ferreira. 1970. "A Amazônia no Contexto Cultural do Brasil." *Antologia da cultura amazônica*. Ed. Carlos Roque and Arthur César Ferreira Reis. Vol. 1. Belém: Amazônia Edições Culturais. 21–37.

Salles, Vicente. 1971. *O Negro no Pará*. Rio de Janeiro: Fundação Getúlio Vargas/Editora da Universidade Federal do Pará.

——. 1980. *A Música e o Tempo no Grão-Pará*. Belém: Conselho Estadual de Cultura.

——. 1992. *Memorial da Cabanagem*. Belém: Editora CEJUP.

——. 1994. *Épocas do Teatro no Grão-Pará ou Apresentação do Teatro de Época*. 2 vols. Belém: Editora da Universidade Federal do Pará.

Santos, Roberto. 1980. *Historia Econômica da Amazônia (1800–1920)*. São Paulo: T.A. Queiroz.

Sousa, Herculano Marcos Inglês de. 1988. *Contos Amazônicos*. Rio de Janeiro: Editora Presença.

Veríssimo, José. 1886. *Scenas da vida amazónica com um estudo das populações indígenas e mestiças da Amazonia*. Lisbon: n.p. Rpt. 1970. Belem: Editora da Universidade Federal do Pará.

——. 1894. *Estudos Brazileiros (segunda série)*. Rio de Janeiro/São Paulo: Laemmert & C. Editores.

——. 1970a. *Estudos amazônicos*. [Jacarepaguá]: Universidade Federal do Pará.

——. 1970b. *A Pesca na Amazônia*. [Jacarepaguá]: Universidade Federal do Pará.

——. 1994. *Que é Literatura? e outros escriptos*. Belém: SECULT.

Vieira, Antônio. 1971. *Cartas*. Vol. I.. Ed. João Lúcio de Azevedo. Lisbon: Imprensa Nacional.

CHAPTER 44

DOCUMENT: THE VIEW FROM MANAUS

Milton Hatoum

Whoever flies over Manaus, traveling in a westward direction, will notice that the city is located on Brazil's main river navigation axis. The geographer Áziz Ab'Saber rightly observed that Manaus "is a kind of link between river navigation, which is rudimentary and extensive, and the great coastal-sailing routes. For this reason, it enjoys an absolutely privileged geographical situation facing the Amazonian expanse and the huge drainage of the regional hydrographic basin" (18). From a geographical and topographical point of view, Manaus is a truly privileged city of confluence, lying on an area of soft hills on the left shore of the Negro River 20 kilometers away from the Solimões River.

The Portuguese colonizers knew how to reconcile their military strategy with a charming landscape. At the heart of the Amazonian hinterland, the São José do Rio Negro Fort was founded in 1669, eight years after the Jesuit missionaries were expelled by the slaveholding colonists (Azevedo 144). Without the Jesuits around, the "rescue" troops of *entradistas* who enslaved the Indians had more freedom of movement, and it is just possible that the absence of missions slowed down the development of the settlement built around the fort. It is well known that the missions founded agricultural colonies next to the villages. The Jesuits suffered the sometimes violent opposition of local power, but acted as mediators for the indigenous workforce. By having a spiritual quest and striving to succeed in the process of colonization, they became an equilibrating factor between the capturing of Indians and the real development of villages (Ab'Saber 23). The purpose of the military presence of the Portuguese at this strategic point was to stop the Spanish advance along the Solimões River and the Dutch advance along the Orinoco. For more than two centuries, the small village called Lugar da Barra "não dependeu de nenhuma rota terrestre, mas tão somente dos rios de planície e de uma história econômica ligada intimamente à navegação fluvial" ("did not depend on any inland route; it only depended on the plains rivers and on an economic history intimately linked to river navigation," Ab'Saber 19).

The fort was just an "imitation of Fortaleza" (according to Monteiro), much more rustic and precarious than the other forts built in the Amazon region and along the coastline. The Manaos, Tarumã, and Baré Indians were captured by the "rescue troops" and taken to Belém. Many Indians remained *aldeados*, that is, they were enslaved to work locally. A brief digression is needed here to recount the fate of these indigenous peoples, not only because they give the city its name (Manaus), which in itself carries a significant symbolic meaning, but also because, for a long time, the population of the Lugar da Barra was basically Indian. The Manaos Indians occupied both shores of the low Negro River and were the most important ethnic group of the fort's area of influence. The Tarumã Indians inhabited the rivers Tarumã and Ajurim, affluents of the left tributary of the Negro River, which were not far from the fort. The Baré

Indians lived in the upper region of the Negro River and some tribes were neighbours to the Manaos, who were largely exterminated during the 1720s, when manpower was scarce in Belém. The extermination was the result of bloody battles between Portuguese soldiers and Manaos Indians. From this uneven confrontation, the collective memory of the Amazonians has given rise to the image of Ajuricaba, the fighting leader of this indigenous people (see Freire).

In 1757, another rebellion took place along the Negro River, where the Portuguese had founded several villages, the most important of which was Mariuá, located in the lower part of the river; a year later it became the Vila de Barcelos, a city that still possesses among its vegetation-covered ruins the signs of a far from edifying past. The second defeat of the Manaos sealed their destiny as part of the tragedy of the mistakes and horrors of colonization. The Tarumãs managed to escape from the liberation troops and undertook a long journey of thousands of kilometers upriver. In 1837, a German naturalist discovered their existence along the Essequibo and Cuyuwini rivers, in today's Guyana. The Baré Indians, or large numbers of them, went into the Cassiquiare and settled in the Orinoco basin. Today the descendants of those who participated in this exodus live in the Negro River Department in Venezuela (see Freire). Upon spending some hours in Barcelos, German ethnographer Theodor Koch-Grünberg (1872–1924) wrote on 4 July 1903: "that they went ashore to bury a Baré Indian who had died on board their boat during the trip." The settlement that gave rise to the city is, therefore, related to the brutal and violent system of Indian slavery, a practice which decimated thousands of human beings as well as leaving everlasting marks of humiliation and social exclusion. The slaves of the villages of yore are, in a way, the marginalized groups of the modern city.

It was only in 1695 that the Carmelite missionaries (who took the place of the Jesuits) began to evangelize the region, taught the Indians of the new village how to read and write, and exerted a moral influence in the life of the Lugar da Barra. Free and unregulated interracial relations among Indian women and soldiers were replaced by marriage—a new social, moral, and religious order that became part of a policy to consolidate the settlement process. Something which slowed down the development of the future city of Manaus, however, was the transference of the Captaincy of São José do Rio Negro from Lugar da Barra to the Vila de Barcelos. From 1758 on, the new captaincy overshadowed the significance of Lugar da Barra, which, for a long time, became merely a place of passage, a stopping point for the expeditions and the liberation troops going up the Negro River. Until the last quarter of the eighteenth century, the population of the village comprised some 300 people. In truth, the feared Dutch and Spanish incursions were more an illusion than a real threat. Thus, the fort and the small settlement founded in 1669 were not very different from the hamlet of 1783 when the fort was abandoned. This urban inertia was related to the fact that Western Amazonia was a dependency of the Captaincy of Grão-Pará, the capital of which, Belém, attracted all the political and economic activities of the region. A large part of the Indian workforce was taken to Belém, the crossroads for goods and the spice trade in the region. In the meantime, from 1788 to 1799, there were some significant economic and physical changes during the Lobo de Almada administration: "Em poucos anos fez-se masi que em todo o século de vida do povoado" ["More was done in a few years than in the entire previous life of the village," Ab'Saber 25].

In 1791, Governor Manoel Lobo de Almada, rebelling against the governor of Grão-Pará, transferred the Captaincy of São José do Rio Negro from Barcelos to Lugar da Barra. This political decision and the administrative functions which arose from it had a great influence upon the rhythm of growth of the city, which was characterized by a small but significant economic activity based on cotton fabric, candle and net factories, a rope workshop, a pottery maker, a dockyard, sugarcane plantations, a gunpowder depot, a slaughter house, and a bakery. In addition, the Governor's Palace was built, a structure whose significance is more symbolic than architectural. Still a modest village, Lugar da Barra lost once again the seat of the Captaincy in 1799, but regained it in 1804. This brief period of relative prosperity was interrupted by the removal of governor Lobo d'Almada for political reasons: Francisco de Souza Coutinho, governor of Grão-Pará, felt threatened by Lobo de Almada's enterprising boldness. Coutinho had close family links with the Portuguese Court, which allowed him to weave a number of plots and intrigues in which Almada was involved. He was finally removed from his post as Governor of the Negro River (Reis 54). As a parenthesis, it may be added that such plots and intrigues are part of the regional and even national political life, undermining and disrupting social projects. It is too hasty to say whether—had he been able to continue with his work—Lobo d'Almada would have transformed the small urban settlement as well as the commercial and industrial activities that were so scarce in the Captaincy of São José do Rio Negro. In the meantime, it can be said that his wish for progress was not inherited by any of his successors during the first half of the nineteenth century.

In 1833, the Pará government divided its territory into three provinces: Grão-Pará, Baixo Amazonas, and Alto Amazonas. The latter replaced the Captaincy of Rio Negro, and its capital was promoted to the category of *vila*: Vila de Manaos. The city had eleven streets and a square. The inhabited area did not go far beyond the 1821 to 1825 limits, and its population was around 3,000 people. In 1848 (two years before the Comarca do Alto Amazonas was transformed into a province), the Vila de Manaos was renamed Cidade da Barra do Rio Negro. The name exchange ended in 1856, when it was definitely called Manaus. Until the 1860s, when the rubber economy was already preparing the ground for a radical transformation of the urban scene, Manaus preserved the same look it had during the first half of the century. From that decade onward demographic growth "remained constant, but was not spectacular" as it would be during the 1890s (Weinstein 90). The late 1870s were the beginning of the expansion of the rubber economy, but the raw rubber exports had already almost tripled during the 1860s. This fact had a significant impact on a stagnant economy like that of the Amazon Province and of the region as a whole.

During that period, construction projects were either started or reformed, such as those of the Main Office or of the Church of the Remedios; others were barely conceived, such as the Quays of Tamandaré Square, a steam tile factory, and the pavement of several streets and of the ramp of the Empress Quay, which was then the main port in the city (Mesquita 31). The speeches given by the president of the province and by members of the city council showed the will to turn Manaus into a hygienic and civilized place, a project which was finally achieved, even if it was after thirty years. Around 1860, the people of Manaus were able to enjoy the images of the Cosmorama or Polyorama (as was advertised by the newspaper *Estrela do Amazonas*, on 24 August 1862). And one wonders about the sense of awe caused by the Cosmorama views, which included winter in Savoy, New York's Crystal Palace, a market day in Switzerland, Saint Cloud's castle, and Rousseau teaching botany in Ermeville. The discordance between the civilizing endeavor and Amazonian reality is actually evident in the portrayals of several foreign travelers and naturalists who visited Manaus throughout the nineteenth century. All of them refer to the rusticity of the small village. Most see the place with an objective eye, not short-sighted or distorted as in certain idealized images of the "Other" that are present in some of these travel books, especially when they ponder native societies. When observing and perceiving the "Other", travellers lose their objectivity, it seems, and the discourse becomes Eurocentric insofar as the image of the Indian and the *mestizo* is always negatively compared to that of the European (see Gondim).

Therefore, the impressions recorded by Alfred Wallace in 1850, Henry Bates in 1850 and 1859, Avé-Lallement in 1859, François Biard in 1856, the Agassiz couple in 1865, and Franz Keller-Leuzinger in 1867 are all characterized by descriptions of the city as a small settlement of rustic and tumble-down buildings, with streets that are neither paved nor aligned—a place, in short, devoid of the minimum standards of hygiene and infrastructure. The illustrations made by Paul Marcoy and Franz Keller reiterate the coarse urban physiognomy mentioned in the travelers' reports: There is a chaotic conglomerate; that is, there is no planned design. Wooden and palm huts stand side by side with clay houses and tiled roofs, and the omnipresence of water is represented by the *igarapés*—narrow natural canals—which were partially banished from the urban scene during the rubber boom. Rather than suggesting a city with its complexity, and a diversity of functions and uses, the landscape reminds the observer of a bucolic, agreeable place. In truth, as Ab'Saber has remarked:

> a cidadezinha, em 1865, possuía todos os defeitos urbanos e sociais de um povoado amazô, minúsculo e segregado, nascido e crescido de um aldeamento de índios e à sombra de uma rústica fortaleza de soldados-colonos . . . . Manaus a esse tempo, era sobretudo uma cidade índia, onde a população de origem índia e os resíduos de costumes e atividades do índio, eram um fato na movimentação da vida urbana. (27)

> in 1865, the little town embodied all the urban and social defects of an Amazonian village: minute and segregated, originated and developed from an Indian hamlet and under the shadow of a rustic fort of soldier-settlers. . . . Manaus was above all an Indian city, where the population of Indian descent and Indian activities and customs made up most of urban life.

In the meantime, the objective record of the travelers contains a yearning for modernity, or at least the promise of an urban world attuned to the European capitals. Around 1825, naturalists Spix and Martius were impressed by the healthy situation (of the city), and its peaceful altitude overlooking the Negro River and close to the Amazon River. For the German travelers, once the lands around the Negro River and its main tributaries (Uapés and Branco) were inhabited and cultivated, they would be "ennobled by industry and civilization." The Lugar da Barra would "flourish and turn into a rich and powerful commercial city" and would become the "key to open the Western region of the country" (Spix 212; qtd. in Ab'Saber 11). These comments reveal a mixture of historic foresight and exaggerated optimism. Other travelers, like Elizabeth Agassiz, shared the optimistic attitude. In fact, from a certain perspective, the city did become rich and powerful, although the foresight and optimism tended to diminish the complexity of reality. The travelers were not able to perceive the abyss created between the capitalist development of the more advanced European centers and their more distant periphery. The same yearning for modernity would mark the tone of the speeches of the politicians and administrators of the Amazon during the rubber boom. The conception of a planned and hygienic urban growth excluded the cultural tradition of the native people.

The presence of an Indian culture is significant not only in Manaus, but in all Amazonian cities as well. Sometimes it is buried, a past that would be better dead, like Manaus' Indian cemeteries, symbols of the architecture of power and civilization, over which several buildings were constructed. However, their mores, housing, culinary traditions, body language, and even the Portuguese language—where one can find the origins of several linguistic branches of Indian groups–are all part of a cultural tradition with deep roots in the Amazonian cities. It is enough to pronounce the name of a fish, a fruit, a tree, or the very name of the city Manaus in order to feel within the inner fire of Indian tradition, of that absence which enlivens us and, which, even if we rebel, becomes a presence as well as present reality.

"On commença tout, on termina   Everything begins. Few things
  peu de choses..."   are completed.
                                   (Paul Le Cointe, "L'Amazonie
                                   Brésilienne")

At the turn of the century, Manaus became the second largest Brazilian city in the Amazon region. From 1889 to 1920, its population grew from 10,000 to 75,000 inhabitants. The modest urban settlement gave way to a purportedly planned city, built as a rational and efficient project in which, in fact, nature and the urban space were not fully integrated: Some *igarapés* which remained in the center of the old city were filled with earth and, unlike the city of Belém, no part of the forest was transformed into a park. The transplanted urban project divided the city from its environment, and this partition is visible even today. Between 1880 and 1910, Manaus's architecture and urban design were substantially transformed. The power of the capital determined a new concept of the city, and the urban functions and the use of space were redefined, as the historian Ednéa Mascarenhas Dias has rightly remarked:

Para cada igarapé aterrado, o surgimento de uma avenida ou o alargamento de uma antiga viela. Uma forma de arruamento harmônico e uso de espaço é imposta nos planos de embelezamento

de Manaus. O tecido urbano passa a configurar um novo desenho de cidade, contando com movos grupos sociais em suas mais diferentes relações, situações e conflitos. (11)

For each earth-filled *igarapé*, a new avenue emerged or an old narrow lane was extended. The harmonic disposition of streets and the use of space were imposed upon the beautifying layout of Manaus. The urban texture configured the new city design, and new social groups evinced the most diverse relations, situations and conflicts.

Manaus's huge transformation took place during the regime of governor Eduardo Ribeiro (1892–1896) and was further continued by his successors. The infrastructure of the new city included drainage and water supply systems, telephone lines, electricity, and trams. Apart from the covering of the *igarapés* (areas which became public roads), more things were built–squares, a central park, bridges, two large hospitals, luxurious mansions (like the Scholz family palace, which today houses a cultural center), and monumental public buildings such as the Amazon Theater or Opera House, the Palace of Justice, the Municipal Market, the Custom House, the Benjamin Constant Institute, the Amazonian High School, the Public Library, and many others. (See **Figure 1**.)

For Euclides da Cunha (1866–1909), Manaus became the tumultuous mecca for the *seringueiros* (the rubber tappers), as

Figure 1.

JARDIM DA MATRIZ
(LADO ORIENTAL)

Photograph by G. Heubner and Amaral of Central Park in Manaus, 1910. (Archive of the author)

well as for many immigrants, both from Brazil and from abroad. Apart from the native population (Indians and *mestizos*), a large number of people from the northeastern region came to the city escaping from the drought of the *sertão* and settled in the rubber-tapping areas and the cities of the Amazon region. Many foreigners (Portuguese, Spaniards, Italians, Germans, British, Moroccans, Syrians, and Lebanese) landed in Manaus well into the 1880s. Ten years later, these immigrants were responsible for the dynamism of trade, urban services, and tertiary activities in the city where 50,000 people then lived. Some were river merchants and established a bridge between the capital and the Amazonian interior. Many of them, especially the poorest, worked in civil construction. Some Italians, skilled craftsmen who had worked decorating the Amazon Opera House, remained in the city.

The sudden demographic growth of Manaus also revealed the perverse side of an incomplete or maimed modernization: social stratification (Dias 3). Rustic huts and the remains of clay houses predominated in the old city: Huts in wood and straw (which were elements of the native architecture but also signs of poverty) were next to clay constructions and tiled roofs. In the new city, Indians and poor immigrants became urban laborers, men and women excluded from a modernizing project that only pertained to the elites and an incipient middle class. It was then that the town saw the emergence of shelters, collective lodgings, and camps of northeastern immigrants awaiting the arrival of a ship which would take them to a distant rubber plantation. Manaus had many poor people, as well as many diseases and epidemics. That is why the state claimed it needed to exclude the sick and the wretched. In the city planned according to a bourgeois idea badly acclimatized to the equator, it was necessary to think about ways of isolating the outcasts (see Foucault).

The poorest of them were confined to districts such as Mocó, Colônia Oliveira Machado, São Raimundo, and Constantinópolis, which are far from the historical town center. The structural apparatus to shelter the marginalized, the destitute, and the outcast included a penitentiary, homes for beggars and the insane, and an agricultural colony. The aim of these premises was to exert control mechanisms at a time when there was an increase in the population of the poor—considered a threat or a danger to bourgeois order and wellbeing. When we witness, today, the deplorable living conditions of dozens of peripheral districts in Manaus, we forget that this urban misery originates in the economic vacuum of the Amazonian inland, although it is also part of the city's historical process and its excluding policies. During the 1914 recession, the Municipal Superintendent said, upon visiting a suburb of the city: "Se fosse possível a existência de uma necrópole de vivos, de cadáveres ambulantes, tê-la-íeis naquele subúrbio" ["If there could exist a necropolis of living people, of walking corpses, it would be found down there", in Dias 92].

It is not by chance that the glorious times of the rubber boom saw the foundation of the Beneficent Society in Favor of the Poor, the Poverty Protection League, and the Institute Benjamin Constant, which was destined to shelter poor and orphan girls and to turn them into good housewives. Its male companion was the Institute of Arts and Crafts, where the skilled labor force needed by the market was trained. Thus, philanthropy and the guilty conscience of the Manaus elite established deep roots in Amazonian ground. When the Refuge for Homeless People was founded, the state government,

through the First Decree of 29 January 1910, banned begging in Manaus. On the other hand, bathing in the *igarapés*, which was an old and pleasurable habit in all Amazonian cities, was the theme of an article in *O Norte*, 4 November 1912: "Prática que ofende a moral: Homens e Mulheres que tomam banho na Usina Elétrica em franca promiscuidade como a reviverem toda a primitividade dos costumes passados" ["It is a practice which offends the morality of the people: men and women bathing in the electricity plant, in evident promiscuity, an act which recreates the primitive instincts of past habits," in Dias 32]. The last words of this edifying comment refer to the Indian habits inherited by the city's *mestizo* population.

Manaus's modernity was really short-lived and destined for the very few. The common view that it was an exact equatorial copy of Paris is rather exaggerated. Baron Haussmann ("the demolishing artist," according to Walter Benjamin) transformed the face of an already industrialized city; Zola's Paris was poor and grandiose at the same time—the run-down, destroyed, and rebuilt capital city, where ruins and great works mingled, like an arena of never-ending metamorphoses. This was the Paris evoked by Baudelaire. In the case of Manaus, the "demolisher" Eduardo Ribeiro built and urbanized an area deprived of industries and whose wealth was generated by a fragile, extractive economy threatened and later undermined by the British intervention in Asia. The regional elite was too slow to understand the significance of the threat, as it never seriously reflected upon the consequences of Henry Wickham's removal of the thousands of seeds of the *Hevea brasiliensis*, an action which, far from being a legend, was all too real. In 1872, Wickham, a botanist in the service of the British empire, smuggled out the rubber plant seeds which were first taken to Kew Gardens to be acclimatized and later transported to Asia. Forty years after his exploit, Wickham was execrated by journalists, rubber plantation owners, and rubber barons. However, this hard-working, cunning botanist deserves a less undignified place in this tale of the *Hevea* smuggling: His biography should be included in Jorge Luis Borges's (1899–1986) "Universal History of Infamy."

Manaus wanted to see its reflection in Paris or Liverpool, but the image in the mirror only showed the disjunction between the advanced capitalism of France and England and the backwardness of a non-industrialized economy of a peripheral region. The disconnection was even manifest in relation to São Paulo, as noted by Ab'Saber:

> Guardadas as proporções, aconteceu com Manaus um pouco daquilo que se passou com São Paulo, mais ou menos durante a mesma época. São Paulo, à sombra do desenvolvimento econômico do café, cresceu desmesuradamente, controlando a um tempo a uma industrialização crescente. Manaus, ao contrário, cresceu sob o impulso de uma "economia de coleta" extensiva, dependendo de correntes de imigração interna, de um mecanismo de circulação moroso ligado exclusivamente aos rios e, tendo que dividir as glórias de metrópole com a cidade de Belém, a maior cidade do norte do país. (30)

> What happened with Manaus is more or less similar to what happened with São Paulo during that period. Thanks to the economic development related to coffee production, São Paulo burgeoned disproportionately, controlling at the same time the railway expansion of the plateau, foreign immigration, and an increasing industrialization. On the other hand, Manaus grew out of an extensive economy which depended on a strong national

immigration, a slow currency flow which was only dependent on the river economy, and having to divide the glories of being a metropolis with the city of Belém, Brazil's largest city in the Northern region.

Although Manaus shared (and continues to share) its metropolitan prestige with Belém, the latter was Amazonia's trading hub well before the rubber period. The sense of perplexity expressed by those who visited Manaus at the turn of the twentieth century reflects the contrast between the small urban nucleus (almost a wooden port) and the planned city. In 1908, Paul Walle compared the large borough of twenty years before with the "recently-built city.... Today it is a large navigation and trade center" (29).

From the Wooden Port to Manaos Harbor

In Amazonia, almost everything is seen in a hyperbolical way. The superlative nouns used to express its greatness and exuberance hide the ground of everyday life, of prosaic things. Official and iconoclastic rhetoric attributed to the city the lushness and profusion of Nature. Manaus's urban and architectural luxuriance was portrayed with those adjectives previously employed only to describe the surrounding forest. Many myths were created around this ostentatious urbanism. Caruso and Sarah Bernhardt, for instance, never performed at the Amazon Opera House. And if the Theater's design suggests that of the Scala of Milan or the Opera in Paris, the comparison only applies to the facade and the interiors. (See **Figure 2**.) There is only a superficial likeness because, in fact, there are plenty of differences that are evident to the eyes and the ears. In spite of this, Manaus did have a dynamic cultural life with plenty of theaters, cinemas, photographic studios, newspapers, publishing houses, and bookshops.

Figure 2.

Photograph by G. Huebner and Amaral of Teatro Amazonas, The Amazon Opera House, Manaus, 1902. (Archive of the author)

Figure 3.

Photograph by G. Huebner and Amaral of Elegent Department Store "Au Bon Marché" Manaus, 1900. (Archive of the author)

For a foreign observer, the more impressive feature of Manaus was its vocation for trade: exports and imports. The consumer goods acquired by the elite came from the United States and, above all, from Europe: from champagne to Marseilles fabric, from Italian marble stones to wheat meal, from metallic structures to clothes. European fashion was exhibited in the windows of the shops: La Ville de Paris, Maison Chic, Old England, Au Bon Marché, and Aux Cent Mille Paletots, stores which were located on the city's main streets (the avenues Eduardo Ribeiro and Sete de Setembro) and in the surrounding area–between the wharf and the Amazon Theater (see **Figure 3**). Around the same place, one could find the main hotels, bars, casinos, and night clubs where cancan dancing, vaudeville, gambling, fun, and carnal lust all found a common home.

Rapture's euphoria (or euphoria's rapture) drove the rubber barons and the great importers and exporters to wild speculation. Apart from blinding them to the imminent economic collapse, the illusions of ostentation stimulated certain practices which cannot be considered as exquisite (although there is something sublime in this) as well as delirious attitudes caused by a sense of disproportion. It is as if economic wealth overshadowed forever the experience of scarcity; this was the blindness by means of which the elite introjected a feeling of extravagance. Clothes tailored in Paris were sent to be laundered in Lisbon–an instance of the extravagant madness which links the Colonial past to the projection of the elite's desires. That is, Paris becomes the metonym of a civilized Europe. In this sense, Manaus endeavored to mimic the Parisian scene, starting by its architecture.

The neo-Classical style prevailed in most mansions and public works, whereas the façades and interiors of several buildings showed eclectic Baroque, and Art-Nouveau elements. Manaus's urban plan–which dates from 1893–is at least five times larger than the original 1852 plan. Bordered on the south by the bay of the Negro River, Manaus expanded toward the north and the east. To the north, the city reached the Amazonas Boulevard and the São João Batista cemetery. Further up, one could find the huge gardens and wooden chalets and villas where wealthy families spent their weekends. Some of these mansions still exist and in one of them, which belonged to writer Alberto Rangel (1871–1945), Euclides da Cunha lived, in 1905, before leaving for High Purus as Head of the Commission to establish the limits of the border between Brazil and Peru. The construction of the two main avenues of the city, Eduardo Ribeiro and Getulio Vargas, was possible because the waterways or *igarapés* were filled with earth. In order to make the expansion toward the east possible, iron bridges were built over the *igarapés* Cachoeirinha and Cachoeira Grande, and Roman bridges over the *igarapés* Manaus and Bittencourt.

It was a rational project which included structural axes, as well as secondary, parallel and perpendicular streets. The squared outline went against the winding path of the *igarapés'* bed, so that Nature became a real problem in the beautifying project of the city. Once the *igarapés* were filled, it was impossible to turn Manaus into an Amazonian Venice. In 1909, governor Antônio Ribeiro Bittencourt criticized the earth-filling of the *igarapés*, "one of the charms" of the city. For him, if left undrained, the igarapés could make of Manaus "not only the beautiful princess of the Negro River, but even a more poetic, pleasant, and less gloomy Venice, adorned by the lush Amazonian vegetation" (in Mesquita 206).

The poetic spaces imagined by Bittencourt were nothing but a chimera before the 1910 crisis. In the meantime, the margins of the small waterways of this unfulfilled Venice were occupied by *palafittes* (houses built over the water). In the end, popular architecture–in the form of wooden houses covered with straw–was always part of the Manaus landscape. In this sense, one could think of Alejo Carpentier's idea of a third-style city in which native architecture stands side by side with a transplanted one. In spite of the efforts to keep the poor houses away from the central area, the urban space of Manaus was (and continues to be) a mixed space where yesterday's mansions and today's bourgeois lodgings cannot be completely isolated from the popular quarters. It is as if the periphery, with its marginalized population, insisted on remaining in the center–a stubbornness due, above all, to the fact that the poor continue to occupy the margins of the *igarapés*. It is not by chance that in the recent project for modern Manaus, the aim is to transform the *igarapés* (which are now open-air sewers) into wide avenues. That is to say, one hundred years later, Nature has not yet found its place in the city.

The 1893 layout included a series of squares full of trees, with an iron bandstand and statues of Greek gods, imported from Liverpool and Paris, respectively. These were large gardens, some even with stone paths, and ponds with fish and animals. When I was a teenager, as a student of the Pedro II Amazonian High School (the imposing neo-Classical building which, together with the headquarters of the Military Police, formed the two walls of the Heliodoro Balbi square), the lessons given by our science teacher were often outdoors. She used to name the water plants, the orchids nested on top of the trees, the fish and animals which inhabited the garden. In a way, the samples of Amazonian fauna and flora belonged to the city, just as nowadays they only belong to our memory. An engineering student might be able to learn quite a lot about metal structures by studying the Municipal Market, the

Figure 4.

Photograph by G. Huebner and Amaral of Municipal market "Mercado municipal" Manaus, 1910. (Archive of the author)

iron bridge over the Cachoeira Grande *igarapé* and, above all, from the plasticity and the technical solution of the hanging bridge over the Cachoeirinha *igarapé*. (See **Figure 4**.)

If the symbol of the culture of the elite was the Amazon Theater, the most significant icon of the commercial vocation of the city was the port, Manaos Harbor, or just Roadway, as it was called by the inhabitants of Manaus. The port of Manaus is a masterpiece of European engineering (Scottish, Belgian, and British) and technically conveys England's commercial interests in the purchase and sale of Amazonian rubber. It was one of the largest river ports of Latin America (with a length of 1,313 meters of fluctuating quays at a depth of twenty meters), and it reflected the significance of the *Hevea brasiliensis* in world trade. Constructing buildings with huge metallic structures demanded the presence of English engineers and technicians. The English were also responsible for the management and maintenance of the harbor, the drainage and water-treatment systems, the municipal market, the public slaughterhouse, the urban road services, and the trams and electricity services. That is why the elderly still nostalgically remember the "English Manaus."

If it is true that Euclides da Cunha does not mention even once the cultural life of Manaus during the almost three months that he spent in the city in 1905, it is also true that his correspondence to friends and relatives is full of observations about the commercial and predatory character of the Amazonian capital during the boom of the extractive economy. In a letter to a friend he wrote:

caí na vulgaridade de uma grande cidade estritamente comercial de aviadores solertes, zangões vertiginosos e ingleses de sapatos brancos. Comerical e insuportável. O crescimento abrupto levantou-se de chofre fazendo que trouxesse, aqui, ali, salteadamente entre as roupagens civilizadoras, os restos das tangas esfiapadas dos tapuias. Cidade meio caipira, meio européia, onde o tejupar se achata ao lado de palácios e o cosmopolitismo exagerado põe ao lado do ianque espigado . . . o seringueiro achamboado, a impressão que ela nos incute é a de uma maloca transformada em Gand. (256)

I have fallen into the vulgarity of a strictly commercial big city, full of cunning rubber traders (called *"aviadores"* in the Amazon region), giddy idlers and white-shoed Englishmen. Commercial and unbearable. Here and there, sudden growth finds, among its civilized vestments, the remains of the palm-skirted loincloths of the *tapuias*. A city half rural, half European, where the straw hut is disappearing amidst the mansions, and the exaggerated cosmopolitanism places the ill-bred rubbertapper next to the slender yankee. . . ; the impression given by the city is that of a hamlet turned Ghent.

Euclides felt annoyed by the heat and humidity of Amazonia, although later he became reconciled to the climate. In a letter to José Veríssimo, dated 2 February 1905, he quotes with some irony the "glorious climate" of Henry Bates and the delightful climate of Alfred Wallace. He was upset, however, by the fact that he had to start his trip to Alto Purus some months before planned. Many things went wrong during his long stay in the city, so it is understandable that he was critical toward it. Lightly, he wrote to Afonso Arinos on 12 January 1905:

Somente hoje posso mandar-te uma breve notícia—tais as atrapalhações, tais os embaraços que nos saltearam aqui, nesta ruidosa, ampla, mal-arranjada, monstruosa e opulenta capital dos seringueiros. Eu escrevo-te doente. Conseqüências do "glorious climate" de não seir se ilustre ou se ingênuo Bates. (250)

Only today can I send you a brief note . . . such have been the mishaps and inconveniences that I have had in this noisy, large, poorly-arranged, monstrous, and opulent capital of the rubbertappers. I write to you while being ill. Consequences of the "glorious climate" of the illustrious or naive—I do not know which—Bates.

Apart from the harsh climate, his problems, and his feverish state, something else bothered the renowned and learned writer. When writing about Belém—"com seus edifícios desmesurados, as suas praças imcomparáveis e com a sua gente de hábitos europeus, cavalheira e generosa" ("with its huge buildings, its incomparable squares, and its generous, courteous and European-like inhabitants," 249)–Euclides praises a city whose order, progress, and hygiene were in accordance with his own positivist ideal. For him, Belém could be the reincarnation of civilized Europe, whereas Manaus—"capital of the rubbertappers" and a city "half rural, half European"–still had a strong native cultural element, perhaps primitive and backward from Euclides' point of view which was already formed by triumphant science and progress.

Even so, it is extraordinary that the author of *Os Sertões* never mentioned the cultural atmosphere of the city in which he lived for eleven weeks, and even more so when one considers that, in 1905, Manaus had an intense cultural vitality. The cultural contrasts which annoyed Euclides: ("o tejupar que se achata ao lado de palácios" [the straw hut . . . disappearing amidst the mansions]) were more visible in Manaus than Belém ("desde o século XVIII uma cidade cêntrica" [from the eighteenth century a central city"] (see Nunes, this volume), a city that had a long and continuous urbanization history due to its urban design as well as to the greatness of its spaces and monuments. Even after Manaus's beautifying project, its urban space could hide neither the native architecture nor the Indian population, whose presence came to be included in the cauldron of cultures, languages and ethnic groups: Euclides da Cunha's exaggerated cosmopolitanism. At the time, many Indians still spoke *nheengatu* (*língua geral*), which is still alive in the area of the Negro River. Cosmopolitan, but not a great, strictly-commercial city, Manaus did become, from the last decade of the nineteenth century, a significant cultural center in Amazonia.

Foreign travelers, such as ethnographer Theodor Koch-Grünberg (1872–1924) and French writer and poet Henri Michaux (1899–1984), did not ignore some significant aspects of this cultural life. Around 1905, after listening to the musical band of the Military Police in the Praza de matriz, Koch-Grünberg commented upon the skill of the musicians who were, for the most part, "dark or black young men, who play quite well not only some rhythmic marches and dances, but operas by Wagner and some other composers, all of which they master with ease." (See **Figure 5**.) Further on, the ethnologist states: "In this and in many other things, Manaus has something of the big cities" (16). In 1928, travelling from Iquitos to Belém, Henri Michaux captured in his logbook the sense of temporariness and fragility of the modern city, its ephemeral condition, in which the monuments of a recent and glorious past began to show signs of coming oblivion. "The inhabitants of Manaus look at their city as a heap of ruins. Nevertheless, it has very recent buildings, a theater worthy of a great capital, and it irradiates beams of luxury everywhere" (166).

Figure 5.

Photograph by G. Huebner and Amaral of Central Plaza "Praza da matriz" Manaus, 1910. (Archive of the author)

Of the great architectural works built during that period, the Amazon Theater is the most ostentatious. It is possible to imagine the wealth of the elite of that period with a single visit to the Opera House. Its very wealth reflects also its obverse: the isolated life and the toilsome tasks of thousands of *seringueiros* in the rubber plantations. What is more impressive in this eclectic building is its iron and glass dome covered with green, yellow, blue, and red tiles. The dome was not included in the original project, and constitutes a daring detail, a surprising element for such architectural work. It is like a visual noise in a predominantly neo-Classical quiet plan. The inner side of the dome, which is the ceiling of the concert hall is also surprising: Its lining was painted in Paris by the Capezot House and is full of allegories of the arts; its central focus is on Carlos Gomes and, right in the middle, the Eiffel Tower seen from below. Paris and the arts are in the heights, amid the ethereal clouds of a piece of artificial heaven, as if the spectator, looking upward, were touched by a vision of the sublime.

The stage drop cloth, a painting by Crispim do Amaral, represents the Meeting of the Waters of the Negro and the Solimões rivers (which form the Amazon) in an attempt to bring the spectator closer to nature. However, the dark waters of the Negro River are not there, and this goes against the very subject of the picture, thus reducing the "Meeting of the Waters" to a singly-nuanced flowing horizon: Was it the myopia of the craftsmen from the Capezot House or that of the Brazilian artist trained at the Saint Luke Academy in Italy? The ceiling of the Noble Room, painted by Domenico De Angelis and his team, portrays the "Glorification of the Arts in Amazonia", and on the walls of this magnificent room the paintings describe the flora and fauna of the region, as well as the Indian characters of writer José de Alencar. Thus, the profusion of decorative elements in which one can also find Baroque sculptures and Rococo cherubs aims at combining the Fine Arts with Amazonian motifs, a combination that, in itself, suggests the opposition between the Amazonian "primitive world" and European art.

Manaus's cultural events took place precisely around the Opera House, which was inaugurated on 31 December 1896 with a concert performed by the Italian Lyric Company. From that date onward, the number and variety of lyric and dramatic companies that performed in the theater are really impressive. However, quantity prevailed over quality. If, on the one hand, the Manaus elite attended several performances given by the French and Italian lyric companies; on the other, the same stage was also used for magicians, psychics, hypnotists, operettas, *zarzuelas* (Spanish operettas), musical bands, and circus exhibitions. Because of its decorative and architectural significance, the Amazon Opera House was the central attraction for opera and drama, but other theaters also offered a variety of shows. Several Manaus drama companies, such as the Arcadia Dramática (Dramatic Arcadia, 1895), the Grupo Dramático de Manaus (Manaus Drama Company, 1896), and the Sociedade Dramática Familiar (Family Dramatic Society, 1897) competed with the foreign companies and with groups from other cities of Brazil. But dancing was the most popular entertainment: Dozens of dancing societies, clubs, cabarets, and café-concerts animated the night life of the city.

An exciting novelty was the cinema, which had a real impact in the early 1910s, because Manaus did not really have a deeply-rooted lyrical tradition, unlike Belém, where the

people had been used to hearing the best Italian repertory since 1880. It is also probable that the Pará capital became interested in opera thanks to Carlos Gomes, who sang several times in that city. The first film screening took place at the Amazon Theater on 11 April 1897 and returned three years later. Various cinemas, such as the Alhambra, Olympia, Alcazar, Odeon, Avenida, Polytheama, Rio Negro, and Rio Branco exhibited films distributed by Pathé and Gaumont. Some of these cinemas did not survive long, and few overcame the 1910 crisis and the subsequent economic stagnation which lasted up to the late 1960s. During the brief 1910 boom, several schools and colleges were opened such as the Manaus Free University College which had five faculties: Letters and Sciences, Engineering, Pharmacy, and Law (Burns 18). This was the base from which the Amazon Federal University developed. It was founded in 1965, and today has a faculty of 800 professors and 10,000 students.

From the turn of the nineteenth century, fine arts and photography also enlivened the cultural atmosphere of the city. The Amazon Academy of Art was created in 1899 with state support. Joaquim Franco presided over the academy, which offered courses in subjects such as music, reading, recitation, oratory, drawing, painting, sculpture, and architecture, as well as several workshops in areas like engraving, lithography, photography, photoengraving, and phototypy. Most of the lecturers were Italian craftsmen and artists who had decorated the local mansions and city monuments. Some of them founded the great studios and photo galleries. Fidanza, Arturo Luciani, Lyra, Huebner and Amaral are some of the names linked to painting and photography. Many of the newspapers of the time advertised them, especially the German Photographic Studio of Huebner & Amaral, which was considered one of the most modern workshops of the Northern region. Many of the artists, actors, and musicians who took part in the city's cultural flourishment traveled between Manaus and Belém. The Italians De Angelis and Capranesi left works of art in both capitals. So did the photographers Fidanza and Arturo Luciani.

Because of its geographical location, Manaus attracted people from the frontier cities of Bolivia, Peru, Colombia, and Venezuela. San Carlos, the Venezuelan town on the high Negro River, had trade contacts with Manaus, in spite of the huge distance that separates them. The steam ships of the English Booth Line company sailed as far as Iquitos, bringing wood (above all mahogany) and rubber to be exported to Europe and to the United States. The press of Manaus and Iquitos published news related to the main events which occurred in the Peruvian and Brazilian Amazonia. One example is the famous case known as the "horrors of the Putumayo River"–the massacre of thousands of Peruvian Indians carried out by the overseers of Júlio César Arana, one of the largest stockholders of the Peruvian Amazon Rubber Company. Denounced in London by the U.S. engineer Walter Hardenburg, the slaughter had a significant impact on the English anti-slavery movement and for the British Aborigines Protection Society. From 1907 onward, the newspapers, *La Sanción* of Iquitos and *Jornal do Commercio* of Manaus, published the testimony of the victims, which usually incriminated Arana (Costa 157).

Literature and cinema have had an almost obsessive fascination with the Amazon. The movie *Fitzcarraldo* (1982) immediately comes to mind. The film deals with a delirious protagonist, an opera fan, and is almost equally delirious as the vision of Werner Herzog, the film director who is fascinated with Manaus, Iquitos, and the winding rapids of the Amazon tributaries from the landscape of this huge and varied Amazonian world. It is also worth remembering that Manaus, Iquitos, and the Brazilian and Colombian regions of the Negro River are the settings of the novel *La Vorágine* (1924; *The Vortex*, 1935), by José Eustasio Rivera (1888–1928) and that Mario Vargas Llosa's (b. 1936) *La Casa Verde* [1966; *The Green House*, 1968] is partially concerned with Iquitos and the Marañon River. Another important novel dealing with southern Venezuela's Amazon is Alejo Carpentier's *Los Pasos Perdidos* [1953; The Lost Steps], which features the upper Orinoco.

Today, many Colombians and Peruvians live in Manaus, most of them migrant workers who have been attracted by the economic euphoria generated by the tax-free zone in Manaus. However, there are also students and researchers from Peru and Colombia at the Federal University of the Amazon and at the Amazon National Research Institute, both established in Manaus. Highway number BR-174 (Manaus–Boa Vista–Caracas) might just tighten the cultural and economic links between the Brazilian and Venezuelan Amazon. In the year 2000, the city's population exceeded 1.5 million inhabitants but, unfortunately, there has been no plan to organize an urban region where more than 300 industries and dozens of thousands of trade companies have been established; the city has grown excessively. In 1967 (when the tax-free zone was created), Manaus was a city with a population verging on one quarter of a million inhabitants. It was still possible to recognize the urban and architectural features of the 1893 project in this peaceful city, which always awaits some kind of economic miracle—or collapse. It was possible to distinguish the squares, the monuments, the mansions, the statues, the century-old mango trees that give shade to the wide boulevards. People who walk around attentively can still enjoy the beauties of the past: the beauty of immortal ruins in the words of Marcel Proust.

Today, however, the modernity of Manaus (as well as of many other Brazilian cities) remains an unachieved fact, something perhaps even impossible or at least marginal to a wide social welfare project. The arrogant greed of real estate speculation (which goes hand in hand with a lack of planning on the part of ineffective and populist politicians and administrators) has given rise to a large and violent area of absolute poverty both in the outskirts and in the center of the city. For a handful of privileged people, modernity is perhaps the ominous inheritance of a past of slavery that mirrors, in the city, the impossibility of a dignified life for the large majority of people. "How to be modern and civilized within the conditions generated by slavery?" asks Roberto Schwarz in an essay dealing with social order in the novel *Don Casmurro* (19). The impasse suggested by the question, and which was cleverly captured by Machado de Assis, is the central test of our modernity. It is a lasting impasse, always latent in the social tensions and inequalities of Brazilian cities, of which Manaus and Belém are examples.

Without traces of nostalgia, I think that this Manaus does not belong to me anymore. The number of metamorphoses undergone by the city during the past three decades emit fatal signs, suggesting something far too mortal. What will remain from the ruins of such a recent past which was brutally, suddenly extinguished?

Reminiscences . . .

Perhaps, also, leisurely strolls searching for images, because the city has become an "image of thought and of the unconscious" (Gagnebin 160). It has become, in short, a moving text, pages which are always being written, a palimpsest to be revealed by the flight of memory and imagination.

Translation by Nair María Anaya Ferreira

Works Cited

Ab'Saber, Aziz Nacib. 1953. "A cidade de Manaus." *Boletim Paulista de Geografia* 15:18–45.

Burns, E. Bradford. 1966. *Manaus 1910: Retrato de uma cidade em expansão*. Trans. Ruy Alencar. Manaus: Governo do Estado do Amazonas.

Carpentier, Alejo. 1959. *Los pasos perdidos*. Mexico City: Compañía General de Ediciones.

Costa, Selda Vale da. 1996. *El Dorado das Ilusões: Cinema & Sociedade/Manaus 1897–1935*. Manaus: Editora da Universidade do Amazonas.

Cunha, Euclides da. 1997. *Correspondência de Euclides da Cunha*. Ed. Walnice Nogueira Galvão and Oswaldo Galotti. São Paulo: Editora da Universidade de São Paulo.

Dias, Ednea Mascarenhas. 1998. *A ilusão do fausto*. Diss. PUC-São Paulo.

Fitzcarraldo. 1982. Written and Dir. Werner Herzog. Werner-Herzog Filmproduktion.

Foucault, Michel. 1984. *Microfísica do Poder*. Trans. Roberto Machado. Río de Janeiro: Graal.

Freire, José Ribamar Bessa. 1993–94. "Barés, Manaos e Tarumãs." *Manaus: História em Novos Cenários* 2-3: 163-73.

Gagnebin, Jeanne Marie. 1997. *Sete aulas sobre linguagem, memória e história*. Rio de Janeiro: Imago.

Gondim, Neide. 1994. *A Invençao da Amazônia*. São Paulo: Ed. Marco Zero.

Koch-Grünberg, Theodor. n.d. *Dois anos entre os indígenas. Viagem no noroeste do Brasil, (1903–1905)*. Manaus: CEDEM.

Mesquita, Otoni Moreira. 1997. *Manaus: história e arquitetura (1852–1910)*. Manaus: Editora da Universidade do Amazonas.

Michaux, Henri. 1968. *Ecuador: Journal de voyage*. Paris, Gallimard.

Monteiro, Mário Ypiranga. 1952. *Fundaçao de Manaus: aspectos do panorama histórico-social do antigo Lugar da Barra*. 2nd ed. Manaus: n.p.

Reis, Arthur Cezar Ferreira. 1934. *Manáos e outras Villas*. Manaus: Revista do Instituto Geográfico e Histórico de Amazonas.

Rivera, José Eustasio. 1938. *La vorágine*. Mexico City: Espasa-Calpe.

Schwarz, Roberto. 1997. *Duas meninas*. São Paulo: Companhia das Letras.

Spix, Johann Baptist von and Carl Friedrich Philipp von Martius. 1938. *Viagem pelo Brasil*. Vol. 3. Trans. Lúcia Furquim Lahmeyer. Rio de Janeiro: Imprensa Nacional.

Vargas Llosa, Mario. 1967. *La casa verde*. Barcelona: Seix Barral.

Walle, Paul. 1909. *Au Pays de l'Or Noir: Para, Amazonas, Matto Grosso*. Paris: Guilmoto/Librairie Orientale & Americaine.

Weinstein, Barbara. 1993. *A borracha na Amazônia: expansão e decadência 1850–1920*. Trans. Lólio Lourenço de Oliveira. São Paulo, HUCITEC/Editora da Universidade de São Paulo.

CHAPTER 45

AMAZONIAN CULTURAL CENTERS OF BOLIVIA

Nicomedes Suárez Araúz

Bolivia's Amazonia at the beginning of the twenty-first century is in the process of determining or redefining the identity of its culture and cultural centers. During the past four centuries regionalistic tendencies, as well as social, political, and historical factors, have prevented it from arriving at a stable sense of identity. Five key motifs that have characterized Bolivia's Amazonia have been: (1) the archeological discoveries of a pre-history of the region whose antiquity is still under debate; (2) the mythical concept of the land as El Dorado, or Paititi, as the myth was known locally, and the actual search for it by conquistadors, adventurers, and neo-colonial capitalists; (3) the foundational role of religious missions; (4) the effects of the political, economic, social, educational, and cultural policies of the central government; (5) past indigenous rebellions and vindicatory proclamations in the present. These factors have in turn shaped the development of Bolivian Amazonia's cultural production.

The region in question comprises the major part of the so-called *Oriente boliviano* (Eastern Bolivia), which extends from the last foothills of the Andes, to the east, up to the region of Mato Grosso in Brazil, and from the Madeira and Abuná rivers, in the north, to the plains of the Chaco Boreal to the south (Parejas 19). Of the nine departments into which Bolivia is divided, the Amazonian region spans all of Beni and Pando. It also extends into the Iturralde province of the Department of La Paz, the Chapare province of Cochabamba, and the Northern section of three provinces of the Department of Santa Cruz: Ñuflo de Chávez, Guarayos and Velasco. Its population is approximately 344,000 (Pirson 3). The key cultural centers of the region are Santa Cruz de la Sierra, Trinidad, and Riberalta; these were founded in 1561, 1686, and 1894, respectively. They thus represent three key periods in the development of Eastern Bolivia: the age of the conquest, the Jesuit mission period, and the neo-colonial era of international capitalism. Since its foundation, Santa Cruz de la Sierra, the largest of them, was the principal center and the gateway to the rest of the Eastern lands.

We should note that Bolivia's geographic and ethnographic maps have not been fully established (see **Map 1**). Revisions of them sometimes have displaced towns and cities geographically. For example, Santa Cruz de la Sierra, with a population of 697,278 (Nogales, Rosquellas and Montecinos 193), is situated within the Amazonian basin, yet ethnically and culturally has been held to be a fundamental part of the La Plata River Basin. Precise particulars aside, it is now accepted that Bolivia's Amazonia covers 75 percent of its national territory and is equivalent to 11.2 percent of the Amazonian basin area (Pirson 3). This fact calls into question the monolithic denomination of Bolivia as an *Andean nation*, as it has been universally identified. This issue has progressively emerged as a source of pride among Bolivian Amazonians and has fueled the persistent struggle of the region to counter the hegemonic discourse of the highland centers (see Suárez Araúz 1994; Verde Ramo Costas). A revitalized historical consciousness in the region, as well as

Map 1.

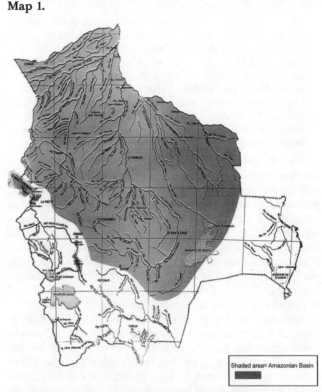

Map of Bolivian Amazon Basin. (Archive of the author)

national changes in the central government's policies, has resulted in a cultural transformation of Bolivia's Amazonia.

The region of Moxos, also known in the sixteenth century as Chunchos, Musu or Muju (Chávez Suárez 3–4), comprises most of Bolivia's Amazonia. The oldest evidence of the history of Moxos is in the fragments of a distant and literally buried past. The traces of this past were first revealed in the early twentieth century by the archeological excavations of Erland Nordenskiöld, who published his conclusions in *L'archéologie de bassin de l'Amazone* (1930). On the basis of his work, Donald Lathrap in *The Upper Amazon* (1970) propounded the view that the pre-Hispanic inhabitants of Moxos had come from the center of the Amazonian basin. William Denevan, Victor Bustos, Max Portugal Ortíz, Clark L. Erickson, Kenneth Lee, Bernard Dougherty, and Horacio A. Calandra are among the noteworthy contributors to the study and elucidation of the traces of the ancient Moxos civilization. Since the 1960s research on this region has been an active force in Amazonian identity formation in the area. Local historians with regionalistic pride present its scientific evidence to challenge the national mystique of an advanced highland civilization antedating all lowland civilizations (Pinto Parada 301–302).

The El Dorado historical marker began with the Conquest and remains a persistent myth. In Bolivia it came to inhabit the province of Moxos, and the discovery of El Dorado became a major objective of the Spaniards (Denevan 28). The first expedition in search of the nation some called "Ambaya," headed by Pedro de Candia, set off from Cuzco in 1538 or 1539 (Chávez Suárez 49). Insurmountable difficulties led him to abandon the expedition and return to Cuzco. In the sixteenth century alone fourteen more expeditions followed (see Chávez Suárez; Métraux; Parejas and Suárez; Finot). The justification for the myth may be found in the fact that the Spaniards saw evidence that in ancient times there had been a great chiefdom with a highly developed civilization (Palau and Sáiz 14):

> This theory is suggested by several things: (1) Many of the rumors about Paititi, Mojos and the *Tierra Rica* of the lowlands did not begin in Asunción and Santa Cruz but rather with Spaniards in Cuzco and La Paz, whose source was the highland Indians; (2) the Incas sent an expedition of conquest to the Río Madre de Dios and the borders of Northern Mojos; (3) the Jesuits believed the Cayuvava region was Paititi; (4) the Jesuits found large, politically unified villages; and (5) there are numerous remnants of large raised fields and trenches in the Cayuvava region, suggesting a former large and well-organized population. (Denevan 51)

This myth that engaged so much human energy and devotion associates Bolivia's Amazonia with all secret lands of unimaginable riches, which throughout history have taken hold of the human imagination. It is not surprising then that the arrival of international capitalism in the region, with the Rubber Boom era (1870–1920), was seen by some as heralding a new El Dorado. Two books on the era evoke the magnetic persistence of the myth: *Le pays des Amazones: l'El Dorado, les terres à cauoutchouc* [1885; The Land of the Amazons] by F. J. de Santa-Anna Nery (1849–1902) and *En busca de El Dorado* [1958; In Search of El Dorado] by Hernando Sanabria Fernández (1909–1986).

Beginning in the 1850s rumors of riches to be made in Bolivia's Amazonia set in motion a massive migration from the West, which thus began a succession of economic cycles that sowed astonishment, confusion, and euphoria at the riches achieved and dejection in the face of sudden economic collapse. Cinchona, rubber, Brazil nuts, cattle, gold, timber, and oil are words that abbreviate more than a century of Amazonian vicissitudes. Each of these cycles can be analogically viewed, in the terminology of the scientific theory of chaos, as an *attractor*, or a point of temporary stability. That is, they were sudden bonanzas, concentrations of capital in a few hands, booms that cyclically exhausted themselves into incoherence and dissolution. Each cycle, and especially the most lasting one, the Rubber Boom, brought constellations of foreign cultural products, primarily European and North American, to the region. These were transported along roads, and by canoes and steam paddle boats that sailed the San Matio, Beni, Madre de Dios, Mamoré, Apere, and Yacuma rivers (see **Figure 1**). Foreign influence was evinced in certain imitated customs, in the multiple imported articles of daily use, and in hunts that the neo-Colonial aristocrats organized, dressed like English lords even in such a tropical climate. The adoption of European customs was complemented by the prestige of being educated in Europe, especially England and France. The dominant presence of British economic power was evinced by the sterling pounds commonly used for most transactions until the 1920s.

The extractivist boom cycles in Eastern Bolivia were initiated by *cruceños* (citizens of Santa Cruz) seeking a better livelihood. The emigration toward the East represented an adventure into a last frontier and the possibility of acquiring prodigious fortunes. Before its 1903–1904 war against Brazil, Bolivia's Amazonian territory extended north up to the Acre

Figure 1.

Photograph of anonymous nineteenth-century painting of the San Matio River near Cochabamba, Bolivia, and the Amazon's source. (Archive of the author)

River: It was 72,000 square kilometers greater than it is nowadays. Bolivia's war effort was funded by Nicolás Suárez, one of the *cruceños* who took to the Eastern Trail in the 1850s. Suárez Hermanos, the company that Nicolás Suárez and two of his older brothers founded, was established close to the Brazilian border town of Guajará Mirim. On the banks of the Madre de Dios River they set up their central post, Cachuela Esperanza. The empire they built revolutionized the economy of the region. Suárez *barracas* (posts) lined the Acre region at intervals below Cobija for about 100 miles. Cachuela Esperanza, by the early 1900s:

> had indeed become the capital of an empire; to the office buildings, radio telegraph station, villas, residential blocks, school and chapel had been added a hotel, restaurant, cinema, theater, club, billiards saloon and skittle alley. Tennis courts illuminated by electricity, and a football pitch, defied the surrounding jungle. A library stocked with books and periodicals in Spanish, German, French and English was added, together with a hospital which under Swiss direction, became famous throughout the Oriente. (Fifer 136–37)

Another rubber baron, Antonio Vaca Díez, a physician and intellectual born in Trinidad, established his headquarters at the confluence of the Orton River with the Beni: "There he had built an imposing villa, warehouses, a hospital and a school"

(Fifer 130). Beginning in 1887 he published the only local newspaper in Northern Bolivia, *Gaceta del Norte*, and launched a journalistic tradition of cultural promotion in the region. Vaca Díez advocated the humane treatment of indigenous people, general education of the poor, and ecological preservation. He condemned the centralist policies of the national government, noting they were a major cause of the penury of the masses of Amazonia. As a medical doctor, Vaca Díez contributed to the clinical definition and therapeutic treatment of tropical diseases (Lijerón Casanovas 1990, 107–133).

The clamorous Rubber Era dramatically transformed the economy of the area. It also increased the separation between the exploited native population and the *mestizo-criollo* class. Its legacy was a number of new urban centers, paramount among them the city of Riberalta, founded in 1894. The mercantilistic practices of the times, with rare exceptions, were indifferent to cultural aspirations. The iterative element in each of those cycles was the social and economic transformations fueled by neo-colonial powers. Manifesting the participation of international capitalism, Bolivia's Amazonia became a sort of frontier between the spheres of influence of Great Britain and the United States (see Otero Reiche). The surnames associated with financial power during those years represent other foreign presences in the region: the French Braillard and Picollet; the Germans Demmer, Willinger, Wichtendahl, Reis, and Getsmann; and the Arabs Essabá and Hamid (Araúz 1912). The largest company, The House of Suárez, left a legacy of cattle raising that, after the collapse of the Rubber Boom, became the mainstay of Moxos's economy.

The Mission Period represents another determining factor in the formation of Bolivia's Amazonia. The missions flourished under Jesuit control from 1682 until 1767, the year of the expulsion of the Jesuits from the territory of the Audiencia de Charcas. By 1754 the Jesuits had founded twenty-seven reductions (missions) in Moxos (Chávez Suárez; Barnadas); in Chiquitos, from 1691 to 1760, they erected eleven (see Parejas and Suárez). Chiquitos forms part of the Department of Santa Cruz and partakes, in its Northern area, of the Amazonian Basin, and to the southeast, of the Plata River Basin. The missions of Chiquitos and Moxos, as Alcides Parejas Moreno and Virgilio Suárez point out, live on in the urban and cultural structures of Amazonian Bolivia. The mission is the foundation of an iterative town, repeated, on different scales, with local turbulences of ethnic hybridness and syncretic religious beliefs and rituals specific to each region. In the missions the present syncretism inherited by modern culture was wrought.

The system of *reductions* comprised three fundamental parameters: the technical enhancement of indigenous communities based on their own capabilities and resources; the implementation of a legal system that would guarantee the rights of the Indian participants; and the preaching of the gospel to create indigenous Christian communities (González Dorado 23). Alcides Parejas notes that–seen from that perspective–the reduction represents the spatial structure in which the spirit of the community developed (75). Virgilio Suárez, co-author with Parejas of *Chiquitos: Historia de una utopía* [1992; Chiquitos: History of a Utopia], notes that as far as urban planning goes, the Jesuit mission:

Se trata del único modelo urbano colonial debidamente planificado, que fue llevado a la práctica globalmente, reinterpretando la rigurosidad del *régimen indiano*, adecuándose a los condicionantes ambientales del ecosistema regional, respetando ciertos valores de la cultura indígena, retomando la tradición ciudadana y humanista, en el marco de los ideales utópicos agustinos y socráticos de *la ciudad de dios en la tierra.* (315)

...

Los nuevos pueblos se constituyeron en núcleos aglutinantes de diversas razas, superando por primera vez los conflictos de segregación racial–tan proverbial en la zona. Ninguna reducción se fundaba especialmente o destinaba para una determinada etnia, sino que el nacimiento de los barrios garantizaba la convivencia de distintas parcialidades, facilitando la conservación–de acuerdo a su desarrollo y fortaleza–hasta hoy de sus lenguas nativas, posibilitando el surgimiento de una verdadera sociedad bilingüe. (319)

It is the only colonial urban model duly planned that was put into practice globally, reinterpreting the rigorousness of the Colonial regime, adapting it to the climatological elements of the regional ecosystem. It respected certain values of Indigenous culture, and took up the civic and humanist tradition, within the framework of Augustine and Socratic ideals of the *City of God on Earth.*

...

The new towns gathered into groups made up of various races, overcoming for the first time the conflicts of racial segregation, so proverbial in the area. None of the reductions founded were especially intended for a particular ethnic group, but rather the set up of the neighborhoods guaranteed the coexistence of various ethnic components, facilitating the preservation–depending on their degree of development and vitality–until today of their native languages, making possible the emergence of a true bilingual society in which one of the native languages was chosen as a lingua franca together with Spanish.

Laudatory opinions of the accomplishments of the mission system (of which the most successful missions were the Jesuit) are countered by criticism of the cultural disruption it caused among indigenous societies (Riester 1975, 18).

According to David Block the centuries of mission culture had three subperiods: the first (1660–1767) was Jesuit, the second (1767–1825) was under the influence of a secular Spanish government, and the third (1825–1880) was under the Bolivian government. "After two hundred years of vitality, mission culture collapsed in the mid-nineteenth century. The onset of international capitalism in Moxos provided the final shock to the system . . . . The rubber boom, which completed the process of native dispossession begun under Spanish administration, marks the end of mission culture in Moxos" (Block 173). During the last three decades the government of Santa Cruz de la Sierra, with the cooperation of international cultural organizations such as UNESCO, has retrieved the past glory and accomplishments of the Jesuit missions of Chiquitos. The restoration of the churches and urban structures has been undertaken. An archival research project yielded numerous documents, which have helped complement knowledge of the history, social and religious organization, and cultural production of the missions (see Querejazu 1995). Musical scores found in the 1970s were transcribed into modern musical notation and performed in 1996 at the "Primer Festival de Música Renacentista y Barroca Americana Misiones de Chiquitos." This conservationist effort has brought a renewed interest in the regional cultural patrimony.

The post-Independence years represent a fourth period with what would be far reaching change in Bolivia's Amazonia. The Andean primacy, based on a concept of geographic determinism, dominated as much in the Pacific region as in the rest of the country (Roca García 1980, 166). The policies based on that Andeanist thesis kept Eastern Bolivia economically depressed and culturally cut off from national life. It was not until the 1950s that a new order emerged in which the central government favored the Department of Santa Cruz. In the 1960s and 1970s Bolivia entered a boom cycle, which led to a dramatic increase in the construction of highways and railways. Since Santa Cruz is rich in oil and agricultural products, especially sugar, cotton, and rice, rising prices of these products propelled the region into frantic modernization. The department also gained in political power when, in 1972, it supported Colonel Hugo Banzer Suárez in his successful takeover of Bolivia's presidency (Klein 258–59). The Banzer regime abruptly relinquished the traditional alliance with Argentina in favor of a new and close relationship with Brazil. Santa Cruz's economic bonanza and the better means of communication with the highland cities and Argentina led to a temporary cultural distancing from the rest of the Amazonian region. However, a recently built road to Trinidad with connections to Riberalta and Cobija emphasized the geo-cultural kinship of Santa Cruz with the rest of Amazonia.

In 1987 Santa Cruz's main state university, Gabriel René Moreno (UGRM), participated as an Amazonian member in the founding of UNAMAZ (Association of Amazonian Universities). Significantly, only 10 percent of UGRM's library materials pertain to Amazonian themes. The technical university Mariscal José Ballivian of Trinidad, the capital of the Department of Beni in the heart of Moxos, did not become a member until 1991 (Pirson 9, 17). In Riberalta there is an Institute of Amazonian Studies and an Amazonian House of Culture.

Amazonian institutions of higher learning concentrate on scientific studies of the regional environment while its literature and arts are only tangentially studied. It is remarkable how recent the growth of a full-fledged historical consciousness in Bolivian Amazonia has been; its process of identity formation, in fact, continues. This process is epitomized, for example, by the creation of new foundational myths such as that of Pedro Ignacio Muiba, a Moxos chieftain who in 1975 was canonized as a hero of Bolivian Independence on the basis of research done by Antonio Carvalho Urey (1977). Through documents found in the *Archivo de Mojos y Chiquitos* (Public Records of Mojos and Chiquitos), Muiba is credited with launching a proclamation in October 1810 addressed to the then governor of Moxos. Testimony by his adversaries shows that Muiba, much like Juan Maraza, another Moxos chieftain, besides calling for the independence of Bolivia from Spain, intended to set up an autonomous indigenous government, an event perhaps without precedent in the annals of Bolivia and possibly in the rest of Spanish America (Roca García 1991, 17).

The resistance of indigenous cultures to the dominant *criollo* and *mestizo* classes is the fifth cultural fact shaping the identity formation of Amazonia. The many rebellions of these classes against the extreme abuse and exploitation they had endured since the conquest have taken the form of either passive or violent resistance. The former is evident after the 1840s in the indigenous retreat to remote regions between the Mamoré and Securé Rivers of the Department of Beni (Lehm, Lijerón Casanovas, and Varech 10). A notable violent reaction after Muiba's rebellion was led by a native priest, Andrés Guayocho, in 1887. It was brutally quashed and ended with the death of Guayocho and another leader, Juan Masupija (Aguilar 163). José Santos Noco Guaji followed in Guayocho's steps and until 1926 led the indigenous towns of San Lorenzo

and San Francisco in creating a social fortress of indigenous life and culture in the face of Bolivian authorities and hordes of traders. In 1990 a vindicatory "Marcha Indígena por el Territorio y la Dignidad" ("Indigenous March for Land and Dignity") was launched by Moxo, Sirionó, Yuracaré, and Movima Indians. In an act of protest for past and present abuses and the usurpation of their lands, they walked for thirty-four days from Trinidad to La Paz (Lijerón Casanovas 1993). Another march followed in 1996 from Santa Cruz to La Paz, led by Moxo Indians. The Bolivian government acceded to their requests by passing decrees, granting legality to their land claims, in addition to their political and cultural organizations. Because of these movements and others, cultural issues have been reconsidered on the basis of the region's traditional elements. The indigenous component has gained such importance that the educational reform of 1996 is based on multicultural and bilingual principles.

Yet the task of recognizing and resolving Amazonia's cultural identity is by no means complete. The regional literature of Amazonia written in Spanish has been traditionally classified as literature *del oriente boliviano* (Eastern Bolivia) or *del trópico boliviano* (Tropical Bolivia). The former simply points to a geographic position–eastern–in relation to the Andean centers of power; the other–"tropical"–is a climatological and ecological appellative. *Amazonian* denotes a specific geo-cultural identity and a historical destiny (see Suárez Araúz 1994). No anthology of Amazonian writing has been published; nor has autochthonous oral literature been incorporated within regional anthologies. Its transcription and compilation have been primarily undertaken by national and foreign anthropologists. Nonetheless, Indian lore and references to Indian languages are present in many regional writers.

Among the earlier writers of the twentieth century, Raúl Otero Reiche (1906–1976) was the first major poet from the region to focus on Amazonia, which he represented as "la selva" [the jungle] or "Moxitania" [the land of the Moxos]. Otero Reiche is part of the Americanist impulse to name one's environment. He is also the foremost exponent of the transition from the Parnassian and symbolist-inspired Spanish American *modernismo* to the avant-garde styles. In the 1930s he was already writing poems with expressionist and surrealist overtones. He was thus one of the precursors of future generations who viewed their surroundings with care, avoiding a commonplace *costumbrismo* and rhetoric and, at the same time, continuing to develop a more universal poetic vision. Julio de la Vega (b. 1924), Pedro Shimose (b. 1940), and Nicomedes Suárez Araúz (b. 1946) are poets representative of that tendency (Shimose 10). Suárez is also the author of *Amnesis*, an Amazonian-inspired aesthetics of amnesia as a creative and structural metaphor and theme in the arts (see Suárez Araúz 1988).

As for fiction, some foundational writers are Enrique Finot (1891–1952), Alfredo Flores Suárez (b. 1897), and Luciano Durán Boger (b. 1904). The newer generations include José Wolfgang Montes Vanucci (b. 1951) and Homero Carvalho Oliva (b. 1957). In fiction, as in poetry, there is a tendency to social protest together with a representation of place and customs. Often the Spanish means of expression bears the watermark of native languages, thus revealing the complex identity of the land. The privileged language of the regional literature has been Spanish. Yet the following indigenous oral text evinces the awareness of a separation of identities. It is a Chimane song translated into Spanish by Juerguen Riester and Gisela Roeckl:

Mira, mira cómo se arrastra el caimán sobre la arena.
Estoy muerto: el convento es ahora mi morada;
Estoy muerto: el convento es mi casa y canto.
Hosana, hosana, hosana,
Hosana, estoy borracho,
¡Hosana en las alturas! (1978, 11)

Look, look at the alligator drag itself over the sand.
I'm dead, the convent is now my dwelling;
I'm dead, the convent is now my house and song.
Hosanna, hosanna, hosanna,
Hosanna, I'm drunk,
Hosanna, in the highest!

And thus into the Chimane world enter European references, the convent and beer (which the author mentions later in his text), and in the process they take on an autochthonous intonation. The graft of one linguistic code onto another fractures the peaceful coherence of both. Yet it is important to emphasize that linguistic *mestizaje* does not imply fusion, but rather a superimposition of cultural signs. The cannibalization of Christian liturgy ("Hosana en las alturas") is incorporated as a parodic element, in a sort of Bakhtinian process (also professed by Brazilian *modernismo's* anthropophagic aesthetics) of incorporating a foreign culture. The above poem expresses the Chimane (dissembling) belief that Christians upon dying end up in a convent, where they spend their time drinking beer. The poem goes on to equate metaphorically a Christian to an alligator, an animal they consider ugly (Riester 1978, 32).

Amazonia in its diverse aspects–social, political, economical and cultural–is a land in the process of reviewing itself, attempting to bring to consciousness the diverse historical factors that come together in a heterogeneity that almost defies grasping as a whole. That process implies the retrieval and vindication of elements that for centuries lay mute, distorted, or forgotten. The incipient awareness of Amazonia's identity as a dialectic of differences always shaped by the land will, no doubt, become stronger in the new millennium as it faces the threat of ecological devastation and the continued erosion of its traditional cultures.

Works Cited

Aguilar, Gonzalo. 1993. "Los pueblos indígenas de las tierras bajas en el siglo XIX." *Data* 4: 153–65.

Araúz, Rodolfo. 1912. *Informe que eleva al Ministerio de Guerra y Colonización el Delegado Nacional en el Territorio de Colonias, Riberalta, 1912.* La Paz: Velarde.

Barnadas, Josep M. 1984. "The Catholic Church in Colonial Spanish America." *The Cambridge History of Latin America.* Ed. Leslie Bethell. Vol 1: *Colonial Latin America.* Cambridge: Cambridge University Press. 511–40.

Block, David. 1994. *Mission Culture on the Upper Amazon: Native Tradition, Jesuit Enterprise and Secular Policy in Moxos, 1660–1880.* Lincoln: University of Nebraska Press.

Carvalho Urey, Antonio. 1977. *Pedro Ignacio Muiba: el héroe.* Santa Cruz: "Los huérfanos."

Chávez Suárez, José. 1944. *Historia de Moxos.* La Paz: Editorial Fenix.

Denevan, William M. 1966. *The Aboriginal Cultural Geography of the Llanos de Mojos of Bolivia.* Berkeley and Los Angeles: University of California Press.

Fifer, J. Valerie. 1970. "The Empire Builders: A History of the Bolivian Rubber Boom and the Rise of the House of Suárez." *Journal of Latin American Studies* 2.2: 113–46.

Finot, Enrique. 1978. *Historia de la conquista del oriente boliviano.* La Paz: Librería Editorial "Juventud."

González Dorado, Antonio. 1979. "Las reducciones jesuíticas: Un sistema de evangelización." *La evangelización en el Paraguay. Cuatro siglos de historia.* Luis Cano, et. al. Asunción del Paraguay: Ediciones Loyola. 23–34.

Klein, Herbert S. 1982. *Bolivia: The Evolution of a Multi-ethnic Society.* New York: Oxford University Press.

Lathrap, Donald W. 1970. *The Upper Amazon.* New York: Praeger.

Lehm A., Zulema, Arnaldo Lijerón Casanovas, and Lorenzo Varech. 1990. *Diagnóstico de los indígenas mojeños en la ciudad de Trinidad.* Trinidad: Centro de Investigación y Documentación para el Desarrollo del Beni.

Lijerón Casanovas, Arnaldo. 1990. "Apuntes de un diario inédito del doctor Vaca Díez sobre la situación social y económica de Mojos en el siglo XIX." *Signo* 29: 107–33.

———. 1993. *Marcha indígena por el territorio y la dignidad.* Trinidad: Centro de Investigación y Documentación para el Desarrollo del Beni.

Métraux, Alfred. 1948. "Tribes of Eastern Bolivia and the Madeira Headwaters." *Handbook of South American Indians.* Ed. Julian Stewart. Vol 3: *The Tropical Forest Tribes.* Washington, DC: U.S. Government Printing Office. 351–454.

Nogales, Graciela Q., Rosa E. Rosquellas, and Germán Montecinos. 1995. *Nueva geografía de Bolivia.* 6th ed. La Paz: Centro Geográfico "Estrella Nueva."

Nordenskiöld, Erland. 1930. *L' archéologie de bassin de l' Amazone.* Paris: Les Editions G. Van Oest.

Otero Reiche, Raúl. 1988. *Cantos del hombre de la selva: Antología poética.* Santa Cruz: Casa de la Cultura "Raul Otero Reiche."

Palau, Mercedes, and Blanca Sáiz. 1989. *Moxos por Lázaro de Ribera, 1786–1794.* Torrejón de Ardoz: Ediciones El Viso.

Parejas Moreno, Alcides, and Virgilio Suárez Salas. 1992. *Chiquitos: Historia de una utopía.* Santa Cruz de la Sierra: Universidad Privada de Santa Cruz.

Pinto Parada, Rodolfo. 1987. *Pueblo de leyenda.* Trinidad: Editorial Tiempo del Beni.

Pirson, Bernard. 1993. *Directorio de centros de capacitación y de investigación de la pan-amazonia; miembros de la UNAMAZ.* Belém do Pará: Vanguardia Editorial.

Querejazu, Pedro, ed. 1995. *Las misiones jesuíticas de Chiquitos.* La Paz: Fundación Banco Hipotecario Nacional.

Riester, Jurgen. 1975. *Indians of Eastern Bolivia: Aspects of their Present Situation.* Copenhagen: International Work Group for Indigenous Affairs.

———. 1978. *Canción y producción en la vida de un pueblo indígena (los chimane: tribu de la selva oriental).* Trans. Claudio Solari T. La Paz: Editorial "Los Amigos del Libro."

Roca García, José Luis. 1980. *Fisonomía del regionalismo boliviano.* La Paz: Los Amigos del Libro.

———. 1991. *Mojos en los albores de la independencia boliviana (1810–1811).* 2nd ed. La Paz: Editorial Don Bosco.

Sanabria Fernández, Fernando. 1958. *En busca de El Dorado: la colonización del oriente boliviano por los cruceños.* Buenos Aires: Imprenta López.

Santa-Anna Nery, Federico José de. 1885. *Le pays des Amazones: l' El Dorado, les terres à cauoutchouc.* Paris: L. Frinzine.

Shimose, Pedro. 1995. "Apuntes sobre poesía boliviana." *Presencia Literaria* (April 16): 8–10.

Suárez Araúz, Nicomedes. 1988. *Amnesis: The Art of the Lost Object.* New York: Lascaux Publishers.

———. 1994. "Hacia una identidad literaria amazónica boliviana." Harvard University: New England Council of Latin American Studies. (October).

Verde Ramo Costas, Eugenio. 1994. "Bolivia, ¿país altiplánico o amazónico?" *Revista de la Sociedad de Estudios Geográficos e Históricos* 46: 9–12.

SECTION VI
EAST AND CENTRAL BRAZIL
INTRODUCTION

Ângela Maria Dias

The Portuguese policy of Brazilian colonization, according to Sérgio Buarque de Hollanda (1902–1982), privileged the foundation of port-cities–understood as catalyzing centers of commercial ambition and territorial defense. For this reason they are aptly described as communities of sowers; that is, they rise and grow spontaneously according to daily whims and urgent needs. Contrary to Spanish America, whose colonization was based mostly on the planning of cities as instruments of the Spanish will for domination and the imposition of a rational plan, Portuguese colonization of the large Brazilian territory shows, by its administrative character, the greater economic importance of large plantations over the development of cities.

The reasons for the preference of the administration for the coast are the obvious ease in communication, control over exportation of materials, and the possibility of defensive measures to protect the vulnerable colony from the English, French, Spanish, and especially Dutch forces. In the seventeenth century Frei Vicente do Salvador (1564–1639?) called this practice the Portuguese habit of living by "arranhando as costas como caranguejos" (Hollanda 155) ("scratching the coast like crabs"). These fundamental factors make the Portuguese position the opposite of the Spanish strategy of determined force and insistent effort in making the New World in the image of the metropolis. In this sense the

Map 1.

Map of the cultural centers of Brazil and their spheres of influence c. 1940: Manaus, Belem, Recife, Salvador (Bahia), Belo Horizonte (Minas Gerais), Rio de Janeiro, Sâo Paulo, and Porto Alegre. In Fernando de Azevedo, A cultura brasileira *(3 vols., Rio de Janeiro, 1943).*

531

contrast that Sérgio Buarque de Hollanda makes between communities of sowers for Colonial Brazil and the cities of bricklayers for the Spanish possessions highlights the distinguishing Portuguese pragmatism, indifferent to the Spanish obsession with rational order and its units. (On the one hand, this latter policy accounts for the amazing   expanse of Spanish Colonial settlements and, on the other hand, it underlines the artifice of their written chronicles with an implicit but powerful domination of all aspects of life in New Spain, New Granada, etc.)

This attempt at laying down roots in and stabilizing the new land explains the priority of the Spanish enterprise for settling and building in order to bring all the natives into the bosom of the Roman Catholic Church and obedient to the civil authorities (Hollanda 62). This was exactly the opposite of the Portuguese practice of immediate strategic conquest of the coastal peoples in order to mobilize all forces in the exploitation of the natural resources. Yet, if this mercantile and strictly utilitarian character in the beginning made for a careless look to the city, spontaneous and "enlaçada na linha da paisagem" (Hollanda 76) ("entwined in the landscape"), it does not really diverge from Spanish practice at least with respect to the preeminent role of the elite peninsular educated groups in the so-called "civilizing" enterprise. The famous "aversão congênita a qualquer ordenação impessoal da existência" (Hollanda 75) ("congenital aversion to any impersonal ordering of existence") did not prevent the Portuguese from developing a vast Colonial administration based on "la fuerza operativa del grupo letrado (y las exigencias de la evangelización [transculturación] de una población indígena) que debía transmitir su mensaje persuasivo a vastísimos públicos analfabetos" (Rama 1984, 27–28) ("Presented with the huge task of carrying its persuasive message to the colonized masses of the New World, [and the project of evangelizing and overseeing the transculturation of an indigenous population] the specialized cadre of letrados took on correspondingly greater operative force" 1996, 19–20).

The Baroque era, whose Brazilian zenith was in the eighteenth century in Minas Gerais (owing to the exploitation of gold and precious stones), is seen in the splendor of its festivals, in terms of scenography and the power of audiovisual resources—one of the greatest investments in ideology and propaganda in Western history until today's cultural industry. In fact, the spectacular and promotional force of the absolutist Church and state in the atmosphere of the enthusiasm of the Counter-Reformation, in both Spanish and Portuguese America, affirms throughout the history of colonization the crucial importance of the educated groups "como diseñadores de modelos culturales, destinados a la conformación de ideologías públicas" (Rama 1984, 30) ("as intellectual producers, who elaborate [rather than merely transmitting] ideological messages, the designers of cultural models raised up for public conformity" 1996, 22).

In this sense Ángel Rama (1926–1983) speaks to us of the "cidade letrada" (Lettered City), not less walled in than the citadel city or the port city, yet more aggressive and redemptivist in the making of collective myths and in the naturalizing of domination:

En el centro de toda ciudad, . . . hubo una ciudad letrada que componía el anillo protector del poder y el ejecutor de sus órdenes: Una plébaye de religiosos, administradores, educadores, profesionales, escritores y múltiples servidores intelectuales, todos

esos que manejaban la pluma, estaban estrechamente asociados a las funciones del poder y componían lo que Georg Friederici ha visto como un país modelo de funcionariado y de burocracia. Desde su consolidación en el último tercio del XVI, ese equipo mostró dimensiones desmesuradas, que no se compadecían con el reducido número de los alfabetizados a los cuales podía llegar su palabra escrita . . . obteniendo por lo tanto una parte nada despreciable de su abundante surplus económico.
(Rama 1984, 25)

At the center of each colonial city, . . . nestled a corresponding version of the city of letters to attend to the mechanisms of political power. The viceregal capitals housed a myriad of administrators, educators, professionals, notaries, religious personnel, and other wielders of pen and paper-whom Georg Friederici thought a model of bureaucratic development. From the time of its consolidation in the final third of the sixteenth century, the activities of the lettered city took on huge proportions, apparently unrelated to the tiny number of literate persons who could read its voluminous writings . . . naturally made them large consumers of the colonies' economic surplus. (1996, 17–18)

The functionality of this intellectual field–"desde el púlpito, la cátedra, la administración, el teatro, los plurales géneros ensayísticos" (Rama 1984, 29) ("in pulpits, universities, and administrative offices, as well as in the theater and various genres of essay writing" 1996, 21)–for the symbolic invention of a space shared by people of all social levels, allowed the formation of a public, though uneducated or illiterate, and transformed the cities (regardless of their style or appearance) into catalyzing poles capable of transposing the social order into physical reality (Rama 1984, 6). Precisely because "the chief function of the city is to convert power into form, energy into culture" (Mumford 571), the temporality of each cultural center, especially during the period of Hispanic-Portuguese colonialism, united with myriad politicoeconomic factors, was deeply marked by the logic of domination.

If we view the notion of a cultural center as a circle of influence around an axis-city, capable of transforming a given region into a magnetic pole of attraction, we will certainly observe some recurring elements in this dynamic of successive and simultaneous events, occurring in the course of time during which such events have influence. Thus, in Brazil, the golden age of the Recôncavo Baiano (Salvador Bahia) as a cultural center extends from its nomination as royal captaincy of Brazil in the sixteenth century to the middle of the eighteenth century, when the colony went into an economic depression due to the sugar market crisis and, later, the decline in the production of gold. (More precisely, this period lasted between 1540 and 1763.)

The geopolitical factors for the choice of Bahia as the center of the colony during the period mentioned were numerous. According to Manoel Maurício de Albuquerque, the following aspects were taken into consideration:

- the geographical location, almost in the center of the inhabited coast and near two captaincies in the process of development: Pernambuco and Ilheus;

- the relative proximity of commercial centers and European and African ports;

- the fertility of the lands of the Recôncavo and the wide hydrographic network;

- the existence of a defensible acclivity on the waterfront, a condition that strengthened the resistance to attacks from foreigners and Amerindians;

- the presence of colonists arriving with the proprietary appointee or even before him. (Alburquerque 182)

Simultaneously with Bahia's zenith, the colony's interests shifted to the south in recognition of the growth of the city of Rio de Janeiro, which would eventually in 1763 become the seat of the government of the State of Brazil by order of the Marquis Pombal; he justified this action with the following reasons:

- the need to control the export of gold and diamonds from Minas Gerais in order to avoid smuggling and evasion of taxes;
- the economic importance of the region, which was the productive center of sugar and stock-raising, as well as the port connected to Europe, Africa, and the Plate River;
- the interest in attending more efficiently to the border problems with the Spanish to the south of Brazil, owing to the conflicts resulting from the Treaty of Madrid, in 1750. (Albuquerque 174)

The expulsion of the Portuguese Jesuits from Paraguay and its dominions was seen by the newly empowered intellectual elite, under the leadership of the controversial Marquis Pombal, as the opportunity to centralize the Portuguese administration and prevent any areas from considering autonomous activity (Fausto 109, 112); in this sense the Colonial administration ended up by clearly recording its determination by choosing a new site for the concentration and diffusion of power. The dynamic of the creation and development of cultural centers in Latin America, inserted in the context of the historicopoliticoeconomic interests of the metropoles, reveals with clarity the lettered city ordering the physical world, normalizing collective life, and socially organizing the system of power.

It is perhaps worthwhile giving the cases of São Paulo and Minas Gerais a closer examination; here, at different times, independent initiatives quite independent of the crown forced a move to the interior of the country, a move that was only officially recognized because of the economic imperative of the discovery of gold at the end of the seventeenth century. As Sérgio Buarque de Hollanda emphatically comments, the civil disobedience of the obstinate pioneers of São Paulo is probably explained by cultural factors resulting from their few contacts with Portugal and much mixing of blood with foreigners and Amerindians; this resulted in a population of "esses audaciosos caçadores de índios, farejadores e exploradores de riqueza . . . antes do mais, puros aventureiros . . . que, desafiando todas as leis e todos os perigos vai dar ao Brasil sua atual silhueta geográfica" (Hollanda 68) ("bold hunters of Indians, trackers and explorers of riches . . . who were more than anything, pure adventurers . . . who, defying all laws and dangers, would give Brazil its present geographical outline"). Even if one disregards the excessive drive of these adventurers, the fact is that the discovery of gold in Minas Gerais by the men of São Paulo not only forced the metropolis to create the captaincy of São Paulo and Minas at Ouro Preto (1709)–and a little later elevate the Vila de São Paulo to the category of city (in 1711) and transform Minas Gerais into a separate captaincy (in 1720) (Fausto 100)–but was also responsible for the creation of a busy cultural center in the interior of Minas that hosted the great Baroque festivals and at the same time gave rise to the most advanced movement of insurrection against colonial oppression in all Brazilian history: the Inconfidência Mineira.

In effect, the formation of such a differentiated, urban society–made up not only of miners but of businessmen, lawyers, priests, farmers, artisans, bureaucrats, and soldiers (Fausto 102)–that was capable of vigorous cultural manifestations, entwining various artistic fields within the splendor of religious celebrations, contributed to an understanding of the development of a reflective community mature enough to produce an oppositional political voice despite overwhelming difficulties. This was the "invisible city" constituted by the lettered, articulate, cultured, and thinking elite–"mineradores, fazendeiros, padres envolvidos em negócios, funcionários, advogados de prestígio e uma alta patente militar, o comandante dos Dragões" (Fausto 115) ("miners, farmers, priests involved in business, civil servants, prestigious lawyers, and a high-ranking soldier, the commander of the Dragoons"), as well as those in the teaching profession. All of them, on one side, were connected to Colonial authorities and, on the other, were profoundly dissatisfied with the course of the regime's decisions, which proved ever more harmful to their interests.

In the strictly artistic practice of writing the purely nativist sentiment present, for example, in the lyrical works of Cláudio Manoel da Costa (1729–1789) in his transfigurations of nature in Minas which gradually took on a critical hue, until eventually one could see "um esboço do que seria a consciência nacional propriamente dita" (Candido 1987, 171) ("a sketch of what would be the national consciousness itself"), whose culminating point, in terms of literary production and critical potential, was attained by Tomás Antônio Gonzaga (1744–1807) in As cartas chilenas [1863; The Chilean Letters]. The local discontent and the growing feeling of contradiction in the system joined in this propitious setting with the resonant ideology of the Enlightenment and Liberal political ideas, thereby creating a syndrome whose double nature–caught between the internal stimulus and the external influence–would consist of a kind of ever-active dynamic on the national scene: the dialectic, already pointed out by Antônio Cândido (b. 1918), between the local and the cosmopolitan. Minas, as the prodigious cultural center of the eighteenth century, was certainly exemplary in this respect. In a radical and eminently practical manner, the great values of the Enlightenment–Reason, Progress, Freedom–and the utopian formation of a free and sovereign country are joined for the first time in Brazilian history. There was, on the one hand, an axis of modernization–the most advanced sociopolitical-economic theories that were incorporated into a body of revolutionary proposals (such as, for example, the republican form of government and the abolition of slavery)–and, on the other, there was an axis of identity that stresses the feeling of belonging to the land and the solidarity of its people.

In the eighteenth century one finds the basis for the future discourse of Brazilian culture and, also, because of an affinity of interests (and obstacles) with Spanish America the basis for nascent discourse on Latin American identity. It is precisely this counterpointed dialogue between external stimulus and internal reality–inherent in the Colonial condition and in a country in formation–that tended to create, in the educated community (beginning with the Inconfidência), the pioneering appropriation of the emblems of the Enlightenment and the tireless civilizing effort to dissipate the darkness of backwardness. Especially after Independence (1822) the public genres (oratory, journalism, essay writing) fostered the goal of uniting the citizen, the intellectual, and the politician (Candido 1969, 234), and conflating the image of the Portuguese university graduate with that of the patriot. It was at this time that the educated class earnestly applied themselves to the transformation of the landowner-slaveowner empire through Liberal ideas imported from bourgeois Europe–despite the obvious "torcicolo cultural" (cultural arrogance) of the European (see Schwarz), or even the open disregard for the very real differences between the imported principles and the local, provincial, and pre-bourgeois context.

In this respect the moment of the Proclamation of the Republic (1889) is crucial and serves as a significant line of division in relation to the whole Imperial period (1822–1889), insofar as it tries to turn the mere change of political regime from the Imperial to the Republican (as devised by the elite dissatisfied with the abolition of slavery) into a sign of the entrance of the country into modernity. As Nicolau Sevcenko points out:

> Era como se a instauração do novo regime implicasse pelo mesmo ato o cancelamento de toda a herança do passado histórico do país e pela mera reforma institucional ele tivesse fixado um nexo so-extensivo com a cultura e a sociedade das potências industrializadas. (27)
>
> It was as if the installation of the new regime implied by the same act the cancellation of the entire inheritance of the historical past of the country and by mere institutional reform it had fixed a nexus co-extensive with the culture and societies of the industrialized powers.

The case of Rio de Janeiro, as Renato Cordeiro Gomes argues, offered a kind of "síntese sociológica e cultural do país" ("sociological and cultural synthesis of the country") in "seu papel de cidade-capital" ("its role of capital-city"); a highly problematic horizon characterizes the determination of the new elites to impose, in the name of modernization, the abstract standards of advanced urban planning on a highly needy, uncultured, and unprotected population, in which many had only recently been released from slavery. In this sense 1860 constitutes the historical moment chosen as the demarcation line between a retrospective view of the Colonial past and the impetus toward the future. The already mentioned progressive vortex of the period from 1870 to 1920, when the process of modernization of the Latin American city took place, would confirm Rio de Janeiro as the mirror for the symbolic identity of Brazil, both in the learned discourses and in those that became national movements and as such were accessible to a larger public: For example, the establishment of the *Jornal do Brasil*, with its suggestive title, is important for the generalization that it manifests. It was housed in a building "encimado por um fantástico minarete em forma de Torre Eifel, no mais cobiçado dos endereços da cidade, a Avenida Central" ("topped by a fantastic minaret in the form of an Eiffel Tower, at one of the most coveted addresses of the city, the Avenida Central").

In effect, Rio as capital, understood as monumental representation of a national project or even as allegory of Republican modernity, was incarnated in an exemplary way during the period of the remodeling of the city, promoted by Pereira Passos (1836–1913), in the name of hygiene, good taste, and art, according to Olavo Bilac's (1865–1918) patriotic note of 1904. If the interventions in the urban landscape of Rio–the construction of the Avenida Central, the reform of the port quay, the Mangue Canal, and the redesigning of Botafogo Bay–are in fact much more timid than such enthusiasm might make one believe, the truth was that the dictatorship of the state inflicted brutal violence against the poor, homeless population, who did not have the alternatives of indemnization or relocation. As a consequence there was an uncontrollable growth in the slums, the drastic repression of the so-called Vaccine Revolt (1904), the prohibition of the central city areas for the homeless, and the deportation of those who resisted to the Amazon. In ironic contrast to this policy of social regeneration is the triumphal inauguration of the Avenida Central, the indelible mark of the progressivist mythology: "A civilização do Brasil divide-se em duas épocas: antes e depois da Avenida Central. Entre a Rua Ouvidor e a Avenida vai uma distância assim como de Sabará a Marselha" ("The civilization of Brazil is divided into two eras: before and after the Avenida Central. The distance between the Rua do Ouvidor and the Avenida is the same as that between Sabará and Marseilles"), according to Renato C. Gomes, one of the chroniclers of the period. In this way the dream of making Rio de Janeiro a tropical Paris marked the fate of all the great Brazilian capitals, dramatizing the pitiless contradiction between obstinate urban modernization–understood as spatial specialization and social segregation–and the compulsive erasure of the past (in the insistent suppression of the marks produced by colonial status and the system of slavery).

Thus the new Republic's obsessive fixation on Paris as "modelo de cirurgia material e social" (Marins 134) ("model of material and social surgery")–from the Haussmann era (1853–1870)–introduces the ideal standards of urban civilized life, set against the tradition of turmoil, carelessness, and instability of Brazilian cities, which had been greatly aggravated by the abolition of slavery without a plan to incorporate the former slaves into society; this lack of social planning was the fault of the Republic at the end of the Empire. Salvador, for example, according to the "padrões de controle necessários às cidades portuárias" ("standards of control necessary for port cities") for their integration into international commerce (Marins 164), adopted, according to Eneida Leal Cunha, the "urbanismo demolidor" ("demolishing urbanism") of J. J. Seabra in 1912. As it was announced at the time, the plan was to make the Colonial city of three centuries ago disappear to make room for a modern city, built according to the rigorous precepts of progress. The passionate controversy over the demolition of the old Sé da Bahia, built during the first General Government of the Colony, constitutes, in this respect, a key to the historical reconstruction of Salvador; since the debate lasted from 1912 to 1932, it brought into an extensive discussion broad social groups, including the public administration, the bureaucracy of the Catholic Church, and the English franchise for streetcar service, and also involved a large part of the population. It was not only intellectuals and artists who were concerned with the defense of the Bahian imaginary and its principal monument; Bahia's entire population responded.

The outcome of the demolition, despite those sweet promises of progress, sounded threatening in the Bahian intellectual context, which–under the aegis of the Medical School–proposed a dialogue among the various interest groups. The proposal was taken up by the Arco & Flexa ("Bow and Arrow") group, in order to mediate the dialogue between the dominant conservative view and the need for literary renewal–through a kind of dynamic traditionalism. The unique character of the aesthetic experimentation in the Modernist project of São Paulo is not in fact exclusive to Bahia. In Recife, as well, the Regionalist Manifesto, signed by Gilberto Freyre (1900–1987) in 1926, offers a reflection on the country from the point of view of the Northeastern tradition of master/slave partnership and of the myths of racial democracy and luso-tropicalism.

Nevertheless, the Northeastern Colonial tradition did not always work within this ideology of Brazilian culture that was acritical and strongly marked by the conciliation of socioeconomic conflicts and interests. In the seventeenth century colonial Bahia would produce Gregório de Matos (1633?–1696), a poet working within a cycle of production, circulation, and dissemination (of cruel and angry satires) in the nonprint mode of distribution of orality and manuscripts. As a result of widespread popular dissemination, there was no guarantee of the authorial authenticity of this entire corpus. In spite of its being ignored throughout the eighteenth century and only rediscovered in the middle of the nineteenth century, the fact is that the satirical work of Gregório de Matos began one of the most authentic currents of reflection on Brazilian culture–a very fertile and long-lasting one, which continued into the twentieth century with the critical–a parodical current that would emerge in the Modernist revolution of Mário de Andrade (1893–1945) and Oswald de Andrade (1890–1954) and appear again in the Tropicalism of the end of the 1960s.

In what specifically concerns Bahian culture, according to Eneida Leal Cunha, the poetic alchemy of Gregório de Matos was a mediation between the lettered elite and the street, within the complex reality of the seventeenth-century city; it put down strong roots, because it captured and represented visions of the past-miscegenation, social differences, economic exploitation, elitist prejudice–and portrayed scenes of Brazilian origins that still have repercussions even in the present-day Bahian imaginary. In fact the prodigality of the seventeenth century in conceiving the continuity of images and values of Bahian Colonial life–produced by the works of Gregório de Matos, Antônio Vieira (1608–1697), and Frei Vicente do Salvador–not only shapes a long history but also founds a kind of imagined community of Brazil.

This same hybrid and popular imaginary was recreated, beginning in the 1930s, in the fictional universe of Jorge Amado (b. 1912) who–in the struggle against cultural racism, through his mixed race, sensual, and irreverent heroes–succeeded in recovering for Bahia a central role in the production of images of identity that are disseminated throughout the country and abroad. In the genealogy of the ideological inspiration of his praise for the African contribution to the formation of Bahian culture, the importance of the truly epic work of Gilberto Freyre is undeniable, according to César Leal. This is because Northeastern regionalism, combined with a thesis about the "assimilation of cultural inheritance," would end up bringing about a new sense of the value of popular cultural elements (religion, music, dance, martial arts, the oral tradition) as a deviant and unforeseen derivation of the myth of racial democracy. On the other hand, from the beginning of the avant-garde period in the 1930s:

> a estruturação do populismo como retórica nacionalista de integração política das massas ao discurso oficial e às prerrogativas do Estado . . . marca o momento crucial da criação de um tipo de hegemonia profundamente atuate na vida sócio-cultural brasileira. (Dias 17)

> the structuring of populism as a nationalist rhetoric of political integration of the masses into the official discourse and the prerogatives of the State . . . marks the crucial moment of the creation of a type of hegemony deeply active in sociocultural Brazilian life.

For precisely this reason, Rio de Janeiro as capital city becomes a privileged showcase where all significant changes in the socioeconomic life of the country take place. As Renato C. Gomes acknowledges, in the context of macrophenomena such as industrialization and urbanization, mass communications and the emergence of a public avid for information and leisure generated the golden age of popular music and radio programs, while the theatrical revue established itself as the trademark of Rio culture; the cinema (the first musical films–a mixed genre of comedy and carnival) became more popular; the carnival and samba gained international recognition; and the Cinelândia neighborhood (Lapa and surroundings) was transformed into Rio's Broadway.

This cultural dynamic, at the crossroads of the cosmopolitanism of the artistic avant-gardes and manifestations of a very rich popular culture (the samba, which was the music of the working classes living in Rio's slums) was reappropriated by the Vargas dictatorship, in its "prática inédita de produzir o consenso por meio de apelos sensoriais e conotações afetivas" ("unprecedented determination to produce consensus by means of sensorial appeals and affective connotations"), through "doses complementares de repressão e doutrinação" ("complementary doses of repression and indoctrination" Sevcenko 38). In this sense "o nacional-popular como construção da intelectualidade incorporada ao aparelho estatal certamente constitui a primeira formação ideológica brasileira com alcance hegemônico" (Dias 18) ("the popular-national, as the construction of the intellectual elite, incorporated into the state apparatus, certainly constitutes the first Brazilian ideological formation of hegemomic scope"), which ended up asserting Rio de Janeiro's role as "província-nação" ("nation-province"), a "espécie de arquiprovíncia, lugar de convergência de todas as partes do Brasil . . . centro de irradiação e locus da diáspora de escritores, artistas e produtores da cultura" (Dias 18) ("kind of arch-province, a place of convergence for all parts of Brazil . . . center of dissemination and locus of the diaspora of writers, artists, and producers of culture").

In effect, the construction of the image of an urban Brazil, cosmopolitan and multiracial, molded in and by Rio de Janeiro, while forming one of the most important and long-lasting ideologies within Brazilian culture–which, with its Leftist features, would reign supreme from the 1930s until the end of the 1960s–went perfectly well with another type of portrait of Brazil, the one painted by the regionalist novel of the 1930s, a rural, realist, and sociologically complex country, welcomed and sponsored by the publisher Editora José Olympio. It is interesting here to note the observation of Sevcenko on the exclusion of any trace of São Paulo localism from the "modelo de cultura nacional abstrata" ("model of abstract national culture") manufactured in Rio de Janeiro to serve the centralist nationalism of Getúlio Vargas:

> Numa peça de teatro musical de grande sucesso, como Chouchou e Balangadãs, se configura o ideal da fusão abstrata pretendida, através da fusão entre o samba e a estética hollywoodiana das escolas-de-samba cariocas, o modelo estilizado da baiana, com sua conotação afro-brasileira e um cenário que evocava as cidades históricas de Minas Gerais. A ausência conspícua era a de qualquer referência a São Paulo, cujo surto industrial, comandado em grande parte por empresários de origem imigrante estrangeira, a estigmatizava como sendo uma ameaça potencial à unidade e cristalização da nova consciência nacional. (Sevcenko 39)

In a highly successful musical, like Chouchou e Balangandãs, the ideal of the intended abstract fusion is formed through the fusion of samba and the Hollywood aesthetic of Rio samba-schools, the stylized model of the Baiana [Bahian woman], with its Afro-Brazilian connotations, and a background that evoked the historical cities of Minas Gerais. One noted the conspicuous absence of any reference to São Paulo, whose industrial surge, mostly led by industrialists of foreign immigrant origins, stigmatized it as a potential threat to the unity and crystallization of the new national consciousness.

Also according to Sevcenko, intimately connected to this erasure of São Paulo-ness by the Getulian regime was the rise of an essentially critical culture, concentrated especially in the investigation and denunciation of authoritarian traditions and structures of domination and social oppression represented by Sérgio Buarque de Hollanda's and Caio Prado Júnior's (1907–1990) interpretations of Brazil, and, above all, incarnated in the founding of the University of São Paulo in 1934. Only in the 1950s, during the postwar redemocratization, does Sevcenko see what can be called the São Paulo renaissance, based on industrialization as a symbol of the expansive possibilities of Brazilian progress, as developed in a series of important and lasting cultural initiatives—the creation of the Museum of Modern Art of São Paulo (1949), the organization of the Biennial Art Exhibitions (1951), architecture, and theater—and, especially, crowned by the apotheosis of the celebrations of the city's four-hundredth anniversary in 1954.

In the first years of the 1960s, the spiral of uncontrolled development in São Paulo did not consist of a single factor but of multiple forces that came together in the building of Brasília. Brasília was a great landmark, since, according to Maria Zilda Cury, it intended to merge "o sonho secular da entrada na terra prometida–o centro inexplorado do país ainda jovem" ("the secular dream of entrance into the promised land–the unexplored center of the still young country") to the "utopia arquitetônica moderna da urbanização aberta e voltada para o social" ("modern architectural utopia of urbanization, open and socially conscious"). If its inauguration in April 1960 takes the title of Federal District away from Rio de Janeiro, it still does not deprive it de facto of its condition as capital city. Throughout the decade, Rio's culture would unquestionably be the leader in the vigorous and highly politicized discussions about the direction of the nation and would shelter the two dominant theoretical-formal currents: the popular-national, which originated in the 1930s, and the performative-experimental, present at least since the 1950s. In the former there was a continuation of Vargas's populism by some intellectuals, like Leon Hirzman, Vianinha, and Carlos Estevam Martins (b. 1936), who deepened the projects of the socially committed theater and popular art that matured with the Teatro de Arena Paulista. They founded the Popular Center for Culture–incorporated by the National Union of Students in December 1961–which later developed various experiments in engagé drama. In the latter the doctrinal-theoretical militance of São Paulo Concretism developed into the neo-Concretism of Rio in the 1960s and, especially, in the revolutionary works of Lygia Clark (1920–1988) and Hélio Oiticica (1937–1980). Cinema Novo was established at this time by the convergence of Rio's intellectual landscape with Glauber Rocha (1939–1981) and the rich heritage of Bahian experimentalism, as well as, after 1967, with the explosive and violent theater of José Celso Martinez Correa (b. 1937) and the Tropicalist movement, which integrated popular music, cinema, theater, and other diverse manifestations of cultural criticism.

On the one hand, the double character of these theoretical-formal tendencies in literary and cultural criticism (despite differences) covered the most diverse range and, through multiple exchanges and negotiations, expanded and encompassed diverse cultural manifestations in search of a greater ideal of communicability. Thus, literature, cinema, popular music, and theater went hand in hand with the social sciences in the analysis of the transformation of national life. The socialization of culture was seen as a program of action and a basic premise of the formal examination of culture. This is because the truly dominant factor, in the Brazilian 1960s, consisted of an educated elite in cultural-artistic fields; they were the major force determining cultural legitimacy and social prestige. In this sense the hegemony of this educated group characterized Brazilian uniqueness in relation to the Euro-American 1960s, which were already dominated by the new sensibility and more attuned to techno-visual culture.

On the other hand, the distinction that has been drawn between the popular-national and the performative-experimental may also be examined from the viewpoint of the interchange (inter-regional) among the various cultural centers of the country. The popular-national shaped the pioneering hegemonic formation of the modernized country as a product of mass politics produced in the heart of the country–the capital city, Rio. The performative and constructivist movement that engulfed all the arts had originated in São Paulo in the Modernist movement of 1922; it had subsequently spread throughout Brazil undergoing modifications and sometimes radical innovations especially in the artistic renaissance of Bahia in the 1960s.

In fact, the founding of the Federal University of Bahia in 1947 played a crucial role in the process of institutional construction. After a century and a half of insular existence, in the 1960s Bahia opened up to a cosmopolitan dialogue with the postwar avant-gardes, taking advantage of the Atlantic diaspora of European intellectuals such as Lina Bo Bardi (1914–1992), Hans Joachim Koellreutter (b. 1915), Yanka Rudzka, and Agostinho da Silva (1906–1996). Thus, as Eneida Leal Cunha notes, the dialectic between cosmopolitan information (brought by the University) and the anthropological reality of the city were linked when university research became part of the daily life and traditions of the city (see Risério). This resulted in the transformation of Bahia into a powerful and active cultural center that now had enough power to reverse the flow of the Brazilian cultural imaginary (which, since the end of the eighteenth century, had been a one-way flow from the south-central region to the northeast). In this sense the contrast between the preservationist popular-national culture, sponsored by the authoritarianism of the Estado Novo and then reappropriated by the populism of the political Left, on the one hand, and the aesthetic-cultural theories and practices inherent in Bahian production–Glauber Rocha's Cinema Novo, Caetano Veloso's (b. 1942) and Gilberto Gil's (b. 1942) popular music, Tropicalism–on the other, constitutes the problematic horizon traced by these two highly reflexive currents.

Recently, with a view to recovering the environment, the purposes, and the aims of the Tropicalist movement, Caetano Veloso took up the cause in his testimonial in which he characterizes the conflict implicit in the aggressiveness and violence of the tropicalist images as part of the imaginary of Bahia–a move that negates the idea of a homogeneous Brazil (Veloso 50). Currently, if the generic and standardized logic of the internationalization of culture and the globalization of the economy, on the one hand, contributes to the surprising speed with which cultural exchanges take place, on the other, it also prevents the survival of regional accents, at least without the mediation of new resources. For this reason Bahian-Central Brazil opposition has ended; the appearance of a "super-Rio internacional-paulistizado" ("São Paulized-international super-Rio")–to use the expression of Caetano Veloso to describe the culture of the two most important cultural centers in the country, polarized by the language of the media–no longer produces the same conflictive relation to Bahia. After all, the creative explosion of the new, contemporary black culture and identity–based on color, on color consciousness, on pride, on the status of the black body (see Sansone)–owes the undeniable national and international consecration of its exotic difference to the assertive promotion of its products, such as Bahian carnival, the performing groups (and carnival blocos) Olodumand Timbalada, as well as its idols, via the efficacy of the media and the cultural industry. The symbolic-economic reconversion (García Canclini 14) of regional characteristics by the dominant media and cultural complex not only creates the fetishized image of an integrated, mosaic country for consumption and export but also tries to stabilize deeper differences and cover over distortions of a socioeconomic order that are responsible for terrible social and economic discrepancies in Brazilian social life.

In a recent essay, Barbara Freitag develops a conceptual distinction between metropolis and megalopolis, arguing that the second term does not refer only to the quantitative dimension of urban life, but also to a specific form of social life in huge cities, which is typical of the end of the twentieth century. She then lists some essential features of the contemporary megalopolis, attempting to outline its macroform: cities with a population of around 10 million; dizzying urban growth (basically from the 1970s on); a population enlarged by migrants of the most-varied origins; and multiculturalism, according to various criteria of characterization (among which are social class, ethnicity, gender, sexual practices, etc.). With that in mind, the metropoles are then said to denote historical cities of a centenary tradition, mostly European, transformed into centers of modern industrialization and archives of world culture, from the end of the nineteenth century and into the beginning of the twentieth. Concluding that in Brazil megalopolization is the most recent form of urbanization, owing to the massive rural exodus that began in the 1960s, the author names Rio de Janeiro, São Paulo, and Brasília as three of the most relevant contemporary examples in the Southern Hemisphere. Commenting on their respective forms of sociability through evidence in contemporary novels, the author finds common denominators in the apocalyptic visions of Brazilian society and in the myth of the megalopolis as the cyclopean monster that destroys its inhabitants and will end by devouring itself. In relation to Brasília, specifically, she even comments that not even its uniqueness as a planned city, laid out in the shape of an airplane, cradle of novelty in Brazil in the 1960s, succeeds in reversing this scenario of the terminal city, locus of death and sterility.

In a less dramatic way but from an equally disillusioned perspective, Maria Zilda Cury, writing on Ouro Preto, Belo Horizonte, and Brasília in the present volume, points out a similar frustration between Brasília, "cidade do Brasil" ("city of Brazil"), "centro da modernidade com igualdade" ("center of modernity with equality"), "ponta de irradiação do novo . . . para todo o país" ("point of dissemination of novelty . . . for the whole country"), and Belo Horizonte, "mediação moderna entre o arcaico que permanece . . . e o futuro de igualdade democrática que não se consubstanciou" ("modern mediation between the archaic that remains . . . and the future of democratic equality that has not been consolidated"). In fact, since its creation, Belo Horizonte, as bride of the Republic (recently proclaimed in the country), has made concrete the Brazilian obsession with the negation of the past through the modernizing utopia of urbanization and the sanitation of space. Once again the positivist dream of Republican thought mixes with the blueprints of the first planned city of the country, a model of authoritarian modernization with its Conservative and exclusionary social practices.

At the end of the twentieth century, in the middle of the latest outbreak of capitalist globalization, the socioeconomic deterioration of the country's main megalopoles, the systematic introduction of the newest mechanisms of urban segregation in Rio de Janeiro and São Paulo–the private condominiums, the fortified enclaves, the discretionary privatization of streets–as well as the elitist and excluding forms of modern architecture in Brasília, without a doubt mark a return of old arbitrary formulas of exclusivist civility, aggravated by the failure of the developmentist paradigm and its failed promises of incorporating excluded groups. On the other hand, that highly proclaimed postmodernity–with its ever-increasing inventory of images, like a chain of viral organisms and their consequent replication–paralyzes the immunological resistance of the social body and prevents these images from formulating any critical program capable of making connections between the disempowered tradition, the diffuse present, and the possibility of a cultural imaginary of the future.

Cury's conclusion is interesting, though profoundly bitter: However much time has passed, the ironic simultaneity of the creation of Belo Horizonte and the destruction of Canudos only proves, on the one hand, the peculiar anachronistic character of this history and, on the other, the sad present condition, at this turn of the new century, of the antipodal cities born in the nineteenth century; destruction and construction, occurring in the same year, explain the apparent end of a modernizing process that, imposed from the top on the bottom, inexorably indicates those worthy of citizenship and those who ought, in the name of order and progress–an infallible emblem–to be swept out of the social intercourse and denied the right to life.

**Translation by Thomas LaBorie Burns
and Gláucia Gonçalves**

Works Cited

Albuquerque, Manoel Maurício. 1981. *Pequena história da formação social brasileira.* Rio de Janeiro: Edições Graal Ltda.

Candido, Antonio. 1969. *Formação da literatura brasileira; momentos decisivos.* Vol. 1: (1750–1836). São Paulo: Livraria Martins Editora.

——. 1987. *A educação pela noite e outros ensaios.* São Paulo: Ática.

Dias, Ângela Maria. 1996. "A questão cultural: cenários-Brasil 2020." *Comunicação & política.* Rio de Janeiro: Cebela. 8.3: 16–30.

Fausto, Boris. 1994. *História do Brasil.* São Paulo: Editora da USP/ Fundação do Desenvolvimento da Educação.

Freitag, Barbara. 1998. "O mito da megalópole na literatura brasileira." *Tempo Brasileiro.* Cidade e Literatura. 132: 143–58.

García, Canclini, Néstor. 1990. *Culturas híbridas: estrategias para entrar y salir de la modernidad.* Mexico City: Grijalbo/Consejo Nacional para la Cultura y las Artes.

Hollanda, Sérgio Buarque de. 1969. *Raízes do Brasil.* Rio de Janeiro: José Olympio.

Marins, Paulo César Garcez. 1998. "Habitação e vizinhança: limites da privacidade no surgimento das metrópoles brasileiras." *História da vida privada no Brasil.* Vol. 3: *República: da Belle Époque à era do rádio.* Ed. Nicolau Sevcenko. São Paulo: Companhia das Letras. 131–214.

Mumford, Lewis. 1961. *The City in History: Its Origins, its Transformations, and its Prospects.* New York: Harcourt, Brace & World.

Rama, Ángel. 1984. *La ciudad letrada.* Hanover, NH: Ediciones del Norte.

———. 1996. *The Lettered City.* Trans. and ed. John Charles Chasteen. Durham, NC: Duke University Press.

Risério, Antonio. 1995. *Avant-garde na Bahia.* São Paulo: Instituto Lina Bo and P.M. Bardi.

Sansone, Livio. 1995. "O local e o global na Afro-Bahia contemporânea." *Revista Brasileira de Ciências Sociais* 29: 65–84.

Schwarz, Roberto. 1988. *Ao vencedor as batatas: forma literária e processo social nos inícios do romance brasileiro.* São Paulo: Livraria Duas Cidades.

Sevcenko, Nicolau. 1998. "Introdução: O período republicano, astúcias da ordem e ilusões do progresso." *História da vida privada no Brasil.* Vol. 3: *República: da Belle Époque à era do rádio.* Ed. Nicolau Sevcenko. São Paulo: Companhia das Letras. 7–48.

Veloso, Caetano. 1997. *Verdade tropical.* São Paulo: Companhia das Letras.

CHAPTER 46

RECIFE AS A CULTURAL CENTER

César Leal

Velhas e tantas igrejas,
tantas pontes inventadas
sobre as pontes, velozmente,
pasa a vida em disparada.
Soperbo perfil de touro,
burgo velho enfeudalado:
Eis Recife, um vasto império,
por mocambos coroado.

The many aged churches,
many invented bridges,
over those bridges, dashing,
life flashes in a stampede.
Superb profile of a bull,
the old feudal burg:
Such is Recife, a vast empire,
crowned by the mocambos.

–César Leal 434

How can we define Recife within the context of Brazilian, or even Latin American culture? What geographic, ethnic, religious, economic, social, and political factors have contributed to ensuring the uniqueness of this urban complex during its formative process and the creation of its symbolic values? At the outset of his monumental work–*European Literature and the Latin Middle Ages*–Ernst Robert Curtius shows us that the progress of historical knowledge does not alter the ways of thinking of those who were part of it: "They lead to a widening and a clarification of consciousness" (3). And it is Curtius, again, who reminds us of the difference that should be observed between the human and natural sciences, if considered from the standpoint of the interests of modern industrial technological societies. The progress of the natural sciences is clear and depends upon resources denied the human sciences by "interested egoism embodied in powerful agencies" (3). Might these considerations be outside our debates? Yes. In the case of other modern centers such as Belo Horizonte and Brasília, they might render discussion unnecessary, but not when one speaks of "early" cities as cultural centers, and especially of Recife, whose history and culture are indissolubly linked to the history and the culture of the whole of Brazilian society, with elements not observed in other centers. Gilberto Freyre (1900–1987), the most complete interpreter of this culture from its beginnings, has written: "No Recife a futura cultura nacional do Brasil absorveu de norte-europeus Protestantes e de Judeus sefardins, nos grandes dias do conde alemão Maurício de Nassau, governador desta parte da América, valores que não lhe teriam vindo nunca das gentes ibéricas e Católicas . . . sem perder o essencial de sua cristandade. Criando suas próprias formas de cultura e até desenvolvendo seus próprios modos de ser religioso e até de ser cristão" (1969, 27) ("In Recife, in the grand days of the Count Maurice of Nassau, governor of the Dutch Brazilian colony, the city absorbed values from Northern European Protestants and Sephardic Jews which could never have come from the Iberian and Catholic peoples . . . without losing the essence of their Christianity. The city created its own forms of culture and developed its own religious practices and even ways of being Christian").

Duarte Coelho, Pernambuco's first grantee, arrived there in 1535. He was the grandson of a cavalryman who had fought in India and served at sea under Vasco da Gama. The grantee's powers nearly rivaled those of the king: He was permitted to dispose of the natives as he pleased and even to send some of them into exile if he wished. He was allowed the privilege of "dar sesmarias, condenar em muitos casos sem apelação nem agravo, investir tabeliães e alcaides ou governadores militares das vilas e até possiur a faculdade de não anuir às eleições dos juizes e mais oficiais dos conselhos, feitas pelos homens bons" (Lima 10) ("bestowing land grants, of sentencing, in many cases without appeal or recourse; he could appoint notary publics and provincial governors, and possessed even the power to disagree with judges and council officials elected by good men").

As may be observed from these brief indications, the organization of the Brazilian provinces was that of a feudal society, stronger and more structured than in those regions previously conquered by the Portuguese in Africa and India. Duarte Coelho's first acts were the founding of the townships of Igarassu and Olinda. The structure of that society has been described with unique eloquence by Gilberto Freyre in his classic book *Casa Grande & Senzala* [1933; *The Masters and the Slaves*, 1946]. During the nineteenth century, the feudal, patriarchal society that the Portuguese had set up with Duarte Coelho was based on two centuries of experience in adapting to tropical regions–in India and Africa. Definitive proof of the colonizer's aptitude for life in the tropics "fizera no Brasil em bases mais sólidas e em condições mais estáveis que na Índia e nas feitorias africanas" (Freyre 1956, 3) ("took place in Brazil on more solid bases and under more stable conditions than in India or in the African trading posts"). Such facts might well be set aside in this brief study, were it not for the need to demonstrate what is singular about Recife as a cultural center, with a character of its own, throughout the nearly five centuries of its existence, and how this character, this identity was formed. For if one were to judge Recife solely on its cultural traces, in the same way as any other Brazilian or Latin American metropolis, one would be making a mistake. Turning once again to Gilberto Freyre:

Formou-se na América tropical uma sociedade agrária na estrutura, escravocrata na técnica de exploração econômica, híbrida de índio–e mais tarde de negro–na composição. Sociedade que se desenvolveria defendida menos pela consciência de raça, quase nenhuma no português cosmopolita e plástico, do que pelo exclusivismo religioso desdobrado em profilaxia social e política. Mas tudo isso aqui, como em Portugal, foi desde o primeiro século elemento de formação nacional; sendo entre nós através das grandes famílias proprietárias e autônomas: senhores de engenho com altar e capelão dentro de casa e Índios armados de arco e flecha ou negro de arcabuz às suas ordens; donos de terras e de escravos que dos senados das Câmaras falaram alto e grosso aos representantes d'el Rei e pela voz liberal dos filhos padres ou doutores clamaram contra toda sorte de abusos da Metrópole e da própria Madre Igreja. Bem diversos dos *criollos* ricos e dos bacharéis letrados da América Espanhola–por longo tempo inérmes à sombra das catedrais e dos palácios dos vice-reis, ou constituídos em *cabildos* que em geral só faziam servir de mangação aos reinóis todo-poderosos. (1956, 3–4)

In tropical America there was formed a society agrarian in structure, slave-holding in its technique of economic exploitation, and hybrid in composition, with an admixture of the Indian and later of the Black. This was a society that in its evolution was protected less by a consciousness of race, which was practically nonexistent in the cosmopolitan and plastic-minded Portuguese, than it was by a religious exclusiveness given expression in a system of social and political prophylaxis; less by official action than by the arm and the sword of the individual. All this, however, was subordinated to a spirit of political, economic, and juridical realism that here as in Portugal, from the first century on, was the decisive element in the forming of the nation. What we had in our country was great landowning and autonomous families, lords of the plantation, with an altar and a chaplain in the house and Indians armed with bow and arrow or Blacks armed with muskets at their command; and from their seats in the municipal council chamber these masters of the earth and of the slaves that tilled it always spoke up boldly to the representatives of the crown, while through the liberal-toned voices of their sons who were priests or doctors of the law they cried out against every species of abuse on the part of the Metropolis and of Mother Church itself. In this they were quite different from the rich *criollos* and learned bachelors of Spanish America, who for so long were inert in the dominant shadow of the cathedrals and the palaces of the viceroys, or who, when gathered in *cabildos*, did little more than serve as a laughing-stock for the all-powerful lords of the realm.

According to Manoel de Oliveira Lima (1867–1928), the choice of Olinda and Igarassu showed that the Portuguese were commercially inept: Igarassu is a central town, and the principal city Olinda–capital of the province–was erected on a hill covered with thick vegetation, a difficult location in terms of military defense and also distant from the port of Recife, whose naturally privileged harbor the Dutch transformed into the capital of Dutch Brazil. Under attack, the Portuguese were unable to save Olinda, which was taken by the Dutch by storm.

From Bleak Town to Maurisstad

It would be impossible to imagine Recife at the end of the seventeenth century as a cultural center without considering Dutch colonization. In the beginning, Recife was a settlement dominated by a strange melancholy. Not even as "*la tierra de más sol de la Tierra*" ("the land of most sun on Earth"), in the words of Vicente Pinzon (when he sailed past the coast, three months before Pedro Alvares Cabral landed in Brazil), nothing could cheer the settlers of this small dot on the map where, a little further south, a strip of land met the sea and was named "Cabo del rostro hermoso" ("Cape of the Beautiful Face") by the Spanish navigator: "Burgo triste nos primeiros anos do século XVII. Burgo triste e abandonado, que os bobres de Olinda deviam atravessar pisando em ponta de pé, receando alagados e mangues; burgo triste de marinheiros e de gente ligada ao serviço do porto; burgo triste, sem vida, onde até a água tinha de vir de Olinda" (Mello 41) ("A bleak town in the first years of the seventeenth century. A bleak and neglected town which the noblemen of Olinda would have to cross on tiptoe in fear of marshes and swamps; a bleak town of sailors and people to service the port; a bleak, lifeless town to which even water had to come from Olinda").

During the early moments of the Dutch invasion, panic gripped Olinda. The population abandoned the city, giving the Dutch commander the impression that he had won an overwhelming victory. But resistance was soon organized and the Dutch realized they had been mistaken. The letters of the military commander Weendenburch to the Dutch government show the violence of the war in Pernambuco, not merely that of the Portuguese and the Spanish against the Dutch, but principally that of the first generation of Brazilians whose feeling for their country provided them with the strength to fight for a land they already considered their own. The heat of the blazing sun in summer was not lessened by the constant breezes that blew from the sea, and was intensified by the continual firing of muskets, short rifles, and, occasionally, the intermittent roar of the cannons echoing over the tall hills of Olinda like distant thunder. A few trees provided shade and shelter for the Dutch soldiers, although as soon as they sought protection from the sun they would fall to the ground, riddled with bullets from fighters who ambushed them from the marshes. Dutch morale, however, was not affected by the struggle against an invisible enemy. The invaders were well aware that Holland was, at that time, one of the greatest maritime powers in the world, with one hundred thousand sailors who, although they were for the most part largely undisciplined mercenaries, had experience in battle in every ocean and on every continent. At that moment, however, all their power and experience were to no avail. They had taken the capital but were constantly ambushed by an implacable enemy. Had the Brazilians and the Portuguese been better armed, they might well have pushed them back into the sea, for the Dutch encampment lacked everything except arms. The soldiers did not know what to do in order to cook their food. Some tried to dig the ground in search of roots to serve as firewood. Others, exhausted, like animals, took their daily rations raw. The dispatches of the Political Council and the officials, in letters to Holland, explained: "Aqui não há víveres da Terra, de modo que nós e todos os que aqui estamos depositamos todas as esperanças de vida em pronta remessa de víveres quanto VV.SSª. possam imaginar que temos precisão; queiram mandar vinho da Espanha, um forte vinho francês, tanto branco quanto tinto, alguma cerveja, . . . e especialmente aparas de madeira ["rigs," para lenha] favas turcas [isto é, milho] passas de Corinto e sobretudo grande quantidade de trigo" (Mello 42) ("Here there are no provisions, so that we and all those who are here place all our life on hopes of the ready remittance of however many provisions your lordships may imagine we are in need; please send wine from Spain, a strong French wine, either white or red, some beer, . . . and especially wood shavings ["rigs," for fuel], Turkish fava beans [that is, corn] Corinthian raisins and, above all, a large amount of wheat").

This was the situation in Recife, situated at the end of the isthmus of Olinda, at the confluence of the Beberibe and Capibaribe rivers. Here, at the end of the sixteenth century, the first Brazilian poem in the Portuguese language written in America was produced–Bento Teixeira's (ca. 1560–1618) *Prosopopéia*–which describes the port thus:

> Junta da Nova Lusitânia ordena
> A natureza, mãe bem alentada,
> Um porto tão quieto e tão seguro
> Que para as curvas naus serve de muro.
>
> Close to New Lusitania is the ruling
> Of nature, the hearty mother,
> Such a quiet and safe harbour
> Walls for curved vessels.

(7)

When the first of the land grants were given in 1630, available land in the space that is currently Recife was so limited that it was called a *languette* (or "small tongue"): some 30 meters wide by a few kilometers in length. Across the town moved tax collectors, stevedores, soldiers with their armaments, artillery to confront enemies who might appear by land or by sea, and a few fishermen. There was even a small chapel. After taking Olinda, the Dutch found themselves in a paradoxical position. Although the city's inhabitants had fled, they maintained contact with the invaders, who were now trapped between the tall hills and the port. The pressure of the war was strongly felt on all sides except from the sea, where the Dutch fleet, commanded by an experienced admiral, provided powerful cover for the thousands of soldiers and sailors on land.

Led by engineers van Bueren and Drewsch, the Dutch drew up plans for landfills in the swamps and marshes, starting at the peninsula where the harbor was located, and including, as part of the future urban grid, wide spaces that were connected by bridges to the Island of Antonio Vaz. The Dutch, however, had not forgotten to make the necessary reinforcements of their military positions. The old Portuguese three-door defense, of the type used in medieval European cities, was replaced by modern fortifications with trenches and forts that soon enclosed the settlement's entire territorial area. Dutch technology slowly transformed the sea of black mud into a territory that each day progressed further until it was ready for buildings. Large canals protected the landfills against water and rain. On the military side, the bridgehead established at Pau Amarelo beach grew monthly, then yearly, diminishing the resistance of Portuguese and Brazilian combatants. The fighting, however, did not abate. As it moved away from Recife, it grew in violence. Other land grants were being occupied and Dutch power extended from the Sergipe to Maranhão. Nearly two years after the invasion, in November of 1631, the governor and military commander, though countermanding orders from the Dutch government, set fire to Olinda, alleging reasons of defense.

After their defeat in the skirmishes with the guerrillas and with no further need to struggle for position, the Dutch proceeded to employ methods of torture directly upon the civilian population. Women and children had their feet dipped in tar and boiling oil. Accounts note that Lieutenant-General von Schkoppe was "*dur jusqu'à la cruauté*" ("hard man, even cruel") (Lima 82). Nail-studded planks compressed the bodies of civilians before they were handed over to cannibal tribes as banquet fare. With the arrival of Count Maurice of Nassau, the war grew more intense, but the worst torture was stopped and some officials were sent back to Holland. Nonetheless, since he was a military man respected by the prince, Sigismund von Schkoppe was never indicted for his crimes against the civilian population.

After gaining a victory over the Portuguese, the governor of Dutch Brazil turned to the administration and urbanization of the city. Great changes were introduced into Recife. Architect Piet Post (the brother of painter Franz Post, considered to be the father of Brazilian painting) arrived and drew up the plans for the governor's residences. He sought to escape from the influence of the Gothic on Dutch art: "Grandes cômodos realistas" ("Large realistic rooms")—says Lima—"como toda a arte holandesa" ("like those in Dutch art") (86). Thus, Vrijburg and Schoonzigt (*Sem Cuidado* [Without Care] and *Boa Vista* [Good View], in Portuguese) rose up in the center of the Island of Antonio Vaz. A heavenly landscape surrounded the Palácio de Friburgo [Vrijburg], around which was built a botanical garden. Rembrandt, two years younger than his friend Nassau, accepted an invitation to accompany him to Brazil but was unable to travel because of illness. The prince arrived with painters Albert Eckhout and Franz Post and four other masters of Flemish painting. Here is Frei Manoel Calado's (1584–1654) account of the botanical garden:

> Em um jardim de tão preciosas coleções, enriquecidas ainda pelas viagens empreendidas por Piso e Marggraf ao interior do Brasil Holandês, encontravam os sábios e artistas da comitiva do governador ampla matéria para seus estudos e pinturas. Maurício, dizia Piso com entusiasmo, lembra Alexandre Magno fornecendo a Aristóteles os materiais para os seus trabalhos. Com efeito, o jardim do Príncipe por si só podia ter fornecido o assunto, não somente dos livros de história natural dos dois citados escritores, livros que conservam hoje a primitiva importância, como dos numerosos desenhos e quadros que o Príncipe, de volta com seus lauréis, carregou para Haia. Esta coleção antes de sua morte se dispersou, em momentos de aperto pecuniário, parte vendida ao eleitor de Bradenburgo, parte interesseiramente oferecida a Luiz XIV . . . Quando menos se perdessem aquelas produções artísticas bastariam para abonar a memória do ilustre protetor das ciências e das artes, as obervações astronômicas, de geografia, matemática, zoológicas, botânicas, climatológicas, higiências, etnográficas. (quoted in Lima 88)

In a garden of such precious collections, further enriched by the travels of Piso and Marggraf to the interior of Dutch Brazil, artists and scholars of the governor's entourage could find ample material for their studies and paintings. Piso, with his enthusiasm, reminds one of Alexander the Great providing Aristotle with the material for his studies. Indeed, the Prince's garden alone was subject enough, not only for the volumes on natural history, books which even today retain their original importance, but also for the numerous drawings and paintings that the Prince took back to the Hague. Before his death the collection was dispersed at different moments of financial need, partly sold off to the Brandenburg electorate and also to Louis XIV. . . . The more of those artistic creations saved, the better was perpetuated the memory of that illustrious protector of art and science, anatomical observations, mathematical geography, zoology, botany, climatology, hygiene, and ethnography.

All this contributed to the appearance, in this century, of forms of poetry and painting in which are reflected the different aspects of Recife as a cultural center with a well-defined identity of its own.

The other house, Schoonzigt, was decorated with huge paintings by Franz Post (1612–1680) and his companions–six of the most notable painters. Today Franz Post's paintings may be found in the museums of Amsterdam and Copenhagen, at the Prado in Madrid, and, of course, in Recife itself. In his letters to friends in Holland, Nassau expressed his enchantment with the journey he had undertaken to the São Francisco River. Maurice of Nassau's education was reflected in his cultural interests. For a time, in Holland, he had been tutored by Descartes, who developed in the prince a taste for mathematics and science in general. His education took place in the finest European universities, making him a typical product of the Renaissance. The fact that Descartes was also his fencing coach has been a source of some surprise to those unaware of the fact that the author of the *Discourse on Method* was also expert in the use of the sword and the foil. In his company, Nassau brought together men from many areas of knowledge, such as the Evangelical minister Plante, a poet and Latinist, the botanist Marggraf, and the mathematician and geographer Cralitz, not to mention the painters whose works today are universally renowned. A tolerant man in matters of religion, he extended freedom of religious worship to include Catholics and Jews, along with their churches and convents; during his time in Recife, the first synagogue in the Americas was constructed. He built an astronomical observatory, also the first on the continent, planned the installation of a printing press, drew up topographical maps of Dutch Brazil, and planned the University of Pernambuco (Lima 118).

Thus, it is that we may trace Recife's beginnings as a cultural center to the first half of the seventeenth century, under John Maurice of Nassau. (See **Figure 1.**) Nassau sought to pacify his territory, by creating a legislative assembly in which natives, Portuguese, and Dutch were all participants. It was the first parliament of the Americas. Outstanding among its administrative members was João Fernandes Vieira, a wealthy plantation owner who had arrived from the Island of Madeira in his early youth. After Nassau's return to the Netherlands in May 1644, Vieira commanded the insurrection that effectively ended Dutch rule in Brazil. The nucleus of the great cultural center that Recife was to become over the next centuries was made up ethnically of Portuguese, Dutch, Portuguese Jews, Germans, Amerindians, and Africans. After ten years of struggle that followed upon Nassau's return to Europe, the Dutch capitulated. The war, the longest in the history of the Americas, had lasted twenty-four years.

With the end of the war in 1654, the Jews, who had formed in Recife one of the largest Jewish colonies in the world, abandoned the city, moving on variously to Holland, Surinam, and

Figure 1.

Lithograph of Johannes Mauritus (John Mauritus of Nassau-Siegen), Dutch governor of Recife 1637–1644. (Archive of the author)

the United States, where they settled on the island of New Amsterdam, which is today known as New York. In 1710, the population of New York was 10,000 compared to Recife's nearly 13,000. The plantations were in need of reconstruction after the forces of the general from the state of Paraíba, André Vidal de Negreiros, had set fire to them during the war. With the destruction of the plantations, production of sugar ceased and, without this economic element, there was no reason for the continued presence of the Dutch West India Company in Brazil.

Colonial Literature

What can we say of seventeenth-century Colonial literature? It would appear that, during the period of the Dutch occupation, literary production developed almost exclusively in Bahia and Recife. The presence of great writers, some of whom might be considered better than those in Portugal, renders unjust the critiques of literary historians on seventeenth- and eighteenth-century Brazilian literature. Padre Antonio Vieira (1608–1697) ought to be considered a Brazilian writer, for the greater part of his life was lived in Brazil, and it was in Recife that he wrote his best work, *Os Sermões* [1679; *The Sermons*]. The sermon was not an Iberian genre, but rather a European Catholic one, and had one of its greatest representatives in Saint Augustine, a writer of the end of Classical Antiquity. If one bears in mind the idea of a "European" literature, nationalist, provincial, or local sentiments disappear, for they were created by Romanticism and its concept of a "national literature." This is why a great poet such as Manuel Botelho de Oliveira (1636–1711) was praised here only for his worst work: "A Ilha da Maré" [1705; Maré Isle], while his best work, so representative of the poetry of his time, was held up as imitative of Iberian literature, when the Baroque as a style of culture intensified the cosmic significance of its lines in Europe and especially in Spain.

Referring to Gregório de Matos (1633?–1696), who lived in Recife after his exile from Angola, Lima speaks of his merciless irony and implacable sarcasm, motivated by his dislike of a governor general who figured in his satirical poems about the rich of Recife (195–96). His work featured both the malicious intrigue of the idle rich and racial antagonism. According to Lima, the reasons for de Matos's popularity during the seventeenth century were similar to those of Bocage in eighteenth-century Portugal: He displayed satiric wit that entertained the very same people it satirized. In the eyes of Sílvio Romero (1851–1914), he was the real founder of Brazilian literature, no doubt an exaggeration of the critic–historian. Even so, the colony's literary production was among the strongest and oldest in South America. This is hardly surprising for, as Antero de Quental (1842–1891) denounced in a lecture on 27 May 1871 at the Lisbon Casino, on the decadence of the peninsular peoples during the past three centuries, Portuguese literature of the period was insignificant. Criticizing the literary customs of the period, Quental accused Portuguese poets of merely copying the past, interested only in translation and devoid of any inventive spark. Poetic invention was a spirit the Portuguese regarded as dangerous; according to Quental, invention was considered both dangerous and inferior. The greater the number of verses translated from Horace and Ovid, the more perfect the work of poetry was considered, and tragedy, the Pindaric ode, and the comic heroic poem were flourishing. In other words, this was the final degradation of poetry in Quental's view, confirming the view that, during the Colonial period, Brazil had nothing to learn from the Portuguese (see Quental).

Besides Gregório de Matos, buried at the Church of Penha in Recife, the following century saw the rise of a group of poets in Minas well-situated in the history of this literature: Thomaz Antônio Gonzaga (1744–1807), Cláudio Manoel da Costa (1729–1789), Inácio da Silva Alvarenga (1749–1814), Alvarenga Peixoto (1748–1798), and José Basílio da Gama (1740–1795). During this period, Portugal has only Manuel Maria do Bocage (1765–1805), as a poet whose place is definitively assured in the history of Portuguese poetry. This does not mean that Recife or Brazil had a literature already formed before Independence, or rather, in the national phase that begins with Romanticism. Five or six poets—even if they are considered great because of their language, ideas, and general force of the presentation of their work—would not be sufficient to make a literature.

I believe that observations such as these contribute to a wider understanding of not only Brazilian literature but also others in Latin America. Gilberto Freyre, in an essay published in the *Revista Estudos Universitários* in 1966, lamented that the more varied expressions of Latin American culture have not been studied with an eye to the characterization of a supranational Latin American style rather than Brazilian, Paraguayan, Mexican, Haitian, or Bolivian expression. He wrote: "É para lamentar que o assunto não tenha sido ainda versado, de modo sistemático, por antropólogos ou sociólogos da cultura constituídos em *equipe*–pois só continentais, seguindo ou desenvolvendo métodos já inaugurados por Kroeber" (13, 14) ("It is too bad that the subject has not yet been systematically discussed by *teams* of anthropologists or cultural sociologists– for only a *team* could account for such a diverse subject matter and commit to a task of continental proportions, following or developing methods already set out by Kroeber").

To a degree, I believe that this current project responds, more completely and inclusively, to this need for understanding the Latin American *ethos*, and thus produces a better understanding of its national literatures.

From the Olinda Seminary to the School of Recife

In the last year of the eighteenth century, Bishop Azeredo Coutinho (1742–1821) developed an infrastructure for advanced studies in Recife–the Olinda Seminary–which would eventually lead to the creation, in the early nineteenth century, of juridical studies at both Olinda and São Paulo. The Seminary became a center of dissemination of new social and political ideas that would eventually form the revolutionary elite that commanded the Pernambucan Rebellions of 1817 and 1824. The Pernambuco *Confederação do Equador*, as it became known, had its martyr in the humanist poet and orator, Friar Caneca (Joaquim do Amor Divino Caneca, 1779–1825), executed in Recife in 1825 by order of the Emperor Pedro I. The execution of this Pernambucan hero motivated some of the most beautiful creations of modern poetry, including the *Auto do Frade* (463), by poet and diplomat João Cabral de Melo Neto, who was born in Recife in 1920. The *Auto*'s composition was begun in Quito in 1981 and concluded in Tegucigalpa in 1983, and its version of Friar Caneca's death is powerful. As the Friar is escorted by an official to the fort where he will be executed, the people are heard on the sidewalks asking if Don Pedro is aware of what is happening. The Friar speaks as he walks:

Dentro desta cela móvel
do curral da gente viva,
dentro da cela ambulante

que me prende mais caminha
posso olhar de cada lado,
para baixo e para cima.
Eis as pedras do Recife
Que o professo carmelita,
Embora frade calçado
Sente na sola despida

Inside the mobile cell
corral of living people
inside the walking cell
which constricts yet moves
I can look on either side,
downwards and upwards.
These are the stones of Recife
That the professed Carmelite,
In spite of wearing shoes
Can feel on his naked soles.

(quoted in Melo Neto 491–92)

Recife in 1827 still echoed with the voice of Caneca's civic preaching, when the juridical courses of Olinda and São Paulo were created on August 11. This was to be the nucleus of the school of law, the most modern expression of humanist culture, a way of thinking that would transform Recife into a strong cultural center. In 1854, the Olinda Academy of Juridical Sciences was granted institutional status by the creation of the College of Law, in Recife, which was, by then, capital of the province. The city became urbanized, possessing even a modern theater–the Santa Isabel. The city plan was developed by the French cultural mission directed by architect Louis Leger Vauthier and his team of engineers, and included libraries, numerous bridges connecting the different quarters, and many educational and cultural institutions. Young men from all parts of Brazil came to its law school. The city also had a cultural organ of the greatest importance, the *Diário de Pernambuco*, the oldest circulating newspaper in Brazil and one of the country's finest newspapers to this day. It was in such a cultural climate that the Recife school of writers (so named by Brazilian literary historian Silvio Romero) came about during the latter half of the century. In his book *Medo à Utopia* [1985; Fear of Utopia], writer Evaristo de Moraes Filho (b. 1914), of the Brazilian Academy of Letters, rightly contests the existence of a *school* (41). Others too, like José Veríssimo (1857–1916), do not consider the intense artistic and literary activity of Recife, under the leadership of Tobias Barreto (1839–1889) and Silvio Romero, to be aptly characterized as a school; be that as it may, the fact is that Recife had a notable and distinguishing role in Brazilian letters in the nineteenth century. In earlier studies, José Veríssimo had denied the existence of the Bahia and Minas Gerais schools along with so many others that had supposedly cropped up in different cities throughout colonial Brazil. According to Evaristo de Moraes Filho, Silvio Romero's work represented, above all else, a desire to establish himself at the royal court. When, in 1879, he published the essay "Prioridades de Pernambuco no movimento espiritual brasileiro" ("Priorities of Pernambuco in the Brazilian Spiritual Movement") in the *Revista do Brasil*, Romero represented himself as the initiator of a spiritual and ideological patrimony that Olinda and Recife had bequeathed to Brazil from the very beginning of their early history. The so-called Recife School claimed to have the support of Joaquim Nabuco (1849–1910), nineteenth-century Pernambuco's most complete intellectual, a writer, politician, humanist, and biographer with a broad knowledge of literature.

It is unfortunate, however, that the unjustified attacks on Machado de Assis (1839–1908) came from Recife. If Machado is not recognized today as one of the great Brazilian poets, it is not because his poetry is overshadowed by his achievement as a novelist but largely because of Sílvio Romero's critical criteria and the influence these exerted. Romero's understanding of poetry was hampered by a rather impoverished erudition when it came to a theory of poetry. In 1966, in the Federal University of Pernambuco's journal *Estudos Universitários*, I published an essay on the poetry of Machado de Assis where I argued that Sílvio Romero, a celebrated historian but rather limited critic of literature, was always dominated by an almost morbid prejudice against Machado's work. Whatever he said about him, even in praise, went against his own literary and philosophical principles, not to mention the purported rigor of his criticism. He stated that Machado was not intimate with great natural phenomena, that he lacked kinship with trees and animals, mountains, fields, and woods, that he did not display feeling inebriated at the spectacle of deep, dark or shining skies, or of leaden or blue or starry ones. Such criticism need not be aimed only at Machado himself: It should probably include all the philosophers and theoreticians of art from Aristotle to Hegel. Literary criticism should be directed to the work of art in itself. The fact that a poet is not interested in natural elements signifies nothing in terms of the richness or poverty of his expression.

In contrast, when Joaquim Nabuco lectured on Camões at both Yale and Cornell, in discussing certain aspects of the lyric and the epic in Luis de Camões (1524?–1580), he proved to be a good critic of poetry. He justified Camões's *choice*, and in this he revealed that wisdom to which Ezra Pound refers: the wisdom of choice. Nabuco owed nothing to the celebrated Recife writers whose sense of self-importance has already been noted. Neither Tobias Barreto nor Sílvio Romero were familiar with the intense theorizing that took place in Europe toward the end of the eighteenth century, with Lessing, Novalis, Schelling, the brothers Schlegel, Coleridge, Wordsworth, Diderot, Hegel, and all the others who made poetry and criticism modern. They knew nothing of these writers' critical theories. When one realizes that Joaquim Nabuco's lectures took place in 1908, and that it was in that year that Pound moved to Europe, one should not forget that it was possible that he may have influenced Ezra Pound to write his famous essay on Camões. Many elements considered in those American lectures were also used by Pound and the two may well have known each other: Nabuco–with his rigorous English education–an old man, and Ezra Pound, the young man interested in poetry.

Earlier, in the 1860s, attracted by its Law School, Castro Alves (1847–1871) arrived in Recife where, at the age of sixteen, he began to write poetry. Perhaps, had he remained in Bahia, he could have been an even more complete poet. He owes his great fame, however, to the vision of social justice that he acquired through his relationship with the abolitionist struggle in Recife. He was admired more for his ideas than for his technique, but there are a few studies that examine the uniqueness and power of his poetry. His imagery is almost always empyrean: The cosmic reach of his great images emanates from a search for the "celestial sapphire." (Undeniably, among the Romantics, he is rivaled by Gonçalves Dias (1823–1864), who, though not as famous, was the better poet.) It was Recife, the city of republican revolutions, that awakened in Castro Alves the yearning for freedom, the

search for the infinite. His typically Latin American style, *condoreirismo*, takes its name from South America's largest bird, the condor, and has marked association with the style of Victor Hugo's poetry. (But of the 140,000 verses written by Hugo, only 4000 are in what could be compared to the condor style.) In Castro Alves the cosmic images resemble some of the timeless images of Henry Wells's classification in *Poetic Imagery*, images that effectively elicit the reader's experience. Some of the images of the so-called metaphors of the masses are popular images without the complexity of the more expansive and radical images studied by Wells in Elizabethan poetry.

All this critical commentary serves as testimony to Recife as a cultural center of great attraction. The very founders of the School of Recife, speaking particularly of Tobias Barreto and Sílvio Romero, were erudite men who were not originally from Pernambuco. These two, along with many others from various regions, were attracted by the libraries–frequently not put to their best use–the art, the painters, the architecture with its Portuguese, Arab, or French influences, the churches, the old Golden Chapel in the Convent of São Francisco. (See **Figure 2**.) They were attracted, above all, by the Faculty of Law where Professor Gláucio Veiga wrote the history of his ideas, a vast project that will consist of twelve volumes, nine of which have already been published. The people of Pernambuco believe in their School, not as the creation of Tobias Barreto and Sílvio Romero, but as the product of that revolutionary liberalism that has produced heroes and martyrs, especially the constitutional liberalism of the *Confederação do Equador*, whose prophet and martyr was that Friar Joaquim do Amor Divino (or Caneca), never forgotten by historians, poets, and painters. They have also not forgotten that one of their sons left Brazil after the execution of his father, in 1817, to become a general of Bolivar: Abreu e Lima. He later returned to Recife, where he continued to participate in its struggles. When he died, religious intolerance denied him a grave, but his body was not abandoned. He rests in Recife in the English Cemetery–as the poet Manuel Bandeira (1886–1968) would write.

The Argentinean writer Jorge Meyers argues that the differences between the regional literatures of Romanticism were based on various factors, but the main one appeared to be "el problema de la institucionalidad cultural" ("the problem of institutionalizing culture"), a very acute observation that seems to me to go beyond Romanticism. Even if Tobias Barreto and Sílvio Romero did not consider themselves part of the Romantic movement, it is possible that the so-called School of Recife may have contributed to preventing the isolation observed by the Bolivian Gabriel René-Moreno (which Jorge Meyers mentions in his essay). The Faculty of Law of Recife was the nucleus of the Federal University of Pernambuco, the magnet that attracted so many young poets and essayists, from places as distant as Belém and São Paulo. The Romantic poet Luís Nicolau Fagundes Varela (1841–1875) was one of many who pursued the study of law in the Faculty of Law of Recife.

Modernism

During the last two decades of the nineteenth century, three of the greatest writers of the twentieth century were born in Recife: Manuel Bandeira (1886–1968), Joaquim Cardozo (1897–1978), and Gilberto Freyre (1900–1987). All three are associated with *modernity*, and not the *Modernism* related to the Modern Art Week of 1922 that took place in São Paulo. This

Figure 2.

Photograph of the old city Recife by Stille. (Archive of the author)

idea of Modernism was only peripheral to the literary movements occurring in the world at large from the second half of the nineteenth century to today. Outside Brazil, only a small number of Brazilianists understood the implications of the Modern Art Week of 1922. The term *Modernism* itself was deeply ambiguous when applied to the Brazilian movement whose theoretical bases did not exist. The expression *modernismo,* applied to the study of Hispanic American literature, is understood in Europe and particularly in Spain as a poetic revolution that, despite its beginnings in Mexico in 1880, affirms itself definitively only with *Azul* (1888) by Rubén Darío (1867–1916), the Nicaraguan who, at twenty-one, became the undisputed leader of that school from its beginning (in 1888) until his death in 1916. In France, England, Italy, Germany, and North America–somewhat later than in Spanish America–a type of Modernism was being cultivated that encompassed wide sectors of culture. However, the term *Modernism* is almost never used, appearing only as an expression of *modernity* and its various developments and ramifications: Futurism, Vorticism, Imagism, Dadaism, Surrealism, and so on. Recent documents show that in 1906 Rubén Darío wrote to Graça Aranha (1868–1931) to propose a Modernist revolution in Brazilian literature. Everything indicates that Graça Aranha demonstrated no interest in the theses of Rubén Darío, at least not until 1922, when Spanish American *modernismo* had already run its course, though it had arrived with great power, as can be seen in the work of the Uruguayan Julio Herrera y Reissig (1875–1910) and the Colombian José Asunción Silva (1865–1896). Brazilian *Modernism* had nothing in common with Spanish American *modernismo,* or even with Baudelaire's theories about *modernity* in his essay of 1859, but only with elements of the avant-garde movements.

Invited to participate in São Paulo's Modern Art Week of 1922, Manuel Bandeira first refused, but he then contributed his famous poem, "Os Sapos" ["The Toads"]. He became an intimate friend of the São Paulo Modernists, and of Mário de Andrade (1893–1945) in particular. Bandeira, who had been a friend of Paul Éluard when they were together at Clavadel's Sanatorium in Switzerland, wound up writing Modernist "joke poems" in 1922, the year in which James Joyce published *Ulysses* and T.S. Eliot, *The Waste Land.* Breton, Aragon, and Éluard himself, as well as Hugo Ball, Tzara, and all the founders of the Cabaret Voltaire in Zurich, were all quite active at this time, as well. In 1924, Breton published the *Surrealist Manifesto.* In the *Itinerário de Pasárgada* ["Itinerary of Pasárgada"], Manuel Bandeira mentions the influence on him of the Modernism of 1922, but does not forget to mention the stronger, almost wholly European influence, as well he should, especially if one does not work with the narrow Romantic idea of a national literature. The poetic oeuvre of Manuel Bandeira is extensive and of the highest quality. He wrote a good deal about his native land, including one of his most famous poems, "Evocação do Recife" ["Evocation of Recife"].

In 1923, after his graduate studies at Columbia and Baylor, Gilberto Freyre (1900–1987) returned to Pernambuco. He was well informed about the various Modernist currents in Europe and the United States. The day after the *Diário de Pernambuco* announced W.B. Yeats's 1923 victory over Thomas Hardy in the fight for the Nobel prize, Freyre wrote an article that demonstrated both his powerful style and strong visual imagery:

> Conheci o grande poeta irlandês há quatro anos ou cinco anos. Parece que eu o estou vendo, alto e branco, as mãos cumpridas, o cabelo prateado, uns olhos cismadores por trás de umas lunetas de pedagogo, e os dedos finos e brincarem com a fita de seda preta das lunetas. Parece que o estou ouvindo falar de Dublin, de Wilde, de Lionel Johnson, um grande místico católico e grande intelectual das camaradagens da "Young Ireland" que bebia muito e mentia como um desadorado . . . Mas ninguém me deu até hoje como William Butler Yeats a impressão de um poeta. (1926, 49 and 50)

> I met the great Irish poet four or five years ago. I can see him now, tall and pale, long hands, silver hair, suspicious eyes behind a teacher's eyeglasses, his thin fingers toying with the black silk of the eyeglass. I can almost hear him talking of Dublin, of Wilde, of Lionel Johnson, a great Catholic mystic and intellectual from his 'Young Ireland' who drank a great deal and lied like mad . . . . But no one has ever impressed me so strongly as a poet as William Butler Yeats.

Further on, Gilberto Freyre speaks of Yeats's melodic Irish accent and "uma voz de moça que parecia ir sumir-se" (50) ("a girlish voice that seemed to trail off"). He remembered Yeats had recently accepted a chair in the Irish Senate and says he can barely imagine the poet among the senators of Ireland, with their auctioneer voices. "Que diria a eles a voz quase de moça de Yeats?" (51) ("What could Yeats's girlish voice say to them?"), asked Gilberto Freyre. This question, asked in 1923, was to be answered many years later by Prof. G.S. Fraser, in his introduction to the selected works of Yeats; Yeats's time in the Irish Senate was a failure.

Such considerations are necessary to explain why, with the exception of two or three poets, Recife did not become associated with the Modern Art Week of 1922, many of whose participants would remain tied to Marinetti's Futurist Manifesto of

1929. I believe Gilberto Freyre, through his influence, maintained Recife's individual character by supporting what was best in its intellectual life. His regionalism, so badly interpreted by Mário de Andrade, was the expression of one of modernity's strongest currents. In demonstrating that the regionalism he defended was an expression of modernity present in the regionalism of Joyce (about whom he wrote in 1923) and of W.B. Yeats (whom he met before 1920), Freyre kept Recife distant from the principle of the Modern Art Week of 1922. He knew that both Joyce and Yeats were regionalists and traditionalists and yet, at the same time, that they were essentially modern. When the concept of *post-Modernism* appeared in North American criticism during the 1960s, it was used by critics like Ihab Hassan to characterize the works of fiction–the model was William S. Burroughs–that intend to break with the Modernism of Joyce in particular (see Ferry 325). Gilberto Freyre also used the term *post-Modernism* in the sense intended by North American and European critics and architects in an essay on Latin America published in the magazine *Diogène* in Paris in 1963 and reproduced in *Estudos Universitários* in Recife in 1966. There Freyre writes: "Estamos neste particular, diante de um paradoxo que é o da América Latina tornar-se de repente sob certos aspectos, pós-moderna, e a América Inglesa, arcaica em suas atitudes e em seus hábitos, criados por três séculos de progresso à base de um sentido econômico de tempo: o tempo–dinheiro" (1966, 15) ("Here is a paradox, in which all of a sudden, under certain aspects, Latin America becomes postmodern and English America archaic, with attitudes and habits created by three centuries of progress based on an economic meaning of time: time-money").

The Modernism to which Gilberto Freyre here refers is the Modernism of T.S. Eliot (1888–1965), Paul Valéry (1871–1945), Eugenio Montale (1896–1981), Jorge Guillén (1893–1984), Carlos Drummond de Andrade (1902–1987), and Elizabeth Bishop (1911–1979), and not the peripheral Brazilian Modernism of 1922. So long as Modernism is read through the eyes of the Brazilianists, it will be bound within severe limits, a concept with no possible leverage in discussions about Modernism or post-Modernism on a worldwide scale. Brazilian Modernism does not possess the enormous critical achievement of that of Spanish American writers, heirs to the modern tradition of Rubén Darío. This tradition was ultimately integrated to European Modernism, which had its origins in Baudelaire's *modernité*. This, too, is the Modernism that Recife cultivates, ever distant from the theorizing that marked the São Paulo Modern Art Week of 1922, the Modernism of the Brazilianists, also heirs–though there are exceptions–of this impoverished literary tradition in the twentieth century: "Nesta particular é possível que a América Latina venha a ser considerada antes pós-moderna que arcaica em suas atitudes e em seu comportamento: com relação à atual valorização que se processa em algumas áreas de atividades tradicionalistas e valores tradicionais corrigindo-se assim excessos modernistas da parte de alguns povos modernos ou excessivos desejos de modernização com sacrifício de tudo o mais, da parte de populações das chamadas subdesenvolvidas" (Freyre 1966, 16) ("In this manner, Latin America may possibly be considered postmodern rather than archaic in its attitudes and behavior: with regard to the current valorization which is processed in some areas of traditionalist activity and traditional values thus correcting the Modernist excesses . . . or excessive desires of modernization . . . of the so-called underdeveloped world").

Since I am here being guided by a comparative perspective, it is up to me to say whether we are Modern or post-Modern because we are knowledgeable of the natural phenomena of literary reception and transmission, travelers, translations, journals, and so on. All this rapidly internationalizes theories, ideas, and techniques, disassociating them from the names of their alleged creators through the simultaneity of manifestations in different countries and in diverse linguistic contexts. Regionalism? Modernism of 1922? Brazil's best writers abolished such concepts from their creative minds as early on as the first half of the twentieth century. They knew that the raw material of literature is language as an instrument of the expression of nature and the inner world of each individual person: Sun and moon, life and death are neither regionalist nor modernist. Thus, it would appear to me that the great works of Gilberto Freyre are those in which he interprets the formation of our patriarchal society. *Casa grande & senzala* [1933; *The Masters and the Slaves*] and *Sobrados e mucambos* [1935; *The Mansions and the Shanties*] demonstrate that one of his greatest ambitions was to be recognized as a writer situated within the scope of modernity. In the preface to the third edition of *Sobrados e mucambos*, he develops the thesis that the Brazilian family "sociologicamente cristocêntrica é que foi a unidade" (1981, xxxiii) ("sociologically Christocentric was the prime unit"). He adds that the family was also the economic factor and the base of an expansion that the State only sanctioned or confirmed. This civilization, which had been transplanted from Europe by families and individuals more than by the Church and by the efficient representatives of the kings of Portugal and Spain themselves, would, for reasons explained in the preface, cause the regional differences that to this day exist in Brazilian society.

In some aspects, the position assumed by Gilberto Freyre anticipates some of the issues dealt with, in 1948, by T.S. Eliot in *Notes Towards the Definition of Culture*, in particular the chapter entitled "Unity and Diversity: The Region." Freyre argues that the source of critical divergence lies in the ideological orientation of the most distinguished Brazilian interpreters of Marxism, such as Caio Prado Júnior, Astrogildo Pereira, and Nelson Werneck Sodré, and even among such sociologists as Raymundo Faoro, in his book *Os Donos do Poder* [The Owners of Power], these have denied the feudal aspects of the power of the great patriarchal families in the development of Brazil, and have argued instead that the colonizing State was the true power (see Freyre 1956). As it may be observed from these brief examples, the work of Gilberto Freyre differs from that of specific segments of the Brazilian intelligentsia, engaged with questions of (Marxist) historical continuity/discontinuity, and even that of more moderate groups, as is the case with Professor Alfredo Bosi, of the University of São Paulo (USP). Although Bosi appears to be integrated in these currents, he seems to hold in great esteem the work of Gilberto Freyre, perhaps because he is part of USP's Department of Brazilian Literature, rather than its celebrated Centre for Social Sciences.

I believe these considerations are necessary for any discussion of an almost tautological theme such as "language" and regionalism in *Sobrados e mucambos*. Language is to be understood here in a wide sense: the sum of numerous languages, such as the language of anthropologists, physicists, poets, and social scientists, among others. Each language will speak of something not dealt with by another language, with the exception of the poet; the language of the poet can be described by expressions like "the poetic language of

Gonçalves Dias," "the poetic language of Drummond," and "the poetic language of Jorge de Lima." This signifies that in the sphere of these different languages, poetry has its own status, different from that of any other language, although there are languages with very strong pretensions, such as that of the so-called exact sciences. With respect to that, Cassirer wrote: "Without reservation or epistemological dogma, we must attempt to understand each sort of language–the language of science, the language of art, of religion, and so on–in its particularity; we must determine what each contributes to the construction of a 'common world'" (42). Already in its first pages, the language of *Sobrados e mucambos* announces the artistic intentions of Gilberto Freyre. Throughout this work, the presence of alliteration is frequent, an aesthetic artifice used to intensify the meaning and suggest to the reader something that is not in the text but that can be made visible through images. Adjectives almost always transparent are frequently elongated to serve as adverbs, a process used by Joaquim Cardozo in some of his poems with impressive efficacy. The reader of *Sobrados e mucambos* encounters an attempt to achieve an awareness of the culture Brazil is building; there is the desire to build a society in which there will be civilizing, cultured, orderly integration between the city and the countryside.

Cardozo: The Engineer Poet

In referring to the construction of Brasília in his essay on *La ciudad letrada* [1984; The Lettered City], Ángel Rama (1926–1983) cites the names of Lúcio Costa (1902–1998) and Oscar Niemeyer (b. 1907) but omits that of Joaquim Cardozo (1897–1978), the brilliant engineer of the monuments and palaces of Brasília. A great engineer and an even greater poet, he creates in his work a series of forms comparable to a planetary system held in perfect equilibrium. Cardozo was born in Recife and lived in the city to the age of 50 when he moved to Rio. His first book was published by friends and contained a preface by Carlos Drummond de Andrade. *Trivium 1952–1970* (1971) is his fourth book, and one of the three or four greatest expressions of Brazilian poetry in the twentieth century. *Trivium* signifies the point of intersection of three paths, the meeting place where things or beings speak the same language. It also signifies the three liberal arts that made up the first part of university learning during the Middle Ages: grammar, logic, and rhetoric. It also signifies the ordering of the poem's three parts. In it, the "Prelúdio e Elegia de uma Despedida" ["Prelude and Elegy to a Farewell"] presents the theme of "dehumanization," also important in the poem "Congresso dos Ventos" ["Congress of the Winds"]. The poet describes hearing in "seio da noite um choro prolongado" (Cardozo 1971, 117) ("the heart of the night a prolonged weeping"). Nevertheless, it is not children, nor women or men, who weep; the agents of human action are absent. At first it seems to him that these are the sounds of wind in the trees in the garden or even of distant serenading voices. But the weeping is too heartfelt and perfect. It seems to him now that it came down from the stars, the mountains, "ou como se subisse da terra fria ou da noite da águas" (Cardozo 1971, 117) ("or as if it came up from the cold earth or the watery night"). The poet asks himself why stars, waters, and mountains might cry. Soon, the elegy moves into a transcendent language, with the universe as the primordial fountain of emotions where are hidden the secrets and mysteries of the origins of life:

Em vão! Por toda a parte o vulto da recusa
O Avesso, o Detrás, o Por baixo, o de permeio
Multidão de velados rostos, luz voltada.

In vain! Everywhere the shadow of refusal
Inside-out, Backwards, Underneath, Admixtured
Crowd of veiled faces, reflected light.

(118)

Observe the enigmatic capitalized words of the second line as they induce in the reader an emotional effect in preparation for the appearance of fantastic images, utterly alien to a receptive experience, such as "Luz voltada" ("reflected light"). He goes on to speak of the sleep that comes over roofs and horses "em trajetória e agitação de crinas batendo as patas surdas e macias" (119) ("in trajectory and agitation of manes beating silent deaf, soft hooves"). He asks us what language will come out of this perfect, plaintive weeping? Using anaphorical serial forms: "Eis a face . . . Eis o culto . . . Eis o pranto . . . Eis a noite . . ." (119) ("Here is the face . . . Here is the cult . . . Here is the weeping . . . Here is the night"), he speaks to us of black diamonds, starry beaches, and "lâmpada de Korf, suspensa dos abismos" ("the lamp of Korf, suspended above chasms") (119), breaking the walls of the days and erasing the trail of death. Images of comparable power occur frequently, as in "seres sepultos em profundos espelhos" ("beings buried in deep mirrors") (119). At the start of the elegy's third part, he says he must leave while it is still night, preparing the reader for the "Visão do Último Trem Subindo ao Céu" [Vision of the Last Train Going Up to Heaven]. (Hence, my thesis that the *Trivium* is a poem divided in three parts.) Also in the "Prelúdio e uma Elegia de Despedida" we find that image whose psychological drawing of form confers exactitude, truth, and beauty in speaking of a journey "beyond the air": "Do ar–plâncton do espaço, alimento das asas/–casulo da luz–crisálida" (121) ("From the air–space plankton, food of wings/–cocoon of light–chrysalis"). Here, apparently simple language hides something much more complex, increasing the pleasure of reading the poem, especially when one figures out what Joaquim Cardozo wanted to say in these verses, through an image whose meaning is expressed in the contour of its perfect geometry. The song ends with an announcement of the journey on the train, headed not for the Empyrean, as with Dante, but to a place without space and a time without time:

É partir!
É partir e partir para o fim das memórias . . .
Arcturus, Antares, Altair! Capitâneas
Dessa navegação taciturna e para sempre
E para além da verdade e grandeza da vida.

It is to leave!
It is to leave and depart to the end of memories . . .
Arcturus, Antares, Altair! Colonies
Of this taciturn navigation, forever,
And beyond truth and the grandiosity of life.

(122)

The relationship between the "Prelúdio e uma Elegia de Despedida" and the "Visão do Último Trem Subindo ao Céu" [Vision of the Last Train Going Up to Heaven] is clear in the allusion to the "end of memories." In line 365 of the ""Visão do Último Trem," Cardozo demonstrates how writing his poem is submitted to "technical reflection": "Poeira da memória, da memória dos homens/que irá perder-se no universo" (136) ("Dust of memory, of the memory of men/that will lose itself in the universe"). At this point in the poem, he is speaking more directly of Werner Heisenberg's quantum mechanics or particle physics, than to Einstein's theory of relativity, without which it would be impossible to narrate the events witnessed by the passengers (foreseen in the equation $E= mc^2$, in which E represents energy, m mass and c the speed of light). Joaquim Cardozo succeeds in exploring these themes in language redolent of the highest poetry. The travelers on the train look from on high at the changes men have made of what is cosmic and permanent about the nature of things of the Earth

> Olham para os homens cheios de
>   orgulho e de glória
> Os rostos voltados para o alto, para as
>   estrelas longínquas.
>
> They look at men filled with
>   pride and glory
> The faces looking up at the distant stars.

(Cardozo 1971, 129)

Philosophical reflection is constant and at the highest level here.

Almost without referring to the theory of relativity, Cardozo can explain it. In all its rigor, his train obeys the postulates of Einstein during its dislocation in the geodesic, as Euclidian space is no longer considered. Aware of the poet's mission, Cardozo knows that the train, as a material object, shall never achieve the speed of light, but the fabular function of language, which belongs exclusively to humanity, allows him to merge science with myth; this occurs precisely in line 457, when "O trem ultrapassa a velocidade da luz" ("The train surpasses the speed of light") and is no longer an "objeto do universo" ("object of the universe") (139).

> O trem e os seus passageiros
> Romperam os vínculos da inércia
> Rasgaram as cortinas da gravitação
> Suas formas ponderáveis recuaram
>   para seus contornos
> Para as nébulas mais leves das origens.
>
> The train and its passengers
> Broke away from the roots of inertia
> They tore the curtains of gravitation
> To the slightest mist of origin.
> Their imaginable forms receded to contours

(139–40).

In part IX of the "Visão," the train enters the region of the dead and, among the many who once lived on earth, he sees Mahatma Gandhi:

> E as cabrinhas que lhe derem o saboroso leite;
> Nas gotas da clara nuvem, dos homens
> Que ele não pode impedir de morrerem famintos.
>
> And the little goats who gave him the tasty milk;
> In the drops of the light cloud, of men
> Whom he cannot prevent from dying hungry.

(142)

In the dream region, he writes that "viver é saber sentir, sonhar. O sonho é o gás da Razão fictícia" (145) ("living is knowing how to feel, and dream. The dream is the gas of fictitious Reason"). He teaches us that if the train had not departed on its endless journey to infinity in the middle of the night, if it had left at dawn, or in the blue sun of noon,

> outros seriam os ponto-acontecimentos
> De sua viagem seriam os outros o sonho
> e os pontos do sonho,
> Outra a visão do, ao céu chegando,
> o último Trem.
>
> there would have been other events [points of trajectory]
> On its journey there would be other dreams and
> stops in the dream,
> Another vision of, in Heaven arriving,
> the last Train.

(145)

It might be best to refer the reader to the end of this part of the *Trivium*, where the poet writes:

> —No centro dos centros, do anúncio
> de todos os possíveis
> Erguido em Glória, em Majestade,
> em Grandeza
> O acontecimento Branco.
> Divino? Eterno.
>
> The centre of all centres, banner of all
> possibilities
> Raised in Glory, in Majesty,
> in Grandness
> The White event.
> Divine? Eternal.

(147)

And the book concludes with the personification of the Serra dos Órgãos mountain range; the mountain narrates the beginning of everything that has happened on the planet until the appearance of life and of humanity and offers a prophecy of its end–the end of humanity–well before that of other living beings, including spiders and ants.

Recife Today

At the start of the 1960s, a revolutionary literacy campaign began in Recife, created by Paulo Freire. The objective was to teach adolescents and adults how to read, preparing the region for the tasks of economic, social, and political development. The beneficiaries of this method, particularly the peasants, acquired a high degree of awareness of their roles in the struggle against misery and economic stagnation. Germano Coelho, along with other educators, created the Movement for Popular Culture counting on the support of the community and those intellectuals most committed to the industrialization of the Northeast and its integration into the process of the country's global development. Pernambuco's political establishment, which grew out of the feudal system implanted here by the colonizers during the sixteenth century, saw one great danger in these two instruments for the education of the masses: the loss of its privileges and of its almost hereditary political power based on the possession of large properties. This was communism transforming Recife into the most powerful base of subversive ideas put into practice, and so these two movements were considered dangerously subversive. The military movement of 1964 was soon to make its appearance, establishing the Brazilian military dictatorship that lasted for over two decades. Paulo Freire's method and the Movement for Popular Culture were both outlawed.

But Recife's humanistic tradition prevailed. In spite of the authoritarian regime, the Federal University of Pernambuco succeeded in transforming itself into a center for the creation of knowledge, with roughly sixty-three departments. The Literature Department is part of the Center for Arts and Communication, where the master's and doctoral courses in literary science and linguistics offer research possibilities and advanced studies. The research within the field of literature and the science of language is sustained by an infrastructure of the highest level, as observed by evaluators from the Ministry of Education. Today, Recife has four universities, a public library, and many museums: the Museum of Modern Art, the Recife Museum, the State Museum, the Northeastern Man Museum, maintained by the Joaquim Nabuco Foundation, an organ of the Ministry of Education and one of the best and most highly regarded research institutions of the region. The Federal University of Pernambuco has its own publishing imprint, operates educational television and radio stations, as well as two theaters, and edits a journal called *Estudos Universitários*, a publication of international quality. A strong oral literature maintains the constant relationship between expressions of popular and scholarly writing at every level. During the 1960s and 1970s, the graduate studies program and the *Diário de Pernambuco* became the principal centers for the activities of the poets of the Generation of 1965. The Federal University employs a large number of foreign scientists and researchers in its various departments. It was here that Professor Didier Lamaison translated 211 of Carlos Drummond de Andrade's poems into French, subsequently published in Paris by Gallimard. The University is also enriched with the work of the Canadian literary theorist Sébastien Joachim (b. 1933), a specialist in cybernetic imagination in the poetry and the poetics of the imaginary. Among works by poets from the Generation of 1965, the following are outstanding: *Livro de Olinda* [1982; The Book of Olinda] and *Comarca da memória* [1944; District of Memory] by Jaci Bezerra (b. 1944), *Poemas anteriores* [1989; Previous Poems] and *Oração pelo poema* [1969; Prayer for the Poem] by Alberto Cunha Melo (b. 1942), *Sísifo* [1969; Sisyphus] and *Nordestinados* [1971; Northeast Bound] by Marcus Accioly (b. 1943), *Quasar* (1987) by Lucila Nogueira (b. 1950), *Poemaceso* [1985; Lighted Poem] by Tereza Tenório (b. 1949), *Livrório-Opus-Zero* (1981) by Mário Hélio Gomes de Lima (b. 1964), *O Aedo* [1989; The Poet] by Weydson Barros Leal (b. 1921), *Armorial de um caçador de nuvens* [1971; A Cloud Hunter] by Ângelo Monteiro (b. 1942), and *Pomar de sombras* [1995; Shadow Grove] and *Claridade* [1996; Clarity] by Débora Brennand (b. 1928), creator of poetry of great beauty.

Among contemporary books that contribute to a knowledge of Recife as a cultural center, I should mention *A tradição humanística* [1981; The Humanist Tradition] by Nelson Saldanha (b. 1933), professor, essayist, and poet; *Tempo dos Flamengos* [1947; Time of the Flemish] by José Antônio Gonsalves de Mello (b. 1916); the books of historian Evaldo Cabral de Mello (b. 1936), *Rubro veio* [1986; Red Streak], *A fronda dos Mazombos* [1995; The Mazombo Rebellion], and *Olinda restaurada* [1975; Olinda Restored]. Among writers of fiction, there are Fernando Monteiro (b. 1949) with his *Aspades* (1997); Ariano Suassuna (b. 1927) writing *Romance d'a Pedra do reino e o príncipe do sangue do vai-e-volta; romance armorial-popular brasileiro* [1971; The Novel about the Stone of the

Kingdom and the Prince of Blood of the Comings and Goings: Novel on Popular Brazilian Heraldy], Raimundo Carrero (b. 1947) author of *Somos pedras que se consomem* [1995; We are Stones that Consume Themselves], Osman Lins (1924–1978) with his *Avalovara* (1973) and *Nove Novena* [1966; Nine Novena]; Cláudio Aguiar (b. 1944) author of *Caldeirão* [1982; Cauldron], and Maria Cristina Cavalcanti de Albuquerque (b. 1943) who wrote *Luz do Abismo* [1996; Light of the Abyss], the novel that finally lays regionalism to rest, as it brings Brazil into the international debate about post-Modernism in the terms defined by Linda Hutcheon.

There are, in Recife, a number of visual artists, many of them internationally renowned, such as Cícero Dias (1907–2003) who lived in Paris since 1937, and Francisco Brennand (b. 1927) whose roughly 17,000-square-meter ceramics factory is also an enormous museum admired and known around the world. In 1993, Brennand was awarded the Gabriela Mistral Prize for science and visual arts by the Organization of American States. His beautiful sculptures and paintings have been studied by many art critics in Brazil and abroad. Other great painters from Recife are Vicente do Rego Monteiro (1899–1970), João Câmara (b. 1944), Reynaldo Fonseca (b. 1925), José Cláudio, Lula Cardoso Ayres (1910–1987), and, among the younger generation, painter Gil Vicente (b. 1958).

Despite all these details, I do not believe I have given the reader a complete picture of Recife as a cultural center. What I have shown is necessarily fragmentary when compared to the enormously rich creations of the human spirit.

Translation by Stephen A. Berg

Works Cited

Cardozo, Joaquim. 1971. "Trivium." *Poesias completas*. Rio de Janeiro: Editora Civilização Brasileira. 116–54.

——. 1996. "Trivium." *Poemas selecionados*. Ed. César Leal. Recife: Editora Bagaço. 123–70.

Cassirer, Ernst. 2000. *The Logic of the Cultural Sciences: Five Studies*. Trans. S.G. Lofts. New Haven: Yale University Press.

Curtius, Ernst Robert. 1953. *European Literature and the Latin Middle Ages*. Trans. Willard R. Trask. New York: Pantheon Books.

Eliot, T.S. 1923. "The Function of Criticism." *The Criterion: A Quarterly Review* 2.5: 31–42.

——. 1948. *Notes Towards the Definition of Culture*. London: Faber and Faber.

Ferry, Luc. 1994. *Homo Aestheticus: A invenção do gosto na era democrática*. Trans. Eliana Maria de Melo e Souza. São Paulo: Editora Ensaio.

Freyre, Gilberto. 1935. *Artigos de Jornal*. Ed. Luís Jardim. Recife: Edições Mozart.

——. 1956. *The Masters and the Slaves*. 2nd ed. Trans. Samuel Putman. New York: Knopf.

——. 1966. "Latinidade e Americanidade da América Latina: crescente interpretação e decrescente desagregação." *Revista Estudos Universitários* 6.1: 5–21.

——. 1969. "Conselho Estadual de Cultura." *Revista do Conselho Estadual de Cultura de Pernambuco* 1.1: 27–33.

——. 1981. *Sobrados e mucambos*. 6th ed. Vol. 1. Rio de Janeiro: José Olympio Editora. 2 vols.

——. 1984. *Casa grande & senzala*. 23rd ed. Rio de Janeiro: José Olympio Editora.

Hutcheon, Linda. 1988. *The Poetics of Postmodernism: History, Theory, Fiction*. London and New York: Routledge.

Leal, César. 1966. "Machado de Assis: poeta." *Estudos Universitários* 6.1: 61–78.

——. 1998. "Poemas não datados." *Tempo e vida na terra*. Rio de Janeiro: Editora Imago.

Lima, Manoel de Oliveira. 1975. *Pernambuco, seu desenvolvimento histórico*. 2nd ed. Recife: Governo do Estado de Pernambuco, Secretaria de Educação e Cultura.

Mello, José Antonio Gonsalves. 1987. *Tempo dos Flamengos*. 3rd ed. Preface by Gilberto Freyre. Recife: Editora Massangana.

Melo Neto, João Cabral de. 1994. "O Auto de Frade." *Obras completas*. Ed. Marly de Oliveira. Rio de Janeiro: Nova Aguilar. 463–513.

Meyers, Jorge. 1994. "Literatura romántica y proyeto social." *América Latina: Palavra, literatura e cultura*. Vol. I. Ed. Ana Pizarro. Campinas: Editora da Unicamp. 221–50.

Moraes Filho, Evaristo de. 1985. *Medo à utopia*. Rio de Janeiro: Editora Nova Fronteira.

Pound, Ezra. 1976. *A arte da poesia*. Trans. Heloysa de Lima Dantas and José Paulo Paes. São Paulo: Editora Cultrix and EDUSP.

Quental, Antero de. 1987. *Causas de decadência dos povos peninsulares*. Lisboa: Ulmeiro.

Rama, Ángel. 1984. *La ciudad letrada*. Montevideo: Fundación Angel Rama.

Teixeira, Bento. 1969. *Prosopopéia*. Recife: Editora Universitária.

Veríssimo, José. 1998. *História da literatura brasileira: De Bento Teixeira (1601) a Machado de Assis (1908)*. Ed. Luiz Roberto S.S. Malta. São Paulo: Letras & Letras.

Wells, Henry. 1924. *Poetic Imagery: Illustrated from Elizabethan Literature*. New York: Columbia University Press.

CHAPTER 47

BAHIA
COLONIZATION AND CULTURES

Eneida Leal Cunha, Jeferson Bacelar, and Lizir Arcanjo Alves

Toma esta capitania o nome da Bahia por ter uma tão grande que por autonomásia e excelência se levanta com o nome comum e apropriando-se a si se chama Bahia, e com razão, porque tem maior recôncavo, mais ilhas e rios dentro de si que quantas são descobertas em o mundo.... Está esta baia em treze graus e um terço, e tem em seu circuito a melhor terra do Brasil.

This captaincy is named Bahia after a bay so large, so excellent and so self-sufficient that it rises with a common name and, appropriating it, is called Bahia with reason, for it possesses a greater expanse of land and more islands and rivers within it than may be found anywhere in the world.... This bay lies at thirteen and one third degrees, and possesses the best land in Brazil.

−Fr. Vicente do Salvador, História do Brasil: 1500–1627

In 1501, Americo Vespucio, pilot of the Portuguese land reconnaissance expedition to the place where Pedro Alvares Cabral's fleet had landed a year earlier, gave the name of Bahia de Todos os Santos (Bay of All Saints) to the natural port and large, safe bay that greeted him. On 29 March 1549, when the age of captaincies (or hereditary land grants) during Brazil's first administrative division was still in force, the nobleman Tomé de Souza disembarked in this same bay, charged with the creation of an administrative center for the general government of the colony and the founding of a city to be called São Salvador da Bahia de Todos os Santos. From that day, Salvador has been a secondary name that appears in formal political circumstances. The city and the administrative region−the captaincy (or land grant), later the province, and later still the state−are fused in the short word Bahia, for all those who inhabit, narrate, and describe it.

Bahia, as both port and an allusion to the mercantile importance of the Colonial metropolis, acquired nearly unshakable symbolic and textual consistency. It has been successively described in superlative tones by early chroniclers, both execrated and loved in the verses of the seventeenth-century Baroque poet Gregório de Matos (1633?–1696) (when, through metonymy, it signified the entire colony), exalted in the Romantic-Libertarian poems of the abolitionist Castro Alves (1847–1871), and fictionalized in the widely read novels of Jorge Amado (1912–2001). At present, the sounds, images, and colors of "Afro-Bahianness" are disseminated by the media to the rest of the country. One may read in the way in which it is designated the fixation in the social imaginary of resistant identity traces that conceive and reiterate Bahia as an ancestral center, as the natural place of reception, transit, exchange, and admixture.

Between 1549 and the beginning of the nineteenth century, the city of Bahia was the colony's prominent political, cultural, and economic center. Installed on a rocky coast 70 meters above sea level, with hills and low grasslands alternating, it offered various points from which the entrance to the bay could be watched; that is, it offered favorable conditions of vigilance and access. A natural ecology favored settlement; abundant drinking water guaranteed survival; winds were determined by the diversified orientation of the valleys; and easy communication enhanced agricultural production and distribution of indispensable imports. In the *recôncavo* (the land surrounding the port or the city), 300 kilometers of

shoreline of the interior sea provided the fertile land where the sugar economy was established.

The city was founded as a result of administrative and economic imperatives that, from the start, configured these Colonial cities destined to exert the function of receiving and distribution; these port cities, whose principal activity was the forwarding of consumer goods produced in the colony to the metropolis, were marked as much by the influence of the rural area to which they were connected as by the intense contact with the exterior (Mattoso 75–6). The profile of agro-mercantile economy–the "wealth"–from the seventeenth to the nineteenth centuries, was primarily associated with the monoculture of sugar, the principal export product, and with the trading of slaves from Africa, which made Bahia the largest market for blacks in Brazil; it formed an interdependent pairing responsible for the city's prominence through the beginning of the nineteenth century and also for its economic decline.

At the time of the general government's establishment, there were approximately fifty inhabitants of European origin in the area, under the protection of Diogo Alvares Correia, a legendary figure treated with reticence by historiography but of great importance according to the first accounts of the encounter between the Portuguese and the natural inhabitants of the land and thus the imaginary of miscegenation. Nicknamed Caramuru, he probably arrived in 1513, and imposed himself upon the Tupinambá Indians, among whom he lived and had children. Roughly 1000 men arrived with Tomé de Souza in 1549 to build and populate the city. At the end of the seventeenth century Jesuit accounts record 3000 Portuguese living in Bahia, along with 4000 blacks and 8000 catechized Indians; this still does not represent the total population, as there is no reference to the number of *mestizos* (Mattoso 119), whose invisibility was to persist, if not in terms of demographic information, then at least in the majority of accounts that describe Bahia during and after its Colonial history. The continuous arrival of new contingents of blacks and Portuguese, the successive incorporation of catechized Indians into slave labor, and the exercise of a multiethnic sexuality (which appropriated to itself the subordinated bodies as violently as it did the conquered land) were the matrices of population, leading to the rapid growth of the colonial and *mestizo* population. The intense miscegenation and subsequent double acculturation made for social relationships in which the ambiguity between closeness and domination (between profoundly hierarchized classes and races) became the rule in a society split between masters and slaves who interpenetrated intensely in everyday life but were repeatedly separated in discourse.

From the end of the seventeenth to the beginning of the eighteenth century, when the Company of Jesus was expelled from Portuguese territory, cultural life centered around the Jesuit College. Founded in 1556, it was principally responsible for the transference of lettered culture to the colony. The College offered a primary course for white boys, sons of settlers, and for newly baptized Christians, and a course in arts, letters, and theology that graduated its first bachelors and masters in arts in 1575 (Calmon 14). Despite the scarcity of books in circulation within the colony (limited to religious books, Virgil, Seneca, and Horace), the college, which instigated contact between priests and men of letters, stimulated the first literary productions of the colony. From this came, for example, the poet Gregório de Matos (1633?–1696) and the Jesuit Antônio Vieira (1608–1697).

Read by Brazilian historiographers in the late seventeenth century as symptoms of an emerging patriotic sentiment, the descriptive texts written in the earlier centuries, whether directly or indirectly related to Bahia, dealt primarily with giving symbolic existence to the land and its "barbarian inhabitants," and instituting them as possessions and extensions of the European metropolis. They are minute and systematic reports both in their description of the physical aspects with which the Europeans should deal and the natural wealth that could be of immediate commercial use, as well as (and especially) in their description of the autochthonous population (Cunha 1995, 63–4). Exemplary of the resulting ethnography so necessary to the efficacy of Portuguese colonization (as may be inferred from their very titles) are *Tratado descritivo do Brasil* [The Descriptive Treatise of Brazil] by Gabriel Soares de Sousa (ca. 1540–ca. 1591), the *Tratado da terra do Brasil* [Treatise of the Land of Brazil] by Pero de Magalhães Gândavo (d. 1576), the *Tratados da terra e da gente do Brasil* [Treatises of the Land and People of Brazil] by Fernão Cardim (d. 1625), and the *Diálogo sobre a conversão do gentio* [Dialogue on the Conversion of the People] by Manóel de Nóbrega (1517–1570), all dating from the sixteenth century.

Seventeenth-century writing went beyond these descriptive or prescriptive evaluations of Colonial life. In 1618 Ambrósio Fernandes Brandão (b. ca. 1555), a new Portuguese Christian who had settled in Paraíba, wrote the *Diálogos das grandezas do Brasil* [Dialogues on the Treasures of Brazil], a systematic advertisement for the possibilities of wealth in the colony, enumerating the "seis coisas, com as quais seus povoadores se fazem muito ricos: a primeira a lavoura do açúcar, a segunda a mercancia, a terceira o pau a que chamam Brasil, a quarta os algodões e madeira, a quinta a lavoura de mantimentos, a sexta e última a criação de gados. De todas essas coisas o principal nervo e substância da riqueza da terra é a lavoura dos açúcares" (Bosi 28) ("six things which may bring wealth to its settlers: first the cultivation of sugar, secondly trade, thirdly the wood which is called Brazil, fourth the cottons and the lumber, fifth the cultivation of staples, sixth, and last, the breeding of cattle. Among all these things the principal nerve and substance of land's wealth is the farming of sugars").

As the emphasis on the sugar economy indicates, the land referred to by Fernandes Brandão includes the large strip of northeastern territory where sugar was planted. Even

then the principal texts that expose and comment on the ethos of the Colonial society note the umbilical connection to the city of Bahia.

Frei Vicente do Salvador's (1564–1639?) *História do Brasil 1500–1627* [1886–1887; History of Brazil: 1500–1627] offers an unsystematic account, similar to that of the first chronicles but rich in significant commentary about the first hundred years of colonization. An accurate observer of detail, he was able to establish surprising connections between small, everyday events and the great lines of colonial history that distinguish the society and the country. "Porque tudo querem para lá. E isto não tem só os que de lá vieram, mas ainda os que cá nasceram, que uns e outros usam da terra não como senhores, mas como usufrutuários, só para a desfrutarem e deixarem destruída" ("Because they want to have all things for Portugal. And this is so not only with those who come from Portugal, but also those who were born in Brazil and who work the land not as owners, but as farmers who merely want to exploit it and leave the land destroyed"), thus concluding that "nem um homem nesta terra é república, nem zela ou cuida do bem comum, senão cada um do bem particular" ("not a man in this land is republican, nor cares for the common good, but only for his personal advantage") (Salvador 59).

Frei Vicente do Salvador's criticism of Colonial society would be radically intensified in the vast satirical oeuvre of Gregório de Matos, the most important poet of those first centuries, but in the introduction to his text, Frei Vicente do Salvador exposes the nostalgia for a stable order founded upon divine transcendence, attributing unfortunate events in the colony's future to the heresy, namely the substitution of the sacred name of the Land of Santa Cruz–"o divino pau, que deu tinta e virtude a todos os sacramentos da Igreja" ("the divine wood, which has given foundation and virtue to all the sacraments of the church")–for the profane and commercial Brazil "por causa de um pau assim chamado de cor abrasada e vermelha com que tingem panos, do qual há muito, nesta terra" ("because of an abundant, ember-like, reddish colored wood with which cloth is dyed") (58). For historian and priest, all "disorders" stem from this transgression, the fruit of material greed and the easy, uncompromised wealth of the colony's possessors (Cunha 1993b, 112). In the verses of Gregório de Matos a similar nostalgia may also be inferred in criticisms almost indiscriminately aimed at all aspects and personages of colonial society; this is a similar nostalgia for an order that would transcend the values of a mercantile culture:

> Notável desventura
> de um povo néscio e sandeu,
> que não sabe que o perdeu
> Negócio, Ambição e Usura.

> Notable misfortune
> of ignorant and foolish people,
> who know not what they have lost
> Trade, Ambition and Usury.

> *(Mendes 54)*

Gregório de Matos Guerra was born in Bahia in 1636 into a well-to-do family of plantation owners, studied in the Jesuit College and graduated in law from the University of Coimbra, remaining in Portugal until 1681, when he returned to Bahia. He practiced law, held ecclesiastical positions, and led a popular poet's life of bohemian dissipation, improvising caustic verses on his violin, as he roamed city streets and the plantations of the surrounding area singing to his contemporaries, as a poem says, of his "musa praguejadora" ("cursing muse"), which earned him, during his lifetime, the nickname of "Boca do Inferno" ("Mouth of Hell"). Due to friction with the local powers that be, he was exiled to Angola and eventually permitted to return to Brazil, so long as he did not return to Bahia and agreed to silence his slandering, evil-speaking lyre. He died in Recife in 1695.

Poetry attributed to Gregório de Matos, usually considered among the highest expressions of either religious or romantic lyrics or satirical verse of unmeasured virulence, whose targets were public personalities and circumstances of the Colonial metropolis, point to a man educated in the classical humanist tradition, familiar with the Iberian Baroque and the satirical tradition, at once profoundly immersed in the everyday life of his city and supported by an oral tradition that went beyond the frontiers of the lettered community. Not one of the roughly 700 poems attributed to Gregório de Matos was published in his lifetime and his autograph is not known. Available manuscripts (even these were ignored until 1881, when forty poems were first published) consisted of copies made by admirers. The repetition of Iberian models, the uncertainties about authorship, as well as the immediate (and future) local recognition that made possible the preservation of the work–all of these are at the heart of the restrictions on account of Gregório de Matos in Brazilian historiography, and result from discrepancies between the Colonial author and the emphasis of literary modernity on originality, on authenticity of the written text, on the value of individual signature, and, especially, on the confinement of literary production to the sphere of *written* literature as its exclusive instance of circulation, reproduction, and legitimation.

For a cultural history of Bahia, and especially for an understanding of the symbolic productions that trigger the chemistry between identity and the imaginary, Gregório de Matos is of great importance, first, because within the inconsistency of the work's limits and the permanent suspicion of inauthenticity of its verse lies the merit of a name that, in fact, designates a collective creation, one that has been made and unmade for three centuries, creating a dialogue (sometimes a conflict-ridden dialogue) between the lettered tradition and erudite appreciation and popular memory; second, because in his verses it is possible to read, beyond the exceptional verbal and ideological constructions of the baroque, a minute and acid documentation of Colonial life in eighteenth-century Bahia; third, because these verses both shaped and established a vision of the past–primal scenes–that reverberate to this day in the Bahian imaginary. The poems depict a city at once prosperous and hungry, sumptuous and degraded, exclusive and promiscuous, moralistic and licentious, simultaneously exposing the tensions (and shared experiences) between the moralism and the irreverence of the seventeenth-century poet. The principal social actors of the period are characterized in the verses of Gregório de Matos. Here are representatives of the Colonial administration, plantation owners, merchants, the military, friars and nuns, Indians catechized and enslaved, in addition to frequent allusions to a large urban population without specific definition, predominantly classified as adventurers of European origin and mulattos (when born in the colony). The documentary link to their time also allows the poems to be read as a record of relevant events of the day such as plague and hunger, epidemics that victimized and diminished the city's population, stupefaction at the passage of a comet,

petitions to the local authorities and the Portuguese court, balls, and other events of domestic life in the city.

This mediation between the lettered elite and the street effected by the poetry of Gregório de Matos established strong roots in the literary culture of Bahia, less as direct influence on the following centuries than as the historical and imaginary contingency of a society marked by both qualitatively and quantitatively intense unbalance and inequality. For centuries what might be generically and imprecisely designated as Bahian culture provided peculiar ways of connecting social, ethnic, and racial segments that Colonial slaveholding society indelibly marked as antagonistic. Both target of and most interested party in this mediation appears always to have been the majority group of *mestizos*, for whom the sharing of white lettered culture was the minimum demand for the conquest of a social status that might differentiate them from blacks and slaves. For these, the irreverence of Gregório de Matos's verses toward the dominant figures or "the men," as is symptomatically said to this day in Bahia when referring to the rich and powerful, may have signified the necessary space for the projection of repression and resentment. One cannot, however, neglect the fact that the ugly disparagement of blacks, mulattos, and *caboclos*, and the abundant and frequently pornographic references to black and *mestizo* women in the poet's verses, have been collectively introjected, contributing to the sedimentary formation of the particular forms of racism still persistent in Bahian society.

In the most recent edition of Gregório de Matos's satirical poetry, *Senhora Dona Bahia* [1658/1996; Mrs. Bahia], the critical essay that accompanies the poems underscores as "Gregorian alchemy" a rhetoric that does not reduce distances but which articulates the symmetrical oppositions in identity, as much on the thematic level as on the lexical plane, by incorporating Latinisms, indigenous and African words, Castillianisms, slang, and colloquialisms of his time (in Mendes 255). Another result of this Baroque rhetorical alchemy is the enormous repercussions of Gregório de Matos's seventeenth-century verses on the discourses of identity produced and reproduced in Bahia, which articulated so well both libertarian spirit and racism, exclusion and inclusion, moralism and lasciviousness, verbal irreverence and political subservience, and praise and depreciation of *mestizaje* itself.

The second most important name on the list of the creators of the greatest expressions of the literary and Colonial Baroque is that of religious orator Padre Antônio Vieira. Born in Lisbon in 1608, he came to Bahia with his family at the age of six, studied at the Jesuit College, entered the Company of Jesus novitiate in 1623, and was ordained in the priesthood ten years later. He was in Lisbon between 1641 and 1652, in the reign of João IV, as ambassador and mediator in the internal and external politics of the Portuguese Crown in relation to the holy Office of the Inquisition and the new Christians. In Brazil, he lived in Maranhão and in Pará, returning to Bahia in 1681, where he organized for publication the volumes of his vast work, and died in 1697. In Colonial Bahia the famous sermons of Vieira performed a complementary function to the libel of Gregório de Matos and the diagnosis of Frei Vicente do Salvador. The sermons are based on the same recognition of vices and disorder but, in this genre, regarded as venial and mortal sins. Vieira dedicated himself to correcting these transgressions or "patching" them up, as the Bahians would say. His sermons, although written, were part of the oral tradition like the verses of Gregório de Matos, and were shared among the general public through oratory. The sermons of Vieira had, through the pulpit of the principal churches of the city and in the small private chapels of the sugar plantations, a privileged space of dissemination among both the lettered and unlettered. They possessed, however, over and above the caustic and subversive word of the poet, the extraordinary advantage of the legitimacy of the place of enunciation, the Catholic Church, and the benefit of the convergence between the pragmatic Jesuit pedagogy and Baroque rhetoric, masterfully operated by the orator, to articulate divine designation and mundane interests.

Vieira's work covered all the principal subjects of his century, from the greater matters of the Portuguese empire with regard to Europe and the conquered territories to specifically colonial matters of religious, sociopolitical, and economic import. His sermons in defense of the empire's territorial integrity are well known, as are those directed at landowners against the illicit enslavement of the populace in Maranhão. Less well known are the sermons preached to the blacks in churches such as the Brotherhood of Our Lady of the Black Rosary in Bahia, or in the chapels of the sugar plantations in the Bahian Recôncavo–the "doce inferno" ("sweet hell"), as he said in the Fourteenth Sermon of the Rosary in 1633. In these, the Baroque-Jesuit alchemy was a model of efficiency in simultaneously condemning and preserving slavocratic order, the separation of men–all equal in the eyes of God–the separation of masters and slaves, the former destined to riches and enjoyment, the latter to work, hunger, and suffering. Vieira did not stint in his flashy Baroque words to point to the torment of slavery, the extraordinary dimension of which was to be equalled only by the suffering of Jesus Christ. To speak to the blacks–this is the word used by Vieira–as closest to Christ, by demonstrating the same line of descent from Abraham, in the Fourteenth Sermon of the Rosary, or by exposing the equality of martyrdom on the cross and the whipping post, in the Seventeenth Sermon of the Rosary.

Along with the remaining cultural production of the seventeenth century, these three major figures were excluded from Antonio Candido's (b. 1918) *Formação da Literatura Brasileira: Momentos Decisivos* [1959; Formation of Brazilian Literature: Decisive Moments], admittedly the most noble version of Brazilian literary historiography, for being prior to the existence of "um conjunto de produtores literários, mais ou menos conscientes do seu papel; um conjunto de receptores, formando os diferentes tipos de público, sem os quais a obra não vive; um mecanismo transmissor . . . que liga uns a outros" ("a set of literary producers, more or less conscious of their role; a set of receivers, forming different types of public without whom the work does not live; a mechanism of transmission . . . which connects one to another"), forming a "sistema simbólico" ("symbolic system") which would ensure "continuidade literária" ("literary continuity") (Candido 25). Such elements certainly did not exist in the Colonial metropolis–in particular, the desire to produce Brazilian literature did not exist. But the continuity of the images and values of Bahian Colonial life found in the texts of Frei Vicente do Salvador, Gregório de Matos, and Antônio Vieira makes up a lengthy history and shapes an imaginary whose resistance is perhaps greater than may be desirable. They were not making literature–textual production during that time was actually something quite different–and, overall, they were

not published or circulated among their contemporaries; but they were no less efficacious in the symbolic institution of the land. Bahia, the colony, was the unequivocal theme of this early discourse, produced by men of letters confronted by a human, social, and moral landscape that exceeded the order or desirable values to the secular, Eurocentric spirit. These writers committed themselves to describing, criticizing, and correcting "as terras viciosas" ("the corrupt lands")–a superb expression, recovered one century later by José de Santa Rita Durão (1720–1784) in the epic poem *Caramuru* (1781), to inscribe the resemblance of a society where everything occurred in unacceptable differences: This means to colonize.

Until the early nineteenth century Bahia continued to be one of the largest cities of the Portuguese empire, although, by the end of the eighteenth century, it yielded political prominence to Rio de Janeiro. Docking and commercial activities were intense and diversified, but sugar continued to be the basic product, corresponding to 70 percent of all exports, followed by tobacco, which, in 1850, represented 13 percent of export products. Imports supplied the city, much of the surrounding regions, and other provinces with manufactured products and slaves. The economic dimension of the sugar industry, from the sixteenth century to the 1870s, assured the permanent imbalance and social separation in a population divided between a small fraction of plantation owners and merchants and their slaves and, among them, a significant contingent, with the largest growth throughout the nineteenth century, of the poor and freed blacks who populated the city streets–living a life in contrast to the magnificence of the installations of the administration of public life, churches, and rich residences. In racial terms, the most complete data about the population of Bahia and its distribution by color pertain to the years 1808 and 1872, which, at any rate, allows for an understanding of a broad picture of the century. In the beginning, only one-fifth of the free population was composed of whites; 43 percent were mulattos or free blacks, and the slaves represented 35 percent of the population, as the percentage of Indians and *caboclos* had, by that time, become insignificant. The picture is altered at the end of that century, with 24 percent white, 12 percent slaves, and 60 percent blacks and free mulattos (Mattoso 97).

Given the radical nature of economic stratification and social separation, writing the history of Bahia as a cultural center in the nineteenth century, when the lettered institutional processes were being structured in Brazil, demands that we go beyond the recorded activities of the intellectualized elite in their own exclusive means and spaces–published books and periodicals, literary or scientific associations that have traditionally been the object of Bahian historiography, particularly since the mid-twentieth century. For a larger picture, however, less exclusive cultural formations should be considered. The most inclusive view of cultural life in nineteenth-century Bahia may be gained through the Teatro São João, the first theater built in Brazil. Built to be the largest theater in America, with four tiers of boxes and seating 2000, it was inaugurated while still unfinished on 13 May 1812. From the top of the hill upon which it was built, it witnessed major and minor political and artistic events, revolts, compromises, the splendor and decline of the monarchy, the advent of the republic, literary and scientific progress, the smallness and greatness of the men of its time, and was finally extinguished in a fire during the second decade of the twentieth century.

Just as in the city's cultural and political life, at least three important phases may be distinguished for the Teatro São João, synchronic with the development in Bahia, the young national state: The first was an educational vocation, aiming at the formation of a public and the introduction of Europeanized good taste, which lasted until the early 1850s; the second, more political phase, was marked by the local production of nationalist ideology and includes the creation, in 1857, of the Dramatic Conservatory, which took over police censorship of the theater productions. In this regard the figure of the most important Bahian writer of the day, Agrário de Menezes (1834–1863), may be singled out as particularly significant. The third phase, the most effervescent and agitated, spans the years of the abolitionist campaign, from the end of the 1860s to the 1880s; it was in 1880 when conductor Carlos Gomes (1836–1896) visited Bahia, after a production of *O Guarani*–an affirmation of national culture.

The 1808 arrival of the Portuguese royal family in Brazil, when the seat of the kingdom passed from Portugal to Brazil, brought about political alterations that reinforced what had been the precarious relations between the colonial nuclei and the growing urban life, in all its aspects and in all regions. The opening of the theater corresponded to the demand for a sociocultural space for the provincial aristocracy and the expectations of median and *mestizo* segments for sharing the cultural environment that would legitimate them, promoting their artistic education based on the reiteration of current European models, from dress codes to theatrical programming.

Foreign travelers of the time favorably compare the architecture of Bahia to the best in Europe, and point out other material aspects in which the city had customs similar to their own (see **Figure 1**). It is possible to read in these texts, however, as in the Eurocentric appreciation of Maria Graham, contrasts between the suitability of physical apparatus and the unsuitability of sociocultural habits of the provincial capital that would be compelled to modernize itself. They are unanimous in ironically reporting on actors' performances and in pointing out the ridiculousness of Classical theater performances with inadequate casting. On the other hand, the *intermezzos* (entertainments), and above all the *lundu* dance of black origin that filled the intermissions, were described with detailed enthusiasm by Tollenare as "a mais cínica que se possa imaginar" ("the most cynical imaginable"), "a representação a mais crua do ato de amor carnal" ("the crudest representation of carnal love") (Verger 200).

Although these *intermezzos* were consonant with the actors and with local standards of morality, they were considered to be incompatible with public decorum and were prohibited by city officials. In 1835, the theater's administrator held discussions with the chief of police about "se reprovaria inteiramente que se pusesse em cena, em algum intervalo dos espetáculos do Teatro público, a dança denomindada–lundu–por ser instado para a apresentar, por diversos amadores, e porque disso reputava depender o interesse do mesmo teatro" (Boccanera 117) ("whether or not to condemn fully the staging of the dance named lundu during the intervals of public theatrical spectacles, after having been persuaded to permit the dance by several amateurs, and because the interest of the theater was reputed to depend on it").

The administrator insisted that the new chief of police allow the *lundu* back onstage, alleging that the public continually requested it and promising that the dance "sem as contorções que, por indecentes, chocam a moralidade, poderia ser exibida

Figure 1.

Photograph by Voltaire Fraga of the Church of the Rua dos Passos c. 1700 in Salvador Bahia. (Courtesy of John P. Robarts Research Library, University of Toronto)

durante a representação das farsas e nunca durante a dos dramas, que é o que, pela maior parte, assistem as famílias espectadoras nos camarotes" (Boccanera 117) ("would be performed without the usual contortions that shocked morality through their indecency, and that it would be exhibited in the intervals of farces and never during those of dramas, which is what, for the most part, family audiences attended").

Prohibition was reiterated: "a dança devia ser evitada, de qualquer maneira, porque as executantes excediam, sempre, os seus limites, tornando-a, assim, imoral, ofensiva ao pudor das famílias, sobre demonstrarem, atos dessa natureza, sancionados, menosprezo ao teatro" (Boccanera 117) ("the dance should be avoided at all costs, as dancers always exceeded limits, thus rendering it immoral, offensive to family modesty, and demonstrating, through sanctioned acts of this nature, contempt for the theater").

In 1854 the chief of police's guidelines for the operation of the theater prohibited "ingresso, nas noites de espetáculo, os africanos de um e outro sexo, livres ou escravos, e em geral os escravos de qualquer cor" (Boccanera 117) ("entry, on performance nights, of Africans of either sex, whether freemen or slaves, and generally slaves of any color").

The prohibition of the *lundu* in Bahian theaters of the last century is symptomatic of the permanent tension between word and body, between the occidental cultural matrix (the lettered culture, the Eurocentric propriety of the *mestizo* elites

of the provinces) and the embarrassing emergence of an African hybrid cultural expression, which, from the sixteenth to
the nineteenth century, had persisted as popular culture and
now challenged the elite for spaces of prestige in the city,
especially the institutional processes of culture. Considering
its date, this prohibition of black dance indicates the exasperation of the *mestizo* populations in promoting their cultural
whitening through the erasure of the black race at least in
terms of culture.

The creation of the Dramatic Conservatory in 1857
marked the beginning of a particular phase for the São João
Theater. The Conservatory became the principal meeting
place for intellectuals, playwrights, critics, poets, journalists,
and orators. It was there that ideas and works were discussed
and the culture of letters propagated the composition of his-
torical-literary erudition, cultural nationalism, and communication with the public, in the open readings of plays.
Agrário de Menezes (1834–1863), the most important name
of this time in Bahia, lived in and died for the theater. He left
many dramatic works, all of which were staged and few of
which were published; among them were the historical dramas *Calabar* and *Dia da Independência* [Independence Day],
both dated 1858. For him, the task of "doutrinar as turbas"
("indoctrinating the masses") through the theater needed
"pelo menos nas suas primeiras fases, de mais alguma coisa,
que constitui a lição moral, tanto mais profícua e tanto mais
fácil, quando se aparenta com os hábitos e com os costumes
do povo" (Sá Menezes 166) ("something more than the
moral lesson; the lesson would be more effective if it
appeared together with the customs and habits of the people"). Contemporary authors contributed to the development of Brazilian nationalism in a manner that was different
from what was being done at court, through its emphasis on
provincial life and history. Some local contributions were *A
legenda de um pariá: Drama histórico sobre a nossa independência*
[The Legend of a Pariah: A Historical Drama of Our Inde-
pendence] by Francisco Antônio Filgueiras Sobrinho (1842–
1878); *Os tempos de independência* [1861; Times of Independ-
ence] by Constantino do Amaral Tavares (1828–1890); and
Calabar, o mameluco [Calabar, The Mameluke], *Pedro I,* and
Dois de Julio [The Second of July] by Antônio Joaquim Rodrigues da Costa (b. 1833). According to Pedro Calmon, in
those days "nenhum poeta moco, novelista de talento ou
redator de folha política se consideraria completo sem passar pelo teatro" (Calmon 135) ("no young poet, novelist of
talent or editor of a political sheet would be considered complete without having taken part in the theater"). It is important that it was not only the dramatic text but the staging of
the nineteenth-century theater that was an important cultural
fact and offered a shared societal experience. Unfortunately,
this major cultural development has been relegated to secondary status by Brazilian literary historians.

The unfolding of a cultural nationalism in Bahia's Dramatic Conservatory (which was different from that which was
being developed in Rio de Janeiro) can be clearly discerned
in the years leading up to 2 July 1823, when the Bahians concluded the country's process of independence. This spirit of
intellectual independence—and the so-called liberal political
perspective—was present in the theatrical notices that some
members of the Conservatory wrote for the newspapers,
whether with regard to the ideas defended by the conservatives at court in Rio, or to the performances of foreign companies. In 1857, in reaction to harsh criticism by Rio de Janeiro

critics against the staging of Realist plays, a Bahian critic
responded that in Bahia they were not interested in "aos olhos
do povo os desmandos e imoralidades das cortes, e as apreen-
sões ambiciosas dos frades . . . . A missão atual do drama é
copiar o mundo tal qual é, e como é. Apresentá-lo às turbas sob o
aspecto da realidade, é, na frase de um escritor hodierno—bater o
vício com sua própria palabra" (*Diário da Bahia*, 11 September 1857) ("the outrages and immoralities at court, and the
ambitious apprehensions of the monks. . . . The theater's current mission is to present a faithful copy of the world as it is.
To present the world to the masses as it really exists is to
defeat vice with its own face").

In 1874, Vittorio de Alfieri's (1749–1803) tragedy *Orestes*
was performed at the São João. In the 17 September 1874
issue of the *Diário da Bahia*, Belarmino Barreto (1840–1882), a
member of the conservatory who then wrote its theatrical column, claimed that *Orestes* was out of step with the demands of
the time.

The impetus of Bahian intellectuals in maintaining a singular cultural identity (when the national policy was aiming
toward unity and homogeneity and was repressing the differences between the provinces, their past, and their present
conditions) was the cause of continual controversy with the
court. The fall of the Liberal Party in 1848, the defeat of the
Beach Revolution in Pernambuco shortly afterward, the
repercussions of the revolutionary movements that raged in
several European countries (above all France, Hungary, and
Italy) greatly marked the face of politics in the north of Brazil, as all of the provinces above Minas Gerais were generically named. Independence and the National State brought
the politics of a strong, central government to Brazil, after
nearly three centuries of a quasi-autonomous existence, more
or less isolated from distant Lisbon or Rio. Dissatisfaction
with the new central power had a significant impact on the
cultural area and thus reaction manifested itself in various
forms.

In 1867 Antônio de Castro Alves (1847–1871), the most
influential Bahian poet of the nineteenth century, arrived on
the scene of the Teatro São João. In June he was elected honorary member of the Dramatic Conservatory, where he gave
a reading of his drama *Gonzaga ou a Revolução de Minas* [1867;
Gonzaga or the Minas Revolution], and on July 2 he was
acclaimed for his recitation of the "Ode to the Second of
July." His play opened to triumphant notices on September 7.
His intense abolitionist campaign also began at this time with
the publication of *Espumas Flutuantes* [1870; Floating Foam].
As a result of the actions of powerful slaveholders and the
Catholic Church itself, the abolitionist campaign in Bahia was
difficult and conflict ridden, but it was continued and amplified through cultural productions: Abolitionist societies, albeit
ephemeral ones, were created, and periodicals, pamphlets,
speeches, poems, and plays were published. Abolitionism
took over civic celebrations such as that of Bahia's Independence celebration on July 2, and was especially prominent on
the stage of the Teatro São João, with the presentation of abolitionist works. Public banquets and auctions raised funds that
added considerably to the growing private donations for the
campaign to free the slaves. The principal emancipation association, the 512-member "Sociedade Libertadora 7 de Setembro" (September 7 Liberationist Society) freed roughly 500
slaves between 1869 and 1878. In1871, it published the periodical *O Abolicionista* [The Abolitionist], in whose fourth issue,
dated April 30, Castro Alves's "Carta às Senhoras Baianas"

[Letter to the Ladies of Bahia] was printed with an appeal for collaboration with one of the auctions in favor of abolitionism.

Doubtless the most agitated phase of the abolitionist campaign in Bahia was that of the "Sociedade Libertadora 7 de Setembro," following immediately upon the circulation of Castro Alves's first poems published in Recife—"Canção do Africano" ["Song of the African"], "A Cachoeira de Paulo Afonso" ["Paulo Afonso's Falls"] and "Os Escravos" ["The Slaves"]. For Xavier Marques (1861–1942), "sua maior e justa glória" ("his greatest glory") lay in having been "um precursor, uma sentinela perdida, literalmente um João Batista—sem faltar o deserto, que se estendia, mudo, árido, asfixiante, à volta da sua singular figura de pregador" ("a precursor, a lost guard, literally a John the Baptist—who did not lack a desert, which extended itself, mute, arid, asphyxiating, around his singular preacher's figure"). Although other writers had already touched upon the theme of slavery, only Castro Alves "teve a inspiração bastante vigorosa, torrencial e iterativa para compor a sinfonia . . . formando uma consciência nacional acessível à injustiça da escravidão, ou, pelo menos, deslocando da periferia para o centro da nossa consciência a monstruosa iniquidade do fato" (Marques 131) ("had sufficiently vigorous inspiration, torrential and iterative inspiration to compose the symphony. . . forging a national awareness of the injustice of slavery, or at least dislocating from the periphery to the center of our consciousness the monstrous iniquity of it").

Although Castro Alves lived the greater part of his productive life between Recife, São Paulo, and Rio de Janeiro, there is no doubt that his public advocacy centered around his abolitionist manifestations in Bahia. Even after his premature death at the age of twenty-three in 1871, his words resonated throughout the country. Ten years after his death, homage was paid him at the Teatro São João: As a result of Law Number 2146 of 14 May 1881, theatrical support of the emancipation fund for liberation of provincial slaves became compulsory. Established by the provincial assembly, the law demanded, for this purpose, the liquid earnings of one performance or recital of any lyric or dramatic company working in a public theater. During the tenth anniversary festivities on 6 July 1881, certificates of freedom were granted and Salvador newspapers reaffirmed the 1872 agreement not to publish advertisements of the commerce or escape of slaves.

Action in support of the liberation of the slaves in Bahia, however, if compared with other cities, was not terribly efficacious. Abolitionist societies, "depois de uma existência curta, enlanguesciam, definhavam e morriam, sem ter conseguido exercer a menor influência sobre a população" (Fonseca 135) ("after a brief existence, languished, wasted away and died, without having managed to exert the slightest influence upon the population"). Slavery had penetrated every segment of society (*Falla* 118). There were economic interests involved in the preservation of rural slavery. More important, however, was the "imaginary" value of maintaining slavery, involving almost all segments of society: The slave proved the degraded, inferior position of the black in society, legitimizing the divisions between the freemen and slaves. Hence, the duplicity of the abolitionist celebration and the resistance of slave owners that marked the century's end.

To Sílio Boccanera (b. 1863) the fall of the monarchy was responsible for the decline of the Teatro São João (Boccanera 118). This lamented decline corresponded to the changes in the genres of theatrical programming: The domain of revues arrived and dominated, substituting for opera and drama.

The Theater finally gave in to the old, repressed forms of the humoristic genres—comedies and malicious songs. Also in the last decades of the nineteenth century, Bahia entered an economic decline caused by its products' loss of position in the international market. The depression of the Bahian economy and the modernizing signs of the new century's culture are mutually contrasting factors that contributed to the decline of the Teatro São João. The setting for the cultural affirmation of the emerging Brazilian nationalism in Bahia of the twentieth century was suddenly part of the plan for the urban reform of 1912. The Theater escaped from the destruction planned in the modernizing project of the municipal administration but was finally ravaged by a great fire on the night of 6 June 1923, right in the midst of Brazilian cultural Modernism.

A secondary setting for cultural life in the nineteenth century, inhabited by a more restricted elite of society, was the Bahia School of Medicine, thus named in 1832 as the result of the restructuring of the Surgical College of Medicine of 1808, and installed in the place where the Jesuit College had functioned from the sixteenth to the eighteenth centuries. Its importance as a center for receiving and disseminating scientific ideas of the day is notable from 1840 onward, when Positivist ideas began to be discussed as a result of Justiniano da Silva Gomes's thesis presentation in 1844 for the chair of physiology. Azevedo writes: "O sistema de concursos para as escolas superiores favorecia, à época, esse caráter de disputa e exibição de saber, sobretudo de mostra de atualidade, de modernidade e afoiteza de posições intelectuais e políticas" (Azevedo 131) ("At the time, the system of competition for academic chairs favored the exhibition of learning, and above all else of a display of actuality, modernity, and courageous intellectual and political stances"). The university associated the teaching of medicine with both reflections on society and belles lettres, thus developing a didactic tradition of spectacular lectures performed for applause. Doctoral dissertations, which signaled mandatory course completion, contributed to the elaboration of a medical culture in which science and literature were linked. Some of the dissertation titles are illustrative: "Considerações médico-filosóficas sobre a mulher" ["Medical-Philosophic Considerations on Women"], "Reflexões sobre a saudade" ["Reflections on Nostalgia"], "Sobre a influência das relgiões e particularmente da religião sobre a saúde pública" ["On the Influence of Religions and in Particular of Religion on Public Health"]. Even within the most rigorously deterministic Eurocentric perspective, blacks and Indians, peculiarities of climate, flora, fauna, and tropical society became objects of interest and academic investigation to the naturalists who had incessantly visited Bahia since the eighteenth century. Bahia is situated on the margins of these central foci, but through the fissures it is possible to observe a city inhabited by the poor, blacks, and *mestizos* who populated its streets, gave it color, a sound, and a flavor different from the rest of the country. The secular project of knowledge and nationalization of society did not take into consideration the cultural expression of nonwhite cultures and did not foresee the strength and force of their resistance. To stop the relaxation of European customs, to polish manners, and to purify language—these were the pragmatic preoccupations of the lettered classes.

During the first decades of the twentieth century, the most representative locus of the cultural milieu in Bahia was still the old School of Medicine, where grandiloquence and traditionalism were predominant. The beginning of the new century did not alter the crisis in the Bahian agro-mercantile economy, which had been deteriorating steadily since 1879. The city, however, was not immune to the ideology of progress, to the modernizing impulse that dominated the mentality of the ruling elites of the young republic. The politics and the liberalizing of credit implemented by Bahian Minister of the Treasury Rui Barbosa gave the old provinces ample autonomy that resulted in an abundant money supply, and, with republican federalism, was a stimulus for urban reform. The essence of the ideology of urban progress was the strategy of substituting the new for the old (Barbosa 17). "Tearing down," as the administration of Rio de Janeiro's Francisco Pereira Passos became known, arrived in Bahia in 1912 during José Joaquim Seabra's administration with the aim of urban demolition: "Bahia material, que guarda ainda todos os característicos de uma cidade colonial de três séculos atraz, vae desapparecer para ceder lugar a uma cidade moderna, construída sob os preceitos rigorosos do progresso" ("Material Bahia, which still retains all the characteristics of a Colonial city of three centuries ago, will disappear to give way to a modern city, built by the rigorous precepts of progress"). The full program published by the *Gazeta do Povo* [People's Gazette], on 29 June 1912, gives us a good idea of the beginnings of an intense campaign to present the state government's project; the campaign to win over public opinion was thus initiated by the press of the day. Also in 1912, improvements were carried out in the city, and rows of old houses made way for avenues, widening the narrow strip between the city and the sea in the docks region, so as to allow for the circulation of motor vehicles, but also in the name of "aformoseamento e higiene" ("beautification and hygiene"), as Bahians were informed in that year's June 13 edition of the *Diário de Notícias* (Peres 36–8). The nucleus of the old Colonial metropolis, where the most expressive architectural monuments were located in narrow, winding streets, constituted the most problematic area for the city's modernization and the circulation of vehicles, especially streetcars. The reform plan called for the demolition, among many others, of sixteenth-century buildings such as the Igreja da Ajuda–without much protest except from the Geographical and Historical Institute–and the Diocese Church, and beyond these many more recent constructions no less relevant to the cultural history of the city, such as the Teatro São João.

In June 1912, on five consecutive days, the *Jornal de Notícias* presented its readers with an insert coupon that asked "What does the city need most?" Within the context of arguments in favor of the progressive sanitizing and beautifying of the city, the question received symptomatic and articulate responses that document the opinion of an anonymous, diffuse, and broad segment of the culture–the dwellers of the Lettered City reached by the written media. Suggestions for the demolition of the Teatro São João–"filthy, despicable"–demonstrate both an unpredictable contempt and the changes that were taking place in mentalities and social institutions. The exceptional value of the results of this survey as an expression of the social imaginary, however, lies in a vein other than the reformist and sanitizing one that emerges from the responses: that of the racial. In an inquiry into public opinion on the urban reform in question, reader response recommended: that the government encourage the emigration of blacks or resort to the expulsion or to deportation of the black race. This was the change Bahia needed the most, they said, revealing the rejection by the lettered class of the social reality of Bahia.

According to available records on this public survey, there is no direct reference in the answers to the old Diocese of Bahia, built during the colony's first general government (Peres 44), but it is with regard to it that, between 1912 and the beginning of its destruction in 1932, a heated debate began in Bahia, involving multiple elements of society and different perspectives, revealing a broad and complex clash of ideologies that gave expression to all of the city's lettered forces. Recovered and publicized by the contemporary poet and researcher Fernando da Rocha Peres (b. 1936) in his book *Memória da Sé* [Record of the Cathedral], this long controversy may be read as a moment in which literati, intellectuals, liberal professionals, politicians, merchants, entrepreneurs, priests and the faithful, the press and its reading public–all of civil society with access to the written word–sees itself compelled to articulate a point of view about the historical memory of the city, its present reality, and the societal expectations for the future. Center stage in this cathartic spectacle of unusual duration is the conflict between, on the one hand, forces favorable to the demolition: the public administration wanting to carry out its conception of city government; the bureaucracy of the Catholic Church set on defining the material value of the building and ways in which it would be compensated; the English concessionaire of the streetcar services, Companhia Circular de Carris da Bahia (the railway company), seeking an effective and economical path for its vehicles, willing to pay the costs for the transfer of the diocese; and spokesmen for modernizing rationality, progress, and technical solutions. To these could be added an articulate fraction of the population mobilized by the expectation of improvement in the quality of urban life, in a city with a heritage of nearly four centuries of neglect of its streets and of the public welfare, as Frei Vicente Salvador had pointed out. On the other hand, the opposite reaction was intense and its voices various, led by intellectuals and artists, but encompassing a wide spectrum of society, for the chief value of the Bahian imaginary was at stake, its institutional and cultural difference–the memory and prominence of the Colonial metropolis, given material form in the old Diocese of Bahia. To the general cultural imaginary, its demolition meant a destruction of the symbolic value of Bahia itself.

In the traditionalist and rhetorical Bahian context, under the aegis of the School of Medicine and to the echoes of controversy throughout the diocese, the Modernist revolution and the repertory of ideas of São Paulo's Modern Art Week of 1922 had no immediate repercussions. The first signs of aesthetic renewal did not appear in Bahia until 1927, with the publication of *Moema* by Eugênio Gomes (1897–1972) and the *Balada de Outro Preto* [Ballad of Another Black Man], the poet Godofredo Filho's (1904–1992) first book. Literary societies continued to insist on cultural change and, among these, there were groups with Modernist links but with divergences from the cultural hegemony of São Paulo Modernism and its self-appointed role as arbiter of literary modernization. In Bahia the common objective was the renewal of Bahian literature and participation in the construction of a national literature.

From 1928 to 1929, the *Arco & Flexa* (Bow and Arrow) group, led by Carlos Chiacchio–who had experience writing book reviews for various newspapers–published five issues in two volumes of a magazine by the same name. The group's intentions were collected in a manifesto entitled "Tradicionalismo Dinâmico" ["Dynamic Traditionalism"]. Devoid of the aggressive tone and inaugural posturing typical of the avant-garde that had inspired the São Paulo movement, the manifesto clearly announced its intention to establish a dialogue with Bahia's predominantly conservative lettered population in pursuit of literary renewal (Chiacchio 2–3). Carlos Chiacchio's manifesto criticized the aesthetic experimentation of São Paulo 1922 as showing undesirable European influence, and instead advocated cultural ties with other Latin American countries, particularly Mexico and Uruguay, but referring also to the United States–"all America seeks itself," he claimed. In short, what was called for was a dynamic, reelaborated continuity of tradition, deemed indispensable to the preservation of the country as an American culture. The Indian allusion in the group's self-designation as well as in the title of its magazine–*Arco & Flexa*–did not bring them any closer, as might seem to be the case at first glance, to the "primitivism" that had stimulated part of Brazilian Modernism. Chiacchio's essay-manifesto rejected any resemblance with the anthropophagic cultural logic of Oswald de Andrade (1890–1954), considering it insensitive to the elapsed historical interval and thus nothing more than the impoverished expression of a constructed and artificial tradition. The literary stand taken in *Arco & Flexa* clearly translated into a refusal of a rupture of any sort and offered a broad diversity of degrees of commitment to aesthetic renewal in its attempt to include various modernizing attempts of the end of the century (Alves 44).

In the spirit of controversy (which appears to have become a strong trait in Bahian intellectual history), a second Modernist group was formed at about the same time, which combined literary concerns with political criticism. Made up of young writers, artists, and intellectuals, it was led by the older João Amaro Pinheiro Viegas (1865–1937), an epigrammatist much esteemed by his contemporaries who had been an active participant in the abolitionist and republican campaigns. Even their name–Academia dos Rebeldes (The Academy of Rebels)–contrasted with the older generation gathered around Carlos Chiacchio (1884–1947). Among its members were novelists Clóvis Amorim (1911–1970), João Cordeiro (b. 1914), and Dias da Costa (1878–1935), folklorist Édison de Sousa Carneiro (1912–1972), poet Sosígenes Costa (1901–1968), and the young Jorge Amado (1912–2001), who was not yet an active participant in any literary activities but who, a short while later, was to shake the cultural scene by gaining for Bahia the recognition of its cultural centrality in Brazilian literature through novels that would be disseminated throughout the country and abroad. The importance of this group in the cultural history of Bahia is in large part owed to him (*Jorge Amado* 1961). As a result of its irreverent posture, quite different from that of *Arco & Flexa*, this group did not have much influence on the literary life of the decade, and was considered a sort of underground movement more attentive to Bahia's masses and especially to the city's black population.

During the hundred years between the last decades of the nineteenth century and the last of the twentieth century, divergent images of identity were developed in Bahia, emerging from the tension between the Portuguese Colonial matrix and the *banto* and especially the *jèje-nagô* African repertories. The current recognition, in the social reality of Bahia, of cultural practices and representations of black African roots is the result of this fertile process.

On 13 May 1888, along with the rest of the country, Bahia commemorated the abolition of slavery. In a conservative society that mythicized its past as a Colonial metropolis, this moment of institutional rupture with the master–slave polarity was when the free black became a fundamental question to be elaborated on at length by the Lettered City. Neither the important import–export merchants nor the proprietor landowners of the local oligarchy had any interest in altering the social and economic structure, and the city did not undergo any significant change in its demographic composition. It remained the most miscegenated of Brazilian cities; it was still the "black citadel" that received millions of Africans annually throughout the nineteenth century. At the end of that century, the development of cocoa farming attracted large numbers of workers and spared the city from having to accept more migration from rural zones. Since blacks made up a majority of the population and its workforce, and the frightening example of past slave rebellions was still present in the collective memory, the policy of *escamotear* or minimizing the racial issue was an efficient mechanism in discouraging the organization of nonwhites (see Reis 1986). It is within this context that the assimilationist discourse of racial harmony begins. Simultaneously, however, in order to maintain current social order without altering the positions occupied by blacks and whites and while preventing the social mobilization of Afro-Brazilians, it became indispensable to reaffirm white supremacy and the inferiority of ex-slaves. Color was a preeminent element in discourses, and racial terms indicated not only skin color but also acted as a sign of status in the organization of society and the distribution of power. Racial hierarchy situated whites at the top, blacks at the bottom, and, in the intermediate position, mulattos or *mestizos*, objectively closer to the blacks yet differentiated enough to encourage the belief in mobility and the project of assimilation (see Bacelar 1997a).

The dominant white politics regarding black cultural practices were quite diverse, especially toward those of African origin. The problem was not in the cultural differences, which were tolerable and even necessary, but in the fear of a rupture with regard to the instituted cultural order. Thus began a politics of exclusion of all African presence in the city's scenery, expressly visible in the systematic repression of the *candomblés* during the first decades of the century (see Braga; Luhning). The prohibition was not aimed at the culture itself or actual African-born individuals who were, after all, few and elderly in 1888 (see Bacelar 1997b), but at the black population in general as bearer of backwardness and barbarism and symbolic of incivility. As long as they did not break the rules of public behavior and expose their "abominable" practices, blacks were allowed to keep their bit of space, yet stay invisible to the city's minority white population. The autonomous formulation of a black Bahian world took place under these circumstances. During the sixteenth and seventeenth centuries, the slave trade brought the Bantu of Angola and the old Congo kingdom. Starting at the end of the eighteenth century, however, the slave trade turned to the coast of Senegal and the Gulf of Benin, and then to subequatorial Africa; the Bantu slaves lost their majority (see Verger). However, despite the continuous process of acculturation, the Bantu have left deep marks on Bahian society. It was the Bantu who instituted the important Brotherhood of the Black Rosary in the Pelourinho, created during the sixteenth century and which exists to the present day; the Bantu languages were very much present in popular speech (see Yedda Pessoa Castro; Riserio 1988, 154) and were present in the carnival, toward the end of the nineteenth century, in groups such as the Pândegos da Africa (the African Revelers) (Rodrigues 180); the Bantu were also responsible for the introduction of *capoeira* and samba in Bahia and maintained their religious traditions through the "angola" and "congo" *candomblés*. A period of marked Sudanese influence began at the end of the eighteenth century with the arrival of the *fon* of Benin, identified as *jèjes*, and the *yoruba*, better known as *nagos*. Because they came in larger numbers, and because of the constant interchange with the West African coast, they quickly exerted considerable influence and in the nineteenth century came to occupy a central place in Brazilian African cultures, making Bahia an Africanized city and taking up a dominant place among the workforce and in street culture (Querino 87–9; see also Reis 1993).

Despite the persecution and prohibition of the *candomblé* at the beginning of the twentieth century, it was around the *família-de-santo*, the *terreiros*, and the religious communities, with their *orixás* and *voduns*, that a new model of social organization was created that would become the mark of black cultural survival in Bahia (see Rodrigues; Bastide; Lima 1977). Religion and rituals of initiation, were major elements in black Bahia; in these they recreated their dances, music, chant, sacrifices, and offerings. Transformative and dynamic, these elements spread throughout the city's homes and streets. The *afoxés* of carnival, the percussion music, the "food of the gods" (which transformed "Bahian cuisine"), the popular tales, artistic traditions of woodcutting and metal engraving, forms of expressing affection, familial matriarchy, and extended forms of kinship and solidarity—all are the common and constant aspects of everyday life for black Bahian society since the end of the nineteenth century (Herskovits 92; Bacelar 1997a, 24); this culture has been strengthened by the ethnodemographic stability of the population and by the cultural separation of Bahia from the culture of southern Brazil (Risério 1988, 163–64). The politics of de-Africanization of Bahia, although always desired by the dominant white groups, was not capable of supplanting the popular, cultural world of the blacks with its solid African roots. The city of Bahia maintained its Colonial Portuguese traditions but also became irreversibly Afro-Brazilian.

From 1930 to 1950 Bahia underwent no substantial alterations to its economy beyond the exchange, in the agro-export sector, of cocoa for sugar as the principal product. In politics, with the Revolution of 1930, there was a greater centralization of power and the opposition, which appeared during the period, belonged to an influential elite formed by traditional political forces, maintaining the same political style of the old republic—based on violence and on the pact with the "colonels." For the workers, with the exception of some new employment opportunities resulting from the growth of the state's bureaucratic machine and a marginal increase in access to education, what remained was the same degradation of impoverished living and work conditions for much of the population of Bahia. Blacks and *mestizos* continued to be a majority—a constant 70 percent of workers throughout the city's history—and were the greatest victims of white domination. *Candomblé* continued to be the object of police persecution, and another stigmatizing designation was added to those of the past: "Ninhos da propaganda comunista" (Landes 70; Dantas 97–115) ("nests of Communist propaganda"). In spite of this, "os candomblés cresciam em número e afirmavam-se com a apropriação de valores da sociedade inclusiva, capitalizavam-se, compravam terrenos nos limites do centro urbano, construíam terreiros que se tornariam centros comunitários,

com organização hierárquica bem definida e rigorosa, em que a autoridade do líder e a solidariedade interfrupal eram a norma dominante e indiscutível" (Lima 1987, 40) ("the candomblé grew in number and affirmed itself with accumulated capital, purchased land on the outskirts of the urban center, constructed *terreiros* which later became community centers, with a well-defined and rigorous hierarchical organization in which the authority of the leader and intergroup solidarity were the dominant, undisputed norm").

At the same time they transformed themselves into civil societies, "com diretorias executivas que se encarregavam das relações efetivas de cada grupo com o sistema de poder do Estado e, sobretudo, estendiam a rede do parentesco espiritual para além das fronteiras étnicas e de classe" (Lima 1987, 40) ("with executive boards in charge of effective relationships between each group and with the State's power system and, above all, they extended the network of spiritual kinship beyond ethnic and class boundaries"). African religions were "nationalized," transformed into the religions of Bahian blacks.

As this social reality imposed another interpretation of Brazil, foreign racial theories that had been adapted to describe the Brazilian situation now became outmoded (see Skidmore; Schwarz). The work of Gilberto Freyre (1900–1987), with its myth of three races fused in the construction of a harmonious *mestizo* society, was also challenged by the social demands for multicultural diversity (Ortiz 1985, 40). The effective result of such an interpretation–divulged and ritually celebrated in everyday relationships and major events such as carnival and soccer–was the camouflaging of relations of power and growing violence between racial groups. The official government propagation of the myth of racial democracy, greeted positively by all the intellectual and political currents of Brazil, represented for Bahia the reiteration of the old stance taken by the dominant groups; it was nothing more than the continuation of the party line of the old republic. What was innovative on the national scene was, for the government of Bahia and its dominant white population, merely a reiteration of the politics of the "old mulatta"–the pejorative name by which Bahia was referred to in the country's southern press as far back as the beginning of the nineteenth century.

In the case of Bahia, however, a new element was added. An intellectual avant-garde–which included Jorge Amado, Édison de Sousa Carneiro, and Artur Ramos (1903–1949)–largely opposed to both local and national government, initiated a discourse laudatory of the African contribution to the formation of Bahian culture. In varying degrees and with different nuances, these discourses reflected the multiple stimuli of Gilberto Freyre, northeastern regionalism, and the Brazilian Communist Party's 1935 manifesto of assimilation of cultural heritage by proposing the privileged taking of elements present in the popular manifestations with the aim of creating a new nationalism that would oppose the particular elements of popular culture to the cosmopolitanism of the dominant classes (see Almeida).

In 1936, in keeping with this concept of the assimilation of popular cultural heritage, Jorge Amado, by now a nationally renowned Communist Party member, published *Jubiabá*, which, aside from incorporating elements of Afro-Bahian culture–religion, music, dance, martial arts, and oral tradition–had a black fictional character at the center of its narrative, young Antônio Balduíno, articulating, with the predictable hierarchy of Marxist postulates, issues ranging from that of race to the process of conscience raising and proletarian struggle. According to Amado himself, *Jubiabá* represented the poverty and resistance of the blacks: "o meu novo romance procura refletir a vida dos pretos da Bahia, poetas que vivem à miséria maior, sofrendo todos os pre-conceitos de raça que ainda dominam no Brasil e resistem a tudo bravamente sem perder aquela gargalhada clara, aquele poder de rir, de cantar, de lutar, que só os negros possuem" (in Tati 77) ("my new novel seeks to reflect the life of blacks in Bahia, poets who live in the greatest misery, suf-fering every racial prejudice still extant in Brazil and strug-gling bravely without losing that clear laugh, that ability to laugh, to sing, to fight, which only blacks possess").

Given the novel's immediate repercussions, the heroic image of the black man resulted in a powerful instrument of interethnic communication, revealing racial relationships more effectively than those previously admitted and dis-cussed by lettered Bahian society, confronting it with a pluri-secular racism (see Ramos). At the same time, both in Brazil and abroad, *Jubiabá* strengthened and disseminated the image of Bahia as a black city–an epithet repeated throughout the novel and transformed into the title in many of its transla-tions. This could be read, on the one hand, as an ethnocentric move to exoticism, or on the other hand, as an intellectual challenge for the state, in a society symptomatic of the ambi-guities and intensities of the racial questions inherited from the Colonial and slavocratic times.

One year after the novel was published, the markedly cul-turalist and political orientation of the second Afro-Brazilian Congress reiterated the role of Bahia as a center of dissemina-tion of a differentiated perspective on racial matters. The Con-gress was held during the difficult political time of the inauguration of the Estado Novo (Vargas's New State) and the government's position, *tomada de posição*, in favor of the Ger-man and Italian fascists; under white gaze and official supervi-sion, the Second Congress was a great event in the union of races, with authorities, men of science and the people valoriz-ing the cultural manifestations of African origin–*capoeira*, *batu-que*, samba and cuisine, and especially *candomblé* (Oliveira 28–30). As in the First Congress (which had taken place in 1934 at the Regionalist Center for the Northeast, in Recife), the Com-munist Party participated in the event (see Carneiro), influenc-ing congressional approval of resolutions on popular culture and motions in support of freedom of religious expression for Afro-Brazilian religions. Besides demonstrating a strong con-cern with the preservation and valuing of black culture in Bra-zil, this position stimulated the taking of political stands against the rise of racism in Europe and against discrimination against blacks in Brazil. From this Congress came the creation of the Union of Afro-Brazilian Sects of Bahia, but only in 1947 did the struggle against discrimination receive formal attention in the State Legislature, when Jorge Amado, then a Federal Dep-uty of the Constitutional Assembly, presented and managed to win approval of the amendment which assured freedom of reli-gious expression throughout the country.

In the social context created by the Second Congress in the late thirties there was a decline in political expressions of exclusion of Afro-Brazilian culture in the Lettered City of offi-cial and academic Bahia. Bahia became black, African and, above all, *jèje-nagô*; a constant repertory of intellectuals and politicians strived to recognize its unique character. At the same time, its African-ness was discovered by the interna-tional intelligentsia, including people such as Donald Pierson, Melville Herskovits, Ruth Landes, Roger Bastide and Pierre Verger. Intellectuals and politicians, however, did not work with a blank slate. Black culture crossed various fields, forged allegiances among black leaders who developed an intelligent politics of negotiation for the affirmation of their culture in an inclusive society (Lima 1987, 39–65). Bahia consisted of an active world, seeking mutual respect and dialogue with white society, although it still maintained itself, in a certain sense, in a parallel mode, without manifesting its differences very visi-bly. Literary, academic, or scientific recognition of the Afri-can presence in a society where Africans no longer existed served as a defining element of Bahian uniqueness, but could not reverse, let alone radically separate itself from, the histori-cal legacy of slavery.

Starting in the 1950s, and above all in the 1960s, a com-plete transformation took place in Bahia which had manifest repercussions on the lives of blacks in society. The new indus-trialization, an extension of the industrial development of the southeast, sparked profound changes in the city and its space. Modern industry was installed in the industrial center of Aratu and later in the Camaçarí petrochemical complex, with a large concentration of capital, dedicated to the production of intermediary goods; this soon became the dynamic core of the regional economy. With the expansion of industrial employment and opportunities for advancement in both pub-lic and commercial jobs, blacks were able to obtain formal employment and thus have some chance at social mobility. Unlike the past when they "knew their place" and, in a way, kept themselves invisible, upward social mobility now brought them into direct contact with color barriers until then unnoticed (Sansone 72). They knew the subtle mechanisms of discrimination still in force within Bahian society, notwith-standing the ideological apparatus of the state in its multiple diffusions, which emphasized the equality of relations between individuals and distinct groups, and promoted, at the national and international levels, its image as a model of racial harmony. The myths of racial democracy and cultural democracy allied themselves with the celebration of Africa and the foreign black, which was to the liking of the local intelligentsia. This perspective, though rooted in the ambigu-ity of the forces of exaltation and control of black pride, made room for traditional organizations and the cultural practices of blacks. *Candomblé* had become an increasingly synchretized and pluralistic popular religion, with initiates and followers of all races and social classes. At the same time, however, an articulate segment of the *terreiros*, above all of the oldest fami-lies, began to react against religious synchretism and valorize the return to ancient African roots. The *cozinha de azeite* became the typical cuisine of Bahia. *Capoeira* regained its Angolan roots. High and low art openly explored Bahia's African roots. And, in the words of black songwriter Gilberto Gil, all these elements were including everything, remaking the imaginary of *Baianidade* (Bahiana people).

Institutionalized culture and the arts were also being remade in the fifties. In 1947 the Federal University of Bahia was built and led by its creator Edgard Santos, principal agent of the transformations in his fifteen years as dean. In the multiple paths emerging in the renewal of race relations in society, cul-ture and knowledge, the university played a crucial, catalyzing role in confirming the modernizing values in three basic disci-plines: geology, geophysics and chemistry (stimulated by the new petroleum economy), the arts, and the human and social sciences. In the latter, the School of Philosophy explored a par-adoxical heritage, benefiting from the tradition of ethnographic studies developed in the old School of Medicine. Anthropology and sociology expanded, notably with the stimulus of names such as Roger Bastide and Pierre Verger.

However, the principal merit of this process of institutional construction lies in the opening up of Bahia itself; after a century and a half of isolation, the city entered into a cosmopolitan dialogue with the postwar avant-garde (Risério 1995, 21), brought to Bahia through skilful utilization of the post-war diaspora of European intellectuals such as Italian architect and designer Lina Bo Bardi, the classical music and atonal-dodecaphonic aesthetic proponent Austrian Joachim Koellreuter, the modern dance choreographer Yanka Rudzka of Poland, and the Portuguese anthropologist Agostinho da Silva, whose development of cultural and political connections with contemporary Africa resulted in the creation of the Centro de Estudos Afro-Orientais (Center for Afro-Oriental Studies). Among the countless new centers for cultural interchange with foreign countries, such as the Franco-Brasileiro, Estudos Norte Americanos, Cultura Hispánica, Estudos Portugueses, created by the university, the CEAO was of special relevance because of its influence on Brazilian foreign politics, the institutionalization of Brazil's relations with Africa, and the inauguration of an institutional base for continued dialogue among the academy, the black diaspora, and marginalized social groups in Bahia. What had formerly been done, for example, through the free iorubá courses which brought together social scientists and members of the black community interested in exploring their roots or, through the mediation of foreign intellectuals, was now centered in the University from which came the invigorating linkages and transit between erudite forms of the avant-garde and popular traditions (Castro and Cunha 49).

The "dialética entre informação cosmopolitas" ("dialectic between cosmopolitan information") brought in by the university and "a realidade antropológica que encontrou" ("the anthropological reality which was found in the city's everyday life and traditions") (Risério 1995, 25; 75) resulted in creative effervescence and experimentalism, and in the transformation of Bahia into an active cultural center, renewed and renewing, with sufficient power to invert, at least temporarily, the inward direction of the flow of cultural influence (which since the end of the eighteenth century had been fixed in the direction south central to northeast). Bahia's culture indelibly marked Brazilian cultural production, bringing onto the main stage aesthetic, political, and cultural theories and practices which dislocated the reactionary national-popular culture, sponsored by the authoritarianism of the New State during Getúlio Vargas's first administration, and which were reappropriated and transformed in the sixties (by the populism of the Left in the Popular Centers for Culture), into instruments of mass conscientização (consciousness raising).

The experimentalism generated in Bahia proved itself capable of creative production even while the country was submerged in its most violent and repressive military dictatorship (which began in 1964); such cultural innovation broke through the customary limitations of the traditional settings—theater, literature, concerts, and recitals—and opened itself to the developments of the mass communications media and the culture industry. Filmmaker Glauber Rocha and songwriter Caetano Veloso are among its most renowned heirs. They studied at the Universidade Federal da Bahia and enjoyed its climate of open cultural debate, as well as the theatrical productions, film showings and music recitals promoted or stimulated by that institution. The films of the Cinema Novo—with its significant Terra em Transe [Land in Danger] and Deus e o Diabo na Terra do Sol [God and the Devil in the Land of the Sun] by Glauber Rocha—and popular music—the tropicalismo of Caetano Veloso—are expressions of the desire to reshape innovatively and creatively the mixture of the traditional and the new, the rural and the urban, the erudite and the popular, the latter already understood as a heritage of the ancestral cultures of black slaves. These cultural expressions, coming out of Bahia through the media, especially radio, television and cinema, had great impact on a Brazilian culture saturated with North American products. The old and the modern coexisted in Bahia without any implied backwardness or difficulty in elaborating cultural products for an urban, industrialized society. Hence the tropicalist artistic movement, through its innovative appropriation of the historical legacy, and its high standing in the cultural market (as well as its anthropophagic appropriation of foreign influences), has made for itself an appreciable place in the Brazilian life and has become the Brazilian contribution to the debate about postmodern aesthetic and cultural globalization (see Sovik). Invigorating artistic modernization and connections with the media and the culture industry created a favorable environment for the social legitimation for the powerful Afro-black cultural movements being developed and strengthened in Bahia, though these were never immediately or directly affected by the popularity the derivative expressions achieved in the south of Brazil and abroad.

Starting in 1970, the blacks in Bahia elaborated a new expression for carnival, reviving the old dance afoxés but in a contemporary form and creating Afro blocos such as the Ilê-Aiyê, in a reaction to white carnival; the aim was to celebrate Brazilian as well as international black culture. In a dynamic way, these reinvented African roots were revived in the display of massed drums, in the songs, dress, and dance, creating a sentiment of blackness as an identifying signature. Culture thus took its place in the ideology and politics of the construction of black social identity in the city of Bahia. It was during the 1980s that it became dominant among black and mulatto youth. The affirmation of black pride, however, spread throughout the entire social body: the pride in being black, as well as the creation of black spaces, invaded the city, symbolically occupying the historical center and the old Pelourinho Square, restored by the state government as part of an urban mega-project with clearly touristic-commercial intentions. A new, contemporary black culture and identity was configured, less involved with traditional African aspects—although, on many levels, these are still the basic, reinterpreted reference points—but, rather, it is now "pautada na cor, na consciência da cor, no orgulho, no modo de disposição e apresentação original do corpo negro" (Sansone 75) ("based on color, on awareness of color, on pride, on original ways of arranging and presenting the black body"); these are ethnic symbols which not only sprang from the Afro-Brazilian world, but also from the black populations of other countries or of modern international black culture, above all in music, hair styling, and attire (Sansone 75–77). These symbols were the fruit of the real and imaginary dialogues which black youth, through organized movements and cultural production, initially established with Portuguese Africa, soon after the Colonial liberation in 1975 and, subsequently, with the United States and, more closely and intensely, with Jamaica. This movement of cultural globalization rejected belonging to a nationality—a nationality which, in fact, had never included them.

Cultural production here in the postmodern era, with the economy as its axis, follows a globalizing, standardizing logic, but is also sensitive to individual identities and connections with the local (Ortiz 1994, 181–82). Receptiveness to foreign countries was not new to the dominant groups which had always imported foreign trends and manners, whether in the merely imitative way of the nineteenth century, or as part of an anthropophagic strategy of appropriation, as in the Bahia during the sixties. What is new is the counterpart to this glo-balized stimulus, a valorization of the local and of cultural dif-ference which affects all layers of society (given the efficacy of the media and the cultural industry) and thus moves Bahians of all races to assimilate, in a positive sense, the creative explosion of the blacks, above all, in dance and music, into a picture of Bahian-ness, an identifying mark of society. For those groups that only identify with whites, the response to this contemporary cultural explosion had two sides: a rein-forcement of the old myth of Bahia as a racial paradise, reject-ing any form of ethnic polarization, seeking to make both traditional culture and the new black culture a symbol of the Bahian life and, simultaneously, and perhaps primarily, the recognition of Bahia's insertion within the capitalist circuit of symbolic goods, transmuted into merchandise at home and abroad.

The year 1993, for example, was one of both national (Bra-zilian) and international acclaim for Bahian carnival; there was extensive media exposure of the exotic difference of *Olo-dum*, and *axé* music of *Timbalada*, and the urban music of Dan-iela Mercury, the self-described "blackest white girl in Bahia." Carnival in Bahia is basically a black event, but it also brings with it a sense of egalitarian celebration; it is an extraordinary expression of racial and cultural democracy, in spite of the rigid norms by which it is organized and the separations established and maintained by the police lines, which isolate middle class spectators and the thousands of tourists from the *blocos* ("groups of dancers") of blacks and the black-*mestizo* population which make up the celebration. This transforma-tion of black art into a commercial product of the culture industry has had great impact as a differentiator of status among the distinct schools; those elected "winners," whose work is eminently exportable, have great access to the inter-national market—as has been the case with the *Olodum* and *Areketu* groups and the songwriter Carlinhos Brown. The art-ists are representatives of "sincretismos desconsagrados" (Canevacci 173) ("noncanonic syncretism"), but surprisingly they have also provoked the flourishing of nonsyncretic forms, those based on purity, originality, and a denial of syn-cretism, such as the *candomblés* of the traditional homes and the primitive *Ilê Aiyê*.

Access to the international market of symbolic goods has generated contrasting visions and continued disputes in the black community and, in time, institutionalization trans-formed the divisions into interest groups geared to fundrais-ing for their social group or for personal benefit. The status of black groups and individuals began to be measured by their acceptance on the international market and not by traditional values. Another serious problem was generated by the super-valorization of the limited economy born of the culture indus-try, confusing it with effective black participation in the labor force. Furthermore, the meager participation in the profits of cultural production coming to local artists, the dominant white groups reiterated the stigmatization of inferiority and described blacks as incapable of reason, thus justifying the nonmobility of blacks in society and their exclusion from the work force. However, the longstanding historical racism of a Bahia which would prefer to see itself as white has been obliged to restrict its pejorative articulation to a controlled closet, albeit one that is overflowing; ironically this is the inverse movement to the one which, for over four centuries, has compelled the Afro-Bahian population to express its rejection of white domination. Precious little though this self-restriction may seem, it still distinguishes the city of Bahia from other Brazilian cities, where not even progressive intel-lectuals oppose the use of historically pejorative terms to des-ignate blacks.

Although the current state of affairs (with its increased unemployment and a downturn in economic activity) does not favor the transformation of living conditions for Bahian blacks or other Brazilians, the primordial fact for Bahia as a cultural center and in terms of its identity construction, is that its black cultural forms have been imposed on the life of the city, bestowing upon it an exportable physiognomy all its own, forcing the white elites to recognize it "sob pena de se transformarem em estrangeiras na sua própia terra e de serem vistas, pelo que nos visitam, como segmentos não-baianos da Bahia" (Risério 1997, 56) ("under penalty of becoming stran-gers in their own land and being seen, by those who visit us, as non-Bahian segments of Bahia"). There have been, how-ever, more effective results. Culture has given visibility to blacks as an historical group, to the point that the Brazilian State has recognized racism as a social problem and devel-oped specific public policies, such as the inclusion of a national black hero, Zumbi dos Palmares, in the official histo-ries taught in schools. Even so, full-rights citizenship remains a remote concept for blacks and *mestizos* who make up the majority of the low income population. The flagrant contra-diction of Bahia–where "negromestiços ocupam todo o espaço e quase todo o tempo dos *mass media* . . . suas mani-festações e seus produtos estéticos reinam de forma pratica-mente absoluta" (Risério 1997, 66) ("black mestizos occupy all the space and almost all the time in the mass media . . . their manifestations and their aesthetic products reign to all intents and purposes almost absolutely")–received a lucid diagnosis by poet and anthropologist Antônio Risério, when he said "que, usando livremente os conceitos de Gramsci, podemos afirmar tranqüilamente que, na Bahia de hoje, a cultura negro-mestiça não é dominante, mas é, certamente, hegemônica" ("that, by freely employing Gramsci's concepts, we may safely state that, in Bahia today, black mestizo culture is not dominant but it is certainly hegemonic") (1997, 66). Such lucidity is made possible precisely by giving primacy to local complexity in the interpretive scheme.

The cultural hegemony of noncitizens has been fictionally reconstituted by Bahian writer João Ubaldo Ribeiro (b. 1941) in *Viva o povo brasileiro* [Long Live the Brazilian Race] published in 1984, a daring, polyphonic narrative which restages the social and cultural history of Brazil from the perspective of Bahia, from the sixteenth to the twentieth centuries, through the story of two families. Both the discourse and the imaginary expressed by the white and *mestizo* characters (whose voices were historically repressed) come together to trace a panorama in which the accent is always on the imaginary and symboli-cally legitimized violence of the white over the black mestizo, in social relations as well as in the expression of cultural hybridism. This is the Bahian story which the novel, from its very title, transforms into the saga of a people in search of their affirmation, in the words of the jacket blurb. Ribeiro's novel may be read as a literary contribution to a roster of initiatives which today project the imaginary and cultural production of Bahia, and which privilege the black matrices of Brazilian identity. In it are visible both the destabilizing intention against instituted tradition and the transference of value to the black-*mestizo* cultural expression (see Cunha 1993a).

It was in the eighties that the novels and short stories of Bahian writers like Sonia Coutinho (b. 1939) and Helena Parente Cunha (b. 1929) began to appear on the Brazilian cultural scene. Their narratives single out the reversal of Western values in privileging the strong articulation of relationships of gender and inter-ethnic relationships which lie at the heart of Bahian lived experience. Published in 1980, Coutinho's *O Jogo do Ifá* [The Ifá Game] tells the cultural history of Bahia in the last decades through one woman's personal story, exploring both the interchange between an intellectualized white middle class and the city's black culture and the gaps between men and women, between the hegemonic culture and Afro-Bahian culture. In *Atire em Sofia* [1989; Shoot Sofia], Sonia Coutinho dispenses with the mediation of the white middle class; the principal characters are women who accept their blackness, middle-class Afro-descendents, and spokespersons for local culture. The nexus between an overcoming of the limits of the feminine condition (forged by white, patriarchal, conservative society) and inter-ethnic experience on the sexual plane may also be read in Helena Parente Cunha's novel *A mulher no espelho* [1983; *The Woman Between Mirrors*, 1989], which updates and rewrites the relationships between the mansion and the slave's quarters (topoi given great significance in the modern Brazilian tradition by Gilberto Freyre) from the perspective of a white woman.

Poetry by black writers has begun to gain ground; it is published predominantly in the journals of organized social groups and movements such as the *Boletim Informativo do Movimento Negro Unificado*–MNU (Informative Bulletin of the Unified Black Movement). Both Jônatas Conceição da Silva (b. 1952), in his collections *Miragens do Engenho* [1984; Plantation Mirages] and *Outras Miragens* [1989; Other Mirages], and José Carlos Limeira (b. 1951), in *O arco íris negro* [1979; The Black Rainbow] and *Atabaques* (1984), have established themselves as voices with great resonance, though their poetry is, symptomatically, still labeled as alternative poetry. Published in 1996, in the *Cadernos Negros: Poemas Afro-Brasileiros* [Black Books: Afro-Brazilian Poems], Jônatas Conceição's poem "Porto sem mar" ["Port without Sea"] is powerful in its deconstructive turning upon the principal and primordial image of the port of the city of São Salvador da Bahia de Todos os Santos. Bahia, the place of reception, transit, exchange and admixture, when described from the perspective of black lived experience, it is also the place of exclusion and confinement:

Como um rio que não deságua
O porto desta cidade não me transporta....
Cá, nas campinas,
O porto inexiste, não por faltar o mar
Mas o amar.

O porto da minha cidade
Não me leva a um ponto salvador.
O porto que gostaria que tivesse na minha cidade
Carrego conmigo, à procura de um mar.

Like a river which does not flow
The port of this city does not transport me....
Here, in the grasslands,
The port does not exist, not because there is no sea
But because there is no love.

[Unfortunately, the wordplay between o mar (the sea) and amar (to love) is quite irretrievably lost in translation)]

The port of my city
Leads me not to a saving place.
The port I wished my city had
I carry with me, in search of the sea.

Despite the dissonance in expressing the instituted imaginary which may be read in João Ubaldo Ribeiro's novel or, more acutely, in the black poems, the most potent reproductions, absorptions or appropriations of Afro-Bahian cultural production which currently occur in Brazil project by inference the limits of the Lettered City, although they preserve and amplify the historical ambiguity between the inclusion and exclusion of blackness. This could be seen, for example, in the media coverage of the year 2000, the 500th anniversary of Brazil's discovery, and the city's 450th anniversary. Today the images, music, and artists predominantly chosen to represent Brazilian-ness to millions of spectators are of Afro-Bahian origin. It is the drums of *Olodum* and *Ilê Aiyê*, the body movements and interrupted sounds of Carlinhos Brown, the urban song of Daniela Mercury, the musicality of Gilberto Gil which brings the roots of a more traditional African-ness to contemporary pop, the voice of Caetano Veloso, that have a greater resonance in the current debate on Brazilian identity. From this boom in references to Afro-Bahian-ness, launched upon the country and exported with technological competence by the national media, one might simultaneously deduce the emergence of the cultural value of blackness and a will to invert a history of domination. The intense visibility won by Afro-Bahian culture is not immune to the domesticating, nationalizing effect but, despite all the mediations and negotiations imposed by the culture industry, this culture still retains a peculiar and latent threatening potential, through the ethnic imaginary which it stimulates, and through the alternative of recognition and belonging it offers. All of these are adverse to the primary loyalties which nationality or the national state demand that society as a whole recognize in a "fictional" and homogeneous ethnicity which has been created in Brazil through the repression of profound ethnic and social tensions, social separations, and the memory of the violence of slavery.

During its first centuries, the formative images and discourses of the Brazilian imaginary spread from the city of Bahia, the old Colonial, slaveholding *mestizo* metropolis, to the rest of the country and to Europe. In the nineteenth century, when the young nation appropriated this imaginary, Bahians had little to offer beyond the small, provincial insurrections and a nostalgia for the old cultural and political hegemonies. In the twentieth century, without freeing itself from a peripheral economic and political condition with regard to the rest of the country, the city of Bahia has returned as a center for the production of cultural identity, no longer that of Colonial nostalgia, but of another Bahia, one which attempts to rescue in its Baroque matrix the alchemy of the play between alterity and identity, the power of the hybrid voice which has been formed in this dialectic and is to be located between the texts of the Lettered City and the social fabric of the streets of the black city.

Translation by Stephen A. Berg

Works Cited

Almeida, Alfredo Wagner Berno de. 1979. *Jorge Amado. Política y literatura: um estudo sobre a trajetória intelectual de Jorge Amado*. Rio de Janeiro: Campus.

Alves, Ivia. 1978. *Arco e flexa*. Salvador: Fundação Cultural do Estado da Bahia.

Azevedo, Thales de. 1991. *A guerra aos páracos*. Salvador: Empresa Gráfica da Bahia.

Bacelar, Jeferson. 1997a. "A hierarquia das raças–cor, trabalho e riqueza após a Abolição em Salvador. Raça e família." *Estudos Cedhal* 9 (São Paulo): 9–52.

——. 1997b. "Os últimos africanos em Salvador ." *Exu*. 36 (Salvador): 20–33.

Barbosa, Francisco Assis. 1974. Preface. *Memória da Sé* by Fernando da Rocha Peres. Salvador: Macunaíma/Governo do Estado da Bahia. i–viii.

Barreto, Belarmino. 1874. "Conservatório dramático." *Diário da Bahia*. September 17.

Bastide, Roger. 1978. *O cadomblé da Bahia*. Trans. Maria Isaura Pereira de Queiroz. São Paulo: Editora Nacional.

Boccanera Júnior, Sílio. 1924. *O teatro na Baia: Da colônia à República (1800–1923)*. Bahia: Imprensa Oficial.

Bosi, Alfredo. 1970. *História concisa da Literatura Brasileira*. São Paulo: Cultrix.

Braga, Júlio. 1995. *Na gamela do feitiço: Repressão e resistência nos candomblés da Bahia*. Salvador: Edufba.

Calmon, Pedro. 1949. *História da literatura Baiana*. Salvador: Prefeitura Municipal de Salvador.

Candido, Antonio. 1964. *Formação da literatura brasileira: Momentos decisivos*. 2nd ed. Vol 1. São Paulo: Martins.

Canevacci, Massimo. 1990. *Antropologia da comunicação visual*. São Paulo: Brasiliense.

Carneiro, Édison de Sousa. 1980. *Ursa Maior*. Salvador: Centro Editorial e Didático da Universidade Federal da Bahia.

Castro, Mary, and Eneida Leal Cunha. 1996. *Diálogos trans-atlânticos: Identidades, margens e fronteiras em latinidades*. Salvador: Universidade Federal da Bahia.

Castro, Yeda Pessoa. 1980. *Os falares africanos na interação social do Brasil colônia*. Salvador: Centro de Estudos Baianos.

Chiacchio, Carlos. 1928. "Tradicionalismo dinâmico." *Arco e Flexa*. 1 (Salvador-Bahia): 3–8.

Conceição da Silva, Jônatas. 1996. "Port without Sea." *Cadernos Negros: Poemas Afro-Brasileiros/Black Cadernos: Afro-Brazilian Poems* 19.

Cunha, Eneida Leal. 1993a. "A cruz e o pau Brasil: Imaginário e história no século XVII." *Revista Internacional de Língua Portuguesa* 8 (Lisboa): 109–13.

——. 1993b. "Estampas do imaginário: Literatura, cultura, histórica e identidade." Diss. Pontifícia Universidade Católica do Rio de Janeiro.

——. 1995 "A estampa originária da dependência." *Revista Brasil/Brazil*. 13 (Porto Alegre): 61–70.

Dantas, Beatriz Góis. 1984. "De feiticeiros a comunistas: Acusações sobre o candomblé." *Dédalo* (São Paulo) 23: 97–115.

——. 1988. *Vovó Nagô e Papai Branco: Usos e abusos da África no Brasil*. Rio de Janeiro: Graal.

Diario da Bahia. 1857 (Sept. 11).

Falla da 20 Sessão da 26 a Legislatura da Assembléia Legislativa Provincial. 1887. October 4. Salvador: Assembléia Provincial.

Fonseca, Luis Anselmo da. 1988. *A escravidão, o clero e o abolicionismo*. Recife: Editora Massangana.

Graham, Maria. 1956. *Diário de uma viagem ao Brasil e de uma estada nesse país durane parte dos anos de 1821, 1822 e 1823*. São Paulo: Ed. Nacional.

Herskovits, Melville. 1967. "Pesquisas etnológicas na Bahia." *Afro-Ásia* 4–5 (Salvador): 89–106.

Jorge Amado na Academia. 1961. São Paulo: Martins.

Landes, Ruth 1967. *A cidade das mulheres*. Rio de Janeiro: Civilização Brasileira.

Lima, Vivaldo da Costa. 1977. "A familia-de-santo nos candomblés jêje-nagôs do Bahia." Diss. Universidade Federal da Bahia.

——. 1987. "O Candomble da Bahia." *Cartas de Édison Carneiro a Artur Ramos: De 4 de janeiro de 1936 a 6 de dezembro de 1938*. Ed. Valdir Freitas Oliveira and Vivaldo da Costa Lima. São Paulo: Corrupio. 39–45.

Luhning, Angela. 1995–96. "Acabe com este santo, Pedrito vem aí." *Revista USP: Dossiê Pavo Negro-300 anos* 28 (São Paulo): 194–220.

Mariotti, Giorgio. 1972. *Il nero nel romanzo braziliano*. Roma: Bulzoni.

Marques, Xavier. 1997. *Vida de Castro Alves*. 3rd ed. Rio de Janeiro: Topbooks.

Mattoso, Kátia. 1992. *Bahia século XIX: Uma província no império*. Rio de Janeiro: Nova Fronteira.

Mendes, Cleise Furtado, ed. 1996. *Senhora Dona Bahia: Poesia satírica de Gregório de Matos*. Salvador: Ed. Universidade Federal da Bahia.

Oliveira, Waldir Freitas. 1987. "Os estudos africanistas na Bahia dos anos 30." *Cartas de Édison Carneiro a Artur Ramos: De 4 de janeiro de 1936 a 6 de dezembro de 1938*. Ed. Vivlado da Costa Lima. São Paulo: Corrupio. 23–35.

Ortiz, Renato. 1985. *Cultura brasileira e identidade nacional*. São Paulo: Brasiliense.

——. 1994. *Mundialização e cultura*. São Paulo: Brasiliense.

Peres, Fernando da Rocha. 1974. *Memória da Sé*. Salvador: Macunaíma/Governo do Estado da Bahia.

Querino, Manuel. 1955. *A raça africana e os seus costumes*. Salvador: Livraria Progresso.

Ramos, Ana Rosa Neves. 1992. "L'idée du peuple chez Jorge Amado: Engagement politique et création romanesque." Diss. Université de Sorbonne Nouvelle Paris III.

Reis, João José. 1986. *Rebelião escrava no brasil: A história do levante dos Malês*. São Paulo: Brasiliense.

——. 1993. "A greve negra de 1857." *Revista USP. Dossiê Brasil/África* (São Paulo): 6–29.

Risério, Antônio, ed. 1988. *Escravidão e invenção da liberdade: Estudos sobre o negro no Brasil*. São Paulo: Brasiliense.

——. 1995. *Avant-Garde na Bahia*. São Paulo: Instituto Lina Bo and P. M. Bardi.

——. 1997. *Um mundo afrobarroco*. Salvador: Fundação Casa de Jorge Amado.

Rodrigues, Nina. 1977. *Os africanos no Brasil*. São Paulo: Companhia Editora Nacional

Salvador, Vicente do. 1965. *História do Brasil: 1500–1627*. 5th ed. São Paulo: Melhoramentos.

Sá Menezes, Jayme de. 1983. *Agrário de Menezes: Um liberal do império*. 2nd ed. Rio de Janeiro: Cátedra-Brasília.

Sansone, Livio. 1995. "O local e o global na Afro-Bahia contemporânea." *Revista Brasileira de Ciências Sociais*. 29: 65–84.

Schwarcz, Lilia Moritz. 1993. *O espetáculo das raças: Cientistas, instituições e questão racial no Brasil (1870–1930)*. São Paulo: Companhia das Letras.

Skidmore, Thomas. 1976. *Preto no Branco: Raça e nacionalidade no pensamento brasileiro*. Trans. Raul da Sá Barbosa. Rio de Janeiro: Paz e Terra.

Sovik, Liv. 1994. "Vaca profana: Teoria pós-moderna e tropicália." Diss. Universidade de São Paulo.

Tati, Miécio. 1961. *Jorge Amado: Vida e obra*. Belo Horizonte: Itatiaia.

Verger, Pierre. 1966. *O fumo da Bahia e o tráfico de escravos no Golfo de Benin*. Salvador: Centro Estudos Afro-Orientais.

CHAPTER 48

RIO DE JANEIRO

CAPITAL CITY

Renato Cordeiro Gomes, Margarida de Souza Neves,
and Mónica Pimento Velloso

Uruguayan critic Ángel Rama conceives of the city as a sign in his famous 1985 study *La ciudad letrada* [*The Lettered City*, 1996], where he defines the Latin American city in particular as the unique embodiment of the colonizing dream of order and of power. "Born of intelligence," he writes, the continent's cities are ruled by "una razón ordenadora que se revela en un orden social jerárquico transpuesto a un orden distributivo geométrico" (1984, 4) ("their ordering principle revealed itself as a hierarchical society transposed by analogy into a hierarchical design of urban space. . . . so that in the geometrical distribution we can read the social morphology of the planners" [1996, 3]). Coupled with a process of centralization that aims to discipline society through a structuring hierarchy, this order makes possible the concentration of power. Latin American cities live a double life in this dream of order: The first corresponds to the material order, and the second to the order of signs. A city's material life is physical and palpable, and it is subject to circumstance and to changes resulting from construction and destruction throughout time. This life alone is the object of material redress. In contrast, the city of signs operates on a symbolic level even before it is made concrete in the form of the material life of the city (Rama 32). The realm of signs and its order pertains to the "city of letters," which is strictly associated with the functions of power. The city of letters controls the symbolic languages that perform the cultural functions of the structures of power.

The process of modernization undergone by the Latin American city roughly between 1870 and 1920 did not alter the fundamental indicator of its origin–the prevalence of the order of signs over the material order, or rather, the prevalence of the reason of the state over individual interests and local creativity and imagination (Resende 22). Hervé Théry is indeed right to affirm that the genesis of Latin America's cultural centers is confused with that of its nations, its peripheries and centers of gravity. Nonetheless the city proved a catalyst for this process of modernization as it sought to integrate the national territory as a whole under the urban standards of the capital. Territorial integration confirmed a determined city's role as a cultural center, and as such it constituted a political act of the utmost importance.

From this vantage point we can read the city of Rio de Janeiro as a cultural center and understand the role it fulfilled and continues to fulfill with respect to the rest of the country. If the metropolis represents the most complete expression of Brazil's social formation, Rio de Janeiro proves an exemplary case. Rio reflects both the coherence and contradictions of Brazil's dominant economic, institutional, and ideological systems. Not only did Rio de Janeiro serve as the nation's capital from 1822 to 1960, but it remained the country's most heavily populated city until the 1950s. Rio de Janeiro provided the urban model for the nation's other cities for a considerable time, and the city still retains its function as a model for other urban centers, continuing to reflect the nation's social and cultural make-up (Abreu 16).

Rio de Janeiro's central role in the convergence and dissemination. of Brazilian culture began to be established in 1763, when it became the capital of the then State of Brazil and a strategic point for trade in the gold originating in Minas Gerais. Following a pattern established by other Colonial cities, Rio de Janeiro only gained recognizably urban contours as a function of its role as a port city. It is through this port that Portugal reinforced its ties to Brazil and consolidated colonial practices and institutions. Rio de Janeiro's civil, military, and ecclesiastical bureaucracies embodied the presence of Portuguese power in the colony. Unlike the cities and towns of Minas Gerais, Rio de Janeiro would follow the example of other Portuguese Colonial cities in America and transcend its original function as a military base for defense to form a metropolis. Like other Portuguese Colonial centers in South America, Rio de Janeiro would come to embody what the historian of Colonial Brazil, Sérgio Buarque de Hollanda (1902–1982), has termed the logic of carelessness.

In *Raízes do Brasil* [1936; The Roots of Brazil] Buarque de Hollanda accentuates the belatedness of the process of urbanization in Brazil. Even after independence from Portugal in 1822, Brazilian cities represented no more than small nuclei that exerted little influence compared to the main areas of production, non-governmental rural properties that were the site of permanent activity. This belated urbanization underscores the importance of the rural inheritance to the formation of Brazilian society. Family sugar plantations, farms, and ranches were constituted in space through colonial practices. Urban centers in contrast resisted abstract norms and the formation of a public sphere. Though the fruit of the project of colonization, cities developed in an unattended and irregular fashion. Portuguese cities in America did not grow in the tiled fashion of Spanish American cities, the product of a rigid order reflected in their geometric plans. Rather, Portuguese cities were scattered throughout America in accordance to the dictates of nature and in function of an adaptation to immediate circumstances. Sérgio Buarque de Hollanda demonstrates this point by contrasting the rigorous grid system of Spanish cities to the modest but fanciful improvisation of the Portuguese city. (See **Figure 1**.) In this regard he anticipates the force of similar arguments that were later to be expounded by Rama.

Only in the nineteenth century did Rio de Janeiro undergo a radical transformation in its urban structure and begin to betray stratification along the lines of social class. Until then Rio was a city squeezed between four mountains. Its very ground had been wrenched from nature with great difficulty, through the draining of marshes and mangrove swamps for more than three centuries of the city's history (Abreu 35). Nineteenth-century Rio de Janeiro witnessed substantial change of both a physical and a symbolic order. Key to this change was the relocation of the Portuguese royal family and

566

Figure 1.

Lithograph of "Rua Direita" Rio de Janeiro in Rugendas, Voyage pittoresque au Brésil. *Paris, 1835, plate 3/13. (Courtesy of John P. Robarts Research Library, University of Toronto)*

Figure 2.

Photograph by Marc Ferrez c. 1875 of the port of Rio de Janeiro. (Courtesy of John P. Robarts Research Library, University of Toronto)

court to Rio in 1808 following Napoleon's occupation of Portugal. The presence of Portuguese royalty in Rio lent the city a degree of social complexity hitherto practically unknown in the city. Not the least of the unprecedented demands of the royal family and state bureaucracy were those of a material nature. Most significantly, the relocation of the Portuguese court and state to Rio empowered the city to exercise a vast array of new symbolic functions, from the realms of politics and economics to those of culture and ideology. As the capital of the United Kingdom of Portugal, Brazil, the Algarve, and Overseas possessions, Rio de Janeiro underwent a series of reforms that sought to civilize the city under the sign of Europe. As capital of the Portuguese kingdom, Rio de Janeiro enjoyed a centrality that immeasurably surpassed the bounds of its province and region and even the importance of the Colony of Brazil itself. Statutes governing the political status of Brazil had to be modified to reflect Rio's new significance. Rio de Janeiro was transformed before the eyes of José Hipólito da Costa and his contemporaries in a "New Lisbon," the seat and center of the Portuguese Colonial Empire (see Rizzini).

Political independence in 1822 forged the image of Rio de Janeiro as capital of Brazil. Rio's court marked the imaginary of the new empire of Brazil, and in the 1830s the court became politically and administratively distinguished from the empire in the form of the Neutral Municipality. Rio de

Janeiro's political and economic development projected the city as a cultural center and as the model for the urban spaces and systems of the new empire. Rio's successes as a capital city only served to reinforce the city as the axis upon which the new imperial state turned. (See **Figure 2**.) Thus, Rio de Janeiro came to represent a kind of sociological synthesis of Brazil, a convenient metonymy that marks the legitimization of its role as capital city. This metonymy demonstrates the vast resonance of Rio's capital as capital: Rio de Janeiro was the focus for the nation's culture, its centrifugal and centripetal point. Its public institutions disseminated its influence throughout the Brazilian empire's territory. The city became Brazil's literary capital, the rock and foundation for its culture.

It is in this respect that it makes sense to write of Rio de Janeiro as a capital city even after the transfer of the seat of political power to Brasilia in 1960. Here we do not identify the concept of the capital city exclusively with the realm of political power but rather use it more broadly to denote Rio de Janeiro's centrality to both the political and cultural identity of the nation. Perhaps no period demonstrates Rio's central function in Brazilian culture better than the beginning of the twentieth century, when the whole of Brazil took direction from the federal capital then engaged in a rapid process of modernization. To indulge in a metaphor of Rio as keeping time for the nation, the pace set in motion in the capital gave the clock of the whole nation nothing less than a new time. From Rio de Janeiro those in power sought to accelerate the workings of time under the sign of the vertigo of progress. In this regard the concept of a capital city illuminates the significance of Rio de Janeiro with respect to the motto (and project) of Brazil's New Republic since its inception in 1889: "Order and Progress." It is this period of

Republicanism and modernization that would prove Rio de Janeiro's *belle époque* and provide the most striking contrast to the city as a site of cultural enunciation in past and future epochs, from the Colonial and imperial Rio to the Rio of the second half of the twentieth century.

The Capital of Progress

At the turn of the century, texts often eloquently conflated Rio de Janeiro with Brazil. Texts that refer to the city in particular come to include reflections on the nation in its entirety, moving seamlessly from the part to the whole, and vice-versa. The frequent recourse to this process of metonymy allowed Brazil and Rio de Janeiro to become interchangeable terms. In this spirit Rio's mayor Pereira Passos brought into being the stylish magazine *Kosmos* to court public opinion and gain support for his civic reforms. Within its pages columnist Gil praised the president's own plan "dignificar a Capital, dignificando o Brasil" ("to dignify the Capital, to dignify Brazil"). Gil affirmed that while the "grande artéria" ("great artery") of the Avenida Central dominated Rio, "Rio sugestionava o Brasil" ("Rio represented Brazil") (Dimas 301). (See **Figure 3**.) The semantic elision of Rio de Janeiro and Brazil preceded even the proclamation of the Republic in 1889. Then the reference to the artery that symbolically dominated the city was to Rua do Ouvidor, the focus of Rio's social, cultural, and everyday life before it was dethroned by Avenida Central. When German writer and journalist Carl von Koseritz returned to Rio de Janeiro in April 1883, after living in the south of Brazil for thirty-two years, he chronicled the life of the city for his *Imagens do Brasil*:

> É certo que aqui sentimos o pulsar a vida do Império–aqui nos encontramos no ponto central e mais importante dele e vê-se diariamente na rua do Ouvidor os homens que governam o país e conduzem a opinião pública– mas o caráter geral da sociedade local é muito especial e eu firia frívolo. O Rio de Janeiro é o Brasil, e a rua do Ouvidor é o Rio de Janeiro–eis uma sentença cheia de verdade. Quem quiser aprender a maneira por que o Brasil é governado e os negócios públicos conduzidos, não tem mais que passar algumas horas por dia na rua do Ouvidor. (Koseritz 31)

> Certainly here we feel the pulse of the life of Empire–here we find ourselves in its most focal and important point. At the Rua do Ouvidor we witness daily the men who govern the nation and lead public opinion. And yet the overall character of local society is quite special and I would say frivolous. Rio de Janeiro is Brazil, and the Rua do Ouvidor is Rio–here is a sentence full of truth. He who wishes to learn the manner in which Brazil is governed and its public affairs conducted need do no more than spend a few hours a day at the Rua do Ouvidor.

Gil's and Koseritz's chronicles of Rio in the pages of *Kosmos* and *Imagens do Brasil* figure among innumerable examples of the symbolic identification of Brazil with its capital, both in the writing aimed at the cultured classes and in the civic monuments aimed at the population at large. On 9 April 1891, the daily *O Jornal do Brasil* became the third newspaper published by the city's printing presses to invoke the nation in name and in the range of its coverage and circulation. Years later the daily moved into the most sought after addresses in the city, the Avenida Central, in a building that boasted a fantastic minaret in the form of the Eiffel Tower. The city's great artery also became the site of another daily that boasted of its national import already in its masthead, *O País*. The Brazilian Press Association was founded in its newsroom in 1918. Many of the institutions that sprouted in Rio de Janeiro evoked in

Figure 3.

Photograph Avenida Central by Mar Ferrez c. 1910. (Courtesy of John P. Robarts Research Library, University of Toronto)

their titles the ambition to represent not just Rio, but Brazil. Rio's Central Avenue also housed the National Library, the National Museum of Fine Arts, the Brazilian wing of the Lloyd's of London, and the insurance company *A Equitativa do Brasil*. The National Observatory was located a bit further away in São Cristóvão, the neighborhood previously chosen for the construction of the imperial palace. Rio's center also housed the National Historical Museum (first founded under the suggestive title *A Casa do Brasil*), the Bank of Brazil, and the Brazilian Academy of Letters, founded in emulation of the *Académie Française* in 1896.

Hence it is not without cause that Luiz Edmundo Costa (1878–1961) begins his 1938 chronicle of the Rio de Janeiro of his time by referring to the country to describe the nature of the city: "O Brasil, dentro da natureza como dentro de um sonho, palpitava e floria" (Luiz Edmundo Costa 12) ("Located in nature as if within a dream, Brazil pulsated and flourished"). Luiz Edmundo Costa and other writers of his day frequently make recourse to this metonymy to express the city's role as representative of the country. In this vein he portrays Rio's mayor Pereira Passos as the great catalyst for Brazil's progress: "Passos fez a coisa de vulto ainda maior, porque, além de remodelar materialmente a cidade, transformou-a até em seus usos e costumes, vendo projetar-se, depois no resto do país, como reflexo natural e profícuo, os benefícios que criara" (47) ("Passos's feats were of even greater import, for he not only remodeled the city in concrete and material terms, but transformed Rio in its uses and customs, overseeing the city's emergence as Brazil's most natural and flattering reflection"). One certainly cannot suppose that these constant allusions to Brazil as the natural reflection of its capital were immediately detected and deciphered by Passos's contemporaries. Nonetheless these allusions constitute discursive markers–what Carlo Ginzburg might call clues to a collective and individual imaginary (143–49). At the turn of the century these constant allusions to Brazil as Rio stressed the importance of the city's status as capital to the Republican construction of order as progress. Thus the Republic confirmed Rio as the cultural site that proved central to the order of signs in turn of the century Brazil.

Would it not thus be possible to conceive of Rio de Janeiro as it was reconstructed at the turn of the century as a monument to the Republican project of modernity? Can Rio be interpreted as an embodiment of the Republic's motto and as an allegory of order as progress? Did this turn-of-the-century reconstruction of Rio represent a modern process of construction? How is the city's mark as capital city reflected in its status as cultural center? These questions are answered in part in the work of anthropologist Georges Balandier, in particular in his volume *O poder em cena* [The Scene of Power]. Balandier stresses what he terms a city's liturgical or pedagogical function. He describes the city as a site for the production of images aimed at the education of its inhabitants. Striking a balance between coercion and consent, the city seeks to impose upon its citizens a vision of order. In this vein Balandier observes:

O poder estabelecido unicamente sobre a força ou sobre a violência não controlada teria uma existência constantemente ameaçada. O poder exposto debaixo da iluminação exclusiva da razão teria pouca credibilidade: ele não consegue manter-se nem pelo domínio brutal, nem pela justificativa racional. Ele só se realiza e se conserva pela transposição, pela produção de imagens, pela manipulação de símbolos e sua organização em um quadro cerimonial. (7)

If power were established through force and violence alone, it would be vulnerable, its very existence constantly subject to threats. In turn the exercise of power under the banner of an Enlightenment that is exclusively the product of reason would possess little credibility: This power could be maintained neither through the exercise of brute force, nor through its recourse to reason. Power only succeeds and conserves itself through the production of images, the manipulation of symbols, and ceremony.

In this light the city can be read as a form of discourse, a veritable language. As already noted, Ángel Rama has pointed to the superimposed layers of the city's palimpsestic discourse: the material and the symbolic.

Thus the consolidation of the Republic at the turn of the century saw an unprecedented celebration of the rhythm of *carioca* life and the implementation of a modernizing plan for its then capital, Rio de Janeiro. Until this moment Rio still preserved the character of a Colonial city, though it already constituted Brazil's foremost political and financial center and its most populous and important market. Rio de Janeiro betrayed the anachronism of its old urban structures. For the Republic's motto of order and progress to be set in motion and staged, it was paramount that the old city be remodeled and reconstructed. In the words of Luiz Edmundo Costa in his chronicle of his Rio de Janeiro, it was necessary to transform

a cidade pocilga em Éden maravilhoso, fonte suave de beleza e de saúde, centro para onde afluem estrangeiros que, até então, medrosamente nos visitavam, apavorados, todos com a febre amarela: americanos, ingleses, italianos, alemães, que aqui chegam trazendo-nos além de um esforço pessoal apreciável, capitais, estímulo, e o que é melhor ainda, a visão civilizadora de pátrias adiantadas e progressistas. (Luiz Edmundo Costa 1: 25)

the pigsty into a marvelous Eden, into a natural source of health and beauty that would welcome foreigners, hitherto afraid to visit us on account of fear of contracting yellow fever. One appreciates the formidable effort of Americans, Englishmen, Italians, and Germans to bring their capital and stimulus to this shore, and above all the civilizing vision of their progressive and advanced nations.

In synchronicity with official government policy, Luiz Edmundo Costa urged Brazil to rid itself of its "morrinha colonial" ("colonial stench") and to embrace the models propagated by the hegemonic powers associated with civilization and progress. As a peripheral country Brazil was to overcome its state of arrested development and embrace modernity according to its own schedule. Nothing less than a messianic belief in the destiny of Brazil was required for the obtainment of this goal. For Brazil to keep pace with the march of Western civilization, it was first necessary to set the pace of the Republic in accordance with the rhythm of its capital, Rio de Janeiro. And yet Republican power was exercised in a form that contradicted these goals, as is evident in the Republic's oligarchic and paternalistic practices.

Rio was thus civilized under the patronage of this Republican power and its bourgeois elites. Official government policy called for the attraction of foreign capital and the establishment of credibility vis-à-vis the civilized regard of Europe and the United States. Keeping pace with progress entailed situating Brazil within the same paradigms, standards, and rhythms of European economies. According to Nicolau Sevcenko, the transformation of Rio's public spaces, public consciousness, and manners was conducted according to four basic principles: the condemnation of habits and customs associated in the popular imagination with traditional society; the negation of any and all element of popular culture that might stain the civilized image of the dominant classes; a rigorous policy of removing the poor from the city's center for the benefit of its exclusive enjoyment by the bourgeoisie; and an aggressive cosmopolitanism modeled after the experience of Paris (Sevcenko 30).

The performance of modernity in the tropics required a sumptuous and pompous stage. It required, in the ironic vision of João do Rio, new costumes that revealed an imitative fury. João do Rio (1881–1921) gave a lecture on the costume that was subsequently published in the volume *Psicologia Urbana* [1911; Urban Psychology] and from that beginning developed his law of social psychology. This world of artificiality and copy gave currency to the buzz words *chic* and *smart*, nowhere more prominent than in Figueiredo Pimentel's column "Binóculo" for the daily *Gazeta de Notícias* (see Broca 14). The title of his column, "Binoculars," played upon the idea of simultaneously bringing into focus the near and the far to create a complete picture. With one eye on Paris and the other on Rio, this famous column attempted to reconcile the disparate realities of these cities. Figueiredo Pimental's column even boasted a "a bíblia das elegâncias da terra" ("bible of the earth's elegances") that was devoured by good society and read by all, according to the recollection of Luiz Edmundo Costa. It was in this column that Pimental coined the slogan that came to define Rio de Janeiro during its *belle époque*, "o Rio civiliza-se" ("Rio is getting civilized").

One should not underestimate the symbolic dimension inherent in these transformations. It is the communication of symbols that indicates how Brazil could stage modernity in its peripheral capital. The aim was to erase the traces of the colonial city and erect in its place a metropolis, even if in the end this metropolis was no more than a sub-metropolis that still orbited around Paris. Rio had to be transformed into a forest of symbols in order for it be read as a site of modernity. Thus an exclusive and authoritarian progress was superimposed upon the city: Given a policy of progress and evolution defined solely in material terms, Rio submitted to a constant program of demolition that sought to erase the old city in pursuit of an ever-new modernity. In this context one can observe, along with Giuglio Carlo Argan, that the struggle was not the traditional confrontation between culture and the forces of ignorance, but rather it was much more destructive because this was a battle between two cultures and no matter which side won, culture lost. The second culture was intent on destroying the first which it considered to be its negation and the greatest obstacle to the realization of its goals. In a 1904 column for *Kosmos* Bilac chronicled mayor Pereira Passos's policy of demolition of the old Rio as the action of regenerative pick-axes that celebrated the victory of hygiene, good taste, and art. The reconstruction of Rio de Janeiro altered not only its urban and natural landscape, but the range of experiences of its inhabitants. Rio occupied at once a physical and mythical space—it became both a place and a metaphor.

Rio de Janeiro emerged as a modern city because it was physically and ideologically reconstructed by the lettered class: by engineers, the functionaries of reason, and hygienists who were organically linked to the state. Its modernity at the turn of the century was sculpted not only by pickaxes, but also by hygienic campaigns that sought to cleanse the capital of the old and impose the new. Integral to this process was the labor of newspaper and magazine columnists who toiled in the vast construction site that was the press of the time. Photographer Augusto Malta documented the old city that was left to rot: the kiosks and slums of the Morro do Castelo (or Castle Hill). But he also registered the new sites of the modern capital: the Avenida Central, the remodeled port, the Mangue Canal, and the refashioned bay of Botafogo, where the exuberance of tropical nature was tamed and framed by French mansions and gardens. Nonetheless these interventions in Rio de Janeiro's urban profile fell short of Luiz Edmundo Costa's goals of materially refashioning the city and of transforming it in its uses and customs.

Indeed, it is important not to underestimate the brutal demolition of the old Rio in the first years of the twentieth century, above all with respect to the lives of those who inhabited the colonial side streets that were cleared so as to open up almost two kilometers for the Central Avenue. Nonetheless the reform of the capital was limited to two fundamental projects. The first was the construction of the Parisian (if not Faustian) great stage of the Avenida Central over the city center's network of small streets. The Avenue's imposing rooftops concealed the fragile roofs of almost all buildings in the city center (Luiz Edmundo Costa 25). The second project pertained to the new installations in the city's port, and it required no less than 175,000 square meters of landfill to unite the Mangue Canal to Mauá Square over a distance of 3,500 meters. The new avenue and the new port became the city's new axes, replacing the old Rua Direita and the old quay of Paço Square. Rio's new axes did not, however, displace the mercantile logic that defined society's dynamic: New forms (or reforms) of this mercantile logic did arise, but these were significant transformations that did not change the fundamental logic of the city or the social classes of its inhabitants. Despite these new forms of architecture and of government, modern Rio de Janeiro remained colonial Rio.

Certainly the principle symbol of Rio's *belle époque* remains the Avenida Central, the great boulevard conceived by Lauro Müller based on the old designs from mayor Pereira Passos's tenure in the 1870s. Paulo de Frontin was entrusted with the planning and construction of the new avenue which was to cut the old city along a north-south axis, from Prainha Square (now Mauá) until it reached another projected avenue, the Beira-Mar. The Avenida Central was ready in eighteen months. Its length (1,966 meters) and width (33 meters) required the demolition of 590 buildings in the old city and of small sections of the hills of São Bento and Castelo. Rio's population did not remain indifferent to the ensuing social upheavals. The underprivileged classes suffered in particular, as they were literally erased from the map of the city center. The Central Avenue became the great metaphor for modern times: In 1904, the end of the period of demolitions was celebrated on the anniversary of Independence, September 7, and in 1905 the Avenue was inaugurated anew on the anniversary of the Proclamation of the Republic, November 15. As Jeffrey Needell observes in his work on Rio de Janeiro's culture and society at the turn of the century, *Belle Époque Tropical*: "Quando, em 1910, seus edifícios ficaram prontos, e o conceito da avenida se completou, uma magnífica paisagem urbana passou a embelezar o Rio. A Capital Federal possuía agora um *boulevard* verdadeiramente "civilizado"—duas muralhas paralelas de edifícios que refletiam o máximo de bom gosto existente—e um monumento ao progresso do país" (60–61) ("When the concept of the Avenue became a reality and its buildings were ready in 1910, a magnificent urban landscape lent added beauty to Rio. The federal capital now possessed a truly civilized boulevard—two parallel walls of buildings that fully reflected the time's most sophisticated taste—and thus a monument to the country's progress"). This monumental axis represented the dream of the rational city made concrete by the leaders of the Republic, a symbol of the new, of progress, and of change. This ideology of the lettered city suggested an utopian future. A new urban mythology is formed and consolidated around this central axis: the euphoric mythology of the Avenue that seeks to rewrite the past that is being destroyed and to point to the future and utopia. This mythology marks the city's imaginary and is disseminated in the texts of its scribes. As one of the city's most famous chroniclers Paulo Barreto (João do Rio) would observe in the guise of the pseudonym Godofredo de Alencar that Brazilian civilization can be taken as two distinct periods: before Avenida Central was built and after. Such was the dimension of change that between Rua do Ouvidor and Avenida Central one could experience the distance between Sabará and Marseilles.

The refashioning of space implies an acceleration in time: The rupture with the past manifests an optimism with regard to the future. The inauguration of the Central Avenue marked the beginning of this future for capital and country. With its new design Rio de Janeiro became the *Cidade Maravilhosa*, or marvelous city, after the phrase coined by French poet Jeanne Catulle Mendès following her visit to Rio in 1912. In one respect the denomination of Rio as a "marvelous city" reflects the positive descriptions of Rio from the first chronicles of the city dating back to the sixteenth century. Yet while the earlier texts refer primarily to the city's paradisiacal setting, Jeanne Catulle Mendès's homage refers not only to the divine creation of nature but the human hand that completes it—to Rio's process of urbanization through rationalist visions and technologies. Coming from a foreigner—and a French poet at that—these words of praise acquired a legitimizing force and help offset previous unflattering juxtapositions of Rio with other modern cities. The denomination of Rio as *Cidade Maravilhosa* became integral to both the official and the popular imaginary and became a cliché, immortalized in André

Filho's 1936 carnival song which became the city's official anthem. Filho's song enshrines Rio de Janeiro as the "coração do meu Brasil"–"the heart of my Brazil."

On the other hand, the scene of the great Avenue diverted attention away from both the jewels and the blemishes of the alleys of the colonial city, concealing behind the fantastic façade of its buildings the often masterful architecture of Rio's colonial houses. The great Avenue also withdrew from the city center those *cariocas* whose presence was considered incompatible with the city's Parisian pretensions. Turned out of their slums in the city center, many of these underprivileged *cariocas* fled to the suburbs that sprouted along the railways that led out of the city. The underprivileged were effectively banned from the Avenida Central through municipal bylaws that barred from the center anyone not wearing a suit, tie, and dress shoes. The mythology of the Avenida Central took root and was cultivated despite these blemishes.

Along the refashioned port modern warehouses, fifty-two electrically operated cranes performed a similar symbolic function to the elegant façades of the Central Avenue. While they represented a symbolic opening of Rio de Janeiro to the world and to the influx of new and modern goods, they also performed the analogous function of concealing the fact that Brazil's peripheral economy had not undergone a significant structural change. Bourgeois forms could ill disguise the continued predominance of mercantile capital. While the city would liken itself to a European metropolis, Rio was ordered less along the dictates of the market than in accordance to more palpable and forceful instruments of coercion. The police upheld the city's sartorial laws and maintained order throughout Rio. Engineering clubs and commissions for public hygiene ordered the city's body politic, its customs, and urban logic. A Code of Appearances crystallized in the letter of the law what could and could not be done in the city's public spaces. This formed the hidden engine behind the beautiful clocks that marked the time of Rio's modernity: a civic policy of federalism as the corollary to the city's Republican forms. This federalism nourished and gave new dimensions to old and new elites. Under the sign of oligarchy it recuperated regional alliances, the politics of favor, and the practices of paternalism.

Nonetheless, despite these contradictions, the reconstruction of the port and the Central Avenue did represent a symbolic reinvention of the capital as a whole. Among Rio's labyrinth of streets and alleys the Avenida Central functioned as an Ariadne's thread that pointed to the idea of progress. Following this tenuous thread of progress, many believed in the illusion that the defeat of the monsters of underdevelopment and barbarism was at hand. Few perceived the fragility of this dream. For the order that was yielded by this labyrinth of new forms and signifiers was the old and familiar exclusive hierarchy of Colonial society. Yet the ostentatiousness of the reforms succeeded in underscoring discontinuities at the expense of permanence: The city articulated a new discourse with great efficiency, and the capital emerged as a metaphor for the nation. Thus understood as a ceremonial stage, the city dramatized the Republic's equation of order with progress. In effect Rio de Janeiro came to embody a pedagogy of order that was assimilated as a requisite for progress. This discourse had a double meaning: On the one hand, it affirmed the possibility of realizing in the present the dream of a civilized, progressive, and orderly metropolis; and on the other, it anticipated for the rest of the country a model of utopia for the future.

It is not without cause that one finds constant allusions to Rio as Brazil's postcard abroad and for Europe in particular. The great social and financial cost of refashioning the capital along the lines of a European metropolis was justified in the pursuit of the goal of demonstrating of what the country was capable. Brazilians and eminent foreigners alike dreamed of seeing Rio become a tropical Paris, or at least–in the João do Rio's happy phrase–"tal qual Buenos Aires, que é o esforço despedaçante de ser Paris" (1909, 215) ("just like Buenos Aires, which represents the smashing effort to be Paris"). The European design of some sections of Rio renders palpable the frustrations of Brazilians who felt like exiles in their own land. In turn, eminent foreigners in Rio saw in the dream of a Parisian Rio the possibility of a synthesis between the exuberance of nature and the advantages of progress. Paris may possess the Eiffel Tower, but it does not boast Sugar Loaf Mountain. Paris may have boulevards, but it does not boast Botafogo Bay. In the eyes of proud *cariocas* and Brazilians the capital appeared civilized, beautiful, progressive, and modern. Further they believed Rio capable of incorporating into its modernizing project that which remains specific to its latitude: its lush and splendorous nature.

For the country as a whole, Rio de Janeiro was the capital to the extent that the provinces and provincial cities saw the city as the projection of what was to come for them: the dream of reproducing, perhaps on a smaller scale, the French gardens of the capital, its imposing buildings, monuments, tram, and electric light–in sum, its progress. Rio de Janeiro was the capital as a function of its subordination of social relations to the ideal of progress and the maintenance of order. While the Republic proclaimed the equal importance of order and progress in its rhetoric and its flag, in practice this parity evaporated. Republican policy on the capital subjected all other demands to the maintenance of order. Everything was channeled or reduced to order: administration and reforms, public customs and habits, social practices and agents, feasts and celebrations. The imposition of order as prerequisite for progress justified a strong judicial system and a rigid hierarchy with all its exclusions.

Though the Rio de Janeiro of the turn of the century was far from the modern and bourgeois city that some imagine, it represented nonetheless an allegory of the first Republic's discourse of the new: The rhetoric of novelty was nothing more than the façade for the old political practices, the old compromises, and the old dominant interests. Like the façades of Avenida Central, Rio represented a simulacrum of modernity. Physically and ideologically reconstructed Rio possesses the function of legitimizing, before the nation and the world, an order that–though nominally identified with progress–remained hierarchical and exclusive. Constructed as a metaphor for the future, the Avenida Central cut through the city like a partition between two distinct epochs. To complement the vision of a promising future, it was necessary to destroy remnants of the past: the task that remained was the erasure of memory of the Colonial city.

It is within this context that one must interpret the 1921 demolition of Castelo Hill, which journalist Paulo Barreto (João do Rio) had come to refer to in his column as one of Rio's "livres acampamentos da miséria" ("free harbors of misery"). Once the heart of the Colonial city, the hill was torn down by order of mayor Carlos Sampaio under the pretext of facilitating the circulation of air in the city. Castelo Hill was razed with the assistance of the latest American machinery and technology, but not before Augusto Malta, city hall's official photographer, registered every one of its slopes, the historic Jesuit school, the observatory, and the last mass said at the old church of Sé. Malta also photographed the old Colonial mansion that had been transformed into make-shift housing for the poor and registered many of the anonymous faces of those who lived there. In the vast esplanade of 431,000 square meters cleared by the demolition of Castelo Hill, Epitácio Pessoa would inaugurate in 1922 the International Exhibition that marked the centenary of Brazil's independence. This exhibition furthered the illusion of Rio de Janeiro as the capital of progress, even though the complex and fragile oligarchy of the old Republic was already starting to betray its fissures.

From Colonial City to Imperial Court

Gilberto Velho notes that a national project and memory are associated with the articulation and construction of identity (101). The identity that the Republican government and the cultured elites intended to construct for Rio at the turn of the century resulted not only from a project, but from the reconstruction of memory. As a matter of course, the mastery of memory entails both a remembering and a forgetting. The government and elites alike encouraged the recollection of a generous and exuberant nature as a new Eden. In accordance with the Romantic tradition in Brazil, the original inhabitants of the land were idealized in a process that allowed for a heroic link to the distant past. Conversely both the country's origin as a Portuguese colony and the African presence in its cities and fields was to be forgotten. Above all, the order to flatten Castelo Hill in the beginning of the 1920s sought to erase memory of the Rio de Janeiro of Colonial times. J. A. Maravall notes how the defenders of modernity in Brazil at the beginning of the twentieth century sought to establish a difference with respect to history and old values and make of the past a *tabula rasa*. Since the past was associated with backwardness and primitivism, it was paramount to superimpose upon the past a present that already anticipated the future.

The destruction of Rio de Janeiro's past in the first decades of the twentieth century took place on two fronts: On the one hand, it entailed the reformulation of the city so as to rid it of Colonial markers, be it through their concealment behind the eclectic façades of the Central Avenue or through the destruction of that first stable settlement following the Portuguese victory over the French in 1565. Estácio de Sá had first established this enclosure along the hills at the entry to Guanabara Bay, and it was replaced by a fortress soon named the Castelo (or Castle) by the villa's inhabitants who were busy building the first make-shift houses under its shade and protection. The second front for the destruction of the city's past was discursive and pertained to historiography. For the advocates of a new modernity in the first decades of the twentieth century, it became necessary to extend Brazil's Colonial period past its chronological dates to include almost a century of the country's history after the Proclamation of Independence in 1822. It was in this vein that Luiz Edmundo Costa argued that Brazil's colonial backwardness was only overcome with the Proclamation of the Republic in 1889 and Pereira Passos's urban reforms (25).

Thus extended to encompass the entirety of Brazil's history in the nineteenth century, this refashioned colonial memory elided the differences between Brazil as a Portuguese colony and Brazil as an independent empire; it negated the historical specificity of nineteenth-century Brazilian history and retrospectively projected the notion of Brazilian unity and Rio's

centrality back to the period that preceded the political emancipation of the Republic. It was not without cause that in his description of the founding of Rio de Janeiro, Francisco Adolpho de Varnhagen found that the Brazilian Empire as a whole resembled the physical contour of Guanabara Bay: "a configuração geral de um mapa deste porto do globo, é, em ponto diminuto, a mesma que apresenta o Brasil todo" (Visconde de Porto Seguro 409) ("the general configuration of this part of the globe is, on a smaller scale, the same that Brazil presents as a whole"). It should come as no surprise that in Varnhagen's history of the city as a symbolic synthesis of the nation's nature which itself seems to underscore this metonymy. For the Viscount, the bay that shields the colonial city anticipates and prefigures the shape of the Brazilian empire's territorial unity.

In the first instance, Rio de Janeiro's centrality to Colonial Brazil was a function of its status as the nexus with Lisbon. From 1763 onward, the city, without losing the characteristics of a regional capital, took on the function of the administrative center for the State of Brazil (then complementary to the State of Maranhão in the political configuration of the Portuguese Colonial Empire). It was only with the arrival of the Portuguese court in Rio in 1808 that Rio's political and administrative centrality gained the contours befitting a capital city. The city's new status was the function not only of the relocation of the government of the Portuguese metropolis and realm to Brazil, but of the city's ability to take on (even before independence) functions of paramount importance to the future Empire of Brazil. Colonial Rio de Janeiro demarcated a base for the Portuguese colonists and navy, strategically situated as it was between a narrow stretch on the coast and a hinterland ruled by untamed natives (Mariella da Silva 78–110). By settling in Rio the Portuguese sought to defend themselves against competing colonists, in particular the French Calvinists who sought to found an Antarctic France on the islands of the bay's interior.

With the discovery of mines in the seventeenth century, Rio de Janeiro became the capital of a colonial province, performing functions analogous to those performed by Recife with respect to the sugar industry, São Luis with respect to cotton plantations, and by Belém in relation to the innumerable medicines of the vast Amazon basin. Rio represented a bastion for military defense, a strategic port for all Portuguese routes in the Atlantic, and a site for the establishment of various religious orders (Antonio Vieira 12), then in charge of converting the natives and preaching doctrine to Portuguese subjects in the city. Rio was key to the export of sugar and spirits produced in the sugar plantations that multiplied in proximity to the city, along the contour of Guanabara Bay, in Angra dos Reis, Ilha Grande, Cabo Frio, and above all in Campos de Goitacazes. Rio and its region thus entered into a new era that was at the same time asymmetrical with regard to the other cities and regions of Brazil but also in a deeper sense was complementary to what the other regions contributed.

In the case of the mining region, the belated discovery of gold deposits—belated relative to similar developments in Spanish America—resulted in an unprecedented movement of people to the Gerais (the general mines) and thus in the complex stratification of the region's populations. An infinite number of occupations and positions emerged with reference to the activities surrounding the extraction of gold: the transport of the extracted metal to the port, commerce, agriculture and cattle-ranching, the service sector, the construction and decoration of private and public buildings, the maintenance of civil, ecclesiastic, and military order, and the incipient intellectual life that took root in towns and cities. A scarcity characterized the organization of economic and social activity pertaining to the mining zones: Paths had to be opened to connect the port of Rio to the mines, and the colonial administration (in particular the financial administration) needed to be reinforced. Towns and cities proliferated in the interior of the region with the emergence of agricultural areas to supply the basic needs for subsistence in the Gerais and supply provisions for Rio de Janeiro.

Second we must consider Rio de Janeiro as a Colonial city. In the seventeenth century the city still possessed the profile of a quaint and unsanitary town, lacking in urban machinery—a profile that would still characterize it until the nineteenth century. Only in 1633 did the senate erect the new House for the Chamber and Prison of Rio de Janeiro on a plot of land adjacent to the wilds of Carmo. Until then, the Colonial city occupied the meadows and the fields. Nonetheless, despite the city's modest dimensions, a population numbering in a few dozen thousands and a very limited cultural life, Rio de Janeiro adequately fulfilled the functions allocated to the Colonial cities of Portuguese America:

Os monopólios de colonizadores e colonos tinham seu ponto de interseção na cidade colonial. De modo diverso da cidade clássica, que se distingue por ser núcleo político e mercado, sendo assim um local referido às noções de liberdade e igualdade, a cidade colonial se distingue, antes de tudo pelas funções de porto e centro administrativo, caracterizando, desta forma, o poder do colonizador e expressando a assimetria do pacto colonial. Num certo sentido ela sintetiza o exercício da dominação metropolitana sobre a região colonial: ela é sobretudo núcleo administrativo—isto é, fiscal e militar—na região de mineração-escravista; e s obretudo porto—pólo de convergência obrigatório de portos menores—na região de agricultura-mercantil-escravista.
(Ilmar Mattos 29–30)

The monopolies of colonists and settlers met in the colonial city. In contrast to the classical city which was distinguished by a political nucleus and a market and, by extension, by notions of liberty and equality, the colonial city is differentiated above all by the functions of the port and the administrative center. It characterized the colonizer's power and expressed the asymmetry of the colonial pact. In a certain sense the colonial city synthesizes the exercise of metropolitan power over the colonial region: It forms an administrative, fiscal, and military nucleus in an economy characterized by mining and slavery. Above all the colonial city was a port, a pole for the obligatory convergence of minor ports in a region dominated by a mercantile and agricultural slave economy.

Rio was the port and the door of a colonial region and as such the target of disputes between the Portuguese, the French, and corsairs of all nationalities. Rio de Janeiro formed the fundamental nexus between region and metropolis, established through a commercial monopoly conducted by merchants acting in the name of the Portuguese Crown, who transformed colonial production into a metropolitan business.

Rio de Janeiro housed the headquarters for the region's military, civil, and ecclesiastic administration and was the stage for the many colonial monopolies exercised in name of the Portuguese king: the monopoly over arms (manned by the military bureaucracy), the monopoly over civil and specifically financial administration (manned by civil servants), and the monopoly over souls (exercised by the clergy). Among the colonizers, Ilmar Mattos counts merchants, the military, civil administrators, and the secular and regular clergy—all those who acted in the colony and held monopolies in place of the king, the primary holder of all monopolies and colonizer *par excellence*. Yet colonizers were not the only ones to circulate on the Rua Direita (the city's main artery—which was anything but straight, as the Portuguese name suggests), through the salons of the Chamber House, the Terreiro da Polé, through the Ladeira da Misericórdia, and to the confessionals at the Jesuit schools on Castle Hill, the Benedictine monastery atop São Bento hill, the Fransiscan convent on Santo Antônio Hill, and the Carmelite convent on Conceição in the proximity of São Tiago. Also circulating within the city were the settlers who exercised a monopoly over the land and the means of production on behalf of the Portuguese Crown and supplied Portuguese trade with raw materials. The settlers spent most of their time in the region's interior extracting gold or else producing sugar and other food items on their plantations and farms, supplying both the city and the Portuguese ships docked at Guanabara Bay. Settlers kept a base in Rio for their forays into the city, where they sold their products, purchased slaves, or participated in the religious celebrations that were the great social events of the city's calendar. Settlers and colonizers enjoyed complementary and at times antagonistic relations in the Colonial city. It is in the city that the settlers sold to the colonists their products, paid their taxes, and sought military and religious assistance. It is also in the city that they measured forces against each other in the Chamber House and through the exhibition of the external signs of their personal wealth and prestige. Finally, it is in the city that the mercantile logic that gives meaning to the old system of colonization is expressed most clearly.

However, settlers and colonizers were also not the only ones to frequent the streets and the houses of the city: Seated on the floor or amassed together by the church door, by Marrecas fountain, and performing the public works and domestic service throughout the city were free men, the poor, and black slaves. Above all, it was slave labor that supported and sustained the city and region's colonial activity, the mining and agricultural production that fed colonial commerce and the subsistence of the Colonial cities. While free men, the poor, and black slaves constituted the labor force monopolized by the settlers, they also circulated throughout the city, inscribing in it the marks of subordination imposed on them. In Mattos's vision, they constitute the members of the colonized class.

Finally we must underscore a third spatial dimension to the Colonial dynamic: the imperial metropolis of Lisbon, the seat of the Portuguese realm, the symbolic and physical space where all monopolies originated, and the temporal and historical source of legitimization for the kingdom's transcendent expansion. Lisbon was the seat for the king's two bodies, both that of his person and that of the body politic of his people scattered across the four corners of a globe that Portugal helped expand in braving real and imaginary dangers in "oceans where none had ventured," to quote Camões ("por mares nunca dantes navegados"). In 1808 the poor and quaint city of Rio de Janeiro was transformed not only into the center for the Portuguese colony in America but into the seat for the Portuguese Empire itself, as a function of the dispute for European hegemony between England and France and in particular because of the advance of Napoleon's troops. Occupied by Napoleon, Lisbon saw the Portuguese court relocate to Rio de Janeiro. Even if the material transformation of the city was modest, despite the plans of Grandjean and Montigny, the transfer of power to Rio nonetheless lent the city a new centrality. This was not only as a function of its role as political and administrative capital–with the presence of the monarch, the queen, the court, and the realm's bureaucratic apparatus. Rather one must note a transformation of Rio's relationship to Brazil with respect to the more complex universe of representations and the collective imaginary, and the prefigurement of Brazil's political emancipation and the breaking of colonial ties.

Paramount to this process was the opening of the colony's ports to friendly nations in 1808 and the signing of treaties of friendship and alliance, commerce and navigation with England in 1810. The Crown decreed the opening of the colony's ports already in this passage through Bahia before its arrival in Rio, and this urgent measure proved the death of a fundamental mechanism of colonial dependence: Portugal's monopoly on trade with the colony of Brazil. The opening of the port of Rio is also of great relevance within the context of the economic blockade decreed by Napoleon on the continent in an attempt to asphyxiate England: English commerce gained access not only to the incipient markets in Portuguese America, but to the much broader market formed by the Spanish colonies in the entire continent, in particular to those along the River Plate. As C.G. Mota notes (1970), the opening of the port of Rio made the colony international. In 1810 diplomatic treaties precociously placed the Portuguese colony within the sphere of English influence and into a state of dependency on the European power then exercising its greatest expansion overseas. The routine and mercantile dynamic of the port of Rio (as of the remainder of the colony's ports) would be forever changed.

Rio de Janeiro's *raison d'être* was thus transformed, both in terms of its social make-up and in relation to the realm of representation and the collective imaginary. The city's hitherto somnolent daily life gave way to the bustle of intrigue and feasting, to the demands and rituals that accompanied the presence of the court. Rio grew and gained in complexity with respect to both its increase in territory and population and its role in history. Maria Odila Silva Dias called this process the "interiorization of the metropolis": the slow process whereby metropolitan roots and agents took root in Rio and in the Portuguese colony's Southeast region (in Mota 1972, 160–184). And it was on the shores of Rio de Janeiro that natural scientists and travel writers disembarked: among them Debret, Saint Hilaire, Luccock, Mawe, and Eschwege.

With the court's presence in Rio, various citadels of culture came into being concerning the arts, history, and administration: the Military Archive, the Navy's Academy, the Royal Press, the Library, the Royal Gardens, the Medical School, Brazil's bank, the S. João Royal Theater, and the school of Fine Arts which in 1815 welcomed members of a French mission, following the example of Taunay, Debret, and Grandjean de Montigny. In this fashion Rio de Janeiro became the theater of the principal events that anticipated and laid the groundwork for the colony's political independence (Falcon and Mattos in Mota 1972, 297). In the first quarter of the nineteenth century, Rio also became the center of gravity for a new empire: Brazil. In the 1830s Auguste de Saint-Hilaire noted that "havia um pais chamado Brasil, mas absolutamente não havia brasileiros" (qtd. in Sussekind 21) ("there was a country named Brazil, but there were absolutely no

Brazilians"). Rio gained historical significance as a capital in a Brazil that was founded by the heir to the Portuguese Crown, distant from its people and formed an empire more than a nation, governed by a nominally liberal and enlightened constitution (though the economy was based on slave labor).

As the capital city of the independent Empire of Brazil, Rio de Janeiro witnessed the rituals of the proclamation in Campo de Santana and the coronation of D. Pedro as first Emperor of Brazil in 1822, both carefully registered in the descriptions and images of Jean Baptiste Debret. Once Debret had painted an allegory of Portuguese supremacy for the court theater curtain in which the King of Portugal was surrounded by his kneeling subjects; now the same Debret replaced this painting with one depicting the allegory of the new Empire of Brazil. At the center of the new allegory, a crowned queen bearing the Imperial scepter and mantle holds up stone tablets representing the constitution and a shield with the coat of arms of the young emperor. Though the painter's sketch envisioned her throne being supported by the tops of two palm trees, José Bonifácio–weary that these might betray a touch of wilderness in the allegory of the new state–insisted that these be replaced in the allegory by golden caryatids. The background was made up of a mountain range, a dense vegetation, and the ocean. In the foreground, to the left, one observes an anchored ship loaded with bags of coffee and bundles of sugarcane. The steps leading to the throne boast a cornucopia of the country's fruits. Surrounding the throne Brazilians of all types pledge their loyalty to the new throne: an old man and a young naval officer, whites and blacks, natives of Minas Gerais and of São Paulo. According to Debret's own description of the allegory, "caboclos ajoelhados mostram com sua atitude respeitosa o primeiro grau de civilização que os aproxima do soberano" ("kneeling *mestizos* display a respectful attitude worthy of their sovereign"), while in the sumptuous natural vista of the background "Indios armados e voluntariamente reunidos aos soldados brasileiros" (Debret 326 and 329) ("armed Indians voluntarily join Brazilian soldiers").

This new allegory for the court theater is rich and expressive in meaning. The Imperial throne dominates the scene and the land, while the three races are presented as compatible and complementary both to Brazil's prodigious nature and its European inheritance. Mattos reads the significance of the sugar and coffee loaded onto the anchored ship as the guarantee that the old mercantile order would continue to prey on Brazil's agriculture and the presentation of the tablets of the constitution as an allegorical elision of citizenship with the hierarchy of Empire which shields the interests of the elite class (Ilmar Mattos 109–29). The curtain already anticipates the applause and support of members of the good society that frequented the theater.

As the theater itself staged the meaning of the new imperial state, the city of Rio de Janeiro constructed its centrality within the empire on both a political and symbolic level and reinforced its status as capital. Politically this represented no small achievement in the construction of national unity within the vast territory of the old Portuguese colony. In 1822 São Paulo's representative before the court at Lisbon, future leader Father Diogo Antonio Feijó, remarked "Não somos deputados do Brasil. . . porque cada Província se governa hoje independente (qtd. in Mota 1972, 185) ("We are not deputies of Brazil. . . for currently every province governs itself independently"). In effect before the relocation of the Portuguese court to Rio de Janeiro in 1808, each colonial region (or administrative province, to use Feijó's term) reported directly to Lisbon. The centralization of power in the capital along with the recognition of Rio's centrality on behalf of each part of the territory was the result of a long period of consolidation that only concluded in the second half of the nineteenth century. Most acute during the period of regency, demands for provincial autonomy and manifestations of regional difference continued into the reigns of D. Pedro I and D. Pedro II.

The struggles concerning the new empire's unity were forged both on the battlefield and in the political arena. Unity was made possible only by the common interest of the elites in each of the Empire's provinces. Anti-slavery lobbies from within and from abroad (principally from England) made the local elites rally around the goal of guaranteeing, preserving, and reproducing the order of the slave economy. In 1834 the city of Rio de Janeiro was differentiated from the administrative body of the Brazilian empire through the Additional Act which transformed Rio into a Neutral Municipality, reinforcing its capital importance to the construction of the new imperial order. Representations of the Empire's unity abounded in Rio de Janeiro, be they to the empire as a whole or to the person of the emperor, which the 1824 constitution deemed to be sacred and inviolable. Interprovincial arrangements were to be orchestrated in the capital. From Rio armed forces and the battle of ideas were set in motion to quash autonomous movements and further Federalist ideals. When the coffee from Paraíba Valley transformed the city into an economic and financial center, the city consolidated its historical function as capital and center of order.

Rio also came to embody the center of empire in the realm of representation and the collective imaginary. Those who lived in the provinces regarded the city as an irradiating focus of civilization. Rio de Janeiro was also perceived as a marvelous realm far from the rustic world of the farm, as evident in the comedies of Martins Pena (1815–1848) such as *O Juiz de Paz na roça* [1842; The Rural Justice of the Peace], *Um sertanejo na Corte* [From the Hinterland to the Court], *Os Dous ou o inglês machinista* [The Two, or the English Machinist]. Martins Pena's protagonist in *O Juiz de Paz na roça*, Aninha, demonstrates this conflation of the court in Rio with the world of the fantastic, in particular, when she mixes up her boyfriend's news about the beauty and grandeur of the capital city: "Como é bonita a Corte! Lá é que a gente se pode divertir, e não aqui, onde não se ouve senão os sapos e as entanhas cantarem. Teatros, mágicas, cavalos que dançam, cabeças com dous cabritos, macaco major. . . . Quanta cosa! Quero ir para a Corte!" (Pena 41)("How the court is beautiful! There people can amuse themselves, but not here, where we can only hear the songs of frogs and rustic creatures. Theaters, magic, dancing horses, two-headed goats, monkeys. . . . How many things! I want to go to the Court!").

At once the microcosm and synthesis of empire, Rio represented the empire in its totality. The Rua do Ouvidor was the site of a constant pageantry of the elegant ladies of the city, the province, and the rest of the empire—all in search of the latest Parisian fashions in local stores bearing French names. Government officials made the rounds followed closely by snippets of political gossip and rumor. Those less privileged gathered in kiosks that constituted meeting points for casual socializing, perhaps seeking fortune through the purchase of a lottery ticket or simply oblivion in a drink from their grinding routine. While Rio's Institute for Geography and History

forged the discourse of the consolidation of the nation's unity, slaves and free black men in the city celebrated in their own belief systems the true historical rationale for this same unity. While the journalists, ad men, and the literati sought the divine portal to the Garnier bookstore or even the doors to the less sacred Leuzinger and Laemmert bookstores, beggars took to the streets, just as in Colonial times. Slave children were sold at the market in Valongo, while the children from the elites throughout the Empire learned their lessons from Joaquim Manoel de Macedo and prepared to become good citizens of the Republic at the Imperial school named after D. Pedro II (see Selma Mattos). While the emperor corresponded with Victor Hugo, Dom Obá II D' África, the free descendent of the enslaved Alafim de Oió, circulated within city streets, always bearing an umbrella that few knew to be a sign of his noble lineage in Africa (see Silva). Engineers were taught to forge progress through their own art at the old Escola Central, later (in 1874) renamed the Escola Politécnica (Turazzi 154), while discontented members of the military planned the fall of the monarchy and the rise of a Republic, no less identified with progress. While the fall of the empire was planned, members of good society waltzed at Ilha Grande under the eyes of the emperor and the princess, the heir to the throne. After the fall of the monarchy this same good society would waltz at the inauguration of Catete Palace, the old house of the Barons of Nova Friburgo that was converted into the Presidential Palace. Once, an anonymous crowd gathered at D. Pedro II Square to see the entry of Imperial high society for the ball at Ilha Fiscal; now that the square was renamed after the date of the Proclamation of the Republic, November 15, an anonymous crowd gathered to see the same high society enter the salons of the Republic (see Ferreira Netto).

Order continued to guide the Republican project even after Brazil's territorial unity was consolidated in the nineteenth century. Now identified with progress, order remained the fulcrum of the concerns that shaped state policy. The passage from monarchy to Republic represents another transformation without change: The Republic did not broaden the notion of citizenship or incorporate those previous excluded from the political arena. Rather the Republic sought to differentiate itself from the empire through a double gesture: First, it tried to identify the empire with the backwardness of Colonial times, as a memory to be erased. In turn, the capital was sanitized and illuminated as an example to the country and the world that Brazil had already entered into the era of progress and civilization. Nonetheless, the old oligarchies and paternalistic practices continued. This led to the modernizing reforms of the first decades of the twentieth century and the consolidation of Rio de Janeiro as the nation's cultural center and capital. The modernizing process stressed other features key to Rio's centrality: the aspiration to the cosmopolitanism worthy of a metropolis, the discourse of Rio as the seat of power, and the discourse of Rio as metonym for Brazil in its entirety (Resende 124).

The International Exhibition of 1922, celebrating the centenary of independence, served as a mark of modernity in the tropics. Erected on the site where the city had been founded and Castelo Hill had been razed, the exhibition served as an occasion for the city to be founded anew. Nonetheless it also drew attention to the dueling forces of nationalism and cosmopolitanism: Ever since Pereira Passos's first project, this duality in directives and values had marked the city's cultural tradition. This tension was evident in Brazilian modernism as a whole, but in particular in the modernity that characterized the reconstructed Rio de Janeiro. Republican Rio was meant to embody at once a model for the nation and a possible new Europe. Many writers, such as Lima Barreto and João do Rio, lamented the disappearance of popular traditions and even of the city's own cultural memory. But the International Exhibition presented these regionalist and traditional markers of cultural identity in tension with an emergent cosmopolitanism.

María Alice Carvalho observes that Rio's modernity took place outside of the unifying logic of the market. No significant restructuring of society occurred to incorporate intellectuals and the underprivileged alike. Rather, modern Rio reinforced the exclusive quality of the city's social fragmentation: No mechanisms were set in place to allow Rio's citizens to come to recognize themselves as citizens and thus as participants in a polis and hence sprang the fascination of carioca intellectuals with the underworld, their attempt to capture in the streets an alternative social organization and environment. Only in this fashion could intellectuals identify themselves with the underprivileged and see the city as a constitutive element of their own identify. While some intellectuals were, for a variety of reasons, co-opted by the art sanctioned by the official bureaucracy, others sought to conceive of the city, and by extension of country, through Rio's streets. The streets were interpreted as a space rich in meaning, the origin of novel cultural forms. They revealed the existence of a segment of the population hitherto neglected in the eyes of the modernizing republic. Those intellectuals who emphasized what could be learned from street life and society refuted the possibility of an organized literary movement along the lines of official policy and bureaucracy. Rather they preferred to speak of a discovery of the city, of its places and its types as the starting point for a broader reflection on society.

While São Paulo's 1922 Week of Modern Art was conducted under the sign of the aesthetic, Rio de Janeiro, at the time, did not possess an avant-garde movement centered on an aesthetic ideal of modernity proper, but rather one constructed through an informal network based on the everyday life of the city. Brazilian modernism transcended the realm of the aesthetic and possessed a political dimension, as is evident in the meeting of the Constituent Assembly of Brazil's Communist Party on 25 March 1922. Though the rebellion of the young officers stationed in the fort at Copacabana was defeated, it reflected a dissatisfaction with Brazil's political tradition that culminated in the Revolution of 1930. One should not neglect the force of conservative thought in this period: Figures associated with the Catholic Church–among them Jackson de Figueiredo, Rio's Archbishop Sebastião Leme, and Alceu Amoroso Lima–founded the Dom Vital center and the magazine A Ordem.

Rio was the site of Brazil's first radio transmission on 7 September 1922, as part of the commemoration of the centenary of independence, and in 1923 Henrique Morize and Edgard Roquette Pinto created at the Brazilian Academy of Science the Rádio Sociedade do Rio de Janeiro (today the station owned by the Ministry of Education). Brazil's first cinematographers were present in Rio from the end of the nineteenth century. Ademar Gonzaga founded the magazine Cinearte in 1926 and the studio Cinédia in 1931 to further the notion of a quality national cinema. It was in Rio that samba first developed:

According to legend it originated at the house of Bahia native Tia Ciata, next to Onze Square. And it was here that the first samba song was recorded, "Pelo Telefone" (the composition is attributed to Donga). Toward the end of the 1920s emerged the carnivalesque song or marchinha, a typical manifestation of Rio's carnival and above all of the cariocas's malicious sense of humor. During the same period the revelers who gathered in Estácio, next to the Normal School, forged the first samba school. With the passing of time, samba schools came to be at the center of the experience of carnival both in Rio and throughout Brazil. Vinyl records made their Brazilian debut in Rio, and the nucleus for the evolution of Brazilian popular music remained in Rio with the era of the great composers and singers. In Rio enthusiasm for samba and the music of carnival topped that demonstrated in any other Brazilian city. In 1924 Blaise Cendras and the São Paulo modernists came to Rio to experience carnival. Writer Oswald de Andrade (1890–1954) would register this pilgrimage in his Manifesto Pau-brasil [Brazil-wood Manifesto]: For the modernists carnival would signify the race's great religious event. Beholding this traditional pageantry afresh and under the sign of the new, they undertook no less than a discovery of Brazil. Six of every ten Brazilian books edited in 1929 were published in Rio: The means of cultural production tended to be strongly concentrated there (Miceli 84). In Brazil the advance of modernism was vertiginous: While Anita Malfatti's avant-garde exhibition had been poorly received in São Paulo in December 1917, Tarsila do Amaral's thirty-five modernist paintings were successfully exhibited in Rio in September 1929. If the bastions of tradition and anti-intellectual sentiment were defeated or at least neutralized, the success of Tarsila do Amaral pointed to the incipient institutionalization of modernism in Rio de Janeiro, a process that was to be completed through the cultural policy of President Getúlio Vargas.

Rio's Urban Culture during Vargas's Presidency and Afterward

Historians classify the country's radical transformations of the 1930s and 1940s as marks of a new period in Brazil's history: the Vargas era. From the 1930 Revolution onward, urbanization and industrialization were accelerated, and the lower classes gained increasing political power. A new social dynamic arose, defined by the emergence of a public hungry for information and leisure and by the rise of mass media. In Rio de Janeiro these transformations coincided with the golden age of popular music and radio. Among the most influential radio stations one may single out the station Mayrink Veiga do Rio de Janeiro, founded in 1934; the station established by the daily Jornal do Brasil in 1935; and the Rádio Nacional. First created by the daily A Noite in 1936, the Nacional became the property of the federal government in 1940 and fulfilled an important role in Brazilian culture as a unifying force from its location at Mauá Square (Rio de Janeiro's kilometer zero). Theater revues (a carioca trademark) and films came to attract a large public, while samba and carnival acquired international significance. Rio's role as capital was only reinforced by its status as a center for the production and dissemination of culture, beamed to the rest of the country through instruments of mass communication.

Much of this cultural effervescence took place in the vicinity of Lapa and in Cinelândia, which could be termed Rio's Broadway with its proliferation of movie theaters, tea-houses, and cafés. Rio Branco Avenue was the site for the great pageantry of the samba school processions during carnival. The first musicals premiered at the movie theaters along its neighboring streets–representatives of a hybrid genre of film that mixed comedy and carnival and that would mark the trajectory of Brazilian cinema for more than twenty years in works such as *Coisas Nossas* [1931; Our Things], *A voz do carnaval* [1933; The Voice of the Carnival], and *Alô, Alô, Carnaval* [1936; Hello, Hello, Carnival]. Ademar Gonzaga, who released these three films, tried to concentrate in Rio some of the more talented filmmakers (such as Humberto Mauro) from the country's other regions. In the 1930s Brazilian cinema was fundamentally the cinema of Rio, although it was still too precarious to compete with imported films.

In turn the neighborhood of Lapa encompassed alleys, Colonial houses, bordellos, cafés, and dance clubs, bringing together intellectuals, politicians, artists, and the *bas fond* made up of gamblers, prostitutes, and the streetwise *malandros*. If the Avenida Central was intended as its Parisian boulevard in the imaginary of the writers, Lapa represented Rio's Montmartre: there art, literature, and journalism mingled in a bohemian existence. For many intellectuals the experience of Lapa nightlife seemed to guarantee the modernity of their work. In his 1954 memoir *Itinerário de Pasárgada* [Itinerary of Pasárgada], poet Manuel Bandeira (1886–1968) stressed contact with the common man and the education of street life as the paths to understanding not only the city, but national identity. While it remained the national capital, Rio de Janeiro was characterized by a cultural dynamic that fused avant-garde cosmopolitanism with the expressions of a formidably rich popular culture.

Vargas's administration (1930–1945) was intent on capitalizing on this dynamic. Through the creation of the Ministry of Education and the Department for News and Propaganda, the Vargas regime constructed an efficient apparatus to reach both the elites and the entirety of society. While research and academic inquiry were encouraged by the intellectuals surrounding Capanema's ministry, the regime exercised strict control over the media of mass communication and over manifestations of popular culture. Minister Gustavo Capanema appointed the poet Carlos Drummond de Andrade (1902–1987) as his chief of staff. Drummond de Andrade surrounded himself with prestigious intellectuals such as Mário de Andrade (1893–1945), Rodrigo de Mello Franco de Andrade (1898–1969), Anísio Teixeira (1900–1971), Heitor Villa Lobos (1887–1959), Fernando de Azevedo (1894–1974), and Manuel Bandeira. With the support of this group, Drummond was able to undertake bold and innovative projects: the creation of Brazil's Federal University (currently the Federal University in Rio), the National Historical and Artistic Heritage Foundation, the National Institute for the Book, and the construction of the headquarters for the Ministry of Health and Education (today Rio's Palácio da Cultura). Designed by Lúcio Costa and a team of nine architects who submitted their preliminary sketches to be reviewed by Le Corbusier, the building also boasted murals by Cândido Portinari (1903–1962) and gardens by Burle Marx (1909–1994). It remains one of the landmarks of modernist architecture in Brazil.

Already in 1930 the government arranged for a collective exhibition of traditional and modernist painters at New York's Roerich Museum. This official support for the arts would only increase, making of Rio an important center for the dissemination of art to rival São Paulo. As director of the National School of Fine Arts, Luiz Edmundo Costa organized–along with Manuel Bandeira and Anita Malfatti–the 1931 revolutionary salon in which the government first presented modern art to the general public. Theater also benefited from the support of the intellectuals affiliated with Capanema's ministry. In December 1943 the troupe "Os comediantes" premiered Nelson Rodrigues's landmark *Vestido de Noiva* [1943; The Wedding Dress] at Rio's Municipal Theater with the official sanction of the government and the attendance of President Vargas and his entourage. Influenced by European avant-garde theater and directed by Ziembinsky, the play represented the genesis of modern Brazilian theater.

Research into the past and into questions of national identity were key to this quest for modernity. The publishing market witnesses the emergence of series specifically dedicated to these themes: the series *Brasiliana*, edited by Fernando de Azevedo for São Paulo's Editora Nacional, and the series *Documentos Brasileiros* for Rio's Livraria José Olympio Editora, edited by Gilberto Freire (1900–1987), Afonso Arinos de Mello Franco (1905–1990) and Otávio Tarquínio de Sousa (1889–1959). During this period Olympio, one of the country's three largest publishing houses, came to take the prominent place that belonged to Garnier in the nineteenth century. Olympio's headquarters in Rio were a meeting point for the intelligentsia. Olympio's role was not, however, limited to intellectual matters. Its most secure investments pertained to the genre of the romance novel and its strongest backers occupied important posts in the Brazilian Academy of Letters and in the councils, institutes, and other decision-making bodies affiliated with the federal government (Miceli 89). In addition to the intellectuals who were recently co-opted by the state and formed an organic part of the regime, Olympio attracted to Rio a large range of modernist writers who depended on the publishing house for their distribution and prestige: Among them were Graciliano Ramos (1892–1953), José Lins do Rêgo (1901–1957), Rachel de Queiróz (b. 1910), and others who excelled in writing the regionalist fiction of the 1930s. In this fashion a publishing house situated in Rio played a principal role in the formation of the canon of modern Brazilian literature.

While the Vargas regime embraced quite diverse interpretations of Brazilian identity, it did not do so uncritically. The regime sanctioned portraits of Brazil so long as they remained rural, realistic, objective, and sociological (in this vein one can interpret the second-generation modern novel of the Northeast). Consequently, the literature of the city of Rio met with the criticism that it was too urban. Thus Machado de Assis, the nineteenth-century master who had hitherto been the model for the *carioca* narrative tradition, came to embody a sort of anti-paradigm characterized by a dissipating cosmopolitanism and excessive subjectivity. According to the official magazine *Cultura Política*, to emulate Machado and focus on the Rua do Ouvidor, the aristocratic salons of Botafogo, or even the more humble suburbs represented turning one's back on the real Brazil. As M. Velloso observes (1988), the regime encouraged writers to interpret national experience through the vantage point of rural and regionalist perspectives.

Albeit one of the greatest targets for official control and censure, Rio's popular culture nonetheless became a prime inspiration for Brazil's national culture. One should understand the state's relationship to popular culture as a dynamic where repression and domination did not rule out the mutual construction of new modes of popular cultural expression. In Rio de Janeiro, for example, the pageantry of the samba schools during carnivals became an officially sanctioned event. The government went as far as making exacting requirements for the procession and interfering in the make-up of the schools, although the *sambistas* did well to guarantee a space for their survival (see M. Augras).

It is through the Department for News and Propaganda that the state imposed its doctrines and its authority. Under the direction of Lourival Fontes, this department channeled the conservative wing of São Paulo's modernists, a wing known by the name *verde-amarelos* (green-yellow, in a nod to the colors of Brazil's flag). Cassiano Ricardo became the editor of the official newspaper, *A Manhã*, and head of the cultural department of the National Radio. It was this radio station that blacked out all other signals throughout Brazil for an hour every day for the compulsory transmission of *A Voz do Brasil*, known for its signature opening melody, the prelude to Carlos Gomes's nationalist opera *O Guarani*. In 1941 Herón Domingues created the radio news program *Repórter Esso*, inspired by American news programs and dependent on the press releases from United Press International (UPI). This program gained such credibility that the public came to deem the *Esso* report synonymous with news. In the 1930s, radio brought something unprecedented to Brazil's increasingly urban society: the possibility of mass leisure free of charge. Live programs recorded before studio audiences on National Radio attracted veritable multitudes. Radio mania ensued, bringing about a revolution in customs, dictating fashion and behavior, inventing expressions, and provoking consumer demand. Dozens of programs focused on these themes emerged during the 1940s, among them *A Revista do Rádio* and *Radiolândia*.

Vargas's regime was attentive to the great impact of mass media on the general population which relied on the radio almost exclusively for news and leisure. Radio and carnival merited particular attention from the Department for News and Propaganda. Not infrequently the department would allow a carnival song to be featured in a film soundtrack, but not to be played on radio during carnival. Radio stations and newspapers were considered frontline means for the dissemination of the authoritarian regime's ideology. Only intellectuals of the right were appointed to the key posts in these stations and dailies, as a guarantee of cultural homogeneity. As in Hannah Arendt's description of totalitarianism, in Brazil the government co-opted society from within: Ideology was woven into the fabric of everyday life through textbooks, national newspapers, cinema, theater, popular music, carnival, and official and popular festivities. Vargas's 1937 Constitution deemed public service and the public good to be the goal of communication and decreed an end to freedom of speech. The government seized the dailies *A Manhã* and *A Noite* in a measure which betrayed its control of the flow of information. And yet, despite the rigid control exercised by the Department for News and Propaganda, the greater part of the press in Rio sided with the opposition and succeeded not infrequently in evading censure.

Composers of Brazilian popular music likewise reacted against government policy as implemented through the Brazilian Society for Theater Actors. Dissatisfied with the law governing authorial rights, a group of composers led by Lamartine Babo, Eratóstenes Frazão, and Mário Lago founded the Brazilian Association of Composers of Music. In 1942, writers led by Tarquínio de Sousa (1889–1959) founded the Association of Brazilian Writers to defend their freedom of speech: Among

the founding members were Sérgio Buarque de Hollanda, Graciliano Ramos, José Lins do Rêgo, Mário de Andrade, Oswald de Andrade (1890–1954), Astrogildo Pereira Duarte Silva (1890–1965), and Érico Veríssimo (1905–1975). The initiatives of writers and composers clearly demonstrated the limits of the cultural policy instituted by Vargas's authoritarian regime, the *Estado Novo*. The period's cultural dynamic was marked by tensions between force and consent, between repression and acceptance. No consideration of propaganda in 1940s Brazil can neglect Walt Disney's creation of the Brazilian character Zé Carioca ("Joe from Rio") with the aim of gaining the support of Brazilian public for the U.S. entry into World War II and Brazil's possible move in the same direction. The 1942 U.S. film featuring Zé Carioca–released in Brazil under the title *Alô, Amigos*–included Ari Barroso's song "Aquarela do Brasil," a samba which uncritically and grandiloquently exalted Brazilian patriotism. In 1941 the regime's official magazine *Cultura Política* had ominously praised Barroso's song as "the samba of legitimacy."

At this point Rio de Janeiro's popular culture already constituted a framework of reference for the rest of the country, even if the nation's embrace of *carioca* popular culture was by no means always uncritical. Among the Vargas's regime most significant strategies for co-opting the power of popular culture were the aforementioned legitimization of samba, the transformation of carnival pageants and balls into official events, the institution of a national day in honor of the composer of popular music, and the dissemination abroad of Brazilian and in particular *carioca* music: *samba* and *chorinho*. Gilberto Freyre and other academics came to Rio to experience first-hand Afro-Brazilian music. H. Vianna observes that in the 1930s all Brazil recognized in Rio the emblem of the nation's *sambista* people. Samba certainly was the center of the cultural debates of the time. In the Northeast, novelist José Lins do Rego and historian Pedro Calmon discussed the question of samba in the pages of the dailies *A Noite* and *O Jornal* in June and July 1939. While Rego defended samba as an expression of Brazilian culture, Calmon countered that the people and nation of Brazil could not be reduced to Salgueiro Hill in Rio de Janeiro. In turn Fransisco Guimarães, a columnist for Rio's *Jornal do Brasil*, defended the hills of Rio as the true havens for authentic samba and criticized the participation of intellectuals (see Cabral and Guimarães).

The debate on samba raises a question key to construction of Brazilian cultural identity: How to integrate popular culture into a synthesis that might represent the entirety of Brazilian culture? At the time mainstream culture integrated elements of popular culture most successfully and dynamically in Rio's bohemian circles, where the educated and uneducated often collaborated in composing samba for theater revues and carnival. Rio's bohemian circles demonstrated that, alongside state repression and censure, there was also a mutual collaboration between representatives of the state and society at large. In the 1930s and 1940s philosophical meditations and expressions of popular culture alike stressed the fundamental syncretism underlying Brazilian culture: The force of Afro-Brazilian culture and samba came to form part of national identity. Rio then provided rich soil for such elaboration in its capacity as cultural capital.

The tension between local and cosmopolitan culture was a frequent topic in the discussions over national identity that then took place in Rio. A characteristic intervention in this debate is Álvaro Lins's 1942 essay "É uma saga do Rio de Janeiro em termos de provincia-naçao" ["A Saga of Rio de Janeiro in Terms of the Province-Nation"] which insists on the primacy of the local and provincial experience. Considering the work of *carioca* writer Marques Rebelo, Lins calls into question the existence of an urban literary tradition in Brazil. Lins argues that national identity should be staked on local experience at the expense of cosmopolitanism; otherwise Brazilian identity would descend to the level of the *déraciné*, the fake, the artificial and the cosmopolitan. By *déraciné* Lins meant everything that was anemic and undernourished, bereft of the vigor and blood of the earth. Note how he resorted to the language of pathology to diagnose cosmopolitanism as devoid of life and health. For Lins, a universal sensibility must be first rooted in the provincial, the national spirit being itself no more than the combination of provincial spirits. At the center of this national spirit stood Rio de Janeiro as the sum of all the provinces—as an archprovince that would represent everything that was purely and authentically Brazilian. Diverse traditions would converge and enter into dialogue in Rio, the city which welcomed so many writers, artists, and producers of other cultural life.

If Brazilian modernism originated in São Paulo, out of necessity the movement was only institutionalized in the federal capital, Rio de Janeiro, during the Vargas regime. It was at Rio's Itamarati Palace and with the benefit of twenty years of retrospective experience that writer and São Paulo native Mário de Andrade described São Paulo's 1922 Week of Modern Art as a modernist movement and came to terms with its shortcomings. With this statement in Rio of his ultimate disappointment with Brazilian Modernism, Mário de Andrade symbolically closed the cycle started in 1922 in São Paulo. In 1942 Andrade helped found the Brazilian Association of Writers, and in 1945 the association organized the first Brazilian Congress of Writers in São Paulo. Both landmarks were associated with the call for a return to a fully democratic state.

After Vargas's dictatorship Brazil experienced a new and not entirely stable democratic order characterized by rapid development and industrialization and widespread optimism among the country's elites. In the immediate aftermath of World War II and the return of democracy the newly urban and industrialized Brazil witnessed the emergence of a true mass culture (Ortiz, 1988, 38). Rio's Rádio Nacional gained a large audience with its variety shows and soap operas. In the 1940s and 1950s film became a consumer good of mass consumption in Brazil. During this period Cine Atlântida consolidated its position as the most prolific studio in Rio and by extension in Brazil. Above all, Atlântida's success was due to the *chanchadas*, a popular genre which fused comedy and musical and which incorporated radio's most renowned actors into productions reminiscent of light melodrama (Ortiz 1988, 70). In 1951 Diários Associados introduced TV Tupi, Rio de Janeiro's first television station. In 1953 Rio saw the emergence of the tabloid magazine *Manchete*, which came to rival in circulation the weekly review *O Cruzeiro*, though the latter retained the largest circulation in the country, as its slogan suggested—the largest and best magazine in Latin America.

Though this period in Brazilian history was characterized by a sharp increase in the influence of the United States and the growth of its cultural industry, it also proved a dynamic and stimulating moment for Brazil's own project of national development and for the articulation of Brazilian cultural production in many areas (Hollanda and Gonçalves 33). An Advanced Institute for Brazilian Studies was founded in Rio in 1955 with the aim of encouraging its scholars to interpret Brazil and its ideological productions. The city's entrepreneurial class also responded to this new optimism concerning the state of arts and culture in Brazil, and in May 1948 art patron and collector Raymundo de Castro Maia founded Rio's Museum of Modern Art. The museum's aim was to instill in the general public a taste for modern art, to introduce and educate the public to understand that contemporary artists do not aim to mystify, but rather seek to explore what they feel. Its first exhibit showcased contemporary European painting at the headquarters of Bank Boa Vista in Rio. The Museum of Modern Art soon gained the support of Niomar Moniz Sodré, representing a group that held a proprietary interest in one of the most important national dailies, the *Correio da Manhã*. In 1952 the museum found a home at the headquarters for the Ministry of Education and Health, and in 1955 it opened its own cinemathèque. The Museum of Modern Art has consistently defended the avant-garde in the arts before the city's public for over half a century. In 1957 the museum opened the First National Exhibit of Concrete Art, soon after welcoming dissidents from the São Paulo Concretist movement with individual shows devoted to Lygia Clark, Amilcar de Castro, and others who were affiliated with poet and art critic Ferreira Gullar, theorist of Neo-Concrete art. In 1967 the museum was transferred to its current site in Flamengo in a building designed by Affonso Eduardo Heidy which remains a landmark of modern architecture in Brazil.

This same climate of optimism toward the end of the 1950s saw the emergence of bossa nova, the meeting of samba with modern jazz, according to Antônio Carlos Jobim. Alongside the poet Vinicius de Moraes and singer João Gilberto, Jobim was the protagonist of the new phenomenon typical of the culture of south Rio's bourgeois middle class. Bossa nova gave continuity to the city's tradition of seeking a synthesis between its popular culture and its cosmopolitan ambitions. The optimism of these times was also reflected in the publication (between 1957 and 1961) in the daily *Jornal do Brasil* of a weekly special supplement devoted to the most recent developments in the arts both in Brazil and abroad.

The dream of Brazil as a developed nation was embodied in the construction of the new capital Brasília by modernist visionary President Juscelino Kubtschek. Though Rio ceased to be the nation's capital, it did not lose the traits of a capital city. In 1960 Brasília became the federal capital and the new state of Guanabara was created around the former capital of Rio de Janeiro. Despite the emergence of other cultural centers and the continued importance of São Paulo, Brazil's most significant events continued to resonate most sharply in Rio. In fact the culture generated and disseminated in Rio in the turbulent 1960s was strictly linked to the decade's political developments, and the city's dynamic culture gained a radical force after the 1964 military coup in Brasília. In Rio in 1961, the National Federation of Students created the first Center for Popular Culture to build a "national, popular, and democratic" culture and to defend Revolutionary art as an instrument of social revolution. The young intellectuals of these Centers for Popular Culture interacted directly with the masses, staging plays at shanty towns, factories, and unions, publishing the poetry series *Violão de rua* [Street Guitar], and producing self-financed films such as *Cinco vezes favela* [Five Times Shanty Town] (Hollanda and Gonçalves 10; Ortiz 68–78).

After the imposition of a military regime in 1964 the intelligentsia became a focus for political resistance. In this context one notes the landmark December 1964 premiere in Rio of the musical *Opinião* [Opinion] with a libretto by Oduvaldo Vianna, Armando Costa, and Paulo Pontes, music by popular black composers Zé Kéti and João do Vale, and featuring the muse of bossa nova and south Rio's upper middle class, Nara Leão (later replaced by Maria Betânia in her first starring role). The audience was made up largely from Rio's middle class. An art form of political opinion proved fundamental for the times, as evident in Arnoldo Jabor's film *Opinião Pública* [Public Opinion], and in the exhibits of an art renovated by urban themes and use of mass media, *Opinião 65* and *Opinião 66*. At *Opinião 65* Hélio Oiticica experimented with the first of his radical events termed *Parangolés*, bringing to the Museum of Modern Art members of the Mangueira samba school. Oiticica was also the subject of the 1967 exhibit of the Brazilian New Objectivity at the Museum of Modern Art. Within the context of the intellectual response to the military regime, Carlos Guilherme Mota singles out the publication between 1965 and 1968 of the *Revista Civilização Brasileira* [Brazilian Civilization Review] as a landmark in Brazil's progressive thinking and its cultural history. Brazil's *Cinema Novo* movement of the 1960s also stressed culture and politics as the flipsides of the same coin, as for example in Nelson Pereira dos Santos's (b. 1928) work *Rio, 40 graus* (1955) and *Rio Zona Norte* (1957). Centered in Rio, Brazil's new cinema emerged in opposition to what it deemed to be the colonialist tradition of Brazil's old cinema.

The military regime moved to suppress dissent and resistance with the passage and implementation of the Fifth Institutional Act in 1968, which brought into being a much cruder system of censorship and repression. Paradoxically the Brazilian market for cultural products modernized and expanded between 1964 and 1980 gave rise to a new socioeconomic reality. It was in this atmosphere of the youth's disillusion with alternatives to the military regime and with the political projects of the left that the country saw the emergence of a new counterculture. Perhaps best situated to reflect the contradictions of the time, late 1960s Rio de Janeiro gives rise to the *Tropicalismo* movement, which sought a fertile dialogue with the new cultural industry and its international ambitions. The youth counterculture and *Tropicalismo* channeled political rebellion into attitudes with respect to the body and to desire. In turn, reactionary and official culture found allies among printing presses and record labels and in TV Globo, which embraced the authoritarian regime's goal of national integration through culture (Ortiz 159). The country experienced an increasing institutionalization of its culture through the aggressive initiative of private enterprise and state agencies (such as Rio's National Theater Service and EMBRAFILME, the state film studio). Political censorship stimulated the search for new alternatives, be it at the level of an accessible alternative cultural production or at the underlying level of language (Hollanda and Gonçalves 96). If this phenomenon was discernible throughout Brazil, it was nonetheless most visible in Rio: The daily *O Pasquim* returned to the irreverent tradition that had characterized Rio's modernism in the first decades of the century (Velloso 1997). An alternative poetry thrived in the production of hand-crafted books and the practice of reading poetry as a spectacle. This was a poetry of everyday life that sought the development of an informal and humorous language (Heloisa Buarque de Hollanda 1980). In 1975

Leblon's Casa Grande Theater was the site for a series of debates before a large audience between intellectuals and artists on the nation's political and cultural predicament. With the benefit of retrospect, it has become the norm to refer to this forum as suggestive of an incipient re-democratization of the country which would only take place in the decade commencing in 1980. It is curious to note that these debates did not contemplate as a topic the consolidation of Brazil's cultural industry and market for cultural goods. During this time Rio de Janeiro was the country's cultural capital in respect to the broadcasts of its phenomenally influential TV Globo.

A discernible slowdown characterized Rio's economy in the 1980s, a malaise that was reflected in the city's cultural scene. A sharp increase in violent crime helped corrode the myth of Rio as a marvelous city, reactivating in the city's collective imaginary a strong nostalgia for better times in the past. Carnival still marked the city's calendar, albeit in a more commercial incarnation and facing competition from the carnival in Bahia. The visual arts remained strong, in particular thanks to the young artists that form the Generation of 80 that emerged from Lage Park's School of Visual Arts. Once more Rio's principal manifestation as a national cultural center was dependent on the journalism and soap operas on TV Globo, the largest station in Brazil and one of major significance in the international market. If Rio was no longer the hegemonic force it once was in the field of letters, it nonetheless remained a capital city with respect to the production and dissemination of mass culture.

In the 1990s the municipality sought to reverse this cultural decline and re-establish Rio as cultural center. With the help of the private sector, the municipality succeeded in revitalizing the city's historical center. Banco do Brasil, the Post Office, and other buildings converted their beautiful old headquarters in the heart of the city into cultural centers. Museums and art galleries renovated their sites to make space for pedagogical seminars and new cultural production aimed at the formation of a new public. The National Museum of Fine Arts and the Museum of Modern Art welcomed exhibitions from the international circuit of great museums. The Museum of Modern Art in particular made a new commitment to contemporary art and resumed its place in the city's cultural life. In this cultural landscape one should also note the programs of the Museu da República, the Paço Imperial, the Gávea Planetarium, the Maison France-Brazil, and the Federal University's Forum for Science and Culture. New theaters were established and Brazilian cinema attracted greater audiences. Seeking to become the greatest hub for audio-visual production, the municipality created RioFilme.

In its synthesis of exaltation and criticism, Veloso's song "Fora da ordem" supplied images that paradigmatically indicate how Rio is portrayed in literature. The song functions as a sort of collage that uncannily juxtaposes various fragments and clichés to create an allegory of the city in crisis. Little by little images of horror come to mix with images of joy. At first Veloso presents the city's urban spaces as segregated, fractured, and disharmonious: "Aqui tudo parece que é ainda construção e já é ruína" ("Everything seems to be in construction but is already in ruins"). A precarious order is never quite finished, but rather unravels in ruins. Yet the song also reveals hints of an intense life: The cacophony of the song's beginning contrasts with the static calm of the postcard city. Veloso captures the city through images that have been made banal due to their repetition in everyday life and on television: drug trafficking, street kids, a mulatto, the viaducts, the garbage. Finally he unites the contrary elements of his portrait:

> E o cano da pistola que as crianças mord
> Reflete todas as cores da paisagem da cidade
> Que é muito mais bonita
> E muito mais intensa que no cartão postal.

> And the children bite the barrel of a gun
> That reflects the city landscape in all its colors
> A landscape much more beautiful
> And much more intense than the postcard city.

In the song this vision of pessimism and catastrophe is balanced by the glimpse of an "excess of joy" that engages the spectator's sympathy. Nothing remains outside of the spectacle; the song accumulates bits from the multiple realities Veloso perceives in the city's human and urban landscape. From the raw material of its tensions, the city manufactures diverse beautiful harmonies. Images of catastrophe do not add up to an apocalyptic vision; the future is not filled with horror; nor does it deliver a final judgment. Yet neither does the song—the fruit of a time that no longer believes in utopias—point to a naïve utopia around which men and women might build a consensus. The narrator's voice is rooted in the present and does not betray a nostalgia for the city's golden age. Rather, a creative energy is born from the clash of construction and ruin. Another city and another order are made possible from the tense harmony that arises from the meeting of violence and joy.

Thus Veloso's song "Fora de Ordem" combines two visions that almost always occurred separately in literary representations of the metropolis, from the first moment that texts began to ask what it means to read and write the city of Rio de Janeiro. Two poems by Carlos Drummond de Andrade's 1978 collection *Discursos de primavera e outras sombras* [Discourses of Spring and Other Shadows] prove representative of this split between darker and more celebratory visions of the city: "Retrato de uma cidade" ["Portrait of a City"] and "Elegia carioca" ["An Elegy for Rio"]. "Retrato de uma cidade" celebrates Rio as an erotic and colorful revelry, reborn each day along with the nature to which it is indissolubly linked. In the poem an underlying sensuality holds together popular cultural manifestations such as carnival, soccer, religious practices, and the cult of woman and landscape. To decipher the code city (*cidade código*) one must remain attuned to the language specific to the city: "Cada cidade tem sua linguagem/nas dobras da linguagem transparente" ("Each city possesses its language/in the folds of its transparent language"). The poem concludes with a luminous portrait of the city which confuses night and light as signals of brightness: "Anoitece no Rio. A noite é luz sonhando" ("Night falls in Rio. Night is the dream of light"). "Elegia carioca," on the other hand, is a kind of chronicle of nostalgia in which the narrator of the poem embodies the city's decay: Both are marked by the changes brought about by progress and are corroded by the passage of time. And so the poem begins: "Nesta cidade vivi há quarenta anos/há 40 anos vivo esta cidade/a cidade me vive há 40 anos" ("In this city I have lived for forty years/for forty years I live this city/the city has lived me for forty years"). The poem soon becomes a lament for the loss of an affective cartography, for the passing of friends and the social and political facts and personalities that marked the life of the poet and the city. The poem is clearly autobiographical: The poet attempts to recuperate his experiences through memory and comes to renounce the possibility of fulfillment. Like the poet, the city is fragmented, and it is revealed as "O Rio diverso múltiplo/desordenado sob tantos planos" ("Rio diverse and multiple/out of order in so many planes").

Concomitant with the exaltation of Rio as the *Cidade Maravilhosa* or marvelous city is a nostalgic vision of the city that is reinforced in the face of the present's real or imaginary evils. Faced with the violence of the present, the collective imaginary projects into the past a vision of a beautiful and superior Rio de Janeiro. For alongside references to the city's beauty, it is the theme of violence that is most frequent in literary and mass media representations of the city: in Chico Buarque's (b. 1944) novel *Estorvo* [1992; Disturbance], Sérgio Sant' Anna's (b. 1942) *Contos e novelas reunidos* [1977; Collected Short Fiction and Novellas], and in the detective novels of Luiz Alfredo Garcia Roza (b. 1936) *O silêncio da chuva* [1996; The Rain's Silence], *Achados e perdidos*, [1998; Lost and Found], and *Vento sudoeste*, [1999; Southwestern Wind]. Violence is also the reigning theme in Paulo Lins's (b. 1958) 1997 novel *Cidade de Deus* [City of God] which describes the spread of crime in the *neofavela* (or neo-shanty-town) that answers to this name in west Rio de Janeiro. What distinguishes the *neofavela* as an urban space is its transformation by the war between drug traffickers and the corresponding violence and corruption within the police force. Violence also permeates the short stories and novels of José Rubem Fonseca (b. 1925), perhaps the city's most significant literary chronicler in the last three decades.

While Rubem Fonseca's fervor for Rio is obvious, it is necessary to qualify this statement and ask which Rio inspired Fonseca's passion. For as he writes in the opening of "O caso F.A." from the 1969 collection *Lúcia McCartney*, "The city is not what you see from the Sugar Loaf (mountain)" ("A cidade não é aquilo que se vê do Pão de Açúcar"). The phrase is characteristic of Fonseca's representation of Rio elsewhere in his work, and it is decidedly at odds with Drummond's portrait of Rio as a "Cidade feita de montanhas/em casamento indissolúvel/com o mar" ("City made of mountains/in indissoluble matrimony/with the sea"). Fonseca's phrase alerts his reader not to expect a postcard representation of Rio that would stress its monumental beauty at the expense of its human conflicts. Rather he presents Rio in an extreme close-up: Each small object gains an enormous dimension, and the city becomes an immense arena of disperse and wasted signs, a city of disproportionate weight in its relation with its inhabitants. Fonseca's Rio de Janeiro burns with violence and crisis. It is a problematic megalopolis characterized by the logic of exclusion and the destabilization of ethical and human values. In sum, it is the product of the process of modernization that characterizes the peripheral metropolis.

Fonseca views Rio under the sign of perversion, thus entering into dialogue with a long line of urban narratives of Rio that includes the work of José de Alencar (1829–1877), Joaquim Manuel de Macedo (1820–1882), Manuel Antônio de Almeida (1831–1861), Machado de Assis (1839–1908), Lima Barreto, João do Rio, and Marques Rebelo (1907–1973). He is at once faithful to this tradition and deliberately unfaithful, so as to recycle it to represent a perverse polis that includes everything that it rejects, excludes, segregates, disdains, and destroys. Fonseca's hyper-realist fiction follows the already classic partition of the city between its South and

North, and the differentiation of the latter from the former regarding aspects of social, economic, and cultural order. These are the markers of "The Partitioned City," to borrow the title of Zuenir Ventura's 1994 book-length expose (*A Cidade Partida*). As demonstrated in the first part of this study, the archeology of the city's partition dates to the period of Mayor Pereira Passos at the beginning of the twentieth century and his imposition on the city of a modernity at once exclusive and authoritarian. Rio's borders have been blurred over the course of time through the geography of crime which draws together rich and poor, the powerful and the marginalized, those who possess teeth and those who do not (the destitute and toothless man is a constant image in Fonseca's fiction). As Vera Follain de Figueiredo notes in a 1996 essay on the city and the geography of crime in Rubem Fonseca's fiction, "O crime ultrapassa qualquer fronteira ou limite, até proque Rubem Fonseca se nega a tematizar a vilência dos oprimidos. A geografia da violência se impõe a outros possíveis recortes da cidade, diluindo contornos, embaralhando as linhas do mapa" (89) ("Crime surpasses any frontier or limit, perhaps because Fonseca refuses to take as his theme the violence of the oppressed. The geography of violence superimposes itself upon other possible partitions for the city, blurring contours, and shuffling the lines on the map").

Fonseca's eminently urban fiction thus composes a broad mural on the subject of violence and establishes a constant dialogue with the non-literary world. All the while Fonseca breaks with mass media's daily exposition of violence as a banal spectacle. Fonseca's Rio is divided not by class struggle but by the fear and incomprehension of populations that do not possess a common language. He reveals violence as the common trait that permeates all segments of society. In this respect one might read the stories "Passeio Noturno I" ["Night Drive I"] and "Passeio Noturno II" ["Night Drive II"] in contrast to "Feliz Ano Novo" ["Happy New Year"] in which criminals rob an elegant upper-middle-class house in São Conrado on New Year's Eve (from the volume 1975 *Feliz Ano Novo*). In "Feliz Ano Novo," Fonseca envisions a band of criminals excluded from citizenship, the right to the city, and consumer society (which does violence to them via television), but united in destitution, hunger, and violence. While they suffer the institutional violence perpetrated by the police, they are agents of violence with respect to the bodies and properties of others. In contrast, in the two versions of "Passeio," Fonseca focuses on a rich yet disunited family caught up in the game of appearances of bourgeois society. Only consumer goods and the money that provides access to these unite the family. The concise and bruising tale concerns a millionaire who gives in to his solitary and sadist desire for violence after a stressful day at his company job. He has fashioned his own rituals where he becomes a man-machine. Leaving his wife and children to their own individualistic routines, the millionaire goes for a drive in his expensive car and deliberately runs over defenseless women. The two tales conclude with his return home, where he finds everything in its place—including the sight of his wife, as always, watching television—and is ready for "um dia terrível na companhia" ("one more terrible day at work"). Violence permeates the city from the realm of the individual to that of the group, the family and the institution (as evident in the 1983 detective novel, *A grande arte* [The Great Art]).

Fonseca's fiction is also concerned with the failure and shattering of love as a form of violence and in particular with the city's loss of an affective cartography. "Vivem empilhadas na cidade enquanto os tecnocratas afiam o arame farpado" (1975, 143) ("We live piled up in the city while the technocrats sharpen the barbed wire"), declares the protagonist interviewed in the story "Intestino Grosso" ["Large Intestine"], which closes the collection *Feliz Ano Novo*. Underlying Fonseca's understanding of Rio's urban reality there seems nonetheless to be a romantic and nostalgic vein and the vision of a city once civil and cordial, as evident in "A arte de andar nas ruas do Rio de Janeiro" ["The Art of Walking through the Streets of Rio de Janeiro"] in the 1992 collection *Romance negro e outras histórias* [The Black Novel and Other Stories]. Above all "A arte de andar nas ruas do Rio de Janeiro" provides an itinerary for its protagonist's wandering through the city. In his walks he recreates a cartography of meetings and confrontations, coincidences and surprises, stories and fragments of stories. His movement is determined not by the logic of a plot that might order these fragments and give them meaning but rather by that of the history of Rio de Janeiro and its protagonists. The text plays upon the relationship between memory and the city, between a writer (such as the protagonist of this and other stories) and his work.

In the tradition of Rio's urban fiction "A arte de andar nas ruas do Rio de Janeiro" chronicles the trajectory of Augusto, a dilettante who fashions himself as a writer after winning the lottery. Augusto sets himself up in an abandoned house in the old city center, the origin of both the protagonist and of Rio, to write a work also entitled *A arte de andar nas ruas do Rio de Janeiro*. He does not see the city through the eyes of the crowd but beholds it from within his own settled patterns of thinking. Without knowing it, this false *flaneur* is exiled in postmodernity: The narrative depicts scenes of proliferating urban violence and underscores the state of neglect and abandon that corroded the myth of the once *Cidade Maravilhosa*. While he observes and writes, the itinerant writer registers the presence of those who are at the margin of society and who speak with voices that do not communicate with each other. While he registers this polyphonic city, its visage at once concealed and visible, he believes he can solve the problems of the divided and perverted city. His objective is not to represent the city as an exotic spectacle of horror, crime, and misery; rather he focuses on the loss of civility, the corrosion of dialogue, the loss of points of reference for his affective cartography, and the violence of the destruction of Rio's collective memory. Walking through the city's historical center, Augusto wants to find a peripatetic art and philosophy that might help him establish a better communion with the city, a walking solution.

In his attempt to articulate text, city, and memory, Augusto notes the loss of the charming soul (registered by João do Rio) of a city reduced to places molded by habit. Augusto observes that the city is no longer in communion with its inhabitants and wants to go in search of the trace of this lost city. He wants his work in progress to discover and reinvent Rio. Driven by nostalgia, he ignores the dissonance between the rhythm of the metropolis and his own affective sensibility. Augusto's project is to resist up-rootedness, the dispersion of Babel, the vision of a city abandoned to graffiti. Augusto seeks to recover his roots, and that is why he moves into the center of the city into a space of social pulverization in a time of a destabilized subjectivity, where communication is difficult. Glued to the reality he observes from the ground floor, a prisoner in an urban environment that by definition does not encourage continued attention, the writer cannot escape the ruins and the remains of the city he reads. While he walks through a city with no aura, he is overtaken by the aura of nostalgia. While he pretends to construct his ideal reader and teaches prostitutes how to read, he indicates he is in need of a reader who will understand him. He seeks a reader who could stand in for the city, become its sign. He wants to teach the city to read, so it can recognize itself in Augusto's words and design for it. The art of walking through Rio's streets is also that of preparing someone to receive the city in turn, as recreated through literature. Augusto's project simultaneously sustains a nostalgic tone and a post-utopian disillusion: It feeds the desire to render urban space legible, saving its writing from the phantom of death, a writing that would pervert the perversions of political practices–that is to say, would include those that the city produced but has excluded.

Fonseca seeks to escape the exclusive demands of modernity by conceiving of the city as a series of discontinuous fragments, a patchwork of styles captured by a multiplicity of signs. He seeks to decipher the city which exists in the porous border between fiction and reality. In literary descriptions cities are confused with the words used to describe them. Yet the writing of the city on the page indicates that cities are not merely the product of memory or desire, as many of Italo Calvino's invisible cities are; rather they are complex objects that include both reality and its description. It is from this vantage point that Rubem Fonseca constructs a burning Rio de Janeiro with his writerly fervor, and it is from this vantage that Caetano Veloso sings the city "that is much more beautiful and much more intense than the postcard city." It is not the city seen from the Sugar Loaf.

Translation by Paulo Horta

Works Cited

A Era Vargas I. 1996. Cd-Rom. Rio de Janeiro: Cpdoc.

Abreu, Maurício de A. 1987. *Evolução urbana do Rio de Janeiro*. Rio de Janeiro: Iplanario/Zahar.

Andrade, Carlos Drummond de. 1978. *Discurso de primavera e algumas sombras*. Rio de Janeiro: José Olympio.

Arendt, Hannah. 1979. *Totalitarismo, o paroxismo do poder*. Rio de Janeiro: Documentário.

Argan, Giulio Carlo. 1964. *L'Europe des capitales (1600–1700)*. Genève: Skira.

Augras, Monique. 1998. *O Brasil do samba-enredo*. Rio de Janeiro: Fundação Getúlio Vargas.

Balandier, Georges. 1982. *O poder em cena*. Brasília: Ed. da UNB.

Bandeira, Manuel. 1957. *Itinerário de Pasárgada*. Rio de Janeiro: Jornal de Letras.

Broca, Brito. 1956. *A vida literária no Brasil–1900*. Rio de Janeiro: Ministério da Educação e Cultura, Serviço de Documentação.

Cabral, Sérgio. 1996. *A MPB na era do rádio*. Rio de Janeiro: Moderna.

Carvalho, Maria Alice Resende de. 1994. *Quatro vezes cidade*. Rio de Janeiro: Sette Letras.

Costa, Luiz Edmundo de Melo Pimenta da. 1983. *O Rio de Janeiro do meu tempo*. Rio de Janeiro: Imprensa Nacional.

Debret, Jean Baptiste. 1978. *Viagem pitoresca e histórica ao Brasil* (I & II). Belo Horizonte/São Paulo: Itatiaia/EDUSP.

Dimas, Antonio. 1983. *Tempos Eufóricos: análise da Revista Kosmos, 1904–1909*. São Paulo: Ática.

Ferreira Neto, Edgard Leite. 1989. *O improviso da civilização: A Nação Republicana e a construção da ordem social no final do século XIX*. Niterói: UFF, (mimeo).

Figueiredo, Vera Follain de. 1996. "A geografia do crime na ficção de Rubem Fonseca." *Revista Literatuara e Sociedade* (Universidade São Paulo) 1: 88–93.

Fonseca, Rubem. 1975. *Feliz Ano Novo*. Rio de Janeiro: Artenova.

———. 1983. *A grande arte*. Rio de Janeiro: Francisco Alves.

———. 1992. *Romance negro e outras histórias*. São Paulo: Companhia das Letras.

Garcia Roza, Luis Alfredo. 1996. *O silêncio da chuva*. São Paulo: Companhia das Letras.

———. 1999. *Vento sudoeste*. São Paulo: Companhia das Letras.

Ginzburg, Carlo. 1989. *Mitos, emblemas, sinais. Morfologia e história*. Trans. Federico Carotti. São Paulo: Companhia das Letras.

Gomes, Renato Cordeiro. 1994. *Todas as cidades, a cidade: Literatura e experiência urbana*. Rio de Janeiro: Rocco.

———. 1996. *João do Rio: Vielas do vício, ruas da graça*. Rio de Janeiro: Relume-Dumará: RioArte.

Guimarães, Francisco. 1978. *Na roda do samba*. Rio de Janeiro: Funarte.

Hollanda, Chico Buarque de. 1992. *Estorvo*. Lisboa: Dom Quixote.

Hollanda, Heloísa Buarque de. 1980. *Impressões de viagem–CPC, vanguarda e desbunde: 1960/1970*. São Paulo: Brasiliense.

——— and Marcos Augusto Gonçalves. 1982. *Cultura e participação no anos 60*. São Paulo: Brasiliense.

Hollanda, Sérgio Buarque de. 1948. *Raízes do Brazil*. Rio de Janeiro: José Olympio.

João Do Rio (Paulo Barreto). 1909. *Cinematógrapho*. Porto: Chardon.

———. 1911. *Psicologia urbana: O amor carioca; O figurino; O flirt; A delicia de mentir; Discurso de recepção as Academia brazileira*. Rio de Janeiro: H. Garnier.

Koseritz, Carl Von. *Imagens do Brasil*. 1980. Belo Horizonte/São Paulo: Itatiaia/Edusp.

Lins, Álvaro. 1963. "E uma saga do Rio de Janeiro em termos de província-nação." *Os mortos de sobrecasaca: Ensaios e estudos*. Rio de Janeiro: Civilização Brasileira. 269–78.

Lins, Paulo. 1997. *Cidade de Deus*. São Paulo: Companhia das Letras.

Maravall, Jose Antonio. 1966. *Antiguos y modernos*. Madrid: Sociedad de Estudios y Publicaciones.

Mariella da Silva, Ricardo. 1996. *São Sebastião do Rio de Janeiro. Religiosidade e segurança no século XVI*. Rio de Janeiro: PUC-Rio (mimeo).

Mattos, Ilmar Rohloff de. 1987. *O tempo Saquarema*. São Paulo: Hucitec/I.N.L.

Mattos, Selma Rinaldi de. 1993. *Brasil em lições. A História do Brasil no Império_através dos manuais de Joaquim Manoel de Macedo*. Rio de Janeiro: IESAE/FGV (mimeo).

Máximo, João and Carlos Didier. 1990. *Noel Rosa, uma biografia*. Brasilia: UnB.

——— and Carlos Secchin. 1997. *Cinelândia: história breve de um sonho*. Rio de Janeiro: Salamandra.

Miceli, Sérgio. 1979. *Intelectuais e classe dirigente no Brasil (1920–1945)*. São Paulo: Difel.

Mota, Carlos Guilherme. 1970. *Atitudes de inovação no Brasil. (1789–1801)*. Lisboa: Livros Horizonte.

———, ed. 1992. *1822. Dimensões*. São Paulo: Perspectiva.

Needell, Jeffrey D. 1993. *Belle époque tropical*. São Paulo: Companhia das Letras.

Neves, Margarida de Souza and Alda Heizer. 1991. *A ordem é o progresso: O Brasil de 1870 a 1910*. São Paulo: Atual.

Neves, Margarida de Souza. 1994. "O povo na rua: um conto de duas cidades." *Olhares sobre a cidade*. Ed. Robert M. Pechman. Rio de Janeiro: Ed. UFRJ. 135-55.

Novais, Fernando Antonio. 1979. *Portugal e o Brasil na crise do Antigo Sistema Colonial (1777-1808)*. São Paulo: Hucitec.

Ortiz, Renato. 1988. *A moderna tradição brasileira*. São Paulo: Ed. Brasiliense.

Pena, Martins. N.d. *Comédias*. Rio de Janeiro: Edições Ouro.

Pereira, Victor Hugo Adler. 1998. *A musa carrancuda: Estado Novo e política cultural*. Rio de Janeiro: Fundação Getúlio Vargas.

Rama, Ángel. 1984. *La ciudad letrada*. Hanover, N.H.: Ediciones del Norte.

——. 1996. *The Lettered City*. Trans. John Charles Chasteen. Durham: Duke University Press.

Resende, Beatriz. 1994. "Rio de Janeiro, cidade de modernismos." *Olhares sobre a cidade*. Ed. Robert Pechman Moses. Rio de Janeiro: Ed. UFRJ. 121-33.

Rizzini, Carlos. 1957. *Hipólito da Costa e o Correio Brasiliense*. Rio de Janeiro: Companhia Editora Nacional.

Rodrigues, Nelson. 1946. *Álbum de Família e Vestido de Noiva*. Rio de Janeiro: Edições do Povo.

Sant'Anna, Sérgio. 1997. *Contos e novelas reunidos*. São Paulo. Companhia das Letras.

Sevcenko, Nicolau. 1980. *Literatura como Missão*. São Paulo: Brasiliense.

Severiano, Jairo e Mello, Zuza Homem de. 1997. *A canção no tempo: 85 anos de música brasileira* . São Paulo: Ed. 34.

Silva, Eduardo. 1997. *Dom Obá II D'Africa, o príncipe do povo. Vida, tempo e pensamento de um homem livre de cor*. São Paulo: Companhia das Letras.

Sussekind, Flora. 1990. *O Brasil não é longe daqui. O narrador, a viagem*. São Paulo: Companhia das Letras.

Théry, Hervé. 1992. "Des Amériques au Sud." *Géographie Universelle*. Vol. 3. *Amérique Latine*. Ed. Claude Bataillon, Jean-Paul Deler, and Hervé Théry. Paris: Hachette/Reclus. 6-87.

Velho, Gilberto. 1994. *Projeto e metamorfose*. Rio de Janeiro: Jorge Zahar.

Velloso, Mônica Pimenta. 1988. "A literatura como espelho da nação." *Estudos Históricos* (Rio de Janeiro) 2: 57-74.

——. 1996. *Modernismo no Rio de Janeiro: Turunas e quixotes*. Rio de Janeiro: Fundação Getúlio Vargas.

——. 1997. "Os intelectuais e a política cultural no Estado Novo." *Revista de Sociologia e Política* (Curitiba: Universidade Federal do Paraná) 9: 57-74.

Vianna, Hermano. 1995. *Os mistérios do samba*. Rio de Janeiro: Zahar/UFRJ.

Vieira, Lúcia Gouveia. 1984. *Salão de 31, marco da revelação da arte moderna*. Rio de Janeiro: Funarte.

Vieira, Pe. Antonio. 1959. *Obras Completas do Padre Antonio Vieira*. Vol. 1 Porto: Lello & Irmão Editores.

Visconde De Porto Seguro [Francisco Adolfo Varnhagen]. 1927. *História Geral do Brasil*. 3.ed. São Paulo: Melhoramentos.

CHAPTER 49

SÃO PAULO
THE CULTURAL LABORATORY
AND ITS CLOSE

Nicolau Sevcenko

How do I know what Order brings
Me into being?
I only know, if you do certain things,
I must become your Hearing and your Seeing;
Also your Strength, to make great wheels go round,
And save your sons from toil, while I am bound!

What do I care how you dispose
The powers that move me?
I only know that I am one with those
True Powers which rend the firmament above me,
And, harrying earth, would save me at the last
But that your coward foresight holds me fast!

–Rudyard Kipling, "Song of the Dinamo,"
written in 1927 upon his visit to Cubatão's Hydroelectric
Plant, built to supply energy to the city of São Paulo.

Early morning 26 July 1968, in São Paulo an extreme right-wing terrorist group carried out a dreadful attack on Federico García Lorca (1898–1936)–not against his person this time but rather against the monument conceived in homage to him by architect and artist Flávio de Carvalho (Leite and Zanini 83; Toledo). Protected by the night's darkness, an armed horde charged the memorial and attacked the work of art in a frenzy, working with large steel hammers and electric saws until the monument was reduced to a deformed mass of scrap metal with pieces of twisted metal scattered throughout the garden. The horde saluted the end of its labor with salvoes of gunshots and rounds of machine gun fire into the air. The monument had been installed at Guianas Square, at the center of a peaceful residential area and close to a grade school and a church, in a central area of São Paulo where the diametrical axes represented by Nove de Julho and Brasil avenues intersect in the direction of the popular Ibirapuera Park. Occurring in the very heart of the city, this tragic episode is richly significant and perhaps the most telling revelation of São Paulo's transformation into a space of discord in the course of the twentieth century.

Carvalho's (1899–1973) monument to Lorca was itself extremely evocative. From its concrete base an intricate set of rectilinear tubes flourished up in disconcerting geometric angles, partially enveloped by iron plates molded into sinuous curves, culminating in three bright red plates formed like amoebas, one at each end, and the largest suspended at the center of the composition. On the surface of the largest plate Carvalho painted in black letters verses from the beautiful poem "Los Alamos de Plata" ["The Silver Poplar Trees"] from Lorca's 1921 *Libro de Poemas* [Book of Poems]:

¡Hay que abrirse del todo
frente a la noche negra,
para que nos llenemos del rocío inmortal!

We must open up completely
before the black night
so that we can be filled with immortal dew.

(173–74)

In its basic structure Carvalho's monument strongly evoked the memorial Pablo Picasso created to honor his friend Guillaume Apollinaire, dead in 1918 as a consequence of wounds received in the trenches in World War I. (Lorca's poem was composed in 1919.) Picasso had wished to build the memorial upon the tomb of his friend but was forbidden to raise it at Père Lachaise cemetery or anywhere else in Paris (Steegmuller 298–308). Carvalho's bright red iron surfaces suggested the amorphous shapes developed by Miró in images of pure color and ethereal space. In turn the unstable equilibrium in which these were suspended–as if in virtual flotation–recalled Calder's experiments with mobile and stabile painted metal plates.

As a whole Carvalho's monument represented not only a homage to García Lorca but a kind of laudatory manifesto to the project of Modernism, an expression of solidarity with the cosmopolitan movement of artists and intellectuals engaged in the transformation of culture and society set in motion by World War I. The initiative for the construction of an artistic memorial linking Lorca to São Paulo came from the Spanish Democratic Center and received the support of a group of São Paulo's notable artists and intellectuals. Picasso, Buñuel, and Arrabal among other celebrated colleagues abroad welcomed the idea of the memorial with brotherly enthusiasm. Chilean poet Pablo Neruda (1904–1973) presided over the inauguration of the memorial, which also boasted the presence of Lorca's brother, Paco García. Already in his first sketch for the memorial, Carvalho had included the following rationale for the project: The monument sought to capture in iron the dynamic spirit of the Spanish poet. It was to be a sculpture that would explode before the viewer in living universal poetry. The long metal tubes represented arrows shot into space; like so many efforts of humanity to find freedom and dignity, the piece symbolized García Lorca's life force and the struggle against tyranny and oppression.

Curiously all the artists who seem to have inspired Carvalho's monument to Lorca–Picasso, Apollinaire, Miró, and Calder–were friends themselves, and they were all associated with French-Swiss poet Blaise Cendrars, who along with Apollinaire was one of the creators of Cubist poetry in 1913. With the death of Apollinaire, Cendrars became a kind of center of the post-war art scene in Paris, encouraging both the neo-Plasticism of Le Corbusier and Léger and the Surrealism of Picabia, Cocteau, and Masson. It was in his capacity as spokesman for the city's radical initiatives in aesthetic innovation that Cendrars was approached by Paulo Prado in Paris and brought to São Paulo for a long sojourn in 1923 with many return trips during the 1920s (Sevcenko 1993). Also in 1923 Flávio de Carvalho returned to São Paulo after eleven years in France and England receiving degrees in engineering and architecture at the University of Durham (Leite and Zanini 77). Carvalho returned a convert to modern art and preached of its achievements; in Cendrars he met the most celebrated spokesman for the movement.

The architect of this encounter was Paulo Prado, the city's arts patron and supporter *par excellence*. His power and prestige derived above all from a family fortune (then the largest in the country) made by coffee plantations and multiple investments in industry, export houses, railways, and banks. Prado's prestige was augmented further by the singular status of his father Counselor Antônio Prado, ex-personal consultant to the emperor and, since the advent of the Republic, the most eminent and admired political figure in the country, who played a decisive role in the selection of candidates for the presidency (see Levi). During his long tenure as mayor of São Paulo, Antônio Prado developed a prodigious plan of re-urbanization that completely transformed the city. He possessed an intimate knowledge of the great European capitals, having in his youth enthusiastically accompanied the process of urban reform in Paris commanded by Baron Haussmann during the Second Empire. As mayor of São Paulo, Antônio Prado sought to adapt Haussmann's project of urban reform to a city which retained the quaint features of a Colonial city despite its enormous concentration of wealth.

São Paulo was founded by Jesuit priests in 1554, one of the pioneer settlements of the recently claimed colony and the first to be established not along the coast but in the interior. The Jesuits conceived of this post in the interior as a catalyst for the catechism of the natives who lived deeper in the colony's territory. In this respect the location of the settlement of São Paulo could not have been more propitious: Located at the height of the Serra do Mar range, it was flanked on the one side by a river that flowed to the maritime ports of Santos and São Vicente. On the range's other side water flowed into the Tietê River that flows through the interior's dryland to connect with the River Plate basin and other hydrographic basins to the south, facilitating access to the São Fransisco River for the colony's center and the colony's west and north in the direction of the Amazonas's basin. From their settlement in São Paulo the Jesuits could dream of a gigantic Tupi-Guarani Catholic empire that would extend from the River Plate in the south to the immensity of the Amazon forest in the north.

Thus the small settlement of São Paulo was established in a group of hills surrounded by the Tietê River and its affluents, the Pinheiros and Tamanduateí. Its strategic importance lay in part in the easy access it provided to the sinuous Ganha-almas River but no less to considerations of defense: The high hills afforded the isolated white settlers an ample view of the movements of the hordes of hostile natives below. If it was convenient from the vantage point of defense and communication, nonetheless São Paulo proved a horrible site for human habitation. Since the hills were surrounded by swamp, they were subject to periodic floods and were a focal point for the most morbid of tropical diseases. Because the hills were steep and intercut by streams, they afforded scarce communication from one to the next. The settlement had been conceived as a refuge for Portuguese settlers and a site for the catechism of the native people. Given its harsh topography, severe floods, and drastically insalubrious conditions, the little settlement seemed as far

removed as possible from a location that would encourage an urban agglomeration. And yet what seemed both undesirable and impossible would be imposed by the random vicissitudes of history (Sevcenko 1992, 106–107).

São Paulo remained extremely poor until the middle of the nineteenth century. Constrained by the permanent lack of the resources requisite for survival, young men systematically abandoned the small village to try their luck in the dry lands of the interior, be it by imprisoning natives to sell them as slaves to the farmers on the coast, by digging in mines for precious metals, or through the cultivation of modest crops of cassava or the raising of pigs for their own consumption (Buarque 25–48). For this reason São Paulo's population was mostly constituted by women and their children, mostly *mestizos* born of the union of whites and natives, though there was also a smaller presence of mulattoes (see Dias). And so the life of the village continued without great change for centuries. But, industrialization in Europe and in the United States and, in particular, the scientific and technological revolution circa 1870 transformed the market for raw materials. Industrialization generated an increasing demand for stimulants from the tropics. In this manner coffee–hitherto an obscure, scarcely known, and little consumed product–suddenly became indispensable to the conditions of modern life. The rapid expansion in consumption meant proportionately high profits for producers. Production expanded quickly as the empire's farmers became cognizant of the favorable ecology for coffee planting in the geographic corridor linking the capital Rio de Janeiro to São Paulo, the Rio Paraíba Valley. The expansion of coffee production became a boom when it reached the soil of São Paulo, particularly rich in its volcanic decomposition. From the last quarter of the nineteenth century to the end of 1920s, São Paulo would control 70 percent of the world's coffee market (Saliba 33–35).

Or rather, São Paulo produced 70 percent of the world's coffee, but English merchants controlled the markets. English middlemen controlled the process of production, from the product's transportation to its commercialization. Due to their control of financing and the lines of credit, English merchants financed the planting of coffee and purchased the entire production at low prices before the harvest. Merchants released small quotas for export at any one time in order to maintain sale prices at the highest possible levels in the international market. For English investors the planting and exporting of coffee entailed a gigantic speculative manipulation on a global scale. In a vertiginous rhythm of metropolitanization, São Paulo–an insignificant town until the mid-nineteenth century–became a city. Since the English required an intermediary point between the coffee plantations in the state's interior and the port of Santos on the coast, they chose São Paulo as the strategic point of its export network, a place of convergence for the railways they themselves financed and built. The merchants kept the coffee in São Paulo and let small amounts out into the international market. Thus the bulk of the wealth generated by the coffee economy was concentrated in São Paulo, attracting legions of immigrants from all parts of Brazil and the four corners of the globe, in what came to be known–with reference to the color of the coffee plant–as the "green gold run." The considerable resources accumulated by coffee-related business were rapidly reinvested in other commercial, financial, and industrial ventures, including the most lucrative investment in a city with an exploding population: real estate speculation (Sevcenko 1989, 160–61). **Table 1** gives the basic data of the demographic expansion of São Paulo from 1872 to 2000, an almost unprecedented development (with the possible exception of Mexico City during this same period):

Table 1. *Demographic Growth of the City of São Paulo*

Year	Population
1872	19,347
1890	64,934
1905	279,000
1920	579,000
1934	1,060,120
1940	1,568,045
1950	2,662,786
1960	4,739,406
1970	8,139,730
1980	12,588,745
1990	17,448,600
2000	21,416,700 (estimated)

Source: Petrone 125; Araújo Filho 175–79; Vilaça 38; Prado Jr. 122; Rolnik et al. 32

Thus when Counselor Antônio Prado became the city's mayor, he sought to channel this fund of concentrated wealth into a civilizing project reminiscent of the sophisticated urbanism of Paris during the Second Empire. With this aim in mind he hired the services of two specialists with a long list of services rendered to the city of Paris and the landscape projects of its world fairs, engineer-architects Buvard and Couchet. The result had a great impact: Practically everything that remained from the old Colonial town was destroyed and the whole of the city's physiognomy altered to transform São Paulo into a modern metropolis with a European profile. The two basic hills that make up the city's center—hitherto separated by steep inclines, swamps, and the Anhangabaú River—were united by two broad and solemn viaducts made with iron arches imported from Germany. The Anhangabaú River was channeled and above it an elegant park boasting splendid gardens was created. A series of great public buildings were built as civic marks of reference, among them the Ipiranga Historical Museum (in French neo-Classical style), the Light Station (in imitation of Paddington and imported entirely from England), and the imposing Municipal Theater (inspired by the Italian neo-Renaissance style). A dense corridor of adjoining green spaces linked parks on the city's fringe (Ipiranga and Aclimação) to the English-style Dom Pedro II Park at the foot of the central hills, culminating in the impressive landscape of Anhangabaú Valley (Bruno 3: 1001–95).

Citizens were astonished by the results. Antônio Prado ambitiously sought not only the modernization of the city, but the dissemination of a new standard of democratic civility within the growing population. His ideal was to promote social interaction across class lines in the new vast public spaces and to encourage practices of courtesy, elegance, mutual respect, and civic awareness. To this end he programmed a series of concerts for the stages installed in public parks and gardens. In a ritual rich in meaning, Prado would promenade with his family through the green avenues composed of complex flower arrangements and Amazonian, North American, and European trees, refresh himself in the shade and by the public fountains, and attend the public performances exhibiting a most respectful degree of concentration (Americano 259–61). Given the expectation that the country's richest and most powerful family would prefer to promenade through the avenues of Paris or remain enclosed within their palisades, Prado's attitude gave an enormous boost of confidence in the consolidation not only of new and hitherto inexistent public spaces, but of new and liberal standards of sociability. Further, Prado's bearing demonstrated his confidence in the liberalizing potential of the city's new-found wealth. In sum, the city's population—once circumspect and imprisoned within domestic space—now demonstrated a contagious enthusiasm for the city's green salons. On the weekend legions of citizens would convene in these new gardens and parks for promenades, exercise, and picnics.

De rigueur these promenades generated a fervor for European fashion: for French models in the case of women and for English models in the case of men. Coupled with the local penchant for European décor, architecture, and urban design, the enthusiasm for European fashion confused foreign visitors to the city. Thus in his travel writing Georges Clemanceau, former president of the French Republic's council, records his visit to São Paulo before the Great War: "The city of São Paulo is so curiously French in certain respects that in the course of a whole week I do not remember having the impression of being abroad" (in Amaral 38). In turn writer Paul Adam would record a somewhat different impression of the city at almost the same moment in time. From the vantage point of the bottom of São Paulo's hills Adam notes the architecture of the popular houses that were generally the work of Italian foremen: "A luminous city exists in São Paulo, in the rise and fall of its hills, a city of red roof-tops superimposed upon each other, in the slopes that pile up in the background. Doting upon the colors of the same sun and the sketch of its streets, memories of Verona and other Italian cities come to mind" (in Bruno 182). Yet from the top of the hills overlooking the city center, Paul Adam saw a different city: "The city centre and its narrow streets clogged with trams and automobiles, the small houses, open stores, and light-colored warehouses all suggest certain features of London" (in Bruno 182). This curious mixture of elements reminiscent of the Mediterranean and Northern Europe was captured with remarkable spontaneity by the verses Blaise Cendrars (pseud., Fréderic Sausir-Hall, 1887–1961) composed to describe his arrival in the city. The city felt familiar and Cendrars was immediately at ease:

Enfin voici des usines une banlieue un gentil
petit tramway
Des conduites électriques
Une rue populeuse avec des gens qui vont faire
leurs emplettes du soir
Un gazomètre
Enfin on entre en gare
Saint-Paul
Je crois être en garde de Nice
Ou débarquer à Charring-Cross à Londres
Je trouve tous mes amis
Bonjour
C'est moi

Finally here are some factories a suburb a nice little trolley
Electric lines

A street crowded with people doing their evening
shopping
A natural gas tank
Finally we pull into the station
São Paulo
I feel like I'm in the station in Nice
Or getting off at Charing Cross in London
I find all my friends
Hello
It's me

(1947, 59–60) (1992, 178)

In contrast French ethnographer Claude Lévi-Strauss (b. 1908) described São Paulo in the early 1930s as "a wild city, as are all American cities. . . . São Paulo was then untamed" (87–88). Indeed the city then bore the appearance of a patchwork quilt of cosmopolitan fragments. The population was composed by the descendents of various peoples: the original native inhabitants; Afro-Brazilians who had gained their freedom by escaping from plantations or later with the abolition of slavery; migrants from Central and Northern Brazil, and from the River Plate region; European peoples, in particular Italian, Portuguese, Spanish, German, and Slav; and immigrants from the Near and Far East: among them Arabs, Turks, Armenians, Jews, Japanese, and Chinese. In their architecture, the houses tended to reflect elements of these different traditions. The architecture of official and governmental buildings varied across a broad eclectic spectrum that almost constituted a compressed history of European art: from the gothic of the great cathedral at Sé Square, modeled after the Cathedral in Cologne, to the Martinelli building at Antônio Prado Square, a concrete skyscraper standing 130 meters tall. São Paulo's geographical location only contributed to this confusion: Cut through by the Tropic of Capricorn, São Paulo was at once a tropical and a semi-tropical city; though close to the coast, the city rested atop a plateau. While the hills were characterized by the tall and dense vegetation of the Atlantic woods, vast swamplands and flooded fields were invaded by low-lying ivies, bushes, weeds, aquatic plants, and algae; though a brilliant sun and blue sky shone over the city during the day, a light drizzle tended to fall during the late afternoon and a thick cloud of fog arrived with the night and lingered until dawn. Having eliminated its past, metropolitan São Paulo was born an enigma. Its only markers of identification were not stable elements but processes existing in a vertiginous course: fusion, growth, acceleration, speculation. Though the municipality's official symbol featured two branches of a coffee tree, for the population at large it was rather the image of a locomotive in full acceleration (Sevcenko 1993b).

No one understood the impetuous nature of the phenomenon of São Paulo better than Blaise Cendrars. The poet's empathy for the city was immediate and complete. The role that befell him in São Paulo was decisive. Cendrars was himself an energetic phenomenon, an uprooted creature, an emissary for the emancipatory potential of the technologies new to the twentieth century. John dos Passos extolled him as the "Trans-Siberian Man" with reference to Cendrars's poem "La Prose du Transsibérien et de la Petite Jeanne de France" ["The Prose of the Trans-Siberian and of the Little Jeanne of France"]. Jean Bhuler would call him "the twentieth-century Marco Polo," and Rainer Maria Rilke would refer to his poems as "supreme ballads of the songs of the street," associating Cendrars with Walt Whitman and his lyric intensity (with reference

to Cendrars's broad democratic appeal) (see Chefdor 16, 23–24; Bochner 7).

While still an adolescent Cendrars left his Swiss home to wander through Russia, determined to live in the wagons of the recently inaugurated Trans-Siberian railway. He lived in permanent transit between Western and Eastern Europe, writing his first book of poetry and smuggling goods until he was expelled by the Russian authorities for his involvement with anarchist groups. Always attracted to the most extraordinary manifestations of new technological wonders, Cendrars traveled to New York to glimpse the multiplication of skyscrapers in Manhattan. He wandered through the streets of the great metropolis cold and hungry, a witness to the influx of legions of human beings disembarking at the city's port from all corners of the globe. The migrants arrived mute, emaciated, and clothed in rags. They moved like automatons, propelled only by the blind hope for a better future. It was their experience that Cendrars portrayed with compassion and sympathy in *Les Pâques à New York* [Easter in New York], which alongside Apollinaire's *Alcools* [Alcohols] launched Cubist poetry in Paris in 1913. In the California gold rush, Cendrars witnessed cities being born out of nothing, like mushrooms after rain. At the recently opened Panama Canal he observed how men now linked oceans together. He enlisted for history's first technological war and was wounded during a bombardment, losing his right hand. Despite this mutilation he became a race car driver after the war. Alongside Cocteau and Darius Milhaud he opened the cabaret "Le Boeuf sur le toit" ("The Ox on the Roof"), which became the dynamic focus for cultural debate and creation in Paris (Wiser 133–42). It was in this context that Paulo Prado approached him.

And it was thus that Cendrars came to São Paulo. Just as Antônio Prado had once presided over the city's urban reform, his son Paulo was in charge of the subsequent project for cultural reform. The outbreak of war forced Paulo to leave Paris and return to São Paulo, and from that point on he became the city's principal arts patron and advocate. His plan was to project São Paulo–both the city and the state–as the irradiating center of modernity and the cosmopolitan culture that would emancipate Brazil from the backward historical condition that remained the legacy of its Colonial past. To this end Paulo Prado and his family stimulated initiatives that promoted a militant nativism and sought to establish the ideological roots for São Paulo's position of cultural leadership within Brazil: the 1919–1920 sumptuous production of the *Diamond Contractor* and the 1922 Week of Modern Art that involved concerts, exhibitions, lectures, and recitals of poetry. The Week of Modern Art sought to demonstrate that São Paulo was in tune with the most recent and daring manifestations of European art. Prado conceived of Cendrars's visit to São Paulo within the framework of this second project. The poet had his own motives for coming, seduced by the possibility of observing first-hand the effervescence of the fastest growing city in the world. He would not regret this decision, as he recorded in his journal (1976, 73).

Dispensing with the aid of guides or translators, Cendrars–who possessed no knowledge of Portuguese–walked through the city's streets collecting impressions at random, quickly registering them in spontaneous and crystalline verses under the direct impact of city scenes and landscapes. This was the aesthetic he would establish with his last book *Kodak*. The immediate impact of external reality should reverberate on the poet's sensorial organs, without allowing time for consciousness or imagination to dilute that fragmentary instant through symbolic representation or the language of cultural tradition. The poet captures the uniqueness of the new just as a photographic camera fixes a fragment of lived time on paper soaked in photosensitive solution. This poetic method proved particularly appropriate for Cendrars to describe the bewildering atmosphere of the young metropolis in the poem "São Paulo":

> J'adore cette ville
> Saint-Paul est selon mon Coeur
> Ici nulle tradition
> Aucun préjugé
> Ni ancien ni moderne
> Seuls comptent cet appétit furieux cette confiance
> absolue cet optimisme cette audace ce travail ce
> labeur cette spéculation qui font construire dix
> maisons par heure de tous styles ridicules
> grotesques beaux grands petits nord sud
> égyptien yankee cubiste
> Sans autre préoccupation que de suivre les
> statistiques prévoir l'avenir le confort l'utilité
> la plus-value et d'attirer une grosse immigration population
> Tous les pays
> Tous les peuples
> J'aime ça
> Les deux trois vieilles maisons portugaises
> qui restent sont des faïences bleues.

> I adore this city
> São Paulo is after my own heart
> No tradition here
> No prejudice
> Ancient or modern
> All that matters is this furious appetite this absolute confidence
> this optimism this daring this work
> this labor this speculation which builds ten houses
> per hour in all styles ridiculous
> grotesque beautiful big small northern southern
> Egyptian Yankee Cubist
> With no other concern than to follow the
> statistics foresee the future the comfort the utility
> the increment value and to attract a large immigrant population
> All countries
> All peoples
> I love that
> The two or three old Portuguese houses that remain
> are blue china

> *(1947, 63–64) (1992, 180–81)*

In Cendrars's vision São Paulo was itself a gigantic work of modern art, a social experiment on a colossal scale. His unpunctuated poetry of quick notes and a fluid syntax, full of prompt and concrete references, accentuate the frenetic rhythm and the fragmented character of the reality described. The enormous verses 6, 7, and 11 embody the multiple and cumulative effect of the energy flowing through the city–these verses bury the last architectural relics from the Colonial past under an avalanche of foreign peoples and cultures. In the poem "Paysage" ["Landscape"] Cendrars's vision captures and fixes the Babel-like bustle of the city center:

> Le mur ripoliné de la PENSION MILANESE
> s'encadre
> Je vois une tranche de l'avenue S[ã]o-João
> Trams autos trams
> Trams-trams trams trams
> Des mules jaunes attelés par trois tirent de toutes

> petites charrettes vides
> Au-dessus des poivriers de l'avenue se détache
> l'enseigne géante de la CASA TOKIO
> Le soleil verse du vernis

> The high-gloss wall of the PENSION MILANESE
> is framed by my window
> I see a slice of São Jo[ã]o Avenue
> Trolleys cars trolleys
> Trolleys-trolleys trolleys trolleys
> Yellow mules harnessed in threes pull tiny empty
> carts
> Above the avenue's pepper trees the giant sign of the
> CASA TOKIO stands out
> The sun spilling varnish

> *(1947, 63) (1992, 180)*

Cendrars is always attracted to the popular neighborhoods and humble suburbs inhabited by those who like him are denied roots, possessions, and an inheritance. There the poet can observe the tragic consequences of this strange encounter between technological marvel and destitution, the destitution of those who have lived on the periphery of colonialism and modernity and now embody the hope, misery, and ruin of citizenship. Cendrars signals the destiny of these foundlings in a single scene captured by his *Kodak* sensibility in the dry composition "O Menu de Bagatela" ["A Menu of Trifles"]. Here he links the fate of these waifs to the unmerciful rigors of a frugal diet and tropical climate:

> Le ciel est d'un bleu vru
> Le mur d'en face est d'un blanc cru
> Le soleil cru me tape sur la tête
> Une négresse installée sur une petite terrasse fait
> frire de tout petits poissons sur un réchaud
> découpé dans une vieille boîte à biscuits
> Deux négrillons rongent une tige de canne à sucre

> The sky is a harsh blue
> The wall across is a harsh white
> The harsh sun is beating down on my head
> A black woman on a little terrace is frying tiny fish
> on a portable stove made out of an old cookie tin
> Two little black kids chew on a stalk of sugarcane

> *(1947, 62) (1992, 180)*

Eager to be acquainted with the country's most disparate elements, Cendrars exhorted his hosts to embark on unheard of voyages to understand and share experiences hitherto snubbed by the elites. Alongside some of his hosts and a small group of artists Cendrars visited Minas Gerais's historic mining towns during Holy Week. Soon after the same group led him to visit Rio de Janeiro during carnival. In both cases he parted company with his hosts and set out alone to visit the poor houses and prisons of Minas and the shanty-towns in the hills surrounding Rio de Janeiro. In the slums of Rio he befriended black composers of samba and other forms of popular music (Amaral 1970b, 39–79). Returning to São Paulo, Cendrars preferred the life of the streets to the salons of the local bourgeoisie–where he was anxiously expected to appear in the capacity of Paris's cultural ambassador. At Paissandu Square, Cendrars liked to attend the performances of the extremely popular circus of the clown Piolim, whom he considered Brazil's greatest artist (Lara 110–11).

The presence in São Paulo of one who was considered–alongside his friend Picasso–a pioneer and foremost representative of modern art's avant-garde (Morand 12) served to reinforce the convictions of the city's young Modernists and to confirm the preeminence of the new aesthetic before the local public. With his solitary wandering and impulsive curiosity about local conditions, Cendrars provided for the city's young artists the desired thread of identification with popular culture and Brazilian society's unique cultural history. His presence proved a decisive incentive for innovative intellectuals to break with the belletristic and academic impediments typical of a hitherto incipient culture, a culture that had depended for its survival on the support of government institutions and of a public that saw culture as the varnish over its affiliation with the matrix of European civilization.

Upon his return to Europe Cendrars would continue to play a crucial role in Modernist Brazilian culture. He would welcome Brazilian artists and intellectuals, introduce them to his friends, and make possible their interaction with the most irreverent and creative representatives of modern art. In this respect one need only consider the example of composer Heitor Villa-Lobos (1887–1959). A native of Rio de Janeiro, Villa-Lobos had followed from his youth the movements for the renovation of European music, above all through the scores and recordings of Debussy and Stravinsky. He was stimulated by the presence of Paul Claudel and Darius Milhaud in Rio in 1919, when they came to discuss the clauses of the Treaty of Versailles that pertained to Brazil. Having performed to great acclaim during São Paulo's 1922 Week of Modern Art, Villa-Lobos came to enjoy the patronage of the Prado family and had the chance to meet Cendrars in Europe. Cendrars introduced Villa-Lobos as a star in consecutive performances in the cabaret "Le boeuf sur le toit," where he took turns with other young composers, including the Spaniard Manuel de Falla and the Austrian Arnold Schoenberg. Among the other Brazilian artists of note who took residence in Paris from 1923 to 1924, we can single out the poet Oswald de Andrade (1890–1954) and his then companion Tarsila do Amaral (1886–1973), the São Paulo sculptor of Italian descent Victor Brecheret (1894–1955), and filmmaker Alberto Cavalcante (1897–1982). Cendrars introduced Oswald to Cocteau, Tarsila to Léger, Brecheret to Brancusi, and Cavalcante to the Surrealists, facilitating a cross-pollination that directly linked art in São Paulo to the European scene. Cendrars further planned a monumental Amazonian Ballet that he was to produce alongside Cocteau and Milhaud, and which was to boast a score by Villa-Lobos, a libretto by Oswald de Andrade, and set design and costumes by Tarsila do Amaral. Though financial difficulties prevented the trio of producers from bringing the Amazonian Ballet into being, it remained an enormous source of inspiration for São Paulo's art scene throughout the next decade (Amaral 1970b, 39–79).

Upon his return to Brazil in 1924, Oswald de Andrade co-wrote with the writer Mário de Andrade (no relation) (1893–1945) an ambitious manifesto that called on the new generation to seek inspiration in modern aesthetics and salvage Brazil's popular traditions of black and native origin. Oswald de Andrade sought to define an unmistakably Brazilian aesthetic with the term *Pau-Brasil* poetry (Brazil-wood poetry), in a reference to the stained wood that gave the nation its name and was the first resource exploited by Portuguese colonizers (through the labor of the natives):

Poetry exists in facts. Saffron and ochre shacks amid the green of the hills and under the blue sky constitute aesthetic facts. In Rio carnival is a religious event of race. Brazil-wood. Wagner is submerged before the carnival groups in Botafogo, barbarous and ours. A rich ethnic formation. A rich flora. Mines. Cuisine. The vatapá, the gold, the dance. . . .

Elevators shafts, towers of skyscrapers, and the wise solar sloth. Prayer. Carnival. An intimate energy. The song-thrush. A somewhat amorous and sensual hospitality. The nostalgia for medicine men and the airforce landing field. Brazil-wood. . .

Barbarous credulous picturesque and gentle. Newspaper readers. Brazil-wood. The forest and the school. The National Museum. Cuisine, mines, dance. The vegetation. Brazil-wood.
(Oswald de Andrade 203–208)

Mário de Andrade's effort to assemble emblematic images of Brazil's specific historical and cultural experiences was even more systematic, and he conducted a series of research trips into the country's most remote areas in search of vestiges of popular traditions. In 1924–the year of the *Brazil-Wood Manifesto*–Mário de Andrade also published his volume of poetry *O Clã do Jabuti* [The Jabuti Clan] that culminates with a long poem of nationalist exhaltation, "Noturno de Belo Horizonte" ["Nocturne of Belo Horizonte"]. Andrade's poem exalts the nation under the sign of the permanent communion of humanity with others and with the surrounding environment:

Nós somos na Terra o grande milagre do amor!
E embora tão diversa nossa vida
Dançamos juntos no carnaval das gentes. . .
Nós somos os brasileiros auriverdes!
As esmeraldas das araras
O rubi dos colibris
Os abacaxis as mangas os cajus
Atravessam amorosamente
A fremente celebração do Universal! . . .
Juntos formamos esse assombro de misérias e grandeza,
Brasil, nome de vegetal! . . .

On Earth we are the great miracle of love!
And though our life be so diverse
We dance together in the carnival of peoples. . .
We are Brazilians in gold and green!
The emerald of the parrot
The ruby of the hummingbird
The pineapples the mangoes the cashew
Amorously cross
A rousing celebration of the Universal! . . .
Together we form this marvel of misery and grandeur,
Brazil, name of a wood!. . .

(Mário de Andrade 164)

With an impact parallel to the intervention of Cendrars and of his circle of friends in the circle of Brazilian artists in Paris and São Paulo, two notable artists representative of other innovative schools of modern art arrived in São Paulo: the Russians Lasar Segall and Gregori Warchavchik. Segall's formation as an artist took place in Dresden and Berlin, where he participated in the experiments of the Expressionists, became a member of *Die Brücke,* and was particularly known for his engravings, following the social criticism and democratic political program of *Neue Sachlichkeit* (The New Objectivity). A graduate of Rome's Institute of Fine Arts in the field of architecture, Warchavchik pioneered Neo-Plasticist Functionalism in Brazil. The presence of both Segall and Warchavchik fed the flames of São Paulo's artistic circles. In 1927 Flávio de Carvalho's architectural plans for São Paulo's State Governmental Palace reflected the influence of their work and started a formidable controversy. Among the polemical elements of Flávio de Carvalho's blueprint for the palace were its rigorous geometry and rhythmic effects, and the fragmented, discontinuous, and asymmetrical nature of the whole composition–Flávio de Carvalho's palace remained at once elegant and disconcerting, monumental and playful, solemn, and irreverent. If his versatile visual syntax owed its inspiration to *De Stijl*, the plastic daring of the whole evoked the sketches of the Futurist-Cubist Russian Tchernikhov. In 1929, at Paulo Prado's house, these three artists–Flávio de Carvalho, Lasar Segall, and Gregori Warchavchik–would meet their greatest interlocutor in the architect Le Corbusier (Leite and Zanini 77).

The meeting proved auspicious despite the unfavorable historical circumstances. Ominous signs were accumulating, and São Paulo and Brazil felt the imminent approach of a catastrophe. It would strike in three related blows: the economic crisis of 1929, the collapse of the coffee economy, and the coup d'état that would bring Getúlio Vargas to power. The experiment with Modernism would be aborted. The daring historical adventure that characterized the construction of Brazil's new political order following the declaration of the Republic in 1889 would dissipate along with the collapse of its organic basis of support, the prodigious wealth afforded by the coffee economy. In 1870 the coffee plantation owners' rapid and unprecedented prosperity had led them to create and invest in the Republican Party, eager to retain the profits that the Imperial government insisted should be transferred by way of taxation to the seat of the crown in Rio de Janeiro. Dissatisfied with the slow political process, these same agents conspired with the leaders of the army to abolish the monarchy in 1889. Once they had pushed aside the military leaders with whom they had allied themselves and become masters of the situation, they assumed control of the federal government through a two-fold system of coercion over the party machines throughout the Republic's states: This was the policy of the governors, which imposed loyalty to the federal government in return for stability for local governments and the so-called "elections by bludgeoning," which manipulated voting through violence exerted by hired thugs against voters. Having thus consolidated their hold on a power from which they could not be removed, the coffee plantation owners delivered their *coup de grace* in 1904 by securing substantial financing from London's Rothschilds. Thus they retained and controlled their stocks of coffee, encouraged an artificially high price of the commodity, and promoted the most extraordinary currency devaluation then known to the financial world with the aim of generating a highly favorable exchange for the export of coffee. While the profits were to be shared exclusively among the barons of the coffee economy, the interest on the Rothschilds loan and the increased cost of all imports were shared by the Brazilian population at large. When France's former Prime Minister Georges Clemanceau was informed of this scheme during a visit to Brazil, he declared with astonishment that it represented "un coup d'audace sans pareil!" (Love 1980, 44; Love 1982, 71).

It should come as no surprise that during the course of this period of complete supremacy, São Paulo government officials and their allies harbored an obstinate hatred for broad sectors of society. When, at the height of the protests against this oppressive scheme, in 1924, a group of young army officers mutinied to restore trust in public institutions and freedom in the electoral process, the symbolic act they decided upon was the invasion of São Paulo. On a single night–5 July 1924–the young officers from Rio de Janeiro conquered São Paulo. After offering some resistance, the president of the state of São Paulo fled with the battalions that remained faithful to him to the city's distant environs. There he awaited the reinforcements that were to be sent by the President Washington Luís, also a native of the state of São Paulo. As soon as the reinforcements arrived, the president of the state ordered, without any advance notice, the massive and continuous bombardment of the city of São Paulo, for he could not determine the rebel's positions. Thus the city was systematically bombed for a month, with no regard for buildings, residences, public services, and utilities, or for the fate of men, women, children, and the elderly. The city was destroyed and thousands of civilians were killed, mutilated, or wounded. Upon receiving a plea from the citizens to halt the bombing, the president of the state answered: "Let São Paulo burn, afterwards we will build the city anew!" (in Cendrars 1976, 88).

This event is symptomatic of the attitude of the dominant elite with regard to the population at large. The wealth of the coffee economy afforded the emergence of a robust metropolis, but the severe disequilibrium in the distribution of wealth and opportunity stunted the development of a notion of citizenship. The topographical allocation of the population betrayed this social inequality: While the elites lived a healthy life on the dry top of the hills, the mass of population inhabited swampy plains where no public money was spent on sanitation, hygiene, or leisure. Two thirds of the babies born in the city died before reaching two years of age (Sevcenko 1992, 127–51). The work-day could be as long as fourteen hours, for men, women, and children alike. Unions and strikes were repressed with brutal violence. "The social problem," in the words of President Washington Luís, "is a police problem." To compensate for oscillations in the price of coffee, many coffee growers also operated in the city's most lucrative business: real estate speculation. A collusion among landowners, political authorities, and international speculators allowed a single company–The City of São Paulo Improvements, with headquarters in London–to control more than a third of the total area of the city. In turn this company was associated with American-Canadian Light and Power, which possessed a complete monopoly over the distribution of electricity, gas, and telephone services, and which subjected the population to extortionist rates. Although its use of the sources of São Paulo's rivers for the purpose of propelling the turbines of its hydroelectric plants provoked periodic floods with catastrophic consequences for the poor dwellers of the plains, Light and Power never had to worry about compensation (Sevcenko 1992, 122–27).

It is this context of social tension and political instability that prevailed in 1928, the year in which Paulo Prado welcomed Le Corbusier to the city and Paulo's father, Antônio Prado founded the Democratic Party to fight electoral fraud and the political manipulations of the state of São Paulo's Republican Party. The world economic crisis of 1929 would destroy the fragile speculative basis of the coffee economy, weaken the power of the Republican Party, and create the necessary conditions for opposition forces to converge around the leadership of Getúlio Vargas, then president of the state of Rio Grande do Sul. This process would culminate in the 1930 coup which deposed Washington Luís's hand-picked successor (also a native of São Paulo) and catapulting the leader from Rio Grande do Sul into the presidency. The nation's honeymoon with Vargas, however, would not last. When in 1932 the president's allies in São Paulo realized that he intended to remain in power indefinitely, they mutinied and attempted an aborted war for the secession of the state of São Paulo from the federal government in Rio. Once victorious, Vargas appointed a military governor for the state of São Paulo and relegated both city and state to a long period of political ostracism.

Nonetheless, Vargas sought to associate himself with the prestige of São Paulo's Modernist culture from the moment he took federal office. Already in his inaugural address he affirmed his intention to incorporate São Paulo's Modernism into his government policies (Vargas 828). Reality would not bear this out. Vargas was obsessed with a nationalism anchored in a strong cultural policy of centralism, particularly after the new *coup d'état* of 1937 through which he established a dictatorship with a fascist profile. Vargas sought to forge an abstract model for Brazil's culture, imposed from above and determined in all its instances by the authorities in Rio de Janeiro. To this end, it was necessary to extinguish the Republican experience and erase all local culture: He ordered all symbols and insignia of state and municipal autonomy to be burned. Once this was accomplished, Vargas invested heavily in select cultural manifestations: samba as the bearer of official ideology in the form of the *samba-exaltação*; the samba schools transformed in Hollywood-like spectacles of a patriotic and nationalist orientation; the cinema, and the theater revue. A representative musical play of great success, such as *Chouchou e Balangandãs*, fused samba and the Hollywood aesthetic of Rio's samba schools with a stylized presentation of the *baiana* and Afro-Brazilian culture, on a stage that evoked the historic cities in Minas Gerais. Here there was a conspicuous absence of any reference to São Paulo and its industrial growth, led in great part by foreign-born entrepreneurs: São Paulo represented a potential threat to the unity and crystallization of the new national consciousness (see Sevcenko 1995).

While São Paulo's most significant painter during this period—Cândido Portinari—would orient his career with reference to activities associated with the federal government in Rio, Flávio de Carvalho met with a different fate by remaining in São Paulo. His Teatro da Experiência (Theater of Experience) was closed by police in 1933, and his first exhibition of paintings was also closed in 1934 by the police, who also confiscated many of his paintings and prohibited the display of his work. Events such as these encouraged the development in São Paulo of an essentially critical culture which privileged above all the denunciation of authoritarian traditions and structures of social discrimination and oppression. Among its most notable representatives, we can single out the young intellectuals Sérgio Buarque de Hollanda (1902–1982) and Caio Prado Júnior (1907–1990). In 1936 Sérgio Buarque de Hollanda published his *Raízes do Brasil* [Roots of Brazil], seeking in the country's Iberian origins and in the process of colonization an explanation for the obstacles to the construction of democratic institutions and a democratic society in Brazil. In turn Caio Prado's works on *Evolução Política do Brasil* [1934; Brazil's Political Evolution] and *Formação do Brasil Contemporâneo* [1942; Formation of Contemporary Brazil] pioneered the use of Marxist categories to forward a

critical analysis of colonialism, slavery, and the resulting social evils that marked the country's history. In response to the state's defeat in 1932 and its consequent political marginalization, the University of São Paulo was created (in 1934) and emerged as a site for a critical reconsideration of the transformations in Brazilian society. The nucleus for this new university was constituted by a group of eminent professors from the Sorbonne, among them Claude Lévi Strauss and Fernand Braudel. The new generations of social scientists who apprenticed with these masters would come to mix their teaching with those of Sérgio Buarque de Hollanda and Caio Prado, giving birth to the so-called São Paulo school of sociology that would be responsible for the formulation of dependency theory (enormously influential in the international politics of the 1960s and 1970s).

During this period, the city of São Paulo not only maintained, but increased its accelerated process of industrial and economic growth. Yet from the moment Washington Luís became mayor at the beginning of the1920s, the municipality's administrative emphasis shifted from Prado's project of urbanization, inspired in the French Second Empire, to privilege a technical vision that favored the circulation of the automobile at the expense of pedestrians. Obviously the natural culmination of this process coincided with the 1930 coup d'état and the adoption of the first technical plan for the city: the Plano Avenidas (Avenues Plan), based on the idea of broad corridors for express lanes along the margins of the city's rivers. Gardens and public spaces were, from this moment on, sacrificed for the benefit of the circulation and parking of cars. (See **Figure 1**.) From the vantage point of architecture, the new speculative logic prevalent in the real estate market dictated the construction of vertical buildings to the detriment of horizontal accommodations on a human scale. It is this arid, rude and smothering city, where millions of solitary hopes converge, that Mário de Andrade sings of in his 1945 "Meditação Sobre o Tietê" ["Meditation on the River Tietê"]–where multiple expressions of a stunted sensibility characterize the parties in poor neighborhoods and the football played in peripheral fields. Incorporating the sinuous image of the river that silently curves through the poor neighborhoods and painting the distant glow of the buildings and the rectilinear express ways, Andrade laments the frustration of the unrealized dream of emancipation:

Porque os homens não me escutam! Porque os governadores
Não me escutam? Por não me escutam
Os plutocratas e todos os que são chefes e são fezes?
Todos os donos da vida?
Eu lhes daria o impossível e lhes daria o segredo.
Eu lhes dava tudo aquilo que fica pra cá do grito
Metálico dos números. e tudo
O que está além da
insinuação cruenta da posse. . .
Por que os donos da vida não me escutam?
Eu só seir que eu não sei por mim! Sabem por mim
as fonts
Da água e eu bailo de ignorâncias inventivas
Meu baile é solto como a dor que range, meu
Baile é tão vário que possui mil sambas insonhados!
Eu converteria o humano crime num baile mais denso
Que estas ondas negras de água
pesada e oliosa,
Porque os meus gestos e os meus ritmos nascem
Do incêndio puro do amor . . .
Eu me acho tão cansado em meu furor.
As águas apenas murmuram hostis, água vil mas

turrona paulista
Que sobe e se espraia, levando as auroras represadas
Para o peito do sofrimento dos homens.
. . . e tudo é noite. Sob o arco admirável
Da Ponte das Bandeiras, morta, dissoluta, fraca.
Uma lágrima apenas, uma lágrima
eu sigo alga escusa nas águas do meu Tietê.

Why do the men not hear me? Why do the governors
not hear me? Why do they not listen
The plutocrats and all who are bosses and are faeces?
All the proprietors of life?
I would give them the impossible and the secret,
I gave them everything this side of the metallic
Shout of numbers, and everything
That is beyond the bloody insinuation of possession. . .
Why do the proprietors of life not hear me?
I alone know that I know nothing by myself. On my
behalf
Sources of water know, and I dance out of an inventive ignorance
My dance is as loose as the pain that afflicts me, my
Dance is so various that I posses a thousand undreamt sambas!
I would convert the human crime in a dance more dense
Than these black waves of heavy and oily water,
Because my gestures and my rhythms are born
From the pure combustion of love . . .
I find myself so tired in my furor.
The waters merely murmur in their hostility,
São Paulo water vile but contentious
It rises and washes against the beach, bringing the dammed
aurora
To the core of the suffering of men.
. . . and all is night. Under the admirable arch
Of Bandeiras Bridge, dead, dissolute and weak
A tear, a single tear
I follow some excuse in the waters of my Tietê.

(1976, 368–70)

The hostility to the defeated fascist regimes after World War II allowed opposition forces in Brazil to combine efforts to dethrone Vargas and his regime in 1945. Re-democratization followed the dictatorship and was marked by the policy of a drive for a self-sufficient development, best symbolized by the construction of the Modernist city of Brasília (inaugurated in 1960). Brasília was meant to be the engine for national economic redemption. But if Brasília was the symbol, than São Paulo was the reality. A city that numbered 230,000 inhabitants in 1900 bounded to 2,662,000 at the middle of the century, becoming the largest Brazilian metropolis and the largest Latin American industrial center, responsible for more than 50 percent of the country's industrial production. Industry thus replaced the cultivation of coffee as the anchor of São Paulo's prosperity, and already the capital amalgamated with its neighboring municipalities to create Greater São Paulo. The local elite now included a new component: industrial entrepreneurs, most of them recent immigrants to Brazil.

It is within this new context that Francisco Matarazzo Sobrinho (known by his nickname "Ciccillo") (see Almeida) emerged as the patron who would make possible the city's resurgence during this period. He belonged to a family that controlled one of the largest industrial holdings in São Paulo, built by founder Francesco Matarazzo (a native of Castellabate, Salerno, who arrived in Brazil in 1882). Ciccillo completed elementary school in São Paulo, high school in Italy, and university in Belgium, where he graduated with a degree

Figure 1.

Photograph of São Paulo, Anhangabaú Park, the Chá Viaduct and the Municipal Theater in Fernando de Azevedo's A Cultura brasileira *1943. (Courtesy of John P. Robarts Research Library, University of Toronto)*

in engineering from Liège University. Upon his return to Brazil he became the successful director of one of the family's most profitable businesses, Matarazzo Metal Works. Most significantly Ciccillo became São Paulo's most influential arts patron, having a significant if not decisive role in practically all the initiatives that restored the creative energies that had been suffocated during the Vargas regime.

Intimate with the circle of artists who were the protagonists of the city's Modernist movement in the 1920s, Ciccillo headed the effort to found a Museum of Modern Art in the city. In his efforts he was aided by the advice of Nierendorf, then director of the Guggenheim in New York. Ciccillo inaugurated São Paulo's Museum in 1949 with an exhibition of abstract art, a movement hitherto practically unknown to Brazil, given the cultural policies of the dictatorship. To consolidate São Paulo as a center of convergence for international debates on the arts, Ciccillo set in motion biannual exhibitions of fine art, architecture, and theater. For the first Biannual Exhibition of Fine Art in 1951, Ciccillo could count on the decisive support of New York's Museum of Modern Art and Tokyo's Kokusai Bunka Shinkokai. Ciccillo's prestige in the international art scene was such that, for the second biannual in 1953, he secured the loan of *Guernica* and eighty other works for a retrospective of Picasso. Ciccillo was central to the creation of both permanent collections and temporary exhibits in the city, featuring the work of the greatest exponents of contemporary art in Brazil, Latin America, and from abroad. Ciccillo also headed the foundation of the Teatro Brasileiro de Comedia (Brazilian Theater Company)–instrumental in the renovation of Brazilian theater–and the Vera Cruz Cinematographic Company, which boasted the most advanced equipment and the expertise of European technicians and which proved central to the technical advances in Brazilian post-war cinema. Other initiatives along these lines included the International Film Festival (first held in 1951), the University of São Paulo's Museu de Arqueologia e Etnologia (Museum of Archeology and Ethnology; founded in 1964), and the Bienal Internacional do Livro (International Book Fair; first held in 1969). Ciccillo's support for innovation in the arts transcended the institutional realm. When, in 1956, Flávio de Carvalho created a men's fashion adapted to Brazil's climate–consisting of flowing shirts and skirts in brilliant fabrics–Ciccillo accompanied Carvalho on the public fashion show that crossed the city, attracting a scandalized crowd.

The height of Ciccillo's activity is associated with his tenure as president of the organizing committee for the celebration of São Paulo's fourth centenary in 1954. Over the objections of city hall, Ciccillo proposed a project to recuperate a vast swampy area in the meadows along the Pinheiros River in the city's south end and create a public garden, leisure area, and cultural center. The project brought into being Ibirapuera Park, encompassing 18 square kilometers of green space and a complex of buildings designed by Oscar Niemayer, the future architect of Brasília. Among the various activities and initiatives commemorating the city's fourth centenary, we can single out the creation of the fourth centenary Ballet Company, the first great stride toward the development of choreography in Brazil. The ballet company was directed by celebrated Hungarian choreographer Aurel Milloss–former director of the Paris, Berlin, Vienna, and La Scala ballet companies–and performances were open to the public at large. Guest conductors included Germany's Paul Hindemith, France's Pierre Dervaux, and Italy's Nino Stinco; the repertory featured Brazilian composers and, in particular, Villa-Lobos; costumes and set design were commissioned from Brazilian artists such as Flávio de Carvalho.

A total of more than a hundred cultural events were presented before popular audiences during the commemoration of the fourth centenary, featuring about 350 Brazilian artists. In return for his efforts, Ciccillo was presented by members of the city's artistic community with a painting by De Chirico, which he donated to the Museum of Modern Art's permanent collection. This contribution to the museum led to a curious coincidence. One of Ciccillo's first collaborators was the journalist and communications tycoon Assis Chateaubriand, a veteran of the aborted secession war of 1932. Chateaubriand had his own claims to being the city's chief arts patron. In collaboration with Italian art critic Pietro Maria Bardi and his wife, the architect Lina Bo Bardi (1914–1992), Chateaubriand was responsible for the creation of the city's most sophisticated permanent art collection, comprising works of the masters from the Renaissance to contemporary art. Lina Bo Bardi's father Enrico Bo was a Surrealist painter and close friend and neighbor of De Chirico on Gesu Street in Milan. Strongly influenced by the Italian master of metaphysical painting, Lina Bo Bardi was commissioned in 1968 to design São Paulo's Museum of Art in the city's most central and visible core on Paulista Avenue. Her designs, original from the vantage point of both museology and architecture, were influenced by De Chirico's aesthetic of dreamlike displacement. Thus the Museum of Art, along with Lina Bo Bardi's other creations, helped lend a peculiar tone to São Paulo architecture in this period (Oliveira 82–87).

Once the basic frameworks of reference and general atmosphere of São Paulo's cultural renaissance were established, the city's art scene acquired a radical and dynamic force in the 1960s. Following the establishment of the Brazilian Cinemathèque from the Museum of Modern Art's film archive in 1956 and with the critical engagement of Paulo Emílio Salles Gomes, the first Convention of Film Critics was held in 1960. It set in motion the series of reflections and debates on the aesthetic of Brazilian cinema that led to the emergence of the Cinema Novo (New Cinema). In the realm of theater, Gian Francesco Guarnieri (b. 1934) launched the Theater of Arena and radicalized the theatrical scene by directing factory workers in the production of *Eles Não Usam Black Tie* [They Don't Use Black Tie]. In 1967 TV Record's third festival of Brazilian popular music launched *tropicalismo*–a movement that fused the innovations of bossa nova with the electronic distortions and visual iconography of the international pop scene. At the forefront of *tropicalismo* were Caetano Veloso (b. 1942) and Gilberto Gil (b. 1942) with their respective compositions "Alegria, alegria" ["Delight, Delight"] and "Domingo no parque" ["Sunday in the Park"]. In the same year José Celso Martinez Corrêa (b. 1937) caused a commotion with his anarchic production of Oswald de Andrade's *O rei de vela* [The Candle King]. And 1968 saw the release of Rogério Sganzerla's (b. 1946) film *O Bandido da luz vermelha* [Red Light District Bandit], which presented a tragic picture of a life of crime and cultural transgression.

This critical and creative wave would acquire a somber backdrop with the military coup d'état of 1964, the consequence of the intolerant and reductive logic that governed American and Soviet policy toward the world's peripheral regions during the Cold War. With the implementation of the fifth Institutional Act in 1967, this military regime gained the full contours of a dictatorship. This act revoked the constitution, abolished the autonomy of the legislature, and suspended individual human rights. It is within this context that reactionary forces invaded the stage of the Ruth Escobar Theater during a performance of Chico Buarque's *Roda Viva* [Live Wheel] and proceeded to assault the actors and members of the audience. A few days later these same forces attacked the heart of the city and destroyed the Dream of García Lorca, which was also the dream of Flávio de Carvalho and of many more in the city who sought inspiration in Lorca. Once more the great cultural laboratory of São Paulo was shut down, precisely at the climax of its unpredictable momentum.

Earlier in the century, writer Mário de Andrade had envisioned a grove of jacaranda trees that would follow São Luís Avenue along to the Municipal Library and provide a gentle shade over the stands that sold used books and the countless anonymous readers who sat on the park benches at Dom José Gaspar Square. In the late 1960s this grove represented one of the last green spaces extant from Antônio Prado's tenure as the city's mayor. Then, symbolically, with a timing and accuracy befitting one of these tests that measure the limits of asphyxiation, these jacaranda trees were cut down with axes and electric saws to open space for a new set of express lanes. A technocratic nightmare engulfed the city to fill the vacuum left by political repression: Viaducts and overpasses ran in parallel lines, crossed each other, and were superimposed; public spaces were closed, and concrete four-story public squares were built for the convenience of automobiles; massive misappropriation of what had been green space and demolitions ensued; a process of unrestrained verticalization transformed the cityscape. This technocratic nightmare was composed of supermarkets, private condominiums, business centers, protective fences, and a jungle of antennas punctuated by massively tall towers for radio transmission. A new landscape of asphalt, concrete, steel, aluminum, and crystal was quickly created where once the Jesuits had envisioned a picturesque vista of hills, rivers, and lakes, and where the Tietê River curved through broad green valleys until it disappeared under a blue cloud of fine mist.

The gradual process of overcoming the various obstacles put in place by the dictatorial regime would only be complete by the mid-1980s, when the city would resume the synergistic experiments of this laboratory without boundaries or center. Entering the twenty-first century as the globe's third largest urban area, São Paulo is once again becoming a site for cultural syncretism–between the extremes of wealth and poverty, speculation and segregation, global culture and local popular tradition, mass society and isolation, avarice and solidarity, the suppression of human rights and the aspiration for democracy. In a cultural landscape predominantly composed of migrant and rootless people, the only common ground seems to rest in a future immersed in the light fog that envelops the city. This is why we are touched by the echo of Paulo Mendes Campos's (1922–1991) "Ode to Federico García Lorca," once read on the garden intended as the memorial to Lorca by one of the finest Brazilian poets:

> Há uma orfandade enorme.
> Sei que conheces todos os caminhos como se
> foras um menino, mas, ao meio de todas
> as vozes que te cercaram, colaste teus ovidos
> aos pulmões enfermos da cidade e não ficaste
> indiferente aos arquejos que captaste.
> um pedaço de voz entrecortado, um coro sem música,
> sem tranqüilidade
> nenhuma, que irrompia de gargantas humanas submersas . . . .
> Seria agora inútil e patético, Garcia Lorca, suspender
> minha voz no céu irresponsável e indagar
> onde estás.
> Estás à sombra das oliveiras, talvez, nos olhos sem tempo
> dos bois, no teu túmulo, talvez,
> à beira dos riachos, à beira dos pensamentos de
> misericórdia, nos versos melhores que fazemos,
> acompanhando a lua na visita às cidades destruidas,
> no soluço definitivo dos moribundos fuzilados,
> no ar, no vento, na chuva, estás por toda parte,
> porque a palavra amor não desmorona nunca.

> There is an enormous orphaning
> I know that you are acquainted with all these paths as
> if you were a boy, but in the midst of all the
> voices that surround you, you pressed your
> ear to the diseased lungs of the city and did
> Not remain indifferent to the gasps you apprehended,
> a piece of a voice cut, a choir without music, without
> any tranquility
> That erupted from submersed human throats. . . .
> Now it would be useless and pathetic, García Lorca, to
> suspend my voice in the sky that does not
> answer and to inquire of your whereabouts.
> You are under the shade of the olive trees, perhaps, in
> the timeless stare of bulls, In your grave, perhaps,
> on the margins of rivulets, on the margin of thoughts
> of mercy, in our better verses,
> Accompanying the moon in a visit to the destroyed

> cities, the definitive sob of the dying that are
> gunned down, in the air, in the wind, in the
> rain, you are everywhere,
> because the word love never falls apart.

(25)

Translation by Paulo Horta

Works Cited

Almeida, Fernando Azevedo de. 1976. *O Franciscano Ciccillo*. São Paulo: Pioneira.

Amaral, Aracy. 1970a. *Artes Plásticas na Semana de 22*. São Paulo: Perspectiva.

——. 1970b. *Blaise Cendrars no Brasil e os Modernistas*. São Paulo: Martins.

Americano, Jorge. 1962. *São Paulo Naquele Tempo, 1895–1915*. São Paulo: Melhoramentos.

Andrade, Mário de. 1976. *Poesias Completas*. São Paulo: Círculo do Livro.

Andrade, Oswalde de. 1972. "Manifesto da Poesia Pau-Brasil." *Vanguarda Européia e Modernismo Brasileiro*. Rio de Janeiro: Vozes. 203–208.

Araújo Filho, José de Ribeiro. 1958. "A População Paulistana." *A Cidade de São Paulo: Estudos de geografia urbana*. Ed. Aroldo de Azevedo. 4 vols. São Paulo: Nacional. 2: 167–247.

Bochner, Jay. 1978. *Blaise Cendrars: Discovery and Re-creation*. Toronto: University of Toronto Press.

Bruno, Ernani Silva. 1954. *História e Tradições da Cidade de São Paulo*. Vol. 3. Rio de Janeiro: José Olympio.

——. 1981. *Depoimentos de Moradores e Visitantes 1553–1958*. São Paulo: Secretaria Municipal de Cultura.

Campos, Paulo Mendes. 1990. *Os Melhores Poemas*. São Paulo: Global, Secretaria Municipal de Cultura.

Cendrars, Blaise. 1947. *Au coeur du monde. Poésies complètes: 1924–1929*. Paris: Gallimard.

——. 1976. *Etc...Etc... (Um Livro 100% Brasileiro)*. São Paulo: Perspectiva.

——. 1992. *Complete Poems*. Trans. Ron Padgett. Berkeley: University of California Press.

Chefdor, Monique. 1980. *Blaise Cendrars*. Boston: Twayne Publishers.

Dias, Maria Odila Leite da Silva. 1995. "*Quotidiano e Poder.*" 2nd ed. São Paulo: Brasiliense.

García Lorca, Frederico. 1983. "Los Alamos de plata." *Libro de poemas (1921)*. Ed. Ian Gibson. Barcelona: Editorial Ariel. 173–74.

Hollanda, Sérgio Buarque de. 1986. *O Extremo Oeste*. São Paulo: Brasiliense.

Lara, Cecília de. 1987. *De Pirandello a Piolin. Alcântara Machado e o teatro no modernismo*. Rio de Janeiro: INACEN.

Leite, R. M. and Walter Zanini. 1983. *Catálogo da Exposição Flávio de Carvalho*. 17th ed. São Paulo: Bienal de São Paulo.

Levi, Darrell E. 1974. *A Família Prado*. São Paulo: Cultura.

Lévi-Strauss, Claude. 1993. *Tristes Trópicos*. Trans. Rosa Freire D'Aguiar. São Paulo: Companhia das Letras.

Love, Joseph Leroy. 1980. *São Paulo in the Brazilian Federation: 1889–1937*. Stanford: Stanford University Press.

——. 1982. *A Locomotiva: São Paulo na federação brasileira, 1889–1937*. Rio de Janeiro: Paz e Terra.

Morand, Paul. 1967. Preface. *Du Monde Entier, poésies complètes: 1912–1924* by Blaise Cendrars. Paris: Gallimard. 9–12.

Oliveira, Olívia Fernandes de. 1995. "Quarto de Arquiteto, Lina Bo Bardi e a história." *Óculum: Revista universitária de arquitetura, urbanismo e cultura* 5.6: 82–87.

Petrone, Pasquale. 1958. "São Paulo no Século XX." *A Cidade de São Paulo: Estudos de geografia urbana*. Ed. Aroldo de Azevedo. 4 vols. São Paulo: Companhia Editora Nacional. 2: 101–105.

Prado Jr., Caio. 1977. *A Evolução Política do Brasil e Outros Estudos.* 10th ed. São Paulo: Brasiliense.

Rolnik, Raquel, Lúcio Kowarik, and Nadia Somekh, eds. 1992. *São Paulo: Crise e mudança.* São Paulo: Prefeitura do Município, Brasiliense.

Saliba, Elias Thomé, ed. 1983. *Idéias Econômicas de Cincinato Braga.* Rio de Janeiro: Casa de Rui Barbosa, Senado Federal, MEC.

Sevcenko, Nicolau. 1989. "Rio de Janeiro y San Pablo: Desarrollo social y cultural comparativo, 1900–1930." *Nuevas Perspectivas en los Estudios Sobre Historia Urbana.* Ed. Jorge Enrique Hardoy and Richard McGee Morse. Buenos Aires: Grupo Editora Latinoamericano. 149–67.

——. 1992. *Orfeu Extático na Metrópole, São Paulo sociedade e cultura nos frementes anos 20.* São Paulo: Companhia das Letras.

——. 1993a. "São Paulo: The Quintessential, Uninhibited Megalopolis as Seen by Blaise Cendrars in the 1920s." *Megalopolis: The Giant City in History.* Ed. Theo Barker and Anthony Sutcliffe. London: Macmillan. 175–93.

——. 1993b. "Transformações da Linguagem e Advento da Cultura Modernista no Brasil." *Estudos Históricos* 5.11: 78–88.

——. 1995. "Brazilian Follies: The Casting, Broadcasting and Consumption of Images of Brazil on Both Sides of the Continent, 1930–1950." Paper delivered at *International Seminar on Ways of Working in Latin American Cultural Studies*, University College, University of London.

Steegmuller, Francis. 1986. *Apollinaire: Poet among the Painters.* New York: Penguin.

Toledo, J. 1994. *Flávio de Carvalho: O comedor de emoções.* São Paulo: Brasiliense.

Vargas, Getúlio. 1952. *O Governo Trabalhista do Brasil.* Rio de Janeiro: José Olympio.

Vilaça, F. 1978. "A Estrutura Territorial da Metrópole Brasileira." Diss. Universidade de São Paulo, Departamento de Geografia.

Wiser, William. 1990. *The Crazy Years: Paris in the Twenties.* London: Thames and Hudson.

CHAPTER 50

OURO PRETO, BELO HORIZONTE, BRASÍLIA

THE UTOPIA OF MODERNITY

Maria Zilda Ferreira Cury

The building of a city is always an incomplete, never-ending work. A cultural center, far from taking on the fixedness that the word *center* suggests, involves, quite to the contrary, spatial and temporal dislocations, ever new and different configurations. This is what has happened to Belo Horizonte, capital of Minas Gerais, a cultural center that presents itself as unique in relation to others in the country. The campaign of Juscelino Kubitschek de Oliveira for presidency of the republic in the 1950s insisted on the acceleration of Brazil's industrial development. He created for the country the image of vectorial time–arrow-time–that advances in the direction of a stage that ought necessarily to surpass those of former times (see Bosi 1992). As president, with objectives that involved moving the capital of the country from Rio de Janeiro to the idealized Brasília, he began to establish the famous "fifty years in five." On 21 April 1960 Brasília was inaugurated. The date chosen, far from being random, had been set in homage to the Inconfidentes (revolutionary conspirators of Minas Gerais) and gave new meaning to 21 April 1792, date of the death of Tiradentes, hero of the Inconfidência Mineira, who had been hanged, drawn, and quartered.

The move to the interior was precisely one of the objectives of the Inconfidentes, who at the end of the eighteenth century rose against the Portuguese Crown in an attempted revolt to make the region of Minas independent. Tiradentes himself had chosen São João del Rei to become the new capital, after the proclamation of the republic proposed by the conspirators, thus substituting Ouro Preto, which was then called Vila Rica. The Inconfidentes, especially Tiradentes–leader and martyr of the revolt–would be appropriated by the recently proclaimed Brazilian Republican Regime of 1889 as national heroes–a dimension that was absolutely not in their plans–and transformed into points of reference for collective identification for the edification of the myth of origin of the new regime. Since the republic lacked an effective involvement of the people in its establishment, a founding symbol had to be created for it, a myth that would confer on it a glorious past and an heroic tradition. Taking advantage of the figure of Tiradentes, who in the Brazilian collective imaginary, and in literary and artistic representations, was already conflated with the figure of Christ, it raised him to the status of national myth, founding hero, and civic totem. Tiradentes, drawn and quartered in the arms of Our Lady Aparecida–patroness of Brazil–would be the perfect civic-religious *pietà*, the nation showing (in pieces) the body of its people whom the Republic was still not able to recompose (see Carvalho 1990). This, a representation of Tiradentes, has had a long life, even today efficiently surviving as a foundational figure, especially in the discourse of politicians of Minas, both as in the example just cited of Juscelino, but also up to the present day with Tancredo Neves, not to mention Getúlio Vargas of the Estado Novo and so many others.

The great national holiday is April 21, a date which also serves to commemorate the death of the Brazilian president who introduced the new Republic, Tancredo Neves, and who died on 21 April 1985.

Since its origin Belo Horizonte has revealed, in its historic process of formation, a character distinct from the other Brazilian capitals: It came into existence to be modern, with the obligation to rapidly become a great political and cultural center. A city planned on paper, it responded to the ideals of sanitation and regulation of space that so marked the urban reforms of European cities of the middle of the nineteenth century. In the recently proclaimed "Bride of the Republic," Belo Horizonte expressed the new regime's ideal come true. In its inaugural year the state president's report recorded that, with the construction of the city, the republic had been consolidated. It stated that in six years the new regime had done more for Brazil than the old one had in sixty-seven years. As can be seen, the idea of surpassing the past is not new; nor did it come with the idealization of Brasília. Responding to the Positivist spirit that was the basis of republican thought in Brazil, Belo Horizonte was the first modern Brazilian capital that resulted from the desire for the creation of a planned space. The character of the city defined ideals of urbanism and shaped from the beginning the modernizing utopia of the republican project. In this sense Belo Horizonte is paradoxically like its opposite, Canudos, which was destroyed in the name of the republic by the same modernizing process that singled out, from top to bottom in an authoritarian way, those worthy of becoming citizens and those that ought, in the name of progress, be swept away as backward by the inexorable course of history (see Paula 1997).

Rising under the sign of the modern, cautiously envisioned to favor a city of order, Belo Horizonte–in a contradictory way–carries with it from its foundation the heavy tradition of the old capital of Minas. This is a tradition which also characterized republican projects in general. Without breaking with the past, the utopia of the modernizing republican project was formed out of tradition, since it brought with it the sacred space of Ouro Preto, a primordial space of the Brazilian Republic (see Mello 1996). (See **Figure 1**.) The new capital of Minas Gerais from its original design has revealed a face on which a recomposition of historical time has been articulated, legitimated by the juxtaposition of tradition and the future, by the ancient and the modern. Thus, to understand Belo Horizonte as a cultural center, one needs to take the city as a point of inflection of both the Colonial past of the eighteenth-century tradition of Ouro Preto, as well as the future, the contradictory modernity of Brasília.

The Seduction/Sedition of Minas Gerais

Minas Gerais, the central region of Brazil, had mining as its base; this too gave it its name. With the discovery of gold at the end of the seventeenth century, the settlement of the mining

Figure 1.

Photograph of Ouro Preto by Radio Iconfidência, Minas Gerais in Fernando de Azevedo A cultura brasileira, *1943. (Courtesy of John P. Robarts Research Library, University of Toronto)*

region began. Minas was late in development compared to the regions along the Brazilian coast; it was characterized as a place of passage or connection, where inter-regional commercial interests crossed. The region developed close contacts with the coast, São Paulo, and Goiás, as well as with Pernambuco and Bahia by way of the São Francisco River. The area displayed more complex contours, with rapid urbanization and settlement and with features markedly differentiated from those of other regions, thanks to the development of unique artistic manifestations and the emergence of new social agents. As the central region of Brazil, it already incorporated the idea that it would be a point of cohesion for a sense of nationality to which the discourse on the Inconfidência would give weight and substance. The importance of Ouro Preto, declared part of the cultural patrimony of humanity by UNESCO, goes beyond this national scope. Such cultural patrimonies in themselves fulfill a mediating role among different temporal dimensions, because they evoke the past but as a reinforcement of a collective identity, which is experienced at the present moment. Vila Rica–as the present Ouro Preto was first known–is thus a symbol-city, a synthesis of the colonizing experience of Minas, a prismatic confluence of the various historical times of the country.

The center of colonial settlement was the urban seat where the civil servants, military, and ecclesiastical personnel were concentrated, constituting a bureaucratic space and a place of the appropriation of the excess production of goods in the form of tribute, profit, soldier's pay, and so forth. This was where power multiplied itself in many different spheres, both in its coercive and persuasive forms. Vila Rica was a place of order, a result of the colonizing work of the state and the Church, whose motive force for progress was gold. Vila Rica was also a place of disorder, insurrections, slavery, and conspiracies. The administrative regulation of the village began in 1711; after 1720 small centers formed along the way that led from Vila Rica to Sabará and other villages of Minas. Vila Rica was then transformed into the capital of the Captaincy of

Minas Gerais. Its settlement evolved somewhat chaotically, with precarious dwelling places, since the village was still noted for the nomadism that characterized the gold extraction of the period. Slaves, in increasing numbers, were preferred from Benin or Costa da Mina, for they were reputed to be strongest and most resistant to the diseases that were very common in the mines. The high mortality rate among slaves was a contributing factor to the unrest, rebellion, and the creation of many *quilombos* (maroon communities), which led to the region being characterized as violent. In this Colonial region the masculine presence predominated, a factor that made it different from the sugar-cane zone of the Brazilian Northeast. Family ties were as a result weak, and there was a high incidence of prostitution. The lack of food supplies was great; this contributed, after 1710, to the cultivation of lands near the mining areas and to trade with São Paulo, Bahia, and Rio de Janeiro, thus conferring more stability to the villages.

Religious orders were not allowed in Minas for political and economic reasons, since only they, and not individual priests, could be proprietors. There was, then, a proliferation of associations and mediators of the religious order of St. Francis. On the mining roads the first explorers took portable *oratórios* (shrines) with them, with images and improvised altars, until the discovery of gold when crude chapels of stucco and wood–though with richly ornamented interiors–were erected (see Ávila 1996). As primitive seeds of urbanization, these chapels make clear that the colonizing work of the Church preceded that of the Portuguese Crown. At the end of the eighteenth century, due to the temptation of gold, Minas Gerais already displayed the greatest population density among the Brazilian captaincies. There was also a large concentration of slaves, the intense commerce in whom attracted even more capital to the region.

If Vila Rica's history was related to the production of wealth, it was also marked by taxation and social control and, above all, as happened in general with the life of Minas, by ideals of liberty and rebellion. In the reports of the governing officials the people of Minas were represented countless times as ungovernable, rebellious, and dangerous, because they were prone to movements of sedition and confrontation with the authorities. From the middle of the century there was a greater frequency of revolts: silent, daily, and disseminated (see Souza 1992). The mining adventure was in itself a repeated invitation to disputes and confrontations. In Brazil, because the colonial state preceded the idea of nation, rebellion was fostered by the view that the Empire prevented the Brazilian nation from attaining its true destiny.

In 1711 the villages of Antônio Dias and Ouro Preto were joined, forming Vila Rica. The mother churches of Nossa Senhora do Pilar and Nossa Senhora da Conceição face opposite directions, revealing by this location the independent formation of the two groups of parishioners. In 1712 the plaza on the Santa Quitéria Hill was created to establish a new central space. There the Pelourinho (pillory) was established as a symbolic sign of temporal power, reinforced by the Municipal Government and the jail, imposed by the appointed force of the metropolitan state. The plaza slowly set a new architectural standard (with greater refinement) and also allowed new expansion, with the erection of houses and many business establishments. As a city, Vila Rica dates from 1737; as a city of power, it began with the construction of the town hall. The process of expansion was being realized in an urban plan that is close to that of the city today.

In 1733 a very important event took place: The festival of the Eucharistic Triumph was celebrated, with great pomp and luxury, with the inauguration of the new church of Nossa Senhora do Pilar, which initiated the aesthetic process of integration of the decorative into architectural elements. The festival was a sign of Counter-Reformist propaganda and of the temporal power of the Church. Beyond that, it was the representative expression of the hierarchized functioning of society in Minas. The Pilar church, completed at the initial phase of the Baroque when mining was still abundant, had its altars coated in gold. For six consecutive nights houses were illuminated, and the streets were richly decorated with silks and satins in the windows. Dances and floats appeared on the streets, and, most important of all, there was a procession in which the clergy, numerous brotherhoods, the Governor Conde de Galvêas, the military and literary elite, the Senate, and the Company of Dragoons all took part, arranged according to their position in the social hierarchy. At the end of the procession were the people. Vila Rica was in fact celebrating the success of the mining enterprise, resorting, as was common in Baroque festivals, to visual language, joining together theater, dance, and music. The entire city was mobilized in procession. A "rhetorical" spectacle was created, intended to persuade the people through visual excess. Although the festival was mostly attended by impoverished people, the image it projected was that of an opulent society (see Ávila 1980). Through the magical spectacle of the Baroque, the supremacy of authority over the precariousness of the mining adventure–the supremacy of order over disorder–was affirmed. The liturgical festivals, of which this is an example, expressed the Baroque style to which the population of the eighteenth century was viscerally attached. The Baroque, far from being content with words, was woven into a sophisticated net of performances, a shining and lasting discoursive tissue emanating from the center of the colony's soul.

The fiscal tax on the metropolis, known as the poll tax, was created in 1736; and in 1742 the boundaries of the city were completed. But the vigilance over Vila Rica went beyond fiscal control because of fear of colonial uprisings. The town, although at a very high cost, was relatively independent, a generator of wealth, power, and culture. It developed an effective urban life, quite distinct from that in the cities of the Brazilian coast more connected to the rural world. The metropolis, which before was little concerned with the organization of the city, now wanted to control the population, since the city was a source of revenue. Portuguese control would be made manifest, and, if there were an uprising, it would be possible to check it. The city was a place where disobedience and discontent could arise at any time, so the role of the municipal government was to exercise order over the population and to control problems.

Between 1730 and 1770 a relative stability can be discerned, which coincided with the highest point of urbanization and the peak of gold production. Between 1740 and 1760 bridges and fountains were built; in 1744 the Governor's Palace was completed, an affirmation of the solidity of power, with its military architecture like that of the coastal cities, symptomatically indicating how great a risk of rebellion the region showed. In 1766 the renovation of the Carmo Church, made by Manuel Francisco Lisboa, with changes on the façade and in interior ornamentation, pointed toward the advent of the Rococo. The redesigned urban space made explicit the presence of temporal power, and the buildings gave the appearance of permanence to Vila Rica.

The introduction of the Rococo style in the architecture of Manoel Francisco had a major influence on the work of his son, Antônio Francisco Lisboa (1730–1814), known as Aleijadinho. Brilliant creator of the masterpiece, the Church of São Francisco de Assis, in Ouro Preto (with altars, pulpits, and panels also made by him), Aleijadinho guaranteed for Minas the highest level of Baroque art. The importance of this work is that it represents an architectural imagination of fully Brazilian character, a fact which would make the church an object of reappropriation at various times in the history of Brazilian art. As gold mining was already dwindling, the artists compensated for the lack of the metal with artistic technique, as was the case in this church. Aleijadinho was also the creator of countless other architectural and sculptural works spread over Minas Gerais. Another particularity of the Colonial art of Minas, and of which Aleijadinho was an undisputed master, can be found in wood and soapstone carving. Statues, as well as ornamental figures on arcades, pulpits, portals, and altarpieces, offer impressive examples of his visual conception. Some historians have proposed the hypothesis of a connection between the artist and the conspirators, strengthened by the Phrygian cap worn by the Prophets sculpted in soapstone, which are found in the city of Congonhas do Campo. Another proposed link is the cut on the neck of the Christ sculpted in wood, which would recall the mark of the rope of the hanging of Tiradentes.

Another outstanding artist was Manoel da Costa Ataíde, who would make a notable contribution to the painting of the interior of the churches. Thus the Church signaled its place of power with many buildings of a monumental nature erected by the brotherhoods. If the public buildings occupied the central space of the town, the churches, for their part, were spread over the city, delimiting the territories of the parishioners. In the 1950s many musical scores were discovered in churches of cities in Minas, attesting to the rich musical flowering of the eighteenth century. The most important composers of this time were Inácio Parreiras Neves (1730–1793), Marcos Coelho Neto (1740–1806), and especially José Joaquim Emerico Lobo de Mesquita (1746–1805); they were mainly church music directors, influenced by the pre-Classical repertoire, Neapolitan operas, and Portuguese religious music of a polyphonic character.

From the first decades of the eighteenth century, experienced master-builders and artists, who were in charge of building the first churches, came to Minas. Their buildings are examples of the Baroque not only in architecture, but also in sculpture, painting, and ornamentation (see Ávila 1967). In a search for legitimation and autonomy, buildings with greater architectural ambition were constructed. The construction sites and shops were transformed into true schools of specialization, preparing artists who would contribute with their talent to the grandeur of Colonial art in Minas. As Nicolau Sevcenko emphasizes, the importance of Baroque art, with its mystical aura, has contributed to the creation of Brazilian sensibility. The Brazilian Baroque was not a passing style, but the basic substance of a whole new cultural synthesis (see Sevcenko 1998). As Sevcenko shows, the Baroque was not an art exclusively for the illustrious elite, but an art that aimed at the emotional enthusiasm of the general population. The specificity of religious architecture in Minas can be noted in the tradition that the Baroque here manifested a preference for the curved line, for the contorted and unexpected elements, from the plan of the building to decoration, as can be seen in the profile of columns and the delineation of façades.

The houses in the region of Minas also displayed modifications in the eighteenth century, with a larger number of rooms and more elaborate façades, although the interior remained plain. Built in alignment with the streets, they form the background of the urban landscape, compactly and uniformly. The proximity of one to another and the fact of their being inhabited by a large number of people indicate a lack of privacy. (The latter was gradually valued.) The refinement of table settings–recorded in travelogues–can be documented by the silver pieces, such as cutlery, mentioned in the inventories, although the reduced number indicates perhaps that they were only used on special occasions. Beginning in the second half of the eighteenth century, furniture became more refined and the houses had a more sophisticated decoration. According to what was reported by nineteenth-century travelers, the beds were especially noted for their opulence, proof of a new concept of privacy. The daily life of Vila was rather simple with respect to food, with meals consisting of meat, bacon, beans, corn, manioc, and fruit. For the slaves there was corn and beans, with tobacco and cachaça (sugar-cane liquor), considered stimulants.

Social differentiation was clear in clothing, a distinctive sign of class, through an impressive variety in quality and a large investment in jewelry. There was not, in domestic life, great care with hygiene, and the city did not even offer basic services of sanitation, such as running water, sewers, or adequate paving. The autonomy of the street was revealed by the separation from the main road, which was the road used by caravans and merchants. House and street both depended on the work of numerous slaves. The streets were filthy, full of animals and abandoned children, a place of slaves and vagrants. The streets constituted the space of disorder–only used by the population in religious and civic festivals. If the festivals were a cause for joy, they could also be transformed into the site of violent quarrels, the occasion for revenge, and for the overflow of the population's resentment of the authorities. For the slaves–who were frequently involved in violent conflicts–it was the place of drum beating, fighting, and other violent altercations. Although the "urban spectacle" codified the borders between the classes, mining allowed for the emergence of a great number of free workers, blacks, and mulattoes, all potentially dangerous to the power of the Crown. Throughout the century slave revolts broke out. Thus it came to be that the house was the locus of affirmation of the family; the street was the locus of consolidation of the hierarchies–constantly disturbed, however, by the human convergence of adventurers, soldiers, bureaucrats, vagrants, artists, and artisans, all sharing the space of the town. There was also a notion that there was a *war* going on in Minas between colonists and slaves. The fugitive slaves, for example, gathered in isolated communities or along the paths to the mines and attacked the white population on the roads. A number of expeditions were organized for their recapture. When they were caught alive, the slaves had their owner's mark branded on their bodies or even had an ear cut off to expose, publicly and spectacularly, their infraction (see Souza 1992). In a society entirely based on the exploitation of slave labor and therefore on the need for slaves in great numbers, the black population was also seen as a constant threat. The eighteenth century also witnessed several manifestations against metropolitan politics, in most cases because of excessive tax levies and the resistance to taxation promoted by the powerful men of the colony (see Anastasia 1995). In the last quarter of the eighteenth century gold supplies had already dwindled, making the region less prosperous than in the past and the population more restless, with the few alternatives proposed by the metropolis. Although such a scenario of decline was increasingly evident, the Portuguese crown continued to levy taxes with an iron hand but did not work to prevent lawlessness, disobedience, and contraband.

Doctors and scholars who graduated from the most important European universities circulated through the economic centers of Minas. With their diplomas they also brought in their baggage the most advanced literature, filled with Enlightenment ideas that considered the struggle for political freedom fundamental. Enlightenment ideas spread in Brazil, especially the proposals for substituting a constitutional monarchy or a democratic republic, based on liberal economic politics, for the power of the monarchy. Even without a significant number of bookstores, the intellectuals of Minas had access to the texts that discussed the independence of English America, a great inspiration as a practical example of liberation that truly fascinated the conspirators of Minas (see Rouanet 1992). The Inconfidência Mineira, as the most important movement of sedition in Minas became known, was planned by a group of wealthy men: farmers, slave-owners, and mine-owners. Some historians say that, owing to their social status as proprietors, the conspiracy was a revolt of an elitist nature against taxation. For this reason the rebels criticized Colonialism and not the ostentation and luxury of the life of the Colonial rich. The conspirators were, with the exception of Tiradentes, men of wealth who paid heavy taxes to the crown; notable among them were: Francisco de Paula Freire de Andrada, José Álvares Maciel, Padre Toledo, Ignácio José de Alvarenga Peixoto (1744–1793), and Padre Rolim–the activists; Tomás Antônio Gonzaga (1744–1807?), Luís Vieira da Silva, and Cláudio Manoel da Costa (1729–1789)–the ideologues; as well as Domingos de Abreu Vieira, Joaquim Silvério dos Reis, and João Rodrigues de Macedo. The intellectual mentors of the movement–the poets Cláudio Manoel da Costa, Tomás Antônio Gonzaga, and Alvarenga Peixoto–had been friends since their school days in Coimbra. When they met again in Minas, they established a strict relation of daily sociability in which, besides literature, Enlightenment principles were discussed. Through the study of the papers regarding the confiscation of conspirators' goods, it has been confirmed that there were books by Enlightenment authors in their libraries. The new ideas also permeated their works. Cláudio Manoel da Costa, for example, creates landscapes with political themes. In the *Canto genetlíaco* [Genethliatic Song] of Alvarenga Peixoto the protagonists are slaves, and in the *Cartas chilenas* [Chilean Letters] of Tomás Antônio Gonzaga there is sympathy for the suffering of the colonials and anger against the genocide of natives, although the poet, closer to European standards, shows a biased and excluding perception in relation to exploited groups. In the work of the three poets, verses with a tone of accusation against the politics of the metropolis in relation to the colony can be found. In this way they moved from the literary to the political, from a theoretical vision to a proposal for action.

The moment that would unleash the movement was the beginning of the compulsory collection of the debts of mine-owners–the *derrama* (literally, the spill)–a propitious occasion for the incitement of the people of Minas to revolt. Their plan foresaw the death of the governor, the establishment of a Provisional Council, and the Declaration of Independence of the Captaincy of Minas Gerais. Even though they desired to break with the metropolis, they did not question property, and, although often condemning cruelties against blacks, they feared that abolition would cause serious economic problems. They proposed, however, the freedom of slaves born in the country. The pro-abolition arguments of the conspirators, far from being linked to humanitarian reasons, were tempered by the fear of slave revolts. The point of view here continues to be that of the white property-owner, who fears the more radical revolt of the numerous blacks and vagrants. Priests would directly receive their tithe, as long as they provided social welfare work, and women who were disposed to have more children would be rewarded. The people's militias would take the place of the army on a permanent basis, and there would be freedom in the mining of diamonds and iron. There was also a project for the creation of a mint. After independence the capital would be transferred to São João del Rei, where a university was founded. In the 1920s, when the Federal University of Minas Gerais was created in Belo Horizonte, republican discourse took it to be the fulfillment of the dream of the Inconfidentes, as payment of a debt with the past. Another example, along the same lines, was the creation of the Foundation of Higher Education of São João del Rei, soon after the death of Tancredo Neves.

The rebels were arrested and condemned, banished to Africa by the Jurisdiction Commission, especially created for the judgment of the conspirators. The only exception was Joaquim José da Silva Xavier, nicknamed Tiradentes, condemned to being hanged, drawn, and quartered as an example to the inhabitants of Minas of the power of the Crown. On the Largo da Lampadosa in Rio de Janeiro, on 21 April 1792, Tiradentes was hanged. The contrition shown by him at the hour of his death, the exhibition of his body, quartered and hung on posts along the roads into Minas, the thanksgiving mass celebrated for the failure of the episode, the lamps lighted for three nights in Vila Rica—all this transformed the execution into a Baroque spectacle. Note, once again, the didactic character that such spectacles had in the colony (see Campos 1992). Both Tiradentes's revolutionary views and his death profoundly affected the imaginary of the people of Minas. If the formal revolt had been secret, in the pamphlets of Minas, it was made public (see Souza 1992). Publications on the Inconfidentes gradually appeared and increased in number. When the debates between monarchists and republicans heated up in the nineteenth century, the rebellion occupied an ever more significant place in theatrical performances, novels, and even the building of monuments. One must single out the work of Joaquim Norberto de Souza e Silva (1820–1891), *História da conjuração mineira* [1873; History of the Minas Conspiracy], as fundamental, for it was the first substantial work on the movement and was based on the inquest documents. The author, a staunch monarchist, paradoxically broadened the perspectives for studies on the Inconfidência, the basis for the republican appropriation of the myth of Tiradentes as the precursor of nationalism. Norberto's work played a decisive role in integrating the Inconfidência into the foundations of the Brazilian nation. For the historiography of the republic, the Inconfidência Mineira was a decisive step in the process of the formation of nationality under the aegis of the elites. From having generated great interest in the Romantics, Nativists *par excellence*, the theme of the conspiracy ended up being incorporated into the patriotism of Brazilians. From the literary point of view, the Nativist tone of many of Cláudio Manoel da Costa's and Tomás Antônio Gonzaga's poems

would influence the concept of nation and independence that stimulated Romantic poetry.

The poetic production of Costa, Gonzaga, and Alvarenga Peixoto made up what was conventionally called the Brazilian Arcadia. The Arcadian movement, in the second half of the century, took the place of the cultist and conceptual tendencies so characteristic of the still current Baroque canon, introducing a style more musically smooth and more adequate to new themes. The imitation of nature and the bucolic pastoral atmosphere of their poetry, witness to an often successful articulation of lyrical and epic themes, greatly influenced the Brazilian literature of the future, both in the poetry of Romantic tradition and in Parnassian poetry. The Arcadian poets, influenced by English, North American, and French ideas, also express in their writings a will for independence and autonomy determined by the local environment, a critique by the more enlightened bourgeoisie of the excesses of the nobility and the clergy (see Bosi 1994). Regarded by Antônio Candido (in 1993) as being on the threshold of the new style, Cláudio Manoel da Costa is considered to be deeply associated with the sentiments and values of the land. One can say that in his writings he articulates the Minas regionalist style, devoted to his "native river" (Riberão do Carmo), the rocky landscape of Minas, and the intellectual tradition of Europe.

The episode of the Inconfidência resonates even in contemporary literature, as in the 1974 novel *Os sinos da agonia* [The Bells of Agony] by Autran Dourado (b. 1926), a writer from Minas, who obsessively thematizes the decadence of Minas Gerais in his works (see Picchio 1997). Recreating Vila Rica, Dourado gives different meaning to the Inconfidência, turning it into an allegory of the dictatorship in Brazil during the 1970s. The nineteenth century, considered the "dark ages" by the republicans interested in disqualifying the monarchy, displayed a scenario of great decline in Minas Gerais. The accounts of travelers who passed through Ouro Preto already noted a city in decay. With antiquated methods of farming, little variety of products, and technical limitations of every order, the Minas of the nineteenth century lagged behind the ideals of scientific progress that characterized the era. The republicans who praised Ouro Preto as the foundation of the nation paradoxically designated the city as backward and criticized its architecture.

After the Proclamation of the Republic there were disputes in every Brazilian province over the political positions opened up by the new regime. It was no different in Minas, leading even to a proposal for the restructuring of the state, suggested several times by some parliamentarians. Ouro Preto was no longer the main economic center of the state. There were separatist movements coming from the southern coffee-growing region, which already had important urban centers, railroads, and its own commercial development. The intention was to create a new state, Minas do Sul (South Minas), where the exclusiveness of coffee growers' interests could be represented. It was important to Minas Gerais to maintain the physical integrity of the old Colonial Captaincy because with it was preserved a historical partrimony, a synthesis and convergent union that created a nationality (see Mello 1996). In his address of 1891 Augusto de Lima, state president, spoke about the different problems of Minas Gerais. To the threat of political destruction of the state, he proposed the urgent creating of a new capital, with a mission to be the center of intellectual, industrial, and financial activity, as well as a point of support for the spatial integrity of Minas. It is clear that the republic also feared that the break-up of Minas could mean the beginning of the fragmentation of Brazil into several countries, as had occurred elsewhere in Spanish America. The discussions that occupied congress about which region ought to be chosen to be the seat of the new state capital soon took up space in the newspapers, mobilized the population, and put into dispute varied political interests. The proposal for a new capital as a point of economic and cultural convergence was consolidated in this context of political effervescence at the beginning of the republic, in the context of the cult of progress and the conservation of the tradition of Ouro Preto as the cradle of nativism and Brazilian identity. As already noted above, the transfer of the capital of Minas was already a part of the plan of the Inconfidentes.

Belo Horizonte: The City on Paper

Belo Horizonte, in the previous century, was a dream built on paper; it was also announced as the great city. "The capital is transferred to a place that, offering the necessary sanitation conditions, is apt for the construction of a big city," the first Republican Constitution of the State of Minas Gerais announced in 1891. This statement conveyed the ideas that shaped the project for creating the new capital of Minas, transferred from the traditional Ouro Preto. The initial settlement, where Belo Horizonte would later be built, was established by the *bandeirante* (frontiersman) from São Paulo, João Leite da Silva Ortiz, who set up a farm in a place called Cercado. There in 1701 he settled with many slaves, attracting new residents and adventurers to the farm that would become the embryo of the hamlet of Nossa Senhora da Boa Viagem do Curral del-Rei, as it was already called in 1707. The social and cultural life of the hamlet developed around the mother church Nossa Senhora da Boa Viagem, built in the beginning of the eighteenth century (razed in the beginning of the twentieth century to make way for the current mother-church, built in a Gothic style). Little by little other leisure and social options and new cultural spaces were created, and the mother-church lost its centralizing character. The daily life of the hamlet was extremely simple, and its cultural and social life comes to us, in a fragmented form, through the accounts of chroniclers and scholars.

Thus Curral del Rei, in 1891, began to be known by the name of Belo Horizonte. In 1893, based on the studies of the engineer Aarão Reis, congress determined that the new capital would be built. For this a building commission was created presided over by Aarão Reis and composed of important names in engineering and architecture. Engineers were considered the most advanced intellectual group of Brazil at that time, especially as the schools of engineering were seats of Positivist and Republican thought. The small settlement of Curral del Rei, with its eight streets, ten alleys, two squares, and three hundred houses, was completely demolished. Under the sign of the modern, the new city would have wide streets, running water, electric power, trains, and imposing buildings. The urban model was European, still present were the radical reforms of London and especially Paris, but it was also inspired by Argentinean cities. The city emerged on paper (see Rama 1985) as a technical utopia envisioned by the elites without any contestation by the inhabitants, present or future. Work was begun and continued at an accelerated pace, especially after the inauguration of the railway branch line of General Carneiro. The urban area was designed to consist of sixty-five streets, twelve avenues, and twenty-four

plazas. In 1895 the foundation stones of the most important buildings, such as the Secretary of the Interior, Finances, and Agriculture and the Presidential Palace, were laid.

To the sound of two bands that marched about the city and twenty-one sticks of dynamite, on 12 December 1897, one day after electrical power became available, the Cidade de Minas (City of Minas) was inaugurated. For the creators of the capital the name would bring cultural unification and overcome the diversity that historically went along with the region. This choice provoked such controversy that it later went back to being called Belo Horizonte, a name blessed by the populace. Construction had taken four years, the same time as the construction of Brasília would take. Several planned establishments of learning and leisure helped the old hamlet come alive. In July 1897, even before the official inauguration of the new capital, the press announced to great acclaim the opening of the Café Mineiro, one of the first coffee houses in Belo Horizonte. With these coffee houses, Belo Horizonte would be a "Petite Paris," the press insisted, and it would soon be transformed into the most important cultural center of the state. The desire for cosmopolitanism, for the city to be transformed into a Paris of the tropics, would make its bars and cafés acquire enormous importance in the life of the city. In 1898 the first bicycle race took place in the capital, and in 1902 a route of cable cars was inaugurated, with the first automobile appearing in the city in 1908. For the city to go beyond the limits of a political center and be transformed into an economic and cultural center, what had to occur was a well-constructed mobilization effort, detectable in the reports of the mayors, the periodicals that circulated since the city's founding, and in the speeches of politicians in general.

From the blueprints of the city, a proposal for the segregated occupation of the city was drawn up; the lots were owned by a few, among them the state itself, and the intention of the elites to make of the urban space one of the instruments of domination was evident (Faria and Grossi 1982, 176). The project corresponded to the ideals of the Brazilian elites, who wished for the country to join the group of developed nations in the adventure of modernity, at the end of the century. Such a modernizing model was imposed from above, since it brought together the ideas of modernization and conservative social practices. It was a question of a model of modernism amidst underdevelopment, anchored in the utopian illusion of the elites, who modeled themselves on their European counterparts. All this conferred on the city a form of hybrid life, undecided between past and future (see Julião 1996), a feature that even today can be seen in its profile as a cultural center.

The planning and building of the capital activated an interdisciplinary knowledge—judicial, medical, sanitary, and architectural—trying to avoid through prevention the problems that had ravaged great urban centers. It was necessary to occupy the space in a disciplined manner, to create a city on the model of Bentham's panopticon, with its vigilance and control. To this end, a city was born on the drawing boards that was literate and technical, conceived without taking into consideration social dictates, and rising out of the utopia of a scientific administration of space. To build the exact, correct city, planned with ruler and compass, it was not necessary to listen to the citizens, who would certainly be ignorant of the high scientific aims of the creators. Therefore zoning was an essential instrument: By establishing the limits of the urban space, zoning imposed a hierarchical division of its use immediately self-evident to the occupants in its restraining and regimenting of social contacts. To urban sanitation was conceded a power nearly unlimited. The sanitation ideal, which so marked the turn-of-century ideologies, was imposed in an authoritative manner mainly on the suburban population but also creating firm rules for the occupation of the city center. To create order meant to exclude. The rigorous measures put in place for the sanitized and clean central space contrasted with the suburbs, which lacked an infrastructure, water supply, and sewers. The blueprint of the city included an avenue in the shape of a ring, inspired by the *Ringstrasse* of Vienna, although according to the account of Aarão Reis the actual nearest model had been the Argentinean city of La Plata. An urban organization, which would create a social order where conflict and disorder would be eliminated, was envisioned. The Avenida 17 de Dezembro–later called *Contorno*–encompassing the whole central area, established the limits between the urban and suburban zones, privileging only the internal area. In that urban zone, as on a chessboard, two planes were geometrically joined: one squared and another diagonal, with large avenues and tree-lined sidewalks 4 meters wide and with the center left free for automobile traffic. The ideal location for public buildings was also established as being at crossings and plazas, with the aim of directing attention to them. Ouro Preto would only be remembered as a monument. For Drummond de Andrade (1902–1987), the poet from Itabira, the *Itacolomi de cimento* (polished sandstone ornamented buildings) would be a nostalgic reminder of his hometown.

The long and wide avenues, inspired by Haussmann's Parisian boulevards, were counterposed to the narrow and winding streets of Ouro Preto and allowed for an unobstructed view, thereby connecting the opposite ends of the city and controlling the circulation of people. The street organized both movement and landscape; it was the space of order, contrasted to the disorder that characterized the Colonial street. Alleys and backstreets, like Rococo ornaments, were elements of the Colonial past; the era now demanded boulevards, plazas, and ample spaces, a garden city. The new urban space wanted to stimulate "footing" (jogging) and the use of the avenues (especially Avenida Afonso Pena) by bourgeois families, but such a use would only become common practice over time. The creation of sectors designed for institutions, such as schools and hospitals, as well as a railroad station, slaughterhouse, cemetery, and water-treatment station, was foreseen. The Building Commission put special emphasis on the location of the railroad station, building it near the Praça Rui Barbosa, the doorway to the city, since it was the railway that connected the capital of Minas to the rest of the country. The train was the symbol of modernity and thus a major concern at the beginning of the century. In the context of the 1920s and 1930s, the importance of that place was reiterated by the presence of a gazebo for concerts and of the luminous fountain Independência. Even today this plaza is the stage for the most varied of performances. The seats of power, both civil (as represented by the Governor's Palace) and clerical (as embodied in the cathedral), were designated. Avenida Afonso Pena was conceived as the main artery, as the only north-south connection, with the function of promoting growth toward the periphery and guaranteeing the sanitation of the downtown area.

In architecture Belo Horizonte was the symbol of aesthetic tendencies in vogue, displaying the confluence of neo-Gothic, neo-Colonial, and neo-Classical styles with ornamental and decorative elements of Art Nouveau. With the transfer of the capital of Minas, civil servants of various kinds came to the city. The Building Commission established six types of houses from A to F. All building projects followed catalogues of samples of ornaments to be used on the façades, with side gardens, romanticized flower beds, and porches with columns of various types. This eclectic local architecture was the model followed for the proposed capital city. The success was so great that it would later co-exist with the Modernism of the architectural project of Pampulha.

The urban planning of the city favored an increase in the price of lots and rents in the central area, with its greater share of the services of infrastructure, land-leveling, and urbanization. With an authoritarian paternalism, the city was administered like a large farm, spatially separate from its population, a mirror of social inequality, thus establishing a vertical relation between the people and the state. The overt political domination and the already mentioned segregated character would in themselves be the causes of social conflicts. The state offered to mediate–coercively or paternalistically–the conflicts, at least in the first phase of Belo Horizonte's history. The state paved the way for capitalist real-estate speculation, regulating the process of spatial growth in the periphery by bringing into the city population clusters that insisted on escaping its control (see Faria). All this building thus aimed at inscribing in the urban space, but above all in people's souls, the project of modernity that would make of Belo Horizonte a marvelous, cosmopolitan, elegant space. But the inhabitants took a long time to accept the role that was imposed on them; the rigid division of space, far from favoring social interaction, was a constriction that hindered integration into public life. The first residents of the city witnessed how difficult it was to get used to the noise, to the dust resulting from endless construction, and especially to an exposed city, which would not allow any privacy. For a long time the press noted the unease of the Belo Horizonte residents, who kept up old habits and customs. It was the city of civil servants, a bureaucratic seat of political power but no importance as a cultural center. Symptomatically, the neighborhood nearest the Governor's Palace was called Funcionários (civil servants). In the words of the writer José Bento Monteiro Lobato (1882–1948), its inhabitants were "public passers-by," that is, civil servants regarded as mere passers-by. The original planning of the city, on the other hand, was gradually but systematically altered, since the real city insisted on invading the ideal city. Suburbs grew in relative disorder, invading the spaces of the sanitized city. The rapid and uncontrolled growth of the city, from the periphery toward the center, took place therefore in total opposition to the original plan.

With the transfer of the capital to Belo Horizonte, independent schools of higher education were created: the Dental School in 1907, the Medical School in 1911–1912, the School of Engineering in 1911, all private and autonomous establishments. The Rua da Bahia housed cafés, very important for the life of the city, especially the Café e Confeitaria Estrela (inspired by the famous Confeitaria Colombo of Rio de Janeiro), which would be a gathering place for modern artists in the 1920s, the group also known as the Grupo do Estrela. Others were the Café Martini, the High-Life, and, perhaps the most famous, the Café e Bar do Ponto. Open as a place of transit, at the *ponto* (stop) from which the cable cars started out, the latter had the most democratic group of customers, ranging from politicians and intellectuals to common people; it became a strategic place in the city for dropping by and obtaining information (see Silveira). In the first decades of the century the Rua da Bahia possessed what existed of refinement in the city, remaining in the collective memory of generations of writers. It is remembered, throughout the years, as a place for intellectuals, bohemian writers, and politicians. But it was also the setting for barricades against police, as occurred during the workers' strike of 1912 (see Paula).

Many families from Ouro Preto came to Belo Horizonte; just as the stones of the old capital were brought to build the pavements of the new. The Colonial past was thus "transplanted" to the new capital. Artists and intellectuals, such as Aleijadinho, Ataíde, Cláudio Manoel da Costa, and Gonzaga, also brought their journalistic tradition to the capital, and this contributed to a rapid flourishing of literary activity. From the city's foundation, significant literary manifestations were witnessed in Belo Horizonte, and the reading public from Ouro Preto came to be the public (of intellectuals) of the new capital (see Dias 1971). Newspapers and literary clubs appeared everywhere. The novel *A Capital* [1893; The Capital] by the anarchist writer Avelino Fóscolo (1864–1944) deserves mention in this respect; it shows the building of Belo Horizonte as the reverse of that modernity that had aimed to impose culture on the population from the top. The text was published in 1903, a few years after the inauguration of the city. Minas Gerais also witnessed the creation of the newspapers *Abelha do Itacolomy* and *Compilador Mineiro* (1824) and *O Universal* (1825). Over the course of the nineteenth century there were 163 publications in Vila Rica.

Artists and artisans, many of whom were foreigners, moved to the capital during the construction period. It is with their work that one can speak of the first artistic manifestations in Belo Horizonte; as well, there were musical concerts, operas, and exhibitions (see Santos), which meant some cultural continuity with the life of the old capital. Nevertheless, such artistic work still had the problem of becoming known outside Minas, since there was no effective exchange with other centers. Various foreign families, mostly Italian, also came to the capital. Although they did not form organized groups of immigrants, they contributed to culture in an interesting way—as seen for instance in their strong influence on the city's cinema production and on soccer teams. The Palestra Itália, which later came to be called Palestra Mineiro, the present Cruzeiro, was an important team for the capital, with thousands of fans, and was of Italian origin.

Photography was used as an instrument by the Building Commission, anxious to document the works and the localities on which the city had been erected. The Portuguese Francisco Soucasseaux, who was also a pioneer of film in Minas, was the man who took these photographs. The interest in this activity is what would pave the way for the movie industry. The town hall received on 2 July 1898 the proposal sent by the businessman Oscar Trompowski for the theater owner William Mardock to establish a motion-picture theater in the city. In the same year several films of the cinematographer Lumière were projected, and there is also evidence of new showings in 1900 and 1903. In 1908 the press announced the showing of two films that had Belo Horizonte as a theme: the panorama of the city and the departure of a train. Both were shown at the Colosso Movie-Theater, which also showed the work of Raimundo Alves Pinto, who filmed the Rua da Bahia

from a cable car in motion. The latter seems to have been the first person to film Belo Horizonte. At first the cinema was regarded as cheap entertainment by the city's inhabitants, like popular spectacles considered less refined, more like carnival and circus shows. This fact did not prevent the establishment of newspaper columns and specific publications about the new art: the company Borges e Cia., for example, had a little paper, *O Biógrafo*, for news about cinema; in 1912 the newspaper *A Tarde* created the column "Stages and Screens"; and in 1915 the newspaper *O Momento* began the column "Films and Stages." They all featured announcements of film showings, and gave public attendance figures, reported news about the actors, and even held a contest to choose the most beautiful woman attending the theaters. The cinema was rapidly being transformed into an important factor of social life in the city. Charlie Chaplin, for example, was a passion, but the public also delighted in the popular films of Max Linder. In the 1910s the foreign film industry had already begun to dominate the market, and gradually North American cinema took over. Brazilian film showings were restricted to Rio de Janeiro and local film-making was limited to topics in praise of the military or ecclesiastical authorities, to the propaganda of politicians, and, as has already been seen, to portraits of interesting corners of the city.

The theater also experienced good attendance figures. A municipal law of 1911 prohibited the wearing of hats in the audience of the Municipal Theater, aiming chiefly at women who overdid the size of their head adornments. This theater was razed in the 1940s to make place for the Cine Metrópole, whose demolition, in its turn, took place in 1983, despite a great movement against it on the part of intellectuals and the population in general. As this episode illustrates, the points of spatial reference of urban centers are transitory indeed. Belo Horizonte was still under construction when the First World War broke out, and, because importation of materials became extremely difficult, there was a suspension of public works. But this crisis did not hinder the development of industry, although it could not be said that the capital was yet the center of the state economy.

The 1920s and 1930s: Modernity and Tradition

By the 1920s Belo Horizonte was still noticeably bureaucratic; it had a politicoadministrative role but was already becoming industrialized in a more and more accelerated way, with a surprising economic thrust. It was to be expected that the ruling class and its mediators would insist on the idea of a great center and of the need to make its residents less provincial; the local press often set itself up as the rhetorical advocate of modernization and sought to influence readers so that they might participate more fully in the civilizing process that would make the state capital equal to other principal centers. If we recall the elitist attitude of the Belo Horizonte press of the period, the insistence on this theme fulfills a specific ideological goal: to help transform the city into a center of economic and political decision-making, through the mediation of activities more strictly connected to culture. In 1920 the city received Belgium's royal family, an initial step toward the negotiations for establishing the Belgo-Mineira industry. The visit attracted thousands of people, even from other parts of the state, to receive King Albert, and brought about a number of renovations in the gardens and plazas in order to impress the guests. The building of the first soccer stadiums of the city began in this decade. A greater affluence in the public in the cafés was noticeable, and the Rua da Bahia, with its many bars and coffee houses, attracted intellectuals and politicians.

The renovating artistic drive of the 1920s in Brazil did not manage to touch theatrical production. This would all change rapidly: The theater-going public of the big cities would soon be transformed into an artistic axis capable of attracting national and foreign companies. The character of the then provincial Belo Horizonte did not prevent the capital from boasting significant attendance in its theaters. Newspapers provide abundant documentation of the fact that the area of theatrical culture soon aroused great interest on the part of the population. The excessive reservedness of the public in Minas–revealing the still provincial profile of the city–is also registered in the criticism, which makes frequent comments about the fact that women, for example, did not applaud the performances. The preferences of the public were notable–not only in Belo Horizonte, but, according to studies, also in other Brazilian capitals–for the so-called "light theater" of comedies and operettas. The success of the genre is explained by the fact that its staging was meant for a basically popular audience, since the elites enjoyed themselves abroad. The dominant popular Brazilian productions of the period were vaudevilles (see Dória). Little by little the capital of Minas was also becoming a venue increasingly attractive to theater companies, which, after Rio de Janeiro, São Paulo, or Porto Alegre, would stage performances there. The theater could not remain indifferent to the nationalistic atmosphere of the period. The theme of "nationalization" caused controversy, and it was common for the press to discuss the need, even the duty, for writers and the public to turn to national productions, even in the sense of winning over the petit-bourgeois audience excessively attracted to foreign dramas and casts. The period was notable for a greater national self-affirmation and therefore for an increased demand both for Brazilian casts and playwrighting.

The upscale social classes in Belo Horizonte met in the cinemas, whose interiors were the places where people of means paraded. A testimony of the provinciality that still characterized Belo Horizonte society was the daily publication in the newspapers of lists of films censored or recommended by the League of Morality, an association connected to the Catholic Church, which watched over the good habits in the city. In 1920 the Cine Pathé and Pathé Jornal were inaugurated with a view to bringing films to public notice. The theater room was perfumed according to the film being shown. During this period the cinema continued to be a passion in the city and the newspapers offered commentaries on the change in people's behavior. Nevertheless, tickets to see the shows were expensive, a fact that caused a large demonstration also involving protests against poor cable car service on 19 June 1922.

In the 1920s an outstanding cultural figure was Igino Bonfioli (1886–1965), an Italian living in Belo Horizonte, where he became a famous and much sought-after photographer. In 1920 he made his first documentary, O Enterrado Vivo [Buried Alive], focusing on a fakir who had come to perform in the city; this was soon followed by another film, A Visita do Rei Alberto da Bélgica a Belo Horizonte [The Visit of King Albert to Belo Horizonte]. In 1925 he completed his full-length film, Minas Antiga [Old Minas], intended for showing in schools. The recovery of the historical past, as can be seen, was already a theme for the movies. During the 1920s Bonfioli filmed a number of events in the city, organizing a project for the fortnightly documentation of its urban life in 1927. The

shortcomings of the national cinema, and the cinema of Minas in particular, began to be discussed at this time. In the middle of 1923 Aníbal Mattos (1889–1969) completed the first dramatic film in Minas–in fact, the first full-length Brazilian film–filmed by Bonfioli, with many color sequences. This was the transposition to the screen of the play Canção da primavera [Spring Song] by Aníbal Mattos himself; this is the oldest feature-length Brazilian film preserved in its entirety. The actors were from the Theater Group Silvestre Moreira, and the première took place, with great success, at the Ciné Pathé on 11 July 1923. With the Argentinean Manuel Talon, Bonfioli would even make an imitation of a U.S. western, Entre as montanhas de Minas [Among the Mountains of Minas], in 1928. Filming at that time was not too expensive, because the films were silent and the local film-making was of a solid quality, even in the towns of the interior such as Cataguases, which embraced the pioneering projects of Humberto Mauro (1897–1983). This filmmaker from Cataguases came to Belo Horizonte in 1927, where he filmed the action of Tesouro perdido [Lost Treasure], the last film of the Cataguases Cycle. It should be noted, however, that local films were almost exclusively made by immigrants.

In 1920 the pioneering exhibition of the painter Zina Aita (1900–1968) was held; this can be considered the first individual Modernist event in Belo Horizonte. Her art was described as Futurist by the newspapers, which praised the exhibition as proof that Belo Horizonte was modern. Her painting was notable for its chromatic "disharmony" that shocked the Belo Horizonte public. The modern spirit–prior to São Paulo's Week of Modern Art, in which Zina Aita took part (see Amaral)–manifested itself in the city at the same time as in other centers and was covered in the press (see Cury 1998). The break with conservatism was important, but the use of pure colors by Aita, especially red, can also be associated with Mestre Ataíde of eighteenth-century Minas (see Vieira 1997).

In the field of education during this period, the state, while conservative, was open to the educational reforms the country was proposing. The Francisco Campos reform associated Minas with the ideas of the so-called New School (see Peixoto) and brought several foreign educators to the state, among whom was Helena Antipoff (1892–1973), who would play an important part in special and rural education. The Institute of Education was created, a model for the formation of teachers. An important fact was the establishment of the University of Minas Gerais (UMG) in 1927–the fulfillment of a dream of the Inconfidentes–which created for the state a modern space for higher education. The university became a center for political-cultural initiatives, undoubtedly responsible for many changes. There had been several plans for universities in the nineteenth century, but they were only realized in the twentieth century, when it was in the interest of the ruling class to support independent schools, with a view to the professionalization of new generations. In Ouro Preto, in 1839, the College of Pharmacy was founded, the first in Brazil; the School of Mines was founded in 1875; and the Free School of Law was created in 1892 (transferred to Belo Horizonte in 1898). The pro-university movement increased in the 1920s. In the first place, the independent schools began to produce their first fruits; the majority of the Belo Horizonte Modernists, for example, attended the School of Law and constituted a homogeneous group interested in recovering the cultural regionalism of Minas and bringing back the cultural tradition of the eighteenth century. If, on the one hand, Belo Horizonte continued to be, politically and administratively, a quiet city, on the other hand, it took in people from all over the state, quickening the urban and commercial life and gradually centralizing the cultural life of Minas.

During this period Belo Horizonte attracted a large number of writers, all anxious to take part in the cultural life of the young capital of Minas and of its ambiance, which was at once progressive and conservative. Carlos Drummond de Andrade, Emílio Guimãraes Moura (1902–1971), João Alphonsus (1901–1944), Pedro Nava (1903–1984), Aníbal Machado (1894–1964), Abgar Renault (1901–1995), Milton Campos (1900–1972), and Mário Casassanta (1898–1963), all very young, wanted to move the city beyond its provincial and conservative academic environment. The 1920s would remain forever inscribed in their later writings. Many of them later held prominent places in Brazilian literature—Drummond, João Alphonsus, and Emílio Moura. They were young intellectuals engaged in vigorous debate. All of them worked for the press, eager to show off their writing—and their anxieties of modernity.

They were different from the Modernist group of São Paulo in that they did not travel to Europe in search of contact with the avant-garde of the Old World. Their cultural modernization took place through the books that arrived weekly in crates at the Livraria Alves. Although part of the process of cultural and literary modernization that occurred in the most important cities of the country, this generation revealed a shift from the Rio-São Paulo cultural axis, inscribing itself specifically in the renovating process set in motion by the avant-gardes within the country and abroad; this was despite the fact that, like the Modernists of São Paulo, they published in politically conservative newspapers. In the case of the intellectuals of Minas, the opportunities that opened up for them in the newspapers of the capital were, in fact, part of the strategy devised by certain sectors of the oligarchy to transmit some modernization but basically aiming at maintaining power and at continuing the social exclusion of other classes. There was a head-on collision between the old (represented by the traditional sectors of the oligarchy), the modern (represented by the industrializing tendencies), and the emergence of the new (represented by the greater participation of the popular classes). These young intellectuals were not men of letters from the interior lost in the big city, but rather a generation that was well-born and well-educated, with aspirations to influence and power; they formed an intelligentsia that was eager to attain political power. All of them held positions in the state apparatus (see Schwartzman, Bomeny, and Costa), and all left the city, most going to Rio de Janeiro.

Yet, with or without the knowledge of the groups in power, and responding in its own way to the modernizing conditions of the city and Modernist literary influences, the group from Belo Horizonte did have a spirit of renewal: It made public the works of writers from other states, probed into the situation in other capitals, and gave its own, original response. These intellectuals played the role of "modernizers" of the cultural milieu in which they lived. A fascination with urban space was the main characteristic of Modernism, an attraction rooted in the real conditions of rapid change and development of the Brazilian cities of the period.

The seduction of the city can be seen among the Belo Horizonte Modernists in the first poems published in the newspaper. But it was not only the Futurist city, noisy and busy, which endured in the work of the group of Minas; tradition also appeared quite markedly, often represented by the mountains of Minas—in the poetry of Carlos Drummond de Andrade, in the fiction of João Alphonsus, and in Nava's memoirs of maturity. "Por que ruas tão largas?/Por que ruas tão retas?/Meu passo torto/foi regulado pelos becos tortos/de onde eu venho./Não sei andar na vastidão simétrica/implacável," wrote Carlos Drummond (Andrade 1979, 129) ("Why such wide streets?/Why such straight streets?/My crooked gait/was regulated by the crooked alleys/from where I come./I don't know how to walk in the symmetrical/implacable vastness"). The *gauche* poet would walk in the modernized space of the symmetrical city with the crooked gait molded by tradition. Belo Horizonte has a fundamental presence in the development of the rooted "Minas-style" of the Modernists: It was the city—linking the regional and the universal, modernity, and tradition—which served as the backdrop for the formation of writers and intellectuals. Belo Horizonte was the place to both read the classics and love the new arts. This atmosphere accompanied the Modernists even outside of Minas, or rather, perhaps *because* they were outside of Minas.

But also present in their writing was an enchantment with Rio de Janeiro; the attraction of the coast is also a part of the people of Minas. This fascination drew generations of writers, who formed a true Diaspora, away from Minas. The first Modernists moved there: Pedro Nava, Aníbal Machado, Martins de Almeida, and Drummond de Andrade. Other generations would leave in the following decades: Fernando Sabino (b. 1923), Otto Lara Rezende (1922–1992), Paulo Mendes Campos (1922–1991), and Hélio Pellegrino (1924–1988). This continuing migration to Rio reaffirmed the understandable magnet attraction of the capital of the republic but also, perhaps, pointed to a certain provincialism in Belo Horizonte that prevented the more mature flowering of a cohesive and articulate intellectual life. Thus, in John Wirth's view, Belo Horizonte ended up being transformed by these young men into a good place to be from. Cosmopolitan Rio offered the possibility of political appointments and social status, while the capital of Minas would only slowly and gradually become a cultural center. For those who stayed in Minas the sense of inferiority in relation to the capital of the country had a subtle, penetrating, sometimes pernicious, influence. People from Rio still say, in reference to the people from Minas, "the best ones always leave" (Wirth 99). And yet, all of these emigrant intellectuals remained true to their origins, taking Belo Horizonte and Minas with them, writing about their regions, sharing a common sense of their Minas culture. If Belo Horizonte is a good place to be from, it is in addition to this (and above all) the place that you carry with you, that insistently resounds, echoes like concentric circles in the waters of the memory of all of the intellectuals' writings.

The young writers of the 1920s formed what has conventionally been called a "generation." In the cultural life of Belo Horizonte this is common: Its intellectuals are often recognized as belonging to generations, usually grouping around the publication of periodicals. In 1925 Modernists showed themselves to the world in a publication that became their signature: *A Revista* [The Magazine] (see Cury 1994). A publication of only four issues, short-lived like others at the time, it was nevertheless important as a place to show to Minas and the rest of the country that Belo Horizonte also had a group of "futurists," a qualification that did not always have positive connotations. *A Revista* also had a direct contact with the renovating group of São Paulo. Its influence, however, would not have turned out to be as effective and creative as it was, had the young intellectuals of Minas not had their own strong cultural core from which to respect and develop their own ideas on literary modernization.

A relevant event helped the Modernist proposals of the Week of Modern Art in São Paulo to reach the Belo Horizonte group and have repercussions in it: This was the visit to Minas made in 1924 by the so-called caravan from São Paulo. This was a trip undertaken by Mário de Andrade (1893–1945) and Oswald de Andrade (1890–1954), Blaise Cendrars (1887–1961), and Tarsila do Amaral (1886–1973). On the occasion of the Swiss-French poet's (Cendrars's) coming to Brazil, the group from São Paulo, playing at being tourists, decided to show him the country. They went to Rio and the historical cities of Minas, with a stopover in Belo Horizonte, where they met with local writers. In reality they were showing Brazil less to the foreign visitor than to themselves, motivated by their desire to grasp the Brazilian and the popular. It is this that made possible the (heretofore absent) influence of the Baroque art of Minas on the people from Minas as well as on the writers from São Paulo. Cultural discourse was stimulated (see Santiago) through a rereading of the Baroque of Minas, seen through the eyes of the avant-garde. Revisited in this way, Ouro Preto constituted a gaze that turned to the interior of Brazil to the search for a genuinely national identity. This trip to discover Brazil made by the Brazilians showed a different attitude from that of radical rupture that had characterized the earlier phase of Modernism; in 1924 the reconciliation between the old and the new developed through the revising of traditions that until then had been disregarded. Before the visit of the caravan, the Baroque was considered a crude tropical style and Aleijadhinho a local sculptor of no importance.

This discovery of the Brazilian past as expressed in the Baroque was not entirely new; it had been touched on once before, in 1919, on the occasion of the first visit of Mário de Andrade, the Modernist from São Paulo, to Minas, to see the Colonial cities and visit Alphonsus de Guimarãens (1870–1921), the great Symbolist poet of Minas. Mario de Andrade's trip is worthy of note since it marks the way in which the Modernists found themselves linked to tradition and to Symbolist poetry. The intellectual presence of Alphonsus de Guimaraens in Minas Gerais was of great significance to the work of the Modernists of Belo Horizonte; it demonstrated the importance of preserving the historical continuity of the intellectual life of the region. This central notion was renewed later with their return to the works of the Arcadians, as well as, on another level, to the work of Aleijadinho (see Dias 1975). The publication in 1923 of the book *Pastoral aos crentes do amor e da morte* [Pastoral for Believers in Love and Death] by Guimaraens caused great astonishment in the literary circles of Minas. The admiration that the young had for him gave great cultural value to the renovating aspect of Alphonsus's poetry. Mário de Andrade, after his visit to the poet, wrote an article in which he discussed the originality of the Baroque of Minas. The trip undertaken in 1924 therefore marked the consolidation of this new value given to Colonial art; it was perhaps the most significant example of the involvement of the Modernists with the tradition of the eighteenth-century Baroque of Minas (see Santiago). The topic of landscape of Minas now appeared to the Modernists as something original, satisfying their taste for newness and at the same time for a truly Brazilian art. The excursion of the São Paulo

artists remained strongly in the memory of the Modernist writers of Belo Horizonte and was to be the trigger for the artistic process that would characterize their work. Modernists of Belo Horizonte established long-lasting ties with the São Paulo writers; they explained their own views on modernity, and they were at the same time deeply influenced by the São Paulo Modernist movement. It is also worth recalling the influence of Tarsila do Amaral's "primitivism" on Pedro Nava, who illustrated the cover of Oswald's book, *Pau-Brasil* [Brazilwood], with a stylized flag.

The conditions were effectively present by then for the group from Belo Horizonte to define itself and relate to others who shared the same spirit of renewal. It was time for the Week of Modern Art of the Belo Horizonte artists. Tarsila do Amaral, Oswald de Andrade, and Mário de Andrade revealed Minas to the people of Minas. The close ties that were established by correspondence between the artists of São Paulo and those of Minas, especially between Mário de Andrade and Drummond, were of vital importance to the development of Modernism in Minas and lasted through generations of writers. In great part this 1924 connection explains the association of the young artists of Minas with the Modernism of São Paulo. Although the influence of Rio de Janeiro–the center of politics during the old republic–was naturally greater, one could notice the shift in cultural influence to São Paulo. It is noteworthy that the caravan did not limit itself to influencing Minas, but also was influenced by the colors and shapes of Colonial architecture that characterize Oswald de Andrade's poems, the "Belo Horizonte Nocturne" of Mário de Andrade, the lines and naive colors of Tarsila do Amaral's paintings. In her paintings Tarsila recovered the popular roots, the mobility of curves of Baroque architecture, and the pink and blue of the *baús* (chests) in Colonial houses of Minas.

Soon after this visit, the Brazilian Society of Fine Arts created an architectural commission to undertake studies of the buildings of the historical cities, with the express desire of conserving and protecting the patrimony. Jair Lins wrote a careful, erudite report in which he discussed the legislation and proposed a formula for the official protection of cultural property in Brazil; this work was the basis, years later, for the solution suggested by Mário de Andrade to the project for creating the Commission for National Historical and Artistic Patrimony. Mello Vianna, then governor of the state, gave an important start to aesthetic renewal, especially in relation to associating nineteenth-century traditions with the art of Aleijadinho, resignified by the cosmopolitanism of the Belo Horizonte *belle époque*.

The ideas of the nation's construction manifested in the preservation of the national culture would be taken over by the authoritarian Estado Novo after the 1930s, during the period of office of the Minister of Education and Public Health, Gustavo Capanema, from Minas. Many intellectuals entered the national political system, which began the institutionalization of a strategy for preserving the national patrimony. Mário de Andrade and Rodrigo de Mello Franco from Minas would be responsible for directing the Service of National Historical and Artistic Patrimony (SPAHN). This policy was what would determine the fate of many historical cities of Minas, especially of Ouro Preto, which in 1933 became national patrimony, with its nucleus protected, as the greatest collection of Baroque art in the country. Its architectural and artistic patrimony was once again consecrated as a symbol of the national artistic past. Ouro Preto was once again constituted as a monument to a past forged to justify a state that was looking for and pretentiously attributing to itself the historical antecedents of Brazilian nationalism. Although Brazilian Modernism proposed a break with the past, its modernizing project actually worked to recover the past. While Belo Horizonte rapidly changed its image, the city that was historically contrasted with it, Ouro Preto, had to be maintained intact as the cultural memory of the nation. Ouro Preto was the past; Belo Horizonte was the future.

The poetry of the Modernists of Minas was also imbued with this nationalist flavor in its rereading of tradition and explaining of themes that looked back to the little towns of the interior. The modernity and tradition duality, we should recall, was the predominant characteristic in their writings. At this moment of strong manifestation of cultural and political regionalism in the whole country, people spoke of the civilization of Minas and the Minas style. Minas would offer a vision of the world of which the Baroque was the greatest expression. Throughout Brazil diverse centers were being formed to expand the Week of Modern Art, giving the movement features that, though common, were enriched by the peculiarities of each region and thus decentered from the exclusive, polarizing cultural influence of Rio de Janeiro. Two days after the publication of *A Revista*, a group of young writers of Cataguases, a city in the Zona da Mata in Minas, under the influence of the Belo Horizonte Modernists, published the radical and rash *Verde* [Green] with the subtitle *Revista mensal de arte e cultura* [Monthly Review of Art and Culture] (with each S backward, as Futurist ideas prescribed in those days), run by the young Guilhermino César (1908–1993), Rosário Fusco (1910–1977), Ascânio Lopes (1906–1929), and Enrique de Resende (1899–1973). *Verde* basically took on the two currents of São Paulo Modernism: the pursuit of freedom of expression and the search for the national. The cultural renewal of Belo Horizonte rapidly widened its scope of influence, encompassing the artistic manifestations of other cities in Minas. The periodical also counted on contributions by people from other areas, since it not only called attention to the renovating group from Belo Horizonte that collaborated with it, but also seduced the Modernists of São Paulo and Rio. How can one explain a "Modernist outbreak" in Cataguases, a town in the interior, and, moreover, chronologically simultaneous with the manifestations in large centers like the Week of Modern Art in São Paulo? There could be many causes. The bulk of the town's economy was based on the textile industry. The modernization process, as in other larger centers, seemed connected to the local bourgeoisie, vigorous for the period, which took on for itself the role of patron, financing and stimulating the projects of the new generation. Years later the town would be the home to one of the first works of Niemeyer, to Brecheret's sculptures, to Portinari's and Djanira's murals, and to Burle Marx's landscapes; these are the result of the financing of emerging artists. It cannot be forgotten that there, in the same period, the bold, modern filmmaking of Humberto Mauro came into existence.

Belo Horizonte writers would see their texts published as books in the 1930s, a more tangible result of the intellectual renewal for which they fought. With the books they would go beyond the circuit of cafés and of Rua da Bahia to reach a larger audience. It was a moment of strong regionalist fervor in Minas. The proof was that in January 1929, with the idea of strengthening regional culture, an edition of the *Jornal do Brasil* of Rio de Janeiro came out that was entirely dedicated to

Minas Gerais. To use the expression of Antonio Candido, the curious modernity of Minas was thus formed, a mix of classics read with humor and of the most up-to-date prose in the country. Note that the governor Antonio Carlos, associated with the Modernists, was a likely candidate for president of the republic, given the political scheme of the "Old Brazilian Republic" (known as "café au lait") that alternated the power between Minas and São Paulo. When the pact with São Paulo was broken, Minas joined the Revolution of the Thirties, which caused tumult in the life of the capital of Minas. A period of disordered growth followed, with an increasingly deficient infrastructure much in evidence.

In 1930 the book *Alguma poesia* [Some Poetry] was published by Carlos Drummond de Andrade, the most important poet of this generation, who would distinguish himself on the national literary scene and become a lasting influence on the constitution of an ethos in Minas. Essentially modern (see Bosi 1994), he revealed himself from his early work on to be an antirhetorical poet, with a strong touch of irony and humor. The city of Belo Horizonte, a constantly reinvented Minas, the return to the paternal home, the Minas family and its strong tradition—these would be recurrent themes in his poetry. In the same decade Cyro dos Anjos enters the scene with the novel *O amanusense Belmiro* [1936; Belmiro the Amanuensis], which describes life in the capital of Minas using a stream of consciousness narrative mode.

The visual arts in the 1920s and 1930s revealed the hegemony of academic culture, which was closely associated with the official system, and was therefore elitist in tune with the status quo. The most dominant figure was Aníbal Mattos, who also devoted himself to theater, literature, and cinema. He was connected to practically every initiative in the visual arts: the coordination of the system of fine arts in the city (1918), the establishment of the Minas Society of Fine Arts, whose annual exhibition was incorporated into the city's calendar of events (1918), the opening of the School of Arts (1927), and the establishment of the Fine Art State Picture Gallery (1928). But a confrontation between those who held key posts in cultural institutions and those who pursued modernization as a way to change the structure of support for artistic production was already visible. The following are notable for the modernity of their works: Domingos Xavier Andrade (Malsã), Érico de Paula, Jeanne Milde, Delpino Júnior, and Julius Kaukal, even though they worked as individuals and did not constitute a school. In the 1920s Érico and Malsã, pioneer designers, founded the first advertising agency in the city with an important visual program. A European pedagogical mission in 1929 brought Jeanne Milde to the city; she stayed and contributed to the formation of groups connected to Modernism. The Exhibition of Modern Art, also known as the Salão Bar Brasil, coordinated by Delpino Júnior, opened in 1936. The Cubist and Expressionist paintings, with strong traces of Art Deco, opposed institutional art, still represented in the city by Aníbal Mattos. Delpino, Pierucetti, Genesco Murta, Milde were among the notable Modernist artists.

The original eclecticism that characterized the architecture of Belo Horizonte was modified in the 1930s, making way for the Cubist and Art Deco style, as the city witnessed the construction of the first skyscrapers. The demolitions reiterate the old and modern dichotomy, this time allegorically marking the face of the city with the new (which was already its future ruins); this was a city that was renovated practically every twenty-five years. More and more the contrast was intensified: Ouro Preto, the monument city, should remain unchanged, and Belo Horizonte, the garden city, as it was known, swiftly yielded green space to concrete. In this period, too, public works were built that would be read as signs of modernity: the Santa Tereza automobile overpass (1930)—at the time the largest span of reinforced concrete in Latin America—the Floresta overpass (1936), and the fountains in the Praça Rui Barbosa and Praça Raul Soares (1936), which were completed with luminous neon signs that were becoming a commonplace in the city. In 1932 the Cine Brasil was inaugurated, the largest cinema in the country at the time. Two years later the city would enthusiastically witness the introduction of sound film. With it, the panorama of cinematographic productions was radically altered. Given the high cost of installing laboratories, these productions could only be created in the large cities.

One of the leisure activities of the 1930s was swimming in the Rio Arrudas, which runs through the city. The present image of the river, even after the canalization, reveals the amount of change the city has undergone. Today, swimming in its polluted waters is equal to suicide by infection. Belo Horizonte already constituted a polarizing center of the state, culturally and economically speaking. The Modernist movement in the capital of Minas, which has its beginning in the 1920s, attained its climax in the 1940s, winning national recognition as the center of cultural and artistic tendencies.

The 1940s and 1950s: Pampulha and the Modernity of Juscelino Kubitschek

The city changed rapidly, prey to real-estate speculation, and witnessed the destruction of its traditional areas and thus an intense housing crisis. At the opening of the Exhibition of Modern Art in 1944, Juscelino Kubitschek, then mayor of Belo Horizonte, referring to the creation of the city, said that it had been the result of a great and profound Modernist movement and related it to the dream of the Inconfidentes. Superimposing anachronistic images, he proclaimed a new moment of modernity, offering the country the architectural and urbanistic boldness of the Pampulha complex. The synchronizing of such far-distanced times once again reinforced the defining idea of Belo Horizonte as a center that, while pointing to the future, simultaneously reordered the past to better serve the political moment. Juscelino Kubitschek, as city mayor from 1940 to 1945, was associated with the cultural politics of the Vargas Estado Novo, as a conciliator between conservatism and Modernism. At the same time academic art gained space in the National School of Fine Arts, modernity was served when minister Capanema invited Mário de Andrade to create the Commission of National Artistic Patrimony.

This city of 211,000 inhabitants possessed an impressive number of architectural works of great daring for the period, which gained international recognition. The mayor prepared to transform Belo Horizonte into a Modernist architectural showcase, bringing to fruition architectural, landscaping, and urban planning projects quite bold for the period, including the work of Lúcio Costa, Oscar Niemeyer, Portinari, Burle Marx, Santa Rosa, and Alfredo Cesciatti—artists who became well-known after they became involved in the construction of Brasília. From the architectural point of view Brasília began in Belo Horizonte. There were many material results of these urban projects: the Pampulha complex (the

Cassino, the São Francisco Church, Casa do Baile, Iate Golf Club, the creation of a reservoir, and the paving of the Avenida Getúlio Vargas introduced a new cycle of works. The Pampulha site became the greatest symbol of the city. This architectural complex anticipated—by twenty years—the architectural dream of the new federal capital.

In Pampulha, as can be seen, for example, in the São Francisco Church, the curves and waves in concrete (Niemeyer's trademark in the buildings of Brasília) were inspired by the mountains of Minas. In a statement on his project the architect admitted that he was uninterested in orthodox functionalism, affirming that beauty was one of the most important functions of architecture. He repeated his preference for the curve, with its "Baroque sensuality," so present in the Colonial tradition and now recovered in reinforced concrete (see Lamare). If the São Francisco Church was extremely bold as a whole, it nevertheless resembled in some details the Colonial churches of Minas: the lateral spire, like that found on the Padre Faria Chapel in Ouro Preto, and the use of latticed wood on the spire, which suggests Baroque trellises (see Campos 1983). For fourteen years the Church's beauty was not recognized by the Catholic Church, whose clergy seemed to lack the artistic sensibility to understand it. The Archbishop of Belo Horizonte, Dom Cabral, refused to consecrate it, because in addition to being designed by a confessed communist, it had frescos, tiles, and an altar painted by Portinari, who was also a communist. Furthermore, St. Francis, painted behind the main altar, has deformed hands, and, what seemed most scandalous for the period, he was shown in the company of a dog; in addition, the stations of the cross were "deformed" because of the Expressionism of the painting. The press also noted that the shadow of the church, when reflected in the lake, recalled the hammer and sickle, a symbol of Soviet Communism. The same connection was made years later when the monument in homage to Kubitschek, also done by Niemeyer, was erected in Brasília. The consecration of the church finally took place after the change of the archbishop of Belo Horizonte in 1959.

Nevertheless, Pampulha turned out to be effectively an elitist enterprise, a neighborhood built for the richest classes, even though it was proclaimed in a populist political discourse that referred to it as a democratic opening of the suburbs, with spaces for popular leisure. A reading of the periodicals of the 1940s and 1950s shows that there was a dispute between the supporters of progress and the conservatives in terms of criticizing the project for its intended public, in effect, the elite. The modeling of the lake in 1938, for example, had its counterpart in the creation of the Lake Paranoá in Brasília. Both served to increase real estate values in surrounding areas. Pampulha also had a promotional purpose for the politician Juscelino Kubitschek, since, from the viewpoint of his political rise after being governor of Minas in the 1950s, it was the first step toward the presidency in Brasília. Another architectural project of Niemeyer's that is worthy of mention is the JK Residential Complex, since it was the first in the country that would offer residents a number of services, a type of apartment-hotel *avant la lettre*. Completed after twenty years, it represented, in opposition to the initial project intended for the middle classes, a more economic and popular residential option.

As mayor, Kubitschek had a surprising number of works built and in 1944 created the Industrial District, already taking up at this point what would be the substance of his discourse later for the presidency: development, progress, and modernization. The city saw the opening up of urban streets, introducing a new rhythm to other changes that were taking place more rapidly. Skyscrapers proliferated, confirming what Oswald de Andrade had predicted in 1924: "O cimento armado matará com certeza os versalhes de estuque. E como a cidade foi possantemente rasgada e o seu local muito bem escolhido, os arranha-céus se instalarão admiravelmente aqui. Assim tenho a esperança de que Belo Horizonte virá a ser uma das mais belas cidades do século 20. Sendo do seu tempo, entrará por isso mesmo na tradição" (*Diário de Minas,* April 27, 1924) ("Reinforced concrete will certainly destroy the stucco buildings. And since the city will be extended and its locale is very well chosen, the skyscrapers will be admirably situated here. Thus, I have the hope that Belo Horizonte will come to be one of the most beautiful cities of the twentieth century. Being of its time, it will become a part of tradition for this very reason").

In the field of arts there was a strengthening of modern tendencies, signifying a break with the local academic tradition. The capital of Minas showed a great openness to the artistic avant-gardes of the country. In the 1940s and 1950s the university was consolidated, incorporating the College of Philosophy and Human Sciences, as well as the School of Fine Arts and Architecture. In 1949 the university was federated. Currently, the Universidade Federal de Minas Gerais is one of the most fertile centers of scientific, social, and philosophical research in the country. It was always a center of democratic ideals and resistance to the great upheavals in the history of education in Brazil. In the decade of the 1940s the educational network of the capital of Minas was famous all over the country, receiving students from the most varied places. In 1943 the Abílio Barreto Historical Museum was inaugurated in the last remaining building of the old village. Kubitschek's project also included the building of the Municipal Theater in the city park; the creation of the Museum of Belo Horizonte in the old Curral del Rei Farm; the founding of the Institute of Fine Arts; and the establishment of the Belo Horizonte Symphonic Orchestra. The research of Curt Lange on the music of the Colonial period of Minas was part of the enhanced status of music gained by the symphony orchestra with whom he was so closely identified.

The Exhibition of Modern Art of 1944, with lectures in the main hall of the public library, as already mentioned, had great repercussion in the press. The debates between defenders of modern art and traditionalists were heated. Modernist art was accused of being elitist and intellectualized with regard to the people. There were several incidents, including some in which paintings were damaged. Tendencies in the exhibited works–drawings, engravings, and paintings–were varied: Cubism, Expressionism, and Surrealism. A very important work was the São Paulo Modernist Brecheret's "Monument to the Flag," a project commissioned by the mayor of Belo Horizonte. Troops of artists from Rio and São Paulo came to the city, and the presence of important intellectuals from the whole country was noted, people who would take the intellectual debate to Belo Horizonte, turning the city into a cultural center. For the occasion the following artists of Brazilian Modernism came: Tarsila do Amaral, Volpi, Anita Malfatti, Pancetti, Lasar Segall (1891–1957), and others. The lectures turned to reflections on the consolidation of the Brazilian Modernist movement and on the political meaning of modern art. Sérgio Milliet (1898–1966), Álvaro Moreyra

(1888–1964), and Jorge Amado (1912–2001) were present. Oswald de Andrade's lecture (1972) deserves special mention, since it once again pointed out the need for the artists of Belo Horizonte, following the example of the Modernists Carlos Drummond de Andrade and Aníbal Machado, to maintain a commitment to the Inconfidentes. Again modernity and the past of Ouro Preto were juxtaposed. Once more, it is the imaginary of the Inconfidência that is used to express the modern. Such discourse reevaluated the modernization of the 1920s, but yoked it to the colonial past.

The casino, after the prohibition of gambling, would be transformed into the Museum of Modern Art in 1957. In 1955 Itacolomi TV was established, making Belo Horizonte the fifth city in the country to have television. It was an important event for the new generation of intellectuals. In the 1950s, with an enterprising governor such as Kubitschek, the city already had the atmosphere of a metropolis, with its intense development of civil construction and with the problems typical of the great urban conglomerates: slums, not enough openings in schools and beds in hospitals, and a periphery with a lack of social services. By the end of the decade the first supermarkets were opened in a city that was already made up of more demanding consumers and was a center of attraction for migrants from other regions. It is important to remember that the groups of intellectuals who formed and were identified with literary journals continued to leave Belo Horizonte in pursuit of better opportunities in Rio and São Paulo. There was no shortage of new journals on art, cinema, and literature in the 1950s; almost all were short-lived but were the means by which new generations of Belo Horizonte intellectuals were launched into Brazililan culture. These included *Edifício, Vocação, Tendência, Ptyx,* and the *Suplemento Literário,* which is still in circulation.

The figure of Carlos Drummond de Andrade, regarded as an important figure for this generation, would gain more importance, especially because of the publication of *A Rosa do povo* [1945; The Rose of the People]. Intellectuals such as Autran Dourado (b. 1926), Wilson Figueiredo, Francisco Iglésias (1923–1999), Sábato Magaldi, and Edmur Fonseca were all members of the Communist Party; they formed a heterogeneous group of students of history and law together with poets and film critics. The journal *Edifício* (four issues published in 1946) was shared by the new poets, anxious for affirmation on the local and national scenes, and by writers already well-known. Historically, the group is important because of its social and political militancy and notable for its vision of literature that was also militant. In the same year, 1946, Guimarães Rosa (1908–1967) published the collection of stories called *Sagarana,* a book that demonstrated that he was a unique writer in Brazilian literature, with a style known for its syntactic disjointedness, verbal invention, and the recovery of popular usage as a living language. Making of the world of the backlands a microcosm that escaped conventional regionalism, he offered a lyrical-metaphysical reflection that would also distinguish later literature in Minas.

Complemento also deserves mention; it was published from 1955 to 1958. Its organizers and even those who gravitated around them, the *Complemento* Generation, were young men extremely active in the culture of the city, who would later hold important positions in the cultural panorama of the country: Silviano Santiago (b. 1936), Frederico Morais (b. 1936), Ivan Ângelo (b. 1936), Ezequiel Neves, Maurício Gomes Leite (b. 1936), José Nilo Tavares (1935–1997), Theotônio dos Santos

(b. 1937), and Heitor Martins. One fundamental spot for the consolidation of modern space where the group worked was the Center of Cinematographic Studies (CEC), the first, perhaps the most important, organized film-club in the country, known even abroad. The Clube de Cinema, founded in 1951 but whose peak was from 1955 to 1964, was the place where they held their meetings. The film clubs all over the country were centers of debates and study and were focal points for cultural development, since in this period central importance was given to the visual image. One must not forget that the Brazil of the 1950s was feeling the spell of the novelty of television and was under the impact of the creation of visual theories that helped expand the study of literature beyond the strictly verbal. For the *Complemento* generation, and for other contemporary and even later generations, cinema represented one of the ways to take part in a national and international art form. The CEC, besides dominating film criticism in all the newspapers, was also on television, which was still produced locally, and forged a connection with the university, inviting professors for lectures and debates. Many of the filmmakers who would form the so-called Cinema Novo came to Belo Horizonte to give lectures: Glauber Rocha, Nelson Pereira dos Santos, and Joaquim Pedro. Humberto Mauro would film the city as well in 1957.

This importance conferred on the visual image was shared by the group's concept of modernity, proof of which is the connection with the Guignard Art School, the Experimental Theater—the first group to stage Beckett's *End Game*—the dance-group directed by Klauss Vianna—the dancer-choreographer responsible for the renewal of Brazilian dance—the Renaissance Madrigal. All these are recognized as belonging to the *Complemento* generation, identified with a more universal position that aimed beyond a strict Minas-style. It was no longer necessary to "discover" Ouro Preto in order to affirm oneself as being from Minas. The idea of Minas-style was not as important, because the former generations, as well as the Modernists (such as Fernando Sabino, Paulo M. Campos, and Otto Lara, who took Minas with them wherever they went), already had, in a way, surpassed the previous barriers of ostracism. In the revolutionary choreographies of the Klauss Vianna Dance Company, the national themes associated with contemporary literature made their mark. Klauss said that new directions for modern Brazilian dance should avoid folk and popular themes, although they could not dispense with the cultivated national themes, present mainly in the writers of Minas—according to him, a "summary" of Brazilianness. The people of *Complemento* worked in this renewed space, guided by the desire to create a new, more open cultural ethos; they were attracted especially by the visual changes the city displayed, so in tune with a fundamentally visual aesthetic.

Another important initiative of Mayor Kubitschek was the establishment of the Institute of Fine Arts, where Alberto da Veiga Guignard's courses, financed by the city government, were taught. The aim was to create a center that would disseminate the culture of Minas. The institute operated for only two years before it was transferred to the Municipal Park. Guignard came to Belo Horizonte at Kubitschek's invitation and his work represented a true landmark for the modern art of the city, giving a new dimension to the teaching of the arts (see Vieira 1988). His school was not limited to the employment of new techniques, but promoted student exchanges, visits to historical cities of Minas, and constant contact with groups of artists from other areas and with the press of Belo

Horizonte and Rio de Janeiro, thus proposing more open forms of art and more freedom of expression. The Guignard School, responsible for the formation and promotion of important artists in the capital, as well as for pioneering new educational methods, was closed down despite an avalanche of protests around 1948. Artistic manifestations continued to take place, as in the 1920s, under the sponsorship of the state, a patron that fulfilled the function of exercising a certain control and conferred a touch of conservatism on even the most transgressive initiatives.

All of Juscelino Kubitscheck's enterprises created for himself the image of a modern, dynamic, *Futurist* administrator. This would continue to be the image of this politician when he was president of the country, thanks to a well-constructed marketing strategy that presented him as a man of his time, the smiling builder of the futurist Brasília, a regular jet setter. As a popular song in the period of his presidency had it, he was "our bossa-nova president." His great political weapon was development, associated with the construction of Brasília and the symbolic strategy of his goals (see Maranhão 1994).

From Belo Horizonte to Brasília

In January 1956 Juscelino Kubitschek took office as president of the republic. In April he underwrote a new project, together with the bill that delimited the area for the Federal District and created the Urbanizing Company of the New Capital. Voted in as Law 2874, its final article gave a name to the projected capital: Brasília. In the same year the planning commission was dissolved and an edict was published for the pilot plan. Israel Pinheiro, an engineer from Minas, was put at the head of the project and the works were begun under the technical direction of Oscar Niemeyer. Guimarães Rosa in his *Grande Sertão: Veredas* [1956; *The Devil to Pay in the Backlands*] retraces the path from backlands to city, rereading the urban beginnings through the rural tradition, thus negotiating between the traditional and the modern (see Vasconcelos), mixing the two worlds of local tradition and urban modernizing impulse (see Rama 1982). This is also the year in which the construction of Brasilia was begun: "A grande cidade apenas começava a fazer-se, num semi-ermo, no chapadão: a mágica monotonia, os diluídos ares" (Rosa 390) ("The great city began to be made, in a semi-wasteland, on the plateau: the magical monotony, the diluted airs"). Brasilia, where *candangos* (workers) coming from the most diverse rural areas of Brazil, produced the icons of modernity on the country's central plateau: "Outra era a vez. . . . Os mil e mil homens muitamente trabalhavam fazendo a grande cidade" (Rosa 512) ("This was the time . . . thousand, upon thousand of men worked to build the great city"). The leveling of the ground necessary for raising the new capital began in November 1956, creating a space of estrangement:

> um horizonte, homens no trabalho de terraplenagem, os caminhões de cascalho, as vagas árvores, um ribeirão de águas cinzentas, o velame-do-campo apenas uma planta desbotada, o encantamento morto e sem pássaros, o ar cheio de poeira. Sua fadiga, de impedida emoção, formava um medo secreto: descobria o possível de outras adversidades, no muno maquinal, no hostil espaço; e que entre o contentamento e a desilusão, na balança infidelíssima quase nada medeia. (Rosa 391)

> a horizon, men levelling the ground, the gravel trucks, the sparse trees, a stream of gray waters, the *velame-do-campo* merely a discolored plant, the enchantment dead and birdless, the air filled with dust. Fatigue, with blocked emotions, created a secret fear:

one would discover the possibility of other adversities, in the machine world, in the hostile space; and that between contentment and disillusion, in the most unfaithful balance, almost nothing can be interposed.

The master plan of Brasília was organized around two axes that crossed at the bus station, the whole taking the shape of an airplane or a large bird with open wings right in the center of the country. As with Belo Horizonte at the beginning of the century, Brasília also had in its initial planning a place of arrival and departure as the major point of intersection. The axis goes from the Plaza of the Three Powers, where ministry buildings and the supreme legislative, executive, and judicial divisions of government were built. Intersecting this axis, on the north and south wings, the residential blocks are laid out, grouped in super-blocks that are independent with respect to commerce, schools, and recreation. A bureaucratic city, like Belo Horizonte in the early decades, Brasília envisioned these super-blocks to be inhabited democratically by civil servants at the most varied levels. The very modern cathedral in glass and concrete, however, displayed an archaic iconography: It was the shape of a flower or hands joined in prayer (see Eco). Like Colonial Ouro Preto, Brasília would also be declared by UNESCO (on 7 December 1987) part of the Cultural Patrimony of Humanity for its daring architecture and for being the first city built in the twentieth century to serve as a capital.

What compelled the rural man onto the road to this city can be associated with the biblical image of passing from the Garden of Eden to the City of the Apocalypse, a space of new skies and new lands. In this sense the urban planning proposed for Brasília was in a direction that was projected for the development of Brazil as a whole. Such a projected architectural utopia (see Furter) wished to model the whole country within a space of openness, combining fine-living (green, leisure spaces, safety) with the human sociability (blocks, super-blocks) in which the collective and the social would set the tone. Brasília as a project announced the secular dream of entering the Promised Land. The shift to the interior, to occupy the unexplored heart of a country still young, called forth a pioneering spirit open to the risk of a still inconclusive yet promising identity for the country (see Eco). "Sobre as cabeças os aviões. Sob os meus pés os caminhões. Aponta contra os chapadões meu nariz . . ." ("Overhead the airplanes. Under my feet the roads. My nose rises to the plateau . . .," (sang Caetano Veloso in "Tropicália"). Whether or not this spirit–planned fine-living and sociability as indices of an urbanized democratic living experience–was adopted would determine the most progressive or reactionary directions of national development. The noblest American dream of a modern city (see Rama 1985), a civilizing utopia, a gliding frontier in a scenario of late and unequal modernity, was thus repeated.

"Eu inauguro um monumento no planalto central do país" ("I inaugurate a monument of the central plateau of the country")–in these parodic words of Caetano Veloso, his tropicalist vision of modernity in a country that is stubbornly anachronistic–the monument is made of "papel crepom e prata, sem porta e cuja entrada é uma rua estreita e torta e no joelho uma criança sorridente feia e morta estende a mão" ("crepe paper and silver, without a door, whose entrance is a narrow, crooked street and on his knees a child smiling, ugly, and dead, holds out his hand"). Brasília, which would unveil the big, beautiful horizon of modernity for Brazil, was turned into a monument of democratic utopia but let itself be invaded by slums, ignoring the project of social equality proposed in its

architectural and urban planning. The Brazilian artist Siron Franco made a collage of the national flag with little children's coffins a few years ago. This image of nationality was set up in front of the seat of government, the Palácio do Planalto, in the political heart of the nation. Creating a dramatic statement with this flag, he powerfully revealed the rawness of the face of death behind it. The child, the "hope of the nation," represented by the little casket, is a symbol of an aborted future. Also tainted by death is the visage of the national identity, again, ironically, symbolized by an Indian; in the political center of power white hands set fire to him, causing his death. The Pataxó Indian and the dead child, in Caetano's song and in Siron Franco's contemporary art, deconstruct in their carnivalized way the utopia of the city.

What does it take to make a cultural center? In fact, the center is a void in which memories and accounts are woven. Of how many cities is the city made, and how many ways can they be understood? This essay offers no conclusions: Reality never stops its revolving motion, and the idea of a cultural center leads to various ways of thinking about this perpetually unfinished state of the real. Center is an inner point, "inside" a circumference, equidistant from the lines that encompass it (from Latin *centrum*). Is it not curious that the three cities focused on here–all situated in the geographical center–are interior cities opposed, physically and culturally speaking, to coastal centers? But a center is also a point (from Greek *kentrón*), the sharp extremity of a materialized sign, which indicates the exit from a closed center. The circle is transmuted, then, into a spiral in the plan of the architect, in the work of the engineer, in the discourse of the student of culture.

Ouro Preto, "pantheon of heroes," was also one of the centers of the slave-holding regime by which the mines were exploited and exhausted. There, in the suffering of slavery and colonialist exploitation, a Colonial monument of rare beauty was erected, a center for contesting the reigning order. If reality reveals its limits through change, Ouro Preto became the doubly symbolic center of both a desire for newness, which the city could not maintain, and an undesirable archaic image. The point decentralizes and points to another center. Belo Horizonte was to be the new center of the Minas that began as the City of Minas and pointed to a new, beautiful horizon:

Belo Horizonte, que lindo nome! Fiquei a repeti-lo e a enroscar-me na sua sonoridade. Era longo, sinuoso, tinha de pássaro e sua cauda repetia rimas belas e amenas. Fonte. Monte. Era refrescante. Continha fáceis ascensões e aladas evasões. Sugeria associações cheias de bobreza na riqueza das homofonias. Belerofonte. Laocoonte. Caronte. Era bom de repetir–Belorizonte, Belorizonte, Belorizonte–e ir despojando aos poucos a palavra: das arestas de suas consoantes e ir deixando apenas suas vogais ondularem molemente. Belo Horizonte. Belorizonte. Beorizonte. Beoizonte, Beoionte. Fui à nossa sala de visitas e apliquei no ouvido a concha mágica que me abria aos caminhos da distância. Ouvi sem ruído helênico e o apelo longínquo–beoiooooooo–prolongado como o silvo dos trens que subiam de Caminho Novo acima, dobrando o canto dos apitos na pauta das noites divididas. (Nava 107–08)

Belo Horizonte, what a beautiful name! I repeated it and entwined myself in its sonority. It was long, sinuous, like a bird and its tail; I repeated soft, lovely rhymes: *fonte, monte, ponte*. It was refreshing. It contained easy ascents and winged evasions. It suggested associations of nobility in the richness of the homophones. *Belerofonte, Laocoonte, Caronte*. It was good to repeat–Belorizonte, Belorizonte, Belorizonte—and to strip the word little by little from the edges of its consonants, leaving only its vowels to undulate softly. Belo Horizonte, Belorizonte, Beorizonte, Beoizonte, Beoionte. I went to our parlor and put to my ear the magic conch that would open the paths of distance. I heard the Hellenic roar and the distant call—beoiooooo—prolonged like the whistle of the trains that climb up Caminho Novo, doubling the song of the whistles in the musical staff of shared nights.

A large horizon disclosed for all, Brasília is the city of Brazil, created to be the future in the present, center of modernity with equality, the result of national development, the irradiating point of the newness that would be extended to the whole country. As a cultural center, Belo Horizonte, on the other hand, sought to be the modern mediator between the archaic, which persists in those constant reappropriations and the future of democratic equality that has not yet been consolidated.

Translation by Glaucia Gonçalves and Thomas LaBorie Burns

Works Cited

Amaral, Aracy. 1979. *Artes plásticas na Semana de 22: subsídios para uma história da renovação das artes no Brasil.* 4th ed. São Paulo: Perspectiva.

Anastasia, Carla. 1995. *Vassalos rebeldes: Violência coletiva nas Minas na primeira metade do século XVIII.* Belo Horizonte: Universidade Federal de Minas Gerais.

Andrade, Oswald de. 1924. *Diário de Minas.* (April 27).

——. 1972. "O caminho percorrido." *Obras completas.* Vol 5. *Ponta de lança.* Rio de Janeiro: Civilizaçao Brasileira. 93–110.

Andrade, Carlos Drummond de. 1979. *Poesia e Prosa.* Rio de Janeiro: Nova Aguilar.

——. 1986. "Dormir na Floresta." *Meningo Antigo: Boitempo II.* Rio de Janeiro: Editora Record. 183.

Ávila, Affonso. 1967. *Resíduos seiscentistas em Minas Gerais.* Vol. 1. Belo Horizonte: Centro de Estudos Mineiros.

——. 1980. *O lúdico e as projeções do barroco.* São Paulo: Perspectiva.

——. 1996. "O que é o barroco mineiro." *Barroco mineiro: glossário de arquitetura e ornamentação.* 3rd ed. Ed. Affonso Ávila, João Marcos Machado Gotinjo and Reinaldo Guedes Machado. Belo Horizonte: Fundação João Pinheiro, Centro de Estudios Históricos e Culturais. 2–10.

Bosi, Alfredo. 1992. "O tempo e os tempos." *Tempo e História.* Ed. Adauto Novaes. São Paulo: Companhia das Letras: Secretaria Municipal de Cultura. 19–32.

——. 1994. *História Concisa da Literatura Brasileira.* 35th ed. São Paulo: Cultrix.

Campos, Adalgisa Arantes. 1983. "Pampulha: uma proposta estética e ideológica." *Revista da Fundação João Pinheiro* 13 (May–June): 69–90.

——. 1992. "Execuções na Colônia: a morte de Tiradentes e a cultura barroca." *Tempo Brasileiro* 1.1:141–67.

Candido, Antonio. 1993. *Formação da Literatura Brasileira: momentos decisivos.* 7th ed. Belo Horizonte: Itatiaia.

Carvalho, José Murilo de. 1990. *A formação das almas: o imaginário da República no Brasil.* São Paulo: Companhia das Letras.

Cury, Maria Zilda Ferreira. 1994. "Manifestos Mineiros: a Revista em revista." *Vertentes: Revista da Fundação de Ensino Superior de São João del-Rei* 3: 14–22.

——. 1998. *Horizontes modernistas: o jovem Drummond em papel jornal.* Belo Horizonte: Autêntica.

Dias, Fernando Correia. 1971. *O movimento modernista em Minas: uma interpretação sociológica.* Brasilia: Ed. Universidade de Brasília.

——. 1975. "Gênese e expressão grupal do modernismo em Minas." *O modernismo.* Ed. Affonso Ávilla. São Paulo: Perspectiva, Secretaria de Cultural Ciência e Tecnologia. 165–77.

Dória, Gustavo A. 1975. *Moderno teatro brasileiro: crônica de suas raízes.* Rio de Janeiro: Serviço Nacional de Teatro.

Eco, Umberto. 1976. *A estrutura ausente: introdução à pesquisa semiológica.* Trans. Pérola del Carvalho. São Paulo: Perspectiva.

Faria, Maria Auxiliadora. 1985. "Belo Horizonte: espaço urbano e dominação política." *Varia Historia:* Revista do Departamento de História Universidade Federal de Minas Gerais. 1 (November): 26–43.

Faria, Maria Auxiliadora, and Yone de Souza Grossi. 1982. "A classe operária em Belo Horizonte: 1897–1920." *A república velha em Minas Gerais. Seminário de Estudos Mineiros.* Ed. Norma de Góes Monteiro. Belo Horizonte: Universidade Federal de Minas Gerais. 165–99.

Furter, Pierre. 1974. *Dialética da Esperança: uma interpretação do pensamento utópico de Ernest Bloch.* Rio de Janeiro: Paz e Terra.

Julião, Letícia. 1996. "Belo Horizonte: itinerários da cidade moderna (1891–1920)." *BH: Horizontes Históricos.* Ed. Eliana de Freitas Druta. Belo Horizonte: C/Arte. 49–118.

Lamare, G. 1968. "Oscar Niemeyer: quase memória." *Correio da Manhã.* Rio de Janeiro (May 1).

Maranhão, Ricardo. 1994. *O governo Juscelino Kubitschek.* São Paulo: Brasiliiense.

Mello, Ciro Flávio Bandeira. 1996. "A noiva do trabalho–uma capital para a República." *BH: Horizontes Históricos.* Ed. Eliana de Freitas Druta. Belo Horizonte: C/Arte. 11–47.

Nava, Pedro. 1986. *Balão cativo: memorias 2.* Rio de Janeiro: Nova Fronteira.

Paula, João Antônio de. 1997. "Memória e esquecimento, Belo Horizonte e Canudos: encontros e estranhamento." *Varia Historia:* Revista do Departamento de História Universidade Federal de Minas Gerais. 18: 43–67.

Peixoto, Anamaria Casassanta. 1983. *Educação no Brasil, anos vinte.* São Paulo: Loyola.

Picchio, Luciana S. 1997. *História da literatura Brasileira: do descobrimento aos dias de hoje.* Rio de Janeiro: Nova Aguilar.

Rama, Angel. 1982. "Literatura y cultura." *Transculturación Narrativa en América Latina.* Mexico City: Siglo Veintiuno. 34–37.

——. 1985. *A cidade das letras.* Trans. Emir Sader. São Paulo: Brasiliense.

Rosa, João Guimarães. 1994. *Ficção Completa em dois volumes.* Rio de Janeiro: Nova Aguilar.

Rouanet, Sérgio Paulo. 1992. "As Minas Iluminadas: a Ilustração e a Inconfidência." *Tempo e História.* Ed. Adauto Novaes. São Paulo: Companhia das Letras. 329–45.

Santiago, Silviano. 1989. *Nas malhas da letra.* São Paulo: Companhia das Letras.

Santos, Cristina Ávila. 1986. "Modernismo em Minas. Literatura e artes plásticas: um paradoxo, uma questão em aberto." *Análise e conjuntura.* Belo Horizonte: Fundação João Pinheiro. 1: 165–200.

Schwartzman, Simon, Helena Maria B. Bomeny, and Wanda Maria R. Costa. 1984. *Tempos de Capanema.* Rio de Janeiro: Paz e Terra; São Paulo: Universidade do São Paulo.

Sevcenko, Nicolau. 1998. "A cultura brasileira foi gerada pelo sopro místico do Barroco." *O Estado de São Paulo.* (March 28): D4.

Silva, Joaquim Norberto de Souza e. 1948. *História da conjuração mineira.* 2nd ed. 2 vols. Rio de Janeiro: Biblioteca Nacional.

Silveira, Anny J. T. 1996. "O sonho de uma petite Paris: os cafés no cotidiano da capital." *BH: Horizontes Históricos.* Ed. Eliana de Freitas Dutra. Belo Horizonte: C/Arte. 119–82.

Souza, Laura de Mello e. 1992. "Tensões sociais em Minas na segunda metade do século XVIII." *Tempo e história*. Ed. Adauto Novaes. São Paulo: Companhia das Letras. 347–66.

Vasconcelos, Sandra G. Teixeira. 1997–1998. "Os mundos de Rosa." *Revista USP* 36. (Dec.–Jan.–Feb.): 79–88.

Vieira, Ivone Luzia. 1988. *A Escola Guignard na cultura modernista de Minas, 1944-1962*. Minas Gerais: Companhia Empreendimento Sabará.

——. 1997. "Emergência do modernismo." *Um século de artes plásticas em Belo Horizonte*. Ed. Marília Andrés Ribeiro and Fernando Pedro da Silva. Belo Horizonte: C/Arte/Fundação João Pinheiro/Centro de Estudos Históricos e Culturais. 114–67.

Wirth, John. 1982. "Minas e a nação: um estudo de poder e dependência regional 1889–1937." *O Brasil republicano: estrutura de poder e economia (1889–1930)*. Ed. Boris Fausto. São Paulo: Difel. 76-99.

THE PAMPAS, THE SOUTHERN BORDERLANDS
INTRODUCTION

Mario J. Valdés

The territory that today comprises the southernmost Brazilian state, Rio Grande do Sul, as well as Paraguay and Uruguay was a war zone of intermittent intensity over much of the seventeenth, eighteenth, and nineteenth centuries. It was not until 1828 that a British-brokered treaty was signed between Brazil and Argentina, establishing the buffer state of the Republic of Uruguay, and it was not until Paraguay's defeat in 1870 in a disastrous war against the armies of the Triple Alliance (Argentina, Brazil, and Uruguay) that the two buffer states of Uruguay and Paraguay were accepted by all parties (Burns 235; Quesada 214–223). This extended period of constant warfare left a lasting mark on both Rio Grande do Sul and Paraguay. In the former it led directly to gaucho political influence in Brazil far in excess of the state's size–3 percent of Brazilian territory and 8 percent of the population. Getulio Vargas, Brazil's populist dictator (1930–1937), dictator once again (1937–1945), and finally president (1951–1954), made much of the gaucho cultural tradition of his native Rio Grande do Sul. In Paraguay the disaster led to a renewed passionate nationalism, making Francisco Solano López, the Paraguayan leader who had led the nation into the war, a national hero in spite of everything.

This war zone of the borderlands between the Spanish and Portuguese Colonial empires–later the two most powerful states in South America–as had a complex cultural history. There are as many links as there are differences and as many similarities as sharp divisions between Asunción and Porto Alegre. As Rita Schmidt explains in her text, Rio Grande do Sul stands apart in Brazil much as Paraguay does in Spanish America:

> [E]mblematic of a region whose imaginary was developed in the shadow of a collective and conflicting feeling of belonging to a land almost apart, an island in the middle of three countries, the city therefore pursued its legitimation under the influence of opposite movements: local versus national, regional versus cosmopolitan, autonomy versus belonging, Brazilianness versus Latin Americanism. (This volume, 646)

The same can be said in general terms about Paraguay–a state in almost constant isolation trying to negotiate its Guaraní and Spanish polarities within its cultural imaginary.

Another significant feature that is common to the area is the cultivated cultural imaginary of "gaucho-ness," which in Brazil has been denied by writers from Rio de Janeiro and São Paulo but clearly recognized by critics like João Pinto da Silva from Porto Alegre, who had identified relations and influences of the Plate region on Rio Grande do Sul literature in his *Historia literaria do Rio Grande do Sul* [Literary History of Rio Grande do Sul]. It goes without saying that the image of the gaucho was converted into a state symbol by political leaders. The shared popular gaucho-ness is a transnational and translinguistic imaginary that dominates most of the nineteenth and twentieth centuries in the area (Levine and Crocitti 115 and, especially, Love 3–5). Carlos E. Cortes puts it this way in explaining the cultural imaginary of Porto Alegre:

> Climaxing in the Paraguayan War, the more than a century of strife had an enduring effect on the gaucho psyche and on future gaucho political behavior. These years of immense human and economic sacrifice made the gaucho intensely proud of and defensive about his state and its history. He came to believe that his suffering and blood shed on his country's behalf, and his decision to be Brazilian rather than Argentine, had made him a better citizen than his "involuntary Brazilian" fellow countrymen. (5)

In her essay on Asunción, Olga Araujo-Mendieta outlines almost a parallel reaction to the war within Paraguay in spite of the devastating destruction and loss of life. Paraguay is unique in Latin American history not only because of the extreme isolation imposed by the dictator José Gaspar de Francia shortly after Independence in 1812 (which ended only with his death in 1840), but also–and, in terms of literary culture, primarily–because it is the only fully bilingual nation in Latin America (Spanish-Guaraní). In fact, Rodríguez de Francia drew his support from the strong sense of identity of the Guaraní-speaking *mestizo* majority, an identity that is rooted in the pre-Hispanic structure of the Guaraní communities and the reinforcement of the Jesuit missions, which thrived until the expulsion of the order from all Spanish possessions in 1767. From 1812 to 1840 the only contacts for Asunción and Paraguay as a whole with the outside world came through a select few Brazilian merchants from Porto Alegre and southern Brazil. By the mid-nineteenth century southern Brazil had began to receive the same large-scale immigration that was affecting Argentina and Uruguay, but this did not affect Asunción. Thus in the 1870s Asunción and Porto Alegre are a study in contrasts.

Porto Alegre was founded in 1742 by immigrants from the Azores; its population vastly increased in the last decades of the nineteenth century with German and Italian immigration. As the capital of Brazil's southern-most state of Rio Grande do Sul, it is and has been the borderland between Portuguese and Spanish South America. Asunción, in contrast, is inland on the Paraguay River and is much older than the Brazilian city, but its relative importance to the Spanish Crown diminished as Buenos Aires rose in prominence. It is almost entirely made up of a *mestizo* population.

Asunción has felt the brunt of borderland strife caught in the middle between Argentinean and Brazilian expansionism. It was devastated by the war with the Triple Alliance (1864–1870) against Brazil, Argentina, and Uruguay. The forces of the three neighboring states overwhelmed the heroic defense of the Paraguayans; the destruction was extensive, but the human loss was paramount: The Paraguayan population was reduced by half. In the aftermath of the war, neo-Colonialism entered Paraguay, and power passed to a landowning oligarchy. The new economy was oriented to the international market so that by the end of the nineteenth century there were extensive exports of hides to Europe and tobacco and the tealike yerba maté to the River Plate region. The commercial links between southern Brazil and Asunción were now firmly established and almost exclusively benefited the ruling class.

On a cultural level the unusual history of this war-torn borderland (there was another exhausting war in the Chaco [1932–1935], this time with Bolivia), has meant that the most interesting links between the cultural centers have been at the level of popular culture, in which there is extensive cross-fertilization in *gaucho* literature and, today, in popular music. Of course, the rich storehouse of the Guaraní oral tradition has also left a mark in the Argentinean Pampas and Chaco regions, and to a certain extent in Brazilian popular culture of the backlands. The recent development of a regional trading bloc, *Mercosur*, has as yet not produced the expected economic upturn, but on the cultural level it has made a difference in terms of increased access to cultural products, especially from Brazil's thriving popular music industry.

The key issue of cultural identity in this southern Brazilian capital has been described with consummate care by Rita Schmidt:

> [T]he border as a zone of permeabilities, affiliations, and social/textual exchanges that do not coincide with the line arbitrarily imposed by the geopolitical borders of the nation-state . . . apprehends the double movement of conflict and acceptance between the Rio Grande do Sul *gaucho* and that of the River Plate. (This volume, 654)

In a striking statement concluding his seminal book, *Gaucho Politics in Brazil*, Cortes portrays the Rio Grande do Sul gaucho in words that could easily be applied to Paraguay:

> As well as pride, gauchos have *saudades* for their political past. A beautiful, nearly intranslatable Portuguese word, *saudade* approximates longing, remembrance, yearning nostalgia . . . and more. Gauchos look back on their political history with *saudades*–the knowledge that the old gaucho politics is gone. And as much as the deeply romantic gaucho might wish, it will never return. (214)

Paraguayan cultural identity is ethnic (*mestizo*) but above all linguistic (Guaraní and Spanish); this has been so deeply rooted that a non-Guaraní-speaking person is not considered Paraguayan, while a non-Spanish-speaking person is simply considered uneducated. The vast majority of the population is bilingual and bicultural. Part of the strength of the Guaraní language is religious and part is historical, since it was this language that was chosen as the lingua franca by the Jesuits and was dominant in large sections of Brazil until it was banned in the eighteenth century.

Borders throughout Latin America still mark limits of contested sovereignty, and nowhere has this been more acutely felt than in Paraguay in two crushing wars (1864–1870 and 1932–1935), but it is also too easy to forget that borders are also zones of intense cultural interaction and of complex creativity in the everyday life of those who live and learn to negotiate this liminal space. The southern borderlands between Portuguese-speaking Brazil, Spanish-speaking Argentina and Uruguay, and bilingual Paraguay are as complex and painful as any on the continent, but through it all the literary cultures have survived and have grown. Homi Bhabha's discussion of culture in the borderlands is appropriate here: "Culture becomes as much an uncomfortable, disturbing practice of survival and supplementarity–between art and politics, past and present, the public and the private–as its resplendent being is a moment of pleasure, enlightenment or liberation" (175).

Works Cited

Bhabha, Homi K. 1994. *The Location of Culture.* London: Routledge.

Burns, E. Bradford. 1980. *A History of Brazil.* New York: Columbia University Press.

Cortes, Carlos E. 1974. *Gaucho Politics in Brazil.* Albuquerque: University of New Mexico Press.

Levine, Robert M., and John J. Crocitti, eds. 1999. *The Brazil Reader: History, Culture, Politics.* Durham: Duke University Press.

Love, Joseph L. 1971. *Rio Grande do Sul and Brazilian Regionalism.* Stanford: Stanford University Press.

Quesada, Vicente Gregorio. 1920. *La política imperialista del Brasil y las cuestiones de límites de las repúblicas sudamericanas.* Buenos Aires: Administración General.

CHAPTER 51

ASUNCIÓN AS A CULTURAL CENTER

Olga V. Araujo-Mendieta

Figure 1.

Paraguay is divided into two major regions: the eastern region and the western, or Chaco Paraguayo, region, separated by the Paraguay River. The Chaco zone, with its tropical climate, scant vegetation, scarcity of navigable rivers, and shortage of drinking water, is hardly conducive to a sedentary life. At the time of the Spaniards' arrival, it was inhabited by the most belligerent tribes in the area, the Guaycurú and the Payaguá. In contrast with the Chaco Paraguayo, the eastern region had extremely fertile soil, suitable for a wide range of crops, and a mild climate virtually all year round. These lands were owned by the Cario Indians, members of the Guaraní family. Unlike the Indians from the Chaco Paraguayo, they were less hostile toward the Spaniards. At the same time, according to the geographical concepts of the sixteenth century, the Paraguay River lay very close to upper Peru, in other words, to the coveted Incan wealth. Asunción was founded on the banks of this river on 15 August 1537 by Juan de Salazar de Espinoza (1508–1556) under the name of Nuestra Señora Santa María de la Asunción; it was regarded as a strategic point and a sort of stopover on the route to upper Peru. (See **Figure 1.**) These geographic and logistic factors encouraged the Spaniards to settle in the eastern zone.

In 1541, owing to the shortage of provisions caused by constant attacks by the Indians, all the settlers in Buenos Aires moved to Asunción, which offered more favorable living conditions. This contributed to the growth and development of Asunción, which became the base for the conquest of the vast Río de la Plata basin. On the Spaniards' arrival in what was to become Asunción, the Cario Indians had already settled in farming communities. Hunting and fishing were their primary means of subsistence. The Cario lived in small tribes, generally formed on the basis of consanguinity. As a sign of friendship and respect the Indians used to offer their daughters as wives for the *caciques*. In the view of certain historians (Cardozo 12), perhaps in accordance with this tradition, the Cario gave some of their women to the newly arrived Spaniards, even though the great majority was forced to serve the conquistadors. Those born of the unions between Spaniards and Guaraní Indian women came to be known as "mancebos de la tierra" [sons of the earth]. The Cario tradition of creating tribes on the basis of consanguinity meant that the Cario regarded the Spaniards as their brothers-in-law (*tovayás*), since the women belonging to their tribes were the wives of the Spaniards. Moreover, mutual aid between relatives was customary among the Indians, and both of these factors were later used by the Spaniards to facilitate the exploitation and enslavement of the Indians. The economic and political system of these Indians contained the following features that were subsequently utilized by the Spaniards: the cultivation of crops, which meant that a community was able to remain in the same place; the special role in agriculture of women, who were experts in this field; and certain forms of collective work, particularly in farming.

Drawing by Guamán Poma de Ayala depicting the foundation of Asunción in 1536 in his El primer nueva corónica y buen gobierno, *1615. (Courtesy of John P. Robarts Research Library, University of Toronto)*

As we shall see throughout this study, Paraguayan national identity was formed around the Guaraní language. The survival of this autochthonous language (and its subsequent acceptance as an official language) is due to three main factors: the role of Guaraní women during the Colonial period; the Guaraní religion; and the use made of the indigenous language by the missionaries for the purpose of evangelization on which I shall elaborate further. Once they were of marriageable age, Guaraní women began to serve the Spaniards as slaves and mistresses. Thus their role was doubly important: They were both agricultural specialists–the Spaniards needed crops to survive–and reproducers of the labor force. Illegitimate *mestizo* children were given back to their mothers, who assumed the responsibility of educating them; their children therefore learned the native language. When a young indigenous woman joined a Spaniard's household, she also brought her Guaraní traditions with her, which were immediately incorporated into the nascent-hybrid culture. Although her youth prevented her from having a profound knowledge of the philosophical and ritual aspects of her tribe—which were in any case reserved for men—through her language, the Guaraní woman also transmitted her religious beliefs, whose principles are based on the divine origin of the spoken word. It was not until the beginning of the twentieth century that non-Guaranís, slowly and perhaps still only partially, began to understand the sacred value of the spoken word for the Guaraní through Guaraní literature. According to this philosophy, the word is of divine origin, which is why it plays an extremely important role in their culture. For the Guaraní language is more than a means of communication; it is a reflection of the soul. A person capable of finding a new word with greater meaning and depth than an existing one will be very close to perfection. Losing the word would therefore mean losing one's soul, whereas maintaining and enhancing speech becomes synonymous with spiritual enrichment. Human beings have the ability to immortalize themselves in the words of others, thereby perpetuating themselves through the language of subsequent generations. This was the religious principle that kept alive the spoken word: Guaraní.

It is estimated that the first group of settlers in the entire Rio de la Plata region, of which Asunción formed part, comprised approximately 1000 to 1200 Spaniards. In the sixteenth century the Spanish population of Asunción fluctuated between 400 and 500 (Meliá 56). During the second half of this century no important group of immigrants reached Asunción. The lack of gold and silver mines made this area unattractive to new immigrants. The Spaniards aged; and as the *mestizo* "sons of the earth" came of age, they sought the same privileges as their parents, such as, for example, becoming *encomenderos*, which involved being allocated a certain number of Indians who would either pay them tribute or work for free. This system, widely practiced during the Colonial period, is commonly known as an *encomienda* of Indians (Mora Mérida 211–12). As the *encomiendas* grew, however, the number of Indians decreased. This shortage of Indians was further exacerbated by the exodus of conquistadors in search of mines in Peru, taking a vast number of Indians with them.

The reduction of both the Spanish and the indigenous populations strengthened the growth of the *mestizos* and, consequently, their power. The *mestizos* began to fill posts that had hitherto been solely occupied by Spaniards. Over the years *mestizos* and *criollos* gradually distanced themselves from the few remaining Spaniards in Asunción and felt remote from the authorities who arrived from Spain. The cultural distance between conquistadors and Indians was gradually eliminated, as the number of *mestizos* grew and the number of Spaniards diminished. However, there was no Spanish acculturation of the Indian population; instead, *mestizos* began to identify more closely with the Indian culture. As we shall see shortly, this rapport with Guaraní culture and particularly the language would be constantly reinforced and reaffirmed as a symbol of national identity.

In 1617 Spain decreed the separation of the dependency of Asunción from Buenos Aires. The coveted route from Asunción to the mines of Peru failed to materialize, and, consequently, the idea of creating one was also abandoned; the crown's interest in the city declined considerably, while Buenos Aires, with its river port, became increasingly important. Although it continued to supply provisions for the settlers, Asunción became a fort, whose main function was to prevent the entry of the Portuguese from Brazil into the Río de la Plata region.

Around 1580, the number of priests in Asunción had risen to twenty, still a small number in relation to the Indian population. For this reason the *encomenderos* were responsible for disseminating Catholicism. That same year the Franciscans implemented the system of *reducciones* or reductions (Indian towns ruled by priests) in Paraguay. Regardless of sex or age, the Indian converts lived and worked under the strict supervision of the priests who in exchange fed, clothed, and protected them from the *encomiendas*. The arrival of the Jesuits in 1610 helped to boost and expand the reductions. Although the Jesuits' work focused on religious matters, it also fostered the development of other important aspects that enabled the community to become self-sufficient, such as weaving linen to clothe themselves, the slaves, and the poor. Likewise, the production of ironwork and silverware was restricted to the needs of each reduction, while the development of other cultural forms, such as sculpture, painting, music, and theater, concentrated on the propagation of Catholicism. Some of the Jesuits learnt Guaraní and transmitted their religion to certain *caciques*, who in turn spread it among the rest of the community in their native language.

Thus the first printing press in Río de la Plata was operated in the Jesuit missions in Paraguay in about 1700 (Cardozo 42). However, its role in the cultural life of the colony was restricted to the propagation of religion. The Guaraní translation of the catechism, entitled *Catecismo breve para rudos y ocupados* [1583; Brief Catechism for Uneducated Workers], by Father Luis Bolaños (1539?–1629), reflected a new cultural and religious process that led to the Synod of Asunción in 1603. The Synod "manda que los curas enseñen la doctrina en guaraní y tengan la Doctrina de Catecismo que hizo el Padre Fr. Luis Bolaños" (Meliá 72) ("ordered priests to teach the doctrine in Guaraní and to have the Doctrine of Catechism by Fr. Luis Bolaños"). *De la diferencia entre lo temporal y lo eterno* [1705; A Treatise of the Difference Between the Temporal and the Eternal, 1775?] by Father Juan Eusebio Nieremberg (1595–1658) was translated directly from Latin into Guaraní and printed in the mission towns. *Araporú*, a sort of Christian Bible in Guaraní, translated by Father Antonio Garrida, was published in 1713.

It is important to point out the distinction between *Guaraní literature* and *literature in Guaraní*. The former refers to texts created exclusively by the Guaraní, whereas the latter corresponds to any text written in the Guaraní language. The earliest texts written in Guaraní are translations of Christian texts, although this changed with the arrival of Nicolás Yapuguay (b. 1680), who wrote in Guaraní. The importance of this writer does not lie in the purely religious content of his works, but rather in the fact he was the first indigenous Guaraní writer to have written in Guaraní. His first book, *La explicación del catequismo en lengua guaraní* [1724; The Explanation of the Catechism in the Guarani Language], was written under the supervision of Father Paulo Restivo (1658–1741) of the Society of Jesus. Three years later the Jesuits published another of his works: *Sermones y exemplos en lengua guaraní* [1727; Sermons and Examples in the Guarani Language].

Although, at the outset, the Jesuits' work focused on religious aspects, as time went by, they undertook valuable historiographical work in Paraguay. Foremost among the Jesuit historians was Father Pedro Lozano (1697–1752), whose most famous works include *Descripción chorographica del terreno, ríos, árboles, animales de las dilatadísimas provincias del Gran Chaco* [1733; Chorographic Description of the Land, Rivers, Fauna, and Flora of the Extensive Provinces of the Gran Chaco]; *Historia de la Compañía de Jesús en la provincia del Paraguay* [1754–1755; History of the Society of Jesus in the Province of Paraguay]; and *Historia de las revoluciones del Paraguay* [1905; History of the Revolution of Paraguay].

In *La conquista espiritual* [The Spiritual Conquest], published in Madrid in 1639, Father Antonio Ruiz de Montoya (1585–1652) described the work of the Society of Jesus at the start of the Conquest in Río de la Plata. However, his main legacy is the dictionary entitled *El tesoro de la lengua guaraní* [The Treasure of the Guarani Language], published in Madrid that same year. (See **Figure 2.**) Father Ruiz de Montoya demonstrated his mastery of the native language in this book, which is more of a treatise on ethnography than a dictionary. The historiographical work of the Jesuit fathers continued even after their expulsion from Paraguay, decreed by Charles III in 1767, which was carried out the following year.

Outside the Missions, cultural activity during the Colonial period was extremely limited. In Asunción, for example, the city's founder, Juan de Salazar de Espinoza, on his death "dejó doce o catorce libros casi todos de religión y un platero fallecido también por esos años, dejó dos libros, uno de ellos El Lazarillo de Tormes" (Plá 1985, 45) ("left a mere twelve or fourteen books, virtually all on religion, while a silversmith, who died at about the same time, left two books, one of which was *El Lazarillo de Tormes*"). The first poem to the city of Asunción, composed by Martín Barco de Centenera (1535–1601), is entitled *La Argentina* (Lisbon, 1602), while the only eighteenth-century Paraguayan sonnet is attributed to the leader of the *Comunera* Revolution, José de Antequera y Castro (1690–1731).

At the start of the emancipation of the Spanish colonies, Paraguay found itself in a sociopolitical situation that would prepare it for independence (Romero 133). In 1810 Buenos Aires broke off relations with the Spanish Crown and sought to establish itself as the new metropolis of Río de la Plata. For its part, Paraguay declared its allegiance to Fernando VII and rejected Buenos Aires' proposals. In order to ensure that its conditions were accepted, Buenos Aires sent an army led by Manuel Belgrano (1770–1820) into Paraguay. The governor of Asunción, Bernardo Velazco, warning that Buenos Aires intended to conquer Paraguay, urged citizens to defend their territory. Thousands of Paraguayans responded to his call, thereby demonstrating their awareness of being Paraguayan for the first time ever (Williams 24–26). Belgrano's army was defeated by the Paraguayans on the banks of the Tacuarí River. Nevertheless, Belgrano managed to turn his military defeat into a political victory by convincing the Paraguayan officers Manuel Antonio Cabañas and Fulgencio Yegros of the irrationality of their position toward Spain, since independence would bring numerous economic benefits, such as the elimination of heavy taxes on Paraguayan exports.

The Paraguayan *criollos* who were in favor of independence from Spain rose up on 14 May 1811 under the command of Captain Pedro Juan Caballero, demanding that Governor Velazco incorporate two new members into his government.

Figure 2.

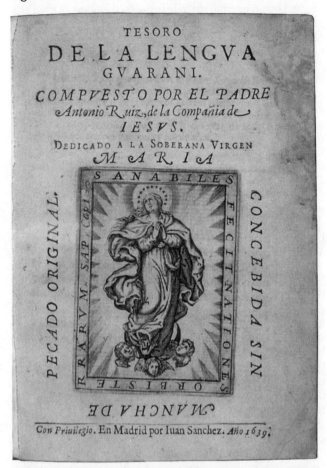

Cover page of Tesoro de la lengua guarani *by Antonio Ruiz of the Jesuit order published in 1639. (Courtesy of the The Thomas Fisher Library, University of Toronto)*

Two days later the Triumvirate of Asunción was formed, with the participation of the government of Captain Juan Valeriano de Zeballos, Dr. Gaspar Rodríguez de Francia (1766–1840), and Velazco himself, although now with limited functions. However, Velazco's days as governor were numbered, and on 9 June 1811 he was deposed by a coalition led by Rodríguez de Francia, who accused him of subversive conspiracy with the Spaniards in Montevideo.

The achievement of independence brought with it a cultural movement that had immediate repercussions on Asunción society–the center of political, economic, and cultural power in Paraguay. In 1812 the government announced the creation of the Sociedad Patriótica Literaria, the organization responsible for public education. That same year witnessed the opening of the first public library and the establishment of the military academy. In 1812 the Real Colegio Seminario de San Carlos, the principal cultural center of Colonial Paraguay, was reopened on the occasion of the war with Buenos Aires. One of the tacit aims of reopening the prestigious college was to turn it into a university, but the first Paraguayan university, the National University, was not in fact opened until 1890. Another important cultural event at this time was the implementation by decree of compulsory public education throughout the country.

The political scene immediately after independence was marked by an internal struggle between members of the Paraguayan junta over the position they should adopt toward the attitude of Buenos Aires, which now insisted on a confederation. Certain members of the Paraguayan junta were inclined to accept Buenos Aires' policy as the most viable option, although the majority rejected it. Buenos Aires therefore sent Nicolás de Herrera to Asunción on a mission to convince the junta in Asunción of the need to join the federal system. Buenos Aires threatened to paralyze Paraguay economically if it refused. However, all its efforts at repression proved fruitless. On 12 October 1813 the Asunción Congress, which had met to discuss this complex political situation, voted to declare Paraguay an independent republic. The government of Buenos Aires therefore decided to levy prohibitive new taxes on *yerba maté* [yerba maté tea] and tobacco—the principal Paraguayan export products—thereby fulfilling its threat and beginning Paraguay's long period of isolation (Guerra Vilaboy 48–68).

In Asunción, Gaspar Rodríguez de Francia and Fulgencio Yegros were appointed consuls and would take turns leading the government. Paraguay thus rejected the authority of either Spain or Buenos Aires. Dr. Francia, as he was usually known, gradually increased his power. In 1814 he had himself appointed Supreme Dictator of the republic, and in 1816 he was nominated Perpetual Dictator of the republic by congress. Thereafter, he ruled with an iron hand until his death in 1840. (This dominating figure is the subject of Roa Bastos's *Yo, el Supremo* [1974; *I, the Supreme*, 1986]. One of the first measures taken by the Perpetual Dictator was to close the river port at Pilar, thereby severing ties with the only province in Río de la Plata, Corrientes, which still maintained a few trade links with Paraguay. Itapua thereby became the only point of contact with the outside world, although when Paraguay experienced political problems with Brazil, this port was also closed. Buenos Aires constantly attempted to reduce Paraguay to its authority, which also contributed to its isolation. Thus the First Republic of the South was virtually isolated from the rest of the world. These constant threats from Buenos Aires provided Dr. Francia with the necessary justification for subordinating individual freedoms to the need for national freedom. The country's total isolation was the most outstanding feature of Paraguayan history during this period. The absolute power attained by Dr. Francia produced drastic changes in the politics of the country. According to the historian Fulgencio Moreno (252), throughout this period, the only books and printed matter imported into Paraguay were those received by Dr. Francia, while both private and monastery libraries were converted into playing card factories, which, owing to the shortage of paper, were compelled to use the leaves out of books for this purpose. Other historians, such as White, have highlighted certain redeeming features of the government of Dr. Francia, such as popular education and the equitable distribution of land and goods. This practice was born of Dr. Francia's belief that "[p]rivate interest should be subordinated to the common and general welfare" (White 125).

On the one hand, the country's isolation curbed cultural development, and all the cultural institutions founded in 1812 were subsequently abolished. On the other hand, Dr. Francia focused his efforts on forming an army that would defend the country from attacks from its neighbors, particularly Buenos Aires. He therefore created an army of 5000 active soldiers,

with reserve troops of 30,000 who could be called up in the event of an emergency. Under the government of Dr. Francia, the Church lost its status. In 1824 this governor decreed the "Reforma de los Regulares" [Reform of the Regular Clergy], ordering the closure of monasteries and houses of refuge and the transfer of all Church land and property to the state. Dr. Francia regarded the Church as part of the state, which meant that priests continued to be citizens and were as such subject to the laws of the state.

With the death of Gaspar Rodríguez de Francia in 1840, a military junta was established, and, in March 1841, the second consulate was formed, consisting of Mariano Roque Alonso and Carlos Antonio López (1792–1862). This consulate initiated a process aimed at restricting state power, marked by the release of political prisoners, and allowing foreigners to enter and leave the country freely (a right hitherto denied by Dr. Francia). One of the first priorities of this government was to free Paraguay from the isolation in which it had lived for so long, and as a result the Port of Villa Pilar was fitted out for river trade. The Seminario San Carlos—closed by Dr. Francia—was not immediately reopened. Instead, it was replaced by the Academia Literaria (1842) under the direction of Father Marco Antonio Maíz. On its inauguration this first lay institution in Paraguay had a total enrolment of 149 students. At the same time, given the need to defend its independence and free navigation, and in order to compel the Argentinean government to recognize Paraguay's fundamental rights, this government founded the first newspaper: *El paraguayo independiente* (1845). When Argentina finally recognized Paraguayan independence in 1852, *El paraguayo independiente* was replaced by *El Semanario* (1853). The political changes implemented by the second consulate also contributed to the recognition of Paraguayan independence by certain European countries. In 1852 several European diplomatic representatives who recognized the country's independence came to Asunción and signed trade and free navigation agreements with Paraguay (Cardozo 75). After many years of isolation the country was incorporated into the international community.

This new openness to the outside world, together with the political changes within the country, encouraged many Paraguayans who had fled during the administration of Gaspar Rodríguez de Francia to return to their native land. Among these was Juan Andrés Gelly (1815–1904), who had left Paraguay in 1813 and returned in 1845. Gelly made a substantial contribution to Paraguayan culture: He wrote for *El paraguayo independiente* and was subsequently director of *El Semanario*. He was also responsible for founding the School of Civil and Political Law (1850). The government of Carlos Antonio López was characterized by its dedication to the economic and cultural growth of the country. In order to promote the development of national industry, López contracted over 200 technicians, the majority of whom were English. In 1853 he authorized the founding of the first school of mathematics in Asunción. In addition to opening the earliest national printing press (1844) and publishing the first Paraguayan newspaper, he promoted the foundation of cultural institutions such as the School of Philosophy (1856). This secondary school, directed by Ildefonso Antonio Bermejo (1820–1882), who had been hired from Spain by the Paraguayan government in 1855, produced the first literary generation in independent Paraguay that in turn spawned the group of writers for the first journal in the country, *La Aurora* (1860). This journal was responsible for disseminating the earliest essays and writings of the School of Philosophy. Bermejo also founded the Teacher Training College, wrote for the newspapers *El Eco del Paraguay* and *El Semanario*, and was the director of *La Aurora*. He founded the National Theater, formed a pioneering group of actors, and, between 1858 and 1864, co-authored the first plays performed in the country with Cornelio Porter Bliss. This period also saw the emergence of the earliest expressions of art and architecture with the Asunción Theater and Oratorium. Although the expression of ideas was subject to a certain amount of censorship, the spirit could be freely cultivated, and, according to Fulgencio Moreno, the most advanced authors in political and economic principles were freely read in Asunción (277).

Natalicio Talavera (1839–1867) is regarded as the earliest poet in independent Paraguay. He initially attracted attention as writer for the journal *La Aurora* and subsequently for newspapers, particularly as a correspondent for *El Semanario*. His best-known poetry is contained in a collection entitled *Reflexiones de un centinela en la víspera del combate* [A Centinel's Reflections on the Eve of Battle]. Another member of this generation was Juan Crisóstomo Centurión (1840–1902), whose work, *Viaje Nocturno* [Nocturnal Journey], published in New York in 1877, established him as a precursor of the novel in Paraguay. This florescence in the intellectual and economic sphere would be brutally interrupted by the war against Argentina, Brazil, and Uruguay, known as the War of the Triple Alliance (1865). The government of Carlos Antonio López demonstrated its command of diplomacy by resisting continuous attempts by Argentina and Brazil to claim Paraguayan territory. On his death López was succeeded by his son, Francisco Solano López, whose view of Paraguay's position in Río de la Plata affairs differed sharply from the cautious position of his father. The younger López insisted on Paraguay's right to intervene in regional matters and was keen for the country to play a more active role in Río de la Plata. A series of plots and treason eventually led to the Great War.

Rather than examining the political and economic reasons that led to this tragic war that ruined Paraguay, I shall focus on the cultural aspect and its impact on national identity. The war drew Paraguayans closer to their autochthonous roots. For the first time since the era of the Jesuit missions, texts were printed in Guaraní, and a new type of literature was forged in this language: journalistic writing. A number of newspapers were founded to support the war against the alliance, the most important of which was *Cabichuí* (1867–1868). Although this newspaper was published in Guaraní and Spanish, its name *Cabichuí* is a reflection of the dominant social position attained by the indigenous language within Paraguayan society. The sections written in Guaraní served to echo popular feelings. This language was also used in the satirical poems that ended each issue, in popular colloquia, and as an expression of linguistic reality, with its frequent, colorful Guaraní expressions (Meliá 197). *Cacique Lambaré*, founded in 1867, the same year as *El Centinela*, was a satirical newspaper; its main contributor was Father S. Espinoza. Popular Guaraní, known today as *yopará*, was the expressive means used to provide an ironic commentary on the events of the war. Guaraní became in this sense the language of national defense. Major-General Francisco Solano López, aware that the Paraguayan people regarded Guaraní as a symbol of national identity, delivered several of his speeches in this language during his campaign for the war.

In addition to this journalistic production, the War of the Triple Alliance also inspired a considerable number of songs in Guaraní, which would last until and subsequently be reinforced by another war, known as the Chaco War (1932–1935). In his discussion of the role of the War of the Triple Alliance, the great scholar of Guaraní culture, Bartomeu Meliá (b. 1932), suggests that it lent Paraguayan literature renewed creative vigor: "Si en la época colonial la literatura en guaraní se identifica con la sociedad de guaraníes de los pueblos jesuíticos a la que ofrece apenas textos religiosos y políticos, a partir de la nueva situación creada con la guerra esta literatura se da a sí misma otro destino y función: el registro poético de las vivencias del pueblo" (203) ("Although during the Colonial era, literature in Guaraní was identified with the Guaraní societies in the Jesuit mission towns, who were only offered religious and political texts, as a result of the new situation created by the war, this literature acquired a different purpose and function: the poetic recording of the experiences of the people").

The Guaraní language was transformed into an expression of the identity of one people as opposed to another, while at the same time becoming a catalyst for national identity. In practical terms, however, the war devastated Paraguay. Its population was decimated; the country was looted, and over half its territory was lost. Moreover, the Guaraní warriors did not hesitate to take the war to its ultimate extremes. In the battle of Pirebebuy, Major-General Francisco Solano López was accompanied by an army of old men, women, the disabled, and children. And at the battle of Acosta Ñú, children, disguised with false beards, fought bravely against the enemy forces. Their defeat was compounded by the death of Francisco Solano López at the head of a starving, ragged army on 1 March 1870.

The tragic events of the war with Paraguay pricked the consciences of a number of intellectuals, including the Argentinean poet, Carlos Guido y Spano (1827–1918), who wrote the following in "Nenia" (Funeral Oration):

Llora, llora, ûrutaú
Ya no existe el Paraguay
Donde nací como tú–
Llora, llora ûrutaú! (189)

Weep, weep, ûrutaú
Paraguay no longer exists
Where I, like you, was born–
Weep, weep ûrutaú!

The allied army that entered Asunción in 1869 looted everything in its path, including churches and tombs. The Brazilians took away all they could find, from fine works of art, pianos, marble, and doors, to even the door frames of the finest buildings (Guerra Vilaboy 165–66). The war had catastrophic consequences for Paraguay: Agriculture was abandoned; all cattle-raising was virtually eliminated; and industry was destroyed. In the economic sphere the market collapsed, with foreign capital replacing state capital. According to some historians, including Efraim Cardozo, so many able-bodied men had died that polygamy had to be authorized to overcome the demographic losses. After the war, large numbers of Italian, Spanish, and Argentinean immigrants, together with Paraguayans who had lived outside the country, particularly in Argentina, began to settle in Paraguay. It fell to the few surviving Paraguayans, especially women, together with the new inhabitants of the region, to reconstruct a country in ruins.

The first president elected after the War of the Triple Alliance was Cirilo Antonio Rivarola (1870). The conquering army that occupied the country remained there until 1876 and continued to be politically active. Far from being a passive observer, it intervened regularly in civil struggles, either to put down revolts or to impose its policies. This great sociopolitical instability caused successive coups d'état and revolutions. Despite this, however, cultural expression made great strides. In 1870 the first post-war newspaper, entitled *La Regeneración*, was founded, followed by others such as *El látigo inmortal*, a satirical Asunción newspaper, and *La Verdad autógrafa*. The latter experimented with a sort of collective and pluralistic writing open to general participation. In 1877 the National College was established, and in 1880 the San Carlos Seminario was re-opened. This was followed by the creation of the Law School two years later, while 1890 saw the opening of the Graduate School of Teachers, which became the Normal School in 1896. The year 1890 was particularly important for Asunción culture, since it marked the opening of the first university in the country: the Universidad Nacional. This university received many of the students who had trained at the National College. During this period Paraguayan writers particularly cultivated the historical genre; historical writing was used to praise or vilify national leaders such as Gaspar Rodríguez de Francia and Carlos and Francisco Solano López. This nationalistic position is reflected in *Tres ensayos sobre la historia del Paraguay* [1942; Three Essays on Paraguayan History] by Blas Garay (1873–1899), a graduate of the National College, and in the work of Juan Silvano Godoy (1850–1926), particularly *Monografías Históricas* [1893; Historical Monographs] and *Últimas operaciones de guerra del general José Edivigis Díaz* [1897; Last War Manoeuver of General José Edivigis Díaz].

It is worth noting that Silvano Godoy belonged to the generation of Paraguayan expatriates who returned to Asunción following the War of the Triple Alliance. Godoy studied in Buenos Aires and traveled through Europe, where he came into contact with European, particularly French, culture. On his return to Paraguay in 1895 he brought his valuable library and his collection of paintings by European artists. Foremost among these works was "La virgen con el niño" [The Madonna with Child] by the Spanish painter Murillo, acquired in Rome in 1904. Using part of Godoy's collection, together with other private collections, the Asunción Museum was opened in 1909, exhibiting works by Murillo, Tintoretto, Fabritius, Rusiñol, and Cardi (Plá 1970, 11–14). Because of his great contribution to culture, Godoy is recognized today as one of the leading intellectuals in Paraguay, who formed part of the generation that emerged in the early twentieth century.

The golden age of Paraguayan literature occurred at the beginning of the twentieth century, when a group of intellectuals comprising the so-called "generación del 1900" appeared on the Paraguayan cultural scene. Members of this generation, like the Spanish members of the generation of 1898, wished to contribute to the spiritual reconstruction of the country through their literature. To this end they resorted to the reinterpretation and revindication of certain aspects of Paraguayan history and the reaffirmation of national values. According to Raúl Amaral, "El novecentismo ha querido ser o significar, en el Paraguay, la renovación de modos de vida, de sistemas de orientación intelectual y, por sobre todo, un método distinto para enfocar los desencuentros de la historia, latentes aún a treinta años de terminada la guerra de la Triple Alianza" (29) ("In Paraguay, *novecentismo* attempted to embody or signify the renewal of ways of life, systems of intellectual guidance, and above all, a different method for focusing on unresolved historical issues, still latent thirty years after the end of the War of the Triple Alliance"). The leading exponents of this generation were Juan E. O'Leary (1879–1969), Ignacio A. Pane (1880–1919), and Narciso R. Colmán (1878–1954), known as Rosicrán, whose teacher was the Spanish-born writer Victoriano Abente (1846–1935). Other members of this generation included Manuel Domínguez (1869–1935), Manuel Gondra (1871–1927), Fulgencio Moreno (1872–1933), Arsenio López Decoud (1867–1945), Eloy Fariña Nuñez (1885–1929), Eligio Ayala (1879–1930), Eusebio Ayala (1875–1942), Francisco L. Bareiro (1877–1930), and Alejandro Guanes (1872–1925). These prose writers sought to find a balance that was missing in a nation traumatized and worn down by the lengthy war. During this search they shifted from historical revisionism to a critical analysis of the country's sociopolitical position.

With Juan E. O'Leary, this generation of 1900 included the cultured poets in Guaraní and reinforced the worship of national heroes. Some writers used the indigenous language as an act of symbolic affirmation, with defiant compositions such as a Guaraní version of *Don Quijote* by Juan E. O'Leary (Plá 1985, 204). This time the Guaraní language became a new discoursive tool. Guaraní had hitherto served as the means of expression for the feelings of the Paraguayan people. More immediately it had reinforced national sentiment during the War of the Triple Alliance. But this generation of writers used Guaraní to develop a cultured, and therefore elitist, literature, whose point of reference was European rather than autochthonous culture. Foremost among these writers in the Guaraní language was Narciso R. Colmán, whose pen name was Rosicrán, who, with his new poetry in Guaraní, sought to create a sort of mythical epic entitled *Ñandé Yppycuéra* (1929). Ironically, the original version of this book in Guaraní failed to receive the expected public acclaim, whereas its translation into the dominant, minority language, Spanish published in 1973, was far more widely circulated. Rosicrán's main contribution, however, was not in the genre of poetry, but in the dissemination of a vigorous, active language, which sought idiomatic purity (Meliá 208–13), the utopia of all writers; as Lotman points out (12), language, like any living being, is unable to escape the influence of its environment, and in this specific case Guaraní is inevitably influenced by Spanish. In his work, Rosicrán, as a representative of the movement of this period, showed that the cultural identity of Paraguayan men and women revolved around the core of the Guaraní language. He devoted himself to compiling proverbs that he grouped into two series–the first, published in 1921, entitled *Ñe'éngá roviú* [Dark Green Proverbs], and the second, called *Ñe'enga* [A Thousand Guaraní Proverbs], issued in 1928.

Not all the literary production of this period was in Guaraní, however, but those who wrote in Spanish emphasized the romantic image of Paraguayan traditions and customs. Among these were Cecilio Báez (1862–1941), precursor and teacher of the young generation of 1900. His best-known works include *Ensayo sobre la libertad civil* [1893; Essay on Civil Liberties]; *Bosquejo histórico del Brasil* [1940; Historical Outline of Brazil]; and *Ensayo sobre el doctor Francia y la dictadura en Sudamérica* [1910; Essay on Dr. Francia and Dictatorship in South America]. Another movement that arose during this period emerged at the same time as the literary journal *Crónica* (1913–1915). Although this group of writers strove to establish links with its environment, it failed to penetrate with the desired depth, and the group disintegrated. Members of this group included Pablo Max Ynsfrán (1894–1972) and Guillermo Molinas Rolón (1892–1945). The leading figures in the field of historical research were Arturo Bray (1898–1974), Natalicio González (1897–1966), and Justo Pastor Benítez (1895–1967).

The journal *Juventud* (1923–26) subsequently took up the *modernista* banner of *Crónica*. We believe that Josefina Plá's analysis (1976, 13) of the characteristics of this group is correct: She points out that cultural disconnection from the outside world prevented growth and made the members of the group feel asphyxiated. At the same time the First World War ideology that reached Paraguay lacked the essential historical-cultural background, and, lastly, the proximity of the Chaco War made young people feel disoriented. Like the members of *Crónica,* the majority of the members of this group disappeared from cultural view. Nevertheless, those who survived the search for identity with their environment became profoundly integrated into it. At this point Herib Campos Cervera (1908–1953) and Julio Correa (1890–1953) rose to prominence, subsequently to be acknowledged as among the most important figures in the cycle of the Chaco War. This war provided poets in the Guaraní language with lyrical material that would be linked to the previous war in epic form. Campos Cervera was the principal exponent of post-Chaco War poetry, with *Ceniza redimida* [1950; Redeeming Ashes], and Elvio Romero (b. 1926) was the second.

As a result of the Chaco War, the Guaraní language reemerged on the national scene, where it was regarded as the pivotal point of Paraguayan identity. Guaraní indeed experienced a boom throughout the country. Its widespread use was due to the fact that people tended to regard it as part of *ñadé reko,* "la manera de ser paraguayo" ("the Paraguayan way of life"). The role of musicians and poets on the battle-front was undoubtedly crucial, since their songs and poetry fed the spirit of war daily. Emiliano R. Fernández (1894–1949) and Herminio Giménez (1905–1991) were the two great poets and musicians of this period. Nowadays, their compositions are regarded as epic poetry since they celebrate the heroism of the Paraguayan people. Emiliano R. Fernández played a key role during this period, leaving a cultural legacy that can be felt to this day. At least three recordings with selections from the most famous songs of the Chaco War, entitled "Chácore purahéi," are now available. Fernández was an enormously successful poet at the popular level, his discourse reflecting colloquial speech. He was not only a poet, but he actually fought in the Chaco War and most of his famous compositions date from this period. His work also contains a deep vein of social criticism, as reflected in "*Mboriahu memby*" [Son of a Poor Mother] (Meliá 214–15). The journal *Ocara poty Cue-mi: Revista de composiciones populares* (1922) widely disseminated popular poetry and Guaraní songs, particularly those on the Chaco War.

Another aspect of the cultural movement of this period was expressed in the emergence of theater in Guaraní by Julio Correa, which caused a radical change in the prevailing aesthetic perspectives of the time. The enormous success of his play *Sandía Yvyguay*–first performed at the beginning of the war and published with a Spanish translation in 1965– transformed him into a leading figure in Guaraní theater. Thereafter, he produced a number of works that brilliantly reflected the Paraguayan *Zeitgeist.* His theater in Guaraní

opened the doors not only to a new dramatic experience, but also to a new aesthetic experience. Indeed, his works totally replaced plays in Spanish. For the first time ever Paraguayan theater broke its traditional mold and freed itself from foreign influences by seeking a form of expression more in keeping with *ñadé rekó* (the Paraguayan manner). The success of Correa's work showed that the conventional depiction of Paraguayans, particularly peasants, in both literature and theater, was a fallacy, and that it was only through the accurate portrayal of reality that Paraguayans could break the mold into which they had been forced, reaffirm themselves as human beings through their language, and recover lost ground. Although Correa touched on the issue of war, he was primarily concerned with the violation of fundamental human rights of freedom and justice. In the violent, post-war environment, Correa wrote protest poems that were publicly recited. Later on, Roa Bastos (b. 1917) and Hérib Campos Cervera (1908–1953) would write poetry in Guaraní, although this cultured poetry failed to achieve the same power as did Correa's plays. The success of his plays led certain Paraguayan intellectuals to suggest that only theater in Guaraní was viable in Paraguay, and thereafter the country's supposed bilingualism became a problem for Paraguayan writers who therefore reformulated the prevailing aesthetic values and experimented with new prose styles. It is worth noting at this point that Paraguay continued to be an essentially Guaraní-speaking country. In the words of Roa Bastos, "[el guaraní] una lengua oral cuyo prodominio continúa siendo neto frente al idioma heredado en una proporción de aproximadamente un 50% de guaraní-hablantes y un 43% de bilingües, es decir de hablantes que dominan y practican por igual las dos lenguas, y sólo un 7% de castellano-hablantes que no hablan guaraní" (11) ("Guaraní is an oral language which continues to hold sway over the inherited language, since 50% of the population are Guaraní-speakers, and 43% are bilingual, in other words, they are equally fluent in both languages, while only 7% are Spanish speakers who do not speak Guaraní").

Thus some authors, such as Gabriel Casaccia Bibolini (1907–1980), incorporated entire sentences of Guaraní into their work, with footnoted translations; while others, such as Roa Bastos, experimented by inserting Paraguayan words or expressions whose meaning could be deduced from the context, or utilized the commonly used Guaraní Spanish, known today as *Yopará.* The theme of war continued to be present in the limited narrative production of this period. Thus, for example, the work of José Santiago Villarejo (b. 1907), *Ocho hombres* [1934; Eight Men], like *Cruces de Quebracho* [1943; Crosses of Wood] by Arnaldo Valdovinos (1908–1991), describes man in the tragic situation of war. In *El Guajhú* [The Shout], published in 1938, Casaccia Bibolini broke the Romantic mold into which the Paraguayan peasant had been forced.

At the end of the war with Bolivia (1935) (in other words, the Chaco War), Paraguay was on the verge of economic collapse, its human resources having once again been virtually exhausted. Nevertheless, peace abroad did not mean domestic peace. In February 1936 a coup d´état ousted the Liberal Party government under J. F. Estigarribia, who was sent into exile, and prohibited any political activity that was not directly sponsored by the state. At the same time, however, this military government lacked support and was deposed in 1937. President Estigarribia returned triumphantly from exile and remained in power until his death in 1940, as a result of a plane accident. Thereafter, Paraguay entered a period of even greater political instability, which led to the consolidation of the Colorado Party, supported by Argentina during the 1947 Revolution (Cardozo 153). This party unleashed an unprecedented wave of repression against political opponents who were either imprisoned or exiled. The internal struggle within the Colorado Party itself eventually culminated in the triumph of Federico Chaves (1881–1978) in 1949, who governed the country until 1954, when General Alfredo Stroessner came to power as a result of a coup d'état.

Given the cultural movement that began with the Chaco War, the end of the war marked the beginning of a new stage in Paraguayan cultural life. Due to the repression in the country, many Paraguayan intellectuals were forced to emigrate, the majority to Argentina. Buenos Aires became the center of dissemination of Paraguayan thought, and the best-known works of this period were created and published in exile. Although the historical genre continued to be cultivated, a new type of narrative fiction emerged, which brought with it numerous direct references to Paraguay. A leading exponent of this historical trend was Natalicio González (1897–1966). In his first essay, *El Paraguay eterno* [1935; Eternal Paraguay], he argues in favor of state socialism, while his book *Proceso de la formación de la cultura paraguaya* [1938; Process of the Cultural Formation of Paraguay] made him one of the great Paraguayan prose writers. He also published *Motivos de tierra escarlata* [1938; Motifs of Scarlet Landscape] and *El Estado servidor del hombre libre* [1960; The State, Servant of Free Men]. Another writer of this period was Justo Prieto (1897–1982), who, in addition to writing sociological essays, such as *Síntesis sociológica* [1944; Sociological Synthesis], attempted to provide a liberal interpretation of Paraguayan history through *Paraguay, la provincia gigante de las Indias* [1951; Paraguay, the Giant Province of the Indies].

One of the best-known post-war figures was Justo Pastor Benítez (1895–1967), who wrote historicosociological essays. All his work was produced in exile, his most famous being *Formación social del pueblo paraguayo* [1955; Social Formation of the Paraguayan People]. Certain writers of this period sought a solution to Paraguayan problems: Carlos Pastore, for example, in *La Lucha por la tierra en el Paraguay* [1949; Struggle for Land in Paraguay], believed that the solution to the problems of his country lay in agrarian issues, whereas Luis J. González (1912–1990) in *Paraguay, prisionero geopolítico* [1947; Paraguay, Geopolitical Prisoner] explored the evils of continuing to regard the Mediterranean as the sole point of reference. Within this historical genre, a new trend emerged that strove to be more objective in its interpretative analysis by attempting to reach the truth at all costs, as in the works of Julio César Chaves (1907–1989), Arturo Bray (1898–1974), Efraím Cardozo (1906–1973), and Hipólito Sánchez Quell (1907–1986). The Chaco War also gave rise to a form of testimonial literature, in which war veterans documented their experiences.

The 1950s saw the emergence of a group of intellectuals who met in the context of the journal *Alcor,* founded in 1955 by Rubén Bareiro Saguier (b. 1930) and Julio César Troche (b. 1927). Most of these writers had witnessed the violence unleashed during the civil war of 1947, and themes of love and death predominate in their work. Among the works of fiction that proliferated abroad during this period was *La babosa* [Sentimental Woman] by Gabriel Casaccia Bibolini, published in 1952. This novel, which lacks a specific protagonist, yet embodies profound social criticism, elicited an unenthusiastic, highly negative response in Asunción. Abroad, however, it met with considerable critical acclaim. In 1963 Gabriel Casaccia Bibolini was awarded the first prize by Kraft publishers for *La llaga* [The Wound]. This short novel combines two of Casaccia's main themes: the social and the psychological. The other Paraguayan writer who appeared on the international literary scene was Augusto Roa Bastos, whose novel *Hijo de hombre* [1959; *Son of Man,* 1965] won first prize in the Losada publishers' competition. The theme of the Chaco War is fully represented in this novel, which traces the history of Paraguay from the era of Independence until 1959. The second great novel by this author, *Yo el Supremo* [*I, the Supreme,* 1986], was published in 1974. Here, political and historical discourse is stripped of its temporal dimension and portrayed as the discourse of power.

The Paraguayan sociopolitical scenario of the past few decades has undoubtedly had a negative impact on the country's cultural development. Much of the literary production of this period has been published abroad, since the 1959–1989 dictatorship of Alfredo Stroessner cruelly punished anyone who dared operate outside the limits of his doctrine. The theme of persecution and repression is present in works such as *Rebelión después* [1970; Rebellion After] by Lincoln Silva (b. 1945), *Ojo por diente* [1973; An Eye for a Tooth] by Rubén Bareiro Saguier (b. 1930), and *Entrevista* [1978; Interview] by Rodrigo Díaz-Pérez (b. 1924).

As for the narrative produced within the country during this period, there are stories that touch on certain sociopolitical and cultural issues, as well as *costumbrista* tales. Leading writers of the period include José-Luis Appleyard (b. 1927), author of *Imágenes sin tierra* [1965; Landless Images]; Augusto Casola (b. 1944), who published *El laberinto* [1972; The Labyrinth]; Josefina Plá (1903–1999), author of *La mano en la tierra* [1963; Hand on the Earth]; Jorge Ritter (1907–1977), who wrote *El pecho y la espalda* [1962; Back and Breast]; and Carlos Zubizarreta (1904–1972), who published *Los grillos de la duda* [1966; The Shackles of Doubt]. The journal *Criterio* attracted a generation of poets, eager for freedom and knowledge, which became known as the "Grupo Criterio" (1966–1971). Leading members of the group included Juan Manuel Marcos (b. 1950), Emilio Pérez Chaves (b. 1950), and René Dávalos (1945–1968), while Lourdes Espínola (b. 1954), Nila Lópes (b. 1954), and Mabel Pedrozo (b. 1965) were some of the principal female poets. Despite the repression suffered by several of these intellectuals, internal literary production intensified in subsequent years, as did the denunciation of the longest and most brutal dictatorship in South America. Works such as *Celda 12* [1991; Cell #12] by Moncho Azuaga (b. 1953), *Los nudos del silencio* [1988; Knots of Silence] by Renée Ferrer (b. 1944), and *La isla sin mar* [1987; Island Without a Sea] by Juan Bautista Rivarola Matto (1933–1991) document the experience of Stroessner's dictatorship.

According to Guaraní tradition, the male was the sole depository of the knowledge of his tribe, and, consequently, poetry has always been a male attribute. Nevertheless, this idea began to change in the 1980s, which led to the emergence of a number of female writers besides Renée Ferrer, such as Neida Bonnet de Mendoça (b. 1933), Raquel Saguier (b. 1940), Sara Karlik (b. 1935), Lucy Mendonça de Spinzi (b. 1932), Milia Gayoso (b. 1962), Chiquita Barreto (b. 1947), Margot Ayala de Michelagnoli (b. 1935), Luisa Moreno de Gabaglio (b. 1949), Maybell Lebrón (b. 1923), and Dirma de Caraguti (b. 1922).

As mentioned earlier, poetry in Guaraní has been frequently composed by Paraguayan intellectuals, while prose in Guaraní was primarily used to express religious matters. However, there were no works of fiction in Guaraní until 1972, when Carlos Martínez Gamba (b. 1939) published *Amombeúta avañe'~eme* [I'm Going to Tell You a Story in Guaraní]; after this other writers began to write narrative works in Guaraní, such as Juan Rivarola Matto's (1933–1991) *Karai Réi oha'~aramo guare tuka'~ kañy* [1980; About the Time when Karai Rey Played Hide-and-Seek]. However, the first novel in Guaraní, *Kalaíto Pombero* [Calixto Pombero] by Tadeo Zarratea (b. 1947), was not published until 1981. Another of his works, *Araundú kaaty* [1989; Wisdom of the Forest], belongs to the testimonial genre of popular Paraguayan culture, while *Kásos Ahendu, ahai* [1989; I Listen and Write) by Rubén Rolandi is a collection of folk tales, known as "cases." The "cases," compiled by David A. Galeano Olivera in *Jakavere ypykue* [1989; The Jakavere Origins] (Meliá 237–39), belongs to the same category of folktale.

Nevertheless, Guaraní prose, by which we specifically mean literature written *in* Guaraní, would not emerge until even later. As Meliá notes, ignorance denied the possibility of discovering Guaraní texts until well into the twentieth century: "sólo hemos tenido conocimiento de la literatura guaraní indígena en este siglo, esto es, 400 años después del primer contacto con los guaraníes y cuando hacía más de tres siglos que se producían textos en lengua guaraní" (253) ("we are only familiar with the indigenous Guaraní literature of this century, that is, four hundred years after the first contact with the Guaraní, when texts in the Guaraní language had been produced for over three centuries"). In other words, the texts that had hitherto been produced in the Guaraní language reflected an alien culture. Western culture—particularly that of Spanish origin—had somehow been transcribed into the Guaraní language, although this written language lacked the philosophical values of its culture which had remained buried in that other text, that "texto primero" ("first text"), which is the oral tradition (Roa Bastos 15).

The German ethnologist, Curt Unkel (1883–1945), who was known by his Guaraní name, Nimuendajú Curt, was the first to record the philosophical-mythical texts of the Apapokúva-Guaraní: *Die Sagen von der Erschaffund und Vernichtung der Welt als Grundlagen der Religion der Apapocúva-Guaraní* (1914), translated into Spanish as *La leyenda de la creación del mundo* [The Legend of the Creation of the World]. This work is unusual in that, rather than being a mere transcription of a Guaraní text, it has been assimilated and retold by the author himself. At the same time it provides a description of Guaraní philosophy, hitherto unknown, whose religious basis was the word. Thus Guaraní religion is revealed as a religion of the word. In 1946 León Cadogan (1899–1973), through the texts of the Mbyá-Guaraní, highlighted the importance of the word in this culture. His best-known works are *Ayvu Rapyta* [1959; Mythical Texts of the Guairá], *Ywyrá ñeéry; fluye del árbol la palabra* [1970; The Word Flows from the Tree], and *La literatura de los guaraníes* [1965; Literature of the Guaraní]. Nimuendajú Curt and León Cadogan opened the doors to Guaraní literature; since then, several researchers have studied Guaraní culture, including Egon Schaden, Miguel A. Bartolomé, Pierre Clastres, and, more recently, Lorenzo Ramos, Benito Ramos, Antonio Martínez, José Antonio Perasso, Miguel Chase-Sardi, and Bartomeu Meliá.

The geopolitical factors that influenced the establishment of Asunción as a fort in 1537 continued to play a key role in its development as a cultural center. In the years following its independence, Paraguay grew internally, with its customs, traditions, legends, and rich language. Until the arrival of the airplane, the only route linking Asunción with the outside world was the train to Buenos Aires. Political implications aside, although the country's isolation delayed the economic and social development of the region, it also contributed to strengthening national identity and preserving the Guaraní language, of which Paraguayans of today are so proud.

Translation by Suzanne Stephens

Works Cited

Amaral, Raúl. 1968. "El novecentismo paraguayo." *Comentario* 15.61 (Buenos Aires): 29.

Cardozo, Efraím. 1965. *Breve historia del Paraguay.* Buenos Aires: Editorial Universitaria de Buenos Aires.

Guerra Vilaboy, Sergio. 1984. *Paraguay: de la independencia a la dominación imperialista, 1811–1870.* Havana: Editorial de Ciencias Sociales.

Guido y Spano, Carlos. 1911. "Nenia." *Poesías completas.* Buenos Aires: Maucci Hnos. 187–89.

Lotman, Jurij. 1977. *The Structure of the Artistic Text.* Trans. Gail Lenhoff and Ronald Vroom. Ann Arbor: University of Michigan.

Meliá, Bartomeu. 1992. *La lengua guaraní del Paraguay: historia, sociedad y literatura.* Madrid: Mapfre.

Mora Mérida, José Luis. 1973. *Historia social de Paraguay, 1600-1650.* Seville: Escuela de Estudios Hispanoamericanos.

Moreno, Fulgencio Ricardo. 1922. *La ciudad de Asunción.* Buenos Aires: J. Suarez.

Plá, Josefina. 1970. *Historia y catálogo del Museo de Bellas Artes.* Asuncion: Museo Nacional de Bellas Artes.

———. 1976. *Literatura paraguaya en el siglo XX.* Asuncion: Ediciones Comuneros.

———. 1985. *Españoles en la cultura del Paraguay.* Asuncion: Araverá.

Roa Bastos, Augusto. 1984. "La narrativa paraguaya en el contexto de la narrativa hispanoamericana actual." *Revista de crítica literaria latinoamericana* 9–10 (Lima): 7–21.

Romero, Roberto. 1988. *Dr. José Gaspar Rodríguez de Francia: ideólogo de la independencia del Paraguay.* Asuncion: A.R. Impresiones.

White, Richard Alan. 1978. *Paraguay's Autonomous Revolution, 1810–1840.* Albuquerque: University of New Mexico Press.

Williams, John Hoyt. 1979. *The Rise and Fall of the Paraguayan Republic, 1800–1870.* Austin: University of Texas Press.

CHAPTER 52

PORTO ALEGRE
CULTURAL CENTER OF SOUTHERN BRAZIL

Rita Terezinha Schmidt

In addition to being the capital of the southernmost state of Brazil, the state of Rio Grande do Sul, the city of Porto Alegre is strategically located at an equal distance between the two largest Brazilian metropoles–Rio de Janeiro and São Paulo–and the River Plate capitals–Buenos Aires and Montevideo. This peculiarity of place, with its effect on historical developments, inscribes a unique landscape whose shape mixes space and metaphor in a rich web of relations, which, signaling a zone that is regionally marked by geographical and political connections, also accumulates the symbolic signs of its historical process and cultural times. As a marginal space determined by national limits and therefore at a distance from the metropolitan axis of the country, this city constitutes an "other," with its difference defined in relation to the monopolizing and homogeneous center. As a border space and therefore a transit zone and point of contact between important points of neighboring countries, the city itself is configured as a passage. This space of superimposition destabilizes its own marginal condition and forges an oscillating image of the city that resists totalization; it is internally crossed and strained by the continuous dislocation of similarity and difference.

Inasmuch as the margin/boundary image points to the contingencies and sociabilities that are divided in layers of memory and that compose the constitutive traits of the city's identity, it can be thought of as a kind of empirical model for the city's setting. To make its meanings emerge in the reconstitution of the material, intellectual, and aesthetic construction of the community presupposes a historicizing of this model in terms of its context of production, which in turn implies showing how to configure the forms of that making in terms of the construction of the city as a social and cultural space. In the words of Hayden White: "A specifically historical inquiry is born less of the necessity to establish that certain events occurred than of the desire to determine what certain events might mean for a given group, society, or culture's conception of its present tasks and future prospects" (487). To historicize is to bring up the problem of the narrative, since the formation of an account presupposes the processing of the real into a discursive reality, which is the product of a narrative act on the part of a subject who, for his/her part, selects, organizes, and interprets the oral and written data from his/her own position, that is, from his/her own insertion in space and time, as well as language, gender, class, ethnicity, and nationality. In other words, the subject of the narrative is necessarily conditioned by the partiality of his/her viewpoint, with a resulting account that is always relative, provisional, and approximate. Therefore, the act of narrativizing the city offers as many readings as can be made of it. This means that the referential city dissolves into a discursive network where as Roger Chartier well puts it: "Le réel prend ainsi un sens nouveau: ce qui est réel, en effet, n'est pas (ou pas seulement) la réalité visée par le texte, mais la manière même

dont il la vise, dans l'historicité de sa production et la stratégie de son écriture" (1983, 304) ("Reality thus takes on a new meaning. What is real, in fact, is not [or is not only] the reality that the text aims at, but the very manner in which it aims at it in the historic setting of its production and the strategy used in its writing" [1988, 44]). Starting from these notions, I wish to propose an empirical model for the representation of the margin/border city as a narrative paradigm of the city-text.

The configuration of Porto Alegre is inseparable from that which led the city for two centuries to become distinguished in terms of local and regional historical processes, whose confluences and political clashes determined the development of its social landscape, its ways of being, and its values, in short, the cultural environment of the community. From the eighteenth-century Colonial period onward, the city's life was predicated on the conditions of insularity of a community with a transplanted and doubly decentralized culture–from its European origins and from the dominant axis of the country. An added complication was its insertion into a space of geographical, political, and linguistic borders which fix the contrasting limits between the two Iberian cultures–the Portuguese and the Spanish–and which, so to speak, suggest a vertically imposed nationality. Thus it is emblematic of a region whose imaginary was developed in the shadow of a collective and conflicting feeling of belonging to a land almost apart, an island in the middle of three countries. The city therefore pursued its legitimation under the influence of opposite movements: local versus national, regional versus cosmopolitan, autonomy versus belonging, and Brazilianness versus Latin Americanism.

It is curious that the city grew up at the meeting of waters, a sign of its transitoriness *par excellence* but a fact which by force of political necessity was converted into an auxiliary agent of its founding. Located on the banks of the Guaíba River, a link joining two large navigable rivers–the Jacuí, which receives the waters of the Taquari, Caí, Gravataí, and Rio dos Sinos rivers, and the Lagoa dos Patos, which empties into the Atlantic Ocean 250 kilometers to the south–Porto Alegre marked the provisional camp of Azorian immigrants–established at the tip of the peninsula (today the central area of the city)–who were abandoned to their own fate, en route to the Jesuit missions in the northwest of the state. It was set up in a period of bloody disputes between the Portuguese and Spanish Crowns for the possession of the lands of the River Plate. With the signing of the Treaty of Madrid (1750), which determined the exchange of the Colônia do Sacramento, founded by Portuguese on the banks of the River Plate, facing the city of Buenos Aires, for the missions under Spanish control, it became imperative to hasten the occupation of the interior by the swiftest and most accessible route: the Jacuí River. In 1752, Azorian couples from Santa Catarina arrived at the tip of the peninsula, where they began preparing to go up-river. With the failure to demarcate territorial limits and the added failure of the Treaty of Madrid, the islanders were forced to remain there, where they improvised housing and started small businesses, taking advantage of the natural port located at the tip of the peninsula.

The elevation of the small settlement, called Porto dos Casais (Port of the Couples), to the status of village and administrative seat of what was then called the Continent of Rio Grande de São Pedro occurred for military reasons, that is, because of the need to contain the advances of Spaniards who had taken the village of Rio Grande to the south and threatened to take the village of Rio Pardo. The fortification erected on the highest point of the peninsula on the Guaíba River, which joined the two villages by the Lagoa dos Patos and the Jacuí River, respectively, was of vital importance for maintaining the Portuguese dominion in the region. Porto dos Casais was thus formed as a geographical center point between the two conflicting borders, being formed, in the words of the historian Francisco R. de Macedo (b. 1921), on the "esquina do continente de São Pedro" (1982, 48) ("corner of the continent of São Pedro"). The establishing of its limits and the first public services took place with the founding of the Parish of São Francisco de Chagas on 26 March 1772, a date officially recognized by the Historical and Geographical Institute of Rio Grande do Sul as being the date of the foundation of the city.

A year later, the governor, who was from Lisbon, transferred the seat of his administration from Viamão to that parish, giving it the name of Porto Alegre, a name that evoked the city of the same name in Alto Além Tejo, in Portugal (Laytano 1974, 50). Other Portuguese immigrants joined the original group of Azorian couples, thus consolidating the political power of the Portuguese descendants; their importance on the local scene thus favored the development of a culture based on Portuguese values, something important to the national formation. The influence of the Portuguese colonizer is visibly present, even today, in the southern Rio Grande's folklore, mainly in the *gaucho* dances like the *chula*, which comes from the Minho and the Douro regions, and the *maçarico*. Specifically of Azorian tradition are the *pezinho* and the *chimarrita* dances, as well as songs like the *prenda minha*. The vocabulary of the local idiom, for its part, incorporates many words of Azorian origin, such as *bandana* (sheep), *peão* (ranch-hand), *bombacha* (wide pants of the *gaucho*), *obrigação* (in the sense of family), *computo* (to compute), and *hostar* (host) (Laytano 1975, 21). The Azorians valued the traditional family structure and maintained a strong religious feeling, manifested in the religious processions on the occasion of the celebrations of the Holy Ghost and Easter, held on the square built on the Alto da Praia. But they also cultivated secular amusements, such as the games of the carnival, like the rubber ball filled with perfumed water and flour, that now have a long tradition in the city. Particularly fond of theater and music, they built the Casa da Comédia in 1794, where farces and pantomimes were put on, besides plays originating from Portuguese folklore, like *Inês de Castro*, *A Princesa Magalona*, and the *Auto da Lusitânia* (Ferreira 1956, 3). In 1803, the building was renovated and renamed Casa da Ópera. Using common sense, one would think that the peaceful nature of the Azorians would have calmed the over-excited spirit of the *gaucho caudillo* from the River Plate. If one considers, however, that the region lived through five revolutions in a little more than 100 years, such assumptions could be put into question.

In the first decades of the nineteenth century, the local population, made up of Portuguese and slaves, was increased by immigrants of German, English, Italian, and French origin, who devoted themselves to the most varied kinds of work. The society's elite, however, was composed of officers of the Portuguese Guard and the Portuguese merchants responsible for the expansion of business in the port, which received ships from the River Plate and from Europe and thus was the port with the largest market in southern Brazil, according to reports of the period. With the independence of Brazil in 1822, this village, a seat of the government, with approximately 10,000 inhabitants, gained the status of a city, which provided incentives to investment in the area of urbanization. The traits of Portuguese Colonial-style architecture were visible signs of prosperity and today make up a significant part of the visual cultural patrimony of the city. One example is the customs complex: the building whose popular name was Casa da Junta, where the annex of the Casa Civil of the state government operates; the oldest church, the Igreja das Dores, with its large stairway by the Rua da Praia; the hospital Santa Casa de Misericórdia, inaugurated in 1826; and the oldest residential building, called Solar dos Câmaras, completed in 1818 and today a site for recitals, exhibitions, and cultural events. Details of the city's appearance did not escape the foreign eye. The French botanist Auguste de Saint Hilaire, who traveled around the region from 1820 to 1821, referred in his book *Journey to Rio Grande do Sul* to the tall, sturdy, and lively men whom he found here, the boldness of the women, who, contrary to the women from the interior, talked without embarrassment to the men at social gatherings, the well-built and furnished houses, and the great bustle of people on the Rua da Praia.

The instability and isolation that characterized the organization of the physical framework of the city had repercussions on the unfolding of a sociopolitical process aligned with the liberal ideas of the Enlightenment that had spread around the world from the middle of the eighteenth century onward, in the wake of the signing of the Declaration of Independence in the United States in 1776 and the outbreak of the French Revolution in 1789. In Brazil, these ideas, associated with the action of the Latin American liberators Bolívar, San Martin, and Artigas, were received in a special way in Rio Grande do Sul, above all in the capital, where republican propaganda intensified. With the establishment of the press in 1827 and the publication of the first newspaper, *Diário de Porto Alegre*, the city watched its vocation for militancy in ideas awaken. It is important to emphasize the "surto extraordinário, dificilmente igualado, no mesmo período, em outras regiões brasileiras da imprensa" (César 1956, 89) ("extraordinary emergence, hardly equaled during the same period in other regions of Brazil, of the press"), mainly in the decade following. The press was committed to arousing the provincial consciousness, while it promoted a debate on ideas about the economic policy imposed by the center which was regarded as a sign of indifference on the part of the imperial government about the fate of the province. The city that still lived under the threat of war on the River Plate border began to experience the turbulent days of growing resistance to the central government. The thirty-five newspapers that proliferated in the city (Franco 1988, 215) classified people into republicans (or *farrapos*) or into imperials (or legalists). The outbreak of the Farroupilha Revolution in 1835, the greatest civil war in the history of the country, led to the aggravation of an aggressive nationalism, which, if in the recent past had been a response to the threat of the

River Plate, at that moment responded to the imperial power of the center.

In the understanding of the *farrapos*, Rio Grande do Sul had been converted into an exploited dependency of the empire, for besides supplying soldiers, horses, and food during the frontier wars, it had to deal with the losses resulting from the organization of its agricultural and cattle-raising modes of production without receiving any compensation from the central government. The situation grew worse with the high taxes on salt, a product indispensable to the southern jerked-beef, while the River Plate area, its chief competitor in that market, paid a low salt tariff. According to the historian Sandra Pesavento, "por trás deste tratamento preferencial ao produto estrangeiro, que forçava a baixa de preço do artigo rio-grandense, manifestavam-se os interesses do centro e norte do país, que queriam comprar o alimento para seus escravos a baixo custo" (1984, 38) ("behind this preferential treatment to the foreign product, which forced the low price for the Rio Grande product, the interests of the center and north of the country, which wanted to buy the food for its slaves at low cost, were manifest"). At the time, the imperials accused local politicians of conspiring with Uruguayans and Argentineans to separate the province from the rest of the country, since Bento Gonçalves, one of the *farroupilha* leaders, was accused by the governor, Fernando Braga, of keeping counsel with Juan Lavalleja, who fought in Uruguay against Oribe (Lazzaroto 65). In fact, the *farroupilhas* could always count on the port of Montevideo for their business (Flores 84), which, in a way, directly exposed them to the influence of republican and federalist ideas that also circulated in the River Plate region, particularly in Uruguay, which was struggling for autonomy from the Spanish government.

From the viewpoint of the intellectual development of the city, the internal struggle favored the circulation of ideas which came either from the River Plate, through books (translated into Spanish) about eighteenth-century liberal ideology or through politicians coming from Italy, like Giuseppe Garibaldi, Luigi Rosseti, and Tito Zambecari (César 1956, 70). During the ten-year conflict, the city was under siege three times and lived the horror of the trenches and the lack of food, but not even these conditions could reduce it to a mere battlefield. The atmosphere of civic exaltation was an opportunity for the emergence of the first local poets, many of them inspired to sing of the heroic deeds of the armed rebels, others to proclaim the order of the empire. As it could not be otherwise, the passion that divided the city into political factions was also extended to the intellectuals who were aligned with the two groups: the imperials, a smaller group belonging to the ruling class of Portuguese descent, and the *farroupilhas*, a much larger group but with less influence on the sociopolitical scene. Following the line of historical continuity under Portuguese domination, the imperial group effectively left its mark on the intellectual life of the city. The first book printed on local presses was in 1834, *Poesias oferecidas às senhoras rio-grandenses* [Poems Offered to Rio-Grande Ladies], by Delfina Benigna da Cunha (1791–1857). In many of her panegyric sonnets, whose topics were independence, Benigna da Cunha conveys a feeling of nationality obsessively based on the idealized image of the emperor, equated with the values of reason and order in the aristocratic tradition of the Portuguese Arcadians. Although her work displays a thematic diversity not reducible to one political current, it is undeniable that her political ideology hindered the development of a view capable

of articulating a critical perspective on the colonial status–contrary to the Arcadian poets of Minas Gerais, such as Alvarenga Peixoto (1748–1798) and Silva Alvarenga (1749–1814).

Despite the inhospitable and generally uncultured environment of the province, the post-Revolutionary period witnessed a series of initiatives which successively established the city as the irradiating center of culture in the south of the country. The São Pedro Theater, situated on the Praça da Matriz and whose construction had been suspended because of the revolution, was grandly and ceremoniously inaugurated in 1859. This neo-Classical project had been ordered by the court, which designated the architect Felipe de Normann to build it. Its original beauty recovered, the theater offered the best acoustics in the country, in addition to being a theater that was uniquely open during the day with recitals of serious and popular music and artistic exhibitions. Literature, for its part, received a substantial push in this period with the publication, in 1847, of what is considered the first Rio Grande do Sul novel, *A divina pastora* [The Divine Shepherdess] by José Antonio do Vale Caldre e Fião (1821–1876), a work also evoked for being the first literary representation of Porto Alegre. The novel has a Romantic plot against the background of a real historical situation, the war of the *farrapos*. In this scenario of epic dimensions, the novelist does not linger on the rural landscape around the city but, more importantly, draws on the cartography of a provincial Porto Alegre in which notes on social habits and customs are added to the minute descriptions of the city space. The novel effectively describes the social symbol that would receive the name *gaucho*, a prototype of the rural worker and fighter, idealized in the collective consciousness as the repository of audacity, rusticity, virility, and hospitality, and who a decade later would receive the epithet of "monarch of the grassy hills" in the fiction of José de Alencar (1829–1877). In this sense, the novel not only registers "o ingresso do gaúcho no território da ficção brasileira" (Chaves 15) ("the entrance of the *gaucho* into the territory of Brazilian fiction") but from the ideological point of view inaugurates one of the most constant traits of the Rio Grande do Sul novel–regionalism–even if the regionalism of Caldre e Fião is shown in an embryonic form when compared to the more elaborate regionalism of the writers at the turn of the century, like João Simões Lopes Neto (1865–1916) and Alcides Maya (1878–1944). In the national literature, it is important to note that regionalism would only be consolidated in the 1870s as a dominant literary project, which puts Caldre e Fião in the position of the founder of Brazilian regionalism (César 1979).

From the generation of Caldre e Fião, an urban elite appeared that was responsible for an active literary press which made an important contribution to the intellectual development of the city and the province in general in the second half of the nineteenth century, particularly in the sense of disseminating foreign ideas and establishing limits for the directions of local and regional literature. The pioneering newspaper, *O Guayba*, appeared in 1856, and the exponents of the first generation of Romantic writers of the province gravitated around it. Besides promoting local writers, *O Guayba* offered in its pages transcribed passages of European authors, a revealing indication not only of the predominant taste of the period (Ferreira 1975, 17), but mainly of the desire of the local intellectuals to establish affiliations with that literature as a form of legitimizing local production. Among the writers of this generation, the poet Rita Barém de Melo

(1840–1868) should be mentioned, as her work *Sorrisos e prantos* [Smiles and Tears], posthumously published in 1868, establishes her as "uma das intérpretes mais luminosas da poesia brasileira" (César 1956, 160) ("one of the most luminous writers of Brazilian poetry"). A perceptive reader of the great Portuguese and French Romantic poets (like Camões, Almeida Garret, Lamartine, and Victor Hugo, among others), Barém de Melo did not forget her Brazilian contemporaries, Manuel Antônio Álvares de Azevedo (1831–1852), Antônio Gonçalves Dias (1823–1864), and Casimiro José Marques de Abreu (1839–1860), whose words appear in epigraphs that operate in the manner of mottoes for many of her poems. With a lyricism sung in a sonorous, light, and graceful tone, the poet sings the city, conveying the appeal that the local landscape arouses in her visual sensibility in elegiac verses, which evoke the sensuous experience of a place and a time, as in the first lines of the long poem "Uma tarde no Guaíba" ["An Afternoon on the Guaíba"]:

Era uma tarde encantada,
Que tinha a face espelhada
Nas águas vindas do mar:
Era uma tarde de rosas,
Passavam brisas queixosas
Com prantos do cismar.

It was an enchanted afternoon
Whose face was mirrored
in the waters from the sea:
It was an afternoon of roses,
Lamenting breezes wafted
Like the weeping of daydreams.

(in Melo 1998, 76)

The pioneering and unifying quality of the work developed by the group from *O Guayba* had consequences in the realm of the longest-lasting literary association in imperial Brazil, which was the *Sociedade Partenon Literário* (Parthenon Literary Society), proof of a growing cultural vitality of the city in the period from 1868 to 1885. Caldre e Fião, its first president, and Apolinário Porto Alegre (1844–1904), Múcio Scóevola Lopes Teixeira (1858–1926), and Luciana de Abreu (1847–1880), among others, gave the society a profile aligned with a liberal set of ideas in the tradition of the Enlightenment, from which the association defined its broad plan action.

Besides revitalizing the local literary productivity through contests, readings, and dramatic performances, the Parthenon created a free evening school and a library with more than 6000 volumes, which made possible the pioneering initiative of bibliographical research and the collection of Rio Grande do Sul legends and traditions. In this debate forum, its members established a fertile context for the exchange of ideas around controversial issues like the abolition of slavery, republican principles, women's rights—in short, the democratization of culture—thus promoting the city to the position of a place where values of civilization and democracy were put into practice. In these debates, accomplishments of Madame de Stäel, Madame de Sevigné, and George Sand were alluded to in the context of the emancipatory ideas of the English philosopher John Stuart Mill, a reader of Mary Wollstonecraft, who was seen as one of the early ideologues of the feminist movement. One of the notable things about the Parthenon was undoubtedly the integration of theory and practice. Frequently, the sponsorship of dramatic performances had the aim of raising funds used for purchasing the freedom of slaves

(Hessel 3). For the first time on its debate platform, a woman gave a speech in Rio Grande do Sul. Speaking for the emancipation of women, of their access to knowledge, and their place in literature, Luciana de Abreu aroused some commotion among the members, the majority of whom were male, but the Parthenon conferred on her the homage of the society, published in the *Revista do Partenon Literário*, in its December 1873 and June 1875 issues. This periodical, supported by the association, was the vehicle of publication for its political and aesthetic ideas. Circulating throughout the state for ten years with only a few interruptions, it was responsible for "pela unificação do processo literário sul-rio-grandense, até então caracterizado pela presença de manifestações esparsas e isoladas" (Baumgarten 71) ("the unification of the Rio Grande do Sul literary process, until then characterized by the presence of sparse and isolated manifestations").

In effect, the literary production of the writers assembled round the Parthenon determined the two aesthetic trends that guided the later development of literature in the south: the Romantic, tied to erudite forms of Brazilian Romanticism, under the influence of Gonçalves Dias and Casimiro de Abreu, both of whom had a close relation to Iberian peninsular lyricism, and the regionalist, which incorporated local color, the linguistic peculiarities and literary use of the southern type. If, on the one hand, regionalism expressed the valuing of the local, the basis of the Romantic movement that dominated the national scenario, on the other, it also represented political separatism that had always existed and that was manifest in several regional rebellions, from the regency period to the outbreak of the war with Paraguay (Zilberman 46). But it was not in this direction that Apolinário Porto Alegre (one of the creators of the Parthenon and one of the early voices of local intellectuals in terms of articulating the integration of *gaucho* Rio Grande do Sul literature into the larger context of national literary production) aimed his critical work. In the first critical essay of breadth published in the south that focuses on a particular literary work, "José de Alencar–Estudo biográfico" ["José de Alencar–A Biographical Study"], published in the *Revista do Partenon Literário* in 1873 and 1874, Apolinário Porto Alegre set up a dialogue with the great themes of the literary critics of central Brazil: the question of nationality and the importance of originality, related to the valuing of the uniqueness of the means, as a form of affirming the independence of Brazilian from Portuguese literature. In an arrogant tone, the article presents an anthropologically based argument for the literary use of a Brazilian language, in which the neologisms and regional terms constitute defining criteria for a distinctly national literature.

In this period, during which Porto Alegre began to leave behind its Colonial atmosphere and flourish as an urban center, cultural development responded to the slow socio-economic transformations and an emerging elite. Even in the difficult times of the city's daily life during the War of the Triple Alliance, the city resisted inertia. The historian Athos Damasceno Ferreira (1975, 15) notes the existence of ten literary associations from 1868 to 1880, in addition to the recreational and cultural societies associated with German and Italian immigrants, who cultivated in a special way the taste for serious and popular music. That is why there were frequent concerts with artists generally going from the center of the country out toward Montevideo and Buenos Aires; Porto Alegre, as a zone of passage, constituted thereby an obligatory stop on the itinerary to the River Plate. On the stage of the Teatro São Pedro, performances of operas and important plays from Europe were staged. In other ways as well, geographical insularity did not impose serious limitation on the city's everyday life. As the sixth Brazilian city to offer the services of the Telephone Company (and the first one outside the residential area of the Emperor Dom Pedro II), Porto Alegre established its links with the rest of the world in 1886.

From the turn of the twentieth century to the early decades, the city underwent a new phase in its flowering, beginning with the transformation of its urban appearance under the impact of the ideology of the Rio-Grande Republican Party (inspired by philosophicopolitical Positivism) which had taken power in the Revolution of 1893. Comte's Positivism, conceived in the European context out of a mature capitalism, was transplanted and adjusted to the local and regional reality, guaranteeing the doctrinal basis for carrying out a project of industrialization and rationalization of production; the objective of this was to get the city and the state into the rhythm of modernity, following the model of industrialized capitalist countries and their large urban centers. As a result of this project, a new urban-industrial order was progressively consolidated, and the city (as capital) began to be the center from which values spread, according to the bourgeois maxims of order and progress. The construction of a cultural imaginary was imperative; it projected the image of the ideal city as "higiênica, bela, ordenada. A Porto Alegre dos sonhos, culta e civilizada, progressista e industriosa" (Pesavento 1994, 139) ("sanitary, beautiful, ordered. The Porto Alegre of dreams, cultured and civilized, progressive and industrious"). The image of grandeur, corresponding to the concept of a powerful and all-present state, appears in the official buildings of the government, all of which followed the style of Positivist architecture, whose eclectic forms recreated a synthesis of European culture. It is estimated that three hundred architects came from Europe—no surprise, given the proliferation of buildings in the city center. The School of Engineering, founded in 1897, the second college of what would later come to be the Federal University of Rio Grande do Sul, was the first Positivist building to be erected. The Public Library and the Positivist Temple itself are among the most representative of the period. (See **Figure 1**.)

The visible signs of the city's growth, for their part, determined the organization of space and the enlarging of the urban perimeter. The Parque da Redenção, an area of 700,000 square meters in the heart of the city, was transformed into a main center, with its numerous gardens, bullfight arena, and velodrome. Seat of the International Exhibition of 1901, the park impressed its visitors, including foreigners, with the audacity of its pavilions, artificial waterfalls, restaurants, and theater (Macedo 1973, 107). Thirty-four years later, the same park would be the setting for one of the most memorable events of the city's history: the Centennial Farroupilha Revolution Exhibition, visited by a million people. The exhibition proposed to show the country the strength of the state economy, no longer restricted to agriculture and live stock-raising, as well as to reinforce the integration of the state into the national consciousness. From September to December, the park (renamed Parque Farroupilha) was transformed into a fantasy scene, with theaters and casinos built in the architectural style then in vogue—Art-Deco—with six times more lighting than all of the streets in the city. (See **Figure 2**.)

Amidst the socioeconomic transformations that altered the shape of the city, the street gained a new dimension, becoming the stage where "o espetáculo burguês do 'viver em cidades'"

Figure 1.

Photograph of the Public Library of Porto Alegre. (Archive of the author)

(Pesavento 1991, 44) [the bourgeois spectacle of 'living in cities' was held]. Bars, cafés, and cinemas proliferated, especially around the city center. The Rua da Praia became a showcase for the prosperity of the elite, for whom the ritual of *footing* (jogging) became the basic condition of affirming social status. In one night of 1936, on the brightly lit and colorful "little Broadway," as it was called, a film premiered in great style: Charlie Chaplin's *Modern Times*. But it was not only on the screen that modern times were discerned. On the horizon, over the waters of the Guaíba, the Zeppelin on its Rio de Janeiro-Buenos Aires route could be seen, as could the descent of the hydroplanes of Varig Airlines. In 1938, in the São Pedro Theater, there were unforgettable nights with the pianist Artur Rubenstein, as well as shows with nationally famous artists, such as Noel Rosa, Francisco Alves, and Pixinguinha. Porto Alegre already had a symphonic orchestra, the OSPA, the second oldest orchestra in uninterrupted performing in the country.

The city then took on the appearance of a metropolis and channeled its critical expression into the daily press, where cultural journalism became an instrument of intervention in the public sphere, mediating the conflicts and affiliations among the local intellectuals. In an environment where the borders between artistic and political creation were always closely related, one expected that political stands were part of the cultural and aesthetic debate. In the period following the Federalist Revolution of 1893, separatism was made official as the program of the government that had assumed power, and this set off a strong reaction in local political and intellectual

Figure 2.

Photograph of the Theatro São Pedro, Porto Alegre.
(Archive of the author)

circles. The radicalization of difference once more called attention to the question of belonging, which, from the point of view of nationality, encompassed two opposing perspectives: the segregationist, nourished by a feeling rooted in subalterity and ostracism vis-à-vis the political and cultural practices of the center, and the integrationist, which presupposed associating with the defining values of national unity. It was in the pages of the newspapers *A República, O Rio Grande Independente, A Federação,* the *Correio do Povo,* and *O Diário de Notícias* that the critical discourse reconverted the regionalism of a separatist type into a cohesive element of nationality, starting from the understanding that peculiarities of the popular and regional cultures were presented as ways of constructing the autonomy of a national culture.

Under the strong impact of the scientific ideas in fashion at the time, the theories formulated by Comte, Taine, Buckle, and especially Spencer, critical essay writing reached its maturity in the work of Alcides Maya (1878–1943). Directly refuting separatism, as editor of *A República* and as writer of *O Rio Grande Independente,* Maya raised the level of thought on literary nationalism, establishing a controversial dialogue with the ideas defended by important critics largely responsible for the renewal of national thought at the turn of the century, such as Araripe Junior (1848–1911), Tobias Barreto (1840–1882), and especially Silvio Romero (1851–1914). If Maya ratified the principles that founded Romero's explanation of the cultural formation of Brazil as being the result of the milieu,

the social environment, and the racial fusion from which the national type emerged, he was opposed to Romero's critical judgements in relation to the Romantics José de Alencar and Castro Alves (1847–1871), and to Machado de Assis (1839–1908). The progressive distancing of orthodoxy with respect to the application of scientific concepts to literary phenomena, and, consequently, the repudiation of the reigning biographism, which is at the base of Maya's emphasis on the contribution of the Romantic authors to the nationalizing process of Brazilian literature, conferred on his thought a critical depth that made possible the understanding of the relation of Machado's work within the national context, from an absolutely original point of view, in which he combined psychological approach and comparative method. With his work *Machado de Assis–algumas notas sobre o humor* [Machado de Assis: Some Notes on Humor] in 1912 Maya's name became nationally renowned, a fact which would later guarantee him a seat in the Brazilian Academy of Letters. As the first Rio Grande do Sul critic to be known outside the region, Maya enriched a discourse that decentered hardened hegemonies and made viable a dialectical exegesis of the center and margin. On the one hand, he fiercely contested reductive nativism, while preserving his loyalty to his southern roots. On the other hand, he postulated the universalization of Rio Grande do Sul thought, without, however, losing an awareness of the conditions of a transplanted and peripheral culture, in the double sense of a national and regional culture. Nevertheless, it is important to point out that in his discourse there was a constant dialogue with France. The acceptance of the models of French culture, in obvious opposition to the dominant Portuguese fashion was a way to legitimize local production, since the French, in his view, offered the means of access to universal culture.

The dialectic of fascination and repulsion vis-à-vis the influx of European cultures that nourished the ambivalent positions on the autonomy of Brazilian literature was always inscribed in a contradictory movement of nationalization and internationalization–thus, in some ways, reinforcing the idea of a center. In the south, the center represented a matrix of influences and models, first of Portuguese culture, then of French and also German cultures. In cultural journalism, one should mention the role of Carlos von Koseritz (1834–1890), a member of the German militia hired to help Brazilians arm against the dictator Rosas, who ended up living in Porto Alegre and played an important role in articulating ideas "naturalmente impregnadas de alemanismo" (César 1956, 252) ("naturally impregnated with Germanism"). He was the great disseminator, in the south, of the works of Tobias Barreto of the Recife School, another Germanist with whom he shared the ideas of critical scienficism as well as enthusiasm about his culture of origin (presented as advantageous compared to French culture). Through his political-cultural journalism, he won an audience all over the state: "para os intelectuais nativos, o publicista parecia o mensageiro mais autorizado de todo o saber europeu; para os habitantes da região colonial alemã, católicos ou protestantes, era o patrício que lhes falava, na língua da origem, de coisas inatingíveis ou simplesmente pitorescas" (César 1956, 254) [for the native intellectuals, the journalist seemed like the most authorized messenger of all European thought; for the inhabitants of the German colonial region, Catholics or Protestants, he was the fellow-countryman who spoke to them, in their language of origin, of unattainable or simply picturesque things]. In this newspaper *A Gazeta de Porto*

Alegre, he made public his extensive research on the Rio Grande do Sul song collections, quoting verses that Sílvio Romero would incorporate in *Cantos Populares do Brazil* [1897; Popular Songs of Brazil]. In 1883 he founded a German-language newspaper *Neue Deutsche Zeitung*, which soon had wide circulation in the area settled by German immigrants and lasted until the 1940s. A sharp observer, brilliant in his play of ideas, he developed in his essays a genre classified by himself as *kulturhistoriker*. With the so-called "generation of the thirties" an urban literature emerged, in which the legacy of the city was reshaped and brought up to date in an imaginary that definitively broke with the Romantic and provincial image of the turn of the century. In 1935, three important works were published: *Os ratos* [The Rats], by Dyonélio Machado (1895–1985); *A ronda dos anjos sensuais* [The Rounds of the Sensual Angels], by Reynaldo Moura (1900–1965); and *Caminhos cruzados* [*Crossroads*], by Érico Veríssimo (1905–1975). In these novels, the city's geography is represented as problematic seen from the angle of its political implications and social consequences: the dislocation and progressive decline of a ruling class of rural origin, the rise of a new urban bourgeoisie, as well as the social stratification resulting from an economic model that promoted crime in the slums that rapidly grew in the outskirts of the city. The image of city is associated here with the local, but is not reduced to the effect of a localism, which implies that it defines the new order of the "modern city," whose context is aligned to the urban social landscape of Brazilian novels of the thirties which are set in Rio de Janeiro, São Paulo, or Belo Horizonte.

In the following year, 1936, *Poemas da minha cidade*, by Athos Damasceno Ferreira (1902–1975), was published, a poetic landmark in the same transformations signaled by the novelists. Here, the eye of the poet captures the gap between the city of today and the city of the past, imaginatively reconstructed by affective memory. The streets, roads, and alleys become the stations of the cross of the poet, who walks through them with the weariness of one who meditates "em solidão, sobre a Paixão e Morte de Porto Alegre de outrora, extinta e sepultada em nome de uma pretensa modernidade" [in solitude, on the Passion and Death of a former Porto Alegre, extinct and buried in the name of a false modernity] (Papaleo 103):

Que é dos poetas que, num dia, ó velha praça morta,
embriagaste com o filtro amável dos teus luares,
das tuas sombras cariciosas,
dos teus silêncios confidentes?

És um deserto só . . . Ninguém mais te procura!
Nem sequer o fantasma andejo da saudade
Vem percorrer, à noite, as tuas alamedas. . . .

What has become of the poets who, one day, old dead plaza,
you made drunk on the friendly filter of your moonlights,
on your caressing shadows,
on your trusting silences?

You are a vast desert alone . . . Nobody looks for you anymore!
Not even the roving ghost of homesickness
comes to walk down your avenues, at night. . . .

The realization of loss facing an urban scene, one that mirrors the ever more accelerated changes in social life, contributes to a new view of the Rio Grande do Sul past in prose fiction–a view whose focus is no longer a synchronic one on the farroupilha past, converted by the regionalist view into the privileged theme of a fiction with patriotic traits that looked back to the first literary experiments of Caldre e Fião, but instead on a diachronic take on a warrior past, whose epic strength is evoked as a form of combating "o esquecimento provocado pelo silêncio dos brasileiros sobre o seu passado de lutas, na conquista do território e no trabalho da civilização" (Chiappini 100) ("the forgetfulness caused by the silence of Brazilians about their past of fighting, the conquest of territory, and the work of civilization"). It is based on the argument (extended to the realm of historical formation and development) that Érico Veríssimo sketched about southern history in his work *O tempo e o vento* [Time and the Wind], composed of the trilogy *O continente* [The Continent], *O retrato* [The Portrait], and *O arquipélago* [The Archipelago], written between 1949 and 1962; this covers a 200-year span of the history of Rio Grande do Sul, from its origins in the Guarani war, even before its incorporation by the Portuguese Crown, to the end of the dictatorship of Getúlio Vargas in 1945, a period which roughly corresponds to the beginning of the political decline of the state on the national scene.

The diachronic line of this work is punctuated by successive generations of the Terra Cambará family, as the destiny of each of them is interwoven with the events of the decisive periods of local history: the frontier fighting, the *Farroupilha* War, the war with Paraguay, the Revolutions of 1893 and 1930. The rise and fall of the Terra Cambará, in whose roots the indigenous and Portuguese are mingled (resulting in the gaucho type), is thus intertwined with the history of the southern continent. If, on the one hand, the thematic axis of history is inscribed in the orbit of the large landowners, holders of power, on the other it is evident that the narrative program of the work juxtaposes the ruling elite and marginalized groups, like the blacks, the ranch-workers, and distinct groups of immigrants, who appear in the composition of the social spectrum and who activate by their presence a critical position vis-à-vis the process of the racial and social formation of the southern (and ultimately all) Brazilian society. Considered Érico Veríssimo's most important work, *O tempo e o vento* figures among the ten most recognized and valued works of Brazilian culture, according to a survey made by the magazine *Veja* in 1994. Because of criticism focusing on the first part of *O continente*, the work was taken, in a restrictive way, as representing the regional expression of Rio Grande do Sul literature. As a whole, however, *O tempo e o vento* problematizes the heroic version of official history, calling attention to the limits of the ideology that legitimated the structure of power and the established order. In this way, Érico Veríssimo emptied the idealized and promotional representation of the *gaucho*, making possible the representation of the cultural difference of Rio Grande do Sul within the complex of the Brazilian nation as intergrated "novos assuntos históricos, cujo resultado será o estabelecimento do leque de etnias que formam a nação sulina" (Zilberman 112) [new historical subjects, whose result will be the establishment of the number of ethnicities that forms the southern nation].

In the style of large urban centers, the intellectual generation of the 1930s–in which are included Augusto Meyer (1902–1970), Moyses Vellinho (1902–1980), Theodomiro Tostes (1903–1986), Dyonélio Machado, Mario Quintana (1906–1994), Athos Damasceno Ferreira, and Érico Veríssimo, among others–met in bohemian spots such as the Chalé da Praça XV or in a bookstore like the Livraria do Globo, a place for literary conversation and political talk, in the fashion of the Livraria Garnier in Rio de Janeiro. The Livraria do

Globo, which had begun as a modest stationery store in 1883, was transformed in the 1940s into a company with an important press that played a significant role in the cultural movement of the city, first with the publication of the *Almanaque do Globo* and, after 1929, with the *Revista do Globo*, of which Erico Veríssimo was secretary for a period. For forty-eight years, the *Revista* offered a social, political, and cultural x-ray of the city with a wide thematic spectrum, covering everything from aspects of everyday life to essays of writers from the Rio Grande do Sul and other states. As a vehicle for diffusion, its great merit lay in the publication of passages in translation from foreign authors. Actually, the *Revista* served as a showcase for the publisher, whose work in the line of translations with the collection *Biblioteca dos Séculos* broadened the literary and scientific horizons, not only of the regional but also the national community.

To give an example, the incomparable translation of Balzac's *La comédie humaine* by Paulo Ronai (1907–1992), under the supervision of the writer and critic Maurício Rosenblatt, deserves mention, as well as the translation by the poet Mário Quintana of the novel *La princesse de Clèves* by Madame de Lafayette. The appearance, in 1945, of the *Revista Província de São Pedro* (also an initiative of the Editora do Globo) filled the need for a differentiated and specialized magazine that could respond to the demands of a more sophisticated public that was not in tune with the more popular *Revista do Globo*. The aim of the magazine, whose editor was Moysés Vellinho, was to promote literary exchange with the rest of the country, moving away from regionalist narrowness without denying Rio Grande do Sul singularities. In other words, Rio Grande do Sul regionalism would be the southern version of the construction of nationality. About the title of the magazine, Theodomiro Tostes said: "Debalde o Brasil mudou, as províncias passaram a ser estados. O Rio Grande guardou sempre para ele o nome caseiro de província. Como esses parentes que envelhecem, mudam de situação e de importância mas continuam a ser tratados com carinho pelo velho apelido de família" (Tostes 18) ("Brazil changed, the provinces became states. Rio Grande always kept for itself the home name of the province. Like relatives who age, change their situation and status but continue to be affectionately called by the old family nickname").

With a national circulation and recognition by São Paulo critics like Mário da Silva Brito and Osmar Pimental of the *Diário de São Paulo*, the *Província de São Pedro* maintained for thirteen years an ambitious publishing program, directed toward the works and criticism of the south's best writers, inspiring a necessarily combative attitude regarding the impermeability of the publishing market of the center of the country for Rio Grande do Sul writers. To appraise the role of the Livraria do Globo in the culture of Porto Alegre, however, it is necessary to mention the fact that it involved from its conception, a vast undertaking, which came to be realized in one of the most important cultural events that formed part of the official calendar of the city: the Porto Alegre Book Fair. Held in the Praça da Alfândega, it was one of the few fairs to take place outdoors (not counting the transparent awnings of polycarbonate). In its forty-three year history, the Fair has mobilized the community in a collective ritual each spring, during which the interest in books and the habit of reading is renewed. In one of its latest occurrences, it had 147 stands, with nine from foreign countries (four of which were from Latin American countries). Besides local writers, the participation of writers from the rest of the country and abroad in the book-signings and round-table discussions before a quite heterogeneous public has turned the Fair into an effective channel for democratizing what could be defined as the most advanced "book culture" of the Mercosul.

The uprising of 1961, referred to as the Legality Campaign, a resistance movement organized by the then state governor Leonel Brizola in defense of the Vice-President-elect João Goulart (taking office after the resignation of Jânio Quadros), was the last "war" that took place within the city limits. Under the threat of bombardment of the Palácio Piratini, the seat of the government, by the Ministry of War, the city lived through turbulent days, with the central areas of the Campus of the Federal University transformed into zones of open conflict between civilians and the military. It was a reoccurrence, in a certain sense and with historical proportions duly measured, of the conflict between the southern will and the central power. The growing social, political, and economic crises affecting national life resulted in the military coup of '64 and a period of undemocratic government. The year 1968, which in the great European capitals was notable for intense mass demonstrations and intellectual ferment driven by the desire to redemocratize institutions, represented for the city the institutionalization of repression. The country found itself in a state of siege thanks to the Institutional Act No. 5; the city was "in readiness." The intellectual activity continued even in a climate of tight censorship of the press; ideas were expressed in the pages of the *Caderno de Sábado*, the literary supplement of the *Correio do Povo*, the oldest newspaper of the city, founded in 1895 and still in circulation. As the writer Antonio Hohlfeldt makes clear, "durante as décadas de 60/70 . . . , os suplementos culturais foram o local para o debate e a discussão de idéais e de resistência à ditadura então vigente como nenhum outro locus jornalístico poderia ser (61) ("during the decades of the sixties and seventies . . . the cultural supplements were the place for debate and discussion of ideas and resistance to the then reigning dictatorship as no other journalistic locus could have been"). In the case of the *Caderno de Sábado*, "a pressão e o controle censorial eram menos fortes do que, por exemplo, no 'Suplemento Cultural' da Tribuna da Imprensa, do Rio de Janeiro" (Hohlfeldt 61) ("the pressure and censor's control were less strong than, for example, in the 'Cultural Supplement' of the *Tribuna da Imprensa*, in Rio de Janeiro").

From its first issue in September 1967, the *Caderno de Sábado* established itself as an interdisciplinary medium, with articles on arts and letters but also with incursions into the most varied areas of knowledge. At the same time, it was concerned with preserving the memory of Porto Alegre, with articles on events associated with the city's history. Tânia Carvalhal thus defines the mixed wealth of the *Caderno*'s profile: "nem tão regional, que ao Rio Grande se restringisse, nem tão cosmopolita que se voltasse apenas para o que fosse produzido fora de suas fronteiras" (11) ("neither too regional to be restricted to Rio Grande, nor so cosmopolitan that it was aimed only at what was produced outside its borders"). Among all its contributors, one name especially stands out: that of the critic, historian, and poet Guilhermino César (1908–1993). Keeping in mind the heterogeneity of the subjects César discussed, many of his pieces were in the form of chronicles of daily life, weekly from 1971, for a period of twenty years; his historical and critical reflection on the cultural and literary process in the context of the south of Brazil developed and deepened in his texts written about the works of Rio Grande do Sul writers whom he had studied in his *História da literatura do Rio Grande do Sul* [History of the Literature of Rio Grande do Sul].

Following some leads of critics like João Pinto da Silva (b. 1889), who, in his *História literária do Rio Grande do Sul* [Literary History of Rio Grande do Sul] had identified relations and influences of the River Plate region on Rio Grande do Sul literature, associating the fiction of Augusto Maya with this literary culture, Guilhermino César brought to the surface the question of cross-border cultural exchanges. This essential part of the region's culture had been completely ignored by literary criticism under the pressure of an anti–River Plate politics, which had historically taken shape as a way of preserving Portuguese autonomy with regards to the proximity of the Spanish colonies. He also problematized regionalism in his texts on *gaucho* literary culture; writing about one of the most constant trends of Rio Grande do Sul literature (that built around the image of the gaucho and the values of the pastoral life), César penetrated the complexities and reconstructed the frame for differentiating the particular aspects of a great part of the literary production of the south. Viewing it through the angle of the border as a zone of permeabilities, affiliations, and social/textual exchanges that do not coincide with the line arbitrarily imposed by the geopolitical borders of the nation-state, César apprehends the double movement of conflict and acceptance between the Rio Grande do Sul *gaucho* and that of the River Plate, "sob e sobre o denominador comum de determinado território, sua conquista e evolução histórica, exatamente pontilhado pelas lutas de fronteiras, quer dizer, de opção de identidade" (Castello 1994, 8) ("over and above the common denominator of a specific territory, its conquest and historical evolution, precisely delineated by border struggles, that is, the option of identity"). It is worth mentioning that the valuing of the cultural border of the River Plate significantly destabilizes the almost naturalized dimension of the margin/center relation which conditioned the historical and cultural development of the southernmost region of the country, by placing all within a referential framework of identification with Brazilian nationalism and its Luso-European inheritance.

The paths of the border's imaginary opened by writers at the turn of the century are taken up again by one of the most renowned story-tellers of the south, one whose career began exactly in 1968 with his first publications in the *Caderno de Sábado*. The regional stories of Sérgio Faraco (b. 1940) succeed in affirming the process of transculturation typical of the contact zone between cultures with differentiated linguistic and literary systems, as in the case of Brazil and the River Plate. Faraco's devotion to his rural birthplace, Alegrete, allowed him to capture this process not simply through the language and the customs, but through the ethos of the border gaucho. In this lies one of the great merits of his work: the renewal of the very meaning of the term regionalism, tarnished by the force of a tradition whose store of imagery, especially by the turn of the century, had been based on a conservative world dominated by the ranch-owning oligarchy (today defeated by history). Even when his characters go from the country to the city, where they are abandoned or marginalized, as in the situation of many in the texts that compose *Manilha de Espadas* [Bracelet of Swords] of 1984, "se singularizam por manterem uma relação de origens com a campanha, com o interior do Estado, com as zonas provincianas" (Masina 1994, 75) ("they are unique in maintaining a relation to their rural

origins, the interior of the state, the provincial zones"). The constant negotiations of one culture with the other, in the making of an intercultural space that defines one of the axes of this practical aesthetics, are also extended to activities related to translation. Having translated over twenty-five works of Uruguayan, Argentine, and Paraguayan writers, such as Juan Morosoli, Mario Arregui, Tomás de Mattos, Horacio Quiroga, and Mempo Giardinelli, among others, Faraco wove together in his unique manner the threads that highlighted the multifaceted and superimposed identity of this "third margin," the intercultural zone of the Southern Cone countries.

Since the 1970s, in the atmosphere of the political opening up of the military regime, Porto Alegre, too, has began to breath fresh air–to the rhythm of "Deu prá ti anos 70" [It Gave to You the 70s], a song of Kleiton and Kledir which made the national hit-parade and which became a popular hymn of celebration of and passion for the city. Urban development is not encouraging a reflection of the pauperization of the state. The city is undergoing the problems resulting from the rural exodus, with pockets of misery on the outskirts and no hope for investment in a zone of strangled transportation–the port's activities ended in frustration; the railway was deactivated; and the highway system is stagnant. The motives for collective pride are not lacking, however, and in the words of the historian Sérgio da Costa Franco,

> não cansamos de os apregoar. Tomamos o Brasil de assalto em 1930 e amarramos os cavalos no obelisco da Avenida. Salvamos (ou tentou se salvar) a democracia em 1961, bailando a dança das fações na Praça da Matriz. Ensinamos samba e dor-de-cotovelo ao país com Lupicínio Rodrigues e como nunca padecemos do vício da modéstia . . . nos jactamos de possuir o eleitorado mais politizado do Brasil, mesmo sem ter prova nenhuma para sustentar a fanfarrice. (1997, 192)

> we do not get tired of proclaiming them. We took Brazil by storm in 1930 and tied our horses to the avenue's obelisk. We saved (or tried to save) democracy in 1961, dancing to the machetes on the Praça da Matriz. We taught the country samba and heartsickness with Lupicínio Rodrigues and as we never suffered from the vice of modesty . . . we boast of having the most politicized electorate in the country, even without having any proof at all to sustain the boasting.

It is clear that this pride, which is to a certain extent defensive, contains residual elements of the political inheritance of the Farrapos, which, in fact, is made material in the name of many of the city's streets; September 20, the date of the rebels' proclamation of the Republic of Piratini, is a state holiday and celebrated with solemn parades; the Governor's Palace is called Piratini and the building of the Legislative Assembly is called Farroupilha, which is also the name of the city's main park, the oldest radio station, and one of the more prestigious schools. The ideals of the first Republicans are evoked in the design of the flag and state seal and their names are found on more than a dozen streets. Surrounded by its ghosts, the old Porto dos Casais generated, however, a happy people, perhaps a little *xucro* (untamed), a regional term used by Sérgio da Costa Franco when defining the profile of the natives of Porto Alegre, since it is they who selected the *Laçador* [Man with a Lasso], the statue of the *gaucho* located at the main entrance to the city, as symbol of the city. Sign of a "primitive" bellicose nature, root of the alleged southern arrogance for many, to others it is rather the sign of the backwardness which "literalmente nos aparta de uma identidade urbana e nos encurrala em um potreiro do mais deplorável dos passados: o da legitimação ideológica da exploração" (Guedes 69) ("literally separates us from an urban identity and traps us in a corral of the most deplorable of the past: the ideological legitimation of exploitation"). The *Laçador* seems to fit into the history of mistakes that accompanies the city, as the writer Luís Fernando Veríssimo humorously observed: in the city where its inhabitants refer to the Guaíba River, which is not a river, to the Rua da Praia (Beach Street), which has no beach and which is officially called Rua dos Andradas, to the Praça da Alfândega (Customs Plaza), which has no Customs, to the Parque da Redenção (Redemption Park), which is called Farroupilha, the fact of a rural symbol representing the most cosmopolitan city of the south does not seem to be an inconsistency. Differences aside, the image that truly captures the affection of the community, exercising a real seduction on its imaginary, is that of the abundant waters of the river, which, as the greatest poet Mário Quintana taught everyone, has one of the loveliest twilights of the world.

Leaving aside any provincial pretension, the city at the 30 degrees parallel south has won an enviable profile since the 1920s, when the people saluted the arrival of the Minuano south wind as the only force of nature able to remove the bad smell that threatened to disturb the life of the citizens. Research carried out at a national level by the magazine *Exame*, with results appearing in its twenty-sixth issue in December 1996, indicated that Porto Alegre is the city that displays the highest standard of living in the country, the greatest purchasing power per capita–200 dollars above the São Paulo average–and the lowest rate of infant mortality–less than twenty per 1,000–well below the rate of Rio de Janeiro (at thirty-six), against a Brazilian average of forty-four. Added to this picture the growing ecological consciousness of the community, which is reflected in administrative acts that have placed the city first in the national scene to have garbage collection extended to all its neighborhoods, with recycling centers at eight strategic locations.

Given these positively stimulating data attesting to the city's tendency to overcome the limitations of its development, there is one significant factor that makes it an important model of innovative practices with respect to the managing of public funds. This factor is the Orçamento Participativo (Participatory Budget), a process of popular representation through which civil society assures the distribution of public resources to the poorer areas, according to priorities established by their legitimate representatives. Throughout the ten years since its inauguration by the Municipal Administration in 1989, the Participatory Budget has undergone several adjustments and its evolution points towards a growing sophistication and operational complexity (Navarro 7). As a politicoadministrative model, the OP, as it is called, has attracted the attention of social scientists, political analysts, and mayors from other Brazilian cities interested in the viability of adopting the model in their respective cities. The repercussions beyond national borders have led the OP to be chosen as one of the forty urban innovations selected by the United Nations and presented in the II Conference on Human Settlement, which took place in Istanbul, Turkey, in June 1996. With the opening up of the means of exchange between Mercosur countries, it can be said that the city has exported the first product of its political culture: The OP is in use in the constitution of Buenos Aires.

To speak of Mercosur (the economic integration of Argentina, Paraguay, Uruguay, and Brazil made viable by the Treaty of Asuncion, signed in 1991) today is to refer to the consolidation of important political articulations and decisions of an economic nature which yielded to these countries an appreciable sum of 20.33 billion dollars in 1997. No less important than the exchange between the sectors of industry and commerce is surely the cooperation in the areas of science and culture, axes whose integration offers a field of representations with meanings and values that are signs of social solidarity and collective development. As the main center on the Mercosur route, Porto Alegre has confronted the historical challenge of overcoming its geographically and metaphorically marginal condition through efforts that attempt to reconstruct the links with the other side of its river, with its southern margins, forgotten and repressed by the logic of Portuguese domination. One of the first products jointly produced by the countries of Mercosur was the film *Lua de Outono* [Autumn Moon], based on three stories by the Uruguayan writer Mario Arregui, and with a cast made up of actors from the countries involved. Of the series of initiatives which have already marked Porto Alegre and the capitals of the River Plate, involving dozens of artists, intellectuals, and journalists in the areas of cinema, literature, theater, dance, music, and the visual arts, we should mention the annual Porto Alegre events in Buenos Aires, and the corresponding Buenos Aires in Porto Alegre, the First Exhibition of Uruguayan Theater and, of course, the First Mercosur Biennial Arts Exhibition, which took place in 1997 and gathered 275 artists from seven countries. Considered the third market for art in Brazil, the city experienced a unique moment in its history, with works exhibited in public places, including parks and plazas, allowing the community direct contact with these works. The fact that the city was able to count on and feel pride in its Institute of Arts, founded in 1908 (one of the first in the country at the university level), partly explains the dynamism of this particular market, in spite of its isolation from those at the center of the country.

It would be impossible to conceive of Porto Alegre apart from its university base, which was created by the strong will of the community and which has made it one of the national centers of reference in terms of the formation and development of human resources, as well as scientific and technological production. The Universidade Federal do Rio Grande do Sul (Federal University of Rio Grande do Sul), with its fifty-four undergraduate programs and ninety-five post-graduate programs (fifty-seven masters and thirty-eight doctoral), is second among the public universities of the federal system of Brazil's higher education in the preparation of masters and doctors; thus it plays an important role in the preparation of professors and researchers for the entire system, be it regional or national. As one of the nerve-centers of Mercosur, within the concept of a harmonious and balanced integration in the areas of economics, science, and culture, UFRGS is an active member of the Association of Universities of the Montevideo Group, founded in 1992, which is comprised of twelve public universities from Paraguay, Uruguay, Argentina, and Brazil. The Montevideo Group is a non-governmental organization whose primary aim is to establish a public academic forum for incentives in and strengthening of critical thought and human resources that may advance the development of the region. With more than 15,000 researchers, students, and teachers involved, "a integração de nossas universidades, neste final de século, quando a pesquisa científica é reconhe-cida como mola propulsora do desenvolvimento tecnológico, econômico e social, se constitui em fator essencial para a afir-mação da identidade, da potencialidade produtiva e da sobe-rania dos países do Cone Sul" (Panizzi 25) ("the integration of our universities, at this turn of the [twenty-first] century, when scientific research is recognized as the springboard for tech-nological, economic, and social development, constitutes an essential factor for the affirmation of identity, productive potentiality, and the sovereignty of the countries of the South-ern Cone").

Returning to my initial image of the margin/border, from the point-of-view of cultural politics, the regional tendency to open the borders in the south makes visible, by contrast and as far as it is possible to generalize, the marginality of the cul-tural production of the south, from the viewpoint of the center of the country–a center which has the cultural and discour-sive authority to strengthen the south and, therefore, ratify and legitimate its own position of authority as center. If today separatism constitutes nothing more than old-fashioned, rar-efied rhetoric in Rio Grande do Sul political folklore, contrib-uting to the veneration of a past which for a long time has not supported collective representation, the feeling of exclusion as a consequence of geopolitical location and historical speci-ficity has been renewed among southern intellectuals vis-à-vis the centralizing logic that rationalizes the authoritarian and normative tendency in culture by inscribing regional cultural difference in a hierarchical and reductionist relation between metropolis (hegemony) and periphery (dependence). This relation presupposes the definition of aesthetic parameters of originality and belatedness, a distinction which confers a canonical status on the production of the center in relation to which the production of the margin is seen as reduced to insignificance. In this logic, the cultural construction of the nation necessarily involves the silencing of the margin (in this case, the south) or its *nordestização* (northeasternization), a term which, rooted in prejudice, points toward an elitist and exclusionary conception of art and culture. Such is the pub-licly declared position of Otávio Farias Filho, chief editor of one of the most prestigious newspapers of the country, who, while making remarks on the *gaucho* film production *Anahy de las missiones* [Anahy of the Missions], referred to the south in this way in concluding his editorial: "a região mais desen-volvida do país, do pronto de vista social e político, é também aquela de menor contribuição foi capaz de dar do pronto de vista cultural e artístico; nesse sentido, o nordeste é o sul" (2) ("the most developed region in the country, from the social and political point of view, is also that which has made the least contribution from the cultural and artistic point of view; in this sense, the *northeast* is the south"). Invisibility like this is also present in the *História da vida privada no Brasil: a corte e a modernidade nacional* [History of Private Life in Brazil: The Court and National Modernity], in which, along with the extremely reduced space given to Rio Grande do Sul, there is no reference at all to the Farroupilha Revolution, a histori-cally unacceptable exclusion considering that one of the sec-tions of the work deals especially with Liberal revolutions.

Misplaced and outside history in the map of Brazilian cul-tural production, the south carries the paradoxically distress-ing and calming consciousness of *otherness*, living with the certainty that a great part of its cultural production finds no space on the national scene and is therefore restricted to a zone of regional influence. Of the new generation of writers,

some have been able to transgress the limits of the margin, people like João Gilberto Noll (b. 1946), Lya Luft (b. 1938), Luis Fernando Veríssimo (b. 1936), and Moacyr Scliar (b. 1937). Others have not succeeded in becoming known in the rest of the country, although their production is significant and is praised by the best local critics. Names like Luiz Antônio de Assis Brasil (b. 1945), Tabajara Ruas (b. 1942), and Sérgio Faraco (b. 1940), in the words of the critic José Castello:

> ainda se conservam injustamente restritios no cenário literário gaúcho ou ao gosto mais refinado de uma minoria de leitores. Sinal de uma vitalidade regional, mas sinal também, de um cerco ainda cruel, que contradiz as teses sobre a globalização crescente da cultura e a informação instantânea que caracterizam a nossa época. (1997, 10)

are still unjustly restricted to the gaucho literary scene or to the more refined taste of a minority of readers. This is the sign of a regional vitality, but also of a cruel restriction, which contradicts the thesis about the growing globalization of culture and instantaneous information that are said to characterize our era.

Seen through the angle of resistance as a strategy of sur-vival, the fact is that a literary market exists today in Porto Alegre which is defined as autonomous and independent, and which sustains a surprising number of small and large pub-lishers, responsible for launching talented writers and for the production of their best-sellers. Under the influence of the his-tory of immigration that is peculiar to the Rio Grande do Sul social formation, this market is nourished in great part by a significant literary production which explores the theme of colonization, from the viewpoint of various ethnic groups that have their roots in southern lands.

The differentiated aspects of the Rio Grande do Sul cul-ture are present in the literary production of the nineties, a period of affirmation for local literary culture, thanks to the consolidation of the prestige of writers who have come onto the scene in the last three decades and who have main-tained a regular production of work of quality, which has assured them from the beginning an outstanding place in the city's cultural scene and in the literary historiography of Rio Grande do Sul. In terms of the development of Rio Grande do Sul letters, this work articulates the permanent characteristics that vouch for the specificity of the literature produced in the south and that authorize the term *gaucho lit-erature*, as disseminated beyond national borders. While such an expression refers to a different field in relation to Brazilian literature, it inscribes a spatial and historical inheritance whose representations represent genuine criti-cal-interpretive research into history and its imaginaries. It is understandable that fictional narrative has gained prece-dence over the lyric and dramatic genres, since it is the local social history, its political confrontations, and cultural transformations that provide the raw material for the important novels of the period.

The theme of immigration–in a memorialist trend in which history becomes a thematic source and is often fore-grounded as a structuring element of the narrative–is partic-ularly emphasized in the works of Luiz Antônio de Assis Brasil. Since his debut with *Um quarto de légua em quatro* [1976; A Quarter League in Four], in which he explores the saga of the Azorian immigrant in the first years of the forma-tion of the state, to *Videiras de cristal* [1990; Crystal Vines], whose focus is the messianic episode of the Muckers, the reli-gious war in the zone of the German colonization of the Vale do Rio dos Sinos in the middle of the nineteenth century, Assis

Brasil's *oeuvre* is remarkably unified, and he is recognized as one of the most important gaucho novelists. His latest three novels, *Perversas famílias* [1992; Perverse Families] , *Pedra da memória* [1993; Rock of Memory], and *Os senhores do século* [1994; Lords of the Century] make up the trilogy *Un castelo no pampa* [A Castle in the Pampas], which is noted in the *Encyclopedia Britannica* yearbook. Here, the historical fact is found within the histories of private life, in a modulation that unites the social and the subjective worlds under the sign of a culture in turmoil. Still on the subject of immigration, other representative works include *Valsa para Bruno Stein* [1986; Waltz for Bruno Stein], by Charles Kiefer (b. 1958). The history of German colonization is here approached through a problematic relation of loss, conflict, and transformation. The acculturation process, the country-city displacements, and the transformations of values resulting from economic changes provide the narrative with a dramatic component whose energy comes from critical and social denunciation.

The option of reflection on the present without any historicist preoccupation is what distinguishes the recent fiction of Moacyr Scliar from his first works published in the seventies, like *A guerra no Bom Fim* [1972; The War in Bom Fim] and *Exército de um homem só* [1973; One-Man Army]. Although the theme of the Jewish colonization is present in his plots, the angle adopted points towards another trend of modern Rio-Grande fiction, that is, the urban novel, where the city scene thoroughly reveals the effects of a social order marked by growing social differences, daily frustrations, and existential restlessness. Another writer who is an example of this trend is Caio Fernando Abreu (1948–1996), whose fiction is characterized by an intimist mode with an existential tone. Identified with the generation who lived through the 1964 military *coup*, the repression of the student movements of 1968, and the effects of AI-5, Caio chooses characters from marginalized social groups for whom the disillusion with life is overcome through one of two paths: the anarchist or the mystical. The two works published before his premature death, *Onde andará Dulce Veiga* [1990; Where Is Dulce Veiga] and *Ovelhas negras* [1995; Black Sheep], confirmed his reputation as a short story writer of the first rank, even by the critics from the center of the country.

The intimist narrative, a branch of the tradition of psychological analysis, gains power in the works of Lya Luft and Patrícia Bins, two writers who return to the problematic of female identity by emphasizing the reinvention of memory as a poetic-narrative resource in order to strip naked the state of marginality—the affective, sexual, and cultural exile which accompanies the life of characters under a repressive patriarchal order that paralyzes and incapacitates them in their search for desire and self-fulfillment. The predominant figure in their novels is therefore the female protagonist-narrator, whose narrative usually tells of the painful and liberating experience from which it becomes possible to reinvent oneself. Among Lya Luft's recent novels are *O exílio* [1987; The Exile] and *A sentinela* [1994; The Sentinel]. After concluding her "Passion Trilogy" in 1991, Patrícia Bins has begun her "Eros Trilogy" with the novel *Caçador de memórias* [Hunter of Memories], published in 1995.

The rise of fictional narrative has not, however, prevented the city from producing its poets and playwrights. Contemporary poetry is characterized, along general lines, by the continuity of the Symbolist influence allied to the Modernist renovation of language, mainly when one refers to the work of Mário Quintana, the city's poet *par excellence*. During a long career begun in the forties with the publication of *A rua dos cataventos* [The Street of the Weathervanes], Quintana opposed a poetry of a social type in order to explore a more individualist line, framed in an urban context and concentrating on the relation of the outer and the inner self. With a vast output throughout four decades, Quintana is still considered the brightest star in the constellation of contemporary poets, within which group Armindo Trevisan (b. 1933), Paulo Hecker Filho (b. 1926), and Luiz de Miranda (b. 1945) are also noteworthy. In drama, we should mention the figure of Ivo Bender (b. 1938), who premiered in 1975 with *Teatro escolhido* [Selected Theater], and today still writes pieces for children's and adult's theater, from the perspective of a critical view of Brazilian reality where there is evidence of German, colonial, and rural culture.

Thus has Porto Alegre, through the creative vitality of its writers, overcome and renewed itself in the crossing over to peripheral modernity. While it avoids the subservience implicit in the marginal condition, it is, however, from it that the city molds its difference—by transforming it into the nourishing power of a cultural option whose directions flow back into and de-essentialize the margin, working against the hegemonic and the identity that appropriates the other. Even if it is still the hostage of the subtle play between remembering and forgetting, which (as a result of historical vicissitudes) persists in imposing itself on its imaginary. This in its turn, perhaps for this very reason has not dared to project itself in terms of avant-garde paradigms defined by the center. This means that the violence underlying the idea of a center produces a monological coloring which is also a form of imprisonment: The city remakes its associations and rearticulates its signs of identification through the literal and metaphorical axis of the border. Initially as an area of dispute, later as a mere passage, the border today refers to a mapping of meeting points, a heterogeneous space of living experiences, affective networks, and cultural and aesthetic affiliations which create potential reconfigurations of the national and the regional on the dramatic horizon of cultural practices under the siege of globalization.

**Translation by Thomas La Borie Burns and
Glaucia Renate Gonçalves**

Works Cited

Balzac, Honoré de. 1989. *A comédia humana.* Trans., ed Paulo Ronai. Porto Alegre: Globo.

Baumgarten, Carlos Alexandre. 1997. *A crítica literária no Rio grande do Sul: do romantismo ao modernismo.* Porto Alegre: IEL/EDIPUCRS.

Carvalhal, Tania Franco. 1994. "Guilhermino César: do efêmero ao permanente." *Notícia do Rio Grande.* By Guilhermino César. Porto Alegre: IEL/Editora da Universidade Federal do Rio Grande do Sul. 9–15.

Castello, José Aderaldo. 1994. "Apresentação." *Notícia do Rio Grande.* By Guilhermino César. Porto Alegre: IEL/Editora da Universidade Federal do Rio Grande do Sul. 7–8.

——. 1997. "Sérgio Faraco reflete seu silêncio nas letras." *O Estado de São Paulo. Caderno* 2 (June 28).

César, Guilhermino. 1956. *História da literatura do Rio Grande do Sul.* Porto Alegre: Globo.

——. 1979. "Introdução." *O corsário.* By José Antônio do Vale Caldre e Fião. Porto Alegre: Movimento. 5–32.

Chartier, Roger. 1983. "Histoire intellectuelle et histoire des mentalités. Trajectoires et questions." *Revue de synthèse* 104.111–112: 277–307.

———. 1988. "Intellectual History and the History of Mentalités: A Dual Re-evaluation." *Cultural History: Between Practices and Representations*. Trans. Lydia G. Cochrane. Cambridge: Polity P. 19–52.

Chaves, Flávio Loureiro. 1992. "Um texto resgatado." *A divina pastora*. José Antônio do Vale Caldre e Fião, et al. 2nd ed. Porto Alegre: L & PM editora. 9–17.

Chiappini, Ligia. 1988. *No entretanto dos tempos*. São Paulo: Martins Fontes.

Cunha, Delfina Benigna da. 1834. *Poemas oferecidos às senhoras rio-grandenses*. Porto Alegre: Typografia da Fonseca & Cia.

Faraco, Sergio. 1984. *Manilha de espadas: Contos*. Rio de Janeiro: Philobiblion.

Ferreira, Athos Damasceno. 1936. *Poemas da Minha Cidade*. Porto Alegre: Globo.

———. 1956. *Palco, Salão e Picadeiro em Porto Alegre no Século XIX*. Porto Alegre: Editora Globo.

———. 1975. *Imprensa Literária de Porto Alegre no Século XIX*. Porto Alegre: Editora da Universidade Federal do Rio Grande do Sul.

Filho, Otavio Farias. 1997. "Na fronteira do sul." Opinião. *Folha de São Paulo*. (December 11): 2.

Flores, Moacyr. 1978. *Modelo político dos farrapos*. Porto Alegre: Mercado Aberto.

Franco, Sérgio da Costa. 1988. *Porto Alegre: Guia histórico*. Porto Alegre: Editora da Universidade Federal do Rio Grande do Sul.

———. 1997. *Alegres, mas meio xucros. História ilustrada de Porto Alegre*. Porto Alegre: [np].

Guedes, Paulo. 1993. "Apesar de você, não é o Laçador." *Sobre Porto Alegre*. Ed. Carlos Augusto Bissán. Porto Alegre: Editora da Universidade Federal do Rio Grande do Sul. 65–69.

Hessel, Lothar F., et al. 1976. *O Partenon Literário e sua obra*. Porto Alegre: Edição Flama.

Hohlfeldt, Antônio. 1996. "Jornalismo cultural: Uma perspectiva permanente." *Continente sul sur*. Porto Alegre: Revista do IEL. (November) 2: 57–64.

Lafayette, Madame de. 1987. *La princesa de Clèves*. Trans. Mário Quintana. 2nd ed. Porto Alegre: Globo.

Laytano, Dante. 1974. *Legado luso-açoriano na formação do RS*. Porto Alegre: Centro Regional de Pesquisas Educacionais do Sul.

———. 1975. "Legado étnico das populações do Rio Grande do Sul através da história e da tradição." *Relatório do Banco do estado do Rio do Sul B 1974*. Porto Alegre: Banco do Estado do Rio do Sul. [np].

Lazzaroto, Danilo. 1971. *História do Rio Grande do Sul*. Porto Alegre: Sulina.

Macedo, Francisco Riopardense de. 1973. *Porto Alegre: História e vida da cidade*. Porto Alegre: Editora da Universidade Federal do Rio Grande do Sul.

———. 1982. *Porto Alegre: aspectos culturais*. Porto Alegre: SMEC.

Machado, Dyonélio. 1980. *Os ratos*. 7th ed. São Paulo: Ática.

Masina, Léa. 1994. *Percursos de leitura*. Porto Alegre: Movimento/IEL.

Maya, Alcydes de Castilho. 1912. *Machado de Assis: Algumas notas sobre o humor*. Rio de Janeiro: Casa Editorial Jacinto da Silva.

Melo, Rita Barém de. 1868. *Sorrisos e prantos*. Rio Grande: Tipografia Eco do Sul.

———. 1998. *Sorrisos e prantos*. Florianópolis: Mulheres, Porto Alegre: Movimento.

Navarro, Zander. 1997. "'Affirmative democracy' and Redistributive Development: The Case of 'Participatory Budgeting' in Porto Alegre, Brasil (1989–1997)." Porto Alegre: Universidade Federal do Rio Grande do Sul [Unpublished].

Panizzi, Wrana. 1998. "Integração no Cone Sul." Opinião. *Zero Hora*. Porto Alegre. (April 22): 25.

Papaleo, Maria Beatriz Meurer. 1996. "Athos Damasceno Ferreira: Rivarol da província." Diss. Porto Alegre: Universidade Federal do Rio Grande do Sul.

Pesavento, Sandra. 1984. *História do Rio Grande do Sul*. 3rd ed. Porto Alegre: Mercado Aberto.

———, ed. 1991. *Memória Porto Alegre: Espaços e vivências*. Porto Alegre: Editora da Universidade Federal do Rio Grande do Sul/Prefeitura Municipal de Porto Alegre.

———. 1994. "Um novo olhar sobre a cidade: A nova história cultural e as representações do urbano." *Porto Alegre na virada do século 19: Cultura e sociedade*. Anderson Zalewski Vargas, et al. Porto Alegre: Editora da UFRGS. 126–43.

Porto Alegre, Apolinário José Gomes. 1873–1874. "José de Alencar: Estudo biográfico." *Revista mensal da sociedade Partenon Literário*. [Porto Alegre] (1873) 9: 371–73; (1873) 10: 422–26; (1873) 11: 480–84; (1873) 12: 520–24; (1874) [n.n]: 629–33.

Romero, Silvio. 1977. *Estudos sobre a poesia popular do Brasil*. 2nd ed. Petrópolis: Vozes.

Tostes, Theodomiro. 1979. "Notas sobre Moysés Vellinho." Caderno de Sábado. *Correio do Povo*. [Porto Alegre] (January 6).

Veríssimo, Érico. 1935. *Caminhos cruzados*. Porto Alegre: [np].

———. 1979. *O continente*. 18th ed. Porto Alegre: Globo.

———. 1981. *O arquipélago*. Porto Alegre: Globo.

———. 1981. *O retrato*. Porto Alegre: Globo.

White, Hayden. 1986. "Historical Pluralism." *Critical Inquiry*. 12.3: 480–93.

Zilberman, Regina. 1992. *A literatura no Rio Grande do Sul*. 3rd ed. Porto Alegre: Mercado Aberto.

SECTION VIII
RIO DE LA PLATA AND CHILE
INTRODUCTION

Richard J. Walter

Buenos Aires, Montevideo, and Santiago are the three predominant capital cities of the southern cone of South America. Buenos Aires and Montevideo, linked by geography and history, are–except for differences in scale–almost carbon copies of one another. As national capitals, main ports, and predominant commercial, industrial, and governmental centers, they have dominated their respective nations for centuries. Santiago, Chile's capital, has also been predominant in that nation, but, due to geography and other factors, has evolved somewhat differently from its Atlantic counterparts. Landlocked, Santiago has shared national importance to a certain extent with the main port city of Valparaíso some 80 miles to its west. Nonetheless, despite certain differences, all three cities share significant similarities as they have evolved over the course of the Spanish Colonial period into the modern era. As the essays in this volume indicate, all three were and continued to be important centers of culture, not only nationally but also to some extent internationally. In this essay I shall note some of the similarities in their development as cultural centers, focusing on some of the common features of this process. In addition, I shall try to add a bit more historical context, again trying to do so in a comparative manner. Given the practical limitations, the generalizations made will be rather broad.

All three cities were founded as frontier outposts on the margins of the Spanish Colonial empire in the Americas: Santiago in 1541, Buenos Aires in 1580, and Montevideo in 1730. As with all Spanish Colonial cities, they were laid out in a gridiron pattern around a central plaza. In the case of Buenos Aires, the main plaza was close to the river, while in Montevideo it was in the center of a peninsula in a city that was–unlike its counterparts–surrounded by a wall to protect it against foreign attacks. Over the course of the Colonial period, all three cities emerged as commercial and governmental centers and by the time of independence in the early nineteenth century had clearly gained the predominance they continue to enjoy. By 1800, with a population of 40,000, Buenos Aires was a thriving commercial center, the capital of the Viceroyalty of La Plata created in 1776, and the largest city in the region. In Chile, "although Santiago had only 30,000 residents at the time of independence, it overshadowed the other towns and villages, all of which had fewer than 5000 residents" (Scarpaci 112–13); "by 1800, Montevideo was Uruguay, with a population of some 15,000, roughly half the entire population of the banda oriental" (Sargent 473).

Home to much of the educated *criollo* elite who fomented Independence from Spain, all three cities played important roles in that process. Immediately following Independence, the three new nations of which these cities were the capitals

took divergent political paths. Argentina suffered a period of anarchy and confusion from about 1810 to 1835, when dictator Juan Manuel de Rosas (1793–1877) imposed a repressive regime that lasted until 1852. In Uruguay, liberal Colorados fought conservative Blancos for dominance in an unresolved and difficult struggle that persisted until the early twentieth century. These internal difficulties were complicated by external pressures from Argentina and Brazil that led to long sieges of the city of Montevideo in the first half of the nineteenth century. After some initial turmoil in the 1820s, the Chilean state was consolidated under the Constitution of 1833, and relative political order was established. Chile was spared the direct foreign interventions that afflicted Argentina and Uruguay, and especially Buenos Aires and Montevideo, during this period.

A result of these developments was the beginning of an exile experience that would affect all three capitals. In the first half of the nineteenth century, most of the exiles came from Argentina and found refuge in Montevideo or Santiago. As many of the exiles were men of letters and learning, such as Domingo Sarmiento, they often enriched the culture of their host cities. Over time the exile peregrinations would become more fluid and complex, depending on political and economic circumstances in each country and its capital. In the twentieth century Chilean politicians–such as former presidents Arturo Alessandri and his main nemesis Carlos Ibáñez–took up residence in Buenos Aires (not simultaneously), while politicians and intellectuals fleeing the repressive regime of Juan Perón moved to Montevideo in the 1940s. The movement of exiles among all three cities became even more complex in the 1960s and 1970s, as Chileans, first of the Right and then of the Left, settled in Buenos Aires, accompanied–until 1976–by numerous Uruguayans who either were forced out of their country or left voluntarily. By 1976 all three cities and countries were controlled by repressive right-wing military regimes and were therefore avoided by exiles, who found refuge elsewhere.

Despite their differing developments, all three cities saw the emergence of important cultural institutions in the first half of the nineteenth century. National universities were established during this period (Buenos Aires, 1821; Santiago, 1842; Montevideo, 1849), and a vital and expanding press began to appear. Newspapers and magazines, the major ones published in the national capitals, helped to create an "imagined community," and contributed to the development of national identity. In addition to reporting the news and providing editorial opinion, most newspapers devoted much of their space to essays, poems, short stories, and other literature as a way to ensure the diffusion of the cultural products of both national and foreign authors. All three cities also became the center of book publishing, and various important nineteenth-century novels were both produced in and described the life of these major urban centers. As the three essays on these cities clearly describe, these were cultural developments that continued and expanded throughout the twentieth century.

As with most major cities in the Americas and Europe, Buenos Aires, Montevideo, and Santiago all began to undergo significant modernization and transformation in the second half of the nineteenth century. Gas, electricity, and telephones were introduced; sewer and water systems were established; streets were paved and lighted; and, in the cases of Buenos Aires and Montevideo, ports were modernized. Concerted efforts were made to improve sanitation and public health, and police forces were professionalized and expanded to ensure public safety and order. Impressive new public and private buildings were constructed, many of which were designed by foreign architects (mostly French and Italian), and many of which still exist today. Plazas and parks, such as the Cerro Santa Lucía in Santiago and Palermo in Buenos Aires, were created as attractive public spaces, originally much favored by the city's elite but increasingly open to the popular classes as well. Following the influence of Haussmann, broad, new, monumental avenues–the Alameda O'Higgins in Santiago, the Avenida 25 de Mayo in Buenos Aires, the Avenida 18 de Julio in Montevideo–were constructed, not only symbolizing the attempt to imitate the Parisian model but also serving to commemorate important events and individuals in the struggle for national Independence and identity. Street widening and efforts to break up the rigid Colonial gridiron pattern accompanied the expansion of public transportation, at first by way of horse-drawn streetcars and increasingly–by the end of the century–with an electrified system. In 1913 Buenos Aires inaugurated Latin America's first subway, a feat not duplicated in Chile until the 1970s and not yet repeated in Montevideo.

Phenomenal demographic growth characterized all three cities. Montevideo grew from 50,000 in 1860 to 248,000 by 1908; Buenos Aires from 187,000 in 1870 to 1,500,000 by 1914; and Santiago from 130,000 in 1875 to 333,000 in 1907. By 1930 Buenos Aires contained 18.3 percent of all Argentineans; Santiago contained 16.2 percent of all Chileans; and Montevideo contained 33 percent of all Uruguayans (Scobie 1989). This demographic growth reflected improved public health standards and the decline of mortality rates, leading to a natural increase in urban residents. More important factors, however, were the movements of people from the rest of the country into the national capital and, most notably in the cases of Buenos Aires and Montevideo, from abroad. By 1908 about one-third of the population of Montevideo was foreign-born, coming mostly from Spain and Italy. By 1914 half of Buenos Aires's 1.5 million were also foreign-born, also mostly from Spain and Italy, although representatives of many other important nationalities (for example, large numbers of Russian and Polish Jews). The impact of foreign immigration on Santiago was less great. In 1907 the province of Santiago had a total population of 384,989, of whom only 12,219 were foreign-born, with most of the foreigners coming from Italy, Spain, and France (1907 Census). One result of the relatively minor impact of immigrants was that there were significantly more females than males in Santiago, while the reverse was true in Buenos Aires and Montevideo.

Some industrialization occurred in all three cities during this period, but unlike the case in the United States and Europe, where large manufacturing establishments appeared in these years, most industry in the southern cone capitals–and Latin America generally–was predominantly of the small-scale, family-owned variety, employing relatively few workers. Exceptions were the foreign-owned meat-packing plants in Buenos Aires and Montevideo. These three capitals, as James Scobie described Buenos Aires, remained primarily commercial–bureaucratic cities until the beginnings of import-substitution industrialization in the 1930s (Scobie 1972).

With the transformations that occurred over the course of the second half of the nineteenth century, new social groups were created and began to emerge to play significant roles in the lives of all three cities. Stimulated to some extent by what industrialization did occur, but also by the building boom of the period and the expansion and elaboration of urban services, an urban working class began to organize and mobilize for improved working and living conditions. Anarchism and socialism provided ideological inspiration for these movements, and, increasingly, all three capitals began to experience militant protests that often evolved into general strikes and serious disruptions of urban life. In the latter part of the century, socialist parties were created in Argentina and Uruguay, and in 1904 Alfredo L. Palacios, elected from Buenos Aires's Italian district of La Boca, became the first Socialist congressman of the Americas, soon joined by his Uruguayan compatriot Emilio Frugoni. In Chile the Democratic party was formed in the 1880s to represent the interests of that nation's working class.

The turn of the century also witnessed the appearance of a growing and increasingly influential middle class in all three cities. With government employees making up a large component of this group, the middle class sought to advance its interests through political parties (the Radicals in Argentina and Chile and the Colorados in Uruguay), an expanded suffrage, and honest elections. This group and the parties they represented were important factors in the reform administrations of José Batlle y Ordóñez in Uruguay (1903–1907; 1911–1915), Hipólito Yrigoyen in Argentina (1916–1922), and Arturo Alessandri in Chile (1920–1925).

Foreign influences and interests played crucial roles in driving many of these developments. This could be clearly seen in the remodeling of the three capitals along Parisian lines, as well as the impact of French and Italian architects and architecture. Most significant in affecting urban growth, however, were the British, who were the largest direct investors in all three countries and who controlled many of the most important economic activities. British construction of the main railways of Argentina and Uruguay–all of which centered on the capital port cities, for example–did much to enhance the predominance of Buenos Aires and Montevideo. British banks, import-export firms, and department stores such as Harrods and Gath & Chaves were prominent in Buenos Aires and Santiago, and British interests owned and operated many of the municipal services in all three capitals. For the most part the British were welcomed and their contributions appreciated. By the end of World War I, however, a growing sense of economic nationalism–mostly among intellectuals and political groups in the capitals–began to assert itself in all three countries and there was a call for greater national control over economic life and the services foreigners provided. Particular targets were the

British-owned streetcar companies, all of which ran into financial and political difficulties in the inter-war period and all of which were eventually nationalized. While the British impact on high culture was less great than that of the French, the influence on popular culture through the introduction of soccer at the end of the century was certainly considerable. Certain urban habits of dress and of eating and entertainment, such as the afternoon tea, also bore an unmistakable British stamp.

Over the course of the twentieth century, the transformations and growth that began in the late nineteenth century continued and accelerated. By 1990 the city of Buenos Aires contained almost 3 million inhabitants, and the Greater Buenos Aires area, which included the city, almost 12 million (one in three of all Argentineans). Montevideo continued to dominate Uruguay, reaching a population of 1.25 million in 1985, also representing about one-third of the national total. By 1989 Santiago's greater metropolitan area had reached to over 5 million persons in a total national population of about 13 million (Scarpaci 120). In this case most of this growth was due–as it had been in the nineteenth century–to internal migration. For Buenos Aires and Montevideo foreign immigration fueled much of the growth, as it had earlier. However, by the 1930s, foreign immigration declined dramatically and internal migration played the major role in urban expansion in these two cases as well. In all three the growth of large-scale industry located in and around the national capitals after the 1930s (somewhat less the case in Montevideo) was a powerful factor in attracting the native-born to what were becoming megacities.

One of the major problems accompanying such massive growth was housing. Throughout much of the twentieth century, each capital was characterized by the presence, usually in the downtown area, of crowded tenement dwellings, called *conventillos*. While some of the details differed, these dwellings usually lacked adequate space, heat, light, and sanitary facilities and thus were breeding grounds of poverty, crime, and disease. Particularly in the post-World War II era, shantytowns–*villas miserias* in Buenos Aires and Montevideo, *callampas* and *poblaciones* in Santiago–have appeared on the outskirts of all three cities and sometimes in abandoned areas near the downtown as well. Social segregation has occurred in all three. From the late nineteenth century, certain neighborhoods have housed the elite–the Barrio Norte and Palermo Chico in Buenos Aires, the area around the Plaza Prado in Montevideo as well as the beach-front neighborhoods to the east of downtown, the center of the city and then the Barrio Alto to the east in Santiago–while others have become working-class districts–La Boca and Barracas in Buenos Aires, the Cerro in Montevideo, the western and southern districts of Santiago. While these are some of the clearest examples of social stratification, there are also many neighborhoods and districts where the boundaries are not so clear and where representatives of the entire class structure can be found.

Another common feature shared by all three has been the rapid growth of surrounding suburbs. As was the case throughout the Americas and elsewhere, this growth was stimulated in large measures by improvements in public transportation, first railroads, then streetcars, and, from the 1920s on, by more flexible (i.e., not limited to rails) buses of various kinds. Beginning most notably in the 1920s, too, the private automobile started to have the dramatic impact on the southern cone capitals that it was having elsewhere, forcing new accommodations and new construction patterns and further accelerating the development of suburbs. Over the past few decades, the building of modern superhighways to accommodate ever-expanding automobile and truck traffic has been one of the most notable features of all three cities.

Much of the growth of these cities over the twentieth century was directed by a combination of national, provincial, and local governments. Struggling to bring order to what was often a chaotic situation, as private interests strove to respond to and to take advantage of this growth, these governments frequently called on experts in the growing field of urbanism to devise plans for more orderly development. Some of these were crafted by European and North American specialists, others by homegrown architects and engineers, and many had at least some influence over how the various cities evolved. For the most part, however, these plans were at best only partially carried out and in most instances ignored altogether. Most urban growth was more ad hoc and spontaneous than it was rational and controlled (Hardoy).

By the 1920s the Parisian model that had so influenced the patterns of urban development in the three capitals was replaced to a large extent by North American examples, especially New York and Chicago and particularly in the growth of skyscrapers, as vertical expansion began to accompany horizontal spread. By the 1920s, as well, North American influences could be seen clearly in the growth of urban popular culture in the three capitals, influences that expanded over the remainder of the century. Most notable early on was the impact of Hollywood films and popular music, especially jazz. By the 1920s U.S. investments and U.S. products were beginning to challenge the British commercial dominance of southern cone countries. Perhaps most important in this regard was the introduction and successful sale of U.S. automobiles, which came to dominate the market, with the popular Ford Model T leading the way. At the same time, soccer, or *fútbol*, became professionalized and internationalized, and during the 1920s and 1930s many of the massive stadiums that housed these teams were constructed and became important city landmarks. As work days and work hours were gradually reduced, more and more of the urban population had the opportunity to take advantage of leisure time activities, not only as spectators but also as participants in various sporting and recreational activities—in some instances in facilities provided by local governments and, in other cases, through an ever-growing number of private clubs. An especially popular pastime in all three cities was horse racing, which catered to both elite and popular audiences and which flourished particularly in the first half of the twentieth century. By the 1920s and 1930s auto and bicycle racing also became popular, as did professional boxing. In the summer months urban residents often fled to the well-known beach resorts of Mar del Plata in Argentina, Punta del Este in Uruguay, and Viña del Mar in Chile. At first designed by and for the elite, these resorts became increasingly accessible to the middle classes as the century progressed and became sites–to one degree or another–for tourists from all three countries.

Throughout the twentieth century, all three cities remained, as they had been almost from their founding, the main political centers of the nation. Home to the national government, they were also home to the main headquarters of all national parties as well as some local groups. In Buenos Aires, at both the national and local level, the city has generally been a principal stronghold of the middle-class Radical party, with some occasional competition from Conservatives and, since the 1940s, Peronists. In 1996 Radical Fernando de la Rúa became the first elected mayor of Buenos Aires. In Uruguay the Colorado party, with a middle-class and working-class constituency, has generally dominated Montevideo. In Chile, with a more complex political party structure, Santiago has seen more competition among various groups, although for a good part of the twentieth century the Radical party was an important force at both the national and local levels. In all three capitals Socialists occasionally have played significant roles in local government. In Buenos Aires representatives of the Socialist party often held between one third and one half of the seats on the city council in the 1920s and 1930s (see Walter). In Santiago Socialists were also present on the city council, and in 1939 Socialist Graciela Contreras de Schnake was appointed the first female mayor of a major Latin American city. In 1989, in Uruguay, a Leftist coalition, the Frente Amplio, captured the plurality in the capital and its leader, Socialist Tabaré Vázquez, became the head of local government (Dietz and Shidlo).

In addition to being main centers of political party organization and activity, all three cities also have been characterized by the development of local neighborhood organizations that have petitioned local and national governments for specific improvements in specific *barrios*. All three, too, have been the arenas of the mass mobilizations of hundreds of thousands–if not millions–of citizens rallying for one cause or another. Throughout the twentieth century the broad avenues and principal plazas of the three capitals have been the arenas for the city's citizens to demonstrate their political sentiments and not infrequently to clash violently with the police and the army. Especially prominent in such mobilizations have been political parties, labor organizations, and other special interest groups such as teachers and other government employees. The University Reform movement, which had its origins in Argentina and Uruguay and spread to Chile, helped stimulate student protest movements centered in the main national universities and helped make university students prominent actors in many public demonstrations.

Some of the most violent episodes in the history of all three capitals occurred in the 1960s and 1970s. In the cases of Buenos Aires and Montevideo, the emergence of urban guerrilla organizations–such as the Montoneros and the People's Revolutionary Army in Argentina and the Tupamaros in Uruguay–severely disrupted urban life. In Chile urban guerrillas were less numerous and influential, but the polarization between groups–such as the Movimiento de Izquierda Revolucionario (MIR) on the Left and Patria y Libertad on the Right–produced increasingly violent confrontations in Santiago in the late 1960s and early 1970s. As is well known, these revolutionary activities were significant factors in creating the conditions that led to military takeovers in all three countries and the imposition of brutal, repressive regimes. In Argentina military governments ruled from 1966 to 1973 and from 1976 to 1983. In Uruguay the military gained control in the early 1970s and ruled until the mid-1980s. In Chile the dictatorship of Augusto Pinochet came to power in 1973 and lasted until 1990.

As the three separate essays on the cities note, this period of repression had especially deleterious effects on culture.

Intellectuals and students were singled out for arrest, detention, and "disappearance." The more fortunate were forced into exile. Censorship was imposed on the printed press and the electronic media, and severe restrictions were placed on academic freedom. Despite the many difficulties imposed by these regimes, as the essays also note, an important culture of resistance appeared in all three countries and capitals, which played an important role in the ultimate end of these repressive regimes and which aided in the transition to and apparent consolidation of democracy in the 1980s and 1990s. Much of the cultural activity in all three cities and countries in this period has been directed toward coming to grips with the legacy of the period of military rule and the many human rights abuses associated with that experience.

Over the past two decades, all three capitals have served as the primary centers of the transition to democracy and a free society. They have continued to be the principal arena for the kinds of mass mobilizations that have characterized them throughout the century, although in these years generally more peaceful than in the past. All three, too, are the major showcases for the economic neo-Liberalism and globalization that came to dominate the 1990s throughout Latin America (perhaps less in Uruguay than in Chile and Argentina). While all three cities retain many aspects of European influences and character, the impact of North American culture is particularly prominent, most visibly perhaps in changing clothing styles, taste in music, and the proliferation of U.S.-based fast-food chains. The enclosed shopping mall has also become a notable presence in all three cities–in some cases repeating the U.S. pattern of a new center located in the suburbs, in other instances involving the refurbishing of existing downtown buildings. While modern steel and glass multistory buildings increasingly characterize the urban landscape in all three capitals, there also have been many attempts to renovate and preserve established landmarks, such as the Galerías Pacífico in Buenos Aires and the Estación Mapocho in Santiago, following the model of similar efforts in the United States and Europe.

The recent growth in all three cities has been accompanied by the intensification and accentuation of problems that have deep historical roots. Even with certain improvements in public transportation and the creation of new avenues and highways, the downtowns of all three cities remain crowded and difficult to negotiate, and monumental traffic jams are frequent occurrences. Environmental problems have grown and deepened in all three capitals, with Santiago suffering some of the worst air pollution in the world, and Buenos Aires and Montevideo forced to deal with the contamination of its rivers as well as air quality issues. Crime has become an increasing concern. While criminal activity–notably burglaries and robberies–has always been present, the growth in the number of violent incidents in cities that traditionally had been considered relatively safe is an issue of great public preoccupation. The Neo-Liberalism of the 1990s has also been accompanied by rising urban unemployment and the growth of the so-called *informal sector* of the economy throughout Latin America and including the southern cone capitals.

As the three capital cities enter the twenty-first century, several things seem fairly certain. All will continue into the foreseeable future as the main political centers of their respective nations, although efforts to disperse authority–such as the relocation of Chile's national Congress to Valparaíso and the attempt to move the capital of Argentina from Buenos Aires to Viedma—may reoccur from time to time. Their size, location, infrastructure, and built environment assure that they will remain economic, social, and cultural centers as well. Population growth and concentration in the future may not equal the pace of the twentieth century, but it seems assured that all three capitals will continue to grow, moving ever outward beyond the present-day suburbs, while trying to maintain a vital downtown core. Interest in politics may wax and wane, but it seems likely that all three will continue as the main arenas of mass mobilization and that local neighborhood associations will continue to play important roles in city life. National and city leaders will be obliged to address the ever-present problems of traffic flow and control, the provision of adequate housing, the regulation of construction, and concerns over environmental deterioration and public safety. In the process they will have to balance the desire for continued growth and modernization with the need to retain the special character of all three cities in the face of the homogenization—that seems an inevitable part of globalization—as well as to ensure that a city's greatness is measured not only by its size and beauty but also by the quality of life for every one of its inhabitants.

Works Cited

Censo de la República de Chile, levantado el 28 de noviembre de 1907. [n.d] (Santiago).

Dietz, Henry A., and Gil Shidlo, ed. 1998. *Urban Elections in Democratic Latin America.* Wilmington: Scholarly Resources.

Hardoy, Jorge. 1987. "Teorías y prácticas urbanísticas en Europa entre 1850 y 1930: su traslado a América Latina." *Revista de Indias* [Madrid] 47.179: 187–224.

Sargent, Charles S. 1994. "Uruguay." *Latin American Urbanization: Historical Profiles of Major Cities.* Ed. Michael Gerald Greenfield. Westport: Greenwood Press. 468–85.

Scarpaci, Joseph L. 1994. "Chile." *Latin American Urbanization: Historical Profiles of Major Cities.* Ed. Michael Gerald Greenfield. Westport: Greenwood Press. 106–33.

Scobie, James R. 1972. "Buenos Aires as a Commercial-Bureaucratic City, 1880–1910: Characteristics of a City's Orientation." *American Historical Review* 77. 4: 1035–73.

——. 1989. "The Growth of Cities." *Latin American Economy and Society, 1870–1930.* Ed. Leslie Bethell. Cambridge: Cambridge University Press. 149–81.

Walter, Richard J. 1993. *Politics and Urban Growth in Buenos Aires: 1910–1942.* Cambridge: Cambridge University Press.

CHAPTER 53

MONTEVIDEO
FROM FRONTIER CITY TO MERCOSUR

Hugo Achugar

As is well known, every overview, like every attempt to narrate the passage of a historical current, whether in literature or culture, involves an interpretation and a translation, and thus an act of betrayal. The act of narrating an account of Montevidean or Uruguayan culture or, for that matter, any other culture, not only cannot escape from this compound interpretation-betrayal, it must perforce fall into fiction–among others the fiction of the origins. Although this description of Montevideo as a cultural center was conceived around the notion of culture and not exclusively or principally around the idea of Montevideo as a literary center, it has had nevertheless to engage in a risky negotiation between chronicling the literary and the cultural. The other danger in such a description is that of falling into an enumerative litany, but how else can one account for the variety of cultural events and sites in a historical panorama that covers more than two and a half centuries without running this risk, which is to say, ending in failure? The plethora of dates, however, is something more than a risk: It is a wager placed upon the present interpretation of the history of Montevideo as a cultural center. It is, in short, the edification of a failure.

The Origins: Frontier City, Garrison City

With respect to the origins of Montevideo, its invention stems from or is limited to the name of Montevideo itself. According to tradition, the name Montevideo would have the following origins: It refers to the Spanish geographic designation of Monte VI De E. O. (Monte Sexto de Este a Oeste/The Sixth Peak from East to West); or, it refers to the observation made by a Portuguese explorer upon identifying the hill that overlooked the bay: Monte Vide Eu (I see the peak–in a mixed idiom composed of Portuguese and Latin). These fictional origins notwithstanding, it is a fact that the city was founded in 1724 by Bruno Mauricio de Zabala. Before the arrival of the Europeans, the present site of the city of Montevideo and its geographical zone of influence were supposedly inhabited by nomadic communities of indigenous peoples. Save for some tools, arms, a number of symbolic pictographic records, and the so-called *cerritos* (mounds), no other manifestations of this culture have been found. However, this scarcity of cultural records can in no way be taken as evidence of a cultural absence in the formation of what would later be Montevideo or, indeed, of Uruguay itself. In fact, the natives have been associated both with a number of military episodes relating to the struggle for Uruguayan independence and with the construction of various Uruguayan cities; this was particularly the case with the *tapes* from the Jesuit missions who participated in the construction of Montevideo in 1724.

Thus, it was not a fear of the natives or the necessity of subduing them that caused the Spanish authorities to establish the city of Montevideo on the north shore of the River Plate. The late colonization of the Banda Oriental (east bank of the Plate) was motivated by geopolitical reasons antedating the decision to found the city of San Felipe y Santiago de Montevideo. We might even venture the affirmation that Montevideo was, in a certain sense, established as an after-effect of the Treaty of Tordesillas (1494) and the later treaties of Utrecht (1713). San Felipe y Santiago de Montevideo was not the first settlement constructed in what is today Uruguay and what was then known as the Banda Oriental. In 1527 Gaboto had raised a small fort at the site he called the Port of San Lázaro, which was soon abandoned; in the seventeenth century the Dominican friars established what they called Santo Domingo de Soriano; and further inland, Jesuits were establishing missions–all of which encouraged colonization in the Banda Oriental. The Portuguese, for their part, were also in the process of establishing themselves in the region, in 1680, founding the Colonia do Sacramento almost opposite Buenos Aires. It was this presence of the Portuguese, as well as their intention to establish another city in the Banda Oriental near present-day Montevideo that convinced the governor of Buenos Aires to stop postponing his decision on settling the opposite shore of the Plate. According to the accounts of Bauzá and Pérez Santarcieri, Captain Pedro Gronardo, the River Plate pilot who had settled in the region of what would later become Montevideo, warned the authorities in Buenos Aires of Portuguese intentions to settle the area. Unlike other cities, Montevideo was not founded in a single gesture but rather as the result of a long process: In November 1723 the Spanish confronted the Banda Oriental Portuguese and soon after began the process of founding the city when they erected a fort in Montevideo Bay. The military garrison of 1724 was followed by the arrival of a civilian population, first from Buenos Aires, later from the Canary Islands, in 1726 and 1729, and this phase was capped when a municipal government was installed on 1 January 1730.

As a fortified outpost against Portuguese incursions and as a frontier city, Montevideo thrived. This frontier status–geographic destiny having placed the city on or near the boundary between the Spanish and Portuguese empires–marked the cultural and political history of Montevideo and what would later become Uruguay; this has been true since its inception and, across the centuries, continues to mark it today. It was precisely this buffer-state function that encouraged Lord Ponsomby, in the name of the English government, to call for the creation of an independent nation-state between Argentina and Brazil, a nation that since 1830–the same year in which Ponsomby promoted the independence of Belgium as another independent buffer state–has been known as the República Oriental de Uruguay. Today, at the start of the twenty-first century and for the first time since the Treaty of Tordesillas (that is, with the end of the hostilities between, first, the traditional imperial antagonists of Spain and Portugal and, later, Argentina and Brazil), the geopolitical particularity of Uruguay has made it possible that, in the same moment that Uruguay lost its historic identity as a buffer state, Montevideo was been chosen as the administrative seat of the Mercosur, the economic union of Argentina, Uruguay, Paraguay, and Brazil.

The initial confrontation between Colonia do Sacramento and Montevideo, and not the later competition between the ports of Montevideo and Buenos Aires, is what lay behind the founding of the city in 1730. These military origins marked the city not only at its foundation but for a long time: "During the entire eighteenth century, Montevideo was considered nothing more than a simple fortified outpost and naval station, and, in reality, a military garrison whose civil life was rudimentary" (Zum Felde I: 27–28). Although the city's frontier status was the *raison d'être* for the Spanish presence, it was also to give the city an extra-military destiny. Commercial activity, whether legitimate or illegitimate, would be fundamental to the growth of the new city and the region which surrounded it. The special consideration with which the Spanish Crown regarded the port of Montevideo was made evident in 1791 when the Crown named the port as the sole point of entry for slaves into the River Plate.

Every frontier is, by definition, not only a limit and a barrier, but also a place of transit, a space of negotiation and hybridity, a porous zone. The frontier region that Montevideo occupied did not escape these characteristics and for much of its history the city lived off the avails of illegal commerce, which is to say, contraband. Even the regime of free trade instituted by Carlos III in 1778 did not put an end to this underground economy of the River Plate. Legitimate economic activity was based almost exclusively in the production of hides and leathers from the livestock herds that the then Governor of Asunción Hernando Arias de Saavedra o Hernandarias had introduced into the Banda Oriental in the early decades of the seventeenth century and which in the eighteenth century underwent a spectacular development. This introduction of (beef) livestock has been seen by certain historians (Zum Felde; Caetano and Rilla) as an emblem of Uruguayan economic and cultural identity and an event that would determine its future. The great boom of the leather epoch financed a large part of the early economic and cultural development of the Banda Oriental. It would give way only much later to another stage in which, in addition to hides, Uruguay would become a major producer of jerked beef. Throughout the twentieth century a meat-curing industry of particular importance would develop.

Given that Montevideo was originally considered to be neither a commercial nor an administrative center, the initial cultural and educational development of the city was rather meager. Up until just before the era of the independence struggles, there were only a few educational institutions in Montevideo and its zone of influence. At first only Santo Domingo de Soriano, Colonia do Sacramento, and Montevideo had schools where literacy and the catechism were taught. With the expulsion of the Jesuits in 1767 and the rout of the Portuguese in the Colonia do Sacramento in 1777, the development of literate culture in the region was even more limited and indeed retarded. During this entire period up until the end of the eighteenth century, rather than being a city of letters, Montevideo was, as it had been from the beginning, a militarized or garrison city.

From Colony to Republic

Discounting the cultural production of the Portuguese in Colonia do Sacramento, where the cultural activity of the literate was relatively significant, we can say that, although there was not a complete absence of either literate or written culture, life in the Banda Oriental territory during the Colonial era did develop one particularly relevant form of cultural production. The large majority of the first inhabitants of the city were illiterate and Montevidean daily life toward the end of the eighteenth century did not differ much from that experienced in any village on the Iberian peninsula, save for the presence of the natives. The population of the entire Banda Oriental territory around 1796 numbered less than 30,000 individuals, with Montevideo home to less than one tenth of them. These numbers notwithstanding, the cultural production of the city during the almost 100 years of the Colonial era was manifest in a symbolic elaboration of local life that can be read as much in the Municipal Records (see Milán) as in the accounts that various ecclesiastics, functionaries of the Crown, and occasional visitors to the city left during the period. The image of the Colonial era of Montevideo that the historians have bequeathed to us is one of a society without a significant cultural depth or density, largely composed of soldiers, laborers, merchants, artisans, priests, slaves and slave traders, as well as a few plantation owners and smugglers.

However, the Municipal Records–the sole written record of what transpired in the first decades of Montevideo's history–tell a story of the vicissitudes of daily life and of the struggles for power in a city whose inhabitants had nothing of great importance to do and who seem to have passed their leisure time in conversation. This oral character of the early city life appears to have been linked not only to the debates in the municipal government, but also to the fact that the overwhelming majority of the residents were illiterate (see Milán). It is not only the Municipal Records that demonstrate the pronounced orality of Colonial Montevideo; Guillermo Milán links this hegemonic orality to the organization of sociability in which, according to the account of the traveler Pernetty, the majority of the population whiled away the time in smoking and conversing:

> Es así que muy a menudo, se les encuentra delante de la puerta de una casa conversando y fumando. Otros en cambio, montan a caballo, pero no para hacer un paseo por los alrededores, sino simplemente para dar una vuelta por las calles. Si el deseo los lleva, descienden del caballo, se juntan con algunos amigos, hablan dos horas, sin decirse nada, fuman, toman mate, y vuelven a montar a caballo de regreso. (qtd. in Milán 80)

> Such is the situation that very often one encounters groups of people on the front steps of the houses smoking and conversing. Others, by contrast, get into the saddle, not, however, in order to view the surrounding countryside, but rather simply to take the air in the streets. Should the desire overtake them, they dismount, join in with their fellows, pass a couple of hours in conversation without saying anything of import, smoke, drink maté, and then remount their horses and return home.

In addition to the register of the Municipal Records, there exists another form of public writing, chronicling the first decades of Colonial life that we may call judicial writing (see Ferrés). However, although this form of public writing has, like the private writing of personal letters and diaries, recently begun to be studied, it has not yet entered into the collective cultural memory, whether official or popular, of Uruguay. However, between the end of the eighteenth and the beginning of the nineteenth century, it is possible to sketch the outlines of what, within a belletristic concept of literature, might be called if not a national, at the very least, a local literature. It is this latter category that the majority of literary historians have employed in their consideration of the works of Eusebio Valdenegro (1781–1818), Bartolomé Hidalgo (1788–1822),

Manuel Pérez Castellanos (1743–1815), and Juan Francisco Martínez (fl. 1807) (see Roxlo; Zum Felde I). While this writing generally goes unmentioned in literary dictionaries and histories, its grounding in military life, administrative activity, and geographic surveys formed the basis for some of the first descriptions of the natural and cultural environment of the region. The accounts realized by Félix de Azara are particularly relevant in this context (see Bauzá; Verdesio). These public forms of writing–governmental, judicial, administrative, military, or literary–bear testimony to the intentions of the ruling classes (and administrative apparatus of the state) to shape a society that had been born relatively late in the life of the Spanish imperial colonial regime. José Pedro Barrán (b. 1934) in his *Historia de la sensibilidad en el Uruguay* (History of Uruguayan Sensibility) has pointed out that: "las clases dirigentes españolas y orientales. . . ya en el siglo XVIII describían la sexualidad vigente como una '*inclinación a la barbarie*' y en 1809 calificaban a los sectores populares de '*República de Carives*,' utilizando la antinomia civilización y barbarie en un sentido cultural más vasto que el de Sarmiento. (su énfasis; I:15) ("already in the eighteenth century the Spanish ruling classes had described the prevailing sexuality in terms of an '*inclination towards barbarism*'; and [that] by 1809, employing the cultural antinomy of civilization and barbarism in a sense far more sweeping than had Sarmiento, the [Banda Oriental] masses had been branded a '*Republic of Savages*'") [author's emphasis].

In Barrán's usage the notion of barbarism refers to:

> . . . la sensibilidad de los "excesos" en el juego y el ocio (su consecuencia improductiva), en la sexualidad, en la violencia, en la exhibición "irrespetuosa" de la muerte, la "barbarie" que practicó también buena parte, a veces la mayoría de las clases dominantes en su vida cotidiana, fue opuesta, sobre todo por los dirigentes de la política y el saber–cabildantes, gobernadores, presidentes, ministros, legisladores, periodistas y fundamentalmente el clero–a la "civilización," en el sentido de represión de la violencia, el juego, la sexualidad y la "fiesta" de la muerte. (I, 15)

> the sensibility of "excess" in amusement and leisure (its non-productive consequences), in sexuality, in violence, and in the "lawless and crude" display of death. The "barbarism" that was also practiced by a good part, at times the majority, of the ruling classes in their daily lives was by political and opinion leaders– aldermen, governors, presidents, ministers, legislators, journalists, and above all by the clergy–opposed to a notion of "civilization," standing for the repression of violence, amusement, sexuality, and the "fiesta" of death.

This barbarous sensibility of which Barrán writes, if only to condemn it, is passed over in silence by the learned and public writing of colonial Montevideo. The aforementioned Félix de Azara pointed out around 1800 that the inhabitants of the colony "know no restraint in anything, nor demonstrate any sense of modesty, discretion or shame" (qtd. in Barrán I: 21–22). This licentiousness on the part of the inhabitants of Montevideo and its environs makes one think not so much of a peaceful Iberian village transplanted to the New World, but of a frontier post governed by the immanence or the proximity of the non-European, uncivilized world of the natives, however decimated or subdued, and especially by the Spanish inhabitants' ever-present fears of an imminent rebellion on the part of the numerically superior black population.

The barely 1,000 inhabitants of Montevideo, according to the estimate made by Concolorcorvo around 1773, did not pass their leisure hours in literary salons or philosophical discussions. If we are to believe the account of the Abbé Pernetty, who arrived in the city as part of Bougainville's expedition in 1767, the principal diversion of Montevidean society consisted of family reunions where guitars were played, occasionally accompanied by *zapateo* dancing and hand-clapping. Of particular interest in this context was the *calenda*, a dance bearing some similarities to the Andalusian *zapateo* but more probably the product of the African presence in Montevidean society. Supposedly imported from Guinea by the slaves, the *calenda* was danced not only by the blacks and mulattos, but, as Pernetty points out, by the Spanish immigrants, including the monks. According to Ruben Cotelo, the music of the *calenda* was characterized by the intermixing of musical instruments and the human voice. The dancers would line up in two lines, the men facing the women, and the spectators would form a circle around them. Someone sang the verses, and the spectators would repeat the refrain while clapping their hands. Holding their arms raised half up and turning, the dancers would approach one another until such time as the force of the instruments or the tone of the singer's voice signaled that they should draw near their partner and strike his or her belly, two or three times. From time to time the dancers would lock arms in a pair and slowly drawing their bellies together would kiss each other without losing the rhythm. Monks, too, would dance the *calenda* in religious ceremonies. On the evening of Christmas Day a platform or theater stage would be erected in the choir in front of the screen which would be kept open so that the public could view the spectacle. Except for the fact that the townsmen did not dance with the monks, the holy *calenda* did not differ from the profane (Cotelo 127).

Up until the years preceding the struggles for independence, daily life in the colony hardly favored cultural development (in the sense of high culture) of the city. The disproportionate number of men in the population, both in Montevideo and in the rest of the Banda Oriental, led the anonymous editor of the *Noticia sobre el estado de los campos de la Banda Oriental* (Report on Rural Conditions in the Banda Oriental), submitted to the Spanish Crown in 1794, to describe the colony as being populated by "men in appearance only. . . men bearing in matters of religion no resemblance to their likenesses elsewhere" (Barrán-Alpini 76). Although the barbarous society–or the culture of barbarity–of Montevideo that was the object of the astonished gaze of the occasional sheltered European visitor did not, despite the best intentions of the literate few, develop a self-conscious image of itself, it was at least fully aware of the debates surrounding new ideas. The struggle for independence makes this clear. Despite Spanish government censorship, the diffusion of Enlightenment and North American and French revolutionary ideas made possible the emergence of a consciousness that was, if not properly speaking revolutionary, at least independence-oriented in nature. Figures such as José Gervasio Artigas, leader of the independence plot, and the writers who surrounded him, especially Dámaso Antonio Larrañaga (1771–1848), would be examples of this new mode of thought in the Banda Oriental. In this context, it is possible to highlight yet another, more civilized kind of cultural manifestation taking place in eighteenth-century Montevideo. The ludic, pleasure-loving spirit of Montevidean Colonial society found an outlet in the festivities surrounding the coronation of Carlos

IV in 1789, as well as in the performances at the Casa de Comedias theater which opened its doors in 1793, well before the first patriotic representations of Juan Francisco Martínez were mounted in the early years of the nineteenth century.

The brief period of English rule between 1806 and 1807 was without major consequence. However, beyond the exacerbation of the confrontation with Buenos Aires, the English presence did facilitate the appearance in 1807 of the first Uruguayan newspaper, *The Southern Star*, published in English. In this same line of development, we can say that the Siege of Montevideo and the independence campaign mobilized the literary imagination of the colony and forged powerful links between that imagination and political and historical referents. Both the *Diario histórico* [Chronicle of My Times] of Francisco Acuña de Figueroa (1791–1862)–the writer who later, in addition to a diverse and abundant corpus of works, would compose the words to the national anthem–and the "Cielitos" ["Poems to the Beloved"] and *Diálogos* [Dialogues] of Bartolomé Hidalgo testify to the nascent independence sentiment and to the historical-cultural transformations then underway in Montevidean society.

The Cisplatine Republic, the name under which Uruguay was known during the period of Brazilian domination from 1816 to 1821, demonstrated that Brazilian influence in Uruguayan affairs had not ceased with the expulsion of the Portuguese from Colonia do Sacramento. And, indeed, we may say that Brazilian influence was fundamental to the emergence of the new nation-state. The establishment of this new state was realized in 1828, although it wasn't until 1830 that the constitution of the República Oriental del Uruguay was approved. The pageantry with which the Montevideans celebrated the event closed the book not only on a period of political turbulence, but on what the title of Francisco Bauzá's (1849–1899) book called *La historia de la dominación española en el Uruguay* [1880; The History of the Spanish Domination of Uruguay]. The 14,500 inhabitants of Montevideo, of which 2,489 were slaves, began their newly independent life with an outpouring of fiestas, patriotic celebrations, and theatrical performances that together set the incipient cultural life of the city in motion. It was not long thereafter that the first anthology of nationalist poetry, edited by Luciano Lira (d. 1840?), was published, *El Parnaso Oriental* [1835; The Eastern Parnassus], a collection that brought to light the work of the first Uruguayan poet of significance, Petrona Rosende de la Sierra (1787–1845). Cultural activity in the theater of the day, however, was much more important: In May 1830 a Spanish version of Rossini's *El engaño feliz* [The Happily Deceived] was mounted by the Tanni company, continuing the succession of visiting theatrical companies from Buenos Aires (the Buenos Aires Theatrical Society had mounted a production in 1829) and Spain that had recently passed through Montevideo.

From New Troy to the End of the Century (1838–1900)

Independence was followed by a period of political turbulence in which the struggles between local leaders involved not only the Uruguayans, but the region as a whole. This period from 1839 to 1851, known as the Great War, had a special effect on the city of Montevideo, transforming it into a place of exile for Argentineans fleeing the Rosas dictatorship and a site of discussion for European politics, particularly those of England and France. The slow rate of local demographic increase in this era did not stop the actual population from growing precipitously; the total population of Uruguay rose from 74,000 inhabitants in 1830 to 224,430 in 1860, 34 percent of whom were foreigners. The city had become a center of international intrigues, witnessing through her gates the passage of every kind of agent, spy, politician, and soldier from both the New and Old World. It was in this period, for example, that the Italian Guisseppe Garibaldi commanded the Eastern Squadron and perfected his battle tactics in the military campaigns of the epoch. Above and beyond these intrigues and conflicts, Montevideo became the intellectual and cultural center of the River Plate region. As Alberto Zum Felde (1889–1976) has affirmed, "De 1840 a 1851, la mayor parte de la intelectualidad argentina refugiada en Montevideo, convirtió a esta ciudad en el centro único de las letras platenses" (I: 129) ("from 1840 to 1851, with the greater part of the Argentinean intelligentsia taking refuge in Montevideo, the city was transformed into the extraordinary center of River Plate letters").

In 1838 *El Iniciador* began publishing under the directorship of Andrés Lamas (1817–1891) and Miguel Cané (1851–1905), marking the beginning of the presence of the Argentinean exiles and confirming the establishment of Romanticism that had arrived in Uruguay at the beginning of the decade. In 1816 the library created by Larrañaga out of the former personal collection of Pérez Castellano was chartered as the National Library; the Universidad de la República was established in 1838, although it did not commence activities until 1849. Other exiles arriving with Cané from Buenos Aires were Bartolomé Mitre (1821–1906) and Juan Bautista Alberdi (1810–1884); later, José Mármol (1818–1871), Vicente Fidel López (1815–1903), Juan de la Cruz Varela (1794–1839), and Juan María Gutiérrez (1809–1878) would arrive; and in 1846 Domingo Sarmiento (1811–1888) himself would pass through Montevideo. The presence of exiled Argentinean intellectuals and politicians in this period played a particularly important role in the cultural and political development of Uruguay and above all Montevideo. Not only did the exiles edit numerous periodicals and newspapers, they published a number of key books, including Echeverría's *Dogma socialista de la Asociación de Mayo* [1846; The Socialist Doctrine of the May Association] and Alberdi's *Plan de filosofía* [1840; Philosophical Program], as well as instituting a number of literary prizes, especially the one founded in 1841, of which Alberdi noted "La victoria del nuevo movimiento [romántico] ha sido completa. . . . Sin la tiranía de Rosas, todo el romanticismo platense no hubiera sido más que un concierto de gritos inútiles; la tiranía hizo de él una idealidad viva" (Zum Felde I: 119) ("the victory of the new (Romantic) movement is now complete. . . . Without the Rosas's tyranny, the entire movement of River Plate Romanticism would have been nothing more than a chorus of vain proclamations; with it, River Plate Romanticism acquired a living ideality"). Zum Felde's affirmation not only gives us an indication of the highly charged political nature of the moment that he himself lived through, but of the common experience shared by those on both sides of the River Plate. Montevideo was besieged–or at least that is what many Argentineans and Uruguayans felt–and the image of Troy asserted itself in the minds of many. In 1849, with the dispatch of Melchor Pacheco y Obes as envoy to Paris, Alexandre Dumas (1802–1870) took up the task of casting this national drama in literature. The result was *Montévideo ou la nouvelle Troie* [1850; Montevideo or The New Troy], a novel which, as the title indicates, drew a parallel between the confrontation of the federalist supporters and the unitarian antagonists of Rosas, and the conflict between the Argives and the Trojans. The Montevidean elites and the exiled Argentinean unitarians felt perhaps flattered by Dumas's imaginative representation, although the parallel of their plight with that of ancient Trojans cannot have filled them with much enthusiasm.

To the Montevidean besieged, the words of Manuel Herrera y Obes (1806–1890) painted a bleak picture:

> Figuráos vencedor dentro de la plaza de Montevideo al ejército que la cerca y, qué divisáis entonces dentro de la Capital del Estado? La dictadura personal, sea bajo el nombre de Rosas o de Oribe, la clase bárbara de la sociedad sofocando con su mayor número la inteligencia y las intenciones de la clase civilizada, el comercio inteligente con Europa, obstruido por una muralla de preocupaciones insensatas. (in Caetano and Rilla 58)

> Let us imagine for ourselves the unimaginable: that the army which encircles us was victorious here in the main square of Montevideo. What then would await us in the capital of the state? The personal dictatorship, whether of Rosas or Oribe; the barbarous majority of society smothering beneath their superior numbers the intelligence and the promise of the civilized minority; our intellectual commerce with Europe cut off by a rampart of senseless prejudices.

To the ears of the besiegers, the voice of Bernardo Prudencio Berro (1803–1868) presented another view:

> Pero, ¿qué ciudad es ésa?, ¿es la ciudad de América, es la ciudad oriental? No, es la ciudad de los europeos; es la ciudad abandonada de sus vecinos, la ciudad de Thiebaut o Garibaldi, la ciudad que sirve de apoyo a las pretensiones europeas, la ciudad finalmente donde un puñado de rebeldes contumaces apenas se descubre entre la multitud extranjera que los tiene absorbidos y los defiende y ampara. ¿Qué se puede atribuir de oriental ni de americano a todo lo que ha hecho Montevideo durante la lucha que sostiene contra los verdaderos americanos y orientales? (qtd. in Caetano and Rilla 59)

> What kind of city is this? Is it an American city, a Banda Oriental city? No: It is a European city; a city abandoned by its inhabitants; a city propped up by European pretensions, by Thiebaut and Garibaldi; a city in which a handful of contemptible rebels, s urrounded by a great mass of foreigners, find themselves absorbed, sheltered, and defended. I ask you this: What can be found that is Banda Oriental or American in all that Montevideo has done during the struggle they have mounted against the real Americans and the true Banda Oriental patriots?

During all this the city had become, if not totally cosmopolitan, at least an international center sheltering some 30,000 souls. Primary schools continued to multiply, and musicians, painters, sculptors, and theatrical companies continued to arrive, despite the siege. For their part, the besiegers, commanded by the former President Oribe, faced up to the stalemate with resolve, building churches, customs houses, and relatively ostentatious residences in small villages on the outskirts of Montevideo that would become, in the decades after the walls had been demolished, the new neighborhoods of the enlarged city. While life outside the walls was not as intense or as cosmopolitan as inside the city, it did develop a significant profile of cultural activity and included a number of booksellers.

The peace of April 1852 opened the doors to a new wave of foreign immigrants (then making up 21 percent of the population). It also saw the creation of the College of Medicine (the first scientific society in the country), and, for the more than 700 graduates of the elementary school system, the expansion of higher education with the establishment of a Faculty of Civil Law. The years that followed witnessed a boom in public architectural projects, including the construction of the Solís Theater (overtaking in importance the old Casa de Comedias and soon to be amalgamated with the San Felipe) the creation of the first Hospital Italiano (1857), the construction of the Plaza Independencia, as well as the renovation and expansion of the old Hospital Maciel. Despite the political turbulence that continued up until the first decades of the twentieth century, the constructive spirit born in the Independence movement did not abate. International, regional, and national politics continued to mark in large part life in Montevideo and Uruguay. French and English demands for indemnification following the Great War, treaties signed with Argentina and Brazil, the Brazilian incursion into Uruguayan territory (1864), and the Triple Alliance between Argentina, Brazil, and Uruguay against Paraguay (1865) were the major events guiding the direction of a society that had doubled in population since 1852.

In 1843, immigrants of French origin (in the majority, Basques) composed one third of the Uruguayan population, although this was to change in the decades that followed. Between 1825 and 1851 European immigrants to Uruguay were mostly Basques; however, in the period following and up until 1870, Brazilians outnumbered Spaniards, Basques, and Italians. In the last third of the century, the Italians were by far the largest group (see Marenales), although by the turn of the twentieth century Spaniards, and in particular Galicians, had decisive presence in Montevidean and Uruguayan society and cultural activity. The high rate of immigration in these years was manifest not only in the publication of French, Italian, and even English language newspapers, but also in the formation of a solid cosmopolitan consciousness that became even more evident at the end of the nineteenth century when the modernization of the country, and in particular of Montevideo, had been consolidated. The immigrant presence would play an important role in the physical construction of Montevideo itself, for, in addition to architects and builders–the majority of whom were Catalan, Italian, and French in origin (Víctor Rabú, Eduardo Canstatt, Luis Andreoni, Juan Lukasiewicks, Juan Tossi, Aquiles Monzani), although the work of the Uruguayan Juan A. Capurro is also important–masons and artisans of European origin would be responsible for the construction of the civic face of the city in the final third of the nineteenth century.

The process of modernizing a pastoral, mercantile, and autocratic Uruguay began to take off around 1870, following the end of the War of the Triple Alliance, through the consolidation of the nation's cultural, scientific, and religious institutions. The 1877 Public Education Bill, tabled during the Lorenzo Latorre dictatorship, instituted a set of educational reforms under the direction of José Pedro Varela and mandated a free and non-religious system of instruction, measures that were to play a definitive role in the shaping of Uruguayan society. This 1877 bill would become a cornerstone of national cultural pride and an affirmative instrument not only of the project to amalgamate a heterogeneous Uruguayan society, but of the consolidation of its identity. Indeed, we can go so far as to say that a part of the present national imaginary directly stems from this secularization of instruction under the Varela reforms. Parallel to the educational reforms that were to be central to the consolidation of the country, a series of celebrations of national achievements was initiated, beginning with the inauguration on 18 May 1879, just as the Varela reforms began to take effect, of a monument commemorating the 1825 Congress of Florida.

This event is particularly important to the cultural history of Uruguay for several reasons. On the one hand, it demonstrated the desire of the hegemonic elites to fashion an ensemble of cultural emblems concretizing the national identity; however, it also served as the pretext for a series of incidents that are particularly resonant in Uruguayan intellectual and artistic history. The inauguration of the monument was accompanied by a reading of poems that had won an open competition held in conjunction with the event. Following the reading of the winning poems by Aurelio Berro and Joaquín de Salterain (1856–1926), José Zorrilla de San Martín's (1855–1931) "La leyenda patria" ["The Legend of the Motherland"] was read, a piece that had not been considered because of its excessive length. Zorrilla de San Martín's poem was so enthusiastically received by the multitude present–or so historical memory informs us–that it was declared the winner of the competition by popular vote, and the official winner Aurelio Berro gave the golden medallion that had been bestowed on him to Zorrilla de San Martín. The later works (such as *Tabaré* (1888) and *La epopeya de Artigas* [1910; The Epic of Artigas]) of Zorrilla de San Martín, Uruguay's national poet, as he was known from this moment forward, would fortify the then prevailing literary nationalist project. The artistic production of these years was not limited to poetry and monuments. Juan Manuel Blanes (1830–1901), the most important painter of the era, presented his monumental canvas "El desembarco de los treinta y tres orientales" ["The Landing of the Thirty-Three Patriots"] to the Governor Lorenzo Latorre in the same year (1879). Together with *Tabaré* and "La leyenda patria," Blanes's historical canvas depicting a milestone of the independence campaign would become one of the emblematic representations of the Uruguayan national imaginary.

The significance of the inauguration of the Congress of Florida monument in May 1879 went much further than a mere celebration of independence. It was precisely from this date on that a series of polemics developed between various intellectuals of the Montevidean elites with respect to the meaning of independence (Acevedo 125–27). The refusal of Juan Carlos Gómez (1820–1844) to participate in the inauguration, on the pretext that the Congress of Florida in 1825 had not declared independence, provoked a debate in Montevideo's Ateneo del Uruguay cultural center between José Pedro Ramírez and Pedro Bustamante. Education, the monument itself, painting, and poetry were the principal points of contention in an intellectual and political debate that raged against the backdrop of the government's attempts to consolidate the organization of the state. In the years following the foundation (around 1880) of the Ateneo del Uruguay, in the epoch that came to be known as that of the second Romantic generation, Uruguayan intellectual life began to manifest a special dynamism. This was the generation that rejected positivism and realism, "considering them to be two negative expressions of the human spirit and the meaning of life" (Zum Felde I: 163). However, the intellectual ferment surrounding the Ateneo also coincided with the militarism of the Latorre–Santos regime in which, according to Zum Felde, "outside the Ateneo. . . life in the city was a lamentable spectacle. Military rule meant that unruly militia men in their tightly cinched *kepis* and thugs sporting neckerchiefs were permanent fixtures on every street corner" (165).

The picture painted by Zum Felde, while certainly appropriate, is also revealing of a certain literate optic in which cultural manifestations other than those of the Ateneo were hardly esteemed or, for that matter, even taken notice of. Parallel to the high culture incarnated by the Ateneo, there developed in Montevideo in these same years a popular culture that, as an involuntary legatee of the Colonial *calenda*, had definitively incorporated the African-inspired *candombe*; this slowly began to take shape as the Uruguayan carnival. The masquerade groups or *comparsas*, as they were called, that formed the backbone of the carnival included among their numbers women–a rather scandalous development from the point of view of the social codes in force amongst Uruguay's literate classes. The *comparsas* were responsible for creating the first images of an urban culture that bore little resemblance to the traditions of the *payadores* (gaucho minstrels), the gauchos, or *criollo* or *gaucho* literature. These same years also saw the popular circus (which included theatrical representations) delight those "barbarous" Montevideans who resisted the "civilizing" projects of the hegemonic classes, projects which included the demolition of both the old Fort, where the Government House was located, and the Old Market, and the construction of a boulevard girding the periphery of a city that could still count more than 10,000 in attendance at the bullfights: "En los palcos (de la plaza de toros, H.A.) estaban las principales familias de Montevideo que, contagiadas por el entusiasmo de la madre patria, intentaban dar hondo arraigo al bárbaro espectáculo que hasta entonces sólo los hombres de Montevideo se resolvían a presenciar (Acevedo 145) ("The principal families of Montevideo could be found on a regular basis in the boxes [of the arena] where, swept up in the enthusiasm for the motherland, they attempted to peer deep into the heart of a barbarous spectacle that until then only the men of Montevideo had resolved to attend"). In addition to the *comparsas*, the circus, the theaters, the concerts, and the bullfights, Montevideans of all classes were also drawn to the rat pit located near the then center of the city. How many rats a dog could or would kill in a given fight was the subject of heated wagers, much like the horse races. After 1877 the jockeys at the races were obliged to ride sporting a jockey costume (Acevedo 145).

It was also in these years that a powerful movement for the creation of artistic symbols reinforcing the national identity arose among the producers of high culture, a movement that would win important popular recognition: José Zorrilla de San Martín in the domain of poetry, with his "La leyenda patria" and *Tabaré* (1888); Eduardo Acevedo Díaz (1851–1921), with his series of historical novels, *Brenda* (1884), *Ismael* (1888), and *El combate de la tapera* [1892; The Battle for the Abandoned Village]; Manuel Blanes with his numerous canvases and especially his enormous *El juramento de los treinta y tres orientales* [1878; The Oath of the Thirty-Three Patriots], as well as with his series of "Gauchos" and historical paintings; the première of G. Grasso's musical composition, *Pericón Nacional* [1887; National Pericon]. All these works contributed to ongoing attempts to affix an emotional charge and consolidate a sense of national belonging and patriotism. This political decision to enhance such sentiments was prompted by the fact that at the end of the nineteenth century a sense of nation had not yet solidified and the heterogeneity of Uruguayan society, with its high percentage of immigrants, put unity in some measure of danger. The disputes between the nationalist party, the *blancos*, and the liberal or *colorado* party–or, put in another way, the opposition between those who were said to represent rural interests and those representing the well-heeled Montevideans–came to a head in the Civil Wars of 1897 and 1904 which, far from threatening to derail the national consolidation project, can be said to have signaled the completion of the process of national constitution. Uruguay entered the twentieth century with a capital city that represented one-third of the total population and which was poised to complete its urban transformation. In this sense, it can be said that the institution of nationalist artistic representation created in the final decades of the nineteenth century–Zorrilla in poetry, Blanes in painting, Acevedo Díaz in narrative, and Grasso, Fabini, Broqua, and Clouzeau-Mortet in music–coincided with the urban transformations and the physical modernization of the civic face of Montevideo.

Between the end of the Great War (1851) and the census of 1908, the national population rose from 33,994 inhabitants to 309,231. In an epoch of interminable political battles between the *blancos* and the *colorados* and an ever-rising rate of foreign immigration (with immigrants comprising 47 percent of the population in 1889), nothing remained of the sentiments that had animated the era of the New Troy, save the memory. The walls of the old city had been demolished in 1876, and the urban transformations introduced by the public works projects of Emilio Reus–the inauguration of the Plaza Zabala in 1890, the construction of a boulevard ring-road, and the Parque Urbano (later named Parque Rodó)–would make of Montevideo a city that in desiring to be modern and European and by negating its Hispanic origins, had transformed itself from its isolated, fortified, self-absorbed, and inward-looking origins into a truly urban center with the unmistakable gloss of modernity (see Schelotto). It was this cosmopolitan city of modernity that welcomed Sarah Bernhardt to the Solís Theater in 1886 and that staged, one after the other, the operas of Verdi sung by the Italian tenors and sopranos who toured the River Plate region. Two late-century events summed up the new life of Montevideo's *fin-de-siècle* modernity: the proliferation of cafés, such as the Tupí Nambá (1889), that were to become particularly important cultural and artistic centers and the exhibition, just a few months after their premières in Paris, of the first Lumière short-subject films on 18 August 1896.

It was in this climate of cosmopolitanism and pretensions to modernity that the Generation of the 900 or the *modernista* Generation developed their works. José Enrique Rodó (1871–1917), Julio Herrera y Reissig (1875–1910), Carlos Reyles (1868–1938), Florencio Sánchez (1875–1910), Delmira Agustini (1886–1914), María Eugenia Vaz Ferreira (1875–1924), Víctor Pérez Petit (1871–1947), and Roberto de las Carreras (1875–1963) are but a few of the writers who published in the years around 1900 and who constituted one of the most exceptional movements of Uruguayan high culture. It was in this Montevideo that José Enrique Rodó, anxious about the advance of a mania for Anglo-Saxon values, as well as about the presence in his city of a foreign population whose numbers placed traditional values in jeopardy, wrote his *Ariel* (1900). The Montevideo that would receive Ramón Menéndez Pidal (1869–1968) and Rubén Darío (1867–1916) was already a city in which approximately 80,000 received primary schooling, in which the First Latin American Scientific Congress would be held, in which Arturo Toscanini had directed Richard Wagner's *Die Meistersinger von Nürnberg* (in which Enrico Caruso sang) (1903), *Lohengrin* (1904), and

Tristan und Isolde (1906), in which the compositions of Camille Saint-Saëns had been performed (1904), as had Giacomo Puccini's *Edgar* (1905)–and in which the anarchist trade unionists exiled from Argentina had taken up residence. This city of cosmopolitan aspirations had little in common with the rest of the country: In the same year that Toscanini conducted Wagner, in the distant department of Cerro Largo approximately 400 kilometers from Montevideo, Aparicio Saravia was mounting an insurrection against the *dotores* in the capital. Civilized Montevideo lived cheek by jowl with a barbarous hinterland.

The Modern City, The Centenary, The Society of Felicity, and Its Dark Side (1910–1950)

When the U.S. Secretary of State Elliot Rott arrived in Montevideo in 1906 for talks with President José Batlle y Ordoñez, the first electric trams had only recently been introduced in the city, and Syrians had only recently been allowed entry to the country. Public education continued the process of integrating foreigners into the national project, a project that, under Batlle y Ordoñez, would include a series of social reforms (the eight-hour workday, legalized divorce, old age pensions), as well as the orchestration of a cultural policy (public concerts by Luis Sambuccetti; the institution, inspired by Pedro Figari [1861–1938], of the School of Arts and Crafts) that together would characterize the political tenor of the era as, if not advanced and populist, at the very least progressive. However, strikes by tramway workers, coach drivers, and bakers, coeval with the prohibition of religious images in hospitality establishments–a prohibition that provoked José Enrique Rodó to register his disagreement with Batlle y Ordoñez–demonstrated that the process of democratization and the concern to advance Uruguayan society were not easily accomplished in a Montevideo that now sheltered trade unions and socialist associations. These were new times for Montevideans: The swearing in of Parliamentary deputies on the Bible was eliminated (1908); religious practice and instruction in public schools were suppressed (1909); the first woman to study medicine, Paulina Luisi, received her certification as a medical doctor (1908), while another woman, Delmira Agustini (1886–1914), after having published her *Cantos de la mañana* [1910; Morning Songs], was assassinated a few years later by her ex-husband to the scandal of the city. It was also in these years that the Women's University was founded (1912). New times, new ideas, advanced politics (in 1911 tramway companies were obliged to offer discounts to workers), new poetry, and above all new people characterized Montevideo and Uruguay. Immigration to Uruguay continued to increase, and in these years the Spanish Galicians outstripped all others. This was also a time of new artistic forms: In 1911 there were twenty-five cinemas in Montevideo and a couple of years later a modest film-production industry started producing news reports (Glucksman's Newsreels were the talk of the town) and documentaries.

In a certain manner, this first golden age of national culture–and especially the national high culture of which Rodó, Herrera y Reissig, Sánchez, Horacio Quiroga (1878–1937), and Agustini were some of the principal artists–would survive and dominate the national imaginary from Montevideo until well into the reign of the man the Uruguayans of the epoch considered the giant of the century, José

Batlle y Ordoñez (1856–1929). Although long before Batlle died, Montevidean society was no longer the same society that had witnessed the birth of the new century three decades earlier; the Uruguayan cultural imaginary that had developed in the shadow cast by his figure persisted in more than one manner of speaking. The crowning image of this happy society of the first decades of the twentieth century would be embraced by the many sectors of Montevidean society; World War I would merely confirm the advantages of Montevidean life and of Uruguayan society in its entirety. The publication in 1917 of *La agonía de Europa* [The Agony of Europe] by Adolfo Agorio (1888–1965) is an eloquent testimony to this belief. Thus it can be said that with the initiation of the celebrations surrounding Uruguay's centenary, (including the 1925 publication of *El libro del centenario del Uruguay* [The Book of the Uruguayan Centenary]) which, given the heated argument between those who considered 1825 to mark the foundation of Uruguay and those who favored 1830, lasted from 1925 to 1930, Montevideo presented a self-image of a modern and content society.

The organization of executive power in the form of collegiate government, the implementation of social reforms, the rising rates of literacy, the urban development, and the public works projects that added new plazas, avenues, buildings, and monuments to the city–all served to justify in the eyes of Montevideans their pride in having created a peaceable "Switzerland in the Americas." It was this city that received world-renowned scientists (Albert Einstein, 1924), presidents (Hoover, 1928; Franklin Delano Roosevelt and Getulio Vargas, 1935), musicians and conductors (Rubinstein, 1928; Ottorino Respighi, Lily Pons, and Tito Schipa in 1934; Marian Anderson and Pablo Casals in 1937), poets (Gabriela Mistral [1889–1957] in 1925; Alfonso Reyes [1899–1959] in 1928), playwrights (Pirandello, 1927), and politicians (Enrique Díez Canedo, Minister of the Spanish Republic, 1931). Montevideo in the 1920s and 1930s not only saw the publication of journals like *La Pluma, La Cruz del Sur*, and *Cartel*–manifestations of the modest face of the Uruguayan avant-garde–but also saw the completion of the Centenary Stadium (1930) which hosted the World Cup of soccer in which the Uruguayan team won the championship. In 1930 the SODRE (Servicio Oficial de Radiodifusión del Estado–the state broadcaster) began transmitting and the International Congress of Medicine was held in Montevideo.

Another event of significance in these years was the coronation, presided over by Alfonso Reyes, of Juana de Ibarbourou (1892–1979) as "Juana of the Américas." The ceremony was held in the recently inaugurated Legislature Palace (1925), a neo-Classical edifice that both symbolized the reign of representative democracy in Uruguay and aspired to a personification of Montevideo's modern urbanist yearnings. There is a relative consensus that Uruguayan society of the 1920s was both content and peaceable. A feeling of euphoria stemming from the economic boom and world peace marked many of the cultural manifestations of the epoch. The idea of a triumphant modernity combined with a sense of new beginnings was manifest in the titles of journals such as *Los nuevos* [1920; The Moderns] or in books of verse such as *Alas nuevas* [1922; New Wings], as well as in the many celebratory anthems, such as Juan Parra del Riego's (1894–1925) work *Himnos del cielo y los ferrocarriles* [1925; Anthems of Paradise and Locomotives]: "This was a time of happiness not only for Uruguay, but for the whole of the River Plate" (Díaz

88). This optimism also informed the technological transformations of the era and the momentum of a city in which social mobility, the already mentioned emergence of new social classes, and the accumulated effect of the successive waves of immigration seemed to sanction dreams of a paradise on earth.

The *locus amoenus*, the abode of pleasure presupposed in the imaginary of this period, was not drawn with reference to the *Georgics* of Virgil but rather after the scenography or scenario of a triumphant machine aesthetic that had arisen in Europe in the years before the 1914 war. The *Himnos of Parra del Riego*, the poems of Enrique Ricardo Garet (1904–1979) collected in *Paracaídas* [1927; Parachutes], and the celebrations of the new urban monuments, especially the Palacio Salvo skyscraper eulogized in Juvenal Ortiz Saralegui's (1907–1959) poem of the same name or even Alfredo Mario Ferreiro's (1899–1959) work, *El hombre que se comió un autobús* [1927; The Man who Devoured an Omnibus], show a few of the modes in which this imagined landscape of felicity was manifest in these years. This imaginary landscape combined aspects of cosmopolitanism with a reclamation of the local. Indeed, the Uruguayan and Latin American local was exalted in the writings and paintings of Pedro Figari (1861–1938), in the works of poets like Fernán Silva Valdés (1887–1975), in essays like Emilio Frugoni's (1880–1969) *La sensibilidad americana* [1927; The Sensibility of the Americas], as well as in the African-inspired poems of Ildefonso Pereda Valdés (1899–1996) and the cosmic *gauchismo* of Pedro Leandro Ipuche (1889–1976).

While the exaltation of the local can be observed in many of the works of Figari, where it functioned as part of an ideological-aesthetic project, such rhapsodies clearly expressed the sensations of optimism and contentment that Montevidean society was experiencing. Thus Garet, in his poem "Playa Ramírez" ["Ramírez Beach"], paints a picture of public happiness in which "Vienen chorros de gente/de los tranvías,/y mujeres y niños/tiemblan un arcoiris triunfal sobre la arena. . . "(37) ("Oceans of people/come streaming from trams,/mothers with children/a triumphant rainbow shimmers the sands. . . "). The exaltation of the beach and the *leitmotif* of the poem, "un arcoiris triunfal sobre la playa," are the incarnations of the *locus amoenus* that animated Montevidean society in the 1920s when the preparations for the centenary and the fireworks and the dances of the celebrations were in full swing on every corner of the city. Garet's rhapsody on the sands of Ramírez's beach inspired the development of a series of beaches and spas that bestowed on the official capital of the Republic something of the air of a summer resort.

The 1930s, however, would bring about a radical transformation in this happy landscape. The repression of the unions, the suppression of the Communist daily *Justicia*, and the interruption of old age pension payments in 1932 were all like preannouncements of the *coup d'état* that President Gabriel Terra would effect the following year by closing the parliament. Montevideo watched stupefied as the ex-President Baltasar Brum took his own life in public, and as agents-provocateurs disturbed the funeral of the anti-oligarch leader Julio César Grauert who had been assassinated on orders from the dictator. Despite the turmoil, however, foreign artists continued to visit. In this same year Pirandello returned again, as did David Alfaro Siqueiros who marked the occasion by painting a brutal portrait of the Dictator Terra's wife. The following year Federico García Lorca (1898–1939) arrived in Montevideo to deliver a lecture at the Teatro 18 de Julio (1934) and lodged in the Hotel Carrasco where he wrote the second act of *Bodas de sangre* [Blood Wedding]. This was also the year in which the painter Joaquín Torres García returned to Uruguay; immediately upon his return he began the lecture series that would later form the basis of his *Universalismo constructivo* [1943; Constructive Universalism], in which he outlined his theory of the Southern school and coined the phrase *Nuestro es el Sur* (the South is ours) that would accompany his celebrated upside down map of South America (1935 and 1943).

Even in these times in which the world began to experience the shock waves that emanated from the economic crisis of 1929 and the ideological confrontations that were created by both the Spanish Civil War and World War II, Montevidean society was involved in intense cultural activity. Illustrious visitors continued to arrive (Pablo Neruda [1904–1973], Igor Stravinsky, Margarita Xirgu [1888–1969]); summer courses in 1938 brought together Juana de Ibarbourou, Gabriela Mistral, and Alfonsina Storni (1892–1938); and the 1935 Latin American Festival of Music was held in Montevideo. The intensity of the cultural scene was not limited to high culture, for this same era saw the development of the golden years of the traditional Uruguayan carnival. Further, the intensification of political and cultural activity, the growth in the number of publications, and the construction of theaters and cinemas that occurred in these years was accompanied by increasing restrictions on immigration and limitations on the freedom of the press.

Parallel with the committees of support that were organized all across Montevideo in solidarity with the Republican cause in the Spanish Civil War, a resurgence began to be felt in the artistic, intellectual, and political panorama of Montevideo that brought to prominence a number of the cultural institutions which were to dominate Montevidean and Uruguayan cultural life until the advent of the dictatorship of 1973. In 1939 Juan Carlos Onetti (1909–1994) published *El pozo* [The Well]. In the same year *Marcha*, the weekly to which Onetti would contribute from the time of its inception and which was directed by Carlos Quijano for thirty-five years (1939–1974) hit the stands. The advent of *Marcha* marked the beginning not only of an era, but also of a generation, what two of its key figures, Ángel Rama (1926–1983) and Emir Rodríguez Monegal (1921–1985), would later dub the generation of '45,' the critical generation, or the *Marcha* generation. *Marcha* brought together not only the best of the Uruguayan intellectual scene, but also those of Latin America and Europe, publishing writers such as Gabriel García Márquez (b. 1927), Julio Cortázar (1914–1984), Mario Vargas Llosa (b. 1936), José Donoso (1925–1996), Carlos Fuentes (b. 1928), Augusto Roa Bastos (b. 1917), Ernesto "Che" Guevara, Jean Paul Sartre, and Pierre Mendes-France.

These were, without a doubt, years of both inception and closure. Hardly a trace remained of the satisfied Montevideo of the 1920s; if it had been still possible to speak of Uruguay as the "land of milk and honey," the end of World War II would announce the gray Montevideo of crisis that Mario Benedetti (b. 1920), a few years later, would describe in his *Poemas de la oficina* [1956; Poems from the Office] and in *Montevideanos* [1959; Montevideans]. Despite such omens as the deaths of a good number of the central figures of the previous era, including Julio Vilamajó (1894–1948), Joaquín Torres García (1874–1949), and Eduardo Fabini (1882–1950), the

society of happiness would not disappear so quickly, even as the dark side began to rear its head. The immediate reception of Juan Carlos Onetti's *El pozo* (1939) is instructive in this context. Onetti had leveled a brutal and demolishing irony at the trivial and obsolete nationalism of the official imaginary, invoking and parodying the emblematic image of the "Treinta y tres" that Blanes painted and, thus, the sacralization of official history in a country with a slender past and, an uncertain future:

¿[Q]ué se puede hacer en este país? Nada, ni dejarse engañar. Si uno fuera una bestia rubia, acaso comprendiera a Hitler. Hay posibilidades para una fe en Alemania; existe un antiguo pasado y un futuro cualquiera que sea. Si uno fuera voluntarioso imbécil se dejaría ganar sin esfuerzos por la nueva mística germana. ¿Pero aquí? Detrás de nosotros no hay nada. Un gaucho, dos gauchos, treinta y tres gauchos. (42)

What are we to do in this country? Nothing, clearly, but not even will we let ourselves be deceived. If we were blond beasts, perhaps we would embrace Hitler. There are possibilities for faith in Germany; an ancient past and a future, of sorts. If we were voluntary idiots we'd let ourselves be wooed by the new German mysticism. But, here? With our past? There's nothing behind us. What does it amount to, one gaucho, two gauchos, thirty-three gauchos?

Yet Onetti's critique made few inroads into the collective imaginary. As late as 1950, the Uruguayan imaginary of a happy and contented society would renew itself in the image of the national football team triumphing over the Brazilians in their own stadium of Maracaná. Since then and up until today, to utter the word Maracaná is to invoke, for the generation that high culture preferred to label the critical generation (Rama) or the generation of '45', the symbol and popular identifier of the happy society (see Rodríguez Monegal).

From Maracaná to the Dictatorship: The Zenith and Decline of the "Land of Milk and Honey" (1950–1985)

The festivities that greeted the returning football players in Montevideo in January 1950 were spectacular. Packing the Avenida 18 de Julio, the city's principal thoroughfare, was a crowd whose numbers had only rarely been seen in Montevideo, a multitude that showered the team with flowers, songs, and their collective elation, as if they were the victors in some bloody war. The economic crisis had yet to declare itself, and in the aftermath of World War II and with the opening of the Korean War, it seemed as though exports would continue to rise. Now a metropolis of one million inhabitants, with ever-rising levels of schooling, Montevideo was a city which had recently established a Faculty of Humanities and Sciences, as well as a Comedia Nacional (theater), under the direction of Margarita Xirgu. These years also saw the publication of a number of new journals articulating the concerns of the generation of '45'– *Escritura*, *Clinamen*, *La Licorne*, *Asir*, *Número*–journals which grouped together writers like Idea Vilariño (b. 1920), Amanda Berenguer (b. 1921), Ángel Rama, Emir Rodríguez Monegal, Ida Vitale, Mario Benedetti, Carlos Maggi (b. 1922), Carlos Martínez Moreno (1917–1986), Carlos Real de Azúa (1916–1977), Arturo Sergio Visca (1917–1993), Domingo Bordoli (b. 1919), Susana Soca (1907–1959), and Armonía Somers (1914–1994). This generation, like these journals did not limit its concerns to literature, but included as well philosophers and historians of ideas such as Arturo Ardao and Mario Sambarino, historians such as Bentancourt Díaz, Alfredo Castellanos, and

Pivel Devoto, musicologists like Lauro Ayestarán, and anthropologists such as Daniel Vidart, among many others.

The impact of the generation that Juan Carlos Onetti acknowledged as the most significant of the first half of the twentieth century and which had discovered the world of Felisberto Hernández (1902–1964), made itself felt over the following decades. Further, we can say that for many this generation constituted the second golden age of Uruguay's short cultural history, an age that would, only after the end of the dictatorship in 1985, begin to be questioned. The society of happiness, created under the reign of and in the image of Batlle y Ordóñez, would be subject to question by these men and women who demanded rigor in all things and who opened themselves to the world in their search for excellence. Profoundly influenced by the Spanish Civil War and World War II, this was the generation that received not only the European Jewish refugees fleeing Hitler, some of the more recent who bore the tattoos of the concentration camps, but also the Spanish Republican intellectuals and Argentinean anti-Peronists (Margarita Xirgu, José Bergamín [1895–1983], Pablo Serrano [1908–1985], José Estruch) who would integrate into the cultural and academic life of the city.

For the next few years, up until the end of the 1950s when the economic crisis began to make itself felt, Montevideo continued to grow. The signs were everywhere: new office buildings and monuments; cinema and theater festivals; carnivals with multicolored troupes–such as those organized by Carmelo Imperio, for example–and allegorical floats that were both creatively extravagant and materially lavish; new cultural associations; the inauguration of mass primary and secondary education; and visits by musicians (Kachaturian), and theater and ballet groups from Latin America and Europe (Alicia Alonso, Louis Jouvet, Piccolo Teatro di Milano); the buzz created by the Punta del Este Cinema Festival and the rhythms of Xavier Cugat and the "Lecuona Cuban Boys" who, having been invited to "up" the voltage in the carnival celebrations, were to write the emblematic song of the era, "Al carnaval del Uruguay" ("At the Uruguay Carnival"). All of this cultural activity allowed Montevideans to continue to believe that they possessed that certain something and that, as the saying goes, "Como el Uruguay no hay" ("There's nothing like Uruguay"). And, social and economic indicators did not prove them wrong: Immigration continued, although with lower numbers; Montevideans continued to feel secure and relatively safe from violence; the welfare state system continued to function, the civil service to expand, and retirees to make the dreamed trip to Europe; the textile industry continued to boast that the cashmere garments knitted in Montevideo were still sold in England with a false label claiming they were "Made in Lancastershire." It was at this moment of contentment, however, that the self-satisfied society of happiness was on the point of disappearing.

The first manifestations of the crisis began to appear in 1957 and 1958 with the closure of the Swift and Artigas meatpacking plants and the strikes that followed, the 100 percent devaluation of the Uruguayan currency, and the suppression of the university students who had demanded and obtained the passage of a constitutional amendment that had strengthened internal democratic politics. In 1958, after ninety years of uninterrupted rule by the *Colorado* party, the National party won the national elections. It was from this moment on that the crisis became a reality, and in Montevideo at least (the countryside was another story) unmistakable signs became

more than evident. Onetti's 1961 novel *El astillero* [The Dockyard] recounts, perhaps involuntarily, the transformations then operative in society. The transmission of television broadcasting–which had begun in 1958, although the first limited emission had begun two years earlier–did not do any major damage to the cinema-going audience or the radio listenership that would continue for a time to play a key role in Uruguayan mass culture. Radio serials, avidly followed by large sectors of the Montevidean population, would continue to be one of the most important mass cultural phenomena until the end of the 1950s. However, if the culture industry reached its height and maturity at the end of the 1950s and the beginning of the 1960s, this did not mean that the traditional culture of *belles lettres* and fine arts was on the wane. On the contrary, the book publishing industry augmented its production and editorial houses like Arca (directed by Ángel Rama), Banda Oriental (directed by Heber Raviolo), and Alfa (directed by Benito Milla) blossomed, together with institutions and art galleries like the Instituto General Electric (under the directorship of Ángel Kalenberg), Galería U (under Enrique Gómez), and Galería Losada, which contained the editorial house of the same name and the visual arts space directed by Quela Viloró. The international festivals of experimental and art cinema sponsored by the SODRE bolstered the Montevidean inclination for high culture, and in particular, for the consumption of imported products, since local productions were limited to short- or medium-length documentary films. However, if Uruguayan film production was meager, cinema criticism flourished, and, in 1964, the same year in which Charles de Gaulle visited the city, Montevideo was honored with the world première of Ingmar Bergman's *The Silence* in recognition of the fact that several years earlier the Punta del Este Festival had bestowed world recognition on the Swedish filmmaker.

The political events of the 1960s would introduce a series of important changes into this climate of cultural effervescence, and it is to this that Ángel Rama referred when he spoke of the rise of the crisis generation or the 1960s generation. These political events would produce an inflection of the national culture that would leave no aspect of it–high or low, popular or mass–untouched. The Book and Recorded Music Fair, the new poetry and the new journalism, the graphic arts, the creation of the Third World Cinematheque, and the transformation of the carnival bands, as well as their approbation by large sectors of the middle class and by the leftist intelligentsia (see Alfaro), were all signs of the change that the crisis and the political radicalization of society had brought. In the wake of the Cuban Revolution, Uruguayan society would develop its own urban guerrilla movements–the MLN and the Tupamaros–as well as the constitution of the Congress of the People, the first serious and successful attempt to unite the progressive forces of society both on the intellectual and trade-union levels. Uruguayan society had entered the prolegomenon of what would, in a very short time, lead to the full-scale confrontation with the armed forces that erupted in the *coup d'état* of 1973.

Many of the books published in the years preceding 1973–*Diario del cuartel* [1970; Barracks Diary] by Carlos María Gutiérrez (b. 1926), *Las venas abiertas de América Latina* [1971; *Open Veins of Latin America,* 1973] by Eduardo Galeano (b. 1940), *Indicios pánicos* [1970; *Panic Signs,* 2002] by Cristina Peri Rossi (b. 1941)–as well as the plays then produced, those of Uruguayan authors, as well as adaptations from the classics like Lope de Vega's

Fuenteovejuna (1619) and various versions of the works of Brecht, exemplify the new *zeitgeist* of a culture that had turned militant. Social and political militancy was the watchword of the times, and we can say that if, not the culture in its totality, at least the major part of it, particularly the producers of artistic and social scientific knowledge and research, found it necessary to synchronize their works with the charged, profoundly ethical rhythm of the times. That said, however, much of the literary and cultural production of the era was not straight-forwardly militant but rather sought to embrace the practice of a writing or a painting that avoided the provisionality of political and social engagement.

The government continued to close down newspapers throughout the 1960s, thus partly explaining the key status of the new journalism in the era, and by the end of the decade not only were diaries, books, and performances being banned, but even words: In these years the use of the words "guerrilla," "tupamaro," and "revolution" were subject to strict prohibition. The Universidad de la República (and above all its students) engaged in a bloody confrontation with the forces of repression and, symbolically, on 14 August 1968, the student Liber Arce, whose name was meant to encapsulate an entire political program of liberation, was killed by government forces suppressing a student demonstration. In this same year a new U.S. embassy was constructed in Montevideo, designed by the celebrated architect I. M. Pei, who would later oversee the transformation of the Louvre in Paris and the erection of its glass pyramid. Given the nature of the times in which it was built, however, Pei's embassy was associated in the minds of many Montevideans with a bunker.

From the late 1960s through to June 1973, when a *coup d'état* overthrew the elected government, Montevideo lived through a virtual civil war. Despite the turmoil of these years, cultural life did in a way continue, and in 1973 the National Museum of Fine Arts mounted a Picasso Exposition exhibiting more than 100 of the Spanish master's engravings. The resistance or militant culture that figures so prominently in the historical investigations of Lucía Sala, Julio Rodríguez, and José Pedro Barrán, as well as in the works of the Uruguayan intelligentsia as a whole, lead to a number of undertakings and research projects that transformed intellectual Montevideo into an immense laboratory for the analysis and study of the national past and present. Two publications appeared at this time bringing together the best fruits of this research into and reflection upon the national condition: *Capítulo Oriental* [1968; Eastern Chapter], directed by Carlos Maggi, Carlos Martínez Moreno, and Carlos Real de Azúa, and *Enciclopedia uruguaya* [1968; Uruguayan Encyclopedia], edited by Ángel Rama. Both publications brought to the city's newsstands an analysis and re-reading of national letters and national culture. These publications, together with the appearance of the University's Economic Institute's *Proceso económico del Uruguay* [1969; Economic Progress of Uruguay], gave evidence of the local intelligentsia's attempts to interpret the state of a nation in crisis and on the edge of collapse.

During these years, immigration to Uruguay and Montevideo, which had been continuous for over a century, practically ceased. Uruguayan demographics now made an about-face: Economic migrants began to leave the country in search of employment and, shortly thereafter, a wave of political refugees fleeing the dictatorship initiated the era of the Uruguayan exiles and their diaspora. Bars and restaurants with names evoking Montevideo or aspects of its culture began to open up

in New Jersey, in the United States, and in Sydney, Australia. The Uruguayan diaspora is still a fact of national life today and is so prevalent that a number of Uruguayan writers have now lived the major part of their lives in exile. This is the case, for example, with Cristina Peri Rossi, whose works are particularly influential and not only in Spain, where she has resided since the beginning of the 1970s, and with Eduardo Milán (b. 1952), a poet of growing influence, residing in Mexico. These two, among others, are well-known examples of an unusual and unheralded phenomenon in the cultural history of Uruguay, one which has not been limited to writers but also includes scientists and literary and art critics (Carlos Capelán, Julio Alpuy, Luis Camnitzer, among others) who now reside in the various countries of Europe and both North and South America. Juan Carlos Onetti, who ended his days in Spain, where he published his final great novels, can also be considered a part of this wave of exiles, this diasporic community.

Much has been written about the "cultural blackout" that occurred during the dictatorship. While descriptive of policy, the expression is not entirely factual, for, despite the difficulties, cultural activity did continue. Novels, poems, and plays went on being published, works of theater continued to be staged, and carnival festivities, as well as popular and youth music, can be said to have experienced a certain boom. The term *cultural blackout* simply refers to the conditions of cultural and political repression that were a daily reality during the period, as well as to the rise of dominance of groups that had until then been marginal in the sphere of cultural power, groups that had rejected the Uruguayan high culture reigning in the 1950s and 1960s. As a result of this change in leadership, Uruguayan literary culture saw the republication of a number of works of poetic *modernismo* and some of the works of the centenary generation. In 1974, after thirty-five years of repeated closures and reopenings, the journal *Marcha* finally ceased publication, and its editor (along with many of its collaborators) went into exile. This was the year in which the Universidad de la República lost its autonomy and became subject to state control; many of its professors were either expelled or detained. Political terror had descended upon the city: Libraries were confiscated; the books of prohibited authors were placed in hiding in the back rooms of bookstores; a portion of the remaining intelligentsia (in the preceding years Benedetti, Galeano, Ángel Rama, Cristina Peri Rossi, Alfredo Zitarrosa (1936–1989), to name only a few, had already sought refuge outside the country) was forced to leave the country; and Carlos Quijano, the editor of *Marcha*, started up the second epoch of *Cuadernos de Marcha* in Mexico.

Despite these bleak conditions, Uruguayan youth culture and the popular music called *canto popu* became one of the most dynamic vehicles for the articulation of both the culture of this era and resistance to the dictatorship. The group and solo concerts that were held in these years were public events of the first magnitude—especially the "Candombe del 31," "Los que iban cantando," and "Canto nuestro" concerts of 1977—and constituted popular expressions of the reclamation of freedom and national culture. In addition, the *canto popu* groups often included *cantautores*, poets from the sphere of high culture such as Idea Vilariño or Washington Benavides (b. 1930). Another phenomenon of importance in these years was the growth of art cinema and experimental film production as an increase in the number of cinemas in the Cinemateca chain, a nonprofit private body created in the 1970s that became a focal point for Montevidean high culture. After the restitution of democracy, the Cinemateca continued its cultural leadership and began organizing international film festivals, making it more than a purely Montevidean center of attraction. These years also saw the emergence of new generations of artists–Musso, Seveso, Patrone, and so forth–and of writers. A number of the latter, grouped around the Ediciones de Uno publishing house, endeavored to launch a Neo-avant-garde movement through a series of alternative publications and distribution systems. The neo-avant-garde theater movement reached its own apogee, and a number of independent groups mounted productions that became, relatively speaking, popular successes. There were, in addition, several reviews, supplements, and literary pages that arose at this time, including *Correo de los viernes* (1981), *Jaque* (1983), *Cuadernos de Granaldea* (1980), and *Foro literario* (1977), among others.

It was also in these years that a number of other cultural transformations began to be felt. The militant affirmation of certain aspects of the national popular culture led to a public cultivation of old traditions that now acquired a new significance, such as, for example, the drinking of *maté* and the use of certain popular objects. The nationalist Banda Oriental patriotism trumpeted by the dictatorship was rejected by both Montevideans and Uruguayans at large; by means of these symbolic practices, however, people expressed their opposition to the officially sanctioned conception of national popular culture and embraced, instead, the local. Parallel with these developments, there was an increase in evangelical sects, as well as growing participation in *umbanda* rites, in particular, those celebrating Iemanjá, the African American marine deity that had acquired a special importance in Brazil. In the 1970s the Iemanjá cult spread to the formerly unfrequented beaches of Montevideo; this phenomenon, together with the rise in Christian fundamentalism, revealed that Montevideans' traditionally limited interest in religion was undergoing a change.

A significant part of the high cultural activity in these years revolved around foreign cultural institutions such as the Alliance Française, the Goethe Institute, the Alianza Uruguay-Estados Unidos, and the Institute of Italian Culture. Likewise, an equally important portion of the scientific and social and human sciences research was centered around institutes, private foundations, and NGOs (non-governmental organizations) supported by international foundations and organizations: Among the research centers, the CIEDUR (Centro Indisciplinario de Estudios sobre el Desarrollo, Uruguay) and the CLAEH (Centro Latinoamericano de Economía Humana) deserve mention, while the PLEMUU (Plenario de Mujeres del Uruguay) and the GRECMU (Grupo de Estudios sobre la Condición de la Mujer en el Uruguay)–both taking up women's issues and the new feminism–were two of the NGOs of the period.

It was only in the 1990s that the cultural transformations effected during the dictatorship, as well as the regime's manipulation of national history and symbolism, came under scrutiny (see Markarian y Cosse). These studies focused on aspects of the political culture of the military dictatorship such as the attempts to rewrite history, the erection of monuments, and the change of street names in the capital in line with the interests of militarist historiography. By the beginning of the 1980s, the civic face of Montevideo had changed. Land speculation had led to the demolition of part of the architectural patrimony of the city, while the economic crisis of 1982, bringing in its wake a sharp devaluation of the currency and the bankruptcy of a number of construction firms, meant that the building of dozens of office buildings was suspended before they were finished; when democracy returned several years later, the city appeared as if its development had been interrupted. Other important urban phenomena in these years were the migration of the impoverished sectors of the middle class to the Montevidean suburbs and neighboring cities and the collecting of the poor in slums or shanty-towns, also known as *asentamientos* (townships). The growth of an informal economy also contributed to changing the face of the city. Seeking to supplement their meager incomes, large numbers of Montevideans opened street stalls selling everything from contraband to home made or artisanal goods. The "river of liberty," as the final wave of resistance to the dictatorship was known, was, according to some commentators, the largest concentration of public activity in Montevidean history. It was also, perhaps, the symbol of the cultural movement of the era, a movement that was, despite military repression, in essence political. Thus, when the free elections that would re-open the doors to democracy, were held toward the end of 1984, Montevideo was a city whose fundamental cultural activity was political through and through.

From the End of the Dictatorship to the Mercosur (1985–1998)

When the democratic government of President Julio María Sanguinetti assumed power on 1 March 1985, twelve years of dictatorship came to an end. Loudspeakers set up in the main streets of Montevideo announced the entrance of the president, the ministers, and special envoys at the ceremony commemorating the restoration of democracy; they also proclaimed some of the first acts of the government, including the creation of the Fundación Ángel Rama, named in homage of the intellectual who had tragically died in November 1983. The democratic government faced a nation divided, and a country, and above all a capital city, ravaged by the economic crisis of 1982. In 1985, however, the first of what would later be a series of shopping malls scattered throughout Montevideo opened, a symbol, perhaps, in more than one sense, of a new era. Montevideo's population was then 1.5 million, and this new phenomenon would mark a transformation both in the organization of the city's commercial traffic and in the daily practices of the population. In a certain sense, these shopping malls were to offer Montevideans an alternative streetscape to the traditional plazas, as well as contributing to the decline of Montevideo's urban core and signaling a much more lasting and profound cultural change.

The sensation of euphoria that the return to democracy appeared to bring in its wake was manifest in numerous ways. It produced not only a kind of publishing boom in which works that had been suppressed during the dictatorship–novels, essays, and above all, testimonials–began to appear, but also the establishment of new periodicals and the revitalization of old cultural institutions: *Brecha* (1985), for example, and the return to Uruguay of the *Cuadernos de Marcha*. All this activity took place within the context of a double movement that can be characterized by, on the one hand, a reconstructive will aspiring to a return to the state of affairs prior to the dictatorship and, on the other hand, a consciousness of the necessary changes demanded as much by the new times as by the new democracy. Samuel Lichtenstein, for example, the rector of the Universidad de la República who had been forced to abandon the country, resumed his leadership. But this was not the only example: The return of a good number of the exiles (as well as the restitution to their former positions as functionaries and professors) who had been removed—many of them imprisoned—by the dictatorship, also contributed to the spirit of restoration.

Things, however, were not going to be easy. The dialogue between the ex-prisoners, the exiles, and the *insiliados*, as Mario Benedetti called them, would be a difficult one, and during the first years of democracy Montevideans and Uruguayans struggled to establish or re-establish a cultural dialogue that was representative of actual complexities. This climate would change, however, with the first outbreak of demonstrations over the referendum that would have foreclosed the Statutory Limitations Law (1989), the law that offered the possibility of amnesty for the perpetrators of human rights violations during the dictatorship. The impact of these demonstrations and of the campaign around the referendum was deeply felt not only on the streets: An entire series of high and low cultural manifestations would find themselves affected. Testimonials, historical revisionist works, and sociopolitical analyses, together with carnival presentations, works of theater and fine art, and a series of historical novels, all sought to raise questions about the problems of the dictatorship and the violation of human rights, and together initiated a rethinking of the nation's traditional history and a discussion of the viability of the country as a nation-state. Three of the many texts published in these years are emblematic of the then state of cultural affairs: Tomás de Mattos's (b. 1947) novel, *Bernabé, Bernabé . . .* (1988), the psychoanalysts Maren and Marcelo Viñar's essay, *Fracturas de memoria* [1990; Fractures of Memory], and José Pedro Barrán's two-volume history, *La historia de la sensibilidad* [1988–1990; The History of Sensibility].

The other development that profoundly affected the cultural and political climate of these years was the process of economic integration into the regional free-trade block, the Mercosur, a process that posed a significant challenge to the future of the country. Although the Mercosur would affect the country as a whole, it had a particular impact on Montevideo since it was declared the administrative headquarters of the trading block; the old Parque Hotel, where Amado Nervo had died in 1919, was transformed into an office complex housing the Mercosur bureaucracy. In one way or another, with the advent of the Mercosur, Uruguay's old buffer-state function has been reformulated such that Montevideo now has adopted into its civic imaginary the possibility of being the Brussels of the River Plate. But the city aspires to much more: The Cinemateca film festival, the International Biennial Theater Festival, public sculptures, classical and popular music concerts, and the abbreviated opera season, all form part of a project seeking to convert Montevideo into the cultural center of the Mercosur. In 1996 the city held the title of the "Cultural Capital" of Ibero-America.

Montevideo's transformation is more than evident. Although the luxurious, brand new "Punta Carretas Shopping Center," one of the numerous such centers that have been constructed in recent years, is housed in the former prison from which the Tupamaro guerrillas escaped in the late 1970s, and although Plácido Domingo, José Carreras, Pavarotti, Liza Minelli, and other international stars pass through the city on a regular basis, the feeling persists in the city that time passes slowly. Modernity in Montevideo continues to be a slow-motion modernity. The reconstruction of the SODRE's Estudio Auditorio theater, which had burnt down symbolically shortly before the dictatorial *coup d'état*, has still not been completed.

The new private universities that arose with the restoration of democracy have not yet been completely accepted by the Universidad de la República. Many young people bereft of employment continue to emigrate abroad, while the state telephone company's construction of a new headquarters—within the context of the BID financed "Phoenix Plan" for the renovation of certain depressed zones of the city—has generated multiple polemics both for and against (*for* the Montevideo of the twenty-first century; *against* the squandering of public moneys in an architectural wonder that the city does not need).

At the start of the new century, Montevideo appears to be, once again, trapped in the snares of time. This condition notwithstanding, there are signs that the process of change continues unabated: Gay Pride Day has brought transvestites, lesbians, and gays parading out into the streets, and the old cinemas which had been abandoned or converted into evangelical churches or parking garages are now returning as micro-cinema complexes that reveal the renaissance of the local film industry. New bookstores and museums are opening up, and a sculpture garden has been created on the grounds of the government office complex. Not only is annual attendance at the Iemanjá festivities on Montevideo's beaches on the rise, but African-Uruguayans are organizing themselves, creating associations like the Mundo Afro, and making efforts to reclaim their history. And, restoration of the Old City is underway: Buildings that for years had been derelict and dilapidated have begun to be renovated.

These transformations, however, do not affect all Montevideans equally; while they all share, if not the same space at least the same historical times, some Montevideans are more affected by the changes than others. At the same time that the horse-drawn wagons of the junk sellers and garbage recyclers patrol the streets and the number of shanty-towns and townships is on the increase, the city has also begun, in the last five years, to navigate the media space of MTV hand-in-hand with various groups. Thus, in the local videos "Pendeja" ["Ass Hole"] by the group Plátano Macho (Macho Banana) and "Himno a Montevideo" ["Montevidean Anthem"] by Mauricio Ubal, the city is portrayed as the stage for a new form of artistic expression seeking to synchronize slow-motion modernity with the virtual space of television. Further, the audio-visual image of Montevideo has been adopted by others from outside the country, by the Argentinean group Las pelotas (The Balls), in a video entitled "Para qué?" ["What for?"], and by the film director Christien Laurent for his film *Transatlántico* [Transatlantic] since, as he himself has said, "Montevideo is for the cinema a virgin city" (a personal comment made to the author). The question posed by the Las pelotas's video goes beyond the audio-visual format to address the future of a city that was born as a frontier port and has constantly aspired to geopolitical centrality which in real terms and up until the present, has never been more than accidental or occasional. It addresses, ultimately, the cultural history of a city which, despite its multiple roles as frontier city, port city, and present administrative center of the Mercosur, has not completed its performance.

Translation by Colman Hogan

Works Cited

Acevedo, Eduardo. 1934. *Anales históricos del Uruguay. Abarca los gobiernos de Latorre, Vidal, Santos, Tajes y Herrera y Obes desde 1876 hasta 1894.* Vol. 4. Montevideo: Casa Barreiro y Ramos.

Alfaro, Milita. 1991. *Carnaval: Una historia social de Montevideo desde la perspectiva de la fiesta.* Montevideo: Ediciones Trilce.

Barrán, José Pedro. 1989 and 1990. *La historia de la sensibilidad en el Uruguay.* 2 Vols. Montevideo: Ediciones de la Banda Oriental/Facultad de Humanidades y Ciencias.

——. and Alfredo Alpini. 1997. "Las formas de la Venus." *Historias de la vida privada.* Ed. José Pedro Barrán, Gerardo Caetano and Teresa Porzecanski. Vol. 1. Montevideo: Alfaguara. 75–95.

Bauzá, Francisco. 1929. *La historia de la dominación española en el Uruguay.* 2 Vols. Montevideo: El Demócrata.

Caetano, Gerardo and José Rilla. 1998. *Historia contemporánea del Uruguay: De la colonia al Mercosur.* Montevideo: Fin de siglo.

Díaz, José Pedro. 1987. "Las letras." *Vida y cultura en el Río de la Plata.* Ed. Germán D'Elía et al. Montevideo: Universidad de la República. 87–97.

Ferrés, Carlos. 1975. *Época colonial: La compañia de Jesús en Montevideo.* Montevideo: Ministerio de Educación y Cultura.

Garet, Enrique Ricardo. 1927. *Paracaídas.* Montevideo: "La Facultad," Casa Editora de Maximo García.

Irigoyen, Emilio. 2000. "Fiesta y representación en Montevideo, durante la primera mitad del siglo XIX." *Cultura y campo intelectual en Uruguay.* Vol. 1. Ed. Hugo Achugar and Mabel Moraña. Montevideo: Trilce. 95–124.

Marenales, Martha and Juan Carlos Luzuriaga. 1990. *Vascos en el Uruguay.* Montevideo: Editorial Nuestra Tierra.

Milán, Guillermo. 2000. "Letra 'oscura' contra habla 'transparente': Los valores de la palabra oral y la palabra escrita en el Montevideo colonial." *Cultura y campo intelectual.* Vol. 1. Ed. Hugo Achugar and Mabel Moraña. Montevideo: Trilce. 67–94.

Onetti, Juan Carlos. 1967. *El pozo.* 4th ed. Montevideo: Arca.

Pérez Santarcieri, María Emilia. 1996. *Montevideo, escenas de la vida y la historia de la ciudad.* Montevideo: Ediciones L. Ametrano.

Rama, Ángel. 1965. "Origen de un novelista y una generación literaria." In *El pozo* by Juan Carlos Onetti. Montevideo: Arca. 57–110.

Rodríguez Monegal, Emir. 1966. *Literatura uruguaya del medio siglo.* Montevideo: Alfa.

Roxlo, Carlos. 1912. *Historia crítica de la literatura uruguaya: El romanticismo.* Vol. 1. Montevideo: Barreiro y Ramos.

Schelotto, Salvador. 2000. "Montevideo 1829–1890: Una urbanidad se gesta entre la civilización y la barbarie." *Cultura y campo intelectual.* Ed. Hugo Achugar and Mabel Moraña. Montevideo: Trilce. 203–20.

Verdesio, Gustavo. 1996. *La invención del Uruguay: La entrada del territorio y sus habitantes a la cultura occidental.* Montevideo: Editorial Graffiti.

Zum Felde, Alberto. 1985. *Proceso intelectual del Uruguay.* 3 vols. Montevideo: Librosur.

CHAPTER 54

BUENOS AIRES
CULTURAL CENTER OF RIVER PLATE

Noemí Ulla

The federalization of Buenos Aires was achieved in 1880 under the presidency (1880–1886) of Julio Argentino Roca, a young military officer who had gained a name for himself in the extermination campaign against the natives of the Argentinean hinterland. This act of federalization conferred on the city a legal status corresponding to what it had in fact been considered for some time—the cultural and political center; it also brought to an end the old disputes between the inhabitants of the inland provinces and those of the River Plate area that had been in effect since the generation of 1837, known as *los proscriptos* (the interdicted writers in exile). Among this group a number stand out: Esteban Echeverría (1805–1851), author of *El matadero* [*The Slaughter House*, 1959], the first Argentinean work of fiction (written circa 1838; but only published in 1871); Juan Bautista Alberdi (1810–1884), the customs and manners critic of the periodical *La Moda*; Domingo Faustino Sarmiento (1811–1888), author of the novel-essay *Facundo. Civilización y barbarie* [1845; *Facundo: Civilization and Barbarism*, 1961]; Juan María Gutiérrez (1809–1878), founder of Argentinean literary criticism; José Mármol (1817–1871), author of the historical novel *Amalia* [1851; *Amalia*, 2001], with its numerous editions and translations into, for example, French and Russian; Vicente Fidel López (1815–1903), one of the founders of national historiography; and Bartolomé Mitre (1821–1906), historian and founder of the daily *La Nación* (1889). These were the men who laid the sociopolitical foundations of the country and the city of Buenos Aires through the discussion and diffusion of their ideas in the Literary Salon held at the Buenos Aires bookshop of Marcos Sastre in 1837, forerunner of the *May Association*. This association met clandestinely during 1838 when the Rosas tyranny closed down the Literary Salon where these young men gathered (with the exception of Sarmiento, resident in San Juan and later exiled in Chile). Almost all of the exiled sought asylum in Uruguay, where many of them remained permanent residents, and as such this constituted, according to the historian Félix Weinberg, the first of a series of exiles that would disperse Argentinean writers to Brazil, Chile, Bolivia, and Peru (217–18). These writers were the founders of what the historian José Luis Romero (1909–1977) would call Argentinean conservative liberalism, by that term designating the ideology that dominated Argentina in the years following the fall of Juan Manuel de Rosas (1793–1877) in 1852.

Las Bases [1852; The Fundaments] of Juan Bautista Alberdi, the foundation of the ideology of the generation of the exiles, would encounter its perfect executor thirty years later in President Julio A. Roca (1843–1914). As the essayist Adolfo Prieto (b. 1928) has stated, the new political order established in 1880, "far from guaranteeing the fitting completion of representative democracy, aspired rather to the consolidation of a kind of enlightened despotism, a special form of oligarchy in which power was shared by its various members up until the beginning of the twentieth century when the secret ballot confirmed the triumph of Hipólito Yrigoyen in

1916" (1980, 54). As was the case with other cities in South America such as Rio de Janeiro and Montevideo, Buenos Aires was influenced by the urban planning that Baron Haussmann had brought to bear on the transformation of Paris. The First Intendant of Buenos Aires (1880), Torcuato de Alvear, made a large contribution to the remodeling of the city. A part of the Colonial Cabildo district was demolished in order to make room for the avenue that would link the plaza where the fort once stood and where the presidential palace, the Casa Rosada, can now be found, with another plaza where the Palacio del Congreso would be built. According to official statistics, the inhabitants of the city numbered 305,285 in 1880. The Recova Vieja (Old Market) that had divided the old Plaza de Mayo in two was also demolished in 1884, and the two plazas became one, the new present-day Plaza de Mayo. The original paraíso trees of the plaza were replaced by palm trees and much later by banana trees. The Avenida de Mayo was thus created: a huge thoroughfare where modern buildings would soon be erected, some of them in the Art Nouveau style. Also constructed in the French style were the residences of the upper bourgeoisie, described by José Luis Romero (1986, 280). (See **Figure 1.**) Around 1883 the construction of a drainage and sewer system began and was completed in 1886 for a large section of the central core of the city; a few years later it was extended to the entire city. In 1896 electric street lighting was instituted, replacing gas lamps, and soon thereafter the public tramway system was also electrified.

The alacrity with which Buenos Aires modernized did not escape the notice of Argentineans and foreigners alike, and a number of them left records of this. Among the most notable of these records were those of José Antonio Wilde (1813–1885) detailed in his 1881 book *Buenos Aires, desde setenta años atrás* [Buenos Aires, Seventy Years of History], a smashing success with a reading public that recognized in Wilde's nostalgic evocations that the Colonial city was already fading into oblivion. A couple of years later Lucio V. López (1848–1894) published in installments his sole contribution to literature, *La gran aldea* [1884; The Great Village], whose subtitle "Costumbres bonaerenses" ["Customs of Buenos Aires"] alerted the reader to the book's realist character. López's description of the customs and manners of the society in a state of transformation paralleled the city itself; it was marked by an ironic and sarcastic style that evoked the simplicity of the Colonial city of 1860 and critically exposed the growth of the modern capital in the early years of the 1880s. (See **Figure 2.**)

López's literary model, and indeed that of most of the writers of his generation, was a combination of French realism and Mariano José de Larra's (1809–1837) *Artículos de costumbres* [1835-37; Articles on Costumes and Manners]. The world of European culture was an intense part of the lives of the writers of the 1880s, who were openly disposed to artistic and cultural borrowing. Most of them traveled a great deal, frequented the artistic coteries of London and Paris, and

Figure 1.

Photograph of Avenida de Mayo, Buenos Aires. (Archive of the author)

Figure 2.

*Photograph of Plaza Victoria, Buenos Aires 1880–1890.
(Archive of the author)*

adopted upon their return a pronounced dandyism that was not only manifest in their social comportment at the Progreso Club (founded 1852), but also in the literature that many of them wrote. The French critic Paul Groussac (1848–1929) lived in Buenos Aires from his youth, edited the review *La Biblioteca*, and enjoyed the respect of writers well into the second decade of the twentieth century. Groussac was a man of professional conscientiousness that he exercised above all in his writing on history; he was a characteristic figure of the period and served from 1885 until his death in 1929 as the director of the National Library (founded in 1812 as the Public Library–its name was changed following the federalization of the city).

Groussac himself defined with precision and impartiality the distinguishing traits of the 1880s generation in an article he wrote on Miguel Cané's (1851–1905) *En viaje* [1884; En Route], and on the works of Pedro Goyena (1843–1892), Eduardo Wilde (1844–1913), Eduardo Gutiérrez (1851–1889), and Aristóbulo Del Valle (1845–1896):

> Their knowledge of letters extends to the most minute details; and they enjoy the finest and most up-to-date understanding of the world's intellectual movements. If there is anything about which they are ignorant it is their own idiom and their own country.

> They have savored Sainte-Beuve and Macaulay. . . . They know the art of writing, intimately; they are erudite dandies; and they wear their learning lightly. A little refined, somewhat discontent and ironic, their metier is for surfaces; they prefer a page, from which results a dispersion, an enormous squandering of talent to the four winds of journalism or conversation. (2–5)

Under the presidency of Julio A. Roca the capital and the country enjoyed an institutional stability and economic well-being that had not been seen before. This phase of the Roca administration, whose motto was "peace and good government," saw the building of railroads, the establishment of free trade, and the foundation of provincial capitals, as well as the integration of the hinterlands into economic production and the arrival of hundreds of thousands of immigrants, swelling the pool of labor. If, in one sense, the Roca administration carried out the aims and objectives that Alberdi had outlined in *Las Bases*, in another sense the changes did not turn out as hoped for in populating such an enormous country, since by far the majority of the mass of immigrants either struck roots in the federal capital or in the moist and temperate pampas traversed by the new railroads.

In 1882 the government passed legislation providing for the creation of the Port of Madero, and construction began in 1887; to this end they contracted the firm of Eduardo

Madero and Sons who began work on the southern docks, and in 1889 they opened for business. (See **Figure 3**.) Successive projects would contribute to the expansion of the port of Buenos Aires, such as the law of 1908 authorizing the construction of the New Port, although the work did not begin until 1920 (Cánepa 106–107). The working classes, largely Spaniards and Italians, formed a mass of identities in constant change, speaking an idiom that became integrated with the River Plate dialect of Argentina and was named *cocoliche*, pidgin Spanish, Italian. This name, according to the linguist Beatriz Lavandera (b. 1942), was given in Uruguay and Argentina to the variety of Spanish of the Italian immigrants (61). The resulting culture was always in a state of flux. José S. Alvarez (1858–1903) who was born in the province of Entre Ríos (to the immediate north-east of the capital) but was resident in Buenos Aires since 1876, and who became popular under the name of "Fray Mocho" ("Brother Lock-less"), was one of the most popular commentators of the city at the turn of the century. While the group of writers that formed the generation of the 1880s were readers in constant contact with the literatures of France and England and adopted a number of very different European perspectives (e.g. Eugenio Cambacérès [1843–1890], Lucio V. López [1848–1894], Eduardo Wilde [1844–1913], Lucio V. Mansilla [1831–1913], and Fray Mocho [1858–1903]), they opened Argentinean literature to a description of the conditions, behavior, and idioms of the lower middle classes and the mass of immigrants who arrived at the port of Buenos Aires, swelling the numbers of the capital day after day, with a resultant overcrowding in the 2,462 tenement houses that then existed.

In a colloquial idiom, the stories of Fray Mocho bore witness to the popular Spanish as it was spoken in the streets, portraying not only the older *criollo* culture but the newer culture of the Italian immigrants, the *cocoliches*. The 1879 novel *Juan Moreira*, by Eduardo Gutiérrez (1851–1889), a portrayal of a Neapolitan immigrant, was an important precedent. These popular texts, by means of their different registers and their interlacing of discourses, painted a portrait of the changing identity of Buenos Aires, fruit of the surge in immigration and the contrasts between tradition and modern life. The *Cuentos* [The Tales] of Fray Mocho, most of them collected in the journal *Caras y Caretas* (1898–1939), as well as in his chronicles and articles, presented a gallery of the diverse "characters" rooted in the realist literature of the nineteenth century whose great masters were Balzac, Dickens, Zola, Pérez Galdós, and Tolstoy. *Caras y Caretas* was a popular journal directed by Fray Mocho in collaboration with two Spaniards, the cartoonist Manuel Mayor and the editor Eustaquio Pellicer; *Caras y Caretas* was a publication of enormous print runs and readership. Thanks to the popularity of Fray Mocho and to the journal's visual presentation, making use of chromolithographs and photo-engravings, and to the space it gave to national and international events, *Caras y Caretas* soon distinguished itself by the professional recognition it gave to the writer. Literary collaborators were paid, and writers were drawn, not only from the River Plate region, but from other regions of the continent, including the Peruvian Ricardo Palma (1833–1919), the Brazilian Olavo Bilac (1865–1918), as well as the Spaniard Miguel de Unamuno (1864–1936) (Rufinelli 9–10).

As a result of the diverse and numerous waves of immigrants who continually arrived in Buenos Aires (see **Figure 4**),

Figure 3.

Photograph by Rimathe of an anonymous painting "Muelle de pasajeros" [Passenger docks] c. 1890, Buenos Aires. (Archive of the author)

the city's elites adopted the custom, brought to the city by English traders (Troncoso 18–19), of taking summer holidays in country villas. The so-called European landscape artists designed the majority of the sumptuous gardens that dotted the suburbs of the city: Adrogué, Belgrano, San Isidro, San José de Flores, Quilmes, Tigre, and Lomas de Zamora. The yellow fever epidemic that found Buenos Aires sanitarily unprepared, commencing in January 1871 and not abating until April of that year, increased the elite classes desire to retreat to the countryside. In these protected residences the English game of croquet was the preferred pastime of men and women. Today, Lezama Park, former villa of Fair Mackinley, Avellaneda Park, formerly of the Olivera family, and Rivadavia Park, former villa of the Lezicas, evoke the atmosphere of those times. A well-known poem by Rafael Obligado (1851–1920) has also recorded the *douceur* of those tranquil sites of diversion: "Juro, Fabio, por todos los poetas,/ que no hay porteñas hoy mas regaladas/que aquellas que acudían en bandadas/a nuestras quintas a juntar violetas" (Obligado 184) ("I swear, Fabio, by all the poets, that there are none today more carefree than those women who flocked to our villas to gather violets"). On the eve of 1890 Carlos D'Amico, former governor of Buenos Aires, noted that with respect to leisure time the horse-racing tracks and polo fields of the western and southern suburbs attracted more people than the northern coastal towns, as evidenced by railway

Figure 4.

Photograph of the Port of Buenos Aires 1907 by E. Arcuri.
(Archive of the author)

passenger statistics–Northern Railway: 30,000 passengers; Western Railway to Moreno: 40,000 passengers; Southern Railway to Lomas, Quilmes, and Adrogué: 20,000 passengers (see Troncoso). The southern quarters of the city also saw a large nocturnal influx of city dwellers eager to dance tango at the famous corner of Suárez and Necochea in the 1870s. It was there in 1878 that the Tuscan José Tancredi had opened the doors of his establishment to a solicitous clientele (Bossio 82–83). Underworld figures and their friends would stroll down Necochea street to Olavarría, where, although entrance to the dance hall was free, dancing itself cost five centavos a number, and José Tancredi himself took the collection with the aid of a blunderbuss for those dancers who were remiss in their payment.

If, on the one hand, popular music opened up a space populated with the proletarian suburban archetypes of *el malevo* (the tough) and *la mina* (the sweetheart; a contraction of *menina*, a term originating with the Portuguese smugglers who plied the River Plate riversides between Buenos Aires and Uruguay) (Goldar 2), on the other hand, the majority of the Argentinean writers of this generation were informed by reading French literature. Lucio V. Mansilla, for example, in his *Una*

excursión a los indios ranqueles [1870; An Excursion to the Ranquel Indians], writes that French influence was "most visible in narrative modes and dialogue" (qtd. in Gándara 66). Mansilla, for his part, saw himself as the commandant of the frontier between "civilization" and the "Indian lands." During this epoch President Sarmiento had ordered that the border be extended up to the banks of the Quinto River in the province of Córdoba. Mansilla's narratives develop against the backdrop of native frontier villages, but his writing is markedly influenced by French modes and idioms.

The arrival of the Nicaraguan poet Rubén Darío (1867–1916) in Buenos Aires constituted a singular development in Argentinean letters, destined to liberate the nation's poetry from its Spanish typologies and Romantic remainders. Under Darío's influence Argentinean literature, and especially its poetry, was revolutionized, and the already existent links to French literature were affirmed and strengthened. French language and culture had already been influential in the work of Argentinean prose narratives, and now with the advent of *modernismo* and the example of Darío, Argentinean poetry became intimately related with the French Parnassan and Symbolist poets. Pedro Henríquez Ureña (1884–1946) has written of Darío's influence that "of any poem written in Spanish that you care to mention, it can be stated with precision whether it was written prior to or after his arrival" (173). The great *modernista* poet arrived preceded by *Azul* [Azure], published in Chile in 1888, in which he portrays in a number of stories, as Rafael Gutiérrez Girardot (b. 1928) has observed, the marginal situation of the artist in bourgeois bureaucratic society (40–54). Although the professionalization of the artist is still some years in the future, there did begin at this time a certain specialization that was to modify the figure of the poet, who in River Plate and Spanish American society acquired a manifold of tasks and exigencies (Rama 40–46). This was the epoch in which a literary clique of young post-Romantics that included Leopoldo Lugones (1874–1938), José Ingenieros (1877–1925), and Luis Berisso (1866–1944) gathered around Darío at the famous Aue's Keller. Buenos Aires, christened Cosmópolis by Darío, was a meeting place for a diverse group of cultural figures, and the cafés and cliques of the city received an array of actors, poets, artists, and politicians, increasing the floating population of the Buenos Aires bohemians. It was also in these years that photography appeared on the scene and had an incomparable impact on painting and literary culture. The ferment of the city can be in part explained by the first census which was completed in 1887; it recorded a total population of 433,375 of which 204,734 were Argentineans and 228,651 were foreigners.

The playwrights Enrique García Velloso (1880–1938), Rodolfo González Pacheco (1882–1949), and the Uruguayan Florencio Sánchez (1875–1910) often met at the café-bar Piaggio, while the La Brasileña café was the meeting place for the playwright Samuel Eichelbaum (1894–1967) and the poet Evaristo Carriego (1883–1912), a friend of the Borges family. The lyricist Samuel Linning (1888–1925), author of the celebrated tango "Milonguita," was a regular, along with Belisario Roldán (1873–1922), at the café known as the Seminario, next to the Sarmiento and Comedia theaters. This milieu of intense interchange between the realms of bohemia and high culture was gradually bringing the tango into the center of the city's culture (Giusti 13).

At the same time, the tango lyrics themselves were changing–from "La Morocha" [1905; "The Brunette"] (lyrics by Angel G. Villoldo, music by Enrique Saborido), a rural flavored song that painted a picture of a city whose urban limits were not well defined and blurred into the countryside (as appears, for example, in Borges's story "Hombre de la esquina rosada" ["Man on the Pink Corner"]) to tangos like "Mi noche triste" ["My Sad Night"]. This tango (lyrics by Pascal Contursi, music by Samuel Castriota) is the first tango of an entirely urban character; it premiered in 1917 in the cabaret review *Los dientes del perro* [The Teeth of the Dog] and initiated a long series of lyrics in which the *amurado* or the abandoned lover lamented the loss of his *mina* sweetheart. The French language also had its influence on the tango. If Rubén Darío took from French poetry new scansions, rhythms, and accents that transformed and made poetry written in Spanish more diverse, influencing also the poets from Spain, the tango, on the other hand, appropriated from the French lexicon a number of terms (in many cases giving them a Castilian orthography) such as *satén* (sateen), *mishé* (prostitute's john), *chiqué* (feign), *champán* (champagne), *vuaturé* (car), and so on (Ulla 1986, 126–27).

These were the years in which was spawned the poetic and narrative work of Leopoldo Lugones, a controversial public figure whose end was tragic. Born in the interior of the country in Villa María del Río Seco in the province of Córdoba, he took up residence in the capital in 1896. A friend of Darío, Lugones shared an inclination toward anarchist political ideas with a number of other writers, including Alberto Gerchunoff (1883–1950), Manuel Ugarte (1878–1951), Alberto Ghiraldo (1874–1946), and Roberto Payró (1867–1928); he would later break ranks with them and pass, first to the socialist camp and then later to German and Italian fascism. Together with Darío, the Bolivian Ricardo Jaimes Freyre (1868–1933) and Enrique Larreta (1875–1961), Lugones disseminated *modernismo* in the River Plate region; Freyre was the author of *Castalia bárbara* [1897; Barbaric Castalia], while Larreta was the author of a famous historical novel about Vespucci's final voyage to America and the subsequent epoch of Philip II of Spain (1556–1598), *La gloria de Don Ramiro* [1908; The Glory of Don Ramiro] (Anderson Imbert 464–65).

Lugones rendered homage to Spain's May 1808 Revolution against Napoleon (the event that precipitated Argentina's independence) on its centenary in his *Odas seculares* [1910; Secular Odes]. In this collection Lugones abandoned the French influence that marked his *Lunario sentimental* [1909; Soulful Moon Book], his most *modernista* work, while his collection of stories *La guerra gaucha* [1905; The Gaucho War] bore witness to the struggles for independence in a dense and labored style that Valle-Inclán would call "esperpéntico" (or parodic caricatures) (Anderson Imbert 410–17). Lugones's more than forty years of literary labor created a corpus of poems, narratives, philological studies, polemics, and histories. These works are animated by the passion that was his constant inspiration, "the passion of the ideologue and the agitator who fought to make a place for the man of letters in the social and political process of his times" (Prieto 1968, 98), offering an indisputable if controversial model for the poets who would follow him, Lugones's verse is characterized by a tone and an accent from which Borges would keep his distance.

However, the poetic work that best typifies the historical period of *modernismo* is Rubén Darío's "Canto a la Argentina" [1914; "Song to Argentina"]. Argentina received the world's third largest number of immigrants in the period 1857–1914, a whopping 3,330,000 people; they were the labor force that built refrigerated meat packing plants and the transportation network linking the zones of cattle production with the capital-port. The wide scope of these changes were poetically recorded, as Ángel Rama (1926–1983) has accurately analyzed, in Darío's poem (122–25): the restoration of an economy that had been based on a cereal monoculture, the development of livestock production, the expansion of the port industrial zone and the growth of the ports themselves, the development of an agriculture oriented toward the provisioning of beef to the world, the development of crafts and skills, a progressive social and cultural reformation, the advent of inexpensive consumer goods, the disciplined organization of work and leisure, and a general sensation of modern vitality. Darío expresses this in the "Canto," anticipating what was to occur in the not too distant future, as: "Tráfagos, fuerzas urbanas,/trajín de hierro y fragores,/veloz, acerado hipogrifo,/rosales eléctricos, flores/miliunanochescas, pompas/babilónicas, timbres, trompas" (1914, 42) ("Traffic, the city's bustle,/clattering iron carriages,/swift steel hippogriffs,/electric roses, flowers/of a thousand and one nights,/Babylonian pomps and trumpets" [1973, 124]).

During the course of World War I the value of Argentinean exports effectively rose by a magnitude of 40 percent compared to 1914 values; by the end of the war this figure had vaulted to 300 percent of the 1914 values (Cantón 24). In 1913, at the apogee of the boom in foreign investment, almost half of the total invested was fixed capital. By 1929, the year of the stock market crash, the percentage of foreign investment was still very high at 35 percent. This period saw the rise to power of political radicals by means of the ballot box, with the radicals holding power from 1916 to 1930. With the advent of universal suffrage brought into law by Sáenz Peña in 1912, radicals were elected to the presidency in quick succession: Hipólito Yrigoyen (1852–1933), Marcelo T. de Alvear (1922–1928), and Yrigoyen again from 1928 to 6 September 1930, when he was overthrown by the army. Within this radical period the Alvear presidency was rather distant from the policies of his predecessor and successor Yrigoyen (Cantón 13), but in general the radical governments can be characterized as resulting from a pronounced social mobility promoted in large part by the marked increase in all levels of education. The Uruguayan dramatist Florencio Sánchez's play *M'hijo el dotor* [M'boy the Doc] illustrated at the turn of the century what would be recreated some time later in the words of the popular tango "Giuseppe el zapatero" ["Joseph the Cobbler"]: social climbing through university education. The immigrants who had arrived in Argentina brought with them a knowledge and experience of the politicoideological currents that characterized the various European workers' movements, and during the period of radical government, reformist policies were strongly promoted in the trade union and socialist camps. For the first time in Argentinean political history the president, Yrigoyen, received a delegation of striking workers. Under the same administration, the Córdoba University student movement came to a head and forced university reform at the most conservative of the nation's three universities in June 1918; the movement spread to Buenos Aires and La Plata universities almost immediately. The Yrigoyen administration distinguished itself not only by entering into dialogue with the students, but also in its international stance of neutrality during World War I, contrary to the openly bellicose position advocated by figures such as Lugones.

The years of radical government coincided with the widespread diffusion of the tango and the cabaret review–the rage in London, Paris, and New York since 1913, while in Buenos Aires the tango was danced in the public dance halls known as *ollas populares*, where a number of women were kept on salary to dance with the customers. Making inroads into the upper classes, the Montmartre, Royal Pigale, and Armenonville cabarets showcased tango orchestras. The important collaboration of the tango and the theatrical farce persisted until 1930, when radio and cinema slowly began to replace the popular theater. The tango lyricists recorded the appearance in the city of the *milongueras*, or women from the proletarian suburbs who, to escape from misery, flocked to the cabarets as nocturnal professionals and were exploited by a *caften*. It was Samuel Linning who with his tango "Milonguita" (1920; music by Enrique Delfino) first designated this new phenomena of urban displacement; among its most famous interpreters were Pascual Contursi, Celedonio Flores, Enrique Cadícamo, and Discépolo. The plain language of the majority of the tango lyrics was often entwined with terminology borrowed from the argot of the suburbs that was one of the most singular and felicitous expressions of Buenos Airean language use. This local usage did not, however, impede the tangos from conquering provincial listeners; they, like the city dwellers, were rhapsodized by the irresistible tones of Carlos Gardel (1890–1935), known as "El Mago" ("The Wizard") because of his graceful voice and figure. Gardel traversed the world with his stage shows until 1935 when he tragically died in the city of Medellín, Colombia (Ulla 1982, 80–81).

The tango and the *milongas* exploited the language of the underworld, the world of bravado that exalted proletarian suburban life and thus had a profound impact on society's cultural imaginary. The melodrama that smoldered in many of the tango lyrics, as well as the familiar exaltation of River Plate machismo, was cinematographically captured by the film director Manuel Romero (1897–1954), himself a writer of many tangos, in his many filmscripts and his best films of the 1930s. No sooner had Jorge Luis Borges (1899–1986) returned from Europe where he had spent a number of years than he published his first book of poems, *Fervor de Buenos Aires* [1923; Adoration of Buenos Aires], deeply inspired by the Ultraist school and River Plate realities.

The literary journals of the period, *Prisma* (1921–1922), *Proa, Inicial*, and *Martín Fierro* (2nd series: 1924–1927) brought together the poets inspired by the discovery of the suburbs and celebrated European post-war literature under the name of the *Florida* group, named after the most opulent and cosmopolitan street in Buenos Aires (see **Figure 5**). Borges, Evar Méndez (1888–1955), Oliverio Girondo (1891–1967), Raúl González Tuñón (1905–1974), Eduardo González Lanuza (1900–1984), Leopoldo Marechal (1900–1970), Pablo Rojas Paz (1896–1956), Luis Leopoldo Franco (1898–1988), Ernesto Palacio (1900–1979) (the historian), Brandán Caraffa (1898–1987), and Sergio Piñero (d. 1931) were all collaborators to *Martín Fierro* and, in politics, were sympathizers of Hipólito Yrigoyen. Standing in opposition to the *Florida* was the *Boedo* group, named after a neighborhood street that symbolized the literature of commitment to social causes, whose journals were *Los Pensadores* (1922) and *Claridad* (1926). The most distinguished representatives of this group were the writers Elías Castelnuovo (1893–1982), Roberto Mariani (1892–1946), Alvaro Yunque (1889–1982), César Tiempo (1906–1980), and Leónidas Barletta (1902–1975), founder and director of the

Figure 5.

Photograph of "Calle Florida," Buenos Aires, c. 1890 by Samuel Boote. (Archive of the author)

People's Theater in 1930. Although the *Boedo-Florida* polemics began as a discussion of the distinction between wit and humor, they were to end up being crucial to the Argentinean literature of these years and to have ideological repercussions for many years to come.

The polemics on the unity or diversity of the Spanish language initiated in the nineteenth century by Domingo Faustino Sarmiento and the Chilean scholar Andrés Bello (1781–1865) continued to be active in the 1920s–with Rafael Obligado (1851–1920), Juan Antonio Argerich (1862–1924), Alberto del Solar (1860–1921), Mariano de Vedia (1880–1958), Ernesto Quesada (1858–1934), Estanislao S. Zeballos (1854–1923)–and in the 1930s, notably turning on the issue of the River Plate written language. The combative Uruguayan philologist Vicente Rossi (1871–1945) championed nationalist ideas of language usage that had resulted in the development of the *American Standard Dictionary* at the end of the eighteenth century in the United States under the direction of Noah Webster. The young Argentinean writers Jorge Luis Borges and Roberto Arlt (1900–1942) and the Uruguayans Felisberto Hernández (1902–1964) and Juan Carlos Onetti (1909–1994) took up the task of establishing a River Plate written language that was more representative of the spoken language and differentiated from the canon of rigorously Iberian Spanish. Borges and Arlt, perhaps unaware of the role that their fiction would play in the formation of future writers, established models of probity and craftsmanship that were unquestioned for almost six decades. The novel *El juguete rabioso* [1926; *Mad Toy,* 2002] by Roberto Arlt was composed as a veritable hybrid of discourses in a style impregnated by the multiple registers of immigrant Spanish, the high Spanish of translations and dialectics, criollisms, Italianisms, underworld argot, and literary constructions that functioned as fixed rhetorical formulae. Although the colloquial idiom was not predominant in it, *El juguete rabioso* was, up until the 1970s, one of the most read works of Argentinean fiction for its absolutely popular and enigmatic character. Its success initiated the lively literary and ideological opposition between Borges and Arlt, in which Borges represented the educated imagination, Europe, and erudition, while Arlt represented popular concerns and realism. Both in his fictional works as well as in his journalism, Arlt discovered a Buenos Aires in a constant state of transformation vis-à-vis its customs and its woes. For his part, Borges, relinquishing his initial enthusiasm for Ultraism, published in 1933 a story that would for more than thirty years be a touchstone of the River Platan narrative, "Hombre de la esquina rosada" ["Man on the Pink Corner"]. Distancing himself from traditional models, Borges chose a style in this story that strives to adopt the likeness of its protagonist's voice, a pretty-boy (*guapo*) who speaks the local dialect. The diction is larded with the criollisms of a braggart, only a few of which, notably the underworld terms (*quilombo* [brothel], *lengue* [scarf], *biaba* [a thrashing]) and the Italianism (*facha* [fascist]), are written without quotation marks or italics. This text shows Borges in the combative light of the times, the era in which the Argentinean Academy of Letters was founded (1931) and in which the issues of criollism, argot, and pure Spanish were hotly contested by writers, linguists, academics, and students. In the *Folletos lenguaraces* (1932), one of the philologist Vicente Rossi's linguistic-nationalist proposals was taken up in a redefinition of the "River Plate voice" as the language of Uruguayan-Argentinean fraternity and joint participation, due to their common history and folklore.

The Uruguayan writer Felisberto Hernández (1902–1964), in his first books *Fulano de tal* [1925; Some So and So], *Libro sin tapas* [1929; Coverless Book], *La cara de Ana* [1930; Ana's Face], and *La envenenada* [1931; The Poisoned Woman] also opened up the linguistic question of a River Plate Spanish but purged of Italianisms, criollisms, and underworld argot. And this despite the fact that in these books a colloquial style and a first-person narration (similar to the style of Borges) are, in his quite particular kind of fantasy, the predominant leitmotifs. On the other side of this issue was the Uruguayan writer Juan Carlos Onetti, whose novel *El pozo* [1939; *The Pit,* 1991] made him one of the founders of the River Plate language. This novel abounds with Italianisms, underworld argot, and other oral registers on both the lexical and syntactic levels. Close to Roberto Arlt, Onetti had a profound impact on the writers of the 1970s. Rebelling against academic literary tradition, Onetti, who lived for many years in Buenos Aires, introduced what has been called an "un-literary" discourse, in which the narrative voice relates its tale with the spontaneity of orality (Ulla 1990, 219–235). Although it was through these writers that the use of the River Plate language became a standard in the region's literature, the hesitations and vacillations of the use of the term have meant that it has designated very different modes of expression. In 1852 the subject of a "National Language" was introduced into the cultural scene, a term that reappears in the language laws of 1884, 1887, 1888, 1898, and

1900. The rising levels of literacy in this period gave rise in Buenos Aires to a daily press that included the morning papers, *La Prensa* and *La Nación,* and in 1931 *Noticias Gráficas,* and the evening paper *Crítica,* to whose cultural section Borges was a regular contributor. In addition, *La Capital* published in Rosario, and *Los Principios* published in Córdoba, were dailies of recognized importance.

The military *coup d'état* of 4 June 1943, which overthrew the presidency of Dr. Ramón Castillo, opened the door to a new mode of Argentinean politics that was soon to be incarnated in the figure of the then colonel, Juan Domingo Perón (1895–1974). During his reign (1946–1955), there was a clear division, both in Buenos Aires and in the provincial cities, between the Peronist majority and the opposition. According to Tulio Halperín Donghi (b. 1926), the only phase of Argentinean political history remotely comparable to Perón's in terms of populism was the reign of Yrigoyen (64–65). Thanks to the favorable foreign exchange rate and gold reserves accumulated during World War II, the new regime was able to raise salaries to the highest levels ever seen in the country and to establish a system of social security (Bagú 100). Thus for the working class, the Peronist state delivered access to consumer goods, to political decision-making, and to the formerly inaccessible sites of pleasure and leisure, sites like the *La enramada* dance hall and Retiro Park in the capital where folkloric musical spectacles began to be held. According to Luis Alberto Romero, the working classes took over the city, the center, and "made use of everything" (159). The trade unions, working class institutions *par excellence,* were the site from which workers were able to integrate themselves into society under the mantle of a new popular figure, the *descamisado* (literally the shirtless referring to the militant proletarian supporters of Perón). Television broadcasting was introduced into the country by a radio pioneer, Jaime Yankelevich, backed by state subventions, and the first images were transmitted in Buenos Aires by Channel 7 on on 17 October 1951. In 1952 the rank of Liberator of the Republic was conferred upon Perón and that of Spiritual Leader (*Jefa Espiritual*) of the Nation upon his wife María Eva Duarte de Perón (Evita; 1919–1952), at a time when the nation was in the throes of devotion to the "*justicialismo*" national doctrine. A series of reforms were instituted, including unconditional divorce, the equality of legitimate and extra-matrimonial children, the legalization of brothels, and the suppression of religious instruction in public education (the effect of which was to undermine the support that the Church had from the beginning lent the government). This was to precipitate the fall of the Peronist regime in a new military *coup d'état* and, with it, the dreams of prosperity that had been the main concern of the masses.

Cultural activity in these years was in large measure under the rule of government directives that tended to impose an established national and popular tradition by setting limits on press and radio freedom, closing political weeklies, and progressively infiltrating the universities, depriving them of autonomy. According to Alberto Ciria (b. 1943), the Peronist state began the take over and rule of the majority of the nation's broadcasters from 1945 onward, so that by 1954 four national networks ("El Mundo," "Splendid," "Belgrano," and "LRA Radio del Estado") constituted the bulk of official radio transmissions, broadcasting a major dose of political propaganda to the listening public (15). Many of the nation's writers and thinkers, caught up in the conflict between the "popular" and what Perón called the "oligarchy," either officially supported the government or closed ranks with the critical stance adopted by the Colegio Libre de Estudios Superiores and the journal *Sur*. The Colegio, one of whose founders was the philosopher and politician Aníbal Ponce (1898–1938), author of (among other works) *La vejez de Sarmiento* [1927; Sarmiento's Old Age], acted as a surrogate university for Buenos Aires and some of the provincial cities. Having arisen out of the dialogue between Waldo Frank (1889–1967) and Eduardo Mallea (1903–1982) (*Historia de una pasión argentina* [1937; *History of an Argentine Passion,* 1983]; *La bahía del silencio* [1940; *Bay of Silence,* 1944]), the journal *Sur* was founded and directed by the writer Victoria Ocampo (1890–1979) from 1931 until her death; it distinguished itself by being a vehicle for young Argentinean writers and for the diffusion of foreign writers, both Anglo American and European, often translating them into Spanish for the first time (Paz Leston 1). José Bianco (1908–1986), author of the novels *Sombras suele vestir* [1941; *Shadow Play,* 1983], *Las ratas* [1943; *The Rats,* 1983], and *La pérdida del reino* [1972; The Loss of the Kingdom], succeeded Guillermo de Torre as *Sur*'s editor and from 1938 to 1961 and pursued an editorial policy of opting for originality and meticulous editorial revisions of the works published. The editorial house of *Sur*, founded in 1933, adopted a similar role as a disseminator of new work. Eduardo Mallea, an essayist and prose fiction writer closely linked to the house of *Sur*, was for many years the editor of the literary supplement of *La Nación* which also celebrated the collaboration of young writers. A notable exception to the discursive climate of these years, dominated by *Sur*, was Ezequiel Martínez Estrada (1895–1964), author of *Radiografía de la pampa* [1933; *X-Ray of the Pampa,* 1971], *La cabeza de Goliat* [1940; Goliath's Head], *Muerte y transfiguración de Martín Fierro* [1948; Martin Fierro: Death and Transfiguration], and *Qué es esto?* [1956; What is This?]. In the latter book, Estrada initiated a study of his times from a point of view critical of Peronism. For many years resident in Mexico and Cuba, from where he defended the Cuban Revolution, Estrada took an active interest in Latin American literature as a whole.

One of the most distinguished writers sympathetic to the Peronist government was Leopoldo Marechal (1900–1970). Although in his first book of poetry, *Días como flechas* [1926; Days Like Arrows], he appeared to share ties with the Ultraist school, in his later poetry, *El centauro* [1940; The Centaur], *Sonetos a Sophia* [1940; Sonnets to Sophia], *Viaje de primavera* [1945; Spring Voyage], and *Heptamerón* [1966; Heptameron], he developed his aesthetic preoccupations in the direction of the Platonic tradition. He continued this quest in his later novels *Adán Buenosayres* [1948; Adam BuenosAyres] and *El banquete de Severo Arcángelo* [1965; The Symposium of Severo Archangel]. *Adán Buenosayres*, an allegory of literary production charged with the comic vision characteristic of the Martín Fierro group, is one of the most celebrated novels of contemporary Argentinean letters. Among Marechal's dramatic works are *Antígona Vélez* [1951; Antigone Velez] and *Las tres caras de Venus* [1966; The Three Faces of Venus]. Marechal's support for Peronism, as Adolfo Prieto has reminded us, was clearly visible in his holding of various national government administrative posts concerning education and cultural diffusion (103–105); during the 1970s Marechal was one the literary models of the young Peronist writers. The same can be said of the group of Catholic traditionalist writers, as Rodolfo Borello (1930–1996) has defined them (31), among whom

were included: Ignacio Anzoátegui (1905–1978); Arturo Cambours Ocampo (1908–1996); Horacio Rega Molina (1899–1957); José María Castiñeira de Dios (b. 1920), a former member of the *Boedo* group; Elías Castelnuovo (1893–1982), author of *Tinieblas* [1923; Darkness], *Malditos* [1924; The Accursed], and *El arte y las masas* [1935; Art and the Masses]; Homero Manzi (1905–1951), whose numerous and memorable tango and *milonga* lyrics, "Sur" ["The South"], "Malena", "El último organito" ["The Last Squeeze Box"], "Che Bandoneón" ["Hey Accordion!"], "Viejo ciego" ["The Old Blind Man"], "Fuimos" ["We Were. . ."]) painted a picture of a bygone ambiance and its typical figures; and the poet and fiction writer Nicolás Olivari (1900–1966), author of *La musa de la mala pata* [1926; Bad Luck Muse, or The Clubfooted Muse], *El gato escaldado* [1929; The Wary Cat], *La mosca verde* [1933; Dirty Money], and *Mi Buenos Aires querido* [1966; The Buenos Aires I Love]. Like the philosopher Carlos Astrada (1894–1970), Raúl Scalabrini Ortiz (1898–1959) also adhered to the ruling *justicialista* ideology. Author of the essay *El hombre que está solo y espera* [1931; The Solitary Man, Waiting], in which he painted the portrait of the average person from the River Plate who, after immigration, would incarnate the national spirit (Prieto 144), Ortiz was also responsible for studies in an economic nationalist vein, including *Política británica en el Río de la Plata* [1936; British Influence in the River Plate] and *Historia de los ferrocarriles argentinos* [1944; History of Argentinean Railways]. Another development of note in the 1940s was the professionalization of the nation's musicians, singers, lyricists, and composers under the auspices of the SADAIC (Sociedad Argentina de Autores y Compositores de Música), an organization which, although founded in 1936 during the Peronist era, took up a strong trade unionist position of advocacy on behalf of the professionals of the tango. With the fall of the Perón regime in 1955, a veritable cultural euphoria ensued that continued into the following years of the radical presidencies of Arturo Frondizi (1958–1962) and Arturo H. Illia (1963–1966) until a new military coup brought down Illia's administration. The Frondizi adminstration's "developmentalist" policies saw new foreign capital invested in the country and an upsurge in the production of coal, steel, and oil. In the cultural domain, a truly inspiring moment in the history of Buenos Aires was capped with the inauguration of the Instituto Torquato Di Tella, a cultural center bringing together avant-garde artists and writers. Jorge Romero Brest (1905–1989), one of the art critics linked to the center, took on the task of establishing close ties between the arts and artists of the world and those of the River Plate region. Located in the city center, the so-called *manzana loca* (crazy block), the Institute became a focal point for the avant-garde fine arts and, in the performing arts, the theater of the absurd.

Under the rectorship of José Luis Romero, the University of Buenos Aires began to modernize its curriculum and practices. It opened its doors to the new social sciences with programs in sociology and psychiatry; its biology and biochemical laboratories were staffed by researchers and scientists; the study of physics and agronomy was encouraged, and, in contrast to the previous Peronist period, the humanities recovered their previous prestige and sense of moving forward. The new openness of the university was symbolized in a fundamental development, the founding of the EUDEBA (Editorial universitaria de Buenos Aires), whose series of inexpensive editions sold in curb-side kiosks fostered the expansion of understanding in science, philosophy, and literature. Boris Spivacow was one of the principal promoters of EUDEBA and oversaw its program of getting books to the reading public, as well as being responsible for reviving a number of forgotten authors, such as Macedonio Fernández (1874–1952), author of *No toda es vigilia la de los ojos abiertos* [1928; Not Everything is Watched Over with Eyes Open]; *Poemas* [1953; Poems] and *Museo de la novela de la eterna* [1967; Museum of the Novel of Eternal] and a writer whose influence on Borges should be noted. As Luis Alberto Romero has pointed out, the EUDEBA in this manner continued the work began by a number of editorial houses of the 1930s and 1940s (221).

The Cuban Revolution of 1959 created in Argentina, as it did in the rest of Latin America, an ideological furor and inspired the development of a militant popular culture in the capital and throughout the country. Most Argentinean progressive thinkers rallied behind the revolutionary dreams unleashed by events, and the Left, bolstered by the Cuban triumph, paraded its support of Cuba and its ideology. Young River Plate writers of the Left, in full agreement with the revolutionary doctrine and the literary "engagement" that Sartean existentialism had championed, began to reopen other roads to literary and artistic creation. With the return of General Perón to the country and the new Peronist government (1972–1976) that culminated with Perón's second wife, Isabel Martínez de Perón, assuming power after his death (in July 1974), the intellectuals and above all the writers, stimulated by the Cuban example of the possibility of change, sought ideologically to construct a cultural identity in a period of exultant and complete politicization.

During this third Peronist period of nationalism and traditionalism in the 1970s, the University of Buenos Aires discovered in Borges—the writer most harassed by the previous Peronist government—a representative of a sentiment to its liking: the author of the story "Hombre de la esquina rosada" [1935; "Man on the Pink Corner," 1954], *El idioma de los argentinos* [1928; Argentinean Language], and the essay *Evaristo Carriego* (1930). This was a Borges who gave the lie to the rest of his *oeuvre*, a *criollista* Borges, that young irreverent writer who in the 1930s had written in a *criolledá* and *dualidá* manner. Against the elite Borges, the popular (and populist) culture of the 1970s fired its own volleys, proposing a different aesthetic and a direct discourse of the people, desirous of giving voice to those social groups lacking the legitimacy of representation in Argentinean culture. It soon became apparent that the artificial paradox of the supposed Borges-Arlt dichotomy—with which critics had designated the two poles of the European fantastic, on the one hand, and the literary realist and the denunciation of social conditions, on the other—required a point of conciliation between these extremities, and it was soon found in the works of Julio Cortázar (1914–1984), whose works disseminated the special features that had so characterized the writers of the Argentinean 1930s: the informal form of address (*el voseo*), the River Plate forms corresponding to this informality, a common lexicon, at times indecipherable, and a colloquial syntax. Although Silvina Ocampo (1903–1993) had employed, timidly, a number of characteristic features of River Plate speech in her stories in *La Furia* [1959; Rage], Cortázar, a devoted reader of Borges and Arlt and an admirer of Felisberto Hernández and Juan Carlos Onetti, appeared to resolve the duality of the Borges-Arlt antagonism by fusing the socialist ideology that had been attributed to Arlt with the Borgesean constructions of the fantastic tale. Thus, with the reevaluation of Macedonio Fernández, the opponent of poetic traditionalism, and the

glowing reception of the work of Cortázar, the 1970s decade was opened up to the question of the possibility of a liberation from the reductionism of academic literary genres. Following in the footsteps of Fernández's rupture of narrative form, Cortázar stamped his narratives like *Rayuela* [1963; Hopscotch] and his theoretical texts (for example, his study of the short story included in *Ultimo Round* [1969]) with a special license.

In Cortázar's fiction, as in that of David Viñas (b. 1929), Manuel Puig (1932–1990), and Germán Rozenmacher (1936–1971), there is a clear attempt to disembowel the Argentinean cultural imaginary. In this, they are all responding to what the Uruguayan critic Ángel Rama has called transculturation, the Latin American desire to uncover the particularities of each culture. And for a writer in the River Plate region and in all of Latin America, the intimate identity of each culture consists of signposting the linguistic particularities of the local spoken idiom. Thus, for the young writers, the colloquial register of Borges's "Hombre de la esquina rosada" was appropriated and charged with another signification: the sociopolitical. And such was the force of this proposition that the major writers, those who had already a number of books behind them, were carried away by the social construction that is language, adopting the modality of giving speech the upper hand over the written language. This was the case with Manuel Mujica Láinez (1910–1984), Silvina Ocampo, and Adolfo Bioy Casares (1914–1999). However, each of these writers in their diverse ways imposed their own stamp on their discourse: the mimesis of the popular speech in Silvina Ocampo's characters in *Enumeración de la patria* [1942; Reckoning of the Homeland], *Autobiografía de Irene* [1948; Irene's Own Story], *Los días de la noche* [1970; The Days of the Night], and *Cornelia frente al espejo* [1988; Cornelia at the Mirror] is quite different than that of Germán Rozenmacher (*Cabecita negra* [1962; Little Black Head], *Los ojos del tigre* [1968; The Eyes of the Tiger]), Manuel Puig (*La traición de Rita Hayworth* [1968; Betrayed by Rita Hayworth*, 1971], *Boquitas pintadas* [1970; Heartbreak Tango]), and David Viñas (*Los dueños de la tierra* [1958; The Landlords], *Las malas costumbres* [1964; Bad Habits], *Claudia conversa* [1966; Claudia Relates]), or Adolfo Bioy Casares (*La invención de Morel* [1940; The Invention of Morel, 1985], *Guirnalda con amores* [1959; Garland of Love], *Dormir al sol* [1973; Asleep in the Sun, 1976], *La aventura de un fotógrafo en La Plata* [1985; The Adventures of a Photographer in La Plata, 1989]); but in every case the language of the texts is the language of Argentinean orality.

This intense period of variegated, prolific, intellectual, critical, and polemic activity, the product of a whole range of both mature and young writers, was abruptly interrupted by the last military dictatorship (1976–1983). Many writers, including Rodolfo Walsh (1927–1977), Haroldo Conti (1925–1976?), and Roberto Santoro (1939–1976) were "disappeared" and murdered during this malignant period of Argentina's self-mutilation, and others opted for exile in other Latin American or European countries. The youngest writers, those who had not yet lived through a period of cultural politicization, sought, in the face of censorship and almost as a cultural retort to the repression, to resuscitate the ancient literary genre of parody and to revive popular music as a poetic genre. These writers, writing and publishing in the 1970s and 1980s under the eyes of the military dictatorship, viewed realist aesthetics as an authoritarian project, the shackling of imaginative development. Some took Borges for a model; others unleashed what they considered to be an avant-garde movement, the writing of parody. As had Borges and Bioy

Casares in the 1940s with their *Seis problemas para don Isidro Parodi* [1942; *Six Problems for Don Isidro Parodi*, 1981], these young writers attempted to recuperate in their narrative voices the diverse intonations of River Plate social groups, idiomatic clichés, and both consecrated and ridiculed writers. In these difficult years, when the mere mention of Russian formalism in academic and university contexts unleashed open persecution, many young people eagerly digested the parodic theories of Bakhtin and Julia Kristeva, while others, without knowing of these theories but nonetheless writing and breathing in this same atmosphere, were dazzled by the work of Osvaldo Lamborghini (1940–1985), a writer who enjoyed a great influence among certain groups of River Plate writers. César Aira (b. 1949) and Arturo Carrera (b. 1948) were also producing parodic poetry during these dark years. In a nutshell the repression imposed by the dictatorship had renewed parody as a genre, that in certain texts was not in any sense ideological but rather discursive and as such operated on a comic, reflexive, and critical level. In 1981 Aira published his novel *Emma, la cautiva* [Emma, the Captive], the proper noun of the title invoking a humorous game of double significance: on the one hand referring to Flaubert's protagonist Madame Bovary, while on the other hand, echoing Esteban Echeverría's *La cautiva* (1837). The captive of Aira's novel takes part in a strange voyage that is at the same time a parody of Mansilla's *Una excursión a los indios ranqueles*. Through the use of anachronisms and hyperbole, the landscape of the pampas becomes in the narrator's hands a new literary domain, infused with intertextuality. The historical referents of the text are woven in such a way that the credible appears within a number of conceits simulating the improbable. In this novel and through these techniques, Aira mocks not only novels of customs and manners, the psychological novel, and the discourse of feminism, but all the conventions of realism.

The theory and practice of psychoanalysis, which in the 1970s bore its most influential fruit in the city of Buenos Aires, also suffered a serious setback under the military dictatorship. Despite the well-known persecutions and murders of leading figures among Argentina's psychoanalysts, however, the seed of psychoanalytic knowledge had already found a fertile bed in many literary groups and thus survived. Certain psychoanalytic theories made deep inroads into Argentinean letters, one of the premier examples of which was Arturo Carrera's book of poems, *La partera canta* [1982; The Midwife Sings]. In the years immediately previous to this publication a number of diverse writers had grouped themselves around the journal *Literal*—Germán Leopoldo García (b. 1944), Osvaldo Lamborghini, Luis Gusmán (b. 1944), and Lorenzo Quinteros (b. 1945)—and had adopted the position of opposing not only realism, but the subjection to the referent, all in order to champion the site of desire. The title of an article published in *Literal* in its first issue of 1973, "No matar la palabra. No dejarse matar por ella" ["Do not kill the word: nor let oneself be killed by it"], reminded its readers that by pontification on the supremacy of the real, realism had moralized the superficiality of desire. These texts and these writers proposed, contrary to the committed, testimonial, and denunciatory literature prevalent outside of Argentina, Chile, and Uruguay (all subject to the terror of military dictatorship), a writing in which desire could claim for itself its own true space.

Literary discourses were in large measure saturated by different ideological and cultural viewpoints, and the 1980 bestseller *Flores robadas en los jardines de Quilmes* [1980; Flowers Stolen from the Quilmes Gardens] awakened the most impassioned and contradictory criticism. Its author, Jorge Asís (b. 1946), attempted by means of a newspaper-reporting style to fashion a poetics that repudiated any attempt at historical solutions to the problems faced by the complex social groups it described. *Flores robadas* was a realistic view of life in Buenos Aires, but it was much more. In a manner similar to Oscar Hermes Villordo's (1928–1994) novel *La brasa en la mano* [1983; Hot Potato] on the world of homosexuals, Asís's picaresque narrative insinuated itself into a number of diverse social milieus that it describes in a cynical mocking voice. Preoccupied with the discourse of history, a number of critics saw Asís's book as a work of indignation and his slight of hand with historical referents as satisfactory without realizing that the book's total mockery–of every ideology and politics, whether it be communist, Peronist, Leftist, or any other cultural trend–stressed (and this in middle of a dictatorship) sexual liberation and the critique of the machismo proper to the petit-bourgeois behavior of the protagonist. With a highly atuned ear, the protagonist-narrator records the distinct social discourses of society, making reference as he does so to an immense array of ideological and axiological connotations. What is demonstrated in this intensely mimetic writing–the novel is practically a document of this modality–is that language has ceased to be a contingency.

In a prior story, "Las FAC" ["The CAF"] in his collection *Fe de ratas* [1976; Rat Faith], Asís had painted a picture of the Leftist intellectuals or guerilla fighters of Peronism. Evincing the same high mockery we saw in *Flores robadas*, with the emphasis, however, more on the ideological, this story follows the CAF, or Cultural Armed Forces, who are charged with the task of hunting down and scapegoating artists and writers, those the story ironically designates as the "poetas de choque" ("poetic warriors"); it ends with a denouement reminiscent of Borges's tale "La espera" ["The Wait," 1949] in *El Aleph* [1949; The Aleph]. It seems clear that the author intended to scandalize by putting Borges up to ridicule through a number of descriptions; what was also clear was that Asís was saturated with Borges, as we can see in his story "Fe de Ratas" ["Rat Faith"] in the collection of that name. Asís has also demonstrated, as few can, a dexterity in the creation of charlatan or confident male figures whose function is to privilege communication at any cost.

Among the young poets of those years who found in parody a form of the rupture of verisimilitude, Arturo Carrera manifests a change of tack toward the end of the 1980s. After the already mentioned *La partera canta* [1982; The Midwife Sings] and *Mi padre* [1985; My Father], in which Carrera works the referent of psychoanalysis into his literary discourse, he began to probe into the Argentinean poetic tradition with Juan L. Ortiz (1896–1978) and Baldomero Fernández Moreno (1886–1950), and in the Hispano American tradition with César Vallejo (1892–1938). His next books, however, *Arturo y yo* [1984; Arthur and I] and *Animaciones suspendidas* [1986; Suspended Animations] are interrogations into the sense of his own expression in which the poet proposes to ignore the voices of the past. The traditional rhetorical figures of hyperbaton and anaphora–poetic characteristics that Mercedes Roffé (b. 1954) employed in *El tapiz de Ferdinand Oziel* [1983; Ferdinand Oziel's Tapestry] and *Cámara baja* [1987; The Lower Chamber]–take, in these books of poetry, the place previously occupied by linguistic play with the signifier, so that the poet ruptures literal meaning, in much the same way that Néstor Perlongher (1949–1992) and Emeterio

Cerro (b. 1952) had done. The intertexts of *Arturo y yo* and *Animaciones suspendidas* are, perhaps, a modernity without limits, including a number of reminiscences of Giovanni Pascoli and Fernando Pessoa; their lexicon encompasses English and astronomical terms, vulgarisms, children's constructions, the expression of the extraterrestrial, various forms of informal verbal address, intertextuality–always in search of the possible word and the speech that finds the right expression. In his most recent books, *Children's Corner* (1989), *La banda oscura de Alejandro* [1994; Alexander's Indistinct Side], and *El vespertillo de las Parcas* [1997; The Evening of the Fates], Carrera appears to have reached the highest pitch of his poetic register. In recent years, those poets known for their work since the 1950s, then considered avant-garde, have continued to realize a singular body of work. Among this group we would include Alberto Girri (1919–1991), Enrique Molina (1910–1997), and Olga Orozco (1920–1999) whose *También la luz es un abismo* [1995; Light Is Also an Abyss] won the Juan Rulfo Prize (1998).

Among the Argentinean writers living in exile, Daniel Moyano (1930–1992) and Blas Matamoro (b. 1942) took up residence in Spain. Moyano, the author of a highly representative body of narrative work (*El fuego interrumpido* [1967; Interrupted Fire], *Mi música es para gente* [1970; My Music Is for People], *El trino del diablo* [1974; The Devil's Warble]), died in Madrid. Matamoro has also lived there since 1975 and his literary reputation in Argentina has suffered as a result of the censorship imposed since 1982 on his book of short stories *Nieblas* [1982; Mists]. The title story, an allegory of the violent death and destruction of a city that nonetheless eludes historical and geographic referents, can also be read as representing the annihilation of thought and culture. As such, this story stands apart from the other stories in the collection and substantiates, in the malaise of this nation of "Mists" the intimate demolition of the condition of exile. The tensions between life and death, quietude and violence, peace and war, and a sentiment that is never named–fear–serve to charge this important story of exile with a singular eloquence (Ulla 1996, 152–53). Another of the Madrid exiles Reina Roffé (b. 1951), who first spent several years in the United States, authored *La rompiente* [1987; The Reef]. *El cielo dividido* [1996; The Divided Heavens] is her most recent work, which is also about the shattering condition of exile.

With its defeat in the Malvinas/Falkland Islands War (April to June 1982), a tragic military farce in which many lives were lost, the military regime entered a period of crisis. The exhaustion of the dictatorship had as a necessary consequence free elections in 1983 that made the return to democracy possible. With the end of the junta, censorship, which had been the most stringent in the period 1980–1983, was lifted and a large quantity of literary works began to see the light of day. In this context of political-cultural difficulties, the publication of the second, revised and augmented, edition of the *Historia de la literatura argentina* [The History of Argentine Literature] (by CEAL, *Centro Editor de América Latina*) made a famous contribution to and an impact upon Argentinean writers and readers.

Among the diverse narrative strategies prevalent in these years, the novels of Adolfo Bioy Casares (1914–1999) stand out as a singular expression distinguishing them from the ensemble of novels by other authors. Works such as *La aventura de un fotógrafo en La Plata* [1985; *The Adventures of a Photographer in La Plata*] and *Historias desaforadas* [1986; Outrageous Stories] challenged Bioy Casares's own earlier writing, condensing and perfecting his prose; this is also true of his most recent works, *Una muñeca rusa* [1991; *A Russian Doll*, 1992], *Una magia modesta* [1997; Modest Magic], and *De un mundo a otro* [1998; From One World to Another]. The use these narratives make of dialogue, almost without commentary, is one of the most salient features of their narrative construction and distinguishes Bioy Casares as the most accomplished inheritor in River Plate literature of Hemingway's sharp ear for cutting dialogue. Moreover, it is surprising that Bioy Casares, formed by his reading of Stevenson and Spanish literature, has been the one to best highlight the effectiveness of the Hemingway-style dialogue and not those writers who began publishing in the 1970s, for whom U.S. literature and Hemingway in particular was their preferred reading. For Bioy Casares, who always thinks of the reader, dialogue is a constant preoccupation. The jointly written works of Bioy Casares and Borges demonstrate their mutual accord with respect to the language form of choice employed in their fictions: conversation. However, and despite their avowed intentions toward naturalness, it would take each of them many years before their individual narrative works were able to reach this objective. In 1970, with his *El informe de Brodie* [Dr. Brodie's Report], Borges returned to the simplicity of a colloquial style that had marked "Hombre de la esquina rosada." For his part, starting with his *Diario de la guerra del cerdo* [1969; *Diary of the War of Pigs*, 1975] (as well as the already mentioned *Las aventuras de un fotógrafo en La Plata*), Bioy Casares truly began to realize the spoken language style that he had championed. In this novel we follow a male protagonist seduced and vanquished several times over by a certain kind of woman who attracts him. The reader's sympathy is awoken for a quasi-Chaplinesque hero who, because of his weaknesses, appears to be in need of protection. As for Bioy Casares's female characters, who in previous novels conversed in a less than direct fashion, they tend in these later novels to be so informal, concrete, and sharp-witted, that we can say it is as if they have definitively abandoned the courtly drawing room. In large measure, as a writer Bioy Casares continues to maintain his position in literary life, facing up to the demands of language and its articulations, its forcefulness and its gravity, with a sense of conviction and belief in the power of communication. With respect to his dramatic dialogues, the narrator attains an immediacy in the give-and-take of questions and replies without commentary and without the discourse of the dialogue appearing to be a performance or a transcription (Ulla 1996, 147–73).

One of the novels that captured the terror of the last dictatorship was *Respiración artificial* [1980; *Artificial Respiration*, 1994] by Ricardo Piglia (b. 1940), a writer who also published *La invasión* [1967; The Invasion], *Nombre falso* [1994; *Assumed Name*, 1995], and a number of critical interpretations of Argentinean writers such as Roberto Arlt and Jorge Luis Borges, whom he has contrasted in such a way that it has engendered much resistance. Most recently, his novel *Plata quemada* [1997; Burnt Silver], winner of the Planeta Prize in 1997, sets out within the frame of a detective story to reclaim the language spoken in the capital in the 1970s.

What Martínez Estrada has called the "Goliath's head," the capital's growth and domination over the rest of the country, has not, nonetheless, impeded the cultural and literary movements of the provinces that, almost always with an invaluable effort, have been able to evolve, thanks to the efforts of their writers and artists. Many of these have opted to live in Buenos Aires, which, for the writers, has often meant the illusion, in many cases, of having their work published and disseminated, since in general the work of provincial writers is slighted, when it is not completely overlooked in the capital, especially by the media. Even in the mid-twentieth century, the provincial writers continued to endure difficulties with diffusion, distribution, and communication that hindered their recognition by and access to readers, as, for example, Uruguayan writers were also hindered.

New modes of writing have arisen in recent times—since the last military dictatorship (1976–1983)—practices that feature reflexive introspection, the interchange of ideas, and the engagement with texts from less repressive environments which have been the inspiration behind the literary presses that have started throughout Argentina in a kind of spontaneous defense of freedom of thought. Thus, all the cities and regions of the country, even those most distant from the capital, have played an equal part in this resurgence of intellectual and literary activity. The same can be said of the significant function that the Teatro Abierto (Open Theater) played during this same period and in cities far from the capital. Practicing an active form of resistance characterized by free expression that challenged the censors in the final years of the dictatorship, Teatro Abierto's actor-based productions matched political import with aesthetic significance. Clearly, if we were to draw up a balance sheet of the *fin de siècle*, it would record that in Argentinean literature and literary life of the century's last thirty years there has been a determined and noticeable participation of writers in poetry, essays, drama, and fiction. Today, if a writer adopts the first person in the name of the feminist discourse, she is campaigning less for the claims of her gender than evoking a literary aesthetic.

Translation by Colman Hogan

Works Cited

Alberdi, Juan Bautista and Ricardo Rojas. 1915. *Las bases*. Buenos Aires: La Facultad.

Anderson Imbert, Enrique. 1970. *Historia de la literatura hispanoamericana*. Mexico City: Fondo de Cultura Económica.

Bagú, Sergio. 1971. *Argentina en el mundo*. Vol. 3. Mexico City: Fondo de Cultura Económica.

Borello, Rodolfo. 1991. *El peronismo (1943–1955) en la narrativa argentina*. Ottawa: Dovehouse, Editions Canada.

Bossio, Jorge. 1968. *Los cafés de Buenos Aires*. Buenos Aires: Shapire.

Cánepa, Luis. 1936. *El Buenos Aires de antaño*. Buenos Aires: Talleres Gráficos Linari & Cía.

Cantón, Darío, José L. Moreno and Alberto Ciria. 1980. *Argentina. La democracia constitucional y su crisis*. Vol. 6. *Historia Argentina*. Buenos Aires: Paidós.

Ciria, Alberto. 1990. *Treinta años de política y cultura*. Buenos Aires: De la Flor.

Darío, Rubén. 1914. *Canto a la Argentina y otros poemas*. Madrid: Biblioteca Corona.

——. 1973. *Selected Poems of Rubén Darío*. Trans. Lysander Kemp. Austin: University of Texas Press.

Gándara, Carmen. 1968. *El mundo del narrador*. Buenos Aires: Sudamericana.

Giusti, Juan Carlos. 1982. "Los cafés." *La vida de nuestro pueblo*. Vol 2. Buenos Aires: CEAL. 1–20.

Goldar, Ernesto. 1982. "El burdel." *La vida de nuestro pueblo*. Vol 1. Buenos Aires: CEAL. 1–20.

Groussac, Paul. 1884. "M. Cané (*En viaje*)." *El Diario*. 722 (Buenos Aires, 8 feb) 1 col. 2–5.

Gutiérrez Girardot, Rafael. 1976. "Teoría social de la literatura." *Escritura* 1.1. 40–56.

Halperín Donghi, Tulio. 1972. *La democracia de masas*. Vol. 7. *Historia Argentina*. Buenos Aires: Paidós.

Henríquez Ureña, Pedro. 1949. *Las corrientes literarias en América Hispánica*. Mexico City: Fondo de Cultura Económica.

Lavandera, Beatriz R. 1984. *Variación y significado*. Buenos Aires: Hachette.

Obligado, Rafael. 1951. "Las quintas de mi tiempo." *Poesías completas*. Buenos Aires: Editorial Sopena. 63–65.

Paz Leston, Eduardo. 1981. *Sur*. I-VIII. Buenos Aires: CEAL.

Prieto, Adolfo. 1968. *Diccionario básico de la literatura argentina*. Buenos Aires: CEAL.

——. 1980. "La generación del ochenta. Las ideas y el ensayo." *Historia de la Literatura Argentina*. Vol 2. Buenos Aires: CEAL. 49–72.

Rama, Ángel. 1985. *Rubén Darío y el Modernismo*. Caracas: Alfadil.

Romero, José Luis. 1959. *Las ideas políticas en la Argentina*. Mexico City: Buenos Aires, Fondo de Cultura Económica.

——. 1986. "Las ciudades burguesas. " *Latinoamérica: Las ciudades y las ideas*. Buenos Aires: Siglo XXI. 247–318.

Romero, Luis Alberto. 1995. *Breve historia contemporánea de la Argentina*. México-Buenos Aires: Fondo de Cultura Económica.

Rufinelli, Jorge. 1968. *La revista "Caras y Caretas"*. Buenos Aires: Galerna.

Troncoso, Oscar. 1982. "Juegos y diversiones de la gran aldea." *La vida de nuestro pueblo*. Vol. 1. Buenos Aires: CEAL. 1–20.

Ulla, Noemí. 1982. *Tango, rebelión y nostalgia*. Buenos Aires: Jorge Álvarez. Rev. Ed. Buenos Aires: CEAL.

——. 1986. "La hibridación en la letra de tango: El francés marginal." *Le Tango. Hommage à Carlos Gardel*. Toulouse: Université de Toulouse-Le Mirail: Eché Editeur. 123–30.

——. 1990. *Identidad rioplatense, 1930. La escritura coloquial (Borges, Arlt, Hernández, Onetti)*. Buenos Aires: Torres Agüero.

——. 1996. *La insurrección literaria. De lo coloquial en la narrativa de los años 1960 y 1970*. Buenos Aires: Torres Agüero.

Weinberg, Félix. 1980. "La época de Rosas. El romanticismo." *Historia de la literatura Argentina*, Vol. 1. Buenos Aires: CEAL. 217–40.

CHAPTER 55

SANTIAGO

Marcela Orellana

España entró hasta el Sur del Mundo, Agobiados
exploraron la nieve los altos españoles.
El bosque de maitenes cuyos hilos
verdes como temblor de lluvia
Dijo a España: "No sigas"
Pero hasta el fondo de la patria mía,
puño y puñal, el invasor llegaba
"Avanzando en las tierras de Chile"
—Pablo Neruda 1997, 72

Spain drove into the South of the World.
Overwhelmed, the tall Spaniards explored the snow.
The forest of maytens whose green
threads weep like a tremor of rain
told Spain: "Stop here."
But the invader kept coming, fist and dagger,
down to the bottom of my country.
"Advancing in the Lands of Chile"
—Pablo Neruda 1991, 77

The history of Santiago begins when the Spanish entered the hostile lands controlled by indigenous warriors. In the middle of the sixteenth century, Pedro de Valdivia (1500?–1554?), knowing full well that this was "la tierra más mal infamada de cuantas hay en las Indias" (Valdivia 87) (the most infamous land of all in the Indies), invaded the same region, to the south of Peru, that 500 men on horseback under Diego de Almagro had tried unsuccessfully to conquer several years earlier (Valdivia 87). In 1541 he founded a city in the Mapocho Valley, at the foot of the Andes. (See **Figure 1**.) Wishing to seek protection against the daily threat of war against the Indians, and to avoid repeating Almagro's story, "púsole por nombre Santiago, tomándolo por abogado, como patrón de España" (Góngora Marmolejo 41) ("he gave it the name of Santiago, taking him as the defender, as the Spanish patron saint").

The city of Santiago was created according to the checkerboard model imposed in Colonial America. This model represented to its founder the symbolic act of domination over a new, unknown, and wild space on which, when the city came into being, he would stamp the definitive presence of Spain: "The checkerboard model represented the intention of change and domination; it served persuasive and rhetorical purposes; it attempted to modify the mode of thought and conduct of its 'public' and to convert the inhabitants to Christianity and propriety" (Durston 93). In accordance with this model, land was apportioned outward from the plaza, the center of all political and social activity, so that those landowners who were closest to it were the richest and most aristocratic. Pedro de Valdivia attempted to organize and control this new reality by instituting order from the moment of the city's foundation to prevent any future disorder.

In order to interest people in this venture, Valdivia wrote attractive descriptions of the spot, for it appeared to be difficult to populate the region:

Y para que haga saber a los mercaderes y gentes que se quisieren avecindar, que vengan, porque esta tierra es tal, que para poder vivir en ella y perpetuarse no la hay mejor en el mundo; dígolo porque es muy llana, sanísima, de mucho contento; tiene cuatro meses de invierno no más, que en ellos, si no es cuando hace cuarto la luna, que llueve un día o dos, todos los demás hacen tan lindos soles, que no hay para que llegarse al fuego. El verano es tan templado y corren tan deleitosos aires, que todo el día se puede el hombre andar al sol, que no le es inoportuno. Es la más abundante de pastos y sementeras, y para darse todo género de ganado y plantas que se puede pintar; mucha y muy linda madera para hacer casas, infinidad otra de leña para el servicio dellas, y las minas riquísimas

Figure 1.

Drawing by Guamán Poma de Ayala depicting the foundation of Santiago de Chile in 1541 in El primer nueva corónica y buen gobierno, *1615. (Courtesy of John P. Robarts Research Library, University of Toronto)*

de oro, y toda la tierra está llena de ello, y donde quieran sacarlo allí hallarán en qué sembrar y con qué edificar y agua, leña y yerba para sus ganados, que parece la creó Dios a posta. (43)

Let the merchants and people who wish to settle here know that they should come, for there is no better place in the world than this land to live in and multiply; I say this because it is very flat, extremely healthy, and full of contentment; winter lasts only four months. During this time, if the moon is not in its quarter when it rains for a day or two, the days are so lovely and sunny that one does not need to go near a fire. The summer is so temperate and the breeze so gentle that man can spend all day in the sun, which is by no means inauspicious. The land abounds in pasture and fertile land where every breed of cattle and plant imaginable can flourish; there is much beautiful wood to make houses with, an infinity of other wood for household purposes, and mines rich in gold; and the land is full of it, and wherever they wish to extract it, there they will find land they can cultivate and material to build with and water, wood and grass for their cattle, which it seems God created for this purpose.

Thus he wrote to the Holy Roman Emperor Charles V in 1545. In a letter to Hernando Pizarro during the same year, he insisted on the virtues of the place, comparing it to that popular image of the time of the land of milk and honey: "Y de las dos cochinillas y el cochino se han dado tantos puercos, que hay más de ocho mil cabezas en la tierra, y de la gallina y pollo hay tantos como yerbas, y en invierno y verano se crían sin cuento, y cómese de todo en abundancia" (67) ("And the two young sows and the boar have produced so many piglets that there are more than eight thousand head in the land, and there are as many hens and chicks as there is grass, and they go on breeding in winter and summer without end, and we eat of all in abundance").

However, the hostility of the Indians persisted. The permanence of war to the south made Santiago the safest place in the region. It supplied other cities with provisions, soldiers, clothing, and money, as well as welcoming refugees from those lands in strife. From the time that the Spaniards settled south of Peru, Santiago thus had become the dominant city. The war in Araucania, around which the life of Santiago revolved, inspired Alonso de Ercilla y Zúñiga (1533–1594), who fought in the campaigns against the Mapuche, to write an epic poem entitled *La Araucana* [The Araucaniad]. Published in parts in Spain in 1569, 1578, and 1589, it recounts the bloody battles between the Spaniards and the Araucanians, expressing admiration for the courage of the enemy. Alongside the Spanish figures of Valdivia, Villagrán, Hurtado de Mendoza, he exalts the Araucanian heroes: Tucapel, Lautaro, Galvarino, and Caupolicán. *La Araucana* was the first book printed about Chile and justly received great praise. For example, when the priest is investigating the mad knight's library in Miguel de Cervantes's *Don Quixote* (1605), he says: "Los tres libros–La Araucana, de Alonso de Ercilla, la Austríada, de Juan Rufo, y el Monserrat, de Cristóbal de Virués– son los mejores que se han escrito en lengua castellana; guárdense como las más ricas prendas de poesía que tiene España" (Cervantes 1054 in Fernández 83) ("Now here come three together: *The Araucana* of Don Alonso de Ercilla, *The Austriada* of Juan Rufo, and *The Monserrat* of Cristóbal de Virués, the Valencian poet. These three books are the best ever written in Castilian. Let them be preserved as the richest treasures of poetry Spain possesses").

In this context, it is worth mentioning a seventeenth-century work which narrates the captivity of Francisco Núñez de Pineda y Bascuñán by the Mapuche. "El Cautiverio Feliz y Razón individual de las Guerras Dilatadas del Reino de Chile" ["The Felicitous Captivity and Personal Account of the Extended Wars of the Kingdom of Chile"] reveals a friendly and understanding attitude toward the Mapuche people and their history. What characterizes the descriptions of the landscape and the indigenous customs is the narrator's new feeling for the land in which he was born, although he does not forget to acknowledge Spain.

At the beginning of the seventeenth century, there was great racial heterogeneity in Santiago as in many other American cities: 7.59 percent of the population was of Spanish origin; 18.84 percent were *mestizos* (of mixed Spanish and Indian parentage); 67.67 percent were pure Indian; and 6 percent were of African origin (Ramón 48). In the eighteenth century, the peace agreed upon in the Araucanian war guaranteed greater stability to everyday life in the city of Santiago. Concern was expressed about the differences in the education provided for men and women. Whereas women were taught to read, write, and pray, men, "who did not intend to become men of the cloth or gown, were taught to read by rote, to write ungrammatically, and to learn their multiplication tables by heart" (Pérez Rosales 14). Many years later, Judge Irigoyen visited nine schools in Santiago, where 399 pupils were enrolled, a visit which did not include the numerous schools that had no subsidy.

The growth of the construction industry improved the physical appearance of the city. Haymhausen, a Jesuit priest, started an artisan workshop for silversmiths, founders, and painters who then left their mark on the churches of the order in Chile. The expulsion of the Company of Jesus from America interrupted this work until the arrival in 1780 of Joaquín Toesca who is associated with Santiago's changing physiognomy, which included the Cathedral and the Casa de la Moneda, the current presidential palace. The mansions of the Colonial aristocracy and the wealthy bourgeoisie did not undergo great changes. Built on one floor, they were distinguished by the iron gratings over the windows and the family crest sculpted in stone. The most important room was the decorative hall, known as the *cuadra*, in which Venetian looking-glasses or religious paintings hung on the brocaded walls. Lighting was provided by glass chandeliers holding tallow candles. Beside the window leading to the first patio there was a drawing room, covered in cushions, where the housewives would sit with their legs crossed in Moorish fashion. Assorted furniture was arranged around the room: tooled leather armchairs, a clavichord, and side tables on which sat a Quito-type Virgin. During social gatherings, which would take place in this room, the guests would dance, sing, and play games; forfeit games, such as blind man's buff and pass the ring, were among the most popular.

Music and painting also acquired a space in everyday life. In 1740, there were about twenty clavichords in the city; guitars and harps, which were made locally, were popular among the people. In relation to painting, the German Jesuit priest José Ambrosi left a prodigious *oeuvre* before the expulsion of his order, part of which may still be appreciated today in the sacristy of the Cathedral. The main theme of early paintings was religious, but at the beginning of the nineteenth century this was replaced by the portrait as, for example, in the Peruvian Gil de Castro's work, which marked the transition from the Colonial to the Republican period. His particular style can be observed in his countless portraits of Chilean society, which record the costume and customs of the period. Unfortunately, of the architecture where all this activity took place in Colonial Santiago, only a few vestiges have been conserved. A few Colonial buildings stand side by side with modern ones in what is now the political and administrative city center.

Besides children's games and food, vending is today perhaps the most notable street custom. By 1756 it had become standard practice for vendors to sell their wares around the Plaza de Armas and the Paseo Ahumada, but in that year they were denounced by retail traders. Tailors, shoemakers, and hatters appealed on the grounds that "que desde tiempo inmemorial estamos en posesión de esta especie de comercio con la gente del campo y vulgo" (in Ramón 117) ("from time immemorial we have conducted this kind of trade with common people and those from the country"). During the first decades of the nineteenth century, the issue of the vendors appeared once more: "From the prison door, all along the street that is now called Estado, one observed a line of run-down wooden shacks and dilapidated huts, which going under the name of bric-a-brac stalls were the substitute for the charming and clean little shops that now enhance the bases of the columns of the Fernández Concha 'portal' (covered gallery)" (Pérez Rosales 7).

Alberto Blest Gana (1830–1920) wrote about this custom in *Martin Rivas* (1862), a novel set in the mid-nineteenth century. The protagonist, who has just arrived from the provinces, walks around the Plaza de Armas and is surrounded by vendors: "No fue pequeño su asombro cuando, al hacer esfuerzos para entrar el pie, se vió rodeado de seis individuos, de los cuales cada uno le ofrecía un par de calzado, hablándole todos a un tiempo" (27) ("He was extremely amazed when, attempting to enter, he discovered he was surrounded by six individuals, each of whom offered him a pair of shoes, all talking to him at once"). Street-vending is still common practice, as Enrique Lihn (1929–1988), one of the most representative poets of our times, described it: "Si te ofrecen, Pingüino, tres pares de calcetines por cien pesos, un tomacorrientes por la misma suma, de tres arranques, de esos que se derriten como un queso si se los hace funcionar con toda su capacidad instalada" (8–9) ("They offer you, Pinguino, three pairs of socks for a hundred pesos, an adaptor for the same price with three sockets, those that melt like cheese if they are made to work at full capacity"). He insists on the illegality of this activity (9).

Travel in the eighteenth century was another decisive change that transformed the mentality of those living in the Americas; the people of Santiago were no exception to these influences which engendered ideas of freedom from Spanish colonial tutelage. Traveling to Lima, where there were more books than anywhere else in colonial South America, or to Europe meant being exposed to the ideas of the Enlightenment then in vogue. Manuel de Salas and José Antonio de Rojas brought back selected libraries, which included books by representative authors and scientific works that reflected the thought of the century. Bernardo O'Higgins, who met the Venezuelan revolutionary Francisco de Miranda in London, was so stimulated by his ideas that upon his return to Chile he became, along with Juan Martínez de Rozas, Juan Egaña, and Manuel de Salas, one of the prime movers in the emancipation of his country. These ideas took shape on different social, educational, and political levels, as well as involving such measures as equality before the law for all born on Chilean soil, the abolition of slavery, and the freedom of commerce and of the press.

Santiago Since Independence

A quest for long-awaited political stability marked the first decades of independent life. Unlike other Latin American countries, this had been achieved in Chile by the 1840s, and the country thus became a refuge for Bolivian partisans of the deposed Santa Cruz, Argentineans persecuted by Rosas, and other foreigners who gathered there. The project common to American intellectuals–overcoming centuries of colonial

rule and the search for new national identities–created, due to the presence of these foreigners, a continental environment which produced the most fruitful results in Chile. The Spaniard Joaquín de Mora, who came from Argentina as a guest of President Francisco Antonio Pinto, opened the Liceo de Chile, where José J. Vallejo and José Victorino Lastarria, distinguished national cultural figures, were educated. His wife, in turn, opened a college for young women. The Venezuelan Andrés Bello (1781–1865), the most influential of the foreigners, arrived in Chile in 1829. A colleague of Alexander von Humboldt on his naturalist expedition through the Americas and the tutor of Simón Bolívar, he went to London after the revolution in his country in 1810 to follow his intellectual pursuits. Among his many other contributions to Latin American culture are his poems *Silvas americanas* (1823 and 1826). His acceptance of the post of Minister of Foreign Affairs brought him to Santiago, where he took a prominent part in cultural and political life. He wrote or translated articles for the newspaper *El araucano* on literature, philosophy, mathematics, and the natural sciences, while giving lectures at home in the humanities and law. Although he expressed his deep concern for education in his numerous publications, perhaps his major contribution was the report he wrote that formed the basis for the foundation of the University of Chile, of which he was the first rector after its inauguration in 1843. One cannot help but link Bello's life to the history of national education; not only was he mainly responsible for the writing of the Chilean Civil Code, but he was also the author of many educational works.

Domingo Faustino Sarmiento (1811–1888), an Argentinean intellectual, future president, and author of *Facundo: Civilización y barbarie* [1845; *Civilization and Barbarism*], who spent several years of exile in Chile, made an important contribution to the national press. At the time of his arrival in the beginning of the 1840s, the press was a propaganda machine and weapon used by the political parties. Acutely aware of these shortcomings, he sought to develop Chilean journalism by moving beyond confrontational party politics. Sarmiento had a more global understanding of the press as a means of communication and believed its function to be to promote liberty and progress. It should, in his opinion, be used to educate the people and to draw the attention of the government and the public to matters needing reform. In this productive environment, the University of Chile, the Normal School for Teachers, the School of Arts and Craft, and the School of Architecture were all founded. Likewise, a mode of thought was stimulated that sought to locate itself within the new context of independence, in which literary and political discourses converged in the joint project of founding a national identity. Lastarria made this clear in a speech which is considered the manifesto of his generation: "nada será Chile, la América toda, sin las luces. . . . nosotros debemos sacrificarnos por la patria. Hemos tenido la fortuna de recibir una mediana ilustración: pues bien, sirvamos al pueblo, alumbrémosle en su marcha social para que nuestros hijos le vean un día feliz, libre y poderoso" (in Promis 76) ("Chile, like all America, will be nothing, without enlightenment. . . . We must sacrifice ourselves for the fatherland. Fortunately, we have received partial enlightenment: Let us then serve the people and shed light upon their social progress so that our children one day can see themselves happy, free, and powerful"). According to Lastarria, the role of literature was crucial to the construction of the new independent society. Not only would it serve to educate the people, but it would also fashion a national language: "La literatura debe, pues, dirigirse a todo un pueblo, representarlo todo entero, así como los gobiernos deben ser el resumen de todas las fuerzas sociales, la expresión de todas las necesidades, los representantes de todas las superioridades: con estas condiciones sólo puede ser una literatura verdaderamente *nacional*". (in Promis 90) "Literature should address the entire nation, represent it all, just as governments should be the sum of all social forces, the expression of all needs, the representatives of all ranks: Only under these conditions can a literature be truly *national*"). During the first half of the nineteenth century, culture was understood in broader terms: One spoke of American culture rather than confining it to one's country. This notion of culture was largely responsible for the incorporation of a technical innovation which changed the life of those living in Chilean cities, particularly in Santiago: the printing press and the subsequent development of newspapers. The government acquired the first Chilean printing press from a Swedish merchant who disembarked in Valparaiso in 1811. On 13 February 1812, the first issue of the *Aurora de Chile*, a ministerial and political newspaper, appeared. The oral tradition of disseminating information was gradually overtaken, but in 1839 both oral and written means were still in use: "El intendente ha tomado medidas muy arbitrarias a consecuencia de las cuales se han hecho versos, se han puesto pasquines, etc. El hijo de Palacios está en la cárcel más de 15 días sólo porque recibió un paquete de versos y los leyó sin saber quien se los mandaba" (Pinochet de la Barra 242–43) ("The intendant has taken very arbitrary measures as a result of which verses have been made, broadsheets have been posted, etc. Palacios's son is in prison for more than fifteen days merely because he received a package of verses and read them without knowing who had sent them"). In 1855 when *El ferrocarril* first appeared, it rapidly gained control over the field with a virtual monopoly over *El independiente*, *La libertad*, and the weekly *El araucano*; this situation lasted until the beginning of the twentieth century when, for technological reasons, it could not compete with *El mercurio* and *El diario ilustrado*.

Urban development, new ideas, and the press changed Santiago enormously during the nineteenth century. Vicente Pérez Rosales (1807–1886), a traveler, intellectual, and statesman who wrote some sixty years after the country gained independence in 1818, romantically narrates in his *Recuerdos del Pasado* [Memories of the Past] the rapidity with which the city grew during the first half of the century, becoming "de aventajada estatura para su corta edad" ("exceptionally tall for its tender years"):

> ¡Quién... hubiera podido adivinar entonces, que andando el tiempo, esos inútiles eriazos visitados por primera vez el año [18]20 por el turbio Maipo, ... habían de ser los mismos por donde ahora brama y corre la locomotora al través de las frescas arboledas que circundan mil valiosas heredades rústicas, en cada una de las cuales la industria, el arte y las comodidades de la vida, parece que hubiesen encontrado su natural asiento! Quién hubiera imaginado que aquellos inmundos ranchos que acrecían la ciudad tras el basural de la Cañada, se habían de convertir en parques, en suntuosas y regias residencias, y lo que es más que el mismo basural se habría de tornar en Alameda de las Delicias. (6)

> Who... could have guessed then that, as time went by, the useless untilled land, visited for the first time in 1820 by the muddy river Maipo,... would be that along which the locomotive now roars and runs through the cool groves which surround a thousand valuable country estates, in each of which industry, art, and the commodities of life seem to have found their natural home! Who would have imagined that those foul smelling ranches, which enlarged the city behind the rubbish dump of the *cañada*, would be converted into parks, into sumptuous and splendid residences, and, what is more, that the dump itself would become the Alameda de las Delicias.

The face of the city really did change during those years. Chile's prosperity between 1840 and 1870 could be seen on the streets of Santiago which were lined with the huge mansions and palaces of the men of power. What Pérez Rosales forgets to point out is that the poor areas on the outskirts were growing at the same rate. There were unequivocal signs of progress, such as the construction of the Municipal Theater in the 1850s and the installation of public street lighting, inaugurated in 1857 with 600 gas lamps; that same year the urban tramway system was created, linking the railway station to the center of Santiago (as well as further rail developments which began to link the capital with other important destinations in the country). Meanwhile, the shanty towns proliferated:

> The poverty-stricken made their homes close to their possible sources of income: Chuchunco, opposite the railway station, ... the *guangualí*... whose inhabitants offered domestic services to the area, the Ovalle district next to the Arenal, that is, the depots for sand, debris, and stones used for building in Santiago, the Conventillo or "Ranch of Death" close to the city slaughterhouse, and the borders of the agricultural and vineyard belt running round the south of Santiago where in the 1820s and 1830s the San Carlos canal began to function. All these offered temporary but plentiful work... which enabled the poor to survive even if employment was unpredictable and badly paid. (Ramón 172)

Demographic trends in the country were another indicator of change; the urban population grew significantly to 42 percent in 1913 from 10 percent in 1813 (Salazar 228), bringing labor in search of new opportunities to Santiago and other cities. Even if this influx of people was marginalized by official circles (and their intellectual and artistic ideas), they brought a new worldview with them and an individual artistic sense. Their initial creativity has continued to grow, at times in parallel, at times in conflict, or at times in convergence with the educated sectors, blossoming into urban expressions of the twentieth century, such as the new *canto* or song and the *arpilleras*, the murals of protest during the dictatorship from 1973 to 1989. Besides offering manpower to Santiago during the second half of the nineteenth century, some immigrants became involved in the secular activity of creating poetry following the oral tradition. The city provided not only a new and unknown context for these poets, but also a creative space which united them, imposed its dynamics on them, obliged them to turn to writing, to immerse themselves within urban history, and thus to abandon the timelessness of rural life. This gave rise to the publication of loose sheets, or *literatura de cordel* (popular narratives in verse), starting as popular urban poetry and leading to the birth of the popular press.

The practice of printing the poetry of the traditional bards began around 1860 and continued until 1920. Printed on low-grade paper, these publications, illustrated with engravings and vignettes, were sold wherever there were people, such as in the markets, the railway station, and so forth. Over the years the *lira popular* became the means of expression for those who did not have access to official channels or a voice in the newspapers or magazines of the period. This opened a new space which, though influenced by the educated press, presented events from a specific point of view. One of the most important "events" related was the War of the Pacific against Peru and Bolivia (1789) because educated poets were able to use the medium of popular poetry to express their patriotic sentiments. This produced the first conjunction of popular and lettered poetry. The journalist José Rafael Allende and the poet Carlos Pezoa Véliz (1879–1908) published sheets of *lira popular* under the pseudonyms of El Pequén and Juan Mauro Bío Bío respectively. This merging of modes gave rise to new artistic creations, such as the poetry sung to peasants and workers for the first time by Carlos Pezoa Véliz at the beginning of the new century.

In the last decades of the nineteenth century, Santiago had a population of 230,000 inhabitants (Subercaseaux 41) and had become a center for different cultural manifestations which interfused with and influenced each other. (See **Figure 2**.) The literacy campaigns created a new reader who had a variety of interests. The *lira popular* was sold on the streets to the cry of "Vamos comprando, vamos pagando, vamos leyendo, vamos vendiendo" ("Let's buy, let's pay, let's read, let's sell"); newspapers offered their readership serial novels before it appeared in book form. They also printed articles from the newspapers and magazines of neighboring countries, which was an effective means of diffusing Latin American culture. Bookshops played an active cultural role as well: "Since one spent hours and hours looking for books in second-hand bookshops, some of them soon became meeting places. Such was the Miranda bookshop for more than twenty years. . . . *The Chilean magazine* and the University Printing Press emerged from there" (Subercaseaux 49).

Toward the end of the nineteenth century there were many possibilities in Santiago for those seeking a profession. Besides attending one of the five schools at the University of Chile (law, humanities, mathematics, medicine, and theology), one could also enter the seminary, the schools of agriculture or of mining, the school of fine arts, the school of arts and crafts, or the school of music, the naval and military schools, telegraphy school, veterinary school, the Normal schools for men and women, and even cooking and sewing schools. In 1889, the Catholic University was founded with the schools of jurisprudence and of physical and mathematical sciences.

There was now enough of a public to create large and spectacular events for it. The eighty-performance opera season at the Municipal Theater sold out its (capacity) 2000 seats every night year after year. The production of *zarzuelas* at the Politeama Theater, the Santa Lucía Theatre, and the Romea Theater met with similar success. Walks through such parks as the Quinta Normal and the Cousiño also provided diversion and recreation.

If the literature of the nineteenth century had been largely associated with the process of the creation of a national identity, politics and letters gradually drifted apart. This meant that literary discourses could become autonomous and strike out into new territory. After the turn of the century, the journal *Musa Joven* appeared (in 1912), edited by Jorge Hubner and the nineteen-year-old Vicente Huidobro (1893–1948). In it, national poets were published and new voices, such as those of Amado Nervo (1870–1919), Ramón del Valle Inclán (1866–1936), and Juan Ramón Jimenez (1881–1958), were heard. One issue was dedicated to Baudelaire and another to Rubén Darío

Figure 2.

Lithograph of a Sunday afternoon in Santiago, c. 1890.
(Courtesy of Gwen Kirkpatrick)

(1867–1916). In 1914, for the first time, a woman writer, Gabriela Mistral (1889–1957), won the prize awarded at the Florales de Santiago festival for her collection of poetry *Sonetos de la muerte* [Sonnets on Death]. In 1945, she was the first Latin American to be awarded the Nobel Prize for Literature, thereby opening the world's eyes to Latin American literary sensibilities. She would continue to promote the literature of Latin America throughout her life during her travels and meetings with intellectuals outside Chile.

There was a convergence of voices and different languages in literary circles in the early part of the twentieth century. A social gathering that took place in 1925 highlights this particularly well: "Vicente spoke of looking toward Cosmopolis. He spoke of *criollismo*. This should be inspired by the homeland, by the well-known Tolstoyan recipe: 'Depict your village and you depict the world.' At these Mapuche fiestas, amidst drinking and chatting, schools and tendencies began to take shape and coalesce. As time went by, these two would become leaders of opposing camps" (Teitelboim 1993:77). The two leaders referred to above are Mariano Latorre and Vicente Huidobro, who created *criollismo* and the vanguard movement of *creacionismo* or creationism respectively.

Huidobro made claims for a universal poetry expressed in a new language, and in 1916 he went to Europe where he kept company with Juan Gris, Pierre Reverdy, Max Jacob, and many other artists seeking to break with tradition. His manifesto *Non serviam* read in the Atheneum in Santiago in 1914 reveals his theory of autonomous, non-mimetic art: "No he de ser tu esclavo, madre Natura; seré tu amo. . . . Y ya no podrás decirme: 'Ese árbol está mal, no me gusta ese cielo. . . los míos son mejores' Yo te responderé que mis cielos y mis árboles son los míos y no los tuyos y que no tienen por qué parecerse"(Schwartz 73)("I will not be your slave, Mother Nature; I will be your master. . . . And you cannot tell me: 'That tree is wrong, I don't like that sky. . . mine are better.' I will tell you that my skies and my trees are mine and not yours and that they do not have to be alike"). This new sensitivity influenced intellectuals and produced in the 1920s such experimental journals as *Elipse, Dionysios, Dínamo, Andamio, Caballo de Bastos,* and so on (Schwartz 73). At the other end of the cultural spectrum, Mariano Latorre's (1886–1955) *criollismo* aspired to establish the essence of the Americas in explicit contrast to that of Europe. In his article, "Algunas preguntas que no me han hecho sobre el criollismo" ["Some Questions I Have Not Been Asked About Criollismo"], he gives advice to younger generations: "Renunciar a lo extranjero, hacer propios, con la técnica de países más viejos o más evolucionados, los temas de Chile. . . . Ahondar en el rincón es la única manera de ser entendido por el mundo" (in Promis 198) ("Abandon everything foreign, use the techniques of the oldest or most developed countries to make the themes of Chile your own. . . . Only by delving deeply into one's corner can one be understood by the world"). This concern was brought to the fore by another cultural group, the generation of painters known as the "Generation of 13," which included, among others, Exequiel Plaza (1892–1944), Arturo Gordon (1883–1944), and Pedro Luna (1896–1956).

Thus, the external gaze of the avant-garde coexisted with the internal gaze of *criollismo.* The realist tendency of depicting Chilean life persisted, even if the perception of the regional changed. The literary generation of 1938, which started in the Pedagogic Institute and included such writers as Manuel Rojas (1896–1973), Nicomedes Guzmán (1914–1964), and Carlos Sepúlveda Leyton (1895–1941), rejected the *criollista* idea that Chilean life could be summed up by the geographical context and a series of customs. This group believed that the function of literature went beyond realist representation: "It is a kind of political praxis that does not depend necessarily on a realistic form and, in this sense, the text as a denunciation which contributes to social change represents a true aesthetic challenge. . . . It was proposed that in works of social protest the proletarian space should not only be depicted from within, but should also be given an aesthetic appeal that would emerge from the experiences themselves set in an urban area" (Guerra 106).

The *Antología de poesía chilena nueva* [Anthology of New Chilean Poetry], published in 1935 and compiled by Eduardo Anguita and Volodia Teitelboim, promoted the distinct poetic voices of the time; they were not all from Santiago. It was here that many young poets first gained recognition and a space for their expression. Mistral, Neruda (1904–1973), Huidobro, and de Rokha (1894–1968), four key figures of Chilean poetry of the twentieth century, were included in this text: By 1938 Santiago had become an international center for intellectuals of diverse nationalities, who were persecuted by the numerous dictatorships that scarred the political map of America (Ramón 240). Pablo Neruda presided over the Alliance of Intellectuals of Chile which was founded in November 1937, and to its credit included members who came from all fields of art and knowledge. By this time Neruda was a famous poet and stood at the center of the nation's intellectual life. His first work, *Crepusculario,*

appeared in 1923, followed by his collection of love poetry, *Veinte poemas de amor y una canción desesperada* [*Twenty Love Poems and a Song of Despair*] and the surrealism of *Residencia en la tierra* [*Residence on Earth*]. In 1937 he returned from Spain and published *España en el corazón* [*Spain in the Heart*] in support of the Republican side in the Spanish Civil War. His poetic vision changed radically when he joined the Marxist cause and decided to commit his life and his work to the defense of these ideals. This vision ruled his longest work, *Canto general,* published in 1950, in which he celebrated the human and natural life of Latin America and roused its peoples to liberty and independence. Neruda was awarded the Nobel Prize for Literature in 1971, two years before his death in September 1973.

By 1939 Neruda had been appointed consul for Spanish émigrés and organized the arrival of Spanish refugees on board the *Winnipeg.* In September, the Spaniards, who had landed at the port of Valparaiso, arrived by train at Mapocho station to large and welcoming crowds. Their integration proved most fruitful and their contribution enormous: "En las artes musicales, plásticas y escénicas se dió, no como un aporte foráneo, sino como un aporte desde dentro y para adentro. En el área académica, pasa exactamente lo mismo. Profesores de las universidades chilenas, en las áreas científicas y literarias, en el área de las ciencias sociales han producido y sido considerados como nacionales" (Vázquez 66) ("In the musical, visual, and dramatic arts, they contributed not as foreigners, but as those working from and for within. Exactly the same happened in academia. Professors at Chilean universities were regarded as nationals, as a result of their work in the fields of science, literature, and social sciences"). The painters Gracia Barrios (b. 1927), José Balmes (b. 1927), and Roser Bru (b. 1923) are instances of this phenomenon in the visual arts. The Mexican muralists Xavier Guerrero and David Alfaro Siqueiros visited Santiago in 1940. Their influence had already inspired the founding of the Chair in Mural Painting in 1938, which formed a generation of muralists who wished to promote culture through an artistic mode accessible to all. The Minister of Education commissioned them to decorate Chilean schools with frescos. The first work to be completed was at the Liceo de la Ciudad del Niño with murals painted by Osvaldo Reyes (b. 1919), Laureano Guevara (1889–1968), Orlando Silva, and Fernando Marcos. This tradition of official public murals gave way, in the 1960s, to the work of the popular brigades and the muralist workshops, which continues to this day. The accessibility of art to all has its parallel in Nicanor Parra's (b. 1914) *Poemas y antipoemas* (Poems and Antipoems*)*, published in 1954. It had a tremendous impact: His new mode of expression stressed the poetry of everyday life, and his personal and unadorned view of the world resisted preconceived poetic conventions.

In the 1960s the streets of Santiago overflowed with cultural expression. The state subsidized, either directly or indirectly, two theater companies, two symphony orchestras, three ballet companies, and a series of other artistic activities. Toward the end of the decade, an attempt was made to take art to the streets. Occasional dramatic, musical, and dance events were performed in the popular quarters. There were popular demonstrations, and the streets became a privileged place for expression. The city was alive. The Bar El Bosco in the center of the city became a meeting-place for the "Generation of the 50s." This literary group did not recognize local predecessors; it turned instead to European and North American prose, and its writing reflected themes of existential anxiety. Claudio Giaconi (b. 1927) defined his generation, which includes the novelists José Donoso (1924–1996) and Jorge Edwards (b. 1931) and the poet Enrique Lihn: "Éramos típicos outsiders, mucho antes que el vocablo se pusiese de moda. No comulgábamos con intereses de grupos ni partidos; no adheríamos a convencionalismo, realizábamos un proceso de lenta maduración personal, observando el mundo al margen del núcleo social al cual pertenecíamos, éramos poseedores de un sentido crítico sobremanera desarrollado" (Promis 364) ("We were outsiders long before the term came into fashion. We did not agree with the interests of groups or parties; we did not ally ourselves to conventional ideas but underwent a gradual process of personal development, and, observing the world from the fringes of the social nucleus to which we belonged, we were exceedingly critical"). José Donoso is one of the most outstanding writers of this generation; his first novel, *Coronación* [1957; *Coronation*, 1965], was awarded the William Faulkner Foundation prize in 1961. His other novels, such as the excellent *Este domingo* [1965; *This Sunday*, 1967], *El obsceno pájaro de la noche* [1970; *The Obscene Bird of Night*, 1973], and *Casa de campo* [1978; *A House in the Country*, 1983] unmask the absurdities of social conventions in Chilean society. A member of the "boom" in Latin American narrative, he left his personal history of it in *Historia personal del boom* [1972; *The Boom in Spanish American Literature: A Personal History*, 1977].

The streets were also a center for the electoral battle of the years 1963 to 1964, which gave rise to a new kind of wall-painting, which was popular rather than official; this was subsequently given full expression from 1970 to 1973 as much by recognized painters as by art students, workers, and residents. Muralist brigades under the names of "Ramona Parra," "Inti Paredo," and "Elmo Catalán" painted the city in colorful, "didactic, social, and political" language (Bellange 46). Murals on the 200-meter-long dykes of the Mapocho River, which crosses the city, told the story of the Chilean Communist Party and of the workers' movement. This great diversity of expression depicted a city that brought together a multiplicity of voices weaving stories that unwittingly intertwined and mixed with each other. The streets had become the focus of the expression both of discontent against the government and of the festivities and dances which year after year mark 18 September, Independence Day.

Urban space was thus transformed into a stage for creative expression. Santiago sang to itself with "Il Bosco" by Gonzalo "Payo" Grondon (b. 1945):

Seis de la mañana
Parque Forestal
entre gatos mapochinos
tuve que pensar
no hay un metro cuadrado
Donde se pueda amar?

Six in the morning
Forestal Park
amongst Mapochine cats
I had to think
is there one square meter
where one can love?

The new Chilean song found a niche for itself in Santiago in such places as the musical bar, Peña de los Parra (340 Carmen Street), where a distinctive popular urban expression, which had repercussions for national creativity, grew around Isabel (b. 1937) and Angel Parra (b. 1943), Rolando Alarcón (1929–1973),

and Patricio Manns (b. 1937). This atmosphere was felt once more during the presidential campaign of 1970 when supporters of the candidate of the Popular Unity Party, Salvador Allende, organized a 24-hour reading marathon led by Pablo Neruda. Left-wing painters installed a large awning next to the Museum of Fine Arts where they sold at ridiculously low prices, engravings and posters alluding to the social situation of the country.

This habit of using the street was interrupted on 11 September 1973, the day of the *coup d'état*; the imposition of a curfew prohibiting anyone from being on the streets after a given hour meant that people had to stay at home and maintain an urban silence. One could no longer appropriate street space; the walls covered with collective messages and colored by the painting brigades were scrubbed, and the graffiti whitewashed. But walls also have memory; they were perused in silence and fearful evidence was stamped upon them. Enrique Lihn (1929–1988) reflected the fear and the life of this Santiago in *El paseo ahumada* (1983):

Como si el Ahumada fuera un pantano
eso se ha llenado de zancudos helicopteros infinitesmales
que vuelan aquí sin un zumbido
exangües.

As if the Ahumada were a swamp
it has been filled with infinitesimal helicopter mosquitoes
which fly here weak without blood
buzzing.

(14)

In response to this text, Gloria Favi has linked Santiago's past with its present: "The heroic space–the colonial center–is now the shelter for vagabonds, beggars, the unemployed, artists, speakers, magicians; all moving–disregarding the geographical axis of the conquest–from the Alameda de las Delicias to the Plaza de Armas, understandably fleeing from the police, and it is this glorious march that has enabled them–without any real mandate–to record and study in detail the topography, climate, products, flora and fauna of this Kingdom of Chile" (133). The *arpilleras*, or motifs, embroidered or stuck on sackcloth, also denounced what cannot be shouted out in the street: the pain felt for what was missing.

Most of Santiago's residents lived as if they had been invaded, but others found it to be a haven of peace, as the posters in the airport confirmed: "Chile avanza en orden y paz" ("Chile advances in order and peace"). For many others, it was an absent city because, as Grínor Rojo (b. 1941) stated: "Aun cuando no somos los pobladores visibles de la patria, la seguimos construyendo en tierra ajena" (94) ("Even when we are not visible residents of the fatherland, we still construct its city in foreign lands"). Gonzalo Millán (b. 1947) was another exile. His poem "La ciudad" ["The City"] is constructed on the basis of autonomous lines, linked by repetition or association, so that each line is a statement. This creates an accelerated, urban rhythm, which stresses the idea at once of discord and of fragmentation characteristic of the city he alludes to:

Se abarca la ciudad desde aquí
Un funicular lleva a la cumbre
En la cumbre hay una virgen.
La procesión asciende el cerro.
Ascienden a oficiales.
Los oficiales llevan charreteras.

La espada se lleva al cinto.
La espada hace sangre.
La procesión lleva estandartes.
La procesión canta salmos
La procesión va por dentro.

One takes in the city from here.
A cable car goes up to the summit.
On the summit there is a virgin.
The procession ascends the hill.
The officers ascend.
The officers wear epaulettes.
The sword is worn at the belt.
The sword draws blood.
The procession carries banners.
The procession sings psalms.
The procession is kept within ourselves.

(62)

Midway through the 1980s, the curfew was lifted, and the streets were gradually reclaimed. A new popular expression burst forth. People took their demonstrations into the streets; they organized new groups of muralists, who, even if their murals were immediately erased, began again their silent work: An association of young people (the A.P.J.), the muralist brigade known as "América Latina" from Villa Portales in the district of La Victoria and the "Chacón" brigade from the Villa Robert Kennedy filled the streets with phrases; the walls began to speak again.

Censorship of cultural activity was undermined in different ways. Clandestine publications multiplied and alternative means of expression were sought beyond the closed structure of the book form. This led to a displacement of the literary by other types of discourse. Experimental journals, such as *La Castaña, El organillo*, and *Noreste*, which were sold to the masses, proposed their contestation in off-beat language. Nevertheless, the recuperation of urban space is often painful. After the restoration of the democratic regime in 1990, the many exiles who returned and those who had never left met once again in their city. Carlos Cerda (b. 1942) speaks about this in his novel *Una casa vacía* [1996; *An Empty House*, 2003]. At the end, a character, who slowly finds out that the house he had lived in Santiago had been a torture chamber, joins the narrator in reflecting: "Fue bueno entrar en la casa para escuchar lo que nos decía desde sus rincones. Había que hacerlo no sólo por el respeto al dolor de quienes habían sufrido allí, sino porque ese dolor tenía mucho que ver con las penurias que la seguían persiguiendo afuera" (Cerda 324) ("It was good to enter the house in order to hear what it told us from its corners. It had to be done not only out of respect for the pain of those who had suffered there, but also because that pain had a lot to do with the penury that persecuted others outside").

Translation by Charlotte Broad

Works Cited

Anguita Eduardo and Volodia Teitelboim. 1935. *Antología de poesía chilena nueva*. Santiago de Chile: Zig-Zag.

Bellange, Ebe. 1995. *El mural como reflejo de la realidad social en Chile*. Santiago: LOM Ediciones.

Blest Gana, Alberto. 1981. *Martín Rivas*. Madrid: Cátedra.

Cerda, Carlos. 1996. *Una casa vacía*. Santiago: Aguilar chilena de Ediciones.

Cervantes, Miguel de. 1949. *Obras completas*. Madrid: Aguilar.

Durston, Alan. 1994. "Un régimen urbanístico en la América Hispana colonial: El trazado en damero durante los siglos XVI y XVII" *Historia 28*. Santiago: Instituto de Historia, Pontificia Universidad Católica de Chile. 59–115.

Ercilla y Zúñiga, Alonso de. 1979. *La araucana*. Madrid: Editorial Castalia.

Favi, Gloria. 1993. "Enrique Lihn, cronista de ciudad." *Revista chilena de literatura*. (Santiago) 43: 131–36.

Fernández Fraile, Maximino. 1994. *Historia de la literatura chilena*. Vol. 1. Santiago: Editorial Salesiana.

Góngora Marmolejo, Alonso. 1969. *Historia de Chile desde su descubrimiento hasta el año 1575*. Santiago de Chile: Editorial Universitaria.

Guerra, Lucía. 1987. "Estética y compromiso social de la generación de 1938." *Ideologies and Literature*. Minnesota: University of Minnesota Press. 101–32.

Lihn, Enrique. 1983. *El paseo Ahumada*. Santiago de Chile: Ediciones Minga.

Millán, Gonzalo. 1979. *La ciudad*. [Quebec]: Les Editions Maison Culturelle Québec-Amérique Latine.

Neruda, Pablo. 1991. *Canto general*. Trans. Jack Schmitt. Berkeley: University of California Press, 1991.

——. 1997. *Canto general*. Buenos Aires: Seix Barral.

Parra, Nicanor. 1967. *Poems and Antipoems*. Trans. Fernando Alegría et al. New York: New Directions.

——. 1971 [1954]. *Poemas y antipoemas*. Santiago: Editorial Nascimiento.

Pérez Rosales, Vicente. 1969. *Recuerdos del pasado (1814–1860)*. Buenos Aires: Ed. Francisco de Aguirre.

Pinochet de la Barra, Oscar. 1990. *Carmen Arriagada: Cartas de una mujer apasionada*. Santiago: Editorial Universitaria.

Promis, José. 1995. *Testimonio y documentos de la literatura chilena*. Santiago: Editorial Andrés Bello.

Ramón, Armando de. 1992. *Santiago de Chile (1541–1991)*. Madrid: Ed. MAPRE.

Rojo, Grínor. 1988. *Crítica del exilio*. Santiago: Pehuén Editores.

Salazar, Gabriel. 1985. *Labradores, peones y proletarios*. Santiago: Ediciones Sur.

Schwartz, Jorge. 1991. *Las vanguardias latinoamericanas*. Madrid: Cátedra.

Subercaseaux, Bernardo. 1992. *La cultura en la época de Balmaceda (1880–1900)* Santiago: Dirección de Bibliotecas Archivos y Museos, Centro de Investigaciones Diego Barros Arana.

Teitelboim, Volodia. 1993. *Huidobro: La marcha infinita*. Santiago: Bat.

——. 1995. *Neruda*. Buenos Aires: Losada.

Valdivia, Pedro de. 1970. *Cartas de relación del reyno de Chile*. Ed. Mario Ferrecio Podesta. Santiago: Col. Escritores Coloniales de Chile, Editorial Universitaria.

Vázquez Riviero, Antelina. 1989. *Winnipeg: Cuando la libertad tuvo nombre de barco*. Madrid: Ediciones Meigas.

CHAPTER 56

NEW YORK CITY
CENTER AND TRANSIT POINT FOR HISPANIC CULTURAL NOMADISM

**Dionisio Cañas, with contributions by Orlando Hernández,
Doris Schnabel, and Luisa García Conde**

This essay will explore from a historical point of view the coordinates legitimating the contention that New York City is an important Hispanic cultural center. To this end we have explored the following themes: first, the trajectory of Hispanic immigration, the use of the Spanish language, and the establishment and evolution of the principal Hispanic sociocultural institutions in the city, and second, the production of Hispanic culture in the New York City region. Within this second theme, we will examine publications and the media, many of the genres of literature, popular music, graffiti, and the arts. For reasons of space, we will not explore Hispanic classical music, opera, ballet, dance, and other performance arts, or the manifestations of religious culture, architecture, or academic scholarship. A number of factors ought to be borne in mind by the reader. First, in this study of New York City as a Hispanic cultural center and as a point of transit for the same, we have given equal consideration to Hispano-American and peninsular Spanish figures, institutions, and publications. Second, because in the United States these people have been designated, generally and statistically, as Spanish people–Latin Americans, Hispanics and, finally (whether or not they speak Spanish), Latinos–we have, therefore (regardless of whether the name or label "Latino" is the preferred term today) indiscriminately employed all of these terms. Third, the important literary and humanistic production made by this Hispanic or Latino population in English will only be considered here as a point of reference and not to the full extent it deserves. And, finally, nomadism and cultural cross-fertilization (*mestizaje*) appear to have taken hold in the twentieth century, and as a consequence the cultural products under discussion here are marked by the coexistence of different traditions–for Hispanics or Latinos–Spanish, Latin American, English, Anglo-American, Native American, African, Jewish, Arabic, Chinese, and many other cultures.

On the basis of these considerations, we can state that New York City is, at the same time, both a fixed and nomadic Hispanic or Latino cultural center. These terms have been carefully chosen: *center*, because the city is a geographic and cultural space that has attracted and has accommodated, temporarily or permanently, persons of Hispanic origin; *cultural*, in this site where cultural products and expressions are generated by these same people; *nomadic*, because the protagonists of this cultural travel (in reality or in their minds) move between different localities and traditions; and *Hispanic* or *Latino* because, for better or for worse, this is how people of a Hispano-American background are known in the United States, even though a part of this community was born in the United States.

Population, Language, and Sociocultural Institutions

Ever since 1527, when Diego Ribero sketched the outlines of "The Bay," in which present-day New York City is located, the Hispanic imagination has been constantly entranced with the space and the city that would become not only the cultural capital of the world in the second half of the twentieth century, but one of the most important and vital Latino cultural centers in existence. In those early days the present-day Hudson was known as the San Antonio River because a Spanish ship captained by the black Portuguese navigator Esteban Gómez explored the mouth of this river on 17 January (the feast of St. Anthony) 1526, one year after its sighting by the first European explorer, the Italian Giovanni da Verrazano.

In 1612, Dutch merchants constructed the first trading post in Manhattes (present-day Manhattan); their interpreter was a free African, Jan Rodríguez, who would eventually settle on the island. Visiting New Amsterdam in 1643, the French Jesuit missionary Isaac Jogues noted that eighteen different languages were spoken in the town, including Spanish. The historical documents show that the origins of the use of Spanish in New York are tied to three marginalized groups of Iberian extraction: Spanish-Portuguese Jews; Spanish sailors, locally known as "Spanish negroes"; and a group of slaves identified as the "Spanish Indians," although it is not known if these latter actually spoke Spanish (Goodfriend 114). The first historically important reference to a Spanish presence in New York is dated August 1654. In that month a group of twenty-three Jews of Spanish-Portuguese origin arrived in the city from Recife, Brazil. In the same month the Spanish and Portuguese

Figure 1.

Photograph by Ricardo Blanco. (Archive of the author)

Synagogue was founded in secret, the first Jewish congregation in what was to become the United States. Since then (and until today), a part of the Spanish-Jewish community in the city has continued to use the Ladino dialect of Spanish, not only in daily life, but also in literary expression, as a vehicle for the transmission of the Sephardic oral tradition. (See **Figure 1**.)

In 1741, the population of New York numbered 10,000, 2,000 of which were slaves, many of these being "Spanish negroes." The term "Spanish negroes" refers to the formerly free crewmen of Spanish ships captured in the Caribbean by the English, who were brought to New York and there traded as slaves. Documents show that some, but not all, of these Africans spoke Spanish, although at a very rudimentary level. Five "Spanish negroes" were accused of arson in 1741. This accusation was, in part, thanks to the fact that a witness is said to have overheard someone say in Spanish, "*Ven aquí, señor*" (Come here, sir), at the beginning of the fire (Davis 81). While four of the accused were pardoned, the fifth, pleading his innocence, was sentenced to death; at the moment of execution he broke into prayer in Spanish (Davis 226; Ellis 129–37).

The same year (1741) saw the publication in New York of the first Spanish grammar for use in the Thirteen Colonies. In 1835 Francis Lieber (1800–1872) stated that Spanish, among other languages, could be heard on a daily basis on the principal street of the city, Broadway. Already by this date New York had three Spanish newspapers (García 22), and it is known that a Spanish guide to the city was published in 1876. (Later we will examine the cultural activities related to the Spanish language in nineteenth-century New York.)

In this register of the dates related to New York's Hispanic population and their culture, the floating, vague, and nomadic aspect of their existence as well as the more stable side, their anchorage at the heart of U.S. society, ought to be kept in mind. For this reason we wish to stress two fundamental perspectives that have informed our research: the official view, based on census data and historical documents, and the extra-official view, based on sources which are less scientific but form part of an empirical and oral history of the very same facts and events. In this sense the memoirs written by the Puerto Rican Bernardo Vega (1885–1965) have been indispensable for a better understanding of the Latino ambiance of the Big Apple during the first half of the twentieth century. The novel *Windmills in Brooklyn* (1960), written in English by the Spaniard

Prudencio de Pereda (b. 1912), has also been an interesting source of information on the Latino community in the same time period.

The various censuses taken in New York in the nineteenth century can only be considered approximations and not entirely trustworthy. Nevertheless, there are documents showing that between 5 May 1847 and 31 December 1860, 4,537 "Spanish," 1,376 "South American," and 324 "Mexican" immigrants arrived at the port of New York City, for a total of 6,237 Hispanics in less than two decades (Ernst 188). Over the course of the nineteenth century and up until the 1920s, the Spanish community would be the largest among all immigrant communities in New York. Toward the end of the nineteenth century Spanish sailors began to take up residence in the Chelsea district of Manhattan also known as "Little Spain" (La pequeña España), between West 14th and 23rd streets. However, Spaniards also lived in other sections of the city: in lower Manhattan, at the foot of the present day Brooklyn Bridge, resided some 25,000–30,000 Spaniards; in Brooklyn, 5,000–6,000; and in Astoria, Queens, a sizable number also resided (Rueda 85–92). Starting from 1920, political refugees, in the majority socialists and anarchists, came to live in New York, fleeing the Spanish dictatorship of Primo de Rivera; during the Spanish Civil War (1936–1939) a new wave of Spanish refugees arrived, and it would not be until the end of the Franco dictatorship in 1975 that this flow of immigrants from Spain would begin to fall off. By and large the Spaniards who came to New York in these waves were artists and intellectuals, and, as we shall see, very few would make the city their permanent place of residence; in fact, today there are less than 25,000 New Yorkers who were born in Spain.

Toward the middle of the nineteenth century a wave of Cuban refugees began to make itself felt. In general, these Cubans had a high level of education and were mostly white; thus, many of them and their children integrated into U.S. society, despite their initial plan to return to their homeland once Spanish colonial rule had been ended. Later, in the 1860s and 1870s, Cuban tobacco workers began to show up in New York. In the twentieth century, another wave of exiles was seen at the time of the Batista dictatorship–in 1959 more than fifteen thousand Cubans lived on the Upper West Side. During the 1970s, fleeing yet another regime, that of Fidel Castro, Cubans continued to arrive in New York. It is to be noted that among this last wave were significant numbers of a very particular group, the Cuban-Chinese, a group speaking not only English, but Chinese and Spanish as well, and who have kept alive the traditions linked to these two languages (Leeds 375–79).

What is today known as Spanish Harlem (*el barrio latino*) began taking shape during the last quarter of the nineteenth century, in the Upper East Side of Manhattan, from 96th Street to 124th Street. According to Bernardo Vega, this area already contained at that time a considerable Cuban community. In 1904 the first Puerto Rican families, approximately 150 people, established themselves there, with a similar number being scattered around other parts of the city. Spanish Harlem in those days was an area where the Sephardic Jews had established many businesses, shops, and restaurants, and while they spoke Ladino among themselves, their clientele were mostly Latin Americans and peninsular Spaniards. Vega notes that already by 1913, even though the Hispanics were not concentrated in any specific district and were to be found scattered here and there throughout the city, "había un sector de profesionales y familias acaudaladas en el Oeste, al otro lado del Parque Central" ("There was a community of professionals and affluent families living in the West on the other side of Central Park") and that by 1916 "la población de habla hispana se calculaba en 16.000 personas" (Vega 132, 30) ("the Spanish-speaking population of the city was reckoned to be 16,000 people").

About this time, Juan Flores, one of the intellectuals whose works are indispensable for learning about the Puerto Rican community of New York, wrote: "Years ago, back in the 1920s and [19]30s, you used to be able to tell where the Puerto Rican families lived by the green plants and colored flowers on their windowsills. Of all the immigrant nationalities settling in New York in those times, it was the Puerto Ricans who would freshen up their humble tenement walls with splashes of nature and provide themselves, neighbors, and passers-by some relief from the dreary grays and browns of the big-city streets" (331). In effect, already by the 1920s and 1930s, "los puertorriqueños se habían extendido desde la Avenida Lexington, entre las Calles 96 y 107, hasta el borde del barrio italiano de la Primera Avenida. En todo ese sector se vivía a la usanza criolla.... En tiendas y calles sólo se oía hablar en español" (Vega 183) ("the Puerto Ricans had extended themselves from Lexington Avenue, between 96th and 107th Street, up to the border of the Italian neighborhood at First Avenue. All throughout this district the *criollo* way of life was lived.... In shops and on the streets the only language you would hear was Spanish"). Around the beginning of 1929, "el viejo vencindario integrado en su mayoría por tabaqueros, al Este de Manhattan, se desplazó hacia Harlem. Definitivamente, el Barrio Latino se consolidó como el corazón de la comunidad puertorriqueña en Nueva York" (Vega 187) ("the old neighborhood on the East Side of Manhattan, composed of largely Cuban tobacco workers, moved to Harlem. From this moment, Spanish Harlem was definitively constituted as the heart of the New York Puerto Rican community"). Vega goes on to point out, citing census figures, that Puerto Rican immigration grew from 2,000 in 1904 to 26,000 in 1947, and that during the 1940s 60,000 Puerto Rican children were born in New York City (267). This phenomenal growth in the immigration and population of the Puerto Rican community also brought with it some pernicious consequences that, despite the quasi-poetic description that Flores paints today of the Puerto Ricans, began to create a much more negative image of them in the eyes of other New Yorkers. This unfair simplification of how the Puerto Ricans in New York live unfortunately has obscured the important contributions they have made. In the final account, the fact that Spanish language and culture enjoys a well-deserved privileged status in the city today is largely due to them.

The first and still the best study about immigrants from the Dominican Republic to New York City is "Dominicans in New York: Men, Women and Prospects" by Ramona Hernandez and Silvio Torres-Saillant. The first to arrive in the city from what is now the Dominican Republic were the relatively small number of whites and mulattos who fled a slave revolt in the capital, Santo Domingo, at the end of the eighteenth century (Leeds 368). However, in the 1970s, Dominican immigration would become massive: "The largest numbers of post-1970 immigrants came from the Caribbean. After the 1960s, Puerto Rican migrants declined, but the figures for other Caribbean newcomers increased. Whereas in the 1950s about 90 percent of the city's Hispanics were Puerto Ricans, by 1990 only about 50 percent were" (Binder and Reimers 227). Dominican

immigrants and their children, born in the city, would take up residence in the Washington Heights area of the city at the northern end of the island of Manhattan, and in certain areas of Queens. While in 1967 there were only 125,000 Dominicans in the city (Hendricks 153), by 1990 the Dominican community would be estimated at 300,000–evidence of an extremely rapid rate of immigration. Although the Trujillo dictatorship had prohibited emigration to the United States from its beginnings in 1930, after the assassination of Trujillo in 1961, Dominicans began arriving in the Big Apple in considerable numbers (Leeds 369; Ugalde and Larson 98). Despite their large numbers the Dominicans "have yet to produce solid institutions with the power of transmitting social values, practices, and norms aimed at ensuring the protection and preservation of the community" (Leeds 46). In 1998 Hernández and Torres-Saillant published *The Dominican Americans* and Francisco Rodriguez de León published *El furioso merengue del Norte. Una historia de la comunidad dominicana en los Estados Unidos* [The Furious Merengue of the North: A History of the Dominican Community in the United States]. The establishment of an Institute of Dominican Studies at the City University of New York in 1992 in part demonstrates that the community is in the process of legitimating, with resolution and rigor, its own cultural values.

Colombian and Mexican immigrants are two other groups who have added to the numbers of New York's Hispanic community. It is difficult to ascertain the exact number of Mexicans and Colombians in the city since a large number of them, especially the Mexicans, are illegal immigrants and thus do not appear in census figures. However, the Colombians, principally living in the Jackson Heights area of Queens, began arriving at the beginning of the 1990s and now number around three hundred thousand. Anneris Goris and José Hernández, in their *Latin Communities in New York City*, offer a panoramic overview of these two communities as well as other groups that we will not deal with here.

In 1990 the Hispanic population of the city was 1,783,511. This number is of course approximate, for the already mentioned reason that the census does not include those Latinos who reside in New York illegally. As well, many Hispanics who do figure in the census classify themselves as belonging to other ethnic groups–African-American, for example–or do not identify with the official census denominations. It is thought that in reality there are about 2 million Latinos living in the city, more than a quarter of the total population, and that by the year 2010 that figure will rise to 35 percent. Approximately 50 percent of New York's Hispanics are of Puerto Rican origin, 20 percent Dominican, 5 percent Colombian, and the remaining 25 percent are people from all the Latin American countries and Spain (Zentella 167–72).

New York Spanish has a decidedly Caribbean flavor, not only because the largest group of Spanish speakers come from that region–73 percent if we add up Puerto Ricans, Dominicans, and Cubans–but also because, in marriages between Latin Americans in New York, one of the two is frequently of Caribbean origin. The tendency of New York Spanish is to adapt to the vocabulary established principally by the Puerto Ricans. At the same time, however, the general phonology in use by the majority of the Spanish speakers in the city demonstrates a desire to employ and learn a standardized Spanish, or better put, an idiom in which Americanisms and Anglicisms do not hinder its comprehension at a national or international level. In the Spanish media, especially television and periodicals, there is a tendency toward the use of a Spanish that can be comprehended without difficulty by all Spanish-speaking groups in the city and the nation in general. In addition to the variations in pronunciation, intonation, lexicon, and grammar, Spanish as it is spoken in New York City is significantly marked, to varying degrees and depending on the country of origin of the speaker, by the influence or interference of English. However, the influence of English on New York Spanish, while subject to much criticism from linguistic purists, is not that different from the English influence felt by the various Spanish idioms spoken in Latin America and Spain. Nevertheless, the Spanish spoken in the city, and the Spanish used by American Hispanics in general, possesses its own characteristic features.

"Spanglish" is one of the most extreme and interesting modalities of the Spanish spoken in New York and in the U.S. Spanglish is composed of the following constituents: First, a number of English loan-words have been Hispanicized (e.g., "to have lunch" has become "*lonchar*"); second, those Spanish words bearing a phonetic similarity to English words are used with their English signification (e.g., *librería* means "library" instead of "bookstore," because of its resemblance to the English word); third, words and phrases are translated literally from English into Spanish (e.g., "I'll call you back" is in New York Spanish *te llamo pa tras*). In a similar manner, while conversing in English, for example, it is not uncommon for New York Hispanics to introduce fragments of Spanish speech, and vice versa. However, as numerous linguists have demonstrated, these changes or substitutions of codes are not arbitrary or chaotic but rather possess certain very concrete and coherent guidelines, with specific reasons and intentions. Those who employ this mix of English and Spanish assume that their interlocutors understand the two languages perfectly and, in general, when the other speaks only one language (whether it be Spanish or English), the bilingual speakers do everything possible to sustain the dialogue within the parameters of that language (Zentella 179–81).

According to a report by the Modern Language Association of America, in 1998 Spanish continued to be the foreign language most studied in U.S. universities: A total of 656,590 students were registered in Spanish courses in that year (Brod and Welles 23). This interest on the part of U.S. students to make Spanish their second language is due, in part, to the Hispanic presence in the United States, as well as to the geographic proximity of Latin America and the fact that many institutions, in addition to the Hispanics and the Latino media, have kept Hispanic language and culture alive.

Although evidence of a significant Anglo-Saxon culture was already present in the 1730s (theatrical performances and periodical publication), 1750 is the date traditionally assigned to the initiation of an autonomous New York City cultural life. In 1754, for example, the first New York Society Library was established. In the following decade children's books and Latin and Spanish school texts began to be published (Kammen 243–48). Given that toward the beginning of the nineteenth century the first Spanish periodicals edited in New York began to appear and during these same years a number of Hispanic sociocultural associations were founded, it can be seen that the formation of New York as a Hispanic cultural center is tied, from a chronological point of view (with a half-century lag), to the birth of an autonomous U.S. cultural life in the metropolis. Nineteenth-century Hispanic sociocultural

Figure 2.

One of the most active Caribbean cultural associations is El Museo del Barrio. Photograph by Rícardo Blanco. (Archive of the author)

enclaves were of an almost exclusively political, nationalist, and regional character (at times there were cultural centers representing people from a single Spanish or Caribbean town), although there was no lack of cultural activity of a more general nature. Over time these centers have become more "specialized." Today many of them make every possible effort to integrate their programs with the community and its popular cultural expressions. (See **Figure 2**.)

It is possible at the start of the twenty-first century to view the concept of "culture," however inclusive and vague, as no longer having an inherent meaning and, therefore, to deem any selection of cultural points of focus arbitrary. This is to say that, while we mention the Museum of Spanish Harlem (El museo del barrio), we could just as easily have studied the culture of *botánicas*, barber shops, and the mini-marts known as *colmados* and *bodegas*, respectively. However, in a certain sense a large part of the cultural identity of New York Hispanics survives, at least institutionally, thanks to the continual use of the Spanish language and the activities of certain cultural centers. Thus, Gustavo Bueno, in his *El mito de la cultura* [1996; The Myth of Culture], writes: "To invoke cultural identity as a means of justifying a conservationist politics vis-à-vis the language or the institutions of a people is nothing but a vacant, ideological, and propagandistic gesture, because cultural identity is ultimately the product of the persistence of the language and institutions, and not the other way around" (176). In this sense, we can state that if it is legitimate to speak of a Hispanic communal identity in New York City, it is because people have continued to use the Spanish language in an active and dynamic form, not only as a vehicle of communication and creation, but also as a principal point of reference for a Latino sensibility, however latent, in those Hispanics who speak only English. On the other hand, clearly a number of institutions have taken up the task of actively reminding Hispanic New Yorkers not only that they form part of a very rich tradition, but also that Latin American, Spanish, and U.S. Latino cultural expression is just as much a living force in the United States as it is in the other nations of the Hispanic world.

With respect to the peninsular Spanish cultural institutions of the city, Germán Rueda has noted, "New York saw the integration of the majority of the regional cultural centers into national centers toward the end of the 1930s and throughout the 1940s. Thus, one of the Galician centers, the Casa Galicia, united with the Centro Español in 1939, and the same happened to the Centro Montañés (Santander region) and the Centro Aragonés (Aragón). The Centro Asturiano (Asturias) was integrated to La Nacional in 1947" (221). The Casa de España was created later, and in the 1990s came the Instituto Cervantes de Nueva York. The dynamic of transformation from regional to national or international groupings was also seen in many other cases in the Latin American community of the Big Apple. Later, we will examine what form the institutional infrastructure of Hispanic culture in the city takes today.

Reviewing the chronological evolution of the Hispanic population of New York, it can be seen that the most important Hispanic cultural institutions have been directly related, in terms of their resources and the frequency of their activities, to the origin of the majority group resident in the city. In the final decade of the twentieth century this pattern was partially broken because Spain had transformed itself into a developed and economically powerful nation. Spain's newfound cultural maternalism, her desire for an international cultural prestige, and, for some Spaniards, the most antiquated imperialist nostalgia have all combined to mean that the degree of Spain's cultural presence in New York is not related to the number of Spanish citizens in the city but rather to its economic muscle. The names of the most significant and well-funded Spanish cultural institutions in the city speak volumes: Instituto Cervantes (1991) and the Centro Rey Juan Carlos I at the University of New York (1997). During the first four decades of the twentieth century, when the majority of the Spanish-speaking community was of Spanish origin, the Instituto de las Españas (1920, now known as the Hispanic Institute and la Casa de España) and the Hispanic Society of America (1904) were the most relevant Spanish cultural centers. In the 1930s there also existed a Spanish and American Alliance, publisher of the bilingual review, *Alhambra*. Later, the Spanish Institute (1954) would add its weight to those prestigious institutions. However, despite the fact that these institutions are today still in operation, Spanish cultural leadership resides with the Instituto Cervantes and the Centro Rey Juan Carlos I at New York University. (See **Figure 3**.)

In the 1960s, with the Puerto Ricans and other Latin Americans forming the majority of Spanish speakers in the city, two

Figure 3.

The Hispanic Society of America building. Photograph by Ricardo Blanco. (Archive of the author)

new centers were created: The Americas Society (1968) and the Centro de Estudios Puertorriqueños, as part of the Department of Black and Puerto Rican Studies at Hunter College, City University of New York (1969). Starting in these years, the New York public university system began creating on every one of its campuses centers similar to the one at Hunter College, the most recent and significant of these being the already mentioned Instituto de Estudios Dominicanos (1992) at City College, City University of New York. In tandem with these centers, other institutions were created, some of whose efforts and activities we will highlight in each section of this text. The most important of these still active today are: the Museo del Barrio, the OLLANTAY Center for the Arts, the Instituto de Escritores Latinoamericanos (The Institute of Latin American Writers), the Mexican Cultural Institute, the INTAR Hispanic American Arts Center, the Centro Cultural Eugenio María de Hostos, and the Caribbean Cultural Center.

It is to be noted that throughout the entire twentieth century, museums, cultural centers, and galleries have consolidated the image of New York as a platform for the introduction and launching of Spanish and Latin American artists into the cultural marketplace. Hispanic art maintains a presence in New York through expositions of Spanish and Latin American art, the temporary or permanent residence in the city of Latino artists, and through the galleries and institutions that mount and promote this art. These factors notwithstanding, for the enormous number of New York Latinos, Hispanic art is only relatively known. Much more fertile for the knowledge of Hispanic art has been a phenomenon that moves in the opposite direction: the general and popular use of images, symbols, subjects, figures, and materials of a Latin American origin. Beginning in the 1960s, New York became not only a center of attraction and a stopover for Hispanic artists, but was also transformed into an important center of artistic production for the Latinos temporarily or permanently resident in the city, as well as for those born or raised there. At the end of this essay we will concisely trace the trajectory of the presence of Hispanic art in the city.

The First Latin American Congress of New York Visual Arts, a point of reunion for a discussion of various aspects of the Latino art situation in the United States, was held at the OLLANTAY Center for the Arts on 26 May 1990. According to photographer Charles Biasiny-Rivera, U.S. "mainstream institutions come to us now more than they ever have" (Monge-Rafuls 17); and we can second this opinion by pointing to, for example, the "Emerging Latino Artists in New York" exposition, sponsored by AT&T, that was held in July and August 1997 in the Art Gallery at the Queens Theater in the Park.

With the minimal parameters established, it is important for us to ask, "What are the most important institutions for the legitimation of New York as an important center of Latino art?" Lucy R. Lippard, in 1990, laid down a number of coordinates for an approach to the U.S. artistic scene, coordinates representing the situation in which U.S. Latino art found itself at the end of the twentieth century. According to Lippard, we must take into account the fact that "we now look at art within the context of disorder—a far more difficult task than following institutional regulations" (7). However, in order to arrive at this point of disorder, there must necessarily have been a pre-existing order. Let us consider, then, the institutions that, until today, have given us an organized picture of Hispanic art.

The Museo del Barrio, founded by the Puerto Rican artist Rafael Montañez Ortiz in 1969, is perhaps the most significant cultural center in the United States exclusively devoted to Latin American art. Within Manhattan itself, other centers such as the Americas Society and the Spanish Institute have institutionally backed the contemporary art of Spain and Spanish America. Various cultural centers contain galleries that regularly mount shows by Latino and Latin American artists. Among this group, INTAR, Hostos, the OLLANTAY Center, El Taller Latinoamericano, Boricua, GALA, the Mexican Cultural Institute, and the Colombia Center have been the most prominent. Some other museums, by virtue of their multicultural character, have promoted expositions of Latino artists: the Studio Museum in Harlem, the Bronx Museum of Arts, and the Caribbean Cultural Centre, in particular. In addition to these institutions, almost all of New York's art museums have at one time or another, and some with great frequency, put on exhibitions of Spanish or Latin American art because it falls within their general mandate for holding art exhibits. The cultural bulletins and journals put out by the consulates of various Spanish-speaking nations have published monthly notices of the Latino art to be seen in the city. More than any other publication, ¡AHA! Hispanic Art News has kept the Hispanic community abreast of the most important exhibits.

Periodicals, Journals, and Other Media

Around the middle of the eighteenth century, as already mentioned, one can identify the beginnings of an autonomous Anglo-Saxon culture in New York City. Although all evidence indicates a plurality of ethnic groups, languages, and religions within the urban center, little is known about the participation of the Spaniards and Latin Americans in the cultural activity of the city (Kammen 243–45). The first important English-language periodical published in New York, The Independent Reflector (1752), was primarily of a political and social character; similarly, the beginnings of the Spanish-language periodical press in the city in the nineteenth century is also tied to Independence movements, those of Cuba and Puerto Rico. "A clear differentiation between reviews and periodicals during this epoch is very often impossible to make, or at least very difficult to maintain, whether on the grounds of form, content, or frequency, and there is no advantage that we can see in attempting to do so. However, there clearly were newspapers, and plenty, in more or less the modern sense of the term, since these publications came out on a daily basis, were principally occupied with furnishing information and editorial opinions, thus servicing a Spanish speaking public, and carrying out the traditional and fundamental role of the periodical" (Shearer 50). Thus, when we use the term newspaper, it is not to be confused with the modern connotation of the word (i.e., a daily newspaper); similarly, when we refer to reviews or journals, neither should this be associated exclusively with the contemporary notion of literary, or specialized, journals.

The launching of New York Spanish-language periodical publication really began in the 1820s: El Habanero (Philadelphia-New York, 1824–1826), edited by Father Félix Varela; El Redactor (1826?–1831?) concerned itself with literary subjects, information on Latin America, and commercial affairs; El Mensajero Semanal (1828–1831); Espejo Macénico (sic), a Freemason publication; Noticioso de Ambos Mundos (1836–1859?); El Continental (1861), mostly dedicated to business but also containing political and cultural information; El Porvenir (1863); La Voz de la América (1865?); La Voz de Puerto Rico (1874, only

one issue published); El Espejo (1869–1894); El Comercio (1875–1930); and La Crónica (1848–1853 and afterward as El Cronista, possibly as late as 1877):

> None of these papers was as successful as the La crónica which survived their competition and lived beyond the period of the Civil War. From the start, La crónica appealed to Latin American merchants and carried many advertisements of Havana businessmen; its news columns dealt chiefly with events in Spain and Latin America; but after the middle of the century it printed more news of the United States and, as did most of the foreign press, supported the Democratic party and opposed nativism and abolitionism. It was at once the medium of expression of the Hispanic community, the leading political and commercial paper in the Spanish language during the fifties, and the chief source of information for Latin American immigrants. (Ernst 157)

As well as these full-fledged publications, a number of more modest informational broadsides appeared in these years: La Verdad (1848–1860, after 1855 published in New Orleans), a free multi-page circular subsidized by the newspaper The Sun; El Mulato (1854); El Pueblo (1855); and Delta (1882–1885, bilingual).

However, one of the best known periodicals of the era was Patria (14 March 1892–31 December 1898), founded and edited by the Cuban writer and revolutionary José Martí (1853–1895). From its first issue to its last, Patria adopted a position laid out in its first editorial: "Nace este periódico, por la voluntad y con los recursos de los cubanos y puertorriqueños independientes de New York, para contribuir sin premura y sin descanso, a la organización de los hombres libres de Cuba y Puerto Rico" (in Ripoll 18–19) ("Founded by the will and the means of the independent Cubans and Puerto Ricans of New York City, this periodical is devoted, without haste and without rest, to the organization of the free society of Cuba and Puerto Rico").

It can be said, then, that beginning with El Redactor and La Crónica, Latino journalism in New York began to shape its own identity within the Hispanic world. With the end of Spanish colonial rule in Cuba and Puerto Rico (1898), revolutionary matters disappeared from the Hispanic press, and local problems, in addition to Latin American subjects, constituted the bulk of the coverage in the New York Spanish-language press. Parallel to Spanish-language journalism was the translation into Spanish of certain U.S. publications: América Científica (1890–1909), a literal version of Scientific American, and La Gaceta de Policía (1894–1896), a translation of The Police Gazette, are two examples. In addition, there were a number of very specialized publications also published in Spanish that we will not consider here, such as La Moda Ilustrada (1896–1897), El Círculo del Joyero (1876–1877), La Gaceta de Bomberos (1884–1885), Gaceta de Ferrocarriles (1892), El Museo de las Familias (1872–1873?), and El Ateneo (1874–1877) (Shearer 47–48).

Although the twentieth century opened in 1901 with the publication of the Puerto Rico Herald, founded by Luis Muñoz Rivera (1859–1916), the most outstanding Latino daily of the entire century, La Prensa, would begin publishing in the following decade. According to Bernardo Vega:

> La prensa, the longest running Spanish-language daily in the history of New York City, began publication on June 4, 1918, although it had been in circulation [as a weekly] since October 12, 1913. It was founded by Rafael Viera, who established his editorial office at 87 Broad Street. For a time the celebrated Colombian writer José María Vargas Vila (1860–1933) was the editor; later, the

post passed to V. H. Collao, who transformed the paper into a daily; and shortly after that, the Spaniard José Camprubí took the reins. Under the tenacious leadership of Camprubí, and with the backing of the Unión Benéfica Española (The Spanish Benevolent League), *La prensa* achieved financial stability. (125)

In 1948 *El Diario de Nueva York* arrived on the scene and began competing with *La Prensa* until the two were amalgamated in 1962 under the banner *El Diario La Prensa*. Still publishing today, the paper has a print run of 321,000 and some sixty thousand readers in the New York City region. New York's second present-day Spanish-language daily, *Noticias del Mundo*, (founded in 1980) has a readership of 28,000. In 1954, John H. Burma, in his *Spanish-Speaking Groups in the United States*, passed a death sentence on the Spanish press: "The Spanish-language press is on the decline . . . it is probable that in fifteen years the Spanish-language press will virtually die out" (99). Despite Burma's prognostication, precisely the opposite has transpired: The National Association of Hispanic Publications, founded in 1982, represents forty-two Hispanic periodicals (some of which are written in English), with a total circulation in 1986 of 1,340,000 copies (Veciana-Suárez, v).

Throughout the entire twentieth century Spanish-language periodicals were published in New York, but their history has been only partially documented. In his memoirs, Bernardo Vega mentions *Las Novedades, Cultura Proletaria, El Norteamericano, El Corsario, The Tobacco Worker* (bilingual), *El Machete Criollo, Metrópolis, Liberación, Pueblos Hispanos*, and the weekly *Gráfico*, which was bought and run by Vega himself in 1927. Collaborating with Vega were the distinguished Puerto Rican intellectuals Cayetano Coll y Toste (1850–1930) and Jesús Colón (1901–1974).

In addition to the local papers, the major Latin American and Spanish periodicals can be bought in New York; with a circulation of 25,000, the Santo Domingan *El Nacional* is the most read. Also to be found are a number of weeklies, some of them distributed gratis; among these are *El Especial, Resumen* (founded in 1971), *Impacto* (founded in 1975), *El Tiempo, El Continental, Visión Hispana, Eco Latino*, and *Noticiero Colombiano e Hispano* (founded in 1983), *El Sol de México y Latinoamérica*, and *El Sol de Colombia*, now known as simply *El Sol*, and others such as *Nosotros los Latinos* (founded in 1995), and *El Puente Latino* (founded in 1997), a free newspaper with a circulation of 100,000 (Zentella 182–83).

Although, as we have noted, in the nineteenth century it is difficult to distinguish between what was a periodical and what was a review, a number of these publications do draw close to what we mean by a review: *La América* (1871), reappearing the following year as *La América Ilustrada* (1872–1874), and later amalgamated with *El Mundo Nuevo* (1871–1876) under the editorship of Enrique Piñeyro; *Ambos Mundos* (1865?); *La América* (1882–1889?), a journal (different from the previously mentioned review with the same name) dedicated to agricultural and industrial subjects, but which included information about literature, edited and managed for a time by José Martí; and *Cuba y América* (1897–1898, New York; 1899–1917, Havana). Two of the reviews in this category deserve special mention for being literary journals of some significance and longevity: *Las Novedades. España y los Pueblos Hispano-Americanos* (1877–1905; Shearer gives other dates: 1876–1918), where, among others, Leopoldo Alas 'Clarín' and Emilia Pardo Bazán were published; and *La Revista Ilustrada de Nueva York* (1886–1893; Shearer's dates: 1882–1894). (For a fuller study

of the history and import of these two journals, see the book by Vernon A. Chamberlin and Ivan A. Schulman [Sotelo 11]). Other important journals are *Las Tres Américas* (1896–1899; Shearer: 1893–1896), founded by the Venezuelan poet Nicanor Bolet Peraza (d. 1906 in New York), as well as the *La Revista Lustrada*, in which many of the famous Latin American *modernistas* were published: Rubén Darío (1867–1916), Manuel Gutiérrez Nájera (1859–1895), José Martí, Salvador Díaz Mirón (1853–1928), Salvador Rueda (1857–1933), and Enrique José Varona (1849–1933). Some journals followed a complex publishing path, such as *Literatura Americana*, which was founded in Curaçao (1849) by the Guatemalan poet Antonio José Irisarri (1786–1868) and later began publishing in New York in January 1850, the year in which it ceased operations (Shearer 47).

In the first half of the twentieth century, a number of publications with a political character came out in New York, such as *España Libre* and *Ibérica*, but the most comprehensive and rigorous literary journal of the epoch was the *Revista Hispánica Moderna* , founded in 1934 by Federico de Onís (1885–1966) as the "*Boletín del Instituto de las Españas*" (Casa de las Españas, Columbia University). The objective of this latter publication was to "study and disseminate Hispanic culture"; it contained articles, book reviews, and information on contemporary literature, a Spanish-American bibliographic section, and another section devoted to students of Spanish. Today it is almost exclusively a journal of academic scholarship (Sobejano 222).

Other reviews in these first decades worth mentioning are: *El Liberal* (1935–?), New York/Havana, a mostly political journal; *Norte* (1940–1950?), with numerous articles on the painters of Cuba, and among whose collaborators were intellectuals and writers such as Ernest Hemingway–with an article on the Cuban painter Gattorno (February, 1941, n. 32)–Américo Castro, and Ciro Alegría (1909–1967), and in the February 1946 issue several interesting pages devoted to "El Nueva York que vio García Lorca" (Esquenazi 43–44, 50–51) (New York Through the Eyes of García Lorca). Among the more specialized publications were *Cine Mundial* (1916–1935), *Ecos* (1946–?) and, in the 1970s, *Furia*, a journal of politics and current events which, according to its editors, "recoge todas las pasiones que se registran en los distintos sectores: amor, teatro, cine, deportes, televisión, en general" ("gathers together all the passions to be found in distinct sectors: love, theater, cinema, sports, television"); we have only been able to find three issues published in 1974.

In the last half of the twentieth century, New York has seen a large number of Latino reviews and magazines, both in Spanish and English, an account of which must here be limited to a selection. Among those no longer in circulation are: *Exilio* (1966–1973); *Lugar sin Límite* and *Caronte*, both created by the Puerto Rican writer Iván Silén (b. 1944); *Románica*, founded by Rafael Catalá, and *Lyra*, both edited by the Cubans Lourdes Gil (b. 1951) and Iraida Iturralde (b. 1954); *Escandalar*, created by the Cuban poet Octavio Armand (b. 1946); *Emen-Ya, Enlace, De Azur*, edited by the Dominican poet Leandro Morales; *Transimagen, Punto 7*, edited by the Dominican Silvio Torres-Saillant; *Alcance, AREITO; OLLANTAY Theater Magazine*, founded by Pedro R. Monge-Rafuls; *Centro de Estudios Puertorriqueños, Extremos Líricos: del Caribe a la Araucania*, a poetry journal published simultaneously in San Juan, Puerto Rico, Stony Brook, NY, and Concepción, Chile; *Encuentros*, a bilingual journal published by Columbia University students; *Al Aire Libre, Boletín del CEPI (Círculo de Escritores y Poetas*

Iberoamericanos de Nueva York); and *Espacio de Escritores*. Among the journals most active today are *Review: Latin American Literature and Arts*, published by the Americas Society; *Brújula/Compass*, edited by the Peruvian writer Isaac Goldemberg (b. 1945); *Tercer Milenio*, edited by the Puerto Rican poet Pedro López Adorno (b. 1954); *La nuez,* founded by the Cuban poet Rafael Bordao (b. 1951); *Realidad Aparte*, edited by the Colombian poet Gabriel Jaime Caro (b. 1949); and the most recent, *Ñ*, created in 1995 by the Colombian Ricardo Léon Peña-Villa (b. 1962).

In addition to the press, among the other most influential communications media in the Spanish-speaking community of New York are Latino television and radio. The history of these two forms has been recounted in practically every book dedicated to the U.S. Hispanic community. Geoffrey Fox's chapter, "The Image Machine," in his book *Hispanic Nation* (1996), is perhaps the best, in the sense of most informative, of the accounts to date (40–66). The New York television channels 41, 44, 47, MH, ACQ, and BQ offer a total of 557 hours of weekly programming in Spanish (García 34). Serious doubts have been raised about the deplorable state of Hispanic television programming, specifically its propensity to foment a brutalization and alienation of the Latino community rather than promoting the development of greater Latino self-esteem. However, despite these reservations, it is unquestionable that a sentiment of unity, and therefore of mass identity, emerges from these programs–not only because they are realized in a Spanish that is at the same time local and standard, but because the focus that they place on Latino and Latin American subjects is a priority with all these channels. Ana Celia Zentella, in an excellent essay entitled "Spanish in New York," has taken up this subject (181–86) and with respect to radio programming (of the four stations, La Mega and Radio Wado deserve special merit), Zentella has come to the following conclusions: "Overall, Spanish radio is much more reflective of life in New York than Spanish television in programming, advertisements, and in the type of Spanish that is spoken, because most radio programs are produced locally and many people call in" (185).

Literature

Although many of the authors to whom we will refer form an integral part of the literary history of their country of origin, we have deemed it necessary to limit our discussion here to those books that have made significant use of New York City as a theme within Hispanic literature. It can be said that the experience of New York in these works and for these authors has varied: Some have only passed through the city; others stayed for either a short time or a considerable number of years; still others have made the city their permanent place of residence; and finally there are those who arrived as children or were born here, the majority of whom write in English. Although this latter group must be considered an integral part of a history of Latino literature in New York, we treat them here only briefly, largely because this text centers on Hispanic cultural manifestations that have employed Spanish as their principal means of expression. The situation of the Puerto Rican writers of New York–forming part of two histories, that of Puerto Rico and that of the United States–is a fine example of the extent to which circumstances of unrest, uncertainty, crisis, and affirmation of identity can give rise to works that, beyond their historical

significance, have in themselves an aesthetic importance. These works are important because they throw light on the conflict (in the sense of collision and separation, identification and alienation) of the human being with his or her surroundings, society, and institutions, with the historical moment in which it has been their fate to live, with their imposed identity and their inherited identity, and ultimately, with the desire to be oneself, an individual and part of a collective identity within the history of humanity and far beyond a solely national history.

Finally, we wish to alert the reader that we have not arranged the writers by literary genre, but have rather followed a chronological order, grouping these figures into those of a Latin American origin and those who come from Spain. While many of the writers we will mention are much better known within a specific genre (José Martí, for example, in poetry and journalism), some have also been practitioners of other genres and have at times been translators, editors of journals, professors, cultural animators, and so forth. A separate section is devoted to theater, and a number of the names already mentioned will appear there again. In *El poeta y la ciudad: Nueva York y los escritores hispanos* [1994; *The Poet and the City: Hispanic Writers and New York*] the author of this chapter studied numerous authors and works that will be discussed much more briefly in these pages. In addition, the bibliography lists a series of articles and essays that followed that book and in which the author traced in a historical fashion the relation between Hispanic poetry and New York City. Thus, although the pages that follow amount to no more than a very abridged approximation of certain authors and works that, because of their importance, really deserve a much fuller study, what is important here is to give a more panoramic picture of the intellectual and creative activity of New York's Hispanics; this is not, then, an analysis of these works.

The emergence of Latino literature in New York can be dated from the era during which the city saw the publication of the first ever anthology of Hispanic literature in exile, *El laúd del desterrado* [1858; The Outcast Lute] (see Kanellos 1997), and in which José Martí's magnificent book, *Versos libres* [Free Poems] (1882; published much later) and his literary and political journalism were written (1882–1891). The influence of New York City on the works of other nineteenth-century Spanish-American writers resident in the city was a relative one; this is the case with, for example, José María Heredia (1803–1839) (who published the first book of Spanish-language verse in the city in 1825) and Juan Clemente Zenea (1832–1871) (also from Cuba), both of whom were included in the aforementioned anthology, as well as with Juan A. Pérez Bonalde (1846–1892) (Venezuelan) and Lola Rodríguez de Tió (1843–1924) (Puerto Rican). On the other hand, the impress of the city was in the works of the Nicaraguan Rubén Darío (1867–1916) and the Mexican José Juan Tablada (1871–1945), two of whose most important books were published in the city: *El Jarro de Flores* [1922; The Flower Jug] and *La feria* [1928; The Fair, or The Market]. Other works that were first published in New York are the book by the Nicaraguan Salomón de la Selva (1893–1959), written in English, *Tropical Town and Other Poems* (1918), and *Desolación* [1922; Distress] by Gabriela Mistral (1889–1957), who died in Hempstead, New York. Later, the Chileans Humberto Díaz-Casanueva (1907–1992), Rosamel del Valle (1900–1965), and Nicanor Parra (b. 1914), and the Puerto Ricans Clemente Soto Vélez (1905–1993) and Graciany

Miranda Archilla (1908–1993), founders of the avant-garde group Atalaya, would come to New York.

Arriving in 1855 and remaining until 1872 (with a brief return to Colombia in 1856–1857), Rafael Pombo (1833–1912) resided in New York, first as a diplomat and later as a writer. He translated, created, and adapted a number of children's fables that would be published by the New York house Appleton. Pombo knew Ralph Waldo Emerson and counted among his intimates Henry Wadsworth Longfellow, with whom he corresponded for more than nine years, and whose poem "The Psalm of Life" he translated into Spanish. A number of Pombo's most important works were written here, including a Diary [1855; Diario] recounting his experiences in the United States, "Hora de tinieblas" ["The Twilight Hour"], his most representative philosophical poem, and his famous "En el Niágara" ["In the Niagara"]. In addition, Pombo published a sonnet written in English in the U.S. review Post (Orjuela 69–79, 142–49).

As a literary curiosity, the works of the Mexican politician and poet Guillermo Prieto, pseud. Fidel (1818–1897), can also be mentioned; his Viaje a los Estados Unidos [1877; Voyage to the United States] includes some poems composed in the United States. A number of Prieto's journalistic pieces written in New York are of interest because they contain some information about the Hispanic literary ambience of the city. For example, in his diary he writes:

El señor Pérez Bonalde es un hombre de treinta y cinco años, venezolano también [el otro escritor mencionado anteriormente es Jacinto Gutiérrez y Coll], alto, blanco, de frente despejada, insinuante y afable. El señor Bonalde está dedicado al comercio, sus ocios los entrega a la literatura y cultiva con muy buen éxito la poesía. Posee varios idiomas, y entre ellos el alemán, con notable perfección. La dote más sobresaliente de su alma, es la admiración por el ajeno mérito. Exento de toda pretensión, ignorante con sinceridad de su elevado mérito, hizo culto de su cariño a Heine, y el gran poeta ha tenido un intérprete fiel de sus inspiraciones singulares. La traducción de las poesías del Voltaire alemán, hechas por el señor Pérez Bonalde, acaba de ver la luz pública en Nueva York, en medio de los entusiastas elogios de la prensa. (123–24)

Señor Pérez Bonalde is a man of thirty-five years, also Venezuelan (Prieto has just mentioned Jacinto Gutiérrez y Coll), tall and fair, with a clear brow, and a sly and affable disposition. Señor Pérez Bonalde is a man of commerce, but his leisure time is devoted to literature, which he cultivates with great success in his poetry. He speaks a number of languages, among them German, with remarkable perfection. His most outstanding gift, however, is his admiration for the merits of others. Exempt from every pretension, sincerely ignorant of his own great talents, he makes a worship of his affection for Heine, and that great poet has found in him a faithful interpreter of his unique images. The translation of the "German Voltaire's" verse made by Señor Pérez Bonalde has just been published in New York to the most enthusiastic praise in the local press.

The residence in the city of the Cuban writer Cirilo Villaverde (1812–1894) (from 1849 to 23 October, 1894, although with a number of trips of both long and short duration to other places in the United States as well as to Cuba) is very significant because it was in New York that Villaverde wrote his most important novel, a denunciation of slavery, Cecilia Valdés, o la loma del ángel [Cecilia Valdés, or Angel's Hill], published in New York in 1882. Villaverde not only

edited the separatist periodical La verdad, but was the editor of a number of other reviews and periodicals, including La América, Frank Leslie's Magazine, La ilustración americana, and El Espejo, as well as a contributor to the journals La familia, El avisador hispanoamericano, El Fígaro, and Revista cubana. In addition to these journalistic activities, Villaverde was also a translator of a number of writers, including Charles Dickens.

The Cuban writer José Martí towers over the historical panorama of Hispanic literature in New York City as a kind of foundational figure, a literary patriarch. Both in his poetry and in his prose works, Martí established a horizon that will forever be a point of necessary reference. His sharp observations on U.S. society and culture in the 1880s constitute an enormous literary corpus that demonstrates in large measure his modernity. Arriving in the city in the flower of his youth on 3 January 1880, on the cusp of his 27th birthday, Martí would wear many hats during his years in New York: professor, journalist, children's writer, consul, clerk, translator, and political ideologue of Cuban Independence. He would also edit the journal La América, found the revolutionary periodical Patria, publish two books of verse, Ismaelillo (1882) and Versos sencillos [1891; Unaffected Verses], leave behind after his departure two unpublished verse collections, "Versos libres" and "Flores del destierro" ["Flowers of Exile"], as well as write and publish in the city one of his first modernista novels, Amistad funesta: Lucía Jerez [1885; Ill-fated Friendship]. Martí remained in New York (with visits to and periods of residence in other U.S. cities and other countries) until 1895.

Among the Latin American intellectuals who resided in New York during the nineteenth century there are a number of others who should be mentioned: the Puerto Rican Eugenio María de Hostos (1839–1903); the Argentinean Domingo Faustino Sarmiento (1811–1888), who arrived in New York in 1865 and remained in the United States until 1868, and who took a great interest in the institutions and literary life of the nation (his diary Diario de un viaje de Nueva York a Buenos Aires [1944; Diary of a Voyage from New York to Buenos Aires] is based on these experiences); the Venezuelan Nicanor Bolet Peraza (1838–1906), whose cultural mentorship and enthusiasm were important and whose house was the headquarters of the Sociedad Literaria Hispanoamericana de Nueva York (Shearer 49–50); and Arturo Alfonso Schomburg (1874–1938), the Puerto Rican writer and bibliophile (whose English works form part of the African-American intellectual history of the United States).

Rubén Darío visited New York on a number of occasions—in 1893, 1907, and for several months between the end of 1914 and the beginning of 1915—and wrote there a number of poems, some of them taking up the theme of the city. In 1893, Darío was received into New York's Cuban community led by José Martí. In his El viaje a Nicaragua [Voyage to Nicaragua], Darío wrote: "Pasé por la metrópoli yanqui cuando estaba en pleno hervor una crisis financiera. Sentí el huracán de la Bolsa. Vi la omnipotencia del multimillonario y admiré la locura mormónica de la vasta capital del cheque" (1919a, 2) ("I passed through the Yankee metropolis when it was in the full boil of a financial crisis. I experienced the full force of the Stock Market hurricane. I witnessed the omnipotence of the multi-millionaire and admired the mammonic madness of the immense capital of the checkbook"). Darío, despite being endowed with a cosmopolitan outlook, was basically a poet of Parisian sensibility and genuinely Spanish-American sensitivities. Thus, despite all his attempts, Manhattan ultimately remained a lusterless city for Darío; in his essay on Poe written in New York he stated: "Se cree oír la voz de New York, el eco de un vasto soliloquios de cifras. (Cuán distinto de la voz de París. . . !)" (1918, 19) ("One thinks one hears the voice of New York, the echo of an immense soliloquy of ciphers. How distinct from the voice of Paris. . . !"). On his last trip to the city, Darío published a number of pieces in the New York daily *La Prensa*. However, despite having partially integrated into New York cultural life, his poem "La gran cosmópolis" ["The Great Cosmopolis"] well illustrates his discomfort with the city (1919b, 35–39).

In the twentieth century, writers from every country in Latin America took up residence in or passed through New York. Among numerous possible examples, the Dominican Pedro Henríquez Ureña (1884–1946) comes to mind. Editor of the New York periodical *Las novedades*, Ureña published his book *El nacimiento de Dionisos* [The Birth of Dionysus] in the city in 1916. Another important writer, for whom the experience of the great metropolis appears to have been quite different from that of Darío, was the Mexican José Juan Tablada. First arriving in flight from the dictator General Victoriano Huerta, he stayed in New York four years (1914–1918); later, he came back for an extended residence between 1920 and 1935, and finally returned, for reasons of health, in 1944, the year before his death (in New York). Tablada not only published his most significant work in New York, but was also an active Hispanist, re-creating in the city, through various U.S. and Spanish-American journals, a Mexican artistic panorama and opening the bookstore known as Libros Latinos on East 28th Street. In 1945, a month after his death, Octavio Paz delivered a homage to Tablada in Manhattan, highlighting the fascination the poet had for travel and flight, in the sense of continual exile: "fuga de sí mismo y fuga de México" ("flight from himself, flight from Mexico"), Paz wrote. As he describes in his travel diary "Nueva York de día y de noche (313–25) [New York by Day and Night], New York signified for Tablada this condition of flight because it was a permanent jack-in-the-box where nothing was static or definitive. We may see in him the first Latin American literary nomad of the twentieth century, a writer who made the U.S. metropolis his most frequent place of transit.

Within the Spanish American context, the three most important and influential points of reference for the literature written in New York are Puerto Rican, Cuban, and Dominican writers. Arriving in New York by and large because of economic reasons, the Puerto Ricans have had an attitude to the English language that has been one of both resistance and assimilation. For their part, the Cubans, in the majority of cases, came to the Big Apple for political reasons, and although there would be no lack of frustration with the condition of exile, including a critical attitude toward the big city, as refugees they have been much more acquiescent to the host country. If we recall that half of the present-day population of Puerto Rico resides in New York, it can be understood that for these writers the fundamental condition is not that of exile, as it is for the Cubans, but rather that of a "doubling" of the spiritual and intellectual field, divided between Puerto Rico and New York. The Dominicans, for their part, constitute a group whose presence and influence (both in Spanish and in English) is becoming more important day by day.

The figure of Julia de Burgos can be taken as representative of the historical tensions experienced by the Puerto Ricans in New York. On the one hand, in her work we encounter a multi-leveled search for an identity: personal, as a woman; literary, as a poet; and political, as a partisan of Independence. The tempestuous biographical trajectory of her life (1914–1953) is directly tied to her poetic production. Born into a family of modest means in a working-class part of the town of Carolina, she studied at normal school in San Juan, Puerto Rico, where she discovered what would be a lifelong social and political commitment to the people of Puerto Rico. She went through a number of stormy love affairs and ended tragically dying of alcoholism in New York before she was thirty-six. Burgos's long residence in New York (eleven and a half years, first in 1940, and later between 1942 and 1953) is principally reflected in the fourteen poems she wrote in the city and in her correspondence. Margarite Fernández Olmos, in her *Sobre la literatura puertorriqueña de aquí y de allá: aproximaciones feministas* [1989; On the Puerto Rican Literature of Here and There: A Feminist Approach], situates Julia de Burgos at the point of transition between those poets who resided in Puerto Rico and wrote in Spanish, and those poets who lived in New York and who sometimes wrote in English or in a mix of the two languages. This question of a divided Puerto Rican literature has been much debated, and José Luis González (1926–1997), for example, in his *El país de cuatro pisos y otros ensayos* [1980; *Puerto Rico: The Four-Storeyed Country, and Other Essays* (1990)], has demystified the various views of a Puerto Rican cultural homogeneity. Julia de Burgos played a very important role in Puerto Rican literature: Without losing her sense of being completely Puerto Rican, she opened up the possibility for other Puerto Rican writers to compose poetry in English, as she herself had done at the end of her life in her poem "Farewell in Welfare Island." Arcadio Díaz Quiñones, commenting on *Puerto Rican Voices in English. Interviews with Writers* (published in 1997), has remarked: "la fuerza de estas voces hace posible replantear la rigidez de una construcción de la legitimidad cultural fija y prevista exclusivamente en la posesión del espacio insular, en la lengua española o en la ciudadanía norteamericana" (10) ("the vigor of these voices has made it possible to reconceive the rigid construction of a fixed cultural legitimacy, formulated exclusively in terms of the possession of an insular space, and transplant it into the Spanish language and Puerto Rican citizenry in the United States").

The New York poetry of the Cuban writer Eugenio Florit (born in Madrid in 1903, moved to Cuba in 1918, later to New York in 1940, and finally in the 1980s to Miami, where he died in 1999) has grown out of a conversational style evocative of a sharp Catholic-existential consciousness entirely free from any rhetorical tendencies. In his *Antología penúltima* [1970; Penultimate Anthology], in a section entitled "Intermedio de Manhattan" ["Manhattan Interlude"], we can find one of Florit's most important and emblematic poems of the 1960s, "Los poetas solos de Manhattan" ["The Solitary Poets of Manhattan"], in which he portrays the essential solitude of the human condition within the metropolitan multitude. Similarly, in the poem "En la ciudad grande" ["In the Big City"], a poetic response to José Martí's "Amor de ciudad grande" ["Metropolitan Passion"], Florit reflects on the human condition from a position of serenity, solitude, and Christian stoicism that he opposes to the rat-race life–contaminating everything, including love–of New York City. Florit also played an important role in New York cultural life as a translator of U.S. poetry and as a cultural animator from his professorship at Columbia University; his final New York book was *De tiempo y agonía–Versos del hombre solo* [1974; *Of Time and Anguish–Poems of a Solitary Man*].

Following in the footsteps of Rafael Pombo, one of the first Colombian writers to come to New York, many other

Colombian authors would pass through or take up residence in the city. Eduardo Márceles Daconte (b. 1942), in his book *Narradores colombianos en U.S.A.* [1993; *Colombian Writers in the U.S.*], has pointed out that José Eusebio Caro (1817–1853) also spent a time in New York, that José María Vargas Vila (1860–1933) founded there the journal *Hispanoamérica*, published until 1905, and that the poet Porfirio Barba Jacob (1883–1942) made New York his home between 1919 and 1921. Other important Colombian writers to be mentioned in this context are José Eustasio Rivera (1888–1928), author of *La vorágine* [1924; *The Vortex*], who died in the city, and the *Nadaísta* poets Amílkar U (Osorio) (1940–1985) and Elmo Valencia, both of whom lived the life of the Beat generation. Valencia would write an important prose poem on his New York experiences entitled "Extraña visión" ["Strange Vision"].

The position taken by social poetry with New York City as a theme is, at times, overly simplistic and has continually fallen back on the use of platitudes in poems that certainly contain an expected political-social message (as is the case with the Spanish poet Rafael Alberti, although the same can be said of the sporadic allusions to the city in the works of Pablo Neruda [1904–1973]). However, the use of such clichés does little to communicate the real complexity of the U.S. metropolis. In 1971 Nicolás Guillén (1902–1989) composed a sonnet entitled "A las ruinas de Nueva York" ["To the Ruins of New York"], in which he summons up a tradition of meditations on the ruins of great cities, following, in particular, in a genealogy stemming from Rodrigo Caro's (1573–1647) "Canción a las ruinas de Itálica" ["Lyric on the Italic Ruins"]. However, there is little, if anything at all, in the works of these three great writers bearing upon Spanish-language cultural activity in the city of New York.

The Nicaraguan poet Ernesto Cardenal's (b. 1925) poetic chronicle, "Viaje a Nueva York" ["Voyage to New York"], however, is a different case. In this work Cardenal employs a poetic narrative tradition in which the personal, the social, and the religious are intertwined, producing a vision of New York as the diabolical center of capitalism. A number of the topical themes worked into this poem by Cardenal had already been mined by García Lorca in his "Poet in New York" (1940), and would continue to be reproduced in a multitude of books on the city. The significance of this text, perhaps, lies in its documentary value: The poem reflects with a certain fidelity the ambience of 1970s New York, describing Cardenal's experience in the Nixon era and in the Gay Liberation movement; it is addressed to another Spanish American poet and novelist, the Chilean Enrique Lihn (1929–1988), who frequently visited New York and published in 1979 a book entitled *A partir de Manhattan* [*From Manhattan*]. The theme of the subway is Lihn's most constant preoccupation, and already in these texts Lihn signals the arrival of those who would in the 1980s become a multitude: the homeless.

In 1989 it was calculated that some 160 Hispanic writers lived in the New York City area; ten years later this number had likely doubled. In addition to countless poetry, short story, or novel-excerpt readings, as well as innumerable performances, conferences, and book launchings, every year New York holds a Spanish-language book fair. A number of U.S. publishers have begun issuing Spanish-language literary collections, including Penguin U.S.A., Ballantine, and Vintage (the latter in collaboration with Santillana), in which Latino, Latin American, and to a lesser extent Spanish authors are published in their original languages. Small Hispanic editorial houses and bookstores have existed in New York since the nineteenth century; in the twentieth century this situation continued, and two of these, Las Américas and Eliseo Torres (both are publishers and booksellers) have taken up important roles in the Latino cultural life of the city. Today, many would agree that Librería Lectorum and Macondo (both on East 14th Street in Manhattan) are the most important bookstores, although not the only ones. (As for the other Spanish-language editorial houses, given their limited size and publishing efforts, we will pass them by here.) In an article on the changing conditions of New York Hispanic poetic production, Jaime Giordano has written that

> If the Hispanic presence in New York in the 1970s drew attention to itself in the "street fights" of social and political protest groups like the *Young Lords* or the *Real Great Society*, the 1980s has been marked by the invasion of an elite that does not consider itself to be a wave of immigrants and that maintains strong ties to its countries of origin, returning there once or twice a year. This phenomenon is absolutely new in the history of immigration to the United States, and is due not only to the enormous differences between Hispanic and U.S. culture, but also to the great development that has been seen in the means of transportation and communication, as well as to the fact that it has been political conditions (dictatorship, dependency) and academic conditions (unpleasant material working conditions) that have motivated their move, conditions not considered to be irreversible and, thus, conditions favoring an outlook that is much more that of exiles than that of immigrants. The vigor with which these elites defend and cultivate the Spanish language is, in part, a result of the cohesive existence of this community of *foreigners* rooted in the U.S. and their stubborn defence of the cultural oases of the universities. (83)

Although Giordano refers in this article to the Hispanic writers who live in the "area" of New York, this notion of the New York area is somewhat difficult to define, as its coordinates are much more poetic than geographic. What can be said is that some of these writers, even though they do not live in New York City, do orbit around it, its Hispanic cultural centers, its journals, and its universities, and these institutions have, as Giordano points out, from the beginning of the twentieth century until the present day, played a fundamental role in the development of Hispanic literature written in New York.

From a historical point of view, 1977 was extremely significant for the Latino writers of New York, because it was in that year that the Centro para las artes OLLANTAY was founded. From its inception, the center was dedicated to the promotion of Hispanic artists residing in the New York City area, as its mission statement-manifesto published in March of that year underlines:

> We believe that there exists in New York City a poetry unlike the poetry of our countries of origin, a poetry in which the currents of Hispanic verse are transformed into something original and independent. For this reason we seek to uncover the roots of this fugitive and fleeting Tradition of Flight! This tradition perhaps lies buried in the recesses of the poetry of Heredia, Martí, Tablada, García Lorca, Florit, and many more unknown to us. For to create in a linguistic environment and in circumstances that are foreign to us transforms our poetry, and it is in this transformation that it is distinguished from the poetry that is produced in our countries of origin; it is for this reason that we make this announcement. We seek to discover and give a name to the characteristics of a poetry that can be written in the Spanish language in New York. (qtd. in Cañas 1994, 169–70)

Since 1977 OLLANTAY has sponsored a wide variety of meetings, lectures, theatrical presentations, and exhibitions and has published a number of books. This moment in the 1970s signified a particular coming to consciousness for many of the Hispanic writers residing in New York City. This new awareness was tied to the double recognition that they had to reopen the question of their own relation to the poetic tradition of their country of origin, and at the same time that their living in New York made them participants in a tradition that, as a coherent ensemble—and not as a series of isolated works or as works seen from within the poetic perspective of their respective countries—was, let us say, marginalized and forgotten: the tradition of Spanish-language poetry written in New York City. While recognizing that the authentication of place is a necessary and supplementary theme of their work, these writers of Spanish-language U.S. literature have yet to formulate the parameters in which that authentication might be accomplished.

The contingent of New York Puerto Rican, Cuban, and Dominican writers, from three of the city's most important Hispanic groups, calls for an extensive and particularized study of its own. Nevertheless, a number of these poets and prose writers have already appeared in numerous anthologies (some of them published in Spain), and critical attention, both inside and outside the United States, has recently begun to be paid to their works. The account that follows will deal with writers from other Spanish-American countries resident in New York. Before that task can be begun, however, a number of essential writers, and beginning with the Puerto Ricans of this group, must at least be mentioned: Iván Silén (b. 1944), Manuel Ramos Otero (1948–1990), Giannina Braschi (b. 1954), Marithelma Costa (b. 1955), Pedro López Adorno (b. 1954), among others. In 1994 the Ollantay Press of New York published a collection of essays entitled *Lo que no se ha dicho* [That Which Has Been Left Unsaid], in which a significant portion of the Cuban literary production in exile was studied. Of the New York Cubans, Octavio Armand (b. 1946) (no longer, but for some time, resident here) and José Kozer (b. 1940) were singled out for special attention. It needs to be stressed that in both the Cuban and the Puerto Rican literature of today, the poetic work of women constitutes one of the most significant and interesting creative forces. The anthology *Poetas cubanas en Nueva York* [Cuban Women Poets in New York] was published in Spain in 1991; included in it were the five excellent writers Magali Alabau (b. 1945), Alina Galliano (b. 1950), Lourdes Gil (b. 1951), Maya Islas (b. 1947), and Iraida Iturralde (b. 1954). Among Dominican poets, Alexis Gómez Rosa (b. 1950), resident in New York since 1985, is the best known. In the last few years he has published *Contra la pluma la espuma. Poemas 1980–1986* [1990; Foam Against the Feather: Collected Poems 1980–1986], *Tiza & Tinta (Antología poética)* [1991; Chalk & Ink: An Anthology], *New York City en tránsito de pie quebrado* [1990; Crossing New York City on Broken Feet ("feet" in a metrical sense)], and *Si Dios quiere y otros poemas* [1992; God Willing, and Other Poems]. Rosa's poetry is a continual meditation on the poetic phenomenon, writing, language, self-identity, and time. Among the group of Spanish-language Dominican writers, Angel Rafael Lamarche (1900–1962) (who published his first stories in New York in the 1950s), Viriato Sención (b. 1941), Tomás Modesto (b. 1951), Juan Rivero (b. 1940), Daisy Cocco de Filippis (b. 1949), José Carvajal (b. 1961), Juan Torres (b. 1955), and León Félix Batista (b. 1964) are particularly interesting. The New York

journal *Brújula-Compass* dedicated a special issue in the winter of 1998 to Dominican writers living in the United States.

With regard to other parts of Latin America, let us consider the Peruvian novelist and poet Isaac Goldemberg (b. 1945), who took up residence in the city in 1965. Goldemberg's double origin, as a Jew and a Peruvian Amerindian, placed him in the precarious position of being a *Hombre de Paso* (Man of Passage), the title he gave to a book he published in the United States in 1981. With a language that is at once direct and mythic, Goldemberg's work is endowed with the psalmodic power of the Bible and the simple and profound wisdom of the Amerindian oral tradition of the natives of Peru. In 1992, he published another book of poems, *La vida al contado* [Life: Cash on Delivery]. A similar response to the big city life, although at a much more intellectual and hermetic level, has been that of Roberto Echavarren (b. 1944), resident in New York since the middle of the 1970s and a writer who, in recent years, lives with one foot in Uruguay and one in the United States. During the years he lived in New York, Echavarren published two books of verse, *La planicie mojada* [1981; The Moist Plain] and *Animalaccio* [1985; Beast]. The works of Raúl Barrientos (Puerto Montt, Chile, 1942) offer us a more referential world, although one charged with imagination. He published his first book of poetry in the United States in 1981, *Ese mismo sol* [That Sun Itself], and since the fall of Allende in 1973 has wandered throughout various locales of the United States. Closely connected to a group of Spanish American poets writing in New York, where he himself now resides, Barrientos published *Libro de las imágenes* [Image Book], a collection of his most significant work to date, in 1989. Two more books have appeared, *Monarca* [1997; Monarch] and *Llave de néon* [1998; The Key of Neon]. The Colombian writer Jaime Manrique (b. 1949) came to the United States when he was eighteen and has lived in New York since 1982. A number of his novels have been published there, the most recent of which is *Twilight at the Equator* (1997). Although Manrique wrote his latest two novels in English, when it comes to poetry he writes in Spanish; *My Night with Federico García Lorca/Mi noche con Federico García Lorca* (bilingual edition, 1997) is his most recent book of verse. It is also necessary to take note of two more writers from Ecuador who have recently made important contributions to the cultural life of New York City: Jaime Montesinos (b. 1938) and Petrorio Rafael Cevallos (b. 1953). In addition to those writers from other countries we have already mentioned, or will soon mention, the Argentinean Manuel Puig (1932–1990), a large number of whose works were written in New York, and the Cuban Reinaldo Arenas, born in 1943, who took his life in the city in 1990, are among the prominent writers because consideration of their *oeuvres* cannot be reduced solely to a discussion of poetry and prose but must also include an account of their works in other genres such as theater.

One of the most important literary phenomena of the last decades has been the poetry and literature of the "Nuyorican" group. Nuyorican poetry had its origin at the end of the 1960s and the beginning of the 1970s, and culminated in 1975 with the publication of the anthology *Nuyorican Poetry: An Anthology of Puerto Rican Words and Feelings.* On the Lower East Side of Manhattan one can still find the Nuyorican Poet's Café, the former meeting place for these writers. *Aloud: Voices from the Nuyorican Poet's Café* (1994) was the final anthology of works that came out of the scene at this already mythic meeting place. Latino literature written in English is an area of letters that is being assimilated into the U.S. book publishing industry, and it can be said that it has very recently become something of a vogue. Names like Oscar Hijuelos (b. 1951), Julia Álvarez (b. 1950), Ed Vega (b. 1938), Piri Thomas (b. 1928), Cristina García (b. 1958), Sandra Cisneros (b. 1954), and Junot Díaz (b. 1968) are already familiar to U.S. readers. The phenomenon of writers whose background is Hispanic but who either were born or grew up in the United States is so complex that neither the historians nor the literary critics yet have been able to come to a consensus on how to "classify" such figures. Are they U.S. writers whose themes are related to their Hispanic roots, or are they simply writers whose narratives may be in English but whose cultural ambit is Latin American? Arcadio Díaz Quiñones, referring to Puerto Rican English language writers, has advanced a possible answer to this question:

La literatura aquí transita por tiempos y espacios diversos. Hay otra topografía social y cultural que cuestiona los viejos modos de pensar lo *nacional* y desjerarquiza las tradicionales legitimaciones de lo literario. La existencia de las comunidades puertorriqueñas implica, por un lado, la dificultad de imaginar una autosuficiente cultura situada en un único territorio con el tiempo histórico lineal y continuo. Por otro, una nueva espacialización de la memoria que desmiente cualquier ilusión de una *integración* fácil a la cultura norteamericana. (10)

Here, literature moves between diverse times and spaces. There is here another social and cultural topography that questions the old modes of thinking the *national*, and de-hierarchizes the traditional legitimations of the literary. The existence of the U.S. Puerto Rican communities implies, on the one hand, the difficulty of imagining a self sufficient culture situated in a unique place within a linear historical continuum. On the other hand, it also implies a new spatialization of memory that belies every illusion of a facile *integration* into the U.S. culture.

The precursors of this wave of English language novels by U.S. Hispanics were figures like the nineteenth-century María Amparo Ruiz de Burton (1832–1895), with *Who Would Have Thought It?* (1872), and, in the next century, George Santayana (1863–1952) with his novel *The Last Puritan: A Memoir in the Form of a Novel* (1935) (see Kanellos 1997). With the publication in 1989 of *The Mambo Kings Play Songs of Love*, and its garnering the Pulitzer prize that same year, Oscar Hijuelos (b. 1951) raised this strong Latin-flavored tradition to the highest level of respect it has ever seen. There are over a hundred important Hispanic fiction writers, writing in Spanish or English, spread out over the vastness of the continental United States; many of them can be indexed in the *Biographical Dictionary of Hispanic Literature in the United States/Diccionario Biográfico de la Literatura Hispana en los Estados Unidos*.

The peninsular Spanish writers who passed through or remained for a longer time in New York did so for a wide array of reasons, but almost every one of them, sooner or later, has written an account of his/her New York experience. Similarly, the impact of New York has become, within our imagination, a literary commonplace (whether or not the city has been visited), and thus poets such as Rafael Alberti (1902–2002); the novelist Camilo José Cela (1916–2002), with his unfortunate book of poems *Viaje a U.S.A.* [1967; Voyage to the U.S.A.]; José Hierro (b. 1922), in his last book *Cuaderno de Nueva York* [1998; New York Notebook]; and, among others, Luis García Montero (b. 1958) have all written texts whose central theme is some aspect of Manhattan. In the field of

prose, also, many books have been written about New York by Spanish writers: Joaquín Belda's (1883–1935) *En el país del bluff, veinte días en Nueva York* [1926; The Land of the Bluff: 20 Days in New York], Julio Camba's (1882–1962) *Un año en el otro mundo* [1947; A Year in the Other World], Diego Hidalgo's (b. 1888) *Nueva York: impresiones de un español del siglo XIX que no sabe inglés* [1947; New York: Impressions of a Nineteenth-Century Spaniard Who Speaks No English], Josep Pla's (1897–1981) *Viaje a América* [1960; Voyage to America] (the poet lived in New York in 1954 and published in 1987 *Weekend (d'estiu) a Nova York* [Weekend in Nova York]), José María Carrascal's (b. 1930) *Groovy* (1973), Carmen Martín Gaite's (1925–2000) *Caperucita en Manhattan* [1990; The Adventures of Little Red Riding Hood in Manhattan], Carlos Perellón's (b. 1957) *La ciudad doble* [1995; The Double City], and a book by one of the most important cultural promoters of the last decade, José María Conget's (b. 1948) *Cincuenta y tres y Octava* [1997; 53rd and 8th]. The extremely interesting case of the Spaniard Felipe Alfau (1902–1999), who lived in New York from 1916 on and published two novels in English, *Locos* (1936) and *Chromos* (1948), also deserves mention. In the last few years these works have been reissued to considerable critical acclaim. However, while it is difficult to place this author within the U.S. narrative tradition, the same can be said vis-à-vis the Spanish tradition.

Although the two best known Spanish poets to have written pieces on New York are García Lorca and Juan Ramón Jiménez, a number of other Spanish poets have passed through the city, including Dámaso Alonso (1898–1952), León Felipe (1884–1968), Jorge Guillén (1893–1984), Concha Espina (1869–1955), Pedro Salinas (1892–1951), and José Moreno Villa (1887–1955). Moreno Villa, who was in New York on a couple of occasions in 1927 and 1937, published two New York-related books, one in prose, *Pruebas de Nueva York* [1927; New York Proofs], and one in verse, *Jacinta la pelirroja* [1929; Jacinta the Red-Haired Woman]; this latter inaugurated the use of conversational turns of phrase in Spanish poetry. In the last few years a couple of other books of verse have been published: J. M. Fonollosa's (1922–1991) *Ciudad del hombre: New York* [1990; City of Man: New York] and a bilingual book by the previously mentioned Catalan novelist, Felipe Alfau: *Sentimental Songs: La poesía cursi* [1992]. Juan Ramón Jiménez (1881–1958) came to New York on 12 February, 1916, and remained for almost six months. The book he partially wrote during his stay in Manhattan, *Diario de un poeta recién casado* [Diary of a Recently Married Poet], made a significant contribution to the Spanish poetry of the time and became a point of reference for the fundamental shift in Jiménez's work that dates from this moment in his career. Jiménez bequeathed to the Spanish-language poetic tradition of the city, a much less moralistic and less negative vision than that of José Martí (1853–1895) and Rubén Darío (1867–1916), and later García Lorca (1898–1939). Distancing himself from ideological preoccupations, Jiménez traced the outward face of the city with a great deal more freedom than his predecessors. The advertising landscape and illuminated "signscape" of New York produced in Jiménez a sensation of unreality, in which the city was doubled by the mutual reflection of the actuality of the streets and the graphic world of advertising that mocked it, writing its parody in neon signs traced against the nighttime sky. It is hardly surprising, then, that Jiménez writes in his farewell to the city: "New York, como una realidad no vista o como una visión irreal" ("New York, a reality unseen or an unreal vision") "Despedida sin adiós" ("Farewell without Good-bye"). What is more surprising is the characterization in the poem "De Boston a New York" ["From Boston to New York"]: "¡New York, maravillosa New York! ¡Presencia tuya, olvido de todo!" ("New York, marvelous New York! Presence of your own, complete oblivion!"). Contradictions of this sort can also be found in Lorca's *Poet in New York*, poetry between a negative and shattered vision of the city and a positive, childlike exaltation. As Octavio Paz has pointed out, Jiménez's "Espacio" ["Space"] is one of the most important texts of twentieth-century Spanish writing. In 1941, twenty-five years after his visit to the city, Jiménez began his finalization of "Espacio," bringing to completion, in the second fragment of the poem, his vision of the great city.

During his nine-month residence in New York, between 1929 and 1930, Federico García Lorca wrote the poems that would become a fundamental and emblematic work for twentieth-century Hispanic poetry: *Poeta en Nueva York* [*Poet in New York*]. This is a book whose echoes can still be heard today in much of the city's Latino poetry. In 1997 the New York journal *ñ* inaugurated a new award, the Premio Internacional de Poesía–"Poeta en Nueva York" (there already being a Federico García Lorca Prize in the city)—and we can read in this an index of the influence that García Lorca's book has had and continues to have on the Latino writers of the city. García Lorca knew how to capture, better than any other, the commercial violence, the social injustice, the racial discrimination, and the lack of consoling spirituality that characterizes life in New York. On the other hand, both in the letters written from New York and in the lectures he gave introducing his New York poems to the Spanish audience, there is a clearly marked double tension between admiration and contempt animating García Lorca's feelings about New York and New York society in general. This famous book is the subject of many critical studies, including a section of my own *El poeta y la ciudad* [The Poet and the City], and this is not the place to delve deeper into its problematics. What should be underlined, however, is that if José Martí is the founding father of Hispanic literature in New York, García Lorca is the modern poet who best embodies the Hispanic spirit of New York throughout the twentieth century.

In 1956 Odón Palacios Betanzos (b. 1926) arrived in New York, publishing there his first book of verse, *Santidad y Guerrería* [1969; *Sanctity and Belligerence*] and the majority of the rest of his works. Betanzos is the director of the Academia Norteamericana de la Lengua Española (founded in 1973), and plays an important role as a cultural promoter. Beginning in the 1970s a new generation of Spanish writers began establishing themselves in New York. The author of this article, Dionisio Cañas (b. Tomelloso, 1949), has resided in the city since 1972 and written all his critical and literary work here. Octavio Zaya (b. Las Palmas, 1954) has resided in the city since 1978; his first book of verse, *Aproximación de la manera más abrupta* [1982; *The Most Abrupt Approach*] was written in collaboration with his twin brother. While in the last few years Zaya has dedicated himself almost exclusively to art criticism and journalism, a number of his poems (some of them in English) have appeared in exhibition catalogues and art journals.

The abundant tradition of Spanish-language poetry written in or about New York City was enriched in the 1980s with two new books: *Balada de la misericordia* [1989; The Ballad of Mercy]

by Luis Moliner (b. Lumpiaque, 1949) and *Puer Profeta* [Boy Prophet] (winner of the Adonais Prize, 1989) by Juan Carlos Marset (b. Albacete, 1963). These two collections have moved their respective authors to the front ranks of new Spanish poetry, both for their maturity and finesse and for the independent aesthetic they each embody, distancing their works from the known schools, groups, and literary coteries of peninsular Spanish verse. At the same time, however, they form part of the trajectory of Spanish voices that, for very diverse reasons, have found in the subject of the urban space of Manhattan a stimulating challenge, both from a poetic and from a social and personal perspective. The prize-winning collection, *Aquel mar de esta orilla* [That Sea of This Shore] (Premio de Poesía Hiperión, 1990) by Francisco Javier Ávila (b. Madrid/Chozas de Canales, 1961), marked the debut of one of the most interesting poetic voices of the new decade. This book is the product of an artist who, facing his experience of New York City, has opened up the question not only of his own identity as a Spaniard between two worlds (alluded to in the title of the collection, a free paraphrase from Juan Ramón Jiménez), but also of this moment and this place in history. Ávila's response is alternately critical, ironic, tender, and melancholic, but always endowed with a poetic surety and suggestiveness. In 1997 the Catalan poet Gabriel Planella published *New York, obert tota la nit*, and in 1998 the *Premio*. Moliner, Marset, and Ávila were all pursuing doctoral studies in New York when the aforementioned books were written, and have since returned to Spain to continue their careers. In 1998 the Premio Internacional de Poesía Gastón Baquero was awarded to Hilario Barrero (b. 1948), a Toledean poet who resides in New York, for his collection *In tempori belli*.

The subject of literary translations, both from English to Spanish and Spanish to English, is an extremely interesting one and important to an understanding of the role that New York has had and continues to have in the cultural relations between Latin America and the United States.

In the field of literary translation, political exiles and Latin American writers who have lived and still reside in New York and other cities of the eastern United States have made a valuable intellectual contribution to the emerging Spanish Language cultural presence. In the nineteenth century, the contribution of the Cuban writers who brought to the United States a rich wealth of experience in translation has been particularly distinguished. A number of intellectuals including Varela, Saco, Luz, y Caballero, from the island, as well as a large contingent of poets, novelists, journalists, and educators in the United States, have dedicated themselves to this work.

In various journals and periodicals published in New York since the middle of the last century, exiled Cuban writers published translations that aided the dissemination of the mosty outstanding works of world literature of the epoch. Among these translators several deserve mention for having translated into Spanish the works of important authors from English (Tennyson, Byron, Longfellow, Emerson, Poe, William Cullen Bryant), French (Hugo, Lamartine, Musset), and German (Schiller, Heine): José Agustin Quintero, Rafael Maria de Mendive, Juan Clemente Zenea, Rafael María Merchán, the brothers Antonio and Francisco Sellén, and José Martí. The brothers Sellén were particulary active in the diffusion of German lyric poetry: Francisco published in 1875 the first Spanish translation of Heine's *Intermezzo litrico* [Lyrical Intermezzo] and, in 1881 he published in New York the anthology of German Romantic verse, *Ecos del Rin* [Echoes of the Rhine], comprised of translations of 163 poems by 38 poets, a number of which were done by his brother Antonio. In 1875, also in New York, a Spanish version of Heine's *El cancionero* [Buch der Leider] was published, in a translation by the Venezuelan poet José Antonio Pérez Bonalde, who was then resident in the city.

The New York editorial house Appleton deserves mention for the exceptional role it played in engaging many of the exiled Hispanic writers as translators of a wide variety of, in general, technical and pedagogic texts, and as collaborators in the preparation of dictionaries. Figures like the Puerto Rican educator Eugenio María de Hostos, the Colombian Rafael Pombo, and José Martí, as well as other Cubans, were employed in this kind of work by Appleton.

In the twentieth century, the Spanish poet León Felipe's verse translation of Walt Whitman's poetry, known to Federico García Lorca during his residence in New York City before it was published in book form in 1941, seems to have played a seminal part in the writing of *Poeta en Nueva York*. The translations of the Puerto Rican writer Angel Flores, helped to make better known the great modern poets T. S. Eliot and Pablo Neruda. In 1930 Flores published the first authoritative Spanish version of Eliot's *The Waste Land* [*La Tierra baldía*]. Garcia Lorca, who was Flores' friend, read this translation while in New York. In 1946 Flores' English version of Neruda's *Residencia en la tierra* [Residence on Earth and Other Poems] was published.

Two anthologies opened up the readership for U.S. poetry in Latin America and for Latin American poetry in the U.S.: the *Anthology of Contemporary Latin American Poetry*, edited and translated by Dudley Fitts in 1942, and the *Antología de la poesia norteamericana comtemporánea*, edited and translated by the Cuban poet Eugenio Florit in 1954. These two books marked a watershed: they confirmed an interest in Latin American and peninsular Spanish letters that would deepen in the following decades, a body of literature that would occupy an important place in U.S. book sales. During this same period, Harriet de Onís brought out a number of English translations of a diverse array of Hispanic fiction writers, that further contributed to the high level of interest in the English-speaking world for Spanish-language literature.

Beginning in the 1960s an increasing number of Latin American works were translated into English; these versions made by professional translators were both critically well received and commercial best sellers. In this most recent phase of translation (dating up to the present), the contributions of Gregory Rabassa, Helen Lane, Donald Walsh, Robert Bly, Alastair Reid, W. S. Merwin, Ben Belitt, Nathaniel Tarn, and Hardie St. Martin, to mention only the most important, have been outstanding.

—*Orlando José Hernández*

Theater

Theatrical works began to be published in New York in the 1820s. Although the census of 1855 counted 231 actors in the city, three of whom were Spanish and one Latin American (Ernst 216), the first notice of a Hispanic theatrical production would appear in José Martí's periodical *Patria* in 1892. In general, the theater productions advertising in this paper were being staged, often by the Cuban actor Luis Baralt, in order to collect funds for the Cuban Independence movement. As the groups mounting these plays did not have a theater of their own, they were staged in places frequented by Spanish-speaking, and principally Cuban, immigrants: el Club Lírico Dramático Cubano and the Carnegie Lyceum Theater, for example. The last known performance of this kind in the nineteenth century took place in the Central

Opera House on 16 January 1899, with the aim of raising funds for the purchase of a tombstone for José Martí (see Kanellos 1990; 1993).

Latino theater was not seen again in New York until 1916. The promoter of this new wave of performances was the Spanish actor and *zarzuela* singer Manuel Noriega. In this year he founded the first Hispanic theatrical troop in the city, the Compañía Dramática Española, whose repertoire consisted of Spanish *comedias*, farces, and *zarzuelas*. In 1919 Noriega opened New York's first regular Hispanic theater, the Park Theater, which later changed its name to El Teatro Español (see Kanellos 1990; 1993; Miller).

During the 1920s and 1930s the number and frequency of Hispanic theatrical productions grew. A number of companies had their own theaters or signed contracts with theaters that gave them a measure of stability; this was the case with the Dalys, Apollo, San José/Variedades, and Campoamor theaters, as well as with the longest running of them all, El Teatro Hispano. The majority of the works staged, either by local companies such as La Compañía del Teatro Español, Compañía de Bufos Cubanos, Compañía Narcisín, or the Compañía Hispana de Nueva York, or by visiting groups from Cuba, Spain, Mexico, or the U.S. Southwest, continued to be melodramas, *comedias*, farces, and *zarzuelas* (again, see Kanellos 1990; 1993; Miller).

As John V. Antush has pointed out, "[t]he golden age of New York's Hispanic theater came during the 1920s and 1930s when it was predominantly Spanish and a vital part of the international cultural life of the city. The Spanish Civil War dissipated much of that cultural impact, and the Second World War almost snuffed out any cultural exchange between Spain and the United States for a time" (ix). Although the first Puerto Rican play written in New York, Gonzalo O'Neill's *Borinquen o bajo una sola bandera* [Puerto Rico: Under a Single Flag], was staged in 1929, local companies were not that interested in serious works written locally. From time to time works directly related to the local community were mounted, though these were almost always comedies, such as the Cuban farce *En la calle 116* [On 116th Street], by René Borgia. The Apollo Theater, located in the heart of Harlem on 125th Street, was the place where numerous Cuban opera *bufas* on New York Latino daily life were staged: *Mientras Nueva York duerme* [While New York Slumbers], *Bronca entre latinos* [The Quarrel Between Latinos], *Terremoto en Harlem* [The Harlem Earthquake], *Cuadro en el precinto* [Precinct Scenes], *Lo que hace el Black Bottom* [What Black Bottom Does], *Cosas de policías* [Police Business], *Kid Chocolate* (see Kanellos 1990). Despite the ephemeral nature of these productions, they were enjoyed by the working population of the immigrant community, and in their "local content" they did impart a certain unity to the Spanish-speaking community. Plays of this kind were also produced at the Teatro Variedades, works with titles like *Mosaico hispano* [Hispanic Mosaic], *Locuras de Nueva York* [New York Follies], and *Ecos de Harlem* [Harlem Echoes]. Nicolás Kanellos cites a review originally appearing in *La Prensa* (26 September 1933) that gives us a sense of this identification: "*Harlem Arrabalero* [The Other Side of the Tracks in Harlem] paints a picture of a typical night in the Latino quarter of Harlem–a farrago of marijuana, rumbles and stabbings, women, men and misery, cops and whistles, gunfire and blood. Very rarely has there ever been amassed and successfully presented in a single spectacle a more vivid description of what one imagines the Latino quarter of Harlem to be like" (1990, 129). In these theatrical shows and musical reviews (and many others like them: *De Puerto Rico a Nueva York* [From Puerto Rico to New York], *De México vengo* [I Came from Mexico], *Nueva York de noche* [New York Nights], and *Sucedió en Harlem* [It Happened in Harlem]), a tradition of addressing the themes of New York immigrant life began, a tradition that continues in the theatrical and literary works of today.

Although the general keynote struck in Latino theatrical representations of this era was fundamentally one of entertainment, they were not lacking in nationalist elements, in the form of political vindications and grievances over the cause of Puerto Rican Independence, or in social commentary, in general, and on the subject of racism, in particular. This "popular" tendency notwithstanding, local and visiting companies did produce, although without attracting large audiences, plays of a more serious character by authors such as Alejandro Casona (1903–1965) or Miguel de Unamuno (1864–1936). On the other hand, although Cuban and Spanish plays predominated in these decades, during the same years a Puerto Rican theater more committed to social and political causes also emerged, whose principal authors were Franca de Armiño (almost certainly a pseudonym), José Enamorado Cuesta, and Gonzalo O'Neill. In a similar manner, the Spaniard María (or Marita, Merita, or Mariita) Reid Masalla, whose bilingual upbringing (English father, Spanish mother) allowed her to alternate between the English- and Spanish-language theater scenes, played a fundamental role in the development of Hispanic theater in New York. Owing to her efforts, New York's Spanish-speaking audience was exposed to sophisticated theater; during the mid-1930s these performances were frequently in support of the Spanish Republican cause. Other, smaller groups such as Cultura Proletaria and Cuadro Artístico Proletario were, as their names suggest, also producing works inspired by political and social themes. In general, the intention behind the staging of many of these works was not only to entertain the public, but also to expose them, either before or after the performance, to political speeches. Important artists such as David Alfaro Siqueiros (1896–1974), for example, were involved in these events; at the Ateneo Hispano in May 1933, Siqueiros gave a lecture prior to the performance on "Art for the Masses" (see Kanellos 1990). According to the theater historian Pablo Figueroa:

> [t]here are two figures whose contributions to the first two decades of Spanish-speaking theater in New York stand out: the Spaniard Manuel Aparicio and the Cuban Edelmiro Borrás, both of whom continued working as actors into the 1960s and '70s. They were the ones to light the creative spark in the new generations of theatrical artists. Until his death in 1976 Borrás was known in the community as the Father of New York Hispanic theatre. (13)

In the 1940s musical revues continued their dominance of the Latino theater scene. Only a few centers, such as Barnard College (at Columbia University), under the leadership of Ángel del Río, Amelia Agostini, and the Cuban Luis Baralt, produced Spanish works. There was, nonetheless, no shortage of short-lived theater companies, such as the one started by the Dominican Rolando Barrera, Gala, and the Futurist Company. One interesting development in this period was the influence of the San Juan theatrical scene on New York: "During the 1940s one of the most sophisticated

national theaters in all Latin America was developing in Puerto Rico. When large numbers of Puerto Ricans migrated to the mainland in the 1940s and 1950s, they brought with them the seeds for a theater that would blossom in the 1960s and 1970s" (Antush ix). This movement was already in evidence in 1954 when one of the fundamental works on the issue of Puerto Rican immigration to New York was staged, *La carreta* [The Wheelbarrow], by René Marqués, a writer who had been a theater student at Columbia University and at Piscator's Dramatic Workshop in 1940. In 1956 Roberto Rodríguez and Miriam Colón formed El Círculo Dramático, one of the few groups of this epoch having its own theater. In this same year the first play in English on a Latino theme, Walter Anderson's *Innocent Me,* was staged (see Miller).

In the 1960s Hispanic theater maintained its high level of activity. John C. Miller has described the scene:

> The first half of the 1960s saw many theatrical companies and productions appear and disappear in a weekend. New playwrights appeared—Alvarado, Arriví [in Puerto Rico], Anteló, and Rodríguez, among them—as well as a cadre of professional actors and actresses: Miriam Colón, Raúl Juliá, and Carla Pinza. The year 1964 in which the New York Shakespeare Festival initiated plays in Spanish, and 1965 in which *La carreta* was produced off-Broadway and in which Chelsea Theater presented *Las ventanas* [*The Windows*] of Roberto Rodríguez, music re-entered the theater, not as in the review, but integrated into *La jíbara* [The Peasant], music by Bobbie Collazo. (25)

From 1965 on, three broad tendencies that are still in existence began to distinguish themselves: (1) a series of companies frequently related to European and Latin American theater groups and styles (INTAR, Puerto Rican Traveling Theater, Teatro Repertorio Español, Nuestro Teatro, Centro Cultural Cubano, Duo, Instituto Arte Teatral INTI, Latin American Theater Ensemble [LATE], Thalía (in Queens), the Tremont Art Group (in the Bronx), the Theater of Latin America, Inc. [TOLA]); (2) a group of popular and political street-theater companies (Teatro 4, Teatro Orilla, Teatro Jurutungo, Teatro Guazábara, and El Nuevo Teatro Pobre de América); and (3) a group of companies composing the Nuyorican theater movement (Aquarius, Latin Insomniacs, El Teatro Ambulante de Bimbo Rivas, Puerto Rican Organization for Self Advancement, Teatro Otra Cosa, The Family, and the Nuyorican Poet's Café), whose principal characteristic is the use of English, Spanish, or a mix of the two languages and whose greatest achievement has been Miguel Piñero's play *Short Eyes*. One significant aspect of some of these groups is their link to various poets; for example, Magali Alabau and Teatro Duo, Pedro Pietri and Latin Insomniacs, and all the poets of the Nuyorican Poet's Café (Miller).

In its entirety, and especially for those troupes with their own theaters, the range of Latino Spanish- or English-language theatrical productions in these years was very diverse, running the gamut from traditional and modern Spanish peninsular classics (*La Celestina*, Calderón de la Barca, Lope de Vega, Federico García Lorca, Fernando Arrabal) to Latin American plays and works more related to the Latino community of New York, such as *Carmencita, Swallows, Rice and Beans, El super* [The Superintendent], *Canciones de la vellonera* [Jukebox Hits], *Simpson Street, Tiempo de amor y guerra* [The Time of Love and War]. Miller sums up the panorama of recent Hispanic theater in New York thus: "since 1977 the following conclusions can be made. Young, creative playwrights exist and are occasionally produced–for example, Gallardo's *Simpson Street*–but too often their works are limited to staged readings" (32). Miller's conclusions notwithstanding, many of these new playwrights are today in full creative stride and have been produced with success: Randy Barceló (b. 1951), Migdalia Cruz (b. 1958), Moisés Kaufman (b. 1954), Edwin Sánchez (b. 1955), and Pedro R. Monge Rafuls (b. 1943) among them. The last of this group is the editor of the only Hispanic journal in New York dedicated to the theater, *OLLANTAY: Theater Magazine* (first published in January 1993).

In the last two decades of this century there have been a number of developments. Of the previously mentioned companies that got off the ground in the 1960s several are still going strong, including: INTAR (on 42nd Street), Puerto Rican Traveling Theater and the Repertorio Español (on 27th Street), the Thalia Spanish Theater and OLLANTAY (in Queens), the Nuyorican Poet's Café (3rd Street), and a number of cultural centers such as CHARAS (in lower Manhattan), the Centro para las artes y la cultura del Colegio Comunal Eugenio María de Hostos, the African Caribbean Theater, and Pregones Touring Puerto Rican Collective (all in the Bronx), and the Amistad World Theater. In 1988, New York counted thirty-four Hispanic theatrical organizations (Pottlitzer 35). Starting with the La Mama Theater in the 1970s, various organizations have opened their doors to productions realized by Spanish, Latin American, and local Latino theater groups. The support of Joseph Papp made possible the Latin American Popular Theater Festival and El Festival Latino held annually under the umbrella of the New York Shakespeare Festival's Public Theater. In addition, OLLANTAY sponsored the first Festival de Dramaturgia Española in New York in September 1997.

Two new phenomena that characterize the present-day state of Spanish-language theater in the city are the existence of theatrical workshops, held in many of the previously mentioned cultural centers, and the emergence of the genre of "performance" as a medium for the presentation of local Latino works. The Gas Station (now closed), led by the Spaniard Javier Domingo, was a meeting place for experimental productions and "performances" in the final years of the 1980s. A number of alternative spaces in the Tribeca and Soho neighborhoods, as well as the Mabou-Mines-Suite on 9th Street, still offer these kinds of theatrical experiences. In addition to the critics we have already cited in this section, the works of Mario Peña, Pablo Figueroa, José Monleón, Moisés Pérez Coterillo, and Manuel Martín have taken up the task of documenting the history of Spanish-language theater in New York; Martín, in the article (1997) cited in the bibliography to this chapter, lists a large number of the theater groups active today (11–37).

In pace with the rapidity of urban life, new Latino theater groups and organizations appear and disappear, virtually overnight. The strongest institutions, like the Repertorio Español, maintain their base by a combination of high-quality work and shrewd business instincts. Hispanic theater in New York, whether in Spanish, English, or Spanglish, possesses an indisputable vitality. The cosmopolitan and multicultural climate of New York has ensured that the range of Spanish-language theater to be seen in the city is much more varied than what is offered in Miami or Los Angeles. In 1998 the Repertorio Español mounted productions of the Cuban Senel Paz's (b. 1950) *Fresa y chocolate* [Strawberry and Chocolate] and García Lorca's *El público* [The Public], one more indication of the diversity we have referred to and also

of a political and aesthetic openness in New York's Hispanic theater scene. In spite of the spectacular flop of Paul Simon's *Cape Man*, 1998 was a particularly rich year for Hispanic theater. Two works in particular, *Forever Tango* by Luis Bravo and the Colombian John Leguizamo's monologue *Freak*, have received kudos in the English-language mainstream press.

At the beginning of this essay it was mentioned that the Spanish Jews were the first group to establish the presence of the Spanish language in New York, in the seventeenth century. The Ladino-speaking Sephardic community has kept its musical and oral traditions alive, and in February 1998 the Sephardic Home of Brooklyn produced the play *Hank Halio's Ladino Reveries*, interpreted by "The Ladino Players," in the synagogue on West 70th Street in Manhattan. In spite of being a costume drama recounting the experience of the Turkish and Greek Sephardic immigrants to New York in the first half of the twentieth century, the sound of that peculiar mix of fifteenth-century Spanish and English, sprinkled with Turkish and Greek words–something we might call "Ladinoenglish"–did not fail to move all those in attendance. In the final analysis, this modest New York Judeo-Hispanic theatrical event–and the various Judeo-Spanish songs that accompanied the performance, songs (or songs like them) that have been sung in the Sephardic community since their arrival in New York in the seventeenth century–forms part of the Latino theatrical panorama that we have attempted to sketch in these last few pages.

Music and Graffiti

In the first three decades of the twentieth century New York was a veritable laboratory of popular music. At the same time that jazz was invading the night clubs, Hispanic-Caribbean music was making its appearance in Manhattan. This musical movement, which would become common practice by the 1920s, was not viewed sympathetically by those who felt that the commercialization of Afro-Caribbean music undermined its national roots and spirit. Thus, in the 1940s, Alejo Carpentier in his *La música en Cuba* [1946; Music in Cuba] would claim that

> por una rara paradoja, la boga mundial que favoreció ciertos géneros bailables cubanos a partir de 1928, hizo un daño inmenso a la música popular de la isla. Cuando los editores de New York y de París establecieron una demanda continuada de *sones*, de *congas*, y de *rumbas*–designando cualquier cosa bajo este último título– impusieron sus leyes a los autores de una música ligera, hasta entonces llena de gracia y de sabor. Exigieron sencillez en la notación, una menor complicación de ritmos, un estilo *más comercial*. (360)

> by a peculiar paradox, the world's vogue for certain genres of Cuban dance music would, after 1928, do immense damage to the island's popular music. When the publishers of New York and Paris faced a constant demand for *sones*, congas, and rumbas–designating no matter what under this latter rubric–they foisted their laws on the creators of a light music, until then full of grace and agility. They demanded simplicity in the notation, a less complex matrix of rhythms, a *more commercial* style.

Even Rafael Cortijo Verdejo (1928–1982), the prince of Puerto Rican music, appears to have later "disowned salsa" forever, the ultimate consequence of the metamorphosis of Caribbean music into a decidedly New York style (Rodríguez Juliá 71). Despite this opposition to the commercialization of Caribbean rhythms, today it can be said that, thanks in large part to the commercial market and, it goes without saying, popular taste, the music of preference for New York's Latinos is the salsa. Let us examine in more detail how this musical form evolved in the city.

In the early phase of its development, New York Latino music remained confined to the ghetto. Latino musicians played for a Hispanic audience at private parties and at dances sponsored by community organizations. Economic factors, the high degree of technical and creative artistry of these musicians, and the ancestral affinity between Caribbean and African-American musical styles and forms meant that Caribbean musicians made sorties out of the Latin quarter in order to join American combos and orchestras, principally jazz groups. It should be recalled that, before the advent of jazz, in the nineteenth century Cuban rhythms formed part of the sound-scape of New Orleans and that among the pioneers of early jazz at least twenty four had Hispanic family names (Storm Roberts 36–37). These relations between different musicians and different music resulted in what came to be known in the twentieth century as Latin jazz, a style that continues to be played not only by Latinos but also by Anglo American musicians to this day. The Latin-quarter musicians were participants in the Harlem jazz club scene as well as playing at hotels, parties, and concerts for a select white New York audience.

However, popular recognition of the music of the Latino immigrants began with its "dance" forms. Theatrical and cinematic spectacles have contributed to this popularity. A notable development was the inclusion of Latino themes in movie musicals depicting a Hollywood vision of the universe "south of the border." Carmen Miranda, Xavier Cugat, and Desi Arnaz, among others, became North American re-creations and personifications of the Latino world. Already in the 1920s, from Buenos Aires via Paris, Argentine tangos were making a splash on Broadway. The popularity of ballroom dancing in North America opened the door for the easy acceptance throughout the entire twentieth century of the tango, the rumba, the conga, and the samba (in the 1930s) and of the mambo, the cha-cha, and calypso (from the end of the 1940s). The 1950s phenomenon of mambo mania contributed, perhaps, more than any other event to the recognition of a distinct "Latin" sound. What is interesting is that the mambo that was popularized in the Manhattan night club, the Palladium, was already a syncretization of Afro-Cuban rhythmic structures and the "big band" sound (Storm Roberts 123), and that the mambo as a dance form integrated steps from the lindy and other North American dances. In the 1960s the bossa nova arrived from Brazil and left its melodic and rhythmic impression on jazz music. Also in this decade there appeared for a short time the rhythmic form of the "boogaloo," an attempt to combine rhythm and blues with jazz and Latin sounds.

The recording industry, interested in the commercial possibilities, took measures to popularize these musical forms, simplifying and altering the musical structures in order to make Hispanic music a more salable commodity. The result was the "invention" of "Latin music": an exotic musical commodity denoting color and sensuality that corresponded to the stereotype of the Latino as a "natural" musician (just as had been the case with African-American music and musicians). The repertoire of Latin music was commercialized and assimilated in order to attract a North American audience. Songs with Latin names and rhythms ("Papa Loves Mambo," "Italian Mambo"), and English versions of "international" boleros ("Qué será, será," "Quiéreme mucho," "Aquellos ojos verdes," etc.), sung by North American balladeers, began to appear. The complex rhythmic structure of Latin music was converted, thus, into background raw material for pop arrangements.

Meanwhile, in Spanish Harlem and in other Latino ghettos in the city, the immigrants of many countries and from different generations continued singing and dancing to the sound of a diverse array of rhythms: some were traditional and folkloric;

some recently brought to the city by new immigrants; and others marked by a combination of styles. Toward the end of the 1960s, a new sound arose in the Latino musical community, a new manifestation reflecting the ethno-cultural syncretization of New York's Latin quarter: salsa. This was the synthesis and logical result, the unfolding and re-solution [re-solución], of New York's Hispanic urban immigrant stew. Although originally cooked up in the ghettos of New York, salsa has spread throughout all the Americas, and thanks to its open form and improvisational and experimental spirit, it has developed a number of novel combinatory forms and been enriched by new local materials, stylistic variations, and rhythmic ingredients. The New York ghetto has also been the breeding ground for Latino rap (some of the first rap singers were Nuyoricans) and Jamaican reggae, forms that have had strong repercussions for rock music in recent decades. The most recent movement of immigrants from the Caribbean basin to New York has brought with it other rhythms: Dominican *merengue*, Colombian *cumbia* and *ballenato*, Haitian *konpa direk* (*konbit*), Lesser Antillean *zouk*, Jamaican *ska*, and many other forms.

We must ask what impact, if any, this music has had in the non-Latino world. Internationally speaking, these works are known, assimilated, embellished, and studied. The music consortia record, promote, export, and import Latino musical ideas for a Latino public. In both the United States and Latin America there is a captive audience for the commodities purveyed by the recording companies.

However, in the North American context, for the New Yorker who encounters this music at his or her local record shop under the rubric of "Third World" or "World" music, Latin music continues to be something exotic, something other, something foreign. Clearly there is a kind of assimilation within the mass music industry in the use, for example, of congas as rhythmic backdrop, in which stylistic echoes of Latino music form a popular subtrack to pop songs. However, this assimilation is unconscious on the part of the consumer—the ethnic equivalent of Muzak— and as a result salsa, bolero, and all the other Latino musical forms have returned to the ghetto.

—*Doris Schnabel*

Because New York has been a platform for the international launching of salsa and rap, it has also been responsible for the partial image of the Spanish-speaking community that exists in the wider world. In Spain, in Europe in general, and in countries as remote as Japan, salsa is listened to, danced to, and musically recycled. The beginnings of this fusion of Afro-Caribbean music were toward the end of the 1960s. This epoch also saw the rise to consciousness of a Latino self-awareness that no longer desired to be the "other" (neither Anglo nor African American), but rather sought to assert Latino identity as an integral constituent of the U.S. mix. In this sense, salsa from the very beginning played an important role in the movement for social revindication (Manuel 72–79). These former sociopolitical currents have all but disappeared from salsa today, but rap music has taken up the cause and has become the musical witness to many of the problems experienced on a daily basis by the New York Latino community.

It is important to underline the leadership role that Puerto Rican immigrant musicians have played in the origins of salsa and rap music in New York City, without, however, glossing over the Cuban roots of the former. A number of studies have attempted to trace the historical development of salsa, although often from a Cubano-centric point of view. Among these are the works of John Storm Roberts (1979), Miguel

César Rondón (1980), Argeliers León (1984), Isabelle Leymarie (1985), Charley Gerard and Marty Sheller (1989), Peter Manuel (1990, and 1995), Vernon Boggs (1992), Ruth Glasser (1995), and Ángel G. Quintero Rivera's (Salsa, sabor y control! Sociología de la música "tropical" [Salsa, Taste and Control!: Sociology of "Tropical" Music] (Premio Casa de las Américas, 1998). In addition, an important study of Latino rap by Mayra Santos Febres has been completed. Whatever the future holds for salsa (and, in part, for rap), this is the emblematic music of the New York Latino community and, in one way or another, salsa and rap are the two distinguishing marks of the nomadic identity of the city's Hispanics.

It is in this context that we need to consider another form of artistic expression, graffiti, in which the use of language, and particularly the Spanish language, has (as was the case with salsa and rap) both acquired an artistic value and become a means of affirming Hispanic identity.

Graffiti have been another popular artistic form in which New York Latinos have played and continue to play an important role. According to Martha Cooper and Henry Chalfant, "[t]he history of subway graffiti in New York is a brief one, and the phenomenon differs from all other kinds of graffiti, both past and present. In the 1960s, teenagers in New York began to write their names on neighborhood walls" (14). In the 1970s and the 1980s, however, the graffiti craze would reach its apogee. In 1972 Hugo Martínez brought to the City College Department of Art a group of graffiti artists, and at that moment the art world profile of graffiti was born. The "United Graffiti Artists" exhibition at the Artists Space in 1975 was the first attempt to introduce graffiti art into New York galleries. This was followed by the creation of Fashion Moda in the Bronx in 1978, and the open spaces of the collectives Group Material and ABC No Rio, two years later. CUD (Contemporary Urbicultural Documentation) and PADD (Political Art Documentation-Distribution) were other organizations promoting projects related to graffiti in these years. In the 1980s the graffiti movement saw a resurgence, this time in more commercial galleries, and, in one way or another, influenced artists such as Jean Michel Basquiat and Julian Schnabel. Similarly, graffiti artist Keith Haring made the transit from the streets to the galleries and from there to international fame. The phenomenon of graffiti opened up possibilities for collaborations between Latino and non-Latino artists, although the Latinos have frequently been forgotten once these collaborations became the subject of attention. This has been the case in the collaborations between Jenny Holzer and Lady Pink (the Colombian Sandra Fabara, and one of the few female graffiti artists), between Tim Rollins and KOS (Kids of Survival), and that between John Ahearn and Rigoberto Torres (Lippard 158–69). Graffiti continue to be a living phenomenon in New York in the 1990s, but subject to controls. The majority of today's graffiti works are done on commission, at times to adorn some wall or other in the poorest quarters of the city, and especially as a form of street commemoration of the death of someone:

> Latino artists play a predominant role in the development of the New York memorial tradition. . . . The strong Latino presence reveals a historic precedent for the memorial tradition. The walls are updated versions of the simple roadside crosses often erected at the site of an automobile accident in predominantly Catholic countries.
> (Cooper and Sciorra 10)

The municipal government of New York City has erased all the graffiti in the city's subway system and has the intention of doing the same with the graffiti still found on walls. Former Mayor Rudolph Giuliani created in 1995 an Anti Graffiti Unit to pursue the practitioners of graffiti as if they were common delinquents.

Art

In the introduction to this essay it was mentioned that throughout the twentieth century New York has played an important role as both a launching platform and a center of attraction for many Hispanic visual artists. We should now examine this historical trajectory in more detail. One artist who was of fundamental importance to the launching of the avant-garde art movement in New York was Marius de Zayas (1880–1961), the Mexican caricaturist and promoter of aesthetic modernity, who arrived in the city in 1906. Friend and artistic confidant of Alfred Stieglitz, Zayas was instrumental in bringing African and pre-Columbian arts to the attention of the New York art world, particularly through his various galleries, including the Modern Gallery (1915–1918) and the De Zayas Gallery (1918–1921); he was a point of contact through which New York artists established relations with Tristan Tzara and the Zurich Dadaists. In addition, he was a writer and collaborated in the launching of Stieglitz's avant-garde journal, 291, where his article "African Negro Art: Its Influence on Modern Art" was published (Sims 153–54). Furthermore, Zayas opened the door in the New York scene for the introduction of Mexican art, a phenomenon that would become important from the 1930s. In 1928 The Art Center gallery presented the first exhibition of Mexican artists in the city; twenty-two painters were represented, among them Orozco, Siqueiros, and Tamayo. Shortly thereafter, The Metropolitan Museum organized a large exposition entitled "Mexican Arts" (October 1930), in which a number of important contemporary Mexican painters again appeared; in the same year Orozco and Thomas Hart Benton painted the mural in the New School for Social Research. In 1931 a retrospective of the works of Diego Rivera was held at the Museum of Modern Art (MOMA); and in 1933 the Mexican artist completed the famous mural in Rockefeller Center. Another important event of these years was the participation of Orozco and Siqueiros in the Congress of American Artists in February 1936. Frida Kahlo had her first New York show at the Julien Levy Gallery in 1938 and also appeared two years later at the MOMA's "Twenty Centuries of Mexican Art" exposition. A further couple of exhibitions of Mexican contemporary art were held in 1945 (in various New York galleries) and in 1946 at the Grand Central Galleries. A Vital Dialogue: Mexican Artists in New York (November 2000 to January 2001, Gallery of the Mexican Institute of New York) provides a brief, selective look at art produced by fourteen Mexican artists living in New York in the late years of the twentieth century. But the greatest achievement of the century with respect to Mexican art in New York City was without a doubt the 1991 exhibition Mexico: Splendors of Thirty Centuries at the Metropolitan Museum of Art (April to August 1991).

Among the peninsular Spanish artists who enjoyed the most influence with young U.S. painters were Pablo Picasso, Joan Miró, and Salvador Dalí. Miró's work was already to be seen in a large exhibition held at the Brooklyn Museum in

1926; fine examples of Picasso's cubist works formed part of the Gallatin Collection at New York University from 1927 to 1942; and in 1933 the famous Julien Levy Gallery mounted an exhibition of the works of Miró and Dalí, with Dalí giving a very important lecture the following year at MOMA against "logical" art. From the beginning of the Spanish Civil War in 1936, New York artists and intellectuals turned their attention to Spain, and this interest in the Spanish situation culminated in 1939 with the exhibition of Picasso's famous "Guernica" at the Valentine Gallery and the large retrospective of his work at MOMA in the same year, attracting thousands of visitors, including of course almost all artists of New York (see Ashton). From the 1940s, a number of Spanish painters including Esteban Vicente and José Guerrero took up residence in the city and collaborated with their U.S. colleagues in the systematic shift of the center of the international art movement from Paris to New York.

Besides Picasso, Miró, and Dalí, the most germane artist to an understanding of the development of twentieth-century U.S. art (without forgetting, of course, the Mexicans José Clemente Orozco [1883–1949], Alfaro Siqueiros [1896–1974], and Diego Rivera [1886–1957]) was the Chilean Roberto Matta (1911–2002), who arrived in New York in 1939 and remained there until 1947. Together with the surrealist writers and artists who spent much of the decade of the 1940s in New York (e.g., Breton, André Masson, and Max Ernst, among others), Matta had an enormous influence on the group of painters that would later be known as the New York School. Critics have recognized Matta's influence on the work of artists like Arshile Gorky, Jackson Pollock, and Robert Motherwell, and on U.S. abstract expressionism in general; in 1957 MOMA organized a selective exhibition of his work (Sims 162–63). The Cuban Wifredo Lam (1902–1982) was another Hispanic presence in the New York art scene in these years. He first visited the city in 1946, and later came on frequent visits, especially in the 1950s. Lam, Matta, and Frida Kahlo (1907–1954) were the three artists linked to Latin American surrealism whose works received the most attention on the New York scene. Among the other Latin American artists whose contributions enriched the artistic panorama of the city in these years were the Cubans Mario Carreño, Daniel Serra-Badué, and Agustín Fernández, the Brazilian Maria Martins, and the Chilean Nemesio Antúnez.

From the beginning of the 1960s a new generation of Latin American artists established themselves in New York. The 1964 exhibition at the Bonino Gallery, "Magnet: New York," provoked the New York Times critic John Canady to say: "It is not exactly an invasion but there is at least a strong Latin American infiltration into the international strongholds so largely cornered by New York galleries" (Stellweg 284). Canady was referring to the twenty-eight Hispanic artists in the exhibition, most of whom were resident, and some of them are still, in New York. One of these artists was Mathias Goeritz (born in Germany, founder of the Spanish Escuela de Altamira, moved to Mexico) who, during his time in New York, provoked considerable interest with his conceptual art interventions. A student of Goeritz in Mexico City, the Argentinean Liliana Porter, also established herself in New York in the 1960s and, together with the Uruguayan Luis Camnitzer, was able to create a certain community of Latin American sensibility in New York. Jaime Davidovich, also an Argentinean, was another artist associated with the conceptual art movement in these years; in 1970 he created in Soho the "Artists Television Network."

Marta Minujín, another Argentinean, was considered to be the creator of a Hispanicized, or hot-blooded, Pop Art in New York. According to Stellweg, "[a]lthough her media-oriented ideas were already crystallizing in Argentina, her reaction to the U.S. technological society, to the possibility of global communication, allowed her to become very quickly an American technological creation. By choosing the most debated issues of the times and presenting these in media spectacles, Marta Minujín became, more than any other Latin American artist, a media celebrity not unlike Andy Warhol. She adapted to U.S. culture and became an outright proponent of the American dream" (290). Rafael Montañez Ortiz (Ralph Ortiz), born in New York of Puerto Rican and Mexican parents, was the leader behind the Destruction in Art movement, and one of the first Latino (by birth and by education) artists to win an international reputation. Beginning in 1963, with his destruction of a piano and a mattress, Ortiz began to acquire a name for himself. However, despite his Hispanic origins, Ortiz has defined his late 1950s and 1960s stance as one that is "not just the result of my own roots but rather based on questioning diverse historical and aesthetic contexts" (in Stellweg 290–91).

The "kinetic" artist Julio Le Parc, born in Argentina, held his first New York exhibition in 1962 as a part of the Parisian collective Groupe de Recherche d'Art Visuel (GRAV). Since then he has been creating pieces that attempt to enter into dialogue with the community, as a way of overcoming the barriers between the elitist arts and the average citizen. The Chilean Enrique Castro-Cid, who arrived in the city in 1962, exhibited his first robots at the Richard Feigen Gallery in 1965. Another Chilean, Juan Downey, has expressed his reasons for coming to New York: "There wasn't any specific reason for leaving Chile other than I knew that to make art I had to move to a cultural center, one where art is marketed" (Stellweg 291). In 1966 Downey would enter into contact with the circle of artists that had founded the E.A.T. (Experiments in Art and Technology), Billy Klüver and Robert Rauschenberg, and other artists like John Cage. According to Downey, New York is "a city of outsiders, a sort of hospital with an open-door situation like nowhere else in the world," and it promotes nomadic art, about "leaving, going away, and taking off" (Stellweg 293–99). This nomadism is perhaps the best concept for defining the expatriate condition of many of the Hispanic artists who live in New York today, in part because the majority of them have never been very patriotic with respect to their countries of origin, and in part also because the sociocultural circumstances of the large metropolis means that cities like New York assimilate and internationalize every message of a nationalist character.

In 1964 José Guillermo Castillo, Luis Camnitzer, and Liliana Porter founded the New York Graphic Workshop, a collective that would serve as a platform for artistic activities of a social character. Porter has commented on the group that "[w]e gave a lot of consideration to the political and moral aspects of art-making, and through prints there was this idea we were working toward mass culture" (Stellweg 311). In 1970 the workshop disbanded and Castillo returned to Venezuela; however, both Porter and Camnitzer continued to be very active in the realm of political art, and Camnitzer is today leading a similar collective that is not located in New York. Together with other artists, including Julio Le Parc, Mathias Goeritz, José Luis Cuevas, Luis Felipe Noé, and Gordon Matta-Clark, they produced a book attacking the São Paulo Biennial entitled Counter Biennial. Within the group behind this book, known as the Museo para la Independencia Cultural Latinoamericana group, was also to be found a number of other Hispanic artists, including Rafael Ferrer from Puerto Rico, Leandro Katz, Eduardo Costa, and Nicolás Uriburu, all from Argentina, and the Brazilians

Rubens Gerchman, Antonio Dias, Lygia Clark, and Helio Oiticica. The culmination of the Hispanic presence in the New York art scene was reached with the "Information" exhibit in 1970 at MOMA. Among those whose works appeared were twenty-one Latin Americans: "These artists made global communication and nomadic information the centerpieces of their work" (Stellweg 311).

Informational space as a global, transnational site, openly accessible to all, became definitively materialized in the 1990s thanks to the Internet. Today, a number of the Spanish and Latin American artists already mentioned are undertaking cybernetic projects on the World Wide Web, signaling that art is no longer necessarily localized in any particular geographic center. Of course this delocalization must be considered in the context of the fact that New York continues to be, if not the absolute center, one of the most important centers of the world art market.

Also in the 1970s a number of other studios were created whose leaders were the Puerto Rican artists who had resided temporarily or permanently in New York. The well-known organization the Friends of Puerto Rico included figures like Juan Maldonado, Victor Linares, Rafael Tufiño, Carlos Osorio, Domingo López, Domingo García, Rafael Colón-Morales, and Carlos Irizarry. This artists' group also mounted exhibitions in various galleries such as the Caravan House, the Galería Hoy, and the Galería Sudamericana. In 1969 another studio space was set up, the Taller Alma Boricua (known as the Puerto Rican Workshop), continuing the work begun by the Friends of Puerto Rico. A number of Puerto Rican artists established international profiles for themselves without membership in these groups: Olga Albizu, Ralph Ortiz, Rafael Ferrer, and José Morales; Morales emigrated to Europe (Spain, France, and then Sweden), where he no longer had to labor under the label of "Latino artist." Today, in fact, artists such as Pepón Osorio and the painter Juan Sánchez occupy important places in U.S. art for their own accomplishments, although the Latino label reappears whenever they are mentioned.

—*Luisa García Conde*

Photography has been a field of artistic endeavor whose historical trajectory has been similar to that of the other Hispanic visual arts in New York. Although space does not allow us to go into the detail its history merits, the "Photography in Latin America: A Spiritual Journey" show should be mentioned, one of the most important recent exhibitions sponsored by the Brooklyn Museum (September 1996 to January 1997). Also in 1997 (February to May) MoMA presented a retrospective exposition of the Mexican photographer Manuel Álvarez Bravo (1902–2002). Finally, two Latino photographers, both born in New York, have distinguished themselves recently: Andrés Serrano and Joseph Rodríguez.

The most recent mass arrival of Dominicans, in addition to the Dominicans already living in the city for some time, has meant that this community has assumed a tremendous importance in various domains of Hispanic culture and society in New York. The latest evidence of this cultural presence was the "Art in Transit. A Dominican Experience" show held in 1996 (September to October) at the INTAR gallery. Of the innumerable Hispanic artists living and working in New York today, all of them appear to be finding their proper place in the history of U.S. art and that of the national arts of their respective countries. Lucy R. Lippard's book, *Mixed Blessings: New Art in a Multicultural America*, seems to be the best point of reference for

evaluating the importance of Latino artists. However, it remains to be seen whether this phenomenon is only a multicultural fashion or whether it marks in fact a new and definitive opening up of U.S. institutions and markets. Only the twenty-first century will give us the answer to this question.

Let us return to the Spanish presence in the New York art world. According to the critics Octavio Zaya and Carlos E. Pinto, "since the famous exhibition organized by Frank O'Hara at MOMA in 1960, the Spanish artists who appear to most enjoy critical attention and popular consideration are the well known and historically important figures of Tápies and Chillida, artists worthy of the attention reserved for the great masters. Tápies is represented in the most prestigious U.S. collections and museums of contemporary art and is exhibited regularly in New York in internationally renowned and critically recognized galleries. Chillida, together with de Kooning, received the Andrew W. Mellon Prize in 1979; was the subject of a retrospective at the Guggenheim Museum in 1981; and was the only Spanish artist included in the just closed Transformation in Sculpture (Four Decades of European and American Art) exhibition at the Guggenheim" (Zaya and Pinto 1985, 2). If we were to round out a panoramic and reasonably comprehensive picture of the Spanish artists of the 1950s whose work continues to have a presence in the New York art scene, we would have to add to the figures of Tápies and Chillida the names of Manolo Millares, Antonio Saura, Antonio López García, Juan Genovés, Esteban Vicente, Martín Chirino, Senen Ubina, José Guerrero, and César Manrique. In addition, we should mention an exhibition held at the Guggenheim in 1991, "New Images from Spain," as well as many other more recent exhibits by Spanish artists, but to go into all of that would make this essay interminable. In the last three decades several generations of Spanish artists have passed through New York, and a number of these artists have stayed; Antonio Muntadas, Francesco Torres, Juan Uslé, and Francisco Leiro are already distinguished figures in the world art scene. Once again, to be comprehensive we would have to add an extensive list of Spanish artists resident or formerly resident in the city, artists who have, some more than others, made a name for themselves in the international art market or simply returned to Spain to continue their work. As evidence of the vital presence of Spanish artists in the New York scene we might mention Juan Muñoz's installation at the Dia Center for the Arts in 1997 (September–December). As a final point of reference for the new phenomena of decentralization and decolonization in the relations between the New York art world and Spain, we should also note the opening of the monumental Museo Guggenheim, in Bilbao, Spain, in October 1997.

In the 1990s a number of books focusing special attention on Latino art in the United States were published. These books have been preceded by various exhibitions and their respective catalogues. The following exhibition-related publications have stood out from the crowd: *Bridge Between Islands: Retrospective Works by Six Puerto Rican Artists in New York* (Henry Street Settlement, Bronx Museum, and El Museo del Barrio 1979); *Exhibition: Hispanic Artists in New York* (Association of Hispanic Artists 1982); *Hispanic Artists in New York* (City Gallery 1981); *Ten Latin American Artists Working in New York* (International House 1984); *The Latin American Spirit: Art and Artists in the United States, 1920–1970* (Bronx Museum of the Arts 1988); *Taller Alma Boricua 1969–1989: Reflections on Twenty Years of the Puerto Rican Workshop* (El Museo del Barrio 1989); and outside New York, *Latin American Artists in New York Since 1970* (Austin, University of Texas 1987). With respect to critical studies, Lucy R. Lippard's *Mixed Blessings: New Art in a Multicultural America* (1990), was a pioneering work in that it took up the study of Latino artists established in New York in the context of U.S. multiculturalism. Shifra M. Goldman's *Dimensions of the Americas: Art and Social Change in Latin America and the United States* (1994) was also important in this context, particularly its chapter on Latin American art in the United States. The volume *Latin American Art in the Twentieth Century* (1996), edited by Edward J. Sullivan, is a less interesting one in this context in that, although it has a chapter on Chicano art, it has ignored New York City as a center of production for U.S. Latino art.

Conclusions

We have attempted here to trace the path of the word; which is to say, we have lingered over all those aspects of Latino culture in New York in which the Spanish language has been and is the principle tool and referent. Within these geographic limits, limits established not by political powers but rather by language, it can be stated that the cultural manifestations mentioned in this account form part of the general Hispanic domain, but at the same time are also part of the cultural history of the United States. In mapping the coordinates of Latino verbal culture in New York we have paid little attention to its elite manifestations, at the risk of presenting a tiresome or overwhelming crush of facts. However, this account does seek to reflect the cultural activities that have been informed by the Spanish language in general, and not only its most distinguished achievements. While the criterion of "quality" has not determined the selection of information offered, and while it is undeniable that what is presented here is not an index or an exhaustive catalogue, we do hope we have given a series of useful references for the orientation of those readers who seek to deepen their understanding in one or more of the cultural areas we have explored.

In the last week of March 1995 the "Primer Encuentro sobre la Cultura Latina en la frontera de un nuevo siglo" ["First Congress of Latino Culture on the Cusp of the New Century"] was held in Granada, Spain. In a speech before the delegates, Eduardo de Lourenço expressed his hope that "[a]t the very least we dream—and not only in order to amuse the erudite—of a bell tower whose peal reaches farther, a knell which is above all more ours than that one which resounds to the rap of Harlem and the McDonald's hamburger" (Lourenço 19). This simplification of U.S. culture is not only crude, it is unfair.

In 1886, with the publication in New York of his *Bibliotheca Americana Vetustissima* [The Most Venerable American Library], the scholar Henry Harrise (1829–1910) established himself as the "Prince of the Americanists," opening up, thus, the way for the many other U.S. Hispanists who have contributed to the fortification of that culture. Later, in a text entitled "The Spanish Element in Our Nationality" written in the form of a letter dated 20 July 1883, Walt Whitman would declare:

> The seething materialistic and business vortices of the United States, in their present devouring relations, controlling and belittling everything else, are, in my opinion, but a vast and indispensable stage in the new world's development, and are certainly to be follow'd by something entirely different—at least by immense modifications. Character, literature, a society worthy of the name, are yet to be establish'd, through a nationality of noblest spiritual, heroic and democratic attributes—not one of which at present definitely exists—entirely different from the past, though unerringly founded upon it, and to justify it. To that composite American identity of the future, Spanish character will supply some of the most needed parts. (553)

T. S. Eliot, Ezra Pound, Ernest Hemingway, and Wallace Stevens would view Hispanic culture with a similar generosity. These examples, I believe, clearly demonstrate both the error of reducing U.S. culture to the image of a colossal "Big Mac" and that Latino culture forms an integral part of U.S. identity.

When in a poem Rubén Darío described New York City as composed of "fifty storey buildings," he succeeded, perhaps in all innocence, in defining the paradox of being Hispanic in the Big Apple: Hispanics feel themselves to be emotionally tied to the notions of hearth and home, and yet at the same time they live as if in a state of homelessness with respect to any national history, in a world of apartment blocks. It is, thus, hardly surprising that so many immigrants have gathered there, in the beginning, in associations whose names contain the word "casa": Casa de España, Casa de Galicia, Hispanic House, and the phenomenon of "Las Casitas" (small modern sheds) that New York's Puerto Ricans have created in their backyard gardens. In an autobiographical article Isaías Lerner, another nomad, has written: "la casa como fortaleza de la identidad era más que una metáfora" (61) ("the home as the castle of identity is more than a metaphor"); for the Hispanics of New York, including those who express themselves in English, it can be said that "language is the castle of identity." In fact, this essay may be said to work only this vein: the historical presence of the Spanish language as a site and reference point for defining the identity of the Hispanic population of New York. Although those who write in English hear, as it were, inside themselves only the echoes of the Spanish of the Americas in their parents, their grandparents, or their peers, they do not for all that become any less Hispanic than those who still use the maternal language as a means of expression. Let us conclude with the Caribbean words of Arcadio Díaz Quiñones, who with great lucidity has said:

> La experiencia puertorriqueña–al igual que la haitiana, la mexicana, la dominicana o la cubana–ha sido, a lo largo del siglo XX, un caso paradigmático de desplazamiento y diáspora, en medio de las desigualdades que constituye el núcleo central de la democracia norteamericana. Se trata de una cultura viajera, transformada en diversos lugares, cuya extensión es inconmensurable. (10)

> In the midst of the inequalities that constitute the central nucleus of U.S. democracy, the Puerto Rican experience–just like that of the Haitians, Mexicans, Dominicans, or Cubans–has throughout the twentieth century been a paradigmatic case of displacement and diaspora. It is the question of a culture in transit, transformed in diverse places, whose compass is incommensurable.

Translation by Colman Hogan

Works Cited

Antush, John, ed. 1994. Introduction. *Nuestro New York: An Anthology of Puerto Rican Plays*. New York: Penguin Books. ix–xxxii.

Ashton, Dore. 1979. *The New York School: A Cultural Reckoning*. New York: Penguin Books.

Binder, Frederick M. and David M. Reimers. 1995. *All the Nations Under Heaven: An Ethnic and Racial History of New York City*. New York: Columbia University Press.

Brod, Richard, and Elizabeth B. Welles. 2000. "Foreign Language Enrollments in United States Institutions of Higher Education, Fall 1998." *ADFL Bulletin*. 31.2: 22–29.

Bueno, Gustavo. 1997. *El mito de la cultura: ensayo de una filosofía materialista de la cultura.* 4th ed. Barcelona: Prensa Ibérica.

Burma, John H. 1954. *Spanish-Speaking Groups in the United States.* Cambridge: Durham: Duke University Press.

Cañas, Dionisio. 1994. *El poeta y la ciudad. Nueva York y los escritores hispanos.* Madrid: Cátedra.

—. 1995. "Latinos o hispanos?: los escritores hispanos en Nueva York." *Latinos: la cultura latina en la frontera de un nuevo siglo.* Ed. Mariano Maresca and Horacio Rébora. Granada: Comares. 217–227.

Carpentier, Alejo. 1972. *La música en Cuba.* Colección Popular, 109. Mexico City: Fondo de Cultura Económica.

Cooper, Martha, and Joseph Sciorra. 1992. *R.I.P.: Memorial Wall Art.* New York: Henry Holt and Company.

—. and Henry Chalfant. 1984. *Subway Art.* New York: Henry Holt and Company.

Darío, Rubén. 1918. *Los raros. Obras completas.* Vol. 6. Madrid: Mundo Latino.

—. 1919a. *El viaje a Nicaragua.* Obras completas. Vol. 17. Madrid: Mundo Latino.

—. 1919b *Lira póstuma. Obras completas.* Vol. 21. Madrid: Mundo Latino.

Davis, Thomas J. 1985. *A Rumor of Revolt: the "Great Negro Plot" in Colonial New York.* New York: Free Press.

Díaz Quiñones, Arcadio. 1997. "La literatura y la metanación puertorriqueña." *El Nuevo Día.* San Juan. 7 Dec: 10.

Ellis, Edward Robb. 1966. *The Epic of New York City.* New York: Old Town Books.

Ernst, Robert. 1949. *Immigrant Life in New York City.* New York: King's Crown Press, Columbia University Press.

Esquenazi-Mayo, Roberto, ed. 1993. *A Survey of Cuban Revistas, 1902–1958.* Washington: Library of Congress.

Fernández Olmos, Margarite. 1989. *Sobre la literatura puertorriqueña de aquí y de allí: aproximaciones feministas.* Santo Domingo: Alfa & Omega.

Figueroa, Pablo. 1977. *Teatro: Hispanic Theater in New York City, 1920–1976.* New York: Off Off Broadway Alliance, Inc. and El Museo del Barrio.

Flores, Juan. 1996. "Puerto Rican and Latino Culture at the Crossroads." *Latinos in New York: Communities in Transition.* Ed. Gabriel Haslip-Viera and Sherrie L. Baver. Notre Dame, IN: University of Notre Dame Press. pp. 331–338.

Fox, Geoffrey. 1996. *Hispanic Nation: Culture, Politics, and the Constructing of Identity.* Secaucus, NJ: Birch Lane Press, Carol Publishing Group.

García, Ofelia. 1997. "New York's Multilingualism: World Languages and Their Role in a U.S. City." *The Multilingual Apple: Languages in New York City.* Ed. Ofelia García and Joshua A. Fishman. Berlin: Mouton de Gruyter. 3–50.

García Lorca, Federico. 1940. *Poeta en Nueva York.* México City: Séneca.

Giordano, Jaime. 1989–90. "La poesía de los hispanos en el área de Nueva York: una somera introducción." *Extremos.* (New York) 4–5.6: 81–89.

González, José Luis. 1990. *El país de cuatro pisos.* Maplewood: Waterfront Press.

Goodfriend, Joyce D. 1992. *Before the Melting Pot: Society and Culture in Colonial New York City.* Princeton: Princeton University Press.

Goris, Anneris and José Hernández, eds. 1996. *Latin Communities in New York City.* New York: Department of Black and Puerto Rican Studies, Hunter College, City University of New York.

Hendricks, Glenn. 1974. The Dominican Diaspora: From the Dominican Republic to New York City–Villagers in Transition. New York: Teachers College, Columbia.

Hernández, Ramona, and Silvio Torres-Saillant. 1996. "Dominicans in New York: Men, Women, and Prospects." *Latinos in New York: Communities in Transition.* Ed. Gabriel Haslip-Viera and Sherriel L. Baver. Notre Dame, IN: University of Notre Dame Press. 30–56.

Jiménez, Juan Ramón. 1917. *Diario de un poeta recién casado.* Madrid: Calleja.

Kammen, Michael. 1975. *Colonial New York: A History.* Oxford: Oxford University Press.

Kanellos, Nicolás. 1990. *A History of Hispanic Theater in the United States: Origins to 1940.* Austin: University of Texas Press.

—.1993. "Brief History of Hispanic Theater in the United States." *Handbook of Hispanic Cultures in the US: Literature and Art.* Ed. Francisco Lomelí. Houston: Arte Público Press. 248–67.

—. 1997. *Hispanic Firsts: 500 Years of Extraordinary Achievement.* Detroit: Gale.

Katz, William Loren. 1997. *Black Legacy: A History of New York's African Americans.* New York: Ethrac Publications.

Kirking, Clayton. 2000. *A Vital Dialogue: Mexican Artist in New York.* New York: Mexican Cultural Institute of New York.

Leeds, Mark. 1996. *Ethnic New York: A Complete Guide to the Many Faces and Cultures of New York.* 2nd ed. Chicago: Passport Books.

Lerner, Isaías. 1998. "La experiencia judía en la Argentina de hace medio siglo." *Claves de razón práctica* (Madrid) 79: 60–64.

Lippard, Lucy R. 1990. *Mixed Blessings: New Art in a Multicultural America.* New York: Pantheon Books.

Lourenço, Eduardo de. 1995. "Digresión sobre la latinidad." *Latinos: la cultura latina en la frontera de un nuevo siglo.* Mariano Maresca y Horacio Rébora eds. Granada: Comares. 17–23.

Manuel, Peter, Kenneth Bilby and Michael Largy. 1995. *Caribbean Currents: Caribbean Music from Rumba to Reggae.* Philadelphia: Temple University Press.

Márceles Daconte, Eduardo. 1993. *Narradores colombianos en U.S.A.* Bogota: Instituto Colombiano de Cultura.

Martín, Manuel. 1997. "The Development of the Hispanic-American Theater in New York City: from 1960 to the Present." *OLLANTAY: Theater Magazine* 1.2 (Summer/Autumm): 11–37.

Miller, John C. 1984. "Contemporary Hispanic Theater in New York." *Hispanic Theater in the United States.* ed. Nicolás Kanellos. Houston: Arte Público Press. 24–33.

Monge-Rafuls, Pedro R. ed. 1993. *Visual Arts: A Different Approach/ Desde otro punto de vista: Dialogue from the First Latin American Visual Arts Conference in New York on May 26, 1990.* New York: OLLANTAY Press.

Museum of Modern Art. 1940. *Twenty Centuries of Mexican Art.* New York: The Museum of Modern Art.

O'Neill, John P., ed. 1990. *Mexico: Splendors of Thirty Centuries.* New York: Bullfinch Press and the Metropolitan Museum of Art.

Orjuela, Héctor H. 1975. *La obra poética de Rafael Pombo.* Bogota: Institute Caro y Cuervo.

Paz, Octavio. 1987. "Estela de José Juan Tablada." In *Mexico en la obra de Octavio Paz.* Vol 2. eds. Octavio Paz and Luis Mario Schneider. Mexico: Fondo de Cultura Económico.

Pereda, Prudencia de. 1960. *Windmills in Brooklyn.* New York: Atheneum.

Pottlitzer, Joanne. 1988. *Hispanic Theater in the United States and Puerto Rico.* New York: Ford Foundation.

Prieto, Guillermo. 1994. *Obras completas.* Ed. Boris Rosen Jélomer. Vol. 8. Mexico City: Consejo Nacional para la Cultura y las Artes.

Ripoll, Carlos. 1971. *Patria. El periódico de José Martí.* New York: Eliseo Torres.

Rodríguez Juliá, Edgardo. 1985. *El entierro de Cortijo*. Río Piedras: Ediciones Huracán.

Rodríguez de León, Francisco. 1998. *El furioso merengue del norte: una historia de la comunidad dominicana en los Estados Unidos*. New York: Editorial Sitel.

Rueda, Germán. 1993. *La emigración contemporánea de españoles a Estados Unidos, 1820–1950*. Madrid: Editorial MAPFRE.

Shearer, James F. 1954. "Periódicos españoles en los Estados Unidos." *Revista Hispánica Moderna* 20: 45–57.

Sims, Lowery. 1988. "New York Dada and New World Surrealism." *The Latin American Spirit: Art and Artists in the United States, 1920–1970*. New York: Bronx Museum of the Arts. 152–183

Sobejano, Gonzalo. 1988. "Revista Hispánica Moderna." *Romanische Forschungen* 100: 1–3, 222–30.

Sotelo Vázquez, Adolfo. 1994. Introduction. "Los artículos de Leopoldo Alas *Clarín* publicados en *Las Novedades*, Nueva York, 1894–1897." *Cuadernos Hispanoamericanos* (Los complementarios) 13–14: 5–23.

Stellweg, Carla. 1988. "*Magnet-New York*: Conceptual, Performance, Environmental, and Installation Art by Latin American Artists in New York." *The Latin American Spirit: Art and Artists in the United States, 1920–1970*. New York: Bronx Museum of the Arts. 284–311.

Storm Roberts, John. 1979. *The Latin Tinge: The Impact of Latin American Music on the United States*. New York: Oxford University Press.

Torres-Saillant, Silvio, and Ramona Hernández. 1998. *The Dominican Americans*. Westport: Greenwood Press.

Ugalde, Antonio, and Erick Larson. 1988. "Flujo migratorio del Caribe a los Estados Unidos: el caso de la República Dominicana." *EME-EME. Estudios Dominicanos* (Santo Domingo) 15.81: 97–113.

Veciana-Suarez, Ana. 1987. *Hispanic Media, USA: A Narrative Guide to the Print and Electronic Hispanic News Media in the United States*. Washington DC: Media Institute.

Vega, Bernardo. 1994. *Memorias de Bernardo Vega: contribución a la historia de la comunidad puertorriqueña en Nueva York*. Ed. César Andreu Iglesias. 5th ed. Río Piedras, Puerto Rico: Ediciones Huracán.

Whitman, Walt. 1964. *The Collected Writings of Walt Whitman*. Ed. Gay Wilson Allen and Sculley Bradley. Vol. 2. New York: New York University Press.

Zaya, Octavio y Carlos E. Pinto. 1985. "Artistas españoles en Nueva York (Una introducción provisional)." *Hartísimo* (Tenerife) 8–9: 1–8.

Zentella, Ana Celia. 1997. "Spanish in New York." *The Multilingual Apple: Languages in New York City*. Ed. Ofelia García and Joshua A. Fishman. Berlin: Mouton de Gruyter. 167–201.

CHAPTER 57

PARIS AND LATIN AMERICANS, NINETEENTH AND TWENTIETH CENTURIES
FROM CULTURAL METROPOLIS TO CULTURAL MUSEUM?

Denis Rolland

La América del Sur se dió intelectualmente á Francia con la ingenuidad de una virgen, se convirtió en su discípulo respetuoso, la imitó hasta en sus errores y, desde lejos, . . . ató su destino al de aquella nación . . . que parecía reunir todas las excelencias y realizar todos los sueños.
—*Manuel Ugarte xvii–xviii*

Reportons-nous à cinquante ou soixante ans en arrière: l'homme très intelligent, très cultivé, en Amérique, à quoi aspirait-il? Non pas à être Brésilien, mais à être, au Brésil, le représentant de la plus haute et de la plus fine culture intellectuelle.
—*Lucien Febvre 204–205*

South America gave itself intellectually to France with the innocence of a virgin, it became its respectful disciple, it imitated even its errors, and from a far, . . . with that nation's destiny it linked its own . . . since France represented ultimate perfection and could realize all dreams.
Let us think back to fifty or sixty years ago: what did the intellectually gifted and well cultivated man in America aspire to? Not to be Brazilian but to be, in Brazil, the representative of the highest and finest intellectual culture.

The confusion between Paris and France is inevitable for Latin Americans. France is often perceived as the ideal embodiment of a new system of values established in Paris in the nineteenth century (Guerra 171). The elites of Latin America present one of the best reflections of the supposed enlightenment of a city renowned for its encyclopedist and universalist Revolution of 1789: At the end of the nineteenth century and start of the next, Paris represented the world's most important cultural metropolis. First, then, the distinction between Paris and France is not always an easy one to draw. Second, to be precise here would be to attempt the impossible. In the nineteenth and twentieth centuries, a large part of the Latin American elites certainly considered Paris as an oracle. However, with twenty continental states and a vast grouping of Caribbean Islands, Latin America defies any definition that is strictly disciplinary and especially linguistic. The ancient world's perception of a nondistinct group quickly generates the all-embracing and imperfect term, *Latin America*, used in France at the time of the Second Empire. (Although the term appears in France in 1856, it is taken to be the invention of Latin Americans from various countries living in Paris.) One could recall the wealthy Brazilian traveler of Offenbach's *La vie Parisienne* [1866; The Parisian Life] and the half-Mexican, half-Argentinean look about him, a kind of gaucho with his sombrero, in Paris for the World Fair, where France shows itself to the world. Although vague, the perception is lasting, even though Argentineans (often mistaken for Europeans in France) and Haitians (who pass for Africans) hardly feel they belong to a real common cultural group. Third, to examine this attraction for Paris or the mirror it holds up to Latin America, undoubtedly right after the First World War and certainly after the Second World War, is to question the construction of international cultural representations, as well as the decline in French–Latin American relations.

This study therefore begins by briefly considering representations of Latin America and Paris. Then it will trace the evolution and nature of the Latin American presence in Paris during the course of two periods. This part will include a broad survey of the lengthy, nineteenth-century *belle époque*, that lasted into the interim of the two world wars, and a more detailed look at the years after 1945. The study thus seeks to establish a topology of Latin America's paradoxical presence in Paris. From Fidel Castro's arrival in Havana to the end of the major military regimes of Latin America, this presence (though limited) has paradoxically and greatly affected parts of the French cultural and political elite of the nineteenth century, renewing itself in the second half of the twentieth century.

During the nineteenth century, Latin American constitutions were political expressions of Latin America's study of Paris. In 1875 Alexis Peyret drafted the Constitution Project for the Argentinean Republic; although the British contributed to the Brazilian Republican constitution of 1889, the French were still paramount. The influence of Parisian thought was wide-ranging and affected political ideas, the education of citizens, legislation on education (in Mexico and Argentina, for instance, Eugenio Labougle and Paul Groussac had a profound impact, as did the francophile educationalists and legislators of Bahia in Brazil in the 1840s), police and public order, religious legislation on the separation of Church and state (although in Brazil this legislation decidedly anticipated the French decisions of 1891), and state organization, as well as public and military administration (in 1907–1908, France sent a task force to São Paulo for the organization of the military police). In the fields of science and culture, there was also a multiplicity of transpositions and transfers or social introductions: masonic lodges and their rituals, cooperatives, unions, learned or philanthropic societies, leisure centers, religious congregations, Catholic associations (the Association Catholique de la Jeunesse

Française greatly inspired the Mexican Catholic Youth Association, created in 1913), and a variety of other kinds of twentieth-century youth associations.

In almost every political and cultural arena there were signs of a French presence steeped in Parisian culture: In the nineteenth century and at the start of the twentieth, the old continent generated a number of innovations passed down to and applied by the young nations of Latin America. The same can be said about the political and cultural imagination, the concept of society, citizen, and nation, the circulation of language, oral and written discourse as well as symbols and ceremonial language. This European imprint was all the more important because it was socially integrative.

During the nineteenth century, Europe served as a frame of reference that became a factor in the unification of a large part of the Latin American elites; it also contributed to the definition of a social setting that was favorable to the functioning of the elites. French ideas had a formative role in the process of developing the national imaginary through the unfolding of Latin American national histories. Either as a representative of the highest cultural tradition and richness or, in the political arena, of modern man, nineteenth-century fashion was primarily Parisian in Latin America. Like elsewhere in the world, the world of fashion reflected the political revolutions of the nineteenth and twentieth centuries. For instance, the *mestizo* Bahian tailor, militia lieutenant and actor, João de Deus do Nascimento, dressed *à la française* in order to display his desire to build an egalitarian and wealthy society (Carelli 50). At the end of the nineteenth century, the Parisian flavor of European fashion served as a maxim for Latin Americans and introduced a certain social reorganization in the public domain; although, it must be said, Latin American urban centers revealed what was largely a European, rather than strictly French, architecture. However, the first Argentinean school of architecture (University of Buenos Aires, 1901) modeled itself exclusively on the École des Beaux-Arts de Paris (School of Fine Arts of Paris); the multi-talented son of a French immigrant, Pierre Benoit, carried out approximately 1800 projects in Argentina, leaving his mark on the urban scene of the shores of La Plata; the Belgian Jules Dornal (1846–1924), who held a degree from the *École spéciale d'architecture de Paris* (Special Architecture School of Paris), introduced Argentina to *Beaux-Arts* architecture. Most of all, from across the Atlantic the Hausmannian model reached Buenos Aires with the construction of the Avenida de Mayo (1885–1894); it also reached Rio de Janeiro with the idea of large clearings, as well as Fortaleza, with the introduction of exterior boulevards. Neo-Gothic and, later, neo-Roman styles or *Art Nouveau* had a similar impact. As for Brazil, Lima Barreto (1881–1922) described a middle-class style of living in a Parisian decor and at the heart of a Europeanized city–fearing that foreigners might notice what lies behind the scenes (see Rolland 2000). (See **Table 1**.)

According to a complex chronology that varied from one country to the other, the dominant image of France originated in the diffusion of Enlightenment ideas and the principles established by the French Revolution. There are a number of reasons for this, but one is notably the fact that the French Revolution had completely and suddenly broken with absolutism, monarchy, and the entire hierarchical *ancien régime*. Indeed, the revolution had constructed a theoretical and abstract model of the ideal republic, based on a pure notion of modernity. Along with independence and the adoption of

Table 1. *French Imported Products in Argentina Classification in order of Importance (1912)*

- fashion accessories: new fashions, hats, women's outfits, dress fabrics, drapery from Roubaix and silk from Lyon;
- automobiles;
- food, canned foods, chocolate, olive oil, mustard, paté de foie gras, refined sugar, mineral water, cognac, absinthe, bitter, barreled wine, bottled wine;
- furniture, furniture fabrics, carpets, fine jewels, electrical light fixtures from Paris, perfumes, equipment for sugar refineries, coach-building supplies;
- cement, tiles and ceramics from Marseille, girders and tiles, patent medicines, lingerie, novelty items, *objets d'art*, materials for wine cellars and production, fine crystal and glassware, Limoges porcelain, machine tools, pianos, water/oil colors, French toys (in very small quantity);

Source: Huret 442.

the republican model–which revealed the new states' embrace of the French Revolution and liberal thought–the triumphant success of a theoretical modernity that was purer than its contemporary French version was noticeable in Spanish America (especially after the empire and the constitutional monarchy that followed). To a different degree and depending on the country and period, the nineteenth-century model for Latin American nationalism was often powerfully connected to the Enlightenment, as it referred back to Jean-Jacques Rousseau's Social Contract and retained the idea of a nation of free and equal individuals. Similarly, a source of inspiration for the Latin American elites was a Parisian positivism that rested on the political liberalism derived from France's Third Republic (although United States models gave rise to Brazil's own liberalism). Yet, once again, facile generalizations about the continent must be avoided: In Colombia a political conservatism swept aside this Positivism at the end of the 1880s.

From the time of independence, many noted a political and cultural synchronicity between France and Latin America: In particular, Latin American historians repeated (and orchestrated) these links at the end of the nineteenth century. This apparent synchronism of French and Latin American history generated the idea that France had greatly contributed to the birth of the young nations of Latin America after the Revolution. These historians also created the impression that the revolutionary model came from Paris before the concept of *Latinity* created a Latin American unity somewhat tied to Europe–with France in the forefront. It must be remembered that the French definition of *Latinity* oriented itself around the legitimation of French expansion in America rather than reflecting the strictly linguistic fact of proximity of the Romance [Latin] languages. Two Spanish American examples should be sufficient to illustrate this kind of classical discourse on a reconstructed past, prevalent at the outset of the First World War. One is by former Uruguayan senator, Eugène Garzón, and the other is by Francisco García Calderón (1883–1953) at the Sorbonne:

Le sens de la Révolution française avait pénétré au plus profond les hommes de la Révolution américaine, et ils se le communiquaient les uns aux autres comme un évangile de salut. Les pages les plus fameuses qui s'écrivaient en Europe sur la liberté, l'égalité et les droits de l'homme, parvenaient jusqu'à nos rivages et nous apportaient la formule de la future existence que nous devions réaliser. Et c'est après les avoir longuement mûries et s'en être imprégnés, que les hommes du Nouveau-Monde, confiants en leur foi révolutionnaire, se lancèrent dans la lute et obtinrent la victoire. (Garzón 14)

The meaning of the French Revolution had profoundly affected the men of the American Revolution, and they transformed that meaning into an evangelical redemption. The greatest European writings on liberty, equality and the rights of man reached our shores and brought us the formula for our future existence which we had yet to realize. And after they had for a long time nurtured and absorbed these writings, the men of the New World were confident enough and had enough faith in the revolution to launch their battle and obtain their victory.

Notre histoire se développe parallèlement à la vôtre. Nous avons aussi nos Girondins, votre Déclaration des Droits est traduite à l'heure tragique de notre Indépendance. Bolivar médite le Contrat Social dans les premières années de sa mission libératrice. Bilbao demande des inspirations à Edgar Quinet, Montalvo exalte la démocratie chrétienne de Lamartine. Quand la dissolution nous menace, Guizot sera le maître de nos conservateurs angoissés. Auguste Comte donne une religion aux hommes d'Etat du Brésil qui avaient abandonné leurs vieux dogmes. (García Calderón qtd. in Pérez-Pacheco 272)

Our histories develop side by side. We have our own Girondins; your Declaration of Rights is translated upon the tragic hour of our Independence. In the early years of his mission of liberation, Bolivar muses over the Social Contract. Bilbao seeks ideas from Edgar Quinet; Montalvo praises Lamartine's Christian democracy. Upon the threat of dissolution, Guizot is the leader of our anxious conservatives. Having abandoned their old dogmas, the men of the state of Brazil receive a new religion from Auguste Comte.

These representations constructed Latin American political reality, and these imaginary constructs were henceforth preponderant. Even arguments about French Catholicism quickly reverberate throughout Latin America, marking the conservative-liberal split. Of universal significance at the end of the nineteenth century, the myth of Paris is specifically induced by this imaginary construction of it in Latin America.

Moreover, not the French expedition in Mexico (1863–1867), not the War in the Pacific (1879–1887), nor France's failure with the Panama Canal (1878–1889) seriously weakened French influence–except, perhaps, in Colombia, where President Nuñez declared: "Surprisingly Colombia is willing to do what France itself . . . has refused . . . in order to save the French capital from catastrophe . . . . Should we, poor wretches, then sacrifice our precious rights for foreigners?" (in Cartagena, *El Porvenir* 20-04-1889). On the contrary, near the end of the nineteenth century, France's presence was stronger than ever in the urban parts of Latin America, such as Porfirio Díaz's Mexico and Guzmán Blanco's Venezuela–although it varied depending on the country and city. This was also the case in Brazil, where a marine officer remembered in 1912 the republic's years of struggle:

Todas as nossas aspirações, todas as preocupações dos republicanos da propaganda, eram de fato copiadas das tradições francesas. Falávamos na França bem-amada, na influência da cultura francesa, nas menores coisas das nossas lutas políticas relembrávamos a França. A *Marselhesa* era nosso hino de guerra, e sabíamos de cor os episódios da grande revolução. Ao nosso bravado "Viva a República!" seguia-se quase sempre o de "Viva a França! . . . A França era a nossa guiadora, dela falávamos sempre e sob qualquer pretexto. (*O Paiz*, 20-11-1912; qtd. in Murilo de Carvalho 12-13)

All of our aspirations, all the preoccupations of the republican converts were, in fact, copies of French traditions. We spoke of beloved France, of the influence of French culture; we evoked France in the smallest details of our political struggles. The *Marseillaise* was our war hymn and we knew the episodes of the Great Revolution by heart. Our clamor, "Vive la République," was almost always followed with "Vive la France!" . . . France was our guide, and no matter what the pretext, we spoke about her constantly.

In Brazil this model survived rather well France's reluctance and awkwardness during the proclamation of the republic. Indeed, in spite of France's negotiation for its participation in the formation of the Brazilian military at the beginning of the twentieth century, those close to the Emperor William II often heard him voice his distrust of those "Francophile people," always ready to welcome news and novelties from Paris (Blancpain 285).

The French have greatly contributed to this Latin American image of France that has prevailed since the end of the eighteenth century. The view of France as the defender of law and liberty (see Zola), as a nation predestined by her entire history to embrace the world (see Jaurès), was received outside of France as an enlightening dissonance. More or less exaggerated and yet remarkably long-lasting, the late nineteenth-century *afrancesamiento* (francophilism) of an urban, affluent Latin American elite merely reflected a larger world phenomenon–since there is "a constituent imagination" steeped in French culture that played, in many countries, "a central role in the development of the State, and more generally, of its politics" (Bayart 231). The social and cultural influences exerted by an idealized France and a place soon to be known as the City of Light not only reached the elites; evidence can be found everywhere, from Mexico to Argentina, that it reached deep into the national ethos. Meticulous studies show that France provided an imaginary that was followed in Rio de Janeiro, as well as Buenos Aires or Mexico City, and was disseminated in oral cultures where few could write, let alone possess the means to dress *à la française* (see Muzart); the idea of France as a political paradigm therefore seemed to spread throughout the Latin American population and envelop it. Nonetheless, from Voltaire to Comte, French culture markedly and directly influenced a single, restricted area of Latin American culture: the highest level of written culture–the Lettered City. This is the only area that was distinctly open to foreign influences and registered their rise in the ruling elite and subsequent fall as a middle class belatedly developed. French influence predominated as long as the elite and the enlightened oligarchies with access to written culture controlled the various nations. This fact is even more singular in view of some uncertain though telling statistics: When the French influence reached its height in Latin America, less than one out of ten Argentineans (in the best situation in Latin America) and less than one out of forty Colombians had received any primary education. Nevertheless, in both nations French was the language of culture and France was the source of a lifestyle that was copied by the cultural elites. In her diary, the Francophile queen of Argentinean letters, Victoria Ocampo (1890–1979), exclaimed: "Hablo mejor francés que español, y me gusta más. ¿Cómo ha pasado?" (90) ("How is it that I speak better French than Spanish, and that the former pleases me so much more?"). Indeed reflecting, as an Argentinean, the extreme Europeanization of

Latin America, her attitude is far from exceptional: "Esta actitud fue típica de cierta categoría, de argentinos, y constituyó durante mucho tiempo algo tan característicamente argentino como vestirse a la inglesa o tomar el té" (Ernesto Sábato, qtd. in Ayerza de Castilho and Felgine 11) ("This attitude was, for a very long time, typical of a certain class of Argentineans, but it was as characteristically Argentinean as was dressing like the English or having tea"). (See **Table 2**.)

Nicaraguan poet Rubén Darío (1867–1916) stands as a remarkable example of the cosmopolitan *criollo* who fixed his attention on Paris, inventing the concept of "mental gallicism" (Darío 1955, 874). This expression reveals the state of mind of part of the Latin American elite. Considering its exclusive nature, it is also an exaggeration, although it does reveal the eagerness of one part of the Latin American elites to identify with French culture. Within this general context, France was often imagined as the land of progress, a great universal source likened to Athens and Rome. Pérez-Pacheco writes of this fervor for French literature and political thought that has been dominant for more than a century: "Nous avons imité la France avec cette ferveur touchante du jeune peuple romain qui se mit à l'école de la Grèce" (269) ("We have imitated France with the touching fervor of the young Roman people who sought a

Greek education"). Or, as the Mexican intellectual, Mario de la Cueva, put it: "Francia salvó a la América Hispánica. Los pueblos de América vivieron a la francesa y pudieron conservarse latinos. La Universidad de México fu[e] una Universidad francesa, y a Francia le debemos por sobre todo el amor a la libertad . . ." (qtd. in Silva 20) ("France has saved Hispanic America. The nations of America have lived *à la française* and have managed to preserve their Latinity. The University of Mexico has been a French university; and above all else, we owe France our love of freedom . . .").

Thus, when it comes to Paris and France, there was a consensus among the modern elites of Latin America as to their centrality.

Much less economically present than Great Britain, France was still self-invested in a messianic mission and stood as a purveyor of founding ideas, having acceded, before the new Latin American nations, to a political modernity by breaking with old political models. Built to last, the most politically and culturally unifying common denominator of a large part of the Latin American elites was indeed France. A number of Latin American politicians recalled this fact, as did the Brazilian president who–in 1896–spoke of Brazil and France's common "community of origins" and "aspirations" (AMAE, NS, Brazil, 121A [25]). Many cultural institutions in Latin America echoed this idea at the start of the twentieth century: The Brazilian Academy of Letters structured itself according to the French model. Those in law and medicine too revealed an appreciation of Parisian science, a mastery of the French language, and a taste for the voyage to Paris. Produced in Mexico in 1833, the *Establecimiento de Ciencias Médicas* (Establishment of Medical Sciences) listed the texts that are indispensable to student learning: All were in French. The many statues of Pasteur erected in most big Latin American cities reveal French influences over the discipline. It was not rare for those Latin Americans educated in France to settle there: From the early days of the Third Republic to the start of the twentieth century (in 1903), fourteen Venezuelan physicians practiced in Paris, and as many others published their scientific research there (Vannini de Gerulewicz 97). At the start of the century Brazil displayed a particular fondness for French medicine and exact sciences. Indeed, Oswaldo Cruz (1872–1917), a former Brazilian student from the Pasteur Institute, perfected the vaccine for yellow fever; on the eve of the fall of the empire in Brazil (1889), the Emperor Don Pedro II sought medical care in France. In early twentieth century, for certain disciplines, some countries favored France, that is to say, Paris. For instance, young Brazilians moved to Paris to pursue university degrees in literature, engineering, and medicine. Others with engineering and industrial aspirations preferred Switzerland and Germany, while England was the destination for future tradesmen (see Foncin). Chile revealed the same tendencies, although Chileans tended earlier and more widely to opt for the United States.

Arts and letters represented even more the powerful European (and essentially Parisian) direction taken by the Latin American elites (but the common links limited themselves to artistic influences, contrary to common perception stemming from recent events). In 1904 the Francophile review from Caracas, *El Cojo Ilustrado*, organized a literary competition around the theme of "foreign writers having influenced the literary movement of the past decade in Venezuela." Venezuelan writer, José Gil Fortoul (1861–1943) was awarded the prize: The laureate explained that "la

Table 2. *The French Language in South America at the Turn of the Nineteenth Century*

Argentina, 1895/1900
- Elementary, secondary, and university curriculums favor the French language (see Foncin)
- For the first five years (in free public schools) at the elementary level: one theory and practice course in French, games and children's dances in French are compulsory.
- "Today (1895) English is as equally mandatory as French in all Argentinean schools." (Bulletin 03-04-1895).
- In 1897, the teaching of French is declared compulsory–as opposed to Italian and English.
- In 1899–1900, the government contemplates suppressing French from the secondary level since "students inevitably know French already." Because of protests, the idea is revoked.
- Law schools: French entry exam required.

Bolivia, Peru
- "Our influence is undermined" (see Foncin).

Brazil
- French is compulsory for graduate exams. Professors of medicine and most sciences use French textbooks or French translations of German texts.

Chile
- French is not compulsory at any level. There was a decrease in French moral authority; the Germans have "invaded the Chilean university with their own professors, instructors and methods" (see Foncin).

Paraguay
- French is not compulsory at any programed level.

Uruguay
- "The Uruguayan university's Bachelors program (letters and science) requires a certain knowledge of our language": on average, 168 students per year around 1898. French is required for "final exams at the Military Academy and School of Arts and Occupations." In the two teachers' training colleges, French is taught to about 90 students. (Bulletin 15-01-1898)

Source: Foncin; *Bulletin de l'Alliance française*, 03/04-1895; *Bulletin de l'Alliance française*, 15-01-1898.

Table 3. *1900: Teaching of French (Evaluation by the Alliance française)*

Argentina
- "Initially, a Frenchman who arrives in Buenos Aires is under the impression that the French language is widely used . . . . This is partly a mistake." "In the past twenty-five years," French "has lost much of its foothold in social and commercial relations." It is "outstripped by Spanish and English in business, and in certain cases, by Italian . . ., [which has] become the language of immigrants." "It seems inevitable and definite that our language is being eliminated."
- Distinct decline in French colleges for girls because of elementary schools and state colleges.
- "For their French education, elementary students in the capital merely possess a French grammar, translated from English, and/or a spelling vocabulary modified for the most part by Spanish words." The French textbook is translated, imitated, plagiarized—but in Spanish.

Brazil
- The "preponderance" of French "leaves a distinct mark on all other foreign languages." Like the Portuguese, every Brazilian who has received some form of education understands French." "In Brazil, French is taught in most colleges and schools." "Knowledge of French appears almost exclusively in the coastal regions where education is common and relations with European countries are more frequent. Yet, even there, it is the privilege of the upper classes." The influence of French "grows with the increasing expansion of education; this expansion becomes sharply more pronounced."

Chile
- "Our language is not spoken as frequently." It is necessary to organize a "resistance against the growing and threatening expansion and increase of other languages."

Cuba
- "The many private schools . . .do not concern themselves in the slightest with French . . . . Every day, our language loses a bit more ground."

Mexico
- One French high school founded before 1898. "Our cause has progressed greatly." "The teaching staff includes teachers from France and sent by the *Alliance*." Porfirio Diaz visits the school (1898). Twelve instructors offer French courses to all students enrolled in Mexico's national schools. The General Director of primary education lends his support to the diffusion of the French language.

Paraguay
- "French is taught more or less by a few independent teachers and in a few educational establishments." "Larger and wealthier, the German colony has managed to open national schools in Asuncion."

Uruguay
- The capital's public schools offer no French courses (2427 French children, 1600 of whom are in Montevideo). "No schools that are mainly French," except a small school in Carmelo in 1898.
- "French is taught only in independent foreign schools . . .and (in the provinces, unlike Montevideo) the offering of French programs has not been successful": ten in Montevideo, yet some in serious difficulty.
- One French college, the *Lycée Carnot* (established between 1895–1898).
- Italian is "the everyday language, the language of small trade," and is spoken in the city. "Because of transactions with England and the United States, English is above all others the commercial language. "Although in third place, French is . . . the language of literature, arts, science and ideas." Texts and authors used in graduate teaching, notably for law and medicine, are . . . French and do not exist in Spanish translation."

Source: Bulletin de l'Alliance française, 03-04-1895, 15-01-1898, 11-1899; Foncin, 237 ff.

mayor influencia extranjera durante la última década ha sido la de los escritores franceses contemporáneos" (Vannini de Gerulewicz 101) ("the greatest foreign influence has been that of contemporary French writers"). Among the most imitated, he listed Benjamin Constant, Stendhal, the Goncourts, Verlaine, Baudelaire, Mallarmé, Mendés, Bourget, Maupassant, and Barrès. He added that writers from other countries had also influenced the nation's literature, but "hablando en términos generales, Venezuela está viendo las literaturas extranjeras con anteojos franceses" (Vannini de Gerulewicz 101) ("that generally, Venezuela reads foreign literatures with French eyes"). In Argentina the influence of French literature quickly developed through Romanticism and, upon Echeverría's return from France, libraries carried Villemain, Hugo, Dumas, Lamartine, Cousin, and Chateaubriand, along with Lamennais, Montesquieu, Renan, and many others—some of whom are translated by Sarmiento. In Brazil, France's literary influence was a determining factor. In 1909 the academic Rui Barbosa (1849–1923) welcomed Anatole France in French on a visit that was significant for Brazil's culture and its pol-

itics; he proclaimed "le splendeur solaire de cette grande France qui a été la mère intellectuelle de tous le peuples de cette race" (Tavares 236) ("the solar splendor of a majestic France, mother of all nations of this race"). Generally speaking, French influence is also apparent in Latin American demand for French lecturers, artists, or actors (Matthieu 217). Certainly prone to self-satisfaction, the *Groupement des universités et des grandes écoles de France pour les relations avec l'Amérique Latine* (Commission of French Universities and *Grandes écoles* in France [the elite institutes of advanced studies] for relations with Latin America) produces, in 1908, the following report: "La culture française est en honneur dans la plupart des collèges et des universités d'Amérique latine; . . . les jeunes gens s'y instruisent en grande partie dans nos livres et avec nos méthodes; . . . quelques-uns viennent en France pour achever leurs études ou les compléter" (Choncol and Martinière 63) ("French culture is honored by most colleges and universities of Latin America; . . . a good number of young people use our books and methods to educate themselves; . . . some come to France to complete or finish their studies"). (See **Table 3**.)

The plastic arts also undergo French influence, experiencing it either directly or indirectly. Admittedly, such influence cannot necessarily be detected where contemporary culture might expect: in avant-garde art associated with such revolutionaries as Manet, Monet, Degas, Renoir, and Pissaro, who are reduced to and sometimes erroneously identified with the great political movement for democracy. We must recall the two first great Venezuelan painters, Arturo Michelena (1863–1898) and Tito Salas (1887–1974), who were brilliant students of academic French painters: Michelena worked essentially in Paris as the student of Jean-Paul Laurens and retained a deep religious bent (he won a gold medal at the World Fair of 1889 for his "Charlotte Corday"); Salas was also a disciple of Laurens and one of the last masters of historical painting; he received a gold medal at the Salon (in Paris) in 1907. At the start of the twentieth century, many of the innovative movements originated in Paris: Fauvism and Cubism burst forth in Paris, which was where Picasso settled; Paris was chosen for the diffusion of Italian Futurism, the new choreography of Russian ballet, and the beginnings of cinema. (Only six months after the first showings in Paris, the first films were shown in Buenos Aires on 18 July 1896 by the brothers Lumière.) This was also when the French language–used by Frederic II, the Tsar's, and the Brazilian Empire's courts, as well as hesitantly chosen by Goethe–increasingly insinuated itself into the languages of Latin America; now, it is in good form and stylish for proper people to say *la soirée, la matinée, le bouquet, le nécessaire, le buffet* . . . .

Latin Americans in France 1901–1990

A great number of Latin Americans moved to France: "Né du désir d'une vie libre et facile et du besoin d'une enrichissement culturel que le voyageur croyait trouver, à peine parcourus les quais de la Seine" (Séris 1989, 299) ("Sprung from a desire for freedom, ease, and a cultural thirst which the traveler believes to have fulfilled before even reaching the banks of the Seine"). This Parisian complex became deeply entrenched in the years prior to 1914. During the nineteenth century the ritual voyage to Europe undertaken by a part of the elites led to Paris; we need only mention those from Argentina in the first half of the nineteenth century, Bernardino Rivadavia (1780–1845), Esteban Echeverría (1805–1851), Juan Bautista Alberdi (1810–1884), Domingo Faustino Sarmiento (1811–1888), or the *libertador* San Martín (1778–1850), who retired to Paris (Quentin-Mauroy 67–81). Moreover, the Venezuelan Guzmán Blanco went to Paris six times and died there in 1899. In the year of his death the Spaniard Miguel de Unamuno (1864–1936) wrote to the Nicaraguan Rubén Darío: "Debo decirle que no acabo de comprender del todo esa atracción que sobre ustedes ejerce París, ni ese anhelo de que sea precisamente París, y no Londres, o Berlín, o Viena, o Bruselas, o Estocolmo, o . . . Heidelberg" (in Darío 1943, 33) ("I must tell you that I cannot quite understand your attraction for Paris, nor this desire that it be in Paris that we find you and not London, Berlin, Vienna, Brussels, Stockholm or . . . Heidelberg").

Even though encounters with the French along the banks of the Seine were not as fruitful as those among the Latin Americans themselves, the belief in the "nécessité de Paris" [need for Paris], "le rêve immense" [the great dream], "le printemps éternel de la race latine" [the eternal spring of the Latin race], prevailed (Séris 1989, 311). The publication of reviews by

Latin Americans in Paris is a good example. An inventory of only Spanish publications in the last third of the nineteenth century includes *El Americano, La Raza latina*, later *Cristóbal Colón, América en Paris, La Colonia hispano-americana de París, La Estrella de Chile, La Revue illustrée du Rio de la Plata, La República cubana* . . . . Other publications at the start of the twentieth century include Enrique Gómez Carrillo's (1873–1927) *El nuevo Mercurio* (1907), Rubén Darío's *Mundial* (1911–1912) and *Elegancias* (1912), Francisco García Calderón's *La Revista de América* (1912–1914), and Leopoldo Lugones's (1874–1938) *La revue sud-américaine* (1914). At the turn of this century an entire generation of Spanish American intellectuals and artists oscillated between Paris and Madrid–and the latter, according to Manuel Ugarte (1878–1951), representing origins–the blood of their idiom and their essential life. Yet Paris tipped the scales since it offered recognition, publishing opportunities (with Garnier, Bouret, Michaud, and Ollendorff), and arts awards. To a large extent this was also the case in Portuguese-speaking America. Indeed, at the end of the nineteenth century, Brazilian students seemed to prefer Paris over Coimbra; artists journeyed to the banks of the Seine for the *Salon d'automne*, seeking a first triumph, as did the sculptor Victor Brecheret (1894–1955), as well as "os coortes futuristas de São Paulo" (Brito Silva 131) ("the futurist troop of São Paulo"). They were not alone or even first in choosing France: In the early twentieth century, a long, luxurious vacation in the Paris of *la belle époque* was favored by the wealthy *fazendeiros* (landowners), whose currency had been strengthened by the export of coffee. The memoirs of Alceu Amoroso Lima (1893–1983) and Afonso Arinos de Mello Franco (1868–1916) are filled with such accounts, while those of Medeiros e Albuquerque (1867–1934) or Gilberto Amado (1887–1969) demonstrate what Brazilian youths came looking for in Paris–a city whose streets recalled the rivers "da Grécia" (of Greece) (Amado 207). During these stays, only rarely did a less enchanting reality manage to transform seductive illusions about France. Until the time of the First World War, nothing could undermine those illusions: Upon their return to American soil, many Spanish speakers yearned nostalgically (*extrañar*) for the country left behind, just as Portuguese speakers experienced *saudade* (the loss of a far away place). Again, on only the rarest occasion did daily annoyances or disappointments, likely to arise during the stay in France, tarnish this mental construction.

Although it was generally the elites that undertook such journeys, these fortunate, cultivated groups were not alone in embracing Parisian culture. Historians have archival evidence of non-Francophone, nonlearned Latin Americans

Table 4. *Latin Americans in France 1901–1990*

	In 1982		In 1990	
	Paris	*France*	*Paris*	*France*
Latin Americans	6,613	29,180	11,939	45,478
Brazilians	1,427	3,808	2,522	6,069
Argentineans	955	3,724	1,247	3,500
Haitian	819	4,724	2,490	14,343
Colombians	780	1,852	1,831	4,189
Mexicans	549	2,128	769	2,052
Chileans	508	6,272	647	8,212
Venezuelans	453	1,820	341	1,052

Source: Préfecture de Police/INED-INSEE. *Tableaux démographiques.*

who journeyed to France despite their moderate means, driven by the same faith in the opportunity to make their fortune in Europe and especially Paris. During the First World War in particular, Argentinean diplomats attempted to solve some of the problems faced by these travelers and helped to make arrangements for their return home, sometimes even establishing aid programs (AMRE-A, *Secc. diplomática y consular, div. comercial, Francia*, 1918). Until the 1930s, various representatives of the Latin American intellectual elite lived in Paris and were proof of continued French influence on Latin America. Either transient or long-lasting, the stay in Paris might consist of a cultural holiday, an educational experience sought from the intelligentsia of the Latin Quarter, or, at times, a kind of cultural refuge. Many well-known intellectuals traveled to Paris to become aware of their own Latin American identity: Alfonso Reyes (1899–1959), Pablo Neruda (1904–1973), Oswald de Andrade (1890–1954), Gilberto Freyre (1900–1987), Miguel Angel Asturias (1899–1974), Alejo Carpentier (1904–1980), Ernesto Sábato (b. 1911), and Octavio Paz (1914–1998). There were also artists such as Diego Rivera (1886–1957), Tarsila do Amaral (1886–1973), and Heitor Villa-Lobos (1887–1959), technicians and engineers Santos-Dumont (1873–1932), whose grandparents were French, studied mechanical engineering in Bordeaux before his pioneering flights of 1901 and 1906, physicians, and politicians in exile before the Great War, Porfirio Diaz (1830–1915) and the Mexican Francisco de la Barra (1863–1939), or, after that, the Peruvians José Carlos Mariátegui (1894–1930) and Victor Raúl Haya de la Torre (1895–1979) (Neira 155–84). The presence of such various groups underlined the close and perpetual overlapping of the cultural importance and symbolic significance of France's influence.

Prior to 1914 (or between 1901 and 1911), Latin American women and men alike traveled to France; there, their numbers slowly increased, making up 8.2 percent of the Parisian population (although this percentage may also include Canadians). Yet the growth in this Latin American presence was three times less than the global presence of foreigners in France and seven times lower than the increase in U.S. citizens. And, by the start of the twentieth century, Latin Americans contributed progressively less to the total number of foreigners in the capital: Between 1901 and 1911 the percentage of Americans (excluding the United States) dropped from 3.7 percent to 3.3 percent. During the first decades of the twentieth century, France's powerful image began to fade, but without affecting the above statistics. There were at least four factors at work in this waning effect, following in a certain chronological succession: reasons intrinsic to Latin America, a decline in French presence, an evolution in the perception of France, and the competition of other foreign models. The French metaphor was no longer necessary; new reflections on identity reinforced distinctly Latin American politics, and nation-building, as well as identity-formation, no longer required explicit cultural references to an outside source. The process of assimilating French values had been accomplished. Despite an understandable fresh upsurge of Francophilia, signs of France's decline around the First World War were accumulating; but the new interest could be seen in Chile, as Carlos Gutiérrez declares in the name of the Federation of Chilean Students: "Il faut que la France vive, et elle vivra. France de tous les siècles, tu es la mère de toutes les libertés saintes, et c'est pourquoi nous te portons un amour filial" (Martinenche 186) ("France must live, and it will. France of all centuries, you are the mother of all holy rights, and that is why we have such filial love for you").

But in truth, the war contributed to the weakening of such representations. Even though its victorious end temporarily slowed down this decline, the Great War crystallized certain movements and accelerated hidden trends. Admittedly, in 1919, Brazil still chose to train its modest army in Paris, at the expense of the two competing countries, Great Britain and Germany. But it was the U.S. forces that ended the War in Europe, and Washington joined Europe in the training of Latin American armies. During the war, "a veritable spiritual scission" divided the two continents (Duhamel 4). Yet it was only in stages that both Europe and Latin America, each for their own reasons, abandoned the notion of a shared identity and set of values for the West. In Europe, it was the First World War that caused this disillusionment; for example, in France, this could be heard in the echoes of the Third Republic in the regime established at Vichy in 1940, which abandoned loudly and clearly France's revolutionary ideology, whose motto has been "liberty, equality, fraternity." In Latin America the abandonment of shared ideals could be seen in the development of the elites and a growing access to a culture inherited from Europe, as well as in the denunciation of cosmopolitanism and the rise of nationalism.

Before the war Latin Americans still journeyed to France in large numbers; the war essentially stalled these travels. Certain consequences of this interruption are still visible today. Deprived of Europe, Latin Americans accentuate the marks of their European appropriations. For instance, during this period the Argentinean resort Mar del Plata took on a distinctly European guise as Argentina's elite society, prevented from crossing the Atlantic, extended its stay. Only the many Latin American soldiers enlisted in the French army were to be found in France at this time; in most capitals, memorials recall those Latin Americans who died for a Parisian ideal.

When they are spontaneous, foreign cultural phenomena remain unchanged. Yet in the 1920s and 1930s, when France (or the French Enlightenment) still represented a paradigmatic model, Latin American travel to Paris was steady. Paris indeed retained a considerable influence over certain scientific disciplines and remained a powerful general cultural force. But in the 1920s, the City of Liberty, *Paris-femme* or *Paris-nuit*, was no longer the only artistic source of influence. Artistic revolutions took place rather in Berlin or Moscow. Paris did remain, though, a cultural, and particularly artistic, favorite for the young Latin American elites.

After the victory many U.S. travelers were said to "[volver] a París sus miradas como a la nueva Jerusalén" (José E. Machado, qtd. in Vannini de Gerulewicz 112) ("consider Paris as the new Jerusalem"). Between and beyond the two wars, French journals and writers abounded in France, but so did eulogies by foreigners as well as Latin American journals. France was still appreciated for its supposed cultural superiority by a number of Latin American intellectuals who marked their generation, including the Mexican man of letters and diplomat, Alfonso Reyes, the Venezuelan Gil Fortoul, and the Argentinean writer and patron, Victoria Ocampo.

Paris still attracts, but sometimes more ambiguously than in the past. The Surrealist movement may come to mind here, deemed in Latin America as "one of the last great universal movements of expression and creativity" (Fuentes 1986, 118). Strictly speaking, Surrealism is not a French phenomenon; it has sparked intense cultural expression in Spain and been adopted by some parts of German culture. However, Surrealism was widely developed in Paris and considered essentially

Parisian; indeed, in their frequent denunciations of Futurism, Cubism, Dadaism, and Surrealism, Latin Americans have characterized these "isms" as Parisian rubbish. Certainly, Surrealism has manifested itself differently in Latin America, but its influence is noticeable everywhere. In the 1920s a good number of Spanish American intellectuals "continue to funnel through their numerous 'isms' the lesson of a French avant-garde, which they have most often learned from the Parisian milieu of Breton, Aragon and Éluard" (Stegagno Picchio 190). Through this exposure to Surrealism, they also discovered traces of Spanish literature's long tradition of fantasy, embodied in Calderón, Góngora, García Lorca, Rafael Alberti, Dalí, Miró, and Picasso. In the Buenos Aires of the 1920s and 1930s, French influence was felt in painting, especially in the work of the first group of avant-garde painters known as *el grupo de París* or *la escuela de París*, and organized around Aquiles Bali, Héctor Basaldúa, Horacio Butler, Raquel Forner, Emilio Pettoruti, and Juan del Prete. But the genuine Surrealist forerunner was undoubtedly Xul Solar of Argentina, and one of its first representatives was incontestably Antonio Berni. It was especially after the war that a Surrealist poetics spread throughout Argentina, with a second generation of avant-garde artists that included Aldo Pellegrini (1903–1973), Enrique Molina (1910–1996), Francisco Madariaga (1927–2000), Olga Orozco (1920–1999), and Julio Llinás (b. 1929). In the early 1940s, conversations between César Moro (1903–1956) and André Breton generated the International Surrealist Exhibition in Mexico, which was organized with Wolfgang Paalen; later, Octavio Paz made the most of his stay in Paris from 1946 to 1951 by participating in the Surrealist movement, which impacted on the direction of his literary work. In Brazil between 1925 and 1927, Pedro Dantas proposed, without attracting much attention, collective exercises in *écriture automatique*, labeled with the catchall term, "manifestations modernistes" (Stegagno Picchio 192) (modernist expression). But it was especially after 1930 that European Surrealism developed in Brazil: with Vicente do Rego Monteiro (1899–1970) who lived in Paris, Tarsila de Amaral who joined Oswald de Andrade in the Modernist movement, and especially the poets Jorge de Lima (1893–1953) and Murilo Mendes (1901–1975), as well as many others who followed suit.

Paris continued to be the ultimate cosmopolitan center, and representations that favored France slowly evolved. Surely, this French attraction did, in some cases, come to exist out of a certain sense of lack. As Manuel Ugarte, an Argentinean socialist writer devoted to "à révéler à l'Europe l'Amérique exotique" (revealing an exotic America to Europe), wrote: "verité, cette jeunesse ne se sentait pas attirée par un monde nouveau. Elle s'évadait d'un monde où elle étoufait" (qtd. in Séris 1994, 257) ("in truth, this young generation was not attracted to a new world. It was escaping from a world that was suffocating it"). But this evades the question: As nationalisms began to challenge this early-century cosmopolitanism, French influence was not simply assimilated by Latin America's cultural identity constructions. A good example is the Argentinean writer Ricardo Güiraldes (1886–1927), who lived in France from 1910 to 1912 and died there in 1927. Studded with Gallicisms, his most famous novel, *Don Segundo Sombra* (1927), recalls Sarmiento's binary opposition in *Civilización y Barbarie* [1845; *Civilization and Barbarism*], arguing that civilization can be found in the pampas, and barbarism in the city. Yet here, the city in question is not Paris but Buenos Aires. Unshakably, Paris remains the quintessence of civilization. And even when France goes to war in 1939, many Latin Americans living in Paris remained there; the Uruguayan writer and diplomat, Eugenio Garzón (1849–1940), died in Paris during the war, although the hostilities in and defeat of France did cause many to leave.

The City of Light and a developing French cultural diplomacy maintained their attraction; but there were certainly conflicting perceptions about, and exceptions to, the relatively sullen and increasingly unconvincing state of Paris's influence. Part of the cultivated elite continued to appreciate a history that was not their own, to breach the distance, and to see itself through the eyes of others; French presence in Latin America—as a mirroring of Europe—did not erase itself so readily. Moreover, as in most matters, everything depended on perception. Initially, many Latin Americans and an even greater number of French people failed to understand the recessionary impact of the war.

French culture was still a recipient of the highest distinctions, however. In 1921 the anticlerical writer and Dreyfus supporter, Anatole France, received the Nobel Prize for literature. This scholar's notoriety as well as his work had long since reached the other side of the Atlantic, and his writing had known immediate success. In 1909 he visited the South American republics, reaching Rio, São Paulo, Montevideo, and Buenos Aires—which was his ultimate goal; he lectured on François Rabelais, everywhere advocating human rights and the secularization of laws (see Salgado Campos). Apparently, there were numerous translations and more than 100,000 copies printed of his June 29 speech before the Chamber of Deputies in Buenos Aires. With triumphal arches and the French tricolor, Montevideo, Rio, and São Paulo welcomed this visitor who, along with the Third Republic, would incarnate French culture and intelligence for a long time to come. Brazilians were thus subjected to "do feitiço, da coqueluche, da deliciosa peste do anatolismo" (Carelli 95) ("the charm, veneration and wonderful nuisance of Anatolism"). Francophilia continued to touch the right chord; it underlay Claude Lévi-Strauss's account about an encounter with an old Brazilian villager who was overwhelmed about meeting a Frenchman for the first time: "Ah, Monsieur, vous êtes Français! Ah, la France! Anatole, Anatole!" (1955, 30) ("Ah, *Monsieur*, you are French! Ah, France! Anatole, Anatole!"). Selectively at least, French culture penetrated well beyond the civilized shores of the Atlantic.

Another exception to the weakening ties between France and Latin America was the development of Franco-Brazilian cultural relations through the scientific impetus of Georges Dumas. In the 1920s, Franco-Brazilian institutes of high culture were created in Rio de Janeiro (1922) and São Paulo (1925). Of the thirteen professors recruited from Europe by the Faculty of Philosophy, Science and Letters of São Paulo's State University (founded in 1934), six were French, four were Italian, and three were German. Yet the French were predominant only in the humanities and social sciences; the Italians took charge of mathematics and physics; and the Germans organized chemistry, zoology, and botany. Noticeably in Brazil, French influence restricted itself to literary culture and the humanities. Through its training and funding programs with which Europe could hardly compete, the United States dominated these fields from the First World War onward.

Once the First World War had ended, Latin Americans again journeyed to France, although for different reasons. In fact, trips were no longer undertaken by the economic or political elites, as was frequently the case at the end of the nineteenth century. It was especially the members of the literary or artistic elites who crossed the Atlantic, such as the poet of the Chilean avant-garde, Vicente Huidobro (1893–1948), and Argentinean writer Ricardo Güiraldes, who settled in Paris with the help of Valéry Larbaud, and there wrote his gaucho epic, *Don Segundo Sombra*. Others include Victoria Ocampo who, between Buenos Aires and Paris, established relations between Güiraldes, César Fernández Moreno (1919–1985), Borges (1899–1986), and Sábato, as well as a very heterogeneous "European" group featuring Rabindranath Tagore, Keyserling, Drieu La Rochelle, Waldo Frank, Paul Valéry, Roger Caillois, and André Malraux. The Peruvian poet César Vallejo (1892–1938) was buried in Montparnasse Cemetery (1938), as were other men of letters and Latin American politicians, such as President Porfirio Diaz. Finally, the French-Cuban painter Picabia, the pioneer of abstract painting, worked in Paris and scandalized what was left of the polite society responsible for France-Latin American relations. The literary and artistic elites were not alone in traveling to France: Latin American soldiers are sometimes still trained with the French army, although French military schools were not easily accessible to Latin Americans. Since the war, scientific fields are under the influence of other countries (notably Germany and the Anglo-Saxon nations); this was even true of medicine, in which France was still an authority. The education of the children of Brazilian President Vargas was a good indication of the decline in travel to Paris after the First World War. Not one of them was educated in France, but rather, the eldest son studied in Germany and married a German woman. The other son studied chemical engineering in the United States; and although the daughter studied law in Brazil, she was educated mostly in England. Statistics that compared the most likely countries of choice for studies abroad are difficult to come by. On the one hand, France remained a popular destination for North Americans; on the other, between the two world wars, the United States was a strong competitor in the areas of political and social sciences, economics, and engineering.

Germany attracted mostly future physicians or specialists, chemists, and some engineers; even prior to 1914 Berlin was considered to be a "scientific Mecca," to quote Louis Liard. Soon to become a fascist nation, Italy attracted lawyers and artists. These two countries actually promoted their programs in Latin America; they facilitated the transfer of former students, and Germany in particular organized them in social networks that were regularly well-maintained. More globally speaking, statistical data from the Préfecture de Police reveals a renewed presence of Latin Americans in France after the First World War in the early 1930s, although this renewal conceals a number of elements. On the one hand, it was ephemeral: The same numbers do not reappear before the 1970s, when Latin America's own political circumstances (exile caused by the rise of dictatorships) were a motivating factor. On the other hand, the statistic for 1931 must take into account the demographic increase in Latin America (60 million inhabitants in 1900, 82 million in 1914, and 111 million in 1930); increased access to written culture; and the growing ease of travel between America and Europe.

Paris certainly continued to proclaim the superiority of its culture throughout the world and particularly in Latin America. This proclamation did not always include the kind of nonsense spoken by the very racist writer and journalist, Abel Bonnard (Bonnard 74). The French Argentina specialist, Georges Lafond, was one of the most prolific supporters of Latin America in France, but did not hesitate in his writings to imply a similar superiority: "Ce fut une des particularités de l'Amérique latine de solliciter à toutes les époques de son histoire le concours de l'intellectualité européene–c'est-à-dire française" (Lafond 285) ("Throughout its history, one of Latin America's distinctive features has been its appeal to a European–that is to say a French–intellectuality").

In fact, right at the start of the century, the *Groupement des universités et des grandes écoles* (Commission of French universities and *grandes écoles*) noted France's ignorance of Latin America (qtd. in Lesca 430). During his pre-war visit to Latin America, Georges Clémenceau thanked his own ignorance since it protected him from a biased view.

About ten years later in the 1930s, Claude Lévi-Strauss indicated that, before his departure, "le Brésil et l'Amérique du Sud ne signifiaient pas grand-chose" ("Brazil and South America did not mean much") to him: "Le Brésil s'esquissait dans mon imagination comme des gerbes de palmiers contournés, dissimulant des architectures bizarres, le tout baigné dans une odeur de cassolette" ("I imagined Brazil as a torturous collection of palm trees, concealing bizarre architecture, with everything drenched in the odor of incense burners") (1955, 50). And the director of the *École normale supérieure*, who offered Lévi-Strauss a teaching position in São Paulo, imagined a place inhabited by Indians, at least in its outlying districts. The minister of Brazilian External Affairs, Baron de Rio Branco, was not completely wrong in his remark to a foreign diplomat in 1905: "On se conduit avec le Brésil comme avec une peuplade de sauvages" (AMAE, NS, Brazil, 21, 12-12-1905) ("We conduct ourselves with Brazil as we would with a tribe of savages"). Placing Paris at the top of the cultural hierarchy, these stereotypes also originated from a lack of either general or precise knowledge about Latin America–knowledge that would have replaced the global, vague, indeed inaccurate, view of Latin America and recognized the differences among its many countries. "Brazil . . . a small detail," parodied a revolted Gilberto Amado in 1912, a Francophile who was offended by France's vague and all-encompassing view of South America. Thus one of the common denominators of French perceptions was as follows: Latin America had no history; it had gradually been included, within Western historicity, entire Latin American societies, which until then were "slumbering nations 'without history,' silenced by colonial oppression" (Nora 286). The sub-continent was therefore a land almost without culture (or a least an autonomous one), constructed by a set of clichés. However, in contrast, the questioning of Europe's primacy by the educated sectors of Latin America stemmed from their extensive knowledge of the culture of the Old World. Although few in number, these challenges did indeed arise. On the eve of the First World War, the rebellion against flashy foreigners in Latin America had already begun. National feeling had sometimes been concomitant with the consciousness of a spreading Parisian influence, but from this point on, Latin American nationalism grew. In 1914 in Venezuela, for instance, Francisco Pimentel (1889–1942) remarked that until then the style and culture of Paris had completely invaded Venezuela (even though he himself was planning a trip to Paris).

However, during the quarter century separating the two world wars, Europe was still admired, while Latin America experienced a kind of puberty that rectified a hereditary yearning to be other than it was. Nationalisms, on a long-term basis, would undermine the most solid foundations of cosmopolitanism, exposing that curious dialogue between Europe and Latin America, which, on either side, was enthusiastically maintained but resulted in two very different views of each other. After the First World War the sense that Latin America was coming of age weakened, and the idea of original sin or *capitis diminutio* of being American disintegrated. Previously, some believed, as they did in Mexico, that Latin America arrived late at the banquet of European civilization and bypassed the formative stages of historical development, hurrying on, running from one form to the other, without allowing time for anything to mature. But with the affirmation of Latin America's coming of age, there was also the idea that the European rhythm might not be the only historical tempo available, and that Paris might no longer be a necessary point of reference.

After the Second World War Paris seemed to renew its influence, but this impression is a false one. Admittedly, the fall of Paris and then France in 1940 aroused the "mental Gallicism" and what were still the Francophile values of the Nicaraguan poet Rubén Darío; traditionally, members of the most elevated Latin American social groups had been attached to a symbolic country—sometimes through money, but almost always through culture. But henceforth, it was a sense of failure that predominated—the failure of the European democracies and of their system of alliance. Europe was no longer held up as an example, as the war set a complex new stage for the breakdown of European models in Latin America. The tenuous economic relations between Latin America and France were annihilated and journeys to Paris were postponed.

The news of liberation certainly startled most Latin American cultural elites. Preserved from imminent destruction, was Paris really liberated? In street demonstrations, many cities of the subcontinent acclaimed the historical city—this mausoleum of universalist values that originated in the French Revolution. Having worked hard, during the war, to disseminate its culture in Latin America, a liberated France noted that "l'influence spirituelle dont jouissait la France dans ces pays avant la guerre est restée presque intacte" (AMAE, G 1939–1945, Algeria, América 1291 [19] 17-06-1943) ("her spiritual influence in these countries prior to the war was almost intact"). Nevertheless, the defeat, the sight of France's struggle, and the interruption of commercial relations struck a lasting blow against the prestige of the cultural metropolis.

In the early post-war years, concrete or oratorical expressions of Francophilia were still frequent in Latin America (e.g., *Revue de l' IFAL*, 1, 1945). However, these must be compared to the increased cultural and economic presence of the United States. Traditional links to French culture were often recalled, in fact, in order to offset the growing U.S. presence. It is thus easy to understand why a number of Latin American chancellors vowed "in warm friendship" to include France as a permanent member of the United Nations Security Council, "en hommage . . . à son rôle spirituel et à l'élévation de sa culture" (AMAE, G. 1939–1945, Algeria, América 1300 [102], 20-09-1942) ("to pay homage to . . . its spiritual role and the loftiness of its culture"). Thus the ties were apparently renewed.

At the outset of Liberation, Paris and Latin America created a multiplicity of institutions intended mainly for the revitalization of diplomatic and economic relations between the French and the Latin Americans (see Choncol and Martinière). But in the long term, these institutions served above all as a form of cultural conservation, and the results failed to meet high expectations. These initiatives marked a certain renewal of those intellectual affinities from the 1930s interrupted by the war. At the University of São Paulo in Brazil, for example, the connections were solid, with the visits of Fernand Braudel, Claude Lévi-Strauss, Pierre Monbeig, and, to a lesser extent, Georges Bernanos; or with Paul Rivet in Colombia, Jacques Soustelle in Mexico, and Roger Caillois in Argentina. In a revised treaty of Tordesillas, Fernand Braudel's students took on different parts of the Latin American continent: Pierre Chaunu went to Spanish America and Frédéric Mauro moved to Brazil. While French institutions in Latin America were created in order to promote Francophilia (1945, Mexico City, IFAL; 1945, Port-au-Prince; 1947, Santiago, Chile; 1948, Lima, IFEA), in Paris itself, relations with Latin America were also pursued, notably at the *Maison de l'Amérique latine* [1945; Latin American House], the *Chambre de commerce France-Amérique latine* [1946; Chamber of Commerce France-Latin America], and the *Groupe parlementaire d'amitié France-Amérique latine* [1947; Parliamentary Group of French-Latin American Friendship].

Thus, in the early post-war years, and with the active support of many Latin American governments, UNESCO settled in Paris, as the city regained its symbolic meaning through its diplomatic and university networks. Gradually, Paris once again received distinguished Latin Americans, as it had in the nineteenth century. In Brazil, for instance, the honorary president of the newly founded *Maison d'Amérique latine* was the ambassador de Souza Dantas, already posted in Paris and Vichy; Brazil's permanent delegate to UNESCO, Paulo Berredo Carneiro, became the first general representative of a very "French" Latin Union founded in 1954, while the economist and future minister, Celso Furtado, defended his thesis in Paris. Destitute, Brazilian writer and communist member Jorge Amado (1912–2001) finally settled in the bohemian circle of a Latin Quarter hotel. In 1954, this renewal seemed to culminate in the inauguration of the Institut des hautes études de l'Amérique latine (Institute for Advanced Studies on Latin America), symbolically located on the same street that housed the prestigious Institut des études politiques (Institute of Political Studies).

In 1946, the number of Latin Americans in France was at its lowest in the entire century: A census shows 3,791 people, which equals only a quarter of the number counted in 1931 and a third of those recorded in 1901. With an increase to 6,933, according to a 1962 census sixteen years later, the Latin American presence in Paris had not reached the levels of the 1930s, which were, it must be recalled, a time of economic crisis and of serious breakdown in European political stability. As industrial growth resumed in Latin America after the post-war difficulties, France was hardly welcoming during the cold war; for instance it stripped Brazilian Jorge Amado (1912–2001) of his residence permit. Wrapped up in its colonial wars, France aroused criticism and suspicion. Engaged, by turning to the rest of Europe, in its own industrial reconstruction and development, it invested little in distant foreign countries, struggling to renew tenuous commercial relations.

Yet the connection was renewed, reinforced by the stabilization of the Fifth Republic. Paris was again deemed attractive, since it was the capital of an ambitious country that, under General de Gaulle's leadership, drew the world's attention; it was now more open (through André Malraux's intervention, Jorge Amado regained his residence permit), and it developed an open relationship with Latin America. De Gaulle's 1964 visit of ten Latin American capitals revived a traditional discourse centered on the old theme of Franco-Latin American affinities; it also initiated a policy of cultural and technological cooperation, based on an agreement, which meant that France and Latin America would exchange students and researchers. Thus, from 1968 to 1969, 526 Latin Americans (of whom 220 were Brazilian, 111 were Mexican, and 101 were Argentinean) were registered in Parisian schools: They formed the first regional contingent of foreign scholarship holders.

Throughout the 1960s Fidel Castro's ascent to power in Havana, the political development of the Cuban government, and the networks of French Latin-Americanism drastically changed France's perception of Latin America. From then on Latin America was considered to be an exemplary political laboratory. A number of factors radically altered French, Parisian, and Latin American thinking, as well as relations with Latin Americans living in Paris: anti-U.S. and French anti-imperialist protests against the U.S. embargo, the French intelligentsia's journeys to Cuba, and the positive mythology of guerilla revolution surrounding Che Guevara (his name is a rally cry during the Parisian student protest of 1968). Henceforth, the dominant contact characteristics were not so much diplomacy and academia, but militancy and leftist ideology (even though these two were not exclusive to each other); current events were the main focus, attracting journalists, editors, and economists preoccupied with the problems of Latin America's development—as it joined the Third World. Professional and ideological associations, friendships, and sometimes familial links (for example the Debrays, Joxes, and Pisanis) were formed at the heart of militant networks, which were open to contacts and exchanges with Latin America; these relations help to explain why Paris, through its show of solidarity from the end of the 1960s onward, was the destination favored by those Latin Americans forced into exile by the rise of dictatorships. Among the first to arrive were Uruguayans and Brazilians (most notably Celso Furtado), Argentineans (such as the economists Julio Cesar Neffa and Moïse Ikonikof), and a number of Colombians, including the president of the Colombian M19 (Guerrilla Army), Navarro Wolf.

Latin Americans in Paris were still in modest numbers, for as refugees they were without status, and if they held a traditional residence permit, their numbers still could not be recorded in a census. Nevertheless, their presence was deeply felt, due to their more or less easy integration into the heart of France's research and teaching institutions, and thanks to their relations with or immersion in the militant groups of the French Left. With the overthrow of the Social Democratic government of Chile in September 1973, the image of a Latin American community in exile crystallized in Paris and lasted well beyond the reinstatement of democracy in most Spanish American countries as well as the return of Latin Americans in exile to their own countries. During the 1960s, the French Left and parts of the youth rallied around Castro and then experienced much disillusionment. Yet with the political change led by President Allende, the French Left witnessed, in the early 1970s, the real possibility of an elected socialist president, as well as the subsequent socialist structuring of society. Did not a correspondent from Le Monde propagate in France the expression, "Mitterand, the French Allende"? The brutal overthrow of Allende was a dramatic experience that sparked heated and typically French debates, as well as a headline in Le Monde: "Santiago sur Seine." The French (and Swedish) ambassadors' initiatives, the support of the French government, and a rallying around leftist (communist and noncommunist) parties and unions resulted in an emergency plan to accommodate all those in asylum at the French embassy in Santiago.

From 4 November 1973 (the arrival date at Paris Orly Airport of the first twenty-four refugees granted safe conduct passes by the Pinochet junta) until the end of 1974, arrivals at Orly were steady, especially between the months of February and May. How many were there? On 30 January 1975, OFPRA counted 1,021 Latin American refugees registered in France, 63 percent from Chile; at the end of that year, the official number is 1570, but this—it must be remembered—was still quite a small number compared to a total of 127,979 refugees in France. The explosion of reception facilities reflected improvisation and solidarity at work: The coordinating activities and know-how of volunteer organizations, such as CIMADE, the Social Aid Service to Immigrants, and France-Terre d'Asile, were fundamental. Yet, at the same time, the French government also increased its participation under the pressure of events: With the influx of Chilean refugees, the government moved away from a case-by-case system into an organization of collective reception facilities. In this sense the reception of Chilean refugees anticipated the methods that would be used with Vietnamese refugees (see Sáenz Carrete).

With 2,360 of them resident in France in 1975, Chileans ranked among the largest of the Latin American communities in the country (6,272 out of 29,180 in 1982). Nevertheless, out of 4,864 citizens of Latin American descent (who made up only 1.5 percent of foreigners recorded in Paris in 1978), there were fewer than 400 Chileans in the capital by the end of the 1970s. If the Chilean refugees once made up as much as 44.5 percent of the Latin Americans in Paris, they still represented but 4 percent of the total refugees in the capital. But it is important to note that many Latin Americans in exile did not receive or request refugee status. The inflow of Chileans remained at a more or less moderate rate, while the size of the Latin American community remained modest; thus the false generalization that identified every Latin American as a refugee began to fade in the public perception. Since the Second World War the largest group of Latin Americans in Paris were Brazilians and Argentineans, followed quantitatively by Colombians, Venezuelans, and Mexicans. The arrival of Chilean refugees, who accounted for a particularly small number of Latin American residents, did not alter this hierarchy of Latin American presence in the city.

An increasingly important part of the Latin American diaspora became militant, creating a multiplicity of committees, collectives, groups, and associations. With the collaboration of French militants, associations were organized in the suburbs and around key focal points in Paris, such as the Centre international de la culture populaire (International Center of Popular Culture), CEDETIM/Centre d'études anti-impérialistes (Center of Anti-Imperialist Studies), the latter located on the premises of Rue du Théâtre (on loan from Church authorities) or at the Church of Saint Eustache on Montmartre, commonly known as La pointe and organized in 1976 as a rallying point for a dispersed community by the curate, Denis Perrot. In the years between 1968 and 1973, it is possible to locate about seven more or less well-knit groups, and a few years later the Coordination des comités latino-américains (Coordination of Latin American Committees), which combined twenty different committees and associations, was established. In particular, it actively attempted to rally around the boycott of the 1977–1978 World Cup in Argentina; it supported Nicaragua (as well as other causes) by circulating information, supporting the families of missing persons, or acting in the favor of political prisoners, such as the Uruguayan pianist Miguel A. Estrella. What other part of the world was as obviously present in the Parisian ceremonies devised to salute the election victory of President François Mitterrand and his entry into office in May 1981? The nation's capital that, according to its new leaders, "reprend le flambeau de la défense des libertés et des droits de l'homme" (Jacques Lang, *Le Monde* 20-05-1981) ("resumes the defense of man's liberty and rights"), knew the value of symbols: At the socialist president's side was Mexican writer Carlos Fuentes (b. 1928), Colombian writer Gabriel García Márquez (b. 1927), and Venezuelan writer Miguel Otero Silva (1908–1985), as well as the widows of President Allende and of poet (and Chilean ambassador to France) Pablo Neruda.

But who was still traveling to Paris? At the start of the 1990s, foreigners in Paris represented more than 15 percent of the total population; the city was more cosmopolitan than it had ever been in the course of the century, though the mere evolution in transportation alone explains part of this phenomenon common to most capitals of developed countries. Latin Americans have in turn helped in shaping this multicultural aspect of the French capital. From 1978, when 4,864 Latin Americans resided in Paris, to 1990, when their numbers increased to 11,939, they have more than doubled their presence overall, while a slight decrease in the total foreign population can be detected. At the end of the 1970s, Latin Americans made up 1.5 percent of foreigners, and in the early nineties they made up 2.8 percent. The high proportion of Latin American students (representing 10 to 12 percent of foreign students and 1.3 percent of French residents) as well as the high standard of living of Latin American expatriates in France explain this relative and specific increase of Latin Americans in relation to the total foreign population of Paris. Their symbolic presence, however, far outweighs their actual numbers in Paris. In fact, the low numbers would come as a surprise to the cultural French elite of this time; as it crossed paths and even kept company with the Latin American community, this elite ended up overestimating Latin American presence as well as the proportion of refugees–especially in Paris.

Since the Second World War, as we have seen, the number of Latin Americans in France certainly underwent a slow asymptomatic increase. Nonetheless, their contribution to the total foreign population remained relatively small: The total number of Latin Americans increased from approximately 0.5 percent in 1975 to 0.8 percent in 1982, and further increased to 1.3 percent (45,478 Latin Americans out of 3,607,590 foreigners) in 1990. Putting aside any provocative comparisons, we can detect for instance that this number remains inferior to the number of Laotians or Senegalese alone–though admittedly these are two former countries of the French colonial empire.

France has nonetheless strived to preserve its influence: In 1969 Latin Americans constituted the first student contingent of university scholarship holders in France (21.5 percent), and more than half were registered in Paris (Office français pour les refugiés et les apatrides). Yet the numbers have since

dropped, and due to the lack of funding, many students educated in a Latin American-French lycée no longer set out for the City of Light. But Paris continues to be the world capital of arts and letters: According to a 1981 UNESCO inquiry, of the 220 Latin Americans involved in the plastic arts and who supposedly spearhead Latin American art, almost 40 percent undertook or had undertaken the voyage to Paris, often setting up a studio there. Half of them still reside in Paris; at the same time, New York attracts only 9 percent, or half as much, of these artists (see Bayon). In fact, the Denise René Gallery on Boulevard Saint Germain has been a veritable center of expression for a Latin American artistic current in Paris: Argentineans and Venezuelans from Rossi or Tomasello to Soto in particular distinguish themselves there. As a place of emigration or exile, Paris still represents an attractive milieu where one's art gets exposure or is sold and where Latin American literature gets published.

Literature evidently occupies center stage, that is to say, alongside the theater of Georges Lavelli and Alfredo Arias, who are very visible in Nancy (where sixteen plays have been presented by seven Latin American countries in the first ten years of that festival), in Avignon, at Paris's Théâtre des Nations founded by UNESCO, and alongside the cinematic genius of the Chilean theorist Miguel Littin (b. 1942) or the *telenovela* of the Bolivian Ukama group; in 1989 the Institut national de l'audio-visuel invited a well-known Brazilian scriptwriter to offer a writing workshop. While including a range of writers, from Borges to Fuentes, Amado to Carpentier, Asturias to Paz, as well as Rubén Bareiro Saguier (b. 1930), Alfredo Bryce Echenique (b. 1939), Vargas Llosa (b. 1936), García Márquez, Cortázar (1914–1984), and Rulfo (1918–1986), the list of major Latin American writers who have had prolonged stays in Paris is endless. Along with the world of dance, choreography, song, tango, lambada, salsa, or the Quarteto Cedrón and Atahualpa Yupanqui, architecture too cannot be forgotten here: The present Ministry of Finances and the Opéra de la Bastille represent the architectural works of Latin Americans.

The idea of a rich Parisian life was restricted to the nineteenth century, which, in certain cases, overlapped with the first half of the twentieth. If Paris remained the center of fashion and luxury, the French capital no longer had a monopoly, since the wars entailed a new appreciation for North American merchandise and luxury. The uncertainty of the functioning of parliament between the two wars, the wars themselves, and the second post-war period have stripped Paris of its role as the "référence globale de la politique, de la civilisation et

Table 5. *Comparative Statistics of Brazilian and U.S. Students in France*

Disciplines	Average % of foreigners	United States citizens	Brazilian citizens
Literature/Languages	22%	25.9%	46.3%
grandes écoles	6.6%	7.3%	5.9%
Sciences	6.6%	5.5%	0.6%
Medicine	6.4%	7.5%	0.3%
Humanities	5.5%	9.3%	3.0%
Technical Education	4.0%	1.5%	1.4%
Other	48.9%	43.0%	42.5%

Source: Office National de l'Immigration 1991.

de la culture" (Guerra 178) ("global model for politics, civilization and culture"). What has come to pass since? Latin America has experienced a massive return to democracy. From 1976 to 1978, there has been a distinct decline in militant activity involving Latin America; yet within all the disciplines, Latin Americanism retains its militant image, which is not always a noble one, and a number of Latin Americans in exile (or their children, also in exile) have finally integrated so well that there is no evidence of their wish to return to their newly democratizing countries. Thus Latin American presence in Paris returns to its classic form.

Have we come full circle? Is this the age-old cycle of progressive, mutual French-Latin American disinterest? In proportion to the number of Latin Americans living in France, fewer of them travel there as tourists. The few visible displays of France's interest in Latin America, such as in the early days of François Mitterrand's seven-year term, the declarations in Cancún, or the General States of Latin America (1982) in Paris are hardly impressive, considering the ten-year intervals that separate them. Has there not been any evolution, then? Perhaps not: Sometimes confused with the old representations, images of Latin Americans (for example, as *guerrillero*) and Latin America (as instability) endure, despite global refutation of certain ideas and a new exotic interest confirmed by the recent increase in the number of Latin American restaurants. Wearing colorful Peruvian caps or Mexican hats, Latin American musicians perform militant folk songs in the Paris subway tunnels, allowing Parisians to continue to cultivate stereotypes (which certain publicists have understood well).

Thus, since 1945, the intensified presence of Latin Americans in Paris has profoundly marked French, as well as Latin American, culture. At the same time, and along with the political instability and importance of military coups in Latin America, the Latin American's image–acquired in the nineteenth century–has gradually changed from that of the casual and luxurious Parisian attending an Offenbach operetta to the revolutionary who has been one French generation's fantasy since Fidel Castro's entry into Havana. Like the exceptional diffusion of Latin American literature in Europe, the modification of this image marks a distinct shift in the direction of the exportation of models between Paris and Latin America: Indeed "Che" was once the model for Europe's young generation. During the 1960s and 1970s, the image that survived the various transitions was the one transmitted by the media and Latin Americans in political exile: that of the political refugee, the left-winger, the political militant–those (physically and symbolically) at President Mitterrand's side at the Panthéon in 1981. There is also the image of a strongly politicized Chilean community, popularized through its diffusion around Paris and in the provinces.

As Latin America ceases to be a peripheral province of the Western model, the change in the perception of Latin Americans in France and Paris also corresponds to a modification of the various networks of contact between the Latin Americans and the French. From the end of the 1950s to the 1990s, the academic and diplomatic networks–mostly in keeping with a twentieth-century turbulent legacy–seem to embrace militant circles and certain professional associations; meanwhile, the trip to Cuba was becoming a distinct ritual for part of Paris's intelligentsia. In time, with the Brazilians, Argentineans and especially Chileans in exile, the flux is finally limited by administrative or semi-administrative proceedings, while networks of solidarity outside intellectual circles multiply themselves. Is this a factor

in the subsequent decline? A number of topics lose their importance within French society, and often vanish; first and foremost is "Latin Americanism," a view promoted by, but also a prisoner of, a dominant militant movement devoted to surviving from Latin American dictatorships and Latin American communism. Many among the Latin Americans in exile gradually have integrated into or have been integrated by French society (which still thinks, according to *Le Monde*, that Serguei is Argentinean and that Pancho Villa was Venezuelan). Latin America's economic crisis of the 1980s and France's (as well as other principal creditors) indifference to Latin America's economic interests, the School of Chicago's neo-Liberal economic model, are now the unique points of reference for Latin American elites in charge of state affairs (with the possible exception of Venezuela and Cuba). French and especially Parisian networks of contact with Latin America have remained unchanged, with the result that the image of Latin Americans in Paris still remains disproportionate to their actual numbers.

Does Paris retain its influence today? It was not so long ago (1980) that Carlos Fuentes wondered about "ese extraño amor a Francia que supuestamente nos salva a los latinoamericanos de la vieja subordinación hispánica y la nueva subordinación anglosajona" (1980, 163) ("that strange love for France which supposedly saves us Latin Americans from our ancient subordination to Spain and our more recent subordination to the Anglo-Saxon world") (1982,169).

Translation by Marie Carrière

Works Cited

AMAE: Archives du ministère français des affaires étrangères. Paris [1896].

AMRE-A: Ministerio de Relaciones Exteriores. Argentina. Secc. diplomática y consular, div. comercial, Francia [1918].

Alcântara Machado, Antonio de, 1983. *Pathé Baby e Prosa turística: o viajante europeu e platino.* Ed. Cecelia de Lara. Rio de Janeiro, Civilização Brasileira.

Amado, Gilberto. 1956. *Mocidade no Rio e primeira viagem a Europa.* Rio de Janeiro: José Olympio.

Anonymous. 1913. "Nôtre enseignement scientifique et les étudiantes d'Amérique latine." *Bulletin de la bibliothéque américaine* (March): 191.

Ayerza de Castilho, Laura, and Odile Felgine. 1993. *Victoria Ocampo.* Trans. Roser Berdagué. Barcelona: Circe.

Bayart, Jean-Françoise. 1996. *L'illusion identitaire.* Paris: Fayard.

Bayón, Damián. 1981. *Artistas contemporáneos de América Latina.* Paris: UNESCO.

Blancpain, Jean-Pierre. 1999. "Du Chili au Brésil : succès et déboires de la 'coopération' militaire allemande, 1885–1914." *Le Brésil, l'Europe et les équilibres internationaux XVIe–XXe siecles.* Ed. K. de Queirós Mattoso, Idelette Muzart-Fonseca dos Santos, Denis Rolland. Paris: PUPS. 281–92.

Bonnard, Abel. 1929. *Océan et Brésil.* Paris: Flammarion.

Brito Silva, Mario da. 1964. *Historia do modernismo brasileiro: antecedentes da Semana de Arte Moderna.* Rio de Janeiro: Civilização Brasileira.

Bulletin de l'Alliance française. 1895 (April 3). Paris: Association nationale pour la propagation de la langue française dans les colonies et à l'étranger.

——. 1898 (Jan. 15). Paris: Association nationale pour la propagation de la langue française dans les colonies et à l'étranger.

——. 1899 (Nov.). Paris: Association nationale pour la propagation de la langue française dans les colonies et à l'étranger.

Carelli, Mario. 1989. *Brasil-França, cinco séculos de sedução*. Rio de Janeiro: Espaço e Tempo.

Choncol, Jacques, and Guy Martinière. 1985. *L'Amérique latine et le latino-américanisme en France*. Paris: L'Harmattan.

Cortázar, Julio. 1981. *Paris*. Genève: Office du Livre.

Darío, Rubén. 1943. *El Archivo de Rubén Darío*. Ed. Alberto Ghiraldo. Buenos Aires: Losada.

———. 1955. "Los colores del estandarte." *Obras completas*. Vol. 4. Madrid: Afrodisio Aguado. 872–82.

Duhamel, Georges. 1937. *Europa-América Latina*. Buenos Aires: IICI.

Febvre, Lucien. 1955. "Les Lumières de Clio." *Le nouveau monde et l'Europe*. Ed. Lucien Febvre et al. Neuchâtel: Ed. de la Bâconnière. 11–29.

Foncin, Pierre, ed. 1900. *La langue française dans le monde*. Paris: Alliance française.

Fuentes, Carlos. 1980. *Una familia lejana*. Mexico City: Ediciones Era.

———. 1981. *Une certaine parenté*. Trans. Celíne Zins. Paris: Gallimard.

———. 1982. *Distant Relations*. Trans. Margaret Sayers Peden. New York: Farrar, Straus, Giroux.

———. 1986. *Institut français d'Amérique latine, 1945–1985*. Mexico City: IFAL.

Garzón, Eugenio. 1916. "Comité d'action parlementaire à l'étranger." *La Première Semaine de l'Amérique latine*. Paris: n.p. 14.

Guerra, François-Xavier. 1989. "La lumière et ses reflets: Paris et la politique latino-américaine." *Le Paris des étrangers*. Ed. André Kaspi and Antoine Marès. Paris: Editions de l'Imprimerie nationale. 171–81.

Güiraldes, Ricardo. 1927. *Don Segundo Sombra*. Buenos Aires: Ateneo.

Huret, Jules. 1913. *De La Plata à la Cordillère des Andes, avec une carte de la République Argentine*. Paris: Bibliothèque-Carpentier.

Jouvet, Louis. 1945. *Prestige et perspective du théâtre français*. Paris: Gallimard.

Lafond, Georges. 1916. "La librairie française en Amérique latine." *Actes de la Première semaine de l'Amérique latine*. Lyon: [np]. 285–301.

Lesca, Charles. 1939. "Histoire d'une revue." *Hommage à Ernest Martinenche: Etudes hispaniques et américaines*. Paris: Editions d'Artrey. 428–40.

Lévi-Strauss, Claude. 1955. *Tristes Tropiques*. Paris: Plon.

———. 1994. *Saudades do Brasil*. Trans. Paulo Neves. São Paulo: Companhia das Letras.

Martinenche, Ernest. 1918. "L'Amérique latine et la guerre." *Bulletin de l'Amérique latine* (Paris): 03-04-1918.

Matthieu, Gilles. 1991. *Une ambition sud-américaine: politique culturelle de la France, 1914–1940*. Paris: L'Harmattan.

Murilo de Carvalho, José. 1990. *A formação das almas: o imaginario da República no Brasil*. São Paulo: Companhia das Letras.

Muzart Fonseca dos Santos, Idelette. 1997. *La littérature de cordel au Brésil, mémoire des voix, grenier d'histoires*. Paris: L' Harmattan.

Neira, Hugo. 1985. "Un descubrimiento americano: la Europa de los años veinte. El viaje legendario de Haya de la Torre y de José Carlos Mariátegui. Pontencialidades y peligros del discurso anti-occidental." *Les Amériques et l'Europe: Voyage. Emigration. Exil*. Ed. Claire Pailler. Toulouse: U de Toulouse-Le Mirail. 155–84.

Nora, Pierre. 1974. "Le retour de l'évènement." Faire de l'histoire. Vol. I: *Nouveaux problèmes*. Ed. Jacques Le Goff and Pierre Nora. Paris: Gallimard. 210?28.

Ocampo, Victoria. 1979. *Autobiografía*. Vol. I: *El Archipiélago*. Buenos Aires: Sur.

Pérez-Pacheco, Mateo. 1921. "La culture française en Amérique latine." *Bulletin de l'Amérique latine* (Paris) 06-07-1921. 272.

Quentin-Mauroy, Dominique. 1985. "Les jeunes Argentins et le voyage rituel en Europe au milieu du XIXe siècle." *Les Amériques et l'Europe: Voyage*. Emigration. Exil. Ed. Claire Pailler. Toulouse: U de Toulouse-Le Mirail. 67–81.

Reyes, Alfonso. 1917. "A travers quelques journax de l'Amérique latine." *Bulletin de l'Amérique latine* (Paris) 08-11-1917. 55–56.

Rolland, Denis. 1999. *L'Amérique et la crise du modèle français*. Paris: L'Harmattan.

———. 1999. *Mémoire et imaginarie de la France en Amérique latine*. Rennes: PUR/IUF.

———. 2000. *La crise du modèle français, Marianne et l'Amèrique latine*. Rennes: PUR/IUF.

Sáenz Carrete, Erasmo. 1983. "Les cadres socio-politiques de l'adaptation des réfugiés latino-américains en France, 1964–1979." Dissertation. U de Paris III.

Salgado Campo, Regina. 2001. "Anatole France au Brésil." *Modèles politiques et culturels de l'Europe au Brésil*. Ed. K. de Queiros Mattoso, D. Rolland and I. Muzart. Paris: PUPS. 249–69.

Séris, Christiane.1989. "Microcosmes dans la capitale ou l'histoire de la colonie intellectuelle hispano-américaine à Paris entre 1890 et 1914." *Le Paris des étrangers depuis un siècle*. Ed. André Kaspi and Antoine Mares. Paris: Imprimerie nationale. 299–312.

———. 1994. "Les écrivains latino-américains devant la France entre 1885 et 1914." Dissertation [mémoire d'habilitation]. U de Paris V.

Silva, Jorge. 1946. *Viajeros franceses en México*. México City: Editorial América.

Stegagno Picchio, Luciana. 1995. "Deux visages du surréalisme au Brésil, de Murilo Mendes à Jorge de Lima." *Nouveau monde, autres mondes: Surréalisme et Amériques*. Ed. Daniel Lefort, Pierre Rivas and Jacqueline Chénieux-Gendron. Paris: Lachenal & Ritter. 189–203.

Tavares, Aurélio de Lyra. 1979. *Brasil-França: ao longo de 5 séculos*. Rio de Janeiro: Biblioteca do Exército.

Ugarte, Manuel. 1906. *La joven literatura hispano-americana*. Paris: A. Colin.

Vannini de Gerulewicz, Marisa. 1968. *La influencia francesa en Venezuela*. 2nd ed. Maracaibo: Universidad de Zulia.